NEW INTERNATIONAL VERSION

HOLY BIBLE

ZONDERVAN®

NIV Holy Bible
Published by Zondervan
Grand Rapids, Michigan, USA

www.Zondervan.com

Library of Congress Control Number: 2013957114

Printed in the United States of America

N101210

---

25 26 27 28 29 30 31 32 /TRM/ 25 24 23 22 21 20 19

A portion of the purchase price of your NIV® Bible is provided to Biblica so together we support the mission of *Transforming lives through God's Word.*

Biblica provides God's Word to people through translation, publishing and Bible engagement in Africa, Asia Pacific, Europe, Latin America, Middle East, and North America. Through its worldwide reach, Biblica engages people with God's Word so that their lives are transformed through a relationship with Jesus Christ.

Table of Contents

The Old Testament

The New Testament

Preface

The goal of the New International Version (NIV) is to enable English-speaking people from around the world to read and hear God's eternal Word in their own language. Our work as translators is motivated by our conviction that the Bible is God's Word in written form. We believe that the Bible contains the divine answer to the deepest needs of humanity, sheds unique light on our path in a dark world and sets forth the way to our eternal well-being. Out of these deep convictions, we have sought to recreate as far as possible the experience of the original audience—blending transparency to the original text with accessibility for the millions of English speakers around the world. We have prioritized accuracy, clarity and literary quality with the goal of creating a translation suitable for public and private reading, evangelism, teaching, preaching, memorizing and liturgical use. We have also sought to preserve a measure of continuity with the long tradition of translating the Scriptures into English.

The complete NIV Bible was first published in 1978. It was a completely new translation made by over a hundred scholars working directly from the best available Hebrew, Aramaic and Greek texts. The translators came from the United States, Great Britain, Canada, Australia and New Zealand, giving the translation an international scope. They were from many denominations and churches—including Anglican, Assemblies of God, Baptist, Brethren, Christian Reformed, Church of Christ, Evangelical Covenant, Evangelical Free, Lutheran, Mennonite, Methodist, Nazarene, Presbyterian, Wesleyan and others. This breadth of denominational and theological perspective helped to safeguard the translation from sectarian bias. For these reasons, and by the grace of God, the NIV has gained a wide readership in all parts of the English-speaking world.

The work of translating the Bible is never finished. As good as they are, English translations must be regularly updated so that they will continue to communicate accurately the meaning of God's Word. Updates are needed in order to reflect the latest developments in our understanding of the biblical world and its languages and to keep pace with changes in English usage. Recognizing, then, that the NIV would retain its ability to communicate God's Word accurately only if it were regularly updated, the original translators established the Committee on Bible Translation (CBT). The Committee is a self-perpetuating group of biblical scholars charged with keeping abreast of advances in biblical scholarship and changes in English and issuing periodic updates to the NIV. The CBT is an independent, self-governing body and has sole responsibility for the NIV text. The Committee mirrors the original group of translators in its diverse international and denominational makeup and in its unifying commitment to the Bible as God's inspired Word.

In obedience to its mandate, the Committee has issued periodic updates to the NIV. An initial revision was released in 1984. A more thorough revision process was completed in 2005, resulting in the separately published TNIV. The updated NIV you now have in your hands builds on both the original NIV and the TNIV and represents the latest effort of the Committee to articulate God's unchanging Word in the way the original authors might have said it had they been speaking in English to the global English-speaking audience today.

Translation Philosophy

The Committee's translating work has been governed by three widely accepted principles about the way people use words and about the way we understand them.

First, the meaning of words is determined by the way that users of the language actually use them at any given time. For the biblical languages, therefore, the Committee utilizes the best and most recent scholarship on the way Hebrew, Aramaic and Greek words were being used in biblical times. At the same time, the Committee carefully studies the state of modern English. Good translation is like good communication: one must know the target audience so that the appropriate choices can be made about which English words to use to represent the original words of Scripture. From its inception, the NIV has had as its target the general English-speaking population all over the world, the "International" in its title reflecting this concern. The aim of the Committee is to put the Scriptures into natural English that will communicate effectively with the broadest possible audience of English speakers.

Modern technology has enhanced the Committee's ability to choose the right English words to convey the meaning of the original text. The field of computational linguistics harnesses the power of computers to provide broadly applicable and current data about the state of the language. Translators can now access huge databases of modern English to better understand the current meaning and usage of key words. The Committee utilized this resource in preparing the 2011 edition of the NIV. An area of especially rapid and significant change in English is the way certain nouns and pronouns are used to refer to human beings. The Committee therefore requested experts in computational linguistics at Collins Dictionaries to pose some key questions about this usage to its database of English—the largest in the world, with over 4.4 billion words, gathered from several English-speaking countries and including both spoken and written English. (The Collins Study, called "The Development and Use of Gender Language in Contemporary English," can be accessed at *http://www.thenivbible.com/about-the-niv/about-the-2011-edition/.*) The study revealed that the most popular words to describe the human race in modern U.S. English were "humanity," "man" and "mankind." The Committee then used this data in the updated NIV, choosing from among these three words (and occasionally others also) depending on the context.

A related issue creates a larger problem for modern translations: the move away from using the third-person masculine singular pronouns—"he/him/his"—to refer to men and women equally. This usage does persist in some forms of English, and this revision therefore occasionally uses these pronouns in a generic sense. But the tendency, recognized in day-to-day usage and confirmed by the Collins study, is away from the generic use of "he," "him" and "his." In recognition of this shift in language and in an effort to translate into the natural English that people are actually using, this revision of the NIV generally uses other constructions when the biblical text is plainly addressed to men and women equally. The reader will encounter especially frequently a "they," "their" or "them" to express a generic singular idea. Thus, for instance, Mark 8:36 reads: "What good is it for someone to gain the whole world, yet forfeit their soul?" This generic use of the "distributive" or "singular" "they/them/their" has been used for many centuries by respected writers of English and has now become established as standard English, spoken and written, all over the world.

A second linguistic principle that feeds into the Committee's translation work is that meaning is found not in individual words, as vital as they are, but in larger clusters: phrases, clauses, sentences, discourses. Translation is not, as many people think, a matter of word substitution: English word *x* in place of Hebrew word *y*. Translators must first determine the meaning of the words of the biblical languages in the context of the passage and then select English words that accurately communicate that meaning to modern listeners and readers. This means that accurate translation will not always reflect the exact structure of the original language. To be sure, there is debate over the degree to which translators should try to preserve the "form" of the original text in English. From the beginning, the NIV has taken a mediating position on this issue. The manual produced when the translation that became the NIV was first being planned states: "If the Greek or Hebrew syntax has a good parallel in modern English, it should be used. But if there is no good parallel, the English syntax appropriate to the meaning of the original is to be chosen." It is fine, in other words, to carry over the form of the biblical languages into English—but not at the expense of natural expression. The principle that meaning resides in larger clusters of words means that the Committee has not insisted on a "word-for-word" approach to translation. We certainly believe that every word of Scripture is inspired by God and therefore to be carefully studied to determine what God is saying to us. It is for this reason that the Committee labors over every single word of the original texts, working hard to determine how each of those words contributes to what the text is saying. Ultimately, however, it is how these individual words function in combination with other words that determines meaning.

A third linguistic principle guiding the Committee in its translation work is the recognition that words have a spectrum of meaning. It is popular to define a word by using another word, or "gloss," to substitute for it. This substitute word is then sometimes called the "literal" meaning of a word. In fact, however, words have a range of possible meanings. Those meanings will vary depending on the context, and words in one language will usually not occupy the same semantic range as words in another language. The Committee therefore studies each original word of Scripture in its context to identify its meaning in a particular verse and then chooses an appropriate English word (or phrase) to represent it. It is impossible, then, to translate any given Hebrew, Aramaic or Greek word with the same English word all the time. The Committee does try to translate related occurrences of a word in the original languages with the same English word in order to preserve the connection for the English reader. But the Committee generally privileges clear natural meaning over a concern with consistency in rendering particular words.

Textual Basis

For the Old Testament the standard Hebrew text, the Masoretic Text as published in the latest edition of *Biblia Hebraica*, has been used throughout. The Masoretic Text tradition contains marginal notations that offer variant readings. These have sometimes been followed instead of the text itself. Because such instances involve variants within the Masoretic tradition, they have not been indicated in the textual notes. In a few cases, words in the basic consonantal text have been divided differently than in the Masoretic Text. Such cases are usually indicated in the textual footnotes. The Dead Sea Scrolls contain biblical texts that represent an earlier stage of the transmission of the Hebrew text.

They have been consulted, as have been the Samaritan Pentateuch and the ancient scribal traditions concerning deliberate textual changes. The translators also consulted the more important early versions. Readings from these versions, the Dead Sea Scrolls and the scribal traditions were occasionally followed where the Masoretic Text seemed doubtful and where accepted principles of textual criticism showed that one or more of these textual witnesses appeared to provide the correct reading. In rare cases, the translators have emended the Hebrew text where it appears to have become corrupted at an even earlier stage of its transmission. These departures from the Masoretic Text are also indicated in the textual footnotes. Sometimes the vowel indicators (which are later additions to the basic consonantal text) found in the Masoretic Text did not, in the judgment of the translators, represent the correct vowels for the original text. Accordingly, some words have been read with a different set of vowels. These instances are usually not indicated in the footnotes.

The Greek text used in translating the New Testament has been an eclectic one, based on the latest editions of the Nestle-Aland/United Bible Societies' Greek New Testament. The translators have made their choices among the variant readings in accordance with widely accepted principles of New Testament textual criticism. Footnotes call attention to places where uncertainty remains.

The New Testament authors, writing in Greek, often quote the Old Testament from its ancient Greek version, the Septuagint. This is one reason why some of the Old Testament quotations in the NIV New Testament are not identical to the corresponding passages in the NIV Old Testament. Such quotations in the New Testament are indicated with the footnote "(see Septuagint)."

Footnotes and Formatting

Footnotes in this version are of several kinds, most of which need no explanation. Those giving alternative translations begin with "Or" and generally introduce the alternative with the last word preceding it in the text, except when it is a single-word alternative. When poetry is quoted in a footnote a slash mark indicates a line division.

It should be noted that references to diseases, minerals, flora and fauna, architectural details, clothing, jewelry, musical instruments and other articles cannot always be identified with precision. Also, linear measurements and measures of capacity can only be approximated (see the Table of Weights and Measures). Although *Selah*, used mainly in the Psalms, is probably a musical term, its meaning is uncertain. Since it may interrupt reading and distract the reader, this word has not been kept in the English text, but every occurrence has been signaled by a footnote.

As an aid to the reader, sectional headings have been inserted. They are not to be regarded as part of the biblical text and are not intended for oral reading. It is the Committee's hope that these headings may prove more helpful to the reader than the traditional chapter divisions, which were introduced long after the Bible was written.

Sometimes the chapter and/or verse numbering in English translations of the Old Testament differs from that found in published Hebrew texts. This is particularly the case in the Psalms, where the traditional titles are included in the Hebrew verse numbering. Such differences are indicated in the footnotes at the bottom of the page. In the New Testament, verse numbers that marked off portions of the traditional English text not supported by the best Greek manuscripts now appear in brackets, with a footnote indicating the text that has been omitted (see, for example, Matthew 17:[21]).

Mark 16:9–20 and John 7:53—8:11, although long accorded virtually equal status with the rest of the Gospels in which they stand, have a questionable standing in the textual history of the New Testament, as noted in the bracketed annotations with which they are set off. A different typeface has been chosen for these passages to indicate their uncertain status.

Basic formatting of the text, such as lining the poetry, paragraphing (both prose and poetry), setting up of (administrative-like) lists, indenting letters and lengthy prayers within narratives and the insertion of sectional headings, has been the work of the Committee. However, the choice between single-column and double-column formats has been left to the publishers. Also the issuing of "red-letter" editions is a publisher's choice—one that the Committee does not endorse.

The Committee has again been reminded that every human effort is flawed—including this revision of the NIV. We trust, however, that many will find in it an improved representation of the Word of God, through which they hear his call to faith in our Lord Jesus Christ and to service in his kingdom. We offer this version of the Bible to him in whose name and for whose glory it has been made.

The Committee on Bible Translation

The Old Testament

Genesis

The Beginning

1 In the beginning God created the heavens and the earth. 2Now the earth was
formless and empty, darkness was over
the surface of the deep, and the Spirit of
God was hovering over the waters.

3 And God said, "Let there be light," and there
was light. 4God saw that the light was
good, and he separated the light from the
darkness. 5God called the light "day," and
the darkness he called "night." And there
was evening, and there was morning—
the first day.
6 And God said, "Let there be a vault between
the waters to separate water from water."
7So God made the vault and separated
the water under the vault from the water
above it. And it was so. 8God called the
vault "sky." And there was evening, and
there was morning—the second day.
9 And God said, "Let the water under the
sky be gathered to one place, and let dry
ground appear." And it was so. 10God
called the dry ground "land," and the
gathered waters he called "seas." And
God saw that it was good.
11Then God said, "Let the land produce
vegetation: seed-bearing plants and trees
on the land that bear fruit with seed in it,
according to their various kinds." And it
was so. 12The land produced vegetation:
plants bearing seed according to their
kinds and trees bearing fruit with seed
in it according to their kinds. And God
saw that it was good. 13And there was
evening, and there was morning—the
third day.
14 And God said, "Let there be lights in the
vault of the sky to separate the day from
the night, and let them serve as signs to
mark sacred times, and days and years,
15and let them be lights in the vault of
the sky to give light on the earth." And
it was so. 16God made two great lights—
the greater light to govern the day and
the lesser light to govern the night. He
also made the stars. 17God set them in the
vault of the sky to give light on the earth,
18to govern the day and the night, and to
separate light from darkness. And God
saw that it was good. 19And there was
evening, and there was morning—the
fourth day.
20 And God said, "Let the water teem with living creatures, and let birds fly above the
earth across the vault of the sky." 21So
God created the great creatures of the
sea and every living thing with which
the water teems and that moves about
in it, according to their kinds, and every
winged bird according to its kind. And
God saw that it was good. 22God blessed
them and said, "Be fruitful and increase
in number and fill the water in the seas,
and let the birds increase on the earth."
23And there was evening, and there was
morning—the fifth day.
24 And God said, "Let the land produce living creatures according to their kinds:
the livestock, the creatures that move
along the ground, and the wild animals,
each according to its kind." And it was
so. 25God made the wild animals according to their kinds, the livestock according
to their kinds, and all the creatures that
move along the ground according to their
kinds. And God saw that it was good.
26Then God said, "Let us make mankind in our image, in our likeness, so that
they may rule over the fish in the sea and
the birds in the sky, over the livestock
and all the wild animals,[a] and over all the
creatures that move along the ground."

27 So God created mankind in his own
image,
in the image of God he created them;
male and female he created them.

28God blessed them and said to them,
"Be fruitful and increase in number; fill
the earth and subdue it. Rule over the fish
in the sea and the birds in the sky and
over every living creature that moves on
the ground."
29Then God said, "I give you every seed-
bearing plant on the face of the whole
earth and every tree that has fruit with
seed in it. They will be yours for food.
30And to all the beasts of the earth and all
the birds in the sky and all the creatures
that move along the ground—everything
that has the breath of life in it—I give every green plant for food." And it was so.
31God saw all that he had made, and it
was very good. And there was evening,
and there was morning—the sixth day.

2 Thus the heavens and the earth were
completed in all their vast array.

2 By the seventh day God had finished the
work he had been doing; so on the seventh day he rested from all his work.
3Then God blessed the seventh day and
made it holy, because on it he rested from
all the work of creating that he had done.

Adam and Eve

4This is the account of the heavens and the
earth when they were created, when the LORD
God made the earth and the heavens.

[a] *26* Probable reading of the original Hebrew text (see Syriac); Masoretic Text *the earth*

5 Now no shrub had yet appeared on the
earth[a] and no plant had yet sprung up, for
the LORD God had not sent rain on the earth
and there was no one to work the ground,
6 but streams[b] came up from the earth and watered the whole surface of the ground. 7 Then
the LORD God formed a man[c] from the dust
of the ground and breathed into his nostrils
the breath of life, and the man became a living being.
8 Now the LORD God had planted a garden in
the east, in Eden; and there he put the man he
had formed. 9 The LORD God made all kinds of
trees grow out of the ground—trees that were
pleasing to the eye and good for food. In the
middle of the garden were the tree of life and
the tree of the knowledge of good and evil.
10 A river watering the garden flowed from
Eden; from there it was separated into four
headwaters. 11 The name of the first is the
Pishon; it winds through the entire land of
Havilah, where there is gold. 12 (The gold of
that land is good; aromatic resin[d] and onyx
are also there.) 13 The name of the second river
is the Gihon; it winds through the entire land
of Cush.[e] 14 The name of the third river is the
Tigris; it runs along the east side of Ashur.
And the fourth river is the Euphrates.
15 The LORD God took the man and put him
in the Garden of Eden to work it and take
care of it. 16 And the LORD God commanded
the man, "You are free to eat from any tree
in the garden; 17 but you must not eat from the
tree of the knowledge of good and evil, for
when you eat from it you will certainly die."
18 The LORD God said, "It is not good for the
man to be alone. I will make a helper suitable
for him."
19 Now the LORD God had formed out of the
ground all the wild animals and all the birds
in the sky. He brought them to the man to
see what he would name them; and whatever the man called each living creature, that
was its name. 20 So the man gave names to all
the livestock, the birds in the sky and all the
wild animals.
But for Adam[f] no suitable helper was found.
21 So the LORD God caused the man to fall into
a deep sleep; and while he was sleeping, he
took one of the man's ribs[g] and then closed
up the place with flesh. 22 Then the LORD God
made a woman from the rib[h] he had taken out
of the man, and he brought her to the man.
23 The man said,

"This is now bone of my bones
  and flesh of my flesh;
she shall be called 'woman,'
  for she was taken out of man."

24 That is why a man leaves his father and
mother and is united to his wife, and they
become one flesh.
25 Adam and his wife were both naked, and
they felt no shame.

The Fall

3 Now the serpent was more crafty than
any of the wild animals the LORD God
had made. He said to the woman, "Did God
really say, 'You must not eat from any tree in
the garden'?"
2 The woman said to the serpent, "We may
eat fruit from the trees in the garden, 3 but God
did say, 'You must not eat fruit from the tree
that is in the middle of the garden, and you
must not touch it, or you will die.'"
4 "You will not certainly die," the serpent
said to the woman. 5 "For God knows that
when you eat from it your eyes will be opened,
and you will be like God, knowing good and
evil."
6 When the woman saw that the fruit of the
tree was good for food and pleasing to the eye,
and also desirable for gaining wisdom, she
took some and ate it. She also gave some to
her husband, who was with her, and he ate it.
7 Then the eyes of both of them were opened,
and they realized they were naked; so they
sewed fig leaves together and made coverings
for themselves.
8 Then the man and his wife heard the sound
of the LORD God as he was walking in the
garden in the cool of the day, and they hid
from the LORD God among the trees of the
garden. 9 But the LORD God called to the man,
"Where are you?"
10 He answered, "I heard you in the garden,
and I was afraid because I was naked; so I
hid."
11 And he said, "Who told you that you were
naked? Have you eaten from the tree that I
commanded you not to eat from?"
12 The man said, "The woman you put here
with me—she gave me some fruit from the
tree, and I ate it."
13 Then the LORD God said to the woman,
"What is this you have done?"
The woman said, "The serpent deceived
me, and I ate."
14 So the LORD God said to the serpent, "Because you have done this,

"Cursed are you above all livestock
  and all wild animals!
You will crawl on your belly
  and you will eat dust
  all the days of your life.
15 And I will put enmity
  between you and the woman,
  and between your offspring[i] and hers;
he will crush[j] your head,
  and you will strike his heel."

16 To the woman he said,

"I will make your pains in childbearing
    very severe;
  with painful labor you will give birth to
    children.
Your desire will be for your husband,
  and he will rule over you."

[a] 5 Or *land*; also in verse 6 [b] 6 Or *mist* [c] 7 The Hebrew for *man (adam)* sounds like and may be related to the Hebrew for *ground (adamah)*; it is also the name *Adam* (see verse 20). [d] 12 Or *good; pearls* [e] 13 Possibly southeast Mesopotamia [f] 20 Or *the man* [g] 21 Or *took part of the man's side* [h] 22 Or *part* [i] 15 Or *seed* [j] 15 Or *strike*

17To Adam he said, "Because you listened
to your wife and ate fruit from the tree about
which I commanded you, 'You must not eat
from it,'

"Cursed is the ground because of you;
through painful toil you will eat food
from it
all the days of your life.
18 It will produce thorns and thistles for you,
and you will eat the plants of the field.
19 By the sweat of your brow
you will eat your food
until you return to the ground,
since from it you were taken;
for dust you are
and to dust you will return."

20Adam[a] named his wife Eve,[b] because she
would become the mother of all the living.
21The LORD God made garments of skin for
Adam and his wife and clothed them. 22And
the LORD God said, "The man has now become
like one of us, knowing good and evil. He must
not be allowed to reach out his hand and take
also from the tree of life and eat, and live forever." 23So the LORD God banished him from
the Garden of Eden to work the ground from
which he had been taken. 24After he drove
the man out, he placed on the east side[c] of
the Garden of Eden cherubim and a flaming
sword flashing back and forth to guard the
way to the tree of life.

Cain and Abel

4 Adam[a] made love to his wife Eve, and she
became pregnant and gave birth to Cain.[d]
She said, "With the help of the LORD I have
brought forth[e] a man." 2Later she gave birth
to his brother Abel.
Now Abel kept flocks, and Cain worked
the soil. 3In the course of time Cain brought
some of the fruits of the soil as an offering to
the LORD. 4And Abel also brought an offering—fat portions from some of the firstborn
of his flock. The LORD looked with favor on
Abel and his offering, 5but on Cain and his
offering he did not look with favor. So Cain
was very angry, and his face was downcast.
6Then the LORD said to Cain, "Why are you
angry? Why is your face downcast? 7If you do
what is right, will you not be accepted? But if
you do not do what is right, sin is crouching
at your door; it desires to have you, but you
must rule over it."
8Now Cain said to his brother Abel, "Let's go
out to the field."[f] While they were in the field,
Cain attacked his brother Abel and killed him.
9Then the LORD said to Cain, "Where is your
brother Abel?"
"I don't know," he replied. "Am I my brother's keeper?"
10The LORD said, "What have you done?
Listen! Your brother's blood cries out to me
from the ground. 11Now you are under a curse
and driven from the ground, which opened its
mouth to receive your brother's blood from
your hand. 12When you work the ground, it
will no longer yield its crops for you. You will
be a restless wanderer on the earth."
13Cain said to the LORD, "My punishment is
more than I can bear. 14Today you are driving
me from the land, and I will be hidden from
your presence; I will be a restless wanderer on
the earth, and whoever finds me will kill me."
15But the LORD said to him, "Not so[g]; anyone
who kills Cain will suffer vengeance seven
times over." Then the LORD put a mark on Cain
so that no one who found him would kill him.
16So Cain went out from the LORD's presence
and lived in the land of Nod,[h] east of Eden.
17Cain made love to his wife, and she became pregnant and gave birth to Enoch. Cain
was then building a city, and he named it after
his son Enoch. 18To Enoch was born Irad, and
Irad was the father of Mehujael, and Mehujael
was the father of Methushael, and Methushael
was the father of Lamech.
19Lamech married two women, one named
Adah and the other Zillah. 20Adah gave birth
to Jabal; he was the father of those who live in
tents and raise livestock. 21His brother's name
was Jubal; he was the father of all who play
stringed instruments and pipes. 22Zillah also
had a son, Tubal-Cain, who forged all kinds
of tools out of[i] bronze and iron. Tubal-Cain's
sister was Naamah.
23Lamech said to his wives,

"Adah and Zillah, listen to me;
wives of Lamech, hear my words.
I have killed a man for wounding me,
a young man for injuring me.
24 If Cain is avenged seven times,
then Lamech seventy-seven times."

25Adam made love to his wife again, and
she gave birth to a son and named him Seth,[j]
saying, "God has granted me another child in
place of Abel, since Cain killed him." 26Seth
also had a son, and he named him Enosh.
At that time people began to call on[k] the
name of the LORD.

From Adam to Noah

5 This is the written account of Adam's family line.

When God created mankind, he made them
in the likeness of God. 2He created them male
and female and blessed them. And he named
them "Mankind"[l] when they were created.
3When Adam had lived 130 years, he had
a son in his own likeness, in his own image;
and he named him Seth. 4After Seth was born,
Adam lived 800 years and had other sons and

[a] 20,1 Or *The man* [b] 20 *Eve* probably means *living.* [c] 24 Or *placed in front* [d] 1 *Cain* sounds like the Hebrew for *brought forth* or *acquired.* [e] 1 Or *have acquired* [f] 8 Samaritan Pentateuch, Septuagint, Vulgate and Syriac; Masoretic Text does not have *"Let's go out to the field."* [g] 15 Septuagint, Vulgate and Syriac; Hebrew *Very well* [h] 16 *Nod* means *wandering* (see verses 12 and 14). [i] 22 Or *who instructed all who work in* [j] 25 *Seth* probably means *granted.* [k] 26 Or *to proclaim* [l] 2 Hebrew *adam*

daughters. 5Altogether, Adam lived a total of
930 years, and then he died.
6When Seth had lived 105 years, he became
the father[a] of Enosh. 7After he became the father of Enosh, Seth lived 807 years and had
other sons and daughters. 8Altogether, Seth
lived a total of 912 years, and then he died.
9When Enosh had lived 90 years, he became
the father of Kenan. 10After he became the father of Kenan, Enosh lived 815 years and had
other sons and daughters. 11Altogether, Enosh
lived a total of 905 years, and then he died.
12When Kenan had lived 70 years, he became the father of Mahalalel. 13After he became the father of Mahalalel, Kenan lived
840 years and had other sons and daughters.
14Altogether, Kenan lived a total of 910 years,
and then he died.
15When Mahalalel had lived 65 years, he
became the father of Jared. 16After he became
the father of Jared, Mahalalel lived 830 years
and had other sons and daughters. 17Altogeth-
er, Mahalalel lived a total of 895 years, and
then he died.
18When Jared had lived 162 years, he became
the father of Enoch. 19After he became the father of Enoch, Jared lived 800 years and had
other sons and daughters. 20Altogether, Jared
lived a total of 962 years, and then he died.
21When Enoch had lived 65 years, he became the father of Methuselah. 22After he became the father of Methuselah, Enoch walked
faithfully with God 300 years and had other
sons and daughters. 23Altogether, Enoch lived
a total of 365 years. 24Enoch walked faithfully
with God; then he was no more, because God
took him away.
25When Methuselah had lived 187 years, he
became the father of Lamech. 26After he became the father of Lamech, Methuselah lived
782 years and had other sons and daughters.
27Altogether, Methuselah lived a total of 969
years, and then he died.
28When Lamech had lived 182 years, he had
a son. 29He named him Noah[b] and said, "He
will comfort us in the labor and painful toil
of our hands caused by the ground the LORD
has cursed." 30After Noah was born, Lamech
lived 595 years and had other sons and daughters. 31Altogether, Lamech lived a total of 777
years, and then he died.
32After Noah was 500 years old, he became
the father of Shem, Ham and Japheth.

Wickedness in the World

6 When human beings began to increase in
number on the earth and daughters were
born to them, 2the sons of God saw that the
daughters of humans were beautiful, and they
married any of them they chose. 3Then the
LORD said, "My Spirit will not contend with[c]
humans forever, for they are mortal[d]; their
days will be a hundred and twenty years."
4The Nephilim were on the earth in those
days—and also afterward—when the sons
of God went to the daughters of humans and
had children by them. They were the heroes
of old, men of renown.
5The LORD saw how great the wickedness
of the human race had become on the earth,
and that every inclination of the thoughts of
the human heart was only evil all the time.
6The LORD regretted that he had made human
beings on the earth, and his heart was deeply troubled. 7So the LORD said, "I will wipe
from the face of the earth the human race I
have created—and with them the animals, the
birds and the creatures that move along the
ground—for I regret that I have made them."
8But Noah found favor in the eyes of the LORD.

Noah and the Flood

9This is the account of Noah and his family.
Noah was a righteous man, blameless
among the people of his time, and he walked
faithfully with God. 10Noah had three sons:
Shem, Ham and Japheth.
11Now the earth was corrupt in God's sight
and was full of violence. 12God saw how corrupt the earth had become, for all the people on
earth had corrupted their ways. 13So God said
to Noah, "I am going to put an end to all people,
for the earth is filled with violence because of
them. I am surely going to destroy both them
and the earth. 14So make yourself an ark of cypress[e] wood; make rooms in it and coat it with
pitch inside and out. 15This is how you are to
build it: The ark is to be three hundred cubits
long, fifty cubits wide and thirty cubits high.[f]
16Make a roof for it, leaving below the roof an
opening one cubit[g] high all around.[h] Put a door
in the side of the ark and make lower, middle
and upper decks. 17I am going to bring floodwaters on the earth to destroy all life under the
heavens, every creature that has the breath
of life in it. Everything on earth will perish.
18But I will establish my covenant with you,
and you will enter the ark—you and your sons
and your wife and your sons' wives with you.
19You are to bring into the ark two of all living
creatures, male and female, to keep them alive
with you. 20Two of every kind of bird, of every
kind of animal and of every kind of creature
that moves along the ground will come to you
to be kept alive. 21You are to take every kind
of food that is to be eaten and store it away as
food for you and for them."
22Noah did everything just as God commanded him.

7 The LORD then said to Noah, "Go into the
ark, you and your whole family, because I
have found you righteous in this generation.
2Take with you seven pairs of every kind of
clean animal, a male and its mate, and one
pair of every kind of unclean animal, a male
and its mate, 3and also seven pairs of every

[a] 6 *Father* may mean *ancestor*; also in verses 7-26. [b] 29 *Noah* sounds like the Hebrew for *comfort*. [c] 3 Or *My spirit will not remain in* [d] 3 Or *corrupt* [e] 14 The meaning of the Hebrew for this word is uncertain. [f] 15 That is, about 450 feet long, 75 feet wide and 45 feet high or about 135 meters long, 23 meters wide and 14 meters high [g] 16 That is, about 18 inches or about 45 centimeters [h] 16 The meaning of the Hebrew for this clause is uncertain.

kind of bird, male and female, to keep their
various kinds alive throughout the earth.
[4]Seven days from now I will send rain on the
earth for forty days and forty nights, and I
will wipe from the face of the earth every living creature I have made."
[5]And Noah did all that the LORD commanded him.
[6]Noah was six hundred years old when the
floodwaters came on the earth. [7]And Noah
and his sons and his wife and his sons' wives
entered the ark to escape the waters of the
flood. [8]Pairs of clean and unclean animals,
of birds and of all creatures that move along
the ground, [9]male and female, came to Noah
and entered the ark, as God had commanded
Noah. [10]And after the seven days the floodwaters came on the earth.
[11]In the six hundredth year of Noah's life, on
the seventeenth day of the second month—on
that day all the springs of the great deep burst
forth, and the floodgates of the heavens were
opened. [12]And rain fell on the earth forty days
and forty nights.
[13]On that very day Noah and his sons, Shem,
Ham and Japheth, together with his wife and
the wives of his three sons, entered the ark.
[14]They had with them every wild animal according to its kind, all livestock according to
their kinds, every creature that moves along
the ground according to its kind and every bird
according to its kind, everything with wings.
[15]Pairs of all creatures that have the breath of
life in them came to Noah and entered the ark.
[16]The animals going in were male and female
of every living thing, as God had commanded
Noah. Then the LORD shut him in.
[17]For forty days the flood kept coming on
the earth, and as the waters increased they
lifted the ark high above the earth. [18]The waters rose and increased greatly on the earth,
and the ark floated on the surface of the water. [19]They rose greatly on the earth, and all
the high mountains under the entire heavens
were covered. [20]The waters rose and covered
the mountains to a depth of more than fifteen
cubits.[a,b] [21]Every living thing that moved on
land perished—birds, livestock, wild animals,
all the creatures that swarm over the earth,
and all mankind. [22]Everything on dry land
that had the breath of life in its nostrils died.
[23]Every living thing on the face of the earth
was wiped out; people and animals and the
creatures that move along the ground and the
birds were wiped from the earth. Only Noah
was left, and those with him in the ark.
[24]The waters flooded the earth for a hundred and fifty days.

8 But God remembered Noah and all the
wild animals and the livestock that were
with him in the ark, and he sent a wind over
the earth, and the waters receded. [2]Now the
springs of the deep and the floodgates of the
heavens had been closed, and the rain had
stopped falling from the sky. [3]The water receded steadily from the earth. At the end of
the hundred and fifty days the water had
gone down, [4]and on the seventeenth day of
the seventh month the ark came to rest on the
mountains of Ararat. [5]The waters continued
to recede until the tenth month, and on the
first day of the tenth month the tops of the
mountains became visible.
[6]After forty days Noah opened a window
he had made in the ark [7]and sent out a raven,
and it kept flying back and forth until the
water had dried up from the earth. [8]Then he
sent out a dove to see if the water had receded
from the surface of the ground. [9]But the dove
could find nowhere to perch because there
was water over all the surface of the earth;
so it returned to Noah in the ark. He reached
out his hand and took the dove and brought it
back to himself in the ark. [10]He waited seven
more days and again sent out the dove from
the ark. [11]When the dove returned to him in
the evening, there in its beak was a freshly
plucked olive leaf! Then Noah knew that the
water had receded from the earth. [12]He waited
seven more days and sent the dove out again,
but this time it did not return to him.
[13]By the first day of the first month of Noah's six hundred and first year, the water had
dried up from the earth. Noah then removed
the covering from the ark and saw that the
surface of the ground was dry. [14]By the twenty-seventh day of the second month the earth
was completely dry.
[15]Then God said to Noah, [16]"Come out of
the ark, you and your wife and your sons and
their wives. [17]Bring out every kind of living
creature that is with you—the birds, the animals, and all the creatures that move along
the ground—so they can multiply on the earth
and be fruitful and increase in number on it."
[18]So Noah came out, together with his sons
and his wife and his sons' wives. [19]All the animals and all the creatures that move along
the ground and all the birds—everything that
moves on land—came out of the ark, one kind
after another.
[20]Then Noah built an altar to the LORD and,
taking some of all the clean animals and clean
birds, he sacrificed burnt offerings on it. [21]The
LORD smelled the pleasing aroma and said in
his heart: "Never again will I curse the ground
because of humans, even though[c] every inclination of the human heart is evil from childhood. And never again will I destroy all living
creatures, as I have done.

[22]"As long as the earth endures,
seedtime and harvest,
cold and heat,
summer and winter,
day and night
will never cease."

God's Covenant With Noah

9 Then God blessed Noah and his sons,
saying to them, "Be fruitful and increase
in number and fill the earth. [2]The fear and

[a] 20 That is, about 23 feet or about 6.8 meters [b] 20 Or *rose more than fifteen cubits, and the mountains were covered* [c] 21 Or *humans, for*

dread of you will fall on all the beasts of the
earth, and on all the birds in the sky, on every
creature that moves along the ground, and
on all the fish in the sea; they are given into
your hands. 3Everything that lives and moves
about will be food for you. Just as I gave you
the green plants, I now give you everything.
4"But you must not eat meat that has its lifeblood still in it. 5And for your lifeblood I will
surely demand an accounting. I will demand
an accounting from every animal. And from
each human being, too, I will demand an accounting for the life of another human being.

6"Whoever sheds human blood,
by humans shall their blood be shed;
for in the image of God
has God made mankind.

7As for you, be fruitful and increase in number;
multiply on the earth and increase upon it."
8Then God said to Noah and to his sons with
him: 9"I now establish my covenant with you
and with your descendants after you 10and with
every living creature that was with you—the
birds, the livestock and all the wild animals, all
those that came out of the ark with you—every living creature on earth. 11I establish my
covenant with you: Never again will all life
be destroyed by the waters of a flood; never
again will there be a flood to destroy the earth."
12And God said, "This is the sign of the covenant I am making between me and you and
every living creature with you, a covenant
for all generations to come: 13I have set my
rainbow in the clouds, and it will be the sign
of the covenant between me and the earth.
14Whenever I bring clouds over the earth and
the rainbow appears in the clouds, 15I will remember my covenant between me and you
and all living creatures of every kind. Never
again will the waters become a flood to destroy all life. 16Whenever the rainbow appears
in the clouds, I will see it and remember the
everlasting covenant between God and all
living creatures of every kind on the earth."
17So God said to Noah, "This is the sign of
the covenant I have established between me
and all life on the earth."

The Sons of Noah

18The sons of Noah who came out of the ark
were Shem, Ham and Japheth. (Ham was the
father of Canaan.) 19These were the three sons
of Noah, and from them came the people who
were scattered over the whole earth.
20Noah, a man of the soil, proceeded[a] to
plant a vineyard. 21When he drank some of
its wine, he became drunk and lay uncovered
inside his tent. 22Ham, the father of Canaan,
saw his father naked and told his two brothers outside. 23But Shem and Japheth took a
garment and laid it across their shoulders;
then they walked in backward and covered
their father's naked body. Their faces were
turned the other way so that they would not
see their father naked.
24When Noah awoke from his wine and
found out what his youngest son had done to
him, 25he said,

"Cursed be Canaan!
The lowest of slaves
will he be to his brothers."

26He also said,

"Praise be to the LORD, the God of Shem!
May Canaan be the slave of Shem.
27May God extend Japheth's[b] territory;
may Japheth live in the tents of Shem,
and may Canaan be the slave of
Japheth."

28After the flood Noah lived 350 years.
29Noah lived a total of 950 years, and then
he died.

The Table of Nations

10 This is the account of Shem, Ham and
Japheth, Noah's sons, who themselves
had sons after the flood.

The Japhethites

2The sons[c] of Japheth:
Gomer, Magog, Madai, Javan, Tubal,
Meshek and Tiras.
3The sons of Gomer:
Ashkenaz, Riphath and Togarmah.
4The sons of Javan:
Elishah, Tarshish, the Kittites and the
Rodanites.[d] 5(From these the maritime
peoples spread out into their territories
by their clans within their nations, each
with its own language.)

The Hamites

6The sons of Ham:
Cush, Egypt, Put and Canaan.
7The sons of Cush:
Seba, Havilah, Sabtah, Raamah and
Sabteka.
The sons of Raamah:
Sheba and Dedan.

8Cush was the father[e] of Nimrod, who became a mighty warrior on the earth. 9He was
a mighty hunter before the LORD; that is why it
is said, "Like Nimrod, a mighty hunter before
the LORD." 10The first centers of his kingdom
were Babylon, Uruk, Akkad and Kalneh, in[f]
Shinar.[g] 11From that land he went to Assyria,
where he built Nineveh, Rehoboth Ir,[h] Calah
12and Resen, which is between Nineveh and
Calah—which is the great city.

13Egypt was the father of
the Ludites, Anamites, Lehabites,

[a] 20 Or *soil, was the first* [b] 27 *Japheth* sounds like the Hebrew for *extend.* [c] 2 *Sons* may mean *descendants* or *successors* or *nations*; also in verses 3, 4, 6, 7, 20-23, 29 and 31. [d] 4 Some manuscripts of the Masoretic Text and Samaritan Pentateuch (see also Septuagint and 1 Chron. 1:7); most manuscripts of the Masoretic Text *Dodanites* [e] 8 *Father* may mean *ancestor* or *predecessor* or *founder*; also in verses 13, 15, 24 and 26. [f] 10 Or *Uruk and Akkad—all of them in* [g] 10 That is, Babylonia [h] 11 Or *Nineveh with its city squares*

Naphtuhites, 14Pathrusites, Kasluhites
(from whom the Philistines came) and
Caphtorites.
15Canaan was the father of
Sidon his firstborn,[a] and of the Hittites,
16Jebusites, Amorites, Girgashites,
17Hivites, Arkites, Sinites, 18Arvadites,
Zemarites and Hamathites.

Later the Canaanite clans scattered 19and
the borders of Canaan reached from Sidon
toward Gerar as far as Gaza, and then toward
Sodom, Gomorrah, Admah and Zeboyim, as
far as Lasha.
20These are the sons of Ham by their clans
and languages, in their territories and nations.

The Semites

21Sons were also born to Shem, whose older
brother was[b] Japheth; Shem was the ancestor
of all the sons of Eber.

22The sons of Shem:
Elam, Ashur, Arphaxad, Lud and
Aram.
23The sons of Aram:
Uz, Hul, Gether and Meshek.[c]
24Arphaxad was the father of[d] Shelah,
and Shelah the father of Eber.
25Two sons were born to Eber:
One was named Peleg,[e] because in his
time the earth was divided; his brother
was named Joktan.
26Joktan was the father of
Almodad, Sheleph, Hazarmaveth, Jerah, 27Hadoram, Uzal, Diklah, 28Obal,
Abimael, Sheba, 29Ophir, Havilah and
Jobab. All these were sons of Joktan.

30The region where they lived stretched from Mesha toward Sephar, in the eastern hill country.
31These are the sons of Shem by their clans
and languages, in their territories and nations.

32These are the clans of Noah's sons, according to their lines of descent, within their
nations. From these the nations spread out
over the earth after the flood.

The Tower of Babel

11 Now the whole world had one language
and a common speech. 2As people
moved eastward,[f] they found a plain in Shinar[g] and settled there.
3They said to each other, "Come, let's make
bricks and bake them thoroughly." They used
brick instead of stone, and tar for mortar.
4Then they said, "Come, let us build ourselves
a city, with a tower that reaches to the heavens, so that we may make a name for ourselves; otherwise we will be scattered over
the face of the whole earth."
5But the LORD came down to see the city and
the tower the people were building. 6The LORD
said, "If as one people speaking the same language they have begun to do this, then nothing they plan to do will be impossible for them.
7Come, let us go down and confuse their language so they will not understand each other."
8So the LORD scattered them from there over
all the earth, and they stopped building the
city. 9That is why it was called Babel[h]—because there the LORD confused the language
of the whole world. From there the LORD scattered them over the face of the whole earth.

From Shem to Abram

10This is the account of Shem's family line.

Two years after the flood, when Shem was
100 years old, he became the father[i] of Arphaxad. 11And after he became the father of
Arphaxad, Shem lived 500 years and had other sons and daughters.
12When Arphaxad had lived 35 years, he
became the father of Shelah. 13And after he
became the father of Shelah, Arphaxad lived
403 years and had other sons and daughters.[j]
14When Shelah had lived 30 years, he became the father of Eber. 15And after he became the father of Eber, Shelah lived 403
years and had other sons and daughters.
16When Eber had lived 34 years, he became
the father of Peleg. 17And after he became the
father of Peleg, Eber lived 430 years and had
other sons and daughters.
18When Peleg had lived 30 years, he became
the father of Reu. 19And after he became the
father of Reu, Peleg lived 209 years and had
other sons and daughters.
20When Reu had lived 32 years, he became
the father of Serug. 21And after he became the
father of Serug, Reu lived 207 years and had
other sons and daughters.
22When Serug had lived 30 years, he became the father of Nahor. 23And after he became the father of Nahor, Serug lived 200
years and had other sons and daughters.
24When Nahor had lived 29 years, he became the father of Terah. 25And after he became the father of Terah, Nahor lived 119
years and had other sons and daughters.
26After Terah had lived 70 years, he became
the father of Abram, Nahor and Haran.

Abram's Family

27This is the account of Terah's family line.

Terah became the father of Abram, Nahor
and Haran. And Haran became the father of

[a] 15 Or *of the Sidonians, the foremost* [b] 21 Or *Shem, the older brother of* [c] 23 See Septuagint and 1 Chron. 1:17; Hebrew *Mash.* [d] 24 Hebrew; Septuagint *father of Cainan, and Cainan was the father of* [e] 25 *Peleg* means *division.* [f] 2 Or *from the east*; or *in the east* [g] 2 That is, Babylonia [h] 9 That is, Babylon; *Babel* sounds like the Hebrew for *confused.* [i] 10 *Father* may mean *ancestor*; also in verses 11-25. [j] 12,13 Hebrew; Septuagint (see also Luke 3:35, 36 and note at Gen. 10:24) *35 years, he became the father of Cainan. 13And after he became the father of Cainan, Arphaxad lived 430 years and had other sons and daughters, and then he died. When Cainan had lived 130 years, he became the father of Shelah. And after he became the father of Shelah, Cainan lived 330 years and had other sons and daughters*

Lot. 28While his father Terah was still alive,
Haran died in Ur of the Chaldeans, in the land
of his birth. 29Abram and Nahor both married.
The name of Abram's wife was Sarai, and the
name of Nahor's wife was Milkah; she was the
daughter of Haran, the father of both Milkah
and Iskah. 30Now Sarai was childless because
she was not able to conceive.
31Terah took his son Abram, his grandson
Lot son of Haran, and his daughter-in-law Sarai, the wife of his son Abram, and together
they set out from Ur of the Chaldeans to go
to Canaan. But when they came to Harran,
they settled there.
32Terah lived 205 years, and he died in Harran.

The Call of Abram

12 The LORD had said to Abram, "Go from
your country, your people and your father's household to the land I will show you.

2"I will make you into a great nation,
and I will bless you;
I will make your name great,
and you will be a blessing.[a]
3I will bless those who bless you,
and whoever curses you I will curse;
and all peoples on earth
will be blessed through you."[b]

4So Abram went, as the LORD had told him;
and Lot went with him. Abram was seventy-
five years old when he set out from Harran.
5He took his wife Sarai, his nephew Lot, all
the possessions they had accumulated and
the people they had acquired in Harran, and
they set out for the land of Canaan, and they
arrived there.
6Abram traveled through the land as far as
the site of the great tree of Moreh at Shechem.
At that time the Canaanites were in the land.
7The LORD appeared to Abram and said, "To
your offspring[c] I will give this land." So he
built an altar there to the LORD, who had appeared to him.
8From there he went on toward the hills east
of Bethel and pitched his tent, with Bethel on
the west and Ai on the east. There he built
an altar to the LORD and called on the name
of the LORD.
9Then Abram set out and continued toward
the Negev.

Abram in Egypt

10Now there was a famine in the land, and
Abram went down to Egypt to live there for a
while because the famine was severe. 11As he
was about to enter Egypt, he said to his wife
Sarai, "I know what a beautiful woman you
are. 12When the Egyptians see you, they will
say, 'This is his wife.' Then they will kill me
but will let you live. 13Say you are my sister,
so that I will be treated well for your sake and
my life will be spared because of you."
14When Abram came to Egypt, the Egyptians saw that Sarai was a very beautiful
woman. 15And when Pharaoh's officials saw
her, they praised her to Pharaoh, and she was
taken into his palace. 16He treated Abram well
for her sake, and Abram acquired sheep and
cattle, male and female donkeys, male and
female servants, and camels.
17But the LORD inflicted serious diseases
on Pharaoh and his household because of
Abram's wife Sarai. 18So Pharaoh summoned
Abram. "What have you done to me?" he said.
"Why didn't you tell me she was your wife?
19Why did you say, 'She is my sister,' so that
I took her to be my wife? Now then, here is
your wife. Take her and go!" 20Then Pharaoh
gave orders about Abram to his men, and they
sent him on his way, with his wife and everything he had.

Abram and Lot Separate

13 So Abram went up from Egypt to the
Negev, with his wife and everything he
had, and Lot went with him. 2Abram had become very wealthy in livestock and in silver
and gold.
3From the Negev he went from place to place
until he came to Bethel, to the place between
Bethel and Ai where his tent had been earlier
4and where he had first built an altar. There
Abram called on the name of the LORD.
5Now Lot, who was moving about with
Abram, also had flocks and herds and tents.
6But the land could not support them while
they stayed together, for their possessions
were so great that they were not able to stay
together. 7And quarreling arose between
Abram's herders and Lot's. The Canaanites
and Perizzites were also living in the land
at that time.
8So Abram said to Lot, "Let's not have any
quarreling between you and me, or between
your herders and mine, for we are close relatives. 9Is not the whole land before you?
Let's part company. If you go to the left, I'll
go to the right; if you go to the right, I'll go
to the left."
10Lot looked around and saw that the
whole plain of the Jordan toward Zoar was
well watered, like the garden of the LORD,
like the land of Egypt. (This was before the
LORD destroyed Sodom and Gomorrah.) 11So
Lot chose for himself the whole plain of the
Jordan and set out toward the east. The two
men parted company: 12Abram lived in the
land of Canaan, while Lot lived among the
cities of the plain and pitched his tents near
Sodom. 13Now the people of Sodom were
wicked and were sinning greatly against
the LORD.
14The LORD said to Abram after Lot had
parted from him, "Look around from where
you are, to the north and south, to the east
and west. 15All the land that you see I will
give to you and your offspring[d] forever. 16I
will make your offspring like the dust of the
earth, so that if anyone could count the dust,
then your offspring could be counted. 17Go,

[a] 2 Or *be seen as blessed* [b] 3 Or *earth / will use your name in blessings* (see 48:20) [c] 7 Or *seed*
[d] 15 Or *seed*; also in verse 16

walk through the length and breadth of the
land, for I am giving it to you."
18So Abram went to live near the great trees
of Mamre at Hebron, where he pitched his
tents. There he built an altar to the LORD.

Abram Rescues Lot

14 At the time when Amraphel was king of
Shinar,[a] Arioch king of Ellasar, Kedorlaomer king of Elam and Tidal king of Goyim,
2these kings went to war against Bera king
of Sodom, Birsha king of Gomorrah, Shinab
king of Admah, Shemeber king of Zeboyim,
and the king of Bela (that is, Zoar). 3All these
latter kings joined forces in the Valley of Siddim (that is, the Dead Sea Valley). 4For twelve
years they had been subject to Kedorlaomer,
but in the thirteenth year they rebelled.
5In the fourteenth year, Kedorlaomer and
the kings allied with him went out and defeated the Rephaites in Ashteroth Karnaim, the
Zuzites in Ham, the Emites in Shaveh Kiriathaim 6and the Horites in the hill country of
Seir, as far as El Paran near the desert. 7Then
they turned back and went to En Mishpat (that
is, Kadesh), and they conquered the whole territory of the Amalekites, as well as the Amorites who were living in Hazezon Tamar.
8Then the king of Sodom, the king of Gomorrah, the king of Admah, the king of Zeboyim and the king of Bela (that is, Zoar)
marched out and drew up their battle lines
in the Valley of Siddim 9against Kedorlaomer
king of Elam, Tidal king of Goyim, Amraphel
king of Shinar and Arioch king of Ellasar—
four kings against five. 10Now the Valley of
Siddim was full of tar pits, and when the kings
of Sodom and Gomorrah fled, some of the men
fell into them and the rest fled to the hills.
11The four kings seized all the goods of Sodom
and Gomorrah and all their food; then they
went away. 12They also carried off Abram's
nephew Lot and his possessions, since he was
living in Sodom.
13A man who had escaped came and reported this to Abram the Hebrew. Now Abram
was living near the great trees of Mamre the
Amorite, a brother[b] of Eshkol and Aner, all
of whom were allied with Abram. 14When
Abram heard that his relative had been taken
captive, he called out the 318 trained men born
in his household and went in pursuit as far as
Dan. 15During the night Abram divided his
men to attack them and he routed them, pursuing them as far as Hobah, north of Damascus.
16He recovered all the goods and brought back
his relative Lot and his possessions, together
with the women and the other people.
17After Abram returned from defeating
Kedorlaomer and the kings allied with him,
the king of Sodom came out to meet him in the
Valley of Shaveh (that is, the King's Valley).
18Then Melchizedek king of Salem brought
out bread and wine. He was priest of God Most
High, 19and he blessed Abram, saying,

"Blessed be Abram by God Most High,
Creator of heaven and earth.
20 And praise be to God Most High,
who delivered your enemies into your
hand."

Then Abram gave him a tenth of everything.
21The king of Sodom said to Abram, "Give
me the people and keep the goods for yourself."
22But Abram said to the king of Sodom,
"With raised hand I have sworn an oath to the
LORD, God Most High, Creator of heaven and
earth, 23that I will accept nothing belonging to
you, not even a thread or the strap of a sandal,
so that you will never be able to say, 'I made
Abram rich.' 24I will accept nothing but what
my men have eaten and the share that belongs
to the men who went with me—to Aner, Eshkol and Mamre. Let them have their share."

The LORD's Covenant With Abram

15 After this, the word of the LORD came
to Abram in a vision:

"Do not be afraid, Abram.
I am your shield,[c]
your very great reward.[d]"

2But Abram said, "Sovereign LORD, what
can you give me since I remain childless and
the one who will inherit[e] my estate is Eliezer of Damascus?" 3And Abram said, "You
have given me no children; so a servant in
my household will be my heir."
4Then the word of the LORD came to him:
"This man will not be your heir, but a son who
is your own flesh and blood will be your heir."
5He took him outside and said, "Look up at the
sky and count the stars—if indeed you can
count them." Then he said to him, "So shall
your offspring[f] be."
6Abram believed the LORD, and he credited
it to him as righteousness.
7He also said to him, "I am the LORD, who
brought you out of Ur of the Chaldeans to give
you this land to take possession of it."
8But Abram said, "Sovereign LORD, how
can I know that I will gain possession of it?"
9So the LORD said to him, "Bring me a heifer,
a goat and a ram, each three years old, along
with a dove and a young pigeon."
10Abram brought all these to him, cut them
in two and arranged the halves opposite each
other; the birds, however, he did not cut in
half. 11Then birds of prey came down on the
carcasses, but Abram drove them away.
12As the sun was setting, Abram fell into
a deep sleep, and a thick and dreadful darkness came over him. 13Then the LORD said to
him, "Know for certain that for four hundred
years your descendants will be strangers in
a country not their own and that they will
be enslaved and mistreated there. 14But I
will punish the nation they serve as slaves,
and afterward they will come out with great

[a] *1* That is, Babylonia; also in verse 9 [b] *13* Or *a relative;* or *an ally* [c] *1* Or *sovereign*
[d] *1* Or *shield; / your reward will be very great* [e] *2* The meaning of the Hebrew for this phrase is uncertain. [f] *5* Or *seed*

possessions. 15 You, however, will go to your
ancestors in peace and be buried at a good
old age. 16 In the fourth generation your descendants will come back here, for the sin
of the Amorites has not yet reached its full
measure."
17 When the sun had set and darkness had
fallen, a smoking firepot with a blazing torch
appeared and passed between the pieces.
18 On that day the LORD made a covenant
with Abram and said, "To your descendants
I give this land, from the Wadi[a] of Egypt to the
great river, the Euphrates— 19 the land of the
Kenites, Kenizzites, Kadmonites, 20 Hittites,
Perizzites, Rephaites, 21 Amorites, Canaanites,
Girgashites and Jebusites."

Hagar and Ishmael

16 Now Sarai, Abram's wife, had borne him
no children. But she had an Egyptian
slave named Hagar; 2 so she said to Abram,
"The LORD has kept me from having children.
Go, sleep with my slave; perhaps I can build
a family through her."
Abram agreed to what Sarai said. 3 So after
Abram had been living in Canaan ten years,
Sarai his wife took her Egyptian slave Hagar
and gave her to her husband to be his wife. 4 He
slept with Hagar, and she conceived.
When she knew she was pregnant, she began to despise her mistress. 5 Then Sarai said
to Abram, "You are responsible for the wrong
I am suffering. I put my slave in your arms,
and now that she knows she is pregnant, she
despises me. May the LORD judge between
you and me."
6 "Your slave is in your hands," Abram said.
"Do with her whatever you think best." Then
Sarai mistreated Hagar; so she fled from her.
7 The angel of the LORD found Hagar near a
spring in the desert; it was the spring that is
beside the road to Shur. 8 And he said, "Hagar,
slave of Sarai, where have you come from, and
where are you going?"
"I'm running away from my mistress Sarai," she answered.
9 Then the angel of the LORD told her, "Go
back to your mistress and submit to her." 10 The
angel added, "I will increase your descendants
so much that they will be too numerous to
count."
11 The angel of the LORD also said to her:

"You are now pregnant
and you will give birth to a son.
You shall name him Ishmael,[b]
for the LORD has heard of your misery.
12 He will be a wild donkey of a man;
his hand will be against everyone
and everyone's hand against him,
and he will live in hostility
toward[c] all his brothers."

13 She gave this name to the LORD who spoke
to her: "You are the God who sees me," for
she said, "I have now seen[d] the One who sees
me." 14 That is why the well was called Beer
Lahai Roi[e]; it is still there, between Kadesh
and Bered.
15 So Hagar bore Abram a son, and Abram
gave the name Ishmael to the son she had
borne. 16 Abram was eighty-six years old when
Hagar bore him Ishmael.

The Covenant of Circumcision

17 When Abram was ninety-nine years old,
the LORD appeared to him and said, "I
am God Almighty[f]; walk before me faithfully
and be blameless. 2 Then I will make my covenant between me and you and will greatly
increase your numbers."
3 Abram fell facedown, and God said to him,
4 "As for me, this is my covenant with you:
You will be the father of many nations. 5 No
longer will you be called Abram[g]; your name
will be Abraham,[h] for I have made you a father of many nations. 6 I will make you very
fruitful; I will make nations of you, and kings
will come from you. 7 I will establish my covenant as an everlasting covenant between me
and you and your descendants after you for
the generations to come, to be your God and
the God of your descendants after you. 8 The
whole land of Canaan, where you now reside
as a foreigner, I will give as an everlasting
possession to you and your descendants after
you; and I will be their God."
9 Then God said to Abraham, "As for you,
you must keep my covenant, you and your
descendants after you for the generations to
come. 10 This is my covenant with you and
your descendants after you, the covenant you
are to keep: Every male among you shall be
circumcised. 11 You are to undergo circumcision, and it will be the sign of the covenant
between me and you. 12 For the generations
to come every male among you who is eight
days old must be circumcised, including those
born in your household or bought with money from a foreigner—those who are not your
offspring. 13 Whether born in your household
or bought with your money, they must be circumcised. My covenant in your flesh is to be
an everlasting covenant. 14 Any uncircumcised
male, who has not been circumcised in the
flesh, will be cut off from his people; he has
broken my covenant."
15 God also said to Abraham, "As for Sarai
your wife, you are no longer to call her Sarai;
her name will be Sarah. 16 I will bless her and
will surely give you a son by her. I will bless
her so that she will be the mother of nations;
kings of peoples will come from her."
17 Abraham fell facedown; he laughed and
said to himself, "Will a son be born to a man
a hundred years old? Will Sarah bear a child
at the age of ninety?" 18 And Abraham said to
God, "If only Ishmael might live under your
blessing!"
19 Then God said, "Yes, but your wife Sarah will bear you a son, and you will call him

[a] 18 Or *river* [b] 11 *Ishmael* means *God hears.* [c] 12 Or *live to the east of* [d] 13 Or *seen the back of* [e] 14 *Beer Lahai Roi* means *well of the Living One who sees me.* [f] 1 Hebrew *El-Shaddai* [g] 5 *Abram* means *exalted father.* [h] 5 *Abraham* probably means *father of many.*

Isaac.[a] I will establish my covenant with him as an everlasting covenant for his descendants after him. [20]And as for Ishmael, I have heard you: I will surely bless him; I will make him fruitful and will greatly increase his numbers. He will be the father of twelve rulers, and I will make him into a great nation. [21]But my covenant I will establish with Isaac, whom Sarah will bear to you by this time next year." [22]When he had finished speaking with Abraham, God went up from him.

[23]On that very day Abraham took his son Ishmael and all those born in his household or bought with his money, every male in his household, and circumcised them, as God told him. [24]Abraham was ninety-nine years old when he was circumcised, [25]and his son Ishmael was thirteen; [26]Abraham and his son Ishmael were both circumcised on that very day. [27]And every male in Abraham's household, including those born in his household or bought from a foreigner, was circumcised with him.

The Three Visitors

18 The LORD appeared to Abraham near the great trees of Mamre while he was sitting at the entrance to his tent in the heat of the day. [2]Abraham looked up and saw three men standing nearby. When he saw them, he hurried from the entrance of his tent to meet them and bowed low to the ground.

[3]He said, "If I have found favor in your eyes, my lord,[b] do not pass your servant by. [4]Let a little water be brought, and then you may all wash your feet and rest under this tree. [5]Let me get you something to eat, so you can be refreshed and then go on your way—now that you have come to your servant."

"Very well," they answered, "do as you say."

[6]So Abraham hurried into the tent to Sarah. "Quick," he said, "get three seahs[c] of the finest flour and knead it and bake some bread."

[7]Then he ran to the herd and selected a choice, tender calf and gave it to a servant, who hurried to prepare it. [8]He then brought some curds and milk and the calf that had been prepared, and set these before them. While they ate, he stood near them under a tree.

[9]"Where is your wife Sarah?" they asked him.

"There, in the tent," he said.

[10]Then one of them said, "I will surely return to you about this time next year, and Sarah your wife will have a son."

Now Sarah was listening at the entrance to the tent, which was behind him. [11]Abraham and Sarah were already very old, and Sarah was past the age of childbearing. [12]So Sarah laughed to herself as she thought, "After I am worn out and my lord is old, will I now have this pleasure?"

[13]Then the LORD said to Abraham, "Why did Sarah laugh and say, 'Will I really have a child, now that I am old?' [14]Is anything too hard for the LORD? I will return to you at the appointed time next year, and Sarah will have a son."

[15]Sarah was afraid, so she lied and said, "I did not laugh."

But he said, "Yes, you did laugh."

Abraham Pleads for Sodom

[16]When the men got up to leave, they looked down toward Sodom, and Abraham walked along with them to see them on their way. [17]Then the LORD said, "Shall I hide from Abraham what I am about to do? [18]Abraham will surely become a great and powerful nation, and all nations on earth will be blessed through him.[d] [19]For I have chosen him, so that he will direct his children and his household after him to keep the way of the LORD by doing what is right and just, so that the LORD will bring about for Abraham what he has promised him."

[20]Then the LORD said, "The outcry against Sodom and Gomorrah is so great and their sin so grievous [21]that I will go down and see if what they have done is as bad as the outcry that has reached me. If not, I will know."

[22]The men turned away and went toward Sodom, but Abraham remained standing before the LORD.[e] [23]Then Abraham approached him and said: "Will you sweep away the righteous with the wicked? [24]What if there are fifty righteous people in the city? Will you really sweep it away and not spare[f] the place for the sake of the fifty righteous people in it? [25]Far be it from you to do such a thing—to kill the righteous with the wicked, treating the righteous and the wicked alike. Far be it from you! Will not the Judge of all the earth do right?"

[26]The LORD said, "If I find fifty righteous people in the city of Sodom, I will spare the whole place for their sake."

[27]Then Abraham spoke up again: "Now that I have been so bold as to speak to the Lord, though I am nothing but dust and ashes, [28]what if the number of the righteous is five less than fifty? Will you destroy the whole city for lack of five people?"

"If I find forty-five there," he said, "I will not destroy it."

[29]Once again he spoke to him, "What if only forty are found there?"

He said, "For the sake of forty, I will not do it."

[30]Then he said, "May the Lord not be angry, but let me speak. What if only thirty can be found there?"

He answered, "I will not do it if I find thirty there."

[31]Abraham said, "Now that I have been so bold as to speak to the Lord, what if only twenty can be found there?"

[a] *19 Isaac* means *he laughs.* [b] *3* Or *eyes, Lord* [c] *6* That is, probably about 36 pounds or about 16 kilograms [d] *18* Or *will use his name in blessings* (see 48:20) [e] *22* Masoretic Text; an ancient Hebrew scribal tradition *but the LORD remained standing before Abraham* [f] *24* Or *forgive*; also in verse 26

He said, "For the sake of twenty, I will not destroy it."

32Then he said, "May the Lord not be angry, but let me speak just once more. What if only ten can be found there?"

He answered, "For the sake of ten, I will not destroy it."

33When the LORD had finished speaking with Abraham, he left, and Abraham returned home.

Sodom and Gomorrah Destroyed

19 The two angels arrived at Sodom in the evening, and Lot was sitting in the gateway of the city. When he saw them, he got up to meet them and bowed down with his face to the ground. 2"My lords," he said, "please turn aside to your servant's house. You can wash your feet and spend the night and then go on your way early in the morning."

"No," they answered, "we will spend the night in the square."

3But he insisted so strongly that they did go with him and entered his house. He prepared a meal for them, baking bread without yeast, and they ate. 4Before they had gone to bed, all the men from every part of the city of Sodom—both young and old—surrounded the house. 5They called to Lot, "Where are the men who came to you tonight? Bring them out to us so that we can have sex with them."

6Lot went outside to meet them and shut the door behind him 7and said, "No, my friends. Don't do this wicked thing. 8Look, I have two daughters who have never slept with a man. Let me bring them out to you, and you can do what you like with them. But don't do anything to these men, for they have come under the protection of my roof."

9"Get out of our way," they replied. "This fellow came here as a foreigner, and now he wants to play the judge! We'll treat you worse than them." They kept bringing pressure on Lot and moved forward to break down the door.

10But the men inside reached out and pulled Lot back into the house and shut the door. 11Then they struck the men who were at the door of the house, young and old, with blindness so that they could not find the door.

12The two men said to Lot, "Do you have anyone else here—sons-in-law, sons or daughters, or anyone else in the city who belongs to you? Get them out of here, 13because we are going to destroy this place. The outcry to the LORD against its people is so great that he has sent us to destroy it."

14So Lot went out and spoke to his sons-in-law, who were pledged to marry[a] his daughters. He said, "Hurry and get out of this place, because the LORD is about to destroy the city!" But his sons-in-law thought he was joking.

15With the coming of dawn, the angels urged Lot, saying, "Hurry! Take your wife and your two daughters who are here, or you will be swept away when the city is punished."

16When he hesitated, the men grasped his hand and the hands of his wife and of his two daughters and led them safely out of the city, for the LORD was merciful to them. 17As soon as they had brought them out, one of them said, "Flee for your lives! Don't look back, and don't stop anywhere in the plain! Flee to the mountains or you will be swept away!"

18But Lot said to them, "No, my lords,[b] please! 19Your[c] servant has found favor in your[c] eyes, and you[c] have shown great kindness to me in sparing my life. But I can't flee to the mountains; this disaster will overtake me, and I'll die. 20Look, here is a town near enough to run to, and it is small. Let me flee to it—it is very small, isn't it? Then my life will be spared."

21He said to him, "Very well, I will grant this request too; I will not overthrow the town you speak of. 22But flee there quickly, because I cannot do anything until you reach it." (That is why the town was called Zoar.[d])

23By the time Lot reached Zoar, the sun had risen over the land. 24Then the LORD rained down burning sulfur on Sodom and Gomorrah—from the LORD out of the heavens. 25Thus he overthrew those cities and the entire plain, destroying all those living in the cities—and also the vegetation in the land. 26But Lot's wife looked back, and she became a pillar of salt.

27Early the next morning Abraham got up and returned to the place where he had stood before the LORD. 28He looked down toward Sodom and Gomorrah, toward all the land of the plain, and he saw dense smoke rising from the land, like smoke from a furnace.

29So when God destroyed the cities of the plain, he remembered Abraham, and he brought Lot out of the catastrophe that overthrew the cities where Lot had lived.

Lot and His Daughters

30Lot and his two daughters left Zoar and settled in the mountains, for he was afraid to stay in Zoar. He and his two daughters lived in a cave. 31One day the older daughter said to the younger, "Our father is old, and there is no man around here to give us children—as is the custom all over the earth. 32Let's get our father to drink wine and then sleep with him and preserve our family line through our father."

33That night they got their father to drink wine, and the older daughter went in and slept with him. He was not aware of it when she lay down or when she got up.

34The next day the older daughter said to the younger, "Last night I slept with my father. Let's get him to drink wine again tonight, and you go in and sleep with him so we can preserve our family line through our father." 35So they got their father to drink wine that night also, and the younger daughter went in and slept with him. Again he was not aware of it when she lay down or when she got up.

36So both of Lot's daughters became pregnant by their father. 37The older daughter had

[a] 14 Or *were married to* [b] 18 Or *No, Lord*; or *No, my lord* [c] 19 The Hebrew is singular..
[d] 22 *Zoar* means *small*.

a son, and she named him Moab[a]; he is the
father of the Moabites of today. 38The younger
daughter also had a son, and she named him
Ben-Ammi[b]; he is the father of the Ammonites[c] of today.

Abraham and Abimelek

20 Now Abraham moved on from there into
the region of the Negev and lived between Kadesh and Shur. For a while he stayed
in Gerar, 2and there Abraham said of his wife
Sarah, "She is my sister." Then Abimelek king
of Gerar sent for Sarah and took her.
3But God came to Abimelek in a dream one
night and said to him, "You are as good as
dead because of the woman you have taken;
she is a married woman."
4Now Abimelek had not gone near her, so he
said, "Lord, will you destroy an innocent nation? 5Did he not say to me, 'She is my sister,'
and didn't she also say, 'He is my brother'? I
have done this with a clear conscience and
clean hands."
6Then God said to him in the dream, "Yes,
I know you did this with a clear conscience,
and so I have kept you from sinning against
me. That is why I did not let you touch her.
7Now return the man's wife, for he is a prophet, and he will pray for you and you will live.
But if you do not return her, you may be sure
that you and all who belong to you will die."
8Early the next morning Abimelek summoned all his officials, and when he told them
all that had happened, they were very much
afraid. 9Then Abimelek called Abraham in
and said, "What have you done to us? How
have I wronged you that you have brought
such great guilt upon me and my kingdom?
You have done things to me that should never
be done." 10And Abimelek asked Abraham,
"What was your reason for doing this?"
11Abraham replied, "I said to myself, 'There
is surely no fear of God in this place, and they
will kill me because of my wife.' 12Besides, she
really is my sister, the daughter of my father
though not of my mother; and she became my
wife. 13And when God had me wander from
my father's household, I said to her, 'This is
how you can show your love to me: Everywhere we go, say of me, "He is my brother." ' "
14Then Abimelek brought sheep and cattle
and male and female slaves and gave them to
Abraham, and he returned Sarah his wife to
him. 15And Abimelek said, "My land is before
you; live wherever you like."
16To Sarah he said, "I am giving your brother a thousand shekels[d] of silver. This is to cover the offense against you before all who are
with you; you are completely vindicated."
17Then Abraham prayed to God, and God
healed Abimelek, his wife and his female
slaves so they could have children again, 18for
the LORD had kept all the women in Abimelek's household from conceiving because of
Abraham's wife Sarah.

The Birth of Isaac

21 Now the LORD was gracious to Sarah as
he had said, and the LORD did for Sarah what he had promised. 2Sarah became
pregnant and bore a son to Abraham in his
old age, at the very time God had promised
him. 3Abraham gave the name Isaac[e] to the
son Sarah bore him. 4When his son Isaac was
eight days old, Abraham circumcised him,
as God commanded him. 5Abraham was a
hundred years old when his son Isaac was
born to him.
6Sarah said, "God has brought me laughter, and everyone who hears about this will
laugh with me." 7And she added, "Who would
have said to Abraham that Sarah would nurse
children? Yet I have borne him a son in his
old age."

Hagar and Ishmael Sent Away

8The child grew and was weaned, and on
the day Isaac was weaned Abraham held a
great feast. 9But Sarah saw that the son whom
Hagar the Egyptian had borne to Abraham
was mocking, 10and she said to Abraham, "Get
rid of that slave woman and her son, for that
woman's son will never share in the inheritance with my son Isaac."
11The matter distressed Abraham greatly
because it concerned his son. 12But God said
to him, "Do not be so distressed about the
boy and your slave woman. Listen to whatever
Sarah tells you, because it is through Isaac
that your offspring[f] will be reckoned. 13I will
make the son of the slave into a nation also,
because he is your offspring."
14Early the next morning Abraham took
some food and a skin of water and gave them
to Hagar. He set them on her shoulders and
then sent her off with the boy. She went on her
way and wandered in the Desert of Beersheba.
15When the water in the skin was gone, she
put the boy under one of the bushes. 16Then
she went off and sat down about a bowshot
away, for she thought, "I cannot watch the boy
die." And as she sat there, she[g] began to sob.
17God heard the boy crying, and the angel
of God called to Hagar from heaven and said
to her, "What is the matter, Hagar? Do not be
afraid; God has heard the boy crying as he lies
there. 18Lift the boy up and take him by the
hand, for I will make him into a great nation."
19Then God opened her eyes and she saw a
well of water. So she went and filled the skin
with water and gave the boy a drink.
20God was with the boy as he grew up. He
lived in the desert and became an archer.
21While he was living in the Desert of Paran,
his mother got a wife for him from Egypt.

The Treaty at Beersheba

22At that time Abimelek and Phicol the commander of his forces said to Abraham, "God is
with you in everything you do. 23Now swear

[a] *37 Moab* sounds like the Hebrew for *from father.* [b] *38 Ben-Ammi* means *son of my father's people.* [c] *38* Hebrew *Bene-Ammon* [d] *16* That is, about 25 pounds or about 12 kilograms [e] *3 Isaac* means *he laughs.* [f] *12* Or *seed* [g] *16* Hebrew; Septuagint *the child*

to me here before God that you will not deal
falsely with me or my children or my descendants. Show to me and the country where you
now reside as a foreigner the same kindness
I have shown to you."
24Abraham said, "I swear it."
25Then Abraham complained to Abimelek
about a well of water that Abimelek's servants
had seized. 26But Abimelek said, "I don't know
who has done this. You did not tell me, and I
heard about it only today."
27So Abraham brought sheep and cattle and
gave them to Abimelek, and the two men made
a treaty. 28Abraham set apart seven ewe lambs
from the flock, 29and Abimelek asked Abraham, "What is the meaning of these seven
ewe lambs you have set apart by themselves?"
30He replied, "Accept these seven lambs
from my hand as a witness that I dug this
well."
31So that place was called Beersheba,[a] because the two men swore an oath there.
32After the treaty had been made at Beersheba, Abimelek and Phicol the commander
of his forces returned to the land of the Philistines. 33Abraham planted a tamarisk tree
in Beersheba, and there he called on the name
of the LORD, the Eternal God. 34And Abraham stayed in the land of the Philistines for
a long time.

Abraham Tested

22 Some time later God tested Abraham.
He said to him, "Abraham!"
"Here I am," he replied.
2Then God said, "Take your son, your only
son, whom you love—Isaac—and go to the
region of Moriah. Sacrifice him there as a
burnt offering on a mountain I will show you."
3Early the next morning Abraham got up
and loaded his donkey. He took with him two
of his servants and his son Isaac. When he had
cut enough wood for the burnt offering, he set
out for the place God had told him about. 4On
the third day Abraham looked up and saw the
place in the distance. 5He said to his servants,
"Stay here with the donkey while I and the
boy go over there. We will worship and then
we will come back to you."
6Abraham took the wood for the burnt offering and placed it on his son Isaac, and he
himself carried the fire and the knife. As the
two of them went on together, 7Isaac spoke
up and said to his father Abraham, "Father?"
"Yes, my son?" Abraham replied.
"The fire and wood are here," Isaac said,
"but where is the lamb for the burnt offering?"
8Abraham answered, "God himself will provide the lamb for the burnt offering, my son."
And the two of them went on together.
9When they reached the place God had told
him about, Abraham built an altar there and
arranged the wood on it. He bound his son
Isaac and laid him on the altar, on top of the
wood. 10Then he reached out his hand and
took the knife to slay his son. 11But the angel
of the LORD called out to him from heaven,
"Abraham! Abraham!"
"Here I am," he replied.
12"Do not lay a hand on the boy," he said.
"Do not do anything to him. Now I know that
you fear God, because you have not withheld
from me your son, your only son."
13Abraham looked up and there in a thicket
he saw a ram[b] caught by its horns. He went
over and took the ram and sacrificed it as a
burnt offering instead of his son. 14So Abraham called that place The LORD Will Provide.
And to this day it is said, "On the mountain of
the LORD it will be provided."
15The angel of the LORD called to Abraham
from heaven a second time 16and said, "I swear
by myself, declares the LORD, that because you
have done this and have not withheld your
son, your only son, 17I will surely bless you
and make your descendants as numerous as
the stars in the sky and as the sand on the seashore. Your descendants will take possession
of the cities of their enemies, 18and through
your offspring[c] all nations on earth will be
blessed,[d] because you have obeyed me."
19Then Abraham returned to his servants,
and they set off together for Beersheba. And
Abraham stayed in Beersheba.

Nahor's Sons

20Some time later Abraham was told, "Milkah is also a mother; she has borne sons to
your brother Nahor: 21Uz the firstborn, Buz
his brother, Kemuel (the father of Aram),
22Kesed, Hazo, Pildash, Jidlaph and Bethuel." 23Bethuel became the father of Rebekah.
Milkah bore these eight sons to Abraham's
brother Nahor. 24His concubine, whose name
was Reumah, also had sons: Tebah, Gaham,
Tahash and Maakah.

The Death of Sarah

23 Sarah lived to be a hundred and twenty-seven years old. 2She died at Kiriath
Arba (that is, Hebron) in the land of Canaan,
and Abraham went to mourn for Sarah and
to weep over her.
3Then Abraham rose from beside his dead
wife and spoke to the Hittites.[e] He said, 4"I am
a foreigner and stranger among you. Sell me
some property for a burial site here so I can
bury my dead."
5The Hittites replied to Abraham, 6"Sir, listen to us. You are a mighty prince among us.
Bury your dead in the choicest of our tombs.
None of us will refuse you his tomb for burying your dead."
7Then Abraham rose and bowed down before the people of the land, the Hittites. 8He
said to them, "If you are willing to let me bury
my dead, then listen to me and intercede with
Ephron son of Zohar on my behalf 9so he will

[a] *31 Beersheba* can mean *well of seven* and *well of the oath.* [b] *13* Many manuscripts of the Masoretic Text, Samaritan Pentateuch, Septuagint and Syriac; most manuscripts of the Masoretic Text *a ram behind him* [c] *18* Or *seed* [d] *18* Or *and all nations on earth will use the name of your offspring in blessings* (see 48:20) [e] *3* Or *the descendants of Heth*; also in verses 5, 7, 10, 16, 18 and 20

sell me the cave of Machpelah, which belongs to him and is at the end of his field. Ask him to sell it to me for the full price as a burial site among you."

10Ephron the Hittite was sitting among his people and he replied to Abraham in the hearing of all the Hittites who had come to the gate of his city. 11"No, my lord," he said. "Listen to me; I give[a] you the field, and I give[a] you the cave that is in it. I give[a] it to you in the presence of my people. Bury your dead."

12Again Abraham bowed down before the people of the land 13and he said to Ephron in their hearing, "Listen to me, if you will. I will pay the price of the field. Accept it from me so I can bury my dead there."

14Ephron answered Abraham, 15"Listen to me, my lord; the land is worth four hundred shekels[b] of silver, but what is that between you and me? Bury your dead."

16Abraham agreed to Ephron's terms and weighed out for him the price he had named in the hearing of the Hittites: four hundred shekels of silver, according to the weight current among the merchants.

17So Ephron's field in Machpelah near Mamre—both the field and the cave in it, and all the trees within the borders of the field—was deeded 18to Abraham as his property in the presence of all the Hittites who had come to the gate of the city. 19Afterward Abraham buried his wife Sarah in the cave in the field of Machpelah near Mamre (which is at Hebron) in the land of Canaan. 20So the field and the cave in it were deeded to Abraham by the Hittites as a burial site.

Isaac and Rebekah

24 Abraham was now very old, and the LORD had blessed him in every way. 2He said to the senior servant in his household, the one in charge of all that he had, "Put your hand under my thigh. 3I want you to swear by the LORD, the God of heaven and the God of earth, that you will not get a wife for my son from the daughters of the Canaanites, among whom I am living, 4but will go to my country and my own relatives and get a wife for my son Isaac."

5The servant asked him, "What if the woman is unwilling to come back with me to this land? Shall I then take your son back to the country you came from?"

6"Make sure that you do not take my son back there," Abraham said. 7"The LORD, the God of heaven, who brought me out of my father's household and my native land and who spoke to me and promised me on oath, saying, 'To your offspring[c] I will give this land'—he will send his angel before you so that you can get a wife for my son from there. 8If the woman is unwilling to come back with you, then you will be released from this oath of mine. Only do not take my son back there." 9So the servant put his hand under the thigh of his master Abraham and swore an oath to him concerning this matter.

10Then the servant left, taking with him ten of his master's camels loaded with all kinds of good things from his master. He set out for Aram Naharaim[d] and made his way to the town of Nahor. 11He had the camels kneel down near the well outside the town; it was toward evening, the time the women go out to draw water.

12Then he prayed, "LORD, God of my master Abraham, make me successful today, and show kindness to my master Abraham. 13See, I am standing beside this spring, and the daughters of the townspeople are coming out to draw water. 14May it be that when I say to a young woman, 'Please let down your jar that I may have a drink,' and she says, 'Drink, and I'll water your camels too'—let her be the one you have chosen for your servant Isaac. By this I will know that you have shown kindness to my master."

15Before he had finished praying, Rebekah came out with her jar on her shoulder. She was the daughter of Bethuel son of Milkah, who was the wife of Abraham's brother Nahor. 16The woman was very beautiful, a virgin; no man had ever slept with her. She went down to the spring, filled her jar and came up again.

17The servant hurried to meet her and said, "Please give me a little water from your jar."

18"Drink, my lord," she said, and quickly lowered the jar to her hands and gave him a drink.

19After she had given him a drink, she said, "I'll draw water for your camels too, until they have had enough to drink." 20So she quickly emptied her jar into the trough, ran back to the well to draw more water, and drew enough for all his camels. 21Without saying a word, the man watched her closely to learn whether or not the LORD had made his journey successful.

22When the camels had finished drinking, the man took out a gold nose ring weighing a beka[e] and two gold bracelets weighing ten shekels.[f] 23Then he asked, "Whose daughter are you? Please tell me, is there room in your father's house for us to spend the night?"

24She answered him, "I am the daughter of Bethuel, the son that Milkah bore to Nahor." 25And she added, "We have plenty of straw and fodder, as well as room for you to spend the night."

26Then the man bowed down and worshiped the LORD, 27saying, "Praise be to the LORD, the God of my master Abraham, who has not abandoned his kindness and faithfulness to my master. As for me, the LORD has led me on the journey to the house of my master's relatives."

28The young woman ran and told her mother's household about these things. 29Now Rebekah had a brother named Laban, and he hurried out to the man at the spring. 30As soon as he had seen the nose ring, and the bracelets

[a] *11* Or *sell* [b] *15* That is, about 10 pounds or about 4.6 kilograms [c] *7* Or *seed* [d] *10* That is, Northwest Mesopotamia [e] *22* That is, about 1/5 ounce or about 5.7 grams [f] *22* That is, about 4 ounces or about 115 grams

on his sister's arms, and had heard Rebekah tell what the man said to her, he went out to the man and found him standing by the camels near the spring. 31"Come, you who are blessed by the LORD," he said. "Why are you standing out here? I have prepared the house and a place for the camels."

32So the man went to the house, and the camels were unloaded. Straw and fodder were brought for the camels, and water for him and his men to wash their feet. 33Then food was set before him, but he said, "I will not eat until I have told you what I have to say."

"Then tell us," Laban said.

34So he said, "I am Abraham's servant. 35The LORD has blessed my master abundantly, and he has become wealthy. He has given him sheep and cattle, silver and gold, male and female servants, and camels and donkeys. 36My master's wife Sarah has borne him a son in her old age, and he has given him everything he owns. 37And my master made me swear an oath, and said, 'You must not get a wife for my son from the daughters of the Canaanites, in whose land I live, 38but go to my father's family and to my own clan, and get a wife for my son.'

39"Then I asked my master, 'What if the woman will not come back with me?'

40"He replied, 'The LORD, before whom I have walked faithfully, will send his angel with you and make your journey a success, so that you can get a wife for my son from my own clan and from my father's family. 41You will be released from my oath if, when you go to my clan, they refuse to give her to you—then you will be released from my oath.'

42"When I came to the spring today, I said, 'LORD, God of my master Abraham, if you will, please grant success to the journey on which I have come. 43See, I am standing beside this spring. If a young woman comes out to draw water and I say to her, "Please let me drink a little water from your jar," 44and if she says to me, "Drink, and I'll draw water for your camels too," let her be the one the LORD has chosen for my master's son.'

45"Before I finished praying in my heart, Rebekah came out, with her jar on her shoulder. She went down to the spring and drew water, and I said to her, 'Please give me a drink.'

46"She quickly lowered her jar from her shoulder and said, 'Drink, and I'll water your camels too.' So I drank, and she watered the camels also.

47"I asked her, 'Whose daughter are you?'

"She said, 'The daughter of Bethuel son of Nahor, whom Milkah bore to him.'

"Then I put the ring in her nose and the bracelets on her arms, 48and I bowed down and worshiped the LORD. I praised the LORD, the God of my master Abraham, who had led me on the right road to get the granddaughter of my master's brother for his son. 49Now if you will show kindness and faithfulness to my master, tell me; and if not, tell me, so I may know which way to turn."

50Laban and Bethuel answered, "This is from the LORD; we can say nothing to you one way or the other. 51Here is Rebekah; take her and go, and let her become the wife of your master's son, as the LORD has directed."

52When Abraham's servant heard what they said, he bowed down to the ground before the LORD. 53Then the servant brought out gold and silver jewelry and articles of clothing and gave them to Rebekah; he also gave costly gifts to her brother and to her mother. 54Then he and the men who were with him ate and drank and spent the night there.

When they got up the next morning, he said, "Send me on my way to my master."

55But her brother and her mother replied, "Let the young woman remain with us ten days or so; then you[a] may go."

56But he said to them, "Do not detain me, now that the LORD has granted success to my journey. Send me on my way so I may go to my master."

57Then they said, "Let's call the young woman and ask her about it." 58So they called Rebekah and asked her, "Will you go with this man?"

"I will go," she said.

59So they sent their sister Rebekah on her way, along with her nurse and Abraham's servant and his men. 60And they blessed Rebekah and said to her,

"Our sister, may you increase
  to thousands upon thousands;
may your offspring possess
  the cities of their enemies."

61Then Rebekah and her attendants got ready and mounted the camels and went back with the man. So the servant took Rebekah and left.

62Now Isaac had come from Beer Lahai Roi, for he was living in the Negev. 63He went out to the field one evening to meditate,[b] and as he looked up, he saw camels approaching. 64Rebekah also looked up and saw Isaac. She got down from her camel 65and asked the servant, "Who is that man in the field coming to meet us?"

"He is my master," the servant answered. So she took her veil and covered herself.

66Then the servant told Isaac all he had done. 67Isaac brought her into the tent of his mother Sarah, and he married Rebekah. So she became his wife, and he loved her; and Isaac was comforted after his mother's death.

The Death of Abraham

25 Abraham had taken another wife, whose name was Keturah. 2She bore him Zimran, Jokshan, Medan, Midian, Ishbak and Shuah. 3Jokshan was the father of Sheba and Dedan; the descendants of Dedan were the Ashurites, the Letushites and the Leummites. 4The sons of Midian were Ephah, Epher, Hanok, Abida and Eldaah. All these were descendants of Keturah.

5Abraham left everything he owned to

[a] 55 Or *she*   [b] 63 The meaning of the Hebrew for this word is uncertain.

Isaac. 6But while he was still living, he gave
gifts to the sons of his concubines and sent
them away from his son Isaac to the land of
the east.
7Abraham lived a hundred and seventy-five
years. 8Then Abraham breathed his last and
died at a good old age, an old man and full
of years; and he was gathered to his people.
9His sons Isaac and Ishmael buried him in
the cave of Machpelah near Mamre, in the
field of Ephron son of Zohar the Hittite, 10the
field Abraham had bought from the Hittites.[a]
There Abraham was buried with his wife Sarah. 11After Abraham's death, God blessed his
son Isaac, who then lived near Beer Lahai Roi.

Ishmael's Sons

12This is the account of the family line of
Abraham's son Ishmael, whom Sarah's slave,
Hagar the Egyptian, bore to Abraham.

13These are the names of the sons of Ishmael, listed in the order of their birth: Nebaioth the firstborn of Ishmael, Kedar, Adbeel,
Mibsam, 14Mishma, Dumah, Massa, 15Hadad,
Tema, Jetur, Naphish and Kedemah. 16These
were the sons of Ishmael, and these are the
names of the twelve tribal rulers according to
their settlements and camps. 17Ishmael lived a
hundred and thirty-seven years. He breathed
his last and died, and he was gathered to his
people. 18His descendants settled in the area
from Havilah to Shur, near the eastern border of Egypt, as you go toward Ashur. And
they lived in hostility toward[b] all the tribes
related to them.

Jacob and Esau

19This is the account of the family line of
Abraham's son Isaac.

Abraham became the father of Isaac, 20and
Isaac was forty years old when he married
Rebekah daughter of Bethuel the Aramean
from Paddan Aram[c] and sister of Laban the
Aramean.
21Isaac prayed to the LORD on behalf of his
wife, because she was childless. The LORD
answered his prayer, and his wife Rebekah
became pregnant. 22The babies jostled each
other within her, and she said, "Why is this
happening to me?" So she went to inquire of
the LORD.
23The LORD said to her,

"Two nations are in your womb,
  and two peoples from within you will
    be separated;
one people will be stronger than the
    other,
  and the older will serve the younger."

24When the time came for her to give birth,
there were twin boys in her womb. 25The first
to come out was red, and his whole body was
like a hairy garment; so they named him
Esau.[d] 26After this, his brother came out,
with his hand grasping Esau's heel; so he was
named Jacob.[e] Isaac was sixty years old when
Rebekah gave birth to them.
27The boys grew up, and Esau became a
skillful hunter, a man of the open country,
while Jacob was content to stay at home
among the tents. 28Isaac, who had a taste for
wild game, loved Esau, but Rebekah loved
Jacob.
29Once when Jacob was cooking some stew,
Esau came in from the open country, famished. 30He said to Jacob, "Quick, let me have
some of that red stew! I'm famished!" (That
is why he was also called Edom.[f])
31Jacob replied, "First sell me your birthright."
32"Look, I am about to die," Esau said.
"What good is the birthright to me?"
33But Jacob said, "Swear to me first." So he
swore an oath to him, selling his birthright
to Jacob.
34Then Jacob gave Esau some bread and
some lentil stew. He ate and drank, and then
got up and left.
So Esau despised his birthright.

Isaac and Abimelek

26 Now there was a famine in the land—
besides the previous famine in Abraham's time—and Isaac went to Abimelek
king of the Philistines in Gerar. 2The LORD
appeared to Isaac and said, "Do not go down
to Egypt; live in the land where I tell you to
live. 3Stay in this land for a while, and I will
be with you and will bless you. For to you and
your descendants I will give all these lands
and will confirm the oath I swore to your
father Abraham. 4I will make your descendants as numerous as the stars in the sky and
will give them all these lands, and through
your offspring[g] all nations on earth will be
blessed,[h] 5because Abraham obeyed me and
did everything I required of him, keeping my
commands, my decrees and my instructions."
6So Isaac stayed in Gerar.
7When the men of that place asked him
about his wife, he said, "She is my sister," because he was afraid to say, "She is my wife."
He thought, "The men of this place might
kill me on account of Rebekah, because she
is beautiful."
8When Isaac had been there a long time,
Abimelek king of the Philistines looked down
from a window and saw Isaac caressing his
wife Rebekah. 9So Abimelek summoned Isaac
and said, "She is really your wife! Why did
you say, 'She is my sister'?"
Isaac answered him, "Because I thought I
might lose my life on account of her."
10Then Abimelek said, "What is this you
have done to us? One of the men might well
have slept with your wife, and you would have
brought guilt upon us."

[a] 10 Or *the descendants of Heth* [b] 18 Or *lived to the east of* [c] 20 That is, Northwest Mesopotamia
[d] 25 *Esau* may mean *hairy.* [e] 26 *Jacob* means *he grasps the heel,* a Hebrew idiom for *he deceives.*
[f] 30 *Edom* means *red.* [g] 4 Or *seed* [h] 4 Or *and all nations on earth will use the name of your offspring in blessings* (see 48:20)

11So Abimelek gave orders to all the people:
"Anyone who harms this man or his wife shall
surely be put to death."
12Isaac planted crops in that land and the
same year reaped a hundredfold, because
the LORD blessed him. 13The man became
rich, and his wealth continued to grow until
he became very wealthy. 14He had so many
flocks and herds and servants that the Philistines envied him. 15So all the wells that his
father's servants had dug in the time of his
father Abraham, the Philistines stopped up,
filling them with earth.
16Then Abimelek said to Isaac, "Move
away from us; you have become too powerful for us."
17So Isaac moved away from there and encamped in the Valley of Gerar, where he settled. 18Isaac reopened the wells that had been
dug in the time of his father Abraham, which
the Philistines had stopped up after Abraham
died, and he gave them the same names his
father had given them.
19Isaac's servants dug in the valley and discovered a well of fresh water there. 20But the
herders of Gerar quarreled with those of Isaac
and said, "The water is ours!" So he named
the well Esek,[a] because they disputed with
him. 21Then they dug another well, but they
quarreled over that one also; so he named it
Sitnah.[b] 22He moved on from there and dug
another well, and no one quarreled over it.
He named it Rehoboth,[c] saying, "Now the
LORD has given us room and we will flourish
in the land."
23From there he went up to Beersheba.
24That night the LORD appeared to him and
said, "I am the God of your father Abraham.
Do not be afraid, for I am with you; I will
bless you and will increase the number of
your descendants for the sake of my servant
Abraham."
25Isaac built an altar there and called on the
name of the LORD. There he pitched his tent,
and there his servants dug a well.
26Meanwhile, Abimelek had come to him
from Gerar, with Ahuzzath his personal adviser and Phicol the commander of his forces.
27Isaac asked them, "Why have you come to
me, since you were hostile to me and sent me
away?"
28They answered, "We saw clearly that the
LORD was with you; so we said, 'There ought
to be a sworn agreement between us'—between us and you. Let us make a treaty with
you 29that you will do us no harm, just as we
did not harm you but always treated you well
and sent you away peacefully. And now you
are blessed by the LORD."
30Isaac then made a feast for them, and they
ate and drank. 31Early the next morning the
men swore an oath to each other. Then Isaac
sent them on their way, and they went away
peacefully.
32That day Isaac's servants came and told
him about the well they had dug. They said,
"We've found water!" 33He called it Shibah,[d]
and to this day the name of the town has been
Beersheba.[e]

Jacob Takes Esau's Blessing

34When Esau was forty years old, he married Judith daughter of Beeri the Hittite, and
also Basemath daughter of Elon the Hittite.
35They were a source of grief to Isaac and Rebekah.

27 When Isaac was old and his eyes were
so weak that he could no longer see,
he called for Esau his older son and said to
him, "My son."
"Here I am," he answered.
2Isaac said, "I am now an old man and don't
know the day of my death. 3Now then, get
your equipment—your quiver and bow—and
go out to the open country to hunt some wild
game for me. 4Prepare me the kind of tasty
food I like and bring it to me to eat, so that I
may give you my blessing before I die."
5Now Rebekah was listening as Isaac spoke
to his son Esau. When Esau left for the open
country to hunt game and bring it back, 6Re-
bekah said to her son Jacob, "Look, I overheard
your father say to your brother Esau, 7'Bring
me some game and prepare me some tasty food
to eat, so that I may give you my blessing in
the presence of the LORD before I die.' 8Now,
my son, listen carefully and do what I tell you:
9Go out to the flock and bring me two choice
young goats, so I can prepare some tasty food
for your father, just the way he likes it. 10Then
take it to your father to eat, so that he may give
you his blessing before he dies."
11Jacob said to Rebekah his mother, "But
my brother Esau is a hairy man while I have
smooth skin. 12What if my father touches me?
I would appear to be tricking him and would
bring down a curse on myself rather than a
blessing."
13His mother said to him, "My son, let the
curse fall on me. Just do what I say; go and
get them for me."
14So he went and got them and brought
them to his mother, and she prepared some
tasty food, just the way his father liked it.
15Then Rebekah took the best clothes of Esau
her older son, which she had in the house, and
put them on her younger son Jacob. 16She also
covered his hands and the smooth part of his
neck with the goatskins. 17Then she handed
to her son Jacob the tasty food and the bread
she had made.
18He went to his father and said, "My father."
"Yes, my son," he answered. "Who is it?"
19Jacob said to his father, "I am Esau your
firstborn. I have done as you told me. Please
sit up and eat some of my game, so that you
may give me your blessing."
20Isaac asked his son, "How did you find it
so quickly, my son?"
"The LORD your God gave me success," he
replied.
21Then Isaac said to Jacob, "Come near so I

[a] 20 *Esek* means *dispute.* [b] 21 *Sitnah* means *opposition.* [c] 22 *Rehoboth* means *room.*
[d] 33 *Shibah* can mean *oath* or *seven.* [e] 33 *Beersheba* can mean *well of the oath* and *well of seven.*

can touch you, my son, to know whether you
really are my son Esau or not."
22 Jacob went close to his father Isaac, who
touched him and said, "The voice is the voice
of Jacob, but the hands are the hands of Esau."
23 He did not recognize him, for his hands were
hairy like those of his brother Esau; so he
proceeded to bless him. 24 "Are you really my
son Esau?" he asked.
"I am," he replied.
25 Then he said, "My son, bring me some of
your game to eat, so that I may give you my
blessing."
Jacob brought it to him and he ate; and he
brought some wine and he drank. 26 Then his
father Isaac said to him, "Come here, my son,
and kiss me."
27 So he went to him and kissed him. When
Isaac caught the smell of his clothes, he
blessed him and said,

"Ah, the smell of my son
  is like the smell of a field
  that the LORD has blessed.
28 May God give you heaven's dew
  and earth's richness—
  an abundance of grain and new wine.
29 May nations serve you
  and peoples bow down to you.
Be lord over your brothers,
  and may the sons of your mother bow
    down to you.
May those who curse you be cursed
  and those who bless you be blessed."

30 After Isaac finished blessing him, and
Jacob had scarcely left his father's presence,
his brother Esau came in from hunting. 31 He
too prepared some tasty food and brought it
to his father. Then he said to him, "My father,
please sit up and eat some of my game, so that
you may give me your blessing."
32 His father Isaac asked him, "Who are you?"
"I am your son," he answered, "your firstborn, Esau."
33 Isaac trembled violently and said, "Who
was it, then, that hunted game and brought
it to me? I ate it just before you came and I
blessed him—and indeed he will be blessed!"
34 When Esau heard his father's words, he
burst out with a loud and bitter cry and said
to his father, "Bless me—me too, my father!"
35 But he said, "Your brother came deceitfully and took your blessing."
36 Esau said, "Isn't he rightly named Jacob[a]? This is the second time he has taken
advantage of me: He took my birthright, and
now he's taken my blessing!" Then he asked,
"Haven't you reserved any blessing for me?"
37 Isaac answered Esau, "I have made him
lord over you and have made all his relatives
his servants, and I have sustained him with
grain and new wine. So what can I possibly
do for you, my son?"
38 Esau said to his father, "Do you have only
one blessing, my father? Bless me too, my father!" Then Esau wept aloud.
39 His father Isaac answered him,

"Your dwelling will be
  away from the earth's richness,
  away from the dew of heaven above.
40 You will live by the sword
  and you will serve your brother.
But when you grow restless,
  you will throw his yoke
  from off your neck."

41 Esau held a grudge against Jacob because
of the blessing his father had given him. He
said to himself, "The days of mourning for
my father are near; then I will kill my brother Jacob."
42 When Rebekah was told what her older
son Esau had said, she sent for her younger
son Jacob and said to him, "Your brother Esau
is planning to avenge himself by killing you.
43 Now then, my son, do what I say: Flee at once
to my brother Laban in Harran. 44 Stay with
him for a while until your brother's fury sub-
sides. 45 When your brother is no longer angry
with you and forgets what you did to him, I'll
send word for you to come back from there.
Why should I lose both of you in one day?"
46 Then Rebekah said to Isaac, "I'm disgust-
ed with living because of these Hittite women.
If Jacob takes a wife from among the women
of this land, from Hittite women like these,
my life will not be worth living."

28 So Isaac called for Jacob and blessed
him. Then he commanded him: "Do
not marry a Canaanite woman. 2 Go at once
to Paddan Aram,[b] to the house of your mother's father Bethuel. Take a wife for yourself
there, from among the daughters of Laban,
your mother's brother. 3 May God Almighty[c]
bless you and make you fruitful and increase
your numbers until you become a community
of peoples. 4 May he give you and your descendants the blessing given to Abraham, so that
you may take possession of the land where you
now reside as a foreigner, the land God gave to
Abraham." 5 Then Isaac sent Jacob on his way,
and he went to Paddan Aram, to Laban son of
Bethuel the Aramean, the brother of Rebekah,
who was the mother of Jacob and Esau.
6 Now Esau learned that Isaac had blessed
Jacob and had sent him to Paddan Aram to
take a wife from there, and that when he
blessed him he commanded him, "Do not
marry a Canaanite woman," 7 and that Jacob
had obeyed his father and mother and had
gone to Paddan Aram. 8 Esau then realized
how displeasing the Canaanite women were
to his father Isaac; 9 so he went to Ishmael and
married Mahalath, the sister of Nebaioth and
daughter of Ishmael son of Abraham, in addition to the wives he already had.

Jacob's Dream at Bethel

10 Jacob left Beersheba and set out for Harran. 11 When he reached a certain place, he
stopped for the night because the sun had set.
Taking one of the stones there, he put it under

[a] *36* *Jacob* means *he grasps the heel,* a Hebrew idiom for *he takes advantage of* or *he deceives.*
[b] *2* That is, Northwest Mesopotamia; also in verses 5, 6 and 7 [c] *3* Hebrew *El-Shaddai*

his head and lay down to sleep. 12He had a dream in which he saw a stairway resting on the earth, with its top reaching to heaven, and the angels of God were ascending and descending on it. 13There above it[a] stood the LORD, and he said: "I am the LORD, the God of your father Abraham and the God of Isaac. I will give you and your descendants the land on which you are lying. 14Your descendants will be like the dust of the earth, and you will spread out to the west and to the east, to the north and to the south. All peoples on earth will be blessed through you and your offspring.[b] 15I am with you and will watch over you wherever you go, and I will bring you back to this land. I will not leave you until I have done what I have promised you."

16When Jacob awoke from his sleep, he thought, "Surely the LORD is in this place, and I was not aware of it." 17He was afraid and said, "How awesome is this place! This is none other than the house of God; this is the gate of heaven."

18Early the next morning Jacob took the stone he had placed under his head and set it up as a pillar and poured oil on top of it. 19He called that place Bethel,[c] though the city used to be called Luz.

20Then Jacob made a vow, saying, "If God will be with me and will watch over me on this journey I am taking and will give me food to eat and clothes to wear 21so that I return safely to my father's household, then the LORD[d] will be my God 22and[e] this stone that I have set up as a pillar will be God's house, and of all that you give me I will give you a tenth."

Jacob Arrives in Paddan Aram

29 Then Jacob continued on his journey and came to the land of the eastern peoples. 2There he saw a well in the open country, with three flocks of sheep lying near it because the flocks were watered from that well. The stone over the mouth of the well was large. 3When all the flocks were gathered there, the shepherds would roll the stone away from the well's mouth and water the sheep. Then they would return the stone to its place over the mouth of the well.

4Jacob asked the shepherds, "My brothers, where are you from?"

"We're from Harran," they replied.

5He said to them, "Do you know Laban, Nahor's grandson?"

"Yes, we know him," they answered.

6Then Jacob asked them, "Is he well?"

"Yes, he is," they said, "and here comes his daughter Rachel with the sheep."

7"Look," he said, "the sun is still high; it is not time for the flocks to be gathered. Water the sheep and take them back to pasture."

8"We can't," they replied, "until all the flocks are gathered and the stone has been rolled away from the mouth of the well. Then we will water the sheep."

9While he was still talking with them, Rachel came with her father's sheep, for she was a shepherd. 10When Jacob saw Rachel daughter of his uncle Laban, and Laban's sheep, he went over and rolled the stone away from the mouth of the well and watered his uncle's sheep. 11Then Jacob kissed Rachel and began to weep aloud. 12He had told Rachel that he was a relative of her father and a son of Rebekah. So she ran and told her father.

13As soon as Laban heard the news about Jacob, his sister's son, he hurried to meet him. He embraced him and kissed him and brought him to his home, and there Jacob told him all these things. 14Then Laban said to him, "You are my own flesh and blood."

Jacob Marries Leah and Rachel

After Jacob had stayed with him for a whole month, 15Laban said to him, "Just because you are a relative of mine, should you work for me for nothing? Tell me what your wages should be."

16Now Laban had two daughters; the name of the older was Leah, and the name of the younger was Rachel. 17Leah had weak[f] eyes, but Rachel had a lovely figure and was beautiful. 18Jacob was in love with Rachel and said, "I'll work for you seven years in return for your younger daughter Rachel."

19Laban said, "It's better that I give her to you than to some other man. Stay here with me." 20So Jacob served seven years to get Rachel, but they seemed like only a few days to him because of his love for her.

21Then Jacob said to Laban, "Give me my wife. My time is completed, and I want to make love to her."

22So Laban brought together all the people of the place and gave a feast. 23But when evening came, he took his daughter Leah and brought her to Jacob, and Jacob made love to her. 24And Laban gave his servant Zilpah to his daughter as her attendant.

25When morning came, there was Leah! So Jacob said to Laban, "What is this you have done to me? I served you for Rachel, didn't I? Why have you deceived me?"

26Laban replied, "It is not our custom here to give the younger daughter in marriage before the older one. 27Finish this daughter's bridal week; then we will give you the younger one also, in return for another seven years of work."

28And Jacob did so. He finished the week with Leah, and then Laban gave him his daughter Rachel to be his wife. 29Laban gave his servant Bilhah to his daughter Rachel as her attendant. 30Jacob made love to Rachel also, and his love for Rachel was greater than his love for Leah. And he worked for Laban another seven years.

Jacob's Children

31When the LORD saw that Leah was not loved, he enabled her to conceive, but Rachel

[a] 13 Or *There beside him* [b] 14 Or *will use your name and the name of your offspring in blessings* (see 48:20) [c] 19 *Bethel* means *house of God.* [d] 20,21 Or *Since God . . . father's household, the* LORD [e] 21,22 Or *household, and the* LORD *will be my God, 22then* [f] 17 Or *delicate*

remained childless. 32Leah became pregnant
and gave birth to a son. She named him Reuben,[a] for she said, "It is because the LORD has
seen my misery. Surely my husband will love
me now."
33She conceived again, and when she gave
birth to a son she said, "Because the LORD
heard that I am not loved, he gave me this one
too." So she named him Simeon.[b]
34Again she conceived, and when she gave
birth to a son she said, "Now at last my husband will become attached to me, because I
have borne him three sons." So he was named
Levi.[c]
35She conceived again, and when she gave
birth to a son she said, "This time I will praise
the LORD." So she named him Judah.[d] Then
she stopped having children.
30 When Rachel saw that she was not bearing Jacob any children, she became
jealous of her sister. So she said to Jacob,
"Give me children, or I'll die!"
2Jacob became angry with her and said,
"Am I in the place of God, who has kept you
from having children?"
3Then she said, "Here is Bilhah, my servant.
Sleep with her so that she can bear children
for me and I too can build a family through
her."
4So she gave him her servant Bilhah as a
wife. Jacob slept with her, 5and she became
pregnant and bore him a son. 6Then Rachel
said, "God has vindicated me; he has listened
to my plea and given me a son." Because of
this she named him Dan.[e]
7Rachel's servant Bilhah conceived again
and bore Jacob a second son. 8Then Rachel
said, "I have had a great struggle with my
sister, and I have won." So she named him
Naphtali.[f]
9When Leah saw that she had stopped having children, she took her servant Zilpah and
gave her to Jacob as a wife. 10Leah's servant
Zilpah bore Jacob a son. 11Then Leah said,
"What good fortune!"[g] So she named him
Gad.[h]
12Leah's servant Zilpah bore Jacob a second
son. 13Then Leah said, "How happy I am! The
women will call me happy." So she named
him Asher.[i]
14During wheat harvest, Reuben went out
into the fields and found some mandrake
plants, which he brought to his mother Leah.
Rachel said to Leah, "Please give me some of
your son's mandrakes."
15But she said to her, "Wasn't it enough that
you took away my husband? Will you take my
son's mandrakes too?"
"Very well," Rachel said, "he can sleep with
you tonight in return for your son's mandrakes."
16So when Jacob came in from the fields
that evening, Leah went out to meet him. "You
must sleep with me," she said. "I have hired
you with my son's mandrakes." So he slept
with her that night.
17God listened to Leah, and she became
pregnant and bore Jacob a fifth son. 18Then
Leah said, "God has rewarded me for giving
my servant to my husband." So she named
him Issachar.[j]
19Leah conceived again and bore Jacob a
sixth son. 20Then Leah said, "God has presented me with a precious gift. This time my
husband will treat me with honor, because I
have borne him six sons." So she named him
Zebulun.[k]
21Some time later she gave birth to a daughter and named her Dinah.
22Then God remembered Rachel; he listened
to her and enabled her to conceive. 23She became pregnant and gave birth to a son and
said, "God has taken away my disgrace." 24She
named him Joseph,[l] and said, "May the LORD
add to me another son."

Jacob's Flocks Increase

25After Rachel gave birth to Joseph, Jacob
said to Laban, "Send me on my way so I can
go back to my own homeland. 26Give me my
wives and children, for whom I have served
you, and I will be on my way. You know how
much work I've done for you."
27But Laban said to him, "If I have found
favor in your eyes, please stay. I have learned
by divination that the LORD has blessed me
because of you." 28He added, "Name your wages, and I will pay them."
29Jacob said to him, "You know how I have
worked for you and how your livestock has
fared under my care. 30The little you had before I came has increased greatly, and the
LORD has blessed you wherever I have been.
But now, when may I do something for my
own household?"
31"What shall I give you?" he asked.
"Don't give me anything," Jacob replied.
"But if you will do this one thing for me, I will
go on tending your flocks and watching over
them: 32Let me go through all your flocks today and remove from them every speckled or
spotted sheep, every dark-colored lamb and
every spotted or speckled goat. They will be
my wages. 33And my honesty will testify for
me in the future, whenever you check on the
wages you have paid me. Any goat in my possession that is not speckled or spotted, or any
lamb that is not dark-colored, will be considered stolen."
34"Agreed," said Laban. "Let it be as you
have said." 35That same day he removed all
the male goats that were streaked or spotted,
and all the speckled or spotted female goats

[a] 32 *Reuben* sounds like the Hebrew for *he has seen my misery*; the name means *see, a son.*
[b] 33 *Simeon* probably means *one who hears.* [c] 34 *Levi* sounds like and may be derived from the Hebrew for *attached.* [d] 35 *Judah* sounds like and may be derived from the Hebrew for *praise.*
[e] 6 *Dan* here means *he has vindicated.* [f] 8 *Naphtali* means *my struggle.* [g] 11 Or "*A troop is coming!*" [h] 11 *Gad* can mean *good fortune* or *a troop.* [i] 13 *Asher* means *happy.* [j] 18 *Issachar* sounds like the Hebrew for *reward.* [k] 20 *Zebulun* probably means *honor.* [l] 24 *Joseph* means *may he add.*

(all that had white on them) and all the dark-colored lambs, and he placed them in the care of his sons. 36Then he put a three-day journey between himself and Jacob, while Jacob continued to tend the rest of Laban's flocks.

37Jacob, however, took fresh-cut branches from poplar, almond and plane trees and made white stripes on them by peeling the bark and exposing the white inner wood of the branches. 38Then he placed the peeled branches in all the watering troughs, so that they would be directly in front of the flocks when they came to drink. When the flocks were in heat and came to drink, 39they mated in front of the branches. And they bore young that were streaked or speckled or spotted. 40Jacob set apart the young of the flock by themselves, but made the rest face the streaked and dark-colored animals that belonged to Laban. Thus he made separate flocks for himself and did not put them with Laban's animals. 41Whenever the stronger females were in heat, Jacob would place the branches in the troughs in front of the animals so they would mate near the branches, 42but if the animals were weak, he would not place them there. So the weak animals went to Laban and the strong ones to Jacob. 43In this way the man grew exceedingly prosperous and came to own large flocks, and female and male servants, and camels and donkeys.

Jacob Flees From Laban

31 Jacob heard that Laban's sons were saying, "Jacob has taken everything our father owned and has gained all this wealth from what belonged to our father." 2And Jacob noticed that Laban's attitude toward him was not what it had been.

3Then the LORD said to Jacob, "Go back to the land of your fathers and to your relatives, and I will be with you."

4So Jacob sent word to Rachel and Leah to come out to the fields where his flocks were. 5He said to them, "I see that your father's attitude toward me is not what it was before, but the God of my father has been with me. 6You know that I've worked for your father with all my strength, 7yet your father has cheated me by changing my wages ten times. However, God has not allowed him to harm me. 8If he said, 'The speckled ones will be your wages,' then all the flocks gave birth to speckled young; and if he said, 'The streaked ones will be your wages,' then all the flocks bore streaked young. 9So God has taken away your father's livestock and has given them to me.

10"In breeding season I once had a dream in which I looked up and saw that the male goats mating with the flock were streaked, speckled or spotted. 11The angel of God said to me in the dream, 'Jacob.' I answered, 'Here I am.' 12And he said, 'Look up and see that all the male goats mating with the flock are streaked, speckled or spotted, for I have seen all that Laban has been doing to you. 13I am the God of Bethel, where you anointed a pillar and where you made a vow to me. Now leave this land at once and go back to your native land.' "

14Then Rachel and Leah replied, "Do we still have any share in the inheritance of our father's estate? 15Does he not regard us as foreigners? Not only has he sold us, but he has used up what was paid for us. 16Surely all the wealth that God took away from our father belongs to us and our children. So do whatever God has told you."

17Then Jacob put his children and his wives on camels, 18and he drove all his livestock ahead of him, along with all the goods he had accumulated in Paddan Aram,[a] to go to his father Isaac in the land of Canaan.

19When Laban had gone to shear his sheep, Rachel stole her father's household gods. 20Moreover, Jacob deceived Laban the Aramean by not telling him he was running away. 21So he fled with all he had, crossed the Euphrates River, and headed for the hill country of Gilead.

Laban Pursues Jacob

22On the third day Laban was told that Jacob had fled. 23Taking his relatives with him, he pursued Jacob for seven days and caught up with him in the hill country of Gilead. 24Then God came to Laban the Aramean in a dream at night and said to him, "Be careful not to say anything to Jacob, either good or bad."

25Jacob had pitched his tent in the hill country of Gilead when Laban overtook him, and Laban and his relatives camped there too. 26Then Laban said to Jacob, "What have you done? You've deceived me, and you've carried off my daughters like captives in war. 27Why did you run off secretly and deceive me? Why didn't you tell me, so I could send you away with joy and singing to the music of timbrels and harps? 28You didn't even let me kiss my grandchildren and my daughters goodbye. You have done a foolish thing. 29I have the power to harm you; but last night the God of your father said to me, 'Be careful not to say anything to Jacob, either good or bad.' 30Now you have gone off because you longed to return to your father's household. But why did you steal my gods?"

31Jacob answered Laban, "I was afraid, because I thought you would take your daughters away from me by force. 32But if you find anyone who has your gods, that person shall not live. In the presence of our relatives, see for yourself whether there is anything of yours here with me; and if so, take it." Now Jacob did not know that Rachel had stolen the gods.

33So Laban went into Jacob's tent and into Leah's tent and into the tent of the two female servants, but he found nothing. After he came out of Leah's tent, he entered Rachel's tent. 34Now Rachel had taken the household gods and put them inside her camel's saddle and was sitting on them. Laban searched through everything in the tent but found nothing.

[a] *18* That is, Northwest Mesopotamia

35Rachel said to her father, "Don't be angry,
my lord, that I cannot stand up in your presence; I'm having my period." So he searched
but could not find the household gods.
36Jacob was angry and took Laban to task.
"What is my crime?" he asked Laban. "How
have I wronged you that you hunt me down?
37Now that you have searched through all my
goods, what have you found that belongs to
your household? Put it here in front of your
relatives and mine, and let them judge between the two of us.
38"I have been with you for twenty years
now. Your sheep and goats have not miscar-
ried, nor have I eaten rams from your flocks.
39I did not bring you animals torn by wild
beasts; I bore the loss myself. And you demanded payment from me for whatever was
stolen by day or night. 40This was my situation: The heat consumed me in the daytime
and the cold at night, and sleep fled from my
eyes. 41It was like this for the twenty years
I was in your household. I worked for you
fourteen years for your two daughters and
six years for your flocks, and you changed my
wages ten times. 42If the God of my father, the
God of Abraham and the Fear of Isaac, had
not been with me, you would surely have sent
me away empty-handed. But God has seen my
hardship and the toil of my hands, and last
night he rebuked you."
43Laban answered Jacob, "The women are
my daughters, the children are my children,
and the flocks are my flocks. All you see is
mine. Yet what can I do today about these
daughters of mine, or about the children they
have borne? 44Come now, let's make a covenant, you and I, and let it serve as a witness
between us."
45So Jacob took a stone and set it up as a
pillar. 46He said to his relatives, "Gather some
stones." So they took stones and piled them in
a heap, and they ate there by the heap. 47Laban
called it Jegar Sahadutha, and Jacob called
it Galeed.[a]
48Laban said, "This heap is a witness between you and me today." That is why it was
called Galeed. 49It was also called Mizpah,[b]
because he said, "May the LORD keep watch
between you and me when we are away from
each other. 50If you mistreat my daughters or
if you take any wives besides my daughters,
even though no one is with us, remember that
God is a witness between you and me."
51Laban also said to Jacob, "Here is this
heap, and here is this pillar I have set up between you and me. 52This heap is a witness,
and this pillar is a witness, that I will not go
past this heap to your side to harm you and
that you will not go past this heap and pillar to my side to harm me. 53May the God of
Abraham and the God of Nahor, the God of
their father, judge between us."
So Jacob took an oath in the name of the
Fear of his father Isaac. 54He offered a sacrifice there in the hill country and invited his
relatives to a meal. After they had eaten, they
spent the night there.
55Early the next morning Laban kissed his
grandchildren and his daughters and blessed
them. Then he left and returned home.[c]

Jacob Prepares to Meet Esau

32[d] Jacob also went on his way, and the
angels of God met him. 2When Jacob
saw them, he said, "This is the camp of God!"
So he named that place Mahanaim.[e]
3Jacob sent messengers ahead of him to his
brother Esau in the land of Seir, the country
of Edom. 4He instructed them: "This is what
you are to say to my lord Esau: 'Your servant
Jacob says, I have been staying with Laban
and have remained there till now. 5I have
cattle and donkeys, sheep and goats, male
and female servants. Now I am sending this
message to my lord, that I may find favor in
your eyes.'"
6When the messengers returned to Jacob,
they said, "We went to your brother Esau, and
now he is coming to meet you, and four hundred men are with him."
7In great fear and distress Jacob divided the
people who were with him into two groups,[f]
and the flocks and herds and camels as well.
8He thought, "If Esau comes and attacks one
group,[g] the group[g] that is left may escape."
9Then Jacob prayed, "O God of my father
Abraham, God of my father Isaac, LORD, you
who said to me, 'Go back to your country and
your relatives, and I will make you prosper,'
10I am unworthy of all the kindness and faithfulness you have shown your servant. I had
only my staff when I crossed this Jordan, but
now I have become two camps. 11Save me, I
pray, from the hand of my brother Esau, for
I am afraid he will come and attack me, and
also the mothers with their children. 12But you
have said, 'I will surely make you prosper and
will make your descendants like the sand of
the sea, which cannot be counted.'"
13He spent the night there, and from what he
had with him he selected a gift for his brother
Esau: 14two hundred female goats and twenty male goats, two hundred ewes and twenty
rams, 15thirty female camels with their young,
forty cows and ten bulls, and twenty female
donkeys and ten male donkeys. 16He put them
in the care of his servants, each herd by itself,
and said to his servants, "Go ahead of me, and
keep some space between the herds."
17He instructed the one in the lead: "When
my brother Esau meets you and asks, 'Who
do you belong to, and where are you going,
and who owns all these animals in front of
you?' 18then you are to say, 'They belong to
your servant Jacob. They are a gift sent to
my lord Esau, and he is coming behind us.'"
19He also instructed the second, the third
and all the others who followed the herds:
"You are to say the same thing to Esau when

[a] 47 The Aramaic *Jegar Sahadutha* and the Hebrew *Galeed* both mean *witness heap.* [b] 49 *Mizpah* means *watchtower.* [c] 55 In Hebrew texts this verse (31:55) is numbered 32:1. [d] In Hebrew texts 32:1-32 is numbered 32:2-33. [e] 2 *Mahanaim* means *two camps.* [f] 7 Or *camps* [g] 8 Or *camp*

you meet him. 20And be sure to say, 'Your servant Jacob is coming behind us.'" For he thought, "I will pacify him with these gifts I am sending on ahead; later, when I see him, perhaps he will receive me." 21So Jacob's gifts went on ahead of him, but he himself spent the night in the camp.

Jacob Wrestles With God

22That night Jacob got up and took his two wives, his two female servants and his eleven sons and crossed the ford of the Jabbok. 23After he had sent them across the stream, he sent over all his possessions. 24So Jacob was left alone, and a man wrestled with him till daybreak. 25When the man saw that he could not overpower him, he touched the socket of Jacob's hip so that his hip was wrenched as he wrestled with the man. 26Then the man said, "Let me go, for it is daybreak."

But Jacob replied, "I will not let you go unless you bless me."

27The man asked him, "What is your name?"

"Jacob," he answered.

28Then the man said, "Your name will no longer be Jacob, but Israel,[a] because you have struggled with God and with humans and have overcome."

29Jacob said, "Please tell me your name."

But he replied, "Why do you ask my name?" Then he blessed him there.

30So Jacob called the place Peniel,[b] saying, "It is because I saw God face to face, and yet my life was spared."

31The sun rose above him as he passed Peniel,[c] and he was limping because of his hip. 32Therefore to this day the Israelites do not eat the tendon attached to the socket of the hip, because the socket of Jacob's hip was touched near the tendon.

Jacob Meets Esau

33 Jacob looked up and there was Esau, coming with his four hundred men; so he divided the children among Leah, Rachel and the two female servants. 2He put the female servants and their children in front, Leah and her children next, and Rachel and Joseph in the rear. 3He himself went on ahead and bowed down to the ground seven times as he approached his brother.

4But Esau ran to meet Jacob and embraced him; he threw his arms around his neck and kissed him. And they wept. 5Then Esau looked up and saw the women and children. "Who are these with you?" he asked.

Jacob answered, "They are the children God has graciously given your servant."

6Then the female servants and their children approached and bowed down. 7Next, Leah and her children came and bowed down. Last of all came Joseph and Rachel, and they too bowed down.

8Esau asked, "What's the meaning of all these flocks and herds I met?"

"To find favor in your eyes, my lord," he said.

9But Esau said, "I already have plenty, my brother. Keep what you have for yourself."

10"No, please!" said Jacob. "If I have found favor in your eyes, accept this gift from me. For to see your face is like seeing the face of God, now that you have received me favorably. 11Please accept the present that was brought to you, for God has been gracious to me and I have all I need." And because Jacob insisted, Esau accepted it.

12Then Esau said, "Let us be on our way; I'll accompany you."

13But Jacob said to him, "My lord knows that the children are tender and that I must care for the ewes and cows that are nursing their young. If they are driven hard just one day, all the animals will die. 14So let my lord go on ahead of his servant, while I move along slowly at the pace of the flocks and herds before me and the pace of the children, until I come to my lord in Seir."

15Esau said, "Then let me leave some of my men with you."

"But why do that?" Jacob asked. "Just let me find favor in the eyes of my lord."

16So that day Esau started on his way back to Seir. 17Jacob, however, went to Sukkoth, where he built a place for himself and made shelters for his livestock. That is why the place is called Sukkoth.[d]

18After Jacob came from Paddan Aram,[e] he arrived safely at the city of Shechem in Canaan and camped within sight of the city. 19For a hundred pieces of silver,[f] he bought from the sons of Hamor, the father of Shechem, the plot of ground where he pitched his tent. 20There he set up an altar and called it El Elohe Israel.[g]

Dinah and the Shechemites

34 Now Dinah, the daughter Leah had borne to Jacob, went out to visit the women of the land. 2When Shechem son of Hamor the Hivite, the ruler of that area, saw her, he took her and raped her. 3His heart was drawn to Dinah daughter of Jacob; he loved the young woman and spoke tenderly to her. 4And Shechem said to his father Hamor, "Get me this girl as my wife."

5When Jacob heard that his daughter Dinah had been defiled, his sons were in the fields with his livestock; so he did nothing about it until they came home.

6Then Shechem's father Hamor went out to talk with Jacob. 7Meanwhile, Jacob's sons had come in from the fields as soon as they heard what had happened. They were shocked and furious, because Shechem had done an outrageous thing in[h] Israel by sleeping with Jacob's daughter—a thing that should not be done.

[a] 28 *Israel* probably means *he struggles with God.* [b] 30 *Peniel* means *face of God.* [c] 31 Hebrew *Penuel,* a variant of *Peniel* [d] 17 *Sukkoth* means *shelters.* [e] 18 That is, Northwest Mesopotamia [f] 19 Hebrew *hundred kesitahs;* a kesitah was a unit of money of unknown weight and value. [g] 20 *El Elohe Israel* can mean *El is the God of Israel* or *mighty is the God of Israel.* [h] 7 Or *against*

8But Hamor said to them, "My son Shechem has his heart set on your daughter. Please give her to him as his wife. 9Intermarry with us; give us your daughters and take our daughters for yourselves. 10You can settle among us; the land is open to you. Live in it, trade[a] in it, and acquire property in it."

11Then Shechem said to Dinah's father and brothers, "Let me find favor in your eyes, and I will give you whatever you ask. 12Make the price for the bride and the gift I am to bring as great as you like, and I'll pay whatever you ask me. Only give me the young woman as my wife."

13Because their sister Dinah had been defiled, Jacob's sons replied deceitfully as they spoke to Shechem and his father Hamor. 14They said to them, "We can't do such a thing; we can't give our sister to a man who is not circumcised. That would be a disgrace to us. 15We will enter into an agreement with you on one condition only: that you become like us by circumcising all your males. 16Then we will give you our daughters and take your daughters for ourselves. We'll settle among you and become one people with you. 17But if you will not agree to be circumcised, we'll take our sister and go."

18Their proposal seemed good to Hamor and his son Shechem. 19The young man, who was the most honored of all his father's family, lost no time in doing what they said, because he was delighted with Jacob's daughter. 20So Hamor and his son Shechem went to the gate of their city to speak to the men of their city. 21"These men are friendly toward us," they said. "Let them live in our land and trade in it; the land has plenty of room for them. We can marry their daughters and they can marry ours. 22But the men will agree to live with us as one people only on the condition that our males be circumcised, as they themselves are. 23Won't their livestock, their property and all their other animals become ours? So let us agree to their terms, and they will settle among us."

24All the men who went out of the city gate agreed with Hamor and his son Shechem, and every male in the city was circumcised.

25Three days later, while all of them were still in pain, two of Jacob's sons, Simeon and Levi, Dinah's brothers, took their swords and attacked the unsuspecting city, killing every male. 26They put Hamor and his son Shechem to the sword and took Dinah from Shechem's house and left. 27The sons of Jacob came upon the dead bodies and looted the city where[b] their sister had been defiled. 28They seized their flocks and herds and donkeys and everything else of theirs in the city and out in the fields. 29They carried off all their wealth and all their women and children, taking as plunder everything in the houses.

30Then Jacob said to Simeon and Levi, "You have brought trouble on me by making me obnoxious to the Canaanites and Perizzites, the people living in this land. We are few in number, and if they join forces against me and attack me, I and my household will be destroyed."

31But they replied, "Should he have treated our sister like a prostitute?"

Jacob Returns to Bethel

35 Then God said to Jacob, "Go up to Bethel and settle there, and build an altar there to God, who appeared to you when you were fleeing from your brother Esau."

2So Jacob said to his household and to all who were with him, "Get rid of the foreign gods you have with you, and purify yourselves and change your clothes. 3Then come, let us go up to Bethel, where I will build an altar to God, who answered me in the day of my distress and who has been with me wherever I have gone." 4So they gave Jacob all the foreign gods they had and the rings in their ears, and Jacob buried them under the oak at Shechem. 5Then they set out, and the terror of God fell on the towns all around them so that no one pursued them.

6Jacob and all the people with him came to Luz (that is, Bethel) in the land of Canaan. 7There he built an altar, and he called the place El Bethel,[c] because it was there that God revealed himself to him when he was fleeing from his brother.

8Now Deborah, Rebekah's nurse, died and was buried under the oak outside Bethel. So it was named Allon Bakuth.[d]

9After Jacob returned from Paddan Aram,[e] God appeared to him again and blessed him. 10God said to him, "Your name is Jacob,[f] but you will no longer be called Jacob; your name will be Israel.[g]" So he named him Israel.

11And God said to him, "I am God Almighty[h]; be fruitful and increase in number. A nation and a community of nations will come from you, and kings will be among your descendants. 12The land I gave to Abraham and Isaac I also give to you, and I will give this land to your descendants after you." 13Then God went up from him at the place where he had talked with him.

14Jacob set up a stone pillar at the place where God had talked with him, and he poured out a drink offering on it; he also poured oil on it. 15Jacob called the place where God had talked with him Bethel.[i]

The Deaths of Rachel and Isaac

16Then they moved on from Bethel. While they were still some distance from Ephrath, Rachel began to give birth and had great difficulty. 17And as she was having great difficulty in childbirth, the midwife said to her, "Don't despair, for you have another son." 18As she breathed her last—for she was dying—

[a] 10 Or *move about freely*; also in verse 21 [b] 27 Or *because* [c] 7 *El Bethel* means *God of Bethel.*
[d] 8 *Allon Bakuth* means *oak of weeping.* [e] 9 That is, Northwest Mesopotamia; also in verse 26
[f] 10 *Jacob* means *he grasps the heel,* a Hebrew idiom for *he deceives.* [g] 10 *Israel* probably means *he struggles with God.* [h] 11 Hebrew *El-Shaddai* [i] 15 *Bethel* means *house of God.*

she named her son Ben-Oni.[a] But his father
named him Benjamin.[b]
19So Rachel died and was buried on the way
to Ephrath (that is, Bethlehem). 20Over her
tomb Jacob set up a pillar, and to this day that
pillar marks Rachel's tomb.
21Israel moved on again and pitched his tent
beyond Migdal Eder. 22While Israel was living in that region, Reuben went in and slept
with his father's concubine Bilhah, and Israel
heard of it.

Jacob had twelve sons:
23The sons of Leah:
Reuben the firstborn of Jacob,
Simeon, Levi, Judah, Issachar and Zebulun.
24The sons of Rachel:
Joseph and Benjamin.
25The sons of Rachel's servant Bilhah:
Dan and Naphtali.
26The sons of Leah's servant Zilpah:
Gad and Asher.
These were the sons of Jacob, who were
born to him in Paddan Aram.

27Jacob came home to his father Isaac in
Mamre, near Kiriath Arba (that is, Hebron),
where Abraham and Isaac had stayed. 28Isaac
lived a hundred and eighty years. 29Then he
breathed his last and died and was gathered
to his people, old and full of years. And his
sons Esau and Jacob buried him.

Esau's Descendants

36 This is the account of the family line of
Esau (that is, Edom).

2Esau took his wives from the women
of Canaan: Adah daughter of Elon the
Hittite, and Oholibamah daughter of
Anah and granddaughter of Zibeon the
Hivite— 3also Basemath daughter of Ishmael and sister of Nebaioth.
4Adah bore Eliphaz to Esau, Basemath
bore Reuel, 5and Oholibamah bore Jeush,
Jalam and Korah. These were the sons of
Esau, who were born to him in Canaan.
6Esau took his wives and sons and
daughters and all the members of his
household, as well as his livestock and
all his other animals and all the goods he
had acquired in Canaan, and moved to a
land some distance from his brother Jacob.
7Their possessions were too great for them
to remain together; the land where they
were staying could not support them both
because of their livestock. 8So Esau (that
is, Edom) settled in the hill country of Seir.

9This is the account of the family line of
Esau the father of the Edomites in the hill
country of Seir.

10These are the names of Esau's sons:
Eliphaz, the son of Esau's wife Adah,
and Reuel, the son of Esau's wife Basemath.
11The sons of Eliphaz:
Teman, Omar, Zepho, Gatam and Kenaz.
12Esau's son Eliphaz also had a concubine named Timna, who bore him Amalek. These were grandsons of Esau's
wife Adah.
13The sons of Reuel:
Nahath, Zerah, Shammah and Mizzah.
These were grandsons of Esau's wife
Basemath.
14The sons of Esau's wife Oholibamah
daughter of Anah and granddaughter of
Zibeon, whom she bore to Esau:
Jeush, Jalam and Korah.

15These were the chiefs among Esau's descendants:
The sons of Eliphaz the firstborn of Esau:
Chiefs Teman, Omar, Zepho, Kenaz,
16Korah,[c] Gatam and Amalek. These
were the chiefs descended from Eliphaz in Edom; they were grandsons
of Adah.
17The sons of Esau's son Reuel:
Chiefs Nahath, Zerah, Shammah and
Mizzah. These were the chiefs descended from Reuel in Edom; they were
grandsons of Esau's wife Basemath.
18The sons of Esau's wife Oholibamah:
Chiefs Jeush, Jalam and Korah. These
were the chiefs descended from Esau's
wife Oholibamah daughter of Anah.
19These were the sons of Esau (that is,
Edom), and these were their chiefs.

20These were the sons of Seir the Horite,
who were living in the region:
Lotan, Shobal, Zibeon, Anah, 21Dishon,
Ezer and Dishan. These sons of Seir in
Edom were Horite chiefs.
22The sons of Lotan:
Hori and Homam.[d] Timna was Lotan's
sister.
23The sons of Shobal:
Alvan, Manahath, Ebal, Shepho and
Onam.
24The sons of Zibeon:
Aiah and Anah. This is the Anah who
discovered the hot springs[e] in the desert while he was grazing the donkeys
of his father Zibeon.
25The children of Anah:
Dishon and Oholibamah daughter of
Anah.
26The sons of Dishon[f]:
Hemdan, Eshban, Ithran and Keran.
27The sons of Ezer:
Bilhan, Zaavan and Akan.
28The sons of Dishan:
Uz and Aran.
29These were the Horite chiefs:
Lotan, Shobal, Zibeon, Anah, 30Dishon,

[a] 18 *Ben-Oni* means *son of my trouble.* [b] 18 *Benjamin* means *son of my right hand.*
[c] 16 Masoretic Text; Samaritan Pentateuch (also verse 11 and 1 Chron. 1:36) does not have *Korah.*
[d] 22 Hebrew *Hemam,* a variant of *Homam* (see 1 Chron. 1:39) [e] 24 Vulgate; Syriac *discovered water;* the meaning of the Hebrew for this word is uncertain. [f] 26 Hebrew *Dishan,* a variant of *Dishon*

Ezer and Dishan. These were the Horite chiefs, according to their divisions,
in the land of Seir.

The Rulers of Edom

31These were the kings who reigned in
Edom before any Israelite king reigned:
32Bela son of Beor became king of Edom.
His city was named Dinhabah.
33When Bela died, Jobab son of Zerah from
Bozrah succeeded him as king.
34When Jobab died, Husham from the
land of the Temanites succeeded him
as king.
35When Husham died, Hadad son of Bedad,
who defeated Midian in the country of
Moab, succeeded him as king. His city
was named Avith.
36When Hadad died, Samlah from Masrekah succeeded him as king.
37When Samlah died, Shaul from Rehoboth
on the river succeeded him as king.
38When Shaul died, Baal-Hanan son of Akbor succeeded him as king.
39When Baal-Hanan son of Akbor died, Hadad[a] succeeded him as king. His city
was named Pau, and his wife's name
was Mehetabel daughter of Matred, the
daughter of Me-Zahab.

40These were the chiefs descended from
Esau, by name, according to their clans and
regions:
Timna, Alvah, Jetheth, 41Oholibamah,
Elah, Pinon, 42Kenaz, Teman, Mibzar,
43Magdiel and Iram. These were the
chiefs of Edom, according to their settlements in the land they occupied.

This is the family line of Esau, the father
of the Edomites.

Joseph's Dreams

37 Jacob lived in the land where his father
had stayed, the land of Canaan.

2This is the account of Jacob's family line.
Joseph, a young man of seventeen, was
tending the flocks with his brothers, the sons
of Bilhah and the sons of Zilpah, his father's
wives, and he brought their father a bad report about them.
3Now Israel loved Joseph more than any of
his other sons, because he had been born to
him in his old age; and he made an ornate[b]
robe for him. 4When his brothers saw that
their father loved him more than any of them,
they hated him and could not speak a kind
word to him.
5Joseph had a dream, and when he told it
to his brothers, they hated him all the more.
6He said to them, "Listen to this dream I had:
7We were binding sheaves of grain out in the
field when suddenly my sheaf rose and stood
upright, while your sheaves gathered around
mine and bowed down to it."
8His brothers said to him, "Do you intend
to reign over us? Will you actually rule us?"
And they hated him all the more because of
his dream and what he had said.
9Then he had another dream, and he told
it to his brothers. "Listen," he said, "I had another dream, and this time the sun and moon
and eleven stars were bowing down to me."
10When he told his father as well as his
brothers, his father rebuked him and said,
"What is this dream you had? Will your mother and I and your brothers actually come and
bow down to the ground before you?" 11His
brothers were jealous of him, but his father
kept the matter in mind.

Joseph Sold by His Brothers

12Now his brothers had gone to graze their
father's flocks near Shechem, 13and Israel said
to Joseph, "As you know, your brothers are
grazing the flocks near Shechem. Come, I am
going to send you to them."
"Very well," he replied.
14So he said to him, "Go and see if all is well
with your brothers and with the flocks, and
bring word back to me." Then he sent him off
from the Valley of Hebron.
When Joseph arrived at Shechem, 15a man
found him wandering around in the fields and
asked him, "What are you looking for?"
16He replied, "I'm looking for my brothers.
Can you tell me where they are grazing their
flocks?"
17"They have moved on from here," the man
answered. "I heard them say, 'Let's go to Dothan.'"
So Joseph went after his brothers and found
them near Dothan. 18But they saw him in the
distance, and before he reached them, they
plotted to kill him.
19"Here comes that dreamer!" they said to
each other. 20"Come now, let's kill him and
throw him into one of these cisterns and say
that a ferocious animal devoured him. Then
we'll see what comes of his dreams."
21When Reuben heard this, he tried to rescue him from their hands. "Let's not take his
life," he said. 22"Don't shed any blood. Throw
him into this cistern here in the wilderness,
but don't lay a hand on him." Reuben said this
to rescue him from them and take him back
to his father.
23So when Joseph came to his brothers, they
stripped him of his robe—the ornate robe he
was wearing— 24and they took him and threw
him into the cistern. The cistern was empty;
there was no water in it.
25As they sat down to eat their meal, they
looked up and saw a caravan of Ishmaelites coming from Gilead. Their camels were
loaded with spices, balm and myrrh, and they
were on their way to take them down to Egypt.
26Judah said to his brothers, "What will we
gain if we kill our brother and cover up his
blood? 27Come, let's sell him to the Ishmaelites

[a] 39 Many manuscripts of the Masoretic Text, Samaritan Pentateuch and Syriac (see also 1 Chron. 1:50); most manuscripts of the Masoretic Text *Hadar* [b] 3 The meaning of the Hebrew for this word is uncertain; also in verses 23 and 32.

and not lay our hands on him; after all, he is
our brother, our own flesh and blood." His
brothers agreed.
28 So when the Midianite merchants came
by, his brothers pulled Joseph up out of the
cistern and sold him for twenty shekels[a] of silver to the Ishmaelites, who took him to Egypt.
29 When Reuben returned to the cistern and
saw that Joseph was not there, he tore his
clothes. 30 He went back to his brothers and said,
"The boy isn't there! Where can I turn now?"
31 Then they got Joseph's robe, slaughtered a
goat and dipped the robe in the blood. 32 They
took the ornate robe back to their father and
said, "We found this. Examine it to see whether it is your son's robe."
33 He recognized it and said, "It is my son's
robe! Some ferocious animal has devoured
him. Joseph has surely been torn to pieces."
34 Then Jacob tore his clothes, put on sackcloth and mourned for his son many days.
35 All his sons and daughters came to comfort
him, but he refused to be comforted. "No," he
said, "I will continue to mourn until I join my
son in the grave." So his father wept for him.
36 Meanwhile, the Midianites[b] sold Joseph in
Egypt to Potiphar, one of Pharaoh's officials,
the captain of the guard.

Judah and Tamar

38 At that time, Judah left his brothers
and went down to stay with a man of
Adullam named Hirah. 2 There Judah met the
daughter of a Canaanite man named Shua.
He married her and made love to her; 3 she
became pregnant and gave birth to a son, who
was named Er. 4 She conceived again and gave
birth to a son and named him Onan. 5 She gave
birth to still another son and named him Shelah. It was at Kezib that she gave birth to him.
6 Judah got a wife for Er, his firstborn, and
her name was Tamar. 7 But Er, Judah's firstborn, was wicked in the LORD's sight; so the
LORD put him to death.
8 Then Judah said to Onan, "Sleep with your
brother's wife and fulfill your duty to her as a
brother-in-law to raise up offspring for your
brother." 9 But Onan knew that the child would
not be his; so whenever he slept with his brother's wife, he spilled his semen on the ground to
keep from providing offspring for his brother.
10 What he did was wicked in the LORD's sight;
so the LORD put him to death also.
11 Judah then said to his daughter-in-law
Tamar, "Live as a widow in your father's
household until my son Shelah grows up."
For he thought, "He may die too, just like his
brothers." So Tamar went to live in her father's household.
12 After a long time Judah's wife, the daughter of Shua, died. When Judah had recovered
from his grief, he went up to Timnah, to the
men who were shearing his sheep, and his
friend Hirah the Adullamite went with him.
13 When Tamar was told, "Your father-in-law
is on his way to Timnah to shear his sheep,"
14 she took off her widow's clothes, covered
herself with a veil to disguise herself, and then
sat down at the entrance to Enaim, which is on
the road to Timnah. For she saw that, though
Shelah had now grown up, she had not been
given to him as his wife.
15 When Judah saw her, he thought she was a
prostitute, for she had covered her face. 16 Not
realizing that she was his daughter-in-law,
he went over to her by the roadside and said,
"Come now, let me sleep with you."
"And what will you give me to sleep with
you?" she asked.
17 "I'll send you a young goat from my flock,"
he said.
"Will you give me something as a pledge
until you send it?" she asked.
18 He said, "What pledge should I give you?"
"Your seal and its cord, and the staff in your
hand," she answered. So he gave them to her
and slept with her, and she became pregnant
by him. 19 After she left, she took off her veil
and put on her widow's clothes again.
20 Meanwhile Judah sent the young goat by
his friend the Adullamite in order to get his
pledge back from the woman, but he did not
find her. 21 He asked the men who lived there,
"Where is the shrine prostitute who was beside the road at Enaim?"
"There hasn't been any shrine prostitute
here," they said.
22 So he went back to Judah and said, "I
didn't find her. Besides, the men who lived
there said, 'There hasn't been any shrine prostitute here.'"
23 Then Judah said, "Let her keep what she
has, or we will become a laughingstock. After all, I did send her this young goat, but you
didn't find her."
24 About three months later Judah was told,
"Your daughter-in-law Tamar is guilty of prostitution, and as a result she is now pregnant."
Judah said, "Bring her out and have her
burned to death!"
25 As she was being brought out, she sent a
message to her father-in-law. "I am pregnant
by the man who owns these," she said. And
she added, "See if you recognize whose seal
and cord and staff these are."
26 Judah recognized them and said, "She is
more righteous than I, since I wouldn't give
her to my son Shelah." And he did not sleep
with her again.
27 When the time came for her to give birth,
there were twin boys in her womb. 28 As she
was giving birth, one of them put out his hand;
so the midwife took a scarlet thread and tied
it on his wrist and said, "This one came out
first." 29 But when he drew back his hand, his
brother came out, and she said, "So this is how
you have broken out!" And he was named Perez.[c] 30 Then his brother, who had the scarlet
thread on his wrist, came out. And he was
named Zerah.[d]

[a] *28* That is, about 8 ounces or about 230 grams
[b] *36* Samaritan Pentateuch, Septuagint, Vulgate and Syriac (see also verse 28); Masoretic Text *Medanites*
[c] *29 Perez* means *breaking out.*
[d] *30 Zerah* can mean *scarlet* or *brightness.*

Joseph and Potiphar's Wife

39 Now Joseph had been taken down to
Egypt. Potiphar, an Egyptian who was
one of Pharaoh's officials, the captain of the
guard, bought him from the Ishmaelites who
had taken him there.
2The LORD was with Joseph so that he prospered, and he lived in the house of his Egyptian master. 3When his master saw that the
LORD was with him and that the LORD gave
him success in everything he did, 4Joseph
found favor in his eyes and became his attendant. Potiphar put him in charge of his
household, and he entrusted to his care everything he owned. 5From the time he put him
in charge of his household and of all that he
owned, the LORD blessed the household of the
Egyptian because of Joseph. The blessing of
the LORD was on everything Potiphar had,
both in the house and in the field. 6So Potiphar
left everything he had in Joseph's care; with
Joseph in charge, he did not concern himself
with anything except the food he ate.
Now Joseph was well-built and handsome,
7and after a while his master's wife took notice
of Joseph and said, "Come to bed with me!"
8But he refused. "With me in charge," he
told her, "my master does not concern himself with anything in the house; everything
he owns he has entrusted to my care. 9No one
is greater in this house than I am. My master
has withheld nothing from me except you,
because you are his wife. How then could I
do such a wicked thing and sin against God?"
10And though she spoke to Joseph day after
day, he refused to go to bed with her or even
be with her.
11One day he went into the house to attend to
his duties, and none of the household servants
was inside. 12She caught him by his cloak and
said, "Come to bed with me!" But he left his
cloak in her hand and ran out of the house.
13When she saw that he had left his cloak in
her hand and had run out of the house, 14she
called her household servants. "Look," she
said to them, "this Hebrew has been brought
to us to make sport of us! He came in here
to sleep with me, but I screamed. 15When he
heard me scream for help, he left his cloak
beside me and ran out of the house."
16She kept his cloak beside her until his
master came home. 17Then she told him this
story: "That Hebrew slave you brought us
came to me to make sport of me. 18But as soon
as I screamed for help, he left his cloak beside
me and ran out of the house."
19When his master heard the story his wife
told him, saying, "This is how your slave treated me," he burned with anger. 20Joseph's master took him and put him in prison, the place
where the king's prisoners were confined.
But while Joseph was there in the prison,
21the LORD was with him; he showed him kindness and granted him favor in the eyes of the
prison warden. 22So the warden put Joseph in
charge of all those held in the prison, and he
was made responsible for all that was done
there. 23The warden paid no attention to anything under Joseph's care, because the LORD
was with Joseph and gave him success in
whatever he did.

The Cupbearer and the Baker

40 Some time later, the cupbearer and
the baker of the king of Egypt offend-
ed their master, the king of Egypt. 2Pharaoh
was angry with his two officials, the chief
cupbearer and the chief baker, 3and put them
in custody in the house of the captain of the
guard, in the same prison where Joseph was
confined. 4The captain of the guard assigned
them to Joseph, and he attended them.
After they had been in custody for some
time, 5each of the two men—the cupbearer
and the baker of the king of Egypt, who were
being held in prison—had a dream the same
night, and each dream had a meaning of its
own.
6When Joseph came to them the next morning, he saw that they were dejected. 7So he
asked Pharaoh's officials who were in custody
with him in his master's house, "Why do you
look so sad today?"
8"We both had dreams," they answered,
"but there is no one to interpret them."
Then Joseph said to them, "Do not interpre-
tations belong to God? Tell me your dreams."
9So the chief cupbearer told Joseph his
dream. He said to him, "In my dream I saw
a vine in front of me, 10and on the vine were
three branches. As soon as it budded, it blossomed, and its clusters ripened into grapes.
11Pharaoh's cup was in my hand, and I took
the grapes, squeezed them into Pharaoh's cup
and put the cup in his hand."
12"This is what it means," Joseph said to
him. "The three branches are three days.
13Within three days Pharaoh will lift up your
head and restore you to your position, and
you will put Pharaoh's cup in his hand, just as
you used to do when you were his cupbearer.
14But when all goes well with you, remember me and show me kindness; mention me
to Pharaoh and get me out of this prison. 15I
was forcibly carried off from the land of the
Hebrews, and even here I have done nothing
to deserve being put in a dungeon."
16When the chief baker saw that Joseph had
given a favorable interpretation, he said to
Joseph, "I too had a dream: On my head were
three baskets of bread.[a] 17In the top basket
were all kinds of baked goods for Pharaoh,
but the birds were eating them out of the basket on my head."
18"This is what it means," Joseph said. "The
three baskets are three days. 19Within three
days Pharaoh will lift off your head and impale your body on a pole. And the birds will
eat away your flesh."
20Now the third day was Pharaoh's birthday, and he gave a feast for all his officials.
He lifted up the heads of the chief cupbearer
and the chief baker in the presence of his officials: 21He restored the chief cupbearer to

[a] 16 Or *three wicker baskets*

his position, so that he once again put the cup
into Pharaoh's hand— 22but he impaled the
chief baker, just as Joseph had said to them
in his interpretation.
23The chief cupbearer, however, did not remember Joseph; he forgot him.

Pharaoh's Dreams

41 When two full years had passed, Pharaoh had a dream: He was standing by
the Nile, 2when out of the river there came up
seven cows, sleek and fat, and they grazed
among the reeds. 3After them, seven other
cows, ugly and gaunt, came up out of the Nile
and stood beside those on the riverbank. 4And
the cows that were ugly and gaunt ate up the
seven sleek, fat cows. Then Pharaoh woke up.
5He fell asleep again and had a second
dream: Seven heads of grain, healthy and
good, were growing on a single stalk. 6Af-
ter them, seven other heads of grain sprouted—thin and scorched by the east wind. 7The
thin heads of grain swallowed up the seven
healthy, full heads. Then Pharaoh woke up;
it had been a dream.
8In the morning his mind was troubled, so
he sent for all the magicians and wise men of
Egypt. Pharaoh told them his dreams, but no
one could interpret them for him.
9Then the chief cupbearer said to Pharaoh,
"Today I am reminded of my shortcomings.
10Pharaoh was once angry with his servants,
and he imprisoned me and the chief baker in
the house of the captain of the guard. 11Each
of us had a dream the same night, and each
dream had a meaning of its own. 12Now a
young Hebrew was there with us, a servant
of the captain of the guard. We told him our
dreams, and he interpreted them for us, giving each man the interpretation of his dream.
13And things turned out exactly as he interpreted them to us: I was restored to my position, and the other man was impaled."
14So Pharaoh sent for Joseph, and he was
quickly brought from the dungeon. When he
had shaved and changed his clothes, he came
before Pharaoh.
15Pharaoh said to Joseph, "I had a dream,
and no one can interpret it. But I have heard
it said of you that when you hear a dream you
can interpret it."
16"I cannot do it," Joseph replied to Pharaoh, "but God will give Pharaoh the answer
he desires."
17Then Pharaoh said to Joseph, "In my
dream I was standing on the bank of the
Nile, 18when out of the river there came up
seven cows, fat and sleek, and they grazed
among the reeds. 19After them, seven other
cows came up—scrawny and very ugly and
lean. I had never seen such ugly cows in all
the land of Egypt. 20The lean, ugly cows ate
up the seven fat cows that came up first. 21But
even after they ate them, no one could tell that
they had done so; they looked just as ugly as
before. Then I woke up.
22"In my dream I saw seven heads of grain,
full and good, growing on a single stalk. 23Af-
ter them, seven other heads sprouted—withered and thin and scorched by the east wind.
24The thin heads of grain swallowed up the
seven good heads. I told this to the magicians,
but none of them could explain it to me."
25Then Joseph said to Pharaoh, "The
dreams of Pharaoh are one and the same. God
has revealed to Pharaoh what he is about to
do. 26The seven good cows are seven years,
and the seven good heads of grain are seven
years; it is one and the same dream. 27The
seven lean, ugly cows that came up afterward
are seven years, and so are the seven worthless heads of grain scorched by the east wind:
They are seven years of famine.
28"It is just as I said to Pharaoh: God has
shown Pharaoh what he is about to do. 29Sev-
en years of great abundance are coming
throughout the land of Egypt, 30but seven
years of famine will follow them. Then all the
abundance in Egypt will be forgotten, and the
famine will ravage the land. 31The abundance
in the land will not be remembered, because
the famine that follows it will be so severe.
32The reason the dream was given to Pharaoh
in two forms is that the matter has been firmly decided by God, and God will do it soon.
33"And now let Pharaoh look for a discerning and wise man and put him in charge of
the land of Egypt. 34Let Pharaoh appoint commissioners over the land to take a fifth of the
harvest of Egypt during the seven years of
abundance. 35They should collect all the food
of these good years that are coming and store
up the grain under the authority of Pharaoh,
to be kept in the cities for food. 36This food
should be held in reserve for the country, to
be used during the seven years of famine that
will come upon Egypt, so that the country may
not be ruined by the famine."
37The plan seemed good to Pharaoh and
to all his officials. 38So Pharaoh asked them,
"Can we find anyone like this man, one in
whom is the spirit of God[a]?"
39Then Pharaoh said to Joseph, "Since God
has made all this known to you, there is no one
so discerning and wise as you. 40You shall be
in charge of my palace, and all my people are
to submit to your orders. Only with respect to
the throne will I be greater than you."

Joseph in Charge of Egypt

41So Pharaoh said to Joseph, "I hereby put
you in charge of the whole land of Egypt."
42Then Pharaoh took his signet ring from
his finger and put it on Joseph's finger. He
dressed him in robes of fine linen and put
a gold chain around his neck. 43He had him
ride in a chariot as his second-in-command,[b]
and people shouted before him, "Make way[c]!"
Thus he put him in charge of the whole land
of Egypt.
44Then Pharaoh said to Joseph, "I am Pharaoh, but without your word no one will lift

[a] 38 Or *of the gods* [b] 43 Or *in the chariot of his second-in-command*; or *in his second chariot*
[c] 43 Or *Bow down*

hand or foot in all Egypt." 45 Pharaoh gave Joseph the name Zaphenath-Paneah and gave him Asenath daughter of Potiphera, priest of On,[a] to be his wife. And Joseph went throughout the land of Egypt.

46 Joseph was thirty years old when he entered the service of Pharaoh king of Egypt. And Joseph went out from Pharaoh's presence and traveled throughout Egypt. 47 During the seven years of abundance the land produced plentifully. 48 Joseph collected all the food produced in those seven years of abundance in Egypt and stored it in the cities. In each city he put the food grown in the fields surrounding it. 49 Joseph stored up huge quantities of grain, like the sand of the sea; it was so much that he stopped keeping records because it was beyond measure.

50 Before the years of famine came, two sons were born to Joseph by Asenath daughter of Potiphera, priest of On. 51 Joseph named his firstborn Manasseh[b] and said, "It is because God has made me forget all my trouble and all my father's household." 52 The second son he named Ephraim[c] and said, "It is because God has made me fruitful in the land of my suffering."

53 The seven years of abundance in Egypt came to an end, 54 and the seven years of famine began, just as Joseph had said. There was famine in all the other lands, but in the whole land of Egypt there was food. 55 When all Egypt began to feel the famine, the people cried to Pharaoh for food. Then Pharaoh told all the Egyptians, "Go to Joseph and do what he tells you."

56 When the famine had spread over the whole country, Joseph opened all the storehouses and sold grain to the Egyptians, for the famine was severe throughout Egypt. 57 And all the world came to Egypt to buy grain from Joseph, because the famine was severe everywhere.

Joseph's Brothers Go to Egypt

42 When Jacob learned that there was grain in Egypt, he said to his sons, "Why do you just keep looking at each other?" 2 He continued, "I have heard that there is grain in Egypt. Go down there and buy some for us, so that we may live and not die."

3 Then ten of Joseph's brothers went down to buy grain from Egypt. 4 But Jacob did not send Benjamin, Joseph's brother, with the others, because he was afraid that harm might come to him. 5 So Israel's sons were among those who went to buy grain, for there was famine in the land of Canaan also.

6 Now Joseph was the governor of the land, the person who sold grain to all its people. So when Joseph's brothers arrived, they bowed down to him with their faces to the ground. 7 As soon as Joseph saw his brothers, he recognized them, but he pretended to be a stranger and spoke harshly to them. "Where do you come from?" he asked.

"From the land of Canaan," they replied, "to buy food."

8 Although Joseph recognized his brothers, they did not recognize him. 9 Then he remembered his dreams about them and said to them, "You are spies! You have come to see where our land is unprotected."

10 "No, my lord," they answered. "Your servants have come to buy food. 11 We are all the sons of one man. Your servants are honest men, not spies."

12 "No!" he said to them. "You have come to see where our land is unprotected."

13 But they replied, "Your servants were twelve brothers, the sons of one man, who lives in the land of Canaan. The youngest is now with our father, and one is no more."

14 Joseph said to them, "It is just as I told you: You are spies! 15 And this is how you will be tested: As surely as Pharaoh lives, you will not leave this place unless your youngest brother comes here. 16 Send one of your number to get your brother; the rest of you will be kept in prison, so that your words may be tested to see if you are telling the truth. If you are not, then as surely as Pharaoh lives, you are spies!" 17 And he put them all in custody for three days.

18 On the third day, Joseph said to them, "Do this and you will live, for I fear God: 19 If you are honest men, let one of your brothers stay here in prison, while the rest of you go and take grain back for your starving households. 20 But you must bring your youngest brother to me, so that your words may be verified and that you may not die." This they proceeded to do.

21 They said to one another, "Surely we are being punished because of our brother. We saw how distressed he was when he pleaded with us for his life, but we would not listen; that's why this distress has come on us."

22 Reuben replied, "Didn't I tell you not to sin against the boy? But you wouldn't listen! Now we must give an accounting for his blood." 23 They did not realize that Joseph could understand them, since he was using an interpreter.

24 He turned away from them and began to weep, but then came back and spoke to them again. He had Simeon taken from them and bound before their eyes.

25 Joseph gave orders to fill their bags with grain, to put each man's silver back in his sack, and to give them provisions for their journey. After this was done for them, 26 they loaded their grain on their donkeys and left.

27 At the place where they stopped for the night one of them opened his sack to get feed for his donkey, and he saw his silver in the mouth of his sack. 28 "My silver has been returned," he said to his brothers. "Here it is in my sack."

Their hearts sank and they turned to each other trembling and said, "What is this that God has done to us?"

[a] *45* That is, Heliopolis; also in verse 50 [b] *51* *Manasseh* sounds like and may be derived from the Hebrew for *forget.* [c] *52* *Ephraim* sounds like the Hebrew for *twice fruitful.*

29When they came to their father Jacob in
the land of Canaan, they told him all that had
happened to them. They said, 30"The man who
is lord over the land spoke harshly to us and
treated us as though we were spying on the
land. 31But we said to him, 'We are honest
men; we are not spies. 32We were twelve brothers, sons of one father. One is no more, and the
youngest is now with our father in Canaan.'
33"Then the man who is lord over the land
said to us, 'This is how I will know whether you are honest men: Leave one of your
brothers here with me, and take food for your
starving households and go. 34But bring your
youngest brother to me so I will know that
you are not spies but honest men. Then I will
give your brother back to you, and you can
trade[a] in the land.' "
35As they were emptying their sacks, there
in each man's sack was his pouch of silver!
When they and their father saw the money
pouches, they were frightened. 36Their father
Jacob said to them, "You have deprived me of
my children. Joseph is no more and Simeon is
no more, and now you want to take Benjamin.
Everything is against me!"
37Then Reuben said to his father, "You may
put both of my sons to death if I do not bring
him back to you. Entrust him to my care, and
I will bring him back."
38But Jacob said, "My son will not go down
there with you; his brother is dead and he is
the only one left. If harm comes to him on
the journey you are taking, you will bring
my gray head down to the grave in sorrow."

The Second Journey to Egypt

43 Now the famine was still severe in the
land. 2So when they had eaten all the
grain they had brought from Egypt, their father said to them, "Go back and buy us a little
more food."
3But Judah said to him, "The man warned
us solemnly, 'You will not see my face again
unless your brother is with you.' 4If you will
send our brother along with us, we will go
down and buy food for you. 5But if you will
not send him, we will not go down, because
the man said to us, 'You will not see my face
again unless your brother is with you.' "
6Israel asked, "Why did you bring this trouble on me by telling the man you had another
brother?"
7They replied, "The man questioned us
closely about ourselves and our family. 'Is
your father still living?' he asked us. 'Do you
have another brother?' We simply answered
his questions. How were we to know he would
say, 'Bring your brother down here'?"
8Then Judah said to Israel his father, "Send
the boy along with me and we will go at once,
so that we and you and our children may live
and not die. 9I myself will guarantee his safety; you can hold me personally responsible
for him. If I do not bring him back to you and
set him here before you, I will bear the blame
before you all my life. 10As it is, if we had not
delayed, we could have gone and returned
twice."
11Then their father Israel said to them, "If
it must be, then do this: Put some of the best
products of the land in your bags and take
them down to the man as a gift—a little balm
and a little honey, some spices and myrrh,
some pistachio nuts and almonds. 12Take double the amount of silver with you, for you must
return the silver that was put back into the
mouths of your sacks. Perhaps it was a mistake. 13Take your brother also and go back to
the man at once. 14And may God Almighty[b]
grant you mercy before the man so that he
will let your other brother and Benjamin come
back with you. As for me, if I am bereaved, I
am bereaved."
15So the men took the gifts and double the
amount of silver, and Benjamin also. They
hurried down to Egypt and presented themselves to Joseph. 16When Joseph saw Benjamin with them, he said to the steward of his
house, "Take these men to my house, slaughter
an animal and prepare a meal; they are to eat
with me at noon."
17The man did as Joseph told him and took
the men to Joseph's house. 18Now the men
were frightened when they were taken to his
house. They thought, "We were brought here
because of the silver that was put back into
our sacks the first time. He wants to attack
us and overpower us and seize us as slaves
and take our donkeys."
19So they went up to Joseph's steward and
spoke to him at the entrance to the house.
20"We beg your pardon, our lord," they said,
"we came down here the first time to buy food.
21But at the place where we stopped for the
night we opened our sacks and each of us
found his silver—the exact weight—in the
mouth of his sack. So we have brought it back
with us. 22We have also brought additional
silver with us to buy food. We don't know who
put our silver in our sacks."
23"It's all right," he said. "Don't be afraid.
Your God, the God of your father, has given
you treasure in your sacks; I received your
silver." Then he brought Simeon out to them.
24The steward took the men into Joseph's
house, gave them water to wash their feet and
provided fodder for their donkeys. 25They prepared their gifts for Joseph's arrival at noon,
because they had heard that they were to eat
there.
26When Joseph came home, they presented to him the gifts they had brought into the
house, and they bowed down before him to
the ground. 27He asked them how they were,
and then he said, "How is your aged father
you told me about? Is he still living?"
28They replied, "Your servant our father is
still alive and well." And they bowed down,
prostrating themselves before him.
29As he looked about and saw his brother
Benjamin, his own mother's son, he asked, "Is
this your youngest brother, the one you told
me about?" And he said, "God be gracious to

[a] 34 Or *move about freely* [b] 14 Hebrew *El-Shaddai*

you, my son." 30Deeply moved at the sight of
his brother, Joseph hurried out and looked
for a place to weep. He went into his private
room and wept there.
31After he had washed his face, he came
out and, controlling himself, said, "Serve the
food."
32They served him by himself, the brothers by themselves, and the Egyptians who ate
with him by themselves, because Egyptians
could not eat with Hebrews, for that is detestable to Egyptians. 33The men had been
seated before him in the order of their ages,
from the firstborn to the youngest; and they
looked at each other in astonishment. 34When
portions were served to them from Joseph's
table, Benjamin's portion was five times as
much as anyone else's. So they feasted and
drank freely with him.

A Silver Cup in a Sack

44 Now Joseph gave these instructions to
the steward of his house: "Fill the men's
sacks with as much food as they can carry,
and put each man's silver in the mouth of his
sack. 2Then put my cup, the silver one, in the
mouth of the youngest one's sack, along with
the silver for his grain." And he did as Joseph said.
3As morning dawned, the men were sent
on their way with their donkeys. 4They had
not gone far from the city when Joseph said
to his steward, "Go after those men at once,
and when you catch up with them, say to them,
'Why have you repaid good with evil? 5Isn't
this the cup my master drinks from and also
uses for divination? This is a wicked thing
you have done.'"
6When he caught up with them, he repeated
these words to them. 7But they said to him,
"Why does my lord say such things? Far be it
from your servants to do anything like that!
8We even brought back to you from the land of
Canaan the silver we found inside the mouths
of our sacks. So why would we steal silver or
gold from your master's house? 9If any of your
servants is found to have it, he will die; and
the rest of us will become my lord's slaves."
10"Very well, then," he said, "let it be as you
say. Whoever is found to have it will become
my slave; the rest of you will be free from
blame."
11Each of them quickly lowered his sack to
the ground and opened it. 12Then the steward
proceeded to search, beginning with the oldest and ending with the youngest. And the cup
was found in Benjamin's sack. 13At this, they
tore their clothes. Then they all loaded their
donkeys and returned to the city.
14Joseph was still in the house when Judah
and his brothers came in, and they threw
themselves to the ground before him. 15Joseph
said to them, "What is this you have done?
Don't you know that a man like me can find
things out by divination?"
16"What can we say to my lord?" Judah replied. "What can we say? How can we prove
our innocence? God has uncovered your servants' guilt. We are now my lord's slaves—we
ourselves and the one who was found to have
the cup."
17But Joseph said, "Far be it from me to do
such a thing! Only the man who was found
to have the cup will become my slave. The
rest of you, go back to your father in peace."
18Then Judah went up to him and said: "Pardon your servant, my lord, let me speak a word
to my lord. Do not be angry with your servant,
though you are equal to Pharaoh himself.
19My lord asked his servants, 'Do you have
a father or a brother?' 20And we answered,
'We have an aged father, and there is a young
son born to him in his old age. His brother is
dead, and he is the only one of his mother's
sons left, and his father loves him.'
21"Then you said to your servants, 'Bring
him down to me so I can see him for myself.'
22And we said to my lord, 'The boy cannot
leave his father; if he leaves him, his father
will die.' 23But you told your servants, 'Unless
your youngest brother comes down with you,
you will not see my face again.' 24When we
went back to your servant my father, we told
him what my lord had said.
25"Then our father said, 'Go back and buy
a little more food.' 26But we said, 'We cannot
go down. Only if our youngest brother is with
us will we go. We cannot see the man's face
unless our youngest brother is with us.'
27"Your servant my father said to us, 'You
know that my wife bore me two sons. 28One
of them went away from me, and I said, "He
has surely been torn to pieces." And I have not
seen him since. 29If you take this one from me
too and harm comes to him, you will bring
my gray head down to the grave in misery.'
30"So now, if the boy is not with us when I
go back to your servant my father, and if my
father, whose life is closely bound up with the
boy's life, 31sees that the boy isn't there, he will
die. Your servants will bring the gray head
of our father down to the grave in sorrow.
32Your servant guaranteed the boy's safety to
my father. I said, 'If I do not bring him back
to you, I will bear the blame before you, my
father, all my life!'
33"Now then, please let your servant remain
here as my lord's slave in place of the boy, and
let the boy return with his brothers. 34How
can I go back to my father if the boy is not
with me? No! Do not let me see the misery
that would come on my father."

Joseph Makes Himself Known

45 Then Joseph could no longer control
himself before all his attendants, and
he cried out, "Have everyone leave my presence!" So there was no one with Joseph when
he made himself known to his brothers. 2And
he wept so loudly that the Egyptians heard
him, and Pharaoh's household heard about it.
3Joseph said to his brothers, "I am Joseph! Is
my father still living?" But his brothers were
not able to answer him, because they were
terrified at his presence.
4Then Joseph said to his brothers, "Come
close to me." When they had done so, he said,
"I am your brother Joseph, the one you sold

into Egypt! 5And now, do not be distressed
and do not be angry with yourselves for selling me here, because it was to save lives that
God sent me ahead of you. 6For two years now
there has been famine in the land, and for the
next five years there will be no plowing and
reaping. 7But God sent me ahead of you to
preserve for you a remnant on earth and to
save your lives by a great deliverance.[a]

8"So then, it was not you who sent me here,
but God. He made me father to Pharaoh, lord
of his entire household and ruler of all Egypt.
9Now hurry back to my father and say to him,
'This is what your son Joseph says: God has
made me lord of all Egypt. Come down to me;
don't delay. 10You shall live in the region of
Goshen and be near me—you, your children
and grandchildren, your flocks and herds, and
all you have. 11I will provide for you there, because five years of famine are still to come.
Otherwise you and your household and all
who belong to you will become destitute.'

12"You can see for yourselves, and so can
my brother Benjamin, that it is really I who
am speaking to you. 13Tell my father about all
the honor accorded me in Egypt and about everything you have seen. And bring my father
down here quickly."

14Then he threw his arms around his brother Benjamin and wept, and Benjamin embraced him, weeping. 15And he kissed all his
brothers and wept over them. Afterward his
brothers talked with him.

16When the news reached Pharaoh's palace that Joseph's brothers had come, Pharaoh
and all his officials were pleased. 17Pharaoh
said to Joseph, "Tell your brothers, 'Do this:
Load your animals and return to the land of
Canaan, 18and bring your father and your
families back to me. I will give you the best
of the land of Egypt and you can enjoy the
fat of the land.'

19"You are also directed to tell them, 'Do
this: Take some carts from Egypt for your
children and your wives, and get your father
and come. 20Never mind about your belongings, because the best of all Egypt will be
yours.'"

21So the sons of Israel did this. Joseph gave
them carts, as Pharaoh had commanded, and
he also gave them provisions for their journey.
22To each of them he gave new clothing, but
to Benjamin he gave three hundred shekels[b]
of silver and five sets of clothes. 23And this is
what he sent to his father: ten donkeys loaded
with the best things of Egypt, and ten female
donkeys loaded with grain and bread and other provisions for his journey. 24Then he sent
his brothers away, and as they were leaving
he said to them, "Don't quarrel on the way!"

25So they went up out of Egypt and came
to their father Jacob in the land of Canaan.
26They told him, "Joseph is still alive! In fact,
he is ruler of all Egypt." Jacob was stunned;
he did not believe them. 27But when they told
him everything Joseph had said to them, and
when he saw the carts Joseph had sent to carry him back, the spirit of their father Jacob
revived. 28And Israel said, "I'm convinced! My
son Joseph is still alive. I will go and see him
before I die."

Jacob Goes to Egypt

46 So Israel set out with all that was his,
and when he reached Beersheba, he offered sacrifices to the God of his father Isaac.

2And God spoke to Israel in a vision at night
and said, "Jacob! Jacob!"

"Here I am," he replied.

3"I am God, the God of your father," he said.
"Do not be afraid to go down to Egypt, for I
will make you into a great nation there. 4I will
go down to Egypt with you, and I will surely
bring you back again. And Joseph's own hand
will close your eyes."

5Then Jacob left Beersheba, and Israel's
sons took their father Jacob and their children and their wives in the carts that Pharaoh had sent to transport him. 6So Jacob and
all his offspring went to Egypt, taking with
them their livestock and the possessions they
had acquired in Canaan. 7Jacob brought with
him to Egypt his sons and grandsons and his
daughters and granddaughters—all his offspring.

8These are the names of the sons of Israel (Jacob and his descendants) who went to
Egypt:

Reuben the firstborn of Jacob.
9The sons of Reuben:
Hanok, Pallu, Hezron and Karmi.
10The sons of Simeon:
Jemuel, Jamin, Ohad, Jakin, Zohar and
Shaul the son of a Canaanite woman.
11The sons of Levi:
Gershon, Kohath and Merari.
12The sons of Judah:
Er, Onan, Shelah, Perez and Zerah (but
Er and Onan had died in the land of
Canaan).
The sons of Perez:
Hezron and Hamul.
13The sons of Issachar:
Tola, Puah,[c] Jashub[d] and Shimron.
14The sons of Zebulun:
Sered, Elon and Jahleel.

15These were the sons Leah bore to Jacob
in Paddan Aram,[e] besides his daughter Dinah. These sons and daughters of his were
thirty-three in all.

16The sons of Gad:
Zephon,[f] Haggi, Shuni, Ezbon, Eri, Arodi and Areli.
17The sons of Asher:
Imnah, Ishvah, Ishvi and Beriah.

[a] 7 Or *save you as a great band of survivors* [b] 22 That is, about 7 1/2 pounds or about 3.5 kilograms
[c] 13 Samaritan Pentateuch and Syriac (see also 1 Chron. 7:1); Masoretic Text *Puvah* [d] 13 Samaritan Pentateuch and some Septuagint manuscripts (see also Num. 26:24 and 1 Chron. 7:1); Masoretic Text *Iob* [e] 15 That is, Northwest Mesopotamia [f] 16 Samaritan Pentateuch and Septuagint (see also Num. 26:15); Masoretic Text *Ziphion*

Their sister was Serah.
The sons of Beriah:
Heber and Malkiel.

18 These were the children born to Jacob by Zilpah, whom Laban had given to his daughter Leah—sixteen in all.

19 The sons of Jacob's wife Rachel:
Joseph and Benjamin. 20 In Egypt, Manasseh and Ephraim were born to Joseph by Asenath daughter of Potiphera, priest of On.[a]

21 The sons of Benjamin:
Bela, Beker, Ashbel, Gera, Naaman, Ehi, Rosh, Muppim, Huppim and Ard.

22 These were the sons of Rachel who were born to Jacob—fourteen in all.

23 The son of Dan:
Hushim.

24 The sons of Naphtali:
Jahziel, Guni, Jezer and Shillem.

25 These were the sons born to Jacob by Bilhah, whom Laban had given to his daughter Rachel—seven in all.

26 All those who went to Egypt with Jacob—those who were his direct descendants, not counting his sons' wives—numbered sixty-six persons. 27 With the two sons[b] who had been born to Joseph in Egypt, the members of Jacob's family, which went to Egypt, were seventy[c] in all.

28 Now Jacob sent Judah ahead of him to Joseph to get directions to Goshen. When they arrived in the region of Goshen, 29 Joseph had his chariot made ready and went to Goshen to meet his father Israel. As soon as Joseph appeared before him, he threw his arms around his father[d] and wept for a long time.

30 Israel said to Joseph, "Now I am ready to die, since I have seen for myself that you are still alive."

31 Then Joseph said to his brothers and to his father's household, "I will go up and speak to Pharaoh and will say to him, 'My brothers and my father's household, who were living in the land of Canaan, have come to me. 32 The men are shepherds; they tend livestock, and they have brought along their flocks and herds and everything they own.' 33 When Pharaoh calls you in and asks, 'What is your occupation?' 34 you should answer, 'Your servants have tended livestock from our boyhood on, just as our fathers did.' Then you will be allowed to settle in the region of Goshen, for all shepherds are detestable to the Egyptians."

47 Joseph went and told Pharaoh, "My father and brothers, with their flocks and herds and everything they own, have come from the land of Canaan and are now in Goshen." 2 He chose five of his brothers and presented them before Pharaoh.

3 Pharaoh asked the brothers, "What is your occupation?"

"Your servants are shepherds," they replied to Pharaoh, "just as our fathers were." 4 They also said to him, "We have come to live here for a while, because the famine is severe in Canaan and your servants' flocks have no pasture. So now, please let your servants settle in Goshen."

5 Pharaoh said to Joseph, "Your father and your brothers have come to you, 6 and the land of Egypt is before you; settle your father and your brothers in the best part of the land. Let them live in Goshen. And if you know of any among them with special ability, put them in charge of my own livestock."

7 Then Joseph brought his father Jacob in and presented him before Pharaoh. After Jacob blessed[e] Pharaoh, 8 Pharaoh asked him, "How old are you?"

9 And Jacob said to Pharaoh, "The years of my pilgrimage are a hundred and thirty. My years have been few and difficult, and they do not equal the years of the pilgrimage of my fathers." 10 Then Jacob blessed[f] Pharaoh and went out from his presence.

11 So Joseph settled his father and his brothers in Egypt and gave them property in the best part of the land, the district of Rameses, as Pharaoh directed. 12 Joseph also provided his father and his brothers and all his father's household with food, according to the number of their children.

Joseph and the Famine

13 There was no food, however, in the whole region because the famine was severe; both Egypt and Canaan wasted away because of the famine. 14 Joseph collected all the money that was to be found in Egypt and Canaan in payment for the grain they were buying, and he brought it to Pharaoh's palace. 15 When the money of the people of Egypt and Canaan was gone, all Egypt came to Joseph and said, "Give us food. Why should we die before your eyes? Our money is all gone."

16 "Then bring your livestock," said Joseph. "I will sell you food in exchange for your livestock, since your money is gone." 17 So they brought their livestock to Joseph, and he gave them food in exchange for their horses, their sheep and goats, their cattle and donkeys. And he brought them through that year with food in exchange for all their livestock.

18 When that year was over, they came to him the following year and said, "We cannot hide from our lord the fact that since our money is gone and our livestock belongs to you, there is nothing left for our lord except our bodies and our land. 19 Why should we perish before your eyes—we and our land as well? Buy us and our land in exchange for food, and we with our land will be in bondage to Pharaoh. Give us seed so that we may live and not die, and that the land may not become desolate."

20 So Joseph bought all the land in Egypt for Pharaoh. The Egyptians, one and all, sold

[a] 20 That is, Heliopolis [b] 27 Hebrew; Septuagint *the nine children* [c] 27 Hebrew (see also Exodus 1:5 and note); Septuagint (see also Acts 7:14) *seventy-five* [d] 29 Hebrew *around him* [e] 7 Or *greeted* [f] 10 Or *said farewell to*

their fields, because the famine was too severe
for them. The land became Pharaoh's, 21and
Joseph reduced the people to servitude,[a] from
one end of Egypt to the other. 22However, he
did not buy the land of the priests, because
they received a regular allotment from Pharaoh and had food enough from the allotment
Pharaoh gave them. That is why they did not
sell their land.

23Joseph said to the people, "Now that I have
bought you and your land today for Pharaoh, here is seed for you so you can plant the
ground. 24But when the crop comes in, give
a fifth of it to Pharaoh. The other four-fifths
you may keep as seed for the fields and as
food for yourselves and your households and
your children."

25"You have saved our lives," they said.
"May we find favor in the eyes of our lord;
we will be in bondage to Pharaoh."

26So Joseph established it as a law concerning land in Egypt—still in force today—that
a fifth of the produce belongs to Pharaoh. It
was only the land of the priests that did not
become Pharaoh's.

27Now the Israelites settled in Egypt in the
region of Goshen. They acquired property
there and were fruitful and increased greatly in number.

28Jacob lived in Egypt seventeen years, and
the years of his life were a hundred and forty-
seven. 29When the time drew near for Israel
to die, he called for his son Joseph and said
to him, "If I have found favor in your eyes, put
your hand under my thigh and promise that
you will show me kindness and faithfulness.
Do not bury me in Egypt, 30but when I rest
with my fathers, carry me out of Egypt and
bury me where they are buried."

"I will do as you say," he said.

31"Swear to me," he said. Then Joseph swore
to him, and Israel worshiped as he leaned on
the top of his staff.[b]

Manasseh and Ephraim

48 Some time later Joseph was told, "Your
father is ill." So he took his two sons Manasseh and Ephraim along with him. 2When
Jacob was told, "Your son Joseph has come
to you," Israel rallied his strength and sat up
on the bed.

3Jacob said to Joseph, "God Almighty[c] appeared to me at Luz in the land of Canaan,
and there he blessed me 4and said to me, 'I
am going to make you fruitful and increase
your numbers. I will make you a community of peoples, and I will give this land as an
everlasting possession to your descendants
after you.'

5"Now then, your two sons born to you in
Egypt before I came to you here will be reckoned as mine; Ephraim and Manasseh will be
mine, just as Reuben and Simeon are mine.
6Any children born to you after them will be
yours; in the territory they inherit they will be
reckoned under the names of their brothers.
7As I was returning from Paddan,[d] to my sorrow Rachel died in the land of Canaan while
we were still on the way, a little distance from
Ephrath. So I buried her there beside the road
to Ephrath" (that is, Bethlehem).

8When Israel saw the sons of Joseph, he
asked, "Who are these?"

9"They are the sons God has given me here,"
Joseph said to his father.

Then Israel said, "Bring them to me so I
may bless them."

10Now Israel's eyes were failing because of
old age, and he could hardly see. So Joseph
brought his sons close to him, and his father
kissed them and embraced them.

11Israel said to Joseph, "I never expected to
see your face again, and now God has allowed
me to see your children too."

12Then Joseph removed them from Israel's knees and bowed down with his face to
the ground. 13And Joseph took both of them,
Ephraim on his right toward Israel's left hand
and Manasseh on his left toward Israel's right
hand, and brought them close to him. 14But
Israel reached out his right hand and put it on
Ephraim's head, though he was the younger,
and crossing his arms, he put his left hand
on Manasseh's head, even though Manasseh
was the firstborn.

15Then he blessed Joseph and said,

"May the God before whom my fathers
Abraham and Isaac walked faithfully,
the God who has been my shepherd
all my life to this day,
16the Angel who has delivered me from all
harm
—may he bless these boys.
May they be called by my name
and the names of my fathers Abraham
and Isaac,
and may they increase greatly
on the earth."

17When Joseph saw his father placing his
right hand on Ephraim's head he was displeased; so he took hold of his father's hand
to move it from Ephraim's head to Manasseh's
head. 18Joseph said to him, "No, my father,
this one is the firstborn; put your right hand
on his head."

19But his father refused and said, "I know,
my son, I know. He too will become a people,
and he too will become great. Nevertheless,
his younger brother will be greater than he,
and his descendants will become a group of
nations." 20He blessed them that day and said,

"In your[e] name will Israel pronounce this
blessing:
'May God make you like Ephraim and
Manasseh.'"

So he put Ephraim ahead of Manasseh.

21Then Israel said to Joseph, "I am about to
die, but God will be with you[f] and take you[f]

[a] 21 Samaritan Pentateuch and Septuagint (see also Vulgate); Masoretic Text *and he moved the people into the cities* [b] 31 Or *Israel bowed down at the head of his bed* [c] 3 Hebrew *El-Shaddai*
[d] 7 That is, Northwest Mesopotamia [e] 20 The Hebrew is singular. [f] 21 The Hebrew is plural.

back to the land of your[a] fathers. 22And to you
I give one more ridge of land[b] than to your
brothers, the ridge I took from the Amorites
with my sword and my bow."

Jacob Blesses His Sons

49 Then Jacob called for his sons and said: "Gather around so I can tell you what will happen to you in days to come.

2"Assemble and listen, sons of Jacob;
listen to your father Israel.

3"Reuben, you are my firstborn,
my might, the first sign of my strength,
excelling in honor, excelling in power.
4Turbulent as the waters, you will no longer excel,
for you went up onto your father's bed,
onto my couch and defiled it.

5"Simeon and Levi are brothers—
their swords[c] are weapons of violence.
6Let me not enter their council,
let me not join their assembly,
for they have killed men in their anger
and hamstrung oxen as they pleased.
7Cursed be their anger, so fierce,
and their fury, so cruel!
I will scatter them in Jacob
and disperse them in Israel.

8"Judah,[d] your brothers will praise you;
your hand will be on the neck of your enemies;
your father's sons will bow down to you.
9You are a lion's cub, Judah;
you return from the prey, my son.
Like a lion he crouches and lies down,
like a lioness—who dares to rouse him?
10The scepter will not depart from Judah,
nor the ruler's staff from between his feet,[e]
until he to whom it belongs[f] shall come
and the obedience of the nations shall be his.
11He will tether his donkey to a vine,
his colt to the choicest branch;
he will wash his garments in wine,
his robes in the blood of grapes.
12His eyes will be darker than wine,
his teeth whiter than milk.[g]

13"Zebulun will live by the seashore
and become a haven for ships;
his border will extend toward Sidon.

14"Issachar is a rawboned[h] donkey
lying down among the sheep pens.[i]
15When he sees how good is his resting place
and how pleasant is his land,
he will bend his shoulder to the burden
and submit to forced labor.

16"Dan[j] will provide justice for his people
as one of the tribes of Israel.
17Dan will be a snake by the roadside,
a viper along the path,
that bites the horse's heels
so that its rider tumbles backward.

18"I look for your deliverance, LORD.

19"Gad[k] will be attacked by a band of raiders,
but he will attack them at their heels.

20"Asher's food will be rich;
he will provide delicacies fit for a king.

21"Naphtali is a doe set free
that bears beautiful fawns.[l]

22"Joseph is a fruitful vine,
a fruitful vine near a spring,
whose branches climb over a wall.[m]
23With bitterness archers attacked him;
they shot at him with hostility.
24But his bow remained steady,
his strong arms stayed[n] limber,
because of the hand of the Mighty One of Jacob,
because of the Shepherd, the Rock of Israel,
25because of your father's God, who helps you,
because of the Almighty,[o] who blesses you
with blessings of the skies above,
blessings of the deep springs below,
blessings of the breast and womb.
26Your father's blessings are greater
than the blessings of the ancient mountains,
than[p] the bounty of the age-old hills.
Let all these rest on the head of Joseph,
on the brow of the prince among[q] his brothers.

27"Benjamin is a ravenous wolf;
in the morning he devours the prey,
in the evening he divides the plunder."

28All these are the twelve tribes of Israel,
and this is what their father said to them when
he blessed them, giving each the blessing appropriate to him.

The Death of Jacob

29Then he gave them these instructions: "I
am about to be gathered to my people. Bury
me with my fathers in the cave in the field of
Ephron the Hittite, 30the cave in the field of
Machpelah, near Mamre in Canaan, which

[a] 21 The Hebrew is plural. [b] 22 The Hebrew for *ridge of land* is identical with the place name Shechem. [c] 5 The meaning of the Hebrew for this word is uncertain. [d] 8 *Judah* sounds like and may be derived from the Hebrew for *praise*. [e] 10 Or *from his descendants* [f] 10 Or *to whom tribute belongs*; the meaning of the Hebrew for this phrase is uncertain. [g] 12 Or *will be dull from wine, / his teeth white from milk* [h] 14 Or *strong* [i] 14 Or *the campfires*; or *the saddlebags* [j] 16 *Dan* here means *he provides justice*. [k] 19 *Gad* sounds like the Hebrew for *attack* and also for *band of raiders*. [l] 21 Or *free; / he utters beautiful words* [m] 22 Or *Joseph is a wild colt, / a wild colt near a spring, / a wild donkey on a terraced hill* [n] 23,24 Or *archers will attack . . . will shoot . . . will remain . . . will stay* [o] 25 Hebrew *Shaddai* [p] 26 Or *of my progenitors, / as great as* [q] 26 Or *of the one separated from*

Abraham bought along with the field as a
burial place from Ephron the Hittite. 31There
Abraham and his wife Sarah were buried,
there Isaac and his wife Rebekah were buried, and there I buried Leah. 32The field and
the cave in it were bought from the Hittites.[a]"
33When Jacob had finished giving instructions to his sons, he drew his feet up into the
bed, breathed his last and was gathered to
his people.
50 Joseph threw himself on his father and
wept over him and kissed him. 2Then
Joseph directed the physicians in his service
to embalm his father Israel. So the physicians
embalmed him, 3taking a full forty days, for
that was the time required for embalming. And
the Egyptians mourned for him seventy days.
4When the days of mourning had passed,
Joseph said to Pharaoh's court, "If I have
found favor in your eyes, speak to Pharaoh
for me. Tell him, 5'My father made me swear
an oath and said, "I am about to die; bury me
in the tomb I dug for myself in the land of Canaan." Now let me go up and bury my father;
then I will return.'"
6Pharaoh said, "Go up and bury your father,
as he made you swear to do."
7So Joseph went up to bury his father. All
Pharaoh's officials accompanied him—the
dignitaries of his court and all the dignitaries
of Egypt— 8besides all the members of Joseph's household and his brothers and those
belonging to his father's household. Only their
children and their flocks and herds were left
in Goshen. 9Chariots and horsemen[b] also went
up with him. It was a very large company.
10When they reached the threshing floor of
Atad, near the Jordan, they lamented loudly and bitterly; and there Joseph observed a
seven-day period of mourning for his father.
11When the Canaanites who lived there saw
the mourning at the threshing floor of Atad,
they said, "The Egyptians are holding a solemn ceremony of mourning." That is why that
place near the Jordan is called Abel Mizraim.[c]
12So Jacob's sons did as he had commanded
them: 13They carried him to the land of Canaan and buried him in the cave in the field
of Machpelah, near Mamre, which Abraham
had bought along with the field as a burial
place from Ephron the Hittite. 14After burying
his father, Joseph returned to Egypt, together
with his brothers and all the others who had
gone with him to bury his father.

Joseph Reassures His Brothers

15When Joseph's brothers saw that their
father was dead, they said, "What if Joseph
holds a grudge against us and pays us back
for all the wrongs we did to him?" 16So they
sent word to Joseph, saying, "Your father left
these instructions before he died: 17'This is
what you are to say to Joseph: I ask you to
forgive your brothers the sins and the wrongs
they committed in treating you so badly.' Now
please forgive the sins of the servants of the
God of your father." When their message came
to him, Joseph wept.
18His brothers then came and threw themselves down before him. "We are your slaves,"
they said.
19But Joseph said to them, "Don't be afraid.
Am I in the place of God? 20You intended to
harm me, but God intended it for good to accomplish what is now being done, the saving
of many lives. 21So then, don't be afraid. I will
provide for you and your children." And he
reassured them and spoke kindly to them.

The Death of Joseph

22Joseph stayed in Egypt, along with all
his father's family. He lived a hundred and
ten years 23and saw the third generation of
Ephraim's children. Also the children of Makir son of Manasseh were placed at birth on
Joseph's knees.[d]
24Then Joseph said to his brothers, "I am
about to die. But God will surely come to your
aid and take you up out of this land to the
land he promised on oath to Abraham, Isaac
and Jacob." 25And Joseph made the Israelites
swear an oath and said, "God will surely come
to your aid, and then you must carry my bones
up from this place."
26So Joseph died at the age of a hundred
and ten. And after they embalmed him, he
was placed in a coffin in Egypt.

Exodus

The Israelites Oppressed

1 These are the names of the sons of Israel
who went to Egypt with Jacob, each with
his family: 2Reuben, Simeon, Levi and Judah;
3Issachar, Zebulun and Benjamin; 4Dan and
Naphtali; Gad and Asher. 5The descendants of
Jacob numbered seventy[e] in all; Joseph was
already in Egypt.
6Now Joseph and all his brothers and all
that generation died, 7but the Israelites were

[a] 32 Or *the descendants of Heth* [b] 9 Or *charioteers* [c] 11 *Abel Mizraim* means *mourning of the Egyptians.* [d] 23 That is, were counted as his [e] 5 Masoretic Text (see also Gen. 46:27); Dead Sea Scrolls and Septuagint (see also Acts 7:14 and note at Gen. 46:27) *seventy-five*

exceedingly fruitful; they multiplied greatly,
increased in numbers and became so numerous that the land was filled with them.
8Then a new king, to whom Joseph meant
nothing, came to power in Egypt. 9"Look," he
said to his people, "the Israelites have become
far too numerous for us. 10Come, we must deal
shrewdly with them or they will become even
more numerous and, if war breaks out, will
join our enemies, fight against us and leave
the country."
11So they put slave masters over them to
oppress them with forced labor, and they
built Pithom and Rameses as store cities for
Pharaoh. 12But the more they were oppressed,
the more they multiplied and spread; so the
Egyptians came to dread the Israelites 13and
worked them ruthlessly. 14They made their
lives bitter with harsh labor in brick and mortar and with all kinds of work in the fields;
in all their harsh labor the Egyptians worked
them ruthlessly.
15The king of Egypt said to the Hebrew midwives, whose names were Shiphrah and Puah,
16"When you are helping the Hebrew women
during childbirth on the delivery stool, if you
see that the baby is a boy, kill him; but if it is
a girl, let her live." 17The midwives, however,
feared God and did not do what the king of
Egypt had told them to do; they let the boys
live. 18Then the king of Egypt summoned the
midwives and asked them, "Why have you
done this? Why have you let the boys live?"
19The midwives answered Pharaoh, "Hebrew women are not like Egyptian women;
they are vigorous and give birth before the
midwives arrive."
20So God was kind to the midwives and the
people increased and became even more numerous. 21And because the midwives feared
God, he gave them families of their own.
22Then Pharaoh gave this order to all his
people: "Every Hebrew boy that is born you
must throw into the Nile, but let every girl live."

The Birth of Moses

2 Now a man of the tribe of Levi married a
Levite woman, 2and she became pregnant
and gave birth to a son. When she saw that he
was a fine child, she hid him for three months.
3But when she could hide him no longer, she
got a papyrus basket[a] for him and coated it
with tar and pitch. Then she placed the child
in it and put it among the reeds along the bank
of the Nile. 4His sister stood at a distance to
see what would happen to him.
5Then Pharaoh's daughter went down to the
Nile to bathe, and her attendants were walking along the riverbank. She saw the basket
among the reeds and sent her female slave
to get it. 6She opened it and saw the baby. He
was crying, and she felt sorry for him. "This
is one of the Hebrew babies," she said.
7Then his sister asked Pharaoh's daughter,
"Shall I go and get one of the Hebrew women
to nurse the baby for you?"
8"Yes, go," she answered. So the girl went
and got the baby's mother. 9Pharaoh's daughter said to her, "Take this baby and nurse him
for me, and I will pay you." So the woman took
the baby and nursed him. 10When the child
grew older, she took him to Pharaoh's daughter and he became her son. She named him
Moses,[b] saying, "I drew him out of the water."

Moses Flees to Midian

11One day, after Moses had grown up, he
went out to where his own people were and
watched them at their hard labor. He saw an
Egyptian beating a Hebrew, one of his own
people. 12Looking this way and that and seeing no one, he killed the Egyptian and hid
him in the sand. 13The next day he went out
and saw two Hebrews fighting. He asked the
one in the wrong, "Why are you hitting your
fellow Hebrew?"
14The man said, "Who made you ruler and
judge over us? Are you thinking of killing me
as you killed the Egyptian?" Then Moses was
afraid and thought, "What I did must have
become known."
15When Pharaoh heard of this, he tried to
kill Moses, but Moses fled from Pharaoh and
went to live in Midian, where he sat down by
a well. 16Now a priest of Midian had seven
daughters, and they came to draw water and
fill the troughs to water their father's flock.
17Some shepherds came along and drove them
away, but Moses got up and came to their rescue and watered their flock.
18When the girls returned to Reuel their father, he asked them, "Why have you returned
so early today?"
19They answered, "An Egyptian rescued us
from the shepherds. He even drew water for
us and watered the flock."
20"And where is he?" Reuel asked his daughters. "Why did you leave him? Invite him to
have something to eat."
21Moses agreed to stay with the man, who
gave his daughter Zipporah to Moses in marriage. 22Zipporah gave birth to a son, and Moses named him Gershom,[c] saying, "I have become a foreigner in a foreign land."
23During that long period, the king of Egypt
died. The Israelites groaned in their slavery
and cried out, and their cry for help because
of their slavery went up to God. 24God heard
their groaning and he remembered his covenant with Abraham, with Isaac and with
Jacob. 25So God looked on the Israelites and
was concerned about them.

Moses and the Burning Bush

3 Now Moses was tending the flock of Jethro his father-in-law, the priest of Midian,
and he led the flock to the far side of the wilderness and came to Horeb, the mountain of
God. 2There the angel of the LORD appeared
to him in flames of fire from within a bush.
Moses saw that though the bush was on fire
it did not burn up. 3So Moses thought, "I will

[a] *3* The Hebrew can also mean *ark*, as in Gen. 6:14. [b] *10 Moses* sounds like the Hebrew for *draw out*.
[c] *22 Gershom* sounds like the Hebrew for *a foreigner there*.

go over and see this strange sight—why the bush does not burn up."

4When the LORD saw that he had gone over to look, God called to him from within the bush, "Moses! Moses!"

And Moses said, "Here I am."

5"Do not come any closer," God said. "Take off your sandals, for the place where you are standing is holy ground." 6Then he said, "I am the God of your father,[a] the God of Abraham, the God of Isaac and the God of Jacob." At this, Moses hid his face, because he was afraid to look at God.

7The LORD said, "I have indeed seen the misery of my people in Egypt. I have heard them crying out because of their slave drivers, and I am concerned about their suffering. 8So I have come down to rescue them from the hand of the Egyptians and to bring them up out of that land into a good and spacious land, a land flowing with milk and honey—the home of the Canaanites, Hittites, Amorites, Perizzites, Hivites and Jebusites. 9And now the cry of the Israelites has reached me, and I have seen the way the Egyptians are oppressing them. 10So now, go. I am sending you to Pharaoh to bring my people the Israelites out of Egypt."

11But Moses said to God, "Who am I that I should go to Pharaoh and bring the Israelites out of Egypt?"

12And God said, "I will be with you. And this will be the sign to you that it is I who have sent you: When you have brought the people out of Egypt, you[b] will worship God on this mountain."

13Moses said to God, "Suppose I go to the Israelites and say to them, 'The God of your fathers has sent me to you,' and they ask me, 'What is his name?' Then what shall I tell them?"

14God said to Moses, "I AM WHO I AM.[c] This is what you are to say to the Israelites: 'I AM has sent me to you.'"

15God also said to Moses, "Say to the Israelites, 'The LORD,[d] the God of your fathers—the God of Abraham, the God of Isaac and the God of Jacob—has sent me to you.'

"This is my name forever,
the name you shall call me
from generation to generation.

16"Go, assemble the elders of Israel and say to them, 'The LORD, the God of your fathers—the God of Abraham, Isaac and Jacob—appeared to me and said: I have watched over you and have seen what has been done to you in Egypt. 17And I have promised to bring you up out of your misery in Egypt into the land of the Canaanites, Hittites, Amorites, Perizzites, Hivites and Jebusites—a land flowing with milk and honey.'

18"The elders of Israel will listen to you. Then you and the elders are to go to the king of Egypt and say to him, 'The LORD, the God of the Hebrews, has met with us. Let us take a three-day journey into the wilderness to offer sacrifices to the LORD our God.' 19But I know that the king of Egypt will not let you go unless a mighty hand compels him. 20So I will stretch out my hand and strike the Egyptians with all the wonders that I will perform among them. After that, he will let you go.

21"And I will make the Egyptians favorably disposed toward this people, so that when you leave you will not go empty-handed. 22Every woman is to ask her neighbor and any woman living in her house for articles of silver and gold and for clothing, which you will put on your sons and daughters. And so you will plunder the Egyptians."

Signs for Moses

4 Moses answered, "What if they do not believe me or listen to me and say, 'The LORD did not appear to you'?"

2Then the LORD said to him, "What is that in your hand?"

"A staff," he replied.

3The LORD said, "Throw it on the ground."

Moses threw it on the ground and it became a snake, and he ran from it. 4Then the LORD said to him, "Reach out your hand and take it by the tail." So Moses reached out and took hold of the snake and it turned back into a staff in his hand. 5"This," said the LORD, "is so that they may believe that the LORD, the God of their fathers—the God of Abraham, the God of Isaac and the God of Jacob—has appeared to you."

6Then the LORD said, "Put your hand inside your cloak." So Moses put his hand into his cloak, and when he took it out, the skin was leprous[e]—it had become as white as snow.

7"Now put it back into your cloak," he said. So Moses put his hand back into his cloak, and when he took it out, it was restored, like the rest of his flesh.

8Then the LORD said, "If they do not believe you or pay attention to the first sign, they may believe the second. 9But if they do not believe these two signs or listen to you, take some water from the Nile and pour it on the dry ground. The water you take from the river will become blood on the ground."

10Moses said to the LORD, "Pardon your servant, Lord. I have never been eloquent, neither in the past nor since you have spoken to your servant. I am slow of speech and tongue."

11The LORD said to him, "Who gave human beings their mouths? Who makes them deaf or mute? Who gives them sight or makes them blind? Is it not I, the LORD? 12Now go; I will help you speak and will teach you what to say."

13But Moses said, "Pardon your servant, Lord. Please send someone else."

14Then the LORD's anger burned against Moses and he said, "What about your brother,

[a] *6* Masoretic Text; Samaritan Pentateuch (see Acts 7:32) *fathers* [b] *12* The Hebrew is plural. [c] *14* Or *I WILL BE WHAT I WILL BE* [d] *15* The Hebrew for *LORD* sounds like and may be related to the Hebrew for *I AM* in verse 14. [e] *6* The Hebrew word for *leprous* was used for various diseases affecting the skin.

Aaron the Levite? I know he can speak well.
He is already on his way to meet you, and he
will be glad to see you. 15You shall speak to
him and put words in his mouth; I will help
both of you speak and will teach you what to
do. 16He will speak to the people for you, and it
will be as if he were your mouth and as if you
were God to him. 17But take this staff in your
hand so you can perform the signs with it."

Moses Returns to Egypt

18Then Moses went back to Jethro his father-in-law and said to him, "Let me return to
my own people in Egypt to see if any of them
are still alive."

Jethro said, "Go, and I wish you well."

19Now the LORD had said to Moses in Midian, "Go back to Egypt, for all those who wanted to kill you are dead." 20So Moses took his
wife and sons, put them on a donkey and
started back to Egypt. And he took the staff
of God in his hand.

21The LORD said to Moses, "When you return to Egypt, see that you perform before
Pharaoh all the wonders I have given you the
power to do. But I will harden his heart so that
he will not let the people go. 22Then say to
Pharaoh, 'This is what the LORD says: Israel is
my firstborn son, 23and I told you, "Let my son
go, so he may worship me." But you refused to
let him go; so I will kill your firstborn son.'"

24At a lodging place on the way, the LORD
met Moses[a] and was about to kill him. 25But
Zipporah took a flint knife, cut off her son's
foreskin and touched Moses' feet with it.[b]
"Surely you are a bridegroom of blood to me,"
she said. 26So the LORD let him alone. (At that
time she said "bridegroom of blood," referring
to circumcision.)

27The LORD said to Aaron, "Go into the wilderness to meet Moses." So he met Moses at
the mountain of God and kissed him. 28Then
Moses told Aaron everything the LORD had
sent him to say, and also about all the signs
he had commanded him to perform.

29Moses and Aaron brought together all the
elders of the Israelites, 30and Aaron told them
everything the LORD had said to Moses. He
also performed the signs before the people,
31and they believed. And when they heard that
the LORD was concerned about them and had
seen their misery, they bowed down and worshiped.

Bricks Without Straw

5 Afterward Moses and Aaron went to Pharaoh and said, "This is what the LORD, the
God of Israel, says: 'Let my people go, so that
they may hold a festival to me in the wilderness.'"

2Pharaoh said, "Who is the LORD, that I
should obey him and let Israel go? I do not
know the LORD and I will not let Israel go."

3Then they said, "The God of the Hebrews
has met with us. Now let us take a three-day
journey into the wilderness to offer sacrifices
to the LORD our God, or he may strike us with
plagues or with the sword."

4But the king of Egypt said, "Moses and
Aaron, why are you taking the people away
from their labor? Get back to your work!"
5Then Pharaoh said, "Look, the people of the
land are now numerous, and you are stopping
them from working."

6That same day Pharaoh gave this order to
the slave drivers and overseers in charge of
the people: 7"You are no longer to supply the
people with straw for making bricks; let them
go and gather their own straw. 8But require
them to make the same number of bricks as
before; don't reduce the quota. They are lazy;
that is why they are crying out, 'Let us go and
sacrifice to our God.' 9Make the work harder
for the people so that they keep working and
pay no attention to lies."

10Then the slave drivers and the overseers
went out and said to the people, "This is what
Pharaoh says: 'I will not give you any more
straw. 11Go and get your own straw wherever you can find it, but your work will not be
reduced at all.'" 12So the people scattered all
over Egypt to gather stubble to use for straw.
13The slave drivers kept pressing them, saying, "Complete the work required of you for
each day, just as when you had straw." 14And
Pharaoh's slave drivers beat the Israelite overseers they had appointed, demanding, "Why
haven't you met your quota of bricks yesterday or today, as before?"

15Then the Israelite overseers went and appealed to Pharaoh: "Why have you treated
your servants this way? 16Your servants are
given no straw, yet we are told, 'Make bricks!'
Your servants are being beaten, but the fault
is with your own people."

17Pharaoh said, "Lazy, that's what you are—
lazy! That is why you keep saying, 'Let us go
and sacrifice to the LORD.' 18Now get to work.
You will not be given any straw, yet you must
produce your full quota of bricks."

19The Israelite overseers realized they were
in trouble when they were told, "You are not to
reduce the number of bricks required of you
for each day." 20When they left Pharaoh, they
found Moses and Aaron waiting to meet them,
21and they said, "May the LORD look on you
and judge you! You have made us obnoxious
to Pharaoh and his officials and have put a
sword in their hand to kill us."

God Promises Deliverance

22Moses returned to the LORD and said,
"Why, Lord, why have you brought trouble
on this people? Is this why you sent me? 23Ever
since I went to Pharaoh to speak in your name,
he has brought trouble on this people, and you
have not rescued your people at all."

6 Then the LORD said to Moses, "Now you
will see what I will do to Pharaoh: Because
of my mighty hand he will let them go; because of my mighty hand he will drive them
out of his country."

2God also said to Moses, "I am the LORD. 3I

[a] 24 Hebrew *him* [b] 25 The meaning of the Hebrew for this clause is uncertain.

appeared to Abraham, to Isaac and to Jacob as God Almighty,[a] but by my name the LORD[b] I did not make myself fully known to them. 4I also established my covenant with them to give them the land of Canaan, where they resided as foreigners. 5Moreover, I have heard the groaning of the Israelites, whom the Egyptians are enslaving, and I have remembered my covenant.

6"Therefore, say to the Israelites: 'I am the LORD, and I will bring you out from under the yoke of the Egyptians. I will free you from being slaves to them, and I will redeem you with an outstretched arm and with mighty acts of judgment. 7I will take you as my own people, and I will be your God. Then you will know that I am the LORD your God, who brought you out from under the yoke of the Egyptians. 8And I will bring you to the land I swore with uplifted hand to give to Abraham, to Isaac and to Jacob. I will give it to you as a possession. I am the LORD.'"

9Moses reported this to the Israelites, but they did not listen to him because of their discouragement and harsh labor.

10Then the LORD said to Moses, 11"Go, tell Pharaoh king of Egypt to let the Israelites go out of his country."

12But Moses said to the LORD, "If the Israelites will not listen to me, why would Pharaoh listen to me, since I speak with faltering lips[c]?"

Family Record of Moses and Aaron

13Now the LORD spoke to Moses and Aaron about the Israelites and Pharaoh king of Egypt, and he commanded them to bring the Israelites out of Egypt.

14These were the heads of their families[d]:

The sons of Reuben the firstborn son of Israel were Hanok and Pallu, Hezron and Karmi. These were the clans of Reuben.

15The sons of Simeon were Jemuel, Jamin, Ohad, Jakin, Zohar and Shaul the son of a Canaanite woman. These were the clans of Simeon.

16These were the names of the sons of Levi according to their records: Gershon, Kohath and Merari. Levi lived 137 years.

17The sons of Gershon, by clans, were Libni and Shimei.

18The sons of Kohath were Amram, Izhar, Hebron and Uzziel. Kohath lived 133 years.

19The sons of Merari were Mahli and Mushi.

These were the clans of Levi according to their records.

20Amram married his father's sister Jochebed, who bore him Aaron and Moses. Amram lived 137 years.

21The sons of Izhar were Korah, Nepheg and Zikri.

22The sons of Uzziel were Mishael, Elzaphan and Sithri.

23Aaron married Elisheba, daughter of Amminadab and sister of Nahshon, and she bore him Nadab and Abihu, Eleazar and Ithamar.

24The sons of Korah were Assir, Elkanah and Abiasaph. These were the Korahite clans.

25Eleazar son of Aaron married one of the daughters of Putiel, and she bore him Phinehas.

These were the heads of the Levite families, clan by clan.

26It was this Aaron and Moses to whom the LORD said, "Bring the Israelites out of Egypt by their divisions." 27They were the ones who spoke to Pharaoh king of Egypt about bringing the Israelites out of Egypt—this same Moses and Aaron.

Aaron to Speak for Moses

28Now when the LORD spoke to Moses in Egypt, 29he said to him, "I am the LORD. Tell Pharaoh king of Egypt everything I tell you."

30But Moses said to the LORD, "Since I speak with faltering lips, why would Pharaoh listen to me?"

7 Then the LORD said to Moses, "See, I have made you like God to Pharaoh, and your brother Aaron will be your prophet. 2You are to say everything I command you, and your brother Aaron is to tell Pharaoh to let the Israelites go out of his country. 3But I will harden Pharaoh's heart, and though I multiply my signs and wonders in Egypt, 4he will not listen to you. Then I will lay my hand on Egypt and with mighty acts of judgment I will bring out my divisions, my people the Israelites. 5And the Egyptians will know that I am the LORD when I stretch out my hand against Egypt and bring the Israelites out of it."

6Moses and Aaron did just as the LORD commanded them. 7Moses was eighty years old and Aaron eighty-three when they spoke to Pharaoh.

Aaron's Staff Becomes a Snake

8The LORD said to Moses and Aaron, 9"When Pharaoh says to you, 'Perform a miracle,' then say to Aaron, 'Take your staff and throw it down before Pharaoh,' and it will become a snake."

10So Moses and Aaron went to Pharaoh and did just as the LORD commanded. Aaron threw his staff down in front of Pharaoh and his officials, and it became a snake. 11Pharaoh then summoned wise men and sorcerers, and the Egyptian magicians also did the same things by their secret arts: 12Each one threw down his staff and it became a snake. But Aaron's staff swallowed up their staffs. 13Yet Pharaoh's heart became hard and he would not listen to them, just as the LORD had said.

The Plague of Blood

14Then the LORD said to Moses, "Pharaoh's heart is unyielding; he refuses to let the people

[a] *3* Hebrew *El-Shaddai* [b] *3* See note at 3:15. [c] *12* Hebrew *I am uncircumcised of lips*; also in verse 30 [d] *14* The Hebrew for *families* here and in verse 25 refers to units larger than clans.

go. 15Go to Pharaoh in the morning as he goes
out to the river. Confront him on the bank of
the Nile, and take in your hand the staff that
was changed into a snake. 16Then say to him,
'The LORD, the God of the Hebrews, has sent
me to say to you: Let my people go, so that they
may worship me in the wilderness. But until
now you have not listened. 17This is what the
LORD says: By this you will know that I am
the LORD: With the staff that is in my hand I
will strike the water of the Nile, and it will be
changed into blood. 18The fish in the Nile will
die, and the river will stink; the Egyptians will
not be able to drink its water.'"

19The LORD said to Moses, "Tell Aaron,
'Take your staff and stretch out your hand
over the waters of Egypt—over the streams
and canals, over the ponds and all the reservoirs—and they will turn to blood.' Blood will
be everywhere in Egypt, even in vessels[a] of
wood and stone."

20Moses and Aaron did just as the LORD had
commanded. He raised his staff in the presence of Pharaoh and his officials and struck
the water of the Nile, and all the water was
changed into blood. 21The fish in the Nile died,
and the river smelled so bad that the Egyptians could not drink its water. Blood was everywhere in Egypt.

22But the Egyptian magicians did the same
things by their secret arts, and Pharaoh's
heart became hard; he would not listen to
Moses and Aaron, just as the LORD had said.
23Instead, he turned and went into his palace,
and did not take even this to heart. 24And all
the Egyptians dug along the Nile to get drinking water, because they could not drink the
water of the river.

The Plague of Frogs

25Seven days passed after the LORD struck
8[b] the Nile. 1Then the LORD said to Moses,
"Go to Pharaoh and say to him, 'This is
what the LORD says: Let my people go, so that
they may worship me. 2If you refuse to let
them go, I will send a plague of frogs on your
whole country. 3The Nile will teem with frogs.
They will come up into your palace and your
bedroom and onto your bed, into the houses
of your officials and on your people, and into
your ovens and kneading troughs. 4The frogs
will come up on you and your people and all
your officials.'"

5Then the LORD said to Moses, "Tell Aaron,
'Stretch out your hand with your staff over
the streams and canals and ponds, and make
frogs come up on the land of Egypt.'"

6So Aaron stretched out his hand over the
waters of Egypt, and the frogs came up and
covered the land. 7But the magicians did the
same things by their secret arts; they also
made frogs come up on the land of Egypt.

8Pharaoh summoned Moses and Aaron and
said, "Pray to the LORD to take the frogs away
from me and my people, and I will let your
people go to offer sacrifices to the LORD."

9Moses said to Pharaoh, "I leave to you the
honor of setting the time for me to pray for
you and your officials and your people that
you and your houses may be rid of the frogs,
except for those that remain in the Nile."

10"Tomorrow," Pharaoh said.

Moses replied, "It will be as you say, so that
you may know there is no one like the LORD
our God. 11The frogs will leave you and your
houses, your officials and your people; they
will remain only in the Nile."

12After Moses and Aaron left Pharaoh, Moses cried out to the LORD about the frogs he
had brought on Pharaoh. 13And the LORD did
what Moses asked. The frogs died in the houses, in the courtyards and in the fields. 14They
were piled into heaps, and the land reeked of
them. 15But when Pharaoh saw that there was
relief, he hardened his heart and would not
listen to Moses and Aaron, just as the LORD
had said.

The Plague of Gnats

16Then the LORD said to Moses, "Tell Aaron,
'Stretch out your staff and strike the dust of
the ground,' and throughout the land of Egypt
the dust will become gnats." 17They did this,
and when Aaron stretched out his hand with
the staff and struck the dust of the ground,
gnats came on people and animals. All the
dust throughout the land of Egypt became
gnats. 18But when the magicians tried to produce gnats by their secret arts, they could not.

Since the gnats were on people and animals
everywhere, 19the magicians said to Pharaoh,
"This is the finger of God." But Pharaoh's
heart was hard and he would not listen, just
as the LORD had said.

The Plague of Flies

20Then the LORD said to Moses, "Get up early in the morning and confront Pharaoh as he
goes to the river and say to him, 'This is what
the LORD says: Let my people go, so that they
may worship me. 21If you do not let my people
go, I will send swarms of flies on you and your
officials, on your people and into your houses.
The houses of the Egyptians will be full of flies;
even the ground will be covered with them.

22" 'But on that day I will deal differently
with the land of Goshen, where my people
live; no swarms of flies will be there, so that
you will know that I, the LORD, am in this
land. 23I will make a distinction[c] between my
people and your people. This sign will occur
tomorrow.'"

24And the LORD did this. Dense swarms of
flies poured into Pharaoh's palace and into
the houses of his officials; throughout Egypt
the land was ruined by the flies.

25Then Pharaoh summoned Moses and Aaron and said, "Go, sacrifice to your God here
in the land."

26But Moses said, "That would not be right.
The sacrifices we offer the LORD our God
would be detestable to the Egyptians. And

[a] *19* Or *even on their idols* [b] In Hebrew texts 8:1-4 is numbered 7:26-29, and 8:5-32 is numbered 8:1-28. [c] *23* Septuagint and Vulgate; Hebrew *will put a deliverance*

if we offer sacrifices that are detestable in their eyes, will they not stone us? [27]We must take a three-day journey into the wilderness to offer sacrifices to the LORD our God, as he commands us."

[28]Pharaoh said, "I will let you go to offer sacrifices to the LORD your God in the wilderness, but you must not go very far. Now pray for me."

[29]Moses answered, "As soon as I leave you, I will pray to the LORD, and tomorrow the flies will leave Pharaoh and his officials and his people. Only let Pharaoh be sure that he does not act deceitfully again by not letting the people go to offer sacrifices to the LORD."

[30]Then Moses left Pharaoh and prayed to the LORD, [31]and the LORD did what Moses asked. The flies left Pharaoh and his officials and his people; not a fly remained. [32]But this time also Pharaoh hardened his heart and would not let the people go.

The Plague on Livestock

9 Then the LORD said to Moses, "Go to Pharaoh and say to him, 'This is what the LORD, the God of the Hebrews, says: "Let my people go, so that they may worship me." [2]If you refuse to let them go and continue to hold them back, [3]the hand of the LORD will bring a terrible plague on your livestock in the field—on your horses, donkeys and camels and on your cattle, sheep and goats. [4]But the LORD will make a distinction between the livestock of Israel and that of Egypt, so that no animal belonging to the Israelites will die.'"

[5]The LORD set a time and said, "Tomorrow the LORD will do this in the land." [6]And the next day the LORD did it: All the livestock of the Egyptians died, but not one animal belonging to the Israelites died. [7]Pharaoh investigated and found that not even one of the animals of the Israelites had died. Yet his heart was unyielding and he would not let the people go.

The Plague of Boils

[8]Then the LORD said to Moses and Aaron, "Take handfuls of soot from a furnace and have Moses toss it into the air in the presence of Pharaoh. [9]It will become fine dust over the whole land of Egypt, and festering boils will break out on people and animals throughout the land."

[10]So they took soot from a furnace and stood before Pharaoh. Moses tossed it into the air, and festering boils broke out on people and animals. [11]The magicians could not stand before Moses because of the boils that were on them and on all the Egyptians. [12]But the LORD hardened Pharaoh's heart and he would not listen to Moses and Aaron, just as the LORD had said to Moses.

The Plague of Hail

[13]Then the LORD said to Moses, "Get up early in the morning, confront Pharaoh and say to him, 'This is what the LORD, the God of the Hebrews, says: Let my people go, so that they may worship me, [14]or this time I will send the full force of my plagues against you and against your officials and your people, so you may know that there is no one like me in all the earth. [15]For by now I could have stretched out my hand and struck you and your people with a plague that would have wiped you off the earth. [16]But I have raised you up[a] for this very purpose, that I might show you my power and that my name might be proclaimed in all the earth. [17]You still set yourself against my people and will not let them go. [18]Therefore, at this time tomorrow I will send the worst hailstorm that has ever fallen on Egypt, from the day it was founded till now. [19]Give an order now to bring your livestock and everything you have in the field to a place of shelter, because the hail will fall on every person and animal that has not been brought in and is still out in the field, and they will die.'"

[20]Those officials of Pharaoh who feared the word of the LORD hurried to bring their slaves and their livestock inside. [21]But those who ignored the word of the LORD left their slaves and livestock in the field.

[22]Then the LORD said to Moses, "Stretch out your hand toward the sky so that hail will fall all over Egypt—on people and animals and on everything growing in the fields of Egypt." [23]When Moses stretched out his staff toward the sky, the LORD sent thunder and hail, and lightning flashed down to the ground. So the LORD rained hail on the land of Egypt; [24]hail fell and lightning flashed back and forth. It was the worst storm in all the land of Egypt since it had become a nation. [25]Throughout Egypt hail struck everything in the fields—both people and animals; it beat down everything growing in the fields and stripped every tree. [26]The only place it did not hail was the land of Goshen, where the Israelites were.

[27]Then Pharaoh summoned Moses and Aaron. "This time I have sinned," he said to them. "The LORD is in the right, and I and my people are in the wrong. [28]Pray to the LORD, for we have had enough thunder and hail. I will let you go; you don't have to stay any longer."

[29]Moses replied, "When I have gone out of the city, I will spread out my hands in prayer to the LORD. The thunder will stop and there will be no more hail, so you may know that the earth is the LORD's. [30]But I know that you and your officials still do not fear the LORD God."

[31](The flax and barley were destroyed, since the barley had headed and the flax was in bloom. [32]The wheat and spelt, however, were not destroyed, because they ripen later.)

[33]Then Moses left Pharaoh and went out of the city. He spread out his hands toward the LORD; the thunder and hail stopped, and the rain no longer poured down on the land. [34]When Pharaoh saw that the rain and hail and thunder had stopped, he sinned again: He and his officials hardened their hearts. [35]So Pharaoh's heart was hard and he would not

[a] 16 Or *have spared you*

let the Israelites go, just as the LORD had said through Moses.

The Plague of Locusts

10 Then the LORD said to Moses, "Go to Pharaoh, for I have hardened his heart and the hearts of his officials so that I may perform these signs of mine among them 2that you may tell your children and grandchildren how I dealt harshly with the Egyptians and how I performed my signs among them, and that you may know that I am the LORD."

3So Moses and Aaron went to Pharaoh and said to him, "This is what the LORD, the God of the Hebrews, says: 'How long will you refuse to humble yourself before me? Let my people go, so that they may worship me. 4If you refuse to let them go, I will bring locusts into your country tomorrow. 5They will cover the face of the ground so that it cannot be seen. They will devour what little you have left after the hail, including every tree that is growing in your fields. 6They will fill your houses and those of all your officials and all the Egyptians—something neither your parents nor your ancestors have ever seen from the day they settled in this land till now.'" Then Moses turned and left Pharaoh.

7Pharaoh's officials said to him, "How long will this man be a snare to us? Let the people go, so that they may worship the LORD their God. Do you not yet realize that Egypt is ruined?"

8Then Moses and Aaron were brought back to Pharaoh. "Go, worship the LORD your God," he said. "But tell me who will be going."

9Moses answered, "We will go with our young and our old, with our sons and our daughters, and with our flocks and herds, because we are to celebrate a festival to the LORD."

10Pharaoh said, "The LORD be with you—if I let you go, along with your women and children! Clearly you are bent on evil.[a] 11No! Have only the men go and worship the LORD, since that's what you have been asking for." Then Moses and Aaron were driven out of Pharaoh's presence.

12And the LORD said to Moses, "Stretch out your hand over Egypt so that locusts swarm over the land and devour everything growing in the fields, everything left by the hail."

13So Moses stretched out his staff over Egypt, and the LORD made an east wind blow across the land all that day and all that night. By morning the wind had brought the locusts; 14they invaded all Egypt and settled down in every area of the country in great numbers. Never before had there been such a plague of locusts, nor will there ever be again. 15They covered all the ground until it was black. They devoured all that was left after the hail—everything growing in the fields and the fruit on the trees. Nothing green remained on tree or plant in all the land of Egypt.

16Pharaoh quickly summoned Moses and Aaron and said, "I have sinned against the LORD your God and against you. 17Now forgive my sin once more and pray to the LORD your God to take this deadly plague away from me."

18Moses then left Pharaoh and prayed to the LORD. 19And the LORD changed the wind to a very strong west wind, which caught up the locusts and carried them into the Red Sea.[b] Not a locust was left anywhere in Egypt. 20But the LORD hardened Pharaoh's heart, and he would not let the Israelites go.

The Plague of Darkness

21Then the LORD said to Moses, "Stretch out your hand toward the sky so that darkness spreads over Egypt—darkness that can be felt." 22So Moses stretched out his hand toward the sky, and total darkness covered all Egypt for three days. 23No one could see anyone else or move about for three days. Yet all the Israelites had light in the places where they lived.

24Then Pharaoh summoned Moses and said, "Go, worship the LORD. Even your women and children may go with you; only leave your flocks and herds behind."

25But Moses said, "You must allow us to have sacrifices and burnt offerings to present to the LORD our God. 26Our livestock too must go with us; not a hoof is to be left behind. We have to use some of them in worshiping the LORD our God, and until we get there we will not know what we are to use to worship the LORD."

27But the LORD hardened Pharaoh's heart, and he was not willing to let them go. 28Pharaoh said to Moses, "Get out of my sight! Make sure you do not appear before me again! The day you see my face you will die."

29"Just as you say," Moses replied. "I will never appear before you again."

The Plague on the Firstborn

11 Now the LORD had said to Moses, "I will bring one more plague on Pharaoh and on Egypt. After that, he will let you go from here, and when he does, he will drive you out completely. 2Tell the people that men and women alike are to ask their neighbors for articles of silver and gold." 3(The LORD made the Egyptians favorably disposed toward the people, and Moses himself was highly regarded in Egypt by Pharaoh's officials and by the people.)

4So Moses said, "This is what the LORD says: 'About midnight I will go throughout Egypt. 5Every firstborn son in Egypt will die, from the firstborn son of Pharaoh, who sits on the throne, to the firstborn son of the female slave, who is at her hand mill, and all the firstborn of the cattle as well. 6There will be loud wailing throughout Egypt—worse than there has ever been or ever will be again. 7But among the Israelites not a dog will bark at any person or animal.' Then you will know that the LORD makes a distinction between Egypt and Israel. 8All these officials of yours will come to me, bowing down before me and saying,

[a] 10 Or *Be careful, trouble is in store for you!* [b] 19 Or *the Sea of Reeds*

'Go, you and all the people who follow you!' After that I will leave." Then Moses, hot with anger, left Pharaoh.

9The LORD had said to Moses, "Pharaoh will refuse to listen to you—so that my wonders may be multiplied in Egypt." 10Moses and Aaron performed all these wonders before Pharaoh, but the LORD hardened Pharaoh's heart, and he would not let the Israelites go out of his country.

The Passover and the Festival of Unleavened Bread

12 The LORD said to Moses and Aaron in Egypt, 2"This month is to be for you the first month, the first month of your year. 3Tell the whole community of Israel that on the tenth day of this month each man is to take a lamb[a] for his family, one for each household. 4If any household is too small for a whole lamb, they must share one with their nearest neighbor, having taken into account the number of people there are. You are to determine the amount of lamb needed in accordance with what each person will eat. 5The animals you choose must be year-old males without defect, and you may take them from the sheep or the goats. 6Take care of them until the fourteenth day of the month, when all the members of the community of Israel must slaughter them at twilight. 7Then they are to take some of the blood and put it on the sides and tops of the doorframes of the houses where they eat the lambs. 8That same night they are to eat the meat roasted over the fire, along with bitter herbs, and bread made without yeast. 9Do not eat the meat raw or boiled in water, but roast it over a fire—with the head, legs and internal organs. 10Do not leave any of it till morning; if some is left till morning, you must burn it. 11This is how you are to eat it: with your cloak tucked into your belt, your sandals on your feet and your staff in your hand. Eat it in haste; it is the LORD's Passover.

12"On that same night I will pass through Egypt and strike down every firstborn of both people and animals, and I will bring judgment on all the gods of Egypt. I am the LORD. 13The blood will be a sign for you on the houses where you are, and when I see the blood, I will pass over you. No destructive plague will touch you when I strike Egypt.

14"This is a day you are to commemorate; for the generations to come you shall celebrate it as a festival to the LORD—a lasting ordinance. 15For seven days you are to eat bread made without yeast. On the first day remove the yeast from your houses, for whoever eats anything with yeast in it from the first day through the seventh must be cut off from Israel. 16On the first day hold a sacred assembly, and another one on the seventh day. Do no work at all on these days, except to prepare food for everyone to eat; that is all you may do.

17"Celebrate the Festival of Unleavened Bread, because it was on this very day that I brought your divisions out of Egypt. Celebrate this day as a lasting ordinance for the generations to come. 18In the first month you are to eat bread made without yeast, from the evening of the fourteenth day until the evening of the twenty-first day. 19For seven days no yeast is to be found in your houses. And anyone, whether foreigner or native-born, who eats anything with yeast in it must be cut off from the community of Israel. 20Eat nothing made with yeast. Wherever you live, you must eat unleavened bread."

21Then Moses summoned all the elders of Israel and said to them, "Go at once and select the animals for your families and slaughter the Passover lamb. 22Take a bunch of hyssop, dip it into the blood in the basin and put some of the blood on the top and on both sides of the doorframe. None of you shall go out of the door of your house until morning. 23When the LORD goes through the land to strike down the Egyptians, he will see the blood on the top and sides of the doorframe and will pass over that doorway, and he will not permit the destroyer to enter your houses and strike you down.

24"Obey these instructions as a lasting ordinance for you and your descendants. 25When you enter the land that the LORD will give you as he promised, observe this ceremony. 26And when your children ask you, 'What does this ceremony mean to you?' 27then tell them, 'It is the Passover sacrifice to the LORD, who passed over the houses of the Israelites in Egypt and spared our homes when he struck down the Egyptians.'" Then the people bowed down and worshiped. 28The Israelites did just what the LORD commanded Moses and Aaron.

29At midnight the LORD struck down all the firstborn in Egypt, from the firstborn of Pharaoh, who sat on the throne, to the firstborn of the prisoner, who was in the dungeon, and the firstborn of all the livestock as well. 30Pharaoh and all his officials and all the Egyptians got up during the night, and there was loud wailing in Egypt, for there was not a house without someone dead.

The Exodus

31During the night Pharaoh summoned Moses and Aaron and said, "Up! Leave my people, you and the Israelites! Go, worship the LORD as you have requested. 32Take your flocks and herds, as you have said, and go. And also bless me."

33The Egyptians urged the people to hurry and leave the country. "For otherwise," they said, "we will all die!" 34So the people took their dough before the yeast was added, and carried it on their shoulders in kneading troughs wrapped in clothing. 35The Israelites did as Moses instructed and asked the Egyptians for articles of silver and gold and for clothing. 36The LORD had made the Egyptians favorably disposed toward the people, and they gave them what they asked for; so they plundered the Egyptians.

37The Israelites journeyed from Rameses to Sukkoth. There were about six hundred

[a] *3* The Hebrew word can mean *lamb* or *kid*; also in verse 4.

thousand men on foot, besides women and children. 38Many other people went up with them, and also large droves of livestock, both flocks and herds. 39With the dough the Israelites had brought from Egypt, they baked loaves of unleavened bread. The dough was without yeast because they had been driven out of Egypt and did not have time to prepare food for themselves.

40Now the length of time the Israelite people lived in Egypt[a] was 430 years. 41At the end of the 430 years, to the very day, all the LORD's divisions left Egypt. 42Because the LORD kept vigil that night to bring them out of Egypt, on this night all the Israelites are to keep vigil to honor the LORD for the generations to come.

Passover Restrictions

43The LORD said to Moses and Aaron, "These are the regulations for the Passover meal:

"No foreigner may eat it. 44Any slave you have bought may eat it after you have circumcised him, 45but a temporary resident or a hired worker may not eat it.

46"It must be eaten inside the house; take none of the meat outside the house. Do not break any of the bones. 47The whole community of Israel must celebrate it.

48"A foreigner residing among you who wants to celebrate the LORD's Passover must have all the males in his household circumcised; then he may take part like one born in the land. No uncircumcised male may eat it. 49The same law applies both to the native-born and to the foreigner residing among you."

50All the Israelites did just what the LORD had commanded Moses and Aaron. 51And on that very day the LORD brought the Israelites out of Egypt by their divisions.

Consecration of the Firstborn

13 The LORD said to Moses, 2"Consecrate to me every firstborn male. The first offspring of every womb among the Israelites belongs to me, whether human or animal."

3Then Moses said to the people, "Commemorate this day, the day you came out of Egypt, out of the land of slavery, because the LORD brought you out of it with a mighty hand. Eat nothing containing yeast. 4Today, in the month of Aviv, you are leaving. 5When the LORD brings you into the land of the Canaanites, Hittites, Amorites, Hivites and Jebusites—the land he swore to your ancestors to give you, a land flowing with milk and honey—you are to observe this ceremony in this month: 6For seven days eat bread made without yeast and on the seventh day hold a festival to the LORD. 7Eat unleavened bread during those seven days; nothing with yeast in it is to be seen among you, nor shall any yeast be seen anywhere within your borders. 8On that day tell your son, 'I do this because of what the LORD did for me when I came out of Egypt.' 9This observance will be for you like a sign on your hand and a reminder on your forehead that this law of the LORD is to be on your lips. For the LORD brought you out of Egypt with his mighty hand. 10You must keep this ordinance at the appointed time year after year.

11"After the LORD brings you into the land of the Canaanites and gives it to you, as he promised on oath to you and your ancestors, 12you are to give over to the LORD the first offspring of every womb. All the firstborn males of your livestock belong to the LORD. 13Redeem with a lamb every firstborn donkey, but if you do not redeem it, break its neck. Redeem every firstborn among your sons.

14"In days to come, when your son asks you, 'What does this mean?' say to him, 'With a mighty hand the LORD brought us out of Egypt, out of the land of slavery. 15When Pharaoh stubbornly refused to let us go, the LORD killed the firstborn of both people and animals in Egypt. This is why I sacrifice to the LORD the first male offspring of every womb and redeem each of my firstborn sons.' 16And it will be like a sign on your hand and a symbol on your forehead that the LORD brought us out of Egypt with his mighty hand."

Crossing the Sea

17When Pharaoh let the people go, God did not lead them on the road through the Philistine country, though that was shorter. For God said, "If they face war, they might change their minds and return to Egypt." 18So God led the people around by the desert road toward the Red Sea.[b] The Israelites went up out of Egypt ready for battle.

19Moses took the bones of Joseph with him because Joseph had made the Israelites swear an oath. He had said, "God will surely come to your aid, and then you must carry my bones up with you from this place."[c]

20After leaving Sukkoth they camped at Etham on the edge of the desert. 21By day the LORD went ahead of them in a pillar of cloud to guide them on their way and by night in a pillar of fire to give them light, so that they could travel by day or night. 22Neither the pillar of cloud by day nor the pillar of fire by night left its place in front of the people.

14 Then the LORD said to Moses, 2"Tell the Israelites to turn back and encamp near Pi Hahiroth, between Migdol and the sea. They are to encamp by the sea, directly opposite Baal Zephon. 3Pharaoh will think, 'The Israelites are wandering around the land in confusion, hemmed in by the desert.' 4And I will harden Pharaoh's heart, and he will pursue them. But I will gain glory for myself through Pharaoh and all his army, and the Egyptians will know that I am the LORD." So the Israelites did this.

5When the king of Egypt was told that the people had fled, Pharaoh and his officials changed their minds about them and said,

[a] *40* Masoretic Text; Samaritan Pentateuch and Septuagint *Egypt and Canaan* [b] *18* Or *the Sea of Reeds* [c] *19* See Gen. 50:25.

"What have we done? We have let the Israelites go and have lost their services!" 6So he
had his chariot made ready and took his army
with him. 7He took six hundred of the best
chariots, along with all the other chariots of
Egypt, with officers over all of them. 8The
LORD hardened the heart of Pharaoh king of
Egypt, so that he pursued the Israelites, who
were marching out boldly. 9The Egyptians—
all Pharaoh's horses and chariots, horsemen[a]
and troops—pursued the Israelites and overtook them as they camped by the sea near Pi
Hahiroth, opposite Baal Zephon.

10As Pharaoh approached, the Israelites
looked up, and there were the Egyptians,
marching after them. They were terrified
and cried out to the LORD. 11They said to Moses, "Was it because there were no graves in
Egypt that you brought us to the desert to die?
What have you done to us by bringing us out
of Egypt? 12Didn't we say to you in Egypt,
'Leave us alone; let us serve the Egyptians'?
It would have been better for us to serve the
Egyptians than to die in the desert!"

13Moses answered the people, "Do not be
afraid. Stand firm and you will see the deliverance the LORD will bring you today. The
Egyptians you see today you will never see
again. 14The LORD will fight for you; you need
only to be still."

15Then the LORD said to Moses, "Why are
you crying out to me? Tell the Israelites to
move on. 16Raise your staff and stretch out
your hand over the sea to divide the water so
that the Israelites can go through the sea on
dry ground. 17I will harden the hearts of the
Egyptians so that they will go in after them.
And I will gain glory through Pharaoh and all
his army, through his chariots and his horsemen. 18The Egyptians will know that I am the
LORD when I gain glory through Pharaoh, his
chariots and his horsemen."

19Then the angel of God, who had been
traveling in front of Israel's army, withdrew
and went behind them. The pillar of cloud
also moved from in front and stood behind
them, 20coming between the armies of Egypt
and Israel. Throughout the night the cloud
brought darkness to the one side and light to
the other side; so neither went near the other
all night long.

21Then Moses stretched out his hand over
the sea, and all that night the LORD drove the
sea back with a strong east wind and turned
it into dry land. The waters were divided,
22and the Israelites went through the sea on
dry ground, with a wall of water on their right
and on their left.

23The Egyptians pursued them, and all
Pharaoh's horses and chariots and horsemen followed them into the sea. 24During the
last watch of the night the LORD looked down
from the pillar of fire and cloud at the Egyptian army and threw it into confusion. 25He
jammed[b] the wheels of their chariots so that
they had difficulty driving. And the Egyptians
said, "Let's get away from the Israelites! The
LORD is fighting for them against Egypt."

26Then the LORD said to Moses, "Stretch out
your hand over the sea so that the waters may
flow back over the Egyptians and their chariots and horsemen." 27Moses stretched out his
hand over the sea, and at daybreak the sea
went back to its place. The Egyptians were
fleeing toward[c] it, and the LORD swept them
into the sea. 28The water flowed back and covered the chariots and horsemen—the entire
army of Pharaoh that had followed the Israelites into the sea. Not one of them survived.

29But the Israelites went through the sea
on dry ground, with a wall of water on their
right and on their left. 30That day the LORD
saved Israel from the hands of the Egyptians,
and Israel saw the Egyptians lying dead on
the shore. 31And when the Israelites saw the
mighty hand of the LORD displayed against
the Egyptians, the people feared the LORD
and put their trust in him and in Moses his
servant.

The Song of Moses and Miriam

15 Then Moses and the Israelites sang this
song to the LORD:

"I will sing to the LORD,
for he is highly exalted.
Both horse and driver
he has hurled into the sea.

2 "The LORD is my strength and my
defense[d];
he has become my salvation.
He is my God, and I will praise him,
my father's God, and I will exalt him.
3 The LORD is a warrior;
the LORD is his name.
4 Pharaoh's chariots and his army
he has hurled into the sea.
The best of Pharaoh's officers
are drowned in the Red Sea.[e]
5 The deep waters have covered them;
they sank to the depths like a stone.
6 Your right hand, LORD,
was majestic in power.
Your right hand, LORD,
shattered the enemy.

7 "In the greatness of your majesty
you threw down those who opposed
you.
You unleashed your burning anger;
it consumed them like stubble.
8 By the blast of your nostrils
the waters piled up.
The surging waters stood up like a wall;
the deep waters congealed in the heart
of the sea.
9 The enemy boasted,
'I will pursue, I will overtake them.
I will divide the spoils;
I will gorge myself on them.

[a] 9 Or *charioteers*; also in verses 17, 18, 23, 26 and 28
[b] 25 See Samaritan Pentateuch, Septuagint and Syriac; Masoretic Text *removed*
[c] 27 Or *from*
[d] 2 Or *song*
[e] 4 Or *the Sea of Reeds*; also in verse 22

I will draw my sword
and my hand will destroy them.'
10 But you blew with your breath,
and the sea covered them.
They sank like lead
in the mighty waters.
11 Who among the gods
is like you, LORD?
Who is like you—
majestic in holiness,
awesome in glory,
working wonders?

12 "You stretch out your right hand,
and the earth swallows your enemies.
13 In your unfailing love you will lead
the people you have redeemed.
In your strength you will guide them
to your holy dwelling.
14 The nations will hear and tremble;
anguish will grip the people of
Philistia.
15 The chiefs of Edom will be terrified,
the leaders of Moab will be seized with
trembling,
the people[a] of Canaan will melt away;
16 terror and dread will fall on them.
By the power of your arm
they will be as still as a stone—
until your people pass by, LORD,
until the people you bought[b] pass by.
17 You will bring them in and plant them
on the mountain of your
inheritance—
the place, LORD, you made for your
dwelling,
the sanctuary, Lord, your hands
established.

18 "The LORD reigns
for ever and ever."

19 When Pharaoh's horses, chariots and
horsemen[c] went into the sea, the LORD brought
the waters of the sea back over them, but the
Israelites walked through the sea on dry
ground. 20 Then Miriam the prophet, Aaron's
sister, took a timbrel in her hand, and all the
women followed her, with timbrels and dancing. 21 Miriam sang to them:

"Sing to the LORD,
for he is highly exalted.
Both horse and driver
he has hurled into the sea."

The Waters of Marah and Elim

22 Then Moses led Israel from the Red Sea
and they went into the Desert of Shur. For
three days they traveled in the desert without
finding water. 23 When they came to Marah,
they could not drink its water because it was
bitter. (That is why the place is called Marah.[d])
24 So the people grumbled against Moses, saying, "What are we to drink?"
25 Then Moses cried out to the LORD, and
the LORD showed him a piece of wood. He
threw it into the water, and the water became
fit to drink.

There the LORD issued a ruling and instruction for them and put them to the test. 26 He
said, "If you listen carefully to the LORD your
God and do what is right in his eyes, if you
pay attention to his commands and keep all
his decrees, I will not bring on you any of the
diseases I brought on the Egyptians, for I am
the LORD, who heals you."
27 Then they came to Elim, where there were
twelve springs and seventy palm trees, and
they camped there near the water.

Manna and Quail

16 The whole Israelite community set out
from Elim and came to the Desert of Sin,
which is between Elim and Sinai, on the fifteenth day of the second month after they had
come out of Egypt. 2 In the desert the whole
community grumbled against Moses and Aaron. 3 The Israelites said to them, "If only we
had died by the LORD's hand in Egypt! There
we sat around pots of meat and ate all the
food we wanted, but you have brought us out
into this desert to starve this entire assembly
to death."
4 Then the LORD said to Moses, "I will rain
down bread from heaven for you. The people
are to go out each day and gather enough for
that day. In this way I will test them and see
whether they will follow my instructions. 5 On
the sixth day they are to prepare what they
bring in, and that is to be twice as much as
they gather on the other days."
6 So Moses and Aaron said to all the Israelites, "In the evening you will know that it was
the LORD who brought you out of Egypt, 7 and
in the morning you will see the glory of the
LORD, because he has heard your grumbling
against him. Who are we, that you should
grumble against us?" 8 Moses also said, "You
will know that it was the LORD when he gives
you meat to eat in the evening and all the
bread you want in the morning, because he
has heard your grumbling against him. Who
are we? You are not grumbling against us, but
against the LORD."
9 Then Moses told Aaron, "Say to the entire
Israelite community, 'Come before the LORD,
for he has heard your grumbling.'"
10 While Aaron was speaking to the whole
Israelite community, they looked toward the
desert, and there was the glory of the LORD
appearing in the cloud.
11 The LORD said to Moses, 12 "I have heard
the grumbling of the Israelites. Tell them, 'At
twilight you will eat meat, and in the morning
you will be filled with bread. Then you will
know that I am the LORD your God.'"
13 That evening quail came and covered the
camp, and in the morning there was a layer of dew around the camp. 14 When the dew
was gone, thin flakes like frost on the ground
appeared on the desert floor. 15 When the Israelites saw it, they said to each other, "What is
it?" For they did not know what it was.
Moses said to them, "It is the bread the LORD
has given you to eat. 16 This is what the LORD

[a] 15 Or *rulers* [b] 16 Or *created* [c] 19 Or *charioteers* [d] 23 *Marah* means *bitter.*

has commanded: 'Everyone is to gather as
much as they need. Take an omer[a] for each
person you have in your tent.'"
17The Israelites did as they were told; some
gathered much, some little. 18And when they
measured it by the omer, the one who gathered
much did not have too much, and the one who
gathered little did not have too little. Everyone
had gathered just as much as they needed.
19Then Moses said to them, "No one is to
keep any of it until morning."
20However, some of them paid no attention
to Moses; they kept part of it until morning,
but it was full of maggots and began to smell.
So Moses was angry with them.
21Each morning everyone gathered as much
as they needed, and when the sun grew hot,
it melted away. 22On the sixth day, they gathered twice as much—two omers[b] for each
person—and the leaders of the community
came and reported this to Moses. 23He said
to them, "This is what the LORD commanded: 'Tomorrow is to be a day of sabbath rest,
a holy sabbath to the LORD. So bake what
you want to bake and boil what you want to
boil. Save whatever is left and keep it until
morning.'"
24So they saved it until morning, as Moses
commanded, and it did not stink or get maggots in it. 25"Eat it today," Moses said, "because today is a sabbath to the LORD. You will
not find any of it on the ground today. 26Six
days you are to gather it, but on the seventh
day, the Sabbath, there will not be any."
27Nevertheless, some of the people went out
on the seventh day to gather it, but they found
none. 28Then the LORD said to Moses, "How
long will you[c] refuse to keep my commands
and my instructions? 29Bear in mind that the
LORD has given you the Sabbath; that is why
on the sixth day he gives you bread for two
days. Everyone is to stay where they are on
the seventh day; no one is to go out." 30So the
people rested on the seventh day.
31The people of Israel called the bread manna.[d] It was white like coriander seed and tasted like wafers made with honey. 32Moses said,
"This is what the LORD has commanded: 'Take
an omer of manna and keep it for the generations to come, so they can see the bread I gave
you to eat in the wilderness when I brought
you out of Egypt.'"
33So Moses said to Aaron, "Take a jar and
put an omer of manna in it. Then place it before the LORD to be kept for the generations
to come."
34As the LORD commanded Moses, Aaron
put the manna with the tablets of the covenant
law, so that it might be preserved. 35The Israelites ate manna forty years, until they came to
a land that was settled; they ate manna until
they reached the border of Canaan.
36(An omer is one-tenth of an ephah.)

Water From the Rock

17 The whole Israelite community set out
from the Desert of Sin, traveling from
place to place as the LORD commanded. They
camped at Rephidim, but there was no water
for the people to drink. 2So they quarreled
with Moses and said, "Give us water to drink."
Moses replied, "Why do you quarrel with
me? Why do you put the LORD to the test?"
3But the people were thirsty for water there,
and they grumbled against Moses. They said,
"Why did you bring us up out of Egypt to
make us and our children and livestock die
of thirst?"
4Then Moses cried out to the LORD, "What
am I to do with these people? They are almost
ready to stone me."
5The LORD answered Moses, "Go out in
front of the people. Take with you some of
the elders of Israel and take in your hand the
staff with which you struck the Nile, and go.
6I will stand there before you by the rock at
Horeb. Strike the rock, and water will come
out of it for the people to drink." So Moses
did this in the sight of the elders of Israel.
7And he called the place Massah[e] and Meribah[f] because the Israelites quarreled and
because they tested the LORD saying, "Is the
LORD among us or not?"

The Amalekites Defeated

8The Amalekites came and attacked the Israelites at Rephidim. 9Moses said to Joshua,
"Choose some of our men and go out to fight
the Amalekites. Tomorrow I will stand on top
of the hill with the staff of God in my hands."
10So Joshua fought the Amalekites as Moses
had ordered, and Moses, Aaron and Hur went
to the top of the hill. 11As long as Moses held
up his hands, the Israelites were winning, but
whenever he lowered his hands, the Amalekites were winning. 12When Moses' hands grew
tired, they took a stone and put it under him
and he sat on it. Aaron and Hur held his hands
up—one on one side, one on the other—so
that his hands remained steady till sunset.
13So Joshua overcame the Amalekite army
with the sword.
14Then the LORD said to Moses, "Write this
on a scroll as something to be remembered
and make sure that Joshua hears it, because
I will completely blot out the name of Amalek
from under heaven."
15Moses built an altar and called it The LORD
is my Banner. 16He said, "Because hands were
lifted up against[g] the throne of the LORD,[h] the
LORD will be at war against the Amalekites
from generation to generation."

Jethro Visits Moses

18 Now Jethro, the priest of Midian and
father-in-law of Moses, heard of everything God had done for Moses and for his

[a] *16* That is, possibly about 3 pounds or about 1.4 kilograms; also in verses 18, 32, 33 and 36
[b] *22* That is, possibly about 6 pounds or about 2.8 kilograms [c] *28* The Hebrew is plural.
[d] *31* *Manna* sounds like the Hebrew for *What is it?* (see verse 15). [e] *7* *Massah* means *testing.*
[f] *7* *Meribah* means *quarreling.* [g] *16* Or *to* [h] *16* The meaning of the Hebrew for this clause is
uncertain.

people Israel, and how the LORD had brought
Israel out of Egypt.
2After Moses had sent away his wife Zipporah, his father-in-law Jethro received her 3and
her two sons. One son was named Gershom,[a]
for Moses said, "I have become a foreigner
in a foreign land"; 4and the other was named
Eliezer,[b] for he said, "My father's God was
my helper; he saved me from the sword of
Pharaoh."
5Jethro, Moses' father-in-law, together
with Moses' sons and wife, came to him in
the wilderness, where he was camped near
the mountain of God. 6Jethro had sent word
to him, "I, your father-in-law Jethro, am coming to you with your wife and her two sons."
7So Moses went out to meet his father-in-
law and bowed down and kissed him. They
greeted each other and then went into the
tent. 8Moses told his father-in-law about everything the LORD had done to Pharaoh and
the Egyptians for Israel's sake and about all
the hardships they had met along the way and
how the LORD had saved them.
9Jethro was delighted to hear about all the
good things the LORD had done for Israel in
rescuing them from the hand of the Egyptians. 10He said, "Praise be to the LORD, who
rescued you from the hand of the Egyptians
and of Pharaoh, and who rescued the people
from the hand of the Egyptians. 11Now I know
that the LORD is greater than all other gods, for
he did this to those who had treated Israel arrogantly." 12Then Jethro, Moses' father-in-law,
brought a burnt offering and other sacrifices
to God, and Aaron came with all the elders of
Israel to eat a meal with Moses' father-in-law
in the presence of God.
13The next day Moses took his seat to serve
as judge for the people, and they stood around
him from morning till evening. 14When his
father-in-law saw all that Moses was doing
for the people, he said, "What is this you are
doing for the people? Why do you alone sit as
judge, while all these people stand around you
from morning till evening?"
15Moses answered him, "Because the people
come to me to seek God's will. 16Whenever
they have a dispute, it is brought to me, and I
decide between the parties and inform them
of God's decrees and instructions."
17Moses' father-in-law replied, "What you
are doing is not good. 18You and these people
who come to you will only wear yourselves
out. The work is too heavy for you; you cannot
handle it alone. 19Listen now to me and I will
give you some advice, and may God be with
you. You must be the people's representative
before God and bring their disputes to him.
20Teach them his decrees and instructions,
and show them the way they are to live and
how they are to behave. 21But select capable
men from all the people—men who fear God,
trustworthy men who hate dishonest gain—
and appoint them as officials over thousands,
hundreds, fifties and tens. 22Have them serve
as judges for the people at all times, but have
them bring every difficult case to you; the simple cases they can decide themselves. That
will make your load lighter, because they
will share it with you. 23If you do this and
God so commands, you will be able to stand
the strain, and all these people will go home
satisfied."
24Moses listened to his father-in-law and did
everything he said. 25He chose capable men
from all Israel and made them leaders of the
people, officials over thousands, hundreds,
fifties and tens. 26They served as judges for
the people at all times. The difficult cases they
brought to Moses, but the simple ones they
decided themselves.
27Then Moses sent his father-in-law on his
way, and Jethro returned to his own country.

At Mount Sinai

19 On the first day of the third month after
the Israelites left Egypt—on that very
day—they came to the Desert of Sinai. 2After
they set out from Rephidim, they entered the
Desert of Sinai, and Israel camped there in
the desert in front of the mountain.
3Then Moses went up to God, and the LORD
called to him from the mountain and said,
"This is what you are to say to the descendants
of Jacob and what you are to tell the people
of Israel: 4'You yourselves have seen what I
did to Egypt, and how I carried you on eagles'
wings and brought you to myself. 5Now if you
obey me fully and keep my covenant, then out
of all nations you will be my treasured possession. Although the whole earth is mine,
6you[c] will be for me a kingdom of priests and
a holy nation.' These are the words you are
to speak to the Israelites."
7So Moses went back and summoned the
elders of the people and set before them all
the words the LORD had commanded him to
speak. 8The people all responded together,
"We will do everything the LORD has said." So
Moses brought their answer back to the LORD.
9The LORD said to Moses, "I am going to
come to you in a dense cloud, so that the people will hear me speaking with you and will
always put their trust in you." Then Moses told
the LORD what the people had said.
10And the LORD said to Moses, "Go to the
people and consecrate them today and tomorrow. Have them wash their clothes 11and be
ready by the third day, because on that day
the LORD will come down on Mount Sinai in
the sight of all the people. 12Put limits for the
people around the mountain and tell them, 'Be
careful that you do not approach the mountain
or touch the foot of it. Whoever touches the
mountain is to be put to death. 13They are to
be stoned or shot with arrows; not a hand is to
be laid on them. No person or animal shall be
permitted to live.' Only when the ram's horn
sounds a long blast may they approach the
mountain."
14After Moses had gone down the mountain

[a] 3 *Gershom* sounds like the Hebrew for *a foreigner there.* [b] 4 *Eliezer* means *my God is helper.*
[c] 5,6 Or *possession, for the whole earth is mine.* 6*You*

to the people, he consecrated them, and they
washed their clothes. 15Then he said to the
people, "Prepare yourselves for the third day.
Abstain from sexual relations."
16On the morning of the third day there was
thunder and lightning, with a thick cloud over
the mountain, and a very loud trumpet blast.
Everyone in the camp trembled. 17Then Moses
led the people out of the camp to meet with
God, and they stood at the foot of the mountain. 18Mount Sinai was covered with smoke,
because the LORD descended on it in fire. The
smoke billowed up from it like smoke from a
furnace, and the whole mountain[a] trembled
violently. 19As the sound of the trumpet grew
louder and louder, Moses spoke and the voice
of God answered him.[b]
20The LORD descended to the top of Mount
Sinai and called Moses to the top of the mountain. So Moses went up 21and the LORD said
to him, "Go down and warn the people so
they do not force their way through to see
the LORD and many of them perish. 22Even the
priests, who approach the LORD, must consecrate themselves, or the LORD will break out
against them."
23Moses said to the LORD, "The people cannot come up Mount Sinai, because you yourself warned us, 'Put limits around the mountain and set it apart as holy.'"
24The LORD replied, "Go down and bring
Aaron up with you. But the priests and the
people must not force their way through to
come up to the LORD, or he will break out
against them."
25So Moses went down to the people and
told them.

The Ten Commandments

20 And God spoke all these words:

2"I am the LORD your God, who
brought you out of Egypt, out of the
land of slavery.
3"You shall have no other gods before[c] me.
4"You shall not make for yourself an image
in the form of anything in heaven
above or on the earth beneath or in
the waters below. 5You shall not bow
down to them or worship them; for
I, the LORD your God, am a jealous
God, punishing the children for the
sin of the parents to the third and
fourth generation of those who hate
me, 6but showing love to a thousand
generations of those who love me and
keep my commandments.
7"You shall not misuse the name of the
LORD your God, for the LORD will not
hold anyone guiltless who misuses
his name.
8"Remember the Sabbath day by keeping it
holy. 9Six days you shall labor and do
all your work, 10but the seventh day
is a sabbath to the LORD your God.
On it you shall not do any work, neither you, nor your son or daughter,
nor your male or female servant,
nor your animals, nor any foreigner
residing in your towns. 11For in six
days the LORD made the heavens and
the earth, the sea, and all that is in
them, but he rested on the seventh
day. Therefore the LORD blessed the
Sabbath day and made it holy.
12"Honor your father and your mother, so
that you may live long in the land the
LORD your God is giving you.
13"You shall not murder.
14"You shall not commit adultery.
15"You shall not steal.
16"You shall not give false testimony
against your neighbor.
17"You shall not covet your neighbor's
house. You shall not covet your
neighbor's wife, or his male or female servant, his ox or donkey, or
anything that belongs to your neighbor."

18When the people saw the thunder and
lightning and heard the trumpet and saw the
mountain in smoke, they trembled with fear.
They stayed at a distance 19and said to Moses,
"Speak to us yourself and we will listen. But
do not have God speak to us or we will die."
20Moses said to the people, "Do not be
afraid. God has come to test you, so that the
fear of God will be with you to keep you from
sinning."
21The people remained at a distance, while
Moses approached the thick darkness where
God was.

Idols and Altars

22Then the LORD said to Moses, "Tell the
Israelites this: 'You have seen for yourselves
that I have spoken to you from heaven: 23Do
not make any gods to be alongside me; do not
make for yourselves gods of silver or gods
of gold.
24"'Make an altar of earth for me and sacrifice on it your burnt offerings and fellowship
offerings, your sheep and goats and your cattle. Wherever I cause my name to be honored,
I will come to you and bless you. 25If you make
an altar of stones for me, do not build it with
dressed stones, for you will defile it if you use
a tool on it. 26And do not go up to my altar on
steps, or your private parts may be exposed.'

21 "These are the laws you are to set before them:

Hebrew Servants

2"If you buy a Hebrew servant, he is to serve
you for six years. But in the seventh year, he
shall go free, without paying anything. 3If he
comes alone, he is to go free alone; but if he
has a wife when he comes, she is to go with
him. 4If his master gives him a wife and she
bears him sons or daughters, the woman and

[a] 18 Most Hebrew manuscripts; a few Hebrew manuscripts and Septuagint *and all the people*
[b] 19 Or *and God answered him with thunder* [c] 3 Or *besides*

her children shall belong to her master, and
only the man shall go free.
5“But if the servant declares, ‘I love my master and my wife and children and do not want
to go free,’ 6then his master must take him
before the judges.[a] He shall take him to the
door or the doorpost and pierce his ear with
an awl. Then he will be his servant for life.
7“If a man sells his daughter as a servant,
she is not to go free as male servants do. 8If
she does not please the master who has selected her for himself,[b] he must let her be
redeemed. He has no right to sell her to foreigners, because he has broken faith with her.
9If he selects her for his son, he must grant
her the rights of a daughter. 10If he marries
another woman, he must not deprive the first
one of her food, clothing and marital rights.
11If he does not provide her with these three
things, she is to go free, without any payment
of money.

Personal Injuries

12“Anyone who strikes a person with a fatal
blow is to be put to death. 13However, if it is
not done intentionally, but God lets it happen,
they are to flee to a place I will designate.
14But if anyone schemes and kills someone
deliberately, that person is to be taken from
my altar and put to death.
15“Anyone who attacks[c] their father or
mother is to be put to death.
16“Anyone who kidnaps someone is to be put
to death, whether the victim has been sold or
is still in the kidnapper’s possession.
17“Anyone who curses their father or mother
is to be put to death.
18“If people quarrel and one person hits
another with a stone or with their fist[d] and the
victim does not die but is confined to bed, 19the
one who struck the blow will not be held liable
if the other can get up and walk around outside
with a staff; however, the guilty party must
pay the injured person for any loss of time
and see that the victim is completely healed.
20“Anyone who beats their male or female
slave with a rod must be punished if the slave
dies as a direct result, 21but they are not to be
punished if the slave recovers after a day or
two, since the slave is their property.
22“If people are fighting and hit a pregnant
woman and she gives birth prematurely[e] but
there is no serious injury, the offender must
be fined whatever the woman’s husband demands and the court allows. 23But if there
is serious injury, you are to take life for life,
24eye for eye, tooth for tooth, hand for hand,
foot for foot, 25burn for burn, wound for
wound, bruise for bruise.
26“An owner who hits a male or female slave
in the eye and destroys it must let the slave
go free to compensate for the eye. 27And an
owner who knocks out the tooth of a male
or female slave must let the slave go free to
compensate for the tooth.
28“If a bull gores a man or woman to death,
the bull is to be stoned to death, and its meat
must not be eaten. But the owner of the bull
will not be held responsible. 29If, however,
the bull has had the habit of goring and the
owner has been warned but has not kept it
penned up and it kills a man or woman, the
bull is to be stoned and its owner also is to
be put to death. 30However, if payment is demanded, the owner may redeem his life by the
payment of whatever is demanded. 31This law
also applies if the bull gores a son or daughter. 32If the bull gores a male or female slave,
the owner must pay thirty shekels[f] of silver
to the master of the slave, and the bull is to
be stoned to death.
33“If anyone uncovers a pit or digs one and
fails to cover it and an ox or a donkey falls into
it, 34the one who opened the pit must pay the
owner for the loss and take the dead animal
in exchange.
35“If anyone’s bull injures someone else’s
bull and it dies, the two parties are to sell
the live one and divide both the money and
the dead animal equally. 36However, if it was
known that the bull had the habit of goring,
yet the owner did not keep it penned up, the
owner must pay, animal for animal, and take
the dead animal in exchange.

Protection of Property

22[g] “Whoever steals an ox or a sheep and
slaughters it or sells it must pay back
five head of cattle for the ox and four sheep
for the sheep.
2“If a thief is caught breaking in at night
and is struck a fatal blow, the defender is not
guilty of bloodshed; 3but if it happens after
sunrise, the defender is guilty of bloodshed.
“Anyone who steals must certainly make
restitution, but if they have nothing, they must
be sold to pay for their theft. 4If the stolen
animal is found alive in their possession—
whether ox or donkey or sheep—they must
pay back double.
5“If anyone grazes their livestock in a field
or vineyard and lets them stray and they
graze in someone else’s field, the offender
must make restitution from the best of their
own field or vineyard.
6“If a fire breaks out and spreads into
thornbushes so that it burns shocks of grain
or standing grain or the whole field, the one
who started the fire must make restitution.
7“If anyone gives a neighbor silver or goods
for safekeeping and they are stolen from the
neighbor’s house, the thief, if caught, must pay
back double. 8But if the thief is not found, the
owner of the house must appear before the
judges, and they must[h] determine whether
the owner of the house has laid hands on the
other person’s property. 9In all cases of illegal
possession of an ox, a donkey, a sheep, a garment, or any other lost property about which
somebody says, ‘This is mine,’ both parties

[a] 6 Or *before God* [b] 8 Or *master so that he does not choose her* [c] 15 Or *kills* [d] 18 Or *with a tool* [e] 22 Or *she has a miscarriage* [f] 32 That is, about 12 ounces or about 345 grams [g] In Hebrew texts 22:1 is numbered 21:37, and 22:2-31 is numbered 22:1-30. [h] 8 Or *before God, and he will*

are to bring their cases before the judges.[a] The one whom the judges declare[b] guilty must pay back double to the other.

10“If anyone gives a donkey, an ox, a sheep or any other animal to their neighbor for safekeeping and it dies or is injured or is taken away while no one is looking, 11the issue between them will be settled by the taking of an oath before the LORD that the neighbor did not lay hands on the other person's property. The owner is to accept this, and no restitution is required. 12But if the animal was stolen from the neighbor, restitution must be made to the owner. 13If it was torn to pieces by a wild animal, the neighbor shall bring in the remains as evidence and shall not be required to pay for the torn animal.

14“If anyone borrows an animal from their neighbor and it is injured or dies while the owner is not present, they must make restitution. 15But if the owner is with the animal, the borrower will not have to pay. If the animal was hired, the money paid for the hire covers the loss.

Social Responsibility

16“If a man seduces a virgin who is not pledged to be married and sleeps with her, he must pay the bride-price, and she shall be his wife. 17If her father absolutely refuses to give her to him, he must still pay the bride-price for virgins.

18“Do not allow a sorceress to live.

19“Anyone who has sexual relations with an animal is to be put to death.

20“Whoever sacrifices to any god other than the LORD must be destroyed.[c]

21“Do not mistreat or oppress a foreigner, for you were foreigners in Egypt.

22“Do not take advantage of the widow or the fatherless. 23If you do and they cry out to me, I will certainly hear their cry. 24My anger will be aroused, and I will kill you with the sword; your wives will become widows and your children fatherless.

25“If you lend money to one of my people among you who is needy, do not treat it like a business deal; charge no interest. 26If you take your neighbor's cloak as a pledge, return it by sunset, 27because that cloak is the only covering your neighbor has. What else can they sleep in? When they cry out to me, I will hear, for I am compassionate.

28“Do not blaspheme God[d] or curse the ruler of your people.

29“Do not hold back offerings from your granaries or your vats.[e]

“You must give me the firstborn of your sons. 30Do the same with your cattle and your sheep. Let them stay with their mothers for seven days, but give them to me on the eighth day.

31“You are to be my holy people. So do not eat the meat of an animal torn by wild beasts; throw it to the dogs.

Laws of Justice and Mercy

23 “Do not spread false reports. Do not help a guilty person by being a malicious witness.

2“Do not follow the crowd in doing wrong. When you give testimony in a lawsuit, do not pervert justice by siding with the crowd, 3and do not show favoritism to a poor person in a lawsuit.

4“If you come across your enemy's ox or donkey wandering off, be sure to return it. 5If you see the donkey of someone who hates you fallen down under its load, do not leave it there; be sure you help them with it.

6“Do not deny justice to your poor people in their lawsuits. 7Have nothing to do with a false charge and do not put an innocent or honest person to death, for I will not acquit the guilty.

8“Do not accept a bribe, for a bribe blinds those who see and twists the words of the innocent.

9“Do not oppress a foreigner; you yourselves know how it feels to be foreigners, because you were foreigners in Egypt.

Sabbath Laws

10“For six years you are to sow your fields and harvest the crops, 11but during the seventh year let the land lie unplowed and unused. Then the poor among your people may get food from it, and the wild animals may eat what is left. Do the same with your vineyard and your olive grove.

12“Six days do your work, but on the seventh day do not work, so that your ox and your donkey may rest, and so that the slave born in your household and the foreigner living among you may be refreshed.

13“Be careful to do everything I have said to you. Do not invoke the names of other gods; do not let them be heard on your lips.

The Three Annual Festivals

14“Three times a year you are to celebrate a festival to me.

15“Celebrate the Festival of Unleavened Bread; for seven days eat bread made without yeast, as I commanded you. Do this at the appointed time in the month of Aviv, for in that month you came out of Egypt.

“No one is to appear before me empty-handed.

16“Celebrate the Festival of Harvest with the firstfruits of the crops you sow in your field.

“Celebrate the Festival of Ingathering at the end of the year, when you gather in your crops from the field.

17“Three times a year all the men are to appear before the Sovereign LORD.

18“Do not offer the blood of a sacrifice to me along with anything containing yeast.

“The fat of my festival offerings must not be kept until morning.

19“Bring the best of the firstfruits of your soil to the house of the LORD your God.

[a] 9 Or *before God* [b] 9 Or *whom God declares* [c] 20 The Hebrew term refers to the irrevocable giving over of things or persons to the LORD, often by totally destroying them. [d] 28 Or *Do not revile the judges* [e] 29 The meaning of the Hebrew for this phrase is uncertain.

"Do not cook a young goat in its mother's milk.

God's Angel to Prepare the Way

20"See, I am sending an angel ahead of you to guard you along the way and to bring you to the place I have prepared. 21Pay attention to him and listen to what he says. Do not rebel against him; he will not forgive your rebellion, since my Name is in him. 22If you listen carefully to what he says and do all that I say, I will be an enemy to your enemies and will oppose those who oppose you. 23My angel will go ahead of you and bring you into the land of the Amorites, Hittites, Perizzites, Canaanites, Hivites and Jebusites, and I will wipe them out. 24Do not bow down before their gods or worship them or follow their practices. You must demolish them and break their sacred stones to pieces. 25Worship the LORD your God, and his blessing will be on your food and water. I will take away sickness from among you, 26and none will miscarry or be barren in your land. I will give you a full life span.

27"I will send my terror ahead of you and throw into confusion every nation you encounter. I will make all your enemies turn their backs and run. 28I will send the hornet ahead of you to drive the Hivites, Canaanites and Hittites out of your way. 29But I will not drive them out in a single year, because the land would become desolate and the wild animals too numerous for you. 30Little by little I will drive them out before you, until you have increased enough to take possession of the land.

31"I will establish your borders from the Red Sea[a] to the Mediterranean Sea,[b] and from the desert to the Euphrates River. I will give into your hands the people who live in the land, and you will drive them out before you. 32Do not make a covenant with them or with their gods. 33Do not let them live in your land or they will cause you to sin against me, because the worship of their gods will certainly be a snare to you."

The Covenant Confirmed

24 Then the LORD said to Moses, "Come up to the LORD, you and Aaron, Nadab and Abihu, and seventy of the elders of Israel. You are to worship at a distance, 2but Moses alone is to approach the LORD; the others must not come near. And the people may not come up with him."

3When Moses went and told the people all the LORD's words and laws, they responded with one voice, "Everything the LORD has said we will do." 4Moses then wrote down everything the LORD had said.

He got up early the next morning and built an altar at the foot of the mountain and set up twelve stone pillars representing the twelve tribes of Israel. 5Then he sent young Israelite men, and they offered burnt offerings and sacrificed young bulls as fellowship offerings to the LORD. 6Moses took half of the blood and put it in bowls, and the other half he splashed against the altar. 7Then he took the Book of the Covenant and read it to the people. They responded, "We will do everything the LORD has said; we will obey."

8Moses then took the blood, sprinkled it on the people and said, "This is the blood of the covenant that the LORD has made with you in accordance with all these words."

9Moses and Aaron, Nadab and Abihu, and the seventy elders of Israel went up 10and saw the God of Israel. Under his feet was something like a pavement made of lapis lazuli, as bright blue as the sky. 11But God did not raise his hand against these leaders of the Israelites; they saw God, and they ate and drank.

12The LORD said to Moses, "Come up to me on the mountain and stay here, and I will give you the tablets of stone with the law and commandments I have written for their instruction."

13Then Moses set out with Joshua his aide, and Moses went up on the mountain of God. 14He said to the elders, "Wait here for us until we come back to you. Aaron and Hur are with you, and anyone involved in a dispute can go to them."

15When Moses went up on the mountain, the cloud covered it, 16and the glory of the LORD settled on Mount Sinai. For six days the cloud covered the mountain, and on the seventh day the LORD called to Moses from within the cloud. 17To the Israelites the glory of the LORD looked like a consuming fire on top of the mountain. 18Then Moses entered the cloud as he went on up the mountain. And he stayed on the mountain forty days and forty nights.

Offerings for the Tabernacle

25 The LORD said to Moses, 2"Tell the Israelites to bring me an offering. You are to receive the offering for me from everyone whose heart prompts them to give. 3These are the offerings you are to receive from them: gold, silver and bronze; 4blue, purple and scarlet yarn and fine linen; goat hair; 5ram skins dyed red and another type of durable leather[c]; acacia wood; 6olive oil for the light; spices for the anointing oil and for the fragrant incense; 7and onyx stones and other gems to be mounted on the ephod and breastpiece.

8"Then have them make a sanctuary for me, and I will dwell among them. 9Make this tabernacle and all its furnishings exactly like the pattern I will show you.

The Ark

10"Have them make an ark[d] of acacia wood—two and a half cubits long, a cubit and a half wide, and a cubit and a half high.[e] 11Overlay it with pure gold, both inside and out, and make a gold molding around it. 12Cast four gold rings for it and fasten them to its

[a] 31 Or *the Sea of Reeds* [b] 31 Hebrew *to the Sea of the Philistines* [c] 5 Possibly the hides of large aquatic mammals [d] 10 That is, a chest [e] 10 That is, about 3 3/4 feet long and 2 1/4 feet wide and high or about 1.1 meters long and 68 centimeters wide and high; similarly in verse 17

four feet, with two rings on one side and two rings on the other. 13Then make poles of acacia wood and overlay them with gold. 14Insert the poles into the rings on the sides of the ark to carry it. 15The poles are to remain in the rings of this ark; they are not to be removed. 16Then put in the ark the tablets of the covenant law, which I will give you.

17"Make an atonement cover of pure gold—two and a half cubits long and a cubit and a half wide. 18And make two cherubim out of hammered gold at the ends of the cover. 19Make one cherub on one end and the second cherub on the other; make the cherubim of one piece with the cover, at the two ends. 20The cherubim are to have their wings spread upward, overshadowing the cover with them. The cherubim are to face each other, looking toward the cover. 21Place the cover on top of the ark and put in the ark the tablets of the covenant law that I will give you. 22There, above the cover between the two cherubim that are over the ark of the covenant law, I will meet with you and give you all my commands for the Israelites.

The Table

23"Make a table of acacia wood—two cubits long, a cubit wide and a cubit and a half high.[a] 24Overlay it with pure gold and make a gold molding around it. 25Also make around it a rim a handbreadth[b] wide and put a gold molding on the rim. 26Make four gold rings for the table and fasten them to the four corners, where the four legs are. 27The rings are to be close to the rim to hold the poles used in carrying the table. 28Make the poles of acacia wood, overlay them with gold and carry the table with them. 29And make its plates and dishes of pure gold, as well as its pitchers and bowls for the pouring out of offerings. 30Put the bread of the Presence on this table to be before me at all times.

The Lampstand

31"Make a lampstand of pure gold. Hammer out its base and shaft, and make its flowerlike cups, buds and blossoms of one piece with them. 32Six branches are to extend from the sides of the lampstand—three on one side and three on the other. 33Three cups shaped like almond flowers with buds and blossoms are to be on one branch, three on the next branch, and the same for all six branches extending from the lampstand. 34And on the lampstand there are to be four cups shaped like almond flowers with buds and blossoms. 35One bud shall be under the first pair of branches extending from the lampstand, a second bud under the second pair, and a third bud under the third pair—six branches in all. 36The buds and branches shall all be of one piece with the lampstand, hammered out of pure gold.

37"Then make its seven lamps and set them up on it so that they light the space in front of it. 38Its wick trimmers and trays are to be of pure gold. 39A talent[c] of pure gold is to be used for the lampstand and all these accessories. 40See that you make them according to the pattern shown you on the mountain.

The Tabernacle

26 "Make the tabernacle with ten curtains of finely twisted linen and blue, purple and scarlet yarn, with cherubim woven into them by a skilled worker. 2All the curtains are to be the same size—twenty-eight cubits long and four cubits wide.[d] 3Join five of the curtains together, and do the same with the other five. 4Make loops of blue material along the edge of the end curtain in one set, and do the same with the end curtain in the other set. 5Make fifty loops on one curtain and fifty loops on the end curtain of the other set, with the loops opposite each other. 6Then make fifty gold clasps and use them to fasten the curtains together so that the tabernacle is a unit.

7"Make curtains of goat hair for the tent over the tabernacle—eleven altogether. 8All eleven curtains are to be the same size—thirty cubits long and four cubits wide.[e] 9Join five of the curtains together into one set and the other six into another set. Fold the sixth curtain double at the front of the tent. 10Make fifty loops along the edge of the end curtain in one set and also along the edge of the end curtain in the other set. 11Then make fifty bronze clasps and put them in the loops to fasten the tent together as a unit. 12As for the additional length of the tent curtains, the half curtain that is left over is to hang down at the rear of the tabernacle. 13The tent curtains will be a cubit[f] longer on both sides; what is left will hang over the sides of the tabernacle so as to cover it. 14Make for the tent a covering of ram skins dyed red, and over that a covering of the other durable leather.[g]

15"Make upright frames of acacia wood for the tabernacle. 16Each frame is to be ten cubits long and a cubit and a half wide,[h] 17with two projections set parallel to each other. Make all the frames of the tabernacle in this way. 18Make twenty frames for the south side of the tabernacle 19and make forty silver bases to go under them—two bases for each frame, one under each projection. 20For the other side, the north side of the tabernacle, make twenty frames 21and forty silver bases—two under each frame. 22Make six frames for the far end, that is, the west end of the tabernacle, 23and make two frames for the corners at

[a] *23* That is, about 3 feet long, 1 1/2 feet wide and 2 1/4 feet high or about 90 centimeters long, 45 centimeters wide and 68 centimeters high [b] *25* That is, about 3 inches or about 7.5 centimeters
[c] *39* That is, about 75 pounds or about 34 kilograms [d] *2* That is, about 42 feet long and 6 feet wide or about 13 meters long and 1.8 meters wide [e] *8* That is, about 45 feet long and 6 feet wide or about 13.5 meters long and 1.8 meters wide [f] *13* That is, about 18 inches or about 45 centimeters
[g] *14* Possibly the hides of large aquatic mammals (see 25:5) [h] *16* That is, about 15 feet long and 2 1/4 feet wide or about 4.5 meters long and 68 centimeters wide

the far end. 24At these two corners they must
be double from the bottom all the way to the
top and fitted into a single ring; both shall be
like that. 25So there will be eight frames and
sixteen silver bases—two under each frame.
26"Also make crossbars of acacia wood: five
for the frames on one side of the tabernacle,
27five for those on the other side, and five for
the frames on the west, at the far end of the
tabernacle. 28The center crossbar is to extend
from end to end at the middle of the frames.
29Overlay the frames with gold and make gold
rings to hold the crossbars. Also overlay the
crossbars with gold.
30"Set up the tabernacle according to the
plan shown you on the mountain.
31"Make a curtain of blue, purple and scarlet
yarn and finely twisted linen, with cherubim
woven into it by a skilled worker. 32Hang it
with gold hooks on four posts of acacia wood
overlaid with gold and standing on four silver
bases. 33Hang the curtain from the clasps and
place the ark of the covenant law behind the
curtain. The curtain will separate the Holy
Place from the Most Holy Place. 34Put the
atonement cover on the ark of the covenant
law in the Most Holy Place. 35Place the table
outside the curtain on the north side of the
tabernacle and put the lampstand opposite it
on the south side.
36"For the entrance to the tent make a curtain of blue, purple and scarlet yarn and finely
twisted linen—the work of an embroiderer.
37Make gold hooks for this curtain and five
posts of acacia wood overlaid with gold. And
cast five bronze bases for them.

The Altar of Burnt Offering

27 "Build an altar of acacia wood, three
cubits[a] high; it is to be square, five cubits long and five cubits wide.[b] 2Make a horn
at each of the four corners, so that the horns
and the altar are of one piece, and overlay
the altar with bronze. 3Make all its utensils
of bronze—its pots to remove the ashes, and
its shovels, sprinkling bowls, meat forks and
firepans. 4Make a grating for it, a bronze network, and make a bronze ring at each of the
four corners of the network. 5Put it under the
ledge of the altar so that it is halfway up the
altar. 6Make poles of acacia wood for the altar
and overlay them with bronze. 7The poles are
to be inserted into the rings so they will be on
two sides of the altar when it is carried. 8Make
the altar hollow, out of boards. It is to be made
just as you were shown on the mountain.

The Courtyard

9"Make a courtyard for the tabernacle. The
south side shall be a hundred cubits[c] long and
is to have curtains of finely twisted linen,
10with twenty posts and twenty bronze bases
and with silver hooks and bands on the posts.
11The north side shall also be a hundred cubits long and is to have curtains, with twenty
posts and twenty bronze bases and with silver
hooks and bands on the posts.
12"The west end of the courtyard shall be
fifty cubits[d] wide and have curtains, with ten
posts and ten bases. 13On the east end, toward
the sunrise, the courtyard shall also be fifty
cubits wide. 14Curtains fifteen cubits[e] long are
to be on one side of the entrance, with three
posts and three bases, 15and curtains fifteen
cubits long are to be on the other side, with
three posts and three bases.
16"For the entrance to the courtyard, provide a curtain twenty cubits[f] long, of blue,
purple and scarlet yarn and finely twisted lin-
en—the work of an embroiderer—with four
posts and four bases. 17All the posts around
the courtyard are to have silver bands and
hooks, and bronze bases. 18The courtyard
shall be a hundred cubits long and fifty cubits wide,[g] with curtains of finely twisted lin-
en five cubits[h] high, and with bronze bases.
19All the other articles used in the service of
the tabernacle, whatever their function, including all the tent pegs for it and those for
the courtyard, are to be of bronze.

Oil for the Lampstand

20"Command the Israelites to bring you
clear oil of pressed olives for the light so that
the lamps may be kept burning. 21In the tent
of meeting, outside the curtain that shields
the ark of the covenant law, Aaron and his
sons are to keep the lamps burning before the
LORD from evening till morning. This is to be
a lasting ordinance among the Israelites for
the generations to come.

The Priestly Garments

28 "Have Aaron your brother brought to
you from among the Israelites, along
with his sons Nadab and Abihu, Eleazar and
Ithamar, so they may serve me as priests.
2Make sacred garments for your brother
Aaron to give him dignity and honor. 3Tell
all the skilled workers to whom I have giv-
en wisdom in such matters that they are to
make garments for Aaron, for his consecration, so he may serve me as priest. 4These are
the garments they are to make: a breastpiece,
an ephod, a robe, a woven tunic, a turban and
a sash. They are to make these sacred garments for your brother Aaron and his sons,
so they may serve me as priests. 5Have them
use gold, and blue, purple and scarlet yarn,
and fine linen.

The Ephod

6"Make the ephod of gold, and of blue,
purple and scarlet yarn, and of finely twisted linen—the work of skilled hands. 7It is to
have two shoulder pieces attached to two of

[a] *1* That is, about 4 1/2 feet or about 1.4 meters [b] *1* That is, about 7 1/2 feet or about 2.3 meters long and wide [c] *9* That is, about 150 feet or about 45 meters; also in verse 11 [d] *12* That is, about 75 feet or about 23 meters; also in verse 13 [e] *14* That is, about 23 feet or about 6.8 meters; also in verse 15 [f] *16* That is, about 30 feet or about 9 meters [g] *18* That is, about 150 feet long and 75 feet wide or about 45 meters long and 23 meters wide [h] *18* That is, about 7 1/2 feet or about 2.3 meters

its corners, so it can be fastened. 8 Its skillfully woven waistband is to be like it—of one piece with the ephod and made with gold, and with blue, purple and scarlet yarn, and with finely twisted linen.

9 “Take two onyx stones and engrave on them the names of the sons of Israel 10 in the order of their birth—six names on one stone and the remaining six on the other. 11 Engrave the names of the sons of Israel on the two stones the way a gem cutter engraves a seal. Then mount the stones in gold filigree settings 12 and fasten them on the shoulder pieces of the ephod as memorial stones for the sons of Israel. Aaron is to bear the names on his shoulders as a memorial before the LORD. 13 Make gold filigree settings 14 and two braided chains of pure gold, like a rope, and attach the chains to the settings.

The Breastpiece

15 “Fashion a breastpiece for making decisions—the work of skilled hands. Make it like the ephod: of gold, and of blue, purple and scarlet yarn, and of finely twisted linen. 16 It is to be square—a span[a] long and a span wide—and folded double. 17 Then mount four rows of precious stones on it. The first row shall be carnelian, chrysolite and beryl; 18 the second row shall be turquoise, lapis lazuli and emerald; 19 the third row shall be jacinth, agate and amethyst; 20 the fourth row shall be topaz, onyx and jasper.[b] Mount them in gold filigree settings. 21 There are to be twelve stones, one for each of the names of the sons of Israel, each engraved like a seal with the name of one of the twelve tribes.

22 “For the breastpiece make braided chains of pure gold, like a rope. 23 Make two gold rings for it and fasten them to two corners of the breastpiece. 24 Fasten the two gold chains to the rings at the corners of the breastpiece, 25 and the other ends of the chains to the two settings, attaching them to the shoulder pieces of the ephod at the front. 26 Make two gold rings and attach them to the other two corners of the breastpiece on the inside edge next to the ephod. 27 Make two more gold rings and attach them to the bottom of the shoulder pieces on the front of the ephod, close to the seam just above the waistband of the ephod. 28 The rings of the breastpiece are to be tied to the rings of the ephod with blue cord, connecting it to the waistband, so that the breastpiece will not swing out from the ephod.

29 “Whenever Aaron enters the Holy Place, he will bear the names of the sons of Israel over his heart on the breastpiece of decision as a continuing memorial before the LORD. 30 Also put the Urim and the Thummim in the breastpiece, so they may be over Aaron's heart whenever he enters the presence of the LORD. Thus Aaron will always bear the means of making decisions for the Israelites over his heart before the LORD.

Other Priestly Garments

31 “Make the robe of the ephod entirely of blue cloth, 32 with an opening for the head in its center. There shall be a woven edge like a collar[c] around this opening, so that it will not tear. 33 Make pomegranates of blue, purple and scarlet yarn around the hem of the robe, with gold bells between them. 34 The gold bells and the pomegranates are to alternate around the hem of the robe. 35 Aaron must wear it when he ministers. The sound of the bells will be heard when he enters the Holy Place before the LORD and when he comes out, so that he will not die.

36 “Make a plate of pure gold and engrave on it as on a seal: HOLY TO THE LORD. 37 Fasten a blue cord to it to attach it to the turban; it is to be on the front of the turban. 38 It will be on Aaron's forehead, and he will bear the guilt involved in the sacred gifts the Israelites consecrate, whatever their gifts may be. It will be on Aaron's forehead continually so that they will be acceptable to the LORD.

39 “Weave the tunic of fine linen and make the turban of fine linen. The sash is to be the work of an embroiderer. 40 Make tunics, sashes and caps for Aaron's sons to give them dignity and honor. 41 After you put these clothes on your brother Aaron and his sons, anoint and ordain them. Consecrate them so they may serve me as priests.

42 “Make linen undergarments as a covering for the body, reaching from the waist to the thigh. 43 Aaron and his sons must wear them whenever they enter the tent of meeting or approach the altar to minister in the Holy Place, so that they will not incur guilt and die.

“This is to be a lasting ordinance for Aaron and his descendants.

Consecration of the Priests

29 “This is what you are to do to consecrate them, so they may serve me as priests: Take a young bull and two rams without defect. 2 And from the finest wheat flour make round loaves without yeast, thick loaves without yeast and with olive oil mixed in, and thin loaves without yeast and brushed with olive oil. 3 Put them in a basket and present them along with the bull and the two rams. 4 Then bring Aaron and his sons to the entrance to the tent of meeting and wash them with water. 5 Take the garments and dress Aaron with the tunic, the robe of the ephod, the ephod itself and the breastpiece. Fasten the ephod on him by its skillfully woven waistband. 6 Put the turban on his head and attach the sacred emblem to the turban. 7 Take the anointing oil and anoint him by pouring it on his head. 8 Bring his sons and dress them in tunics 9 and fasten caps on them. Then tie sashes on Aaron and his sons.[d] The priesthood is theirs by a lasting ordinance.

“Then you shall ordain Aaron and his sons.

10 “Bring the bull to the front of the tent of

[a] *16* That is, about 9 inches or about 23 centimeters [b] *20* The precise identification of some of these precious stones is uncertain. [c] *32* The meaning of the Hebrew for this word is uncertain.
[d] *9* Hebrew; Septuagint *on them*

meeting, and Aaron and his sons shall lay their hands on its head. 11Slaughter it in the LORD's presence at the entrance to the tent of meeting. 12Take some of the bull's blood and put it on the horns of the altar with your finger, and pour out the rest of it at the base of the altar. 13Then take all the fat on the internal organs, the long lobe of the liver, and both kidneys with the fat on them, and burn them on the altar. 14But burn the bull's flesh and its hide and its intestines outside the camp. It is a sin offering.[a]

15"Take one of the rams, and Aaron and his sons shall lay their hands on its head. 16Slaughter it and take the blood and splash it against the sides of the altar. 17Cut the ram into pieces and wash the internal organs and the legs, putting them with the head and the other pieces. 18Then burn the entire ram on the altar. It is a burnt offering to the LORD, a pleasing aroma, a food offering presented to the LORD.

19"Take the other ram, and Aaron and his sons shall lay their hands on its head. 20Slaughter it, take some of its blood and put it on the lobes of the right ears of Aaron and his sons, on the thumbs of their right hands, and on the big toes of their right feet. Then splash blood against the sides of the altar. 21And take some blood from the altar and some of the anointing oil and sprinkle it on Aaron and his garments and on his sons and their garments. Then he and his sons and their garments will be consecrated.

22"Take from this ram the fat, the fat tail, the fat on the internal organs, the long lobe of the liver, both kidneys with the fat on them, and the right thigh. (This is the ram for the ordination.) 23From the basket of bread made without yeast, which is before the LORD, take one round loaf, one thick loaf with olive oil mixed in, and one thin loaf. 24Put all these in the hands of Aaron and his sons and have them wave them before the LORD as a wave offering. 25Then take them from their hands and burn them on the altar along with the burnt offering for a pleasing aroma to the LORD, a food offering presented to the LORD. 26After you take the breast of the ram for Aaron's ordination, wave it before the LORD as a wave offering, and it will be your share.

27"Consecrate those parts of the ordination ram that belong to Aaron and his sons: the breast that was waved and the thigh that was presented. 28This is always to be the perpetual share from the Israelites for Aaron and his sons. It is the contribution the Israelites are to make to the LORD from their fellowship offerings.

29"Aaron's sacred garments will belong to his descendants so that they can be anointed and ordained in them. 30The son who succeeds him as priest and comes to the tent of meeting to minister in the Holy Place is to wear them seven days.

31"Take the ram for the ordination and cook the meat in a sacred place. 32At the entrance to the tent of meeting, Aaron and his sons are to eat the meat of the ram and the bread that is in the basket. 33They are to eat these offerings by which atonement was made for their ordination and consecration. But no one else may eat them, because they are sacred. 34And if any of the meat of the ordination ram or any bread is left over till morning, burn it up. It must not be eaten, because it is sacred.

35"Do for Aaron and his sons everything I have commanded you, taking seven days to ordain them. 36Sacrifice a bull each day as a sin offering to make atonement. Purify the altar by making atonement for it, and anoint it to consecrate it. 37For seven days make atonement for the altar and consecrate it. Then the altar will be most holy, and whatever touches it will be holy.

38"This is what you are to offer on the altar regularly each day: two lambs a year old. 39Offer one in the morning and the other at twilight. 40With the first lamb offer a tenth of an ephah[b] of the finest flour mixed with a quarter of a hin[c] of oil from pressed olives, and a quarter of a hin of wine as a drink offering. 41Sacrifice the other lamb at twilight with the same grain offering and its drink offering as in the morning—a pleasing aroma, a food offering presented to the LORD.

42"For the generations to come this burnt offering is to be made regularly at the entrance to the tent of meeting, before the LORD. There I will meet you and speak to you; 43there also I will meet with the Israelites, and the place will be consecrated by my glory.

44"So I will consecrate the tent of meeting and the altar and will consecrate Aaron and his sons to serve me as priests. 45Then I will dwell among the Israelites and be their God. 46They will know that I am the LORD their God, who brought them out of Egypt so that I might dwell among them. I am the LORD their God.

The Altar of Incense

30 "Make an altar of acacia wood for burning incense. 2It is to be square, a cubit long and a cubit wide, and two cubits high[d]—its horns of one piece with it. 3Overlay the top and all the sides and the horns with pure gold, and make a gold molding around it. 4Make two gold rings for the altar below the molding—two on each of the opposite sides—to hold the poles used to carry it. 5Make the poles of acacia wood and overlay them with gold. 6Put the altar in front of the curtain that shields the ark of the covenant law—before the atonement cover that is over the tablets of the covenant law—where I will meet with you.

7"Aaron must burn fragrant incense on the altar every morning when he tends the lamps. 8He must burn incense again when he lights the lamps at twilight so incense will burn regularly before the LORD for the generations to

[a] *14* Or *purification offering*; also in verse 36 [b] *40* That is, probably about 3 1/2 pounds or about 1.6 kilograms [c] *40* That is, probably about 1 quart or about 1 liter [d] *2* That is, about 1 1/2 feet long and wide and 3 feet high or about 45 centimeters long and wide and 90 centimeters high

come. 9Do not offer on this altar any other incense or any burnt offering or grain offering, and do not pour a drink offering on it. 10Once a year Aaron shall make atonement on its horns. This annual atonement must be made with the blood of the atoning sin offering[a] for the generations to come. It is most holy to the LORD."

Atonement Money

11Then the LORD said to Moses, 12"When you take a census of the Israelites to count them, each one must pay the LORD a ransom for his life at the time he is counted. Then no plague will come on them when you number them. 13Each one who crosses over to those already counted is to give a half shekel,[b] according to the sanctuary shekel, which weighs twenty gerahs. This half shekel is an offering to the LORD. 14All who cross over, those twenty years old or more, are to give an offering to the LORD. 15The rich are not to give more than a half shekel and the poor are not to give less when you make the offering to the LORD to atone for your lives. 16Receive the atonement money from the Israelites and use it for the service of the tent of meeting. It will be a memorial for the Israelites before the LORD, making atonement for your lives."

Basin for Washing

17Then the LORD said to Moses, 18"Make a bronze basin, with its bronze stand, for washing. Place it between the tent of meeting and the altar, and put water in it. 19Aaron and his sons are to wash their hands and feet with water from it. 20Whenever they enter the tent of meeting, they shall wash with water so that they will not die. Also, when they approach the altar to minister by presenting a food offering to the LORD, 21they shall wash their hands and feet so that they will not die. This is to be a lasting ordinance for Aaron and his descendants for the generations to come."

Anointing Oil

22Then the LORD said to Moses, 23"Take the following fine spices: 500 shekels[c] of liquid myrrh, half as much (that is, 250 shekels) of fragrant cinnamon, 250 shekels[d] of fragrant calamus, 24500 shekels of cassia—all according to the sanctuary shekel—and a hin[e] of olive oil. 25Make these into a sacred anointing oil, a fragrant blend, the work of a perfumer. It will be the sacred anointing oil. 26Then use it to anoint the tent of meeting, the ark of the covenant law, 27the table and all its articles, the lampstand and its accessories, the altar of incense, 28the altar of burnt offering and all its utensils, and the basin with its stand. 29You shall consecrate them so they will be most holy, and whatever touches them will be holy.

30"Anoint Aaron and his sons and consecrate them so they may serve me as priests. 31Say to the Israelites, 'This is to be my sacred anointing oil for the generations to come. 32Do not pour it on anyone else's body and do not make any other oil using the same formula. It is sacred, and you are to consider it sacred. 33Whoever makes perfume like it and puts it on anyone other than a priest must be cut off from their people.' "

Incense

34Then the LORD said to Moses, "Take fragrant spices—gum resin, onycha and galbanum—and pure frankincense, all in equal amounts, 35and make a fragrant blend of incense, the work of a perfumer. It is to be salted and pure and sacred. 36Grind some of it to powder and place it in front of the ark of the covenant law in the tent of meeting, where I will meet with you. It shall be most holy to you. 37Do not make any incense with this formula for yourselves; consider it holy to the LORD. 38Whoever makes incense like it to enjoy its fragrance must be cut off from their people."

Bezalel and Oholiab

31 Then the LORD said to Moses, 2"See, I have chosen Bezalel son of Uri, the son of Hur, of the tribe of Judah, 3and I have filled him with the Spirit of God, with wisdom, with understanding, with knowledge and with all kinds of skills— 4to make artistic designs for work in gold, silver and bronze, 5to cut and set stones, to work in wood, and to engage in all kinds of crafts. 6Moreover, I have appointed Oholiab son of Ahisamak, of the tribe of Dan, to help him. Also I have given ability to all the skilled workers to make everything I have commanded you: 7the tent of meeting, the ark of the covenant law with the atonement cover on it, and all the other furnishings of the tent— 8the table and its articles, the pure gold lampstand and all its accessories, the altar of incense, 9the altar of burnt offering and all its utensils, the basin with its stand— 10and also the woven garments, both the sacred garments for Aaron the priest and the garments for his sons when they serve as priests, 11and the anointing oil and fragrant incense for the Holy Place. They are to make them just as I commanded you."

The Sabbath

12Then the LORD said to Moses, 13"Say to the Israelites, 'You must observe my Sabbaths. This will be a sign between me and you for the generations to come, so you may know that I am the LORD, who makes you holy.

14" 'Observe the Sabbath, because it is holy to you. Anyone who desecrates it is to be put to death; those who do any work on that day must be cut off from their people. 15For six days work is to be done, but the seventh day is a day of sabbath rest, holy to the LORD. Who-

[a] *10* Or *purification offering* [b] *13* That is, about 1/5 ounce or about 5.8 grams; also in verse 15
[c] *23* That is, about 12 1/2 pounds or about 5.8 kilograms; also in verse 24 [d] *23* That is, about 6 1/4 pounds or about 2.9 kilograms [e] *24* That is, probably about 1 gallon or about 3.8 liters

ever does any work on the Sabbath day is to be
put to death. 16The Israelites are to observe the
Sabbath, celebrating it for the generations to
come as a lasting covenant. 17It will be a sign
between me and the Israelites forever, for in
six days the LORD made the heavens and the
earth, and on the seventh day he rested and
was refreshed.'"

18When the LORD finished speaking to Moses on Mount Sinai, he gave him the two tablets of the covenant law, the tablets of stone
inscribed by the finger of God.

The Golden Calf

32 When the people saw that Moses was
so long in coming down from the mountain, they gathered around Aaron and said,
"Come, make us gods[a] who will go before us.
As for this fellow Moses who brought us up
out of Egypt, we don't know what has happened to him."

2Aaron answered them, "Take off the gold
earrings that your wives, your sons and your
daughters are wearing, and bring them to me."
3So all the people took off their earrings and
brought them to Aaron. 4He took what they
handed him and made it into an idol cast in
the shape of a calf, fashioning it with a tool.
Then they said, "These are your gods,[b] Israel,
who brought you up out of Egypt."

5When Aaron saw this, he built an altar in
front of the calf and announced, "Tomorrow
there will be a festival to the LORD." 6So the
next day the people rose early and sacrificed
burnt offerings and presented fellowship offerings. Afterward they sat down to eat and
drink and got up to indulge in revelry.

7Then the LORD said to Moses, "Go down,
because your people, whom you brought up
out of Egypt, have become corrupt. 8They
have been quick to turn away from what I
commanded them and have made themselves
an idol cast in the shape of a calf. They have
bowed down to it and sacrificed to it and
have said, 'These are your gods, Israel, who
brought you up out of Egypt.'

9"I have seen these people," the LORD said
to Moses, "and they are a stiff-necked people. 10Now leave me alone so that my anger
may burn against them and that I may destroy them. Then I will make you into a great
nation."

11But Moses sought the favor of the LORD
his God. "LORD," he said, "why should your
anger burn against your people, whom you
brought out of Egypt with great power and
a mighty hand? 12Why should the Egyptians
say, 'It was with evil intent that he brought
them out, to kill them in the mountains and
to wipe them off the face of the earth'? Turn
from your fierce anger; relent and do not bring
disaster on your people. 13Remember your servants Abraham, Isaac and Israel, to whom
you swore by your own self: 'I will make your
descendants as numerous as the stars in the
sky and I will give your descendants all this
land I promised them, and it will be their inheritance forever.'" 14Then the LORD relented
and did not bring on his people the disaster
he had threatened.

15Moses turned and went down the mountain with the two tablets of the covenant law
in his hands. They were inscribed on both
sides, front and back. 16The tablets were the
work of God; the writing was the writing of
God, engraved on the tablets.

17When Joshua heard the noise of the people shouting, he said to Moses, "There is the
sound of war in the camp."

18Moses replied:

"It is not the sound of victory,
  it is not the sound of defeat;
  it is the sound of singing that I hear."

19When Moses approached the camp and
saw the calf and the dancing, his anger
burned and he threw the tablets out of his
hands, breaking them to pieces at the foot of
the mountain. 20And he took the calf the people had made and burned it in the fire; then he
ground it to powder, scattered it on the water
and made the Israelites drink it.

21He said to Aaron, "What did these people
do to you, that you led them into such great
sin?"

22"Do not be angry, my lord," Aaron answered. "You know how prone these people
are to evil. 23They said to me, 'Make us gods
who will go before us. As for this fellow Moses who brought us up out of Egypt, we don't
know what has happened to him.' 24So I told
them, 'Whoever has any gold jewelry, take it
off.' Then they gave me the gold, and I threw
it into the fire, and out came this calf!"

25Moses saw that the people were running
wild and that Aaron had let them get out of
control and so become a laughingstock to
their enemies. 26So he stood at the entrance to
the camp and said, "Whoever is for the LORD,
come to me." And all the Levites rallied to him.

27Then he said to them, "This is what the
LORD, the God of Israel, says: 'Each man
strap a sword to his side. Go back and forth
through the camp from one end to the other,
each killing his brother and friend and neighbor.'" 28The Levites did as Moses commanded, and that day about three thousand of the
people died. 29Then Moses said, "You have
been set apart to the LORD today, for you were
against your own sons and brothers, and he
has blessed you this day."

30The next day Moses said to the people,
"You have committed a great sin. But now I
will go up to the LORD; perhaps I can make
atonement for your sin."

31So Moses went back to the LORD and said,
"Oh, what a great sin these people have committed! They have made themselves gods of
gold. 32But now, please forgive their sin—but
if not, then blot me out of the book you have
written."

33The LORD replied to Moses, "Whoever has
sinned against me I will blot out of my book.
34Now go, lead the people to the place I spoke

[a] *1* Or *a god*; also in verses 23 and 31 [b] *4* Or *This is your god*; also in verse 8

of, and my angel will go before you. However, when the time comes for me to punish, I will punish them for their sin."

35And the LORD struck the people with a plague because of what they did with the calf Aaron had made.

33 Then the LORD said to Moses, "Leave this place, you and the people you brought up out of Egypt, and go up to the land I promised on oath to Abraham, Isaac and Jacob, saying, 'I will give it to your descendants.' 2I will send an angel before you and drive out the Canaanites, Amorites, Hittites, Perizzites, Hivites and Jebusites. 3Go up to the land flowing with milk and honey. But I will not go with you, because you are a stiff-necked people and I might destroy you on the way."

4When the people heard these distressing words, they began to mourn and no one put on any ornaments. 5For the LORD had said to Moses, "Tell the Israelites, 'You are a stiff-necked people. If I were to go with you even for a moment, I might destroy you. Now take off your ornaments and I will decide what to do with you.'" 6So the Israelites stripped off their ornaments at Mount Horeb.

The Tent of Meeting

7Now Moses used to take a tent and pitch it outside the camp some distance away, calling it the "tent of meeting." Anyone inquiring of the LORD would go to the tent of meeting outside the camp. 8And whenever Moses went out to the tent, all the people rose and stood at the entrances to their tents, watching Moses until he entered the tent. 9As Moses went into the tent, the pillar of cloud would come down and stay at the entrance, while the LORD spoke with Moses. 10Whenever the people saw the pillar of cloud standing at the entrance to the tent, they all stood and worshiped, each at the entrance to their tent. 11The LORD would speak to Moses face to face, as one speaks to a friend. Then Moses would return to the camp, but his young aide Joshua son of Nun did not leave the tent.

Moses and the Glory of the LORD

12Moses said to the LORD, "You have been telling me, 'Lead these people,' but you have not let me know whom you will send with me. You have said, 'I know you by name and you have found favor with me.' 13If you are pleased with me, teach me your ways so I may know you and continue to find favor with you. Remember that this nation is your people."

14The LORD replied, "My Presence will go with you, and I will give you rest."

15Then Moses said to him, "If your Presence does not go with us, do not send us up from here. 16How will anyone know that you are pleased with me and with your people unless you go with us? What else will distinguish me and your people from all the other people on the face of the earth?"

17And the LORD said to Moses, "I will do the very thing you have asked, because I am pleased with you and I know you by name."

18Then Moses said, "Now show me your glory."

19And the LORD said, "I will cause all my goodness to pass in front of you, and I will proclaim my name, the LORD, in your presence. I will have mercy on whom I will have mercy, and I will have compassion on whom I will have compassion. 20But," he said, "you cannot see my face, for no one may see me and live."

21Then the LORD said, "There is a place near me where you may stand on a rock. 22When my glory passes by, I will put you in a cleft in the rock and cover you with my hand until I have passed by. 23Then I will remove my hand and you will see my back; but my face must not be seen."

The New Stone Tablets

34 The LORD said to Moses, "Chisel out two stone tablets like the first ones, and I will write on them the words that were on the first tablets, which you broke. 2Be ready in the morning, and then come up on Mount Sinai. Present yourself to me there on top of the mountain. 3No one is to come with you or be seen anywhere on the mountain; not even the flocks and herds may graze in front of the mountain."

4So Moses chiseled out two stone tablets like the first ones and went up Mount Sinai early in the morning, as the LORD had commanded him; and he carried the two stone tablets in his hands. 5Then the LORD came down in the cloud and stood there with him and proclaimed his name, the LORD. 6And he passed in front of Moses, proclaiming, "The LORD, the LORD, the compassionate and gracious God, slow to anger, abounding in love and faithfulness, 7maintaining love to thousands, and forgiving wickedness, rebellion and sin. Yet he does not leave the guilty unpunished; he punishes the children and their children for the sin of the parents to the third and fourth generation."

8Moses bowed to the ground at once and worshiped. 9"Lord," he said, "if I have found favor in your eyes, then let the Lord go with us. Although this is a stiff-necked people, forgive our wickedness and our sin, and take us as your inheritance."

10Then the LORD said: "I am making a covenant with you. Before all your people I will do wonders never before done in any nation in all the world. The people you live among will see how awesome is the work that I, the LORD, will do for you. 11Obey what I command you today. I will drive out before you the Amorites, Canaanites, Hittites, Perizzites, Hivites and Jebusites. 12Be careful not to make a treaty with those who live in the land where you are going, or they will be a snare among you. 13Break down their altars, smash their sacred stones and cut down their Asherah poles.[a] 14Do not worship any other god, for the LORD, whose name is Jealous, is a jealous God.

[a] 13 That is, wooden symbols of the goddess Asherah

15“Be careful not to make a treaty with those
who live in the land; for when they prostitute
themselves to their gods and sacrifice to them,
they will invite you and you will eat their sacrifices. 16And when you choose some of their
daughters as wives for your sons and those
daughters prostitute themselves to their gods,
they will lead your sons to do the same.
17“Do not make any idols.
18“Celebrate the Festival of Unleavened
Bread. For seven days eat bread made without yeast, as I commanded you. Do this at the
appointed time in the month of Aviv, for in that
month you came out of Egypt.
19“The first offspring of every womb belongs to me, including all the firstborn males
of your livestock, whether from herd or flock.
20Redeem the firstborn donkey with a lamb,
but if you do not redeem it, break its neck.
Redeem all your firstborn sons.
“No one is to appear before me empty-handed.
21“Six days you shall labor, but on the seventh day you shall rest; even during the plowing season and harvest you must rest.
22“Celebrate the Festival of Weeks with the
firstfruits of the wheat harvest, and the Festival of Ingathering at the turn of the year.[a]
23Three times a year all your men are to appear before the Sovereign LORD, the God of
Israel. 24I will drive out nations before you
and enlarge your territory, and no one will
covet your land when you go up three times
each year to appear before the LORD your God.
25“Do not offer the blood of a sacrifice to me
along with anything containing yeast, and do
not let any of the sacrifice from the Passover
Festival remain until morning.
26“Bring the best of the firstfruits of your
soil to the house of the LORD your God.
“Do not cook a young goat in its mother’s
milk.”
27Then the LORD said to Moses, “Write
down these words, for in accordance with
these words I have made a covenant with
you and with Israel.” 28Moses was there with
the LORD forty days and forty nights without
eating bread or drinking water. And he wrote
on the tablets the words of the covenant—the
Ten Commandments.

The Radiant Face of Moses

29When Moses came down from Mount Sinai with the two tablets of the covenant law
in his hands, he was not aware that his face
was radiant because he had spoken with the
LORD. 30When Aaron and all the Israelites saw
Moses, his face was radiant, and they were
afraid to come near him. 31But Moses called
to them; so Aaron and all the leaders of the
community came back to him, and he spoke to
them. 32Afterward all the Israelites came near
him, and he gave them all the commands the
LORD had given him on Mount Sinai.
33When Moses finished speaking to them,
he put a veil over his face. 34But whenever
he entered the LORD’s presence to speak with
him, he removed the veil until he came out.
And when he came out and told the Israelites
what he had been commanded, 35they saw that
his face was radiant. Then Moses would put
the veil back over his face until he went in to
speak with the LORD.

Sabbath Regulations

35 Moses assembled the whole Israelite
community and said to them, “These
are the things the LORD has commanded you
to do: 2For six days, work is to be done, but
the seventh day shall be your holy day, a day
of sabbath rest to the LORD. Whoever does
any work on it is to be put to death. 3Do not
light a fire in any of your dwellings on the
Sabbath day.”

Materials for the Tabernacle

4Moses said to the whole Israelite community, “This is what the LORD has commanded: 5From what you have, take an offering
for the LORD. Everyone who is willing is to
bring to the LORD an offering of gold, silver
and bronze; 6blue, purple and scarlet yarn and
fine linen; goat hair; 7ram skins dyed red and
another type of durable leather[b]; acacia wood;
8olive oil for the light; spices for the anointing
oil and for the fragrant incense; 9and onyx
stones and other gems to be mounted on the
ephod and breastpiece.
10“All who are skilled among you are to
come and make everything the LORD has
commanded: 11the tabernacle with its tent and
its covering, clasps, frames, crossbars, posts
and bases; 12the ark with its poles and the
atonement cover and the curtain that shields
it; 13the table with its poles and all its articles
and the bread of the Presence; 14the lampstand
that is for light with its accessories, lamps and
oil for the light; 15the altar of incense with
its poles, the anointing oil and the fragrant
incense; the curtain for the doorway at the
entrance to the tabernacle; 16the altar of burnt
offering with its bronze grating, its poles and
all its utensils; the bronze basin with its stand;
17the curtains of the courtyard with its posts
and bases, and the curtain for the entrance
to the courtyard; 18the tent pegs for the tabernacle and for the courtyard, and their ropes;
19the woven garments worn for ministering
in the sanctuary—both the sacred garments
for Aaron the priest and the garments for his
sons when they serve as priests.”
20Then the whole Israelite community withdrew from Moses’ presence, 21and everyone
who was willing and whose heart moved them
came and brought an offering to the LORD for
the work on the tent of meeting, for all its service, and for the sacred garments. 22All who
were willing, men and women alike, came and
brought gold jewelry of all kinds: brooches,
earrings, rings and ornaments. They all presented their gold as a wave offering to the
LORD. 23Everyone who had blue, purple or scarlet yarn or fine linen, or goat hair, ram skins

[a] 22 That is, in the autumn [b] 7 Possibly the hides of large aquatic mammals; also in verse 23

dyed red or the other durable leather brought
them. 24Those presenting an offering of silver
or bronze brought it as an offering to the LORD,
and everyone who had acacia wood for any
part of the work brought it. 25Every skilled
woman spun with her hands and brought what
she had spun—blue, purple or scarlet yarn or
fine linen. 26And all the women who were willing and had the skill spun the goat hair. 27The
leaders brought onyx stones and other gems
to be mounted on the ephod and breastpiece.
28They also brought spices and olive oil for
the light and for the anointing oil and for the
fragrant incense. 29All the Israelite men and
women who were willing brought to the LORD
freewill offerings for all the work the LORD
through Moses had commanded them to do.

Bezalel and Oholiab

30Then Moses said to the Israelites, "See, the
LORD has chosen Bezalel son of Uri, the son of
Hur, of the tribe of Judah, 31and he has filled
him with the Spirit of God, with wisdom, with
understanding, with knowledge and with all
kinds of skills— 32to make artistic designs for
work in gold, silver and bronze, 33to cut and
set stones, to work in wood and to engage in
all kinds of artistic crafts. 34And he has given
both him and Oholiab son of Ahisamak, of the
tribe of Dan, the ability to teach others. 35He
has filled them with skill to do all kinds of
work as engravers, designers, embroiderers
in blue, purple and scarlet yarn and fine lin-
en, and weavers—all of them skilled workers
36 and designers. 1So Bezalel, Oholiab
and every skilled person to whom the
LORD has given skill and ability to know how
to carry out all the work of constructing the
sanctuary are to do the work just as the LORD
has commanded."

2Then Moses summoned Bezalel and Oholiab and every skilled person to whom the LORD
had given ability and who was willing to come
and do the work. 3They received from Moses
all the offerings the Israelites had brought to
carry out the work of constructing the sanctuary. And the people continued to bring
freewill offerings morning after morning.
4So all the skilled workers who were doing
all the work on the sanctuary left what they
were doing 5and said to Moses, "The people
are bringing more than enough for doing the
work the LORD commanded to be done."

6Then Moses gave an order and they sent
this word throughout the camp: "No man or
woman is to make anything else as an offering for the sanctuary." And so the people were
restrained from bringing more, 7because what
they already had was more than enough to
do all the work.

The Tabernacle

8All those who were skilled among the
workers made the tabernacle with ten curtains of finely twisted linen and blue, purple
and scarlet yarn, with cherubim woven into
them by expert hands. 9All the curtains were
the same size—twenty-eight cubits long and
four cubits wide.[a] 10They joined five of the curtains together and did the same with the other
five. 11Then they made loops of blue material
along the edge of the end curtain in one set,
and the same was done with the end curtain in
the other set. 12They also made fifty loops on
one curtain and fifty loops on the end curtain
of the other set, with the loops opposite each
other. 13Then they made fifty gold clasps and
used them to fasten the two sets of curtains
together so that the tabernacle was a unit.

14They made curtains of goat hair for the
tent over the tabernacle—eleven altogether.
15All eleven curtains were the same size—
thirty cubits long and four cubits wide.[b]
16They joined five of the curtains into one
set and the other six into another set. 17Then
they made fifty loops along the edge of the end
curtain in one set and also along the edge of
the end curtain in the other set. 18They made
fifty bronze clasps to fasten the tent together
as a unit. 19Then they made for the tent a covering of ram skins dyed red, and over that a
covering of the other durable leather.[c]

20They made upright frames of acacia wood
for the tabernacle. 21Each frame was ten cubits
long and a cubit and a half wide,[d] 22with two
projections set parallel to each other. They
made all the frames of the tabernacle in this
way. 23They made twenty frames for the south
side of the tabernacle 24and made forty silver
bases to go under them—two bases for each
frame, one under each projection. 25For the
other side, the north side of the tabernacle,
they made twenty frames 26and forty silver
bases—two under each frame. 27They made
six frames for the far end, that is, the west
end of the tabernacle, 28and two frames were
made for the corners of the tabernacle at the
far end. 29At these two corners the frames
were double from the bottom all the way to
the top and fitted into a single ring; both were
made alike. 30So there were eight frames and
sixteen silver bases—two under each frame.

31They also made crossbars of acacia wood:
five for the frames on one side of the tabernacle, 32five for those on the other side, and
five for the frames on the west, at the far end
of the tabernacle. 33They made the center
crossbar so that it extended from end to end
at the middle of the frames. 34They overlaid
the frames with gold and made gold rings to
hold the crossbars. They also overlaid the
crossbars with gold.

35They made the curtain of blue, purple and
scarlet yarn and finely twisted linen, with
cherubim woven into it by a skilled worker.
36They made four posts of acacia wood for it
and overlaid them with gold. They made gold
hooks for them and cast their four silver bas-

[a] *9* That is, about 42 feet long and 6 feet wide or about 13 meters long and 1.8 meters wide [b] *15* That is, about 45 feet long and 6 feet wide or about 14 meters long and 1.8 meters wide [c] *19* Possibly the hides of large aquatic mammals (see 35:7) [d] *21* That is, about 15 feet long and 2 1/4 feet wide or about 4.5 meters long and 68 centimeters wide

es. 37For the entrance to the tent they made a curtain of blue, purple and scarlet yarn and finely twisted linen—the work of an embroiderer; 38and they made five posts with hooks for them. They overlaid the tops of the posts and their bands with gold and made their five bases of bronze.

The Ark

37 Bezalel made the ark of acacia wood—two and a half cubits long, a cubit and a half wide, and a cubit and a half high.[a] 2He overlaid it with pure gold, both inside and out, and made a gold molding around it. 3He cast four gold rings for it and fastened them to its four feet, with two rings on one side and two rings on the other. 4Then he made poles of acacia wood and overlaid them with gold. 5And he inserted the poles into the rings on the sides of the ark to carry it.

6He made the atonement cover of pure gold—two and a half cubits long and a cubit and a half wide. 7Then he made two cherubim out of hammered gold at the ends of the cover. 8He made one cherub on one end and the second cherub on the other; at the two ends he made them of one piece with the cover. 9The cherubim had their wings spread upward, overshadowing the cover with them. The cherubim faced each other, looking toward the cover.

The Table

10They[b] made the table of acacia wood—two cubits long, a cubit wide and a cubit and a half high.[c] 11Then they overlaid it with pure gold and made a gold molding around it. 12They also made around it a rim a handbreadth[d] wide and put a gold molding on the rim. 13They cast four gold rings for the table and fastened them to the four corners, where the four legs were. 14The rings were put close to the rim to hold the poles used in carrying the table. 15The poles for carrying the table were made of acacia wood and were overlaid with gold. 16And they made from pure gold the articles for the table—its plates and dishes and bowls and its pitchers for the pouring out of drink offerings.

The Lampstand

17They made the lampstand of pure gold. They hammered out its base and shaft, and made its flowerlike cups, buds and blossoms of one piece with them. 18Six branches extended from the sides of the lampstand—three on one side and three on the other. 19Three cups shaped like almond flowers with buds and blossoms were on one branch, three on the next branch and the same for all six branches extending from the lampstand. 20And on the lampstand were four cups shaped like almond flowers with buds and blossoms. 21One bud was under the first pair of branches extending from the lampstand, a second bud under the second pair, and a third bud under the third pair—six branches in all. 22The buds and the branches were all of one piece with the lampstand, hammered out of pure gold.

23They made its seven lamps, as well as its wick trimmers and trays, of pure gold. 24They made the lampstand and all its accessories from one talent[e] of pure gold.

The Altar of Incense

25They made the altar of incense out of acacia wood. It was square, a cubit long and a cubit wide and two cubits high[f]—its horns of one piece with it. 26They overlaid the top and all the sides and the horns with pure gold, and made a gold molding around it. 27They made two gold rings below the molding—two on each of the opposite sides—to hold the poles used to carry it. 28They made the poles of acacia wood and overlaid them with gold.

29They also made the sacred anointing oil and the pure, fragrant incense—the work of a perfumer.

The Altar of Burnt Offering

38 They[g] built the altar of burnt offering of acacia wood, three cubits[h] high; it was square, five cubits long and five cubits wide.[i] 2They made a horn at each of the four corners, so that the horns and the altar were of one piece, and they overlaid the altar with bronze. 3They made all its utensils of bronze—its pots, shovels, sprinkling bowls, meat forks and firepans. 4They made a grating for the altar, a bronze network, to be under its ledge, halfway up the altar. 5They cast bronze rings to hold the poles for the four corners of the bronze grating. 6They made the poles of acacia wood and overlaid them with bronze. 7They inserted the poles into the rings so they would be on the sides of the altar for carrying it. They made it hollow, out of boards.

The Basin for Washing

8They made the bronze basin and its bronze stand from the mirrors of the women who served at the entrance to the tent of meeting.

The Courtyard

9Next they made the courtyard. The south side was a hundred cubits[j] long and had curtains of finely twisted linen, 10with twenty posts and twenty bronze bases, and with silver hooks and bands on the posts. 11The north side was also a hundred cubits long and had

[a] *1* That is, about 3 3/4 feet long and 2 1/4 feet wide and high or about 1.1 meters long and 68 centimeters wide and high; similarly in verse 6 [b] *10* Or *He*; also in verses 11-29 [c] *10* That is, about 3 feet long, 1 1/2 feet wide and 2 1/4 feet high or about 90 centimeters long, 45 centimeters wide and 68 centimeters high [d] *12* That is, about 3 inches or about 7.5 centimeters [e] *24* That is, about 75 pounds or about 34 kilograms [f] *25* That is, about 1 1/2 feet long and wide and 3 feet high or about 45 centimeters long and wide and 90 centimeters high [g] *1* Or *He*; also in verses 2-9 [h] *1* That is, about 4 1/2 feet or about 1.4 meters [i] *1* That is, about 7 1/2 feet or about 2.3 meters long and wide [j] *9* That is, about 150 feet or about 45 meters

twenty posts and twenty bronze bases, with silver hooks and bands on the posts.

12The west end was fifty cubits[a] wide and had curtains, with ten posts and ten bases, with silver hooks and bands on the posts. 13The east end, toward the sunrise, was also fifty cubits wide. 14Curtains fifteen cubits[b] long were on one side of the entrance, with three posts and three bases, 15and curtains fifteen cubits long were on the other side of the entrance to the courtyard, with three posts and three bases. 16All the curtains around the courtyard were of finely twisted linen. 17The bases for the posts were bronze. The hooks and bands on the posts were silver, and their tops were overlaid with silver; so all the posts of the courtyard had silver bands.

18The curtain for the entrance to the courtyard was made of blue, purple and scarlet yarn and finely twisted linen—the work of an embroiderer. It was twenty cubits[c] long and, like the curtains of the courtyard, five cubits[d] high, 19with four posts and four bronze bases. Their hooks and bands were silver, and their tops were overlaid with silver. 20All the tent pegs of the tabernacle and of the surrounding courtyard were bronze.

The Materials Used

21These are the amounts of the materials used for the tabernacle, the tabernacle of the covenant law, which were recorded at Moses' command by the Levites under the direction of Ithamar son of Aaron, the priest. 22(Bezalel son of Uri, the son of Hur, of the tribe of Judah, made everything the LORD commanded Moses; 23with him was Oholiab son of Ahisamak, of the tribe of Dan—an engraver and designer, and an embroiderer in blue, purple and scarlet yarn and fine linen.) 24The total amount of the gold from the wave offering used for all the work on the sanctuary was 29 talents and 730 shekels,[e] according to the sanctuary shekel.

25The silver obtained from those of the community who were counted in the census was 100 talents[f] and 1,775 shekels,[g] according to the sanctuary shekel— 26one beka per person, that is, half a shekel,[h] according to the sanctuary shekel, from everyone who had crossed over to those counted, twenty years old or more, a total of 603,550 men. 27The 100 talents of silver were used to cast the bases for the sanctuary and for the curtain—100 bases from the 100 talents, one talent for each base. 28They used the 1,775 shekels to make the hooks for the posts, to overlay the tops of the posts, and to make their bands.

29The bronze from the wave offering was 70 talents and 2,400 shekels.[i] 30They used it to make the bases for the entrance to the tent of meeting, the bronze altar with its bronze grating and all its utensils, 31the bases for the surrounding courtyard and those for its entrance and all the tent pegs for the tabernacle and those for the surrounding courtyard.

The Priestly Garments

39 From the blue, purple and scarlet yarn they made woven garments for ministering in the sanctuary. They also made sacred garments for Aaron, as the LORD commanded Moses.

The Ephod

2They[j] made the ephod of gold, and of blue, purple and scarlet yarn, and of finely twisted linen. 3They hammered out thin sheets of gold and cut strands to be worked into the blue, purple and scarlet yarn and fine linen—the work of skilled hands. 4They made shoulder pieces for the ephod, which were attached to two of its corners, so it could be fastened. 5Its skillfully woven waistband was like it—of one piece with the ephod and made with gold, and with blue, purple and scarlet yarn, and with finely twisted linen, as the LORD commanded Moses.

6They mounted the onyx stones in gold filigree settings and engraved them like a seal with the names of the sons of Israel. 7Then they fastened them on the shoulder pieces of the ephod as memorial stones for the sons of Israel, as the LORD commanded Moses.

The Breastpiece

8They fashioned the breastpiece—the work of a skilled craftsman. They made it like the ephod: of gold, and of blue, purple and scarlet yarn, and of finely twisted linen. 9It was square—a span[k] long and a span wide—and folded double. 10Then they mounted four rows of precious stones on it. The first row was carnelian, chrysolite and beryl; 11the second row was turquoise, lapis lazuli and emerald; 12the third row was jacinth, agate and amethyst; 13the fourth row was topaz, onyx and jasper.[l] They were mounted in gold filigree settings. 14There were twelve stones, one for each of the names of the sons of Israel, each engraved like a seal with the name of one of the twelve tribes.

15For the breastpiece they made braided chains of pure gold, like a rope. 16They made two gold filigree settings and two gold rings, and fastened the rings to two of the corners of the breastpiece. 17They fastened the two gold chains to the rings at the corners of the breastpiece, 18and the other ends of the chains to the two settings, attaching them to the shoulder pieces of the ephod at the front. 19They made two gold rings and attached them to the other two corners of the breastpiece on the inside

[a] *12* That is, about 75 feet or about 23 meters [b] *14* That is, about 22 feet or about 6.8 meters [c] *18* That is, about 30 feet or about 9 meters [d] *18* That is, about 7 1/2 feet or about 2.3 meters [e] *24* The weight of the gold was a little over a ton or about 1 metric ton. [f] *25* That is, about 3 3/4 tons or about 3.4 metric tons; also in verse 27 [g] *25* That is, about 44 pounds or about 20 kilograms; also in verse 28 [h] *26* That is, about 1/5 ounce or about 5.7 grams [i] *29* The weight of the bronze was about 2 1/2 tons or about 2.4 metric tons. [j] *2* Or *He*; also in verses 7, 8 and 22 [k] *9* That is, about 9 inches or about 23 centimeters [l] *13* The precise identification of some of these precious stones is uncertain.

edge next to the ephod. 20 Then they made two more gold rings and attached them to the bottom of the shoulder pieces on the front of the ephod, close to the seam just above the waistband of the ephod. 21 They tied the rings of the breastpiece to the rings of the ephod with blue cord, connecting it to the waistband so that the breastpiece would not swing out from the ephod—as the LORD commanded Moses.

Other Priestly Garments

22 They made the robe of the ephod entirely of blue cloth—the work of a weaver— 23 with an opening in the center of the robe like the opening of a collar,[a] and a band around this opening, so that it would not tear. 24 They made pomegranates of blue, purple and scarlet yarn and finely twisted linen around the hem of the robe. 25 And they made bells of pure gold and attached them around the hem between the pomegranates. 26 The bells and pomegranates alternated around the hem of the robe to be worn for ministering, as the LORD commanded Moses.

27 For Aaron and his sons, they made tunics of fine linen—the work of a weaver— 28 and the turban of fine linen, the linen caps and the undergarments of finely twisted linen. 29 The sash was made of finely twisted linen and blue, purple and scarlet yarn—the work of an embroiderer—as the LORD commanded Moses.

30 They made the plate, the sacred emblem, out of pure gold and engraved on it, like an inscription on a seal: HOLY TO THE LORD. 31 Then they fastened a blue cord to it to attach it to the turban, as the LORD commanded Moses.

Moses Inspects the Tabernacle

32 So all the work on the tabernacle, the tent of meeting, was completed. The Israelites did everything just as the LORD commanded Moses. 33 Then they brought the tabernacle to Moses: the tent and all its furnishings, its clasps, frames, crossbars, posts and bases; 34 the covering of ram skins dyed red and the covering of another durable leather[b] and the shielding curtain; 35 the ark of the covenant law with its poles and the atonement cover; 36 the table with all its articles and the bread of the Presence; 37 the pure gold lampstand with its row of lamps and all its accessories, and the olive oil for the light; 38 the gold altar, the anointing oil, the fragrant incense, and the curtain for the entrance to the tent; 39 the bronze altar with its bronze grating, its poles and all its utensils; the basin with its stand; 40 the curtains of the courtyard with its posts and bases, and the curtain for the entrance to the courtyard; the ropes and tent pegs for the courtyard; all the furnishings for the tabernacle, the tent of meeting; 41 and the woven garments worn for ministering in the sanctuary, both the sacred garments for Aaron the priest and the garments for his sons when serving as priests

42 The Israelites had done all the work just as the LORD had commanded Moses. 43 Moses inspected the work and saw that they had done it just as the LORD had commanded. So Moses blessed them.

Setting Up the Tabernacle

40 Then the LORD said to Moses: 2 "Set up the tabernacle, the tent of meeting, on the first day of the first month. 3 Place the ark of the covenant law in it and shield the ark with the curtain. 4 Bring in the table and set out what belongs on it. Then bring in the lampstand and set up its lamps. 5 Place the gold altar of incense in front of the ark of the covenant law and put the curtain at the entrance to the tabernacle.

6 "Place the altar of burnt offering in front of the entrance to the tabernacle, the tent of meeting; 7 place the basin between the tent of meeting and the altar and put water in it. 8 Set up the courtyard around it and put the curtain at the entrance to the courtyard.

9 "Take the anointing oil and anoint the tabernacle and everything in it; consecrate it and all its furnishings, and it will be holy. 10 Then anoint the altar of burnt offering and all its utensils; consecrate the altar, and it will be most holy. 11 Anoint the basin and its stand and consecrate them.

12 "Bring Aaron and his sons to the entrance to the tent of meeting and wash them with water. 13 Then dress Aaron in the sacred garments, anoint him and consecrate him so he may serve me as priest. 14 Bring his sons and dress them in tunics. 15 Anoint them just as you anointed their father, so they may serve me as priests. Their anointing will be to a priesthood that will continue throughout their generations." 16 Moses did everything just as the LORD commanded him.

17 So the tabernacle was set up on the first day of the first month in the second year. 18 When Moses set up the tabernacle, he put the bases in place, erected the frames, inserted the crossbars and set up the posts. 19 Then he spread the tent over the tabernacle and put the covering over the tent, as the LORD commanded him.

20 He took the tablets of the covenant law and placed them in the ark, attached the poles to the ark and put the atonement cover over it. 21 Then he brought the ark into the tabernacle and hung the shielding curtain and shielded the ark of the covenant law, as the LORD commanded him.

22 Moses placed the table in the tent of meeting on the north side of the tabernacle outside the curtain 23 and set out the bread on it before the LORD, as the LORD commanded him.

24 He placed the lampstand in the tent of meeting opposite the table on the south side of the tabernacle 25 and set up the lamps before the LORD, as the LORD commanded him.

26 Moses placed the gold altar in the tent of meeting in front of the curtain 27 and burned

[a] *23* The meaning of the Hebrew for this word is uncertain. [b] *34* Possibly the hides of large aquatic mammals

fragrant incense on it, as the LORD commanded him.

28Then he put up the curtain at the entrance to the tabernacle. 29He set the altar of burnt offering near the entrance to the tabernacle, the tent of meeting, and offered on it burnt offerings and grain offerings, as the LORD commanded him.

30He placed the basin between the tent of meeting and the altar and put water in it for washing, 31and Moses and Aaron and his sons used it to wash their hands and feet. 32They washed whenever they entered the tent of meeting or approached the altar, as the LORD commanded Moses.

33Then Moses set up the courtyard around the tabernacle and altar and put up the curtain at the entrance to the courtyard. And so Moses finished the work.

The Glory of the LORD

34Then the cloud covered the tent of meeting, and the glory of the LORD filled the tabernacle. 35Moses could not enter the tent of meeting because the cloud had settled on it, and the glory of the LORD filled the tabernacle.

36In all the travels of the Israelites, whenever the cloud lifted from above the tabernacle, they would set out; 37but if the cloud did not lift, they did not set out—until the day it lifted. 38So the cloud of the LORD was over the tabernacle by day, and fire was in the cloud by night, in the sight of all the Israelites during all their travels.

Leviticus

The Burnt Offering

1 The LORD called to Moses and spoke to him from the tent of meeting. He said, 2"Speak to the Israelites and say to them: 'When anyone among you brings an offering to the LORD, bring as your offering an animal from either the herd or the flock.

3" 'If the offering is a burnt offering from the herd, you are to offer a male without defect. You must present it at the entrance to the tent of meeting so that it will be acceptable to the LORD. 4You are to lay your hand on the head of the burnt offering, and it will be accepted on your behalf to make atonement for you. 5You are to slaughter the young bull before the LORD, and then Aaron's sons the priests shall bring the blood and splash it against the sides of the altar at the entrance to the tent of meeting. 6You are to skin the burnt offering and cut it into pieces. 7The sons of Aaron the priest are to put fire on the altar and arrange wood on the fire. 8Then Aaron's sons the priests shall arrange the pieces, including the head and the fat, on the wood that is burning on the altar. 9You are to wash the internal organs and the legs with water, and the priest is to burn all of it on the altar. It is a burnt offering, a food offering, an aroma pleasing to the LORD.

10" 'If the offering is a burnt offering from the flock, from either the sheep or the goats, you are to offer a male without defect. 11You are to slaughter it at the north side of the altar before the LORD, and Aaron's sons the priests shall splash its blood against the sides of the altar. 12You are to cut it into pieces, and the priest shall arrange them, including the head and the fat, on the wood that is burning on the altar. 13You are to wash the internal organs and the legs with water, and the priest is to bring all of them and burn them on the altar. It is a burnt offering, a food offering, an aroma pleasing to the LORD.

14" 'If the offering to the LORD is a burnt offering of birds, you are to offer a dove or a young pigeon. 15The priest shall bring it to the altar, wring off the head and burn it on the altar; its blood shall be drained out on the side of the altar. 16He is to remove the crop and the feathers[a] and throw them down east of the altar where the ashes are. 17He shall tear it open by the wings, not dividing it completely, and then the priest shall burn it on the wood that is burning on the altar. It is a burnt offering, a food offering, an aroma pleasing to the LORD.

The Grain Offering

2 " 'When anyone brings a grain offering to the LORD, their offering is to be of the finest flour. They are to pour olive oil on it, put incense on it 2and take it to Aaron's sons the priests. The priest shall take a handful of the flour and oil, together with all the incense, and burn this as a memorial[b] portion on the altar, a food offering, an aroma pleasing to the LORD. 3The rest of the grain offering belongs to Aaron and his sons; it is a most holy part of the food offerings presented to the LORD.

4" 'If you bring a grain offering baked in an oven, it is to consist of the finest flour: either thick loaves made without yeast and with olive oil mixed in or thin loaves made without yeast and brushed with olive oil. 5If your grain offering is prepared on a griddle, it is to be made of the finest flour mixed with oil, and without yeast. 6Crumble it and pour

[a] 16 Or *crop with its contents*; the meaning of the Hebrew for this word is uncertain.
[b] 2 Or *representative*; also in verses 9 and 16

oil on it; it is a grain offering. 7If your grain offering is cooked in a pan, it is to be made of the finest flour and some olive oil. 8Bring the grain offering made of these things to the LORD; present it to the priest, who shall take it to the altar. 9He shall take out the memorial portion from the grain offering and burn it on the altar as a food offering, an aroma pleasing to the LORD. 10The rest of the grain offering belongs to Aaron and his sons; it is a most holy part of the food offerings presented to the LORD.

11“ ‘Every grain offering you bring to the LORD must be made without yeast, for you are not to burn any yeast or honey in a food offering presented to the LORD. 12You may bring them to the LORD as an offering of the firstfruits, but they are not to be offered on the altar as a pleasing aroma. 13Season all your grain offerings with salt. Do not leave the salt of the covenant of your God out of your grain offerings; add salt to all your offerings.

14“ ‘If you bring a grain offering of firstfruits to the LORD, offer crushed heads of new grain roasted in the fire. 15Put oil and incense on it; it is a grain offering. 16The priest shall burn the memorial portion of the crushed grain and the oil, together with all the incense, as a food offering presented to the LORD.

The Fellowship Offering

3 “ ‘If your offering is a fellowship offering, and you offer an animal from the herd, whether male or female, you are to present before the LORD an animal without defect. 2You are to lay your hand on the head of your offering and slaughter it at the entrance to the tent of meeting. Then Aaron’s sons the priests shall splash the blood against the sides of the altar. 3From the fellowship offering you are to bring a food offering to the LORD: the internal organs and all the fat that is connected to them, 4both kidneys with the fat on them near the loins, and the long lobe of the liver, which you will remove with the kidneys. 5Then Aaron’s sons are to burn it on the altar on top of the burnt offering that is lying on the burning wood; it is a food offering, an aroma pleasing to the LORD.

6“ ‘If you offer an animal from the flock as a fellowship offering to the LORD, you are to offer a male or female without defect. 7If you offer a lamb, you are to present it before the LORD, 8lay your hand on its head and slaughter it in front of the tent of meeting. Then Aaron’s sons shall splash its blood against the sides of the altar. 9From the fellowship offering you are to bring a food offering to the LORD: its fat, the entire fat tail cut off close to the backbone, the internal organs and all the fat that is connected to them, 10both kidneys with the fat on them near the loins, and the long lobe of the liver, which you will remove with the kidneys. 11The priest shall burn them on the altar as a food offering presented to the LORD.

12“ ‘If your offering is a goat, you are to present it before the LORD, 13lay your hand on its head and slaughter it in front of the tent of meeting. Then Aaron’s sons shall splash its blood against the sides of the altar. 14From what you offer you are to present this food offering to the LORD: the internal organs and all the fat that is connected to them, 15both kidneys with the fat on them near the loins, and the long lobe of the liver, which you will remove with the kidneys. 16The priest shall burn them on the altar as a food offering, a pleasing aroma. All the fat is the LORD’s.

17“ ‘This is a lasting ordinance for the generations to come, wherever you live: You must not eat any fat or any blood.’ ”

The Sin Offering

4 The LORD said to Moses, 2“Say to the Israelites: ‘When anyone sins unintentionally and does what is forbidden in any of the LORD’s commands—

3“ ‘If the anointed priest sins, bringing guilt on the people, he must bring to the LORD a young bull without defect as a sin offering[a] for the sin he has committed. 4He is to present the bull at the entrance to the tent of meeting before the LORD. He is to lay his hand on its head and slaughter it there before the LORD. 5Then the anointed priest shall take some of the bull’s blood and carry it into the tent of meeting. 6He is to dip his finger into the blood and sprinkle some of it seven times before the LORD, in front of the curtain of the sanctuary. 7The priest shall then put some of the blood on the horns of the altar of fragrant incense that is before the LORD in the tent of meeting. The rest of the bull’s blood he shall pour out at the base of the altar of burnt offering at the entrance to the tent of meeting. 8He shall remove all the fat from the bull of the sin offering—all the fat that is connected to the internal organs, 9both kidneys with the fat on them near the loins, and the long lobe of the liver, which he will remove with the kidneys— 10just as the fat is removed from the ox[b] sacrificed as a fellowship offering. Then the priest shall burn them on the altar of burnt offering. 11But the hide of the bull and all its flesh, as well as the head and legs, the internal organs and the intestines— 12that is, all the rest of the bull—he must take outside the camp to a place ceremonially clean, where the ashes are thrown, and burn it there in a wood fire on the ash heap.

13“ ‘If the whole Israelite community sins unintentionally and does what is forbidden in any of the LORD’s commands, even though the community is unaware of the matter, when they realize their guilt 14and the sin they committed becomes known, the assembly must bring a young bull as a sin offering and present it before the tent of meeting. 15The elders of the community are to lay their hands on the bull’s head before the LORD, and the bull shall be slaughtered before the LORD. 16Then

[a] *3* Or *purification offering*; here and throughout this chapter [b] *10* The Hebrew word can refer to either male or female.

the anointed priest is to take some of the bull's blood into the tent of meeting. 17He shall dip his finger into the blood and sprinkle it before the LORD seven times in front of the curtain. 18He is to put some of the blood on the horns of the altar that is before the LORD in the tent of meeting. The rest of the blood he shall pour out at the base of the altar of burnt offering at the entrance to the tent of meeting. 19He shall remove all the fat from it and burn it on the altar, 20and do with this bull just as he did with the bull for the sin offering. In this way the priest will make atonement for the community, and they will be forgiven. 21Then he shall take the bull outside the camp and burn it as he burned the first bull. This is the sin offering for the community.

22" 'When a leader sins unintentionally and does what is forbidden in any of the commands of the LORD his God, when he realizes his guilt 23and the sin he has committed becomes known, he must bring as his offering a male goat without defect. 24He is to lay his hand on the goat's head and slaughter it at the place where the burnt offering is slaughtered before the LORD. It is a sin offering. 25Then the priest shall take some of the blood of the sin offering with his finger and put it on the horns of the altar of burnt offering and pour out the rest of the blood at the base of the altar. 26He shall burn all the fat on the altar as he burned the fat of the fellowship offering. In this way the priest will make atonement for the leader's sin, and he will be forgiven.

27" 'If any member of the community sins unintentionally and does what is forbidden in any of the LORD's commands, when they realize their guilt 28and the sin they have committed becomes known, they must bring as their offering for the sin they committed a female goat without defect. 29They are to lay their hand on the head of the sin offering and slaughter it at the place of the burnt offering. 30Then the priest is to take some of the blood with his finger and put it on the horns of the altar of burnt offering and pour out the rest of the blood at the base of the altar. 31They shall remove all the fat, just as the fat is removed from the fellowship offering, and the priest shall burn it on the altar as an aroma pleasing to the LORD. In this way the priest will make atonement for them, and they will be forgiven.

32" 'If someone brings a lamb as their sin offering, they are to bring a female without defect. 33They are to lay their hand on its head and slaughter it for a sin offering at the place where the burnt offering is slaughtered. 34Then the priest shall take some of the blood of the sin offering with his finger and put it on the horns of the altar of burnt offering and pour out the rest of the blood at the base of the altar. 35They shall remove all the fat, just as the fat is removed from the lamb of the fellowship offering, and the priest shall burn it on the altar on top of the food offerings presented to the LORD. In this way the priest will make atonement for them for the sin they have committed, and they will be forgiven.

5 " 'If anyone sins because they do not speak up when they hear a public charge to testify regarding something they have seen or learned about, they will be held responsible.

2" 'If anyone becomes aware that they are guilty—if they unwittingly touch anything ceremonially unclean (whether the carcass of an unclean animal, wild or domestic, or of any unclean creature that moves along the ground) and they are unaware that they have become unclean, but then they come to realize their guilt; 3or if they touch human uncleanness (anything that would make them unclean) even though they are unaware of it, but then they learn of it and realize their guilt; 4or if anyone thoughtlessly takes an oath to do anything, whether good or evil (in any matter one might carelessly swear about) even though they are unaware of it, but then they learn of it and realize their guilt— 5when anyone becomes aware that they are guilty in any of these matters, they must confess in what way they have sinned. 6As a penalty for the sin they have committed, they must bring to the LORD a female lamb or goat from the flock as a sin offering[a]; and the priest shall make atonement for them for their sin.

7" 'Anyone who cannot afford a lamb is to bring two doves or two young pigeons to the LORD as a penalty for their sin—one for a sin offering and the other for a burnt offering. 8They are to bring them to the priest, who shall first offer the one for the sin offering. He is to wring its head from its neck, not dividing it completely, 9and is to splash some of the blood of the sin offering against the side of the altar; the rest of the blood must be drained out at the base of the altar. It is a sin offering. 10The priest shall then offer the other as a burnt offering in the prescribed way and make atonement for them for the sin they have committed, and they will be forgiven.

11" 'If, however, they cannot afford two doves or two young pigeons, they are to bring as an offering for their sin a tenth of an ephah[b] of the finest flour for a sin offering. They must not put olive oil or incense on it, because it is a sin offering. 12They are to bring it to the priest, who shall take a handful of it as a memorial[c] portion and burn it on the altar on top of the food offerings presented to the LORD. It is a sin offering. 13In this way the priest will make atonement for them for any of these sins they have committed, and they will be forgiven. The rest of the offering will belong to the priest, as in the case of the grain offering.' "

The Guilt Offering

14The LORD said to Moses: 15"When anyone is unfaithful to the LORD by sinning unintentionally in regard to any of the LORD's holy things, they are to bring to the LORD as a pen-

[a] 6 Or *purification offering*; here and throughout this chapter [b] 11 That is, probably about 3 1/2 pounds or about 1.6 kilograms [c] 12 Or *representative*

alty a ram from the flock, one without defect
and of the proper value in silver, according
to the sanctuary shekel.[a] It is a guilt offering.
16They must make restitution for what they
have failed to do in regard to the holy things,
pay an additional penalty of a fifth of its value and give it all to the priest. The priest will
make atonement for them with the ram as a
guilt offering, and they will be forgiven.
17"If anyone sins and does what is forbidden
in any of the LORD's commands, even though
they do not know it, they are guilty and will
be held responsible. 18They are to bring to the
priest as a guilt offering a ram from the flock,
one without defect and of the proper value.
In this way the priest will make atonement
for them for the wrong they have committed
unintentionally, and they will be forgiven. 19It
is a guilt offering; they have been guilty of[b]
wrongdoing against the LORD."

6[c] The LORD said to Moses: 2"If anyone sins
and is unfaithful to the LORD by deceiving
a neighbor about something entrusted to them
or left in their care or about something stolen,
or if they cheat their neighbor, 3or if they find
lost property and lie about it, or if they swear
falsely about any such sin that people may
commit— 4when they sin in any of these ways
and realize their guilt, they must return what
they have stolen or taken by extortion, or what
was entrusted to them, or the lost property
they found, 5or whatever it was they swore
falsely about. They must make restitution in
full, add a fifth of the value to it and give it all
to the owner on the day they present their guilt
offering. 6And as a penalty they must bring
to the priest, that is, to the LORD, their guilt
offering, a ram from the flock, one without
defect and of the proper value. 7In this way the
priest will make atonement for them before
the LORD, and they will be forgiven for any of
the things they did that made them guilty."

The Burnt Offering

8The LORD said to Moses: 9"Give Aaron and
his sons this command: 'These are the regulations for the burnt offering: The burnt offering
is to remain on the altar hearth throughout the
night, till morning, and the fire must be kept
burning on the altar. 10The priest shall then
put on his linen clothes, with linen undergarments next to his body, and shall remove the
ashes of the burnt offering that the fire has
consumed on the altar and place them beside
the altar. 11Then he is to take off these clothes
and put on others, and carry the ashes outside
the camp to a place that is ceremonially clean.
12The fire on the altar must be kept burning; it
must not go out. Every morning the priest is to
add firewood and arrange the burnt offering
on the fire and burn the fat of the fellowship
offerings on it. 13The fire must be kept burning
on the altar continuously; it must not go out.

The Grain Offering

14" 'These are the regulations for the grain
offering: Aaron's sons are to bring it before
the LORD, in front of the altar. 15The priest
is to take a handful of the finest flour and
some olive oil, together with all the incense
on the grain offering, and burn the memorial[d]
portion on the altar as an aroma pleasing to
the LORD. 16Aaron and his sons shall eat the
rest of it, but it is to be eaten without yeast in
the sanctuary area; they are to eat it in the
courtyard of the tent of meeting. 17It must not
be baked with yeast; I have given it as their
share of the food offerings presented to me.
Like the sin offering[e] and the guilt offering, it
is most holy. 18Any male descendant of Aaron
may eat it. For all generations to come it is his
perpetual share of the food offerings presented to the LORD. Whatever touches them will
become holy.[f] ' "
19The LORD also said to Moses, 20"This is the
offering Aaron and his sons are to bring to the
LORD on the day he[g] is anointed: a tenth of an
ephah[h] of the finest flour as a regular grain
offering, half of it in the morning and half in
the evening. 21It must be prepared with oil on
a griddle; bring it well-mixed and present the
grain offering broken[i] in pieces as an aroma
pleasing to the LORD. 22The son who is to succeed him as anointed priest shall prepare it.
It is the LORD's perpetual share and is to be
burned completely. 23Every grain offering of
a priest shall be burned completely; it must
not be eaten."

The Sin Offering

24The LORD said to Moses, 25"Say to Aaron
and his sons: 'These are the regulations for the
sin offering: The sin offering is to be slaughtered before the LORD in the place the burnt
offering is slaughtered; it is most holy. 26The
priest who offers it shall eat it; it is to be eaten
in the sanctuary area, in the courtyard of the
tent of meeting. 27Whatever touches any of the
flesh will become holy, and if any of the blood
is spattered on a garment, you must wash it in
the sanctuary area. 28The clay pot the meat is
cooked in must be broken; but if it is cooked
in a bronze pot, the pot is to be scoured and
rinsed with water. 29Any male in a priest's
family may eat it; it is most holy. 30But any
sin offering whose blood is brought into the
tent of meeting to make atonement in the Holy
Place must not be eaten; it must be burned up.

The Guilt Offering

7 " 'These are the regulations for the guilt
offering, which is most holy: 2The guilt offering is to be slaughtered in the place where
the burnt offering is slaughtered, and its blood
is to be splashed against the sides of the altar.
3All its fat shall be offered: the fat tail and
the fat that covers the internal organs, 4both

[a] *15* That is, about 2/5 ounce or about 12 grams [b] *19* Or *offering; atonement has been made for their* [c] In Hebrew texts 6:1-7 is numbered 5:20-26, and 6:8-30 is numbered 6:1-23. [d] *15* Or *representative* [e] *17* Or *purification offering*; also in verses 25 and 30 [f] *18* Or *Whoever touches them must be holy*; similarly in verse 27 [g] *20* Or *each* [h] *20* That is, probably about 3 1/2 pounds or about 1.6 kilograms [i] *21* The meaning of the Hebrew for this word is uncertain.

kidneys with the fat on them near the loins, and the long lobe of the liver, which is to be removed with the kidneys. 5The priest shall burn them on the altar as a food offering presented to the LORD. It is a guilt offering. 6Any male in a priest's family may eat it, but it must be eaten in the sanctuary area; it is most holy.

7" 'The same law applies to both the sin offering[a] and the guilt offering: They belong to the priest who makes atonement with them. 8The priest who offers a burnt offering for anyone may keep its hide for himself. 9Every grain offering baked in an oven or cooked in a pan or on a griddle belongs to the priest who offers it, 10and every grain offering, whether mixed with olive oil or dry, belongs equally to all the sons of Aaron.

The Fellowship Offering

11" 'These are the regulations for the fellowship offering anyone may present to the LORD:

12" 'If they offer it as an expression of thankfulness, then along with this thank offering they are to offer thick loaves made without yeast and with olive oil mixed in, thin loaves made without yeast and brushed with oil, and thick loaves of the finest flour well-kneaded and with oil mixed in. 13Along with their fellowship offering of thanksgiving they are to present an offering with thick loaves of bread made with yeast. 14They are to bring one of each kind as an offering, a contribution to the LORD; it belongs to the priest who splashes the blood of the fellowship offering against the altar. 15The meat of their fellowship offering of thanksgiving must be eaten on the day it is offered; they must leave none of it till morning.

16" 'If, however, their offering is the result of a vow or is a freewill offering, the sacrifice shall be eaten on the day they offer it, but anything left over may be eaten on the next day. 17Any meat of the sacrifice left over till the third day must be burned up. 18If any meat of the fellowship offering is eaten on the third day, the one who offered it will not be accepted. It will not be reckoned to their credit, for it has become impure; the person who eats any of it will be held responsible.

19" 'Meat that touches anything ceremonially unclean must not be eaten; it must be burned up. As for other meat, anyone ceremonially clean may eat it. 20But if anyone who is unclean eats any meat of the fellowship offering belonging to the LORD, they must be cut off from their people. 21Anyone who touches something unclean—whether human uncleanness or an unclean animal or any unclean creature that moves along the ground[b]—and then eats any of the meat of the fellowship offering belonging to the LORD must be cut off from their people.' "

Eating Fat and Blood Forbidden

22The LORD said to Moses, 23"Say to the Israelites: 'Do not eat any of the fat of cattle, sheep or goats. 24The fat of an animal found dead or torn by wild animals may be used for any other purpose, but you must not eat it. 25Anyone who eats the fat of an animal from which a food offering may be[c] presented to the LORD must be cut off from their people. 26And wherever you live, you must not eat the blood of any bird or animal. 27Anyone who eats blood must be cut off from their people.' "

The Priests' Share

28The LORD said to Moses, 29"Say to the Israelites: 'Anyone who brings a fellowship offering to the LORD is to bring part of it as their sacrifice to the LORD. 30With their own hands they are to present the food offering to the LORD; they are to bring the fat, together with the breast, and wave the breast before the LORD as a wave offering. 31The priest shall burn the fat on the altar, but the breast belongs to Aaron and his sons. 32You are to give the right thigh of your fellowship offerings to the priest as a contribution. 33The son of Aaron who offers the blood and the fat of the fellowship offering shall have the right thigh as his share. 34From the fellowship offerings of the Israelites, I have taken the breast that is waved and the thigh that is presented and have given them to Aaron the priest and his sons as their perpetual share from the Israelites.' "

35This is the portion of the food offerings presented to the LORD that were allotted to Aaron and his sons on the day they were presented to serve the LORD as priests. 36On the day they were anointed, the LORD commanded that the Israelites give this to them as their perpetual share for the generations to come.

37These, then, are the regulations for the burnt offering, the grain offering, the sin offering, the guilt offering, the ordination offering and the fellowship offering, 38which the LORD gave Moses at Mount Sinai in the Desert of Sinai on the day he commanded the Israelites to bring their offerings to the LORD.

The Ordination of Aaron and His Sons

8 The LORD said to Moses, 2"Bring Aaron and his sons, their garments, the anointing oil, the bull for the sin offering,[d] the two rams and the basket containing bread made without yeast, 3and gather the entire assembly at the entrance to the tent of meeting." 4Moses did as the LORD commanded him, and the assembly gathered at the entrance to the tent of meeting.

5Moses said to the assembly, "This is what the LORD has commanded to be done." 6Then Moses brought Aaron and his sons forward and washed them with water. 7He put the tunic on Aaron, tied the sash around him, clothed him with the robe and put the ephod on him. He also fastened the ephod with a decorative waistband, which he tied around him. 8He placed the breastpiece on him and put

[a] 7 Or *purification offering*; also in verse 37 [b] 21 A few Hebrew manuscripts, Samaritan Pentateuch, Syriac and Targum (see 5:2); most Hebrew manuscripts *any unclean, detestable thing*
[c] 25 Or *offering is* [d] 2 Or *purification offering*; also in verse 14

the Urim and Thummim in the breastpiece. 9 Then he placed the turban on Aaron's head and set the gold plate, the sacred emblem, on the front of it, as the LORD commanded Moses.

10 Then Moses took the anointing oil and anointed the tabernacle and everything in it, and so consecrated them. 11 He sprinkled some of the oil on the altar seven times, anointing the altar and all its utensils and the basin with its stand, to consecrate them. 12 He poured some of the anointing oil on Aaron's head and anointed him to consecrate him. 13 Then he brought Aaron's sons forward, put tunics on them, tied sashes around them and fastened caps on them, as the LORD commanded Moses.

14 He then presented the bull for the sin offering, and Aaron and his sons laid their hands on its head. 15 Moses slaughtered the bull and took some of the blood, and with his finger he put it on all the horns of the altar to purify the altar. He poured out the rest of the blood at the base of the altar. So he consecrated it to make atonement for it. 16 Moses also took all the fat around the internal organs, the long lobe of the liver, and both kidneys and their fat, and burned it on the altar. 17 But the bull with its hide and its flesh and its intestines he burned up outside the camp, as the LORD commanded Moses.

18 He then presented the ram for the burnt offering, and Aaron and his sons laid their hands on its head. 19 Then Moses slaughtered the ram and splashed the blood against the sides of the altar. 20 He cut the ram into pieces and burned the head, the pieces and the fat. 21 He washed the internal organs and the legs with water and burned the whole ram on the altar. It was a burnt offering, a pleasing aroma, a food offering presented to the LORD, as the LORD commanded Moses.

22 He then presented the other ram, the ram for the ordination, and Aaron and his sons laid their hands on its head. 23 Moses slaughtered the ram and took some of its blood and put it on the lobe of Aaron's right ear, on the thumb of his right hand and on the big toe of his right foot. 24 Moses also brought Aaron's sons forward and put some of the blood on the lobes of their right ears, on the thumbs of their right hands and on the big toes of their right feet. Then he splashed blood against the sides of the altar. 25 After that, he took the fat, the fat tail, all the fat around the internal organs, the long lobe of the liver, both kidneys and their fat and the right thigh. 26 And from the basket of bread made without yeast, which was before the LORD, he took one thick loaf, one thick loaf with olive oil mixed in, and one thin loaf, and he put these on the fat portions and on the right thigh. 27 He put all these in the hands of Aaron and his sons, and they waved them before the LORD as a wave offering. 28 Then Moses took them from their hands and burned them on the altar on top of the burnt offering as an ordination offering, a pleasing aroma, a food offering presented to the LORD. 29 Moses also took the breast, which was his share of the ordination ram, and waved it before the LORD as a wave offering, as the LORD commanded Moses.

30 Then Moses took some of the anointing oil and some of the blood from the altar and sprinkled them on Aaron and his garments and on his sons and their garments. So he consecrated Aaron and his garments and his sons and their garments.

31 Moses then said to Aaron and his sons, "Cook the meat at the entrance to the tent of meeting and eat it there with the bread from the basket of ordination offerings, as I was commanded: 'Aaron and his sons are to eat it.' 32 Then burn up the rest of the meat and the bread. 33 Do not leave the entrance to the tent of meeting for seven days, until the days of your ordination are completed, for your ordination will last seven days. 34 What has been done today was commanded by the LORD to make atonement for you. 35 You must stay at the entrance to the tent of meeting day and night for seven days and do what the LORD requires, so you will not die; for that is what I have been commanded."

36 So Aaron and his sons did everything the LORD commanded through Moses.

The Priests Begin Their Ministry

9 On the eighth day Moses summoned Aaron and his sons and the elders of Israel. 2 He said to Aaron, "Take a bull calf for your sin offering[a] and a ram for your burnt offering, both without defect, and present them before the LORD. 3 Then say to the Israelites: 'Take a male goat for a sin offering, a calf and a lamb—both a year old and without defect—for a burnt offering, 4 and an ox[b] and a ram for a fellowship offering to sacrifice before the LORD, together with a grain offering mixed with olive oil. For today the LORD will appear to you.'"

5 They took the things Moses commanded to the front of the tent of meeting, and the entire assembly came near and stood before the LORD. 6 Then Moses said, "This is what the LORD has commanded you to do, so that the glory of the LORD may appear to you."

7 Moses said to Aaron, "Come to the altar and sacrifice your sin offering and your burnt offering and make atonement for yourself and the people; sacrifice the offering that is for the people and make atonement for them, as the LORD has commanded."

8 So Aaron came to the altar and slaughtered the calf as a sin offering for himself. 9 His sons brought the blood to him, and he dipped his finger into the blood and put it on the horns of the altar; the rest of the blood he poured out at the base of the altar. 10 On the altar he burned the fat, the kidneys and the long lobe of the liver from the sin offering, as the LORD commanded Moses; 11 the flesh and the hide he burned up outside the camp.

12 Then he slaughtered the burnt offer-

[a] 2 Or *purification offering*; here and throughout this chapter [b] 4 The Hebrew word can refer to either male or female; also in verses 18 and 19.

ing. His sons handed him the blood, and
he splashed it against the sides of the altar.
13They handed him the burnt offering piece
by piece, including the head, and he burned
them on the altar. 14He washed the internal
organs and the legs and burned them on top
of the burnt offering on the altar.

15Aaron then brought the offering that was
for the people. He took the goat for the people's sin offering and slaughtered it and offered it for a sin offering as he did with the
first one.

16He brought the burnt offering and offered
it in the prescribed way. 17He also brought the
grain offering, took a handful of it and burned
it on the altar in addition to the morning's
burnt offering.

18He slaughtered the ox and the ram as
the fellowship offering for the people. His
sons handed him the blood, and he splashed
it against the sides of the altar. 19But the fat
portions of the ox and the ram—the fat tail,
the layer of fat, the kidneys and the long lobe
of the liver— 20these they laid on the breasts,
and then Aaron burned the fat on the altar.
21Aaron waved the breasts and the right thigh
before the LORD as a wave offering, as Moses
commanded.

22Then Aaron lifted his hands toward the
people and blessed them. And having sacrificed the sin offering, the burnt offering and
the fellowship offering, he stepped down.

23Moses and Aaron then went into the
tent of meeting. When they came out, they
blessed the people; and the glory of the LORD
appeared to all the people. 24Fire came out
from the presence of the LORD and consumed
the burnt offering and the fat portions on the
altar. And when all the people saw it, they
shouted for joy and fell facedown.

The Death of Nadab and Abihu

10 Aaron's sons Nadab and Abihu took
their censers, put fire in them and added incense; and they offered unauthorized fire
before the LORD, contrary to his command.
2So fire came out from the presence of the
LORD and consumed them, and they died before the LORD. 3Moses then said to Aaron,
"This is what the LORD spoke of when he said:

"'Among those who approach me
  I will be proved holy;
in the sight of all the people
  I will be honored.'"

Aaron remained silent.

4Moses summoned Mishael and Elzaphan,
sons of Aaron's uncle Uzziel, and said to them,
"Come here; carry your cousins outside the
camp, away from the front of the sanctuary."
5So they came and carried them, still in their
tunics, outside the camp, as Moses ordered.

6Then Moses said to Aaron and his sons
Eleazar and Ithamar, "Do not let your hair become unkempt[a] and do not tear your clothes,
or you will die and the LORD will be angry
with the whole community. But your relatives, all the Israelites, may mourn for those
the LORD has destroyed by fire. 7Do not leave
the entrance to the tent of meeting or you will
die, because the LORD's anointing oil is on
you." So they did as Moses said.

8Then the LORD said to Aaron, 9"You and
your sons are not to drink wine or other fermented drink whenever you go into the tent
of meeting, or you will die. This is a lasting
ordinance for the generations to come, 10so
that you can distinguish between the holy
and the common, between the unclean and
the clean, 11and so you can teach the Israelites all the decrees the LORD has given them
through Moses."

12Moses said to Aaron and his remaining
sons, Eleazar and Ithamar, "Take the grain
offering left over from the food offerings prepared without yeast and presented to the LORD
and eat it beside the altar, for it is most holy.
13Eat it in the sanctuary area, because it is
your share and your sons' share of the food
offerings presented to the LORD; for so I have
been commanded. 14But you and your sons
and your daughters may eat the breast that
was waved and the thigh that was presented.
Eat them in a ceremonially clean place; they
have been given to you and your children as
your share of the Israelites' fellowship offerings. 15The thigh that was presented and the
breast that was waved must be brought with
the fat portions of the food offerings, to be
waved before the LORD as a wave offering.
This will be the perpetual share for you and
your children, as the LORD has commanded."

16When Moses inquired about the goat of
the sin offering[b] and found that it had been
burned up, he was angry with Eleazar and
Ithamar, Aaron's remaining sons, and asked,
17"Why didn't you eat the sin offering in the
sanctuary area? It is most holy; it was given
to you to take away the guilt of the community by making atonement for them before the
LORD. 18Since its blood was not taken into the
Holy Place, you should have eaten the goat in
the sanctuary area, as I commanded."

19Aaron replied to Moses, "Today they
sacrificed their sin offering and their burnt
offering before the LORD, but such things as
this have happened to me. Would the LORD
have been pleased if I had eaten the sin offering today?" 20When Moses heard this, he
was satisfied.

Clean and Unclean Food

11 The LORD said to Moses and Aaron,
2"Say to the Israelites: 'Of all the animals that live on land, these are the ones you
may eat: 3You may eat any animal that has a
divided hoof and that chews the cud.

4"'There are some that only chew the cud
or only have a divided hoof, but you must not
eat them. The camel, though it chews the cud,
does not have a divided hoof; it is ceremonially unclean for you. 5The hyrax, though it
chews the cud, does not have a divided hoof;
it is unclean for you. 6The rabbit, though it

[a] 6 Or *Do not uncover your heads*   [b] 16 Or *purification offering*; also in verses 17 and 19

chews the cud, does not have a divided hoof;
it is unclean for you. 7And the pig, though it
has a divided hoof, does not chew the cud; it
is unclean for you. 8You must not eat their
meat or touch their carcasses; they are unclean for you.

9“ ‘Of all the creatures living in the water
of the seas and the streams you may eat any
that have fins and scales. 10But all creatures
in the seas or streams that do not have fins
and scales—whether among all the swarming
things or among all the other living creatures
in the water—you are to regard as unclean.
11And since you are to regard them as unclean,
you must not eat their meat; you must regard
their carcasses as unclean. 12Anything living
in the water that does not have fins and scales
is to be regarded as unclean by you.

13“ ‘These are the birds you are to regard as
unclean and not eat because they are unclean:
the eagle,[a] the vulture, the black vulture, 14the
red kite, any kind of black kite, 15any kind of
raven, 16the horned owl, the screech owl, the
gull, any kind of hawk, 17the little owl, the
cormorant, the great owl, 18the white owl, the
desert owl, the osprey, 19the stork, any kind
of heron, the hoopoe and the bat.

20“ ‘All flying insects that walk on all fours
are to be regarded as unclean by you. 21There
are, however, some flying insects that walk
on all fours that you may eat: those that have
jointed legs for hopping on the ground. 22Of
these you may eat any kind of locust, katydid,
cricket or grasshopper. 23But all other flying
insects that have four legs you are to regard
as unclean.

24“ ‘You will make yourselves unclean by
these; whoever touches their carcasses will
be unclean till evening. 25Whoever picks up
one of their carcasses must wash their clothes,
and they will be unclean till evening.

26“ ‘Every animal that does not have a divided hoof or that does not chew the cud is
unclean for you; whoever touches the carcass
of any of them will be unclean. 27Of all the animals that walk on all fours, those that walk
on their paws are unclean for you; whoever
touches their carcasses will be unclean till
evening. 28Anyone who picks up their carcasses must wash their clothes, and they will be
unclean till evening. These animals are unclean for you.

29“ ‘Of the animals that move along the
ground, these are unclean for you: the weasel,
the rat, any kind of great lizard, 30the gecko,
the monitor lizard, the wall lizard, the skink
and the chameleon. 31Of all those that move
along the ground, these are unclean for you.
Whoever touches them when they are dead
will be unclean till evening. 32When one of
them dies and falls on something, that article,
whatever its use, will be unclean, whether it
is made of wood, cloth, hide or sackcloth. Put
it in water; it will be unclean till evening, and
then it will be clean. 33If one of them falls into
a clay pot, everything in it will be unclean,
and you must break the pot. 34Any food you
are allowed to eat that has come into contact
with water from any such pot is unclean, and
any liquid that is drunk from such a pot is unclean. 35Anything that one of their carcasses
falls on becomes unclean; an oven or cooking pot must be broken up. They are unclean,
and you are to regard them as unclean. 36A
spring, however, or a cistern for collecting
water remains clean, but anyone who touches
one of these carcasses is unclean. 37If a carcass falls on any seeds that are to be planted,
they remain clean. 38But if water has been
put on the seed and a carcass falls on it, it is
unclean for you.

39“ ‘If an animal that you are allowed to eat
dies, anyone who touches its carcass will be
unclean till evening. 40Anyone who eats some
of its carcass must wash their clothes, and
they will be unclean till evening. Anyone who
picks up the carcass must wash their clothes,
and they will be unclean till evening.

41“ ‘Every creature that moves along the
ground is to be regarded as unclean; it is not to
be eaten. 42You are not to eat any creature that
moves along the ground, whether it moves
on its belly or walks on all fours or on many
feet; it is unclean. 43Do not defile yourselves
by any of these creatures. Do not make yourselves unclean by means of them or be made
unclean by them. 44I am the LORD your God;
consecrate yourselves and be holy, because I
am holy. Do not make yourselves unclean by
any creature that moves along the ground.
45I am the LORD, who brought you up out of
Egypt to be your God; therefore be holy, because I am holy.

46“ ‘These are the regulations concerning
animals, birds, every living thing that moves
about in the water and every creature that
moves along the ground. 47You must distinguish between the unclean and the clean, between living creatures that may be eaten and
those that may not be eaten.’ ”

Purification After Childbirth

12 The LORD said to Moses, 2“Say to the
Israelites: ‘A woman who becomes pregnant and gives birth to a son will be ceremonially unclean for seven days, just as she
is unclean during her monthly period. 3On
the eighth day the boy is to be circumcised.
4Then the woman must wait thirty-three days
to be purified from her bleeding. She must not
touch anything sacred or go to the sanctuary
until the days of her purification are over. 5If
she gives birth to a daughter, for two weeks
the woman will be unclean, as during her period. Then she must wait sixty-six days to be
purified from her bleeding.

6“ ‘When the days of her purification for a
son or daughter are over, she is to bring to
the priest at the entrance to the tent of meeting a year-old lamb for a burnt offering and
a young pigeon or a dove for a sin offering.[b]
7He shall offer them before the LORD to make

[a] *13* The precise identification of some of the birds, insects and animals in this chapter is uncertain.
[b] *6* Or *purification offering*; also in verse 8

atonement for her, and then she will be ceremonially clean from her flow of blood.

"'These are the regulations for the woman who gives birth to a boy or a girl. 8But if she cannot afford a lamb, she is to bring two doves or two young pigeons, one for a burnt offering and the other for a sin offering. In this way the priest will make atonement for her, and she will be clean.'"

Regulations About Defiling Skin Diseases

13 The LORD said to Moses and Aaron, 2"When anyone has a swelling or a rash or a shiny spot on their skin that may be a defiling skin disease,[a] they must be brought to Aaron the priest or to one of his sons[b] who is a priest. 3The priest is to examine the sore on the skin, and if the hair in the sore has turned white and the sore appears to be more than skin deep, it is a defiling skin disease. When the priest examines that person, he shall pronounce them ceremonially unclean. 4If the shiny spot on the skin is white but does not appear to be more than skin deep and the hair in it has not turned white, the priest is to isolate the affected person for seven days. 5On the seventh day the priest is to examine them, and if he sees that the sore is unchanged and has not spread in the skin, he is to isolate them for another seven days. 6On the seventh day the priest is to examine them again, and if the sore has faded and has not spread in the skin, the priest shall pronounce them clean; it is only a rash. They must wash their clothes, and they will be clean. 7But if the rash does spread in their skin after they have shown themselves to the priest to be pronounced clean, they must appear before the priest again. 8The priest is to examine that person, and if the rash has spread in the skin, he shall pronounce them unclean; it is a defiling skin disease.

9"When anyone has a defiling skin disease, they must be brought to the priest. 10The priest is to examine them, and if there is a white swelling in the skin that has turned the hair white and if there is raw flesh in the swelling, 11it is a chronic skin disease and the priest shall pronounce them unclean. He is not to isolate them, because they are already unclean.

12"If the disease breaks out all over their skin and, so far as the priest can see, it covers all the skin of the affected person from head to foot, 13the priest is to examine them, and if the disease has covered their whole body, he shall pronounce them clean. Since it has all turned white, they are clean. 14But whenever raw flesh appears on them, they will be unclean. 15When the priest sees the raw flesh, he shall pronounce them unclean. The raw flesh is unclean; they have a defiling disease. 16If the raw flesh changes and turns white, they must go to the priest. 17The priest is to examine them, and if the sores have turned white, the priest shall pronounce the affected person clean; then they will be clean.

18"When someone has a boil on their skin and it heals, 19and in the place where the boil was, a white swelling or reddish-white spot appears, they must present themselves to the priest. 20The priest is to examine it, and if it appears to be more than skin deep and the hair in it has turned white, the priest shall pronounce that person unclean. It is a defiling skin disease that has broken out where the boil was. 21But if, when the priest examines it, there is no white hair in it and it is not more than skin deep and has faded, then the priest is to isolate them for seven days. 22If it is spreading in the skin, the priest shall pronounce them unclean; it is a defiling disease. 23But if the spot is unchanged and has not spread, it is only a scar from the boil, and the priest shall pronounce them clean.

24"When someone has a burn on their skin and a reddish-white or white spot appears in the raw flesh of the burn, 25the priest is to examine the spot, and if the hair in it has turned white, and it appears to be more than skin deep, it is a defiling disease that has broken out in the burn. The priest shall pronounce them unclean; it is a defiling skin disease. 26But if the priest examines it and there is no white hair in the spot and if it is not more than skin deep and has faded, then the priest is to isolate them for seven days. 27On the seventh day the priest is to examine that person, and if it is spreading in the skin, the priest shall pronounce them unclean; it is a defiling skin disease. 28If, however, the spot is unchanged and has not spread in the skin but has faded, it is a swelling from the burn, and the priest shall pronounce them clean; it is only a scar from the burn.

29"If a man or woman has a sore on their head or chin, 30the priest is to examine the sore, and if it appears to be more than skin deep and the hair in it is yellow and thin, the priest shall pronounce them unclean; it is a defiling skin disease on the head or chin. 31But if, when the priest examines the sore, it does not seem to be more than skin deep and there is no black hair in it, then the priest is to isolate the affected person for seven days. 32On the seventh day the priest is to examine the sore, and if it has not spread and there is no yellow hair in it and it does not appear to be more than skin deep, 33then the man or woman must shave themselves, except for the affected area, and the priest is to keep them isolated another seven days. 34On the seventh day the priest is to examine the sore, and if it has not spread in the skin and appears to be no more than skin deep, the priest shall pronounce them clean. They must wash their clothes, and they will be clean. 35But if the sore does spread in the skin after they are pronounced clean, 36the priest is to examine them, and if he finds that the sore has spread in the skin, he does not need to look for yellow hair; they are unclean. 37If, however, the sore is unchanged so far as the priest can see, and if black hair has grown in it, the affected per-

[a] 2 The Hebrew word for *defiling skin disease*, traditionally translated "leprosy," was used for various diseases affecting the skin; here and throughout verses 3-46. [b] 2 Or *descendants*

son is healed. They are clean, and the priest
shall pronounce them clean.
38“When a man or woman has white spots
on the skin, 39the priest is to examine them,
and if the spots are dull white, it is a harmless
rash that has broken out on the skin; they
are clean.
40“A man who has lost his hair and is bald is
clean. 41If he has lost his hair from the front of
his scalp and has a bald forehead, he is clean.
42But if he has a reddish-white sore on his
bald head or forehead, it is a defiling disease
breaking out on his head or forehead. 43The
priest is to examine him, and if the swollen
sore on his head or forehead is reddish-white
like a defiling skin disease, 44the man is diseased and is unclean. The priest shall pronounce him unclean because of the sore on
his head.
45“Anyone with such a defiling disease must
wear torn clothes, let their hair be unkempt,[a]
cover the lower part of their face and cry out,
‘Unclean! Unclean!’ 46As long as they have
the disease they remain unclean. They must
live alone; they must live outside the camp.

Regulations About Defiling Molds

47“As for any fabric that is spoiled with a
defiling mold—any woolen or linen clothing,
48any woven or knitted material of linen or
wool, any leather or anything made of leather— 49if the affected area in the fabric, the
leather, the woven or knitted material, or any
leather article, is greenish or reddish, it is a
defiling mold and must be shown to the priest.
50The priest is to examine the affected area
and isolate the article for seven days. 51On
the seventh day he is to examine it, and if the
mold has spread in the fabric, the woven or
knitted material, or the leather, whatever its
use, it is a persistent defiling mold; the article is unclean. 52He must burn the fabric, the
woven or knitted material of wool or linen,
or any leather article that has been spoiled;
because the defiling mold is persistent, the
article must be burned.
53“But if, when the priest examines it, the
mold has not spread in the fabric, the woven
or knitted material, or the leather article, 54he
shall order that the spoiled article be washed.
Then he is to isolate it for another seven days.
55After the article has been washed, the priest
is to examine it again, and if the mold has
not changed its appearance, even though it
has not spread, it is unclean. Burn it, no matter which side of the fabric has been spoiled.
56If, when the priest examines it, the mold has
faded after the article has been washed, he is
to tear the spoiled part out of the fabric, the
leather, or the woven or knitted material. 57But
if it reappears in the fabric, in the woven or
knitted material, or in the leather article, it
is a spreading mold; whatever has the mold
must be burned. 58Any fabric, woven or knitted material, or any leather article that has
been washed and is rid of the mold, must be
washed again. Then it will be clean.”
59These are the regulations concerning
defiling molds in woolen or linen clothing,
woven or knitted material, or any leather article, for pronouncing them clean or unclean.

Cleansing From Defiling Skin Diseases

14 The LORD said to Moses, 2“These are the
regulations for any diseased person at
the time of their ceremonial cleansing, when
they are brought to the priest: 3The priest is
to go outside the camp and examine them. If
they have been healed of their defiling skin
disease,[b] 4the priest shall order that two live
clean birds and some cedar wood, scarlet yarn
and hyssop be brought for the person to be
cleansed. 5Then the priest shall order that one
of the birds be killed over fresh water in a clay
pot. 6He is then to take the live bird and dip it,
together with the cedar wood, the scarlet yarn
and the hyssop, into the blood of the bird that
was killed over the fresh water. 7Seven times
he shall sprinkle the one to be cleansed of the
defiling disease, and then pronounce them
clean. After that, he is to release the live bird
in the open fields.
8“The person to be cleansed must wash their
clothes, shave off all their hair and bathe with
water; then they will be ceremonially clean.
After this they may come into the camp, but
they must stay outside their tent for seven
days. 9On the seventh day they must shave
off all their hair; they must shave their head,
their beard, their eyebrows and the rest of
their hair. They must wash their clothes and
bathe themselves with water, and they will
be clean.
10“On the eighth day they must bring two
male lambs and one ewe lamb a year old, each
without defect, along with three-tenths of an
ephah[c] of the finest flour mixed with olive
oil for a grain offering, and one log[d] of oil.
11The priest who pronounces them clean shall
present both the one to be cleansed and their
offerings before the LORD at the entrance to
the tent of meeting.
12“Then the priest is to take one of the male
lambs and offer it as a guilt offering, along
with the log of oil; he shall wave them before
the LORD as a wave offering. 13He is to slaughter the lamb in the sanctuary area where
the sin offering[e] and the burnt offering are
slaughtered. Like the sin offering, the guilt
offering belongs to the priest; it is most holy.
14The priest is to take some of the blood of the
guilt offering and put it on the lobe of the right
ear of the one to be cleansed, on the thumb
of their right hand and on the big toe of their
right foot. 15The priest shall then take some
of the log of oil, pour it in the palm of his own
left hand, 16dip his right forefinger into the
oil in his palm, and with his finger sprinkle

[a] *45* Or *clothes, uncover their head* [b] *3* The Hebrew word for *defiling skin disease*, traditionally translated “leprosy,” was used for various diseases affecting the skin; also in verses 7, 32, 54 and 57. [c] *10* That is, probably about 11 pounds or about 5 kilograms [d] *10* That is, about 1/3 quart or about 0.3 liter; also in verses 12, 15, 21 and 24 [e] *13* Or *purification offering*; also in verses 19, 22 and 31

some of it before the LORD seven times. 17The
priest is to put some of the oil remaining in his
palm on the lobe of the right ear of the one to
be cleansed, on the thumb of their right hand
and on the big toe of their right foot, on top
of the blood of the guilt offering. 18The rest
of the oil in his palm the priest shall put on
the head of the one to be cleansed and make
atonement for them before the LORD.
19"Then the priest is to sacrifice the sin offering and make atonement for the one to be
cleansed from their uncleanness. After that,
the priest shall slaughter the burnt offering
20and offer it on the altar, together with the
grain offering, and make atonement for them,
and they will be clean.
21"If, however, they are poor and cannot afford these, they must take one male lamb as a
guilt offering to be waved to make atonement
for them, together with a tenth of an ephah[a]
of the finest flour mixed with olive oil for a
grain offering, a log of oil, 22and two doves
or two young pigeons, such as they can afford, one for a sin offering and the other for
a burnt offering.
23"On the eighth day they must bring them
for their cleansing to the priest at the entrance
to the tent of meeting, before the LORD. 24The
priest is to take the lamb for the guilt offering,
together with the log of oil, and wave them
before the LORD as a wave offering. 25He shall
slaughter the lamb for the guilt offering and
take some of its blood and put it on the lobe
of the right ear of the one to be cleansed, on
the thumb of their right hand and on the big
toe of their right foot. 26The priest is to pour
some of the oil into the palm of his own left
hand, 27and with his right forefinger sprinkle
some of the oil from his palm seven times before the LORD. 28Some of the oil in his palm he
is to put on the same places he put the blood
of the guilt offering—on the lobe of the right
ear of the one to be cleansed, on the thumb
of their right hand and on the big toe of their
right foot. 29The rest of the oil in his palm
the priest shall put on the head of the one
to be cleansed, to make atonement for them
before the LORD. 30Then he shall sacrifice the
doves or the young pigeons, such as the person can afford, 31one as a sin offering and
the other as a burnt offering, together with
the grain offering. In this way the priest will
make atonement before the LORD on behalf
of the one to be cleansed."
32These are the regulations for anyone who
has a defiling skin disease and who cannot afford the regular offerings for their cleansing.

Cleansing From Defiling Molds

33The LORD said to Moses and Aaron,
34"When you enter the land of Canaan, which
I am giving you as your possession, and I put
a spreading mold in a house in that land, 35the
owner of the house must go and tell the priest,
'I have seen something that looks like a defiling mold in my house.' 36The priest is to
order the house to be emptied before he goes
in to examine the mold, so that nothing in the
house will be pronounced unclean. After this
the priest is to go in and inspect the house.
37He is to examine the mold on the walls, and
if it has greenish or reddish depressions that
appear to be deeper than the surface of the
wall, 38the priest shall go out the doorway of
the house and close it up for seven days. 39On
the seventh day the priest shall return to inspect the house. If the mold has spread on the
walls, 40he is to order that the contaminated
stones be torn out and thrown into an unclean
place outside the town. 41He must have all the
inside walls of the house scraped and the material that is scraped off dumped into an unclean place outside the town. 42Then they are
to take other stones to replace these and take
new clay and plaster the house.
43"If the defiling mold reappears in the
house after the stones have been torn out and
the house scraped and plastered, 44the priest
is to go and examine it and, if the mold has
spread in the house, it is a persistent defiling
mold; the house is unclean. 45It must be torn
down—its stones, timbers and all the plaster—and taken out of the town to an unclean
place.
46"Anyone who goes into the house while
it is closed up will be unclean till evening.
47Anyone who sleeps or eats in the house must
wash their clothes.
48"But if the priest comes to examine it and
the mold has not spread after the house has
been plastered, he shall pronounce the house
clean, because the defiling mold is gone. 49To
purify the house he is to take two birds and
some cedar wood, scarlet yarn and hyssop.
50He shall kill one of the birds over fresh water in a clay pot. 51Then he is to take the cedar
wood, the hyssop, the scarlet yarn and the live
bird, dip them into the blood of the dead bird
and the fresh water, and sprinkle the house
seven times. 52He shall purify the house with
the bird's blood, the fresh water, the live bird,
the cedar wood, the hyssop and the scarlet
yarn. 53Then he is to release the live bird in
the open fields outside the town. In this way
he will make atonement for the house, and it
will be clean."
54These are the regulations for any defiling
skin disease, for a sore, 55for defiling molds
in fabric or in a house, 56and for a swelling,
a rash or a shiny spot, 57to determine when
something is clean or unclean.
These are the regulations for defiling skin
diseases and defiling molds.

Discharges Causing Uncleanness

15 The LORD said to Moses and Aaron,
2"Speak to the Israelites and say to them:
'When any man has an unusual bodily discharge, such a discharge is unclean. 3Wheth-
er it continues flowing from his body or is
blocked, it will make him unclean. This is how
his discharge will bring about uncleanness:
4" 'Any bed the man with a discharge lies
on will be unclean, and anything he sits on

[a] 21 That is, probably about 3 1/2 pounds or about 1.6 kilograms

will be unclean. 5Anyone who touches his
bed must wash their clothes and bathe with
water, and they will be unclean till evening.
6Whoever sits on anything that the man with
a discharge sat on must wash their clothes and
bathe with water, and they will be unclean
till evening.

7“ ‘Whoever touches the man who has a discharge must wash their clothes and bathe with
water, and they will be unclean till evening.

8“ ‘If the man with the discharge spits on
anyone who is clean, they must wash their
clothes and bathe with water, and they will
be unclean till evening.

9“ ‘Everything the man sits on when riding
will be unclean, 10and whoever touches any of
the things that were under him will be unclean
till evening; whoever picks up those things
must wash their clothes and bathe with water,
and they will be unclean till evening.

11“ ‘Anyone the man with a discharge touches without rinsing his hands with water must
wash their clothes and bathe with water, and
they will be unclean till evening.

12“ ‘A clay pot that the man touches must
be broken, and any wooden article is to be
rinsed with water.

13“ ‘When a man is cleansed from his discharge, he is to count off seven days for his
ceremonial cleansing; he must wash his
clothes and bathe himself with fresh water,
and he will be clean. 14On the eighth day he
must take two doves or two young pigeons
and come before the LORD to the entrance to
the tent of meeting and give them to the priest.
15The priest is to sacrifice them, the one for
a sin offering[a] and the other for a burnt offering. In this way he will make atonement
before the LORD for the man because of his
discharge.

16“ ‘When a man has an emission of semen,
he must bathe his whole body with water, and
he will be unclean till evening. 17Any clothing or leather that has semen on it must be
washed with water, and it will be unclean till
evening. 18When a man has sexual relations
with a woman and there is an emission of
semen, both of them must bathe with water,
and they will be unclean till evening.

19“ ‘When a woman has her regular flow of
blood, the impurity of her monthly period will
last seven days, and anyone who touches her
will be unclean till evening.

20“ ‘Anything she lies on during her period
will be unclean, and anything she sits on will
be unclean. 21Anyone who touches her bed will
be unclean; they must wash their clothes and
bathe with water, and they will be unclean till
evening. 22Anyone who touches anything she
sits on will be unclean; they must wash their
clothes and bathe with water, and they will be
unclean till evening. 23Whether it is the bed
or anything she was sitting on, when anyone
touches it, they will be unclean till evening.

24“ ‘If a man has sexual relations with her
and her monthly flow touches him, he will
be unclean for seven days; any bed he lies on
will be unclean.

25“ ‘When a woman has a discharge of blood
for many days at a time other than her monthly period or has a discharge that continues
beyond her period, she will be unclean as long
as she has the discharge, just as in the days of
her period. 26Any bed she lies on while her discharge continues will be unclean, as is her bed
during her monthly period, and anything she
sits on will be unclean, as during her period.
27Anyone who touches them will be unclean;
they must wash their clothes and bathe with
water, and they will be unclean till evening.

28“ ‘When she is cleansed from her discharge, she must count off seven days, and
after that she will be ceremonially clean. 29On
the eighth day she must take two doves or two
young pigeons and bring them to the priest
at the entrance to the tent of meeting. 30The
priest is to sacrifice one for a sin offering and
the other for a burnt offering. In this way he
will make atonement for her before the LORD
for the uncleanness of her discharge.

31“ ‘You must keep the Israelites separate
from things that make them unclean, so they
will not die in their uncleanness for defiling
my dwelling place,[b] which is among them.’ ”

32These are the regulations for a man with
a discharge, for anyone made unclean by
an emission of semen, 33for a woman in her
monthly period, for a man or a woman with
a discharge, and for a man who has sexual
relations with a woman who is ceremonially
unclean.

The Day of Atonement

16 The LORD spoke to Moses after the death
of the two sons of Aaron who died when
they approached the LORD. 2The LORD said to
Moses: “Tell your brother Aaron that he is not
to come whenever he chooses into the Most
Holy Place behind the curtain in front of the
atonement cover on the ark, or else he will
die. For I will appear in the cloud over the
atonement cover.

3“This is how Aaron is to enter the Most
Holy Place: He must first bring a young bull
for a sin offering[c] and a ram for a burnt offering. 4He is to put on the sacred linen tunic,
with linen undergarments next to his body; he
is to tie the linen sash around him and put on
the linen turban. These are sacred garments;
so he must bathe himself with water before he
puts them on. 5From the Israelite community
he is to take two male goats for a sin offering
and a ram for a burnt offering.

6“Aaron is to offer the bull for his own sin
offering to make atonement for himself and
his household. 7Then he is to take the two
goats and present them before the LORD at
the entrance to the tent of meeting. 8He is to
cast lots for the two goats—one lot for the
LORD and the other for the scapegoat.[d] 9Aaron

[a] 15 Or *purification offering*; also in verse 30 [b] 31 Or *my tabernacle* [c] 3 Or *purification offering*; here and throughout this chapter [d] 8 The meaning of the Hebrew for this word is uncertain; also in verses 10 and 26.

shall bring the goat whose lot falls to the LORD and sacrifice it for a sin offering. 10But the goat chosen by lot as the scapegoat shall be presented alive before the LORD to be used for making atonement by sending it into the wilderness as a scapegoat.

11"Aaron shall bring the bull for his own sin offering to make atonement for himself and his household, and he is to slaughter the bull for his own sin offering. 12He is to take a censer full of burning coals from the altar before the LORD and two handfuls of finely ground fragrant incense and take them behind the curtain. 13He is to put the incense on the fire before the LORD, and the smoke of the incense will conceal the atonement cover above the tablets of the covenant law, so that he will not die. 14He is to take some of the bull's blood and with his finger sprinkle it on the front of the atonement cover; then he shall sprinkle some of it with his finger seven times before the atonement cover.

15"He shall then slaughter the goat for the sin offering for the people and take its blood behind the curtain and do with it as he did with the bull's blood: He shall sprinkle it on the atonement cover and in front of it. 16In this way he will make atonement for the Most Holy Place because of the uncleanness and rebellion of the Israelites, whatever their sins have been. He is to do the same for the tent of meeting, which is among them in the midst of their uncleanness. 17No one is to be in the tent of meeting from the time Aaron goes in to make atonement in the Most Holy Place until he comes out, having made atonement for himself, his household and the whole community of Israel.

18"Then he shall come out to the altar that is before the LORD and make atonement for it. He shall take some of the bull's blood and some of the goat's blood and put it on all the horns of the altar. 19He shall sprinkle some of the blood on it with his finger seven times to cleanse it and to consecrate it from the uncleanness of the Israelites.

20"When Aaron has finished making atonement for the Most Holy Place, the tent of meeting and the altar, he shall bring forward the live goat. 21He is to lay both hands on the head of the live goat and confess over it all the wickedness and rebellion of the Israelites—all their sins—and put them on the goat's head. He shall send the goat away into the wilderness in the care of someone appointed for the task. 22The goat will carry on itself all their sins to a remote place; and the man shall release it in the wilderness.

23"Then Aaron is to go into the tent of meeting and take off the linen garments he put on before he entered the Most Holy Place, and he is to leave them there. 24He shall bathe himself with water in the sanctuary area and put on his regular garments. Then he shall come out and sacrifice the burnt offering for himself and the burnt offering for the people, to make atonement for himself and for the people. 25He shall also burn the fat of the sin offering on the altar.

26"The man who releases the goat as a scapegoat must wash his clothes and bathe himself with water; afterward he may come into the camp. 27The bull and the goat for the sin offerings, whose blood was brought into the Most Holy Place to make atonement, must be taken outside the camp; their hides, flesh and intestines are to be burned up. 28The man who burns them must wash his clothes and bathe himself with water; afterward he may come into the camp.

29"This is to be a lasting ordinance for you: On the tenth day of the seventh month you must deny yourselves[a] and not do any work—whether native-born or a foreigner residing among you— 30because on this day atonement will be made for you, to cleanse you. Then, before the LORD, you will be clean from all your sins. 31It is a day of sabbath rest, and you must deny yourselves; it is a lasting ordinance. 32The priest who is anointed and ordained to succeed his father as high priest is to make atonement. He is to put on the sacred linen garments 33and make atonement for the Most Holy Place, for the tent of meeting and the altar, and for the priests and all the members of the community.

34"This is to be a lasting ordinance for you: Atonement is to be made once a year for all the sins of the Israelites."

And it was done, as the LORD commanded Moses.

Eating Blood Forbidden

17 The LORD said to Moses, 2"Speak to Aaron and his sons and to all the Israelites and say to them: 'This is what the LORD has commanded: 3Any Israelite who sacrifices an ox,[b] a lamb or a goat in the camp or outside of it 4instead of bringing it to the entrance to the tent of meeting to present it as an offering to the LORD in front of the tabernacle of the LORD—that person shall be considered guilty of bloodshed; they have shed blood and must be cut off from their people. 5This is so the Israelites will bring to the LORD the sacrifices they are now making in the open fields. They must bring them to the priest, that is, to the LORD, at the entrance to the tent of meeting and sacrifice them as fellowship offerings. 6The priest is to splash the blood against the altar of the LORD at the entrance to the tent of meeting and burn the fat as an aroma pleasing to the LORD. 7They must no longer offer any of their sacrifices to the goat idols[c] to whom they prostitute themselves. This is to be a lasting ordinance for them and for the generations to come.'

8"Say to them: 'Any Israelite or any foreigner residing among them who offers a burnt offering or sacrifice 9and does not bring it to the entrance to the tent of meeting to sacrifice it to the LORD must be cut off from the people of Israel.

[a] 29 Or *must fast*; also in verse 31 [b] 3 The Hebrew word can refer to either male or female.
[c] 7 Or *the demons*

10“ ‘I will set my face against any Israelite or
any foreigner residing among them who eats
blood, and I will cut them off from the people.
11For the life of a creature is in the blood, and
I have given it to you to make atonement for
yourselves on the altar; it is the blood that
makes atonement for one’s life.[a] 12Therefore
I say to the Israelites, “None of you may eat
blood, nor may any foreigner residing among
you eat blood.”
13“ ‘Any Israelite or any foreigner residing
among you who hunts any animal or bird that
may be eaten must drain out the blood and
cover it with earth, 14because the life of every creature is its blood. That is why I have
said to the Israelites, “You must not eat the
blood of any creature, because the life of every creature is its blood; anyone who eats it
must be cut off.”
15“ ‘Anyone, whether native-born or foreigner, who eats anything found dead or torn by
wild animals must wash their clothes and
bathe with water, and they will be ceremonially unclean till evening; then they will be
clean. 16But if they do not wash their clothes
and bathe themselves, they will be held responsible.’ ”

Unlawful Sexual Relations

18 The LORD said to Moses, 2“Speak to the
Israelites and say to them: ‘I am the
LORD your God. 3You must not do as they
do in Egypt, where you used to live, and you
must not do as they do in the land of Canaan,
where I am bringing you. Do not follow their
practices. 4You must obey my laws and be
careful to follow my decrees. I am the LORD
your God. 5Keep my decrees and laws, for the
person who obeys them will live by them. I
am the LORD.
6“ ‘No one is to approach any close relative
to have sexual relations. I am the LORD.
7“ ‘Do not dishonor your father by having
sexual relations with your mother. She is your
mother; do not have relations with her.
8“ ‘Do not have sexual relations with your
father’s wife; that would dishonor your father.
9“ ‘Do not have sexual relations with your
sister, either your father’s daughter or your
mother’s daughter, whether she was born in
the same home or elsewhere.
10“ ‘Do not have sexual relations with your
son’s daughter or your daughter’s daughter;
that would dishonor you.
11“ ‘Do not have sexual relations with the
daughter of your father’s wife, born to your
father; she is your sister.
12“ ‘Do not have sexual relations with your
father’s sister; she is your father’s close relative.
13“ ‘Do not have sexual relations with your
mother’s sister, because she is your mother’s
close relative.
14“ ‘Do not dishonor your father’s brother by
approaching his wife to have sexual relations;
she is your aunt.
15“ ‘Do not have sexual relations with your
daughter-in-law. She is your son’s wife; do not
have relations with her.
16“ ‘Do not have sexual relations with your
brother’s wife; that would dishonor your
brother.
17“ ‘Do not have sexual relations with both a
woman and her daughter. Do not have sexual
relations with either her son’s daughter or her
daughter’s daughter; they are her close relatives. That is wickedness.
18“ ‘Do not take your wife’s sister as a rival
wife and have sexual relations with her while
your wife is living.
19“ ‘Do not approach a woman to have sexual relations during the uncleanness of her
monthly period.
20“ ‘Do not have sexual relations with your
neighbor’s wife and defile yourself with her.
21“ ‘Do not give any of your children to be
sacrificed to Molek, for you must not profane
the name of your God. I am the LORD.
22“ ‘Do not have sexual relations with a man
as one does with a woman; that is detestable.
23“ ‘Do not have sexual relations with an
animal and defile yourself with it. A woman
must not present herself to an animal to have
sexual relations with it; that is a perversion.
24“ ‘Do not defile yourselves in any of these
ways, because this is how the nations that
I am going to drive out before you became
defiled. 25Even the land was defiled; so I punished it for its sin, and the land vomited out
its inhabitants. 26But you must keep my decrees and my laws. The native-born and the
foreigners residing among you must not do
any of these detestable things, 27for all these
things were done by the people who lived in
the land before you, and the land became defiled. 28And if you defile the land, it will vomit
you out as it vomited out the nations that were
before you.
29“ ‘Everyone who does any of these detestable things—such persons must be cut off
from their people. 30Keep my requirements
and do not follow any of the detestable customs that were practiced before you came and
do not defile yourselves with them. I am the
LORD your God.’ ”

Various Laws

19 The LORD said to Moses, 2“Speak to
the entire assembly of Israel and say to
them: ‘Be holy because I, the LORD your God,
am holy.
3“ ‘Each of you must respect your mother
and father, and you must observe my Sabbaths. I am the LORD your God.
4“ ‘Do not turn to idols or make metal gods
for yourselves. I am the LORD your God.
5“ ‘When you sacrifice a fellowship offering
to the LORD, sacrifice it in such a way that it will
be accepted on your behalf. 6It shall be eaten
on the day you sacrifice it or on the next day;
anything left over until the third day must be
burned up. 7If any of it is eaten on the third day,
it is impure and will not be accepted. 8Whoever
eats it will be held responsible because they

[a] 11 *Or atonement by the life in the blood*

have desecrated what is holy to the LORD; they
must be cut off from their people.
9“ ‘When you reap the harvest of your land,
do not reap to the very edges of your field or
gather the gleanings of your harvest. 10Do not
go over your vineyard a second time or pick
up the grapes that have fallen. Leave them
for the poor and the foreigner. I am the LORD
your God.
11“ ‘Do not steal.
“ ‘Do not lie.
“ ‘Do not deceive one another.
12“ ‘Do not swear falsely by my name and so
profane the name of your God. I am the LORD.
13“ ‘Do not defraud or rob your neighbor.
“ ‘Do not hold back the wages of a hired
worker overnight.
14“ ‘Do not curse the deaf or put a stumbling
block in front of the blind, but fear your God.
I am the LORD.
15“ ‘Do not pervert justice; do not show partiality to the poor or favoritism to the great,
but judge your neighbor fairly.
16“ ‘Do not go about spreading slander
among your people.
“ ‘Do not do anything that endangers your
neighbor’s life. I am the LORD.
17“ ‘Do not hate a fellow Israelite in your
heart. Rebuke your neighbor frankly so you
will not share in their guilt.
18“ ‘Do not seek revenge or bear a grudge
against anyone among your people, but love
your neighbor as yourself. I am the LORD.
19“ ‘Keep my decrees.
“ ‘Do not mate different kinds of animals.
“ ‘Do not plant your field with two kinds
of seed.
“ ‘Do not wear clothing woven of two kinds
of material.
20“ ‘If a man sleeps with a female slave who
is promised to another man but who has not
been ransomed or given her freedom, there
must be due punishment.[a] Yet they are not
to be put to death, because she had not been
freed. 21The man, however, must bring a ram
to the entrance to the tent of meeting for a
guilt offering to the LORD. 22With the ram of
the guilt offering the priest is to make atonement for him before the LORD for the sin he
has committed, and his sin will be forgiven.
23“ ‘When you enter the land and plant any
kind of fruit tree, regard its fruit as forbidden.[b] For three years you are to consider it
forbidden[b]; it must not be eaten. 24In the fourth
year all its fruit will be holy, an offering of
praise to the LORD. 25But in the fifth year you
may eat its fruit. In this way your harvest will
be increased. I am the LORD your God.
26“ ‘Do not eat any meat with the blood still
in it.
“ ‘Do not practice divination or seek omens.
27“ ‘Do not cut the hair at the sides of your
head or clip off the edges of your beard.
28“ ‘Do not cut your bodies for the dead or
put tattoo marks on yourselves. I am the LORD.
29“ ‘Do not degrade your daughter by making her a prostitute, or the land will turn to
prostitution and be filled with wickedness.
30“ ‘Observe my Sabbaths and have reverence for my sanctuary. I am the LORD.
31“ ‘Do not turn to mediums or seek out spiritists, for you will be defiled by them. I am the
LORD your God.
32“ ‘Stand up in the presence of the aged,
show respect for the elderly and revere your
God. I am the LORD.
33“ ‘When a foreigner resides among you in
your land, do not mistreat them. 34The foreigner residing among you must be treated
as your native-born. Love them as yourself,
for you were foreigners in Egypt. I am the
LORD your God.
35“ ‘Do not use dishonest standards when
measuring length, weight or quantity. 36Use
honest scales and honest weights, an honest
ephah[c] and an honest hin.[d] I am the LORD your
God, who brought you out of Egypt.
37“ ‘Keep all my decrees and all my laws and
follow them. I am the LORD.’ ”

Punishments for Sin

20 The LORD said to Moses, 2“Say to the Israelites: ‘Any Israelite or any foreigner
residing in Israel who sacrifices any of his
children to Molek is to be put to death. The
members of the community are to stone him.
3I myself will set my face against him and will
cut him off from his people; for by sacrificing his children to Molek, he has defiled my
sanctuary and profaned my holy name. 4If the
members of the community close their eyes
when that man sacrifices one of his children
to Molek and if they fail to put him to death,
5I myself will set my face against him and his
family and will cut them off from their people
together with all who follow him in prostitut-
ing themselves to Molek.
6“ ‘I will set my face against anyone who
turns to mediums and spiritists to prostitute
themselves by following them, and I will cut
them off from their people.
7“ ‘Consecrate yourselves and be holy, because I am the LORD your God. 8Keep my decrees and follow them. I am the LORD, who
makes you holy.
9“ ‘Anyone who curses their father or mother is to be put to death. Because they have
cursed their father or mother, their blood will
be on their own head.
10“ ‘If a man commits adultery with another
man’s wife—with the wife of his neighbor—
both the adulterer and the adulteress are to
be put to death.
11“ ‘If a man has sexual relations with his
father’s wife, he has dishonored his father.
Both the man and the woman are to be put to
death; their blood will be on their own heads.
12“ ‘If a man has sexual relations with his
daughter-in-law, both of them are to be put to

[a] *20* Or *be an inquiry* [b] *23* Hebrew *uncircumcised* [c] *36* An ephah was a dry measure having the capacity of about 3/5 of a bushel or about 22 liters. [d] *36* A hin was a liquid measure having the capacity of about 1 gallon or about 3.8 liters.

death. What they have done is a perversion;
their blood will be on their own heads.
13“ ‘If a man has sexual relations with a man
as one does with a woman, both of them have
done what is detestable. They are to be put to
death; their blood will be on their own heads.
14“ ‘If a man marries both a woman and her
mother, it is wicked. Both he and they must
be burned in the fire, so that no wickedness
will be among you.
15“ ‘If a man has sexual relations with an
animal, he is to be put to death, and you must
kill the animal.
16“ ‘If a woman approaches an animal to
have sexual relations with it, kill both the
woman and the animal. They are to be put to
death; their blood will be on their own heads.
17“ ‘If a man marries his sister, the daughter
of either his father or his mother, and they
have sexual relations, it is a disgrace. They
are to be publicly removed from their people.
He has dishonored his sister and will be held
responsible.
18“ ‘If a man has sexual relations with a
woman during her monthly period, he has
exposed the source of her flow, and she has
also uncovered it. Both of them are to be cut
off from their people.
19“ ‘Do not have sexual relations with the
sister of either your mother or your father,
for that would dishonor a close relative; both
of you would be held responsible.
20“ ‘If a man has sexual relations with his
aunt, he has dishonored his uncle. They will
be held responsible; they will die childless.
21“ ‘If a man marries his brother’s wife, it
is an act of impurity; he has dishonored his
brother. They will be childless.
22“ ‘Keep all my decrees and laws and follow
them, so that the land where I am bringing you
to live may not vomit you out. 23You must not
live according to the customs of the nations
I am going to drive out before you. Because
they did all these things, I abhorred them.
24But I said to you, “You will possess their
land; I will give it to you as an inheritance, a
land flowing with milk and honey.” I am the
LORD your God, who has set you apart from
the nations.
25“ ‘You must therefore make a distinction
between clean and unclean animals and between unclean and clean birds. Do not defile
yourselves by any animal or bird or anything
that moves along the ground—those that I
have set apart as unclean for you. 26You are
to be holy to me because I, the LORD, am holy,
and I have set you apart from the nations to
be my own.
27“ ‘A man or woman who is a medium or
spiritist among you must be put to death. You
are to stone them; their blood will be on their
own heads.’ ”

Rules for Priests

21 The LORD said to Moses, “Speak to the
priests, the sons of Aaron, and say to
them: ‘A priest must not make himself ceremonially unclean for any of his people who die,
2except for a close relative, such as his mother
or father, his son or daughter, his brother, 3or
an unmarried sister who is dependent on him
since she has no husband—for her he may
make himself unclean. 4He must not make
himself unclean for people related to him by
marriage,[a] and so defile himself.
5“ ‘Priests must not shave their heads or
shave off the edges of their beards or cut their
bodies. 6They must be holy to their God and
must not profane the name of their God. Because they present the food offerings to the
LORD, the food of their God, they are to be
holy.
7“ ‘They must not marry women defiled by
prostitution or divorced from their husbands,
because priests are holy to their God. 8Regard
them as holy, because they offer up the food of
your God. Consider them holy, because I the
LORD am holy—I who make you holy.
9“ ‘If a priest’s daughter defiles herself by
becoming a prostitute, she disgraces her father; she must be burned in the fire.
10“ ‘The high priest, the one among his
brothers who has had the anointing oil poured
on his head and who has been ordained to
wear the priestly garments, must not let his
hair become unkempt[b] or tear his clothes. 11He
must not enter a place where there is a dead
body. He must not make himself unclean, even
for his father or mother, 12nor leave the sanctuary of his God or desecrate it, because he
has been dedicated by the anointing oil of his
God. I am the LORD.
13“ ‘The woman he marries must be a virgin. 14He must not marry a widow, a divorced
woman, or a woman defiled by prostitution,
but only a virgin from his own people, 15so
that he will not defile his offspring among his
people. I am the LORD, who makes him holy.’ ”
16The LORD said to Moses, 17“Say to Aaron:
‘For the generations to come none of your descendants who has a defect may come near
to offer the food of his God. 18No man who
has any defect may come near: no man who
is blind or lame, disfigured or deformed; 19no
man with a crippled foot or hand, 20or who
is a hunchback or a dwarf, or who has any
eye defect, or who has festering or running
sores or damaged testicles. 21No descendant
of Aaron the priest who has any defect is to
come near to present the food offerings to the
LORD. He has a defect; he must not come near
to offer the food of his God. 22He may eat the
most holy food of his God, as well as the holy
food; 23yet because of his defect, he must not
go near the curtain or approach the altar, and
so desecrate my sanctuary. I am the LORD,
who makes them holy.’ ”
24So Moses told this to Aaron and his sons
and to all the Israelites.

22 The LORD said to Moses, 2“Tell Aaron
and his sons to treat with respect the
sacred offerings the Israelites consecrate to
me, so they will not profane my holy name.
I am the LORD.

[a] 4 Or *unclean as a leader among his people* [b] 10 Or *not uncover his head*

3“Say to them: ‘For the generations to come,
if any of your descendants is ceremonially
unclean and yet comes near the sacred offerings that the Israelites consecrate to the
LORD, that person must be cut off from my
presence. I am the LORD.

4“ ‘If a descendant of Aaron has a defiling skin disease[a] or a bodily discharge, he
may not eat the sacred offerings until he is
cleansed. He will also be unclean if he touches something defiled by a corpse or by anyone who has an emission of semen, 5or if he
touches any crawling thing that makes him
unclean, or any person who makes him unclean, whatever the uncleanness may be. 6The
one who touches any such thing will be unclean till evening. He must not eat any of the
sacred offerings unless he has bathed himself
with water. 7When the sun goes down, he will
be clean, and after that he may eat the sacred
offerings, for they are his food. 8He must not
eat anything found dead or torn by wild animals, and so become unclean through it. I
am the LORD.

9“ ‘The priests are to perform my service
in such a way that they do not become guilty
and die for treating it with contempt. I am the
LORD, who makes them holy.

10“ ‘No one outside a priest’s family may
eat the sacred offering, nor may the guest of
a priest or his hired worker eat it. 11But if a
priest buys a slave with money, or if slaves
are born in his household, they may eat his
food. 12If a priest’s daughter marries anyone
other than a priest, she may not eat any of the
sacred contributions. 13But if a priest’s daughter becomes a widow or is divorced, yet has
no children, and she returns to live in her father’s household as in her youth, she may eat
her father’s food. No unauthorized person,
however, may eat it.

14“ ‘Anyone who eats a sacred offering by
mistake must make restitution to the priest
for the offering and add a fifth of the value to
it. 15The priests must not desecrate the sacred
offerings the Israelites present to the LORD
16by allowing them to eat the sacred offerings
and so bring upon them guilt requiring payment. I am the LORD, who makes them holy.’ ”

Unacceptable Sacrifices

17The LORD said to Moses, 18“Speak to Aaron and his sons and to all the Israelites and
say to them: ‘If any of you—whether an Israelite or a foreigner residing in Israel—presents
a gift for a burnt offering to the LORD, either
to fulfill a vow or as a freewill offering, 19you
must present a male without defect from the
cattle, sheep or goats in order that it may be
accepted on your behalf. 20Do not bring anything with a defect, because it will not be accepted on your behalf. 21When anyone brings
from the herd or flock a fellowship offering
to the LORD to fulfill a special vow or as a
freewill offering, it must be without defect or
blemish to be acceptable. 22Do not offer to the
LORD the blind, the injured or the maimed, or
anything with warts or festering or running
sores. Do not place any of these on the altar
as a food offering presented to the LORD. 23You
may, however, present as a freewill offering
an ox[b] or a sheep that is deformed or stunted,
but it will not be accepted in fulfillment of a
vow. 24You must not offer to the LORD an animal whose testicles are bruised, crushed, torn
or cut. You must not do this in your own land,
25and you must not accept such animals from
the hand of a foreigner and offer them as the
food of your God. They will not be accepted
on your behalf, because they are deformed
and have defects.’ ”

26The LORD said to Moses, 27“When a calf, a
lamb or a goat is born, it is to remain with its
mother for seven days. From the eighth day
on, it will be acceptable as a food offering
presented to the LORD. 28Do not slaughter a
cow or a sheep and its young on the same day.

29“When you sacrifice a thank offering to
the LORD, sacrifice it in such a way that it will
be accepted on your behalf. 30It must be eaten
that same day; leave none of it till morning.
I am the LORD.

31“Keep my commands and follow them. I
am the LORD. 32Do not profane my holy name,
for I must be acknowledged as holy by the
Israelites. I am the LORD, who made you holy
33and who brought you out of Egypt to be your
God. I am the LORD.”

The Appointed Festivals

23 The LORD said to Moses, 2“Speak to the
Israelites and say to them: ‘These are
my appointed festivals, the appointed festivals of the LORD, which you are to proclaim
as sacred assemblies.

The Sabbath

3“ ‘There are six days when you may work,
but the seventh day is a day of sabbath rest,
a day of sacred assembly. You are not to do
any work; wherever you live, it is a sabbath
to the LORD.

The Passover and the Festival of Unleavened Bread

4“ ‘These are the LORD’s appointed festivals,
the sacred assemblies you are to proclaim at
their appointed times: 5The LORD’s Passover
begins at twilight on the fourteenth day of
the first month. 6On the fifteenth day of that
month the LORD’s Festival of Unleavened
Bread begins; for seven days you must eat
bread made without yeast. 7On the first day
hold a sacred assembly and do no regular
work. 8For seven days present a food offering to the LORD. And on the seventh day hold
a sacred assembly and do no regular work.’ ”

Offering the Firstfruits

9The LORD said to Moses, 10“Speak to the Israelites and say to them: ‘When you enter the

[a] *4* The Hebrew word for *defiling skin disease*, traditionally translated “leprosy,” was used for various diseases affecting the skin. [b] *23* The Hebrew word can refer to either male or female.

land I am going to give you and you reap its harvest, bring to the priest a sheaf of the first grain you harvest. 11He is to wave the sheaf before the LORD so it will be accepted on your behalf; the priest is to wave it on the day after the Sabbath. 12On the day you wave the sheaf, you must sacrifice as a burnt offering to the LORD a lamb a year old without defect, 13together with its grain offering of two-tenths of an ephah[a] of the finest flour mixed with olive oil—a food offering presented to the LORD, a pleasing aroma—and its drink offering of a quarter of a hin[b] of wine. 14You must not eat any bread, or roasted or new grain, until the very day you bring this offering to your God. This is to be a lasting ordinance for the generations to come, wherever you live.

The Festival of Weeks

15" 'From the day after the Sabbath, the day you brought the sheaf of the wave offering, count off seven full weeks. 16Count off fifty days up to the day after the seventh Sabbath, and then present an offering of new grain to the LORD. 17From wherever you live, bring two loaves made of two-tenths of an ephah of the finest flour, baked with yeast, as a wave offering of firstfruits to the LORD. 18Present with this bread seven male lambs, each a year old and without defect, one young bull and two rams. They will be a burnt offering to the LORD, together with their grain offerings and drink offerings—a food offering, an aroma pleasing to the LORD. 19Then sacrifice one male goat for a sin offering[c] and two lambs, each a year old, for a fellowship offering. 20The priest is to wave the two lambs before the LORD as a wave offering, together with the bread of the firstfruits. They are a sacred offering to the LORD for the priest. 21On that same day you are to proclaim a sacred assembly and do no regular work. This is to be a lasting ordinance for the generations to come, wherever you live.

22" 'When you reap the harvest of your land, do not reap to the very edges of your field or gather the gleanings of your harvest. Leave them for the poor and for the foreigner residing among you. I am the LORD your God.' "

The Festival of Trumpets

23The LORD said to Moses, 24"Say to the Israelites: 'On the first day of the seventh month you are to have a day of sabbath rest, a sacred assembly commemorated with trumpet blasts. 25Do no regular work, but present a food offering to the LORD.' "

The Day of Atonement

26The LORD said to Moses, 27"The tenth day of this seventh month is the Day of Atonement. Hold a sacred assembly and deny yourselves,[d] and present a food offering to the LORD. 28Do not do any work on that day, because it is the Day of Atonement, when atonement is made for you before the LORD your God. 29Those who do not deny themselves on that day must be cut off from their people. 30I will destroy from among their people anyone who does any work on that day. 31You shall do no work at all. This is to be a lasting ordinance for the generations to come, wherever you live. 32It is a day of sabbath rest for you, and you must deny yourselves. From the evening of the ninth day of the month until the following evening you are to observe your sabbath."

The Festival of Tabernacles

33The LORD said to Moses, 34"Say to the Israelites: 'On the fifteenth day of the seventh month the LORD's Festival of Tabernacles begins, and it lasts for seven days. 35The first day is a sacred assembly; do no regular work. 36For seven days present food offerings to the LORD, and on the eighth day hold a sacred assembly and present a food offering to the LORD. It is the closing special assembly; do no regular work.

37(" 'These are the LORD's appointed festivals, which you are to proclaim as sacred assemblies for bringing food offerings to the LORD—the burnt offerings and grain offerings, sacrifices and drink offerings required for each day. 38These offerings are in addition to those for the LORD's Sabbaths and[e] in addition to your gifts and whatever you have vowed and all the freewill offerings you give to the LORD.)

39" 'So beginning with the fifteenth day of the seventh month, after you have gathered the crops of the land, celebrate the festival to the LORD for seven days; the first day is a day of sabbath rest, and the eighth day also is a day of sabbath rest. 40On the first day you are to take branches from luxuriant trees—from palms, willows and other leafy trees—and rejoice before the LORD your God for seven days. 41Celebrate this as a festival to the LORD for seven days each year. This is to be a lasting ordinance for the generations to come; celebrate it in the seventh month. 42Live in temporary shelters for seven days: All native-born Israelites are to live in such shelters 43so your descendants will know that I had the Israelites live in temporary shelters when I brought them out of Egypt. I am the LORD your God.' "

44So Moses announced to the Israelites the appointed festivals of the LORD.

Olive Oil and Bread Set Before the LORD

24 The LORD said to Moses, 2"Command the Israelites to bring you clear oil of pressed olives for the light so that the lamps may be kept burning continually. 3Outside the curtain that shields the ark of the covenant law in the tent of meeting, Aaron is to tend the lamps before the LORD from evening till morning, continually. This is to be a lasting ordinance for the generations to come. 4The

[a] *13* That is, probably about 7 pounds or about 3.2 kilograms; also in verse 17 [b] *13* That is, about 1 quart or about 1 liter [c] *19* Or *purification offering* [d] *27* Or *and fast*; similarly in verses 29 and 32
[e] *38* Or *These festivals are in addition to the LORD's Sabbaths, and these offerings are*

lamps on the pure gold lampstand before the
LORD must be tended continually.
5“Take the finest flour and bake twelve
loaves of bread, using two-tenths of an ephah[a]
for each loaf. 6Arrange them in two stacks,
six in each stack, on the table of pure gold
before the LORD. 7By each stack put some pure
incense as a memorial[b] portion to represent
the bread and to be a food offering presented
to the LORD. 8This bread is to be set out before
the LORD regularly, Sabbath after Sabbath, on
behalf of the Israelites, as a lasting covenant.
9It belongs to Aaron and his sons, who are to
eat it in the sanctuary area, because it is a
most holy part of their perpetual share of the
food offerings presented to the LORD.”

A Blasphemer Put to Death

10Now the son of an Israelite mother and
an Egyptian father went out among the Israelites, and a fight broke out in the camp
between him and an Israelite. 11The son of the
Israelite woman blasphemed the Name with
a curse; so they brought him to Moses. (His
mother’s name was Shelomith, the daughter
of Dibri the Danite.) 12They put him in custody until the will of the LORD should be made
clear to them.
13Then the LORD said to Moses: 14“Take the
blasphemer outside the camp. All those who
heard him are to lay their hands on his head,
and the entire assembly is to stone him. 15Say
to the Israelites: ‘Anyone who curses their God
will be held responsible; 16anyone who blasphemes the name of the LORD is to be put to
death. The entire assembly must stone them.
Whether foreigner or native-born, when they
blaspheme the Name they are to be put to death.
17“ ‘Anyone who takes the life of a human
being is to be put to death. 18Anyone who takes
the life of someone’s animal must make restitution—life for life. 19Anyone who injures
their neighbor is to be injured in the same
manner: 20fracture for fracture, eye for eye,
tooth for tooth. The one who has inflicted the
injury must suffer the same injury. 21Whoev-
er kills an animal must make restitution, but
whoever kills a human being is to be put to
death. 22You are to have the same law for the
foreigner and the native-born. I am the LORD
your God.’ ”
23Then Moses spoke to the Israelites, and
they took the blasphemer outside the camp
and stoned him. The Israelites did as the LORD
commanded Moses.

The Sabbath Year

25 The LORD said to Moses at Mount Sinai, 2“Speak to the Israelites and say
to them: ‘When you enter the land I am going to give you, the land itself must observe a
sabbath to the LORD. 3For six years sow your
fields, and for six years prune your vineyards
and gather their crops. 4But in the seventh
year the land is to have a year of sabbath rest,
a sabbath to the LORD. Do not sow your fields
or prune your vineyards. 5Do not reap what
grows of itself or harvest the grapes of your
untended vines. The land is to have a year
of rest. 6Whatever the land yields during the
sabbath year will be food for you—for yourself, your male and female servants, and the
hired worker and temporary resident who live
among you, 7as well as for your livestock and
the wild animals in your land. Whatever the
land produces may be eaten.

The Year of Jubilee

8“ ‘Count off seven sabbath years—seven
times seven years—so that the seven sabbath
years amount to a period of forty-nine years.
9Then have the trumpet sounded everywhere
on the tenth day of the seventh month; on the
Day of Atonement sound the trumpet throughout your land. 10Consecrate the fiftieth year
and proclaim liberty throughout the land to
all its inhabitants. It shall be a jubilee for you;
each of you is to return to your family property and to your own clan. 11The fiftieth year
shall be a jubilee for you; do not sow and do
not reap what grows of itself or harvest the
untended vines. 12For it is a jubilee and is to
be holy for you; eat only what is taken directly
from the fields.
13“ ‘In this Year of Jubilee everyone is to return to their own property.
14“ ‘If you sell land to any of your own people
or buy land from them, do not take advantage
of each other. 15You are to buy from your own
people on the basis of the number of years
since the Jubilee. And they are to sell to you
on the basis of the number of years left for harvesting crops. 16When the years are many, you
are to increase the price, and when the years
are few, you are to decrease the price, because
what is really being sold to you is the number
of crops. 17Do not take advantage of each other,
but fear your God. I am the LORD your God.
18“ ‘Follow my decrees and be careful to
obey my laws, and you will live safely in the
land. 19Then the land will yield its fruit, and
you will eat your fill and live there in safety.
20You may ask, “What will we eat in the seventh year if we do not plant or harvest our
crops?” 21I will send you such a blessing in
the sixth year that the land will yield enough
for three years. 22While you plant during the
eighth year, you will eat from the old crop and
will continue to eat from it until the harvest
of the ninth year comes in.
23“ ‘The land must not be sold permanently,
because the land is mine and you reside in my
land as foreigners and strangers. 24Through-
out the land that you hold as a possession, you
must provide for the redemption of the land.
25“ ‘If one of your fellow Israelites becomes
poor and sells some of their property, their
nearest relative is to come and redeem what
they have sold. 26If, however, there is no one
to redeem it for them but later on they prosper and acquire sufficient means to redeem it
themselves, 27they are to determine the value
for the years since they sold it and refund the

[a] 5 That is, probably about 7 pounds or about 3.2 kilograms [b] 7 Or *representative*

balance to the one to whom they sold it; they
can then go back to their own property. 28 But
if they do not acquire the means to repay, what
was sold will remain in the possession of the
buyer until the Year of Jubilee. It will be returned in the Jubilee, and they can then go
back to their property.
29 " 'Anyone who sells a house in a walled
city retains the right of redemption a full year
after its sale. During that time the seller may
redeem it. 30 If it is not redeemed before a full
year has passed, the house in the walled city
shall belong permanently to the buyer and the
buyer's descendants. It is not to be returned
in the Jubilee. 31 But houses in villages without walls around them are to be considered
as belonging to the open country. They can
be redeemed, and they are to be returned in
the Jubilee.
32 " 'The Levites always have the right to
redeem their houses in the Levitical towns,
which they possess. 33 So the property of the
Levites is redeemable—that is, a house sold
in any town they hold—and is to be returned
in the Jubilee, because the houses in the towns
of the Levites are their property among the
Israelites. 34 But the pastureland belonging to
their towns must not be sold; it is their permanent possession.
35 " 'If any of your fellow Israelites become
poor and are unable to support themselves
among you, help them as you would a foreigner and stranger, so they can continue to
live among you. 36 Do not take interest or any
profit from them, but fear your God, so that
they may continue to live among you. 37 You
must not lend them money at interest or sell
them food at a profit. 38 I am the LORD your
God, who brought you out of Egypt to give
you the land of Canaan and to be your God.
39 " 'If any of your fellow Israelites become
poor and sell themselves to you, do not make
them work as slaves. 40 They are to be treated as hired workers or temporary residents
among you; they are to work for you until the
Year of Jubilee. 41 Then they and their children
are to be released, and they will go back to
their own clans and to the property of their
ancestors. 42 Because the Israelites are my servants, whom I brought out of Egypt, they must
not be sold as slaves. 43 Do not rule over them
ruthlessly, but fear your God.
44 " 'Your male and female slaves are to come
from the nations around you; from them you
may buy slaves. 45 You may also buy some of
the temporary residents living among you and
members of their clans born in your country,
and they will become your property. 46 You can
bequeath them to your children as inherited
property and can make them slaves for life,
but you must not rule over your fellow Israelites ruthlessly.
47 " 'If a foreigner residing among you becomes rich and any of your fellow Israelites
become poor and sell themselves to the foreigner or to a member of the foreigner's clan,
48 they retain the right of redemption after they
have sold themselves. One of their relatives
may redeem them: 49 An uncle or a cousin or
any blood relative in their clan may redeem
them. Or if they prosper, they may redeem
themselves. 50 They and their buyer are to
count the time from the year they sold themselves up to the Year of Jubilee. The price for
their release is to be based on the rate paid to
a hired worker for that number of years. 51 If
many years remain, they must pay for their
redemption a larger share of the price paid for
them. 52 If only a few years remain until the
Year of Jubilee, they are to compute that and
pay for their redemption accordingly. 53 They
are to be treated as workers hired from year
to year; you must see to it that those to whom
they owe service do not rule over them ruthlessly.
54 " 'Even if someone is not redeemed in any
of these ways, they and their children are to
be released in the Year of Jubilee, 55 for the
Israelites belong to me as servants. They are
my servants, whom I brought out of Egypt. I
am the LORD your God.

Reward for Obedience

26 " 'Do not make idols or set up an image
or a sacred stone for yourselves, and
do not place a carved stone in your land to
bow down before it. I am the LORD your God.
2 " 'Observe my Sabbaths and have reverence for my sanctuary. I am the LORD.
3 " 'If you follow my decrees and are careful
to obey my commands, 4 I will send you rain in
its season, and the ground will yield its crops
and the trees their fruit. 5 Your threshing will
continue until grape harvest and the grape
harvest will continue until planting, and you
will eat all the food you want and live in safety in your land.
6 " 'I will grant peace in the land, and you
will lie down and no one will make you afraid.
I will remove wild beasts from the land, and
the sword will not pass through your country.
7 You will pursue your enemies, and they will
fall by the sword before you. 8 Five of you will
chase a hundred, and a hundred of you will
chase ten thousand, and your enemies will
fall by the sword before you.
9 " 'I will look on you with favor and make
you fruitful and increase your numbers, and
I will keep my covenant with you. 10 You will
still be eating last year's harvest when you
will have to move it out to make room for the
new. 11 I will put my dwelling place[a] among
you, and I will not abhor you. 12 I will walk
among you and be your God, and you will be
my people. 13 I am the LORD your God, who
brought you out of Egypt so that you would
no longer be slaves to the Egyptians; I broke
the bars of your yoke and enabled you to walk
with heads held high.

Punishment for Disobedience

14 " 'But if you will not listen to me and carry
out all these commands, 15 and if you reject my

[a] 11 Or *my tabernacle*

decrees and abhor my laws and fail to carry out all my commands and so violate my covenant, [16]then I will do this to you: I will bring on you sudden terror, wasting diseases and fever that will destroy your sight and sap your strength. You will plant seed in vain, because your enemies will eat it. [17]I will set my face against you so that you will be defeated by your enemies; those who hate you will rule over you, and you will flee even when no one is pursuing you.

[18]" 'If after all this you will not listen to me, I will punish you for your sins seven times over. [19]I will break down your stubborn pride and make the sky above you like iron and the ground beneath you like bronze. [20]Your strength will be spent in vain, because your soil will not yield its crops, nor will the trees of your land yield their fruit.

[21]" 'If you remain hostile toward me and refuse to listen to me, I will multiply your afflictions seven times over, as your sins deserve. [22]I will send wild animals against you, and they will rob you of your children, destroy your cattle and make you so few in number that your roads will be deserted.

[23]" 'If in spite of these things you do not accept my correction but continue to be hostile toward me, [24]I myself will be hostile toward you and will afflict you for your sins seven times over. [25]And I will bring the sword on you to avenge the breaking of the covenant. When you withdraw into your cities, I will send a plague among you, and you will be given into enemy hands. [26]When I cut off your supply of bread, ten women will be able to bake your bread in one oven, and they will dole out the bread by weight. You will eat, but you will not be satisfied.

[27]" 'If in spite of this you still do not listen to me but continue to be hostile toward me, [28]then in my anger I will be hostile toward you, and I myself will punish you for your sins seven times over. [29]You will eat the flesh of your sons and the flesh of your daughters. [30]I will destroy your high places, cut down your incense altars and pile your dead bodies[a] on the lifeless forms of your idols, and I will abhor you. [31]I will turn your cities into ruins and lay waste your sanctuaries, and I will take no delight in the pleasing aroma of your offerings. [32]I myself will lay waste the land, so that your enemies who live there will be appalled. [33]I will scatter you among the nations and will draw out my sword and pursue you. Your land will be laid waste, and your cities will lie in ruins. [34]Then the land will enjoy its sabbath years all the time that it lies desolate and you are in the country of your enemies; then the land will rest and enjoy its sabbaths. [35]All the time that it lies desolate, the land will have the rest it did not have during the sabbaths you lived in it.

[36]" 'As for those of you who are left, I will make their hearts so fearful in the lands of their enemies that the sound of a windblown leaf will put them to flight. They will run as though fleeing from the sword, and they will fall, even though no one is pursuing them. [37]They will stumble over one another as though fleeing from the sword, even though no one is pursuing them. So you will not be able to stand before your enemies. [38]You will perish among the nations; the land of your enemies will devour you. [39]Those of you who are left will waste away in the lands of their enemies because of their sins; also because of their ancestors' sins they will waste away.

[40]" 'But if they will confess their sins and the sins of their ancestors—their unfaithfulness and their hostility toward me, [41]which made me hostile toward them so that I sent them into the land of their enemies—then when their uncircumcised hearts are humbled and they pay for their sin, [42]I will remember my covenant with Jacob and my covenant with Isaac and my covenant with Abraham, and I will remember the land. [43]For the land will be deserted by them and will enjoy its sabbaths while it lies desolate without them. They will pay for their sins because they rejected my laws and abhorred my decrees. [44]Yet in spite of this, when they are in the land of their enemies, I will not reject them or abhor them so as to destroy them completely, breaking my covenant with them. I am the LORD their God. [45]But for their sake I will remember the covenant with their ancestors whom I brought out of Egypt in the sight of the nations to be their God. I am the LORD.' "

[46]These are the decrees, the laws and the regulations that the LORD established at Mount Sinai between himself and the Israelites through Moses.

Redeeming What Is the LORD's

27 The LORD said to Moses, [2]"Speak to the Israelites and say to them: 'If anyone makes a special vow to dedicate a person to the LORD by giving the equivalent value, [3]set the value of a male between the ages of twenty and sixty at fifty shekels[b] of silver, according to the sanctuary shekel[c]; [4]for a female, set her value at thirty shekels[d]; [5]for a person between the ages of five and twenty, set the value of a male at twenty shekels[e] and of a female at ten shekels[f]; [6]for a person between one month and five years, set the value of a male at five shekels[g] of silver and that of a female at three shekels[h] of silver; [7]for a person sixty years old or more, set the value of a male at fifteen shekels[i] and of a female at ten shekels. [8]If anyone making the vow is too poor to pay the specified amount, the person being dedicated is to be presented to the priest, who will set the value according to what the one making the vow can afford.

[9]" 'If what they vowed is an animal that is

[a] *30* Or *your funeral offerings* [b] *3* That is, about 1 1/4 pounds or about 575 grams; also in verse 16 [c] *3* That is, about 2/5 ounce or about 12 grams; also in verse 25 [d] *4* That is, about 12 ounces or about 345 grams [e] *5* That is, about 8 ounces or about 230 grams [f] *5* That is, about 4 ounces or about 115 grams; also in verse 7 [g] *6* That is, about 2 ounces or about 58 grams [h] *6* That is, about 1 1/4 ounces or about 35 grams [i] *7* That is, about 6 ounces or about 175 grams

acceptable as an offering to the LORD, such
an animal given to the LORD becomes holy.
10 They must not exchange it or substitute a
good one for a bad one, or a bad one for a
good one; if they should substitute one animal
for another, both it and the substitute become
holy. 11 If what they vowed is a ceremonially
unclean animal—one that is not acceptable
as an offering to the LORD—the animal must
be presented to the priest, 12 who will judge its
quality as good or bad. Whatever value the
priest then sets, that is what it will be. 13 If the
owner wishes to redeem the animal, a fifth
must be added to its value.

14 " 'If anyone dedicates their house as something holy to the LORD, the priest will judge
its quality as good or bad. Whatever value the
priest then sets, so it will remain. 15 If the one
who dedicates their house wishes to redeem
it, they must add a fifth to its value, and the
house will again become theirs.

16 " 'If anyone dedicates to the LORD part of
their family land, its value is to be set according to the amount of seed required for it—fifty
shekels of silver to a homer[a] of barley seed.
17 If they dedicate a field during the Year of
Jubilee, the value that has been set remains.
18 But if they dedicate a field after the Jubilee,
the priest will determine the value according
to the number of years that remain until the
next Year of Jubilee, and its set value will be
reduced. 19 If the one who dedicates the field
wishes to redeem it, they must add a fifth to its
value, and the field will again become theirs.
20 If, however, they do not redeem the field, or if
they have sold it to someone else, it can never
be redeemed. 21 When the field is released in the
Jubilee, it will become holy, like a field devoted
to the LORD; it will become priestly property.

22 " 'If anyone dedicates to the LORD a field
they have bought, which is not part of their
family land, 23 the priest will determine its value up to the Year of Jubilee, and the owner
must pay its value on that day as something
holy to the LORD. 24 In the Year of Jubilee the
field will revert to the person from whom it
was bought, the one whose land it was. 25 Every value is to be set according to the sanctuary shekel, twenty gerahs to the shekel.

26 " 'No one, however, may dedicate the
firstborn of an animal, since the firstborn
already belongs to the LORD; whether an ox[b]
or a sheep, it is the LORD's. 27 If it is one of the
unclean animals, it may be bought back at its
set value, adding a fifth of the value to it. If it
is not redeemed, it is to be sold at its set value.

28 " 'But nothing that a person owns and de-
votes[c] to the LORD—whether a human being
or an animal or family land—may be sold
or redeemed; everything so devoted is most
holy to the LORD.

29 " 'No person devoted to destruction[d] may
be ransomed; they are to be put to death.

30 " 'A tithe of everything from the land,
whether grain from the soil or fruit from the
trees, belongs to the LORD; it is holy to the
LORD. 31 Whoever would redeem any of their
tithe must add a fifth of the value to it. 32 Every tithe of the herd and flock—every tenth
animal that passes under the shepherd's rod—
will be holy to the LORD. 33 No one may pick
out the good from the bad or make any substitution. If anyone does make a substitution,
both the animal and its substitute become holy
and cannot be redeemed.' "

34 These are the commands the LORD gave
Moses at Mount Sinai for the Israelites.

Numbers

The Census

1 The LORD spoke to Moses in the tent of
meeting in the Desert of Sinai on the first
day of the second month of the second year
after the Israelites came out of Egypt. He said:
2 "Take a census of the whole Israelite community by their clans and families, listing every
man by name, one by one. 3 You and Aaron
are to count according to their divisions all
the men in Israel who are twenty years old or
more and able to serve in the army. 4 One man
from each tribe, each of them the head of his
family, is to help you. 5 These are the names
of the men who are to assist you:

from Reuben, Elizur son of Shedeur;
6 from Simeon, Shelumiel son of Zurishaddai;
7 from Judah, Nahshon son of Amminadab;
8 from Issachar, Nethanel son of Zuar;
9 from Zebulun, Eliab son of Helon;
10 from the sons of Joseph:
from Ephraim, Elishama son of Ammihud;
from Manasseh, Gamaliel son of Pedahzur;
11 from Benjamin, Abidan son of Gideoni;
12 from Dan, Ahiezer son of Ammishaddai;
13 from Asher, Pagiel son of Okran;

[a] *16* That is, probably about 300 pounds or about 135 kilograms [b] *26* The Hebrew word can refer to either male or female. [c] *28* The Hebrew term refers to the irrevocable giving over of things or persons to the LORD. [d] *29* The Hebrew term refers to the irrevocable giving over of things or persons to the LORD, often by totally destroying them.

14 from Gad, Eliasaph son of Deuel;
15 from Naphtali, Ahira son of Enan."

16 These were the men appointed from the
community, the leaders of their ancestral
tribes. They were the heads of the clans of
Israel.
17 Moses and Aaron took these men whose
names had been specified, 18 and they called
the whole community together on the first day
of the second month. The people registered
their ancestry by their clans and families, and
the men twenty years old or more were listed by name, one by one, 19 as the LORD commanded Moses. And so he counted them in
the Desert of Sinai:

20 From the descendants of Reuben the firstborn son of Israel:
All the men twenty years old or more
who were able to serve in the army
were listed by name, one by one, according to the records of their clans
and families. 21 The number from the
tribe of Reuben was 46,500.

22 From the descendants of Simeon:
All the men twenty years old or more
who were able to serve in the army
were counted and listed by name, one
by one, according to the records of their
clans and families. 23 The number from
the tribe of Simeon was 59,300.

24 From the descendants of Gad:
All the men twenty years old or more
who were able to serve in the army
were listed by name, according to the
records of their clans and families.
25 The number from the tribe of Gad
was 45,650.

26 From the descendants of Judah:
All the men twenty years old or more
who were able to serve in the army
were listed by name, according to the
records of their clans and families.
27 The number from the tribe of Judah
was 74,600.

28 From the descendants of Issachar:
All the men twenty years old or more
who were able to serve in the army
were listed by name, according to the
records of their clans and families.
29 The number from the tribe of Issachar was 54,400.

30 From the descendants of Zebulun:
All the men twenty years old or more
who were able to serve in the army
were listed by name, according to the
records of their clans and families.
31 The number from the tribe of Zebulun was 57,400.

32 From the sons of Joseph:
From the descendants of Ephraim:
All the men twenty years old or more
who were able to serve in the army were
listed by name, according to the records
of their clans and families. 33 The number
from the tribe of Ephraim was 40,500.

34 From the descendants of Manasseh:
All the men twenty years old or more
who were able to serve in the army
were listed by name, according to the
records of their clans and families.
35 The number from the tribe of Manasseh was 32,200.

36 From the descendants of Benjamin:
All the men twenty years old or more
who were able to serve in the army
were listed by name, according to the
records of their clans and families.
37 The number from the tribe of Benjamin was 35,400.

38 From the descendants of Dan:
All the men twenty years old or more
who were able to serve in the army
were listed by name, according to the
records of their clans and families.
39 The number from the tribe of Dan
was 62,700.

40 From the descendants of Asher:
All the men twenty years old or more
who were able to serve in the army
were listed by name, according to the
records of their clans and families.
41 The number from the tribe of Asher
was 41,500.

42 From the descendants of Naphtali:
All the men twenty years old or more
who were able to serve in the army
were listed by name, according to the
records of their clans and families.
43 The number from the tribe of Naphtali was 53,400.

44 These were the men counted by Moses
and Aaron and the twelve leaders of Israel,
each one representing his family. 45 All the
Israelites twenty years old or more who were
able to serve in Israel's army were counted
according to their families. 46 The total number was 603,550.
47 The ancestral tribe of the Levites, however,
was not counted along with the others. 48 The
LORD had said to Moses: 49 "You must not count
the tribe of Levi or include them in the census of the other Israelites. 50 Instead, appoint
the Levites to be in charge of the tabernacle
of the covenant law—over all its furnishings
and everything belonging to it. They are to
carry the tabernacle and all its furnishings;
they are to take care of it and encamp around
it. 51 Whenever the tabernacle is to move, the
Levites are to take it down, and whenever the
tabernacle is to be set up, the Levites shall do
it. Anyone else who approaches it is to be put to
death. 52 The Israelites are to set up their tents
by divisions, each of them in their own camp
under their standard. 53 The Levites, however,
are to set up their tents around the tabernacle
of the covenant law so that my wrath will not
fall on the Israelite community. The Levites are
to be responsible for the care of the tabernacle
of the covenant law."
54 The Israelites did all this just as the LORD
commanded Moses.

The Arrangement of the Tribal Camps

2 The LORD said to Moses and Aaron: 2"The
Israelites are to camp around the tent of
meeting some distance from it, each of them
under their standard and holding the banners
of their family."

3On the east, toward the sunrise, the
divisions of the camp of Judah are to encamp under their standard. The leader
of the people of Judah is Nahshon son
of Amminadab. 4His division numbers
74,600.
5The tribe of Issachar will camp next
to them. The leader of the people of Issachar is Nethanel son of Zuar. 6His division numbers 54,400.
7The tribe of Zebulun will be next.
The leader of the people of Zebulun is
Eliab son of Helon. 8His division numbers 57,400.
9All the men assigned to the camp of
Judah, according to their divisions, number 186,400. They will set out first.

10On the south will be the divisions of
the camp of Reuben under their standard.
The leader of the people of Reuben is Elizur son of Shedeur. 11His division numbers 46,500.
12The tribe of Simeon will camp next to
them. The leader of the people of Simeon
is Shelumiel son of Zurishaddai. 13His division numbers 59,300.
14The tribe of Gad will be next. The
leader of the people of Gad is Eliasaph son
of Deuel.[a] 15His division numbers 45,650.
16All the men assigned to the camp
of Reuben, according to their divisions,
number 151,450. They will set out second.

17Then the tent of meeting and the
camp of the Levites will set out in the
middle of the camps. They will set out
in the same order as they encamp, each
in their own place under their standard.

18On the west will be the divisions of
the camp of Ephraim under their standard. The leader of the people of Ephraim is Elishama son of Ammihud. 19His
division numbers 40,500.
20The tribe of Manasseh will be next
to them. The leader of the people of Manasseh is Gamaliel son of Pedahzur. 21His
division numbers 32,200.
22The tribe of Benjamin will be next.
The leader of the people of Benjamin is
Abidan son of Gideoni. 23His division
numbers 35,400.
24All the men assigned to the camp of
Ephraim, according to their divisions,
number 108,100. They will set out third.
25On the north will be the divisions of
the camp of Dan under their standard.
The leader of the people of Dan is Ahiezer son of Ammishaddai. 26His division
numbers 62,700.
27The tribe of Asher will camp next to
them. The leader of the people of Asher is Pagiel son of Okran. 28His division
numbers 41,500.
29The tribe of Naphtali will be next.
The leader of the people of Naphtali is
Ahira son of Enan. 30His division numbers 53,400.
31All the men assigned to the camp of
Dan number 157,600. They will set out
last, under their standards.

32These are the Israelites, counted according to their families. All the men in
the camps, by their divisions, number
603,550. 33The Levites, however, were not
counted along with the other Israelites,
as the LORD commanded Moses.

34So the Israelites did everything the LORD
commanded Moses; that is the way they encamped under their standards, and that is the
way they set out, each of them with their clan
and family.

The Levites

3 This is the account of the family of Aaron
and Moses at the time the LORD spoke to
Moses at Mount Sinai.
2The names of the sons of Aaron were Nadab the firstborn and Abihu, Eleazar and Ithamar. 3Those were the names of Aaron's sons,
the anointed priests, who were ordained to
serve as priests. 4Nadab and Abihu, however, died before the LORD when they made an
offering with unauthorized fire before him
in the Desert of Sinai. They had no sons, so
Eleazar and Ithamar served as priests during
the lifetime of their father Aaron.
5The LORD said to Moses, 6"Bring the tribe
of Levi and present them to Aaron the priest
to assist him. 7They are to perform duties for
him and for the whole community at the tent
of meeting by doing the work of the tabernacle. 8They are to take care of all the furnishings of the tent of meeting, fulfilling the
obligations of the Israelites by doing the work
of the tabernacle. 9Give the Levites to Aaron
and his sons; they are the Israelites who are
to be given wholly to him.[b] 10Appoint Aaron
and his sons to serve as priests; anyone else
who approaches the sanctuary is to be put
to death."
11The LORD also said to Moses, 12"I have
taken the Levites from among the Israelites
in place of the first male offspring of every
Israelite woman. The Levites are mine, 13for
all the firstborn are mine. When I struck down
all the firstborn in Egypt, I set apart for myself
every firstborn in Israel, whether human or
animal. They are to be mine. I am the LORD."
14The LORD said to Moses in the Desert of
Sinai, 15"Count the Levites by their families
and clans. Count every male a month old or

[a] *14* Many manuscripts of the Masoretic Text, Samaritan Pentateuch and Vulgate (see also 1:14); most manuscripts of the Masoretic Text *Reuel* [b] *9* Most manuscripts of the Masoretic Text; some manuscripts of the Masoretic Text, Samaritan Pentateuch and Septuagint (see also 8:16) *to me*

more." 16So Moses counted them, as he was
commanded by the word of the LORD.

17These were the names of the sons of Levi:
Gershon, Kohath and Merari.

18These were the names of the Gershonite
clans:
Libni and Shimei.

19The Kohathite clans:
Amram, Izhar, Hebron and Uzziel.

20The Merarite clans:
Mahli and Mushi.

These were the Levite clans, according to
their families.

21To Gershon belonged the clans of the Lib-
nites and Shimeites; these were the Gershonite
clans. 22The number of all the males a month
old or more who were counted was 7,500.
23The Gershonite clans were to camp on the
west, behind the tabernacle. 24The leader of
the families of the Gershonites was Eliasaph
son of Lael. 25At the tent of meeting the Gershonites were responsible for the care of the
tabernacle and tent, its coverings, the curtain
at the entrance to the tent of meeting, 26the
curtains of the courtyard, the curtain at the
entrance to the courtyard surrounding the
tabernacle and altar, and the ropes—and everything related to their use.

27To Kohath belonged the clans of the Amramites, Izharites, Hebronites and Uzzielites;
these were the Kohathite clans. 28The number of all the males a month old or more was
8,600.[a] The Kohathites were responsible for
the care of the sanctuary. 29The Kohathite
clans were to camp on the south side of the
tabernacle. 30The leader of the families of the
Kohathite clans was Elizaphan son of Uzziel.
31They were responsible for the care of the
ark, the table, the lampstand, the altars, the
articles of the sanctuary used in ministering,
the curtain, and everything related to their
use. 32The chief leader of the Levites was Eleazar son of Aaron, the priest. He was appointed
over those who were responsible for the care
of the sanctuary.

33To Merari belonged the clans of the Mah-
lites and the Mushites; these were the Merarite
clans. 34The number of all the males a month
old or more who were counted was 6,200.
35The leader of the families of the Merarite
clans was Zuriel son of Abihail; they were
to camp on the north side of the tabernacle.
36The Merarites were appointed to take care
of the frames of the tabernacle, its crossbars,
posts, bases, all its equipment, and everything
related to their use, 37as well as the posts of
the surrounding courtyard with their bases,
tent pegs and ropes.

38Moses and Aaron and his sons were to
camp to the east of the tabernacle, toward the
sunrise, in front of the tent of meeting. They
were responsible for the care of the sanctuary on behalf of the Israelites. Anyone else
who approached the sanctuary was to be put
to death.

39The total number of Levites counted at
the LORD's command by Moses and Aaron according to their clans, including every male
a month old or more, was 22,000.

40The LORD said to Moses, "Count all the
firstborn Israelite males who are a month
old or more and make a list of their names.
41Take the Levites for me in place of all the
firstborn of the Israelites, and the livestock
of the Levites in place of all the firstborn of
the livestock of the Israelites. I am the LORD."
42So Moses counted all the firstborn of the
Israelites, as the LORD commanded him. 43The
total number of firstborn males a month old
or more, listed by name, was 22,273.
44The LORD also said to Moses, 45"Take the
Levites in place of all the firstborn of Israel,
and the livestock of the Levites in place of
their livestock. The Levites are to be mine. I
am the LORD. 46To redeem the 273 firstborn Israelites who exceed the number of the Levites,
47collect five shekels[b] for each one, according
to the sanctuary shekel, which weighs twenty
gerahs. 48Give the money for the redemption
of the additional Israelites to Aaron and his
sons."
49So Moses collected the redemption money from those who exceeded the number redeemed by the Levites. 50From the firstborn
of the Israelites he collected silver weighing
1,365 shekels,[c] according to the sanctuary
shekel. 51Moses gave the redemption money
to Aaron and his sons, as he was commanded
by the word of the LORD.

The Kohathites

4 The LORD said to Moses and Aaron: 2"Take
a census of the Kohathite branch of the
Levites by their clans and families. 3Count
all the men from thirty to fifty years of age
who come to serve in the work at the tent of
meeting.
4"This is the work of the Kohathites at the
tent of meeting: the care of the most holy
things. 5When the camp is to move, Aaron
and his sons are to go in and take down the
shielding curtain and put it over the ark of the
covenant law. 6Then they are to cover the curtain with a durable leather,[d] spread a cloth of
solid blue over that and put the poles in place.
7"Over the table of the Presence they are to
spread a blue cloth and put on it the plates,
dishes and bowls, and the jars for drink offerings; the bread that is continually there is
to remain on it. 8They are to spread a scarlet
cloth over them, cover that with the durable
leather and put the poles in place.
9"They are to take a blue cloth and cover the
lampstand that is for light, together with its

[a] *28* Hebrew; some Septuagint manuscripts *8,300*
[b] *47* That is, about 2 ounces or about 58 grams
[c] *50* That is, about 35 pounds or about 16 kilograms
[d] *6* Possibly the hides of large aquatic mammals; also in verses 8, 10, 11, 12, 14 and 25

lamps, its wick trimmers and trays, and all its
jars for the olive oil used to supply it. 10Then
they are to wrap it and all its accessories in a
covering of the durable leather and put it on
a carrying frame.
11"Over the gold altar they are to spread
a blue cloth and cover that with the durable
leather and put the poles in place.
12"They are to take all the articles used for
ministering in the sanctuary, wrap them in a
blue cloth, cover that with the durable leather
and put them on a carrying frame.
13"They are to remove the ashes from the
bronze altar and spread a purple cloth over it.
14Then they are to place on it all the utensils
used for ministering at the altar, including the
firepans, meat forks, shovels and sprinkling
bowls. Over it they are to spread a covering of
the durable leather and put the poles in place.
15"After Aaron and his sons have finished
covering the holy furnishings and all the holy
articles, and when the camp is ready to move,
only then are the Kohathites to come and do
the carrying. But they must not touch the holy
things or they will die. The Kohathites are
to carry those things that are in the tent of
meeting.
16"Eleazar son of Aaron, the priest, is to
have charge of the oil for the light, the fragrant incense, the regular grain offering and
the anointing oil. He is to be in charge of the
entire tabernacle and everything in it, including its holy furnishings and articles."
17The LORD said to Moses and Aaron,
18"See that the Kohathite tribal clans are not
destroyed from among the Levites. 19So that
they may live and not die when they come
near the most holy things, do this for them:
Aaron and his sons are to go into the sanctuary and assign to each man his work and
what he is to carry. 20But the Kohathites must
not go in to look at the holy things, even for a
moment, or they will die."

The Gershonites

21The LORD said to Moses, 22"Take a census
also of the Gershonites by their families and
clans. 23Count all the men from thirty to fifty
years of age who come to serve in the work at
the tent of meeting.
24"This is the service of the Gershonite clans
in their carrying and their other work: 25They
are to carry the curtains of the tabernacle,
that is, the tent of meeting, its covering and
its outer covering of durable leather, the curtains for the entrance to the tent of meeting,
26the curtains of the courtyard surrounding
the tabernacle and altar, the curtain for the
entrance to the courtyard, the ropes and all
the equipment used in the service of the tent.
The Gershonites are to do all that needs to
be done with these things. 27All their service,
whether carrying or doing other work, is to
be done under the direction of Aaron and
his sons. You shall assign to them as their
responsibility all they are to carry. 28This is
the service of the Gershonite clans at the tent
of meeting. Their duties are to be under the
direction of Ithamar son of Aaron, the priest.

The Merarites

29"Count the Merarites by their clans and
families. 30Count all the men from thirty to fifty years of age who come to serve in the work
at the tent of meeting. 31As part of all their
service at the tent, they are to carry the frames
of the tabernacle, its crossbars, posts and bases, 32as well as the posts of the surrounding
courtyard with their bases, tent pegs, ropes,
all their equipment and everything related
to their use. Assign to each man the specific
things he is to carry. 33This is the service of
the Merarite clans as they work at the tent of
meeting under the direction of Ithamar son
of Aaron, the priest."

The Numbering of the Levite Clans

34Moses, Aaron and the leaders of the community counted the Kohathites by their clans
and families. 35All the men from thirty to fifty
years of age who came to serve in the work
at the tent of meeting, 36counted by clans,
were 2,750. 37This was the total of all those
in the Kohathite clans who served at the tent
of meeting. Moses and Aaron counted them
according to the LORD's command through
Moses.
38The Gershonites were counted by their
clans and families. 39All the men from thirty to fifty years of age who came to serve in
the work at the tent of meeting, 40counted by
their clans and families, were 2,630. 41This
was the total of those in the Gershonite clans
who served at the tent of meeting. Moses and
Aaron counted them according to the LORD's
command.
42The Merarites were counted by their clans
and families. 43All the men from thirty to fifty
years of age who came to serve in the work at
the tent of meeting, 44counted by their clans,
were 3,200. 45This was the total of those in
the Merarite clans. Moses and Aaron counted them according to the LORD's command
through Moses.
46So Moses, Aaron and the leaders of Israel
counted all the Levites by their clans and families. 47All the men from thirty to fifty years
of age who came to do the work of serving
and carrying the tent of meeting 48numbered
8,580. 49At the LORD's command through Moses, each was assigned his work and told what
to carry.
Thus they were counted, as the LORD commanded Moses.

The Purity of the Camp

5 The LORD said to Moses, 2"Command the
Israelites to send away from the camp
anyone who has a defiling skin disease[a] or a
discharge of any kind, or who is ceremonially
unclean because of a dead body. 3Send away

[a] 2 The Hebrew word for *defiling skin disease*, traditionally translated "leprosy," was used for various diseases affecting the skin.

male and female alike; send them outside the camp so they will not defile their camp, where I dwell among them." 4The Israelites did so; they sent them outside the camp. They did just as the LORD had instructed Moses.

Restitution for Wrongs

5The LORD said to Moses, 6"Say to the Israelites: 'Any man or woman who wrongs another in any way[a] and so is unfaithful to the LORD is guilty 7and must confess the sin they have committed. They must make full restitution for the wrong they have done, add a fifth of the value to it and give it all to the person they have wronged. 8But if that person has no close relative to whom restitution can be made for the wrong, the restitution belongs to the LORD and must be given to the priest, along with the ram with which atonement is made for the wrongdoer. 9All the sacred contributions the Israelites bring to a priest will belong to him. 10Sacred things belong to their owners, but what they give to the priest will belong to the priest.'"

The Test for an Unfaithful Wife

11Then the LORD said to Moses, 12"Speak to the Israelites and say to them: 'If a man's wife goes astray and is unfaithful to him 13so that another man has sexual relations with her, and this is hidden from her husband and her impurity is undetected (since there is no witness against her and she has not been caught in the act), 14and if feelings of jealousy come over her husband and he suspects his wife and she is impure—or if he is jealous and suspects her even though she is not impure— 15then he is to take his wife to the priest. He must also take an offering of a tenth of an ephah[b] of barley flour on her behalf. He must not pour olive oil on it or put incense on it, because it is a grain offering for jealousy, a reminder-offering to draw attention to wrongdoing.

16" 'The priest shall bring her and have her stand before the LORD. 17Then he shall take some holy water in a clay jar and put some dust from the tabernacle floor into the water. 18After the priest has had the woman stand before the LORD, he shall loosen her hair and place in her hands the reminder-offering, the grain offering for jealousy, while he himself holds the bitter water that brings a curse. 19Then the priest shall put the woman under oath and say to her, "If no other man has had sexual relations with you and you have not gone astray and become impure while married to your husband, may this bitter water that brings a curse not harm you. 20But if you have gone astray while married to your husband and you have made yourself impure by having sexual relations with a man other than your husband"— 21here the priest is to put the woman under this curse—"may the LORD cause you to become a curse[c] among your people when he makes your womb miscarry and your abdomen swell. 22May this water that brings a curse enter your body so that your abdomen swells or your womb miscarries."

" 'Then the woman is to say, "Amen. So be it."

23" 'The priest is to write these curses on a scroll and then wash them off into the bitter water. 24He shall make the woman drink the bitter water that brings a curse, and this water that brings a curse and causes bitter suffering will enter her. 25The priest is to take from her hands the grain offering for jealousy, wave it before the LORD and bring it to the altar. 26The priest is then to take a handful of the grain offering as a memorial[d] offering and burn it on the altar; after that, he is to have the woman drink the water. 27If she has made herself impure and been unfaithful to her husband, this will be the result: When she is made to drink the water that brings a curse and causes bitter suffering, it will enter her, her abdomen will swell and her womb will miscarry, and she will become a curse. 28If, however, the woman has not made herself impure, but is clean, she will be cleared of guilt and will be able to have children.

29" 'This, then, is the law of jealousy when a woman goes astray and makes herself impure while married to her husband, 30or when feelings of jealousy come over a man because he suspects his wife. The priest is to have her stand before the LORD and is to apply this entire law to her. 31The husband will be innocent of any wrongdoing, but the woman will bear the consequences of her sin.' "

The Nazirite

6 The LORD said to Moses, 2"Speak to the Israelites and say to them: 'If a man or woman wants to make a special vow, a vow of dedication to the LORD as a Nazirite, 3they must abstain from wine and other fermented drink and must not drink vinegar made from wine or other fermented drink. They must not drink grape juice or eat grapes or raisins. 4As long as they remain under their Nazirite vow, they must not eat anything that comes from the grapevine, not even the seeds or skins.

5" 'During the entire period of their Nazirite vow, no razor may be used on their head. They must be holy until the period of their dedication to the LORD is over; they must let their hair grow long.

6" 'Throughout the period of their dedication to the LORD, the Nazirite must not go near a dead body. 7Even if their own father or mother or brother or sister dies, they must not make themselves ceremonially unclean on account of them, because the symbol of their dedication to God is on their head. 8Throughout the period of their dedication, they are consecrated to the LORD.

9" 'If someone dies suddenly in the Nazirite's presence, thus defiling the hair that symbolizes their dedication, they must shave their head

[a] *6* Or *woman who commits any wrong common to mankind* [b] *15* That is, probably about 3 1/2 pounds or about 1.6 kilograms [c] *21* That is, may he cause your name to be used in cursing (see Jer. 29:22); or, may others see that you are cursed; similarly in verse 27. [d] *26* Or *representative*

on the seventh day—the day of their cleansing. [10]Then on the eighth day they must bring
two doves or two young pigeons to the priest at
the entrance to the tent of meeting. [11]The priest
is to offer one as a sin offering[a] and the other as a burnt offering to make atonement for
the Nazirite because they sinned by being in
the presence of the dead body. That same day
they are to consecrate their head again. [12]They
must rededicate themselves to the LORD for
the same period of dedication and must bring
a year-old male lamb as a guilt offering. The
previous days do not count, because they became defiled during their period of dedication.
[13]" 'Now this is the law of the Nazirite when
the period of their dedication is over. They
are to be brought to the entrance to the tent
of meeting. [14]There they are to present their
offerings to the LORD: a year-old male lamb
without defect for a burnt offering, a year-old
ewe lamb without defect for a sin offering,
a ram without defect for a fellowship offering, [15]together with their grain offerings and
drink offerings, and a basket of bread made
with the finest flour and without yeast—thick
loaves with olive oil mixed in, and thin loaves
brushed with olive oil.
[16]" 'The priest is to present all these before
the LORD and make the sin offering and the
burnt offering. [17]He is to present the basket of
unleavened bread and is to sacrifice the ram
as a fellowship offering to the LORD, together with its grain offering and drink offering.
[18]" 'Then at the entrance to the tent of meeting, the Nazirite must shave off the hair that
symbolizes their dedication. They are to take
the hair and put it in the fire that is under the
sacrifice of the fellowship offering.
[19]" 'After the Nazirite has shaved off the hair
that symbolizes their dedication, the priest is
to place in their hands a boiled shoulder of the
ram, and one thick loaf and one thin loaf from
the basket, both made without yeast. [20]The
priest shall then wave these before the LORD
as a wave offering; they are holy and belong
to the priest, together with the breast that was
waved and the thigh that was presented. After
that, the Nazirite may drink wine.
[21]" 'This is the law of the Nazirite who vows
offerings to the LORD in accordance with their
dedication, in addition to whatever else they
can afford. They must fulfill the vows they
have made, according to the law of the Nazirite.' "

The Priestly Blessing

[22]The LORD said to Moses, [23]"Tell Aaron and
his sons, 'This is how you are to bless the Israelites. Say to them:

[24]" ' "The LORD bless you
and keep you;
[25]the LORD make his face shine on you
and be gracious to you;
[26]the LORD turn his face toward you
and give you peace." '

[27]"So they will put my name on the Israelites, and I will bless them."

Offerings at the Dedication of the Tabernacle

7 When Moses finished setting up the tabernacle, he anointed and consecrated it and
all its furnishings. He also anointed and consecrated the altar and all its utensils. [2]Then
the leaders of Israel, the heads of families who
were the tribal leaders in charge of those who
were counted, made offerings. [3]They brought
as their gifts before the LORD six covered carts
and twelve oxen—an ox from each leader and
a cart from every two. These they presented
before the tabernacle.
[4]The LORD said to Moses, [5]"Accept these
from them, that they may be used in the work
at the tent of meeting. Give them to the Levites
as each man's work requires."
[6]So Moses took the carts and oxen and gave
them to the Levites. [7]He gave two carts and
four oxen to the Gershonites, as their work
required, [8]and he gave four carts and eight
oxen to the Merarites, as their work required.
They were all under the direction of Ithamar
son of Aaron, the priest. [9]But Moses did not
give any to the Kohathites, because they were
to carry on their shoulders the holy things, for
which they were responsible.
[10]When the altar was anointed, the leaders brought their offerings for its dedication
and presented them before the altar. [11]For the
LORD had said to Moses, "Each day one leader is to bring his offering for the dedication
of the altar."

[12]The one who brought his offering on the
first day was Nahshon son of Amminadab of
the tribe of Judah.
[13]His offering was one silver plate weighing a hundred and thirty shekels[b] and one
silver sprinkling bowl weighing seventy
shekels,[c] both according to the sanctuary
shekel, each filled with the finest flour
mixed with olive oil as a grain offering;
[14]one gold dish weighing ten shekels,[d]
filled with incense; [15]one young bull, one
ram and one male lamb a year old for a
burnt offering; [16]one male goat for a sin
offering[e]; [17]and two oxen, five rams, five
male goats and five male lambs a year old
to be sacrificed as a fellowship offering.
This was the offering of Nahshon son of
Amminadab.

[18]On the second day Nethanel son of Zuar,
the leader of Issachar, brought his offering.
[19]The offering he brought was one silver plate weighing a hundred and thirty
shekels and one silver sprinkling bowl
weighing seventy shekels, both according

[a] *11* Or *purification offering*; also in verses 14 and 16 [b] *13* That is, about 3 1/4 pounds or about 1.5 kilograms; also elsewhere in this chapter [c] *13* That is, about 1 3/4 pounds or about 800 grams; also elsewhere in this chapter [d] *14* That is, about 4 ounces or about 115 grams; also elsewhere in this chapter [e] *16* Or *purification offering*; also elsewhere in this chapter

to the sanctuary shekel, each filled with
the finest flour mixed with olive oil as
a grain offering; [20]one gold dish weighing ten shekels, filled with incense; [21]one
young bull, one ram and one male lamb a
year old for a burnt offering; [22]one male
goat for a sin offering; [23]and two oxen,
five rams, five male goats and five male
lambs a year old to be sacrificed as a fellowship offering. This was the offering
of Nethanel son of Zuar.

[24]On the third day, Eliab son of Helon, the
leader of the people of Zebulun, brought his
offering.

[25]His offering was one silver plate weighing a hundred and thirty shekels and one
silver sprinkling bowl weighing seventy
shekels, both according to the sanctuary
shekel, each filled with the finest flour
mixed with olive oil as a grain offering;
[26]one gold dish weighing ten shekels, filled
with incense; [27]one young bull, one ram
and one male lamb a year old for a burnt
offering; [28]one male goat for a sin offering;
[29]and two oxen, five rams, five male goats
and five male lambs a year old to be sacrificed as a fellowship offering. This was
the offering of Eliab son of Helon.

[30]On the fourth day Elizur son of Shedeur,
the leader of the people of Reuben, brought
his offering.

[31]His offering was one silver plate weighing a hundred and thirty shekels and one
silver sprinkling bowl weighing seventy
shekels, both according to the sanctuary
shekel, each filled with the finest flour
mixed with olive oil as a grain offering;
[32]one gold dish weighing ten shekels,
filled with incense; [33]one young bull, one
ram and one male lamb a year old for a
burnt offering; [34]one male goat for a sin
offering; [35]and two oxen, five rams, five
male goats and five male lambs a year
old to be sacrificed as a fellowship offering. This was the offering of Elizur son
of Shedeur.

[36]On the fifth day Shelumiel son of Zurishaddai, the leader of the people of Simeon,
brought his offering.

[37]His offering was one silver plate weighing a hundred and thirty shekels and one
silver sprinkling bowl weighing seventy
shekels, both according to the sanctuary
shekel, each filled with the finest flour
mixed with olive oil as a grain offering;
[38]one gold dish weighing ten shekels,
filled with incense; [39]one young bull, one
ram and one male lamb a year old for a
burnt offering; [40]one male goat for a sin
offering; [41]and two oxen, five rams, five
male goats and five male lambs a year old
to be sacrificed as a fellowship offering.
This was the offering of Shelumiel son
of Zurishaddai.

[42]On the sixth day Eliasaph son of Deuel, the
leader of the people of Gad, brought his offering.

[43]His offering was one silver plate weighing a hundred and thirty shekels and one
silver sprinkling bowl weighing seventy
shekels, both according to the sanctuary
shekel, each filled with the finest flour
mixed with olive oil as a grain offering;
[44]one gold dish weighing ten shekels,
filled with incense; [45]one young bull, one
ram and one male lamb a year old for a
burnt offering; [46]one male goat for a sin
offering; [47]and two oxen, five rams, five
male goats and five male lambs a year
old to be sacrificed as a fellowship offering. This was the offering of Eliasaph
son of Deuel.

[48]On the seventh day Elishama son of Ammihud, the leader of the people of Ephraim,
brought his offering.

[49]His offering was one silver plate weighing a hundred and thirty shekels and one
silver sprinkling bowl weighing seventy
shekels, both according to the sanctuary
shekel, each filled with the finest flour
mixed with olive oil as a grain offering;
[50]one gold dish weighing ten shekels,
filled with incense; [51]one young bull, one
ram and one male lamb a year old for a
burnt offering; [52]one male goat for a sin
offering; [53]and two oxen, five rams, five
male goats and five male lambs a year old
to be sacrificed as a fellowship offering.
This was the offering of Elishama son
of Ammihud.

[54]On the eighth day Gamaliel son of Pedahzur,
the leader of the people of Manasseh, brought
his offering.

[55]His offering was one silver plate weighing a hundred and thirty shekels and one
silver sprinkling bowl weighing seventy
shekels, both according to the sanctuary
shekel, each filled with the finest flour
mixed with olive oil as a grain offering;
[56]one gold dish weighing ten shekels,
filled with incense; [57]one young bull, one
ram and one male lamb a year old for a
burnt offering; [58]one male goat for a sin
offering; [59]and two oxen, five rams, five
male goats and five male lambs a year old
to be sacrificed as a fellowship offering.
This was the offering of Gamaliel son of
Pedahzur.

[60]On the ninth day Abidan son of Gideoni,
the leader of the people of Benjamin, brought
his offering.

[61]His offering was one silver plate weighing a hundred and thirty shekels and one
silver sprinkling bowl weighing seventy
shekels, both according to the sanctuary
shekel, each filled with the finest flour
mixed with olive oil as a grain offering;
[62]one gold dish weighing ten shekels,
filled with incense; [63]one young bull, one
ram and one male lamb a year old for a
burnt offering; [64]one male goat for a sin
offering; [65]and two oxen, five rams, five
male goats and five male lambs a year
old to be sacrificed as a fellowship offer-

ing. This was the offering of Abidan son
of Gideoni.

66On the tenth day Ahiezer son of Ammishaddai, the leader of the people of Dan, brought
his offering.
67His offering was one silver plate weighing a hundred and thirty shekels and one
silver sprinkling bowl weighing seventy
shekels, both according to the sanctuary
shekel, each filled with the finest flour
mixed with olive oil as a grain offering;
68one gold dish weighing ten shekels,
filled with incense; 69one young bull, one
ram and one male lamb a year old for a
burnt offering; 70one male goat for a sin
offering; 71and two oxen, five rams, five
male goats and five male lambs a year old
to be sacrificed as a fellowship offering.
This was the offering of Ahiezer son of
Ammishaddai.

72On the eleventh day Pagiel son of Okran,
the leader of the people of Asher, brought his
offering.
73His offering was one silver plate weighing a hundred and thirty shekels and one
silver sprinkling bowl weighing seventy
shekels, both according to the sanctuary
shekel, each filled with the finest flour
mixed with olive oil as a grain offering;
74one gold dish weighing ten shekels,
filled with incense; 75one young bull, one
ram and one male lamb a year old for a
burnt offering; 76one male goat for a sin
offering; 77and two oxen, five rams, five
male goats and five male lambs a year
old to be sacrificed as a fellowship offering. This was the offering of Pagiel
son of Okran.

78On the twelfth day Ahira son of Enan, the
leader of the people of Naphtali, brought his
offering.
79His offering was one silver plate weighing a hundred and thirty shekels and one
silver sprinkling bowl weighing seventy
shekels, both according to the sanctuary
shekel, each filled with the finest flour
mixed with olive oil as a grain offering;
80one gold dish weighing ten shekels,
filled with incense; 81one young bull, one
ram and one male lamb a year old for a
burnt offering; 82one male goat for a sin
offering; 83and two oxen, five rams, five
male goats and five male lambs a year
old to be sacrificed as a fellowship offering. This was the offering of Ahira son
of Enan.

84These were the offerings of the Israelite
leaders for the dedication of the altar when
it was anointed: twelve silver plates, twelve
silver sprinkling bowls and twelve gold
dishes. 85Each silver plate weighed a hundred and thirty shekels, and each sprinkling
bowl seventy shekels. Altogether, the silver
dishes weighed two thousand four hundred
shekels,[a] according to the sanctuary shekel.
86The twelve gold dishes filled with incense
weighed ten shekels each, according to the
sanctuary shekel. Altogether, the gold dishes
weighed a hundred and twenty shekels.[b] 87The
total number of animals for the burnt offering
came to twelve young bulls, twelve rams and
twelve male lambs a year old, together with
their grain offering. Twelve male goats were
used for the sin offering. 88The total number of
animals for the sacrifice of the fellowship offering came to twenty-four oxen, sixty rams,
sixty male goats and sixty male lambs a year
old. These were the offerings for the dedication of the altar after it was anointed.
89When Moses entered the tent of meeting
to speak with the LORD, he heard the voice
speaking to him from between the two cherubim above the atonement cover on the ark of
the covenant law. In this way the LORD spoke
to him.

Setting Up the Lamps

8 The LORD said to Moses, 2"Speak to Aaron and say to him, 'When you set up the
lamps, see that all seven light up the area in
front of the lampstand.'"
3Aaron did so; he set up the lamps so that
they faced forward on the lampstand, just as
the LORD commanded Moses. 4This is how the
lampstand was made: It was made of hammered gold—from its base to its blossoms.
The lampstand was made exactly like the
pattern the LORD had shown Moses.

The Setting Apart of the Levites

5The LORD said to Moses: 6"Take the Levites
from among all the Israelites and make them
ceremonially clean. 7To purify them, do this:
Sprinkle the water of cleansing on them; then
have them shave their whole bodies and wash
their clothes. And so they will purify themselves. 8Have them take a young bull with its
grain offering of the finest flour mixed with
olive oil; then you are to take a second young
bull for a sin offering.[c] 9Bring the Levites to
the front of the tent of meeting and assemble
the whole Israelite community. 10You are to
bring the Levites before the LORD, and the Israelites are to lay their hands on them. 11Aar-
on is to present the Levites before the LORD
as a wave offering from the Israelites, so that
they may be ready to do the work of the LORD.
12"Then the Levites are to lay their hands
on the heads of the bulls, using one for a sin
offering to the LORD and the other for a burnt
offering, to make atonement for the Levites.
13Have the Levites stand in front of Aaron
and his sons and then present them as a wave
offering to the LORD. 14In this way you are to
set the Levites apart from the other Israelites,
and the Levites will be mine.
15"After you have purified the Levites and
presented them as a wave offering, they are to
come to do their work at the tent of meeting.
16They are the Israelites who are to be given

[a] *85* That is, about 60 pounds or about 28 kilograms [b] *86* That is, about 3 pounds or about 1.4 kilograms [c] *8* Or *purification offering*; also in verse 12

wholly to me. I have taken them as my own in
place of the firstborn, the first male offspring
from every Israelite woman. [17]Every firstborn
male in Israel, whether human or animal, is
mine. When I struck down all the firstborn
in Egypt, I set them apart for myself. [18]And
I have taken the Levites in place of all the
firstborn sons in Israel. [19]From among all the
Israelites, I have given the Levites as gifts to
Aaron and his sons to do the work at the tent
of meeting on behalf of the Israelites and to
make atonement for them so that no plague
will strike the Israelites when they go near
the sanctuary."

[20]Moses, Aaron and the whole Israelite community did with the Levites just as the LORD
commanded Moses. [21]The Levites purified
themselves and washed their clothes. Then
Aaron presented them as a wave offering before the LORD and made atonement for them
to purify them. [22]After that, the Levites came
to do their work at the tent of meeting under
the supervision of Aaron and his sons. They
did with the Levites just as the LORD commanded Moses.

[23]The LORD said to Moses, [24]"This applies
to the Levites: Men twenty-five years old or
more shall come to take part in the work at
the tent of meeting, [25]but at the age of fifty,
they must retire from their regular service
and work no longer. [26]They may assist their
brothers in performing their duties at the tent
of meeting, but they themselves must not do
the work. This, then, is how you are to assign
the responsibilities of the Levites."

The Passover

9 The LORD spoke to Moses in the Desert
of Sinai in the first month of the second
year after they came out of Egypt. He said,
[2]"Have the Israelites celebrate the Passover
at the appointed time. [3]Celebrate it at the appointed time, at twilight on the fourteenth day
of this month, in accordance with all its rules
and regulations."

[4]So Moses told the Israelites to celebrate
the Passover, [5]and they did so in the Desert
of Sinai at twilight on the fourteenth day of
the first month. The Israelites did everything
just as the LORD commanded Moses.

[6]But some of them could not celebrate the
Passover on that day because they were ceremonially unclean on account of a dead body.
So they came to Moses and Aaron that same
day [7]and said to Moses, "We have become unclean because of a dead body, but why should
we be kept from presenting the LORD's offering with the other Israelites at the appointed
time?"

[8]Moses answered them, "Wait until I find
out what the LORD commands concerning
you."

[9]Then the LORD said to Moses, [10]"Tell the
Israelites: 'When any of you or your descendants are unclean because of a dead body or
are away on a journey, they are still to celebrate the LORD's Passover, [11]but they are to do
it on the fourteenth day of the second month
at twilight. They are to eat the lamb, together with unleavened bread and bitter herbs.
[12]They must not leave any of it till morning or
break any of its bones. When they celebrate
the Passover, they must follow all the regulations. [13]But if anyone who is ceremonially
clean and not on a journey fails to celebrate
the Passover, they must be cut off from their
people for not presenting the LORD's offering
at the appointed time. They will bear the consequences of their sin.

[14]" 'A foreigner residing among you is also to
celebrate the LORD's Passover in accordance
with its rules and regulations. You must have
the same regulations for both the foreigner
and the native-born.' "

The Cloud Above the Tabernacle

[15]On the day the tabernacle, the tent of the
covenant law, was set up, the cloud covered
it. From evening till morning the cloud above
the tabernacle looked like fire. [16]That is how
it continued to be; the cloud covered it, and
at night it looked like fire. [17]Whenever the
cloud lifted from above the tent, the Israelites
set out; wherever the cloud settled, the Israelites encamped. [18]At the LORD's command
the Israelites set out, and at his command
they encamped. As long as the cloud stayed
over the tabernacle, they remained in camp.
[19]When the cloud remained over the tabernacle a long time, the Israelites obeyed the
LORD's order and did not set out. [20]Sometimes
the cloud was over the tabernacle only a few
days; at the LORD's command they would encamp, and then at his command they would
set out. [21]Sometimes the cloud stayed only
from evening till morning, and when it lifted
in the morning, they set out. Whether by day
or by night, whenever the cloud lifted, they
set out. [22]Whether the cloud stayed over the
tabernacle for two days or a month or a year,
the Israelites would remain in camp and not
set out; but when it lifted, they would set out.
[23]At the LORD's command they encamped,
and at the LORD's command they set out. They
obeyed the LORD's order, in accordance with
his command through Moses.

The Silver Trumpets

10 The LORD said to Moses: [2]"Make two
trumpets of hammered silver, and use
them for calling the community together and
for having the camps set out. [3]When both are
sounded, the whole community is to assemble
before you at the entrance to the tent of meeting. [4]If only one is sounded, the leaders—the
heads of the clans of Israel—are to assemble
before you. [5]When a trumpet blast is sounded, the tribes camping on the east are to set
out. [6]At the sounding of a second blast, the
camps on the south are to set out. The blast
will be the signal for setting out. [7]To gather
the assembly, blow the trumpets, but not with
the signal for setting out.

[8]"The sons of Aaron, the priests, are to blow
the trumpets. This is to be a lasting ordinance
for you and the generations to come. [9]When
you go into battle in your own land against an

enemy who is oppressing you, sound a blast on the trumpets. Then you will be remembered by the LORD your God and rescued from your enemies. 10Also at your times of rejoicing—your appointed festivals and New Moon feasts—you are to sound the trumpets over your burnt offerings and fellowship offerings, and they will be a memorial for you before your God. I am the LORD your God."

The Israelites Leave Sinai

11On the twentieth day of the second month of the second year, the cloud lifted from above the tabernacle of the covenant law. 12Then the Israelites set out from the Desert of Sinai and traveled from place to place until the cloud came to rest in the Desert of Paran. 13They set out, this first time, at the LORD's command through Moses.

14The divisions of the camp of Judah went first, under their standard. Nahshon son of Amminadab was in command. 15Nethanel son of Zuar was over the division of the tribe of Issachar, 16and Eliab son of Helon was over the division of the tribe of Zebulun. 17Then the tabernacle was taken down, and the Gershonites and Merarites, who carried it, set out.

18The divisions of the camp of Reuben went next, under their standard. Elizur son of Shedeur was in command. 19Shelumiel son of Zurishaddai was over the division of the tribe of Simeon, 20and Eliasaph son of Deuel was over the division of the tribe of Gad. 21Then the Kohathites set out, carrying the holy things. The tabernacle was to be set up before they arrived.

22The divisions of the camp of Ephraim went next, under their standard. Elishama son of Ammihud was in command. 23Gamaliel son of Pedahzur was over the division of the tribe of Manasseh, 24and Abidan son of Gideoni was over the division of the tribe of Benjamin.

25Finally, as the rear guard for all the units, the divisions of the camp of Dan set out under their standard. Ahiezer son of Ammishaddai was in command. 26Pagiel son of Okran was over the division of the tribe of Asher, 27and Ahira son of Enan was over the division of the tribe of Naphtali. 28This was the order of march for the Israelite divisions as they set out.

29Now Moses said to Hobab son of Reuel the Midianite, Moses' father-in-law, "We are setting out for the place about which the LORD said, 'I will give it to you.' Come with us and we will treat you well, for the LORD has promised good things to Israel."

30He answered, "No, I will not go; I am going back to my own land and my own people."

31But Moses said, "Please do not leave us. You know where we should camp in the wilderness, and you can be our eyes. 32If you come with us, we will share with you whatever good things the LORD gives us."

33So they set out from the mountain of the LORD and traveled for three days. The ark of the covenant of the LORD went before them during those three days to find them a place to rest. 34The cloud of the LORD was over them by day when they set out from the camp.

35Whenever the ark set out, Moses said,

"Rise up, LORD!
 May your enemies be scattered;
 may your foes flee before you."

36Whenever it came to rest, he said,

"Return, LORD,
 to the countless thousands of Israel."

Fire From the LORD

11 Now the people complained about their hardships in the hearing of the LORD, and when he heard them his anger was aroused. Then fire from the LORD burned among them and consumed some of the outskirts of the camp. 2When the people cried out to Moses, he prayed to the LORD and the fire died down. 3So that place was called Taberah,[a] because fire from the LORD had burned among them.

Quail From the LORD

4The rabble with them began to crave other food, and again the Israelites started wailing and said, "If only we had meat to eat! 5We remember the fish we ate in Egypt at no cost—also the cucumbers, melons, leeks, onions and garlic. 6But now we have lost our appetite; we never see anything but this manna!"

7The manna was like coriander seed and looked like resin. 8The people went around gathering it, and then ground it in a hand mill or crushed it in a mortar. They cooked it in a pot or made it into loaves. And it tasted like something made with olive oil. 9When the dew settled on the camp at night, the manna also came down.

10Moses heard the people of every family wailing at the entrance to their tents. The LORD became exceedingly angry, and Moses was troubled. 11He asked the LORD, "Why have you brought this trouble on your servant? What have I done to displease you that you put the burden of all these people on me? 12Did I conceive all these people? Did I give them birth? Why do you tell me to carry them in my arms, as a nurse carries an infant, to the land you promised on oath to their ancestors? 13Where can I get meat for all these people? They keep wailing to me, 'Give us meat to eat!' 14I cannot carry all these people by myself; the burden is too heavy for me. 15If this is how you are going to treat me, please go ahead and kill me—if I have found favor in your eyes—and do not let me face my own ruin."

16The LORD said to Moses: "Bring me seventy of Israel's elders who are known to you as leaders and officials among the people. Have them come to the tent of meeting, that they may stand there with you. 17I will come down and speak with you there, and I will take some of the power of the Spirit that is on you and put it on them. They will share the burden of

[a] 3 *Taberah* means *burning*.

the people with you so that you will not have
to carry it alone.
18“Tell the people: ‘Consecrate yourselves in
preparation for tomorrow, when you will eat
meat. The LORD heard you when you wailed,
“If only we had meat to eat! We were better
off in Egypt!” Now the LORD will give you
meat, and you will eat it. 19You will not eat it
for just one day, or two days, or five, ten or
twenty days, 20but for a whole month—until
it comes out of your nostrils and you loathe
it—because you have rejected the LORD, who
is among you, and have wailed before him,
saying, “Why did we ever leave Egypt?”’”
21But Moses said, “Here I am among six
hundred thousand men on foot, and you say, ‘I
will give them meat to eat for a whole month!’
22Would they have enough if flocks and herds
were slaughtered for them? Would they have
enough if all the fish in the sea were caught
for them?”
23The LORD answered Moses, “Is the LORD’s
arm too short? Now you will see whether or
not what I say will come true for you.”
24So Moses went out and told the people
what the LORD had said. He brought together
seventy of their elders and had them stand
around the tent. 25Then the LORD came down
in the cloud and spoke with him, and he took
some of the power of the Spirit that was on
him and put it on the seventy elders. When the
Spirit rested on them, they prophesied—but
did not do so again.
26However, two men, whose names were Eldad and Medad, had remained in the camp.
They were listed among the elders, but did not
go out to the tent. Yet the Spirit also rested on
them, and they prophesied in the camp. 27A
young man ran and told Moses, “Eldad and
Medad are prophesying in the camp.”
28Joshua son of Nun, who had been Moses’
aide since youth, spoke up and said, “Moses,
my lord, stop them!”
29But Moses replied, “Are you jealous for
my sake? I wish that all the LORD’s people
were prophets and that the LORD would put his
Spirit on them!” 30Then Moses and the elders
of Israel returned to the camp.
31Now a wind went out from the LORD and
drove quail in from the sea. It scattered them
up to two cubits[a] deep all around the camp,
as far as a day’s walk in any direction. 32All
that day and night and all the next day the
people went out and gathered quail. No one
gathered less than ten homers.[b] Then they
spread them out all around the camp. 33But
while the meat was still between their teeth
and before it could be consumed, the anger of
the LORD burned against the people, and he
struck them with a severe plague. 34Therefore
the place was named Kibroth Hattaavah,[c] because there they buried the people who had
craved other food.
35From Kibroth Hattaavah the people traveled to Hazeroth and stayed there.

Miriam and Aaron Oppose Moses

12 Miriam and Aaron began to talk against
Moses because of his Cushite wife, for
he had married a Cushite. 2“Has the LORD spoken only through Moses?” they asked. “Hasn’t
he also spoken through us?” And the LORD
heard this.
3(Now Moses was a very humble man, more
humble than anyone else on the face of the
earth.)
4At once the LORD said to Moses, Aaron and
Miriam, “Come out to the tent of meeting, all
three of you.” So the three of them went out.
5Then the LORD came down in a pillar of cloud;
he stood at the entrance to the tent and summoned Aaron and Miriam. When the two of
them stepped forward, 6he said, “Listen to my
words:

“When there is a prophet among you,
I, the LORD, reveal myself to them in
visions,
I speak to them in dreams.
7But this is not true of my servant Moses;
he is faithful in all my house.
8With him I speak face to face,
clearly and not in riddles;
he sees the form of the LORD.
Why then were you not afraid
to speak against my servant Moses?”

9The anger of the LORD burned against
them, and he left them.
10When the cloud lifted from above the
tent, Miriam’s skin was leprous[d]—it became
as white as snow. Aaron turned toward her
and saw that she had a defiling skin disease,
11and he said to Moses, “Please, my lord, I ask
you not to hold against us the sin we have so
foolishly committed. 12Do not let her be like
a stillborn infant coming from its mother’s
womb with its flesh half eaten away.”
13So Moses cried out to the LORD, “Please,
God, heal her!”
14The LORD replied to Moses, “If her father
had spit in her face, would she not have been
in disgrace for seven days? Confine her outside
the camp for seven days; after that she can
be brought back.” 15So Miriam was confined
outside the camp for seven days, and the people did not move on till she was brought back.
16After that, the people left Hazeroth and
encamped in the Desert of Paran.

Exploring Canaan

13 The LORD said to Moses, 2“Send some
men to explore the land of Canaan,
which I am giving to the Israelites. From each
ancestral tribe send one of its leaders.”
3So at the LORD’s command Moses sent
them out from the Desert of Paran. All of
them were leaders of the Israelites. 4These
are their names:

from the tribe of Reuben, Shammua son
of Zakkur;

[a] *31* That is, about 3 feet or about 90 centimeters [b] *32* That is, possibly about 1 3/4 tons or about 1.6 metric tons [c] *34* *Kibroth Hattaavah* means *graves of craving.* [d] *10* The Hebrew for *leprous* was used for various diseases affecting the skin.

5from the tribe of Simeon, Shaphat son of
Hori;
6from the tribe of Judah, Caleb son of Jephunneh;
7from the tribe of Issachar, Igal son of Joseph;
8from the tribe of Ephraim, Hoshea son of
Nun;
9from the tribe of Benjamin, Palti son of
Raphu;
10from the tribe of Zebulun, Gaddiel son of
Sodi;
11from the tribe of Manasseh (a tribe of Joseph), Gaddi son of Susi;
12from the tribe of Dan, Ammiel son of Ge-
malli;
13from the tribe of Asher, Sethur son of Michael;
14from the tribe of Naphtali, Nahbi son of
Vophsi;
15from the tribe of Gad, Geuel son of Maki.

16These are the names of the men Moses sent
to explore the land. (Moses gave Hoshea son
of Nun the name Joshua.)
17When Moses sent them to explore Canaan,
he said, "Go up through the Negev and on into
the hill country. 18See what the land is like and
whether the people who live there are strong
or weak, few or many. 19What kind of land
do they live in? Is it good or bad? What kind
of towns do they live in? Are they unwalled
or fortified? 20How is the soil? Is it fertile or
poor? Are there trees in it or not? Do your best
to bring back some of the fruit of the land."
(It was the season for the first ripe grapes.)
21So they went up and explored the land
from the Desert of Zin as far as Rehob, toward
Lebo Hamath. 22They went up through the
Negev and came to Hebron, where Ahiman,
Sheshai and Talmai, the descendants of Anak,
lived. (Hebron had been built seven years before Zoan in Egypt.) 23When they reached the
Valley of Eshkol,[a] they cut off a branch bearing a single cluster of grapes. Two of them
carried it on a pole between them, along with
some pomegranates and figs. 24That place was
called the Valley of Eshkol because of the cluster of grapes the Israelites cut off there. 25At
the end of forty days they returned from ex-
ploring the land.

Report on the Exploration

26They came back to Moses and Aaron and
the whole Israelite community at Kadesh in
the Desert of Paran. There they reported to
them and to the whole assembly and showed
them the fruit of the land. 27They gave Moses
this account: "We went into the land to which
you sent us, and it does flow with milk and
honey! Here is its fruit. 28But the people who
live there are powerful, and the cities are fortified and very large. We even saw descendants
of Anak there. 29The Amalekites live in the
Negev; the Hittites, Jebusites and Amorites
live in the hill country; and the Canaanites
live near the sea and along the Jordan."
30Then Caleb silenced the people before Moses and said, "We should go up and take possession of the land, for we can certainly do it."
31But the men who had gone up with him
said, "We can't attack those people; they are
stronger than we are." 32And they spread
among the Israelites a bad report about the
land they had explored. They said, "The land
we explored devours those living in it. All the
people we saw there are of great size. 33We
saw the Nephilim there (the descendants of
Anak come from the Nephilim). We seemed
like grasshoppers in our own eyes, and we
looked the same to them."

The People Rebel

14 That night all the members of the community raised their voices and wept
aloud. 2All the Israelites grumbled against
Moses and Aaron, and the whole assembly
said to them, "If only we had died in Egypt! Or
in this wilderness! 3Why is the LORD bringing
us to this land only to let us fall by the sword?
Our wives and children will be taken as plunder. Wouldn't it be better for us to go back to
Egypt?" 4And they said to each other, "We
should choose a leader and go back to Egypt."
5Then Moses and Aaron fell facedown in
front of the whole Israelite assembly gathered
there. 6Joshua son of Nun and Caleb son of
Jephunneh, who were among those who had
explored the land, tore their clothes 7and said
to the entire Israelite assembly, "The land we
passed through and explored is exceedingly
good. 8If the LORD is pleased with us, he will
lead us into that land, a land flowing with
milk and honey, and will give it to us. 9Only
do not rebel against the LORD. And do not be
afraid of the people of the land, because we
will devour them. Their protection is gone, but
the LORD is with us. Do not be afraid of them."
10But the whole assembly talked about stoning them. Then the glory of the LORD appeared
at the tent of meeting to all the Israelites. 11The
LORD said to Moses, "How long will these people treat me with contempt? How long will
they refuse to believe in me, in spite of all the
signs I have performed among them? 12I will
strike them down with a plague and destroy
them, but I will make you into a nation greater
and stronger than they."
13Moses said to the LORD, "Then the Egyptians will hear about it! By your power you
brought these people up from among them.
14And they will tell the inhabitants of this land
about it. They have already heard that you,
LORD, are with these people and that you,
LORD, have been seen face to face, that your
cloud stays over them, and that you go before
them in a pillar of cloud by day and a pillar
of fire by night. 15If you put all these people
to death, leaving none alive, the nations who
have heard this report about you will say,
16'The LORD was not able to bring these people into the land he promised them on oath, so
he slaughtered them in the wilderness.'
17"Now may the Lord's strength be

[a] 23 *Eshkol* means *cluster*; also in verse 24.

displayed, just as you have declared: 18'The
LORD is slow to anger, abounding in love and
forgiving sin and rebellion. Yet he does not
leave the guilty unpunished; he punishes the
children for the sin of the parents to the third
and fourth generation.' 19In accordance with
your great love, forgive the sin of these people,
just as you have pardoned them from the time
they left Egypt until now."

20The LORD replied, "I have forgiven them,
as you asked. 21Nevertheless, as surely as I
live and as surely as the glory of the LORD fills
the whole earth, 22not one of those who saw
my glory and the signs I performed in Egypt
and in the wilderness but who disobeyed me
and tested me ten times— 23not one of them
will ever see the land I promised on oath to
their ancestors. No one who has treated me
with contempt will ever see it. 24But because
my servant Caleb has a different spirit and
follows me wholeheartedly, I will bring him
into the land he went to, and his descendants
will inherit it. 25Since the Amalekites and the
Canaanites are living in the valleys, turn back
tomorrow and set out toward the desert along
the route to the Red Sea.[a]"

26The LORD said to Moses and Aaron:
27"How long will this wicked community
grumble against me? I have heard the complaints of these grumbling Israelites. 28So tell
them, 'As surely as I live, declares the LORD, I
will do to you the very thing I heard you say:
29In this wilderness your bodies will fall—every one of you twenty years old or more who
was counted in the census and who has grumbled against me. 30Not one of you will enter
the land I swore with uplifted hand to make
your home, except Caleb son of Jephunneh
and Joshua son of Nun. 31As for your children
that you said would be taken as plunder, I will
bring them in to enjoy the land you have rejected. 32But as for you, your bodies will fall in
this wilderness. 33Your children will be shepherds here for forty years, suffering for your
unfaithfulness, until the last of your bodies
lies in the wilderness. 34For forty years—one
year for each of the forty days you explored
the land—you will suffer for your sins and
know what it is like to have me against you.'
35I, the LORD, have spoken, and I will surely
do these things to this whole wicked community, which has banded together against me.
They will meet their end in this wilderness;
here they will die."

36So the men Moses had sent to explore
the land, who returned and made the whole
community grumble against him by spreading a bad report about it— 37these men who
were responsible for spreading the bad report
about the land were struck down and died of
a plague before the LORD. 38Of the men who
went to explore the land, only Joshua son of
Nun and Caleb son of Jephunneh survived.

39When Moses reported this to all the Israelites, they mourned bitterly. 40Early the next
morning they set out for the highest point in
the hill country, saying, "Now we are ready to
go up to the land the LORD promised. Surely
we have sinned!"

41But Moses said, "Why are you disobeying
the LORD's command? This will not succeed!
42Do not go up, because the LORD is not with
you. You will be defeated by your enemies,
43for the Amalekites and the Canaanites will
face you there. Because you have turned away
from the LORD, he will not be with you and
you will fall by the sword."

44Nevertheless, in their presumption they
went up toward the highest point in the hill
country, though neither Moses nor the ark of
the LORD's covenant moved from the camp.
45Then the Amalekites and the Canaanites
who lived in that hill country came down and
attacked them and beat them down all the
way to Hormah.

Supplementary Offerings

15 The LORD said to Moses, 2"Speak to the
Israelites and say to them: 'After you enter the land I am giving you as a home 3and
you present to the LORD food offerings from
the herd or the flock, as an aroma pleasing
to the LORD—whether burnt offerings or sacrifices, for special vows or freewill offerings
or festival offerings— 4then the person who
brings an offering shall present to the LORD
a grain offering of a tenth of an ephah[b] of the
finest flour mixed with a quarter of a hin[c] of
olive oil. 5With each lamb for the burnt offering or the sacrifice, prepare a quarter of a hin
of wine as a drink offering.

6" 'With a ram prepare a grain offering of
two-tenths of an ephah[d] of the finest flour
mixed with a third of a hin[e] of olive oil, 7and
a third of a hin of wine as a drink offering.
Offer it as an aroma pleasing to the LORD.

8" 'When you prepare a young bull as a
burnt offering or sacrifice, for a special vow
or a fellowship offering to the LORD, 9bring
with the bull a grain offering of three-tenths
of an ephah[f] of the finest flour mixed with
half a hin[g] of olive oil, 10and also bring half a
hin of wine as a drink offering. This will be a
food offering, an aroma pleasing to the LORD.
11Each bull or ram, each lamb or young goat,
is to be prepared in this manner. 12Do this for
each one, for as many as you prepare.

13" 'Everyone who is native-born must do
these things in this way when they present
a food offering as an aroma pleasing to the
LORD. 14For the generations to come, whenever
a foreigner or anyone else living among you
presents a food offering as an aroma pleasing
to the LORD, they must do exactly as you do.
15The community is to have the same rules for
you and for the foreigner residing among you;
this is a lasting ordinance for the generations
to come. You and the foreigner shall be the

[a] *25* Or *the Sea of Reeds* [b] *4* That is, probably about 3 1/2 pounds or about 1.6 kilograms [c] *4* That is, about 1 quart or about 1 liter; also in verse 5 [d] *6* That is, probably about 7 pounds or about 3.2 kilograms [e] *6* That is, about 1 1/3 quarts or about 1.3 liters; also in verse 7 [f] *9* That is, probably about 11 pounds or about 5 kilograms [g] *9* That is, about 2 quarts or about 1.9 liters; also in verse 10

same before the LORD: 16The same laws and
regulations will apply both to you and to the
foreigner residing among you.' "
17The LORD said to Moses, 18"Speak to the Israelites and say to them: 'When you enter the
land to which I am taking you 19and you eat
the food of the land, present a portion as an
offering to the LORD. 20Present a loaf from the
first of your ground meal and present it as an
offering from the threshing floor. 21Through-
out the generations to come you are to give
this offering to the LORD from the first of your
ground meal.

Offerings for Unintentional Sins

22" 'Now if you as a community unintentionally fail to keep any of these commands the
LORD gave Moses— 23any of the LORD's commands to you through him, from the day the
LORD gave them and continuing through the
generations to come— 24and if this is done
unintentionally without the community being
aware of it, then the whole community is to
offer a young bull for a burnt offering as an
aroma pleasing to the LORD, along with its
prescribed grain offering and drink offering,
and a male goat for a sin offering.[a] 25The
priest is to make atonement for the whole Israelite community, and they will be forgiven,
for it was not intentional and they have presented to the LORD for their wrong a food offering and a sin offering. 26The whole Israelite community and the foreigners residing
among them will be forgiven, because all the
people were involved in the unintentional
wrong.
27" 'But if just one person sins unintentionally, that person must bring a year-old female
goat for a sin offering. 28The priest is to make
atonement before the LORD for the one who
erred by sinning unintentionally, and when
atonement has been made, that person will be
forgiven. 29One and the same law applies to
everyone who sins unintentionally, whether
a native-born Israelite or a foreigner residing
among you.
30" 'But anyone who sins defiantly, whether
native-born or foreigner, blasphemes the LORD
and must be cut off from the people of Israel.
31Because they have despised the LORD's word
and broken his commands, they must surely
be cut off; their guilt remains on them.' "

The Sabbath-Breaker Put to Death

32While the Israelites were in the wilderness, a man was found gathering wood on
the Sabbath day. 33Those who found him
gathering wood brought him to Moses and
Aaron and the whole assembly, 34and they
kept him in custody, because it was not clear
what should be done to him. 35Then the LORD
said to Moses, "The man must die. The whole
assembly must stone him outside the camp."
36So the assembly took him outside the camp
and stoned him to death, as the LORD commanded Moses.

Tassels on Garments

37The LORD said to Moses, 38"Speak to the
Israelites and say to them: 'Throughout the
generations to come you are to make tassels
on the corners of your garments, with a blue
cord on each tassel. 39You will have these tassels to look at and so you will remember all
the commands of the LORD, that you may obey
them and not prostitute yourselves by chasing
after the lusts of your own hearts and eyes.
40Then you will remember to obey all my commands and will be consecrated to your God.
41I am the LORD your God, who brought you
out of Egypt to be your God. I am the LORD
your God.' "

Korah, Dathan and Abiram

16 Korah son of Izhar, the son of Kohath,
the son of Levi, and certain Reubenites—Dathan and Abiram, sons of Eliab, and
On son of Peleth—became insolent[b] 2and rose
up against Moses. With them were 250 Israelite men, well-known community leaders who
had been appointed members of the council.
3They came as a group to oppose Moses and
Aaron and said to them, "You have gone too
far! The whole community is holy, every one
of them, and the LORD is with them. Why then
do you set yourselves above the LORD's assembly?"
4When Moses heard this, he fell facedown.
5Then he said to Korah and all his followers:
"In the morning the LORD will show who
belongs to him and who is holy, and he will
have that person come near him. The man
he chooses he will cause to come near him.
6You, Korah, and all your followers are to do
this: Take censers 7and tomorrow put burning
coals and incense in them before the LORD.
The man the LORD chooses will be the one
who is holy. You Levites have gone too far!"
8Moses also said to Korah, "Now listen, you
Levites! 9Isn't it enough for you that the God
of Israel has separated you from the rest of
the Israelite community and brought you near
himself to do the work at the LORD's tabernacle and to stand before the community and
minister to them? 10He has brought you and
all your fellow Levites near himself, but now
you are trying to get the priesthood too. 11It is
against the LORD that you and all your followers have banded together. Who is Aaron that
you should grumble against him?"
12Then Moses summoned Dathan and Abiram, the sons of Eliab. But they said, "We
will not come! 13Isn't it enough that you have
brought us up out of a land flowing with milk
and honey to kill us in the wilderness? And
now you also want to lord it over us! 14More-
over, you haven't brought us into a land flowing with milk and honey or given us an inheritance of fields and vineyards. Do you want
to treat these men like slaves[c]? No, we will
not come!"
15Then Moses became very angry and said
to the LORD, "Do not accept their offering. I

[a] 24 Or *purification offering*; also in verses 25 and 27 [b] 1 Or *Peleth—took men* [c] 14 Or *to deceive these men*; Hebrew *Will you gouge out the eyes of these men*

have not taken so much as a donkey from them, nor have I wronged any of them."

16 Moses said to Korah, "You and all your followers are to appear before the LORD tomorrow—you and they and Aaron. 17 Each man is to take his censer and put incense in it—250 censers in all—and present it before the LORD. You and Aaron are to present your censers also." 18 So each of them took his censer, put burning coals and incense in it, and stood with Moses and Aaron at the entrance to the tent of meeting. 19 When Korah had gathered all his followers in opposition to them at the entrance to the tent of meeting, the glory of the LORD appeared to the entire assembly. 20 The LORD said to Moses and Aaron, 21 "Separate yourselves from this assembly so I can put an end to them at once."

22 But Moses and Aaron fell facedown and cried out, "O God, the God who gives breath to all living things, will you be angry with the entire assembly when only one man sins?"

23 Then the LORD said to Moses, 24 "Say to the assembly, 'Move away from the tents of Korah, Dathan and Abiram.' "

25 Moses got up and went to Dathan and Abiram, and the elders of Israel followed him. 26 He warned the assembly, "Move back from the tents of these wicked men! Do not touch anything belonging to them, or you will be swept away because of all their sins." 27 So they moved away from the tents of Korah, Dathan and Abiram. Dathan and Abiram had come out and were standing with their wives, children and little ones at the entrances to their tents.

28 Then Moses said, "This is how you will know that the LORD has sent me to do all these things and that it was not my idea: 29 If these men die a natural death and suffer the fate of all mankind, then the LORD has not sent me. 30 But if the LORD brings about something totally new, and the earth opens its mouth and swallows them, with everything that belongs to them, and they go down alive into the realm of the dead, then you will know that these men have treated the LORD with contempt."

31 As soon as he finished saying all this, the ground under them split apart 32 and the earth opened its mouth and swallowed them and their households, and all those associated with Korah, together with their possessions. 33 They went down alive into the realm of the dead, with everything they owned; the earth closed over them, and they perished and were gone from the community. 34 At their cries, all the Israelites around them fled, shouting, "The earth is going to swallow us too!"

35 And fire came out from the LORD and consumed the 250 men who were offering the incense.

36 The LORD said to Moses, 37 "Tell Eleazar son of Aaron, the priest, to remove the censers from the charred remains and scatter the coals some distance away, for the censers are holy— 38 the censers of the men who sinned at the cost of their lives. Hammer the censers into sheets to overlay the altar, for they were presented before the LORD and have become holy. Let them be a sign to the Israelites."

39 So Eleazar the priest collected the bronze censers brought by those who had been burned to death, and he had them hammered out to overlay the altar, 40 as the LORD directed him through Moses. This was to remind the Israelites that no one except a descendant of Aaron should come to burn incense before the LORD, or he would become like Korah and his followers.

41 The next day the whole Israelite community grumbled against Moses and Aaron. "You have killed the LORD's people," they said.

42 But when the assembly gathered in opposition to Moses and Aaron and turned toward the tent of meeting, suddenly the cloud covered it and the glory of the LORD appeared. 43 Then Moses and Aaron went to the front of the tent of meeting, 44 and the LORD said to Moses, 45 "Get away from this assembly so I can put an end to them at once." And they fell facedown.

46 Then Moses said to Aaron, "Take your censer and put incense in it, along with burning coals from the altar, and hurry to the assembly to make atonement for them. Wrath has come out from the LORD; the plague has started." 47 So Aaron did as Moses said, and ran into the midst of the assembly. The plague had already started among the people, but Aaron offered the incense and made atonement for them. 48 He stood between the living and the dead, and the plague stopped. 49 But 14,700 people died from the plague, in addition to those who had died because of Korah. 50 Then Aaron returned to Moses at the entrance to the tent of meeting, for the plague had stopped.[a]

The Budding of Aaron's Staff

17[b] The LORD said to Moses, 2 "Speak to the Israelites and get twelve staffs from them, one from the leader of each of their ancestral tribes. Write the name of each man on his staff. 3 On the staff of Levi write Aaron's name, for there must be one staff for the head of each ancestral tribe. 4 Place them in the tent of meeting in front of the ark of the covenant law, where I meet with you. 5 The staff belonging to the man I choose will sprout, and I will rid myself of this constant grumbling against you by the Israelites."

6 So Moses spoke to the Israelites, and their leaders gave him twelve staffs, one for the leader of each of their ancestral tribes, and Aaron's staff was among them. 7 Moses placed the staffs before the LORD in the tent of the covenant law.

8 The next day Moses entered the tent and saw that Aaron's staff, which represented the tribe of Levi, had not only sprouted but had budded, blossomed and produced almonds. 9 Then Moses brought out all the staffs from the LORD's presence to all the Israelites. They

[a] *50* In Hebrew texts 16:36-50 is numbered 17:1-15.

[b] In Hebrew texts 17:1-13 is numbered 17:16-28.

looked at them, and each of the leaders took
his own staff.
10The LORD said to Moses, "Put back Aaron's staff in front of the ark of the covenant
law, to be kept as a sign to the rebellious. This
will put an end to their grumbling against me,
so that they will not die." 11Moses did just as
the LORD commanded him.
12The Israelites said to Moses, "We will die!
We are lost, we are all lost! 13Anyone who
even comes near the tabernacle of the LORD
will die. Are we all going to die?"

Duties of Priests and Levites

18 The LORD said to Aaron, "You, your
sons and your family are to bear the responsibility for offenses connected with the
sanctuary, and you and your sons alone are to
bear the responsibility for offenses connected
with the priesthood. 2Bring your fellow Levites from your ancestral tribe to join you and
assist you when you and your sons minister
before the tent of the covenant law. 3They are
to be responsible to you and are to perform
all the duties of the tent, but they must not go
near the furnishings of the sanctuary or the
altar. Otherwise both they and you will die.
4They are to join you and be responsible for
the care of the tent of meeting—all the work
at the tent—and no one else may come near
where you are.
5"You are to be responsible for the care of
the sanctuary and the altar, so that my wrath
will not fall on the Israelites again. 6I myself
have selected your fellow Levites from among
the Israelites as a gift to you, dedicated to the
LORD to do the work at the tent of meeting.
7But only you and your sons may serve as
priests in connection with everything at the
altar and inside the curtain. I am giving you
the service of the priesthood as a gift. Anyone else who comes near the sanctuary is to
be put to death."

Offerings for Priests and Levites

8Then the LORD said to Aaron, "I myself
have put you in charge of the offerings presented to me; all the holy offerings the Israelites give me I give to you and your sons as
your portion, your perpetual share. 9You are
to have the part of the most holy offerings
that is kept from the fire. From all the gifts
they bring me as most holy offerings, whether
grain or sin[a] or guilt offerings, that part belongs to you and your sons. 10Eat it as something most holy; every male shall eat it. You
must regard it as holy.
11"This also is yours: whatever is set aside
from the gifts of all the wave offerings of the
Israelites. I give this to you and your sons and
daughters as your perpetual share. Everyone
in your household who is ceremonially clean
may eat it.
12"I give you all the finest olive oil and all
the finest new wine and grain they give the
LORD as the firstfruits of their harvest. 13All
the land's firstfruits that they bring to the
LORD will be yours. Everyone in your household who is ceremonially clean may eat it.
14"Everything in Israel that is devoted[b] to
the LORD is yours. 15The first offspring of every womb, both human and animal, that is
offered to the LORD is yours. But you must
redeem every firstborn son and every firstborn male of unclean animals. 16When they
are a month old, you must redeem them at the
redemption price set at five shekels[c] of silver, according to the sanctuary shekel, which
weighs twenty gerahs.
17"But you must not redeem the firstborn of
a cow, a sheep or a goat; they are holy. Splash
their blood against the altar and burn their
fat as a food offering, an aroma pleasing to
the LORD. 18Their meat is to be yours, just as
the breast of the wave offering and the right
thigh are yours. 19Whatever is set aside from
the holy offerings the Israelites present to the
LORD I give to you and your sons and daughters as your perpetual share. It is an everlasting covenant of salt before the LORD for both
you and your offspring."
20The LORD said to Aaron, "You will have
no inheritance in their land, nor will you have
any share among them; I am your share and
your inheritance among the Israelites.
21"I give to the Levites all the tithes in Israel
as their inheritance in return for the work they
do while serving at the tent of meeting. 22From
now on the Israelites must not go near the tent
of meeting, or they will bear the consequences
of their sin and will die. 23It is the Levites who
are to do the work at the tent of meeting and
bear the responsibility for any offenses they
commit against it. This is a lasting ordinance
for the generations to come. They will receive
no inheritance among the Israelites. 24Instead,
I give to the Levites as their inheritance the
tithes that the Israelites present as an offering
to the LORD. That is why I said concerning
them: 'They will have no inheritance among
the Israelites.'"
25The LORD said to Moses, 26"Speak to the
Levites and say to them: 'When you receive
from the Israelites the tithe I give you as your
inheritance, you must present a tenth of that
tithe as the LORD's offering. 27Your offering
will be reckoned to you as grain from the
threshing floor or juice from the winepress.
28In this way you also will present an offering
to the LORD from all the tithes you receive from
the Israelites. From these tithes you must give
the LORD's portion to Aaron the priest. 29You
must present as the LORD's portion the best
and holiest part of everything given to you.'
30"Say to the Levites: 'When you present
the best part, it will be reckoned to you as the
product of the threshing floor or the winepress. 31You and your households may eat
the rest of it anywhere, for it is your wages for your work at the tent of meeting. 32By
presenting the best part of it you will not be

[a] *9* Or *purification* [b] *14* The Hebrew term refers to the irrevocable giving over of things or persons to the LORD. [c] *16* That is, about 2 ounces or about 58 grams

guilty in this matter; then you will not defile the holy offerings of the Israelites, and you will not die.’ ”

The Water of Cleansing

19 The LORD said to Moses and Aaron: 2“This is a requirement of the law that the LORD has commanded: Tell the Israelites to bring you a red heifer without defect or blemish and that has never been under a yoke. 3Give it to Eleazar the priest; it is to be taken outside the camp and slaughtered in his presence. 4Then Eleazar the priest is to take some of its blood on his finger and sprinkle it seven times toward the front of the tent of meeting. 5While he watches, the heifer is to be burned—its hide, flesh, blood and intestines. 6The priest is to take some cedar wood, hyssop and scarlet wool and throw them onto the burning heifer. 7After that, the priest must wash his clothes and bathe himself with water. He may then come into the camp, but he will be ceremonially unclean till evening. 8The man who burns it must also wash his clothes and bathe with water, and he too will be unclean till evening.

9“A man who is clean shall gather up the ashes of the heifer and put them in a ceremonially clean place outside the camp. They are to be kept by the Israelite community for use in the water of cleansing; it is for purification from sin. 10The man who gathers up the ashes of the heifer must also wash his clothes, and he too will be unclean till evening. This will be a lasting ordinance both for the Israelites and for the foreigners residing among them.

11“Whoever touches a human corpse will be unclean for seven days. 12They must purify themselves with the water on the third day and on the seventh day; then they will be clean. But if they do not purify themselves on the third and seventh days, they will not be clean. 13If they fail to purify themselves after touching a human corpse, they defile the LORD’s tabernacle. They must be cut off from Israel. Because the water of cleansing has not been sprinkled on them, they are unclean; their uncleanness remains on them.

14“This is the law that applies when a person dies in a tent: Anyone who enters the tent and anyone who is in it will be unclean for seven days, 15and every open container without a lid fastened on it will be unclean.

16“Anyone out in the open who touches someone who has been killed with a sword or someone who has died a natural death, or anyone who touches a human bone or a grave, will be unclean for seven days.

17“For the unclean person, put some ashes from the burned purification offering into a jar and pour fresh water over them. 18Then a man who is ceremonially clean is to take some hyssop, dip it in the water and sprinkle the tent and all the furnishings and the people who were there. He must also sprinkle anyone who has touched a human bone or a grave or anyone who has been killed or anyone who has died a natural death. 19The man who is clean is to sprinkle those who are unclean on the third and seventh days, and on the seventh day he is to purify them. Those who are being cleansed must wash their clothes and bathe with water, and that evening they will be clean. 20But if those who are unclean do not purify themselves, they must be cut off from the community, because they have defiled the sanctuary of the LORD. The water of cleansing has not been sprinkled on them, and they are unclean. 21This is a lasting ordinance for them.

“The man who sprinkles the water of cleansing must also wash his clothes, and anyone who touches the water of cleansing will be unclean till evening. 22Anything that an unclean person touches becomes unclean, and anyone who touches it becomes unclean till evening.”

Water From the Rock

20 In the first month the whole Israelite community arrived at the Desert of Zin, and they stayed at Kadesh. There Miriam died and was buried.

2Now there was no water for the community, and the people gathered in opposition to Moses and Aaron. 3They quarreled with Moses and said, “If only we had died when our brothers fell dead before the LORD! 4Why did you bring the LORD’s community into this wilderness, that we and our livestock should die here? 5Why did you bring us up out of Egypt to this terrible place? It has no grain or figs, grapevines or pomegranates. And there is no water to drink!”

6Moses and Aaron went from the assembly to the entrance to the tent of meeting and fell facedown, and the glory of the LORD appeared to them. 7The LORD said to Moses, 8“Take the staff, and you and your brother Aaron gather the assembly together. Speak to that rock before their eyes and it will pour out its water. You will bring water out of the rock for the community so they and their livestock can drink.”

9So Moses took the staff from the LORD’s presence, just as he commanded him. 10He and Aaron gathered the assembly together in front of the rock and Moses said to them, “Listen, you rebels, must we bring you water out of this rock?” 11Then Moses raised his arm and struck the rock twice with his staff. Water gushed out, and the community and their livestock drank.

12But the LORD said to Moses and Aaron, “Because you did not trust in me enough to honor me as holy in the sight of the Israelites, you will not bring this community into the land I give them.”

13These were the waters of Meribah,[a] where the Israelites quarreled with the LORD and where he was proved holy among them.

Edom Denies Israel Passage

14Moses sent messengers from Kadesh to the king of Edom, saying:

[a] *13 Meribah* means *quarreling.*

"This is what your brother Israel says:
You know about all the hardships that
have come on us. [15]Our ancestors went
down into Egypt, and we lived there
many years. The Egyptians mistreated
us and our ancestors, [16]but when we cried
out to the LORD, he heard our cry and sent
an angel and brought us out of Egypt.

"Now we are here at Kadesh, a town on
the edge of your territory. [17]Please let us
pass through your country. We will not
go through any field or vineyard, or drink
water from any well. We will travel along
the King's Highway and not turn to the
right or to the left until we have passed
through your territory."

[18]But Edom answered:

"You may not pass through here; if you
try, we will march out and attack you
with the sword."

[19]The Israelites replied:

"We will go along the main road, and
if we or our livestock drink any of your
water, we will pay for it. We only want
to pass through on foot—nothing else."

[20]Again they answered:

"You may not pass through."

Then Edom came out against them with a
large and powerful army. [21]Since Edom refused to let them go through their territory,
Israel turned away from them.

The Death of Aaron

[22]The whole Israelite community set out
from Kadesh and came to Mount Hor. [23]At
Mount Hor, near the border of Edom, the LORD
said to Moses and Aaron, [24]"Aaron will be
gathered to his people. He will not enter the
land I give the Israelites, because both of you
rebelled against my command at the waters of
Meribah. [25]Get Aaron and his son Eleazar and
take them up Mount Hor. [26]Remove Aaron's
garments and put them on his son Eleazar,
for Aaron will be gathered to his people; he
will die there."

[27]Moses did as the LORD commanded: They
went up Mount Hor in the sight of the whole
community. [28]Moses removed Aaron's garments and put them on his son Eleazar. And
Aaron died there on top of the mountain.
Then Moses and Eleazar came down from the
mountain, [29]and when the whole community
learned that Aaron had died, all the Israelites
mourned for him thirty days.

Arad Destroyed

21 When the Canaanite king of Arad,
who lived in the Negev, heard that Israel was coming along the road to Atharim,
he attacked the Israelites and captured some
of them. [2]Then Israel made this vow to the
LORD: "If you will deliver these people into our
hands, we will totally destroy[a] their cities."
[3]The LORD listened to Israel's plea and gave
the Canaanites over to them. They completely
destroyed them and their towns; so the place
was named Hormah.[b]

The Bronze Snake

[4]They traveled from Mount Hor along the
route to the Red Sea,[c] to go around Edom.
But the people grew impatient on the way;
[5]they spoke against God and against Moses,
and said, "Why have you brought us up out
of Egypt to die in the wilderness? There is no
bread! There is no water! And we detest this
miserable food!"

[6]Then the LORD sent venomous snakes
among them; they bit the people and many
Israelites died. [7]The people came to Moses
and said, "We sinned when we spoke against
the LORD and against you. Pray that the LORD
will take the snakes away from us." So Moses
prayed for the people.

[8]The LORD said to Moses, "Make a snake
and put it up on a pole; anyone who is bitten
can look at it and live." [9]So Moses made a
bronze snake and put it up on a pole. Then
when anyone was bitten by a snake and
looked at the bronze snake, they lived.

The Journey to Moab

[10]The Israelites moved on and camped at
Oboth. [11]Then they set out from Oboth and
camped in Iye Abarim, in the wilderness that
faces Moab toward the sunrise. [12]From there
they moved on and camped in the Zered Valley. [13]They set out from there and camped
alongside the Arnon, which is in the wilderness extending into Amorite territory. The
Arnon is the border of Moab, between Moab
and the Amorites. [14]That is why the Book of
the Wars of the LORD says:

". . . Zahab[d] in Suphah and the ravines,
the Arnon [15]and[e] the slopes of the
ravines
that lead to the settlement of Ar
and lie along the border of Moab."

[16]From there they continued on to Beer, the
well where the LORD said to Moses, "Gather
the people together and I will give them water."

[17]Then Israel sang this song:

"Spring up, O well!
Sing about it,
[18]about the well that the princes dug,
that the nobles of the people sank—
the nobles with scepters and staffs."

Then they went from the wilderness to Mattanah, [19]from Mattanah to Nahaliel, from
Nahaliel to Bamoth, [20]and from Bamoth to
the valley in Moab where the top of Pisgah
overlooks the wasteland.

[a] 2 The Hebrew term refers to the irrevocable giving over of things or persons to the LORD, often by totally destroying them; also in verse 3. [b] 3 *Hormah* means *destruction.* [c] 4 *Or the Sea of Reeds*
[d] 14 Septuagint; Hebrew *Waheb* [e] 14,15 Or *"I have been given from Suphah and the ravines / of the Arnon* [15]*to*

Defeat of Sihon and Og

21Israel sent messengers to say to Sihon
king of the Amorites:

> 22"Let us pass through your country.
> We will not turn aside into any field or
> vineyard, or drink water from any well.
> We will travel along the King's Highway
> until we have passed through your ter-
> ritory."

23But Sihon would not let Israel pass
through his territory. He mustered his entire
army and marched out into the wilderness
against Israel. When he reached Jahaz, he
fought with Israel. 24Israel, however, put him
to the sword and took over his land from the
Arnon to the Jabbok, but only as far as the
Ammonites, because their border was fortified. 25Israel captured all the cities of the Amorites and occupied them, including Heshbon
and all its surrounding settlements. 26Hesh-
bon was the city of Sihon king of the Amorites, who had fought against the former king
of Moab and had taken from him all his land
as far as the Arnon.
27That is why the poets say:

"Come to Heshbon and let it be rebuilt;
 let Sihon's city be restored.

28"Fire went out from Heshbon,
  a blaze from the city of Sihon.
 It consumed Ar of Moab,
  the citizens of Arnon's heights.
29Woe to you, Moab!
  You are destroyed, people of Chemosh!
 He has given up his sons as fugitives
  and his daughters as captives
  to Sihon king of the Amorites.

30"But we have overthrown them;
  Heshbon's dominion has been
   destroyed all the way to Dibon.
 We have demolished them as far as
   Nophah,
  which extends to Medeba."

31So Israel settled in the land of the Amorites.
32After Moses had sent spies to Jazer, the Israelites captured its surrounding settlements
and drove out the Amorites who were there.
33Then they turned and went up along the road
toward Bashan, and Og king of Bashan and
his whole army marched out to meet them in
battle at Edrei.
34The LORD said to Moses, "Do not be afraid
of him, for I have delivered him into your
hands, along with his whole army and his
land. Do to him what you did to Sihon king
of the Amorites, who reigned in Heshbon."
35So they struck him down, together with
his sons and his whole army, leaving them
no survivors. And they took possession of
his land.

Balak Summons Balaam

22 Then the Israelites traveled to the plains
of Moab and camped along the Jordan
across from Jericho.

2Now Balak son of Zippor saw all that Israel had done to the Amorites, 3and Moab was
terrified because there were so many people.
Indeed, Moab was filled with dread because
of the Israelites.
4The Moabites said to the elders of Midian, "This horde is going to lick up everything
around us, as an ox licks up the grass of the
field."
So Balak son of Zippor, who was king of
Moab at that time, 5sent messengers to summon Balaam son of Beor, who was at Pethor,
near the Euphrates River, in his native land.
Balak said:

> "A people has come out of Egypt; they
> cover the face of the land and have settled
> next to me. 6Now come and put a curse
> on these people, because they are too
> powerful for me. Perhaps then I will be
> able to defeat them and drive them out
> of the land. For I know that whoever you
> bless is blessed, and whoever you curse
> is cursed."

7The elders of Moab and Midian left, taking
with them the fee for divination. When they
came to Balaam, they told him what Balak
had said.
8"Spend the night here," Balaam said to
them, "and I will report back to you with the
answer the LORD gives me." So the Moabite
officials stayed with him.
9God came to Balaam and asked, "Who are
these men with you?"
10Balaam said to God, "Balak son of Zippor, king of Moab, sent me this message: 11'A
people that has come out of Egypt covers the
face of the land. Now come and put a curse
on them for me. Perhaps then I will be able to
fight them and drive them away.'"
12But God said to Balaam, "Do not go with
them. You must not put a curse on those people, because they are blessed."
13The next morning Balaam got up and
said to Balak's officials, "Go back to your
own country, for the LORD has refused to let
me go with you."
14So the Moabite officials returned to Balak
and said, "Balaam refused to come with us."
15Then Balak sent other officials, more numerous and more distinguished than the first.
16They came to Balaam and said:

> "This is what Balak son of Zippor says:
> Do not let anything keep you from com-
> ing to me, 17because I will reward you
> handsomely and do whatever you say.
> Come and put a curse on these people
> for me."

18But Balaam answered them, "Even if Balak gave me all the silver and gold in his palace, I could not do anything great or small to
go beyond the command of the LORD my God.
19Now spend the night here so that I can find
out what else the LORD will tell me."
20That night God came to Balaam and said,
"Since these men have come to summon you,
go with them, but do only what I tell you."

Balaam's Donkey

21 Balaam got up in the morning, saddled his
donkey and went with the Moabite officials.
22 But God was very angry when he went, and
the angel of the LORD stood in the road to oppose him. Balaam was riding on his donkey,
and his two servants were with him. 23 When
the donkey saw the angel of the LORD standing
in the road with a drawn sword in his hand, it
turned off the road into a field. Balaam beat
it to get it back on the road.

24 Then the angel of the LORD stood in a narrow path through the vineyards, with walls
on both sides. 25 When the donkey saw the angel of the LORD, it pressed close to the wall,
crushing Balaam's foot against it. So he beat
the donkey again.

26 Then the angel of the LORD moved on
ahead and stood in a narrow place where
there was no room to turn, either to the right
or to the left. 27 When the donkey saw the angel
of the LORD, it lay down under Balaam, and he
was angry and beat it with his staff. 28 Then
the LORD opened the donkey's mouth, and it
said to Balaam, "What have I done to you to
make you beat me these three times?"

29 Balaam answered the donkey, "You have
made a fool of me! If only I had a sword in my
hand, I would kill you right now."

30 The donkey said to Balaam, "Am I not
your own donkey, which you have always
ridden, to this day? Have I been in the habit
of doing this to you?"

"No," he said.

31 Then the LORD opened Balaam's eyes, and
he saw the angel of the LORD standing in the
road with his sword drawn. So he bowed low
and fell facedown.

32 The angel of the LORD asked him, "Why
have you beaten your donkey these three
times? I have come here to oppose you because your path is a reckless one before me.[a]
33 The donkey saw me and turned away from
me these three times. If it had not turned
away, I would certainly have killed you by
now, but I would have spared it."

34 Balaam said to the angel of the LORD, "I
have sinned. I did not realize you were standing in the road to oppose me. Now if you are
displeased, I will go back."

35 The angel of the LORD said to Balaam, "Go
with the men, but speak only what I tell you."
So Balaam went with Balak's officials.

36 When Balak heard that Balaam was coming, he went out to meet him at the Moabite
town on the Arnon border, at the edge of his
territory. 37 Balak said to Balaam, "Did I not
send you an urgent summons? Why didn't
you come to me? Am I really not able to reward you?"

38 "Well, I have come to you now," Balaam
replied. "But I can't say whatever I please. I
must speak only what God puts in my mouth."

39 Then Balaam went with Balak to Kiriath
Huzoth. 40 Balak sacrificed cattle and sheep,
and gave some to Balaam and the officials
who were with him. 41 The next morning Balak took Balaam up to Bamoth Baal, and from
there he could see the outskirts of the Israelite camp.

Balaam's First Message

23 Balaam said, "Build me seven altars
here, and prepare seven bulls and sev-
en rams for me." 2 Balak did as Balaam said,
and the two of them offered a bull and a ram
on each altar.

3 Then Balaam said to Balak, "Stay here beside your offering while I go aside. Perhaps
the LORD will come to meet with me. Whatever
he reveals to me I will tell you." Then he went
off to a barren height.

4 God met with him, and Balaam said, "I
have prepared seven altars, and on each altar I have offered a bull and a ram."

5 The LORD put a word in Balaam's mouth
and said, "Go back to Balak and give him this
word."

6 So he went back to him and found him
standing beside his offering, with all the
Moabite officials. 7 Then Balaam spoke his
message:

"Balak brought me from Aram,
  the king of Moab from the eastern
    mountains.
'Come,' he said, 'curse Jacob for me;
  come, denounce Israel.'
8 How can I curse
  those whom God has not cursed?
How can I denounce
  those whom the LORD has not
    denounced?
9 From the rocky peaks I see them,
  from the heights I view them.
I see a people who live apart
  and do not consider themselves one of
    the nations.
10 Who can count the dust of Jacob
  or number even a fourth of Israel?
Let me die the death of the righteous,
  and may my final end be like theirs!"

11 Balak said to Balaam, "What have you
done to me? I brought you to curse my enemies, but you have done nothing but bless
them!"

12 He answered, "Must I not speak what the
LORD puts in my mouth?"

Balaam's Second Message

13 Then Balak said to him, "Come with me
to another place where you can see them; you
will not see them all but only the outskirts of
their camp. And from there, curse them for
me." 14 So he took him to the field of Zophim on
the top of Pisgah, and there he built seven altars and offered a bull and a ram on each altar.

15 Balaam said to Balak, "Stay here beside
your offering while I meet with him over
there."

16 The LORD met with Balaam and put a word
in his mouth and said, "Go back to Balak and
give him this word."

[a] 32 The meaning of the Hebrew for this clause is uncertain.

17So he went to him and found him standing
beside his offering, with the Moabite officials.
Balak asked him, "What did the LORD say?"
18Then he spoke his message:

"Arise, Balak, and listen;
hear me, son of Zippor.
19God is not human, that he should lie,
not a human being, that he should
change his mind.
Does he speak and then not act?
Does he promise and not fulfill?
20I have received a command to bless;
he has blessed, and I cannot change it.

21"No misfortune is seen in Jacob,
no misery observed[a] in Israel.
The LORD their God is with them;
the shout of the King is among them.
22God brought them out of Egypt;
they have the strength of a wild ox.
23There is no divination against[b] Jacob,
no evil omens against[b] Israel.
It will now be said of Jacob
and of Israel, 'See what God has
done!'
24The people rise like a lioness;
they rouse themselves like a lion
that does not rest till it devours its prey
and drinks the blood of its victims."

25Then Balak said to Balaam, "Neither curse
them at all nor bless them at all!"
26Balaam answered, "Did I not tell you I
must do whatever the LORD says?"

Balaam's Third Message

27Then Balak said to Balaam, "Come, let
me take you to another place. Perhaps it will
please God to let you curse them for me from
there." 28And Balak took Balaam to the top of
Peor, overlooking the wasteland.
29Balaam said, "Build me seven altars here,
and prepare seven bulls and seven rams for
me." 30Balak did as Balaam had said, and offered a bull and a ram on each altar.

24 Now when Balaam saw that it pleased
the LORD to bless Israel, he did not resort
to divination as at other times, but turned his
face toward the wilderness. 2When Balaam
looked out and saw Israel encamped tribe by
tribe, the Spirit of God came on him 3and he
spoke his message:

"The prophecy of Balaam son of Beor,
the prophecy of one whose eye sees
clearly,
4the prophecy of one who hears the words
of God,
who sees a vision from the Almighty,[c]
who falls prostrate, and whose eyes are
opened:

5"How beautiful are your tents, Jacob,
your dwelling places, Israel!

6"Like valleys they spread out,
like gardens beside a river,
like aloes planted by the LORD,
like cedars beside the waters.
7Water will flow from their buckets;
their seed will have abundant water.

"Their king will be greater than Agag;
their kingdom will be exalted.

8"God brought them out of Egypt;
they have the strength of a wild ox.
They devour hostile nations
and break their bones in pieces;
with their arrows they pierce them.
9Like a lion they crouch and lie down,
like a lioness—who dares to rouse
them?

"May those who bless you be blessed
and those who curse you be cursed!"

10Then Balak's anger burned against Balaam. He struck his hands together and said
to him, "I summoned you to curse my enemies, but you have blessed them these three
times. 11Now leave at once and go home! I said
I would reward you handsomely, but the LORD
has kept you from being rewarded."
12Balaam answered Balak, "Did I not tell
the messengers you sent me, 13'Even if Balak
gave me all the silver and gold in his palace,
I could not do anything of my own accord,
good or bad, to go beyond the command of
the LORD—and I must say only what the LORD
says'? 14Now I am going back to my people,
but come, let me warn you of what this people
will do to your people in days to come."

Balaam's Fourth Message

15Then he spoke his message:

"The prophecy of Balaam son of Beor,
the prophecy of one whose eye sees
clearly,
16the prophecy of one who hears the words
of God,
who has knowledge from the Most High,
who sees a vision from the Almighty,
who falls prostrate, and whose eyes are
opened:

17"I see him, but not now;
I behold him, but not near.
A star will come out of Jacob;
a scepter will rise out of Israel.
He will crush the foreheads of Moab,
the skulls[d] of[e] all the people of Sheth.[f]
18Edom will be conquered;
Seir, his enemy, will be conquered,
but Israel will grow strong.
19A ruler will come out of Jacob
and destroy the survivors of the city."

Balaam's Fifth Message

20Then Balaam saw Amalek and spoke his
message:

"Amalek was first among the nations,
but their end will be utter destruction."

[a] 21 Or *He has not looked on Jacob's offenses / or on the wrongs found* [b] 23 Or *in* [c] 4 Hebrew *Shaddai*; also in verse 16 [d] 17 Samaritan Pentateuch (see also Jer. 48:45); the meaning of the word in the Masoretic Text is uncertain. [e] 17 Or possibly *Moab, / batter* [f] 17 Or *all the noisy boasters*

Balaam's Sixth Message

21Then he saw the Kenites and spoke his
message:

"Your dwelling place is secure,
your nest is set in a rock;
22yet you Kenites will be destroyed
when Ashur takes you captive."

Balaam's Seventh Message

23Then he spoke his message:

"Alas! Who can live when God does this?[a]
24 Ships will come from the shores of
Cyprus;
they will subdue Ashur and Eber,
but they too will come to ruin."

25Then Balaam got up and returned home,
and Balak went his own way.

Moab Seduces Israel

25 While Israel was staying in Shittim, the
men began to indulge in sexual immorality with Moabite women, 2who invited them
to the sacrifices to their gods. The people ate
the sacrificial meal and bowed down before
these gods. 3So Israel yoked themselves to the
Baal of Peor. And the LORD's anger burned
against them.

4The LORD said to Moses, "Take all the leaders of these people, kill them and expose them
in broad daylight before the LORD, so that the
LORD's fierce anger may turn away from Israel."

5So Moses said to Israel's judges, "Each of
you must put to death those of your people
who have yoked themselves to the Baal of
Peor."

6Then an Israelite man brought into the
camp a Midianite woman right before the
eyes of Moses and the whole assembly of Israel while they were weeping at the entrance
to the tent of meeting. 7When Phinehas son
of Eleazar, the son of Aaron, the priest, saw
this, he left the assembly, took a spear in his
hand 8and followed the Israelite into the tent.
He drove the spear into both of them, right
through the Israelite man and into the woman's stomach. Then the plague against the
Israelites was stopped; 9but those who died
in the plague numbered 24,000.

10The LORD said to Moses, 11"Phinehas son
of Eleazar, the son of Aaron, the priest, has
turned my anger away from the Israelites.
Since he was as zealous for my honor among
them as I am, I did not put an end to them in
my zeal. 12Therefore tell him I am making
my covenant of peace with him. 13He and his
descendants will have a covenant of a lasting priesthood, because he was zealous for
the honor of his God and made atonement
for the Israelites."

14The name of the Israelite who was killed
with the Midianite woman was Zimri son of
Salu, the leader of a Simeonite family. 15And
the name of the Midianite woman who was put
to death was Kozbi daughter of Zur, a tribal
chief of a Midianite family.

16The LORD said to Moses, 17"Treat the Midianites as enemies and kill them. 18They treated you as enemies when they deceived you in
the Peor incident involving their sister Kozbi,
the daughter of a Midianite leader, the woman who was killed when the plague came as
a result of that incident."

The Second Census

26 After the plague the LORD said to Moses
and Eleazar son of Aaron, the priest,
2"Take a census of the whole Israelite community by families—all those twenty years old
or more who are able to serve in the army of
Israel." 3So on the plains of Moab by the Jordan across from Jericho, Moses and Eleazar
the priest spoke with them and said, 4"Take a
census of the men twenty years old or more,
as the LORD commanded Moses."

These were the Israelites who came out of
Egypt:

5The descendants of Reuben, the firstborn son
of Israel, were:
through Hanok, the Hanokite clan;
through Pallu, the Palluite clan;
6through Hezron, the Hezronite clan;
through Karmi, the Karmite clan.
7These were the clans of Reuben; those numbered were 43,730.

8The son of Pallu was Eliab, 9and the sons
of Eliab were Nemuel, Dathan and Abiram.
The same Dathan and Abiram were the community officials who rebelled against Moses
and Aaron and were among Korah's followers
when they rebelled against the LORD. 10The
earth opened its mouth and swallowed them
along with Korah, whose followers died when
the fire devoured the 250 men. And they
served as a warning sign. 11The line of Korah, however, did not die out.

12The descendants of Simeon by their clans
were:
through Nemuel, the Nemuelite clan;
through Jamin, the Jaminite clan;
through Jakin, the Jakinite clan;
13through Zerah, the Zerahite clan;
through Shaul, the Shaulite clan.
14These were the clans of Simeon; those numbered were 22,200.

15The descendants of Gad by their clans were:
through Zephon, the Zephonite clan;
through Haggi, the Haggite clan;
through Shuni, the Shunite clan;
16through Ozni, the Oznite clan;
through Eri, the Erite clan;
17through Arodi,[b] the Arodite clan;
through Areli, the Arelite clan.
18These were the clans of Gad; those numbered were 40,500.

19Er and Onan were sons of Judah, but they
died in Canaan.

[a] 23 Masoretic Text; with a different word division of the Hebrew *The people from the islands will gather from the north.* [b] 17 Samaritan Pentateuch and Syriac (see also Gen. 46:16); Masoretic Text *Arod*

20The descendants of Judah by their clans were:
through Shelah, the Shelanite clan;
through Perez, the Perezite clan;
through Zerah, the Zerahite clan.
21The descendants of Perez were:
through Hezron, the Hezronite clan;
through Hamul, the Hamulite clan.
22These were the clans of Judah; those numbered were 76,500.

23The descendants of Issachar by their clans were:
through Tola, the Tolaite clan;
through Puah, the Puite[a] clan;
24through Jashub, the Jashubite clan;
through Shimron, the Shimronite clan.
25These were the clans of Issachar; those numbered were 64,300.

26The descendants of Zebulun by their clans were:
through Sered, the Seredite clan;
through Elon, the Elonite clan;
through Jahleel, the Jahleelite clan.
27These were the clans of Zebulun; those numbered were 60,500.

28The descendants of Joseph by their clans through Manasseh and Ephraim were:

29The descendants of Manasseh:
through Makir, the Makirite clan (Makir was the father of Gilead);
through Gilead, the Gileadite clan.
30These were the descendants of Gilead:
through Iezer, the Iezerite clan;
through Helek, the Helekite clan;
31through Asriel, the Asrielite clan;
through Shechem, the Shechemite clan;
32through Shemida, the Shemidaite clan;
through Hepher, the Hepherite clan.
33(Zelophehad son of Hepher had no sons; he had only daughters, whose names were Mahlah, Noah, Hoglah, Milkah and Tirzah.)
34These were the clans of Manasseh; those numbered were 52,700.

35These were the descendants of Ephraim by their clans:
through Shuthelah, the Shuthelahite clan;
through Beker, the Bekerite clan;
through Tahan, the Tahanite clan.
36These were the descendants of Shuthelah:
through Eran, the Eranite clan.
37These were the clans of Ephraim; those numbered were 32,500.

These were the descendants of Joseph by their clans.

38The descendants of Benjamin by their clans were:
through Bela, the Belaite clan;
through Ashbel, the Ashbelite clan;
through Ahiram, the Ahiramite clan;
39through Shupham,[b] the Shuphamite clan;
through Hupham, the Huphamite clan.
40The descendants of Bela through Ard and Naaman were:
through Ard,[c] the Ardite clan;
through Naaman, the Naamite clan.
41These were the clans of Benjamin; those numbered were 45,600.

42These were the descendants of Dan by their clans:
through Shuham, the Shuhamite clan.
These were the clans of Dan: 43All of them
were Shuhamite clans; and those numbered
were 64,400.

44The descendants of Asher by their clans were:
through Imnah, the Imnite clan;
through Ishvi, the Ishvite clan;
through Beriah, the Beriite clan;
45and through the descendants of Beriah:
through Heber, the Heberite clan;
through Malkiel, the Malkielite clan.
46(Asher had a daughter named Serah.)
47These were the clans of Asher; those numbered were 53,400.

48The descendants of Naphtali by their clans were:
through Jahzeel, the Jahzeelite clan;
through Guni, the Gunite clan;
49through Jezer, the Jezerite clan;
through Shillem, the Shillemite clan.
50These were the clans of Naphtali; those numbered were 45,400.

51The total number of the men of Israel was 601,730.

52The LORD said to Moses, 53"The land is to
be allotted to them as an inheritance based on
the number of names. 54To a larger group give
a larger inheritance, and to a smaller group a
smaller one; each is to receive its inheritance
according to the number of those listed. 55Be
sure that the land is distributed by lot. What
each group inherits will be according to the
names for its ancestral tribe. 56Each inheritance is to be distributed by lot among the
larger and smaller groups."

57These were the Levites who were counted by their clans:
through Gershon, the Gershonite clan;
through Kohath, the Kohathite clan;
through Merari, the Merarite clan.
58These also were Levite clans:
the Libnite clan,
the Hebronite clan,
the Mahlite clan,
the Mushite clan,
the Korahite clan.
(Kohath was the forefather of Amram;
59the name of Amram's wife was Jochebed, a descendant of Levi, who was born

[a] 23 Samaritan Pentateuch, Septuagint, Vulgate and Syriac (see also 1 Chron. 7:1); Masoretic Text *through Puvah, the Punite* [b] 39 A few manuscripts of the Masoretic Text, Samaritan Pentateuch, Vulgate and Syriac (see also Septuagint); most manuscripts of the Masoretic Text *Shephupham*
[c] 40 Samaritan Pentateuch and Vulgate (see also Septuagint); Masoretic Text does not have *through Ard.*

to the Levites[a] in Egypt. To Amram she
bore Aaron, Moses and their sister Miriam. 60Aaron was the father of Nadab
and Abihu, Eleazar and Ithamar. 61But
Nadab and Abihu died when they made
an offering before the LORD with unauthorized fire.)

62All the male Levites a month old or more
numbered 23,000. They were not counted
along with the other Israelites because they
received no inheritance among them.

63These are the ones counted by Moses and
Eleazar the priest when they counted the Israelites on the plains of Moab by the Jordan
across from Jericho. 64Not one of them was
among those counted by Moses and Aaron the
priest when they counted the Israelites in the
Desert of Sinai. 65For the LORD had told those
Israelites they would surely die in the wilderness, and not one of them was left except Caleb son of Jephunneh and Joshua son of Nun.

Zelophehad's Daughters

27 The daughters of Zelophehad son of
Hepher, the son of Gilead, the son of
Makir, the son of Manasseh, belonged to
the clans of Manasseh son of Joseph. The
names of the daughters were Mahlah, Noah,
Hoglah, Milkah and Tirzah. They came forward 2and stood before Moses, Eleazar the
priest, the leaders and the whole assembly at
the entrance to the tent of meeting and said,
3"Our father died in the wilderness. He was
not among Korah's followers, who banded together against the LORD, but he died for his
own sin and left no sons. 4Why should our father's name disappear from his clan because
he had no son? Give us property among our
father's relatives."

5So Moses brought their case before the
LORD, 6and the LORD said to him, 7"What Zelophehad's daughters are saying is right. You
must certainly give them property as an inheritance among their father's relatives and
give their father's inheritance to them.

8"Say to the Israelites, 'If a man dies and
leaves no son, give his inheritance to his
daughter. 9If he has no daughter, give his
inheritance to his brothers. 10If he has no
brothers, give his inheritance to his father's
brothers. 11If his father had no brothers, give
his inheritance to the nearest relative in his
clan, that he may possess it. This is to have
the force of law for the Israelites, as the LORD
commanded Moses.'"

Joshua to Succeed Moses

12Then the LORD said to Moses, "Go up this
mountain in the Abarim Range and see the
land I have given the Israelites. 13After you
have seen it, you too will be gathered to your
people, as your brother Aaron was, 14for when
the community rebelled at the waters in the
Desert of Zin, both of you disobeyed my command to honor me as holy before their eyes."
(These were the waters of Meribah Kadesh,
in the Desert of Zin.)

15Moses said to the LORD, 16"May the LORD,
the God who gives breath to all living things,
appoint someone over this community 17to go
out and come in before them, one who will
lead them out and bring them in, so the LORD's
people will not be like sheep without a shepherd."

18So the LORD said to Moses, "Take Joshua son of Nun, a man in whom is the spirit
of leadership,[b] and lay your hand on him.
19Have him stand before Eleazar the priest
and the entire assembly and commission him
in their presence. 20Give him some of your
authority so the whole Israelite community
will obey him. 21He is to stand before Eleazar
the priest, who will obtain decisions for him
by inquiring of the Urim before the LORD. At
his command he and the entire community of
the Israelites will go out, and at his command
they will come in."

22Moses did as the LORD commanded him.
He took Joshua and had him stand before
Eleazar the priest and the whole assembly.
23Then he laid his hands on him and commis-
sioned him, as the LORD instructed through
Moses.

Daily Offerings

28 The LORD said to Moses, 2"Give this
command to the Israelites and say to
them: 'Make sure that you present to me at
the appointed time my food offerings, as an
aroma pleasing to me.' 3Say to them: 'This
is the food offering you are to present to the
LORD: two lambs a year old without defect,
as a regular burnt offering each day. 4Offer
one lamb in the morning and the other at
twilight, 5together with a grain offering of a
tenth of an ephah[c] of the finest flour mixed
with a quarter of a hin[d] of oil from pressed
olives. 6This is the regular burnt offering
instituted at Mount Sinai as a pleasing aroma, a food offering presented to the LORD.
7The accompanying drink offering is to be a
quarter of a hin of fermented drink with each
lamb. Pour out the drink offering to the LORD
at the sanctuary. 8Offer the second lamb at
twilight, along with the same kind of grain
offering and drink offering that you offer in
the morning. This is a food offering, an aroma pleasing to the LORD.

Sabbath Offerings

9"'On the Sabbath day, make an offering of
two lambs a year old without defect, together
with its drink offering and a grain offering
of two-tenths of an ephah[e] of the finest flour
mixed with olive oil. 10This is the burnt offering for every Sabbath, in addition to the
regular burnt offering and its drink offering.

[a] 59 Or *Jochebed, a daughter of Levi, who was born to Levi* [b] 18 Or *the Spirit* [c] 5 That is, probably about 3 1/2 pounds or about 1.6 kilograms; also in verses 13, 21 and 29 [d] 5 That is, about 1 quart or about 1 liter; also in verses 7 and 14 [e] 9 That is, probably about 7 pounds or about 3.2 kilograms; also in verses 12, 20 and 28

Monthly Offerings

11 “ ‘On the first of every month, present to the LORD a burnt offering of two young bulls, one ram and seven male lambs a year old, all without defect. 12 With each bull there is to be a grain offering of three-tenths of an ephah[a] of the finest flour mixed with oil; with the ram, a grain offering of two-tenths of an ephah of the finest flour mixed with oil; 13 and with each lamb, a grain offering of a tenth of an ephah of the finest flour mixed with oil. This is for a burnt offering, a pleasing aroma, a food offering presented to the LORD. 14 With each bull there is to be a drink offering of half a hin[b] of wine; with the ram, a third of a hin[c]; and with each lamb, a quarter of a hin. This is the monthly burnt offering to be made at each new moon during the year. 15 Besides the regular burnt offering with its drink offering, one male goat is to be presented to the LORD as a sin offering.[d]

The Passover

16 “ ‘On the fourteenth day of the first month the LORD's Passover is to be held. 17 On the fifteenth day of this month there is to be a festival; for seven days eat bread made without yeast. 18 On the first day hold a sacred assembly and do no regular work. 19 Present to the LORD a food offering consisting of a burnt offering of two young bulls, one ram and seven male lambs a year old, all without defect. 20 With each bull offer a grain offering of three-tenths of an ephah of the finest flour mixed with oil; with the ram, two-tenths; 21 and with each of the seven lambs, one-tenth. 22 Include one male goat as a sin offering to make atonement for you. 23 Offer these in addition to the regular morning burnt offering. 24 In this way present the food offering every day for seven days as an aroma pleasing to the LORD; it is to be offered in addition to the regular burnt offering and its drink offering. 25 On the seventh day hold a sacred assembly and do no regular work.

The Festival of Weeks

26 “ ‘On the day of firstfruits, when you present to the LORD an offering of new grain during the Festival of Weeks, hold a sacred assembly and do no regular work. 27 Present a burnt offering of two young bulls, one ram and seven male lambs a year old as an aroma pleasing to the LORD. 28 With each bull there is to be a grain offering of three-tenths of an ephah of the finest flour mixed with oil; with the ram, two-tenths; 29 and with each of the seven lambs, one-tenth. 30 Include one male goat to make atonement for you. 31 Offer these together with their drink offerings, in addition to the regular burnt offering and its grain offering. Be sure the animals are without defect.

The Festival of Trumpets

29 “ ‘On the first day of the seventh month hold a sacred assembly and do no regular work. It is a day for you to sound the trumpets. 2 As an aroma pleasing to the LORD, offer a burnt offering of one young bull, one ram and seven male lambs a year old, all without defect. 3 With the bull offer a grain offering of three-tenths of an ephah[e] of the finest flour mixed with olive oil; with the ram, two-tenths[f]; 4 and with each of the seven lambs, one-tenth.[g] 5 Include one male goat as a sin offering[h] to make atonement for you. 6 These are in addition to the monthly and daily burnt offerings with their grain offerings and drink offerings as specified. They are food offerings presented to the LORD, a pleasing aroma.

The Day of Atonement

7 “ ‘On the tenth day of this seventh month hold a sacred assembly. You must deny yourselves[i] and do no work. 8 Present as an aroma pleasing to the LORD a burnt offering of one young bull, one ram and seven male lambs a year old, all without defect. 9 With the bull offer a grain offering of three-tenths of an ephah of the finest flour mixed with oil; with the ram, two-tenths; 10 and with each of the seven lambs, one-tenth. 11 Include one male goat as a sin offering, in addition to the sin offering for atonement and the regular burnt offering with its grain offering, and their drink offerings.

The Festival of Tabernacles

12 “ ‘On the fifteenth day of the seventh month, hold a sacred assembly and do no regular work. Celebrate a festival to the LORD for seven days. 13 Present as an aroma pleasing to the LORD a food offering consisting of a burnt offering of thirteen young bulls, two rams and fourteen male lambs a year old, all without defect. 14 With each of the thirteen bulls offer a grain offering of three-tenths of an ephah of the finest flour mixed with oil; with each of the two rams, two-tenths; 15 and with each of the fourteen lambs, one-tenth. 16 Include one male goat as a sin offering, in addition to the regular burnt offering with its grain offering and drink offering.

17 “ ‘On the second day offer twelve young bulls, two rams and fourteen male lambs a year old, all without defect. 18 With the bulls, rams and lambs, offer their grain offerings and drink offerings according to the number specified. 19 Include one male goat as a sin offering, in addition to the regular burnt offering with its grain offering, and their drink offerings.

20 “ ‘On the third day offer eleven bulls, two rams and fourteen male lambs a year old, all without defect. 21 With the bulls, rams and

[a] *12* That is, probably about 11 pounds or about 5 kilograms; also in verses 20 and 28 [b] *14* That is, about 2 quarts or about 1.9 liters [c] *14* That is, about 1 1/3 quarts or about 1.3 liters [d] *15* Or *purification offering*; also in verse 22 [e] *3* That is, probably about 11 pounds or about 5 kilograms; also in verses 9 and 14 [f] *3* That is, probably about 7 pounds or about 3.2 kilograms; also in verses 9 and 14 [g] *4* That is, probably about 3 1/2 pounds or about 1.6 kilograms; also in verses 10 and 15 [h] *5* Or *purification offering*; also elsewhere in this chapter [i] *7* Or *must fast*

lambs, offer their grain offerings and drink
offerings according to the number specified.
22Include one male goat as a sin offering, in
addition to the regular burnt offering with its
grain offering and drink offering.
23" 'On the fourth day offer ten bulls, two
rams and fourteen male lambs a year old, all
without defect. 24With the bulls, rams and
lambs, offer their grain offerings and drink
offerings according to the number specified.
25Include one male goat as a sin offering, in
addition to the regular burnt offering with its
grain offering and drink offering.
26" 'On the fifth day offer nine bulls, two
rams and fourteen male lambs a year old, all
without defect. 27With the bulls, rams and
lambs, offer their grain offerings and drink
offerings according to the number specified.
28Include one male goat as a sin offering, in
addition to the regular burnt offering with its
grain offering and drink offering.
29" 'On the sixth day offer eight bulls, two
rams and fourteen male lambs a year old, all
without defect. 30With the bulls, rams and
lambs, offer their grain offerings and drink
offerings according to the number specified.
31Include one male goat as a sin offering, in
addition to the regular burnt offering with its
grain offering and drink offering.
32" 'On the seventh day offer seven bulls,
two rams and fourteen male lambs a year old,
all without defect. 33With the bulls, rams and
lambs, offer their grain offerings and drink
offerings according to the number specified.
34Include one male goat as a sin offering, in
addition to the regular burnt offering with its
grain offering and drink offering.
35" 'On the eighth day hold a closing special
assembly and do no regular work. 36Present as
an aroma pleasing to the LORD a food offering
consisting of a burnt offering of one bull, one
ram and seven male lambs a year old, all without defect. 37With the bull, the ram and the
lambs, offer their grain offerings and drink
offerings according to the number specified.
38Include one male goat as a sin offering, in
addition to the regular burnt offering with its
grain offering and drink offering.
39" 'In addition to what you vow and your
freewill offerings, offer these to the LORD at
your appointed festivals: your burnt offerings,
grain offerings, drink offerings and fellowship offerings.' "
40Moses told the Israelites all that the LORD
commanded him.[a]

Vows

30[b] Moses said to the heads of the tribes
of Israel: "This is what the LORD commands: 2When a man makes a vow to the
LORD or takes an oath to obligate himself by
a pledge, he must not break his word but must
do everything he said.
3"When a young woman still living in her
father's household makes a vow to the LORD
or obligates herself by a pledge 4and her father hears about her vow or pledge but says
nothing to her, then all her vows and every
pledge by which she obligated herself will
stand. 5But if her father forbids her when he
hears about it, none of her vows or the pledges by which she obligated herself will stand;
the LORD will release her because her father
has forbidden her.
6"If she marries after she makes a vow or
after her lips utter a rash promise by which
she obligates herself 7and her husband hears
about it but says nothing to her, then her vows
or the pledges by which she obligated herself will stand. 8But if her husband forbids
her when he hears about it, he nullifies the
vow that obligates her or the rash promise
by which she obligates herself, and the LORD
will release her.
9"Any vow or obligation taken by a widow
or divorced woman will be binding on her.
10"If a woman living with her husband
makes a vow or obligates herself by a pledge
under oath 11and her husband hears about it
but says nothing to her and does not forbid
her, then all her vows or the pledges by which
she obligated herself will stand. 12But if her
husband nullifies them when he hears about
them, then none of the vows or pledges that
came from her lips will stand. Her husband
has nullified them, and the LORD will release
her. 13Her husband may confirm or nullify any
vow she makes or any sworn pledge to deny
herself.[c] 14But if her husband says nothing to
her about it from day to day, then he confirms
all her vows or the pledges binding on her.
He confirms them by saying nothing to her
when he hears about them. 15If, however, he
nullifies them some time after he hears about
them, then he must bear the consequences of
her wrongdoing."
16These are the regulations the LORD gave
Moses concerning relationships between a
man and his wife, and between a father and
his young daughter still living at home.

Vengeance on the Midianites

31 The LORD said to Moses, 2"Take vengeance on the Midianites for the Israelites. After that, you will be gathered to your
people."
3So Moses said to the people, "Arm some
of your men to go to war against the Midianites so that they may carry out the LORD's
vengeance on them. 4Send into battle a thousand men from each of the tribes of Israel."
5So twelve thousand men armed for battle, a
thousand from each tribe, were supplied from
the clans of Israel. 6Moses sent them into battle, a thousand from each tribe, along with
Phinehas son of Eleazar, the priest, who took
with him articles from the sanctuary and the
trumpets for signaling.
7They fought against Midian, as the LORD
commanded Moses, and killed every man.
8Among their victims were Evi, Rekem, Zur,
Hur and Reba—the five kings of Midian. They

[a] *40* In Hebrew texts this verse (29:40) is numbered 30:1. [b] In Hebrew texts 30:1-16 is numbered 30:2-17.
[c] *13* Or *to fast*

also killed Balaam son of Beor with the sword. [9]The Israelites captured the Midianite women and children and took all the Midianite herds, flocks and goods as plunder. [10]They burned all the towns where the Midianites had settled, as well as all their camps. [11]They took all the plunder and spoils, including the people and animals, [12]and brought the captives, spoils and plunder to Moses and Eleazar the priest and the Israelite assembly at their camp on the plains of Moab, by the Jordan across from Jericho.

[13]Moses, Eleazar the priest and all the leaders of the community went to meet them outside the camp. [14]Moses was angry with the officers of the army—the commanders of thousands and commanders of hundreds—who returned from the battle.

[15]"Have you allowed all the women to live?" he asked them. [16]"They were the ones who followed Balaam's advice and enticed the Israelites to be unfaithful to the LORD in the Peor incident, so that a plague struck the LORD's people. [17]Now kill all the boys. And kill every woman who has slept with a man, [18]but save for yourselves every girl who has never slept with a man.

[19]"Anyone who has killed someone or touched someone who was killed must stay outside the camp seven days. On the third and seventh days you must purify yourselves and your captives. [20]Purify every garment as well as everything made of leather, goat hair or wood."

[21]Then Eleazar the priest said to the soldiers who had gone into battle, "This is what is required by the law that the LORD gave Moses: [22]Gold, silver, bronze, iron, tin, lead [23]and anything else that can withstand fire must be put through the fire, and then it will be clean. But it must also be purified with the water of cleansing. And whatever cannot withstand fire must be put through that water. [24]On the seventh day wash your clothes and you will be clean. Then you may come into the camp."

Dividing the Spoils

[25]The LORD said to Moses, [26]"You and Eleazar the priest and the family heads of the community are to count all the people and animals that were captured. [27]Divide the spoils equally between the soldiers who took part in the battle and the rest of the community. [28]From the soldiers who fought in the battle, set apart as tribute for the LORD one out of every five hundred, whether people, cattle, donkeys or sheep. [29]Take this tribute from their half share and give it to Eleazar the priest as the LORD's part. [30]From the Israelites' half, select one out of every fifty, whether people, cattle, donkeys, sheep or other animals. Give them to the Levites, who are responsible for the care of the LORD's tabernacle." [31]So Moses and Eleazar the priest did as the LORD commanded Moses.

[32]The plunder remaining from the spoils that the soldiers took was 675,000 sheep, [33]72,000 cattle, [34]61,000 donkeys [35]and 32,000 women who had never slept with a man.

[36]The half share of those who fought in the battle was:

337,500 sheep, [37]of which the tribute for the LORD was 675;
[38]36,000 cattle, of which the tribute for the LORD was 72;
[39]30,500 donkeys, of which the tribute for the LORD was 61;
[40]16,000 people, of whom the tribute for the LORD was 32.

[41]Moses gave the tribute to Eleazar the priest as the LORD's part, as the LORD commanded Moses.

[42]The half belonging to the Israelites, which Moses set apart from that of the fighting men— [43]the community's half—was 337,500 sheep, [44]36,000 cattle, [45]30,500 donkeys [46]and 16,000 people. [47]From the Israelites' half, Moses selected one out of every fifty people and animals, as the LORD commanded him, and gave them to the Levites, who were responsible for the care of the LORD's tabernacle.

[48]Then the officers who were over the units of the army—the commanders of thousands and commanders of hundreds—went to Moses [49]and said to him, "Your servants have counted the soldiers under our command, and not one is missing. [50]So we have brought as an offering to the LORD the gold articles each of us acquired—armlets, bracelets, signet rings, earrings and necklaces—to make atonement for ourselves before the LORD."

[51]Moses and Eleazar the priest accepted from them the gold—all the crafted articles. [52]All the gold from the commanders of thousands and commanders of hundreds that Moses and Eleazar presented as a gift to the LORD weighed 16,750 shekels.[a] [53]Each soldier had taken plunder for himself. [54]Moses and Eleazar the priest accepted the gold from the commanders of thousands and commanders of hundreds and brought it into the tent of meeting as a memorial for the Israelites before the LORD.

The Transjordan Tribes

32 The Reubenites and Gadites, who had very large herds and flocks, saw that the lands of Jazer and Gilead were suitable for livestock. [2]So they came to Moses and Eleazar the priest and to the leaders of the community, and said, [3]"Ataroth, Dibon, Jazer, Nimrah, Heshbon, Elealeh, Sebam, Nebo and Beon— [4]the land the LORD subdued before the people of Israel—are suitable for livestock, and your servants have livestock. [5]If we have found favor in your eyes," they said, "let this land be given to your servants as our possession. Do not make us cross the Jordan."

[6]Moses said to the Gadites and Reubenites, "Should your fellow Israelites go to war while you sit here? [7]Why do you discourage the Israelites from crossing over into the land the LORD has given them? [8]This is what your fa-

[a] *52* That is, about 420 pounds or about 190 kilograms

thers did when I sent them from Kadesh Barnea to look over the land. 9After they went up
to the Valley of Eshkol and viewed the land,
they discouraged the Israelites from entering the land the LORD had given them. 10The
LORD's anger was aroused that day and he
swore this oath: 11'Because they have not followed me wholeheartedly, not one of those
who were twenty years old or more when
they came up out of Egypt will see the land
I promised on oath to Abraham, Isaac and
Jacob— 12not one except Caleb son of Jephunneh the Kenizzite and Joshua son of Nun, for
they followed the LORD wholeheartedly.' 13The
LORD's anger burned against Israel and he
made them wander in the wilderness forty
years, until the whole generation of those who
had done evil in his sight was gone.

14"And here you are, a brood of sinners,
standing in the place of your fathers and making the LORD even more angry with Israel. 15If
you turn away from following him, he will
again leave all this people in the wilderness,
and you will be the cause of their destruction."

16Then they came up to him and said, "We
would like to build pens here for our livestock
and cities for our women and children. 17But
we will arm ourselves for battle[a] and go ahead
of the Israelites until we have brought them to
their place. Meanwhile our women and children will live in fortified cities, for protection
from the inhabitants of the land. 18We will not
return to our homes until each of the Israelites
has received their inheritance. 19We will not
receive any inheritance with them on the other side of the Jordan, because our inheritance
has come to us on the east side of the Jordan."

20Then Moses said to them, "If you will do
this—if you will arm yourselves before the
LORD for battle 21and if all of you who are
armed cross over the Jordan before the LORD
until he has driven his enemies out before
him— 22then when the land is subdued before the LORD, you may return and be free
from your obligation to the LORD and to Israel. And this land will be your possession
before the LORD.

23"But if you fail to do this, you will be sinning against the LORD; and you may be sure
that your sin will find you out. 24Build cities
for your women and children, and pens for
your flocks, but do what you have promised."

25The Gadites and Reubenites said to Moses,
"We your servants will do as our lord commands. 26Our children and wives, our flocks
and herds will remain here in the cities of
Gilead. 27But your servants, every man who is
armed for battle, will cross over to fight before
the LORD, just as our lord says."

28Then Moses gave orders about them to
Eleazar the priest and Joshua son of Nun and
to the family heads of the Israelite tribes. 29He
said to them, "If the Gadites and Reubenites,
every man armed for battle, cross over the
Jordan with you before the LORD, then when
the land is subdued before you, you must give
them the land of Gilead as their possession.
30But if they do not cross over with you armed,
they must accept their possession with you
in Canaan."

31The Gadites and Reubenites answered,
"Your servants will do what the LORD has said.
32We will cross over before the LORD into Canaan armed, but the property we inherit will
be on this side of the Jordan."

33Then Moses gave to the Gadites, the Reubenites and the half-tribe of Manasseh son
of Joseph the kingdom of Sihon king of the
Amorites and the kingdom of Og king of Bashan—the whole land with its cities and the
territory around them.

34The Gadites built up Dibon, Ataroth, Aroer, 35Atroth Shophan, Jazer, Jogbehah, 36Beth
Nimrah and Beth Haran as fortified cities, and
built pens for their flocks. 37And the Reubenites rebuilt Heshbon, Elealeh and Kiriathaim,
38as well as Nebo and Baal Meon (these names
were changed) and Sibmah. They gave names
to the cities they rebuilt.

39The descendants of Makir son of Manasseh went to Gilead, captured it and drove out
the Amorites who were there. 40So Moses gave
Gilead to the Makirites, the descendants of
Manasseh, and they settled there. 41Jair, a descendant of Manasseh, captured their settlements and called them Havvoth Jair.[b] 42And
Nobah captured Kenath and its surrounding
settlements and called it Nobah after himself.

Stages in Israel's Journey

33 Here are the stages in the journey of the
Israelites when they came out of Egypt
by divisions under the leadership of Moses
and Aaron. 2At the LORD's command Moses
recorded the stages in their journey. This is
their journey by stages:

3The Israelites set out from Rameses
on the fifteenth day of the first month,
the day after the Passover. They marched
out defiantly in full view of all the Egyptians, 4who were burying all their firstborn, whom the LORD had struck down
among them; for the LORD had brought
judgment on their gods.

5The Israelites left Rameses and
camped at Sukkoth.

6They left Sukkoth and camped at
Etham, on the edge of the desert.

7They left Etham, turned back to Pi Hahiroth, to the east of Baal Zephon, and
camped near Migdol.

8They left Pi Hahiroth[c] and passed
through the sea into the desert, and when
they had traveled for three days in the
Desert of Etham, they camped at Marah.

9They left Marah and went to Elim,
where there were twelve springs and seventy palm trees, and they camped there.

10They left Elim and camped by the
Red Sea.[d]

[a] 17 Septuagint; Hebrew *will be quick to arm ourselves* [b] 41 Or *them the settlements of Jair*
[c] 8 Many manuscripts of the Masoretic Text, Samaritan Pentateuch and Vulgate; most manuscripts of
the Masoretic Text *left from before Hahiroth* [d] 10 Or *the Sea of Reeds*; also in verse 11

11They left the Red Sea and camped in
the Desert of Sin.
12They left the Desert of Sin and
camped at Dophkah.
13They left Dophkah and camped at
Alush.
14They left Alush and camped at Rephidim, where there was no water for the
people to drink.
15They left Rephidim and camped in
the Desert of Sinai.
16They left the Desert of Sinai and
camped at Kibroth Hattaavah.
17They left Kibroth Hattaavah and
camped at Hazeroth.
18They left Hazeroth and camped at
Rithmah.
19They left Rithmah and camped at
Rimmon Perez.
20They left Rimmon Perez and camped
at Libnah.
21They left Libnah and camped at Rissah.
22They left Rissah and camped at Kehelathah.
23They left Kehelathah and camped at
Mount Shepher.
24They left Mount Shepher and camped
at Haradah.
25They left Haradah and camped at
Makheloth.
26They left Makheloth and camped at
Tahath.
27They left Tahath and camped at Terah.
28They left Terah and camped at Mithkah.
29They left Mithkah and camped at
Hashmonah.
30They left Hashmonah and camped
at Moseroth.
31They left Moseroth and camped at
Bene Jaakan.
32They left Bene Jaakan and camped
at Hor Haggidgad.
33They left Hor Haggidgad and camped
at Jotbathah.
34They left Jotbathah and camped at
Abronah.
35They left Abronah and camped at
Ezion Geber.
36They left Ezion Geber and camped at
Kadesh, in the Desert of Zin.
37They left Kadesh and camped at
Mount Hor, on the border of Edom. 38At
the LORD's command Aaron the priest
went up Mount Hor, where he died on
the first day of the fifth month of the fortieth year after the Israelites came out
of Egypt. 39Aaron was a hundred and
twenty-three years old when he died on
Mount Hor.
40The Canaanite king of Arad, who
lived in the Negev of Canaan, heard that
the Israelites were coming.
41They left Mount Hor and camped at
Zalmonah.
42They left Zalmonah and camped at
Punon.
43They left Punon and camped at Oboth.
44They left Oboth and camped at Iye
Abarim, on the border of Moab.
45They left Iye Abarim and camped at
Dibon Gad.
46They left Dibon Gad and camped at
Almon Diblathaim.
47They left Almon Diblathaim and
camped in the mountains of Abarim,
near Nebo.
48They left the mountains of Abarim
and camped on the plains of Moab by the
Jordan across from Jericho. 49There on the
plains of Moab they camped along the Jordan from Beth Jeshimoth to Abel Shittim.

50On the plains of Moab by the Jordan
across from Jericho the LORD said to Moses,
51"Speak to the Israelites and say to them:
'When you cross the Jordan into Canaan,
52drive out all the inhabitants of the land
before you. Destroy all their carved images
and their cast idols, and demolish all their
high places. 53Take possession of the land
and settle in it, for I have given you the land
to possess. 54Distribute the land by lot, according to your clans. To a larger group give
a larger inheritance, and to a smaller group
a smaller one. Whatever falls to them by lot
will be theirs. Distribute it according to your
ancestral tribes.
55" 'But if you do not drive out the inhabitants of the land, those you allow to remain
will become barbs in your eyes and thorns in
your sides. They will give you trouble in the
land where you will live. 56And then I will do
to you what I plan to do to them.' "

Boundaries of Canaan

34 The LORD said to Moses, 2"Command
the Israelites and say to them: 'When
you enter Canaan, the land that will be allotted to you as an inheritance is to have these
boundaries:

3" 'Your southern side will include some of
the Desert of Zin along the border of Edom.
Your southern boundary will start in the east
from the southern end of the Dead Sea, 4cross
south of Scorpion Pass, continue on to Zin and
go south of Kadesh Barnea. Then it will go to
Hazar Addar and over to Azmon, 5where it
will turn, join the Wadi of Egypt and end at
the Mediterranean Sea.
6" 'Your western boundary will be the coast
of the Mediterranean Sea. This will be your
boundary on the west.
7" 'For your northern boundary, run a line
from the Mediterranean Sea to Mount Hor
8and from Mount Hor to Lebo Hamath. Then
the boundary will go to Zedad, 9continue to
Ziphron and end at Hazar Enan. This will be
your boundary on the north.
10" 'For your eastern boundary, run a line
from Hazar Enan to Shepham. 11The boundary will go down from Shepham to Riblah on
the east side of Ain and continue along the
slopes east of the Sea of Galilee.[a] 12Then the

[a] 11 Hebrew *Kinnereth*

boundary will go down along the Jordan and
end at the Dead Sea.
"'This will be your land, with its boundaries
on every side.'"
13 Moses commanded the Israelites: "Assign
this land by lot as an inheritance. The LORD
has ordered that it be given to the nine and a
half tribes, 14 because the families of the tribe
of Reuben, the tribe of Gad and the half-tribe
of Manasseh have received their inheritance.
15 These two and a half tribes have received
their inheritance east of the Jordan across
from Jericho, toward the sunrise."
16 The LORD said to Moses, 17 "These are the
names of the men who are to assign the land
for you as an inheritance: Eleazar the priest
and Joshua son of Nun. 18 And appoint one
leader from each tribe to help assign the land.
19 These are their names:

Caleb son of Jephunneh,
from the tribe of Judah;
20 Shemuel son of Ammihud,
from the tribe of Simeon;
21 Elidad son of Kislon,
from the tribe of Benjamin;
22 Bukki son of Jogli,
the leader from the tribe of Dan;
23 Hanniel son of Ephod,
the leader from the tribe of Manasseh
son of Joseph;
24 Kemuel son of Shiphtan,
the leader from the tribe of Ephraim
son of Joseph;
25 Elizaphan son of Parnak,
the leader from the tribe of Zebulun;
26 Paltiel son of Azzan,
the leader from the tribe of Issachar;
27 Ahihud son of Shelomi,
the leader from the tribe of Asher;
28 Pedahel son of Ammihud,
the leader from the tribe of Naphtali."

29 These are the men the LORD commanded
to assign the inheritance to the Israelites in
the land of Canaan.

Towns for the Levites

35 On the plains of Moab by the Jordan
across from Jericho, the LORD said to
Moses, 2 "Command the Israelites to give the
Levites towns to live in from the inheritance
the Israelites will possess. And give them pasturelands around the towns. 3 Then they will
have towns to live in and pasturelands for the
cattle they own and all their other animals.
4 "The pasturelands around the towns that
you give the Levites will extend a thousand
cubits[a] from the town wall. 5 Outside the
town, measure two thousand cubits[b] on the
east side, two thousand on the south side, two
thousand on the west and two thousand on the
north, with the town in the center. They will
have this area as pastureland for the towns.

Cities of Refuge

6 "Six of the towns you give the Levites will
be cities of refuge, to which a person who has
killed someone may flee. In addition, give
them forty-two other towns. 7 In all you must
give the Levites forty-eight towns, together with their pasturelands. 8 The towns you
give the Levites from the land the Israelites
possess are to be given in proportion to the
inheritance of each tribe: Take many towns
from a tribe that has many, but few from one
that has few."
9 Then the LORD said to Moses: 10 "Speak
to the Israelites and say to them: 'When you
cross the Jordan into Canaan, 11 select some
towns to be your cities of refuge, to which a
person who has killed someone accidentally
may flee. 12 They will be places of refuge from
the avenger, so that anyone accused of murder
may not die before they stand trial before the
assembly. 13 These six towns you give will be
your cities of refuge. 14 Give three on this side
of the Jordan and three in Canaan as cities of
refuge. 15 These six towns will be a place of refuge for Israelites and for foreigners residing
among them, so that anyone who has killed
another accidentally can flee there.
16 "'If anyone strikes someone a fatal blow
with an iron object, that person is a murderer; the murderer is to be put to death. 17 Or if
anyone is holding a stone and strikes someone
a fatal blow with it, that person is a murderer; the murderer is to be put to death. 18 Or if
anyone is holding a wooden object and strikes
someone a fatal blow with it, that person is a
murderer; the murderer is to be put to death.
19 The avenger of blood shall put the murderer
to death; when the avenger comes upon the
murderer, the avenger shall put the murderer
to death. 20 If anyone with malice aforethought
shoves another or throws something at them
intentionally so that they die 21 or if out of enmity one person hits another with their fist so
that the other dies, that person is to be put to
death; that person is a murderer. The avenger of blood shall put the murderer to death
when they meet.
22 "'But if without enmity someone suddenly
pushes another or throws something at them
unintentionally 23 or, without seeing them,
drops on them a stone heavy enough to kill
them, and they die, then since that other person was not an enemy and no harm was intended, 24 the assembly must judge between the
accused and the avenger of blood according to
these regulations. 25 The assembly must protect
the one accused of murder from the avenger of
blood and send the accused back to the city of
refuge to which they fled. The accused must
stay there until the death of the high priest,
who was anointed with the holy oil.
26 "'But if the accused ever goes outside the
limits of the city of refuge to which they fled
27 and the avenger of blood finds them outside the city, the avenger of blood may kill
the accused without being guilty of murder.
28 The accused must stay in the city of refuge
until the death of the high priest; only after
the death of the high priest may they return
to their own property.

[a] *4* That is, about 1,500 feet or about 450 meters [b] *5* That is, about 3,000 feet or about 900 meters

29 "'This is to have the force of law for you throughout the generations to come, wherever you live.

30 "'Anyone who kills a person is to be put to death as a murderer only on the testimony of witnesses. But no one is to be put to death on the testimony of only one witness.

31 "'Do not accept a ransom for the life of a murderer, who deserves to die. They are to be put to death.

32 "'Do not accept a ransom for anyone who has fled to a city of refuge and so allow them to go back and live on their own land before the death of the high priest.

33 "'Do not pollute the land where you are. Bloodshed pollutes the land, and atonement cannot be made for the land on which blood has been shed, except by the blood of the one who shed it. 34 Do not defile the land where you live and where I dwell, for I, the LORD, dwell among the Israelites.'"

Inheritance of Zelophehad's Daughters

36 The family heads of the clan of Gilead son of Makir, the son of Manasseh, who were from the clans of the descendants of Joseph, came and spoke before Moses and the leaders, the heads of the Israelite families. 2 They said, "When the LORD commanded my lord to give the land as an inheritance to the Israelites by lot, he ordered you to give the inheritance of our brother Zelophehad to his daughters. 3 Now suppose they marry men from other Israelite tribes; then their inheritance will be taken from our ancestral inheritance and added to that of the tribe they marry into. And so part of the inheritance allotted to us will be taken away. 4 When the Year of Jubilee for the Israelites comes, their inheritance will be added to that of the tribe into which they marry, and their property will be taken from the tribal inheritance of our ancestors."

5 Then at the LORD's command Moses gave this order to the Israelites: "What the tribe of the descendants of Joseph is saying is right. 6 This is what the LORD commands for Zelophehad's daughters: They may marry anyone they please as long as they marry within their father's tribal clan. 7 No inheritance in Israel is to pass from one tribe to another, for every Israelite shall keep the tribal inheritance of their ancestors. 8 Every daughter who inherits land in any Israelite tribe must marry someone in her father's tribal clan, so that every Israelite will possess the inheritance of their ancestors. 9 No inheritance may pass from one tribe to another, for each Israelite tribe is to keep the land it inherits."

10 So Zelophehad's daughters did as the LORD commanded Moses. 11 Zelophehad's daughters—Mahlah, Tirzah, Hoglah, Milkah and Noah—married their cousins on their father's side. 12 They married within the clans of the descendants of Manasseh son of Joseph, and their inheritance remained in their father's tribe and clan.

13 These are the commands and regulations the LORD gave through Moses to the Israelites on the plains of Moab by the Jordan across from Jericho.

Deuteronomy

The Command to Leave Horeb

1 These are the words Moses spoke to all Israel in the wilderness east of the Jordan—that is, in the Arabah—opposite Suph, between Paran and Tophel, Laban, Hazeroth and Dizahab. 2 (It takes eleven days to go from Horeb to Kadesh Barnea by the Mount Seir road.)

3 In the fortieth year, on the first day of the eleventh month, Moses proclaimed to the Israelites all that the LORD had commanded him concerning them. 4 This was after he had defeated Sihon king of the Amorites, who reigned in Heshbon, and at Edrei had defeated Og king of Bashan, who reigned in Ashtaroth.

5 East of the Jordan in the territory of Moab, Moses began to expound this law, saying:

6 The LORD our God said to us at Horeb, "You have stayed long enough at this mountain. 7 Break camp and advance into the hill country of the Amorites; go to all the neighboring peoples in the Arabah, in the mountains, in the western foothills, in the Negev and along the coast, to the land of the Canaanites and to Lebanon, as far as the great river, the Euphrates. 8 See, I have given you this land. Go in and take possession of the land the LORD swore he would give to your fathers—to Abraham, Isaac and Jacob—and to their descendants after them."

The Appointment of Leaders

9 At that time I said to you, "You are too heavy a burden for me to carry alone. 10 The LORD your God has increased your numbers so that today you are as numerous as the stars in the sky. 11 May the LORD, the God of your ancestors, increase you a thousand times and bless you as he has promised! 12 But how can I bear your problems and your burdens and your disputes all by myself? 13 Choose some wise, understanding and respected men from each of your tribes, and I will set them over you."

14 You answered me, “What you propose to
do is good.”
15 So I took the leading men of your tribes,
wise and respected men, and appointed them
to have authority over you—as commanders
of thousands, of hundreds, of fifties and of
tens and as tribal officials. 16 And I charged
your judges at that time, “Hear the disputes
between your people and judge fairly, whether
the case is between two Israelites or between
an Israelite and a foreigner residing among
you. 17 Do not show partiality in judging; hear
both small and great alike. Do not be afraid of
anyone, for judgment belongs to God. Bring
me any case too hard for you, and I will hear
it.” 18 And at that time I told you everything
you were to do.

Spies Sent Out

19 Then, as the LORD our God commanded
us, we set out from Horeb and went toward
the hill country of the Amorites through all
that vast and dreadful wilderness that you
have seen, and so we reached Kadesh Barnea.
20 Then I said to you, “You have reached the
hill country of the Amorites, which the LORD
our God is giving us. 21 See, the LORD your
God has given you the land. Go up and take
possession of it as the LORD, the God of your
ancestors, told you. Do not be afraid; do not
be discouraged.”
22 Then all of you came to me and said, “Let
us send men ahead to spy out the land for us
and bring back a report about the route we
are to take and the towns we will come to.”
23 The idea seemed good to me; so I selected twelve of you, one man from each tribe.
24 They left and went up into the hill country,
and came to the Valley of Eshkol and explored
it. 25 Taking with them some of the fruit of the
land, they brought it down to us and reported, “It is a good land that the LORD our God
is giving us.”

Rebellion Against the LORD

26 But you were unwilling to go up; you rebelled against the command of the LORD your
God. 27 You grumbled in your tents and said,
“The LORD hates us; so he brought us out of
Egypt to deliver us into the hands of the Amorites to destroy us. 28 Where can we go? Our
brothers have made our hearts melt in fear.
They say, ‘The people are stronger and taller
than we are; the cities are large, with walls up
to the sky. We even saw the Anakites there.’ ”
29 Then I said to you, “Do not be terrified;
do not be afraid of them. 30 The LORD your
God, who is going before you, will fight for
you, as he did for you in Egypt, before your
very eyes, 31 and in the wilderness. There you
saw how the LORD your God carried you, as
a father carries his son, all the way you went
until you reached this place.”
32 In spite of this, you did not trust in the
LORD your God, 33 who went ahead of you on
your journey, in fire by night and in a cloud by
day, to search out places for you to camp and
to show you the way you should go.
34 When the LORD heard what you said, he
was angry and solemnly swore: 35 “No one
from this evil generation shall see the good
land I swore to give your ancestors, 36 except
Caleb son of Jephunneh. He will see it, and I
will give him and his descendants the land he
set his feet on, because he followed the LORD
wholeheartedly.”
37 Because of you the LORD became angry
with me also and said, “You shall not enter
it, either. 38 But your assistant, Joshua son of
Nun, will enter it. Encourage him, because
he will lead Israel to inherit it. 39 And the little
ones that you said would be taken captive,
your children who do not yet know good from
bad—they will enter the land. I will give it to
them and they will take possession of it. 40 But
as for you, turn around and set out toward
the desert along the route to the Red Sea.[a]”
41 Then you replied, “We have sinned against
the LORD. We will go up and fight, as the LORD
our God commanded us.” So every one of you
put on his weapons, thinking it easy to go up
into the hill country.
42 But the LORD said to me, “Tell them, ‘Do
not go up and fight, because I will not be with
you. You will be defeated by your enemies.’ ”
43 So I told you, but you would not listen. You
rebelled against the LORD’s command and in
your arrogance you marched up into the hill
country. 44 The Amorites who lived in those
hills came out against you; they chased you
like a swarm of bees and beat you down from
Seir all the way to Hormah. 45 You came back
and wept before the LORD, but he paid no attention to your weeping and turned a deaf ear
to you. 46 And so you stayed in Kadesh many
days—all the time you spent there.

Wanderings in the Wilderness

2 Then we turned back and set out toward
the wilderness along the route to the Red
Sea,[a] as the LORD had directed me. For a long
time we made our way around the hill country of Seir.
2 Then the LORD said to me, 3 “You have
made your way around this hill country long
enough; now turn north. 4 Give the people
these orders: ‘You are about to pass through
the territory of your relatives the descendants
of Esau, who live in Seir. They will be afraid
of you, but be very careful. 5 Do not provoke
them to war, for I will not give you any of
their land, not even enough to put your foot
on. I have given Esau the hill country of Seir
as his own. 6 You are to pay them in silver for
the food you eat and the water you drink.’ ”
7 The LORD your God has blessed you in
all the work of your hands. He has watched
over your journey through this vast wilderness. These forty years the LORD your God
has been with you, and you have not lacked
anything.
8 So we went on past our relatives the descendants of Esau, who live in Seir. We turned

[a] *40,1 Or the Sea of Reeds*

from the Arabah road, which comes up from
Elath and Ezion Geber, and traveled along
the desert road of Moab.
9Then the LORD said to me, "Do not harass
the Moabites or provoke them to war, for I
will not give you any part of their land. I have
given Ar to the descendants of Lot as a possession."
10(The Emites used to live there—a people
strong and numerous, and as tall as the Anakites. 11Like the Anakites, they too were considered Rephaites, but the Moabites called
them Emites. 12Horites used to live in Seir,
but the descendants of Esau drove them out.
They destroyed the Horites from before them
and settled in their place, just as Israel did
in the land the LORD gave them as their possession.)
13And the LORD said, "Now get up and cross
the Zered Valley." So we crossed the valley.
14Thirty-eight years passed from the time
we left Kadesh Barnea until we crossed the
Zered Valley. By then, that entire generation
of fighting men had perished from the camp,
as the LORD had sworn to them. 15The LORD's
hand was against them until he had completely eliminated them from the camp.
16Now when the last of these fighting men
among the people had died, 17the LORD said to
me, 18"Today you are to pass by the region of
Moab at Ar. 19When you come to the Ammonites, do not harass them or provoke them to
war, for I will not give you possession of any
land belonging to the Ammonites. I have given
it as a possession to the descendants of Lot."
20(That too was considered a land of the
Rephaites, who used to live there; but the Ammonites called them Zamzummites. 21They
were a people strong and numerous, and as
tall as the Anakites. The LORD destroyed them
from before the Ammonites, who drove them
out and settled in their place. 22The LORD had
done the same for the descendants of Esau,
who lived in Seir, when he destroyed the
Horites from before them. They drove them
out and have lived in their place to this day.
23And as for the Avvites who lived in villages
as far as Gaza, the Caphtorites coming out
from Caphtor[a] destroyed them and settled in
their place.)

Defeat of Sihon King of Heshbon

24"Set out now and cross the Arnon Gorge.
See, I have given into your hand Sihon the
Amorite, king of Heshbon, and his country.
Begin to take possession of it and engage him
in battle. 25This very day I will begin to put the
terror and fear of you on all the nations under
heaven. They will hear reports of you and will
tremble and be in anguish because of you."
26From the Desert of Kedemoth I sent messengers to Sihon king of Heshbon offering
peace and saying, 27"Let us pass through your
country. We will stay on the main road; we
will not turn aside to the right or to the left.
28Sell us food to eat and water to drink for
their price in silver. Only let us pass through
on foot— 29as the descendants of Esau, who
live in Seir, and the Moabites, who live in Ar,
did for us—until we cross the Jordan into the
land the LORD our God is giving us." 30But
Sihon king of Heshbon refused to let us pass
through. For the LORD your God had made
his spirit stubborn and his heart obstinate in
order to give him into your hands, as he has
now done.
31The LORD said to me, "See, I have begun
to deliver Sihon and his country over to you.
Now begin to conquer and possess his land."
32When Sihon and all his army came out to
meet us in battle at Jahaz, 33the LORD our God
delivered him over to us and we struck him
down, together with his sons and his whole
army. 34At that time we took all his towns and
completely destroyed[b] them—men, women
and children. We left no survivors. 35But the
livestock and the plunder from the towns we
had captured we carried off for ourselves.
36From Aroer on the rim of the Arnon Gorge,
and from the town in the gorge, even as far
as Gilead, not one town was too strong for us.
The LORD our God gave us all of them. 37But
in accordance with the command of the LORD
our God, you did not encroach on any of the
land of the Ammonites, neither the land along
the course of the Jabbok nor that around the
towns in the hills.

Defeat of Og King of Bashan

3 Next we turned and went up along the road
toward Bashan, and Og king of Bashan
with his whole army marched out to meet us in
battle at Edrei. 2The LORD said to me, "Do not
be afraid of him, for I have delivered him into
your hands, along with his whole army and
his land. Do to him what you did to Sihon king
of the Amorites, who reigned in Heshbon."
3So the LORD our God also gave into our
hands Og king of Bashan and all his army.
We struck them down, leaving no survivors.
4At that time we took all his cities. There was
not one of the sixty cities that we did not take
from them—the whole region of Argob, Og's
kingdom in Bashan. 5All these cities were
fortified with high walls and with gates and
bars, and there were also a great many unwalled villages. 6We completely destroyed[b]
them, as we had done with Sihon king of
Heshbon, destroying[b] every city—men,
women and children. 7But all the livestock
and the plunder from their cities we carried
off for ourselves.
8So at that time we took from these two
kings of the Amorites the territory east of the
Jordan, from the Arnon Gorge as far as Mount
Hermon. 9(Hermon is called Sirion by the Sidonians; the Amorites call it Senir.) 10We took
all the towns on the plateau, and all Gilead,
and all Bashan as far as Salekah and Edrei,
towns of Og's kingdom in Bashan. 11(Og king
of Bashan was the last of the Rephaites. His
bed was decorated with iron and was more

[a] *23* That is, Crete [b] *34,6* The Hebrew term refers to the irrevocable giving over of things or persons to the LORD, often by totally destroying them.

than nine cubits long and four cubits wide.[a] It is still in Rabbah of the Ammonites.)

Division of the Land

12Of the land that we took over at that time, I gave the Reubenites and the Gadites the territory north of Aroer by the Arnon Gorge, including half the hill country of Gilead, together with its towns. 13The rest of Gilead and also all of Bashan, the kingdom of Og, I gave to the half-tribe of Manasseh. (The whole region of Argob in Bashan used to be known as a land of the Rephaites. 14Jair, a descendant of Manasseh, took the whole region of Argob as far as the border of the Geshurites and the Maakathites; it was named after him, so that to this day Bashan is called Havvoth Jair.[b]) 15And I gave Gilead to Makir. 16But to the Reubenites and the Gadites I gave the territory extending from Gilead down to the Arnon Gorge (the middle of the gorge being the border) and out to the Jabbok River, which is the border of the Ammonites. 17Its western border was the Jordan in the Arabah, from Kinnereth to the Sea of the Arabah (that is, the Dead Sea), below the slopes of Pisgah.

18I commanded you at that time: "The LORD your God has given you this land to take possession of it. But all your able-bodied men, armed for battle, must cross over ahead of the other Israelites. 19However, your wives, your children and your livestock (I know you have much livestock) may stay in the towns I have given you, 20until the LORD gives rest to your fellow Israelites as he has to you, and they too have taken over the land that the LORD your God is giving them across the Jordan. After that, each of you may go back to the possession I have given you."

Moses Forbidden to Cross the Jordan

21At that time I commanded Joshua: "You have seen with your own eyes all that the LORD your God has done to these two kings. The LORD will do the same to all the kingdoms over there where you are going. 22Do not be afraid of them; the LORD your God himself will fight for you."

23At that time I pleaded with the LORD: 24"Sovereign LORD, you have begun to show to your servant your greatness and your strong hand. For what god is there in heaven or on earth who can do the deeds and mighty works you do? 25Let me go over and see the good land beyond the Jordan—that fine hill country and Lebanon."

26But because of you the LORD was angry with me and would not listen to me. "That is enough," the LORD said. "Do not speak to me anymore about this matter. 27Go up to the top of Pisgah and look west and north and south and east. Look at the land with your own eyes, since you are not going to cross this Jordan. 28But commission Joshua, and encourage and strengthen him, for he will lead this people across and will cause them to inherit the land that you will see." 29So we stayed in the valley near Beth Peor.

Obedience Commanded

4 Now, Israel, hear the decrees and laws I am about to teach you. Follow them so that you may live and may go in and take possession of the land the LORD, the God of your ancestors, is giving you. 2Do not add to what I command you and do not subtract from it, but keep the commands of the LORD your God that I give you.

3You saw with your own eyes what the LORD did at Baal Peor. The LORD your God destroyed from among you everyone who followed the Baal of Peor, 4but all of you who held fast to the LORD your God are still alive today.

5See, I have taught you decrees and laws as the LORD my God commanded me, so that you may follow them in the land you are entering to take possession of it. 6Observe them carefully, for this will show your wisdom and understanding to the nations, who will hear about all these decrees and say, "Surely this great nation is a wise and understanding people." 7What other nation is so great as to have their gods near them the way the LORD our God is near us whenever we pray to him? 8And what other nation is so great as to have such righteous decrees and laws as this body of laws I am setting before you today?

9Only be careful, and watch yourselves closely so that you do not forget the things your eyes have seen or let them fade from your heart as long as you live. Teach them to your children and to their children after them. 10Remember the day you stood before the LORD your God at Horeb, when he said to me, "Assemble the people before me to hear my words so that they may learn to revere me as long as they live in the land and may teach them to their children." 11You came near and stood at the foot of the mountain while it blazed with fire to the very heavens, with black clouds and deep darkness. 12Then the LORD spoke to you out of the fire. You heard the sound of words but saw no form; there was only a voice. 13He declared to you his covenant, the Ten Commandments, which he commanded you to follow and then wrote them on two stone tablets. 14And the LORD directed me at that time to teach you the decrees and laws you are to follow in the land that you are crossing the Jordan to possess.

Idolatry Forbidden

15You saw no form of any kind the day the LORD spoke to you at Horeb out of the fire. Therefore watch yourselves very carefully, 16so that you do not become corrupt and make for yourselves an idol, an image of any shape, whether formed like a man or a woman, 17or like any animal on earth or any bird that flies in the air, 18or like any creature that moves along the ground or any fish in the waters below. 19And when you look up to the sky and see

[a] *11* That is, about 14 feet long and 6 feet wide or about 4 meters long and 1.8 meters wide
[b] *14* Or *called the settlements of Jair*

the sun, the moon and the stars—all the heavenly array—do not be enticed into bowing
down to them and worshiping things the LORD
your God has apportioned to all the nations
under heaven. 20But as for you, the LORD took
you and brought you out of the iron-smelting
furnace, out of Egypt, to be the people of his
inheritance, as you now are.
21The LORD was angry with me because of
you, and he solemnly swore that I would not
cross the Jordan and enter the good land the
LORD your God is giving you as your inheritance. 22I will die in this land; I will not cross
the Jordan; but you are about to cross over and
take possession of that good land. 23Be careful
not to forget the covenant of the LORD your
God that he made with you; do not make for
yourselves an idol in the form of anything the
LORD your God has forbidden. 24For the LORD
your God is a consuming fire, a jealous God.
25After you have had children and grandchildren and have lived in the land a long
time—if you then become corrupt and make
any kind of idol, doing evil in the eyes of the
LORD your God and arousing his anger, 26I
call the heavens and the earth as witnesses against you this day that you will quickly
perish from the land that you are crossing
the Jordan to possess. You will not live there
long but will certainly be destroyed. 27The
LORD will scatter you among the peoples,
and only a few of you will survive among
the nations to which the LORD will drive you.
28There you will worship man-made gods of
wood and stone, which cannot see or hear
or eat or smell. 29But if from there you seek
the LORD your God, you will find him if you
seek him with all your heart and with all your
soul. 30When you are in distress and all these
things have happened to you, then in later
days you will return to the LORD your God and
obey him. 31For the LORD your God is a merciful God; he will not abandon or destroy you
or forget the covenant with your ancestors,
which he confirmed to them by oath.

The LORD Is God

32Ask now about the former days, long before your time, from the day God created human beings on the earth; ask from one end
of the heavens to the other. Has anything so
great as this ever happened, or has anything
like it ever been heard of? 33Has any other
people heard the voice of God[a] speaking out
of fire, as you have, and lived? 34Has any god
ever tried to take for himself one nation out
of another nation, by testings, by signs and
wonders, by war, by a mighty hand and an
outstretched arm, or by great and awesome
deeds, like all the things the LORD your God
did for you in Egypt before your very eyes?
35You were shown these things so that you
might know that the LORD is God; besides him
there is no other. 36From heaven he made you
hear his voice to discipline you. On earth he
showed you his great fire, and you heard his
words from out of the fire. 37Because he loved
your ancestors and chose their descendants
after them, he brought you out of Egypt by his
Presence and his great strength, 38to drive out
before you nations greater and stronger than
you and to bring you into their land to give
it to you for your inheritance, as it is today.
39Acknowledge and take to heart this day
that the LORD is God in heaven above and on
the earth below. There is no other. 40Keep his
decrees and commands, which I am giving
you today, so that it may go well with you and
your children after you and that you may live
long in the land the LORD your God gives you
for all time.

Cities of Refuge

41Then Moses set aside three cities east of
the Jordan, 42to which anyone who had killed
a person could flee if they had unintentionally killed a neighbor without malice aforethought. They could flee into one of these cities and save their life. 43The cities were these:
Bezer in the wilderness plateau, for the Reubenites; Ramoth in Gilead, for the Gadites;
and Golan in Bashan, for the Manassites.

Introduction to the Law

44This is the law Moses set before the Israelites. 45These are the stipulations, decrees
and laws Moses gave them when they came
out of Egypt 46and were in the valley near
Beth Peor east of the Jordan, in the land of
Sihon king of the Amorites, who reigned in
Heshbon and was defeated by Moses and the
Israelites as they came out of Egypt. 47They
took possession of his land and the land of Og
king of Bashan, the two Amorite kings east of
the Jordan. 48This land extended from Aroer
on the rim of the Arnon Gorge to Mount Sirion[b] (that is, Hermon), 49and included all the
Arabah east of the Jordan, as far as the Dead
Sea,[c] below the slopes of Pisgah.

The Ten Commandments

5 Moses summoned all Israel and said:
Hear, Israel, the decrees and laws I declare in your hearing today. Learn them and
be sure to follow them. 2The LORD our God
made a covenant with us at Horeb. 3It was not
with our ancestors[d] that the LORD made this
covenant, but with us, with all of us who are
alive here today. 4The LORD spoke to you face
to face out of the fire on the mountain. 5(At
that time I stood between the LORD and you to
declare to you the word of the LORD, because
you were afraid of the fire and did not go up
the mountain.) And he said:

6"I am the LORD your God, who
brought you out of Egypt, out of the
land of slavery.
7"You shall have no other gods before[e] me.
8"You shall not make for yourself an image
in the form of anything in heaven
above or on the earth beneath or in

[a] 33 Or *of a god* [b] 48 Syriac (see also 3:9); Hebrew *Siyon* [c] 49 Hebrew *the Sea of the Arabah*
[d] 3 Or *not only with our parents* [e] 7 Or *besides*

the waters below. 9You shall not bow
down to them or worship them; for
I, the LORD your God, am a jealous
God, punishing the children for the
sin of the parents to the third and
fourth generation of those who hate
me, 10but showing love to a thousand
generations of those who love me and
keep my commandments.
11 "You shall not misuse the name of the
LORD your God, for the LORD will not
hold anyone guiltless who misuses
his name.
12 "Observe the Sabbath day by keeping it
holy, as the LORD your God has commanded you. 13Six days you shall labor and do all your work, 14but the
seventh day is a sabbath to the LORD
your God. On it you shall not do any
work, neither you, nor your son or
daughter, nor your male or female
servant, nor your ox, your donkey
or any of your animals, nor any foreigner residing in your towns, so
that your male and female servants
may rest, as you do. 15Remember
that you were slaves in Egypt and
that the LORD your God brought you
out of there with a mighty hand and
an outstretched arm. Therefore the
LORD your God has commanded you
to observe the Sabbath day.
16 "Honor your father and your mother, as
the LORD your God has commanded
you, so that you may live long and
that it may go well with you in the
land the LORD your God is giving
you.
17 "You shall not murder.
18 "You shall not commit adultery.
19 "You shall not steal.
20 "You shall not give false testimony
against your neighbor.
21 "You shall not covet your neighbor's wife.
You shall not set your desire on your
neighbor's house or land, his male or
female servant, his ox or donkey, or
anything that belongs to your neighbor."

22These are the commandments the LORD
proclaimed in a loud voice to your whole assembly there on the mountain from out of the
fire, the cloud and the deep darkness; and he
added nothing more. Then he wrote them on
two stone tablets and gave them to me.
23When you heard the voice out of the darkness, while the mountain was ablaze with fire,
all the leaders of your tribes and your elders
came to me. 24And you said, "The LORD our
God has shown us his glory and his majesty,
and we have heard his voice from the fire. Today we have seen that a person can live even if
God speaks with them. 25But now, why should
we die? This great fire will consume us, and
we will die if we hear the voice of the LORD our
God any longer. 26For what mortal has ever
heard the voice of the living God speaking out
of fire, as we have, and survived? 27Go near
and listen to all that the LORD our God says.
Then tell us whatever the LORD our God tells
you. We will listen and obey."
28The LORD heard you when you spoke to
me, and the LORD said to me, "I have heard
what this people said to you. Everything they
said was good. 29Oh, that their hearts would
be inclined to fear me and keep all my commands always, so that it might go well with
them and their children forever!
30"Go, tell them to return to their tents. 31But
you stay here with me so that I may give you
all the commands, decrees and laws you are
to teach them to follow in the land I am giving
them to possess."
32So be careful to do what the LORD your
God has commanded you; do not turn aside
to the right or to the left. 33Walk in obedience
to all that the LORD your God has commanded you, so that you may live and prosper and
prolong your days in the land that you will
possess.

Love the LORD Your God

6 These are the commands, decrees and laws
the LORD your God directed me to teach
you to observe in the land that you are crossing the Jordan to possess, 2so that you, your
children and their children after them may
fear the LORD your God as long as you live by
keeping all his decrees and commands that
I give you, and so that you may enjoy long
life. 3Hear, Israel, and be careful to obey so
that it may go well with you and that you may
increase greatly in a land flowing with milk
and honey, just as the LORD, the God of your
ancestors, promised you.
4Hear, O Israel: The LORD our God, the LORD
is one.[a] 5Love the LORD your God with all your
heart and with all your soul and with all your
strength. 6These commandments that I give
you today are to be on your hearts. 7Impress
them on your children. Talk about them when
you sit at home and when you walk along the
road, when you lie down and when you get up.
8Tie them as symbols on your hands and bind
them on your foreheads. 9Write them on the
doorframes of your houses and on your gates.
10When the LORD your God brings you into
the land he swore to your fathers, to Abraham, Isaac and Jacob, to give you—a land
with large, flourishing cities you did not build,
11houses filled with all kinds of good things
you did not provide, wells you did not dig,
and vineyards and olive groves you did not
plant—then when you eat and are satisfied,
12be careful that you do not forget the LORD,
who brought you out of Egypt, out of the land
of slavery.
13Fear the LORD your God, serve him only
and take your oaths in his name. 14Do not follow other gods, the gods of the peoples around
you; 15for the LORD your God, who is among
you, is a jealous God and his anger will burn

[a] 4 Or *The LORD our God is one LORD*; or *The LORD is our God, the LORD is one*; or *The LORD is our God, the LORD alone*

against you, and he will destroy you from the
face of the land. 16Do not put the LORD your God
to the test as you did at Massah. 17Be sure to
keep the commands of the LORD your God and
the stipulations and decrees he has given you.
18Do what is right and good in the LORD's sight,
so that it may go well with you and you may go
in and take over the good land the LORD promised on oath to your ancestors, 19thrusting out
all your enemies before you, as the LORD said.
20In the future, when your son asks you,
"What is the meaning of the stipulations, decrees and laws the LORD our God has commanded you?" 21tell him: "We were slaves of
Pharaoh in Egypt, but the LORD brought us
out of Egypt with a mighty hand. 22Before our
eyes the LORD sent signs and wonders—great
and terrible—on Egypt and Pharaoh and his
whole household. 23But he brought us out from
there to bring us in and give us the land he
promised on oath to our ancestors. 24The LORD
commanded us to obey all these decrees and
to fear the LORD our God, so that we might always prosper and be kept alive, as is the case
today. 25And if we are careful to obey all this
law before the LORD our God, as he has commanded us, that will be our righteousness."

Driving Out the Nations

7 When the LORD your God brings you into
the land you are entering to possess and
drives out before you many nations—the Hittites, Girgashites, Amorites, Canaanites, Perizzites, Hivites and Jebusites, seven nations
larger and stronger than you— 2and when the
LORD your God has delivered them over to you
and you have defeated them, then you must
destroy them totally.[a] Make no treaty with
them, and show them no mercy. 3Do not intermarry with them. Do not give your daughters
to their sons or take their daughters for your
sons, 4for they will turn your children away
from following me to serve other gods, and the
LORD's anger will burn against you and will
quickly destroy you. 5This is what you are to
do to them: Break down their altars, smash
their sacred stones, cut down their Asherah
poles[b] and burn their idols in the fire. 6For
you are a people holy to the LORD your God.
The LORD your God has chosen you out of all
the peoples on the face of the earth to be his
people, his treasured possession.
7The LORD did not set his affection on you
and choose you because you were more numerous than other peoples, for you were the
fewest of all peoples. 8But it was because the
LORD loved you and kept the oath he swore to
your ancestors that he brought you out with a
mighty hand and redeemed you from the land
of slavery, from the power of Pharaoh king
of Egypt. 9Know therefore that the LORD your
God is God; he is the faithful God, keeping his
covenant of love to a thousand generations of
those who love him and keep his commandments. 10But

those who hate him he will repay to their
face by destruction;
he will not be slow to repay to their face
those who hate him.

11Therefore, take care to follow the commands, decrees and laws I give you today.
12If you pay attention to these laws and are
careful to follow them, then the LORD your
God will keep his covenant of love with you,
as he swore to your ancestors. 13He will love
you and bless you and increase your numbers.
He will bless the fruit of your womb, the crops
of your land—your grain, new wine and olive
oil—the calves of your herds and the lambs of
your flocks in the land he swore to your ancestors to give you. 14You will be blessed more
than any other people; none of your men or
women will be childless, nor will any of your
livestock be without young. 15The LORD will
keep you free from every disease. He will not
inflict on you the horrible diseases you knew
in Egypt, but he will inflict them on all who
hate you. 16You must destroy all the peoples
the LORD your God gives over to you. Do not
look on them with pity and do not serve their
gods, for that will be a snare to you.
17You may say to yourselves, "These nations
are stronger than we are. How can we drive
them out?" 18But do not be afraid of them;
remember well what the LORD your God did
to Pharaoh and to all Egypt. 19You saw with
your own eyes the great trials, the signs and
wonders, the mighty hand and outstretched
arm, with which the LORD your God brought
you out. The LORD your God will do the same
to all the peoples you now fear. 20Moreover,
the LORD your God will send the hornet among
them until even the survivors who hide from
you have perished. 21Do not be terrified by
them, for the LORD your God, who is among
you, is a great and awesome God. 22The LORD
your God will drive out those nations before
you, little by little. You will not be allowed to
eliminate them all at once, or the wild animals
will multiply around you. 23But the LORD your
God will deliver them over to you, throwing
them into great confusion until they are destroyed. 24He will give their kings into your
hand, and you will wipe out their names from
under heaven. No one will be able to stand up
against you; you will destroy them. 25The images of their gods you are to burn in the fire.
Do not covet the silver and gold on them, and
do not take it for yourselves, or you will be
ensnared by it, for it is detestable to the LORD
your God. 26Do not bring a detestable thing
into your house or you, like it, will be set apart
for destruction. Regard it as vile and utterly
detest it, for it is set apart for destruction.

Do Not Forget the LORD

8 Be careful to follow every command I am
giving you today, so that you may live and
increase and may enter and possess the land

[a] 2 The Hebrew term refers to the irrevocable giving over of things or persons to the LORD, often by totally destroying them; also in verse 26. [b] 5 That is, wooden symbols of the goddess Asherah; here and elsewhere in Deuteronomy

the LORD promised on oath to your ancestors.
2Remember how the LORD your God led you all
the way in the wilderness these forty years,
to humble and test you in order to know what
was in your heart, whether or not you would
keep his commands. 3He humbled you, causing you to hunger and then feeding you with
manna, which neither you nor your ancestors
had known, to teach you that man does not
live on bread alone but on every word that
comes from the mouth of the LORD. 4Your
clothes did not wear out and your feet did not
swell during these forty years. 5Know then in
your heart that as a man disciplines his son,
so the LORD your God disciplines you.

6Observe the commands of the LORD your
God, walking in obedience to him and revering him. 7For the LORD your God is bringing
you into a good land—a land with brooks,
streams, and deep springs gushing out into
the valleys and hills; 8a land with wheat and
barley, vines and fig trees, pomegranates, olive oil and honey; 9a land where bread will
not be scarce and you will lack nothing; a
land where the rocks are iron and you can
dig copper out of the hills.

10When you have eaten and are satisfied,
praise the LORD your God for the good land he
has given you. 11Be careful that you do not forget the LORD your God, failing to observe his
commands, his laws and his decrees that I am
giving you this day. 12Otherwise, when you eat
and are satisfied, when you build fine houses
and settle down, 13and when your herds and
flocks grow large and your silver and gold
increase and all you have is multiplied, 14then
your heart will become proud and you will forget the LORD your God, who brought you out
of Egypt, out of the land of slavery. 15He led
you through the vast and dreadful wilderness,
that thirsty and waterless land, with its venomous snakes and scorpions. He brought you
water out of hard rock. 16He gave you manna
to eat in the wilderness, something your ancestors had never known, to humble and test
you so that in the end it might go well with
you. 17You may say to yourself, "My power
and the strength of my hands have produced
this wealth for me." 18But remember the LORD
your God, for it is he who gives you the ability to produce wealth, and so confirms his
covenant, which he swore to your ancestors,
as it is today.

19If you ever forget the LORD your God and
follow other gods and worship and bow down
to them, I testify against you today that you
will surely be destroyed. 20Like the nations
the LORD destroyed before you, so you will be
destroyed for not obeying the LORD your God.

Not Because of Israel's Righteousness

9 Hear, Israel: You are now about to cross
the Jordan to go in and dispossess nations
greater and stronger than you, with large cities that have walls up to the sky. 2The people
are strong and tall—Anakites! You know
about them and have heard it said: "Who
can stand up against the Anakites?" 3But be
assured today that the LORD your God is the
one who goes across ahead of you like a devouring fire. He will destroy them; he will
subdue them before you. And you will drive
them out and annihilate them quickly, as the
LORD has promised you.

4After the LORD your God has driven them
out before you, do not say to yourself, "The
LORD has brought me here to take possession
of this land because of my righteousness." No,
it is on account of the wickedness of these
nations that the LORD is going to drive them
out before you. 5It is not because of your righteousness or your integrity that you are going in to take possession of their land; but on
account of the wickedness of these nations,
the LORD your God will drive them out before you, to accomplish what he swore to
your fathers, to Abraham, Isaac and Jacob.
6Understand, then, that it is not because of
your righteousness that the LORD your God is
giving you this good land to possess, for you
are a stiff-necked people.

The Golden Calf

7Remember this and never forget how you
aroused the anger of the LORD your God in the
wilderness. From the day you left Egypt until
you arrived here, you have been rebellious
against the LORD. 8At Horeb you aroused the
LORD's wrath so that he was angry enough to
destroy you. 9When I went up on the mountain to receive the tablets of stone, the tablets of the covenant that the LORD had made
with you, I stayed on the mountain forty days
and forty nights; I ate no bread and drank no
water. 10The LORD gave me two stone tablets
inscribed by the finger of God. On them were
all the commandments the LORD proclaimed
to you on the mountain out of the fire, on the
day of the assembly.

11At the end of the forty days and forty
nights, the LORD gave me the two stone tablets, the tablets of the covenant. 12Then the
LORD told me, "Go down from here at once,
because your people whom you brought out of
Egypt have become corrupt. They have turned
away quickly from what I commanded them
and have made an idol for themselves."

13And the LORD said to me, "I have seen this
people, and they are a stiff-necked people indeed! 14Let me alone, so that I may destroy
them and blot out their name from under heav-
en. And I will make you into a nation stronger
and more numerous than they."

15So I turned and went down from the
mountain while it was ablaze with fire. And
the two tablets of the covenant were in my
hands. 16When I looked, I saw that you had
sinned against the LORD your God; you had
made for yourselves an idol cast in the shape
of a calf. You had turned aside quickly from
the way that the LORD had commanded you.
17So I took the two tablets and threw them out
of my hands, breaking them to pieces before
your eyes.

18Then once again I fell prostrate before the
LORD for forty days and forty nights; I ate
no bread and drank no water, because of all
the sin you had committed, doing what was

evil in the LORD's sight and so arousing his
anger. 19I feared the anger and wrath of the
LORD, for he was angry enough with you to
destroy you. But again the LORD listened to
me. 20And the LORD was angry enough with
Aaron to destroy him, but at that time I prayed
for Aaron too. 21Also I took that sinful thing
of yours, the calf you had made, and burned
it in the fire. Then I crushed it and ground it
to powder as fine as dust and threw the dust
into a stream that flowed down the mountain.

22You also made the LORD angry at Taberah,
at Massah and at Kibroth Hattaavah.

23And when the LORD sent you out from Kadesh Barnea, he said, "Go up and take possession of the land I have given you." But you
rebelled against the command of the LORD
your God. You did not trust him or obey him.
24You have been rebellious against the LORD
ever since I have known you.

25I lay prostrate before the LORD those forty days and forty nights because the LORD
had said he would destroy you. 26I prayed to
the LORD and said, "Sovereign LORD, do not
destroy your people, your own inheritance
that you redeemed by your great power and
brought out of Egypt with a mighty hand.
27Remember your servants Abraham, Isaac
and Jacob. Overlook the stubbornness of this
people, their wickedness and their sin. 28Oth-
erwise, the country from which you brought
us will say, 'Because the LORD was not able to
take them into the land he had promised them,
and because he hated them, he brought them
out to put them to death in the wilderness.'
29But they are your people, your inheritance
that you brought out by your great power and
your outstretched arm."

Tablets Like the First Ones

10 At that time the LORD said to me, "Chisel
out two stone tablets like the first ones
and come up to me on the mountain. Also
make a wooden ark.[a] 2I will write on the tablets the words that were on the first tablets,
which you broke. Then you are to put them
in the ark."

3So I made the ark out of acacia wood and
chiseled out two stone tablets like the first
ones, and I went up on the mountain with the
two tablets in my hands. 4The LORD wrote on
these tablets what he had written before, the
Ten Commandments he had proclaimed to you
on the mountain, out of the fire, on the day of
the assembly. And the LORD gave them to me.
5Then I came back down the mountain and
put the tablets in the ark I had made, as the
LORD commanded me, and they are there now.

6(The Israelites traveled from the wells of
Bene Jaakan to Moserah. There Aaron died
and was buried, and Eleazar his son succeeded him as priest. 7From there they traveled to
Gudgodah and on to Jotbathah, a land with
streams of water. 8At that time the LORD set
apart the tribe of Levi to carry the ark of the
covenant of the LORD, to stand before the LORD
to minister and to pronounce blessings in his
name, as they still do today. 9That is why the
Levites have no share or inheritance among
their fellow Israelites; the LORD is their inheritance, as the LORD your God told them.)

10Now I had stayed on the mountain forty
days and forty nights, as I did the first time,
and the LORD listened to me at this time also.
It was not his will to destroy you. 11"Go," the
LORD said to me, "and lead the people on their
way, so that they may enter and possess the
land I swore to their ancestors to give them."

Fear the LORD

12And now, Israel, what does the LORD your
God ask of you but to fear the LORD your God,
to walk in obedience to him, to love him, to
serve the LORD your God with all your heart
and with all your soul, 13and to observe the
LORD's commands and decrees that I am giving you today for your own good?

14To the LORD your God belong the heavens, even the highest heavens, the earth and
everything in it. 15Yet the LORD set his affection on your ancestors and loved them, and
he chose you, their descendants, above all
the nations—as it is today. 16Circumcise your
hearts, therefore, and do not be stiff-necked
any longer. 17For the LORD your God is God of
gods and Lord of lords, the great God, mighty
and awesome, who shows no partiality and
accepts no bribes. 18He defends the cause of
the fatherless and the widow, and loves the
foreigner residing among you, giving them
food and clothing. 19And you are to love those
who are foreigners, for you yourselves were
foreigners in Egypt. 20Fear the LORD your God
and serve him. Hold fast to him and take your
oaths in his name. 21He is the one you praise;
he is your God, who performed for you those
great and awesome wonders you saw with
your own eyes. 22Your ancestors who went
down into Egypt were seventy in all, and now
the LORD your God has made you as numerous
as the stars in the sky.

Love and Obey the LORD

11 Love the LORD your God and keep his
requirements, his decrees, his laws and
his commands always. 2Remember today that
your children were not the ones who saw and
experienced the discipline of the LORD your
God: his majesty, his mighty hand, his outstretched arm; 3the signs he performed and
the things he did in the heart of Egypt, both
to Pharaoh king of Egypt and to his whole
country; 4what he did to the Egyptian army, to
its horses and chariots, how he overwhelmed
them with the waters of the Red Sea[b] as they
were pursuing you, and how the LORD brought
lasting ruin on them. 5It was not your children
who saw what he did for you in the wilderness
until you arrived at this place, 6and what he
did to Dathan and Abiram, sons of Eliab the
Reubenite, when the earth opened its mouth
right in the middle of all Israel and swallowed
them up with their households, their tents and

[a] *1* That is, a chest [b] *4* Or *the Sea of Reeds*

every living thing that belonged to them. 7But it was your own eyes that saw all these great things the LORD has done.

8Observe therefore all the commands I am giving you today, so that you may have the strength to go in and take over the land that you are crossing the Jordan to possess, 9and so that you may live long in the land the LORD swore to your ancestors to give to them and their descendants, a land flowing with milk and honey. 10The land you are entering to take over is not like the land of Egypt, from which you have come, where you planted your seed and irrigated it by foot as in a vegetable garden. 11But the land you are crossing the Jordan to take possession of is a land of mountains and valleys that drinks rain from heaven. 12It is a land the LORD your God cares for; the eyes of the LORD your God are continually on it from the beginning of the year to its end.

13So if you faithfully obey the commands I am giving you today—to love the LORD your God and to serve him with all your heart and with all your soul— 14then I will send rain on your land in its season, both autumn and spring rains, so that you may gather in your grain, new wine and olive oil. 15I will provide grass in the fields for your cattle, and you will eat and be satisfied.

16Be careful, or you will be enticed to turn away and worship other gods and bow down to them. 17Then the LORD's anger will burn against you, and he will shut up the heavens so that it will not rain and the ground will yield no produce, and you will soon perish from the good land the LORD is giving you. 18Fix these words of mine in your hearts and minds; tie them as symbols on your hands and bind them on your foreheads. 19Teach them to your children, talking about them when you sit at home and when you walk along the road, when you lie down and when you get up. 20Write them on the doorframes of your houses and on your gates, 21so that your days and the days of your children may be many in the land the LORD swore to give your ancestors, as many as the days that the heavens are above the earth.

22If you carefully observe all these commands I am giving you to follow—to love the LORD your God, to walk in obedience to him and to hold fast to him— 23then the LORD will drive out all these nations before you, and you will dispossess nations larger and stronger than you. 24Every place where you set your foot will be yours: Your territory will extend from the desert to Lebanon, and from the Euphrates River to the Mediterranean Sea. 25No one will be able to stand against you. The LORD your God, as he promised you, will put the terror and fear of you on the whole land, wherever you go.

26See, I am setting before you today a blessing and a curse— 27the blessing if you obey the commands of the LORD your God that I am giving you today; 28the curse if you disobey the commands of the LORD your God and turn from the way that I command you today by following other gods, which you have not known. 29When the LORD your God has brought you into the land you are entering to possess, you are to proclaim on Mount Gerizim the blessings, and on Mount Ebal the curses. 30As you know, these mountains are across the Jordan, westward, toward the setting sun, near the great trees of Moreh, in the territory of those Canaanites living in the Arabah in the vicinity of Gilgal. 31You are about to cross the Jordan to enter and take possession of the land the LORD your God is giving you. When you have taken it over and are living there, 32be sure that you obey all the decrees and laws I am setting before you today.

The One Place of Worship

12 These are the decrees and laws you must be careful to follow in the land that the LORD, the God of your ancestors, has given you to possess—as long as you live in the land. 2Destroy completely all the places on the high mountains, on the hills and under every spreading tree, where the nations you are dispossessing worship their gods. 3Break down their altars, smash their sacred stones and burn their Asherah poles in the fire; cut down the idols of their gods and wipe out their names from those places.

4You must not worship the LORD your God in their way. 5But you are to seek the place the LORD your God will choose from among all your tribes to put his Name there for his dwelling. To that place you must go; 6there bring your burnt offerings and sacrifices, your tithes and special gifts, what you have vowed to give and your freewill offerings, and the firstborn of your herds and flocks. 7There, in the presence of the LORD your God, you and your families shall eat and shall rejoice in everything you have put your hand to, because the LORD your God has blessed you.

8You are not to do as we do here today, everyone doing as they see fit, 9since you have not yet reached the resting place and the inheritance the LORD your God is giving you. 10But you will cross the Jordan and settle in the land the LORD your God is giving you as an inheritance, and he will give you rest from all your enemies around you so that you will live in safety. 11Then to the place the LORD your God will choose as a dwelling for his Name—there you are to bring everything I command you: your burnt offerings and sacrifices, your tithes and special gifts, and all the choice possessions you have vowed to the LORD. 12And there rejoice before the LORD your God—you, your sons and daughters, your male and female servants, and the Levites from your towns who have no allotment or inheritance of their own. 13Be careful not to sacrifice your burnt offerings anywhere you please. 14Offer them only at the place the LORD will choose in one of your tribes, and there observe everything I command you.

15Nevertheless, you may slaughter your animals in any of your towns and eat as much of the meat as you want, as if it were gazelle or deer, according to the blessing the LORD your God gives you. Both the ceremonially unclean and the clean may eat it. 16But you must not eat the blood; pour it out on the ground like water. [17]You must not eat in your own towns the tithe of your grain and new wine and olive oil, or the firstborn of your herds and flocks, or whatever you have vowed to give, or your freewill offerings or special gifts. [18]Instead, you are to eat them in the presence of the LORD your God at the place the LORD your God will choose—you, your sons and daughters, your male and female servants, and the Levites from your towns—and you are to rejoice before the LORD your God in everything you put your hand to. [19]Be careful not to neglect the Levites as long as you live in your land.

[20]When the LORD your God has enlarged your territory as he promised you, and you crave meat and say, "I would like some meat," then you may eat as much of it as you want. [21]If the place where the LORD your God chooses to put his Name is too far away from you, you may slaughter animals from the herds and flocks the LORD has given you, as I have commanded you, and in your own towns you may eat as much of them as you want. [22]Eat them as you would gazelle or deer. Both the ceremonially unclean and the clean may eat. [23]But be sure you do not eat the blood, because the blood is the life, and you must not eat the life with the meat. [24]You must not eat the blood; pour it out on the ground like water. [25]Do not eat it, so that it may go well with you and your children after you, because you will be doing what is right in the eyes of the LORD.

[26]But take your consecrated things and whatever you have vowed to give, and go to the place the LORD will choose. [27]Present your burnt offerings on the altar of the LORD your God, both the meat and the blood. The blood of your sacrifices must be poured beside the altar of the LORD your God, but you may eat the meat. [28]Be careful to obey all these regulations I am giving you, so that it may always go well with you and your children after you, because you will be doing what is good and right in the eyes of the LORD your God.

[29]The LORD your God will cut off before you the nations you are about to invade and dispossess. But when you have driven them out and settled in their land, [30]and after they have been destroyed before you, be careful not to be ensnared by inquiring about their gods, saying, "How do these nations serve their gods? We will do the same." [31]You must not worship the LORD your God in their way, because in worshiping their gods, they do all kinds of detestable things the LORD hates. They even burn their sons and daughters in the fire as sacrifices to their gods.

[32]See that you do all I command you; do not add to it or take away from it.[a]

Worshiping Other Gods

13[b] If a prophet, or one who foretells by dreams, appears among you and announces to you a sign or wonder, [2]and if the sign or wonder spoken of takes place, and the prophet says, "Let us follow other gods" (gods you have not known) "and let us worship them," [3]you must not listen to the words of that prophet or dreamer. The LORD your God is testing you to find out whether you love him with all your heart and with all your soul. [4]It is the LORD your God you must follow, and him you must revere. Keep his commands and obey him; serve him and hold fast to him. [5]That prophet or dreamer must be put to death for inciting rebellion against the LORD your God, who brought you out of Egypt and redeemed you from the land of slavery. That prophet or dreamer tried to turn you from the way the LORD your God commanded you to follow. You must purge the evil from among you.

[6]If your very own brother, or your son or daughter, or the wife you love, or your closest friend secretly entices you, saying, "Let us go and worship other gods" (gods that neither you nor your ancestors have known, [7]gods of the peoples around you, whether near or far, from one end of the land to the other), [8]do not yield to them or listen to them. Show them no pity. Do not spare them or shield them. [9]You must certainly put them to death. Your hand must be the first in putting them to death, and then the hands of all the people. [10]Stone them to death, because they tried to turn you away from the LORD your God, who brought you out of Egypt, out of the land of slavery. [11]Then all Israel will hear and be afraid, and no one among you will do such an evil thing again.

[12]If you hear it said about one of the towns the LORD your God is giving you to live in [13]that troublemakers have arisen among you and have led the people of their town astray, saying, "Let us go and worship other gods" (gods you have not known), [14]then you must inquire, probe and investigate it thoroughly. And if it is true and it has been proved that this detestable thing has been done among you, [15]you must certainly put to the sword all who live in that town. You must destroy it completely,[c] both its people and its livestock. [16]You are to gather all the plunder of the town into the middle of the public square and completely burn the town and all its plunder as a whole burnt offering to the LORD your God. That town is to remain a ruin forever, never to be rebuilt, [17]and none of the condemned things[c] are to be found in your hands. Then the LORD will turn from his fierce anger, will show you mercy, and will have compassion on you. He will increase your numbers, as he promised on oath to your ancestors— [18]because you obey the LORD your God by keeping all his commands that I am giving you today and doing what is right in his eyes.

Clean and Unclean Food

14 You are the children of the LORD your God. Do not cut yourselves or shave the front of your heads for the dead, [2]for you are

[a] *32* In Hebrew texts this verse (12:32) is numbered 13:1. [b] In Hebrew texts 13:1-18 is numbered 13:2-19. [c] *15,17* The Hebrew term refers to the irrevocable giving over of things or persons to the LORD, often by totally destroying them.

a people holy to the LORD your God. Out of all the peoples on the face of the earth, the LORD has chosen you to be his treasured possession.

3Do not eat any detestable thing. 4These are the animals you may eat: the ox, the sheep, the goat, 5the deer, the gazelle, the roe deer, the wild goat, the ibex, the antelope and the mountain sheep.[a] 6You may eat any animal that has a divided hoof and that chews the cud. 7However, of those that chew the cud or that have a divided hoof you may not eat the camel, the rabbit or the hyrax. Although they chew the cud, they do not have a divided hoof; they are ceremonially unclean for you. 8The pig is also unclean; although it has a divided hoof, it does not chew the cud. You are not to eat their meat or touch their carcasses.

9Of all the creatures living in the water, you may eat any that has fins and scales. 10But anything that does not have fins and scales you may not eat; for you it is unclean.

11You may eat any clean bird. 12But these you may not eat: the eagle, the vulture, the black vulture, 13the red kite, the black kite, any kind of falcon, 14any kind of raven, 15the horned owl, the screech owl, the gull, any kind of hawk, 16the little owl, the great owl, the white owl, 17the desert owl, the osprey, the cormorant, 18the stork, any kind of heron, the hoopoe and the bat.

19All flying insects are unclean to you; do not eat them. 20But any winged creature that is clean you may eat.

21Do not eat anything you find already dead. You may give it to the foreigner residing in any of your towns, and they may eat it, or you may sell it to any other foreigner. But you are a people holy to the LORD your God.

Do not cook a young goat in its mother's milk.

Tithes

22Be sure to set aside a tenth of all that your fields produce each year. 23Eat the tithe of your grain, new wine and olive oil, and the firstborn of your herds and flocks in the presence of the LORD your God at the place he will choose as a dwelling for his Name, so that you may learn to revere the LORD your God always. 24But if that place is too distant and you have been blessed by the LORD your God and cannot carry your tithe (because the place where the LORD will choose to put his Name is so far away), 25then exchange your tithe for silver, and take the silver with you and go to the place the LORD your God will choose. 26Use the silver to buy whatever you like: cattle, sheep, wine or other fermented drink, or anything you wish. Then you and your household shall eat there in the presence of the LORD your God and rejoice. 27And do not neglect the Levites living in your towns, for they have no allotment or inheritance of their own.

28At the end of every three years, bring all the tithes of that year's produce and store it in your towns, 29so that the Levites (who have no allotment or inheritance of their own) and the foreigners, the fatherless and the widows who live in your towns may come and eat and be satisfied, and so that the LORD your God may bless you in all the work of your hands.

The Year for Canceling Debts

15 At the end of every seven years you must cancel debts. 2This is how it is to be done: Every creditor shall cancel any loan they have made to a fellow Israelite. They shall not require payment from anyone among their own people, because the LORD's time for canceling debts has been proclaimed. 3You may require payment from a foreigner, but you must cancel any debt your fellow Israelite owes you. 4However, there need be no poor people among you, for in the land the LORD your God is giving you to possess as your inheritance, he will richly bless you, 5if only you fully obey the LORD your God and are careful to follow all these commands I am giving you today. 6For the LORD your God will bless you as he has promised, and you will lend to many nations but will borrow from none. You will rule over many nations but none will rule over you.

7If anyone is poor among your fellow Israelites in any of the towns of the land the LORD your God is giving you, do not be hardhearted or tightfisted toward them. 8Rather, be openhanded and freely lend them whatever they need. 9Be careful not to harbor this wicked thought: "The seventh year, the year for canceling debts, is near," so that you do not show ill will toward the needy among your fellow Israelites and give them nothing. They may then appeal to the LORD against you, and you will be found guilty of sin. 10Give generously to them and do so without a grudging heart; then because of this the LORD your God will bless you in all your work and in everything you put your hand to. 11There will always be poor people in the land. Therefore I command you to be openhanded toward your fellow Israelites who are poor and needy in your land.

Freeing Servants

12If any of your people—Hebrew men or women—sell themselves to you and serve you six years, in the seventh year you must let them go free. 13And when you release them, do not send them away empty-handed. 14Supply them liberally from your flock, your threshing floor and your winepress. Give to them as the LORD your God has blessed you. 15Remember that you were slaves in Egypt and the LORD your God redeemed you. That is why I give you this command today.

16But if your servant says to you, "I do not want to leave you," because he loves you and your family and is well off with you, 17then take an awl and push it through his earlobe into the door, and he will become your servant for life. Do the same for your female servant.

18Do not consider it a hardship to set your servant free, because their service to you these six years has been worth twice as much as that of a hired hand. And the LORD your God will bless you in everything you do.

[a] 5 The precise identification of some of the birds and animals in this chapter is uncertain.

The Firstborn Animals

19Set apart for the LORD your God every firstborn male of your herds and flocks. Do not put the firstborn of your cows to work, and do not shear the firstborn of your sheep. 20Each year you and your family are to eat them in the presence of the LORD your God at the place he will choose. 21If an animal has a defect, is lame or blind, or has any serious flaw, you must not sacrifice it to the LORD your God. 22You are to eat it in your own towns. Both the ceremonially unclean and the clean may eat it, as if it were gazelle or deer. 23But you must not eat the blood; pour it out on the ground like water.

The Passover

16 Observe the month of Aviv and celebrate the Passover of the LORD your God, because in the month of Aviv he brought you out of Egypt by night. 2Sacrifice as the Passover to the LORD your God an animal from your flock or herd at the place the LORD will choose as a dwelling for his Name. 3Do not eat it with bread made with yeast, but for seven days eat unleavened bread, the bread of affliction, because you left Egypt in haste—so that all the days of your life you may remember the time of your departure from Egypt. 4Let no yeast be found in your possession in all your land for seven days. Do not let any of the meat you sacrifice on the evening of the first day remain until morning.

5You must not sacrifice the Passover in any town the LORD your God gives you 6except in the place he will choose as a dwelling for his Name. There you must sacrifice the Passover in the evening, when the sun goes down, on the anniversary[a] of your departure from Egypt. 7Roast it and eat it at the place the LORD your God will choose. Then in the morning return to your tents. 8For six days eat unleavened bread and on the seventh day hold an assembly to the LORD your God and do no work.

The Festival of Weeks

9Count off seven weeks from the time you begin to put the sickle to the standing grain. 10Then celebrate the Festival of Weeks to the LORD your God by giving a freewill offering in proportion to the blessings the LORD your God has given you. 11And rejoice before the LORD your God at the place he will choose as a dwelling for his Name—you, your sons and daughters, your male and female servants, the Levites in your towns, and the foreigners, the fatherless and the widows living among you. 12Remember that you were slaves in Egypt, and follow carefully these decrees.

The Festival of Tabernacles

13Celebrate the Festival of Tabernacles for seven days after you have gathered the produce of your threshing floor and your winepress. 14Be joyful at your festival—you, your sons and daughters, your male and female servants, and the Levites, the foreigners, the fatherless and the widows who live in your towns. 15For seven days celebrate the festival to the LORD your God at the place the LORD will choose. For the LORD your God will bless you in all your harvest and in all the work of your hands, and your joy will be complete.

16Three times a year all your men must appear before the LORD your God at the place he will choose: at the Festival of Unleavened Bread, the Festival of Weeks and the Festival of Tabernacles. No one should appear before the LORD empty-handed: 17Each of you must bring a gift in proportion to the way the LORD your God has blessed you.

Judges

18Appoint judges and officials for each of your tribes in every town the LORD your God is giving you, and they shall judge the people fairly. 19Do not pervert justice or show partiality. Do not accept a bribe, for a bribe blinds the eyes of the wise and twists the words of the innocent. 20Follow justice and justice alone, so that you may live and possess the land the LORD your God is giving you.

Worshiping Other Gods

21Do not set up any wooden Asherah pole beside the altar you build to the LORD your God, 22and do not erect a sacred stone, for these the LORD your God hates.

17 Do not sacrifice to the LORD your God an ox or a sheep that has any defect or flaw in it, for that would be detestable to him.

2If a man or woman living among you in one of the towns the LORD gives you is found doing evil in the eyes of the LORD your God in violation of his covenant, 3and contrary to my command has worshiped other gods, bowing down to them or to the sun or the moon or the stars in the sky, 4and this has been brought to your attention, then you must investigate it thoroughly. If it is true and it has been proved that this detestable thing has been done in Israel, 5take the man or woman who has done this evil deed to your city gate and stone that person to death. 6On the testimony of two or three witnesses a person is to be put to death, but no one is to be put to death on the testimony of only one witness. 7The hands of the witnesses must be the first in putting that person to death, and then the hands of all the people. You must purge the evil from among you.

Law Courts

8If cases come before your courts that are too difficult for you to judge—whether bloodshed, lawsuits or assaults—take them to the place the LORD your God will choose. 9Go to the Levitical priests and to the judge who is in office at that time. Inquire of them and they will give you the verdict. 10You must act according to the decisions they give you at the

[a] 6 Or *down, at the time of day*

place the LORD will choose. Be careful to do
everything they instruct you to do. [11]Act according to whatever they teach you and the decisions they give you. Do not turn aside from
what they tell you, to the right or to the left.
[12]Anyone who shows contempt for the judge
or for the priest who stands ministering there
to the LORD your God is to be put to death.
You must purge the evil from Israel. [13]All the
people will hear and be afraid, and will not
be contemptuous again.

The King

[14]When you enter the land the LORD your
God is giving you and have taken possession
of it and settled in it, and you say, "Let us set
a king over us like all the nations around us,"
[15]be sure to appoint over you a king the LORD
your God chooses. He must be from among
your fellow Israelites. Do not place a foreigner over you, one who is not an Israelite. [16]The
king, moreover, must not acquire great numbers of horses for himself or make the people
return to Egypt to get more of them, for the
LORD has told you, "You are not to go back that
way again." [17]He must not take many wives,
or his heart will be led astray. He must not
accumulate large amounts of silver and gold.

[18]When he takes the throne of his kingdom,
he is to write for himself on a scroll a copy
of this law, taken from that of the Levitical
priests. [19]It is to be with him, and he is to read
it all the days of his life so that he may learn
to revere the LORD his God and follow carefully all the words of this law and these decrees [20]and not consider himself better than
his fellow Israelites and turn from the law
to the right or to the left. Then he and his
descendants will reign a long time over his
kingdom in Israel.

Offerings for Priests and Levites

18 The Levitical priests—indeed, the whole
tribe of Levi—are to have no allotment
or inheritance with Israel. They shall live on
the food offerings presented to the LORD, for
that is their inheritance. [2]They shall have no
inheritance among their fellow Israelites; the
LORD is their inheritance, as he promised them.

[3]This is the share due the priests from the
people who sacrifice a bull or a sheep: the
shoulder, the internal organs and the meat
from the head. [4]You are to give them the firstfruits of your grain, new wine and olive oil,
and the first wool from the shearing of your
sheep, [5]for the LORD your God has chosen
them and their descendants out of all your
tribes to stand and minister in the LORD's
name always.

[6]If a Levite moves from one of your towns
anywhere in Israel where he is living, and
comes in all earnestness to the place the LORD
will choose, [7]he may minister in the name of
the LORD his God like all his fellow Levites
who serve there in the presence of the LORD.
[8]He is to share equally in their benefits, even
though he has received money from the sale
of family possessions.

Occult Practices

[9]When you enter the land the LORD your
God is giving you, do not learn to imitate the
detestable ways of the nations there. [10]Let no
one be found among you who sacrifices their
son or daughter in the fire, who practices divination or sorcery, interprets omens, engages
in witchcraft, [11]or casts spells, or who is a
medium or spiritist or who consults the dead.
[12]Anyone who does these things is detestable
to the LORD; because of these same detestable practices the LORD your God will drive
out those nations before you. [13]You must be
blameless before the LORD your God.

The Prophet

[14]The nations you will dispossess listen
to those who practice sorcery or divination.
But as for you, the LORD your God has not
permitted you to do so. [15]The LORD your God
will raise up for you a prophet like me from
among you, from your fellow Israelites. You
must listen to him. [16]For this is what you asked
of the LORD your God at Horeb on the day of
the assembly when you said, "Let us not hear
the voice of the LORD our God nor see this
great fire anymore, or we will die."

[17]The LORD said to me: "What they say is
good. [18]I will raise up for them a prophet like
you from among their fellow Israelites, and
I will put my words in his mouth. He will tell
them everything I command him. [19]I myself
will call to account anyone who does not listen
to my words that the prophet speaks in my
name. [20]But a prophet who presumes to speak
in my name anything I have not commanded,
or a prophet who speaks in the name of other
gods, is to be put to death."

[21]You may say to yourselves, "How can we
know when a message has not been spoken
by the LORD?" [22]If what a prophet proclaims
in the name of the LORD does not take place or
come true, that is a message the LORD has not
spoken. That prophet has spoken presumptu-
ously, so do not be alarmed.

Cities of Refuge

19 When the LORD your God has destroyed
the nations whose land he is giving you,
and when you have driven them out and settled in their towns and houses, [2]then set aside
for yourselves three cities in the land the LORD
your God is giving you to possess. [3]Determine
the distances involved and divide into three
parts the land the LORD your God is giving
you as an inheritance, so that a person who
kills someone may flee for refuge to one of
these cities.

[4]This is the rule concerning anyone who
kills a person and flees there for safety—anyone who kills a neighbor unintentionally,
without malice aforethought. [5]For instance,
a man may go into the forest with his neighbor
to cut wood, and as he swings his ax to fell a
tree, the head may fly off and hit his neighbor and kill him. That man may flee to one of
these cities and save his life. [6]Otherwise, the
avenger of blood might pursue him in a rage,

overtake him if the distance is too great, and kill him even though he is not deserving of death, since he did it to his neighbor without malice aforethought. 7 This is why I command you to set aside for yourselves three cities.

8 If the LORD your God enlarges your territory, as he promised on oath to your ancestors, and gives you the whole land he promised them, 9 because you carefully follow all these laws I command you today—to love the LORD your God and to walk always in obedience to him—then you are to set aside three more cities. 10 Do this so that innocent blood will not be shed in your land, which the LORD your God is giving you as your inheritance, and so that you will not be guilty of bloodshed.

11 But if out of hate someone lies in wait, assaults and kills a neighbor, and then flees to one of these cities, 12 the killer shall be sent for by the town elders, be brought back from the city, and be handed over to the avenger of blood to die. 13 Show no pity. You must purge from Israel the guilt of shedding innocent blood, so that it may go well with you.

14 Do not move your neighbor's boundary stone set up by your predecessors in the inheritance you receive in the land the LORD your God is giving you to possess.

Witnesses

15 One witness is not enough to convict anyone accused of any crime or offense they may have committed. A matter must be established by the testimony of two or three witnesses.

16 If a malicious witness takes the stand to accuse someone of a crime, 17 the two people involved in the dispute must stand in the presence of the LORD before the priests and the judges who are in office at the time. 18 The judges must make a thorough investigation, and if the witness proves to be a liar, giving false testimony against a fellow Israelite, 19 then do to the false witness as that witness intended to do to the other party. You must purge the evil from among you. 20 The rest of the people will hear of this and be afraid, and never again will such an evil thing be done among you. 21 Show no pity: life for life, eye for eye, tooth for tooth, hand for hand, foot for foot.

Going to War

20 When you go to war against your enemies and see horses and chariots and an army greater than yours, do not be afraid of them, because the LORD your God, who brought you up out of Egypt, will be with you. 2 When you are about to go into battle, the priest shall come forward and address the army. 3 He shall say: "Hear, Israel: Today you are going into battle against your enemies. Do not be fainthearted or afraid; do not panic or be terrified by them. 4 For the LORD your God is the one who goes with you to fight for you against your enemies to give you victory."

5 The officers shall say to the army: "Has anyone built a new house and not yet begun to live in it? Let him go home, or he may die in battle and someone else may begin to live in it. 6 Has anyone planted a vineyard and not begun to enjoy it? Let him go home, or he may die in battle and someone else enjoy it. 7 Has anyone become pledged to a woman and not married her? Let him go home, or he may die in battle and someone else marry her." 8 Then the officers shall add, "Is anyone afraid or fainthearted? Let him go home so that his fellow soldiers will not become disheartened too." 9 When the officers have finished speaking to the army, they shall appoint commanders over it.

10 When you march up to attack a city, make its people an offer of peace. 11 If they accept and open their gates, all the people in it shall be subject to forced labor and shall work for you. 12 If they refuse to make peace and they engage you in battle, lay siege to that city. 13 When the LORD your God delivers it into your hand, put to the sword all the men in it. 14 As for the women, the children, the livestock and everything else in the city, you may take these as plunder for yourselves. And you may use the plunder the LORD your God gives you from your enemies. 15 This is how you are to treat all the cities that are at a distance from you and do not belong to the nations nearby.

16 However, in the cities of the nations the LORD your God is giving you as an inheritance, do not leave alive anything that breathes. 17 Completely destroy[a] them—the Hittites, Amorites, Canaanites, Perizzites, Hivites and Jebusites—as the LORD your God has commanded you. 18 Otherwise, they will teach you to follow all the detestable things they do in worshiping their gods, and you will sin against the LORD your God.

19 When you lay siege to a city for a long time, fighting against it to capture it, do not destroy its trees by putting an ax to them, because you can eat their fruit. Do not cut them down. Are the trees people, that you should besiege them?[b] 20 However, you may cut down trees that you know are not fruit trees and use them to build siege works until the city at war with you falls.

Atonement for an Unsolved Murder

21 If someone is found slain, lying in a field in the land the LORD your God is giving you to possess, and it is not known who the killer was, 2 your elders and judges shall go out and measure the distance from the body to the neighboring towns. 3 Then the elders of the town nearest the body shall take a heifer that has never been worked and has never worn a yoke 4 and lead it down to a valley that has not been plowed or planted and where there is a flowing stream. There in the valley they are to break the heifer's neck. 5 The Levitical priests shall step forward, for the LORD your God has chosen them to minister and to pronounce blessings in the name of

[a] *17* The Hebrew term refers to the irrevocable giving over of things or persons to the LORD, often by totally destroying them. [b] *19* Or *down to use in the siege, for the fruit trees are for the benefit of people.*

the LORD and to decide all cases of dispute
and assault. 6Then all the elders of the town
nearest the body shall wash their hands over
the heifer whose neck was broken in the valley, 7and they shall declare: "Our hands did
not shed this blood, nor did our eyes see it
done. 8Accept this atonement for your people
Israel, whom you have redeemed, LORD, and
do not hold your people guilty of the blood
of an innocent person." Then the bloodshed
will be atoned for, 9and you will have purged
from yourselves the guilt of shedding innocent blood, since you have done what is right
in the eyes of the LORD.

Marrying a Captive Woman

10When you go to war against your enemies and the LORD your God delivers them
into your hands and you take captives, 11if you
notice among the captives a beautiful woman and are attracted to her, you may take her
as your wife. 12Bring her into your home and
have her shave her head, trim her nails 13and
put aside the clothes she was wearing when
captured. After she has lived in your house
and mourned her father and mother for a full
month, then you may go to her and be her husband and she shall be your wife. 14If you are
not pleased with her, let her go wherever she
wishes. You must not sell her or treat her as a
slave, since you have dishonored her.

The Right of the Firstborn

15If a man has two wives, and he loves one
but not the other, and both bear him sons but
the firstborn is the son of the wife he does not
love, 16when he wills his property to his sons,
he must not give the rights of the firstborn
to the son of the wife he loves in preference
to his actual firstborn, the son of the wife he
does not love. 17He must acknowledge the son
of his unloved wife as the firstborn by giving
him a double share of all he has. That son is
the first sign of his father's strength. The right
of the firstborn belongs to him.

A Rebellious Son

18If someone has a stubborn and rebellious
son who does not obey his father and mother
and will not listen to them when they discipline him, 19his father and mother shall take
hold of him and bring him to the elders at
the gate of his town. 20They shall say to the
elders, "This son of ours is stubborn and rebellious. He will not obey us. He is a glutton and
a drunkard." 21Then all the men of his town
are to stone him to death. You must purge the
evil from among you. All Israel will hear of
it and be afraid.

Various Laws

22If someone guilty of a capital offense is
put to death and their body is exposed on a
pole, 23you must not leave the body hanging
on the pole overnight. Be sure to bury it that
same day, because anyone who is hung on a
pole is under God's curse. You must not desecrate the land the LORD your God is giving
you as an inheritance.

22 If you see your fellow Israelite's ox or
sheep straying, do not ignore it but be
sure to take it back to its owner. 2If they do not
live near you or if you do not know who owns
it, take it home with you and keep it until they
come looking for it. Then give it back. 3Do
the same if you find their donkey or cloak or
anything else they have lost. Do not ignore it.
4If you see your fellow Israelite's donkey or
ox fallen on the road, do not ignore it. Help
the owner get it to its feet.
5A woman must not wear men's clothing,
nor a man wear women's clothing, for the
LORD your God detests anyone who does this.
6If you come across a bird's nest beside the
road, either in a tree or on the ground, and
the mother is sitting on the young or on the
eggs, do not take the mother with the young.
7You may take the young, but be sure to let
the mother go, so that it may go well with you
and you may have a long life.
8When you build a new house, make a parapet around your roof so that you may not
bring the guilt of bloodshed on your house if
someone falls from the roof.
9Do not plant two kinds of seed in your
vineyard; if you do, not only the crops you
plant but also the fruit of the vineyard will
be defiled.[a]
10Do not plow with an ox and a donkey
yoked together.
11Do not wear clothes of wool and linen woven together.
12Make tassels on the four corners of the
cloak you wear.

Marriage Violations

13If a man takes a wife and, after sleeping
with her, dislikes her 14and slanders her and
gives her a bad name, saying, "I married this
woman, but when I approached her, I did not
find proof of her virginity," 15then the young
woman's father and mother shall bring to the
town elders at the gate proof that she was a
virgin. 16Her father will say to the elders, "I
gave my daughter in marriage to this man, but
he dislikes her. 17Now he has slandered her
and said, 'I did not find your daughter to be a
virgin.' But here is the proof of my daughter's
virginity." Then her parents shall display the
cloth before the elders of the town, 18and the
elders shall take the man and punish him.
19They shall fine him a hundred shekels[b] of
silver and give them to the young woman's
father, because this man has given an Israelite virgin a bad name. She shall continue to
be his wife; he must not divorce her as long
as he lives.
20If, however, the charge is true and no proof
of the young woman's virginity can be found,
21she shall be brought to the door of her father's house and there the men of her town
shall stone her to death. She has done an outrageous thing in Israel by being promiscuous

[a] 9 Or *be forfeited to the sanctuary*   [b] 19 That is, about 2 1/2 pounds or about 1.2 kilograms

while still in her father's house. You must purge the evil from among you.

[22]If a man is found sleeping with another man's wife, both the man who slept with her and the woman must die. You must purge the evil from Israel.

[23]If a man happens to meet in a town a virgin pledged to be married and he sleeps with her, [24]you shall take both of them to the gate of that town and stone them to death—the young woman because she was in a town and did not scream for help, and the man because he violated another man's wife. You must purge the evil from among you.

[25]But if out in the country a man happens to meet a young woman pledged to be married and rapes her, only the man who has done this shall die. [26]Do nothing to the woman; she has committed no sin deserving death. This case is like that of someone who attacks and murders a neighbor, [27]for the man found the young woman out in the country, and though the betrothed woman screamed, there was no one to rescue her.

[28]If a man happens to meet a virgin who is not pledged to be married and rapes her and they are discovered, [29]he shall pay her father fifty shekels[a] of silver. He must marry the young woman, for he has violated her. He can never divorce her as long as he lives.

[30]A man is not to marry his father's wife; he must not dishonor his father's bed.[b]

Exclusion From the Assembly

23[c] No one who has been emasculated by crushing or cutting may enter the assembly of the LORD.

[2]No one born of a forbidden marriage[d] nor any of their descendants may enter the assembly of the LORD, not even in the tenth generation.

[3]No Ammonite or Moabite or any of their descendants may enter the assembly of the LORD, not even in the tenth generation. [4]For they did not come to meet you with bread and water on your way when you came out of Egypt, and they hired Balaam son of Beor from Pethor in Aram Naharaim[e] to pronounce a curse on you. [5]However, the LORD your God would not listen to Balaam but turned the curse into a blessing for you, because the LORD your God loves you. [6]Do not seek a treaty of friendship with them as long as you live.

[7]Do not despise an Edomite, for the Edomites are related to you. Do not despise an Egyptian, because you resided as foreigners in their country. [8]The third generation of children born to them may enter the assembly of the LORD.

Uncleanness in the Camp

[9]When you are encamped against your enemies, keep away from everything impure. [10]If one of your men is unclean because of a nocturnal emission, he is to go outside the camp and stay there. [11]But as evening approaches he is to wash himself, and at sunset he may return to the camp.

[12]Designate a place outside the camp where you can go to relieve yourself. [13]As part of your equipment have something to dig with, and when you relieve yourself, dig a hole and cover up your excrement. [14]For the LORD your God moves about in your camp to protect you and to deliver your enemies to you. Your camp must be holy, so that he will not see among you anything indecent and turn away from you.

Miscellaneous Laws

[15]If a slave has taken refuge with you, do not hand them over to their master. [16]Let them live among you wherever they like and in whatever town they choose. Do not oppress them.

[17]No Israelite man or woman is to become a shrine prostitute. [18]You must not bring the earnings of a female prostitute or of a male prostitute[f] into the house of the LORD your God to pay any vow, because the LORD your God detests them both.

[19]Do not charge a fellow Israelite interest, whether on money or food or anything else that may earn interest. [20]You may charge a foreigner interest, but not a fellow Israelite, so that the LORD your God may bless you in everything you put your hand to in the land you are entering to possess.

[21]If you make a vow to the LORD your God, do not be slow to pay it, for the LORD your God will certainly demand it of you and you will be guilty of sin. [22]But if you refrain from making a vow, you will not be guilty. [23]Whatever your lips utter you must be sure to do, because you made your vow freely to the LORD your God with your own mouth.

[24]If you enter your neighbor's vineyard, you may eat all the grapes you want, but do not put any in your basket. [25]If you enter your neighbor's grainfield, you may pick kernels with your hands, but you must not put a sickle to their standing grain.

24 If a man marries a woman who becomes displeasing to him because he finds something indecent about her, and he writes her a certificate of divorce, gives it to her and sends her from his house, [2]and if after she leaves his house she becomes the wife of another man, [3]and her second husband dislikes her and writes her a certificate of divorce, gives it to her and sends her from his house, or if he dies, [4]then her first husband, who divorced her, is not allowed to marry her again after she has been defiled. That would be detestable in the eyes of the LORD. Do not bring sin upon the land the LORD your God is giving you as an inheritance.

[5]If a man has recently married, he must not be sent to war or have any other duty laid on him. For one year he is to be free to stay

[a] *29* That is, about 1 1/4 pounds or about 575 grams [b] *30* In Hebrew texts this verse (22:30) is numbered 23:1. [c] In Hebrew texts 23:1-25 is numbered 23:2-26. [d] *2* Or *one of illegitimate birth* [e] *4* That is, Northwest Mesopotamia [f] *18* Hebrew *of a dog*

at home and bring happiness to the wife he
has married.
[6]Do not take a pair of millstones—not even
the upper one—as security for a debt, because
that would be taking a person's livelihood as
security.
[7]If someone is caught kidnapping a fellow
Israelite and treating or selling them as a
slave, the kidnapper must die. You must purge
the evil from among you.
[8]In cases of defiling skin diseases,[a] be very
careful to do exactly as the Levitical priests
instruct you. You must follow carefully what
I have commanded them. [9]Remember what
the LORD your God did to Miriam along the
way after you came out of Egypt.
[10]When you make a loan of any kind to
your neighbor, do not go into their house to
get what is offered to you as a pledge. [11]Stay
outside and let the neighbor to whom you are
making the loan bring the pledge out to you.
[12]If the neighbor is poor, do not go to sleep
with their pledge in your possession. [13]Return
their cloak by sunset so that your neighbor
may sleep in it. Then they will thank you, and
it will be regarded as a righteous act in the
sight of the LORD your God.
[14]Do not take advantage of a hired worker
who is poor and needy, whether that worker
is a fellow Israelite or a foreigner residing in
one of your towns. [15]Pay them their wages
each day before sunset, because they are poor
and are counting on it. Otherwise they may
cry to the LORD against you, and you will be
guilty of sin.
[16]Parents are not to be put to death for their
children, nor children put to death for their
parents; each will die for their own sin.
[17]Do not deprive the foreigner or the fatherless of justice, or take the cloak of the widow
as a pledge. [18]Remember that you were slaves
in Egypt and the LORD your God redeemed
you from there. That is why I command you
to do this.
[19]When you are harvesting in your field and
you overlook a sheaf, do not go back to get
it. Leave it for the foreigner, the fatherless
and the widow, so that the LORD your God
may bless you in all the work of your hands.
[20]When you beat the olives from your trees,
do not go over the branches a second time.
Leave what remains for the foreigner, the fatherless and the widow. [21]When you harvest
the grapes in your vineyard, do not go over
the vines again. Leave what remains for the
foreigner, the fatherless and the widow. [22]Re-
member that you were slaves in Egypt. That
is why I command you to do this.

25 When people have a dispute, they are
to take it to court and the judges will
decide the case, acquitting the innocent and
condemning the guilty. [2]If the guilty person
deserves to be beaten, the judge shall make
them lie down and have them flogged in his
presence with the number of lashes the crime
deserves, [3]but the judge must not impose more
than forty lashes. If the guilty party is flogged
more than that, your fellow Israelite will be
degraded in your eyes.
[4]Do not muzzle an ox while it is treading
out the grain.
[5]If brothers are living together and one
of them dies without a son, his widow must
not marry outside the family. Her husband's
brother shall take her and marry her and fulfill the duty of a brother-in-law to her. [6]The
first son she bears shall carry on the name
of the dead brother so that his name will not
be blotted out from Israel.
[7]However, if a man does not want to marry
his brother's wife, she shall go to the elders at
the town gate and say, "My husband's brother
refuses to carry on his brother's name in Israel. He will not fulfill the duty of a brother-in-
law to me." [8]Then the elders of his town shall
summon him and talk to him. If he persists
in saying, "I do not want to marry her," [9]his
brother's widow shall go up to him in the presence of the elders, take off one of his sandals,
spit in his face and say, "This is what is done
to the man who will not build up his brother's
family line." [10]That man's line shall be known
in Israel as The Family of the Unsandaled.
[11]If two men are fighting and the wife of one
of them comes to rescue her husband from
his assailant, and she reaches out and seizes
him by his private parts, [12]you shall cut off
her hand. Show her no pity.
[13]Do not have two differing weights in your
bag—one heavy, one light. [14]Do not have two
differing measures in your house—one large,
one small. [15]You must have accurate and honest weights and measures, so that you may
live long in the land the LORD your God is
giving you. [16]For the LORD your God detests
anyone who does these things, anyone who
deals dishonestly.
[17]Remember what the Amalekites did to you
along the way when you came out of Egypt.
[18]When you were weary and worn out, they
met you on your journey and attacked all who
were lagging behind; they had no fear of God.
[19]When the LORD your God gives you rest from
all the enemies around you in the land he is
giving you to possess as an inheritance, you
shall blot out the name of Amalek from under
heaven. Do not forget!

Firstfruits and Tithes

26 When you have entered the land the
LORD your God is giving you as an inheritance and have taken possession of it and
settled in it, [2]take some of the firstfruits of all
that you produce from the soil of the land the
LORD your God is giving you and put them in
a basket. Then go to the place the LORD your
God will choose as a dwelling for his Name
[3]and say to the priest in office at the time,
"I declare today to the LORD your God that I
have come to the land the LORD swore to our
ancestors to give us." [4]The priest shall take
the basket from your hands and set it down in

[a] 8 The Hebrew word for *defiling skin diseases*, traditionally translated "leprosy," was used for various diseases affecting the skin.

front of the altar of the LORD your God. 5Then you shall declare before the LORD your God: "My father was a wandering Aramean, and he went down into Egypt with a few people and lived there and became a great nation, powerful and numerous. 6But the Egyptians mistreated us and made us suffer, subjecting us to harsh labor. 7Then we cried out to the LORD, the God of our ancestors, and the LORD heard our voice and saw our misery, toil and oppression. 8So the LORD brought us out of Egypt with a mighty hand and an outstretched arm, with great terror and with signs and wonders. 9He brought us to this place and gave us this land, a land flowing with milk and honey; 10and now I bring the firstfruits of the soil that you, LORD, have given me." Place the basket before the LORD your God and bow down before him. 11Then you and the Levites and the foreigners residing among you shall rejoice in all the good things the LORD your God has given to you and your household.

12When you have finished setting aside a tenth of all your produce in the third year, the year of the tithe, you shall give it to the Levite, the foreigner, the fatherless and the widow, so that they may eat in your towns and be satisfied. 13Then say to the LORD your God: "I have removed from my house the sacred portion and have given it to the Levite, the foreigner, the fatherless and the widow, according to all you commanded. I have not turned aside from your commands nor have I forgotten any of them. 14I have not eaten any of the sacred portion while I was in mourning, nor have I removed any of it while I was unclean, nor have I offered any of it to the dead. I have obeyed the LORD my God; I have done everything you commanded me. 15Look down from heaven, your holy dwelling place, and bless your people Israel and the land you have given us as you promised on oath to our ancestors, a land flowing with milk and honey."

Follow the LORD's Commands

16The LORD your God commands you this day to follow these decrees and laws; carefully observe them with all your heart and with all your soul. 17You have declared this day that the LORD is your God and that you will walk in obedience to him, that you will keep his decrees, commands and laws—that you will listen to him. 18And the LORD has declared this day that you are his people, his treasured possession as he promised, and that you are to keep all his commands. 19He has declared that he will set you in praise, fame and honor high above all the nations he has made and that you will be a people holy to the LORD your God, as he promised.

The Altar on Mount Ebal

27 Moses and the elders of Israel commanded the people: "Keep all these commands that I give you today. 2When you have crossed the Jordan into the land the LORD your God is giving you, set up some large stones and coat them with plaster. 3Write on them all the words of this law when you have crossed over to enter the land the LORD your God is giving you, a land flowing with milk and honey, just as the LORD, the God of your ancestors, promised you. 4And when you have crossed the Jordan, set up these stones on Mount Ebal, as I command you today, and coat them with plaster. 5Build there an altar to the LORD your God, an altar of stones. Do not use any iron tool on them. 6Build the altar of the LORD your God with fieldstones and offer burnt offerings on it to the LORD your God. 7Sacrifice fellowship offerings there, eating them and rejoicing in the presence of the LORD your God. 8And you shall write very clearly all the words of this law on these stones you have set up."

Curses From Mount Ebal

9Then Moses and the Levitical priests said to all Israel, "Be silent, Israel, and listen! You have now become the people of the LORD your God. 10Obey the LORD your God and follow his commands and decrees that I give you today."

11On the same day Moses commanded the people:

12When you have crossed the Jordan, these tribes shall stand on Mount Gerizim to bless the people: Simeon, Levi, Judah, Issachar, Joseph and Benjamin. 13And these tribes shall stand on Mount Ebal to pronounce curses: Reuben, Gad, Asher, Zebulun, Dan and Naphtali.

14The Levites shall recite to all the people of Israel in a loud voice:

15"Cursed is anyone who makes an idol—a thing detestable to the LORD, the work of skilled hands—and sets it up in secret."

Then all the people shall say,
"Amen!"

16"Cursed is anyone who dishonors their father or mother."

Then all the people shall say,
"Amen!"

17"Cursed is anyone who moves their neighbor's boundary stone."

Then all the people shall say,
"Amen!"

18"Cursed is anyone who leads the blind astray on the road."

Then all the people shall say,
"Amen!"

19"Cursed is anyone who withholds justice from the foreigner, the fatherless or the widow."

Then all the people shall say,
"Amen!"

20"Cursed is anyone who sleeps with his father's wife, for he dishonors his father's bed."

Then all the people shall say,
"Amen!"

21"Cursed is anyone who has sexual relations with any animal."

Then all the people shall say,
"Amen!"

22"Cursed is anyone who sleeps with

his sister, the daughter of his father or the
daughter of his mother.”
Then all the people shall say,
“Amen!”
23“Cursed is anyone who sleeps with
his mother-in-law.”
Then all the people shall say,
“Amen!”
24“Cursed is anyone who kills their
neighbor secretly.”
Then all the people shall say,
“Amen!”
25“Cursed is anyone who accepts a
bribe to kill an innocent person.”
Then all the people shall say,
“Amen!”
26“Cursed is anyone who does not uphold the words of this law by carrying
them out.”
Then all the people shall say,
“Amen!”

Blessings for Obedience

28 If you fully obey the LORD your God and
carefully follow all his commands I give
you today, the LORD your God will set you
high above all the nations on earth. 2All these
blessings will come on you and accompany
you if you obey the LORD your God:

3You will be blessed in the city and
blessed in the country.
4The fruit of your womb will be blessed,
and the crops of your land and the young
of your livestock—the calves of your
herds and the lambs of your flocks.
5Your basket and your kneading trough
will be blessed.
6You will be blessed when you come in
and blessed when you go out.

7The LORD will grant that the enemies who
rise up against you will be defeated before
you. They will come at you from one direction
but flee from you in seven.
8The LORD will send a blessing on your
barns and on everything you put your hand
to. The LORD your God will bless you in the
land he is giving you.
9The LORD will establish you as his holy
people, as he promised you on oath, if you
keep the commands of the LORD your God
and walk in obedience to him. 10Then all the
peoples on earth will see that you are called
by the name of the LORD, and they will fear
you. 11The LORD will grant you abundant
prosperity—in the fruit of your womb, the
young of your livestock and the crops of your
ground—in the land he swore to your ancestors to give you.
12The LORD will open the heavens, the storehouse of his bounty, to send rain on your land
in season and to bless all the work of your
hands. You will lend to many nations but will
borrow from none. 13The LORD will make you
the head, not the tail. If you pay attention to
the commands of the LORD your God that I
give you this day and carefully follow them,
you will always be at the top, never at the bottom. 14Do not turn aside from any of the commands I give you today, to the right or to the
left, following other gods and serving them.

Curses for Disobedience

15However, if you do not obey the LORD
your God and do not carefully follow all his
commands and decrees I am giving you today, all these curses will come on you and
overtake you:

16You will be cursed in the city and
cursed in the country.
17Your basket and your kneading
trough will be cursed.
18The fruit of your womb will be
cursed, and the crops of your land, and
the calves of your herds and the lambs
of your flocks.
19You will be cursed when you come in
and cursed when you go out.

20The LORD will send on you curses, confusion and rebuke in everything you put your
hand to, until you are destroyed and come to
sudden ruin because of the evil you have done
in forsaking him.[a] 21The LORD will plague you
with diseases until he has destroyed you from
the land you are entering to possess. 22The
LORD will strike you with wasting disease,
with fever and inflammation, with scorching heat and drought, with blight and mildew, which will plague you until you perish.
23The sky over your head will be bronze, the
ground beneath you iron. 24The LORD will turn
the rain of your country into dust and powder;
it will come down from the skies until you
are destroyed.
25The LORD will cause you to be defeated
before your enemies. You will come at them
from one direction but flee from them in sev-
en, and you will become a thing of horror to
all the kingdoms on earth. 26Your carcasses
will be food for all the birds and the wild animals, and there will be no one to frighten
them away. 27The LORD will afflict you with
the boils of Egypt and with tumors, festering
sores and the itch, from which you cannot
be cured. 28The LORD will afflict you with
madness, blindness and confusion of mind.
29At midday you will grope about like a blind
person in the dark. You will be unsuccess-
ful in everything you do; day after day you
will be oppressed and robbed, with no one
to rescue you.
30You will be pledged to be married to a
woman, but another will take her and rape
her. You will build a house, but you will not
live in it. You will plant a vineyard, but you
will not even begin to enjoy its fruit. 31Your ox
will be slaughtered before your eyes, but you
will eat none of it. Your donkey will be forcibly
taken from you and will not be returned. Your
sheep will be given to your enemies, and no
one will rescue them. 32Your sons and daughters will be given to another nation, and you
will wear out your eyes watching for them day

[a] 20 Hebrew *me*

after day, powerless to lift a hand. 33A people that you do not know will eat what your land and labor produce, and you will have nothing but cruel oppression all your days. 34The sights you see will drive you mad. 35The LORD will afflict your knees and legs with painful boils that cannot be cured, spreading from the soles of your feet to the top of your head.

36The LORD will drive you and the king you set over you to a nation unknown to you or your ancestors. There you will worship other gods, gods of wood and stone. 37You will become a thing of horror, a byword and an object of ridicule among all the peoples where the LORD will drive you.

38You will sow much seed in the field but you will harvest little, because locusts will devour it. 39You will plant vineyards and cultivate them but you will not drink the wine or gather the grapes, because worms will eat them. 40You will have olive trees throughout your country but you will not use the oil, because the olives will drop off. 41You will have sons and daughters but you will not keep them, because they will go into captivity. 42Swarms of locusts will take over all your trees and the crops of your land.

43The foreigners who reside among you will rise above you higher and higher, but you will sink lower and lower. 44They will lend to you, but you will not lend to them. They will be the head, but you will be the tail.

45All these curses will come on you. They will pursue you and overtake you until you are destroyed, because you did not obey the LORD your God and observe the commands and decrees he gave you. 46They will be a sign and a wonder to you and your descendants forever. 47Because you did not serve the LORD your God joyfully and gladly in the time of prosperity, 48therefore in hunger and thirst, in nakedness and dire poverty, you will serve the enemies the LORD sends against you. He will put an iron yoke on your neck until he has destroyed you.

49The LORD will bring a nation against you from far away, from the ends of the earth, like an eagle swooping down, a nation whose language you will not understand, 50a fierce-looking nation without respect for the old or pity for the young. 51They will devour the young of your livestock and the crops of your land until you are destroyed. They will leave you no grain, new wine or olive oil, nor any calves of your herds or lambs of your flocks until you are ruined. 52They will lay siege to all the cities throughout your land until the high fortified walls in which you trust fall down. They will besiege all the cities throughout the land the LORD your God is giving you.

53Because of the suffering your enemy will inflict on you during the siege, you will eat the fruit of the womb, the flesh of the sons and daughters the LORD your God has given you. 54Even the most gentle and sensitive man among you will have no compassion on his own brother or the wife he loves or his surviving children, 55and he will not give to one of them any of the flesh of his children that he is eating. It will be all he has left because of the suffering your enemy will inflict on you during the siege of all your cities. 56The most gentle and sensitive woman among you—so sensitive and gentle that she would not venture to touch the ground with the sole of her foot—will begrudge the husband she loves and her own son or daughter 57the afterbirth from her womb and the children she bears. For in her dire need she intends to eat them secretly because of the suffering your enemy will inflict on you during the siege of your cities.

58If you do not carefully follow all the words of this law, which are written in this book, and do not revere this glorious and awesome name—the LORD your God— 59the LORD will send fearful plagues on you and your descendants, harsh and prolonged disasters, and severe and lingering illnesses. 60He will bring on you all the diseases of Egypt that you dreaded, and they will cling to you. 61The LORD will also bring on you every kind of sickness and disaster not recorded in this Book of the Law, until you are destroyed. 62You who were as numerous as the stars in the sky will be left but few in number, because you did not obey the LORD your God. 63Just as it pleased the LORD to make you prosper and increase in number, so it will please him to ruin and destroy you. You will be uprooted from the land you are entering to possess.

64Then the LORD will scatter you among all nations, from one end of the earth to the other. There you will worship other gods—gods of wood and stone, which neither you nor your ancestors have known. 65Among those nations you will find no repose, no resting place for the sole of your foot. There the LORD will give you an anxious mind, eyes weary with longing, and a despairing heart. 66You will live in constant suspense, filled with dread both night and day, never sure of your life. 67In the morning you will say, "If only it were evening!" and in the evening, "If only it were morning!"—because of the terror that will fill your hearts and the sights that your eyes will see. 68The LORD will send you back in ships to Egypt on a journey I said you should never make again. There you will offer yourselves for sale to your enemies as male and female slaves, but no one will buy you.

Renewal of the Covenant

29[a] These are the terms of the covenant the LORD commanded Moses to make with the Israelites in Moab, in addition to the covenant he had made with them at Horeb.

2Moses summoned all the Israelites and said to them:

Your eyes have seen all that the LORD did in Egypt to Pharaoh, to all his officials and to all his land. 3With your own eyes you saw those

[a] In Hebrew texts 29:1 is numbered 28:69, and 29:2-29 is numbered 29:1-28.

great trials, those signs and great wonders.
4But to this day the LORD has not given you
a mind that understands or eyes that see or
ears that hear. 5Yet the LORD says, "During the
forty years that I led you through the wilderness, your clothes did not wear out, nor did
the sandals on your feet. 6You ate no bread
and drank no wine or other fermented drink.
I did this so that you might know that I am the
LORD your God."

7When you reached this place, Sihon king
of Heshbon and Og king of Bashan came out
to fight against us, but we defeated them. 8We
took their land and gave it as an inheritance to
the Reubenites, the Gadites and the half-tribe
of Manasseh.

9Carefully follow the terms of this covenant,
so that you may prosper in everything you do.
10All of you are standing today in the presence
of the LORD your God—your leaders and chief
men, your elders and officials, and all the other men of Israel, 11together with your children
and your wives, and the foreigners living in
your camps who chop your wood and carry
your water. 12You are standing here in order
to enter into a covenant with the LORD your
God, a covenant the LORD is making with you
this day and sealing with an oath, 13to confirm
you this day as his people, that he may be your
God as he promised you and as he swore to
your fathers, Abraham, Isaac and Jacob. 14I
am making this covenant, with its oath, not
only with you 15who are standing here with
us today in the presence of the LORD our God
but also with those who are not here today.

16You yourselves know how we lived in
Egypt and how we passed through the countries on the way here. 17You saw among them
their detestable images and idols of wood and
stone, of silver and gold. 18Make sure there is
no man or woman, clan or tribe among you
today whose heart turns away from the LORD
our God to go and worship the gods of those
nations; make sure there is no root among you
that produces such bitter poison.

19When such a person hears the words of
this oath and they invoke a blessing on themselves, thinking, "I will be safe, even though I
persist in going my own way," they will bring
disaster on the watered land as well as the dry.
20The LORD will never be willing to forgive
them; his wrath and zeal will burn against
them. All the curses written in this book will
fall on them, and the LORD will blot out their
names from under heaven. 21The LORD will
single them out from all the tribes of Israel for disaster, according to all the curses of
the covenant written in this Book of the Law.

22Your children who follow you in later
generations and foreigners who come from
distant lands will see the calamities that have
fallen on the land and the diseases with which
the LORD has afflicted it. 23The whole land will
be a burning waste of salt and sulfur—nothing planted, nothing sprouting, no vegetation
growing on it. It will be like the destruction
of Sodom and Gomorrah, Admah and Zeboyim, which the LORD overthrew in fierce anger. 24All the nations will ask: "Why has the
LORD done this to this land? Why this fierce,
burning anger?"

25And the answer will be: "It is because this
people abandoned the covenant of the LORD,
the God of their ancestors, the covenant he
made with them when he brought them out
of Egypt. 26They went off and worshiped other gods and bowed down to them, gods they
did not know, gods he had not given them.
27Therefore the LORD's anger burned against
this land, so that he brought on it all the curses
written in this book. 28In furious anger and
in great wrath the LORD uprooted them from
their land and thrust them into another land,
as it is now."

29The secret things belong to the LORD our
God, but the things revealed belong to us and
to our children forever, that we may follow all
the words of this law.

Prosperity After Turning to the LORD

30 When all these blessings and curses I
have set before you come on you and
you take them to heart wherever the LORD
your God disperses you among the nations,
2and when you and your children return to
the LORD your God and obey him with all
your heart and with all your soul according
to everything I command you today, 3then the
LORD your God will restore your fortunes[a]
and have compassion on you and gather you
again from all the nations where he scattered
you. 4Even if you have been banished to the
most distant land under the heavens, from
there the LORD your God will gather you and
bring you back. 5He will bring you to the land
that belonged to your ancestors, and you will
take possession of it. He will make you more
prosperous and numerous than your ancestors. 6The LORD your God will circumcise your
hearts and the hearts of your descendants, so
that you may love him with all your heart and
with all your soul, and live. 7The LORD your
God will put all these curses on your enemies
who hate and persecute you. 8You will again
obey the LORD and follow all his commands
I am giving you today. 9Then the LORD your
God will make you most prosperous in all the
work of your hands and in the fruit of your
womb, the young of your livestock and the
crops of your land. The LORD will again delight in you and make you prosperous, just as
he delighted in your ancestors, 10if you obey
the LORD your God and keep his commands
and decrees that are written in this Book of
the Law and turn to the LORD your God with
all your heart and with all your soul.

The Offer of Life or Death

11Now what I am commanding you today is
not too difficult for you or beyond your reach.
12It is not up in heaven, so that you have to ask,
"Who will ascend into heaven to get it and
proclaim it to us so we may obey it?" 13Nor

[a] 3 Or *will bring you back from captivity*

is it beyond the sea, so that you have to ask, "Who will cross the sea to get it and proclaim it to us so we may obey it?" 14No, the word is very near you; it is in your mouth and in your heart so you may obey it.

15See, I set before you today life and prosperity, death and destruction. 16For I command you today to love the LORD your God, to walk in obedience to him, and to keep his commands, decrees and laws; then you will live and increase, and the LORD your God will bless you in the land you are entering to possess.

17But if your heart turns away and you are not obedient, and if you are drawn away to bow down to other gods and worship them, 18I declare to you this day that you will certainly be destroyed. You will not live long in the land you are crossing the Jordan to enter and possess.

19This day I call the heavens and the earth as witnesses against you that I have set before you life and death, blessings and curses. Now choose life, so that you and your children may live 20and that you may love the LORD your God, listen to his voice, and hold fast to him. For the LORD is your life, and he will give you many years in the land he swore to give to your fathers, Abraham, Isaac and Jacob.

Joshua to Succeed Moses

31 Then Moses went out and spoke these words to all Israel: 2"I am now a hundred and twenty years old and I am no longer able to lead you. The LORD has said to me, 'You shall not cross the Jordan.' 3The LORD your God himself will cross over ahead of you. He will destroy these nations before you, and you will take possession of their land. Joshua also will cross over ahead of you, as the LORD said. 4And the LORD will do to them what he did to Sihon and Og, the kings of the Amorites, whom he destroyed along with their land. 5The LORD will deliver them to you, and you must do to them all that I have commanded you. 6Be strong and courageous. Do not be afraid or terrified because of them, for the LORD your God goes with you; he will never leave you nor forsake you."

7Then Moses summoned Joshua and said to him in the presence of all Israel, "Be strong and courageous, for you must go with this people into the land that the LORD swore to their ancestors to give them, and you must divide it among them as their inheritance. 8The LORD himself goes before you and will be with you; he will never leave you nor forsake you. Do not be afraid; do not be discouraged."

Public Reading of the Law

9So Moses wrote down this law and gave it to the Levitical priests, who carried the ark of the covenant of the LORD, and to all the elders of Israel. 10Then Moses commanded them: "At the end of every seven years, in the year for canceling debts, during the Festival of Tabernacles, 11when all Israel comes to appear before the LORD your God at the place he will choose, you shall read this law before them in their hearing. 12Assemble the people—men, women and children, and the foreigners residing in your towns—so they can listen and learn to fear the LORD your God and follow carefully all the words of this law. 13Their children, who do not know this law, must hear it and learn to fear the LORD your God as long as you live in the land you are crossing the Jordan to possess."

Israel's Rebellion Predicted

14The LORD said to Moses, "Now the day of your death is near. Call Joshua and present yourselves at the tent of meeting, where I will commission him." So Moses and Joshua came and presented themselves at the tent of meeting.

15Then the LORD appeared at the tent in a pillar of cloud, and the cloud stood over the entrance to the tent. 16And the LORD said to Moses: "You are going to rest with your ancestors, and these people will soon prostitute themselves to the foreign gods of the land they are entering. They will forsake me and break the covenant I made with them. 17And in that day I will become angry with them and forsake them; I will hide my face from them, and they will be destroyed. Many disasters and calamities will come on them, and in that day they will ask, 'Have not these disasters come on us because our God is not with us?' 18And I will certainly hide my face in that day because of all their wickedness in turning to other gods.

19"Now write down this song and teach it to the Israelites and have them sing it, so that it may be a witness for me against them. 20When I have brought them into the land flowing with milk and honey, the land I promised on oath to their ancestors, and when they eat their fill and thrive, they will turn to other gods and worship them, rejecting me and breaking my covenant. 21And when many disasters and calamities come on them, this song will testify against them, because it will not be forgotten by their descendants. I know what they are disposed to do, even before I bring them into the land I promised them on oath." 22So Moses wrote down this song that day and taught it to the Israelites.

23The LORD gave this command to Joshua son of Nun: "Be strong and courageous, for you will bring the Israelites into the land I promised them on oath, and I myself will be with you."

24After Moses finished writing in a book the words of this law from beginning to end, 25he gave this command to the Levites who carried the ark of the covenant of the LORD: 26"Take this Book of the Law and place it beside the ark of the covenant of the LORD your God. There it will remain as a witness against you. 27For I know how rebellious and stiff-necked you are. If you have been rebellious against the LORD while I am still alive and with you, how much more will you rebel after I die! 28Assemble before me all the elders of your tribes and all your officials, so that I can speak these

words in their hearing and call the heavens
and the earth to testify against them. 29For
I know that after my death you are sure to
become utterly corrupt and to turn from the
way I have commanded you. In days to come,
disaster will fall on you because you will do
evil in the sight of the LORD and arouse his
anger by what your hands have made."

The Song of Moses

30And Moses recited the words of this song
from beginning to end in the hearing of the
whole assembly of Israel:

32 Listen, you heavens, and I will speak;
hear, you earth, the words of my
mouth.
2 Let my teaching fall like rain
and my words descend like dew,
like showers on new grass,
like abundant rain on tender plants.

3 I will proclaim the name of the LORD.
Oh, praise the greatness of our God!
4 He is the Rock, his works are perfect,
and all his ways are just.
A faithful God who does no wrong,
upright and just is he.

5 They are corrupt and not his children;
to their shame they are a warped and
crooked generation.
6 Is this the way you repay the LORD,
you foolish and unwise people?
Is he not your Father, your Creator,[a]
who made you and formed you?

7 Remember the days of old;
consider the generations long past.
Ask your father and he will tell you,
your elders, and they will explain to you.
8 When the Most High gave the nations
their inheritance,
when he divided all mankind,
he set up boundaries for the peoples
according to the number of the sons of
Israel.[b]
9 For the LORD's portion is his people,
Jacob his allotted inheritance.

10 In a desert land he found him,
in a barren and howling waste.
He shielded him and cared for him;
he guarded him as the apple of his eye,
11 like an eagle that stirs up its nest
and hovers over its young,
that spreads its wings to catch them
and carries them aloft.
12 The LORD alone led him;
no foreign god was with him.

13 He made him ride on the heights of the
land
and fed him with the fruit of the fields.
He nourished him with honey from the
rock,
and with oil from the flinty crag,
14 with curds and milk from herd and flock
and with fattened lambs and goats,
with choice rams of Bashan
and the finest kernels of wheat.
You drank the foaming blood of the
grape.

15 Jeshurun[c] grew fat and kicked;
filled with food, they became heavy
and sleek.
They abandoned the God who made them
and rejected the Rock their Savior.
16 They made him jealous with their foreign
gods
and angered him with their detestable
idols.
17 They sacrificed to false gods, which are
not God—
gods they had not known,
gods that recently appeared,
gods your ancestors did not fear.
18 You deserted the Rock, who fathered you;
you forgot the God who gave you birth.

19 The LORD saw this and rejected them
because he was angered by his sons
and daughters.
20 "I will hide my face from them," he said,
"and see what their end will be;
for they are a perverse generation,
children who are unfaithful.
21 They made me jealous by what is no god
and angered me with their worthless
idols.
I will make them envious by those who
are not a people;
I will make them angry by a nation that
has no understanding.
22 For a fire will be kindled by my wrath,
one that burns down to the realm of the
dead below.
It will devour the earth and its harvests
and set afire the foundations of the
mountains.

23 "I will heap calamities on them
and spend my arrows against them.
24 I will send wasting famine against them,
consuming pestilence and deadly
plague;
I will send against them the fangs of wild
beasts,
the venom of vipers that glide in the
dust.
25 In the street the sword will make them
childless;
in their homes terror will reign.
The young men and young women will
perish,
the infants and those with gray hair.
26 I said I would scatter them
and erase their name from human
memory,
27 but I dreaded the taunt of the enemy,
lest the adversary misunderstand
and say, 'Our hand has triumphed;
the LORD has not done all this.'"

28 They are a nation without sense,
there is no discernment in them.

[a] 6 Or *Father, who bought you* [b] 8 Masoretic Text; Dead Sea Scrolls (see also Septuagint) *sons of God* [c] 15 *Jeshurun* means *the upright one*, that is, Israel.

29 If only they were wise and would
understand this
and discern what their end will be!
30 How could one man chase a thousand,
or two put ten thousand to flight,
unless their Rock had sold them,
unless the LORD had given them up?
31 For their rock is not like our Rock,
as even our enemies concede.
32 Their vine comes from the vine of
Sodom
and from the fields of Gomorrah.
Their grapes are filled with poison,
and their clusters with bitterness.
33 Their wine is the venom of serpents,
the deadly poison of cobras.

34 "Have I not kept this in reserve
and sealed it in my vaults?
35 It is mine to avenge; I will repay.
In due time their foot will slip;
their day of disaster is near
and their doom rushes upon them."

36 The LORD will vindicate his people
and relent concerning his servants
when he sees their strength is gone
and no one is left, slave or free.[a]
37 He will say: "Now where are their gods,
the rock they took refuge in,
38 the gods who ate the fat of their sacrifices
and drank the wine of their drink
offerings?
Let them rise up to help you!
Let them give you shelter!

39 "See now that I myself am he!
There is no god besides me.
I put to death and I bring to life,
I have wounded and I will heal,
and no one can deliver out of my hand.
40 I lift my hand to heaven and solemnly
swear:
As surely as I live forever,
41 when I sharpen my flashing sword
and my hand grasps it in judgment,
I will take vengeance on my adversaries
and repay those who hate me.
42 I will make my arrows drunk with
blood,
while my sword devours flesh:
the blood of the slain and the captives,
the heads of the enemy leaders."

43 Rejoice, you nations, with his people,[b,c]
for he will avenge the blood of his
servants;
he will take vengeance on his enemies
and make atonement for his land and
people.

44 Moses came with Joshua[d] son of Nun and
spoke all the words of this song in the hearing
of the people. 45 When Moses finished reciting
all these words to all Israel, 46 he said to them,
"Take to heart all the words I have solemnly declared to you this day, so that you may
command your children to obey carefully all
the words of this law. 47 They are not just idle
words for you—they are your life. By them
you will live long in the land you are crossing
the Jordan to possess."

Moses to Die on Mount Nebo

48 On that same day the LORD told Moses,
49 "Go up into the Abarim Range to Mount
Nebo in Moab, across from Jericho, and view
Canaan, the land I am giving the Israelites as
their own possession. 50 There on the mountain that you have climbed you will die and be
gathered to your people, just as your brother
Aaron died on Mount Hor and was gathered
to his people. 51 This is because both of you
broke faith with me in the presence of the Israelites at the waters of Meribah Kadesh in the
Desert of Zin and because you did not uphold
my holiness among the Israelites. 52 Therefore,
you will see the land only from a distance;
you will not enter the land I am giving to the
people of Israel."

Moses Blesses the Tribes

33 This is the blessing that Moses the man
of God pronounced on the Israelites before his death. 2 He said:

"The LORD came from Sinai
and dawned over them from Seir;
he shone forth from Mount Paran.
He came with[e] myriads of holy ones
from the south, from his mountain
slopes.[f]
3 Surely it is you who love the people;
all the holy ones are in your hand.
At your feet they all bow down,
and from you receive instruction,
4 the law that Moses gave us,
the possession of the assembly of
Jacob.
5 He was king over Jeshurun[g]
when the leaders of the people
assembled,
along with the tribes of Israel.

6 "Let Reuben live and not die,
nor[h] his people be few."

7 And this he said about Judah:

"Hear, LORD, the cry of Judah;
bring him to his people.
With his own hands he defends his
cause.
Oh, be his help against his foes!"

8 About Levi he said:

"Your Thummim and Urim belong
to your faithful servant.
You tested him at Massah;
you contended with him at the waters
of Meribah.

[a] 36 Or *and they are without a ruler or leader* [b] 43 Or *Make his people rejoice, you nations* [c] 43 Masoretic Text; Dead Sea Scrolls (see also Septuagint) *people, / and let all the angels worship him, /* [d] 44 Hebrew *Hoshea,* a variant of *Joshua* [e] 2 Or *from* [f] 2 The meaning of the Hebrew for this phrase is uncertain. [g] 5 *Jeshurun* means *the upright one,* that is, Israel; also in verse 26. [h] 6 Or *but let*

9 He said of his father and mother,
'I have no regard for them.'
He did not recognize his brothers
or acknowledge his own children,
but he watched over your word
and guarded your covenant.
10 He teaches your precepts to Jacob
and your law to Israel.
He offers incense before you
and whole burnt offerings on your altar.
11 Bless all his skills, LORD,
and be pleased with the work of his hands.
Strike down those who rise against him,
his foes till they rise no more."

12 About Benjamin he said:

"Let the beloved of the LORD rest secure in him,
for he shields him all day long,
and the one the LORD loves rests between his shoulders."

13 About Joseph he said:

"May the LORD bless his land
with the precious dew from heaven above
and with the deep waters that lie below;
14 with the best the sun brings forth
and the finest the moon can yield;
15 with the choicest gifts of the ancient mountains
and the fruitfulness of the everlasting hills;
16 with the best gifts of the earth and its fullness
and the favor of him who dwelt in the burning bush.
Let all these rest on the head of Joseph,
on the brow of the prince among[a] his brothers.
17 In majesty he is like a firstborn bull;
his horns are the horns of a wild ox.
With them he will gore the nations,
even those at the ends of the earth.
Such are the ten thousands of Ephraim;
such are the thousands of Manasseh."

18 About Zebulun he said:

"Rejoice, Zebulun, in your going out,
and you, Issachar, in your tents.
19 They will summon peoples to the mountain
and there offer the sacrifices of the righteous;
they will feast on the abundance of the seas,
on the treasures hidden in the sand."

20 About Gad he said:

"Blessed is he who enlarges Gad's domain!
Gad lives there like a lion,
tearing at arm or head.
21 He chose the best land for himself;
the leader's portion was kept for him.
When the heads of the people assembled,
he carried out the LORD's righteous will,
and his judgments concerning Israel."

22 About Dan he said:

"Dan is a lion's cub,
springing out of Bashan."

23 About Naphtali he said:

"Naphtali is abounding with the favor of the LORD
and is full of his blessing;
he will inherit southward to the lake."

24 About Asher he said:

"Most blessed of sons is Asher;
let him be favored by his brothers,
and let him bathe his feet in oil.
25 The bolts of your gates will be iron and bronze,
and your strength will equal your days.

26 "There is no one like the God of Jeshurun,
who rides across the heavens to help you
and on the clouds in his majesty.
27 The eternal God is your refuge,
and underneath are the everlasting arms.
He will drive out your enemies before you,
saying, 'Destroy them!'
28 So Israel will live in safety;
Jacob will dwell[b] secure
in a land of grain and new wine,
where the heavens drop dew.
29 Blessed are you, Israel!
Who is like you,
a people saved by the LORD?
He is your shield and helper
and your glorious sword.
Your enemies will cower before you,
and you will tread on their heights."

The Death of Moses

34 Then Moses climbed Mount Nebo from
the plains of Moab to the top of Pisgah,
across from Jericho. There the LORD showed
him the whole land—from Gilead to Dan, 2 all
of Naphtali, the territory of Ephraim and Manasseh, all the land of Judah as far as the
Mediterranean Sea, 3 the Negev and the whole
region from the Valley of Jericho, the City of
Palms, as far as Zoar. 4 Then the LORD said
to him, "This is the land I promised on oath
to Abraham, Isaac and Jacob when I said, 'I
will give it to your descendants.' I have let you
see it with your eyes, but you will not cross
over into it."

5 And Moses the servant of the LORD died
there in Moab, as the LORD had said. 6 He buried him[c] in Moab, in the valley opposite Beth
Peor, but to this day no one knows where his
grave is. 7 Moses was a hundred and twenty
years old when he died, yet his eyes were not
weak nor his strength gone. 8 The Israelites

[a] 16 Or *of the one separated from* [b] 28 Septuagint; Hebrew *Jacob's spring is* [c] 6 Or *He was buried*

grieved for Moses in the plains of Moab thirty
days, until the time of weeping and mourning was over.
9Now Joshua son of Nun was filled with
the spirit[a] of wisdom because Moses had laid
his hands on him. So the Israelites listened to
him and did what the LORD had commanded
Moses.
10Since then, no prophet has risen in Israel like Moses, whom the LORD knew face to
face, 11who did all those signs and wonders
the LORD sent him to do in Egypt—to Pharaoh
and to all his officials and to his whole land.
12For no one has ever shown the mighty power
or performed the awesome deeds that Moses
did in the sight of all Israel.

Joshua

Joshua Installed as Leader

1 After the death of Moses the servant of
the LORD, the LORD said to Joshua son of
Nun, Moses' aide: 2"Moses my servant is dead.
Now then, you and all these people, get ready
to cross the Jordan River into the land I am
about to give to them—to the Israelites. 3I will
give you every place where you set your foot,
as I promised Moses. 4Your territory will extend from the desert to Lebanon, and from
the great river, the Euphrates—all the Hittite country—to the Mediterranean Sea in the
west. 5No one will be able to stand against you
all the days of your life. As I was with Moses,
so I will be with you; I will never leave you nor
forsake you. 6Be strong and courageous, because you will lead these people to inherit the
land I swore to their ancestors to give them.
7"Be strong and very courageous. Be careful to obey all the law my servant Moses gave
you; do not turn from it to the right or to the
left, that you may be successful wherever you
go. 8Keep this Book of the Law always on your
lips; meditate on it day and night, so that you
may be careful to do everything written in it.
Then you will be prosperous and successful.
9Have I not commanded you? Be strong and
courageous. Do not be afraid; do not be discouraged, for the LORD your God will be with
you wherever you go."
10So Joshua ordered the officers of the people: 11"Go through the camp and tell the people, 'Get your provisions ready. Three days
from now you will cross the Jordan here to go
in and take possession of the land the LORD
your God is giving you for your own.'"
12But to the Reubenites, the Gadites and the
half-tribe of Manasseh, Joshua said, 13"Remember the command that Moses the servant
of the LORD gave you after he said, 'The LORD
your God will give you rest by giving you this
land.' 14Your wives, your children and your
livestock may stay in the land that Moses gave
you east of the Jordan, but all your fighting
men, ready for battle, must cross over ahead
of your fellow Israelites. You are to help them
15until the LORD gives them rest, as he has
done for you, and until they too have taken
possession of the land the LORD your God is
giving them. After that, you may go back and
occupy your own land, which Moses the servant of the LORD gave you east of the Jordan
toward the sunrise."
16Then they answered Joshua, "Whatever you have commanded us we will do, and
wherever you send us we will go. 17Just as we
fully obeyed Moses, so we will obey you. Only
may the LORD your God be with you as he was
with Moses. 18Whoever rebels against your
word and does not obey it, whatever you may
command them, will be put to death. Only be
strong and courageous!"

Rahab and the Spies

2 Then Joshua son of Nun secretly sent two
spies from Shittim. "Go, look over the
land," he said, "especially Jericho." So they
went and entered the house of a prostitute
named Rahab and stayed there.
2The king of Jericho was told, "Look, some
of the Israelites have come here tonight to spy
out the land." 3So the king of Jericho sent this
message to Rahab: "Bring out the men who
came to you and entered your house, because
they have come to spy out the whole land."
4But the woman had taken the two men and
hidden them. She said, "Yes, the men came to
me, but I did not know where they had come
from. 5At dusk, when it was time to close the
city gate, they left. I don't know which way
they went. Go after them quickly. You may
catch up with them." 6(But she had taken
them up to the roof and hidden them under
the stalks of flax she had laid out on the roof.)
7So the men set out in pursuit of the spies on
the road that leads to the fords of the Jordan,
and as soon as the pursuers had gone out, the
gate was shut.
8Before the spies lay down for the night,
she went up on the roof 9and said to them, "I
know that the LORD has given you this land
and that a great fear of you has fallen on us,
so that all who live in this country are melting
in fear because of you. 10We have heard how
the LORD dried up the water of the Red Sea[b]
for you when you came out of Egypt, and what

[a] 9 Or *Spirit* [b] 10 Or *the Sea of Reeds*

you did to Sihon and Og, the two kings of the
Amorites east of the Jordan, whom you completely destroyed.[a] 11When we heard of it, our
hearts melted in fear and everyone's courage
failed because of you, for the LORD your God is
God in heaven above and on the earth below.
12"Now then, please swear to me by the
LORD that you will show kindness to my family, because I have shown kindness to you.
Give me a sure sign 13that you will spare the
lives of my father and mother, my brothers
and sisters, and all who belong to them—and
that you will save us from death."
14"Our lives for your lives!" the men assured
her. "If you don't tell what we are doing, we
will treat you kindly and faithfully when the
LORD gives us the land."
15So she let them down by a rope through
the window, for the house she lived in was
part of the city wall. 16She said to them, "Go
to the hills so the pursuers will not find you.
Hide yourselves there three days until they
return, and then go on your way."
17Now the men had said to her, "This oath
you made us swear will not be binding on us
18unless, when we enter the land, you have
tied this scarlet cord in the window through
which you let us down, and unless you have
brought your father and mother, your brothers
and all your family into your house. 19If any
of them go outside your house into the street,
their blood will be on their own heads; we will
not be responsible. As for those who are in
the house with you, their blood will be on our
head if a hand is laid on them. 20But if you tell
what we are doing, we will be released from
the oath you made us swear."
21"Agreed," she replied. "Let it be as you say."
So she sent them away, and they departed.
And she tied the scarlet cord in the window.
22When they left, they went into the hills
and stayed there three days, until the pursuers had searched all along the road and
returned without finding them. 23Then the
two men started back. They went down out
of the hills, forded the river and came to Joshua son of Nun and told him everything that
had happened to them. 24They said to Joshua,
"The LORD has surely given the whole land
into our hands; all the people are melting in
fear because of us."

Crossing the Jordan

3 Early in the morning Joshua and all the
Israelites set out from Shittim and went to
the Jordan, where they camped before crossing over. 2After three days the officers went
throughout the camp, 3giving orders to the
people: "When you see the ark of the covenant
of the LORD your God, and the Levitical priests
carrying it, you are to move out from your
positions and follow it. 4Then you will know
which way to go, since you have never been
this way before. But keep a distance of about
two thousand cubits[b] between you and the
ark; do not go near it."
5Joshua told the people, "Consecrate yourselves, for tomorrow the LORD will do amazing
things among you."
6Joshua said to the priests, "Take up the
ark of the covenant and pass on ahead of the
people." So they took it up and went ahead
of them.
7And the LORD said to Joshua, "Today I will
begin to exalt you in the eyes of all Israel,
so they may know that I am with you as I
was with Moses. 8Tell the priests who carry
the ark of the covenant: 'When you reach the
edge of the Jordan's waters, go and stand in
the river.'"
9Joshua said to the Israelites, "Come here
and listen to the words of the LORD your God.
10This is how you will know that the living
God is among you and that he will certainly
drive out before you the Canaanites, Hittites,
Hivites, Perizzites, Girgashites, Amorites and
Jebusites. 11See, the ark of the covenant of the
Lord of all the earth will go into the Jordan
ahead of you. 12Now then, choose twelve men
from the tribes of Israel, one from each tribe.
13And as soon as the priests who carry the ark
of the LORD—the Lord of all the earth—set
foot in the Jordan, its waters flowing down-
stream will be cut off and stand up in a heap."
14So when the people broke camp to cross
the Jordan, the priests carrying the ark of
the covenant went ahead of them. 15Now the
Jordan is at flood stage all during harvest.
Yet as soon as the priests who carried the
ark reached the Jordan and their feet touched
the water's edge, 16the water from upstream
stopped flowing. It piled up in a heap a great
distance away, at a town called Adam in the
vicinity of Zarethan, while the water flowing down to the Sea of the Arabah (that is,
the Dead Sea) was completely cut off. So the
people crossed over opposite Jericho. 17The
priests who carried the ark of the covenant
of the LORD stopped in the middle of the Jordan and stood on dry ground, while all Israel
passed by until the whole nation had completed the crossing on dry ground.

4 When the whole nation had finished crossing the Jordan, the LORD said to Joshua,
2"Choose twelve men from among the people,
one from each tribe, 3and tell them to take up
twelve stones from the middle of the Jordan,
from right where the priests are standing, and
carry them over with you and put them down
at the place where you stay tonight."
4So Joshua called together the twelve men
he had appointed from the Israelites, one from
each tribe, 5and said to them, "Go over before
the ark of the LORD your God into the middle
of the Jordan. Each of you is to take up a stone
on his shoulder, according to the number of
the tribes of the Israelites, 6to serve as a sign
among you. In the future, when your children
ask you, 'What do these stones mean?' 7tell
them that the flow of the Jordan was cut off
before the ark of the covenant of the LORD.
When it crossed the Jordan, the waters of the

[a] *10* The Hebrew term refers to the irrevocable giving over of things or persons to the LORD, often by totally destroying them. [b] *4* That is, about 3,000 feet or about 900 meters

Jordan were cut off. These stones are to be a memorial to the people of Israel forever."

8So the Israelites did as Joshua commanded them. They took twelve stones from the middle of the Jordan, according to the number of the tribes of the Israelites, as the LORD had told Joshua; and they carried them over with them to their camp, where they put them down. 9Joshua set up the twelve stones that had been[a] in the middle of the Jordan at the spot where the priests who carried the ark of the covenant had stood. And they are there to this day.

10Now the priests who carried the ark remained standing in the middle of the Jordan until everything the LORD had commanded Joshua was done by the people, just as Moses had directed Joshua. The people hurried over, 11and as soon as all of them had crossed, the ark of the LORD and the priests came to the other side while the people watched. 12The men of Reuben, Gad and the half-tribe of Manasseh crossed over, ready for battle, in front of the Israelites, as Moses had directed them. 13About forty thousand armed for battle crossed over before the LORD to the plains of Jericho for war.

14That day the LORD exalted Joshua in the sight of all Israel; and they stood in awe of him all the days of his life, just as they had stood in awe of Moses.

15Then the LORD said to Joshua, 16"Command the priests carrying the ark of the covenant law to come up out of the Jordan."

17So Joshua commanded the priests, "Come up out of the Jordan."

18And the priests came up out of the river carrying the ark of the covenant of the LORD. No sooner had they set their feet on the dry ground than the waters of the Jordan returned to their place and ran at flood stage as before.

19On the tenth day of the first month the people went up from the Jordan and camped at Gilgal on the eastern border of Jericho. 20And Joshua set up at Gilgal the twelve stones they had taken out of the Jordan. 21He said to the Israelites, "In the future when your descendants ask their parents, 'What do these stones mean?' 22tell them, 'Israel crossed the Jordan on dry ground.' 23For the LORD your God dried up the Jordan before you until you had crossed over. The LORD your God did to the Jordan what he had done to the Red Sea[b] when he dried it up before us until we had crossed over. 24He did this so that all the peoples of the earth might know that the hand of the LORD is powerful and so that you might always fear the LORD your God."

5 Now when all the Amorite kings west of the Jordan and all the Canaanite kings along the coast heard how the LORD had dried up the Jordan before the Israelites until they[c] had crossed over, their hearts melted in fear and they no longer had the courage to face the Israelites.

Circumcision and Passover at Gilgal

2At that time the LORD said to Joshua, "Make flint knives and circumcise the Israelites again." 3So Joshua made flint knives and circumcised the Israelites at Gibeath Haaraloth.[d]

4Now this is why he did so: All those who came out of Egypt—all the men of military age—died in the wilderness on the way after leaving Egypt. 5All the people that came out had been circumcised, but all the people born in the wilderness during the journey from Egypt had not. 6The Israelites had moved about in the wilderness forty years until all the men who were of military age when they left Egypt had died, since they had not obeyed the LORD. For the LORD had sworn to them that they would not see the land he had solemnly promised their ancestors to give us, a land flowing with milk and honey. 7So he raised up their sons in their place, and these were the ones Joshua circumcised. They were still uncircumcised because they had not been circumcised on the way. 8And after the whole nation had been circumcised, they remained where they were in camp until they were healed.

9Then the LORD said to Joshua, "Today I have rolled away the reproach of Egypt from you." So the place has been called Gilgal[e] to this day.

10On the evening of the fourteenth day of the month, while camped at Gilgal on the plains of Jericho, the Israelites celebrated the Passover. 11The day after the Passover, that very day, they ate some of the produce of the land: unleavened bread and roasted grain. 12The manna stopped the day after[f] they ate this food from the land; there was no longer any manna for the Israelites, but that year they ate the produce of Canaan.

The Fall of Jericho

13Now when Joshua was near Jericho, he looked up and saw a man standing in front of him with a drawn sword in his hand. Joshua went up to him and asked, "Are you for us or for our enemies?"

14"Neither," he replied, "but as commander of the army of the LORD I have now come." Then Joshua fell facedown to the ground in reverence, and asked him, "What message does my Lord[g] have for his servant?"

15The commander of the LORD's army replied, "Take off your sandals, for the place where you are standing is holy." And Joshua did so.

6 Now the gates of Jericho were securely barred because of the Israelites. No one went out and no one came in.

2Then the LORD said to Joshua, "See, I have delivered Jericho into your hands, along with its king and its fighting men. 3March around the city once with all the armed men. Do this for six days. 4Have seven priests carry trum-

[a] 9 Or *Joshua also set up twelve stones* [b] 23 Or *the Sea of Reeds* [c] 1 Another textual tradition *we*
[d] 3 *Gibeath Haaraloth* means *the hill of foreskins.* [e] 9 *Gilgal* sounds like the Hebrew for *roll.*
[f] 12 Or *the day* [g] 14 Or *lord*

pets of rams' horns in front of the ark. On
the seventh day, march around the city seven
times, with the priests blowing the trumpets.
5When you hear them sound a long blast on
the trumpets, have the whole army give a loud
shout; then the wall of the city will collapse
and the army will go up, everyone straight in."
6So Joshua son of Nun called the priests
and said to them, "Take up the ark of the covenant of the LORD and have seven priests carry trumpets in front of it." 7And he ordered
the army, "Advance! March around the city,
with an armed guard going ahead of the ark
of the LORD."
8When Joshua had spoken to the people,
the seven priests carrying the seven trumpets
before the LORD went forward, blowing their
trumpets, and the ark of the LORD's covenant
followed them. 9The armed guard marched
ahead of the priests who blew the trumpets,
and the rear guard followed the ark. All this
time the trumpets were sounding. 10But Joshua had commanded the army, "Do not give a
war cry, do not raise your voices, do not say
a word until the day I tell you to shout. Then
shout!" 11So he had the ark of the LORD carried around the city, circling it once. Then the
army returned to camp and spent the night
there.
12Joshua got up early the next morning
and the priests took up the ark of the LORD.
13The seven priests carrying the seven trumpets went forward, marching before the ark
of the LORD and blowing the trumpets. The
armed men went ahead of them and the rear
guard followed the ark of the LORD, while the
trumpets kept sounding. 14So on the second
day they marched around the city once and returned to the camp. They did this for six days.
15On the seventh day, they got up at daybreak and marched around the city seven
times in the same manner, except that on
that day they circled the city seven times.
16The seventh time around, when the priests
sounded the trumpet blast, Joshua commanded the army, "Shout! For the LORD has given
you the city! 17The city and all that is in it
are to be devoted[a] to the LORD. Only Rahab
the prostitute and all who are with her in her
house shall be spared, because she hid the
spies we sent. 18But keep away from the devoted things, so that you will not bring about
your own destruction by taking any of them.
Otherwise you will make the camp of Israel
liable to destruction and bring trouble on it.
19All the silver and gold and the articles of
bronze and iron are sacred to the LORD and
must go into his treasury."
20When the trumpets sounded, the army
shouted, and at the sound of the trumpet,
when the men gave a loud shout, the wall collapsed; so everyone charged straight in, and
they took the city. 21They devoted the city to
the LORD and destroyed with the sword every
living thing in it—men and women, young
and old, cattle, sheep and donkeys.
22Joshua said to the two men who had spied
out the land, "Go into the prostitute's house
and bring her out and all who belong to her,
in accordance with your oath to her." 23So the
young men who had done the spying went in
and brought out Rahab, her father and mother,
her brothers and sisters and all who belonged
to her. They brought out her entire family and
put them in a place outside the camp of Israel.
24Then they burned the whole city and everything in it, but they put the silver and gold
and the articles of bronze and iron into the
treasury of the LORD's house. 25But Joshua
spared Rahab the prostitute, with her family
and all who belonged to her, because she hid
the men Joshua had sent as spies to Jericho—
and she lives among the Israelites to this day.
26At that time Joshua pronounced this solemn oath: "Cursed before the LORD is the one
who undertakes to rebuild this city, Jericho:

"At the cost of his firstborn son
 he will lay its foundations;
at the cost of his youngest
 he will set up its gates."

27So the LORD was with Joshua, and his
fame spread throughout the land.

Achan's Sin

7 But the Israelites were unfaithful in regard
to the devoted things[b]; Achan son of Karmi, the son of Zimri,[c] the son of Zerah, of
the tribe of Judah, took some of them. So the
LORD's anger burned against Israel.
2Now Joshua sent men from Jericho to Ai,
which is near Beth Aven to the east of Bethel,
and told them, "Go up and spy out the region."
So the men went up and spied out Ai.
3When they returned to Joshua, they said,
"Not all the army will have to go up against
Ai. Send two or three thousand men to take it
and do not weary the whole army, for only a
few people live there." 4So about three thousand went up; but they were routed by the men
of Ai, 5who killed about thirty-six of them.
They chased the Israelites from the city gate
as far as the stone quarries and struck them
down on the slopes. At this the hearts of the
people melted in fear and became like water.
6Then Joshua tore his clothes and fell facedown to the ground before the ark of the LORD,
remaining there till evening. The elders of
Israel did the same, and sprinkled dust on
their heads. 7And Joshua said, "Alas, Sovereign LORD, why did you ever bring this people
across the Jordan to deliver us into the hands
of the Amorites to destroy us? If only we had
been content to stay on the other side of the
Jordan! 8Pardon your servant, Lord. What
can I say, now that Israel has been routed by
its enemies? 9The Canaanites and the other
people of the country will hear about this and

[a] *17* The Hebrew term refers to the irrevocable giving over of things or persons to the LORD, often by totally destroying them; also in verses 18 and 21. [b] *1* The Hebrew term refers to the irrevocable giving over of things or persons to the LORD, often by totally destroying them; also in verses 11, 12, 13 and 15. [c] *1* See Septuagint and 1 Chron. 2:6; Hebrew *Zabdi*; also in verses 17 and 18.

they will surround us and wipe out our name
from the earth. What then will you do for your
own great name?"
10The LORD said to Joshua, "Stand up! What
are you doing down on your face? 11Israel
has sinned; they have violated my covenant,
which I commanded them to keep. They have
taken some of the devoted things; they have
stolen, they have lied, they have put them with
their own possessions. 12That is why the Israelites cannot stand against their enemies;
they turn their backs and run because they
have been made liable to destruction. I will
not be with you anymore unless you destroy
whatever among you is devoted to destruction.
13"Go, consecrate the people. Tell them,
'Consecrate yourselves in preparation for tomorrow; for this is what the LORD, the God of
Israel, says: There are devoted things among
you, Israel. You cannot stand against your
enemies until you remove them.
14" 'In the morning, present yourselves tribe
by tribe. The tribe the LORD chooses shall
come forward clan by clan; the clan the LORD
chooses shall come forward family by family;
and the family the LORD chooses shall come
forward man by man. 15Whoever is caught
with the devoted things shall be destroyed
by fire, along with all that belongs to him. He
has violated the covenant of the LORD and has
done an outrageous thing in Israel!' "
16Early the next morning Joshua had Israel
come forward by tribes, and Judah was chosen. 17The clans of Judah came forward, and
the Zerahites were chosen. He had the clan of
the Zerahites come forward by families, and
Zimri was chosen. 18Joshua had his family
come forward man by man, and Achan son
of Karmi, the son of Zimri, the son of Zerah,
of the tribe of Judah, was chosen.
19Then Joshua said to Achan, "My son, give
glory to the LORD, the God of Israel, and honor
him. Tell me what you have done; do not hide
it from me."
20Achan replied, "It is true! I have sinned
against the LORD, the God of Israel. This is
what I have done: 21When I saw in the plunder a beautiful robe from Babylonia,[a] two
hundred shekels[b] of silver and a bar of gold
weighing fifty shekels,[c] I coveted them and
took them. They are hidden in the ground
inside my tent, with the silver underneath."
22So Joshua sent messengers, and they ran
to the tent, and there it was, hidden in his tent,
with the silver underneath. 23They took the
things from the tent, brought them to Joshua and all the Israelites and spread them out
before the LORD.
24Then Joshua, together with all Israel, took
Achan son of Zerah, the silver, the robe, the
gold bar, his sons and daughters, his cattle,
donkeys and sheep, his tent and all that he
had, to the Valley of Achor. 25Joshua said,
"Why have you brought this trouble on us?
The LORD will bring trouble on you today."
Then all Israel stoned him, and after they
had stoned the rest, they burned them. 26Over
Achan they heaped up a large pile of rocks,
which remains to this day. Then the LORD
turned from his fierce anger. Therefore that
place has been called the Valley of Achor[d]
ever since.

Ai Destroyed

8 Then the LORD said to Joshua, "Do not be
afraid; do not be discouraged. Take the
whole army with you, and go up and attack Ai.
For I have delivered into your hands the king
of Ai, his people, his city and his land. 2You
shall do to Ai and its king as you did to Jericho and its king, except that you may carry
off their plunder and livestock for yourselves.
Set an ambush behind the city."
3So Joshua and the whole army moved out
to attack Ai. He chose thirty thousand of his
best fighting men and sent them out at night
4with these orders: "Listen carefully. You are
to set an ambush behind the city. Don't go
very far from it. All of you be on the alert.
5I and all those with me will advance on the
city, and when the men come out against us,
as they did before, we will flee from them.
6They will pursue us until we have lured them
away from the city, for they will say, 'They
are running away from us as they did before.'
So when we flee from them, 7you are to rise
up from ambush and take the city. The LORD
your God will give it into your hand. 8When
you have taken the city, set it on fire. Do what
the LORD has commanded. See to it; you have
my orders."
9Then Joshua sent them off, and they went
to the place of ambush and lay in wait between
Bethel and Ai, to the west of Ai—but Joshua
spent that night with the people.
10Early the next morning Joshua mustered his army, and he and the leaders of Israel marched before them to Ai. 11The entire
force that was with him marched up and approached the city and arrived in front of it.
They set up camp north of Ai, with the valley
between them and the city. 12Joshua had tak-
en about five thousand men and set them in
ambush between Bethel and Ai, to the west
of the city. 13So the soldiers took up their positions—with the main camp to the north of
the city and the ambush to the west of it. That
night Joshua went into the valley.
14When the king of Ai saw this, he and all
the men of the city hurried out early in the
morning to meet Israel in battle at a certain
place overlooking the Arabah. But he did not
know that an ambush had been set against
him behind the city. 15Joshua and all Israel let
themselves be driven back before them, and
they fled toward the wilderness. 16All the men
of Ai were called to pursue them, and they
pursued Joshua and were lured away from
the city. 17Not a man remained in Ai or Bethel
who did not go after Israel. They left the city
open and went in pursuit of Israel.
18Then the LORD said to Joshua, "Hold out

[a] *21* Hebrew *Shinar* [b] *21* That is, about 5 pounds or about 2.3 kilograms [c] *21* That is, about 1 1/4 pounds or about 575 grams [d] *26* *Achor* means *trouble*.

toward Ai the javelin that is in your hand,
for into your hand I will deliver the city." So
Joshua held out toward the city the javelin that
was in his hand. 19As soon as he did this, the
men in the ambush rose quickly from their
position and rushed forward. They entered the
city and captured it and quickly set it on fire.
20The men of Ai looked back and saw the
smoke of the city rising up into the sky, but
they had no chance to escape in any direction;
the Israelites who had been fleeing toward
the wilderness had turned back against their
pursuers. 21For when Joshua and all Israel
saw that the ambush had taken the city and
that smoke was going up from it, they turned
around and attacked the men of Ai. 22Those in
the ambush also came out of the city against
them, so that they were caught in the middle,
with Israelites on both sides. Israel cut them
down, leaving them neither survivors nor fugitives. 23But they took the king of Ai alive
and brought him to Joshua.
24When Israel had finished killing all the
men of Ai in the fields and in the wilderness
where they had chased them, and when every
one of them had been put to the sword, all the
Israelites returned to Ai and killed those who
were in it. 25Twelve thousand men and women
fell that day—all the people of Ai. 26For Joshua did not draw back the hand that held out his
javelin until he had destroyed[a] all who lived
in Ai. 27But Israel did carry off for themselves
the livestock and plunder of this city, as the
LORD had instructed Joshua.
28So Joshua burned Ai[b] and made it a permanent heap of ruins, a desolate place to this
day. 29He impaled the body of the king of Ai on
a pole and left it there until evening. At sunset,
Joshua ordered them to take the body from
the pole and throw it down at the entrance of
the city gate. And they raised a large pile of
rocks over it, which remains to this day.

The Covenant Renewed at Mount Ebal

30Then Joshua built on Mount Ebal an altar
to the LORD, the God of Israel, 31as Moses the
servant of the LORD had commanded the Israelites. He built it according to what is written
in the Book of the Law of Moses—an altar of
uncut stones, on which no iron tool had been
used. On it they offered to the LORD burnt offerings and sacrificed fellowship offerings.
32There, in the presence of the Israelites, Joshua wrote on stones a copy of the law of Moses.
33All the Israelites, with their elders, officials
and judges, were standing on both sides of
the ark of the covenant of the LORD, facing
the Levitical priests who carried it. Both the
foreigners living among them and the native-
born were there. Half of the people stood in
front of Mount Gerizim and half of them in
front of Mount Ebal, as Moses the servant of
the LORD had formerly commanded when he
gave instructions to bless the people of Israel.
34Afterward, Joshua read all the words of
the law—the blessings and the curses—just
as it is written in the Book of the Law. 35There
was not a word of all that Moses had commanded that Joshua did not read to the whole
assembly of Israel, including the women and
children, and the foreigners who lived among
them.

The Gibeonite Deception

9 Now when all the kings west of the Jordan heard about these things—the kings
in the hill country, in the western foothills,
and along the entire coast of the Mediterranean Sea as far as Lebanon (the kings of the
Hittites, Amorites, Canaanites, Perizzites, Hivites and Jebusites)— 2they came together to
wage war against Joshua and Israel.
3However, when the people of Gibeon heard
what Joshua had done to Jericho and Ai, 4they
resorted to a ruse: They went as a delegation
whose donkeys were loaded[c] with worn-out
sacks and old wineskins, cracked and mend-
ed. 5They put worn and patched sandals on
their feet and wore old clothes. All the bread
of their food supply was dry and moldy. 6Then
they went to Joshua in the camp at Gilgal
and said to him and the Israelites, "We have
come from a distant country; make a treaty
with us."
7The Israelites said to the Hivites, "But perhaps you live near us, so how can we make a
treaty with you?"
8"We are your servants," they said to Joshua.
But Joshua asked, "Who are you and where
do you come from?"
9They answered: "Your servants have come
from a very distant country because of the
fame of the LORD your God. For we have heard
reports of him: all that he did in Egypt, 10and
all that he did to the two kings of the Amorites
east of the Jordan—Sihon king of Heshbon,
and Og king of Bashan, who reigned in Ashtaroth. 11And our elders and all those living
in our country said to us, 'Take provisions
for your journey; go and meet them and say
to them, "We are your servants; make a treaty with us."' 12This bread of ours was warm
when we packed it at home on the day we
left to come to you. But now see how dry and
moldy it is. 13And these wineskins that we
filled were new, but see how cracked they are.
And our clothes and sandals are worn out by
the very long journey."
14The Israelites sampled their provisions
but did not inquire of the LORD. 15Then Joshua
made a treaty of peace with them to let them
live, and the leaders of the assembly ratified
it by oath.
16Three days after they made the treaty with
the Gibeonites, the Israelites heard that they
were neighbors, living near them. 17So the
Israelites set out and on the third day came

[a] *26* The Hebrew term refers to the irrevocable giving over of things or persons to the LORD, often by totally destroying them. [b] *28* Ai means *the ruin.* [c] *4* Most Hebrew manuscripts; some Hebrew manuscripts, Vulgate and Syriac (see also Septuagint) *They prepared provisions and loaded their donkeys*

to their cities: Gibeon, Kephirah, Beeroth and
Kiriath Jearim. 18But the Israelites did not attack them, because the leaders of the assembly had sworn an oath to them by the LORD,
the God of Israel.

The whole assembly grumbled against the
leaders, 19but all the leaders answered, "We
have given them our oath by the LORD, the
God of Israel, and we cannot touch them now.
20This is what we will do to them: We will let
them live, so that God's wrath will not fall on
us for breaking the oath we swore to them."
21They continued, "Let them live, but let them
be woodcutters and water carriers in the service of the whole assembly." So the leaders'
promise to them was kept.

22Then Joshua summoned the Gibeonites
and said, "Why did you deceive us by saying,
'We live a long way from you,' while actually
you live near us? 23You are now under a curse:
You will never be released from service as
woodcutters and water carriers for the house
of my God."

24They answered Joshua, "Your servants
were clearly told how the LORD your God had
commanded his servant Moses to give you the
whole land and to wipe out all its inhabitants
from before you. So we feared for our lives
because of you, and that is why we did this.
25We are now in your hands. Do to us whatever seems good and right to you."

26So Joshua saved them from the Israelites,
and they did not kill them. 27That day he made
the Gibeonites woodcutters and water carriers for the assembly, to provide for the needs
of the altar of the LORD at the place the LORD
would choose. And that is what they are to
this day.

The Sun Stands Still

10 Now Adoni-Zedek king of Jerusalem
heard that Joshua had taken Ai and totally destroyed[a] it, doing to Ai and its king as
he had done to Jericho and its king, and that
the people of Gibeon had made a treaty of
peace with Israel and had become their allies.
2He and his people were very much alarmed
at this, because Gibeon was an important city,
like one of the royal cities; it was larger than
Ai, and all its men were good fighters. 3So
Adoni-Zedek king of Jerusalem appealed to
Hoham king of Hebron, Piram king of Jarmuth, Japhia king of Lachish and Debir king
of Eglon. 4"Come up and help me attack Gibeon," he said, "because it has made peace with
Joshua and the Israelites."

5Then the five kings of the Amorites—the
kings of Jerusalem, Hebron, Jarmuth, Lachish
and Eglon—joined forces. They moved up
with all their troops and took up positions
against Gibeon and attacked it.

6The Gibeonites then sent word to Joshua
in the camp at Gilgal: "Do not abandon your
servants. Come up to us quickly and save us!
Help us, because all the Amorite kings from
the hill country have joined forces against us."

7So Joshua marched up from Gilgal with
his entire army, including all the best fighting men. 8The LORD said to Joshua, "Do not
be afraid of them; I have given them into your
hand. Not one of them will be able to withstand you."

9After an all-night march from Gilgal, Joshua took them by surprise. 10The LORD threw
them into confusion before Israel, so Joshua
and the Israelites defeated them completely
at Gibeon. Israel pursued them along the road
going up to Beth Horon and cut them down all
the way to Azekah and Makkedah. 11As they
fled before Israel on the road down from Beth
Horon to Azekah, the LORD hurled large hailstones down on them, and more of them died
from the hail than were killed by the swords
of the Israelites.

12On the day the LORD gave the Amorites
over to Israel, Joshua said to the LORD in the
presence of Israel:

"Sun, stand still over Gibeon,
and you, moon, over the Valley of
Aijalon."
13So the sun stood still,
and the moon stopped,
till the nation avenged itself on[b] its
enemies,

as it is written in the Book of Jashar.

The sun stopped in the middle of the sky
and delayed going down about a full day.
14There has never been a day like it before
or since, a day when the LORD listened to a
human being. Surely the LORD was fighting
for Israel!

15Then Joshua returned with all Israel to
the camp at Gilgal.

Five Amorite Kings Killed

16Now the five kings had fled and hidden in
the cave at Makkedah. 17When Joshua was told
that the five kings had been found hiding in the
cave at Makkedah, 18he said, "Roll large rocks
up to the mouth of the cave, and post some men
there to guard it. 19But don't stop; pursue your
enemies! Attack them from the rear and don't
let them reach their cities, for the LORD your
God has given them into your hand."

20So Joshua and the Israelites defeated them
completely, but a few survivors managed to
reach their fortified cities. 21The whole army
then returned safely to Joshua in the camp at
Makkedah, and no one uttered a word against
the Israelites.

22Joshua said, "Open the mouth of the cave
and bring those five kings out to me." 23So
they brought the five kings out of the cave—
the kings of Jerusalem, Hebron, Jarmuth, Lachish and Eglon. 24When they had brought
these kings to Joshua, he summoned all the
men of Israel and said to the army commanders who had come with him, "Come here and
put your feet on the necks of these kings." So
they came forward and placed their feet on
their necks.

[a] *1* The Hebrew term refers to the irrevocable giving over of things or persons to the LORD, often by totally destroying them; also in verses 28, 35, 37, 39 and 40. [b] *13* Or *nation triumphed over*

25 Joshua said to them, “Do not be afraid;
do not be discouraged. Be strong and courageous. This is what the LORD will do to all
the enemies you are going to fight.” 26 Then
Joshua put the kings to death and exposed
their bodies on five poles, and they were left
hanging on the poles until evening.
27 At sunset Joshua gave the order and they
took them down from the poles and threw
them into the cave where they had been hiding. At the mouth of the cave they placed large
rocks, which are there to this day.

Southern Cities Conquered

28 That day Joshua took Makkedah. He put
the city and its king to the sword and totally
destroyed everyone in it. He left no survivors.
And he did to the king of Makkedah as he had
done to the king of Jericho.
29 Then Joshua and all Israel with him
moved on from Makkedah to Libnah and attacked it. 30 The LORD also gave that city and
its king into Israel’s hand. The city and everyone in it Joshua put to the sword. He left
no survivors there. And he did to its king as
he had done to the king of Jericho.
31 Then Joshua and all Israel with him
moved on from Libnah to Lachish; he took
up positions against it and attacked it. 32 The
LORD gave Lachish into Israel’s hands, and
Joshua took it on the second day. The city
and everyone in it he put to the sword, just as
he had done to Libnah. 33 Meanwhile, Horam
king of Gezer had come up to help Lachish,
but Joshua defeated him and his army—until
no survivors were left.
34 Then Joshua and all Israel with him
moved on from Lachish to Eglon; they took
up positions against it and attacked it. 35 They
captured it that same day and put it to the
sword and totally destroyed everyone in it,
just as they had done to Lachish.
36 Then Joshua and all Israel with him went
up from Eglon to Hebron and attacked it.
37 They took the city and put it to the sword, together with its king, its villages and everyone
in it. They left no survivors. Just as at Eglon,
they totally destroyed it and everyone in it.
38 Then Joshua and all Israel with him
turned around and attacked Debir. 39 They
took the city, its king and its villages, and
put them to the sword. Everyone in it they totally destroyed. They left no survivors. They
did to Debir and its king as they had done to
Libnah and its king and to Hebron.
40 So Joshua subdued the whole region, including the hill country, the Negev, the western foothills and the mountain slopes, together with all their kings. He left no survivors.
He totally destroyed all who breathed, just as
the LORD, the God of Israel, had commanded.
41 Joshua subdued them from Kadesh Barnea
to Gaza and from the whole region of Goshen
to Gibeon. 42 All these kings and their lands
Joshua conquered in one campaign, because
the LORD, the God of Israel, fought for Israel.
43 Then Joshua returned with all Israel to
the camp at Gilgal.

Northern Kings Defeated

11 When Jabin king of Hazor heard of this,
he sent word to Jobab king of Madon,
to the kings of Shimron and Akshaph, 2 and
to the northern kings who were in the mountains, in the Arabah south of Kinnereth, in
the western foothills and in Naphoth Dor on
the west; 3 to the Canaanites in the east and
west; to the Amorites, Hittites, Perizzites and
Jebusites in the hill country; and to the Hivites below Hermon in the region of Mizpah.
4 They came out with all their troops and a
large number of horses and chariots—a huge
army, as numerous as the sand on the seashore. 5 All these kings joined forces and made
camp together at the Waters of Merom to fight
against Israel.
6 The LORD said to Joshua, “Do not be afraid
of them, because by this time tomorrow I will
hand all of them, slain, over to Israel. You
are to hamstring their horses and burn their
chariots.”
7 So Joshua and his whole army came
against them suddenly at the Waters of Merom and attacked them, 8 and the LORD gave
them into the hand of Israel. They defeated
them and pursued them all the way to Greater
Sidon, to Misrephoth Maim, and to the Valley of Mizpah on the east, until no survivors
were left. 9 Joshua did to them as the LORD
had directed: He hamstrung their horses and
burned their chariots.
10 At that time Joshua turned back and captured Hazor and put its king to the sword. (Hazor had been the head of all these kingdoms.)
11 Everyone in it they put to the sword. They
totally destroyed[a] them, not sparing anyone
that breathed, and he burned Hazor itself.
12 Joshua took all these royal cities and their
kings and put them to the sword. He totally
destroyed them, as Moses the servant of the
LORD had commanded. 13 Yet Israel did not
burn any of the cities built on their mounds—
except Hazor, which Joshua burned. 14 The
Israelites carried off for themselves all the
plunder and livestock of these cities, but all
the people they put to the sword until they
completely destroyed them, not sparing anyone that breathed. 15 As the LORD commanded his servant Moses, so Moses commanded
Joshua, and Joshua did it; he left nothing undone of all that the LORD commanded Moses.
16 So Joshua took this entire land: the hill
country, all the Negev, the whole region of
Goshen, the western foothills, the Arabah
and the mountains of Israel with their foothills, 17 from Mount Halak, which rises toward
Seir, to Baal Gad in the Valley of Lebanon
below Mount Hermon. He captured all their
kings and put them to death. 18 Joshua waged
war against all these kings for a long time.
19 Except for the Hivites living in Gibeon,
not one city made a treaty of peace with the

[a] *11* The Hebrew term refers to the irrevocable giving over of things or persons to the LORD, often by totally destroying them; also in verses 12, 20 and 21.

Israelites, who took them all in battle. [20]For
it was the LORD himself who hardened their
hearts to wage war against Israel, so that he
might destroy them totally, exterminating
them without mercy, as the LORD had commanded Moses.
[21]At that time Joshua went and destroyed
the Anakites from the hill country: from Hebron, Debir and Anab, from all the hill country of Judah, and from all the hill country
of Israel. Joshua totally destroyed them and
their towns. [22]No Anakites were left in Israelite territory; only in Gaza, Gath and Ashdod
did any survive.
[23]So Joshua took the entire land, just as the
LORD had directed Moses, and he gave it as an
inheritance to Israel according to their tribal
divisions. Then the land had rest from war.

List of Defeated Kings

12 These are the kings of the land whom the
Israelites had defeated and whose territory they took over east of the Jordan, from
the Arnon Gorge to Mount Hermon, including
all the eastern side of the Arabah:

[2]Sihon king of the Amorites, who reigned
in Heshbon.
He ruled from Aroer on the rim of the
Arnon Gorge—from the middle of the
gorge—to the Jabbok River, which is
the border of the Ammonites. This included half of Gilead. [3]He also ruled
over the eastern Arabah from the Sea
of Galilee[a] to the Sea of the Arabah
(that is, the Dead Sea), to Beth Jeshimoth, and then southward below the
slopes of Pisgah.

[4]And the territory of Og king of Bashan,
one of the last of the Rephaites, who
reigned in Ashtaroth and Edrei.
[5]He ruled over Mount Hermon, Salekah, all of Bashan to the border of the
people of Geshur and Maakah, and half
of Gilead to the border of Sihon king
of Heshbon.

[6]Moses, the servant of the LORD, and the
Israelites conquered them. And Moses the
servant of the LORD gave their land to the
Reubenites, the Gadites and the half-tribe of
Manasseh to be their possession.
[7]Here is a list of the kings of the land that
Joshua and the Israelites conquered on the
west side of the Jordan, from Baal Gad in the
Valley of Lebanon to Mount Halak, which rises toward Seir. Joshua gave their lands as an
inheritance to the tribes of Israel according to
their tribal divisions. [8]The lands included the
hill country, the western foothills, the Arabah,
the mountain slopes, the wilderness and the
Negev. These were the lands of the Hittites,
Amorites, Canaanites, Perizzites, Hivites and
Jebusites. These were the kings:

[9]the king of Jericho — one
the king of Ai (near Bethel) — one
[10]the king of Jerusalem — one
the king of Hebron — one
[11]the king of Jarmuth — one
the king of Lachish — one
[12]the king of Eglon — one
the king of Gezer — one
[13]the king of Debir — one
the king of Geder — one
[14]the king of Hormah — one
the king of Arad — one
[15]the king of Libnah — one
the king of Adullam — one
[16]the king of Makkedah — one
the king of Bethel — one
[17]the king of Tappuah — one
the king of Hepher — one
[18]the king of Aphek — one
the king of Lasharon — one
[19]the king of Madon — one
the king of Hazor — one
[20]the king of Shimron Meron — one
the king of Akshaph — one
[21]the king of Taanach — one
the king of Megiddo — one
[22]the king of Kedesh — one
the king of Jokneam in Carmel — one
[23]the king of Dor (in Naphoth Dor) — one
the king of Goyim in Gilgal — one
[24]the king of Tirzah — one
thirty-one kings in all.

Land Still to Be Taken

13 When Joshua had grown old, the LORD
said to him, "You are now very old, and
there are still very large areas of land to be
taken over.

[2]"This is the land that remains: all the regions of the Philistines and Geshurites,
[3]from the Shihor River on the east of Egypt
to the territory of Ekron on the north, all
of it counted as Canaanite though held by
the five Philistine rulers in Gaza, Ashdod,
Ashkelon, Gath and Ekron; the territory
of the Avvites [4]on the south; all the land
of the Canaanites, from Arah of the Sidonians as far as Aphek and the border of
the Amorites; [5]the area of Byblos; and all
Lebanon to the east, from Baal Gad below
Mount Hermon to Lebo Hamath.

[6]"As for all the inhabitants of the mountain
regions from Lebanon to Misrephoth Maim,
that is, all the Sidonians, I myself will drive
them out before the Israelites. Be sure to al-
locate this land to Israel for an inheritance,
as I have instructed you, [7]and divide it as an
inheritance among the nine tribes and half of
the tribe of Manasseh."

Division of the Land East of the Jordan

[8]The other half of Manasseh,[b] the Reubenites
and the Gadites had received the inheritance
that Moses had given them east of the Jordan,
as he, the servant of the LORD, had assigned
it to them.

[9]It extended from Aroer on the rim of
the Arnon Gorge, and from the town in

[a] 3 Hebrew *Kinnereth* [b] 8 Hebrew *With it* (that is, with the other half of Manasseh)

the middle of the gorge, and included the
whole plateau of Medeba as far as Dibon,
10 and all the towns of Sihon king of the
Amorites, who ruled in Heshbon, out to
the border of the Ammonites. 11 It also
included Gilead, the territory of the people of Geshur and Maakah, all of Mount
Hermon and all Bashan as far as Salekah— 12 that is, the whole kingdom of Og
in Bashan, who had reigned in Ashtaroth
and Edrei. (He was the last of the Rephaites.) Moses had defeated them and taken
over their land. 13 But the Israelites did
not drive out the people of Geshur and
Maakah, so they continue to live among
the Israelites to this day.

14 But to the tribe of Levi he gave no inheritance, since the food offerings presented to the
LORD, the God of Israel, are their inheritance,
as he promised them.

15 This is what Moses had given to the tribe of
Reuben, according to its clans:

16 The territory from Aroer on the rim of
the Arnon Gorge, and from the town in
the middle of the gorge, and the whole
plateau past Medeba 17 to Heshbon and
all its towns on the plateau, including Dibon, Bamoth Baal, Beth Baal Meon, 18 Jahaz, Kedemoth, Mephaath, 19 Kiriathaim,
Sibmah, Zereth Shahar on the hill in the
valley, 20 Beth Peor, the slopes of Pisgah,
and Beth Jeshimoth— 21 all the towns on
the plateau and the entire realm of Sihon
king of the Amorites, who ruled at Heshbon. Moses had defeated him and the
Midianite chiefs, Evi, Rekem, Zur, Hur
and Reba—princes allied with Sihon—
who lived in that country. 22 In addition
to those slain in battle, the Israelites had
put to the sword Balaam son of Beor, who
practiced divination. 23 The boundary of
the Reubenites was the bank of the Jordan. These towns and their villages were
the inheritance of the Reubenites, according to their clans.

24 This is what Moses had given to the tribe of
Gad, according to its clans:

25 The territory of Jazer, all the towns of
Gilead and half the Ammonite country
as far as Aroer, near Rabbah; 26 and from
Heshbon to Ramath Mizpah and Beto-
nim, and from Mahanaim to the territory of Debir; 27 and in the valley, Beth Ha-
ram, Beth Nimrah, Sukkoth and Zaphon
with the rest of the realm of Sihon king
of Heshbon (the east side of the Jordan,
the territory up to the end of the Sea of
Galilee[a]). 28 These towns and their villages were the inheritance of the Gadites,
according to their clans.

29 This is what Moses had given to the half-
tribe of Manasseh, that is, to half the family
of the descendants of Manasseh, according
to its clans:

30 The territory extending from Mahanaim and including all of Bashan, the entire
realm of Og king of Bashan—all the settlements of Jair in Bashan, sixty towns,
31 half of Gilead, and Ashtaroth and Edrei
(the royal cities of Og in Bashan). This
was for the descendants of Makir son of
Manasseh—for half of the sons of Makir,
according to their clans.

32 This is the inheritance Moses had given
when he was in the plains of Moab across
the Jordan east of Jericho. 33 But to the tribe
of Levi, Moses had given no inheritance; the
LORD, the God of Israel, is their inheritance,
as he promised them.

Division of the Land West of the Jordan

14 Now these are the areas the Israelites
received as an inheritance in the land
of Canaan, which Eleazar the priest, Joshua
son of Nun and the heads of the tribal clans
of Israel allotted to them. 2 Their inheritances were assigned by lot to the nine and a half
tribes, as the LORD had commanded through
Moses. 3 Moses had granted the two and a half
tribes their inheritance east of the Jordan but
had not granted the Levites an inheritance
among the rest, 4 for Joseph's descendants had
become two tribes—Manasseh and Ephraim. The Levites received no share of the land
but only towns to live in, with pasturelands
for their flocks and herds. 5 So the Israelites
divided the land, just as the LORD had commanded Moses.

Allotment for Caleb

6 Now the people of Judah approached Joshua at Gilgal, and Caleb son of Jephunneh the
Kenizzite said to him, "You know what the
LORD said to Moses the man of God at Kadesh
Barnea about you and me. 7 I was forty years
old when Moses the servant of the LORD sent
me from Kadesh Barnea to explore the land.
And I brought him back a report according to
my convictions, 8 but my fellow Israelites who
went up with me made the hearts of the people
melt in fear. I, however, followed the LORD my
God wholeheartedly. 9 So on that day Moses
swore to me, 'The land on which your feet
have walked will be your inheritance and that
of your children forever, because you have
followed the LORD my God wholeheartedly.'[b]

10 "Now then, just as the LORD promised, he
has kept me alive for forty-five years since the
time he said this to Moses, while Israel moved
about in the wilderness. So here I am today,
eighty-five years old! 11 I am still as strong today as the day Moses sent me out; I'm just as
vigorous to go out to battle now as I was then.
12 Now give me this hill country that the LORD
promised me that day. You yourself heard then
that the Anakites were there and their cities
were large and fortified, but, the LORD helping
me, I will drive them out just as he said."

13 Then Joshua blessed Caleb son of Jephunneh and gave him Hebron as his inheritance.

[a] 27 Hebrew *Kinnereth* [b] 9 Deut. 1:36

14So Hebron has belonged to Caleb son of Jephunneh the Kenizzite ever since, because he
followed the LORD, the God of Israel, wholeheartedly. 15(Hebron used to be called Kiriath
Arba after Arba, who was the greatest man
among the Anakites.)

Then the land had rest from war.

Allotment for Judah

15 The allotment for the tribe of Judah, according to its clans, extended down to
the territory of Edom, to the Desert of Zin in
the extreme south.

2Their southern boundary started from
the bay at the southern end of the Dead
Sea, 3crossed south of Scorpion Pass,
continued on to Zin and went over to the
south of Kadesh Barnea. Then it ran past
Hezron up to Addar and curved around
to Karka. 4It then passed along to Azmon
and joined the Wadi of Egypt, ending at
the Mediterranean Sea. This is their[a]
southern boundary.

5The eastern boundary is the Dead Sea
as far as the mouth of the Jordan.

The northern boundary started from
the bay of the sea at the mouth of the Jordan, 6went up to Beth Hoglah and continued north of Beth Arabah to the Stone
of Bohan son of Reuben. 7The boundary
then went up to Debir from the Valley of
Achor and turned north to Gilgal, which
faces the Pass of Adummim south of the
gorge. It continued along to the waters of
En Shemesh and came out at En Rogel.
8Then it ran up the Valley of Ben Hinnom
along the southern slope of the Jebusite
city (that is, Jerusalem). From there it
climbed to the top of the hill west of the
Hinnom Valley at the northern end of the
Valley of Rephaim. 9From the hilltop the
boundary headed toward the spring of
the waters of Nephtoah, came out at the
towns of Mount Ephron and went down
toward Baalah (that is, Kiriath Jearim).
10Then it curved westward from Baalah
to Mount Seir, ran along the northern
slope of Mount Jearim (that is, Kesa-
lon), continued down to Beth Shemesh
and crossed to Timnah. 11It went to the
northern slope of Ekron, turned toward
Shikkeron, passed along to Mount Baalah and reached Jabneel. The boundary
ended at the sea.

12The western boundary is the coast-
line of the Mediterranean Sea.

These are the boundaries around the people
of Judah by their clans.

13In accordance with the LORD's command
to him, Joshua gave to Caleb son of Jephunneh a portion in Judah—Kiriath Arba, that
is, Hebron. (Arba was the forefather of Anak.)
14From Hebron Caleb drove out the three Anakites—Sheshai, Ahiman and Talmai, the sons
of Anak. 15From there he marched against the
people living in Debir (formerly called Kiriath Sepher). 16And Caleb said, "I will give
my daughter Aksah in marriage to the man
who attacks and captures Kiriath Sepher."
17Othniel son of Kenaz, Caleb's brother, took
it; so Caleb gave his daughter Aksah to him
in marriage.

18One day when she came to Othniel, she
urged him[b] to ask her father for a field. When
she got off her donkey, Caleb asked her,
"What can I do for you?"

19She replied, "Do me a special favor. Since
you have given me land in the Negev, give me
also springs of water." So Caleb gave her the
upper and lower springs.

20This is the inheritance of the tribe of Judah, according to its clans:

21The southernmost towns of the tribe of Judah in the Negev toward the boundary of
Edom were:

Kabzeel, Eder, Jagur, 22Kinah, Dimo-
nah, Adadah, 23Kedesh, Hazor, Ithnan,
24Ziph, Telem, Bealoth, 25Hazor Hadattah,
Kerioth Hezron (that is, Hazor), 26Amam,
Shema, Moladah, 27Hazar Gaddah, Hesh-
mon, Beth Pelet, 28Hazar Shual, Beersheba, Biziothiah, 29Baalah, Iyim, Ezem,
30Eltolad, Kesil, Hormah, 31Ziklag, Madmannah, Sansannah, 32Lebaoth, Shilhim,
Ain and Rimmon—a total of twenty-nine
towns and their villages.

33In the western foothills:

Eshtaol, Zorah, Ashnah, 34Zanoah,
En Gannim, Tappuah, Enam, 35Jarmuth,
Adullam, Sokoh, Azekah, 36Shaaraim,
Adithaim and Gederah (or Gederotha-
im)[c]—fourteen towns and their villages.

37Zenan, Hadashah, Migdal Gad, 38Dil-
ean, Mizpah, Joktheel, 39Lachish, Bozkath, Eglon, 40Kabbon, Lahmas, Kitlish,
41Gederoth, Beth Dagon, Naamah and
Makkedah—sixteen towns and their
villages.

42Libnah, Ether, Ashan, 43Iphtah, Ashnah, Nezib, 44Keilah, Akzib and Mareshah—nine towns and their villages.

45Ekron, with its surrounding settlements and villages; 46west of Ekron, all
that were in the vicinity of Ashdod, together with their villages; 47Ashdod, its
surrounding settlements and villages;
and Gaza, its settlements and villages,
as far as the Wadi of Egypt and the coast-
line of the Mediterranean Sea.

48In the hill country:

Shamir, Jattir, Sokoh, 49Dannah, Kir-
iath Sannah (that is, Debir), 50Anab,
Eshtemoh, Anim, 51Goshen, Holon and
Giloh—eleven towns and their villages.

52Arab, Dumah, Eshan, 53Janim, Beth
Tappuah, Aphekah, 54Humtah, Kiriath
Arba (that is, Hebron) and Zior—nine
towns and their villages.

55Maon, Carmel, Ziph, Juttah, 56Jezreel,

[a] *4* Septuagint; Hebrew *your* [b] *18* Hebrew and some Septuagint manuscripts; other Septuagint manuscripts (see also note at Judges 1:14) *Othniel, he urged her* [c] *36* Or *Gederah and Gederothaim*

Jokdeam, Zanoah, 57Kain, Gibeah and
Timnah—ten towns and their villages.
58Halhul, Beth Zur, Gedor, 59Maarath,
Beth Anoth and Eltekon—six towns and
their villages.[a]
60Kiriath Baal (that is, Kiriath Jearim)
and Rabbah—two towns and their villages.

61In the wilderness:
Beth Arabah, Middin, Sekakah, 62Nib-
shan, the City of Salt and En Gedi—six
towns and their villages.
63Judah could not dislodge the Jebusites,
who were living in Jerusalem; to this day the
Jebusites live there with the people of Judah.

Allotment for Ephraim and Manasseh

16 The allotment for Joseph began at
the Jordan, east of the springs of
Jericho, and went up from there through
the desert into the hill country of Bethel.
2It went on from Bethel (that is, Luz),[b]
crossed over to the territory of the Arkites
in Ataroth, 3descended westward to the
territory of the Japhletites as far as the
region of Lower Beth Horon and on to
Gezer, ending at the Mediterranean Sea.
4So Manasseh and Ephraim, the descendants
of Joseph, received their inheritance.

5This was the territory of Ephraim, according to its clans:

The boundary of their inheritance
went from Ataroth Addar in the east to
Upper Beth Horon 6and continued to the
Mediterranean Sea. From Mikmethath
on the north it curved eastward to Taa-
nath Shiloh, passing by it to Janoah on
the east. 7Then it went down from Janoah
to Ataroth and Naarah, touched Jericho
and came out at the Jordan. 8From Tappuah the border went west to the Kanah
Ravine and ended at the Mediterranean Sea. This was the inheritance of the
tribe of the Ephraimites, according to its
clans. 9It also included all the towns and
their villages that were set aside for the
Ephraimites within the inheritance of the
Manassites.
10They did not dislodge the Canaanites living in Gezer; to this day the Canaanites live
among the people of Ephraim but are required
to do forced labor.

17 This was the allotment for the tribe of
Manasseh as Joseph's firstborn, that is,
for Makir, Manasseh's firstborn. Makir was
the ancestor of the Gileadites, who had received Gilead and Bashan because the Makirites were great soldiers. 2So this allotment was
for the rest of the people of Manasseh—the
clans of Abiezer, Helek, Asriel, Shechem, Hepher and Shemida. These are the other male
descendants of Manasseh son of Joseph by
their clans.
3Now Zelophehad son of Hepher, the son of
Gilead, the son of Makir, the son of Manasseh,
had no sons but only daughters, whose names
were Mahlah, Noah, Hoglah, Milkah and Tirzah. 4They went to Eleazar the priest, Joshua
son of Nun, and the leaders and said, "The
LORD commanded Moses to give us an inheritance among our relatives." So Joshua gave
them an inheritance along with the brothers of their father, according to the LORD's
command. 5Manasseh's share consisted of
ten tracts of land besides Gilead and Bashan
east of the Jordan, 6because the daughters of
the tribe of Manasseh received an inheritance
among the sons. The land of Gilead belonged
to the rest of the descendants of Manasseh.

7The territory of Manasseh extended from Asher to Mikmethath east of
Shechem. The boundary ran southward
from there to include the people living
at En Tappuah. 8(Manasseh had the land
of Tappuah, but Tappuah itself, on the
boundary of Manasseh, belonged to the
Ephraimites.) 9Then the boundary continued south to the Kanah Ravine. There
were towns belonging to Ephraim lying
among the towns of Manasseh, but the
boundary of Manasseh was the northern side of the ravine and ended at the
Mediterranean Sea. 10On the south the
land belonged to Ephraim, on the north
to Manasseh. The territory of Manasseh
reached the Mediterranean Sea and bor-
dered Asher on the north and Issachar
on the east.
11Within Issachar and Asher, Manasseh also had Beth Shan, Ibleam and the
people of Dor, Endor, Taanach and Megiddo, together with their surrounding
settlements (the third in the list is Naphoth[c]).
12Yet the Manassites were not able to occupy
these towns, for the Canaanites were determined to live in that region. 13However, when
the Israelites grew stronger, they subjected
the Canaanites to forced labor but did not
drive them out completely.

14The people of Joseph said to Joshua,
"Why have you given us only one allotment
and one portion for an inheritance? We are a
numerous people, and the LORD has blessed
us abundantly."
15"If you are so numerous," Joshua answered, "and if the hill country of Ephraim
is too small for you, go up into the forest and
clear land for yourselves there in the land of
the Perizzites and Rephaites."
16The people of Joseph replied, "The hill
country is not enough for us, and all the Canaanites who live in the plain have chariots
fitted with iron, both those in Beth Shan and
its settlements and those in the Valley of Jezreel."
17But Joshua said to the tribes of Joseph—to
Ephraim and Manasseh—"You are numerous
and very powerful. You will have not only
one allotment 18but the forested hill country

[a] *59* The Septuagint adds another district of eleven towns, including Tekoa and Ephrathah
(Bethlehem). [b] *2* Septuagint; Hebrew *Bethel to Luz* [c] *11* That is, Naphoth Dor

as well. Clear it, and its farthest limits will be
yours; though the Canaanites have chariots
fitted with iron and though they are strong,
you can drive them out."

Division of the Rest of the Land

18 The whole assembly of the Israelites
gathered at Shiloh and set up the tent
of meeting there. The country was brought
under their control, 2 but there were still sev-
en Israelite tribes who had not yet received
their inheritance.
3 So Joshua said to the Israelites: "How long
will you wait before you begin to take possession of the land that the LORD, the God of your
ancestors, has given you? 4 Appoint three men
from each tribe. I will send them out to make
a survey of the land and to write a description of it, according to the inheritance of each.
Then they will return to me. 5 You are to divide
the land into seven parts. Judah is to remain
in its territory on the south and the tribes of
Joseph in their territory on the north. 6 After
you have written descriptions of the seven
parts of the land, bring them here to me and
I will cast lots for you in the presence of the
LORD our God. 7 The Levites, however, do not
get a portion among you, because the priestly
service of the LORD is their inheritance. And
Gad, Reuben and the half-tribe of Manasseh
have already received their inheritance on the
east side of the Jordan. Moses the servant of
the LORD gave it to them."
8 As the men started on their way to map
out the land, Joshua instructed them, "Go and
make a survey of the land and write a description of it. Then return to me, and I will cast lots
for you here at Shiloh in the presence of the
LORD." 9 So the men left and went through the
land. They wrote its description on a scroll,
town by town, in seven parts, and returned to
Joshua in the camp at Shiloh. 10 Joshua then
cast lots for them in Shiloh in the presence of
the LORD, and there he distributed the land
to the Israelites according to their tribal divisions.

Allotment for Benjamin

11 The first lot came up for the tribe of Benjamin according to its clans. Their allotted
territory lay between the tribes of Judah and
Joseph:
12 On the north side their boundary began at the Jordan, passed the northern
slope of Jericho and headed west into the
hill country, coming out at the wilderness
of Beth Aven. 13 From there it crossed to
the south slope of Luz (that is, Bethel) and
went down to Ataroth Addar on the hill
south of Lower Beth Horon.
14 From the hill facing Beth Horon on
the south the boundary turned south
along the western side and came out at
Kiriath Baal (that is, Kiriath Jearim), a
town of the people of Judah. This was the
western side.
15 The southern side began at the outskirts of Kiriath Jearim on the west, and
the boundary came out at the spring of
the waters of Nephtoah. 16 The boundary
went down to the foot of the hill facing
the Valley of Ben Hinnom, north of the
Valley of Rephaim. It continued down the
Hinnom Valley along the southern slope
of the Jebusite city and so to En Rogel.
17 It then curved north, went to En Shemesh, continued to Geliloth, which faces
the Pass of Adummim, and ran down to
the Stone of Bohan son of Reuben. 18 It
continued to the northern slope of Beth
Arabah[a] and on down into the Arabah.
19 It then went to the northern slope of
Beth Hoglah and came out at the northern bay of the Dead Sea, at the mouth
of the Jordan in the south. This was the
southern boundary.
20 The Jordan formed the boundary on
the eastern side.
These were the boundaries that marked out
the inheritance of the clans of Benjamin on
all sides.

21 The tribe of Benjamin, according to its clans,
had the following towns:
Jericho, Beth Hoglah, Emek Keziz,
22 Beth Arabah, Zemaraim, Bethel, 23 Av-
vim, Parah, Ophrah, 24 Kephar Ammoni,
Ophni and Geba—twelve towns and their
villages.
25 Gibeon, Ramah, Beeroth, 26 Mizpah,
Kephirah, Mozah, 27 Rekem, Irpeel, Tar-
alah, 28 Zelah, Haeleph, the Jebusite city
(that is, Jerusalem), Gibeah and Kiriath—
fourteen towns and their villages.
This was the inheritance of Benjamin for its
clans.

Allotment for Simeon

19 The second lot came out for the tribe
of Simeon according to its clans. Their
inheritance lay within the territory of Judah.
2 It included:
Beersheba (or Sheba),[b] Moladah, 3 Hazar Shual, Balah, Ezem, 4 Eltolad, Beth-
ul, Hormah, 5 Ziklag, Beth Markaboth,
Hazar Susah, 6 Beth Lebaoth and Sharu-
hen—thirteen towns and their villages;
7 Ain, Rimmon, Ether and Ashan—four
towns and their villages— 8 and all the
villages around these towns as far as Baalath Beer (Ramah in the Negev).
This was the inheritance of the tribe of the
Simeonites, according to its clans. 9 The inheritance of the Simeonites was taken from
the share of Judah, because Judah's portion
was more than they needed. So the Simeonites
received their inheritance within the territory of Judah.

Allotment for Zebulun

10 The third lot came up for Zebulun according to its clans:

[a] 18 Septuagint; Hebrew *slope facing the Arabah*
have *Sheba*.
[b] 2 Or *Beersheba, Sheba*; 1 Chron. 4:28 does not

The boundary of their inheritance went
as far as Sarid. 11Going west it ran to Mar-
alah, touched Dabbesheth, and extended
to the ravine near Jokneam. 12It turned
east from Sarid toward the sunrise to the
territory of Kisloth Tabor and went on to
Daberath and up to Japhia. 13Then it continued eastward to Gath Hepher and Eth
Kazin; it came out at Rimmon and turned
toward Neah. 14There the boundary went
around on the north to Hannathon and
ended at the Valley of Iphtah El. 15Includ-
ed were Kattath, Nahalal, Shimron, Id-
alah and Bethlehem. There were twelve
towns and their villages.
16These towns and their villages were the inheritance of Zebulun, according to its clans.

Allotment for Issachar

17The fourth lot came out for Issachar according to its clans. 18Their territory included:
Jezreel, Kesulloth, Shunem, 19Hapha-
raim, Shion, Anaharath, 20Rabbith, Kishion, Ebez, 21Remeth, En Gannim, En Had-
dah and Beth Pazzez. 22The boundary
touched Tabor, Shahazumah and Beth
Shemesh, and ended at the Jordan. There
were sixteen towns and their villages.
23These towns and their villages were the inheritance of the tribe of Issachar, according
to its clans.

Allotment for Asher

24The fifth lot came out for the tribe of Asher
according to its clans. 25Their territory included:
Helkath, Hali, Beten, Akshaph, 26Al-
lammelek, Amad and Mishal. On the
west the boundary touched Carmel and
Shihor Libnath. 27It then turned east toward Beth Dagon, touched Zebulun and
the Valley of Iphtah El, and went north
to Beth Emek and Neiel, passing Kabul
on the left. 28It went to Abdon,[a] Rehob,
Hammon and Kanah, as far as Greater
Sidon. 29The boundary then turned back
toward Ramah and went to the fortified
city of Tyre, turned toward Hosah and
came out at the Mediterranean Sea in the
region of Akzib, 30Ummah, Aphek and
Rehob. There were twenty-two towns and
their villages.
31These towns and their villages were the inheritance of the tribe of Asher, according to
its clans.

Allotment for Naphtali

32The sixth lot came out for Naphtali according to its clans:
33Their boundary went from Heleph
and the large tree in Zaanannim, passing Adami Nekeb and Jabneel to Lakkum
and ending at the Jordan. 34The boundary
ran west through Aznoth Tabor and came
out at Hukkok. It touched Zebulun on the
south, Asher on the west and the Jordan[b]
on the east. 35The fortified towns were
Ziddim, Zer, Hammath, Rakkath, Kinnereth, 36Adamah, Ramah, Hazor, 37Ke-
desh, Edrei, En Hazor, 38Iron, Migdal El,
Horem, Beth Anath and Beth Shemesh.
There were nineteen towns and their villages.
39These towns and their villages were the inheritance of the tribe of Naphtali, according
to its clans.

Allotment for Dan

40The seventh lot came out for the tribe of Dan
according to its clans. 41The territory of their
inheritance included:
Zorah, Eshtaol, Ir Shemesh, 42Shaa-
labbin, Aijalon, Ithlah, 43Elon, Timnah,
Ekron, 44Eltekeh, Gibbethon, Baalath,
45Jehud, Bene Berak, Gath Rimmon,
46Me Jarkon and Rakkon, with the area
facing Joppa.
47(When the territory of the Danites was
lost to them, they went up and attacked Leshem, took it, put it to the sword and occupied
it. They settled in Leshem and named it Dan
after their ancestor.)
48These towns and their villages were the inheritance of the tribe of Dan, according to
its clans.

Allotment for Joshua

49When they had finished dividing the land
into its allotted portions, the Israelites gave
Joshua son of Nun an inheritance among
them, 50as the LORD had commanded. They
gave him the town he asked for—Timnath
Serah[c] in the hill country of Ephraim. And he
built up the town and settled there.
51These are the territories that Eleazar the
priest, Joshua son of Nun and the heads of the
tribal clans of Israel assigned by lot at Shiloh
in the presence of the LORD at the entrance
to the tent of meeting. And so they finished
dividing the land.

Cities of Refuge

20 Then the LORD said to Joshua: 2"Tell
the Israelites to designate the cities of
refuge, as I instructed you through Moses,
3so that anyone who kills a person accidentally and unintentionally may flee there and
find protection from the avenger of blood.
4When they flee to one of these cities, they
are to stand in the entrance of the city gate
and state their case before the elders of that
city. Then the elders are to admit the fugitive into their city and provide a place to
live among them. 5If the avenger of blood
comes in pursuit, the elders must not surrender the fugitive, because the fugitive killed
their neighbor unintentionally and without
malice aforethought. 6They are to stay in that
city until they have stood trial before the assembly and until the death of the high priest

[a] *28* Some Hebrew manuscripts (see also 21:30); most Hebrew manuscripts *Ebron* [b] *34* Septuagint; Hebrew *west, and Judah, the Jordan,* [c] *50* Also known as *Timnath Heres* (see Judges 2:9)

who is serving at that time. Then they may
go back to their own home in the town from
which they fled."
7So they set apart Kedesh in Galilee in the
hill country of Naphtali, Shechem in the hill
country of Ephraim, and Kiriath Arba (that
is, Hebron) in the hill country of Judah. 8East
of the Jordan (on the other side from Jericho)
they designated Bezer in the wilderness on
the plateau in the tribe of Reuben, Ramoth
in Gilead in the tribe of Gad, and Golan in
Bashan in the tribe of Manasseh. 9Any of the
Israelites or any foreigner residing among
them who killed someone accidentally could
flee to these designated cities and not be killed
by the avenger of blood prior to standing trial
before the assembly.

Towns for the Levites

21 Now the family heads of the Levites
approached Eleazar the priest, Joshua
son of Nun, and the heads of the other tribal
families of Israel 2at Shiloh in Canaan and
said to them, "The LORD commanded through
Moses that you give us towns to live in, with
pasturelands for our livestock." 3So, as the
LORD had commanded, the Israelites gave the
Levites the following towns and pasturelands
out of their own inheritance:
4The first lot came out for the Kohathites,
according to their clans. The Levites who were
descendants of Aaron the priest were allotted thirteen towns from the tribes of Judah,
Simeon and Benjamin. 5The rest of Kohath's
descendants were allotted ten towns from the
clans of the tribes of Ephraim, Dan and half
of Manasseh.
6The descendants of Gershon were allotted
thirteen towns from the clans of the tribes of
Issachar, Asher, Naphtali and the half-tribe
of Manasseh in Bashan.
7The descendants of Merari, according to
their clans, received twelve towns from the
tribes of Reuben, Gad and Zebulun.
8So the Israelites allotted to the Levites
these towns and their pasturelands, as the
LORD had commanded through Moses.

9From the tribes of Judah and Simeon they
allotted the following towns by name 10(these
towns were assigned to the descendants of
Aaron who were from the Kohathite clans of
the Levites, because the first lot fell to them):
11They gave them Kiriath Arba (that is,
Hebron), with its surrounding pastureland, in the hill country of Judah. (Arba
was the forefather of Anak.) 12But the
fields and villages around the city they
had given to Caleb son of Jephunneh as
his possession.
13So to the descendants of Aaron the
priest they gave Hebron (a city of refuge for one accused of murder), Libnah,
14Jattir, Eshtemoa, 15Holon, Debir, 16Ain,
Juttah and Beth Shemesh, together with
their pasturelands—nine towns from
these two tribes.
17And from the tribe of Benjamin they
gave them Gibeon, Geba, 18Anathoth
and Almon, together with their pasturelands—four towns.
19The total number of towns for the priests,
the descendants of Aaron, came to thirteen,
together with their pasturelands.

20The rest of the Kohathite clans of the Levites
were allotted towns from the tribe of Ephraim:
21In the hill country of Ephraim they
were given Shechem (a city of refuge for
one accused of murder) and Gezer, 22Kib-
zaim and Beth Horon, together with their
pasturelands—four towns.
23Also from the tribe of Dan they received Eltekeh, Gibbethon, 24Aijalon and
Gath Rimmon, together with their pasturelands—four towns.
25From half the tribe of Manasseh they
received Taanach and Gath Rimmon,
together with their pasturelands—two
towns.
26All these ten towns and their pasturelands
were given to the rest of the Kohathite clans.

27The Levite clans of the Gershonites were
given:
from the half-tribe of Manasseh,
Golan in Bashan (a city of refuge for one accused of murder) and Be Eshterah, together
with their pasturelands—two towns;
28from the tribe of Issachar,
Kishion, Daberath, 29Jarmuth and En
Gannim, together with their pasturelands—four towns;
30from the tribe of Asher,
Mishal, Abdon, 31Helkath and Rehob,
together with their pasturelands—four
towns;
32from the tribe of Naphtali,
Kedesh in Galilee (a city of refuge for
one accused of murder), Hammoth Dor
and Kartan, together with their pasturelands—three towns.
33The total number of towns of the Gershonite clans came to thirteen, together with their
pasturelands.

34The Merarite clans (the rest of the Levites)
were given:
from the tribe of Zebulun,
Jokneam, Kartah, 35Dimnah and Nahalal, together with their pasturelands—
four towns;
36from the tribe of Reuben,
Bezer, Jahaz, 37Kedemoth and Mephaath,
together with their pasturelands—four
towns;
38from the tribe of Gad,
Ramoth in Gilead (a city of refuge for one
accused of murder), Mahanaim, 39Hesh-
bon and Jazer, together with their pasturelands—four towns in all.
40The total number of towns allotted to the
Merarite clans, who were the rest of the Levites, came to twelve.
41The towns of the Levites in the territory
held by the Israelites were forty-eight in all,
together with their pasturelands. 42Each of
these towns had pasturelands surrounding
it; this was true for all these towns.

43So the LORD gave Israel all the land he
had sworn to give their ancestors, and they
took possession of it and settled there. 44The
LORD gave them rest on every side, just as he
had sworn to their ancestors. Not one of their
enemies withstood them; the LORD gave all
their enemies into their hands. 45Not one of
all the LORD's good promises to Israel failed;
every one was fulfilled.

Eastern Tribes Return Home

22 Then Joshua summoned the Reubenites,
the Gadites and the half-tribe of Manasseh 2and said to them, "You have done all that
Moses the servant of the LORD commanded,
and you have obeyed me in everything I commanded. 3For a long time now—to this very
day—you have not deserted your fellow Israelites but have carried out the mission the
LORD your God gave you. 4Now that the LORD
your God has given them rest as he promised,
return to your homes in the land that Moses
the servant of the LORD gave you on the other
side of the Jordan. 5But be very careful to keep
the commandment and the law that Moses
the servant of the LORD gave you: to love the
LORD your God, to walk in obedience to him,
to keep his commands, to hold fast to him and
to serve him with all your heart and with all
your soul."

6Then Joshua blessed them and sent them
away, and they went to their homes. 7(To the
half-tribe of Manasseh Moses had given land
in Bashan, and to the other half of the tribe
Joshua gave land on the west side of the Jordan along with their fellow Israelites.) When
Joshua sent them home, he blessed them, 8say-
ing, "Return to your homes with your great
wealth—with large herds of livestock, with
silver, gold, bronze and iron, and a great quantity of clothing—and divide the plunder from
your enemies with your fellow Israelites."

9So the Reubenites, the Gadites and the
half-tribe of Manasseh left the Israelites at
Shiloh in Canaan to return to Gilead, their
own land, which they had acquired in accordance with the command of the LORD through
Moses.

10When they came to Geliloth near the Jordan in the land of Canaan, the Reubenites, the
Gadites and the half-tribe of Manasseh built
an imposing altar there by the Jordan. 11And
when the Israelites heard that they had built
the altar on the border of Canaan at Geliloth
near the Jordan on the Israelite side, 12the
whole assembly of Israel gathered at Shiloh
to go to war against them.

13So the Israelites sent Phinehas son of Eleazar, the priest, to the land of Gilead—to
Reuben, Gad and the half-tribe of Manasseh.
14With him they sent ten of the chief men, one
from each of the tribes of Israel, each the head
of a family division among the Israelite clans.

15When they went to Gilead—to Reuben,
Gad and the half-tribe of Manasseh—they
said to them: 16"The whole assembly of the
LORD says: 'How could you break faith with
the God of Israel like this? How could you turn
away from the LORD and build yourselves an
altar in rebellion against him now? 17Was not
the sin of Peor enough for us? Up to this very
day we have not cleansed ourselves from that
sin, even though a plague fell on the community of the LORD! 18And are you now turning
away from the LORD?

"'If you rebel against the LORD today, tomorrow he will be angry with the whole community of Israel. 19If the land you possess is
defiled, come over to the LORD's land, where
the LORD's tabernacle stands, and share the
land with us. But do not rebel against the
LORD or against us by building an altar for
yourselves, other than the altar of the LORD
our God. 20When Achan son of Zerah was
unfaithful in regard to the devoted things,[a]
did not wrath come on the whole community
of Israel? He was not the only one who died
for his sin.'"

21Then Reuben, Gad and the half-tribe of
Manasseh replied to the heads of the clans of
Israel: 22"The Mighty One, God, the LORD! The
Mighty One, God, the LORD! He knows! And
let Israel know! If this has been in rebellion
or disobedience to the LORD, do not spare us
this day. 23If we have built our own altar to
turn away from the LORD and to offer burnt
offerings and grain offerings, or to sacrifice
fellowship offerings on it, may the LORD himself call us to account.

24"No! We did it for fear that some day your
descendants might say to ours, 'What do you
have to do with the LORD, the God of Israel?
25The LORD has made the Jordan a boundary
between us and you—you Reubenites and
Gadites! You have no share in the LORD.' So
your descendants might cause ours to stop
fearing the LORD.

26"That is why we said, 'Let us get ready and
build an altar—but not for burnt offerings or
sacrifices.' 27On the contrary, it is to be a witness between us and you and the generations
that follow, that we will worship the LORD at
his sanctuary with our burnt offerings, sacrifices and fellowship offerings. Then in the
future your descendants will not be able to
say to ours, 'You have no share in the LORD.'

28"And we said, 'If they ever say this to us,
or to our descendants, we will answer: Look
at the replica of the LORD's altar, which our ancestors built, not for burnt offerings and sacrifices, but as a witness between us and you.'

29"Far be it from us to rebel against the LORD
and turn away from him today by building an
altar for burnt offerings, grain offerings and
sacrifices, other than the altar of the LORD
our God that stands before his tabernacle."

30When Phinehas the priest and the leaders of the community—the heads of the clans
of the Israelites—heard what Reuben, Gad
and Manasseh had to say, they were pleased.
31And Phinehas son of Eleazar, the priest,
said to Reuben, Gad and Manasseh, "Today

[a] *20* The Hebrew term refers to the irrevocable giving over of things or persons to the LORD, often by totally destroying them.

we know that the LORD is with us, because you
have not been unfaithful to the LORD in this
matter. Now you have rescued the Israelites
from the LORD's hand."
32Then Phinehas son of Eleazar, the priest,
and the leaders returned to Canaan from their
meeting with the Reubenites and Gadites in
Gilead and reported to the Israelites. 33They
were glad to hear the report and praised God.
And they talked no more about going to war
against them to devastate the country where
the Reubenites and the Gadites lived.
34And the Reubenites and the Gadites gave
the altar this name: A Witness Between Us—
that the LORD is God.

Joshua's Farewell to the Leaders

23 After a long time had passed and the
LORD had given Israel rest from all
their enemies around them, Joshua, by then
a very old man, 2summoned all Israel—their
elders, leaders, judges and officials—and said
to them: "I am very old. 3You yourselves have
seen everything the LORD your God has done
to all these nations for your sake; it was the
LORD your God who fought for you. 4Remem-
ber how I have allotted as an inheritance for
your tribes all the land of the nations that
remain—the nations I conquered—between
the Jordan and the Mediterranean Sea in the
west. 5The LORD your God himself will push
them out for your sake. He will drive them
out before you, and you will take possession
of their land, as the LORD your God promised you.
6"Be very strong; be careful to obey all that
is written in the Book of the Law of Moses,
without turning aside to the right or to the
left. 7Do not associate with these nations that
remain among you; do not invoke the names
of their gods or swear by them. You must not
serve them or bow down to them. 8But you
are to hold fast to the LORD your God, as you
have until now.
9"The LORD has driven out before you great
and powerful nations; to this day no one has
been able to withstand you. 10One of you routs
a thousand, because the LORD your God fights
for you, just as he promised. 11So be very careful to love the LORD your God.
12"But if you turn away and ally yourselves
with the survivors of these nations that remain among you and if you intermarry with
them and associate with them, 13then you may
be sure that the LORD your God will no longer
drive out these nations before you. Instead,
they will become snares and traps for you,
whips on your backs and thorns in your eyes,
until you perish from this good land, which
the LORD your God has given you.
14"Now I am about to go the way of all the
earth. You know with all your heart and soul
that not one of all the good promises the LORD
your God gave you has failed. Every promise
has been fulfilled; not one has failed. 15But
just as all the good things the LORD your God
has promised you have come to you, so he
will bring on you all the evil things he has
threatened, until the LORD your God has destroyed you from this good land he has given
you. 16If you violate the covenant of the LORD
your God, which he commanded you, and go
and serve other gods and bow down to them,
the LORD's anger will burn against you, and
you will quickly perish from the good land
he has given you."

The Covenant Renewed at Shechem

24 Then Joshua assembled all the tribes of
Israel at Shechem. He summoned the
elders, leaders, judges and officials of Israel,
and they presented themselves before God.
2Joshua said to all the people, "This is what
the LORD, the God of Israel, says: 'Long ago
your ancestors, including Terah the father of
Abraham and Nahor, lived beyond the Euphrates River and worshiped other gods. 3But
I took your father Abraham from the land beyond the Euphrates and led him throughout
Canaan and gave him many descendants. I
gave him Isaac, 4and to Isaac I gave Jacob
and Esau. I assigned the hill country of Seir
to Esau, but Jacob and his family went down
to Egypt.
5" 'Then I sent Moses and Aaron, and I afflicted the Egyptians by what I did there, and
I brought you out. 6When I brought your people out of Egypt, you came to the sea, and
the Egyptians pursued them with chariots
and horsemen[a] as far as the Red Sea.[b] 7But
they cried to the LORD for help, and he put
darkness between you and the Egyptians; he
brought the sea over them and covered them.
You saw with your own eyes what I did to the
Egyptians. Then you lived in the wilderness
for a long time.
8" 'I brought you to the land of the Amorites who lived east of the Jordan. They fought
against you, but I gave them into your hands.
I destroyed them from before you, and you
took possession of their land. 9When Balak
son of Zippor, the king of Moab, prepared to
fight against Israel, he sent for Balaam son
of Beor to put a curse on you. 10But I would
not listen to Balaam, so he blessed you again
and again, and I delivered you out of his hand.
11" 'Then you crossed the Jordan and came
to Jericho. The citizens of Jericho fought
against you, as did also the Amorites, Perizzites, Canaanites, Hittites, Girgashites,
Hivites and Jebusites, but I gave them into
your hands. 12I sent the hornet ahead of you,
which drove them out before you—also the
two Amorite kings. You did not do it with your
own sword and bow. 13So I gave you a land on
which you did not toil and cities you did not
build; and you live in them and eat from vineyards and olive groves that you did not plant.'
14"Now fear the LORD and serve him with
all faithfulness. Throw away the gods your
ancestors worshiped beyond the Euphrates
River and in Egypt, and serve the LORD. 15But
if serving the LORD seems undesirable to you,
then choose for yourselves this day whom you

[a] 6 Or *charioteers* [b] 6 Or *the Sea of Reeds*

will serve, whether the gods your ancestors served beyond the Euphrates, or the gods of the Amorites, in whose land you are living. But as for me and my household, we will serve the LORD."

16Then the people answered, "Far be it from us to forsake the LORD to serve other gods! 17It was the LORD our God himself who brought us and our parents up out of Egypt, from that land of slavery, and performed those great signs before our eyes. He protected us on our entire journey and among all the nations through which we traveled. 18And the LORD drove out before us all the nations, including the Amorites, who lived in the land. We too will serve the LORD, because he is our God."

19Joshua said to the people, "You are not able to serve the LORD. He is a holy God; he is a jealous God. He will not forgive your rebellion and your sins. 20If you forsake the LORD and serve foreign gods, he will turn and bring disaster on you and make an end of you, after he has been good to you."

21But the people said to Joshua, "No! We will serve the LORD."

22Then Joshua said, "You are witnesses against yourselves that you have chosen to serve the LORD."

"Yes, we are witnesses," they replied.

23"Now then," said Joshua, "throw away the foreign gods that are among you and yield your hearts to the LORD, the God of Israel."

24And the people said to Joshua, "We will serve the LORD our God and obey him."

25On that day Joshua made a covenant for the people, and there at Shechem he reaffirmed for them decrees and laws. 26And Joshua recorded these things in the Book of the Law of God. Then he took a large stone and set it up there under the oak near the holy place of the LORD.

27"See!" he said to all the people. "This stone will be a witness against us. It has heard all the words the LORD has said to us. It will be a witness against you if you are untrue to your God."

28Then Joshua dismissed the people, each to their own inheritance.

Buried in the Promised Land

29After these things, Joshua son of Nun, the servant of the LORD, died at the age of a hundred and ten. 30And they buried him in the land of his inheritance, at Timnath Serah[a] in the hill country of Ephraim, north of Mount Gaash.

31Israel served the LORD throughout the lifetime of Joshua and of the elders who outlived him and who had experienced everything the LORD had done for Israel.

32And Joseph's bones, which the Israelites had brought up from Egypt, were buried at Shechem in the tract of land that Jacob bought for a hundred pieces of silver[b] from the sons of Hamor, the father of Shechem. This became the inheritance of Joseph's descendants.

33And Eleazar son of Aaron died and was buried at Gibeah, which had been allotted to his son Phinehas in the hill country of Ephraim.

Judges

Israel Fights the Remaining Canaanites

1 After the death of Joshua, the Israelites asked the LORD, "Who of us is to go up first to fight against the Canaanites?"

2The LORD answered, "Judah shall go up; I have given the land into their hands."

3The men of Judah then said to the Simeonites their fellow Israelites, "Come up with us into the territory allotted to us, to fight against the Canaanites. We in turn will go with you into yours." So the Simeonites went with them.

4When Judah attacked, the LORD gave the Canaanites and Perizzites into their hands, and they struck down ten thousand men at Bezek. 5It was there that they found Adoni-Bezek and fought against him, putting to rout the Canaanites and Perizzites. 6Adoni-Bezek fled, but they chased him and caught him, and cut off his thumbs and big toes.

7Then Adoni-Bezek said, "Seventy kings with their thumbs and big toes cut off have picked up scraps under my table. Now God has paid me back for what I did to them." They brought him to Jerusalem, and he died there.

8The men of Judah attacked Jerusalem also and took it. They put the city to the sword and set it on fire.

9After that, Judah went down to fight against the Canaanites living in the hill country, the Negev and the western foothills. 10They advanced against the Canaanites living in Hebron (formerly called Kiriath Arba) and defeated Sheshai, Ahiman and Talmai. 11From there they advanced against the people living in Debir (formerly called Kiriath Sepher).

12And Caleb said, "I will give my daughter Aksah in marriage to the man who attacks and captures Kiriath Sepher." 13Othniel son

[a] *30* Also known as *Timnath Heres* (see Judges 2:9)

[b] *32* Hebrew *hundred kesitahs*; a kesitah was a unit of money of unknown weight and value.

of Kenaz, Caleb's younger brother, took it; so Caleb gave his daughter Aksah to him in marriage.

14One day when she came to Othniel, she urged him[a] to ask her father for a field. When she got off her donkey, Caleb asked her, "What can I do for you?"

15She replied, "Do me a special favor. Since you have given me land in the Negev, give me also springs of water." So Caleb gave her the upper and lower springs.

16The descendants of Moses' father-in-law, the Kenite, went up from the City of Palms[b] with the people of Judah to live among the inhabitants of the Desert of Judah in the Negev near Arad.

17Then the men of Judah went with the Simeonites their fellow Israelites and attacked the Canaanites living in Zephath, and they totally destroyed[c] the city. Therefore it was called Hormah.[d] 18Judah also took[e] Gaza, Ashkelon and Ekron—each city with its territory.

19The LORD was with the men of Judah. They took possession of the hill country, but they were unable to drive the people from the plains, because they had chariots fitted with iron. 20As Moses had promised, Hebron was given to Caleb, who drove from it the three sons of Anak. 21The Benjamites, however, did not drive out the Jebusites, who were living in Jerusalem; to this day the Jebusites live there with the Benjamites.

22Now the tribes of Joseph attacked Bethel, and the LORD was with them. 23When they sent men to spy out Bethel (formerly called Luz), 24the spies saw a man coming out of the city and they said to him, "Show us how to get into the city and we will see that you are treated well." 25So he showed them, and they put the city to the sword but spared the man and his whole family. 26He then went to the land of the Hittites, where he built a city and called it Luz, which is its name to this day.

27But Manasseh did not drive out the people of Beth Shan or Taanach or Dor or Ibleam or Megiddo and their surrounding settlements, for the Canaanites were determined to live in that land. 28When Israel became strong, they pressed the Canaanites into forced labor but never drove them out completely. 29Nor did Ephraim drive out the Canaanites living in Gezer, but the Canaanites continued to live there among them. 30Neither did Zebulun drive out the Canaanites living in Kitron or Nahalol, so these Canaanites lived among them, but Zebulun did subject them to forced labor. 31Nor did Asher drive out those living in Akko or Sidon or Ahlab or Akzib or Helbah or Aphek or Rehob. 32The Asherites lived among the Canaanite inhabitants of the land because they did not drive them out. 33Neither did Naphtali drive out those living in Beth Shemesh or Beth Anath; but the Naphtalites too lived among the Canaanite inhabitants of the land, and those living in Beth Shemesh and Beth Anath became forced laborers for them. 34The Amorites confined the Danites to the hill country, not allowing them to come down into the plain. 35And the Amorites were determined also to hold out in Mount Heres, Aijalon and Shaalbim, but when the power of the tribes of Joseph increased, they too were pressed into forced labor. 36The boundary of the Amorites was from Scorpion Pass to Sela and beyond.

The Angel of the LORD at Bokim

2 The angel of the LORD went up from Gilgal to Bokim and said, "I brought you up out of Egypt and led you into the land I swore to give to your ancestors. I said, 'I will never break my covenant with you, 2and you shall not make a covenant with the people of this land, but you shall break down their altars.' Yet you have disobeyed me. Why have you done this? 3And I have also said, 'I will not drive them out before you; they will become traps for you, and their gods will become snares to you.'"

4When the angel of the LORD had spoken these things to all the Israelites, the people wept aloud, 5and they called that place Bokim.[f] There they offered sacrifices to the LORD.

Disobedience and Defeat

6After Joshua had dismissed the Israelites, they went to take possession of the land, each to their own inheritance. 7The people served the LORD throughout the lifetime of Joshua and of the elders who outlived him and who had seen all the great things the LORD had done for Israel.

8Joshua son of Nun, the servant of the LORD, died at the age of a hundred and ten. 9And they buried him in the land of his inheritance, at Timnath Heres[g] in the hill country of Ephraim, north of Mount Gaash.

10After that whole generation had been gathered to their ancestors, another generation grew up who knew neither the LORD nor what he had done for Israel. 11Then the Israelites did evil in the eyes of the LORD and served the Baals. 12They forsook the LORD, the God of their ancestors, who had brought them out of Egypt. They followed and worshiped various gods of the peoples around them. They aroused the LORD's anger 13because they forsook him and served Baal and the Ashtoreths. 14In his anger against Israel the LORD gave them into the hands of raiders who plundered them. He sold them into the hands of their enemies all around, whom they were no longer able to resist. 15Whenever Israel went out to fight, the hand of the LORD was against them to defeat them, just as he had sworn to them. They were in great distress.

16Then the LORD raised up judges,[h] who

[a] 14 Hebrew; Septuagint and Vulgate *Othniel, he urged her* [b] 16 That is, Jericho [c] 17 The Hebrew term refers to the irrevocable giving over of things or persons to the LORD, often by totally destroying them. [d] 17 *Hormah* means *destruction.* [e] 18 Hebrew; Septuagint *Judah did not take* [f] 5 *Bokim* means *weepers.* [g] 9 Also known as *Timnath Serah* (see Joshua 19:50 and 24:30) [h] 16 Or *leaders;* similarly in verses 17-19

saved them out of the hands of these raiders. [17]Yet they would not listen to their judges but prostituted themselves to other gods and worshiped them. They quickly turned from the ways of their ancestors, who had been obedient to the LORD's commands. [18]Whenever the LORD raised up a judge for them, he was with the judge and saved them out of the hands of their enemies as long as the judge lived; for the LORD relented because of their groaning under those who oppressed and afflicted them. [19]But when the judge died, the people returned to ways even more corrupt than those of their ancestors, following other gods and serving and worshiping them. They refused to give up their evil practices and stubborn ways.

[20]Therefore the LORD was very angry with Israel and said, "Because this nation has violated the covenant I ordained for their ancestors and has not listened to me, [21]I will no longer drive out before them any of the nations Joshua left when he died. [22]I will use them to test Israel and see whether they will keep the way of the LORD and walk in it as their ancestors did." [23]The LORD had allowed those nations to remain; he did not drive them out at once by giving them into the hands of Joshua.

3 These are the nations the LORD left to test all those Israelites who had not experienced any of the wars in Canaan [2](he did this only to teach warfare to the descendants of the Israelites who had not had previous battle experience): [3]the five rulers of the Philistines, all the Canaanites, the Sidonians, and the Hivites living in the Lebanon mountains from Mount Baal Hermon to Lebo Hamath. [4]They were left to test the Israelites to see whether they would obey the LORD's commands, which he had given their ancestors through Moses.

[5]The Israelites lived among the Canaanites, Hittites, Amorites, Perizzites, Hivites and Jebusites. [6]They took their daughters in marriage and gave their own daughters to their sons, and served their gods.

Othniel

[7]The Israelites did evil in the eyes of the LORD; they forgot the LORD their God and served the Baals and the Asherahs. [8]The anger of the LORD burned against Israel so that he sold them into the hands of Cushan-Rishathaim king of Aram Naharaim,[a] to whom the Israelites were subject for eight years. [9]But when they cried out to the LORD, he raised up for them a deliverer, Othniel son of Kenaz, Caleb's younger brother, who saved them. [10]The Spirit of the LORD came on him, so that he became Israel's judge[b] and went to war. The LORD gave Cushan-Rishathaim king of Aram into the hands of Othniel, who overpowered him. [11]So the land had peace for forty years, until Othniel son of Kenaz died.

Ehud

[12]Again the Israelites did evil in the eyes of the LORD, and because they did this evil the LORD gave Eglon king of Moab power over Israel. [13]Getting the Ammonites and Amalekites to join him, Eglon came and attacked Israel, and they took possession of the City of Palms.[c] [14]The Israelites were subject to Eglon king of Moab for eighteen years.

[15]Again the Israelites cried out to the LORD, and he gave them a deliverer—Ehud, a left-handed man, the son of Gera the Benjamite. The Israelites sent him with tribute to Eglon king of Moab. [16]Now Ehud had made a double-edged sword about a cubit[d] long, which he strapped to his right thigh under his clothing. [17]He presented the tribute to Eglon king of Moab, who was a very fat man. [18]After Ehud had presented the tribute, he sent on their way those who had carried it. [19]But on reaching the stone images near Gilgal he himself went back to Eglon and said, "Your Majesty, I have a secret message for you."

The king said to his attendants, "Leave us!" And they all left.

[20]Ehud then approached him while he was sitting alone in the upper room of his palace[e] and said, "I have a message from God for you." As the king rose from his seat, [21]Ehud reached with his left hand, drew the sword from his right thigh and plunged it into the king's belly. [22]Even the handle sank in after the blade, and his bowels discharged. Ehud did not pull the sword out, and the fat closed in over it. [23]Then Ehud went out to the porch[f]; he shut the doors of the upper room behind him and locked them.

[24]After he had gone, the servants came and found the doors of the upper room locked. They said, "He must be relieving himself in the inner room of the palace." [25]They waited to the point of embarrassment, but when he did not open the doors of the room, they took a key and unlocked them. There they saw their lord fallen to the floor, dead.

[26]While they waited, Ehud got away. He passed by the stone images and escaped to Seirah. [27]When he arrived there, he blew a trumpet in the hill country of Ephraim, and the Israelites went down with him from the hills, with him leading them.

[28]"Follow me," he ordered, "for the LORD has given Moab, your enemy, into your hands." So they followed him down and took possession of the fords of the Jordan that led to Moab; they allowed no one to cross over. [29]At that time they struck down about ten thousand Moabites, all vigorous and strong; not one escaped. [30]That day Moab was made subject to Israel, and the land had peace for eighty years.

Shamgar

[31]After Ehud came Shamgar son of Anath, who struck down six hundred Philistines with an oxgoad. He too saved Israel.

[a] *8* That is, Northwest Mesopotamia [b] *10* Or *leader* [c] *13* That is, Jericho [d] *16* That is, about 18 inches or about 45 centimeters [e] *20* The meaning of the Hebrew for this word is uncertain; also in verse 24. [f] *23* The meaning of the Hebrew for this word is uncertain.

Deborah

4 Again the Israelites did evil in the eyes of
the LORD, now that Ehud was dead. 2So the
LORD sold them into the hands of Jabin king
of Canaan, who reigned in Hazor. Sisera, the
commander of his army, was based in Harosheth Haggoyim. 3Because he had nine hundred chariots fitted with iron and had cruelly
oppressed the Israelites for twenty years, they
cried to the LORD for help.
4Now Deborah, a prophet, the wife of Lap-
pidoth, was leading[a] Israel at that time. 5She
held court under the Palm of Deborah between Ramah and Bethel in the hill country
of Ephraim, and the Israelites went up to her
to have their disputes decided. 6She sent for
Barak son of Abinoam from Kedesh in Naphtali and said to him, "The LORD, the God of
Israel, commands you: 'Go, take with you ten
thousand men of Naphtali and Zebulun and
lead them up to Mount Tabor. 7I will lead Sisera, the commander of Jabin's army, with his
chariots and his troops to the Kishon River
and give him into your hands.'"
8Barak said to her, "If you go with me, I will
go; but if you don't go with me, I won't go."
9"Certainly I will go with you," said Deborah. "But because of the course you are taking, the honor will not be yours, for the LORD
will deliver Sisera into the hands of a woman." So Deborah went with Barak to Kedesh.
10There Barak summoned Zebulun and Naphtali, and ten thousand men went up under his
command. Deborah also went up with him.
11Now Heber the Kenite had left the other
Kenites, the descendants of Hobab, Moses'
brother-in-law,[b] and pitched his tent by the
great tree in Zaanannim near Kedesh.
12When they told Sisera that Barak son of
Abinoam had gone up to Mount Tabor, 13Sis-
era summoned from Harosheth Haggoyim
to the Kishon River all his men and his nine
hundred chariots fitted with iron.
14Then Deborah said to Barak, "Go! This is
the day the LORD has given Sisera into your
hands. Has not the LORD gone ahead of you?"
So Barak went down Mount Tabor, with ten
thousand men following him. 15At Barak's
advance, the LORD routed Sisera and all his
chariots and army by the sword, and Sisera
got down from his chariot and fled on foot.
16Barak pursued the chariots and army as
far as Harosheth Haggoyim, and all Sisera's
troops fell by the sword; not a man was left.
17Sisera, meanwhile, fled on foot to the tent
of Jael, the wife of Heber the Kenite, because
there was an alliance between Jabin king of
Hazor and the family of Heber the Kenite.
18Jael went out to meet Sisera and said to
him, "Come, my lord, come right in. Don't be
afraid." So he entered her tent, and she covered him with a blanket.
19"I'm thirsty," he said. "Please give me
some water." She opened a skin of milk, gave
him a drink, and covered him up.
20"Stand in the doorway of the tent," he told
her. "If someone comes by and asks you, 'Is
anyone in there?' say 'No.'"
21But Jael, Heber's wife, picked up a tent
peg and a hammer and went quietly to him
while he lay fast asleep, exhausted. She drove
the peg through his temple into the ground,
and he died.
22Just then Barak came by in pursuit of Sisera, and Jael went out to meet him. "Come,"
she said, "I will show you the man you're looking for." So he went in with her, and there
lay Sisera with the tent peg through his temple—dead.
23On that day God subdued Jabin king of
Canaan before the Israelites. 24And the hand
of the Israelites pressed harder and harder
against Jabin king of Canaan until they destroyed him.

The Song of Deborah

5 On that day Deborah and Barak son of
Abinoam sang this song:

2 "When the princes in Israel take the lead,
when the people willingly offer
themselves—
praise the LORD!

3 "Hear this, you kings! Listen, you rulers!
I, even I, will sing to[c] the LORD;
I will praise the LORD, the God of Israel,
in song.

4 "When you, LORD, went out from Seir,
when you marched from the land of
Edom,
the earth shook, the heavens poured,
the clouds poured down water.
5 The mountains quaked before the LORD,
the One of Sinai,
before the LORD, the God of Israel.

6 "In the days of Shamgar son of Anath,
in the days of Jael, the highways were
abandoned;
travelers took to winding paths.
7 Villagers in Israel would not fight;
they held back until I, Deborah, arose,
until I arose, a mother in Israel.
8 God chose new leaders
when war came to the city gates,
but not a shield or spear was seen
among forty thousand in Israel.
9 My heart is with Israel's princes,
with the willing volunteers among the
people.
Praise the LORD!

10 "You who ride on white donkeys,
sitting on your saddle blankets,
and you who walk along the road,
consider 11the voice of the singers[d] at the
watering places.
They recite the victories of the LORD,
the victories of his villagers in Israel.

"Then the people of the LORD
went down to the city gates.

[a] 4 Traditionally *judging* [b] 11 Or *father-in-law* [c] 3 Or *of* [d] 11 The meaning of the Hebrew for this word is uncertain.

12 'Wake up, wake up, Deborah!
Wake up, wake up, break out in song!
Arise, Barak!
Take captive your captives, son of Abinoam.'
13 "The remnant of the nobles came down;
the people of the LORD came down to me against the mighty.
14 Some came from Ephraim, whose roots were in Amalek;
Benjamin was with the people who followed you.
From Makir captains came down,
from Zebulun those who bear a commander's[a] staff.
15 The princes of Issachar were with Deborah;
yes, Issachar was with Barak,
sent under his command into the valley.
In the districts of Reuben
there was much searching of heart.
16 Why did you stay among the sheep pens[b]
to hear the whistling for the flocks?
In the districts of Reuben
there was much searching of heart.
17 Gilead stayed beyond the Jordan.
And Dan, why did he linger by the ships?
Asher remained on the coast
and stayed in his coves.
18 The people of Zebulun risked their very lives;
so did Naphtali on the terraced fields.
19 "Kings came, they fought,
the kings of Canaan fought.
At Taanach, by the waters of Megiddo,
they took no plunder of silver.
20 From the heavens the stars fought,
from their courses they fought against Sisera.
21 The river Kishon swept them away,
the age-old river, the river Kishon.
March on, my soul; be strong!
22 Then thundered the horses' hooves—
galloping, galloping go his mighty steeds.
23 'Curse Meroz,' said the angel of the LORD.
'Curse its people bitterly,
because they did not come to help the LORD,
to help the LORD against the mighty.'

24 "Most blessed of women be Jael,
the wife of Heber the Kenite,
most blessed of tent-dwelling women.
25 He asked for water, and she gave him milk;
in a bowl fit for nobles she brought him curdled milk.
26 Her hand reached for the tent peg,
her right hand for the workman's hammer.
She struck Sisera, she crushed his head,
she shattered and pierced his temple.
27 At her feet he sank,
he fell; there he lay.
At her feet he sank, he fell;
where he sank, there he fell—dead.
28 "Through the window peered Sisera's mother;
behind the lattice she cried out,
'Why is his chariot so long in coming?
Why is the clatter of his chariots delayed?'
29 The wisest of her ladies answer her;
indeed, she keeps saying to herself,
30 'Are they not finding and dividing the spoils:
a woman or two for each man,
colorful garments as plunder for Sisera,
colorful garments embroidered,
highly embroidered garments for my neck—
all this as plunder?'

31 "So may all your enemies perish, LORD!
But may all who love you be like the sun
when it rises in its strength."
Then the land had peace forty years.

Gideon

6 The Israelites did evil in the eyes of the
LORD, and for seven years he gave them
into the hands of the Midianites. 2 Because
the power of Midian was so oppressive, the
Israelites prepared shelters for themselves
in mountain clefts, caves and strongholds.
3 Whenever the Israelites planted their crops,
the Midianites, Amalekites and other eastern
peoples invaded the country. 4 They camped
on the land and ruined the crops all the way
to Gaza and did not spare a living thing for
Israel, neither sheep nor cattle nor donkeys.
5 They came up with their livestock and their
tents like swarms of locusts. It was impossible
to count them or their camels; they invaded
the land to ravage it. 6 Midian so impoverished
the Israelites that they cried out to the LORD
for help.
7 When the Israelites cried out to the LORD
because of Midian, 8 he sent them a prophet,
who said, "This is what the LORD, the God of
Israel, says: I brought you up out of Egypt,
out of the land of slavery. 9 I rescued you from
the hand of the Egyptians. And I delivered
you from the hand of all your oppressors; I
drove them out before you and gave you their
land. 10 I said to you, 'I am the LORD your God;
do not worship the gods of the Amorites, in
whose land you live.' But you have not listened to me."
11 The angel of the LORD came and sat down
under the oak in Ophrah that belonged to Joash the Abiezrite, where his son Gideon was
threshing wheat in a winepress to keep it
from the Midianites. 12 When the angel of the
LORD appeared to Gideon, he said, "The LORD
is with you, mighty warrior."
13 "Pardon me, my lord," Gideon replied, "but
if the LORD is with us, why has all this happened to us? Where are all his wonders that

[a] *14* The meaning of the Hebrew for this word is uncertain. [b] *16* Or *the campfires*; or *the saddlebags*

our ancestors told us about when they said,
'Did not the LORD bring us up out of Egypt?'
But now the LORD has abandoned us and given
us into the hand of Midian."
14The LORD turned to him and said, "Go in
the strength you have and save Israel out of
Midian's hand. Am I not sending you?"
15"Pardon me, my lord," Gideon replied, "but
how can I save Israel? My clan is the weakest
in Manasseh, and I am the least in my family."
16The LORD answered, "I will be with you,
and you will strike down all the Midianites,
leaving none alive."
17Gideon replied, "If now I have found favor
in your eyes, give me a sign that it is really
you talking to me. 18Please do not go away
until I come back and bring my offering and
set it before you."
And the LORD said, "I will wait until you
return."
19Gideon went inside, prepared a young
goat, and from an ephah[a] of flour he made
bread without yeast. Putting the meat in a
basket and its broth in a pot, he brought them
out and offered them to him under the oak.
20The angel of God said to him, "Take the
meat and the unleavened bread, place them
on this rock, and pour out the broth." And
Gideon did so. 21Then the angel of the LORD
touched the meat and the unleavened bread
with the tip of the staff that was in his hand.
Fire flared from the rock, consuming the meat
and the bread. And the angel of the LORD disappeared. 22When Gideon realized that it was
the angel of the LORD, he exclaimed, "Alas,
Sovereign LORD! I have seen the angel of the
LORD face to face!"
23But the LORD said to him, "Peace! Do not
be afraid. You are not going to die."
24So Gideon built an altar to the LORD there
and called it The LORD Is Peace. To this day it
stands in Ophrah of the Abiezrites.
25That same night the LORD said to him, "Take
the second bull from your father's herd, the one
seven years old.[b] Tear down your father's altar
to Baal and cut down the Asherah pole[c] beside
it. 26Then build a proper kind of[d] altar to the
LORD your God on the top of this height. Using
the wood of the Asherah pole that you cut down,
offer the second[e] bull as a burnt offering."
27So Gideon took ten of his servants and
did as the LORD told him. But because he was
afraid of his family and the townspeople, he
did it at night rather than in the daytime.
28In the morning when the people of the
town got up, there was Baal's altar, demolished, with the Asherah pole beside it cut
down and the second bull sacrificed on the
newly built altar!
29They asked each other, "Who did this?"
When they carefully investigated, they
were told, "Gideon son of Joash did it."
30The people of the town demanded of Joash, "Bring out your son. He must die, because
he has broken down Baal's altar and cut down
the Asherah pole beside it."
31But Joash replied to the hostile crowd
around him, "Are you going to plead Baal's
cause? Are you trying to save him? Whoever
fights for him shall be put to death by morning! If Baal really is a god, he can defend himself when someone breaks down his altar."
32So because Gideon broke down Baal's altar,
they gave him the name Jerub-Baal[f] that day,
saying, "Let Baal contend with him."
33Now all the Midianites, Amalekites and
other eastern peoples joined forces and
crossed over the Jordan and camped in the
Valley of Jezreel. 34Then the Spirit of the
LORD came on Gideon, and he blew a trumpet, summoning the Abiezrites to follow him.
35He sent messengers throughout Manasseh,
calling them to arms, and also into Asher,
Zebulun and Naphtali, so that they too went
up to meet them.
36Gideon said to God, "If you will save Israel
by my hand as you have promised— 37look, I
will place a wool fleece on the threshing floor.
If there is dew only on the fleece and all the
ground is dry, then I will know that you will
save Israel by my hand, as you said." 38And
that is what happened. Gideon rose early the
next day; he squeezed the fleece and wrung
out the dew—a bowlful of water.
39Then Gideon said to God, "Do not be angry with me. Let me make just one more request. Allow me one more test with the fleece,
but this time make the fleece dry and let the
ground be covered with dew." 40That night
God did so. Only the fleece was dry; all the
ground was covered with dew.

Gideon Defeats the Midianites

7 Early in the morning, Jerub-Baal (that is,
Gideon) and all his men camped at the
spring of Harod. The camp of Midian was
north of them in the valley near the hill of Moreh. 2The LORD said to Gideon, "You have too
many men. I cannot deliver Midian into their
hands, or Israel would boast against me, 'My
own strength has saved me.' 3Now announce
to the army, 'Anyone who trembles with fear
may turn back and leave Mount Gilead.'" So
twenty-two thousand men left, while ten thousand remained.
4But the LORD said to Gideon, "There are
still too many men. Take them down to the
water, and I will thin them out for you there.
If I say, 'This one shall go with you,' he shall
go; but if I say, 'This one shall not go with you,'
he shall not go."
5So Gideon took the men down to the water.
There the LORD told him, "Separate those who
lap the water with their tongues as a dog laps
from those who kneel down to drink." 6Three
hundred of them drank from cupped hands,
lapping like dogs. All the rest got down on
their knees to drink.

[a] *19* That is, probably about 36 pounds or about 16 kilograms [b] *25* Or *Take a full-grown, mature bull from your father's herd* [c] *25* That is, a wooden symbol of the goddess Asherah; also in verses 26, 28 and 30 [d] *26* Or *build with layers of stone an* [e] *26* Or *full-grown*; also in verse 28 [f] *32* *Jerub-Baal* probably means *let Baal contend.*

[7]The LORD said to Gideon, "With the three hundred men that lapped I will save you and give the Midianites into your hands. Let all the others go home." [8]So Gideon sent the rest of the Israelites home but kept the three hundred, who took over the provisions and trumpets of the others.

Now the camp of Midian lay below him in the valley. [9]During that night the LORD said to Gideon, "Get up, go down against the camp, because I am going to give it into your hands. [10]If you are afraid to attack, go down to the camp with your servant Purah [11]and listen to what they are saying. Afterward, you will be encouraged to attack the camp." So he and Purah his servant went down to the outposts of the camp. [12]The Midianites, the Amalekites and all the other eastern peoples had settled in the valley, thick as locusts. Their camels could no more be counted than the sand on the seashore.

[13]Gideon arrived just as a man was telling a friend his dream. "I had a dream," he was saying. "A round loaf of barley bread came tumbling into the Midianite camp. It struck the tent with such force that the tent overturned and collapsed."

[14]His friend responded, "This can be nothing other than the sword of Gideon son of Joash, the Israelite. God has given the Midianites and the whole camp into his hands."

[15]When Gideon heard the dream and its interpretation, he bowed down and worshiped. He returned to the camp of Israel and called out, "Get up! The LORD has given the Midianite camp into your hands." [16]Dividing the three hundred men into three companies, he placed trumpets and empty jars in the hands of all of them, with torches inside.

[17]"Watch me," he told them. "Follow my lead. When I get to the edge of the camp, do exactly as I do. [18]When I and all who are with me blow our trumpets, then from all around the camp blow yours and shout, 'For the LORD and for Gideon.'"

[19]Gideon and the hundred men with him reached the edge of the camp at the beginning of the middle watch, just after they had changed the guard. They blew their trumpets and broke the jars that were in their hands. [20]The three companies blew the trumpets and smashed the jars. Grasping the torches in their left hands and holding in their right hands the trumpets they were to blow, they shouted, "A sword for the LORD and for Gideon!" [21]While each man held his position around the camp, all the Midianites ran, crying out as they fled.

[22]When the three hundred trumpets sounded, the LORD caused the men throughout the camp to turn on each other with their swords. The army fled to Beth Shittah toward Zererah as far as the border of Abel Meholah near Tabbath. [23]Israelites from Naphtali, Asher and all Manasseh were called out, and they pursued the Midianites. [24]Gideon sent messengers throughout the hill country of Ephraim, saying, "Come down against the Midianites and seize the waters of the Jordan ahead of them as far as Beth Barah."

So all the men of Ephraim were called out and they seized the waters of the Jordan as far as Beth Barah. [25]They also captured two of the Midianite leaders, Oreb and Zeeb. They killed Oreb at the rock of Oreb, and Zeeb at the winepress of Zeeb. They pursued the Midianites and brought the heads of Oreb and Zeeb to Gideon, who was by the Jordan.

Zebah and Zalmunna

8 Now the Ephraimites asked Gideon, "Why have you treated us like this? Why didn't you call us when you went to fight Midian?" And they challenged him vigorously.

[2]But he answered them, "What have I accomplished compared to you? Aren't the gleanings of Ephraim's grapes better than the full grape harvest of Abiezer? [3]God gave Oreb and Zeeb, the Midianite leaders, into your hands. What was I able to do compared to you?" At this, their resentment against him subsided.

[4]Gideon and his three hundred men, exhausted yet keeping up the pursuit, came to the Jordan and crossed it. [5]He said to the men of Sukkoth, "Give my troops some bread; they are worn out, and I am still pursuing Zebah and Zalmunna, the kings of Midian."

[6]But the officials of Sukkoth said, "Do you already have the hands of Zebah and Zalmunna in your possession? Why should we give bread to your troops?"

[7]Then Gideon replied, "Just for that, when the LORD has given Zebah and Zalmunna into my hand, I will tear your flesh with desert thorns and briers."

[8]From there he went up to Peniel[a] and made the same request of them, but they answered as the men of Sukkoth had. [9]So he said to the men of Peniel, "When I return in triumph, I will tear down this tower."

[10]Now Zebah and Zalmunna were in Karkor with a force of about fifteen thousand men, all that were left of the armies of the eastern peoples; a hundred and twenty thousand swordsmen had fallen. [11]Gideon went up by the route of the nomads east of Nobah and Jogbehah and attacked the unsuspecting army. [12]Zebah and Zalmunna, the two kings of Midian, fled, but he pursued them and captured them, routing their entire army.

[13]Gideon son of Joash then returned from the battle by the Pass of Heres. [14]He caught a young man of Sukkoth and questioned him, and the young man wrote down for him the names of the seventy-seven officials of Sukkoth, the elders of the town. [15]Then Gideon came and said to the men of Sukkoth, "Here are Zebah and Zalmunna, about whom you taunted me by saying, 'Do you already have the hands of Zebah and Zalmunna in your possession? Why should we give bread to your exhausted men?'" [16]He took the elders of the town and taught the men of Sukkoth a lesson by punishing them with desert thorns

[a] 8 Hebrew *Penuel,* a variant of *Peniel;* also in verses 9 and 17

and briers. 17He also pulled down the tower of
Peniel and killed the men of the town.
18Then he asked Zebah and Zalmunna,
"What kind of men did you kill at Tabor?"
"Men like you," they answered, "each one
with the bearing of a prince."
19Gideon replied, "Those were my brothers, the sons of my own mother. As surely as
the LORD lives, if you had spared their lives,
I would not kill you." 20Turning to Jether, his
oldest son, he said, "Kill them!" But Jether
did not draw his sword, because he was only
a boy and was afraid.
21Zebah and Zalmunna said, "Come, do it
yourself. 'As is the man, so is his strength.'" So
Gideon stepped forward and killed them, and
took the ornaments off their camels' necks.

Gideon's Ephod

22The Israelites said to Gideon, "Rule over
us—you, your son and your grandson—because you have saved us from the hand of
Midian."
23But Gideon told them, "I will not rule over
you, nor will my son rule over you. The LORD
will rule over you." 24And he said, "I do have
one request, that each of you give me an earring from your share of the plunder." (It was
the custom of the Ishmaelites to wear gold
earrings.)
25They answered, "We'll be glad to give
them." So they spread out a garment, and
each of them threw a ring from his plunder
onto it. 26The weight of the gold rings he asked
for came to seventeen hundred shekels,[a] not
counting the ornaments, the pendants and the
purple garments worn by the kings of Midian
or the chains that were on their camels' necks.
27Gideon made the gold into an ephod, which
he placed in Ophrah, his town. All Israel prostituted themselves by worshiping it there, and
it became a snare to Gideon and his family.

Gideon's Death

28Thus Midian was subdued before the Israelites and did not raise its head again. During
Gideon's lifetime, the land had peace forty
years.
29Jerub-Baal son of Joash went back home
to live. 30He had seventy sons of his own,
for he had many wives. 31His concubine,
who lived in Shechem, also bore him a son,
whom he named Abimelek. 32Gideon son of
Joash died at a good old age and was buried
in the tomb of his father Joash in Ophrah of
the Abiezrites.
33No sooner had Gideon died than the Israelites again prostituted themselves to the
Baals. They set up Baal-Berith as their god
34and did not remember the LORD their God,
who had rescued them from the hands of all
their enemies on every side. 35They also failed
to show any loyalty to the family of Jerub-Baal
(that is, Gideon) in spite of all the good things
he had done for them.

Abimelek

9 Abimelek son of Jerub-Baal went to his
mother's brothers in Shechem and said to
them and to all his mother's clan, 2"Ask all
the citizens of Shechem, 'Which is better for
you: to have all seventy of Jerub-Baal's sons
rule over you, or just one man?' Remember, I
am your flesh and blood."
3When the brothers repeated all this to the
citizens of Shechem, they were inclined to follow Abimelek, for they said, "He is related to
us." 4They gave him seventy shekels[b] of silver
from the temple of Baal-Berith, and Abimelek used it to hire reckless scoundrels, who
became his followers. 5He went to his father's
home in Ophrah and on one stone murdered
his seventy brothers, the sons of Jerub-Baal.
But Jotham, the youngest son of Jerub-Baal,
escaped by hiding. 6Then all the citizens of
Shechem and Beth Millo gathered beside the
great tree at the pillar in Shechem to crown
Abimelek king.
7When Jotham was told about this, he
climbed up on the top of Mount Gerizim and
shouted to them, "Listen to me, citizens of Shechem, so that God may listen to you. 8One
day the trees went out to anoint a king for
themselves. They said to the olive tree, 'Be
our king.'
9"But the olive tree answered, 'Should I give
up my oil, by which both gods and humans are
honored, to hold sway over the trees?'
10"Next, the trees said to the fig tree, 'Come
and be our king.'
11"But the fig tree replied, 'Should I give
up my fruit, so good and sweet, to hold sway
over the trees?'
12"Then the trees said to the vine, 'Come
and be our king.'
13"But the vine answered, 'Should I give
up my wine, which cheers both gods and humans, to hold sway over the trees?'
14"Finally all the trees said to the thornbush,
'Come and be our king.'
15"The thornbush said to the trees, 'If you
really want to anoint me king over you, come
and take refuge in my shade; but if not, then
let fire come out of the thornbush and consume the cedars of Lebanon!'
16"Have you acted honorably and in good
faith by making Abimelek king? Have you
been fair to Jerub-Baal and his family? Have
you treated him as he deserves? 17Remem-
ber that my father fought for you and risked
his life to rescue you from the hand of Midian. 18But today you have revolted against my
father's family. You have murdered his seventy sons on a single stone and have made
Abimelek, the son of his female slave, king
over the citizens of Shechem because he is
related to you. 19So have you acted honorably
and in good faith toward Jerub-Baal and his
family today? If you have, may Abimelek be
your joy, and may you be his, too! 20But if you
have not, let fire come out from Abimelek and
consume you, the citizens of Shechem and

[a] *26* That is, about 43 pounds or about 20 kilograms [b] *4* That is, about 1 3/4 pounds or about 800 grams

Beth Millo, and let fire come out from you,
the citizens of Shechem and Beth Millo, and
consume Abimelek!"

21 Then Jotham fled, escaping to Beer, and
he lived there because he was afraid of his
brother Abimelek.

22 After Abimelek had governed Israel three
years, 23 God stirred up animosity between
Abimelek and the citizens of Shechem so that
they acted treacherously against Abimelek.
24 God did this in order that the crime against
Jerub-Baal's seventy sons, the shedding of their
blood, might be avenged on their brother Abimelek and on the citizens of Shechem, who had
helped him murder his brothers. 25 In opposition
to him these citizens of Shechem set men on
the hilltops to ambush and rob everyone who
passed by, and this was reported to Abimelek.

26 Now Gaal son of Ebed moved with his
clan into Shechem, and its citizens put their
confidence in him. 27 After they had gone out
into the fields and gathered the grapes and
trodden them, they held a festival in the temple of their god. While they were eating and
drinking, they cursed Abimelek. 28 Then Gaal
son of Ebed said, "Who is Abimelek, and why
should we Shechemites be subject to him? Isn't
he Jerub-Baal's son, and isn't Zebul his dep-
uty? Serve the family of Hamor, Shechem's
father! Why should we serve Abimelek? 29 If
only this people were under my command!
Then I would get rid of him. I would say to
Abimelek, 'Call out your whole army!'"[a]

30 When Zebul the governor of the city heard
what Gaal son of Ebed said, he was very angry. 31 Under cover he sent messengers to
Abimelek, saying, "Gaal son of Ebed and his
clan have come to Shechem and are stirring
up the city against you. 32 Now then, during
the night you and your men should come and
lie in wait in the fields. 33 In the morning at
sunrise, advance against the city. When Gaal
and his men come out against you, seize the
opportunity to attack them."

34 So Abimelek and all his troops set out by
night and took up concealed positions near
Shechem in four companies. 35 Now Gaal son
of Ebed had gone out and was standing at the
entrance of the city gate just as Abimelek and
his troops came out from their hiding place.

36 When Gaal saw them, he said to Zebul,
"Look, people are coming down from the tops
of the mountains!"

Zebul replied, "You mistake the shadows
of the mountains for men."

37 But Gaal spoke up again: "Look, people
are coming down from the central hill,[b] and
a company is coming from the direction of
the diviners' tree."

38 Then Zebul said to him, "Where is your
big talk now, you who said, 'Who is Abimelek that we should be subject to him?' Aren't
these the men you ridiculed? Go out and fight
them!"

39 So Gaal led out[c] the citizens of Shechem
and fought Abimelek. 40 Abimelek chased him
all the way to the entrance of the gate, and
many were killed as they fled. 41 Then Abimelek stayed in Arumah, and Zebul drove Gaal
and his clan out of Shechem.

42 The next day the people of Shechem went
out to the fields, and this was reported to
Abimelek. 43 So he took his men, divided them
into three companies and set an ambush in the
fields. When he saw the people coming out of
the city, he rose to attack them. 44 Abimelek
and the companies with him rushed forward to
a position at the entrance of the city gate. Then
two companies attacked those in the fields and
struck them down. 45 All that day Abimelek
pressed his attack against the city until he
had captured it and killed its people. Then he
destroyed the city and scattered salt over it.

46 On hearing this, the citizens in the tower
of Shechem went into the stronghold of the
temple of El-Berith. 47 When Abimelek heard
that they had assembled there, 48 he and all his
men went up Mount Zalmon. He took an ax
and cut off some branches, which he lifted to
his shoulders. He ordered the men with him,
"Quick! Do what you have seen me do!" 49 So
all the men cut branches and followed Abimelek. They piled them against the stronghold
and set it on fire with the people still inside.
So all the people in the tower of Shechem,
about a thousand men and women, also died.

50 Next Abimelek went to Thebez and besieged it and captured it. 51 Inside the city,
however, was a strong tower, to which all
the men and women—all the people of the
city—had fled. They had locked themselves
in and climbed up on the tower roof. 52 Abimelek went to the tower and attacked it. But as
he approached the entrance to the tower to
set it on fire, 53 a woman dropped an upper
millstone on his head and cracked his skull.

54 Hurriedly he called to his armor-bearer,
"Draw your sword and kill me, so that they
can't say, 'A woman killed him.'" So his servant ran him through, and he died. 55 When
the Israelites saw that Abimelek was dead,
they went home.

56 Thus God repaid the wickedness that
Abimelek had done to his father by murdering his seventy brothers. 57 God also made the
people of Shechem pay for all their wickedness. The curse of Jotham son of Jerub-Baal
came on them.

Tola

10 After the time of Abimelek, a man of
Issachar named Tola son of Puah, the
son of Dodo, rose to save Israel. He lived in
Shamir, in the hill country of Ephraim. 2 He
led[d] Israel twenty-three years; then he died,
and was buried in Shamir.

Jair

3 He was followed by Jair of Gilead, who led
Israel twenty-two years. 4 He had thirty sons,

[a] 29 Septuagint; Hebrew *him." Then he said to Abimelek, "Call out your whole army!"* [b] 37 The Hebrew for this phrase means *the navel of the earth.* [c] 39 Or *Gaal went out in the sight of* [d] 2 Traditionally *judged*; also in verse 3

who rode thirty donkeys. They controlled
thirty towns in Gilead, which to this day are
called Havvoth Jair.[a] 5When Jair died, he was
buried in Kamon.

Jephthah

6Again the Israelites did evil in the eyes
of the LORD. They served the Baals and the
Ashtoreths, and the gods of Aram, the gods
of Sidon, the gods of Moab, the gods of the
Ammonites and the gods of the Philistines.
And because the Israelites forsook the LORD
and no longer served him, 7he became angry
with them. He sold them into the hands of
the Philistines and the Ammonites, 8who that
year shattered and crushed them. For eighteen
years they oppressed all the Israelites on the
east side of the Jordan in Gilead, the land of
the Amorites. 9The Ammonites also crossed
the Jordan to fight against Judah, Benjamin
and Ephraim; Israel was in great distress.
10Then the Israelites cried out to the LORD,
"We have sinned against you, forsaking our
God and serving the Baals."

11The LORD replied, "When the Egyptians,
the Amorites, the Ammonites, the Philistines,
12the Sidonians, the Amalekites and the Ma-
onites[b] oppressed you and you cried to me for
help, did I not save you from their hands? 13But
you have forsaken me and served other gods,
so I will no longer save you. 14Go and cry out
to the gods you have chosen. Let them save
you when you are in trouble!"

15But the Israelites said to the LORD, "We
have sinned. Do with us whatever you think
best, but please rescue us now." 16Then they
got rid of the foreign gods among them and
served the LORD. And he could bear Israel's
misery no longer.

17When the Ammonites were called to arms
and camped in Gilead, the Israelites assembled and camped at Mizpah. 18The leaders
of the people of Gilead said to each other,
"Whoever will take the lead in attacking the
Ammonites will be head over all who live in
Gilead."

11 Jephthah the Gileadite was a mighty
warrior. His father was Gilead; his mother was a prostitute. 2Gilead's wife also bore
him sons, and when they were grown up, they
drove Jephthah away. "You are not going to
get any inheritance in our family," they said,
"because you are the son of another woman."
3So Jephthah fled from his brothers and settled in the land of Tob, where a gang of scoundrels gathered around him and followed him.

4Some time later, when the Ammonites were
fighting against Israel, 5the elders of Gilead
went to get Jephthah from the land of Tob.
6"Come," they said, "be our commander, so
we can fight the Ammonites."

7Jephthah said to them, "Didn't you hate me
and drive me from my father's house? Why do
you come to me now, when you're in trouble?"

8The elders of Gilead said to him, "Nevertheless, we are turning to you now; come with
us to fight the Ammonites, and you will be
head over all of us who live in Gilead."

9Jephthah answered, "Suppose you take me
back to fight the Ammonites and the LORD
gives them to me—will I really be your head?"

10The elders of Gilead replied, "The LORD is
our witness; we will certainly do as you say."
11So Jephthah went with the elders of Gilead,
and the people made him head and commander over them. And he repeated all his words
before the LORD in Mizpah.

12Then Jephthah sent messengers to the
Ammonite king with the question: "What do
you have against me that you have attacked
my country?"

13The king of the Ammonites answered
Jephthah's messengers, "When Israel came
up out of Egypt, they took away my land from
the Arnon to the Jabbok, all the way to the
Jordan. Now give it back peaceably."

14Jephthah sent back messengers to the Ammonite king, 15saying:

"This is what Jephthah says: Israel did
not take the land of Moab or the land of
the Ammonites. 16But when they came up
out of Egypt, Israel went through the wilderness to the Red Sea[c] and on to Kadesh.
17Then Israel sent messengers to the king
of Edom, saying, 'Give us permission to
go through your country,' but the king
of Edom would not listen. They sent also
to the king of Moab, and he refused. So
Israel stayed at Kadesh.

18"Next they traveled through the wilderness, skirted the lands of Edom and
Moab, passed along the eastern side of
the country of Moab, and camped on the
other side of the Arnon. They did not enter the territory of Moab, for the Arnon
was its border.

19"Then Israel sent messengers to Sihon king of the Amorites, who ruled in
Heshbon, and said to him, 'Let us pass
through your country to our own place.'
20Sihon, however, did not trust Israel[d] to
pass through his territory. He mustered
all his troops and encamped at Jahaz and
fought with Israel.

21"Then the LORD, the God of Israel,
gave Sihon and his whole army into Israel's hands, and they defeated them. Israel
took over all the land of the Amorites who
lived in that country, 22capturing all of it
from the Arnon to the Jabbok and from
the desert to the Jordan.

23"Now since the LORD, the God of Israel, has driven the Amorites out before his
people Israel, what right have you to take
it over? 24Will you not take what your god
Chemosh gives you? Likewise, whatever
the LORD our God has given us, we will
possess. 25Are you any better than Balak
son of Zippor, king of Moab? Did he ever
quarrel with Israel or fight with them?
26For three hundred years Israel occupied Heshbon, Aroer, the surrounding

[a] 4 Or *called the settlements of Jair* [b] 12 Hebrew; some Septuagint manuscripts *Midianites*
[c] 16 Or *the Sea of Reeds* [d] 20 Or *however, would not make an agreement for Israel*

settlements and all the towns along the
Arnon. Why didn't you retake them during that time? 27I have not wronged you,
but you are doing me wrong by waging
war against me. Let the LORD, the Judge,
decide the dispute this day between the
Israelites and the Ammonites."

28The king of Ammon, however, paid no attention to the message Jephthah sent him.

29Then the Spirit of the LORD came on
Jephthah. He crossed Gilead and Manasseh,
passed through Mizpah of Gilead, and from
there he advanced against the Ammonites.
30And Jephthah made a vow to the LORD:
"If you give the Ammonites into my hands,
31whatever comes out of the door of my house
to meet me when I return in triumph from
the Ammonites will be the LORD's, and I will
sacrifice it as a burnt offering."

32Then Jephthah went over to fight the
Ammonites, and the LORD gave them into his
hands. 33He devastated twenty towns from
Aroer to the vicinity of Minnith, as far as Abel
Keramim. Thus Israel subdued Ammon.

34When Jephthah returned to his home in
Mizpah, who should come out to meet him
but his daughter, dancing to the sound of timbrels! She was an only child. Except for her he
had neither son nor daughter. 35When he saw
her, he tore his clothes and cried, "Oh no, my
daughter! You have brought me down and I
am devastated. I have made a vow to the LORD
that I cannot break."

36"My father," she replied, "you have given
your word to the LORD. Do to me just as you
promised, now that the LORD has avenged you
of your enemies, the Ammonites. 37But grant
me this one request," she said. "Give me two
months to roam the hills and weep with my
friends, because I will never marry."

38"You may go," he said. And he let her go
for two months. She and her friends went into
the hills and wept because she would never
marry. 39After the two months, she returned to
her father, and he did to her as he had vowed.
And she was a virgin.

From this comes the Israelite tradition
40that each year the young women of Israel go out for four days to commemorate the
daughter of Jephthah the Gileadite.

Jephthah and Ephraim

12 The Ephraimite forces were called out,
and they crossed over to Zaphon. They
said to Jephthah, "Why did you go to fight
the Ammonites without calling us to go with
you? We're going to burn down your house
over your head."

2Jephthah answered, "I and my people were
engaged in a great struggle with the Ammonites, and although I called, you didn't save
me out of their hands. 3When I saw that you
wouldn't help, I took my life in my hands and
crossed over to fight the Ammonites, and the
LORD gave me the victory over them. Now why
have you come up today to fight me?"

4Jephthah then called together the men of
Gilead and fought against Ephraim. The Gileadites struck them down because the Ephraimites had said, "You Gileadites are renegades
from Ephraim and Manasseh." 5The Gileadites captured the fords of the Jordan leading to Ephraim, and whenever a survivor of
Ephraim said, "Let me cross over," the men of
Gilead asked him, "Are you an Ephraimite?"
If he replied, "No," 6they said, "All right, say
'Shibboleth.'" If he said, "Sibboleth," because
he could not pronounce the word correctly,
they seized him and killed him at the fords of
the Jordan. Forty-two thousand Ephraimites
were killed at that time.

7Jephthah led[a] Israel six years. Then Jephthah the Gileadite died and was buried in a
town in Gilead.

Ibzan, Elon and Abdon

8After him, Ibzan of Bethlehem led Israel.
9He had thirty sons and thirty daughters. He
gave his daughters away in marriage to those
outside his clan, and for his sons he brought
in thirty young women as wives from outside
his clan. Ibzan led Israel seven years. 10Then
Ibzan died and was buried in Bethlehem.

11After him, Elon the Zebulunite led Israel
ten years. 12Then Elon died and was buried
in Aijalon in the land of Zebulun.

13After him, Abdon son of Hillel, from Pirathon, led Israel. 14He had forty sons and thirty
grandsons, who rode on seventy donkeys. He
led Israel eight years. 15Then Abdon son of Hillel died and was buried at Pirathon in Ephraim,
in the hill country of the Amalekites.

The Birth of Samson

13 Again the Israelites did evil in the eyes
of the LORD, so the LORD delivered them
into the hands of the Philistines for forty
years.

2A certain man of Zorah, named Manoah,
from the clan of the Danites, had a wife who
was childless, unable to give birth. 3The angel
of the LORD appeared to her and said, "You
are barren and childless, but you are going
to become pregnant and give birth to a son.
4Now see to it that you drink no wine or other
fermented drink and that you do not eat anything unclean. 5You will become pregnant and
have a son whose head is never to be touched
by a razor because the boy is to be a Nazirite,
dedicated to God from the womb. He will take
the lead in delivering Israel from the hands
of the Philistines."

6Then the woman went to her husband
and told him, "A man of God came to me. He
looked like an angel of God, very awesome.
I didn't ask him where he came from, and he
didn't tell me his name. 7But he said to me,
'You will become pregnant and have a son.
Now then, drink no wine or other fermented
drink and do not eat anything unclean, because the boy will be a Nazirite of God from
the womb until the day of his death.'"

[a] 7 Traditionally *judged*; also in verses 8-14

8Then Manoah prayed to the LORD: "Pardon
your servant, Lord. I beg you to let the man
of God you sent to us come again to teach us
how to bring up the boy who is to be born."
9God heard Manoah, and the angel of God
came again to the woman while she was out
in the field; but her husband Manoah was not
with her. 10The woman hurried to tell her husband, "He's here! The man who appeared to
me the other day!"
11Manoah got up and followed his wife.
When he came to the man, he said, "Are you
the man who talked to my wife?"
"I am," he said.
12So Manoah asked him, "When your words
are fulfilled, what is to be the rule that governs
the boy's life and work?"
13The angel of the LORD answered, "Your
wife must do all that I have told her. 14She
must not eat anything that comes from the
grapevine, nor drink any wine or other fermented drink nor eat anything unclean. She
must do everything I have commanded her."
15Manoah said to the angel of the LORD,
"We would like you to stay until we prepare
a young goat for you."
16The angel of the LORD replied, "Even
though you detain me, I will not eat any of
your food. But if you prepare a burnt offering,
offer it to the LORD." (Manoah did not realize
that it was the angel of the LORD.)
17Then Manoah inquired of the angel of the
LORD, "What is your name, so that we may
honor you when your word comes true?"
18He replied, "Why do you ask my name? It
is beyond understanding.[a]" 19Then Manoah
took a young goat, together with the grain offering, and sacrificed it on a rock to the LORD.
And the LORD did an amazing thing while
Manoah and his wife watched: 20As the flame
blazed up from the altar toward heaven, the
angel of the LORD ascended in the flame. Seeing this, Manoah and his wife fell with their
faces to the ground. 21When the angel of the
LORD did not show himself again to Manoah
and his wife, Manoah realized that it was the
angel of the LORD.
22"We are doomed to die!" he said to his
wife. "We have seen God!"
23But his wife answered, "If the LORD had
meant to kill us, he would not have accepted
a burnt offering and grain offering from our
hands, nor shown us all these things or now
told us this."
24The woman gave birth to a boy and named
him Samson. He grew and the LORD blessed
him, 25and the Spirit of the LORD began to stir
him while he was in Mahaneh Dan, between
Zorah and Eshtaol.

Samson's Marriage

14 Samson went down to Timnah and saw
there a young Philistine woman. 2When
he returned, he said to his father and mother,
"I have seen a Philistine woman in Timnah;
now get her for me as my wife."
3His father and mother replied, "Isn't there
an acceptable woman among your relatives
or among all our people? Must you go to the
uncircumcised Philistines to get a wife?"
But Samson said to his father, "Get her for
me. She's the right one for me." 4(His parents
did not know that this was from the LORD,
who was seeking an occasion to confront the
Philistines; for at that time they were ruling
over Israel.)
5Samson went down to Timnah together with his father and mother. As they approached the vineyards of Timnah, suddenly
a young lion came roaring toward him. 6The
Spirit of the LORD came powerfully upon him
so that he tore the lion apart with his bare
hands as he might have torn a young goat. But
he told neither his father nor his mother what
he had done. 7Then he went down and talked
with the woman, and he liked her.
8Some time later, when he went back to marry her, he turned aside to look at the lion's
carcass, and in it he saw a swarm of bees and
some honey. 9He scooped out the honey with
his hands and ate as he went along. When he
rejoined his parents, he gave them some, and
they too ate it. But he did not tell them that he
had taken the honey from the lion's carcass.
10Now his father went down to see the woman. And there Samson held a feast, as was
customary for young men. 11When the people saw him, they chose thirty men to be his
companions.
12"Let me tell you a riddle," Samson said to
them. "If you can give me the answer within
the seven days of the feast, I will give you thirty linen garments and thirty sets of clothes.
13If you can't tell me the answer, you must
give me thirty linen garments and thirty sets
of clothes."
"Tell us your riddle," they said. "Let's
hear it."
14He replied,

"Out of the eater, something to eat;
out of the strong, something sweet."

For three days they could not give the answer.
15On the fourth[b] day, they said to Samson's
wife, "Coax your husband into explaining the
riddle for us, or we will burn you and your
father's household to death. Did you invite
us here to steal our property?"
16Then Samson's wife threw herself on him,
sobbing, "You hate me! You don't really love
me. You've given my people a riddle, but you
haven't told me the answer."
"I haven't even explained it to my father or
mother," he replied, "so why should I explain
it to you?" 17She cried the whole seven days
of the feast. So on the seventh day he finally
told her, because she continued to press him.
She in turn explained the riddle to her people.
18Before sunset on the seventh day the men
of the town said to him,

"What is sweeter than honey?
What is stronger than a lion?"

Samson said to them,

[a] 18 Or *is wonderful* [b] 15 Some Septuagint manuscripts and Syriac; Hebrew *seventh*

"If you had not plowed with my heifer,
you would not have solved my riddle."

19 Then the Spirit of the LORD came powerfully upon him. He went down to Ashkelon, struck down thirty of their men, stripped them of everything and gave their clothes to those who had explained the riddle. Burning with anger, he returned to his father's home. 20 And Samson's wife was given to one of his companions who had attended him at the feast.

Samson's Vengeance on the Philistines

15 Later on, at the time of wheat harvest, Samson took a young goat and went to visit his wife. He said, "I'm going to my wife's room." But her father would not let him go in.

2 "I was so sure you hated her," he said, "that I gave her to your companion. Isn't her younger sister more attractive? Take her instead."

3 Samson said to them, "This time I have a right to get even with the Philistines; I will really harm them." 4 So he went out and caught three hundred foxes and tied them tail to tail in pairs. He then fastened a torch to every pair of tails, 5 lit the torches and let the foxes loose in the standing grain of the Philistines. He burned up the shocks and standing grain, together with the vineyards and olive groves.

6 When the Philistines asked, "Who did this?" they were told, "Samson, the Timnite's son-in-law, because his wife was given to his companion."

So the Philistines went up and burned her and her father to death. 7 Samson said to them, "Since you've acted like this, I swear that I won't stop until I get my revenge on you." 8 He attacked them viciously and slaughtered many of them. Then he went down and stayed in a cave in the rock of Etam.

9 The Philistines went up and camped in Judah, spreading out near Lehi. 10 The people of Judah asked, "Why have you come to fight us?"

"We have come to take Samson prisoner," they answered, "to do to him as he did to us."

11 Then three thousand men from Judah went down to the cave in the rock of Etam and said to Samson, "Don't you realize that the Philistines are rulers over us? What have you done to us?"

He answered, "I merely did to them what they did to me."

12 They said to him, "We've come to tie you up and hand you over to the Philistines."

Samson said, "Swear to me that you won't kill me yourselves."

13 "Agreed," they answered. "We will only tie you up and hand you over to them. We will not kill you." So they bound him with two new ropes and led him up from the rock. 14 As he approached Lehi, the Philistines came toward him shouting. The Spirit of the LORD came powerfully upon him. The ropes on his arms became like charred flax, and the bindings dropped from his hands. 15 Finding a fresh jawbone of a donkey, he grabbed it and struck down a thousand men.

16 Then Samson said,

"With a donkey's jawbone
I have made donkeys of them.[a]
With a donkey's jawbone
I have killed a thousand men."

17 When he finished speaking, he threw away the jawbone; and the place was called Ramath Lehi.[b]

18 Because he was very thirsty, he cried out to the LORD, "You have given your servant this great victory. Must I now die of thirst and fall into the hands of the uncircumcised?" 19 Then God opened up the hollow place in Lehi, and water came out of it. When Samson drank, his strength returned and he revived. So the spring was called En Hakkore,[c] and it is still there in Lehi.

20 Samson led[d] Israel for twenty years in the days of the Philistines.

Samson and Delilah

16 One day Samson went to Gaza, where he saw a prostitute. He went in to spend the night with her. 2 The people of Gaza were told, "Samson is here!" So they surrounded the place and lay in wait for him all night at the city gate. They made no move during the night, saying, "At dawn we'll kill him."

3 But Samson lay there only until the middle of the night. Then he got up and took hold of the doors of the city gate, together with the two posts, and tore them loose, bar and all. He lifted them to his shoulders and carried them to the top of the hill that faces Hebron.

4 Some time later, he fell in love with a woman in the Valley of Sorek whose name was Delilah. 5 The rulers of the Philistines went to her and said, "See if you can lure him into showing you the secret of his great strength and how we can overpower him so we may tie him up and subdue him. Each one of us will give you eleven hundred shekels[e] of silver."

6 So Delilah said to Samson, "Tell me the secret of your great strength and how you can be tied up and subdued."

7 Samson answered her, "If anyone ties me with seven fresh bowstrings that have not been dried, I'll become as weak as any other man."

8 Then the rulers of the Philistines brought her seven fresh bowstrings that had not been dried, and she tied him with them. 9 With men hidden in the room, she called to him, "Samson, the Philistines are upon you!" But he snapped the bowstrings as easily as a piece of string snaps when it comes close to a flame. So the secret of his strength was not discovered.

10 Then Delilah said to Samson, "You have made a fool of me; you lied to me. Come now, tell me how you can be tied."

11 He said, "If anyone ties me securely with

[a] 16 Or *made a heap or two*; the Hebrew for *donkey* sounds like the Hebrew for *heap*. [b] 17 *Ramath Lehi* means *jawbone hill*. [c] 19 *En Hakkore* means *caller's spring*. [d] 20 Traditionally *judged*
[e] 5 That is, about 28 pounds or about 13 kilograms

new ropes that have never been used, I'll become as weak as any other man."
12So Delilah took new ropes and tied him
with them. Then, with men hidden in the
room, she called to him, "Samson, the Philistines are upon you!" But he snapped the
ropes off his arms as if they were threads.
13Delilah then said to Samson, "All this time
you have been making a fool of me and lying
to me. Tell me how you can be tied."
He replied, "If you weave the seven braids of
my head into the fabric on the loom and tight-
en it with the pin, I'll become as weak as any
other man." So while he was sleeping, Delilah
took the seven braids of his head, wove them
into the fabric 14and[a] tightened it with the pin.
Again she called to him, "Samson, the Philistines are upon you!" He awoke from his
sleep and pulled up the pin and the loom, with
the fabric.
15Then she said to him, "How can you say, 'I
love you,' when you won't confide in me? This
is the third time you have made a fool of me
and haven't told me the secret of your great
strength." 16With such nagging she prodded
him day after day until he was sick to death of it.
17So he told her everything. "No razor has
ever been used on my head," he said, "because
I have been a Nazirite dedicated to God from
my mother's womb. If my head were shaved,
my strength would leave me, and I would become as weak as any other man."
18When Delilah saw that he had told her
everything, she sent word to the rulers of
the Philistines, "Come back once more; he
has told me everything." So the rulers of the
Philistines returned with the silver in their
hands. 19After putting him to sleep on her lap,
she called for someone to shave off the sev-
en braids of his hair, and so began to subdue
him.[b] And his strength left him.
20Then she called, "Samson, the Philistines
are upon you!"
He awoke from his sleep and thought, "I'll
go out as before and shake myself free." But
he did not know that the LORD had left him.
21Then the Philistines seized him, gouged
out his eyes and took him down to Gaza. Binding him with bronze shackles, they set him
to grinding grain in the prison. 22But the hair
on his head began to grow again after it had
been shaved.

The Death of Samson

23Now the rulers of the Philistines assembled to offer a great sacrifice to Dagon their
god and to celebrate, saying, "Our god has
delivered Samson, our enemy, into our hands."
24When the people saw him, they praised
their god, saying,

"Our god has delivered our enemy
into our hands,
the one who laid waste our land
and multiplied our slain."

25While they were in high spirits, they
shouted, "Bring out Samson to entertain us."
So they called Samson out of the prison, and
he performed for them.
When they stood him among the pillars,
26Samson said to the servant who held his
hand, "Put me where I can feel the pillars
that support the temple, so that I may lean
against them." 27Now the temple was crowded with men and women; all the rulers of the
Philistines were there, and on the roof were
about three thousand men and women watching Samson perform. 28Then Samson prayed
to the LORD, "Sovereign LORD, remember me.
Please, God, strengthen me just once more,
and let me with one blow get revenge on the
Philistines for my two eyes." 29Then Samson reached toward the two central pillars
on which the temple stood. Bracing himself
against them, his right hand on the one and his
left hand on the other, 30Samson said, "Let me
die with the Philistines!" Then he pushed with
all his might, and down came the temple on the
rulers and all the people in it. Thus he killed
many more when he died than while he lived.
31Then his brothers and his father's whole
family went down to get him. They brought
him back and buried him between Zorah and
Eshtaol in the tomb of Manoah his father. He
had led[c] Israel twenty years.

Micah's Idols

17 Now a man named Micah from the hill
country of Ephraim 2said to his mother,
"The eleven hundred shekels[d] of silver that
were taken from you and about which I heard
you utter a curse—I have that silver with me;
I took it."
Then his mother said, "The LORD bless you,
my son!"
3When he returned the eleven hundred
shekels of silver to his mother, she said, "I
solemnly consecrate my silver to the LORD for
my son to make an image overlaid with silver.
I will give it back to you."
4So after he returned the silver to his mother, she took two hundred shekels[e] of silver and
gave them to a silversmith, who used them to
make the idol. And it was put in Micah's house.
5Now this man Micah had a shrine, and
he made an ephod and some household gods
and installed one of his sons as his priest. 6In
those days Israel had no king; everyone did
as they saw fit.
7A young Levite from Bethlehem in Judah,
who had been living within the clan of Judah,
8left that town in search of some other place
to stay. On his way[f] he came to Micah's house
in the hill country of Ephraim.
9Micah asked him, "Where are you from?"
"I'm a Levite from Bethlehem in Judah,"
he said, "and I'm looking for a place to stay."
10Then Micah said to him, "Live with me
and be my father and priest, and I'll give you

[a] *13,14* Some Septuagint manuscripts; Hebrew *replied, "I can if you weave the seven braids of my head into the fabric on the loom." 14So she* [b] *19* Hebrew; some Septuagint manuscripts *and he began to weaken* [c] *31* Traditionally *judged* [d] *2* That is, about 28 pounds or about 13 kilograms [e] *4* That is, about 5 pounds or about 2.3 kilograms [f] *8* Or *To carry on his profession*

ten shekels[a] of silver a year, your clothes and your food." 11 So the Levite agreed to live with him, and the young man became like one of his sons to him. 12 Then Micah installed the Levite, and the young man became his priest and lived in his house. 13 And Micah said, "Now I know that the LORD will be good to me, since this Levite has become my priest."

The Danites Settle in Laish

18 In those days Israel had no king. And in those days the tribe of the Danites was seeking a place of their own where they might settle, because they had not yet come into an inheritance among the tribes of Israel. 2 So the Danites sent five of their leading men from Zorah and Eshtaol to spy out the land and explore it. These men represented all the Danites. They told them, "Go, explore the land."

So they entered the hill country of Ephraim and came to the house of Micah, where they spent the night. 3 When they were near Micah's house, they recognized the voice of the young Levite; so they turned in there and asked him, "Who brought you here? What are you doing in this place? Why are you here?"

4 He told them what Micah had done for him, and said, "He has hired me and I am his priest."

5 Then they said to him, "Please inquire of God to learn whether our journey will be successful."

6 The priest answered them, "Go in peace. Your journey has the LORD's approval."

7 So the five men left and came to Laish, where they saw that the people were living in safety, like the Sidonians, at peace and secure. And since their land lacked nothing, they were prosperous.[b] Also, they lived a long way from the Sidonians and had no relationship with anyone else.[c]

8 When they returned to Zorah and Eshtaol, their fellow Danites asked them, "How did you find things?"

9 They answered, "Come on, let's attack them! We have seen the land, and it is very good. Aren't you going to do something? Don't hesitate to go there and take it over. 10 When you get there, you will find an unsuspecting people and a spacious land that God has put into your hands, a land that lacks nothing whatever."

11 Then six hundred men of the Danites, armed for battle, set out from Zorah and Eshtaol. 12 On their way they set up camp near Kiriath Jearim in Judah. This is why the place west of Kiriath Jearim is called Mahaneh Dan[d] to this day. 13 From there they went on to the hill country of Ephraim and came to Micah's house.

14 Then the five men who had spied out the land of Laish said to their fellow Danites, "Do you know that one of these houses has an ephod, some household gods and an image overlaid with silver? Now you know what to do." 15 So they turned in there and went to the house of the young Levite at Micah's place and greeted him. 16 The six hundred Danites, armed for battle, stood at the entrance of the gate. 17 The five men who had spied out the land went inside and took the idol, the ephod and the household gods while the priest and the six hundred armed men stood at the entrance of the gate.

18 When the five men went into Micah's house and took the idol, the ephod and the household gods, the priest said to them, "What are you doing?"

19 They answered him, "Be quiet! Don't say a word. Come with us, and be our father and priest. Isn't it better that you serve a tribe and clan in Israel as priest rather than just one man's household?" 20 The priest was very pleased. He took the ephod, the household gods and the idol and went along with the people. 21 Putting their little children, their livestock and their possessions in front of them, they turned away and left.

22 When they had gone some distance from Micah's house, the men who lived near Micah were called together and overtook the Danites. 23 As they shouted after them, the Danites turned and said to Micah, "What's the matter with you that you called out your men to fight?"

24 He replied, "You took the gods I made, and my priest, and went away. What else do I have? How can you ask, 'What's the matter with you?'"

25 The Danites answered, "Don't argue with us, or some of the men may get angry and attack you, and you and your family will lose your lives." 26 So the Danites went their way, and Micah, seeing that they were too strong for him, turned around and went back home.

27 Then they took what Micah had made, and his priest, and went on to Laish, against a people at peace and secure. They attacked them with the sword and burned down their city. 28 There was no one to rescue them because they lived a long way from Sidon and had no relationship with anyone else. The city was in a valley near Beth Rehob.

The Danites rebuilt the city and settled there. 29 They named it Dan after their ancestor Dan, who was born to Israel—though the city used to be called Laish. 30 There the Danites set up for themselves the idol, and Jonathan son of Gershom, the son of Moses,[e] and his sons were priests for the tribe of Dan until the time of the captivity of the land. 31 They continued to use the idol Micah had made, all the time the house of God was in Shiloh.

A Levite and His Concubine

19 In those days Israel had no king. Now a Levite who lived in a remote area in the hill country of Ephraim took a

[a] *10* That is, about 4 ounces or about 115 grams [b] *7* The meaning of the Hebrew for this clause is uncertain. [c] *7* Hebrew; some Septuagint manuscripts *with the Arameans* [d] *12* *Mahaneh Dan* means *Dan's camp.* [e] *30* Many Hebrew manuscripts, some Septuagint manuscripts and Vulgate; many other Hebrew manuscripts and some other Septuagint manuscripts *Manasseh*

concubine from Bethlehem in Judah. 2But she was unfaithful to him. She left him and went back to her parents' home in Bethlehem, Judah. After she had been there four months, 3her husband went to her to persuade her to return. He had with him his servant and two donkeys. She took him into her parents' home, and when her father saw him, he gladly welcomed him. 4His father-in-law, the woman's father, prevailed on him to stay; so he remained with him three days, eating and drinking, and sleeping there.

5On the fourth day they got up early and he prepared to leave, but the woman's father said to his son-in-law, "Refresh yourself with something to eat; then you can go." 6So the two of them sat down to eat and drink together. Afterward the woman's father said, "Please stay tonight and enjoy yourself." 7And when the man got up to go, his father-in-law persuaded him, so he stayed there that night. 8On the morning of the fifth day, when he rose to go, the woman's father said, "Refresh yourself. Wait till afternoon!" So the two of them ate together.

9Then when the man, with his concubine and his servant, got up to leave, his father-in-law, the woman's father, said, "Now look, it's almost evening. Spend the night here; the day is nearly over. Stay and enjoy yourself. Early tomorrow morning you can get up and be on your way home." 10But, unwilling to stay another night, the man left and went toward Jebus (that is, Jerusalem), with his two saddled donkeys and his concubine.

11When they were near Jebus and the day was almost gone, the servant said to his master, "Come, let's stop at this city of the Jebusites and spend the night."

12His master replied, "No. We won't go into any city whose people are not Israelites. We will go on to Gibeah." 13He added, "Come, let's try to reach Gibeah or Ramah and spend the night in one of those places." 14So they went on, and the sun set as they neared Gibeah in Benjamin. 15There they stopped to spend the night. They went and sat in the city square, but no one took them in for the night.

16That evening an old man from the hill country of Ephraim, who was living in Gibeah (the inhabitants of the place were Benjamites), came in from his work in the fields. 17When he looked and saw the traveler in the city square, the old man asked, "Where are you going? Where did you come from?"

18He answered, "We are on our way from Bethlehem in Judah to a remote area in the hill country of Ephraim where I live. I have been to Bethlehem in Judah and now I am going to the house of the LORD.[a] No one has taken me in for the night. 19We have both straw and fodder for our donkeys and bread and wine for ourselves your servants—me, the woman and the young man with us. We don't need anything."

20"You are welcome at my house," the old man said. "Let me supply whatever you need. Only don't spend the night in the square." 21So he took him into his house and fed his donkeys. After they had washed their feet, they had something to eat and drink.

22While they were enjoying themselves, some of the wicked men of the city surrounded the house. Pounding on the door, they shouted to the old man who owned the house, "Bring out the man who came to your house so we can have sex with him."

23The owner of the house went outside and said to them, "No, my friends, don't be so vile. Since this man is my guest, don't do this outrageous thing. 24Look, here is my virgin daughter, and his concubine. I will bring them out to you now, and you can use them and do to them whatever you wish. But as for this man, don't do such an outrageous thing."

25But the men would not listen to him. So the man took his concubine and sent her outside to them, and they raped her and abused her throughout the night, and at dawn they let her go. 26At daybreak the woman went back to the house where her master was staying, fell down at the door and lay there until daylight.

27When her master got up in the morning and opened the door of the house and stepped out to continue on his way, there lay his concubine, fallen in the doorway of the house, with her hands on the threshold. 28He said to her, "Get up; let's go." But there was no answer. Then the man put her on his donkey and set out for home.

29When he reached home, he took a knife and cut up his concubine, limb by limb, into twelve parts and sent them into all the areas of Israel. 30Everyone who saw it was saying to one another, "Such a thing has never been seen or done, not since the day the Israelites came up out of Egypt. Just imagine! We must do something! So speak up!"

The Israelites Punish the Benjamites

20 Then all Israel from Dan to Beersheba and from the land of Gilead came together as one and assembled before the LORD in Mizpah. 2The leaders of all the people of the tribes of Israel took their places in the assembly of God's people, four hundred thousand men armed with swords. 3(The Benjamites heard that the Israelites had gone up to Mizpah.) Then the Israelites said, "Tell us how this awful thing happened."

4So the Levite, the husband of the murdered woman, said, "I and my concubine came to Gibeah in Benjamin to spend the night. 5During the night the men of Gibeah came after me and surrounded the house, intending to kill me. They raped my concubine, and she died. 6I took my concubine, cut her into pieces and sent one piece to each region of Israel's inheritance, because they committed this lewd and outrageous act in Israel. 7Now, all you Israelites, speak up and tell me what you have decided to do."

8All the men rose up together as one, saying, "None of us will go home. No, not one of

[a] 18 Hebrew, Vulgate, Syriac and Targum; Septuagint *going home*

us will return to his house. 9But now this is what we'll do to Gibeah: We'll go up against it in the order decided by casting lots. 10We'll take ten men out of every hundred from all the tribes of Israel, and a hundred from a thousand, and a thousand from ten thousand, to get provisions for the army. Then, when the army arrives at Gibeah[a] in Benjamin, it can give them what they deserve for this outrageous act done in Israel." 11So all the Israelites got together and united as one against the city.

12The tribes of Israel sent messengers throughout the tribe of Benjamin, saying, "What about this awful crime that was committed among you? 13Now turn those wicked men of Gibeah over to us so that we may put them to death and purge the evil from Israel."

But the Benjamites would not listen to their fellow Israelites. 14From their towns they came together at Gibeah to fight against the Israelites. 15At once the Benjamites mobilized twenty-six thousand swordsmen from their towns, in addition to seven hundred able young men from those living in Gibeah. 16Among all these soldiers there were seven hundred select troops who were left-handed, each of whom could sling a stone at a hair and not miss.

17Israel, apart from Benjamin, mustered four hundred thousand swordsmen, all of them fit for battle.

18The Israelites went up to Bethel[b] and inquired of God. They said, "Who of us is to go up first to fight against the Benjamites?"

The LORD replied, "Judah shall go first."

19The next morning the Israelites got up and pitched camp near Gibeah. 20The Israelites went out to fight the Benjamites and took up battle positions against them at Gibeah. 21The Benjamites came out of Gibeah and cut down twenty-two thousand Israelites on the battlefield that day. 22But the Israelites encouraged one another and again took up their positions where they had stationed themselves the first day. 23The Israelites went up and wept before the LORD until evening, and they inquired of the LORD. They said, "Shall we go up again to fight against the Benjamites, our fellow Israelites?"

The LORD answered, "Go up against them."

24Then the Israelites drew near to Benjamin the second day. 25This time, when the Benjamites came out from Gibeah to oppose them, they cut down another eighteen thousand Israelites, all of them armed with swords.

26Then all the Israelites, the whole army, went up to Bethel, and there they sat weeping before the LORD. They fasted that day until evening and presented burnt offerings and fellowship offerings to the LORD. 27And the Israelites inquired of the LORD. (In those days the ark of the covenant of God was there, 28with Phinehas son of Eleazar, the son of Aaron, ministering before it.) They asked, "Shall we go up again to fight against the Benjamites, our fellow Israelites, or not?"

The LORD responded, "Go, for tomorrow I will give them into your hands."

29Then Israel set an ambush around Gibeah. 30They went up against the Benjamites on the third day and took up positions against Gibeah as they had done before. 31The Benjamites came out to meet them and were drawn away from the city. They began to inflict casualties on the Israelites as before, so that about thirty men fell in the open field and on the roads—the one leading to Bethel and the other to Gibeah. 32While the Benjamites were saying, "We are defeating them as before," the Israelites were saying, "Let's retreat and draw them away from the city to the roads."

33All the men of Israel moved from their places and took up positions at Baal Tamar, and the Israelite ambush charged out of its place on the west[c] of Gibeah.[d] 34Then ten thousand of Israel's able young men made a frontal attack on Gibeah. The fighting was so heavy that the Benjamites did not realize how near disaster was. 35The LORD defeated Benjamin before Israel, and on that day the Israelites struck down 25,100 Benjamites, all armed with swords. 36Then the Benjamites saw that they were beaten.

Now the men of Israel had given way before Benjamin, because they relied on the ambush they had set near Gibeah. 37Those who had been in ambush made a sudden dash into Gibeah, spread out and put the whole city to the sword. 38The Israelites had arranged with the ambush that they should send up a great cloud of smoke from the city, 39and then the Israelites would counterattack.

The Benjamites had begun to inflict casualties on the Israelites (about thirty), and they said, "We are defeating them as in the first battle." 40But when the column of smoke began to rise from the city, the Benjamites turned and saw the whole city going up in smoke. 41Then the Israelites counterattacked, and the Benjamites were terrified, because they realized that disaster had come on them. 42So they fled before the Israelites in the direction of the wilderness, but they could not escape the battle. And the Israelites who came out of the towns cut them down there. 43They surrounded the Benjamites, chased them and easily[e] overran them in the vicinity of Gibeah on the east. 44Eighteen thousand Benjamites fell, all of them valiant fighters. 45As they turned and fled toward the wilderness to the rock of Rimmon, the Israelites cut down five thousand men along the roads. They kept pressing after the Benjamites as far as Gidom and struck down two thousand more.

46On that day twenty-five thousand Benjamite swordsmen fell, all of them valiant fighters. 47But six hundred of them turned and fled into the wilderness to the rock of Rimmon, where they stayed four months. 48The men of Israel went back to Benjamin and put all

[a] *10* One Hebrew manuscript; most Hebrew manuscripts *Geba,* a variant of *Gibeah* [b] *18* Or *to the house of God*; also in verse 26 [c] *33* Some Septuagint manuscripts and Vulgate; the meaning of the Hebrew for this word is uncertain. [d] *33* Hebrew *Geba,* a variant of *Gibeah* [e] *43* The meaning of the Hebrew for this word is uncertain.

the towns to the sword, including the animals
and everything else they found. All the towns
they came across they set on fire.

Wives for the Benjamites

21 The men of Israel had taken an oath
at Mizpah: "Not one of us will give his
daughter in marriage to a Benjamite."
2The people went to Bethel,[a] where they sat
before God until evening, raising their voices
and weeping bitterly. 3"LORD, God of Israel,"
they cried, "why has this happened to Israel?
Why should one tribe be missing from Israel
today?"
4Early the next day the people built an altar
and presented burnt offerings and fellowship
offerings.
5Then the Israelites asked, "Who from all
the tribes of Israel has failed to assemble
before the LORD?" For they had taken a solemn oath that anyone who failed to assemble
before the LORD at Mizpah was to be put to
death.
6Now the Israelites grieved for the tribe of
Benjamin, their fellow Israelites. "Today one
tribe is cut off from Israel," they said. 7"How
can we provide wives for those who are left,
since we have taken an oath by the LORD not to
give them any of our daughters in marriage?"
8Then they asked, "Which one of the tribes of
Israel failed to assemble before the LORD at
Mizpah?" They discovered that no one from
Jabesh Gilead had come to the camp for the
assembly. 9For when they counted the people,
they found that none of the people of Jabesh
Gilead were there.
10So the assembly sent twelve thousand
fighting men with instructions to go to Jabesh
Gilead and put to the sword those living there,
including the women and children. 11"This is
what you are to do," they said. "Kill every male
and every woman who is not a virgin." 12They
found among the people living in Jabesh Gilead four hundred young women who had never
slept with a man, and they took them to the
camp at Shiloh in Canaan.
13Then the whole assembly sent an offer of
peace to the Benjamites at the rock of Rimmon. 14So the Benjamites returned at that time
and were given the women of Jabesh Gilead who had been spared. But there were not
enough for all of them.
15The people grieved for Benjamin, because
the LORD had made a gap in the tribes of Israel.
16And the elders of the assembly said, "With
the women of Benjamin destroyed, how shall
we provide wives for the men who are left?
17The Benjamite survivors must have heirs,"
they said, "so that a tribe of Israel will not be
wiped out. 18We can't give them our daughters
as wives, since we Israelites have taken this
oath: 'Cursed be anyone who gives a wife to a
Benjamite.' 19But look, there is the annual festival of the LORD in Shiloh, which lies north of
Bethel, east of the road that goes from Bethel
to Shechem, and south of Lebonah."
20So they instructed the Benjamites, saying,
"Go and hide in the vineyards 21and watch.
When the young women of Shiloh come out to
join in the dancing, rush from the vineyards
and each of you seize one of them to be your
wife. Then return to the land of Benjamin.
22When their fathers or brothers complain to
us, we will say to them, 'Do us the favor of
helping them, because we did not get wives for
them during the war. You will not be guilty of
breaking your oath because you did not give
your daughters to them.'"
23So that is what the Benjamites did. While
the young women were dancing, each man
caught one and carried her off to be his wife.
Then they returned to their inheritance and
rebuilt the towns and settled in them.
24At that time the Israelites left that place
and went home to their tribes and clans, each
to his own inheritance.
25In those days Israel had no king; everyone
did as they saw fit.

Ruth

Naomi Loses Her Husband and Sons

1 In the days when the judges ruled,[b] there
was a famine in the land. So a man from
Bethlehem in Judah, together with his wife
and two sons, went to live for a while in the
country of Moab. 2The man's name was Elimelek, his wife's name was Naomi, and the
names of his two sons were Mahlon and Kilion. They were Ephrathites from Bethlehem,
Judah. And they went to Moab and lived there.
3Now Elimelek, Naomi's husband, died, and
she was left with her two sons. 4They married
Moabite women, one named Orpah and the
other Ruth. After they had lived there about
ten years, 5both Mahlon and Kilion also died,
and Naomi was left without her two sons and
her husband.

Naomi and Ruth Return to Bethlehem

6When Naomi heard in Moab that the LORD
had come to the aid of his people by providing
food for them, she and her daughters-in-law
prepared to return home from there. 7With
her two daughters-in-law she left the place

[a] 2 Or *to the house of God* [b] 1 Traditionally *judged*

where she had been living and set out on the
road that would take them back to the land
of Judah.
8Then Naomi said to her two daughters-in-
law, "Go back, each of you, to your mother's
home. May the LORD show you kindness, as
you have shown kindness to your dead husbands and to me. 9May the LORD grant that
each of you will find rest in the home of another husband."
Then she kissed them goodbye and they
wept aloud 10and said to her, "We will go back
with you to your people."
11But Naomi said, "Return home, my daughters. Why would you come with me? Am I going to have any more sons, who could become
your husbands? 12Return home, my daughters;
I am too old to have another husband. Even if
I thought there was still hope for me—even if
I had a husband tonight and then gave birth to
sons— 13would you wait until they grew up?
Would you remain unmarried for them? No,
my daughters. It is more bitter for me than
for you, because the LORD's hand has turned
against me!"
14At this they wept aloud again. Then Orpah
kissed her mother-in-law goodbye, but Ruth
clung to her.
15"Look," said Naomi, "your sister-in-law
is going back to her people and her gods. Go
back with her."
16But Ruth replied, "Don't urge me to leave
you or to turn back from you. Where you go
I will go, and where you stay I will stay. Your
people will be my people and your God my
God. 17Where you die I will die, and there I
will be buried. May the LORD deal with me, be
it ever so severely, if even death separates you
and me." 18When Naomi realized that Ruth
was determined to go with her, she stopped
urging her.
19So the two women went on until they came
to Bethlehem. When they arrived in Bethlehem, the whole town was stirred because of
them, and the women exclaimed, "Can this
be Naomi?"
20"Don't call me Naomi,[a]" she told them.
"Call me Mara,[b] because the Almighty[c] has
made my life very bitter. 21I went away full,
but the LORD has brought me back empty.
Why call me Naomi? The LORD has afflicted[d] me; the Almighty has brought misfortune
upon me."
22So Naomi returned from Moab accompanied by Ruth the Moabite, her daughter-in-law,
arriving in Bethlehem as the barley harvest
was beginning.

Ruth Meets Boaz in the Grain Field

2 Now Naomi had a relative on her husband's
side, a man of standing from the clan of
Elimelek, whose name was Boaz.
2And Ruth the Moabite said to Naomi, "Let
me go to the fields and pick up the leftover
grain behind anyone in whose eyes I find favor."
Naomi said to her, "Go ahead, my daughter."
3So she went out, entered a field and began to
glean behind the harvesters. As it turned out,
she was working in a field belonging to Boaz,
who was from the clan of Elimelek.
4Just then Boaz arrived from Bethlehem
and greeted the harvesters, "The LORD be
with you!"
"The LORD bless you!" they answered.
5Boaz asked the overseer of his harvesters,
"Who does that young woman belong to?"
6The overseer replied, "She is the Moabite who came back from Moab with Naomi.
7She said, 'Please let me glean and gather
among the sheaves behind the harvesters.'
She came into the field and has remained here
from morning till now, except for a short rest
in the shelter."
8So Boaz said to Ruth, "My daughter, listen to me. Don't go and glean in another field
and don't go away from here. Stay here with
the women who work for me. 9Watch the field
where the men are harvesting, and follow
along after the women. I have told the men
not to lay a hand on you. And whenever you
are thirsty, go and get a drink from the water
jars the men have filled."
10At this, she bowed down with her face
to the ground. She asked him, "Why have I
found such favor in your eyes that you notice
me—a foreigner?"
11Boaz replied, "I've been told all about what
you have done for your mother-in-law since
the death of your husband—how you left your
father and mother and your homeland and
came to live with a people you did not know
before. 12May the LORD repay you for what
you have done. May you be richly rewarded
by the LORD, the God of Israel, under whose
wings you have come to take refuge."
13"May I continue to find favor in your eyes,
my lord," she said. "You have put me at ease by
speaking kindly to your servant—though I do
not have the standing of one of your servants."
14At mealtime Boaz said to her, "Come over
here. Have some bread and dip it in the wine
vinegar."
When she sat down with the harvesters, he
offered her some roasted grain. She ate all
she wanted and had some left over. 15As she
got up to glean, Boaz gave orders to his men,
"Let her gather among the sheaves and don't
reprimand her. 16Even pull out some stalks for
her from the bundles and leave them for her
to pick up, and don't rebuke her."
17So Ruth gleaned in the field until evening.
Then she threshed the barley she had gathered, and it amounted to about an ephah.[e]
18She carried it back to town, and her mother-in-law saw how much she had gathered.
Ruth also brought out and gave her what she
had left over after she had eaten enough.
19Her mother-in-law asked her, "Where
did you glean today? Where did you work?
Blessed be the man who took notice of you!"
Then Ruth told her mother-in-law about the

[a] 20 *Naomi* means *pleasant.* [b] 20 *Mara* means *bitter.* [c] 20 Hebrew *Shaddai*; also in verse 21
[d] 21 Or *has testified against* [e] 17 That is, probably about 30 pounds or about 13 kilograms

one at whose place she had been working. “The name of the man I worked with today is Boaz,” she said.

20“The LORD bless him!” Naomi said to her daughter-in-law. “He has not stopped showing his kindness to the living and the dead.” She added, “That man is our close relative; he is one of our guardian-redeemers.[a]”

21Then Ruth the Moabite said, “He even said to me, ‘Stay with my workers until they finish harvesting all my grain.’ ”

22Naomi said to Ruth her daughter-in-law, “It will be good for you, my daughter, to go with the women who work for him, because in someone else’s field you might be harmed.”

23So Ruth stayed close to the women of Boaz to glean until the barley and wheat harvests were finished. And she lived with her mother-in-law.

Ruth and Boaz at the Threshing Floor

3 One day Ruth’s mother-in-law Naomi said to her, “My daughter, I must find a home[b] for you, where you will be well provided for. 2Now Boaz, with whose women you have worked, is a relative of ours. Tonight he will be winnowing barley on the threshing floor. 3Wash, put on perfume, and get dressed in your best clothes. Then go down to the threshing floor, but don’t let him know you are there until he has finished eating and drinking. 4When he lies down, note the place where he is lying. Then go and uncover his feet and lie down. He will tell you what to do.”

5“I will do whatever you say,” Ruth answered. 6So she went down to the threshing floor and did everything her mother-in-law told her to do.

7When Boaz had finished eating and drinking and was in good spirits, he went over to lie down at the far end of the grain pile. Ruth approached quietly, uncovered his feet and lay down. 8In the middle of the night something startled the man; he turned—and there was a woman lying at his feet!

9“Who are you?” he asked.

“I am your servant Ruth,” she said. “Spread the corner of your garment over me, since you are a guardian-redeemer[c] of our family.”

10“The LORD bless you, my daughter,” he replied. “This kindness is greater than that which you showed earlier: You have not run after the younger men, whether rich or poor. 11And now, my daughter, don’t be afraid. I will do for you all you ask. All the people of my town know that you are a woman of noble character. 12Although it is true that I am a guardian-redeemer of our family, there is another who is more closely related than I. 13Stay here for the night, and in the morning if he wants to do his duty as your guardian-redeemer, good; let him redeem you. But if he is not willing, as surely as the LORD lives I will do it. Lie here until morning.”

14So she lay at his feet until morning, but got up before anyone could be recognized; and he said, “No one must know that a woman came to the threshing floor.”

15He also said, “Bring me the shawl you are wearing and hold it out.” When she did so, he poured into it six measures of barley and placed the bundle on her. Then he[d] went back to town.

16When Ruth came to her mother-in-law, Naomi asked, “How did it go, my daughter?”

Then she told her everything Boaz had done for her 17and added, “He gave me these six measures of barley, saying, ‘Don’t go back to your mother-in-law empty-handed.’ ”

18Then Naomi said, “Wait, my daughter, until you find out what happens. For the man will not rest until the matter is settled today.”

Boaz Marries Ruth

4 Meanwhile Boaz went up to the town gate and sat down there just as the guardian-redeemer[e] he had mentioned came along. Boaz said, “Come over here, my friend, and sit down.” So he went over and sat down.

2Boaz took ten of the elders of the town and said, “Sit here,” and they did so. 3Then he said to the guardian-redeemer, “Naomi, who has come back from Moab, is selling the piece of land that belonged to our relative Elimelek. 4I thought I should bring the matter to your attention and suggest that you buy it in the presence of these seated here and in the presence of the elders of my people. If you will redeem it, do so. But if you[f] will not, tell me, so I will know. For no one has the right to do it except you, and I am next in line.”

“I will redeem it,” he said.

5Then Boaz said, “On the day you buy the land from Naomi, you also acquire Ruth the Moabite, the[g] dead man’s widow, in order to maintain the name of the dead with his property.”

6At this, the guardian-redeemer said, “Then I cannot redeem it because I might endanger my own estate. You redeem it yourself. I cannot do it.”

7(Now in earlier times in Israel, for the redemption and transfer of property to become final, one party took off his sandal and gave it to the other. This was the method of legalizing transactions in Israel.)

8So the guardian-redeemer said to Boaz, “Buy it yourself.” And he removed his sandal.

9Then Boaz announced to the elders and all the people, “Today you are witnesses that I have bought from Naomi all the property of

[a] *20* The Hebrew word for *guardian-redeemer* is a legal term for one who has the obligation to redeem a relative in serious difficulty (see Lev. 25:25-55). [b] *1* Hebrew *find rest* (see 1:9) [c] *9* The Hebrew word for *guardian-redeemer* is a legal term for one who has the obligation to redeem a relative in serious difficulty (see Lev. 25:25-55); also in verses 12 and 13. [d] *15* Most Hebrew manuscripts; many Hebrew manuscripts, Vulgate and Syriac *she* [e] *1* The Hebrew word for *guardian-redeemer* is a legal term for one who has the obligation to redeem a relative in serious difficulty (see Lev. 25:25-55); also in verses 3, 6, 8 and 14. [f] *4* Many Hebrew manuscripts, Septuagint, Vulgate and Syriac; most Hebrew manuscripts *he* [g] *5* Vulgate and Syriac; Hebrew (see also Septuagint) *Naomi and from Ruth the Moabite, you acquire the*

Elimelek, Kilion and Mahlon. 10I have also acquired Ruth the Moabite, Mahlon's widow, as my wife, in order to maintain the name of the dead with his property, so that his name will not disappear from among his family or from his hometown. Today you are witnesses!"

11Then the elders and all the people at the gate said, "We are witnesses. May the LORD make the woman who is coming into your home like Rachel and Leah, who together built up the family of Israel. May you have standing in Ephrathah and be famous in Bethlehem. 12Through the offspring the LORD gives you by this young woman, may your family be like that of Perez, whom Tamar bore to Judah."

Naomi Gains a Son

13So Boaz took Ruth and she became his wife. When he made love to her, the LORD enabled her to conceive, and she gave birth to a son. 14The women said to Naomi: "Praise be to the LORD, who this day has not left you without a guardian-redeemer. May he become famous throughout Israel! 15He will renew your life and sustain you in your old age. For your daughter-in-law, who loves you and who is better to you than seven sons, has given him birth."

16Then Naomi took the child in her arms and cared for him. 17The women living there said, "Naomi has a son!" And they named him Obed. He was the father of Jesse, the father of David.

The Genealogy of David

18This, then, is the family line of Perez:

Perez was the father of Hezron,
19 Hezron the father of Ram,
Ram the father of Amminadab,
20 Amminadab the father of Nahshon,
Nahshon the father of Salmon,[a]
21 Salmon the father of Boaz,
Boaz the father of Obed,
22 Obed the father of Jesse,
and Jesse the father of David.

1 Samuel

The Birth of Samuel

1 There was a certain man from Ramathaim, a Zuphite[b] from the hill country of Ephraim, whose name was Elkanah son of Jeroham, the son of Elihu, the son of Tohu, the son of Zuph, an Ephraimite. 2He had two wives; one was called Hannah and the other Peninnah. Peninnah had children, but Hannah had none.

3Year after year this man went up from his town to worship and sacrifice to the LORD Almighty at Shiloh, where Hophni and Phinehas, the two sons of Eli, were priests of the LORD. 4Whenever the day came for Elkanah to sacrifice, he would give portions of the meat to his wife Peninnah and to all her sons and daughters. 5But to Hannah he gave a double portion because he loved her, and the LORD had closed her womb. 6Because the LORD had closed Hannah's womb, her rival kept provoking her in order to irritate her. 7This went on year after year. Whenever Hannah went up to the house of the LORD, her rival provoked her till she wept and would not eat. 8Her husband Elkanah would say to her, "Hannah, why are you weeping? Why don't you eat? Why are you downhearted? Don't I mean more to you than ten sons?"

9Once when they had finished eating and drinking in Shiloh, Hannah stood up. Now Eli the priest was sitting on his chair by the doorpost of the LORD's house. 10In her deep anguish Hannah prayed to the LORD, weeping bitterly. 11And she made a vow, saying, "LORD Almighty, if you will only look on your servant's misery and remember me, and not forget your servant but give her a son, then I will give him to the LORD for all the days of his life, and no razor will ever be used on his head."

12As she kept on praying to the LORD, Eli observed her mouth. 13Hannah was praying in her heart, and her lips were moving but her voice was not heard. Eli thought she was drunk 14and said to her, "How long are you going to stay drunk? Put away your wine."

15"Not so, my lord," Hannah replied, "I am a woman who is deeply troubled. I have not been drinking wine or beer; I was pouring out my soul to the LORD. 16Do not take your servant for a wicked woman; I have been praying here out of my great anguish and grief."

17Eli answered, "Go in peace, and may the God of Israel grant you what you have asked of him."

18She said, "May your servant find favor in your eyes." Then she went her way and ate something, and her face was no longer downcast.

19Early the next morning they arose and worshiped before the LORD and then went back to their home at Ramah. Elkanah made love to his wife Hannah, and the LORD

[a] *20* A few Hebrew manuscripts, some Septuagint manuscripts and Vulgate (see also verse 21 and Septuagint of 1 Chron. 2:11); most Hebrew manuscripts *Salma* [b] *1* See Septuagint and 1 Chron. 6:26-27,33-35; or *from Ramathaim Zuphim.*

remembered her. 20 So in the course of time
Hannah became pregnant and gave birth to
a son. She named him Samuel,[a] saying, "Because I asked the LORD for him."

Hannah Dedicates Samuel

21 When her husband Elkanah went up with
all his family to offer the annual sacrifice to
the LORD and to fulfill his vow, 22 Hannah did
not go. She said to her husband, "After the boy
is weaned, I will take him and present him before the LORD, and he will live there always."[b]
23 "Do what seems best to you," her husband
Elkanah told her. "Stay here until you have
weaned him; only may the LORD make good
his[c] word." So the woman stayed at home and
nursed her son until she had weaned him.
24 After he was weaned, she took the boy
with her, young as he was, along with a
three-year-old bull,[d] an ephah[e] of flour and
a skin of wine, and brought him to the house
of the LORD at Shiloh. 25 When the bull had
been sacrificed, they brought the boy to Eli,
26 and she said to him, "Pardon me, my lord.
As surely as you live, I am the woman who
stood here beside you praying to the LORD.
27 I prayed for this child, and the LORD has
granted me what I asked of him. 28 So now I
give him to the LORD. For his whole life he will
be given over to the LORD." And he worshiped
the LORD there.

Hannah's Prayer

2 Then Hannah prayed and said:

"My heart rejoices in the LORD;
in the LORD my horn[f] is lifted high.
My mouth boasts over my enemies,
for I delight in your deliverance.

2 "There is no one holy like the LORD;
there is no one besides you;
there is no Rock like our God.

3 "Do not keep talking so proudly
or let your mouth speak such arrogance,
for the LORD is a God who knows,
and by him deeds are weighed.

4 "The bows of the warriors are broken,
but those who stumbled are armed with strength.
5 Those who were full hire themselves out for food,
but those who were hungry are hungry no more.
She who was barren has borne seven children,
but she who has had many sons pines away.

6 "The LORD brings death and makes alive;
he brings down to the grave and raises up.
7 The LORD sends poverty and wealth;
he humbles and he exalts.
8 He raises the poor from the dust
and lifts the needy from the ash heap;
he seats them with princes
and has them inherit a throne of honor.

"For the foundations of the earth are the LORD's;
on them he has set the world.
9 He will guard the feet of his faithful servants,
but the wicked will be silenced in the place of darkness.

"It is not by strength that one prevails;
10 those who oppose the LORD will be broken.
The Most High will thunder from heaven;
the LORD will judge the ends of the earth.

"He will give strength to his king
and exalt the horn of his anointed."

11 Then Elkanah went home to Ramah, but
the boy ministered before the LORD under Eli
the priest.

Eli's Wicked Sons

12 Eli's sons were scoundrels; they had no
regard for the LORD. 13 Now it was the practice of the priests that, whenever any of the
people offered a sacrifice, the priest's servant
would come with a three-pronged fork in his
hand while the meat was being boiled 14 and
would plunge the fork into the pan or kettle
or caldron or pot. Whatever the fork brought
up the priest would take for himself. This is
how they treated all the Israelites who came to
Shiloh. 15 But even before the fat was burned,
the priest's servant would come and say to the
person who was sacrificing, "Give the priest
some meat to roast; he won't accept boiled
meat from you, but only raw."
16 If the person said to him, "Let the fat be
burned first, and then take whatever you
want," the servant would answer, "No, hand
it over now; if you don't, I'll take it by force."
17 This sin of the young men was very great
in the LORD's sight, for they[g] were treating the
LORD's offering with contempt.
18 But Samuel was ministering before the
LORD—a boy wearing a linen ephod. 19 Each
year his mother made him a little robe and
took it to him when she went up with her husband to offer the annual sacrifice. 20 Eli would
bless Elkanah and his wife, saying, "May the
LORD give you children by this woman to take
the place of the one she prayed for and gave
to[h] the LORD." Then they would go home.
21 And the LORD was gracious to Hannah; she
gave birth to three sons and two daughters.
Meanwhile, the boy Samuel grew up in the
presence of the LORD.

[a] 20 *Samuel* sounds like the Hebrew for *heard by God.* [b] 22 Masoretic Text; Dead Sea Scrolls *always. I have dedicated him as a Nazirite—all the days of his life."* [c] 23 Masoretic Text; Dead Sea Scrolls, Septuagint and Syriac *your* [d] 24 Dead Sea Scrolls, Septuagint and Syriac; Masoretic Text *with three bulls* [e] 24 That is, probably about 36 pounds or about 16 kilograms [f] 1 *Horn* here symbolizes strength; also in verse 10. [g] 17 Dead Sea Scrolls and Septuagint; Masoretic Text *people* [h] 20 Dead Sea Scrolls; Masoretic Text *and asked from*

22Now Eli, who was very old, heard about everything his sons were doing to all Israel and how they slept with the women who served at the entrance to the tent of meeting. 23So he said to them, "Why do you do such things? I hear from all the people about these wicked deeds of yours. 24No, my sons; the report I hear spreading among the LORD's people is not good. 25If one person sins against another, God[a] may mediate for the offender; but if anyone sins against the LORD, who will intercede for them?" His sons, however, did not listen to their father's rebuke, for it was the LORD's will to put them to death.

26And the boy Samuel continued to grow in stature and in favor with the LORD and with people.

Prophecy Against the House of Eli

27Now a man of God came to Eli and said to him, "This is what the LORD says: 'Did I not clearly reveal myself to your ancestor's family when they were in Egypt under Pharaoh? 28I chose your ancestor out of all the tribes of Israel to be my priest, to go up to my altar, to burn incense, and to wear an ephod in my presence. I also gave your ancestor's family all the food offerings presented by the Israelites. 29Why do you[b] scorn my sacrifice and offering that I prescribed for my dwelling? Why do you honor your sons more than me by fattening yourselves on the choice parts of every offering made by my people Israel?'

30"Therefore the LORD, the God of Israel, declares: 'I promised that members of your family would minister before me forever.' But now the LORD declares: 'Far be it from me! Those who honor me I will honor, but those who despise me will be disdained. 31The time is coming when I will cut short your strength and the strength of your priestly house, so that no one in it will reach old age, 32and you will see distress in my dwelling. Although good will be done to Israel, no one in your family line will ever reach old age. 33Every one of you that I do not cut off from serving at my altar I will spare only to destroy your sight and sap your strength, and all your descendants will die in the prime of life.

34" 'And what happens to your two sons, Hophni and Phinehas, will be a sign to you— they will both die on the same day. 35I will raise up for myself a faithful priest, who will do according to what is in my heart and mind. I will firmly establish his priestly house, and they will minister before my anointed one always. 36Then everyone left in your family line will come and bow down before him for a piece of silver and a loaf of bread and plead, "Appoint me to some priestly office so I can have food to eat." ' "

The LORD Calls Samuel

3 The boy Samuel ministered before the LORD under Eli. In those days the word of the LORD was rare; there were not many visions.

2One night Eli, whose eyes were becoming so weak that he could barely see, was lying down in his usual place. 3The lamp of God had not yet gone out, and Samuel was lying down in the house of the LORD, where the ark of God was. 4Then the LORD called Samuel.

Samuel answered, "Here I am." 5And he ran to Eli and said, "Here I am; you called me."

But Eli said, "I did not call; go back and lie down." So he went and lay down.

6Again the LORD called, "Samuel!" And Samuel got up and went to Eli and said, "Here I am; you called me."

"My son," Eli said, "I did not call; go back and lie down."

7Now Samuel did not yet know the LORD: The word of the LORD had not yet been revealed to him.

8A third time the LORD called, "Samuel!" And Samuel got up and went to Eli and said, "Here I am; you called me."

Then Eli realized that the LORD was calling the boy. 9So Eli told Samuel, "Go and lie down, and if he calls you, say, 'Speak, LORD, for your servant is listening.' " So Samuel went and lay down in his place.

10The LORD came and stood there, calling as at the other times, "Samuel! Samuel!"

Then Samuel said, "Speak, for your servant is listening."

11And the LORD said to Samuel: "See, I am about to do something in Israel that will make the ears of everyone who hears about it tingle. 12At that time I will carry out against Eli everything I spoke against his family— from beginning to end. 13For I told him that I would judge his family forever because of the sin he knew about; his sons blasphemed God,[c] and he failed to restrain them. 14Therefore I swore to the house of Eli, 'The guilt of Eli's house will never be atoned for by sacrifice or offering.' "

15Samuel lay down until morning and then opened the doors of the house of the LORD. He was afraid to tell Eli the vision, 16but Eli called him and said, "Samuel, my son."

Samuel answered, "Here I am."

17"What was it he said to you?" Eli asked. "Do not hide it from me. May God deal with you, be it ever so severely, if you hide from me anything he told you." 18So Samuel told him everything, hiding nothing from him. Then Eli said, "He is the LORD; let him do what is good in his eyes."

19The LORD was with Samuel as he grew up, and he let none of Samuel's words fall to the ground. 20And all Israel from Dan to Beersheba recognized that Samuel was attested as a prophet of the LORD. 21The LORD continued to appear at Shiloh, and there he revealed himself to Samuel through his word.

4 And Samuel's word came to all Israel.

The Philistines Capture the Ark

Now the Israelites went out to fight against the Philistines. The Israelites camped at

[a] 25 Or *the judges* [b] 29 The Hebrew is plural. [c] 13 An ancient Hebrew scribal tradition (see also Septuagint); Masoretic Text *sons made themselves contemptible*

Ebenezer, and the Philistines at Aphek. 2The
Philistines deployed their forces to meet Israel, and as the battle spread, Israel was defeated by the Philistines, who killed about four
thousand of them on the battlefield. 3When the
soldiers returned to camp, the elders of Israel
asked, "Why did the LORD bring defeat on us
today before the Philistines? Let us bring the
ark of the LORD's covenant from Shiloh, so
that he may go with us and save us from the
hand of our enemies."

4So the people sent men to Shiloh, and they
brought back the ark of the covenant of the
LORD Almighty, who is enthroned between
the cherubim. And Eli's two sons, Hophni and
Phinehas, were there with the ark of the covenant of God.

5When the ark of the LORD's covenant came
into the camp, all Israel raised such a great
shout that the ground shook. 6Hearing the uproar, the Philistines asked, "What's all this
shouting in the Hebrew camp?"

When they learned that the ark of the LORD
had come into the camp, 7the Philistines were
afraid. "A god has[a] come into the camp," they
said. "Oh no! Nothing like this has happened
before. 8We're doomed! Who will deliver us
from the hand of these mighty gods? They are
the gods who struck the Egyptians with all
kinds of plagues in the wilderness. 9Be strong,
Philistines! Be men, or you will be subject to
the Hebrews, as they have been to you. Be
men, and fight!"

10So the Philistines fought, and the Israelites were defeated and every man fled to his
tent. The slaughter was very great; Israel lost
thirty thousand foot soldiers. 11The ark of God
was captured, and Eli's two sons, Hophni and
Phinehas, died.

Death of Eli

12That same day a Benjamite ran from the
battle line and went to Shiloh with his clothes
torn and dust on his head. 13When he arrived,
there was Eli sitting on his chair by the side of
the road, watching, because his heart feared
for the ark of God. When the man entered the
town and told what had happened, the whole
town sent up a cry.

14Eli heard the outcry and asked, "What is
the meaning of this uproar?"

The man hurried over to Eli, 15who was
ninety-eight years old and whose eyes had
failed so that he could not see. 16He told Eli,
"I have just come from the battle line; I fled
from it this very day."

Eli asked, "What happened, my son?"

17The man who brought the news replied,
"Israel fled before the Philistines, and the
army has suffered heavy losses. Also your
two sons, Hophni and Phinehas, are dead, and
the ark of God has been captured."

18When he mentioned the ark of God, Eli
fell backward off his chair by the side of the
gate. His neck was broken and he died, for he
was an old man, and he was heavy. He had
led[b] Israel forty years.

19His daughter-in-law, the wife of Phinehas,
was pregnant and near the time of delivery.
When she heard the news that the ark of God
had been captured and that her father-in-law
and her husband were dead, she went into labor and gave birth, but was overcome by her
labor pains. 20As she was dying, the women
attending her said, "Don't despair; you have
given birth to a son." But she did not respond
or pay any attention.

21She named the boy Ichabod,[c] saying, "The
Glory has departed from Israel"—because of
the capture of the ark of God and the deaths
of her father-in-law and her husband. 22She
said, "The Glory has departed from Israel, for
the ark of God has been captured."

The Ark in Ashdod and Ekron

5 After the Philistines had captured the ark
of God, they took it from Ebenezer to Ashdod. 2Then they carried the ark into Dagon's
temple and set it beside Dagon. 3When the
people of Ashdod rose early the next day,
there was Dagon, fallen on his face on the
ground before the ark of the LORD! They took
Dagon and put him back in his place. 4But the
following morning when they rose, there was
Dagon, fallen on his face on the ground before the ark of the LORD! His head and hands
had been broken off and were lying on the
threshold; only his body remained. 5That is
why to this day neither the priests of Dagon
nor any others who enter Dagon's temple at
Ashdod step on the threshold.

6The LORD's hand was heavy on the people
of Ashdod and its vicinity; he brought dev-
astation on them and afflicted them with tumors.[d] 7When the people of Ashdod saw what
was happening, they said, "The ark of the god
of Israel must not stay here with us, because
his hand is heavy on us and on Dagon our
god." 8So they called together all the rulers of
the Philistines and asked them, "What shall
we do with the ark of the god of Israel?"

They answered, "Have the ark of the god
of Israel moved to Gath." So they moved the
ark of the God of Israel.

9But after they had moved it, the LORD's
hand was against that city, throwing it into a
great panic. He afflicted the people of the city,
both young and old, with an outbreak of tumors.[e] 10So they sent the ark of God to Ekron.

As the ark of God was entering Ekron, the
people of Ekron cried out, "They have brought
the ark of the god of Israel around to us to kill
us and our people." 11So they called together
all the rulers of the Philistines and said, "Send
the ark of the god of Israel away; let it go back
to its own place, or it[f] will kill us and our people." For death had filled the city with panic;
God's hand was very heavy on it. 12Those who
did not die were afflicted with tumors, and the
outcry of the city went up to heaven.

[a] 7 Or "*Gods have* (see Septuagint) [b] *18* Traditionally *judged* [c] *21 Ichabod* means *no glory.*
[d] *6* Hebrew; Septuagint and Vulgate *tumors. And rats appeared in their land, and there was death and destruction throughout the city* [e] *9* Or *with tumors in the groin* (see Septuagint) [f] *11* Or *he*

The Ark Returned to Israel

6 When the ark of the LORD had been in Philistine territory seven months, [2]the Philistines called for the priests and the diviners and said, "What shall we do with the ark of the LORD? Tell us how we should send it back to its place."

[3]They answered, "If you return the ark of the god of Israel, do not send it back to him without a gift; by all means send a guilt offering to him. Then you will be healed, and you will know why his hand has not been lifted from you."

[4]The Philistines asked, "What guilt offering should we send to him?"

They replied, "Five gold tumors and five gold rats, according to the number of the Philistine rulers, because the same plague has struck both you and your rulers. [5]Make models of the tumors and of the rats that are destroying the country, and give glory to Israel's god. Perhaps he will lift his hand from you and your gods and your land. [6]Why do you harden your hearts as the Egyptians and Pharaoh did? When Israel's god dealt harshly with them, did they not send the Israelites out so they could go on their way?

[7]"Now then, get a new cart ready, with two cows that have calved and have never been yoked. Hitch the cows to the cart, but take their calves away and pen them up. [8]Take the ark of the LORD and put it on the cart, and in a chest beside it put the gold objects you are sending back to him as a guilt offering. Send it on its way, [9]but keep watching it. If it goes up to its own territory, toward Beth Shemesh, then the LORD has brought this great disaster on us. But if it does not, then we will know that it was not his hand that struck us but that it happened to us by chance."

[10]So they did this. They took two such cows and hitched them to the cart and penned up their calves. [11]They placed the ark of the LORD on the cart and along with it the chest containing the gold rats and the models of the tumors. [12]Then the cows went straight up toward Beth Shemesh, keeping on the road and lowing all the way; they did not turn to the right or to the left. The rulers of the Philistines followed them as far as the border of Beth Shemesh.

[13]Now the people of Beth Shemesh were harvesting their wheat in the valley, and when they looked up and saw the ark, they rejoiced at the sight. [14]The cart came to the field of Joshua of Beth Shemesh, and there it stopped beside a large rock. The people chopped up the wood of the cart and sacrificed the cows as a burnt offering to the LORD. [15]The Levites took down the ark of the LORD, together with the chest containing the gold objects, and placed them on the large rock. On that day the people of Beth Shemesh offered burnt offerings and made sacrifices to the LORD. [16]The five rulers of the Philistines saw all this and then returned that same day to Ekron.

[17]These are the gold tumors the Philistines sent as a guilt offering to the LORD—one each for Ashdod, Gaza, Ashkelon, Gath and Ekron. [18]And the number of the gold rats was according to the number of Philistine towns belonging to the five rulers—the fortified towns with their country villages. The large rock on which the Levites set the ark of the LORD is a witness to this day in the field of Joshua of Beth Shemesh.

[19]But God struck down some of the inhabitants of Beth Shemesh, putting seventy[a] of them to death because they looked into the ark of the LORD. The people mourned because of the heavy blow the LORD had dealt them. [20]And the people of Beth Shemesh asked, "Who can stand in the presence of the LORD, this holy God? To whom will the ark go up from here?"

[21]Then they sent messengers to the people of Kiriath Jearim, saying, "The Philistines have returned the ark of the LORD. Come down and

7 take it up to your town." [1]So the men of Kiriath Jearim came and took up the ark of the LORD. They brought it to Abinadab's house on the hill and consecrated Eleazar his son to guard the ark of the LORD. [2]The ark remained at Kiriath Jearim a long time—twenty years in all.

Samuel Subdues the Philistines at Mizpah

Then all the people of Israel turned back to the LORD. [3]So Samuel said to all the Israelites, "If you are returning to the LORD with all your hearts, then rid yourselves of the foreign gods and the Ashtoreths and commit yourselves to the LORD and serve him only, and he will deliver you out of the hand of the Philistines." [4]So the Israelites put away their Baals and Ashtoreths, and served the LORD only.

[5]Then Samuel said, "Assemble all Israel at Mizpah, and I will intercede with the LORD for you." [6]When they had assembled at Mizpah, they drew water and poured it out before the LORD. On that day they fasted and there they confessed, "We have sinned against the LORD." Now Samuel was serving as leader[b] of Israel at Mizpah.

[7]When the Philistines heard that Israel had assembled at Mizpah, the rulers of the Philistines came up to attack them. When the Israelites heard of it, they were afraid because of the Philistines. [8]They said to Samuel, "Do not stop crying out to the LORD our God for us, that he may rescue us from the hand of the Philistines." [9]Then Samuel took a suckling lamb and sacrificed it as a whole burnt offering to the LORD. He cried out to the LORD on Israel's behalf, and the LORD answered him.

[10]While Samuel was sacrificing the burnt offering, the Philistines drew near to engage Israel in battle. But that day the LORD thundered with loud thunder against the Philistines and threw them into such a panic that they were routed before the Israelites. [11]The men of Israel rushed out of Mizpah and pursued the Philistines, slaughtering them along the way to a point below Beth Kar.

[a] *19* A few Hebrew manuscripts; most Hebrew manuscripts and Septuagint *50,070* [b] *6* Traditionally *judge*; also in verse 15

12 Then Samuel took a stone and set it up between Mizpah and Shen. He named it Ebenezer,[a] saying, "Thus far the LORD has helped us."

13 So the Philistines were subdued and they stopped invading Israel's territory. Throughout Samuel's lifetime, the hand of the LORD was against the Philistines. 14 The towns from Ekron to Gath that the Philistines had captured from Israel were restored to Israel, and Israel delivered the neighboring territory from the hands of the Philistines. And there was peace between Israel and the Amorites.

15 Samuel continued as Israel's leader all the days of his life. 16 From year to year he went on a circuit from Bethel to Gilgal to Mizpah, judging Israel in all those places. 17 But he always went back to Ramah, where his home was, and there he also held court for Israel. And he built an altar there to the LORD.

Israel Asks for a King

8 When Samuel grew old, he appointed his sons as Israel's leaders.[b] 2 The name of his firstborn was Joel and the name of his second was Abijah, and they served at Beersheba. 3 But his sons did not follow his ways. They turned aside after dishonest gain and accepted bribes and perverted justice.

4 So all the elders of Israel gathered together and came to Samuel at Ramah. 5 They said to him, "You are old, and your sons do not follow your ways; now appoint a king to lead[c] us, such as all the other nations have."

6 But when they said, "Give us a king to lead us," this displeased Samuel; so he prayed to the LORD. 7 And the LORD told him: "Listen to all that the people are saying to you; it is not you they have rejected, but they have rejected me as their king. 8 As they have done from the day I brought them up out of Egypt until this day, forsaking me and serving other gods, so they are doing to you. 9 Now listen to them; but warn them solemnly and let them know what the king who will reign over them will claim as his rights."

10 Samuel told all the words of the LORD to the people who were asking him for a king. 11 He said, "This is what the king who will reign over you will claim as his rights: He will take your sons and make them serve with his chariots and horses, and they will run in front of his chariots. 12 Some he will assign to be commanders of thousands and commanders of fifties, and others to plow his ground and reap his harvest, and still others to make weapons of war and equipment for his chariots. 13 He will take your daughters to be perfumers and cooks and bakers. 14 He will take the best of your fields and vineyards and olive groves and give them to his attendants. 15 He will take a tenth of your grain and of your vintage and give it to his officials and attendants. 16 Your male and female servants and the best of your cattle[d] and donkeys he will take for his own use. 17 He will take a tenth of your flocks, and you yourselves will become his slaves. 18 When that day comes, you will cry out for relief from the king you have chosen, but the LORD will not answer you in that day."

19 But the people refused to listen to Samuel. "No!" they said. "We want a king over us. 20 Then we will be like all the other nations, with a king to lead us and to go out before us and fight our battles."

21 When Samuel heard all that the people said, he repeated it before the LORD. 22 The LORD answered, "Listen to them and give them a king."

Then Samuel said to the Israelites, "Everyone go back to your own town."

Samuel Anoints Saul

9 There was a Benjamite, a man of standing, whose name was Kish son of Abiel, the son of Zeror, the son of Bekorath, the son of Aphiah of Benjamin. 2 Kish had a son named Saul, as handsome a young man as could be found anywhere in Israel, and he was a head taller than anyone else.

3 Now the donkeys belonging to Saul's father Kish were lost, and Kish said to his son Saul, "Take one of the servants with you and go and look for the donkeys." 4 So he passed through the hill country of Ephraim and through the area around Shalisha, but they did not find them. They went on into the district of Shaalim, but the donkeys were not there. Then he passed through the territory of Benjamin, but they did not find them.

5 When they reached the district of Zuph, Saul said to the servant who was with him, "Come, let's go back, or my father will stop thinking about the donkeys and start worrying about us."

6 But the servant replied, "Look, in this town there is a man of God; he is highly respected, and everything he says comes true. Let's go there now. Perhaps he will tell us what way to take."

7 Saul said to his servant, "If we go, what can we give the man? The food in our sacks is gone. We have no gift to take to the man of God. What do we have?"

8 The servant answered him again. "Look," he said, "I have a quarter of a shekel[e] of silver. I will give it to the man of God so that he will tell us what way to take." 9 (Formerly in Israel, if someone went to inquire of God, they would say, "Come, let us go to the seer," because the prophet of today used to be called a seer.)

10 "Good," Saul said to his servant. "Come, let's go." So they set out for the town where the man of God was.

11 As they were going up the hill to the town, they met some young women coming out to draw water, and they asked them, "Is the seer here?"

12 "He is," they answered. "He's ahead of you. Hurry now; he has just come to our town today, for the people have a sacrifice at the high place. 13 As soon as you enter the town,

[a] 12 *Ebenezer* means *stone of help.* [b] 1 Traditionally *judges* [c] 5 Traditionally *judge*; also in verses 6 and 20 [d] 16 Septuagint; Hebrew *young men* [e] 8 That is, about 1/10 ounce or about 3 grams

you will find him before he goes up to the
high place to eat. The people will not begin
eating until he comes, because he must bless
the sacrifice; afterward, those who are invited will eat. Go up now; you should find him
about this time."
14They went up to the town, and as they
were entering it, there was Samuel, coming
toward them on his way up to the high place.
15Now the day before Saul came, the LORD
had revealed this to Samuel: 16"About this time
tomorrow I will send you a man from the land
of Benjamin. Anoint him ruler over my people
Israel; he will deliver them from the hand of
the Philistines. I have looked on my people,
for their cry has reached me."
17When Samuel caught sight of Saul, the
LORD said to him, "This is the man I spoke to
you about; he will govern my people."
18Saul approached Samuel in the gateway
and asked, "Would you please tell me where
the seer's house is?"
19"I am the seer," Samuel replied. "Go up
ahead of me to the high place, for today you
are to eat with me, and in the morning I will
send you on your way and will tell you all
that is in your heart. 20As for the donkeys you
lost three days ago, do not worry about them;
they have been found. And to whom is all the
desire of Israel turned, if not to you and your
whole family line?"
21Saul answered, "But am I not a Benjamite,
from the smallest tribe of Israel, and is not
my clan the least of all the clans of the tribe
of Benjamin? Why do you say such a thing
to me?"
22Then Samuel brought Saul and his servant into the hall and seated them at the head
of those who were invited—about thirty in
number. 23Samuel said to the cook, "Bring the
piece of meat I gave you, the one I told you to
lay aside."
24So the cook took up the thigh with what
was on it and set it in front of Saul. Samuel
said, "Here is what has been kept for you. Eat,
because it was set aside for you for this occasion from the time I said, 'I have invited
guests.'" And Saul dined with Samuel that
day.
25After they came down from the high place
to the town, Samuel talked with Saul on the
roof of his house. 26They rose about daybreak,
and Samuel called to Saul on the roof, "Get
ready, and I will send you on your way." When
Saul got ready, he and Samuel went outside
together. 27As they were going down to the
edge of the town, Samuel said to Saul, "Tell
the servant to go on ahead of us"—and the
servant did so—"but you stay here for a while,
so that I may give you a message from God."
10 Then Samuel took a flask of olive oil and
poured it on Saul's head and kissed him,
saying, "Has not the LORD anointed you ruler
over his inheritance?[a] 2When you leave me
today, you will meet two men near Rachel's
tomb, at Zelzah on the border of Benjamin.
They will say to you, 'The donkeys you set out
to look for have been found. And now your father has stopped thinking about them and is
worried about you. He is asking, "What shall
I do about my son?"'
3"Then you will go on from there until you
reach the great tree of Tabor. Three men going up to worship God at Bethel will meet you
there. One will be carrying three young goats,
another three loaves of bread, and another a
skin of wine. 4They will greet you and offer
you two loaves of bread, which you will accept from them.
5"After that you will go to Gibeah of God,
where there is a Philistine outpost. As you
approach the town, you will meet a procession
of prophets coming down from the high place
with lyres, timbrels, pipes and harps being
played before them, and they will be prophesying. 6The Spirit of the LORD will come
powerfully upon you, and you will prophesy
with them; and you will be changed into a
different person. 7Once these signs are fulfilled, do whatever your hand finds to do, for
God is with you.
8"Go down ahead of me to Gilgal. I will
surely come down to you to sacrifice burnt
offerings and fellowship offerings, but you
must wait seven days until I come to you and
tell you what you are to do."

Saul Made King

9As Saul turned to leave Samuel, God
changed Saul's heart, and all these signs were
fulfilled that day. 10When he and his servant
arrived at Gibeah, a procession of prophets
met him; the Spirit of God came powerfully
upon him, and he joined in their prophesying.
11When all those who had formerly known
him saw him prophesying with the prophets, they asked each other, "What is this that
has happened to the son of Kish? Is Saul also
among the prophets?"
12A man who lived there answered, "And
who is their father?" So it became a saying:
"Is Saul also among the prophets?" 13After
Saul stopped prophesying, he went to the
high place.
14Now Saul's uncle asked him and his servant, "Where have you been?"
"Looking for the donkeys," he said. "But
when we saw they were not to be found, we
went to Samuel."
15Saul's uncle said, "Tell me what Samuel
said to you."
16Saul replied, "He assured us that the donkeys had been found." But he did not tell his
uncle what Samuel had said about the kingship.
17Samuel summoned the people of Israel to
the LORD at Mizpah 18and said to them, "This
is what the LORD, the God of Israel, says: 'I
brought Israel up out of Egypt, and I delivered you from the power of Egypt and all the

[a] 1 Hebrew; Septuagint and Vulgate *over his people Israel? You will reign over the LORD's people and save them from the power of their enemies round about. And this will be a sign to you that the LORD has anointed you ruler over his inheritance:*

kingdoms that oppressed you.' 19But you have now rejected your God, who saves you out of all your disasters and calamities. And you have said, 'No, appoint a king over us.' So now present yourselves before the LORD by your tribes and clans."

20When Samuel had all Israel come forward by tribes, the tribe of Benjamin was taken by lot. 21Then he brought forward the tribe of Benjamin, clan by clan, and Matri's clan was taken. Finally Saul son of Kish was taken. But when they looked for him, he was not to be found. 22So they inquired further of the LORD, "Has the man come here yet?"

And the LORD said, "Yes, he has hidden himself among the supplies."

23They ran and brought him out, and as he stood among the people he was a head taller than any of the others. 24Samuel said to all the people, "Do you see the man the LORD has chosen? There is no one like him among all the people."

Then the people shouted, "Long live the king!"

25Samuel explained to the people the rights and duties of kingship. He wrote them down on a scroll and deposited it before the LORD. Then Samuel dismissed the people to go to their own homes.

26Saul also went to his home in Gibeah, accompanied by valiant men whose hearts God had touched. 27But some scoundrels said, "How can this fellow save us?" They despised him and brought him no gifts. But Saul kept silent.

Saul Rescues the City of Jabesh

11 Nahash[a] the Ammonite went up and besieged Jabesh Gilead. And all the men of Jabesh said to him, "Make a treaty with us, and we will be subject to you."

2But Nahash the Ammonite replied, "I will make a treaty with you only on the condition that I gouge out the right eye of every one of you and so bring disgrace on all Israel."

3The elders of Jabesh said to him, "Give us seven days so we can send messengers throughout Israel; if no one comes to rescue us, we will surrender to you."

4When the messengers came to Gibeah of Saul and reported these terms to the people, they all wept aloud. 5Just then Saul was returning from the fields, behind his oxen, and he asked, "What is wrong with everyone? Why are they weeping?" Then they repeated to him what the men of Jabesh had said.

6When Saul heard their words, the Spirit of God came powerfully upon him, and he burned with anger. 7He took a pair of oxen, cut them into pieces, and sent the pieces by messengers throughout Israel, proclaiming, "This is what will be done to the oxen of anyone who does not follow Saul and Samuel." Then the terror of the LORD fell on the people, and they came out together as one. 8When Saul mustered them at Bezek, the men of Israel numbered three hundred thousand and those of Judah thirty thousand.

9They told the messengers who had come, "Say to the men of Jabesh Gilead, 'By the time the sun is hot tomorrow, you will be rescued.'" When the messengers went and reported this to the men of Jabesh, they were elated. 10They said to the Ammonites, "Tomorrow we will surrender to you, and you can do to us whatever you like."

11The next day Saul separated his men into three divisions; during the last watch of the night they broke into the camp of the Ammonites and slaughtered them until the heat of the day. Those who survived were scattered, so that no two of them were left together.

Saul Confirmed as King

12The people then said to Samuel, "Who was it that asked, 'Shall Saul reign over us?' Turn these men over to us so that we may put them to death."

13But Saul said, "No one will be put to death today, for this day the LORD has rescued Israel."

14Then Samuel said to the people, "Come, let us go to Gilgal and there renew the kingship." 15So all the people went to Gilgal and made Saul king in the presence of the LORD. There they sacrificed fellowship offerings before the LORD, and Saul and all the Israelites held a great celebration.

Samuel's Farewell Speech

12 Samuel said to all Israel, "I have listened to everything you said to me and have set a king over you. 2Now you have a king as your leader. As for me, I am old and gray, and my sons are here with you. I have been your leader from my youth until this day. 3Here I stand. Testify against me in the presence of the LORD and his anointed. Whose ox have I taken? Whose donkey have I taken? Whom have I cheated? Whom have I oppressed? From whose hand have I accepted a bribe to make me shut my eyes? If I have done any of these things, I will make it right."

4"You have not cheated or oppressed us," they replied. "You have not taken anything from anyone's hand."

5Samuel said to them, "The LORD is witness against you, and also his anointed is witness this day, that you have not found anything in my hand."

"He is witness," they said.

6Then Samuel said to the people, "It is the LORD who appointed Moses and Aaron and brought your ancestors up out of Egypt. 7Now then, stand here, because I am going to confront you with evidence before the LORD as to all the righteous acts performed by the LORD for you and your ancestors.

[a] *1* Masoretic Text; Dead Sea Scrolls *gifts. Now Nahash king of the Ammonites oppressed the Gadites and Reubenites severely. He gouged out all their right eyes and struck terror and dread in Israel. Not a man remained among the Israelites beyond the Jordan whose right eye was not gouged out by Nahash king of the Ammonites, except that seven thousand men fled from the Ammonites and entered Jabesh Gilead. About a month later,* [1]*Nahash*

8“After Jacob entered Egypt, they cried to
the LORD for help, and the LORD sent Moses
and Aaron, who brought your ancestors out
of Egypt and settled them in this place.
9“But they forgot the LORD their God; so he
sold them into the hand of Sisera, the commander of the army of Hazor, and into the
hands of the Philistines and the king of Moab,
who fought against them. 10They cried out
to the LORD and said, ‘We have sinned; we
have forsaken the LORD and served the Baals
and the Ashtoreths. But now deliver us from
the hands of our enemies, and we will serve
you.’ 11Then the LORD sent Jerub-Baal,[a] Barak,[b] Jephthah and Samuel,[c] and he delivered
you from the hands of your enemies all around
you, so that you lived in safety.
12“But when you saw that Nahash king of
the Ammonites was moving against you,
you said to me, ‘No, we want a king to rule
over us’—even though the LORD your God
was your king. 13Now here is the king you
have chosen, the one you asked for; see, the
LORD has set a king over you. 14If you fear
the LORD and serve and obey him and do not
rebel against his commands, and if both you
and the king who reigns over you follow the
LORD your God—good! 15But if you do not
obey the LORD, and if you rebel against his
commands, his hand will be against you, as
it was against your ancestors.
16“Now then, stand still and see this great
thing the LORD is about to do before your eyes!
17Is it not wheat harvest now? I will call on
the LORD to send thunder and rain. And you
will realize what an evil thing you did in the
eyes of the LORD when you asked for a king.”
18Then Samuel called on the LORD, and that
same day the LORD sent thunder and rain. So
all the people stood in awe of the LORD and
of Samuel.
19The people all said to Samuel, “Pray to the
LORD your God for your servants so that we
will not die, for we have added to all our other
sins the evil of asking for a king.”
20“Do not be afraid,” Samuel replied. “You
have done all this evil; yet do not turn away
from the LORD, but serve the LORD with all
your heart. 21Do not turn away after useless
idols. They can do you no good, nor can they
rescue you, because they are useless. 22For
the sake of his great name the LORD will
not reject his people, because the LORD was
pleased to make you his own. 23As for me,
far be it from me that I should sin against
the LORD by failing to pray for you. And I
will teach you the way that is good and right.
24But be sure to fear the LORD and serve him
faithfully with all your heart; consider what
great things he has done for you. 25Yet if you
persist in doing evil, both you and your king
will perish.”

Samuel Rebukes Saul

13 Saul was thirty[d] years old when he became king, and he reigned over Israel
forty-[e] two years.
2Saul chose three thousand men from Israel; two thousand were with him at Mikmash and in the hill country of Bethel, and
a thousand were with Jonathan at Gibeah in
Benjamin. The rest of the men he sent back
to their homes.
3Jonathan attacked the Philistine outpost at
Geba, and the Philistines heard about it. Then
Saul had the trumpet blown throughout the
land and said, “Let the Hebrews hear!” 4So all
Israel heard the news: “Saul has attacked the
Philistine outpost, and now Israel has become
obnoxious to the Philistines.” And the people
were summoned to join Saul at Gilgal.
5The Philistines assembled to fight Israel,
with three thousand[f] chariots, six thousand
charioteers, and soldiers as numerous as the
sand on the seashore. They went up and camped
at Mikmash, east of Beth Aven. 6When the Israelites saw that their situation was critical and
that their army was hard pressed, they hid in
caves and thickets, among the rocks, and in pits
and cisterns. 7Some Hebrews even crossed the
Jordan to the land of Gad and Gilead.
Saul remained at Gilgal, and all the troops
with him were quaking with fear. 8He waited
seven days, the time set by Samuel; but Samuel did not come to Gilgal, and Saul's men
began to scatter. 9So he said, “Bring me the
burnt offering and the fellowship offerings.”
And Saul offered up the burnt offering. 10Just
as he finished making the offering, Samuel
arrived, and Saul went out to greet him.
11“What have you done?” asked Samuel.
Saul replied, “When I saw that the men were
scattering, and that you did not come at the set
time, and that the Philistines were assembling
at Mikmash, 12I thought, ‘Now the Philistines
will come down against me at Gilgal, and I
have not sought the LORD's favor.’ So I felt
compelled to offer the burnt offering.”
13“You have done a foolish thing,” Samuel
said. “You have not kept the command the LORD
your God gave you; if you had, he would have established your kingdom over Israel for all time.
14But now your kingdom will not endure; the
LORD has sought out a man after his own heart
and appointed him ruler of his people, because
you have not kept the LORD's command.”
15Then Samuel left Gilgal[g] and went up to
Gibeah in Benjamin, and Saul counted the
men who were with him. They numbered
about six hundred.

Israel Without Weapons

16Saul and his son Jonathan and the
men with them were staying in Gibeah[h] in

[a] *11* Also called *Gideon* [b] *11* Some Septuagint manuscripts and Syriac; Hebrew *Bedan*
[c] *11* Hebrew; some Septuagint manuscripts and Syriac *Samson* [d] *1* A few late manuscripts of the Septuagint; Hebrew does not have *thirty.* [e] *1* Probable reading of the original Hebrew text (see Acts 13:21); Masoretic Text does not have *forty-.* [f] *5* Some Septuagint manuscripts and Syriac; Hebrew *thirty thousand* [g] *15* Hebrew; Septuagint *Gilgal and went his way; the rest of the people went after Saul to meet the army, and they went out of Gilgal* [h] *16* Two Hebrew manuscripts; most Hebrew manuscripts *Geba,* a variant of *Gibeah*

Benjamin, while the Philistines camped at Mikmash. 17Raiding parties went out from the Philistine camp in three detachments. One turned toward Ophrah in the vicinity of Shual, 18another toward Beth Horon, and the third toward the borderland overlooking the Valley of Zeboyim facing the wilderness.

19Not a blacksmith could be found in the whole land of Israel, because the Philistines had said, "Otherwise the Hebrews will make swords or spears!" 20So all Israel went down to the Philistines to have their plow points, mattocks, axes and sickles[a] sharpened. 21The price was two-thirds of a shekel[b] for sharpening plow points and mattocks, and a third of a shekel[c] for sharpening forks and axes and for repointing goads.

22So on the day of the battle not a soldier with Saul and Jonathan had a sword or spear in his hand; only Saul and his son Jonathan had them.

Jonathan Attacks the Philistines

23Now a detachment of Philistines had gone

14

out to the pass at Mikmash. 1One day Jonathan son of Saul said to his young armor-bearer, "Come, let's go over to the Philistine outpost on the other side." But he did not tell his father.

2Saul was staying on the outskirts of Gibeah under a pomegranate tree in Migron. With him were about six hundred men, 3among whom was Ahijah, who was wearing an ephod. He was a son of Ichabod's brother Ahitub son of Phinehas, the son of Eli, the LORD's priest in Shiloh. No one was aware that Jonathan had left.

4On each side of the pass that Jonathan intended to cross to reach the Philistine outpost was a cliff; one was called Bozez and the other Seneh. 5One cliff stood to the north toward Mikmash, the other to the south toward Geba.

6Jonathan said to his young armor-bearer, "Come, let's go over to the outpost of those uncircumcised men. Perhaps the LORD will act in our behalf. Nothing can hinder the LORD from saving, whether by many or by few."

7"Do all that you have in mind," his armor-bearer said. "Go ahead; I am with you heart and soul."

8Jonathan said, "Come on, then; we will cross over toward them and let them see us. 9If they say to us, 'Wait there until we come to you,' we will stay where we are and not go up to them. 10But if they say, 'Come up to us,' we will climb up, because that will be our sign that the LORD has given them into our hands."

11So both of them showed themselves to the Philistine outpost. "Look!" said the Philistines. "The Hebrews are crawling out of the holes they were hiding in." 12The men of the outpost shouted to Jonathan and his armor-bearer, "Come up to us and we'll teach you a lesson."

So Jonathan said to his armor-bearer, "Climb up after me; the LORD has given them into the hand of Israel."

13Jonathan climbed up, using his hands and feet, with his armor-bearer right behind him. The Philistines fell before Jonathan, and his armor-bearer followed and killed behind him. 14In that first attack Jonathan and his armor-bearer killed some twenty men in an area of about half an acre.

Israel Routs the Philistines

15Then panic struck the whole army—those in the camp and field, and those in the outposts and raiding parties—and the ground shook. It was a panic sent by God.[d]

16Saul's lookouts at Gibeah in Benjamin saw the army melting away in all directions. 17Then Saul said to the men who were with him, "Muster the forces and see who has left us." When they did, it was Jonathan and his armor-bearer who were not there.

18Saul said to Ahijah, "Bring the ark of God." (At that time it was with the Israelites.)[e] 19While Saul was talking to the priest, the tumult in the Philistine camp increased more and more. So Saul said to the priest, "Withdraw your hand."

20Then Saul and all his men assembled and went to the battle. They found the Philistines in total confusion, striking each other with their swords. 21Those Hebrews who had previously been with the Philistines and had gone up with them to their camp went over to the Israelites who were with Saul and Jonathan. 22When all the Israelites who had hidden in the hill country of Ephraim heard that the Philistines were on the run, they joined the battle in hot pursuit. 23So on that day the LORD saved Israel, and the battle moved on beyond Beth Aven.

Jonathan Eats Honey

24Now the Israelites were in distress that day, because Saul had bound the people under an oath, saying, "Cursed be anyone who eats food before evening comes, before I have avenged myself on my enemies!" So none of the troops tasted food.

25The entire army entered the woods, and there was honey on the ground. 26When they went into the woods, they saw the honey oozing out; yet no one put his hand to his mouth, because they feared the oath. 27But Jonathan had not heard that his father had bound the people with the oath, so he reached out the end of the staff that was in his hand and dipped it into the honeycomb. He raised his hand to his mouth, and his eyes brightened.[f] 28Then one of the soldiers told him, "Your father bound the army under a strict oath, saying, 'Cursed be anyone who eats food today!' That is why the men are faint."

29Jonathan said, "My father has made trou-

[a] *20* Septuagint; Hebrew *plow points* [b] *21* That is, about 1/4 ounce or about 8 grams [c] *21* That is, about 1/8 ounce or about 4 grams [d] *15* Or *a terrible panic* [e] *18* Hebrew; Septuagint *"Bring the ephod." (At that time he wore the ephod before the Israelites.)* [f] *27* Or *his strength was renewed*; similarly in verse 29

ble for the country. See how my eyes brightened when I tasted a little of this honey. 30How
much better it would have been if the men
had eaten today some of the plunder they took
from their enemies. Would not the slaughter
of the Philistines have been even greater?"
31That day, after the Israelites had struck
down the Philistines from Mikmash to Aijalon, they were exhausted. 32They pounced
on the plunder and, taking sheep, cattle and
calves, they butchered them on the ground
and ate them, together with the blood. 33Then
someone said to Saul, "Look, the men are sinning against the LORD by eating meat that
has blood in it."
"You have broken faith," he said. "Roll a
large stone over here at once." 34Then he said,
"Go out among the men and tell them, 'Each
of you bring me your cattle and sheep, and
slaughter them here and eat them. Do not sin
against the LORD by eating meat with blood
still in it.'"
So everyone brought his ox that night and
slaughtered it there. 35Then Saul built an altar to the LORD; it was the first time he had
done this.
36Saul said, "Let us go down and pursue
the Philistines by night and plunder them till
dawn, and let us not leave one of them alive."
"Do whatever seems best to you," they replied.
But the priest said, "Let us inquire of God
here."
37So Saul asked God, "Shall I go down and
pursue the Philistines? Will you give them
into Israel's hand?" But God did not answer
him that day.
38Saul therefore said, "Come here, all you
who are leaders of the army, and let us find
out what sin has been committed today. 39As
surely as the LORD who rescues Israel lives,
even if the guilt lies with my son Jonathan,
he must die." But not one of them said a word.
40Saul then said to all the Israelites, "You
stand over there; I and Jonathan my son will
stand over here."
"Do what seems best to you," they replied.
41Then Saul prayed to the LORD, the God
of Israel, "Why have you not answered your
servant today? If the fault is in me or my son
Jonathan, respond with Urim, but if the men
of Israel are at fault,[a] respond with Thummim." Jonathan and Saul were taken by lot,
and the men were cleared. 42Saul said, "Cast
the lot between me and Jonathan my son."
And Jonathan was taken.
43Then Saul said to Jonathan, "Tell me what
you have done."
So Jonathan told him, "I tasted a little honey
with the end of my staff. And now I must die!"
44Saul said, "May God deal with me, be it
ever so severely, if you do not die, Jonathan."
45But the men said to Saul, "Should Jonathan die—he who has brought about this
great deliverance in Israel? Never! As surely
as the LORD lives, not a hair of his head will
fall to the ground, for he did this today with
God's help." So the men rescued Jonathan,
and he was not put to death.
46Then Saul stopped pursuing the Philistines, and they withdrew to their own land.
47After Saul had assumed rule over Israel, he fought against their enemies on every
side: Moab, the Ammonites, Edom, the kings[b]
of Zobah, and the Philistines. Wherever he
turned, he inflicted punishment on them.[c]
48He fought valiantly and defeated the Amalekites, delivering Israel from the hands of
those who had plundered them.

Saul's Family

49Saul's sons were Jonathan, Ishvi and Malki-Shua. The name of his older daughter was
Merab, and that of the younger was Michal.
50His wife's name was Ahinoam daughter of
Ahimaaz. The name of the commander of
Saul's army was Abner son of Ner, and Ner
was Saul's uncle. 51Saul's father Kish and Abner's father Ner were sons of Abiel.
52All the days of Saul there was bitter war
with the Philistines, and whenever Saul saw
a mighty or brave man, he took him into his
service.

The LORD Rejects Saul as King

15 Samuel said to Saul, "I am the one the
LORD sent to anoint you king over his
people Israel; so listen now to the message
from the LORD. 2This is what the LORD Almighty says: 'I will punish the Amalekites
for what they did to Israel when they waylaid
them as they came up from Egypt. 3Now go,
attack the Amalekites and totally destroy[d] all
that belongs to them. Do not spare them; put to
death men and women, children and infants,
cattle and sheep, camels and donkeys.'"
4So Saul summoned the men and mustered
them at Telaim—two hundred thousand foot
soldiers and ten thousand from Judah. 5Saul
went to the city of Amalek and set an ambush
in the ravine. 6Then he said to the Kenites, "Go
away, leave the Amalekites so that I do not
destroy you along with them; for you showed
kindness to all the Israelites when they came
up out of Egypt." So the Kenites moved away
from the Amalekites.
7Then Saul attacked the Amalekites all the
way from Havilah to Shur, near the eastern
border of Egypt. 8He took Agag king of the
Amalekites alive, and all his people he totally
destroyed with the sword. 9But Saul and the
army spared Agag and the best of the sheep
and cattle, the fat calves[e] and lambs—everything that was good. These they were unwilling to destroy completely, but everything that
was despised and weak they totally destroyed.

[a] *41* Septuagint; Hebrew does not have "*Why . . . at fault.*" [b] *47* Masoretic Text; Dead Sea Scrolls and Septuagint *king* [c] *47* Hebrew; Septuagint *he was victorious* [d] *3* The Hebrew term refers to the irrevocable giving over of things or persons to the LORD, often by totally destroying them; also in verses 8, 9, 15, 18, 20 and 21. [e] *9* Or *the grown bulls*; the meaning of the Hebrew for this phrase is uncertain.

10Then the word of the LORD came to Samuel: 11"I regret that I have made Saul king,
because he has turned away from me and
has not carried out my instructions." Samuel was angry, and he cried out to the LORD
all that night.
12Early in the morning Samuel got up and
went to meet Saul, but he was told, "Saul has
gone to Carmel. There he has set up a monument in his own honor and has turned and
gone on down to Gilgal."
13When Samuel reached him, Saul said,
"The LORD bless you! I have carried out the
LORD's instructions."
14But Samuel said, "What then is this bleat-
ing of sheep in my ears? What is this lowing
of cattle that I hear?"
15Saul answered, "The soldiers brought
them from the Amalekites; they spared the
best of the sheep and cattle to sacrifice to the
LORD your God, but we totally destroyed the
rest."
16"Enough!" Samuel said to Saul. "Let me
tell you what the LORD said to me last night."
"Tell me," Saul replied.
17Samuel said, "Although you were once
small in your own eyes, did you not become
the head of the tribes of Israel? The LORD
anointed you king over Israel. 18And he sent
you on a mission, saying, 'Go and completely
destroy those wicked people, the Amalekites;
wage war against them until you have wiped
them out.' 19Why did you not obey the LORD?
Why did you pounce on the plunder and do
evil in the eyes of the LORD?"
20"But I did obey the LORD," Saul said. "I
went on the mission the LORD assigned me.
I completely destroyed the Amalekites and
brought back Agag their king. 21The soldiers
took sheep and cattle from the plunder, the
best of what was devoted to God, in order to
sacrifice them to the LORD your God at Gilgal."
22But Samuel replied:

"Does the LORD delight in burnt offerings
and sacrifices
as much as in obeying the LORD?
To obey is better than sacrifice,
and to heed is better than the fat of
rams.
23For rebellion is like the sin of divination,
and arrogance like the evil of idolatry.
Because you have rejected the word of the
LORD,
he has rejected you as king."

24Then Saul said to Samuel, "I have sinned.
I violated the LORD's command and your instructions. I was afraid of the men and so I
gave in to them. 25Now I beg you, forgive my
sin and come back with me, so that I may worship the LORD."
26But Samuel said to him, "I will not go back
with you. You have rejected the word of the
LORD, and the LORD has rejected you as king
over Israel!"
27As Samuel turned to leave, Saul caught
hold of the hem of his robe, and it tore. 28Sam-
uel said to him, "The LORD has torn the kingdom of Israel from you today and has given it
to one of your neighbors—to one better than
you. 29He who is the Glory of Israel does not
lie or change his mind; for he is not a human
being, that he should change his mind."
30Saul replied, "I have sinned. But please
honor me before the elders of my people and
before Israel; come back with me, so that I
may worship the LORD your God." 31So Samuel went back with Saul, and Saul worshiped
the LORD.
32Then Samuel said, "Bring me Agag king
of the Amalekites."
Agag came to him in chains.[a] And he
thought, "Surely the bitterness of death is
past."
33But Samuel said,

"As your sword has made women
childless,
so will your mother be childless among
women."

And Samuel put Agag to death before the
LORD at Gilgal.
34Then Samuel left for Ramah, but Saul
went up to his home in Gibeah of Saul. 35Un-
til the day Samuel died, he did not go to see
Saul again, though Samuel mourned for him.
And the LORD regretted that he had made Saul
king over Israel.

Samuel Anoints David

16 The LORD said to Samuel, "How long will
you mourn for Saul, since I have rejected
him as king over Israel? Fill your horn with
oil and be on your way; I am sending you to
Jesse of Bethlehem. I have chosen one of his
sons to be king."
2But Samuel said, "How can I go? If Saul
hears about it, he will kill me."
The LORD said, "Take a heifer with you and
say, 'I have come to sacrifice to the LORD.' 3In-
vite Jesse to the sacrifice, and I will show you
what to do. You are to anoint for me the one
I indicate."
4Samuel did what the LORD said. When he
arrived at Bethlehem, the elders of the town
trembled when they met him. They asked, "Do
you come in peace?"
5Samuel replied, "Yes, in peace; I have come
to sacrifice to the LORD. Consecrate yourselves
and come to the sacrifice with me." Then he
consecrated Jesse and his sons and invited
them to the sacrifice.
6When they arrived, Samuel saw Eliab and
thought, "Surely the LORD's anointed stands
here before the LORD."
7But the LORD said to Samuel, "Do not consider his appearance or his height, for I have
rejected him. The LORD does not look at the
things people look at. People look at the outward appearance, but the LORD looks at the
heart."
8Then Jesse called Abinadab and had him
pass in front of Samuel. But Samuel said, "The
LORD has not chosen this one either." 9Jesse

[a] *32* The meaning of the Hebrew for this phrase is uncertain.

then had Shammah pass by, but Samuel said,
"Nor has the LORD chosen this one." 10Jesse
had seven of his sons pass before Samuel, but
Samuel said to him, "The LORD has not chosen
these." 11So he asked Jesse, "Are these all the
sons you have?"

"There is still the youngest," Jesse answered. "He is tending the sheep."

Samuel said, "Send for him; we will not sit
down until he arrives."

12So he sent for him and had him brought
in. He was glowing with health and had a fine
appearance and handsome features.

Then the LORD said, "Rise and anoint him;
this is the one."

13So Samuel took the horn of oil and anointed him in the presence of his brothers, and
from that day on the Spirit of the LORD came
powerfully upon David. Samuel then went to
Ramah.

David in Saul's Service

14Now the Spirit of the LORD had departed
from Saul, and an evil[a] spirit from the LORD
tormented him.

15Saul's attendants said to him, "See, an evil
spirit from God is tormenting you. 16Let our
lord command his servants here to search for
someone who can play the lyre. He will play
when the evil spirit from God comes on you,
and you will feel better."

17So Saul said to his attendants, "Find someone who plays well and bring him to me."

18One of the servants answered, "I have
seen a son of Jesse of Bethlehem who knows
how to play the lyre. He is a brave man and a
warrior. He speaks well and is a fine-looking
man. And the LORD is with him."

19Then Saul sent messengers to Jesse and
said, "Send me your son David, who is with
the sheep." 20So Jesse took a donkey loaded
with bread, a skin of wine and a young goat
and sent them with his son David to Saul.

21David came to Saul and entered his service. Saul liked him very much, and David
became one of his armor-bearers. 22Then Saul
sent word to Jesse, saying, "Allow David to
remain in my service, for I am pleased with
him."

23Whenever the spirit from God came on
Saul, David would take up his lyre and play.
Then relief would come to Saul; he would feel
better, and the evil spirit would leave him.

David and Goliath

17 Now the Philistines gathered their forces
for war and assembled at Sokoh in Judah. They pitched camp at Ephes Dammim,
between Sokoh and Azekah. 2Saul and the
Israelites assembled and camped in the Valley
of Elah and drew up their battle line to meet
the Philistines. 3The Philistines occupied one
hill and the Israelites another, with the valley
between them.

4A champion named Goliath, who was from
Gath, came out of the Philistine camp. His
height was six cubits and a span.[b] 5He had a
bronze helmet on his head and wore a coat of
scale armor of bronze weighing five thousand
shekels[c]; 6on his legs he wore bronze greaves,
and a bronze javelin was slung on his back.
7His spear shaft was like a weaver's rod, and
its iron point weighed six hundred shekels.[d]
His shield bearer went ahead of him.

8Goliath stood and shouted to the ranks of
Israel, "Why do you come out and line up for
battle? Am I not a Philistine, and are you not
the servants of Saul? Choose a man and have
him come down to me. 9If he is able to fight and
kill me, we will become your subjects; but if I
overcome him and kill him, you will become
our subjects and serve us." 10Then the Philistine said, "This day I defy the armies of Israel!
Give me a man and let us fight each other."
11On hearing the Philistine's words, Saul and
all the Israelites were dismayed and terrified.

12Now David was the son of an Ephrathite
named Jesse, who was from Bethlehem in Judah. Jesse had eight sons, and in Saul's time
he was very old. 13Jesse's three oldest sons had
followed Saul to the war: The firstborn was
Eliab; the second, Abinadab; and the third,
Shammah. 14David was the youngest. The
three oldest followed Saul, 15but David went
back and forth from Saul to tend his father's
sheep at Bethlehem.

16For forty days the Philistine came forward every morning and evening and took
his stand.

17Now Jesse said to his son David, "Take
this ephah[e] of roasted grain and these ten
loaves of bread for your brothers and hurry
to their camp. 18Take along these ten cheeses
to the commander of their unit. See how your
brothers are and bring back some assurance[f]
from them. 19They are with Saul and all the
men of Israel in the Valley of Elah, fighting
against the Philistines."

20Early in the morning David left the flock
in the care of a shepherd, loaded up and set
out, as Jesse had directed. He reached the
camp as the army was going out to its battle
positions, shouting the war cry. 21Israel and
the Philistines were drawing up their lines
facing each other. 22David left his things with
the keeper of supplies, ran to the battle lines
and asked his brothers how they were. 23As
he was talking with them, Goliath, the Philistine champion from Gath, stepped out from
his lines and shouted his usual defiance, and
David heard it. 24Whenever the Israelites saw
the man, they all fled from him in great fear.

25Now the Israelites had been saying, "Do
you see how this man keeps coming out? He
comes out to defy Israel. The king will give
great wealth to the man who kills him. He will
also give him his daughter in marriage and
will exempt his family from taxes in Israel."

[a] 14 Or *and a harmful*; similarly in verses 15, 16 and 23 [b] 4 That is, about 9 feet 9 inches or about 3 meters [c] 5 That is, about 125 pounds or about 58 kilograms [d] 7 That is, about 15 pounds or about 6.9 kilograms [e] 17 That is, probably about 36 pounds or about 16 kilograms [f] 18 Or *some token*; or *some pledge of spoils*

26David asked the men standing near him, "What will be done for the man who kills this Philistine and removes this disgrace from Israel? Who is this uncircumcised Philistine that he should defy the armies of the living God?"

27They repeated to him what they had been saying and told him, "This is what will be done for the man who kills him."

28When Eliab, David's oldest brother, heard him speaking with the men, he burned with anger at him and asked, "Why have you come down here? And with whom did you leave those few sheep in the wilderness? I know how conceited you are and how wicked your heart is; you came down only to watch the battle."

29"Now what have I done?" said David. "Can't I even speak?" 30He then turned away to someone else and brought up the same matter, and the men answered him as before. 31What David said was overheard and reported to Saul, and Saul sent for him.

32David said to Saul, "Let no one lose heart on account of this Philistine; your servant will go and fight him."

33Saul replied, "You are not able to go out against this Philistine and fight him; you are only a young man, and he has been a warrior from his youth."

34But David said to Saul, "Your servant has been keeping his father's sheep. When a lion or a bear came and carried off a sheep from the flock, 35I went after it, struck it and rescued the sheep from its mouth. When it turned on me, I seized it by its hair, struck it and killed it. 36Your servant has killed both the lion and the bear; this uncircumcised Philistine will be like one of them, because he has defied the armies of the living God. 37The LORD who rescued me from the paw of the lion and the paw of the bear will rescue me from the hand of this Philistine."

Saul said to David, "Go, and the LORD be with you."

38Then Saul dressed David in his own tunic. He put a coat of armor on him and a bronze helmet on his head. 39David fastened on his sword over the tunic and tried walking around, because he was not used to them.

"I cannot go in these," he said to Saul, "because I am not used to them." So he took them off. 40Then he took his staff in his hand, chose five smooth stones from the stream, put them in the pouch of his shepherd's bag and, with his sling in his hand, approached the Philistine.

41Meanwhile, the Philistine, with his shield bearer in front of him, kept coming closer to David. 42He looked David over and saw that he was little more than a boy, glowing with health and handsome, and he despised him. 43He said to David, "Am I a dog, that you come at me with sticks?" And the Philistine cursed David by his gods. 44"Come here," he said, "and I'll give your flesh to the birds and the wild animals!"

45David said to the Philistine, "You come against me with sword and spear and javelin, but I come against you in the name of the LORD Almighty, the God of the armies of Israel, whom you have defied. 46This day the LORD will deliver you into my hands, and I'll strike you down and cut off your head. This very day I will give the carcasses of the Philistine army to the birds and the wild animals, and the whole world will know that there is a God in Israel. 47All those gathered here will know that it is not by sword or spear that the LORD saves; for the battle is the LORD's, and he will give all of you into our hands."

48As the Philistine moved closer to attack him, David ran quickly toward the battle line to meet him. 49Reaching into his bag and taking out a stone, he slung it and struck the Philistine on the forehead. The stone sank into his forehead, and he fell facedown on the ground.

50So David triumphed over the Philistine with a sling and a stone; without a sword in his hand he struck down the Philistine and killed him.

51David ran and stood over him. He took hold of the Philistine's sword and drew it from the sheath. After he killed him, he cut off his head with the sword.

When the Philistines saw that their hero was dead, they turned and ran. 52Then the men of Israel and Judah surged forward with a shout and pursued the Philistines to the entrance of Gath[a] and to the gates of Ekron. Their dead were strewn along the Shaaraim road to Gath and Ekron. 53When the Israelites returned from chasing the Philistines, they plundered their camp.

54David took the Philistine's head and brought it to Jerusalem; he put the Philistine's weapons in his own tent.

55As Saul watched David going out to meet the Philistine, he said to Abner, commander of the army, "Abner, whose son is that young man?"

Abner replied, "As surely as you live, Your Majesty, I don't know."

56The king said, "Find out whose son this young man is."

57As soon as David returned from killing the Philistine, Abner took him and brought him before Saul, with David still holding the Philistine's head.

58"Whose son are you, young man?" Saul asked him.

David said, "I am the son of your servant Jesse of Bethlehem."

Saul's Growing Fear of David

18 After David had finished talking with Saul, Jonathan became one in spirit with David, and he loved him as himself. 2From that day Saul kept David with him and did not let him return home to his family. 3And Jonathan made a covenant with David because he loved him as himself. 4Jonathan took off the robe he was wearing and gave it to David, along with his tunic, and even his sword, his bow and his belt.

5Whatever mission Saul sent him on, David

[a] 52 Some Septuagint manuscripts; Hebrew *of a valley*

was so successful that Saul gave him a high rank in the army. This pleased all the troops, and Saul's officers as well.

6When the men were returning home after David had killed the Philistine, the women came out from all the towns of Israel to meet King Saul with singing and dancing, with joyful songs and with timbrels and lyres. 7As they danced, they sang:

"Saul has slain his thousands,
  and David his tens of thousands."

8Saul was very angry; this refrain displeased him greatly. "They have credited David with tens of thousands," he thought, "but me with only thousands. What more can he get but the kingdom?" 9And from that time on Saul kept a close eye on David.

10The next day an evil[a] spirit from God came forcefully on Saul. He was prophesying in his house, while David was playing the lyre, as he usually did. Saul had a spear in his hand 11and he hurled it, saying to himself, "I'll pin David to the wall." But David eluded him twice.

12Saul was afraid of David, because the LORD was with David but had departed from Saul. 13So he sent David away from him and gave him command over a thousand men, and David led the troops in their campaigns. 14In everything he did he had great success, because the LORD was with him. 15When Saul saw how successful he was, he was afraid of him. 16But all Israel and Judah loved David, because he led them in their campaigns.

17Saul said to David, "Here is my older daughter Merab. I will give her to you in marriage; only serve me bravely and fight the battles of the LORD." For Saul said to himself, "I will not raise a hand against him. Let the Philistines do that!"

18But David said to Saul, "Who am I, and what is my family or my clan in Israel, that I should become the king's son-in-law?" 19So[b] when the time came for Merab, Saul's daughter, to be given to David, she was given in marriage to Adriel of Meholah.

20Now Saul's daughter Michal was in love with David, and when they told Saul about it, he was pleased. 21"I will give her to him," he thought, "so that she may be a snare to him and so that the hand of the Philistines may be against him." So Saul said to David, "Now you have a second opportunity to become my son-in-law."

22Then Saul ordered his attendants: "Speak to David privately and say, 'Look, the king likes you, and his attendants all love you; now become his son-in-law.'"

23They repeated these words to David. But David said, "Do you think it is a small matter to become the king's son-in-law? I'm only a poor man and little known."

24When Saul's servants told him what David had said, 25Saul replied, "Say to David, 'The king wants no other price for the bride than a hundred Philistine foreskins, to take revenge on his enemies.'" Saul's plan was to have David fall by the hands of the Philistines.

26When the attendants told David these things, he was pleased to become the king's son-in-law. So before the allotted time elapsed, 27David took his men with him and went out and killed two hundred Philistines and brought back their foreskins. They counted out the full number to the king so that David might become the king's son-in-law. Then Saul gave him his daughter Michal in marriage.

28When Saul realized that the LORD was with David and that his daughter Michal loved David, 29Saul became still more afraid of him, and he remained his enemy the rest of his days.

30The Philistine commanders continued to go out to battle, and as often as they did, David met with more success than the rest of Saul's officers, and his name became well known.

Saul Tries to Kill David

19 Saul told his son Jonathan and all the attendants to kill David. But Jonathan had taken a great liking to David 2and warned him, "My father Saul is looking for a chance to kill you. Be on your guard tomorrow morning; go into hiding and stay there. 3I will go out and stand with my father in the field where you are. I'll speak to him about you and will tell you what I find out."

4Jonathan spoke well of David to Saul his father and said to him, "Let not the king do wrong to his servant David; he has not wronged you, and what he has done has benefited you greatly. 5He took his life in his hands when he killed the Philistine. The LORD won a great victory for all Israel, and you saw it and were glad. Why then would you do wrong to an innocent man like David by killing him for no reason?"

6Saul listened to Jonathan and took this oath: "As surely as the LORD lives, David will not be put to death."

7So Jonathan called David and told him the whole conversation. He brought him to Saul, and David was with Saul as before.

8Once more war broke out, and David went out and fought the Philistines. He struck them with such force that they fled before him.

9But an evil[c] spirit from the LORD came on Saul as he was sitting in his house with his spear in his hand. While David was playing the lyre, 10Saul tried to pin him to the wall with his spear, but David eluded him as Saul drove the spear into the wall. That night David made good his escape.

11Saul sent men to David's house to watch it and to kill him in the morning. But Michal, David's wife, warned him, "If you don't run for your life tonight, tomorrow you'll be killed." 12So Michal let David down through a window, and he fled and escaped. 13Then Michal took an idol and laid it on the bed, covering it with a garment and putting some goats' hair at the head.

[a] 10 Or *a harmful* [b] 19 Or *However,* [c] 9 Or *But a harmful*

14When Saul sent the men to capture David, Michal said, "He is ill."

15Then Saul sent the men back to see David and told them, "Bring him up to me in his bed so that I may kill him." 16But when the men entered, there was the idol in the bed, and at the head was some goats' hair.

17Saul said to Michal, "Why did you deceive me like this and send my enemy away so that he escaped?"

Michal told him, "He said to me, 'Let me get away. Why should I kill you?' "

18When David had fled and made his escape, he went to Samuel at Ramah and told him all that Saul had done to him. Then he and Samuel went to Naioth and stayed there. 19Word came to Saul: "David is in Naioth at Ramah"; 20so he sent men to capture him. But when they saw a group of prophets prophesying, with Samuel standing there as their leader, the Spirit of God came on Saul's men, and they also prophesied. 21Saul was told about it, and he sent more men, and they prophesied too. Saul sent men a third time, and they also prophesied. 22Finally, he himself left for Ramah and went to the great cistern at Seku. And he asked, "Where are Samuel and David?"

"Over in Naioth at Ramah," they said.

23So Saul went to Naioth at Ramah. But the Spirit of God came even on him, and he walked along prophesying until he came to Naioth. 24He stripped off his garments, and he too prophesied in Samuel's presence. He lay naked all that day and all that night. This is why people say, "Is Saul also among the prophets?"

David and Jonathan

20 Then David fled from Naioth at Ramah and went to Jonathan and asked, "What have I done? What is my crime? How have I wronged your father, that he is trying to kill me?"

2"Never!" Jonathan replied. "You are not going to die! Look, my father doesn't do anything, great or small, without letting me know. Why would he hide this from me? It isn't so!"

3But David took an oath and said, "Your father knows very well that I have found favor in your eyes, and he has said to himself, 'Jonathan must not know this or he will be grieved.' Yet as surely as the LORD lives and as you live, there is only a step between me and death."

4Jonathan said to David, "Whatever you want me to do, I'll do for you."

5So David said, "Look, tomorrow is the New Moon feast, and I am supposed to dine with the king; but let me go and hide in the field until the evening of the day after tomorrow. 6If your father misses me at all, tell him, 'David earnestly asked my permission to hurry to Bethlehem, his hometown, because an annual sacrifice is being made there for his whole clan.' 7If he says, 'Very well,' then your servant is safe. But if he loses his temper, you can be sure that he is determined to harm me. 8As for you, show kindness to your servant, for you have brought him into a covenant with you before the LORD. If I am guilty, then kill me yourself! Why hand me over to your father?"

9"Never!" Jonathan said. "If I had the least inkling that my father was determined to harm you, wouldn't I tell you?"

10David asked, "Who will tell me if your father answers you harshly?"

11"Come," Jonathan said, "let's go out into the field." So they went there together.

12Then Jonathan said to David, "I swear by the LORD, the God of Israel, that I will surely sound out my father by this time the day after tomorrow! If he is favorably disposed toward you, will I not send you word and let you know? 13But if my father intends to harm you, may the LORD deal with Jonathan, be it ever so severely, if I do not let you know and send you away in peace. May the LORD be with you as he has been with my father. 14But show me unfailing kindness like the LORD's kindness as long as I live, so that I may not be killed, 15and do not ever cut off your kindness from my family—not even when the LORD has cut off every one of David's enemies from the face of the earth."

16So Jonathan made a covenant with the house of David, saying, "May the LORD call David's enemies to account." 17And Jonathan had David reaffirm his oath out of love for him, because he loved him as he loved himself.

18Then Jonathan said to David, "Tomorrow is the New Moon feast. You will be missed, because your seat will be empty. 19The day after tomorrow, toward evening, go to the place where you hid when this trouble began, and wait by the stone Ezel. 20I will shoot three arrows to the side of it, as though I were shooting at a target. 21Then I will send a boy and say, 'Go, find the arrows.' If I say to him, 'Look, the arrows are on this side of you; bring them here,' then come, because, as surely as the LORD lives, you are safe; there is no danger. 22But if I say to the boy, 'Look, the arrows are beyond you,' then you must go, because the LORD has sent you away. 23And about the matter you and I discussed—remember, the LORD is witness between you and me forever."

24So David hid in the field, and when the New Moon feast came, the king sat down to eat. 25He sat in his customary place by the wall, opposite Jonathan,[a] and Abner sat next to Saul, but David's place was empty. 26Saul said nothing that day, for he thought, "Something must have happened to David to make him ceremonially unclean—surely he is unclean." 27But the next day, the second day of the month, David's place was empty again. Then Saul said to his son Jonathan, "Why hasn't the son of Jesse come to the meal, either yesterday or today?"

28Jonathan answered, "David earnestly asked me for permission to go to Bethlehem. 29He said, 'Let me go, because our family is observing a sacrifice in the town and my brother

[a] 25 Septuagint; Hebrew *wall. Jonathan arose*

has ordered me to be there. If I have found
favor in your eyes, let me get away to see my
brothers.' That is why he has not come to the
king's table."
30Saul's anger flared up at Jonathan and he
said to him, "You son of a perverse and rebellious woman! Don't I know that you have sided
with the son of Jesse to your own shame and
to the shame of the mother who bore you? 31As
long as the son of Jesse lives on this earth,
neither you nor your kingdom will be established. Now send someone to bring him to me,
for he must die!"
32"Why should he be put to death? What has
he done?" Jonathan asked his father. 33But
Saul hurled his spear at him to kill him. Then
Jonathan knew that his father intended to kill
David.
34Jonathan got up from the table in fierce
anger; on that second day of the feast he did
not eat, because he was grieved at his father's
shameful treatment of David.
35In the morning Jonathan went out to the
field for his meeting with David. He had a
small boy with him, 36and he said to the boy,
"Run and find the arrows I shoot." As the boy
ran, he shot an arrow beyond him. 37When
the boy came to the place where Jonathan's
arrow had fallen, Jonathan called out after
him, "Isn't the arrow beyond you?" 38Then he
shouted, "Hurry! Go quickly! Don't stop!" The
boy picked up the arrow and returned to his
master. 39(The boy knew nothing about all
this; only Jonathan and David knew.) 40Then
Jonathan gave his weapons to the boy and
said, "Go, carry them back to town."
41After the boy had gone, David got up from
the south side of the stone and bowed down
before Jonathan three times, with his face to
the ground. Then they kissed each other and
wept together—but David wept the most.
42Jonathan said to David, "Go in peace, for
we have sworn friendship with each other in
the name of the LORD, saying, 'The LORD is
witness between you and me, and between
your descendants and my descendants forever.'" Then David left, and Jonathan went
back to the town.[a]

David at Nob

21[b] David went to Nob, to Ahimelek the
priest. Ahimelek trembled when he met
him, and asked, "Why are you alone? Why is
no one with you?"
2David answered Ahimelek the priest, "The
king sent me on a mission and said to me, 'No
one is to know anything about the mission I
am sending you on.' As for my men, I have
told them to meet me at a certain place. 3Now
then, what do you have on hand? Give me five
loaves of bread, or whatever you can find."
4But the priest answered David, "I don't
have any ordinary bread on hand; however,
there is some consecrated bread here—provided the men have kept themselves from
women."
5David replied, "Indeed women have been
kept from us, as usual whenever[c] I set out.
The men's bodies are holy even on missions
that are not holy. How much more so today!"
6So the priest gave him the consecrated
bread, since there was no bread there except
the bread of the Presence that had been removed from before the LORD and replaced by
hot bread on the day it was taken away.
7Now one of Saul's servants was there that
day, detained before the LORD; he was Doeg
the Edomite, Saul's chief shepherd.
8David asked Ahimelek, "Don't you have
a spear or a sword here? I haven't brought
my sword or any other weapon, because the
king's mission was urgent."
9The priest replied, "The sword of Goliath
the Philistine, whom you killed in the Valley
of Elah, is here; it is wrapped in a cloth behind
the ephod. If you want it, take it; there is no
sword here but that one."
David said, "There is none like it; give it
to me."

David at Gath

10That day David fled from Saul and went
to Achish king of Gath. 11But the servants of
Achish said to him, "Isn't this David, the king
of the land? Isn't he the one they sing about
in their dances:

"'Saul has slain his thousands,
and David his tens of thousands'?"

12David took these words to heart and was
very much afraid of Achish king of Gath. 13So
he pretended to be insane in their presence;
and while he was in their hands he acted like
a madman, making marks on the doors of the
gate and letting saliva run down his beard.
14Achish said to his servants, "Look at the
man! He is insane! Why bring him to me?
15Am I so short of madmen that you have to
bring this fellow here to carry on like this
in front of me? Must this man come into my
house?"

David at Adullam and Mizpah

22 David left Gath and escaped to the cave
of Adullam. When his brothers and his
father's household heard about it, they went
down to him there. 2All those who were in
distress or in debt or discontented gathered
around him, and he became their commander. About four hundred men were with him.
3From there David went to Mizpah in Moab
and said to the king of Moab, "Would you let
my father and mother come and stay with you
until I learn what God will do for me?" 4So
he left them with the king of Moab, and they
stayed with him as long as David was in the
stronghold.
5But the prophet Gad said to David, "Do
not stay in the stronghold. Go into the land
of Judah." So David left and went to the forest of Hereth.

[a] 42 In Hebrew texts this sentence (20:42b) is numbered 21:1. [b] In Hebrew texts 21:1-15 is numbered 21:2-16. [c] 5 Or *from us in the past few days since*

Saul Kills the Priests of Nob

[6]Now Saul heard that David and his men
had been discovered. And Saul was seated,
spear in hand, under the tamarisk tree on the
hill at Gibeah, with all his officials standing
at his side. [7]He said to them, "Listen, men of
Benjamin! Will the son of Jesse give all of you
fields and vineyards? Will he make all of you
commanders of thousands and commanders
of hundreds? [8]Is that why you have all conspired against me? No one tells me when my
son makes a covenant with the son of Jesse.
None of you is concerned about me or tells
me that my son has incited my servant to lie
in wait for me, as he does today."

[9]But Doeg the Edomite, who was standing
with Saul's officials, said, "I saw the son of
Jesse come to Ahimelek son of Ahitub at Nob.
[10]Ahimelek inquired of the LORD for him; he
also gave him provisions and the sword of
Goliath the Philistine."

[11]Then the king sent for the priest Ahimelek
son of Ahitub and all the men of his family, who were the priests at Nob, and they all
came to the king. [12]Saul said, "Listen now,
son of Ahitub."

"Yes, my lord," he answered.

[13]Saul said to him, "Why have you conspired against me, you and the son of Jesse,
giving him bread and a sword and inquiring
of God for him, so that he has rebelled against
me and lies in wait for me, as he does today?"

[14]Ahimelek answered the king, "Who of all
your servants is as loyal as David, the king's
son-in-law, captain of your bodyguard and
highly respected in your household? [15]Was
that day the first time I inquired of God for
him? Of course not! Let not the king accuse
your servant or any of his father's family, for
your servant knows nothing at all about this
whole affair."

[16]But the king said, "You will surely die,
Ahimelek, you and your whole family."

[17]Then the king ordered the guards at his
side: "Turn and kill the priests of the LORD,
because they too have sided with David. They
knew he was fleeing, yet they did not tell me."

But the king's officials were unwilling to
raise a hand to strike the priests of the LORD.

[18]The king then ordered Doeg, "You turn
and strike down the priests." So Doeg the
Edomite turned and struck them down. That
day he killed eighty-five men who wore the
linen ephod. [19]He also put to the sword Nob,
the town of the priests, with its men and wom-
en, its children and infants, and its cattle, donkeys and sheep.

[20]But one son of Ahimelek son of Ahitub,
named Abiathar, escaped and fled to join David. [21]He told David that Saul had killed the
priests of the LORD. [22]Then David said to Abiathar, "That day, when Doeg the Edomite was
there, I knew he would be sure to tell Saul. I
am responsible for the death of your whole
family. [23]Stay with me; don't be afraid. The
man who wants to kill you is trying to kill me
too. You will be safe with me."

David Saves Keilah

23 When David was told, "Look, the Philistines are fighting against Keilah and
are looting the threshing floors," [2]he inquired
of the LORD, saying, "Shall I go and attack
these Philistines?"

The LORD answered him, "Go, attack the
Philistines and save Keilah."

[3]But David's men said to him, "Here in Judah we are afraid. How much more, then, if
we go to Keilah against the Philistine forces!"

[4]Once again David inquired of the LORD,
and the LORD answered him, "Go down to
Keilah, for I am going to give the Philistines
into your hand." [5]So David and his men went
to Keilah, fought the Philistines and carried
off their livestock. He inflicted heavy losses on the Philistines and saved the people of
Keilah. [6](Now Abiathar son of Ahimelek had
brought the ephod down with him when he
fled to David at Keilah.)

Saul Pursues David

[7]Saul was told that David had gone to Keilah, and he said, "God has delivered him into
my hands, for David has imprisoned himself
by entering a town with gates and bars." [8]And
Saul called up all his forces for battle, to go
down to Keilah to besiege David and his men.

[9]When David learned that Saul was plotting
against him, he said to Abiathar the priest,
"Bring the ephod." [10]David said, "LORD, God of
Israel, your servant has heard definitely that
Saul plans to come to Keilah and destroy the
town on account of me. [11]Will the citizens of
Keilah surrender me to him? Will Saul come
down, as your servant has heard? LORD, God
of Israel, tell your servant."

And the LORD said, "He will."

[12]Again David asked, "Will the citizens of
Keilah surrender me and my men to Saul?"

And the LORD said, "They will."

[13]So David and his men, about six hundred
in number, left Keilah and kept moving from
place to place. When Saul was told that David
had escaped from Keilah, he did not go there.

[14]David stayed in the wilderness strongholds and in the hills of the Desert of Ziph.
Day after day Saul searched for him, but God
did not give David into his hands.

[15]While David was at Horesh in the Desert of Ziph, he learned that[a] Saul had come
out to take his life. [16]And Saul's son Jonathan
went to David at Horesh and helped him find
strength in God. [17]"Don't be afraid," he said.
"My father Saul will not lay a hand on you.
You will be king over Israel, and I will be second to you. Even my father Saul knows this."
[18]The two of them made a covenant before the
LORD. Then Jonathan went home, but David
remained at Horesh.

[19]The Ziphites went up to Saul at Gibeah
and said, "Is not David hiding among us in
the strongholds at Horesh, on the hill of Hakilah, south of Jeshimon? [20]Now, Your Majesty,
come down whenever it pleases you to do so,

[a] 15 Or *he was afraid because*

and we will be responsible for giving him into your hands."

21 Saul replied, "The LORD bless you for your concern for me. 22 Go and get more information. Find out where David usually goes and who has seen him there. They tell me he is very crafty. 23 Find out about all the hiding places he uses and come back to me with definite information. Then I will go with you; if he is in the area, I will track him down among all the clans of Judah."

24 So they set out and went to Ziph ahead of Saul. Now David and his men were in the Desert of Maon, in the Arabah south of Jeshimon. 25 Saul and his men began the search, and when David was told about it, he went down to the rock and stayed in the Desert of Maon. When Saul heard this, he went into the Desert of Maon in pursuit of David.

26 Saul was going along one side of the mountain, and David and his men were on the other side, hurrying to get away from Saul. As Saul and his forces were closing in on David and his men to capture them, 27 a messenger came to Saul, saying, "Come quickly! The Philistines are raiding the land." 28 Then Saul broke off his pursuit of David and went to meet the Philistines. That is why they call this place Sela Hammahlekoth.[a] 29 And David went up from there and lived in the strongholds of En Gedi.[b]

David Spares Saul's Life

24[c] After Saul returned from pursuing the Philistines, he was told, "David is in the Desert of En Gedi." 2 So Saul took three thousand able young men from all Israel and set out to look for David and his men near the Crags of the Wild Goats.

3 He came to the sheep pens along the way; a cave was there, and Saul went in to relieve himself. David and his men were far back in the cave. 4 The men said, "This is the day the LORD spoke of when he said[d] to you, 'I will give your enemy into your hands for you to deal with as you wish.'" Then David crept up unnoticed and cut off a corner of Saul's robe.

5 Afterward, David was conscience-stricken for having cut off a corner of his robe. 6 He said to his men, "The LORD forbid that I should do such a thing to my master, the LORD's anointed, or lay my hand on him; for he is the anointed of the LORD." 7 With these words David sharply rebuked his men and did not allow them to attack Saul. And Saul left the cave and went his way.

8 Then David went out of the cave and called out to Saul, "My lord the king!" When Saul looked behind him, David bowed down and prostrated himself with his face to the ground. 9 He said to Saul, "Why do you listen when men say, 'David is bent on harming you'? 10 This day you have seen with your own eyes how the LORD delivered you into my hands in the cave. Some urged me to kill you, but I spared you; I said, 'I will not lay my hand on my lord, because he is the LORD's anointed.' 11 See, my father, look at this piece of your robe in my hand! I cut off the corner of your robe but did not kill you. See that there is nothing in my hand to indicate that I am guilty of wrongdoing or rebellion. I have not wronged you, but you are hunting me down to take my life. 12 May the LORD judge between you and me. And may the LORD avenge the wrongs you have done to me, but my hand will not touch you. 13 As the old saying goes, 'From evildoers come evil deeds,' so my hand will not touch you.

14 "Against whom has the king of Israel come out? Who are you pursuing? A dead dog? A flea? 15 May the LORD be our judge and decide between us. May he consider my cause and uphold it; may he vindicate me by delivering me from your hand."

16 When David finished saying this, Saul asked, "Is that your voice, David my son?" And he wept aloud. 17 "You are more righteous than I," he said. "You have treated me well, but I have treated you badly. 18 You have just now told me about the good you did to me; the LORD delivered me into your hands, but you did not kill me. 19 When a man finds his enemy, does he let him get away unharmed? May the LORD reward you well for the way you treated me today. 20 I know that you will surely be king and that the kingdom of Israel will be established in your hands. 21 Now swear to me by the LORD that you will not kill off my descendants or wipe out my name from my father's family."

22 So David gave his oath to Saul. Then Saul returned home, but David and his men went up to the stronghold.

David, Nabal and Abigail

25 Now Samuel died, and all Israel assembled and mourned for him; and they buried him at his home in Ramah. Then David moved down into the Desert of Paran.[e]

2 A certain man in Maon, who had property there at Carmel, was very wealthy. He had a thousand goats and three thousand sheep, which he was shearing in Carmel. 3 His name was Nabal and his wife's name was Abigail. She was an intelligent and beautiful woman, but her husband was surly and mean in his dealings—he was a Calebite.

4 While David was in the wilderness, he heard that Nabal was shearing sheep. 5 So he sent ten young men and said to them, "Go up to Nabal at Carmel and greet him in my name. 6 Say to him: 'Long life to you! Good health to you and your household! And good health to all that is yours!

7 " 'Now I hear that it is sheep-shearing time. When your shepherds were with us, we did not mistreat them, and the whole time they were at Carmel nothing of theirs was missing. 8 Ask your own servants and they will tell

[a] *28 Sela Hammahlekoth* means *rock of parting.* [b] *29* In Hebrew texts this verse (23:29) is numbered 24:1. [c] In Hebrew texts 24:1-22 is numbered 24:2-23. [d] *4* Or *"Today the LORD is saying*
[e] *1* Hebrew and some Septuagint manuscripts; other Septuagint manuscripts *Maon*

you. Therefore be favorable toward my men,
since we come at a festive time. Please give
your servants and your son David whatever
you can find for them.'"
9When David's men arrived, they gave Nabal this message in David's name. Then they
waited.
10Nabal answered David's servants, "Who
is this David? Who is this son of Jesse? Many
servants are breaking away from their masters these days. 11Why should I take my bread
and water, and the meat I have slaughtered for
my shearers, and give it to men coming from
who knows where?"
12David's men turned around and went
back. When they arrived, they reported every
word. 13David said to his men, "Each of you
strap on your sword!" So they did, and David
strapped his on as well. About four hundred
men went up with David, while two hundred
stayed with the supplies.
14One of the servants told Abigail, Nabal's
wife, "David sent messengers from the wilderness to give our master his greetings, but he
hurled insults at them. 15Yet these men were
very good to us. They did not mistreat us, and
the whole time we were out in the fields near
them nothing was missing. 16Night and day
they were a wall around us the whole time
we were herding our sheep near them. 17Now
think it over and see what you can do, because
disaster is hanging over our master and his
whole household. He is such a wicked man
that no one can talk to him."
18Abigail acted quickly. She took two hundred loaves of bread, two skins of wine, five
dressed sheep, five seahs[a] of roasted grain,
a hundred cakes of raisins and two hundred
cakes of pressed figs, and loaded them on
donkeys. 19Then she told her servants, "Go
on ahead; I'll follow you." But she did not tell
her husband Nabal.
20As she came riding her donkey into a
mountain ravine, there were David and his
men descending toward her, and she met
them. 21David had just said, "It's been useless—all my watching over this fellow's property in the wilderness so that nothing of his
was missing. He has paid me back evil for
good. 22May God deal with David,[b] be it ever
so severely, if by morning I leave alive one
male of all who belong to him!"
23When Abigail saw David, she quickly got
off her donkey and bowed down before David
with her face to the ground. 24She fell at his
feet and said: "Pardon your servant, my lord,
and let me speak to you; hear what your servant has to say. 25Please pay no attention, my
lord, to that wicked man Nabal. He is just like
his name—his name means Fool, and folly
goes with him. And as for me, your servant,
I did not see the men my lord sent. 26And now,
my lord, as surely as the LORD your God lives
and as you live, since the LORD has kept you
from bloodshed and from avenging yourself
with your own hands, may your enemies and
all who are intent on harming my lord be like
Nabal. 27And let this gift, which your servant
has brought to my lord, be given to the men
who follow you.
28"Please forgive your servant's presumption. The LORD your God will certainly make
a lasting dynasty for my lord, because you
fight the LORD's battles, and no wrongdoing
will be found in you as long as you live. 29Even
though someone is pursuing you to take your
life, the life of my lord will be bound securely
in the bundle of the living by the LORD your
God, but the lives of your enemies he will hurl
away as from the pocket of a sling. 30When
the LORD has fulfilled for my lord every good
thing he promised concerning him and has
appointed him ruler over Israel, 31my lord
will not have on his conscience the staggering burden of needless bloodshed or of having
avenged himself. And when the LORD your
God has brought my lord success, remember
your servant."
32David said to Abigail, "Praise be to the
LORD, the God of Israel, who has sent you
today to meet me. 33May you be blessed for
your good judgment and for keeping me from
bloodshed this day and from avenging myself
with my own hands. 34Otherwise, as surely
as the LORD, the God of Israel, lives, who has
kept me from harming you, if you had not
come quickly to meet me, not one male belonging to Nabal would have been left alive
by daybreak."
35Then David accepted from her hand what
she had brought him and said, "Go home in
peace. I have heard your words and granted
your request."
36When Abigail went to Nabal, he was in the
house holding a banquet like that of a king. He
was in high spirits and very drunk. So she told
him nothing at all until daybreak. 37Then in
the morning, when Nabal was sober, his wife
told him all these things, and his heart failed
him and he became like a stone. 38About ten
days later, the LORD struck Nabal and he died.
39When David heard that Nabal was dead,
he said, "Praise be to the LORD, who has upheld my cause against Nabal for treating me
with contempt. He has kept his servant from
doing wrong and has brought Nabal's wrongdoing down on his own head."
Then David sent word to Abigail, asking
her to become his wife. 40His servants went to
Carmel and said to Abigail, "David has sent us
to you to take you to become his wife."
41She bowed down with her face to the
ground and said, "I am your servant and am
ready to serve you and wash the feet of my
lord's servants." 42Abigail quickly got on a
donkey and, attended by her five female servants, went with David's messengers and
became his wife. 43David had also married
Ahinoam of Jezreel, and they both were his
wives. 44But Saul had given his daughter Michal, David's wife, to Paltiel[c] son of Laish,
who was from Gallim.

[a] *18* That is, probably about 60 pounds or about 27 kilograms [b] *22* Some Septuagint manuscripts; Hebrew *with David's enemies* [c] *44* Hebrew *Palti*, a variant of *Paltiel*

David Again Spares Saul's Life

26 The Ziphites went to Saul at Gibeah and
said, "Is not David hiding on the hill of
Hakilah, which faces Jeshimon?"
2So Saul went down to the Desert of Ziph,
with his three thousand select Israelite troops,
to search there for David. 3Saul made his
camp beside the road on the hill of Hakilah
facing Jeshimon, but David stayed in the wilderness. When he saw that Saul had followed
him there, 4he sent out scouts and learned that
Saul had definitely arrived.
5Then David set out and went to the place
where Saul had camped. He saw where Saul
and Abner son of Ner, the commander of the
army, had lain down. Saul was lying inside the
camp, with the army encamped around him.
6David then asked Ahimelek the Hittite and
Abishai son of Zeruiah, Joab's brother, "Who
will go down into the camp with me to Saul?"
"I'll go with you," said Abishai.
7So David and Abishai went to the army by
night, and there was Saul, lying asleep inside
the camp with his spear stuck in the ground
near his head. Abner and the soldiers were
lying around him.
8Abishai said to David, "Today God has delivered your enemy into your hands. Now let
me pin him to the ground with one thrust of
the spear; I won't strike him twice."
9But David said to Abishai, "Don't destroy
him! Who can lay a hand on the LORD's anointed and be guiltless? 10As surely as the LORD
lives," he said, "the LORD himself will strike
him, or his time will come and he will die,
or he will go into battle and perish. 11But the
LORD forbid that I should lay a hand on the
LORD's anointed. Now get the spear and water
jug that are near his head, and let's go."
12So David took the spear and water jug
near Saul's head, and they left. No one saw or
knew about it, nor did anyone wake up. They
were all sleeping, because the LORD had put
them into a deep sleep.
13Then David crossed over to the other side
and stood on top of the hill some distance
away; there was a wide space between them.
14He called out to the army and to Abner son of
Ner, "Aren't you going to answer me, Abner?"
Abner replied, "Who are you who calls to
the king?"
15David said, "You're a man, aren't you?
And who is like you in Israel? Why didn't you
guard your lord the king? Someone came to
destroy your lord the king. 16What you have
done is not good. As surely as the LORD lives,
you and your men must die, because you did
not guard your master, the LORD's anointed.
Look around you. Where are the king's spear
and water jug that were near his head?"
17Saul recognized David's voice and said,
"Is that your voice, David my son?"
David replied, "Yes it is, my lord the king."
18And he added, "Why is my lord pursuing his
servant? What have I done, and what wrong
am I guilty of? 19Now let my lord the king
listen to his servant's words. If the LORD has
incited you against me, then may he accept
an offering. If, however, people have done it,
may they be cursed before the LORD! They
have driven me today from my share in the
LORD's inheritance and have said, 'Go, serve
other gods.' 20Now do not let my blood fall
to the ground far from the presence of the
LORD. The king of Israel has come out to look
for a flea—as one hunts a partridge in the
mountains."
21Then Saul said, "I have sinned. Come
back, David my son. Because you considered
my life precious today, I will not try to harm
you again. Surely I have acted like a fool and
have been terribly wrong."
22"Here is the king's spear," David answered. "Let one of your young men come
over and get it. 23The LORD rewards everyone
for their righteousness and faithfulness. The
LORD delivered you into my hands today, but
I would not lay a hand on the LORD's anointed. 24As surely as I valued your life today, so
may the LORD value my life and deliver me
from all trouble."
25Then Saul said to David, "May you be
blessed, David my son; you will do great
things and surely triumph."
So David went on his way, and Saul returned home.

David Among the Philistines

27 But David thought to himself, "One of
these days I will be destroyed by the
hand of Saul. The best thing I can do is to escape to the land of the Philistines. Then Saul
will give up searching for me anywhere in
Israel, and I will slip out of his hand."
2So David and the six hundred men with
him left and went over to Achish son of Maok
king of Gath. 3David and his men settled in
Gath with Achish. Each man had his family with him, and David had his two wives:
Ahinoam of Jezreel and Abigail of Carmel,
the widow of Nabal. 4When Saul was told that
David had fled to Gath, he no longer searched
for him.
5Then David said to Achish, "If I have found
favor in your eyes, let a place be assigned to
me in one of the country towns, that I may
live there. Why should your servant live in
the royal city with you?"
6So on that day Achish gave him Ziklag,
and it has belonged to the kings of Judah ever
since. 7David lived in Philistine territory a
year and four months.
8Now David and his men went up and raided
the Geshurites, the Girzites and the Amalekites. (From ancient times these peoples had
lived in the land extending to Shur and Egypt.)
9Whenever David attacked an area, he did not
leave a man or woman alive, but took sheep
and cattle, donkeys and camels, and clothes.
Then he returned to Achish.
10When Achish asked, "Where did you go
raiding today?" David would say, "Against
the Negev of Judah" or "Against the Negev
of Jerahmeel" or "Against the Negev of the
Kenites." 11He did not leave a man or woman
alive to be brought to Gath, for he thought,
"They might inform on us and say, 'This is
what David did.'" And such was his practice

as long as he lived in Philistine territory. 12 Achish trusted David and said to himself, "He has become so obnoxious to his people, the Israelites, that he will be my servant for life."

28 In those days the Philistines gathered their forces to fight against Israel. Achish said to David, "You must understand that you and your men will accompany me in the army."

2 David said, "Then you will see for yourself what your servant can do."

Achish replied, "Very well, I will make you my bodyguard for life."

Saul and the Medium at Endor

3 Now Samuel was dead, and all Israel had mourned for him and buried him in his own town of Ramah. Saul had expelled the mediums and spiritists from the land.

4 The Philistines assembled and came and set up camp at Shunem, while Saul gathered all Israel and set up camp at Gilboa. 5 When Saul saw the Philistine army, he was afraid; terror filled his heart. 6 He inquired of the LORD, but the LORD did not answer him by dreams or Urim or prophets. 7 Saul then said to his attendants, "Find me a woman who is a medium, so I may go and inquire of her."

"There is one in Endor," they said.

8 So Saul disguised himself, putting on other clothes, and at night he and two men went to the woman. "Consult a spirit for me," he said, "and bring up for me the one I name."

9 But the woman said to him, "Surely you know what Saul has done. He has cut off the mediums and spiritists from the land. Why have you set a trap for my life to bring about my death?"

10 Saul swore to her by the LORD, "As surely as the LORD lives, you will not be punished for this."

11 Then the woman asked, "Whom shall I bring up for you?"

"Bring up Samuel," he said.

12 When the woman saw Samuel, she cried out at the top of her voice and said to Saul, "Why have you deceived me? You are Saul!"

13 The king said to her, "Don't be afraid. What do you see?"

The woman said, "I see a ghostly figure[a] coming up out of the earth."

14 "What does he look like?" he asked.

"An old man wearing a robe is coming up," she said.

Then Saul knew it was Samuel, and he bowed down and prostrated himself with his face to the ground.

15 Samuel said to Saul, "Why have you disturbed me by bringing me up?"

"I am in great distress," Saul said. "The Philistines are fighting against me, and God has departed from me. He no longer answers me, either by prophets or by dreams. So I have called on you to tell me what to do."

16 Samuel said, "Why do you consult me, now that the LORD has departed from you and become your enemy? 17 The LORD has done what he predicted through me. The LORD has torn the kingdom out of your hands and given it to one of your neighbors—to David. 18 Because you did not obey the LORD or carry out his fierce wrath against the Amalekites, the LORD has done this to you today. 19 The LORD will deliver both Israel and you into the hands of the Philistines, and tomorrow you and your sons will be with me. The LORD will also give the army of Israel into the hands of the Philistines."

20 Immediately Saul fell full length on the ground, filled with fear because of Samuel's words. His strength was gone, for he had eaten nothing all that day and all that night.

21 When the woman came to Saul and saw that he was greatly shaken, she said, "Look, your servant has obeyed you. I took my life in my hands and did what you told me to do. 22 Now please listen to your servant and let me give you some food so you may eat and have the strength to go on your way."

23 He refused and said, "I will not eat."

But his men joined the woman in urging him, and he listened to them. He got up from the ground and sat on the couch.

24 The woman had a fattened calf at the house, which she butchered at once. She took some flour, kneaded it and baked bread without yeast. 25 Then she set it before Saul and his men, and they ate. That same night they got up and left.

Achish Sends David Back to Ziklag

29 The Philistines gathered all their forces at Aphek, and Israel camped by the spring in Jezreel. 2 As the Philistine rulers marched with their units of hundreds and thousands, David and his men were marching at the rear with Achish. 3 The commanders of the Philistines asked, "What about these Hebrews?"

Achish replied, "Is this not David, who was an officer of Saul king of Israel? He has already been with me for over a year, and from the day he left Saul until now, I have found no fault in him."

4 But the Philistine commanders were angry with Achish and said, "Send the man back, that he may return to the place you assigned him. He must not go with us into battle, or he will turn against us during the fighting. How better could he regain his master's favor than by taking the heads of our own men? 5 Isn't this the David they sang about in their dances:

"'Saul has slain his thousands,
and David his tens of thousands'?"

6 So Achish called David and said to him, "As surely as the LORD lives, you have been reliable, and I would be pleased to have you serve with me in the army. From the day you came to me until today, I have found no fault in you, but the rulers don't approve of you. 7 Now turn back and go in peace; do nothing to displease the Philistine rulers."

[a] 13 Or *see spirits*; or *see gods*

8“But what have I done?” asked David.
“What have you found against your servant
from the day I came to you until now? Why
can’t I go and fight against the enemies of my
lord the king?”
9Achish answered, “I know that you have
been as pleasing in my eyes as an angel of
God; nevertheless, the Philistine commanders have said, ‘He must not go up with us into
battle.’ 10Now get up early, along with your
master’s servants who have come with you,
and leave in the morning as soon as it is light.”
11So David and his men got up early in the
morning to go back to the land of the Philistines, and the Philistines went up to Jezreel.

David Destroys the Amalekites

30 David and his men reached Ziklag on
the third day. Now the Amalekites had
raided the Negev and Ziklag. They had attacked Ziklag and burned it, 2and had taken
captive the women and everyone else in it,
both young and old. They killed none of them,
but carried them off as they went on their way.
3When David and his men reached Ziklag,
they found it destroyed by fire and their wives
and sons and daughters taken captive. 4So
David and his men wept aloud until they had
no strength left to weep. 5David’s two wives
had been captured—Ahinoam of Jezreel and
Abigail, the widow of Nabal of Carmel. 6David
was greatly distressed because the men were
talking of stoning him; each one was bitter in
spirit because of his sons and daughters. But
David found strength in the LORD his God.
7Then David said to Abiathar the priest, the
son of Ahimelek, “Bring me the ephod.” Abiathar brought it to him, 8and David inquired of
the LORD, “Shall I pursue this raiding party?
Will I overtake them?”
“Pursue them,” he answered. “You will
certainly overtake them and succeed in the
rescue.”
9David and the six hundred men with him
came to the Besor Valley, where some stayed
behind. 10Two hundred of them were too exhausted to cross the valley, but David and the
other four hundred continued the pursuit.
11They found an Egyptian in a field and
brought him to David. They gave him water
to drink and food to eat— 12part of a cake of
pressed figs and two cakes of raisins. He ate
and was revived, for he had not eaten any
food or drunk any water for three days and
three nights.
13David asked him, “Who do you belong to?
Where do you come from?”
He said, “I am an Egyptian, the slave of an
Amalekite. My master abandoned me when
I became ill three days ago. 14We raided the
Negev of the Kerethites, some territory belonging to Judah and the Negev of Caleb. And
we burned Ziklag.”
15David asked him, “Can you lead me down
to this raiding party?”
He answered, “Swear to me before God that
you will not kill me or hand me over to my
master, and I will take you down to them.”
16He led David down, and there they were,
scattered over the countryside, eating, drinking and reveling because of the great amount
of plunder they had taken from the land of the
Philistines and from Judah. 17David fought
them from dusk until the evening of the next
day, and none of them got away, except four
hundred young men who rode off on camels and fled. 18David recovered everything
the Amalekites had taken, including his two
wives. 19Nothing was missing: young or old,
boy or girl, plunder or anything else they had
taken. David brought everything back. 20He
took all the flocks and herds, and his men
drove them ahead of the other livestock, saying, “This is David’s plunder.”
21Then David came to the two hundred men
who had been too exhausted to follow him and
who were left behind at the Besor Valley. They
came out to meet David and the men with him.
As David and his men approached, he asked
them how they were. 22But all the evil men
and troublemakers among David’s followers
said, “Because they did not go out with us,
we will not share with them the plunder we
recovered. However, each man may take his
wife and children and go.”
23David replied, “No, my brothers, you must
not do that with what the LORD has given us.
He has protected us and delivered into our
hands the raiding party that came against us.
24Who will listen to what you say? The share
of the man who stayed with the supplies is to
be the same as that of him who went down to
the battle. All will share alike.” 25David made
this a statute and ordinance for Israel from
that day to this.
26When David reached Ziklag, he sent some
of the plunder to the elders of Judah, who were
his friends, saying, “Here is a gift for you from
the plunder of the LORD’s enemies.”
27David sent it to those who were in Bethel,
Ramoth Negev and Jattir; 28to those in Aroer,
Siphmoth, Eshtemoa 29and Rakal; to those in
the towns of the Jerahmeelites and the Kenites; 30to those in Hormah, Bor Ashan, Athak
31and Hebron; and to those in all the other
places where he and his men had roamed.

Saul Takes His Life

31 Now the Philistines fought against Israel; the Israelites fled before them, and
many fell dead on Mount Gilboa. 2The Philistines were in hot pursuit of Saul and his sons,
and they killed his sons Jonathan, Abinadab
and Malki-Shua. 3The fighting grew fierce
around Saul, and when the archers overtook
him, they wounded him critically.
4Saul said to his armor-bearer, “Draw your
sword and run me through, or these uncircumcised fellows will come and run me
through and abuse me.”
But his armor-bearer was terrified and
would not do it; so Saul took his own sword
and fell on it. 5When the armor-bearer saw
that Saul was dead, he too fell on his sword
and died with him. 6So Saul and his three
sons and his armor-bearer and all his men
died together that same day.
7When the Israelites along the valley and

those across the Jordan saw that the Israelite
army had fled and that Saul and his sons had
died, they abandoned their towns and fled.
And the Philistines came and occupied them.
8 The next day, when the Philistines came to
strip the dead, they found Saul and his three
sons fallen on Mount Gilboa. 9 They cut off his
head and stripped off his armor, and they sent
messengers throughout the land of the Philistines to proclaim the news in the temple of
their idols and among their people. 10 They put
his armor in the temple of the Ashtoreths and
fastened his body to the wall of Beth Shan.
11 When the people of Jabesh Gilead heard
what the Philistines had done to Saul, 12 all
their valiant men marched through the night
to Beth Shan. They took down the bodies of
Saul and his sons from the wall of Beth Shan
and went to Jabesh, where they burned them.
13 Then they took their bones and buried them
under a tamarisk tree at Jabesh, and they fasted seven days.

2 Samuel

David Hears of Saul's Death

1 After the death of Saul, David returned
from striking down the Amalekites and
stayed in Ziklag two days. 2 On the third day a
man arrived from Saul's camp with his clothes
torn and dust on his head. When he came to
David, he fell to the ground to pay him honor.
3 "Where have you come from?" David asked
him.

He answered, "I have escaped from the Israelite camp."
4 "What happened?" David asked. "Tell me."

"The men fled from the battle," he replied.
"Many of them fell and died. And Saul and
his son Jonathan are dead."
5 Then David said to the young man who
brought him the report, "How do you know
that Saul and his son Jonathan are dead?"
6 "I happened to be on Mount Gilboa," the
young man said, "and there was Saul, leaning
on his spear, with the chariots and their drivers in hot pursuit. 7 When he turned around
and saw me, he called out to me, and I said,
'What can I do?'
8 "He asked me, 'Who are you?'

"'An Amalekite,' I answered.
9 "Then he said to me, 'Stand here by me
and kill me! I'm in the throes of death, but
I'm still alive.'
10 "So I stood beside him and killed him, because I knew that after he had fallen he could
not survive. And I took the crown that was on
his head and the band on his arm and have
brought them here to my lord."
11 Then David and all the men with him took
hold of their clothes and tore them. 12 They
mourned and wept and fasted till evening for
Saul and his son Jonathan, and for the army of
the LORD and for the nation of Israel, because
they had fallen by the sword.
13 David said to the young man who brought
him the report, "Where are you from?"

"I am the son of a foreigner, an Amalekite,"
he answered.
14 David asked him, "Why weren't you afraid
to lift your hand to destroy the LORD's anointed?"
15 Then David called one of his men and
said, "Go, strike him down!" So he struck him
down, and he died. 16 For David had said to
him, "Your blood be on your own head. Your
own mouth testified against you when you
said, 'I killed the LORD's anointed.'"

David's Lament for Saul and Jonathan

17 David took up this lament concerning Saul
and his son Jonathan, 18 and he ordered that
the people of Judah be taught this lament of
the bow (it is written in the Book of Jashar):

19 "A gazelle[a] lies slain on your heights,
Israel.
How the mighty have fallen!

20 "Tell it not in Gath,
proclaim it not in the streets of Ashkelon,
lest the daughters of the Philistines be
glad,
lest the daughters of the uncircumcised
rejoice.

21 "Mountains of Gilboa,
may you have neither dew nor rain,
may no showers fall on your terraced
fields.[b]
For there the shield of the mighty was
despised,
the shield of Saul—no longer rubbed
with oil.

22 "From the blood of the slain,
from the flesh of the mighty,
the bow of Jonathan did not turn back,
the sword of Saul did not return
unsatisfied.
23 Saul and Jonathan—
in life they were loved and admired,
and in death they were not parted.
They were swifter than eagles,
they were stronger than lions.

[a] 19 *Gazelle* here symbolizes a human dignitary.

[b] 21 Or / *nor fields that yield grain for offerings*

24 "Daughters of Israel,
weep for Saul,
who clothed you in scarlet and finery,
who adorned your garments with
ornaments of gold.

25 "How the mighty have fallen in battle!
Jonathan lies slain on your heights.
26 I grieve for you, Jonathan my brother;
you were very dear to me.
Your love for me was wonderful,
more wonderful than that of women.

27 "How the mighty have fallen!
The weapons of war have perished!"

David Anointed King Over Judah

2 In the course of time, David inquired of the
LORD. "Shall I go up to one of the towns of
Judah?" he asked.
The LORD said, "Go up."
David asked, "Where shall I go?"
"To Hebron," the LORD answered.
2 So David went up there with his two wives,
Ahinoam of Jezreel and Abigail, the widow
of Nabal of Carmel. 3 David also took the men
who were with him, each with his family, and
they settled in Hebron and its towns. 4 Then the
men of Judah came to Hebron, and there they
anointed David king over the tribe of Judah.
When David was told that it was the men
from Jabesh Gilead who had buried Saul, 5 he
sent messengers to them to say to them, "The
LORD bless you for showing this kindness to
Saul your master by burying him. 6 May the
LORD now show you kindness and faithfulness, and I too will show you the same favor
because you have done this. 7 Now then, be
strong and brave, for Saul your master is dead,
and the people of Judah have anointed me
king over them."

War Between the Houses of David and Saul

8 Meanwhile, Abner son of Ner, the commander of Saul's army, had taken Ish-Bosheth son of Saul and brought him over to
Mahanaim. 9 He made him king over Gilead,
Ashuri and Jezreel, and also over Ephraim,
Benjamin and all Israel.
10 Ish-Bosheth son of Saul was forty years
old when he became king over Israel, and he
reigned two years. The tribe of Judah, however, remained loyal to David. 11 The length
of time David was king in Hebron over Judah
was seven years and six months.
12 Abner son of Ner, together with the men of
Ish-Bosheth son of Saul, left Mahanaim and
went to Gibeon. 13 Joab son of Zeruiah and David's men went out and met them at the pool
of Gibeon. One group sat down on one side
of the pool and one group on the other side.
14 Then Abner said to Joab, "Let's have some
of the young men get up and fight hand to
hand in front of us."
"All right, let them do it," Joab said.
15 So they stood up and were counted off—
twelve men for Benjamin and Ish-Bosheth son
of Saul, and twelve for David. 16 Then each
man grabbed his opponent by the head and
thrust his dagger into his opponent's side, and
they fell down together. So that place in Gibeon was called Helkath Hazzurim.[a]
17 The battle that day was very fierce, and
Abner and the Israelites were defeated by David's men.
18 The three sons of Zeruiah were there:
Joab, Abishai and Asahel. Now Asahel was
as fleet-footed as a wild gazelle. 19 He chased
Abner, turning neither to the right nor to the
left as he pursued him. 20 Abner looked behind
him and asked, "Is that you, Asahel?"
"It is," he answered.
21 Then Abner said to him, "Turn aside to the
right or to the left; take on one of the young
men and strip him of his weapons." But Asahel would not stop chasing him.
22 Again Abner warned Asahel, "Stop chasing me! Why should I strike you down? How
could I look your brother Joab in the face?"
23 But Asahel refused to give up the pursuit;
so Abner thrust the butt of his spear into Asahel's stomach, and the spear came out through
his back. He fell there and died on the spot.
And every man stopped when he came to the
place where Asahel had fallen and died.
24 But Joab and Abishai pursued Abner, and
as the sun was setting, they came to the hill of
Ammah, near Giah on the way to the wasteland of Gibeon. 25 Then the men of Benjamin
rallied behind Abner. They formed themselves
into a group and took their stand on top of
a hill.
26 Abner called out to Joab, "Must the sword
devour forever? Don't you realize that this
will end in bitterness? How long before you
order your men to stop pursuing their fellow
Israelites?"
27 Joab answered, "As surely as God lives, if
you had not spoken, the men would have continued pursuing them until morning."
28 So Joab blew the trumpet, and all the
troops came to a halt; they no longer pursued
Israel, nor did they fight anymore.
29 All that night Abner and his men marched
through the Arabah. They crossed the Jordan,
continued through the morning hours[b] and
came to Mahanaim.
30 Then Joab stopped pursuing Abner and
assembled the whole army. Besides Asahel,
nineteen of David's men were found missing.
31 But David's men had killed three hundred
and sixty Benjamites who were with Abner.
32 They took Asahel and buried him in his father's tomb at Bethlehem. Then Joab and his
men marched all night and arrived at Hebron
by daybreak.

3 The war between the house of Saul and the
house of David lasted a long time. David
grew stronger and stronger, while the house
of Saul grew weaker and weaker.
2 Sons were born to David in Hebron:
His firstborn was Amnon the son of
Ahinoam of Jezreel;

[a] 16 *Helkath Hazzurim* means *field of daggers* or *field of hostilities.* [b] 29 See Septuagint; the meaning of the Hebrew for this phrase is uncertain.

3his second, Kileab the son of Abigail
the widow of Nabal of Carmel;
the third, Absalom the son of Maakah
daughter of Talmai king of Geshur;
4the fourth, Adonijah the son of Haggith;
the fifth, Shephatiah the son of Abital;
5and the sixth, Ithream the son of David's wife Eglah.
These were born to David in Hebron.

Abner Goes Over to David

6During the war between the house of
Saul and the house of David, Abner had been
strengthening his own position in the house of
Saul. 7Now Saul had had a concubine named
Rizpah daughter of Aiah. And Ish-Bosheth
said to Abner, "Why did you sleep with my
father's concubine?"
8Abner was very angry because of what
Ish-Bosheth said. So he answered, "Am I a
dog's head—on Judah's side? This very day I
am loyal to the house of your father Saul and
to his family and friends. I haven't handed
you over to David. Yet now you accuse me of
an offense involving this woman! 9May God
deal with Abner, be it ever so severely, if I do
not do for David what the LORD promised him
on oath 10and transfer the kingdom from the
house of Saul and establish David's throne
over Israel and Judah from Dan to Beersheba." 11Ish-Bosheth did not dare to say another
word to Abner, because he was afraid of him.
12Then Abner sent messengers on his behalf
to say to David, "Whose land is it? Make an
agreement with me, and I will help you bring
all Israel over to you."
13"Good," said David. "I will make an agreement with you. But I demand one thing of
you: Do not come into my presence unless
you bring Michal daughter of Saul when you
come to see me." 14Then David sent messengers to Ish-Bosheth son of Saul, demanding,
"Give me my wife Michal, whom I betrothed
to myself for the price of a hundred Philistine
foreskins."
15So Ish-Bosheth gave orders and had her
taken away from her husband Paltiel son of
Laish. 16Her husband, however, went with her,
weeping behind her all the way to Bahurim.
Then Abner said to him, "Go back home!" So
he went back.
17Abner conferred with the elders of Israel
and said, "For some time you have wanted to
make David your king. 18Now do it! For the
LORD promised David, 'By my servant David
I will rescue my people Israel from the hand
of the Philistines and from the hand of all
their enemies.'"
19Abner also spoke to the Benjamites in
person. Then he went to Hebron to tell David
everything that Israel and the whole tribe of
Benjamin wanted to do. 20When Abner, who
had twenty men with him, came to David at
Hebron, David prepared a feast for him and
his men. 21Then Abner said to David, "Let me
go at once and assemble all Israel for my lord
the king, so that they may make a covenant
with you, and that you may rule over all that
your heart desires." So David sent Abner
away, and he went in peace.

Joab Murders Abner

22Just then David's men and Joab returned
from a raid and brought with them a great
deal of plunder. But Abner was no longer with
David in Hebron, because David had sent him
away, and he had gone in peace. 23When Joab
and all the soldiers with him arrived, he was
told that Abner son of Ner had come to the
king and that the king had sent him away and
that he had gone in peace.
24So Joab went to the king and said, "What
have you done? Look, Abner came to you.
Why did you let him go? Now he is gone! 25You
know Abner son of Ner; he came to deceive
you and observe your movements and find
out everything you are doing."
26Joab then left David and sent messengers
after Abner, and they brought him back from
the cistern at Sirah. But David did not know it.
27Now when Abner returned to Hebron, Joab
took him aside into an inner chamber, as if to
speak with him privately. And there, to avenge
the blood of his brother Asahel, Joab stabbed
him in the stomach, and he died.
28Later, when David heard about this, he
said, "I and my kingdom are forever innocent before the LORD concerning the blood of
Abner son of Ner. 29May his blood fall on the
head of Joab and on his whole family! May
Joab's family never be without someone who
has a running sore or leprosy[a] or who leans
on a crutch or who falls by the sword or who
lacks food."
30(Joab and his brother Abishai murdered
Abner because he had killed their brother Asahel in the battle at Gibeon.)
31Then David said to Joab and all the people with him, "Tear your clothes and put on
sackcloth and walk in mourning in front of
Abner." King David himself walked behind
the bier. 32They buried Abner in Hebron, and
the king wept aloud at Abner's tomb. All the
people wept also.
33The king sang this lament for Abner:

"Should Abner have died as the lawless
die?
34 Your hands were not bound,
your feet were not fettered.
You fell as one falls before the wicked."

And all the people wept over him again.
35Then they all came and urged David to
eat something while it was still day; but David took an oath, saying, "May God deal with
me, be it ever so severely, if I taste bread or
anything else before the sun sets!"
36All the people took note and were pleased;
indeed, everything the king did pleased them.
37So on that day all the people there and all
Israel knew that the king had no part in the
murder of Abner son of Ner.
38Then the king said to his men, "Do you not

[a] *29* The Hebrew for *leprosy* was used for various diseases affecting the skin.

realize that a commander and a great man has fallen in Israel this day? 39And today, though I am the anointed king, I am weak, and these sons of Zeruiah are too strong for me. May the LORD repay the evildoer according to his evil deeds!"

Ish-Bosheth Murdered

4 When Ish-Bosheth son of Saul heard that Abner had died in Hebron, he lost courage, and all Israel became alarmed. 2Now Saul's son had two men who were leaders of raiding bands. One was named Baanah and the other Rekab; they were sons of Rimmon the Beerothite from the tribe of Benjamin—Beeroth is considered part of Benjamin, 3because the people of Beeroth fled to Gittaim and have resided there as foreigners to this day.

4(Jonathan son of Saul had a son who was lame in both feet. He was five years old when the news about Saul and Jonathan came from Jezreel. His nurse picked him up and fled, but as she hurried to leave, he fell and became disabled. His name was Mephibosheth.)

5Now Rekab and Baanah, the sons of Rimmon the Beerothite, set out for the house of Ish-Bosheth, and they arrived there in the heat of the day while he was taking his noonday rest. 6They went into the inner part of the house as if to get some wheat, and they stabbed him in the stomach. Then Rekab and his brother Baanah slipped away.

7They had gone into the house while he was lying on the bed in his bedroom. After they stabbed and killed him, they cut off his head. Taking it with them, they traveled all night by way of the Arabah. 8They brought the head of Ish-Bosheth to David at Hebron and said to the king, "Here is the head of Ish-Bosheth son of Saul, your enemy, who tried to kill you. This day the LORD has avenged my lord the king against Saul and his offspring."

9David answered Rekab and his brother Baanah, the sons of Rimmon the Beerothite, "As surely as the LORD lives, who has delivered me out of every trouble, 10when someone told me, 'Saul is dead,' and thought he was bringing good news, I seized him and put him to death in Ziklag. That was the reward I gave him for his news! 11How much more—when wicked men have killed an innocent man in his own house and on his own bed—should I not now demand his blood from your hand and rid the earth of you!"

12So David gave an order to his men, and they killed them. They cut off their hands and feet and hung the bodies by the pool in Hebron. But they took the head of Ish-Bosheth and buried it in Abner's tomb at Hebron.

David Becomes King Over Israel

5 All the tribes of Israel came to David at Hebron and said, "We are your own flesh and blood. 2In the past, while Saul was king over us, you were the one who led Israel on their military campaigns. And the LORD said to you, 'You will shepherd my people Israel, and you will become their ruler.'"

3When all the elders of Israel had come to King David at Hebron, the king made a covenant with them at Hebron before the LORD, and they anointed David king over Israel.

4David was thirty years old when he became king, and he reigned forty years. 5In Hebron he reigned over Judah seven years and six months, and in Jerusalem he reigned over all Israel and Judah thirty-three years.

David Conquers Jerusalem

6The king and his men marched to Jerusalem to attack the Jebusites, who lived there. The Jebusites said to David, "You will not get in here; even the blind and the lame can ward you off." They thought, "David cannot get in here." 7Nevertheless, David captured the fortress of Zion—which is the City of David.

8On that day David had said, "Anyone who conquers the Jebusites will have to use the water shaft to reach those 'lame and blind' who are David's enemies.[a]" That is why they say, "The 'blind and lame' will not enter the palace."

9David then took up residence in the fortress and called it the City of David. He built up the area around it, from the terraces[b] inward. 10And he became more and more powerful, because the LORD God Almighty was with him.

11Now Hiram king of Tyre sent envoys to David, along with cedar logs and carpenters and stonemasons, and they built a palace for David. 12Then David knew that the LORD had established him as king over Israel and had exalted his kingdom for the sake of his people Israel.

13After he left Hebron, David took more concubines and wives in Jerusalem, and more sons and daughters were born to him. 14These are the names of the children born to him there: Shammua, Shobab, Nathan, Solomon, 15Ibhar, Elishua, Nepheg, Japhia, 16Elishama, Eliada and Eliphelet.

David Defeats the Philistines

17When the Philistines heard that David had been anointed king over Israel, they went up in full force to search for him, but David heard about it and went down to the stronghold. 18Now the Philistines had come and spread out in the Valley of Rephaim; 19so David inquired of the LORD, "Shall I go and attack the Philistines? Will you deliver them into my hands?"

The LORD answered him, "Go, for I will surely deliver the Philistines into your hands."

20So David went to Baal Perazim, and there he defeated them. He said, "As waters break out, the LORD has broken out against my enemies before me." So that place was called Baal Perazim.[c] 21The Philistines abandoned their idols there, and David and his men carried them off.

[a] 8 Or *are hated by David* [b] 9 Or *the Millo* [c] 20 *Baal Perazim* means *the lord who breaks out.*

22Once more the Philistines came up and spread out in the Valley of Rephaim; 23so David inquired of the LORD, and he answered, "Do not go straight up, but circle around behind them and attack them in front of the poplar trees. 24As soon as you hear the sound of marching in the tops of the poplar trees, move quickly, because that will mean the LORD has gone out in front of you to strike the Philistine army." 25So David did as the LORD commanded him, and he struck down the Philistines all the way from Gibeon[a] to Gezer.

The Ark Brought to Jerusalem

6 David again brought together all the able young men of Israel—thirty thousand. 2He and all his men went to Baalah[b] in Judah to bring up from there the ark of God, which is called by the Name,[c] the name of the LORD Almighty, who is enthroned between the cherubim on the ark. 3They set the ark of God on a new cart and brought it from the house of Abinadab, which was on the hill. Uzzah and Ahio, sons of Abinadab, were guiding the new cart 4with the ark of God on it,[d] and Ahio was walking in front of it. 5David and all Israel were celebrating with all their might before the LORD, with castanets,[e] harps, lyres, timbrels, sistrums and cymbals.

6When they came to the threshing floor of Nakon, Uzzah reached out and took hold of the ark of God, because the oxen stumbled. 7The LORD's anger burned against Uzzah because of his irreverent act; therefore God struck him down, and he died there beside the ark of God.

8Then David was angry because the LORD's wrath had broken out against Uzzah, and to this day that place is called Perez Uzzah.[f]

9David was afraid of the LORD that day and said, "How can the ark of the LORD ever come to me?" 10He was not willing to take the ark of the LORD to be with him in the City of David. Instead, he took it to the house of Obed-Edom the Gittite. 11The ark of the LORD remained in the house of Obed-Edom the Gittite for three months, and the LORD blessed him and his entire household.

12Now King David was told, "The LORD has blessed the household of Obed-Edom and everything he has, because of the ark of God." So David went to bring up the ark of God from the house of Obed-Edom to the City of David with rejoicing. 13When those who were carrying the ark of the LORD had taken six steps, he sacrificed a bull and a fattened calf. 14Wearing a linen ephod, David was dancing before the LORD with all his might, 15while he and all Israel were bringing up the ark of the LORD with shouts and the sound of trumpets.

16As the ark of the LORD was entering the City of David, Michal daughter of Saul watched from a window. And when she saw King David leaping and dancing before the LORD, she despised him in her heart.

17They brought the ark of the LORD and set it in its place inside the tent that David had pitched for it, and David sacrificed burnt offerings and fellowship offerings before the LORD. 18After he had finished sacrificing the burnt offerings and fellowship offerings, he blessed the people in the name of the LORD Almighty. 19Then he gave a loaf of bread, a cake of dates and a cake of raisins to each person in the whole crowd of Israelites, both men and women. And all the people went to their homes.

20When David returned home to bless his household, Michal daughter of Saul came out to meet him and said, "How the king of Israel has distinguished himself today, going around half-naked in full view of the slave girls of his servants as any vulgar fellow would!"

21David said to Michal, "It was before the LORD, who chose me rather than your father or anyone from his house when he appointed me ruler over the LORD's people Israel—I will celebrate before the LORD. 22I will become even more undignified than this, and I will be humiliated in my own eyes. But by these slave girls you spoke of, I will be held in honor."

23And Michal daughter of Saul had no children to the day of her death.

God's Promise to David

7 After the king was settled in his palace and the LORD had given him rest from all his enemies around him, 2he said to Nathan the prophet, "Here I am, living in a house of cedar, while the ark of God remains in a tent."

3Nathan replied to the king, "Whatever you have in mind, go ahead and do it, for the LORD is with you."

4But that night the word of the LORD came to Nathan, saying:

> 5"Go and tell my servant David, 'This is what the LORD says: Are you the one to build me a house to dwell in? 6I have not dwelt in a house from the day I brought the Israelites up out of Egypt to this day. I have been moving from place to place with a tent as my dwelling. 7Wherever I have moved with all the Israelites, did I ever say to any of their rulers whom I commanded to shepherd my people Israel, "Why have you not built me a house of cedar?"'
>
> 8"Now then, tell my servant David, 'This is what the LORD Almighty says: I took you from the pasture, from tending the flock, and appointed you ruler over my people Israel. 9I have been with you wherever you have gone, and I have cut off all your enemies from before you. Now I will make your name great, like the names of the greatest men on earth.

[a] 25 Septuagint (see also 1 Chron. 14:16); Hebrew *Geba* [b] 2 That is, Kiriath Jearim (see 1 Chron. 13:6) [c] 2 Hebrew; Septuagint and Vulgate do not have *the Name.* [d] 3,4 Dead Sea Scrolls and some Septuagint manuscripts; Masoretic Text *cart* 4*and they brought it with the ark of God from the house of Abinadab, which was on the hill* [e] 5 Masoretic Text; Dead Sea Scrolls and Septuagint (see also 1 Chron. 13:8) *songs* [f] 8 *Perez Uzzah* means *outbreak against Uzzah.*

10And I will provide a place for my people
Israel and will plant them so that they can
have a home of their own and no longer
be disturbed. Wicked people will not oppress them anymore, as they did at the
beginning 11and have done ever since the
time I appointed leaders[a] over my people
Israel. I will also give you rest from all
your enemies.
"'The LORD declares to you that the
LORD himself will establish a house for
you: 12When your days are over and you
rest with your ancestors, I will raise up
your offspring to succeed you, your own
flesh and blood, and I will establish his
kingdom. 13He is the one who will build
a house for my Name, and I will establish the throne of his kingdom forever. 14I
will be his father, and he will be my son.
When he does wrong, I will punish him
with a rod wielded by men, with floggings
inflicted by human hands. 15But my love
will never be taken away from him, as I
took it away from Saul, whom I removed
from before you. 16Your house and your
kingdom will endure forever before me[b];
your throne will be established forever.'"

17Nathan reported to David all the words of
this entire revelation.

David's Prayer

18Then King David went in and sat before
the LORD, and he said:

"Who am I, Sovereign LORD, and what
is my family, that you have brought me
this far? 19And as if this were not enough
in your sight, Sovereign LORD, you have
also spoken about the future of the house
of your servant—and this decree, Sovereign LORD, is for a mere human![c]
20"What more can David say to you?
For you know your servant, Sovereign
LORD. 21For the sake of your word and
according to your will, you have done
this great thing and made it known to
your servant.
22"How great you are, Sovereign LORD!
There is no one like you, and there is no
God but you, as we have heard with our
own ears. 23And who is like your people Israel—the one nation on earth that
God went out to redeem as a people for
himself, and to make a name for himself, and to perform great and awesome
wonders by driving out nations and their
gods from before your people, whom you
redeemed from Egypt?[d] 24You have established your people Israel as your very
own forever, and you, LORD, have become
their God.
25"And now, LORD God, keep forever
the promise you have made concerning
your servant and his house. Do as you
promised, 26so that your name will be
great forever. Then people will say, 'The
LORD Almighty is God over Israel!' And
the house of your servant David will be
established in your sight.
27"LORD Almighty, God of Israel, you
have revealed this to your servant, saying, 'I will build a house for you.' So your
servant has found courage to pray this
prayer to you. 28Sovereign LORD, you are
God! Your covenant is trustworthy, and
you have promised these good things to
your servant. 29Now be pleased to bless
the house of your servant, that it may
continue forever in your sight; for you,
Sovereign LORD, have spoken, and with
your blessing the house of your servant
will be blessed forever."

David's Victories

8 In the course of time, David defeated the
Philistines and subdued them, and he took
Metheg Ammah from the control of the Philistines.
2David also defeated the Moabites. He made
them lie down on the ground and measured
them off with a length of cord. Every two
lengths of them were put to death, and the
third length was allowed to live. So the Moabites became subject to David and brought
him tribute.
3Moreover, David defeated Hadadezer son
of Rehob, king of Zobah, when he went to restore his monument at[e] the Euphrates River.
4David captured a thousand of his chariots,
seven thousand charioteers[f] and twenty thousand foot soldiers. He hamstrung all but a
hundred of the chariot horses.
5When the Arameans of Damascus came to
help Hadadezer king of Zobah, David struck
down twenty-two thousand of them. 6He put
garrisons in the Aramean kingdom of Damascus, and the Arameans became subject
to him and brought tribute. The LORD gave
David victory wherever he went.
7David took the gold shields that belonged
to the officers of Hadadezer and brought them
to Jerusalem. 8From Tebah[g] and Berothai,
towns that belonged to Hadadezer, King David took a great quantity of bronze.
9When Tou[h] king of Hamath heard that David had defeated the entire army of Hadadezer, 10he sent his son Joram[i] to King David to
greet him and congratulate him on his victory
in battle over Hadadezer, who had been at war
with Tou. Joram brought with him articles of
silver, of gold and of bronze.
11King David dedicated these articles to the

[a] *11* Traditionally *judges* [b] *16* Some Hebrew manuscripts and Septuagint; most Hebrew manuscripts *you* [c] *19* Or *for the human race* [d] *23* See Septuagint and 1 Chron. 17:21; Hebrew *wonders for your land and before your people, whom you redeemed from Egypt, from the nations and their gods.* [e] *3* Or *his control along* [f] *4* Septuagint (see also Dead Sea Scrolls and 1 Chron. 18:4); Masoretic Text *captured seventeen hundred of his charioteers* [g] *8* See some Septuagint manuscripts (see also 1 Chron. 18:8); Hebrew *Betah.* [h] *9* Hebrew *Toi,* a variant of *Tou;* also in verse 10 [i] *10* A variant of *Hadoram*

LORD, as he had done with the silver and gold from all the nations he had subdued: 12Edom[a] and Moab, the Ammonites and the Philistines, and Amalek. He also dedicated the plunder taken from Hadadezer son of Rehob, king of Zobah.

13And David became famous after he returned from striking down eighteen thousand Edomites[b] in the Valley of Salt.

14He put garrisons throughout Edom, and all the Edomites became subject to David. The LORD gave David victory wherever he went.

David's Officials

15David reigned over all Israel, doing what was just and right for all his people. 16Joab son of Zeruiah was over the army; Jehoshaphat son of Ahilud was recorder; 17Zadok son of Ahitub and Ahimelek son of Abiathar were priests; Seraiah was secretary; 18Benaiah son of Jehoiada was over the Kerethites and Pelethites; and David's sons were priests.[c]

David and Mephibosheth

9 David asked, "Is there anyone still left of the house of Saul to whom I can show kindness for Jonathan's sake?"

2Now there was a servant of Saul's household named Ziba. They summoned him to appear before David, and the king said to him, "Are you Ziba?"

"At your service," he replied.

3The king asked, "Is there no one still alive from the house of Saul to whom I can show God's kindness?"

Ziba answered the king, "There is still a son of Jonathan; he is lame in both feet."

4"Where is he?" the king asked.

Ziba answered, "He is at the house of Makir son of Ammiel in Lo Debar."

5So King David had him brought from Lo Debar, from the house of Makir son of Ammiel.

6When Mephibosheth son of Jonathan, the son of Saul, came to David, he bowed down to pay him honor.

David said, "Mephibosheth!"

"At your service," he replied.

7"Don't be afraid," David said to him, "for I will surely show you kindness for the sake of your father Jonathan. I will restore to you all the land that belonged to your grandfather Saul, and you will always eat at my table."

8Mephibosheth bowed down and said, "What is your servant, that you should notice a dead dog like me?"

9Then the king summoned Ziba, Saul's steward, and said to him, "I have given your master's grandson everything that belonged to Saul and his family. 10You and your sons and your servants are to farm the land for him and bring in the crops, so that your master's grandson may be provided for. And Mephibosheth, grandson of your master, will always eat at my table." (Now Ziba had fifteen sons and twenty servants.)

11Then Ziba said to the king, "Your servant will do whatever my lord the king commands his servant to do." So Mephibosheth ate at David's[d] table like one of the king's sons.

12Mephibosheth had a young son named Mika, and all the members of Ziba's household were servants of Mephibosheth. 13And Mephibosheth lived in Jerusalem, because he always ate at the king's table; he was lame in both feet.

David Defeats the Ammonites

10 In the course of time, the king of the Ammonites died, and his son Hanun succeeded him as king. 2David thought, "I will show kindness to Hanun son of Nahash, just as his father showed kindness to me." So David sent a delegation to express his sympathy to Hanun concerning his father.

When David's men came to the land of the Ammonites, 3the Ammonite commanders said to Hanun their lord, "Do you think David is honoring your father by sending envoys to you to express sympathy? Hasn't David sent them to you only to explore the city and spy it out and overthrow it?" 4So Hanun seized David's envoys, shaved off half of each man's beard, cut off their garments at the buttocks, and sent them away.

5When David was told about this, he sent messengers to meet the men, for they were greatly humiliated. The king said, "Stay at Jericho till your beards have grown, and then come back."

6When the Ammonites realized that they had become obnoxious to David, they hired twenty thousand Aramean foot soldiers from Beth Rehob and Zobah, as well as the king of Maakah with a thousand men, and also twelve thousand men from Tob.

7On hearing this, David sent Joab out with the entire army of fighting men. 8The Ammonites came out and drew up in battle formation at the entrance of their city gate, while the Arameans of Zobah and Rehob and the men of Tob and Maakah were by themselves in the open country.

9Joab saw that there were battle lines in front of him and behind him; so he selected some of the best troops in Israel and deployed them against the Arameans. 10He put the rest of the men under the command of Abishai his brother and deployed them against the Ammonites. 11Joab said, "If the Arameans are too strong for me, then you are to come to my rescue; but if the Ammonites are too strong for you, then I will come to rescue you. 12Be strong, and let us fight bravely for our people and the cities of our God. The LORD will do what is good in his sight."

13Then Joab and the troops with him advanced to fight the Arameans, and they fled

[a] *12* Some Hebrew manuscripts, Septuagint and Syriac (see also 1 Chron. 18:11); most Hebrew manuscripts *Aram* [b] *13* A few Hebrew manuscripts, Septuagint and Syriac (see also 1 Chron. 18:12); most Hebrew manuscripts *Aram* (that is, Arameans) [c] *18* Or *were chief officials* (see Septuagint and Targum; see also 1 Chron. 18:17) [d] *11* Septuagint; Hebrew *my*

before him. 14When the Ammonites realized that the Arameans were fleeing, they fled before Abishai and went inside the city. So Joab returned from fighting the Ammonites and came to Jerusalem.

15After the Arameans saw that they had been routed by Israel, they regrouped. 16Hadadezer had Arameans brought from beyond the Euphrates River; they went to Helam, with Shobak the commander of Hadadezer's army leading them.

17When David was told of this, he gathered all Israel, crossed the Jordan and went to Helam. The Arameans formed their battle lines to meet David and fought against him. 18But they fled before Israel, and David killed seven hundred of their charioteers and forty thousand of their foot soldiers.[a] He also struck down Shobak the commander of their army, and he died there. 19When all the kings who were vassals of Hadadezer saw that they had been routed by Israel, they made peace with the Israelites and became subject to them.

So the Arameans were afraid to help the Ammonites anymore.

David and Bathsheba

11 In the spring, at the time when kings go off to war, David sent Joab out with the king's men and the whole Israelite army. They destroyed the Ammonites and besieged Rabbah. But David remained in Jerusalem.

2One evening David got up from his bed and walked around on the roof of the palace. From the roof he saw a woman bathing. The woman was very beautiful, 3and David sent someone to find out about her. The man said, "She is Bathsheba, the daughter of Eliam and the wife of Uriah the Hittite." 4Then David sent messengers to get her. She came to him, and he slept with her. (Now she was purifying herself from her monthly uncleanness.) Then she went back home. 5The woman conceived and sent word to David, saying, "I am pregnant."

6So David sent this word to Joab: "Send me Uriah the Hittite." And Joab sent him to David. 7When Uriah came to him, David asked him how Joab was, how the soldiers were and how the war was going. 8Then David said to Uriah, "Go down to your house and wash your feet." So Uriah left the palace, and a gift from the king was sent after him. 9But Uriah slept at the entrance to the palace with all his master's servants and did not go down to his house.

10David was told, "Uriah did not go home." So he asked Uriah, "Haven't you just come from a military campaign? Why didn't you go home?"

11Uriah said to David, "The ark and Israel and Judah are staying in tents,[b] and my commander Joab and my lord's men are camped in the open country. How could I go to my house to eat and drink and make love to my wife? As surely as you live, I will not do such a thing!"

12Then David said to him, "Stay here one more day, and tomorrow I will send you back." So Uriah remained in Jerusalem that day and the next. 13At David's invitation, he ate and drank with him, and David made him drunk. But in the evening Uriah went out to sleep on his mat among his master's servants; he did not go home.

14In the morning David wrote a letter to Joab and sent it with Uriah. 15In it he wrote, "Put Uriah out in front where the fighting is fiercest. Then withdraw from him so he will be struck down and die."

16So while Joab had the city under siege, he put Uriah at a place where he knew the strongest defenders were. 17When the men of the city came out and fought against Joab, some of the men in David's army fell; moreover, Uriah the Hittite died.

18Joab sent David a full account of the battle. 19He instructed the messenger: "When you have finished giving the king this account of the battle, 20the king's anger may flare up, and he may ask you, 'Why did you get so close to the city to fight? Didn't you know they would shoot arrows from the wall? 21Who killed Abimelek son of Jerub-Besheth[c]? Didn't a woman drop an upper millstone on him from the wall, so that he died in Thebez? Why did you get so close to the wall?' If he asks you this, then say to him, 'Moreover, your servant Uriah the Hittite is dead.' "

22The messenger set out, and when he arrived he told David everything Joab had sent him to say. 23The messenger said to David, "The men overpowered us and came out against us in the open, but we drove them back to the entrance of the city gate. 24Then the archers shot arrows at your servants from the wall, and some of the king's men died. Moreover, your servant Uriah the Hittite is dead."

25David told the messenger, "Say this to Joab: 'Don't let this upset you; the sword devours one as well as another. Press the attack against the city and destroy it.' Say this to encourage Joab."

26When Uriah's wife heard that her husband was dead, she mourned for him. 27After the time of mourning was over, David had her brought to his house, and she became his wife and bore him a son. But the thing David had done displeased the LORD.

Nathan Rebukes David

12 The LORD sent Nathan to David. When he came to him, he said, "There were two men in a certain town, one rich and the other poor. 2The rich man had a very large number of sheep and cattle, 3but the poor man had nothing except one little ewe lamb he had bought. He raised it, and it grew up with him and his children. It shared his food, drank from his cup and even slept in his arms. It was like a daughter to him.

4"Now a traveler came to the rich man, but the rich man refrained from taking one of his own sheep or cattle to prepare a meal for the traveler who had come to him. Instead,

[a] *18* Some Septuagint manuscripts (see also 1 Chron. 19:18); Hebrew *horsemen* [b] *11* Or *staying at Sukkoth* [c] *21* Also known as *Jerub-Baal* (that is, Gideon)

he took the ewe lamb that belonged to the poor man and prepared it for the one who had come to him."

5 David burned with anger against the man and said to Nathan, "As surely as the LORD lives, the man who did this must die! 6 He must pay for that lamb four times over, because he did such a thing and had no pity."

7 Then Nathan said to David, "You are the man! This is what the LORD, the God of Israel, says: 'I anointed you king over Israel, and I delivered you from the hand of Saul. 8 I gave your master's house to you, and your master's wives into your arms. I gave you all Israel and Judah. And if all this had been too little, I would have given you even more. 9 Why did you despise the word of the LORD by doing what is evil in his eyes? You struck down Uriah the Hittite with the sword and took his wife to be your own. You killed him with the sword of the Ammonites. 10 Now, therefore, the sword will never depart from your house, because you despised me and took the wife of Uriah the Hittite to be your own.'

11 "This is what the LORD says: 'Out of your own household I am going to bring calamity on you. Before your very eyes I will take your wives and give them to one who is close to you, and he will sleep with your wives in broad daylight. 12 You did it in secret, but I will do this thing in broad daylight before all Israel.'"

13 Then David said to Nathan, "I have sinned against the LORD."

Nathan replied, "The LORD has taken away your sin. You are not going to die. 14 But because by doing this you have shown utter contempt for[a] the LORD, the son born to you will die."

15 After Nathan had gone home, the LORD struck the child that Uriah's wife had borne to David, and he became ill. 16 David pleaded with God for the child. He fasted and spent the nights lying in sackcloth[b] on the ground. 17 The elders of his household stood beside him to get him up from the ground, but he refused, and he would not eat any food with them.

18 On the seventh day the child died. David's attendants were afraid to tell him that the child was dead, for they thought, "While the child was still living, he wouldn't listen to us when we spoke to him. How can we now tell him the child is dead? He may do something desperate."

19 David noticed that his attendants were whispering among themselves, and he realized the child was dead. "Is the child dead?" he asked.

"Yes," they replied, "he is dead."

20 Then David got up from the ground. After he had washed, put on lotions and changed his clothes, he went into the house of the LORD and worshiped. Then he went to his own house, and at his request they served him food, and he ate.

21 His attendants asked him, "Why are you acting this way? While the child was alive, you fasted and wept, but now that the child is dead, you get up and eat!"

22 He answered, "While the child was still alive, I fasted and wept. I thought, 'Who knows? The LORD may be gracious to me and let the child live.' 23 But now that he is dead, why should I go on fasting? Can I bring him back again? I will go to him, but he will not return to me."

24 Then David comforted his wife Bathsheba, and he went to her and made love to her. She gave birth to a son, and they named him Solomon. The LORD loved him; 25 and because the LORD loved him, he sent word through Nathan the prophet to name him Jedidiah.[c]

26 Meanwhile Joab fought against Rabbah of the Ammonites and captured the royal citadel. 27 Joab then sent messengers to David, saying, "I have fought against Rabbah and taken its water supply. 28 Now muster the rest of the troops and besiege the city and capture it. Otherwise I will take the city, and it will be named after me."

29 So David mustered the entire army and went to Rabbah, and attacked and captured it. 30 David took the crown from their king's[d] head, and it was placed on his own head. It weighed a talent[e] of gold, and it was set with precious stones. David took a great quantity of plunder from the city 31 and brought out the people who were there, consigning them to labor with saws and with iron picks and axes, and he made them work at brickmaking.[f] David did this to all the Ammonite towns. Then he and his entire army returned to Jerusalem.

Amnon and Tamar

13 In the course of time, Amnon son of David fell in love with Tamar, the beautiful sister of Absalom son of David.

2 Amnon became so obsessed with his sister Tamar that he made himself ill. She was a virgin, and it seemed impossible for him to do anything to her.

3 Now Amnon had an adviser named Jonadab son of Shimeah, David's brother. Jonadab was a very shrewd man. 4 He asked Amnon, "Why do you, the king's son, look so haggard morning after morning? Won't you tell me?"

Amnon said to him, "I'm in love with Tamar, my brother Absalom's sister."

5 "Go to bed and pretend to be ill," Jonadab said. "When your father comes to see you, say to him, 'I would like my sister Tamar to come and give me something to eat. Let her prepare the food in my sight so I may watch her and then eat it from her hand.'"

6 So Amnon lay down and pretended to be ill. When the king came to see him, Amnon said to him, "I would like my sister Tamar to come and make some special bread in my sight, so I may eat from her hand."

[a] *14* An ancient Hebrew scribal tradition; Masoretic Text *for the enemies of* [b] *16* Dead Sea Scrolls and Septuagint; Masoretic Text does not have *in sackcloth.* [c] *25* *Jedidiah* means *loved by the LORD.* [d] *30* Or *from Milkom's* (that is, Molek's) [e] *30* That is, about 75 pounds or about 34 kilograms [f] *31* The meaning of the Hebrew for this clause is uncertain.

[7]David sent word to Tamar at the palace: "Go to the house of your brother Amnon and prepare some food for him." [8]So Tamar went to the house of her brother Amnon, who was lying down. She took some dough, kneaded it, made the bread in his sight and baked it. [9]Then she took the pan and served him the bread, but he refused to eat.

"Send everyone out of here," Amnon said. So everyone left him. [10]Then Amnon said to Tamar, "Bring the food here into my bedroom so I may eat from your hand." And Tamar took the bread she had prepared and brought it to her brother Amnon in his bedroom. [11]But when she took it to him to eat, he grabbed her and said, "Come to bed with me, my sister."

[12]"No, my brother!" she said to him. "Don't force me! Such a thing should not be done in Israel! Don't do this wicked thing. [13]What about me? Where could I get rid of my disgrace? And what about you? You would be like one of the wicked fools in Israel. Please speak to the king; he will not keep me from being married to you." [14]But he refused to listen to her, and since he was stronger than she, he raped her.

[15]Then Amnon hated her with intense hatred. In fact, he hated her more than he had loved her. Amnon said to her, "Get up and get out!"

[16]"No!" she said to him. "Sending me away would be a greater wrong than what you have already done to me."

But he refused to listen to her. [17]He called his personal servant and said, "Get this woman out of my sight and bolt the door after her." [18]So his servant put her out and bolted the door after her. She was wearing an ornate[a] robe, for this was the kind of garment the virgin daughters of the king wore. [19]Tamar put ashes on her head and tore the ornate robe she was wearing. She put her hands on her head and went away, weeping aloud as she went.

[20]Her brother Absalom said to her, "Has that Amnon, your brother, been with you? Be quiet for now, my sister; he is your brother. Don't take this thing to heart." And Tamar lived in her brother Absalom's house, a desolate woman.

[21]When King David heard all this, he was furious. [22]And Absalom never said a word to Amnon, either good or bad; he hated Amnon because he had disgraced his sister Tamar.

Absalom Kills Amnon

[23]Two years later, when Absalom's sheepshearers were at Baal Hazor near the border of Ephraim, he invited all the king's sons to come there. [24]Absalom went to the king and said, "Your servant has had shearers come. Will the king and his attendants please join me?"

[25]"No, my son," the king replied. "All of us should not go; we would only be a burden to you." Although Absalom urged him, he still refused to go but gave him his blessing.

[26]Then Absalom said, "If not, please let my brother Amnon come with us."

The king asked him, "Why should he go with you?" [27]But Absalom urged him, so he sent with him Amnon and the rest of the king's sons.

[28]Absalom ordered his men, "Listen! When Amnon is in high spirits from drinking wine and I say to you, 'Strike Amnon down,' then kill him. Don't be afraid. Haven't I given you this order? Be strong and brave." [29]So Absalom's men did to Amnon what Absalom had ordered. Then all the king's sons got up, mounted their mules and fled.

[30]While they were on their way, the report came to David: "Absalom has struck down all the king's sons; not one of them is left." [31]The king stood up, tore his clothes and lay down on the ground; and all his attendants stood by with their clothes torn.

[32]But Jonadab son of Shimeah, David's brother, said, "My lord should not think that they killed all the princes; only Amnon is dead. This has been Absalom's express intention ever since the day Amnon raped his sister Tamar. [33]My lord the king should not be concerned about the report that all the king's sons are dead. Only Amnon is dead."

[34]Meanwhile, Absalom had fled.

Now the man standing watch looked up and saw many people on the road west of him, coming down the side of the hill. The watchman went and told the king, "I see men in the direction of Horonaim, on the side of the hill."[b]

[35]Jonadab said to the king, "See, the king's sons have come; it has happened just as your servant said."

[36]As he finished speaking, the king's sons came in, wailing loudly. The king, too, and all his attendants wept very bitterly.

[37]Absalom fled and went to Talmai son of Ammihud, the king of Geshur. But King David mourned many days for his son.

[38]After Absalom fled and went to Geshur, he stayed there three years. [39]And King David longed to go to Absalom, for he was consoled concerning Amnon's death.

Absalom Returns to Jerusalem

14 Joab son of Zeruiah knew that the king's heart longed for Absalom. [2]So Joab sent someone to Tekoa and had a wise woman brought from there. He said to her, "Pretend you are in mourning. Dress in mourning clothes, and don't use any cosmetic lotions. Act like a woman who has spent many days grieving for the dead. [3]Then go to the king and speak these words to him." And Joab put the words in her mouth.

[4]When the woman from Tekoa went[c] to the king, she fell with her face to the ground to pay him honor, and she said, "Help me, Your Majesty!"

[5]The king asked her, "What is troubling you?"

[a] *18* The meaning of the Hebrew for this word is uncertain; also in verse 19. [b] *34* Septuagint; Hebrew does not have this sentence. [c] *4* Many Hebrew manuscripts, Septuagint, Vulgate and Syriac; most Hebrew manuscripts *spoke*

She said, "I am a widow; my husband is
dead. 6I your servant had two sons. They got
into a fight with each other in the field, and
no one was there to separate them. One struck
the other and killed him. 7Now the whole clan
has risen up against your servant; they say,
'Hand over the one who struck his brother
down, so that we may put him to death for the
life of his brother whom he killed; then we will
get rid of the heir as well.' They would put out
the only burning coal I have left, leaving my
husband neither name nor descendant on the
face of the earth."

8The king said to the woman, "Go home,
and I will issue an order in your behalf."

9But the woman from Tekoa said to him,
"Let my lord the king pardon me and my family, and let the king and his throne be without
guilt."

10The king replied, "If anyone says anything to you, bring them to me, and they will
not bother you again."

11She said, "Then let the king invoke the
LORD his God to prevent the avenger of blood
from adding to the destruction, so that my son
will not be destroyed."

"As surely as the LORD lives," he said, "not
one hair of your son's head will fall to the
ground."

12Then the woman said, "Let your servant
speak a word to my lord the king."

"Speak," he replied.

13The woman said, "Why then have you devised a thing like this against the people of
God? When the king says this, does he not
convict himself, for the king has not brought
back his banished son? 14Like water spilled
on the ground, which cannot be recovered, so
we must die. But that is not what God desires;
rather, he devises ways so that a banished
person does not remain banished from him.

15"And now I have come to say this to my
lord the king because the people have made
me afraid. Your servant thought, 'I will speak
to the king; perhaps he will grant his servant's
request. 16Perhaps the king will agree to deliver his servant from the hand of the man who
is trying to cut off both me and my son from
God's inheritance.'

17"And now your servant says, 'May the
word of my lord the king secure my inheritance, for my lord the king is like an angel
of God in discerning good and evil. May the
LORD your God be with you.'"

18Then the king said to the woman, "Don't
keep from me the answer to what I am going
to ask you."

"Let my lord the king speak," the woman
said.

19The king asked, "Isn't the hand of Joab
with you in all this?"

The woman answered, "As surely as you
live, my lord the king, no one can turn to the
right or to the left from anything my lord the
king says. Yes, it was your servant Joab who
instructed me to do this and who put all these
words into the mouth of your servant. 20Your
servant Joab did this to change the present
situation. My lord has wisdom like that of an
angel of God—he knows everything that happens in the land."

21The king said to Joab, "Very well, I will do
it. Go, bring back the young man Absalom."

22Joab fell with his face to the ground to pay
him honor, and he blessed the king. Joab said,
"Today your servant knows that he has found
favor in your eyes, my lord the king, because
the king has granted his servant's request."

23Then Joab went to Geshur and brought
Absalom back to Jerusalem. 24But the king
said, "He must go to his own house; he must
not see my face." So Absalom went to his own
house and did not see the face of the king.

25In all Israel there was not a man so highly
praised for his handsome appearance as Absalom. From the top of his head to the sole of
his foot there was no blemish in him. 26When-
ever he cut the hair of his head—he used to
cut his hair once a year because it became
too heavy for him—he would weigh it, and
its weight was two hundred shekels[a] by the
royal standard.

27Three sons and a daughter were born to
Absalom. His daughter's name was Tamar,
and she became a beautiful woman.

28Absalom lived two years in Jerusalem
without seeing the king's face. 29Then Absalom sent for Joab in order to send him to the
king, but Joab refused to come to him. So he
sent a second time, but he refused to come.
30Then he said to his servants, "Look, Joab's
field is next to mine, and he has barley there.
Go and set it on fire." So Absalom's servants
set the field on fire.

31Then Joab did go to Absalom's house, and
he said to him, "Why have your servants set
my field on fire?"

32Absalom said to Joab, "Look, I sent word
to you and said, 'Come here so I can send you
to the king to ask, "Why have I come from
Geshur? It would be better for me if I were
still there!"' Now then, I want to see the king's
face, and if I am guilty of anything, let him
put me to death."

33So Joab went to the king and told him this.
Then the king summoned Absalom, and he
came in and bowed down with his face to the
ground before the king. And the king kissed
Absalom.

Absalom's Conspiracy

15 In the course of time, Absalom provided himself with a chariot and horses
and with fifty men to run ahead of him. 2He
would get up early and stand by the side of
the road leading to the city gate. Whenever
anyone came with a complaint to be placed
before the king for a decision, Absalom would
call out to him, "What town are you from?"
He would answer, "Your servant is from one
of the tribes of Israel." 3Then Absalom would
say to him, "Look, your claims are valid and
proper, but there is no representative of the
king to hear you." 4And Absalom would add,

[a] *26* That is, about 5 pounds or about 2.3 kilograms

"If only I were appointed judge in the land!
Then everyone who has a complaint or case
could come to me and I would see that they
receive justice."
5 Also, whenever anyone approached him to
bow down before him, Absalom would reach
out his hand, take hold of him and kiss him.
6 Absalom behaved in this way toward all the
Israelites who came to the king asking for
justice, and so he stole the hearts of the people of Israel.
7 At the end of four[a] years, Absalom said to
the king, "Let me go to Hebron and fulfill a
vow I made to the LORD. 8 While your servant
was living at Geshur in Aram, I made this
vow: 'If the LORD takes me back to Jerusalem,
I will worship the LORD in Hebron.[b]'"
9 The king said to him, "Go in peace." So he
went to Hebron.
10 Then Absalom sent secret messengers
throughout the tribes of Israel to say, "As soon
as you hear the sound of the trumpets, then
say, 'Absalom is king in Hebron.'" 11 Two hundred men from Jerusalem had accompanied
Absalom. They had been invited as guests
and went quite innocently, knowing nothing
about the matter. 12 While Absalom was offering sacrifices, he also sent for Ahithophel
the Gilonite, David's counselor, to come from
Giloh, his hometown. And so the conspiracy
gained strength, and Absalom's following
kept on increasing.

David Flees

13 A messenger came and told David, "The
hearts of the people of Israel are with Absalom."
14 Then David said to all his officials who
were with him in Jerusalem, "Come! We must
flee, or none of us will escape from Absalom.
We must leave immediately, or he will move
quickly to overtake us and bring ruin on us
and put the city to the sword."
15 The king's officials answered him, "Your
servants are ready to do whatever our lord the
king chooses."
16 The king set out, with his entire household
following him; but he left ten concubines to
take care of the palace. 17 So the king set out,
with all the people following him, and they
halted at the edge of the city. 18 All his men
marched past him, along with all the Kerethites and Pelethites; and all the six hundred
Gittites who had accompanied him from Gath
marched before the king.
19 The king said to Ittai the Gittite, "Why
should you come along with us? Go back and
stay with King Absalom. You are a foreigner,
an exile from your homeland. 20 You came only
yesterday. And today shall I make you wander about with us, when I do not know where
I am going? Go back, and take your people
with you. May the LORD show you kindness
and faithfulness."[c]
21 But Ittai replied to the king, "As surely as
the LORD lives, and as my lord the king lives,
wherever my lord the king may be, whether
it means life or death, there will your servant be."
22 David said to Ittai, "Go ahead, march on."
So Ittai the Gittite marched on with all his
men and the families that were with him.
23 The whole countryside wept aloud as all
the people passed by. The king also crossed
the Kidron Valley, and all the people moved
on toward the wilderness.
24 Zadok was there, too, and all the Levites
who were with him were carrying the ark of
the covenant of God. They set down the ark
of God, and Abiathar offered sacrifices until
all the people had finished leaving the city.
25 Then the king said to Zadok, "Take the
ark of God back into the city. If I find favor in
the LORD's eyes, he will bring me back and let
me see it and his dwelling place again. 26 But
if he says, 'I am not pleased with you,' then I
am ready; let him do to me whatever seems
good to him."
27 The king also said to Zadok the priest, "Do
you understand? Go back to the city with my
blessing. Take your son Ahimaaz with you,
and also Abiathar's son Jonathan. You and
Abiathar return with your two sons. 28 I will
wait at the fords in the wilderness until word
comes from you to inform me." 29 So Zadok
and Abiathar took the ark of God back to Jerusalem and stayed there.
30 But David continued up the Mount of Olives, weeping as he went; his head was covered and he was barefoot. All the people with
him covered their heads too and were weeping as they went up. 31 Now David had been
told, "Ahithophel is among the conspirators
with Absalom." So David prayed, "LORD, turn
Ahithophel's counsel into foolishness."
32 When David arrived at the summit, where
people used to worship God, Hushai the Arkite was there to meet him, his robe torn and
dust on his head. 33 David said to him, "If you
go with me, you will be a burden to me. 34 But
if you return to the city and say to Absalom,
'Your Majesty, I will be your servant; I was
your father's servant in the past, but now I
will be your servant,' then you can help me
by frustrating Ahithophel's advice. 35 Won't
the priests Zadok and Abiathar be there with
you? Tell them anything you hear in the king's
palace. 36 Their two sons, Ahimaaz son of Zadok and Jonathan son of Abiathar, are there
with them. Send them to me with anything
you hear."
37 So Hushai, David's confidant, arrived at
Jerusalem as Absalom was entering the city.

David and Ziba

16 When David had gone a short distance
beyond the summit, there was Ziba, the
steward of Mephibosheth, waiting to meet
him. He had a string of donkeys saddled and
loaded with two hundred loaves of bread, a

[a] 7 Some Septuagint manuscripts, Syriac and Josephus; Hebrew *forty* [b] 8 Some Septuagint manuscripts; Hebrew does not have *in Hebron.* [c] 20 Septuagint; Hebrew *May kindness and faithfulness be with you*

hundred cakes of raisins, a hundred cakes of
figs and a skin of wine.
2The king asked Ziba, “Why have you
brought these?”
Ziba answered, “The donkeys are for the
king’s household to ride on, the bread and
fruit are for the men to eat, and the wine is to
refresh those who become exhausted in the
wilderness.”
3The king then asked, “Where is your master’s grandson?”
Ziba said to him, “He is staying in Jerusalem, because he thinks, ‘Today the Israelites
will restore to me my grandfather’s kingdom.’ ”
4Then the king said to Ziba, “All that belonged to Mephibosheth is now yours.”
“I humbly bow,” Ziba said. “May I find favor
in your eyes, my lord the king.”

Shimei Curses David

5As King David approached Bahurim, a
man from the same clan as Saul’s family came
out from there. His name was Shimei son of
Gera, and he cursed as he came out. 6He pelted
David and all the king’s officials with stones,
though all the troops and the special guard
were on David’s right and left. 7As he cursed,
Shimei said, “Get out, get out, you murderer, you scoundrel! 8The LORD has repaid you
for all the blood you shed in the household of
Saul, in whose place you have reigned. The
LORD has given the kingdom into the hands
of your son Absalom. You have come to ruin
because you are a murderer!”
9Then Abishai son of Zeruiah said to the
king, “Why should this dead dog curse my
lord the king? Let me go over and cut off his
head.”
10But the king said, “What does this have
to do with you, you sons of Zeruiah? If he is
cursing because the LORD said to him, ‘Curse
David,’ who can ask, ‘Why do you do this?’ ”
11David then said to Abishai and all his officials, “My son, my own flesh and blood, is
trying to kill me. How much more, then, this
Benjamite! Leave him alone; let him curse,
for the LORD has told him to. 12It may be that
the LORD will look upon my misery and restore to me his covenant blessing instead of
his curse today.”
13So David and his men continued along
the road while Shimei was going along the
hillside opposite him, cursing as he went and
throwing stones at him and showering him
with dirt. 14The king and all the people with
him arrived at their destination exhausted.
And there he refreshed himself.

The Advice of Ahithophel and Hushai

15Meanwhile, Absalom and all the men of
Israel came to Jerusalem, and Ahithophel was
with him. 16Then Hushai the Arkite, David’s
confidant, went to Absalom and said to him,
“Long live the king! Long live the king!”
17Absalom said to Hushai, “So this is the
love you show your friend? If he’s your friend,
why didn’t you go with him?”
18Hushai said to Absalom, “No, the one chosen by the LORD, by these people, and by all
the men of Israel—his I will be, and I will remain with him. 19Furthermore, whom should
I serve? Should I not serve the son? Just as I
served your father, so I will serve you.”
20Absalom said to Ahithophel, “Give us your
advice. What should we do?”
21Ahithophel answered, “Sleep with your
father’s concubines whom he left to take care
of the palace. Then all Israel will hear that you
have made yourself obnoxious to your father,
and the hands of everyone with you will be
more resolute.” 22So they pitched a tent for
Absalom on the roof, and he slept with his
father’s concubines in the sight of all Israel.
23Now in those days the advice Ahithophel
gave was like that of one who inquires of God.
That was how both David and Absalom regarded all of Ahithophel’s advice.
17 Ahithophel said to Absalom, “I would[a]
choose twelve thousand men and set
out tonight in pursuit of David. 2I would attack him while he is weary and weak. I would
strike him with terror, and then all the people
with him will flee. I would strike down only
the king 3and bring all the people back to you.
The death of the man you seek will mean the
return of all; all the people will be unharmed.”
4This plan seemed good to Absalom and to all
the elders of Israel.
5But Absalom said, “Summon also Hushai
the Arkite, so we can hear what he has to say
as well.” 6When Hushai came to him, Absalom said, “Ahithophel has given this advice.
Should we do what he says? If not, give us
your opinion.”
7Hushai replied to Absalom, “The advice
Ahithophel has given is not good this time.
8You know your father and his men; they are
fighters, and as fierce as a wild bear robbed
of her cubs. Besides, your father is an experienced fighter; he will not spend the night with
the troops. 9Even now, he is hidden in a cave
or some other place. If he should attack your
troops first,[b] whoever hears about it will say,
‘There has been a slaughter among the troops
who follow Absalom.’ 10Then even the bravest
soldier, whose heart is like the heart of a lion,
will melt with fear, for all Israel knows that
your father is a fighter and that those with
him are brave.
11“So I advise you: Let all Israel, from Dan
to Beersheba—as numerous as the sand on
the seashore—be gathered to you, with you
yourself leading them into battle. 12Then we
will attack him wherever he may be found,
and we will fall on him as dew settles on the
ground. Neither he nor any of his men will be
left alive. 13If he withdraws into a city, then all
Israel will bring ropes to that city, and we will
drag it down to the valley until not so much
as a pebble is left.”
14Absalom and all the men of Israel said,
“The advice of Hushai the Arkite is better than

[a] 1 Or *Let me* [b] 9 Or *When some of the men fall at the first attack*

that of Ahithophel." For the LORD had determined to frustrate the good advice of Ahithophel in order to bring disaster on Absalom.

15Hushai told Zadok and Abiathar, the priests, "Ahithophel has advised Absalom and the elders of Israel to do such and such, but I have advised them to do so and so. 16Now send a message at once and tell David, 'Do not spend the night at the fords in the wilderness; cross over without fail, or the king and all the people with him will be swallowed up.'"

17Jonathan and Ahimaaz were staying at En Rogel. A female servant was to go and inform them, and they were to go and tell King David, for they could not risk being seen entering the city. 18But a young man saw them and told Absalom. So the two of them left at once and went to the house of a man in Bahurim. He had a well in his courtyard, and they climbed down into it. 19His wife took a covering and spread it out over the opening of the well and scattered grain over it. No one knew anything about it.

20When Absalom's men came to the woman at the house, they asked, "Where are Ahimaaz and Jonathan?"

The woman answered them, "They crossed over the brook."[a] The men searched but found no one, so they returned to Jerusalem.

21After they had gone, the two climbed out of the well and went to inform King David. They said to him, "Set out and cross the river at once; Ahithophel has advised such and such against you." 22So David and all the people with him set out and crossed the Jordan. By daybreak, no one was left who had not crossed the Jordan.

23When Ahithophel saw that his advice had not been followed, he saddled his donkey and set out for his house in his hometown. He put his house in order and then hanged himself. So he died and was buried in his father's tomb.

Absalom's Death

24David went to Mahanaim, and Absalom crossed the Jordan with all the men of Israel. 25Absalom had appointed Amasa over the army in place of Joab. Amasa was the son of Jether,[b] an Ishmaelite[c] who had married Abigail,[d] the daughter of Nahash and sister of Zeruiah the mother of Joab. 26The Israelites and Absalom camped in the land of Gilead.

27When David came to Mahanaim, Shobi son of Nahash from Rabbah of the Ammonites, and Makir son of Ammiel from Lo Debar, and Barzillai the Gileadite from Rogelim 28brought bedding and bowls and articles of pottery. They also brought wheat and barley, flour and roasted grain, beans and lentils,[e] 29honey and curds, sheep, and cheese from cows' milk for David and his people to eat. For they said, "The people have become exhausted and hungry and thirsty in the wilderness."

18 David mustered the men who were with him and appointed over them commanders of thousands and commanders of hundreds. 2David sent out his troops, a third under the command of Joab, a third under Joab's brother Abishai son of Zeruiah, and a third under Ittai the Gittite. The king told the troops, "I myself will surely march out with you."

3But the men said, "You must not go out; if we are forced to flee, they won't care about us. Even if half of us die, they won't care; but you are worth ten thousand of us.[f] It would be better now for you to give us support from the city."

4The king answered, "I will do whatever seems best to you."

So the king stood beside the gate while all his men marched out in units of hundreds and of thousands. 5The king commanded Joab, Abishai and Ittai, "Be gentle with the young man Absalom for my sake." And all the troops heard the king giving orders concerning Absalom to each of the commanders.

6David's army marched out of the city to fight Israel, and the battle took place in the forest of Ephraim. 7There Israel's troops were routed by David's men, and the casualties that day were great—twenty thousand men. 8The battle spread out over the whole countryside, and the forest swallowed up more men that day than the sword.

9Now Absalom happened to meet David's men. He was riding his mule, and as the mule went under the thick branches of a large oak, Absalom's hair got caught in the tree. He was left hanging in midair, while the mule he was riding kept on going.

10When one of the men saw what had happened, he told Joab, "I just saw Absalom hanging in an oak tree."

11Joab said to the man who had told him this, "What! You saw him? Why didn't you strike him to the ground right there? Then I would have had to give you ten shekels[g] of silver and a warrior's belt."

12But the man replied, "Even if a thousand shekels[h] were weighed out into my hands, I would not lay a hand on the king's son. In our hearing the king commanded you and Abishai and Ittai, 'Protect the young man Absalom for my sake.[i]' 13And if I had put my life in jeopardy[j]—and nothing is hidden from the king—you would have kept your distance from me."

14Joab said, "I'm not going to wait like this for you." So he took three javelins in his hand and plunged them into Absalom's heart while Absalom was still alive in the oak tree. 15And ten of Joab's armor-bearers surrounded Absalom, struck him and killed him.

[a] 20 Or *"They passed by the sheep pen toward the water."* [b] 25 Hebrew *Ithra,* a variant of *Jether* [c] 25 Some Septuagint manuscripts (see also 1 Chron. 2:17); Hebrew and other Septuagint manuscripts *Israelite* [d] 25 Hebrew *Abigal,* a variant of *Abigail* [e] 28 Most Septuagint manuscripts and Syriac; Hebrew *lentils, and roasted grain* [f] 3 Two Hebrew manuscripts, some Septuagint manuscripts and Vulgate; most Hebrew manuscripts *care; for now there are ten thousand like us* [g] 11 That is, about 4 ounces or about 115 grams [h] 12 That is, about 25 pounds or about 12 kilograms [i] 12 A few Hebrew manuscripts, Septuagint, Vulgate and Syriac; most Hebrew manuscripts may be translated *Absalom, whoever you may be.* [j] 13 Or *Otherwise, if I had acted treacherously toward him*

[16]Then Joab sounded the trumpet, and the
troops stopped pursuing Israel, for Joab halted them. [17]They took Absalom, threw him into
a big pit in the forest and piled up a large heap
of rocks over him. Meanwhile, all the Israelites fled to their homes.

[18]During his lifetime Absalom had taken a
pillar and erected it in the King's Valley as a
monument to himself, for he thought, "I have
no son to carry on the memory of my name."
He named the pillar after himself, and it is
called Absalom's Monument to this day.

David Mourns

[19]Now Ahimaaz son of Zadok said, "Let me
run and take the news to the king that the
LORD has vindicated him by delivering him
from the hand of his enemies."

[20]"You are not the one to take the news today," Joab told him. "You may take the news
another time, but you must not do so today,
because the king's son is dead."

[21]Then Joab said to a Cushite, "Go, tell the
king what you have seen." The Cushite bowed
down before Joab and ran off.

[22]Ahimaaz son of Zadok again said to Joab,
"Come what may, please let me run behind
the Cushite."

But Joab replied, "My son, why do you want
to go? You don't have any news that will bring
you a reward."

[23]He said, "Come what may, I want to run."

So Joab said, "Run!" Then Ahimaaz ran
by way of the plain[a] and outran the Cushite.

[24]While David was sitting between the inner and outer gates, the watchman went up
to the roof of the gateway by the wall. As he
looked out, he saw a man running alone.
[25]The watchman called out to the king and
reported it.

The king said, "If he is alone, he must have
good news." And the runner came closer and
closer.

[26]Then the watchman saw another runner,
and he called down to the gatekeeper, "Look,
another man running alone!"

The king said, "He must be bringing good
news, too."

[27]The watchman said, "It seems to me that
the first one runs like Ahimaaz son of Zadok."

"He's a good man," the king said. "He comes
with good news."

[28]Then Ahimaaz called out to the king, "All
is well!" He bowed down before the king with
his face to the ground and said, "Praise be
to the LORD your God! He has delivered up
those who lifted their hands against my lord
the king."

[29]The king asked, "Is the young man Absalom safe?"

Ahimaaz answered, "I saw great confusion
just as Joab was about to send the king's servant and me, your servant, but I don't know
what it was."

[30]The king said, "Stand aside and wait
here." So he stepped aside and stood there.

[31]Then the Cushite arrived and said, "My
lord the king, hear the good news! The LORD
has vindicated you today by delivering you
from the hand of all who rose up against you."

[32]The king asked the Cushite, "Is the young
man Absalom safe?"

The Cushite replied, "May the enemies of
my lord the king and all who rise up to harm
you be like that young man."

[33]The king was shaken. He went up to the
room over the gateway and wept. As he went,
he said: "O my son Absalom! My son, my son
Absalom! If only I had died instead of you—O
Absalom, my son, my son!"[b]

19[c] Joab was told, "The king is weeping and
mourning for Absalom." [2]And for the
whole army the victory that day was turned
into mourning, because on that day the troops
heard it said, "The king is grieving for his
son." [3]The men stole into the city that day as
men steal in who are ashamed when they flee
from battle. [4]The king covered his face and
cried aloud, "O my son Absalom! O Absalom,
my son, my son!"

[5]Then Joab went into the house to the king
and said, "Today you have humiliated all your
men, who have just saved your life and the
lives of your sons and daughters and the lives
of your wives and concubines. [6]You love those
who hate you and hate those who love you.
You have made it clear today that the commanders and their men mean nothing to you. I
see that you would be pleased if Absalom were
alive today and all of us were dead. [7]Now go
out and encourage your men. I swear by the
LORD that if you don't go out, not a man will be
left with you by nightfall. This will be worse
for you than all the calamities that have come
on you from your youth till now."

[8]So the king got up and took his seat in
the gateway. When the men were told, "The
king is sitting in the gateway," they all came
before him.

Meanwhile, the Israelites had fled to their
homes.

David Returns to Jerusalem

[9]Throughout the tribes of Israel, all the people were arguing among themselves, saying,
"The king delivered us from the hand of our
enemies; he is the one who rescued us from
the hand of the Philistines. But now he has
fled the country to escape from Absalom;
[10]and Absalom, whom we anointed to rule
over us, has died in battle. So why do you
say nothing about bringing the king back?"

[11]King David sent this message to Zadok
and Abiathar, the priests: "Ask the elders of
Judah, 'Why should you be the last to bring
the king back to his palace, since what is being
said throughout Israel has reached the king
at his quarters? [12]You are my relatives, my
own flesh and blood. So why should you be
the last to bring back the king?' [13]And say to
Amasa, 'Are you not my own flesh and blood?
May God deal with me, be it ever so severely,

[a] *23* That is, the plain of the Jordan [b] *33* In Hebrew texts this verse (18:33) is numbered 19:1. [c] In Hebrew texts 19:1-43 is numbered 19:2-44.

if you are not the commander of my army for
life in place of Joab.'"
14He won over the hearts of the men of Judah so that they were all of one mind. They
sent word to the king, "Return, you and all
your men." 15Then the king returned and went
as far as the Jordan.
Now the men of Judah had come to Gilgal
to go out and meet the king and bring him
across the Jordan. 16Shimei son of Gera, the
Benjamite from Bahurim, hurried down with
the men of Judah to meet King David. 17With
him were a thousand Benjamites, along with
Ziba, the steward of Saul's household, and
his fifteen sons and twenty servants. They
rushed to the Jordan, where the king was.
18They crossed at the ford to take the king's
household over and to do whatever he wished.
When Shimei son of Gera crossed the Jordan, he fell prostrate before the king 19and said
to him, "May my lord not hold me guilty. Do not
remember how your servant did wrong on the
day my lord the king left Jerusalem. May the
king put it out of his mind. 20For I your servant
know that I have sinned, but today I have come
here as the first from the tribes of Joseph to
come down and meet my lord the king."
21Then Abishai son of Zeruiah said,
"Shouldn't Shimei be put to death for this?
He cursed the LORD's anointed."
22David replied, "What does this have to do
with you, you sons of Zeruiah? What right do
you have to interfere? Should anyone be put
to death in Israel today? Don't I know that
today I am king over Israel?" 23So the king
said to Shimei, "You shall not die." And the
king promised him on oath.
24Mephibosheth, Saul's grandson, also went
down to meet the king. He had not taken care
of his feet or trimmed his mustache or washed
his clothes from the day the king left until
the day he returned safely. 25When he came
from Jerusalem to meet the king, the king
asked him, "Why didn't you go with me, Mephibosheth?"
26He said, "My lord the king, since I your
servant am lame, I said, 'I will have my donkey saddled and will ride on it, so I can go with
the king.' But Ziba my servant betrayed me.
27And he has slandered your servant to my
lord the king. My lord the king is like an angel of God; so do whatever you wish. 28All my
grandfather's descendants deserved nothing
but death from my lord the king, but you gave
your servant a place among those who eat at
your table. So what right do I have to make
any more appeals to the king?"
29The king said to him, "Why say more? I
order you and Ziba to divide the land."
30Mephibosheth said to the king, "Let him
take everything, now that my lord the king
has returned home safely."
31Barzillai the Gileadite also came down
from Rogelim to cross the Jordan with the
king and to send him on his way from there.
32Now Barzillai was very old, eighty years of
age. He had provided for the king during his
stay in Mahanaim, for he was a very wealthy
man. 33The king said to Barzillai, "Cross over
with me and stay with me in Jerusalem, and
I will provide for you."
34But Barzillai answered the king, "How
many more years will I live, that I should go
up to Jerusalem with the king? 35I am now
eighty years old. Can I tell the difference between what is enjoyable and what is not? Can
your servant taste what he eats and drinks?
Can I still hear the voices of male and female
singers? Why should your servant be an added burden to my lord the king? 36Your servant
will cross over the Jordan with the king for
a short distance, but why should the king reward me in this way? 37Let your servant return, that I may die in my own town near the
tomb of my father and mother. But here is your
servant Kimham. Let him cross over with my
lord the king. Do for him whatever you wish."
38The king said, "Kimham shall cross over
with me, and I will do for him whatever you
wish. And anything you desire from me I will
do for you."
39So all the people crossed the Jordan, and
then the king crossed over. The king kissed
Barzillai and bid him farewell, and Barzillai
returned to his home.
40When the king crossed over to Gilgal,
Kimham crossed with him. All the troops of
Judah and half the troops of Israel had taken
the king over.
41Soon all the men of Israel were coming
to the king and saying to him, "Why did our
brothers, the men of Judah, steal the king
away and bring him and his household across
the Jordan, together with all his men?"
42All the men of Judah answered the men of
Israel, "We did this because the king is closely related to us. Why are you angry about it?
Have we eaten any of the king's provisions?
Have we taken anything for ourselves?"
43Then the men of Israel answered the men
of Judah, "We have ten shares in the king;
so we have a greater claim on David than
you have. Why then do you treat us with
contempt? Weren't we the first to speak of
bringing back our king?"
But the men of Judah pressed their claims
even more forcefully than the men of Israel.

Sheba Rebels Against David

20 Now a troublemaker named Sheba son
of Bikri, a Benjamite, happened to be
there. He sounded the trumpet and shouted,

"We have no share in David,
no part in Jesse's son!
Every man to his tent, Israel!"

2So all the men of Israel deserted David to
follow Sheba son of Bikri. But the men of Judah stayed by their king all the way from the
Jordan to Jerusalem.
3When David returned to his palace in Jerusalem, he took the ten concubines he had
left to take care of the palace and put them in
a house under guard. He provided for them
but had no sexual relations with them. They
were kept in confinement till the day of their
death, living as widows.
4Then the king said to Amasa, "Summon

the men of Judah to come to me within three days, and be here yourself." 5But when Amasa went to summon Judah, he took longer than the time the king had set for him.

6David said to Abishai, "Now Sheba son of Bikri will do us more harm than Absalom did. Take your master's men and pursue him, or he will find fortified cities and escape from us."[a] 7So Joab's men and the Kerethites and Pelethites and all the mighty warriors went out under the command of Abishai. They marched out from Jerusalem to pursue Sheba son of Bikri.

8While they were at the great rock in Gibeon, Amasa came to meet them. Joab was wearing his military tunic, and strapped over it at his waist was a belt with a dagger in its sheath. As he stepped forward, it dropped out of its sheath.

9Joab said to Amasa, "How are you, my brother?" Then Joab took Amasa by the beard with his right hand to kiss him. 10Amasa was not on his guard against the dagger in Joab's hand, and Joab plunged it into his belly, and his intestines spilled out on the ground. Without being stabbed again, Amasa died. Then Joab and his brother Abishai pursued Sheba son of Bikri.

11One of Joab's men stood beside Amasa and said, "Whoever favors Joab, and whoever is for David, let him follow Joab!" 12Amasa lay wallowing in his blood in the middle of the road, and the man saw that all the troops came to a halt there. When he realized that everyone who came up to Amasa stopped, he dragged him from the road into a field and threw a garment over him. 13After Amasa had been removed from the road, everyone went on with Joab to pursue Sheba son of Bikri.

14Sheba passed through all the tribes of Israel to Abel Beth Maakah and through the entire region of the Bikrites,[b] who gathered together and followed him. 15All the troops with Joab came and besieged Sheba in Abel Beth Maakah. They built a siege ramp up to the city, and it stood against the outer fortifications. While they were battering the wall to bring it down, 16a wise woman called from the city, "Listen! Listen! Tell Joab to come here so I can speak to him." 17He went toward her, and she asked, "Are you Joab?"

"I am," he answered.

She said, "Listen to what your servant has to say."

"I'm listening," he said.

18She continued, "Long ago they used to say, 'Get your answer at Abel,' and that settled it. 19We are the peaceful and faithful in Israel. You are trying to destroy a city that is a mother in Israel. Why do you want to swallow up the LORD's inheritance?"

20"Far be it from me!" Joab replied, "Far be it from me to swallow up or destroy! 21That is not the case. A man named Sheba son of Bikri, from the hill country of Ephraim, has lifted up his hand against the king, against David. Hand over this one man, and I'll withdraw from the city."

The woman said to Joab, "His head will be thrown to you from the wall."

22Then the woman went to all the people with her wise advice, and they cut off the head of Sheba son of Bikri and threw it to Joab. So he sounded the trumpet, and his men dispersed from the city, each returning to his home. And Joab went back to the king in Jerusalem.

David's Officials

23Joab was over Israel's entire army; Benaiah son of Jehoiada was over the Kerethites and Pelethites; 24Adoniram[c] was in charge of forced labor; Jehoshaphat son of Ahilud was recorder; 25Sheva was secretary; Zadok and Abiathar were priests; 26and Ira the Jairite[d] was David's priest.

The Gibeonites Avenged

21 During the reign of David, there was a famine for three successive years; so David sought the face of the LORD. The LORD said, "It is on account of Saul and his blood-stained house; it is because he put the Gibeonites to death."

2The king summoned the Gibeonites and spoke to them. (Now the Gibeonites were not a part of Israel but were survivors of the Amorites; the Israelites had sworn to spare them, but Saul in his zeal for Israel and Judah had tried to annihilate them.) 3David asked the Gibeonites, "What shall I do for you? How shall I make atonement so that you will bless the LORD's inheritance?"

4The Gibeonites answered him, "We have no right to demand silver or gold from Saul or his family, nor do we have the right to put anyone in Israel to death."

"What do you want me to do for you?" David asked.

5They answered the king, "As for the man who destroyed us and plotted against us so that we have been decimated and have no place anywhere in Israel, 6let seven of his male descendants be given to us to be killed and their bodies exposed before the LORD at Gibeah of Saul—the LORD's chosen one."

So the king said, "I will give them to you."

7The king spared Mephibosheth son of Jonathan, the son of Saul, because of the oath before the LORD between David and Jonathan son of Saul. 8But the king took Armoni and Mephibosheth, the two sons of Aiah's daughter Rizpah, whom she had borne to Saul, together with the five sons of Saul's daughter Merab,[e] whom she had borne to Adriel son of Barzillai the Meholathite. 9He handed them over to the Gibeonites, who killed them and

[a] *6* Or *and do us serious injury* [b] *14* See Septuagint and Vulgate; Hebrew *Berites.* [c] *24* Some Septuagint manuscripts (see also 1 Kings 4:6 and 5:14); Hebrew *Adoram* [d] *26* Hebrew; some Septuagint manuscripts and Syriac (see also 23:38) *Ithrite* [e] *8* Two Hebrew manuscripts, some Septuagint manuscripts and Syriac (see also 1 Samuel 18:19); most Hebrew and Septuagint manuscripts *Michal*

exposed their bodies on a hill before the LORD.
All seven of them fell together; they were put
to death during the first days of the harvest,
just as the barley harvest was beginning.
10Rizpah daughter of Aiah took sackcloth
and spread it out for herself on a rock. From
the beginning of the harvest till the rain
poured down from the heavens on the bodies,
she did not let the birds touch them by day or
the wild animals by night. 11When David was
told what Aiah's daughter Rizpah, Saul's concubine, had done, 12he went and took the bones
of Saul and his son Jonathan from the citizens of Jabesh Gilead. (They had stolen their
bodies from the public square at Beth Shan,
where the Philistines had hung them after they
struck Saul down on Gilboa.) 13David brought
the bones of Saul and his son Jonathan from
there, and the bones of those who had been
killed and exposed were gathered up.
14They buried the bones of Saul and his son
Jonathan in the tomb of Saul's father Kish,
at Zela in Benjamin, and did everything the
king commanded. After that, God answered
prayer in behalf of the land.

Wars Against the Philistines

15Once again there was a battle between the
Philistines and Israel. David went down with
his men to fight against the Philistines, and
he became exhausted. 16And Ishbi-Benob, one
of the descendants of Rapha, whose bronze
spearhead weighed three hundred shekels[a]
and who was armed with a new sword, said
he would kill David. 17But Abishai son of Zeruiah came to David's rescue; he struck the
Philistine down and killed him. Then David's
men swore to him, saying, "Never again will
you go out with us to battle, so that the lamp
of Israel will not be extinguished."
18In the course of time, there was another
battle with the Philistines, at Gob. At that time
Sibbekai the Hushathite killed Saph, one of
the descendants of Rapha.
19In another battle with the Philistines at
Gob, Elhanan son of Jair[b] the Bethlehemite
killed the brother of[c] Goliath the Gittite, who
had a spear with a shaft like a weaver's rod.
20In still another battle, which took place at
Gath, there was a huge man with six fingers
on each hand and six toes on each foot—twenty-four in all. He also was descended from
Rapha. 21When he taunted Israel, Jonathan
son of Shimeah, David's brother, killed him.
22These four were descendants of Rapha
in Gath, and they fell at the hands of David
and his men.

David's Song of Praise

22 David sang to the LORD the words of this
song when the LORD delivered him from
the hand of all his enemies and from the hand
of Saul. 2He said:

"The LORD is my rock, my fortress and
my deliverer;
3 my God is my rock, in whom I take
refuge,
my shield[d] and the horn[e] of my
salvation.
He is my stronghold, my refuge and my
savior—
from violent people you save me.

4 "I called to the LORD, who is worthy of
praise,
and have been saved from my enemies.
5 The waves of death swirled about me;
the torrents of destruction
overwhelmed me.
6 The cords of the grave coiled around me;
the snares of death confronted me.

7 "In my distress I called to the LORD;
I called out to my God.
From his temple he heard my voice;
my cry came to his ears.
8 The earth trembled and quaked,
the foundations of the heavens[f]
shook;
they trembled because he was angry.
9 Smoke rose from his nostrils;
consuming fire came from his mouth,
burning coals blazed out of it.
10 He parted the heavens and came down;
dark clouds were under his feet.
11 He mounted the cherubim and flew;
he soared[g] on the wings of the wind.
12 He made darkness his canopy around
him—
the dark[h] rain clouds of the sky.
13 Out of the brightness of his presence
bolts of lightning blazed forth.
14 The LORD thundered from heaven;
the voice of the Most High resounded.
15 He shot his arrows and scattered the
enemy,
with great bolts of lightning he routed
them.
16 The valleys of the sea were exposed
and the foundations of the earth laid
bare
at the rebuke of the LORD,
at the blast of breath from his nostrils.

17 "He reached down from on high and took
hold of me;
he drew me out of deep waters.
18 He rescued me from my powerful
enemy,
from my foes, who were too strong for
me.
19 They confronted me in the day of my
disaster,
but the LORD was my support.
20 He brought me out into a spacious
place;
he rescued me because he delighted in
me.

[a] *16* That is, about 7 1/2 pounds or about 3.5 kilograms [b] *19* See 1 Chron. 20:5; Hebrew *Jaare-Oregim.* [c] *19* See 1 Chron. 20:5; Hebrew does not have *the brother of.* [d] *3* Or *sovereign*
[e] *3* *Horn* here symbolizes strength. [f] *8* Hebrew; Vulgate and Syriac (see also Psalm 18:7) *mountains*
[g] *11* Many Hebrew manuscripts (see also Psalm 18:10); most Hebrew manuscripts *appeared*
[h] *12* Septuagint (see also Psalm 18:11); Hebrew *massed*

21 "The LORD has dealt with me according to
my righteousness;
according to the cleanness of my hands
he has rewarded me.
22 For I have kept the ways of the LORD;
I am not guilty of turning from my God.
23 All his laws are before me;
I have not turned away from his
decrees.
24 I have been blameless before him
and have kept myself from sin.
25 The LORD has rewarded me according to
my righteousness,
according to my cleanness[a] in his sight.

26 "To the faithful you show yourself
faithful,
to the blameless you show yourself
blameless,
27 to the pure you show yourself pure,
but to the devious you show yourself
shrewd.
28 You save the humble,
but your eyes are on the haughty to
bring them low.
29 You, LORD, are my lamp;
the LORD turns my darkness into light.
30 With your help I can advance against a
troop[b];
with my God I can scale a wall.

31 "As for God, his way is perfect:
The LORD's word is flawless;
he shields all who take refuge in him.
32 For who is God besides the LORD?
And who is the Rock except our God?
33 It is God who arms me with strength[c]
and keeps my way secure.
34 He makes my feet like the feet of a deer;
he causes me to stand on the heights.
35 He trains my hands for battle;
my arms can bend a bow of bronze.
36 You make your saving help my shield;
your help has made[d] me great.
37 You provide a broad path for my feet,
so that my ankles do not give way.

38 "I pursued my enemies and crushed them;
I did not turn back till they were
destroyed.
39 I crushed them completely, and they
could not rise;
they fell beneath my feet.
40 You armed me with strength for battle;
you humbled my adversaries before me.
41 You made my enemies turn their backs in
flight,
and I destroyed my foes.
42 They cried for help, but there was no one
to save them—
to the LORD, but he did not answer.
43 I beat them as fine as the dust of the
earth;
I pounded and trampled them like mud
in the streets.

44 "You have delivered me from the attacks
of the peoples;
you have preserved me as the head of
nations.
People I did not know now serve me,
45 foreigners cower before me;
as soon as they hear of me, they obey
me.
46 They all lose heart;
they come trembling[e] from their
strongholds.

47 "The LORD lives! Praise be to my Rock!
Exalted be my God, the Rock, my
Savior!
48 He is the God who avenges me,
who puts the nations under me,
49 who sets me free from my enemies.
You exalted me above my foes;
from a violent man you rescued me.
50 Therefore I will praise you, LORD, among
the nations;
I will sing the praises of your name.

51 "He gives his king great victories;
he shows unfailing kindness to his
anointed,
to David and his descendants forever."

David's Last Words

23 These are the last words of David:

"The inspired utterance of David son of
Jesse,
the utterance of the man exalted by the
Most High,
the man anointed by the God of Jacob,
the hero of Israel's songs:

2 "The Spirit of the LORD spoke through me;
his word was on my tongue.
3 The God of Israel spoke,
the Rock of Israel said to me:
'When one rules over people in
righteousness,
when he rules in the fear of God,
4 he is like the light of morning at sunrise
on a cloudless morning,
like the brightness after rain
that brings grass from the earth.'

5 "If my house were not right with God,
surely he would not have made with me
an everlasting covenant,
arranged and secured in every part;
surely he would not bring to fruition my
salvation
and grant me my every desire.
6 But evil men are all to be cast aside like
thorns,
which are not gathered with the hand.
7 Whoever touches thorns
uses a tool of iron or the shaft of a
spear;
they are burned up where they lie."

[a] 25 Hebrew; Septuagint and Vulgate (see also Psalm 18:24) *to the cleanness of my hands*
[b] 30 Or *can run through a barricade* [c] 33 Dead Sea Scrolls, some Septuagint manuscripts, Vulgate and Syriac (see also Psalm 18:32); Masoretic Text *who is my strong refuge* [d] 36 Dead Sea Scrolls; Masoretic Text *shield; / you stoop down to make* [e] 46 Some Septuagint manuscripts and Vulgate (see also Psalm 18:45); Masoretic Text *they arm themselves*

David's Mighty Warriors

8These are the names of David's mighty
warriors:
Josheb-Basshebeth,[a] a Tahkemonite,[b] was
chief of the Three; he raised his spear against
eight hundred men, whom he killed[c] in one
encounter.
9Next to him was Eleazar son of Dodai the
Ahohite. As one of the three mighty warriors,
he was with David when they taunted the Philistines gathered at Pas Dammim[d] for battle.
Then the Israelites retreated, 10but Eleazar
stood his ground and struck down the Philistines till his hand grew tired and froze to
the sword. The LORD brought about a great
victory that day. The troops returned to Eleazar, but only to strip the dead.
11Next to him was Shammah son of Agee the
Hararite. When the Philistines banded together
at a place where there was a field full of lentils,
Israel's troops fled from them. 12But Shammah
took his stand in the middle of the field. He
defended it and struck the Philistines down,
and the LORD brought about a great victory.
13During harvest time, three of the thirty
chief warriors came down to David at the cave
of Adullam, while a band of Philistines was
encamped in the Valley of Rephaim. 14At that
time David was in the stronghold, and the
Philistine garrison was at Bethlehem. 15David
longed for water and said, "Oh, that someone
would get me a drink of water from the well
near the gate of Bethlehem!" 16So the three
mighty warriors broke through the Philistine
lines, drew water from the well near the gate
of Bethlehem and carried it back to David.
But he refused to drink it; instead, he poured
it out before the LORD. 17"Far be it from me,
LORD, to do this!" he said. "Is it not the blood
of men who went at the risk of their lives?"
And David would not drink it.
Such were the exploits of the three mighty
warriors.
18Abishai the brother of Joab son of Zeruiah
was chief of the Three.[e] He raised his spear
against three hundred men, whom he killed,
and so he became as famous as the Three.
19Was he not held in greater honor than the
Three? He became their commander, even
though he was not included among them.
20Benaiah son of Jehoiada, a valiant fighter from Kabzeel, performed great exploits.
He struck down Moab's two mightiest warriors. He also went down into a pit on a snowy
day and killed a lion. 21And he struck down
a huge Egyptian. Although the Egyptian had
a spear in his hand, Benaiah went against
him with a club. He snatched the spear from
the Egyptian's hand and killed him with his
own spear. 22Such were the exploits of Benaiah son of Jehoiada; he too was as famous as
the three mighty warriors. 23He was held in
greater honor than any of the Thirty, but he
was not included among the Three. And David
put him in charge of his bodyguard.

24Among the Thirty were:
Asahel the brother of Joab,
Elhanan son of Dodo from Bethlehem,
25Shammah the Harodite,
Elika the Harodite,
26Helez the Paltite,
Ira son of Ikkesh from Tekoa,
27Abiezer from Anathoth,
Sibbekai[f] the Hushathite,
28Zalmon the Ahohite,
Maharai the Netophathite,
29Heled[g] son of Baanah the Netophathite,
Ithai son of Ribai from Gibeah in Benjamin,
30Benaiah the Pirathonite,
Hiddai[h] from the ravines of Gaash,
31Abi-Albon the Arbathite,
Azmaveth the Barhumite,
32Eliahba the Shaalbonite,
the sons of Jashen,
Jonathan 33son of[i] Shammah the Hararite,
Ahiam son of Sharar[j] the Hararite,
34Eliphelet son of Ahasbai the Maakathite,
Eliam son of Ahithophel the Gilonite,
35Hezro the Carmelite,
Paarai the Arbite,
36Igal son of Nathan from Zobah,
the son of Hagri,[k]
37Zelek the Ammonite,
Naharai the Beerothite, the armor-
bearer of Joab son of Zeruiah,
38Ira the Ithrite,
Gareb the Ithrite
39and Uriah the Hittite.
There were thirty-seven in all.

David Enrolls the Fighting Men

24 Again the anger of the LORD burned
against Israel, and he incited David
against them, saying, "Go and take a census
of Israel and Judah."
2So the king said to Joab and the army commanders[l] with him, "Go throughout the tribes
of Israel from Dan to Beersheba and enroll
the fighting men, so that I may know how
many there are."

[a] 8 Hebrew; some Septuagint manuscripts suggest *Ish-Bosheth*, that is, *Esh-Baal* (see also 1 Chron. 11:11 *Jashobeam*). [b] 8 Probably a variant of *Hakmonite* (see 1 Chron. 11:11) [c] 8 Some Septuagint manuscripts (see also 1 Chron. 11:11); Hebrew and other Septuagint manuscripts *Three; it was Adino the Eznite who killed eight hundred men* [d] 9 See 1 Chron. 11:13; Hebrew *gathered there.*
[e] 18 Most Hebrew manuscripts (see also 1 Chron. 11:20); two Hebrew manuscripts and Syriac *Thirty*
[f] 27 Some Septuagint manuscripts (see also 21:18; 1 Chron. 11:29); Hebrew *Mebunnai* [g] 29 Some Hebrew manuscripts and Vulgate (see also 1 Chron. 11:30); most Hebrew manuscripts *Heleb*
[h] 30 Hebrew; some Septuagint manuscripts (see also 1 Chron. 11:32) *Hurai* [i] 33 Some Septuagint manuscripts (see also 1 Chron. 11:34); Hebrew does not have *son of.* [j] 33 Hebrew; some Septuagint manuscripts (see also 1 Chron. 11:35) *Sakar* [k] 36 Some Septuagint manuscripts (see also 1 Chron. 11:38); Hebrew *Haggadi* [l] 2 Septuagint (see also verse 4 and 1 Chron. 21:2); Hebrew *Joab the army commander*

3But Joab replied to the king, "May the LORD your God multiply the troops a hundred times over, and may the eyes of my lord the king see it. But why does my lord the king want to do such a thing?"

4The king's word, however, overruled Joab and the army commanders; so they left the presence of the king to enroll the fighting men of Israel.

5After crossing the Jordan, they camped near Aroer, south of the town in the gorge, and then went through Gad and on to Jazer. 6They went to Gilead and the region of Tahtim Hodshi, and on to Dan Jaan and around toward Sidon. 7Then they went toward the fortress of Tyre and all the towns of the Hivites and Canaanites. Finally, they went on to Beersheba in the Negev of Judah.

8After they had gone through the entire land, they came back to Jerusalem at the end of nine months and twenty days.

9Joab reported the number of the fighting men to the king: In Israel there were eight hundred thousand able-bodied men who could handle a sword, and in Judah five hundred thousand.

10David was conscience-stricken after he had counted the fighting men, and he said to the LORD, "I have sinned greatly in what I have done. Now, LORD, I beg you, take away the guilt of your servant. I have done a very foolish thing."

11Before David got up the next morning, the word of the LORD had come to Gad the prophet, David's seer: 12"Go and tell David, 'This is what the LORD says: I am giving you three options. Choose one of them for me to carry out against you.'"

13So Gad went to David and said to him, "Shall there come on you three[a] years of famine in your land? Or three months of fleeing from your enemies while they pursue you? Or three days of plague in your land? Now then, think it over and decide how I should answer the one who sent me."

14David said to Gad, "I am in deep distress. Let us fall into the hands of the LORD, for his mercy is great; but do not let me fall into human hands."

15So the LORD sent a plague on Israel from that morning until the end of the time designated, and seventy thousand of the people from Dan to Beersheba died. 16When the angel stretched out his hand to destroy Jerusalem, the LORD relented concerning the disaster and said to the angel who was afflicting the people, "Enough! Withdraw your hand." The angel of the LORD was then at the threshing floor of Araunah the Jebusite.

17When David saw the angel who was striking down the people, he said to the LORD, "I have sinned; I, the shepherd,[b] have done wrong. These are but sheep. What have they done? Let your hand fall on me and my family."

David Builds an Altar

18On that day Gad went to David and said to him, "Go up and build an altar to the LORD on the threshing floor of Araunah the Jebusite." 19So David went up, as the LORD had commanded through Gad. 20When Araunah looked and saw the king and his officials coming toward him, he went out and bowed down before the king with his face to the ground.

21Araunah said, "Why has my lord the king come to his servant?"

"To buy your threshing floor," David answered, "so I can build an altar to the LORD, that the plague on the people may be stopped."

22Araunah said to David, "Let my lord the king take whatever he wishes and offer it up. Here are oxen for the burnt offering, and here are threshing sledges and ox yokes for the wood. 23Your Majesty, Araunah[c] gives all this to the king." Araunah also said to him, "May the LORD your God accept you."

24But the king replied to Araunah, "No, I insist on paying you for it. I will not sacrifice to the LORD my God burnt offerings that cost me nothing."

So David bought the threshing floor and the oxen and paid fifty shekels[d] of silver for them. 25David built an altar to the LORD there and sacrificed burnt offerings and fellowship offerings. Then the LORD answered his prayer in behalf of the land, and the plague on Israel was stopped.

1 Kings

Adonijah Sets Himself Up as King

1 When King David was very old, he could not keep warm even when they put covers over him. 2So his attendants said to him, "Let us look for a young virgin to serve the king and take care of him. She can lie beside him so that our lord the king may keep warm."

3Then they searched throughout Israel for a beautiful young woman and found Abishag, a Shunammite, and brought her to the king.

[a] 13 Septuagint (see also 1 Chron. 21:12); Hebrew *seven* [b] 17 Dead Sea Scrolls and Septuagint; Masoretic Text does not have *the shepherd.* [c] 23 Some Hebrew manuscripts and Septuagint; most Hebrew manuscripts *King Araunah* [d] 24 That is, about 1 1/4 pounds or about 575 grams

4The woman was very beautiful; she took care
of the king and waited on him, but the king
had no sexual relations with her.
5Now Adonijah, whose mother was Haggith, put himself forward and said, "I will be
king." So he got chariots and horses[a] ready,
with fifty men to run ahead of him. 6(His father had never rebuked him by asking, "Why
do you behave as you do?" He was also very
handsome and was born next after Absalom.)
7Adonijah conferred with Joab son of Zeruiah and with Abiathar the priest, and they
gave him their support. 8But Zadok the priest,
Benaiah son of Jehoiada, Nathan the prophet,
Shimei and Rei and David's special guard did
not join Adonijah.
9Adonijah then sacrificed sheep, cattle
and fattened calves at the Stone of Zoheleth
near En Rogel. He invited all his brothers, the
king's sons, and all the royal officials of Judah, 10but he did not invite Nathan the prophet
or Benaiah or the special guard or his brother
Solomon.
11Then Nathan asked Bathsheba, Solomon's
mother, "Have you not heard that Adonijah,
the son of Haggith, has become king, and our
lord David knows nothing about it? 12Now
then, let me advise you how you can save your
own life and the life of your son Solomon. 13Go
in to King David and say to him, 'My lord the
king, did you not swear to me your servant:
"Surely Solomon your son shall be king after
me, and he will sit on my throne"? Why then
has Adonijah become king?' 14While you are
still there talking to the king, I will come in
and add my word to what you have said."
15So Bathsheba went to see the aged king
in his room, where Abishag the Shunammite
was attending him. 16Bathsheba bowed down,
prostrating herself before the king.
"What is it you want?" the king asked.
17She said to him, "My lord, you yourself
swore to me your servant by the LORD your
God: 'Solomon your son shall be king after
me, and he will sit on my throne.' 18But now
Adonijah has become king, and you, my lord
the king, do not know about it. 19He has sacrificed great numbers of cattle, fattened calves,
and sheep, and has invited all the king's sons,
Abiathar the priest and Joab the commander
of the army, but he has not invited Solomon
your servant. 20My lord the king, the eyes of
all Israel are on you, to learn from you who
will sit on the throne of my lord the king after
him. 21Otherwise, as soon as my lord the king
is laid to rest with his ancestors, I and my son
Solomon will be treated as criminals."
22While she was still speaking with the
king, Nathan the prophet arrived. 23And the
king was told, "Nathan the prophet is here."
So he went before the king and bowed with
his face to the ground.
24Nathan said, "Have you, my lord the king,
declared that Adonijah shall be king after you,
and that he will sit on your throne? 25Today he
has gone down and sacrificed great numbers
of cattle, fattened calves, and sheep. He has
invited all the king's sons, the commanders
of the army and Abiathar the priest. Right
now they are eating and drinking with him
and saying, 'Long live King Adonijah!' 26But
me your servant, and Zadok the priest, and
Benaiah son of Jehoiada, and your servant
Solomon he did not invite. 27Is this something
my lord the king has done without letting his
servants know who should sit on the throne
of my lord the king after him?"

David Makes Solomon King

28Then King David said, "Call in Bathsheba." So she came into the king's presence and
stood before him.
29The king then took an oath: "As surely
as the LORD lives, who has delivered me out
of every trouble, 30I will surely carry out this
very day what I swore to you by the LORD,
the God of Israel: Solomon your son shall be
king after me, and he will sit on my throne
in my place."
31Then Bathsheba bowed down with her
face to the ground, prostrating herself before
the king, and said, "May my lord King David
live forever!"
32King David said, "Call in Zadok the priest,
Nathan the prophet and Benaiah son of Jehoiada." When they came before the king,
33he said to them: "Take your lord's servants
with you and have Solomon my son mount
my own mule and take him down to Gihon.
34There have Zadok the priest and Nathan the
prophet anoint him king over Israel. Blow the
trumpet and shout, 'Long live King Solomon!'
35Then you are to go up with him, and he is to
come and sit on my throne and reign in my
place. I have appointed him ruler over Israel
and Judah."
36Benaiah son of Jehoiada answered the
king, "Amen! May the LORD, the God of my
lord the king, so declare it. 37As the LORD was
with my lord the king, so may he be with Solomon to make his throne even greater than
the throne of my lord King David!"
38So Zadok the priest, Nathan the prophet,
Benaiah son of Jehoiada, the Kerethites and
the Pelethites went down and had Solomon
mount King David's mule, and they escorted him to Gihon. 39Zadok the priest took the
horn of oil from the sacred tent and anointed
Solomon. Then they sounded the trumpet and
all the people shouted, "Long live King Solomon!" 40And all the people went up after him,
playing pipes and rejoicing greatly, so that the
ground shook with the sound.
41Adonijah and all the guests who were with
him heard it as they were finishing their feast.
On hearing the sound of the trumpet, Joab
asked, "What's the meaning of all the noise
in the city?"
42Even as he was speaking, Jonathan son
of Abiathar the priest arrived. Adonijah said,
"Come in. A worthy man like you must be
bringing good news."
43"Not at all!" Jonathan answered. "Our lord
King David has made Solomon king. 44The

[a] 5 Or *charioteers*

king has sent with him Zadok the priest, Nathan the prophet, Benaiah son of Jehoiada, the
Kerethites and the Pelethites, and they have
put him on the king's mule, 45and Zadok the
priest and Nathan the prophet have anointed him king at Gihon. From there they have
gone up cheering, and the city resounds with
it. That's the noise you hear. 46Moreover, Solomon has taken his seat on the royal throne.
47Also, the royal officials have come to congratulate our lord King David, saying, 'May
your God make Solomon's name more famous
than yours and his throne greater than yours!'
And the king bowed in worship on his bed
48and said, 'Praise be to the LORD, the God
of Israel, who has allowed my eyes to see a
successor on my throne today.'"

49At this, all Adonijah's guests rose in alarm
and dispersed. 50But Adonijah, in fear of Solomon, went and took hold of the horns of the
altar. 51Then Solomon was told, "Adonijah is
afraid of King Solomon and is clinging to the
horns of the altar. He says, 'Let King Solomon
swear to me today that he will not put his servant to death with the sword.'"

52Solomon replied, "If he shows himself to
be worthy, not a hair of his head will fall to
the ground; but if evil is found in him, he will
die." 53Then King Solomon sent men, and they
brought him down from the altar. And Adonijah came and bowed down to King Solomon,
and Solomon said, "Go to your home."

David's Charge to Solomon

2 When the time drew near for David to die,
he gave a charge to Solomon his son.

2"I am about to go the way of all the earth,"
he said. "So be strong, act like a man, 3and observe what the LORD your God requires: Walk
in obedience to him, and keep his decrees and
commands, his laws and regulations, as written in the Law of Moses. Do this so that you
may prosper in all you do and wherever you
go 4and that the LORD may keep his promise to
me: 'If your descendants watch how they live,
and if they walk faithfully before me with all
their heart and soul, you will never fail to have
a successor on the throne of Israel.'

5"Now you yourself know what Joab son
of Zeruiah did to me—what he did to the two
commanders of Israel's armies, Abner son of
Ner and Amasa son of Jether. He killed them,
shedding their blood in peacetime as if in battle, and with that blood he stained the belt
around his waist and the sandals on his feet.
6Deal with him according to your wisdom,
but do not let his gray head go down to the
grave in peace.

7"But show kindness to the sons of Barzillai
of Gilead and let them be among those who
eat at your table. They stood by me when I
fled from your brother Absalom.

8"And remember, you have with you Shimei son of Gera, the Benjamite from Bahurim,
who called down bitter curses on me the day
I went to Mahanaim. When he came down to
meet me at the Jordan, I swore to him by the
LORD: 'I will not put you to death by the sword.'
9But now, do not consider him innocent. You
are a man of wisdom; you will know what to
do to him. Bring his gray head down to the
grave in blood."

10Then David rested with his ancestors
and was buried in the City of David. 11He had
reigned forty years over Israel—seven years
in Hebron and thirty-three in Jerusalem. 12So
Solomon sat on the throne of his father David,
and his rule was firmly established.

Solomon's Throne Established

13Now Adonijah, the son of Haggith, went
to Bathsheba, Solomon's mother. Bathsheba
asked him, "Do you come peacefully?"

He answered, "Yes, peacefully." 14Then he
added, "I have something to say to you."

"You may say it," she replied.

15"As you know," he said, "the kingdom was
mine. All Israel looked to me as their king. But
things changed, and the kingdom has gone to
my brother; for it has come to him from the
LORD. 16Now I have one request to make of
you. Do not refuse me."

"You may make it," she said.

17So he continued, "Please ask King Solomon—he will not refuse you—to give me
Abishag the Shunammite as my wife."

18"Very well," Bathsheba replied, "I will
speak to the king for you."

19When Bathsheba went to King Solomon
to speak to him for Adonijah, the king stood
up to meet her, bowed down to her and sat
down on his throne. He had a throne brought
for the king's mother, and she sat down at his
right hand.

20"I have one small request to make of you,"
she said. "Do not refuse me."

The king replied, "Make it, my mother; I
will not refuse you."

21So she said, "Let Abishag the Shunammite be given in marriage to your brother
Adonijah."

22King Solomon answered his mother,
"Why do you request Abishag the Shunammite for Adonijah? You might as well request
the kingdom for him—after all, he is my older
brother—yes, for him and for Abiathar the
priest and Joab son of Zeruiah!"

23Then King Solomon swore by the LORD:
"May God deal with me, be it ever so severely, if Adonijah does not pay with his life for
this request! 24And now, as surely as the LORD
lives—he who has established me securely on
the throne of my father David and has founded
a dynasty for me as he promised—Adonijah
shall be put to death today!" 25So King Solomon gave orders to Benaiah son of Jehoiada,
and he struck down Adonijah and he died.

26To Abiathar the priest the king said, "Go
back to your fields in Anathoth. You deserve
to die, but I will not put you to death now, because you carried the ark of the Sovereign
LORD before my father David and shared all
my father's hardships." 27So Solomon removed Abiathar from the priesthood of the
LORD, fulfilling the word the LORD had spoken
at Shiloh about the house of Eli.

28When the news reached Joab, who had
conspired with Adonijah though not with Ab-

salom, he fled to the tent of the LORD and took hold of the horns of the altar. 29King Solomon was told that Joab had fled to the tent of the LORD and was beside the altar. Then Solomon ordered Benaiah son of Jehoiada, "Go, strike him down!"

30So Benaiah entered the tent of the LORD and said to Joab, "The king says, 'Come out!'"

But he answered, "No, I will die here."

Benaiah reported to the king, "This is how Joab answered me."

31Then the king commanded Benaiah, "Do as he says. Strike him down and bury him, and so clear me and my whole family of the guilt of the innocent blood that Joab shed. 32The LORD will repay him for the blood he shed, because without my father David knowing it he attacked two men and killed them with the sword. Both of them—Abner son of Ner, commander of Israel's army, and Amasa son of Jether, commander of Judah's army—were better men and more upright than he. 33May the guilt of their blood rest on the head of Joab and his descendants forever. But on David and his descendants, his house and his throne, may there be the LORD's peace forever."

34So Benaiah son of Jehoiada went up and struck down Joab and killed him, and he was buried at his home out in the country. 35The king put Benaiah son of Jehoiada over the army in Joab's position and replaced Abiathar with Zadok the priest.

36Then the king sent for Shimei and said to him, "Build yourself a house in Jerusalem and live there, but do not go anywhere else. 37The day you leave and cross the Kidron Valley, you can be sure you will die; your blood will be on your own head."

38Shimei answered the king, "What you say is good. Your servant will do as my lord the king has said." And Shimei stayed in Jerusalem for a long time.

39But three years later, two of Shimei's slaves ran off to Achish son of Maakah, king of Gath, and Shimei was told, "Your slaves are in Gath." 40At this, he saddled his donkey and went to Achish at Gath in search of his slaves. So Shimei went away and brought the slaves back from Gath.

41When Solomon was told that Shimei had gone from Jerusalem to Gath and had returned, 42the king summoned Shimei and said to him, "Did I not make you swear by the LORD and warn you, 'On the day you leave to go anywhere else, you can be sure you will die'? At that time you said to me, 'What you say is good. I will obey.' 43Why then did you not keep your oath to the LORD and obey the command I gave you?"

44The king also said to Shimei, "You know in your heart all the wrong you did to my father David. Now the LORD will repay you for your wrongdoing. 45But King Solomon will be blessed, and David's throne will remain secure before the LORD forever."

46Then the king gave the order to Benaiah son of Jehoiada, and he went out and struck Shimei down and he died.

The kingdom was now established in Solomon's hands.

Solomon Asks for Wisdom

3 Solomon made an alliance with Pharaoh king of Egypt and married his daughter. He brought her to the City of David until he finished building his palace and the temple of the LORD, and the wall around Jerusalem. 2The people, however, were still sacrificing at the high places, because a temple had not yet been built for the Name of the LORD. 3Solomon showed his love for the LORD by walking according to the instructions given him by his father David, except that he offered sacrifices and burned incense on the high places.

4The king went to Gibeon to offer sacrifices, for that was the most important high place, and Solomon offered a thousand burnt offerings on that altar. 5At Gibeon the LORD appeared to Solomon during the night in a dream, and God said, "Ask for whatever you want me to give you."

6Solomon answered, "You have shown great kindness to your servant, my father David, because he was faithful to you and righteous and upright in heart. You have continued this great kindness to him and have given him a son to sit on his throne this very day.

7"Now, LORD my God, you have made your servant king in place of my father David. But I am only a little child and do not know how to carry out my duties. 8Your servant is here among the people you have chosen, a great people, too numerous to count or number. 9So give your servant a discerning heart to govern your people and to distinguish between right and wrong. For who is able to govern this great people of yours?"

10The Lord was pleased that Solomon had asked for this. 11So God said to him, "Since you have asked for this and not for long life or wealth for yourself, nor have asked for the death of your enemies but for discernment in administering justice, 12I will do what you have asked. I will give you a wise and discerning heart, so that there will never have been anyone like you, nor will there ever be. 13Moreover, I will give you what you have not asked for—both wealth and honor—so that in your lifetime you will have no equal among kings. 14And if you walk in obedience to me and keep my decrees and commands as David your father did, I will give you a long life." 15Then Solomon awoke—and he realized it had been a dream.

He returned to Jerusalem, stood before the ark of the Lord's covenant and sacrificed burnt offerings and fellowship offerings. Then he gave a feast for all his court.

A Wise Ruling

16Now two prostitutes came to the king and stood before him. 17One of them said, "Pardon me, my lord. This woman and I live in the same house, and I had a baby while she was there with me. 18The third day after my child was born, this woman also had a baby.

We were alone; there was no one in the house
but the two of us.
19“During the night this woman’s son died
because she lay on him. 20So she got up in the
middle of the night and took my son from my
side while I your servant was asleep. She put
him by her breast and put her dead son by my
breast. 21The next morning, I got up to nurse
my son—and he was dead! But when I looked
at him closely in the morning light, I saw that
it wasn’t the son I had borne.”
22The other woman said, “No! The living
one is my son; the dead one is yours.”
But the first one insisted, “No! The dead one
is yours; the living one is mine.” And so they
argued before the king.
23The king said, “This one says, ‘My son
is alive and your son is dead,’ while that one
says, ‘No! Your son is dead and mine is alive.’ ”
24Then the king said, “Bring me a sword.”
So they brought a sword for the king. 25He
then gave an order: “Cut the living child in
two and give half to one and half to the other.”
26The woman whose son was alive was
deeply moved out of love for her son and said
to the king, “Please, my lord, give her the living baby! Don’t kill him!”
But the other said, “Neither I nor you shall
have him. Cut him in two!”
27Then the king gave his ruling: “Give the
living baby to the first woman. Do not kill
him; she is his mother.”
28When all Israel heard the verdict the king
had given, they held the king in awe, because
they saw that he had wisdom from God to
administer justice.

Solomon’s Officials and Governors

4 So King Solomon ruled over all Israel.
2And these were his chief officials:

Azariah son of Zadok—the priest;
3Elihoreph and Ahijah, sons of Shisha—secretaries;
Jehoshaphat son of Ahilud—recorder;
4Benaiah son of Jehoiada—commander in chief;
Zadok and Abiathar—priests;
5Azariah son of Nathan—in charge of the district governors;
Zabud son of Nathan—a priest and adviser to the king;
6Ahishar—palace administrator;
Adoniram son of Abda—in charge of forced labor.

7Solomon had twelve district governors
over all Israel, who supplied provisions for
the king and the royal household. Each one
had to provide supplies for one month in the
year. 8These are their names:

Ben-Hur—in the hill country of Ephraim;
9Ben-Deker—in Makaz, Shaalbim, Beth Shemesh and Elon Bethhanan;
10Ben-Hesed—in Arubboth (Sokoh and all the land of Hepher were his);
11Ben-Abinadab—in Naphoth Dor (he was married to Taphath daughter of Solomon);
12Baana son of Ahilud—in Taanach and Megiddo, and in all of Beth Shan next to Zarethan below Jezreel, from Beth Shan to Abel Meholah across to Jokmeam;
13Ben-Geber—in Ramoth Gilead (the settlements of Jair son of Manasseh in Gilead were his, as well as the region of Argob in Bashan and its sixty large walled cities with bronze gate bars);
14Ahinadab son of Iddo—in Mahanaim;
15Ahimaaz—in Naphtali (he had married Basemath daughter of Solomon);
16Baana son of Hushai—in Asher and in Aloth;
17Jehoshaphat son of Paruah—in Issachar;
18Shimei son of Ela—in Benjamin;
19Geber son of Uri—in Gilead (the country of Sihon king of the Amorites and the country of Og king of Bashan). He was the only governor over the district.

Solomon’s Daily Provisions

20The people of Judah and Israel were as
numerous as the sand on the seashore; they
ate, they drank and they were happy. 21And
Solomon ruled over all the kingdoms from the
Euphrates River to the land of the Philistines,
as far as the border of Egypt. These countries
brought tribute and were Solomon’s subjects
all his life.
22Solomon’s daily provisions were thirty
cors[a] of the finest flour and sixty cors[b] of
meal, 23ten head of stall-fed cattle, twenty of
pasture-fed cattle and a hundred sheep and
goats, as well as deer, gazelles, roebucks
and choice fowl. 24For he ruled over all the
kingdoms west of the Euphrates River, from
Tiphsah to Gaza, and had peace on all sides.
25During Solomon’s lifetime Judah and Israel,
from Dan to Beersheba, lived in safety, everyone under their own vine and under their
own fig tree.
26Solomon had four[c] thousand stalls for
chariot horses, and twelve thousand horses.[d]
27The district governors, each in his month,
supplied provisions for King Solomon and
all who came to the king’s table. They saw
to it that nothing was lacking. 28They also
brought to the proper place their quotas of
barley and straw for the chariot horses and
the other horses.

Solomon’s Wisdom

29God gave Solomon wisdom and very great
insight, and a breadth of understanding as
measureless as the sand on the seashore.
30Solomon’s wisdom was greater than the wisdom of all the people of the East, and greater
than all the wisdom of Egypt. 31He was wiser
than anyone else, including Ethan the Ezrahite—wiser than Heman, Kalkol and Darda,

[a] *22* That is, probably about 5 1/2 tons or about 5 metric tons [b] *22* That is, probably about 11 tons or about 10 metric tons [c] *26* Some Septuagint manuscripts (see also 2 Chron. 9:25); Hebrew *forty*
[d] *26* Or *charioteers*

the sons of Mahol. And his fame spread to
all the surrounding nations. 32He spoke three
thousand proverbs and his songs numbered
a thousand and five. 33He spoke about plant
life, from the cedar of Lebanon to the hyssop
that grows out of walls. He also spoke about
animals and birds, reptiles and fish. 34From
all nations people came to listen to Solomon's
wisdom, sent by all the kings of the world,
who had heard of his wisdom.[a]

Preparations for Building the Temple

5[b] When Hiram king of Tyre heard that Solomon had been anointed king to succeed
his father David, he sent his envoys to Solomon, because he had always been on friendly
terms with David. 2Solomon sent back this
message to Hiram:

> 3"You know that because of the wars
> waged against my father David from all
> sides, he could not build a temple for the
> Name of the LORD his God until the LORD
> put his enemies under his feet. 4But now
> the LORD my God has given me rest on
> every side, and there is no adversary or
> disaster. 5I intend, therefore, to build a
> temple for the Name of the LORD my God,
> as the LORD told my father David, when
> he said, 'Your son whom I will put on the
> throne in your place will build the temple
> for my Name.'
>
> 6"So give orders that cedars of Leba-
> non be cut for me. My men will work with
> yours, and I will pay you for your men
> whatever wages you set. You know that
> we have no one so skilled in felling timber
> as the Sidonians."

7When Hiram heard Solomon's message,
he was greatly pleased and said, "Praise be to
the LORD today, for he has given David a wise
son to rule over this great nation."
8So Hiram sent word to Solomon:

> "I have received the message you sent
> me and will do all you want in provid-
> ing the cedar and juniper logs. 9My men
> will haul them down from Lebanon to the
> Mediterranean Sea, and I will float them
> as rafts by sea to the place you specify.
> There I will separate them and you can
> take them away. And you are to grant
> my wish by providing food for my royal
> household."

10In this way Hiram kept Solomon supplied
with all the cedar and juniper logs he wanted,
11and Solomon gave Hiram twenty thousand
cors[c] of wheat as food for his household, in addition to twenty thousand baths[d,e] of pressed
olive oil. Solomon continued to do this for Hiram year after year. 12The LORD gave Solomon
wisdom, just as he had promised him. There
were peaceful relations between Hiram and
Solomon, and the two of them made a treaty.
13King Solomon conscripted laborers from
all Israel—thirty thousand men. 14He sent
them off to Lebanon in shifts of ten thousand a month, so that they spent one month in
Lebanon and two months at home. Adoniram
was in charge of the forced labor. 15Solomon
had seventy thousand carriers and eighty
thousand stonecutters in the hills, 16as well
as thirty-three hundred[f] foremen who supervised the project and directed the workers.
17At the king's command they removed from
the quarry large blocks of high-grade stone
to provide a foundation of dressed stone for
the temple. 18The craftsmen of Solomon and
Hiram and workers from Byblos cut and prepared the timber and stone for the building
of the temple.

Solomon Builds the Temple

6 In the four hundred and eightieth[g] year after the Israelites came out of Egypt, in the
fourth year of Solomon's reign over Israel, in
the month of Ziv, the second month, he began
to build the temple of the LORD.
2The temple that King Solomon built for the
LORD was sixty cubits long, twenty wide and
thirty high.[h] 3The portico at the front of the
main hall of the temple extended the width of
the temple, that is twenty cubits,[i] and project-
ed ten cubits[j] from the front of the temple. 4He
made narrow windows high up in the temple
walls. 5Against the walls of the main hall and
inner sanctuary he built a structure around
the building, in which there were side rooms.
6The lowest floor was five cubits[k] wide, the
middle floor six cubits[l] and the third floor sev-
en.[m] He made offset ledges around the outside
of the temple so that nothing would be inserted into the temple walls.
7In building the temple, only blocks dressed
at the quarry were used, and no hammer, chisel or any other iron tool was heard at the temple site while it was being built.
8The entrance to the lowest[n] floor was on
the south side of the temple; a stairway led
up to the middle level and from there to the
third. 9So he built the temple and completed it,
roofing it with beams and cedar planks. 10And
he built the side rooms all along the temple.
The height of each was five cubits, and they
were attached to the temple by beams of cedar.
11The word of the LORD came to Solomon:
12"As for this temple you are building, if you
follow my decrees, observe my laws and keep
all my commands and obey them, I will fulfill
through you the promise I gave to David your

[a] *34* In Hebrew texts 4:21-34 is numbered 5:1-14. [b] In Hebrew texts 5:1-18 is numbered 5:15-32. [c] *11* That is, probably about 3,600 tons or about 3,250 metric tons [d] *11* Septuagint (see also 2 Chron. 2:10); Hebrew *twenty cors* [e] *11* That is, about 120,000 gallons or about 440,000 liters [f] *16* Hebrew; some Septuagint manuscripts (see also 2 Chron. 2:2,18) *thirty-six hundred* [g] *1* Hebrew; Septuagint *four hundred and fortieth* [h] *2* That is, about 90 feet long, 30 feet wide and 45 feet high or about 27 meters long, 9 meters wide and 14 meters high [i] *3* That is, about 30 feet or about 9 meters; also in verses 16 and 20 [j] *3* That is, about 15 feet or about 4.5 meters; also in verses 23-26 [k] *6* That is, about 7 1/2 feet or about 2.3 meters; also in verses 10 and 24 [l] *6* That is, about 9 feet or about 2.7 meters [m] *6* That is, about 11 feet or about 3.2 meters [n] *8* Septuagint; Hebrew *middle*

father. 13And I will live among the Israelites and will not abandon my people Israel."

14So Solomon built the temple and completed it. 15He lined its interior walls with cedar boards, paneling them from the floor of the temple to the ceiling, and covered the floor of the temple with planks of juniper. 16He partitioned off twenty cubits at the rear of the temple with cedar boards from floor to ceiling to form within the temple an inner sanctuary, the Most Holy Place. 17The main hall in front of this room was forty cubits[a] long. 18The inside of the temple was cedar, carved with gourds and open flowers. Everything was cedar; no stone was to be seen.

19He prepared the inner sanctuary within the temple to set the ark of the covenant of the LORD there. 20The inner sanctuary was twenty cubits long, twenty wide and twenty high. He overlaid the inside with pure gold, and he also overlaid the altar of cedar. 21Solomon covered the inside of the temple with pure gold, and he extended gold chains across the front of the inner sanctuary, which was overlaid with gold. 22So he overlaid the whole interior with gold. He also overlaid with gold the altar that belonged to the inner sanctuary.

23For the inner sanctuary he made a pair of cherubim out of olive wood, each ten cubits high. 24One wing of the first cherub was five cubits long, and the other wing five cubits—ten cubits from wing tip to wing tip. 25The second cherub also measured ten cubits, for the two cherubim were identical in size and shape. 26The height of each cherub was ten cubits. 27He placed the cherubim inside the innermost room of the temple, with their wings spread out. The wing of one cherub touched one wall, while the wing of the other touched the other wall, and their wings touched each other in the middle of the room. 28He overlaid the cherubim with gold.

29On the walls all around the temple, in both the inner and outer rooms, he carved cherubim, palm trees and open flowers. 30He also covered the floors of both the inner and outer rooms of the temple with gold.

31For the entrance to the inner sanctuary he made doors out of olive wood that were one fifth of the width of the sanctuary. 32And on the two olive-wood doors he carved cherubim, palm trees and open flowers, and overlaid the cherubim and palm trees with hammered gold. 33In the same way, for the entrance to the main hall he made doorframes out of olive wood that were one fourth of the width of the hall. 34He also made two doors out of juniper wood, each having two leaves that turned in sockets. 35He carved cherubim, palm trees and open flowers on them and overlaid them with gold hammered evenly over the carvings.

36And he built the inner courtyard of three courses of dressed stone and one course of trimmed cedar beams.

37The foundation of the temple of the LORD was laid in the fourth year, in the month of Ziv. 38In the eleventh year in the month of Bul, the eighth month, the temple was finished in all its details according to its specifications. He had spent seven years building it.

Solomon Builds His Palace

7 It took Solomon thirteen years, however, to complete the construction of his palace. 2He built the Palace of the Forest of Lebanon a hundred cubits long, fifty wide and thirty high,[b] with four rows of cedar columns supporting trimmed cedar beams. 3It was roofed with cedar above the beams that rested on the columns—forty-five beams, fifteen to a row. 4Its windows were placed high in sets of three, facing each other. 5All the doorways had rectangular frames; they were in the front part in sets of three, facing each other.[c]

6He made a colonnade fifty cubits long and thirty wide.[d] In front of it was a portico, and in front of that were pillars and an overhanging roof.

7He built the throne hall, the Hall of Justice, where he was to judge, and he covered it with cedar from floor to ceiling.[e] 8And the palace in which he was to live, set farther back, was similar in design. Solomon also made a palace like this hall for Pharaoh's daughter, whom he had married.

9All these structures, from the outside to the great courtyard and from foundation to eaves, were made of blocks of high-grade stone cut to size and smoothed on their inner and outer faces. 10The foundations were laid with large stones of good quality, some measuring ten cubits[f] and some eight.[g] 11Above were high-grade stones, cut to size, and cedar beams. 12The great courtyard was surrounded by a wall of three courses of dressed stone and one course of trimmed cedar beams, as was the inner courtyard of the temple of the LORD with its portico.

The Temple's Furnishings

13King Solomon sent to Tyre and brought Huram,[h] 14whose mother was a widow from the tribe of Naphtali and whose father was from Tyre and a skilled craftsman in bronze. Huram was filled with wisdom, with understanding and with knowledge to do all kinds of bronze work. He came to King Solomon and did all the work assigned to him.

15He cast two bronze pillars, each eighteen cubits high and twelve cubits in circumference.[i] 16He also made two capitals of cast bronze to set on the tops of the pillars; each capital was five cubits[j] high. 17A network of

[a] *17* That is, about 60 feet or about 18 meters [b] *2* That is, about 150 feet long, 75 feet wide and 45 feet high or about 45 meters long, 23 meters wide and 14 meters high [c] *5* The meaning of the Hebrew for this verse is uncertain. [d] *6* That is, about 75 feet long and 45 feet wide or about 23 meters long and 14 meters wide [e] *7* Vulgate and Syriac; Hebrew *floor* [f] *10* That is, about 15 feet or about 4.5 meters; also in verse 23 [g] *10* That is, about 12 feet or about 3.6 meters [h] *13* Hebrew *Hiram,* a variant of *Huram;* also in verses 40 and 45 [i] *15* That is, about 27 feet high and 18 feet in circumference or about 8.1 meters high and 5.4 meters in circumference [j] *16* That is, about 7 1/2 feet or about 2.3 meters; also in verse 23

interwoven chains adorned the capitals on top of the pillars, seven for each capital. 18He made pomegranates in two rows[a] encircling each network to decorate the capitals on top of the pillars.[b] He did the same for each capital. 19The capitals on top of the pillars in the portico were in the shape of lilies, four cubits[c] high. 20On the capitals of both pillars, above the bowl-shaped part next to the network, were the two hundred pomegranates in rows all around. 21He erected the pillars at the portico of the temple. The pillar to the south he named Jakin[d] and the one to the north Boaz.[e] 22The capitals on top were in the shape of lilies. And so the work on the pillars was completed.

23He made the Sea of cast metal, circular in shape, measuring ten cubits from rim to rim and five cubits high. It took a line of thirty cubits[f] to measure around it. 24Below the rim, gourds encircled it—ten to a cubit. The gourds were cast in two rows in one piece with the Sea.

25The Sea stood on twelve bulls, three facing north, three facing west, three facing south and three facing east. The Sea rested on top of them, and their hindquarters were toward the center. 26It was a handbreadth[g] in thickness, and its rim was like the rim of a cup, like a lily blossom. It held two thousand baths.[h]

27He also made ten movable stands of bronze; each was four cubits long, four wide and three high.[i] 28This is how the stands were made: They had side panels attached to uprights. 29On the panels between the uprights were lions, bulls and cherubim—and on the uprights as well. Above and below the lions and bulls were wreaths of hammered work. 30Each stand had four bronze wheels with bronze axles, and each had a basin resting on four supports, cast with wreaths on each side. 31On the inside of the stand there was an opening that had a circular frame one cubit[j] deep. This opening was round, and with its basework it measured a cubit and a half.[k] Around its opening there was engraving. The panels of the stands were square, not round. 32The four wheels were under the panels, and the axles of the wheels were attached to the stand. The diameter of each wheel was a cubit and a half. 33The wheels were made like chariot wheels; the axles, rims, spokes and hubs were all of cast metal.

34Each stand had four handles, one on each corner, projecting from the stand. 35At the top of the stand there was a circular band half a cubit[l] deep. The supports and panels were attached to the top of the stand. 36He engraved cherubim, lions and palm trees on the surfaces of the supports and on the panels, in every available space, with wreaths all around. 37This is the way he made the ten stands. They were all cast in the same molds and were identical in size and shape.

38He then made ten bronze basins, each holding forty baths[m] and measuring four cubits across, one basin to go on each of the ten stands. 39He placed five of the stands on the south side of the temple and five on the north. He placed the Sea on the south side, at the southeast corner of the temple. 40He also made the pots[n] and shovels and sprinkling bowls.

So Huram finished all the work he had undertaken for King Solomon in the temple of the LORD:

41the two pillars;
the two bowl-shaped capitals on top of the pillars;
the two sets of network decorating the two bowl-shaped capitals on top of the pillars;
42the four hundred pomegranates for the two sets of network (two rows of pomegranates for each network decorating the bowl-shaped capitals on top of the pillars);
43the ten stands with their ten basins;
44the Sea and the twelve bulls under it;
45the pots, shovels and sprinkling bowls.

All these objects that Huram made for King Solomon for the temple of the LORD were of burnished bronze. 46The king had them cast in clay molds in the plain of the Jordan between Sukkoth and Zarethan. 47Solomon left all these things unweighed, because there were so many; the weight of the bronze was not determined.

48Solomon also made all the furnishings that were in the LORD's temple:

the golden altar;
the golden table on which was the bread of the Presence;
49the lampstands of pure gold (five on the right and five on the left, in front of the inner sanctuary);
the gold floral work and lamps and tongs;
50the pure gold basins, wick trimmers, sprinkling bowls, dishes and censers;
and the gold sockets for the doors of the innermost room, the Most Holy Place, and also for the doors of the main hall of the temple.

51When all the work King Solomon had done for the temple of the LORD was finished,

[a] *18* Two Hebrew manuscripts and Septuagint; most Hebrew manuscripts *made the pillars, and there were two rows* [b] *18* Many Hebrew manuscripts and Syriac; most Hebrew manuscripts *pomegranates* [c] *19* That is, about 6 feet or about 1.8 meters; also in verse 38 [d] *21* *Jakin* probably means *he establishes.* [e] *21* *Boaz* probably means *in him is strength.* [f] *23* That is, about 45 feet or about 14 meters [g] *26* That is, about 3 inches or about 7.5 centimeters [h] *26* That is, about 12,000 gallons or about 44,000 liters; the Septuagint does not have this sentence. [i] *27* That is, about 6 feet long and wide and about 4 1/2 feet high or about 1.8 meters long and wide and 1.4 meters high [j] *31* That is, about 18 inches or about 45 centimeters [k] *31* That is, about 2 1/4 feet or about 68 centimeters; also in verse 32 [l] *35* That is, about 9 inches or about 23 centimeters [m] *38* That is, about 240 gallons or about 880 liters [n] *40* Many Hebrew manuscripts, Septuagint, Syriac and Vulgate (see also verse 45 and 2 Chron. 4:11); many other Hebrew manuscripts *basins*

he brought in the things his father David had
dedicated—the silver and gold and the furnishings—and he placed them in the treasuries of the LORD's temple.

The Ark Brought to the Temple

8 Then King Solomon summoned into his
presence at Jerusalem the elders of Israel,
all the heads of the tribes and the chiefs of the
Israelite families, to bring up the ark of the
LORD's covenant from Zion, the City of David.
2All the Israelites came together to King Solomon at the time of the festival in the month
of Ethanim, the seventh month.

3When all the elders of Israel had arrived,
the priests took up the ark, 4and they brought
up the ark of the LORD and the tent of meeting
and all the sacred furnishings in it. The priests
and Levites carried them up, 5and King Solomon and the entire assembly of Israel that
had gathered about him were before the ark,
sacrificing so many sheep and cattle that they
could not be recorded or counted.

6The priests then brought the ark of the
LORD's covenant to its place in the inner sanctuary of the temple, the Most Holy Place, and
put it beneath the wings of the cherubim. 7The
cherubim spread their wings over the place
of the ark and overshadowed the ark and its
carrying poles. 8These poles were so long that
their ends could be seen from the Holy Place
in front of the inner sanctuary, but not from
outside the Holy Place; and they are still there
today. 9There was nothing in the ark except the
two stone tablets that Moses had placed in it at
Horeb, where the LORD made a covenant with
the Israelites after they came out of Egypt.

10When the priests withdrew from the Holy
Place, the cloud filled the temple of the LORD.
11And the priests could not perform their service because of the cloud, for the glory of the
LORD filled his temple.

12Then Solomon said, "The LORD has said
that he would dwell in a dark cloud; 13I have
indeed built a magnificent temple for you, a
place for you to dwell forever."

14While the whole assembly of Israel was
standing there, the king turned around and
blessed them. 15Then he said:

> "Praise be to the LORD, the God of Isra-
> el, who with his own hand has fulfilled
> what he promised with his own mouth
> to my father David. For he said, 16'Since
> the day I brought my people Israel out
> of Egypt, I have not chosen a city in any
> tribe of Israel to have a temple built so
> that my Name might be there, but I have
> chosen David to rule my people Israel.'
>
> 17"My father David had it in his heart to
> build a temple for the Name of the LORD,
> the God of Israel. 18But the LORD said to
> my father David, 'You did well to have
> it in your heart to build a temple for my
> Name. 19Nevertheless, you are not the one
> to build the temple, but your son, your
> own flesh and blood—he is the one who
> will build the temple for my Name.'
>
> 20"The LORD has kept the promise he
> made: I have succeeded David my father
> and now I sit on the throne of Israel, just
> as the LORD promised, and I have built
> the temple for the Name of the LORD, the
> God of Israel. 21I have provided a place
> there for the ark, in which is the covenant
> of the LORD that he made with our ances-
> tors when he brought them out of Egypt."

Solomon's Prayer of Dedication

22Then Solomon stood before the altar of
the LORD in front of the whole assembly of
Israel, spread out his hands toward heaven
23and said:

> "LORD, the God of Israel, there is no
> God like you in heaven above or on earth
> below—you who keep your covenant of
> love with your servants who continue
> wholeheartedly in your way. 24You have
> kept your promise to your servant Da-
> vid my father; with your mouth you have
> promised and with your hand you have
> fulfilled it—as it is today.
>
> 25"Now LORD, the God of Israel, keep
> for your servant David my father the
> promises you made to him when you said,
> 'You shall never fail to have a successor
> to sit before me on the throne of Israel, if
> only your descendants are careful in all
> they do to walk before me faithfully as
> you have done.' 26And now, God of Israel,
> let your word that you promised your ser-
> vant David my father come true.
>
> 27"But will God really dwell on earth?
> The heavens, even the highest heaven,
> cannot contain you. How much less this
> temple I have built! 28Yet give attention
> to your servant's prayer and his plea for
> mercy, LORD my God. Hear the cry and
> the prayer that your servant is praying in
> your presence this day. 29May your eyes
> be open toward this temple night and day,
> this place of which you said, 'My Name
> shall be there,' so that you will hear the
> prayer your servant prays toward this
> place. 30Hear the supplication of your
> servant and of your people Israel when
> they pray toward this place. Hear from
> heaven, your dwelling place, and when
> you hear, forgive.
>
> 31"When anyone wrongs their neighbor
> and is required to take an oath and they
> come and swear the oath before your al-
> tar in this temple, 32then hear from heav-
> en and act. Judge between your servants,
> condemning the guilty by bringing down
> on their heads what they have done, and
> vindicating the innocent by treating them
> in accordance with their innocence.
>
> 33"When your people Israel have been
> defeated by an enemy because they have
> sinned against you, and when they turn
> back to you and give praise to your name,
> praying and making supplication to you
> in this temple, 34then hear from heaven
> and forgive the sin of your people Israel
> and bring them back to the land you gave
> to their ancestors.

35“When the heavens are shut up and there is no rain because your people have sinned against you, and when they pray toward this place and give praise to your name and turn from their sin because you have afflicted them, 36then hear from heaven and forgive the sin of your servants, your people Israel. Teach them the right way to live, and send rain on the land you gave your people for an inheritance.

37“When famine or plague comes to the land, or blight or mildew, locusts or grasshoppers, or when an enemy besieges them in any of their cities, whatever disaster or disease may come, 38and when a prayer or plea is made by anyone among your people Israel—being aware of the afflictions of their own hearts, and spreading out their hands toward this temple— 39then hear from heaven, your dwelling place. Forgive and act; deal with everyone according to all they do, since you know their hearts (for you alone know every human heart), 40so that they will fear you all the time they live in the land you gave our ancestors.

41“As for the foreigner who does not belong to your people Israel but has come from a distant land because of your name— 42for they will hear of your great name and your mighty hand and your outstretched arm—when they come and pray toward this temple, 43then hear from heaven, your dwelling place. Do whatever the foreigner asks of you, so that all the peoples of the earth may know your name and fear you, as do your own people Israel, and may know that this house I have built bears your Name.

44“When your people go to war against their enemies, wherever you send them, and when they pray to the LORD toward the city you have chosen and the temple I have built for your Name, 45then hear from heaven their prayer and their plea, and uphold their cause.

46“When they sin against you—for there is no one who does not sin—and you become angry with them and give them over to their enemies, who take them captive to their own lands, far away or near; 47and if they have a change of heart in the land where they are held captive, and repent and plead with you in the land of their captors and say, ‘We have sinned, we have done wrong, we have acted wickedly’; 48and if they turn back to you with all their heart and soul in the land of their enemies who took them captive, and pray to you toward the land you gave their ancestors, toward the city you have chosen and the temple I have built for your Name; 49then from heaven, your dwelling place, hear their prayer and their plea, and uphold their cause. 50And forgive your people, who have sinned against you; forgive all the offenses they have committed against you, and cause their captors to show them mercy; 51for they are your people and your inheritance, whom you brought out of Egypt, out of that iron-smelting furnace.

52“May your eyes be open to your servant’s plea and to the plea of your people Israel, and may you listen to them whenever they cry out to you. 53For you singled them out from all the nations of the world to be your own inheritance, just as you declared through your servant Moses when you, Sovereign LORD, brought our ancestors out of Egypt.”

54When Solomon had finished all these prayers and supplications to the LORD, he rose from before the altar of the LORD, where he had been kneeling with his hands spread out toward heaven. 55He stood and blessed the whole assembly of Israel in a loud voice, saying:

56“Praise be to the LORD, who has given rest to his people Israel just as he promised. Not one word has failed of all the good promises he gave through his servant Moses. 57May the LORD our God be with us as he was with our ancestors; may he never leave us nor forsake us. 58May he turn our hearts to him, to walk in obedience to him and keep the commands, decrees and laws he gave our ancestors. 59And may these words of mine, which I have prayed before the LORD, be near to the LORD our God day and night, that he may uphold the cause of his servant and the cause of his people Israel according to each day’s need, 60so that all the peoples of the earth may know that the LORD is God and that there is no other. 61And may your hearts be fully committed to the LORD our God, to live by his decrees and obey his commands, as at this time.”

The Dedication of the Temple

62Then the king and all Israel with him offered sacrifices before the LORD. 63Solomon offered a sacrifice of fellowship offerings to the LORD: twenty-two thousand cattle and a hundred and twenty thousand sheep and goats. So the king and all the Israelites dedicated the temple of the LORD.

64On that same day the king consecrated the middle part of the courtyard in front of the temple of the LORD, and there he offered burnt offerings, grain offerings and the fat of the fellowship offerings, because the bronze altar that stood before the LORD was too small to hold the burnt offerings, the grain offerings and the fat of the fellowship offerings.

65So Solomon observed the festival at that time, and all Israel with him—a vast assembly, people from Lebo Hamath to the Wadi of Egypt. They celebrated it before the LORD our God for seven days and seven days more, fourteen days in all. 66On the following day he sent the people away. They blessed the king and then went home, joyful and glad in heart for all the good things the LORD had done for his servant David and his people Israel.

The LORD Appears to Solomon

9 When Solomon had finished building the temple of the LORD and the royal palace, and had achieved all he had desired to do, 2the LORD appeared to him a second time, as he had appeared to him at Gibeon. 3The LORD said to him:

> "I have heard the prayer and plea you have made before me; I have consecrated this temple, which you have built, by putting my Name there forever. My eyes and my heart will always be there.
>
> 4"As for you, if you walk before me faithfully with integrity of heart and uprightness, as David your father did, and do all I command and observe my decrees and laws, 5I will establish your royal throne over Israel forever, as I promised David your father when I said, 'You shall never fail to have a successor on the throne of Israel.'
>
> 6"But if you[a] or your descendants turn away from me and do not observe the commands and decrees I have given you[a] and go off to serve other gods and worship them, 7then I will cut off Israel from the land I have given them and will reject this temple I have consecrated for my Name. Israel will then become a byword and an object of ridicule among all peoples. 8This temple will become a heap of rubble. All[b] who pass by will be appalled and will scoff and say, 'Why has the LORD done such a thing to this land and to this temple?' 9People will answer, 'Because they have forsaken the LORD their God, who brought their ancestors out of Egypt, and have embraced other gods, worshiping and serving them—that is why the LORD brought all this disaster on them.'"

Solomon's Other Activities

10At the end of twenty years, during which Solomon built these two buildings—the temple of the LORD and the royal palace— 11King Solomon gave twenty towns in Galilee to Hiram king of Tyre, because Hiram had supplied him with all the cedar and juniper and gold he wanted. 12But when Hiram went from Tyre to see the towns that Solomon had given him, he was not pleased with them. 13"What kind of towns are these you have given me, my brother?" he asked. And he called them the Land of Kabul,[c] a name they have to this day. 14Now Hiram had sent to the king 120 talents[d] of gold.

15Here is the account of the forced labor King Solomon conscripted to build the LORD's temple, his own palace, the terraces,[e] the wall of Jerusalem, and Hazor, Megiddo and Gezer. 16(Pharaoh king of Egypt had attacked and captured Gezer. He had set it on fire. He killed its Canaanite inhabitants and then gave it as a wedding gift to his daughter, Solomon's wife. 17And Solomon rebuilt Gezer.) He built up Lower Beth Horon, 18Baalath, and Tadmor[f] in the desert, within his land, 19as well as all his store cities and the towns for his chariots and for his horses[g]—whatever he desired to build in Jerusalem, in Lebanon and throughout all the territory he ruled.

20There were still people left from the Amorites, Hittites, Perizzites, Hivites and Jebusites (these peoples were not Israelites). 21Solomon conscripted the descendants of all these peoples remaining in the land—whom the Israelites could not exterminate[h]—to serve as slave labor, as it is to this day. 22But Solomon did not make slaves of any of the Israelites; they were his fighting men, his government officials, his officers, his captains, and the commanders of his chariots and charioteers. 23They were also the chief officials in charge of Solomon's projects—550 officials supervising those who did the work.

24After Pharaoh's daughter had come up from the City of David to the palace Solomon had built for her, he constructed the terraces.

25Three times a year Solomon sacrificed burnt offerings and fellowship offerings on the altar he had built for the LORD, burning incense before the LORD along with them, and so fulfilled the temple obligations.

26King Solomon also built ships at Ezion Geber, which is near Elath in Edom, on the shore of the Red Sea.[i] 27And Hiram sent his men—sailors who knew the sea—to serve in the fleet with Solomon's men. 28They sailed to Ophir and brought back 420 talents[j] of gold, which they delivered to King Solomon.

The Queen of Sheba Visits Solomon

10 When the queen of Sheba heard about the fame of Solomon and his relationship to the LORD, she came to test Solomon with hard questions. 2Arriving at Jerusalem with a very great caravan—with camels carrying spices, large quantities of gold, and precious stones—she came to Solomon and talked with him about all that she had on her mind. 3Solomon answered all her questions; nothing was too hard for the king to explain to her. 4When the queen of Sheba saw all the wisdom of Solomon and the palace he had built, 5the food on his table, the seating of his officials, the attending servants in their robes, his cupbearers, and the burnt offerings he made at[k] the temple of the LORD, she was overwhelmed.

6She said to the king, "The report I heard in my own country about your achievements and your wisdom is true. 7But I did not believe

[a] *6* The Hebrew is plural. [b] *8* See some Septuagint manuscripts, Old Latin, Syriac, Arabic and Targum; Hebrew *And though this temple is now imposing, all* [c] *13* *Kabul* sounds like the Hebrew for *good-for-nothing.* [d] *14* That is, about 4 1/2 tons or about 4 metric tons [e] *15* Or *the Millo*; also in verse 24 [f] *18* The Hebrew may also be read *Tamar.* [g] *19* Or *charioteers* [h] *21* The Hebrew term refers to the irrevocable giving over of things or persons to the LORD, often by totally destroying them. [i] *26* Or *the Sea of Reeds* [j] *28* That is, about 16 tons or about 14 metric tons [k] *5* Or *the ascent by which he went up to*

these things until I came and saw with my own eyes. Indeed, not even half was told me; in wisdom and wealth you have far exceeded the report I heard. 8How happy your people must be! How happy your officials, who continually stand before you and hear your wisdom! 9Praise be to the LORD your God, who has delighted in you and placed you on the throne of Israel. Because of the LORD's eternal love for Israel, he has made you king to maintain justice and righteousness."

10And she gave the king 120 talents[a] of gold, large quantities of spices, and precious stones. Never again were so many spices brought in as those the queen of Sheba gave to King Solomon.

11(Hiram's ships brought gold from Ophir; and from there they brought great cargoes of almugwood[b] and precious stones. 12The king used the almugwood to make supports[c] for the temple of the LORD and for the royal palace, and to make harps and lyres for the musicians. So much almugwood has never been imported or seen since that day.)

13King Solomon gave the queen of Sheba all she desired and asked for, besides what he had given her out of his royal bounty. Then she left and returned with her retinue to her own country.

Solomon's Splendor

14The weight of the gold that Solomon received yearly was 666 talents,[d] 15not including the revenues from merchants and traders and from all the Arabian kings and the governors of the territories.

16King Solomon made two hundred large shields of hammered gold; six hundred shekels[e] of gold went into each shield. 17He also made three hundred small shields of hammered gold, with three minas[f] of gold in each shield. The king put them in the Palace of the Forest of Lebanon.

18Then the king made a great throne covered with ivory and overlaid with fine gold. 19The throne had six steps, and its back had a rounded top. On both sides of the seat were armrests, with a lion standing beside each of them. 20Twelve lions stood on the six steps, one at either end of each step. Nothing like it had ever been made for any other kingdom. 21All King Solomon's goblets were gold, and all the household articles in the Palace of the Forest of Lebanon were pure gold. Nothing was made of silver, because silver was considered of little value in Solomon's days. 22The king had a fleet of trading ships[g] at sea along with the ships of Hiram. Once every three years it returned, carrying gold, silver and ivory, and apes and baboons.

23King Solomon was greater in riches and wisdom than all the other kings of the earth. 24The whole world sought audience with Solomon to hear the wisdom God had put in his heart. 25Year after year, everyone who came brought a gift—articles of silver and gold, robes, weapons and spices, and horses and mules.

26Solomon accumulated chariots and horses; he had fourteen hundred chariots and twelve thousand horses,[h] which he kept in the chariot cities and also with him in Jerusalem. 27The king made silver as common in Jerusalem as stones, and cedar as plentiful as sycamore-fig trees in the foothills. 28Solomon's horses were imported from Egypt and from Kue[i]—the royal merchants purchased them from Kue at the current price. 29They imported a chariot from Egypt for six hundred shekels of silver, and a horse for a hundred and fifty.[j] They also exported them to all the kings of the Hittites and of the Arameans.

Solomon's Wives

11 King Solomon, however, loved many foreign women besides Pharaoh's daughter—Moabites, Ammonites, Edomites, Sidonians and Hittites. 2They were from nations about which the LORD had told the Israelites, "You must not intermarry with them, because they will surely turn your hearts after their gods." Nevertheless, Solomon held fast to them in love. 3He had seven hundred wives of royal birth and three hundred concubines, and his wives led him astray. 4As Solomon grew old, his wives turned his heart after other gods, and his heart was not fully devoted to the LORD his God, as the heart of David his father had been. 5He followed Ashtoreth the goddess of the Sidonians, and Molek the detestable god of the Ammonites. 6So Solomon did evil in the eyes of the LORD; he did not follow the LORD completely, as David his father had done.

7On a hill east of Jerusalem, Solomon built a high place for Chemosh the detestable god of Moab, and for Molek the detestable god of the Ammonites. 8He did the same for all his foreign wives, who burned incense and offered sacrifices to their gods.

9The LORD became angry with Solomon because his heart had turned away from the LORD, the God of Israel, who had appeared to him twice. 10Although he had forbidden Solomon to follow other gods, Solomon did not keep the LORD's command. 11So the LORD said to Solomon, "Since this is your attitude and you have not kept my covenant and my decrees, which I commanded you, I will most certainly tear the kingdom away from you and give it to one of your subordinates. 12Nevertheless, for the sake of David your father, I will not do it during your lifetime. I will tear it out of the hand of your son. 13Yet I will not

[a] *10* That is, about 4 1/2 tons or about 4 metric tons [b] *11* Probably a variant of *algumwood*; also in verse 12 [c] *12* The meaning of the Hebrew for this word is uncertain. [d] *14* That is, about 25 tons or about 23 metric tons [e] *16* That is, about 15 pounds or about 6.9 kilograms; also in verse 29 [f] *17* That is, about 3 3/4 pounds or about 1.7 kilograms; or perhaps reference is to double minas, that is, about 7 1/2 pounds or about 3.5 kilograms. [g] *22* Hebrew *of ships of Tarshish* [h] *26* Or *charioteers* [i] *28* Probably *Cilicia* [j] *29* That is, about 3 3/4 pounds or about 1.7 kilograms

tear the whole kingdom from him, but will give him one tribe for the sake of David my servant and for the sake of Jerusalem, which I have chosen."

Solomon's Adversaries

14Then the LORD raised up against Solomon an adversary, Hadad the Edomite, from the royal line of Edom. 15Earlier when David was fighting with Edom, Joab the commander of the army, who had gone up to bury the dead, had struck down all the men in Edom. 16Joab and all the Israelites stayed there for six months, until they had destroyed all the men in Edom. 17But Hadad, still only a boy, fled to Egypt with some Edomite officials who had served his father. 18They set out from Midian and went to Paran. Then taking people from Paran with them, they went to Egypt, to Pharaoh king of Egypt, who gave Hadad a house and land and provided him with food.

19Pharaoh was so pleased with Hadad that he gave him a sister of his own wife, Queen Tahpenes, in marriage. 20The sister of Tahpenes bore him a son named Genubath, whom Tahpenes brought up in the royal palace. There Genubath lived with Pharaoh's own children.

21While he was in Egypt, Hadad heard that David rested with his ancestors and that Joab the commander of the army was also dead. Then Hadad said to Pharaoh, "Let me go, that I may return to my own country."

22"What have you lacked here that you want to go back to your own country?" Pharaoh asked.

"Nothing," Hadad replied, "but do let me go!"

23And God raised up against Solomon another adversary, Rezon son of Eliada, who had fled from his master, Hadadezer king of Zobah. 24When David destroyed Zobah's army, Rezon gathered a band of men around him and became their leader; they went to Damascus, where they settled and took control. 25Rezon was Israel's adversary as long as Solomon lived, adding to the trouble caused by Hadad. So Rezon ruled in Aram and was hostile toward Israel.

Jeroboam Rebels Against Solomon

26Also, Jeroboam son of Nebat rebelled against the king. He was one of Solomon's officials, an Ephraimite from Zeredah, and his mother was a widow named Zeruah.

27Here is the account of how he rebelled against the king: Solomon had built the terraces[a] and had filled in the gap in the wall of the city of David his father. 28Now Jeroboam was a man of standing, and when Solomon saw how well the young man did his work, he put him in charge of the whole labor force of the tribes of Joseph.

29About that time Jeroboam was going out of Jerusalem, and Ahijah the prophet of Shiloh met him on the way, wearing a new cloak. The two of them were alone out in the country, 30and Ahijah took hold of the new cloak he was wearing and tore it into twelve pieces. 31Then he said to Jeroboam, "Take ten pieces for yourself, for this is what the LORD, the God of Israel, says: 'See, I am going to tear the kingdom out of Solomon's hand and give you ten tribes. 32But for the sake of my servant David and the city of Jerusalem, which I have chosen out of all the tribes of Israel, he will have one tribe. 33I will do this because they have[b] forsaken me and worshiped Ashtoreth the goddess of the Sidonians, Chemosh the god of the Moabites, and Molek the god of the Ammonites, and have not walked in obedience to me, nor done what is right in my eyes, nor kept my decrees and laws as David, Solomon's father, did.

34" 'But I will not take the whole kingdom out of Solomon's hand; I have made him ruler all the days of his life for the sake of David my servant, whom I chose and who obeyed my commands and decrees. 35I will take the kingdom from his son's hands and give you ten tribes. 36I will give one tribe to his son so that David my servant may always have a lamp before me in Jerusalem, the city where I chose to put my Name. 37However, as for you, I will take you, and you will rule over all that your heart desires; you will be king over Israel. 38If you do whatever I command you and walk in obedience to me and do what is right in my eyes by obeying my decrees and commands, as David my servant did, I will be with you. I will build you a dynasty as enduring as the one I built for David and will give Israel to you. 39I will humble David's descendants because of this, but not forever.' "

40Solomon tried to kill Jeroboam, but Jeroboam fled to Egypt, to Shishak the king, and stayed there until Solomon's death.

Solomon's Death

41As for the other events of Solomon's reign—all he did and the wisdom he displayed—are they not written in the book of the annals of Solomon? 42Solomon reigned in Jerusalem over all Israel forty years. 43Then he rested with his ancestors and was buried in the city of David his father. And Rehoboam his son succeeded him as king.

Israel Rebels Against Rehoboam

12 Rehoboam went to Shechem, for all Israel had gone there to make him king. 2When Jeroboam son of Nebat heard this (he was still in Egypt, where he had fled from King Solomon), he returned from[c] Egypt. 3So they sent for Jeroboam, and he and the whole assembly of Israel went to Rehoboam and said to him: 4"Your father put a heavy yoke on us, but now lighten the harsh labor and the heavy yoke he put on us, and we will serve you."

5Rehoboam answered, "Go away for three days and then come back to me." So the people went away.

[a] 27 Or *the Millo* [b] 33 Hebrew; Septuagint, Vulgate and Syriac *because he has* [c] 2 Or *he remained in*

6Then King Rehoboam consulted the elders
who had served his father Solomon during his
lifetime. "How would you advise me to answer
these people?" he asked.
7They replied, "If today you will be a servant to these people and serve them and give
them a favorable answer, they will always be
your servants."
8But Rehoboam rejected the advice the elders gave him and consulted the young men
who had grown up with him and were serving
him. 9He asked them, "What is your advice?
How should we answer these people who say to
me, 'Lighten the yoke your father put on us'?"
10The young men who had grown up with
him replied, "These people have said to you,
'Your father put a heavy yoke on us, but make
our yoke lighter.' Now tell them, 'My little finger is thicker than my father's waist. 11My
father laid on you a heavy yoke; I will make
it even heavier. My father scourged you with
whips; I will scourge you with scorpions.'"
12Three days later Jeroboam and all the people returned to Rehoboam, as the king had
said, "Come back to me in three days." 13The
king answered the people harshly. Rejecting
the advice given him by the elders, 14he followed the advice of the young men and said,
"My father made your yoke heavy; I will make
it even heavier. My father scourged you with
whips; I will scourge you with scorpions." 15So
the king did not listen to the people, for this
turn of events was from the LORD, to fulfill
the word the LORD had spoken to Jeroboam
son of Nebat through Ahijah the Shilonite.
16When all Israel saw that the king refused
to listen to them, they answered the king:

"What share do we have in David,
  what part in Jesse's son?
To your tents, Israel!
  Look after your own house, David!"

So the Israelites went home. 17But as for the
Israelites who were living in the towns of Judah, Rehoboam still ruled over them.
18King Rehoboam sent out Adoniram,[a] who
was in charge of forced labor, but all Israel
stoned him to death. King Rehoboam, however, managed to get into his chariot and escape
to Jerusalem. 19So Israel has been in rebellion
against the house of David to this day.
20When all the Israelites heard that Jeroboam had returned, they sent and called him
to the assembly and made him king over all
Israel. Only the tribe of Judah remained loyal
to the house of David.
21When Rehoboam arrived in Jerusalem,
he mustered all Judah and the tribe of Benjamin—a hundred and eighty thousand able
young men—to go to war against Israel and
to regain the kingdom for Rehoboam son of
Solomon.
22But this word of God came to Shemaiah
the man of God: 23"Say to Rehoboam son of
Solomon king of Judah, to all Judah and Benjamin, and to the rest of the people, 24'This
is what the LORD says: Do not go up to fight
against your brothers, the Israelites. Go home,
every one of you, for this is my doing.'" So
they obeyed the word of the LORD and went
home again, as the LORD had ordered.

Golden Calves at Bethel and Dan

25Then Jeroboam fortified Shechem in the
hill country of Ephraim and lived there. From
there he went out and built up Peniel.[b]
26Jeroboam thought to himself, "The kingdom will now likely revert to the house of David. 27If these people go up to offer sacrifices
at the temple of the LORD in Jerusalem, they
will again give their allegiance to their lord,
Rehoboam king of Judah. They will kill me
and return to King Rehoboam."
28After seeking advice, the king made two
golden calves. He said to the people, "It is too
much for you to go up to Jerusalem. Here are
your gods, Israel, who brought you up out
of Egypt." 29One he set up in Bethel, and the
other in Dan. 30And this thing became a sin;
the people came to worship the one at Bethel
and went as far as Dan to worship the other.[c]
31Jeroboam built shrines on high places
and appointed priests from all sorts of people, even though they were not Levites. 32He
instituted a festival on the fifteenth day of the
eighth month, like the festival held in Judah,
and offered sacrifices on the altar. This he
did in Bethel, sacrificing to the calves he had
made. And at Bethel he also installed priests
at the high places he had made. 33On the fifteenth day of the eighth month, a month of
his own choosing, he offered sacrifices on the
altar he had built at Bethel. So he instituted
the festival for the Israelites and went up to
the altar to make offerings.

The Man of God From Judah

13 By the word of the LORD a man of God
came from Judah to Bethel, as Jeroboam
was standing by the altar to make an offering.
2By the word of the LORD he cried out against
the altar: "Altar, altar! This is what the LORD
says: 'A son named Josiah will be born to the
house of David. On you he will sacrifice the
priests of the high places who make offerings here, and human bones will be burned on
you.'" 3That same day the man of God gave a
sign: "This is the sign the LORD has declared:
The altar will be split apart and the ashes on
it will be poured out."
4When King Jeroboam heard what the man
of God cried out against the altar at Bethel,
he stretched out his hand from the altar and
said, "Seize him!" But the hand he stretched
out toward the man shriveled up, so that he
could not pull it back. 5Also, the altar was split
apart and its ashes poured out according to
the sign given by the man of God by the word
of the LORD.

[a] *18* Some Septuagint manuscripts and Syriac (see also 4:6 and 5:14); Hebrew *Adoram* [b] *25* Hebrew *Penuel,* a variant of *Peniel* [c] *30* Probable reading of the original Hebrew text; Masoretic Text *people went to the one as far as Dan*

6 Then the king said to the man of God, "Intercede with the LORD your God and pray for me that my hand may be restored." So the man of God interceded with the LORD, and the king's hand was restored and became as it was before.

7 The king said to the man of God, "Come home with me for a meal, and I will give you a gift."

8 But the man of God answered the king, "Even if you were to give me half your possessions, I would not go with you, nor would I eat bread or drink water here. 9 For I was commanded by the word of the LORD: 'You must not eat bread or drink water or return by the way you came.'" 10 So he took another road and did not return by the way he had come to Bethel.

11 Now there was a certain old prophet living in Bethel, whose sons came and told him all that the man of God had done there that day. They also told their father what he had said to the king. 12 Their father asked them, "Which way did he go?" And his sons showed him which road the man of God from Judah had taken. 13 So he said to his sons, "Saddle the donkey for me." And when they had saddled the donkey for him, he mounted it 14 and rode after the man of God. He found him sitting under an oak tree and asked, "Are you the man of God who came from Judah?"

"I am," he replied.

15 So the prophet said to him, "Come home with me and eat."

16 The man of God said, "I cannot turn back and go with you, nor can I eat bread or drink water with you in this place. 17 I have been told by the word of the LORD: 'You must not eat bread or drink water there or return by the way you came.'"

18 The old prophet answered, "I too am a prophet, as you are. And an angel said to me by the word of the LORD: 'Bring him back with you to your house so that he may eat bread and drink water.'" (But he was lying to him.) 19 So the man of God returned with him and ate and drank in his house.

20 While they were sitting at the table, the word of the LORD came to the old prophet who had brought him back. 21 He cried out to the man of God who had come from Judah, "This is what the LORD says: 'You have defied the word of the LORD and have not kept the command the LORD your God gave you. 22 You came back and ate bread and drank water in the place where he told you not to eat or drink. Therefore your body will not be buried in the tomb of your ancestors.'"

23 When the man of God had finished eating and drinking, the prophet who had brought him back saddled his donkey for him. 24 As he went on his way, a lion met him on the road and killed him, and his body was left lying on the road, with both the donkey and the lion standing beside it. 25 Some people who passed by saw the body lying there, with the lion standing beside the body, and they went and reported it in the city where the old prophet lived.

26 When the prophet who had brought him back from his journey heard of it, he said, "It is the man of God who defied the word of the LORD. The LORD has given him over to the lion, which has mauled him and killed him, as the word of the LORD had warned him."

27 The prophet said to his sons, "Saddle the donkey for me," and they did so. 28 Then he went out and found the body lying on the road, with the donkey and the lion standing beside it. The lion had neither eaten the body nor mauled the donkey. 29 So the prophet picked up the body of the man of God, laid it on the donkey, and brought it back to his own city to mourn for him and bury him. 30 Then he laid the body in his own tomb, and they mourned over him and said, "Alas, my brother!"

31 After burying him, he said to his sons, "When I die, bury me in the grave where the man of God is buried; lay my bones beside his bones. 32 For the message he declared by the word of the LORD against the altar in Bethel and against all the shrines on the high places in the towns of Samaria will certainly come true."

33 Even after this, Jeroboam did not change his evil ways, but once more appointed priests for the high places from all sorts of people. Anyone who wanted to become a priest he consecrated for the high places. 34 This was the sin of the house of Jeroboam that led to its downfall and to its destruction from the face of the earth.

Ahijah's Prophecy Against Jeroboam

14 At that time Abijah son of Jeroboam became ill, 2 and Jeroboam said to his wife, "Go, disguise yourself, so you won't be recognized as the wife of Jeroboam. Then go to Shiloh. Ahijah the prophet is there—the one who told me I would be king over this people. 3 Take ten loaves of bread with you, some cakes and a jar of honey, and go to him. He will tell you what will happen to the boy." 4 So Jeroboam's wife did what he said and went to Ahijah's house in Shiloh.

Now Ahijah could not see; his sight was gone because of his age. 5 But the LORD had told Ahijah, "Jeroboam's wife is coming to ask you about her son, for he is ill, and you are to give her such and such an answer. When she arrives, she will pretend to be someone else."

6 So when Ahijah heard the sound of her footsteps at the door, he said, "Come in, wife of Jeroboam. Why this pretense? I have been sent to you with bad news. 7 Go, tell Jeroboam that this is what the LORD, the God of Israel, says: 'I raised you up from among the people and appointed you ruler over my people Israel. 8 I tore the kingdom away from the house of David and gave it to you, but you have not been like my servant David, who kept my commands and followed me with all his heart, doing only what was right in my eyes. 9 You have done more evil than all who lived before you. You have made for yourself other gods, idols made of metal; you have aroused my anger and turned your back on me.

10 "'Because of this, I am going to bring di-

saster on the house of Jeroboam. I will cut off from Jeroboam every last male in Israel—slave or free.[a] I will burn up the house of Jeroboam as one burns dung, until it is all gone. 11Dogs will eat those belonging to Jeroboam who die in the city, and the birds will feed on those who die in the country. The LORD has spoken!'

12"As for you, go back home. When you set foot in your city, the boy will die. 13All Israel will mourn for him and bury him. He is the only one belonging to Jeroboam who will be buried, because he is the only one in the house of Jeroboam in whom the LORD, the God of Israel, has found anything good.

14"The LORD will raise up for himself a king over Israel who will cut off the family of Jeroboam. Even now this is beginning to happen.[b] 15And the LORD will strike Israel, so that it will be like a reed swaying in the water. He will uproot Israel from this good land that he gave to their ancestors and scatter them beyond the Euphrates River, because they aroused the LORD's anger by making Asherah poles.[c] 16And he will give Israel up because of the sins Jeroboam has committed and has caused Israel to commit."

17Then Jeroboam's wife got up and left and went to Tirzah. As soon as she stepped over the threshold of the house, the boy died. 18They buried him, and all Israel mourned for him, as the LORD had said through his servant the prophet Ahijah.

19The other events of Jeroboam's reign, his wars and how he ruled, are written in the book of the annals of the kings of Israel. 20He reigned for twenty-two years and then rested with his ancestors. And Nadab his son succeeded him as king.

Rehoboam King of Judah

21Rehoboam son of Solomon was king in Judah. He was forty-one years old when he became king, and he reigned seventeen years in Jerusalem, the city the LORD had chosen out of all the tribes of Israel in which to put his Name. His mother's name was Naamah; she was an Ammonite.

22Judah did evil in the eyes of the LORD. By the sins they committed they stirred up his jealous anger more than those who were before them had done. 23They also set up for themselves high places, sacred stones and Asherah poles on every high hill and under every spreading tree. 24There were even male shrine prostitutes in the land; the people engaged in all the detestable practices of the nations the LORD had driven out before the Israelites.

25In the fifth year of King Rehoboam, Shishak king of Egypt attacked Jerusalem. 26He carried off the treasures of the temple of the LORD and the treasures of the royal palace. He took everything, including all the gold shields Solomon had made. 27So King Rehoboam made bronze shields to replace them and assigned these to the commanders of the guard on duty at the entrance to the royal palace. 28Whenever the king went to the LORD's temple, the guards bore the shields, and afterward they returned them to the guardroom.

29As for the other events of Rehoboam's reign, and all he did, are they not written in the book of the annals of the kings of Judah? 30There was continual warfare between Rehoboam and Jeroboam. 31And Rehoboam rested with his ancestors and was buried with them in the City of David. His mother's name was Naamah; she was an Ammonite. And Abijah[d] his son succeeded him as king.

Abijah King of Judah

15 In the eighteenth year of the reign of Jeroboam son of Nebat, Abijah[e] became king of Judah, 2and he reigned in Jerusalem three years. His mother's name was Maakah daughter of Abishalom.[f]

3He committed all the sins his father had done before him; his heart was not fully devoted to the LORD his God, as the heart of David his forefather had been. 4Nevertheless, for David's sake the LORD his God gave him a lamp in Jerusalem by raising up a son to succeed him and by making Jerusalem strong. 5For David had done what was right in the eyes of the LORD and had not failed to keep any of the LORD's commands all the days of his life—except in the case of Uriah the Hittite.

6There was war between Abijah[g] and Jeroboam throughout Abijah's lifetime. 7As for the other events of Abijah's reign, and all he did, are they not written in the book of the annals of the kings of Judah? There was war between Abijah and Jeroboam. 8And Abijah rested with his ancestors and was buried in the City of David. And Asa his son succeeded him as king.

Asa King of Judah

9In the twentieth year of Jeroboam king of Israel, Asa became king of Judah, 10and he reigned in Jerusalem forty-one years. His grandmother's name was Maakah daughter of Abishalom.

11Asa did what was right in the eyes of the LORD, as his father David had done. 12He expelled the male shrine prostitutes from the land and got rid of all the idols his ancestors had made. 13He even deposed his grandmother Maakah from her position as queen mother, because she had made a repulsive image for the worship of Asherah. Asa cut it down and burned it in the Kidron Valley. 14Although he did not remove the high places, Asa's heart was fully committed to the LORD all his life.

[a] *10* Or *Israel—every ruler or leader* [b] *14* The meaning of the Hebrew for this sentence is uncertain. [c] *15* That is, wooden symbols of the goddess Asherah; here and elsewhere in 1 Kings [d] *31* Some Hebrew manuscripts and Septuagint (see also 2 Chron. 12:16); most Hebrew manuscripts *Abijam* [e] *1* Some Hebrew manuscripts and Septuagint (see also 2 Chron. 12:16); most Hebrew manuscripts *Abijam*; also in verses 7 and 8 [f] *2* A variant of *Absalom*; also in verse 10 [g] *6* Some Hebrew manuscripts and Syriac *Abijam* (that is, Abijah); most Hebrew manuscripts *Rehoboam*

15 He brought into the temple of the LORD the silver and gold and the articles that he and his father had dedicated.

16 There was war between Asa and Baasha king of Israel throughout their reigns. 17 Baasha king of Israel went up against Judah and fortified Ramah to prevent anyone from leaving or entering the territory of Asa king of Judah.

18 Asa then took all the silver and gold that was left in the treasuries of the LORD's temple and of his own palace. He entrusted it to his officials and sent them to Ben-Hadad son of Tabrimmon, the son of Hezion, the king of Aram, who was ruling in Damascus. 19 "Let there be a treaty between me and you," he said, "as there was between my father and your father. See, I am sending you a gift of silver and gold. Now break your treaty with Baasha king of Israel so he will withdraw from me."

20 Ben-Hadad agreed with King Asa and sent the commanders of his forces against the towns of Israel. He conquered Ijon, Dan, Abel Beth Maakah and all Kinnereth in addition to Naphtali. 21 When Baasha heard this, he stopped building Ramah and withdrew to Tirzah. 22 Then King Asa issued an order to all Judah—no one was exempt—and they carried away from Ramah the stones and timber Baasha had been using there. With them King Asa built up Geba in Benjamin, and also Mizpah.

23 As for all the other events of Asa's reign, all his achievements, all he did and the cities he built, are they not written in the book of the annals of the kings of Judah? In his old age, however, his feet became diseased. 24 Then Asa rested with his ancestors and was buried with them in the city of his father David. And Jehoshaphat his son succeeded him as king.

Nadab King of Israel

25 Nadab son of Jeroboam became king of Israel in the second year of Asa king of Judah, and he reigned over Israel two years. 26 He did evil in the eyes of the LORD, following the ways of his father and committing the same sin his father had caused Israel to commit.

27 Baasha son of Ahijah from the tribe of Issachar plotted against him, and he struck him down at Gibbethon, a Philistine town, while Nadab and all Israel were besieging it. 28 Baasha killed Nadab in the third year of Asa king of Judah and succeeded him as king.

29 As soon as he began to reign, he killed Jeroboam's whole family. He did not leave Jeroboam anyone that breathed, but destroyed them all, according to the word of the LORD given through his servant Ahijah the Shilonite. 30 This happened because of the sins Jeroboam had committed and had caused Israel to commit, and because he aroused the anger of the LORD, the God of Israel.

31 As for the other events of Nadab's reign, and all he did, are they not written in the book of the annals of the kings of Israel? 32 There was war between Asa and Baasha king of Israel throughout their reigns.

Baasha King of Israel

33 In the third year of Asa king of Judah, Baasha son of Ahijah became king of all Israel in Tirzah, and he reigned twenty-four years. 34 He did evil in the eyes of the LORD, following the ways of Jeroboam and committing the same sin Jeroboam had caused Israel to commit.

16 Then the word of the LORD came to Jehu son of Hanani concerning Baasha: 2 "I lifted you up from the dust and appointed you ruler over my people Israel, but you followed the ways of Jeroboam and caused my people Israel to sin and to arouse my anger by their sins. 3 So I am about to wipe out Baasha and his house, and I will make your house like that of Jeroboam son of Nebat. 4 Dogs will eat those belonging to Baasha who die in the city, and birds will feed on those who die in the country."

5 As for the other events of Baasha's reign, what he did and his achievements, are they not written in the book of the annals of the kings of Israel? 6 Baasha rested with his ancestors and was buried in Tirzah. And Elah his son succeeded him as king.

7 Moreover, the word of the LORD came through the prophet Jehu son of Hanani to Baasha and his house, because of all the evil he had done in the eyes of the LORD, arousing his anger by the things he did, becoming like the house of Jeroboam—and also because he destroyed it.

Elah King of Israel

8 In the twenty-sixth year of Asa king of Judah, Elah son of Baasha became king of Israel, and he reigned in Tirzah two years.

9 Zimri, one of his officials, who had command of half his chariots, plotted against him. Elah was in Tirzah at the time, getting drunk in the home of Arza, the palace administrator at Tirzah. 10 Zimri came in, struck him down and killed him in the twenty-seventh year of Asa king of Judah. Then he succeeded him as king.

11 As soon as he began to reign and was seated on the throne, he killed off Baasha's whole family. He did not spare a single male, whether relative or friend. 12 So Zimri destroyed the whole family of Baasha, in accordance with the word of the LORD spoken against Baasha through the prophet Jehu— 13 because of all the sins Baasha and his son Elah had committed and had caused Israel to commit, so that they aroused the anger of the LORD, the God of Israel, by their worthless idols.

14 As for the other events of Elah's reign, and all he did, are they not written in the book of the annals of the kings of Israel?

Zimri King of Israel

15 In the twenty-seventh year of Asa king of Judah, Zimri reigned in Tirzah seven days. The army was encamped near Gibbethon, a Philistine town. 16 When the Israelites in the camp heard that Zimri had plotted against the king and murdered him, they proclaimed

Omri, the commander of the army, king over
Israel that very day there in the camp. 17Then
Omri and all the Israelites with him withdrew
from Gibbethon and laid siege to Tirzah.
18When Zimri saw that the city was taken,
he went into the citadel of the royal palace and
set the palace on fire around him. So he died,
19because of the sins he had committed, doing
evil in the eyes of the LORD and following the
ways of Jeroboam and committing the same
sin Jeroboam had caused Israel to commit.
20As for the other events of Zimri's reign,
and the rebellion he carried out, are they not
written in the book of the annals of the kings
of Israel?

Omri King of Israel

21Then the people of Israel were split into
two factions; half supported Tibni son of Ginath for king, and the other half supported
Omri. 22But Omri's followers proved stronger
than those of Tibni son of Ginath. So Tibni
died and Omri became king.
23In the thirty-first year of Asa king of
Judah, Omri became king of Israel, and he
reigned twelve years, six of them in Tirzah.
24He bought the hill of Samaria from Shemer
for two talents[a] of silver and built a city on
the hill, calling it Samaria, after Shemer, the
name of the former owner of the hill.
25But Omri did evil in the eyes of the LORD
and sinned more than all those before him.
26He followed completely the ways of Jeroboam son of Nebat, committing the same sin
Jeroboam had caused Israel to commit, so that
they aroused the anger of the LORD, the God
of Israel, by their worthless idols.
27As for the other events of Omri's reign,
what he did and the things he achieved, are
they not written in the book of the annals of
the kings of Israel? 28Omri rested with his
ancestors and was buried in Samaria. And
Ahab his son succeeded him as king.

Ahab Becomes King of Israel

29In the thirty-eighth year of Asa king of
Judah, Ahab son of Omri became king of Israel, and he reigned in Samaria over Israel
twenty-two years. 30Ahab son of Omri did
more evil in the eyes of the LORD than any of
those before him. 31He not only considered it
trivial to commit the sins of Jeroboam son of
Nebat, but he also married Jezebel daughter
of Ethbaal king of the Sidonians, and began
to serve Baal and worship him. 32He set up
an altar for Baal in the temple of Baal that he
built in Samaria. 33Ahab also made an Asherah pole and did more to arouse the anger of
the LORD, the God of Israel, than did all the
kings of Israel before him.
34In Ahab's time, Hiel of Bethel rebuilt Jericho. He laid its foundations at the cost of his
firstborn son Abiram, and he set up its gates
at the cost of his youngest son Segub, in accordance with the word of the LORD spoken
by Joshua son of Nun.

Elijah Announces a Great Drought

17 Now Elijah the Tishbite, from Tishbe[b] in
Gilead, said to Ahab, "As the LORD, the
God of Israel, lives, whom I serve, there will
be neither dew nor rain in the next few years
except at my word."

Elijah Fed by Ravens

2Then the word of the LORD came to Elijah:
3"Leave here, turn eastward and hide in the
Kerith Ravine, east of the Jordan. 4You will
drink from the brook, and I have directed the
ravens to supply you with food there."
5So he did what the LORD had told him. He
went to the Kerith Ravine, east of the Jordan,
and stayed there. 6The ravens brought him
bread and meat in the morning and bread
and meat in the evening, and he drank from
the brook.

Elijah and the Widow at Zarephath

7Some time later the brook dried up because
there had been no rain in the land. 8Then the
word of the LORD came to him: 9"Go at once
to Zarephath in the region of Sidon and stay
there. I have directed a widow there to supply
you with food." 10So he went to Zarephath.
When he came to the town gate, a widow was
there gathering sticks. He called to her and
asked, "Would you bring me a little water in a
jar so I may have a drink?" 11As she was going
to get it, he called, "And bring me, please, a
piece of bread."
12"As surely as the LORD your God lives,"
she replied, "I don't have any bread—only a
handful of flour in a jar and a little olive oil
in a jug. I am gathering a few sticks to take
home and make a meal for myself and my son,
that we may eat it—and die."
13Elijah said to her, "Don't be afraid. Go
home and do as you have said. But first make a
small loaf of bread for me from what you have
and bring it to me, and then make something
for yourself and your son. 14For this is what
the LORD, the God of Israel, says: 'The jar of
flour will not be used up and the jug of oil will
not run dry until the day the LORD sends rain
on the land.'"
15She went away and did as Elijah had told
her. So there was food every day for Elijah
and for the woman and her family. 16For the
jar of flour was not used up and the jug of oil
did not run dry, in keeping with the word of
the LORD spoken by Elijah.
17Some time later the son of the woman
who owned the house became ill. He grew
worse and worse, and finally stopped breathing. 18She said to Elijah, "What do you have
against me, man of God? Did you come to
remind me of my sin and kill my son?"
19"Give me your son," Elijah replied. He took
him from her arms, carried him to the upper
room where he was staying, and laid him on
his bed. 20Then he cried out to the LORD, "LORD
my God, have you brought tragedy even on
this widow I am staying with, by causing her

[a] *24* That is, about 150 pounds or about 68 kilograms [b] *1* Or *Tishbite, of the settlers*

son to die?" [21]Then he stretched himself out on the boy three times and cried out to the LORD, "LORD my God, let this boy's life return to him!"

[22]The LORD heard Elijah's cry, and the boy's life returned to him, and he lived. [23]Elijah picked up the child and carried him down from the room into the house. He gave him to his mother and said, "Look, your son is alive!"

[24]Then the woman said to Elijah, "Now I know that you are a man of God and that the word of the LORD from your mouth is the truth."

Elijah and Obadiah

18 After a long time, in the third year, the word of the LORD came to Elijah: "Go and present yourself to Ahab, and I will send rain on the land." [2]So Elijah went to present himself to Ahab.

Now the famine was severe in Samaria, [3]and Ahab had summoned Obadiah, his palace administrator. (Obadiah was a devout believer in the LORD. [4]While Jezebel was killing off the LORD's prophets, Obadiah had taken a hundred prophets and hidden them in two caves, fifty in each, and had supplied them with food and water.) [5]Ahab had said to Obadiah, "Go through the land to all the springs and valleys. Maybe we can find some grass to keep the horses and mules alive so we will not have to kill any of our animals." [6]So they divided the land they were to cover, Ahab going in one direction and Obadiah in another.

[7]As Obadiah was walking along, Elijah met him. Obadiah recognized him, bowed down to the ground, and said, "Is it really you, my lord Elijah?"

[8]"Yes," he replied. "Go tell your master, 'Elijah is here.'"

[9]"What have I done wrong," asked Obadiah, "that you are handing your servant over to Ahab to be put to death? [10]As surely as the LORD your God lives, there is not a nation or kingdom where my master has not sent someone to look for you. And whenever a nation or kingdom claimed you were not there, he made them swear they could not find you. [11]But now you tell me to go to my master and say, 'Elijah is here.' [12]I don't know where the Spirit of the LORD may carry you when I leave you. If I go and tell Ahab and he doesn't find you, he will kill me. Yet I your servant have worshiped the LORD since my youth. [13]Haven't you heard, my lord, what I did while Jezebel was killing the prophets of the LORD? I hid a hundred of the LORD's prophets in two caves, fifty in each, and supplied them with food and water. [14]And now you tell me to go to my master and say, 'Elijah is here.' He will kill me!"

[15]Elijah said, "As the LORD Almighty lives, whom I serve, I will surely present myself to Ahab today."

Elijah on Mount Carmel

[16]So Obadiah went to meet Ahab and told him, and Ahab went to meet Elijah. [17]When he saw Elijah, he said to him, "Is that you, you troubler of Israel?"

[18]"I have not made trouble for Israel," Elijah replied. "But you and your father's family have. You have abandoned the LORD's commands and have followed the Baals. [19]Now summon the people from all over Israel to meet me on Mount Carmel. And bring the four hundred and fifty prophets of Baal and the four hundred prophets of Asherah, who eat at Jezebel's table."

[20]So Ahab sent word throughout all Israel and assembled the prophets on Mount Carmel. [21]Elijah went before the people and said, "How long will you waver between two opinions? If the LORD is God, follow him; but if Baal is God, follow him."

But the people said nothing.

[22]Then Elijah said to them, "I am the only one of the LORD's prophets left, but Baal has four hundred and fifty prophets. [23]Get two bulls for us. Let Baal's prophets choose one for themselves, and let them cut it into pieces and put it on the wood but not set fire to it. I will prepare the other bull and put it on the wood but not set fire to it. [24]Then you call on the name of your god, and I will call on the name of the LORD. The god who answers by fire—he is God."

Then all the people said, "What you say is good."

[25]Elijah said to the prophets of Baal, "Choose one of the bulls and prepare it first, since there are so many of you. Call on the name of your god, but do not light the fire." [26]So they took the bull given them and prepared it.

Then they called on the name of Baal from morning till noon. "Baal, answer us!" they shouted. But there was no response; no one answered. And they danced around the altar they had made.

[27]At noon Elijah began to taunt them. "Shout louder!" he said. "Surely he is a god! Perhaps he is deep in thought, or busy, or traveling. Maybe he is sleeping and must be awakened." [28]So they shouted louder and slashed themselves with swords and spears, as was their custom, until their blood flowed. [29]Midday passed, and they continued their frantic prophesying until the time for the evening sacrifice. But there was no response, no one answered, no one paid attention.

[30]Then Elijah said to all the people, "Come here to me." They came to him, and he repaired the altar of the LORD, which had been torn down. [31]Elijah took twelve stones, one for each of the tribes descended from Jacob, to whom the word of the LORD had come, saying, "Your name shall be Israel." [32]With the stones he built an altar in the name of the LORD, and he dug a trench around it large enough to hold two seahs[a] of seed. [33]He arranged the wood, cut the bull into pieces and laid it on the wood. Then he said to them, "Fill four large jars with water and pour it on the offering and on the wood."

[a] *32* That is, probably about 24 pounds or about 11 kilograms

[34]"Do it again," he said, and they did it again.

"Do it a third time," he ordered, and they did it the third time. [35]The water ran down around the altar and even filled the trench.

[36]At the time of sacrifice, the prophet Elijah stepped forward and prayed: "LORD, the God of Abraham, Isaac and Israel, let it be known today that you are God in Israel and that I am your servant and have done all these things at your command. [37]Answer me, LORD, answer me, so these people will know that you, LORD, are God, and that you are turning their hearts back again."

[38]Then the fire of the LORD fell and burned up the sacrifice, the wood, the stones and the soil, and also licked up the water in the trench.

[39]When all the people saw this, they fell prostrate and cried, "The LORD—he is God! The LORD—he is God!"

[40]Then Elijah commanded them, "Seize the prophets of Baal. Don't let anyone get away!" They seized them, and Elijah had them brought down to the Kishon Valley and slaughtered there.

[41]And Elijah said to Ahab, "Go, eat and drink, for there is the sound of a heavy rain." [42]So Ahab went off to eat and drink, but Elijah climbed to the top of Carmel, bent down to the ground and put his face between his knees.

[43]"Go and look toward the sea," he told his servant. And he went up and looked.

"There is nothing there," he said.

Seven times Elijah said, "Go back."

[44]The seventh time the servant reported, "A cloud as small as a man's hand is rising from the sea."

So Elijah said, "Go and tell Ahab, 'Hitch up your chariot and go down before the rain stops you.'"

[45]Meanwhile, the sky grew black with clouds, the wind rose, a heavy rain started falling and Ahab rode off to Jezreel. [46]The power of the LORD came on Elijah and, tucking his cloak into his belt, he ran ahead of Ahab all the way to Jezreel.

Elijah Flees to Horeb

19 Now Ahab told Jezebel everything Elijah had done and how he had killed all the prophets with the sword. [2]So Jezebel sent a messenger to Elijah to say, "May the gods deal with me, be it ever so severely, if by this time tomorrow I do not make your life like that of one of them."

[3]Elijah was afraid[a] and ran for his life. When he came to Beersheba in Judah, he left his servant there, [4]while he himself went a day's journey into the wilderness. He came to a broom bush, sat down under it and prayed that he might die. "I have had enough, LORD," he said. "Take my life; I am no better than my ancestors." [5]Then he lay down under the bush and fell asleep.

All at once an angel touched him and said, "Get up and eat." [6]He looked around, and there by his head was some bread baked over hot coals, and a jar of water. He ate and drank and then lay down again.

[7]The angel of the LORD came back a second time and touched him and said, "Get up and eat, for the journey is too much for you." [8]So he got up and ate and drank. Strengthened by that food, he traveled forty days and forty nights until he reached Horeb, the mountain of God. [9]There he went into a cave and spent the night.

The LORD Appears to Elijah

And the word of the LORD came to him: "What are you doing here, Elijah?"

[10]He replied, "I have been very zealous for the LORD God Almighty. The Israelites have rejected your covenant, torn down your altars, and put your prophets to death with the sword. I am the only one left, and now they are trying to kill me too."

[11]The LORD said, "Go out and stand on the mountain in the presence of the LORD, for the LORD is about to pass by."

Then a great and powerful wind tore the mountains apart and shattered the rocks before the LORD, but the LORD was not in the wind. After the wind there was an earthquake, but the LORD was not in the earthquake. [12]After the earthquake came a fire, but the LORD was not in the fire. And after the fire came a gentle whisper. [13]When Elijah heard it, he pulled his cloak over his face and went out and stood at the mouth of the cave.

Then a voice said to him, "What are you doing here, Elijah?"

[14]He replied, "I have been very zealous for the LORD God Almighty. The Israelites have rejected your covenant, torn down your altars, and put your prophets to death with the sword. I am the only one left, and now they are trying to kill me too."

[15]The LORD said to him, "Go back the way you came, and go to the Desert of Damascus. When you get there, anoint Hazael king over Aram. [16]Also, anoint Jehu son of Nimshi king over Israel, and anoint Elisha son of Shaphat from Abel Meholah to succeed you as prophet. [17]Jehu will put to death any who escape the sword of Hazael, and Elisha will put to death any who escape the sword of Jehu. [18]Yet I reserve seven thousand in Israel—all whose knees have not bowed down to Baal and whose mouths have not kissed him."

The Call of Elisha

[19]So Elijah went from there and found Elisha son of Shaphat. He was plowing with twelve yoke of oxen, and he himself was driving the twelfth pair. Elijah went up to him and threw his cloak around him. [20]Elisha then left his oxen and ran after Elijah. "Let me kiss my father and mother goodbye," he said, "and then I will come with you."

"Go back," Elijah replied. "What have I done to you?"

[21]So Elisha left him and went back. He took

[a] 3 Or *Elijah saw*

his yoke of oxen and slaughtered them. He burned the plowing equipment to cook the meat and gave it to the people, and they ate. Then he set out to follow Elijah and became his servant.

Ben-Hadad Attacks Samaria

20 Now Ben-Hadad king of Aram mustered his entire army. Accompanied by thirty-two kings with their horses and chariots, he went up and besieged Samaria and attacked it. [2]He sent messengers into the city to Ahab king of Israel, saying, "This is what Ben-Hadad says: [3]'Your silver and gold are mine, and the best of your wives and children are mine.'"

[4]The king of Israel answered, "Just as you say, my lord the king. I and all I have are yours."

[5]The messengers came again and said, "This is what Ben-Hadad says: 'I sent to demand your silver and gold, your wives and your children. [6]But about this time tomorrow I am going to send my officials to search your palace and the houses of your officials. They will seize everything you value and carry it away.'"

[7]The king of Israel summoned all the elders of the land and said to them, "See how this man is looking for trouble! When he sent for my wives and my children, my silver and my gold, I did not refuse him."

[8]The elders and the people all answered, "Don't listen to him or agree to his demands."

[9]So he replied to Ben-Hadad's messengers, "Tell my lord the king, 'Your servant will do all you demanded the first time, but this demand I cannot meet.'" They left and took the answer back to Ben-Hadad.

[10]Then Ben-Hadad sent another message to Ahab: "May the gods deal with me, be it ever so severely, if enough dust remains in Samaria to give each of my men a handful."

[11]The king of Israel answered, "Tell him: 'One who puts on his armor should not boast like one who takes it off.'"

[12]Ben-Hadad heard this message while he and the kings were drinking in their tents,[a] and he ordered his men: "Prepare to attack." So they prepared to attack the city.

Ahab Defeats Ben-Hadad

[13]Meanwhile a prophet came to Ahab king of Israel and announced, "This is what the LORD says: 'Do you see this vast army? I will give it into your hand today, and then you will know that I am the LORD.'"

[14]"But who will do this?" asked Ahab.

The prophet replied, "This is what the LORD says: 'The junior officers under the provincial commanders will do it.'"

"And who will start the battle?" he asked.

The prophet answered, "You will."

[15]So Ahab summoned the 232 junior officers under the provincial commanders. Then he assembled the rest of the Israelites, 7,000 in all. [16]They set out at noon while Ben-Hadad and the 32 kings allied with him were in their tents getting drunk. [17]The junior officers under the provincial commanders went out first.

Now Ben-Hadad had dispatched scouts, who reported, "Men are advancing from Samaria."

[18]He said, "If they have come out for peace, take them alive; if they have come out for war, take them alive."

[19]The junior officers under the provincial commanders marched out of the city with the army behind them [20]and each one struck down his opponent. At that, the Arameans fled, with the Israelites in pursuit. But Ben-Hadad king of Aram escaped on horseback with some of his horsemen. [21]The king of Israel advanced and overpowered the horses and chariots and inflicted heavy losses on the Arameans.

[22]Afterward, the prophet came to the king of Israel and said, "Strengthen your position and see what must be done, because next spring the king of Aram will attack you again."

[23]Meanwhile, the officials of the king of Aram advised him, "Their gods are gods of the hills. That is why they were too strong for us. But if we fight them on the plains, surely we will be stronger than they. [24]Do this: Remove all the kings from their commands and replace them with other officers. [25]You must also raise an army like the one you lost—horse for horse and chariot for chariot—so we can fight Israel on the plains. Then surely we will be stronger than they." He agreed with them and acted accordingly.

[26]The next spring Ben-Hadad mustered the Arameans and went up to Aphek to fight against Israel. [27]When the Israelites were also mustered and given provisions, they marched out to meet them. The Israelites camped opposite them like two small flocks of goats, while the Arameans covered the countryside.

[28]The man of God came up and told the king of Israel, "This is what the LORD says: 'Because the Arameans think the LORD is a god of the hills and not a god of the valleys, I will deliver this vast army into your hands, and you will know that I am the LORD.'"

[29]For seven days they camped opposite each other, and on the seventh day the battle was joined. The Israelites inflicted a hundred thousand casualties on the Aramean foot soldiers in one day. [30]The rest of them escaped to the city of Aphek, where the wall collapsed on twenty-seven thousand of them. And Ben-Hadad fled to the city and hid in an inner room.

[31]His officials said to him, "Look, we have heard that the kings of Israel are merciful. Let us go to the king of Israel with sackcloth around our waists and ropes around our heads. Perhaps he will spare your life."

[32]Wearing sackcloth around their waists and ropes around their heads, they went to the king of Israel and said, "Your servant Ben-Hadad says: 'Please let me live.'"

The king answered, "Is he still alive? He is my brother."

[33]The men took this as a good sign and were

[a] *12* Or *in Sukkoth*; also in verse 16

quick to pick up his word. “Yes, your brother Ben-Hadad!” they said.

“Go and get him,” the king said. When Ben-Hadad came out, Ahab had him come up into his chariot.

34“I will return the cities my father took from your father,” Ben-Hadad offered. “You may set up your own market areas in Damascus, as my father did in Samaria.”

Ahab said, “On the basis of a treaty I will set you free.” So he made a treaty with him, and let him go.

A Prophet Condemns Ahab

35By the word of the LORD one of the company of the prophets said to his companion, “Strike me with your weapon,” but he refused.

36So the prophet said, “Because you have not obeyed the LORD, as soon as you leave me a lion will kill you.” And after the man went away, a lion found him and killed him.

37The prophet found another man and said, “Strike me, please.” So the man struck him and wounded him. 38Then the prophet went and stood by the road waiting for the king. He disguised himself with his headband down over his eyes. 39As the king passed by, the prophet called out to him, “Your servant went into the thick of the battle, and someone came to me with a captive and said, ‘Guard this man. If he is missing, it will be your life for his life, or you must pay a talent[a] of silver.’ 40While your servant was busy here and there, the man disappeared.”

“That is your sentence,” the king of Israel said. “You have pronounced it yourself.”

41Then the prophet quickly removed the headband from his eyes, and the king of Israel recognized him as one of the prophets. 42He said to the king, “This is what the LORD says: ‘You have set free a man I had determined should die.[b] Therefore it is your life for his life, your people for his people.’ ” 43Sullen and angry, the king of Israel went to his palace in Samaria.

Naboth’s Vineyard

21 Some time later there was an incident involving a vineyard belonging to Naboth the Jezreelite. The vineyard was in Jezreel, close to the palace of Ahab king of Samaria. 2Ahab said to Naboth, “Let me have your vineyard to use for a vegetable garden, since it is close to my palace. In exchange I will give you a better vineyard or, if you prefer, I will pay you whatever it is worth.”

3But Naboth replied, “The LORD forbid that I should give you the inheritance of my ancestors.”

4So Ahab went home, sullen and angry because Naboth the Jezreelite had said, “I will not give you the inheritance of my ancestors.” He lay on his bed sulking and refused to eat.

5His wife Jezebel came in and asked him, “Why are you so sullen? Why won’t you eat?”

6He answered her, “Because I said to Naboth the Jezreelite, ‘Sell me your vineyard; or if you prefer, I will give you another vineyard in its place.’ But he said, ‘I will not give you my vineyard.’ ”

7Jezebel his wife said, “Is this how you act as king over Israel? Get up and eat! Cheer up. I’ll get you the vineyard of Naboth the Jezreelite.”

8So she wrote letters in Ahab’s name, placed his seal on them, and sent them to the elders and nobles who lived in Naboth’s city with him. 9In those letters she wrote:

> “Proclaim a day of fasting and seat Naboth in a prominent place among the people. 10But seat two scoundrels opposite him and have them bring charges that he has cursed both God and the king. Then take him out and stone him to death.”

11So the elders and nobles who lived in Naboth’s city did as Jezebel directed in the letters she had written to them. 12They proclaimed a fast and seated Naboth in a prominent place among the people. 13Then two scoundrels came and sat opposite him and brought charges against Naboth before the people, saying, “Naboth has cursed both God and the king.” So they took him outside the city and stoned him to death. 14Then they sent word to Jezebel: “Naboth has been stoned to death.”

15As soon as Jezebel heard that Naboth had been stoned to death, she said to Ahab, “Get up and take possession of the vineyard of Naboth the Jezreelite that he refused to sell you. He is no longer alive, but dead.” 16When Ahab heard that Naboth was dead, he got up and went down to take possession of Naboth’s vineyard.

17Then the word of the LORD came to Elijah the Tishbite: 18“Go down to meet Ahab king of Israel, who rules in Samaria. He is now in Naboth’s vineyard, where he has gone to take possession of it. 19Say to him, ‘This is what the LORD says: Have you not murdered a man and seized his property?’ Then say to him, ‘This is what the LORD says: In the place where dogs licked up Naboth’s blood, dogs will lick up your blood—yes, yours!’ ”

20Ahab said to Elijah, “So you have found me, my enemy!”

“I have found you,” he answered, “because you have sold yourself to do evil in the eyes of the LORD. 21He says, ‘I am going to bring disaster on you. I will wipe out your descendants and cut off from Ahab every last male in Israel—slave or free.[c] 22I will make your house like that of Jeroboam son of Nebat and that of Baasha son of Ahijah, because you have aroused my anger and have caused Israel to sin.’

23“And also concerning Jezebel the LORD says: ‘Dogs will devour Jezebel by the wall of[d] Jezreel.’

[a] *39* That is, about 75 pounds or about 34 kilograms [b] *42* The Hebrew term refers to the irrevocable giving over of things or persons to the LORD, often by totally destroying them. [c] *21* Or *Israel—every ruler or leader* [d] *23* Most Hebrew manuscripts; a few Hebrew manuscripts, Vulgate and Syriac (see also 2 Kings 9:26) *the plot of ground at*

24“Dogs will eat those belonging to Ahab
who die in the city, and the birds will feed on
those who die in the country.”
25(There was never anyone like Ahab, who
sold himself to do evil in the eyes of the LORD,
urged on by Jezebel his wife. 26He behaved in
the vilest manner by going after idols, like the
Amorites the LORD drove out before Israel.)
27When Ahab heard these words, he tore his
clothes, put on sackcloth and fasted. He lay in
sackcloth and went around meekly.
28Then the word of the LORD came to Elijah
the Tishbite: 29“Have you noticed how Ahab
has humbled himself before me? Because he
has humbled himself, I will not bring this
disaster in his day, but I will bring it on his
house in the days of his son.”

Micaiah Prophesies Against Ahab

22 For three years there was no war between Aram and Israel. 2But in the third
year Jehoshaphat king of Judah went down
to see the king of Israel. 3The king of Israel had said to his officials, “Don’t you know
that Ramoth Gilead belongs to us and yet we
are doing nothing to retake it from the king
of Aram?”
4So he asked Jehoshaphat, “Will you go
with me to fight against Ramoth Gilead?”
Jehoshaphat replied to the king of Israel,
“I am as you are, my people as your people,
my horses as your horses.” 5But Jehoshaphat
also said to the king of Israel, “First seek the
counsel of the LORD.”
6So the king of Israel brought together the
prophets—about four hundred men—and
asked them, “Shall I go to war against Ramoth Gilead, or shall I refrain?”
“Go,” they answered, “for the Lord will give
it into the king’s hand.”
7But Jehoshaphat asked, “Is there no longer a prophet of the LORD here whom we can
inquire of?”
8The king of Israel answered Jehoshaphat,
“There is still one prophet through whom we
can inquire of the LORD, but I hate him because he never prophesies anything good
about me, but always bad. He is Micaiah son
of Imlah.”
“The king should not say such a thing,” Jehoshaphat replied.
9So the king of Israel called one of his officials and said, “Bring Micaiah son of Imlah
at once.”
10Dressed in their royal robes, the king of
Israel and Jehoshaphat king of Judah were
sitting on their thrones at the threshing floor
by the entrance of the gate of Samaria, with
all the prophets prophesying before them.
11Now Zedekiah son of Kenaanah had made
iron horns and he declared, “This is what the
LORD says: ‘With these you will gore the Arameans until they are destroyed.’ ”
12All the other prophets were prophesying
the same thing. “Attack Ramoth Gilead and
be victorious,” they said, “for the LORD will
give it into the king’s hand.”
13The messenger who had gone to summon
Micaiah said to him, “Look, the other prophets without exception are predicting success
for the king. Let your word agree with theirs,
and speak favorably.”
14But Micaiah said, “As surely as the LORD
lives, I can tell him only what the LORD
tells me.”
15When he arrived, the king asked him,
“Micaiah, shall we go to war against Ramoth
Gilead, or not?”
“Attack and be victorious,” he answered,
“for the LORD will give it into the king’s hand.”
16The king said to him, “How many times
must I make you swear to tell me nothing but
the truth in the name of the LORD?”
17Then Micaiah answered, “I saw all Israel scattered on the hills like sheep without
a shepherd, and the LORD said, ‘These people have no master. Let each one go home in
peace.’ ”
18The king of Israel said to Jehoshaphat,
“Didn’t I tell you that he never prophesies anything good about me, but only bad?”
19Micaiah continued, “Therefore hear the
word of the LORD: I saw the LORD sitting on
his throne with all the multitudes of heaven
standing around him on his right and on his
left. 20And the LORD said, ‘Who will entice
Ahab into attacking Ramoth Gilead and going
to his death there?’
“One suggested this, and another that. 21Fi-
nally, a spirit came forward, stood before the
LORD and said, ‘I will entice him.’
22“ ‘By what means?’ the LORD asked.
“ ‘I will go out and be a deceiving spirit in
the mouths of all his prophets,’ he said.
“ ‘You will succeed in enticing him,’ said the
LORD. ‘Go and do it.’
23“So now the LORD has put a deceiving spirit in the mouths of all these prophets of yours.
The LORD has decreed disaster for you.”
24Then Zedekiah son of Kenaanah went up
and slapped Micaiah in the face. “Which way
did the spirit from[a] the LORD go when he went
from me to speak to you?” he asked.
25Micaiah replied, “You will find out on the
day you go to hide in an inner room.”
26The king of Israel then ordered, “Take Micaiah and send him back to Amon the ruler of
the city and to Joash the king’s son 27and say,
‘This is what the king says: Put this fellow in
prison and give him nothing but bread and
water until I return safely.’ ”
28Micaiah declared, “If you ever return safely, the LORD has not spoken through me.” Then
he added, “Mark my words, all you people!”

Ahab Killed at Ramoth Gilead

29So the king of Israel and Jehoshaphat king
of Judah went up to Ramoth Gilead. 30The
king of Israel said to Jehoshaphat, “I will enter the battle in disguise, but you wear your
royal robes.” So the king of Israel disguised
himself and went into battle.
31Now the king of Aram had ordered his
thirty-two chariot commanders, “Do not fight

[a] *24* Or *Spirit of*

with anyone, small or great, except the king of
Israel." 32When the chariot commanders saw
Jehoshaphat, they thought, "Surely this is the
king of Israel." So they turned to attack him,
but when Jehoshaphat cried out, 33the chariot
commanders saw that he was not the king of
Israel and stopped pursuing him.
34But someone drew his bow at random and
hit the king of Israel between the sections of
his armor. The king told his chariot driver,
"Wheel around and get me out of the fighting.
I've been wounded." 35All day long the battle
raged, and the king was propped up in his
chariot facing the Arameans. The blood from
his wound ran onto the floor of the chariot,
and that evening he died. 36As the sun was
setting, a cry spread through the army: "Every man to his town. Every man to his land!"
37So the king died and was brought to Samaria, and they buried him there. 38They
washed the chariot at a pool in Samaria
(where the prostitutes bathed),[a] and the dogs
licked up his blood, as the word of the LORD
had declared.
39As for the other events of Ahab's reign,
including all he did, the palace he built and
adorned with ivory, and the cities he fortified,
are they not written in the book of the annals
of the kings of Israel? 40Ahab rested with his
ancestors. And Ahaziah his son succeeded
him as king.

Jehoshaphat King of Judah

41Jehoshaphat son of Asa became king of
Judah in the fourth year of Ahab king of Israel. 42Jehoshaphat was thirty-five years old
when he became king, and he reigned in Jerusalem twenty-five years. His mother's name
was Azubah daughter of Shilhi. 43In everything he followed the ways of his father Asa
and did not stray from them; he did what was
right in the eyes of the LORD. The high places,
however, were not removed, and the people
continued to offer sacrifices and burn incense
there.[b] 44Jehoshaphat was also at peace with
the king of Israel.
45As for the other events of Jehoshaphat's
reign, the things he achieved and his military
exploits, are they not written in the book of
the annals of the kings of Judah? 46He rid the
land of the rest of the male shrine prostitutes
who remained there even after the reign of
his father Asa. 47There was then no king in
Edom; a provincial governor ruled.
48Now Jehoshaphat built a fleet of trading
ships[c] to go to Ophir for gold, but they never
set sail—they were wrecked at Ezion Geber.
49At that time Ahaziah son of Ahab said to
Jehoshaphat, "Let my men sail with yours,"
but Jehoshaphat refused.
50Then Jehoshaphat rested with his ancestors and was buried with them in the city of
David his father. And Jehoram his son succeeded him as king.

Ahaziah King of Israel

51Ahaziah son of Ahab became king of Israel in Samaria in the seventeenth year of
Jehoshaphat king of Judah, and he reigned
over Israel two years. 52He did evil in the eyes
of the LORD, because he followed the ways of
his father and mother and of Jeroboam son of
Nebat, who caused Israel to sin. 53He served
and worshiped Baal and aroused the anger
of the LORD, the God of Israel, just as his father had done.

2 Kings

The LORD's Judgment on Ahaziah

1 After Ahab's death, Moab rebelled against
Israel. 2Now Ahaziah had fallen through
the lattice of his upper room in Samaria and
injured himself. So he sent messengers, saying to them, "Go and consult Baal-Zebub, the
god of Ekron, to see if I will recover from this
injury."
3But the angel of the LORD said to Elijah
the Tishbite, "Go up and meet the messengers of the king of Samaria and ask them, 'Is
it because there is no God in Israel that you
are going off to consult Baal-Zebub, the god
of Ekron?' 4Therefore this is what the LORD
says: 'You will not leave the bed you are lying
on. You will certainly die!'" So Elijah went.
5When the messengers returned to the king,
he asked them, "Why have you come back?"
6"A man came to meet us," they replied.
"And he said to us, 'Go back to the king who
sent you and tell him, "This is what the LORD
says: Is it because there is no God in Israel
that you are sending messengers to consult
Baal-Zebub, the god of Ekron? Therefore you
will not leave the bed you are lying on. You
will certainly die!"'"
7The king asked them, "What kind of man
was it who came to meet you and told you
this?"
8They replied, "He had a garment of hair[d]
and had a leather belt around his waist."
The king said, "That was Elijah the Tishbite."

[a] 38 Or *Samaria and cleaned the weapons* [b] 43 In Hebrew texts this sentence (22:43b) is numbered 22:44, and 22:44-53 is numbered 22:45-54. [c] 48 Hebrew *of ships of Tarshish* [d] 8 Or *He was a hairy man*

9Then he sent to Elijah a captain with his company of fifty men. The captain went up to Elijah, who was sitting on the top of a hill, and said to him, "Man of God, the king says, 'Come down!' "

10Elijah answered the captain, "If I am a man of God, may fire come down from heaven and consume you and your fifty men!" Then fire fell from heaven and consumed the captain and his men.

11At this the king sent to Elijah another captain with his fifty men. The captain said to him, "Man of God, this is what the king says, 'Come down at once!' "

12"If I am a man of God," Elijah replied, "may fire come down from heaven and consume you and your fifty men!" Then the fire of God fell from heaven and consumed him and his fifty men.

13So the king sent a third captain with his fifty men. This third captain went up and fell on his knees before Elijah. "Man of God," he begged, "please have respect for my life and the lives of these fifty men, your servants! 14See, fire has fallen from heaven and consumed the first two captains and all their men. But now have respect for my life!"

15The angel of the LORD said to Elijah, "Go down with him; do not be afraid of him." So Elijah got up and went down with him to the king.

16He told the king, "This is what the LORD says: Is it because there is no God in Israel for you to consult that you have sent messengers to consult Baal-Zebub, the god of Ekron? Because you have done this, you will never leave the bed you are lying on. You will certainly die!" 17So he died, according to the word of the LORD that Elijah had spoken.

Because Ahaziah had no son, Joram[a] succeeded him as king in the second year of Jehoram son of Jehoshaphat king of Judah. 18As for all the other events of Ahaziah's reign, and what he did, are they not written in the book of the annals of the kings of Israel?

Elijah Taken Up to Heaven

2 When the LORD was about to take Elijah up to heaven in a whirlwind, Elijah and Elisha were on their way from Gilgal. 2Elijah said to Elisha, "Stay here; the LORD has sent me to Bethel."

But Elisha said, "As surely as the LORD lives and as you live, I will not leave you." So they went down to Bethel.

3The company of the prophets at Bethel came out to Elisha and asked, "Do you know that the LORD is going to take your master from you today?"

"Yes, I know," Elisha replied, "so be quiet."

4Then Elijah said to him, "Stay here, Elisha; the LORD has sent me to Jericho."

And he replied, "As surely as the LORD lives and as you live, I will not leave you." So they went to Jericho.

5The company of the prophets at Jericho went up to Elisha and asked him, "Do you know that the LORD is going to take your master from you today?"

"Yes, I know," he replied, "so be quiet."

6Then Elijah said to him, "Stay here; the LORD has sent me to the Jordan."

And he replied, "As surely as the LORD lives and as you live, I will not leave you." So the two of them walked on.

7Fifty men from the company of the prophets went and stood at a distance, facing the place where Elijah and Elisha had stopped at the Jordan. 8Elijah took his cloak, rolled it up and struck the water with it. The water divided to the right and to the left, and the two of them crossed over on dry ground.

9When they had crossed, Elijah said to Elisha, "Tell me, what can I do for you before I am taken from you?"

"Let me inherit a double portion of your spirit," Elisha replied.

10"You have asked a difficult thing," Elijah said, "yet if you see me when I am taken from you, it will be yours—otherwise, it will not."

11As they were walking along and talking together, suddenly a chariot of fire and horses of fire appeared and separated the two of them, and Elijah went up to heaven in a whirlwind. 12Elisha saw this and cried out, "My father! My father! The chariots and horsemen of Israel!" And Elisha saw him no more. Then he took hold of his garment and tore it in two.

13Elisha then picked up Elijah's cloak that had fallen from him and went back and stood on the bank of the Jordan. 14He took the cloak that had fallen from Elijah and struck the water with it. "Where now is the LORD, the God of Elijah?" he asked. When he struck the water, it divided to the right and to the left, and he crossed over.

15The company of the prophets from Jericho, who were watching, said, "The spirit of Elijah is resting on Elisha." And they went to meet him and bowed to the ground before him. 16"Look," they said, "we your servants have fifty able men. Let them go and look for your master. Perhaps the Spirit of the LORD has picked him up and set him down on some mountain or in some valley."

"No," Elisha replied, "do not send them."

17But they persisted until he was too embarrassed to refuse. So he said, "Send them." And they sent fifty men, who searched for three days but did not find him. 18When they returned to Elisha, who was staying in Jericho, he said to them, "Didn't I tell you not to go?"

Healing of the Water

19The people of the city said to Elisha, "Look, our lord, this town is well situated, as you can see, but the water is bad and the land is unproductive."

20"Bring me a new bowl," he said, "and put salt in it." So they brought it to him.

21Then he went out to the spring and threw the salt into it, saying, "This is what the LORD says: 'I have healed this water. Never again will it cause death or make the land unpro-

[a] 17 Hebrew *Jehoram*, a variant of *Joram*

ductive.'" 22And the water has remained pure to this day, according to the word Elisha had spoken.

Elisha Is Jeered

23From there Elisha went up to Bethel. As he was walking along the road, some boys came out of the town and jeered at him. "Get out of here, baldy!" they said. "Get out of here, baldy!" 24He turned around, looked at them and called down a curse on them in the name of the LORD. Then two bears came out of the woods and mauled forty-two of the boys. 25And he went on to Mount Carmel and from there returned to Samaria.

Moab Revolts

3 Joram[a] son of Ahab became king of Israel in Samaria in the eighteenth year of Jehoshaphat king of Judah, and he reigned twelve years. 2He did evil in the eyes of the LORD, but not as his father and mother had done. He got rid of the sacred stone of Baal that his father had made. 3Nevertheless he clung to the sins of Jeroboam son of Nebat, which he had caused Israel to commit; he did not turn away from them.

4Now Mesha king of Moab raised sheep, and he had to pay the king of Israel a tribute of a hundred thousand lambs and the wool of a hundred thousand rams. 5But after Ahab died, the king of Moab rebelled against the king of Israel. 6So at that time King Joram set out from Samaria and mobilized all Israel. 7He also sent this message to Jehoshaphat king of Judah: "The king of Moab has rebelled against me. Will you go with me to fight against Moab?"

"I will go with you," he replied. "I am as you are, my people as your people, my horses as your horses."

8"By what route shall we attack?" he asked.

"Through the Desert of Edom," he answered.

9So the king of Israel set out with the king of Judah and the king of Edom. After a roundabout march of seven days, the army had no more water for themselves or for the animals with them.

10"What!" exclaimed the king of Israel. "Has the LORD called us three kings together only to deliver us into the hands of Moab?"

11But Jehoshaphat asked, "Is there no prophet of the LORD here, through whom we may inquire of the LORD?"

An officer of the king of Israel answered, "Elisha son of Shaphat is here. He used to pour water on the hands of Elijah.[b]"

12Jehoshaphat said, "The word of the LORD is with him." So the king of Israel and Jehoshaphat and the king of Edom went down to him.

13Elisha said to the king of Israel, "Why do you want to involve me? Go to the prophets of your father and the prophets of your mother."

"No," the king of Israel answered, "because it was the LORD who called us three kings together to deliver us into the hands of Moab."

14Elisha said, "As surely as the LORD Almighty lives, whom I serve, if I did not have respect for the presence of Jehoshaphat king of Judah, I would not pay any attention to you. 15But now bring me a harpist."

While the harpist was playing, the hand of the LORD came on Elisha 16and he said, "This is what the LORD says: I will fill this valley with pools of water. 17For this is what the LORD says: You will see neither wind nor rain, yet this valley will be filled with water, and you, your cattle and your other animals will drink. 18This is an easy thing in the eyes of the LORD; he will also deliver Moab into your hands. 19You will overthrow every fortified city and every major town. You will cut down every good tree, stop up all the springs, and ruin every good field with stones."

20The next morning, about the time for offering the sacrifice, there it was—water flowing from the direction of Edom! And the land was filled with water.

21Now all the Moabites had heard that the kings had come to fight against them; so every man, young and old, who could bear arms was called up and stationed on the border. 22When they got up early in the morning, the sun was shining on the water. To the Moabites across the way, the water looked red—like blood. 23"That's blood!" they said. "Those kings must have fought and slaughtered each other. Now to the plunder, Moab!"

24But when the Moabites came to the camp of Israel, the Israelites rose up and fought them until they fled. And the Israelites invaded the land and slaughtered the Moabites. 25They destroyed the towns, and each man threw a stone on every good field until it was covered. They stopped up all the springs and cut down every good tree. Only Kir Hareseth was left with its stones in place, but men armed with slings surrounded it and attacked it.

26When the king of Moab saw that the battle had gone against him, he took with him seven hundred swordsmen to break through to the king of Edom, but they failed. 27Then he took his firstborn son, who was to succeed him as king, and offered him as a sacrifice on the city wall. The fury against Israel was great; they withdrew and returned to their own land.

The Widow's Olive Oil

4 The wife of a man from the company of the prophets cried out to Elisha, "Your servant my husband is dead, and you know that he revered the LORD. But now his creditor is coming to take my two boys as his slaves."

2Elisha replied to her, "How can I help you? Tell me, what do you have in your house?"

"Your servant has nothing there at all," she said, "except a small jar of olive oil."

3Elisha said, "Go around and ask all your neighbors for empty jars. Don't ask for just a

[a] *1* Hebrew *Jehoram*, a variant of *Joram*; also in verse 6 [b] *11* That is, he was Elijah's personal servant.

few. 4Then go inside and shut the door behind
you and your sons. Pour oil into all the jars,
and as each is filled, put it to one side."
5She left him and shut the door behind her
and her sons. They brought the jars to her and
she kept pouring. 6When all the jars were full,
she said to her son, "Bring me another one."
But he replied, "There is not a jar left." Then
the oil stopped flowing.
7She went and told the man of God, and he
said, "Go, sell the oil and pay your debts. You
and your sons can live on what is left."

The Shunammite's Son Restored to Life

8One day Elisha went to Shunem. And a
well-to-do woman was there, who urged him
to stay for a meal. So whenever he came by,
he stopped there to eat. 9She said to her husband, "I know that this man who often comes
our way is a holy man of God. 10Let's make
a small room on the roof and put in it a bed
and a table, a chair and a lamp for him. Then
he can stay there whenever he comes to us."
11One day when Elisha came, he went up to
his room and lay down there. 12He said to his
servant Gehazi, "Call the Shunammite." So he
called her, and she stood before him. 13Elisha
said to him, "Tell her, 'You have gone to all
this trouble for us. Now what can be done for
you? Can we speak on your behalf to the king
or the commander of the army?'"
She replied, "I have a home among my own
people."
14"What can be done for her?" Elisha asked.
Gehazi said, "She has no son, and her husband is old."
15Then Elisha said, "Call her." So he called
her, and she stood in the doorway. 16"About
this time next year," Elisha said, "you will
hold a son in your arms."
"No, my lord!" she objected. "Please, man
of God, don't mislead your servant!"
17But the woman became pregnant, and the
next year about that same time she gave birth
to a son, just as Elisha had told her.
18The child grew, and one day he went out
to his father, who was with the reapers. 19He
said to his father, "My head! My head!"
His father told a servant, "Carry him to his
mother." 20After the servant had lifted him up
and carried him to his mother, the boy sat on
her lap until noon, and then he died. 21She
went up and laid him on the bed of the man of
God, then shut the door and went out.
22She called her husband and said, "Please
send me one of the servants and a donkey so I
can go to the man of God quickly and return."
23"Why go to him today?" he asked. "It's not
the New Moon or the Sabbath."
"That's all right," she said.
24She saddled the donkey and said to her
servant, "Lead on; don't slow down for me
unless I tell you." 25So she set out and came
to the man of God at Mount Carmel.
When he saw her in the distance, the man of
God said to his servant Gehazi, "Look! There's
the Shunammite! 26Run to meet her and ask
her, 'Are you all right? Is your husband all
right? Is your child all right?'"
"Everything is all right," she said.
27When she reached the man of God at the
mountain, she took hold of his feet. Gehazi
came over to push her away, but the man of
God said, "Leave her alone! She is in bitter
distress, but the LORD has hidden it from me
and has not told me why."
28"Did I ask you for a son, my lord?" she said.
"Didn't I tell you, 'Don't raise my hopes'?"
29Elisha said to Gehazi, "Tuck your cloak
into your belt, take my staff in your hand and
run. Don't greet anyone you meet, and if anyone greets you, do not answer. Lay my staff
on the boy's face."
30But the child's mother said, "As surely as
the LORD lives and as you live, I will not leave
you." So he got up and followed her.
31Gehazi went on ahead and laid the staff
on the boy's face, but there was no sound or
response. So Gehazi went back to meet Elisha
and told him, "The boy has not awakened."
32When Elisha reached the house, there was
the boy lying dead on his couch. 33He went in,
shut the door on the two of them and prayed to
the LORD. 34Then he got on the bed and lay on
the boy, mouth to mouth, eyes to eyes, hands
to hands. As he stretched himself out on him,
the boy's body grew warm. 35Elisha turned
away and walked back and forth in the room
and then got on the bed and stretched out on
him once more. The boy sneezed seven times
and opened his eyes.
36Elisha summoned Gehazi and said, "Call
the Shunammite." And he did. When she
came, he said, "Take your son." 37She came
in, fell at his feet and bowed to the ground.
Then she took her son and went out.

Death in the Pot

38Elisha returned to Gilgal and there was a
famine in that region. While the company of
the prophets was meeting with him, he said
to his servant, "Put on the large pot and cook
some stew for these prophets."
39One of them went out into the fields to
gather herbs and found a wild vine and picked
as many of its gourds as his garment could
hold. When he returned, he cut them up into
the pot of stew, though no one knew what
they were. 40The stew was poured out for the
men, but as they began to eat it, they cried
out, "Man of God, there is death in the pot!"
And they could not eat it.
41Elisha said, "Get some flour." He put it into
the pot and said, "Serve it to the people to eat."
And there was nothing harmful in the pot.

Feeding of a Hundred

42A man came from Baal Shalishah, bringing the man of God twenty loaves of barley
bread baked from the first ripe grain, along
with some heads of new grain. "Give it to the
people to eat," Elisha said.
43"How can I set this before a hundred
men?" his servant asked.
But Elisha answered, "Give it to the people
to eat. For this is what the LORD says: 'They
will eat and have some left over.'" 44Then he

set it before them, and they ate and had some left over, according to the word of the LORD.

Naaman Healed of Leprosy

5 Now Naaman was commander of the army of the king of Aram. He was a great man in the sight of his master and highly regarded, because through him the LORD had given victory to Aram. He was a valiant soldier, but he had leprosy.[a]

2 Now bands of raiders from Aram had gone out and had taken captive a young girl from Israel, and she served Naaman's wife. 3 She said to her mistress, "If only my master would see the prophet who is in Samaria! He would cure him of his leprosy."

4 Naaman went to his master and told him what the girl from Israel had said. 5 "By all means, go," the king of Aram replied. "I will send a letter to the king of Israel." So Naaman left, taking with him ten talents[b] of silver, six thousand shekels[c] of gold and ten sets of clothing. 6 The letter that he took to the king of Israel read: "With this letter I am sending my servant Naaman to you so that you may cure him of his leprosy."

7 As soon as the king of Israel read the letter, he tore his robes and said, "Am I God? Can I kill and bring back to life? Why does this fellow send someone to me to be cured of his leprosy? See how he is trying to pick a quarrel with me!"

8 When Elisha the man of God heard that the king of Israel had torn his robes, he sent him this message: "Why have you torn your robes? Have the man come to me and he will know that there is a prophet in Israel." 9 So Naaman went with his horses and chariots and stopped at the door of Elisha's house. 10 Elisha sent a messenger to say to him, "Go, wash yourself seven times in the Jordan, and your flesh will be restored and you will be cleansed."

11 But Naaman went away angry and said, "I thought that he would surely come out to me and stand and call on the name of the LORD his God, wave his hand over the spot and cure me of my leprosy. 12 Are not Abana and Pharpar, the rivers of Damascus, better than all the waters of Israel? Couldn't I wash in them and be cleansed?" So he turned and went off in a rage.

13 Naaman's servants went to him and said, "My father, if the prophet had told you to do some great thing, would you not have done it? How much more, then, when he tells you, 'Wash and be cleansed'!" 14 So he went down and dipped himself in the Jordan seven times, as the man of God had told him, and his flesh was restored and became clean like that of a young boy.

15 Then Naaman and all his attendants went back to the man of God. He stood before him and said, "Now I know that there is no God in all the world except in Israel. So please accept a gift from your servant."

16 The prophet answered, "As surely as the LORD lives, whom I serve, I will not accept a thing." And even though Naaman urged him, he refused.

17 "If you will not," said Naaman, "please let me, your servant, be given as much earth as a pair of mules can carry, for your servant will never again make burnt offerings and sacrifices to any other god but the LORD. 18 But may the LORD forgive your servant for this one thing: When my master enters the temple of Rimmon to bow down and he is leaning on my arm and I have to bow there also—when I bow down in the temple of Rimmon, may the LORD forgive your servant for this."

19 "Go in peace," Elisha said.

After Naaman had traveled some distance, 20 Gehazi, the servant of Elisha the man of God, said to himself, "My master was too easy on Naaman, this Aramean, by not accepting from him what he brought. As surely as the LORD lives, I will run after him and get something from him."

21 So Gehazi hurried after Naaman. When Naaman saw him running toward him, he got down from the chariot to meet him. "Is everything all right?" he asked.

22 "Everything is all right," Gehazi answered. "My master sent me to say, 'Two young men from the company of the prophets have just come to me from the hill country of Ephraim. Please give them a talent[d] of silver and two sets of clothing.'"

23 "By all means, take two talents," said Naaman. He urged Gehazi to accept them, and then tied up the two talents of silver in two bags, with two sets of clothing. He gave them to two of his servants, and they carried them ahead of Gehazi. 24 When Gehazi came to the hill, he took the things from the servants and put them away in the house. He sent the men away and they left.

25 When he went in and stood before his master, Elisha asked him, "Where have you been, Gehazi?"

"Your servant didn't go anywhere," Gehazi answered.

26 But Elisha said to him, "Was not my spirit with you when the man got down from his chariot to meet you? Is this the time to take money or to accept clothes—or olive groves and vineyards, or flocks and herds, or male and female slaves? 27 Naaman's leprosy will cling to you and to your descendants forever." Then Gehazi went from Elisha's presence and his skin was leprous—it had become as white as snow.

An Axhead Floats

6 The company of the prophets said to Elisha, "Look, the place where we meet with you is too small for us. 2 Let us go to the Jordan, where each of us can get a pole; and let us build a place there for us to meet."

And he said, "Go."

[a] *1* The Hebrew for *leprosy* was used for various diseases affecting the skin; also in verses 3, 6, 7, 11 and 27. [b] *5* That is, about 750 pounds or about 340 kilograms [c] *5* That is, about 150 pounds or about 69 kilograms [d] *22* That is, about 75 pounds or about 34 kilograms

3Then one of them said, "Won't you please
come with your servants?"
"I will," Elisha replied. 4And he went with
them.
They went to the Jordan and began to cut
down trees. 5As one of them was cutting down
a tree, the iron axhead fell into the water. "Oh
no, my lord!" he cried out. "It was borrowed!"
6The man of God asked, "Where did it fall?"
When he showed him the place, Elisha cut a
stick and threw it there, and made the iron
float. 7"Lift it out," he said. Then the man
reached out his hand and took it.

Elisha Traps Blinded Arameans

8Now the king of Aram was at war with
Israel. After conferring with his officers, he
said, "I will set up my camp in such and such
a place."
9The man of God sent word to the king of
Israel: "Beware of passing that place, because
the Arameans are going down there." 10So the
king of Israel checked on the place indicated
by the man of God. Time and again Elisha
warned the king, so that he was on his guard
in such places.
11This enraged the king of Aram. He summoned his officers and demanded of them,
"Tell me! Which of us is on the side of the
king of Israel?"
12"None of us, my lord the king," said one of
his officers, "but Elisha, the prophet who is in
Israel, tells the king of Israel the very words
you speak in your bedroom."
13"Go, find out where he is," the king ordered, "so I can send men and capture him."
The report came back: "He is in Dothan."
14Then he sent horses and chariots and a
strong force there. They went by night and
surrounded the city.
15When the servant of the man of God got up
and went out early the next morning, an army
with horses and chariots had surrounded the
city. "Oh no, my lord! What shall we do?" the
servant asked.
16"Don't be afraid," the prophet answered.
"Those who are with us are more than those
who are with them."
17And Elisha prayed, "Open his eyes, LORD,
so that he may see." Then the LORD opened
the servant's eyes, and he looked and saw
the hills full of horses and chariots of fire all
around Elisha.
18As the enemy came down toward him, Elisha prayed to the LORD, "Strike this army with
blindness." So he struck them with blindness,
as Elisha had asked.
19Elisha told them, "This is not the road and
this is not the city. Follow me, and I will lead
you to the man you are looking for." And he
led them to Samaria.
20After they entered the city, Elisha said,
"LORD, open the eyes of these men so they
can see." Then the LORD opened their eyes
and they looked, and there they were, inside
Samaria.
21When the king of Israel saw them, he
asked Elisha, "Shall I kill them, my father?
Shall I kill them?"
22"Do not kill them," he answered. "Would
you kill those you have captured with your
own sword or bow? Set food and water before them so that they may eat and drink and
then go back to their master." 23So he prepared a great feast for them, and after they
had finished eating and drinking, he sent
them away, and they returned to their master. So the bands from Aram stopped raiding
Israel's territory.

Famine in Besieged Samaria

24Some time later, Ben-Hadad king of Aram
mobilized his entire army and marched up
and laid siege to Samaria. 25There was a great
famine in the city; the siege lasted so long
that a donkey's head sold for eighty shekels[a]
of silver, and a quarter of a cab[b] of seed pods[c]
for five shekels.[d]
26As the king of Israel was passing by on
the wall, a woman cried to him, "Help me, my
lord the king!"
27The king replied, "If the LORD does not
help you, where can I get help for you? From
the threshing floor? From the winepress?"
28Then he asked her, "What's the matter?"
She answered, "This woman said to me,
'Give up your son so we may eat him today,
and tomorrow we'll eat my son.' 29So we
cooked my son and ate him. The next day I
said to her, 'Give up your son so we may eat
him,' but she had hidden him."
30When the king heard the woman's words,
he tore his robes. As he went along the wall,
the people looked, and they saw that, under
his robes, he had sackcloth on his body. 31He
said, "May God deal with me, be it ever so
severely, if the head of Elisha son of Shaphat
remains on his shoulders today!"
32Now Elisha was sitting in his house, and
the elders were sitting with him. The king
sent a messenger ahead, but before he arrived,
Elisha said to the elders, "Don't you see how
this murderer is sending someone to cut off
my head? Look, when the messenger comes,
shut the door and hold it shut against him. Is
not the sound of his master's footsteps behind
him?" 33While he was still talking to them, the
messenger came down to him.
The king said, "This disaster is from the
LORD. Why should I wait for the LORD any
longer?"
7 Elisha replied, "Hear the word of the LORD.
This is what the LORD says: About this time
tomorrow, a seah[e] of the finest flour will sell
for a shekel[f] and two seahs[g] of barley for a
shekel at the gate of Samaria."

[a] *25* That is, about 2 pounds or about 920 grams [b] *25* That is, probably about 1/4 pound or about 100 grams [c] *25* Or *of doves' dung* [d] *25* That is, about 2 ounces or about 58 grams [e] *1* That is, probably about 12 pounds or about 5.5 kilograms of flour; also in verses 16 and 18 [f] *1* That is, about 2/5 ounce or about 12 grams; also in verses 16 and 18 [g] *1* That is, probably about 20 pounds or about 9 kilograms of barley; also in verses 16 and 18

2The officer on whose arm the king was
leaning said to the man of God, "Look, even
if the LORD should open the floodgates of the
heavens, could this happen?"
"You will see it with your own eyes," answered Elisha, "but you will not eat any of it!"

The Siege Lifted

3Now there were four men with leprosy[a]
at the entrance of the city gate. They said to
each other, "Why stay here until we die? 4If
we say, 'We'll go into the city'—the famine
is there, and we will die. And if we stay here,
we will die. So let's go over to the camp of the
Arameans and surrender. If they spare us, we
live; if they kill us, then we die."
5At dusk they got up and went to the camp
of the Arameans. When they reached the edge
of the camp, no one was there, 6for the Lord
had caused the Arameans to hear the sound
of chariots and horses and a great army, so
that they said to one another, "Look, the king
of Israel has hired the Hittite and Egyptian
kings to attack us!" 7So they got up and fled in
the dusk and abandoned their tents and their
horses and donkeys. They left the camp as it
was and ran for their lives.
8The men who had leprosy reached the edge
of the camp, entered one of the tents and ate
and drank. Then they took silver, gold and
clothes, and went off and hid them. They
returned and entered another tent and took
some things from it and hid them also.
9Then they said to each other, "What we're
doing is not right. This is a day of good news
and we are keeping it to ourselves. If we wait
until daylight, punishment will overtake us.
Let's go at once and report this to the royal
palace."
10So they went and called out to the city
gatekeepers and told them, "We went into the
Aramean camp and no one was there—not a
sound of anyone—only tethered horses and
donkeys, and the tents left just as they were."
11The gatekeepers shouted the news, and it
was reported within the palace.
12The king got up in the night and said to
his officers, "I will tell you what the Arameans
have done to us. They know we are starving; so they have left the camp to hide in the
countryside, thinking, 'They will surely come
out, and then we will take them alive and get
into the city.'"
13One of his officers answered, "Have some
men take five of the horses that are left in the
city. Their plight will be like that of all the Israelites left here—yes, they will only be like
all these Israelites who are doomed. So let us
send them to find out what happened."
14So they selected two chariots with their
horses, and the king sent them after the Aramean army. He commanded the drivers, "Go
and find out what has happened." 15They followed them as far as the Jordan, and they
found the whole road strewn with the clothing and equipment the Arameans had thrown
away in their headlong flight. So the messen
gers returned and reported to the king. 16Then
the people went out and plundered the camp
of the Arameans. So a seah of the finest flour
sold for a shekel, and two seahs of barley sold
for a shekel, as the LORD had said.
17Now the king had put the officer on whose
arm he leaned in charge of the gate, and the
people trampled him in the gateway, and he
died, just as the man of God had foretold when
the king came down to his house. 18It happened as the man of God had said to the king:
"About this time tomorrow, a seah of the finest
flour will sell for a shekel and two seahs of
barley for a shekel at the gate of Samaria."
19The officer had said to the man of God,
"Look, even if the LORD should open the floodgates of the heavens, could this happen?" The
man of God had replied, "You will see it with
your own eyes, but you will not eat any of it!"
20And that is exactly what happened to him,
for the people trampled him in the gateway,
and he died.

The Shunammite's Land Restored

8 Now Elisha had said to the woman whose
son he had restored to life, "Go away with
your family and stay for a while wherever you
can, because the LORD has decreed a famine in
the land that will last seven years." 2The woman proceeded to do as the man of God said.
She and her family went away and stayed in
the land of the Philistines seven years.
3At the end of the seven years she came back
from the land of the Philistines and went to
appeal to the king for her house and land. 4The
king was talking to Gehazi, the servant of the
man of God, and had said, "Tell me about all
the great things Elisha has done." 5Just as Gehazi was telling the king how Elisha had restored the dead to life, the woman whose son
Elisha had brought back to life came to appeal
to the king for her house and land.
Gehazi said, "This is the woman, my lord
the king, and this is her son whom Elisha restored to life." 6The king asked the woman
about it, and she told him.
Then he assigned an official to her case and
said to him, "Give back everything that belonged to her, including all the income from
her land from the day she left the country
until now."

Hazael Murders Ben-Hadad

7Elisha went to Damascus, and Ben-Hadad
king of Aram was ill. When the king was told,
"The man of God has come all the way up
here," 8he said to Hazael, "Take a gift with you
and go to meet the man of God. Consult the
LORD through him; ask him, 'Will I recover
from this illness?'"
9Hazael went to meet Elisha, taking with
him as a gift forty camel-loads of all the finest wares of Damascus. He went in and stood
before him, and said, "Your son Ben-Hadad
king of Aram has sent me to ask, 'Will I recover from this illness?'"

[a] 3 The Hebrew for *leprosy* was used for various diseases affecting the skin; also in verse 8.

10Elisha answered, "Go and say to him,
'You will certainly recover.' Nevertheless,[a]
the LORD has revealed to me that he will in
fact die." 11He stared at him with a fixed gaze
until Hazael was embarrassed. Then the man
of God began to weep.
12"Why is my lord weeping?" asked Hazael.
"Because I know the harm you will do to
the Israelites," he answered. "You will set fire
to their fortified places, kill their young men
with the sword, dash their little children to the
ground, and rip open their pregnant women."
13Hazael said, "How could your servant, a
mere dog, accomplish such a feat?"
"The LORD has shown me that you will become king of Aram," answered Elisha.
14Then Hazael left Elisha and returned to
his master. When Ben-Hadad asked, "What
did Elisha say to you?" Hazael replied, "He
told me that you would certainly recover."
15But the next day he took a thick cloth,
soaked it in water and spread it over the king's
face, so that he died. Then Hazael succeeded
him as king.

Jehoram King of Judah

16In the fifth year of Joram son of Ahab
king of Israel, when Jehoshaphat was king
of Judah, Jehoram son of Jehoshaphat began
his reign as king of Judah. 17He was thirty-
two years old when he became king, and he
reigned in Jerusalem eight years. 18He followed the ways of the kings of Israel, as the
house of Ahab had done, for he married a
daughter of Ahab. He did evil in the eyes of
the LORD. 19Nevertheless, for the sake of his
servant David, the LORD was not willing to
destroy Judah. He had promised to maintain
a lamp for David and his descendants forever.
20In the time of Jehoram, Edom rebelled
against Judah and set up its own king. 21So Jehoram[b] went to Zair with all his chariots. The
Edomites surrounded him and his chariot commanders, but he rose up and broke through by
night; his army, however, fled back home. 22To
this day Edom has been in rebellion against
Judah. Libnah revolted at the same time.
23As for the other events of Jehoram's reign,
and all he did, are they not written in the book
of the annals of the kings of Judah? 24Jehoram
rested with his ancestors and was buried with
them in the City of David. And Ahaziah his
son succeeded him as king.

Ahaziah King of Judah

25In the twelfth year of Joram son of Ahab
king of Israel, Ahaziah son of Jehoram king
of Judah began to reign. 26Ahaziah was twenty-two years old when he became king, and
he reigned in Jerusalem one year. His mother's name was Athaliah, a granddaughter of
Omri king of Israel. 27He followed the ways of
the house of Ahab and did evil in the eyes of
the LORD, as the house of Ahab had done, for
he was related by marriage to Ahab's family.
28Ahaziah went with Joram son of Ahab to
war against Hazael king of Aram at Ramoth
Gilead. The Arameans wounded Joram; 29so
King Joram returned to Jezreel to recover
from the wounds the Arameans had inflicted
on him at Ramoth[c] in his battle with Hazael
king of Aram.
Then Ahaziah son of Jehoram king of Judah went down to Jezreel to see Joram son of
Ahab, because he had been wounded.

Jehu Anointed King of Israel

9 The prophet Elisha summoned a man from
the company of the prophets and said to
him, "Tuck your cloak into your belt, take this
flask of olive oil with you and go to Ramoth
Gilead. 2When you get there, look for Jehu
son of Jehoshaphat, the son of Nimshi. Go
to him, get him away from his companions
and take him into an inner room. 3Then take
the flask and pour the oil on his head and
declare, 'This is what the LORD says: I anoint
you king over Israel.' Then open the door and
run; don't delay!"
4So the young prophet went to Ramoth Gilead. 5When he arrived, he found the army
officers sitting together. "I have a message
for you, commander," he said.
"For which of us?" asked Jehu.
"For you, commander," he replied.
6Jehu got up and went into the house. Then
the prophet poured the oil on Jehu's head and
declared, "This is what the LORD, the God of
Israel, says: 'I anoint you king over the LORD's
people Israel. 7You are to destroy the house of
Ahab your master, and I will avenge the blood
of my servants the prophets and the blood of
all the LORD's servants shed by Jezebel. 8The
whole house of Ahab will perish. I will cut off
from Ahab every last male in Israel—slave
or free.[d] 9I will make the house of Ahab like
the house of Jeroboam son of Nebat and like
the house of Baasha son of Ahijah. 10As for
Jezebel, dogs will devour her on the plot of
ground at Jezreel, and no one will bury her.'"
Then he opened the door and ran.
11When Jehu went out to his fellow officers, one of them asked him, "Is everything
all right? Why did this maniac come to you?"
"You know the man and the sort of things
he says," Jehu replied.
12"That's not true!" they said. "Tell us."
Jehu said, "Here is what he told me: 'This
is what the LORD says: I anoint you king over
Israel.'"
13They quickly took their cloaks and spread
them under him on the bare steps. Then they
blew the trumpet and shouted, "Jehu is king!"

Jehu Kills Joram and Ahaziah

14So Jehu son of Jehoshaphat, the son of
Nimshi, conspired against Joram. (Now Joram and all Israel had been defending Ramoth Gilead against Hazael king of Aram,
15but King Joram[e] had returned to Jezreel to

[a] *10* The Hebrew may also be read *Go and say, 'You will certainly not recover,' for.* [b] *21* Hebrew *Joram,* a variant of *Jehoram;* also in verses 23 and 24 [c] *29* Hebrew *Ramah,* a variant of *Ramoth* [d] *8* Or *Israel—every ruler or leader* [e] *15* Hebrew *Jehoram,* a variant of *Joram;* also in verses 17 and 21-24

recover from the wounds the Arameans had inflicted on him in the battle with Hazael king of Aram.) Jehu said, "If you desire to make me king, don't let anyone slip out of the city to go and tell the news in Jezreel." 16 Then he got into his chariot and rode to Jezreel, because Joram was resting there and Ahaziah king of Judah had gone down to see him.

17 When the lookout standing on the tower in Jezreel saw Jehu's troops approaching, he called out, "I see some troops coming."

"Get a horseman," Joram ordered. "Send him to meet them and ask, 'Do you come in peace?'"

18 The horseman rode off to meet Jehu and said, "This is what the king says: 'Do you come in peace?'"

"What do you have to do with peace?" Jehu replied. "Fall in behind me."

The lookout reported, "The messenger has reached them, but he isn't coming back."

19 So the king sent out a second horseman. When he came to them he said, "This is what the king says: 'Do you come in peace?'"

Jehu replied, "What do you have to do with peace? Fall in behind me."

20 The lookout reported, "He has reached them, but he isn't coming back either. The driving is like that of Jehu son of Nimshi—he drives like a maniac."

21 "Hitch up my chariot," Joram ordered. And when it was hitched up, Joram king of Israel and Ahaziah king of Judah rode out, each in his own chariot, to meet Jehu. They met him at the plot of ground that had belonged to Naboth the Jezreelite. 22 When Joram saw Jehu he asked, "Have you come in peace, Jehu?"

"How can there be peace," Jehu replied, "as long as all the idolatry and witchcraft of your mother Jezebel abound?"

23 Joram turned about and fled, calling out to Ahaziah, "Treachery, Ahaziah!"

24 Then Jehu drew his bow and shot Joram between the shoulders. The arrow pierced his heart and he slumped down in his chariot. 25 Jehu said to Bidkar, his chariot officer, "Pick him up and throw him on the field that belonged to Naboth the Jezreelite. Remember how you and I were riding together in chariots behind Ahab his father when the LORD spoke this prophecy against him: 26 'Yesterday I saw the blood of Naboth and the blood of his sons, declares the LORD, and I will surely make you pay for it on this plot of ground, declares the LORD.'[a] Now then, pick him up and throw him on that plot, in accordance with the word of the LORD."

27 When Ahaziah king of Judah saw what had happened, he fled up the road to Beth Haggan.[b] Jehu chased him, shouting, "Kill him too!" They wounded him in his chariot on the way up to Gur near Ibleam, but he escaped to Megiddo and died there. 28 His servants took him by chariot to Jerusalem and buried him with his ancestors in his tomb in the City of David. 29 (In the eleventh year of Joram son of Ahab, Ahaziah had become king of Judah.)

Jezebel Killed

30 Then Jehu went to Jezreel. When Jezebel heard about it, she put on eye makeup, arranged her hair and looked out of a window. 31 As Jehu entered the gate, she asked, "Have you come in peace, you Zimri, you murderer of your master?"[c]

32 He looked up at the window and called out, "Who is on my side? Who?" Two or three eunuchs looked down at him. 33 "Throw her down!" Jehu said. So they threw her down, and some of her blood spattered the wall and the horses as they trampled her underfoot.

34 Jehu went in and ate and drank. "Take care of that cursed woman," he said, "and bury her, for she was a king's daughter." 35 But when they went out to bury her, they found nothing except her skull, her feet and her hands. 36 They went back and told Jehu, who said, "This is the word of the LORD that he spoke through his servant Elijah the Tishbite: On the plot of ground at Jezreel dogs will devour Jezebel's flesh.[d] 37 Jezebel's body will be like dung on the ground in the plot at Jezreel, so that no one will be able to say, 'This is Jezebel.'"

Ahab's Family Killed

10 Now there were in Samaria seventy sons of the house of Ahab. So Jehu wrote letters and sent them to Samaria: to the officials of Jezreel,[e] to the elders and to the guardians of Ahab's children. He said, 2 "You have your master's sons with you and you have chariots and horses, a fortified city and weapons. Now as soon as this letter reaches you, 3 choose the best and most worthy of your master's sons and set him on his father's throne. Then fight for your master's house."

4 But they were terrified and said, "If two kings could not resist him, how can we?"

5 So the palace administrator, the city governor, the elders and the guardians sent this message to Jehu: "We are your servants and we will do anything you say. We will not appoint anyone as king; you do whatever you think best."

6 Then Jehu wrote them a second letter, saying, "If you are on my side and will obey me, take the heads of your master's sons and come to me in Jezreel by this time tomorrow."

Now the royal princes, seventy of them, were with the leading men of the city, who were rearing them. 7 When the letter arrived, these men took the princes and slaughtered all seventy of them. They put their heads in baskets and sent them to Jehu in Jezreel. 8 When the messenger arrived, he told Jehu, "They have brought the heads of the princes."

Then Jehu ordered, "Put them in two piles at the entrance of the city gate until morning."

[a] *26* See 1 Kings 21:19. [b] *27* Or *fled by way of the garden house* [c] *31* Or *"Was there peace for Zimri, who murdered his master?"* [d] *36* See 1 Kings 21:23. [e] *1* Hebrew; some Septuagint manuscripts and Vulgate *of the city*

9The next morning Jehu went out. He stood before all the people and said, "You are innocent. It was I who conspired against my master and killed him, but who killed all these? 10Know, then, that not a word the LORD has spoken against the house of Ahab will fail. The LORD has done what he announced through his servant Elijah." 11So Jehu killed everyone in Jezreel who remained of the house of Ahab, as well as all his chief men, his close friends and his priests, leaving him no survivor.

12Jehu then set out and went toward Samaria. At Beth Eked of the Shepherds, 13he met some relatives of Ahaziah king of Judah and asked, "Who are you?"

They said, "We are relatives of Ahaziah, and we have come down to greet the families of the king and of the queen mother."

14"Take them alive!" he ordered. So they took them alive and slaughtered them by the well of Beth Eked—forty-two of them. He left no survivor.

15After he left there, he came upon Jehonadab son of Rekab, who was on his way to meet him. Jehu greeted him and said, "Are you in accord with me, as I am with you?"

"I am," Jehonadab answered.

"If so," said Jehu, "give me your hand." So he did, and Jehu helped him up into the chariot. 16Jehu said, "Come with me and see my zeal for the LORD." Then he had him ride along in his chariot.

17When Jehu came to Samaria, he killed all who were left there of Ahab's family; he destroyed them, according to the word of the LORD spoken to Elijah.

Servants of Baal Killed

18Then Jehu brought all the people together and said to them, "Ahab served Baal a little; Jehu will serve him much. 19Now summon all the prophets of Baal, all his servants and all his priests. See that no one is missing, because I am going to hold a great sacrifice for Baal. Anyone who fails to come will no longer live." But Jehu was acting deceptively in order to destroy the servants of Baal.

20Jehu said, "Call an assembly in honor of Baal." So they proclaimed it. 21Then he sent word throughout Israel, and all the servants of Baal came; not one stayed away. They crowded into the temple of Baal until it was full from one end to the other. 22And Jehu said to the keeper of the wardrobe, "Bring robes for all the servants of Baal." So he brought out robes for them.

23Then Jehu and Jehonadab son of Rekab went into the temple of Baal. Jehu said to the servants of Baal, "Look around and see that no one who serves the LORD is here with you—only servants of Baal." 24So they went in to make sacrifices and burnt offerings. Now Jehu had posted eighty men outside with this warning: "If one of you lets any of the men I am placing in your hands escape, it will be your life for his life."

25As soon as Jehu had finished making the burnt offering, he ordered the guards and officers: "Go in and kill them; let no one escape." So they cut them down with the sword. The guards and officers threw the bodies out and then entered the inner shrine of the temple of Baal. 26They brought the sacred stone out of the temple of Baal and burned it. 27They demolished the sacred stone of Baal and tore down the temple of Baal, and people have used it for a latrine to this day.

28So Jehu destroyed Baal worship in Israel. 29However, he did not turn away from the sins of Jeroboam son of Nebat, which he had caused Israel to commit—the worship of the golden calves at Bethel and Dan.

30The LORD said to Jehu, "Because you have done well in accomplishing what is right in my eyes and have done to the house of Ahab all I had in mind to do, your descendants will sit on the throne of Israel to the fourth generation." 31Yet Jehu was not careful to keep the law of the LORD, the God of Israel, with all his heart. He did not turn away from the sins of Jeroboam, which he had caused Israel to commit.

32In those days the LORD began to reduce the size of Israel. Hazael overpowered the Israelites throughout their territory 33east of the Jordan in all the land of Gilead (the region of Gad, Reuben and Manasseh), from Aroer by the Arnon Gorge through Gilead to Bashan.

34As for the other events of Jehu's reign, all he did, and all his achievements, are they not written in the book of the annals of the kings of Israel?

35Jehu rested with his ancestors and was buried in Samaria. And Jehoahaz his son succeeded him as king. 36The time that Jehu reigned over Israel in Samaria was twenty-eight years.

Athaliah and Joash

11 When Athaliah the mother of Ahaziah saw that her son was dead, she proceeded to destroy the whole royal family. 2But Jehosheba, the daughter of King Jehoram[a] and sister of Ahaziah, took Joash son of Ahaziah and stole him away from among the royal princes, who were about to be murdered. She put him and his nurse in a bedroom to hide him from Athaliah; so he was not killed. 3He remained hidden with his nurse at the temple of the LORD for six years while Athaliah ruled the land.

4In the seventh year Jehoiada sent for the commanders of units of a hundred, the Carites and the guards and had them brought to him at the temple of the LORD. He made a covenant with them and put them under oath at the temple of the LORD. Then he showed them the king's son. 5He commanded them, saying, "This is what you are to do: You who are in the three companies that are going on duty on the Sabbath—a third of you guarding the royal palace, 6a third at the Sur Gate, and a third at the gate behind the guard, who take turns guarding the temple— 7and you who

[a] 2 Hebrew *Joram,* a variant of *Jehoram*

are in the other two companies that normally go off Sabbath duty are all to guard the temple for the king. 8Station yourselves around the king, each of you with weapon in hand. Anyone who approaches your ranks[a] is to be put to death. Stay close to the king wherever he goes."

9The commanders of units of a hundred did just as Jehoiada the priest ordered. Each one took his men—those who were going on duty on the Sabbath and those who were going off duty—and came to Jehoiada the priest. 10Then he gave the commanders the spears and shields that had belonged to King David and that were in the temple of the LORD. 11The guards, each with weapon in hand, stationed themselves around the king—near the altar and the temple, from the south side to the north side of the temple.

12Jehoiada brought out the king's son and put the crown on him; he presented him with a copy of the covenant and proclaimed him king. They anointed him, and the people clapped their hands and shouted, "Long live the king!"

13When Athaliah heard the noise made by the guards and the people, she went to the people at the temple of the LORD. 14She looked and there was the king, standing by the pillar, as the custom was. The officers and the trumpeters were beside the king, and all the people of the land were rejoicing and blowing trumpets. Then Athaliah tore her robes and called out, "Treason! Treason!"

15Jehoiada the priest ordered the commanders of units of a hundred, who were in charge of the troops: "Bring her out between the ranks[b] and put to the sword anyone who follows her." For the priest had said, "She must not be put to death in the temple of the LORD." 16So they seized her as she reached the place where the horses enter the palace grounds, and there she was put to death.

17Jehoiada then made a covenant between the LORD and the king and people that they would be the LORD's people. He also made a covenant between the king and the people. 18All the people of the land went to the temple of Baal and tore it down. They smashed the altars and idols to pieces and killed Mattan the priest of Baal in front of the altars.

Then Jehoiada the priest posted guards at the temple of the LORD. 19He took with him the commanders of hundreds, the Carites, the guards and all the people of the land, and together they brought the king down from the temple of the LORD and went into the palace, entering by way of the gate of the guards. The king then took his place on the royal throne. 20All the people of the land rejoiced, and the city was calm, because Athaliah had been slain with the sword at the palace.

21Joash[c] was seven years old when he began to reign.[d]

Joash Repairs the Temple

12[e] In the seventh year of Jehu, Joash[f] became king, and he reigned in Jerusalem forty years. His mother's name was Zibiah; she was from Beersheba. 2Joash did what was right in the eyes of the LORD all the years Jehoiada the priest instructed him. 3The high places, however, were not removed; the people continued to offer sacrifices and burn incense there.

4Joash said to the priests, "Collect all the money that is brought as sacred offerings to the temple of the LORD—the money collected in the census, the money received from personal vows and the money brought voluntarily to the temple. 5Let every priest receive the money from one of the treasurers, then use it to repair whatever damage is found in the temple."

6But by the twenty-third year of King Joash the priests still had not repaired the temple. 7Therefore King Joash summoned Jehoiada the priest and the other priests and asked them, "Why aren't you repairing the damage done to the temple? Take no more money from your treasurers, but hand it over for repairing the temple." 8The priests agreed that they would not collect any more money from the people and that they would not repair the temple themselves.

9Jehoiada the priest took a chest and bored a hole in its lid. He placed it beside the altar, on the right side as one enters the temple of the LORD. The priests who guarded the entrance put into the chest all the money that was brought to the temple of the LORD. 10Whenever they saw that there was a large amount of money in the chest, the royal secretary and the high priest came, counted the money that had been brought into the temple of the LORD and put it into bags. 11When the amount had been determined, they gave the money to the men appointed to supervise the work on the temple. With it they paid those who worked on the temple of the LORD—the carpenters and builders, 12the masons and stonecutters. They purchased timber and blocks of dressed stone for the repair of the temple of the LORD, and met all the other expenses of restoring the temple.

13The money brought into the temple was not spent for making silver basins, wick trimmers, sprinkling bowls, trumpets or any other articles of gold or silver for the temple of the LORD; 14it was paid to the workers, who used it to repair the temple. 15They did not require an accounting from those to whom they gave the money to pay the workers, because they acted with complete honesty. 16The money from the guilt offerings and sin offerings[g] was not brought into the temple of the LORD; it belonged to the priests.

17About this time Hazael king of Aram went up and attacked Gath and captured it. Then he

[a] *8* Or *approaches the precincts* [b] *15* Or *out from the precincts* [c] *21* Hebrew *Jehoash,* a variant of *Joash* [d] *21* In Hebrew texts this verse (11:21) is numbered 12:1. [e] In Hebrew texts 12:1-21 is numbered 12:2-22. [f] *1* Hebrew *Jehoash,* a variant of *Joash;* also in verses 2, 4, 6, 7 and 18
[g] *16* Or *purification offerings*

turned to attack Jerusalem. 18But Joash king
of Judah took all the sacred objects dedicated
by his predecessors—Jehoshaphat, Jehoram
and Ahaziah, the kings of Judah—and the
gifts he himself had dedicated and all the gold
found in the treasuries of the temple of the
LORD and of the royal palace, and he sent them
to Hazael king of Aram, who then withdrew
from Jerusalem.
19As for the other events of the reign of Joash, and all he did, are they not written in the
book of the annals of the kings of Judah? 20His
officials conspired against him and assassinated him at Beth Millo, on the road down to
Silla. 21The officials who murdered him were
Jozabad son of Shimeath and Jehozabad son
of Shomer. He died and was buried with his
ancestors in the City of David. And Amaziah
his son succeeded him as king.

Jehoahaz King of Israel

13 In the twenty-third year of Joash son
of Ahaziah king of Judah, Jehoahaz
son of Jehu became king of Israel in Samaria, and he reigned seventeen years. 2He did
evil in the eyes of the LORD by following the
sins of Jeroboam son of Nebat, which he had
caused Israel to commit, and he did not turn
away from them. 3So the LORD's anger burned
against Israel, and for a long time he kept
them under the power of Hazael king of Aram
and Ben-Hadad his son.
4Then Jehoahaz sought the LORD's favor,
and the LORD listened to him, for he saw how
severely the king of Aram was oppressing Israel. 5The LORD provided a deliverer for Israel,
and they escaped from the power of Aram. So
the Israelites lived in their own homes as they
had before. 6But they did not turn away from
the sins of the house of Jeroboam, which he
had caused Israel to commit; they continued
in them. Also, the Asherah pole[a] remained
standing in Samaria.
7Nothing had been left of the army of Jehoahaz except fifty horsemen, ten chariots
and ten thousand foot soldiers, for the king of
Aram had destroyed the rest and made them
like the dust at threshing time.
8As for the other events of the reign of Jehoahaz, all he did and his achievements, are
they not written in the book of the annals of
the kings of Israel? 9Jehoahaz rested with his
ancestors and was buried in Samaria. And
Jehoash[b] his son succeeded him as king.

Jehoash King of Israel

10In the thirty-seventh year of Joash king of
Judah, Jehoash son of Jehoahaz became king
of Israel in Samaria, and he reigned sixteen
years. 11He did evil in the eyes of the LORD
and did not turn away from any of the sins of
Jeroboam son of Nebat, which he had caused
Israel to commit; he continued in them.
12As for the other events of the reign of Jehoash, all he did and his achievements, including his war against Amaziah king of Judah,
are they not written in the book of the annals
of the kings of Israel? 13Jehoash rested with
his ancestors, and Jeroboam succeeded him
on the throne. Jehoash was buried in Samaria
with the kings of Israel.
14Now Elisha had been suffering from the
illness from which he died. Jehoash king of
Israel went down to see him and wept over
him. "My father! My father!" he cried. "The
chariots and horsemen of Israel!"
15Elisha said, "Get a bow and some arrows,"
and he did so. 16"Take the bow in your hands,"
he said to the king of Israel. When he had tak-
en it, Elisha put his hands on the king's hands.
17"Open the east window," he said, and he
opened it. "Shoot!" Elisha said, and he shot.
"The LORD's arrow of victory, the arrow of
victory over Aram!" Elisha declared. "You will
completely destroy the Arameans at Aphek."
18Then he said, "Take the arrows," and the
king took them. Elisha told him, "Strike the
ground." He struck it three times and stopped.
19The man of God was angry with him and
said, "You should have struck the ground five
or six times; then you would have defeated
Aram and completely destroyed it. But now
you will defeat it only three times."
20Elisha died and was buried.
Now Moabite raiders used to enter the country every spring. 21Once while some Israelites were burying a man, suddenly they saw a
band of raiders; so they threw the man's body
into Elisha's tomb. When the body touched
Elisha's bones, the man came to life and stood
up on his feet.
22Hazael king of Aram oppressed Israel
throughout the reign of Jehoahaz. 23But the
LORD was gracious to them and had compassion and showed concern for them because of
his covenant with Abraham, Isaac and Jacob.
To this day he has been unwilling to destroy
them or banish them from his presence.
24Hazael king of Aram died, and Ben-Hadad
his son succeeded him as king. 25Then Jehoash son of Jehoahaz recaptured from Ben-Hadad son of Hazael the towns he had taken in
battle from his father Jehoahaz. Three times
Jehoash defeated him, and so he recovered
the Israelite towns.

Amaziah King of Judah

14 In the second year of Jehoash[c] son of
Jehoahaz king of Israel, Amaziah son
of Joash king of Judah began to reign. 2He
was twenty-five years old when he became
king, and he reigned in Jerusalem twenty-
nine years. His mother's name was Jehoaddan; she was from Jerusalem. 3He did what
was right in the eyes of the LORD, but not as
his father David had done. In everything he
followed the example of his father Joash. 4The
high places, however, were not removed; the
people continued to offer sacrifices and burn
incense there.

[a] 6 That is, a wooden symbol of the goddess Asherah; here and elsewhere in 2 Kings [b] 9 Hebrew *Joash*, a variant of *Jehoash*; also in verses 12-14 and 25 [c] 1 Hebrew *Joash*, a variant of *Jehoash*; also in verses 13, 23 and 27

5After the kingdom was firmly in his grasp,
he executed the officials who had murdered
his father the king. 6Yet he did not put the children of the assassins to death, in accordance
with what is written in the Book of the Law of
Moses where the LORD commanded: "Parents
are not to be put to death for their children,
nor children put to death for their parents;
each will die for their own sin."[a]
7He was the one who defeated ten thousand
Edomites in the Valley of Salt and captured
Sela in battle, calling it Joktheel, the name it
has to this day.
8Then Amaziah sent messengers to Jehoash son of Jehoahaz, the son of Jehu, king of
Israel, with the challenge: "Come, let us face
each other in battle."
9But Jehoash king of Israel replied to Amaziah king of Judah: "A thistle in Lebanon sent
a message to a cedar in Lebanon, 'Give your
daughter to my son in marriage.' Then a wild
beast in Lebanon came along and trampled
the thistle underfoot. 10You have indeed defeated Edom and now you are arrogant. Glory
in your victory, but stay at home! Why ask for
trouble and cause your own downfall and that
of Judah also?"
11Amaziah, however, would not listen, so
Jehoash king of Israel attacked. He and Amaziah king of Judah faced each other at Beth
Shemesh in Judah. 12Judah was routed by Israel, and every man fled to his home. 13Jeho-
ash king of Israel captured Amaziah king of
Judah, the son of Joash, the son of Ahaziah,
at Beth Shemesh. Then Jehoash went to Jerusalem and broke down the wall of Jerusalem
from the Ephraim Gate to the Corner Gate—a
section about four hundred cubits long.[b] 14He
took all the gold and silver and all the articles
found in the temple of the LORD and in the
treasuries of the royal palace. He also took
hostages and returned to Samaria.
15As for the other events of the reign of
Jehoash, what he did and his achievements,
including his war against Amaziah king of
Judah, are they not written in the book of the
annals of the kings of Israel? 16Jehoash rested
with his ancestors and was buried in Samaria
with the kings of Israel. And Jeroboam his
son succeeded him as king.
17Amaziah son of Joash king of Judah lived
for fifteen years after the death of Jehoash
son of Jehoahaz king of Israel. 18As for the
other events of Amaziah's reign, are they not
written in the book of the annals of the kings
of Judah?
19They conspired against him in Jerusalem,
and he fled to Lachish, but they sent men after
him to Lachish and killed him there. 20He was
brought back by horse and was buried in Jerusalem with his ancestors, in the City of David.
21Then all the people of Judah took Azariah,[c] who was sixteen years old, and made him
king in place of his father Amaziah. 22He was
the one who rebuilt Elath and restored it to Judah after Amaziah rested with his ancestors.

Jeroboam II King of Israel

23In the fifteenth year of Amaziah son of
Joash king of Judah, Jeroboam son of Jehoash king of Israel became king in Samaria,
and he reigned forty-one years. 24He did evil
in the eyes of the LORD and did not turn away
from any of the sins of Jeroboam son of Nebat,
which he had caused Israel to commit. 25He
was the one who restored the boundaries of
Israel from Lebo Hamath to the Dead Sea,[d]
in accordance with the word of the LORD, the
God of Israel, spoken through his servant Jonah son of Amittai, the prophet from Gath
Hepher.
26The LORD had seen how bitterly everyone
in Israel, whether slave or free, was suffering;[e]
there was no one to help them. 27And since
the LORD had not said he would blot out the
name of Israel from under heaven, he saved
them by the hand of Jeroboam son of Jehoash.
28As for the other events of Jeroboam's
reign, all he did, and his military achievements, including how he recovered for Israel
both Damascus and Hamath, which had belonged to Judah, are they not written in the
book of the annals of the kings of Israel? 29Jer-
oboam rested with his ancestors, the kings
of Israel. And Zechariah his son succeeded
him as king.

Azariah King of Judah

15 In the twenty-seventh year of Jeroboam king of Israel, Azariah[f] son of Amaziah king of Judah began to reign. 2He was
sixteen years old when he became king, and
he reigned in Jerusalem fifty-two years. His
mother's name was Jekoliah; she was from
Jerusalem. 3He did what was right in the eyes
of the LORD, just as his father Amaziah had
done. 4The high places, however, were not removed; the people continued to offer sacrifices
and burn incense there.
5The LORD afflicted the king with leprosy[g] until the day he died, and he lived in a
separate house.[h] Jotham the king's son had
charge of the palace and governed the people
of the land.
6As for the other events of Azariah's reign,
and all he did, are they not written in the book
of the annals of the kings of Judah? 7Azariah
rested with his ancestors and was buried near
them in the City of David. And Jotham his son
succeeded him as king.

Zechariah King of Israel

8In the thirty-eighth year of Azariah king
of Judah, Zechariah son of Jeroboam became
king of Israel in Samaria, and he reigned six

[a] *6* Deut. 24:16 [b] *13* That is, about 600 feet or about 180 meters [c] *21* Also called *Uzziah*
[d] *25* Hebrew *the Sea of the Arabah* [e] *26* Or *Israel was suffering. They were without a ruler or leader, and* [f] *1* Also called *Uzziah*; also in verses 6, 7, 8, 17, 23 and 27 [g] *5* The Hebrew for *leprosy* was used for various diseases affecting the skin. [h] *5* Or *in a house where he was relieved of responsibilities*

months. 9He did evil in the eyes of the LORD,
as his predecessors had done. He did not turn
away from the sins of Jeroboam son of Nebat,
which he had caused Israel to commit.
10Shallum son of Jabesh conspired against
Zechariah. He attacked him in front of the
people,[a] assassinated him and succeeded him
as king. 11The other events of Zechariah's
reign are written in the book of the annals of
the kings of Israel. 12So the word of the LORD
spoken to Jehu was fulfilled: "Your descendants will sit on the throne of Israel to the
fourth generation."[b]

Shallum King of Israel

13Shallum son of Jabesh became king in
the thirty-ninth year of Uzziah king of Judah,
and he reigned in Samaria one month. 14Then
Menahem son of Gadi went from Tirzah up to
Samaria. He attacked Shallum son of Jabesh
in Samaria, assassinated him and succeeded
him as king.
15The other events of Shallum's reign, and
the conspiracy he led, are written in the book
of the annals of the kings of Israel.
16At that time Menahem, starting out from
Tirzah, attacked Tiphsah and everyone in
the city and its vicinity, because they refused
to open their gates. He sacked Tiphsah and
ripped open all the pregnant women.

Menahem King of Israel

17In the thirty-ninth year of Azariah king of
Judah, Menahem son of Gadi became king of
Israel, and he reigned in Samaria ten years.
18He did evil in the eyes of the LORD. During
his entire reign he did not turn away from the
sins of Jeroboam son of Nebat, which he had
caused Israel to commit.
19Then Pul[c] king of Assyria invaded the
land, and Menahem gave him a thousand
talents[d] of silver to gain his support and
strengthen his own hold on the kingdom.
20Menahem exacted this money from Israel.
Every wealthy person had to contribute fifty
shekels[e] of silver to be given to the king of
Assyria. So the king of Assyria withdrew and
stayed in the land no longer.
21As for the other events of Menahem's
reign, and all he did, are they not written in
the book of the annals of the kings of Israel?
22Menahem rested with his ancestors. And
Pekahiah his son succeeded him as king.

Pekahiah King of Israel

23In the fiftieth year of Azariah king of
Judah, Pekahiah son of Menahem became
king of Israel in Samaria, and he reigned
two years. 24Pekahiah did evil in the eyes
of the LORD. He did not turn away from the
sins of Jeroboam son of Nebat, which he had
caused Israel to commit. 25One of his chief
officers, Pekah son of Remaliah, conspired
against him. Taking fifty men of Gilead with
him, he assassinated Pekahiah, along with
Argob and Arieh, in the citadel of the royal
palace at Samaria. So Pekah killed Pekahiah
and succeeded him as king.
26The other events of Pekahiah's reign, and
all he did, are written in the book of the annals
of the kings of Israel.

Pekah King of Israel

27In the fifty-second year of Azariah king of
Judah, Pekah son of Remaliah became king
of Israel in Samaria, and he reigned twenty
years. 28He did evil in the eyes of the LORD.
He did not turn away from the sins of Jeroboam son of Nebat, which he had caused Israel
to commit.
29In the time of Pekah king of Israel, Tiglath-Pileser king of Assyria came and took
Ijon, Abel Beth Maakah, Janoah, Kedesh and
Hazor. He took Gilead and Galilee, including all the land of Naphtali, and deported the
people to Assyria. 30Then Hoshea son of Elah
conspired against Pekah son of Remaliah. He
attacked and assassinated him, and then succeeded him as king in the twentieth year of
Jotham son of Uzziah.
31As for the other events of Pekah's reign,
and all he did, are they not written in the book
of the annals of the kings of Israel?

Jotham King of Judah

32In the second year of Pekah son of Remaliah king of Israel, Jotham son of Uzziah
king of Judah began to reign. 33He was twenty-five years old when he became king, and
he reigned in Jerusalem sixteen years. His
mother's name was Jerusha daughter of Zadok. 34He did what was right in the eyes of
the LORD, just as his father Uzziah had done.
35The high places, however, were not removed;
the people continued to offer sacrifices and
burn incense there. Jotham rebuilt the Upper
Gate of the temple of the LORD.
36As for the other events of Jotham's reign,
and what he did, are they not written in the
book of the annals of the kings of Judah? 37(In
those days the LORD began to send Rezin king
of Aram and Pekah son of Remaliah against
Judah.) 38Jotham rested with his ancestors
and was buried with them in the City of David, the city of his father. And Ahaz his son
succeeded him as king.

Ahaz King of Judah

16 In the seventeenth year of Pekah son of
Remaliah, Ahaz son of Jotham king of
Judah began to reign. 2Ahaz was twenty years
old when he became king, and he reigned in
Jerusalem sixteen years. Unlike David his
father, he did not do what was right in the
eyes of the LORD his God. 3He followed the
ways of the kings of Israel and even sacrificed
his son in the fire, engaging in the detestable
practices of the nations the LORD had driven

[a] *10* Hebrew; some Septuagint manuscripts *in Ibleam* [b] *12* 2 Kings 10:30 [c] *19* Also called *Tiglath-Pileser* [d] *19* That is, about 38 tons or about 34 metric tons [e] *20* That is, about 1 1/4 pounds or about 575 grams

out before the Israelites. 4He offered sacrifices and burned incense at the high places, on
the hilltops and under every spreading tree.
5Then Rezin king of Aram and Pekah son
of Remaliah king of Israel marched up to fight
against Jerusalem and besieged Ahaz, but
they could not overpower him. 6At that time,
Rezin king of Aram recovered Elath for Aram
by driving out the people of Judah. Edomites
then moved into Elath and have lived there
to this day.
7Ahaz sent messengers to say to Tiglath-
Pileser king of Assyria, "I am your servant
and vassal. Come up and save me out of the
hand of the king of Aram and of the king of
Israel, who are attacking me." 8And Ahaz took
the silver and gold found in the temple of the
LORD and in the treasuries of the royal palace
and sent it as a gift to the king of Assyria.
9The king of Assyria complied by attacking
Damascus and capturing it. He deported its
inhabitants to Kir and put Rezin to death.
10Then King Ahaz went to Damascus to
meet Tiglath-Pileser king of Assyria. He
saw an altar in Damascus and sent to Uriah the priest a sketch of the altar, with detailed plans for its construction. 11So Uriah
the priest built an altar in accordance with
all the plans that King Ahaz had sent from
Damascus and finished it before King Ahaz
returned. 12When the king came back from
Damascus and saw the altar, he approached it
and presented offerings[a] on it. 13He offered up
his burnt offering and grain offering, poured
out his drink offering, and splashed the blood
of his fellowship offerings against the altar.
14As for the bronze altar that stood before
the LORD, he brought it from the front of the
temple—from between the new altar and the
temple of the LORD—and put it on the north
side of the new altar.
15King Ahaz then gave these orders to Uriah the priest: "On the large new altar, offer
the morning burnt offering and the evening
grain offering, the king's burnt offering and
his grain offering, and the burnt offering of all
the people of the land, and their grain offering
and their drink offering. Splash against this
altar the blood of all the burnt offerings and
sacrifices. But I will use the bronze altar for
seeking guidance." 16And Uriah the priest did
just as King Ahaz had ordered.
17King Ahaz cut off the side panels and removed the basins from the movable stands.
He removed the Sea from the bronze bulls
that supported it and set it on a stone base.
18He took away the Sabbath canopy[b] that had
been built at the temple and removed the royal
entryway outside the temple of the LORD, in
deference to the king of Assyria.
19As for the other events of the reign of
Ahaz, and what he did, are they not written
in the book of the annals of the kings of Judah? 20Ahaz rested with his ancestors and
was buried with them in the City of David.
And Hezekiah his son succeeded him as king.

Hoshea Last King of Israel

17 In the twelfth year of Ahaz king of Judah, Hoshea son of Elah became king of
Israel in Samaria, and he reigned nine years.
2He did evil in the eyes of the LORD, but not
like the kings of Israel who preceded him.
3Shalmaneser king of Assyria came up
to attack Hoshea, who had been Shalmaneser's vassal and had paid him tribute. 4But the
king of Assyria discovered that Hoshea was
a traitor, for he had sent envoys to So[c] king
of Egypt, and he no longer paid tribute to the
king of Assyria, as he had done year by year.
Therefore Shalmaneser seized him and put
him in prison. 5The king of Assyria invaded
the entire land, marched against Samaria and
laid siege to it for three years. 6In the ninth
year of Hoshea, the king of Assyria captured
Samaria and deported the Israelites to Assyria. He settled them in Halah, in Gozan on the
Habor River and in the towns of the Medes.

Israel Exiled Because of Sin

7All this took place because the Israelites
had sinned against the LORD their God, who
had brought them up out of Egypt from under
the power of Pharaoh king of Egypt. They
worshiped other gods 8and followed the practices of the nations the LORD had driven out
before them, as well as the practices that the
kings of Israel had introduced. 9The Israelites secretly did things against the LORD their
God that were not right. From watchtower to
fortified city they built themselves high places in all their towns. 10They set up sacred
stones and Asherah poles on every high hill
and under every spreading tree. 11At every
high place they burned incense, as the nations whom the LORD had driven out before
them had done. They did wicked things that
aroused the LORD's anger. 12They worshiped
idols, though the LORD had said, "You shall not
do this."[d] 13The LORD warned Israel and Judah
through all his prophets and seers: "Turn from
your evil ways. Observe my commands and
decrees, in accordance with the entire Law
that I commanded your ancestors to obey and
that I delivered to you through my servants
the prophets."
14But they would not listen and were as
stiff-necked as their ancestors, who did not
trust in the LORD their God. 15They rejected
his decrees and the covenant he had made
with their ancestors and the statutes he had
warned them to keep. They followed worthless idols and themselves became worthless.
They imitated the nations around them although the LORD had ordered them, "Do not
do as they do."
16They forsook all the commands of the
LORD their God and made for themselves two
idols cast in the shape of calves, and an Asherah pole. They bowed down to all the starry
hosts, and they worshiped Baal. 17They sacrificed their sons and daughters in the fire.
They practiced divination and sought omens

[a] 12 Or *and went up* [b] 18 Or *the dais of his throne* (see Septuagint) [c] 4 *So* is probably an abbreviation for *Osorkon.* [d] 12 Exodus 20:4,5

and sold themselves to do evil in the eyes of
the LORD, arousing his anger.
18So the LORD was very angry with Israel
and removed them from his presence. Only
the tribe of Judah was left, 19and even Judah
did not keep the commands of the LORD their
God. They followed the practices Israel had
introduced. 20Therefore the LORD rejected all
the people of Israel; he afflicted them and gave
them into the hands of plunderers, until he
thrust them from his presence.
21When he tore Israel away from the house
of David, they made Jeroboam son of Nebat
their king. Jeroboam enticed Israel away from
following the LORD and caused them to commit a great sin. 22The Israelites persisted in all
the sins of Jeroboam and did not turn away
from them 23until the LORD removed them
from his presence, as he had warned through
all his servants the prophets. So the people
of Israel were taken from their homeland into
exile in Assyria, and they are still there.

Samaria Resettled

24The king of Assyria brought people from
Babylon, Kuthah, Avva, Hamath and Sepharvaim and settled them in the towns of Samaria
to replace the Israelites. They took over Samaria and lived in its towns. 25When they first
lived there, they did not worship the LORD;
so he sent lions among them and they killed
some of the people. 26It was reported to the
king of Assyria: "The people you deported
and resettled in the towns of Samaria do not
know what the god of that country requires.
He has sent lions among them, which are killing them off, because the people do not know
what he requires."
27Then the king of Assyria gave this order:
"Have one of the priests you took captive from
Samaria go back to live there and teach the
people what the god of the land requires." 28So
one of the priests who had been exiled from
Samaria came to live in Bethel and taught
them how to worship the LORD.
29Nevertheless, each national group made
its own gods in the several towns where they
settled, and set them up in the shrines the
people of Samaria had made at the high places. 30The people from Babylon made Sukkoth
Benoth, those from Kuthah made Nergal, and
those from Hamath made Ashima; 31the Avvites made Nibhaz and Tartak, and the Se-
pharvites burned their children in the fire as
sacrifices to Adrammelek and Anammelek,
the gods of Sepharvaim. 32They worshiped the
LORD, but they also appointed all sorts of their
own people to officiate for them as priests in
the shrines at the high places. 33They worshiped the LORD, but they also served their
own gods in accordance with the customs
of the nations from which they had been
brought.
34To this day they persist in their former
practices. They neither worship the LORD
nor adhere to the decrees and regulations,
the laws and commands that the LORD gave
the descendants of Jacob, whom he named
Israel. 35When the LORD made a covenant
with the Israelites, he commanded them: "Do
not worship any other gods or bow down to
them, serve them or sacrifice to them. 36But
the LORD, who brought you up out of Egypt
with mighty power and outstretched arm, is
the one you must worship. To him you shall
bow down and to him offer sacrifices. 37You
must always be careful to keep the decrees
and regulations, the laws and commands he
wrote for you. Do not worship other gods. 38Do
not forget the covenant I have made with you,
and do not worship other gods. 39Rather, worship the LORD your God; it is he who will deliver you from the hand of all your enemies."
40They would not listen, however, but persisted in their former practices. 41Even while
these people were worshiping the LORD, they
were serving their idols. To this day their children and grandchildren continue to do as their
ancestors did.

Hezekiah King of Judah

18 In the third year of Hoshea son of Elah
king of Israel, Hezekiah son of Ahaz
king of Judah began to reign. 2He was twenty-five years old when he became king, and
he reigned in Jerusalem twenty-nine years.
His mother's name was Abijah[a] daughter of
Zechariah. 3He did what was right in the eyes
of the LORD, just as his father David had done.
4He removed the high places, smashed the sacred stones and cut down the Asherah poles.
He broke into pieces the bronze snake Moses
had made, for up to that time the Israelites
had been burning incense to it. (It was called
Nehushtan.[b])
5Hezekiah trusted in the LORD, the God of
Israel. There was no one like him among all
the kings of Judah, either before him or after him. 6He held fast to the LORD and did not
stop following him; he kept the commands
the LORD had given Moses. 7And the LORD
was with him; he was successful in whatever
he undertook. He rebelled against the king of
Assyria and did not serve him. 8From watchtower to fortified city, he defeated the Philistines, as far as Gaza and its territory.
9In King Hezekiah's fourth year, which was
the seventh year of Hoshea son of Elah king of
Israel, Shalmaneser king of Assyria marched
against Samaria and laid siege to it. 10At the
end of three years the Assyrians took it. So
Samaria was captured in Hezekiah's sixth
year, which was the ninth year of Hoshea king
of Israel. 11The king of Assyria deported Israel to Assyria and settled them in Halah, in
Gozan on the Habor River and in towns of the
Medes. 12This happened because they had not
obeyed the LORD their God, but had violated
his covenant—all that Moses the servant of
the LORD commanded. They neither listened
to the commands nor carried them out.
13In the fourteenth year of King Hezekiah's

[a] 2 Hebrew *Abi*, a variant of *Abijah* [b] 4 *Nehushtan* sounds like the Hebrew for both *bronze* and *snake*.

reign, Sennacherib king of Assyria attacked
all the fortified cities of Judah and captured
them. 14So Hezekiah king of Judah sent this
message to the king of Assyria at Lachish: "I
have done wrong. Withdraw from me, and I
will pay whatever you demand of me." The
king of Assyria exacted from Hezekiah king
of Judah three hundred talents[a] of silver and
thirty talents[b] of gold. 15So Hezekiah gave him
all the silver that was found in the temple of
the LORD and in the treasuries of the royal
palace.
16At this time Hezekiah king of Judah
stripped off the gold with which he had covered the doors and doorposts of the temple of
the LORD, and gave it to the king of Assyria.

Sennacherib Threatens Jerusalem

17The king of Assyria sent his supreme commander, his chief officer and his field commander with a large army, from Lachish to
King Hezekiah at Jerusalem. They came up to
Jerusalem and stopped at the aqueduct of the
Upper Pool, on the road to the Washerman's
Field. 18They called for the king; and Eliakim
son of Hilkiah the palace administrator, Shebna the secretary, and Joah son of Asaph the
recorder went out to them.
19The field commander said to them, "Tell
Hezekiah:

> "'This is what the great king, the king
> of Assyria, says: On what are you bas-
> ing this confidence of yours? 20You say
> you have the counsel and the might for
> war—but you speak only empty words.
> On whom are you depending, that you
> rebel against me? 21Look, I know you
> are depending on Egypt, that splintered
> reed of a staff, which pierces the hand of
> anyone who leans on it! Such is Pharaoh
> king of Egypt to all who depend on him.
> 22But if you say to me, "We are depending
> on the LORD our God"—isn't he the one
> whose high places and altars Hezekiah
> removed, saying to Judah and Jerusalem,
> "You must worship before this altar in
> Jerusalem"?
> 23"'Come now, make a bargain with my
> master, the king of Assyria: I will give
> you two thousand horses—if you can put
> riders on them! 24How can you repulse
> one officer of the least of my master's of-
> ficials, even though you are depending
> on Egypt for chariots and horsemen[c]?
> 25Furthermore, have I come to attack and
> destroy this place without word from the
> LORD? The LORD himself told me to march
> against this country and destroy it.'"

26Then Eliakim son of Hilkiah, and Shebna
and Joah said to the field commander, "Please
speak to your servants in Aramaic, since we
understand it. Don't speak to us in Hebrew in
the hearing of the people on the wall."
27But the commander replied, "Was it only
to your master and you that my master sent
me to say these things, and not to the people
sitting on the wall—who, like you, will have
to eat their own excrement and drink their
own urine?"
28Then the commander stood and called
out in Hebrew, "Hear the word of the great
king, the king of Assyria! 29This is what the
king says: Do not let Hezekiah deceive you.
He cannot deliver you from my hand. 30Do not
let Hezekiah persuade you to trust in the LORD
when he says, 'The LORD will surely deliver
us; this city will not be given into the hand of
the king of Assyria.'
31"Do not listen to Hezekiah. This is what
the king of Assyria says: Make peace with
me and come out to me. Then each of you will
eat fruit from your own vine and fig tree and
drink water from your own cistern, 32until I
come and take you to a land like your own—a
land of grain and new wine, a land of bread
and vineyards, a land of olive trees and honey.
Choose life and not death!
"Do not listen to Hezekiah, for he is misleading you when he says, 'The LORD will
deliver us.' 33Has the god of any nation ever
delivered his land from the hand of the king of
Assyria? 34Where are the gods of Hamath and
Arpad? Where are the gods of Sepharvaim,
Hena and Ivvah? Have they rescued Samaria
from my hand? 35Who of all the gods of these
countries has been able to save his land from
me? How then can the LORD deliver Jerusalem
from my hand?"
36But the people remained silent and said
nothing in reply, because the king had commanded, "Do not answer him."
37Then Eliakim son of Hilkiah the palace
administrator, Shebna the secretary, and Joah
son of Asaph the recorder went to Hezekiah,
with their clothes torn, and told him what the
field commander had said.

Jerusalem's Deliverance Foretold

19 When King Hezekiah heard this, he tore
his clothes and put on sackcloth and
went into the temple of the LORD. 2He sent
Eliakim the palace administrator, Shebna the
secretary and the leading priests, all wearing
sackcloth, to the prophet Isaiah son of Amoz.
3They told him, "This is what Hezekiah says:
This day is a day of distress and rebuke and
disgrace, as when children come to the moment of birth and there is no strength to deliver them. 4It may be that the LORD your God
will hear all the words of the field commander,
whom his master, the king of Assyria, has sent
to ridicule the living God, and that he will
rebuke him for the words the LORD your God
has heard. Therefore pray for the remnant
that still survives."
5When King Hezekiah's officials came to
Isaiah, 6Isaiah said to them, "Tell your master,
'This is what the LORD says: Do not be afraid
of what you have heard—those words with
which the underlings of the king of Assyria
have blasphemed me. 7Listen! When he hears

[a] *14* That is, about 11 tons or about 10 metric tons
[b] *14* That is, about 1 ton or about 1 metric ton
[c] *24* Or *charioteers*

a certain report, I will make him want to return to his own country, and there I will have him cut down with the sword.'"

8When the field commander heard that the king of Assyria had left Lachish, he withdrew and found the king fighting against Libnah.

9Now Sennacherib received a report that Tirhakah, the king of Cush,[a] was marching out to fight against him. So he again sent messengers to Hezekiah with this word: 10"Say to Hezekiah king of Judah: Do not let the god you depend on deceive you when he says, 'Jerusalem will not be given into the hands of the king of Assyria.' 11Surely you have heard what the kings of Assyria have done to all the countries, destroying them completely. And will you be delivered? 12Did the gods of the nations that were destroyed by my predecessors deliver them—the gods of Gozan, Harran, Rezeph and the people of Eden who were in Tel Assar? 13Where is the king of Hamath or the king of Arpad? Where are the kings of Lair, Sepharvaim, Hena and Ivvah?"

Hezekiah's Prayer

14Hezekiah received the letter from the messengers and read it. Then he went up to the temple of the LORD and spread it out before the LORD. 15And Hezekiah prayed to the LORD: "LORD, the God of Israel, enthroned between the cherubim, you alone are God over all the kingdoms of the earth. You have made heaven and earth. 16Give ear, LORD, and hear; open your eyes, LORD, and see; listen to the words Sennacherib has sent to ridicule the living God.

17"It is true, LORD, that the Assyrian kings have laid waste these nations and their lands. 18They have thrown their gods into the fire and destroyed them, for they were not gods but only wood and stone, fashioned by human hands. 19Now, LORD our God, deliver us from his hand, so that all the kingdoms of the earth may know that you alone, LORD, are God."

Isaiah Prophesies Sennacherib's Fall

20Then Isaiah son of Amoz sent a message to Hezekiah: "This is what the LORD, the God of Israel, says: I have heard your prayer concerning Sennacherib king of Assyria. 21This is the word that the LORD has spoken against him:

"'Virgin Daughter Zion
despises you and mocks you.
Daughter Jerusalem
tosses her head as you flee.
22Who is it you have ridiculed and blasphemed?
Against whom have you raised your voice
and lifted your eyes in pride?
Against the Holy One of Israel!
23By your messengers
you have ridiculed the Lord.
And you have said,
"With my many chariots
I have ascended the heights of the mountains,
the utmost heights of Lebanon.
I have cut down its tallest cedars,
the choicest of its junipers.
I have reached its remotest parts,
the finest of its forests.
24I have dug wells in foreign lands
and drunk the water there.
With the soles of my feet
I have dried up all the streams of Egypt."

25"'Have you not heard?
Long ago I ordained it.
In days of old I planned it;
now I have brought it to pass,
that you have turned fortified cities
into piles of stone.
26Their people, drained of power,
are dismayed and put to shame.
They are like plants in the field,
like tender green shoots,
like grass sprouting on the roof,
scorched before it grows up.

27"'But I know where you are
and when you come and go
and how you rage against me.
28Because you rage against me
and because your insolence has reached my ears,
I will put my hook in your nose
and my bit in your mouth,
and I will make you return
by the way you came.'

29"This will be the sign for you, Hezekiah:

"This year you will eat what grows by itself,
and the second year what springs from that.
But in the third year sow and reap,
plant vineyards and eat their fruit.
30Once more a remnant of the kingdom of Judah
will take root below and bear fruit above.
31For out of Jerusalem will come a remnant,
and out of Mount Zion a band of survivors.

"The zeal of the LORD Almighty will accomplish this.

32"Therefore this is what the LORD says concerning the king of Assyria:

"'He will not enter this city
or shoot an arrow here.
He will not come before it with shield
or build a siege ramp against it.
33By the way that he came he will return;
he will not enter this city,
declares the LORD.
34I will defend this city and save it,
for my sake and for the sake of David
my servant.'"

[a] 9 That is, the upper Nile region

35 That night the angel of the LORD went out
and put to death a hundred and eighty-five
thousand in the Assyrian camp. When the
people got up the next morning—there were
all the dead bodies! 36 So Sennacherib king
of Assyria broke camp and withdrew. He returned to Nineveh and stayed there.

37 One day, while he was worshiping in the
temple of his god Nisrok, his sons Adrammelek and Sharezer killed him with the sword,
and they escaped to the land of Ararat. And
Esarhaddon his son succeeded him as king.

Hezekiah's Illness

20 In those days Hezekiah became ill and
was at the point of death. The prophet Isaiah son of Amoz went to him and said,
"This is what the LORD says: Put your house
in order, because you are going to die; you
will not recover."

2 Hezekiah turned his face to the wall and
prayed to the LORD, 3 "Remember, LORD, how
I have walked before you faithfully and with
wholehearted devotion and have done what
is good in your eyes." And Hezekiah wept
bitterly.

4 Before Isaiah had left the middle court, the
word of the LORD came to him: 5 "Go back and
tell Hezekiah, the ruler of my people, 'This is
what the LORD, the God of your father David,
says: I have heard your prayer and seen your
tears; I will heal you. On the third day from
now you will go up to the temple of the LORD.
6 I will add fifteen years to your life. And I will
deliver you and this city from the hand of the
king of Assyria. I will defend this city for my
sake and for the sake of my servant David.'"

7 Then Isaiah said, "Prepare a poultice of
figs." They did so and applied it to the boil,
and he recovered.

8 Hezekiah had asked Isaiah, "What will be
the sign that the LORD will heal me and that
I will go up to the temple of the LORD on the
third day from now?"

9 Isaiah answered, "This is the LORD's sign to
you that the LORD will do what he has promised: Shall the shadow go forward ten steps,
or shall it go back ten steps?"

10 "It is a simple matter for the shadow to go
forward ten steps," said Hezekiah. "Rather,
have it go back ten steps."

11 Then the prophet Isaiah called on the
LORD, and the LORD made the shadow go back
the ten steps it had gone down on the stairway of Ahaz.

Envoys From Babylon

12 At that time Marduk-Baladan son of Baladan king of Babylon sent Hezekiah letters
and a gift, because he had heard of Hezekiah's
illness. 13 Hezekiah received the envoys and
showed them all that was in his storehouses—the silver, the gold, the spices and the fine
olive oil—his armory and everything found
among his treasures. There was nothing in
his palace or in all his kingdom that Hezekiah
did not show them.

14 Then Isaiah the prophet went to King Hezekiah and asked, "What did those men say,
and where did they come from?"

"From a distant land," Hezekiah replied.
"They came from Babylon."

15 The prophet asked, "What did they see
in your palace?"

"They saw everything in my palace," Hezekiah said. "There is nothing among my treasures that I did not show them."

16 Then Isaiah said to Hezekiah, "Hear the
word of the LORD: 17 The time will surely come
when everything in your palace, and all that
your predecessors have stored up until this
day, will be carried off to Babylon. Nothing
will be left, says the LORD. 18 And some of your
descendants, your own flesh and blood who
will be born to you, will be taken away, and
they will become eunuchs in the palace of the
king of Babylon."

19 "The word of the LORD you have spoken
is good," Hezekiah replied. For he thought,
"Will there not be peace and security in my
lifetime?"

20 As for the other events of Hezekiah's
reign, all his achievements and how he made
the pool and the tunnel by which he brought
water into the city, are they not written in
the book of the annals of the kings of Judah?
21 Hezekiah rested with his ancestors. And
Manasseh his son succeeded him as king.

Manasseh King of Judah

21 Manasseh was twelve years old when
he became king, and he reigned in Jerusalem fifty-five years. His mother's name
was Hephzibah. 2 He did evil in the eyes of
the LORD, following the detestable practices
of the nations the LORD had driven out before
the Israelites. 3 He rebuilt the high places his
father Hezekiah had destroyed; he also erected altars to Baal and made an Asherah pole,
as Ahab king of Israel had done. He bowed
down to all the starry hosts and worshiped
them. 4 He built altars in the temple of the
LORD, of which the LORD had said, "In Jerusalem I will put my Name." 5 In the two courts
of the temple of the LORD, he built altars to all
the starry hosts. 6 He sacrificed his own son in
the fire, practiced divination, sought omens,
and consulted mediums and spiritists. He did
much evil in the eyes of the LORD, arousing
his anger.

7 He took the carved Asherah pole he had
made and put it in the temple, of which the
LORD had said to David and to his son Solomon, "In this temple and in Jerusalem, which
I have chosen out of all the tribes of Israel, I
will put my Name forever. 8 I will not again
make the feet of the Israelites wander from
the land I gave their ancestors, if only they
will be careful to do everything I commanded them and will keep the whole Law that my
servant Moses gave them." 9 But the people did
not listen. Manasseh led them astray, so that
they did more evil than the nations the LORD
had destroyed before the Israelites.

10 The LORD said through his servants the
prophets: 11 "Manasseh king of Judah has
committed these detestable sins. He has done

more evil than the Amorites who preceded him and has led Judah into sin with his idols. [12]Therefore this is what the LORD, the God of Israel, says: I am going to bring such disaster on Jerusalem and Judah that the ears of everyone who hears of it will tingle. [13]I will stretch out over Jerusalem the measuring line used against Samaria and the plumb line used against the house of Ahab. I will wipe out Jerusalem as one wipes a dish, wiping it and turning it upside down. [14]I will forsake the remnant of my inheritance and give them into the hands of enemies. They will be looted and plundered by all their enemies; [15]they have done evil in my eyes and have aroused my anger from the day their ancestors came out of Egypt until this day."

[16]Moreover, Manasseh also shed so much innocent blood that he filled Jerusalem from end to end—besides the sin that he had caused Judah to commit, so that they did evil in the eyes of the LORD.

[17]As for the other events of Manasseh's reign, and all he did, including the sin he committed, are they not written in the book of the annals of the kings of Judah? [18]Manasseh rested with his ancestors and was buried in his palace garden, the garden of Uzza. And Amon his son succeeded him as king.

Amon King of Judah

[19]Amon was twenty-two years old when he became king, and he reigned in Jerusalem two years. His mother's name was Meshullemeth daughter of Haruz; she was from Jotbah. [20]He did evil in the eyes of the LORD, as his father Manasseh had done. [21]He followed completely the ways of his father, worshiping the idols his father had worshiped, and bowing down to them. [22]He forsook the LORD, the God of his ancestors, and did not walk in obedience to him.

[23]Amon's officials conspired against him and assassinated the king in his palace. [24]Then the people of the land killed all who had plotted against King Amon, and they made Josiah his son king in his place.

[25]As for the other events of Amon's reign, and what he did, are they not written in the book of the annals of the kings of Judah? [26]He was buried in his tomb in the garden of Uzza. And Josiah his son succeeded him as king.

The Book of the Law Found

22 Josiah was eight years old when he became king, and he reigned in Jerusalem thirty-one years. His mother's name was Jedidah daughter of Adaiah; she was from Bozkath. [2]He did what was right in the eyes of the LORD and followed completely the ways of his father David, not turning aside to the right or to the left.

[3]In the eighteenth year of his reign, King Josiah sent the secretary, Shaphan son of Azaliah, the son of Meshullam, to the temple of the LORD. He said: [4]"Go up to Hilkiah the high priest and have him get ready the money that has been brought into the temple of the LORD, which the doorkeepers have collected from the people. [5]Have them entrust it to the men appointed to supervise the work on the temple. And have these men pay the workers who repair the temple of the LORD— [6]the carpenters, the builders and the masons. Also have them purchase timber and dressed stone to repair the temple. [7]But they need not account for the money entrusted to them, because they are honest in their dealings."

[8]Hilkiah the high priest said to Shaphan the secretary, "I have found the Book of the Law in the temple of the LORD." He gave it to Shaphan, who read it. [9]Then Shaphan the secretary went to the king and reported to him: "Your officials have paid out the money that was in the temple of the LORD and have entrusted it to the workers and supervisors at the temple." [10]Then Shaphan the secretary informed the king, "Hilkiah the priest has given me a book." And Shaphan read from it in the presence of the king.

[11]When the king heard the words of the Book of the Law, he tore his robes. [12]He gave these orders to Hilkiah the priest, Ahikam son of Shaphan, Akbor son of Micaiah, Shaphan the secretary and Asaiah the king's attendant: [13]"Go and inquire of the LORD for me and for the people and for all Judah about what is written in this book that has been found. Great is the LORD's anger that burns against us because those who have gone before us have not obeyed the words of this book; they have not acted in accordance with all that is written there concerning us."

[14]Hilkiah the priest, Ahikam, Akbor, Shaphan and Asaiah went to speak to the prophet Huldah, who was the wife of Shallum son of Tikvah, the son of Harhas, keeper of the wardrobe. She lived in Jerusalem, in the New Quarter.

[15]She said to them, "This is what the LORD, the God of Israel, says: Tell the man who sent you to me, [16]'This is what the LORD says: I am going to bring disaster on this place and its people, according to everything written in the book the king of Judah has read. [17]Because they have forsaken me and burned incense to other gods and aroused my anger by all the idols their hands have made,[a] my anger will burn against this place and will not be quenched.' [18]Tell the king of Judah, who sent you to inquire of the LORD, 'This is what the LORD, the God of Israel, says concerning the words you heard: [19]Because your heart was responsive and you humbled yourself before the LORD when you heard what I have spoken against this place and its people—that they would become a curse[b] and be laid waste—and because you tore your robes and wept in my presence, I also have heard you, declares the LORD. [20]Therefore I will gather you to your ancestors, and you will be buried in peace.

[a] 17 Or *by everything they have done* [b] 19 That is, their names would be used in cursing (see Jer. 29:22); or, others would see that they are cursed.

Your eyes will not see all the disaster I am
going to bring on this place.'"
So they took her answer back to the king.

Josiah Renews the Covenant

23 Then the king called together all the elders of Judah and Jerusalem. 2He went
up to the temple of the LORD with the people of Judah, the inhabitants of Jerusalem,
the priests and the prophets—all the people
from the least to the greatest. He read in their
hearing all the words of the Book of the Covenant, which had been found in the temple
of the LORD. 3The king stood by the pillar
and renewed the covenant in the presence of
the LORD—to follow the LORD and keep his
commands, statutes and decrees with all his
heart and all his soul, thus confirming the
words of the covenant written in this book.
Then all the people pledged themselves to
the covenant.
4The king ordered Hilkiah the high priest,
the priests next in rank and the doorkeepers
to remove from the temple of the LORD all the
articles made for Baal and Asherah and all
the starry hosts. He burned them outside Jerusalem in the fields of the Kidron Valley and
took the ashes to Bethel. 5He did away with
the idolatrous priests appointed by the kings
of Judah to burn incense on the high places
of the towns of Judah and on those around Jerusalem—those who burned incense to Baal,
to the sun and moon, to the constellations and
to all the starry hosts. 6He took the Asherah
pole from the temple of the LORD to the Kidron Valley outside Jerusalem and burned it
there. He ground it to powder and scattered
the dust over the graves of the common people. 7He also tore down the quarters of the
male shrine prostitutes that were in the temple
of the LORD, the quarters where women did
weaving for Asherah.
8Josiah brought all the priests from the
towns of Judah and desecrated the high places, from Geba to Beersheba, where the priests
had burned incense. He broke down the gateway at the entrance of the Gate of Joshua, the
city governor, which was on the left of the
city gate. 9Although the priests of the high
places did not serve at the altar of the LORD
in Jerusalem, they ate unleavened bread with
their fellow priests.
10He desecrated Topheth, which was in the
Valley of Ben Hinnom, so no one could use it
to sacrifice their son or daughter in the fire to
Molek. 11He removed from the entrance to the
temple of the LORD the horses that the kings of
Judah had dedicated to the sun. They were in
the court[a] near the room of an official named
Nathan-Melek. Josiah then burned the chariots dedicated to the sun.
12He pulled down the altars the kings of
Judah had erected on the roof near the upper
room of Ahaz, and the altars Manasseh had
built in the two courts of the temple of the
LORD. He removed them from there, smashed
them to pieces and threw the rubble into the
Kidron Valley. 13The king also desecrated
the high places that were east of Jerusalem
on the south of the Hill of Corruption—the
ones Solomon king of Israel had built for Ashtoreth the vile goddess of the Sidonians, for
Chemosh the vile god of Moab, and for Molek
the detestable god of the people of Ammon.
14Josiah smashed the sacred stones and cut
down the Asherah poles and covered the sites
with human bones.
15Even the altar at Bethel, the high place
made by Jeroboam son of Nebat, who had
caused Israel to sin—even that altar and high
place he demolished. He burned the high place
and ground it to powder, and burned the Asherah pole also. 16Then Josiah looked around,
and when he saw the tombs that were there
on the hillside, he had the bones removed
from them and burned on the altar to defile
it, in accordance with the word of the LORD
proclaimed by the man of God who foretold
these things.
17The king asked, "What is that tombstone
I see?"
The people of the city said, "It marks the
tomb of the man of God who came from Judah
and pronounced against the altar of Bethel the
very things you have done to it."
18"Leave it alone," he said. "Don't let anyone
disturb his bones." So they spared his bones
and those of the prophet who had come from
Samaria.
19Just as he had done at Bethel, Josiah removed all the shrines at the high places that
the kings of Israel had built in the towns of
Samaria and that had aroused the LORD's
anger. 20Josiah slaughtered all the priests of
those high places on the altars and burned
human bones on them. Then he went back
to Jerusalem.
21The king gave this order to all the people:
"Celebrate the Passover to the LORD your God,
as it is written in this Book of the Covenant."
22Neither in the days of the judges who led
Israel nor in the days of the kings of Israel
and the kings of Judah had any such Passover
been observed. 23But in the eighteenth year
of King Josiah, this Passover was celebrated
to the LORD in Jerusalem.
24Furthermore, Josiah got rid of the mediums and spiritists, the household gods, the
idols and all the other detestable things seen
in Judah and Jerusalem. This he did to fulfill the requirements of the law written in the
book that Hilkiah the priest had discovered
in the temple of the LORD. 25Neither before
nor after Josiah was there a king like him
who turned to the LORD as he did—with all
his heart and with all his soul and with all
his strength, in accordance with all the Law
of Moses.
26Nevertheless, the LORD did not turn
away from the heat of his fierce anger, which
burned against Judah because of all that Manasseh had done to arouse his anger. 27So the
LORD said, "I will remove Judah also from
my presence as I removed Israel, and I will

[a] *11* The meaning of the Hebrew for this word is uncertain.

reject Jerusalem, the city I chose, and this temple, about which I said, 'My Name shall be there.'[a]"

28 As for the other events of Josiah's reign, and all he did, are they not written in the book of the annals of the kings of Judah?

29 While Josiah was king, Pharaoh Necho king of Egypt went up to the Euphrates River to help the king of Assyria. King Josiah marched out to meet him in battle, but Necho faced him and killed him at Megiddo. 30 Josiah's servants brought his body in a chariot from Megiddo to Jerusalem and buried him in his own tomb. And the people of the land took Jehoahaz son of Josiah and anointed him and made him king in place of his father.

Jehoahaz King of Judah

31 Jehoahaz was twenty-three years old when he became king, and he reigned in Jerusalem three months. His mother's name was Hamutal daughter of Jeremiah; she was from Libnah. 32 He did evil in the eyes of the LORD, just as his predecessors had done. 33 Pharaoh Necho put him in chains at Riblah in the land of Hamath so that he might not reign in Jerusalem, and he imposed on Judah a levy of a hundred talents[b] of silver and a talent[c] of gold. 34 Pharaoh Necho made Eliakim son of Josiah king in place of his father Josiah and changed Eliakim's name to Jehoiakim. But he took Jehoahaz and carried him off to Egypt, and there he died. 35 Jehoiakim paid Pharaoh Necho the silver and gold he demanded. In order to do so, he taxed the land and exacted the silver and gold from the people of the land according to their assessments.

Jehoiakim King of Judah

36 Jehoiakim was twenty-five years old when he became king, and he reigned in Jerusalem eleven years. His mother's name was Zebidah daughter of Pedaiah; she was from Rumah. 37 And he did evil in the eyes of the LORD, just as his predecessors had done.

24 During Jehoiakim's reign, Nebuchadnezzar king of Babylon invaded the land, and Jehoiakim became his vassal for three years. But then he turned against Nebuchadnezzar and rebelled. 2 The LORD sent Babylonian,[d] Aramean, Moabite and Ammonite raiders against him to destroy Judah, in accordance with the word of the LORD proclaimed by his servants the prophets. 3 Surely these things happened to Judah according to the LORD's command, in order to remove them from his presence because of the sins of Manasseh and all he had done, 4 including the shedding of innocent blood. For he had filled Jerusalem with innocent blood, and the LORD was not willing to forgive.

5 As for the other events of Jehoiakim's reign, and all he did, are they not written in the book of the annals of the kings of Judah? 6 Jehoiakim rested with his ancestors. And Jehoiachin his son succeeded him as king.

7 The king of Egypt did not march out from his own country again, because the king of Babylon had taken all his territory, from the Wadi of Egypt to the Euphrates River.

Jehoiachin King of Judah

8 Jehoiachin was eighteen years old when he became king, and he reigned in Jerusalem three months. His mother's name was Nehushta daughter of Elnathan; she was from Jerusalem. 9 He did evil in the eyes of the LORD, just as his father had done.

10 At that time the officers of Nebuchadnezzar king of Babylon advanced on Jerusalem and laid siege to it, 11 and Nebuchadnezzar himself came up to the city while his officers were besieging it. 12 Jehoiachin king of Judah, his mother, his attendants, his nobles and his officials all surrendered to him.

In the eighth year of the reign of the king of Babylon, he took Jehoiachin prisoner. 13 As the LORD had declared, Nebuchadnezzar removed the treasures from the temple of the LORD and from the royal palace, and cut up the gold articles that Solomon king of Israel had made for the temple of the LORD. 14 He carried all Jerusalem into exile: all the officers and fighting men, and all the skilled workers and artisans—a total of ten thousand. Only the poorest people of the land were left.

15 Nebuchadnezzar took Jehoiachin captive to Babylon. He also took from Jerusalem to Babylon the king's mother, his wives, his officials and the prominent people of the land. 16 The king of Babylon also deported to Babylon the entire force of seven thousand fighting men, strong and fit for war, and a thousand skilled workers and artisans. 17 He made Mattaniah, Jehoiachin's uncle, king in his place and changed his name to Zedekiah.

Zedekiah King of Judah

18 Zedekiah was twenty-one years old when he became king, and he reigned in Jerusalem eleven years. His mother's name was Hamutal daughter of Jeremiah; she was from Libnah. 19 He did evil in the eyes of the LORD, just as Jehoiakim had done. 20 It was because of the LORD's anger that all this happened to Jerusalem and Judah, and in the end he thrust them from his presence.

The Fall of Jerusalem

Now Zedekiah rebelled against the king of Babylon.

25 So in the ninth year of Zedekiah's reign, on the tenth day of the tenth month, Nebuchadnezzar king of Babylon marched against Jerusalem with his whole army. He encamped outside the city and built siege works all around it. 2 The city was kept under siege until the eleventh year of King Zedekiah.

[a] *27* 1 Kings 8:29 [b] *33* That is, about 3 3/4 tons or about 3.4 metric tons [c] *33* That is, about 75 pounds or about 34 kilograms [d] *2* Or *Chaldean*

3By the ninth day of the fourth[a] month the famine in the city had become so severe that there was no food for the people to eat. 4Then the city wall was broken through, and the whole army fled at night through the gate between the two walls near the king's garden, though the Babylonians[b] were surrounding the city. They fled toward the Arabah,[c] 5but the Babylonian[d] army pursued the king and overtook him in the plains of Jericho. All his soldiers were separated from him and scattered, 6and he was captured.

He was taken to the king of Babylon at Riblah, where sentence was pronounced on him. 7They killed the sons of Zedekiah before his eyes. Then they put out his eyes, bound him with bronze shackles and took him to Babylon.

8On the seventh day of the fifth month, in the nineteenth year of Nebuchadnezzar king of Babylon, Nebuzaradan commander of the imperial guard, an official of the king of Babylon, came to Jerusalem. 9He set fire to the temple of the LORD, the royal palace and all the houses of Jerusalem. Every important building he burned down. 10The whole Babylonian army under the commander of the imperial guard broke down the walls around Jerusalem. 11Nebuzaradan the commander of the guard carried into exile the people who remained in the city, along with the rest of the populace and those who had deserted to the king of Babylon. 12But the commander left behind some of the poorest people of the land to work the vineyards and fields.

13The Babylonians broke up the bronze pillars, the movable stands and the bronze Sea that were at the temple of the LORD and they carried the bronze to Babylon. 14They also took away the pots, shovels, wick trimmers, dishes and all the bronze articles used in the temple service. 15The commander of the imperial guard took away the censers and sprinkling bowls—all that were made of pure gold or silver.

16The bronze from the two pillars, the Sea and the movable stands, which Solomon had made for the temple of the LORD, was more than could be weighed. 17Each pillar was eighteen cubits[e] high. The bronze capital on top of one pillar was three cubits[f] high and was decorated with a network and pomegranates of bronze all around. The other pillar, with its network, was similar.

18The commander of the guard took as prisoners Seraiah the chief priest, Zephaniah the priest next in rank and the three doorkeepers. 19Of those still in the city, he took the officer in charge of the fighting men, and five royal advisers. He also took the secretary who was chief officer in charge of conscripting the people of the land and sixty of the conscripts who were found in the city. 20Nebuzaradan the commander took them all and brought them to the king of Babylon at Riblah. 21There at Riblah, in the land of Hamath, the king had them executed.

So Judah went into captivity, away from her land.

22Nebuchadnezzar king of Babylon appointed Gedaliah son of Ahikam, the son of Shaphan, to be over the people he had left behind in Judah. 23When all the army officers and their men heard that the king of Babylon had appointed Gedaliah as governor, they came to Gedaliah at Mizpah—Ishmael son of Nethaniah, Johanan son of Kareah, Seraiah son of Tanhumeth the Netophathite, Jaazaniah the son of the Maakathite, and their men. 24Gedaliah took an oath to reassure them and their men. "Do not be afraid of the Babylonian officials," he said. "Settle down in the land and serve the king of Babylon, and it will go well with you."

25In the seventh month, however, Ishmael son of Nethaniah, the son of Elishama, who was of royal blood, came with ten men and assassinated Gedaliah and also the men of Judah and the Babylonians who were with him at Mizpah. 26At this, all the people from the least to the greatest, together with the army officers, fled to Egypt for fear of the Babylonians.

Jehoiachin Released

27In the thirty-seventh year of the exile of Jehoiachin king of Judah, in the year Awel-Marduk became king of Babylon, he released Jehoiachin king of Judah from prison. He did this on the twenty-seventh day of the twelfth month. 28He spoke kindly to him and gave him a seat of honor higher than those of the other kings who were with him in Babylon. 29So Jehoiachin put aside his prison clothes and for the rest of his life ate regularly at the king's table. 30Day by day the king gave Jehoiachin a regular allowance as long as he lived.

[a] *3* Probable reading of the original Hebrew text (see Jer. 52:6); Masoretic Text does not have *fourth*.
[b] *4* Or *Chaldeans*; also in verses 13, 25 and 26 [c] *4* Or *the Jordan Valley* [d] *5* Or *Chaldean*; also in verses 10 and 24 [e] *17* That is, about 27 feet or about 8.1 meters [f] *17* That is, about 4 1/2 feet or about 1.4 meters

1 Chronicles

Historical Records From Adam to Abraham

To Noah's Sons

1 Adam, Seth, Enosh, 2Kenan, Mahalalel,
Jared, 3Enoch, Methuselah, Lamech, Noah.

4The sons of Noah:[a]
Shem, Ham and Japheth.

The Japhethites

5The sons[b] of Japheth:
Gomer, Magog, Madai, Javan, Tubal, Meshek and Tiras.
6The sons of Gomer:
Ashkenaz, Riphath[c] and Togarmah.
7The sons of Javan:
Elishah, Tarshish, the Kittites and the Rodanites.

The Hamites

8The sons of Ham:
Cush, Egypt, Put and Canaan.
9The sons of Cush:
Seba, Havilah, Sabta, Raamah and Sabteka.
The sons of Raamah:
Sheba and Dedan.
10Cush was the father[d] of
Nimrod, who became a mighty warrior on earth.
11Egypt was the father of
the Ludites, Anamites, Lehabites,
Naphtuhites, 12Pathrusites, Kasluhites
(from whom the Philistines came) and Caphtorites.
13Canaan was the father of
Sidon his firstborn,[e] and of the Hittites,
14Jebusites, Amorites, Girgashites,
15Hivites, Arkites, Sinites, 16Arvadites,
Zemarites and Hamathites.

The Semites

17The sons of Shem:
Elam, Ashur, Arphaxad, Lud and Aram.
The sons of Aram:[f]
Uz, Hul, Gether and Meshek.
18Arphaxad was the father of Shelah,
and Shelah the father of Eber.
19Two sons were born to Eber:
One was named Peleg,[g] because in his time the earth was divided; his brother was named Joktan.
20Joktan was the father of
Almodad, Sheleph, Hazarmaveth, Jerah, 21Hadoram, Uzal, Diklah, 22Obal,[h]
Abimael, Sheba, 23Ophir, Havilah and Jobab. All these were sons of Joktan.

24Shem, Arphaxad,[i] Shelah,
25Eber, Peleg, Reu,
26Serug, Nahor, Terah
27and Abram (that is, Abraham).

The Family of Abraham

28The sons of Abraham:
Isaac and Ishmael.

Descendants of Hagar

29These were their descendants:
Nebaioth the firstborn of Ishmael, Kedar, Adbeel, Mibsam, 30Mishma, Dumah, Massa, Hadad, Tema, 31Jetur,
Naphish and Kedemah. These were the sons of Ishmael.

Descendants of Keturah

32The sons born to Keturah, Abraham's concubine:
Zimran, Jokshan, Medan, Midian, Ishbak and Shuah.
The sons of Jokshan:
Sheba and Dedan.
33The sons of Midian:
Ephah, Epher, Hanok, Abida and Eldaah.
All these were descendants of Keturah.

Descendants of Sarah

34Abraham was the father of Isaac.
The sons of Isaac:
Esau and Israel.

Esau's Sons

35The sons of Esau:
Eliphaz, Reuel, Jeush, Jalam and Korah.
36The sons of Eliphaz:
Teman, Omar, Zepho,[j] Gatam and Kenaz;
by Timna: Amalek.[k]
37The sons of Reuel:
Nahath, Zerah, Shammah and Mizzah.

The People of Seir in Edom

38The sons of Seir:
Lotan, Shobal, Zibeon, Anah, Dishon, Ezer and Dishan.

[a] 4 Septuagint; Hebrew does not have this line. [b] 5 *Sons* may mean *descendants* or *successors* or *nations*; also in verses 6-9, 17 and 23. [c] 6 Many Hebrew manuscripts and Vulgate (see also Septuagint and Gen. 10:3); most Hebrew manuscripts *Diphath* [d] 10 *Father* may mean *ancestor* or *predecessor* or *founder*; also in verses 11, 13, 18 and 20. [e] 13 Or *of the Sidonians, the foremost* [f] 17 One Hebrew manuscript and some Septuagint manuscripts (see also Gen. 10:23); most Hebrew manuscripts do not have this line. [g] 19 *Peleg* means *division.* [h] 22 Some Hebrew manuscripts and Syriac (see also Gen. 10:28); most Hebrew manuscripts *Ebal* [i] 24 Hebrew; some Septuagint manuscripts *Arphaxad, Cainan* (see also note at Gen. 11:10) [j] 36 Many Hebrew manuscripts, some Septuagint manuscripts and Syriac (see also Gen. 36:11); most Hebrew manuscripts *Zephi* [k] 36 Some Septuagint manuscripts (see also Gen. 36:12); Hebrew *Gatam, Kenaz, Timna and Amalek*

39 The sons of Lotan:
Hori and Homam. Timna was Lotan's sister.
40 The sons of Shobal:
Alvan,[a] Manahath, Ebal, Shepho and Onam.
The sons of Zibeon:
Aiah and Anah.
41 The son of Anah:
Dishon.
The sons of Dishon:
Hemdan,[b] Eshban, Ithran and Keran.
42 The sons of Ezer:
Bilhan, Zaavan and Akan.[c]
The sons of Dishan[d]:
Uz and Aran.

The Rulers of Edom

43 These were the kings who reigned in Edom before any Israelite king reigned:
Bela son of Beor, whose city was named Dinhabah.
44 When Bela died, Jobab son of Zerah from Bozrah succeeded him as king.
45 When Jobab died, Husham from the land of the Temanites succeeded him as king.
46 When Husham died, Hadad son of Bedad, who defeated Midian in the country of Moab, succeeded him as king. His city was named Avith.
47 When Hadad died, Samlah from Masrekah succeeded him as king.
48 When Samlah died, Shaul from Rehoboth on the river[e] succeeded him as king.
49 When Shaul died, Baal-Hanan son of Akbor succeeded him as king.
50 When Baal-Hanan died, Hadad succeeded him as king. His city was named Pau,[f] and his wife's name was Mehetabel daughter of Matred, the daughter
of Me-Zahab. 51 Hadad also died.

The chiefs of Edom were:
Timna, Alvah, Jetheth, 52 Oholibamah,
Elah, Pinon, 53 Kenaz, Teman, Mibzar,
54 Magdiel and Iram. These were the chiefs of Edom.

Israel's Sons

2 These were the sons of Israel:
Reuben, Simeon, Levi, Judah, Issachar,
Zebulun, 2 Dan, Joseph, Benjamin, Naphtali, Gad and Asher.

Judah

To Hezron's Sons

3 The sons of Judah:
Er, Onan and Shelah. These three were born to him by a Canaanite woman, the daughter of Shua. Er, Judah's firstborn, was wicked in the LORD's sight; so the LORD put him to death.
4 Judah's daughter-in-law Tamar bore Perez and Zerah to Judah. He had five sons in all.

5 The sons of Perez:
Hezron and Hamul.
6 The sons of Zerah:
Zimri, Ethan, Heman, Kalkol and Darda[g]—five in all.
7 The son of Karmi:
Achar,[h] who brought trouble on Israel by violating the ban on taking devoted things.[i]
8 The son of Ethan:
Azariah.
9 The sons born to Hezron were:
Jerahmeel, Ram and Caleb.[j]

From Ram Son of Hezron

10 Ram was the father of
Amminadab, and Amminadab the father of Nahshon, the leader of the people of Judah. 11 Nahshon was the father
of Salmon,[k] Salmon the father of Boaz,
12 Boaz the father of Obed and Obed the father of Jesse.
13 Jesse was the father of
Eliab his firstborn; the second son
was Abinadab, the third Shimea, 14 the
fourth Nethanel, the fifth Raddai, 15 the
sixth Ozem and the seventh David.
16 Their sisters were Zeruiah and Abigail. Zeruiah's three sons were Abishai, Joab and Asahel. 17 Abigail was the
mother of Amasa, whose father was Jether the Ishmaelite.

Caleb Son of Hezron

18 Caleb son of Hezron had children by his wife Azubah (and by Jerioth). These were her sons: Jesher, Shobab and Ar-
don. 19 When Azubah died, Caleb mar-
ried Ephrath, who bore him Hur. 20 Hur
was the father of Uri, and Uri the father of Bezalel.
21 Later, Hezron, when he was sixty years old, married the daughter of Makir the father of Gilead. He made love to her,
and she bore him Segub. 22 Segub was
the father of Jair, who controlled twenty-three towns in Gilead. 23 (But Geshur
and Aram captured Havvoth Jair,[l] as well as Kenath with its surrounding settlements—sixty towns.) All these

[a] *40* Many Hebrew manuscripts and some Septuagint manuscripts (see also Gen. 36:23); most Hebrew manuscripts *Alian* [b] *41* Many Hebrew manuscripts and some Septuagint manuscripts (see also Gen. 36:26); most Hebrew manuscripts *Hamran* [c] *42* Many Hebrew and Septuagint manuscripts (see also Gen. 36:27); most Hebrew manuscripts *Zaavan, Jaakan* [d] *42* See Gen. 36:28; Hebrew *Dishon,* a variant of *Dishan* [e] *48* Possibly the Euphrates [f] *50* Many Hebrew manuscripts, some Septuagint manuscripts, Vulgate and Syriac (see also Gen. 36:39); most Hebrew manuscripts *Pai* [g] *6* Many Hebrew manuscripts, some Septuagint manuscripts and Syriac (see also 1 Kings 4:31); most Hebrew manuscripts *Dara* [h] *7 Achar* means *trouble*; *Achar* is called *Achan* in Joshua. [i] *7* The Hebrew term refers to the irrevocable giving over of things or persons to the LORD, often by totally destroying them. [j] *9* Hebrew *Kelubai,* a variant of *Caleb* [k] *11* Septuagint (see also Ruth 4:21); Hebrew *Salma* [l] *23* Or *captured the settlements of Jair*

were descendants of Makir the father of Gilead.

24 After Hezron died in Caleb Ephrathah, Abijah the wife of Hezron bore him Ashhur the father[a] of Tekoa.

Jerahmeel Son of Hezron

25 The sons of Jerahmeel the firstborn of Hezron:
Ram his firstborn, Bunah, Oren, Ozem and[b] Ahijah.
26 Jerahmeel had another wife, whose name was Atarah; she was the mother of Onam.
27 The sons of Ram the firstborn of Jerahmeel:
Maaz, Jamin and Eker.
28 The sons of Onam:
Shammai and Jada.
The sons of Shammai:
Nadab and Abishur.
29 Abishur's wife was named Abihail, who bore him Ahban and Molid.
30 The sons of Nadab:
Seled and Appaim. Seled died without children.
31 The son of Appaim:
Ishi, who was the father of Sheshan.
Sheshan was the father of Ahlai.
32 The sons of Jada, Shammai's brother:
Jether and Jonathan. Jether died without children.
33 The sons of Jonathan:
Peleth and Zaza.
These were the descendants of Jerahmeel.
34 Sheshan had no sons—only daughters. He had an Egyptian servant named Jarha.
35 Sheshan gave his daughter in marriage to his servant Jarha, and she bore him Attai.
36 Attai was the father of Nathan,
Nathan the father of Zabad,
37 Zabad the father of Ephlal,
Ephlal the father of Obed,
38 Obed the father of Jehu,
Jehu the father of Azariah,
39 Azariah the father of Helez,
Helez the father of Eleasah,
40 Eleasah the father of Sismai,
Sismai the father of Shallum,
41 Shallum the father of Jekamiah,
and Jekamiah the father of Elishama.

The Clans of Caleb

42 The sons of Caleb the brother of Jerahmeel:
Mesha his firstborn, who was the father of Ziph, and his son Mareshah,[c] who was the father of Hebron.
43 The sons of Hebron:
Korah, Tappuah, Rekem and Shema.
44 Shema was the father of Raham, and Raham the father of Jorkeam. Rekem was the father of Shammai.
45 The son of Shammai was Maon, and Maon was the father of Beth Zur.
46 Caleb's concubine Ephah was the mother of Haran, Moza and Gazez. Haran was the father of Gazez.
47 The sons of Jahdai:
Regem, Jotham, Geshan, Pelet, Ephah and Shaaph.
48 Caleb's concubine Maakah was the mother of Sheber and Tirhanah.
49 She also gave birth to Shaaph the father of Madmannah and to Sheva the father of Makbenah and Gibea. Caleb's daughter was Aksah.
50 These were the descendants of Caleb.

The sons of Hur the firstborn of Ephrathah:
Shobal the father of Kiriath Jearim,
51 Salma the father of Bethlehem, and Hareph the father of Beth Gader.
52 The descendants of Shobal the father of Kiriath Jearim were:
Haroeh, half the Manahathites,
53 and the clans of Kiriath Jearim: the Ithrites, Puthites, Shumathites and Mishraites. From these descended the Zorathites and Eshtaolites.
54 The descendants of Salma:
Bethlehem, the Netophathites, Atroth Beth Joab, half the Manahathites, the Zorites,
55 and the clans of scribes[d] who lived at Jabez: the Tirathites, Shimeathites and Sucathites. These are the Kenites who came from Hammath, the father of the Rekabites.[e]

The Sons of David

3 These were the sons of David born to him in Hebron:
The firstborn was Amnon the son of Ahinoam of Jezreel;
the second, Daniel the son of Abigail of Carmel;
2 the third, Absalom the son of Maakah daughter of Talmai king of Geshur;
the fourth, Adonijah the son of Haggith;
3 the fifth, Shephatiah the son of Abital;
and the sixth, Ithream, by his wife Eglah.
4 These six were born to David in Hebron, where he reigned seven years and six months.
David reigned in Jerusalem thirty-three years,
5 and these were the children born to him there:
Shammua,[f] Shobab, Nathan and Solomon. These four were by Bathsheba[g] daughter of Ammiel.
6 There were also Ibhar, Elishua,[h] Eliphelet,
7 Nogah, Nepheg, Japhia,
8 Elishama, Eliada and

[a] 24 *Father* may mean *civic leader* or *military leader*; also in verses 42, 45, 49-52 and possibly elsewhere. [b] 25 Or *Oren and Ozem, by* [c] 42 The meaning of the Hebrew for this phrase is uncertain. [d] 55 Or *of the Sopherites* [e] 55 Or *father of Beth Rekab* [f] 5 Hebrew *Shimea,* a variant of *Shammua* [g] 5 One Hebrew manuscript and Vulgate (see also Septuagint and 2 Samuel 11:3); most Hebrew manuscripts *Bathshua* [h] 6 Two Hebrew manuscripts (see also 2 Samuel 5:15 and 1 Chron. 14:5); most Hebrew manuscripts *Elishama*

Eliphelet—nine in all. 9All these were
the sons of David, besides his sons by his
concubines. And Tamar was their sister.

The Kings of Judah

10 Solomon's son was Rehoboam,
Abijah his son,
Asa his son,
Jehoshaphat his son,
11 Jehoram[a] his son,
Ahaziah his son,
Joash his son,
12 Amaziah his son,
Azariah his son,
Jotham his son,
13 Ahaz his son,
Hezekiah his son,
Manasseh his son,
14 Amon his son,
Josiah his son.
15 The sons of Josiah:
Johanan the firstborn,
Jehoiakim the second son,
Zedekiah the third,
Shallum the fourth.
16 The successors of Jehoiakim:
Jehoiachin[b] his son,
and Zedekiah.

The Royal Line After the Exile

17 The descendants of Jehoiachin the captive:
Shealtiel his son, 18Malkiram, Pedaiah,
Shenazzar, Jekamiah, Hoshama and
Nedabiah.
19 The sons of Pedaiah:
Zerubbabel and Shimei.
The sons of Zerubbabel:
Meshullam and Hananiah.
Shelomith was their sister.
20 There were also five others:
Hashubah, Ohel, Berekiah, Hasadiah
and Jushab-Hesed.
21 The descendants of Hananiah:
Pelatiah and Jeshaiah, and the sons of
Rephaiah, of Arnan, of Obadiah and of
Shekaniah.
22 The descendants of Shekaniah:
Shemaiah and his sons:
Hattush, Igal, Bariah, Neariah and
Shaphat—six in all.
23 The sons of Neariah:
Elioenai, Hizkiah and Azrikam—three
in all.
24 The sons of Elioenai:
Hodaviah, Eliashib, Pelaiah, Akkub,
Johanan, Delaiah and Anani—seven
in all.

Other Clans of Judah

4 The descendants of Judah:
Perez, Hezron, Karmi, Hur and Shobal.
2 Reaiah son of Shobal was the father of
Jahath, and Jahath the father of Ahu-
mai and Lahad. These were the clans
of the Zorathites.
3 These were the sons[c] of Etam:
Jezreel, Ishma and Idbash. Their sister
was named Hazzelelponi. 4Penuel was
the father of Gedor, and Ezer the father
of Hushah.
These were the descendants of Hur, the
firstborn of Ephrathah and father[d] of
Bethlehem.
5 Ashhur the father of Tekoa had two
wives, Helah and Naarah.
6 Naarah bore him Ahuzzam, Hepher, Tem-
eni and Haahashtari. These were the
descendants of Naarah.
7 The sons of Helah:
Zereth, Zohar, Ethnan, 8and Koz, who
was the father of Anub and Hazzobe-
bah and of the clans of Aharhel son of
Harum.

9 Jabez was more honorable than his brothers. His mother had named him Jabez,[e] saying, "I gave birth to him in pain." 10Jabez cried
out to the God of Israel, "Oh, that you would
bless me and enlarge my territory! Let your
hand be with me, and keep me from harm so
that I will be free from pain." And God granted his request.

11 Kelub, Shuhah's brother, was the father
of Mehir, who was the father of Eshton.
12Eshton was the father of Beth Rapha,
Paseah and Tehinnah the father of Ir
Nahash.[f] These were the men of Rekah.
13 The sons of Kenaz:
Othniel and Seraiah.
The sons of Othniel:
Hathath and Meonothai.[g] 14Meonothai
was the father of Ophrah.
Seraiah was the father of Joab,
the father of Ge Harashim.[h] It was
called this because its people were
skilled workers.
15 The sons of Caleb son of Jephunneh:
Iru, Elah and Naam.
The son of Elah:
Kenaz.
16 The sons of Jehallelel:
Ziph, Ziphah, Tiria and Asarel.
17 The sons of Ezrah:
Jether, Mered, Epher and Jalon. One
of Mered's wives gave birth to Miriam,
Shammai and Ishbah the father of Eshtemoa. 18(His wife from the tribe of Judah gave birth to Jered the father of
Gedor, Heber the father of Soko, and
Jekuthiel the father of Zanoah.) These
were the children of Pharaoh's daughter Bithiah, whom Mered had married.
19 The sons of Hodiah's wife, the sister of
Naham:

[a] *11* Hebrew *Joram*, a variant of *Jehoram* [b] *16* Hebrew *Jeconiah*, a variant of *Jehoiachin*; also in verse 17 [c] *3* Some Septuagint manuscripts (see also Vulgate); Hebrew *father* [d] *4* *Father* may mean *civic leader* or *military leader*; also in verses 12, 14, 17, 18 and possibly elsewhere. [e] *9* *Jabez* sounds like the Hebrew for *pain*. [f] *12* Or *of the city of Nahash* [g] *13* Some Septuagint manuscripts and Vulgate; Hebrew does not have *and Meonothai*. [h] *14* *Ge Harashim* means *valley of skilled workers*.

the father of Keilah the Garmite, and
Eshtemoa the Maakathite.
20The sons of Shimon:
Amnon, Rinnah, Ben-Hanan and Tilon.
The descendants of Ishi:
Zoheth and Ben-Zoheth.
21The sons of Shelah son of Judah:
Er the father of Lekah, Laadah the father of Mareshah and the clans of the
linen workers at Beth Ashbea, 22Jokim,
the men of Kozeba, and Joash and Sa-
raph, who ruled in Moab and Jashubi
Lehem. (These records are from ancient times.) 23They were the potters
who lived at Netaim and Gederah; they
stayed there and worked for the king.

Simeon

24The descendants of Simeon:
Nemuel, Jamin, Jarib, Zerah and Shaul;
25Shallum was Shaul's son, Mibsam his
son and Mishma his son.
26The descendants of Mishma:
Hammuel his son, Zakkur his son and
Shimei his son.
27Shimei had sixteen sons and six daughters, but his brothers did not have many children; so their entire clan did not become as
numerous as the people of Judah. 28They lived
in Beersheba, Moladah, Hazar Shual, 29Bil-
hah, Ezem, Tolad, 30Bethuel, Hormah, Ziklag,
31Beth Markaboth, Hazar Susim, Beth Biri
and Shaaraim. These were their towns until
the reign of David. 32Their surrounding villages were Etam, Ain, Rimmon, Token and
Ashan—five towns— 33and all the villages
around these towns as far as Baalath.[a] These
were their settlements. And they kept a genealogical record.

34Meshobab, Jamlech, Joshah son of Amaziah, 35Joel, Jehu son of Joshibiah, the
son of Seraiah, the son of Asiel, 36also
Elioenai, Jaakobah, Jeshohaiah, Asaiah, Adiel, Jesimiel, Benaiah, 37and Ziza
son of Shiphi, the son of Allon, the son
of Jedaiah, the son of Shimri, the son of
Shemaiah.

38The men listed above by name were leaders of their clans. Their families increased
greatly, 39and they went to the outskirts of
Gedor to the east of the valley in search of
pasture for their flocks. 40They found rich,
good pasture, and the land was spacious,
peaceful and quiet. Some Hamites had lived
there formerly.
41The men whose names were listed came
in the days of Hezekiah king of Judah. They
attacked the Hamites in their dwellings and
also the Meunites who were there and completely destroyed[b] them, as is evident to this
day. Then they settled in their place, because
there was pasture for their flocks. 42And five
hundred of these Simeonites, led by Pelatiah, Neariah, Rephaiah and Uzziel, the sons of
Ishi, invaded the hill country of Seir. 43They
killed the remaining Amalekites who had escaped, and they have lived there to this day.

Reuben

5 The sons of Reuben the firstborn of Israel
(he was the firstborn, but when he defiled
his father's marriage bed, his rights as firstborn were given to the sons of Joseph son of
Israel; so he could not be listed in the genealogical record in accordance with his birthright, 2and though Judah was the strongest of
his brothers and a ruler came from him, the
rights of the firstborn belonged to Joseph)—
3the sons of Reuben the firstborn of Israel:
Hanok, Pallu, Hezron and Karmi.
4The descendants of Joel:
Shemaiah his son, Gog his son,
Shimei his son, 5Micah his son,
Reaiah his son, Baal his son,
6and Beerah his son, whom Tiglath-Pileser[c] king of Assyria took into exile.
Beerah was a leader of the Reubenites.
7Their relatives by clans, listed according
to their genealogical records:
Jeiel the chief, Zechariah, 8and Bela son
of Azaz, the son of Shema, the son of
Joel. They settled in the area from Aroer to Nebo and Baal Meon. 9To the east
they occupied the land up to the edge of
the desert that extends to the Euphrates River, because their livestock had
increased in Gilead.
10During Saul's reign they waged war
against the Hagrites, who were defeated
at their hands; they occupied the dwellings of the Hagrites throughout the entire
region east of Gilead.

Gad

11The Gadites lived next to them in Bashan,
as far as Salekah:
12Joel was the chief, Shapham the second, then Janai and Shaphat, in Bashan.
13Their relatives, by families, were:
Michael, Meshullam, Sheba, Jorai, Ja-
kan, Zia and Eber—seven in all.
14These were the sons of Abihail son
of Huri, the son of Jaroah, the son of
Gilead, the son of Michael, the son of
Jeshishai, the son of Jahdo, the son of
Buz.
15Ahi son of Abdiel, the son of Guni, was
head of their family.
16The Gadites lived in Gilead, in Bashan
and its outlying villages, and on all the
pasturelands of Sharon as far as they
extended.
17All these were entered in the genealogical
records during the reigns of Jotham king of
Judah and Jeroboam king of Israel.

18The Reubenites, the Gadites and the half-
tribe of Manasseh had 44,760 men ready for

[a] *33* Some Septuagint manuscripts (see also Joshua 19:8); Hebrew *Baal* [b] *41* The Hebrew term refers to the irrevocable giving over of things or persons to the LORD, often by totally destroying them.
[c] *6* Hebrew *Tilgath-Pilneser*, a variant of *Tiglath-Pileser*; also in verse 26

military service—able-bodied men who could
handle shield and sword, who could use a bow,
and who were trained for battle. 19They waged
war against the Hagrites, Jetur, Naphish and
Nodab. 20They were helped in fighting them,
and God delivered the Hagrites and all their
allies into their hands, because they cried out
to him during the battle. He answered their
prayers, because they trusted in him. 21They
seized the livestock of the Hagrites—fifty
thousand camels, two hundred fifty thousand
sheep and two thousand donkeys. They also
took one hundred thousand people captive,
22and many others fell slain, because the battle was God's. And they occupied the land
until the exile.

The Half-Tribe of Manasseh

23The people of the half-tribe of Manasseh were numerous; they settled in the land
from Bashan to Baal Hermon, that is, to Senir
(Mount Hermon).

24These were the heads of their families:
Epher, Ishi, Eliel, Azriel, Jeremiah, Hodaviah
and Jahdiel. They were brave warriors, famous men, and heads of their families. 25But
they were unfaithful to the God of their ancestors and prostituted themselves to the gods
of the peoples of the land, whom God had destroyed before them. 26So the God of Israel
stirred up the spirit of Pul king of Assyria
(that is, Tiglath-Pileser king of Assyria), who
took the Reubenites, the Gadites and the half-
tribe of Manasseh into exile. He took them to
Halah, Habor, Hara and the river of Gozan,
where they are to this day.

Levi

6 [a] The sons of Levi:
Gershon, Kohath and Merari.
2The sons of Kohath:
Amram, Izhar, Hebron and Uzziel.
3The children of Amram:
Aaron, Moses and Miriam.
The sons of Aaron:
Nadab, Abihu, Eleazar and Ithamar.
4Eleazar was the father of Phinehas,
Phinehas the father of Abishua,
5Abishua the father of Bukki,
Bukki the father of Uzzi,
6Uzzi the father of Zerahiah,
Zerahiah the father of Meraioth,
7Meraioth the father of Amariah,
Amariah the father of Ahitub,
8Ahitub the father of Zadok,
Zadok the father of Ahimaaz,
9Ahimaaz the father of Azariah,
Azariah the father of Johanan,
10Johanan the father of Azariah (it was
he who served as priest in the temple
Solomon built in Jerusalem),
11Azariah the father of Amariah,
Amariah the father of Ahitub,
12Ahitub the father of Zadok,
Zadok the father of Shallum,
13Shallum the father of Hilkiah,
Hilkiah the father of Azariah,
14Azariah the father of Seraiah,
and Seraiah the father of Jozadak.[b]
15Jozadak was deported when the LORD
sent Judah and Jerusalem into exile by
the hand of Nebuchadnezzar.

16The sons of Levi:
Gershon,[c] Kohath and Merari.
17These are the names of the sons of Ger-
shon:
Libni and Shimei.
18The sons of Kohath:
Amram, Izhar, Hebron and Uzziel.
19The sons of Merari:
Mahli and Mushi.
These are the clans of the Levites listed
according to their fathers:
20Of Gershon:
Libni his son, Jahath his son,
Zimmah his son, 21Joah his son,
Iddo his son, Zerah his son
and Jeatherai his son.
22The descendants of Kohath:
Amminadab his son, Korah his son,
Assir his son, 23Elkanah his son,
Ebiasaph his son, Assir his son,
24Tahath his son, Uriel his son,
Uzziah his son and Shaul his son.
25The descendants of Elkanah:
Amasai, Ahimoth,
26Elkanah his son,[d] Zophai his son,
Nahath his son, 27Eliab his son,
Jeroham his son, Elkanah his son
and Samuel his son.[e]
28The sons of Samuel:
Joel[f] the firstborn
and Abijah the second son.
29The descendants of Merari:
Mahli, Libni his son,
Shimei his son, Uzzah his son,
30Shimea his son, Haggiah his son
and Asaiah his son.

The Temple Musicians

31These are the men David put in charge of
the music in the house of the LORD after the
ark came to rest there. 32They ministered with
music before the tabernacle, the tent of meeting, until Solomon built the temple of the LORD
in Jerusalem. They performed their duties according to the regulations laid down for them.
33Here are the men who served, together
with their sons:
From the Kohathites:
Heman, the musician,
the son of Joel, the son of Samuel,
34the son of Elkanah, the son of Jeroham,
the son of Eliel, the son of Toah,

[a] In Hebrew texts 6:1-15 is numbered 5:27-41, and 6:16-81 is numbered 6:1-66. [b] *14* Hebrew *Jehozadak*, a variant of *Jozadak*; also in verse 15 [c] *16* Hebrew *Gershom*, a variant of *Gershon*; also in verses 17, 20, 43, 62 and 71 [d] *26* Some Hebrew manuscripts, Septuagint and Syriac; most Hebrew manuscripts *Ahimoth* [26]*and Elkanah. The sons of Elkanah:* [e] *27* Some Septuagint manuscripts (see also 1 Samuel 1:19,20 and 1 Chron. 6:33,34); Hebrew does not have *and Samuel his son.* [f] *28* Some Septuagint manuscripts and Syriac (see also 1 Samuel 8:2 and 1 Chron. 6:33); Hebrew does not have *Joel*.

35 the son of Zuph, the son of Elkanah,
the son of Mahath, the son of Amasai,
36 the son of Elkanah, the son of Joel,
the son of Azariah, the son of Zephaniah,
37 the son of Tahath, the son of Assir,
the son of Ebiasaph, the son of Korah,
38 the son of Izhar, the son of Kohath,
the son of Levi, the son of Israel;
39 and Heman's associate Asaph, who served at his right hand:
Asaph son of Berekiah, the son of Shimea,
40 the son of Michael, the son of Baaseiah,[a]
the son of Malkijah, 41 the son of Ethni,
the son of Zerah, the son of Adaiah,
42 the son of Ethan, the son of Zimmah,
the son of Shimei, 43 the son of Jahath,
the son of Gershon, the son of Levi;
44 and from their associates, the Merarites, at his left hand:
Ethan son of Kishi, the son of Abdi,
the son of Malluk, 45 the son of Hashabiah,
the son of Amaziah, the son of Hilkiah,
46 the son of Amzi, the son of Bani,
the son of Shemer, 47 the son of Mahli,
the son of Mushi, the son of Merari,
the son of Levi.

48 Their fellow Levites were assigned to all the other duties of the tabernacle, the house of God. 49 But Aaron and his descendants were the ones who presented offerings on the altar of burnt offering and on the altar of incense in connection with all that was done in the Most Holy Place, making atonement for Israel, in accordance with all that Moses the servant of God had commanded.

50 These were the descendants of Aaron:
Eleazar his son, Phinehas his son,
Abishua his son, 51 Bukki his son,
Uzzi his son, Zerahiah his son,
52 Meraioth his son, Amariah his son,
Ahitub his son, 53 Zadok his son
and Ahimaaz his son.

54 These were the locations of their settlements allotted as their territory (they were assigned to the descendants of Aaron who were from the Kohathite clan, because the first lot was for them):

55 They were given Hebron in Judah
with its surrounding pasturelands. 56 But
the fields and villages around the city were given to Caleb son of Jephunneh.
57 So the descendants of Aaron were given Hebron (a city of refuge), and Libnah,[b] Jattir, Eshtemoa, 58 Hilen, Debir,
59 Ashan, Juttah[c] and Beth Shemesh,
together with their pasturelands. 60 And
from the tribe of Benjamin they were given Gibeon,[d] Geba, Alemeth and Anathoth, together with their pasturelands.

The total number of towns distributed among the Kohathite clans came to thirteen.

61 The rest of Kohath's descendants were allotted ten towns from the clans of half the tribe of Manasseh.

62 The descendants of Gershon, clan by clan, were allotted thirteen towns from the tribes of Issachar, Asher and Naphtali, and from the part of the tribe of Manasseh that is in Bashan.

63 The descendants of Merari, clan by clan, were allotted twelve towns from the tribes of Reuben, Gad and Zebulun.

64 So the Israelites gave the Levites these
towns and their pasturelands. 65 From the
tribes of Judah, Simeon and Benjamin they allotted the previously named towns.

66 Some of the Kohathite clans were given as their territory towns from the tribe of Ephraim.

67 In the hill country of Ephraim they were given Shechem (a city of refuge),
and Gezer,[e] 68 Jokmeam, Beth Horon,
69 Aijalon and Gath Rimmon, together with their pasturelands.
70 And from half the tribe of Manasseh the Israelites gave Aner and Bileam, together with their pasturelands, to the rest of the Kohathite clans.

71 The Gershonites received the following:
From the clan of the half-tribe of Manasseh
they received Golan in Bashan and also Ashtaroth, together with their pasturelands;
72 from the tribe of Issachar
they received Kedesh, Daberath, 73 Ramoth and Anem, together with their pasturelands;
74 from the tribe of Asher
they received Mashal, Abdon, 75 Hukok and Rehob, together with their pasturelands;
76 and from the tribe of Naphtali
they received Kedesh in Galilee, Hammon and Kiriathaim, together with their pasturelands.

77 The Merarites (the rest of the Levites) received the following:
From the tribe of Zebulun
they received Jokneam, Kartah,[f] Rimmono and Tabor, together with their pasturelands;
78 from the tribe of Reuben across the Jordan east of Jericho
they received Bezer in the wilderness,
Jahzah, 79 Kedemoth and Mephaath,
together with their pasturelands;
80 and from the tribe of Gad
they received Ramoth in Gilead, Mahanaim, 81 Heshbon and Jazer, together with their pasturelands.

[a] *40* Most Hebrew manuscripts; some Hebrew manuscripts, one Septuagint manuscript and Syriac *Maaseiah* [b] *57* See Joshua 21:13; Hebrew *given the cities of refuge: Hebron, Libnah.* [c] *59* Syriac (see also Septuagint and Joshua 21:16); Hebrew does not have *Juttah.* [d] *60* See Joshua 21:17; Hebrew does not have *Gibeon.* [e] *67* See Joshua 21:21; Hebrew *given the cities of refuge: Shechem, Gezer.* [f] *77* See Septuagint and Joshua 21:34; Hebrew does not have *Jokneam, Kartah.*

Issachar

7 The sons of Issachar:
Tola, Puah, Jashub and Shimron—four in all.
2 The sons of Tola:
Uzzi, Rephaiah, Jeriel, Jahmai, Ibsam and Samuel—heads of their families. During the reign of David, the descendants of Tola listed as fighting men in their genealogy numbered 22,600.
3 The son of Uzzi:
Izrahiah.
The sons of Izrahiah:
Michael, Obadiah, Joel and Ishiah. All
five of them were chiefs. 4According to
their family genealogy, they had 36,000 men ready for battle, for they had many wives and children.
5 The relatives who were fighting men belonging to all the clans of Issachar, as listed in their genealogy, were 87,000 in all.

Benjamin

6 Three sons of Benjamin:
Bela, Beker and Jediael.
7 The sons of Bela:
Ezbon, Uzzi, Uzziel, Jerimoth and Iri, heads of families—five in all. Their genealogical record listed 22,034 fighting men.
8 The sons of Beker:
Zemirah, Joash, Eliezer, Elioenai, Omri, Jeremoth, Abijah, Anathoth and Alemeth. All these were the sons
of Beker. 9Their genealogical record
listed the heads of families and 20,200 fighting men.
10 The son of Jediael:
Bilhan.
The sons of Bilhan:
Jeush, Benjamin, Ehud, Kenaanah, Zethan, Tarshish and Ahishahar.
11All these sons of Jediael were heads
of families. There were 17,200 fighting men ready to go out to war.
12 The Shuppites and Huppites were the descendants of Ir, and the Hushites[a] the descendants of Aher.

Naphtali

13 The sons of Naphtali:
Jahziel, Guni, Jezer and Shillem[b]—the descendants of Bilhah.

Manasseh

14 The descendants of Manasseh:
Asriel was his descendant through his Aramean concubine. She gave birth
to Makir the father of Gilead. 15Makir
took a wife from among the Huppites and Shuppites. His sister's name was Maakah.
Another descendant was named Zelophehad, who had only daughters.
16Makir's wife Maakah gave birth to a son and named him Peresh. His brother was named Sheresh, and his sons were Ulam and Rakem.
17 The son of Ulam:
Bedan.
These were the sons of Gilead son of Makir, the son of Manasseh. 18His sister
Hammoleketh gave birth to Ishhod, Abiezer and Mahlah.
19 The sons of Shemida were:
Ahian, Shechem, Likhi and Aniam.

Ephraim

20 The descendants of Ephraim:
Shuthelah, Bered his son,
Tahath his son, Eleadah his son,
Tahath his son, 21Zabad his son
and Shuthelah his son.
Ezer and Elead were killed by the native-born men of Gath, when they went
down to seize their livestock. 22Their fa-
ther Ephraim mourned for them many days, and his relatives came to comfort
him. 23Then he made love to his wife
again, and she became pregnant and gave birth to a son. He named him Beriah,[c] because there had been misfortune in
his family. 24His daughter was Sheerah,
who built Lower and Upper Beth Horon as well as Uzzen Sheerah.
25 Rephah was his son, Resheph his son,[d]
Telah his son, Tahan his son,
26 Ladan his son, Ammihud his son,
Elishama his son, 27Nun his son
and Joshua his son.
28Their lands and settlements included Bethel and its surrounding villages, Naaran to the east, Gezer and its villages to the west, and Shechem and its villages all the way to
Ayyah and its villages. 29Along the borders
of Manasseh were Beth Shan, Taanach, Megiddo and Dor, together with their villages. The descendants of Joseph son of Israel lived in these towns.

Asher

30 The sons of Asher:
Imnah, Ishvah, Ishvi and Beriah. Their sister was Serah.
31 The sons of Beriah:
Heber and Malkiel, who was the father of Birzaith.
32 Heber was the father of Japhlet, Shomer and Hotham and of their sister Shua.
33 The sons of Japhlet:
Pasak, Bimhal and Ashvath.
These were Japhlet's sons.
34 The sons of Shomer:
Ahi, Rohgah,[e] Hubbah and Aram.
35 The sons of his brother Helem:
Zophah, Imna, Shelesh and Amal.

[a] 12 Or *Ir. The sons of Dan: Hushim,* (see Gen. 46:23); Hebrew does not have *The sons of Dan.*
[b] 13 Some Hebrew and Septuagint manuscripts (see also Gen. 46:24 and Num. 26:49); most Hebrew manuscripts *Shallum*
[c] 23 *Beriah* sounds like the Hebrew for *misfortune.*
[d] 25 Some Septuagint manuscripts; Hebrew does not have *his son.*
[e] 34 Or *of his brother Shomer: Rohgah*

36 The sons of Zophah:
Suah, Harnepher, Shual, Beri, Imrah,
37 Bezer, Hod, Shamma, Shilshah, Ithran[a] and Beera.
38 The sons of Jether:
Jephunneh, Pispah and Ara.
39 The sons of Ulla:
Arah, Hanniel and Rizia.
40 All these were descendants of Asher—
heads of families, choice men, brave warriors
and outstanding leaders. The number of men
ready for battle, as listed in their genealogy,
was 26,000.

The Genealogy of Saul the Benjamite

8 Benjamin was the father of Bela his firstborn,
Ashbel the second son, Aharah the
third,
2 Nohah the fourth and Rapha the fifth.
3 The sons of Bela were:
Addar, Gera, Abihud,[b] 4 Abishua, Naaman, Ahoah, 5 Gera, Shephuphan and
Huram.
6 These were the descendants of Ehud, who
were heads of families of those living in
Geba and were deported to Manahath:
7 Naaman, Ahijah, and Gera, who deported them and who was the father
of Uzza and Ahihud.
8 Sons were born to Shaharaim in Moab
after he had divorced his wives Hushim
and Baara. 9 By his wife Hodesh he had
Jobab, Zibia, Mesha, Malkam, 10 Jeuz,
Sakia and Mirmah. These were his
sons, heads of families. 11 By Hushim
he had Abitub and Elpaal.
12 The sons of Elpaal:
Eber, Misham, Shemed (who built Ono
and Lod with its surrounding villages), 13 and Beriah and Shema, who were
heads of families of those living in Aijalon and who drove out the inhabitants
of Gath.
14 Ahio, Shashak, Jeremoth, 15 Zebadiah,
Arad, Eder, 16 Michael, Ishpah and Joha
were the sons of Beriah.
17 Zebadiah, Meshullam, Hizki, Heber,
18 Ishmerai, Izliah and Jobab were the
sons of Elpaal.
19 Jakim, Zikri, Zabdi, 20 Elienai, Zillethai,
Eliel, 21 Adaiah, Beraiah and Shimrath
were the sons of Shimei.
22 Ishpan, Eber, Eliel, 23 Abdon, Zikri, Hanan, 24 Hananiah, Elam, Anthothijah,
25 Iphdeiah and Penuel were the sons of
Shashak.
26 Shamsherai, Shehariah, Athaliah, 27 Jaa-
reshiah, Elijah and Zikri were the sons
of Jeroham.
28 All these were heads of families, chiefs
as listed in their genealogy, and they lived
in Jerusalem.

29 Jeiel[c] the father[d] of Gibeon lived in Gibeon.
His wife's name was Maakah, 30 and his
firstborn son was Abdon, followed by
Zur, Kish, Baal, Ner,[e] Nadab, 31 Gedor,
Ahio, Zeker 32 and Mikloth, who was
the father of Shimeah. They too lived
near their relatives in Jerusalem.
33 Ner was the father of Kish, Kish the father
of Saul, and Saul the father of Jonathan, Malki-Shua, Abinadab and Esh-
Baal.[f]
34 The son of Jonathan:
Merib-Baal,[g] who was the father of Micah.
35 The sons of Micah:
Pithon, Melek, Tarea and Ahaz.
36 Ahaz was the father of Jehoaddah, Jehoaddah was the father of Alemeth,
Azmaveth and Zimri, and Zimri was
the father of Moza. 37 Moza was the
father of Binea; Raphah was his son,
Eleasah his son and Azel his son.
38 Azel had six sons, and these were their
names:
Azrikam, Bokeru, Ishmael, Sheariah,
Obadiah and Hanan. All these were the
sons of Azel.
39 The sons of his brother Eshek:
Ulam his firstborn, Jeush the second
son and Eliphelet the third. 40 The sons
of Ulam were brave warriors who could
handle the bow. They had many sons
and grandsons—150 in all.
All these were the descendants of Benjamin.

9 All Israel was listed in the genealogies recorded in the book of the kings of Israel
and Judah. They were taken captive to Babylon because of their unfaithfulness.

The People in Jerusalem

2 Now the first to resettle on their own property in their own towns were some Israelites,
priests, Levites and temple servants.
3 Those from Judah, from Benjamin, and
from Ephraim and Manasseh who lived in
Jerusalem were:
4 Uthai son of Ammihud, the son of Omri,
the son of Imri, the son of Bani, a descendant of Perez son of Judah.
5 Of the Shelanites[h]:
Asaiah the firstborn and his sons.
6 Of the Zerahites:
Jeuel.
The people from Judah numbered 690.
7 Of the Benjamites:
Sallu son of Meshullam, the son of Hodaviah, the son of Hassenuah;
8 Ibneiah son of Jeroham; Elah son of
Uzzi, the son of Mikri; and Meshullam
son of Shephatiah, the son of Reuel, the
son of Ibnijah.

[a] 37 Possibly a variant of *Jether* [b] 3 Or *Gera the father of Ehud* [c] 29 Some Septuagint manuscripts (see also 9:35); Hebrew does not have *Jeiel.* [d] 29 *Father* may mean *civic leader* or *military leader.* [e] 30 Some Septuagint manuscripts (see also 9:36); Hebrew does not have *Ner.* [f] 33 Also known as *Ish-Bosheth* [g] 34 Also known as *Mephibosheth* [h] 5 See Num. 26:20; Hebrew *Shilonites.*

9 The people from Benjamin, as listed
in their genealogy, numbered 956. All
these men were heads of their families.
10 Of the priests:
Jedaiah; Jehoiarib; Jakin;
11 Azariah son of Hilkiah, the son of Meshullam, the son of Zadok, the son of
Meraioth, the son of Ahitub, the official
in charge of the house of God;
12 Adaiah son of Jeroham, the son of
Pashhur, the son of Malkijah; and Ma-
asai son of Adiel, the son of Jahzerah,
the son of Meshullam, the son of Me-
shillemith, the son of Immer.
13 The priests, who were heads of families, numbered 1,760. They were able
men, responsible for ministering in the
house of God.
14 Of the Levites:
Shemaiah son of Hasshub, the son
of Azrikam, the son of Hashabiah, a
Merarite; 15 Bakbakkar, Heresh, Galal
and Mattaniah son of Mika, the son of
Zikri, the son of Asaph; 16 Obadiah son
of Shemaiah, the son of Galal, the son
of Jeduthun; and Berekiah son of Asa,
the son of Elkanah, who lived in the
villages of the Netophathites.
17 The gatekeepers:
Shallum, Akkub, Talmon, Ahiman and
their fellow Levites, Shallum their chief
18 being stationed at the King's Gate on
the east, up to the present time. These
were the gatekeepers belonging to the
camp of the Levites. 19 Shallum son
of Kore, the son of Ebiasaph, the son
of Korah, and his fellow gatekeepers
from his family (the Korahites) were
responsible for guarding the thresholds of the tent just as their ancestors
had been responsible for guarding the
entrance to the dwelling of the LORD.
20 In earlier times Phinehas son of Eleazar was the official in charge of the
gatekeepers, and the LORD was with
him. 21 Zechariah son of Meshelemiah
was the gatekeeper at the entrance to
the tent of meeting.
22 Altogether, those chosen to be gatekeepers at the thresholds numbered 212. They were
registered by genealogy in their villages. The
gatekeepers had been assigned to their positions of trust by David and Samuel the seer.
23 They and their descendants were in charge
of guarding the gates of the house of the
LORD—the house called the tent of meeting.
24 The gatekeepers were on the four sides: east,
west, north and south. 25 Their fellow Levites
in their villages had to come from time to time
and share their duties for seven-day periods.
26 But the four principal gatekeepers, who were
Levites, were entrusted with the responsibility for the rooms and treasuries in the house of
God. 27 They would spend the night stationed
around the house of God, because they had to
guard it; and they had charge of the key for
opening it each morning.
28 Some of them were in charge of the articles used in the temple service; they counted
them when they were brought in and when
they were taken out. 29 Others were assigned to
take care of the furnishings and all the other
articles of the sanctuary, as well as the special flour and wine, and the olive oil, incense
and spices. 30 But some of the priests took
care of mixing the spices. 31 A Levite named
Mattithiah, the firstborn son of Shallum the
Korahite, was entrusted with the responsibility for baking the offering bread. 32 Some
of the Kohathites, their fellow Levites, were
in charge of preparing for every Sabbath the
bread set out on the table.
33 Those who were musicians, heads of Levite families, stayed in the rooms of the temple
and were exempt from other duties because
they were responsible for the work day and
night.
34 All these were heads of Levite families,
chiefs as listed in their genealogy, and they
lived in Jerusalem.

The Genealogy of Saul

35 Jeiel the father[a] of Gibeon lived in Gibeon.
His wife's name was Maakah, 36 and his
firstborn son was Abdon, followed by
Zur, Kish, Baal, Ner, Nadab, 37 Gedor,
Ahio, Zechariah and Mikloth. 38 Mikloth was the father of Shimeam. They
too lived near their relatives in Jerusalem.
39 Ner was the father of Kish, Kish the father
of Saul, and Saul the father of Jonathan, Malki-Shua, Abinadab and Esh-
Baal.[b]
40 The son of Jonathan:
Merib-Baal,[c] who was the father of Micah.
41 The sons of Micah:
Pithon, Melek, Tahrea and Ahaz.[d]
42 Ahaz was the father of Jadah, Jadah[e]
was the father of Alemeth, Azmaveth
and Zimri, and Zimri was the father of
Moza. 43 Moza was the father of Binea;
Rephaiah was his son, Eleasah his son
and Azel his son.
44 Azel had six sons, and these were their
names:
Azrikam, Bokeru, Ishmael, Sheariah,
Obadiah and Hanan. These were the
sons of Azel.

Saul Takes His Life

10 Now the Philistines fought against Israel; the Israelites fled before them, and
many fell dead on Mount Gilboa. 2 The Philistines were in hot pursuit of Saul and his sons,
and they killed his sons Jonathan, Abinadab

[a] *35 Father* may mean *civic leader* or *military leader.* [b] *39* Also known as *Ish-Bosheth* [c] *40* Also known as *Mephibosheth* [d] *41* Vulgate and Syriac (see also Septuagint and 8:35); Hebrew does not have *and Ahaz.* [e] *42* Some Hebrew manuscripts and Septuagint (see also 8:36); most Hebrew manuscripts *Jarah, Jarah*

and Malki-Shua. 3The fighting grew fierce
around Saul, and when the archers overtook
him, they wounded him.
4Saul said to his armor-bearer, "Draw your
sword and run me through, or these uncircumcised fellows will come and abuse me."
But his armor-bearer was terrified and
would not do it; so Saul took his own sword
and fell on it. 5When the armor-bearer saw
that Saul was dead, he too fell on his sword
and died. 6So Saul and his three sons died,
and all his house died together.
7When all the Israelites in the valley saw
that the army had fled and that Saul and his
sons had died, they abandoned their towns
and fled. And the Philistines came and occupied them.
8The next day, when the Philistines came to
strip the dead, they found Saul and his sons
fallen on Mount Gilboa. 9They stripped him
and took his head and his armor, and sent
messengers throughout the land of the Philistines to proclaim the news among their idols
and their people. 10They put his armor in the
temple of their gods and hung up his head in
the temple of Dagon.
11When all the inhabitants of Jabesh Gilead heard what the Philistines had done to
Saul, 12all their valiant men went and took
the bodies of Saul and his sons and brought
them to Jabesh. Then they buried their bones
under the great tree in Jabesh, and they fasted seven days.
13Saul died because he was unfaithful to the
LORD; he did not keep the word of the LORD
and even consulted a medium for guidance,
14and did not inquire of the LORD. So the LORD
put him to death and turned the kingdom over
to David son of Jesse.

David Becomes King Over Israel

11 All Israel came together to David at Hebron and said, "We are your own flesh
and blood. 2In the past, even while Saul was
king, you were the one who led Israel on their
military campaigns. And the LORD your God
said to you, 'You will shepherd my people Israel, and you will become their ruler.'"
3When all the elders of Israel had come to
King David at Hebron, he made a covenant
with them at Hebron before the LORD, and
they anointed David king over Israel, as the
LORD had promised through Samuel.

David Conquers Jerusalem

4David and all the Israelites marched to Jerusalem (that is, Jebus). The Jebusites who
lived there 5said to David, "You will not get
in here." Nevertheless, David captured the
fortress of Zion—which is the City of David.
6David had said, "Whoever leads the attack
on the Jebusites will become commander in
chief." Joab son of Zeruiah went up first, and
so he received the command.
7David then took up residence in the fortress, and so it was called the City of David.
8He built up the city around it, from the terraces[a] to the surrounding wall, while Joab
restored the rest of the city. 9And David became more and more powerful, because the
LORD Almighty was with him.

David's Mighty Warriors

10These were the chiefs of David's mighty
warriors—they, together with all Israel, gave
his kingship strong support to extend it over
the whole land, as the LORD had promised—
11this is the list of David's mighty warriors:
Jashobeam,[b] a Hakmonite, was chief of the
officers[c]; he raised his spear against three
hundred men, whom he killed in one encounter.
12Next to him was Eleazar son of Dodai the
Ahohite, one of the three mighty warriors.
13He was with David at Pas Dammim when
the Philistines gathered there for battle. At
a place where there was a field full of barley, the troops fled from the Philistines. 14But
they took their stand in the middle of the field.
They defended it and struck the Philistines
down, and the LORD brought about a great
victory.
15Three of the thirty chiefs came down to
David to the rock at the cave of Adullam,
while a band of Philistines was encamped
in the Valley of Rephaim. 16At that time David was in the stronghold, and the Philistine
garrison was at Bethlehem. 17David longed
for water and said, "Oh, that someone would
get me a drink of water from the well near
the gate of Bethlehem!" 18So the Three broke
through the Philistine lines, drew water from
the well near the gate of Bethlehem and carried it back to David. But he refused to drink
it; instead, he poured it out to the LORD. 19"God
forbid that I should do this!" he said. "Should I
drink the blood of these men who went at the
risk of their lives?" Because they risked their
lives to bring it back, David would not drink it.
Such were the exploits of the three mighty
warriors.
20Abishai the brother of Joab was chief of
the Three. He raised his spear against three
hundred men, whom he killed, and so he became as famous as the Three. 21He was doubly
honored above the Three and became their
commander, even though he was not included
among them.
22Benaiah son of Jehoiada, a valiant fighter
from Kabzeel, performed great exploits. He
struck down Moab's two mightiest warriors.
He also went down into a pit on a snowy day
and killed a lion. 23And he struck down an
Egyptian who was five cubits[d] tall. Although
the Egyptian had a spear like a weaver's rod
in his hand, Benaiah went against him with
a club. He snatched the spear from the Egyptian's hand and killed him with his own spear.
24Such were the exploits of Benaiah son of
Jehoiada; he too was as famous as the three
mighty warriors. 25He was held in greater

[a] *8* Or *the Millo* [b] *11* Possibly a variant of *Jashob-Baal* [c] *11* Or *Thirty*; some Septuagint manuscripts *Three* (see also 2 Samuel 23:8) [d] *23* That is, about 7 feet 6 inches or about 2.3 meters

honor than any of the Thirty, but he was not included among the Three. And David put him in charge of his bodyguard.

26 The mighty warriors were:
Asahel the brother of Joab,
Elhanan son of Dodo from Bethlehem,
27 Shammoth the Harorite,
Helez the Pelonite,
28 Ira son of Ikkesh from Tekoa,
Abiezer from Anathoth,
29 Sibbekai the Hushathite,
Ilai the Ahohite,
30 Maharai the Netophathite,
Heled son of Baanah the Netophathite,
31 Ithai son of Ribai from Gibeah in Benjamin,
Benaiah the Pirathonite,
32 Hurai from the ravines of Gaash,
Abiel the Arbathite,
33 Azmaveth the Baharumite,
Eliahba the Shaalbonite,
34 the sons of Hashem the Gizonite,
Jonathan son of Shagee the Hararite,
35 Ahiam son of Sakar the Hararite,
Eliphal son of Ur,
36 Hepher the Mekerathite,
Ahijah the Pelonite,
37 Hezro the Carmelite,
Naarai son of Ezbai,
38 Joel the brother of Nathan,
Mibhar son of Hagri,
39 Zelek the Ammonite,
Naharai the Berothite, the armor-bearer of Joab son of Zeruiah,
40 Ira the Ithrite,
Gareb the Ithrite,
41 Uriah the Hittite,
Zabad son of Ahlai,
42 Adina son of Shiza the Reubenite, who was chief of the Reubenites, and the thirty with him,
43 Hanan son of Maakah,
Joshaphat the Mithnite,
44 Uzzia the Ashterathite,
Shama and Jeiel the sons of Hotham the Aroerite,
45 Jediael son of Shimri,
his brother Joha the Tizite,
46 Eliel the Mahavite,
Jeribai and Joshaviah the sons of Elnaam,
Ithmah the Moabite,
47 Eliel, Obed and Jaasiel the Mezobaite.

Warriors Join David

12 These were the men who came to David
at Ziklag, while he was banished from
the presence of Saul son of Kish (they were
among the warriors who helped him in battle;
2they were armed with bows and were able to
shoot arrows or to sling stones right-handed
or left-handed; they were relatives of Saul
from the tribe of Benjamin):

3Ahiezer their chief and Joash the sons
of Shemaah the Gibeathite; Jeziel and
Pelet the sons of Azmaveth; Berakah,
Jehu the Anathothite, 4and Ishmaiah the
Gibeonite, a mighty warrior among the
Thirty, who was a leader of the Thirty;
Jeremiah, Jahaziel, Johanan, Jozabad the
Gederathite,[a] 5Eluzai, Jerimoth, Bealiah, Shemariah and Shephatiah the Haruphite; 6Elkanah, Ishiah, Azarel, Joezer
and Jashobeam the Korahites; 7and Joelah and Zebadiah the sons of Jeroham
from Gedor.

8Some Gadites defected to David at his
stronghold in the wilderness. They were brave
warriors, ready for battle and able to handle
the shield and spear. Their faces were the faces of lions, and they were as swift as gazelles
in the mountains.

9 Ezer was the chief,
Obadiah the second in command, Eliab the third,
10 Mishmannah the fourth, Jeremiah the fifth,
11 Attai the sixth, Eliel the seventh,
12 Johanan the eighth, Elzabad the ninth,
13 Jeremiah the tenth and Makbannai the eleventh.

14These Gadites were army commanders;
the least was a match for a hundred, and the
greatest for a thousand. 15It was they who
crossed the Jordan in the first month when it
was overflowing all its banks, and they put
to flight everyone living in the valleys, to the
east and to the west.

16Other Benjamites and some men from
Judah also came to David in his stronghold.
17David went out to meet them and said to
them, "If you have come to me in peace to
help me, I am ready for you to join me. But if
you have come to betray me to my enemies
when my hands are free from violence, may
the God of our ancestors see it and judge
you."

18Then the Spirit came on Amasai, chief of
the Thirty, and he said:

"We are yours, David!
We are with you, son of Jesse!
Success, success to you,
and success to those who help you,
for your God will help you."

So David received them and made them
leaders of his raiding bands.

19Some of the tribe of Manasseh defected
to David when he went with the Philistines
to fight against Saul. (He and his men did
not help the Philistines because, after consultation, their rulers sent him away. They
said, "It will cost us our heads if he deserts
to his master Saul.") 20When David went to
Ziklag, these were the men of Manasseh who
defected to him: Adnah, Jozabad, Jediael, Michael, Jozabad, Elihu and Zillethai, leaders
of units of a thousand in Manasseh. 21They
helped David against raiding bands, for all
of them were brave warriors, and they were
commanders in his army. 22Day after day men

[a] *4* In Hebrew texts the second half of this verse (*Jeremiah . . . Gederathite*) is numbered 12:5, and 12:5-40 is numbered 12:6-41.

came to help David, until he had a great army,
like the army of God.[a]

Others Join David at Hebron

23These are the numbers of the men armed
for battle who came to David at Hebron to
turn Saul's kingdom over to him, as the LORD
had said:
24 from Judah, carrying shield and spear—
6,800 armed for battle;
25 from Simeon, warriors ready for battle—
7,100;
26 from Levi—4,600, 27including Jehoiada, leader of the family of Aaron, with
3,700 men, 28and Zadok, a brave young
warrior, with 22 officers from his family;
29 from Benjamin, Saul's tribe—3,000, most
of whom had remained loyal to Saul's
house until then;
30 from Ephraim, brave warriors, famous
in their own clans—20,800;
31 from half the tribe of Manasseh, designated by name to come and make David
king—18,000;
32 from Issachar, men who understood the
times and knew what Israel should
do—200 chiefs, with all their relatives
under their command;
33 from Zebulun, experienced soldiers
prepared for battle with every type of
weapon, to help David with undivided
loyalty—50,000;
34 from Naphtali—1,000 officers, together
with 37,000 men carrying shields and
spears;
35 from Dan, ready for battle—28,600;
36 from Asher, experienced soldiers prepared for battle—40,000;
37 and from east of the Jordan, from Reuben, Gad and the half-tribe of Manasseh, armed with every type of weapon—120,000.

38All these were fighting men who volunteered to serve in the ranks. They came to
Hebron fully determined to make David king
over all Israel. All the rest of the Israelites
were also of one mind to make David king.
39The men spent three days there with David, eating and drinking, for their families
had supplied provisions for them. 40Also,
their neighbors from as far away as Issachar,
Zebulun and Naphtali came bringing food on
donkeys, camels, mules and oxen. There were
plentiful supplies of flour, fig cakes, raisin
cakes, wine, olive oil, cattle and sheep, for
there was joy in Israel.

Bringing Back the Ark

13 David conferred with each of his officers, the commanders of thousands and
commanders of hundreds. 2He then said to the
whole assembly of Israel, "If it seems good to
you and if it is the will of the LORD our God,
let us send word far and wide to the rest of
our people throughout the territories of Israel, and also to the priests and Levites who are
with them in their towns and pasturelands,
to come and join us. 3Let us bring the ark of
our God back to us, for we did not inquire of[b]
it[c] during the reign of Saul." 4The whole assembly agreed to do this, because it seemed
right to all the people.

5So David assembled all Israel, from the
Shihor River in Egypt to Lebo Hamath, to
bring the ark of God from Kiriath Jearim.
6David and all Israel went to Baalah of Judah (Kiriath Jearim) to bring up from there
the ark of God the LORD, who is enthroned
between the cherubim—the ark that is called
by the Name.

7They moved the ark of God from Abinadab's house on a new cart, with Uzzah and
Ahio guiding it. 8David and all the Israelites
were celebrating with all their might before
God, with songs and with harps, lyres, timbrels, cymbals and trumpets.

9When they came to the threshing floor of
Kidon, Uzzah reached out his hand to steady
the ark, because the oxen stumbled. 10The
LORD's anger burned against Uzzah, and he
struck him down because he had put his hand
on the ark. So he died there before God.

11Then David was angry because the LORD's
wrath had broken out against Uzzah, and to
this day that place is called Perez Uzzah.[d]

12David was afraid of God that day and
asked, "How can I ever bring the ark of God to
me?" 13He did not take the ark to be with him
in the City of David. Instead, he took it to the
house of Obed-Edom the Gittite. 14The ark of
God remained with the family of Obed-Edom
in his house for three months, and the LORD
blessed his household and everything he had.

David's House and Family

14 Now Hiram king of Tyre sent messengers to David, along with cedar logs,
stonemasons and carpenters to build a palace for him. 2And David knew that the LORD
had established him as king over Israel and
that his kingdom had been highly exalted for
the sake of his people Israel.

3In Jerusalem David took more wives and
became the father of more sons and daughters. 4These are the names of the children
born to him there: Shammua, Shobab, Nathan, Solomon, 5Ibhar, Elishua, Elpelet, 6No-
gah, Nepheg, Japhia, 7Elishama, Beeliada[e]
and Eliphelet.

David Defeats the Philistines

8When the Philistines heard that David had
been anointed king over all Israel, they went
up in full force to search for him, but David
heard about it and went out to meet them.
9Now the Philistines had come and raided
the Valley of Rephaim; 10so David inquired
of God: "Shall I go and attack the Philistines?
Will you deliver them into my hands?"

The LORD answered him, "Go, I will deliver
them into your hands."

[a] 22 Or *a great and mighty army* [b] 3 Or *we neglected* [c] 3 Or *him* [d] 11 *Perez Uzzah* means *outbreak against Uzzah.* [e] 7 A variant of *Eliada*

11So David and his men went up to Baal Perazim, and there he defeated them. He said, "As waters break out, God has broken out against my enemies by my hand." So that place was called Baal Perazim.[a] 12The Philistines had abandoned their gods there, and David gave orders to burn them in the fire.

13Once more the Philistines raided the valley; 14so David inquired of God again, and God answered him, "Do not go directly after them, but circle around them and attack them in front of the poplar trees. 15As soon as you hear the sound of marching in the tops of the poplar trees, move out to battle, because that will mean God has gone out in front of you to strike the Philistine army." 16So David did as God commanded him, and they struck down the Philistine army, all the way from Gibeon to Gezer.

17So David's fame spread throughout every land, and the LORD made all the nations fear him.

The Ark Brought to Jerusalem

15 After David had constructed buildings for himself in the City of David, he prepared a place for the ark of God and pitched a tent for it. 2Then David said, "No one but the Levites may carry the ark of God, because the LORD chose them to carry the ark of the LORD and to minister before him forever."

3David assembled all Israel in Jerusalem to bring up the ark of the LORD to the place he had prepared for it. 4He called together the descendants of Aaron and the Levites:

5From the descendants of Kohath,
Uriel the leader and 120 relatives;
6from the descendants of Merari,
Asaiah the leader and 220 relatives;
7from the descendants of Gershon,[b]
Joel the leader and 130 relatives;
8from the descendants of Elizaphan,
Shemaiah the leader and 200 relatives;
9from the descendants of Hebron,
Eliel the leader and 80 relatives;
10from the descendants of Uzziel,
Amminadab the leader and 112 relatives.

11Then David summoned Zadok and Abiathar the priests, and Uriel, Asaiah, Joel, Shemaiah, Eliel and Amminadab the Levites. 12He said to them, "You are the heads of the Levitical families; you and your fellow Levites are to consecrate yourselves and bring up the ark of the LORD, the God of Israel, to the place I have prepared for it. 13It was because you, the Levites, did not bring it up the first time that the LORD our God broke out in anger against us. We did not inquire of him about how to do it in the prescribed way." 14So the priests and Levites consecrated themselves in order to bring up the ark of the LORD, the God of Israel. 15And the Levites carried the ark of God with the poles on their shoulders, as Moses had commanded in accordance with the word of the LORD.

16David told the leaders of the Levites to appoint their fellow Levites as musicians to make a joyful sound with musical instruments: lyres, harps and cymbals.

17So the Levites appointed Heman son of Joel; from his relatives, Asaph son of Berekiah; and from their relatives the Merarites, Ethan son of Kushaiah; 18and with them their relatives next in rank: Zechariah,[c] Jaaziel, Shemiramoth, Jehiel, Unni, Eliab, Benaiah, Maaseiah, Mattithiah, Eliphelehu, Mikneiah, Obed-Edom and Jeiel,[d] the gatekeepers.

19The musicians Heman, Asaph and Ethan were to sound the bronze cymbals; 20Zechariah, Jaaziel,[e] Shemiramoth, Jehiel, Unni, Eliab, Maaseiah and Benaiah were to play the lyres according to *alamoth*,[f] 21and Mattithiah, Eliphelehu, Mikneiah, Obed-Edom, Jeiel and Azaziah were to play the harps, directing according to *sheminith*.[f] 22Kenaniah the head Levite was in charge of the singing; that was his responsibility because he was skillful at it.

23Berekiah and Elkanah were to be doorkeepers for the ark. 24Shebaniah, Joshaphat, Nethanel, Amasai, Zechariah, Benaiah and Eliezer the priests were to blow trumpets before the ark of God. Obed-Edom and Jehiah were also to be doorkeepers for the ark.

25So David and the elders of Israel and the commanders of units of a thousand went to bring up the ark of the covenant of the LORD from the house of Obed-Edom, with rejoicing. 26Because God had helped the Levites who were carrying the ark of the covenant of the LORD, seven bulls and seven rams were sacrificed. 27Now David was clothed in a robe of fine linen, as were all the Levites who were carrying the ark, and as were the musicians, and Kenaniah, who was in charge of the singing of the choirs. David also wore a linen ephod. 28So all Israel brought up the ark of the covenant of the LORD with shouts, with the sounding of rams' horns and trumpets, and of cymbals, and the playing of lyres and harps.

29As the ark of the covenant of the LORD was entering the City of David, Michal daughter of Saul watched from a window. And when she saw King David dancing and celebrating, she despised him in her heart.

Ministering Before the Ark

16 They brought the ark of God and set it inside the tent that David had pitched for it, and they presented burnt offerings and fellowship offerings before God. 2After David had finished sacrificing the burnt offerings and fellowship offerings, he blessed the people in the name of the LORD. 3Then he gave a loaf of bread, a cake of dates and a cake of raisins to each Israelite man and woman.

[a] *11 Baal Perazim* means *the lord who breaks out.* [b] *7* Hebrew *Gershom,* a variant of *Gershon*
[c] *18* Three Hebrew manuscripts and most Septuagint manuscripts (see also verse 20 and 16:5); most Hebrew manuscripts *Zechariah son and* or *Zechariah, Ben and* [d] *18* Hebrew; Septuagint (see also verse 21) *Jeiel and Azaziah* [e] *20* See verse 18; Hebrew *Aziel,* a variant of *Jaaziel.* [f] *20,21* Probably a musical term

4He appointed some of the Levites to minister before the ark of the LORD, to extol,[a] thank,
and praise the LORD, the God of Israel: 5Asaph
was the chief, and next to him in rank were
Zechariah, then Jaaziel,[b] Shemiramoth, Jehiel, Mattithiah, Eliab, Benaiah, Obed-Edom
and Jeiel. They were to play the lyres and
harps, Asaph was to sound the cymbals, 6and
Benaiah and Jahaziel the priests were to blow
the trumpets regularly before the ark of the
covenant of God.

7That day David first appointed Asaph and
his associates to give praise to the LORD in
this manner:

8 Give praise to the LORD, proclaim his
name;
make known among the nations what
he has done.
9 Sing to him, sing praise to him;
tell of all his wonderful acts.
10 Glory in his holy name;
let the hearts of those who seek the
LORD rejoice.
11 Look to the LORD and his strength;
seek his face always.

12 Remember the wonders he has done,
his miracles, and the judgments he
pronounced,
13 you his servants, the descendants of
Israel,
his chosen ones, the children of Jacob.
14 He is the LORD our God;
his judgments are in all the earth.

15 He remembers[c] his covenant forever,
the promise he made, for a thousand
generations,
16 the covenant he made with Abraham,
the oath he swore to Isaac.
17 He confirmed it to Jacob as a decree,
to Israel as an everlasting covenant:
18 "To you I will give the land of Canaan
as the portion you will inherit."

19 When they were but few in number,
few indeed, and strangers in it,
20 they[d] wandered from nation to nation,
from one kingdom to another.
21 He allowed no one to oppress them;
for their sake he rebuked kings:
22 "Do not touch my anointed ones;
do my prophets no harm."

23 Sing to the LORD, all the earth;
proclaim his salvation day after day.
24 Declare his glory among the nations,
his marvelous deeds among all
peoples.

25 For great is the LORD and most worthy of
praise;
he is to be feared above all gods.
26 For all the gods of the nations are idols,
but the LORD made the heavens.
27 Splendor and majesty are before him;
strength and joy are in his dwelling
place.

28 Ascribe to the LORD, all you families of
nations,
ascribe to the LORD glory and strength.
29 Ascribe to the LORD the glory due his
name;
bring an offering and come before him.
Worship the LORD in the splendor of his[e]
holiness.
30 Tremble before him, all the earth!
The world is firmly established; it
cannot be moved.

31 Let the heavens rejoice, let the earth be
glad;
let them say among the nations, "The
LORD reigns!"
32 Let the sea resound, and all that is in it;
let the fields be jubilant, and everything
in them!
33 Let the trees of the forest sing,
let them sing for joy before the LORD,
for he comes to judge the earth.

34 Give thanks to the LORD, for he is good;
his love endures forever.
35 Cry out, "Save us, God our Savior;
gather us and deliver us from the
nations,
that we may give thanks to your holy
name,
and glory in your praise."
36 Praise be to the LORD, the God of Israel,
from everlasting to everlasting.

Then all the people said "Amen" and "Praise
the LORD."

37David left Asaph and his associates before the ark of the covenant of the LORD to
minister there regularly, according to each
day's requirements. 38He also left Obed-Edom
and his sixty-eight associates to minister with
them. Obed-Edom son of Jeduthun, and also
Hosah, were gatekeepers.
39David left Zadok the priest and his fellow
priests before the tabernacle of the LORD at
the high place in Gibeon 40to present burnt
offerings to the LORD on the altar of burnt
offering regularly, morning and evening, in
accordance with everything written in the
Law of the LORD, which he had given Israel.
41With them were Heman and Jeduthun and
the rest of those chosen and designated by
name to give thanks to the LORD, "for his love
endures forever." 42Heman and Jeduthun were
responsible for the sounding of the trumpets
and cymbals and for the playing of the other
instruments for sacred song. The sons of Jeduthun were stationed at the gate.
43Then all the people left, each for their own
home, and David returned home to bless his
family.

[a] 4 Or *petition*; or *invoke* [b] 5 See 15:18,20; Hebrew *Jeiel*, possibly another name for *Jaaziel*.
[c] 15 Some Septuagint manuscripts (see also Psalm 105:8); Hebrew *Remember* [d] 18-20 One Hebrew manuscript, Septuagint and Vulgate (see also Psalm 105:12); most Hebrew manuscripts *inherit, / 19though you are but few in number, / few indeed, and strangers in it." / 20They* [e] 29 Or *LORD with the splendor of*

God's Promise to David

17 After David was settled in his palace,
he said to Nathan the prophet, "Here I
am, living in a house of cedar, while the ark
of the covenant of the LORD is under a tent."
2Nathan replied to David, "Whatever you
have in mind, do it, for God is with you."
3But that night the word of God came to
Nathan, saying:

4"Go and tell my servant David, 'This
is what the LORD says: You are not the
one to build me a house to dwell in. 5I
have not dwelt in a house from the day
I brought Israel up out of Egypt to this
day. I have moved from one tent site to
another, from one dwelling place to another. 6Wherever I have moved with all
the Israelites, did I ever say to any of their
leaders[a] whom I commanded to shepherd
my people, "Why have you not built me a
house of cedar?"'
7"Now then, tell my servant David,
'This is what the LORD Almighty says: I
took you from the pasture, from tending
the flock, and appointed you ruler over
my people Israel. 8I have been with you
wherever you have gone, and I have cut
off all your enemies from before you. Now
I will make your name like the names of
the greatest men on earth. 9And I will provide a place for my people Israel and will
plant them so that they can have a home
of their own and no longer be disturbed.
Wicked people will not oppress them anymore, as they did at the beginning 10and
have done ever since the time I appointed
leaders over my people Israel. I will also
subdue all your enemies.
"'I declare to you that the LORD will
build a house for you: 11When your days
are over and you go to be with your ancestors, I will raise up your offspring to
succeed you, one of your own sons, and
I will establish his kingdom. 12He is the
one who will build a house for me, and I
will establish his throne forever. 13I will
be his father, and he will be my son. I
will never take my love away from him,
as I took it away from your predecessor.
14I will set him over my house and my
kingdom forever; his throne will be established forever.'"

15Nathan reported to David all the words of
this entire revelation.

David's Prayer

16Then King David went in and sat before
the LORD, and he said:

"Who am I, LORD God, and what is my
family, that you have brought me this far?
17And as if this were not enough in your
sight, my God, you have spoken about the
future of the house of your servant. You,
LORD God, have looked on me as though
I were the most exalted of men.
18"What more can David say to you for
honoring your servant? For you know
your servant, 19LORD. For the sake of
your servant and according to your will,
you have done this great thing and made
known all these great promises.
20"There is no one like you, LORD, and
there is no God but you, as we have heard
with our own ears. 21And who is like your
people Israel—the one nation on earth
whose God went out to redeem a people
for himself, and to make a name for yourself, and to perform great and awesome
wonders by driving out nations from before your people, whom you redeemed
from Egypt? 22You made your people
Israel your very own forever, and you,
LORD, have become their God.
23"And now, LORD, let the promise you
have made concerning your servant and
his house be established forever. Do as
you promised, 24so that it will be established and that your name will be great
forever. Then people will say, 'The LORD
Almighty, the God over Israel, is Israel's
God!' And the house of your servant David will be established before you.
25"You, my God, have revealed to your
servant that you will build a house for
him. So your servant has found courage
to pray to you. 26You, LORD, are God! You
have promised these good things to your
servant. 27Now you have been pleased to
bless the house of your servant, that it
may continue forever in your sight; for
you, LORD, have blessed it, and it will be
blessed forever."

David's Victories

18 In the course of time, David defeated the
Philistines and subdued them, and he
took Gath and its surrounding villages from
the control of the Philistines.
2David also defeated the Moabites, and
they became subject to him and brought him
tribute.
3Moreover, David defeated Hadadezer king
of Zobah, in the vicinity of Hamath, when he
went to set up his monument at[b] the Euphrates
River. 4David captured a thousand of his chariots, seven thousand charioteers and twenty
thousand foot soldiers. He hamstrung all but
a hundred of the chariot horses.
5When the Arameans of Damascus came to
help Hadadezer king of Zobah, David struck
down twenty-two thousand of them. 6He put
garrisons in the Aramean kingdom of Damascus, and the Arameans became subject to
him and brought him tribute. The LORD gave
David victory wherever he went.
7David took the gold shields carried by the
officers of Hadadezer and brought them to
Jerusalem. 8From Tebah[c] and Kun, towns that
belonged to Hadadezer, David took a great

[a] 6 Traditionally *judges*; also in verse 10 [b] 3 Or *to restore his control over* [c] 8 Hebrew *Tibhath*, a variant of *Tebah*

quantity of bronze, which Solomon used to
make the bronze Sea, the pillars and various
bronze articles.
9When Tou king of Hamath heard that David had defeated the entire army of Hadadezer
king of Zobah, 10he sent his son Hadoram to
King David to greet him and congratulate him
on his victory in battle over Hadadezer, who
had been at war with Tou. Hadoram brought all
kinds of articles of gold, of silver and of bronze.
11King David dedicated these articles to the
LORD, as he had done with the silver and gold
he had taken from all these nations: Edom
and Moab, the Ammonites and the Philistines,
and Amalek.
12Abishai son of Zeruiah struck down eighteen thousand Edomites in the Valley of Salt.
13He put garrisons in Edom, and all the Edomites became subject to David. The LORD gave
David victory wherever he went.

David's Officials

14David reigned over all Israel, doing what
was just and right for all his people. 15Joab son
of Zeruiah was over the army; Jehoshaphat
son of Ahilud was recorder; 16Zadok son of
Ahitub and Ahimelek[a] son of Abiathar were
priests; Shavsha was secretary; 17Benaiah son
of Jehoiada was over the Kerethites and Pelethites; and David's sons were chief officials
at the king's side.

David Defeats the Ammonites

19 In the course of time, Nahash king of the
Ammonites died, and his son succeeded him as king. 2David thought, "I will show
kindness to Hanun son of Nahash, because
his father showed kindness to me." So David
sent a delegation to express his sympathy to
Hanun concerning his father.
When David's envoys came to Hanun in the
land of the Ammonites to express sympathy
to him, 3the Ammonite commanders said to
Hanun, "Do you think David is honoring your
father by sending envoys to you to express
sympathy? Haven't his envoys come to you
only to explore and spy out the country and
overthrow it?" 4So Hanun seized David's envoys, shaved them, cut off their garments at
the buttocks, and sent them away.
5When someone came and told David about
the men, he sent messengers to meet them, for
they were greatly humiliated. The king said,
"Stay at Jericho till your beards have grown,
and then come back."
6When the Ammonites realized that they
had become obnoxious to David, Hanun and
the Ammonites sent a thousand talents[b] of
silver to hire chariots and charioteers from
Aram Naharaim,[c] Aram Maakah and Zobah.
7They hired thirty-two thousand chariots and
charioteers, as well as the king of Maakah
with his troops, who came and camped near
Medeba, while the Ammonites were mustered
from their towns and moved out for battle.
8On hearing this, David sent Joab out with
the entire army of fighting men. 9The Ammonites came out and drew up in battle formation at the entrance to their city, while the
kings who had come were by themselves in
the open country.
10Joab saw that there were battle lines in
front of him and behind him; so he selected
some of the best troops in Israel and deployed
them against the Arameans. 11He put the rest
of the men under the command of Abishai his
brother, and they were deployed against the
Ammonites. 12Joab said, "If the Arameans are
too strong for me, then you are to rescue me;
but if the Ammonites are too strong for you,
then I will rescue you. 13Be strong, and let us
fight bravely for our people and the cities of
our God. The LORD will do what is good in
his sight."
14Then Joab and the troops with him advanced to fight the Arameans, and they fled
before him. 15When the Ammonites realized
that the Arameans were fleeing, they too fled
before his brother Abishai and went inside the
city. So Joab went back to Jerusalem.
16After the Arameans saw that they had
been routed by Israel, they sent messengers
and had Arameans brought from beyond the
Euphrates River, with Shophak the commander of Hadadezer's army leading them.
17When David was told of this, he gathered
all Israel and crossed the Jordan; he advanced
against them and formed his battle lines opposite them. David formed his lines to meet the
Arameans in battle, and they fought against
him. 18But they fled before Israel, and David
killed seven thousand of their charioteers and
forty thousand of their foot soldiers. He also
killed Shophak the commander of their army.
19When the vassals of Hadadezer saw that
they had been routed by Israel, they made
peace with David and became subject to him.
So the Arameans were not willing to help
the Ammonites anymore.

The Capture of Rabbah

20 In the spring, at the time when kings go
off to war, Joab led out the armed forces.
He laid waste the land of the Ammonites and
went to Rabbah and besieged it, but David
remained in Jerusalem. Joab attacked Rabbah and left it in ruins. 2David took the crown
from the head of their king[d]—its weight was
found to be a talent[e] of gold, and it was set
with precious stones—and it was placed on
David's head. He took a great quantity of plunder from the city 3and brought out the people
who were there, consigning them to labor with
saws and with iron picks and axes. David did
this to all the Ammonite towns. Then David
and his entire army returned to Jerusalem.

War With the Philistines

4In the course of time, war broke out with
the Philistines, at Gezer. At that time Sibbe-

[a] *16* Some Hebrew manuscripts, Vulgate and Syriac (see also 2 Samuel 8:17); most Hebrew manuscripts *Abimelek* [b] *6* That is, about 38 tons or about 34 metric tons [c] *6* That is, Northwest Mesopotamia [d] *2* Or *of Milkom*, that is, Molek [e] *2* That is, about 75 pounds or about 34 kilograms

kai the Hushathite killed Sippai, one of the
descendants of the Rephaites, and the Philistines were subjugated.
5 In another battle with the Philistines, Elhanan son of Jair killed Lahmi the brother
of Goliath the Gittite, who had a spear with a
shaft like a weaver's rod.
6 In still another battle, which took place at
Gath, there was a huge man with six fingers
on each hand and six toes on each foot—twenty-four in all. He also was descended from
Rapha. 7 When he taunted Israel, Jonathan
son of Shimea, David's brother, killed him.
8 These were descendants of Rapha in Gath,
and they fell at the hands of David and his men.

David Counts the Fighting Men

21 Satan rose up against Israel and incited David to take a census of Israel. 2 So
David said to Joab and the commanders of
the troops, "Go and count the Israelites from
Beersheba to Dan. Then report back to me so
that I may know how many there are."
3 But Joab replied, "May the LORD multiply
his troops a hundred times over. My lord the
king, are they not all my lord's subjects? Why
does my lord want to do this? Why should he
bring guilt on Israel?"
4 The king's word, however, overruled Joab;
so Joab left and went throughout Israel and
then came back to Jerusalem. 5 Joab reported
the number of the fighting men to David: In
all Israel there were one million one hundred
thousand men who could handle a sword, including four hundred and seventy thousand
in Judah.
6 But Joab did not include Levi and Benjamin in the numbering, because the king's
command was repulsive to him. 7 This command was also evil in the sight of God; so he
punished Israel.
8 Then David said to God, "I have sinned
greatly by doing this. Now, I beg you, take
away the guilt of your servant. I have done a
very foolish thing."
9 The LORD said to Gad, David's seer, 10 "Go
and tell David, 'This is what the LORD says: I
am giving you three options. Choose one of
them for me to carry out against you.'"
11 So Gad went to David and said to him,
"This is what the LORD says: 'Take your
choice: 12 three years of famine, three months
of being swept away[a] before your enemies,
with their swords overtaking you, or three
days of the sword of the LORD—days of plague
in the land, with the angel of the LORD rav-
aging every part of Israel.' Now then, decide
how I should answer the one who sent me."
13 David said to Gad, "I am in deep distress.
Let me fall into the hands of the LORD, for his
mercy is very great; but do not let me fall into
human hands."
14 So the LORD sent a plague on Israel, and
seventy thousand men of Israel fell dead.
15 And God sent an angel to destroy Jerusalem.
But as the angel was doing so, the LORD saw it
and relented concerning the disaster and said
to the angel who was destroying the people,
"Enough! Withdraw your hand." The angel of
the LORD was then standing at the threshing
floor of Araunah[b] the Jebusite.
16 David looked up and saw the angel of the
LORD standing between heaven and earth,
with a drawn sword in his hand extended
over Jerusalem. Then David and the elders,
clothed in sackcloth, fell facedown.
17 David said to God, "Was it not I who ordered the fighting men to be counted? I, the
shepherd,[c] have sinned and done wrong.
These are but sheep. What have they done?
LORD my God, let your hand fall on me and
my family, but do not let this plague remain
on your people."

David Builds an Altar

18 Then the angel of the LORD ordered Gad
to tell David to go up and build an altar to the
LORD on the threshing floor of Araunah the
Jebusite. 19 So David went up in obedience to
the word that Gad had spoken in the name
of the LORD.
20 While Araunah was threshing wheat, he
turned and saw the angel; his four sons who
were with him hid themselves. 21 Then David approached, and when Araunah looked
and saw him, he left the threshing floor and
bowed down before David with his face to
the ground.
22 David said to him, "Let me have the site
of your threshing floor so I can build an altar to the LORD, that the plague on the people
may be stopped. Sell it to me at the full price."
23 Araunah said to David, "Take it! Let my
lord the king do whatever pleases him. Look,
I will give the oxen for the burnt offerings, the
threshing sledges for the wood, and the wheat
for the grain offering. I will give all this."
24 But King David replied to Araunah, "No,
I insist on paying the full price. I will not take
for the LORD what is yours, or sacrifice a burnt
offering that costs me nothing."
25 So David paid Araunah six hundred shekels[d] of gold for the site. 26 David built an altar
to the LORD there and sacrificed burnt offerings and fellowship offerings. He called on
the LORD, and the LORD answered him with
fire from heaven on the altar of burnt offering.
27 Then the LORD spoke to the angel, and
he put his sword back into its sheath. 28 At
that time, when David saw that the LORD had
answered him on the threshing floor of Araunah the Jebusite, he offered sacrifices there.
29 The tabernacle of the LORD, which Moses
had made in the wilderness, and the altar of
burnt offering were at that time on the high
place at Gibeon. 30 But David could not go before it to inquire of God, because he was afraid
of the sword of the angel of the LORD.

[a] *12* Hebrew; Septuagint and Vulgate (see also 2 Samuel 24:13) *of fleeing* [b] *15* Hebrew *Ornan,* a variant of *Araunah;* also in verses 18-28 [c] *17* Probable reading of the original Hebrew text (see 2 Samuel 24:17 and note); Masoretic Text does not have *the shepherd.* [d] *25* That is, about 15 pounds or about 6.9 kilograms

22 Then David said, "The house of the LORD
God is to be here, and also the altar of
burnt offering for Israel."

Preparations for the Temple

2So David gave orders to assemble the foreigners residing in Israel, and from among
them he appointed stonecutters to prepare
dressed stone for building the house of God.
3He provided a large amount of iron to make
nails for the doors of the gateways and for
the fittings, and more bronze than could be
weighed. 4He also provided more cedar logs
than could be counted, for the Sidonians and
Tyrians had brought large numbers of them
to David.
5David said, "My son Solomon is young
and inexperienced, and the house to be built
for the LORD should be of great magnificence
and fame and splendor in the sight of all the
nations. Therefore I will make preparations
for it." So David made extensive preparations
before his death.
6Then he called for his son Solomon and
charged him to build a house for the LORD,
the God of Israel. 7David said to Solomon:
"My son, I had it in my heart to build a house
for the Name of the LORD my God. 8But this
word of the LORD came to me: 'You have shed
much blood and have fought many wars. You
are not to build a house for my Name, because
you have shed much blood on the earth in my
sight. 9But you will have a son who will be a
man of peace and rest, and I will give him rest
from all his enemies on every side. His name
will be Solomon,[a] and I will grant Israel peace
and quiet during his reign. 10He is the one who
will build a house for my Name. He will be my
son, and I will be his father. And I will establish
the throne of his kingdom over Israel forever.'
11"Now, my son, the LORD be with you, and
may you have success and build the house of
the LORD your God, as he said you would. 12May
the LORD give you discretion and understanding when he puts you in command over Israel,
so that you may keep the law of the LORD your
God. 13Then you will have success if you are
careful to observe the decrees and laws that
the LORD gave Moses for Israel. Be strong and
courageous. Do not be afraid or discouraged.
14"I have taken great pains to provide for
the temple of the LORD a hundred thousand
talents[b] of gold, a million talents[c] of silver,
quantities of bronze and iron too great to be
weighed, and wood and stone. And you may
add to them. 15You have many workers: stonecutters, masons and carpenters, as well as
those skilled in every kind of work 16in gold
and silver, bronze and iron—craftsmen beyond number. Now begin the work, and the
LORD be with you."
17Then David ordered all the leaders of Israel to help his son Solomon. 18He said to them,
"Is not the LORD your God with you? And has
he not granted you rest on every side? For he
has given the inhabitants of the land into my
hands, and the land is subject to the LORD and
to his people. 19Now devote your heart and
soul to seeking the LORD your God. Begin to
build the sanctuary of the LORD God, so that
you may bring the ark of the covenant of the
LORD and the sacred articles belonging to God
into the temple that will be built for the Name
of the LORD."

The Levites

23 When David was old and full of years,
he made his son Solomon king over Israel.
2He also gathered together all the leaders of
Israel, as well as the priests and Levites. 3The
Levites thirty years old or more were counted,
and the total number of men was thirty-eight
thousand. 4David said, "Of these, twenty-four
thousand are to be in charge of the work of the
temple of the LORD and six thousand are to be
officials and judges. 5Four thousand are to be
gatekeepers and four thousand are to praise
the LORD with the musical instruments I have
provided for that purpose."
6David separated the Levites into divisions
corresponding to the sons of Levi: Gershon,
Kohath and Merari.

Gershonites

7Belonging to the Gershonites:
Ladan and Shimei.
8The sons of Ladan:
Jehiel the first, Zetham and Joel—
three in all.
9The sons of Shimei:
Shelomoth, Haziel and Haran—three
in all.
These were the heads of the families of
Ladan.
10And the sons of Shimei:
Jahath, Ziza,[d] Jeush and Beriah.
These were the sons of Shimei—four
in all.
11Jahath was the first and Ziza the second, but Jeush and Beriah did not have
many sons; so they were counted as one
family with one assignment.

Kohathites

12The sons of Kohath:
Amram, Izhar, Hebron and Uzziel—
four in all.
13The sons of Amram:
Aaron and Moses.
Aaron was set apart, he and his descendants forever, to consecrate the most
holy things, to offer sacrifices before
the LORD, to minister before him and to
pronounce blessings in his name forever. 14The sons of Moses the man of God
were counted as part of the tribe of Levi.
15The sons of Moses:
Gershom and Eliezer.

[a] 9 *Solomon* sounds like and may be derived from the Hebrew for *peace*. [b] 14 That is, about 3,750 tons or about 3,400 metric tons [c] 14 That is, about 37,500 tons or about 34,000 metric tons
[d] 10 One Hebrew manuscript, Septuagint and Vulgate (see also verse 11); most Hebrew manuscripts *Zina*

16 The descendants of Gershom:
Shubael was the first.
17 The descendants of Eliezer:
Rehabiah was the first.
Eliezer had no other sons, but the sons
of Rehabiah were very numerous.
18 The sons of Izhar:
Shelomith was the first.
19 The sons of Hebron:
Jeriah the first, Amariah the second,
Jahaziel the third and Jekameam the
fourth.
20 The sons of Uzziel:
Micah the first and Ishiah the second.

Merarites

21 The sons of Merari:
Mahli and Mushi.
The sons of Mahli:
Eleazar and Kish.
22 Eleazar died without having sons: he
had only daughters. Their cousins, the
sons of Kish, married them.
23 The sons of Mushi:
Mahli, Eder and Jerimoth—three in all.

24 These were the descendants of Levi by
their families—the heads of families as they
were registered under their names and counted individually, that is, the workers twenty
years old or more who served in the temple
of the LORD. 25 For David had said, "Since the
LORD, the God of Israel, has granted rest to
his people and has come to dwell in Jerusalem
forever, 26 the Levites no longer need to carry
the tabernacle or any of the articles used in its
service." 27 According to the last instructions
of David, the Levites were counted from those
twenty years old or more.
28 The duty of the Levites was to help Aaron's
descendants in the service of the temple of the
LORD: to be in charge of the courtyards, the side
rooms, the purification of all sacred things and
the performance of other duties at the house of
God. 29 They were in charge of the bread set out
on the table, the special flour for the grain offerings, the thin loaves made without yeast, the
baking and the mixing, and all measurements
of quantity and size. 30 They were also to stand
every morning to thank and praise the LORD.
They were to do the same in the evening 31 and
whenever burnt offerings were presented to the
LORD on the Sabbaths, at the New Moon feasts
and at the appointed festivals. They were to
serve before the LORD regularly in the proper
number and in the way prescribed for them.
32 And so the Levites carried out their responsibilities for the tent of meeting, for the
Holy Place and, under their relatives the descendants of Aaron, for the service of the temple of the LORD.

The Divisions of Priests

24 These were the divisions of the descendants of Aaron:
The sons of Aaron were Nadab, Abihu, Eleazar and Ithamar. 2 But Nadab and Abihu
died before their father did, and they had no
sons; so Eleazar and Ithamar served as the
priests. 3 With the help of Zadok a descendant
of Eleazar and Ahimelek a descendant of Ithamar, David separated them into divisions for
their appointed order of ministering. 4 A larger
number of leaders were found among Eleazar's descendants than among Ithamar's, and
they were divided accordingly: sixteen heads
of families from Eleazar's descendants and
eight heads of families from Ithamar's descendants. 5 They divided them impartially
by casting lots, for there were officials of the
sanctuary and officials of God among the descendants of both Eleazar and Ithamar.
6 The scribe Shemaiah son of Nethanel, a Levite, recorded their names in the presence of
the king and of the officials: Zadok the priest,
Ahimelek son of Abiathar and the heads of
families of the priests and of the Levites—one
family being taken from Eleazar and then one
from Ithamar.

7 The first lot fell to Jehoiarib,
the second to Jedaiah,
8 the third to Harim,
the fourth to Seorim,
9 the fifth to Malkijah,
the sixth to Mijamin,
10 the seventh to Hakkoz,
the eighth to Abijah,
11 the ninth to Jeshua,
the tenth to Shekaniah,
12 the eleventh to Eliashib,
the twelfth to Jakim,
13 the thirteenth to Huppah,
the fourteenth to Jeshebeab,
14 the fifteenth to Bilgah,
the sixteenth to Immer,
15 the seventeenth to Hezir,
the eighteenth to Happizzez,
16 the nineteenth to Pethahiah,
the twentieth to Jehezkel,
17 the twenty-first to Jakin,
the twenty-second to Gamul,
18 the twenty-third to Delaiah
and the twenty-fourth to Maaziah.

19 This was their appointed order of ministering when they entered the temple of the
LORD, according to the regulations prescribed
for them by their ancestor Aaron, as the LORD,
the God of Israel, had commanded him.

The Rest of the Levites

20 As for the rest of the descendants of Levi:
from the sons of Amram: Shubael;
from the sons of Shubael: Jehdeiah.
21 As for Rehabiah, from his sons:
Ishiah was the first.
22 From the Izharites: Shelomoth;
from the sons of Shelomoth: Jahath.
23 The sons of Hebron: Jeriah the first,[a] Amariah the second, Jahaziel the third and
Jekameam the fourth.
24 The son of Uzziel: Micah;

[a] *23* Two Hebrew manuscripts and some Septuagint manuscripts (see also 23:19); most Hebrew manuscripts *The sons of Jeriah:*

from the sons of Micah: Shamir.
25 The brother of Micah: Ishiah;
from the sons of Ishiah: Zechariah.
26 The sons of Merari: Mahli and Mushi.
The son of Jaaziah: Beno.
27 The sons of Merari:
from Jaaziah: Beno, Shoham, Zakkur
and Ibri.
28 From Mahli: Eleazar, who had no sons.
29 From Kish: the son of Kish:
Jerahmeel.
30 And the sons of Mushi: Mahli, Eder and
Jerimoth.

These were the Levites, according to their
families. 31 They also cast lots, just as their
relatives the descendants of Aaron did, in the presence of King David and of Zadok, Ahimelek, and the heads of families of the priests and of the Levites. The families of the oldest brother were treated the same as those of the youngest.

The Musicians

25 David, together with the commanders of the army, set apart some of the sons of Asaph, Heman and Jeduthun for the ministry of prophesying, accompanied by harps, lyres and cymbals. Here is the list of the men who performed this service:

2 From the sons of Asaph:
Zakkur, Joseph, Nethaniah and Asarelah. The sons of Asaph were under the supervision of Asaph, who prophesied under the king's supervision.
3 As for Jeduthun, from his sons:
Gedaliah, Zeri, Jeshaiah, Shimei,[a] Hashabiah and Mattithiah, six in all, under the supervision of their father Jeduthun, who prophesied, using the harp in thanking and praising the LORD.
4 As for Heman, from his sons:
Bukkiah, Mattaniah, Uzziel, Shubael and Jerimoth; Hananiah, Hanani, Eliathah, Giddalti and Romamti-Ezer; Joshbekashah, Mallothi, Hothir and Mahazioth.
5 (All these were sons of Heman the king's seer. They were given him through the promises of God to exalt him. God gave Heman fourteen sons and three daughters.)

6 All these men were under the supervision of their father for the music of the temple of the LORD, with cymbals, lyres and harps, for the ministry at the house of God.
Asaph, Jeduthun and Heman were under
the supervision of the king. 7 Along with their
relatives—all of them trained and skilled in music for the LORD—they numbered 288.
8 Young and old alike, teacher as well as student, cast lots for their duties.

9 The first lot, which was for Asaph,
fell to Joseph,
his sons and relatives[b] 12[c]
the second to Gedaliah,
him and his relatives and sons 12
10 the third to Zakkur,
his sons and relatives 12
11 the fourth to Izri,[d]
his sons and relatives 12
12 the fifth to Nethaniah,
his sons and relatives 12
13 the sixth to Bukkiah,
his sons and relatives 12
14 the seventh to Jesarelah,[e]
his sons and relatives 12
15 the eighth to Jeshaiah,
his sons and relatives 12
16 the ninth to Mattaniah,
his sons and relatives 12
17 the tenth to Shimei,
his sons and relatives 12
18 the eleventh to Azarel,[f]
his sons and relatives 12
19 the twelfth to Hashabiah,
his sons and relatives 12
20 the thirteenth to Shubael,
his sons and relatives 12
21 the fourteenth to Mattithiah,
his sons and relatives 12
22 the fifteenth to Jerimoth,
his sons and relatives 12
23 the sixteenth to Hananiah,
his sons and relatives 12
24 the seventeenth to Joshbekashah,
his sons and relatives 12
25 the eighteenth to Hanani,
his sons and relatives 12
26 the nineteenth to Mallothi,
his sons and relatives 12
27 the twentieth to Eliathah,
his sons and relatives 12
28 the twenty-first to Hothir,
his sons and relatives 12
29 the twenty-second to Giddalti,
his sons and relatives 12
30 the twenty-third to Mahazioth,
his sons and relatives 12
31 the twenty-fourth to Romamti-Ezer,
his sons and relatives 12.

The Gatekeepers

26 The divisions of the gatekeepers:

From the Korahites: Meshelemiah son of Kore, one of the sons of Asaph.
2 Meshelemiah had sons:
Zechariah the firstborn,
Jediael the second,
Zebadiah the third,
Jathniel the fourth,
3 Elam the fifth,
Jehohanan the sixth
and Eliehoenai the seventh.
4 Obed-Edom also had sons:
Shemaiah the firstborn,

[a] *3* One Hebrew manuscript and some Septuagint manuscripts (see also verse 17); most Hebrew manuscripts do not have *Shimei.* [b] *9* See Septuagint; Hebrew does not have *his sons and relatives.* [c] *9* See the total in verse 7; Hebrew does not have *twelve.* [d] *11* A variant of *Zeri* [e] *14* A variant of *Asarelah* [f] *18* A variant of *Uzziel*

Jehozabad the second,
Joah the third,
Sakar the fourth,
Nethanel the fifth,
5 Ammiel the sixth,
Issachar the seventh
and Peullethai the eighth.
(For God had blessed Obed-Edom.)

6 Obed-Edom's son Shemaiah also had
sons, who were leaders in their father's family because they were very
capable men. 7The sons of Shemaiah:
Othni, Rephael, Obed and Elzabad; his
relatives Elihu and Semakiah were also
able men. 8All these were descendants
of Obed-Edom; they and their sons and
their relatives were capable men with
the strength to do the work—descendants of Obed-Edom, 62 in all.
9 Meshelemiah had sons and relatives, who
were able men—18 in all.

10 Hosah the Merarite had sons: Shimri the
first (although he was not the firstborn,
his father had appointed him the first),
11Hilkiah the second, Tabaliah the third
and Zechariah the fourth. The sons and
relatives of Hosah were 13 in all.

12These divisions of the gatekeepers, through
their leaders, had duties for ministering in the
temple of the LORD, just as their relatives had.
13Lots were cast for each gate, according to
their families, young and old alike.

14The lot for the East Gate fell to Shelemiah.[a] Then lots were cast for his son Zechariah,
a wise counselor, and the lot for the North
Gate fell to him. 15The lot for the South Gate
fell to Obed-Edom, and the lot for the storehouse fell to his sons. 16The lots for the West
Gate and the Shalleketh Gate on the upper
road fell to Shuppim and Hosah.

Guard was alongside of guard: 17There were
six Levites a day on the east, four a day on
the north, four a day on the south and two at
a time at the storehouse. 18As for the court[b]
to the west, there were four at the road and
two at the court[b] itself.

19These were the divisions of the gatekeepers who were descendants of Korah and Merari.

The Treasurers and Other Officials

20Their fellow Levites were[c] in charge of
the treasuries of the house of God and the
treasuries for the dedicated things.

21The descendants of Ladan, who were Gershonites through Ladan and who were heads
of families belonging to Ladan the Gershonite,
were Jehieli, 22the sons of Jehieli, Zetham and
his brother Joel. They were in charge of the
treasuries of the temple of the LORD.

23From the Amramites, the Izharites, the
Hebronites and the Uzzielites:

24 Shubael, a descendant of Gershom son
of Moses, was the official in charge of
the treasuries. 25His relatives through
Eliezer: Rehabiah his son, Jeshaiah his
son, Joram his son, Zikri his son and
Shelomith his son. 26Shelomith and his
relatives were in charge of all the treasuries for the things dedicated by King
David, by the heads of families who
were the commanders of thousands
and commanders of hundreds, and by
the other army commanders. 27Some
of the plunder taken in battle they dedicated for the repair of the temple of
the LORD. 28And everything dedicated
by Samuel the seer and by Saul son of
Kish, Abner son of Ner and Joab son
of Zeruiah, and all the other dedicated
things were in the care of Shelomith
and his relatives.
29 From the Izharites: Kenaniah and his
sons were assigned duties away from
the temple, as officials and judges over
Israel.
30 From the Hebronites: Hashabiah and his
relatives—seventeen hundred able
men—were responsible in Israel west
of the Jordan for all the work of the
LORD and for the king's service. 31As for
the Hebronites, Jeriah was their chief
according to the genealogical records
of their families. In the fortieth year
of David's reign a search was made in
the records, and capable men among
the Hebronites were found at Jazer in
Gilead. 32Jeriah had twenty-seven hundred relatives, who were able men and
heads of families, and King David put
them in charge of the Reubenites, the
Gadites and the half-tribe of Manasseh
for every matter pertaining to God and
for the affairs of the king.

Army Divisions

27 This is the list of the Israelites—heads
of families, commanders of thousands
and commanders of hundreds, and their officers, who served the king in all that concerned
the army divisions that were on duty month
by month throughout the year. Each division
consisted of 24,000 men.

2 In charge of the first division, for the first
month, was Jashobeam son of Zabdi-
el. There were 24,000 men in his division. 3He was a descendant of Perez and
chief of all the army officers for the first
month.
4 In charge of the division for the second
month was Dodai the Ahohite; Mikloth
was the leader of his division. There were
24,000 men in his division.
5 The third army commander, for the third
month, was Benaiah son of Jehoiada the
priest. He was chief and there were 24,000
men in his division. 6This was the Benaiah who was a mighty warrior among the

[a] *14* A variant of *Meshelemiah* [b] *18* The meaning of the Hebrew for this word is uncertain.
[c] *20* Septuagint; Hebrew *As for the Levites, Ahijah was*

Thirty and was over the Thirty. His son
Ammizabad was in charge of his division.
7 The fourth, for the fourth month, was Asahel the brother of Joab; his son Zebadiah
was his successor. There were 24,000 men
in his division.
8 The fifth, for the fifth month, was the commander Shamhuth the Izrahite. There
were 24,000 men in his division.
9 The sixth, for the sixth month, was Ira the
son of Ikkesh the Tekoite. There were
24,000 men in his division.
10 The seventh, for the seventh month, was
Helez the Pelonite, an Ephraimite. There
were 24,000 men in his division.
11 The eighth, for the eighth month, was Sibbekai the Hushathite, a Zerahite. There
were 24,000 men in his division.
12 The ninth, for the ninth month, was Abiezer
the Anathothite, a Benjamite. There were
24,000 men in his division.
13 The tenth, for the tenth month, was Maharai
the Netophathite, a Zerahite. There were
24,000 men in his division.
14 The eleventh, for the eleventh month, was
Benaiah the Pirathonite, an Ephraimite.
There were 24,000 men in his division.
15 The twelfth, for the twelfth month, was Heldai the Netophathite, from the family of
Othniel. There were 24,000 men in his
division.

Leaders of the Tribes

16 The leaders of the tribes of Israel:

over the Reubenites: Eliezer son of Zikri;
over the Simeonites: Shephatiah son of
Maakah;
17 over Levi: Hashabiah son of Kemuel;
over Aaron: Zadok;
18 over Judah: Elihu, a brother of David;
over Issachar: Omri son of Michael;
19 over Zebulun: Ishmaiah son of Obadiah;
over Naphtali: Jerimoth son of Azriel;
20 over the Ephraimites: Hoshea son of Azaziah;
over half the tribe of Manasseh: Joel son
of Pedaiah;
21 over the half-tribe of Manasseh in Gilead:
Iddo son of Zechariah;
over Benjamin: Jaasiel son of Abner;
22 over Dan: Azarel son of Jeroham.
These were the leaders of the tribes of Israel.

23 David did not take the number of the men
twenty years old or less, because the LORD
had promised to make Israel as numerous as
the stars in the sky. 24 Joab son of Zeruiah began to count the men but did not finish. God's
wrath came on Israel on account of this numbering, and the number was not entered in the
book[a] of the annals of King David.

The King's Overseers

25 Azmaveth son of Adiel was in charge of
the royal storehouses.
Jonathan son of Uzziah was in charge of
the storehouses in the outlying districts, in
the towns, the villages and the watchtowers.
26 Ezri son of Kelub was in charge of the
workers who farmed the land.
27 Shimei the Ramathite was in charge of
the vineyards.
Zabdi the Shiphmite was in charge of the
produce of the vineyards for the wine vats.
28 Baal-Hanan the Gederite was in charge of
the olive and sycamore-fig trees in the western foothills.
Joash was in charge of the supplies of olive oil.
29 Shitrai the Sharonite was in charge of the
herds grazing in Sharon.
Shaphat son of Adlai was in charge of the
herds in the valleys.
30 Obil the Ishmaelite was in charge of the
camels.
Jehdeiah the Meronothite was in charge of
the donkeys.
31 Jaziz the Hagrite was in charge of the
flocks.
All these were the officials in charge of
King David's property.

32 Jonathan, David's uncle, was a counselor,
a man of insight and a scribe. Jehiel son of
Hakmoni took care of the king's sons.
33 Ahithophel was the king's counselor.
Hushai the Arkite was the king's confidant.
34 Ahithophel was succeeded by Jehoiada son
of Benaiah and by Abiathar.
Joab was the commander of the royal army.

David's Plans for the Temple

28 David summoned all the officials of
Israel to assemble at Jerusalem: the
officers over the tribes, the commanders of
the divisions in the service of the king, the
commanders of thousands and commanders
of hundreds, and the officials in charge of
all the property and livestock belonging to
the king and his sons, together with the palace officials, the warriors and all the brave
fighting men.
2 King David rose to his feet and said: "Listen to me, my fellow Israelites, my people. I
had it in my heart to build a house as a place
of rest for the ark of the covenant of the LORD,
for the footstool of our God, and I made plans
to build it. 3 But God said to me, 'You are not
to build a house for my Name, because you
are a warrior and have shed blood.'
4 "Yet the LORD, the God of Israel, chose me
from my whole family to be king over Israel
forever. He chose Judah as leader, and from
the tribe of Judah he chose my family, and
from my father's sons he was pleased to make
me king over all Israel. 5 Of all my sons—and
the LORD has given me many—he has chosen
my son Solomon to sit on the throne of the
kingdom of the LORD over Israel. 6 He said to
me: 'Solomon your son is the one who will
build my house and my courts, for I have chosen him to be my son, and I will be his father.
7 I will establish his kingdom forever if he is

[a] 24 Septuagint; Hebrew *number*

unswerving in carrying out my commands
and laws, as is being done at this time.'
8"So now I charge you in the sight of all Israel and of the assembly of the LORD, and in
the hearing of our God: Be careful to follow
all the commands of the LORD your God, that
you may possess this good land and pass it on
as an inheritance to your descendants forever.
9"And you, my son Solomon, acknowledge
the God of your father, and serve him with
wholehearted devotion and with a willing
mind, for the LORD searches every heart and
understands every desire and every thought.
If you seek him, he will be found by you; but
if you forsake him, he will reject you forever.
10Consider now, for the LORD has chosen you
to build a house as the sanctuary. Be strong
and do the work."
11Then David gave his son Solomon the
plans for the portico of the temple, its buildings, its storerooms, its upper parts, its inner
rooms and the place of atonement. 12He gave
him the plans of all that the Spirit had put
in his mind for the courts of the temple of
the LORD and all the surrounding rooms, for
the treasuries of the temple of God and for
the treasuries for the dedicated things. 13He
gave him instructions for the divisions of the
priests and Levites, and for all the work of
serving in the temple of the LORD, as well as
for all the articles to be used in its service. 14He
designated the weight of gold for all the gold
articles to be used in various kinds of service,
and the weight of silver for all the silver articles to be used in various kinds of service:
15the weight of gold for the gold lampstands
and their lamps, with the weight for each
lampstand and its lamps; and the weight of
silver for each silver lampstand and its lamps,
according to the use of each lampstand; 16the
weight of gold for each table for consecrated
bread; the weight of silver for the silver tables;
17the weight of pure gold for the forks, sprinkling bowls and pitchers; the weight of gold
for each gold dish; the weight of silver for each
silver dish; 18and the weight of the refined gold
for the altar of incense. He also gave him the
plan for the chariot, that is, the cherubim of
gold that spread their wings and overshadow
the ark of the covenant of the LORD.
19"All this," David said, "I have in writing
as a result of the LORD's hand on me, and he
enabled me to understand all the details of
the plan."
20David also said to Solomon his son, "Be
strong and courageous, and do the work. Do
not be afraid or discouraged, for the LORD
God, my God, is with you. He will not fail
you or forsake you until all the work for the
service of the temple of the LORD is finished.
21The divisions of the priests and Levites are
ready for all the work on the temple of God,
and every willing person skilled in any craft
will help you in all the work. The officials and
all the people will obey your every command."

Gifts for Building the Temple

29 Then King David said to the whole
assembly: "My son Solomon, the one
whom God has chosen, is young and inexperienced. The task is great, because this palatial
structure is not for man but for the LORD God.
2With all my resources I have provided for the
temple of my God—gold for the gold work, silver for the silver, bronze for the bronze, iron
for the iron and wood for the wood, as well
as onyx for the settings, turquoise,[a] stones
of various colors, and all kinds of fine stone
and marble—all of these in large quantities.
3Besides, in my devotion to the temple of my
God I now give my personal treasures of gold
and silver for the temple of my God, over and
above everything I have provided for this holy
temple: 4three thousand talents[b] of gold (gold
of Ophir) and seven thousand talents[c] of refined silver, for the overlaying of the walls of
the buildings, 5for the gold work and the silver
work, and for all the work to be done by the
craftsmen. Now, who is willing to consecrate
themselves to the LORD today?"
6Then the leaders of families, the officers of
the tribes of Israel, the commanders of thousands and commanders of hundreds, and the
officials in charge of the king's work gave
willingly. 7They gave toward the work on the
temple of God five thousand talents[d] and ten
thousand darics[e] of gold, ten thousand talents[f] of silver, eighteen thousand talents[g] of
bronze and a hundred thousand talents[h] of
iron. 8Anyone who had precious stones gave
them to the treasury of the temple of the LORD
in the custody of Jehiel the Gershonite. 9The
people rejoiced at the willing response of their
leaders, for they had given freely and wholeheartedly to the LORD. David the king also
rejoiced greatly.

David's Prayer

10David praised the LORD in the presence
of the whole assembly, saying,

"Praise be to you, LORD,
the God of our father Israel,
from everlasting to everlasting.
11 Yours, LORD, is the greatness and the power
and the glory and the majesty and the splendor,
for everything in heaven and earth is yours.
Yours, LORD, is the kingdom;
you are exalted as head over all.
12 Wealth and honor come from you;
you are the ruler of all things.
In your hands are strength and power
to exalt and give strength to all.

[a] 2 The meaning of the Hebrew for this word is uncertain. [b] 4 That is, about 110 tons or about 100 metric tons [c] 4 That is, about 260 tons or about 235 metric tons [d] 7 That is, about 190 tons or about 170 metric tons [e] 7 That is, about 185 pounds or about 84 kilograms [f] 7 That is, about 380 tons or about 340 metric tons [g] 7 That is, about 675 tons or about 610 metric tons [h] 7 That is, about 3,800 tons or about 3,400 metric tons

13 Now, our God, we give you thanks,
and praise your glorious name.

14“But who am I, and who are my people,
that we should be able to give as generously
as this? Everything comes from you, and we
have given you only what comes from your
hand. 15We are foreigners and strangers in
your sight, as were all our ancestors. Our
days on earth are like a shadow, without hope.
16LORD our God, all this abundance that we
have provided for building you a temple for
your Holy Name comes from your hand, and
all of it belongs to you. 17I know, my God, that
you test the heart and are pleased with integrity. All these things I have given willingly
and with honest intent. And now I have seen
with joy how willingly your people who are
here have given to you. 18LORD, the God of our
fathers Abraham, Isaac and Israel, keep these
desires and thoughts in the hearts of your people forever, and keep their hearts loyal to you.
19And give my son Solomon the wholehearted devotion to keep your commands, statutes
and decrees and to do everything to build the
palatial structure for which I have provided.”
20Then David said to the whole assembly, “Praise the LORD your God.” So they all
praised the LORD, the God of their fathers;
they bowed down, prostrating themselves
before the LORD and the king.

Solomon Acknowledged as King

21The next day they made sacrifices to the
LORD and presented burnt offerings to him: a
thousand bulls, a thousand rams and a thousand male lambs, together with their drink
offerings, and other sacrifices in abundance
for all Israel. 22They ate and drank with great
joy in the presence of the LORD that day.
Then they acknowledged Solomon son of
David as king a second time, anointing him
before the LORD to be ruler and Zadok to be
priest. 23So Solomon sat on the throne of the
LORD as king in place of his father David. He
prospered and all Israel obeyed him. 24All the
officers and warriors, as well as all of King
David’s sons, pledged their submission to
King Solomon.
25The LORD highly exalted Solomon in the
sight of all Israel and bestowed on him royal splendor such as no king over Israel ever
had before.

The Death of David

26David son of Jesse was king over all Israel.
27He ruled over Israel forty years—seven in
Hebron and thirty-three in Jerusalem. 28He
died at a good old age, having enjoyed long
life, wealth and honor. His son Solomon succeeded him as king.
29As for the events of King David’s reign,
from beginning to end, they are written in
the records of Samuel the seer, the records of
Nathan the prophet and the records of Gad the
seer, 30together with the details of his reign
and power, and the circumstances that surrounded him and Israel and the kingdoms of
all the other lands.

2 Chronicles

Solomon Asks for Wisdom

1 Solomon son of David established himself
firmly over his kingdom, for the LORD his
God was with him and made him exceedingly great.
2Then Solomon spoke to all Israel—to the
commanders of thousands and commanders of hundreds, to the judges and to all the
leaders in Israel, the heads of families— 3and
Solomon and the whole assembly went to the
high place at Gibeon, for God’s tent of meeting
was there, which Moses the LORD’s servant
had made in the wilderness. 4Now David had
brought up the ark of God from Kiriath Jearim
to the place he had prepared for it, because
he had pitched a tent for it in Jerusalem. 5But
the bronze altar that Bezalel son of Uri, the
son of Hur, had made was in Gibeon in front
of the tabernacle of the LORD; so Solomon and
the assembly inquired of him there. 6Solomon
went up to the bronze altar before the LORD
in the tent of meeting and offered a thousand
burnt offerings on it.
7That night God appeared to Solomon and
said to him, “Ask for whatever you want me
to give you.”
8Solomon answered God, “You have shown
great kindness to David my father and have
made me king in his place. 9Now, LORD God,
let your promise to my father David be confirmed, for you have made me king over a
people who are as numerous as the dust of
the earth. 10Give me wisdom and knowledge,
that I may lead this people, for who is able to
govern this great people of yours?”
11God said to Solomon, “Since this is your
heart’s desire and you have not asked for
wealth, possessions or honor, nor for the
death of your enemies, and since you have
not asked for a long life but for wisdom and
knowledge to govern my people over whom I
have made you king, 12therefore wisdom and
knowledge will be given you. And I will also
give you wealth, possessions and honor, such
as no king who was before you ever had and
none after you will have.”

13 Then Solomon went to Jerusalem from the
high place at Gibeon, from before the tent of
meeting. And he reigned over Israel.
14 Solomon accumulated chariots and horses; he had fourteen hundred chariots and
twelve thousand horses,[a] which he kept in the
chariot cities and also with him in Jerusalem.
15 The king made silver and gold as common
in Jerusalem as stones, and cedar as plentiful
as sycamore-fig trees in the foothills. 16 Solomon's horses were imported from Egypt and
from Kue[b]—the royal merchants purchased
them from Kue at the current price. 17 They
imported a chariot from Egypt for six hundred
shekels[c] of silver, and a horse for a hundred
and fifty.[d] They also exported them to all the
kings of the Hittites and of the Arameans.

Preparations for Building the Temple

2[e] Solomon gave orders to build a temple for
the Name of the LORD and a royal palace
for himself. 2 He conscripted 70,000 men as
carriers and 80,000 as stonecutters in the hills
and 3,600 as foremen over them.
3 Solomon sent this message to Hiram[f] king
of Tyre:

"Send me cedar logs as you did for my
father David when you sent him cedar
to build a palace to live in. 4 Now I am
about to build a temple for the Name of
the LORD my God and to dedicate it to
him for burning fragrant incense before
him, for setting out the consecrated bread
regularly, and for making burnt offerings
every morning and evening and on the
Sabbaths, at the New Moons and at the
appointed festivals of the LORD our God.
This is a lasting ordinance for Israel.
5 "The temple I am going to build will
be great, because our God is greater than
all other gods. 6 But who is able to build a
temple for him, since the heavens, even
the highest heavens, cannot contain him?
Who then am I to build a temple for him,
except as a place to burn sacrifices before him?
7 "Send me, therefore, a man skilled to
work in gold and silver, bronze and iron,
and in purple, crimson and blue yarn, and
experienced in the art of engraving, to
work in Judah and Jerusalem with my
skilled workers, whom my father David
provided.
8 "Send me also cedar, juniper and
algum[g] logs from Lebanon, for I know
that your servants are skilled in cutting
timber there. My servants will work
with yours 9 to provide me with plenty
of lumber, because the temple I build
must be large and magnificent. 10 I will
give your servants, the woodsmen who
cut the timber, twenty thousand cors[h] of
ground wheat, twenty thousand cors[i] of
barley, twenty thousand baths[j] of wine
and twenty thousand baths of olive oil."

11 Hiram king of Tyre replied by letter to
Solomon:

"Because the LORD loves his people, he
has made you their king."

12 And Hiram added:

"Praise be to the LORD, the God of Israel, who made heaven and earth! He has
given King David a wise son, endowed
with intelligence and discernment, who
will build a temple for the LORD and a
palace for himself.
13 "I am sending you Huram-Abi, a man
of great skill, 14 whose mother was from
Dan and whose father was from Tyre.
He is trained to work in gold and silver,
bronze and iron, stone and wood, and
with purple and blue and crimson yarn
and fine linen. He is experienced in all
kinds of engraving and can execute any
design given to him. He will work with
your skilled workers and with those of
my lord, David your father.
15 "Now let my lord send his servants
the wheat and barley and the olive oil
and wine he promised, 16 and we will cut
all the logs from Lebanon that you need
and will float them as rafts by sea down
to Joppa. You can then take them up to
Jerusalem."

17 Solomon took a census of all the foreigners residing in Israel, after the census his father David had taken; and they were found
to be 153,600. 18 He assigned 70,000 of them
to be carriers and 80,000 to be stonecutters
in the hills, with 3,600 foremen over them to
keep the people working.

Solomon Builds the Temple

3 Then Solomon began to build the temple of
the LORD in Jerusalem on Mount Moriah,
where the LORD had appeared to his father David. It was on the threshing floor of Araunah[k]
the Jebusite, the place provided by David. 2 He
began building on the second day of the second month in the fourth year of his reign.
3 The foundation Solomon laid for building
the temple of God was sixty cubits long and
twenty cubits wide[l] (using the cubit of the old
standard). 4 The portico at the front of the temple was twenty cubits[m] long across the width
of the building and twenty[n] cubits high.

[a] *14* Or *charioteers* [b] *16* Probably Cilicia [c] *17* That is, about 15 pounds or about 6.9 kilograms
[d] *17* That is, about 3 3/4 pounds or about 1.7 kilograms [e] In Hebrew texts 2:1 is numbered 1:18, and
2:2-18 is numbered 2:1-17. [f] *3* Hebrew *Huram*, a variant of *Hiram*; also in verses 11 and 12
[g] *8* Probably a variant of *almug* [h] *10* That is, probably about 3,600 tons or about 3,200 metric tons of
wheat [i] *10* That is, probably about 3,000 tons or about 2,700 metric tons of barley [j] *10* That is,
about 120,000 gallons or about 440,000 liters [k] *1* Hebrew *Ornan*, a variant of *Araunah* [l] *3* That is,
about 90 feet long and 30 feet wide or about 27 meters long and 9 meters wide [m] *4* That is, about 30
feet or about 9 meters; also in verses 8, 11 and 13 [n] *4* Some Septuagint and Syriac manuscripts;
Hebrew *and a hundred and twenty*

He overlaid the inside with pure gold. 5He paneled the main hall with juniper and covered it with fine gold and decorated it with palm tree and chain designs. 6He adorned the temple with precious stones. And the gold he used was gold of Parvaim. 7He overlaid the ceiling beams, doorframes, walls and doors of the temple with gold, and he carved cherubim on the walls.

8He built the Most Holy Place, its length corresponding to the width of the temple—twenty cubits long and twenty cubits wide. He overlaid the inside with six hundred talents[a] of fine gold. 9The gold nails weighed fifty shekels.[b] He also overlaid the upper parts with gold.

10For the Most Holy Place he made a pair of sculptured cherubim and overlaid them with gold. 11The total wingspan of the cherubim was twenty cubits. One wing of the first cherub was five cubits[c] long and touched the temple wall, while its other wing, also five cubits long, touched the wing of the other cherub. 12Similarly one wing of the second cherub was five cubits long and touched the other temple wall, and its other wing, also five cubits long, touched the wing of the first cherub. 13The wings of these cherubim extended twenty cubits. They stood on their feet, facing the main hall.[d]

14He made the curtain of blue, purple and crimson yarn and fine linen, with cherubim worked into it.

15For the front of the temple he made two pillars, which together were thirty-five cubits[e] long, each with a capital five cubits high. 16He made interwoven chains[f] and put them on top of the pillars. He also made a hundred pomegranates and attached them to the chains. 17He erected the pillars in the front of the temple, one to the south and one to the north. The one to the south he named Jakin[g] and the one to the north Boaz.[h]

The Temple's Furnishings

4 He made a bronze altar twenty cubits long, twenty cubits wide and ten cubits high.[i] 2He made the Sea of cast metal, circular in shape, measuring ten cubits from rim to rim and five cubits[j] high. It took a line of thirty cubits[k] to measure around it. 3Below the rim, figures of bulls encircled it—ten to a cubit.[l] The bulls were cast in two rows in one piece with the Sea.

4The Sea stood on twelve bulls, three facing north, three facing west, three facing south and three facing east. The Sea rested on top of them, and their hindquarters were toward the center. 5It was a handbreadth[m] in thickness, and its rim was like the rim of a cup, like a lily blossom. It held three thousand baths.[n]

6He then made ten basins for washing and placed five on the south side and five on the north. In them the things to be used for the burnt offerings were rinsed, but the Sea was to be used by the priests for washing.

7He made ten gold lampstands according to the specifications for them and placed them in the temple, five on the south side and five on the north.

8He made ten tables and placed them in the temple, five on the south side and five on the north. He also made a hundred gold sprinkling bowls.

9He made the courtyard of the priests, and the large court and the doors for the court, and overlaid the doors with bronze. 10He placed the Sea on the south side, at the southeast corner.

11And Huram also made the pots and shovels and sprinkling bowls.

So Huram finished the work he had undertaken for King Solomon in the temple of God:

12the two pillars;
the two bowl-shaped capitals on top of the pillars;
the two sets of network decorating the two bowl-shaped capitals on top of the pillars;
13the four hundred pomegranates for the two sets of network (two rows of pomegranates for each network, decorating the bowl-shaped capitals on top of the pillars);
14the stands with their basins;
15the Sea and the twelve bulls under it;
16the pots, shovels, meat forks and all related articles.

All the objects that Huram-Abi made for King Solomon for the temple of the LORD were of polished bronze. 17The king had them cast in clay molds in the plain of the Jordan between Sukkoth and Zarethan.[o] 18All these things that Solomon made amounted to so much that the weight of the bronze could not be calculated.

19Solomon also made all the furnishings that were in God's temple:

the golden altar;
the tables on which was the bread of the Presence;
20the lampstands of pure gold with their lamps, to burn in front of the inner sanctuary as prescribed;
21the gold floral work and lamps and tongs (they were solid gold);
22the pure gold wick trimmers, sprinkling bowls, dishes and censers; and the gold doors of the temple: the inner doors to the Most Holy Place and the doors of the main hall.

[a] *8* That is, about 23 tons or about 21 metric tons [b] *9* That is, about 1 1/4 pounds or about 575 grams [c] *11* That is, about 7 1/2 feet or about 2.3 meters; also in verse 15 [d] *13* Or *facing inward* [e] *15* That is, about 53 feet or about 16 meters [f] *16* Or possibly *made chains in the inner sanctuary*; the meaning of the Hebrew for this phrase is uncertain. [g] *17* *Jakin* probably means *he establishes.* [h] *17* *Boaz* probably means *in him is strength.* [i] *1* That is, about 30 feet long and wide and 15 feet high or about 9 meters long and wide and 4.5 meters high [j] *2* That is, about 7 1/2 feet or about 2.3 meters [k] *2* That is, about 45 feet or about 14 meters [l] *3* That is, about 18 inches or about 45 centimeters [m] *5* That is, about 3 inches or about 7.5 centimeters [n] *5* That is, about 18,000 gallons or about 66,000 liters [o] *17* Hebrew *Zeredatha*, a variant of *Zarethan*

5 When all the work Solomon had done for the temple of the LORD was finished, he brought in the things his father David had dedicated—the silver and gold and all the furnishings—and he placed them in the treasuries of God's temple.

The Ark Brought to the Temple

2Then Solomon summoned to Jerusalem the elders of Israel, all the heads of the tribes and the chiefs of the Israelite families, to bring up the ark of the LORD's covenant from Zion, the City of David. 3And all the Israelites came together to the king at the time of the festival in the seventh month.

4When all the elders of Israel had arrived, the Levites took up the ark, 5and they brought up the ark and the tent of meeting and all the sacred furnishings in it. The Levitical priests carried them up; 6and King Solomon and the entire assembly of Israel that had gathered about him were before the ark, sacrificing so many sheep and cattle that they could not be recorded or counted.

7The priests then brought the ark of the LORD's covenant to its place in the inner sanctuary of the temple, the Most Holy Place, and put it beneath the wings of the cherubim. 8The cherubim spread their wings over the place of the ark and covered the ark and its carrying poles. 9These poles were so long that their ends, extending from the ark, could be seen from in front of the inner sanctuary, but not from outside the Holy Place; and they are still there today. 10There was nothing in the ark except the two tablets that Moses had placed in it at Horeb, where the LORD made a covenant with the Israelites after they came out of Egypt.

11The priests then withdrew from the Holy Place. All the priests who were there had consecrated themselves, regardless of their divisions. 12All the Levites who were musicians—Asaph, Heman, Jeduthun and their sons and relatives—stood on the east side of the altar, dressed in fine linen and playing cymbals, harps and lyres. They were accompanied by 120 priests sounding trumpets. 13The trumpeters and musicians joined in unison to give praise and thanks to the LORD. Accompanied by trumpets, cymbals and other instruments, the singers raised their voices in praise to the LORD and sang:

"He is good;
his love endures forever."

Then the temple of the LORD was filled with the cloud, 14and the priests could not perform their service because of the cloud, for the glory of the LORD filled the temple of God.

6 Then Solomon said, "The LORD has said that he would dwell in a dark cloud; 2I have built a magnificent temple for you, a place for you to dwell forever."

3While the whole assembly of Israel was standing there, the king turned around and blessed them. 4Then he said:

"Praise be to the LORD, the God of Israel, who with his hands has fulfilled what he promised with his mouth to my father David. For he said, 5'Since the day I brought my people out of Egypt, I have not chosen a city in any tribe of Israel to have a temple built so that my Name might be there, nor have I chosen anyone to be ruler over my people Israel. 6But now I have chosen Jerusalem for my Name to be there, and I have chosen David to rule my people Israel.'

7"My father David had it in his heart to build a temple for the Name of the LORD, the God of Israel. 8But the LORD said to my father David, 'You did well to have it in your heart to build a temple for my Name. 9Nevertheless, you are not the one to build the temple, but your son, your own flesh and blood—he is the one who will build the temple for my Name.'

10"The LORD has kept the promise he made. I have succeeded David my father and now I sit on the throne of Israel, just as the LORD promised, and I have built the temple for the Name of the LORD, the God of Israel. 11There I have placed the ark, in which is the covenant of the LORD that he made with the people of Israel."

Solomon's Prayer of Dedication

12Then Solomon stood before the altar of the LORD in front of the whole assembly of Israel and spread out his hands. 13Now he had made a bronze platform, five cubits long, five cubits wide and three cubits high,[a] and had placed it in the center of the outer court. He stood on the platform and then knelt down before the whole assembly of Israel and spread out his hands toward heaven. 14He said:

"LORD, the God of Israel, there is no God like you in heaven or on earth—you who keep your covenant of love with your servants who continue wholeheartedly in your way. 15You have kept your promise to your servant David my father; with your mouth you have promised and with your hand you have fulfilled it—as it is today.

16"Now, LORD, the God of Israel, keep for your servant David my father the promises you made to him when you said, 'You shall never fail to have a successor to sit before me on the throne of Israel, if only your descendants are careful in all they do to walk before me according to my law, as you have done.' 17And now, LORD, the God of Israel, let your word that you promised your servant David come true.

18"But will God really dwell on earth with humans? The heavens, even the highest heavens, cannot contain you. How much less this temple I have built! 19Yet, LORD my God, give attention to your

[a] *13* That is, about 7 1/2 feet long and wide and 4 1/2 feet high or about 2.3 meters long and wide and 1.4 meters high

servant's prayer and his plea for mercy.
Hear the cry and the prayer that your servant is praying in your presence. [20]May
your eyes be open toward this temple day
and night, this place of which you said
you would put your Name there. May you
hear the prayer your servant prays toward this place. [21]Hear the supplications
of your servant and of your people Israel
when they pray toward this place. Hear
from heaven, your dwelling place; and
when you hear, forgive.

[22]"When anyone wrongs their neighbor
and is required to take an oath and they
come and swear the oath before your altar in this temple, [23]then hear from heav-
en and act. Judge between your servants,
condemning the guilty and bringing
down on their heads what they have done,
and vindicating the innocent by treating
them in accordance with their innocence.

[24]"When your people Israel have been
defeated by an enemy because they have
sinned against you and when they turn
back and give praise to your name, praying and making supplication before you
in this temple, [25]then hear from heaven
and forgive the sin of your people Israel
and bring them back to the land you gave
to them and their ancestors.

[26]"When the heavens are shut up and
there is no rain because your people
have sinned against you, and when they
pray toward this place and give praise
to your name and turn from their sin
because you have afflicted them, [27]then
hear from heaven and forgive the sin of
your servants, your people Israel. Teach
them the right way to live, and send rain
on the land you gave your people for an
inheritance.

[28]"When famine or plague comes to
the land, or blight or mildew, locusts or
grasshoppers, or when enemies besiege
them in any of their cities, whatever disaster or disease may come, [29]and when a
prayer or plea is made by anyone among
your people Israel—being aware of their
afflictions and pains, and spreading out
their hands toward this temple— [30]then
hear from heaven, your dwelling place.
Forgive, and deal with everyone according to all they do, since you know their
hearts (for you alone know the human
heart), [31]so that they will fear you and
walk in obedience to you all the time they
live in the land you gave our ancestors.

[32]"As for the foreigner who does not
belong to your people Israel but has come
from a distant land because of your great
name and your mighty hand and your
outstretched arm—when they come and
pray toward this temple, [33]then hear from
heaven, your dwelling place. Do whatever
the foreigner asks of you, so that all the
peoples of the earth may know your name
and fear you, as do your own people Israel, and may know that this house I have
built bears your Name.

[34]"When your people go to war against
their enemies, wherever you send them,
and when they pray to you toward this
city you have chosen and the temple I
have built for your Name, [35]then hear
from heaven their prayer and their plea,
and uphold their cause.

[36]"When they sin against you—for
there is no one who does not sin—and you
become angry with them and give them
over to the enemy, who takes them captive
to a land far away or near; [37]and if they
have a change of heart in the land where
they are held captive, and repent and
plead with you in the land of their captivity and say, 'We have sinned, we have done
wrong and acted wickedly'; [38]and if they
turn back to you with all their heart and
soul in the land of their captivity where
they were taken, and pray toward the land
you gave their ancestors, toward the city
you have chosen and toward the temple
I have built for your Name; [39]then from
heaven, your dwelling place, hear their
prayer and their pleas, and uphold their
cause. And forgive your people, who have
sinned against you.

[40]"Now, my God, may your eyes be open
and your ears attentive to the prayers offered in this place.

[41]"Now arise, LORD God, and come to
your resting place,
you and the ark of your might.
May your priests, LORD God, be
clothed with salvation,
may your faithful people rejoice
in your goodness.
[42]LORD God, do not reject your
anointed one.
Remember the great love
promised to David your
servant."

The Dedication of the Temple

7 When Solomon finished praying, fire
came down from heaven and consumed
the burnt offering and the sacrifices, and
the glory of the LORD filled the temple. [2]The
priests could not enter the temple of the LORD
because the glory of the LORD filled it. [3]When
all the Israelites saw the fire coming down
and the glory of the LORD above the temple,
they knelt on the pavement with their faces
to the ground, and they worshiped and gave
thanks to the LORD, saying,

"He is good;
his love endures forever."

[4]Then the king and all the people offered sacrifices before the LORD. [5]And King Solomon
offered a sacrifice of twenty-two thousand
head of cattle and a hundred and twenty thousand sheep and goats. So the king and all
the people dedicated the temple of God. [6]The
priests took their positions, as did the Levites
with the LORD's musical instruments, which
King David had made for praising the LORD
and which were used when he gave thanks,

saying, "His love endures forever." Opposite the Levites, the priests blew their trumpets, and all the Israelites were standing.

7Solomon consecrated the middle part of the courtyard in front of the temple of the LORD, and there he offered burnt offerings and the fat of the fellowship offerings, because the bronze altar he had made could not hold the burnt offerings, the grain offerings and the fat portions.

8So Solomon observed the festival at that time for seven days, and all Israel with him—a vast assembly, people from Lebo Hamath to the Wadi of Egypt. 9On the eighth day they held an assembly, for they had celebrated the dedication of the altar for seven days and the festival for seven days more. 10On the twenty-third day of the seventh month he sent the people to their homes, joyful and glad in heart for the good things the LORD had done for David and Solomon and for his people Israel.

The LORD Appears to Solomon

11When Solomon had finished the temple of the LORD and the royal palace, and had succeeded in carrying out all he had in mind to do in the temple of the LORD and in his own palace, 12the LORD appeared to him at night and said:

"I have heard your prayer and have chosen this place for myself as a temple for sacrifices.

13"When I shut up the heavens so that there is no rain, or command locusts to devour the land or send a plague among my people, 14if my people, who are called by my name, will humble themselves and pray and seek my face and turn from their wicked ways, then I will hear from heaven, and I will forgive their sin and will heal their land. 15Now my eyes will be open and my ears attentive to the prayers offered in this place. 16I have chosen and consecrated this temple so that my Name may be there forever. My eyes and my heart will always be there.

17"As for you, if you walk before me faithfully as David your father did, and do all I command, and observe my decrees and laws, 18I will establish your royal throne, as I covenanted with David your father when I said, 'You shall never fail to have a successor to rule over Israel.'

19"But if you[a] turn away and forsake the decrees and commands I have given you[a] and go off to serve other gods and worship them, 20then I will uproot Israel from my land, which I have given them, and will reject this temple I have consecrated for my Name. I will make it a byword and an object of ridicule among all peoples. 21This temple will become a heap of rubble. All[b] who pass by will be appalled and say, 'Why has the LORD done such a thing to this land and to this temple?' 22People will answer, 'Because they have forsaken the LORD, the God of their ancestors, who brought them out of Egypt, and have embraced other gods, worshiping and serving them—that is why he brought all this disaster on them.'"

Solomon's Other Activities

8 At the end of twenty years, during which Solomon built the temple of the LORD and his own palace, 2Solomon rebuilt the villages that Hiram[c] had given him, and settled Israelites in them. 3Solomon then went to Hamath Zobah and captured it. 4He also built up Tadmor in the desert and all the store cities he had built in Hamath. 5He rebuilt Upper Beth Horon and Lower Beth Horon as fortified cities, with walls and with gates and bars, 6as well as Baalath and all his store cities, and all the cities for his chariots and for his horses[d]—whatever he desired to build in Jerusalem, in Lebanon and throughout all the territory he ruled.

7There were still people left from the Hittites, Amorites, Perizzites, Hivites and Jebusites (these people were not Israelites). 8Solomon conscripted the descendants of all these people remaining in the land—whom the Israelites had not destroyed—to serve as slave labor, as it is to this day. 9But Solomon did not make slaves of the Israelites for his work; they were his fighting men, commanders of his captains, and commanders of his chariots and charioteers. 10They were also King Solomon's chief officials—two hundred and fifty officials supervising the men.

11Solomon brought Pharaoh's daughter up from the City of David to the palace he had built for her, for he said, "My wife must not live in the palace of David king of Israel, because the places the ark of the LORD has entered are holy."

12On the altar of the LORD that he had built in front of the portico, Solomon sacrificed burnt offerings to the LORD, 13according to the daily requirement for offerings commanded by Moses for the Sabbaths, the New Moons and the three annual festivals—the Festival of Unleavened Bread, the Festival of Weeks and the Festival of Tabernacles. 14In keeping with the ordinance of his father David, he appointed the divisions of the priests for their duties, and the Levites to lead the praise and to assist the priests according to each day's requirement. He also appointed the gatekeepers by divisions for the various gates, because this was what David the man of God had ordered. 15They did not deviate from the king's commands to the priests or to the Levites in any matter, including that of the treasuries.

16All Solomon's work was carried out, from the day the foundation of the temple of the LORD was laid until its completion. So the temple of the LORD was finished.

[a] *19* The Hebrew is plural. [b] *21* See some Septuagint manuscripts, Old Latin, Syriac, Arabic and Targum; Hebrew *And though this temple is now so imposing, all* [c] *2* Hebrew *Huram*, a variant of *Hiram*; also in verse 18 [d] *6* Or *charioteers*

17Then Solomon went to Ezion Geber and
Elath on the coast of Edom. 18And Hiram sent
him ships commanded by his own men, sailors who knew the sea. These, with Solomon's
men, sailed to Ophir and brought back four
hundred and fifty talents[a] of gold, which they
delivered to King Solomon.

The Queen of Sheba Visits Solomon

9 When the queen of Sheba heard of Solomon's fame, she came to Jerusalem to
test him with hard questions. Arriving with
a very great caravan—with camels carrying
spices, large quantities of gold, and precious
stones—she came to Solomon and talked with
him about all she had on her mind. 2Solomon
answered all her questions; nothing was too
hard for him to explain to her. 3When the
queen of Sheba saw the wisdom of Solomon,
as well as the palace he had built, 4the food
on his table, the seating of his officials, the
attending servants in their robes, the cupbearers in their robes and the burnt offerings
he made at[b] the temple of the LORD, she was
overwhelmed.

5She said to the king, "The report I heard
in my own country about your achievements
and your wisdom is true. 6But I did not believe
what they said until I came and saw with my
own eyes. Indeed, not even half the greatness
of your wisdom was told me; you have far exceeded the report I heard. 7How happy your
people must be! How happy your officials,
who continually stand before you and hear
your wisdom! 8Praise be to the LORD your
God, who has delighted in you and placed you
on his throne as king to rule for the LORD your
God. Because of the love of your God for Israel
and his desire to uphold them forever, he has
made you king over them, to maintain justice
and righteousness."

9Then she gave the king 120 talents[c] of gold,
large quantities of spices, and precious stones.
There had never been such spices as those the
queen of Sheba gave to King Solomon.

10(The servants of Hiram and the servants of Solomon brought gold from Ophir;
they also brought algumwood[d] and precious
stones. 11The king used the algumwood to
make steps for the temple of the LORD and
for the royal palace, and to make harps and
lyres for the musicians. Nothing like them had
ever been seen in Judah.)

12King Solomon gave the queen of Sheba all
she desired and asked for; he gave her more
than she had brought to him. Then she left and
returned with her retinue to her own country.

Solomon's Splendor

13The weight of the gold that Solomon received yearly was 666 talents,[e] 14not including
the revenues brought in by merchants and
traders. Also all the kings of Arabia and the
governors of the territories brought gold and
silver to Solomon.

15King Solomon made two hundred large
shields of hammered gold; six hundred shekels[f] of hammered gold went into each shield.
16He also made three hundred small shields of
hammered gold, with three hundred shekels[g]
of gold in each shield. The king put them in
the Palace of the Forest of Lebanon.

17Then the king made a great throne covered
with ivory and overlaid with pure gold. 18The
throne had six steps, and a footstool of gold
was attached to it. On both sides of the seat
were armrests, with a lion standing beside
each of them. 19Twelve lions stood on the six
steps, one at either end of each step. Nothing
like it had ever been made for any other kingdom. 20All King Solomon's goblets were gold,
and all the household articles in the Palace of
the Forest of Lebanon were pure gold. Nothing
was made of silver, because silver was considered of little value in Solomon's day. 21The
king had a fleet of trading ships[h] manned by
Hiram's[i] servants. Once every three years it
returned, carrying gold, silver and ivory, and
apes and baboons.

22King Solomon was greater in riches and
wisdom than all the other kings of the earth.
23All the kings of the earth sought audience
with Solomon to hear the wisdom God had
put in his heart. 24Year after year, everyone
who came brought a gift—articles of silver
and gold, and robes, weapons and spices, and
horses and mules.

25Solomon had four thousand stalls for
horses and chariots, and twelve thousand
horses,[j] which he kept in the chariot cities
and also with him in Jerusalem. 26He ruled
over all the kings from the Euphrates River to
the land of the Philistines, as far as the border
of Egypt. 27The king made silver as common
in Jerusalem as stones, and cedar as plentiful
as sycamore-fig trees in the foothills. 28Solo-
mon's horses were imported from Egypt and
from all other countries.

Solomon's Death

29As for the other events of Solomon's reign,
from beginning to end, are they not written
in the records of Nathan the prophet, in the
prophecy of Ahijah the Shilonite and in the
visions of Iddo the seer concerning Jeroboam
son of Nebat? 30Solomon reigned in Jerusalem
over all Israel forty years. 31Then he rested
with his ancestors and was buried in the city
of David his father. And Rehoboam his son
succeeded him as king.

Israel Rebels Against Rehoboam

10 Rehoboam went to Shechem, for all Israel had gone there to make him king.
2When Jeroboam son of Nebat heard this (he
was in Egypt, where he had fled from King

[a] *18* That is, about 17 tons or about 15 metric tons [b] *4* Or *and the ascent by which he went up to* [c] *9* That is, about 4 1/2 tons or about 4 metric tons [d] *10* Probably a variant of *almugwood* [e] *13* That is, about 25 tons or about 23 metric tons [f] *15* That is, about 15 pounds or about 6.9 kilograms [g] *16* That is, about 7 1/2 pounds or about 3.5 kilograms [h] *21* Hebrew *of ships that could go to Tarshish* [i] *21* Hebrew *Huram*, a variant of *Hiram* [j] *25* Or *charioteers*

Solomon), he returned from Egypt. 3So they
sent for Jeroboam, and he and all Israel went
to Rehoboam and said to him: 4"Your father
put a heavy yoke on us, but now lighten the
harsh labor and the heavy yoke he put on us,
and we will serve you."
5Rehoboam answered, "Come back to me in
three days." So the people went away.
6Then King Rehoboam consulted the elders
who had served his father Solomon during his
lifetime. "How would you advise me to answer
these people?" he asked.
7They replied, "If you will be kind to these
people and please them and give them a favorable answer, they will always be your servants."
8But Rehoboam rejected the advice the elders gave him and consulted the young men
who had grown up with him and were serving
him. 9He asked them, "What is your advice?
How should we answer these people who
say to me, 'Lighten the yoke your father put
on us'?"
10The young men who had grown up with
him replied, "The people have said to you,
'Your father put a heavy yoke on us, but make
our yoke lighter.' Now tell them, 'My little finger is thicker than my father's waist. 11My
father laid on you a heavy yoke; I will make
it even heavier. My father scourged you with
whips; I will scourge you with scorpions.'"
12Three days later Jeroboam and all the people returned to Rehoboam, as the king had
said, "Come back to me in three days." 13The
king answered them harshly. Rejecting the
advice of the elders, 14he followed the advice
of the young men and said, "My father made
your yoke heavy; I will make it even heavier. My father scourged you with whips; I will
scourge you with scorpions." 15So the king
did not listen to the people, for this turn of
events was from God, to fulfill the word the
LORD had spoken to Jeroboam son of Nebat
through Ahijah the Shilonite.
16When all Israel saw that the king refused
to listen to them, they answered the king:

"What share do we have in David,
  what part in Jesse's son?
To your tents, Israel!
  Look after your own house, David!"

So all the Israelites went home. 17But as for
the Israelites who were living in the towns of
Judah, Rehoboam still ruled over them.
18King Rehoboam sent out Adoniram,[a] who
was in charge of forced labor, but the Israelites
stoned him to death. King Rehoboam, however, managed to get into his chariot and escape
to Jerusalem. 19So Israel has been in rebellion
against the house of David to this day.
11 When Rehoboam arrived in Jerusalem,
he mustered Judah and Benjamin—a
hundred and eighty thousand able young
men—to go to war against Israel and to regain the kingdom for Rehoboam.
2But this word of the LORD came to Shemaiah the man of God: 3"Say to Rehoboam son
of Solomon king of Judah and to all Israel in
Judah and Benjamin, 4'This is what the LORD
says: Do not go up to fight against your fellow Israelites. Go home, every one of you, for
this is my doing.'" So they obeyed the words
of the LORD and turned back from marching
against Jeroboam.

Rehoboam Fortifies Judah

5Rehoboam lived in Jerusalem and built
up towns for defense in Judah: 6Bethlehem,
Etam, Tekoa, 7Beth Zur, Soko, Adullam,
8Gath, Mareshah, Ziph, 9Adoraim, Lachish,
Azekah, 10Zorah, Aijalon and Hebron. These
were fortified cities in Judah and Benjamin.
11He strengthened their defenses and put commanders in them, with supplies of food, olive
oil and wine. 12He put shields and spears in
all the cities, and made them very strong. So
Judah and Benjamin were his.
13The priests and Levites from all their districts throughout Israel sided with him. 14The
Levites even abandoned their pasturelands
and property and came to Judah and Jerusalem, because Jeroboam and his sons had
rejected them as priests of the LORD 15when
he appointed his own priests for the high
places and for the goat and calf idols he had
made. 16Those from every tribe of Israel who
set their hearts on seeking the LORD, the God
of Israel, followed the Levites to Jerusalem to
offer sacrifices to the LORD, the God of their
ancestors. 17They strengthened the kingdom
of Judah and supported Rehoboam son of Solomon three years, following the ways of David
and Solomon during this time.

Rehoboam's Family

18Rehoboam married Mahalath, who was
the daughter of David's son Jerimoth and of
Abihail, the daughter of Jesse's son Eliab.
19She bore him sons: Jeush, Shemariah and
Zaham. 20Then he married Maakah daughter
of Absalom, who bore him Abijah, Attai, Ziza
and Shelomith. 21Rehoboam loved Maakah
daughter of Absalom more than any of his
other wives and concubines. In all, he had
eighteen wives and sixty concubines, twenty-eight sons and sixty daughters.
22Rehoboam appointed Abijah son of Maakah as crown prince among his brothers, in
order to make him king. 23He acted wisely,
dispersing some of his sons throughout the
districts of Judah and Benjamin, and to all
the fortified cities. He gave them abundant
provisions and took many wives for them.

Shishak Attacks Jerusalem

12 After Rehoboam's position as king was
established and he had become strong,
he and all Israel[b] with him abandoned the
law of the LORD. 2Because they had been unfaithful to the LORD, Shishak king of Egypt
attacked Jerusalem in the fifth year of King
Rehoboam. 3With twelve hundred chariots and sixty thousand horsemen and the
innumerable troops of Libyans, Sukkites and

[a] 18 Hebrew *Hadoram*, a variant of *Adoniram*
[b] 1 That is, Judah, as frequently in 2 Chronicles

Cushites[a] that came with him from Egypt,
4he captured the fortified cities of Judah and
came as far as Jerusalem.
5Then the prophet Shemaiah came to Rehoboam and to the leaders of Judah who had
assembled in Jerusalem for fear of Shishak,
and he said to them, "This is what the LORD
says, 'You have abandoned me; therefore, I
now abandon you to Shishak.'"
6The leaders of Israel and the king humbled
themselves and said, "The LORD is just."
7When the LORD saw that they humbled
themselves, this word of the LORD came to Shemaiah: "Since they have humbled themselves,
I will not destroy them but will soon give them
deliverance. My wrath will not be poured out
on Jerusalem through Shishak. 8They will,
however, become subject to him, so that they
may learn the difference between serving me
and serving the kings of other lands."
9When Shishak king of Egypt attacked Jerusalem, he carried off the treasures of the
temple of the LORD and the treasures of the
royal palace. He took everything, including
the gold shields Solomon had made. 10So King
Rehoboam made bronze shields to replace
them and assigned these to the commanders of the guard on duty at the entrance to
the royal palace. 11Whenever the king went
to the LORD's temple, the guards went with
him, bearing the shields, and afterward they
returned them to the guardroom.
12Because Rehoboam humbled himself, the
LORD's anger turned from him, and he was
not totally destroyed. Indeed, there was some
good in Judah.
13King Rehoboam established himself firmly in Jerusalem and continued as king. He was
forty-one years old when he became king, and
he reigned seventeen years in Jerusalem, the
city the LORD had chosen out of all the tribes of
Israel in which to put his Name. His mother's
name was Naamah; she was an Ammonite.
14He did evil because he had not set his heart
on seeking the LORD.
15As for the events of Rehoboam's reign,
from beginning to end, are they not written
in the records of Shemaiah the prophet and of
Iddo the seer that deal with genealogies? There
was continual warfare between Rehoboam and
Jeroboam. 16Rehoboam rested with his ancestors and was buried in the City of David. And
Abijah his son succeeded him as king.

Abijah King of Judah

13 In the eighteenth year of the reign of Jeroboam, Abijah became king of Judah,
2and he reigned in Jerusalem three years. His
mother's name was Maakah,[b] a daughter[c] of
Uriel of Gibeah.
There was war between Abijah and Jeroboam. 3Abijah went into battle with an army
of four hundred thousand able fighting men,
and Jeroboam drew up a battle line against
him with eight hundred thousand able troops.
4Abijah stood on Mount Zemaraim, in the
hill country of Ephraim, and said, "Jeroboam
and all Israel, listen to me! 5Don't you know
that the LORD, the God of Israel, has given
the kingship of Israel to David and his descendants forever by a covenant of salt? 6Yet
Jeroboam son of Nebat, an official of Solomon son of David, rebelled against his master.
7Some worthless scoundrels gathered around
him and opposed Rehoboam son of Solomon
when he was young and indecisive and not
strong enough to resist them.
8"And now you plan to resist the kingdom
of the LORD, which is in the hands of David's
descendants. You are indeed a vast army and
have with you the golden calves that Jeroboam made to be your gods. 9But didn't you
drive out the priests of the LORD, the sons of
Aaron, and the Levites, and make priests of
your own as the peoples of other lands do?
Whoever comes to consecrate himself with
a young bull and seven rams may become a
priest of what are not gods.
10"As for us, the LORD is our God, and we
have not forsaken him. The priests who serve
the LORD are sons of Aaron, and the Levites
assist them. 11Every morning and evening
they present burnt offerings and fragrant
incense to the LORD. They set out the bread
on the ceremonially clean table and light the
lamps on the gold lampstand every evening.
We are observing the requirements of the
LORD our God. But you have forsaken him.
12God is with us; he is our leader. His priests
with their trumpets will sound the battle cry
against you. People of Israel, do not fight
against the LORD, the God of your ancestors,
for you will not succeed."
13Now Jeroboam had sent troops around
to the rear, so that while he was in front of
Judah the ambush was behind them. 14Judah
turned and saw that they were being attacked
at both front and rear. Then they cried out
to the LORD. The priests blew their trumpets
15and the men of Judah raised the battle cry.
At the sound of their battle cry, God routed
Jeroboam and all Israel before Abijah and
Judah. 16The Israelites fled before Judah, and
God delivered them into their hands. 17Abijah
and his troops inflicted heavy losses on them,
so that there were five hundred thousand casualties among Israel's able men. 18The Israelites were subdued on that occasion, and the
people of Judah were victorious because they
relied on the LORD, the God of their ancestors.
19Abijah pursued Jeroboam and took
from him the towns of Bethel, Jeshanah
and Ephron, with their surrounding villages. 20Jeroboam did not regain power during
the time of Abijah. And the LORD struck him
down and he died.
21But Abijah grew in strength. He married
fourteen wives and had twenty-two sons and
sixteen daughters.
22The other events of Abijah's reign, what
he did and what he said, are written in the
annotations of the prophet Iddo.

[a] 3 That is, people from the upper Nile region [b] 2 Most Septuagint manuscripts and Syriac (see also 11:20 and 1 Kings 15:2); Hebrew *Micaiah* [c] 2 Or *granddaughter*

14[a] And Abijah rested with his ancestors
and was buried in the City of David.
Asa his son succeeded him as king, and in his
days the country was at peace for ten years.

Asa King of Judah

2Asa did what was good and right in the
eyes of the LORD his God. 3He removed the
foreign altars and the high places, smashed
the sacred stones and cut down the Asherah poles.[b] 4He commanded Judah to seek
the LORD, the God of their ancestors, and to
obey his laws and commands. 5He removed
the high places and incense altars in every
town in Judah, and the kingdom was at peace
under him. 6He built up the fortified cities of
Judah, since the land was at peace. No one
was at war with him during those years, for
the LORD gave him rest.

7"Let us build up these towns," he said to Judah, "and put walls around them, with towers,
gates and bars. The land is still ours, because
we have sought the LORD our God; we sought
him and he has given us rest on every side."
So they built and prospered.

8Asa had an army of three hundred thousand men from Judah, equipped with large
shields and with spears, and two hundred and
eighty thousand from Benjamin, armed with
small shields and with bows. All these were
brave fighting men.

9Zerah the Cushite marched out against
them with an army of thousands upon thousands and three hundred chariots, and came
as far as Mareshah. 10Asa went out to meet
him, and they took up battle positions in the
Valley of Zephathah near Mareshah.

11Then Asa called to the LORD his God and
said, "LORD, there is no one like you to help
the powerless against the mighty. Help us,
LORD our God, for we rely on you, and in your
name we have come against this vast army.
LORD, you are our God; do not let mere mortals
prevail against you."

12The LORD struck down the Cushites before
Asa and Judah. The Cushites fled, 13and Asa
and his army pursued them as far as Gerar.
Such a great number of Cushites fell that they
could not recover; they were crushed before
the LORD and his forces. The men of Judah
carried off a large amount of plunder. 14They
destroyed all the villages around Gerar, for
the terror of the LORD had fallen on them.
They looted all these villages, since there was
much plunder there. 15They also attacked the
camps of the herders and carried off droves
of sheep and goats and camels. Then they returned to Jerusalem.

Asa's Reform

15 The Spirit of God came on Azariah son
of Oded. 2He went out to meet Asa and
said to him, "Listen to me, Asa and all Judah
and Benjamin. The LORD is with you when you
are with him. If you seek him, he will be found
by you, but if you forsake him, he will forsake
you. 3For a long time Israel was without the
true God, without a priest to teach and without
the law. 4But in their distress they turned to
the LORD, the God of Israel, and sought him,
and he was found by them. 5In those days it
was not safe to travel about, for all the inhabitants of the lands were in great turmoil. 6One
nation was being crushed by another and one
city by another, because God was troubling
them with every kind of distress. 7But as for
you, be strong and do not give up, for your
work will be rewarded."

8When Asa heard these words and the
prophecy of Azariah son of[c] Oded the prophet,
he took courage. He removed the detestable
idols from the whole land of Judah and Benjamin and from the towns he had captured
in the hills of Ephraim. He repaired the altar
of the LORD that was in front of the portico of
the LORD's temple.

9Then he assembled all Judah and Benjamin and the people from Ephraim, Manasseh
and Simeon who had settled among them, for
large numbers had come over to him from
Israel when they saw that the LORD his God
was with him.

10They assembled at Jerusalem in the third
month of the fifteenth year of Asa's reign. 11At
that time they sacrificed to the LORD seven
hundred head of cattle and seven thousand
sheep and goats from the plunder they had
brought back. 12They entered into a covenant
to seek the LORD, the God of their ancestors,
with all their heart and soul. 13All who would
not seek the LORD, the God of Israel, were
to be put to death, whether small or great,
man or woman. 14They took an oath to the
LORD with loud acclamation, with shouting
and with trumpets and horns. 15All Judah rejoiced about the oath because they had sworn
it wholeheartedly. They sought God eagerly,
and he was found by them. So the LORD gave
them rest on every side.

16King Asa also deposed his grandmother
Maakah from her position as queen mother, because she had made a repulsive image
for the worship of Asherah. Asa cut it down,
broke it up and burned it in the Kidron Valley.
17Although he did not remove the high places
from Israel, Asa's heart was fully committed
to the LORD all his life. 18He brought into the
temple of God the silver and gold and the articles that he and his father had dedicated.

19There was no more war until the thirty-
fifth year of Asa's reign.

Asa's Last Years

16 In the thirty-sixth year of Asa's reign
Baasha king of Israel went up against
Judah and fortified Ramah to prevent anyone
from leaving or entering the territory of Asa
king of Judah.

2Asa then took the silver and gold out of the
treasuries of the LORD's temple and of his own

[a] In Hebrew texts 14:1 is numbered 13:23, and 14:2-15 is numbered 14:1-14. [b] *3* That is, wooden symbols of the goddess Asherah; here and elsewhere in 2 Chronicles [c] *8* Vulgate and Syriac (see also Septuagint and verse 1); Hebrew does not have *Azariah son of.*

palace and sent it to Ben-Hadad king of Aram,
who was ruling in Damascus. 3"Let there be a
treaty between me and you," he said, "as there
was between my father and your father. See,
I am sending you silver and gold. Now break
your treaty with Baasha king of Israel so he
will withdraw from me."

4Ben-Hadad agreed with King Asa and
sent the commanders of his forces against
the towns of Israel. They conquered Ijon, Dan,
Abel Maim[a] and all the store cities of Naphtali. 5When Baasha heard this, he stopped building Ramah and abandoned his work. 6Then
King Asa brought all the men of Judah, and
they carried away from Ramah the stones and
timber Baasha had been using. With them he
built up Geba and Mizpah.

7At that time Hanani the seer came to Asa
king of Judah and said to him: "Because you
relied on the king of Aram and not on the
LORD your God, the army of the king of Aram
has escaped from your hand. 8Were not the
Cushites[b] and Libyans a mighty army with
great numbers of chariots and horsemen[c]?
Yet when you relied on the LORD, he delivered them into your hand. 9For the eyes of the
LORD range throughout the earth to strength-
en those whose hearts are fully committed to
him. You have done a foolish thing, and from
now on you will be at war."

10Asa was angry with the seer because of
this; he was so enraged that he put him in prison. At the same time Asa brutally oppressed
some of the people.

11The events of Asa's reign, from beginning
to end, are written in the book of the kings of
Judah and Israel. 12In the thirty-ninth year of
his reign Asa was afflicted with a disease in
his feet. Though his disease was severe, even
in his illness he did not seek help from the
LORD, but only from the physicians. 13Then in
the forty-first year of his reign Asa died and
rested with his ancestors. 14They buried him
in the tomb that he had cut out for himself
in the City of David. They laid him on a bier
covered with spices and various blended perfumes, and they made a huge fire in his honor.

Jehoshaphat King of Judah

17 Jehoshaphat his son succeeded him as
king and strengthened himself against
Israel. 2He stationed troops in all the fortified
cities of Judah and put garrisons in Judah and
in the towns of Ephraim that his father Asa
had captured.

3The LORD was with Jehoshaphat because
he followed the ways of his father David before him. He did not consult the Baals 4but
sought the God of his father and followed his
commands rather than the practices of Israel. 5The LORD established the kingdom under
his control; and all Judah brought gifts to Jehoshaphat, so that he had great wealth and
honor. 6His heart was devoted to the ways of
the LORD; furthermore, he removed the high
places and the Asherah poles from Judah.

7In the third year of his reign he sent his officials Ben-Hail, Obadiah, Zechariah, Nethanel and Micaiah to teach in the towns of Judah.
8With them were certain Levites—Shemaiah,
Nethaniah, Zebadiah, Asahel, Shemiramoth,
Jehonathan, Adonijah, Tobijah and Tob-Ad-
onijah—and the priests Elishama and Jehoram. 9They taught throughout Judah, taking
with them the Book of the Law of the LORD;
they went around to all the towns of Judah
and taught the people.

10The fear of the LORD fell on all the kingdoms of the lands surrounding Judah, so that
they did not go to war against Jehoshaphat.
11Some Philistines brought Jehoshaphat gifts
and silver as tribute, and the Arabs brought
him flocks: seven thousand seven hundred
rams and seven thousand seven hundred
goats.

12Jehoshaphat became more and more powerful; he built forts and store cities in Judah
13and had large supplies in the towns of Judah. He also kept experienced fighting men
in Jerusalem. 14Their enrollment by families
was as follows:

From Judah, commanders of units of 1,000:
Adnah the commander, with 300,000 fighting men;
15next, Jehohanan the commander, with 280,000;
16next, Amasiah son of Zikri, who volunteered himself for the service of the LORD, with 200,000.
17From Benjamin:
Eliada, a valiant soldier, with 200,000 men armed with bows and shields;
18next, Jehozabad, with 180,000 men armed for battle.

19These were the men who served the king,
besides those he stationed in the fortified cities throughout Judah.

Micaiah Prophesies Against Ahab

18 Now Jehoshaphat had great wealth and
honor, and he allied himself with Ahab
by marriage. 2Some years later he went down
to see Ahab in Samaria. Ahab slaughtered
many sheep and cattle for him and the people
with him and urged him to attack Ramoth Gilead. 3Ahab king of Israel asked Jehoshaphat
king of Judah, "Will you go with me against
Ramoth Gilead?"

Jehoshaphat replied, "I am as you are, and
my people as your people; we will join you in
the war." 4But Jehoshaphat also said to the
king of Israel, "First seek the counsel of the
LORD."

5So the king of Israel brought together the
prophets—four hundred men—and asked
them, "Shall we go to war against Ramoth
Gilead, or shall I not?"

"Go," they answered, "for God will give it
into the king's hand."

6But Jehoshaphat asked, "Is there no lon-

[a] 4 Also known as *Abel Beth Maakah* [b] 8 That is, people from the upper Nile region
[c] 8 Or *charioteers*

ger a prophet of the LORD here whom we can
inquire of?"
7 The king of Israel answered Jehoshaphat,
"There is still one prophet through whom we
can inquire of the LORD, but I hate him because he never prophesies anything good
about me, but always bad. He is Micaiah son
of Imlah."
"The king should not say such a thing," Jehoshaphat replied.
8 So the king of Israel called one of his officials and said, "Bring Micaiah son of Imlah
at once."
9 Dressed in their royal robes, the king of
Israel and Jehoshaphat king of Judah were
sitting on their thrones at the threshing floor
by the entrance of the gate of Samaria, with
all the prophets prophesying before them.
10 Now Zedekiah son of Kenaanah had made
iron horns, and he declared, "This is what
the LORD says: 'With these you will gore the
Arameans until they are destroyed.'"
11 All the other prophets were prophesying
the same thing. "Attack Ramoth Gilead and
be victorious," they said, "for the LORD will
give it into the king's hand."
12 The messenger who had gone to summon
Micaiah said to him, "Look, the other prophets without exception are predicting success
for the king. Let your word agree with theirs,
and speak favorably."
13 But Micaiah said, "As surely as the LORD
lives, I can tell him only what my God says."
14 When he arrived, the king asked him, "Micaiah, shall we go to war against Ramoth Gilead, or shall I not?"
"Attack and be victorious," he answered,
"for they will be given into your hand."
15 The king said to him, "How many times
must I make you swear to tell me nothing but
the truth in the name of the LORD?"
16 Then Micaiah answered, "I saw all Israel scattered on the hills like sheep without
a shepherd, and the LORD said, 'These people have no master. Let each one go home in
peace.'"
17 The king of Israel said to Jehoshaphat,
"Didn't I tell you that he never prophesies anything good about me, but only bad?"
18 Micaiah continued, "Therefore hear the
word of the LORD: I saw the LORD sitting on
his throne with all the multitudes of heaven
standing on his right and on his left. 19 And
the LORD said, 'Who will entice Ahab king
of Israel into attacking Ramoth Gilead and
going to his death there?'
"One suggested this, and another that. 20 Finally, a spirit came forward, stood before the
LORD and said, 'I will entice him.'
"'By what means?' the LORD asked.
21 "'I will go and be a deceiving spirit in the
mouths of all his prophets,' he said.
"'You will succeed in enticing him,' said the
LORD. 'Go and do it.'
22 "So now the LORD has put a deceiving spirit in the mouths of these prophets of yours.
The LORD has decreed disaster for you."
23 Then Zedekiah son of Kenaanah went up
and slapped Micaiah in the face. "Which way
did the spirit from[a] the LORD go when he went
from me to speak to you?" he asked.
24 Micaiah replied, "You will find out on the
day you go to hide in an inner room."
25 The king of Israel then ordered, "Take Micaiah and send him back to Amon the ruler
of the city and to Joash the king's son, 26 and
say, 'This is what the king says: Put this fellow
in prison and give him nothing but bread and
water until I return safely.'"
27 Micaiah declared, "If you ever return safely, the LORD has not spoken through me." Then
he added, "Mark my words, all you people!"

Ahab Killed at Ramoth Gilead

28 So the king of Israel and Jehoshaphat king
of Judah went up to Ramoth Gilead. 29 The
king of Israel said to Jehoshaphat, "I will enter the battle in disguise, but you wear your
royal robes." So the king of Israel disguised
himself and went into battle.
30 Now the king of Aram had ordered his
chariot commanders, "Do not fight with anyone, small or great, except the king of Israel."
31 When the chariot commanders saw Jehoshaphat, they thought, "This is the king of Israel."
So they turned to attack him, but Jehoshaphat
cried out, and the LORD helped him. God drew
them away from him, 32 for when the chariot
commanders saw that he was not the king of
Israel, they stopped pursuing him.
33 But someone drew his bow at random and
hit the king of Israel between the breastplate
and the scale armor. The king told the chariot driver, "Wheel around and get me out of
the fighting. I've been wounded." 34 All day
long the battle raged, and the king of Israel propped himself up in his chariot facing
the Arameans until evening. Then at sunset
he died.

19 When Jehoshaphat king of Judah returned safely to his palace in Jerusalem,
2 Jehu the seer, the son of Hanani, went out to
meet him and said to the king, "Should you
help the wicked and love[b] those who hate the
LORD? Because of this, the wrath of the LORD is
on you. 3 There is, however, some good in you,
for you have rid the land of the Asherah poles
and have set your heart on seeking God."

Jehoshaphat Appoints Judges

4 Jehoshaphat lived in Jerusalem, and he
went out again among the people from Beersheba to the hill country of Ephraim and
turned them back to the LORD, the God of their
ancestors. 5 He appointed judges in the land,
in each of the fortified cities of Judah. 6 He
told them, "Consider carefully what you do,
because you are not judging for mere mortals
but for the LORD, who is with you whenever
you give a verdict. 7 Now let the fear of the
LORD be on you. Judge carefully, for with the
LORD our God there is no injustice or partiality or bribery."

[a] 23 Or *Spirit of* [b] 2 Or *and make alliances with*

8 In Jerusalem also, Jehoshaphat appointed some of the Levites, priests and heads of Israelite families to administer the law of the LORD and to settle disputes. And they lived in Jerusalem. 9 He gave them these orders: "You must serve faithfully and wholeheartedly in the fear of the LORD. 10 In every case that comes before you from your people who live in the cities—whether bloodshed or other concerns of the law, commands, decrees or regulations—you are to warn them not to sin against the LORD; otherwise his wrath will come on you and your people. Do this, and you will not sin.

11 "Amariah the chief priest will be over you in any matter concerning the LORD, and Zebadiah son of Ishmael, the leader of the tribe of Judah, will be over you in any matter concerning the king, and the Levites will serve as officials before you. Act with courage, and may the LORD be with those who do well."

Jehoshaphat Defeats Moab and Ammon

20 After this, the Moabites and Ammonites with some of the Meunites[a] came to wage war against Jehoshaphat.

2 Some people came and told Jehoshaphat, "A vast army is coming against you from Edom,[b] from the other side of the Dead Sea. It is already in Hazezon Tamar" (that is, En Gedi). 3 Alarmed, Jehoshaphat resolved to inquire of the LORD, and he proclaimed a fast for all Judah. 4 The people of Judah came together to seek help from the LORD; indeed, they came from every town in Judah to seek him.

5 Then Jehoshaphat stood up in the assembly of Judah and Jerusalem at the temple of the LORD in the front of the new courtyard 6 and said:

> "LORD, the God of our ancestors, are you not the God who is in heaven? You rule over all the kingdoms of the nations. Power and might are in your hand, and no one can withstand you. 7 Our God, did you not drive out the inhabitants of this land before your people Israel and give it forever to the descendants of Abraham your friend? 8 They have lived in it and have built in it a sanctuary for your Name, saying, 9 'If calamity comes upon us, whether the sword of judgment, or plague or famine, we will stand in your presence before this temple that bears your Name and will cry out to you in our distress, and you will hear us and save us.'
>
> 10 "But now here are men from Ammon, Moab and Mount Seir, whose territory you would not allow Israel to invade when they came from Egypt; so they turned away from them and did not destroy them. 11 See how they are repaying us by coming to drive us out of the possession you gave us as an inheritance. 12 Our God, will you not judge them? For we have no power to face this vast army that is attacking us. We do not know what to do, but our eyes are on you."

13 All the men of Judah, with their wives and children and little ones, stood there before the LORD.

14 Then the Spirit of the LORD came on Jahaziel son of Zechariah, the son of Benaiah, the son of Jeiel, the son of Mattaniah, a Levite and descendant of Asaph, as he stood in the assembly.

15 He said: "Listen, King Jehoshaphat and all who live in Judah and Jerusalem! This is what the LORD says to you: 'Do not be afraid or discouraged because of this vast army. For the battle is not yours, but God's. 16 Tomorrow march down against them. They will be climbing up by the Pass of Ziz, and you will find them at the end of the gorge in the Desert of Jeruel. 17 You will not have to fight this battle. Take up your positions; stand firm and see the deliverance the LORD will give you, Judah and Jerusalem. Do not be afraid; do not be discouraged. Go out to face them tomorrow, and the LORD will be with you.'"

18 Jehoshaphat bowed down with his face to the ground, and all the people of Judah and Jerusalem fell down in worship before the LORD. 19 Then some Levites from the Kohathites and Korahites stood up and praised the LORD, the God of Israel, with a very loud voice.

20 Early in the morning they left for the Desert of Tekoa. As they set out, Jehoshaphat stood and said, "Listen to me, Judah and people of Jerusalem! Have faith in the LORD your God and you will be upheld; have faith in his prophets and you will be successful." 21 After consulting the people, Jehoshaphat appointed men to sing to the LORD and to praise him for the splendor of his[c] holiness as they went out at the head of the army, saying:

> "Give thanks to the LORD,
> for his love endures forever."

22 As they began to sing and praise, the LORD set ambushes against the men of Ammon and Moab and Mount Seir who were invading Judah, and they were defeated. 23 The Ammonites and Moabites rose up against the men from Mount Seir to destroy and annihilate them. After they finished slaughtering the men from Seir, they helped to destroy one another.

24 When the men of Judah came to the place that overlooks the desert and looked toward the vast army, they saw only dead bodies lying on the ground; no one had escaped. 25 So Jehoshaphat and his men went to carry off their plunder, and they found among them a great amount of equipment and clothing[d] and also articles of value—more than they could take away. There was so much plunder that it took three days to collect it. 26 On the fourth day they assembled in the Valley of Berakah,

[a] *1* Some Septuagint manuscripts; Hebrew *Ammonites* [b] *2* One Hebrew manuscript; most Hebrew manuscripts, Septuagint and Vulgate *Aram* [c] *21* Or *him with the splendor of* [d] *25* Some Hebrew manuscripts and Vulgate; most Hebrew manuscripts *corpses*

where they praised the LORD. This is why it is called the Valley of Berakah[a] to this day.

27 Then, led by Jehoshaphat, all the men of Judah and Jerusalem returned joyfully to Jerusalem, for the LORD had given them cause to rejoice over their enemies. 28 They entered Jerusalem and went to the temple of the LORD with harps and lyres and trumpets.

29 The fear of God came on all the surrounding kingdoms when they heard how the LORD had fought against the enemies of Israel. 30 And the kingdom of Jehoshaphat was at peace, for his God had given him rest on every side.

The End of Jehoshaphat's Reign

31 So Jehoshaphat reigned over Judah. He was thirty-five years old when he became king of Judah, and he reigned in Jerusalem twenty-five years. His mother's name was Azubah daughter of Shilhi. 32 He followed the ways of his father Asa and did not stray from them; he did what was right in the eyes of the LORD. 33 The high places, however, were not removed, and the people still had not set their hearts on the God of their ancestors.

34 The other events of Jehoshaphat's reign, from beginning to end, are written in the annals of Jehu son of Hanani, which are recorded in the book of the kings of Israel.

35 Later, Jehoshaphat king of Judah made an alliance with Ahaziah king of Israel, whose ways were wicked. 36 He agreed with him to construct a fleet of trading ships.[b] After these were built at Ezion Geber, 37 Eliezer son of Dodavahu of Mareshah prophesied against Jehoshaphat, saying, "Because you have made an alliance with Ahaziah, the LORD will destroy what you have made." The ships were wrecked and were not able to set sail to trade.[c]

21 Then Jehoshaphat rested with his ancestors and was buried with them in the City of David. And Jehoram his son succeeded him as king. 2 Jehoram's brothers, the sons of Jehoshaphat, were Azariah, Jehiel, Zechariah, Azariahu, Michael and Shephatiah. All these were sons of Jehoshaphat king of Israel.[d] 3 Their father had given them many gifts of silver and gold and articles of value, as well as fortified cities in Judah, but he had given the kingdom to Jehoram because he was his firstborn son.

Jehoram King of Judah

4 When Jehoram established himself firmly over his father's kingdom, he put all his brothers to the sword along with some of the officials of Israel. 5 Jehoram was thirty-two years old when he became king, and he reigned in Jerusalem eight years. 6 He followed the ways of the kings of Israel, as the house of Ahab had done, for he married a daughter of Ahab. He did evil in the eyes of the LORD. 7 Nevertheless, because of the covenant the LORD had made with David, the LORD was not willing to destroy the house of David. He had promised to maintain a lamp for him and his descendants forever.

8 In the time of Jehoram, Edom rebelled against Judah and set up its own king. 9 So Jehoram went there with his officers and all his chariots. The Edomites surrounded him and his chariot commanders, but he rose up and broke through by night. 10 To this day Edom has been in rebellion against Judah.

Libnah revolted at the same time, because Jehoram had forsaken the LORD, the God of his ancestors. 11 He had also built high places on the hills of Judah and had caused the people of Jerusalem to prostitute themselves and had led Judah astray.

12 Jehoram received a letter from Elijah the prophet, which said:

> "This is what the LORD, the God of your father David, says: 'You have not followed the ways of your father Jehoshaphat or of Asa king of Judah. 13 But you have followed the ways of the kings of Israel, and you have led Judah and the people of Jerusalem to prostitute themselves, just as the house of Ahab did. You have also murdered your own brothers, members of your own family, men who were better than you. 14 So now the LORD is about to strike your people, your sons, your wives and everything that is yours, with a heavy blow. 15 You yourself will be very ill with a lingering disease of the bowels, until the disease causes your bowels to come out.'"

16 The LORD aroused against Jehoram the hostility of the Philistines and of the Arabs who lived near the Cushites. 17 They attacked Judah, invaded it and carried off all the goods found in the king's palace, together with his sons and wives. Not a son was left to him except Ahaziah,[e] the youngest.

18 After all this, the LORD afflicted Jehoram with an incurable disease of the bowels. 19 In the course of time, at the end of the second year, his bowels came out because of the disease, and he died in great pain. His people made no funeral fire in his honor, as they had for his predecessors.

20 Jehoram was thirty-two years old when he became king, and he reigned in Jerusalem eight years. He passed away, to no one's regret, and was buried in the City of David, but not in the tombs of the kings.

Ahaziah King of Judah

22 The people of Jerusalem made Ahaziah, Jehoram's youngest son, king in his place, since the raiders, who came with the Arabs into the camp, had killed all the older sons. So Ahaziah son of Jehoram king of Judah began to reign.

2 Ahaziah was twenty-two[f] years old when he became king, and he reigned in Jerusalem

[a] *26 Berakah* means *praise.* [b] *36* Hebrew *of ships that could go to Tarshish* [c] *37* Hebrew *sail for Tarshish* [d] *2* That is, Judah, as frequently in 2 Chronicles [e] *17* Hebrew *Jehoahaz,* a variant of *Ahaziah* [f] *2* Some Septuagint manuscripts and Syriac (see also 2 Kings 8:26); Hebrew *forty-two*

one year. His mother's name was Athaliah, a granddaughter of Omri.

3He too followed the ways of the house of Ahab, for his mother encouraged him to act wickedly. 4He did evil in the eyes of the LORD, as the house of Ahab had done, for after his father's death they became his advisers, to his undoing. 5He also followed their counsel when he went with Joram[a] son of Ahab king of Israel to wage war against Hazael king of Aram at Ramoth Gilead. The Arameans wounded Joram; 6so he returned to Jezreel to recover from the wounds they had inflicted on him at Ramoth[b] in his battle with Hazael king of Aram.

Then Ahaziah[c] son of Jehoram king of Judah went down to Jezreel to see Joram son of Ahab because he had been wounded.

7Through Ahaziah's visit to Joram, God brought about Ahaziah's downfall. When Ahaziah arrived, he went out with Joram to meet Jehu son of Nimshi, whom the LORD had anointed to destroy the house of Ahab. 8While Jehu was executing judgment on the house of Ahab, he found the officials of Judah and the sons of Ahaziah's relatives, who had been attending Ahaziah, and he killed them. 9He then went in search of Ahaziah, and his men captured him while he was hiding in Samaria. He was brought to Jehu and put to death. They buried him, for they said, "He was a son of Jehoshaphat, who sought the LORD with all his heart." So there was no one in the house of Ahaziah powerful enough to retain the kingdom.

Athaliah and Joash

10When Athaliah the mother of Ahaziah saw that her son was dead, she proceeded to destroy the whole royal family of the house of Judah. 11But Jehosheba,[d] the daughter of King Jehoram, took Joash son of Ahaziah and stole him away from among the royal princes who were about to be murdered and put him and his nurse in a bedroom. Because Jehosheba,[d] the daughter of King Jehoram and wife of the priest Jehoiada, was Ahaziah's sister, she hid the child from Athaliah so she could not kill him. 12He remained hidden with them at the temple of God for six years while Athaliah ruled the land.

23 In the seventh year Jehoiada showed his strength. He made a covenant with the commanders of units of a hundred: Azariah son of Jeroham, Ishmael son of Jehohanan, Azariah son of Obed, Maaseiah son of Adaiah, and Elishaphat son of Zikri. 2They went throughout Judah and gathered the Levites and the heads of Israelite families from all the towns. When they came to Jerusalem, 3the whole assembly made a covenant with the king at the temple of God.

Jehoiada said to them, "The king's son shall reign, as the LORD promised concerning the descendants of David. 4Now this is what you are to do: A third of you priests and Levites who are going on duty on the Sabbath are to keep watch at the doors, 5a third of you at the royal palace and a third at the Foundation Gate, and all the others are to be in the courtyards of the temple of the LORD. 6No one is to enter the temple of the LORD except the priests and Levites on duty; they may enter because they are consecrated, but all the others are to observe the LORD's command not to enter.[e] 7The Levites are to station themselves around the king, each with weapon in hand. Anyone who enters the temple is to be put to death. Stay close to the king wherever he goes."

8The Levites and all the men of Judah did just as Jehoiada the priest ordered. Each one took his men—those who were going on duty on the Sabbath and those who were going off duty—for Jehoiada the priest had not released any of the divisions. 9Then he gave the commanders of units of a hundred the spears and the large and small shields that had belonged to King David and that were in the temple of God. 10He stationed all the men, each with his weapon in his hand, around the king—near the altar and the temple, from the south side to the north side of the temple.

11Jehoiada and his sons brought out the king's son and put the crown on him; they presented him with a copy of the covenant and proclaimed him king. They anointed him and shouted, "Long live the king!"

12When Athaliah heard the noise of the people running and cheering the king, she went to them at the temple of the LORD. 13She looked, and there was the king, standing by his pillar at the entrance. The officers and the trumpeters were beside the king, and all the people of the land were rejoicing and blowing trumpets, and musicians with their instruments were leading the praises. Then Athaliah tore her robes and shouted, "Treason! Treason!"

14Jehoiada the priest sent out the commanders of units of a hundred, who were in charge of the troops, and said to them: "Bring her out between the ranks[f] and put to the sword anyone who follows her." For the priest had said, "Do not put her to death at the temple of the LORD." 15So they seized her as she reached the entrance of the Horse Gate on the palace grounds, and there they put her to death.

16Jehoiada then made a covenant that he, the people and the king[g] would be the LORD's people. 17All the people went to the temple of Baal and tore it down. They smashed the altars and idols and killed Mattan the priest of Baal in front of the altars.

18Then Jehoiada placed the oversight of the temple of the LORD in the hands of the Levitical priests, to whom David had made assignments in the temple, to present the burnt

[a] 5 Hebrew *Jehoram,* a variant of *Joram*; also in verses 6 and 7 [b] 6 Hebrew *Ramah,* a variant of *Ramoth* [c] 6 Some Hebrew manuscripts, Septuagint, Vulgate and Syriac (see also 2 Kings 8:29); most Hebrew manuscripts *Azariah* [d] 11 Hebrew *Jehoshabeath,* a variant of *Jehosheba* [e] 6 Or *are to stand guard where the LORD has assigned them* [f] 14 Or *out from the precincts* [g] 16 Or *covenant between the LORD and the people and the king that they* (see 2 Kings 11:17)

offerings of the LORD as written in the Law of Moses, with rejoicing and singing, as David had ordered. 19 He also stationed gatekeepers at the gates of the LORD's temple so that no one who was in any way unclean might enter.

20 He took with him the commanders of hundreds, the nobles, the rulers of the people and all the people of the land and brought the king down from the temple of the LORD. They went into the palace through the Upper Gate and seated the king on the royal throne. 21 All the people of the land rejoiced, and the city was calm, because Athaliah had been slain with the sword.

Joash Repairs the Temple

24 Joash was seven years old when he became king, and he reigned in Jerusalem forty years. His mother's name was Zibiah; she was from Beersheba. 2 Joash did what was right in the eyes of the LORD all the years of Jehoiada the priest. 3 Jehoiada chose two wives for him, and he had sons and daughters.

4 Some time later Joash decided to restore the temple of the LORD. 5 He called together the priests and Levites and said to them, "Go to the towns of Judah and collect the money due annually from all Israel, to repair the temple of your God. Do it now." But the Levites did not act at once.

6 Therefore the king summoned Jehoiada the chief priest and said to him, "Why haven't you required the Levites to bring in from Judah and Jerusalem the tax imposed by Moses the servant of the LORD and by the assembly of Israel for the tent of the covenant law?"

7 Now the sons of that wicked woman Athaliah had broken into the temple of God and had used even its sacred objects for the Baals.

8 At the king's command, a chest was made and placed outside, at the gate of the temple of the LORD. 9 A proclamation was then issued in Judah and Jerusalem that they should bring to the LORD the tax that Moses the servant of God had required of Israel in the wilderness. 10 All the officials and all the people brought their contributions gladly, dropping them into the chest until it was full. 11 Whenever the chest was brought in by the Levites to the king's officials and they saw that there was a large amount of money, the royal secretary and the officer of the chief priest would come and empty the chest and carry it back to its place. They did this regularly and collected a great amount of money. 12 The king and Jehoiada gave it to those who carried out the work required for the temple of the LORD. They hired masons and carpenters to restore the LORD's temple, and also workers in iron and bronze to repair the temple.

13 The men in charge of the work were diligent, and the repairs progressed under them. They rebuilt the temple of God according to its original design and reinforced it. 14 When they had finished, they brought the rest of the money to the king and Jehoiada, and with it were made articles for the LORD's temple: articles for the service and for the burnt offerings, and also dishes and other objects of gold and silver. As long as Jehoiada lived, burnt offerings were presented continually in the temple of the LORD.

15 Now Jehoiada was old and full of years, and he died at the age of a hundred and thirty. 16 He was buried with the kings in the City of David, because of the good he had done in Israel for God and his temple.

The Wickedness of Joash

17 After the death of Jehoiada, the officials of Judah came and paid homage to the king, and he listened to them. 18 They abandoned the temple of the LORD, the God of their ancestors, and worshiped Asherah poles and idols. Because of their guilt, God's anger came on Judah and Jerusalem. 19 Although the LORD sent prophets to the people to bring them back to him, and though they testified against them, they would not listen.

20 Then the Spirit of God came on Zechariah son of Jehoiada the priest. He stood before the people and said, "This is what God says: 'Why do you disobey the LORD's commands? You will not prosper. Because you have forsaken the LORD, he has forsaken you.'"

21 But they plotted against him, and by order of the king they stoned him to death in the courtyard of the LORD's temple. 22 King Joash did not remember the kindness Zechariah's father Jehoiada had shown him but killed his son, who said as he lay dying, "May the LORD see this and call you to account."

23 At the turn of the year,[a] the army of Aram marched against Joash; it invaded Judah and Jerusalem and killed all the leaders of the people. They sent all the plunder to their king in Damascus. 24 Although the Aramean army had come with only a few men, the LORD delivered into their hands a much larger army. Because Judah had forsaken the LORD, the God of their ancestors, judgment was executed on Joash. 25 When the Arameans withdrew, they left Joash severely wounded. His officials conspired against him for murdering the son of Jehoiada the priest, and they killed him in his bed. So he died and was buried in the City of David, but not in the tombs of the kings.

26 Those who conspired against him were Zabad,[b] son of Shimeath an Ammonite woman, and Jehozabad, son of Shimrith[c] a Moabite woman. 27 The account of his sons, the many prophecies about him, and the record of the restoration of the temple of God are written in the annotations on the book of the kings. And Amaziah his son succeeded him as king.

Amaziah King of Judah

25 Amaziah was twenty-five years old when he became king, and he reigned in Jerusalem twenty-nine years. His mother's name was Jehoaddan; she was from Jerusalem. 2 He did what was right in the eyes of the LORD, but not wholeheartedly. 3 After the

[a] 23 Probably in the spring [b] 26 A variant of *Jozabad* [c] 26 A variant of *Shomer*

kingdom was firmly in his control, he executed the officials who had murdered his father
the king. 4Yet he did not put their children
to death, but acted in accordance with what
is written in the Law, in the Book of Moses,
where the LORD commanded: "Parents shall
not be put to death for their children, nor children be put to death for their parents; each
will die for their own sin."[a]

5Amaziah called the people of Judah together and assigned them according to their
families to commanders of thousands and
commanders of hundreds for all Judah and
Benjamin. He then mustered those twenty
years old or more and found that there were
three hundred thousand men fit for military
service, able to handle the spear and shield.
6He also hired a hundred thousand fighting
men from Israel for a hundred talents[b] of silver.

7But a man of God came to him and said,
"Your Majesty, these troops from Israel must
not march with you, for the LORD is not with
Israel—not with any of the people of Ephraim. 8Even if you go and fight courageously
in battle, God will overthrow you before the
enemy, for God has the power to help or to
overthrow."

9Amaziah asked the man of God, "But what
about the hundred talents I paid for these Israelite troops?"

The man of God replied, "The LORD can give
you much more than that."

10So Amaziah dismissed the troops who
had come to him from Ephraim and sent them
home. They were furious with Judah and left
for home in a great rage.

11Amaziah then marshaled his strength and
led his army to the Valley of Salt, where he
killed ten thousand men of Seir. 12The army of
Judah also captured ten thousand men alive,
took them to the top of a cliff and threw them
down so that all were dashed to pieces.

13Meanwhile the troops that Amaziah had
sent back and had not allowed to take part
in the war raided towns belonging to Judah
from Samaria to Beth Horon. They killed
three thousand people and carried off great
quantities of plunder.

14When Amaziah returned from slaughtering the Edomites, he brought back the gods
of the people of Seir. He set them up as his
own gods, bowed down to them and burned
sacrifices to them. 15The anger of the LORD
burned against Amaziah, and he sent a prophet to him, who said, "Why do you consult this
people's gods, which could not save their own
people from your hand?"

16While he was still speaking, the king said
to him, "Have we appointed you an adviser to
the king? Stop! Why be struck down?"

So the prophet stopped but said, "I know
that God has determined to destroy you, because you have done this and have not listened
to my counsel."

17After Amaziah king of Judah consulted
his advisers, he sent this challenge to Jehoash[c] son of Jehoahaz, the son of Jehu, king of
Israel: "Come, let us face each other in battle."

18But Jehoash king of Israel replied to Amaziah king of Judah: "A thistle in Lebanon sent
a message to a cedar in Lebanon, 'Give your
daughter to my son in marriage.' Then a wild
beast in Lebanon came along and trampled
the thistle underfoot. 19You say to yourself
that you have defeated Edom, and now you are
arrogant and proud. But stay at home! Why
ask for trouble and cause your own downfall
and that of Judah also?"

20Amaziah, however, would not listen, for
God so worked that he might deliver them into
the hands of Jehoash, because they sought the
gods of Edom. 21So Jehoash king of Israel attacked. He and Amaziah king of Judah faced
each other at Beth Shemesh in Judah. 22Judah
was routed by Israel, and every man fled to his
home. 23Jehoash king of Israel captured Amaziah king of Judah, the son of Joash, the son
of Ahaziah,[d] at Beth Shemesh. Then Jehoash
brought him to Jerusalem and broke down the
wall of Jerusalem from the Ephraim Gate to
the Corner Gate—a section about four hundred cubits[e] long. 24He took all the gold and
silver and all the articles found in the temple
of God that had been in the care of Obed-
Edom, together with the palace treasures and
the hostages, and returned to Samaria.

25Amaziah son of Joash king of Judah lived
for fifteen years after the death of Jehoash son
of Jehoahaz king of Israel. 26As for the other
events of Amaziah's reign, from beginning to
end, are they not written in the book of the
kings of Judah and Israel? 27From the time
that Amaziah turned away from following
the LORD, they conspired against him in Jerusalem and he fled to Lachish, but they sent
men after him to Lachish and killed him there.
28He was brought back by horse and was buried with his ancestors in the City of Judah.[f]

Uzziah King of Judah

26 Then all the people of Judah took Uzziah,[g] who was sixteen years old, and
made him king in place of his father Amaziah. 2He was the one who rebuilt Elath and
restored it to Judah after Amaziah rested with
his ancestors.

3Uzziah was sixteen years old when he became king, and he reigned in Jerusalem fifty-
two years. His mother's name was Jekoliah;
she was from Jerusalem. 4He did what was
right in the eyes of the LORD, just as his father
Amaziah had done. 5He sought God during
the days of Zechariah, who instructed him
in the fear[h] of God. As long as he sought the
LORD, God gave him success.

[a] *4* Deut. 24:16 [b] *6* That is, about 3 3/4 tons or about 3.4 metric tons; also in verse 9 [c] *17* Hebrew *Joash*, a variant of *Jehoash*; also in verses 18, 21, 23 and 25 [d] *23* Hebrew *Jehoahaz*, a variant of *Ahaziah* [e] *23* That is, about 600 feet or about 180 meters [f] *28* Most Hebrew manuscripts; some Hebrew manuscripts, Septuagint, Vulgate and Syriac (see also 2 Kings 14:20) *David* [g] *1* Also called *Azariah* [h] *5* Many Hebrew manuscripts, Septuagint and Syriac; other Hebrew manuscripts *vision*

6He went to war against the Philistines and broke down the walls of Gath, Jabneh and Ashdod. He then rebuilt towns near Ashdod and elsewhere among the Philistines. 7God helped him against the Philistines and against the Arabs who lived in Gur Baal and against the Meunites. 8The Ammonites brought tribute to Uzziah, and his fame spread as far as the border of Egypt, because he had become very powerful.

9Uzziah built towers in Jerusalem at the Corner Gate, at the Valley Gate and at the angle of the wall, and he fortified them. 10He also built towers in the wilderness and dug many cisterns, because he had much livestock in the foothills and in the plain. He had people working his fields and vineyards in the hills and in the fertile lands, for he loved the soil.

11Uzziah had a well-trained army, ready to go out by divisions according to their numbers as mustered by Jeiel the secretary and Maaseiah the officer under the direction of Hananiah, one of the royal officials. 12The total number of family leaders over the fighting men was 2,600. 13Under their command was an army of 307,500 men trained for war, a powerful force to support the king against his enemies. 14Uzziah provided shields, spears, helmets, coats of armor, bows and slingstones for the entire army. 15In Jerusalem he made devices invented for use on the towers and on the corner defenses so that soldiers could shoot arrows and hurl large stones from the walls. His fame spread far and wide, for he was greatly helped until he became powerful.

16But after Uzziah became powerful, his pride led to his downfall. He was unfaithful to the LORD his God, and entered the temple of the LORD to burn incense on the altar of incense. 17Azariah the priest with eighty other courageous priests of the LORD followed him in. 18They confronted King Uzziah and said, "It is not right for you, Uzziah, to burn incense to the LORD. That is for the priests, the descendants of Aaron, who have been consecrated to burn incense. Leave the sanctuary, for you have been unfaithful; and you will not be honored by the LORD God."

19Uzziah, who had a censer in his hand ready to burn incense, became angry. While he was raging at the priests in their presence before the incense altar in the LORD's temple, leprosy[a] broke out on his forehead. 20When Azariah the chief priest and all the other priests looked at him, they saw that he had leprosy on his forehead, so they hurried him out. Indeed, he himself was eager to leave, because the LORD had afflicted him.

21King Uzziah had leprosy until the day he died. He lived in a separate house[b]—leprous, and banned from the temple of the LORD. Jotham his son had charge of the palace and governed the people of the land.

22The other events of Uzziah's reign, from beginning to end, are recorded by the prophet Isaiah son of Amoz. 23Uzziah rested with his ancestors and was buried near them in a cemetery that belonged to the kings, for people said, "He had leprosy." And Jotham his son succeeded him as king.

Jotham King of Judah

27 Jotham was twenty-five years old when he became king, and he reigned in Jerusalem sixteen years. His mother's name was Jerusha daughter of Zadok. 2He did what was right in the eyes of the LORD, just as his father Uzziah had done, but unlike him he did not enter the temple of the LORD. The people, however, continued their corrupt practices. 3Jotham rebuilt the Upper Gate of the temple of the LORD and did extensive work on the wall at the hill of Ophel. 4He built towns in the hill country of Judah and forts and towers in the wooded areas.

5Jotham waged war against the king of the Ammonites and conquered them. That year the Ammonites paid him a hundred talents[c] of silver, ten thousand cors[d] of wheat and ten thousand cors[e] of barley. The Ammonites brought him the same amount also in the second and third years.

6Jotham grew powerful because he walked steadfastly before the LORD his God.

7The other events in Jotham's reign, including all his wars and the other things he did, are written in the book of the kings of Israel and Judah. 8He was twenty-five years old when he became king, and he reigned in Jerusalem sixteen years. 9Jotham rested with his ancestors and was buried in the City of David. And Ahaz his son succeeded him as king.

Ahaz King of Judah

28 Ahaz was twenty years old when he became king, and he reigned in Jerusalem sixteen years. Unlike David his father, he did not do what was right in the eyes of the LORD. 2He followed the ways of the kings of Israel and also made idols for worshiping the Baals. 3He burned sacrifices in the Valley of Ben Hinnom and sacrificed his children in the fire, engaging in the detestable practices of the nations the LORD had driven out before the Israelites. 4He offered sacrifices and burned incense at the high places, on the hilltops and under every spreading tree.

5Therefore the LORD his God delivered him into the hands of the king of Aram. The Arameans defeated him and took many of his people as prisoners and brought them to Damascus.

He was also given into the hands of the king of Israel, who inflicted heavy casualties on him. 6In one day Pekah son of Remaliah killed a hundred and twenty thousand soldiers in Judah—because Judah had forsaken the LORD, the God of their ancestors. 7Zikri,

[a] *19* The Hebrew for *leprosy* was used for various diseases affecting the skin; also in verses 20, 21 and 23. [b] *21* Or *in a house where he was relieved of responsibilities* [c] *5* That is, about 3 3/4 tons or about 3.4 metric tons [d] *5* That is, probably about 1,800 tons or about 1,600 metric tons of wheat [e] *5* That is, probably about 1,500 tons or about 1,350 metric tons of barley

an Ephraimite warrior, killed Maaseiah the
king's son, Azrikam the officer in charge of
the palace, and Elkanah, second to the king.
8The men of Israel took captive from their
fellow Israelites who were from Judah two
hundred thousand wives, sons and daughters.
They also took a great deal of plunder, which
they carried back to Samaria.
9But a prophet of the LORD named Oded was
there, and he went out to meet the army when
it returned to Samaria. He said to them, "Because the LORD, the God of your ancestors,
was angry with Judah, he gave them into your
hand. But you have slaughtered them in a rage
that reaches to heaven. 10And now you intend
to make the men and women of Judah and Jerusalem your slaves. But aren't you also guilty
of sins against the LORD your God? 11Now listen to me! Send back your fellow Israelites you
have taken as prisoners, for the LORD's fierce
anger rests on you."
12Then some of the leaders in Ephraim—
Azariah son of Jehohanan, Berekiah son of
Meshillemoth, Jehizkiah son of Shallum, and
Amasa son of Hadlai—confronted those who
were arriving from the war. 13"You must not
bring those prisoners here," they said, "or we
will be guilty before the LORD. Do you intend
to add to our sin and guilt? For our guilt is
already great, and his fierce anger rests on
Israel."
14So the soldiers gave up the prisoners and
plunder in the presence of the officials and
all the assembly. 15The men designated by
name took the prisoners, and from the plunder they clothed all who were naked. They
provided them with clothes and sandals, food
and drink, and healing balm. All those who
were weak they put on donkeys. So they took
them back to their fellow Israelites at Jericho,
the City of Palms, and returned to Samaria.
16At that time King Ahaz sent to the kings[a]
of Assyria for help. 17The Edomites had again
come and attacked Judah and carried away
prisoners, 18while the Philistines had raided
towns in the foothills and in the Negev of Judah. They captured and occupied Beth Shemesh, Aijalon and Gederoth, as well as Soko,
Timnah and Gimzo, with their surrounding
villages. 19The LORD had humbled Judah because of Ahaz king of Israel,[b] for he had promoted wickedness in Judah and had been
most unfaithful to the LORD. 20Tiglath-Pileser[c]
king of Assyria came to him, but he gave him
trouble instead of help. 21Ahaz took some of
the things from the temple of the LORD and
from the royal palace and from the officials
and presented them to the king of Assyria,
but that did not help him.
22In his time of trouble King Ahaz became
even more unfaithful to the LORD. 23He offered sacrifices to the gods of Damascus, who
had defeated him; for he thought, "Since the
gods of the kings of Aram have helped them,
I will sacrifice to them so they will help me."
But they were his downfall and the downfall
of all Israel.
24Ahaz gathered together the furnishings
from the temple of God and cut them in pieces. He shut the doors of the LORD's temple and
set up altars at every street corner in Jerusalem. 25In every town in Judah he built high
places to burn sacrifices to other gods and
aroused the anger of the LORD, the God of
his ancestors.
26The other events of his reign and all his
ways, from beginning to end, are written in
the book of the kings of Judah and Israel.
27Ahaz rested with his ancestors and was
buried in the city of Jerusalem, but he was
not placed in the tombs of the kings of Israel.
And Hezekiah his son succeeded him as king.

Hezekiah Purifies the Temple

29 Hezekiah was twenty-five years old
when he became king, and he reigned
in Jerusalem twenty-nine years. His mother's
name was Abijah daughter of Zechariah. 2He
did what was right in the eyes of the LORD, just
as his father David had done.
3In the first month of the first year of his
reign, he opened the doors of the temple of the
LORD and repaired them. 4He brought in the
priests and the Levites, assembled them in the
square on the east side 5and said: "Listen to
me, Levites! Consecrate yourselves now and
consecrate the temple of the LORD, the God of
your ancestors. Remove all defilement from
the sanctuary. 6Our parents were unfaithful; they did evil in the eyes of the LORD our
God and forsook him. They turned their faces away from the LORD's dwelling place and
turned their backs on him. 7They also shut
the doors of the portico and put out the lamps.
They did not burn incense or present any burnt
offerings at the sanctuary to the God of Israel.
8Therefore, the anger of the LORD has fallen
on Judah and Jerusalem; he has made them
an object of dread and horror and scorn, as
you can see with your own eyes. 9This is why
our fathers have fallen by the sword and why
our sons and daughters and our wives are in
captivity. 10Now I intend to make a covenant
with the LORD, the God of Israel, so that his
fierce anger will turn away from us. 11My sons,
do not be negligent now, for the LORD has chosen you to stand before him and serve him,
to minister before him and to burn incense."
12Then these Levites set to work:
from the Kohathites,
Mahath son of Amasai and Joel son of Azariah;
from the Merarites,
Kish son of Abdi and Azariah son of Jehallelel;
from the Gershonites,
Joah son of Zimmah and Eden son of Joah;
13from the descendants of Elizaphan,
Shimri and Jeiel;

[a] *16* Most Hebrew manuscripts; one Hebrew manuscript, Septuagint and Vulgate (see also 2 Kings 16:7) *king* [b] *19* That is, Judah, as frequently in 2 Chronicles [c] *20* Hebrew *Tilgath-Pilneser,* a variant of *Tiglath-Pileser*

from the descendants of Asaph,
Zechariah and Mattaniah;
14from the descendants of Heman,
Jehiel and Shimei;
from the descendants of Jeduthun,
Shemaiah and Uzziel.
15When they had assembled their fellow Levites and consecrated themselves, they went
in to purify the temple of the LORD, as the
king had ordered, following the word of the
LORD. 16The priests went into the sanctuary
of the LORD to purify it. They brought out to
the courtyard of the LORD's temple everything
unclean that they found in the temple of the
LORD. The Levites took it and carried it out to
the Kidron Valley. 17They began the consecration on the first day of the first month, and by
the eighth day of the month they reached the
portico of the LORD. For eight more days they
consecrated the temple of the LORD itself, finishing on the sixteenth day of the first month.
18Then they went in to King Hezekiah and
reported: "We have purified the entire temple
of the LORD, the altar of burnt offering with
all its utensils, and the table for setting out the
consecrated bread, with all its articles. 19We
have prepared and consecrated all the articles
that King Ahaz removed in his unfaithfulness
while he was king. They are now in front of
the LORD's altar."
20Early the next morning King Hezekiah
gathered the city officials together and went
up to the temple of the LORD. 21They brought
seven bulls, seven rams, seven male lambs
and seven male goats as a sin offering[a] for
the kingdom, for the sanctuary and for Judah. The king commanded the priests, the descendants of Aaron, to offer these on the altar
of the LORD. 22So they slaughtered the bulls,
and the priests took the blood and splashed
it against the altar; next they slaughtered the
rams and splashed their blood against the
altar; then they slaughtered the lambs and
splashed their blood against the altar. 23The
goats for the sin offering were brought before
the king and the assembly, and they laid their
hands on them. 24The priests then slaughtered
the goats and presented their blood on the
altar for a sin offering to atone for all Israel,
because the king had ordered the burnt offering and the sin offering for all Israel.
25He stationed the Levites in the temple of the
LORD with cymbals, harps and lyres in the way
prescribed by David and Gad the king's seer
and Nathan the prophet; this was commanded by the LORD through his prophets. 26So the
Levites stood ready with David's instruments,
and the priests with their trumpets.
27Hezekiah gave the order to sacrifice the
burnt offering on the altar. As the offering
began, singing to the LORD began also, accompanied by trumpets and the instruments
of David king of Israel. 28The whole assembly
bowed in worship, while the musicians played
and the trumpets sounded. All this continued
until the sacrifice of the burnt offering was
completed.
29When the offerings were finished, the
king and everyone present with him knelt
down and worshiped. 30King Hezekiah and
his officials ordered the Levites to praise the
LORD with the words of David and of Asaph
the seer. So they sang praises with gladness
and bowed down and worshiped.
31Then Hezekiah said, "You have now dedicated yourselves to the LORD. Come and bring
sacrifices and thank offerings to the temple of
the LORD." So the assembly brought sacrifices and thank offerings, and all whose hearts
were willing brought burnt offerings.
32The number of burnt offerings the assembly brought was seventy bulls, a hundred
rams and two hundred male lambs—all of
them for burnt offerings to the LORD. 33The
animals consecrated as sacrifices amounted
to six hundred bulls and three thousand sheep
and goats. 34The priests, however, were too
few to skin all the burnt offerings; so their
relatives the Levites helped them until the task
was finished and until other priests had been
consecrated, for the Levites had been more
conscientious in consecrating themselves
than the priests had been. 35There were burnt
offerings in abundance, together with the fat
of the fellowship offerings and the drink offerings that accompanied the burnt offerings.
So the service of the temple of the LORD was
reestablished. 36Hezekiah and all the people
rejoiced at what God had brought about for
his people, because it was done so quickly.

Hezekiah Celebrates the Passover

30 Hezekiah sent word to all Israel and Judah and also wrote letters to Ephraim
and Manasseh, inviting them to come to the
temple of the LORD in Jerusalem and celebrate
the Passover to the LORD, the God of Israel.
2The king and his officials and the whole assembly in Jerusalem decided to celebrate the
Passover in the second month. 3They had not
been able to celebrate it at the regular time
because not enough priests had consecrated
themselves and the people had not assembled
in Jerusalem. 4The plan seemed right both
to the king and to the whole assembly. 5They
decided to send a proclamation throughout
Israel, from Beersheba to Dan, calling the
people to come to Jerusalem and celebrate
the Passover to the LORD, the God of Israel.
It had not been celebrated in large numbers
according to what was written.
6At the king's command, couriers went
throughout Israel and Judah with letters from
the king and from his officials, which read:

"People of Israel, return to the LORD, the
God of Abraham, Isaac and Israel, that
he may return to you who are left, who
have escaped from the hand of the kings
of Assyria. 7Do not be like your parents
and your fellow Israelites, who were unfaithful to the LORD, the God of their ancestors, so that he made them an object of
horror, as you see. 8Do not be stiff-necked,

[a] 21 Or *purification offering*; also in verses 23 and 24

as your ancestors were; submit to the LORD. Come to his sanctuary, which he has consecrated forever. Serve the LORD your God, so that his fierce anger will turn away from you. 9If you return to the LORD, then your fellow Israelites and your children will be shown compassion by their captors and will return to this land, for the LORD your God is gracious and compassionate. He will not turn his face from you if you return to him."

10The couriers went from town to town in Ephraim and Manasseh, as far as Zebulun, but people scorned and ridiculed them. 11Nevertheless, some from Asher, Manasseh and Zebulun humbled themselves and went to Jerusalem. 12Also in Judah the hand of God was on the people to give them unity of mind to carry out what the king and his officials had ordered, following the word of the LORD.

13A very large crowd of people assembled in Jerusalem to celebrate the Festival of Unleavened Bread in the second month. 14They removed the altars in Jerusalem and cleared away the incense altars and threw them into the Kidron Valley.

15They slaughtered the Passover lamb on the fourteenth day of the second month. The priests and the Levites were ashamed and consecrated themselves and brought burnt offerings to the temple of the LORD. 16Then they took up their regular positions as prescribed in the Law of Moses the man of God. The priests splashed against the altar the blood handed to them by the Levites. 17Since many in the crowd had not consecrated themselves, the Levites had to kill the Passover lambs for all those who were not ceremonially clean and could not consecrate their lambs[a] to the LORD. 18Although most of the many people who came from Ephraim, Manasseh, Issachar and Zebulun had not purified themselves, yet they ate the Passover, contrary to what was written. But Hezekiah prayed for them, saying, "May the LORD, who is good, pardon everyone 19who sets their heart on seeking God—the LORD, the God of their ancestors—even if they are not clean according to the rules of the sanctuary." 20And the LORD heard Hezekiah and healed the people.

21The Israelites who were present in Jerusalem celebrated the Festival of Unleavened Bread for seven days with great rejoicing, while the Levites and priests praised the LORD every day with resounding instruments dedicated to the LORD.[b]

22Hezekiah spoke encouragingly to all the Levites, who showed good understanding of the service of the LORD. For the seven days they ate their assigned portion and offered fellowship offerings and praised[c] the LORD, the God of their ancestors.

23The whole assembly then agreed to celebrate the festival seven more days; so for another seven days they celebrated joyfully. 24Hezekiah king of Judah provided a thousand bulls and seven thousand sheep and goats for the assembly, and the officials provided them with a thousand bulls and ten thousand sheep and goats. A great number of priests consecrated themselves. 25The entire assembly of Judah rejoiced, along with the priests and Levites and all who had assembled from Israel, including the foreigners who had come from Israel and also those who resided in Judah. 26There was great joy in Jerusalem, for since the days of Solomon son of David king of Israel there had been nothing like this in Jerusalem. 27The priests and the Levites stood to bless the people, and God heard them, for their prayer reached heaven, his holy dwelling place.

31 When all this had ended, the Israelites who were there went out to the towns of Judah, smashed the sacred stones and cut down the Asherah poles. They destroyed the high places and the altars throughout Judah and Benjamin and in Ephraim and Manasseh. After they had destroyed all of them, the Israelites returned to their own towns and to their own property.

Contributions for Worship

2Hezekiah assigned the priests and Levites to divisions—each of them according to their duties as priests or Levites—to offer burnt offerings and fellowship offerings, to minister, to give thanks and to sing praises at the gates of the LORD's dwelling. 3The king contributed from his own possessions for the morning and evening burnt offerings and for the burnt offerings on the Sabbaths, at the New Moons and at the appointed festivals as written in the Law of the LORD. 4He ordered the people living in Jerusalem to give the portion due the priests and Levites so they could devote themselves to the Law of the LORD. 5As soon as the order went out, the Israelites generously gave the firstfruits of their grain, new wine, olive oil and honey and all that the fields produced. They brought a great amount, a tithe of everything. 6The people of Israel and Judah who lived in the towns of Judah also brought a tithe of their herds and flocks and a tithe of the holy things dedicated to the LORD their God, and they piled them in heaps. 7They began doing this in the third month and finished in the seventh month. 8When Hezekiah and his officials came and saw the heaps, they praised the LORD and blessed his people Israel.

9Hezekiah asked the priests and Levites about the heaps; 10and Azariah the chief priest, from the family of Zadok, answered, "Since the people began to bring their contributions to the temple of the LORD, we have had enough to eat and plenty to spare, because the LORD has blessed his people, and this great amount is left over."

11Hezekiah gave orders to prepare storerooms in the temple of the LORD, and this was done. 12Then they faithfully brought in the contributions, tithes and dedicated gifts. Kon-

[a] 17 Or *consecrate themselves* [b] 21 Or *priests sang to the LORD every day, accompanied by the LORD's instruments of praise* [c] 22 Or *and confessed their sins to*

aniah, a Levite, was the overseer in charge of
these things, and his brother Shimei was next
in rank. 13 Jehiel, Azaziah, Nahath, Asahel,
Jerimoth, Jozabad, Eliel, Ismakiah, Mahath
and Benaiah were assistants of Konaniah
and Shimei his brother. All these served by
appointment of King Hezekiah and Azariah
the official in charge of the temple of God.
14 Kore son of Imnah the Levite, keeper
of the East Gate, was in charge of the freewill offerings given to God, distributing the
contributions made to the LORD and also the
consecrated gifts. 15 Eden, Miniamin, Jeshua,
Shemaiah, Amariah and Shekaniah assisted
him faithfully in the towns of the priests, distributing to their fellow priests according to
their divisions, old and young alike.
16 In addition, they distributed to the males
three years old or more whose names were
in the genealogical records—all who would
enter the temple of the LORD to perform the
daily duties of their various tasks, according
to their responsibilities and their divisions.
17 And they distributed to the priests enrolled
by their families in the genealogical records
and likewise to the Levites twenty years old or
more, according to their responsibilities and
their divisions. 18 They included all the little
ones, the wives, and the sons and daughters
of the whole community listed in these genealogical records. For they were faithful in
consecrating themselves.
19 As for the priests, the descendants of
Aaron, who lived on the farmlands around
their towns or in any other towns, men were
designated by name to distribute portions to
every male among them and to all who were
recorded in the genealogies of the Levites.
20 This is what Hezekiah did throughout
Judah, doing what was good and right and
faithful before the LORD his God. 21 In everything that he undertook in the service of God's
temple and in obedience to the law and the
commands, he sought his God and worked
wholeheartedly. And so he prospered.

Sennacherib Threatens Jerusalem

32 After all that Hezekiah had so faithfully done, Sennacherib king of Assyria
came and invaded Judah. He laid siege to the
fortified cities, thinking to conquer them for
himself. 2 When Hezekiah saw that Sennacherib had come and that he intended to wage
war against Jerusalem, 3 he consulted with
his officials and military staff about block-
ing off the water from the springs outside the
city, and they helped him. 4 They gathered a
large group of people who blocked all the
springs and the stream that flowed through
the land. "Why should the kings[a] of Assyria
come and find plenty of water?" they said.
5 Then he worked hard repairing all the broken sections of the wall and building towers
on it. He built another wall outside that one
and reinforced the terraces[b] of the City of David. He also made large numbers of weapons
and shields.
6 He appointed military officers over the
people and assembled them before him in
the square at the city gate and encouraged
them with these words: 7 "Be strong and courageous. Do not be afraid or discouraged because of the king of Assyria and the vast army
with him, for there is a greater power with us
than with him. 8 With him is only the arm of
flesh, but with us is the LORD our God to help
us and to fight our battles." And the people
gained confidence from what Hezekiah the
king of Judah said.
9 Later, when Sennacherib king of Assyria and all his forces were laying siege to Lachish, he sent his officers to Jerusalem with
this message for Hezekiah king of Judah and
for all the people of Judah who were there:

> 10 "This is what Sennacherib king of As-
> syria says: On what are you basing your
> confidence, that you remain in Jerusalem
> under siege? 11 When Hezekiah says, 'The
> LORD our God will save us from the hand
> of the king of Assyria,' he is misleading
> you, to let you die of hunger and thirst.
> 12 Did not Hezekiah himself remove this
> god's high places and altars, saying to
> Judah and Jerusalem, 'You must wor-
> ship before one altar and burn sacrific-
> es on it'?
> 13 "Do you not know what I and my pre-
> decessors have done to all the peoples of
> the other lands? Were the gods of those
> nations ever able to deliver their land
> from my hand? 14 Who of all the gods of
> these nations that my predecessors de-
> stroyed has been able to save his people
> from me? How then can your god deliv-
> er you from my hand? 15 Now do not let
> Hezekiah deceive you and mislead you
> like this. Do not believe him, for no god
> of any nation or kingdom has been able
> to deliver his people from my hand or the
> hand of my predecessors. How much less
> will your god deliver you from my hand!"

16 Sennacherib's officers spoke further
against the LORD God and against his servant Hezekiah. 17 The king also wrote letters
ridiculing the LORD, the God of Israel, and
saying this against him: "Just as the gods
of the peoples of the other lands did not rescue their people from my hand, so the god of
Hezekiah will not rescue his people from my
hand." 18 Then they called out in Hebrew to the
people of Jerusalem who were on the wall, to
terrify them and make them afraid in order
to capture the city. 19 They spoke about the
God of Jerusalem as they did about the gods
of the other peoples of the world—the work
of human hands.
20 King Hezekiah and the prophet Isaiah
son of Amoz cried out in prayer to heaven
about this. 21 And the LORD sent an angel,
who annihilated all the fighting men and the
commanders and officers in the camp of the
Assyrian king. So he withdrew to his own
land in disgrace. And when he went into the

[a] 4 Hebrew; Septuagint and Syriac *king* [b] 5 Or *the Millo*

temple of his god, some of his sons, his own flesh and blood, cut him down with the sword.

22 So the LORD saved Hezekiah and the people of Jerusalem from the hand of Sennacherib king of Assyria and from the hand of all others. He took care of them[a] on every side. 23 Many brought offerings to Jerusalem for the LORD and valuable gifts for Hezekiah king of Judah. From then on he was highly regarded by all the nations.

Hezekiah's Pride, Success and Death

24 In those days Hezekiah became ill and was at the point of death. He prayed to the LORD, who answered him and gave him a miraculous sign. 25 But Hezekiah's heart was proud and he did not respond to the kindness shown him; therefore the LORD's wrath was on him and on Judah and Jerusalem. 26 Then Hezekiah repented of the pride of his heart, as did the people of Jerusalem; therefore the LORD's wrath did not come on them during the days of Hezekiah.

27 Hezekiah had very great wealth and honor, and he made treasuries for his silver and gold and for his precious stones, spices, shields and all kinds of valuables. 28 He also made buildings to store the harvest of grain, new wine and olive oil; and he made stalls for various kinds of cattle, and pens for the flocks. 29 He built villages and acquired great numbers of flocks and herds, for God had given him very great riches.

30 It was Hezekiah who blocked the upper outlet of the Gihon spring and channeled the water down to the west side of the City of David. He succeeded in everything he undertook. 31 But when envoys were sent by the rulers of Babylon to ask him about the miraculous sign that had occurred in the land, God left him to test him and to know everything that was in his heart.

32 The other events of Hezekiah's reign and his acts of devotion are written in the vision of the prophet Isaiah son of Amoz in the book of the kings of Judah and Israel. 33 Hezekiah rested with his ancestors and was buried on the hill where the tombs of David's descendants are. All Judah and the people of Jerusalem honored him when he died. And Manasseh his son succeeded him as king.

Manasseh King of Judah

33 Manasseh was twelve years old when he became king, and he reigned in Jerusalem fifty-five years. 2 He did evil in the eyes of the LORD, following the detestable practices of the nations the LORD had driven out before the Israelites. 3 He rebuilt the high places his father Hezekiah had demolished; he also erected altars to the Baals and made Asherah poles. He bowed down to all the starry hosts and worshiped them. 4 He built altars in the temple of the LORD, of which the LORD had said, "My Name will remain in Jerusalem forever." 5 In both courts of the temple of the LORD, he built altars to all the starry hosts. 6 He sacrificed his children in the fire in the Valley of Ben Hinnom, practiced divination and witchcraft, sought omens, and consulted mediums and spiritists. He did much evil in the eyes of the LORD, arousing his anger.

7 He took the image he had made and put it in God's temple, of which God had said to David and to his son Solomon, "In this temple and in Jerusalem, which I have chosen out of all the tribes of Israel, I will put my Name forever. 8 I will not again make the feet of the Israelites leave the land I assigned to your ancestors, if only they will be careful to do everything I commanded them concerning all the laws, decrees and regulations given through Moses." 9 But Manasseh led Judah and the people of Jerusalem astray, so that they did more evil than the nations the LORD had destroyed before the Israelites.

10 The LORD spoke to Manasseh and his people, but they paid no attention. 11 So the LORD brought against them the army commanders of the king of Assyria, who took Manasseh prisoner, put a hook in his nose, bound him with bronze shackles and took him to Babylon. 12 In his distress he sought the favor of the LORD his God and humbled himself greatly before the God of his ancestors. 13 And when he prayed to him, the LORD was moved by his entreaty and listened to his plea; so he brought him back to Jerusalem and to his kingdom. Then Manasseh knew that the LORD is God.

14 Afterward he rebuilt the outer wall of the City of David, west of the Gihon spring in the valley, as far as the entrance of the Fish Gate and encircling the hill of Ophel; he also made it much higher. He stationed military commanders in all the fortified cities in Judah.

15 He got rid of the foreign gods and removed the image from the temple of the LORD, as well as all the altars he had built on the temple hill and in Jerusalem; and he threw them out of the city. 16 Then he restored the altar of the LORD and sacrificed fellowship offerings and thank offerings on it, and told Judah to serve the LORD, the God of Israel. 17 The people, however, continued to sacrifice at the high places, but only to the LORD their God.

18 The other events of Manasseh's reign, including his prayer to his God and the words the seers spoke to him in the name of the LORD, the God of Israel, are written in the annals of the kings of Israel.[b] 19 His prayer and how God was moved by his entreaty, as well as all his sins and unfaithfulness, and the sites where he built high places and set up Asherah poles and idols before he humbled himself—all these are written in the records of the seers.[c] 20 Manasseh rested with his ancestors and was buried in his palace. And Amon his son succeeded him as king.

Amon King of Judah

21 Amon was twenty-two years old when he became king, and he reigned in Jerusalem two

[a] 22 Hebrew; Septuagint and Vulgate *He gave them rest* [b] 18 That is, Judah, as frequently in 2 Chronicles [c] 19 One Hebrew manuscript and Septuagint; most Hebrew manuscripts *of Hozai*

years. 22He did evil in the eyes of the LORD,
as his father Manasseh had done. Amon worshiped and offered sacrifices to all the idols
Manasseh had made. 23But unlike his father
Manasseh, he did not humble himself before
the LORD; Amon increased his guilt.
24Amon's officials conspired against him
and assassinated him in his palace. 25Then the
people of the land killed all who had plotted
against King Amon, and they made Josiah
his son king in his place.

Josiah's Reforms

34 Josiah was eight years old when he became king, and he reigned in Jerusalem
thirty-one years. 2He did what was right in
the eyes of the LORD and followed the ways
of his father David, not turning aside to the
right or to the left.
3In the eighth year of his reign, while he
was still young, he began to seek the God of
his father David. In his twelfth year he began
to purge Judah and Jerusalem of high places,
Asherah poles and idols. 4Under his direction
the altars of the Baals were torn down; he cut
to pieces the incense altars that were above
them, and smashed the Asherah poles and the
idols. These he broke to pieces and scattered
over the graves of those who had sacrificed
to them. 5He burned the bones of the priests
on their altars, and so he purged Judah and
Jerusalem. 6In the towns of Manasseh, Ephraim and Simeon, as far as Naphtali, and in the
ruins around them, 7he tore down the altars
and the Asherah poles and crushed the idols
to powder and cut to pieces all the incense
altars throughout Israel. Then he went back
to Jerusalem.
8In the eighteenth year of Josiah's reign, to
purify the land and the temple, he sent Shaphan son of Azaliah and Maaseiah the ruler of
the city, with Joah son of Joahaz, the recorder, to repair the temple of the LORD his God.
9They went to Hilkiah the high priest and
gave him the money that had been brought
into the temple of God, which the Levites who
were the gatekeepers had collected from the
people of Manasseh, Ephraim and the entire
remnant of Israel and from all the people of
Judah and Benjamin and the inhabitants of
Jerusalem. 10Then they entrusted it to the men
appointed to supervise the work on the LORD's
temple. These men paid the workers who repaired and restored the temple. 11They also
gave money to the carpenters and builders to
purchase dressed stone, and timber for joists
and beams for the buildings that the kings of
Judah had allowed to fall into ruin.
12The workers labored faithfully. Over them
to direct them were Jahath and Obadiah, Levites descended from Merari, and Zechariah
and Meshullam, descended from Kohath. The
Levites—all who were skilled in playing musical instruments— 13had charge of the laborers and supervised all the workers from job
to job. Some of the Levites were secretaries,
scribes and gatekeepers.

The Book of the Law Found

14While they were bringing out the money that had been taken into the temple of the
LORD, Hilkiah the priest found the Book of the
Law of the LORD that had been given through
Moses. 15Hilkiah said to Shaphan the secretary, "I have found the Book of the Law in the
temple of the LORD." He gave it to Shaphan.
16Then Shaphan took the book to the king
and reported to him: "Your officials are doing
everything that has been committed to them.
17They have paid out the money that was in the
temple of the LORD and have entrusted it to the
supervisors and workers." 18Then Shaphan
the secretary informed the king, "Hilkiah the
priest has given me a book." And Shaphan
read from it in the presence of the king.
19When the king heard the words of the
Law, he tore his robes. 20He gave these orders
to Hilkiah, Ahikam son of Shaphan, Abdon
son of Micah,[a] Shaphan the secretary and
Asaiah the king's attendant: 21"Go and inquire of the LORD for me and for the remnant
in Israel and Judah about what is written in
this book that has been found. Great is the
LORD's anger that is poured out on us because
those who have gone before us have not kept
the word of the LORD; they have not acted
in accordance with all that is written in this
book."
22Hilkiah and those the king had sent with
him[b] went to speak to the prophet Huldah,
who was the wife of Shallum son of Tokhath,[c]
the son of Hasrah,[d] keeper of the wardrobe.
She lived in Jerusalem, in the New Quarter.
23She said to them, "This is what the LORD,
the God of Israel, says: Tell the man who sent
you to me, 24'This is what the LORD says: I am
going to bring disaster on this place and its
people—all the curses written in the book
that has been read in the presence of the king
of Judah. 25Because they have forsaken me
and burned incense to other gods and aroused
my anger by all that their hands have made,[e]
my anger will be poured out on this place
and will not be quenched.' 26Tell the king of
Judah, who sent you to inquire of the LORD,
'This is what the LORD, the God of Israel, says
concerning the words you heard: 27Because
your heart was responsive and you humbled
yourself before God when you heard what he
spoke against this place and its people, and
because you humbled yourself before me and
tore your robes and wept in my presence, I
have heard you, declares the LORD. 28Now I
will gather you to your ancestors, and you will
be buried in peace. Your eyes will not see all
the disaster I am going to bring on this place
and on those who live here.'"
So they took her answer back to the king.
29Then the king called together all the elders
of Judah and Jerusalem. 30He went up to the

[a] 20 Also called *Akbor son of Micaiah* [b] 22 One Hebrew manuscript, Vulgate and Syriac; most Hebrew manuscripts do not have *had sent with him.* [c] 22 Also called *Tikvah* [d] 22 Also called *Harhas* [e] 25 Or *by everything they have done*

temple of the LORD with the people of Judah,
the inhabitants of Jerusalem, the priests and
the Levites—all the people from the least to the
greatest. He read in their hearing all the words
of the Book of the Covenant, which had been
found in the temple of the LORD. 31The king
stood by his pillar and renewed the covenant in
the presence of the LORD—to follow the LORD
and keep his commands, statutes and decrees
with all his heart and all his soul, and to obey
the words of the covenant written in this book.
32Then he had everyone in Jerusalem and
Benjamin pledge themselves to it; the people
of Jerusalem did this in accordance with the
covenant of God, the God of their ancestors.
33Josiah removed all the detestable idols
from all the territory belonging to the Israelites, and he had all who were present in Israel
serve the LORD their God. As long as he lived,
they did not fail to follow the LORD, the God
of their ancestors.

Josiah Celebrates the Passover

35 Josiah celebrated the Passover to the
LORD in Jerusalem, and the Passover
lamb was slaughtered on the fourteenth day
of the first month. 2He appointed the priests
to their duties and encouraged them in the
service of the LORD's temple. 3He said to the
Levites, who instructed all Israel and who
had been consecrated to the LORD: "Put the
sacred ark in the temple that Solomon son of
David king of Israel built. It is not to be carried about on your shoulders. Now serve the
LORD your God and his people Israel. 4Prepare
yourselves by families in your divisions, according to the instructions written by David
king of Israel and by his son Solomon.
5"Stand in the holy place with a group of
Levites for each subdivision of the families of your fellow Israelites, the lay people.
6Slaughter the Passover lambs, consecrate
yourselves and prepare the lambs for your
fellow Israelites, doing what the LORD commanded through Moses."
7Josiah provided for all the lay people who
were there a total of thirty thousand lambs
and goats for the Passover offerings, and also
three thousand cattle—all from the king's
own possessions.
8His officials also contributed voluntarily to
the people and the priests and Levites. Hilkiah,
Zechariah and Jehiel, the officials in charge
of God's temple, gave the priests twenty-six
hundred Passover offerings and three hundred
cattle. 9Also Konaniah along with Shemaiah
and Nethanel, his brothers, and Hashabiah,
Jeiel and Jozabad, the leaders of the Levites,
provided five thousand Passover offerings and
five hundred head of cattle for the Levites.
10The service was arranged and the priests
stood in their places with the Levites in their
divisions as the king had ordered. 11The Passover lambs were slaughtered, and the priests
splashed against the altar the blood handed to
them, while the Levites skinned the animals.
12They set aside the burnt offerings to give
them to the subdivisions of the families of the
people to offer to the LORD, as it is written in
the Book of Moses. They did the same with
the cattle. 13They roasted the Passover animals over the fire as prescribed, and boiled
the holy offerings in pots, caldrons and pans
and served them quickly to all the people.
14After this, they made preparations for themselves and for the priests, because the priests,
the descendants of Aaron, were sacrificing
the burnt offerings and the fat portions until
nightfall. So the Levites made preparations
for themselves and for the Aaronic priests.
15The musicians, the descendants of Asaph,
were in the places prescribed by David,
Asaph, Heman and Jeduthun the king's seer.
The gatekeepers at each gate did not need to
leave their posts, because their fellow Levites
made the preparations for them.
16So at that time the entire service of the
LORD was carried out for the celebration of
the Passover and the offering of burnt offerings on the altar of the LORD, as King Josiah
had ordered. 17The Israelites who were present celebrated the Passover at that time and
observed the Festival of Unleavened Bread
for seven days. 18The Passover had not been
observed like this in Israel since the days of
the prophet Samuel; and none of the kings of
Israel had ever celebrated such a Passover as
did Josiah, with the priests, the Levites and
all Judah and Israel who were there with the
people of Jerusalem. 19This Passover was celebrated in the eighteenth year of Josiah's reign.

The Death of Josiah

20After all this, when Josiah had set the temple in order, Necho king of Egypt went up to
fight at Carchemish on the Euphrates, and Josiah marched out to meet him in battle. 21But
Necho sent messengers to him, saying, "What
quarrel is there, king of Judah, between you
and me? It is not you I am attacking at this
time, but the house with which I am at war.
God has told me to hurry; so stop opposing
God, who is with me, or he will destroy you."
22Josiah, however, would not turn away
from him, but disguised himself to engage
him in battle. He would not listen to what Necho had said at God's command but went to
fight him on the plain of Megiddo.
23Archers shot King Josiah, and he told his
officers, "Take me away; I am badly wounded." 24So they took him out of his chariot, put
him in his other chariot and brought him to
Jerusalem, where he died. He was buried in
the tombs of his ancestors, and all Judah and
Jerusalem mourned for him.
25Jeremiah composed laments for Josiah,
and to this day all the male and female singers
commemorate Josiah in the laments. These
became a tradition in Israel and are written
in the Laments.
26The other events of Josiah's reign and
his acts of devotion in accordance with what
is written in the Law of the LORD— 27all the
events, from beginning to end, are written
in the book of the kings of Israel and Judah.

36 1And the people of the land took Jehoahaz son of Josiah and made him king
in Jerusalem in place of his father.

Jehoahaz King of Judah

2Jehoahaz[a] was twenty-three years old when
he became king, and he reigned in Jerusalem
three months. 3The king of Egypt dethroned
him in Jerusalem and imposed on Judah a levy
of a hundred talents[b] of silver and a talent[c]
of gold. 4The king of Egypt made Eliakim, a
brother of Jehoahaz, king over Judah and Jerusalem and changed Eliakim's name to Jehoiakim. But Necho took Eliakim's brother
Jehoahaz and carried him off to Egypt.

Jehoiakim King of Judah

5Jehoiakim was twenty-five years old when
he became king, and he reigned in Jerusalem eleven years. He did evil in the eyes of
the LORD his God. 6Nebuchadnezzar king of
Babylon attacked him and bound him with
bronze shackles to take him to Babylon. 7Neb-
uchadnezzar also took to Babylon articles
from the temple of the LORD and put them in
his temple[d] there.
8The other events of Jehoiakim's reign, the
detestable things he did and all that was found
against him, are written in the book of the
kings of Israel and Judah. And Jehoiachin
his son succeeded him as king.

Jehoiachin King of Judah

9Jehoiachin was eighteen[e] years old when he
became king, and he reigned in Jerusalem three
months and ten days. He did evil in the eyes of
the LORD. 10In the spring, King Nebuchadnezzar sent for him and brought him to Babylon,
together with articles of value from the temple
of the LORD, and he made Jehoiachin's uncle,[f]
Zedekiah, king over Judah and Jerusalem.

Zedekiah King of Judah

11Zedekiah was twenty-one years old when
he became king, and he reigned in Jerusalem eleven years. 12He did evil in the eyes of
the LORD his God and did not humble himself
before Jeremiah the prophet, who spoke the
word of the LORD. 13He also rebelled against
King Nebuchadnezzar, who had made him
take an oath in God's name. He became
stiff-necked and hardened his heart and
would not turn to the LORD, the God of Israel. 14Furthermore, all the leaders of the priests
and the people became more and more unfaithful, following all the detestable practices
of the nations and defiling the temple of the
LORD, which he had consecrated in Jerusalem.

The Fall of Jerusalem

15The LORD, the God of their ancestors, sent
word to them through his messengers again
and again, because he had pity on his people
and on his dwelling place. 16But they mocked
God's messengers, despised his words and
scoffed at his prophets until the wrath of the
LORD was aroused against his people and
there was no remedy. 17He brought up against
them the king of the Babylonians,[g] who killed
their young men with the sword in the sanctuary, and did not spare young men or young
women, the elderly or the infirm. God gave
them all into the hands of Nebuchadnezzar.
18He carried to Babylon all the articles from
the temple of God, both large and small, and
the treasures of the LORD's temple and the
treasures of the king and his officials. 19They
set fire to God's temple and broke down the
wall of Jerusalem; they burned all the palaces and destroyed everything of value there.
20He carried into exile to Babylon the remnant, who escaped from the sword, and they
became servants to him and his successors
until the kingdom of Persia came to power.
21The land enjoyed its sabbath rests; all the
time of its desolation it rested, until the seventy years were completed in fulfillment of
the word of the LORD spoken by Jeremiah.
22In the first year of Cyrus king of Persia, in
order to fulfill the word of the LORD spoken by
Jeremiah, the LORD moved the heart of Cyrus
king of Persia to make a proclamation throughout his realm and also to put it in writing:

> 23"This is what Cyrus king of Persia says:
> "'The LORD, the God of heaven, has
> given me all the kingdoms of the earth
> and he has appointed me to build a tem-
> ple for him at Jerusalem in Judah. Any
> of his people among you may go up, and
> may the LORD their God be with them.'"

Ezra

Cyrus Helps the Exiles to Return

1 In the first year of Cyrus king of Persia, in
order to fulfill the word of the LORD spoken by Jeremiah, the LORD moved the heart
of Cyrus king of Persia to make a proclamation throughout his realm and also to put it
in writing:

> 2"This is what Cyrus king of Persia says:
> "'The LORD, the God of heaven, has giv-
> en me all the kingdoms of the earth and

[a] 2 Hebrew *Joahaz,* a variant of *Jehoahaz;* also in verse 4 [b] 3 That is, about 3 3/4 tons or about 3.4 metric tons [c] 3 That is, about 75 pounds or about 34 kilograms [d] 7 Or *palace* [e] 9 One Hebrew manuscript, some Septuagint manuscripts and Syriac (see also 2 Kings 24:8); most Hebrew manuscripts *eight* [f] 10 Hebrew *brother,* that is, relative (see 2 Kings 24:17) [g] 17 Or *Chaldeans*

he has appointed me to build a temple
for him at Jerusalem in Judah. 3 Any of
his people among you may go up to Jerusalem in Judah and build the temple
of the LORD, the God of Israel, the God
who is in Jerusalem, and may their God
be with them. 4 And in any locality where
survivors may now be living, the people
are to provide them with silver and gold,
with goods and livestock, and with freewill offerings for the temple of God in
Jerusalem.'"

5 Then the family heads of Judah and Benjamin, and the priests and Levites—everyone
whose heart God had moved—prepared to
go up and build the house of the LORD in Jerusalem. 6 All their neighbors assisted them
with articles of silver and gold, with goods and
livestock, and with valuable gifts, in addition
to all the freewill offerings.
7 Moreover, King Cyrus brought out the
articles belonging to the temple of the LORD,
which Nebuchadnezzar had carried away
from Jerusalem and had placed in the temple
of his god.[a] 8 Cyrus king of Persia had them
brought by Mithredath the treasurer, who
counted them out to Sheshbazzar the prince
of Judah.
9 This was the inventory:

gold dishes	30
silver dishes	1,000
silver pans[b]	29
10 gold bowls	30
matching silver bowls	410
other articles	1,000

11 In all, there were 5,400 articles of gold
and of silver. Sheshbazzar brought all these
along with the exiles when they came up from
Babylon to Jerusalem.

The List of the Exiles Who Returned

2 Now these are the people of the province
who came up from the captivity of the exiles, whom Nebuchadnezzar king of Babylon
had taken captive to Babylon (they returned
to Jerusalem and Judah, each to their own
town, 2 in company with Zerubbabel, Joshua,
Nehemiah, Seraiah, Reelaiah, Mordecai, Bil-
shan, Mispar, Bigvai, Rehum and Baanah):

The list of the men of the people of Israel:

3 the descendants of Parosh	2,172
4 of Shephatiah	372
5 of Arah	775
6 of Pahath-Moab (through the line of Jeshua and Joab)	2,812
7 of Elam	1,254
8 of Zattu	945
9 of Zakkai	760
10 of Bani	642
11 of Bebai	623
12 of Azgad	1,222
13 of Adonikam	666
14 of Bigvai	2,056
15 of Adin	454
16 of Ater (through Hezekiah)	98
17 of Bezai	323
18 of Jorah	112
19 of Hashum	223
20 of Gibbar	95
21 the men of Bethlehem	123
22 of Netophah	56
23 of Anathoth	128
24 of Azmaveth	42
25 of Kiriath Jearim,[c] Kephirah and Beeroth	743
26 of Ramah and Geba	621
27 of Mikmash	122
28 of Bethel and Ai	223
29 of Nebo	52
30 of Magbish	156
31 of the other Elam	1,254
32 of Harim	320
33 of Lod, Hadid and Ono	725
34 of Jericho	345
35 of Senaah	3,630

36 The priests:

the descendants of Jedaiah (through the family of Jeshua)	973
37 of Immer	1,052
38 of Pashhur	1,247
39 of Harim	1,017

40 The Levites:

the descendants of Jeshua and Kadmiel (of the line of Hodaviah)	74

41 The musicians:

the descendants of Asaph	128

42 The gatekeepers of the temple:

the descendants of Shallum, Ater, Talmon, Akkub, Hatita and Shobai	139

43 The temple servants:

the descendants of
Ziha, Hasupha, Tabbaoth,
44 Keros, Siaha, Padon,
45 Lebanah, Hagabah, Akkub,
46 Hagab, Shalmai, Hanan,
47 Giddel, Gahar, Reaiah,
48 Rezin, Nekoda, Gazzam,
49 Uzza, Paseah, Besai,
50 Asnah, Meunim, Nephusim,
51 Bakbuk, Hakupha, Harhur,
52 Bazluth, Mehida, Harsha,
53 Barkos, Sisera, Temah,
54 Neziah and Hatipha

55 The descendants of the servants of Solomon:

the descendants of
Sotai, Hassophereth, Peruda,
56 Jaala, Darkon, Giddel,
57 Shephatiah, Hattil,
Pokereth-Hazzebaim and Ami

[a] 7 Or *gods* [b] 9 The meaning of the Hebrew for this word is uncertain. [c] 25 See Septuagint (see also Neh. 7:29); Hebrew *Kiriath Arim.*

58The temple servants and the
descendants of the servants
of Solomon 392

59The following came up from the
towns of Tel Melah, Tel Harsha, Kerub,
Addon and Immer, but they could not
show that their families were descended
from Israel:

60The descendants of
Delaiah, Tobiah and Nekoda 652

61And from among the priests:

The descendants of
Hobaiah, Hakkoz and Barzillai (a
man who had married a daughter
of Barzillai the Gileadite and was
called by that name).

62These searched for their family records, but they could not find them and
so were excluded from the priesthood as
unclean. 63The governor ordered them not
to eat any of the most sacred food until
there was a priest ministering with the
Urim and Thummim.

64The whole company numbered
42,360, 65besides their 7,337 male and
female slaves; and they also had 200
male and female singers. 66They had
736 horses, 245 mules, 67435 camels and
6,720 donkeys.

68When they arrived at the house of the
LORD in Jerusalem, some of the heads of the
families gave freewill offerings toward the
rebuilding of the house of God on its site. 69Ac-
cording to their ability they gave to the treasury for this work 61,000 darics[a] of gold, 5,000
minas[b] of silver and 100 priestly garments.

70The priests, the Levites, the musicians,
the gatekeepers and the temple servants settled in their own towns, along with some of
the other people, and the rest of the Israelites
settled in their towns.

Rebuilding the Altar

3 When the seventh month came and the Israelites had settled in their towns, the people assembled together as one in Jerusalem.
2Then Joshua son of Jozadak and his fellow
priests and Zerubbabel son of Shealtiel and
his associates began to build the altar of the
God of Israel to sacrifice burnt offerings on
it, in accordance with what is written in the
Law of Moses the man of God. 3Despite their
fear of the peoples around them, they built the
altar on its foundation and sacrificed burnt
offerings on it to the LORD, both the morning
and evening sacrifices. 4Then in accordance
with what is written, they celebrated the Festival of Tabernacles with the required number
of burnt offerings prescribed for each day.
5After that, they presented the regular burnt
offerings, the New Moon sacrifices and the
sacrifices for all the appointed sacred festivals
of the LORD, as well as those brought as freewill offerings to the LORD. 6On the first day of
the seventh month they began to offer burnt
offerings to the LORD, though the foundation
of the LORD's temple had not yet been laid.

Rebuilding the Temple

7Then they gave money to the masons and
carpenters, and gave food and drink and olive oil to the people of Sidon and Tyre, so that
they would bring cedar logs by sea from Lebanon to Joppa, as authorized by Cyrus king
of Persia.

8In the second month of the second year
after their arrival at the house of God in Jerusalem, Zerubbabel son of Shealtiel, Joshua son of Jozadak and the rest of the people
(the priests and the Levites and all who had
returned from the captivity to Jerusalem) began the work. They appointed Levites twenty
years old and older to supervise the building of the house of the LORD. 9Joshua and his
sons and brothers and Kadmiel and his sons
(descendants of Hodaviah[c]) and the sons of
Henadad and their sons and brothers—all Levites—joined together in supervising those
working on the house of God.

10When the builders laid the foundation of
the temple of the LORD, the priests in their
vestments and with trumpets, and the Levites
(the sons of Asaph) with cymbals, took their
places to praise the LORD, as prescribed by David king of Israel. 11With praise and thanksgiving they sang to the LORD:

"He is good;
his love toward Israel endures forever."

And all the people gave a great shout of praise
to the LORD, because the foundation of the
house of the LORD was laid. 12But many of the
older priests and Levites and family heads,
who had seen the former temple, wept aloud
when they saw the foundation of this temple
being laid, while many others shouted for joy.
13No one could distinguish the sound of the
shouts of joy from the sound of weeping, because the people made so much noise. And
the sound was heard far away.

Opposition to the Rebuilding

4 When the enemies of Judah and Benjamin
heard that the exiles were building a temple for the LORD, the God of Israel, 2they came
to Zerubbabel and to the heads of the families
and said, "Let us help you build because, like
you, we seek your God and have been sacrificing to him since the time of Esarhaddon king
of Assyria, who brought us here."

3But Zerubbabel, Joshua and the rest of the
heads of the families of Israel answered, "You
have no part with us in building a temple to
our God. We alone will build it for the LORD,
the God of Israel, as King Cyrus, the king of
Persia, commanded us."

4Then the peoples around them set out to
discourage the people of Judah and make
them afraid to go on building.[d] 5They bribed

[a] *69* That is, about 1,100 pounds or about 500 kilograms [b] *69* That is, about 3 tons or about 2.8 metric tons [c] *9* Hebrew *Yehudah*, a variant of *Hodaviah* [d] *4* Or *and troubled them as they built*

officials to work against them and frustrate their plans during the entire reign of Cyrus king of Persia and down to the reign of Darius king of Persia.

Later Opposition Under Xerxes and Artaxerxes

[6]At the beginning of the reign of Xerxes,[a] they lodged an accusation against the people of Judah and Jerusalem.

[7]And in the days of Artaxerxes king of Persia, Bishlam, Mithredath, Tabeel and the rest of his associates wrote a letter to Artaxerxes. The letter was written in Aramaic script and in the Aramaic language.[b,c]

[8]Rehum the commanding officer and Shimshai the secretary wrote a letter against Jerusalem to Artaxerxes the king as follows:

[9]Rehum the commanding officer and Shimshai the secretary, together with the rest of their associates—the judges, officials and administrators over the people from Persia, Uruk and Babylon, the Elamites of Susa, [10]and the other people whom the great and honorable Ashurbanipal deported and settled in the city of Samaria and elsewhere in Trans-Euphrates.

[11](This is a copy of the letter they sent him.)

To King Artaxerxes,

From your servants in Trans-Euphrates:

[12]The king should know that the people who came up to us from you have gone to Jerusalem and are rebuilding that rebellious and wicked city. They are restoring the walls and repairing the foundations.

[13]Furthermore, the king should know that if this city is built and its walls are restored, no more taxes, tribute or duty will be paid, and eventually the royal revenues will suffer.[d] [14]Now since we are under obligation to the palace and it is not proper for us to see the king dishonored, we are sending this message to inform the king, [15]so that a search may be made in the archives of your predecessors. In these records you will find that this city is a rebellious city, troublesome to kings and provinces, a place with a long history of sedition. That is why this city was destroyed. [16]We inform the king that if this city is built and its walls are restored, you will be left with nothing in Trans-Euphrates.

[17]The king sent this reply:

To Rehum the commanding officer, Shimshai the secretary and the rest of their associates living in Samaria and elsewhere in Trans-Euphrates:

Greetings.

[18]The letter you sent us has been read and translated in my presence. [19]I issued an order and a search was made, and it was found that this city has a long history of revolt against kings and has been a place of rebellion and sedition. [20]Jerusalem has had powerful kings ruling over the whole of Trans-Euphrates, and taxes, tribute and duty were paid to them. [21]Now issue an order to these men to stop work, so that this city will not be rebuilt until I so order. [22]Be careful not to neglect this matter. Why let this threat grow, to the detriment of the royal interests?

[23]As soon as the copy of the letter of King Artaxerxes was read to Rehum and Shimshai the secretary and their associates, they went immediately to the Jews in Jerusalem and compelled them by force to stop.

[24]Thus the work on the house of God in Jerusalem came to a standstill until the second year of the reign of Darius king of Persia.

Tattenai's Letter to Darius

5 Now Haggai the prophet and Zechariah the prophet, a descendant of Iddo, prophesied to the Jews in Judah and Jerusalem in the name of the God of Israel, who was over them. [2]Then Zerubbabel son of Shealtiel and Joshua son of Jozadak set to work to rebuild the house of God in Jerusalem. And the prophets of God were with them, supporting them.

[3]At that time Tattenai, governor of Trans-Euphrates, and Shethar-Bozenai and their associates went to them and asked, "Who authorized you to rebuild this temple and to finish it?" [4]They[e] also asked, "What are the names of those who are constructing this building?" [5]But the eye of their God was watching over the elders of the Jews, and they were not stopped until a report could go to Darius and his written reply be received.

[6]This is a copy of the letter that Tattenai, governor of Trans-Euphrates, and Shethar-Bozenai and their associates, the officials of Trans-Euphrates, sent to King Darius. [7]The report they sent him read as follows:

To King Darius:

Cordial greetings.

[8]The king should know that we went to the district of Judah, to the temple of the great God. The people are building it with large stones and placing the timbers in the walls. The work is being carried on with diligence and is making rapid progress under their direction.

[9]We questioned the elders and asked them, "Who authorized you to rebuild this temple and to finish it?" [10]We also asked them their names, so that we could write down the names of their leaders for your information.

[11]This is the answer they gave us:

[a] 6 Hebrew *Ahasuerus* [b] 7 Or *written in Aramaic and translated* [c] 7 The text of 4:8–6:18 is in Aramaic. [d] 13 The meaning of the Aramaic for this clause is uncertain. [e] 4 See Septuagint; Aramaic *We*.

"We are the servants of the God of heaven and earth, and we are rebuilding the temple that was built many years ago, one that a great king of Israel built and finished. 12But because our ancestors angered the God of heaven, he gave them into the hands of Nebuchadnezzar the Chaldean, king of Babylon, who destroyed this temple and deported the people to Babylon.

13"However, in the first year of Cyrus king of Babylon, King Cyrus issued a decree to rebuild this house of God. 14He even removed from the temple[a] of Babylon the gold and silver articles of the house of God, which Nebuchadnezzar had taken from the temple in Jerusalem and brought to the temple[a] in Babylon. Then King Cyrus gave them to a man named Sheshbazzar, whom he had appointed governor, 15and he told him, 'Take these articles and go and deposit them in the temple in Jerusalem. And rebuild the house of God on its site.'

16"So this Sheshbazzar came and laid the foundations of the house of God in Jerusalem. From that day to the present it has been under construction but is not yet finished."

17Now if it pleases the king, let a search be made in the royal archives of Babylon to see if King Cyrus did in fact issue a decree to rebuild this house of God in Jerusalem. Then let the king send us his decision in this matter.

The Decree of Darius

6 King Darius then issued an order, and they searched in the archives stored in the treasury at Babylon. 2A scroll was found in the citadel of Ecbatana in the province of Media, and this was written on it:

Memorandum:

3In the first year of King Cyrus, the king issued a decree concerning the temple of God in Jerusalem:

Let the temple be rebuilt as a place to present sacrifices, and let its foundations be laid. It is to be sixty cubits[b] high and sixty cubits wide, 4with three courses of large stones and one of timbers. The costs are to be paid by the royal treasury. 5Also, the gold and silver articles of the house of God, which Nebuchadnezzar took from the temple in Jerusalem and brought to Babylon, are to be returned to their places in the temple in Jerusalem; they are to be deposited in the house of God.

6Now then, Tattenai, governor of Trans-Euphrates, and Shethar-Bozenai and you other officials of that province, stay away from there. 7Do not interfere with the work on this temple of God. Let the governor of the Jews and the Jewish elders rebuild this house of God on its site.

8Moreover, I hereby decree what you are to do for these elders of the Jews in the construction of this house of God:

Their expenses are to be fully paid out of the royal treasury, from the revenues of Trans-Euphrates, so that the work will not stop. 9Whatever is needed—young bulls, rams, male lambs for burnt offerings to the God of heaven, and wheat, salt, wine and olive oil, as requested by the priests in Jerusalem—must be given them daily without fail, 10so that they may offer sacrifices pleasing to the God of heaven and pray for the well-being of the king and his sons.

11Furthermore, I decree that if anyone defies this edict, a beam is to be pulled from their house and they are to be impaled on it. And for this crime their house is to be made a pile of rubble. 12May God, who has caused his Name to dwell there, overthrow any king or people who lifts a hand to change this decree or to destroy this temple in Jerusalem.

I Darius have decreed it. Let it be carried out with diligence.

Completion and Dedication of the Temple

13Then, because of the decree King Darius had sent, Tattenai, governor of Trans-Euphrates, and Shethar-Bozenai and their associates carried it out with diligence. 14So the elders of the Jews continued to build and prosper under the preaching of Haggai the prophet and Zechariah, a descendant of Iddo. They finished building the temple according to the command of the God of Israel and the decrees of Cyrus, Darius and Artaxerxes, kings of Persia. 15The temple was completed on the third day of the month Adar, in the sixth year of the reign of King Darius.

16Then the people of Israel—the priests, the Levites and the rest of the exiles—celebrated the dedication of the house of God with joy. 17For the dedication of this house of God they offered a hundred bulls, two hundred rams, four hundred male lambs and, as a sin offering[c] for all Israel, twelve male goats, one for each of the tribes of Israel. 18And they installed the priests in their divisions and the Levites in their groups for the service of God at Jerusalem, according to what is written in the Book of Moses.

The Passover

19On the fourteenth day of the first month, the exiles celebrated the Passover. 20The priests and Levites had purified themselves and were all ceremonially clean. The Levites slaughtered the Passover lamb for all the exiles, for their relatives the priests and for themselves. 21So the Israelites who had returned from the exile ate it, together with all who had separated themselves from the unclean practices of their Gentile neighbors

[a] 14 Or *palace* [b] 3 That is, about 90 feet or about 27 meters [c] 17 Or *purification offering*

in order to seek the LORD, the God of Israel. 22For seven days they celebrated with joy the Festival of Unleavened Bread, because the LORD had filled them with joy by changing the attitude of the king of Assyria so that he assisted them in the work on the house of God, the God of Israel.

Ezra Comes to Jerusalem

7 After these things, during the reign of Artaxerxes king of Persia, Ezra son of Seraiah, the son of Azariah, the son of Hilkiah, 2the son of Shallum, the son of Zadok, the son of Ahitub, 3the son of Amariah, the son of Azariah, the son of Meraioth, 4the son of Zerahiah, the son of Uzzi, the son of Bukki, 5the son of Abishua, the son of Phinehas, the son of Eleazar, the son of Aaron the chief priest— 6this Ezra came up from Babylon. He was a teacher well versed in the Law of Moses, which the LORD, the God of Israel, had given. The king had granted him everything he asked, for the hand of the LORD his God was on him. 7Some of the Israelites, including priests, Levites, musicians, gatekeepers and temple servants, also came up to Jerusalem in the seventh year of King Artaxerxes.

8Ezra arrived in Jerusalem in the fifth month of the seventh year of the king. 9He had begun his journey from Babylon on the first day of the first month, and he arrived in Jerusalem on the first day of the fifth month, for the gracious hand of his God was on him. 10For Ezra had devoted himself to the study and observance of the Law of the LORD, and to teaching its decrees and laws in Israel.

King Artaxerxes' Letter to Ezra

11This is a copy of the letter King Artaxerxes had given to Ezra the priest, a teacher of the Law, a man learned in matters concerning the commands and decrees of the LORD for Israel:

12Artaxerxes, king of kings,

To Ezra the priest, teacher of the Law of the God of heaven:

Greetings.

13Now I decree that any of the Israelites in my kingdom, including priests and Levites, who volunteer to go to Jerusalem with you, may go. 14You are sent by the king and his seven advisers to inquire about Judah and Jerusalem with regard to the Law of your God, which is in your hand. 15Moreover, you are to take with you the silver and gold that the king and his advisers have freely given to the God of Israel, whose dwelling is in Jerusalem, 16together with all the silver and gold you may obtain from the province of Babylon, as well as the freewill offerings of the people and priests for the temple of their God in Jerusalem. 17With this money be sure to buy bulls, rams and male lambs, together with their grain offerings and drink offerings, and sacrifice them on the altar of the temple of your God in Jerusalem.

18You and your fellow Israelites may then do whatever seems best with the rest of the silver and gold, in accordance with the will of your God. 19Deliver to the God of Jerusalem all the articles entrusted to you for worship in the temple of your God. 20And anything else needed for the temple of your God that you are responsible to supply, you may provide from the royal treasury.

21Now I, King Artaxerxes, decree that all the treasurers of Trans-Euphrates are to provide with diligence whatever Ezra the priest, the teacher of the Law of the God of heaven, may ask of you— 22up to a hundred talents[a] of silver, a hundred cors[b] of wheat, a hundred baths[c] of wine, a hundred baths[c] of olive oil, and salt without limit. 23Whatever the God of heaven has prescribed, let it be done with diligence for the temple of the God of heaven. Why should his wrath fall on the realm of the king and of his sons? 24You are also to know that you have no authority to impose taxes, tribute or duty on any of the priests, Levites, musicians, gatekeepers, temple servants or other workers at this house of God.

25And you, Ezra, in accordance with the wisdom of your God, which you possess, appoint magistrates and judges to administer justice to all the people of Trans-Euphrates—all who know the laws of your God. And you are to teach any who do not know them. 26Whoever does not obey the law of your God and the law of the king must surely be punished by death, banishment, confiscation of property, or imprisonment.[d]

27Praise be to the LORD, the God of our ancestors, who has put it into the king's heart to bring honor to the house of the LORD in Jerusalem in this way 28and who has extended his good favor to me before the king and his advisers and all the king's powerful officials. Because the hand of the LORD my God was on me, I took courage and gathered leaders from Israel to go up with me.

List of the Family Heads Returning With Ezra

8 These are the family heads and those registered with them who came up with me from Babylon during the reign of King Artaxerxes:

2 of the descendants of Phinehas, Gershom;
of the descendants of Ithamar, Daniel;
of the descendants of David, Hattush 3of
the descendants of Shekaniah;

[a] 22 That is, about 3 3/4 tons or about 3.4 metric tons [b] 22 That is, probably about 18 tons or about 16 metric tons [c] 22 That is, about 600 gallons or about 2,200 liters [d] 26 The text of 7:12-26 is in Aramaic.

of the descendants of Parosh, Zechariah,
and with him were registered 150 men;
4 of the descendants of Pahath-Moab, Eliehoenai son of Zerahiah, and with him
200 men;
5 of the descendants of Zattu,[a] Shekaniah
son of Jahaziel, and with him 300 men;
6 of the descendants of Adin, Ebed son of
Jonathan, and with him 50 men;
7 of the descendants of Elam, Jeshaiah son
of Athaliah, and with him 70 men;
8 of the descendants of Shephatiah, Zebadiah son of Michael, and with him 80
men;
9 of the descendants of Joab, Obadiah son
of Jehiel, and with him 218 men;
10 of the descendants of Bani,[b] Shelomith son
of Josiphiah, and with him 160 men;
11 of the descendants of Bebai, Zechariah
son of Bebai, and with him 28 men;
12 of the descendants of Azgad, Johanan son
of Hakkatan, and with him 110 men;
13 of the descendants of Adonikam, the last
ones, whose names were Eliphelet, Jeuel
and Shemaiah, and with them 60 men;
14 of the descendants of Bigvai, Uthai and
Zakkur, and with them 70 men.

The Return to Jerusalem

15 I assembled them at the canal that flows toward Ahava, and we camped there three days.
When I checked among the people and the
priests, I found no Levites there. 16 So I summoned Eliezer, Ariel, Shemaiah, Elnathan,
Jarib, Elnathan, Nathan, Zechariah and Meshullam, who were leaders, and Joiarib and
Elnathan, who were men of learning, 17 and I
ordered them to go to Iddo, the leader in Ka-
siphia. I told them what to say to Iddo and his
fellow Levites, the temple servants in Kasiph-
ia, so that they might bring attendants to us for
the house of our God. 18 Because the gracious
hand of our God was on us, they brought us
Sherebiah, a capable man, from the descendants of Mahli son of Levi, the son of Israel,
and Sherebiah's sons and brothers, 18 in all;
19 and Hashabiah, together with Jeshaiah from
the descendants of Merari, and his brothers
and nephews, 20 in all. 20 They also brought
220 of the temple servants—a body that David
and the officials had established to assist the
Levites. All were registered by name.

21 There, by the Ahava Canal, I proclaimed a
fast, so that we might humble ourselves before
our God and ask him for a safe journey for us
and our children, with all our possessions.
22 I was ashamed to ask the king for soldiers
and horsemen to protect us from enemies on
the road, because we had told the king, "The
gracious hand of our God is on everyone who
looks to him, but his great anger is against
all who forsake him." 23 So we fasted and petitioned our God about this, and he answered
our prayer.

24 Then I set apart twelve of the leading
priests, namely, Sherebiah, Hashabiah and
ten of their brothers, 25 and I weighed out to
them the offering of silver and gold and the articles that the king, his advisers, his officials
and all Israel present there had donated for
the house of our God. 26 I weighed out to them
650 talents[c] of silver, silver articles weighing
100 talents,[d] 100 talents[d] of gold, 27 20 bowls of
gold valued at 1,000 darics,[e] and two fine articles of polished bronze, as precious as gold.

28 I said to them, "You as well as these articles are consecrated to the LORD. The silver
and gold are a freewill offering to the LORD,
the God of your ancestors. 29 Guard them carefully until you weigh them out in the chambers
of the house of the LORD in Jerusalem before
the leading priests and the Levites and the
family heads of Israel." 30 Then the priests and
Levites received the silver and gold and sacred articles that had been weighed out to be
taken to the house of our God in Jerusalem.

31 On the twelfth day of the first month we
set out from the Ahava Canal to go to Jerusalem. The hand of our God was on us, and he
protected us from enemies and bandits along
the way. 32 So we arrived in Jerusalem, where
we rested three days.

33 On the fourth day, in the house of our God,
we weighed out the silver and gold and the
sacred articles into the hands of Meremoth
son of Uriah, the priest. Eleazar son of Phinehas was with him, and so were the Levites
Jozabad son of Jeshua and Noadiah son of
Binnui. 34 Everything was accounted for by
number and weight, and the entire weight was
recorded at that time.

35 Then the exiles who had returned from
captivity sacrificed burnt offerings to the God
of Israel: twelve bulls for all Israel, ninety-six
rams, seventy-seven male lambs and, as a sin
offering,[f] twelve male goats. All this was a
burnt offering to the LORD. 36 They also delivered the king's orders to the royal satraps
and to the governors of Trans-Euphrates, who
then gave assistance to the people and to the
house of God.

Ezra's Prayer About Intermarriage

9 After these things had been done, the leaders came to me and said, "The people of
Israel, including the priests and the Levites,
have not kept themselves separate from the
neighboring peoples with their detestable
practices, like those of the Canaanites, Hittites, Perizzites, Jebusites, Ammonites, Moabites, Egyptians and Amorites. 2 They have
taken some of their daughters as wives for
themselves and their sons, and have mingled
the holy race with the peoples around them.
And the leaders and officials have led the way
in this unfaithfulness."

3 When I heard this, I tore my tunic and
cloak, pulled hair from my head and beard

[a] 5 Some Septuagint manuscripts (also 1 Esdras 8:32); Hebrew does not have *Zattu.* [b] 10 Some Septuagint manuscripts (also 1 Esdras 8:36); Hebrew does not have *Bani.* [c] 26 That is, about 24 tons or about 22 metric tons [d] 26 That is, about 3 3/4 tons or about 3.4 metric tons [e] 27 That is, about 19 pounds or about 8.4 kilograms [f] 35 Or *purification offering*

and sat down appalled. 4Then everyone who trembled at the words of the God of Israel gathered around me because of this unfaithfulness of the exiles. And I sat there appalled until the evening sacrifice.

5Then, at the evening sacrifice, I rose from my self-abasement, with my tunic and cloak torn, and fell on my knees with my hands spread out to the LORD my God 6and prayed:

"I am too ashamed and disgraced, my God, to lift up my face to you, because our sins are higher than our heads and our guilt has reached to the heavens. 7From the days of our ancestors until now, our guilt has been great. Because of our sins, we and our kings and our priests have been subjected to the sword and captivity, to pillage and humiliation at the hand of foreign kings, as it is today.

8"But now, for a brief moment, the LORD our God has been gracious in leaving us a remnant and giving us a firm place[a] in his sanctuary, and so our God gives light to our eyes and a little relief in our bondage. 9Though we are slaves, our God has not forsaken us in our bondage. He has shown us kindness in the sight of the kings of Persia: He has granted us new life to rebuild the house of our God and repair its ruins, and he has given us a wall of protection in Judah and Jerusalem.

10"But now, our God, what can we say after this? For we have forsaken the commands 11you gave through your servants the prophets when you said: 'The land you are entering to possess is a land polluted by the corruption of its peoples. By their detestable practices they have filled it with their impurity from one end to the other. 12Therefore, do not give your daughters in marriage to their sons or take their daughters for your sons. Do not seek a treaty of friendship with them at any time, that you may be strong and eat the good things of the land and leave it to your children as an everlasting inheritance.'

13"What has happened to us is a result of our evil deeds and our great guilt, and yet, our God, you have punished us less than our sins deserved and have given us a remnant like this. 14Shall we then break your commands again and intermarry with the peoples who commit such detestable practices? Would you not be angry enough with us to destroy us, leaving us no remnant or survivor? 15LORD, the God of Israel, you are righteous! We are left this day as a remnant. Here we are before you in our guilt, though because of it not one of us can stand in your presence."

The People's Confession of Sin

10 While Ezra was praying and confessing, weeping and throwing himself down before the house of God, a large crowd of Israelites—men, women and children—gathered around him. They too wept bitterly. 2Then Shekaniah son of Jehiel, one of the descendants of Elam, said to Ezra, "We have been unfaithful to our God by marrying foreign women from the peoples around us. But in spite of this, there is still hope for Israel. 3Now let us make a covenant before our God to send away all these women and their children, in accordance with the counsel of my lord and of those who fear the commands of our God. Let it be done according to the Law. 4Rise up; this matter is in your hands. We will support you, so take courage and do it."

5So Ezra rose up and put the leading priests and Levites and all Israel under oath to do what had been suggested. And they took the oath. 6Then Ezra withdrew from before the house of God and went to the room of Jehohanan son of Eliashib. While he was there, he ate no food and drank no water, because he continued to mourn over the unfaithfulness of the exiles.

7A proclamation was then issued throughout Judah and Jerusalem for all the exiles to assemble in Jerusalem. 8Anyone who failed to appear within three days would forfeit all his property, in accordance with the decision of the officials and elders, and would himself be expelled from the assembly of the exiles.

9Within the three days, all the men of Judah and Benjamin had gathered in Jerusalem. And on the twentieth day of the ninth month, all the people were sitting in the square before the house of God, greatly distressed by the occasion and because of the rain. 10Then Ezra the priest stood up and said to them, "You have been unfaithful; you have married foreign women, adding to Israel's guilt. 11Now honor[b] the LORD, the God of your ancestors, and do his will. Separate yourselves from the peoples around you and from your foreign wives."

12The whole assembly responded with a loud voice: "You are right! We must do as you say. 13But there are many people here and it is the rainy season; so we cannot stand outside. Besides, this matter cannot be taken care of in a day or two, because we have sinned greatly in this thing. 14Let our officials act for the whole assembly. Then let everyone in our towns who has married a foreign woman come at a set time, along with the elders and judges of each town, until the fierce anger of our God in this matter is turned away from us." 15Only Jonathan son of Asahel and Jahzeiah son of Tikvah, supported by Meshullam and Shabbethai the Levite, opposed this.

16So the exiles did as was proposed. Ezra the priest selected men who were family heads, one from each family division, and all of them designated by name. On the first day of the tenth month they sat down to investigate the cases, 17and by the first day of the first month they finished dealing with all the men who had married foreign women.

[a] 8 Or *a foothold* [b] 11 Or *Now make confession to*

Those Guilty of Intermarriage

[18]Among the descendants of the priests, the following had married foreign women:

From the descendants of Joshua son of Jozadak, and his brothers: Maaseiah,
Eliezer, Jarib and Gedaliah. [19](They
all gave their hands in pledge to put away their wives, and for their guilt they each presented a ram from the flock as a guilt offering.)

[20]From the descendants of Immer:
Hanani and Zebadiah.

[21]From the descendants of Harim:
Maaseiah, Elijah, Shemaiah, Jehiel and Uzziah.

[22]From the descendants of Pashhur:
Elioenai, Maaseiah, Ishmael, Nethanel, Jozabad and Elasah.

[23]Among the Levites:

Jozabad, Shimei, Kelaiah (that is, Kelita), Pethahiah, Judah and Eliezer.

[24]From the musicians:
Eliashib.
From the gatekeepers:
Shallum, Telem and Uri.

[25]And among the other Israelites:

From the descendants of Parosh:
Ramiah, Izziah, Malkijah, Mijamin, Eleazar, Malkijah and Benaiah.

[26]From the descendants of Elam:
Mattaniah, Zechariah, Jehiel, Abdi, Jeremoth and Elijah.

[27]From the descendants of Zattu:
Elioenai, Eliashib, Mattaniah, Jeremoth, Zabad and Aziza.

[28]From the descendants of Bebai:
Jehohanan, Hananiah, Zabbai and Athlai.

[29]From the descendants of Bani:
Meshullam, Malluk, Adaiah, Jashub, Sheal and Jeremoth.

[30]From the descendants of Pahath-Moab:
Adna, Kelal, Benaiah, Maaseiah, Mattaniah, Bezalel, Binnui and Manasseh.

[31]From the descendants of Harim:
Eliezer, Ishijah, Malkijah, Shemaiah,
Shimeon, [32]Benjamin, Malluk and
Shemariah.

[33]From the descendants of Hashum:
Mattenai, Mattattah, Zabad, Eliphelet, Jeremai, Manasseh and Shimei.

[34]From the descendants of Bani:
Maadai, Amram, Uel, [35]Benaiah, Be-
deiah, Keluhi, [36]Vaniah, Meremoth,
Eliashib, [37]Mattaniah, Mattenai and
Jaasu.

[38]From the descendants of Binnui:[a]
Shimei, [39]Shelemiah, Nathan, Adaiah,
[40]Maknadebai, Shashai, Sharai, [41]Aza-
rel, Shelemiah, Shemariah, [42]Shallum,
Amariah and Joseph.

[43]From the descendants of Nebo:
Jeiel, Mattithiah, Zabad, Zebina, Jaddai, Joel and Benaiah.

[44]All these had married foreign women, and some of them had children by these wives.[b]

Nehemiah

Nehemiah's Prayer

1 The words of Nehemiah son of Hakaliah:

In the month of Kislev in the twentieth year,
while I was in the citadel of Susa, [2]Hanani, one
of my brothers, came from Judah with some other men, and I questioned them about the Jewish remnant that had survived the exile, and also about Jerusalem.

[3]They said to me, "Those who survived the exile and are back in the province are in great trouble and disgrace. The wall of Jerusalem is broken down, and its gates have been burned with fire."

[4]When I heard these things, I sat down and wept. For some days I mourned and fasted and
prayed before the God of heaven. [5]Then I said:

"LORD, the God of heaven, the great and awesome God, who keeps his covenant of love with those who love him and keep his commandments, [6]let your ear be attentive and your eyes open to hear the prayer your servant is praying before you day and night for your servants, the people of Israel. I confess the sins we Israelites, including myself and my father's family,
have committed against you. [7]We have
acted very wickedly toward you. We have not obeyed the commands, decrees and laws you gave your servant Moses.

[8]"Remember the instruction you gave your servant Moses, saying, 'If you are unfaithful, I will scatter you among the
nations, [9]but if you return to me and obey
my commands, then even if your exiled people are at the farthest horizon, I will gather them from there and bring them to the place I have chosen as a dwelling for my Name.'

[10]"They are your servants and your people, whom you redeemed by your

[a] 37,38 See Septuagint (also 1 Esdras 9:34); Hebrew *Jaasu* [38]*and Bani and Binnui,* [b] 44 Or *and they sent them away with their children*

great strength and your mighty hand.
11Lord, let your ear be attentive to the
prayer of this your servant and to the
prayer of your servants who delight in
revering your name. Give your servant
success today by granting him favor in
the presence of this man."

I was cupbearer to the king.

Artaxerxes Sends Nehemiah to Jerusalem

2 In the month of Nisan in the twentieth
year of King Artaxerxes, when wine was
brought for him, I took the wine and gave it
to the king. I had not been sad in his presence
before, 2so the king asked me, "Why does your
face look so sad when you are not ill? This can
be nothing but sadness of heart."

I was very much afraid, 3but I said to the
king, "May the king live forever! Why should
my face not look sad when the city where my
ancestors are buried lies in ruins, and its gates
have been destroyed by fire?"

4The king said to me, "What is it you want?"

Then I prayed to the God of heaven, 5and I
answered the king, "If it pleases the king and
if your servant has found favor in his sight,
let him send me to the city in Judah where my
ancestors are buried so that I can rebuild it."

6Then the king, with the queen sitting
beside him, asked me, "How long will your
journey take, and when will you get back?"
It pleased the king to send me; so I set a time.

7I also said to him, "If it pleases the king,
may I have letters to the governors of Trans-
Euphrates, so that they will provide me safe-
conduct until I arrive in Judah? 8And may I
have a letter to Asaph, keeper of the royal
park, so he will give me timber to make beams
for the gates of the citadel by the temple and
for the city wall and for the residence I will
occupy?" And because the gracious hand of
my God was on me, the king granted my requests. 9So I went to the governors of Trans-
Euphrates and gave them the king's letters.
The king had also sent army officers and
cavalry with me.

10When Sanballat the Horonite and Tobiah
the Ammonite official heard about this, they
were very much disturbed that someone had
come to promote the welfare of the Israelites.

Nehemiah Inspects Jerusalem's Walls

11I went to Jerusalem, and after staying
there three days 12I set out during the night
with a few others. I had not told anyone what
my God had put in my heart to do for Jerusalem. There were no mounts with me except
the one I was riding on.

13By night I went out through the Valley
Gate toward the Jackal[a] Well and the Dung
Gate, examining the walls of Jerusalem,
which had been broken down, and its gates,
which had been destroyed by fire. 14Then I
moved on toward the Fountain Gate and the
King's Pool, but there was not enough room
for my mount to get through; 15so I went up the
valley by night, examining the wall. Finally,
I turned back and reentered through the Valley Gate. 16The officials did not know where I
had gone or what I was doing, because as yet
I had said nothing to the Jews or the priests
or nobles or officials or any others who would
be doing the work.

17Then I said to them, "You see the trouble we are in: Jerusalem lies in ruins, and its
gates have been burned with fire. Come, let
us rebuild the wall of Jerusalem, and we will
no longer be in disgrace." 18I also told them
about the gracious hand of my God on me and
what the king had said to me.

They replied, "Let us start rebuilding." So
they began this good work.

19But when Sanballat the Horonite, Tobiah
the Ammonite official and Geshem the Arab
heard about it, they mocked and ridiculed us.
"What is this you are doing?" they asked. "Are
you rebelling against the king?"

20I answered them by saying, "The God of
heaven will give us success. We his servants
will start rebuilding, but as for you, you have
no share in Jerusalem or any claim or historic
right to it."

Builders of the Wall

3 Eliashib the high priest and his fellow
priests went to work and rebuilt the Sheep
Gate. They dedicated it and set its doors in
place, building as far as the Tower of the Hundred, which they dedicated, and as far as the
Tower of Hananel. 2The men of Jericho built
the adjoining section, and Zakkur son of Imri
built next to them.

3The Fish Gate was rebuilt by the sons of
Hassenaah. They laid its beams and put its
doors and bolts and bars in place. 4Meremoth
son of Uriah, the son of Hakkoz, repaired the
next section. Next to him Meshullam son of
Berekiah, the son of Meshezabel, made repairs, and next to him Zadok son of Baana
also made repairs. 5The next section was repaired by the men of Tekoa, but their nobles
would not put their shoulders to the work under their supervisors.[b]

6The Jeshanah[c] Gate was repaired by Joiada
son of Paseah and Meshullam son of Besode-
iah. They laid its beams and put its doors with
their bolts and bars in place. 7Next to them,
repairs were made by men from Gibeon and
Mizpah—Melatiah of Gibeon and Jadon of
Meronoth—places under the authority of the
governor of Trans-Euphrates. 8Uzziel son of
Harhaiah, one of the goldsmiths, repaired the
next section; and Hananiah, one of the per-
fume-makers, made repairs next to that. They
restored Jerusalem as far as the Broad Wall.
9Rephaiah son of Hur, ruler of a half-district
of Jerusalem, repaired the next section. 10Ad-
joining this, Jedaiah son of Harumaph made
repairs opposite his house, and Hattush son
of Hashabneiah made repairs next to him.
11Malkijah son of Harim and Hasshub son of
Pahath-Moab repaired another section and

[a] 13 Or *Serpent* or *Fig* [b] 5 Or *their Lord* or *the governor* [c] 6 Or *Old*

the Tower of the Ovens. 12Shallum son of Hallohesh, ruler of a half-district of Jerusalem,
repaired the next section with the help of his
daughters.

13The Valley Gate was repaired by Hanun
and the residents of Zanoah. They rebuilt it
and put its doors with their bolts and bars in
place. They also repaired a thousand cubits[a]
of the wall as far as the Dung Gate.

14The Dung Gate was repaired by Malkijah son of Rekab, ruler of the district of Beth
Hakkerem. He rebuilt it and put its doors with
their bolts and bars in place.

15The Fountain Gate was repaired by Shal-
lun son of Kol-Hozeh, ruler of the district of
Mizpah. He rebuilt it, roofing it over and putting its doors and bolts and bars in place. He
also repaired the wall of the Pool of Siloam,[b]
by the King's Garden, as far as the steps going
down from the City of David. 16Beyond him,
Nehemiah son of Azbuk, ruler of a half-district of Beth Zur, made repairs up to a point
opposite the tombs[c] of David, as far as the
artificial pool and the House of the Heroes.
17Next to him, the repairs were made by the
Levites under Rehum son of Bani. Beside him,
Hashabiah, ruler of half the district of Keilah,
carried out repairs for his district. 18Next to
him, the repairs were made by their fellow
Levites under Binnui[d] son of Henadad, ruler
of the other half-district of Keilah. 19Next to
him, Ezer son of Jeshua, ruler of Mizpah, repaired another section, from a point facing
the ascent to the armory as far as the angle of
the wall. 20Next to him, Baruch son of Zabbai
zealously repaired another section, from the
angle to the entrance of the house of Eliashib
the high priest. 21Next to him, Meremoth son
of Uriah, the son of Hakkoz, repaired another
section, from the entrance of Eliashib's house
to the end of it.
22The repairs next to him were made by the
priests from the surrounding region. 23Beyond
them, Benjamin and Hasshub made repairs
in front of their house; and next to them, Azariah son of Maaseiah, the son of Ananiah,
made repairs beside his house. 24Next to him,
Binnui son of Henadad repaired another section, from Azariah's house to the angle and
the corner, 25and Palal son of Uzai worked
opposite the angle and the tower projecting
from the upper palace near the court of the
guard. Next to him, Pedaiah son of Parosh
26and the temple servants living on the hill of
Ophel made repairs up to a point opposite the
Water Gate toward the east and the projecting tower. 27Next to them, the men of Tekoa
repaired another section, from the great projecting tower to the wall of Ophel.

28Above the Horse Gate, the priests made
repairs, each in front of his own house. 29Next
to them, Zadok son of Immer made repairs
opposite his house. Next to him, Shemaiah
son of Shekaniah, the guard at the East Gate,
made repairs. 30Next to him, Hananiah son of
Shelemiah, and Hanun, the sixth son of Za-
laph, repaired another section. Next to them,
Meshullam son of Berekiah made repairs opposite his living quarters. 31Next to him, Malkijah, one of the goldsmiths, made repairs as
far as the house of the temple servants and
the merchants, opposite the Inspection Gate,
and as far as the room above the corner; 32and
between the room above the corner and the
Sheep Gate the goldsmiths and merchants
made repairs.

Opposition to the Rebuilding

4[e] When Sanballat heard that we were rebuilding the wall, he became angry and
was greatly incensed. He ridiculed the Jews,
2and in the presence of his associates and the
army of Samaria, he said, "What are those
feeble Jews doing? Will they restore their
wall? Will they offer sacrifices? Will they finish in a day? Can they bring the stones back
to life from those heaps of rubble—burned
as they are?"
3Tobiah the Ammonite, who was at his side,
said, "What they are building—even a fox
climbing up on it would break down their wall
of stones!"

4Hear us, our God, for we are despised. Turn
their insults back on their own heads. Give
them over as plunder in a land of captivity.
5Do not cover up their guilt or blot out their
sins from your sight, for they have thrown
insults in the face of[f] the builders.

6So we rebuilt the wall till all of it reached
half its height, for the people worked with
all their heart.
7But when Sanballat, Tobiah, the Arabs, the
Ammonites and the people of Ashdod heard
that the repairs to Jerusalem's walls had gone
ahead and that the gaps were being closed,
they were very angry. 8They all plotted together to come and fight against Jerusalem
and stir up trouble against it. 9But we prayed
to our God and posted a guard day and night
to meet this threat.
10Meanwhile, the people in Judah said,
"The strength of the laborers is giving out,
and there is so much rubble that we cannot
rebuild the wall."
11Also our enemies said, "Before they know
it or see us, we will be right there among them
and will kill them and put an end to the work."
12Then the Jews who lived near them came
and told us ten times over, "Wherever you
turn, they will attack us."
13Therefore I stationed some of the people
behind the lowest points of the wall at the
exposed places, posting them by families,

[a] *13* That is, about 1,500 feet or about 450 meters [b] *15* Hebrew *Shelah,* a variant of *Shiloah,* that is, Siloam [c] *16* Hebrew; Septuagint, some Vulgate manuscripts and Syriac *tomb* [d] *18* Two Hebrew manuscripts and Syriac (see also Septuagint and verse 24); most Hebrew manuscripts *Bavvai* [e] In Hebrew texts 4:1-6 is numbered 3:33-38, and 4:7-23 is numbered 4:1-17. [f] *5* Or *have aroused your anger before*

with their swords, spears and bows. 14After I
looked things over, I stood up and said to the
nobles, the officials and the rest of the people,
"Don't be afraid of them. Remember the Lord,
who is great and awesome, and fight for your
families, your sons and your daughters, your
wives and your homes."
15When our enemies heard that we were
aware of their plot and that God had frustrated it, we all returned to the wall, each to
our own work.
16From that day on, half of my men did the
work, while the other half were equipped with
spears, shields, bows and armor. The officers
posted themselves behind all the people of
Judah 17who were building the wall. Those
who carried materials did their work with one
hand and held a weapon in the other, 18and
each of the builders wore his sword at his side
as he worked. But the man who sounded the
trumpet stayed with me.
19Then I said to the nobles, the officials and
the rest of the people, "The work is extensive
and spread out, and we are widely separated
from each other along the wall. 20Wherever
you hear the sound of the trumpet, join us
there. Our God will fight for us!"
21So we continued the work with half the
men holding spears, from the first light of
dawn till the stars came out. 22At that time I
also said to the people, "Have every man and
his helper stay inside Jerusalem at night, so
they can serve us as guards by night and as
workers by day." 23Neither I nor my brothers
nor my men nor the guards with me took off
our clothes; each had his weapon, even when
he went for water.[a]

Nehemiah Helps the Poor

5 Now the men and their wives raised a great
outcry against their fellow Jews. 2Some
were saying, "We and our sons and daughters
are numerous; in order for us to eat and stay
alive, we must get grain."
3Others were saying, "We are mortgaging
our fields, our vineyards and our homes to get
grain during the famine."
4Still others were saying, "We have had to
borrow money to pay the king's tax on our
fields and vineyards. 5Although we are of the
same flesh and blood as our fellow Jews and
though our children are as good as theirs, yet
we have to subject our sons and daughters to
slavery. Some of our daughters have already
been enslaved, but we are powerless, because
our fields and our vineyards belong to others."
6When I heard their outcry and these charges, I was very angry. 7I pondered them in my
mind and then accused the nobles and officials. I told them, "You are charging your own
people interest!" So I called together a large
meeting to deal with them 8and said: "As far
as possible, we have bought back our fellow
Jews who were sold to the Gentiles. Now you
are selling your own people, only for them to
be sold back to us!" They kept quiet, because
they could find nothing to say.
9So I continued, "What you are doing is not
right. Shouldn't you walk in the fear of our
God to avoid the reproach of our Gentile enemies? 10I and my brothers and my men are
also lending the people money and grain. But
let us stop charging interest! 11Give back to
them immediately their fields, vineyards, olive groves and houses, and also the interest
you are charging them—one percent of the
money, grain, new wine and olive oil."
12"We will give it back," they said. "And we
will not demand anything more from them.
We will do as you say."
Then I summoned the priests and made the
nobles and officials take an oath to do what
they had promised. 13I also shook out the folds
of my robe and said, "In this way may God
shake out of their house and possessions anyone who does not keep this promise. So may
such a person be shaken out and emptied!"
At this the whole assembly said, "Amen,"
and praised the LORD. And the people did as
they had promised.
14Moreover, from the twentieth year of King
Artaxerxes, when I was appointed to be their
governor in the land of Judah, until his thirty-
second year—twelve years—neither I nor my
brothers ate the food allotted to the governor.
15But the earlier governors—those preceding
me—placed a heavy burden on the people and
took forty shekels[b] of silver from them in addition to food and wine. Their assistants also
lorded it over the people. But out of reverence
for God I did not act like that. 16Instead, I devoted myself to the work on this wall. All my
men were assembled there for the work; we[c]
did not acquire any land.
17Furthermore, a hundred and fifty Jews
and officials ate at my table, as well as those
who came to us from the surrounding nations.
18Each day one ox, six choice sheep and some
poultry were prepared for me, and every ten
days an abundant supply of wine of all kinds.
In spite of all this, I never demanded the food
allotted to the governor, because the demands
were heavy on these people.
19Remember me with favor, my God, for all
I have done for these people.

Further Opposition to the Rebuilding

6 When word came to Sanballat, Tobiah, Geshem the Arab and the rest of our enemies
that I had rebuilt the wall and not a gap was
left in it—though up to that time I had not
set the doors in the gates— 2Sanballat and
Geshem sent me this message: "Come, let us
meet together in one of the villages[d] on the
plain of Ono."
But they were scheming to harm me; 3so I
sent messengers to them with this reply: "I
am carrying on a great project and cannot go
down. Why should the work stop while I leave
it and go down to you?" 4Four times they sent

[a] *23* The meaning of the Hebrew for this clause is uncertain. [b] *15* That is, about 1 pound or about 460 grams [c] *16* Most Hebrew manuscripts; some Hebrew manuscripts, Septuagint, Vulgate and Syriac *I* [d] *2* Or *in Kephirim*

me the same message, and each time I gave
them the same answer.
5 Then, the fifth time, Sanballat sent his aide
to me with the same message, and in his hand
was an unsealed letter 6 in which was written:

> "It is reported among the nations—and
> Geshem[a] says it is true—that you and the
> Jews are plotting to revolt, and therefore
> you are building the wall. Moreover, ac-
> cording to these reports you are about
> to become their king 7 and have even
> appointed prophets to make this procla-
> mation about you in Jerusalem: 'There
> is a king in Judah!' Now this report will
> get back to the king; so come, let us meet
> together."

8 I sent him this reply: "Nothing like what
you are saying is happening; you are just
making it up out of your head."
9 They were all trying to frighten us, thinking, "Their hands will get too weak for the
work, and it will not be completed."
But I prayed, "Now strengthen my hands."
10 One day I went to the house of Shemaiah
son of Delaiah, the son of Mehetabel, who was
shut in at his home. He said, "Let us meet in
the house of God, inside the temple, and let
us close the temple doors, because men are
coming to kill you—by night they are coming to kill you."
11 But I said, "Should a man like me run
away? Or should someone like me go into
the temple to save his life? I will not go!" 12 I
realized that God had not sent him, but that
he had prophesied against me because Tobiah
and Sanballat had hired him. 13 He had been
hired to intimidate me so that I would commit
a sin by doing this, and then they would give
me a bad name to discredit me.

14 Remember Tobiah and Sanballat, my God,
because of what they have done; remember
also the prophet Noadiah and how she and
the rest of the prophets have been trying to
intimidate me. 15 So the wall was completed
on the twenty-fifth of Elul, in fifty-two days.

Opposition to the Completed Wall

16 When all our enemies heard about this,
all the surrounding nations were afraid and
lost their self-confidence, because they realized that this work had been done with the
help of our God.
17 Also, in those days the nobles of Judah
were sending many letters to Tobiah, and
replies from Tobiah kept coming to them.
18 For many in Judah were under oath to him,
since he was son-in-law to Shekaniah son of
Arah, and his son Jehohanan had married
the daughter of Meshullam son of Berekiah.
19 Moreover, they kept reporting to me his good
deeds and then telling him what I said. And
Tobiah sent letters to intimidate me.
7 After the wall had been rebuilt and I had
set the doors in place, the gatekeepers, the
musicians and the Levites were appointed. 2 I
put in charge of Jerusalem my brother Hanani, along with Hananiah the commander of
the citadel, because he was a man of integrity
and feared God more than most people do. 3 I
said to them, "The gates of Jerusalem are not
to be opened until the sun is hot. While the
gatekeepers are still on duty, have them shut
the doors and bar them. Also appoint residents of Jerusalem as guards, some at their
posts and some near their own houses."

The List of the Exiles Who Returned

4 Now the city was large and spacious, but
there were few people in it, and the houses had
not yet been rebuilt. 5 So my God put it into my
heart to assemble the nobles, the officials and
the common people for registration by families. I found the genealogical record of those
who had been the first to return. This is what
I found written there:

> 6 These are the people of the province
> who came up from the captivity of the ex-
> iles whom Nebuchadnezzar king of Bab-
> ylon had taken captive (they returned to
> Jerusalem and Judah, each to his own
> town, 7 in company with Zerubbabel,
> Joshua, Nehemiah, Azariah, Raamiah,
> Nahamani, Mordecai, Bilshan, Mispe-
> reth, Bigvai, Nehum and Baanah):

The list of the men of Israel:

8 the descendants of Parosh	2,172
9 of Shephatiah	372
10 of Arah	652
11 of Pahath-Moab (through the line of Jeshua and Joab)	2,818
12 of Elam	1,254
13 of Zattu	845
14 of Zakkai	760
15 of Binnui	648
16 of Bebai	628
17 of Azgad	2,322
18 of Adonikam	667
19 of Bigvai	2,067
20 of Adin	655
21 of Ater (through Hezekiah)	98
22 of Hashum	328
23 of Bezai	324
24 of Hariph	112
25 of Gibeon	95

26 the men of Bethlehem and Netophah	188
27 of Anathoth	128
28 of Beth Azmaveth	42
29 of Kiriath Jearim, Kephirah and Beeroth	743
30 of Ramah and Geba	621
31 of Mikmash	122
32 of Bethel and Ai	123
33 of the other Nebo	52
34 of the other Elam	1,254
35 of Harim	320
36 of Jericho	345
37 of Lod, Hadid and Ono	721
38 of Senaah	3,930

[a] 6 Hebrew *Gashmu,* a variant of *Geshem*

39 The priests:

the descendants of Jedaiah
(through the family of Jeshua) 973
40 of Immer 1,052
41 of Pashhur 1,247
42 of Harim 1,017

43 The Levites:

the descendants of Jeshua
(through Kadmiel through the
line of Hodaviah) 74

44 The musicians:

the descendants of Asaph 148

45 The gatekeepers:

the descendants of
Shallum, Ater, Talmon, Akkub,
Hatita and Shobai 138

46 The temple servants:

the descendants of
Ziha, Hasupha, Tabbaoth,
47 Keros, Sia, Padon,
48 Lebana, Hagaba, Shalmai,
49 Hanan, Giddel, Gahar,
50 Reaiah, Rezin, Nekoda,
51 Gazzam, Uzza, Paseah,
52 Besai, Meunim, Nephusim,
53 Bakbuk, Hakupha, Harhur,
54 Bazluth, Mehida, Harsha,
55 Barkos, Sisera, Temah,
56 Neziah and Hatipha

57 The descendants of the servants of Solomon:

the descendants of
Sotai, Sophereth, Perida,
58 Jaala, Darkon, Giddel,
59 Shephatiah, Hattil,
Pokereth-Hazzebaim and Amon
60 The temple servants and the
descendants of the servants of
Solomon 392

61 The following came up from the
towns of Tel Melah, Tel Harsha, Kerub,
Addon and Immer, but they could not
show that their families were descended
from Israel:

62 the descendants of
Delaiah, Tobiah and Nekoda 642

63 And from among the priests:

the descendants of
Hobaiah, Hakkoz and Barzillai (a
man who had married a daughter
of Barzillai the Gileadite and was
called by that name).

64 These searched for their family records, but they could not find them and so
were excluded from the priesthood as unclean. 65 The governor, therefore, ordered
them not to eat any of the most sacred
food until there should be a priest ministering with the Urim and Thummim.

66 The whole company numbered
42,360, 67 besides their 7,337 male and
female slaves; and they also had 245
male and female singers. 68 There were
736 horses, 245 mules,[a] 69 435 camels and
6,720 donkeys.

70 Some of the heads of the families
contributed to the work. The governor
gave to the treasury 1,000 darics[b] of gold,
50 bowls and 530 garments for priests.
71 Some of the heads of the families gave
to the treasury for the work 20,000 darics[c]
of gold and 2,200 minas[d] of silver. 72 The
total given by the rest of the people was
20,000 darics of gold, 2,000 minas[e] of silver and 67 garments for priests.

73 The priests, the Levites, the gatekeepers, the musicians and the temple
servants, along with certain of the people and the rest of the Israelites, settled
in their own towns.

Ezra Reads the Law

When the seventh month came and the
8 Israelites had settled in their towns, 1 all the
people came together as one in the square
before the Water Gate. They told Ezra the
teacher of the Law to bring out the Book of
the Law of Moses, which the LORD had commanded for Israel.

2 So on the first day of the seventh month
Ezra the priest brought the Law before the
assembly, which was made up of men and
women and all who were able to understand.
3 He read it aloud from daybreak till noon as he
faced the square before the Water Gate in the
presence of the men, women and others who
could understand. And all the people listened
attentively to the Book of the Law.

4 Ezra the teacher of the Law stood on a high
wooden platform built for the occasion. Beside him on his right stood Mattithiah, Shema,
Anaiah, Uriah, Hilkiah and Maaseiah; and
on his left were Pedaiah, Mishael, Malkijah,
Hashum, Hashbaddanah, Zechariah and Meshullam.

5 Ezra opened the book. All the people could
see him because he was standing above them;
and as he opened it, the people all stood up.
6 Ezra praised the LORD, the great God; and
all the people lifted their hands and responded, "Amen! Amen!" Then they bowed down
and worshiped the LORD with their faces to
the ground.

7 The Levites—Jeshua, Bani, Sherebiah, Jamin, Akkub, Shabbethai, Hodiah, Maaseiah,
Kelita, Azariah, Jozabad, Hanan and Pelaiah—instructed the people in the Law while
the people were standing there. 8 They read
from the Book of the Law of God, making it

[a] *68* Some Hebrew manuscripts (see also Ezra 2:66); most Hebrew manuscripts do not have this verse.
[b] *70* That is, about 19 pounds or about 8.4 kilograms
[c] *71* That is, about 375 pounds or about 170 kilograms; also in verse 72
[d] *71* That is, about 1 1/3 tons or about 1.2 metric tons
[e] *72* That is, about 1 1/4 tons or about 1.1 metric tons

clear[a] and giving the meaning so that the people understood what was being read.
9Then Nehemiah the governor, Ezra the
priest and teacher of the Law, and the Levites
who were instructing the people said to them
all, "This day is holy to the LORD your God.
Do not mourn or weep." For all the people had
been weeping as they listened to the words
of the Law.
10Nehemiah said, "Go and enjoy choice food
and sweet drinks, and send some to those who
have nothing prepared. This day is holy to our
Lord. Do not grieve, for the joy of the LORD is
your strength."
11The Levites calmed all the people, saying,
"Be still, for this is a holy day. Do not grieve."
12Then all the people went away to eat and
drink, to send portions of food and to celebrate
with great joy, because they now understood
the words that had been made known to them.
13On the second day of the month, the heads
of all the families, along with the priests and
the Levites, gathered around Ezra the teacher to give attention to the words of the Law.
14They found written in the Law, which the
LORD had commanded through Moses, that
the Israelites were to live in temporary shelters during the festival of the seventh month
15and that they should proclaim this word and
spread it throughout their towns and in Jerusalem: "Go out into the hill country and bring
back branches from olive and wild olive trees,
and from myrtles, palms and shade trees, to
make temporary shelters"—as it is written.[b]
16So the people went out and brought back
branches and built themselves temporary
shelters on their own roofs, in their courtyards, in the courts of the house of God and
in the square by the Water Gate and the one
by the Gate of Ephraim. 17The whole company
that had returned from exile built temporary
shelters and lived in them. From the days of
Joshua son of Nun until that day, the Israelites
had not celebrated it like this. And their joy
was very great.
18Day after day, from the first day to the last,
Ezra read from the Book of the Law of God.
They celebrated the festival for seven days,
and on the eighth day, in accordance with the
regulation, there was an assembly.

The Israelites Confess Their Sins

9 On the twenty-fourth day of the same
month, the Israelites gathered together,
fasting and wearing sackcloth and putting
dust on their heads. 2Those of Israelite descent
had separated themselves from all foreigners. They stood in their places and confessed
their sins and the sins of their ancestors.
3They stood where they were and read from
the Book of the Law of the LORD their God
for a quarter of the day, and spent another
quarter in confession and in worshiping the
LORD their God. 4Standing on the stairs of the
Levites were Jeshua, Bani, Kadmiel, Shebaniah, Bunni, Sherebiah, Bani and Kenani.
They cried out with loud voices to the LORD
their God. 5And the Levites—Jeshua, Kadmiel, Bani, Hashabneiah, Sherebiah, Hodiah,
Shebaniah and Pethahiah—said: "Stand up
and praise the LORD your God, who is from
everlasting to everlasting.[c]"

"Blessed be your glorious name, and
may it be exalted above all blessing and
praise. 6You alone are the LORD. You
made the heavens, even the highest heavens, and all their starry host, the earth
and all that is on it, the seas and all that is
in them. You give life to everything, and
the multitudes of heaven worship you.
7"You are the LORD God, who chose
Abram and brought him out of Ur of the
Chaldeans and named him Abraham.
8You found his heart faithful to you, and
you made a covenant with him to give
to his descendants the land of the Canaanites, Hittites, Amorites, Perizzites,
Jebusites and Girgashites. You have kept
your promise because you are righteous.
9"You saw the suffering of our ancestors in Egypt; you heard their cry at the
Red Sea.[d] 10You sent signs and wonders
against Pharaoh, against all his officials and all the people of his land, for
you knew how arrogantly the Egyptians
treated them. You made a name for yourself, which remains to this day. 11You divided the sea before them, so that they
passed through it on dry ground, but you
hurled their pursuers into the depths, like
a stone into mighty waters. 12By day you
led them with a pillar of cloud, and by
night with a pillar of fire to give them
light on the way they were to take.
13"You came down on Mount Sinai; you
spoke to them from heaven. You gave
them regulations and laws that are just
and right, and decrees and commands
that are good. 14You made known to them
your holy Sabbath and gave them commands, decrees and laws through your
servant Moses. 15In their hunger you
gave them bread from heaven and in their
thirst you brought them water from the
rock; you told them to go in and take possession of the land you had sworn with
uplifted hand to give them.
16"But they, our ancestors, became arrogant and stiff-necked, and they did not
obey your commands. 17They refused to
listen and failed to remember the miracles you performed among them. They
became stiff-necked and in their rebellion appointed a leader in order to return
to their slavery. But you are a forgiving
God, gracious and compassionate, slow to
anger and abounding in love. Therefore
you did not desert them, 18even when they
cast for themselves an image of a calf and
said, 'This is your god, who brought you
up out of Egypt,' or when they committed
awful blasphemies.

[a] 8 Or *God, translating it* [b] 15 See Lev. 23:37-40. [c] 5 Or *God for ever and ever* [d] 9 Or *the Sea of Reeds*

19“Because of your great compassion
you did not abandon them in the wilderness. By day the pillar of cloud did
not fail to guide them on their path, nor
the pillar of fire by night to shine on the
way they were to take. 20You gave your
good Spirit to instruct them. You did not
withhold your manna from their mouths,
and you gave them water for their thirst.
21For forty years you sustained them in
the wilderness; they lacked nothing, their
clothes did not wear out nor did their feet
become swollen.

22“You gave them kingdoms and nations, allotting to them even the remotest
frontiers. They took over the country of
Sihon[a] king of Heshbon and the country
of Og king of Bashan. 23You made their
children as numerous as the stars in the
sky, and you brought them into the land
that you told their parents to enter and
possess. 24Their children went in and took
possession of the land. You subdued before them the Canaanites, who lived in the
land; you gave the Canaanites into their
hands, along with their kings and the peoples of the land, to deal with them as they
pleased. 25They captured fortified cities
and fertile land; they took possession of
houses filled with all kinds of good things,
wells already dug, vineyards, olive groves
and fruit trees in abundance. They ate to
the full and were well-nourished; they reveled in your great goodness.

26“But they were disobedient and rebelled against you; they turned their backs
on your law. They killed your prophets,
who had warned them in order to turn
them back to you; they committed awful
blasphemies. 27So you delivered them into
the hands of their enemies, who oppressed
them. But when they were oppressed they
cried out to you. From heaven you heard
them, and in your great compassion you
gave them deliverers, who rescued them
from the hand of their enemies.

28“But as soon as they were at rest, they
again did what was evil in your sight.
Then you abandoned them to the hand of
their enemies so that they ruled over them.
And when they cried out to you again, you
heard from heaven, and in your compassion you delivered them time after time.

29“You warned them in order to turn
them back to your law, but they became
arrogant and disobeyed your commands.
They sinned against your ordinances, of
which you said, ‘The person who obeys
them will live by them.’ Stubbornly
they turned their backs on you, became
stiff-necked and refused to listen. 30For
many years you were patient with them.
By your Spirit you warned them through
your prophets. Yet they paid no attention,
so you gave them into the hands of the
neighboring peoples. 31But in your great
mercy you did not put an end to them or
abandon them, for you are a gracious and
merciful God.

32“Now therefore, our God, the great
God, mighty and awesome, who keeps his
covenant of love, do not let all this hardship seem trifling in your eyes—the hardship that has come on us, on our kings
and leaders, on our priests and prophets, on our ancestors and all your people,
from the days of the kings of Assyria until today. 33In all that has happened to us,
you have remained righteous; you have
acted faithfully, while we acted wickedly. 34Our kings, our leaders, our priests
and our ancestors did not follow your law;
they did not pay attention to your commands or the statutes you warned them
to keep. 35Even while they were in their
kingdom, enjoying your great goodness
to them in the spacious and fertile land
you gave them, they did not serve you or
turn from their evil ways.

36“But see, we are slaves today, slaves
in the land you gave our ancestors so
they could eat its fruit and the other good
things it produces. 37Because of our sins,
its abundant harvest goes to the kings
you have placed over us. They rule over
our bodies and our cattle as they please.
We are in great distress.

The Agreement of the People

38“In view of all this, we are making a binding agreement, putting it in writing, and our
leaders, our Levites and our priests are affix-
ing their seals to it.”[b]

10[c] Those who sealed it were:

Nehemiah the governor, the son of Hakaliah.

Zedekiah, 2Seraiah, Azariah, Jeremiah,
3Pashhur, Amariah, Malkijah,
4Hattush, Shebaniah, Malluk,
5Harim, Meremoth, Obadiah,
6Daniel, Ginnethon, Baruch,
7Meshullam, Abijah, Mijamin,
8Maaziah, Bilgai and Shemaiah.
These were the priests.

9The Levites:

Jeshua son of Azaniah, Binnui of the sons
of Henadad, Kadmiel,
10and their associates: Shebaniah,
Hodiah, Kelita, Pelaiah, Hanan,
11Mika, Rehob, Hashabiah,
12Zakkur, Sherebiah, Shebaniah,
13Hodiah, Bani and Beninu.

14The leaders of the people:

Parosh, Pahath-Moab, Elam, Zattu, Bani,
15Bunni, Azgad, Bebai,
16Adonijah, Bigvai, Adin,

[a] 22 One Hebrew manuscript and Septuagint; most Hebrew manuscripts *Sihon, that is, the country of the* [b] 38 In Hebrew texts this verse (9:38) is numbered 10:1. [c] In Hebrew texts 10:1-39 is numbered 10:2-40.

17 Ater, Hezekiah, Azzur,
18 Hodiah, Hashum, Bezai,
19 Hariph, Anathoth, Nebai,
20 Magpiash, Meshullam, Hezir,
21 Meshezabel, Zadok, Jaddua,
22 Pelatiah, Hanan, Anaiah,
23 Hoshea, Hananiah, Hasshub,
24 Hallohesh, Pilha, Shobek,
25 Rehum, Hashabnah, Maaseiah,
26 Ahiah, Hanan, Anan,
27 Malluk, Harim and Baanah.

28“The rest of the people—priests, Levites, gatekeepers, musicians, temple servants and all who separated themselves
from the neighboring peoples for the sake
of the Law of God, together with their
wives and all their sons and daughters
who are able to understand— 29all these
now join their fellow Israelites the nobles,
and bind themselves with a curse and
an oath to follow the Law of God given
through Moses the servant of God and to
obey carefully all the commands, regulations and decrees of the LORD our Lord.

30“We promise not to give our daughters in marriage to the peoples around
us or take their daughters for our sons.

31“When the neighboring peoples bring
merchandise or grain to sell on the Sabbath, we will not buy from them on the
Sabbath or on any holy day. Every seventh year we will forgo working the land
and will cancel all debts.

32“We assume the responsibility for
carrying out the commands to give a
third of a shekel[a] each year for the service
of the house of our God: 33for the bread
set out on the table; for the regular grain
offerings and burnt offerings; for the offerings on the Sabbaths, at the New Moon
feasts and at the appointed festivals; for
the holy offerings; for sin offerings[b] to
make atonement for Israel; and for all the
duties of the house of our God.

34“We—the priests, the Levites and
the people—have cast lots to determine
when each of our families is to bring to
the house of our God at set times each
year a contribution of wood to burn on the
altar of the LORD our God, as it is written
in the Law.

35“We also assume responsibility for
bringing to the house of the LORD each
year the firstfruits of our crops and of
every fruit tree.

36“As it is also written in the Law, we
will bring the firstborn of our sons and of
our cattle, of our herds and of our flocks
to the house of our God, to the priests
ministering there.

37“Moreover, we will bring to the storerooms of the house of our God, to the
priests, the first of our ground meal, of our
grain offerings, of the fruit of all our trees
and of our new wine and olive oil. And we
will bring a tithe of our crops to the Levites, for it is the Levites who collect the
tithes in all the towns where we work. 38A
priest descended from Aaron is to accompany the Levites when they receive the
tithes, and the Levites are to bring a tenth
of the tithes up to the house of our God,
to the storerooms of the treasury. 39The
people of Israel, including the Levites, are
to bring their contributions of grain, new
wine and olive oil to the storerooms, where
the articles for the sanctuary and for the
ministering priests, the gatekeepers and
the musicians are also kept.

“We will not neglect the house of our
God.”

The New Residents of Jerusalem

11 Now the leaders of the people settled in
Jerusalem. The rest of the people cast
lots to bring one out of every ten of them to
live in Jerusalem, the holy city, while the remaining nine were to stay in their own towns.
2The people commended all who volunteered
to live in Jerusalem.

3These are the provincial leaders who settled in Jerusalem (now some Israelites, priests,
Levites, temple servants and descendants of
Solomon’s servants lived in the towns of Judah, each on their own property in the various
towns, 4while other people from both Judah
and Benjamin lived in Jerusalem):

From the descendants of Judah:

Athaiah son of Uzziah, the son of Zechariah, the son of Amariah, the son of
Shephatiah, the son of Mahalalel, a descendant of Perez; 5and Maaseiah son of
Baruch, the son of Kol-Hozeh, the son of
Hazaiah, the son of Adaiah, the son of
Joiarib, the son of Zechariah, a descendant of Shelah. 6The descendants of Perez
who lived in Jerusalem totaled 468 men
of standing.

7From the descendants of Benjamin:

Sallu son of Meshullam, the son of Joed,
the son of Pedaiah, the son of Kolaiah, the
son of Maaseiah, the son of Ithiel, the son
of Jeshaiah, 8and his followers, Gabbai
and Sallai—928 men. 9Joel son of Zikri
was their chief officer, and Judah son of
Hassenuah was over the New Quarter of
the city.

10From the priests:

Jedaiah; the son of Joiarib; Jakin; 11Sera-
iah son of Hilkiah, the son of Meshullam,
the son of Zadok, the son of Meraioth, the
son of Ahitub, the official in charge of
the house of God, 12and their associates,
who carried on work for the temple—822
men; Adaiah son of Jeroham, the son of
Pelaliah, the son of Amzi, the son of
Zechariah, the son of Pashhur, the son of
Malkijah, 13and his associates, who were
heads of families—242 men; Amashsai
son of Azarel, the son of Ahzai, the son

[a] *32* That is, about 1/8 ounce or about 4 grams   [b] *33* Or *purification offerings*

of Meshillemoth, the son of Immer, 14and
his[a] associates, who were men of standing—128. Their chief officer was Zabdiel
son of Haggedolim.

15From the Levites:

Shemaiah son of Hasshub, the son of Azrikam, the son of Hashabiah, the son of
Bunni; 16Shabbethai and Jozabad, two of
the heads of the Levites, who had charge
of the outside work of the house of God;
17Mattaniah son of Mika, the son of Zabdi, the son of Asaph, the director who led
in thanksgiving and prayer; Bakbukiah,
second among his associates; and Abda
son of Shammua, the son of Galal, the
son of Jeduthun. 18The Levites in the holy
city totaled 284.

19The gatekeepers:

Akkub, Talmon and their associates, who
kept watch at the gates—172 men.

20The rest of the Israelites, with the priests
and Levites, were in all the towns of Judah,
each on their ancestral property.

21The temple servants lived on the hill of
Ophel, and Ziha and Gishpa were in charge
of them.

22The chief officer of the Levites in Jerusalem
was Uzzi son of Bani, the son of Hashabiah, the
son of Mattaniah, the son of Mika. Uzzi was
one of Asaph's descendants, who were the musicians responsible for the service of the house
of God. 23The musicians were under the king's
orders, which regulated their daily activity.

24Pethahiah son of Meshezabel, one of the
descendants of Zerah son of Judah, was the
king's agent in all affairs relating to the people.

25As for the villages with their fields, some
of the people of Judah lived in Kiriath Arba
and its surrounding settlements, in Dibon and
its settlements, in Jekabzeel and its villages,
26in Jeshua, in Moladah, in Beth Pelet, 27in Hazar Shual, in Beersheba and its settlements,
28in Ziklag, in Mekonah and its settlements,
29in En Rimmon, in Zorah, in Jarmuth, 30Za-
noah, Adullam and their villages, in Lachish
and its fields, and in Azekah and its settlements. So they were living all the way from
Beersheba to the Valley of Hinnom.

31The descendants of the Benjamites from
Geba lived in Mikmash, Aija, Bethel and its
settlements, 32in Anathoth, Nob and Ananiah,
33in Hazor, Ramah and Gittaim, 34in Hadid,
Zeboim and Neballat, 35in Lod and Ono, and
in Ge Harashim.

36Some of the divisions of the Levites of Judah settled in Benjamin.

Priests and Levites

12 These were the priests and Levites who
returned with Zerubbabel son of Shealtiel and with Joshua:

Seraiah, Jeremiah, Ezra,
2 Amariah, Malluk, Hattush,
3 Shekaniah, Rehum, Meremoth,
4 Iddo, Ginnethon,[b] Abijah,
5 Mijamin,[c] Moadiah, Bilgah,
6 Shemaiah, Joiarib, Jedaiah,
7 Sallu, Amok, Hilkiah and Jedaiah.

These were the leaders of the priests and their
associates in the days of Joshua.

8The Levites were Jeshua, Binnui, Kadmiel,
Sherebiah, Judah, and also Mattaniah, who,
together with his associates, was in charge of
the songs of thanksgiving. 9Bakbukiah and
Unni, their associates, stood opposite them
in the services.

10Joshua was the father of Joiakim, Joiakim
the father of Eliashib, Eliashib the father of
Joiada, 11Joiada the father of Jonathan, and
Jonathan the father of Jaddua.

12In the days of Joiakim, these were the
heads of the priestly families:

of Seraiah's family, Meraiah;
of Jeremiah's, Hananiah;
13 of Ezra's, Meshullam;
of Amariah's, Jehohanan;
14 of Malluk's, Jonathan;
of Shekaniah's,[d] Joseph;
15 of Harim's, Adna;
of Meremoth's,[e] Helkai;
16 of Iddo's, Zechariah;
of Ginnethon's, Meshullam;
17 of Abijah's, Zikri;
of Miniamin's and of Moadiah's, Piltai;
18 of Bilgah's, Shammua;
of Shemaiah's, Jehonathan;
19 of Joiarib's, Mattenai;
of Jedaiah's, Uzzi;
20 of Sallu's, Kallai;
of Amok's, Eber;
21 of Hilkiah's, Hashabiah;
of Jedaiah's, Nethanel.

22The family heads of the Levites in the days
of Eliashib, Joiada, Johanan and Jaddua, as
well as those of the priests, were recorded in
the reign of Darius the Persian. 23The family
heads among the descendants of Levi up to the
time of Johanan son of Eliashib were recorded
in the book of the annals. 24And the leaders
of the Levites were Hashabiah, Sherebiah,
Jeshua son of Kadmiel, and their associates,
who stood opposite them to give praise and
thanksgiving, one section responding to the
other, as prescribed by David the man of God.

25Mattaniah, Bakbukiah, Obadiah, Meshullam, Talmon and Akkub were gatekeepers
who guarded the storerooms at the gates.
26They served in the days of Joiakim son of
Joshua, the son of Jozadak, and in the days
of Nehemiah the governor and of Ezra the
priest, the teacher of the Law.

Dedication of the Wall of Jerusalem

27At the dedication of the wall of Jerusalem, the Levites were sought out from where

[a] *14* Most Septuagint manuscripts; Hebrew *their* [b] *4* Many Hebrew manuscripts and Vulgate (see also verse 16); most Hebrew manuscripts *Ginnethoi* [c] *5* A variant of *Miniamin* [d] *14* Very many Hebrew manuscripts, some Septuagint manuscripts and Syriac (see also verse 3); most Hebrew manuscripts *Shebaniah's* [e] *15* Some Septuagint manuscripts (see also verse 3); Hebrew *Meraioth's*

they lived and were brought to Jerusalem to celebrate joyfully the dedication with songs of thanksgiving and with the music of cymbals, harps and lyres. 28The musicians also were brought together from the region around Jerusalem—from the villages of the Netophathites, 29from Beth Gilgal, and from the area of Geba and Azmaveth, for the musicians had built villages for themselves around Jerusalem. 30When the priests and Levites had purified themselves ceremonially, they purified the people, the gates and the wall.

31I had the leaders of Judah go up on top of[a] the wall. I also assigned two large choirs to give thanks. One was to proceed on top of[b] the wall to the right, toward the Dung Gate. 32Hoshaiah and half the leaders of Judah followed them, 33along with Azariah, Ezra, Meshullam, 34Judah, Benjamin, Shemaiah, Jeremiah, 35as well as some priests with trumpets, and also Zechariah son of Jonathan, the son of Shemaiah, the son of Mattaniah, the son of Micaiah, the son of Zakkur, the son of Asaph, 36and his associates—Shemaiah, Azarel, Milalai, Gilalai, Maai, Nethanel, Judah and Hanani—with musical instruments prescribed by David the man of God. Ezra the teacher of the Law led the procession. 37At the Fountain Gate they continued directly up the steps of the City of David on the ascent to the wall and passed above the site of David's palace to the Water Gate on the east.

38The second choir proceeded in the opposite direction. I followed them on top of[c] the wall, together with half the people—past the Tower of the Ovens to the Broad Wall, 39over the Gate of Ephraim, the Jeshanah[d] Gate, the Fish Gate, the Tower of Hananel and the Tower of the Hundred, as far as the Sheep Gate. At the Gate of the Guard they stopped.

40The two choirs that gave thanks then took their places in the house of God; so did I, together with half the officials, 41as well as the priests—Eliakim, Maaseiah, Miniamin, Micaiah, Elioenai, Zechariah and Hananiah with their trumpets— 42and also Maaseiah, Shemaiah, Eleazar, Uzzi, Jehohanan, Malkijah, Elam and Ezer. The choirs sang under the direction of Jezrahiah. 43And on that day they offered great sacrifices, rejoicing because God had given them great joy. The women and children also rejoiced. The sound of rejoicing in Jerusalem could be heard far away.

44At that time men were appointed to be in charge of the storerooms for the contributions, firstfruits and tithes. From the fields around the towns they were to bring into the storerooms the portions required by the Law for the priests and the Levites, for Judah was pleased with the ministering priests and Levites. 45They performed the service of their God and the service of purification, as did also the musicians and gatekeepers, according to the commands of David and his son Solomon. 46For long ago, in the days of David and Asaph, there had been directors for the musicians and for the songs of praise and thanksgiving to God. 47So in the days of Zerubbabel and of Nehemiah, all Israel contributed the daily portions for the musicians and the gatekeepers. They also set aside the portion for the other Levites, and the Levites set aside the portion for the descendants of Aaron.

Nehemiah's Final Reforms

13 On that day the Book of Moses was read aloud in the hearing of the people and there it was found written that no Ammonite or Moabite should ever be admitted into the assembly of God, 2because they had not met the Israelites with food and water but had hired Balaam to call a curse down on them. (Our God, however, turned the curse into a blessing.) 3When the people heard this law, they excluded from Israel all who were of foreign descent.

4Before this, Eliashib the priest had been put in charge of the storerooms of the house of our God. He was closely associated with Tobiah, 5and he had provided him with a large room formerly used to store the grain offerings and incense and temple articles, and also the tithes of grain, new wine and olive oil prescribed for the Levites, musicians and gatekeepers, as well as the contributions for the priests.

6But while all this was going on, I was not in Jerusalem, for in the thirty-second year of Artaxerxes king of Babylon I had returned to the king. Some time later I asked his permission 7and came back to Jerusalem. Here I learned about the evil thing Eliashib had done in providing Tobiah a room in the courts of the house of God. 8I was greatly displeased and threw all Tobiah's household goods out of the room. 9I gave orders to purify the rooms, and then I put back into them the equipment of the house of God, with the grain offerings and the incense.

10I also learned that the portions assigned to the Levites had not been given to them, and that all the Levites and musicians responsible for the service had gone back to their own fields. 11So I rebuked the officials and asked them, "Why is the house of God neglected?" Then I called them together and stationed them at their posts.

12All Judah brought the tithes of grain, new wine and olive oil into the storerooms. 13I put Shelemiah the priest, Zadok the scribe, and a Levite named Pedaiah in charge of the storerooms and made Hanan son of Zakkur, the son of Mattaniah, their assistant, because they were considered trustworthy. They were made responsible for distributing the supplies to their fellow Levites.

14Remember me for this, my God, and do not blot out what I have so faithfully done for the house of my God and its services.

15In those days I saw people in Judah treading winepresses on the Sabbath and bringing in grain and loading it on donkeys, together with wine, grapes, figs and all other kinds of

[a] 31 Or *go alongside* [b] 31 Or *proceed alongside* [c] 38 Or *them alongside* [d] 39 Or *Old*

loads. And they were bringing all this into Jerusalem on the Sabbath. Therefore I warned
them against selling food on that day. [16]Peo-
ple from Tyre who lived in Jerusalem were
bringing in fish and all kinds of merchandise
and selling them in Jerusalem on the Sabbath to the people of Judah. [17]I rebuked the
nobles of Judah and said to them, "What is
this wicked thing you are doing—desecrating
the Sabbath day? [18]Didn't your ancestors do
the same things, so that our God brought all
this calamity on us and on this city? Now you
are stirring up more wrath against Israel by
desecrating the Sabbath."

[19]When evening shadows fell on the gates
of Jerusalem before the Sabbath, I ordered
the doors to be shut and not opened until the
Sabbath was over. I stationed some of my
own men at the gates so that no load could
be brought in on the Sabbath day. [20]Once or
twice the merchants and sellers of all kinds
of goods spent the night outside Jerusalem.
[21]But I warned them and said, "Why do you
spend the night by the wall? If you do this
again, I will arrest you." From that time on
they no longer came on the Sabbath. [22]Then I
commanded the Levites to purify themselves
and go and guard the gates in order to keep
the Sabbath day holy.

Remember me for this also, my God, and
show mercy to me according to your great love.

[23]Moreover, in those days I saw men of Judah who had married women from Ashdod,
Ammon and Moab. [24]Half of their children
spoke the language of Ashdod or the language
of one of the other peoples, and did not know
how to speak the language of Judah. [25]I rebuked them and called curses down on them.
I beat some of the men and pulled out their
hair. I made them take an oath in God's name
and said: "You are not to give your daughters
in marriage to their sons, nor are you to take
their daughters in marriage for your sons or
for yourselves. [26]Was it not because of mar-
riages like these that Solomon king of Israel
sinned? Among the many nations there was
no king like him. He was loved by his God,
and God made him king over all Israel, but
even he was led into sin by foreign women.
[27]Must we hear now that you too are doing
all this terrible wickedness and are being
unfaithful to our God by marrying foreign
women?"

[28]One of the sons of Joiada son of Eliashib
the high priest was son-in-law to Sanballat
the Horonite. And I drove him away from me.

[29]Remember them, my God, because they
defiled the priestly office and the covenant of
the priesthood and of the Levites.

[30]So I purified the priests and the Levites of
everything foreign, and assigned them duties,
each to his own task. [31]I also made provision
for contributions of wood at designated times,
and for the firstfruits.

Remember me with favor, my God.

Esther

Queen Vashti Deposed

1 This is what happened during the time of
Xerxes,[a] the Xerxes who ruled over 127
provinces stretching from India to Cush[b]: [2]At
that time King Xerxes reigned from his royal
throne in the citadel of Susa, [3]and in the third
year of his reign he gave a banquet for all his
nobles and officials. The military leaders of
Persia and Media, the princes, and the nobles
of the provinces were present.

[4]For a full 180 days he displayed the vast
wealth of his kingdom and the splendor and
glory of his majesty. [5]When these days were
over, the king gave a banquet, lasting sev-
en days, in the enclosed garden of the king's
palace, for all the people from the least to the
greatest who were in the citadel of Susa. [6]The
garden had hangings of white and blue linen,
fastened with cords of white linen and purple material to silver rings on marble pillars.
There were couches of gold and silver on a
mosaic pavement of porphyry, marble, moth-
er-of-pearl and other costly stones. [7]Wine was
served in goblets of gold, each one different
from the other, and the royal wine was abundant, in keeping with the king's liberality. [8]By
the king's command each guest was allowed
to drink with no restrictions, for the king instructed all the wine stewards to serve each
man what he wished.

[9]Queen Vashti also gave a banquet for the
women in the royal palace of King Xerxes.

[10]On the seventh day, when King Xerxes
was in high spirits from wine, he commanded the seven eunuchs who served him—Me-
human, Biztha, Harbona, Bigtha, Abagtha,
Zethar and Karkas— [11]to bring before him
Queen Vashti, wearing her royal crown, in order to display her beauty to the people and nobles, for she was lovely to look at. [12]But when
the attendants delivered the king's command,
Queen Vashti refused to come. Then the king
became furious and burned with anger.

[13]Since it was customary for the king to con-

[a] *1* Hebrew *Ahasuerus*; here and throughout Esther

[b] *1* That is, the upper Nile region

sult experts in matters of law and justice, he
spoke with the wise men who understood the
times 14and were closest to the king—Kar-
shena, Shethar, Admatha, Tarshish, Meres,
Marsena and Memukan, the seven nobles of
Persia and Media who had special access to
the king and were highest in the kingdom.
15"According to law, what must be done to
Queen Vashti?" he asked. "She has not obeyed
the command of King Xerxes that the eunuchs
have taken to her."
16Then Memukan replied in the presence of
the king and the nobles, "Queen Vashti has
done wrong, not only against the king but also
against all the nobles and the peoples of all the
provinces of King Xerxes. 17For the queen's
conduct will become known to all the women,
and so they will despise their husbands and
say, 'King Xerxes commanded Queen Vashti
to be brought before him, but she would not
come.' 18This very day the Persian and Median
women of the nobility who have heard about
the queen's conduct will respond to all the
king's nobles in the same way. There will be
no end of disrespect and discord.
19"Therefore, if it pleases the king, let him
issue a royal decree and let it be written in the
laws of Persia and Media, which cannot be
repealed, that Vashti is never again to enter
the presence of King Xerxes. Also let the king
give her royal position to someone else who is
better than she. 20Then when the king's edict
is proclaimed throughout all his vast realm,
all the women will respect their husbands,
from the least to the greatest."
21The king and his nobles were pleased with
this advice, so the king did as Memukan proposed. 22He sent dispatches to all parts of the
kingdom, to each province in its own script
and to each people in their own language, proclaiming that every man should be ruler over
his own household, using his native tongue.

Esther Made Queen

2 Later when King Xerxes' fury had subsided, he remembered Vashti and what
she had done and what he had decreed about
her. 2Then the king's personal attendants
proposed, "Let a search be made for beautiful young virgins for the king. 3Let the king
appoint commissioners in every province of
his realm to bring all these beautiful young
women into the harem at the citadel of Susa.
Let them be placed under the care of Hegai, the king's eunuch, who is in charge of the
women; and let beauty treatments be given to
them. 4Then let the young woman who pleases
the king be queen instead of Vashti." This advice appealed to the king, and he followed it.
5Now there was in the citadel of Susa a Jew
of the tribe of Benjamin, named Mordecai son
of Jair, the son of Shimei, the son of Kish,
6who had been carried into exile from Jerusalem by Nebuchadnezzar king of Babylon,
among those taken captive with Jehoiachin[a]
king of Judah. 7Mordecai had a cousin named
Hadassah, whom he had brought up because
she had neither father nor mother. This young
woman, who was also known as Esther, had
a lovely figure and was beautiful. Mordecai
had taken her as his own daughter when her
father and mother died.
8When the king's order and edict had
been proclaimed, many young women were
brought to the citadel of Susa and put under
the care of Hegai. Esther also was taken to the
king's palace and entrusted to Hegai, who had
charge of the harem. 9She pleased him and
won his favor. Immediately he provided her
with her beauty treatments and special food.
He assigned to her seven female attendants
selected from the king's palace and moved
her and her attendants into the best place in
the harem.
10Esther had not revealed her nationality
and family background, because Mordecai
had forbidden her to do so. 11Every day he
walked back and forth near the courtyard of
the harem to find out how Esther was and
what was happening to her.
12Before a young woman's turn came to go
in to King Xerxes, she had to complete twelve
months of beauty treatments prescribed for
the women, six months with oil of myrrh and
six with perfumes and cosmetics. 13And this
is how she would go to the king: Anything she
wanted was given her to take with her from
the harem to the king's palace. 14In the evening she would go there and in the morning
return to another part of the harem to the care
of Shaashgaz, the king's eunuch who was in
charge of the concubines. She would not return to the king unless he was pleased with
her and summoned her by name.
15When the turn came for Esther (the young
woman Mordecai had adopted, the daughter
of his uncle Abihail) to go to the king, she
asked for nothing other than what Hegai,
the king's eunuch who was in charge of the
harem, suggested. And Esther won the favor
of everyone who saw her. 16She was taken to
King Xerxes in the royal residence in the tenth
month, the month of Tebeth, in the seventh
year of his reign.
17Now the king was attracted to Esther more
than to any of the other women, and she won
his favor and approval more than any of the
other virgins. So he set a royal crown on her
head and made her queen instead of Vashti.
18And the king gave a great banquet, Esther's
banquet, for all his nobles and officials. He
proclaimed a holiday throughout the provinces and distributed gifts with royal liberality.

Mordecai Uncovers a Conspiracy

19When the virgins were assembled a second time, Mordecai was sitting at the king's
gate. 20But Esther had kept secret her family
background and nationality just as Mordecai
had told her to do, for she continued to follow
Mordecai's instructions as she had done when
he was bringing her up.
21During the time Mordecai was sitting at
the king's gate, Bigthana[b] and Teresh, two of

[a] 6 Hebrew *Jeconiah*, a variant of *Jehoiachin* [b] 21 Hebrew *Bigthan*, a variant of *Bigthana*

the king's officers who guarded the doorway, became angry and conspired to assassinate King Xerxes. [22]But Mordecai found out about the plot and told Queen Esther, who in turn reported it to the king, giving credit to Mordecai. [23]And when the report was investigated and found to be true, the two officials were impaled on poles. All this was recorded in the book of the annals in the presence of the king.

Haman's Plot to Destroy the Jews

3 After these events, King Xerxes honored Haman son of Hammedatha, the Agagite, elevating him and giving him a seat of honor higher than that of all the other nobles. [2]All the royal officials at the king's gate knelt down and paid honor to Haman, for the king had commanded this concerning him. But Mordecai would not kneel down or pay him honor.

[3]Then the royal officials at the king's gate asked Mordecai, "Why do you disobey the king's command?" [4]Day after day they spoke to him but he refused to comply. Therefore they told Haman about it to see whether Mordecai's behavior would be tolerated, for he had told them he was a Jew.

[5]When Haman saw that Mordecai would not kneel down or pay him honor, he was enraged. [6]Yet having learned who Mordecai's people were, he scorned the idea of killing only Mordecai. Instead Haman looked for a way to destroy all Mordecai's people, the Jews, throughout the whole kingdom of Xerxes.

[7]In the twelfth year of King Xerxes, in the first month, the month of Nisan, the *pur* (that is, the lot) was cast in the presence of Haman to select a day and month. And the lot fell on[a] the twelfth month, the month of Adar.

[8]Then Haman said to King Xerxes, "There is a certain people dispersed among the peoples in all the provinces of your kingdom who keep themselves separate. Their customs are different from those of all other people, and they do not obey the king's laws; it is not in the king's best interest to tolerate them. [9]If it pleases the king, let a decree be issued to destroy them, and I will give ten thousand talents[b] of silver to the king's administrators for the royal treasury."

[10]So the king took his signet ring from his finger and gave it to Haman son of Hammedatha, the Agagite, the enemy of the Jews. [11]"Keep the money," the king said to Haman, "and do with the people as you please."

[12]Then on the thirteenth day of the first month the royal secretaries were summoned. They wrote out in the script of each province and in the language of each people all Haman's orders to the king's satraps, the governors of the various provinces and the nobles of the various peoples. These were written in the name of King Xerxes himself and sealed with his own ring. [13]Dispatches were sent by couriers to all the king's provinces with the order to destroy, kill and annihilate all the Jews—young and old, women and children—on a single day, the thirteenth day of the twelfth month, the month of Adar, and to plunder their goods. [14]A copy of the text of the edict was to be issued as law in every province and made known to the people of every nationality so they would be ready for that day.

[15]The couriers went out, spurred on by the king's command, and the edict was issued in the citadel of Susa. The king and Haman sat down to drink, but the city of Susa was bewildered.

Mordecai Persuades Esther to Help

4 When Mordecai learned of all that had been done, he tore his clothes, put on sackcloth and ashes, and went out into the city, wailing loudly and bitterly. [2]But he went only as far as the king's gate, because no one clothed in sackcloth was allowed to enter it. [3]In every province to which the edict and order of the king came, there was great mourning among the Jews, with fasting, weeping and wailing. Many lay in sackcloth and ashes.

[4]When Esther's eunuchs and female attendants came and told her about Mordecai, she was in great distress. She sent clothes for him to put on instead of his sackcloth, but he would not accept them. [5]Then Esther summoned Hathak, one of the king's eunuchs assigned to attend her, and ordered him to find out what was troubling Mordecai and why.

[6]So Hathak went out to Mordecai in the open square of the city in front of the king's gate. [7]Mordecai told him everything that had happened to him, including the exact amount of money Haman had promised to pay into the royal treasury for the destruction of the Jews. [8]He also gave him a copy of the text of the edict for their annihilation, which had been published in Susa, to show to Esther and explain it to her, and he told him to instruct her to go into the king's presence to beg for mercy and plead with him for her people.

[9]Hathak went back and reported to Esther what Mordecai had said. [10]Then she instructed him to say to Mordecai, [11]"All the king's officials and the people of the royal provinces know that for any man or woman who approaches the king in the inner court without being summoned the king has but one law: that they be put to death unless the king extends the gold scepter to them and spares their lives. But thirty days have passed since I was called to go to the king."

[12]When Esther's words were reported to Mordecai, [13]he sent back this answer: "Do not think that because you are in the king's house you alone of all the Jews will escape. [14]For if you remain silent at this time, relief and deliverance for the Jews will arise from another place, but you and your father's family will perish. And who knows but that you have come to your royal position for such a time as this?"

[15]Then Esther sent this reply to Mordecai: [16]"Go, gather together all the Jews who are in

[a] 7 Septuagint; Hebrew does not have *And the lot fell on*. [b] 9 That is, about 375 tons or about 340 metric tons

Susa, and fast for me. Do not eat or drink for
three days, night or day. I and my attendants
will fast as you do. When this is done, I will
go to the king, even though it is against the
law. And if I perish, I perish."
17 So Mordecai went away and carried out
all of Esther's instructions.

Esther's Request to the King

5 On the third day Esther put on her royal
robes and stood in the inner court of the
palace, in front of the king's hall. The king
was sitting on his royal throne in the hall,
facing the entrance. 2 When he saw Queen
Esther standing in the court, he was pleased
with her and held out to her the gold scepter
that was in his hand. So Esther approached
and touched the tip of the scepter.
3 Then the king asked, "What is it, Queen
Esther? What is your request? Even up to half
the kingdom, it will be given you."
4 "If it pleases the king," replied Esther, "let
the king, together with Haman, come today
to a banquet I have prepared for him."
5 "Bring Haman at once," the king said, "so
that we may do what Esther asks."
So the king and Haman went to the banquet
Esther had prepared. 6 As they were drinking
wine, the king again asked Esther, "Now what
is your petition? It will be given you. And what
is your request? Even up to half the kingdom,
it will be granted."
7 Esther replied, "My petition and my request is this: 8 If the king regards me with
favor and if it pleases the king to grant my
petition and fulfill my request, let the king
and Haman come tomorrow to the banquet I
will prepare for them. Then I will answer the
king's question."

Haman's Rage Against Mordecai

9 Haman went out that day happy and in
high spirits. But when he saw Mordecai at the
king's gate and observed that he neither rose
nor showed fear in his presence, he was filled
with rage against Mordecai. 10 Nevertheless,
Haman restrained himself and went home.
Calling together his friends and Zeresh,
his wife, 11 Haman boasted to them about his
vast wealth, his many sons, and all the ways
the king had honored him and how he had
elevated him above the other nobles and officials. 12 "And that's not all," Haman added.
"I'm the only person Queen Esther invited to
accompany the king to the banquet she gave.
And she has invited me along with the king
tomorrow. 13 But all this gives me no satisfaction as long as I see that Jew Mordecai sitting
at the king's gate."
14 His wife Zeresh and all his friends said to
him, "Have a pole set up, reaching to a height
of fifty cubits,[a] and ask the king in the morning to have Mordecai impaled on it. Then go
with the king to the banquet and enjoy yourself." This suggestion delighted Haman, and
he had the pole set up.

Mordecai Honored

6 That night the king could not sleep; so
he ordered the book of the chronicles,
the record of his reign, to be brought in and
read to him. 2 It was found recorded there that
Mordecai had exposed Bigthana and Teresh,
two of the king's officers who guarded the
doorway, who had conspired to assassinate
King Xerxes.
3 "What honor and recognition has Mordecai received for this?" the king asked.
"Nothing has been done for him," his attendants answered.
4 The king said, "Who is in the court?" Now
Haman had just entered the outer court of the
palace to speak to the king about impaling
Mordecai on the pole he had set up for him.
5 His attendants answered, "Haman is
standing in the court."
"Bring him in," the king ordered.
6 When Haman entered, the king asked him,
"What should be done for the man the king
delights to honor?"
Now Haman thought to himself, "Who is
there that the king would rather honor than
me?" 7 So he answered the king, "For the man
the king delights to honor, 8 have them bring
a royal robe the king has worn and a horse
the king has ridden, one with a royal crest
placed on its head. 9 Then let the robe and
horse be entrusted to one of the king's most
noble princes. Let them robe the man the king
delights to honor, and lead him on the horse
through the city streets, proclaiming before
him, 'This is what is done for the man the king
delights to honor!'"
10 "Go at once," the king commanded Haman. "Get the robe and the horse and do just
as you have suggested for Mordecai the Jew,
who sits at the king's gate. Do not neglect anything you have recommended."
11 So Haman got the robe and the horse. He
robed Mordecai, and led him on horseback
through the city streets, proclaiming before
him, "This is what is done for the man the
king delights to honor!"
12 Afterward Mordecai returned to the
king's gate. But Haman rushed home, with
his head covered in grief, 13 and told Zeresh
his wife and all his friends everything that
had happened to him.
His advisers and his wife Zeresh said to him,
"Since Mordecai, before whom your downfall
has started, is of Jewish origin, you cannot
stand against him—you will surely come to
ruin!" 14 While they were still talking with him,
the king's eunuchs arrived and hurried Haman
away to the banquet Esther had prepared.

Haman Impaled

7 So the king and Haman went to Queen Esther's banquet, 2 and as they were drinking
wine on the second day, the king again asked,
"Queen Esther, what is your petition? It will
be given you. What is your request? Even up
to half the kingdom, it will be granted."

[a] 14 That is, about 75 feet or about 23 meters

3 Then Queen Esther answered, "If I have
found favor with you, Your Majesty, and if
it pleases you, grant me my life—this is my
petition. And spare my people—this is my request. 4 For I and my people have been sold to
be destroyed, killed and annihilated. If we had
merely been sold as male and female slaves, I
would have kept quiet, because no such distress would justify disturbing the king.[a]"
5 King Xerxes asked Queen Esther, "Who is
he? Where is he—the man who has dared to
do such a thing?"
6 Esther said, "An adversary and enemy!
This vile Haman!"
Then Haman was terrified before the king
and queen. 7 The king got up in a rage, left his
wine and went out into the palace garden. But
Haman, realizing that the king had already
decided his fate, stayed behind to beg Queen
Esther for his life.
8 Just as the king returned from the palace
garden to the banquet hall, Haman was falling on the couch where Esther was reclining.
The king exclaimed, "Will he even molest
the queen while she is with me in the house?"
As soon as the word left the king's mouth,
they covered Haman's face. 9 Then Harbona,
one of the eunuchs attending the king, said,
"A pole reaching to a height of fifty cubits[b]
stands by Haman's house. He had it set up
for Mordecai, who spoke up to help the king."
The king said, "Impale him on it!" 10 So they
impaled Haman on the pole he had set up for
Mordecai. Then the king's fury subsided.

The King's Edict in Behalf of the Jews

8 That same day King Xerxes gave Queen
Esther the estate of Haman, the enemy of
the Jews. And Mordecai came into the presence of the king, for Esther had told how he
was related to her. 2 The king took off his
signet ring, which he had reclaimed from
Haman, and presented it to Mordecai. And
Esther appointed him over Haman's estate.
3 Esther again pleaded with the king, falling
at his feet and weeping. She begged him to put
an end to the evil plan of Haman the Agagite,
which he had devised against the Jews. 4 Then
the king extended the gold scepter to Esther
and she arose and stood before him.
5 "If it pleases the king," she said, "and if he
regards me with favor and thinks it the right
thing to do, and if he is pleased with me, let
an order be written overruling the dispatches
that Haman son of Hammedatha, the Agagite,
devised and wrote to destroy the Jews in all
the king's provinces. 6 For how can I bear to
see disaster fall on my people? How can I bear
to see the destruction of my family?"
7 King Xerxes replied to Queen Esther and to
Mordecai the Jew, "Because Haman attacked
the Jews, I have given his estate to Esther, and
they have impaled him on the pole he set up.
8 Now write another decree in the king's name
in behalf of the Jews as seems best to you,
and seal it with the king's signet ring—for
no document written in the king's name and
sealed with his ring can be revoked."
9 At once the royal secretaries were summoned—on the twenty-third day of the third
month, the month of Sivan. They wrote out all
Mordecai's orders to the Jews, and to the satraps, governors and nobles of the 127 provinces stretching from India to Cush.[c] These
orders were written in the script of each
province and the language of each people
and also to the Jews in their own script and
language. 10 Mordecai wrote in the name of
King Xerxes, sealed the dispatches with the
king's signet ring, and sent them by mounted couriers, who rode fast horses especially
bred for the king.
11 The king's edict granted the Jews in every city the right to assemble and protect
themselves; to destroy, kill and annihilate
the armed men of any nationality or province who might attack them and their women
and children,[d] and to plunder the property
of their enemies. 12 The day appointed for the
Jews to do this in all the provinces of King
Xerxes was the thirteenth day of the twelfth
month, the month of Adar. 13 A copy of the text
of the edict was to be issued as law in every
province and made known to the people of
every nationality so that the Jews would be
ready on that day to avenge themselves on
their enemies.
14 The couriers, riding the royal horses, went
out, spurred on by the king's command, and
the edict was issued in the citadel of Susa.

The Triumph of the Jews

15 When Mordecai left the king's presence,
he was wearing royal garments of blue and
white, a large crown of gold and a purple robe
of fine linen. And the city of Susa held a joy-
ous celebration. 16 For the Jews it was a time
of happiness and joy, gladness and honor.
17 In every province and in every city to which
the edict of the king came, there was joy and
gladness among the Jews, with feasting and
celebrating. And many people of other nationalities became Jews because fear of the Jews
had seized them.
9 On the thirteenth day of the twelfth month,
the month of Adar, the edict commanded
by the king was to be carried out. On this day
the enemies of the Jews had hoped to overpower them, but now the tables were turned
and the Jews got the upper hand over those
who hated them. 2 The Jews assembled in their
cities in all the provinces of King Xerxes to attack those determined to destroy them. No one
could stand against them, because the people
of all the other nationalities were afraid of
them. 3 And all the nobles of the provinces,
the satraps, the governors and the king's administrators helped the Jews, because fear
of Mordecai had seized them. 4 Mordecai was
prominent in the palace; his reputation spread

[a] *4* Or *quiet, but the compensation our adversary offers cannot be compared with the loss the king would suffer* [b] *9* That is, about 75 feet or about 23 meters [c] *9* That is, the upper Nile region
[d] *11* Or *province, together with their women and children, who might attack them;*

throughout the provinces, and he became more and more powerful.

5 The Jews struck down all their enemies with the sword, killing and destroying them, and they did what they pleased to those who hated them. 6 In the citadel of Susa, the Jews killed and destroyed five hundred men. 7 They also killed Parshandatha, Dalphon, Aspatha, 8 Poratha, Adalia, Aridatha, 9 Parmashta, Arisai, Aridai and Vaizatha, 10 the ten sons of Haman son of Hammedatha, the enemy of the Jews. But they did not lay their hands on the plunder.

11 The number of those killed in the citadel of Susa was reported to the king that same day. 12 The king said to Queen Esther, "The Jews have killed and destroyed five hundred men and the ten sons of Haman in the citadel of Susa. What have they done in the rest of the king's provinces? Now what is your petition? It will be given you. What is your request? It will also be granted."

13 "If it pleases the king," Esther answered, "give the Jews in Susa permission to carry out this day's edict tomorrow also, and let Haman's ten sons be impaled on poles."

14 So the king commanded that this be done. An edict was issued in Susa, and they impaled the ten sons of Haman. 15 The Jews in Susa came together on the fourteenth day of the month of Adar, and they put to death in Susa three hundred men, but they did not lay their hands on the plunder.

16 Meanwhile, the remainder of the Jews who were in the king's provinces also assembled to protect themselves and get relief from their enemies. They killed seventy-five thousand of them but did not lay their hands on the plunder. 17 This happened on the thirteenth day of the month of Adar, and on the fourteenth they rested and made it a day of feasting and joy.

18 The Jews in Susa, however, had assembled on the thirteenth and fourteenth, and then on the fifteenth they rested and made it a day of feasting and joy.

19 That is why rural Jews—those living in villages—observe the fourteenth of the month of Adar as a day of joy and feasting, a day for giving presents to each other.

Purim Established

20 Mordecai recorded these events, and he sent letters to all the Jews throughout the provinces of King Xerxes, near and far, 21 to have them celebrate annually the fourteenth and fifteenth days of the month of Adar 22 as the time when the Jews got relief from their enemies, and as the month when their sorrow was turned into joy and their mourning into a day of celebration. He wrote them to observe the days as days of feasting and joy and giving presents of food to one another and gifts to the poor.

23 So the Jews agreed to continue the celebration they had begun, doing what Mordecai had written to them. 24 For Haman son of Hammedatha, the Agagite, the enemy of all the Jews, had plotted against the Jews to destroy them and had cast the *pur* (that is, the lot) for their ruin and destruction. 25 But when the plot came to the king's attention,[a] he issued written orders that the evil scheme Haman had devised against the Jews should come back onto his own head, and that he and his sons should be impaled on poles. 26 (Therefore these days were called Purim, from the word *pur*.) Because of everything written in this letter and because of what they had seen and what had happened to them, 27 the Jews took it on themselves to establish the custom that they and their descendants and all who join them should without fail observe these two days every year, in the way prescribed and at the time appointed. 28 These days should be remembered and observed in every generation by every family, and in every province and in every city. And these days of Purim should never fail to be celebrated by the Jews—nor should the memory of these days die out among their descendants.

29 So Queen Esther, daughter of Abihail, along with Mordecai the Jew, wrote with full authority to confirm this second letter concerning Purim. 30 And Mordecai sent letters to all the Jews in the 127 provinces of Xerxes' kingdom—words of goodwill and assurance— 31 to establish these days of Purim at their designated times, as Mordecai the Jew and Queen Esther had decreed for them, and as they had established for themselves and their descendants in regard to their times of fasting and lamentation. 32 Esther's decree confirmed these regulations about Purim, and it was written down in the records.

The Greatness of Mordecai

10 King Xerxes imposed tribute throughout the empire, to its distant shores. 2 And all his acts of power and might, together with a full account of the greatness of Mordecai, whom the king had promoted, are they not written in the book of the annals of the kings of Media and Persia? 3 Mordecai the Jew was second in rank to King Xerxes, preeminent among the Jews, and held in high esteem by his many fellow Jews, because he worked for the good of his people and spoke up for the welfare of all the Jews.

[a] 25 Or *when Esther came before the king*

Job

Prologue

1 In the land of Uz there lived a man whose
name was Job. This man was blameless
and upright; he feared God and shunned evil.
2He had seven sons and three daughters, 3and
he owned seven thousand sheep, three thousand camels, five hundred yoke of oxen and
five hundred donkeys, and had a large number
of servants. He was the greatest man among
all the people of the East.
4His sons used to hold feasts in their homes
on their birthdays, and they would invite their
three sisters to eat and drink with them.
5When a period of feasting had run its course,
Job would make arrangements for them to
be purified. Early in the morning he would
sacrifice a burnt offering for each of them,
thinking, "Perhaps my children have sinned
and cursed God in their hearts." This was
Job's regular custom.
6One day the angels[a] came to present themselves before the LORD, and Satan[b] also came
with them. 7The LORD said to Satan, "Where
have you come from?"
Satan answered the LORD, "From roaming
throughout the earth, going back and forth
on it."
8Then the LORD said to Satan, "Have you
considered my servant Job? There is no one
on earth like him; he is blameless and upright,
a man who fears God and shuns evil."
9"Does Job fear God for nothing?" Satan replied. 10"Have you not put a hedge around him
and his household and everything he has? You
have blessed the work of his hands, so that
his flocks and herds are spread throughout
the land. 11But now stretch out your hand and
strike everything he has, and he will surely
curse you to your face."
12The LORD said to Satan, "Very well, then,
everything he has is in your power, but on the
man himself do not lay a finger."
Then Satan went out from the presence of
the LORD.
13One day when Job's sons and daughters
were feasting and drinking wine at the oldest brother's house, 14a messenger came to
Job and said, "The oxen were plowing and
the donkeys were grazing nearby, 15and the
Sabeans attacked and made off with them.
They put the servants to the sword, and I am
the only one who has escaped to tell you!"
16While he was still speaking, another messenger came and said, "The fire of God fell
from the heavens and burned up the sheep
and the servants, and I am the only one who
has escaped to tell you!"
17While he was still speaking, another messenger came and said, "The Chaldeans formed
three raiding parties and swept down on your
camels and made off with them. They put the
servants to the sword, and I am the only one
who has escaped to tell you!"
18While he was still speaking, yet another messenger came and said, "Your sons and
daughters were feasting and drinking wine
at the oldest brother's house, 19when suddenly
a mighty wind swept in from the desert and
struck the four corners of the house. It collapsed on them and they are dead, and I am
the only one who has escaped to tell you!"
20At this, Job got up and tore his robe and
shaved his head. Then he fell to the ground
in worship 21and said:

"Naked I came from my mother's womb,
and naked I will depart.[c]
The LORD gave and the LORD has taken
away;
may the name of the LORD be praised."

22In all this, Job did not sin by charging God
with wrongdoing.

2 On another day the angels[a] came to present themselves before the LORD, and Satan also came with them to present himself
before him. 2And the LORD said to Satan,
"Where have you come from?"
Satan answered the LORD, "From roaming
throughout the earth, going back and forth
on it."
3Then the LORD said to Satan, "Have you
considered my servant Job? There is no one
on earth like him; he is blameless and upright,
a man who fears God and shuns evil. And
he still maintains his integrity, though you
incited me against him to ruin him without
any reason."
4"Skin for skin!" Satan replied. "A man
will give all he has for his own life. 5But now
stretch out your hand and strike his flesh and
bones, and he will surely curse you to your
face."
6The LORD said to Satan, "Very well, then, he
is in your hands; but you must spare his life."
7So Satan went out from the presence of
the LORD and afflicted Job with painful sores
from the soles of his feet to the crown of his
head. 8Then Job took a piece of broken pottery
and scraped himself with it as he sat among
the ashes.
9His wife said to him, "Are you still main-
taining your integrity? Curse God and die!"
10He replied, "You are talking like a foolish[d]
woman. Shall we accept good from God, and
not trouble?"
In all this, Job did not sin in what he said.

11When Job's three friends, Eliphaz the Temanite, Bildad the Shuhite and Zophar the
Naamathite, heard about all the troubles that

[a] 6,1 Hebrew *the sons of God* [b] 6 Hebrew *satan* means *adversary.* [c] 21 Or *will return there*
[d] 10 The Hebrew word rendered *foolish* denotes moral deficiency.

had come upon him, they set out from their
homes and met together by agreement to go
and sympathize with him and comfort him.
12 When they saw him from a distance, they
could hardly recognize him; they began to
weep aloud, and they tore their robes and
sprinkled dust on their heads. 13 Then they
sat on the ground with him for seven days
and seven nights. No one said a word to him,
because they saw how great his suffering was.

Job Speaks

3 After this, Job opened his mouth and
cursed the day of his birth. 2 He said:

3 "May the day of my birth perish,
and the night that said, 'A boy is conceived!'
4 That day—may it turn to darkness;
may God above not care about it;
may no light shine on it.
5 May gloom and utter darkness claim it once more;
may a cloud settle over it;
may blackness overwhelm it.
6 That night—may thick darkness seize it;
may it not be included among the days of the year
nor be entered in any of the months.
7 May that night be barren;
may no shout of joy be heard in it.
8 May those who curse days[a] curse that day,
those who are ready to rouse Leviathan.
9 May its morning stars become dark;
may it wait for daylight in vain
and not see the first rays of dawn,
10 for it did not shut the doors of the womb on me
to hide trouble from my eyes.

11 "Why did I not perish at birth,
and die as I came from the womb?
12 Why were there knees to receive me
and breasts that I might be nursed?
13 For now I would be lying down in peace;
I would be asleep and at rest
14 with kings and rulers of the earth,
who built for themselves places now lying in ruins,
15 with princes who had gold,
who filled their houses with silver.
16 Or why was I not hidden away in the ground like a stillborn child,
like an infant who never saw the light of day?
17 There the wicked cease from turmoil,
and there the weary are at rest.
18 Captives also enjoy their ease;
they no longer hear the slave driver's shout.
19 The small and the great are there,
and the slaves are freed from their owners.

20 "Why is light given to those in misery,
and life to the bitter of soul,
21 to those who long for death that does not come,
who search for it more than for hidden treasure,
22 who are filled with gladness
and rejoice when they reach the grave?
23 Why is life given to a man
whose way is hidden,
whom God has hedged in?
24 For sighing has become my daily food;
my groans pour out like water.
25 What I feared has come upon me;
what I dreaded has happened to me.
26 I have no peace, no quietness;
I have no rest, but only turmoil."

Eliphaz

4 Then Eliphaz the Temanite replied:

2 "If someone ventures a word with you,
will you be impatient?
But who can keep from speaking?
3 Think how you have instructed many,
how you have strengthened feeble hands.
4 Your words have supported those who stumbled;
you have strengthened faltering knees.
5 But now trouble comes to you, and you are discouraged;
it strikes you, and you are dismayed.
6 Should not your piety be your confidence
and your blameless ways your hope?

7 "Consider now: Who, being innocent, has ever perished?
Where were the upright ever destroyed?
8 As I have observed, those who plow evil
and those who sow trouble reap it.
9 At the breath of God they perish;
at the blast of his anger they are no more.
10 The lions may roar and growl,
yet the teeth of the great lions are broken.
11 The lion perishes for lack of prey,
and the cubs of the lioness are scattered.

12 "A word was secretly brought to me,
my ears caught a whisper of it.
13 Amid disquieting dreams in the night,
when deep sleep falls on people,
14 fear and trembling seized me
and made all my bones shake.
15 A spirit glided past my face,
and the hair on my body stood on end.
16 It stopped,
but I could not tell what it was.
A form stood before my eyes,
and I heard a hushed voice:
17 'Can a mortal be more righteous than God?
Can even a strong man be more pure than his Maker?
18 If God places no trust in his servants,
if he charges his angels with error,

[a] 8 Or *curse the sea*

19 how much more those who live in houses
of clay,
whose foundations are in the dust,
who are crushed more readily than a
moth!
20 Between dawn and dusk they are broken
to pieces;
unnoticed, they perish forever.
21 Are not the cords of their tent pulled up,
so that they die without wisdom?'

5 "Call if you will, but who will answer
you?
To which of the holy ones will you turn?
2 Resentment kills a fool,
and envy slays the simple.
3 I myself have seen a fool taking root,
but suddenly his house was cursed.
4 His children are far from safety,
crushed in court without a defender.
5 The hungry consume his harvest,
taking it even from among thorns,
and the thirsty pant after his wealth.
6 For hardship does not spring from the soil,
nor does trouble sprout from the ground.
7 Yet man is born to trouble
as surely as sparks fly upward.

8 "But if I were you, I would appeal to God;
I would lay my cause before him.
9 He performs wonders that cannot be
fathomed,
miracles that cannot be counted.
10 He provides rain for the earth;
he sends water on the countryside.
11 The lowly he sets on high,
and those who mourn are lifted to safety.
12 He thwarts the plans of the crafty,
so that their hands achieve no success.
13 He catches the wise in their craftiness,
and the schemes of the wily are swept
away.
14 Darkness comes upon them in the
daytime;
at noon they grope as in the night.
15 He saves the needy from the sword in
their mouth;
he saves them from the clutches of the
powerful.
16 So the poor have hope,
and injustice shuts its mouth.

17 "Blessed is the one whom God corrects;
so do not despise the discipline of the
Almighty.[a]
18 For he wounds, but he also binds up;
he injures, but his hands also heal.
19 From six calamities he will rescue you;
in seven no harm will touch you.
20 In famine he will deliver you from death,
and in battle from the stroke of the
sword.
21 You will be protected from the lash of the
tongue,
and need not fear when destruction
comes.
22 You will laugh at destruction and famine,
and need not fear the wild animals.
23 For you will have a covenant with the
stones of the field,
and the wild animals will be at peace
with you.
24 You will know that your tent is secure;
you will take stock of your property
and find nothing missing.
25 You will know that your children will be
many,
and your descendants like the grass of
the earth.
26 You will come to the grave in full vigor,
like sheaves gathered in season.

27 "We have examined this, and it is true.
So hear it and apply it to yourself."

Job

6 Then Job replied:

2 "If only my anguish could be weighed
and all my misery be placed on the
scales!
3 It would surely outweigh the sand of the
seas—
no wonder my words have been
impetuous.
4 The arrows of the Almighty are in me,
my spirit drinks in their poison;
God's terrors are marshaled against me.
5 Does a wild donkey bray when it has
grass,
or an ox bellow when it has fodder?
6 Is tasteless food eaten without salt,
or is there flavor in the sap of the
mallow[b]?
7 I refuse to touch it;
such food makes me ill.

8 "Oh, that I might have my request,
that God would grant what I hope for,
9 that God would be willing to crush me,
to let loose his hand and cut off my life!
10 Then I would still have this consolation—
my joy in unrelenting pain—
that I had not denied the words of the
Holy One.

11 "What strength do I have, that I should
still hope?
What prospects, that I should be patient?
12 Do I have the strength of stone?
Is my flesh bronze?
13 Do I have any power to help myself,
now that success has been driven from
me?

14 "Anyone who withholds kindness from a
friend
forsakes the fear of the Almighty.
15 But my brothers are as undependable as
intermittent streams,
as the streams that overflow
16 when darkened by thawing ice
and swollen with melting snow,
17 but that stop flowing in the dry season,
and in the heat vanish from their
channels.

[a] 17 Hebrew *Shaddai*; here and throughout Job
[b] 6 The meaning of the Hebrew for this phrase is
uncertain.

18 Caravans turn aside from their routes;
they go off into the wasteland and perish.
19 The caravans of Tema look for water,
the traveling merchants of Sheba look in hope.
20 They are distressed, because they had been confident;
they arrive there, only to be disappointed.
21 Now you too have proved to be of no help;
you see something dreadful and are afraid.
22 Have I ever said, 'Give something on my behalf,
pay a ransom for me from your wealth,
23 deliver me from the hand of the enemy,
rescue me from the clutches of the ruthless'?

24 "Teach me, and I will be quiet;
show me where I have been wrong.
25 How painful are honest words!
But what do your arguments prove?
26 Do you mean to correct what I say,
and treat my desperate words as wind?
27 You would even cast lots for the fatherless
and barter away your friend.

28 "But now be so kind as to look at me.
Would I lie to your face?
29 Relent, do not be unjust;
reconsider, for my integrity is at stake.[a]
30 Is there any wickedness on my lips?
Can my mouth not discern malice?

7 "Do not mortals have hard service on earth?
Are not their days like those of hired laborers?
2 Like a slave longing for the evening shadows,
or a hired laborer waiting to be paid,
3 so I have been allotted months of futility,
and nights of misery have been assigned to me.
4 When I lie down I think, 'How long before I get up?'
The night drags on, and I toss and turn until dawn.
5 My body is clothed with worms and scabs,
my skin is broken and festering.

6 "My days are swifter than a weaver's shuttle,
and they come to an end without hope.
7 Remember, O God, that my life is but a breath;
my eyes will never see happiness again.
8 The eye that now sees me will see me no longer;
you will look for me, but I will be no more.
9 As a cloud vanishes and is gone,
so one who goes down to the grave does not return.
10 He will never come to his house again;
his place will know him no more.

11 "Therefore I will not keep silent;
I will speak out in the anguish of my spirit,
I will complain in the bitterness of my soul.
12 Am I the sea, or the monster of the deep,
that you put me under guard?
13 When I think my bed will comfort me
and my couch will ease my complaint,
14 even then you frighten me with dreams
and terrify me with visions,
15 so that I prefer strangling and death,
rather than this body of mine.
16 I despise my life; I would not live forever.
Let me alone; my days have no meaning.

17 "What is mankind that you make so much of them,
that you give them so much attention,
18 that you examine them every morning
and test them every moment?
19 Will you never look away from me,
or let me alone even for an instant?
20 If I have sinned, what have I done to you,
you who see everything we do?
Why have you made me your target?
Have I become a burden to you?[b]
21 Why do you not pardon my offenses
and forgive my sins?
For I will soon lie down in the dust;
you will search for me, but I will be no more."

Bildad

8 Then Bildad the Shuhite replied:

2 "How long will you say such things?
Your words are a blustering wind.
3 Does God pervert justice?
Does the Almighty pervert what is right?
4 When your children sinned against him,
he gave them over to the penalty of their sin.
5 But if you will seek God earnestly
and plead with the Almighty,
6 if you are pure and upright,
even now he will rouse himself on your behalf
and restore you to your prosperous state.
7 Your beginnings will seem humble,
so prosperous will your future be.

8 "Ask the former generation
and find out what their ancestors learned,
9 for we were born only yesterday and know nothing,
and our days on earth are but a shadow.
10 Will they not instruct you and tell you?
Will they not bring forth words from their understanding?

[a] 29 Or *my righteousness still stands* [b] 20 A few manuscripts of the Masoretic Text, an ancient Hebrew scribal tradition and Septuagint; most manuscripts of the Masoretic Text *I have become a burden to myself.*

[11] Can papyrus grow tall where there is no marsh?
Can reeds thrive without water?
[12] While still growing and uncut,
they wither more quickly than grass.
[13] Such is the destiny of all who forget God;
so perishes the hope of the godless.
[14] What they trust in is fragile[a];
what they rely on is a spider's web.
[15] They lean on the web, but it gives way;
they cling to it, but it does not hold.
[16] They are like a well-watered plant in the sunshine,
spreading its shoots over the garden;
[17] it entwines its roots around a pile of rocks
and looks for a place among the stones.
[18] But when it is torn from its spot,
that place disowns it and says, 'I never saw you.'
[19] Surely its life withers away,
and[b] from the soil other plants grow.

[20] "Surely God does not reject one who is blameless
or strengthen the hands of evildoers.
[21] He will yet fill your mouth with laughter
and your lips with shouts of joy.
[22] Your enemies will be clothed in shame,
and the tents of the wicked will be no more."

Job

9 Then Job replied:

[2] "Indeed, I know that this is true.
But how can mere mortals prove their innocence before God?
[3] Though they wished to dispute with him,
they could not answer him one time out of a thousand.
[4] His wisdom is profound, his power is vast.
Who has resisted him and come out unscathed?
[5] He moves mountains without their knowing it
and overturns them in his anger.
[6] He shakes the earth from its place
and makes its pillars tremble.
[7] He speaks to the sun and it does not shine;
he seals off the light of the stars.
[8] He alone stretches out the heavens
and treads on the waves of the sea.
[9] He is the Maker of the Bear[c] and Orion,
the Pleiades and the constellations of the south.
[10] He performs wonders that cannot be fathomed,
miracles that cannot be counted.
[11] When he passes me, I cannot see him;
when he goes by, I cannot perceive him.
[12] If he snatches away, who can stop him?
Who can say to him, 'What are you doing?'
[13] God does not restrain his anger;
even the cohorts of Rahab cowered at his feet.

[14] "How then can I dispute with him?
How can I find words to argue with him?
[15] Though I were innocent, I could not answer him;
I could only plead with my Judge for mercy.
[16] Even if I summoned him and he responded,
I do not believe he would give me a hearing.
[17] He would crush me with a storm
and multiply my wounds for no reason.
[18] He would not let me catch my breath
but would overwhelm me with misery.
[19] If it is a matter of strength, he is mighty!
And if it is a matter of justice, who can challenge him[d]?
[20] Even if I were innocent, my mouth would condemn me;
if I were blameless, it would pronounce me guilty.

[21] "Although I am blameless,
I have no concern for myself;
I despise my own life.
[22] It is all the same; that is why I say,
'He destroys both the blameless and the wicked.'
[23] When a scourge brings sudden death,
he mocks the despair of the innocent.
[24] When a land falls into the hands of the wicked,
he blindfolds its judges.
If it is not he, then who is it?

[25] "My days are swifter than a runner;
they fly away without a glimpse of joy.
[26] They skim past like boats of papyrus,
like eagles swooping down on their prey.
[27] If I say, 'I will forget my complaint,
I will change my expression, and smile,'
[28] I still dread all my sufferings,
for I know you will not hold me innocent.
[29] Since I am already found guilty,
why should I struggle in vain?
[30] Even if I washed myself with soap
and my hands with cleansing powder,
[31] you would plunge me into a slime pit
so that even my clothes would detest me.

[32] "He is not a mere mortal like me that I might answer him,
that we might confront each other in court.
[33] If only there were someone to mediate between us,
someone to bring us together,
[34] someone to remove God's rod from me,
so that his terror would frighten me no more.
[35] Then I would speak up without fear of him,
but as it now stands with me, I cannot.

[a] 14 The meaning of the Hebrew for this word is uncertain. [b] 19 Or *Surely all the joy it has / is that* [c] 9 Or *of Leo* [d] 19 See Septuagint; Hebrew *me.*

10 "I loathe my very life;
therefore I will give free rein to my complaint
and speak out in the bitterness of my soul.
2 I say to God: Do not declare me guilty,
but tell me what charges you have against me.
3 Does it please you to oppress me,
to spurn the work of your hands,
while you smile on the plans of the wicked?
4 Do you have eyes of flesh?
Do you see as a mortal sees?
5 Are your days like those of a mortal
or your years like those of a strong man,
6 that you must search out my faults
and probe after my sin—
7 though you know that I am not guilty
and that no one can rescue me from your hand?

8 "Your hands shaped me and made me.
Will you now turn and destroy me?
9 Remember that you molded me like clay.
Will you now turn me to dust again?
10 Did you not pour me out like milk
and curdle me like cheese,
11 clothe me with skin and flesh
and knit me together with bones and sinews?
12 You gave me life and showed me kindness,
and in your providence watched over my spirit.

13 "But this is what you concealed in your heart,
and I know that this was in your mind:
14 If I sinned, you would be watching me
and would not let my offense go unpunished.
15 If I am guilty—woe to me!
Even if I am innocent, I cannot lift my head,
for I am full of shame
and drowned in[a] my affliction.
16 If I hold my head high, you stalk me like a lion
and again display your awesome power against me.
17 You bring new witnesses against me
and increase your anger toward me;
your forces come against me wave upon wave.

18 "Why then did you bring me out of the womb?
I wish I had died before any eye saw me.
19 If only I had never come into being,
or had been carried straight from the womb to the grave!
20 Are not my few days almost over?
Turn away from me so I can have a moment's joy
21 before I go to the place of no return,
to the land of gloom and utter darkness,
22 to the land of deepest night,
of utter darkness and disorder,
where even the light is like darkness."

Zophar

11 Then Zophar the Naamathite replied:

2 "Are all these words to go unanswered?
Is this talker to be vindicated?
3 Will your idle talk reduce others to silence?
Will no one rebuke you when you mock?
4 You say to God, 'My beliefs are flawless
and I am pure in your sight.'
5 Oh, how I wish that God would speak,
that he would open his lips against you
6 and disclose to you the secrets of wisdom,
for true wisdom has two sides.
Know this: God has even forgotten some of your sin.

7 "Can you fathom the mysteries of God?
Can you probe the limits of the Almighty?
8 They are higher than the heavens above—what can you do?
They are deeper than the depths below—what can you know?
9 Their measure is longer than the earth
and wider than the sea.

10 "If he comes along and confines you in prison
and convenes a court, who can oppose him?
11 Surely he recognizes deceivers;
and when he sees evil, does he not take note?
12 But the witless can no more become wise
than a wild donkey's colt can be born human.[b]

13 "Yet if you devote your heart to him
and stretch out your hands to him,
14 if you put away the sin that is in your hand
and allow no evil to dwell in your tent,
15 then, free of fault, you will lift up your face;
you will stand firm and without fear.
16 You will surely forget your trouble,
recalling it only as waters gone by.
17 Life will be brighter than noonday,
and darkness will become like morning.
18 You will be secure, because there is hope;
you will look about you and take your rest in safety.
19 You will lie down, with no one to make you afraid,
and many will court your favor.
20 But the eyes of the wicked will fail,
and escape will elude them;
their hope will become a dying gasp."

Job

12 Then Job replied:

2 "Doubtless you are the only people who matter,
and wisdom will die with you!

[a] 15 Or *and aware of* [b] 12 Or *wild donkey can be born tame*

3 But I have a mind as well as you;
I am not inferior to you.
Who does not know all these things?

4 "I have become a laughingstock to my friends,
though I called on God and he answered—
a mere laughingstock, though righteous and blameless!
5 Those who are at ease have contempt for misfortune
as the fate of those whose feet are slipping.
6 The tents of marauders are undisturbed,
and those who provoke God are secure—
those God has in his hand.[a]

7 "But ask the animals, and they will teach you,
or the birds in the sky, and they will tell you;
8 or speak to the earth, and it will teach you,
or let the fish in the sea inform you.
9 Which of all these does not know
that the hand of the LORD has done this?
10 In his hand is the life of every creature
and the breath of all mankind.
11 Does not the ear test words
as the tongue tastes food?
12 Is not wisdom found among the aged?
Does not long life bring understanding?

13 "To God belong wisdom and power;
counsel and understanding are his.
14 What he tears down cannot be rebuilt;
those he imprisons cannot be released.
15 If he holds back the waters, there is drought;
if he lets them loose, they devastate the land.
16 To him belong strength and insight;
both deceived and deceiver are his.
17 He leads rulers away stripped
and makes fools of judges.
18 He takes off the shackles put on by kings
and ties a loincloth[b] around their waist.
19 He leads priests away stripped
and overthrows officials long established.
20 He silences the lips of trusted advisers
and takes away the discernment of elders.
21 He pours contempt on nobles
and disarms the mighty.
22 He reveals the deep things of darkness
and brings utter darkness into the light.
23 He makes nations great, and destroys them;
he enlarges nations, and disperses them.
24 He deprives the leaders of the earth of their reason;
he makes them wander in a trackless waste.
25 They grope in darkness with no light;
he makes them stagger like drunkards.

13 "My eyes have seen all this,
my ears have heard and understood it.
2 What you know, I also know;
I am not inferior to you.
3 But I desire to speak to the Almighty
and to argue my case with God.
4 You, however, smear me with lies;
you are worthless physicians, all of you!
5 If only you would be altogether silent!
For you, that would be wisdom.
6 Hear now my argument;
listen to the pleas of my lips.
7 Will you speak wickedly on God's behalf?
Will you speak deceitfully for him?
8 Will you show him partiality?
Will you argue the case for God?
9 Would it turn out well if he examined you?
Could you deceive him as you might deceive a mortal?
10 He would surely call you to account
if you secretly showed partiality.
11 Would not his splendor terrify you?
Would not the dread of him fall on you?
12 Your maxims are proverbs of ashes;
your defenses are defenses of clay.

13 "Keep silent and let me speak;
then let come to me what may.
14 Why do I put myself in jeopardy
and take my life in my hands?
15 Though he slay me, yet will I hope in him;
I will surely[c] defend my ways to his face.
16 Indeed, this will turn out for my deliverance,
for no godless person would dare come before him!
17 Listen carefully to what I say;
let my words ring in your ears.
18 Now that I have prepared my case,
I know I will be vindicated.
19 Can anyone bring charges against me?
If so, I will be silent and die.

20 "Only grant me these two things, God,
and then I will not hide from you:
21 Withdraw your hand far from me,
and stop frightening me with your terrors.
22 Then summon me and I will answer,
or let me speak, and you reply to me.
23 How many wrongs and sins have I committed?
Show me my offense and my sin.
24 Why do you hide your face
and consider me your enemy?
25 Will you torment a windblown leaf?
Will you chase after dry chaff?
26 For you write down bitter things against me
and make me reap the sins of my youth.
27 You fasten my feet in shackles;
you keep close watch on all my paths
by putting marks on the soles of my feet.

[a] 6 Or *those whose god is in their own hand* [b] 18 Or *shackles of kings / and ties a belt* [c] 15 Or *He will surely slay me; I have no hope — / yet I will*

[28]"So man wastes away like something
rotten,
like a garment eaten by moths.

14 "Mortals, born of woman,
are of few days and full of trouble.
[2]They spring up like flowers and wither
away;
like fleeting shadows, they do not
endure.
[3]Do you fix your eye on them?
Will you bring them[a] before you for
judgment?
[4]Who can bring what is pure from the
impure?
No one!
[5]A person's days are determined;
you have decreed the number of his
months
and have set limits he cannot exceed.
[6]So look away from him and let him alone,
till he has put in his time like a hired
laborer.

[7]"At least there is hope for a tree:
If it is cut down, it will sprout again,
and its new shoots will not fail.
[8]Its roots may grow old in the ground
and its stump die in the soil,
[9]yet at the scent of water it will bud
and put forth shoots like a plant.
[10]But a man dies and is laid low;
he breathes his last and is no more.
[11]As the water of a lake dries up
or a riverbed becomes parched and dry,
[12]so he lies down and does not rise;
till the heavens are no more, people will
not awake
or be roused from their sleep.

[13]"If only you would hide me in the grave
and conceal me till your anger has
passed!
If only you would set me a time
and then remember me!
[14]If someone dies, will they live again?
All the days of my hard service
I will wait for my renewal[b] to come.
[15]You will call and I will answer you;
you will long for the creature your
hands have made.
[16]Surely then you will count my steps
but not keep track of my sin.
[17]My offenses will be sealed up in a bag;
you will cover over my sin.

[18]"But as a mountain erodes and crumbles
and as a rock is moved from its place,
[19]as water wears away stones
and torrents wash away the soil,
so you destroy a person's hope.
[20]You overpower them once for all, and
they are gone;
you change their countenance and send
them away.
[21]If their children are honored, they do not
know it;
if their offspring are brought low, they
do not see it.
[22]They feel but the pain of their own bodies
and mourn only for themselves."

Eliphaz

15 Then Eliphaz the Temanite replied:
[2]"Would a wise person answer with empty
notions
or fill their belly with the hot east wind?
[3]Would they argue with useless words,
with speeches that have no value?
[4]But you even undermine piety
and hinder devotion to God.
[5]Your sin prompts your mouth;
you adopt the tongue of the crafty.
[6]Your own mouth condemns you, not
mine;
your own lips testify against you.

[7]"Are you the first man ever born?
Were you brought forth before the
hills?
[8]Do you listen in on God's council?
Do you have a monopoly on wisdom?
[9]What do you know that we do not know?
What insights do you have that we do
not have?
[10]The gray-haired and the aged are on our
side,
men even older than your father.
[11]Are God's consolations not enough for
you,
words spoken gently to you?
[12]Why has your heart carried you away,
and why do your eyes flash,
[13]so that you vent your rage against God
and pour out such words from your
mouth?

[14]"What are mortals, that they could be
pure,
or those born of woman, that they could
be righteous?
[15]If God places no trust in his holy ones,
if even the heavens are not pure in his
eyes,
[16]how much less mortals, who are vile and
corrupt,
who drink up evil like water!

[17]"Listen to me and I will explain to you;
let me tell you what I have seen,
[18]what the wise have declared,
hiding nothing received from their
ancestors
[19](to whom alone the land was given
when no foreigners moved among
them):
[20]All his days the wicked man suffers
torment,
the ruthless man through all the years
stored up for him.
[21]Terrifying sounds fill his ears;
when all seems well, marauders attack
him.
[22]He despairs of escaping the realm of
darkness;
he is marked for the sword.

[a] *3* Septuagint, Vulgate and Syriac; Hebrew *me*
[b] *14* Or *release*

23 He wanders about for food like a vulture;
he knows the day of darkness is at hand.
24 Distress and anguish fill him with terror;
troubles overwhelm him, like a king poised to attack,
25 because he shakes his fist at God
and vaunts himself against the Almighty,
26 defiantly charging against him
with a thick, strong shield.

27 "Though his face is covered with fat
and his waist bulges with flesh,
28 he will inhabit ruined towns
and houses where no one lives,
houses crumbling to rubble.
29 He will no longer be rich and his wealth will not endure,
nor will his possessions spread over the land.
30 He will not escape the darkness;
a flame will wither his shoots,
and the breath of God's mouth will carry him away.
31 Let him not deceive himself by trusting what is worthless,
for he will get nothing in return.
32 Before his time he will wither,
and his branches will not flourish.
33 He will be like a vine stripped of its unripe grapes,
like an olive tree shedding its blossoms.
34 For the company of the godless will be barren,
and fire will consume the tents of those who love bribes.
35 They conceive trouble and give birth to evil;
their womb fashions deceit."

Job

16 Then Job replied:

2 "I have heard many things like these;
you are miserable comforters, all of you!
3 Will your long-winded speeches never end?
What ails you that you keep on arguing?
4 I also could speak like you,
if you were in my place;
I could make fine speeches against you
and shake my head at you.
5 But my mouth would encourage you;
comfort from my lips would bring you relief.

6 "Yet if I speak, my pain is not relieved;
and if I refrain, it does not go away.
7 Surely, God, you have worn me out;
you have devastated my entire household.
8 You have shriveled me up—and it has become a witness;
my gauntness rises up and testifies against me.
9 God assails me and tears me in his anger
and gnashes his teeth at me;
my opponent fastens on me his piercing eyes.
10 People open their mouths to jeer at me;
they strike my cheek in scorn
and unite together against me.
11 God has turned me over to the ungodly
and thrown me into the clutches of the wicked.
12 All was well with me, but he shattered me;
he seized me by the neck and crushed me.
He has made me his target;
13 his archers surround me.
Without pity, he pierces my kidneys
and spills my gall on the ground.
14 Again and again he bursts upon me;
he rushes at me like a warrior.

15 "I have sewed sackcloth over my skin
and buried my brow in the dust.
16 My face is red with weeping,
dark shadows ring my eyes;
17 yet my hands have been free of violence
and my prayer is pure.

18 "Earth, do not cover my blood;
may my cry never be laid to rest!
19 Even now my witness is in heaven;
my advocate is on high.
20 My intercessor is my friend[a]
as my eyes pour out tears to God;
21 on behalf of a man he pleads with God
as one pleads for a friend.

22 "Only a few years will pass
before I take the path of no return.

17 1 My spirit is broken,
my days are cut short,
the grave awaits me.
2 Surely mockers surround me;
my eyes must dwell on their hostility.

3 "Give me, O God, the pledge you demand.
Who else will put up security for me?
4 You have closed their minds to understanding;
therefore you will not let them triumph.
5 If anyone denounces their friends for reward,
the eyes of their children will fail.

6 "God has made me a byword to everyone,
a man in whose face people spit.
7 My eyes have grown dim with grief;
my whole frame is but a shadow.
8 The upright are appalled at this;
the innocent are aroused against the ungodly.
9 Nevertheless, the righteous will hold to their ways,
and those with clean hands will grow stronger.

10 "But come on, all of you, try again!
I will not find a wise man among you.
11 My days have passed, my plans are shattered.
Yet the desires of my heart

[a] 20 Or *My friends treat me with scorn*

[12]turn night into day;
in the face of the darkness light is near.
[13]If the only home I hope for is the grave,
if I spread out my bed in the realm of darkness,
[14]if I say to corruption, 'You are my father,'
and to the worm, 'My mother' or 'My sister,'
[15]where then is my hope—
who can see any hope for me?
[16]Will it go down to the gates of death?
Will we descend together into the dust?"

Bildad

18 Then Bildad the Shuhite replied:

[2]"When will you end these speeches?
Be sensible, and then we can talk.
[3]Why are we regarded as cattle
and considered stupid in your sight?
[4]You who tear yourself to pieces in your anger,
is the earth to be abandoned for your sake?
Or must the rocks be moved from their place?

[5]"The lamp of a wicked man is snuffed out;
the flame of his fire stops burning.
[6]The light in his tent becomes dark;
the lamp beside him goes out.
[7]The vigor of his step is weakened;
his own schemes throw him down.
[8]His feet thrust him into a net;
he wanders into its mesh.
[9]A trap seizes him by the heel;
a snare holds him fast.
[10]A noose is hidden for him on the ground;
a trap lies in his path.
[11]Terrors startle him on every side
and dog his every step.
[12]Calamity is hungry for him;
disaster is ready for him when he falls.
[13]It eats away parts of his skin;
death's firstborn devours his limbs.
[14]He is torn from the security of his tent
and marched off to the king of terrors.
[15]Fire resides[a] in his tent;
burning sulfur is scattered over his dwelling.
[16]His roots dry up below
and his branches wither above.
[17]The memory of him perishes from the earth;
he has no name in the land.
[18]He is driven from light into the realm of darkness
and is banished from the world.
[19]He has no offspring or descendants among his people,
no survivor where once he lived.
[20]People of the west are appalled at his fate;
those of the east are seized with horror.
[21]Surely such is the dwelling of an evil man;
such is the place of one who does not know God."

Job

19 Then Job replied:

[2]"How long will you torment me
and crush me with words?
[3]Ten times now you have reproached me;
shamelessly you attack me.
[4]If it is true that I have gone astray,
my error remains my concern alone.
[5]If indeed you would exalt yourselves above me
and use my humiliation against me,
[6]then know that God has wronged me
and drawn his net around me.

[7]"Though I cry, 'Violence!' I get no response;
though I call for help, there is no justice.
[8]He has blocked my way so I cannot pass;
he has shrouded my paths in darkness.
[9]He has stripped me of my honor
and removed the crown from my head.
[10]He tears me down on every side till I am gone;
he uproots my hope like a tree.
[11]His anger burns against me;
he counts me among his enemies.
[12]His troops advance in force;
they build a siege ramp against me
and encamp around my tent.

[13]"He has alienated my family from me;
my acquaintances are completely estranged from me.
[14]My relatives have gone away;
my closest friends have forgotten me.
[15]My guests and my female servants count me a foreigner;
they look on me as on a stranger.
[16]I summon my servant, but he does not answer,
though I beg him with my own mouth.
[17]My breath is offensive to my wife;
I am loathsome to my own family.
[18]Even the little boys scorn me;
when I appear, they ridicule me.
[19]All my intimate friends detest me;
those I love have turned against me.
[20]I am nothing but skin and bones;
I have escaped only by the skin of my teeth.[b]

[21]"Have pity on me, my friends, have pity,
for the hand of God has struck me.
[22]Why do you pursue me as God does?
Will you never get enough of my flesh?

[23]"Oh, that my words were recorded,
that they were written on a scroll,
[24]that they were inscribed with an iron tool on[c] lead,
or engraved in rock forever!
[25]I know that my redeemer[d] lives,
and that in the end he will stand on the earth.[e]
[26]And after my skin has been destroyed,
yet[f] in[g] my flesh I will see God;

[a] 15 Or *Nothing he had remains* [b] 20 Or *only by my gums* [c] 24 Or *and* [d] 25 Or *vindicator*
[e] 25 Or *on my grave* [f] 26 Or *And after I awake, / though this body has been destroyed, / then*
[g] 26 Or *destroyed, / apart from*

27 I myself will see him
with my own eyes—I, and not another.
How my heart yearns within me!

28 "If you say, 'How we will hound him,
since the root of the trouble lies in him,[a]'
29 you should fear the sword yourselves;
for wrath will bring punishment by the sword,
and then you will know that there is judgment.[b]"

Zophar

20

Then Zophar the Naamathite replied:

2 "My troubled thoughts prompt me to answer
because I am greatly disturbed.
3 I hear a rebuke that dishonors me,
and my understanding inspires me to reply.

4 "Surely you know how it has been from of old,
ever since mankind[c] was placed on the earth,
5 that the mirth of the wicked is brief,
the joy of the godless lasts but a moment.
6 Though the pride of the godless person reaches to the heavens
and his head touches the clouds,
7 he will perish forever, like his own dung;
those who have seen him will say, 'Where is he?'
8 Like a dream he flies away, no more to be found,
banished like a vision of the night.
9 The eye that saw him will not see him again;
his place will look on him no more.
10 His children must make amends to the poor;
his own hands must give back his wealth.
11 The youthful vigor that fills his bones
will lie with him in the dust.

12 "Though evil is sweet in his mouth
and he hides it under his tongue,
13 though he cannot bear to let it go
and lets it linger in his mouth,
14 yet his food will turn sour in his stomach;
it will become the venom of serpents within him.
15 He will spit out the riches he swallowed;
God will make his stomach vomit them up.
16 He will suck the poison of serpents;
the fangs of an adder will kill him.
17 He will not enjoy the streams,
the rivers flowing with honey and cream.
18 What he toiled for he must give back uneaten;
he will not enjoy the profit from his trading.
19 For he has oppressed the poor and left them destitute;
he has seized houses he did not build.

20 "Surely he will have no respite from his craving;
he cannot save himself by his treasure.
21 Nothing is left for him to devour;
his prosperity will not endure.
22 In the midst of his plenty, distress will overtake him;
the full force of misery will come upon him.
23 When he has filled his belly,
God will vent his burning anger against him
and rain down his blows on him.
24 Though he flees from an iron weapon,
a bronze-tipped arrow pierces him.
25 He pulls it out of his back,
the gleaming point out of his liver.
Terrors will come over him;
26 total darkness lies in wait for his treasures.
A fire unfanned will consume him
and devour what is left in his tent.
27 The heavens will expose his guilt;
the earth will rise up against him.
28 A flood will carry off his house,
rushing waters[d] on the day of God's wrath.
29 Such is the fate God allots the wicked,
the heritage appointed for them by God."

Job

21

Then Job replied:

2 "Listen carefully to my words;
let this be the consolation you give me.
3 Bear with me while I speak,
and after I have spoken, mock on.

4 "Is my complaint directed to a human being?
Why should I not be impatient?
5 Look at me and be appalled;
clap your hand over your mouth.
6 When I think about this, I am terrified;
trembling seizes my body.
7 Why do the wicked live on,
growing old and increasing in power?
8 They see their children established around them,
their offspring before their eyes.
9 Their homes are safe and free from fear;
the rod of God is not on them.
10 Their bulls never fail to breed;
their cows calve and do not miscarry.
11 They send forth their children as a flock;
their little ones dance about.
12 They sing to the music of timbrel and lyre;
they make merry to the sound of the pipe.
13 They spend their years in prosperity
and go down to the grave in peace.[e]

[a] 28 Many Hebrew manuscripts, Septuagint and Vulgate; most Hebrew manuscripts *me*
[b] 29 Or *sword, / that you may come to know the Almighty*
[c] 4 Or *Adam*
[d] 28 Or *The possessions in his house will be carried off, / washed away*
[e] 13 Or *in an instant*

14 Yet they say to God, 'Leave us alone!
We have no desire to know your ways.
15 Who is the Almighty, that we should serve him?
What would we gain by praying to him?'
16 But their prosperity is not in their own hands,
so I stand aloof from the plans of the wicked.

17 "Yet how often is the lamp of the wicked snuffed out?
How often does calamity come upon them,
the fate God allots in his anger?
18 How often are they like straw before the wind,
like chaff swept away by a gale?
19 It is said, 'God stores up the punishment of the wicked for their children.'
Let him repay the wicked, so that they themselves will experience it!
20 Let their own eyes see their destruction;
let them drink the cup of the wrath of the Almighty.
21 For what do they care about the families they leave behind
when their allotted months come to an end?

22 "Can anyone teach knowledge to God,
since he judges even the highest?
23 One person dies in full vigor,
completely secure and at ease,
24 well nourished in body,[a]
bones rich with marrow.
25 Another dies in bitterness of soul,
never having enjoyed anything good.
26 Side by side they lie in the dust,
and worms cover them both.

27 "I know full well what you are thinking,
the schemes by which you would wrong me.
28 You say, 'Where now is the house of the great,
the tents where the wicked lived?'
29 Have you never questioned those who travel?
Have you paid no regard to their accounts—
30 that the wicked are spared from the day of calamity,
that they are delivered from[b] the day of wrath?
31 Who denounces their conduct to their face?
Who repays them for what they have done?
32 They are carried to the grave,
and watch is kept over their tombs.
33 The soil in the valley is sweet to them;
everyone follows after them,
and a countless throng goes[c] before them.

34 "So how can you console me with your nonsense?
Nothing is left of your answers but falsehood!"

Eliphaz

22 Then Eliphaz the Temanite replied:

2 "Can a man be of benefit to God?
Can even a wise person benefit him?
3 What pleasure would it give the Almighty if you were righteous?
What would he gain if your ways were blameless?

4 "Is it for your piety that he rebukes you
and brings charges against you?
5 Is not your wickedness great?
Are not your sins endless?
6 You demanded security from your relatives for no reason;
you stripped people of their clothing, leaving them naked.
7 You gave no water to the weary
and you withheld food from the hungry,
8 though you were a powerful man, owning land—
an honored man, living on it.
9 And you sent widows away empty-handed
and broke the strength of the fatherless.
10 That is why snares are all around you,
why sudden peril terrifies you,
11 why it is so dark you cannot see,
and why a flood of water covers you.

12 "Is not God in the heights of heaven?
And see how lofty are the highest stars!
13 Yet you say, 'What does God know?
Does he judge through such darkness?
14 Thick clouds veil him, so he does not see us
as he goes about in the vaulted heavens.'
15 Will you keep to the old path
that the wicked have trod?
16 They were carried off before their time,
their foundations washed away by a flood.
17 They said to God, 'Leave us alone!
What can the Almighty do to us?'
18 Yet it was he who filled their houses with good things,
so I stand aloof from the plans of the wicked.
19 The righteous see their ruin and rejoice;
the innocent mock them, saying,
20 'Surely our foes are destroyed,
and fire devours their wealth.'

21 "Submit to God and be at peace with him;
in this way prosperity will come to you.
22 Accept instruction from his mouth
and lay up his words in your heart.
23 If you return to the Almighty, you will be restored:
If you remove wickedness far from your tent
24 and assign your nuggets to the dust,
your gold of Ophir to the rocks in the ravines,

[a] 24 The meaning of the Hebrew for this word is uncertain. [b] 30 Or *wicked are reserved for the day of calamity, / that they are brought forth to* [c] 33 Or *them, / as a countless throng went*

25 then the Almighty will be your gold,
the choicest silver for you.
26 Surely then you will find delight in the Almighty
and will lift up your face to God.
27 You will pray to him, and he will hear you,
and you will fulfill your vows.
28 What you decide on will be done,
and light will shine on your ways.
29 When people are brought low and you say, 'Lift them up!'
then he will save the downcast.
30 He will deliver even one who is not innocent,
who will be delivered through the cleanness of your hands."

Job

23 Then Job replied:

2 "Even today my complaint is bitter;
his hand[a] is heavy in spite of[b] my groaning.
3 If only I knew where to find him;
if only I could go to his dwelling!
4 I would state my case before him
and fill my mouth with arguments.
5 I would find out what he would answer me,
and consider what he would say to me.
6 Would he vigorously oppose me?
No, he would not press charges against me.
7 There the upright can establish their innocence before him,
and there I would be delivered forever from my judge.

8 "But if I go to the east, he is not there;
if I go to the west, I do not find him.
9 When he is at work in the north, I do not see him;
when he turns to the south, I catch no glimpse of him.
10 But he knows the way that I take;
when he has tested me, I will come forth as gold.
11 My feet have closely followed his steps;
I have kept to his way without turning aside.
12 I have not departed from the commands of his lips;
I have treasured the words of his mouth more than my daily bread.

13 "But he stands alone, and who can oppose him?
He does whatever he pleases.
14 He carries out his decree against me,
and many such plans he still has in store.
15 That is why I am terrified before him;
when I think of all this, I fear him.
16 God has made my heart faint;
the Almighty has terrified me.
17 Yet I am not silenced by the darkness,
by the thick darkness that covers my face.

24 "Why does the Almighty not set times for judgment?
Why must those who know him look in vain for such days?
2 There are those who move boundary stones;
they pasture flocks they have stolen.
3 They drive away the orphan's donkey
and take the widow's ox in pledge.
4 They thrust the needy from the path
and force all the poor of the land into hiding.
5 Like wild donkeys in the desert,
the poor go about their labor of foraging food;
the wasteland provides food for their children.
6 They gather fodder in the fields
and glean in the vineyards of the wicked.
7 Lacking clothes, they spend the night naked;
they have nothing to cover themselves in the cold.
8 They are drenched by mountain rains
and hug the rocks for lack of shelter.
9 The fatherless child is snatched from the breast;
the infant of the poor is seized for a debt.
10 Lacking clothes, they go about naked;
they carry the sheaves, but still go hungry.
11 They crush olives among the terraces[c];
they tread the winepresses, yet suffer thirst.
12 The groans of the dying rise from the city,
and the souls of the wounded cry out for help.
But God charges no one with wrongdoing.

13 "There are those who rebel against the light,
who do not know its ways
or stay in its paths.
14 When daylight is gone, the murderer rises up,
kills the poor and needy,
and in the night steals forth like a thief.
15 The eye of the adulterer watches for dusk;
he thinks, 'No eye will see me,'
and he keeps his face concealed.
16 In the dark, thieves break into houses,
but by day they shut themselves in;
they want nothing to do with the light.
17 For all of them, midnight is their morning;
they make friends with the terrors of darkness.

18 "Yet they are foam on the surface of the water;
their portion of the land is cursed,
so that no one goes to the vineyards.

[a] 2 Septuagint and Syriac; Hebrew / *the hand on me* [b] 2 Or *heavy on me in* [c] 11 The meaning of the Hebrew for this word is uncertain.

19 As heat and drought snatch away the
melted snow,
so the grave snatches away those who
have sinned.
20 The womb forgets them,
the worm feasts on them;
the wicked are no longer remembered
but are broken like a tree.
21 They prey on the barren and childless
woman,
and to the widow they show no
kindness.
22 But God drags away the mighty by his
power;
though they become established, they
have no assurance of life.
23 He may let them rest in a feeling of
security,
but his eyes are on their ways.
24 For a little while they are exalted, and
then they are gone;
they are brought low and gathered up
like all others;
they are cut off like heads of grain.

25 "If this is not so, who can prove me false
and reduce my words to nothing?"

Bildad

25 Then Bildad the Shuhite replied:

2 "Dominion and awe belong to God;
he establishes order in the heights of
heaven.
3 Can his forces be numbered?
On whom does his light not rise?
4 How then can a mortal be righteous
before God?
How can one born of woman be pure?
5 If even the moon is not bright
and the stars are not pure in his eyes,
6 how much less a mortal, who is but a
maggot—
a human being, who is only a worm!"

Job

26 Then Job replied:

2 "How you have helped the powerless!
How you have saved the arm that is
feeble!
3 What advice you have offered to one
without wisdom!
And what great insight you have
displayed!
4 Who has helped you utter these words?
And whose spirit spoke from your
mouth?

5 "The dead are in deep anguish,
those beneath the waters and all that
live in them.
6 The realm of the dead is naked before God;
Destruction[a] lies uncovered.
7 He spreads out the northern skies over
empty space;
he suspends the earth over nothing.
8 He wraps up the waters in his clouds,
yet the clouds do not burst under their
weight.
9 He covers the face of the full moon,
spreading his clouds over it.
10 He marks out the horizon on the face of
the waters
for a boundary between light and
darkness.
11 The pillars of the heavens quake,
aghast at his rebuke.
12 By his power he churned up the sea;
by his wisdom he cut Rahab to pieces.
13 By his breath the skies became fair;
his hand pierced the gliding serpent.
14 And these are but the outer fringe of his
works;
how faint the whisper we hear of him!
Who then can understand the thunder
of his power?"

Job's Final Word to His Friends

27 And Job continued his discourse:

2 "As surely as God lives, who has denied
me justice,
the Almighty, who has made my life
bitter,
3 as long as I have life within me,
the breath of God in my nostrils,
4 my lips will not say anything wicked,
and my tongue will not utter lies.
5 I will never admit you are in the right;
till I die, I will not deny my integrity.
6 I will maintain my innocence and never
let go of it;
my conscience will not reproach me as
long as I live.

7 "May my enemy be like the wicked,
my adversary like the unjust!
8 For what hope have the godless when
they are cut off,
when God takes away their life?
9 Does God listen to their cry
when distress comes upon them?
10 Will they find delight in the Almighty?
Will they call on God at all times?

11 "I will teach you about the power of God;
the ways of the Almighty I will not
conceal.
12 You have all seen this yourselves.
Why then this meaningless talk?

13 "Here is the fate God allots to the wicked,
the heritage a ruthless man receives
from the Almighty:
14 However many his children, their fate is
the sword;
his offspring will never have enough to
eat.
15 The plague will bury those who survive
him,
and their widows will not weep for
them.
16 Though he heaps up silver like dust
and clothes like piles of clay,

[a] 6 Hebrew *Abaddon*

17 what he lays up the righteous will wear,
and the innocent will divide his silver.
18 The house he builds is like a moth's cocoon,
like a hut made by a watchman.
19 He lies down wealthy, but will do so no more;
when he opens his eyes, all is gone.
20 Terrors overtake him like a flood;
a tempest snatches him away in the night.
21 The east wind carries him off, and he is gone;
it sweeps him out of his place.
22 It hurls itself against him without mercy
as he flees headlong from its power.
23 It claps its hands in derision
and hisses him out of his place."

Interlude: Where Wisdom Is Found

28 There is a mine for silver
and a place where gold is refined.
2 Iron is taken from the earth,
and copper is smelted from ore.
3 Mortals put an end to the darkness;
they search out the farthest recesses
for ore in the blackest darkness.
4 Far from human dwellings they cut a shaft,
in places untouched by human feet;
far from other people they dangle and sway.
5 The earth, from which food comes,
is transformed below as by fire;
6 lapis lazuli comes from its rocks,
and its dust contains nuggets of gold.
7 No bird of prey knows that hidden path,
no falcon's eye has seen it.
8 Proud beasts do not set foot on it,
and no lion prowls there.
9 People assault the flinty rock with their hands
and lay bare the roots of the mountains.
10 They tunnel through the rock;
their eyes see all its treasures.
11 They search[a] the sources of the rivers
and bring hidden things to light.

12 But where can wisdom be found?
Where does understanding dwell?
13 No mortal comprehends its worth;
it cannot be found in the land of the living.
14 The deep says, "It is not in me";
the sea says, "It is not with me."
15 It cannot be bought with the finest gold,
nor can its price be weighed out in silver.
16 It cannot be bought with the gold of Ophir,
with precious onyx or lapis lazuli.
17 Neither gold nor crystal can compare with it,
nor can it be had for jewels of gold.
18 Coral and jasper are not worthy of mention;
the price of wisdom is beyond rubies.
19 The topaz of Cush cannot compare with it;
it cannot be bought with pure gold.

20 Where then does wisdom come from?
Where does understanding dwell?
21 It is hidden from the eyes of every living thing,
concealed even from the birds in the sky.
22 Destruction[b] and Death say,
"Only a rumor of it has reached our ears."
23 God understands the way to it
and he alone knows where it dwells,
24 for he views the ends of the earth
and sees everything under the heavens.
25 When he established the force of the wind
and measured out the waters,
26 when he made a decree for the rain
and a path for the thunderstorm,
27 then he looked at wisdom and appraised it;
he confirmed it and tested it.
28 And he said to the human race,
"The fear of the Lord—that is wisdom,
and to shun evil is understanding."

Job's Final Defense

29 Job continued his discourse:

2 "How I long for the months gone by,
for the days when God watched over me,
3 when his lamp shone on my head
and by his light I walked through darkness!
4 Oh, for the days when I was in my prime,
when God's intimate friendship blessed my house,
5 when the Almighty was still with me
and my children were around me,
6 when my path was drenched with cream
and the rock poured out for me streams of olive oil.

7 "When I went to the gate of the city
and took my seat in the public square,
8 the young men saw me and stepped aside
and the old men rose to their feet;
9 the chief men refrained from speaking
and covered their mouths with their hands;
10 the voices of the nobles were hushed,
and their tongues stuck to the roof of their mouths.
11 Whoever heard me spoke well of me,
and those who saw me commended me,
12 because I rescued the poor who cried for help,
and the fatherless who had none to assist them.
13 The one who was dying blessed me;
I made the widow's heart sing.
14 I put on righteousness as my clothing;
justice was my robe and my turban.
15 I was eyes to the blind
and feet to the lame.

[a] 11 Septuagint, Aquila and Vulgate; Hebrew *They dam up* [b] 22 Hebrew *Abaddon*

16 I was a father to the needy;
I took up the case of the stranger.
17 I broke the fangs of the wicked
and snatched the victims from their teeth.

18 "I thought, 'I will die in my own house,
my days as numerous as the grains of sand.
19 My roots will reach to the water,
and the dew will lie all night on my branches.
20 My glory will not fade;
the bow will be ever new in my hand.'

21 "People listened to me expectantly,
waiting in silence for my counsel.
22 After I had spoken, they spoke no more;
my words fell gently on their ears.
23 They waited for me as for showers
and drank in my words as the spring rain.
24 When I smiled at them, they scarcely believed it;
the light of my face was precious to them.[a]
25 I chose the way for them and sat as their chief;
I dwelt as a king among his troops;
I was like one who comforts mourners.

30 "But now they mock me,
men younger than I,
whose fathers I would have disdained
to put with my sheep dogs.
2 Of what use was the strength of their hands to me,
since their vigor had gone from them?
3 Haggard from want and hunger,
they roamed[b] the parched land
in desolate wastelands at night.
4 In the brush they gathered salt herbs,
and their food[c] was the root of the broom bush.
5 They were banished from human society,
shouted at as if they were thieves.
6 They were forced to live in the dry stream beds,
among the rocks and in holes in the ground.
7 They brayed among the bushes
and huddled in the undergrowth.
8 A base and nameless brood,
they were driven out of the land.

9 "And now those young men mock me in song;
I have become a byword among them.
10 They detest me and keep their distance;
they do not hesitate to spit in my face.
11 Now that God has unstrung my bow and afflicted me,
they throw off restraint in my presence.
12 On my right the tribe[d] attacks;
they lay snares for my feet,
they build their siege ramps against me.
13 They break up my road;
they succeed in destroying me.
'No one can help him,' they say.
14 They advance as through a gaping breach;
amid the ruins they come rolling in.
15 Terrors overwhelm me;
my dignity is driven away as by the wind,
my safety vanishes like a cloud.

16 "And now my life ebbs away;
days of suffering grip me.
17 Night pierces my bones;
my gnawing pains never rest.
18 In his great power God becomes like clothing to me[e];
he binds me like the neck of my garment.
19 He throws me into the mud,
and I am reduced to dust and ashes.

20 "I cry out to you, God, but you do not answer;
I stand up, but you merely look at me.
21 You turn on me ruthlessly;
with the might of your hand you attack me.
22 You snatch me up and drive me before the wind;
you toss me about in the storm.
23 I know you will bring me down to death,
to the place appointed for all the living.

24 "Surely no one lays a hand on a broken man
when he cries for help in his distress.
25 Have I not wept for those in trouble?
Has not my soul grieved for the poor?
26 Yet when I hoped for good, evil came;
when I looked for light, then came darkness.
27 The churning inside me never stops;
days of suffering confront me.
28 I go about blackened, but not by the sun;
I stand up in the assembly and cry for help.
29 I have become a brother of jackals,
a companion of owls.
30 My skin grows black and peels;
my body burns with fever.
31 My lyre is tuned to mourning,
and my pipe to the sound of wailing.

31 "I made a covenant with my eyes
not to look lustfully at a young woman.
2 For what is our lot from God above,
our heritage from the Almighty on high?
3 Is it not ruin for the wicked,
disaster for those who do wrong?
4 Does he not see my ways
and count my every step?

5 "If I have walked with falsehood
or my foot has hurried after deceit—
6 let God weigh me in honest scales
and he will know that I am blameless—

[a] *24* The meaning of the Hebrew for this clause is uncertain. [b] *3* Or *gnawed* [c] *4* Or *fuel*
[d] *12* The meaning of the Hebrew for this word is uncertain. [e] *18* Hebrew; Septuagint *power he grasps my clothing*

7 if my steps have turned from the path,
if my heart has been led by my eyes,
or if my hands have been defiled,
8 then may others eat what I have sown,
and may my crops be uprooted.

9 "If my heart has been enticed by a
woman,
or if I have lurked at my neighbor's
door,
10 then may my wife grind another man's
grain,
and may other men sleep with her.
11 For that would have been wicked,
a sin to be judged.
12 It is a fire that burns to Destruction[a];
it would have uprooted my harvest.

13 "If I have denied justice to any of my
servants,
whether male or female,
when they had a grievance against me,
14 what will I do when God confronts me?
What will I answer when called to
account?
15 Did not he who made me in the womb
make them?
Did not the same one form us both
within our mothers?

16 "If I have denied the desires of the poor
or let the eyes of the widow grow
weary,
17 if I have kept my bread to myself,
not sharing it with the fatherless—
18 but from my youth I reared them as a
father would,
and from my birth I guided the
widow—
19 if I have seen anyone perishing for lack of
clothing,
or the needy without garments,
20 and their hearts did not bless me
for warming them with the fleece from
my sheep,
21 if I have raised my hand against the
fatherless,
knowing that I had influence in court,
22 then let my arm fall from the shoulder,
let it be broken off at the joint.
23 For I dreaded destruction from God,
and for fear of his splendor I could not
do such things.

24 "If I have put my trust in gold
or said to pure gold, 'You are my
security,'
25 if I have rejoiced over my great wealth,
the fortune my hands had gained,
26 if I have regarded the sun in its radiance
or the moon moving in splendor,
27 so that my heart was secretly enticed
and my hand offered them a kiss of
homage,
28 then these also would be sins to be
judged,
for I would have been unfaithful to God
on high.

29 "If I have rejoiced at my enemy's
misfortune
or gloated over the trouble that came to
him—
30 I have not allowed my mouth to sin
by invoking a curse against their life—
31 if those of my household have never said,
'Who has not been filled with Job's
meat?'—
32 but no stranger had to spend the night in
the street,
for my door was always open to the
traveler—
33 if I have concealed my sin as people do,[b]
by hiding my guilt in my heart
34 because I so feared the crowd
and so dreaded the contempt of the clans
that I kept silent and would not go
outside—

35 ("Oh, that I had someone to hear me!
I sign now my defense—let the
Almighty answer me;
let my accuser put his indictment in
writing.
36 Surely I would wear it on my shoulder,
I would put it on like a crown.
37 I would give him an account of my every
step;
I would present it to him as to a ruler.)—

38 "if my land cries out against me
and all its furrows are wet with tears,
39 if I have devoured its yield without
payment
or broken the spirit of its tenants,
40 then let briers come up instead of wheat
and stinkweed instead of barley."

The words of Job are ended.

Elihu

32 So these three men stopped answering Job, because he was righteous in
his own eyes. 2 But Elihu son of Barakel the
Buzite, of the family of Ram, became very
angry with Job for justifying himself rather
than God. 3 He was also angry with the three
friends, because they had found no way to refute Job, and yet had condemned him.[c] 4 Now
Elihu had waited before speaking to Job because they were older than he. 5 But when he
saw that the three men had nothing more to
say, his anger was aroused.
6 So Elihu son of Barakel the Buzite said:

"I am young in years,
and you are old;
that is why I was fearful,
not daring to tell you what I know.
7 I thought, 'Age should speak;
advanced years should teach wisdom.'
8 But it is the spirit[d] in a person,
the breath of the Almighty, that gives
them understanding.
9 It is not only the old[e] who are wise,
not only the aged who understand what
is right.

[a] 12 Hebrew *Abaddon* [b] 33 Or *as Adam did* [c] 3 Masoretic Text; an ancient Hebrew scribal tradition *Job, and so had condemned God* [d] 8 Or *Spirit*; also in verse 18 [e] 9 Or *many*; or *great*

10 "Therefore I say: Listen to me;
I too will tell you what I know.
11 I waited while you spoke,
I listened to your reasoning;
while you were searching for words,
12 I gave you my full attention.
But not one of you has proved Job wrong;
none of you has answered his arguments.
13 Do not say, 'We have found wisdom;
let God, not a man, refute him.'
14 But Job has not marshaled his words against me,
and I will not answer him with your arguments.

15 "They are dismayed and have no more to say;
words have failed them.
16 Must I wait, now that they are silent,
now that they stand there with no reply?
17 I too will have my say;
I too will tell what I know.
18 For I am full of words,
and the spirit within me compels me;
19 inside I am like bottled-up wine,
like new wineskins ready to burst.
20 I must speak and find relief;
I must open my lips and reply.
21 I will show no partiality,
nor will I flatter anyone;
22 for if I were skilled in flattery,
my Maker would soon take me away.

33 "But now, Job, listen to my words;
pay attention to everything I say.
2 I am about to open my mouth;
my words are on the tip of my tongue.
3 My words come from an upright heart;
my lips sincerely speak what I know.
4 The Spirit of God has made me;
the breath of the Almighty gives me life.
5 Answer me then, if you can;
stand up and argue your case before me.
6 I am the same as you in God's sight;
I too am a piece of clay.
7 No fear of me should alarm you,
nor should my hand be heavy on you.

8 "But you have said in my hearing—
I heard the very words—
9 'I am pure, I have done no wrong;
I am clean and free from sin.
10 Yet God has found fault with me;
he considers me his enemy.
11 He fastens my feet in shackles;
he keeps close watch on all my paths.'

12 "But I tell you, in this you are not right,
for God is greater than any mortal.
13 Why do you complain to him
that he responds to no one's words[a]?
14 For God does speak—now one way, now another—
though no one perceives it.
15 In a dream, in a vision of the night,
when deep sleep falls on people
as they slumber in their beds,
16 he may speak in their ears
and terrify them with warnings,
17 to turn them from wrongdoing
and keep them from pride,
18 to preserve them from the pit,
their lives from perishing by the sword.[b]

19 "Or someone may be chastened on a bed of pain
with constant distress in their bones,
20 so that their body finds food repulsive
and their soul loathes the choicest meal.
21 Their flesh wastes away to nothing,
and their bones, once hidden, now stick out.
22 They draw near to the pit,
and their life to the messengers of death.[c]
23 Yet if there is an angel at their side,
a messenger, one out of a thousand,
sent to tell them how to be upright,
24 and he is gracious to that person and says to God,
'Spare them from going down to the pit;
I have found a ransom for them—
25 let their flesh be renewed like a child's;
let them be restored as in the days of their youth'—
26 then that person can pray to God and find favor with him,
they will see God's face and shout for joy;
he will restore them to full well-being.
27 And they will go to others and say,
'I have sinned, I have perverted what is right,
but I did not get what I deserved.
28 God has delivered me from going down to the pit,
and I shall live to enjoy the light of life.'

29 "God does all these things to a person—
twice, even three times—
30 to turn them back from the pit,
that the light of life may shine on them.

31 "Pay attention, Job, and listen to me;
be silent, and I will speak.
32 If you have anything to say, answer me;
speak up, for I want to vindicate you.
33 But if not, then listen to me;
be silent, and I will teach you wisdom."

34 Then Elihu said:

2 "Hear my words, you wise men;
listen to me, you men of learning.
3 For the ear tests words
as the tongue tastes food.
4 Let us discern for ourselves what is right;
let us learn together what is good.

5 "Job says, 'I am innocent,
but God denies me justice.

[a] 13 *Or that he does not answer for any of his actions* [b] 18 *Or from crossing the river* [c] 22 *Or to the place of the dead*

6 Although I am right,
I am considered a liar;
although I am guiltless,
his arrow inflicts an incurable wound.'
7 Is there anyone like Job,
who drinks scorn like water?
8 He keeps company with evildoers;
he associates with the wicked.
9 For he says, 'There is no profit
in trying to please God.'

10 "So listen to me, you men of
understanding.
Far be it from God to do evil,
from the Almighty to do wrong.
11 He repays everyone for what they have
done;
he brings on them what their conduct
deserves.
12 It is unthinkable that God would do
wrong,
that the Almighty would pervert
justice.
13 Who appointed him over the earth?
Who put him in charge of the whole
world?
14 If it were his intention
and he withdrew his spirit[a] and breath,
15 all humanity would perish together
and mankind would return to the dust.

16 "If you have understanding, hear this;
listen to what I say.
17 Can someone who hates justice govern?
Will you condemn the just and mighty
One?
18 Is he not the One who says to kings, 'You
are worthless,'
and to nobles, 'You are wicked,'
19 who shows no partiality to princes
and does not favor the rich over the
poor,
for they are all the work of his hands?
20 They die in an instant, in the middle of
the night;
the people are shaken and they pass
away;
the mighty are removed without human
hand.

21 "His eyes are on the ways of mortals;
he sees their every step.
22 There is no deep shadow, no utter
darkness,
where evildoers can hide.
23 God has no need to examine people
further,
that they should come before him for
judgment.
24 Without inquiry he shatters the mighty
and sets up others in their place.
25 Because he takes note of their deeds,
he overthrows them in the night and
they are crushed.
26 He punishes them for their wickedness
where everyone can see them,
27 because they turned from following him
and had no regard for any of his ways.
28 They caused the cry of the poor to come
before him,
so that he heard the cry of the needy.
29 But if he remains silent, who can
condemn him?
If he hides his face, who can see him?
Yet he is over individual and nation alike,
30 to keep the godless from ruling,
from laying snares for the people.

31 "Suppose someone says to God,
'I am guilty but will offend no more.
32 Teach me what I cannot see;
if I have done wrong, I will not do so
again.'
33 Should God then reward you on your
terms,
when you refuse to repent?
You must decide, not I;
so tell me what you know.

34 "Men of understanding declare,
wise men who hear me say to me,
35 'Job speaks without knowledge;
his words lack insight.'
36 Oh, that Job might be tested to the utmost
for answering like a wicked man!
37 To his sin he adds rebellion;
scornfully he claps his hands among us
and multiplies his words against God."

35

Then Elihu said:

2 "Do you think this is just?
You say, 'I am in the right, not God.'
3 Yet you ask him, 'What profit is it to me,[b]
and what do I gain by not sinning?'

4 "I would like to reply to you
and to your friends with you.
5 Look up at the heavens and see;
gaze at the clouds so high above you.
6 If you sin, how does that affect him?
If your sins are many, what does that
do to him?
7 If you are righteous, what do you give to
him,
or what does he receive from your hand?
8 Your wickedness only affects humans
like yourself,
and your righteousness only other
people.

9 "People cry out under a load of
oppression;
they plead for relief from the arm of the
powerful.
10 But no one says, 'Where is God my
Maker,
who gives songs in the night,
11 who teaches us more than he teaches[c] the
beasts of the earth
and makes us wiser than[d] the birds in
the sky?'
12 He does not answer when people cry out
because of the arrogance of the wicked.
13 Indeed, God does not listen to their empty
plea;
the Almighty pays no attention to it.

[a] 14 Or *Spirit* [b] 3 Or *you* [c] 10,11 Or *night,* / [11]*who teaches us by* [d] 11 Or *us wise by*

14 How much less, then, will he listen
when you say that you do not see him,
that your case is before him
and you must wait for him,
15 and further, that his anger never
punishes
and he does not take the least notice of
wickedness.[a]
16 So Job opens his mouth with empty talk;
without knowledge he multiplies
words."

36 Elihu continued:

2 "Bear with me a little longer and I will
show you
that there is more to be said in God's
behalf.
3 I get my knowledge from afar;
I will ascribe justice to my Maker.
4 Be assured that my words are not false;
one who has perfect knowledge is with
you.

5 "God is mighty, but despises no one;
he is mighty, and firm in his purpose.
6 He does not keep the wicked alive
but gives the afflicted their rights.
7 He does not take his eyes off the
righteous;
he enthrones them with kings
and exalts them forever.
8 But if people are bound in chains,
held fast by cords of affliction,
9 he tells them what they have done—
that they have sinned arrogantly.
10 He makes them listen to correction
and commands them to repent of their
evil.
11 If they obey and serve him,
they will spend the rest of their days in
prosperity
and their years in contentment.
12 But if they do not listen,
they will perish by the sword[b]
and die without knowledge.

13 "The godless in heart harbor resentment;
even when he fetters them, they do not
cry for help.
14 They die in their youth,
among male prostitutes of the shrines.
15 But those who suffer he delivers in their
suffering;
he speaks to them in their affliction.

16 "He is wooing you from the jaws of
distress
to a spacious place free from
restriction,
to the comfort of your table laden with
choice food.
17 But now you are laden with the judgment
due the wicked;
judgment and justice have taken hold of
you.
18 Be careful that no one entices you by
riches;
do not let a large bribe turn you aside.
19 Would your wealth or even all your
mighty efforts
sustain you so you would not be in
distress?
20 Do not long for the night,
to drag people away from their homes.[c]
21 Beware of turning to evil,
which you seem to prefer to affliction.

22 "God is exalted in his power.
Who is a teacher like him?
23 Who has prescribed his ways for him,
or said to him, 'You have done wrong'?
24 Remember to extol his work,
which people have praised in song.
25 All humanity has seen it;
mortals gaze on it from afar.
26 How great is God—beyond our
understanding!
The number of his years is past finding
out.

27 "He draws up the drops of water,
which distill as rain to the streams[d];
28 the clouds pour down their moisture
and abundant showers fall on mankind.
29 Who can understand how he spreads out
the clouds,
how he thunders from his pavilion?
30 See how he scatters his lightning about
him,
bathing the depths of the sea.
31 This is the way he governs[e] the nations
and provides food in abundance.
32 He fills his hands with lightning
and commands it to strike its mark.
33 His thunder announces the coming storm;
even the cattle make known its
approach.[f]

37 "At this my heart pounds
and leaps from its place.
2 Listen! Listen to the roar of his voice,
to the rumbling that comes from his
mouth.
3 He unleashes his lightning beneath the
whole heaven
and sends it to the ends of the earth.
4 After that comes the sound of his roar;
he thunders with his majestic voice.
When his voice resounds,
he holds nothing back.
5 God's voice thunders in marvelous ways;
he does great things beyond our
understanding.
6 He says to the snow, 'Fall on the earth,'
and to the rain shower, 'Be a mighty
downpour.'
7 So that everyone he has made may know
his work,
he stops all people from their labor.[g]
8 The animals take cover;
they remain in their dens.

[a] *15* Symmachus, Theodotion and Vulgate; the meaning of the Hebrew for this word is uncertain.
[b] *12* Or *will cross the river* [c] *20* The meaning of the Hebrew for verses 18-20 is uncertain.
[d] *27* Or *distill from the mist as rain* [e] *31* Or *nourishes* [f] *33* Or *announces his coming— / the One zealous against evil* [g] *7* Or *work, / he fills all people with fear by his power*

9 The tempest comes out from its chamber,
the cold from the driving winds.
10 The breath of God produces ice,
and the broad waters become frozen.
11 He loads the clouds with moisture;
he scatters his lightning through them.
12 At his direction they swirl around
over the face of the whole earth
to do whatever he commands them.
13 He brings the clouds to punish people,
or to water his earth and show his love.

14 "Listen to this, Job;
stop and consider God's wonders.
15 Do you know how God controls the clouds
and makes his lightning flash?
16 Do you know how the clouds hang poised,
those wonders of him who has perfect knowledge?
17 You who swelter in your clothes
when the land lies hushed under the south wind,
18 can you join him in spreading out the skies,
hard as a mirror of cast bronze?

19 "Tell us what we should say to him;
we cannot draw up our case because of our darkness.
20 Should he be told that I want to speak?
Would anyone ask to be swallowed up?
21 Now no one can look at the sun,
bright as it is in the skies
after the wind has swept them clean.
22 Out of the north he comes in golden splendor;
God comes in awesome majesty.
23 The Almighty is beyond our reach and exalted in power;
in his justice and great righteousness,
he does not oppress.
24 Therefore, people revere him,
for does he not have regard for all the wise in heart?[a]"

The LORD Speaks

38 Then the LORD spoke to Job out of the storm. He said:

2 "Who is this that obscures my plans
with words without knowledge?
3 Brace yourself like a man;
I will question you,
and you shall answer me.

4 "Where were you when I laid the earth's foundation?
Tell me, if you understand.
5 Who marked off its dimensions? Surely you know!
Who stretched a measuring line across it?
6 On what were its footings set,
or who laid its cornerstone—
7 while the morning stars sang together
and all the angels[b] shouted for joy?

8 "Who shut up the sea behind doors
when it burst forth from the womb,
9 when I made the clouds its garment
and wrapped it in thick darkness,
10 when I fixed limits for it
and set its doors and bars in place,
11 when I said, 'This far you may come and no farther;
here is where your proud waves halt'?

12 "Have you ever given orders to the morning,
or shown the dawn its place,
13 that it might take the earth by the edges
and shake the wicked out of it?
14 The earth takes shape like clay under a seal;
its features stand out like those of a garment.
15 The wicked are denied their light,
and their upraised arm is broken.

16 "Have you journeyed to the springs of the sea
or walked in the recesses of the deep?
17 Have the gates of death been shown to you?
Have you seen the gates of the deepest darkness?
18 Have you comprehended the vast expanses of the earth?
Tell me, if you know all this.

19 "What is the way to the abode of light?
And where does darkness reside?
20 Can you take them to their places?
Do you know the paths to their dwellings?
21 Surely you know, for you were already born!
You have lived so many years!

22 "Have you entered the storehouses of the snow
or seen the storehouses of the hail,
23 which I reserve for times of trouble,
for days of war and battle?
24 What is the way to the place where the lightning is dispersed,
or the place where the east winds are scattered over the earth?
25 Who cuts a channel for the torrents of rain,
and a path for the thunderstorm,
26 to water a land where no one lives,
an uninhabited desert,
27 to satisfy a desolate wasteland
and make it sprout with grass?
28 Does the rain have a father?
Who fathers the drops of dew?
29 From whose womb comes the ice?
Who gives birth to the frost from the heavens
30 when the waters become hard as stone,
when the surface of the deep is frozen?

31 "Can you bind the chains[c] of the Pleiades?
Can you loosen Orion's belt?

[a] 24 Or *for he does not have regard for any who think they are wise.* [b] 7 Hebrew *the sons of God*
[c] 31 Septuagint; Hebrew *beauty*

32 Can you bring forth the constellations in
their seasons[a]
or lead out the Bear[b] with its cubs?
33 Do you know the laws of the heavens?
Can you set up God's[c] dominion over
the earth?

34 "Can you raise your voice to the clouds
and cover yourself with a flood of
water?
35 Do you send the lightning bolts on their
way?
Do they report to you, 'Here we are'?
36 Who gives the ibis wisdom[d]
or gives the rooster understanding?[e]
37 Who has the wisdom to count the
clouds?
Who can tip over the water jars of the
heavens
38 when the dust becomes hard
and the clods of earth stick together?

39 "Do you hunt the prey for the lioness
and satisfy the hunger of the lions
40 when they crouch in their dens
or lie in wait in a thicket?
41 Who provides food for the raven
when its young cry out to God
and wander about for lack of food?

39

"Do you know when the mountain
goats give birth?
Do you watch when the doe bears her
fawn?
2 Do you count the months till they bear?
Do you know the time they give birth?
3 They crouch down and bring forth their
young;
their labor pains are ended.
4 Their young thrive and grow strong in
the wilds;
they leave and do not return.

5 "Who let the wild donkey go free?
Who untied its ropes?
6 I gave it the wasteland as its home,
the salt flats as its habitat.
7 It laughs at the commotion in the town;
it does not hear a driver's shout.
8 It ranges the hills for its pasture
and searches for any green thing.

9 "Will the wild ox consent to serve you?
Will it stay by your manger at night?
10 Can you hold it to the furrow with a
harness?
Will it till the valleys behind you?
11 Will you rely on it for its great strength?
Will you leave your heavy work to it?
12 Can you trust it to haul in your grain
and bring it to your threshing floor?

13 "The wings of the ostrich flap joyfully,
though they cannot compare
with the wings and feathers of the
stork.
14 She lays her eggs on the ground
and lets them warm in the sand,
15 unmindful that a foot may crush them,
that some wild animal may trample
them.
16 She treats her young harshly, as if they
were not hers;
she cares not that her labor was in vain,
17 for God did not endow her with wisdom
or give her a share of good sense.
18 Yet when she spreads her feathers to run,
she laughs at horse and rider.

19 "Do you give the horse its strength
or clothe its neck with a flowing mane?
20 Do you make it leap like a locust,
striking terror with its proud snorting?
21 It paws fiercely, rejoicing in its strength,
and charges into the fray.
22 It laughs at fear, afraid of nothing;
it does not shy away from the sword.
23 The quiver rattles against its side,
along with the flashing spear and lance.
24 In frenzied excitement it eats up the
ground;
it cannot stand still when the trumpet
sounds.
25 At the blast of the trumpet it snorts,
'Aha!'
It catches the scent of battle from afar,
the shout of commanders and the battle
cry.

26 "Does the hawk take flight by your
wisdom
and spread its wings toward the south?
27 Does the eagle soar at your command
and build its nest on high?
28 It dwells on a cliff and stays there at
night;
a rocky crag is its stronghold.
29 From there it looks for food;
its eyes detect it from afar.
30 Its young ones feast on blood,
and where the slain are, there it is."

40

The LORD said to Job:

2 "Will the one who contends with the
Almighty correct him?
Let him who accuses God answer him!"

3 Then Job answered the LORD:

4 "I am unworthy—how can I reply to you?
I put my hand over my mouth.
5 I spoke once, but I have no answer—
twice, but I will say no more."

6 Then the LORD spoke to Job out of the storm:

7 "Brace yourself like a man;
I will question you,
and you shall answer me.

8 "Would you discredit my justice?
Would you condemn me to justify
yourself?
9 Do you have an arm like God's,
and can your voice thunder like his?

[a] 32 Or *the morning star in its season* [b] 32 Or *out Leo* [c] 33 Or *their* [d] 36 That is, wisdom about the flooding of the Nile [e] 36 That is, understanding of when to crow; the meaning of the Hebrew for this verse is uncertain.

10 Then adorn yourself with glory and splendor,
and clothe yourself in honor and majesty.
11 Unleash the fury of your wrath,
look at all who are proud and bring them low,
12 look at all who are proud and humble them,
crush the wicked where they stand.
13 Bury them all in the dust together;
shroud their faces in the grave.
14 Then I myself will admit to you
that your own right hand can save you.

15 "Look at Behemoth,
which I made along with you
and which feeds on grass like an ox.
16 What strength it has in its loins,
what power in the muscles of its belly!
17 Its tail sways like a cedar;
the sinews of its thighs are close-knit.
18 Its bones are tubes of bronze,
its limbs like rods of iron.
19 It ranks first among the works of God,
yet its Maker can approach it with his sword.
20 The hills bring it their produce,
and all the wild animals play nearby.
21 Under the lotus plants it lies,
hidden among the reeds in the marsh.
22 The lotuses conceal it in their shadow;
the poplars by the stream surround it.
23 A raging river does not alarm it;
it is secure, though the Jordan should surge against its mouth.
24 Can anyone capture it by the eyes,
or trap it and pierce its nose?

41[a] "Can you pull in Leviathan with a fishhook
or tie down its tongue with a rope?
2 Can you put a cord through its nose
or pierce its jaw with a hook?
3 Will it keep begging you for mercy?
Will it speak to you with gentle words?
4 Will it make an agreement with you
for you to take it as your slave for life?
5 Can you make a pet of it like a bird
or put it on a leash for the young women in your house?
6 Will traders barter for it?
Will they divide it up among the merchants?
7 Can you fill its hide with harpoons
or its head with fishing spears?
8 If you lay a hand on it,
you will remember the struggle and never do it again!
9 Any hope of subduing it is false;
the mere sight of it is overpowering.
10 No one is fierce enough to rouse it.
Who then is able to stand against me?
11 Who has a claim against me that I must pay?
Everything under heaven belongs to me.
12 "I will not fail to speak of Leviathan's limbs,
its strength and its graceful form.
13 Who can strip off its outer coat?
Who can penetrate its double coat of armor[b]?
14 Who dares open the doors of its mouth,
ringed about with fearsome teeth?
15 Its back has[c] rows of shields
tightly sealed together;
16 each is so close to the next
that no air can pass between.
17 They are joined fast to one another;
they cling together and cannot be parted.
18 Its snorting throws out flashes of light;
its eyes are like the rays of dawn.
19 Flames stream from its mouth;
sparks of fire shoot out.
20 Smoke pours from its nostrils
as from a boiling pot over burning reeds.
21 Its breath sets coals ablaze,
and flames dart from its mouth.
22 Strength resides in its neck;
dismay goes before it.
23 The folds of its flesh are tightly joined;
they are firm and immovable.
24 Its chest is hard as rock,
hard as a lower millstone.
25 When it rises up, the mighty are terrified;
they retreat before its thrashing.
26 The sword that reaches it has no effect,
nor does the spear or the dart or the javelin.
27 Iron it treats like straw
and bronze like rotten wood.
28 Arrows do not make it flee;
slingstones are like chaff to it.
29 A club seems to it but a piece of straw;
it laughs at the rattling of the lance.
30 Its undersides are jagged potsherds,
leaving a trail in the mud like a threshing sledge.
31 It makes the depths churn like a boiling caldron
and stirs up the sea like a pot of ointment.
32 It leaves a glistening wake behind it;
one would think the deep had white hair.
33 Nothing on earth is its equal—
a creature without fear.
34 It looks down on all that are haughty;
it is king over all that are proud."

Job

42 Then Job replied to the LORD:
2 "I know that you can do all things;
no purpose of yours can be thwarted.
3 You asked, 'Who is this that obscures my plans without knowledge?'
Surely I spoke of things I did not understand,
things too wonderful for me to know.

[a] In Hebrew texts 41:1-8 is numbered 40:25-32, and 41:9-34 is numbered 41:1-26. [b] *13* Septuagint; Hebrew *double bridle* [c] *15* Or *Its pride is its*

4 "You said, 'Listen now, and I will speak;
I will question you,
and you shall answer me.'
5 My ears had heard of you
but now my eyes have seen you.
6 Therefore I despise myself
and repent in dust and ashes."

Epilogue

7 After the LORD had said these things to
Job, he said to Eliphaz the Temanite, "I am
angry with you and your two friends, because
you have not spoken the truth about me, as
my servant Job has. 8 So now take seven bulls
and seven rams and go to my servant Job and
sacrifice a burnt offering for yourselves. My
servant Job will pray for you, and I will accept
his prayer and not deal with you according
to your folly. You have not spoken the truth
about me, as my servant Job has." 9 So Eliphaz
the Temanite, Bildad the Shuhite and Zophar
the Naamathite did what the LORD told them;
and the LORD accepted Job's prayer.

10 After Job had prayed for his friends, the
LORD restored his fortunes and gave him twice
as much as he had before. 11 All his brothers
and sisters and everyone who had known him
before came and ate with him in his house.
They comforted and consoled him over all the
trouble the LORD had brought on him, and each
one gave him a piece of silver[a] and a gold ring.

12 The LORD blessed the latter part of Job's
life more than the former part. He had fourteen thousand sheep, six thousand camels, a
thousand yoke of oxen and a thousand donkeys. 13 And he also had seven sons and three
daughters. 14 The first daughter he named
Jemimah, the second Keziah and the third
Keren-Happuch. 15 Nowhere in all the land
were there found women as beautiful as Job's
daughters, and their father granted them an
inheritance along with their brothers.

16 After this, Job lived a hundred and forty
years; he saw his children and their children
to the fourth generation. 17 And so Job died,
an old man and full of years.

Psalms

BOOK I

Psalms 1–41

Psalm 1

1 Blessed is the one
who does not walk in step with the wicked
or stand in the way that sinners take
or sit in the company of mockers,
2 but whose delight is in the law of the LORD,
and who meditates on his law day and night.
3 That person is like a tree planted by streams of water,
which yields its fruit in season
and whose leaf does not wither—
whatever they do prospers.

4 Not so the wicked!
They are like chaff
that the wind blows away.
5 Therefore the wicked will not stand in the judgment,
nor sinners in the assembly of the righteous.

6 For the LORD watches over the way of the righteous,
but the way of the wicked leads to destruction.

Psalm 2

1 Why do the nations conspire[b]
and the peoples plot in vain?
2 The kings of the earth rise up
and the rulers band together
against the LORD and against his anointed, saying,
3 "Let us break their chains
and throw off their shackles."

4 The One enthroned in heaven laughs;
the Lord scoffs at them.
5 He rebukes them in his anger
and terrifies them in his wrath, saying,
6 "I have installed my king
on Zion, my holy mountain."

7 I will proclaim the LORD's decree:

He said to me, "You are my son;
today I have become your father.
8 Ask me,
and I will make the nations your inheritance,
the ends of the earth your possession.
9 You will break them with a rod of iron[c];
you will dash them to pieces like pottery."

10 Therefore, you kings, be wise;
be warned, you rulers of the earth.
11 Serve the LORD with fear
and celebrate his rule with trembling.

[a] *11* Hebrew *him a kesitah;* a kesitah was a unit of money of unknown weight and value.
[b] *1* Hebrew; Septuagint *rage*
[c] *9* Or *will rule them with an iron scepter* (see Septuagint and Syriac)

12 Kiss his son, or he will be angry
and your way will lead to your destruction,
for his wrath can flare up in a moment.
Blessed are all who take refuge in him.

Psalm 3[a]

A psalm of David. When he fled from his son Absalom.

1 LORD, how many are my foes!
How many rise up against me!
2 Many are saying of me,
"God will not deliver him."[b]

3 But you, LORD, are a shield around me,
my glory, the One who lifts my head high.
4 I call out to the LORD,
and he answers me from his holy mountain.

5 I lie down and sleep;
I wake again, because the LORD sustains me.
6 I will not fear though tens of thousands
assail me on every side.

7 Arise, LORD!
Deliver me, my God!
Strike all my enemies on the jaw;
break the teeth of the wicked.

8 From the LORD comes deliverance.
May your blessing be on your people.

Psalm 4[c]

For the director of music. With stringed instruments. A psalm of David.

1 Answer me when I call to you,
my righteous God.
Give me relief from my distress;
have mercy on me and hear my prayer.

2 How long will you people turn my glory into shame?
How long will you love delusions and seek false gods[d]?[e]
3 Know that the LORD has set apart his faithful servant for himself;
the LORD hears when I call to him.

4 Tremble and[f] do not sin;
when you are on your beds,
search your hearts and be silent.
5 Offer the sacrifices of the righteous
and trust in the LORD.

6 Many, LORD, are asking, "Who will bring us prosperity?"
Let the light of your face shine on us.
7 Fill my heart with joy
when their grain and new wine abound.

8 In peace I will lie down and sleep,
for you alone, LORD,
make me dwell in safety.

Psalm 5[g]

For the director of music. For pipes. A psalm of David.

1 Listen to my words, LORD,
consider my lament.
2 Hear my cry for help,
my King and my God,
for to you I pray.

3 In the morning, LORD, you hear my voice;
in the morning I lay my requests before you
and wait expectantly.
4 For you are not a God who is pleased with wickedness;
with you, evil people are not welcome.
5 The arrogant cannot stand
in your presence.
You hate all who do wrong;
6 you destroy those who tell lies.
The bloodthirsty and deceitful
you, LORD, detest.
7 But I, by your great love,
can come into your house;
in reverence I bow down
toward your holy temple.

8 Lead me, LORD, in your righteousness
because of my enemies—
make your way straight before me.
9 Not a word from their mouth can be trusted;
their heart is filled with malice.
Their throat is an open grave;
with their tongues they tell lies.
10 Declare them guilty, O God!
Let their intrigues be their downfall.
Banish them for their many sins,
for they have rebelled against you.
11 But let all who take refuge in you be glad;
let them ever sing for joy.
Spread your protection over them,
that those who love your name may rejoice in you.

12 Surely, LORD, you bless the righteous;
you surround them with your favor as with a shield.

Psalm 6[h]

For the director of music. With stringed instruments. According to sheminith.[i] *A psalm of David.*

1 LORD, do not rebuke me in your anger
or discipline me in your wrath.
2 Have mercy on me, LORD, for I am faint;
heal me, LORD, for my bones are in agony.
3 My soul is in deep anguish.
How long, LORD, how long?

4 Turn, LORD, and deliver me;
save me because of your unfailing love.

[a] In Hebrew texts 3:1-8 is numbered 3:2-9. [b] 2 The Hebrew has *Selah* (a word of uncertain meaning) here and at the end of verses 4 and 8. [c] In Hebrew texts 4:1-8 is numbered 4:2-9. [d] 2 Or *seek lies* [e] 2 The Hebrew has *Selah* (a word of uncertain meaning) here and at the end of verse 4. [f] 4 Or *In your anger* (see Septuagint) [g] In Hebrew texts 5:1-12 is numbered 5:2-13. [h] In Hebrew texts 6:1-10 is numbered 6:2-11. [i] Title: Probably a musical term

5 Among the dead no one proclaims your name.
Who praises you from the grave?

6 I am worn out from my groaning.
All night long I flood my bed with weeping
and drench my couch with tears.
7 My eyes grow weak with sorrow;
they fail because of all my foes.

8 Away from me, all you who do evil,
for the LORD has heard my weeping.
9 The LORD has heard my cry for mercy;
the LORD accepts my prayer.
10 All my enemies will be overwhelmed with shame and anguish;
they will turn back and suddenly be put to shame.

Psalm 7[a]

A shiggaion[b] of David, which he sang to the LORD concerning Cush, a Benjamite.

1 LORD my God, I take refuge in you;
save and deliver me from all who pursue me,
2 or they will tear me apart like a lion
and rip me to pieces with no one to rescue me.

3 LORD my God, if I have done this
and there is guilt on my hands—
4 if I have repaid my ally with evil
or without cause have robbed my foe—
5 then let my enemy pursue and overtake me;
let him trample my life to the ground
and make me sleep in the dust.[c]

6 Arise, LORD, in your anger;
rise up against the rage of my enemies.
Awake, my God; decree justice.
7 Let the assembled peoples gather around you,
while you sit enthroned over them on high.
8 Let the LORD judge the peoples.
Vindicate me, LORD, according to my righteousness,
according to my integrity, O Most High.
9 Bring to an end the violence of the wicked
and make the righteous secure—
you, the righteous God
who probes minds and hearts.

10 My shield[d] is God Most High,
who saves the upright in heart.
11 God is a righteous judge,
a God who displays his wrath every day.
12 If he does not relent,
he[e] will sharpen his sword;
he will bend and string his bow.
13 He has prepared his deadly weapons;
he makes ready his flaming arrows.

14 Whoever is pregnant with evil
conceives trouble and gives birth to disillusionment.
15 Whoever digs a hole and scoops it out
falls into the pit they have made.
16 The trouble they cause recoils on them;
their violence comes down on their own heads.

17 I will give thanks to the LORD because of his righteousness;
I will sing the praises of the name of the LORD Most High.

Psalm 8[f]

For the director of music. According to gittith.[g] *A psalm of David.*

1 LORD, our Lord,
how majestic is your name in all the earth!

You have set your glory
in the heavens.
2 Through the praise of children and infants
you have established a stronghold against your enemies,
to silence the foe and the avenger.
3 When I consider your heavens,
the work of your fingers,
the moon and the stars,
which you have set in place,
4 what is mankind that you are mindful of them,
human beings that you care for them?[h]

5 You have made them[i] a little lower than the angels[j]
and crowned them[i] with glory and honor.
6 You made them rulers over the works of your hands;
you put everything under their[k] feet:
7 all flocks and herds,
and the animals of the wild,
8 the birds in the sky,
and the fish in the sea,
all that swim the paths of the seas.

9 LORD, our Lord,
how majestic is your name in all the earth!

Psalm 9[l,m]

For the director of music. To the tune of "The Death of the Son." A psalm of David.

1 I will give thanks to you, LORD, with all my heart;
I will tell of all your wonderful deeds.

[a] In Hebrew texts 7:1-17 is numbered 7:2-18. [b] Title: Probably a literary or musical term [c] 5 The Hebrew has *Selah* (a word of uncertain meaning) here. [d] *10* Or *sovereign* [e] *12* Or *If anyone does not repent, / God* [f] In Hebrew texts 8:1-9 is numbered 8:2-10. [g] Title: Probably a musical term [h] *4* Or *what is a human being that you are mindful of him, / a son of man that you care for him?* [i] *5* Or *him* [j] *5* Or *than God* [k] *6* Or *made him ruler . . . ; / . . . his* [l] Psalms 9 and 10 may originally have been a single acrostic poem in which alternating lines began with the successive letters of the Hebrew alphabet. In the Septuagint they constitute one psalm. [m] In Hebrew texts 9:1-20 is numbered 9:2-21.

2 I will be glad and rejoice in you;
I will sing the praises of your name,
O Most High.

3 My enemies turn back;
they stumble and perish before you.
4 For you have upheld my right and my cause,
sitting enthroned as the righteous judge.
5 You have rebuked the nations and destroyed the wicked;
you have blotted out their name for ever and ever.
6 Endless ruin has overtaken my enemies,
you have uprooted their cities;
even the memory of them has perished.

7 The LORD reigns forever;
he has established his throne for judgment.
8 He rules the world in righteousness
and judges the peoples with equity.
9 The LORD is a refuge for the oppressed,
a stronghold in times of trouble.
10 Those who know your name trust in you,
for you, LORD, have never forsaken those who seek you.

11 Sing the praises of the LORD, enthroned in Zion;
proclaim among the nations what he has done.
12 For he who avenges blood remembers;
he does not ignore the cries of the afflicted.

13 LORD, see how my enemies persecute me!
Have mercy and lift me up from the gates of death,
14 that I may declare your praises
in the gates of Daughter Zion,
and there rejoice in your salvation.

15 The nations have fallen into the pit they have dug;
their feet are caught in the net they have hidden.
16 The LORD is known by his acts of justice;
the wicked are ensnared by the work of their hands.[a]
17 The wicked go down to the realm of the dead,
all the nations that forget God.
18 But God will never forget the needy;
the hope of the afflicted will never perish.

19 Arise, LORD, do not let mortals triumph;
let the nations be judged in your presence.
20 Strike them with terror, LORD;
let the nations know they are only mortal.

Psalm 10[b]

1 Why, LORD, do you stand far off?
Why do you hide yourself in times of trouble?

2 In his arrogance the wicked man hunts down the weak,
who are caught in the schemes he devises.
3 He boasts about the cravings of his heart;
he blesses the greedy and reviles the LORD.
4 In his pride the wicked man does not seek him;
in all his thoughts there is no room for God.
5 His ways are always prosperous;
your laws are rejected by[c] him;
he sneers at all his enemies.
6 He says to himself, "Nothing will ever shake me."
He swears, "No one will ever do me harm."

7 His mouth is full of lies and threats;
trouble and evil are under his tongue.
8 He lies in wait near the villages;
from ambush he murders the innocent.
His eyes watch in secret for his victims;
9 like a lion in cover he lies in wait.
He lies in wait to catch the helpless;
he catches the helpless and drags them off in his net.
10 His victims are crushed, they collapse;
they fall under his strength.
11 He says to himself, "God will never notice;
he covers his face and never sees."

12 Arise, LORD! Lift up your hand, O God.
Do not forget the helpless.
13 Why does the wicked man revile God?
Why does he say to himself,
"He won't call me to account"?
14 But you, God, see the trouble of the afflicted;
you consider their grief and take it in hand.
The victims commit themselves to you;
you are the helper of the fatherless.
15 Break the arm of the wicked man;
call the evildoer to account for his wickedness
that would not otherwise be found out.

16 The LORD is King for ever and ever;
the nations will perish from his land.
17 You, LORD, hear the desire of the afflicted;
you encourage them, and you listen to their cry,
18 defending the fatherless and the oppressed,
so that mere earthly mortals
will never again strike terror.

Psalm 11

For the director of music. Of David.

1 In the LORD I take refuge.
How then can you say to me:
"Flee like a bird to your mountain.

[a] *16* The Hebrew has *Higgaion* and *Selah* (words of uncertain meaning) here; *Selah* occurs also at the end of verse 20. [b] Psalms 9 and 10 may originally have been a single acrostic poem in which alternating lines began with the successive letters of the Hebrew alphabet. In the Septuagint they constitute one psalm. [c] *5* See Septuagint; Hebrew / *they are haughty, and your laws are far from*

2 For look, the wicked bend their bows;
they set their arrows against the strings
to shoot from the shadows
at the upright in heart.
3 When the foundations are being destroyed,
what can the righteous do?"

4 The LORD is in his holy temple;
the LORD is on his heavenly throne.
He observes everyone on earth;
his eyes examine them.
5 The LORD examines the righteous,
but the wicked, those who love violence,
he hates with a passion.
6 On the wicked he will rain
fiery coals and burning sulfur;
a scorching wind will be their lot.

7 For the LORD is righteous,
he loves justice;
the upright will see his face.

Psalm 12[a]

For the director of music. According to sheminith.[b] A psalm of David.

1 Help, LORD, for no one is faithful anymore;
those who are loyal have vanished from the human race.
2 Everyone lies to their neighbor;
they flatter with their lips
but harbor deception in their hearts.

3 May the LORD silence all flattering lips
and every boastful tongue—
4 those who say,
"By our tongues we will prevail;
our own lips will defend us—who is lord over us?"

5 "Because the poor are plundered and the needy groan,
I will now arise," says the LORD.
"I will protect them from those who malign them."
6 And the words of the LORD are flawless,
like silver purified in a crucible,
like gold[c] refined seven times.

7 You, LORD, will keep the needy safe
and will protect us forever from the wicked,
8 who freely strut about
when what is vile is honored by the human race.

Psalm 13[d]

For the director of music. A psalm of David.

1 How long, LORD? Will you forget me forever?
How long will you hide your face from me?
2 How long must I wrestle with my thoughts
and day after day have sorrow in my heart?
How long will my enemy triumph over me?

3 Look on me and answer, LORD my God.
Give light to my eyes, or I will sleep in death,
4 and my enemy will say, "I have overcome him,"
and my foes will rejoice when I fall.

5 But I trust in your unfailing love;
my heart rejoices in your salvation.
6 I will sing the LORD's praise,
for he has been good to me.

Psalm 14

For the director of music. Of David.

1 The fool[e] says in his heart,
"There is no God."
They are corrupt, their deeds are vile;
there is no one who does good.

2 The LORD looks down from heaven
on all mankind
to see if there are any who understand,
any who seek God.
3 All have turned away, all have become corrupt;
there is no one who does good,
not even one.

4 Do all these evildoers know nothing?

They devour my people as though eating bread;
they never call on the LORD.
5 But there they are, overwhelmed with dread,
for God is present in the company of the righteous.
6 You evildoers frustrate the plans of the poor,
but the LORD is their refuge.

7 Oh, that salvation for Israel would come out of Zion!
When the LORD restores his people,
let Jacob rejoice and Israel be glad!

Psalm 15

A psalm of David.

1 LORD, who may dwell in your sacred tent?
Who may live on your holy mountain?

2 The one whose walk is blameless,
who does what is righteous,
who speaks the truth from their heart;
3 whose tongue utters no slander,
who does no wrong to a neighbor,
and casts no slur on others;
4 who despises a vile person
but honors those who fear the LORD;

[a] In Hebrew texts 12:1-8 is numbered 12:2-9. [b] Title: Probably a musical term [c] *6* Probable reading of the original Hebrew text; Masoretic Text *earth* [d] In Hebrew texts 13:1-6 is numbered 13:2-6.
[e] *1* The Hebrew words rendered *fool* in Psalms denote one who is morally deficient.

who keeps an oath even when it hurts,
and does not change their mind;
5 who lends money to the poor without interest;
who does not accept a bribe against the innocent.

Whoever does these things
will never be shaken.

Psalm 16

A miktam[a] of David.

1 Keep me safe, my God,
for in you I take refuge.

2 I say to the LORD, "You are my Lord;
apart from you I have no good thing."
3 I say of the holy people who are in the land,
"They are the noble ones in whom is all my delight."
4 Those who run after other gods will suffer more and more.
I will not pour out libations of blood to such gods
or take up their names on my lips.

5 LORD, you alone are my portion and my cup;
you make my lot secure.
6 The boundary lines have fallen for me in pleasant places;
surely I have a delightful inheritance.
7 I will praise the LORD, who counsels me;
even at night my heart instructs me.
8 I keep my eyes always on the LORD.
With him at my right hand, I will not be shaken.

9 Therefore my heart is glad and my tongue rejoices;
my body also will rest secure,
10 because you will not abandon me to the realm of the dead,
nor will you let your faithful[b] one see decay.
11 You make known to me the path of life;
you will fill me with joy in your presence,
with eternal pleasures at your right hand.

Psalm 17

A prayer of David.

1 Hear me, LORD, my plea is just;
listen to my cry.
Hear my prayer—
it does not rise from deceitful lips.
2 Let my vindication come from you;
may your eyes see what is right.

3 Though you probe my heart,
though you examine me at night and test me,
you will find that I have planned no evil;
my mouth has not transgressed.
4 Though people tried to bribe me,
I have kept myself from the ways of the violent
through what your lips have commanded.
5 My steps have held to your paths;
my feet have not stumbled.

6 I call on you, my God, for you will answer me;
turn your ear to me and hear my prayer.
7 Show me the wonders of your great love,
you who save by your right hand
those who take refuge in you from their foes.
8 Keep me as the apple of your eye;
hide me in the shadow of your wings
9 from the wicked who are out to destroy me,
from my mortal enemies who surround me.

10 They close up their callous hearts,
and their mouths speak with arrogance.
11 They have tracked me down, they now surround me,
with eyes alert, to throw me to the ground.
12 They are like a lion hungry for prey,
like a fierce lion crouching in cover.

13 Rise up, LORD, confront them, bring them down;
with your sword rescue me from the wicked.
14 By your hand save me from such people, LORD,
from those of this world whose reward is in this life.
May what you have stored up for the wicked fill their bellies;
may their children gorge themselves on it,
and may there be leftovers for their little ones.

15 As for me, I will be vindicated and will see your face;
when I awake, I will be satisfied with seeing your likeness.

Psalm 18[c]

For the director of music. Of David the servant of the LORD. He sang to the LORD the words of this song when the LORD delivered him from the hand of all his enemies and from the hand of Saul. He said:

1 I love you, LORD, my strength.

2 The LORD is my rock, my fortress and my deliverer;
my God is my rock, in whom I take refuge,
my shield[d] and the horn[e] of my salvation, my stronghold.

[a] Title: Probably a literary or musical term [b] 10 Or *holy* [c] In Hebrew texts 18:1-50 is numbered 18:2-51. [d] 2 Or *sovereign* [e] 2 *Horn* here symbolizes strength.

3 I called to the LORD, who is worthy of
praise,
and I have been saved from my enemies.
4 The cords of death entangled me;
the torrents of destruction
overwhelmed me.
5 The cords of the grave coiled around me;
the snares of death confronted me.

6 In my distress I called to the LORD;
I cried to my God for help.
From his temple he heard my voice;
my cry came before him, into his ears.
7 The earth trembled and quaked,
and the foundations of the mountains
shook;
they trembled because he was angry.
8 Smoke rose from his nostrils;
consuming fire came from his mouth,
burning coals blazed out of it.
9 He parted the heavens and came down;
dark clouds were under his feet.
10 He mounted the cherubim and flew;
he soared on the wings of the wind.
11 He made darkness his covering, his
canopy around him—
the dark rain clouds of the sky.
12 Out of the brightness of his presence
clouds advanced,
with hailstones and bolts of lightning.
13 The LORD thundered from heaven;
the voice of the Most High resounded.[a]
14 He shot his arrows and scattered the
enemy,
with great bolts of lightning he routed
them.
15 The valleys of the sea were exposed
and the foundations of the earth laid
bare
at your rebuke, LORD,
at the blast of breath from your nostrils.

16 He reached down from on high and took
hold of me;
he drew me out of deep waters.
17 He rescued me from my powerful enemy,
from my foes, who were too strong for
me.
18 They confronted me in the day of my
disaster,
but the LORD was my support.
19 He brought me out into a spacious place;
he rescued me because he delighted in
me.

20 The LORD has dealt with me according to
my righteousness;
according to the cleanness of my hands
he has rewarded me.
21 For I have kept the ways of the LORD;
I am not guilty of turning from my God.
22 All his laws are before me;
I have not turned away from his
decrees.
23 I have been blameless before him
and have kept myself from sin.
24 The LORD has rewarded me according to
my righteousness,
according to the cleanness of my hands
in his sight.

25 To the faithful you show yourself faithful,
to the blameless you show yourself
blameless,
26 to the pure you show yourself pure,
but to the devious you show yourself
shrewd.
27 You save the humble
but bring low those whose eyes are
haughty.
28 You, LORD, keep my lamp burning;
my God turns my darkness into light.
29 With your help I can advance against a
troop[b];
with my God I can scale a wall.

30 As for God, his way is perfect:
The LORD's word is flawless;
he shields all who take refuge in him.
31 For who is God besides the LORD?
And who is the Rock except our God?
32 It is God who arms me with strength
and keeps my way secure.
33 He makes my feet like the feet of a deer;
he causes me to stand on the heights.
34 He trains my hands for battle;
my arms can bend a bow of bronze.
35 You make your saving help my shield,
and your right hand sustains me;
your help has made me great.
36 You provide a broad path for my feet,
so that my ankles do not give way.

37 I pursued my enemies and overtook them;
I did not turn back till they were
destroyed.
38 I crushed them so that they could not rise;
they fell beneath my feet.
39 You armed me with strength for battle;
you humbled my adversaries before me.
40 You made my enemies turn their backs in
flight,
and I destroyed my foes.
41 They cried for help, but there was no one
to save them—
to the LORD, but he did not answer.
42 I beat them as fine as windblown dust;
I trampled them[c] like mud in the
streets.
43 You have delivered me from the attacks
of the people;
you have made me the head of nations.
People I did not know now serve me,
44 foreigners cower before me;
as soon as they hear of me, they obey
me.
45 They all lose heart;
they come trembling from their
strongholds.

46 The LORD lives! Praise be to my Rock!
Exalted be God my Savior!

[a] *13* Some Hebrew manuscripts and Septuagint (see also 2 Samuel 22:14); most Hebrew manuscripts *resounded, / amid hailstones and bolts of lightning* [b] *29* Or *can run through a barricade*
[c] *42* Many Hebrew manuscripts, Septuagint, Syriac and Targum (see also 2 Samuel 22:43); Masoretic Text *I poured them out*

[47] He is the God who avenges me,
who subdues nations under me,
[48] who saves me from my enemies.
You exalted me above my foes;
from a violent man you rescued me.
[49] Therefore I will praise you, LORD, among the nations;
I will sing the praises of your name.

[50] He gives his king great victories;
he shows unfailing love to his anointed,
to David and to his descendants forever.

Psalm 19[a]

For the director of music. A psalm of David.

[1] The heavens declare the glory of God;
the skies proclaim the work of his hands.
[2] Day after day they pour forth speech;
night after night they reveal knowledge.
[3] They have no speech, they use no words;
no sound is heard from them.
[4] Yet their voice[b] goes out into all the earth,
their words to the ends of the world.
In the heavens God has pitched a tent for the sun.
[5] It is like a bridegroom coming out of his chamber,
like a champion rejoicing to run his course.
[6] It rises at one end of the heavens
and makes its circuit to the other;
nothing is deprived of its warmth.

[7] The law of the LORD is perfect,
refreshing the soul.
The statutes of the LORD are trustworthy,
making wise the simple.
[8] The precepts of the LORD are right,
giving joy to the heart.
The commands of the LORD are radiant,
giving light to the eyes.
[9] The fear of the LORD is pure,
enduring forever.
The decrees of the LORD are firm,
and all of them are righteous.

[10] They are more precious than gold,
than much pure gold;
they are sweeter than honey,
than honey from the honeycomb.
[11] By them your servant is warned;
in keeping them there is great reward.
[12] But who can discern their own errors?
Forgive my hidden faults.
[13] Keep your servant also from willful sins;
may they not rule over me.
Then I will be blameless,
innocent of great transgression.

[14] May these words of my mouth and this meditation of my heart
be pleasing in your sight,
LORD, my Rock and my Redeemer.

Psalm 20[c]

For the director of music. A psalm of David.

[1] May the LORD answer you when you are in distress;
may the name of the God of Jacob protect you.
[2] May he send you help from the sanctuary
and grant you support from Zion.
[3] May he remember all your sacrifices
and accept your burnt offerings.[d]
[4] May he give you the desire of your heart
and make all your plans succeed.
[5] May we shout for joy over your victory
and lift up our banners in the name of our God.

May the LORD grant all your requests.

[6] Now this I know:
The LORD gives victory to his anointed.
He answers him from his heavenly sanctuary
with the victorious power of his right hand.
[7] Some trust in chariots and some in horses,
but we trust in the name of the LORD our God.
[8] They are brought to their knees and fall,
but we rise up and stand firm.
[9] LORD, give victory to the king!
Answer us when we call!

Psalm 21[e]

For the director of music. A psalm of David.

[1] The king rejoices in your strength, LORD.
How great is his joy in the victories you give!

[2] You have granted him his heart's desire
and have not withheld the request of his lips.[d]
[3] You came to greet him with rich blessings
and placed a crown of pure gold on his head.
[4] He asked you for life, and you gave it to him—
length of days, for ever and ever.
[5] Through the victories you gave, his glory is great;
you have bestowed on him splendor and majesty.
[6] Surely you have granted him unending blessings
and made him glad with the joy of your presence.
[7] For the king trusts in the LORD;
through the unfailing love of the Most High
he will not be shaken.

[8] Your hand will lay hold on all your enemies;
your right hand will seize your foes.

[a] In Hebrew texts 19:1-14 is numbered 19:2-15. [b] *4* Septuagint, Jerome and Syriac; Hebrew *measuring line* [c] In Hebrew texts 20:1-9 is numbered 20:2-10. [d] *3,2* The Hebrew has *Selah* (a word of uncertain meaning) here. [e] In Hebrew texts 21:1-13 is numbered 21:2-14.

9 When you appear for battle,
you will burn them up as in a blazing furnace.
The LORD will swallow them up in his wrath,
and his fire will consume them.
10 You will destroy their descendants from the earth,
their posterity from mankind.
11 Though they plot evil against you
and devise wicked schemes, they cannot succeed.
12 You will make them turn their backs
when you aim at them with drawn bow.

13 Be exalted in your strength, LORD;
we will sing and praise your might.

Psalm 22[a]

For the director of music. To the tune of "The Doe of the Morning." A psalm of David.

1 My God, my God, why have you forsaken me?
Why are you so far from saving me,
so far from my cries of anguish?
2 My God, I cry out by day, but you do not answer,
by night, but I find no rest.[b]

3 Yet you are enthroned as the Holy One;
you are the one Israel praises.[c]
4 In you our ancestors put their trust;
they trusted and you delivered them.
5 To you they cried out and were saved;
in you they trusted and were not put to shame.

6 But I am a worm and not a man,
scorned by everyone, despised by the people.
7 All who see me mock me;
they hurl insults, shaking their heads.
8 "He trusts in the LORD," they say,
"let the LORD rescue him.
Let him deliver him,
since he delights in him."

9 Yet you brought me out of the womb;
you made me trust in you, even at my mother's breast.
10 From birth I was cast on you;
from my mother's womb you have been my God.

11 Do not be far from me,
for trouble is near
and there is no one to help.

12 Many bulls surround me;
strong bulls of Bashan encircle me.
13 Roaring lions that tear their prey
open their mouths wide against me.
14 I am poured out like water,
and all my bones are out of joint.
My heart has turned to wax;
it has melted within me.
15 My mouth[d] is dried up like a potsherd,
and my tongue sticks to the roof of my mouth;
you lay me in the dust of death.

16 Dogs surround me,
a pack of villains encircles me;
they pierce[e] my hands and my feet.
17 All my bones are on display;
people stare and gloat over me.
18 They divide my clothes among them
and cast lots for my garment.

19 But you, LORD, do not be far from me.
You are my strength; come quickly to help me.
20 Deliver me from the sword,
my precious life from the power of the dogs.
21 Rescue me from the mouth of the lions;
save me from the horns of the wild oxen.

22 I will declare your name to my people;
in the assembly I will praise you.
23 You who fear the LORD, praise him!
All you descendants of Jacob, honor him!
Revere him, all you descendants of Israel!
24 For he has not despised or scorned
the suffering of the afflicted one;
he has not hidden his face from him
but has listened to his cry for help.

25 From you comes the theme of my praise
in the great assembly;
before those who fear you[f] I will fulfill my vows.
26 The poor will eat and be satisfied;
those who seek the LORD will praise him—
may your hearts live forever!

27 All the ends of the earth
will remember and turn to the LORD,
and all the families of the nations
will bow down before him,
28 for dominion belongs to the LORD
and he rules over the nations.

29 All the rich of the earth will feast and worship;
all who go down to the dust will kneel before him—
those who cannot keep themselves alive.
30 Posterity will serve him;
future generations will be told about the Lord.
31 They will proclaim his righteousness,
declaring to a people yet unborn:
He has done it!

Psalm 23

A psalm of David.

1 The LORD is my shepherd, I lack nothing.
2 He makes me lie down in green pastures,

[a] In Hebrew texts 22:1-31 is numbered 22:2-32. [b] *2* Or *night, and am not silent* [c] *3* Or *Yet you are holy, / enthroned on the praises of Israel* [d] *15* Probable reading of the original Hebrew text; Masoretic Text *strength* [e] *16* Dead Sea Scrolls and some manuscripts of the Masoretic Text, Septuagint and Syriac; most manuscripts of the Masoretic Text *me, / like a lion* [f] *25* Hebrew *him*

he leads me beside quiet waters,
3 he refreshes my soul.
He guides me along the right paths
for his name's sake.
4 Even though I walk
through the darkest valley,[a]
I will fear no evil,
for you are with me;
your rod and your staff,
they comfort me.

5 You prepare a table before me
in the presence of my enemies.
You anoint my head with oil;
my cup overflows.
6 Surely your goodness and love will follow me
all the days of my life,
and I will dwell in the house of the LORD
forever.

Psalm 24

Of David. A psalm.

1 The earth is the LORD's, and everything in it,
the world, and all who live in it;
2 for he founded it on the seas
and established it on the waters.

3 Who may ascend the mountain of the LORD?
Who may stand in his holy place?
4 The one who has clean hands and a pure heart,
who does not trust in an idol
or swear by a false god.[b]

5 They will receive blessing from the LORD
and vindication from God their Savior.
6 Such is the generation of those who seek him,
who seek your face, God of Jacob.[c,d]

7 Lift up your heads, you gates;
be lifted up, you ancient doors,
that the King of glory may come in.
8 Who is this King of glory?
The LORD strong and mighty,
the LORD mighty in battle.
9 Lift up your heads, you gates;
lift them up, you ancient doors,
that the King of glory may come in.
10 Who is he, this King of glory?
The LORD Almighty—
he is the King of glory.

Psalm 25[e]

Of David.

1 In you, LORD my God,
I put my trust.

2 I trust in you;
do not let me be put to shame,
nor let my enemies triumph over me.
3 No one who hopes in you
will ever be put to shame,
but shame will come on those
who are treacherous without cause.

4 Show me your ways, LORD,
teach me your paths.
5 Guide me in your truth and teach me,
for you are God my Savior,
and my hope is in you all day long.
6 Remember, LORD, your great mercy and love,
for they are from of old.
7 Do not remember the sins of my youth
and my rebellious ways;
according to your love remember me,
for you, LORD, are good.

8 Good and upright is the LORD;
therefore he instructs sinners in his ways.
9 He guides the humble in what is right
and teaches them his way.
10 All the ways of the LORD are loving and faithful
toward those who keep the demands of his covenant.
11 For the sake of your name, LORD,
forgive my iniquity, though it is great.

12 Who, then, are those who fear the LORD?
He will instruct them in the ways they should choose.[f]
13 They will spend their days in prosperity,
and their descendants will inherit the land.
14 The LORD confides in those who fear him;
he makes his covenant known to them.
15 My eyes are ever on the LORD,
for only he will release my feet from the snare.

16 Turn to me and be gracious to me,
for I am lonely and afflicted.
17 Relieve the troubles of my heart
and free me from my anguish.
18 Look on my affliction and my distress
and take away all my sins.
19 See how numerous are my enemies
and how fiercely they hate me!

20 Guard my life and rescue me;
do not let me be put to shame,
for I take refuge in you.
21 May integrity and uprightness protect me,
because my hope, LORD,[g] is in you.

22 Deliver Israel, O God,
from all their troubles!

Psalm 26

Of David.

1 Vindicate me, LORD,
for I have led a blameless life;

[a] 4 Or *the valley of the shadow of death* [b] 4 Or *swear falsely* [c] 6 Two Hebrew manuscripts and Syriac (see also Septuagint); most Hebrew manuscripts *face, Jacob* [d] 6 The Hebrew has *Selah* (a word of uncertain meaning) here and at the end of verse 10. [e] This psalm is an acrostic poem, the verses of which begin with the successive letters of the Hebrew alphabet. [f] 12 Or *ways he chooses* [g] 21 Septuagint; Hebrew does not have LORD.

I have trusted in the LORD
and have not faltered.
2 Test me, LORD, and try me,
examine my heart and my mind;
3 for I have always been mindful of your unfailing love
and have lived in reliance on your faithfulness.
4 I do not sit with the deceitful,
nor do I associate with hypocrites.
5 I abhor the assembly of evildoers
and refuse to sit with the wicked.
6 I wash my hands in innocence,
and go about your altar, LORD,
7 proclaiming aloud your praise
and telling of all your wonderful deeds.

8 LORD, I love the house where you live,
the place where your glory dwells.
9 Do not take away my soul along with sinners,
my life with those who are bloodthirsty,
10 in whose hands are wicked schemes,
whose right hands are full of bribes.
11 I lead a blameless life;
deliver me and be merciful to me.
12 My feet stand on level ground;
in the great congregation I will praise the LORD.

Psalm 27

Of David.

1 The LORD is my light and my salvation—
whom shall I fear?
The LORD is the stronghold of my life—
of whom shall I be afraid?

2 When the wicked advance against me
to devour[a] me,
it is my enemies and my foes
who will stumble and fall.
3 Though an army besiege me,
my heart will not fear;
though war break out against me,
even then I will be confident.

4 One thing I ask from the LORD,
this only do I seek:
that I may dwell in the house of the LORD
all the days of my life,
to gaze on the beauty of the LORD
and to seek him in his temple.
5 For in the day of trouble
he will keep me safe in his dwelling;
he will hide me in the shelter of his sacred tent
and set me high upon a rock.

6 Then my head will be exalted
above the enemies who surround me;
at his sacred tent I will sacrifice with shouts of joy;
I will sing and make music to the LORD.

7 Hear my voice when I call, LORD;
be merciful to me and answer me.
8 My heart says of you, "Seek his face!"
Your face, LORD, I will seek.
9 Do not hide your face from me,
do not turn your servant away in anger;
you have been my helper.
Do not reject me or forsake me,
God my Savior.
10 Though my father and mother forsake me,
the LORD will receive me.
11 Teach me your way, LORD;
lead me in a straight path
because of my oppressors.
12 Do not turn me over to the desire of my foes,
for false witnesses rise up against me,
spouting malicious accusations.

13 I remain confident of this:
I will see the goodness of the LORD
in the land of the living.
14 Wait for the LORD;
be strong and take heart
and wait for the LORD.

Psalm 28

Of David.

1 To you, LORD, I call;
you are my Rock,
do not turn a deaf ear to me.
For if you remain silent,
I will be like those who go down to the pit.
2 Hear my cry for mercy
as I call to you for help,
as I lift up my hands
toward your Most Holy Place.

3 Do not drag me away with the wicked,
with those who do evil,
who speak cordially with their neighbors
but harbor malice in their hearts.
4 Repay them for their deeds
and for their evil work;
repay them for what their hands have done
and bring back on them what they deserve.

5 Because they have no regard for the deeds of the LORD
and what his hands have done,
he will tear them down
and never build them up again.

6 Praise be to the LORD,
for he has heard my cry for mercy.
7 The LORD is my strength and my shield;
my heart trusts in him, and he helps me.
My heart leaps for joy,
and with my song I praise him.

8 The LORD is the strength of his people,
a fortress of salvation for his anointed one.
9 Save your people and bless your inheritance;
be their shepherd and carry them forever.

[a] 2 Or *slander*

Psalm 29

A psalm of David.

[1]Ascribe to the LORD, you heavenly beings,
ascribe to the LORD glory and strength.
[2]Ascribe to the LORD the glory due his name;
worship the LORD in the splendor of his[a] holiness.

[3]The voice of the LORD is over the waters;
the God of glory thunders,
the LORD thunders over the mighty waters.
[4]The voice of the LORD is powerful;
the voice of the LORD is majestic.
[5]The voice of the LORD breaks the cedars;
the LORD breaks in pieces the cedars of Lebanon.
[6]He makes Lebanon leap like a calf,
Sirion[b] like a young wild ox.
[7]The voice of the LORD strikes
with flashes of lightning.
[8]The voice of the LORD shakes the desert;
the LORD shakes the Desert of Kadesh.
[9]The voice of the LORD twists the oaks[c]
and strips the forests bare.
And in his temple all cry, "Glory!"

[10]The LORD sits enthroned over the flood;
the LORD is enthroned as King forever.
[11]The LORD gives strength to his people;
the LORD blesses his people with peace.

Psalm 30[d]

A psalm. A song. For the dedication of the temple.[e] Of David.

[1]I will exalt you, LORD,
for you lifted me out of the depths
and did not let my enemies gloat over me.
[2]LORD my God, I called to you for help,
and you healed me.
[3]You, LORD, brought me up from the realm of the dead;
you spared me from going down to the pit.

[4]Sing the praises of the LORD, you his faithful people;
praise his holy name.
[5]For his anger lasts only a moment,
but his favor lasts a lifetime;
weeping may stay for the night,
but rejoicing comes in the morning.

[6]When I felt secure, I said,
"I will never be shaken."
[7]LORD, when you favored me,
you made my royal mountain[f] stand firm;
but when you hid your face,
I was dismayed.

[8]To you, LORD, I called;
to the Lord I cried for mercy:
[9]"What is gained if I am silenced,
if I go down to the pit?
Will the dust praise you?
Will it proclaim your faithfulness?
[10]Hear, LORD, and be merciful to me;
LORD, be my help."

[11]You turned my wailing into dancing;
you removed my sackcloth and clothed me with joy,
[12]that my heart may sing your praises and not be silent.
LORD my God, I will praise you forever.

Psalm 31[g]

For the director of music. A psalm of David.

[1]In you, LORD, I have taken refuge;
let me never be put to shame;
deliver me in your righteousness.
[2]Turn your ear to me,
come quickly to my rescue;
be my rock of refuge,
a strong fortress to save me.
[3]Since you are my rock and my fortress,
for the sake of your name lead and guide me.
[4]Keep me free from the trap that is set for me,
for you are my refuge.
[5]Into your hands I commit my spirit;
deliver me, LORD, my faithful God.

[6]I hate those who cling to worthless idols;
as for me, I trust in the LORD.
[7]I will be glad and rejoice in your love,
for you saw my affliction
and knew the anguish of my soul.
[8]You have not given me into the hands of the enemy
but have set my feet in a spacious place.

[9]Be merciful to me, LORD, for I am in distress;
my eyes grow weak with sorrow,
my soul and body with grief.
[10]My life is consumed by anguish
and my years by groaning;
my strength fails because of my affliction,[h]
and my bones grow weak.
[11]Because of all my enemies,
I am the utter contempt of my neighbors
and an object of dread to my closest friends—
those who see me on the street flee from me.
[12]I am forgotten as though I were dead;
I have become like broken pottery.
[13]For I hear many whispering,
"Terror on every side!"
They conspire against me
and plot to take my life.

[14]But I trust in you, LORD;
I say, "You are my God."

[a] 2 Or *LORD with the splendor of* [b] 6 That is, Mount Hermon [c] 9 Or *LORD makes the deer give birth* [d] In Hebrew texts 30:1-12 is numbered 30:2-13. [e] Title: Or *palace* [f] 7 That is, Mount Zion [g] In Hebrew texts 31:1-24 is numbered 31:2-25. [h] 10 Or *guilt*

15 My times are in your hands;
deliver me from the hands of my enemies,
from those who pursue me.
16 Let your face shine on your servant;
save me in your unfailing love.
17 Let me not be put to shame, LORD,
for I have cried out to you;
but let the wicked be put to shame
and be silent in the realm of the dead.
18 Let their lying lips be silenced,
for with pride and contempt
they speak arrogantly against the righteous.

19 How abundant are the good things
that you have stored up for those who fear you,
that you bestow in the sight of all,
on those who take refuge in you.
20 In the shelter of your presence you hide them
from all human intrigues;
you keep them safe in your dwelling
from accusing tongues.

21 Praise be to the LORD,
for he showed me the wonders of his love
when I was in a city under siege.
22 In my alarm I said,
"I am cut off from your sight!"
Yet you heard my cry for mercy
when I called to you for help.

23 Love the LORD, all his faithful people!
The LORD preserves those who are true to him,
but the proud he pays back in full.
24 Be strong and take heart,
all you who hope in the LORD.

Psalm 32

Of David. A maskil.[a]

1 Blessed is the one
whose transgressions are forgiven,
whose sins are covered.
2 Blessed is the one
whose sin the LORD does not count against them
and in whose spirit is no deceit.

3 When I kept silent,
my bones wasted away
through my groaning all day long.
4 For day and night
your hand was heavy on me;
my strength was sapped
as in the heat of summer.[b]

5 Then I acknowledged my sin to you
and did not cover up my iniquity.
I said, "I will confess
my transgressions to the LORD."
And you forgave
the guilt of my sin.

6 Therefore let all the faithful pray to you
while you may be found;
surely the rising of the mighty waters
will not reach them.
7 You are my hiding place;
you will protect me from trouble
and surround me with songs of deliverance.

8 I will instruct you and teach you in the way you should go;
I will counsel you with my loving eye on you.
9 Do not be like the horse or the mule,
which have no understanding
but must be controlled by bit and bridle
or they will not come to you.
10 Many are the woes of the wicked,
but the LORD's unfailing love
surrounds the one who trusts in him.

11 Rejoice in the LORD and be glad, you righteous;
sing, all you who are upright in heart!

Psalm 33

1 Sing joyfully to the LORD, you righteous;
it is fitting for the upright to praise him.
2 Praise the LORD with the harp;
make music to him on the ten-stringed lyre.
3 Sing to him a new song;
play skillfully, and shout for joy.
4 For the word of the LORD is right and true;
he is faithful in all he does.
5 The LORD loves righteousness and justice;
the earth is full of his unfailing love.

6 By the word of the LORD the heavens were made,
their starry host by the breath of his mouth.
7 He gathers the waters of the sea into jars[c];
he puts the deep into storehouses.
8 Let all the earth fear the LORD;
let all the people of the world revere him.
9 For he spoke, and it came to be;
he commanded, and it stood firm.

10 The LORD foils the plans of the nations;
he thwarts the purposes of the peoples.
11 But the plans of the LORD stand firm forever,
the purposes of his heart through all generations.

12 Blessed is the nation whose God is the LORD,
the people he chose for his inheritance.
13 From heaven the LORD looks down
and sees all mankind;
14 from his dwelling place he watches
all who live on earth—
15 he who forms the hearts of all,
who considers everything they do.

16 No king is saved by the size of his army;
no warrior escapes by his great strength.

[a] Title: Probably a literary or musical term here and at the end of verses 5 and 7. [b] 4 The Hebrew has *Selah* (a word of uncertain meaning) [c] 7 Or *sea as into a heap*

17 A horse is a vain hope for deliverance;
despite all its great strength it cannot save.
18 But the eyes of the LORD are on those who fear him,
on those whose hope is in his unfailing love,
19 to deliver them from death
and keep them alive in famine.
20 We wait in hope for the LORD;
he is our help and our shield.
21 In him our hearts rejoice,
for we trust in his holy name.
22 May your unfailing love be with us, LORD,
even as we put our hope in you.

Psalm 34[a,b]

Of David. When he pretended to be insane before Abimelek, who drove him away, and he left.

1 I will extol the LORD at all times;
his praise will always be on my lips.
2 I will glory in the LORD;
let the afflicted hear and rejoice.
3 Glorify the LORD with me;
let us exalt his name together.

4 I sought the LORD, and he answered me;
he delivered me from all my fears.
5 Those who look to him are radiant;
their faces are never covered with shame.
6 This poor man called, and the LORD heard him;
he saved him out of all his troubles.
7 The angel of the LORD encamps around those who fear him,
and he delivers them.

8 Taste and see that the LORD is good;
blessed is the one who takes refuge in him.
9 Fear the LORD, you his holy people,
for those who fear him lack nothing.
10 The lions may grow weak and hungry,
but those who seek the LORD lack no good thing.
11 Come, my children, listen to me;
I will teach you the fear of the LORD.
12 Whoever of you loves life
and desires to see many good days,
13 keep your tongue from evil
and your lips from telling lies.
14 Turn from evil and do good;
seek peace and pursue it.

15 The eyes of the LORD are on the righteous,
and his ears are attentive to their cry;
16 but the face of the LORD is against those who do evil,
to blot out their name from the earth.

17 The righteous cry out, and the LORD hears them;
he delivers them from all their troubles.
18 The LORD is close to the brokenhearted
and saves those who are crushed in spirit.

19 The righteous person may have many troubles,
but the LORD delivers him from them all;
20 he protects all his bones,
not one of them will be broken.

21 Evil will slay the wicked;
the foes of the righteous will be condemned.
22 The LORD will rescue his servants;
no one who takes refuge in him will be condemned.

Psalm 35

Of David.

1 Contend, LORD, with those who contend with me;
fight against those who fight against me.
2 Take up shield and armor;
arise and come to my aid.
3 Brandish spear and javelin[c]
against those who pursue me.
Say to me,
"I am your salvation."

4 May those who seek my life
be disgraced and put to shame;
may those who plot my ruin
be turned back in dismay.
5 May they be like chaff before the wind,
with the angel of the LORD driving them away;
6 may their path be dark and slippery,
with the angel of the LORD pursuing them.

7 Since they hid their net for me without cause
and without cause dug a pit for me,
8 may ruin overtake them by surprise—
may the net they hid entangle them,
may they fall into the pit, to their ruin.
9 Then my soul will rejoice in the LORD
and delight in his salvation.
10 My whole being will exclaim,
"Who is like you, LORD?
You rescue the poor from those too strong for them,
the poor and needy from those who rob them."

11 Ruthless witnesses come forward;
they question me on things I know nothing about.
12 They repay me evil for good
and leave me like one bereaved.
13 Yet when they were ill, I put on sackcloth
and humbled myself with fasting.
When my prayers returned to me unanswered,
14 I went about mourning
as though for my friend or brother.
I bowed my head in grief
as though weeping for my mother.

[a] This psalm is an acrostic poem, the verses of which begin with the successive letters of the Hebrew alphabet. [b] In Hebrew texts 34:1-22 is numbered 34:2-23. [c] 3 Or *and block the way*

[15] But when I stumbled, they gathered in glee;
assailants gathered against me without my knowledge.
They slandered me without ceasing.
[16] Like the ungodly they maliciously mocked;[a]
they gnashed their teeth at me.

[17] How long, Lord, will you look on?
Rescue me from their ravages,
my precious life from these lions.
[18] I will give you thanks in the great assembly;
among the throngs I will praise you.
[19] Do not let those gloat over me
who are my enemies without cause;
do not let those who hate me without reason
maliciously wink the eye.
[20] They do not speak peaceably,
but devise false accusations
against those who live quietly in the land.
[21] They sneer at me and say, "Aha! Aha!
With our own eyes we have seen it."

[22] LORD, you have seen this; do not be silent.
Do not be far from me, Lord.
[23] Awake, and rise to my defense!
Contend for me, my God and Lord.
[24] Vindicate me in your righteousness, LORD my God;
do not let them gloat over me.
[25] Do not let them think, "Aha, just what we wanted!"
or say, "We have swallowed him up."

[26] May all who gloat over my distress
be put to shame and confusion;
may all who exalt themselves over me
be clothed with shame and disgrace.
[27] May those who delight in my vindication
shout for joy and gladness;
may they always say, "The LORD be exalted,
who delights in the well-being of his servant."

[28] My tongue will proclaim your righteousness,
your praises all day long.

Psalm 36[b]

For the director of music. Of David the servant of the LORD.

[1] I have a message from God in my heart
concerning the sinfulness of the wicked:[c]
There is no fear of God
before their eyes.

[2] In their own eyes they flatter themselves
too much to detect or hate their sin.
[3] The words of their mouths are wicked and deceitful;
they fail to act wisely or do good.
[4] Even on their beds they plot evil;
they commit themselves to a sinful course
and do not reject what is wrong.

[5] Your love, LORD, reaches to the heavens,
your faithfulness to the skies.
[6] Your righteousness is like the highest mountains,
your justice like the great deep.
You, LORD, preserve both people and animals.
[7] How priceless is your unfailing love, O God!
People take refuge in the shadow of your wings.
[8] They feast on the abundance of your house;
you give them drink from your river of delights.
[9] For with you is the fountain of life;
in your light we see light.

[10] Continue your love to those who know you,
your righteousness to the upright in heart.
[11] May the foot of the proud not come against me,
nor the hand of the wicked drive me away.
[12] See how the evildoers lie fallen—
thrown down, not able to rise!

Psalm 37[d]

Of David.

[1] Do not fret because of those who are evil
or be envious of those who do wrong;
[2] for like the grass they will soon wither,
like green plants they will soon die away.

[3] Trust in the LORD and do good;
dwell in the land and enjoy safe pasture.
[4] Take delight in the LORD,
and he will give you the desires of your heart.

[5] Commit your way to the LORD;
trust in him and he will do this:
[6] He will make your righteous reward shine like the dawn,
your vindication like the noonday sun.

[7] Be still before the LORD
and wait patiently for him;
do not fret when people succeed in their ways,
when they carry out their wicked schemes.

[8] Refrain from anger and turn from wrath;
do not fret—it leads only to evil.
[9] For those who are evil will be destroyed,
but those who hope in the LORD will inherit the land.

[a] *16* Septuagint; Hebrew may mean *Like an ungodly circle of mockers,* [b] In Hebrew texts 36:1-12 is numbered 36:2-13. [c] *1* Or *A message from God: The transgression of the wicked / resides in their hearts.* [d] This psalm is an acrostic poem, the stanzas of which begin with the successive letters of the Hebrew alphabet.

10 A little while, and the wicked will be no more;
though you look for them, they will not be found.
11 But the meek will inherit the land
and enjoy peace and prosperity.

12 The wicked plot against the righteous
and gnash their teeth at them;
13 but the Lord laughs at the wicked,
for he knows their day is coming.

14 The wicked draw the sword
and bend the bow
to bring down the poor and needy,
to slay those whose ways are upright.
15 But their swords will pierce their own hearts,
and their bows will be broken.

16 Better the little that the righteous have
than the wealth of many wicked;
17 for the power of the wicked will be broken,
but the LORD upholds the righteous.

18 The blameless spend their days under the LORD's care,
and their inheritance will endure forever.
19 In times of disaster they will not wither;
in days of famine they will enjoy plenty.

20 But the wicked will perish:
Though the LORD's enemies are like the flowers of the field,
they will be consumed, they will go up in smoke.

21 The wicked borrow and do not repay,
but the righteous give generously;
22 those the LORD blesses will inherit the land,
but those he curses will be destroyed.

23 The LORD makes firm the steps
of the one who delights in him;
24 though he may stumble, he will not fall,
for the LORD upholds him with his hand.

25 I was young and now I am old,
yet I have never seen the righteous forsaken
or their children begging bread.
26 They are always generous and lend freely;
their children will be a blessing.[a]

27 Turn from evil and do good;
then you will dwell in the land forever.
28 For the LORD loves the just
and will not forsake his faithful ones.

Wrongdoers will be completely destroyed[b];
the offspring of the wicked will perish.
29 The righteous will inherit the land
and dwell in it forever.

30 The mouths of the righteous utter wisdom,
and their tongues speak what is just.
31 The law of their God is in their hearts;
their feet do not slip.

32 The wicked lie in wait for the righteous,
intent on putting them to death;
33 but the LORD will not leave them in the power of the wicked
or let them be condemned when brought to trial.

34 Hope in the LORD
and keep his way.
He will exalt you to inherit the land;
when the wicked are destroyed, you will see it.

35 I have seen a wicked and ruthless man
flourishing like a luxuriant native tree,
36 but he soon passed away and was no more;
though I looked for him, he could not be found.

37 Consider the blameless, observe the upright;
a future awaits those who seek peace.[c]
38 But all sinners will be destroyed;
there will be no future[d] for the wicked.

39 The salvation of the righteous comes from the LORD;
he is their stronghold in time of trouble.
40 The LORD helps them and delivers them;
he delivers them from the wicked and saves them,
because they take refuge in him.

Psalm 38[e]

A psalm of David. A petition.

1 LORD, do not rebuke me in your anger
or discipline me in your wrath.
2 Your arrows have pierced me,
and your hand has come down on me.
3 Because of your wrath there is no health in my body;
there is no soundness in my bones
because of my sin.
4 My guilt has overwhelmed me
like a burden too heavy to bear.

5 My wounds fester and are loathsome
because of my sinful folly.
6 I am bowed down and brought very low;
all day long I go about mourning.
7 My back is filled with searing pain;
there is no health in my body.
8 I am feeble and utterly crushed;
I groan in anguish of heart.

9 All my longings lie open before you, Lord;
my sighing is not hidden from you.
10 My heart pounds, my strength fails me;
even the light has gone from my eyes.

[a] 26 Or *freely; / the names of their children will be used in blessings* (see Gen. 48:20); or *freely; / others will see that their children are blessed* [b] 28 See Septuagint; Hebrew *They will be protected forever* [c] 37 Or *upright; / those who seek peace will have posterity* [d] 38 Or *posterity* [e] In Hebrew texts 38:1-22 is numbered 38:2-23.

[11] My friends and companions avoid me
because of my wounds;
my neighbors stay far away.
[12] Those who want to kill me set their traps,
those who would harm me talk of my
ruin;
all day long they scheme and lie.

[13] I am like the deaf, who cannot hear,
like the mute, who cannot speak;
[14] I have become like one who does not hear,
whose mouth can offer no reply.
[15] LORD, I wait for you;
you will answer, Lord my God.
[16] For I said, "Do not let them gloat
or exalt themselves over me when my
feet slip."

[17] For I am about to fall,
and my pain is ever with me.
[18] I confess my iniquity;
I am troubled by my sin.
[19] Many have become my enemies without
cause[a];
those who hate me without reason are
numerous.
[20] Those who repay my good with evil
lodge accusations against me,
though I seek only to do what is good.

[21] LORD, do not forsake me;
do not be far from me, my God.
[22] Come quickly to help me,
my Lord and my Savior.

Psalm 39[b]

For the director of music. For Jeduthun.
A psalm of David.

[1] I said, "I will watch my ways
and keep my tongue from sin;
I will put a muzzle on my mouth
while in the presence of the wicked."
[2] So I remained utterly silent,
not even saying anything good.
But my anguish increased;
[3] my heart grew hot within me.
While I meditated, the fire burned;
then I spoke with my tongue:

[4] "Show me, LORD, my life's end
and the number of my days;
let me know how fleeting my life is.
[5] You have made my days a mere
handbreadth;
the span of my years is as nothing
before you.
Everyone is but a breath,
even those who seem secure.[c]

[6] "Surely everyone goes around like a mere
phantom;
in vain they rush about, heaping up
wealth
without knowing whose it will finally
be.

[7] "But now, Lord, what do I look for?
My hope is in you.
[8] Save me from all my transgressions;
do not make me the scorn of fools.
[9] I was silent; I would not open my mouth,
for you are the one who has done this.
[10] Remove your scourge from me;
I am overcome by the blow of your hand.
[11] When you rebuke and discipline anyone
for their sin,
you consume their wealth like a moth—
surely everyone is but a breath.

[12] "Hear my prayer, LORD,
listen to my cry for help;
do not be deaf to my weeping.
I dwell with you as a foreigner,
a stranger, as all my ancestors were.
[13] Look away from me, that I may enjoy life
again
before I depart and am no more."

Psalm 40[d]

For the director of music. Of David. A psalm.

[1] I waited patiently for the LORD;
he turned to me and heard my cry.
[2] He lifted me out of the slimy pit,
out of the mud and mire;
he set my feet on a rock
and gave me a firm place to stand.
[3] He put a new song in my mouth,
a hymn of praise to our God.
Many will see and fear the LORD
and put their trust in him.

[4] Blessed is the one
who trusts in the LORD,
who does not look to the proud,
to those who turn aside to false gods.[e]
[5] Many, LORD my God,
are the wonders you have done,
the things you planned for us.
None can compare with you;
were I to speak and tell of your deeds,
they would be too many to declare.

[6] Sacrifice and offering you did not
desire—
but my ears you have opened[f]—
burnt offerings and sin offerings[g] you
did not require.
[7] Then I said, "Here I am, I have come—
it is written about me in the scroll.[h]
[8] I desire to do your will, my God;
your law is within my heart."

[9] I proclaim your saving acts in the great
assembly;
I do not seal my lips, LORD,
as you know.
[10] I do not hide your righteousness in my
heart;
I speak of your faithfulness and your
saving help.

[a] *19* One Dead Sea Scrolls manuscript; Masoretic Text *my vigorous enemies* [b] In Hebrew texts 39:1-13 is numbered 39:2-14. [c] *5* The Hebrew has *Selah* (a word of uncertain meaning) here and at the end of verse 11. [d] In Hebrew texts 40:1-17 is numbered 40:2-18. [e] *4* Or *to lies* [f] *6* Hebrew; some Septuagint manuscripts *but a body you have prepared for me* [g] *6* Or *purification offerings* [h] *7* Or *come / with the scroll written for me*

I do not conceal your love and your faithfulness
from the great assembly.
11 Do not withhold your mercy from me, LORD;
may your love and faithfulness always protect me.
12 For troubles without number surround me;
my sins have overtaken me, and I cannot see.
They are more than the hairs of my head,
and my heart fails within me.
13 Be pleased to save me, LORD;
come quickly, LORD, to help me.

14 May all who want to take my life
be put to shame and confusion;
may all who desire my ruin
be turned back in disgrace.
15 May those who say to me, "Aha! Aha!"
be appalled at their own shame.
16 But may all who seek you
rejoice and be glad in you;
may those who long for your saving help always say,
"The LORD is great!"

17 But as for me, I am poor and needy;
may the Lord think of me.
You are my help and my deliverer;
you are my God, do not delay.

Psalm 41[a]

For the director of music. A psalm of David.

1 Blessed are those who have regard for the weak;
the LORD delivers them in times of trouble.
2 The LORD protects and preserves them—
they are counted among the blessed in the land—
he does not give them over to the desire of their foes.
3 The LORD sustains them on their sickbed
and restores them from their bed of illness.

4 I said, "Have mercy on me, LORD;
heal me, for I have sinned against you."
5 My enemies say of me in malice,
"When will he die and his name perish?"
6 When one of them comes to see me,
he speaks falsely, while his heart gathers slander;
then he goes out and spreads it around.
7 All my enemies whisper together against me;
they imagine the worst for me, saying,
8 "A vile disease has afflicted him;
he will never get up from the place where he lies."
9 Even my close friend,
someone I trusted,
one who shared my bread,
has turned[b] against me.

10 But may you have mercy on me, LORD;
raise me up, that I may repay them.
11 I know that you are pleased with me,
for my enemy does not triumph over me.
12 Because of my integrity you uphold me
and set me in your presence forever.

13 Praise be to the LORD, the God of Israel,
from everlasting to everlasting.
Amen and Amen.

BOOK II

Psalms 42–72

Psalm 42[c,d]

For the director of music. A maskil[e] of the Sons of Korah.

1 As the deer pants for streams of water,
so my soul pants for you, my God.
2 My soul thirsts for God, for the living God.
When can I go and meet with God?
3 My tears have been my food
day and night,
while people say to me all day long,
"Where is your God?"
4 These things I remember
as I pour out my soul:
how I used to go to the house of God
under the protection of the Mighty One[f]
with shouts of joy and praise
among the festive throng.

5 Why, my soul, are you downcast?
Why so disturbed within me?
Put your hope in God,
for I will yet praise him,
my Savior and my God.

6 My soul is downcast within me;
therefore I will remember you
from the land of the Jordan,
the heights of Hermon—from Mount Mizar.
7 Deep calls to deep
in the roar of your waterfalls;
all your waves and breakers
have swept over me.

8 By day the LORD directs his love,
at night his song is with me—
a prayer to the God of my life.

9 I say to God my Rock,
"Why have you forgotten me?
Why must I go about mourning,
oppressed by the enemy?"
10 My bones suffer mortal agony
as my foes taunt me,

[a] In Hebrew texts 41:1-13 is numbered 41:2-14. [b] 9 Hebrew *has lifted up his heel* [c] In many Hebrew manuscripts Psalms 42 and 43 constitute one psalm. [d] In Hebrew texts 42:1-11 is numbered 42:2-12. [e] Title: Probably a literary or musical term [f] 4 See Septuagint and Syriac; the meaning of the Hebrew for this line is uncertain.

saying to me all day long,
"Where is your God?"

11 Why, my soul, are you downcast?
Why so disturbed within me?
Put your hope in God,
for I will yet praise him,
my Savior and my God.

Psalm 43[a]

1 Vindicate me, my God,
and plead my cause
against an unfaithful nation.
Rescue me from those who are
deceitful and wicked.
2 You are God my stronghold.
Why have you rejected me?
Why must I go about mourning,
oppressed by the enemy?
3 Send me your light and your faithful care,
let them lead me;
let them bring me to your holy mountain,
to the place where you dwell.
4 Then I will go to the altar of God,
to God, my joy and my delight.
I will praise you with the lyre,
O God, my God.

5 Why, my soul, are you downcast?
Why so disturbed within me?
Put your hope in God,
for I will yet praise him,
my Savior and my God.

Psalm 44[b]

For the director of music. Of the Sons of Korah. A maskil.[c]

1 We have heard it with our ears, O God;
our ancestors have told us
what you did in their days,
in days long ago.
2 With your hand you drove out the
nations
and planted our ancestors;
you crushed the peoples
and made our ancestors flourish.
3 It was not by their sword that they won
the land,
nor did their arm bring them victory;
it was your right hand, your arm,
and the light of your face, for you loved
them.
4 You are my King and my God,
who decrees[d] victories for Jacob.
5 Through you we push back our enemies;
through your name we trample our
foes.
6 I put no trust in my bow,
my sword does not bring me victory;
7 but you give us victory over our enemies,
you put our adversaries to shame.
8 In God we make our boast all day long,
and we will praise your name forever.[e]

9 But now you have rejected and humbled
us;
you no longer go out with our armies.
10 You made us retreat before the enemy,
and our adversaries have plundered us.
11 You gave us up to be devoured like sheep
and have scattered us among the
nations.
12 You sold your people for a pittance,
gaining nothing from their sale.

13 You have made us a reproach to our
neighbors,
the scorn and derision of those around
us.
14 You have made us a byword among the
nations;
the peoples shake their heads at us.
15 I live in disgrace all day long,
and my face is covered with shame
16 at the taunts of those who reproach and
revile me,
because of the enemy, who is bent on
revenge.

17 All this came upon us,
though we had not forgotten you;
we had not been false to your covenant.
18 Our hearts had not turned back;
our feet had not strayed from your path.
19 But you crushed us and made us a haunt
for jackals;
you covered us over with deep darkness.

20 If we had forgotten the name of our God
or spread out our hands to a foreign
god,
21 would not God have discovered it,
since he knows the secrets of the heart?
22 Yet for your sake we face death all day
long;
we are considered as sheep to be
slaughtered.

23 Awake, Lord! Why do you sleep?
Rouse yourself! Do not reject us
forever.
24 Why do you hide your face
and forget our misery and oppression?

25 We are brought down to the dust;
our bodies cling to the ground.
26 Rise up and help us;
rescue us because of your unfailing love.

Psalm 45[f]

For the director of music. To the tune of "Lilies." Of the Sons of Korah. A maskil.[c] *A wedding song.*

1 My heart is stirred by a noble theme
as I recite my verses for the king;
my tongue is the pen of a skillful writer.

2 You are the most excellent of men
and your lips have been anointed with
grace,
since God has blessed you forever.

[a] In many Hebrew manuscripts Psalms 42 and 43 constitute one psalm. [b] In Hebrew texts 44:1-26 is numbered 44:2-27. [c] Title: Probably a literary or musical term [d] 4 Septuagint, Aquila and Syriac; Hebrew *King, O God; / command* [e] 8 The Hebrew has *Selah* (a word of uncertain meaning) here.
[f] In Hebrew texts 45:1-17 is numbered 45:2-18.

3 Gird your sword on your side, you mighty
one;
clothe yourself with splendor and
majesty.
4 In your majesty ride forth victoriously
in the cause of truth, humility and
justice;
let your right hand achieve awesome
deeds.
5 Let your sharp arrows pierce the hearts
of the king's enemies;
let the nations fall beneath your feet.
6 Your throne, O God,[a] will last for ever
and ever;
a scepter of justice will be the scepter of
your kingdom.
7 You love righteousness and hate
wickedness;
therefore God, your God, has set you
above your companions
by anointing you with the oil of joy.
8 All your robes are fragrant with myrrh
and aloes and cassia;
from palaces adorned with ivory
the music of the strings makes you glad.
9 Daughters of kings are among your
honored women;
at your right hand is the royal bride in
gold of Ophir.

10 Listen, daughter, and pay careful attention:
Forget your people and your father's
house.
11 Let the king be enthralled by your beauty;
honor him, for he is your lord.
12 The city of Tyre will come with a gift,[b]
people of wealth will seek your favor.
13 All glorious is the princess within her
chamber;
her gown is interwoven with gold.
14 In embroidered garments she is led to the
king;
her virgin companions follow her—
those brought to be with her.
15 Led in with joy and gladness,
they enter the palace of the king.

16 Your sons will take the place of your
fathers;
you will make them princes throughout
the land.

17 I will perpetuate your memory through
all generations;
therefore the nations will praise you for
ever and ever.

Psalm 46[c]

*For the director of music. Of the Sons of Korah.
According to alamoth.[d] A song.*

1 God is our refuge and strength,
an ever-present help in trouble.
2 Therefore we will not fear, though the
earth give way
and the mountains fall into the heart of
the sea,
3 though its waters roar and foam
and the mountains quake with their
surging.[e]

4 There is a river whose streams make glad
the city of God,
the holy place where the Most High
dwells.
5 God is within her, she will not fall;
God will help her at break of day.
6 Nations are in uproar, kingdoms fall;
he lifts his voice, the earth melts.

7 The LORD Almighty is with us;
the God of Jacob is our fortress.

8 Come and see what the LORD has done,
the desolations he has brought on the
earth.
9 He makes wars cease
to the ends of the earth.
He breaks the bow and shatters the spear;
he burns the shields[f] with fire.
10 He says, "Be still, and know that I am God;
I will be exalted among the nations,
I will be exalted in the earth."

11 The LORD Almighty is with us;
the God of Jacob is our fortress.

Psalm 47[g]

*For the director of music. Of the Sons of Korah.
A psalm.*

1 Clap your hands, all you nations;
shout to God with cries of joy.

2 For the LORD Most High is awesome,
the great King over all the earth.
3 He subdued nations under us,
peoples under our feet.
4 He chose our inheritance for us,
the pride of Jacob, whom he loved.[h]

5 God has ascended amid shouts of joy,
the LORD amid the sounding of trumpets.
6 Sing praises to God, sing praises;
sing praises to our King, sing praises.
7 For God is the King of all the earth;
sing to him a psalm of praise.

8 God reigns over the nations;
God is seated on his holy throne.
9 The nobles of the nations assemble
as the people of the God of Abraham,
for the kings[i] of the earth belong to God;
he is greatly exalted.

Psalm 48[j]

A song. A psalm of the Sons of Korah.

1 Great is the LORD, and most worthy of
praise,
in the city of our God, his holy
mountain.

[a] 6 Here the king is addressed as God's representative. [b] 12 Or *A Tyrian robe is among the gifts*
[c] In Hebrew texts 46:1-11 is numbered 46:2-12. [d] Title: Probably a musical term [e] 3 The Hebrew has *Selah* (a word of uncertain meaning) here and at the end of verses 7 and 11. [f] 9 Or *chariots*
[g] In Hebrew texts 47:1-9 is numbered 47:2-10. [h] 4 The Hebrew has *Selah* (a word of uncertain meaning) here. [i] 9 Or *shields* [j] In Hebrew texts 48:1-14 is numbered 48:2-15.

2 Beautiful in its loftiness,
the joy of the whole earth,
like the heights of Zaphon[a] is Mount Zion,
the city of the Great King.
3 God is in her citadels;
he has shown himself to be her fortress.

4 When the kings joined forces,
when they advanced together,
5 they saw her and were astounded;
they fled in terror.
6 Trembling seized them there,
pain like that of a woman in labor.
7 You destroyed them like ships of Tarshish
shattered by an east wind.

8 As we have heard,
so we have seen
in the city of the LORD Almighty,
in the city of our God:
God makes her secure
forever.[b]

9 Within your temple, O God,
we meditate on your unfailing love.
10 Like your name, O God,
your praise reaches to the ends of the earth;
your right hand is filled with righteousness.
11 Mount Zion rejoices,
the villages of Judah are glad
because of your judgments.

12 Walk about Zion, go around her,
count her towers,
13 consider well her ramparts,
view her citadels,
that you may tell of them
to the next generation.

14 For this God is our God for ever and ever;
he will be our guide even to the end.

Psalm 49[c]

For the director of music. Of the Sons of Korah. A psalm.

1 Hear this, all you peoples;
listen, all who live in this world,
2 both low and high,
rich and poor alike:
3 My mouth will speak words of wisdom;
the meditation of my heart will give you understanding.
4 I will turn my ear to a proverb;
with the harp I will expound my riddle:

5 Why should I fear when evil days come,
when wicked deceivers surround me—
6 those who trust in their wealth
and boast of their great riches?
7 No one can redeem the life of another
or give to God a ransom for them—
8 the ransom for a life is costly,
no payment is ever enough—
9 so that they should live on forever
and not see decay.
10 For all can see that the wise die,
that the foolish and the senseless also perish,
leaving their wealth to others.
11 Their tombs will remain their houses[d] forever,
their dwellings for endless generations,
though they had[e] named lands after themselves.

12 People, despite their wealth, do not endure;
they are like the beasts that perish.

13 This is the fate of those who trust in themselves,
and of their followers, who approve their sayings.[f]
14 They are like sheep and are destined to die;
death will be their shepherd
(but the upright will prevail over them in the morning).
Their forms will decay in the grave,
far from their princely mansions.
15 But God will redeem me from the realm of the dead;
he will surely take me to himself.
16 Do not be overawed when others grow rich,
when the splendor of their houses increases;
17 for they will take nothing with them when they die,
their splendor will not descend with them.
18 Though while they live they count themselves blessed—
and people praise you when you prosper—
19 they will join those who have gone before them,
who will never again see the light of life.

20 People who have wealth but lack understanding
are like the beasts that perish.

Psalm 50

A psalm of Asaph.

1 The Mighty One, God, the LORD,
speaks and summons the earth
from the rising of the sun to where it sets.
2 From Zion, perfect in beauty,
God shines forth.
3 Our God comes
and will not be silent;
a fire devours before him,
and around him a tempest rages.
4 He summons the heavens above,
and the earth, that he may judge his people:

[a] 2 *Zaphon* was the most sacred mountain of the Canaanites. [b] 8 The Hebrew has *Selah* (a word of uncertain meaning) here. [c] In Hebrew texts 49:1-20 is numbered 49:2-21. [d] 11 Septuagint and Syriac; Hebrew *In their thoughts their houses will remain* [e] 11 Or *generations, / for they have* [f] 13 The Hebrew has *Selah* (a word of uncertain meaning) here and at the end of verse 15.

5 "Gather to me this consecrated people,
who made a covenant with me by sacrifice."
6 And the heavens proclaim his righteousness,
for he is a God of justice.[a,b]

7 "Listen, my people, and I will speak;
I will testify against you, Israel:
I am God, your God.
8 I bring no charges against you
concerning your sacrifices
or concerning your burnt offerings,
which are ever before me.
9 I have no need of a bull from your stall
or of goats from your pens,
10 for every animal of the forest is mine,
and the cattle on a thousand hills.
11 I know every bird in the mountains,
and the insects in the fields are mine.
12 If I were hungry I would not tell you,
for the world is mine, and all that is in it.
13 Do I eat the flesh of bulls
or drink the blood of goats?

14 "Sacrifice thank offerings to God,
fulfill your vows to the Most High,
15 and call on me in the day of trouble;
I will deliver you, and you will honor me."

16 But to the wicked person, God says:

"What right have you to recite my laws
or take my covenant on your lips?
17 You hate my instruction
and cast my words behind you.
18 When you see a thief, you join with him;
you throw in your lot with adulterers.
19 You use your mouth for evil
and harness your tongue to deceit.
20 You sit and testify against your brother
and slander your own mother's son.
21 When you did these things and I kept silent,
you thought I was exactly[c] like you.
But I now arraign you
and set my accusations before you.

22 "Consider this, you who forget God,
or I will tear you to pieces, with no one to rescue you:
23 Those who sacrifice thank offerings honor me,
and to the blameless[d] I will show my salvation."

Psalm 51[e]

For the director of music. A psalm of David. When the prophet Nathan came to him after David had committed adultery with Bathsheba.

1 Have mercy on me, O God,
according to your unfailing love;
according to your great compassion
blot out my transgressions.
2 Wash away all my iniquity
and cleanse me from my sin.

3 For I know my transgressions,
and my sin is always before me.
4 Against you, you only, have I sinned
and done what is evil in your sight;
so you are right in your verdict
and justified when you judge.
5 Surely I was sinful at birth,
sinful from the time my mother conceived me.
6 Yet you desired faithfulness even in the womb;
you taught me wisdom in that secret place.

7 Cleanse me with hyssop, and I will be clean;
wash me, and I will be whiter than snow.
8 Let me hear joy and gladness;
let the bones you have crushed rejoice.
9 Hide your face from my sins
and blot out all my iniquity.

10 Create in me a pure heart, O God,
and renew a steadfast spirit within me.
11 Do not cast me from your presence
or take your Holy Spirit from me.
12 Restore to me the joy of your salvation
and grant me a willing spirit, to sustain me.

13 Then I will teach transgressors your ways,
so that sinners will turn back to you.
14 Deliver me from the guilt of bloodshed, O God,
you who are God my Savior,
and my tongue will sing of your righteousness.
15 Open my lips, Lord,
and my mouth will declare your praise.
16 You do not delight in sacrifice, or I would bring it;
you do not take pleasure in burnt offerings.
17 My sacrifice, O God, is[f] a broken spirit;
a broken and contrite heart
you, God, will not despise.

18 May it please you to prosper Zion,
to build up the walls of Jerusalem.
19 Then you will delight in the sacrifices of the righteous,
in burnt offerings offered whole;
then bulls will be offered on your altar.

Psalm 52[g]

For the director of music. A maskil[h] of David. When Doeg the Edomite had gone to Saul and told him: "David has gone to the house of Ahimelek."

1 Why do you boast of evil, you mighty hero?
Why do you boast all day long,

[a] *6* With a different word division of the Hebrew; Masoretic Text *for God himself is judge*
[b] *6* The Hebrew has *Selah* (a word of uncertain meaning) here.
[c] *21* Or *thought the 'I AM' was*
[d] *23* Probable reading of the original Hebrew text; the meaning of the Masoretic Text for this phrase is uncertain.
[e] In Hebrew texts 51:1-19 is numbered 51:3-21.
[f] *17* Or *The sacrifices of God are*
[g] In Hebrew texts 52:1-9 is numbered 52:3-11.
[h] Title: Probably a literary or musical term

you who are a disgrace in the eyes of
God?
[2]You who practice deceit,
your tongue plots destruction;
it is like a sharpened razor.
[3]You love evil rather than good,
falsehood rather than speaking the
truth.[a]
[4]You love every harmful word,
you deceitful tongue!
[5]Surely God will bring you down to
everlasting ruin:
He will snatch you up and pluck you
from your tent;
he will uproot you from the land of the
living.
[6]The righteous will see and fear;
they will laugh at you, saying,
[7]"Here now is the man
who did not make God his stronghold
but trusted in his great wealth
and grew strong by destroying others!"
[8]But I am like an olive tree
flourishing in the house of God;
I trust in God's unfailing love
for ever and ever.
[9]For what you have done I will always
praise you
in the presence of your faithful people.
And I will hope in your name,
for your name is good.

Psalm 53[b]

For the director of music. According to mahalath.[c] *A* maskil[d] *of David.*

[1]The fool says in his heart,
"There is no God."
They are corrupt, and their ways are vile;
there is no one who does good.
[2]God looks down from heaven
on all mankind
to see if there are any who understand,
any who seek God.
[3]Everyone has turned away, all have
become corrupt;
there is no one who does good,
not even one.
[4]Do all these evildoers know nothing?
They devour my people as though eating
bread;
they never call on God.
[5]But there they are, overwhelmed with
dread,
where there was nothing to dread.
God scattered the bones of those who
attacked you;
you put them to shame, for God
despised them.
[6]Oh, that salvation for Israel would come
out of Zion!
When God restores his people,
let Jacob rejoice and Israel be glad!

Psalm 54[e]

For the director of music. With stringed instruments. A maskil[d] *of David. When the Ziphites had gone to Saul and said, "Is not David hiding among us?"*

[1]Save me, O God, by your name;
vindicate me by your might.
[2]Hear my prayer, O God;
listen to the words of my mouth.
[3]Arrogant foes are attacking me;
ruthless people are trying to kill me—
people without regard for God.[f]
[4]Surely God is my help;
the Lord is the one who sustains me.
[5]Let evil recoil on those who slander me;
in your faithfulness destroy them.
[6]I will sacrifice a freewill offering to you;
I will praise your name, LORD, for it is
good.
[7]You have delivered me from all my
troubles,
and my eyes have looked in triumph on
my foes.

Psalm 55[g]

For the director of music. With stringed instruments. A maskil[d] *of David.*

[1]Listen to my prayer, O God,
do not ignore my plea;
[2] hear me and answer me.
My thoughts trouble me and I am
distraught
[3] because of what my enemy is saying,
because of the threats of the wicked;
for they bring down suffering on me
and assail me in their anger.
[4]My heart is in anguish within me;
the terrors of death have fallen on me.
[5]Fear and trembling have beset me;
horror has overwhelmed me.
[6]I said, "Oh, that I had the wings of a
dove!
I would fly away and be at rest.
[7]I would flee far away
and stay in the desert;[h]
[8]I would hurry to my place of shelter,
far from the tempest and storm."
[9]Lord, confuse the wicked, confound their
words,
for I see violence and strife in the city.
[10]Day and night they prowl about on its
walls;
malice and abuse are within it.
[11]Destructive forces are at work in the city;
threats and lies never leave its streets.

[a] 3 The Hebrew has *Selah* (a word of uncertain meaning) here and at the end of verse 5. [b] In Hebrew texts 53:1-6 is numbered 53:2-7. [c] Title: Probably a musical term [d] Title: Probably a literary or musical term [e] In Hebrew texts 54:1-7 is numbered 54:3-9. [f] 3 The Hebrew has *Selah* (a word of uncertain meaning) here. [g] In Hebrew texts 55:1-23 is numbered 55:2-24. [h] 7 The Hebrew has *Selah* (a word of uncertain meaning) here and in the middle of verse 19.

12 If an enemy were insulting me,
I could endure it;
if a foe were rising against me,
I could hide.
13 But it is you, a man like myself,
my companion, my close friend,
14 with whom I once enjoyed sweet fellowship
at the house of God,
as we walked about
among the worshipers.

15 Let death take my enemies by surprise;
let them go down alive to the realm of the dead,
for evil finds lodging among them.

16 As for me, I call to God,
and the LORD saves me.
17 Evening, morning and noon
I cry out in distress,
and he hears my voice.
18 He rescues me unharmed
from the battle waged against me,
even though many oppose me.
19 God, who is enthroned from of old,
who does not change—
he will hear them and humble them,
because they have no fear of God.

20 My companion attacks his friends;
he violates his covenant.
21 His talk is smooth as butter,
yet war is in his heart;
his words are more soothing than oil,
yet they are drawn swords.

22 Cast your cares on the LORD
and he will sustain you;
he will never let
the righteous be shaken.
23 But you, God, will bring down the wicked
into the pit of decay;
the bloodthirsty and deceitful
will not live out half their days.

But as for me, I trust in you.

Psalm 56[a]

For the director of music. To the tune of "A Dove on Distant Oaks." Of David. A miktam.[b] *When the Philistines had seized him in Gath.*

1 Be merciful to me, my God,
for my enemies are in hot pursuit;
all day long they press their attack.
2 My adversaries pursue me all day long;
in their pride many are attacking me.

3 When I am afraid, I put my trust in you.
4 In God, whose word I praise—
in God I trust and am not afraid.
What can mere mortals do to me?

5 All day long they twist my words;
all their schemes are for my ruin.
6 They conspire, they lurk,
they watch my steps,
hoping to take my life.
7 Because of their wickedness do not[c] let them escape;
in your anger, God, bring the nations down.

8 Record my misery;
list my tears on your scroll[d]—
are they not in your record?
9 Then my enemies will turn back
when I call for help.
By this I will know that God is for me.

10 In God, whose word I praise,
in the LORD, whose word I praise—
11 in God I trust and am not afraid.
What can man do to me?

12 I am under vows to you, my God;
I will present my thank offerings to you.
13 For you have delivered me from death
and my feet from stumbling,
that I may walk before God
in the light of life.

Psalm 57[e]

For the director of music. To the tune of "Do Not Destroy." Of David. A miktam.[b] *When he had fled from Saul into the cave.*

1 Have mercy on me, my God, have mercy on me,
for in you I take refuge.
I will take refuge in the shadow of your wings
until the disaster has passed.

2 I cry out to God Most High,
to God, who vindicates me.
3 He sends from heaven and saves me,
rebuking those who hotly pursue me—[f]
God sends forth his love and his faithfulness.

4 I am in the midst of lions;
I am forced to dwell among ravenous beasts—
men whose teeth are spears and arrows,
whose tongues are sharp swords.

5 Be exalted, O God, above the heavens;
let your glory be over all the earth.

6 They spread a net for my feet—
I was bowed down in distress.
They dug a pit in my path—
but they have fallen into it themselves.

7 My heart, O God, is steadfast,
my heart is steadfast;
I will sing and make music.
8 Awake, my soul!
Awake, harp and lyre!
I will awaken the dawn.

9 I will praise you, Lord, among the nations;
I will sing of you among the peoples.

[a] In Hebrew texts 56:1-13 is numbered 56:2-14. [b] Title: Probably a literary or musical term
[c] 7 Probable reading of the original Hebrew text; Masoretic Text does not have *do not.*
[d] 8 Or *misery; / put my tears in your wineskin* [e] In Hebrew texts 57:1-11 is numbered 57:2-12.
[f] 3 The Hebrew has *Selah* (a word of uncertain meaning) here and at the end of verse 6.

10 For great is your love, reaching to the
heavens;
your faithfulness reaches to the skies.

11 Be exalted, O God, above the heavens;
let your glory be over all the earth.

Psalm 58[a]

For the director of music. To the tune of "Do Not Destroy." Of David. A miktam.[b]

1 Do you rulers indeed speak justly?
Do you judge people with equity?
2 No, in your heart you devise injustice,
and your hands mete out violence on
the earth.

3 Even from birth the wicked go astray;
from the womb they are wayward,
spreading lies.
4 Their venom is like the venom of a snake,
like that of a cobra that has stopped its
ears,
5 that will not heed the tune of the charmer,
however skillful the enchanter may be.

6 Break the teeth in their mouths, O God;
LORD, tear out the fangs of those lions!
7 Let them vanish like water that flows away;
when they draw the bow, let their
arrows fall short.
8 May they be like a slug that melts away as
it moves along,
like a stillborn child that never sees the
sun.

9 Before your pots can feel the heat of the
thorns—
whether they be green or dry—the
wicked will be swept away.[c]
10 The righteous will be glad when they are
avenged,
when they dip their feet in the blood of
the wicked.
11 Then people will say,
"Surely the righteous still are
rewarded;
surely there is a God who judges the
earth."

Psalm 59[d]

For the director of music. To the tune of "Do Not Destroy." Of David. A miktam.[b] *When Saul had sent men to watch David's house in order to kill him.*

1 Deliver me from my enemies, O God;
be my fortress against those who are
attacking me.
2 Deliver me from evildoers
and save me from those who are after
my blood.

3 See how they lie in wait for me!
Fierce men conspire against me
for no offense or sin of mine, LORD.
4 I have done no wrong, yet they are ready
to attack me.
Arise to help me; look on my plight!
5 You, LORD God Almighty,
you who are the God of Israel,
rouse yourself to punish all the nations;
show no mercy to wicked traitors.[e]

6 They return at evening,
snarling like dogs,
and prowl about the city.
7 See what they spew from their mouths—
the words from their lips are sharp as
swords,
and they think, "Who can hear us?"
8 But you laugh at them, LORD;
you scoff at all those nations.

9 You are my strength, I watch for you;
you, God, are my fortress,
10 my God on whom I can rely.

God will go before me
and will let me gloat over those who
slander me.
11 But do not kill them, Lord our shield,[f]
or my people will forget.
In your might uproot them
and bring them down.
12 For the sins of their mouths,
for the words of their lips,
let them be caught in their pride.
For the curses and lies they utter,
13 consume them in your wrath,
consume them till they are no more.
Then it will be known to the ends of the
earth
that God rules over Jacob.

14 They return at evening,
snarling like dogs,
and prowl about the city.
15 They wander about for food
and howl if not satisfied.
16 But I will sing of your strength,
in the morning I will sing of your love;
for you are my fortress,
my refuge in times of trouble.

17 You are my strength, I sing praise to you;
you, God, are my fortress,
my God on whom I can rely.

Psalm 60[g]

For the director of music. To the tune of "The Lily of the Covenant." A miktam[b] *of David. For teaching. When he fought Aram Naharaim*[h] *and Aram Zobah,*[i] *and when Joab returned and struck down twelve thousand Edomites in the Valley of Salt.*

1 You have rejected us, God, and burst
upon us;
you have been angry—now restore us!
2 You have shaken the land and torn it open;
mend its fractures, for it is quaking.

[a] In Hebrew texts 58:1-11 is numbered 58:2-12. [b] Title: Probably a literary or musical term [c] *9* The meaning of the Hebrew for this verse is uncertain. [d] In Hebrew texts 59:1-17 is numbered 59:2-18. [e] *5* The Hebrew has *Selah* (a word of uncertain meaning) here and at the end of verse 13. [f] *11* Or *sovereign* [g] In Hebrew texts 60:1-12 is numbered 60:3-14. [h] Title: That is, Arameans of Northwest Mesopotamia [i] Title: That is, Arameans of central Syria

3 You have shown your people desperate times;
you have given us wine that makes us stagger.
4 But for those who fear you, you have raised a banner
to be unfurled against the bow.[a]

5 Save us and help us with your right hand,
that those you love may be delivered.
6 God has spoken from his sanctuary:
"In triumph I will parcel out Shechem
and measure off the Valley of Sukkoth.
7 Gilead is mine, and Manasseh is mine;
Ephraim is my helmet,
Judah is my scepter.
8 Moab is my washbasin,
on Edom I toss my sandal;
over Philistia I shout in triumph."

9 Who will bring me to the fortified city?
Who will lead me to Edom?
10 Is it not you, God, you who have now rejected us
and no longer go out with our armies?
11 Give us aid against the enemy,
for human help is worthless.
12 With God we will gain the victory,
and he will trample down our enemies.

Psalm 61[b]

For the director of music. With stringed instruments. Of David.

1 Hear my cry, O God;
listen to my prayer.

2 From the ends of the earth I call to you,
I call as my heart grows faint;
lead me to the rock that is higher than I.
3 For you have been my refuge,
a strong tower against the foe.

4 I long to dwell in your tent forever
and take refuge in the shelter of your wings.[a]
5 For you, God, have heard my vows;
you have given me the heritage of those who fear your name.

6 Increase the days of the king's life,
his years for many generations.
7 May he be enthroned in God's presence forever;
appoint your love and faithfulness to protect him.

8 Then I will ever sing in praise of your name
and fulfill my vows day after day.

Psalm 62[c]

For the director of music. For Jeduthun. A psalm of David.

1 Truly my soul finds rest in God;
my salvation comes from him.
2 Truly he is my rock and my salvation;
he is my fortress, I will never be shaken.

3 How long will you assault me?
Would all of you throw me down—
this leaning wall, this tottering fence?
4 Surely they intend to topple me
from my lofty place;
they take delight in lies.
With their mouths they bless,
but in their hearts they curse.[d]

5 Yes, my soul, find rest in God;
my hope comes from him.
6 Truly he is my rock and my salvation;
he is my fortress, I will not be shaken.
7 My salvation and my honor depend on God[e];
he is my mighty rock, my refuge.
8 Trust in him at all times, you people;
pour out your hearts to him,
for God is our refuge.

9 Surely the lowborn are but a breath,
the highborn are but a lie.
If weighed on a balance, they are nothing;
together they are only a breath.
10 Do not trust in extortion
or put vain hope in stolen goods;
though your riches increase,
do not set your heart on them.

11 One thing God has spoken,
two things I have heard:
"Power belongs to you, God,
12 and with you, Lord, is unfailing love";
and, "You reward everyone
according to what they have done."

Psalm 63[f]

A psalm of David. When he was in the Desert of Judah.

1 You, God, are my God,
earnestly I seek you;
I thirst for you,
my whole being longs for you,
in a dry and parched land
where there is no water.

2 I have seen you in the sanctuary
and beheld your power and your glory.
3 Because your love is better than life,
my lips will glorify you.
4 I will praise you as long as I live,
and in your name I will lift up my hands.
5 I will be fully satisfied as with the richest of foods;
with singing lips my mouth will praise you.

6 On my bed I remember you;
I think of you through the watches of the night.

[a] 4,4 The Hebrew has *Selah* (a word of uncertain meaning) here. [b] In Hebrew texts 61:1-8 is numbered 61:2-9. [c] In Hebrew texts 62:1-12 is numbered 62:2-13. [d] 4 The Hebrew has *Selah* (a word of uncertain meaning) here and at the end of verse 8. [e] 7 Or / *God Most High is my salvation and my honor* [f] In Hebrew texts 63:1-11 is numbered 63:2-12.

7 Because you are my help,
I sing in the shadow of your wings.
8 I cling to you;
your right hand upholds me.

9 Those who want to kill me will be destroyed;
they will go down to the depths of the earth.
10 They will be given over to the sword
and become food for jackals.

11 But the king will rejoice in God;
all who swear by God will glory in him,
while the mouths of liars will be silenced.

Psalm 64[a]

For the director of music. A psalm of David.

1 Hear me, my God, as I voice my complaint;
protect my life from the threat of the enemy.

2 Hide me from the conspiracy of the wicked,
from the plots of evildoers.
3 They sharpen their tongues like swords
and aim cruel words like deadly arrows.
4 They shoot from ambush at the innocent;
they shoot suddenly, without fear.

5 They encourage each other in evil plans,
they talk about hiding their snares;
they say, "Who will see it[b]?"
6 They plot injustice and say,
"We have devised a perfect plan!"
Surely the human mind and heart are cunning.

7 But God will shoot them with his arrows;
they will suddenly be struck down.
8 He will turn their own tongues against them
and bring them to ruin;
all who see them will shake their heads in scorn.
9 All people will fear;
they will proclaim the works of God
and ponder what he has done.

10 The righteous will rejoice in the LORD
and take refuge in him;
all the upright in heart will glory in him!

Psalm 65[c]

For the director of music. A psalm of David. A song.

1 Praise awaits[d] you, our God, in Zion;
to you our vows will be fulfilled.
2 You who answer prayer,
to you all people will come.
3 When we were overwhelmed by sins,
you forgave[e] our transgressions.
4 Blessed are those you choose
and bring near to live in your courts!
We are filled with the good things of your house,
of your holy temple.

5 You answer us with awesome and righteous deeds,
God our Savior,
the hope of all the ends of the earth
and of the farthest seas,
6 who formed the mountains by your power,
having armed yourself with strength,
7 who stilled the roaring of the seas,
the roaring of their waves,
and the turmoil of the nations.
8 The whole earth is filled with awe at your wonders;
where morning dawns, where evening fades,
you call forth songs of joy.

9 You care for the land and water it;
you enrich it abundantly.
The streams of God are filled with water
to provide the people with grain,
for so you have ordained it.[f]
10 You drench its furrows and level its ridges;
you soften it with showers and bless its crops.
11 You crown the year with your bounty,
and your carts overflow with abundance.
12 The grasslands of the wilderness overflow;
the hills are clothed with gladness.
13 The meadows are covered with flocks
and the valleys are mantled with grain;
they shout for joy and sing.

Psalm 66

For the director of music. A song. A psalm.

1 Shout for joy to God, all the earth!
2 Sing the glory of his name;
make his praise glorious.
3 Say to God, "How awesome are your deeds!
So great is your power
that your enemies cringe before you.
4 All the earth bows down to you;
they sing praise to you,
they sing the praises of your name."[g]

5 Come and see what God has done,
his awesome deeds for mankind!
6 He turned the sea into dry land,
they passed through the waters on foot—
come, let us rejoice in him.
7 He rules forever by his power,
his eyes watch the nations—
let not the rebellious rise up against him.

[a] In Hebrew texts 64:1-10 is numbered 64:2-11. [b] 5 Or *us* [c] In Hebrew texts 65:1-13 is numbered 65:2-14. [d] 1 Or *befits*; the meaning of the Hebrew for this word is uncertain. [e] 3 Or *made atonement for* [f] 9 Or *for that is how you prepare the land* [g] 4 The Hebrew has *Selah* (a word of uncertain meaning) here and at the end of verses 7 and 15.

8 Praise our God, all peoples,
let the sound of his praise be heard;
9 he has preserved our lives
and kept our feet from slipping.
10 For you, God, tested us;
you refined us like silver.
11 You brought us into prison
and laid burdens on our backs.
12 You let people ride over our heads;
we went through fire and water,
but you brought us to a place of
abundance.

13 I will come to your temple with burnt
offerings
and fulfill my vows to you—
14 vows my lips promised and my mouth spoke
when I was in trouble.
15 I will sacrifice fat animals to you
and an offering of rams;
I will offer bulls and goats.

16 Come and hear, all you who fear God;
let me tell you what he has done for me.
17 I cried out to him with my mouth;
his praise was on my tongue.
18 If I had cherished sin in my heart,
the Lord would not have listened;
19 but God has surely listened
and has heard my prayer.
20 Praise be to God,
who has not rejected my prayer
or withheld his love from me!

Psalm 67[a]

For the director of music. With stringed instruments. A psalm. A song.

1 May God be gracious to us and bless us
and make his face shine on us—[b]
2 so that your ways may be known on earth,
your salvation among all nations.

3 May the peoples praise you, God;
may all the peoples praise you.
4 May the nations be glad and sing for joy,
for you rule the peoples with equity
and guide the nations of the earth.
5 May the peoples praise you, God;
may all the peoples praise you.

6 The land yields its harvest;
God, our God, blesses us.
7 May God bless us still,
so that all the ends of the earth will fear
him.

Psalm 68[c]

For the director of music. Of David. A psalm. A song.

1 May God arise, may his enemies be
scattered;
may his foes flee before him.
2 May you blow them away like smoke—
as wax melts before the fire,
may the wicked perish before God.
3 But may the righteous be glad
and rejoice before God;
may they be happy and joyful.

4 Sing to God, sing in praise of his name,
extol him who rides on the clouds[d];
rejoice before him—his name is the
LORD.
5 A father to the fatherless, a defender of
widows,
is God in his holy dwelling.
6 God sets the lonely in families,[e]
he leads out the prisoners with
singing;
but the rebellious live in a sun-scorched
land.

7 When you, God, went out before your
people,
when you marched through the
wilderness,[f]
8 the earth shook, the heavens poured
down rain,
before God, the One of Sinai,
before God, the God of Israel.
9 You gave abundant showers, O God;
you refreshed your weary inheritance.
10 Your people settled in it,
and from your bounty, God, you
provided for the poor.

11 The Lord announces the word,
and the women who proclaim it are a
mighty throng:
12 "Kings and armies flee in haste;
the women at home divide the
plunder.
13 Even while you sleep among the sheep
pens,[g]
the wings of my dove are sheathed with
silver,
its feathers with shining gold."
14 When the Almighty[h] scattered the kings
in the land,
it was like snow fallen on Mount
Zalmon.

15 Mount Bashan, majestic mountain,
Mount Bashan, rugged mountain,
16 why gaze in envy, you rugged mountain,
at the mountain where God chooses to
reign,
where the LORD himself will dwell
forever?
17 The chariots of God are tens of
thousands
and thousands of thousands;
the Lord has come from Sinai into his
sanctuary.[i]
18 When you ascended on high,
you took many captives;
you received gifts from people,

[a] In Hebrew texts 67:1-7 is numbered 67:2-8. [b] *1* The Hebrew has *Selah* (a word of uncertain meaning) here and at the end of verse 4. [c] In Hebrew texts 68:1-35 is numbered 68:2-36. [d] *4* Or *name, / prepare the way for him who rides through the deserts* [e] *6* Or *the desolate in a homeland* [f] *7* The Hebrew has *Selah* (a word of uncertain meaning) here and at the end of verses 19 and 32. [g] *13* Or *the campfires;* or *the saddlebags* [h] *14* Hebrew *Shaddai* [i] *17* Probable reading of the original Hebrew text; Masoretic Text *Lord is among them at Sinai in holiness*

even from[a] the rebellious—
that you,[b] LORD God, might dwell there.

19 Praise be to the Lord, to God our Savior,
who daily bears our burdens.
20 Our God is a God who saves;
from the Sovereign LORD comes escape from death.
21 Surely God will crush the heads of his enemies,
the hairy crowns of those who go on in their sins.
22 The Lord says, "I will bring them from Bashan;
I will bring them from the depths of the sea,
23 that your feet may wade in the blood of your foes,
while the tongues of your dogs have their share."

24 Your procession, God, has come into view,
the procession of my God and King into the sanctuary.
25 In front are the singers, after them the musicians;
with them are the young women playing the timbrels.
26 Praise God in the great congregation;
praise the LORD in the assembly of Israel.
27 There is the little tribe of Benjamin, leading them,
there the great throng of Judah's princes,
and there the princes of Zebulun and of Naphtali.

28 Summon your power, God[c];
show us your strength, our God, as you have done before.
29 Because of your temple at Jerusalem
kings will bring you gifts.
30 Rebuke the beast among the reeds,
the herd of bulls among the calves of the nations.
Humbled, may the beast bring bars of silver.
Scatter the nations who delight in war.
31 Envoys will come from Egypt;
Cush[d] will submit herself to God.

32 Sing to God, you kingdoms of the earth,
sing praise to the Lord,
33 to him who rides across the highest heavens, the ancient heavens,
who thunders with mighty voice.
34 Proclaim the power of God,
whose majesty is over Israel,
whose power is in the heavens.
35 You, God, are awesome in your sanctuary;
the God of Israel gives power and strength to his people.

Praise be to God!

Psalm 69[e]

For the director of music. To the tune of "Lilies." Of David.

1 Save me, O God,
for the waters have come up to my neck.
2 I sink in the miry depths,
where there is no foothold.
I have come into the deep waters;
the floods engulf me.
3 I am worn out calling for help;
my throat is parched.
My eyes fail,
looking for my God.
4 Those who hate me without reason
outnumber the hairs of my head;
many are my enemies without cause,
those who seek to destroy me.
I am forced to restore
what I did not steal.

5 You, God, know my folly;
my guilt is not hidden from you.

6 Lord, the LORD Almighty,
may those who hope in you
not be disgraced because of me;
God of Israel,
may those who seek you
not be put to shame because of me.
7 For I endure scorn for your sake,
and shame covers my face.
8 I am a foreigner to my own family,
a stranger to my own mother's children;
9 for zeal for your house consumes me,
and the insults of those who insult you fall on me.
10 When I weep and fast,
I must endure scorn;
11 when I put on sackcloth,
people make sport of me.
12 Those who sit at the gate mock me,
and I am the song of the drunkards.

13 But I pray to you, LORD,
in the time of your favor;
in your great love, O God,
answer me with your sure salvation.
14 Rescue me from the mire,
do not let me sink;
deliver me from those who hate me,
from the deep waters.
15 Do not let the floodwaters engulf me
or the depths swallow me up
or the pit close its mouth over me.

16 Answer me, LORD, out of the goodness of your love;
in your great mercy turn to me.
17 Do not hide your face from your servant;
answer me quickly, for I am in trouble.
18 Come near and rescue me;
deliver me because of my foes.

19 You know how I am scorned, disgraced and shamed;
all my enemies are before you.

[a] 18 Or *gifts for people, / even* [b] 18 Or *they* [c] 28 Many Hebrew manuscripts, Septuagint and Syriac; most Hebrew manuscripts *Your God has summoned power for you* [d] 31 That is, the upper Nile region [e] In Hebrew texts 69:1-36 is numbered 69:2-37.

20 Scorn has broken my heart
and has left me helpless;
I looked for sympathy, but there was none,
for comforters, but I found none.
21 They put gall in my food
and gave me vinegar for my thirst.

22 May the table set before them become a snare;
may it become retribution and[a] a trap.
23 May their eyes be darkened so they cannot see,
and their backs be bent forever.
24 Pour out your wrath on them;
let your fierce anger overtake them.
25 May their place be deserted;
let there be no one to dwell in their tents.
26 For they persecute those you wound
and talk about the pain of those you hurt.
27 Charge them with crime upon crime;
do not let them share in your salvation.
28 May they be blotted out of the book of life
and not be listed with the righteous.

29 But as for me, afflicted and in pain—
may your salvation, God, protect me.

30 I will praise God's name in song
and glorify him with thanksgiving.
31 This will please the LORD more than an ox,
more than a bull with its horns and hooves.
32 The poor will see and be glad—
you who seek God, may your hearts live!
33 The LORD hears the needy
and does not despise his captive people.

34 Let heaven and earth praise him,
the seas and all that move in them,
35 for God will save Zion
and rebuild the cities of Judah.
Then people will settle there and possess it;
36 the children of his servants will inherit it,
and those who love his name will dwell there.

Psalm 70[b]

For the director of music. Of David. A petition.

1 Hasten, O God, to save me;
come quickly, LORD, to help me.

2 May those who want to take my life
be put to shame and confusion;
may all who desire my ruin
be turned back in disgrace.
3 May those who say to me, "Aha! Aha!"
turn back because of their shame.
4 But may all who seek you
rejoice and be glad in you;
may those who long for your saving help
always say,
"The LORD is great!"

5 But as for me, I am poor and needy;
come quickly to me, O God.
You are my help and my deliverer;
LORD, do not delay.

Psalm 71

1 In you, LORD, I have taken refuge;
let me never be put to shame.
2 In your righteousness, rescue me and deliver me;
turn your ear to me and save me.
3 Be my rock of refuge,
to which I can always go;
give the command to save me,
for you are my rock and my fortress.
4 Deliver me, my God, from the hand of the wicked,
from the grasp of those who are evil and cruel.

5 For you have been my hope, Sovereign LORD,
my confidence since my youth.
6 From birth I have relied on you;
you brought me forth from my mother's womb.
I will ever praise you.
7 I have become a sign to many;
you are my strong refuge.
8 My mouth is filled with your praise,
declaring your splendor all day long.

9 Do not cast me away when I am old;
do not forsake me when my strength is gone.
10 For my enemies speak against me;
those who wait to kill me conspire together.
11 They say, "God has forsaken him;
pursue him and seize him,
for no one will rescue him."
12 Do not be far from me, my God;
come quickly, God, to help me.
13 May my accusers perish in shame;
may those who want to harm me
be covered with scorn and disgrace.

14 As for me, I will always have hope;
I will praise you more and more.
15 My mouth will tell of your righteous deeds,
of your saving acts all day long—
though I know not how to relate them all.
16 I will come and proclaim your mighty acts, Sovereign LORD;
I will proclaim your righteous deeds, yours alone.
17 Since my youth, God, you have taught me,
and to this day I declare your marvelous deeds.
18 Even when I am old and gray,
do not forsake me, my God,
till I declare your power to the next generation,
your mighty acts to all who are to come.

[a] 22 Or *snare / and their fellowship become*

[b] In Hebrew texts 70:1-5 is numbered 70:2-6.

19 Your righteousness, God, reaches to the heavens,
you who have done great things.
Who is like you, God?
20 Though you have made me see troubles,
many and bitter,
you will restore my life again;
from the depths of the earth
you will again bring me up.
21 You will increase my honor
and comfort me once more.

22 I will praise you with the harp
for your faithfulness, my God;
I will sing praise to you with the lyre,
Holy One of Israel.
23 My lips will shout for joy
when I sing praise to you—
I whom you have delivered.
24 My tongue will tell of your righteous acts
all day long,
for those who wanted to harm me
have been put to shame and confusion.

Psalm 72

Of Solomon.

1 Endow the king with your justice, O God,
the royal son with your righteousness.
2 May he judge your people in righteousness,
your afflicted ones with justice.

3 May the mountains bring prosperity to the people,
the hills the fruit of righteousness.
4 May he defend the afflicted among the people
and save the children of the needy;
may he crush the oppressor.
5 May he endure[a] as long as the sun,
as long as the moon, through all generations.
6 May he be like rain falling on a mown field,
like showers watering the earth.
7 In his days may the righteous flourish
and prosperity abound till the moon is no more.

8 May he rule from sea to sea
and from the River[b] to the ends of the earth.
9 May the desert tribes bow before him
and his enemies lick the dust.
10 May the kings of Tarshish and of distant shores
bring tribute to him.
May the kings of Sheba and Seba
present him gifts.
11 May all kings bow down to him
and all nations serve him.

12 For he will deliver the needy who cry out,
the afflicted who have no one to help.
13 He will take pity on the weak and the needy
and save the needy from death.
14 He will rescue them from oppression and violence,
for precious is their blood in his sight.

15 Long may he live!
May gold from Sheba be given him.
May people ever pray for him
and bless him all day long.
16 May grain abound throughout the land;
on the tops of the hills may it sway.
May the crops flourish like Lebanon
and thrive[c] like the grass of the field.
17 May his name endure forever;
may it continue as long as the sun.

Then all nations will be blessed through him,[d]
and they will call him blessed.

18 Praise be to the LORD God, the God of Israel,
who alone does marvelous deeds.
19 Praise be to his glorious name forever;
may the whole earth be filled with his glory.
Amen and Amen.

20 This concludes the prayers of David son of Jesse.

BOOK III

Psalms 73–89

Psalm 73

A psalm of Asaph.

1 Surely God is good to Israel,
to those who are pure in heart.

2 But as for me, my feet had almost slipped;
I had nearly lost my foothold.
3 For I envied the arrogant
when I saw the prosperity of the wicked.

4 They have no struggles;
their bodies are healthy and strong.[e]
5 They are free from common human burdens;
they are not plagued by human ills.
6 Therefore pride is their necklace;
they clothe themselves with violence.
7 From their callous hearts comes iniquity[f];
their evil imaginations have no limits.
8 They scoff, and speak with malice;
with arrogance they threaten oppression.
9 Their mouths lay claim to heaven,
and their tongues take possession of the earth.

[a] 5 Septuagint; Hebrew *You will be feared* [b] 8 That is, the Euphrates [c] 16 Probable reading of the original Hebrew text; Masoretic Text *Lebanon, / from the city* [d] 17 Or *will use his name in blessings* (see Gen. 48:20) [e] 4 With a different word division of the Hebrew; Masoretic Text *struggles at their death; / their bodies are healthy* [f] 7 Syriac (see also Septuagint); Hebrew *Their eyes bulge with fat*

[10]Therefore their people turn to them
and drink up waters in abundance.[a]
[11]They say, "How would God know?
Does the Most High know anything?"

[12]This is what the wicked are like—
always free of care, they go on
amassing wealth.
[13]Surely in vain I have kept my heart pure
and have washed my hands in innocence.
[14]All day long I have been afflicted,
and every morning brings new
punishments.

[15]If I had spoken out like that,
I would have betrayed your children.
[16]When I tried to understand all this,
it troubled me deeply
[17]till I entered the sanctuary of God;
then I understood their final destiny.

[18]Surely you place them on slippery ground;
you cast them down to ruin.
[19]How suddenly are they destroyed,
completely swept away by terrors!
[20]They are like a dream when one awakes;
when you arise, Lord,
you will despise them as fantasies.

[21]When my heart was grieved
and my spirit embittered,
[22]I was senseless and ignorant;
I was a brute beast before you.

[23]Yet I am always with you;
you hold me by my right hand.
[24]You guide me with your counsel,
and afterward you will take me into
glory.
[25]Whom have I in heaven but you?
And earth has nothing I desire besides
you.
[26]My flesh and my heart may fail,
but God is the strength of my heart
and my portion forever.

[27]Those who are far from you will perish;
you destroy all who are unfaithful to you.
[28]But as for me, it is good to be near God.
I have made the Sovereign LORD my
refuge;
I will tell of all your deeds.

Psalm 74

A maskil[b] *of Asaph.*

[1]O God, why have you rejected us forever?
Why does your anger smolder against
the sheep of your pasture?
[2]Remember the nation you purchased long
ago,
the people of your inheritance, whom
you redeemed—
Mount Zion, where you dwelt.
[3]Turn your steps toward these everlasting
ruins,
all this destruction the enemy has
brought on the sanctuary.

[4]Your foes roared in the place where you
met with us;
they set up their standards as signs.
[5]They behaved like men wielding axes
to cut through a thicket of trees.
[6]They smashed all the carved paneling
with their axes and hatchets.
[7]They burned your sanctuary to the
ground;
they defiled the dwelling place of your
Name.
[8]They said in their hearts, "We will crush
them completely!"
They burned every place where God
was worshiped in the land.

[9]We are given no signs from God;
no prophets are left,
and none of us knows how long this
will be.
[10]How long will the enemy mock you, God?
Will the foe revile your name forever?
[11]Why do you hold back your hand, your
right hand?
Take it from the folds of your garment
and destroy them!

[12]But God is my King from long ago;
he brings salvation on the earth.

[13]It was you who split open the sea by your
power;
you broke the heads of the monster in
the waters.
[14]It was you who crushed the heads of
Leviathan
and gave it as food to the creatures of
the desert.
[15]It was you who opened up springs and
streams;
you dried up the ever-flowing rivers.
[16]The day is yours, and yours also the night;
you established the sun and moon.
[17]It was you who set all the boundaries of
the earth;
you made both summer and winter.

[18]Remember how the enemy has mocked
you, LORD,
how foolish people have reviled your
name.
[19]Do not hand over the life of your dove to
wild beasts;
do not forget the lives of your afflicted
people forever.
[20]Have regard for your covenant,
because haunts of violence fill the dark
places of the land.
[21]Do not let the oppressed retreat in disgrace;
may the poor and needy praise your
name.
[22]Rise up, O God, and defend your cause;
remember how fools mock you all day
long.
[23]Do not ignore the clamor of your
adversaries,
the uproar of your enemies, which rises
continually.

[a] *10* The meaning of the Hebrew for this verse is uncertain. [b] Title: Probably a literary or musical term

Psalm 75[a]

For the director of music. To the tune of "Do Not Destroy." A psalm of Asaph. A song.

1 We praise you, God,
we praise you, for your Name is near;
people tell of your wonderful deeds.

2 You say, "I choose the appointed time;
it is I who judge with equity.
3 When the earth and all its people quake,
it is I who hold its pillars firm.[b]
4 To the arrogant I say, 'Boast no more,'
and to the wicked, 'Do not lift up your horns.[c]
5 Do not lift your horns against heaven;
do not speak so defiantly.'"

6 No one from the east or the west
or from the desert can exalt themselves.
7 It is God who judges:
He brings one down, he exalts another.
8 In the hand of the LORD is a cup
full of foaming wine mixed with spices;
he pours it out, and all the wicked of the earth
drink it down to its very dregs.

9 As for me, I will declare this forever;
I will sing praise to the God of Jacob,
10 who says, "I will cut off the horns of all the wicked,
but the horns of the righteous will be lifted up."

Psalm 76[d]

For the director of music. With stringed instruments. A psalm of Asaph. A song.

1 God is renowned in Judah;
in Israel his name is great.
2 His tent is in Salem,
his dwelling place in Zion.
3 There he broke the flashing arrows,
the shields and the swords, the weapons of war.[e]

4 You are radiant with light,
more majestic than mountains rich with game.
5 The valiant lie plundered,
they sleep their last sleep;
not one of the warriors
can lift his hands.
6 At your rebuke, God of Jacob,
both horse and chariot lie still.

7 It is you alone who are to be feared.
Who can stand before you when you are angry?
8 From heaven you pronounced judgment,
and the land feared and was quiet—
9 when you, God, rose up to judge,
to save all the afflicted of the land.
10 Surely your wrath against mankind brings you praise,
and the survivors of your wrath are restrained.[f]

11 Make vows to the LORD your God and fulfill them;
let all the neighboring lands
bring gifts to the One to be feared.
12 He breaks the spirit of rulers;
he is feared by the kings of the earth.

Psalm 77[g]

For the director of music. For Jeduthun. Of Asaph. A psalm.

1 I cried out to God for help;
I cried out to God to hear me.
2 When I was in distress, I sought the Lord;
at night I stretched out untiring hands,
and I would not be comforted.

3 I remembered you, God, and I groaned;
I meditated, and my spirit grew faint.[h]
4 You kept my eyes from closing;
I was too troubled to speak.
5 I thought about the former days,
the years of long ago;
6 I remembered my songs in the night.
My heart meditated and my spirit asked:

7 "Will the Lord reject forever?
Will he never show his favor again?
8 Has his unfailing love vanished forever?
Has his promise failed for all time?
9 Has God forgotten to be merciful?
Has he in anger withheld his compassion?"

10 Then I thought, "To this I will appeal:
the years when the Most High stretched out his right hand.
11 I will remember the deeds of the LORD;
yes, I will remember your miracles of long ago.
12 I will consider all your works
and meditate on all your mighty deeds."

13 Your ways, God, are holy.
What god is as great as our God?
14 You are the God who performs miracles;
you display your power among the peoples.
15 With your mighty arm you redeemed your people,
the descendants of Jacob and Joseph.

16 The waters saw you, God,
the waters saw you and writhed;
the very depths were convulsed.
17 The clouds poured down water,
the heavens resounded with thunder;
your arrows flashed back and forth.

[a] In Hebrew texts 75:1-10 is numbered 75:2-11. [b] *3* The Hebrew has *Selah* (a word of uncertain meaning) here. [c] *4* *Horns* here symbolize strength; also in verses 5 and 10. [d] In Hebrew texts 76:1-12 is numbered 76:2-13. [e] *3* The Hebrew has *Selah* (a word of uncertain meaning) here and at the end of verse 9. [f] *10* Or *Surely the wrath of mankind brings you praise, / and with the remainder of wrath you arm yourself* [g] In Hebrew texts 77:1-20 is numbered 77:2-21. [h] *3* The Hebrew has *Selah* (a word of uncertain meaning) here and at the end of verses 9 and 15.

18 Your thunder was heard in the whirlwind,
your lightning lit up the world;
the earth trembled and quaked.
19 Your path led through the sea,
your way through the mighty waters,
though your footprints were not seen.

20 You led your people like a flock
by the hand of Moses and Aaron.

Psalm 78

A maskil[a] *of Asaph.*

1 My people, hear my teaching;
listen to the words of my mouth.
2 I will open my mouth with a parable;
I will utter hidden things, things from of old—
3 things we have heard and known,
things our ancestors have told us.
4 We will not hide them from their descendants;
we will tell the next generation
the praiseworthy deeds of the LORD,
his power, and the wonders he has done.
5 He decreed statutes for Jacob
and established the law in Israel,
which he commanded our ancestors
to teach their children,
6 so the next generation would know them,
even the children yet to be born,
and they in turn would tell their children.
7 Then they would put their trust in God
and would not forget his deeds
but would keep his commands.
8 They would not be like their ancestors—
a stubborn and rebellious generation,
whose hearts were not loyal to God,
whose spirits were not faithful to him.

9 The men of Ephraim, though armed with bows,
turned back on the day of battle;
10 they did not keep God's covenant
and refused to live by his law.
11 They forgot what he had done,
the wonders he had shown them.
12 He did miracles in the sight of their ancestors
in the land of Egypt, in the region of Zoan.
13 He divided the sea and led them through;
he made the water stand up like a wall.
14 He guided them with the cloud by day
and with light from the fire all night.
15 He split the rocks in the wilderness
and gave them water as abundant as the seas;
16 he brought streams out of a rocky crag
and made water flow down like rivers.

17 But they continued to sin against him,
rebelling in the wilderness against the Most High.
18 They willfully put God to the test
by demanding the food they craved.
19 They spoke against God;
they said, "Can God really
spread a table in the wilderness?
20 True, he struck the rock,
and water gushed out,
streams flowed abundantly,
but can he also give us bread?
Can he supply meat for his people?"
21 When the LORD heard them, he was furious;
his fire broke out against Jacob,
and his wrath rose against Israel,
22 for they did not believe in God
or trust in his deliverance.
23 Yet he gave a command to the skies above
and opened the doors of the heavens;
24 he rained down manna for the people to eat,
he gave them the grain of heaven.
25 Human beings ate the bread of angels;
he sent them all the food they could eat.
26 He let loose the east wind from the heavens
and by his power made the south wind blow.
27 He rained meat down on them like dust,
birds like sand on the seashore.
28 He made them come down inside their camp,
all around their tents.
29 They ate till they were gorged—
he had given them what they craved.
30 But before they turned from what they craved,
even while the food was still in their mouths,
31 God's anger rose against them;
he put to death the sturdiest among them,
cutting down the young men of Israel.

32 In spite of all this, they kept on sinning;
in spite of his wonders, they did not believe.
33 So he ended their days in futility
and their years in terror.
34 Whenever God slew them, they would seek him;
they eagerly turned to him again.
35 They remembered that God was their Rock,
that God Most High was their Redeemer.
36 But then they would flatter him with their mouths,
lying to him with their tongues;
37 their hearts were not loyal to him,
they were not faithful to his covenant.
38 Yet he was merciful;
he forgave their iniquities
and did not destroy them.
Time after time he restrained his anger
and did not stir up his full wrath.
39 He remembered that they were but flesh,
a passing breeze that does not return.

40 How often they rebelled against him in the wilderness
and grieved him in the wasteland!

[a] Title: Probably a literary or musical term

41 Again and again they put God to the test;
they vexed the Holy One of Israel.
42 They did not remember his power—
the day he redeemed them from the
oppressor,
43 the day he displayed his signs in Egypt,
his wonders in the region of Zoan.
44 He turned their river into blood;
they could not drink from their streams.
45 He sent swarms of flies that devoured
them,
and frogs that devastated them.
46 He gave their crops to the grasshopper,
their produce to the locust.
47 He destroyed their vines with hail
and their sycamore-figs with sleet.
48 He gave over their cattle to the hail,
their livestock to bolts of lightning.
49 He unleashed against them his hot anger,
his wrath, indignation and hostility—
a band of destroying angels.
50 He prepared a path for his anger;
he did not spare them from death
but gave them over to the plague.
51 He struck down all the firstborn of Egypt,
the firstfruits of manhood in the tents
of Ham.
52 But he brought his people out like a flock;
he led them like sheep through the
wilderness.
53 He guided them safely, so they were
unafraid;
but the sea engulfed their enemies.
54 And so he brought them to the border of
his holy land,
to the hill country his right hand had
taken.
55 He drove out nations before them
and allotted their lands to them as an
inheritance;
he settled the tribes of Israel in their
homes.

56 But they put God to the test
and rebelled against the Most High;
they did not keep his statutes.
57 Like their ancestors they were disloyal
and faithless,
as unreliable as a faulty bow.
58 They angered him with their high places;
they aroused his jealousy with their
idols.
59 When God heard them, he was furious;
he rejected Israel completely.
60 He abandoned the tabernacle of Shiloh,
the tent he had set up among humans.
61 He sent the ark of his might into captivity,
his splendor into the hands of the
enemy.
62 He gave his people over to the sword;
he was furious with his inheritance.
63 Fire consumed their young men,
and their young women had no
wedding songs;
64 their priests were put to the sword,
and their widows could not weep.

65 Then the Lord awoke as from sleep,
as a warrior wakes from the stupor of
wine.
66 He beat back his enemies;
he put them to everlasting shame.
67 Then he rejected the tents of Joseph,
he did not choose the tribe of Ephraim;
68 but he chose the tribe of Judah,
Mount Zion, which he loved.
69 He built his sanctuary like the heights,
like the earth that he established
forever.
70 He chose David his servant
and took him from the sheep pens;
71 from tending the sheep he brought him
to be the shepherd of his people Jacob,
of Israel his inheritance.
72 And David shepherded them with
integrity of heart;
with skillful hands he led them.

Psalm 79

A psalm of Asaph.

1 O God, the nations have invaded your
inheritance;
they have defiled your holy temple,
they have reduced Jerusalem to
rubble.
2 They have left the dead bodies of your
servants
as food for the birds of the sky,
the flesh of your own people for the
animals of the wild.
3 They have poured out blood like water
all around Jerusalem,
and there is no one to bury the dead.
4 We are objects of contempt to our
neighbors,
of scorn and derision to those around
us.

5 How long, LORD? Will you be angry
forever?
How long will your jealousy burn like
fire?
6 Pour out your wrath on the nations
that do not acknowledge you,
on the kingdoms
that do not call on your name;
7 for they have devoured Jacob
and devastated his homeland.
8 Do not hold against us the sins of past
generations;
may your mercy come quickly to meet
us,
for we are in desperate need.
9 Help us, God our Savior,
for the glory of your name;
deliver us and forgive our sins
for your name's sake.
10 Why should the nations say,
"Where is their God?"

Before our eyes, make known among the
nations
that you avenge the outpoured blood of
your servants.
11 May the groans of the prisoners come
before you;
with your strong arm preserve those
condemned to die.

12 Pay back into the laps of our neighbors
seven times
the contempt they have hurled at you,
Lord.
13 Then we your people, the sheep of your
pasture,
will praise you forever;
from generation to generation
we will proclaim your praise.

Psalm 80[a]

For the director of music. To the tune of "The Lilies of the Covenant." Of Asaph. A psalm.

1 Hear us, Shepherd of Israel,
you who lead Joseph like a flock.
You who sit enthroned between the
cherubim,
shine forth 2 before Ephraim, Benjamin
and Manasseh.
Awaken your might;
come and save us.

3 Restore us, O God;
make your face shine on us,
that we may be saved.

4 How long, LORD God Almighty,
will your anger smolder
against the prayers of your people?
5 You have fed them with the bread of
tears;
you have made them drink tears by the
bowlful.
6 You have made us an object of derision[b]
to our neighbors,
and our enemies mock us.

7 Restore us, God Almighty;
make your face shine on us,
that we may be saved.

8 You transplanted a vine from Egypt;
you drove out the nations and planted
it.
9 You cleared the ground for it,
and it took root and filled the land.
10 The mountains were covered with its
shade,
the mighty cedars with its branches.
11 Its branches reached as far as the Sea,[c]
its shoots as far as the River.[d]

12 Why have you broken down its walls
so that all who pass by pick its grapes?
13 Boars from the forest ravage it,
and insects from the fields feed on it.
14 Return to us, God Almighty!
Look down from heaven and see!
Watch over this vine,
15 the root your right hand has planted,
the son[e] you have raised up for
yourself.

16 Your vine is cut down, it is burned with
fire;
at your rebuke your people perish.
17 Let your hand rest on the man at your
right hand,
the son of man you have raised up for
yourself.
18 Then we will not turn away from you;
revive us, and we will call on your
name.

19 Restore us, LORD God Almighty;
make your face shine on us,
that we may be saved.

Psalm 81[f]

For the director of music. According to gittith.[g] Of Asaph.

1 Sing for joy to God our strength;
shout aloud to the God of Jacob!
2 Begin the music, strike the timbrel,
play the melodious harp and lyre.

3 Sound the ram's horn at the New Moon,
and when the moon is full, on the day
of our festival;
4 this is a decree for Israel,
an ordinance of the God of Jacob.
5 When God went out against Egypt,
he established it as a statute for Joseph.

I heard an unknown voice say:

6 "I removed the burden from their
shoulders;
their hands were set free from the
basket.
7 In your distress you called and I rescued
you,
I answered you out of a thundercloud;
I tested you at the waters of Meribah.[h]
8 Hear me, my people, and I will warn
you—
if you would only listen to me, Israel!
9 You shall have no foreign god among you;
you shall not worship any god other
than me.
10 I am the LORD your God,
who brought you up out of Egypt.
Open wide your mouth and I will fill it.

11 "But my people would not listen to me;
Israel would not submit to me.
12 So I gave them over to their stubborn
hearts
to follow their own devices.

13 "If my people would only listen to me,
if Israel would only follow my ways,
14 how quickly I would subdue their enemies
and turn my hand against their foes!
15 Those who hate the LORD would cringe
before him,
and their punishment would last
forever.
16 But you would be fed with the finest of
wheat;
with honey from the rock I would
satisfy you."

[a] In Hebrew texts 80:1-19 is numbered 80:2-20. [b] *6* Probable reading of the original Hebrew text; Masoretic Text *contention* [c] *11* Probably the Mediterranean [d] *11* That is, the Euphrates [e] *15* Or *branch* [f] In Hebrew texts 81:1-16 is numbered 81:2-17. [g] Title: Probably a musical term [h] *7* The Hebrew has *Selah* (a word of uncertain meaning) here.

Psalm 82

A psalm of Asaph.

1 God presides in the great assembly;
he renders judgment among the "gods":
2 "How long will you[a] defend the unjust
and show partiality to the wicked?[b]
3 Defend the weak and the fatherless;
uphold the cause of the poor and the oppressed.
4 Rescue the weak and the needy;
deliver them from the hand of the wicked.

5 "The 'gods' know nothing, they understand nothing.
They walk about in darkness;
all the foundations of the earth are shaken.

6 "I said, 'You are "gods";
you are all sons of the Most High.'
7 But you will die like mere mortals;
you will fall like every other ruler."

8 Rise up, O God, judge the earth,
for all the nations are your inheritance.

Psalm 83[c]

A song. A psalm of Asaph.

1 O God, do not remain silent;
do not turn a deaf ear,
do not stand aloof, O God.
2 See how your enemies growl,
how your foes rear their heads.
3 With cunning they conspire against your people;
they plot against those you cherish.
4 "Come," they say, "let us destroy them as a nation,
so that Israel's name is remembered no more."

5 With one mind they plot together;
they form an alliance against you—
6 the tents of Edom and the Ishmaelites,
of Moab and the Hagrites,
7 Byblos, Ammon and Amalek,
Philistia, with the people of Tyre.
8 Even Assyria has joined them
to reinforce Lot's descendants.[b]

9 Do to them as you did to Midian,
as you did to Sisera and Jabin at the river Kishon,
10 who perished at Endor
and became like dung on the ground.
11 Make their nobles like Oreb and Zeeb,
all their princes like Zebah and Zalmunna,
12 who said, "Let us take possession
of the pasturelands of God."

13 Make them like tumbleweed, my God,
like chaff before the wind.
14 As fire consumes the forest
or a flame sets the mountains ablaze,
15 so pursue them with your tempest
and terrify them with your storm.
16 Cover their faces with shame, LORD,
so that they will seek your name.

17 May they ever be ashamed and dismayed;
may they perish in disgrace.
18 Let them know that you, whose name is the LORD—
that you alone are the Most High over all the earth.

Psalm 84[d]

For the director of music. According to gittith.[e] *Of the Sons of Korah. A psalm.*

1 How lovely is your dwelling place,
LORD Almighty!
2 My soul yearns, even faints,
for the courts of the LORD;
my heart and my flesh cry out
for the living God.
3 Even the sparrow has found a home,
and the swallow a nest for herself,
where she may have her young—
a place near your altar,
LORD Almighty, my King and my God.
4 Blessed are those who dwell in your house;
they are ever praising you.[f]

5 Blessed are those whose strength is in you,
whose hearts are set on pilgrimage.
6 As they pass through the Valley of Baka,
they make it a place of springs;
the autumn rains also cover it with pools.[g]
7 They go from strength to strength,
till each appears before God in Zion.

8 Hear my prayer, LORD God Almighty;
listen to me, God of Jacob.
9 Look on our shield,[h] O God;
look with favor on your anointed one.

10 Better is one day in your courts
than a thousand elsewhere;
I would rather be a doorkeeper in the house of my God
than dwell in the tents of the wicked.
11 For the LORD God is a sun and shield;
the LORD bestows favor and honor;
no good thing does he withhold
from those whose walk is blameless.

12 LORD Almighty,
blessed is the one who trusts in you.

Psalm 85[i]

For the director of music. Of the Sons of Korah. A psalm.

1 You, LORD, showed favor to your land;
you restored the fortunes of Jacob.
2 You forgave the iniquity of your people
and covered all their sins.[b]

[a] 2 The Hebrew is plural. [b] 2,8,2 The Hebrew has *Selah* (a word of uncertain meaning) here. [c] In Hebrew texts 83:1-18 is numbered 83:2-19. [d] In Hebrew texts 84:1-12 is numbered 84:2-13. [e] Title: Probably a musical term [f] 4 The Hebrew has *Selah* (a word of uncertain meaning) here and at the end of verse 8. [g] 6 Or *blessings* [h] 9 Or *sovereign* [i] In Hebrew texts 85:1-13 is numbered 85:2-14.

3 You set aside all your wrath
and turned from your fierce anger.

4 Restore us again, God our Savior,
and put away your displeasure toward us.
5 Will you be angry with us forever?
Will you prolong your anger through all generations?
6 Will you not revive us again,
that your people may rejoice in you?
7 Show us your unfailing love, LORD,
and grant us your salvation.

8 I will listen to what God the LORD says;
he promises peace to his people, his faithful servants—
but let them not turn to folly.
9 Surely his salvation is near those who fear him,
that his glory may dwell in our land.

10 Love and faithfulness meet together;
righteousness and peace kiss each other.
11 Faithfulness springs forth from the earth,
and righteousness looks down from heaven.
12 The LORD will indeed give what is good,
and our land will yield its harvest.
13 Righteousness goes before him
and prepares the way for his steps.

Psalm 86

A prayer of David.

1 Hear me, LORD, and answer me,
for I am poor and needy.
2 Guard my life, for I am faithful to you;
save your servant who trusts in you.
You are my God; 3 have mercy on me, Lord,
for I call to you all day long.
4 Bring joy to your servant, Lord,
for I put my trust in you.

5 You, Lord, are forgiving and good,
abounding in love to all who call to you.
6 Hear my prayer, LORD;
listen to my cry for mercy.
7 When I am in distress, I call to you,
because you answer me.

8 Among the gods there is none like you, Lord;
no deeds can compare with yours.
9 All the nations you have made
will come and worship before you, Lord;
they will bring glory to your name.
10 For you are great and do marvelous deeds;
you alone are God.

11 Teach me your way, LORD,
that I may rely on your faithfulness;
give me an undivided heart,
that I may fear your name.
12 I will praise you, Lord my God, with all my heart;
I will glorify your name forever.
13 For great is your love toward me;
you have delivered me from the depths,
from the realm of the dead.

14 Arrogant foes are attacking me, O God;
ruthless people are trying to kill me—
they have no regard for you.
15 But you, Lord, are a compassionate and gracious God,
slow to anger, abounding in love and faithfulness.
16 Turn to me and have mercy on me;
show your strength in behalf of your servant;
save me, because I serve you
just as my mother did.
17 Give me a sign of your goodness,
that my enemies may see it and be put to shame,
for you, LORD, have helped me and comforted me.

Psalm 87

Of the Sons of Korah. A psalm. A song.

1 He has founded his city on the holy mountain.
2 The LORD loves the gates of Zion
more than all the other dwellings of Jacob.
3 Glorious things are said of you,
city of God:[a]
4 "I will record Rahab[b] and Babylon
among those who acknowledge me—
Philistia too, and Tyre, along with Cush[c]—
and will say, 'This one was born in Zion.' "[d]
5 Indeed, of Zion it will be said,
"This one and that one were born in her,
and the Most High himself will establish her."
6 The LORD will write in the register of the peoples:
"This one was born in Zion."
7 As they make music they will sing,
"All my fountains are in you."

Psalm 88[e]

A song. A psalm of the Sons of Korah. For the director of music. According to mahalath leannoth.[f] *A* maskil[g] *of Heman the Ezrahite.*

1 LORD, you are the God who saves me;
day and night I cry out to you.
2 May my prayer come before you;
turn your ear to my cry.

[a] 3 The Hebrew has *Selah* (a word of uncertain meaning) here and at the end of verse 6. [b] 4 A poetic name for Egypt [c] 4 That is, the upper Nile region [d] 4 Or *"I will record concerning those who acknowledge me: / 'This one was born in Zion.' / Hear this, Rahab and Babylon, / and you too, Philistia, Tyre and Cush."* [e] In Hebrew texts 88:1-18 is numbered 88:2-19. [f] Title: Possibly a tune, "The Suffering of Affliction" [g] Title: Probably a literary or musical term

3 I am overwhelmed with troubles
and my life draws near to death.
4 I am counted among those who go down
to the pit;
I am like one without strength.
5 I am set apart with the dead,
like the slain who lie in the grave,
whom you remember no more,
who are cut off from your care.

6 You have put me in the lowest pit,
in the darkest depths.
7 Your wrath lies heavily on me;
you have overwhelmed me with all
your waves.[a]
8 You have taken from me my closest
friends
and have made me repulsive to them.
I am confined and cannot escape;
9 my eyes are dim with grief.

I call to you, LORD, every day;
I spread out my hands to you.
10 Do you show your wonders to the dead?
Do their spirits rise up and praise you?
11 Is your love declared in the grave,
your faithfulness in Destruction[b]?
12 Are your wonders known in the place of
darkness,
or your righteous deeds in the land of
oblivion?

13 But I cry to you for help, LORD;
in the morning my prayer comes before
you.
14 Why, LORD, do you reject me
and hide your face from me?

15 From my youth I have suffered and been
close to death;
I have borne your terrors and am in
despair.
16 Your wrath has swept over me;
your terrors have destroyed me.
17 All day long they surround me like a
flood;
they have completely engulfed me.
18 You have taken from me friend and
neighbor—
darkness is my closest friend.

Psalm 89[c]

A maskil[d] of Ethan the Ezrahite.

1 I will sing of the LORD's great love forever;
with my mouth I will make your
faithfulness known
through all generations.
2 I will declare that your love stands firm
forever,
that you have established your
faithfulness in heaven itself.
3 You said, "I have made a covenant with
my chosen one,
I have sworn to David my servant,
4 'I will establish your line forever
and make your throne firm through all
generations.' "[e]

5 The heavens praise your wonders, LORD,
your faithfulness too, in the assembly
of the holy ones.
6 For who in the skies above can compare
with the LORD?
Who is like the LORD among the
heavenly beings?
7 In the council of the holy ones God is
greatly feared;
he is more awesome than all who
surround him.
8 Who is like you, LORD God Almighty?
You, LORD, are mighty, and your
faithfulness surrounds you.

9 You rule over the surging sea;
when its waves mount up, you still them.
10 You crushed Rahab like one of the slain;
with your strong arm you scattered
your enemies.
11 The heavens are yours, and yours also
the earth;
you founded the world and all that is in
it.
12 You created the north and the south;
Tabor and Hermon sing for joy at your
name.
13 Your arm is endowed with power;
your hand is strong, your right hand
exalted.

14 Righteousness and justice are the
foundation of your throne;
love and faithfulness go before you.
15 Blessed are those who have learned to
acclaim you,
who walk in the light of your presence,
LORD.
16 They rejoice in your name all day long;
they celebrate your righteousness.
17 For you are their glory and strength,
and by your favor you exalt our horn.[f]
18 Indeed, our shield[g] belongs to the LORD,
our king to the Holy One of Israel.

19 Once you spoke in a vision,
to your faithful people you said:
"I have bestowed strength on a warrior;
I have raised up a young man from
among the people.
20 I have found David my servant;
with my sacred oil I have anointed him.
21 My hand will sustain him;
surely my arm will strengthen him.
22 The enemy will not get the better of him;
the wicked will not oppress him.
23 I will crush his foes before him
and strike down his adversaries.
24 My faithful love will be with him,
and through my name his horn[h] will be
exalted.

[a] 7 The Hebrew has *Selah* (a word of uncertain meaning) here and at the end of verse 10.
[b] *11* Hebrew *Abaddon* [c] In Hebrew texts 89:1-52 is numbered 89:2-53. [d] Title: Probably a literary or musical term [e] *4* The Hebrew has *Selah* (a word of uncertain meaning) here and at the end of verses 37, 45 and 48. [f] *17 Horn* here symbolizes strong one. [g] *18* Or *sovereign* [h] *24 Horn* here symbolizes strength.

[25] I will set his hand over the sea,
his right hand over the rivers.
[26] He will call out to me, 'You are my Father,
my God, the Rock my Savior.'
[27] And I will appoint him to be my firstborn,
the most exalted of the kings of the
earth.
[28] I will maintain my love to him forever,
and my covenant with him will never
fail.
[29] I will establish his line forever,
his throne as long as the heavens endure.

[30] "If his sons forsake my law
and do not follow my statutes,
[31] if they violate my decrees
and fail to keep my commands,
[32] I will punish their sin with the rod,
their iniquity with flogging;
[33] but I will not take my love from him,
nor will I ever betray my faithfulness.
[34] I will not violate my covenant
or alter what my lips have uttered.
[35] Once for all, I have sworn by my
holiness—
and I will not lie to David—
[36] that his line will continue forever
and his throne endure before me like
the sun;
[37] it will be established forever like the
moon,
the faithful witness in the sky."

[38] But you have rejected, you have spurned,
you have been very angry with your
anointed one.
[39] You have renounced the covenant with
your servant
and have defiled his crown in the dust.
[40] You have broken through all his walls
and reduced his strongholds to ruins.
[41] All who pass by have plundered him;
he has become the scorn of his
neighbors.
[42] You have exalted the right hand of his
foes;
you have made all his enemies rejoice.
[43] Indeed, you have turned back the edge of
his sword
and have not supported him in battle.
[44] You have put an end to his splendor
and cast his throne to the ground.
[45] You have cut short the days of his youth;
you have covered him with a mantle of
shame.

[46] How long, LORD? Will you hide yourself
forever?
How long will your wrath burn like fire?
[47] Remember how fleeting is my life.
For what futility you have created all
humanity!
[48] Who can live and not see death,
or who can escape the power of the
grave?
[49] Lord, where is your former great love,
which in your faithfulness you swore to
David?
[50] Remember, Lord, how your servant has[a]
been mocked,
how I bear in my heart the taunts of all
the nations,
[51] the taunts with which your enemies,
LORD, have mocked,
with which they have mocked every
step of your anointed one.

[52] Praise be to the LORD forever!
Amen and Amen.

BOOK IV

Psalms 90–106

Psalm 90

A prayer of Moses the man of God.

[1] Lord, you have been our dwelling place
throughout all generations.
[2] Before the mountains were born
or you brought forth the whole world,
from everlasting to everlasting you are
God.

[3] You turn people back to dust,
saying, "Return to dust, you mortals."
[4] A thousand years in your sight
are like a day that has just gone by,
or like a watch in the night.
[5] Yet you sweep people away in the sleep of
death—
they are like the new grass of the
morning:
[6] In the morning it springs up new,
but by evening it is dry and withered.

[7] We are consumed by your anger
and terrified by your indignation.
[8] You have set our iniquities before you,
our secret sins in the light of your
presence.
[9] All our days pass away under your wrath;
we finish our years with a moan.
[10] Our days may come to seventy years,
or eighty, if our strength endures;
yet the best of them are but trouble and
sorrow,
for they quickly pass, and we fly away.
[11] If only we knew the power of your anger!
Your wrath is as great as the fear that
is your due.
[12] Teach us to number our days,
that we may gain a heart of wisdom.

[13] Relent, LORD! How long will it be?
Have compassion on your servants.
[14] Satisfy us in the morning with your
unfailing love,
that we may sing for joy and be glad all
our days.
[15] Make us glad for as many days as you
have afflicted us,
for as many years as we have seen
trouble.

[a] 50 Or *your servants have*

16 May your deeds be shown to your servants,
your splendor to their children.

17 May the favor[a] of the Lord our God rest on us;
establish the work of our hands for us—
yes, establish the work of our hands.

Psalm 91

1 Whoever dwells in the shelter of the Most High
will rest in the shadow of the Almighty.[b]
2 I will say of the LORD, "He is my refuge and my fortress,
my God, in whom I trust."

3 Surely he will save you
from the fowler's snare
and from the deadly pestilence.
4 He will cover you with his feathers,
and under his wings you will find refuge;
his faithfulness will be your shield and rampart.
5 You will not fear the terror of night,
nor the arrow that flies by day,
6 nor the pestilence that stalks in the darkness,
nor the plague that destroys at midday.
7 A thousand may fall at your side,
ten thousand at your right hand,
but it will not come near you.
8 You will only observe with your eyes
and see the punishment of the wicked.

9 If you say, "The LORD is my refuge,"
and you make the Most High your dwelling,
10 no harm will overtake you,
no disaster will come near your tent.
11 For he will command his angels concerning you
to guard you in all your ways;
12 they will lift you up in their hands,
so that you will not strike your foot against a stone.
13 You will tread on the lion and the cobra;
you will trample the great lion and the serpent.

14 "Because he[c] loves me," says the LORD, "I will rescue him;
I will protect him, for he acknowledges my name.
15 He will call on me, and I will answer him;
I will be with him in trouble,
I will deliver him and honor him.
16 With long life I will satisfy him
and show him my salvation."

Psalm 92[d]

A psalm. A song. For the Sabbath day.

1 It is good to praise the LORD
and make music to your name, O Most High,
2 proclaiming your love in the morning
and your faithfulness at night,
3 to the music of the ten-stringed lyre
and the melody of the harp.

4 For you make me glad by your deeds, LORD;
I sing for joy at what your hands have done.
5 How great are your works, LORD,
how profound your thoughts!
6 Senseless people do not know,
fools do not understand,
7 that though the wicked spring up like grass
and all evildoers flourish,
they will be destroyed forever.

8 But you, LORD, are forever exalted.

9 For surely your enemies, LORD,
surely your enemies will perish;
all evildoers will be scattered.
10 You have exalted my horn[e] like that of a wild ox;
fine oils have been poured on me.
11 My eyes have seen the defeat of my adversaries;
my ears have heard the rout of my wicked foes.

12 The righteous will flourish like a palm tree,
they will grow like a cedar of Lebanon;
13 planted in the house of the LORD,
they will flourish in the courts of our God.
14 They will still bear fruit in old age,
they will stay fresh and green,
15 proclaiming, "The LORD is upright;
he is my Rock, and there is no wickedness in him."

Psalm 93

1 The LORD reigns, he is robed in majesty;
the LORD is robed in majesty and armed with strength;
indeed, the world is established, firm and secure.
2 Your throne was established long ago;
you are from all eternity.

3 The seas have lifted up, LORD,
the seas have lifted up their voice;
the seas have lifted up their pounding waves.
4 Mightier than the thunder of the great waters,
mightier than the breakers of the sea—
the LORD on high is mighty.

5 Your statutes, LORD, stand firm;
holiness adorns your house
for endless days.

Psalm 94

1 The LORD is a God who avenges.
O God who avenges, shine forth.

[a] 17 Or *beauty* [b] 1 Hebrew *Shaddai* [c] 14 That is, probably the king [d] In Hebrew texts 92:1-15 is numbered 92:2-16. [e] 10 *Horn* here symbolizes strength.

2 Rise up, Judge of the earth;
pay back to the proud what they deserve.
3 How long, LORD, will the wicked,
how long will the wicked be jubilant?

4 They pour out arrogant words;
all the evildoers are full of boasting.
5 They crush your people, LORD;
they oppress your inheritance.
6 They slay the widow and the foreigner;
they murder the fatherless.
7 They say, "The LORD does not see;
the God of Jacob takes no notice."

8 Take notice, you senseless ones among the people;
you fools, when will you become wise?
9 Does he who fashioned the ear not hear?
Does he who formed the eye not see?
10 Does he who disciplines nations not punish?
Does he who teaches mankind lack knowledge?
11 The LORD knows all human plans;
he knows that they are futile.

12 Blessed is the one you discipline, LORD,
the one you teach from your law;
13 you grant them relief from days of trouble,
till a pit is dug for the wicked.
14 For the LORD will not reject his people;
he will never forsake his inheritance.
15 Judgment will again be founded on righteousness,
and all the upright in heart will follow it.

16 Who will rise up for me against the wicked?
Who will take a stand for me against evildoers?
17 Unless the LORD had given me help,
I would soon have dwelt in the silence of death.
18 When I said, "My foot is slipping,"
your unfailing love, LORD, supported me.
19 When anxiety was great within me,
your consolation brought me joy.

20 Can a corrupt throne be allied with you—
a throne that brings on misery by its decrees?
21 The wicked band together against the righteous
and condemn the innocent to death.
22 But the LORD has become my fortress,
and my God the rock in whom I take refuge.
23 He will repay them for their sins
and destroy them for their wickedness;
the LORD our God will destroy them.

Psalm 95

1 Come, let us sing for joy to the LORD;
let us shout aloud to the Rock of our salvation.
2 Let us come before him with thanksgiving
and extol him with music and song.

3 For the LORD is the great God,
the great King above all gods.
4 In his hand are the depths of the earth,
and the mountain peaks belong to him.
5 The sea is his, for he made it,
and his hands formed the dry land.

6 Come, let us bow down in worship,
let us kneel before the LORD our Maker;
7 for he is our God
and we are the people of his pasture,
the flock under his care.

Today, if only you would hear his voice,
8 "Do not harden your hearts as you did at Meribah,[a]
as you did that day at Massah[b] in the wilderness,
9 where your ancestors tested me;
they tried me, though they had seen what I did.
10 For forty years I was angry with that generation;
I said, 'They are a people whose hearts go astray,
and they have not known my ways.'
11 So I declared on oath in my anger,
'They shall never enter my rest.' "

Psalm 96

1 Sing to the LORD a new song;
sing to the LORD, all the earth.
2 Sing to the LORD, praise his name;
proclaim his salvation day after day.
3 Declare his glory among the nations,
his marvelous deeds among all peoples.

4 For great is the LORD and most worthy of praise;
he is to be feared above all gods.
5 For all the gods of the nations are idols,
but the LORD made the heavens.
6 Splendor and majesty are before him;
strength and glory are in his sanctuary.

7 Ascribe to the LORD, all you families of nations,
ascribe to the LORD glory and strength.
8 Ascribe to the LORD the glory due his name;
bring an offering and come into his courts.
9 Worship the LORD in the splendor of his[c] holiness;
tremble before him, all the earth.
10 Say among the nations, "The LORD reigns."
The world is firmly established, it cannot be moved;
he will judge the peoples with equity.

11 Let the heavens rejoice, let the earth be glad;
let the sea resound, and all that is in it.
12 Let the fields be jubilant, and everything in them;
let all the trees of the forest sing for joy.

[a] 8 *Meribah* means *quarreling.* [b] 8 *Massah* means *testing.* [c] 9 Or *LORD with the splendor of*

[13]Let all creation rejoice before the LORD,
for he comes,
he comes to judge the earth.
He will judge the world in righteousness
and the peoples in his faithfulness.

Psalm 97

[1]The LORD reigns, let the earth be glad;
let the distant shores rejoice.
[2]Clouds and thick darkness surround him;
righteousness and justice are the
foundation of his throne.
[3]Fire goes before him
and consumes his foes on every side.
[4]His lightning lights up the world;
the earth sees and trembles.
[5]The mountains melt like wax before the
LORD,
before the Lord of all the earth.
[6]The heavens proclaim his righteousness,
and all peoples see his glory.

[7]All who worship images are put to shame,
those who boast in idols—
worship him, all you gods!

[8]Zion hears and rejoices
and the villages of Judah are glad
because of your judgments, LORD.
[9]For you, LORD, are the Most High over all
the earth;
you are exalted far above all gods.
[10]Let those who love the LORD hate evil,
for he guards the lives of his faithful ones
and delivers them from the hand of the
wicked.
[11]Light shines[a] on the righteous
and joy on the upright in heart.
[12]Rejoice in the LORD, you who are
righteous,
and praise his holy name.

Psalm 98

A psalm.

[1]Sing to the LORD a new song,
for he has done marvelous things;
his right hand and his holy arm
have worked salvation for him.
[2]The LORD has made his salvation known
and revealed his righteousness to the
nations.
[3]He has remembered his love
and his faithfulness to Israel;
all the ends of the earth have seen
the salvation of our God.

[4]Shout for joy to the LORD, all the earth,
burst into jubilant song with music;
[5]make music to the LORD with the harp,
with the harp and the sound of singing,
[6]with trumpets and the blast of the ram's
horn—
shout for joy before the LORD, the King.

[7]Let the sea resound, and everything in it,
the world, and all who live in it.
[8]Let the rivers clap their hands,
let the mountains sing together for joy;
[9]let them sing before the LORD,
for he comes to judge the earth.
He will judge the world in righteousness
and the peoples with equity.

Psalm 99

[1]The LORD reigns,
let the nations tremble;
he sits enthroned between the cherubim,
let the earth shake.
[2]Great is the LORD in Zion;
he is exalted over all the nations.
[3]Let them praise your great and awesome
name—
he is holy.

[4]The King is mighty, he loves justice—
you have established equity;
in Jacob you have done
what is just and right.
[5]Exalt the LORD our God
and worship at his footstool;
he is holy.

[6]Moses and Aaron were among his priests,
Samuel was among those who called
on his name;
they called on the LORD
and he answered them.
[7]He spoke to them from the pillar of cloud;
they kept his statutes and the decrees
he gave them.

[8]LORD our God,
you answered them;
you were to Israel a forgiving God,
though you punished their misdeeds.[b]
[9]Exalt the LORD our God
and worship at his holy mountain,
for the LORD our God is holy.

Psalm 100

A psalm. For giving grateful praise.

[1]Shout for joy to the LORD, all the earth.
[2] Worship the LORD with gladness;
come before him with joyful songs.
[3]Know that the LORD is God.
It is he who made us, and we are his[c];
we are his people, the sheep of his
pasture.

[4]Enter his gates with thanksgiving
and his courts with praise;
give thanks to him and praise his
name.
[5]For the LORD is good and his love endures
forever;
his faithfulness continues through all
generations.

Psalm 101

Of David. A psalm.

[1]I will sing of your love and justice;
to you, LORD, I will sing praise.

[a] 11 One Hebrew manuscript and ancient versions (see also 112:4); most Hebrew manuscripts *Light is sown* [b] 8 Or *God, / an avenger of the wrongs done to them* [c] 3 Or *and not we ourselves*

2 I will be careful to lead a blameless life—
when will you come to me?

I will conduct the affairs of my house
with a blameless heart.
3 I will not look with approval
on anything that is vile.

I hate what faithless people do;
I will have no part in it.
4 The perverse of heart shall be far from
me;
I will have nothing to do with what is
evil.

5 Whoever slanders their neighbor in
secret,
I will put to silence;
whoever has haughty eyes and a proud
heart,
I will not tolerate.

6 My eyes will be on the faithful in the
land,
that they may dwell with me;
the one whose walk is blameless
will minister to me.

7 No one who practices deceit
will dwell in my house;
no one who speaks falsely
will stand in my presence.

8 Every morning I will put to silence
all the wicked in the land;
I will cut off every evildoer
from the city of the LORD.

Psalm 102[a]

A prayer of an afflicted person who has grown weak and pours out a lament before the LORD.

1 Hear my prayer, LORD;
let my cry for help come to you.
2 Do not hide your face from me
when I am in distress.
Turn your ear to me;
when I call, answer me quickly.

3 For my days vanish like smoke;
my bones burn like glowing embers.
4 My heart is blighted and withered like
grass;
I forget to eat my food.
5 In my distress I groan aloud
and am reduced to skin and bones.
6 I am like a desert owl,
like an owl among the ruins.
7 I lie awake; I have become
like a bird alone on a roof.
8 All day long my enemies taunt me;
those who rail against me use my name
as a curse.
9 For I eat ashes as my food
and mingle my drink with tears
10 because of your great wrath,
for you have taken me up and thrown
me aside.
11 My days are like the evening shadow;
I wither away like grass.

12 But you, LORD, sit enthroned forever;
your renown endures through all
generations.
13 You will arise and have compassion on
Zion,
for it is time to show favor to her;
the appointed time has come.
14 For her stones are dear to your servants;
her very dust moves them to pity.
15 The nations will fear the name of the
LORD,
all the kings of the earth will revere
your glory.
16 For the LORD will rebuild Zion
and appear in his glory.
17 He will respond to the prayer of the
destitute;
he will not despise their plea.

18 Let this be written for a future
generation,
that a people not yet created may praise
the LORD:
19 "The LORD looked down from his
sanctuary on high,
from heaven he viewed the earth,
20 to hear the groans of the prisoners
and release those condemned to
death."
21 So the name of the LORD will be declared
in Zion
and his praise in Jerusalem
22 when the peoples and the kingdoms
assemble to worship the LORD.

23 In the course of my life[b] he broke my
strength;
he cut short my days.
24 So I said:
"Do not take me away, my God, in the
midst of my days;
your years go on through all
generations.
25 In the beginning you laid the foundations
of the earth,
and the heavens are the work of your
hands.
26 They will perish, but you remain;
they will all wear out like a garment.
Like clothing you will change them
and they will be discarded.
27 But you remain the same,
and your years will never end.
28 The children of your servants will live in
your presence;
their descendants will be established
before you."

Psalm 103

Of David.

1 Praise the LORD, my soul;
all my inmost being, praise his holy
name.
2 Praise the LORD, my soul,
and forget not all his benefits—
3 who forgives all your sins
and heals all your diseases,

[a] In Hebrew texts 102:1-28 is numbered 102:2-29.
[b] 23 Or *By his power*

[4]who redeems your life from the pit
and crowns you with love and compassion,
[5]who satisfies your desires with good things
so that your youth is renewed like the eagle's.

[6]The LORD works righteousness
and justice for all the oppressed.

[7]He made known his ways to Moses,
his deeds to the people of Israel:
[8]The LORD is compassionate and gracious,
slow to anger, abounding in love.
[9]He will not always accuse,
nor will he harbor his anger forever;
[10]he does not treat us as our sins deserve
or repay us according to our iniquities.
[11]For as high as the heavens are above the earth,
so great is his love for those who fear him;
[12]as far as the east is from the west,
so far has he removed our transgressions from us.

[13]As a father has compassion on his children,
so the LORD has compassion on those who fear him;
[14]for he knows how we are formed,
he remembers that we are dust.
[15]The life of mortals is like grass,
they flourish like a flower of the field;
[16]the wind blows over it and it is gone,
and its place remembers it no more.
[17]But from everlasting to everlasting
the LORD's love is with those who fear him,
and his righteousness with their children's children—
[18]with those who keep his covenant
and remember to obey his precepts.

[19]The LORD has established his throne in heaven,
and his kingdom rules over all.

[20]Praise the LORD, you his angels,
you mighty ones who do his bidding,
who obey his word.
[21]Praise the LORD, all his heavenly hosts,
you his servants who do his will.
[22]Praise the LORD, all his works
everywhere in his dominion.

Praise the LORD, my soul.

Psalm 104

[1]Praise the LORD, my soul.

LORD my God, you are very great;
you are clothed with splendor and majesty.

[2]The LORD wraps himself in light as with a garment;
he stretches out the heavens like a tent
[3]and lays the beams of his upper chambers on their waters.
He makes the clouds his chariot
and rides on the wings of the wind.
[4]He makes winds his messengers,[a]
flames of fire his servants.

[5]He set the earth on its foundations;
it can never be moved.
[6]You covered it with the watery depths as with a garment;
the waters stood above the mountains.
[7]But at your rebuke the waters fled,
at the sound of your thunder they took to flight;
[8]they flowed over the mountains,
they went down into the valleys,
to the place you assigned for them.
[9]You set a boundary they cannot cross;
never again will they cover the earth.

[10]He makes springs pour water into the ravines;
it flows between the mountains.
[11]They give water to all the beasts of the field;
the wild donkeys quench their thirst.
[12]The birds of the sky nest by the waters;
they sing among the branches.
[13]He waters the mountains from his upper chambers;
the land is satisfied by the fruit of his work.
[14]He makes grass grow for the cattle,
and plants for people to cultivate—
bringing forth food from the earth:
[15]wine that gladdens human hearts,
oil to make their faces shine,
and bread that sustains their hearts.
[16]The trees of the LORD are well watered,
the cedars of Lebanon that he planted.
[17]There the birds make their nests;
the stork has its home in the junipers.
[18]The high mountains belong to the wild goats;
the crags are a refuge for the hyrax.

[19]He made the moon to mark the seasons,
and the sun knows when to go down.
[20]You bring darkness, it becomes night,
and all the beasts of the forest prowl.
[21]The lions roar for their prey
and seek their food from God.
[22]The sun rises, and they steal away;
they return and lie down in their dens.
[23]Then people go out to their work,
to their labor until evening.

[24]How many are your works, LORD!
In wisdom you made them all;
the earth is full of your creatures.
[25]There is the sea, vast and spacious,
teeming with creatures beyond number—
living things both large and small.
[26]There the ships go to and fro,
and Leviathan, which you formed to frolic there.

[a] 4 Or *angels*

27 All creatures look to you
to give them their food at the proper time.
28 When you give it to them,
they gather it up;
when you open your hand,
they are satisfied with good things.
29 When you hide your face,
they are terrified;
when you take away their breath,
they die and return to the dust.
30 When you send your Spirit,
they are created,
and you renew the face of the ground.

31 May the glory of the LORD endure forever;
may the LORD rejoice in his works—
32 he who looks at the earth, and it trembles,
who touches the mountains, and they smoke.

33 I will sing to the LORD all my life;
I will sing praise to my God as long as I live.
34 May my meditation be pleasing to him,
as I rejoice in the LORD.
35 But may sinners vanish from the earth
and the wicked be no more.

Praise the LORD, my soul.
Praise the LORD.[a]

Psalm 105

1 Give praise to the LORD, proclaim his name;
make known among the nations what he has done.
2 Sing to him, sing praise to him;
tell of all his wonderful acts.
3 Glory in his holy name;
let the hearts of those who seek the LORD rejoice.
4 Look to the LORD and his strength;
seek his face always.
5 Remember the wonders he has done,
his miracles, and the judgments he pronounced,
6 you his servants, the descendants of Abraham,
his chosen ones, the children of Jacob.
7 He is the LORD our God;
his judgments are in all the earth.

8 He remembers his covenant forever,
the promise he made, for a thousand generations,
9 the covenant he made with Abraham,
the oath he swore to Isaac.
10 He confirmed it to Jacob as a decree,
to Israel as an everlasting covenant:
11 "To you I will give the land of Canaan
as the portion you will inherit."

12 When they were but few in number,
few indeed, and strangers in it,
13 they wandered from nation to nation,
from one kingdom to another.
14 He allowed no one to oppress them;
for their sake he rebuked kings:
15 "Do not touch my anointed ones;
do my prophets no harm."

16 He called down famine on the land
and destroyed all their supplies of food;
17 and he sent a man before them—
Joseph, sold as a slave.
18 They bruised his feet with shackles,
his neck was put in irons,
19 till what he foretold came to pass,
till the word of the LORD proved him true.
20 The king sent and released him,
the ruler of peoples set him free.
21 He made him master of his household,
ruler over all he possessed,
22 to instruct his princes as he pleased
and teach his elders wisdom.

23 Then Israel entered Egypt;
Jacob resided as a foreigner in the land of Ham.
24 The LORD made his people very fruitful;
he made them too numerous for their foes,
25 whose hearts he turned to hate his people,
to conspire against his servants.
26 He sent Moses his servant,
and Aaron, whom he had chosen.
27 They performed his signs among them,
his wonders in the land of Ham.
28 He sent darkness and made the land dark—
for had they not rebelled against his words?
29 He turned their waters into blood,
causing their fish to die.
30 Their land teemed with frogs,
which went up into the bedrooms of their rulers.
31 He spoke, and there came swarms of flies,
and gnats throughout their country.
32 He turned their rain into hail,
with lightning throughout their land;
33 he struck down their vines and fig trees
and shattered the trees of their country.
34 He spoke, and the locusts came,
grasshoppers without number;
35 they ate up every green thing in their land,
ate up the produce of their soil.
36 Then he struck down all the firstborn in their land,
the firstfruits of all their manhood.
37 He brought out Israel, laden with silver and gold,
and from among their tribes no one faltered.
38 Egypt was glad when they left,
because dread of Israel had fallen on them.
39 He spread out a cloud as a covering,
and a fire to give light at night.

[a] 35 Hebrew *Hallelu Yah*; in the Septuagint this line stands at the beginning of Psalm 105.

40 They asked, and he brought them quail;
he fed them well with the bread of heaven.
41 He opened the rock, and water gushed out;
it flowed like a river in the desert.

42 For he remembered his holy promise
given to his servant Abraham.
43 He brought out his people with rejoicing,
his chosen ones with shouts of joy;
44 he gave them the lands of the nations,
and they fell heir to what others had toiled for—
45 that they might keep his precepts
and observe his laws.

Praise the LORD.[a]

Psalm 106

1 Praise the LORD.[b]

Give thanks to the LORD, for he is good;
his love endures forever.
2 Who can proclaim the mighty acts of the LORD
or fully declare his praise?
3 Blessed are those who act justly,
who always do what is right.

4 Remember me, LORD, when you show favor to your people,
come to my aid when you save them,
5 that I may enjoy the prosperity of your chosen ones,
that I may share in the joy of your nation
and join your inheritance in giving praise.

6 We have sinned, even as our ancestors did;
we have done wrong and acted wickedly.
7 When our ancestors were in Egypt,
they gave no thought to your miracles;
they did not remember your many kindnesses,
and they rebelled by the sea, the Red Sea.[c]
8 Yet he saved them for his name's sake,
to make his mighty power known.
9 He rebuked the Red Sea, and it dried up;
he led them through the depths as through a desert.
10 He saved them from the hand of the foe;
from the hand of the enemy he redeemed them.
11 The waters covered their adversaries;
not one of them survived.
12 Then they believed his promises
and sang his praise.

13 But they soon forgot what he had done
and did not wait for his plan to unfold.
14 In the desert they gave in to their craving;
in the wilderness they put God to the test.
15 So he gave them what they asked for,
but sent a wasting disease among them.
16 In the camp they grew envious of Moses
and of Aaron, who was consecrated to the LORD.
17 The earth opened up and swallowed Dathan;
it buried the company of Abiram.
18 Fire blazed among their followers;
a flame consumed the wicked.
19 At Horeb they made a calf
and worshiped an idol cast from metal.
20 They exchanged their glorious God
for an image of a bull, which eats grass.
21 They forgot the God who saved them,
who had done great things in Egypt,
22 miracles in the land of Ham
and awesome deeds by the Red Sea.
23 So he said he would destroy them—
had not Moses, his chosen one,
stood in the breach before him
to keep his wrath from destroying them.

24 Then they despised the pleasant land;
they did not believe his promise.
25 They grumbled in their tents
and did not obey the LORD.
26 So he swore to them with uplifted hand
that he would make them fall in the wilderness,
27 make their descendants fall among the nations
and scatter them throughout the lands.

28 They yoked themselves to the Baal of Peor
and ate sacrifices offered to lifeless gods;
29 they aroused the LORD's anger by their wicked deeds,
and a plague broke out among them.
30 But Phinehas stood up and intervened,
and the plague was checked.
31 This was credited to him as righteousness
for endless generations to come.
32 By the waters of Meribah they angered the LORD,
and trouble came to Moses because of them;
33 for they rebelled against the Spirit of God,
and rash words came from Moses' lips.[d]

34 They did not destroy the peoples
as the LORD had commanded them,
35 but they mingled with the nations
and adopted their customs.
36 They worshiped their idols,
which became a snare to them.
37 They sacrificed their sons
and their daughters to false gods.
38 They shed innocent blood,
the blood of their sons and daughters,
whom they sacrificed to the idols of Canaan,
and the land was desecrated by their blood.
39 They defiled themselves by what they did;
by their deeds they prostituted themselves.

[a] 45 Hebrew *Hallelu Yah* [b] 1 Hebrew *Hallelu Yah*; also in verse 48 [c] 7 Or *the Sea of Reeds*; also in verses 9 and 22 [d] 33 Or *against his spirit, / and rash words came from his lips*

40 Therefore the LORD was angry with his
people
and abhorred his inheritance.
41 He gave them into the hands of the nations,
and their foes ruled over them.
42 Their enemies oppressed them
and subjected them to their power.
43 Many times he delivered them,
but they were bent on rebellion
and they wasted away in their sin.
44 Yet he took note of their distress
when he heard their cry;
45 for their sake he remembered his
covenant
and out of his great love he relented.
46 He caused all who held them captive
to show them mercy.

47 Save us, LORD our God,
and gather us from the nations,
that we may give thanks to your holy name
and glory in your praise.

48 Praise be to the LORD, the God of Israel,
from everlasting to everlasting.

Let all the people say, "Amen!"

Praise the LORD.

BOOK V

Psalms 107–150

Psalm 107

1 Give thanks to the LORD, for he is good;
his love endures forever.

2 Let the redeemed of the LORD tell their
story—
those he redeemed from the hand of the
foe,
3 those he gathered from the lands,
from east and west, from north and
south.[a]

4 Some wandered in desert wastelands,
finding no way to a city where they
could settle.
5 They were hungry and thirsty,
and their lives ebbed away.
6 Then they cried out to the LORD in their
trouble,
and he delivered them from their
distress.
7 He led them by a straight way
to a city where they could settle.
8 Let them give thanks to the LORD for his
unfailing love
and his wonderful deeds for mankind,
9 for he satisfies the thirsty
and fills the hungry with good things.

10 Some sat in darkness, in utter darkness,
prisoners suffering in iron chains,
11 because they rebelled against God's
commands
and despised the plans of the Most High.
12 So he subjected them to bitter labor;
they stumbled, and there was no one to
help.
13 Then they cried to the LORD in their
trouble,
and he saved them from their distress.
14 He brought them out of darkness, the
utter darkness,
and broke away their chains.
15 Let them give thanks to the LORD for his
unfailing love
and his wonderful deeds for mankind,
16 for he breaks down gates of bronze
and cuts through bars of iron.

17 Some became fools through their
rebellious ways
and suffered affliction because of their
iniquities.
18 They loathed all food
and drew near the gates of death.
19 Then they cried to the LORD in their trouble,
and he saved them from their distress.
20 He sent out his word and healed them;
he rescued them from the grave.
21 Let them give thanks to the LORD for his
unfailing love
and his wonderful deeds for mankind.
22 Let them sacrifice thank offerings
and tell of his works with songs of joy.

23 Some went out on the sea in ships;
they were merchants on the mighty
waters.
24 They saw the works of the LORD,
his wonderful deeds in the deep.
25 For he spoke and stirred up a tempest
that lifted high the waves.
26 They mounted up to the heavens and
went down to the depths;
in their peril their courage melted away.
27 They reeled and staggered like
drunkards;
they were at their wits' end.
28 Then they cried out to the LORD in their
trouble,
and he brought them out of their distress.
29 He stilled the storm to a whisper;
the waves of the sea[b] were hushed.
30 They were glad when it grew calm,
and he guided them to their desired
haven.
31 Let them give thanks to the LORD for his
unfailing love
and his wonderful deeds for mankind.
32 Let them exalt him in the assembly of the
people
and praise him in the council of the
elders.

33 He turned rivers into a desert,
flowing springs into thirsty ground,
34 and fruitful land into a salt waste,
because of the wickedness of those who
lived there.
35 He turned the desert into pools of water
and the parched ground into flowing
springs;

[a] 3 Hebrew *north and the sea* [b] 29 Dead Sea Scrolls; Masoretic Text / *their waves*

36 there he brought the hungry to live,
and they founded a city where they could settle.
37 They sowed fields and planted vineyards
that yielded a fruitful harvest;
38 he blessed them, and their numbers greatly increased,
and he did not let their herds diminish.

39 Then their numbers decreased, and they were humbled
by oppression, calamity and sorrow;
40 he who pours contempt on nobles
made them wander in a trackless waste.
41 But he lifted the needy out of their affliction
and increased their families like flocks.
42 The upright see and rejoice,
but all the wicked shut their mouths.

43 Let the one who is wise heed these things
and ponder the loving deeds of the LORD.

Psalm 108[a]

A song. A psalm of David.

1 My heart, O God, is steadfast;
I will sing and make music with all my soul.
2 Awake, harp and lyre!
I will awaken the dawn.
3 I will praise you, LORD, among the nations;
I will sing of you among the peoples.
4 For great is your love, higher than the heavens;
your faithfulness reaches to the skies.
5 Be exalted, O God, above the heavens;
let your glory be over all the earth.

6 Save us and help us with your right hand,
that those you love may be delivered.
7 God has spoken from his sanctuary:
"In triumph I will parcel out Shechem
and measure off the Valley of Sukkoth.
8 Gilead is mine, Manasseh is mine;
Ephraim is my helmet,
Judah is my scepter.
9 Moab is my washbasin,
on Edom I toss my sandal;
over Philistia I shout in triumph."

10 Who will bring me to the fortified city?
Who will lead me to Edom?
11 Is it not you, God, you who have rejected us
and no longer go out with our armies?
12 Give us aid against the enemy,
for human help is worthless.
13 With God we will gain the victory,
and he will trample down our enemies.

Psalm 109

For the director of music. Of David. A psalm.

1 My God, whom I praise,
do not remain silent,
2 for people who are wicked and deceitful
have opened their mouths against me;
they have spoken against me with lying tongues.
3 With words of hatred they surround me;
they attack me without cause.
4 In return for my friendship they accuse me,
but I am a man of prayer.
5 They repay me evil for good,
and hatred for my friendship.

6 Appoint someone evil to oppose my enemy;
let an accuser stand at his right hand.
7 When he is tried, let him be found guilty,
and may his prayers condemn him.
8 May his days be few;
may another take his place of leadership.
9 May his children be fatherless
and his wife a widow.
10 May his children be wandering beggars;
may they be driven[b] from their ruined homes.
11 May a creditor seize all he has;
may strangers plunder the fruits of his labor.
12 May no one extend kindness to him
or take pity on his fatherless children.
13 May his descendants be cut off,
their names blotted out from the next generation.
14 May the iniquity of his fathers be remembered before the LORD;
may the sin of his mother never be blotted out.
15 May their sins always remain before the LORD,
that he may blot out their name from the earth.

16 For he never thought of doing a kindness,
but hounded to death the poor
and the needy and the brokenhearted.
17 He loved to pronounce a curse—
may it come back on him.
He found no pleasure in blessing—
may it be far from him.
18 He wore cursing as his garment;
it entered into his body like water,
into his bones like oil.
19 May it be like a cloak wrapped about him,
like a belt tied forever around him.
20 May this be the LORD's payment to my accusers,
to those who speak evil of me.

21 But you, Sovereign LORD,
help me for your name's sake;
out of the goodness of your love, deliver me.
22 For I am poor and needy,
and my heart is wounded within me.
23 I fade away like an evening shadow;
I am shaken off like a locust.
24 My knees give way from fasting;
my body is thin and gaunt.

[a] In Hebrew texts 108:1-13 is numbered 108:2-14.
[b] *10* Septuagint; Hebrew *sought*

25 I am an object of scorn to my accusers;
when they see me, they shake their heads.
26 Help me, LORD my God;
save me according to your unfailing love.
27 Let them know that it is your hand,
that you, LORD, have done it.
28 While they curse, may you bless;
may those who attack me be put to shame,
but may your servant rejoice.
29 May my accusers be clothed with disgrace
and wrapped in shame as in a cloak.
30 With my mouth I will greatly extol the LORD;
in the great throng of worshipers I will praise him.
31 For he stands at the right hand of the needy,
to save their lives from those who would condemn them.

Psalm 110

Of David. A psalm.

1 The LORD says to my lord:[a]

"Sit at my right hand
until I make your enemies
a footstool for your feet."

2 The LORD will extend your mighty scepter from Zion, saying,
"Rule in the midst of your enemies!"
3 Your troops will be willing
on your day of battle.
Arrayed in holy splendor,
your young men will come to you
like dew from the morning's womb.[b]

4 The LORD has sworn
and will not change his mind:
"You are a priest forever,
in the order of Melchizedek."

5 The Lord is at your right hand[c];
he will crush kings on the day of his wrath.
6 He will judge the nations, heaping up the dead
and crushing the rulers of the whole earth.
7 He will drink from a brook along the way,[d]
and so he will lift his head high.

Psalm 111[e]

1 Praise the LORD.[f]

I will extol the LORD with all my heart
in the council of the upright and in the assembly.

2 Great are the works of the LORD;
they are pondered by all who delight in them.
3 Glorious and majestic are his deeds,
and his righteousness endures forever.
4 He has caused his wonders to be remembered;
the LORD is gracious and compassionate.
5 He provides food for those who fear him;
he remembers his covenant forever.

6 He has shown his people the power of his works,
giving them the lands of other nations.
7 The works of his hands are faithful and just;
all his precepts are trustworthy.
8 They are established for ever and ever,
enacted in faithfulness and uprightness.
9 He provided redemption for his people;
he ordained his covenant forever—
holy and awesome is his name.

10 The fear of the LORD is the beginning of wisdom;
all who follow his precepts have good understanding.
To him belongs eternal praise.

Psalm 112[e]

1 Praise the LORD.[f]

Blessed are those who fear the LORD,
who find great delight in his commands.

2 Their children will be mighty in the land;
the generation of the upright will be blessed.
3 Wealth and riches are in their houses,
and their righteousness endures forever.
4 Even in darkness light dawns for the upright,
for those who are gracious and compassionate and righteous.
5 Good will come to those who are generous and lend freely,
who conduct their affairs with justice.

6 Surely the righteous will never be shaken;
they will be remembered forever.
7 They will have no fear of bad news;
their hearts are steadfast, trusting in the LORD.
8 Their hearts are secure, they will have no fear;
in the end they will look in triumph on their foes.
9 They have freely scattered their gifts to the poor,
their righteousness endures forever;
their horn[g] will be lifted high in honor.

[a] *1* Or *Lord* [b] *3* The meaning of the Hebrew for this sentence is uncertain. [c] *5* Or *My lord is at your right hand, LORD* [d] *7* The meaning of the Hebrew for this clause is uncertain. [e] This psalm is an acrostic poem, the lines of which begin with the successive letters of the Hebrew alphabet.
[f] *1,1* Hebrew *Hallelu Yah* [g] *9* *Horn* here symbolizes dignity.

10 The wicked will see and be vexed,
they will gnash their teeth and waste away;
the longings of the wicked will come to nothing.

Psalm 113

1 Praise the LORD.[a]

Praise the LORD, you his servants;
praise the name of the LORD.
2 Let the name of the LORD be praised,
both now and forevermore.
3 From the rising of the sun to the place where it sets,
the name of the LORD is to be praised.

4 The LORD is exalted over all the nations,
his glory above the heavens.
5 Who is like the LORD our God,
the One who sits enthroned on high,
6 who stoops down to look
on the heavens and the earth?

7 He raises the poor from the dust
and lifts the needy from the ash heap;
8 he seats them with princes,
with the princes of his people.
9 He settles the childless woman in her home
as a happy mother of children.

Praise the LORD.

Psalm 114

1 When Israel came out of Egypt,
Jacob from a people of foreign tongue,
2 Judah became God's sanctuary,
Israel his dominion.

3 The sea looked and fled,
the Jordan turned back;
4 the mountains leaped like rams,
the hills like lambs.

5 Why was it, sea, that you fled?
Why, Jordan, did you turn back?
6 Why, mountains, did you leap like rams,
you hills, like lambs?

7 Tremble, earth, at the presence of the Lord,
at the presence of the God of Jacob,
8 who turned the rock into a pool,
the hard rock into springs of water.

Psalm 115

1 Not to us, LORD, not to us
but to your name be the glory,
because of your love and faithfulness.

2 Why do the nations say,
"Where is their God?"
3 Our God is in heaven;
he does whatever pleases him.
4 But their idols are silver and gold,
made by human hands.
5 They have mouths, but cannot speak,
eyes, but cannot see.
6 They have ears, but cannot hear,
noses, but cannot smell.
7 They have hands, but cannot feel,
feet, but cannot walk,
nor can they utter a sound with their throats.
8 Those who make them will be like them,
and so will all who trust in them.

9 All you Israelites, trust in the LORD—
he is their help and shield.
10 House of Aaron, trust in the LORD—
he is their help and shield.
11 You who fear him, trust in the LORD—
he is their help and shield.

12 The LORD remembers us and will bless us:
He will bless his people Israel,
he will bless the house of Aaron,
13 he will bless those who fear the LORD—
small and great alike.

14 May the LORD cause you to flourish,
both you and your children.
15 May you be blessed by the LORD,
the Maker of heaven and earth.

16 The highest heavens belong to the LORD,
but the earth he has given to mankind.
17 It is not the dead who praise the LORD,
those who go down to the place of silence;
18 it is we who extol the LORD,
both now and forevermore.

Praise the LORD.[b]

Psalm 116

1 I love the LORD, for he heard my voice;
he heard my cry for mercy.
2 Because he turned his ear to me,
I will call on him as long as I live.

3 The cords of death entangled me,
the anguish of the grave came over me;
I was overcome by distress and sorrow.
4 Then I called on the name of the LORD:
"LORD, save me!"

5 The LORD is gracious and righteous;
our God is full of compassion.
6 The LORD protects the unwary;
when I was brought low, he saved me.

7 Return to your rest, my soul,
for the LORD has been good to you.

8 For you, LORD, have delivered me from death,
my eyes from tears,
my feet from stumbling,
9 that I may walk before the LORD
in the land of the living.

10 I trusted in the LORD when I said,
"I am greatly afflicted";
11 in my alarm I said,
"Everyone is a liar."

12 What shall I return to the LORD
for all his goodness to me?

[a] 1 Hebrew *Hallelu Yah*; also in verse 9 [b] 18 Hebrew *Hallelu Yah*

13 I will lift up the cup of salvation
and call on the name of the LORD.
14 I will fulfill my vows to the LORD
in the presence of all his people.

15 Precious in the sight of the LORD
is the death of his faithful servants.
16 Truly I am your servant, LORD;
I serve you just as my mother did;
you have freed me from my chains.

17 I will sacrifice a thank offering to you
and call on the name of the LORD.
18 I will fulfill my vows to the LORD
in the presence of all his people,
19 in the courts of the house of the LORD—
in your midst, Jerusalem.

Praise the LORD.[a]

Psalm 117

1 Praise the LORD, all you nations;
extol him, all you peoples.
2 For great is his love toward us,
and the faithfulness of the LORD
endures forever.

Praise the LORD.[a]

Psalm 118

1 Give thanks to the LORD, for he is good;
his love endures forever.

2 Let Israel say:
"His love endures forever."
3 Let the house of Aaron say:
"His love endures forever."
4 Let those who fear the LORD say:
"His love endures forever."

5 When hard pressed, I cried to the LORD;
he brought me into a spacious place.
6 The LORD is with me; I will not be afraid.
What can mere mortals do to me?
7 The LORD is with me; he is my helper.
I look in triumph on my enemies.

8 It is better to take refuge in the LORD
than to trust in humans.
9 It is better to take refuge in the LORD
than to trust in princes.
10 All the nations surrounded me,
but in the name of the LORD I cut them
down.
11 They surrounded me on every side,
but in the name of the LORD I cut them
down.
12 They swarmed around me like bees,
but they were consumed as quickly as
burning thorns;
in the name of the LORD I cut them
down.
13 I was pushed back and about to fall,
but the LORD helped me.
14 The LORD is my strength and my defense[b];
he has become my salvation.

15 Shouts of joy and victory
resound in the tents of the righteous:
"The LORD's right hand has done mighty
things!
16 The LORD's right hand is lifted high;
the LORD's right hand has done mighty
things!"
17 I will not die but live,
and will proclaim what the LORD has
done.
18 The LORD has chastened me severely,
but he has not given me over to death.
19 Open for me the gates of the righteous;
I will enter and give thanks to the LORD.
20 This is the gate of the LORD
through which the righteous may enter.
21 I will give you thanks, for you answered me;
you have become my salvation.

22 The stone the builders rejected
has become the cornerstone;
23 the LORD has done this,
and it is marvelous in our eyes.
24 The LORD has done it this very day;
let us rejoice today and be glad.

25 LORD, save us!
LORD, grant us success!

26 Blessed is he who comes in the name of
the LORD.
From the house of the LORD we bless
you.[c]
27 The LORD is God,
and he has made his light shine on us.
With boughs in hand, join in the festal
procession
up[d] to the horns of the altar.

28 You are my God, and I will praise you;
you are my God, and I will exalt you.

29 Give thanks to the LORD, for he is good;
his love endures forever.

Psalm 119[e]

א Aleph

1 Blessed are those whose ways are
blameless,
who walk according to the law of the
LORD.
2 Blessed are those who keep his statutes
and seek him with all their heart—
3 they do no wrong
but follow his ways.
4 You have laid down precepts
that are to be fully obeyed.
5 Oh, that my ways were steadfast
in obeying your decrees!
6 Then I would not be put to shame
when I consider all your commands.
7 I will praise you with an upright heart
as I learn your righteous laws.
8 I will obey your decrees;
do not utterly forsake me.

[a] *19,2* Hebrew *Hallelu Yah* [b] *14* Or *song* [c] *26* The Hebrew is plural. [d] *27* Or *Bind the festal sacrifice with ropes / and take it* [e] This psalm is an acrostic poem, the stanzas of which begin with successive letters of the Hebrew alphabet; moreover, the verses of each stanza begin with the same letter of the Hebrew alphabet.

ב Beth

[9]How can a young person stay on the path
of purity?
By living according to your word.
[10]I seek you with all my heart;
do not let me stray from your
commands.
[11]I have hidden your word in my heart
that I might not sin against you.
[12]Praise be to you, LORD;
teach me your decrees.
[13]With my lips I recount
all the laws that come from your
mouth.
[14]I rejoice in following your statutes
as one rejoices in great riches.
[15]I meditate on your precepts
and consider your ways.
[16]I delight in your decrees;
I will not neglect your word.

ג Gimel

[17]Be good to your servant while I live,
that I may obey your word.
[18]Open my eyes that I may see
wonderful things in your law.
[19]I am a stranger on earth;
do not hide your commands from me.
[20]My soul is consumed with longing
for your laws at all times.
[21]You rebuke the arrogant, who are
accursed,
those who stray from your commands.
[22]Remove from me their scorn and
contempt,
for I keep your statutes.
[23]Though rulers sit together and slander me,
your servant will meditate on your
decrees.
[24]Your statutes are my delight;
they are my counselors.

ד Daleth

[25]I am laid low in the dust;
preserve my life according to your word.
[26]I gave an account of my ways and you
answered me;
teach me your decrees.
[27]Cause me to understand the way of your
precepts,
that I may meditate on your wonderful
deeds.
[28]My soul is weary with sorrow;
strengthen me according to your word.
[29]Keep me from deceitful ways;
be gracious to me and teach me your
law.
[30]I have chosen the way of faithfulness;
I have set my heart on your laws.
[31]I hold fast to your statutes, LORD;
do not let me be put to shame.
[32]I run in the path of your commands,
for you have broadened my
understanding.

ה He

[33]Teach me, LORD, the way of your
decrees,
that I may follow it to the end.[a]
[34]Give me understanding, so that I may
keep your law
and obey it with all my heart.
[35]Direct me in the path of your commands,
for there I find delight.
[36]Turn my heart toward your statutes
and not toward selfish gain.
[37]Turn my eyes away from worthless
things;
preserve my life according to your
word.[b]
[38]Fulfill your promise to your servant,
so that you may be feared.
[39]Take away the disgrace I dread,
for your laws are good.
[40]How I long for your precepts!
In your righteousness preserve my life.

ו Waw

[41]May your unfailing love come to me,
LORD,
your salvation, according to your
promise;
[42]then I can answer anyone who taunts me,
for I trust in your word.
[43]Never take your word of truth from my
mouth,
for I have put my hope in your laws.
[44]I will always obey your law,
for ever and ever.
[45]I will walk about in freedom,
for I have sought out your precepts.
[46]I will speak of your statutes before
kings
and will not be put to shame,
[47]for I delight in your commands
because I love them.
[48]I reach out for your commands, which I
love,
that I may meditate on your decrees.

ז Zayin

[49]Remember your word to your servant,
for you have given me hope.
[50]My comfort in my suffering is this:
Your promise preserves my life.
[51]The arrogant mock me unmercifully,
but I do not turn from your law.
[52]I remember, LORD, your ancient laws,
and I find comfort in them.
[53]Indignation grips me because of the
wicked,
who have forsaken your law.
[54]Your decrees are the theme of my song
wherever I lodge.
[55]In the night, LORD, I remember your
name,
that I may keep your law.
[56]This has been my practice:
I obey your precepts.

[a] *33* Or *follow it for its reward* [b] *37* Two manuscripts of the Masoretic Text and Dead Sea Scrolls; most manuscripts of the Masoretic Text *life in your way*

ח Heth

57 You are my portion, LORD;
I have promised to obey your words.
58 I have sought your face with all my heart;
be gracious to me according to your promise.
59 I have considered my ways
and have turned my steps to your statutes.
60 I will hasten and not delay
to obey your commands.
61 Though the wicked bind me with ropes,
I will not forget your law.
62 At midnight I rise to give you thanks
for your righteous laws.
63 I am a friend to all who fear you,
to all who follow your precepts.
64 The earth is filled with your love, LORD;
teach me your decrees.

ט Teth

65 Do good to your servant
according to your word, LORD.
66 Teach me knowledge and good judgment,
for I trust your commands.
67 Before I was afflicted I went astray,
but now I obey your word.
68 You are good, and what you do is good;
teach me your decrees.
69 Though the arrogant have smeared me with lies,
I keep your precepts with all my heart.
70 Their hearts are callous and unfeeling,
but I delight in your law.
71 It was good for me to be afflicted
so that I might learn your decrees.
72 The law from your mouth is more precious to me
than thousands of pieces of silver and gold.

י Yodh

73 Your hands made me and formed me;
give me understanding to learn your commands.
74 May those who fear you rejoice when they see me,
for I have put my hope in your word.
75 I know, LORD, that your laws are righteous,
and that in faithfulness you have afflicted me.
76 May your unfailing love be my comfort,
according to your promise to your servant.
77 Let your compassion come to me that I may live,
for your law is my delight.
78 May the arrogant be put to shame for wronging me without cause;
but I will meditate on your precepts.
79 May those who fear you turn to me,
those who understand your statutes.
80 May I wholeheartedly follow your decrees,
that I may not be put to shame.

כ Kaph

81 My soul faints with longing for your salvation,
but I have put my hope in your word.
82 My eyes fail, looking for your promise;
I say, "When will you comfort me?"
83 Though I am like a wineskin in the smoke,
I do not forget your decrees.
84 How long must your servant wait?
When will you punish my persecutors?
85 The arrogant dig pits to trap me,
contrary to your law.
86 All your commands are trustworthy;
help me, for I am being persecuted without cause.
87 They almost wiped me from the earth,
but I have not forsaken your precepts.
88 In your unfailing love preserve my life,
that I may obey the statutes of your mouth.

ל Lamedh

89 Your word, LORD, is eternal;
it stands firm in the heavens.
90 Your faithfulness continues through all generations;
you established the earth, and it endures.
91 Your laws endure to this day,
for all things serve you.
92 If your law had not been my delight,
I would have perished in my affliction.
93 I will never forget your precepts,
for by them you have preserved my life.
94 Save me, for I am yours;
I have sought out your precepts.
95 The wicked are waiting to destroy me,
but I will ponder your statutes.
96 To all perfection I see a limit,
but your commands are boundless.

מ Mem

97 Oh, how I love your law!
I meditate on it all day long.
98 Your commands are always with me
and make me wiser than my enemies.
99 I have more insight than all my teachers,
for I meditate on your statutes.
100 I have more understanding than the elders,
for I obey your precepts.
101 I have kept my feet from every evil path
so that I might obey your word.
102 I have not departed from your laws,
for you yourself have taught me.
103 How sweet are your words to my taste,
sweeter than honey to my mouth!
104 I gain understanding from your precepts;
therefore I hate every wrong path.

נ Nun

105 Your word is a lamp for my feet,
a light on my path.
106 I have taken an oath and confirmed it,
that I will follow your righteous laws.

107 I have suffered much;
preserve my life, LORD, according to your word.
108 Accept, LORD, the willing praise of my mouth,
and teach me your laws.
109 Though I constantly take my life in my hands,
I will not forget your law.
110 The wicked have set a snare for me,
but I have not strayed from your precepts.
111 Your statutes are my heritage forever;
they are the joy of my heart.
112 My heart is set on keeping your decrees
to the very end.[a]

ס Samekh

113 I hate double-minded people,
but I love your law.
114 You are my refuge and my shield;
I have put my hope in your word.
115 Away from me, you evildoers,
that I may keep the commands of my God!
116 Sustain me, my God, according to your promise, and I will live;
do not let my hopes be dashed.
117 Uphold me, and I will be delivered;
I will always have regard for your decrees.
118 You reject all who stray from your decrees,
for their delusions come to nothing.
119 All the wicked of the earth you discard like dross;
therefore I love your statutes.
120 My flesh trembles in fear of you;
I stand in awe of your laws.

ע Ayin

121 I have done what is righteous and just;
do not leave me to my oppressors.
122 Ensure your servant's well-being;
do not let the arrogant oppress me.
123 My eyes fail, looking for your salvation,
looking for your righteous promise.
124 Deal with your servant according to your love
and teach me your decrees.
125 I am your servant; give me discernment
that I may understand your statutes.
126 It is time for you to act, LORD;
your law is being broken.
127 Because I love your commands
more than gold, more than pure gold,
128 and because I consider all your precepts right,
I hate every wrong path.

פ Pe

129 Your statutes are wonderful;
therefore I obey them.
130 The unfolding of your words gives light;
it gives understanding to the simple.
131 I open my mouth and pant,
longing for your commands.
132 Turn to me and have mercy on me,
as you always do to those who love your name.
133 Direct my footsteps according to your word;
let no sin rule over me.
134 Redeem me from human oppression,
that I may obey your precepts.
135 Make your face shine on your servant
and teach me your decrees.
136 Streams of tears flow from my eyes,
for your law is not obeyed.

צ Tsadhe

137 You are righteous, LORD,
and your laws are right.
138 The statutes you have laid down are righteous;
they are fully trustworthy.
139 My zeal wears me out,
for my enemies ignore your words.
140 Your promises have been thoroughly tested,
and your servant loves them.
141 Though I am lowly and despised,
I do not forget your precepts.
142 Your righteousness is everlasting
and your law is true.
143 Trouble and distress have come upon me,
but your commands give me delight.
144 Your statutes are always righteous;
give me understanding that I may live.

ק Qoph

145 I call with all my heart; answer me, LORD,
and I will obey your decrees.
146 I call out to you; save me
and I will keep your statutes.
147 I rise before dawn and cry for help;
I have put my hope in your word.
148 My eyes stay open through the watches of the night,
that I may meditate on your promises.
149 Hear my voice in accordance with your love;
preserve my life, LORD, according to your laws.
150 Those who devise wicked schemes are near,
but they are far from your law.
151 Yet you are near, LORD,
and all your commands are true.
152 Long ago I learned from your statutes
that you established them to last forever.

ר Resh

153 Look on my suffering and deliver me,
for I have not forgotten your law.
154 Defend my cause and redeem me;
preserve my life according to your promise.

[a] 112 Or *decrees / for their enduring reward*

155 Salvation is far from the wicked,
for they do not seek out your decrees.
156 Your compassion, LORD, is great;
preserve my life according to your laws.
157 Many are the foes who persecute me,
but I have not turned from your statutes.
158 I look on the faithless with loathing,
for they do not obey your word.
159 See how I love your precepts;
preserve my life, LORD, in accordance with your love.
160 All your words are true;
all your righteous laws are eternal.

ש Sin and Shin

161 Rulers persecute me without cause,
but my heart trembles at your word.
162 I rejoice in your promise
like one who finds great spoil.
163 I hate and detest falsehood
but I love your law.
164 Seven times a day I praise you
for your righteous laws.
165 Great peace have those who love your law,
and nothing can make them stumble.
166 I wait for your salvation, LORD,
and I follow your commands.
167 I obey your statutes,
for I love them greatly.
168 I obey your precepts and your statutes,
for all my ways are known to you.

ת Taw

169 May my cry come before you, LORD;
give me understanding according to your word.
170 May my supplication come before you;
deliver me according to your promise.
171 May my lips overflow with praise,
for you teach me your decrees.
172 May my tongue sing of your word,
for all your commands are righteous.
173 May your hand be ready to help me,
for I have chosen your precepts.
174 I long for your salvation, LORD,
and your law gives me delight.
175 Let me live that I may praise you,
and may your laws sustain me.
176 I have strayed like a lost sheep.
Seek your servant,
for I have not forgotten your commands.

Psalm 120

A song of ascents.

1 I call on the LORD in my distress,
and he answers me.
2 Save me, LORD,
from lying lips
and from deceitful tongues.

3 What will he do to you,
and what more besides,
you deceitful tongue?
4 He will punish you with a warrior's sharp arrows,
with burning coals of the broom bush.

5 Woe to me that I dwell in Meshek,
that I live among the tents of Kedar!
6 Too long have I lived
among those who hate peace.
7 I am for peace;
but when I speak, they are for war.

Psalm 121

A song of ascents.

1 I lift up my eyes to the mountains—
where does my help come from?
2 My help comes from the LORD,
the Maker of heaven and earth.

3 He will not let your foot slip—
he who watches over you will not slumber;
4 indeed, he who watches over Israel
will neither slumber nor sleep.

5 The LORD watches over you—
the LORD is your shade at your right hand;
6 the sun will not harm you by day,
nor the moon by night.

7 The LORD will keep you from all harm—
he will watch over your life;
8 the LORD will watch over your coming and going
both now and forevermore.

Psalm 122

A song of ascents. Of David.

1 I rejoiced with those who said to me,
"Let us go to the house of the LORD."
2 Our feet are standing
in your gates, Jerusalem.

3 Jerusalem is built like a city
that is closely compacted together.
4 That is where the tribes go up—
the tribes of the LORD—
to praise the name of the LORD
according to the statute given to Israel.
5 There stand the thrones for judgment,
the thrones of the house of David.

6 Pray for the peace of Jerusalem:
"May those who love you be secure.
7 May there be peace within your walls
and security within your citadels."
8 For the sake of my family and friends,
I will say, "Peace be within you."
9 For the sake of the house of the LORD our God,
I will seek your prosperity.

Psalm 123

A song of ascents.

1 I lift up my eyes to you,
to you who sit enthroned in heaven.

2 As the eyes of slaves look to the hand of
their master,
as the eyes of a female slave look to the
hand of her mistress,
so our eyes look to the LORD our God,
till he shows us his mercy.
3 Have mercy on us, LORD, have mercy on
us,
for we have endured no end of
contempt.
4 We have endured no end
of ridicule from the arrogant,
of contempt from the proud.

Psalm 124

A song of ascents. Of David.

1 If the LORD had not been on our side—
let Israel say—
2 if the LORD had not been on our side
when people attacked us,
3 they would have swallowed us alive
when their anger flared against us;
4 the flood would have engulfed us,
the torrent would have swept over us,
5 the raging waters
would have swept us away.
6 Praise be to the LORD,
who has not let us be torn by their
teeth.
7 We have escaped like a bird
from the fowler's snare;
the snare has been broken,
and we have escaped.
8 Our help is in the name of the LORD,
the Maker of heaven and earth.

Psalm 125

A song of ascents.

1 Those who trust in the LORD are like
Mount Zion,
which cannot be shaken but endures
forever.
2 As the mountains surround Jerusalem,
so the LORD surrounds his people
both now and forevermore.
3 The scepter of the wicked will not remain
over the land allotted to the righteous,
for then the righteous might use
their hands to do evil.
4 LORD, do good to those who are good,
to those who are upright in heart.
5 But those who turn to crooked ways
the LORD will banish with the evildoers.

Peace be on Israel.

Psalm 126

A song of ascents.

1 When the LORD restored the fortunes of[a]
Zion,
we were like those who dreamed.[b]
2 Our mouths were filled with laughter,
our tongues with songs of joy.
Then it was said among the nations,
"The LORD has done great things for
them."
3 The LORD has done great things for us,
and we are filled with joy.
4 Restore our fortunes,[c] LORD,
like streams in the Negev.
5 Those who sow with tears
will reap with songs of joy.
6 Those who go out weeping,
carrying seed to sow,
will return with songs of joy,
carrying sheaves with them.

Psalm 127

A song of ascents. Of Solomon.

1 Unless the LORD builds the house,
the builders labor in vain.
Unless the LORD watches over the city,
the guards stand watch in vain.
2 In vain you rise early
and stay up late,
toiling for food to eat—
for he grants sleep to[d] those he loves.
3 Children are a heritage from the LORD,
offspring a reward from him.
4 Like arrows in the hands of a warrior
are children born in one's youth.
5 Blessed is the man
whose quiver is full of them.
They will not be put to shame
when they contend with their
opponents in court.

Psalm 128

A song of ascents.

1 Blessed are all who fear the LORD,
who walk in obedience to him.
2 You will eat the fruit of your labor;
blessings and prosperity will be yours.
3 Your wife will be like a fruitful vine
within your house;
your children will be like olive shoots
around your table.
4 Yes, this will be the blessing
for the man who fears the LORD.
5 May the LORD bless you from Zion;
may you see the prosperity of
Jerusalem
all the days of your life.
6 May you live to see your children's
children—
peace be on Israel.

Psalm 129

A song of ascents.

1 "They have greatly oppressed me from
my youth,"
let Israel say;

[a] *1* Or *LORD brought back the captives to* [b] *1* Or *those restored to health* [c] *4* Or *Bring back our captives* [d] *2* Or *eat— / for while they sleep he provides for*

2 "they have greatly oppressed me from my youth,
but they have not gained the victory over me.
3 Plowmen have plowed my back
and made their furrows long.
4 But the LORD is righteous;
he has cut me free from the cords of the wicked."

5 May all who hate Zion
be turned back in shame.
6 May they be like grass on the roof,
which withers before it can grow;
7 a reaper cannot fill his hands with it,
nor one who gathers fill his arms.
8 May those who pass by not say to them,
"The blessing of the LORD be on you;
we bless you in the name of the LORD."

Psalm 130

A song of ascents.

1 Out of the depths I cry to you, LORD;
2 Lord, hear my voice.
Let your ears be attentive
to my cry for mercy.

3 If you, LORD, kept a record of sins,
Lord, who could stand?
4 But with you there is forgiveness,
so that we can, with reverence, serve you.

5 I wait for the LORD, my whole being waits,
and in his word I put my hope.
6 I wait for the Lord
more than watchmen wait for the morning,
more than watchmen wait for the morning.

7 Israel, put your hope in the LORD,
for with the LORD is unfailing love
and with him is full redemption.
8 He himself will redeem Israel
from all their sins.

Psalm 131

A song of ascents. Of David.

1 My heart is not proud, LORD,
my eyes are not haughty;
I do not concern myself with great matters
or things too wonderful for me.
2 But I have calmed and quieted myself,
I am like a weaned child with its mother;
like a weaned child I am content.

3 Israel, put your hope in the LORD
both now and forevermore.

Psalm 132

A song of ascents.

1 LORD, remember David
and all his self-denial.

2 He swore an oath to the LORD,
he made a vow to the Mighty One of Jacob:
3 "I will not enter my house
or go to my bed,
4 I will allow no sleep to my eyes
or slumber to my eyelids,
5 till I find a place for the LORD,
a dwelling for the Mighty One of Jacob."

6 We heard it in Ephrathah,
we came upon it in the fields of Jaar:[a]
7 "Let us go to his dwelling place,
let us worship at his footstool, saying,
8 'Arise, LORD, and come to your resting place,
you and the ark of your might.
9 May your priests be clothed with your righteousness;
may your faithful people sing for joy.'"

10 For the sake of your servant David,
do not reject your anointed one.

11 The LORD swore an oath to David,
a sure oath he will not revoke:
"One of your own descendants
I will place on your throne.
12 If your sons keep my covenant
and the statutes I teach them,
then their sons will sit
on your throne for ever and ever."

13 For the LORD has chosen Zion,
he has desired it for his dwelling, saying,
14 "This is my resting place for ever and ever;
here I will sit enthroned, for I have desired it.
15 I will bless her with abundant provisions;
her poor I will satisfy with food.
16 I will clothe her priests with salvation,
and her faithful people will ever sing for joy.

17 "Here I will make a horn[b] grow for David
and set up a lamp for my anointed one.
18 I will clothe his enemies with shame,
but his head will be adorned with a radiant crown."

Psalm 133

A song of ascents. Of David.

1 How good and pleasant it is
when God's people live together in unity!

2 It is like precious oil poured on the head,
running down on the beard,
running down on Aaron's beard,
down on the collar of his robe.
3 It is as if the dew of Hermon
were falling on Mount Zion.
For there the LORD bestows his blessing,
even life forevermore.

[a] 6 Or *heard of it in Ephrathah, / we found it in the fields of Jearim.* (See 1 Chron. 13:5,6) (And no quotation marks around verses 7-9) [b] 17 *Horn* here symbolizes strong one, that is, king.

Psalm 134

A song of ascents.

1 Praise the LORD, all you servants of the LORD
who minister by night in the house of the LORD.
2 Lift up your hands in the sanctuary
and praise the LORD.

3 May the LORD bless you from Zion,
he who is the Maker of heaven and earth.

Psalm 135

1 Praise the LORD.[a]

Praise the name of the LORD;
praise him, you servants of the LORD,
2 you who minister in the house of the LORD,
in the courts of the house of our God.

3 Praise the LORD, for the LORD is good;
sing praise to his name, for that is pleasant.
4 For the LORD has chosen Jacob to be his own,
Israel to be his treasured possession.

5 I know that the LORD is great,
that our Lord is greater than all gods.
6 The LORD does whatever pleases him,
in the heavens and on the earth,
in the seas and all their depths.
7 He makes clouds rise from the ends of the earth;
he sends lightning with the rain
and brings out the wind from his storehouses.

8 He struck down the firstborn of Egypt,
the firstborn of people and animals.
9 He sent his signs and wonders into your midst, Egypt,
against Pharaoh and all his servants.
10 He struck down many nations
and killed mighty kings—
11 Sihon king of the Amorites,
Og king of Bashan,
and all the kings of Canaan—
12 and he gave their land as an inheritance,
an inheritance to his people Israel.

13 Your name, LORD, endures forever,
your renown, LORD, through all generations.
14 For the LORD will vindicate his people
and have compassion on his servants.

15 The idols of the nations are silver and gold,
made by human hands.
16 They have mouths, but cannot speak,
eyes, but cannot see.
17 They have ears, but cannot hear,
nor is there breath in their mouths.
18 Those who make them will be like them,
and so will all who trust in them.

19 All you Israelites, praise the LORD;
house of Aaron, praise the LORD;
20 house of Levi, praise the LORD;
you who fear him, praise the LORD.
21 Praise be to the LORD from Zion,
to him who dwells in Jerusalem.

Praise the LORD.

Psalm 136

1 Give thanks to the LORD, for he is good.
His love endures forever.
2 Give thanks to the God of gods.
His love endures forever.
3 Give thanks to the Lord of lords:
His love endures forever.

4 to him who alone does great wonders,
His love endures forever.
5 who by his understanding made the heavens,
His love endures forever.
6 who spread out the earth upon the waters,
His love endures forever.
7 who made the great lights—
His love endures forever.
8 the sun to govern the day,
His love endures forever.
9 the moon and stars to govern the night;
His love endures forever.

10 to him who struck down the firstborn of Egypt
His love endures forever.
11 and brought Israel out from among them
His love endures forever.
12 with a mighty hand and outstretched arm;
His love endures forever.

13 to him who divided the Red Sea[b] asunder
His love endures forever.
14 and brought Israel through the midst of it,
His love endures forever.
15 but swept Pharaoh and his army into the Red Sea;
His love endures forever.

16 to him who led his people through the wilderness;
His love endures forever.

17 to him who struck down great kings,
His love endures forever.
18 and killed mighty kings—
His love endures forever.
19 Sihon king of the Amorites
His love endures forever.
20 and Og king of Bashan—
His love endures forever.
21 and gave their land as an inheritance,
His love endures forever.
22 an inheritance to his servant Israel.
His love endures forever.

23 He remembered us in our low estate
His love endures forever.
24 and freed us from our enemies.
His love endures forever.
25 He gives food to every creature.
His love endures forever.

26 Give thanks to the God of heaven.
His love endures forever.

[a] *1* Hebrew *Hallelu Yah*; also in verses 3 and 21 [b] *13* Or *the Sea of Reeds*; also in verse 15

Psalm 137

1 By the rivers of Babylon we sat and wept
when we remembered Zion.
2 There on the poplars
we hung our harps,
3 for there our captors asked us for songs,
our tormentors demanded songs of joy;
they said, "Sing us one of the songs of Zion!"

4 How can we sing the songs of the LORD
while in a foreign land?
5 If I forget you, Jerusalem,
may my right hand forget its skill.
6 May my tongue cling to the roof of my mouth
if I do not remember you,
if I do not consider Jerusalem
my highest joy.

7 Remember, LORD, what the Edomites did
on the day Jerusalem fell.
"Tear it down," they cried,
"tear it down to its foundations!"
8 Daughter Babylon, doomed to destruction,
happy is the one who repays you
according to what you have done to us.
9 Happy is the one who seizes your infants
and dashes them against the rocks.

Psalm 138

Of David.

1 I will praise you, LORD, with all my heart;
before the "gods" I will sing your praise.
2 I will bow down toward your holy temple
and will praise your name
for your unfailing love and your faithfulness,
for you have so exalted your solemn decree
that it surpasses your fame.
3 When I called, you answered me;
you greatly emboldened me.

4 May all the kings of the earth praise you, LORD,
when they hear what you have decreed.
5 May they sing of the ways of the LORD,
for the glory of the LORD is great.

6 Though the LORD is exalted, he looks kindly on the lowly;
though lofty, he sees them from afar.
7 Though I walk in the midst of trouble,
you preserve my life.
You stretch out your hand against the anger of my foes;
with your right hand you save me.
8 The LORD will vindicate me;
your love, LORD, endures forever—
do not abandon the works of your hands.

Psalm 139

For the director of music. Of David. A psalm.

1 You have searched me, LORD,
and you know me.
2 You know when I sit and when I rise;
you perceive my thoughts from afar.
3 You discern my going out and my lying down;
you are familiar with all my ways.
4 Before a word is on my tongue
you, LORD, know it completely.
5 You hem me in behind and before,
and you lay your hand upon me.
6 Such knowledge is too wonderful for me,
too lofty for me to attain.

7 Where can I go from your Spirit?
Where can I flee from your presence?
8 If I go up to the heavens, you are there;
if I make my bed in the depths, you are there.
9 If I rise on the wings of the dawn,
if I settle on the far side of the sea,
10 even there your hand will guide me,
your right hand will hold me fast.
11 If I say, "Surely the darkness will hide me
and the light become night around me,"
12 even the darkness will not be dark to you;
the night will shine like the day,
for darkness is as light to you.

13 For you created my inmost being;
you knit me together in my mother's womb.
14 I praise you because I am fearfully and wonderfully made;
your works are wonderful,
I know that full well.
15 My frame was not hidden from you
when I was made in the secret place,
when I was woven together in the depths of the earth.
16 Your eyes saw my unformed body;
all the days ordained for me were written in your book
before one of them came to be.
17 How precious to me are your thoughts,[a] God!
How vast is the sum of them!
18 Were I to count them,
they would outnumber the grains of sand—
when I awake, I am still with you.

19 If only you, God, would slay the wicked!
Away from me, you who are bloodthirsty!
20 They speak of you with evil intent;
your adversaries misuse your name.
21 Do I not hate those who hate you, LORD,
and abhor those who are in rebellion against you?
22 I have nothing but hatred for them;
I count them my enemies.
23 Search me, God, and know my heart;
test me and know my anxious thoughts.
24 See if there is any offensive way in me,
and lead me in the way everlasting.

[a] 17 Or *How amazing are your thoughts concerning me*

Psalm 140[a]

For the director of music. A psalm of David.

1 Rescue me, LORD, from evildoers;
protect me from the violent,
2 who devise evil plans in their hearts
and stir up war every day.
3 They make their tongues as sharp as a serpent's;
the poison of vipers is on their lips.[b]

4 Keep me safe, LORD, from the hands of the wicked;
protect me from the violent,
who devise ways to trip my feet.
5 The arrogant have hidden a snare for me;
they have spread out the cords of their net
and have set traps for me along my path.

6 I say to the LORD, "You are my God."
Hear, LORD, my cry for mercy.
7 Sovereign LORD, my strong deliverer,
you shield my head in the day of battle.
8 Do not grant the wicked their desires, LORD;
do not let their plans succeed.

9 Those who surround me proudly rear their heads;
may the mischief of their lips engulf them.
10 May burning coals fall on them;
may they be thrown into the fire,
into miry pits, never to rise.
11 May slanderers not be established in the land;
may disaster hunt down the violent.

12 I know that the LORD secures justice for the poor
and upholds the cause of the needy.
13 Surely the righteous will praise your name,
and the upright will live in your presence.

Psalm 141

A psalm of David.

1 I call to you, LORD, come quickly to me;
hear me when I call to you.
2 May my prayer be set before you like incense;
may the lifting up of my hands be like the evening sacrifice.

3 Set a guard over my mouth, LORD;
keep watch over the door of my lips.
4 Do not let my heart be drawn to what is evil
so that I take part in wicked deeds
along with those who are evildoers;
do not let me eat their delicacies.

5 Let a righteous man strike me—that is a kindness;
let him rebuke me—that is oil on my head.
My head will not refuse it,
for my prayer will still be against the deeds of evildoers.

6 Their rulers will be thrown down from the cliffs,
and the wicked will learn that my words were well spoken.
7 They will say, "As one plows and breaks up the earth,
so our bones have been scattered at the mouth of the grave."

8 But my eyes are fixed on you, Sovereign LORD;
in you I take refuge—do not give me over to death.
9 Keep me safe from the traps set by evildoers,
from the snares they have laid for me.
10 Let the wicked fall into their own nets,
while I pass by in safety.

Psalm 142[c]

A maskil[d] of David. When he was in the cave. A prayer.

1 I cry aloud to the LORD;
I lift up my voice to the LORD for mercy.
2 I pour out before him my complaint;
before him I tell my trouble.

3 When my spirit grows faint within me,
it is you who watch over my way.
In the path where I walk
people have hidden a snare for me.
4 Look and see, there is no one at my right hand;
no one is concerned for me.
I have no refuge;
no one cares for my life.

5 I cry to you, LORD;
I say, "You are my refuge,
my portion in the land of the living."

6 Listen to my cry,
for I am in desperate need;
rescue me from those who pursue me,
for they are too strong for me.
7 Set me free from my prison,
that I may praise your name.
Then the righteous will gather about me
because of your goodness to me.

Psalm 143

A psalm of David.

1 LORD, hear my prayer,
listen to my cry for mercy;
in your faithfulness and righteousness
come to my relief.
2 Do not bring your servant into judgment,
for no one living is righteous before you.
3 The enemy pursues me,
he crushes me to the ground;

[a] In Hebrew texts 140:1-13 is numbered 140:2-14. [b] *3* The Hebrew has *Selah* (a word of uncertain meaning) here and at the end of verses 5 and 8. [c] In Hebrew texts 142:1-7 is numbered 142:2-8. [d] Title: Probably a literary or musical term

he makes me dwell in the darkness
like those long dead.
4 So my spirit grows faint within me;
my heart within me is dismayed.
5 I remember the days of long ago;
I meditate on all your works
and consider what your hands have done.
6 I spread out my hands to you;
I thirst for you like a parched land.[a]

7 Answer me quickly, LORD;
my spirit fails.
Do not hide your face from me
or I will be like those who go down to the pit.
8 Let the morning bring me word of your unfailing love,
for I have put my trust in you.
Show me the way I should go,
for to you I entrust my life.
9 Rescue me from my enemies, LORD,
for I hide myself in you.
10 Teach me to do your will,
for you are my God;
may your good Spirit
lead me on level ground.

11 For your name's sake, LORD, preserve my life;
in your righteousness, bring me out of trouble.
12 In your unfailing love, silence my enemies;
destroy all my foes,
for I am your servant.

Psalm 144

Of David.

1 Praise be to the LORD my Rock,
who trains my hands for war,
my fingers for battle.
2 He is my loving God and my fortress,
my stronghold and my deliverer,
my shield, in whom I take refuge,
who subdues peoples[b] under me.

3 LORD, what are human beings that you care for them,
mere mortals that you think of them?
4 They are like a breath;
their days are like a fleeting shadow.

5 Part your heavens, LORD, and come down;
touch the mountains, so that they smoke.
6 Send forth lightning and scatter the enemy;
shoot your arrows and rout them.
7 Reach down your hand from on high;
deliver me and rescue me
from the mighty waters,
from the hands of foreigners
8 whose mouths are full of lies,
whose right hands are deceitful.

9 I will sing a new song to you, my God;
on the ten-stringed lyre I will make music to you,
10 to the One who gives victory to kings,
who delivers his servant David.

From the deadly sword 11 deliver me;
rescue me from the hands of foreigners
whose mouths are full of lies,
whose right hands are deceitful.

12 Then our sons in their youth
will be like well-nurtured plants,
and our daughters will be like pillars
carved to adorn a palace.
13 Our barns will be filled
with every kind of provision.
Our sheep will increase by thousands,
by tens of thousands in our fields;
14 our oxen will draw heavy loads.[c]
There will be no breaching of walls,
no going into captivity,
no cry of distress in our streets.
15 Blessed is the people of whom this is true;
blessed is the people whose God is the LORD.

Psalm 145[d]

A psalm of praise. Of David.

1 I will exalt you, my God the King;
I will praise your name for ever and ever.
2 Every day I will praise you
and extol your name for ever and ever.
3 Great is the LORD and most worthy of praise;
his greatness no one can fathom.
4 One generation commends your works to another;
they tell of your mighty acts.
5 They speak of the glorious splendor of your majesty—
and I will meditate on your wonderful works.[e]
6 They tell of the power of your awesome works—
and I will proclaim your great deeds.
7 They celebrate your abundant goodness
and joyfully sing of your righteousness.
8 The LORD is gracious and compassionate,
slow to anger and rich in love.
9 The LORD is good to all;
he has compassion on all he has made.
10 All your works praise you, LORD;
your faithful people extol you.
11 They tell of the glory of your kingdom
and speak of your might,
12 so that all people may know of your mighty acts
and the glorious splendor of your kingdom.

[a] 6 The Hebrew has *Selah* (a word of uncertain meaning) here. [b] 2 Many manuscripts of the Masoretic Text, Dead Sea Scrolls, Aquila, Jerome and Syriac; most manuscripts of the Masoretic Text *subdues my people* [c] 14 Or *our chieftains will be firmly established* [d] This psalm is an acrostic poem, the verses of which (including verse 13b) begin with the successive letters of the Hebrew alphabet. [e] 5 Dead Sea Scrolls and Syriac (see also Septuagint); Masoretic Text *On the glorious splendor of your majesty / and on your wonderful works I will meditate*

13 Your kingdom is an everlasting kingdom,
and your dominion endures through all generations.

The LORD is trustworthy in all he promises
and faithful in all he does.[a]
14 The LORD upholds all who fall
and lifts up all who are bowed down.
15 The eyes of all look to you,
and you give them their food at the proper time.
16 You open your hand
and satisfy the desires of every living thing.

17 The LORD is righteous in all his ways
and faithful in all he does.
18 The LORD is near to all who call on him,
to all who call on him in truth.
19 He fulfills the desires of those who fear him;
he hears their cry and saves them.
20 The LORD watches over all who love him,
but all the wicked he will destroy.

21 My mouth will speak in praise of the LORD.
Let every creature praise his holy name
for ever and ever.

Psalm 146

1 Praise the LORD.[b]

Praise the LORD, my soul.

2 I will praise the LORD all my life;
I will sing praise to my God as long as I live.
3 Do not put your trust in princes,
in human beings, who cannot save.
4 When their spirit departs, they return to the ground;
on that very day their plans come to nothing.
5 Blessed are those whose help is the God of Jacob,
whose hope is in the LORD their God.

6 He is the Maker of heaven and earth,
the sea, and everything in them—
he remains faithful forever.
7 He upholds the cause of the oppressed
and gives food to the hungry.
The LORD sets prisoners free,
8 the LORD gives sight to the blind,
the LORD lifts up those who are bowed down,
the LORD loves the righteous.
9 The LORD watches over the foreigner
and sustains the fatherless and the widow,
but he frustrates the ways of the wicked.

10 The LORD reigns forever,
your God, O Zion, for all generations.

Praise the LORD.

Psalm 147

1 Praise the LORD.[c]

How good it is to sing praises to our God,
how pleasant and fitting to praise him!

2 The LORD builds up Jerusalem;
he gathers the exiles of Israel.
3 He heals the brokenhearted
and binds up their wounds.
4 He determines the number of the stars
and calls them each by name.
5 Great is our Lord and mighty in power;
his understanding has no limit.
6 The LORD sustains the humble
but casts the wicked to the ground.

7 Sing to the LORD with grateful praise;
make music to our God on the harp.

8 He covers the sky with clouds;
he supplies the earth with rain
and makes grass grow on the hills.
9 He provides food for the cattle
and for the young ravens when they call.

10 His pleasure is not in the strength of the horse,
nor his delight in the legs of the warrior;
11 the LORD delights in those who fear him,
who put their hope in his unfailing love.

12 Extol the LORD, Jerusalem;
praise your God, Zion.

13 He strengthens the bars of your gates
and blesses your people within you.
14 He grants peace to your borders
and satisfies you with the finest of wheat.

15 He sends his command to the earth;
his word runs swiftly.
16 He spreads the snow like wool
and scatters the frost like ashes.
17 He hurls down his hail like pebbles.
Who can withstand his icy blast?
18 He sends his word and melts them;
he stirs up his breezes, and the waters flow.

19 He has revealed his word to Jacob,
his laws and decrees to Israel.
20 He has done this for no other nation;
they do not know his laws.[d]

Praise the LORD.

Psalm 148

1 Praise the LORD.[e]

Praise the LORD from the heavens;
praise him in the heights above.
2 Praise him, all his angels;
praise him, all his heavenly hosts.

[a] *13* One manuscript of the Masoretic Text, Dead Sea Scrolls and Syriac (see also Septuagint); most manuscripts of the Masoretic Text do not have the last two lines of verse 13. [b] *1* Hebrew *Hallelu Yah*; also in verse 10 [c] *1* Hebrew *Hallelu Yah*; also in verse 20 [d] *20* Masoretic Text; Dead Sea Scrolls and Septuagint *nation; / he has not made his laws known to them* [e] *1* Hebrew *Hallelu Yah*; also in verse 14

3 Praise him, sun and moon;
praise him, all you shining stars.
4 Praise him, you highest heavens
and you waters above the skies.

5 Let them praise the name of the LORD,
for at his command they were created,
6 and he established them for ever and ever—
he issued a decree that will never pass away.

7 Praise the LORD from the earth,
you great sea creatures and all ocean depths,
8 lightning and hail, snow and clouds,
stormy winds that do his bidding,
9 you mountains and all hills,
fruit trees and all cedars,
10 wild animals and all cattle,
small creatures and flying birds,
11 kings of the earth and all nations,
you princes and all rulers on earth,
12 young men and women,
old men and children.

13 Let them praise the name of the LORD,
for his name alone is exalted;
his splendor is above the earth and the heavens.
14 And he has raised up for his people a horn,[a]
the praise of all his faithful servants,
of Israel, the people close to his heart.

Praise the LORD.

Psalm 149

1 Praise the LORD.[b]

Sing to the LORD a new song,
his praise in the assembly of his faithful people.

2 Let Israel rejoice in their Maker;
let the people of Zion be glad in their King.
3 Let them praise his name with dancing
and make music to him with timbrel and harp.
4 For the LORD takes delight in his people;
he crowns the humble with victory.
5 Let his faithful people rejoice in this honor
and sing for joy on their beds.

6 May the praise of God be in their mouths
and a double-edged sword in their hands,
7 to inflict vengeance on the nations
and punishment on the peoples,
8 to bind their kings with fetters,
their nobles with shackles of iron,
9 to carry out the sentence written against them—
this is the glory of all his faithful people.

Praise the LORD.

Psalm 150

1 Praise the LORD.[c]

Praise God in his sanctuary;
praise him in his mighty heavens.
2 Praise him for his acts of power;
praise him for his surpassing greatness.
3 Praise him with the sounding of the trumpet,
praise him with the harp and lyre,
4 praise him with timbrel and dancing,
praise him with the strings and pipe,
5 praise him with the clash of cymbals,
praise him with resounding cymbals.

6 Let everything that has breath praise the LORD.

Praise the LORD.

Proverbs

Purpose and Theme

1 The proverbs of Solomon son of David, king of Israel:

2 for gaining wisdom and instruction;
for understanding words of insight;
3 for receiving instruction in prudent behavior,
doing what is right and just and fair;
4 for giving prudence to those who are simple,[d]
knowledge and discretion to the young—
5 let the wise listen and add to their learning,
and let the discerning get guidance—
6 for understanding proverbs and parables,
the sayings and riddles of the wise.[e]

[a] 14 *Horn* here symbolizes strength. [b] 1 Hebrew *Hallelu Yah*; also in verse 9 [c] 1 Hebrew *Hallelu Yah*; also in verse 6 [d] 4 The Hebrew word rendered *simple* in Proverbs denotes a person who is gullible, without moral direction and inclined to evil. [e] 6 Or *understanding a proverb, namely, a parable, / and the sayings of the wise, their riddles*

7 The fear of the LORD is the beginning of
knowledge,
but fools[a] despise wisdom and
instruction.

Prologue: Exhortations to Embrace Wisdom

Warning Against the Invitation of Sinful Men

8 Listen, my son, to your father's
instruction
and do not forsake your mother's
teaching.
9 They are a garland to grace your head
and a chain to adorn your neck.

10 My son, if sinful men entice you,
do not give in to them.
11 If they say, "Come along with us;
let's lie in wait for innocent blood,
let's ambush some harmless soul;
12 let's swallow them alive, like the grave,
and whole, like those who go down to
the pit;
13 we will get all sorts of valuable things
and fill our houses with plunder;
14 cast lots with us;
we will all share the loot"—
15 my son, do not go along with them,
do not set foot on their paths;
16 for their feet rush into evil,
they are swift to shed blood.
17 How useless to spread a net
where every bird can see it!
18 These men lie in wait for their own blood;
they ambush only themselves!
19 Such are the paths of all who go after ill-
gotten gain;
it takes away the life of those who get
it.

Wisdom's Rebuke

20 Out in the open wisdom calls aloud,
she raises her voice in the public
square;
21 on top of the wall[b] she cries out,
at the city gate she makes her speech:
22 "How long will you who are simple love
your simple ways?
How long will mockers delight in
mockery
and fools hate knowledge?
23 Repent at my rebuke!
Then I will pour out my thoughts to
you,
I will make known to you my teachings.
24 But since you refuse to listen when I call
and no one pays attention when I
stretch out my hand,
25 since you disregard all my advice
and do not accept my rebuke,
26 I in turn will laugh when disaster strikes
you;
I will mock when calamity overtakes
you—
27 when calamity overtakes you like a
storm,
when disaster sweeps over you like a
whirlwind,
when distress and trouble overwhelm
you.
28 "Then they will call to me but I will not
answer;
they will look for me but will not find
me,
29 since they hated knowledge
and did not choose to fear the LORD.
30 Since they would not accept my advice
and spurned my rebuke,
31 they will eat the fruit of their ways
and be filled with the fruit of their
schemes.
32 For the waywardness of the simple will
kill them,
and the complacency of fools will
destroy them;
33 but whoever listens to me will live in
safety
and be at ease, without fear of harm."

Moral Benefits of Wisdom

2 My son, if you accept my words
and store up my commands within you,
2 turning your ear to wisdom
and applying your heart to
understanding—
3 indeed, if you call out for insight
and cry aloud for understanding,
4 and if you look for it as for silver
and search for it as for hidden treasure,
5 then you will understand the fear of the
LORD
and find the knowledge of God.
6 For the LORD gives wisdom;
from his mouth come knowledge and
understanding.
7 He holds success in store for the upright,
he is a shield to those whose walk is
blameless,
8 for he guards the course of the just
and protects the way of his faithful
ones.

9 Then you will understand what is right
and just
and fair—every good path.
10 For wisdom will enter your heart,
and knowledge will be pleasant to your
soul.
11 Discretion will protect you,
and understanding will guard you.

12 Wisdom will save you from the ways of
wicked men,
from men whose words are perverse,
13 who have left the straight paths
to walk in dark ways,
14 who delight in doing wrong
and rejoice in the perverseness of evil,
15 whose paths are crooked
and who are devious in their ways.

[a] 7 The Hebrew words rendered *fool* in Proverbs, and often elsewhere in the Old Testament, denote a person who is morally deficient. [b] 21 Septuagint; Hebrew / *at noisy street corners*

16 Wisdom will save you also from the
adulterous woman,
from the wayward woman with her
seductive words,
17 who has left the partner of her youth
and ignored the covenant she made
before God.[a]
18 Surely her house leads down to death
and her paths to the spirits of the dead.
19 None who go to her return
or attain the paths of life.

20 Thus you will walk in the ways of the good
and keep to the paths of the righteous.
21 For the upright will live in the land,
and the blameless will remain in it;
22 but the wicked will be cut off from the
land,
and the unfaithful will be torn from it.

Wisdom Bestows Well-Being

3 My son, do not forget my teaching,
but keep my commands in your heart,
2 for they will prolong your life many
years
and bring you peace and prosperity.

3 Let love and faithfulness never leave you;
bind them around your neck,
write them on the tablet of your heart.
4 Then you will win favor and a good name
in the sight of God and man.

5 Trust in the LORD with all your heart
and lean not on your own
understanding;
6 in all your ways submit to him,
and he will make your paths straight.[b]

7 Do not be wise in your own eyes;
fear the LORD and shun evil.
8 This will bring health to your body
and nourishment to your bones.

9 Honor the LORD with your wealth,
with the firstfruits of all your crops;
10 then your barns will be filled to
overflowing,
and your vats will brim over with new
wine.

11 My son, do not despise the LORD's
discipline,
and do not resent his rebuke,
12 because the LORD disciplines those he
loves,
as a father the son he delights in.[c]

13 Blessed are those who find wisdom,
those who gain understanding,
14 for she is more profitable than silver
and yields better returns than gold.
15 She is more precious than rubies;
nothing you desire can compare with
her.
16 Long life is in her right hand;
in her left hand are riches and honor.
17 Her ways are pleasant ways,
and all her paths are peace.
18 She is a tree of life to those who take hold
of her;
those who hold her fast will be blessed.

19 By wisdom the LORD laid the earth's
foundations,
by understanding he set the heavens in
place;
20 by his knowledge the watery depths were
divided,
and the clouds let drop the dew.

21 My son, do not let wisdom and
understanding out of your sight,
preserve sound judgment and discretion;
22 they will be life for you,
an ornament to grace your neck.
23 Then you will go on your way in safety,
and your foot will not stumble.
24 When you lie down, you will not be
afraid;
when you lie down, your sleep will be
sweet.
25 Have no fear of sudden disaster
or of the ruin that overtakes the
wicked,
26 for the LORD will be at your side
and will keep your foot from being
snared.

27 Do not withhold good from those to
whom it is due,
when it is in your power to act.
28 Do not say to your neighbor,
"Come back tomorrow and I'll give it to
you"—
when you already have it with you.
29 Do not plot harm against your neighbor,
who lives trustfully near you.
30 Do not accuse anyone for no reason—
when they have done you no harm.

31 Do not envy the violent
or choose any of their ways.

32 For the LORD detests the perverse
but takes the upright into his
confidence.
33 The LORD's curse is on the house of the
wicked,
but he blesses the home of the righteous.
34 He mocks proud mockers
but shows favor to the humble and
oppressed.
35 The wise inherit honor,
but fools get only shame.

Get Wisdom at Any Cost

4 Listen, my sons, to a father's instruction;
pay attention and gain understanding.
2 I give you sound learning,
so do not forsake my teaching.
3 For I too was a son to my father,
still tender, and cherished by my mother.
4 Then he taught me, and he said to me,
"Take hold of my words with all your
heart;
keep my commands, and you will live.

[a] 17 Or *covenant of her God* [b] 6 Or *will direct your paths* [c] 12 Hebrew; Septuagint *loves, / and he chastens everyone he accepts as his child*

[5]Get wisdom, get understanding;
do not forget my words or turn away from them.
[6]Do not forsake wisdom, and she will protect you;
love her, and she will watch over you.
[7]The beginning of wisdom is this: Get[a] wisdom.
Though it cost all you have,[b] get understanding.
[8]Cherish her, and she will exalt you;
embrace her, and she will honor you.
[9]She will give you a garland to grace your head
and present you with a glorious crown."

[10]Listen, my son, accept what I say,
and the years of your life will be many.
[11]I instruct you in the way of wisdom
and lead you along straight paths.
[12]When you walk, your steps will not be hampered;
when you run, you will not stumble.
[13]Hold on to instruction, do not let it go;
guard it well, for it is your life.
[14]Do not set foot on the path of the wicked
or walk in the way of evildoers.
[15]Avoid it, do not travel on it;
turn from it and go on your way.
[16]For they cannot rest until they do evil;
they are robbed of sleep till they make someone stumble.
[17]They eat the bread of wickedness
and drink the wine of violence.
[18]The path of the righteous is like the morning sun,
shining ever brighter till the full light of day.
[19]But the way of the wicked is like deep darkness;
they do not know what makes them stumble.

[20]My son, pay attention to what I say;
turn your ear to my words.
[21]Do not let them out of your sight,
keep them within your heart;
[22]for they are life to those who find them
and health to one's whole body.
[23]Above all else, guard your heart,
for everything you do flows from it.
[24]Keep your mouth free of perversity;
keep corrupt talk far from your lips.
[25]Let your eyes look straight ahead;
fix your gaze directly before you.
[26]Give careful thought to the[c] paths for your feet
and be steadfast in all your ways.
[27]Do not turn to the right or the left;
keep your foot from evil.

Warning Against Adultery

5 My son, pay attention to my wisdom,
turn your ear to my words of insight,
[2]that you may maintain discretion
and your lips may preserve knowledge.
[3]For the lips of the adulterous woman drip honey,
and her speech is smoother than oil;
[4]but in the end she is bitter as gall,
sharp as a double-edged sword.
[5]Her feet go down to death;
her steps lead straight to the grave.
[6]She gives no thought to the way of life;
her paths wander aimlessly, but she does not know it.

[7]Now then, my sons, listen to me;
do not turn aside from what I say.
[8]Keep to a path far from her,
do not go near the door of her house,
[9]lest you lose your honor to others
and your dignity[d] to one who is cruel,
[10]lest strangers feast on your wealth
and your toil enrich the house of another.
[11]At the end of your life you will groan,
when your flesh and body are spent.
[12]You will say, "How I hated discipline!
How my heart spurned correction!
[13]I would not obey my teachers
or turn my ear to my instructors.
[14]And I was soon in serious trouble
in the assembly of God's people."

[15]Drink water from your own cistern,
running water from your own well.
[16]Should your springs overflow in the streets,
your streams of water in the public squares?
[17]Let them be yours alone,
never to be shared with strangers.
[18]May your fountain be blessed,
and may you rejoice in the wife of your youth.
[19]A loving doe, a graceful deer—
may her breasts satisfy you always,
may you ever be intoxicated with her love.
[20]Why, my son, be intoxicated with another man's wife?
Why embrace the bosom of a wayward woman?

[21]For your ways are in full view of the LORD,
and he examines all your paths.
[22]The evil deeds of the wicked ensnare them;
the cords of their sins hold them fast.
[23]For lack of discipline they will die,
led astray by their own great folly.

Warnings Against Folly

6 My son, if you have put up security for your neighbor,
if you have shaken hands in pledge for a stranger,
[2]you have been trapped by what you said,
ensnared by the words of your mouth.
[3]So do this, my son, to free yourself,
since you have fallen into your neighbor's hands:

[a] 7 Or *Wisdom is supreme; therefore get* [b] 7 Or *wisdom. / Whatever else you get* [c] 26 Or *Make level* [d] 9 Or *years*

Go—to the point of exhaustion—[a]
and give your neighbor no rest!
4 Allow no sleep to your eyes,
no slumber to your eyelids.
5 Free yourself, like a gazelle from the hand of the hunter,
like a bird from the snare of the fowler.

6 Go to the ant, you sluggard;
consider its ways and be wise!
7 It has no commander,
no overseer or ruler,
8 yet it stores its provisions in summer
and gathers its food at harvest.

9 How long will you lie there, you sluggard?
When will you get up from your sleep?
10 A little sleep, a little slumber,
a little folding of the hands to rest—
11 and poverty will come on you like a thief
and scarcity like an armed man.

12 A troublemaker and a villain,
who goes about with a corrupt mouth,
13 who winks maliciously with his eye,
signals with his feet
and motions with his fingers,
14 who plots evil with deceit in his heart—
he always stirs up conflict.
15 Therefore disaster will overtake him in an instant;
he will suddenly be destroyed—without remedy.

16 There are six things the LORD hates,
seven that are detestable to him:
17 haughty eyes,
a lying tongue,
hands that shed innocent blood,
18 a heart that devises wicked schemes,
feet that are quick to rush into evil,
19 a false witness who pours out lies
and a person who stirs up conflict in the community.

Warning Against Adultery

20 My son, keep your father's command
and do not forsake your mother's teaching.
21 Bind them always on your heart;
fasten them around your neck.
22 When you walk, they will guide you;
when you sleep, they will watch over you;
when you awake, they will speak to you.
23 For this command is a lamp,
this teaching is a light,
and correction and instruction
are the way to life,
24 keeping you from your neighbor's wife,
from the smooth talk of a wayward woman.

25 Do not lust in your heart after her beauty
or let her captivate you with her eyes.

26 For a prostitute can be had for a loaf of bread,
but another man's wife preys on your very life.
27 Can a man scoop fire into his lap
without his clothes being burned?
28 Can a man walk on hot coals
without his feet being scorched?
29 So is he who sleeps with another man's wife;
no one who touches her will go unpunished.

30 People do not despise a thief if he steals
to satisfy his hunger when he is starving.
31 Yet if he is caught, he must pay sevenfold,
though it costs him all the wealth of his house.
32 But a man who commits adultery has no sense;
whoever does so destroys himself.
33 Blows and disgrace are his lot,
and his shame will never be wiped away.
34 For jealousy arouses a husband's fury,
and he will show no mercy when he takes revenge.
35 He will not accept any compensation;
he will refuse a bribe, however great it is.

Warning Against the Adulterous Woman

7 My son, keep my words
and store up my commands within you.
2 Keep my commands and you will live;
guard my teachings as the apple of your eye.
3 Bind them on your fingers;
write them on the tablet of your heart.
4 Say to wisdom, "You are my sister,"
and to insight, "You are my relative."
5 They will keep you from the adulterous woman,
from the wayward woman with her seductive words.

6 At the window of my house
I looked down through the lattice.
7 I saw among the simple,
I noticed among the young men,
a youth who had no sense.
8 He was going down the street near her corner,
walking along in the direction of her house
9 at twilight, as the day was fading,
as the dark of night set in.

10 Then out came a woman to meet him,
dressed like a prostitute and with crafty intent.
11 (She is unruly and defiant,
her feet never stay at home;
12 now in the street, now in the squares,
at every corner she lurks.)
13 She took hold of him and kissed him
and with a brazen face she said:

14 "Today I fulfilled my vows,
and I have food from my fellowship offering at home.
15 So I came out to meet you;
I looked for you and have found you!

[a] 3 Or *Go and humble yourself,*

16 I have covered my bed
with colored linens from Egypt.
17 I have perfumed my bed
with myrrh, aloes and cinnamon.
18 Come, let's drink deeply of love till morning;
let's enjoy ourselves with love!
19 My husband is not at home;
he has gone on a long journey.
20 He took his purse filled with money
and will not be home till full moon."

21 With persuasive words she led him astray;
she seduced him with her smooth talk.
22 All at once he followed her
like an ox going to the slaughter,
like a deer[a] stepping into a noose[b]
23 till an arrow pierces his liver,
like a bird darting into a snare,
little knowing it will cost him his life.

24 Now then, my sons, listen to me;
pay attention to what I say.
25 Do not let your heart turn to her ways
or stray into her paths.
26 Many are the victims she has brought down;
her slain are a mighty throng.
27 Her house is a highway to the grave,
leading down to the chambers of death.

Wisdom's Call

8 Does not wisdom call out?
Does not understanding raise her voice?
2 At the highest point along the way,
where the paths meet, she takes her stand;
3 beside the gate leading into the city,
at the entrance, she cries aloud:
4 "To you, O people, I call out;
I raise my voice to all mankind.
5 You who are simple, gain prudence;
you who are foolish, set your hearts on it.[c]
6 Listen, for I have trustworthy things to say;
I open my lips to speak what is right.
7 My mouth speaks what is true,
for my lips detest wickedness.
8 All the words of my mouth are just;
none of them is crooked or perverse.
9 To the discerning all of them are right;
they are upright to those who have found knowledge.
10 Choose my instruction instead of silver,
knowledge rather than choice gold,
11 for wisdom is more precious than rubies,
and nothing you desire can compare with her.

12 "I, wisdom, dwell together with prudence;
I possess knowledge and discretion.
13 To fear the LORD is to hate evil;
I hate pride and arrogance,
evil behavior and perverse speech.
14 Counsel and sound judgment are mine;
I have insight, I have power.
15 By me kings reign
and rulers issue decrees that are just;
16 by me princes govern,
and nobles—all who rule on earth.[d]
17 I love those who love me,
and those who seek me find me.
18 With me are riches and honor,
enduring wealth and prosperity.
19 My fruit is better than fine gold;
what I yield surpasses choice silver.
20 I walk in the way of righteousness,
along the paths of justice,
21 bestowing a rich inheritance on those who love me
and making their treasuries full.

22 "The LORD brought me forth as the first of his works,[e,f]
before his deeds of old;
23 I was formed long ages ago,
at the very beginning, when the world came to be.
24 When there were no watery depths, I was given birth,
when there were no springs overflowing with water;
25 before the mountains were settled in place,
before the hills, I was given birth,
26 before he made the world or its fields
or any of the dust of the earth.
27 I was there when he set the heavens in place,
when he marked out the horizon on the face of the deep,
28 when he established the clouds above
and fixed securely the fountains of the deep,
29 when he gave the sea its boundary
so the waters would not overstep his command,
and when he marked out the foundations of the earth.
30 Then I was constantly[g] at his side.
I was filled with delight day after day,
rejoicing always in his presence,
31 rejoicing in his whole world
and delighting in mankind.

32 "Now then, my children, listen to me;
blessed are those who keep my ways.
33 Listen to my instruction and be wise;
do not disregard it.
34 Blessed are those who listen to me,
watching daily at my doors,
waiting at my doorway.
35 For those who find me find life
and receive favor from the LORD.
36 But those who fail to find me harm themselves;
all who hate me love death."

[a] 22 Syriac (see also Septuagint); Hebrew *fool* [b] 22 The meaning of the Hebrew for this line is uncertain. [c] 5 Septuagint; Hebrew *foolish, instruct your minds* [d] 16 Some Hebrew manuscripts and Septuagint; other Hebrew manuscripts *all righteous rulers* [e] 22 Or *way*; or *dominion* [f] 22 Or *The LORD possessed me at the beginning of his work*; or *The LORD brought me forth at the beginning of his work* [g] 30 Or *was the artisan*; or *was a little child*

Invitations of Wisdom and Folly

9 Wisdom has built her house;
she has set up[a] its seven pillars.
2 She has prepared her meat and mixed her wine;
she has also set her table.
3 She has sent out her servants, and she calls
from the highest point of the city,
4 "Let all who are simple come to my house!"
To those who have no sense she says,
5 "Come, eat my food
and drink the wine I have mixed.
6 Leave your simple ways and you will live;
walk in the way of insight."

7 Whoever corrects a mocker invites insults;
whoever rebukes the wicked incurs abuse.
8 Do not rebuke mockers or they will hate you;
rebuke the wise and they will love you.
9 Instruct the wise and they will be wiser still;
teach the righteous and they will add to their learning.

10 The fear of the LORD is the beginning of wisdom,
and knowledge of the Holy One is understanding.
11 For through wisdom[b] your days will be many,
and years will be added to your life.
12 If you are wise, your wisdom will reward you;
if you are a mocker, you alone will suffer.

13 Folly is an unruly woman;
she is simple and knows nothing.
14 She sits at the door of her house,
on a seat at the highest point of the city,
15 calling out to those who pass by,
who go straight on their way,
16 "Let all who are simple come to my house!"
To those who have no sense she says,
17 "Stolen water is sweet;
food eaten in secret is delicious!"
18 But little do they know that the dead are there,
that her guests are deep in the realm of the dead.

Proverbs of Solomon

10 The proverbs of Solomon:

A wise son brings joy to his father,
but a foolish son brings grief to his mother.

2 Ill-gotten treasures have no lasting value,
but righteousness delivers from death.

3 The LORD does not let the righteous go hungry,
but he thwarts the craving of the wicked.

4 Lazy hands make for poverty,
but diligent hands bring wealth.

5 He who gathers crops in summer is a prudent son,
but he who sleeps during harvest is a disgraceful son.

6 Blessings crown the head of the righteous,
but violence overwhelms the mouth of the wicked.[c]

7 The name of the righteous is used in blessings,[d]
but the name of the wicked will rot.

8 The wise in heart accept commands,
but a chattering fool comes to ruin.

9 Whoever walks in integrity walks securely,
but whoever takes crooked paths will be found out.

10 Whoever winks maliciously causes grief,
and a chattering fool comes to ruin.

11 The mouth of the righteous is a fountain of life,
but the mouth of the wicked conceals violence.

12 Hatred stirs up conflict,
but love covers over all wrongs.

13 Wisdom is found on the lips of the discerning,
but a rod is for the back of one who has no sense.

14 The wise store up knowledge,
but the mouth of a fool invites ruin.

15 The wealth of the rich is their fortified city,
but poverty is the ruin of the poor.

16 The wages of the righteous is life,
but the earnings of the wicked are sin and death.

17 Whoever heeds discipline shows the way to life,
but whoever ignores correction leads others astray.

18 Whoever conceals hatred with lying lips
and spreads slander is a fool.

19 Sin is not ended by multiplying words,
but the prudent hold their tongues.

20 The tongue of the righteous is choice silver,
but the heart of the wicked is of little value.

21 The lips of the righteous nourish many,
but fools die for lack of sense.

22 The blessing of the LORD brings wealth,
without painful toil for it.

23 A fool finds pleasure in wicked schemes,
but a person of understanding delights in wisdom.

[a] *1* Septuagint, Syriac and Targum; Hebrew *has hewn out* [b] *11* Septuagint, Syriac and Targum; Hebrew *me* [c] *6* Or *righteous, / but the mouth of the wicked conceals violence* [d] *7* See Gen. 48:20.

24 What the wicked dread will overtake them;
what the righteous desire will be granted.

25 When the storm has swept by, the wicked are gone,
but the righteous stand firm forever.

26 As vinegar to the teeth and smoke to the eyes,
so are sluggards to those who send them.

27 The fear of the LORD adds length to life,
but the years of the wicked are cut short.

28 The prospect of the righteous is joy,
but the hopes of the wicked come to nothing.

29 The way of the LORD is a refuge for the blameless,
but it is the ruin of those who do evil.

30 The righteous will never be uprooted,
but the wicked will not remain in the land.

31 From the mouth of the righteous comes the fruit of wisdom,
but a perverse tongue will be silenced.

32 The lips of the righteous know what finds favor,
but the mouth of the wicked only what is perverse.

11 The LORD detests dishonest scales,
but accurate weights find favor with him.

2 When pride comes, then comes disgrace,
but with humility comes wisdom.

3 The integrity of the upright guides them,
but the unfaithful are destroyed by their duplicity.

4 Wealth is worthless in the day of wrath,
but righteousness delivers from death.

5 The righteousness of the blameless makes their paths straight,
but the wicked are brought down by their own wickedness.

6 The righteousness of the upright delivers them,
but the unfaithful are trapped by evil desires.

7 Hopes placed in mortals die with them;
all the promise of[a] their power comes to nothing.

8 The righteous person is rescued from trouble,
and it falls on the wicked instead.

9 With their mouths the godless destroy their neighbors,
but through knowledge the righteous escape.

10 When the righteous prosper, the city rejoices;
when the wicked perish, there are shouts of joy.

11 Through the blessing of the upright a city is exalted,
but by the mouth of the wicked it is destroyed.

12 Whoever derides their neighbor has no sense,
but the one who has understanding holds their tongue.

13 A gossip betrays a confidence,
but a trustworthy person keeps a secret.

14 For lack of guidance a nation falls,
but victory is won through many advisers.

15 Whoever puts up security for a stranger will surely suffer,
but whoever refuses to shake hands in pledge is safe.

16 A kindhearted woman gains honor,
but ruthless men gain only wealth.

17 Those who are kind benefit themselves,
but the cruel bring ruin on themselves.

18 A wicked person earns deceptive wages,
but the one who sows righteousness reaps a sure reward.

19 Truly the righteous attain life,
but whoever pursues evil finds death.

20 The LORD detests those whose hearts are perverse,
but he delights in those whose ways are blameless.

21 Be sure of this: The wicked will not go unpunished,
but those who are righteous will go free.

22 Like a gold ring in a pig's snout
is a beautiful woman who shows no discretion.

23 The desire of the righteous ends only in good,
but the hope of the wicked only in wrath.

24 One person gives freely, yet gains even more;
another withholds unduly, but comes to poverty.

25 A generous person will prosper;
whoever refreshes others will be refreshed.

26 People curse the one who hoards grain,
but they pray God's blessing on the one who is willing to sell.

27 Whoever seeks good finds favor,
but evil comes to one who searches for it.

[a] 7 Two Hebrew manuscripts; most Hebrew manuscripts, Vulgate, Syriac and Targum *When the wicked die, their hope perishes; / all they expected from*

28 Those who trust in their riches will fall,
but the righteous will thrive like a green leaf.

29 Whoever brings ruin on their family will inherit only wind,
and the fool will be servant to the wise.

30 The fruit of the righteous is a tree of life,
and the one who is wise saves lives.

31 If the righteous receive their due on earth,
how much more the ungodly and the sinner!

12 Whoever loves discipline loves knowledge,
but whoever hates correction is stupid.

2 Good people obtain favor from the LORD,
but he condemns those who devise wicked schemes.

3 No one can be established through wickedness,
but the righteous cannot be uprooted.

4 A wife of noble character is her husband's crown,
but a disgraceful wife is like decay in his bones.

5 The plans of the righteous are just,
but the advice of the wicked is deceitful.

6 The words of the wicked lie in wait for blood,
but the speech of the upright rescues them.

7 The wicked are overthrown and are no more,
but the house of the righteous stands firm.

8 A person is praised according to their prudence,
and one with a warped mind is despised.

9 Better to be a nobody and yet have a servant
than pretend to be somebody and have no food.

10 The righteous care for the needs of their animals,
but the kindest acts of the wicked are cruel.

11 Those who work their land will have abundant food,
but those who chase fantasies have no sense.

12 The wicked desire the stronghold of evildoers,
but the root of the righteous endures.

13 Evildoers are trapped by their sinful talk,
and so the innocent escape trouble.

14 From the fruit of their lips people are filled with good things,
and the work of their hands brings them reward.

15 The way of fools seems right to them,
but the wise listen to advice.

16 Fools show their annoyance at once,
but the prudent overlook an insult.

17 An honest witness tells the truth,
but a false witness tells lies.

18 The words of the reckless pierce like swords,
but the tongue of the wise brings healing.

19 Truthful lips endure forever,
but a lying tongue lasts only a moment.

20 Deceit is in the hearts of those who plot evil,
but those who promote peace have joy.

21 No harm overtakes the righteous,
but the wicked have their fill of trouble.

22 The LORD detests lying lips,
but he delights in people who are trustworthy.

23 The prudent keep their knowledge to themselves,
but a fool's heart blurts out folly.

24 Diligent hands will rule,
but laziness ends in forced labor.

25 Anxiety weighs down the heart,
but a kind word cheers it up.

26 The righteous choose their friends carefully,
but the way of the wicked leads them astray.

27 The lazy do not roast[a] any game,
but the diligent feed on the riches of the hunt.

28 In the way of righteousness there is life;
along that path is immortality.

13 A wise son heeds his father's instruction,
but a mocker does not respond to rebukes.

2 From the fruit of their lips people enjoy good things,
but the unfaithful have an appetite for violence.

3 Those who guard their lips preserve their lives,
but those who speak rashly will come to ruin.

4 A sluggard's appetite is never filled,
but the desires of the diligent are fully satisfied.

5 The righteous hate what is false,
but the wicked make themselves a stench
and bring shame on themselves.

6 Righteousness guards the person of integrity,
but wickedness overthrows the sinner.

[a] 27 The meaning of the Hebrew for this word is uncertain.

[7]One person pretends to be rich, yet has nothing;
another pretends to be poor, yet has great wealth.

[8]A person's riches may ransom their life,
but the poor cannot respond to threatening rebukes.

[9]The light of the righteous shines brightly,
but the lamp of the wicked is snuffed out.

[10]Where there is strife, there is pride,
but wisdom is found in those who take advice.

[11]Dishonest money dwindles away,
but whoever gathers money little by little makes it grow.

[12]Hope deferred makes the heart sick,
but a longing fulfilled is a tree of life.

[13]Whoever scorns instruction will pay for it,
but whoever respects a command is rewarded.

[14]The teaching of the wise is a fountain of life,
turning a person from the snares of death.

[15]Good judgment wins favor,
but the way of the unfaithful leads to their destruction.[a]

[16]All who are prudent act with[b] knowledge,
but fools expose their folly.

[17]A wicked messenger falls into trouble,
but a trustworthy envoy brings healing.

[18]Whoever disregards discipline comes to poverty and shame,
but whoever heeds correction is honored.

[19]A longing fulfilled is sweet to the soul,
but fools detest turning from evil.

[20]Walk with the wise and become wise,
for a companion of fools suffers harm.

[21]Trouble pursues the sinner,
but the righteous are rewarded with good things.

[22]A good person leaves an inheritance for their children's children,
but a sinner's wealth is stored up for the righteous.

[23]An unplowed field produces food for the poor,
but injustice sweeps it away.

[24]Whoever spares the rod hates their children,
but the one who loves their children is careful to discipline them.

[25]The righteous eat to their hearts' content,
but the stomach of the wicked goes hungry.

14 The wise woman builds her house,
but with her own hands the foolish one tears hers down.

[2]Whoever fears the LORD walks uprightly,
but those who despise him are devious in their ways.

[3]A fool's mouth lashes out with pride,
but the lips of the wise protect them.

[4]Where there are no oxen, the manger is empty,
but from the strength of an ox come abundant harvests.

[5]An honest witness does not deceive,
but a false witness pours out lies.

[6]The mocker seeks wisdom and finds none,
but knowledge comes easily to the discerning.

[7]Stay away from a fool,
for you will not find knowledge on their lips.

[8]The wisdom of the prudent is to give thought to their ways,
but the folly of fools is deception.

[9]Fools mock at making amends for sin,
but goodwill is found among the upright.

[10]Each heart knows its own bitterness,
and no one else can share its joy.

[11]The house of the wicked will be destroyed,
but the tent of the upright will flourish.

[12]There is a way that appears to be right,
but in the end it leads to death.

[13]Even in laughter the heart may ache,
and rejoicing may end in grief.

[14]The faithless will be fully repaid for their ways,
and the good rewarded for theirs.

[15]The simple believe anything,
but the prudent give thought to their steps.

[16]The wise fear the LORD and shun evil,
but a fool is hotheaded and yet feels secure.

[17]A quick-tempered person does foolish things,
and the one who devises evil schemes is hated.

[18]The simple inherit folly,
but the prudent are crowned with knowledge.

[19]Evildoers will bow down in the presence of the good,
and the wicked at the gates of the righteous.

[a] *15* Septuagint and Syriac; the meaning of the Hebrew for this phrase is uncertain. [b] *16* Or *prudent protect themselves through*

[20] The poor are shunned even by their
neighbors,
but the rich have many friends.

[21] It is a sin to despise one's neighbor,
but blessed is the one who is kind to the
needy.

[22] Do not those who plot evil go astray?
But those who plan what is good find[a]
love and faithfulness.

[23] All hard work brings a profit,
but mere talk leads only to poverty.

[24] The wealth of the wise is their crown,
but the folly of fools yields folly.

[25] A truthful witness saves lives,
but a false witness is deceitful.

[26] Whoever fears the LORD has a secure
fortress,
and for their children it will be a refuge.

[27] The fear of the LORD is a fountain of life,
turning a person from the snares of
death.

[28] A large population is a king's glory,
but without subjects a prince is ruined.

[29] Whoever is patient has great
understanding,
but one who is quick-tempered displays
folly.

[30] A heart at peace gives life to the body,
but envy rots the bones.

[31] Whoever oppresses the poor shows
contempt for their Maker,
but whoever is kind to the needy honors
God.

[32] When calamity comes, the wicked are
brought down,
but even in death the righteous seek
refuge in God.

[33] Wisdom reposes in the heart of the
discerning
and even among fools she lets herself
be known.[b]

[34] Righteousness exalts a nation,
but sin condemns any people.

[35] A king delights in a wise servant,
but a shameful servant arouses his
fury.

15 A gentle answer turns away wrath,
but a harsh word stirs up anger.

[2] The tongue of the wise adorns
knowledge,
but the mouth of the fool gushes folly.

[3] The eyes of the LORD are everywhere,
keeping watch on the wicked and the
good.

[4] The soothing tongue is a tree of life,
but a perverse tongue crushes the
spirit.

[5] A fool spurns a parent's discipline,
but whoever heeds correction shows
prudence.

[6] The house of the righteous contains great
treasure,
but the income of the wicked brings
ruin.

[7] The lips of the wise spread knowledge,
but the hearts of fools are not upright.

[8] The LORD detests the sacrifice of the
wicked,
but the prayer of the upright pleases
him.

[9] The LORD detests the way of the wicked,
but he loves those who pursue
righteousness.

[10] Stern discipline awaits anyone who
leaves the path;
the one who hates correction will die.

[11] Death and Destruction[c] lie open before
the LORD—
how much more do human hearts!

[12] Mockers resent correction,
so they avoid the wise.

[13] A happy heart makes the face cheerful,
but heartache crushes the spirit.

[14] The discerning heart seeks knowledge,
but the mouth of a fool feeds on folly.

[15] All the days of the oppressed are
wretched,
but the cheerful heart has a continual
feast.

[16] Better a little with the fear of the LORD
than great wealth with turmoil.

[17] Better a small serving of vegetables with
love
than a fattened calf with hatred.

[18] A hot-tempered person stirs up conflict,
but the one who is patient calms a
quarrel.

[19] The way of the sluggard is blocked with
thorns,
but the path of the upright is a highway.

[20] A wise son brings joy to his father,
but a foolish man despises his mother.

[21] Folly brings joy to one who has no sense,
but whoever has understanding keeps a
straight course.

[22] Plans fail for lack of counsel,
but with many advisers they succeed.

[23] A person finds joy in giving an apt
reply—
and how good is a timely word!

[24] The path of life leads upward for the
prudent
to keep them from going down to the
realm of the dead.

[a] *22* Or *show* [b] *33* Hebrew; Septuagint and Syriac *discerning / but in the heart of fools she is not known* [c] *11* Hebrew *Abaddon*

25 The LORD tears down the house of the
proud,
but he sets the widow's boundary
stones in place.

26 The LORD detests the thoughts of the
wicked,
but gracious words are pure in his sight.

27 The greedy bring ruin to their
households,
but the one who hates bribes will live.

28 The heart of the righteous weighs its
answers,
but the mouth of the wicked gushes
evil.

29 The LORD is far from the wicked,
but he hears the prayer of the
righteous.

30 Light in a messenger's eyes brings joy to
the heart,
and good news gives health to the
bones.

31 Whoever heeds life-giving correction
will be at home among the wise.

32 Those who disregard discipline despise
themselves,
but the one who heeds correction gains
understanding.

33 Wisdom's instruction is to fear the LORD,
and humility comes before honor.

16 To humans belong the plans of the
heart,
but from the LORD comes the proper
answer of the tongue.

2 All a person's ways seem pure to them,
but motives are weighed by the LORD.

3 Commit to the LORD whatever you do,
and he will establish your plans.

4 The LORD works out everything to its
proper end—
even the wicked for a day of disaster.

5 The LORD detests all the proud of heart.
Be sure of this: They will not go
unpunished.

6 Through love and faithfulness sin is
atoned for;
through the fear of the LORD evil is
avoided.

7 When the LORD takes pleasure in
anyone's way,
he causes their enemies to make peace
with them.

8 Better a little with righteousness
than much gain with injustice.

9 In their hearts humans plan their course,
but the LORD establishes their steps.

10 The lips of a king speak as an oracle,
and his mouth does not betray justice.

11 Honest scales and balances belong to the
LORD;
all the weights in the bag are of his
making.

12 Kings detest wrongdoing,
for a throne is established through
righteousness.

13 Kings take pleasure in honest lips;
they value the one who speaks what is
right.

14 A king's wrath is a messenger of death,
but the wise will appease it.

15 When a king's face brightens, it means
life;
his favor is like a rain cloud in spring.

16 How much better to get wisdom than gold,
to get insight rather than silver!

17 The highway of the upright avoids evil;
those who guard their ways preserve
their lives.

18 Pride goes before destruction,
a haughty spirit before a fall.

19 Better to be lowly in spirit along with the
oppressed
than to share plunder with the proud.

20 Whoever gives heed to instruction
prospers,[a]
and blessed is the one who trusts in the
LORD.

21 The wise in heart are called discerning,
and gracious words promote
instruction.[b]

22 Prudence is a fountain of life to the
prudent,
but folly brings punishment to fools.

23 The hearts of the wise make their mouths
prudent,
and their lips promote instruction.[c]

24 Gracious words are a honeycomb,
sweet to the soul and healing to the
bones.

25 There is a way that appears to be right,
but in the end it leads to death.

26 The appetite of laborers works for them;
their hunger drives them on.

27 A scoundrel plots evil,
and on their lips it is like a scorching
fire.

28 A perverse person stirs up conflict,
and a gossip separates close friends.

29 A violent person entices their neighbor
and leads them down a path that is not
good.

30 Whoever winks with their eye is plotting
perversity;
whoever purses their lips is bent on
evil.

[a] 20 Or *whoever speaks prudently finds what is good* [b] 21 Or *words make a person persuasive*
[c] 23 Or *prudent / and make their lips persuasive*

[31] Gray hair is a crown of splendor;
it is attained in the way of righteousness.

[32] Better a patient person than a warrior,
one with self-control than one who takes a city.

[33] The lot is cast into the lap,
but its every decision is from the LORD.

17 Better a dry crust with peace and quiet
than a house full of feasting, with strife.

[2] A prudent servant will rule over a disgraceful son
and will share the inheritance as one of the family.

[3] The crucible for silver and the furnace for gold,
but the LORD tests the heart.

[4] A wicked person listens to deceitful lips;
a liar pays attention to a destructive tongue.

[5] Whoever mocks the poor shows contempt for their Maker;
whoever gloats over disaster will not go unpunished.

[6] Children's children are a crown to the aged,
and parents are the pride of their children.

[7] Eloquent lips are unsuited to a godless fool—
how much worse lying lips to a ruler!

[8] A bribe is seen as a charm by the one who gives it;
they think success will come at every turn.

[9] Whoever would foster love covers over an offense,
but whoever repeats the matter separates close friends.

[10] A rebuke impresses a discerning person
more than a hundred lashes a fool.

[11] Evildoers foster rebellion against God;
the messenger of death will be sent against them.

[12] Better to meet a bear robbed of her cubs
than a fool bent on folly.

[13] Evil will never leave the house
of one who pays back evil for good.

[14] Starting a quarrel is like breaching a dam;
so drop the matter before a dispute breaks out.

[15] Acquitting the guilty and condemning the innocent—
the LORD detests them both.

[16] Why should fools have money in hand to buy wisdom,
when they are not able to understand it?

[17] A friend loves at all times,
and a brother is born for a time of adversity.

[18] One who has no sense shakes hands in pledge
and puts up security for a neighbor.

[19] Whoever loves a quarrel loves sin;
whoever builds a high gate invites destruction.

[20] One whose heart is corrupt does not prosper;
one whose tongue is perverse falls into trouble.

[21] To have a fool for a child brings grief;
there is no joy for the parent of a godless fool.

[22] A cheerful heart is good medicine,
but a crushed spirit dries up the bones.

[23] The wicked accept bribes in secret
to pervert the course of justice.

[24] A discerning person keeps wisdom in view,
but a fool's eyes wander to the ends of the earth.

[25] A foolish son brings grief to his father
and bitterness to the mother who bore him.

[26] If imposing a fine on the innocent is not good,
surely to flog honest officials is not right.

[27] The one who has knowledge uses words with restraint,
and whoever has understanding is even-tempered.

[28] Even fools are thought wise if they keep silent,
and discerning if they hold their tongues.

18 An unfriendly person pursues selfish ends
and against all sound judgment starts quarrels.

[2] Fools find no pleasure in understanding
but delight in airing their own opinions.

[3] When wickedness comes, so does contempt,
and with shame comes reproach.

[4] The words of the mouth are deep waters,
but the fountain of wisdom is a rushing stream.

[5] It is not good to be partial to the wicked
and so deprive the innocent of justice.

[6] The lips of fools bring them strife,
and their mouths invite a beating.

[7] The mouths of fools are their undoing,
and their lips are a snare to their very lives.

[8] The words of a gossip are like choice morsels;
they go down to the inmost parts.

[9] One who is slack in his work
is brother to one who destroys.

10 The name of the LORD is a fortified tower;
the righteous run to it and are safe.

11 The wealth of the rich is their fortified city;
they imagine it a wall too high to scale.

12 Before a downfall the heart is haughty,
but humility comes before honor.

13 To answer before listening—
that is folly and shame.

14 The human spirit can endure in sickness,
but a crushed spirit who can bear?

15 The heart of the discerning acquires knowledge,
for the ears of the wise seek it out.

16 A gift opens the way
and ushers the giver into the presence of the great.

17 In a lawsuit the first to speak seems right,
until someone comes forward and cross-examines.

18 Casting the lot settles disputes
and keeps strong opponents apart.

19 A brother wronged is more unyielding than a fortified city;
disputes are like the barred gates of a citadel.

20 From the fruit of their mouth a person's stomach is filled;
with the harvest of their lips they are satisfied.

21 The tongue has the power of life and death,
and those who love it will eat its fruit.

22 He who finds a wife finds what is good
and receives favor from the LORD.

23 The poor plead for mercy,
but the rich answer harshly.

24 One who has unreliable friends soon comes to ruin,
but there is a friend who sticks closer than a brother.

19

Better the poor whose walk is blameless
than a fool whose lips are perverse.

2 Desire without knowledge is not good—
how much more will hasty feet miss the way!

3 A person's own folly leads to their ruin,
yet their heart rages against the LORD.

4 Wealth attracts many friends,
but even the closest friend of the poor person deserts them.

5 A false witness will not go unpunished,
and whoever pours out lies will not go free.

6 Many curry favor with a ruler,
and everyone is the friend of one who gives gifts.

7 The poor are shunned by all their relatives—
how much more do their friends avoid them!
Though the poor pursue them with pleading,
they are nowhere to be found.[a]

8 The one who gets wisdom loves life;
the one who cherishes understanding will soon prosper.

9 A false witness will not go unpunished,
and whoever pours out lies will perish.

10 It is not fitting for a fool to live in luxury—
how much worse for a slave to rule over princes!

11 A person's wisdom yields patience;
it is to one's glory to overlook an offense.

12 A king's rage is like the roar of a lion,
but his favor is like dew on the grass.

13 A foolish child is a father's ruin,
and a quarrelsome wife is like
the constant dripping of a leaky roof.

14 Houses and wealth are inherited from parents,
but a prudent wife is from the LORD.

15 Laziness brings on deep sleep,
and the shiftless go hungry.

16 Whoever keeps commandments keeps their life,
but whoever shows contempt for their ways will die.

17 Whoever is kind to the poor lends to the LORD,
and he will reward them for what they have done.

18 Discipline your children, for in that there is hope;
do not be a willing party to their death.

19 A hot-tempered person must pay the penalty;
rescue them, and you will have to do it again.

20 Listen to advice and accept discipline,
and at the end you will be counted among the wise.

21 Many are the plans in a person's heart,
but it is the LORD's purpose that prevails.

22 What a person desires is unfailing love[b];
better to be poor than a liar.

23 The fear of the LORD leads to life;
then one rests content, untouched by trouble.

24 A sluggard buries his hand in the dish;
he will not even bring it back to his mouth!

[a] 7 The meaning of the Hebrew for this sentence is uncertain. [b] 22 Or *Greed is a person's shame*

25 Flog a mocker, and the simple will learn prudence;
rebuke the discerning, and they will gain knowledge.

26 Whoever robs their father and drives out their mother
is a child who brings shame and disgrace.

27 Stop listening to instruction, my son,
and you will stray from the words of knowledge.

28 A corrupt witness mocks at justice,
and the mouth of the wicked gulps down evil.

29 Penalties are prepared for mockers,
and beatings for the backs of fools.

20 Wine is a mocker and beer a brawler;
whoever is led astray by them is not wise.

2 A king's wrath strikes terror like the roar of a lion;
those who anger him forfeit their lives.

3 It is to one's honor to avoid strife,
but every fool is quick to quarrel.

4 Sluggards do not plow in season;
so at harvest time they look but find nothing.

5 The purposes of a person's heart are deep waters,
but one who has insight draws them out.

6 Many claim to have unfailing love,
but a faithful person who can find?

7 The righteous lead blameless lives;
blessed are their children after them.

8 When a king sits on his throne to judge,
he winnows out all evil with his eyes.

9 Who can say, "I have kept my heart pure;
I am clean and without sin"?

10 Differing weights and differing measures—
the LORD detests them both.

11 Even small children are known by their actions,
so is their conduct really pure and upright?

12 Ears that hear and eyes that see—
the LORD has made them both.

13 Do not love sleep or you will grow poor;
stay awake and you will have food to spare.

14 "It's no good, it's no good!" says the buyer—
then goes off and boasts about the purchase.

15 Gold there is, and rubies in abundance,
but lips that speak knowledge are a rare jewel.

16 Take the garment of one who puts up security for a stranger;
hold it in pledge if it is done for an outsider.

17 Food gained by fraud tastes sweet,
but one ends up with a mouth full of gravel.

18 Plans are established by seeking advice;
so if you wage war, obtain guidance.

19 A gossip betrays a confidence;
so avoid anyone who talks too much.

20 If someone curses their father or mother,
their lamp will be snuffed out in pitch darkness.

21 An inheritance claimed too soon
will not be blessed at the end.

22 Do not say, "I'll pay you back for this wrong!"
Wait for the LORD, and he will avenge you.

23 The LORD detests differing weights,
and dishonest scales do not please him.

24 A person's steps are directed by the LORD.
How then can anyone understand their own way?

25 It is a trap to dedicate something rashly
and only later to consider one's vows.

26 A wise king winnows out the wicked;
he drives the threshing wheel over them.

27 The human spirit is[a] the lamp of the LORD
that sheds light on one's inmost being.

28 Love and faithfulness keep a king safe;
through love his throne is made secure.

29 The glory of young men is their strength,
gray hair the splendor of the old.

30 Blows and wounds scrub away evil,
and beatings purge the inmost being.

21 In the LORD's hand the king's heart is a stream of water
that he channels toward all who please him.

2 A person may think their own ways are right,
but the LORD weighs the heart.

3 To do what is right and just
is more acceptable to the LORD than sacrifice.

4 Haughty eyes and a proud heart—
the unplowed field of the wicked—
produce sin.

5 The plans of the diligent lead to profit
as surely as haste leads to poverty.

6 A fortune made by a lying tongue
is a fleeting vapor and a deadly snare.[b]

7 The violence of the wicked will drag them away,
for they refuse to do what is right.

[a] 27 Or *A person's words are* [b] 6 Some Hebrew manuscripts, Septuagint and Vulgate; most Hebrew manuscripts *vapor for those who seek death*

8 The way of the guilty is devious,
but the conduct of the innocent is upright.

9 Better to live on a corner of the roof
than share a house with a quarrelsome wife.

10 The wicked crave evil;
their neighbors get no mercy from them.

11 When a mocker is punished, the simple gain wisdom;
by paying attention to the wise they get knowledge.

12 The Righteous One[a] takes note of the house of the wicked
and brings the wicked to ruin.

13 Whoever shuts their ears to the cry of the poor
will also cry out and not be answered.

14 A gift given in secret soothes anger,
and a bribe concealed in the cloak pacifies great wrath.

15 When justice is done, it brings joy to the righteous
but terror to evildoers.

16 Whoever strays from the path of prudence
comes to rest in the company of the dead.

17 Whoever loves pleasure will become poor;
whoever loves wine and olive oil will never be rich.

18 The wicked become a ransom for the righteous,
and the unfaithful for the upright.

19 Better to live in a desert
than with a quarrelsome and nagging wife.

20 The wise store up choice food and olive oil,
but fools gulp theirs down.

21 Whoever pursues righteousness and love
finds life, prosperity[b] and honor.

22 One who is wise can go up against the city of the mighty
and pull down the stronghold in which they trust.

23 Those who guard their mouths and their tongues
keep themselves from calamity.

24 The proud and arrogant person—
"Mocker" is his name—
behaves with insolent fury.

25 The craving of a sluggard will be the death of him,
because his hands refuse to work.

26 All day long he craves for more,
but the righteous give without sparing.

27 The sacrifice of the wicked is detestable—
how much more so when brought with evil intent!

28 A false witness will perish,
but a careful listener will testify successfully.

29 The wicked put up a bold front,
but the upright give thought to their ways.

30 There is no wisdom, no insight, no plan
that can succeed against the LORD.

31 The horse is made ready for the day of battle,
but victory rests with the LORD.

22 A good name is more desirable than great riches;
to be esteemed is better than silver or gold.

2 Rich and poor have this in common:
The LORD is the Maker of them all.

3 The prudent see danger and take refuge,
but the simple keep going and pay the penalty.

4 Humility is the fear of the LORD;
its wages are riches and honor and life.

5 In the paths of the wicked are snares and pitfalls,
but those who would preserve their life stay far from them.

6 Start children off on the way they should go,
and even when they are old they will not turn from it.

7 The rich rule over the poor,
and the borrower is slave to the lender.

8 Whoever sows injustice reaps calamity,
and the rod they wield in fury will be broken.

9 The generous will themselves be blessed,
for they share their food with the poor.

10 Drive out the mocker, and out goes strife;
quarrels and insults are ended.

11 One who loves a pure heart and who speaks with grace
will have the king for a friend.

12 The eyes of the LORD keep watch over knowledge,
but he frustrates the words of the unfaithful.

13 The sluggard says, "There's a lion outside!
I'll be killed in the public square!"

14 The mouth of an adulterous woman is a deep pit;
a man who is under the LORD's wrath falls into it.

[a] 12 Or *The righteous person* [b] 21 Or *righteousness*

15 Folly is bound up in the heart of a child,
but the rod of discipline will drive it far away.
16 One who oppresses the poor to increase his wealth
and one who gives gifts to the rich—
both come to poverty.

Thirty Sayings of the Wise

Saying 1

17 Pay attention and turn your ear to the sayings of the wise;
apply your heart to what I teach,
18 for it is pleasing when you keep them in your heart
and have all of them ready on your lips.
19 So that your trust may be in the LORD,
I teach you today, even you.
20 Have I not written thirty sayings for you,
sayings of counsel and knowledge,
21 teaching you to be honest and to speak the truth,
so that you bring back truthful reports
to those you serve?

Saying 2

22 Do not exploit the poor because they are poor
and do not crush the needy in court,
23 for the LORD will take up their case
and will exact life for life.

Saying 3

24 Do not make friends with a hot-tempered person,
do not associate with one easily angered,
25 or you may learn their ways
and get yourself ensnared.

Saying 4

26 Do not be one who shakes hands in pledge
or puts up security for debts;
27 if you lack the means to pay,
your very bed will be snatched from under you.

Saying 5

28 Do not move an ancient boundary stone
set up by your ancestors.

Saying 6

29 Do you see someone skilled in their work?
They will serve before kings;
they will not serve before officials of low rank.

Saying 7

23 When you sit to dine with a ruler,
note well what[a] is before you,
2 and put a knife to your throat
if you are given to gluttony.
3 Do not crave his delicacies,
for that food is deceptive.

Saying 8

4 Do not wear yourself out to get rich;
do not trust your own cleverness.
5 Cast but a glance at riches, and they are gone,
for they will surely sprout wings
and fly off to the sky like an eagle.

Saying 9

6 Do not eat the food of a begrudging host,
do not crave his delicacies;
7 for he is the kind of person
who is always thinking about the cost.[b]
"Eat and drink," he says to you,
but his heart is not with you.
8 You will vomit up the little you have eaten
and will have wasted your compliments.

Saying 10

9 Do not speak to fools,
for they will scorn your prudent words.

Saying 11

10 Do not move an ancient boundary stone
or encroach on the fields of the fatherless,
11 for their Defender is strong;
he will take up their case against you.

Saying 12

12 Apply your heart to instruction
and your ears to words of knowledge.

Saying 13

13 Do not withhold discipline from a child;
if you punish them with the rod, they will not die.
14 Punish them with the rod
and save them from death.

Saying 14

15 My son, if your heart is wise,
then my heart will be glad indeed;
16 my inmost being will rejoice
when your lips speak what is right.

Saying 15

17 Do not let your heart envy sinners,
but always be zealous for the fear of the LORD.
18 There is surely a future hope for you,
and your hope will not be cut off.

Saying 16

19 Listen, my son, and be wise,
and set your heart on the right path:
20 Do not join those who drink too much wine
or gorge themselves on meat,
21 for drunkards and gluttons become poor,
and drowsiness clothes them in rags.

[a] *1* Or *who* [b] *7* Or *for as he thinks within himself, / so he is*; or *for as he puts on a feast, / so he is*

Saying 17

22 Listen to your father, who gave you life,
and do not despise your mother when she is old.
23 Buy the truth and do not sell it—
wisdom, instruction and insight as well.
24 The father of a righteous child has great joy;
a man who fathers a wise son rejoices in him.
25 May your father and mother rejoice;
may she who gave you birth be joyful!

Saying 18

26 My son, give me your heart
and let your eyes delight in my ways,
27 for an adulterous woman is a deep pit,
and a wayward wife is a narrow well.
28 Like a bandit she lies in wait
and multiplies the unfaithful among men.

Saying 19

29 Who has woe? Who has sorrow?
Who has strife? Who has complaints?
Who has needless bruises? Who has bloodshot eyes?
30 Those who linger over wine,
who go to sample bowls of mixed wine.
31 Do not gaze at wine when it is red,
when it sparkles in the cup,
when it goes down smoothly!
32 In the end it bites like a snake
and poisons like a viper.
33 Your eyes will see strange sights,
and your mind will imagine confusing things.
34 You will be like one sleeping on the high seas,
lying on top of the rigging.
35 "They hit me," you will say, "but I'm not hurt!
They beat me, but I don't feel it!
When will I wake up
so I can find another drink?"

Saying 20

24 Do not envy the wicked,
do not desire their company;
2 for their hearts plot violence,
and their lips talk about making trouble.

Saying 21

3 By wisdom a house is built,
and through understanding it is established;
4 through knowledge its rooms are filled
with rare and beautiful treasures.

Saying 22

5 The wise prevail through great power,
and those who have knowledge muster their strength.
6 Surely you need guidance to wage war,
and victory is won through many advisers.

Saying 23

7 Wisdom is too high for fools;
in the assembly at the gate they must not open their mouths.

Saying 24

8 Whoever plots evil
will be known as a schemer.
9 The schemes of folly are sin,
and people detest a mocker.

Saying 25

10 If you falter in a time of trouble,
how small is your strength!
11 Rescue those being led away to death;
hold back those staggering toward slaughter.
12 If you say, "But we knew nothing about this,"
does not he who weighs the heart perceive it?
Does not he who guards your life know it?
Will he not repay everyone according to what they have done?

Saying 26

13 Eat honey, my son, for it is good;
honey from the comb is sweet to your taste.
14 Know also that wisdom is like honey for you:
If you find it, there is a future hope for you,
and your hope will not be cut off.

Saying 27

15 Do not lurk like a thief near the house of the righteous,
do not plunder their dwelling place;
16 for though the righteous fall seven times, they rise again,
but the wicked stumble when calamity strikes.

Saying 28

17 Do not gloat when your enemy falls;
when they stumble, do not let your heart rejoice,
18 or the LORD will see and disapprove
and turn his wrath away from them.

Saying 29

19 Do not fret because of evildoers
or be envious of the wicked,
20 for the evildoer has no future hope,
and the lamp of the wicked will be snuffed out.

Saying 30

21 Fear the LORD and the king, my son,
and do not join with rebellious officials,
22 for those two will send sudden destruction on them,
and who knows what calamities they can bring?

Further Sayings of the Wise

23 These also are sayings of the wise:

To show partiality in judging is not good:
24 Whoever says to the guilty, "You are innocent,"
will be cursed by peoples and denounced by nations.
25 But it will go well with those who convict the guilty,
and rich blessing will come on them.

26 An honest answer
is like a kiss on the lips.

27 Put your outdoor work in order
and get your fields ready;
after that, build your house.

28 Do not testify against your neighbor without cause—
would you use your lips to mislead?
29 Do not say, "I'll do to them as they have done to me;
I'll pay them back for what they did."

30 I went past the field of a sluggard,
past the vineyard of someone who has no sense;
31 thorns had come up everywhere,
the ground was covered with weeds,
and the stone wall was in ruins.
32 I applied my heart to what I observed
and learned a lesson from what I saw:
33 A little sleep, a little slumber,
a little folding of the hands to rest—
34 and poverty will come on you like a thief
and scarcity like an armed man.

More Proverbs of Solomon

25 These are more proverbs of Solomon, compiled by the men of Hezekiah king of Judah:

2 It is the glory of God to conceal a matter;
to search out a matter is the glory of kings.
3 As the heavens are high and the earth is deep,
so the hearts of kings are unsearchable.

4 Remove the dross from the silver,
and a silversmith can produce a vessel;
5 remove wicked officials from the king's presence,
and his throne will be established through righteousness.

6 Do not exalt yourself in the king's presence,
and do not claim a place among his great men;
7 it is better for him to say to you, "Come up here,"
than for him to humiliate you before his nobles.

What you have seen with your eyes
8 do not bring[a] hastily to court,
for what will you do in the end
if your neighbor puts you to shame?

9 If you take your neighbor to court,
do not betray another's confidence,
10 or the one who hears it may shame you
and the charge against you will stand.

11 Like apples[b] of gold in settings of silver
is a ruling rightly given.
12 Like an earring of gold or an ornament of fine gold
is the rebuke of a wise judge to a listening ear.

13 Like a snow-cooled drink at harvest time
is a trustworthy messenger to the one who sends him;
he refreshes the spirit of his master.
14 Like clouds and wind without rain
is one who boasts of gifts never given.

15 Through patience a ruler can be persuaded,
and a gentle tongue can break a bone.

16 If you find honey, eat just enough—
too much of it, and you will vomit.
17 Seldom set foot in your neighbor's house—
too much of you, and they will hate you.

18 Like a club or a sword or a sharp arrow
is one who gives false testimony against a neighbor.
19 Like a broken tooth or a lame foot
is reliance on the unfaithful in a time of trouble.
20 Like one who takes away a garment on a cold day,
or like vinegar poured on a wound,
is one who sings songs to a heavy heart.

21 If your enemy is hungry, give him food to eat;
if he is thirsty, give him water to drink.
22 In doing this, you will heap burning coals on his head,
and the LORD will reward you.

23 Like a north wind that brings unexpected rain
is a sly tongue—which provokes a horrified look.

24 Better to live on a corner of the roof
than share a house with a quarrelsome wife.

25 Like cold water to a weary soul
is good news from a distant land.
26 Like a muddied spring or a polluted well
are the righteous who give way to the wicked.

27 It is not good to eat too much honey,
nor is it honorable to search out matters that are too deep.

28 Like a city whose walls are broken through
is a person who lacks self-control.

[a] 7,8 Or *nobles / on whom you had set your eyes. / 8Do not go*   [b] *11* Or possibly *apricots*

26 Like snow in summer or rain in
harvest,
honor is not fitting for a fool.
2 Like a fluttering sparrow or a darting
swallow,
an undeserved curse does not come to
rest.
3 A whip for the horse, a bridle for the
donkey,
and a rod for the backs of fools!
4 Do not answer a fool according to his
folly,
or you yourself will be just like him.
5 Answer a fool according to his folly,
or he will be wise in his own eyes.
6 Sending a message by the hands of a fool
is like cutting off one's feet or drinking
poison.
7 Like the useless legs of one who is lame
is a proverb in the mouth of a fool.
8 Like tying a stone in a sling
is the giving of honor to a fool.
9 Like a thornbush in a drunkard's hand
is a proverb in the mouth of a fool.
10 Like an archer who wounds at random
is one who hires a fool or any passer-
by.
11 As a dog returns to its vomit,
so fools repeat their folly.
12 Do you see a person wise in their own
eyes?
There is more hope for a fool than for
them.

13 A sluggard says, "There's a lion in the
road,
a fierce lion roaming the streets!"
14 As a door turns on its hinges,
so a sluggard turns on his bed.
15 A sluggard buries his hand in the dish;
he is too lazy to bring it back to his
mouth.
16 A sluggard is wiser in his own eyes
than seven people who answer
discreetly.

17 Like one who grabs a stray dog by the
ears
is someone who rushes into a quarrel
not their own.
18 Like a maniac shooting
flaming arrows of death
19 is one who deceives their neighbor
and says, "I was only joking!"

20 Without wood a fire goes out;
without a gossip a quarrel dies down.
21 As charcoal to embers and as wood to
fire,
so is a quarrelsome person for kindling
strife.
22 The words of a gossip are like choice
morsels;
they go down to the inmost parts.

23 Like a coating of silver dross on
earthenware
are fervent[a] lips with an evil heart.
24 Enemies disguise themselves with their
lips,
but in their hearts they harbor deceit.
25 Though their speech is charming, do not
believe them,
for seven abominations fill their hearts.
26 Their malice may be concealed by
deception,
but their wickedness will be exposed in
the assembly.
27 Whoever digs a pit will fall into it;
if someone rolls a stone, it will roll back
on them.
28 A lying tongue hates those it hurts,
and a flattering mouth works ruin.

27 Do not boast about tomorrow,
for you do not know what a day may
bring.

2 Let someone else praise you, and not your
own mouth;
an outsider, and not your own lips.

3 Stone is heavy and sand a burden,
but a fool's provocation is heavier than
both.

4 Anger is cruel and fury overwhelming,
but who can stand before jealousy?

5 Better is open rebuke
than hidden love.

6 Wounds from a friend can be trusted,
but an enemy multiplies kisses.

7 One who is full loathes honey from the
comb,
but to the hungry even what is bitter
tastes sweet.

8 Like a bird that flees its nest
is anyone who flees from home.

9 Perfume and incense bring joy to the
heart,
and the pleasantness of a friend
springs from their heartfelt advice.

10 Do not forsake your friend or a friend of
your family,
and do not go to your relative's house
when disaster strikes you—
better a neighbor nearby than a relative
far away.

11 Be wise, my son, and bring joy to my
heart;
then I can answer anyone who treats
me with contempt.

12 The prudent see danger and take refuge,
but the simple keep going and pay the
penalty.

13 Take the garment of one who puts up
security for a stranger;
hold it in pledge if it is done for an
outsider.

14 If anyone loudly blesses their neighbor
early in the morning,
it will be taken as a curse.

[a] 23 Hebrew; Septuagint *smooth*

15 A quarrelsome wife is like the dripping
of a leaky roof in a rainstorm;
16 restraining her is like restraining the wind
or grasping oil with the hand.

17 As iron sharpens iron,
so one person sharpens another.

18 The one who guards a fig tree will eat its
fruit,
and whoever protects their master will
be honored.

19 As water reflects the face,
so one's life reflects the heart.[a]

20 Death and Destruction[b] are never
satisfied,
and neither are human eyes.

21 The crucible for silver and the furnace for
gold,
but people are tested by their praise.

22 Though you grind a fool in a mortar,
grinding them like grain with a pestle,
you will not remove their folly from
them.

23 Be sure you know the condition of your
flocks,
give careful attention to your herds;
24 for riches do not endure forever,
and a crown is not secure for all
generations.
25 When the hay is removed and new
growth appears
and the grass from the hills is gathered
in,
26 the lambs will provide you with clothing,
and the goats with the price of a field.
27 You will have plenty of goats' milk to feed
your family
and to nourish your female servants.

28 The wicked flee though no one
pursues,
but the righteous are as bold as a lion.

2 When a country is rebellious, it has many
rulers,
but a ruler with discernment and
knowledge maintains order.

3 A ruler[c] who oppresses the poor
is like a driving rain that leaves no
crops.

4 Those who forsake instruction praise the
wicked,
but those who heed it resist them.

5 Evildoers do not understand what is
right,
but those who seek the LORD
understand it fully.

6 Better the poor whose walk is blameless
than the rich whose ways are perverse.

7 A discerning son heeds instruction,
but a companion of gluttons disgraces
his father.

8 Whoever increases wealth by taking
interest or profit from the poor
amasses it for another, who will be
kind to the poor.

9 If anyone turns a deaf ear to my
instruction,
even their prayers are detestable.

10 Whoever leads the upright along an evil
path
will fall into their own trap,
but the blameless will receive a good
inheritance.

11 The rich are wise in their own eyes;
one who is poor and discerning sees
how deluded they are.

12 When the righteous triumph, there is
great elation;
but when the wicked rise to power,
people go into hiding.

13 Whoever conceals their sins does not
prosper,
but the one who confesses and
renounces them finds mercy.

14 Blessed is the one who always trembles
before God,
but whoever hardens their heart falls
into trouble.

15 Like a roaring lion or a charging bear
is a wicked ruler over a helpless
people.

16 A tyrannical ruler practices extortion,
but one who hates ill-gotten gain will
enjoy a long reign.

17 Anyone tormented by the guilt of
murder
will seek refuge in the grave;
let no one hold them back.

18 The one whose walk is blameless is kept
safe,
but the one whose ways are perverse
will fall into the pit.[d]

19 Those who work their land will have
abundant food,
but those who chase fantasies will have
their fill of poverty.

20 A faithful person will be richly blessed,
but one eager to get rich will not go
unpunished.

21 To show partiality is not good—
yet a person will do wrong for a piece
of bread.

22 The stingy are eager to get rich
and are unaware that poverty awaits
them.

23 Whoever rebukes a person will in the end
gain favor
rather than one who has a flattering
tongue.

[a] 19 Or *so others reflect your heart back to you* [b] 20 Hebrew *Abaddon* [c] 3 Or *A poor person*
[d] 18 Syriac (see Septuagint); Hebrew *into one*

[24]Whoever robs their father or mother
and says, "It's not wrong,"
is partner to one who destroys.

[25]The greedy stir up conflict,
but those who trust in the LORD will
prosper.

[26]Those who trust in themselves are fools,
but those who walk in wisdom are kept
safe.

[27]Those who give to the poor will lack
nothing,
but those who close their eyes to them
receive many curses.

[28]When the wicked rise to power, people go
into hiding;
but when the wicked perish, the
righteous thrive.

29 Whoever remains stiff-necked after
many rebukes
will suddenly be destroyed—without
remedy.

[2]When the righteous thrive, the people
rejoice;
when the wicked rule, the people groan.

[3]A man who loves wisdom brings joy to
his father,
but a companion of prostitutes
squanders his wealth.

[4]By justice a king gives a country stability,
but those who are greedy for[a] bribes
tear it down.

[5]Those who flatter their neighbors
are spreading nets for their feet.

[6]Evildoers are snared by their own sin,
but the righteous shout for joy and are
glad.

[7]The righteous care about justice for the
poor,
but the wicked have no such concern.

[8]Mockers stir up a city,
but the wise turn away anger.

[9]If a wise person goes to court with a fool,
the fool rages and scoffs, and there is
no peace.

[10]The bloodthirsty hate a person of
integrity
and seek to kill the upright.

[11]Fools give full vent to their rage,
but the wise bring calm in the end.

[12]If a ruler listens to lies,
all his officials become wicked.

[13]The poor and the oppressor have this in
common:
The LORD gives sight to the eyes of
both.

[14]If a king judges the poor with fairness,
his throne will be established forever.

[15]A rod and a reprimand impart wisdom,
but a child left undisciplined disgraces
its mother.

[16]When the wicked thrive, so does sin,
but the righteous will see their downfall.

[17]Discipline your children, and they will
give you peace;
they will bring you the delights you
desire.

[18]Where there is no revelation, people cast
off restraint;
but blessed is the one who heeds
wisdom's instruction.

[19]Servants cannot be corrected by mere
words;
though they understand, they will not
respond.

[20]Do you see someone who speaks in haste?
There is more hope for a fool than for
them.

[21]A servant pampered from youth
will turn out to be insolent.

[22]An angry person stirs up conflict,
and a hot-tempered person commits
many sins.

[23]Pride brings a person low,
but the lowly in spirit gain honor.

[24]The accomplices of thieves are their own
enemies;
they are put under oath and dare not
testify.

[25]Fear of man will prove to be a snare,
but whoever trusts in the LORD is kept
safe.

[26]Many seek an audience with a ruler,
but it is from the LORD that one gets
justice.

[27]The righteous detest the dishonest;
the wicked detest the upright.

Sayings of Agur

30 The sayings of Agur son of Jakeh—an
inspired utterance.

This man's utterance to Ithiel:

"I am weary, God,
but I can prevail.[b]
[2]Surely I am only a brute, not a man;
I do not have human understanding.
[3]I have not learned wisdom,
nor have I attained to the knowledge of
the Holy One.
[4]Who has gone up to heaven and come
down?
Whose hands have gathered up the
wind?
Who has wrapped up the waters in a cloak?
Who has established all the ends of the
earth?

[a] 4 Or *who give* [b] 1 With a different word division of the Hebrew; Masoretic Text *utterance to Ithiel, / to Ithiel and Ukal:*

What is his name, and what is the name
of his son?
Surely you know!

5 "Every word of God is flawless;
he is a shield to those who take refuge
in him.
6 Do not add to his words,
or he will rebuke you and prove you a
liar.

7 "Two things I ask of you, LORD;
do not refuse me before I die:
8 Keep falsehood and lies far from me;
give me neither poverty nor riches,
but give me only my daily bread.
9 Otherwise, I may have too much and
disown you
and say, 'Who is the LORD?'
Or I may become poor and steal,
and so dishonor the name of my God.

10 "Do not slander a servant to their master,
or they will curse you, and you will pay
for it.

11 "There are those who curse their fathers
and do not bless their mothers;
12 those who are pure in their own eyes
and yet are not cleansed of their filth;
13 those whose eyes are ever so haughty,
whose glances are so disdainful;
14 those whose teeth are swords
and whose jaws are set with knives
to devour the poor from the earth
and the needy from among mankind.

15 "The leech has two daughters.
'Give! Give!' they cry.

"There are three things that are never
satisfied,
four that never say, 'Enough!':
16 the grave, the barren womb,
land, which is never satisfied with
water,
and fire, which never says, 'Enough!'

17 "The eye that mocks a father,
that scorns an aged mother,
will be pecked out by the ravens of the
valley,
will be eaten by the vultures.

18 "There are three things that are too
amazing for me,
four that I do not understand:
19 the way of an eagle in the sky,
the way of a snake on a rock,
the way of a ship on the high seas,
and the way of a man with a young
woman.

20 "This is the way of an adulterous woman:
She eats and wipes her mouth
and says, 'I've done nothing wrong.'

21 "Under three things the earth trembles,
under four it cannot bear up:
22 a servant who becomes king,
a godless fool who gets plenty to eat,
23 a contemptible woman who gets married,
and a servant who displaces her
mistress.

24 "Four things on earth are small,
yet they are extremely wise:
25 Ants are creatures of little strength,
yet they store up their food in the summer;
26 hyraxes are creatures of little power,
yet they make their home in the crags;
27 locusts have no king,
yet they advance together in ranks;
28 a lizard can be caught with the hand,
yet it is found in kings' palaces.

29 "There are three things that are stately in
their stride,
four that move with stately bearing:
30 a lion, mighty among beasts,
who retreats before nothing;
31 a strutting rooster, a he-goat,
and a king secure against revolt.[a]

32 "If you play the fool and exalt yourself,
or if you plan evil,
clap your hand over your mouth!
33 For as churning cream produces butter,
and as twisting the nose produces
blood,
so stirring up anger produces strife."

Sayings of King Lemuel

31 The sayings of King Lemuel—an inspired utterance his mother taught him.

2 Listen, my son! Listen, son of my womb!
Listen, my son, the answer to my prayers!
3 Do not spend your strength[b] on women,
your vigor on those who ruin kings.

4 It is not for kings, Lemuel—
it is not for kings to drink wine,
not for rulers to crave beer,
5 lest they drink and forget what has been
decreed,
and deprive all the oppressed of their
rights.
6 Let beer be for those who are perishing,
wine for those who are in anguish!
7 Let them drink and forget their poverty
and remember their misery no more.

8 Speak up for those who cannot speak for
themselves,
for the rights of all who are destitute.
9 Speak up and judge fairly;
defend the rights of the poor and needy.

Epilogue: The Wife of Noble Character

10 [c]A wife of noble character who can find?
She is worth far more than rubies.
11 Her husband has full confidence in her
and lacks nothing of value.
12 She brings him good, not harm,
all the days of her life.
13 She selects wool and flax
and works with eager hands.

[a] *31* The meaning of the Hebrew for this phrase is uncertain. [b] *3* Or *wealth* [c] *10* Verses 10-31 are an acrostic poem, the verses of which begin with the successive letters of the Hebrew alphabet.

[14] She is like the merchant ships,
bringing her food from afar.
[15] She gets up while it is still night;
she provides food for her family
and portions for her female servants.
[16] She considers a field and buys it;
out of her earnings she plants a
vineyard.
[17] She sets about her work vigorously;
her arms are strong for her tasks.
[18] She sees that her trading is profitable,
and her lamp does not go out at night.
[19] In her hand she holds the distaff
and grasps the spindle with her fingers.
[20] She opens her arms to the poor
and extends her hands to the needy.
[21] When it snows, she has no fear for her
household;
for all of them are clothed in scarlet.
[22] She makes coverings for her bed;
she is clothed in fine linen and purple.
[23] Her husband is respected at the city gate,
where he takes his seat among the
elders of the land.
[24] She makes linen garments and sells
them,
and supplies the merchants with
sashes.
[25] She is clothed with strength and dignity;
she can laugh at the days to come.
[26] She speaks with wisdom,
and faithful instruction is on her
tongue.
[27] She watches over the affairs of her
household
and does not eat the bread of idleness.
[28] Her children arise and call her blessed;
her husband also, and he praises her:
[29] "Many women do noble things,
but you surpass them all."
[30] Charm is deceptive, and beauty is
fleeting;
but a woman who fears the LORD is to
be praised.
[31] Honor her for all that her hands have
done,
and let her works bring her praise at
the city gate.

Ecclesiastes

Everything Is Meaningless

1 The words of the Teacher,[a] son of David, king in Jerusalem:

[2] "Meaningless! Meaningless!"
says the Teacher.
"Utterly meaningless!
Everything is meaningless."
[3] What do people gain from all their
labors
at which they toil under the sun?
[4] Generations come and generations go,
but the earth remains forever.
[5] The sun rises and the sun sets,
and hurries back to where it rises.
[6] The wind blows to the south
and turns to the north;
round and round it goes,
ever returning on its course.
[7] All streams flow into the sea,
yet the sea is never full.
To the place the streams come from,
there they return again.
[8] All things are wearisome,
more than one can say.
The eye never has enough of seeing,
nor the ear its fill of hearing.
[9] What has been will be again,
what has been done will be done
again;
there is nothing new under the sun.
[10] Is there anything of which one can say,
"Look! This is something new"?
It was here already, long ago;
it was here before our time.
[11] No one remembers the former
generations,
and even those yet to come
will not be remembered
by those who follow them.

Wisdom Is Meaningless

[12] I, the Teacher, was king over Israel in Jerusalem. [13] I applied my mind to study and to
explore by wisdom all that is done under the
heavens. What a heavy burden God has laid
on mankind! [14] I have seen all the things that
are done under the sun; all of them are meaningless, a chasing after the wind.

[15] What is crooked cannot be straightened;
what is lacking cannot be counted.

[16] I said to myself, "Look, I have increased
in wisdom more than anyone who has ruled
over Jerusalem before me; I have experienced
much of wisdom and knowledge." [17] Then I applied myself to the understanding of wisdom,
and also of madness and folly, but I learned
that this, too, is a chasing after the wind.

[18] For with much wisdom comes much
sorrow;
the more knowledge, the more grief.

[a] 1 Or *the leader of the assembly*; also in verses 2 and 12

Pleasures Are Meaningless

2 I said to myself, "Come now, I will test you with pleasure to find out what is good." But that also proved to be meaningless. 2"Laughter," I said, "is madness. And what does pleasure accomplish?" 3I tried cheering myself with wine, and embracing folly—my mind still guiding me with wisdom. I wanted to see what was good for people to do under the heavens during the few days of their lives.

4I undertook great projects: I built houses for myself and planted vineyards. 5I made gardens and parks and planted all kinds of fruit trees in them. 6I made reservoirs to water groves of flourishing trees. 7I bought male and female slaves and had other slaves who were born in my house. I also owned more herds and flocks than anyone in Jerusalem before me. 8I amassed silver and gold for myself, and the treasure of kings and provinces. I acquired male and female singers, and a harem[a] as well—the delights of a man's heart. 9I became greater by far than anyone in Jerusalem before me. In all this my wisdom stayed with me.

10I denied myself nothing my eyes desired;
  I refused my heart no pleasure.
My heart took delight in all my labor,
  and this was the reward for all my toil.
11Yet when I surveyed all that my hands
    had done
  and what I had toiled to achieve,
everything was meaningless, a chasing
    after the wind;
  nothing was gained under the sun.

Wisdom and Folly Are Meaningless

12Then I turned my thoughts to consider
    wisdom,
  and also madness and folly.
What more can the king's successor do
  than what has already been done?
13I saw that wisdom is better than folly,
  just as light is better than darkness.
14The wise have eyes in their heads,
  while the fool walks in the darkness;
but I came to realize
  that the same fate overtakes them
    both.

15Then I said to myself,

"The fate of the fool will overtake me
    also.
  What then do I gain by being wise?"
I said to myself,
  "This too is meaningless."
16For the wise, like the fool, will not be long
    remembered;
  the days have already come when both
    have been forgotten.
Like the fool, the wise too must die!

Toil Is Meaningless

17So I hated life, because the work that is done under the sun was grievous to me. All of it is meaningless, a chasing after the wind. 18I hated all the things I had toiled for under the sun, because I must leave them to the one who comes after me. 19And who knows whether that person will be wise or foolish? Yet they will have control over all the fruit of my toil into which I have poured my effort and skill under the sun. This too is meaningless. 20So my heart began to despair over all my toilsome labor under the sun. 21For a person may labor with wisdom, knowledge and skill, and then they must leave all they own to another who has not toiled for it. This too is meaningless and a great misfortune. 22What do people get for all the toil and anxious striving with which they labor under the sun? 23All their days their work is grief and pain; even at night their minds do not rest. This too is meaningless.

24A person can do nothing better than to eat and drink and find satisfaction in their own toil. This too, I see, is from the hand of God, 25for without him, who can eat or find enjoyment? 26To the person who pleases him, God gives wisdom, knowledge and happiness, but to the sinner he gives the task of gathering and storing up wealth to hand it over to the one who pleases God. This too is meaningless, a chasing after the wind.

A Time for Everything

3 There is a time for everything,
  and a season for every activity under the
    heavens:

2 a time to be born and a time to die,
  a time to plant and a time to uproot,
3 a time to kill and a time to heal,
  a time to tear down and a time to build,
4 a time to weep and a time to laugh,
  a time to mourn and a time to dance,
5 a time to scatter stones and a time to
    gather them,
  a time to embrace and a time to refrain
    from embracing,
6 a time to search and a time to give up,
  a time to keep and a time to throw
    away,
7 a time to tear and a time to mend,
  a time to be silent and a time to speak,
8 a time to love and a time to hate,
  a time for war and a time for peace.

9What do workers gain from their toil? 10I have seen the burden God has laid on the human race. 11He has made everything beautiful in its time. He has also set eternity in the human heart; yet[b] no one can fathom what God has done from beginning to end. 12I know that there is nothing better for people than to be happy and to do good while they live. 13That each of them may eat and drink, and find satisfaction in all their toil—this is the gift of God. 14I know that everything God does will endure forever; nothing can be added to it and nothing taken from it. God does it so that people will fear him.

[a] *8* The meaning of the Hebrew for this phrase is uncertain. [b] *11* Or *also placed ignorance in the human heart, so that*

[15]Whatever is has already been,
and what will be has been before;
and God will call the past to account.[a]

[16]And I saw something else under the sun:

In the place of judgment—wickedness was there,
in the place of justice—wickedness was there.

[17]I said to myself,

"God will bring into judgment
both the righteous and the wicked,
for there will be a time for every activity,
a time to judge every deed."

[18]I also said to myself, "As for humans, God
tests them so that they may see that they are
like the animals. [19]Surely the fate of human
beings is like that of the animals; the same
fate awaits them both: As one dies, so dies
the other. All have the same breath[b]; humans
have no advantage over animals. Everything
is meaningless. [20]All go to the same place; all
come from dust, and to dust all return. [21]Who
knows if the human spirit rises upward and
if the spirit of the animal goes down into the
earth?"

[22]So I saw that there is nothing better for a
person than to enjoy their work, because that
is their lot. For who can bring them to see what
will happen after them?

Oppression, Toil, Friendlessness

4 Again I looked and saw all the oppression that was taking place under the sun:

I saw the tears of the oppressed—
and they have no comforter;
power was on the side of their oppressors—
and they have no comforter.
[2]And I declared that the dead,
who had already died,
are happier than the living,
who are still alive.
[3]But better than both
is the one who has never been born,
who has not seen the evil
that is done under the sun.

[4]And I saw that all toil and all achievement
spring from one person's envy of another. This
too is meaningless, a chasing after the wind.

[5]Fools fold their hands
and ruin themselves.
[6]Better one handful with tranquillity
than two handfuls with toil
and chasing after the wind.

[7]Again I saw something meaningless under the sun:

[8]There was a man all alone;
he had neither son nor brother.
There was no end to his toil,
yet his eyes were not content with his wealth.
"For whom am I toiling," he asked,
"and why am I depriving myself of enjoyment?"
This too is meaningless—
a miserable business!

[9]Two are better than one,
because they have a good return for their labor:
[10]If either of them falls down,
one can help the other up.
But pity anyone who falls
and has no one to help them up.
[11]Also, if two lie down together, they will keep warm.
But how can one keep warm alone?
[12]Though one may be overpowered,
two can defend themselves.
A cord of three strands is not quickly broken.

Advancement Is Meaningless

[13]Better a poor but wise youth than an old
but foolish king who no longer knows how to
heed a warning. [14]The youth may have come
from prison to the kingship, or he may have
been born in poverty within his kingdom. [15]I
saw that all who lived and walked under the
sun followed the youth, the king's successor.
[16]There was no end to all the people who were
before them. But those who came later were
not pleased with the successor. This too is
meaningless, a chasing after the wind.

Fulfill Your Vow to God

5[c] Guard your steps when you go to the house of God. Go near to listen rather than to offer the sacrifice of fools, who do not know that they do wrong.

[2]Do not be quick with your mouth,
do not be hasty in your heart
to utter anything before God.
God is in heaven
and you are on earth,
so let your words be few.
[3]A dream comes when there are many cares,
and many words mark the speech of a fool.

[4]When you make a vow to God, do not delay to fulfill it. He has no pleasure in fools;
fulfill your vow. [5]It is better not to make a
vow than to make one and not fulfill it. [6]Do
not let your mouth lead you into sin. And do
not protest to the temple messenger, "My vow
was a mistake." Why should God be angry at
what you say and destroy the work of your
hands? [7]Much dreaming and many words are
meaningless. Therefore fear God.

Riches Are Meaningless

[8]If you see the poor oppressed in a district,
and justice and rights denied, do not be surprised at such things; for one official is eyed
by a higher one, and over them both are others

[a] 15 Or *God calls back the past* [b] 19 Or *spirit* [c] In Hebrew texts 5:1 is numbered 4:17, and 5:2-20 is numbered 5:1-19.

higher still. 9The increase from the land is
taken by all; the king himself profits from
the fields.

10 Whoever loves money never has enough;
whoever loves wealth is never satisfied
with their income.
This too is meaningless.

11 As goods increase,
so do those who consume them.
And what benefit are they to the owners
except to feast their eyes on them?

12 The sleep of a laborer is sweet,
whether they eat little or much,
but as for the rich, their abundance
permits them no sleep.

13 I have seen a grievous evil under the sun:

wealth hoarded to the harm of its owners,
14 or wealth lost through some
misfortune,
so that when they have children
there is nothing left for them to inherit.
15 Everyone comes naked from their
mother's womb,
and as everyone comes, so they depart.
They take nothing from their toil
that they can carry in their hands.

16 This too is a grievous evil:

As everyone comes, so they depart,
and what do they gain,
since they toil for the wind?
17 All their days they eat in darkness,
with great frustration, affliction and
anger.

18 This is what I have observed to be good:
that it is appropriate for a person to eat, to
drink and to find satisfaction in their toilsome
labor under the sun during the few days of
life God has given them—for this is their lot.
19 Moreover, when God gives someone wealth
and possessions, and the ability to enjoy them,
to accept their lot and be happy in their toil—
this is a gift of God. 20They seldom reflect on
the days of their life, because God keeps them
occupied with gladness of heart.

6 I have seen another evil under the sun, and
it weighs heavily on mankind: 2God gives
some people wealth, possessions and honor,
so that they lack nothing their hearts desire,
but God does not grant them the ability to enjoy them, and strangers enjoy them instead.
This is meaningless, a grievous evil.
3 A man may have a hundred children and
live many years; yet no matter how long he
lives, if he cannot enjoy his prosperity and
does not receive proper burial, I say that a
stillborn child is better off than he. 4It comes
without meaning, it departs in darkness, and
in darkness its name is shrouded. 5Though it
never saw the sun or knew anything, it has
more rest than does that man— 6even if he
lives a thousand years twice over but fails
to enjoy his prosperity. Do not all go to the
same place?

7 Everyone's toil is for their mouth,
yet their appetite is never satisfied.
8 What advantage have the wise over fools?
What do the poor gain
by knowing how to conduct themselves
before others?
9 Better what the eye sees
than the roving of the appetite.
This too is meaningless,
a chasing after the wind.

10 Whatever exists has already been named,
and what humanity is has been known;
no one can contend
with someone who is stronger.
11 The more the words,
the less the meaning,
and how does that profit anyone?

12 For who knows what is good for a person
in life, during the few and meaningless days
they pass through like a shadow? Who can
tell them what will happen under the sun after
they are gone?

Wisdom

7 A good name is better than fine perfume,
and the day of death better than the day
of birth.
2 It is better to go to a house of mourning
than to go to a house of feasting,
for death is the destiny of everyone;
the living should take this to heart.
3 Frustration is better than laughter,
because a sad face is good for the heart.
4 The heart of the wise is in the house of
mourning,
but the heart of fools is in the house of
pleasure.
5 It is better to heed the rebuke of a wise
person
than to listen to the song of fools.
6 Like the crackling of thorns under the pot,
so is the laughter of fools.
This too is meaningless.

7 Extortion turns a wise person into a fool,
and a bribe corrupts the heart.

8 The end of a matter is better than its
beginning,
and patience is better than pride.
9 Do not be quickly provoked in your spirit,
for anger resides in the lap of fools.

10 Do not say, "Why were the old days better
than these?"
For it is not wise to ask such questions.

11 Wisdom, like an inheritance, is a good
thing
and benefits those who see the sun.
12 Wisdom is a shelter
as money is a shelter,
but the advantage of knowledge is this:
Wisdom preserves those who have it.

13 Consider what God has done:

Who can straighten
what he has made crooked?
14 When times are good, be happy;
but when times are bad, consider this:
God has made the one
as well as the other.

Therefore, no one can discover
anything about their future.

15 In this meaningless life of mine I have seen both of these:

the righteous perishing in their
righteousness,
and the wicked living long in their
wickedness.
16 Do not be overrighteous,
neither be overwise—
why destroy yourself?
17 Do not be overwicked,
and do not be a fool—
why die before your time?
18 It is good to grasp the one
and not let go of the other.
Whoever fears God will avoid all
extremes.[a]
19 Wisdom makes one wise person more
powerful
than ten rulers in a city.
20 Indeed, there is no one on earth who is
righteous,
no one who does what is right and
never sins.
21 Do not pay attention to every word people
say,
or you may hear your servant cursing
you—
22 for you know in your heart
that many times you yourself have
cursed others.

23 All this I tested by wisdom and I said,

"I am determined to be wise"—
but this was beyond me.
24 Whatever exists is far off and most
profound—
who can discover it?
25 So I turned my mind to understand,
to investigate and to search out wisdom
and the scheme of things
and to understand the stupidity of
wickedness
and the madness of folly.

26 I find more bitter than death
the woman who is a snare,
whose heart is a trap
and whose hands are chains.
The man who pleases God will escape her,
but the sinner she will ensnare.

27 "Look," says the Teacher,[b] "this is what I have discovered:

"Adding one thing to another to discover
the scheme of things—
28 while I was still searching
but not finding—
I found one upright man among a
thousand,
but not one upright woman among
them all.
29 This only have I found:
God created mankind upright,
but they have gone in search of many
schemes."

8 Who is like the wise?
Who knows the explanation of things?
A person's wisdom brightens their face
and changes its hard appearance.

Obey the King

2 Obey the king's command, I say, because
you took an oath before God. 3 Do not be in
a hurry to leave the king's presence. Do not
stand up for a bad cause, for he will do whatever he pleases. 4 Since a king's word is supreme,
who can say to him, "What are you doing?"

5 Whoever obeys his command will come
to no harm,
and the wise heart will know the
proper time and procedure.
6 For there is a proper time and procedure
for every matter,
though a person may be weighed down
by misery.

7 Since no one knows the future,
who can tell someone else what is to
come?
8 As no one has power over the wind to
contain it,
so[c] no one has power over the time of
their death.
As no one is discharged in time of war,
so wickedness will not release those
who practice it.

9 All this I saw, as I applied my mind to everything done under the sun. There is a time
when a man lords it over others to his own[d]
hurt. 10 Then too, I saw the wicked buried—
those who used to come and go from the holy
place and receive praise[e] in the city where
they did this. This too is meaningless.
11 When the sentence for a crime is not
quickly carried out, people's hearts are filled
with schemes to do wrong. 12 Although a wicked person who commits a hundred crimes
may live a long time, I know that it will go
better with those who fear God, who are reverent before him. 13 Yet because the wicked do
not fear God, it will not go well with them, and
their days will not lengthen like a shadow.
14 There is something else meaningless that
occurs on earth: the righteous who get what
the wicked deserve, and the wicked who get
what the righteous deserve. This too, I say, is
meaningless. 15 So I commend the enjoyment
of life, because there is nothing better for a
person under the sun than to eat and drink
and be glad. Then joy will accompany them in
their toil all the days of the life God has given
them under the sun.
16 When I applied my mind to know wisdom and to observe the labor that is done
on earth—people getting no sleep day or

[a] 18 Or *will follow them both* [b] 27 Or *the leader of the assembly* [c] 8 Or *over the human spirit to retain it, / and so* [d] 9 Or *to their* [e] 10 Some Hebrew manuscripts and Septuagint (Aquila); most Hebrew manuscripts *and are forgotten*

night— [17]then I saw all that God has done. No one can comprehend what goes on under the sun. Despite all their efforts to search it out, no one can discover its meaning. Even if the wise claim they know, they cannot really comprehend it.

A Common Destiny for All

9 So I reflected on all this and concluded that the righteous and the wise and what they do are in God's hands, but no one knows whether love or hate awaits them. [2]All share a common destiny—the righteous and the wicked, the good and the bad,[a] the clean and the unclean, those who offer sacrifices and those who do not.

As it is with the good,
so with the sinful;
as it is with those who take oaths,
so with those who are afraid to take them.

[3]This is the evil in everything that happens under the sun: The same destiny overtakes all. The hearts of people, moreover, are full of evil and there is madness in their hearts while they live, and afterward they join the dead. [4]Anyone who is among the living has hope[b]—even a live dog is better off than a dead lion!

[5]For the living know that they will die,
but the dead know nothing;
they have no further reward,
and even their name is forgotten.
[6]Their love, their hate
and their jealousy have long since vanished;
never again will they have a part
in anything that happens under the sun.

[7]Go, eat your food with gladness, and drink your wine with a joyful heart, for God has already approved what you do. [8]Always be clothed in white, and always anoint your head with oil. [9]Enjoy life with your wife, whom you love, all the days of this meaningless life that God has given you under the sun—all your meaningless days. For this is your lot in life and in your toilsome labor under the sun. [10]Whatever your hand finds to do, do it with all your might, for in the realm of the dead, where you are going, there is neither working nor planning nor knowledge nor wisdom.

[11]I have seen something else under the sun:

The race is not to the swift
or the battle to the strong,
nor does food come to the wise
or wealth to the brilliant
or favor to the learned;
but time and chance happen to them all.

[12]Moreover, no one knows when their hour will come:

As fish are caught in a cruel net,
or birds are taken in a snare,
so people are trapped by evil times
that fall unexpectedly upon them.

Wisdom Better Than Folly

[13]I also saw under the sun this example of wisdom that greatly impressed me: [14]There was once a small city with only a few people in it. And a powerful king came against it, surrounded it and built huge siege works against it. [15]Now there lived in that city a man poor but wise, and he saved the city by his wisdom. But nobody remembered that poor man. [16]So I said, "Wisdom is better than strength." But the poor man's wisdom is despised, and his words are no longer heeded.

[17]The quiet words of the wise are more to be heeded
than the shouts of a ruler of fools.
[18]Wisdom is better than weapons of war,
but one sinner destroys much good.

10 As dead flies give perfume a bad smell,
so a little folly outweighs wisdom and honor.
[2]The heart of the wise inclines to the right,
but the heart of the fool to the left.
[3]Even as fools walk along the road,
they lack sense
and show everyone how stupid they are.
[4]If a ruler's anger rises against you,
do not leave your post;
calmness can lay great offenses to rest.

[5]There is an evil I have seen under the sun,
the sort of error that arises from a ruler:
[6]Fools are put in many high positions,
while the rich occupy the low ones.
[7]I have seen slaves on horseback,
while princes go on foot like slaves.

[8]Whoever digs a pit may fall into it;
whoever breaks through a wall may be bitten by a snake.
[9]Whoever quarries stones may be injured by them;
whoever splits logs may be endangered by them.

[10]If the ax is dull
and its edge unsharpened,
more strength is needed,
but skill will bring success.

[11]If a snake bites before it is charmed,
the charmer receives no fee.

[12]Words from the mouth of the wise are gracious,
but fools are consumed by their own lips.
[13]At the beginning their words are folly;
at the end they are wicked madness—
[14] and fools multiply words.

No one knows what is coming—
who can tell someone else what will happen after them?

[a] 2 Septuagint (Aquila), Vulgate and Syriac; Hebrew does not have *and the bad.* [b] 4 Or *What then is to be chosen? With all who live, there is hope*

15 The toil of fools wearies them;
they do not know the way to town.

16 Woe to the land whose king was a servant[a]
and whose princes feast in the morning.
17 Blessed is the land whose king is of noble birth
and whose princes eat at a proper time—
for strength and not for drunkenness.

18 Through laziness, the rafters sag;
because of idle hands, the house leaks.

19 A feast is made for laughter,
wine makes life merry,
and money is the answer for everything.

20 Do not revile the king even in your thoughts,
or curse the rich in your bedroom,
because a bird in the sky may carry your words,
and a bird on the wing may report what you say.

Invest in Many Ventures

11 Ship your grain across the sea;
after many days you may receive a return.
2 Invest in seven ventures, yes, in eight;
you do not know what disaster may come upon the land.

3 If clouds are full of water,
they pour rain on the earth.
Whether a tree falls to the south or to the north,
in the place where it falls, there it will lie.
4 Whoever watches the wind will not plant;
whoever looks at the clouds will not reap.

5 As you do not know the path of the wind,
or how the body is formed[b] in a mother's womb,
so you cannot understand the work of God,
the Maker of all things.

6 Sow your seed in the morning,
and at evening let your hands not be idle,
for you do not know which will succeed,
whether this or that,
or whether both will do equally well.

Remember Your Creator While Young

7 Light is sweet,
and it pleases the eyes to see the sun.
8 However many years anyone may live,
let them enjoy them all.
But let them remember the days of darkness,
for there will be many.
Everything to come is meaningless.

9 You who are young, be happy while you are young,
and let your heart give you joy in the days of your youth.
Follow the ways of your heart
and whatever your eyes see,
but know that for all these things
God will bring you into judgment.
10 So then, banish anxiety from your heart
and cast off the troubles of your body,
for youth and vigor are meaningless.

12 Remember your Creator
in the days of your youth,
before the days of trouble come
and the years approach when you will say,
"I find no pleasure in them"—
2 before the sun and the light
and the moon and the stars grow dark,
and the clouds return after the rain;
3 when the keepers of the house tremble,
and the strong men stoop,
when the grinders cease because they are few,
and those looking through the windows grow dim;
4 when the doors to the street are closed
and the sound of grinding fades;
when people rise up at the sound of birds,
but all their songs grow faint;
5 when people are afraid of heights
and of dangers in the streets;
when the almond tree blossoms
and the grasshopper drags itself along
and desire no longer is stirred.
Then people go to their eternal home
and mourners go about the streets.

6 Remember him—before the silver cord is severed,
and the golden bowl is broken;
before the pitcher is shattered at the spring,
and the wheel broken at the well,
7 and the dust returns to the ground it came from,
and the spirit returns to God who gave it.

8 "Meaningless! Meaningless!" says the Teacher.[c]
"Everything is meaningless!"

The Conclusion of the Matter

9 Not only was the Teacher wise, but he also
imparted knowledge to the people. He pondered and searched out and set in order many
proverbs. 10 The Teacher searched to find just
the right words, and what he wrote was upright and true.
11 The words of the wise are like goads,
their collected sayings like firmly embedded
nails—given by one shepherd.[d] 12 Be warned,
my son, of anything in addition to them.
Of making many books there is no end, and
much study wearies the body.

[a] 16 Or *king is a child* [b] 5 Or *know how life* (or *the spirit*) / *enters the body being formed*
[c] 8 Or *the leader of the assembly*; also in verses 9 and 10 [d] 11 Or *Shepherd*

13 Now all has been heard;
here is the conclusion of the matter:
Fear God and keep his commandments,
for this is the duty of all mankind.
14 For God will bring every deed into judgment,
including every hidden thing,
whether it is good or evil.

Song of Songs

1 Solomon's Song of Songs.

She[a]

2 Let him kiss me with the kisses of his mouth—
for your love is more delightful than wine.
3 Pleasing is the fragrance of your perfumes;
your name is like perfume poured out.
No wonder the young women love you!
4 Take me away with you—let us hurry!
Let the king bring me into his chambers.

Friends

We rejoice and delight in you[b];
we will praise your love more than wine.

She

How right they are to adore you!

5 Dark am I, yet lovely,
daughters of Jerusalem,
dark like the tents of Kedar,
like the tent curtains of Solomon.[c]
6 Do not stare at me because I am dark,
because I am darkened by the sun.
My mother's sons were angry with me
and made me take care of the vineyards;
my own vineyard I had to neglect.
7 Tell me, you whom I love,
where you graze your flock
and where you rest your sheep at midday.
Why should I be like a veiled woman
beside the flocks of your friends?

Friends

8 If you do not know, most beautiful of women,
follow the tracks of the sheep
and graze your young goats
by the tents of the shepherds.

He

9 I liken you, my darling, to a mare
among Pharaoh's chariot horses.
10 Your cheeks are beautiful with earrings,
your neck with strings of jewels.
11 We will make you earrings of gold,
studded with silver.

She

12 While the king was at his table,
my perfume spread its fragrance.
13 My beloved is to me a sachet of myrrh
resting between my breasts.
14 My beloved is to me a cluster of henna blossoms
from the vineyards of En Gedi.

He

15 How beautiful you are, my darling!
Oh, how beautiful!
Your eyes are doves.

She

16 How handsome you are, my beloved!
Oh, how charming!
And our bed is verdant.

He

17 The beams of our house are cedars;
our rafters are firs.

She[d]

2 I am a rose[e] of Sharon,
a lily of the valleys.

He

2 Like a lily among thorns
is my darling among the young women.

She

3 Like an apple[f] tree among the trees of the forest
is my beloved among the young men.
I delight to sit in his shade,
and his fruit is sweet to my taste.
4 Let him lead me to the banquet hall,
and let his banner over me be love.
5 Strengthen me with raisins,
refresh me with apples,
for I am faint with love.

[a] The main male and female speakers (identified primarily on the basis of the gender of the relevant Hebrew forms) are indicated by the captions *He* and *She* respectively. The words of others are marked *Friends*. In some instances the divisions and their captions are debatable. [b] *4* The Hebrew is masculine singular. [c] *5* Or *Salma* [d] Or *He* [e] *1* Probably a member of the crocus family [f] *3* Or possibly *apricot*; here and elsewhere in Song of Songs

6 His left arm is under my head,
and his right arm embraces me.
7 Daughters of Jerusalem, I charge you
by the gazelles and by the does of the field:
Do not arouse or awaken love
until it so desires.

8 Listen! My beloved!
Look! Here he comes,
leaping across the mountains,
bounding over the hills.
9 My beloved is like a gazelle or a young stag.
Look! There he stands behind our wall,
gazing through the windows,
peering through the lattice.
10 My beloved spoke and said to me,
"Arise, my darling,
my beautiful one, come with me.
11 See! The winter is past;
the rains are over and gone.
12 Flowers appear on the earth;
the season of singing has come,
the cooing of doves
is heard in our land.
13 The fig tree forms its early fruit;
the blossoming vines spread their fragrance.
Arise, come, my darling;
my beautiful one, come with me."

He

14 My dove in the clefts of the rock,
in the hiding places on the mountainside,
show me your face,
let me hear your voice;
for your voice is sweet,
and your face is lovely.
15 Catch for us the foxes,
the little foxes
that ruin the vineyards,
our vineyards that are in bloom.

She

16 My beloved is mine and I am his;
he browses among the lilies.
17 Until the day breaks
and the shadows flee,
turn, my beloved,
and be like a gazelle
or like a young stag
on the rugged hills.[a]

3 All night long on my bed
I looked for the one my heart loves;
I looked for him but did not find him.
2 I will get up now and go about the city,
through its streets and squares;
I will search for the one my heart loves.
So I looked for him but did not find him.
3 The watchmen found me
as they made their rounds in the city.
"Have you seen the one my heart loves?"
4 Scarcely had I passed them
when I found the one my heart loves.
I held him and would not let him go
till I had brought him to my mother's house,
to the room of the one who conceived me.
5 Daughters of Jerusalem, I charge you
by the gazelles and by the does of the field:
Do not arouse or awaken love
until it so desires.

6 Who is this coming up from the wilderness
like a column of smoke,
perfumed with myrrh and incense
made from all the spices of the merchant?
7 Look! It is Solomon's carriage,
escorted by sixty warriors,
the noblest of Israel,
8 all of them wearing the sword,
all experienced in battle,
each with his sword at his side,
prepared for the terrors of the night.
9 King Solomon made for himself the carriage;
he made it of wood from Lebanon.
10 Its posts he made of silver,
its base of gold.
Its seat was upholstered with purple,
its interior inlaid with love.
Daughters of Jerusalem, 11 come out,
and look, you daughters of Zion.
Look[b] on King Solomon wearing a crown,
the crown with which his mother crowned him
on the day of his wedding,
the day his heart rejoiced.

He

4 How beautiful you are, my darling!
Oh, how beautiful!
Your eyes behind your veil are doves.
Your hair is like a flock of goats
descending from the hills of Gilead.
2 Your teeth are like a flock of sheep just shorn,
coming up from the washing.
Each has its twin;
not one of them is alone.
3 Your lips are like a scarlet ribbon;
your mouth is lovely.
Your temples behind your veil
are like the halves of a pomegranate.
4 Your neck is like the tower of David,
built with courses of stone[c];
on it hang a thousand shields,
all of them shields of warriors.
5 Your breasts are like two fawns,
like twin fawns of a gazelle
that browse among the lilies.
6 Until the day breaks
and the shadows flee,

[a] 17 Or *the hills of Bether* [b] 10,11 Or *interior lovingly inlaid / by the daughters of Jerusalem. / 11 Come out, you daughters of Zion, / and look* [c] 4 The meaning of the Hebrew for this phrase is uncertain.

I will go to the mountain of myrrh
and to the hill of incense.
7 You are altogether beautiful, my darling;
there is no flaw in you.

8 Come with me from Lebanon, my bride,
come with me from Lebanon.
Descend from the crest of Amana,
from the top of Senir, the summit of Hermon,
from the lions' dens
and the mountain haunts of leopards.
9 You have stolen my heart, my sister, my bride;
you have stolen my heart
with one glance of your eyes,
with one jewel of your necklace.
10 How delightful is your love, my sister, my bride!
How much more pleasing is your love than wine,
and the fragrance of your perfume
more than any spice!
11 Your lips drop sweetness as the honeycomb, my bride;
milk and honey are under your tongue.
The fragrance of your garments
is like the fragrance of Lebanon.
12 You are a garden locked up, my sister, my bride;
you are a spring enclosed, a sealed fountain.
13 Your plants are an orchard of pomegranates
with choice fruits,
with henna and nard,
14 nard and saffron,
calamus and cinnamon,
with every kind of incense tree,
with myrrh and aloes
and all the finest spices.
15 You are[a] a garden fountain,
a well of flowing water
streaming down from Lebanon.

She

16 Awake, north wind,
and come, south wind!
Blow on my garden,
that its fragrance may spread everywhere.
Let my beloved come into his garden
and taste its choice fruits.

He

5 I have come into my garden, my sister, my bride;
I have gathered my myrrh with my spice.
I have eaten my honeycomb and my honey;
I have drunk my wine and my milk.

Friends

Eat, friends, and drink;
drink your fill of love.

She

2 I slept but my heart was awake.
Listen! My beloved is knocking:
"Open to me, my sister, my darling,
my dove, my flawless one.
My head is drenched with dew,
my hair with the dampness of the night."
3 I have taken off my robe—
must I put it on again?
I have washed my feet—
must I soil them again?
4 My beloved thrust his hand through the latch-opening;
my heart began to pound for him.
5 I arose to open for my beloved,
and my hands dripped with myrrh,
my fingers with flowing myrrh,
on the handles of the bolt.
6 I opened for my beloved,
but my beloved had left; he was gone.
My heart sank at his departure.[b]
I looked for him but did not find him.
I called him but he did not answer.
7 The watchmen found me
as they made their rounds in the city.
They beat me, they bruised me;
they took away my cloak,
those watchmen of the walls!
8 Daughters of Jerusalem, I charge you—
if you find my beloved,
what will you tell him?
Tell him I am faint with love.

Friends

9 How is your beloved better than others,
most beautiful of women?
How is your beloved better than others,
that you so charge us?

She

10 My beloved is radiant and ruddy,
outstanding among ten thousand.
11 His head is purest gold;
his hair is wavy
and black as a raven.
12 His eyes are like doves
by the water streams,
washed in milk,
mounted like jewels.
13 His cheeks are like beds of spice
yielding perfume.
His lips are like lilies
dripping with myrrh.
14 His arms are rods of gold
set with topaz.
His body is like polished ivory
decorated with lapis lazuli.
15 His legs are pillars of marble
set on bases of pure gold.
His appearance is like Lebanon,
choice as its cedars.
16 His mouth is sweetness itself;
he is altogether lovely.
This is my beloved, this is my friend,
daughters of Jerusalem.

[a] 15 Or *I am* (spoken by *She*) [b] 6 Or *heart had gone out to him when he spoke*

Friends

6 Where has your beloved gone,
most beautiful of women?
Which way did your beloved turn,
that we may look for him with you?

She

2 My beloved has gone down to his garden,
to the beds of spices,
to browse in the gardens
and to gather lilies.
3 I am my beloved's and my beloved is mine;
he browses among the lilies.

He

4 You are as beautiful as Tirzah, my darling,
as lovely as Jerusalem,
as majestic as troops with banners.
5 Turn your eyes from me;
they overwhelm me.
Your hair is like a flock of goats
descending from Gilead.
6 Your teeth are like a flock of sheep
coming up from the washing.
Each has its twin,
not one of them is missing.
7 Your temples behind your veil
are like the halves of a pomegranate.
8 Sixty queens there may be,
and eighty concubines,
and virgins beyond number;
9 but my dove, my perfect one, is unique,
the only daughter of her mother,
the favorite of the one who bore her.
The young women saw her and called her blessed;
the queens and concubines praised her.

Friends

10 Who is this that appears like the dawn,
fair as the moon, bright as the sun,
majestic as the stars in procession?

He

11 I went down to the grove of nut trees
to look at the new growth in the valley,
to see if the vines had budded
or the pomegranates were in bloom.
12 Before I realized it,
my desire set me among the royal chariots of my people.[a]

Friends

13 Come back, come back, O Shulammite;
come back, come back, that we may gaze on you!

He

Why would you gaze on the Shulammite
as on the dance of Mahanaim?[b]

7[c] How beautiful your sandaled feet,
O prince's daughter!
Your graceful legs are like jewels,
the work of an artist's hands.
2 Your navel is a rounded goblet
that never lacks blended wine.
Your waist is a mound of wheat
encircled by lilies.
3 Your breasts are like two fawns,
like twin fawns of a gazelle.
4 Your neck is like an ivory tower.
Your eyes are the pools of Heshbon
by the gate of Bath Rabbim.
Your nose is like the tower of Lebanon
looking toward Damascus.
5 Your head crowns you like Mount Carmel.
Your hair is like royal tapestry;
the king is held captive by its tresses.
6 How beautiful you are and how pleasing,
my love, with your delights!
7 Your stature is like that of the palm,
and your breasts like clusters of fruit.
8 I said, "I will climb the palm tree;
I will take hold of its fruit."
May your breasts be like clusters of grapes on the vine,
the fragrance of your breath like apples,
9 and your mouth like the best wine.

She

May the wine go straight to my beloved,
flowing gently over lips and teeth.[d]
10 I belong to my beloved,
and his desire is for me.
11 Come, my beloved, let us go to the countryside,
let us spend the night in the villages.[e]
12 Let us go early to the vineyards
to see if the vines have budded,
if their blossoms have opened,
and if the pomegranates are in bloom—
there I will give you my love.
13 The mandrakes send out their fragrance,
and at our door is every delicacy,
both new and old,
that I have stored up for you, my beloved.

8 If only you were to me like a brother,
who was nursed at my mother's breasts!
Then, if I found you outside,
I would kiss you,
and no one would despise me.
2 I would lead you
and bring you to my mother's house—
she who has taught me.
I would give you spiced wine to drink,
the nectar of my pomegranates.
3 His left arm is under my head
and his right arm embraces me.
4 Daughters of Jerusalem, I charge you:
Do not arouse or awaken love
until it so desires.

[a] *12* Or *among the chariots of Amminadab*; or *among the chariots of the people of the prince*
[b] *13* In Hebrew texts this verse (6:13) is numbered 7:1. [c] In Hebrew texts 7:1-13 is numbered 7:2-14.
[d] *9* Septuagint, Aquila, Vulgate and Syriac; Hebrew *lips of sleepers* [e] *11* Or *the henna bushes*

Friends

5 Who is this coming up from the
wilderness
leaning on her beloved?

She

Under the apple tree I roused you;
there your mother conceived you,
there she who was in labor gave you
birth.
6 Place me like a seal over your heart,
like a seal on your arm;
for love is as strong as death,
its jealousy[a] unyielding as the grave.
It burns like blazing fire,
like a mighty flame.[b]
7 Many waters cannot quench love;
rivers cannot sweep it away.
If one were to give
all the wealth of one's house for love,
it[c] would be utterly scorned.

Friends

8 We have a little sister,
and her breasts are not yet grown.
What shall we do for our sister
on the day she is spoken for?
9 If she is a wall,
we will build towers of silver on her.
If she is a door,
we will enclose her with panels of
cedar.

She

10 I am a wall,
and my breasts are like towers.
Thus I have become in his eyes
like one bringing contentment.
11 Solomon had a vineyard in Baal Hamon;
he let out his vineyard to tenants.
Each was to bring for its fruit
a thousand shekels[d] of silver.
12 But my own vineyard is mine to give;
the thousand shekels are for you,
Solomon,
and two hundred[e] are for those who
tend its fruit.

He

13 You who dwell in the gardens
with friends in attendance,
let me hear your voice!

She

14 Come away, my beloved,
and be like a gazelle
or like a young stag
on the spice-laden mountains.

Isaiah

1 The vision concerning Judah and Jerusalem that Isaiah son of Amoz saw during the reigns of Uzziah, Jotham, Ahaz and Hezekiah, kings of Judah.

A Rebellious Nation

2 Hear me, you heavens! Listen, earth!
For the LORD has spoken:
"I reared children and brought them up,
but they have rebelled against me.
3 The ox knows its master,
the donkey its owner's manger,
but Israel does not know,
my people do not understand."

4 Woe to the sinful nation,
a people whose guilt is great,
a brood of evildoers,
children given to corruption!
They have forsaken the LORD;
they have spurned the Holy One of Israel
and turned their backs on him.

5 Why should you be beaten anymore?
Why do you persist in rebellion?
Your whole head is injured,
your whole heart afflicted.
6 From the sole of your foot to the top of
your head
there is no soundness—
only wounds and welts
and open sores,
not cleansed or bandaged
or soothed with olive oil.

7 Your country is desolate,
your cities burned with fire;
your fields are being stripped by foreigners
right before you,
laid waste as when overthrown by
strangers.
8 Daughter Zion is left
like a shelter in a vineyard,
like a hut in a cucumber field,
like a city under siege.
9 Unless the LORD Almighty
had left us some survivors,
we would have become like Sodom,
we would have been like Gomorrah.

10 Hear the word of the LORD,
you rulers of Sodom;
listen to the instruction of our God,
you people of Gomorrah!

[a] 6 Or *ardor* [b] 6 Or *fire, / like the very flame of the LORD* [c] 7 Or *he* [d] 11 That is, about 25 pounds or about 12 kilograms; also in verse 12 [e] 12 That is, about 5 pounds or about 2.3 kilograms

11 "The multitude of your sacrifices—
what are they to me?" says the LORD.
"I have more than enough of burnt offerings,
of rams and the fat of fattened animals;
I have no pleasure
in the blood of bulls and lambs and goats.
12 When you come to appear before me,
who has asked this of you,
this trampling of my courts?
13 Stop bringing meaningless offerings!
Your incense is detestable to me.
New Moons, Sabbaths and convocations—
I cannot bear your worthless assemblies.
14 Your New Moon feasts and your appointed festivals
I hate with all my being.
They have become a burden to me;
I am weary of bearing them.
15 When you spread out your hands in prayer,
I hide my eyes from you;
even when you offer many prayers,
I am not listening.

Your hands are full of blood!

16 Wash and make yourselves clean.
Take your evil deeds out of my sight;
stop doing wrong.
17 Learn to do right; seek justice.
Defend the oppressed.[a]
Take up the cause of the fatherless;
plead the case of the widow.

18 "Come now, let us settle the matter,"
says the LORD.
"Though your sins are like scarlet,
they shall be as white as snow;
though they are red as crimson,
they shall be like wool.
19 If you are willing and obedient,
you will eat the good things of the land;
20 but if you resist and rebel,
you will be devoured by the sword."
For the mouth of the LORD has spoken.

21 See how the faithful city
has become a prostitute!
She once was full of justice;
righteousness used to dwell in her—
but now murderers!
22 Your silver has become dross,
your choice wine is diluted with water.
23 Your rulers are rebels,
partners with thieves;
they all love bribes
and chase after gifts.
They do not defend the cause of the fatherless;
the widow's case does not come before them.

24 Therefore the Lord, the LORD Almighty,
the Mighty One of Israel, declares:
"Ah! I will vent my wrath on my foes
and avenge myself on my enemies.
25 I will turn my hand against you;[b]
I will thoroughly purge away your dross
and remove all your impurities.
26 I will restore your leaders as in days of old,
your rulers as at the beginning.
Afterward you will be called
the City of Righteousness,
the Faithful City."

27 Zion will be delivered with justice,
her penitent ones with righteousness.
28 But rebels and sinners will both be broken,
and those who forsake the LORD will perish.

29 "You will be ashamed because of the sacred oaks
in which you have delighted;
you will be disgraced because of the gardens
that you have chosen.
30 You will be like an oak with fading leaves,
like a garden without water.
31 The mighty man will become tinder
and his work a spark;
both will burn together,
with no one to quench the fire."

The Mountain of the LORD

2 This is what Isaiah son of Amoz saw concerning Judah and Jerusalem:

2 In the last days

the mountain of the LORD's temple will be established
as the highest of the mountains;
it will be exalted above the hills,
and all nations will stream to it.

3 Many peoples will come and say,

"Come, let us go up to the mountain of the LORD,
to the temple of the God of Jacob.
He will teach us his ways,
so that we may walk in his paths."
The law will go out from Zion,
the word of the LORD from Jerusalem.
4 He will judge between the nations
and will settle disputes for many peoples.
They will beat their swords into plowshares
and their spears into pruning hooks.
Nation will not take up sword against nation,
nor will they train for war anymore.

5 Come, descendants of Jacob,
let us walk in the light of the LORD.

The Day of the LORD

6 You, LORD, have abandoned your people,
the descendants of Jacob.

[a] 17 Or *justice. / Correct the oppressor* [b] 25 That is, against Jerusalem

They are full of superstitions from the East;
they practice divination like the Philistines
and embrace pagan customs.
7 Their land is full of silver and gold;
there is no end to their treasures.
Their land is full of horses;
there is no end to their chariots.
8 Their land is full of idols;
they bow down to the work of their hands,
to what their fingers have made.
9 So people will be brought low
and everyone humbled—
do not forgive them.[a]

10 Go into the rocks, hide in the ground
from the fearful presence of the LORD
and the splendor of his majesty!
11 The eyes of the arrogant will be humbled
and human pride brought low;
the LORD alone will be exalted in that day.

12 The LORD Almighty has a day in store
for all the proud and lofty,
for all that is exalted
(and they will be humbled),
13 for all the cedars of Lebanon, tall and lofty,
and all the oaks of Bashan,
14 for all the towering mountains
and all the high hills,
15 for every lofty tower
and every fortified wall,
16 for every trading ship[b]
and every stately vessel.
17 The arrogance of man will be brought low
and human pride humbled;
the LORD alone will be exalted in that day,
18 and the idols will totally disappear.

19 People will flee to caves in the rocks
and to holes in the ground
from the fearful presence of the LORD
and the splendor of his majesty,
when he rises to shake the earth.
20 In that day people will throw away
to the moles and bats
their idols of silver and idols of gold,
which they made to worship.
21 They will flee to caverns in the rocks
and to the overhanging crags
from the fearful presence of the LORD
and the splendor of his majesty,
when he rises to shake the earth.

22 Stop trusting in mere humans,
who have but a breath in their nostrils.
Why hold them in esteem?

Judgment on Jerusalem and Judah

3 See now, the Lord,
the LORD Almighty,
is about to take from Jerusalem and Judah
both supply and support:
all supplies of food and all supplies of water,
2 the hero and the warrior,
the judge and the prophet,
the diviner and the elder,
3 the captain of fifty and the man of rank,
the counselor, skilled craftsman and clever enchanter.

4 "I will make mere youths their officials;
children will rule over them."

5 People will oppress each other—
man against man, neighbor against neighbor.
The young will rise up against the old,
the nobody against the honored.

6 A man will seize one of his brothers
in his father's house, and say,
"You have a cloak, you be our leader;
take charge of this heap of ruins!"
7 But in that day he will cry out,
"I have no remedy.
I have no food or clothing in my house;
do not make me the leader of the people."

8 Jerusalem staggers,
Judah is falling;
their words and deeds are against the LORD,
defying his glorious presence.
9 The look on their faces testifies against them;
they parade their sin like Sodom;
they do not hide it.
Woe to them!
They have brought disaster upon themselves.

10 Tell the righteous it will be well with them,
for they will enjoy the fruit of their deeds.
11 Woe to the wicked!
Disaster is upon them!
They will be paid back
for what their hands have done.

12 Youths oppress my people,
women rule over them.
My people, your guides lead you astray;
they turn you from the path.

13 The LORD takes his place in court;
he rises to judge the people.
14 The LORD enters into judgment
against the elders and leaders of his people:
"It is you who have ruined my vineyard;
the plunder from the poor is in your houses.
15 What do you mean by crushing my people
and grinding the faces of the poor?"
declares the Lord,
the LORD Almighty.

16 The LORD says,
"The women of Zion are haughty,

[a] 9 Or *not raise them up* [b] 16 Hebrew *every ship of Tarshish*

walking along with outstretched necks,
flirting with their eyes,
strutting along with swaying hips,
with ornaments jingling on their ankles.
17 Therefore the Lord will bring sores on the heads of the women of Zion;
the LORD will make their scalps bald."

18 In that day the Lord will snatch away their
finery: the bangles and headbands and cres-
cent necklaces, 19 the earrings and bracelets
and veils, 20 the headdresses and anklets and
sashes, the perfume bottles and charms, 21 the
signet rings and nose rings, 22 the fine robes
and the capes and cloaks, the purses 23 and
mirrors, and the linen garments and tiaras
and shawls.

24 Instead of fragrance there will be a stench;
instead of a sash, a rope;
instead of well-dressed hair, baldness;
instead of fine clothing, sackcloth;
instead of beauty, branding.
25 Your men will fall by the sword,
your warriors in battle.
26 The gates of Zion will lament and mourn;
destitute, she will sit on the ground.

4 1 In that day seven women
will take hold of one man
and say, "We will eat our own food
and provide our own clothes;
only let us be called by your name.
Take away our disgrace!"

The Branch of the LORD

2 In that day the Branch of the LORD will be
beautiful and glorious, and the fruit of the
land will be the pride and glory of the survivors in Israel. 3 Those who are left in Zion, who
remain in Jerusalem, will be called holy, all
who are recorded among the living in Jerusalem. 4 The Lord will wash away the filth of
the women of Zion; he will cleanse the blood-
stains from Jerusalem by a spirit[a] of judgment
and a spirit[a] of fire. 5 Then the LORD will create
over all of Mount Zion and over those who
assemble there a cloud of smoke by day and a
glow of flaming fire by night; over everything
the glory[b] will be a canopy. 6 It will be a shelter
and shade from the heat of the day, and a refuge and hiding place from the storm and rain.

The Song of the Vineyard

5 I will sing for the one I love
a song about his vineyard:
My loved one had a vineyard
on a fertile hillside.
2 He dug it up and cleared it of stones
and planted it with the choicest vines.
He built a watchtower in it
and cut out a winepress as well.
Then he looked for a crop of good grapes,
but it yielded only bad fruit.

3 "Now you dwellers in Jerusalem and people of Judah,
judge between me and my vineyard.
4 What more could have been done for my vineyard
than I have done for it?
When I looked for good grapes,
why did it yield only bad?
5 Now I will tell you
what I am going to do to my vineyard:
I will take away its hedge,
and it will be destroyed;
I will break down its wall,
and it will be trampled.
6 I will make it a wasteland,
neither pruned nor cultivated,
and briers and thorns will grow there.
I will command the clouds
not to rain on it."

7 The vineyard of the LORD Almighty
is the nation of Israel,
and the people of Judah
are the vines he delighted in.
And he looked for justice, but saw bloodshed;
for righteousness, but heard cries of distress.

Woes and Judgments

8 Woe to you who add house to house
and join field to field
till no space is left
and you live alone in the land.

9 The LORD Almighty has declared in my
hearing:

"Surely the great houses will become desolate,
the fine mansions left without occupants.
10 A ten-acre vineyard will produce only a bath[c] of wine;
a homer[d] of seed will yield only an ephah[e] of grain."

11 Woe to those who rise early in the morning
to run after their drinks,
who stay up late at night
till they are inflamed with wine.
12 They have harps and lyres at their banquets,
pipes and timbrels and wine,
but they have no regard for the deeds of the LORD,
no respect for the work of his hands.
13 Therefore my people will go into exile
for lack of understanding;
those of high rank will die of hunger
and the common people will be parched with thirst.
14 Therefore Death expands its jaws,
opening wide its mouth;
into it will descend their nobles and masses
with all their brawlers and revelers.

[a] 4 Or *the Spirit* [b] 5 Or *over all the glory there* [c] 10 That is, about 6 gallons or about 22 liters
[d] 10 That is, probably about 360 pounds or about 160 kilograms [e] 10 That is, probably about 36 pounds or about 16 kilograms

15 So people will be brought low
and everyone humbled,
the eyes of the arrogant humbled.
16 But the LORD Almighty will be exalted by
his justice,
and the holy God will be proved holy by
his righteous acts.
17 Then sheep will graze as in their own
pasture;
lambs will feed[a] among the ruins of the
rich.

18 Woe to those who draw sin along with
cords of deceit,
and wickedness as with cart ropes,
19 to those who say, "Let God hurry;
let him hasten his work
so we may see it.
The plan of the Holy One of Israel—
let it approach, let it come into view,
so we may know it."

20 Woe to those who call evil good
and good evil,
who put darkness for light
and light for darkness,
who put bitter for sweet
and sweet for bitter.

21 Woe to those who are wise in their own
eyes
and clever in their own sight.

22 Woe to those who are heroes at drinking
wine
and champions at mixing drinks,
23 who acquit the guilty for a bribe,
but deny justice to the innocent.
24 Therefore, as tongues of fire lick up
straw
and as dry grass sinks down in the
flames,
so their roots will decay
and their flowers blow away like dust;
for they have rejected the law of the LORD
Almighty
and spurned the word of the Holy One
of Israel.
25 Therefore the LORD's anger burns against
his people;
his hand is raised and he strikes them
down.
The mountains shake,
and the dead bodies are like refuse in
the streets.

Yet for all this, his anger is not turned
away,
his hand is still upraised.

26 He lifts up a banner for the distant
nations,
he whistles for those at the ends of the
earth.
Here they come,
swiftly and speedily!
27 Not one of them grows tired or stumbles,
not one slumbers or sleeps;
not a belt is loosened at the waist,
not a sandal strap is broken.
28 Their arrows are sharp,
all their bows are strung;
their horses' hooves seem like flint,
their chariot wheels like a whirlwind.
29 Their roar is like that of the lion,
they roar like young lions;
they growl as they seize their prey
and carry it off with no one to rescue.
30 In that day they will roar over it
like the roaring of the sea.
And if one looks at the land,
there is only darkness and distress;
even the sun will be darkened by
clouds.

Isaiah's Commission

6 In the year that King Uzziah died, I saw
the Lord, high and exalted, seated on a
throne; and the train of his robe filled the temple. 2 Above him were seraphim, each with six
wings: With two wings they covered their faces, with two they covered their feet, and with
two they were flying. 3 And they were calling
to one another:

"Holy, holy, holy is the LORD Almighty;
the whole earth is full of his glory."

4 At the sound of their voices the doorposts and
thresholds shook and the temple was filled
with smoke.
5 "Woe to me!" I cried. "I am ruined! For I
am a man of unclean lips, and I live among a
people of unclean lips, and my eyes have seen
the King, the LORD Almighty."
6 Then one of the seraphim flew to me with
a live coal in his hand, which he had taken
with tongs from the altar. 7 With it he touched
my mouth and said, "See, this has touched
your lips; your guilt is taken away and your
sin atoned for."
8 Then I heard the voice of the Lord saying,
"Whom shall I send? And who will go for us?"
And I said, "Here am I. Send me!"
9 He said, "Go and tell this people:
"'Be ever hearing, but never
understanding;
be ever seeing, but never perceiving.'
10 Make the heart of this people calloused;
make their ears dull
and close their eyes.[b]
Otherwise they might see with their eyes,
hear with their ears,
understand with their hearts,
and turn and be healed."

11 Then I said, "For how long, Lord?"
And he answered:

"Until the cities lie ruined
and without inhabitant,
until the houses are left deserted
and the fields ruined and ravaged,
12 until the LORD has sent everyone far away
and the land is utterly forsaken.

[a] *17* Septuagint; Hebrew / *strangers will eat* [b] *9,10* Hebrew; Septuagint *'You will be ever hearing, but never understanding; / you will be ever seeing, but never perceiving.' / 10 This people's heart has become calloused; / they hardly hear with their ears, / and they have closed their eyes*

13And though a tenth remains in the land,
it will again be laid waste.
But as the terebinth and oak
leave stumps when they are cut down,
so the holy seed will be the stump in
the land."

The Sign of Immanuel

7 When Ahaz son of Jotham, the son of Uzziah, was king of Judah, King Rezin of
Aram and Pekah son of Remaliah king of Israel marched up to fight against Jerusalem,
but they could not overpower it.
2Now the house of David was told, "Aram
has allied itself with[a] Ephraim"; so the hearts
of Ahaz and his people were shaken, as the
trees of the forest are shaken by the wind.
3Then the LORD said to Isaiah, "Go out, you
and your son Shear-Jashub,[b] to meet Ahaz at
the end of the aqueduct of the Upper Pool, on
the road to the Launderer's Field. 4Say to him,
'Be careful, keep calm and don't be afraid. Do
not lose heart because of these two smoldering
stubs of firewood—because of the fierce anger
of Rezin and Aram and of the son of Remaliah.
5Aram, Ephraim and Remaliah's son have plotted your ruin, saying, 6"Let us invade Judah; let
us tear it apart and divide it among ourselves,
and make the son of Tabeel king over it." 7Yet
this is what the Sovereign LORD says:

"'It will not take place,
it will not happen,
8for the head of Aram is Damascus,
and the head of Damascus is only
Rezin.
Within sixty-five years
Ephraim will be too shattered to be a
people.
9The head of Ephraim is Samaria,
and the head of Samaria is only
Remaliah's son.
If you do not stand firm in your faith,
you will not stand at all.'"

10Again the LORD spoke to Ahaz, 11"Ask the
LORD your God for a sign, whether in the deepest depths or in the highest heights."
12But Ahaz said, "I will not ask; I will not
put the LORD to the test."
13Then Isaiah said, "Hear now, you house of
David! Is it not enough to try the patience of
humans? Will you try the patience of my God
also? 14Therefore the Lord himself will give
you[c] a sign: The virgin[d] will conceive and give
birth to a son, and[e] will call him Immanuel.[f]
15He will be eating curds and honey when he
knows enough to reject the wrong and choose
the right, 16for before the boy knows enough
to reject the wrong and choose the right, the
land of the two kings you dread will be laid
waste. 17The LORD will bring on you and on
your people and on the house of your father
a time unlike any since Ephraim broke away
from Judah—he will bring the king of Assyria."

Assyria, the LORD's Instrument

18In that day the LORD will whistle for flies
from the Nile delta in Egypt and for bees from
the land of Assyria. 19They will all come and
settle in the steep ravines and in the crevices
in the rocks, on all the thornbushes and at all
the water holes. 20In that day the Lord will use
a razor hired from beyond the Euphrates River—the king of Assyria—to shave your head
and private parts, and to cut off your beard
also. 21In that day, a person will keep alive a
young cow and two goats. 22And because of
the abundance of the milk they give, there
will be curds to eat. All who remain in the
land will eat curds and honey. 23In that day,
in every place where there were a thousand
vines worth a thousand silver shekels,[g] there
will be only briers and thorns. 24Hunters will
go there with bow and arrow, for the land will
be covered with briers and thorns. 25As for all
the hills once cultivated by the hoe, you will
no longer go there for fear of the briers and
thorns; they will become places where cattle
are turned loose and where sheep run.

Isaiah and His Children as Signs

8 The LORD said to me, "Take a large scroll
and write on it with an ordinary pen: Maher-Shalal-Hash-Baz."[h] 2So I called in Uriah
the priest and Zechariah son of Jeberekiah
as reliable witnesses for me. 3Then I made
love to the prophetess, and she conceived and
gave birth to a son. And the LORD said to me,
"Name him Maher-Shalal-Hash-Baz. 4For before the boy knows how to say 'My father' or
'My mother,' the wealth of Damascus and the
plunder of Samaria will be carried off by the
king of Assyria."
5The LORD spoke to me again:

6"Because this people has rejected
the gently flowing waters of Shiloah
and rejoices over Rezin
and the son of Remaliah,
7therefore the Lord is about to bring
against them
the mighty floodwaters of the
Euphrates—
the king of Assyria with all his pomp.
It will overflow all its channels,
run over all its banks
8and sweep on into Judah, swirling over it,
passing through it and reaching up to
the neck.
Its outspread wings will cover the
breadth of your land,
Immanuel[f]!"
9Raise the war cry,[i] you nations, and be
shattered!
Listen, all you distant lands.

[a] 2 Or *has set up camp in*
[b] 3 *Shear-Jashub* means *a remnant will return.*
[c] 14 The Hebrew is plural.
[d] 14 Or *young woman*
[e] 14 Masoretic Text; Dead Sea Scrolls *son, and he* or *son, and they*
[f] *14,8 Immanuel* means *God with us.*
[g] *23* That is, about 25 pounds or about 12 kilograms
[h] *1 Maher-Shalal-Hash-Baz* means *quick to the plunder, swift to the spoil*; also in verse 3.
[i] *9* Or *Do your worst*

Prepare for battle, and be shattered!
Prepare for battle, and be shattered!
10 Devise your strategy, but it will be thwarted;
propose your plan, but it will not stand,
for God is with us.[a]

11 This is what the LORD says to me with his strong hand upon me, warning me not to follow the way of this people:

12 "Do not call conspiracy
everything this people calls a conspiracy;
do not fear what they fear,
and do not dread it.
13 The LORD Almighty is the one you are to regard as holy,
he is the one you are to fear,
he is the one you are to dread.
14 He will be a holy place;
for both Israel and Judah he will be
a stone that causes people to stumble
and a rock that makes them fall.
And for the people of Jerusalem he will be
a trap and a snare.
15 Many of them will stumble;
they will fall and be broken,
they will be snared and captured."

16 Bind up this testimony of warning
and seal up God's instruction among my disciples.
17 I will wait for the LORD,
who is hiding his face from the descendants of Jacob.
I will put my trust in him.

18 Here am I, and the children the LORD has given me. We are signs and symbols in Israel from the LORD Almighty, who dwells on Mount Zion.

The Darkness Turns to Light

19 When someone tells you to consult mediums and spiritists, who whisper and mutter, should not a people inquire of their God? Why consult the dead on behalf of the living?
20 Consult God's instruction and the testimony of warning. If anyone does not speak according to this word, they have no light of dawn. 21 Distressed and hungry, they will roam through the land; when they are famished, they will become enraged and, looking upward, will curse their king and their God.
22 Then they will look toward the earth and see only distress and darkness and fearful gloom, and they will be thrust into utter darkness.
9[b] Nevertheless, there will be no more gloom for those who were in distress. In the past he humbled the land of Zebulun and the land of Naphtali, but in the future he will honor Galilee of the nations, by the Way of the Sea, beyond the Jordan—

2 The people walking in darkness
have seen a great light;
on those living in the land of deep darkness
a light has dawned.
3 You have enlarged the nation
and increased their joy;
they rejoice before you
as people rejoice at the harvest,
as warriors rejoice
when dividing the plunder.
4 For as in the day of Midian's defeat,
you have shattered
the yoke that burdens them,
the bar across their shoulders,
the rod of their oppressor.
5 Every warrior's boot used in battle
and every garment rolled in blood
will be destined for burning,
will be fuel for the fire.
6 For to us a child is born,
to us a son is given,
and the government will be on his shoulders.
And he will be called
Wonderful Counselor, Mighty God,
Everlasting Father, Prince of Peace.
7 Of the greatness of his government and peace
there will be no end.
He will reign on David's throne
and over his kingdom,
establishing and upholding it
with justice and righteousness
from that time on and forever.
The zeal of the LORD Almighty
will accomplish this.

The LORD's Anger Against Israel

8 The Lord has sent a message against Jacob;
it will fall on Israel.
9 All the people will know it—
Ephraim and the inhabitants of Samaria—
who say with pride
and arrogance of heart,
10 "The bricks have fallen down,
but we will rebuild with dressed stone;
the fig trees have been felled,
but we will replace them with cedars."
11 But the LORD has strengthened Rezin's foes against them
and has spurred their enemies on.
12 Arameans from the east and Philistines from the west
have devoured Israel with open mouth.

Yet for all this, his anger is not turned away,
his hand is still upraised.

13 But the people have not returned to him who struck them,
nor have they sought the LORD Almighty.
14 So the LORD will cut off from Israel both head and tail,
both palm branch and reed in a single day;
15 the elders and dignitaries are the head,
the prophets who teach lies are the tail.

[a] 10 Hebrew *Immanuel* [b] In Hebrew texts 9:1 is numbered 8:23, and 9:2-21 is numbered 9:1-20.

16 Those who guide this people mislead them,
and those who are guided are led astray.
17 Therefore the Lord will take no pleasure in the young men,
nor will he pity the fatherless and widows,
for everyone is ungodly and wicked,
every mouth speaks folly.

Yet for all this, his anger is not turned away,
his hand is still upraised.

18 Surely wickedness burns like a fire;
it consumes briers and thorns,
it sets the forest thickets ablaze,
so that it rolls upward in a column of smoke.
19 By the wrath of the LORD Almighty
the land will be scorched
and the people will be fuel for the fire;
they will not spare one another.
20 On the right they will devour,
but still be hungry;
on the left they will eat,
but not be satisfied.
Each will feed on the flesh of their own offspring[a]:
21 Manasseh will feed on Ephraim, and Ephraim on Manasseh;
together they will turn against Judah.

Yet for all this, his anger is not turned away,
his hand is still upraised.

10 Woe to those who make unjust laws,
to those who issue oppressive decrees,
2 to deprive the poor of their rights
and withhold justice from the oppressed of my people,
making widows their prey
and robbing the fatherless.
3 What will you do on the day of reckoning,
when disaster comes from afar?
To whom will you run for help?
Where will you leave your riches?
4 Nothing will remain but to cringe among the captives
or fall among the slain.

Yet for all this, his anger is not turned away,
his hand is still upraised.

God's Judgment on Assyria

5 "Woe to the Assyrian, the rod of my anger,
in whose hand is the club of my wrath!
6 I send him against a godless nation,
I dispatch him against a people who anger me,
to seize loot and snatch plunder,
and to trample them down like mud in the streets.
7 But this is not what he intends,
this is not what he has in mind;
his purpose is to destroy,
to put an end to many nations.
8 'Are not my commanders all kings?' he says.
9 'Has not Kalno fared like Carchemish?
Is not Hamath like Arpad,
and Samaria like Damascus?
10 As my hand seized the kingdoms of the idols,
kingdoms whose images excelled those of Jerusalem and Samaria—
11 shall I not deal with Jerusalem and her images
as I dealt with Samaria and her idols?' "

12 When the Lord has finished all his work
against Mount Zion and Jerusalem, he will
say, "I will punish the king of Assyria for the
willful pride of his heart and the haughty look
in his eyes. 13 For he says:

" 'By the strength of my hand I have done this,
and by my wisdom, because I have understanding.
I removed the boundaries of nations,
I plundered their treasures;
like a mighty one I subdued[b] their kings.
14 As one reaches into a nest,
so my hand reached for the wealth of the nations;
as people gather abandoned eggs,
so I gathered all the countries;
not one flapped a wing,
or opened its mouth to chirp.' "

15 Does the ax raise itself above the person who swings it,
or the saw boast against the one who uses it?
As if a rod were to wield the person who lifts it up,
or a club brandish the one who is not wood!
16 Therefore, the Lord, the LORD Almighty,
will send a wasting disease upon his sturdy warriors;
under his pomp a fire will be kindled
like a blazing flame.
17 The Light of Israel will become a fire,
their Holy One a flame;
in a single day it will burn and consume
his thorns and his briers.
18 The splendor of his forests and fertile fields
it will completely destroy,
as when a sick person wastes away.
19 And the remaining trees of his forests
will be so few
that a child could write them down.

The Remnant of Israel

20 In that day the remnant of Israel,
the survivors of Jacob,
will no longer rely on him
who struck them down
but will truly rely on the LORD,
the Holy One of Israel.

[a] 20 Or *arm* [b] 13 Or *treasures; / I subdued the mighty,*

21 A remnant will return,[a] a remnant of Jacob
will return to the Mighty God.
22 Though your people be like the sand by the sea, Israel,
only a remnant will return.
Destruction has been decreed,
overwhelming and righteous.
23 The Lord, the LORD Almighty, will carry out
the destruction decreed upon the whole land.

24 Therefore this is what the Lord, the LORD Almighty, says:

"My people who live in Zion,
do not be afraid of the Assyrians,
who beat you with a rod
and lift up a club against you, as Egypt did.
25 Very soon my anger against you will end
and my wrath will be directed to their destruction."
26 The LORD Almighty will lash them with a whip,
as when he struck down Midian at the rock of Oreb;
and he will raise his staff over the waters,
as he did in Egypt.
27 In that day their burden will be lifted
from your shoulders,
their yoke from your neck;
the yoke will be broken
because you have grown so fat.[b]

28 They enter Aiath;
they pass through Migron;
they store supplies at Mikmash.
29 They go over the pass, and say,
"We will camp overnight at Geba."
Ramah trembles;
Gibeah of Saul flees.
30 Cry out, Daughter Gallim!
Listen, Laishah!
Poor Anathoth!
31 Madmenah is in flight;
the people of Gebim take cover.
32 This day they will halt at Nob;
they will shake their fist
at the mount of Daughter Zion,
at the hill of Jerusalem.

33 See, the Lord, the LORD Almighty,
will lop off the boughs with great power.
The lofty trees will be felled,
the tall ones will be brought low.
34 He will cut down the forest thickets with an ax;
Lebanon will fall before the Mighty One.

The Branch From Jesse

11 A shoot will come up from the stump of Jesse;
from his roots a Branch will bear fruit.
2 The Spirit of the LORD will rest on him—
the Spirit of wisdom and of understanding,
the Spirit of counsel and of might,
the Spirit of the knowledge and fear of the LORD—
3 and he will delight in the fear of the LORD.

He will not judge by what he sees with his eyes,
or decide by what he hears with his ears;
4 but with righteousness he will judge the needy,
with justice he will give decisions for the poor of the earth.
He will strike the earth with the rod of his mouth;
with the breath of his lips he will slay the wicked.
5 Righteousness will be his belt
and faithfulness the sash around his waist.

6 The wolf will live with the lamb,
the leopard will lie down with the goat,
the calf and the lion and the yearling[c] together;
and a little child will lead them.
7 The cow will feed with the bear,
their young will lie down together,
and the lion will eat straw like the ox.
8 The infant will play near the cobra's den,
and the young child will put its hand into the viper's nest.
9 They will neither harm nor destroy
on all my holy mountain,
for the earth will be filled with the knowledge of the LORD
as the waters cover the sea.

10 In that day the Root of Jesse will stand as
a banner for the peoples; the nations will rally
to him, and his resting place will be glorious.
11 In that day the Lord will reach out his hand a
second time to reclaim the surviving remnant
of his people from Assyria, from Lower Egypt,
from Upper Egypt, from Cush,[d] from Elam,
from Babylonia,[e] from Hamath and from the
islands of the Mediterranean.

12 He will raise a banner for the nations
and gather the exiles of Israel;
he will assemble the scattered people of Judah
from the four quarters of the earth.
13 Ephraim's jealousy will vanish,
and Judah's enemies[f] will be destroyed;
Ephraim will not be jealous of Judah,
nor Judah hostile toward Ephraim.
14 They will swoop down on the slopes of Philistia to the west;
together they will plunder the people to the east.
They will subdue Edom and Moab,
and the Ammonites will be subject to them.

[a] 21 Hebrew *shear-jashub* (see 7:3 and note); also in verse 22 [b] 27 Hebrew; Septuagint *broken / from your shoulders* [c] 6 Hebrew; Septuagint *lion will feed* [d] 11 That is, the upper Nile region [e] 11 Hebrew *Shinar* [f] 13 Or *hostility*

15 The LORD will dry up
the gulf of the Egyptian sea;
with a scorching wind he will sweep his hand
over the Euphrates River.
He will break it up into seven streams
so that anyone can cross over in sandals.
16 There will be a highway for the remnant of his people
that is left from Assyria,
as there was for Israel
when they came up from Egypt.

Songs of Praise

12 In that day you will say:

"I will praise you, LORD.
Although you were angry with me,
your anger has turned away
and you have comforted me.
2 Surely God is my salvation;
I will trust and not be afraid.
The LORD, the LORD himself, is my strength and my defense[a];
he has become my salvation."
3 With joy you will draw water
from the wells of salvation.

4 In that day you will say:

"Give praise to the LORD, proclaim his name;
make known among the nations what he has done,
and proclaim that his name is exalted.
5 Sing to the LORD, for he has done glorious things;
let this be known to all the world.
6 Shout aloud and sing for joy, people of Zion,
for great is the Holy One of Israel
among you."

A Prophecy Against Babylon

13 A prophecy against Babylon that Isaiah son of Amoz saw:

2 Raise a banner on a bare hilltop,
shout to them;
beckon to them
to enter the gates of the nobles.
3 I have commanded those I prepared for battle;
I have summoned my warriors to carry out my wrath—
those who rejoice in my triumph.

4 Listen, a noise on the mountains,
like that of a great multitude!
Listen, an uproar among the kingdoms,
like nations massing together!
The LORD Almighty is mustering
an army for war.
5 They come from faraway lands,
from the ends of the heavens—
the LORD and the weapons of his wrath—
to destroy the whole country.

6 Wail, for the day of the LORD is near;
it will come like destruction from the Almighty.[b]
7 Because of this, all hands will go limp,
every heart will melt with fear.
8 Terror will seize them,
pain and anguish will grip them;
they will writhe like a woman in labor.
They will look aghast at each other,
their faces aflame.

9 See, the day of the LORD is coming
—a cruel day, with wrath and fierce anger—
to make the land desolate
and destroy the sinners within it.
10 The stars of heaven and their constellations
will not show their light.
The rising sun will be darkened
and the moon will not give its light.
11 I will punish the world for its evil,
the wicked for their sins.
I will put an end to the arrogance of the haughty
and will humble the pride of the ruthless.
12 I will make people scarcer than pure gold,
more rare than the gold of Ophir.
13 Therefore I will make the heavens tremble;
and the earth will shake from its place
at the wrath of the LORD Almighty,
in the day of his burning anger.

14 Like a hunted gazelle,
like sheep without a shepherd,
they will all return to their own people,
they will flee to their native land.
15 Whoever is captured will be thrust through;
all who are caught will fall by the sword.
16 Their infants will be dashed to pieces
before their eyes;
their houses will be looted and their wives violated.

17 See, I will stir up against them the Medes,
who do not care for silver
and have no delight in gold.
18 Their bows will strike down the young men;
they will have no mercy on infants,
nor will they look with compassion on children.
19 Babylon, the jewel of kingdoms,
the pride and glory of the Babylonians,[c]
will be overthrown by God
like Sodom and Gomorrah.
20 She will never be inhabited
or lived in through all generations;
there no nomads will pitch their tents,
there no shepherds will rest their flocks.
21 But desert creatures will lie there,
jackals will fill her houses;
there the owls will dwell,
and there the wild goats will leap about.

[a] 2 Or *song* [b] 6 Hebrew *Shaddai* [c] 19 Or *Chaldeans*

22 Hyenas will inhabit her strongholds,
jackals her luxurious palaces.
Her time is at hand,
and her days will not be prolonged.

14

The LORD will have compassion on Jacob;
once again he will choose Israel
and will settle them in their own land.
Foreigners will join them
and unite with the descendants of Jacob.
2 Nations will take them
and bring them to their own place.
And Israel will take possession of the nations
and make them male and female servants in the LORD's land.
They will make captives of their captors
and rule over their oppressors.

3 On the day the LORD gives you relief from
your suffering and turmoil and from the harsh
labor forced on you, 4 you will take up this
taunt against the king of Babylon:

How the oppressor has come to an end!
How his fury[a] has ended!
5 The LORD has broken the rod of the wicked,
the scepter of the rulers,
6 which in anger struck down peoples
with unceasing blows,
and in fury subdued nations
with relentless aggression.
7 All the lands are at rest and at peace;
they break into singing.
8 Even the junipers and the cedars of Lebanon
gloat over you and say,
"Now that you have been laid low,
no one comes to cut us down."

9 The realm of the dead below is all astir
to meet you at your coming;
it rouses the spirits of the departed to greet you—
all those who were leaders in the world;
it makes them rise from their thrones—
all those who were kings over the nations.
10 They will all respond,
they will say to you,
"You also have become weak, as we are;
you have become like us."
11 All your pomp has been brought down to the grave,
along with the noise of your harps;
maggots are spread out beneath you
and worms cover you.

12 How you have fallen from heaven,
morning star, son of the dawn!
You have been cast down to the earth,
you who once laid low the nations!
13 You said in your heart,
"I will ascend to the heavens;
I will raise my throne
above the stars of God;
I will sit enthroned on the mount of assembly,
on the utmost heights of Mount Zaphon.[b]
14 I will ascend above the tops of the clouds;
I will make myself like the Most High."
15 But you are brought down to the realm of the dead,
to the depths of the pit.

16 Those who see you stare at you,
they ponder your fate:
"Is this the man who shook the earth
and made kingdoms tremble,
17 the man who made the world a wilderness,
who overthrew its cities
and would not let his captives go home?"

18 All the kings of the nations lie in state,
each in his own tomb.
19 But you are cast out of your tomb
like a rejected branch;
you are covered with the slain,
with those pierced by the sword,
those who descend to the stones of the pit.
Like a corpse trampled underfoot,
20 you will not join them in burial,
for you have destroyed your land
and killed your people.

Let the offspring of the wicked
never be mentioned again.
21 Prepare a place to slaughter his children
for the sins of their ancestors;
they are not to rise to inherit the land
and cover the earth with their cities.

22 "I will rise up against them,"
declares the LORD Almighty.
"I will wipe out Babylon's name and survivors,
her offspring and descendants,"
declares the LORD.
23 "I will turn her into a place for owls
and into swampland;
I will sweep her with the broom of destruction,"
declares the LORD Almighty.

24 The LORD Almighty has sworn,

"Surely, as I have planned, so it will be,
and as I have purposed, so it will happen.
25 I will crush the Assyrian in my land;
on my mountains I will trample him down.
His yoke will be taken from my people,
and his burden removed from their shoulders."

26 This is the plan determined for the whole world;
this is the hand stretched out over all nations.

[a] *4* Dead Sea Scrolls, Septuagint and Syriac; the meaning of the word in the Masoretic Text is uncertain. [b] *13* Or *of the north*; Zaphon was the most sacred mountain of the Canaanites.

27 For the LORD Almighty has purposed, and
who can thwart him?
His hand is stretched out, and who can
turn it back?

A Prophecy Against the Philistines

28 This prophecy came in the year King
Ahaz died:

29 Do not rejoice, all you Philistines,
that the rod that struck you is broken;
from the root of that snake will spring up
a viper,
its fruit will be a darting, venomous
serpent.
30 The poorest of the poor will find pasture,
and the needy will lie down in safety.
But your root I will destroy by famine;
it will slay your survivors.
31 Wail, you gate! Howl, you city!
Melt away, all you Philistines!
A cloud of smoke comes from the north,
and there is not a straggler in its ranks.
32 What answer shall be given
to the envoys of that nation?
"The LORD has established Zion,
and in her his afflicted people will find
refuge."

A Prophecy Against Moab

15 A prophecy against Moab:

Ar in Moab is ruined,
destroyed in a night!
Kir in Moab is ruined,
destroyed in a night!
2 Dibon goes up to its temple,
to its high places to weep;
Moab wails over Nebo and Medeba.
Every head is shaved
and every beard cut off.
3 In the streets they wear sackcloth;
on the roofs and in the public squares
they all wail,
prostrate with weeping.
4 Heshbon and Elealeh cry out,
their voices are heard all the way to
Jahaz.
Therefore the armed men of Moab cry out,
and their hearts are faint.

5 My heart cries out over Moab;
her fugitives flee as far as Zoar,
as far as Eglath Shelishiyah.
They go up the hill to Luhith,
weeping as they go;
on the road to Horonaim
they lament their destruction.
6 The waters of Nimrim are dried up
and the grass is withered;
the vegetation is gone
and nothing green is left.
7 So the wealth they have acquired and
stored up
they carry away over the Ravine of the
Poplars.
8 Their outcry echoes along the border of
Moab;
their wailing reaches as far as Eglaim,
their lamentation as far as Beer Elim.
9 The waters of Dimon[a] are full of blood,
but I will bring still more upon
Dimon[a]—
a lion upon the fugitives of Moab
and upon those who remain in the land.

16 Send lambs as tribute
to the ruler of the land,
from Sela, across the desert,
to the mount of Daughter Zion.
2 Like fluttering birds
pushed from the nest,
so are the women of Moab
at the fords of the Arnon.

3 "Make up your mind," Moab says.
"Render a decision.
Make your shadow like night—
at high noon.
Hide the fugitives,
do not betray the refugees.
4 Let the Moabite fugitives stay with you;
be their shelter from the destroyer."

The oppressor will come to an end,
and destruction will cease;
the aggressor will vanish from the
land.
5 In love a throne will be established;
in faithfulness a man will sit on it—
one from the house[b] of David—
one who in judging seeks justice
and speeds the cause of righteousness.

6 We have heard of Moab's pride—
how great is her arrogance!—
of her conceit, her pride and her
insolence;
but her boasts are empty.
7 Therefore the Moabites wail,
they wail together for Moab.
Lament and grieve
for the raisin cakes of Kir Hareseth.
8 The fields of Heshbon wither,
the vines of Sibmah also.
The rulers of the nations
have trampled down the choicest
vines,
which once reached Jazer
and spread toward the desert.
Their shoots spread out
and went as far as the sea.[c]
9 So I weep, as Jazer weeps,
for the vines of Sibmah.
Heshbon and Elealeh,
I drench you with tears!
The shouts of joy over your ripened fruit
and over your harvests have been
stilled.
10 Joy and gladness are taken away from
the orchards;
no one sings or shouts in the vineyards;
no one treads out wine at the presses,
for I have put an end to the shouting.

[a] 9 *Dimon*, a wordplay on *Dibon* (see verse 2), sounds like the Hebrew for *blood*. [b] 5 Hebrew *tent*
[c] 8 Probably the Dead Sea

11 My heart laments for Moab like a harp,
my inmost being for Kir Hareseth.
12 When Moab appears at her high place,
she only wears herself out;
when she goes to her shrine to pray,
it is to no avail.

13 This is the word the LORD has already spoken concerning Moab. 14 But now the LORD
says: "Within three years, as a servant bound
by contract would count them, Moab's splendor and all her many people will be despised,
and her survivors will be very few and feeble."

A Prophecy Against Damascus

17 A prophecy against Damascus:

"See, Damascus will no longer be a city
but will become a heap of ruins.
2 The cities of Aroer will be deserted
and left to flocks, which will lie down,
with no one to make them afraid.
3 The fortified city will disappear from
Ephraim,
and royal power from Damascus;
the remnant of Aram will be
like the glory of the Israelites,"
declares the LORD Almighty.

4 "In that day the glory of Jacob will fade;
the fat of his body will waste away.
5 It will be as when reapers harvest the
standing grain,
gathering the grain in their arms—
as when someone gleans heads of grain
in the Valley of Rephaim.
6 Yet some gleanings will remain,
as when an olive tree is beaten,
leaving two or three olives on the topmost
branches,
four or five on the fruitful boughs,"
declares the LORD, the God
of Israel.

7 In that day people will look to their
Maker
and turn their eyes to the Holy One of
Israel.
8 They will not look to the altars,
the work of their hands,
and they will have no regard for the
Asherah poles[a]
and the incense altars their fingers
have made.

9 In that day their strong cities, which they
left because of the Israelites, will be like places abandoned to thickets and undergrowth.
And all will be desolation.

10 You have forgotten God your Savior;
you have not remembered the Rock,
your fortress.
Therefore, though you set out the finest
plants
and plant imported vines,
11 though on the day you set them out, you
make them grow,
and on the morning when you plant
them, you bring them to bud,
yet the harvest will be as nothing
in the day of disease and incurable
pain.

12 Woe to the many nations that rage—
they rage like the raging sea!
Woe to the peoples who roar—
they roar like the roaring of great waters!
13 Although the peoples roar like the roar of
surging waters,
when he rebukes them they flee far
away,
driven before the wind like chaff on the
hills,
like tumbleweed before a gale.
14 In the evening, sudden terror!
Before the morning, they are gone!
This is the portion of those who loot us,
the lot of those who plunder us.

A Prophecy Against Cush

18 Woe to the land of whirring wings[b]
along the rivers of Cush,[c]
2 which sends envoys by sea
in papyrus boats over the water.

Go, swift messengers,
to a people tall and smooth-skinned,
to a people feared far and wide,
an aggressive nation of strange speech,
whose land is divided by rivers.

3 All you people of the world,
you who live on the earth,
when a banner is raised on the
mountains,
you will see it,
and when a trumpet sounds,
you will hear it.
4 This is what the LORD says to me:
"I will remain quiet and will look on
from my dwelling place,
like shimmering heat in the sunshine,
like a cloud of dew in the heat of
harvest."
5 For, before the harvest, when the blossom
is gone
and the flower becomes a ripening
grape,
he will cut off the shoots with pruning
knives,
and cut down and take away the
spreading branches.
6 They will all be left to the mountain birds
of prey
and to the wild animals;
the birds will feed on them all summer,
the wild animals all winter.

7 At that time gifts will be brought to the
LORD Almighty

from a people tall and smooth-skinned,
from a people feared far and wide,
an aggressive nation of strange speech,
whose land is divided by rivers—

[a] *8* That is, wooden symbols of the goddess Asherah
[b] *1* Or *of locusts*
[c] *1* That is, the upper Nile region

the gifts will be brought to Mount Zion, the
place of the Name of the LORD Almighty.

A Prophecy Against Egypt

19 A prophecy against Egypt:

See, the LORD rides on a swift cloud
and is coming to Egypt.
The idols of Egypt tremble before him,
and the hearts of the Egyptians melt
with fear.

2 "I will stir up Egyptian against
Egyptian—
brother will fight against brother,
neighbor against neighbor,
city against city,
kingdom against kingdom.
3 The Egyptians will lose heart,
and I will bring their plans to nothing;
they will consult the idols and the spirits
of the dead,
the mediums and the spiritists.
4 I will hand the Egyptians over
to the power of a cruel master,
and a fierce king will rule over them,"
declares the Lord, the LORD Almighty.

5 The waters of the river will dry up,
and the riverbed will be parched and
dry.
6 The canals will stink;
the streams of Egypt will dwindle and
dry up.
The reeds and rushes will wither,
7 also the plants along the Nile,
at the mouth of the river.
Every sown field along the Nile
will become parched, will blow away
and be no more.
8 The fishermen will groan and lament,
all who cast hooks into the Nile;
those who throw nets on the water
will pine away.
9 Those who work with combed flax will
despair,
the weavers of fine linen will lose hope.
10 The workers in cloth will be dejected,
and all the wage earners will be sick at
heart.

11 The officials of Zoan are nothing but fools;
the wise counselors of Pharaoh give
senseless advice.
How can you say to Pharaoh,
"I am one of the wise men,
a disciple of the ancient kings"?

12 Where are your wise men now?
Let them show you and make known
what the LORD Almighty
has planned against Egypt.
13 The officials of Zoan have become fools,
the leaders of Memphis are deceived;
the cornerstones of her peoples
have led Egypt astray.
14 The LORD has poured into them
a spirit of dizziness;
they make Egypt stagger in all that she
does,
as a drunkard staggers around in his
vomit.
15 There is nothing Egypt can do—
head or tail, palm branch or reed.

16 In that day the Egyptians will become
weaklings. They will shudder with fear at
the uplifted hand that the LORD Almighty
raises against them. 17 And the land of Judah
will bring terror to the Egyptians; everyone
to whom Judah is mentioned will be terrified,
because of what the LORD Almighty is planning against them.

18 In that day five cities in Egypt will speak
the language of Canaan and swear allegiance
to the LORD Almighty. One of them will be
called the City of the Sun.[a]

19 In that day there will be an altar to the
LORD in the heart of Egypt, and a monument
to the LORD at its border. 20 It will be a sign and
witness to the LORD Almighty in the land of
Egypt. When they cry out to the LORD because
of their oppressors, he will send them a savior
and defender, and he will rescue them. 21 So the
LORD will make himself known to the Egyptians, and in that day they will acknowledge
the LORD. They will worship with sacrifices
and grain offerings; they will make vows to
the LORD and keep them. 22 The LORD will strike
Egypt with a plague; he will strike them and
heal them. They will turn to the LORD, and he
will respond to their pleas and heal them.

23 In that day there will be a highway from
Egypt to Assyria. The Assyrians will go to
Egypt and the Egyptians to Assyria. The
Egyptians and Assyrians will worship together. 24 In that day Israel will be the third, along
with Egypt and Assyria, a blessing[b] on the
earth. 25 The LORD Almighty will bless them,
saying, "Blessed be Egypt my people, Assyria
my handiwork, and Israel my inheritance."

A Prophecy Against Egypt and Cush

20 In the year that the supreme commander, sent by Sargon king of Assyria, came
to Ashdod and attacked and captured it—
2 at that time the LORD spoke through Isaiah
son of Amoz. He said to him, "Take off the
sackcloth from your body and the sandals
from your feet." And he did so, going around
stripped and barefoot.

3 Then the LORD said, "Just as my servant
Isaiah has gone stripped and barefoot for
three years, as a sign and portent against
Egypt and Cush,[c] 4 so the king of Assyria will
lead away stripped and barefoot the Egyptian captives and Cushite exiles, young and
old, with buttocks bared—to Egypt's shame.
5 Those who trusted in Cush and boasted in
Egypt will be dismayed and put to shame.
6 In that day the people who live on this coast

[a] *18* Some manuscripts of the Masoretic Text, Dead Sea Scrolls, Symmachus and Vulgate; most manuscripts of the Masoretic Text *City of Destruction* [b] *24* Or *Assyria, whose names will be used in blessings* (see Gen. 48:20); or *Assyria, who will be seen by others as blessed* [c] *3* That is, the upper Nile region; also in verse 5

will say, 'See what has happened to those we relied on, those we fled to for help and deliverance from the king of Assyria! How then can we escape?'"

A Prophecy Against Babylon

21 A prophecy against the Desert by the Sea:

Like whirlwinds sweeping through the southland,
an invader comes from the desert,
from a land of terror.

2 A dire vision has been shown to me:
The traitor betrays, the looter takes loot.
Elam, attack! Media, lay siege!
I will bring to an end all the groaning she caused.

3 At this my body is racked with pain,
pangs seize me, like those of a woman in labor;
I am staggered by what I hear,
I am bewildered by what I see.
4 My heart falters,
fear makes me tremble;
the twilight I longed for
has become a horror to me.

5 They set the tables,
they spread the rugs,
they eat, they drink!
Get up, you officers,
oil the shields!

6 This is what the Lord says to me:

"Go, post a lookout
and have him report what he sees.
7 When he sees chariots
with teams of horses,
riders on donkeys
or riders on camels,
let him be alert,
fully alert."

8 And the lookout[a] shouted,

"Day after day, my lord, I stand on the watchtower;
every night I stay at my post.
9 Look, here comes a man in a chariot
with a team of horses.
And he gives back the answer:
'Babylon has fallen, has fallen!
All the images of its gods
lie shattered on the ground!'"

10 My people who are crushed on the threshing floor,
I tell you what I have heard
from the LORD Almighty,
from the God of Israel.

A Prophecy Against Edom

11 A prophecy against Dumah[b]:

Someone calls to me from Seir,
"Watchman, what is left of the night?
Watchman, what is left of the night?"
12 The watchman replies,
"Morning is coming, but also the night.
If you would ask, then ask;
and come back yet again."

A Prophecy Against Arabia

13 A prophecy against Arabia:

You caravans of Dedanites,
who camp in the thickets of Arabia,
14 bring water for the thirsty;
you who live in Tema,
bring food for the fugitives.
15 They flee from the sword,
from the drawn sword,
from the bent bow
and from the heat of battle.

16 This is what the Lord says to me: "Within one year, as a servant bound by contract
would count it, all the splendor of Kedar will
come to an end. 17 The survivors of the archers,
the warriors of Kedar, will be few." The LORD,
the God of Israel, has spoken.

A Prophecy About Jerusalem

22 A prophecy against the Valley of Vision:

What troubles you now,
that you have all gone up on the roofs,
2 you town so full of commotion,
you city of tumult and revelry?
Your slain were not killed by the sword,
nor did they die in battle.
3 All your leaders have fled together;
they have been captured without using the bow.
All you who were caught were taken prisoner together,
having fled while the enemy was still far away.
4 Therefore I said, "Turn away from me;
let me weep bitterly.
Do not try to console me
over the destruction of my people."

5 The Lord, the LORD Almighty, has a day
of tumult and trampling and terror
in the Valley of Vision,
a day of battering down walls
and of crying out to the mountains.
6 Elam takes up the quiver,
with her charioteers and horses;
Kir uncovers the shield.
7 Your choicest valleys are full of chariots,
and horsemen are posted at the city gates.

8 The Lord stripped away the defenses of Judah,
and you looked in that day
to the weapons in the Palace of the Forest.
9 You saw that the walls of the City of David
were broken through in many places;
you stored up water
in the Lower Pool.

[a] 8 Dead Sea Scrolls and Syriac; Masoretic Text *A lion* [b] 11 *Dumah*, a wordplay on *Edom*, means *silence* or *stillness*.

10 You counted the buildings in Jerusalem
and tore down houses to strengthen the wall.
11 You built a reservoir between the two walls
for the water of the Old Pool,
but you did not look to the One who made it,
or have regard for the One who planned it long ago.

12 The Lord, the LORD Almighty,
called you on that day
to weep and to wail,
to tear out your hair and put on sackcloth.
13 But see, there is joy and revelry,
slaughtering of cattle and killing of sheep,
eating of meat and drinking of wine!
"Let us eat and drink," you say,
"for tomorrow we die!"

14 The LORD Almighty has revealed this in
my hearing: "Till your dying day this sin will
not be atoned for," says the Lord, the LORD
Almighty.

15 This is what the Lord, the LORD Almighty,
says:

"Go, say to this steward,
to Shebna the palace administrator:
16 What are you doing here and who gave you permission
to cut out a grave for yourself here,
hewing your grave on the height
and chiseling your resting place in the rock?

17 "Beware, the LORD is about to take firm hold of you
and hurl you away, you mighty man.
18 He will roll you up tightly like a ball
and throw you into a large country.
There you will die
and there the chariots you were so proud of
will become a disgrace to your master's house.
19 I will depose you from your office,
and you will be ousted from your position.

20 "In that day I will summon my servant,
Eliakim son of Hilkiah. 21 I will clothe him
with your robe and fasten your sash around
him and hand your authority over to him. He
will be a father to those who live in Jerusalem
and to the people of Judah. 22 I will place on
his shoulder the key to the house of David;
what he opens no one can shut, and what he
shuts no one can open. 23 I will drive him like
a peg into a firm place; he will become a seat[a]
of honor for the house of his father. 24 All the
glory of his family will hang on him: its offspring and offshoots—all its lesser vessels,
from the bowls to all the jars.

25 "In that day," declares the LORD Almighty,
"the peg driven into the firm place will give
way; it will be sheared off and will fall, and
the load hanging on it will be cut down." The
LORD has spoken.

A Prophecy Against Tyre

23 A prophecy against Tyre:

Wail, you ships of Tarshish!
For Tyre is destroyed
and left without house or harbor.
From the land of Cyprus
word has come to them.

2 Be silent, you people of the island
and you merchants of Sidon,
whom the seafarers have enriched.
3 On the great waters
came the grain of the Shihor;
the harvest of the Nile[b] was the revenue of Tyre,
and she became the marketplace of the nations.

4 Be ashamed, Sidon, and you fortress of the sea,
for the sea has spoken:
"I have neither been in labor nor given birth;
I have neither reared sons nor brought up daughters."
5 When word comes to Egypt,
they will be in anguish at the report from Tyre.

6 Cross over to Tarshish;
wail, you people of the island.
7 Is this your city of revelry,
the old, old city,
whose feet have taken her
to settle in far-off lands?
8 Who planned this against Tyre,
the bestower of crowns,
whose merchants are princes,
whose traders are renowned in the earth?
9 The LORD Almighty planned it,
to bring down her pride in all her splendor
and to humble all who are renowned on the earth.

10 Till[c] your land as they do along the Nile,
Daughter Tarshish,
for you no longer have a harbor.
11 The LORD has stretched out his hand over the sea
and made its kingdoms tremble.
He has given an order concerning Phoenicia
that her fortresses be destroyed.
12 He said, "No more of your reveling,
Virgin Daughter Sidon, now crushed!

"Up, cross over to Cyprus;
even there you will find no rest."

[a] 23 Or *throne* [b] 2,3 Masoretic Text; Dead Sea Scrolls *Sidon, / who cross over the sea; / your envoys 3are on the great waters. / The grain of the Shihor, / the harvest of the Nile,* [c] 10 Dead Sea Scrolls and some Septuagint manuscripts; Masoretic Text *Go through*

13 Look at the land of the Babylonians,[a]
this people that is now of no account!
The Assyrians have made it
a place for desert creatures;
they raised up their siege towers,
they stripped its fortresses bare
and turned it into a ruin.

14 Wail, you ships of Tarshish;
your fortress is destroyed!

15 At that time Tyre will be forgotten for seventy years, the span of a king's life. But at the
end of these seventy years, it will happen to
Tyre as in the song of the prostitute:

16 "Take up a harp, walk through the city,
you forgotten prostitute;
play the harp well, sing many a song,
so that you will be remembered."

17 At the end of seventy years, the LORD will
deal with Tyre. She will return to her lucrative
prostitution and will ply her trade with all the
kingdoms on the face of the earth. 18 Yet her
profit and her earnings will be set apart for
the LORD; they will not be stored up or hoarded. Her profits will go to those who live before
the LORD, for abundant food and fine clothes.

The LORD's Devastation of the Earth

24 See, the LORD is going to lay waste the
earth
and devastate it;
he will ruin its face
and scatter its inhabitants—
2 it will be the same
for priest as for people,
for the master as for his servant,
for the mistress as for her servant,
for seller as for buyer,
for borrower as for lender,
for debtor as for creditor.
3 The earth will be completely laid waste
and totally plundered.
The LORD has spoken this word.

4 The earth dries up and withers,
the world languishes and withers,
the heavens languish with the earth.
5 The earth is defiled by its people;
they have disobeyed the laws,
violated the statutes
and broken the everlasting covenant.
6 Therefore a curse consumes the earth;
its people must bear their guilt.
Therefore earth's inhabitants are burned
up,
and very few are left.
7 The new wine dries up and the vine
withers;
all the merrymakers groan.
8 The joyful timbrels are stilled,
the noise of the revelers has stopped,
the joyful harp is silent.
9 No longer do they drink wine with a song;
the beer is bitter to its drinkers.
10 The ruined city lies desolate;
the entrance to every house is barred.
11 In the streets they cry out for wine;
all joy turns to gloom,
all joyful sounds are banished from the
earth.
12 The city is left in ruins,
its gate is battered to pieces.
13 So will it be on the earth
and among the nations,
as when an olive tree is beaten,
or as when gleanings are left after the
grape harvest.

14 They raise their voices, they shout for joy;
from the west they acclaim the LORD's
majesty.
15 Therefore in the east give glory to the
LORD;
exalt the name of the LORD, the God of
Israel,
in the islands of the sea.
16 From the ends of the earth we hear
singing:
"Glory to the Righteous One."

But I said, "I waste away, I waste away!
Woe to me!
The treacherous betray!
With treachery the treacherous betray!"
17 Terror and pit and snare await you,
people of the earth.
18 Whoever flees at the sound of terror
will fall into a pit;
whoever climbs out of the pit
will be caught in a snare.

The floodgates of the heavens are opened,
the foundations of the earth shake.
19 The earth is broken up,
the earth is split asunder,
the earth is violently shaken.
20 The earth reels like a drunkard,
it sways like a hut in the wind;
so heavy upon it is the guilt of its
rebellion
that it falls—never to rise again.

21 In that day the LORD will punish
the powers in the heavens above
and the kings on the earth below.
22 They will be herded together
like prisoners bound in a dungeon;
they will be shut up in prison
and be punished[b] after many days.
23 The moon will be dismayed,
the sun ashamed;
for the LORD Almighty will reign
on Mount Zion and in Jerusalem,
and before its elders—with great glory.

Praise to the LORD

25 LORD, you are my God;
I will exalt you and praise your name,
for in perfect faithfulness
you have done wonderful things,
things planned long ago.
2 You have made the city a heap of rubble,
the fortified town a ruin,
the foreigners' stronghold a city no more;
it will never be rebuilt.

[a] 13 Or *Chaldeans* [b] 22 Or *released*

³Therefore strong peoples will honor you;
cities of ruthless nations will revere you.
⁴You have been a refuge for the poor,
a refuge for the needy in their distress,
a shelter from the storm
and a shade from the heat.
For the breath of the ruthless
is like a storm driving against a wall
5 and like the heat of the desert.
You silence the uproar of foreigners;
as heat is reduced by the shadow of a cloud,
so the song of the ruthless is stilled.

6 On this mountain the LORD Almighty will prepare
a feast of rich food for all peoples,
a banquet of aged wine—
the best of meats and the finest of wines.
7 On this mountain he will destroy
the shroud that enfolds all peoples,
the sheet that covers all nations;
8 he will swallow up death forever.
The Sovereign LORD will wipe away the tears
from all faces;
he will remove his people's disgrace
from all the earth.
The LORD has spoken.

9 In that day they will say,

"Surely this is our God;
we trusted in him, and he saved us.
This is the LORD, we trusted in him;
let us rejoice and be glad in his salvation."

10 The hand of the LORD will rest on this mountain;
but Moab will be trampled in their land
as straw is trampled down in the manure.
11 They will stretch out their hands in it,
as swimmers stretch out their hands to swim.
God will bring down their pride
despite the cleverness[a] of their hands.
12 He will bring down your high fortified walls
and lay them low;
he will bring them down to the ground,
to the very dust.

A Song of Praise

26 In that day this song will be sung in the land of Judah:

We have a strong city;
God makes salvation
its walls and ramparts.
2 Open the gates
that the righteous nation may enter,
the nation that keeps faith.
3 You will keep in perfect peace
those whose minds are steadfast,
because they trust in you.
4 Trust in the LORD forever,
for the LORD, the LORD himself, is the Rock eternal.
5 He humbles those who dwell on high,
he lays the lofty city low;
he levels it to the ground
and casts it down to the dust.
6 Feet trample it down—
the feet of the oppressed,
the footsteps of the poor.

7 The path of the righteous is level;
you, the Upright One, make the way of the righteous smooth.
8 Yes, LORD, walking in the way of your laws,[b]
we wait for you;
your name and renown
are the desire of our hearts.
9 My soul yearns for you in the night;
in the morning my spirit longs for you.
When your judgments come upon the earth,
the people of the world learn righteousness.
10 But when grace is shown to the wicked,
they do not learn righteousness;
even in a land of uprightness they go on doing evil
and do not regard the majesty of the LORD.
11 LORD, your hand is lifted high,
but they do not see it.
Let them see your zeal for your people
and be put to shame;
let the fire reserved for your enemies
consume them.

12 LORD, you establish peace for us;
all that we have accomplished you have done for us.
13 LORD our God, other lords besides you
have ruled over us,
but your name alone do we honor.
14 They are now dead, they live no more;
their spirits do not rise.
You punished them and brought them to ruin;
you wiped out all memory of them.
15 You have enlarged the nation, LORD;
you have enlarged the nation.
You have gained glory for yourself;
you have extended all the borders of the land.

16 LORD, they came to you in their distress;
when you disciplined them,
they could barely whisper a prayer.[c]
17 As a pregnant woman about to give birth
writhes and cries out in her pain,
so were we in your presence, LORD.
18 We were with child, we writhed in labor,
but we gave birth to wind.
We have not brought salvation to the earth,
and the people of the world have not come to life.

[a] *11* The meaning of the Hebrew for this word is uncertain. [b] *8* Or *judgments* [c] *16* The meaning of the Hebrew for this clause is uncertain.

19 But your dead will live, LORD;
their bodies will rise—
let those who dwell in the dust
wake up and shout for joy—
your dew is like the dew of the morning;
the earth will give birth to her dead.

20 Go, my people, enter your rooms
and shut the doors behind you;
hide yourselves for a little while
until his wrath has passed by.
21 See, the LORD is coming out of his
dwelling
to punish the people of the earth for
their sins.
The earth will disclose the blood shed on it;
the earth will conceal its slain no
longer.

Deliverance of Israel

27 In that day,

the LORD will punish with his sword—
his fierce, great and powerful sword—
Leviathan the gliding serpent,
Leviathan the coiling serpent;
he will slay the monster of the sea.

2 In that day—

"Sing about a fruitful vineyard:
3 I, the LORD, watch over it;
I water it continually.
I guard it day and night
so that no one may harm it.
4 I am not angry.
If only there were briers and thorns
confronting me!
I would march against them in battle;
I would set them all on fire.
5 Or else let them come to me for refuge;
let them make peace with me,
yes, let them make peace with me."

6 In days to come Jacob will take root,
Israel will bud and blossom
and fill all the world with fruit.
7 Has the LORD struck her
as he struck down those who struck
her?
Has she been killed
as those were killed who killed her?
8 By warfare[a] and exile you contend with
her—
with his fierce blast he drives her out,
as on a day the east wind blows.
9 By this, then, will Jacob's guilt be atoned
for,
and this will be the full fruit of the
removal of his sin:
When he makes all the altar stones
to be like limestone crushed to pieces,
no Asherah poles[b] or incense altars
will be left standing.
10 The fortified city stands desolate,
an abandoned settlement, forsaken like
the wilderness;
there the calves graze,
there they lie down;
they strip its branches bare.
11 When its twigs are dry, they are broken
off
and women come and make fires with
them.
For this is a people without
understanding;
so their Maker has no compassion on
them,
and their Creator shows them no favor.

12 In that day the LORD will thresh from
the flowing Euphrates to the Wadi of Egypt,
and you, Israel, will be gathered up one by
one. 13 And in that day a great trumpet will
sound. Those who were perishing in Assyria
and those who were exiled in Egypt will come
and worship the LORD on the holy mountain
in Jerusalem.

Woe to the Leaders of Ephraim and Judah

28 Woe to that wreath, the pride of
Ephraim's drunkards,
to the fading flower, his glorious
beauty,
set on the head of a fertile valley—
to that city, the pride of those laid low
by wine!
2 See, the Lord has one who is powerful
and strong.
Like a hailstorm and a destructive
wind,
like a driving rain and a flooding
downpour,
he will throw it forcefully to the
ground.
3 That wreath, the pride of Ephraim's
drunkards,
will be trampled underfoot.
4 That fading flower, his glorious beauty,
set on the head of a fertile valley,
will be like figs ripe before harvest—
as soon as people see them and take
them in hand,
they swallow them.

5 In that day the LORD Almighty
will be a glorious crown,
a beautiful wreath
for the remnant of his people.
6 He will be a spirit of justice
to the one who sits in judgment,
a source of strength
to those who turn back the battle at the
gate.

7 And these also stagger from wine
and reel from beer:
Priests and prophets stagger from beer
and are befuddled with wine;
they reel from beer,
they stagger when seeing visions,
they stumble when rendering decisions.
8 All the tables are covered with vomit
and there is not a spot without filth.

[a] 8 See Septuagint; the meaning of the Hebrew for this word is uncertain. [b] 9 That is, wooden symbols of the goddess Asherah

9 "Who is it he is trying to teach?
To whom is he explaining his message?
To children weaned from their milk,
to those just taken from the breast?
10 For it is:
Do this, do that,
a rule for this, a rule for that[a];
a little here, a little there."
11 Very well then, with foreign lips and strange tongues
God will speak to this people,
12 to whom he said,
"This is the resting place, let the weary rest";
and, "This is the place of repose"—
but they would not listen.
13 So then, the word of the LORD to them will become:
Do this, do that,
a rule for this, a rule for that;
a little here, a little there—
so that as they go they will fall backward;
they will be injured and snared and captured.

14 Therefore hear the word of the LORD, you scoffers
who rule this people in Jerusalem.
15 You boast, "We have entered into a covenant with death,
with the realm of the dead we have made an agreement.
When an overwhelming scourge sweeps by,
it cannot touch us,
for we have made a lie our refuge
and falsehood[b] our hiding place."

16 So this is what the Sovereign LORD says:

"See, I lay a stone in Zion, a tested stone,
a precious cornerstone for a sure foundation;
the one who relies on it
will never be stricken with panic.
17 I will make justice the measuring line
and righteousness the plumb line;
hail will sweep away your refuge, the lie,
and water will overflow your hiding place.
18 Your covenant with death will be annulled;
your agreement with the realm of the dead will not stand.
When the overwhelming scourge sweeps by,
you will be beaten down by it.
19 As often as it comes it will carry you away;
morning after morning, by day and by night,
it will sweep through."

The understanding of this message
will bring sheer terror.
20 The bed is too short to stretch out on,
the blanket too narrow to wrap around you.
21 The LORD will rise up as he did at Mount Perazim,
he will rouse himself as in the Valley of Gibeon—
to do his work, his strange work,
and perform his task, his alien task.
22 Now stop your mocking,
or your chains will become heavier;
the Lord, the LORD Almighty, has told me
of the destruction decreed against the whole land.

23 Listen and hear my voice;
pay attention and hear what I say.
24 When a farmer plows for planting, does he plow continually?
Does he keep on breaking up and working the soil?
25 When he has leveled the surface,
does he not sow caraway and scatter cumin?
Does he not plant wheat in its place,[c]
barley in its plot,[c]
and spelt in its field?
26 His God instructs him
and teaches him the right way.

27 Caraway is not threshed with a sledge,
nor is the wheel of a cart rolled over cumin;
caraway is beaten out with a rod,
and cumin with a stick.
28 Grain must be ground to make bread;
so one does not go on threshing it forever.
The wheels of a threshing cart may be rolled over it,
but one does not use horses to grind grain.
29 All this also comes from the LORD Almighty,
whose plan is wonderful,
whose wisdom is magnificent.

Woe to David's City

29 Woe to you, Ariel, Ariel,
the city where David settled!
Add year to year
and let your cycle of festivals go on.
2 Yet I will besiege Ariel;
she will mourn and lament,
she will be to me like an altar hearth.[d]
3 I will encamp against you on all sides;
I will encircle you with towers
and set up my siege works against you.
4 Brought low, you will speak from the ground;
your speech will mumble out of the dust.
Your voice will come ghostlike from the earth;
out of the dust your speech will whisper.

[a] 10 Hebrew / *sav lasav sav lasav* / *kav lakav kav lakav* (probably meaningless sounds mimicking the prophet's words); also in verse 13 [b] 15 Or *false gods* [c] 25 The meaning of the Hebrew for this word is uncertain. [d] 2 The Hebrew for *altar hearth* sounds like the Hebrew for *Ariel*.

5 But your many enemies will become like
fine dust,
the ruthless hordes like blown chaff.
Suddenly, in an instant,
6 the LORD Almighty will come
with thunder and earthquake and great
noise,
with windstorm and tempest and
flames of a devouring fire.
7 Then the hordes of all the nations that
fight against Ariel,
that attack her and her fortress and
besiege her,
will be as it is with a dream,
with a vision in the night—
8 as when a hungry person dreams of
eating,
but awakens hungry still;
as when a thirsty person dreams of
drinking,
but awakens faint and thirsty still.
So will it be with the hordes of all the
nations
that fight against Mount Zion.

9 Be stunned and amazed,
blind yourselves and be sightless;
be drunk, but not from wine,
stagger, but not from beer.
10 The LORD has brought over you a deep
sleep:
He has sealed your eyes (the prophets);
he has covered your heads (the seers).

11 For you this whole vision is nothing but
words sealed in a scroll. And if you give the
scroll to someone who can read, and say,
"Read this, please," they will answer, "I
can't; it is sealed." 12 Or if you give the scroll
to someone who cannot read, and say, "Read
this, please," they will answer, "I don't know
how to read."

13 The Lord says:

"These people come near to me with their
mouth
and honor me with their lips,
but their hearts are far from me.
Their worship of me
is based on merely human rules they
have been taught.[a]
14 Therefore once more I will astound these
people
with wonder upon wonder;
the wisdom of the wise will perish,
the intelligence of the intelligent will
vanish."
15 Woe to those who go to great depths
to hide their plans from the LORD,
who do their work in darkness and
think,
"Who sees us? Who will know?"
16 You turn things upside down,
as if the potter were thought to be like
the clay!
Shall what is formed say to the one who
formed it,
"You did not make me"?
Can the pot say to the potter,
"You know nothing"?
17 In a very short time, will not Lebanon be
turned into a fertile field
and the fertile field seem like a forest?
18 In that day the deaf will hear the words of
the scroll,
and out of gloom and darkness
the eyes of the blind will see.
19 Once more the humble will rejoice in the
LORD;
the needy will rejoice in the Holy One
of Israel.
20 The ruthless will vanish,
the mockers will disappear,
and all who have an eye for evil will be
cut down—
21 those who with a word make someone out
to be guilty,
who ensnare the defender in court
and with false testimony deprive the
innocent of justice.

22 Therefore this is what the LORD, who redeemed Abraham, says to the descendants
of Jacob:

"No longer will Jacob be ashamed;
no longer will their faces grow pale.
23 When they see among them their children,
the work of my hands,
they will keep my name holy;
they will acknowledge the holiness of
the Holy One of Jacob,
and will stand in awe of the God of
Israel.
24 Those who are wayward in spirit will
gain understanding;
those who complain will accept
instruction."

Woe to the Obstinate Nation

30 "Woe to the obstinate children,"
declares the LORD,
"to those who carry out plans that are not
mine,
forming an alliance, but not by my Spirit,
heaping sin upon sin;
2 who go down to Egypt
without consulting me;
who look for help to Pharaoh's protection,
to Egypt's shade for refuge.
3 But Pharaoh's protection will be to your
shame,
Egypt's shade will bring you disgrace.
4 Though they have officials in Zoan
and their envoys have arrived in Hanes,
5 everyone will be put to shame
because of a people useless to them,
who bring neither help nor advantage,
but only shame and disgrace."

6 A prophecy concerning the animals of the
Negev:

Through a land of hardship and distress,
of lions and lionesses,
of adders and darting snakes,

[a] 13 Hebrew; Septuagint *They worship me in vain; / their teachings are merely human rules*

the envoys carry their riches on donkeys' backs,
their treasures on the humps of camels,
to that unprofitable nation,
7 to Egypt, whose help is utterly useless.
Therefore I call her
Rahab the Do-Nothing.

8 Go now, write it on a tablet for them,
inscribe it on a scroll,
that for the days to come
it may be an everlasting witness.
9 For these are rebellious people, deceitful children,
children unwilling to listen to the LORD's instruction.
10 They say to the seers,
"See no more visions!"
and to the prophets,
"Give us no more visions of what is right!
Tell us pleasant things,
prophesy illusions.
11 Leave this way,
get off this path,
and stop confronting us
with the Holy One of Israel!"

12 Therefore this is what the Holy One of Israel says:

"Because you have rejected this message,
relied on oppression
and depended on deceit,
13 this sin will become for you
like a high wall, cracked and bulging,
that collapses suddenly, in an instant.
14 It will break in pieces like pottery,
shattered so mercilessly
that among its pieces not a fragment will be found
for taking coals from a hearth
or scooping water out of a cistern."

15 This is what the Sovereign LORD, the Holy One of Israel, says:

"In repentance and rest is your salvation,
in quietness and trust is your strength,
but you would have none of it.
16 You said, 'No, we will flee on horses.'
Therefore you will flee!
You said, 'We will ride off on swift horses.'
Therefore your pursuers will be swift!
17 A thousand will flee
at the threat of one;
at the threat of five
you will all flee away,
till you are left
like a flagstaff on a mountaintop,
like a banner on a hill."

18 Yet the LORD longs to be gracious to you;
therefore he will rise up to show you compassion.
For the LORD is a God of justice.
Blessed are all who wait for him!

19 People of Zion, who live in Jerusalem, you
will weep no more. How gracious he will be
when you cry for help! As soon as he hears,
he will answer you. 20 Although the Lord gives
you the bread of adversity and the water of
affliction, your teachers will be hidden no
more; with your own eyes you will see them.
21 Whether you turn to the right or to the left,
your ears will hear a voice behind you, saying, "This is the way; walk in it." 22 Then you
will desecrate your idols overlaid with silver
and your images covered with gold; you will
throw them away like a menstrual cloth and
say to them, "Away with you!"

23 He will also send you rain for the seed you
sow in the ground, and the food that comes
from the land will be rich and plentiful. In that
day your cattle will graze in broad meadows.
24 The oxen and donkeys that work the soil
will eat fodder and mash, spread out with fork
and shovel. 25 In the day of great slaughter,
when the towers fall, streams of water will
flow on every high mountain and every lofty
hill. 26 The moon will shine like the sun, and
the sunlight will be seven times brighter, like
the light of seven full days, when the LORD
binds up the bruises of his people and heals
the wounds he inflicted.

27 See, the Name of the LORD comes from afar,
with burning anger and dense clouds of smoke;
his lips are full of wrath,
and his tongue is a consuming fire.
28 His breath is like a rushing torrent,
rising up to the neck.
He shakes the nations in the sieve of destruction;
he places in the jaws of the peoples
a bit that leads them astray.
29 And you will sing
as on the night you celebrate a holy festival;
your hearts will rejoice
as when people playing pipes go up
to the mountain of the LORD,
to the Rock of Israel.
30 The LORD will cause people to hear his majestic voice
and will make them see his arm coming down
with raging anger and consuming fire,
with cloudburst, thunderstorm and hail.
31 The voice of the LORD will shatter Assyria;
with his rod he will strike them down.
32 Every stroke the LORD lays on them
with his punishing club
will be to the music of timbrels and harps,
as he fights them in battle with the blows of his arm.
33 Topheth has long been prepared;
it has been made ready for the king.
Its fire pit has been made deep and wide,
with an abundance of fire and wood;
the breath of the LORD,
like a stream of burning sulfur,
sets it ablaze.

Woe to Those Who Rely on Egypt

31 Woe to those who go down to Egypt
for help,
who rely on horses,
who trust in the multitude of their chariots
and in the great strength of their
horsemen,
but do not look to the Holy One of Israel,
or seek help from the LORD.
2 Yet he too is wise and can bring disaster;
he does not take back his words.
He will rise up against that wicked nation,
against those who help evildoers.
3 But the Egyptians are mere mortals and
not God;
their horses are flesh and not spirit.
When the LORD stretches out his hand,
those who help will stumble,
those who are helped will fall;
all will perish together.

4 This is what the LORD says to me:

"As a lion growls,
a great lion over its prey—
and though a whole band of shepherds
is called together against it,
it is not frightened by their shouts
or disturbed by their clamor—
so the LORD Almighty will come down
to do battle on Mount Zion and on its
heights.
5 Like birds hovering overhead,
the LORD Almighty will shield
Jerusalem;
he will shield it and deliver it,
he will 'pass over' it and will rescue it."

6 Return, you Israelites, to the One you have
so greatly revolted against. 7 For in that day
every one of you will reject the idols of silver
and gold your sinful hands have made.

8 "Assyria will fall by no human sword;
a sword, not of mortals, will devour
them.
They will flee before the sword
and their young men will be put to
forced labor.
9 Their stronghold will fall because of
terror;
at the sight of the battle standard their
commanders will panic,"
declares the LORD,
whose fire is in Zion,
whose furnace is in Jerusalem.

The Kingdom of Righteousness

32 See, a king will reign in righteousness
and rulers will rule with justice.
2 Each one will be like a shelter from the
wind
and a refuge from the storm,
like streams of water in the desert
and the shadow of a great rock in a
thirsty land.
3 Then the eyes of those who see will no
longer be closed,
and the ears of those who hear will
listen.
4 The fearful heart will know and
understand,
and the stammering tongue will be
fluent and clear.
5 No longer will the fool be called noble
nor the scoundrel be highly respected.
6 For fools speak folly,
their hearts are bent on evil:
They practice ungodliness
and spread error concerning the LORD;
the hungry they leave empty
and from the thirsty they withhold
water.
7 Scoundrels use wicked methods,
they make up evil schemes
to destroy the poor with lies,
even when the plea of the needy is just.
8 But the noble make noble plans,
and by noble deeds they stand.

The Women of Jerusalem

9 You women who are so complacent,
rise up and listen to me;
you daughters who feel secure,
hear what I have to say!
10 In little more than a year
you who feel secure will tremble;
the grape harvest will fail,
and the harvest of fruit will not come.
11 Tremble, you complacent women;
shudder, you daughters who feel
secure!
Strip off your fine clothes
and wrap yourselves in rags.
12 Beat your breasts for the pleasant fields,
for the fruitful vines
13 and for the land of my people,
a land overgrown with thorns and
briers—
yes, mourn for all houses of merriment
and for this city of revelry.
14 The fortress will be abandoned,
the noisy city deserted;
citadel and watchtower will become a
wasteland forever,
the delight of donkeys, a pasture for
flocks,
15 till the Spirit is poured on us from on
high,
and the desert becomes a fertile field,
and the fertile field seems like a forest.
16 The LORD's justice will dwell in the
desert,
his righteousness live in the fertile
field.
17 The fruit of that righteousness will be
peace;
its effect will be quietness and
confidence forever.
18 My people will live in peaceful dwelling
places,
in secure homes,
in undisturbed places of rest.
19 Though hail flattens the forest
and the city is leveled completely,
20 how blessed you will be,
sowing your seed by every stream,
and letting your cattle and donkeys
range free.

Distress and Help

33 Woe to you, destroyer,
you who have not been destroyed!
Woe to you, betrayer,
you who have not been betrayed!
When you stop destroying,
you will be destroyed;
when you stop betraying,
you will be betrayed.

2 LORD, be gracious to us;
we long for you.
Be our strength every morning,
our salvation in time of distress.
3 At the uproar of your army, the peoples flee;
when you rise up, the nations scatter.
4 Your plunder, O nations, is harvested as by young locusts;
like a swarm of locusts people pounce on it.

5 The LORD is exalted, for he dwells on high;
he will fill Zion with his justice and righteousness.
6 He will be the sure foundation for your times,
a rich store of salvation and wisdom and knowledge;
the fear of the LORD is the key to this treasure.[a]

7 Look, their brave men cry aloud in the streets;
the envoys of peace weep bitterly.
8 The highways are deserted,
no travelers are on the roads.
The treaty is broken,
its witnesses[b] are despised,
no one is respected.
9 The land dries up and wastes away,
Lebanon is ashamed and withers;
Sharon is like the Arabah,
and Bashan and Carmel drop their leaves.

10 "Now will I arise," says the LORD.
"Now will I be exalted;
now will I be lifted up.
11 You conceive chaff,
you give birth to straw;
your breath is a fire that consumes you.
12 The peoples will be burned to ashes;
like cut thornbushes they will be set ablaze."

13 You who are far away, hear what I have done;
you who are near, acknowledge my power!
14 The sinners in Zion are terrified;
trembling grips the godless:
"Who of us can dwell with the consuming fire?
Who of us can dwell with everlasting burning?"
15 Those who walk righteously
and speak what is right,
who reject gain from extortion
and keep their hands from accepting bribes,
who stop their ears against plots of murder
and shut their eyes against contemplating evil—
16 they are the ones who will dwell on the heights,
whose refuge will be the mountain fortress.
Their bread will be supplied,
and water will not fail them.

17 Your eyes will see the king in his beauty
and view a land that stretches afar.
18 In your thoughts you will ponder the former terror:
"Where is that chief officer?
Where is the one who took the revenue?
Where is the officer in charge of the towers?"
19 You will see those arrogant people no more,
people whose speech is obscure,
whose language is strange and incomprehensible.

20 Look on Zion, the city of our festivals;
your eyes will see Jerusalem,
a peaceful abode, a tent that will not be moved;
its stakes will never be pulled up,
nor any of its ropes broken.
21 There the LORD will be our Mighty One.
It will be like a place of broad rivers and streams.
No galley with oars will ride them,
no mighty ship will sail them.
22 For the LORD is our judge,
the LORD is our lawgiver,
the LORD is our king;
it is he who will save us.

23 Your rigging hangs loose:
The mast is not held secure,
the sail is not spread.
Then an abundance of spoils will be divided
and even the lame will carry off plunder.
24 No one living in Zion will say, "I am ill";
and the sins of those who dwell there will be forgiven.

Judgment Against the Nations

34 Come near, you nations, and listen;
pay attention, you peoples!
Let the earth hear, and all that is in it,
the world, and all that comes out of it!
2 The LORD is angry with all nations;
his wrath is on all their armies.
He will totally destroy[c] them,
he will give them over to slaughter.

[a] 6 Or *is a treasure from him* [b] 8 Dead Sea Scrolls; Masoretic Text / *the cities* [c] 2 The Hebrew term refers to the irrevocable giving over of things or persons to the LORD, often by totally destroying them; also in verse 5.

3 Their slain will be thrown out,
their dead bodies will stink;
the mountains will be soaked with their blood.
4 All the stars in the sky will be dissolved
and the heavens rolled up like a scroll;
all the starry host will fall
like withered leaves from the vine,
like shriveled figs from the fig tree.

5 My sword has drunk its fill in the heavens;
see, it descends in judgment on Edom,
the people I have totally destroyed.
6 The sword of the LORD is bathed in blood,
it is covered with fat—
the blood of lambs and goats,
fat from the kidneys of rams.
For the LORD has a sacrifice in Bozrah
and a great slaughter in the land of Edom.
7 And the wild oxen will fall with them,
the bull calves and the great bulls.
Their land will be drenched with blood,
and the dust will be soaked with fat.

8 For the LORD has a day of vengeance,
a year of retribution, to uphold Zion's cause.
9 Edom's streams will be turned into pitch,
her dust into burning sulfur;
her land will become blazing pitch!
10 It will not be quenched night or day;
its smoke will rise forever.
From generation to generation it will lie desolate;
no one will ever pass through it again.
11 The desert owl[a] and screech owl[a] will possess it;
the great owl[a] and the raven will nest there.
God will stretch out over Edom
the measuring line of chaos
and the plumb line of desolation.
12 Her nobles will have nothing there to be called a kingdom,
all her princes will vanish away.
13 Thorns will overrun her citadels,
nettles and brambles her strongholds.
She will become a haunt for jackals,
a home for owls.
14 Desert creatures will meet with hyenas,
and wild goats will bleat to each other;
there the night creatures will also lie down
and find for themselves places of rest.
15 The owl will nest there and lay eggs,
she will hatch them, and care for her young
under the shadow of her wings;
there also the falcons will gather,
each with its mate.

16 Look in the scroll of the LORD and read:

None of these will be missing,
not one will lack her mate.
For it is his mouth that has given the order,
and his Spirit will gather them together.
17 He allots their portions;
his hand distributes them by measure.
They will possess it forever
and dwell there from generation to generation.

Joy of the Redeemed

35 The desert and the parched land will be glad;
the wilderness will rejoice and blossom.
Like the crocus, 2 it will burst into bloom;
it will rejoice greatly and shout for joy.
The glory of Lebanon will be given to it,
the splendor of Carmel and Sharon;
they will see the glory of the LORD,
the splendor of our God.

3 Strengthen the feeble hands,
steady the knees that give way;
4 say to those with fearful hearts,
"Be strong, do not fear;
your God will come,
he will come with vengeance;
with divine retribution
he will come to save you."

5 Then will the eyes of the blind be opened
and the ears of the deaf unstopped.
6 Then will the lame leap like a deer,
and the mute tongue shout for joy.
Water will gush forth in the wilderness
and streams in the desert.
7 The burning sand will become a pool,
the thirsty ground bubbling springs.
In the haunts where jackals once lay,
grass and reeds and papyrus will grow.

8 And a highway will be there;
it will be called the Way of Holiness;
it will be for those who walk on that Way.
The unclean will not journey on it;
wicked fools will not go about on it.
9 No lion will be there,
nor any ravenous beast;
they will not be found there.
But only the redeemed will walk there,
10 and those the LORD has rescued will return.
They will enter Zion with singing;
everlasting joy will crown their heads.
Gladness and joy will overtake them,
and sorrow and sighing will flee away.

Sennacherib Threatens Jerusalem

36 In the fourteenth year of King Hezekiah's reign, Sennacherib king of Assyria
attacked all the fortified cities of Judah and
captured them. 2 Then the king of Assyria sent
his field commander with a large army from
Lachish to King Hezekiah at Jerusalem. When
the commander stopped at the aqueduct of the
Upper Pool, on the road to the Launderer's
Field, 3 Eliakim son of Hilkiah the palace administrator, Shebna the secretary, and Joah
son of Asaph the recorder went out to him.
4 The field commander said to them, "Tell
Hezekiah:

[a] *11* The precise identification of these birds is uncertain.

"'This is what the great king, the king
of Assyria, says: On what are you bas-
ing this confidence of yours? 5You say
you have counsel and might for war—but
you speak only empty words. On whom
are you depending, that you rebel against
me? 6Look, I know you are depending
on Egypt, that splintered reed of a staff,
which pierces the hand of anyone who
leans on it! Such is Pharaoh king of Egypt
to all who depend on him. 7But if you say
to me, "We are depending on the LORD our
God"—isn't he the one whose high places
and altars Hezekiah removed, saying to
Judah and Jerusalem, "You must worship
before this altar"?

8"'Come now, make a bargain with my
master, the king of Assyria: I will give you
two thousand horses—if you can put riders on them! 9How then can you repulse
one officer of the least of my master's officials, even though you are depending
on Egypt for chariots and horsemen[a]?
10Furthermore, have I come to attack and
destroy this land without the LORD? The
LORD himself told me to march against
this country and destroy it.'"

11Then Eliakim, Shebna and Joah said to
the field commander, "Please speak to your
servants in Aramaic, since we understand it.
Don't speak to us in Hebrew in the hearing
of the people on the wall."

12But the commander replied, "Was it only
to your master and you that my master sent
me to say these things, and not to the people
sitting on the wall—who, like you, will have
to eat their own excrement and drink their
own urine?"

13Then the commander stood and called
out in Hebrew, "Hear the words of the great
king, the king of Assyria! 14This is what the
king says: Do not let Hezekiah deceive you.
He cannot deliver you! 15Do not let Hezekiah
persuade you to trust in the LORD when he
says, 'The LORD will surely deliver us; this
city will not be given into the hand of the king
of Assyria.'

16"Do not listen to Hezekiah. This is what
the king of Assyria says: Make peace with
me and come out to me. Then each of you will
eat fruit from your own vine and fig tree and
drink water from your own cistern, 17until I
come and take you to a land like your own—a
land of grain and new wine, a land of bread
and vineyards.

18"Do not let Hezekiah mislead you when he
says, 'The LORD will deliver us.' Have the gods
of any nations ever delivered their lands from
the hand of the king of Assyria? 19Where are
the gods of Hamath and Arpad? Where are
the gods of Sepharvaim? Have they rescued
Samaria from my hand? 20Who of all the gods
of these countries have been able to save their
lands from me? How then can the LORD deliver
Jerusalem from my hand?"

21But the people remained silent and said
nothing in reply, because the king had commanded, "Do not answer him."

22Then Eliakim son of Hilkiah the palace
administrator, Shebna the secretary and Joah
son of Asaph the recorder went to Hezekiah,
with their clothes torn, and told him what the
field commander had said.

Jerusalem's Deliverance Foretold

37 When King Hezekiah heard this, he tore
his clothes and put on sackcloth and
went into the temple of the LORD. 2He sent
Eliakim the palace administrator, Shebna the
secretary, and the leading priests, all wearing
sackcloth, to the prophet Isaiah son of Amoz.
3They told him, "This is what Hezekiah says:
This day is a day of distress and rebuke and
disgrace, as when children come to the moment of birth and there is no strength to deliver them. 4It may be that the LORD your God
will hear the words of the field commander,
whom his master, the king of Assyria, has
sent to ridicule the living God, and that he will
rebuke him for the words the LORD your God
has heard. Therefore pray for the remnant
that still survives."

5When King Hezekiah's officials came to
Isaiah, 6Isaiah said to them, "Tell your master,
'This is what the LORD says: Do not be afraid
of what you have heard—those words with
which the underlings of the king of Assyria
have blasphemed me. 7Listen! When he hears
a certain report, I will make him want to return to his own country, and there I will have
him cut down with the sword.'"

8When the field commander heard that the
king of Assyria had left Lachish, he withdrew
and found the king fighting against Libnah.

9Now Sennacherib received a report that
Tirhakah, the king of Cush,[b] was marching
out to fight against him. When he heard it, he
sent messengers to Hezekiah with this word:
10"Say to Hezekiah king of Judah: Do not let
the god you depend on deceive you when he
says, 'Jerusalem will not be given into the
hands of the king of Assyria.' 11Surely you
have heard what the kings of Assyria have
done to all the countries, destroying them
completely. And will you be delivered? 12Did
the gods of the nations that were destroyed
by my predecessors deliver them—the gods
of Gozan, Harran, Rezeph and the people of
Eden who were in Tel Assar? 13Where is the
king of Hamath or the king of Arpad? Where
are the kings of Lair, Sepharvaim, Hena and
Ivvah?"

Hezekiah's Prayer

14Hezekiah received the letter from the
messengers and read it. Then he went up to
the temple of the LORD and spread it out before the LORD. 15And Hezekiah prayed to the
LORD: 16"LORD Almighty, the God of Israel,
enthroned between the cherubim, you alone
are God over all the kingdoms of the earth.
You have made heaven and earth. 17Give ear,

[a] 9 Or *charioteers* [b] 9 That is, the upper Nile region

LORD, and hear; open your eyes, LORD, and
see; listen to all the words Sennacherib has
sent to ridicule the living God.
18"It is true, LORD, that the Assyrian kings
have laid waste all these peoples and their
lands. 19They have thrown their gods into the
fire and destroyed them, for they were not
gods but only wood and stone, fashioned by
human hands. 20Now, LORD our God, deliver
us from his hand, so that all the kingdoms of
the earth may know that you, LORD, are the
only God.[a]"

Sennacherib's Fall

21Then Isaiah son of Amoz sent a message
to Hezekiah: "This is what the LORD, the God
of Israel, says: Because you have prayed to
me concerning Sennacherib king of Assyria, 22this is the word the LORD has spoken
against him:

"Virgin Daughter Zion
despises and mocks you.
Daughter Jerusalem
tosses her head as you flee.
23 Who is it you have ridiculed and
blasphemed?
Against whom have you raised your
voice
and lifted your eyes in pride?
Against the Holy One of Israel!
24 By your messengers
you have ridiculed the Lord.
And you have said,
'With my many chariots
I have ascended the heights of the
mountains,
the utmost heights of Lebanon.
I have cut down its tallest cedars,
the choicest of its junipers.
I have reached its remotest heights,
the finest of its forests.
25 I have dug wells in foreign lands[b]
and drunk the water there.
With the soles of my feet
I have dried up all the streams of Egypt.'

26 "Have you not heard?
Long ago I ordained it.
In days of old I planned it;
now I have brought it to pass,
that you have turned fortified cities
into piles of stone.
27 Their people, drained of power,
are dismayed and put to shame.
They are like plants in the field,
like tender green shoots,
like grass sprouting on the roof,
scorched[c] before it grows up.

28 "But I know where you are
and when you come and go
and how you rage against me.
29 Because you rage against me
and because your insolence has
reached my ears,
I will put my hook in your nose
and my bit in your mouth,
and I will make you return
by the way you came.

30"This will be the sign for you, Hezekiah:

"This year you will eat what grows by
itself,
and the second year what springs from
that.
But in the third year sow and reap,
plant vineyards and eat their fruit.
31 Once more a remnant of the kingdom of
Judah
will take root below and bear fruit
above.
32 For out of Jerusalem will come a
remnant,
and out of Mount Zion a band of
survivors.
The zeal of the LORD Almighty
will accomplish this.

33"Therefore this is what the LORD says concerning the king of Assyria:

"He will not enter this city
or shoot an arrow here.
He will not come before it with shield
or build a siege ramp against it.
34 By the way that he came he will return;
he will not enter this city,"
declares the LORD.
35 "I will defend this city and save it,
for my sake and for the sake of David
my servant!"

36Then the angel of the LORD went out and
put to death a hundred and eighty-five thousand in the Assyrian camp. When the people
got up the next morning—there were all the
dead bodies! 37So Sennacherib king of Assyria broke camp and withdrew. He returned to
Nineveh and stayed there.
38One day, while he was worshiping in the
temple of his god Nisrok, his sons Adrammelek and Sharezer killed him with the sword,
and they escaped to the land of Ararat. And
Esarhaddon his son succeeded him as king.

Hezekiah's Illness

38 In those days Hezekiah became ill and
was at the point of death. The prophet Isaiah son of Amoz went to him and said,
"This is what the LORD says: Put your house
in order, because you are going to die; you
will not recover."
2Hezekiah turned his face to the wall and
prayed to the LORD, 3"Remember, LORD, how
I have walked before you faithfully and with
wholehearted devotion and have done what
is good in your eyes." And Hezekiah wept
bitterly.
4Then the word of the LORD came to Isaiah: 5"Go and tell Hezekiah, 'This is what the
LORD, the God of your father David, says: I

[a] 20 Dead Sea Scrolls (see also 2 Kings 19:19); Masoretic Text *you alone are the LORD* [b] 25 Dead Sea Scrolls (see also 2 Kings 19:24); Masoretic Text does not have *in foreign lands.* [c] 27 Some manuscripts of the Masoretic Text, Dead Sea Scrolls and some Septuagint manuscripts (see also 2 Kings 19:26); most manuscripts of the Masoretic Text *roof / and terraced fields*

have heard your prayer and seen your tears; I
will add fifteen years to your life. 6And I will
deliver you and this city from the hand of the
king of Assyria. I will defend this city.
7" 'This is the LORD's sign to you that the
LORD will do what he has promised: 8I will
make the shadow cast by the sun go back the
ten steps it has gone down on the stairway
of Ahaz.' " So the sunlight went back the ten
steps it had gone down.

9A writing of Hezekiah king of Judah after
his illness and recovery:

10I said, "In the prime of my life
must I go through the gates of death
and be robbed of the rest of my years?"
11I said, "I will not again see the LORD himself
in the land of the living;
no longer will I look on my fellow man,
or be with those who now dwell in this world.
12Like a shepherd's tent my house
has been pulled down and taken from me.
Like a weaver I have rolled up my life,
and he has cut me off from the loom;
day and night you made an end of me.
13I waited patiently till dawn,
but like a lion he broke all my bones;
day and night you made an end of me.
14I cried like a swift or thrush,
I moaned like a mourning dove.
My eyes grew weak as I looked to the heavens.
I am being threatened; Lord, come to my aid!"

15But what can I say?
He has spoken to me, and he himself has done this.
I will walk humbly all my years
because of this anguish of my soul.
16Lord, by such things people live;
and my spirit finds life in them too.
You restored me to health
and let me live.
17Surely it was for my benefit
that I suffered such anguish.
In your love you kept me
from the pit of destruction;
you have put all my sins
behind your back.
18For the grave cannot praise you,
death cannot sing your praise;
those who go down to the pit
cannot hope for your faithfulness.
19The living, the living—they praise you,
as I am doing today;
parents tell their children
about your faithfulness.

20The LORD will save me,
and we will sing with stringed instruments
all the days of our lives
in the temple of the LORD.

21Isaiah had said, "Prepare a poultice of figs
and apply it to the boil, and he will recover."
22Hezekiah had asked, "What will be the
sign that I will go up to the temple of the LORD?"

Envoys From Babylon

39 At that time Marduk-Baladan son of
Baladan king of Babylon sent Hezekiah letters and a gift, because he had heard of
his illness and recovery. 2Hezekiah received
the envoys gladly and showed them what was
in his storehouses—the silver, the gold, the
spices, the fine olive oil—his entire armory
and everything found among his treasures.
There was nothing in his palace or in all his
kingdom that Hezekiah did not show them.
3Then Isaiah the prophet went to King Hezekiah and asked, "What did those men say,
and where did they come from?"
"From a distant land," Hezekiah replied.
"They came to me from Babylon."
4The prophet asked, "What did they see in
your palace?"
"They saw everything in my palace," Hezekiah said. "There is nothing among my treasures that I did not show them."
5Then Isaiah said to Hezekiah, "Hear the
word of the LORD Almighty: 6The time will
surely come when everything in your palace,
and all that your predecessors have stored up
until this day, will be carried off to Babylon.
Nothing will be left, says the LORD. 7And some
of your descendants, your own flesh and blood
who will be born to you, will be taken away,
and they will become eunuchs in the palace
of the king of Babylon."
8"The word of the LORD you have spoken
is good," Hezekiah replied. For he thought,
"There will be peace and security in my lifetime."

Comfort for God's People

40 Comfort, comfort my people,
says your God.
2Speak tenderly to Jerusalem,
and proclaim to her
that her hard service has been completed,
that her sin has been paid for,
that she has received from the LORD's hand
double for all her sins.

3A voice of one calling:
"In the wilderness prepare
the way for the LORD[a];
make straight in the desert
a highway for our God.[b]
4Every valley shall be raised up,
every mountain and hill made low;
the rough ground shall become level,
the rugged places a plain.
5And the glory of the LORD will be revealed,
and all people will see it together.
For the mouth of the LORD has spoken."

[a] 3 Or *A voice of one calling in the wilderness: / "Prepare the way for the LORD* [b] 3 Hebrew; Septuagint *make straight the paths of our God*

6 A voice says, "Cry out."
And I said, "What shall I cry?"

"All people are like grass,
and all their faithfulness is like the flowers of the field.
7 The grass withers and the flowers fall,
because the breath of the LORD blows on them.
Surely the people are grass.
8 The grass withers and the flowers fall,
but the word of our God endures forever."

9 You who bring good news to Zion,
go up on a high mountain.
You who bring good news to Jerusalem,[a]
lift up your voice with a shout,
lift it up, do not be afraid;
say to the towns of Judah,
"Here is your God!"
10 See, the Sovereign LORD comes with power,
and he rules with a mighty arm.
See, his reward is with him,
and his recompense accompanies him.
11 He tends his flock like a shepherd:
He gathers the lambs in his arms
and carries them close to his heart;
he gently leads those that have young.

12 Who has measured the waters in the hollow of his hand,
or with the breadth of his hand marked off the heavens?
Who has held the dust of the earth in a basket,
or weighed the mountains on the scales
and the hills in a balance?
13 Who can fathom the Spirit[b] of the LORD,
or instruct the LORD as his counselor?
14 Whom did the LORD consult to enlighten him,
and who taught him the right way?
Who was it that taught him knowledge,
or showed him the path of understanding?

15 Surely the nations are like a drop in a bucket;
they are regarded as dust on the scales;
he weighs the islands as though they were fine dust.
16 Lebanon is not sufficient for altar fires,
nor its animals enough for burnt offerings.
17 Before him all the nations are as nothing;
they are regarded by him as worthless
and less than nothing.

18 With whom, then, will you compare God?
To what image will you liken him?
19 As for an idol, a metalworker casts it,
and a goldsmith overlays it with gold
and fashions silver chains for it.
20 A person too poor to present such an offering
selects wood that will not rot;
they look for a skilled worker
to set up an idol that will not topple.

21 Do you not know?
Have you not heard?
Has it not been told you from the beginning?
Have you not understood since the earth was founded?
22 He sits enthroned above the circle of the earth,
and its people are like grasshoppers.
He stretches out the heavens like a canopy,
and spreads them out like a tent to live in.
23 He brings princes to naught
and reduces the rulers of this world to nothing.
24 No sooner are they planted,
no sooner are they sown,
no sooner do they take root in the ground,
than he blows on them and they wither,
and a whirlwind sweeps them away like chaff.

25 "To whom will you compare me?
Or who is my equal?" says the Holy One.
26 Lift up your eyes and look to the heavens:
Who created all these?
He who brings out the starry host one by one
and calls forth each of them by name.
Because of his great power and mighty strength,
not one of them is missing.

27 Why do you complain, Jacob?
Why do you say, Israel,
"My way is hidden from the LORD;
my cause is disregarded by my God"?
28 Do you not know?
Have you not heard?
The LORD is the everlasting God,
the Creator of the ends of the earth.
He will not grow tired or weary,
and his understanding no one can fathom.
29 He gives strength to the weary
and increases the power of the weak.
30 Even youths grow tired and weary,
and young men stumble and fall;
31 but those who hope in the LORD
will renew their strength.
They will soar on wings like eagles;
they will run and not grow weary,
they will walk and not be faint.

The Helper of Israel

41 "Be silent before me, you islands!
Let the nations renew their strength!
Let them come forward and speak;
let us meet together at the place of judgment.

2 "Who has stirred up one from the east,
calling him in righteousness to his service[c]?
He hands nations over to him
and subdues kings before him.

[a] 9 Or *Zion, bringer of good news, / go up on a high mountain. / Jerusalem, bringer of good news*
[b] 13 Or *mind* [c] 2 Or *east, / whom victory meets at every step*

He turns them to dust with his sword,
to windblown chaff with his bow.
3 He pursues them and moves on unscathed,
by a path his feet have not traveled before.
4 Who has done this and carried it through,
calling forth the generations from the beginning?
I, the LORD—with the first of them
and with the last—I am he."

5 The islands have seen it and fear;
the ends of the earth tremble.
They approach and come forward;
6 they help each other
and say to their companions, "Be strong!"
7 The metalworker encourages the goldsmith,
and the one who smooths with the hammer
spurs on the one who strikes the anvil.
One says of the welding, "It is good."
The other nails down the idol so it will not topple.

8 "But you, Israel, my servant,
Jacob, whom I have chosen,
you descendants of Abraham my friend,
9 I took you from the ends of the earth,
from its farthest corners I called you.
I said, 'You are my servant';
I have chosen you and have not rejected you.
10 So do not fear, for I am with you;
do not be dismayed, for I am your God.
I will strengthen you and help you;
I will uphold you with my righteous right hand.

11 "All who rage against you
will surely be ashamed and disgraced;
those who oppose you
will be as nothing and perish.
12 Though you search for your enemies,
you will not find them.
Those who wage war against you
will be as nothing at all.
13 For I am the LORD your God
who takes hold of your right hand
and says to you, Do not fear;
I will help you.
14 Do not be afraid, you worm Jacob,
little Israel, do not fear,
for I myself will help you," declares the LORD,
your Redeemer, the Holy One of Israel.
15 "See, I will make you into a threshing sledge,
new and sharp, with many teeth.
You will thresh the mountains and crush them,
and reduce the hills to chaff.
16 You will winnow them, the wind will pick them up,
and a gale will blow them away.
But you will rejoice in the LORD
and glory in the Holy One of Israel.

17 "The poor and needy search for water,
but there is none;
their tongues are parched with thirst.
But I the LORD will answer them;
I, the God of Israel, will not forsake them.
18 I will make rivers flow on barren heights,
and springs within the valleys.
I will turn the desert into pools of water,
and the parched ground into springs.
19 I will put in the desert
the cedar and the acacia, the myrtle and the olive.
I will set junipers in the wasteland,
the fir and the cypress together,
20 so that people may see and know,
may consider and understand,
that the hand of the LORD has done this,
that the Holy One of Israel has created it.

21 "Present your case," says the LORD.
"Set forth your arguments," says Jacob's King.
22 "Tell us, you idols,
what is going to happen.
Tell us what the former things were,
so that we may consider them
and know their final outcome.
Or declare to us the things to come,
23 tell us what the future holds,
so we may know that you are gods.
Do something, whether good or bad,
so that we will be dismayed and filled with fear.
24 But you are less than nothing
and your works are utterly worthless;
whoever chooses you is detestable.

25 "I have stirred up one from the north, and he comes—
one from the rising sun who calls on my name.
He treads on rulers as if they were mortar,
as if he were a potter treading the clay.
26 Who told of this from the beginning, so we could know,
or beforehand, so we could say, 'He was right'?
No one told of this,
no one foretold it,
no one heard any words from you.
27 I was the first to tell Zion, 'Look, here they are!'
I gave to Jerusalem a messenger of good news.
28 I look but there is no one—
no one among the gods to give counsel,
no one to give answer when I ask them.
29 See, they are all false!
Their deeds amount to nothing;
their images are but wind and confusion.

The Servant of the LORD

42 "Here is my servant, whom I uphold,
my chosen one in whom I delight;
I will put my Spirit on him,
and he will bring justice to the nations.

2 He will not shout or cry out,
or raise his voice in the streets.
3 A bruised reed he will not break,
and a smoldering wick he will not snuff out.
In faithfulness he will bring forth justice;
4 he will not falter or be discouraged
till he establishes justice on earth.
In his teaching the islands will put their hope."

5 This is what God the LORD says—
the Creator of the heavens, who stretches them out,
who spreads out the earth with all that springs from it,
who gives breath to its people,
and life to those who walk on it:
6 "I, the LORD, have called you in righteousness;
I will take hold of your hand.
I will keep you and will make you
to be a covenant for the people
and a light for the Gentiles,
7 to open eyes that are blind,
to free captives from prison
and to release from the dungeon those who sit in darkness.

8 "I am the LORD; that is my name!
I will not yield my glory to another
or my praise to idols.
9 See, the former things have taken place,
and new things I declare;
before they spring into being
I announce them to you."

Song of Praise to the LORD

10 Sing to the LORD a new song,
his praise from the ends of the earth,
you who go down to the sea, and all that is in it,
you islands, and all who live in them.
11 Let the wilderness and its towns raise their voices;
let the settlements where Kedar lives rejoice.
Let the people of Sela sing for joy;
let them shout from the mountaintops.
12 Let them give glory to the LORD
and proclaim his praise in the islands.
13 The LORD will march out like a champion,
like a warrior he will stir up his zeal;
with a shout he will raise the battle cry
and will triumph over his enemies.

14 "For a long time I have kept silent,
I have been quiet and held myself back.
But now, like a woman in childbirth,
I cry out, I gasp and pant.
15 I will lay waste the mountains and hills
and dry up all their vegetation;
I will turn rivers into islands
and dry up the pools.
16 I will lead the blind by ways they have not known,
along unfamiliar paths I will guide them;
I will turn the darkness into light before them
and make the rough places smooth.
These are the things I will do;
I will not forsake them.
17 But those who trust in idols,
who say to images, 'You are our gods,'
will be turned back in utter shame.

Israel Blind and Deaf

18 "Hear, you deaf;
look, you blind, and see!
19 Who is blind but my servant,
and deaf like the messenger I send?
Who is blind like the one in covenant with me,
blind like the servant of the LORD?
20 You have seen many things, but you pay no attention;
your ears are open, but you do not listen."
21 It pleased the LORD
for the sake of his righteousness
to make his law great and glorious.
22 But this is a people plundered and looted,
all of them trapped in pits
or hidden away in prisons.
They have become plunder,
with no one to rescue them;
they have been made loot,
with no one to say, "Send them back."

23 Which of you will listen to this
or pay close attention in time to come?
24 Who handed Jacob over to become loot,
and Israel to the plunderers?
Was it not the LORD,
against whom we have sinned?
For they would not follow his ways;
they did not obey his law.
25 So he poured out on them his burning anger,
the violence of war.
It enveloped them in flames, yet they did not understand;
it consumed them, but they did not take it to heart.

Israel's Only Savior

43 But now, this is what the LORD says—
he who created you, Jacob,
he who formed you, Israel:
"Do not fear, for I have redeemed you;
I have summoned you by name; you are mine.
2 When you pass through the waters,
I will be with you;
and when you pass through the rivers,
they will not sweep over you.
When you walk through the fire,
you will not be burned;
the flames will not set you ablaze.
3 For I am the LORD your God,
the Holy One of Israel, your Savior;
I give Egypt for your ransom,
Cush[a] and Seba in your stead.

[a] 3 That is, the upper Nile region

4 Since you are precious and honored in my sight,
and because I love you,
I will give people in exchange for you,
nations in exchange for your life.
5 Do not be afraid, for I am with you;
I will bring your children from the east
and gather you from the west.
6 I will say to the north, 'Give them up!'
and to the south, 'Do not hold them back.'
Bring my sons from afar
and my daughters from the ends of the earth—
7 everyone who is called by my name,
whom I created for my glory,
whom I formed and made."

8 Lead out those who have eyes but are blind,
who have ears but are deaf.
9 All the nations gather together
and the peoples assemble.
Which of their gods foretold this
and proclaimed to us the former things?
Let them bring in their witnesses to prove they were right,
so that others may hear and say, "It is true."
10 "You are my witnesses," declares the LORD,
"and my servant whom I have chosen,
so that you may know and believe me
and understand that I am he.
Before me no god was formed,
nor will there be one after me.
11 I, even I, am the LORD,
and apart from me there is no savior.
12 I have revealed and saved and proclaimed—
I, and not some foreign god among you.
You are my witnesses," declares the LORD, "that I am God.
13 Yes, and from ancient days I am he.
No one can deliver out of my hand.
When I act, who can reverse it?"

God's Mercy and Israel's Unfaithfulness

14 This is what the LORD says—
your Redeemer, the Holy One of Israel:
"For your sake I will send to Babylon
and bring down as fugitives all the Babylonians,[a]
in the ships in which they took pride.
15 I am the LORD, your Holy One,
Israel's Creator, your King."

16 This is what the LORD says—
he who made a way through the sea,
a path through the mighty waters,
17 who drew out the chariots and horses,
the army and reinforcements together,
and they lay there, never to rise again,
extinguished, snuffed out like a wick:
18 "Forget the former things;
do not dwell on the past.
19 See, I am doing a new thing!
Now it springs up; do you not perceive it?
I am making a way in the wilderness
and streams in the wasteland.
20 The wild animals honor me,
the jackals and the owls,
because I provide water in the wilderness
and streams in the wasteland,
to give drink to my people, my chosen,
21 the people I formed for myself
that they may proclaim my praise.

22 "Yet you have not called on me, Jacob,
you have not wearied yourselves for[b] me, Israel.
23 You have not brought me sheep for burnt offerings,
nor honored me with your sacrifices.
I have not burdened you with grain offerings
nor wearied you with demands for incense.
24 You have not bought any fragrant calamus for me,
or lavished on me the fat of your sacrifices.
But you have burdened me with your sins
and wearied me with your offenses.

25 "I, even I, am he who blots out
your transgressions, for my own sake,
and remembers your sins no more.
26 Review the past for me,
let us argue the matter together;
state the case for your innocence.
27 Your first father sinned;
those I sent to teach you rebelled against me.
28 So I disgraced the dignitaries of your temple;
I consigned Jacob to destruction[c]
and Israel to scorn.

Israel the Chosen

44 "But now listen, Jacob, my servant,
Israel, whom I have chosen.
2 This is what the LORD says—
he who made you, who formed you in the womb,
and who will help you:
Do not be afraid, Jacob, my servant,
Jeshurun,[d] whom I have chosen.
3 For I will pour water on the thirsty land,
and streams on the dry ground;
I will pour out my Spirit on your offspring,
and my blessing on your descendants.
4 They will spring up like grass in a meadow,
like poplar trees by flowing streams.
5 Some will say, 'I belong to the LORD';
others will call themselves by the name of Jacob;
still others will write on their hand, 'The LORD's,'
and will take the name Israel.

[a] 14 Or *Chaldeans* [b] 22 Or *Jacob; / surely you have grown weary of* [c] 28 The Hebrew term refers to the irrevocable giving over of things or persons to the LORD, often by totally destroying them.
[d] 2 *Jeshurun* means *the upright one,* that is, Israel.

The LORD, Not Idols

6 "This is what the LORD says—
Israel's King and Redeemer, the LORD Almighty:
I am the first and I am the last;
apart from me there is no God.
7 Who then is like me? Let him proclaim it.
Let him declare and lay out before me
what has happened since I established my ancient people,
and what is yet to come—
yes, let them foretell what will come.
8 Do not tremble, do not be afraid.
Did I not proclaim this and foretell it long ago?
You are my witnesses. Is there any God besides me?
No, there is no other Rock; I know not one."

9 All who make idols are nothing,
and the things they treasure are worthless.
Those who would speak up for them are blind;
they are ignorant, to their own shame.
10 Who shapes a god and casts an idol,
which can profit nothing?
11 People who do that will be put to shame;
such craftsmen are only human beings.
Let them all come together and take their stand;
they will be brought down to terror and shame.

12 The blacksmith takes a tool
and works with it in the coals;
he shapes an idol with hammers,
he forges it with the might of his arm.
He gets hungry and loses his strength;
he drinks no water and grows faint.
13 The carpenter measures with a line
and makes an outline with a marker;
he roughs it out with chisels
and marks it with compasses.
He shapes it in human form,
human form in all its glory,
that it may dwell in a shrine.
14 He cut down cedars,
or perhaps took a cypress or oak.
He let it grow among the trees of the forest,
or planted a pine, and the rain made it grow.
15 It is used as fuel for burning;
some of it he takes and warms himself,
he kindles a fire and bakes bread.
But he also fashions a god and worships it;
he makes an idol and bows down to it.
16 Half of the wood he burns in the fire;
over it he prepares his meal,
he roasts his meat and eats his fill.
He also warms himself and says,
"Ah! I am warm; I see the fire."
17 From the rest he makes a god, his idol;
he bows down to it and worships.
He prays to it and says,
"Save me! You are my god!"
18 They know nothing, they understand nothing;
their eyes are plastered over so they cannot see,
and their minds closed so they cannot understand.
19 No one stops to think,
no one has the knowledge or understanding to say,
"Half of it I used for fuel;
I even baked bread over its coals,
I roasted meat and I ate.
Shall I make a detestable thing from what is left?
Shall I bow down to a block of wood?"
20 Such a person feeds on ashes; a deluded heart misleads him;
he cannot save himself, or say,
"Is not this thing in my right hand a lie?"

21 "Remember these things, Jacob,
for you, Israel, are my servant.
I have made you, you are my servant;
Israel, I will not forget you.
22 I have swept away your offenses like a cloud,
your sins like the morning mist.
Return to me,
for I have redeemed you."

23 Sing for joy, you heavens, for the LORD has done this;
shout aloud, you earth beneath.
Burst into song, you mountains,
you forests and all your trees,
for the LORD has redeemed Jacob,
he displays his glory in Israel.

Jerusalem to Be Inhabited

24 "This is what the LORD says—
your Redeemer, who formed you in the womb:
I am the LORD,
the Maker of all things,
who stretches out the heavens,
who spreads out the earth by myself,
25 who foils the signs of false prophets
and makes fools of diviners,
who overthrows the learning of the wise
and turns it into nonsense,
26 who carries out the words of his servants
and fulfills the predictions of his messengers,
who says of Jerusalem, 'It shall be inhabited,'
of the towns of Judah, 'They shall be rebuilt,'
and of their ruins, 'I will restore them,'
27 who says to the watery deep, 'Be dry,
and I will dry up your streams,'
28 who says of Cyrus, 'He is my shepherd
and will accomplish all that I please;
he will say of Jerusalem, "Let it be rebuilt,"
and of the temple, "Let its foundations be laid."'

45 "This is what the LORD says to his anointed,
to Cyrus, whose right hand I take hold of

to subdue nations before him
and to strip kings of their armor,
to open doors before him
so that gates will not be shut:
2 I will go before you
and will level the mountains[a];
I will break down gates of bronze
and cut through bars of iron.
3 I will give you hidden treasures,
riches stored in secret places,
so that you may know that I am the LORD,
the God of Israel, who summons you by name.
4 For the sake of Jacob my servant,
of Israel my chosen,
I summon you by name
and bestow on you a title of honor,
though you do not acknowledge me.
5 I am the LORD, and there is no other;
apart from me there is no God.
I will strengthen you,
though you have not acknowledged me,
6 so that from the rising of the sun
to the place of its setting
people may know there is none besides me.
I am the LORD, and there is no other.
7 I form the light and create darkness,
I bring prosperity and create disaster;
I, the LORD, do all these things.

8 "You heavens above, rain down my righteousness;
let the clouds shower it down.
Let the earth open wide,
let salvation spring up,
let righteousness flourish with it;
I, the LORD, have created it.

9 "Woe to those who quarrel with their Maker,
those who are nothing but potsherds
among the potsherds on the ground.
Does the clay say to the potter,
'What are you making?'
Does your work say,
'The potter has no hands'?
10 Woe to the one who says to a father,
'What have you begotten?'
or to a mother,
'What have you brought to birth?'

11 "This is what the LORD says—
the Holy One of Israel, and its Maker:
Concerning things to come,
do you question me about my children,
or give me orders about the work of my hands?
12 It is I who made the earth
and created mankind on it.
My own hands stretched out the heavens;
I marshaled their starry hosts.
13 I will raise up Cyrus[b] in my righteousness:
I will make all his ways straight.
He will rebuild my city
and set my exiles free,
but not for a price or reward,
says the LORD Almighty."

14 This is what the LORD says:

"The products of Egypt and the merchandise of Cush,[c]
and those tall Sabeans—
they will come over to you
and will be yours;
they will trudge behind you,
coming over to you in chains.
They will bow down before you
and plead with you, saying,
'Surely God is with you, and there is no other;
there is no other god.'"

15 Truly you are a God who has been hiding himself,
the God and Savior of Israel.
16 All the makers of idols will be put to shame and disgraced;
they will go off into disgrace together.
17 But Israel will be saved by the LORD
with an everlasting salvation;
you will never be put to shame or disgraced,
to ages everlasting.

18 For this is what the LORD says—
he who created the heavens,
he is God;
he who fashioned and made the earth,
he founded it;
he did not create it to be empty,
but formed it to be inhabited—
he says:
"I am the LORD,
and there is no other.
19 I have not spoken in secret,
from somewhere in a land of darkness;
I have not said to Jacob's descendants,
'Seek me in vain.'
I, the LORD, speak the truth;
I declare what is right.

20 "Gather together and come;
assemble, you fugitives from the nations.
Ignorant are those who carry about idols of wood,
who pray to gods that cannot save.
21 Declare what is to be, present it—
let them take counsel together.
Who foretold this long ago,
who declared it from the distant past?
Was it not I, the LORD?
And there is no God apart from me,
a righteous God and a Savior;
there is none but me.

22 "Turn to me and be saved,
all you ends of the earth;
for I am God, and there is no other.
23 By myself I have sworn,
my mouth has uttered in all integrity
a word that will not be revoked:
Before me every knee will bow;
by me every tongue will swear.
24 They will say of me, 'In the LORD alone
are deliverance and strength.'"

[a] 2 Dead Sea Scrolls and Septuagint; the meaning of the word in the Masoretic Text is uncertain.
[b] 13 Hebrew *him*
[c] 14 That is, the upper Nile region

All who have raged against him
will come to him and be put to shame.
25 But all the descendants of Israel
will find deliverance in the LORD
and will make their boast in him.

Gods of Babylon

46 Bel bows down, Nebo stoops low;
their idols are borne by beasts of burden.[a]
The images that are carried about are burdensome,
a burden for the weary.
2 They stoop and bow down together;
unable to rescue the burden,
they themselves go off into captivity.

3 "Listen to me, you descendants of Jacob,
all the remnant of the people of Israel,
you whom I have upheld since your birth,
and have carried since you were born.
4 Even to your old age and gray hairs
I am he, I am he who will sustain you.
I have made you and I will carry you;
I will sustain you and I will rescue you.

5 "With whom will you compare me or count me equal?
To whom will you liken me that we may be compared?
6 Some pour out gold from their bags
and weigh out silver on the scales;
they hire a goldsmith to make it into a god,
and they bow down and worship it.
7 They lift it to their shoulders and carry it;
they set it up in its place, and there it stands.
From that spot it cannot move.
Even though someone cries out to it, it cannot answer;
it cannot save them from their troubles.

8 "Remember this, keep it in mind,
take it to heart, you rebels.
9 Remember the former things, those of long ago;
I am God, and there is no other;
I am God, and there is none like me.
10 I make known the end from the beginning,
from ancient times, what is still to come.
I say, 'My purpose will stand,
and I will do all that I please.'
11 From the east I summon a bird of prey;
from a far-off land, a man to fulfill my purpose.
What I have said, that I will bring about;
what I have planned, that I will do.
12 Listen to me, you stubborn-hearted,
you who are now far from my righteousness.
13 I am bringing my righteousness near,
it is not far away;
and my salvation will not be delayed.
I will grant salvation to Zion,
my splendor to Israel.

The Fall of Babylon

47 "Go down, sit in the dust,
Virgin Daughter Babylon;
sit on the ground without a throne,
queen city of the Babylonians.[b]
No more will you be called
tender or delicate.
2 Take millstones and grind flour;
take off your veil.
Lift up your skirts, bare your legs,
and wade through the streams.
3 Your nakedness will be exposed
and your shame uncovered.
I will take vengeance;
I will spare no one."

4 Our Redeemer—the LORD Almighty is his name—
is the Holy One of Israel.

5 "Sit in silence, go into darkness,
queen city of the Babylonians;
no more will you be called
queen of kingdoms.
6 I was angry with my people
and desecrated my inheritance;
I gave them into your hand,
and you showed them no mercy.
Even on the aged
you laid a very heavy yoke.
7 You said, 'I am forever—
the eternal queen!'
But you did not consider these things
or reflect on what might happen.

8 "Now then, listen, you lover of pleasure,
lounging in your security
and saying to yourself,
'I am, and there is none besides me.
I will never be a widow
or suffer the loss of children.'
9 Both of these will overtake you
in a moment, on a single day:
loss of children and widowhood.
They will come upon you in full measure,
in spite of your many sorceries
and all your potent spells.
10 You have trusted in your wickedness
and have said, 'No one sees me.'
Your wisdom and knowledge mislead you
when you say to yourself,
'I am, and there is none besides me.'
11 Disaster will come upon you,
and you will not know how to conjure it away.
A calamity will fall upon you
that you cannot ward off with a ransom;
a catastrophe you cannot foresee
will suddenly come upon you.

12 "Keep on, then, with your magic spells
and with your many sorceries,
which you have labored at since childhood.
Perhaps you will succeed,
perhaps you will cause terror.
13 All the counsel you have received has only worn you out!
Let your astrologers come forward,

[a] 1 Or *are but beasts and cattle* [b] 1 Or *Chaldeans*; also in verse 5

those stargazers who make predictions
month by month,
let them save you from what is coming
upon you.
14 Surely they are like stubble;
the fire will burn them up.
They cannot even save themselves
from the power of the flame.
These are not coals for warmth;
this is not a fire to sit by.
15 That is all they are to you—
these you have dealt with
and labored with since childhood.
All of them go on in their error;
there is not one that can save you.

Stubborn Israel

48 "Listen to this, you descendants of
Jacob,
you who are called by the name of
Israel
and come from the line of Judah,
you who take oaths in the name of the
LORD
and invoke the God of Israel—
but not in truth or righteousness—
2 you who call yourselves citizens of the
holy city
and claim to rely on the God of Israel—
the LORD Almighty is his name:
3 I foretold the former things long ago,
my mouth announced them and I made
them known;
then suddenly I acted, and they came to
pass.
4 For I knew how stubborn you were;
your neck muscles were iron,
your forehead was bronze.
5 Therefore I told you these things long ago;
before they happened I announced
them to you
so that you could not say,
'My images brought them about;
my wooden image and metal god
ordained them.'
6 You have heard these things; look at them
all.
Will you not admit them?

"From now on I will tell you of new
things,
of hidden things unknown to you.
7 They are created now, and not long ago;
you have not heard of them before
today.
So you cannot say,
'Yes, I knew of them.'
8 You have neither heard nor understood;
from of old your ears have not been
open.
Well do I know how treacherous you are;
you were called a rebel from birth.
9 For my own name's sake I delay my
wrath;
for the sake of my praise I hold it back
from you,
so as not to destroy you completely.
10 See, I have refined you, though not as
silver;
I have tested you in the furnace of
affliction.
11 For my own sake, for my own sake, I do
this.
How can I let myself be defamed?
I will not yield my glory to another.

Israel Freed

12 "Listen to me, Jacob,
Israel, whom I have called:
I am he;
I am the first and I am the last.
13 My own hand laid the foundations of the
earth,
and my right hand spread out the
heavens;
when I summon them,
they all stand up together.

14 "Come together, all of you, and listen:
Which of the idols has foretold these
things?
The LORD's chosen ally
will carry out his purpose against
Babylon;
his arm will be against the
Babylonians.[a]
15 I, even I, have spoken;
yes, I have called him.
I will bring him,
and he will succeed in his mission.

16 "Come near me and listen to this:

"From the first announcement I have not
spoken in secret;
at the time it happens, I am there."

And now the Sovereign LORD has sent
me,
endowed with his Spirit.

17 This is what the LORD says—
your Redeemer, the Holy One of Israel:
"I am the LORD your God,
who teaches you what is best for you,
who directs you in the way you should
go.
18 If only you had paid attention to my
commands,
your peace would have been like a
river,
your well-being like the waves of the
sea.
19 Your descendants would have been like
the sand,
your children like its numberless
grains;
their name would never be blotted out
nor destroyed from before me."

20 Leave Babylon,
flee from the Babylonians!
Announce this with shouts of joy
and proclaim it.
Send it out to the ends of the earth;
say, "The LORD has redeemed his
servant Jacob."

[a] *14* Or *Chaldeans*; also in verse 20

21 They did not thirst when he led them
through the deserts;
he made water flow for them from the
rock;
he split the rock
and water gushed out.

22 "There is no peace," says the LORD, "for
the wicked."

The Servant of the LORD

49 Listen to me, you islands;
hear this, you distant nations:
Before I was born the LORD called me;
from my mother's womb he has spoken
my name.
2 He made my mouth like a sharpened
sword,
in the shadow of his hand he hid me;
he made me into a polished arrow
and concealed me in his quiver.
3 He said to me, "You are my servant,
Israel, in whom I will display my
splendor."
4 But I said, "I have labored in vain;
I have spent my strength for nothing at
all.
Yet what is due me is in the LORD's hand,
and my reward is with my God."

5 And now the LORD says—
he who formed me in the womb to be
his servant
to bring Jacob back to him
and gather Israel to himself,
for I am[a] honored in the eyes of the LORD
and my God has been my strength—
6 he says:
"It is too small a thing for you to be my
servant
to restore the tribes of Jacob
and bring back those of Israel I have
kept.
I will also make you a light for the
Gentiles,
that my salvation may reach to the ends
of the earth."

7 This is what the LORD says—
the Redeemer and Holy One of Israel—
to him who was despised and abhorred
by the nation,
to the servant of rulers:
"Kings will see you and stand up,
princes will see and bow down,
because of the LORD, who is faithful,
the Holy One of Israel, who has chosen
you."

Restoration of Israel

8 This is what the LORD says:

"In the time of my favor I will answer you,
and in the day of salvation I will help
you;
I will keep you and will make you
to be a covenant for the people,
to restore the land
and to reassign its desolate
inheritances,
9 to say to the captives, 'Come out,'
and to those in darkness, 'Be free!'

"They will feed beside the roads
and find pasture on every barren hill.
10 They will neither hunger nor thirst,
nor will the desert heat or the sun beat
down on them.
He who has compassion on them will
guide them
and lead them beside springs of water.
11 I will turn all my mountains into roads,
and my highways will be raised up.
12 See, they will come from afar—
some from the north, some from the
west,
some from the region of Aswan.[b]"

13 Shout for joy, you heavens;
rejoice, you earth;
burst into song, you mountains!
For the LORD comforts his people
and will have compassion on his
afflicted ones.

14 But Zion said, "The LORD has forsaken me,
the Lord has forgotten me."

15 "Can a mother forget the baby at her
breast
and have no compassion on the child
she has borne?
Though she may forget,
I will not forget you!
16 See, I have engraved you on the palms of
my hands;
your walls are ever before me.
17 Your children hasten back,
and those who laid you waste depart
from you.
18 Lift up your eyes and look around;
all your children gather and come to you.
As surely as I live," declares the LORD,
"you will wear them all as ornaments;
you will put them on, like a bride.

19 "Though you were ruined and made
desolate
and your land laid waste,
now you will be too small for your people,
and those who devoured you will be far
away.
20 The children born during your
bereavement
will yet say in your hearing,
'This place is too small for us;
give us more space to live in.'
21 Then you will say in your heart,
'Who bore me these?
I was bereaved and barren;
I was exiled and rejected.
Who brought these up?
I was left all alone,
but these—where have they come
from?'"

[a] 5 Or *him, / but Israel would not be gathered; / yet I will be*

[b] 12 Dead Sea Scrolls; Masoretic Text *Sinim*

22This is what the Sovereign LORD says:

"See, I will beckon to the nations,
I will lift up my banner to the peoples;
they will bring your sons in their arms
and carry your daughters on their hips.
23Kings will be your foster fathers,
and their queens your nursing mothers.
They will bow down before you with their faces to the ground;
they will lick the dust at your feet.
Then you will know that I am the LORD;
those who hope in me will not be disappointed."

24Can plunder be taken from warriors,
or captives be rescued from the fierce[a]?

25But this is what the LORD says:

"Yes, captives will be taken from warriors,
and plunder retrieved from the fierce;
I will contend with those who contend with you,
and your children I will save.
26I will make your oppressors eat their own flesh;
they will be drunk on their own blood, as with wine.
Then all mankind will know
that I, the LORD, am your Savior,
your Redeemer, the Mighty One of Jacob."

Israel's Sin and the Servant's Obedience

50 This is what the LORD says:

"Where is your mother's certificate of divorce
with which I sent her away?
Or to which of my creditors
did I sell you?
Because of your sins you were sold;
because of your transgressions your mother was sent away.
2When I came, why was there no one?
When I called, why was there no one to answer?
Was my arm too short to deliver you?
Do I lack the strength to rescue you?
By a mere rebuke I dry up the sea,
I turn rivers into a desert;
their fish rot for lack of water
and die of thirst.
3I clothe the heavens with darkness
and make sackcloth its covering."

4The Sovereign LORD has given me a well-instructed tongue,
to know the word that sustains the weary.
He wakens me morning by morning,
wakens my ear to listen like one being instructed.
5The Sovereign LORD has opened my ears;
I have not been rebellious,
I have not turned away.
6I offered my back to those who beat me,
my cheeks to those who pulled out my beard;
I did not hide my face
from mocking and spitting.
7Because the Sovereign LORD helps me,
I will not be disgraced.
Therefore have I set my face like flint,
and I know I will not be put to shame.
8He who vindicates me is near.
Who then will bring charges against me?
Let us face each other!
Who is my accuser?
Let him confront me!
9It is the Sovereign LORD who helps me.
Who will condemn me?
They will all wear out like a garment;
the moths will eat them up.

10Who among you fears the LORD
and obeys the word of his servant?
Let the one who walks in the dark,
who has no light,
trust in the name of the LORD
and rely on their God.
11But now, all you who light fires
and provide yourselves with flaming torches,
go, walk in the light of your fires
and of the torches you have set ablaze.
This is what you shall receive from my hand:
You will lie down in torment.

Everlasting Salvation for Zion

51 "Listen to me, you who pursue righteousness
and who seek the LORD:
Look to the rock from which you were cut
and to the quarry from which you were hewn;
2look to Abraham, your father,
and to Sarah, who gave you birth.
When I called him he was only one man,
and I blessed him and made him many.
3The LORD will surely comfort Zion
and will look with compassion on all her ruins;
he will make her deserts like Eden,
her wastelands like the garden of the LORD.
Joy and gladness will be found in her,
thanksgiving and the sound of singing.

4"Listen to me, my people;
hear me, my nation:
Instruction will go out from me;
my justice will become a light to the nations.
5My righteousness draws near speedily,
my salvation is on the way,
and my arm will bring justice to the nations.
The islands will look to me
and wait in hope for my arm.
6Lift up your eyes to the heavens,
look at the earth beneath;

[a] 24 Dead Sea Scrolls, Vulgate and Syriac (see also Septuagint and verse 25); Masoretic Text *righteous*

the heavens will vanish like smoke,
the earth will wear out like a garment
and its inhabitants die like flies.
But my salvation will last forever,
my righteousness will never fail.

7 "Hear me, you who know what is right,
you people who have taken my
instruction to heart:
Do not fear the reproach of mere mortals
or be terrified by their insults.
8 For the moth will eat them up like a
garment;
the worm will devour them like wool.
But my righteousness will last forever,
my salvation through all generations."

9 Awake, awake, arm of the LORD,
clothe yourself with strength!
Awake, as in days gone by,
as in generations of old.
Was it not you who cut Rahab to pieces,
who pierced that monster through?
10 Was it not you who dried up the sea,
the waters of the great deep,
who made a road in the depths of the sea
so that the redeemed might cross over?
11 Those the LORD has rescued will return.
They will enter Zion with singing;
everlasting joy will crown their heads.
Gladness and joy will overtake them,
and sorrow and sighing will flee away.

12 "I, even I, am he who comforts you.
Who are you that you fear mere
mortals,
human beings who are but grass,
13 that you forget the LORD your Maker,
who stretches out the heavens
and who lays the foundations of the
earth,
that you live in constant terror every day
because of the wrath of the oppressor,
who is bent on destruction?
For where is the wrath of the oppressor?
14 The cowering prisoners will soon be set
free;
they will not die in their dungeon,
nor will they lack bread.
15 For I am the LORD your God,
who stirs up the sea so that its waves
roar—
the LORD Almighty is his name.
16 I have put my words in your mouth
and covered you with the shadow of my
hand—
I who set the heavens in place,
who laid the foundations of the earth,
and who say to Zion, 'You are my
people.'"

The Cup of the LORD's Wrath

17 Awake, awake!
Rise up, Jerusalem,
you who have drunk from the hand of the
LORD
the cup of his wrath,
you who have drained to its dregs
the goblet that makes people stagger.
18 Among all the children she bore
there was none to guide her;
among all the children she reared
there was none to take her by the hand.
19 These double calamities have come upon
you—
who can comfort you?—
ruin and destruction, famine and
sword—
who can[a] console you?
20 Your children have fainted;
they lie at every street corner,
like antelope caught in a net.
They are filled with the wrath of the
LORD,
with the rebuke of your God.

21 Therefore hear this, you afflicted one,
made drunk, but not with wine.
22 This is what your Sovereign LORD says,
your God, who defends his people:
"See, I have taken out of your hand
the cup that made you stagger;
from that cup, the goblet of my wrath,
you will never drink again.
23 I will put it into the hands of your
tormentors,
who said to you,
'Fall prostrate that we may walk on
you.'
And you made your back like the ground,
like a street to be walked on."

52 Awake, awake, Zion,
clothe yourself with strength!
Put on your garments of splendor,
Jerusalem, the holy city.
The uncircumcised and defiled
will not enter you again.
2 Shake off your dust;
rise up, sit enthroned, Jerusalem.
Free yourself from the chains on your
neck,
Daughter Zion, now a captive.

3 For this is what the LORD says:

"You were sold for nothing,
and without money you will be
redeemed."

4 For this is what the Sovereign LORD says:

"At first my people went down to Egypt to
live;
lately, Assyria has oppressed them.

5 "And now what do I have here?" declares
the LORD.

"For my people have been taken away for
nothing,
and those who rule them mock,[b]"
declares the LORD.
"And all day long
my name is constantly blasphemed.
6 Therefore my people will know my name;
therefore in that day they will know

[a] 19 Dead Sea Scrolls, Septuagint, Vulgate and Syriac; Masoretic Text / *how can I* [b] 5 Dead Sea Scrolls and Vulgate; Masoretic Text *wail*

that it is I who foretold it.
Yes, it is I."
7 How beautiful on the mountains
are the feet of those who bring good news,
who proclaim peace,
who bring good tidings,
who proclaim salvation,
who say to Zion,
"Your God reigns!"
8 Listen! Your watchmen lift up their voices;
together they shout for joy.
When the LORD returns to Zion,
they will see it with their own eyes.
9 Burst into songs of joy together,
you ruins of Jerusalem,
for the LORD has comforted his people,
he has redeemed Jerusalem.
10 The LORD will lay bare his holy arm
in the sight of all the nations,
and all the ends of the earth will see
the salvation of our God.

11 Depart, depart, go out from there!
Touch no unclean thing!
Come out from it and be pure,
you who carry the articles of the LORD's house.
12 But you will not leave in haste
or go in flight;
for the LORD will go before you,
the God of Israel will be your rear guard.

The Suffering and Glory of the Servant

13 See, my servant will act wisely[a];
he will be raised and lifted up and highly exalted.
14 Just as there were many who were appalled at him[b]—
his appearance was so disfigured
beyond that of any human being
and his form marred beyond human likeness—
15 so he will sprinkle many nations,[c]
and kings will shut their mouths
because of him.
For what they were not told, they will see,
and what they have not heard, they will understand.

53 Who has believed our message
and to whom has the arm of the LORD been revealed?
2 He grew up before him like a tender shoot,
and like a root out of dry ground.
He had no beauty or majesty to attract us to him,
nothing in his appearance that we should desire him.
3 He was despised and rejected by mankind,
a man of suffering, and familiar with pain.
Like one from whom people hide their faces
he was despised, and we held him in low esteem.

4 Surely he took up our pain
and bore our suffering,
yet we considered him punished by God,
stricken by him, and afflicted.
5 But he was pierced for our transgressions,
he was crushed for our iniquities;
the punishment that brought us peace was on him,
and by his wounds we are healed.
6 We all, like sheep, have gone astray,
each of us has turned to our own way;
and the LORD has laid on him
the iniquity of us all.

7 He was oppressed and afflicted,
yet he did not open his mouth;
he was led like a lamb to the slaughter,
and as a sheep before its shearers is silent,
so he did not open his mouth.
8 By oppression[d] and judgment he was taken away.
Yet who of his generation protested?
For he was cut off from the land of the living;
for the transgression of my people he was punished.[e]
9 He was assigned a grave with the wicked,
and with the rich in his death,
though he had done no violence,
nor was any deceit in his mouth.

10 Yet it was the LORD's will to crush him
and cause him to suffer,
and though the LORD makes[f] his life an offering for sin,
he will see his offspring and prolong his days,
and the will of the LORD will prosper in his hand.
11 After he has suffered,
he will see the light of life[g] and be satisfied[h];
by his knowledge[i] my righteous servant will justify many,
and he will bear their iniquities.
12 Therefore I will give him a portion among the great,[j]
and he will divide the spoils with the strong,[k]
because he poured out his life unto death,
and was numbered with the transgressors.
For he bore the sin of many,
and made intercession for the transgressors.

[a] 13 Or *will prosper* [b] 14 Hebrew *you* [c] 15 Or *so will many nations be amazed at him* (see also Septuagint) [d] 8 Or *From arrest* [e] 8 Or *generation considered / that he was cut off from the land of the living, / that he was punished for the transgression of my people?* [f] 10 Hebrew *though you make* [g] 11 Dead Sea Scrolls (see also Septuagint); Masoretic Text does not have *the light of life.* [h] 11 Or (with Masoretic Text) [11]*He will see the fruit of his suffering / and will be satisfied* [i] 11 Or *by knowledge of him* [j] 12 Or *many* [k] 12 Or *numerous*

The Future Glory of Zion

54 "Sing, barren woman,
you who never bore a child;
burst into song, shout for joy,
you who were never in labor;
because more are the children of the desolate woman
than of her who has a husband,"
says the LORD.
2 "Enlarge the place of your tent,
stretch your tent curtains wide,
do not hold back;
lengthen your cords,
strengthen your stakes.
3 For you will spread out to the right and to the left;
your descendants will dispossess nations
and settle in their desolate cities.

4 "Do not be afraid; you will not be put to shame.
Do not fear disgrace; you will not be humiliated.
You will forget the shame of your youth
and remember no more the reproach of your widowhood.
5 For your Maker is your husband—
the LORD Almighty is his name—
the Holy One of Israel is your Redeemer;
he is called the God of all the earth.
6 The LORD will call you back
as if you were a wife deserted and distressed in spirit—
a wife who married young,
only to be rejected," says your God.
7 "For a brief moment I abandoned you,
but with deep compassion I will bring you back.
8 In a surge of anger
I hid my face from you for a moment,
but with everlasting kindness
I will have compassion on you,"
says the LORD your Redeemer.

9 "To me this is like the days of Noah,
when I swore that the waters of Noah would never again cover the earth.
So now I have sworn not to be angry with you,
never to rebuke you again.
10 Though the mountains be shaken
and the hills be removed,
yet my unfailing love for you will not be shaken
nor my covenant of peace be removed,"
says the LORD, who has compassion on you.

11 "Afflicted city, lashed by storms and not comforted,
I will rebuild you with stones of turquoise,[a]
your foundations with lapis lazuli.
12 I will make your battlements of rubies,
your gates of sparkling jewels,
and all your walls of precious stones.
13 All your children will be taught by the LORD,
and great will be their peace.
14 In righteousness you will be established:
Tyranny will be far from you;
you will have nothing to fear.
Terror will be far removed;
it will not come near you.
15 If anyone does attack you, it will not be my doing;
whoever attacks you will surrender to you.

16 "See, it is I who created the blacksmith
who fans the coals into flame
and forges a weapon fit for its work.
And it is I who have created the destroyer to wreak havoc;
17 no weapon forged against you will prevail,
and you will refute every tongue that accuses you.
This is the heritage of the servants of the LORD,
and this is their vindication from me,"
declares the LORD.

Invitation to the Thirsty

55 "Come, all you who are thirsty,
come to the waters;
and you who have no money,
come, buy and eat!
Come, buy wine and milk
without money and without cost.
2 Why spend money on what is not bread,
and your labor on what does not satisfy?
Listen, listen to me, and eat what is good,
and you will delight in the richest of fare.
3 Give ear and come to me;
listen, that you may live.
I will make an everlasting covenant with you,
my faithful love promised to David.
4 See, I have made him a witness to the peoples,
a ruler and commander of the peoples.
5 Surely you will summon nations you know not,
and nations you do not know will come running to you,
because of the LORD your God,
the Holy One of Israel,
for he has endowed you with splendor."
6 Seek the LORD while he may be found;
call on him while he is near.
7 Let the wicked forsake their ways
and the unrighteous their thoughts.
Let them turn to the LORD, and he will have mercy on them,
and to our God, for he will freely pardon.
8 "For my thoughts are not your thoughts,
neither are your ways my ways,"
declares the LORD.

[a] *11* The meaning of the Hebrew for this word is uncertain.

9 "As the heavens are higher than the earth,
so are my ways higher than your ways
and my thoughts than your thoughts.
10 As the rain and the snow
come down from heaven,
and do not return to it
without watering the earth
and making it bud and flourish,
so that it yields seed for the sower and
bread for the eater,
11 so is my word that goes out from my
mouth:
It will not return to me empty,
but will accomplish what I desire
and achieve the purpose for which I
sent it.
12 You will go out in joy
and be led forth in peace;
the mountains and hills
will burst into song before you,
and all the trees of the field
will clap their hands.
13 Instead of the thornbush will grow the
juniper,
and instead of briers the myrtle will grow.
This will be for the LORD's renown,
for an everlasting sign,
that will endure forever."

Salvation for Others

56 This is what the LORD says:

"Maintain justice
and do what is right,
for my salvation is close at hand
and my righteousness will soon be
revealed.
2 Blessed is the one who does this—
the person who holds it fast,
who keeps the Sabbath without
desecrating it,
and keeps their hands from doing any
evil."

3 Let no foreigner who is bound to the LORD
say,
"The LORD will surely exclude me from
his people."
And let no eunuch complain,
"I am only a dry tree."

4 For this is what the LORD says:

"To the eunuchs who keep my Sabbaths,
who choose what pleases me
and hold fast to my covenant—
5 to them I will give within my temple and
its walls
a memorial and a name
better than sons and daughters;
I will give them an everlasting name
that will endure forever.
6 And foreigners who bind themselves to
the LORD
to minister to him,
to love the name of the LORD,
and to be his servants,
all who keep the Sabbath without
desecrating it
and who hold fast to my covenant—
7 these I will bring to my holy mountain
and give them joy in my house of
prayer.
Their burnt offerings and sacrifices
will be accepted on my altar;
for my house will be called
a house of prayer for all nations."
8 The Sovereign LORD declares—
he who gathers the exiles of Israel:
"I will gather still others to them
besides those already gathered."

God's Accusation Against the Wicked

9 Come, all you beasts of the field,
come and devour, all you beasts of the
forest!
10 Israel's watchmen are blind,
they all lack knowledge;
they are all mute dogs,
they cannot bark;
they lie around and dream,
they love to sleep.
11 They are dogs with mighty appetites;
they never have enough.
They are shepherds who lack
understanding;
they all turn to their own way,
they seek their own gain.
12 "Come," each one cries, "let me get wine!
Let us drink our fill of beer!
And tomorrow will be like today,
or even far better."

57 The righteous perish,
and no one takes it to heart;
the devout are taken away,
and no one understands
that the righteous are taken away
to be spared from evil.
2 Those who walk uprightly
enter into peace;
they find rest as they lie in death.

3 "But you—come here, you children of a
sorceress,
you offspring of adulterers and
prostitutes!
4 Who are you mocking?
At whom do you sneer
and stick out your tongue?
Are you not a brood of rebels,
the offspring of liars?
5 You burn with lust among the oaks
and under every spreading tree;
you sacrifice your children in the ravines
and under the overhanging crags.
6 The idols among the smooth stones of the
ravines are your portion;
indeed, they are your lot.
Yes, to them you have poured out drink
offerings
and offered grain offerings.
In view of all this, should I relent?
7 You have made your bed on a high and
lofty hill;
there you went up to offer your
sacrifices.
8 Behind your doors and your doorposts
you have put your pagan symbols.

Forsaking me, you uncovered your bed,
you climbed into it and opened it wide;
you made a pact with those whose beds you love,
and you looked with lust on their naked bodies.
9 You went to Molek[a] with olive oil
and increased your perfumes.
You sent your ambassadors[b] far away;
you descended to the very realm of the dead!
10 You wearied yourself by such going about,
but you would not say, 'It is hopeless.'
You found renewal of your strength,
and so you did not faint.

11 "Whom have you so dreaded and feared
that you have not been true to me,
and have neither remembered me
nor taken this to heart?
Is it not because I have long been silent
that you do not fear me?
12 I will expose your righteousness and your works,
and they will not benefit you.
13 When you cry out for help,
let your collection of idols save you!
The wind will carry all of them off,
a mere breath will blow them away.
But whoever takes refuge in me
will inherit the land
and possess my holy mountain."

Comfort for the Contrite

14 And it will be said:

"Build up, build up, prepare the road!
Remove the obstacles out of the way of my people."
15 For this is what the high and exalted One says—
he who lives forever, whose name is holy:
"I live in a high and holy place,
but also with the one who is contrite and lowly in spirit,
to revive the spirit of the lowly
and to revive the heart of the contrite.
16 I will not accuse them forever,
nor will I always be angry,
for then they would faint away because of me—
the very people I have created.
17 I was enraged by their sinful greed;
I punished them, and hid my face in anger,
yet they kept on in their willful ways.
18 I have seen their ways, but I will heal them;
I will guide them and restore comfort to Israel's mourners,
19 creating praise on their lips.
Peace, peace, to those far and near,"
says the LORD. "And I will heal them."
20 But the wicked are like the tossing sea,
which cannot rest,
whose waves cast up mire and mud.
21 "There is no peace," says my God, "for the wicked."

True Fasting

58 "Shout it aloud, do not hold back.
Raise your voice like a trumpet.
Declare to my people their rebellion
and to the descendants of Jacob their sins.
2 For day after day they seek me out;
they seem eager to know my ways,
as if they were a nation that does what is right
and has not forsaken the commands of its God.
They ask me for just decisions
and seem eager for God to come near them.
3 'Why have we fasted,' they say,
'and you have not seen it?
Why have we humbled ourselves,
and you have not noticed?'

"Yet on the day of your fasting, you do as you please
and exploit all your workers.
4 Your fasting ends in quarreling and strife,
and in striking each other with wicked fists.
You cannot fast as you do today
and expect your voice to be heard on high.
5 Is this the kind of fast I have chosen,
only a day for people to humble themselves?
Is it only for bowing one's head like a reed
and for lying in sackcloth and ashes?
Is that what you call a fast,
a day acceptable to the LORD?

6 "Is not this the kind of fasting I have chosen:
to loose the chains of injustice
and untie the cords of the yoke,
to set the oppressed free
and break every yoke?
7 Is it not to share your food with the hungry
and to provide the poor wanderer with shelter—
when you see the naked, to clothe them,
and not to turn away from your own flesh and blood?
8 Then your light will break forth like the dawn,
and your healing will quickly appear;
then your righteousness[c] will go before you,
and the glory of the LORD will be your rear guard.
9 Then you will call, and the LORD will answer;
you will cry for help, and he will say: Here am I.

"If you do away with the yoke of oppression,
with the pointing finger and malicious talk,

[a] 9 Or *to the king* [b] 9 Or *idols* [c] 8 Or *your righteous One*

10 and if you spend yourselves in behalf of
the hungry
and satisfy the needs of the oppressed,
then your light will rise in the darkness,
and your night will become like the
noonday.
11 The LORD will guide you always;
he will satisfy your needs in a sun-
scorched land
and will strengthen your frame.
You will be like a well-watered garden,
like a spring whose waters never fail.
12 Your people will rebuild the ancient ruins
and will raise up the age-old
foundations;
you will be called Repairer of Broken
Walls,
Restorer of Streets with Dwellings.

13 "If you keep your feet from breaking the
Sabbath
and from doing as you please on my
holy day,
if you call the Sabbath a delight
and the LORD's holy day honorable,
and if you honor it by not going your own
way
and not doing as you please or
speaking idle words,
14 then you will find your joy in the LORD,
and I will cause you to ride in triumph
on the heights of the land
and to feast on the inheritance of your
father Jacob."
For the mouth of the LORD
has spoken.

Sin, Confession and Redemption

59 Surely the arm of the LORD is not too
short to save,
nor his ear too dull to hear.
2 But your iniquities have separated
you from your God;
your sins have hidden his face from you,
so that he will not hear.
3 For your hands are stained with blood,
your fingers with guilt.
Your lips have spoken falsely,
and your tongue mutters wicked things.
4 No one calls for justice;
no one pleads a case with integrity.
They rely on empty arguments, they utter
lies;
they conceive trouble and give birth to
evil.
5 They hatch the eggs of vipers
and spin a spider's web.
Whoever eats their eggs will die,
and when one is broken, an adder is
hatched.
6 Their cobwebs are useless for clothing;
they cannot cover themselves with
what they make.
Their deeds are evil deeds,
and acts of violence are in their hands.
7 Their feet rush into sin;
they are swift to shed innocent blood.
They pursue evil schemes;
acts of violence mark their ways.
8 The way of peace they do not know;
there is no justice in their paths.
They have turned them into crooked
roads;
no one who walks along them will
know peace.

9 So justice is far from us,
and righteousness does not reach us.
We look for light, but all is darkness;
for brightness, but we walk in deep
shadows.
10 Like the blind we grope along the wall,
feeling our way like people without
eyes.
At midday we stumble as if it were
twilight;
among the strong, we are like the dead.
11 We all growl like bears;
we moan mournfully like doves.
We look for justice, but find none;
for deliverance, but it is far away.

12 For our offenses are many in your sight,
and our sins testify against us.
Our offenses are ever with us,
and we acknowledge our iniquities:
13 rebellion and treachery against the LORD,
turning our backs on our God,
inciting revolt and oppression,
uttering lies our hearts have conceived.
14 So justice is driven back,
and righteousness stands at a distance;
truth has stumbled in the streets,
honesty cannot enter.
15 Truth is nowhere to be found,
and whoever shuns evil becomes a
prey.

The LORD looked and was displeased
that there was no justice.
16 He saw that there was no one,
he was appalled that there was no one
to intervene;
so his own arm achieved salvation for
him,
and his own righteousness sustained
him.
17 He put on righteousness as his
breastplate,
and the helmet of salvation on his head;
he put on the garments of vengeance
and wrapped himself in zeal as in a
cloak.
18 According to what they have done,
so will he repay
wrath to his enemies
and retribution to his foes;
he will repay the islands their due.
19 From the west, people will fear the name
of the LORD,
and from the rising of the sun, they will
revere his glory.
For he will come like a pent-up flood
that the breath of the LORD drives
along.[a]

[a] 19 Or *When enemies come in like a flood, / the Spirit of the LORD will put them to flight*

20 "The Redeemer will come to Zion,
to those in Jacob who repent of their sins,"
declares the LORD.

21 "As for me, this is my covenant with them,"
says the LORD. "My Spirit, who is on you, will
not depart from you, and my words that I have
put in your mouth will always be on your lips,
on the lips of your children and on the lips
of their descendants—from this time on and
forever," says the LORD.

The Glory of Zion

60 "Arise, shine, for your light has come,
and the glory of the LORD rises upon you.
2 See, darkness covers the earth
and thick darkness is over the peoples,
but the LORD rises upon you
and his glory appears over you.
3 Nations will come to your light,
and kings to the brightness of your dawn.

4 "Lift up your eyes and look about you:
All assemble and come to you;
your sons come from afar,
and your daughters are carried on the hip.
5 Then you will look and be radiant,
your heart will throb and swell with joy;
the wealth on the seas will be brought to you,
to you the riches of the nations will come.
6 Herds of camels will cover your land,
young camels of Midian and Ephah.
And all from Sheba will come,
bearing gold and incense
and proclaiming the praise of the LORD.
7 All Kedar's flocks will be gathered to you,
the rams of Nebaioth will serve you;
they will be accepted as offerings on my altar,
and I will adorn my glorious temple.

8 "Who are these that fly along like clouds,
like doves to their nests?
9 Surely the islands look to me;
in the lead are the ships of Tarshish,[a]
bringing your children from afar,
with their silver and gold,
to the honor of the LORD your God,
the Holy One of Israel,
for he has endowed you with splendor.

10 "Foreigners will rebuild your walls,
and their kings will serve you.
Though in anger I struck you,
in favor I will show you compassion.
11 Your gates will always stand open,
they will never be shut, day or night,
so that people may bring you the wealth of the nations—
their kings led in triumphal procession.
12 For the nation or kingdom that will not serve you will perish;
it will be utterly ruined.

13 "The glory of Lebanon will come to you,
the juniper, the fir and the cypress together,
to adorn my sanctuary;
and I will glorify the place for my feet.
14 The children of your oppressors will come bowing before you;
all who despise you will bow down at your feet
and will call you the City of the LORD,
Zion of the Holy One of Israel.

15 "Although you have been forsaken and hated,
with no one traveling through,
I will make you the everlasting pride
and the joy of all generations.
16 You will drink the milk of nations
and be nursed at royal breasts.
Then you will know that I, the LORD, am your Savior,
your Redeemer, the Mighty One of Jacob.
17 Instead of bronze I will bring you gold,
and silver in place of iron.
Instead of wood I will bring you bronze,
and iron in place of stones.
I will make peace your governor
and well-being your ruler.
18 No longer will violence be heard in your land,
nor ruin or destruction within your borders,
but you will call your walls Salvation
and your gates Praise.
19 The sun will no more be your light by day,
nor will the brightness of the moon shine on you,
for the LORD will be your everlasting light,
and your God will be your glory.
20 Your sun will never set again,
and your moon will wane no more;
the LORD will be your everlasting light,
and your days of sorrow will end.
21 Then all your people will be righteous
and they will possess the land forever.
They are the shoot I have planted,
the work of my hands,
for the display of my splendor.
22 The least of you will become a thousand,
the smallest a mighty nation.
I am the LORD;
in its time I will do this swiftly."

The Year of the LORD's Favor

61 The Spirit of the Sovereign LORD is on me,
because the LORD has anointed me
to proclaim good news to the poor.
He has sent me to bind up the brokenhearted,
to proclaim freedom for the captives
and release from darkness for the prisoners,[b]

[a] 9 Or *the trading ships* [b] 1 Hebrew; Septuagint *the blind*

2 to proclaim the year of the LORD's favor
and the day of vengeance of our God,
to comfort all who mourn,
3 and provide for those who grieve in Zion—
to bestow on them a crown of beauty
instead of ashes,
the oil of joy
instead of mourning,
and a garment of praise
instead of a spirit of despair.
They will be called oaks of righteousness,
a planting of the LORD
for the display of his splendor.

4 They will rebuild the ancient ruins
and restore the places long devastated;
they will renew the ruined cities
that have been devastated for generations.
5 Strangers will shepherd your flocks;
foreigners will work your fields and vineyards.
6 And you will be called priests of the LORD,
you will be named ministers of our God.
You will feed on the wealth of nations,
and in their riches you will boast.

7 Instead of your shame
you will receive a double portion,
and instead of disgrace
you will rejoice in your inheritance.
And so you will inherit a double portion
in your land,
and everlasting joy will be yours.

8 "For I, the LORD, love justice;
I hate robbery and wrongdoing.
In my faithfulness I will reward my people
and make an everlasting covenant with them.
9 Their descendants will be known among the nations
and their offspring among the peoples.
All who see them will acknowledge
that they are a people the LORD has blessed."

10 I delight greatly in the LORD;
my soul rejoices in my God.
For he has clothed me with garments of salvation
and arrayed me in a robe of his righteousness,
as a bridegroom adorns his head like a priest,
and as a bride adorns herself with her jewels.
11 For as the soil makes the sprout come up
and a garden causes seeds to grow,
so the Sovereign LORD will make righteousness
and praise spring up before all nations.

Zion's New Name

62 For Zion's sake I will not keep silent,
for Jerusalem's sake I will not remain quiet,
till her vindication shines out like the dawn,
her salvation like a blazing torch.
2 The nations will see your vindication,
and all kings your glory;
you will be called by a new name
that the mouth of the LORD will bestow.
3 You will be a crown of splendor in the LORD's hand,
a royal diadem in the hand of your God.
4 No longer will they call you Deserted,
or name your land Desolate.
But you will be called Hephzibah,[a]
and your land Beulah[b];
for the LORD will take delight in you,
and your land will be married.
5 As a young man marries a young woman,
so will your Builder marry you;
as a bridegroom rejoices over his bride,
so will your God rejoice over you.

6 I have posted watchmen on your walls, Jerusalem;
they will never be silent day or night.
You who call on the LORD,
give yourselves no rest,
7 and give him no rest till he establishes Jerusalem
and makes her the praise of the earth.

8 The LORD has sworn by his right hand
and by his mighty arm:
"Never again will I give your grain
as food for your enemies,
and never again will foreigners drink the new wine
for which you have toiled;
9 but those who harvest it will eat it
and praise the LORD,
and those who gather the grapes will drink it
in the courts of my sanctuary."

10 Pass through, pass through the gates!
Prepare the way for the people.
Build up, build up the highway!
Remove the stones.
Raise a banner for the nations.

11 The LORD has made proclamation
to the ends of the earth:
"Say to Daughter Zion,
'See, your Savior comes!
See, his reward is with him,
and his recompense accompanies him.'"
12 They will be called the Holy People,
the Redeemed of the LORD;
and you will be called Sought After,
the City No Longer Deserted.

God's Day of Vengeance and Redemption

63 Who is this coming from Edom,
from Bozrah, with his garments stained crimson?
Who is this, robed in splendor,
striding forward in the greatness of his strength?

[a] 4 *Hephzibah* means *my delight is in her.* [b] 4 *Beulah* means *married.*

"It is I, proclaiming victory,
mighty to save."
2 Why are your garments red,
like those of one treading the winepress?
3 "I have trodden the winepress alone;
from the nations no one was with me.
I trampled them in my anger
and trod them down in my wrath;
their blood spattered my garments,
and I stained all my clothing.
4 It was for me the day of vengeance;
the year for me to redeem had come.
5 I looked, but there was no one to help,
I was appalled that no one gave support;
so my own arm achieved salvation for me,
and my own wrath sustained me.
6 I trampled the nations in my anger;
in my wrath I made them drunk
and poured their blood on the ground."

Praise and Prayer

7 I will tell of the kindnesses of the LORD,
the deeds for which he is to be praised,
according to all the LORD has done for us—
yes, the many good things
he has done for Israel,
according to his compassion and many kindnesses.
8 He said, "Surely they are my people,
children who will be true to me";
and so he became their Savior.
9 In all their distress he too was distressed,
and the angel of his presence saved them.[a]
In his love and mercy he redeemed them;
he lifted them up and carried them
all the days of old.
10 Yet they rebelled
and grieved his Holy Spirit.
So he turned and became their enemy
and he himself fought against them.
11 Then his people recalled[b] the days of old,
the days of Moses and his people—
where is he who brought them through the sea,
with the shepherd of his flock?
Where is he who set
his Holy Spirit among them,
12 who sent his glorious arm of power
to be at Moses' right hand,
who divided the waters before them,
to gain for himself everlasting renown,
13 who led them through the depths?
Like a horse in open country,
they did not stumble;
14 like cattle that go down to the plain,
they were given rest by the Spirit of the LORD.
This is how you guided your people
to make for yourself a glorious name.

15 Look down from heaven and see,
from your lofty throne, holy and glorious.
Where are your zeal and your might?
Your tenderness and compassion are withheld from us.
16 But you are our Father,
though Abraham does not know us
or Israel acknowledge us;
you, LORD, are our Father,
our Redeemer from of old is your name.
17 Why, LORD, do you make us wander from your ways
and harden our hearts so we do not revere you?
Return for the sake of your servants,
the tribes that are your inheritance.
18 For a little while your people possessed your holy place,
but now our enemies have trampled down your sanctuary.
19 We are yours from of old;
but you have not ruled over them,
they have not been called[c] by your name.

64 [d] Oh, that you would rend the heavens
and come down,
that the mountains would tremble before you!
2 As when fire sets twigs ablaze
and causes water to boil,
come down to make your name known to your enemies
and cause the nations to quake before you!
3 For when you did awesome things that we did not expect,
you came down, and the mountains trembled before you.
4 Since ancient times no one has heard,
no ear has perceived,
no eye has seen any God besides you,
who acts on behalf of those who wait for him.
5 You come to the help of those who gladly do right,
who remember your ways.
But when we continued to sin against them,
you were angry.
How then can we be saved?
6 All of us have become like one who is unclean,
and all our righteous acts are like filthy rags;
we all shrivel up like a leaf,
and like the wind our sins sweep us away.
7 No one calls on your name
or strives to lay hold of you;
for you have hidden your face from us
and have given us over to[e] our sins.
8 Yet you, LORD, are our Father.
We are the clay, you are the potter;
we are all the work of your hand.

[a] 9 Or *Savior* [9]*in their distress. / It was no envoy or angel / but his own presence that saved them*
[b] 11 Or *But may he recall* [c] 19 Or *We are like those you have never ruled, / like those never called*
[d] In Hebrew texts 64:1 is numbered 63:19b, and 64:2-12 is numbered 64:1-11. [e] 7 Septuagint, Syriac and Targum; Hebrew *have made us melt because of*

9 Do not be angry beyond measure, LORD;
do not remember our sins forever.
Oh, look on us, we pray,
for we are all your people.
10 Your sacred cities have become a wasteland;
even Zion is a wasteland, Jerusalem a desolation.
11 Our holy and glorious temple, where our ancestors praised you,
has been burned with fire,
and all that we treasured lies in ruins.
12 After all this, LORD, will you hold yourself back?
Will you keep silent and punish us beyond measure?

Judgment and Salvation

65 "I revealed myself to those who did not ask for me;
I was found by those who did not seek me.
To a nation that did not call on my name,
I said, 'Here am I, here am I.'
2 All day long I have held out my hands
to an obstinate people,
who walk in ways not good,
pursuing their own imaginations—
3 a people who continually provoke me
to my very face,
offering sacrifices in gardens
and burning incense on altars of brick;
4 who sit among the graves
and spend their nights keeping secret vigil;
who eat the flesh of pigs,
and whose pots hold broth of impure meat;
5 who say, 'Keep away; don't come near me,
for I am too sacred for you!'
Such people are smoke in my nostrils,
a fire that keeps burning all day.

6 "See, it stands written before me:
I will not keep silent but will pay back in full;
I will pay it back into their laps—
7 both your sins and the sins of your ancestors,"
says the LORD.
"Because they burned sacrifices on the mountains
and defied me on the hills,
I will measure into their laps
the full payment for their former deeds."

8 This is what the LORD says:

"As when juice is still found in a cluster of grapes
and people say, 'Don't destroy it,
there is still a blessing in it,'
so will I do in behalf of my servants;
I will not destroy them all.
9 I will bring forth descendants from Jacob,
and from Judah those who will possess my mountains;
my chosen people will inherit them,
and there will my servants live.
10 Sharon will become a pasture for flocks,
and the Valley of Achor a resting place for herds,
for my people who seek me.

11 "But as for you who forsake the LORD
and forget my holy mountain,
who spread a table for Fortune
and fill bowls of mixed wine for Destiny,
12 I will destine you for the sword,
and all of you will fall in the slaughter;
for I called but you did not answer,
I spoke but you did not listen.
You did evil in my sight
and chose what displeases me."

13 Therefore this is what the Sovereign LORD says:

"My servants will eat,
but you will go hungry;
my servants will drink,
but you will go thirsty;
my servants will rejoice,
but you will be put to shame.
14 My servants will sing
out of the joy of their hearts,
but you will cry out
from anguish of heart
and wail in brokenness of spirit.
15 You will leave your name
for my chosen ones to use in their curses;
the Sovereign LORD will put you to death,
but to his servants he will give another name.
16 Whoever invokes a blessing in the land
will do so by the one true God;
whoever takes an oath in the land
will swear by the one true God.
For the past troubles will be forgotten
and hidden from my eyes.

New Heavens and a New Earth

17 "See, I will create
new heavens and a new earth.
The former things will not be remembered,
nor will they come to mind.
18 But be glad and rejoice forever
in what I will create,
for I will create Jerusalem to be a delight
and its people a joy.
19 I will rejoice over Jerusalem
and take delight in my people;
the sound of weeping and of crying
will be heard in it no more.

20 "Never again will there be in it
an infant who lives but a few days,
or an old man who does not live out his years;
the one who dies at a hundred
will be thought a mere child;
the one who fails to reach[a] a hundred
will be considered accursed.

[a] 20 Or *the sinner who reaches*

21 They will build houses and dwell in them;
they will plant vineyards and eat their fruit.
22 No longer will they build houses and others live in them,
or plant and others eat.
For as the days of a tree,
so will be the days of my people;
my chosen ones will long enjoy
the work of their hands.
23 They will not labor in vain,
nor will they bear children doomed to misfortune;
for they will be a people blessed by the LORD,
they and their descendants with them.
24 Before they call I will answer;
while they are still speaking I will hear.
25 The wolf and the lamb will feed together,
and the lion will eat straw like the ox,
and dust will be the serpent's food.
They will neither harm nor destroy
on all my holy mountain,"
says the LORD.

Judgment and Hope

66 This is what the LORD says:

"Heaven is my throne,
and the earth is my footstool.
Where is the house you will build for me?
Where will my resting place be?
2 Has not my hand made all these things,
and so they came into being?"
declares the LORD.

"These are the ones I look on with favor:
those who are humble and contrite in spirit,
and who tremble at my word.
3 But whoever sacrifices a bull
is like one who kills a person,
and whoever offers a lamb
is like one who breaks a dog's neck;
whoever makes a grain offering
is like one who presents pig's blood,
and whoever burns memorial incense
is like one who worships an idol.
They have chosen their own ways,
and they delight in their abominations;
4 so I also will choose harsh treatment for them
and will bring on them what they dread.
For when I called, no one answered,
when I spoke, no one listened.
They did evil in my sight
and chose what displeases me."

5 Hear the word of the LORD,
you who tremble at his word:
"Your own people who hate you,
and exclude you because of my name, have said,
'Let the LORD be glorified,
that we may see your joy!'
Yet they will be put to shame.
6 Hear that uproar from the city,
hear that noise from the temple!
It is the sound of the LORD
repaying his enemies all they deserve.
7 "Before she goes into labor,
she gives birth;
before the pains come upon her,
she delivers a son.
8 Who has ever heard of such things?
Who has ever seen things like this?
Can a country be born in a day
or a nation be brought forth in a moment?
Yet no sooner is Zion in labor
than she gives birth to her children.
9 Do I bring to the moment of birth
and not give delivery?" says the LORD.
"Do I close up the womb
when I bring to delivery?" says your God.
10 "Rejoice with Jerusalem and be glad for her,
all you who love her;
rejoice greatly with her,
all you who mourn over her.
11 For you will nurse and be satisfied
at her comforting breasts;
you will drink deeply
and delight in her overflowing abundance."

12 For this is what the LORD says:

"I will extend peace to her like a river,
and the wealth of nations like a flooding stream;
you will nurse and be carried on her arm
and dandled on her knees.
13 As a mother comforts her child,
so will I comfort you;
and you will be comforted over Jerusalem."

14 When you see this, your heart will rejoice
and you will flourish like grass;
the hand of the LORD will be made known to his servants,
but his fury will be shown to his foes.
15 See, the LORD is coming with fire,
and his chariots are like a whirlwind;
he will bring down his anger with fury,
and his rebuke with flames of fire.
16 For with fire and with his sword
the LORD will execute judgment on all people,
and many will be those slain by the LORD.

17 "Those who consecrate and purify themselves to go into the gardens, following one
who is among those who eat the flesh of pigs,
rats and other unclean things—they will meet
their end together with the one they follow,"
declares the LORD.
18 "And I, because of what they have planned
and done, am about to come[a] and gather the
people of all nations and languages, and they
will come and see my glory.
19 "I will set a sign among them, and I will

[a] 18 The meaning of the Hebrew for this clause is uncertain.

send some of those who survive to the nations—to Tarshish, to the Libyans[a] and Lydi-
ans (famous as archers), to Tubal and Greece,
and to the distant islands that have not heard
of my fame or seen my glory. They will proclaim my glory among the nations. 20And they
will bring all your people, from all the nations,
to my holy mountain in Jerusalem as an offering to the LORD—on horses, in chariots and
wagons, and on mules and camels," says the
LORD. "They will bring them, as the Israelites
bring their grain offerings, to the temple of
the LORD in ceremonially clean vessels. 21And
I will select some of them also to be priests
and Levites," says the LORD.

22"As the new heavens and the new earth
that I make will endure before me," declares
the LORD, "so will your name and descendants
endure. 23From one New Moon to another and
from one Sabbath to another, all mankind
will come and bow down before me," says
the LORD. 24"And they will go out and look on
the dead bodies of those who rebelled against
me; the worms that eat them will not die, the
fire that burns them will not be quenched,
and they will be loathsome to all mankind."

Jeremiah

1 The words of Jeremiah son of Hilkiah, one
of the priests at Anathoth in the territory
of Benjamin. 2The word of the LORD came to
him in the thirteenth year of the reign of Josiah son of Amon king of Judah, 3and through
the reign of Jehoiakim son of Josiah king of
Judah, down to the fifth month of the eleventh
year of Zedekiah son of Josiah king of Judah,
when the people of Jerusalem went into exile.

The Call of Jeremiah

4The word of the LORD came to me, saying,

5"Before I formed you in the womb I knew[b]
you,
before you were born I set you apart;
I appointed you as a prophet to the
nations."

6"Alas, Sovereign LORD," I said, "I do not
know how to speak; I am too young."

7But the LORD said to me, "Do not say, 'I am
too young.' You must go to everyone I send you
to and say whatever I command you. 8Do not
be afraid of them, for I am with you and will
rescue you," declares the LORD.

9Then the LORD reached out his hand and
touched my mouth and said to me, "I have
put my words in your mouth. 10See, today I
appoint you over nations and kingdoms to uproot and tear down, to destroy and overthrow,
to build and to plant."

11The word of the LORD came to me: "What
do you see, Jeremiah?"

"I see the branch of an almond tree," I replied.

12The LORD said to me, "You have seen correctly, for I am watching[c] to see that my word
is fulfilled."

13The word of the LORD came to me again:
"What do you see?"

"I see a pot that is boiling," I answered. "It
is tilting toward us from the north."

14The LORD said to me, "From the north disaster will be poured out on all who live in the
land. 15I am about to summon all the peoples
of the northern kingdoms," declares the LORD.

"Their kings will come and set up their
thrones
in the entrance of the gates of
Jerusalem;
they will come against all her
surrounding walls
and against all the towns of Judah.
16I will pronounce my judgments on my
people
because of their wickedness in
forsaking me,
in burning incense to other gods
and in worshiping what their hands
have made.

17"Get yourself ready! Stand up and say to
them whatever I command you. Do not be
terrified by them, or I will terrify you before
them. 18Today I have made you a fortified
city, an iron pillar and a bronze wall to stand
against the whole land—against the kings of
Judah, its officials, its priests and the people
of the land. 19They will fight against you but
will not overcome you, for I am with you and
will rescue you," declares the LORD.

Israel Forsakes God

2 The word of the LORD came to me: 2"Go
and proclaim in the hearing of Jerusalem:

"This is what the LORD says:

"'I remember the devotion of your
youth,
how as a bride you loved me
and followed me through the wilderness,
through a land not sown.
3Israel was holy to the LORD,
the firstfruits of his harvest;

[a] 19 Some Septuagint manuscripts *Put* (Libyans); Hebrew *Pul* [b] 5 Or *chose* [c] 12 The Hebrew for *watching* sounds like the Hebrew for *almond tree.*

all who devoured her were held guilty,
and disaster overtook them,'"
declares the LORD.

4 Hear the word of the LORD, you
descendants of Jacob,
all you clans of Israel.

5 This is what the LORD says:

"What fault did your ancestors find in me,
that they strayed so far from me?
They followed worthless idols
and became worthless themselves.
6 They did not ask, 'Where is the LORD,
who brought us up out of Egypt
and led us through the barren wilderness,
through a land of deserts and ravines,
a land of drought and utter darkness,
a land where no one travels and no one
lives?'
7 I brought you into a fertile land
to eat its fruit and rich produce.
But you came and defiled my land
and made my inheritance detestable.
8 The priests did not ask,
'Where is the LORD?'
Those who deal with the law did not
know me;
the leaders rebelled against me.
The prophets prophesied by Baal,
following worthless idols.

9 "Therefore I bring charges against you
again,"
declares the LORD.
"And I will bring charges against your
children's children.
10 Cross over to the coasts of Cyprus and
look,
send to Kedar[a] and observe closely;
see if there has ever been anything like
this:
11 Has a nation ever changed its gods?
(Yet they are not gods at all.)
But my people have exchanged their
glorious God
for worthless idols.
12 Be appalled at this, you heavens,
and shudder with great horror,"
declares the LORD.
13 "My people have committed two sins:
They have forsaken me,
the spring of living water,
and have dug their own cisterns,
broken cisterns that cannot hold water.
14 Is Israel a servant, a slave by birth?
Why then has he become plunder?
15 Lions have roared;
they have growled at him.
They have laid waste his land;
his towns are burned and deserted.
16 Also, the men of Memphis and Tahpanhes
have cracked your skull.
17 Have you not brought this on yourselves
by forsaking the LORD your God
when he led you in the way?
18 Now why go to Egypt
to drink water from the Nile[b]?
And why go to Assyria
to drink water from the Euphrates?
19 Your wickedness will punish you;
your backsliding will rebuke you.
Consider then and realize
how evil and bitter it is for you
when you forsake the LORD your God
and have no awe of me,"
declares the Lord,
the LORD Almighty.

20 "Long ago you broke off your yoke
and tore off your bonds;
you said, 'I will not serve you!'
Indeed, on every high hill
and under every spreading tree
you lay down as a prostitute.
21 I had planted you like a choice vine
of sound and reliable stock.
How then did you turn against me
into a corrupt, wild vine?
22 Although you wash yourself with soap
and use an abundance of cleansing
powder,
the stain of your guilt is still before me,"
declares the Sovereign LORD.
23 "How can you say, 'I am not defiled;
I have not run after the Baals'?
See how you behaved in the valley;
consider what you have done.
You are a swift she-camel
running here and there,
24 a wild donkey accustomed to the desert,
sniffing the wind in her craving—
in her heat who can restrain her?
Any males that pursue her need not tire
themselves;
at mating time they will find her.
25 Do not run until your feet are bare
and your throat is dry.
But you said, 'It's no use!
I love foreign gods,
and I must go after them.'

26 "As a thief is disgraced when he is caught,
so the people of Israel are disgraced—
they, their kings and their officials,
their priests and their prophets.
27 They say to wood, 'You are my father,'
and to stone, 'You gave me birth.'
They have turned their backs to me
and not their faces;
yet when they are in trouble, they say,
'Come and save us!'
28 Where then are the gods you made for
yourselves?
Let them come if they can save you
when you are in trouble!
For you, Judah, have as many gods
as you have towns.

29 "Why do you bring charges against me?
You have all rebelled against me,"
declares the LORD.
30 "In vain I punished your people;
they did not respond to correction.
Your sword has devoured your prophets
like a ravenous lion.

[a] *10* In the Syro-Arabian desert [b] *18* Hebrew *Shihor*; that is, a branch of the Nile

31 “You of this generation, consider the word
of the LORD:

“Have I been a desert to Israel
or a land of great darkness?
Why do my people say, ‘We are free to
roam;
we will come to you no more’?
32 Does a young woman forget her jewelry,
a bride her wedding ornaments?
Yet my people have forgotten me,
days without number.
33 How skilled you are at pursuing love!
Even the worst of women can learn
from your ways.
34 On your clothes is found
the lifeblood of the innocent poor,
though you did not catch them
breaking in.
Yet in spite of all this
35 you say, ‘I am innocent;
he is not angry with me.’
But I will pass judgment on you
because you say, ‘I have not sinned.’
36 Why do you go about so much,
changing your ways?
You will be disappointed by Egypt
as you were by Assyria.
37 You will also leave that place
with your hands on your head,
for the LORD has rejected those you trust;
you will not be helped by them.

3 “If a man divorces his wife
and she leaves him and marries
another man,
should he return to her again?
Would not the land be completely
defiled?
But you have lived as a prostitute with
many lovers—
would you now return to me?”
declares the LORD.
2 “Look up to the barren heights and see.
Is there any place where you have not
been ravished?
By the roadside you sat waiting for lovers,
sat like a nomad in the desert.
You have defiled the land
with your prostitution and wickedness.
3 Therefore the showers have been
withheld,
and no spring rains have fallen.
Yet you have the brazen look of a
prostitute;
you refuse to blush with shame.
4 Have you not just called to me:
‘My Father, my friend from my youth,
5 will you always be angry?
Will your wrath continue forever?’
This is how you talk,
but you do all the evil you can.”

Unfaithful Israel

6 During the reign of King Josiah, the LORD
said to me, “Have you seen what faithless Israel has done? She has gone up on every high
hill and under every spreading tree and has
committed adultery there. 7 I thought that after
she had done all this she would return to me
but she did not, and her unfaithful sister Judah
saw it. 8 I gave faithless Israel her certificate
of divorce and sent her away because of all
her adulteries. Yet I saw that her unfaithful
sister Judah had no fear; she also went out and
committed adultery. 9 Because Israel’s immorality mattered so little to her, she defiled the
land and committed adultery with stone and
wood. 10 In spite of all this, her unfaithful sister
Judah did not return to me with all her heart,
but only in pretense,” declares the LORD.
11 The LORD said to me, “Faithless Israel is
more righteous than unfaithful Judah. 12 Go,
proclaim this message toward the north:

“ ‘Return, faithless Israel,’ declares the
LORD,
‘I will frown on you no longer,
for I am faithful,’ declares the LORD,
‘I will not be angry forever.
13 Only acknowledge your guilt—
you have rebelled against the LORD
your God,
you have scattered your favors to foreign
gods
under every spreading tree,
and have not obeyed me,’ ”
declares the LORD.

14 “Return, faithless people,” declares the
LORD, “for I am your husband. I will choose
you—one from a town and two from a clan—
and bring you to Zion. 15 Then I will give you
shepherds after my own heart, who will lead
you with knowledge and understanding.
16 In those days, when your numbers have
increased greatly in the land,” declares the
LORD, “people will no longer say, ‘The ark of
the covenant of the LORD.’ It will never enter
their minds or be remembered; it will not be
missed, nor will another one be made. 17 At
that time they will call Jerusalem The Throne
of the LORD, and all nations will gather in Jerusalem to honor the name of the LORD. No
longer will they follow the stubbornness of
their evil hearts. 18 In those days the people
of Judah will join the people of Israel, and
together they will come from a northern land
to the land I gave your ancestors as an inheritance.
19 “I myself said,

“ ‘How gladly would I treat you like my
children
and give you a pleasant land,
the most beautiful inheritance of any
nation.’
I thought you would call me ‘Father’
and not turn away from following me.
20 But like a woman unfaithful to her
husband,
so you, Israel, have been unfaithful to
me,”
declares the LORD.

21 A cry is heard on the barren heights,
the weeping and pleading of the people
of Israel,
because they have perverted their ways
and have forgotten the LORD their God.

22 "Return, faithless people;
I will cure you of backsliding."

"Yes, we will come to you,
for you are the LORD our God.
23 Surely the idolatrous commotion on the hills
and mountains is a deception;
surely in the LORD our God
is the salvation of Israel.
24 From our youth shameful gods have consumed
the fruits of our ancestors' labor—
their flocks and herds,
their sons and daughters.
25 Let us lie down in our shame,
and let our disgrace cover us.
We have sinned against the LORD our God,
both we and our ancestors;
from our youth till this day
we have not obeyed the LORD our God."

4 "If you, Israel, will return,
then return to me,"
declares the LORD.
"If you put your detestable idols out of my sight
and no longer go astray,
2 and if in a truthful, just and righteous way
you swear, 'As surely as the LORD lives,'
then the nations will invoke blessings by him
and in him they will boast."

3 This is what the LORD says to the people of
Judah and to Jerusalem:

"Break up your unplowed ground
and do not sow among thorns.
4 Circumcise yourselves to the LORD,
circumcise your hearts,
you people of Judah and inhabitants of Jerusalem,
or my wrath will flare up and burn like fire
because of the evil you have done—
burn with no one to quench it.

Disaster From the North

5 "Announce in Judah and proclaim in Jerusalem and say:
'Sound the trumpet throughout the land!'
Cry aloud and say:
'Gather together!
Let us flee to the fortified cities!'
6 Raise the signal to go to Zion!
Flee for safety without delay!
For I am bringing disaster from the north,
even terrible destruction."

7 A lion has come out of his lair;
a destroyer of nations has set out.
He has left his place
to lay waste your land.
Your towns will lie in ruins
without inhabitant.
8 So put on sackcloth,
lament and wail,
for the fierce anger of the LORD
has not turned away from us.

9 "In that day," declares the LORD,
"the king and the officials will lose heart,
the priests will be horrified,
and the prophets will be appalled."

10 Then I said, "Alas, Sovereign LORD! How
completely you have deceived this people and
Jerusalem by saying, 'You will have peace,'
when the sword is at our throats!"
11 At that time this people and Jerusalem
will be told, "A scorching wind from the barren heights in the desert blows toward my
people, but not to winnow or cleanse; 12 a wind
too strong for that comes from me. Now I pronounce my judgments against them."

13 Look! He advances like the clouds,
his chariots come like a whirlwind,
his horses are swifter than eagles.
Woe to us! We are ruined!
14 Jerusalem, wash the evil from your heart
and be saved.
How long will you harbor wicked thoughts?
15 A voice is announcing from Dan,
proclaiming disaster from the hills of Ephraim.
16 "Tell this to the nations,
proclaim concerning Jerusalem:
'A besieging army is coming from a distant land,
raising a war cry against the cities of Judah.
17 They surround her like men guarding a field,
because she has rebelled against me,'"
declares the LORD.
18 "Your own conduct and actions
have brought this on you.
This is your punishment.
How bitter it is!
How it pierces to the heart!"

19 Oh, my anguish, my anguish!
I writhe in pain.
Oh, the agony of my heart!
My heart pounds within me,
I cannot keep silent.
For I have heard the sound of the trumpet;
I have heard the battle cry.
20 Disaster follows disaster;
the whole land lies in ruins.
In an instant my tents are destroyed,
my shelter in a moment.
21 How long must I see the battle standard
and hear the sound of the trumpet?

22 "My people are fools;
they do not know me.
They are senseless children;
they have no understanding.
They are skilled in doing evil;
they know not how to do good."

23 I looked at the earth,
and it was formless and empty;
and at the heavens,
and their light was gone.

24 I looked at the mountains,
and they were quaking;
all the hills were swaying.
25 I looked, and there were no people;
every bird in the sky had flown away.
26 I looked, and the fruitful land was a desert;
all its towns lay in ruins
before the LORD, before his fierce anger.

27 This is what the LORD says:

"The whole land will be ruined,
though I will not destroy it completely.
28 Therefore the earth will mourn
and the heavens above grow dark,
because I have spoken and will not relent,
I have decided and will not turn back."

29 At the sound of horsemen and archers
every town takes to flight.
Some go into the thickets;
some climb up among the rocks.
All the towns are deserted;
no one lives in them.

30 What are you doing, you devastated one?
Why dress yourself in scarlet
and put on jewels of gold?
Why highlight your eyes with makeup?
You adorn yourself in vain.
Your lovers despise you;
they want to kill you.

31 I hear a cry as of a woman in labor,
a groan as of one bearing her first child—
the cry of Daughter Zion gasping for breath,
stretching out her hands and saying,
"Alas! I am fainting;
my life is given over to murderers."

Not One Is Upright

5 "Go up and down the streets of Jerusalem,
look around and consider,
search through her squares.
If you can find but one person
who deals honestly and seeks the truth,
I will forgive this city.
2 Although they say, 'As surely as the LORD lives,'
still they are swearing falsely."
3 LORD, do not your eyes look for truth?
You struck them, but they felt no pain;
you crushed them, but they refused correction.
They made their faces harder than stone
and refused to repent.
4 I thought, "These are only the poor;
they are foolish,
for they do not know the way of the LORD,
the requirements of their God.
5 So I will go to the leaders
and speak to them;
surely they know the way of the LORD,
the requirements of their God."
But with one accord they too had broken off the yoke
and torn off the bonds.
6 Therefore a lion from the forest will attack them,
a wolf from the desert will ravage them,
a leopard will lie in wait near their towns
to tear to pieces any who venture out,
for their rebellion is great
and their backslidings many.

7 "Why should I forgive you?
Your children have forsaken me
and sworn by gods that are not gods.
I supplied all their needs,
yet they committed adultery
and thronged to the houses of prostitutes.
8 They are well-fed, lusty stallions,
each neighing for another man's wife.
9 Should I not punish them for this?"
declares the LORD.
"Should I not avenge myself
on such a nation as this?

10 "Go through her vineyards and ravage them,
but do not destroy them completely.
Strip off her branches,
for these people do not belong to the LORD.
11 The people of Israel and the people of Judah
have been utterly unfaithful to me,"
declares the LORD.

12 They have lied about the LORD;
they said, "He will do nothing!
No harm will come to us;
we will never see sword or famine.
13 The prophets are but wind
and the word is not in them;
so let what they say be done to them."

14 Therefore this is what the LORD God Almighty says:

"Because the people have spoken these words,
I will make my words in your mouth a fire
and these people the wood it consumes.
15 People of Israel," declares the LORD,
"I am bringing a distant nation against you—
an ancient and enduring nation,
a people whose language you do not know,
whose speech you do not understand.
16 Their quivers are like an open grave;
all of them are mighty warriors.
17 They will devour your harvests and food,
devour your sons and daughters;
they will devour your flocks and herds,
devour your vines and fig trees.
With the sword they will destroy
the fortified cities in which you trust.

18 "Yet even in those days," declares the
LORD, "I will not destroy you completely.
19 And when the people ask, 'Why has the
LORD our God done all this to us?' you will tell
them, 'As you have forsaken me and served
foreign gods in your own land, so now you
will serve foreigners in a land not your own.'

20 "Announce this to the descendants of
Jacob
and proclaim it in Judah:
21 Hear this, you foolish and senseless
people,
who have eyes but do not see,
who have ears but do not hear:
22 Should you not fear me?" declares the LORD.
"Should you not tremble in my
presence?
I made the sand a boundary for the sea,
an everlasting barrier it cannot cross.
The waves may roll, but they cannot
prevail;
they may roar, but they cannot cross it.
23 But these people have stubborn and
rebellious hearts;
they have turned aside and gone away.
24 They do not say to themselves,
'Let us fear the LORD our God,
who gives autumn and spring rains in
season,
who assures us of the regular weeks of
harvest.'
25 Your wrongdoings have kept these away;
your sins have deprived you of good.

26 "Among my people are the wicked
who lie in wait like men who snare
birds
and like those who set traps to catch
people.
27 Like cages full of birds,
their houses are full of deceit;
they have become rich and powerful
28 and have grown fat and sleek.
Their evil deeds have no limit;
they do not seek justice.
They do not promote the case of the
fatherless;
they do not defend the just cause of the
poor.
29 Should I not punish them for this?"
declares the LORD.
"Should I not avenge myself
on such a nation as this?

30 "A horrible and shocking thing
has happened in the land:
31 The prophets prophesy lies,
the priests rule by their own authority,
and my people love it this way.
But what will you do in the end?

Jerusalem Under Siege

6 "Flee for safety, people of Benjamin!
Flee from Jerusalem!
Sound the trumpet in Tekoa!
Raise the signal over Beth Hakkerem!
For disaster looms out of the north,
even terrible destruction.
2 I will destroy Daughter Zion,
so beautiful and delicate.
3 Shepherds with their flocks will come
against her;
they will pitch their tents around her,
each tending his own portion."

4 "Prepare for battle against her!
Arise, let us attack at noon!
But, alas, the daylight is fading,
and the shadows of evening grow long.
5 So arise, let us attack at night
and destroy her fortresses!"

6 This is what the LORD Almighty says:

"Cut down the trees
and build siege ramps against
Jerusalem.
This city must be punished;
it is filled with oppression.
7 As a well pours out its water,
so she pours out her wickedness.
Violence and destruction resound in her;
her sickness and wounds are ever
before me.
8 Take warning, Jerusalem,
or I will turn away from you
and make your land desolate
so no one can live in it."

9 This is what the LORD Almighty says:

"Let them glean the remnant of Israel
as thoroughly as a vine;
pass your hand over the branches again,
like one gathering grapes."

10 To whom can I speak and give warning?
Who will listen to me?
Their ears are closed[a]
so they cannot hear.
The word of the LORD is offensive to them;
they find no pleasure in it.
11 But I am full of the wrath of the LORD,
and I cannot hold it in.

"Pour it out on the children in the street
and on the young men gathered
together;
both husband and wife will be caught in
it,
and the old, those weighed down with
years.
12 Their houses will be turned over to
others,
together with their fields and their
wives,
when I stretch out my hand
against those who live in the land,"
declares the LORD.
13 "From the least to the greatest,
all are greedy for gain;
prophets and priests alike,
all practice deceit.
14 They dress the wound of my people
as though it were not serious.
'Peace, peace,' they say,
when there is no peace.
15 Are they ashamed of their detestable
conduct?
No, they have no shame at all;
they do not even know how to blush.
So they will fall among the fallen;
they will be brought down when I
punish them,"
says the LORD.

[a] *10* Hebrew *uncircumcised*

16This is what the LORD says:

“Stand at the crossroads and look;
ask for the ancient paths,
ask where the good way is, and walk in it,
and you will find rest for your souls.
But you said, ‘We will not walk in it.’
17I appointed watchmen over you and said,
‘Listen to the sound of the trumpet!’
But you said, ‘We will not listen.’
18Therefore hear, you nations;
you who are witnesses,
observe what will happen to them.
19Hear, you earth:
I am bringing disaster on this people,
the fruit of their schemes,
because they have not listened to my words
and have rejected my law.
20What do I care about incense from Sheba
or sweet calamus from a distant land?
Your burnt offerings are not acceptable;
your sacrifices do not please me.”

21Therefore this is what the LORD says:

“I will put obstacles before this people.
Parents and children alike will stumble
over them;
neighbors and friends will perish.”

22This is what the LORD says:

“Look, an army is coming
from the land of the north;
a great nation is being stirred up
from the ends of the earth.
23They are armed with bow and spear;
they are cruel and show no mercy.
They sound like the roaring sea
as they ride on their horses;
they come like men in battle formation
to attack you, Daughter Zion.”

24We have heard reports about them,
and our hands hang limp.
Anguish has gripped us,
pain like that of a woman in labor.
25Do not go out to the fields
or walk on the roads,
for the enemy has a sword,
and there is terror on every side.
26Put on sackcloth, my people,
and roll in ashes;
mourn with bitter wailing
as for an only son,
for suddenly the destroyer
will come upon us.

27“I have made you a tester of metals
and my people the ore,
that you may observe
and test their ways.
28They are all hardened rebels,
going about to slander.
They are bronze and iron;
they all act corruptly.
29The bellows blow fiercely
to burn away the lead with fire,
but the refining goes on in vain;
the wicked are not purged out.
30They are called rejected silver,
because the LORD has rejected them.”

False Religion Worthless

7 This is the word that came to Jeremiah from
the LORD: 2“Stand at the gate of the LORD’s
house and there proclaim this message:
“ ‘Hear the word of the LORD, all you people of Judah who come through these gates
to worship the LORD. 3This is what the LORD
Almighty, the God of Israel, says: Reform your
ways and your actions, and I will let you live
in this place. 4Do not trust in deceptive words
and say, “This is the temple of the LORD, the
temple of the LORD, the temple of the LORD!”
5If you really change your ways and your actions and deal with each other justly, 6if you
do not oppress the foreigner, the fatherless or
the widow and do not shed innocent blood in
this place, and if you do not follow other gods
to your own harm, 7then I will let you live in
this place, in the land I gave your ancestors
for ever and ever. 8But look, you are trusting
in deceptive words that are worthless.
9“ ‘Will you steal and murder, commit adultery and perjury,[a] burn incense to Baal and
follow other gods you have not known, 10and
then come and stand before me in this house,
which bears my Name, and say, “We are
safe”—safe to do all these detestable things?
11Has this house, which bears my Name, become a den of robbers to you? But I have been
watching! declares the LORD.
12“ ‘Go now to the place in Shiloh where I
first made a dwelling for my Name, and see
what I did to it because of the wickedness of
my people Israel. 13While you were doing all
these things, declares the LORD, I spoke to you
again and again, but you did not listen; I called
you, but you did not answer. 14Therefore, what
I did to Shiloh I will now do to the house that
bears my Name, the temple you trust in, the
place I gave to you and your ancestors. 15I will
thrust you from my presence, just as I did all
your fellow Israelites, the people of Ephraim.’
16“So do not pray for this people nor offer
any plea or petition for them; do not plead with
me, for I will not listen to you. 17Do you not
see what they are doing in the towns of Judah
and in the streets of Jerusalem? 18The children
gather wood, the fathers light the fire, and the
women knead the dough and make cakes to
offer to the Queen of Heaven. They pour out
drink offerings to other gods to arouse my
anger. 19But am I the one they are provoking?
declares the LORD. Are they not rather harming themselves, to their own shame?
20“ ‘Therefore this is what the Sovereign
LORD says: My anger and my wrath will be
poured out on this place—on man and beast,
on the trees of the field and on the crops of your
land—and it will burn and not be quenched.
21“ ‘This is what the LORD Almighty, the God
of Israel, says: Go ahead, add your burnt offerings to your other sacrifices and eat the
meat yourselves! 22For when I brought your
ancestors out of Egypt and spoke to them, I

[a] 9 Or *and swear by false gods*

did not just give them commands about burnt
offerings and sacrifices, 23but I gave them this
command: Obey me, and I will be your God
and you will be my people. Walk in obedience to all I command you, that it may go well
with you. 24But they did not listen or pay attention; instead, they followed the stubborn
inclinations of their evil hearts. They went
backward and not forward. 25From the time
your ancestors left Egypt until now, day after
day, again and again I sent you my servants
the prophets. 26But they did not listen to me
or pay attention. They were stiff-necked and
did more evil than their ancestors.'

27"When you tell them all this, they will not
listen to you; when you call to them, they will
not answer. 28Therefore say to them, 'This is
the nation that has not obeyed the LORD its
God or responded to correction. Truth has
perished; it has vanished from their lips.

29" 'Cut off your hair and throw it away;
take up a lament on the barren heights, for
the LORD has rejected and abandoned this
generation that is under his wrath.

The Valley of Slaughter

30" 'The people of Judah have done evil in
my eyes, declares the LORD. They have set up
their detestable idols in the house that bears
my Name and have defiled it. 31They have built
the high places of Topheth in the Valley of Ben
Hinnom to burn their sons and daughters in
the fire—something I did not command, nor
did it enter my mind. 32So beware, the days
are coming, declares the LORD, when people
will no longer call it Topheth or the Valley
of Ben Hinnom, but the Valley of Slaughter,
for they will bury the dead in Topheth until
there is no more room. 33Then the carcasses
of this people will become food for the birds
and the wild animals, and there will be no one
to frighten them away. 34I will bring an end
to the sounds of joy and gladness and to the
voices of bride and bridegroom in the towns
of Judah and the streets of Jerusalem, for the
land will become desolate.

8 " 'At that time, declares the LORD, the
bones of the kings and officials of Judah,
the bones of the priests and prophets, and
the bones of the people of Jerusalem will be
removed from their graves. 2They will be exposed to the sun and the moon and all the
stars of the heavens, which they have loved
and served and which they have followed and
consulted and worshiped. They will not be
gathered up or buried, but will be like dung
lying on the ground. 3Wherever I banish them,
all the survivors of this evil nation will prefer death to life, declares the LORD Almighty.'

Sin and Punishment

4"Say to them, 'This is what the LORD says:

" 'When people fall down, do they not get
up?
When someone turns away, do they not
return?
5Why then have these people turned
away?
Why does Jerusalem always turn
away?
They cling to deceit;
they refuse to return.
6I have listened attentively,
but they do not say what is right.
None of them repent of their wickedness,
saying, "What have I done?"
Each pursues their own course
like a horse charging into battle.
7Even the stork in the sky
knows her appointed seasons,
and the dove, the swift and the thrush
observe the time of their migration.
But my people do not know
the requirements of the LORD.

8" 'How can you say, "We are wise,
for we have the law of the LORD,"
when actually the lying pen of the scribes
has handled it falsely?
9The wise will be put to shame;
they will be dismayed and trapped.
Since they have rejected the word of the
LORD,
what kind of wisdom do they have?
10Therefore I will give their wives to other
men
and their fields to new owners.
From the least to the greatest,
all are greedy for gain;
prophets and priests alike,
all practice deceit.
11They dress the wound of my people
as though it were not serious.
"Peace, peace," they say,
when there is no peace.
12Are they ashamed of their detestable
conduct?
No, they have no shame at all;
they do not even know how to blush.
So they will fall among the fallen;
they will be brought down when they
are punished,
says the LORD.

13" 'I will take away their harvest,
declares the LORD.
There will be no grapes on the vine.
There will be no figs on the tree,
and their leaves will wither.
What I have given them
will be taken from them.[a]' "

14Why are we sitting here?
Gather together!
Let us flee to the fortified cities
and perish there!
For the LORD our God has doomed us to
perish
and given us poisoned water to drink,
because we have sinned against him.
15We hoped for peace
but no good has come,
for a time of healing
but there is only terror.

[a] *13* The meaning of the Hebrew for this sentence is uncertain.

16 The snorting of the enemy's horses
is heard from Dan;
at the neighing of their stallions
the whole land trembles.
They have come to devour
the land and everything in it,
the city and all who live there.

17 "See, I will send venomous snakes among
you,
vipers that cannot be charmed,
and they will bite you,"
declares the LORD.

18 You who are my Comforter[a] in sorrow,
my heart is faint within me.
19 Listen to the cry of my people
from a land far away:
"Is the LORD not in Zion?
Is her King no longer there?"

"Why have they aroused my anger with
their images,
with their worthless foreign idols?"

20 "The harvest is past,
the summer has ended,
and we are not saved."

21 Since my people are crushed, I am
crushed;
I mourn, and horror grips me.
22 Is there no balm in Gilead?
Is there no physician there?
Why then is there no healing
for the wound of my people?

9[b] 1 Oh, that my head were a spring of water
and my eyes a fountain of tears!
I would weep day and night
for the slain of my people.
2 Oh, that I had in the desert
a lodging place for travelers,
so that I might leave my people
and go away from them;
for they are all adulterers,
a crowd of unfaithful people.

3 "They make ready their tongue
like a bow, to shoot lies;
it is not by truth
that they triumph[c] in the land.
They go from one sin to another;
they do not acknowledge me,"
declares the LORD.
4 "Beware of your friends;
do not trust anyone in your clan.
For every one of them is a deceiver,[d]
and every friend a slanderer.
5 Friend deceives friend,
and no one speaks the truth.
They have taught their tongues to lie;
they weary themselves with sinning.
6 You[e] live in the midst of deception;
in their deceit they refuse to
acknowledge me,"
declares the LORD.

7 Therefore this is what the LORD Almighty
says:

"See, I will refine and test them,
for what else can I do
because of the sin of my people?
8 Their tongue is a deadly arrow;
it speaks deceitfully.
With their mouths they all speak
cordially to their neighbors,
but in their hearts they set traps for
them.
9 Should I not punish them for this?"
declares the LORD.
"Should I not avenge myself
on such a nation as this?"

10 I will weep and wail for the mountains
and take up a lament concerning the
wilderness grasslands.
They are desolate and untraveled,
and the lowing of cattle is not heard.
The birds have all fled
and the animals are gone.

11 "I will make Jerusalem a heap of ruins,
a haunt of jackals;
and I will lay waste the towns of Judah
so no one can live there."

12 Who is wise enough to understand this?
Who has been instructed by the LORD and can
explain it? Why has the land been ruined and
laid waste like a desert that no one can cross?
13 The LORD said, "It is because they have
forsaken my law, which I set before them; they
have not obeyed me or followed my law. 14 Instead, they have followed the stubbornness
of their hearts; they have followed the Baals,
as their ancestors taught them." 15 Therefore
this is what the LORD Almighty, the God of
Israel, says: "See, I will make this people eat
bitter food and drink poisoned water. 16 I will
scatter them among nations that neither they
nor their ancestors have known, and I will
pursue them with the sword until I have made
an end of them."

17 This is what the LORD Almighty says:

"Consider now! Call for the wailing
women to come;
send for the most skillful of them.
18 Let them come quickly
and wail over us
till our eyes overflow with tears
and water streams from our eyelids.
19 The sound of wailing is heard from Zion:
'How ruined we are!
How great is our shame!
We must leave our land
because our houses are in ruins.'"

20 Now, you women, hear the word of the
LORD;
open your ears to the words of his mouth.
Teach your daughters how to wail;
teach one another a lament.
21 Death has climbed in through our
windows
and has entered our fortresses;

[a] *18* The meaning of the Hebrew for this word is uncertain. [b] In Hebrew texts 9:1 is numbered 8:23, and 9:2-26 is numbered 9:1-25. [c] *3* Or *lies; / they are not valiant for truth* [d] *4* Or *a deceiving Jacob*
[e] *6* That is, Jeremiah (the Hebrew is singular)

it has removed the children from the
streets
and the young men from the public
squares.

22 Say, "This is what the LORD declares:

" 'Dead bodies will lie
like dung on the open field,
like cut grain behind the reaper,
with no one to gather them.' "

23 This is what the LORD says:

"Let not the wise boast of their wisdom
or the strong boast of their strength
or the rich boast of their riches,
24 but let the one who boasts boast about
this:
that they have the understanding to
know me,
that I am the LORD, who exercises
kindness,
justice and righteousness on earth,
for in these I delight,"
declares the LORD.

25 "The days are coming," declares the LORD,
"when I will punish all who are circumcised
only in the flesh— 26 Egypt, Judah, Edom, Ammon, Moab and all who live in the wilderness
in distant places.[a] For all these nations are
really uncircumcised, and even the whole
house of Israel is uncircumcised in heart."

God and Idols

10 Hear what the LORD says to you, people
of Israel. 2 This is what the LORD says:

"Do not learn the ways of the nations
or be terrified by signs in the heavens,
though the nations are terrified by
them.
3 For the practices of the peoples are
worthless;
they cut a tree out of the forest,
and a craftsman shapes it with his chisel.
4 They adorn it with silver and gold;
they fasten it with hammer and nails
so it will not totter.
5 Like a scarecrow in a cucumber field,
their idols cannot speak;
they must be carried
because they cannot walk.
Do not fear them;
they can do no harm
nor can they do any good."

6 No one is like you, LORD;
you are great,
and your name is mighty in power.
7 Who should not fear you,
King of the nations?
This is your due.
Among all the wise leaders of the nations
and in all their kingdoms,
there is no one like you.

8 They are all senseless and foolish;
they are taught by worthless wooden
idols.
9 Hammered silver is brought from
Tarshish
and gold from Uphaz.
What the craftsman and goldsmith have
made
is then dressed in blue and purple—
all made by skilled workers.
10 But the LORD is the true God;
he is the living God, the eternal King.
When he is angry, the earth trembles;
the nations cannot endure his wrath.

11 "Tell them this: 'These gods, who did not
make the heavens and the earth, will perish
from the earth and from under the heavens.' "[b]

12 But God made the earth by his power;
he founded the world by his wisdom
and stretched out the heavens by his
understanding.
13 When he thunders, the waters in the
heavens roar;
he makes clouds rise from the ends of
the earth.
He sends lightning with the rain
and brings out the wind from his
storehouses.

14 Everyone is senseless and without
knowledge;
every goldsmith is shamed by his idols.
The images he makes are a fraud;
they have no breath in them.
15 They are worthless, the objects of
mockery;
when their judgment comes, they will
perish.
16 He who is the Portion of Jacob is not like
these,
for he is the Maker of all things,
including Israel, the people of his
inheritance—
the LORD Almighty is his name.

Coming Destruction

17 Gather up your belongings to leave the
land,
you who live under siege.
18 For this is what the LORD says:
"At this time I will hurl out
those who live in this land;
I will bring distress on them
so that they may be captured."

19 Woe to me because of my injury!
My wound is incurable!
Yet I said to myself,
"This is my sickness, and I must endure
it."
20 My tent is destroyed;
all its ropes are snapped.
My children are gone from me and are no
more;
no one is left now to pitch my tent
or to set up my shelter.
21 The shepherds are senseless
and do not inquire of the LORD;
so they do not prosper
and all their flock is scattered.

[a] 26 Or *wilderness and who clip the hair by their foreheads* [b] 11 The text of this verse is in Aramaic.

22 Listen! The report is coming—
a great commotion from the land of the north!
It will make the towns of Judah desolate,
a haunt of jackals.

Jeremiah's Prayer

23 LORD, I know that people's lives are not their own;
it is not for them to direct their steps.
24 Discipline me, LORD, but only in due measure—
not in your anger,
or you will reduce me to nothing.
25 Pour out your wrath on the nations
that do not acknowledge you,
on the peoples who do not call on your name.
For they have devoured Jacob;
they have devoured him completely
and destroyed his homeland.

The Covenant Is Broken

11 This is the word that came to Jeremiah
from the LORD: 2 "Listen to the terms of
this covenant and tell them to the people of Judah and to those who live in Jerusalem. 3 Tell
them that this is what the LORD, the God of
Israel, says: 'Cursed is the one who does not
obey the terms of this covenant— 4 the terms
I commanded your ancestors when I brought
them out of Egypt, out of the iron-smelting
furnace.' I said, 'Obey me and do everything
I command you, and you will be my people,
and I will be your God. 5 Then I will fulfill the
oath I swore to your ancestors, to give them a
land flowing with milk and honey'—the land
you possess today."

I answered, "Amen, LORD."

6 The LORD said to me, "Proclaim all these
words in the towns of Judah and in the streets
of Jerusalem: 'Listen to the terms of this covenant and follow them. 7 From the time I
brought your ancestors up from Egypt until
today, I warned them again and again, saying, "Obey me." 8 But they did not listen or pay
attention; instead, they followed the stubbornness of their evil hearts. So I brought on them
all the curses of the covenant I had commanded them to follow but that they did not keep.'"

9 Then the LORD said to me, "There is a conspiracy among the people of Judah and those
who live in Jerusalem. 10 They have returned
to the sins of their ancestors, who refused to
listen to my words. They have followed other gods to serve them. Both Israel and Judah
have broken the covenant I made with their
ancestors. 11 Therefore this is what the LORD
says: 'I will bring on them a disaster they cannot escape. Although they cry out to me, I will
not listen to them. 12 The towns of Judah and
the people of Jerusalem will go and cry out
to the gods to whom they burn incense, but
they will not help them at all when disaster
strikes. 13 You, Judah, have as many gods as
you have towns; and the altars you have set up
to burn incense to that shameful god Baal are
as many as the streets of Jerusalem.'

14 "Do not pray for this people or offer any
plea or petition for them, because I will not
listen when they call to me in the time of their
distress.

15 "What is my beloved doing in my temple
as she, with many others, works out her evil schemes?
Can consecrated meat avert your punishment?
When you engage in your wickedness,
then you rejoice.[a]"
16 The LORD called you a thriving olive tree
with fruit beautiful in form.
But with the roar of a mighty storm
he will set it on fire,
and its branches will be broken.

17 The LORD Almighty, who planted you, has
decreed disaster for you, because the people
of both Israel and Judah have done evil and
aroused my anger by burning incense to Baal.

Plot Against Jeremiah

18 Because the LORD revealed their plot to
me, I knew it, for at that time he showed me
what they were doing. 19 I had been like a gentle lamb led to the slaughter; I did not realize
that they had plotted against me, saying,

"Let us destroy the tree and its fruit;
let us cut him off from the land of the living,
that his name be remembered no more."
20 But you, LORD Almighty, who judge righteously
and test the heart and mind,
let me see your vengeance on them,
for to you I have committed my cause.

21 Therefore this is what the LORD says about
the people of Anathoth who are threatening to
kill you, saying, "Do not prophesy in the name
of the LORD or you will die by our hands"—
22 therefore this is what the LORD Almighty
says: "I will punish them. Their young men
will die by the sword, their sons and daughters by famine. 23 Not even a remnant will be
left to them, because I will bring disaster on
the people of Anathoth in the year of their
punishment."

Jeremiah's Complaint

12 You are always righteous, LORD,
when I bring a case before you.
Yet I would speak with you about your justice:
Why does the way of the wicked prosper?
Why do all the faithless live at ease?
2 You have planted them, and they have taken root;
they grow and bear fruit.
You are always on their lips
but far from their hearts.

[a] 15 Or *Could consecrated meat avert your punishment? / Then you would rejoice*

3 Yet you know me, LORD;
you see me and test my thoughts about you.
Drag them off like sheep to be butchered!
Set them apart for the day of slaughter!
4 How long will the land lie parched
and the grass in every field be withered?
Because those who live in it are wicked,
the animals and birds have perished.
Moreover, the people are saying,
"He will not see what happens to us."

God's Answer

5 "If you have raced with men on foot
and they have worn you out,
how can you compete with horses?
If you stumble[a] in safe country,
how will you manage in the thickets by[b] the Jordan?
6 Your relatives, members of your own family—
even they have betrayed you;
they have raised a loud cry against you.
Do not trust them,
though they speak well of you.

7 "I will forsake my house,
abandon my inheritance;
I will give the one I love
into the hands of her enemies.
8 My inheritance has become to me
like a lion in the forest.
She roars at me;
therefore I hate her.
9 Has not my inheritance become to me
like a speckled bird of prey
that other birds of prey surround and attack?
Go and gather all the wild beasts;
bring them to devour.
10 Many shepherds will ruin my vineyard
and trample down my field;
they will turn my pleasant field
into a desolate wasteland.
11 It will be made a wasteland,
parched and desolate before me;
the whole land will be laid waste
because there is no one who cares.
12 Over all the barren heights in the desert
destroyers will swarm,
for the sword of the LORD will devour
from one end of the land to the other;
no one will be safe.
13 They will sow wheat but reap thorns;
they will wear themselves out but gain nothing.
They will bear the shame of their harvest
because of the LORD's fierce anger."

14This is what the LORD says: "As for all my
wicked neighbors who seize the inheritance
I gave my people Israel, I will uproot them
from their lands and I will uproot the people of
Judah from among them. 15But after I uproot
them, I will again have compassion and will
bring each of them back to their own inheritance and their own country. 16And if they
learn well the ways of my people and swear
by my name, saying, 'As surely as the LORD
lives'—even as they once taught my people to
swear by Baal—then they will be established
among my people. 17But if any nation does not
listen, I will completely uproot and destroy it,"
declares the LORD.

A Linen Belt

13 This is what the LORD said to me: "Go
and buy a linen belt and put it around
your waist, but do not let it touch water." 2So
I bought a belt, as the LORD directed, and put
it around my waist.
3Then the word of the LORD came to me a
second time: 4"Take the belt you bought and
are wearing around your waist, and go now
to Perath[c] and hide it there in a crevice in the
rocks." 5So I went and hid it at Perath, as the
LORD told me.
6Many days later the LORD said to me, "Go
now to Perath and get the belt I told you to
hide there." 7So I went to Perath and dug up
the belt and took it from the place where I
had hidden it, but now it was ruined and completely useless.
8Then the word of the LORD came to me:
9"This is what the LORD says: 'In the same way
I will ruin the pride of Judah and the great
pride of Jerusalem. 10These wicked people,
who refuse to listen to my words, who follow
the stubbornness of their hearts and go after
other gods to serve and worship them, will be
like this belt—completely useless! 11For as a
belt is bound around the waist, so I bound all
the people of Israel and all the people of Judah
to me,' declares the LORD, 'to be my people for
my renown and praise and honor. But they
have not listened.'

Wineskins

12"Say to them: 'This is what the LORD, the
God of Israel, says: Every wineskin should be
filled with wine.' And if they say to you, 'Don't
we know that every wineskin should be filled
with wine?' 13then tell them, 'This is what the
LORD says: I am going to fill with drunkenness all who live in this land, including the
kings who sit on David's throne, the priests,
the prophets and all those living in Jerusalem.
14I will smash them one against the other, parents and children alike, declares the LORD. I
will allow no pity or mercy or compassion to
keep me from destroying them.'"

Threat of Captivity

15 Hear and pay attention,
do not be arrogant,
for the LORD has spoken.
16 Give glory to the LORD your God
before he brings the darkness,
before your feet stumble
on the darkening hills.

[a] 5 Or *you feel secure only* [b] 5 Or *the flooding of* [c] 4 Or possibly *to the Euphrates*; similarly in verses 5-7

You hope for light,
but he will turn it to utter darkness
and change it to deep gloom.
17 If you do not listen,
I will weep in secret
because of your pride;
my eyes will weep bitterly,
overflowing with tears,
because the LORD's flock will be taken captive.

18 Say to the king and to the queen mother,
"Come down from your thrones,
for your glorious crowns
will fall from your heads."
19 The cities in the Negev will be shut up,
and there will be no one to open them.
All Judah will be carried into exile,
carried completely away.

20 Look up and see
those who are coming from the north.
Where is the flock that was entrusted to you,
the sheep of which you boasted?
21 What will you say when the LORD sets over you
those you cultivated as your special allies?
Will not pain grip you
like that of a woman in labor?
22 And if you ask yourself,
"Why has this happened to me?"—
it is because of your many sins
that your skirts have been torn off
and your body mistreated.
23 Can an Ethiopian[a] change his skin
or a leopard its spots?
Neither can you do good
who are accustomed to doing evil.

24 "I will scatter you like chaff
driven by the desert wind.
25 This is your lot,
the portion I have decreed for you,"
declares the LORD,
"because you have forgotten me
and trusted in false gods.
26 I will pull up your skirts over your face
that your shame may be seen—
27 your adulteries and lustful neighings,
your shameless prostitution!
I have seen your detestable acts
on the hills and in the fields.
Woe to you, Jerusalem!
How long will you be unclean?"

Drought, Famine, Sword

14 This is the word of the LORD that came to Jeremiah concerning the drought:

2 "Judah mourns,
her cities languish;
they wail for the land,
and a cry goes up from Jerusalem.
3 The nobles send their servants for water;
they go to the cisterns
but find no water.
They return with their jars unfilled;
dismayed and despairing,
they cover their heads.
4 The ground is cracked
because there is no rain in the land;
the farmers are dismayed
and cover their heads.
5 Even the doe in the field
deserts her newborn fawn
because there is no grass.
6 Wild donkeys stand on the barren heights
and pant like jackals;
their eyes fail
for lack of food."

7 Although our sins testify against us,
do something, LORD, for the sake of your name.
For we have often rebelled;
we have sinned against you.
8 You who are the hope of Israel,
its Savior in times of distress,
why are you like a stranger in the land,
like a traveler who stays only a night?
9 Why are you like a man taken by surprise,
like a warrior powerless to save?
You are among us, LORD,
and we bear your name;
do not forsake us!

10 This is what the LORD says about this
people:

"They greatly love to wander;
they do not restrain their feet.
So the LORD does not accept them;
he will now remember their wickedness
and punish them for their sins."

11 Then the LORD said to me, "Do not pray
for the well-being of this people. 12 Although
they fast, I will not listen to their cry; though
they offer burnt offerings and grain offerings,
I will not accept them. Instead, I will destroy
them with the sword, famine and plague."

13 But I said, "Alas, Sovereign LORD! The
prophets keep telling them, 'You will not see
the sword or suffer famine. Indeed, I will give
you lasting peace in this place.'"

14 Then the LORD said to me, "The prophets are prophesying lies in my name. I have
not sent them or appointed them or spoken
to them. They are prophesying to you false
visions, divinations, idolatries[b] and the delusions of their own minds. 15 Therefore this is
what the LORD says about the prophets who
are prophesying in my name: I did not send
them, yet they are saying, 'No sword or famine will touch this land.' Those same prophets
will perish by sword and famine. 16 And the
people they are prophesying to will be thrown
out into the streets of Jerusalem because of
the famine and sword. There will be no one
to bury them, their wives, their sons and their
daughters. I will pour out on them the calamity they deserve.

[a] *23* Hebrew *Cushite* (probably a person from the upper Nile region) [b] *14* Or *visions, worthless divinations*

17 "Speak this word to them:

" 'Let my eyes overflow with tears
night and day without ceasing;
for the Virgin Daughter, my people,
has suffered a grievous wound,
a crushing blow.
18 If I go into the country,
I see those slain by the sword;
if I go into the city,
I see the ravages of famine.
Both prophet and priest
have gone to a land they know not.' "

19 Have you rejected Judah completely?
Do you despise Zion?
Why have you afflicted us
so that we cannot be healed?
We hoped for peace
but no good has come,
for a time of healing
but there is only terror.
20 We acknowledge our wickedness, LORD,
and the guilt of our ancestors;
we have indeed sinned against you.
21 For the sake of your name do not despise us;
do not dishonor your glorious throne.
Remember your covenant with us
and do not break it.
22 Do any of the worthless idols of the
nations bring rain?
Do the skies themselves send down
showers?
No, it is you, LORD our God.
Therefore our hope is in you,
for you are the one who does all this.

15 Then the LORD said to me: "Even if Moses
and Samuel were to stand before me, my
heart would not go out to this people. Send
them away from my presence! Let them go!
2 And if they ask you, 'Where shall we go?' tell
them, 'This is what the LORD says:

" 'Those destined for death, to death;
those for the sword, to the sword;
those for starvation, to starvation;
those for captivity, to captivity.'

3 "I will send four kinds of destroyers
against them," declares the LORD, "the sword
to kill and the dogs to drag away and the birds
and the wild animals to devour and destroy. 4 I
will make them abhorrent to all the kingdoms
of the earth because of what Manasseh son
of Hezekiah king of Judah did in Jerusalem.

5 "Who will have pity on you, Jerusalem?
Who will mourn for you?
Who will stop to ask how you are?
6 You have rejected me," declares the LORD.
"You keep on backsliding.
So I will reach out and destroy you;
I am tired of holding back.
7 I will winnow them with a winnowing fork
at the city gates of the land.
I will bring bereavement and destruction
on my people,
for they have not changed their ways.
8 I will make their widows more numerous
than the sand of the sea.
At midday I will bring a destroyer
against the mothers of their young
men;
suddenly I will bring down on them
anguish and terror.
9 The mother of seven will grow faint
and breathe her last.
Her sun will set while it is still day;
she will be disgraced and humiliated.
I will put the survivors to the sword
before their enemies,"
declares the LORD.

10 Alas, my mother, that you gave me birth,
a man with whom the whole land
strives and contends!
I have neither lent nor borrowed,
yet everyone curses me.

11 The LORD said,

"Surely I will deliver you for a good
purpose;
surely I will make your enemies plead
with you
in times of disaster and times of
distress.

12 "Can a man break iron—
iron from the north—or bronze?

13 "Your wealth and your treasures
I will give as plunder, without charge,
because of all your sins
throughout your country.
14 I will enslave you to your enemies
in[a] a land you do not know,
for my anger will kindle a fire
that will burn against you."

15 LORD, you understand;
remember me and care for me.
Avenge me on my persecutors.
You are long-suffering—do not take me
away;
think of how I suffer reproach for your
sake.
16 When your words came, I ate them;
they were my joy and my heart's
delight,
for I bear your name,
LORD God Almighty.
17 I never sat in the company of revelers,
never made merry with them;
I sat alone because your hand was on me
and you had filled me with indignation.
18 Why is my pain unending
and my wound grievous and incurable?
You are to me like a deceptive brook,
like a spring that fails.

19 Therefore this is what the LORD says:

"If you repent, I will restore you
that you may serve me;
if you utter worthy, not worthless,
words,
you will be my spokesman.

[a] *14* Some Hebrew manuscripts, Septuagint and Syriac (see also 17:4); most Hebrew manuscripts *I will cause your enemies to bring you / into*

Let this people turn to you,
but you must not turn to them.
20 I will make you a wall to this people,
a fortified wall of bronze;
they will fight against you
but will not overcome you,
for I am with you
to rescue and save you,"
declares the LORD.
21 "I will save you from the hands of the
wicked
and deliver you from the grasp of the
cruel."

Day of Disaster

16 Then the word of the LORD came to me:
2"You must not marry and have sons
or daughters in this place." 3For this is what
the LORD says about the sons and daughters
born in this land and about the women who
are their mothers and the men who are their
fathers: 4"They will die of deadly diseases.
They will not be mourned or buried but will
be like dung lying on the ground. They will
perish by sword and famine, and their dead
bodies will become food for the birds and the
wild animals."

5For this is what the LORD says: "Do not enter a house where there is a funeral meal; do
not go to mourn or show sympathy, because
I have withdrawn my blessing, my love and
my pity from this people," declares the LORD.
6"Both high and low will die in this land. They
will not be buried or mourned, and no one
will cut themselves or shave their head for
the dead. 7No one will offer food to comfort
those who mourn for the dead—not even for
a father or a mother—nor will anyone give
them a drink to console them.

8"And do not enter a house where there is
feasting and sit down to eat and drink. 9For
this is what the LORD Almighty, the God of
Israel, says: Before your eyes and in your days
I will bring an end to the sounds of joy and
gladness and to the voices of bride and bridegroom in this place.

10"When you tell these people all this and
they ask you, 'Why has the LORD decreed
such a great disaster against us? What wrong
have we done? What sin have we committed
against the LORD our God?' 11then say to them,
'It is because your ancestors forsook me,' declares the LORD, 'and followed other gods and
served and worshiped them. They forsook me
and did not keep my law. 12But you have behaved more wickedly than your ancestors. See
how all of you are following the stubbornness
of your evil hearts instead of obeying me. 13So
I will throw you out of this land into a land
neither you nor your ancestors have known,
and there you will serve other gods day and
night, for I will show you no favor.'

14"However, the days are coming," declares
the LORD, "when it will no longer be said, 'As
surely as the LORD lives, who brought the Israelites up out of Egypt,' 15but it will be said,
'As surely as the LORD lives, who brought the
Israelites up out of the land of the north and
out of all the countries where he had banished
them.' For I will restore them to the land I gave
their ancestors.

16"But now I will send for many fishermen,"
declares the LORD, "and they will catch them.
After that I will send for many hunters, and
they will hunt them down on every mountain
and hill and from the crevices of the rocks.
17My eyes are on all their ways; they are not
hidden from me, nor is their sin concealed
from my eyes. 18I will repay them double for
their wickedness and their sin, because they
have defiled my land with the lifeless forms
of their vile images and have filled my inheritance with their detestable idols."

19 LORD, my strength and my fortress,
my refuge in time of distress,
to you the nations will come
from the ends of the earth and say,
"Our ancestors possessed nothing but
false gods,
worthless idols that did them no good.
20 Do people make their own gods?
Yes, but they are not gods!"

21 "Therefore I will teach them—
this time I will teach them
my power and might.
Then they will know
that my name is the LORD.

17 "Judah's sin is engraved with an iron
tool,
inscribed with a flint point,
on the tablets of their hearts
and on the horns of their altars.
2 Even their children remember
their altars and Asherah poles[a]
beside the spreading trees
and on the high hills.
3 My mountain in the land
and your[b] wealth and all your treasures
I will give away as plunder,
together with your high places,
because of sin throughout your
country.
4 Through your own fault you will lose
the inheritance I gave you.
I will enslave you to your enemies
in a land you do not know,
for you have kindled my anger,
and it will burn forever."

5This is what the LORD says:

"Cursed is the one who trusts in man,
who draws strength from mere flesh
and whose heart turns away from the
LORD.
6 That person will be like a bush in the
wastelands;
they will not see prosperity when it
comes.
They will dwell in the parched places of
the desert,
in a salt land where no one lives.

[a] 2 That is, wooden symbols of the goddess Asherah
[b] 2,3 Or *hills / 3and the mountains of the land. / Your*

7 “But blessed is the one who trusts in the
LORD,
whose confidence is in him.
8 They will be like a tree planted by the
water
that sends out its roots by the stream.
It does not fear when heat comes;
its leaves are always green.
It has no worries in a year of drought
and never fails to bear fruit.”

9 The heart is deceitful above all things
and beyond cure.
Who can understand it?

10 “I the LORD search the heart
and examine the mind,
to reward each person according to their
conduct,
according to what their deeds deserve.”

11 Like a partridge that hatches eggs it did
not lay
are those who gain riches by unjust
means.
When their lives are half gone, their
riches will desert them,
and in the end they will prove to be fools.

12 A glorious throne, exalted from the
beginning,
is the place of our sanctuary.
13 LORD, you are the hope of Israel;
all who forsake you will be put to
shame.
Those who turn away from you will be
written in the dust
because they have forsaken the LORD,
the spring of living water.

14 Heal me, LORD, and I will be healed;
save me and I will be saved,
for you are the one I praise.
15 They keep saying to me,
“Where is the word of the LORD?
Let it now be fulfilled!”
16 I have not run away from being your
shepherd;
you know I have not desired the day of
despair.
What passes my lips is open before you.
17 Do not be a terror to me;
you are my refuge in the day of
disaster.
18 Let my persecutors be put to shame,
but keep me from shame;
let them be terrified,
but keep me from terror.
Bring on them the day of disaster;
destroy them with double destruction.

Keeping the Sabbath Day Holy

19 This is what the LORD said to me: “Go
and stand at the Gate of the People,[a] through
which the kings of Judah go in and out; stand
also at all the other gates of Jerusalem. 20 Say
to them, ‘Hear the word of the LORD, you kings
of Judah and all people of Judah and everyone
living in Jerusalem who come through these
gates. 21 This is what the LORD says: Be careful not to carry a load on the Sabbath day or
bring it through the gates of Jerusalem. 22 Do
not bring a load out of your houses or do any
work on the Sabbath, but keep the Sabbath
day holy, as I commanded your ancestors.
23 Yet they did not listen or pay attention; they
were stiff-necked and would not listen or respond to discipline. 24 But if you are careful to
obey me, declares the LORD, and bring no load
through the gates of this city on the Sabbath,
but keep the Sabbath day holy by not doing
any work on it, 25 then kings who sit on David’s throne will come through the gates of
this city with their officials. They and their
officials will come riding in chariots and on
horses, accompanied by the men of Judah and
those living in Jerusalem, and this city will
be inhabited forever. 26 People will come from
the towns of Judah and the villages around
Jerusalem, from the territory of Benjamin and
the western foothills, from the hill country
and the Negev, bringing burnt offerings and
sacrifices, grain offerings and incense, and
bringing thank offerings to the house of the
LORD. 27 But if you do not obey me to keep the
Sabbath day holy by not carrying any load
as you come through the gates of Jerusalem
on the Sabbath day, then I will kindle an unquenchable fire in the gates of Jerusalem that
will consume her fortresses.’ ”

At the Potter’s House

18 This is the word that came to Jeremiah
from the LORD: 2 “Go down to the potter’s
house, and there I will give you my message.”
3 So I went down to the potter’s house, and I
saw him working at the wheel. 4 But the pot
he was shaping from the clay was marred in
his hands; so the potter formed it into another
pot, shaping it as seemed best to him.
5 Then the word of the LORD came to me. 6 He
said, “Can I not do with you, Israel, as this
potter does?” declares the LORD. “Like clay in
the hand of the potter, so are you in my hand,
Israel. 7 If at any time I announce that a nation
or kingdom is to be uprooted, torn down and
destroyed, 8 and if that nation I warned repents
of its evil, then I will relent and not inflict on it
the disaster I had planned. 9 And if at another
time I announce that a nation or kingdom is
to be built up and planted, 10 and if it does evil
in my sight and does not obey me, then I will
reconsider the good I had intended to do for it.
11 “Now therefore say to the people of Judah
and those living in Jerusalem, ‘This is what
the LORD says: Look! I am preparing a disaster for you and devising a plan against you.
So turn from your evil ways, each one of you,
and reform your ways and your actions.’ 12 But
they will reply, ‘It’s no use. We will continue with our own plans; we will all follow the
stubbornness of our evil hearts.’ ”

13 Therefore this is what the LORD says:

“Inquire among the nations:
Who has ever heard anything like this?

[a] 19 Or *Army*

A most horrible thing has been done
by Virgin Israel.
14 Does the snow of Lebanon
ever vanish from its rocky slopes?
Do its cool waters from distant sources
ever stop flowing?[a]
15 Yet my people have forgotten me;
they burn incense to worthless idols,
which made them stumble in their ways,
in the ancient paths.
They made them walk in byways,
on roads not built up.
16 Their land will be an object of horror
and of lasting scorn;
all who pass by will be appalled
and will shake their heads.
17 Like a wind from the east,
I will scatter them before their enemies;
I will show them my back and not my face
in the day of their disaster."

18 They said, "Come, let's make plans against
Jeremiah; for the teaching of the law by the
priest will not cease, nor will counsel from
the wise, nor the word from the prophets. So
come, let's attack him with our tongues and
pay no attention to anything he says."

19 Listen to me, LORD;
hear what my accusers are saying!
20 Should good be repaid with evil?
Yet they have dug a pit for me.
Remember that I stood before you
and spoke in their behalf
to turn your wrath away from them.
21 So give their children over to famine;
hand them over to the power of the
sword.
Let their wives be made childless and
widows;
let their men be put to death,
their young men slain by the sword in
battle.
22 Let a cry be heard from their houses
when you suddenly bring invaders
against them,
for they have dug a pit to capture me
and have hidden snares for my feet.
23 But you, LORD, know
all their plots to kill me.
Do not forgive their crimes
or blot out their sins from your sight.
Let them be overthrown before you;
deal with them in the time of your
anger.

19 This is what the LORD says: "Go and
buy a clay jar from a potter. Take along
some of the elders of the people and of the
priests 2 and go out to the Valley of Ben Hinnom, near the entrance of the Potsherd Gate.
There proclaim the words I tell you, 3 and say,
'Hear the word of the LORD, you kings of Judah and people of Jerusalem. This is what
the LORD Almighty, the God of Israel, says:
Listen! I am going to bring a disaster on this
place that will make the ears of everyone who
hears of it tingle. 4 For they have forsaken me
and made this a place of foreign gods; they
have burned incense in it to gods that neither
they nor their ancestors nor the kings of Judah
ever knew, and they have filled this place with
the blood of the innocent. 5 They have built
the high places of Baal to burn their children
in the fire as offerings to Baal—something I
did not command or mention, nor did it enter
my mind. 6 So beware, the days are coming,
declares the LORD, when people will no longer
call this place Topheth or the Valley of Ben
Hinnom, but the Valley of Slaughter.
7 " 'In this place I will ruin[b] the plans of Judah and Jerusalem. I will make them fall by
the sword before their enemies, at the hands
of those who want to kill them, and I will give
their carcasses as food to the birds and the
wild animals. 8 I will devastate this city and
make it an object of horror and scorn; all who
pass by will be appalled and will scoff because
of all its wounds. 9 I will make them eat the
flesh of their sons and daughters, and they
will eat one another's flesh because their enemies will press the siege so hard against them
to destroy them.'
10 "Then break the jar while those who go
with you are watching, 11 and say to them,
'This is what the LORD Almighty says: I will
smash this nation and this city just as this potter's jar is smashed and cannot be repaired.
They will bury the dead in Topheth until there
is no more room. 12 This is what I will do to
this place and to those who live here, declares
the LORD. I will make this city like Topheth.
13 The houses in Jerusalem and those of the
kings of Judah will be defiled like this place,
Topheth—all the houses where they burned
incense on the roofs to all the starry hosts and
poured out drink offerings to other gods.' "
14 Jeremiah then returned from Topheth,
where the LORD had sent him to prophesy,
and stood in the court of the LORD's temple
and said to all the people, 15 "This is what the
LORD Almighty, the God of Israel, says: 'Listen! I am going to bring on this city and all the
villages around it every disaster I pronounced
against them, because they were stiff-necked
and would not listen to my words.' "

Jeremiah and Pashhur

20 When the priest Pashhur son of Immer,
the official in charge of the temple of
the LORD, heard Jeremiah prophesying these
things, 2 he had Jeremiah the prophet beaten
and put in the stocks at the Upper Gate of
Benjamin at the LORD's temple. 3 The next day,
when Pashhur released him from the stocks,
Jeremiah said to him, "The LORD's name for
you is not Pashhur, but Terror on Every Side.
4 For this is what the LORD says: 'I will make
you a terror to yourself and to all your friends;
with your own eyes you will see them fall by
the sword of their enemies. I will give all Judah into the hands of the king of Babylon, who
will carry them away to Babylon or put them

[a] 14 The meaning of the Hebrew for this sentence is uncertain. [b] 7 The Hebrew for *ruin* sounds like the Hebrew for *jar* (see verses 1 and 10).

to the sword. 5I will deliver all the wealth of
this city into the hands of their enemies—all
its products, all its valuables and all the treasures of the kings of Judah. They will take it
away as plunder and carry it off to Babylon.
6And you, Pashhur, and all who live in your
house will go into exile to Babylon. There you
will die and be buried, you and all your friends
to whom you have prophesied lies.'"

Jeremiah's Complaint

7 You deceived[a] me, LORD, and I was
deceived[a];
you overpowered me and prevailed.
I am ridiculed all day long;
everyone mocks me.
8 Whenever I speak, I cry out
proclaiming violence and destruction.
So the word of the LORD has brought me
insult and reproach all day long.
9 But if I say, "I will not mention his word
or speak anymore in his name,"
his word is in my heart like a fire,
a fire shut up in my bones.
I am weary of holding it in;
indeed, I cannot.
10 I hear many whispering,
"Terror on every side!
Denounce him! Let's denounce him!"
All my friends
are waiting for me to slip, saying,
"Perhaps he will be deceived;
then we will prevail over him
and take our revenge on him."

11 But the LORD is with me like a mighty
warrior;
so my persecutors will stumble and not
prevail.
They will fail and be thoroughly
disgraced;
their dishonor will never be forgotten.
12 LORD Almighty, you who examine the
righteous
and probe the heart and mind,
let me see your vengeance on them,
for to you I have committed my cause.

13 Sing to the LORD!
Give praise to the LORD!
He rescues the life of the needy
from the hands of the wicked.

14 Cursed be the day I was born!
May the day my mother bore me not be
blessed!
15 Cursed be the man who brought my
father the news,
who made him very glad, saying,
"A child is born to you—a son!"
16 May that man be like the towns
the LORD overthrew without pity.
May he hear wailing in the morning,
a battle cry at noon.
17 For he did not kill me in the womb,
with my mother as my grave,
her womb enlarged forever.
18 Why did I ever come out of the womb
to see trouble and sorrow
and to end my days in shame?

God Rejects Zedekiah's Request

21 The word came to Jeremiah from the
LORD when King Zedekiah sent to him
Pashhur son of Malkijah and the priest Zephaniah son of Maaseiah. They said: 2"Inquire
now of the LORD for us because Nebuchadnezzar[b] king of Babylon is attacking us. Perhaps
the LORD will perform wonders for us as in
times past so that he will withdraw from us."
3But Jeremiah answered them, "Tell Zedekiah, 4'This is what the LORD, the God of
Israel, says: I am about to turn against you
the weapons of war that are in your hands,
which you are using to fight the king of Babylon and the Babylonians[c] who are outside
the wall besieging you. And I will gather them
inside this city. 5I myself will fight against
you with an outstretched hand and a mighty
arm in furious anger and in great wrath. 6I
will strike down those who live in this city—
both man and beast—and they will die of a
terrible plague. 7After that, declares the LORD,
I will give Zedekiah king of Judah, his officials and the people in this city who survive
the plague, sword and famine, into the hands
of Nebuchadnezzar king of Babylon and to
their enemies who want to kill them. He will
put them to the sword; he will show them no
mercy or pity or compassion.'
8"Furthermore, tell the people, 'This is what
the LORD says: See, I am setting before you the
way of life and the way of death. 9Whoever
stays in this city will die by the sword, famine
or plague. But whoever goes out and surrenders to the Babylonians who are besieging you
will live; they will escape with their lives. 10I
have determined to do this city harm and not
good, declares the LORD. It will be given into
the hands of the king of Babylon, and he will
destroy it with fire.'
11"Moreover, say to the royal house of Judah, 'Hear the word of the LORD. 12This is what
the LORD says to you, house of David:

"'Administer justice every morning;
rescue from the hand of the oppressor
the one who has been robbed,
or my wrath will break out and burn like
fire
because of the evil you have done—
burn with no one to quench it.
13 I am against you, Jerusalem,
you who live above this valley
on the rocky plateau, declares the
LORD—
you who say, "Who can come against us?
Who can enter our refuge?"
14 I will punish you as your deeds deserve,
declares the LORD.
I will kindle a fire in your forests
that will consume everything around
you.'"

[a] 7 Or *persuaded* [b] 2 Hebrew *Nebuchadrezzar,* of which *Nebuchadnezzar* is a variant; here and often in Jeremiah and Ezekiel [c] 4 Or *Chaldeans*; also in verse 9

Judgment Against Wicked Kings

22 This is what the LORD says: "Go down to
the palace of the king of Judah and proclaim this message there: 2'Hear the word of
the LORD to you, king of Judah, you who sit on
David's throne—you, your officials and your
people who come through these gates. 3This
is what the LORD says: Do what is just and
right. Rescue from the hand of the oppressor
the one who has been robbed. Do no wrong
or violence to the foreigner, the fatherless or
the widow, and do not shed innocent blood
in this place. 4For if you are careful to carry
out these commands, then kings who sit on
David's throne will come through the gates of
this palace, riding in chariots and on horses,
accompanied by their officials and their people. 5But if you do not obey these commands,
declares the LORD, I swear by myself that this
palace will become a ruin.'"

6For this is what the LORD says about the
palace of the king of Judah:

"Though you are like Gilead to me,
like the summit of Lebanon,
I will surely make you like a wasteland,
like towns not inhabited.
7I will send destroyers against you,
each man with his weapons,
and they will cut up your fine cedar beams
and throw them into the fire.

8"People from many nations will pass by
this city and will ask one another, 'Why has
the LORD done such a thing to this great city?'
9And the answer will be: 'Because they have
forsaken the covenant of the LORD their God
and have worshiped and served other gods.'"

10Do not weep for the dead king or mourn
his loss;
rather, weep bitterly for him who is
exiled,
because he will never return
nor see his native land again.

11For this is what the LORD says about Shallum[a] son of Josiah, who succeeded his father
as king of Judah but has gone from this place:
"He will never return. 12He will die in the place
where they have led him captive; he will not
see this land again."

13"Woe to him who builds his palace by
unrighteousness,
his upper rooms by injustice,
making his own people work for nothing,
not paying them for their labor.
14He says, 'I will build myself a great palace
with spacious upper rooms.'
So he makes large windows in it,
panels it with cedar
and decorates it in red.

15"Does it make you a king
to have more and more cedar?
Did not your father have food and drink?
He did what was right and just,
so all went well with him.
16He defended the cause of the poor and
needy,
and so all went well.
Is that not what it means to know me?"
declares the LORD.
17"But your eyes and your heart
are set only on dishonest gain,
on shedding innocent blood
and on oppression and extortion."

18Therefore this is what the LORD says about
Jehoiakim son of Josiah king of Judah:

"They will not mourn for him:
'Alas, my brother! Alas, my sister!'
They will not mourn for him:
'Alas, my master! Alas, his splendor!'
19He will have the burial of a donkey—
dragged away and thrown
outside the gates of Jerusalem."

20"Go up to Lebanon and cry out,
let your voice be heard in Bashan,
cry out from Abarim,
for all your allies are crushed.
21I warned you when you felt secure,
but you said, 'I will not listen!'
This has been your way from your
youth;
you have not obeyed me.
22The wind will drive all your shepherds
away,
and your allies will go into exile.
Then you will be ashamed and disgraced
because of all your wickedness.
23You who live in 'Lebanon,[b]'
who are nestled in cedar buildings,
how you will groan when pangs come
upon you,
pain like that of a woman in labor!

24"As surely as I live," declares the LORD,
"even if you, Jehoiachin[c] son of Jehoiakim
king of Judah, were a signet ring on my right
hand, I would still pull you off. 25I will deliver
you into the hands of those who want to kill
you, those you fear—Nebuchadnezzar king
of Babylon and the Babylonians.[d] 26I will hurl
you and the mother who gave you birth into
another country, where neither of you was
born, and there you both will die. 27You will
never come back to the land you long to return to."

28Is this man Jehoiachin a despised, broken
pot,
an object no one wants?
Why will he and his children be hurled
out,
cast into a land they do not know?
29O land, land, land,
hear the word of the LORD!
30This is what the LORD says:
"Record this man as if childless,
a man who will not prosper in his
lifetime,
for none of his offspring will prosper,
none will sit on the throne of David
or rule anymore in Judah."

[a] *11* Also called *Jehoahaz* [b] *23* That is, the palace in Jerusalem (see 1 Kings 7:2) [c] *24* Hebrew *Koniah*, a variant of *Jehoiachin*; also in verse 28 [d] *25* Or *Chaldeans*

The Righteous Branch

23 "Woe to the shepherds who are destroying and scattering the sheep of my pasture!" declares the LORD. 2Therefore this is
what the LORD, the God of Israel, says to the
shepherds who tend my people: "Because you
have scattered my flock and driven them away
and have not bestowed care on them, I will
bestow punishment on you for the evil you
have done," declares the LORD. 3"I myself will
gather the remnant of my flock out of all the
countries where I have driven them and will
bring them back to their pasture, where they
will be fruitful and increase in number. 4I will
place shepherds over them who will tend them,
and they will no longer be afraid or terrified,
nor will any be missing," declares the LORD.

5 "The days are coming," declares the LORD,
"when I will raise up for David[a] a
righteous Branch,
a King who will reign wisely
and do what is just and right in the
land.
6 In his days Judah will be saved
and Israel will live in safety.
This is the name by which he will be
called:
The LORD Our Righteous Savior.

7"So then, the days are coming," declares the
LORD, "when people will no longer say, 'As
surely as the LORD lives, who brought the Israelites up out of Egypt,' 8but they will say,
'As surely as the LORD lives, who brought the
descendants of Israel up out of the land of
the north and out of all the countries where
he had banished them.' Then they will live in
their own land."

Lying Prophets

9Concerning the prophets:

My heart is broken within me;
all my bones tremble.
I am like a drunken man,
like a strong man overcome by wine,
because of the LORD
and his holy words.
10 The land is full of adulterers;
because of the curse[b] the land lies
parched
and the pastures in the wilderness are
withered.
The prophets follow an evil course
and use their power unjustly.

11 "Both prophet and priest are godless;
even in my temple I find their
wickedness,"
declares the LORD.
12 "Therefore their path will become
slippery;
they will be banished to darkness
and there they will fall.
I will bring disaster on them
in the year they are punished,"
declares the LORD.

13 "Among the prophets of Samaria
I saw this repulsive thing:
They prophesied by Baal
and led my people Israel astray.
14 And among the prophets of Jerusalem
I have seen something horrible:
They commit adultery and live a lie.
They strengthen the hands of evildoers,
so that not one of them turns from their
wickedness.
They are all like Sodom to me;
the people of Jerusalem are like
Gomorrah."

15Therefore this is what the LORD Almighty
says concerning the prophets:

"I will make them eat bitter food
and drink poisoned water,
because from the prophets of Jerusalem
ungodliness has spread throughout the
land."

16This is what the LORD Almighty says:

"Do not listen to what the prophets are
prophesying to you;
they fill you with false hopes.
They speak visions from their own
minds,
not from the mouth of the LORD.
17 They keep saying to those who despise
me,
'The LORD says: You will have peace.'
And to all who follow the stubbornness of
their hearts
they say, 'No harm will come to you.'
18 But which of them has stood in the
council of the LORD
to see or to hear his word?
Who has listened and heard his word?
19 See, the storm of the LORD
will burst out in wrath,
a whirlwind swirling down
on the heads of the wicked.
20 The anger of the LORD will not turn back
until he fully accomplishes
the purposes of his heart.
In days to come
you will understand it clearly.
21 I did not send these prophets,
yet they have run with their message;
I did not speak to them,
yet they have prophesied.
22 But if they had stood in my council,
they would have proclaimed my words
to my people
and would have turned them from their
evil ways
and from their evil deeds.

23 "Am I only a God nearby,"
declares the LORD,
"and not a God far away?
24 Who can hide in secret places
so that I cannot see them?"
declares the LORD.
"Do not I fill heaven and earth?"
declares the LORD.

[a] 5 Or *up from David's line* [b] 10 Or *because of these things*

25“I have heard what the prophets say who
prophesy lies in my name. They say, ‘I had a
dream! I had a dream!’ 26How long will this continue in the hearts of these lying prophets, who
prophesy the delusions of their own minds?
27They think the dreams they tell one another
will make my people forget my name, just as
their ancestors forgot my name through Baal
worship. 28Let the prophet who has a dream
recount the dream, but let the one who has my
word speak it faithfully. For what has straw to
do with grain?” declares the LORD. 29“Is not my
word like fire,” declares the LORD, “and like a
hammer that breaks a rock in pieces?

30“Therefore,” declares the LORD, “I am
against the prophets who steal from one another words supposedly from me. 31Yes,” declares the LORD, “I am against the prophets
who wag their own tongues and yet declare,
‘The LORD declares.’ 32Indeed, I am against
those who prophesy false dreams,” declares
the LORD. “They tell them and lead my people astray with their reckless lies, yet I did
not send or appoint them. They do not benefit
these people in the least,” declares the LORD.

False Prophecy

33“When these people, or a prophet or a
priest, ask you, ‘What is the message from
the LORD?’ say to them, ‘What message? I will
forsake you, declares the LORD.’ 34If a prophet
or a priest or anyone else claims, ‘This is a
message from the LORD,’ I will punish them
and their household. 35This is what each of
you keeps saying to your friends and other
Israelites: ‘What is the LORD’s answer?’ or
‘What has the LORD spoken?’ 36But you must
not mention ‘a message from the LORD’ again,
because each one’s word becomes their own
message. So you distort the words of the living
God, the LORD Almighty, our God. 37This is
what you keep saying to a prophet: ‘What is
the LORD’s answer to you?’ or ‘What has the
LORD spoken?’ 38Although you claim, ‘This is a
message from the LORD,’ this is what the LORD
says: You used the words, ‘This is a message
from the LORD,’ even though I told you that
you must not claim, ‘This is a message from
the LORD.’ 39Therefore, I will surely forget you
and cast you out of my presence along with
the city I gave to you and your ancestors. 40I
will bring on you everlasting disgrace—everlasting shame that will not be forgotten.”

Two Baskets of Figs

24 After Jehoiachin[a] son of Jehoiakim king
of Judah and the officials, the skilled
workers and the artisans of Judah were carried into exile from Jerusalem to Babylon by
Nebuchadnezzar king of Babylon, the LORD
showed me two baskets of figs placed in front
of the temple of the LORD. 2One basket had
very good figs, like those that ripen early; the
other basket had very bad figs, so bad they
could not be eaten.

3Then the LORD asked me, “What do you
see, Jeremiah?”

“Figs,” I answered. “The good ones are very
good, but the bad ones are so bad they cannot
be eaten.”

4Then the word of the LORD came to me:
5“This is what the LORD, the God of Israel,
says: ‘Like these good figs, I regard as good
the exiles from Judah, whom I sent away from
this place to the land of the Babylonians.[b] 6My
eyes will watch over them for their good, and
I will bring them back to this land. I will build
them up and not tear them down; I will plant
them and not uproot them. 7I will give them
a heart to know me, that I am the LORD. They
will be my people, and I will be their God,
for they will return to me with all their heart.

8“ ‘But like the bad figs, which are so bad
they cannot be eaten,’ says the LORD, ‘so will I
deal with Zedekiah king of Judah, his officials
and the survivors from Jerusalem, whether
they remain in this land or live in Egypt. 9I
will make them abhorrent and an offense
to all the kingdoms of the earth, a reproach
and a byword, a curse[c] and an object of ridicule, wherever I banish them. 10I will send
the sword, famine and plague against them
until they are destroyed from the land I gave
to them and their ancestors.’ ”

Seventy Years of Captivity

25 The word came to Jeremiah concerning all the people of Judah in the fourth
year of Jehoiakim son of Josiah king of Judah,
which was the first year of Nebuchadnezzar
king of Babylon. 2So Jeremiah the prophet said to all the people of Judah and to all
those living in Jerusalem: 3For twenty-three
years—from the thirteenth year of Josiah son
of Amon king of Judah until this very day—
the word of the LORD has come to me and I
have spoken to you again and again, but you
have not listened.

4And though the LORD has sent all his servants the prophets to you again and again,
you have not listened or paid any attention.
5They said, “Turn now, each of you, from your
evil ways and your evil practices, and you can
stay in the land the LORD gave to you and your
ancestors for ever and ever. 6Do not follow
other gods to serve and worship them; do not
arouse my anger with what your hands have
made. Then I will not harm you.”

7“But you did not listen to me,” declares the
LORD, “and you have aroused my anger with
what your hands have made, and you have
brought harm to yourselves.”

8Therefore the LORD Almighty says this:
“Because you have not listened to my words,
9I will summon all the peoples of the north
and my servant Nebuchadnezzar king of Babylon,” declares the LORD, “and I will bring
them against this land and its inhabitants and
against all the surrounding nations. I will
completely destroy[d] them and make them an

[a] *1* Hebrew *Jeconiah,* a variant of *Jehoiachin* [b] *5* Or *Chaldeans* [c] *9* That is, their names will be used in cursing (see 29:22); or, others will see that they are cursed. [d] *9* The Hebrew term refers to the irrevocable giving over of things or persons to the LORD, often by totally destroying them.

object of horror and scorn, and an everlasting
ruin. 10I will banish from them the sounds
of joy and gladness, the voices of bride and
bridegroom, the sound of millstones and the
light of the lamp. 11This whole country will
become a desolate wasteland, and these nations will serve the king of Babylon seventy
years.
12"But when the seventy years are fulfilled,
I will punish the king of Babylon and his nation, the land of the Babylonians,[a] for their
guilt," declares the LORD, "and will make it
desolate forever. 13I will bring on that land
all the things I have spoken against it, all
that are written in this book and prophesied
by Jeremiah against all the nations. 14They
themselves will be enslaved by many nations
and great kings; I will repay them according
to their deeds and the work of their hands."

The Cup of God's Wrath

15This is what the LORD, the God of Israel,
said to me: "Take from my hand this cup filled
with the wine of my wrath and make all the
nations to whom I send you drink it. 16When
they drink it, they will stagger and go mad
because of the sword I will send among them."
17So I took the cup from the LORD's hand
and made all the nations to whom he sent me
drink it: 18Jerusalem and the towns of Judah,
its kings and officials, to make them a ruin
and an object of horror and scorn, a curse[b]—
as they are today; 19Pharaoh king of Egypt,
his attendants, his officials and all his people,
20and all the foreign people there; all the kings
of Uz; all the kings of the Philistines (those
of Ashkelon, Gaza, Ekron, and the people left
at Ashdod); 21Edom, Moab and Ammon; 22all
the kings of Tyre and Sidon; the kings of the
coastlands across the sea; 23Dedan, Tema, Buz
and all who are in distant places[c]; 24all the
kings of Arabia and all the kings of the foreign people who live in the wilderness; 25all
the kings of Zimri, Elam and Media; 26and
all the kings of the north, near and far, one
after the other—all the kingdoms on the face
of the earth. And after all of them, the king of
Sheshak[d] will drink it too.
27"Then tell them, 'This is what the LORD
Almighty, the God of Israel, says: Drink, get
drunk and vomit, and fall to rise no more because of the sword I will send among you.'
28But if they refuse to take the cup from your
hand and drink, tell them, 'This is what the
LORD Almighty says: You must drink it! 29See,
I am beginning to bring disaster on the city
that bears my Name, and will you indeed go
unpunished? You will not go unpunished, for
I am calling down a sword on all who live on
the earth, declares the LORD Almighty.'
30"Now prophesy all these words against
them and say to them:

"'The LORD will roar from on high;
he will thunder from his holy dwelling
and roar mightily against his land.
He will shout like those who tread the
grapes,
shout against all who live on the earth.
31The tumult will resound to the ends of the
earth,
for the LORD will bring charges against
the nations;
he will bring judgment on all mankind
and put the wicked to the sword,'"
declares the LORD.

32This is what the LORD Almighty says:

"Look! Disaster is spreading
from nation to nation;
a mighty storm is rising
from the ends of the earth."

33At that time those slain by the LORD will be
everywhere—from one end of the earth to the
other. They will not be mourned or gathered
up or buried, but will be like dung lying on
the ground.

34Weep and wail, you shepherds;
roll in the dust, you leaders of the flock.
For your time to be slaughtered has come;
you will fall like the best of the rams.[e]
35The shepherds will have nowhere to flee,
the leaders of the flock no place to
escape.
36Hear the cry of the shepherds,
the wailing of the leaders of the flock,
for the LORD is destroying their
pasture.
37The peaceful meadows will be laid waste
because of the fierce anger of the LORD.
38Like a lion he will leave his lair,
and their land will become desolate
because of the sword[f] of the oppressor
and because of the LORD's fierce anger.

Jeremiah Threatened With Death

26 Early in the reign of Jehoiakim son of
Josiah king of Judah, this word came
from the LORD: 2"This is what the LORD says:
Stand in the courtyard of the LORD's house
and speak to all the people of the towns of Judah who come to worship in the house of the
LORD. Tell them everything I command you;
do not omit a word. 3Perhaps they will listen
and each will turn from their evil ways. Then I
will relent and not inflict on them the disaster
I was planning because of the evil they have
done. 4Say to them, 'This is what the LORD
says: If you do not listen to me and follow my
law, which I have set before you, 5and if you
do not listen to the words of my servants the
prophets, whom I have sent to you again and
again (though you have not listened), 6then I
will make this house like Shiloh and this city
a curse[g] among all the nations of the earth.'"
7The priests, the prophets and all the peo-

[a] *12* Or *Chaldeans* [b] *18* That is, their names to be used in cursing (see 29:22); or, to be seen by others as cursed [c] *23* Or *who clip the hair by their foreheads* [d] *26* *Sheshak* is a cryptogram for Babylon. [e] *34* Septuagint; Hebrew *fall and be shattered like fine pottery* [f] *38* Some Hebrew manuscripts and Septuagint (see also 46:16 and 50:16); most Hebrew manuscripts *anger* [g] *6* That is, its name will be used in cursing (see 29:22); or, others will see that it is cursed.

ple heard Jeremiah speak these words in the
house of the LORD. 8But as soon as Jeremiah
finished telling all the people everything the
LORD had commanded him to say, the priests,
the prophets and all the people seized him and
said, "You must die! 9Why do you prophesy in
the LORD's name that this house will be like
Shiloh and this city will be desolate and deserted?" And all the people crowded around
Jeremiah in the house of the LORD.
10When the officials of Judah heard about
these things, they went up from the royal palace to the house of the LORD and took their
places at the entrance of the New Gate of
the LORD's house. 11Then the priests and the
prophets said to the officials and all the people, "This man should be sentenced to death
because he has prophesied against this city.
You have heard it with your own ears!"
12Then Jeremiah said to all the officials and
all the people: "The LORD sent me to prophesy
against this house and this city all the things
you have heard. 13Now reform your ways and
your actions and obey the LORD your God.
Then the LORD will relent and not bring the
disaster he has pronounced against you. 14As
for me, I am in your hands; do with me whatever you think is good and right. 15Be assured,
however, that if you put me to death, you will
bring the guilt of innocent blood on yourselves
and on this city and on those who live in it, for
in truth the LORD has sent me to you to speak
all these words in your hearing."
16Then the officials and all the people said to
the priests and the prophets, "This man should
not be sentenced to death! He has spoken to
us in the name of the LORD our God."
17Some of the elders of the land stepped
forward and said to the entire assembly of
people, 18"Micah of Moresheth prophesied in
the days of Hezekiah king of Judah. He told
all the people of Judah, 'This is what the LORD
Almighty says:

"'Zion will be plowed like a field,
  Jerusalem will become a heap of
    rubble,
  the temple hill a mound overgrown
    with thickets.'[a]

19"Did Hezekiah king of Judah or anyone else
in Judah put him to death? Did not Hezekiah
fear the LORD and seek his favor? And did
not the LORD relent, so that he did not bring
the disaster he pronounced against them?
We are about to bring a terrible disaster on
ourselves!"
20(Now Uriah son of Shemaiah from Kiriath Jearim was another man who prophesied in the name of the LORD; he prophesied
the same things against this city and this
land as Jeremiah did. 21When King Jehoiakim and all his officers and officials heard
his words, the king was determined to put
him to death. But Uriah heard of it and fled
in fear to Egypt. 22King Jehoiakim, however,
sent Elnathan son of Akbor to Egypt, along
with some other men. 23They brought Uriah
out of Egypt and took him to King Jehoiakim,
who had him struck down with a sword and
his body thrown into the burial place of the
common people.)
24Furthermore, Ahikam son of Shaphan
supported Jeremiah, and so he was not handed over to the people to be put to death.

Judah to Serve Nebuchadnezzar

27 Early in the reign of Zedekiah[b] son of
Josiah king of Judah, this word came
to Jeremiah from the LORD: 2This is what the
LORD said to me: "Make a yoke out of straps
and crossbars and put it on your neck. 3Then
send word to the kings of Edom, Moab, Ammon, Tyre and Sidon through the envoys who
have come to Jerusalem to Zedekiah king of
Judah. 4Give them a message for their masters
and say, 'This is what the LORD Almighty, the
God of Israel, says: "Tell this to your masters:
5With my great power and outstretched arm I
made the earth and its people and the animals
that are on it, and I give it to anyone I please.
6Now I will give all your countries into the
hands of my servant Nebuchadnezzar king
of Babylon; I will make even the wild animals
subject to him. 7All nations will serve him
and his son and his grandson until the time
for his land comes; then many nations and
great kings will subjugate him.
8"'"If, however, any nation or kingdom will
not serve Nebuchadnezzar king of Babylon or
bow its neck under his yoke, I will punish that
nation with the sword, famine and plague,
declares the LORD, until I destroy it by his
hand. 9So do not listen to your prophets, your
diviners, your interpreters of dreams, your
mediums or your sorcerers who tell you, 'You
will not serve the king of Babylon.' 10They
prophesy lies to you that will only serve to
remove you far from your lands; I will banish
you and you will perish. 11But if any nation
will bow its neck under the yoke of the king
of Babylon and serve him, I will let that nation remain in its own land to till it and to live
there, declares the LORD."'"
12I gave the same message to Zedekiah king
of Judah. I said, "Bow your neck under the
yoke of the king of Babylon; serve him and
his people, and you will live. 13Why will you
and your people die by the sword, famine
and plague with which the LORD has threatened any nation that will not serve the king
of Babylon? 14Do not listen to the words of the
prophets who say to you, 'You will not serve
the king of Babylon,' for they are prophesying
lies to you. 15'I have not sent them,' declares
the LORD. 'They are prophesying lies in my
name. Therefore, I will banish you and you
will perish, both you and the prophets who
prophesy to you.'"
16Then I said to the priests and all these people, "This is what the LORD says: Do not listen
to the prophets who say, 'Very soon now the
articles from the LORD's house will be brought

[a] *18* Micah 3:12 [b] *1* A few Hebrew manuscripts and Syriac (see also 27:3,12 and 28:1); most Hebrew manuscripts *Jehoiakim* (Most Septuagint manuscripts do not have this verse.)

back from Babylon.' They are prophesying
lies to you. 17Do not listen to them. Serve
the king of Babylon, and you will live. Why
should this city become a ruin? 18If they are
prophets and have the word of the LORD, let
them plead with the LORD Almighty that the
articles remaining in the house of the LORD
and in the palace of the king of Judah and
in Jerusalem not be taken to Babylon. 19For
this is what the LORD Almighty says about the
pillars, the bronze Sea, the movable stands
and the other articles that are left in this city,
20which Nebuchadnezzar king of Babylon did
not take away when he carried Jehoiachin[a]
son of Jehoiakim king of Judah into exile from
Jerusalem to Babylon, along with all the nobles of Judah and Jerusalem— 21yes, this is
what the LORD Almighty, the God of Israel,
says about the things that are left in the house
of the LORD and in the palace of the king of
Judah and in Jerusalem: 22'They will be taken
to Babylon and there they will remain until
the day I come for them,' declares the LORD.
'Then I will bring them back and restore them
to this place.'"

The False Prophet Hananiah

28 In the fifth month of that same year, the
fourth year, early in the reign of Zedekiah king of Judah, the prophet Hananiah son
of Azzur, who was from Gibeon, said to me in
the house of the LORD in the presence of the
priests and all the people: 2"This is what the
LORD Almighty, the God of Israel, says: 'I will
break the yoke of the king of Babylon. 3Within
two years I will bring back to this place all the
articles of the LORD's house that Nebuchadnezzar king of Babylon removed from here
and took to Babylon. 4I will also bring back to
this place Jehoiachin[a] son of Jehoiakim king
of Judah and all the other exiles from Judah
who went to Babylon,' declares the LORD, 'for
I will break the yoke of the king of Babylon.'"

5Then the prophet Jeremiah replied to the
prophet Hananiah before the priests and all
the people who were standing in the house of
the LORD. 6He said, "Amen! May the LORD do
so! May the LORD fulfill the words you have
prophesied by bringing the articles of the
LORD's house and all the exiles back to this
place from Babylon. 7Nevertheless, listen to
what I have to say in your hearing and in the
hearing of all the people: 8From early times
the prophets who preceded you and me have
prophesied war, disaster and plague against
many countries and great kingdoms. 9But the
prophet who prophesies peace will be recognized as one truly sent by the LORD only if his
prediction comes true."

10Then the prophet Hananiah took the yoke
off the neck of the prophet Jeremiah and
broke it, 11and he said before all the people,
"This is what the LORD says: 'In the same way
I will break the yoke of Nebuchadnezzar king
of Babylon off the neck of all the nations within two years.'" At this, the prophet Jeremiah
went on his way.

12After the prophet Hananiah had broken
the yoke off the neck of the prophet Jeremiah, the word of the LORD came to Jeremiah:
13"Go and tell Hananiah, 'This is what the
LORD says: You have broken a wooden yoke,
but in its place you will get a yoke of iron.
14This is what the LORD Almighty, the God
of Israel, says: I will put an iron yoke on the
necks of all these nations to make them serve
Nebuchadnezzar king of Babylon, and they
will serve him. I will even give him control
over the wild animals.'"

15Then the prophet Jeremiah said to Hananiah the prophet, "Listen, Hananiah! The
LORD has not sent you, yet you have persuaded
this nation to trust in lies. 16Therefore this is
what the LORD says: 'I am about to remove you
from the face of the earth. This very year you
are going to die, because you have preached
rebellion against the LORD.'"

17In the seventh month of that same year,
Hananiah the prophet died.

A Letter to the Exiles

29 This is the text of the letter that the
prophet Jeremiah sent from Jerusalem
to the surviving elders among the exiles and
to the priests, the prophets and all the other
people Nebuchadnezzar had carried into exile
from Jerusalem to Babylon. 2(This was after
King Jehoiachin[a] and the queen mother, the
court officials and the leaders of Judah and
Jerusalem, the skilled workers and the artisans had gone into exile from Jerusalem.) 3He
entrusted the letter to Elasah son of Shaphan
and to Gemariah son of Hilkiah, whom Zedekiah king of Judah sent to King Nebuchadnezzar in Babylon. It said:

> 4This is what the LORD Almighty, the
> God of Israel, says to all those I carried
> into exile from Jerusalem to Babylon:
> 5"Build houses and settle down; plant
> gardens and eat what they produce.
> 6Marry and have sons and daughters;
> find wives for your sons and give your
> daughters in marriage, so that they too
> may have sons and daughters. Increase
> in number there; do not decrease. 7Also,
> seek the peace and prosperity of the city
> to which I have carried you into exile.
> Pray to the LORD for it, because if it pros-
> pers, you too will prosper." 8Yes, this is
> what the LORD Almighty, the God of Is-
> rael, says: "Do not let the prophets and
> diviners among you deceive you. Do not
> listen to the dreams you encourage them
> to have. 9They are prophesying lies to
> you in my name. I have not sent them,"
> declares the LORD.
>
> 10This is what the LORD says: "When
> seventy years are completed for Babylon,
> I will come to you and fulfill my good
> promise to bring you back to this place.
> 11For I know the plans I have for you,"
> declares the LORD, "plans to prosper you
> and not to harm you, plans to give you

[a] 20,4,2 Hebrew *Jeconiah*, a variant of *Jehoiachin*

hope and a future. 12 Then you will call
on me and come and pray to me, and I
will listen to you. 13 You will seek me and
find me when you seek me with all your
heart. 14 I will be found by you," declares
the LORD, "and will bring you back from
captivity.[a] I will gather you from all the
nations and places where I have banished
you," declares the LORD, "and will bring
you back to the place from which I carried
you into exile."

15 You may say, "The LORD has raised
up prophets for us in Babylon," 16 but this
is what the LORD says about the king who
sits on David's throne and all the people who remain in this city, your fellow
citizens who did not go with you into
exile— 17 yes, this is what the LORD Almighty says: "I will send the sword, famine and plague against them and I will
make them like figs that are so bad they
cannot be eaten. 18 I will pursue them with
the sword, famine and plague and will
make them abhorrent to all the kingdoms
of the earth, a curse[b] and an object of
horror, of scorn and reproach, among all
the nations where I drive them. 19 For they
have not listened to my words," declares
the LORD, "words that I sent to them again
and again by my servants the prophets.
And you exiles have not listened either,"
declares the LORD.

20 Therefore, hear the word of the
LORD, all you exiles whom I have sent
away from Jerusalem to Babylon. 21 This
is what the LORD Almighty, the God of
Israel, says about Ahab son of Kolaiah
and Zedekiah son of Maaseiah, who are
prophesying lies to you in my name: "I
will deliver them into the hands of Nebuchadnezzar king of Babylon, and he
will put them to death before your very
eyes. 22 Because of them, all the exiles
from Judah who are in Babylon will use
this curse: 'May the LORD treat you like
Zedekiah and Ahab, whom the king of
Babylon burned in the fire.' 23 For they
have done outrageous things in Israel;
they have committed adultery with their
neighbors' wives, and in my name they
have uttered lies—which I did not autho-
rize. I know it and am a witness to it,"
declares the LORD.

Message to Shemaiah

24 Tell Shemaiah the Nehelamite, 25 "This is
what the LORD Almighty, the God of Israel,
says: You sent letters in your own name to all
the people in Jerusalem, to the priest Zephaniah son of Maaseiah, and to all the other
priests. You said to Zephaniah, 26 'The LORD
has appointed you priest in place of Jehoiada to be in charge of the house of the LORD;
you should put any maniac who acts like a
prophet into the stocks and neck-irons. 27 So
why have you not reprimanded Jeremiah from
Anathoth, who poses as a prophet among you?
28 He has sent this message to us in Babylon:
It will be a long time. Therefore build houses
and settle down; plant gardens and eat what
they produce.'"

29 Zephaniah the priest, however, read the
letter to Jeremiah the prophet. 30 Then the
word of the LORD came to Jeremiah: 31 "Send
this message to all the exiles: 'This is what
the LORD says about Shemaiah the Nehelamite: Because Shemaiah has prophesied to
you, even though I did not send him, and has
persuaded you to trust in lies, 32 this is what
the LORD says: I will surely punish Shemaiah
the Nehelamite and his descendants. He will
have no one left among this people, nor will
he see the good things I will do for my people,
declares the LORD, because he has preached
rebellion against me.'"

Restoration of Israel

30 This is the word that came to Jeremiah
from the LORD: 2 "This is what the LORD,
the God of Israel, says: 'Write in a book all
the words I have spoken to you. 3 The days
are coming,' declares the LORD, 'when I will
bring my people Israel and Judah back from
captivity[c] and restore them to the land I gave
their ancestors to possess,' says the LORD."

4 These are the words the LORD spoke concerning Israel and Judah: 5 "This is what the
LORD says:

"'Cries of fear are heard—
  terror, not peace.
6 Ask and see:
  Can a man bear children?
Then why do I see every strong man
  with his hands on his stomach like a
    woman in labor,
  every face turned deathly pale?
7 How awful that day will be!
  No other will be like it.
It will be a time of trouble for Jacob,
  but he will be saved out of it.

8 "'In that day,' declares the LORD
    Almighty,
  'I will break the yoke off their necks
and will tear off their bonds;
  no longer will foreigners enslave them.
9 Instead, they will serve the LORD their
    God
  and David their king,
  whom I will raise up for them.

10 "'So do not be afraid, Jacob my servant;
  do not be dismayed, Israel,'
          declares the LORD.
'I will surely save you out of a distant
    place,
  your descendants from the land of their
    exile.
Jacob will again have peace and security,
  and no one will make him afraid.
11 I am with you and will save you,'
  declares the LORD.

[a] *14* Or *will restore your fortunes* [b] *18* That is, their names will be used in cursing (see verse 22); or, others will see that they are cursed. [c] *3* Or *will restore the fortunes of my people Israel and Judah*

'Though I completely destroy all the nations
among which I scatter you,
I will not completely destroy you.
I will discipline you but only in due measure;
I will not let you go entirely unpunished.'

12"This is what the LORD says:

" 'Your wound is incurable,
your injury beyond healing.
13 There is no one to plead your cause,
no remedy for your sore,
no healing for you.
14 All your allies have forgotten you;
they care nothing for you.
I have struck you as an enemy would
and punished you as would the cruel,
because your guilt is so great
and your sins so many.
15 Why do you cry out over your wound,
your pain that has no cure?
Because of your great guilt and many sins
I have done these things to you.

16 " 'But all who devour you will be devoured;
all your enemies will go into exile.
Those who plunder you will be plundered;
all who make spoil of you I will despoil.
17 But I will restore you to health
and heal your wounds,'
declares the LORD,
'because you are called an outcast,
Zion for whom no one cares.'

18"This is what the LORD says:

" 'I will restore the fortunes of Jacob's tents
and have compassion on his dwellings;
the city will be rebuilt on her ruins,
and the palace will stand in its proper place.
19 From them will come songs of thanksgiving
and the sound of rejoicing.
I will add to their numbers,
and they will not be decreased;
I will bring them honor,
and they will not be disdained.
20 Their children will be as in days of old,
and their community will be established before me;
I will punish all who oppress them.
21 Their leader will be one of their own;
their ruler will arise from among them.
I will bring him near and he will come close to me—
for who is he who will devote himself
to be close to me?'
declares the LORD.
22 " 'So you will be my people,
and I will be your God.' "

23 See, the storm of the LORD
will burst out in wrath,
a driving wind swirling down
on the heads of the wicked.
24 The fierce anger of the LORD will not turn back
until he fully accomplishes
the purposes of his heart.
In days to come
you will understand this.

31 "At that time," declares the LORD, "I will
be the God of all the families of Israel,
and they will be my people."

2This is what the LORD says:

"The people who survive the sword
will find favor in the wilderness;
I will come to give rest to Israel."

3The LORD appeared to us in the past,[a] saying:

"I have loved you with an everlasting love;
I have drawn you with unfailing kindness.
4 I will build you up again,
and you, Virgin Israel, will be rebuilt.
Again you will take up your timbrels
and go out to dance with the joyful.
5 Again you will plant vineyards
on the hills of Samaria;
the farmers will plant them
and enjoy their fruit.
6 There will be a day when watchmen cry out
on the hills of Ephraim,
'Come, let us go up to Zion,
to the LORD our God.' "

7This is what the LORD says:

"Sing with joy for Jacob;
shout for the foremost of the nations.
Make your praises heard, and say,
'LORD, save your people,
the remnant of Israel.'
8 See, I will bring them from the land of the north
and gather them from the ends of the earth.
Among them will be the blind and the lame,
expectant mothers and women in labor;
a great throng will return.
9 They will come with weeping;
they will pray as I bring them back.
I will lead them beside streams of water
on a level path where they will not stumble,
because I am Israel's father,
and Ephraim is my firstborn son.

10 "Hear the word of the LORD, you nations;
proclaim it in distant coastlands:
'He who scattered Israel will gather them
and will watch over his flock like a shepherd.'
11 For the LORD will deliver Jacob
and redeem them from the hand of
those stronger than they.

[a] 3 Or *LORD has appeared to us from afar*

12 They will come and shout for joy on the heights of Zion;
they will rejoice in the bounty of the LORD—
the grain, the new wine and the olive oil,
the young of the flocks and herds.
They will be like a well-watered garden,
and they will sorrow no more.
13 Then young women will dance and be glad,
young men and old as well.
I will turn their mourning into gladness;
I will give them comfort and joy instead of sorrow.
14 I will satisfy the priests with abundance,
and my people will be filled with my bounty,"
declares the LORD.

15 This is what the LORD says:

"A voice is heard in Ramah,
mourning and great weeping,
Rachel weeping for her children
and refusing to be comforted,
because they are no more."

16 This is what the LORD says:

"Restrain your voice from weeping
and your eyes from tears,
for your work will be rewarded,"
declares the LORD.
"They will return from the land of the enemy.
17 So there is hope for your descendants,"
declares the LORD.
"Your children will return to their own land.

18 "I have surely heard Ephraim's moaning:
'You disciplined me like an unruly calf,
and I have been disciplined.
Restore me, and I will return,
because you are the LORD my God.
19 After I strayed,
I repented;
after I came to understand,
I beat my breast.
I was ashamed and humiliated
because I bore the disgrace of my youth.'
20 Is not Ephraim my dear son,
the child in whom I delight?
Though I often speak against him,
I still remember him.
Therefore my heart yearns for him;
I have great compassion for him,"
declares the LORD.

21 "Set up road signs;
put up guideposts.
Take note of the highway,
the road that you take.
Return, Virgin Israel,
return to your towns.
22 How long will you wander,
unfaithful Daughter Israel?
The LORD will create a new thing on earth—
the woman will return to[a] the man."

23 This is what the LORD Almighty, the God
of Israel, says: "When I bring them back from
captivity,[b] the people in the land of Judah and
in its towns will once again use these words:
'The LORD bless you, you prosperous city, you
sacred mountain.' 24 People will live together in Judah and all its towns—farmers and
those who move about with their flocks. 25 I
will refresh the weary and satisfy the faint."
26 At this I awoke and looked around. My
sleep had been pleasant to me.
27 "The days are coming," declares the LORD,
"when I will plant the kingdoms of Israel and
Judah with the offspring of people and of animals. 28 Just as I watched over them to uproot
and tear down, and to overthrow, destroy and
bring disaster, so I will watch over them to
build and to plant," declares the LORD. 29 "In
those days people will no longer say,

'The parents have eaten sour grapes,
and the children's teeth are set on edge.'

30 Instead, everyone will die for their own sin;
whoever eats sour grapes—their own teeth
will be set on edge.

31 "The days are coming," declares the LORD,
"when I will make a new covenant
with the people of Israel
and with the people of Judah.
32 It will not be like the covenant
I made with their ancestors
when I took them by the hand
to lead them out of Egypt,
because they broke my covenant,
though I was a husband to[c] them,[d]"
declares the LORD.
33 "This is the covenant I will make with the people of Israel
after that time," declares the LORD.
"I will put my law in their minds
and write it on their hearts.
I will be their God,
and they will be my people.
34 No longer will they teach their neighbor,
or say to one another, 'Know the LORD,'
because they will all know me,
from the least of them to the greatest,"
declares the LORD.
"For I will forgive their wickedness
and will remember their sins no more."

35 This is what the LORD says,

he who appoints the sun
to shine by day,
who decrees the moon and stars
to shine by night,
who stirs up the sea
so that its waves roar—
the LORD Almighty is his name:
36 "Only if these decrees vanish from my sight,"
declares the LORD,
"will Israel ever cease
being a nation before me."

[a] 22 Or *will protect* [b] 23 Or *I restore their fortunes* [c] 32 Hebrew; Septuagint and Syriac / *and I turned away from* [d] 32 Or *was their master*

37 This is what the LORD says:

"Only if the heavens above can be
measured
and the foundations of the earth below
be searched out
will I reject all the descendants of Israel
because of all they have done,"
declares the LORD.

38 "The days are coming," declares the LORD, "when this city will be rebuilt for me from the Tower of Hananel to the Corner Gate. 39 The measuring line will stretch from there straight to the hill of Gareb and then turn to Goah. 40 The whole valley where dead bodies and ashes are thrown, and all the terraces out to the Kidron Valley on the east as far as the corner of the Horse Gate, will be holy to the LORD. The city will never again be uprooted or demolished."

Jeremiah Buys a Field

32 This is the word that came to Jeremiah from the LORD in the tenth year of Zedekiah king of Judah, which was the eighteenth year of Nebuchadnezzar. 2 The army of the king of Babylon was then besieging Jerusalem, and Jeremiah the prophet was confined in the courtyard of the guard in the royal palace of Judah.

3 Now Zedekiah king of Judah had imprisoned him there, saying, "Why do you prophesy as you do? You say, 'This is what the LORD says: I am about to give this city into the hands of the king of Babylon, and he will capture it. 4 Zedekiah king of Judah will not escape the Babylonians[a] but will certainly be given into the hands of the king of Babylon, and will speak with him face to face and see him with his own eyes. 5 He will take Zedekiah to Babylon, where he will remain until I deal with him, declares the LORD. If you fight against the Babylonians, you will not succeed.' "

6 Jeremiah said, "The word of the LORD came to me: 7 Hanamel son of Shallum your uncle is going to come to you and say, 'Buy my field at Anathoth, because as nearest relative it is your right and duty to buy it.'

8 "Then, just as the LORD had said, my cousin Hanamel came to me in the courtyard of the guard and said, 'Buy my field at Anathoth in the territory of Benjamin. Since it is your right to redeem it and possess it, buy it for yourself.'

"I knew that this was the word of the LORD; 9 so I bought the field at Anathoth from my cousin Hanamel and weighed out for him seventeen shekels[b] of silver. 10 I signed and sealed the deed, had it witnessed, and weighed out the silver on the scales. 11 I took the deed of purchase—the sealed copy containing the terms and conditions, as well as the unsealed copy— 12 and I gave this deed to Baruch son of Neriah, the son of Mahseiah, in the presence of my cousin Hanamel and of the witnesses who had signed the deed and of all the Jews sitting in the courtyard of the guard.

13 "In their presence I gave Baruch these instructions: 14 'This is what the LORD Almighty, the God of Israel, says: Take these documents, both the sealed and unsealed copies of the deed of purchase, and put them in a clay jar so they will last a long time. 15 For this is what the LORD Almighty, the God of Israel, says: Houses, fields and vineyards will again be bought in this land.'

16 "After I had given the deed of purchase to Baruch son of Neriah, I prayed to the LORD:

17 "Ah, Sovereign LORD, you have made the heavens and the earth by your great power and outstretched arm. Nothing is too hard for you. 18 You show love to thousands but bring the punishment for the parents' sins into the laps of their children after them. Great and mighty God, whose name is the LORD Almighty, 19 great are your purposes and mighty are your deeds. Your eyes are open to the ways of all mankind; you reward each person according to their conduct and as their deeds deserve. 20 You performed signs and wonders in Egypt and have continued them to this day, in Israel and among all mankind, and have gained the renown that is still yours. 21 You brought your people Israel out of Egypt with signs and wonders, by a mighty hand and an outstretched arm and with great terror. 22 You gave them this land you had sworn to give their ancestors, a land flowing with milk and honey. 23 They came in and took possession of it, but they did not obey you or follow your law; they did not do what you commanded them to do. So you brought all this disaster on them.

24 "See how the siege ramps are built up to take the city. Because of the sword, famine and plague, the city will be given into the hands of the Babylonians who are attacking it. What you said has happened, as you now see. 25 And though the city will be given into the hands of the Babylonians, you, Sovereign LORD, say to me, 'Buy the field with silver and have the transaction witnessed.' "

26 Then the word of the LORD came to Jeremiah: 27 "I am the LORD, the God of all mankind. Is anything too hard for me? 28 Therefore this is what the LORD says: I am about to give this city into the hands of the Babylonians and to Nebuchadnezzar king of Babylon, who will capture it. 29 The Babylonians who are attacking this city will come in and set it on fire; they will burn it down, along with the houses where the people aroused my anger by burning incense on the roofs to Baal and by pouring out drink offerings to other gods.

30 "The people of Israel and Judah have done nothing but evil in my sight from their youth; indeed, the people of Israel have done nothing but arouse my anger with what their hands have made, declares the LORD. 31 From the day

[a] 4 Or *Chaldeans*; also in verses 5, 24, 25, 28, 29 and 43 [b] 9 That is, about 7 ounces or about 200 grams

it was built until now, this city has so aroused
my anger and wrath that I must remove it
from my sight. 32The people of Israel and Judah have provoked me by all the evil they
have done—they, their kings and officials,
their priests and prophets, the people of Judah
and those living in Jerusalem. 33They turned
their backs to me and not their faces; though I
taught them again and again, they would not
listen or respond to discipline. 34They set up
their vile images in the house that bears my
Name and defiled it. 35They built high places for Baal in the Valley of Ben Hinnom to
sacrifice their sons and daughters to Molek,
though I never commanded—nor did it enter
my mind—that they should do such a detestable thing and so make Judah sin.

36"You are saying about this city, 'By the
sword, famine and plague it will be given into
the hands of the king of Babylon'; but this is
what the LORD, the God of Israel, says: 37I will
surely gather them from all the lands where
I banish them in my furious anger and great
wrath; I will bring them back to this place
and let them live in safety. 38They will be my
people, and I will be their God. 39I will give
them singleness of heart and action, so that
they will always fear me and that all will then
go well for them and for their children after
them. 40I will make an everlasting covenant
with them: I will never stop doing good to
them, and I will inspire them to fear me, so
that they will never turn away from me. 41I
will rejoice in doing them good and will as-
suredly plant them in this land with all my
heart and soul.

42"This is what the LORD says: As I have
brought all this great calamity on this people, so I will give them all the prosperity I
have promised them. 43Once more fields will
be bought in this land of which you say, 'It is a
desolate waste, without people or animals, for
it has been given into the hands of the Babylonians.' 44Fields will be bought for silver, and
deeds will be signed, sealed and witnessed
in the territory of Benjamin, in the villages
around Jerusalem, in the towns of Judah and
in the towns of the hill country, of the western foothills and of the Negev, because I will
restore their fortunes,[a] declares the LORD."

Promise of Restoration

33 While Jeremiah was still confined in
the courtyard of the guard, the word of
the LORD came to him a second time: 2"This is
what the LORD says, he who made the earth,
the LORD who formed it and established it—
the LORD is his name: 3'Call to me and I will
answer you and tell you great and unsearchable things you do not know.' 4For this is what
the LORD, the God of Israel, says about the
houses in this city and the royal palaces of
Judah that have been torn down to be used
against the siege ramps and the sword 5in
the fight with the Babylonians[b]: 'They will be
filled with the dead bodies of the people I will
slay in my anger and wrath. I will hide my face
from this city because of all its wickedness.

6" 'Nevertheless, I will bring health and
healing to it; I will heal my people and will
let them enjoy abundant peace and security.
7I will bring Judah and Israel back from captivity[c] and will rebuild them as they were before. 8I will cleanse them from all the sin they
have committed against me and will forgive
all their sins of rebellion against me. 9Then
this city will bring me renown, joy, praise and
honor before all nations on earth that hear of
all the good things I do for it; and they will
be in awe and will tremble at the abundant
prosperity and peace I provide for it.'

10"This is what the LORD says: 'You say
about this place, "It is a desolate waste, without people or animals." Yet in the towns of
Judah and the streets of Jerusalem that are
deserted, inhabited by neither people nor
animals, there will be heard once more 11the
sounds of joy and gladness, the voices of bride
and bridegroom, and the voices of those who
bring thank offerings to the house of the LORD,
saying,

> "Give thanks to the LORD Almighty,
> for the LORD is good;
> his love endures forever."

For I will restore the fortunes of the land as
they were before,' says the LORD.

12"This is what the LORD Almighty says:
'In this place, desolate and without people or
animals—in all its towns there will again be
pastures for shepherds to rest their flocks. 13In
the towns of the hill country, of the western
foothills and of the Negev, in the territory of
Benjamin, in the villages around Jerusalem
and in the towns of Judah, flocks will again
pass under the hand of the one who counts
them,' says the LORD.

14" 'The days are coming,' declares the LORD,
'when I will fulfill the good promise I made to
the people of Israel and Judah.

> 15" 'In those days and at that time
> I will make a righteous Branch sprout
> from David's line;
> he will do what is just and right in the
> land.
> 16In those days Judah will be saved
> and Jerusalem will live in safety.
> This is the name by which it[d] will be
> called:
> The LORD Our Righteous Savior.'

17For this is what the LORD says: 'David will
never fail to have a man to sit on the throne
of Israel, 18nor will the Levitical priests ever
fail to have a man to stand before me continually to offer burnt offerings, to burn grain
offerings and to present sacrifices.' "

19The word of the LORD came to Jeremiah: 20"This is what the LORD says: 'If you can
break my covenant with the day and my covenant with the night, so that day and night no
longer come at their appointed time, 21then

[a] 44 Or *will bring them back from captivity* [b] 5 Or *Chaldeans* [c] 7 Or *will restore the fortunes of Judah and Israel* [d] 16 Or *he*

my covenant with David my servant—and
my covenant with the Levites who are priests
ministering before me—can be broken and
David will no longer have a descendant to
reign on his throne. 22 I will make the descendants of David my servant and the Levites
who minister before me as countless as the
stars in the sky and as measureless as the
sand on the seashore.'"

23 The word of the LORD came to Jeremiah:
24 "Have you not noticed that these people are
saying, 'The LORD has rejected the two kingdoms[a] he chose'? So they despise my people
and no longer regard them as a nation. 25 This
is what the LORD says: 'If I have not made my
covenant with day and night and established
the laws of heaven and earth, 26 then I will reject the descendants of Jacob and David my
servant and will not choose one of his sons to
rule over the descendants of Abraham, Isaac
and Jacob. For I will restore their fortunes[b]
and have compassion on them.'"

Warning to Zedekiah

34 While Nebuchadnezzar king of Babylon
and all his army and all the kingdoms
and peoples in the empire he ruled were fighting against Jerusalem and all its surrounding
towns, this word came to Jeremiah from the
LORD: 2 "This is what the LORD, the God of Israel, says: Go to Zedekiah king of Judah and tell
him, 'This is what the LORD says: I am about
to give this city into the hands of the king of
Babylon, and he will burn it down. 3 You will
not escape from his grasp but will surely be
captured and given into his hands. You will
see the king of Babylon with your own eyes,
and he will speak with you face to face. And
you will go to Babylon.

4 "'Yet hear the LORD's promise to you, Zedekiah king of Judah. This is what the LORD says
concerning you: You will not die by the sword;
5 you will die peacefully. As people made a
funeral fire in honor of your predecessors,
the kings who ruled before you, so they will
make a fire in your honor and lament, "Alas,
master!" I myself make this promise, declares
the LORD.'"

6 Then Jeremiah the prophet told all this to
Zedekiah king of Judah, in Jerusalem, 7 while
the army of the king of Babylon was fighting
against Jerusalem and the other cities of Judah that were still holding out—Lachish and
Azekah. These were the only fortified cities
left in Judah.

Freedom for Slaves

8 The word came to Jeremiah from the LORD
after King Zedekiah had made a covenant
with all the people in Jerusalem to proclaim
freedom for the slaves. 9 Everyone was to free
their Hebrew slaves, both male and female; no
one was to hold a fellow Hebrew in bondage.
10 So all the officials and people who entered
into this covenant agreed that they would free
their male and female slaves and no longer
hold them in bondage. They agreed, and set
them free. 11 But afterward they changed their
minds and took back the slaves they had freed
and enslaved them again.

12 Then the word of the LORD came to Jeremiah: 13 "This is what the LORD, the God of
Israel, says: I made a covenant with your ancestors when I brought them out of Egypt, out
of the land of slavery. I said, 14 'Every seventh
year each of you must free any fellow Hebrews
who have sold themselves to you. After they
have served you six years, you must let them
go free.'[c] Your ancestors, however, did not listen to me or pay attention to me. 15 Recently you
repented and did what is right in my sight: Each
of you proclaimed freedom to your own people.
You even made a covenant before me in the
house that bears my Name. 16 But now you have
turned around and profaned my name; each of
you has taken back the male and female slaves
you had set free to go where they wished. You
have forced them to become your slaves again.

17 "Therefore this is what the LORD says:
You have not obeyed me; you have not proclaimed freedom to your own people. So I
now proclaim 'freedom' for you, declares the
LORD—'freedom' to fall by the sword, plague
and famine. I will make you abhorrent to all
the kingdoms of the earth. 18 Those who have
violated my covenant and have not fulfilled
the terms of the covenant they made before
me, I will treat like the calf they cut in two and
then walked between its pieces. 19 The leaders
of Judah and Jerusalem, the court officials,
the priests and all the people of the land who
walked between the pieces of the calf, 20 I will
deliver into the hands of their enemies who
want to kill them. Their dead bodies will become food for the birds and the wild animals.

21 "I will deliver Zedekiah king of Judah and
his officials into the hands of their enemies
who want to kill them, to the army of the king
of Babylon, which has withdrawn from you.
22 I am going to give the order, declares the
LORD, and I will bring them back to this city.
They will fight against it, take it and burn it
down. And I will lay waste the towns of Judah
so no one can live there."

The Rekabites

35 This is the word that came to Jeremiah
from the LORD during the reign of Jehoiakim son of Josiah king of Judah: 2 "Go to
the Rekabite family and invite them to come
to one of the side rooms of the house of the
LORD and give them wine to drink."

3 So I went to get Jaazaniah son of Jeremiah, the son of Habazziniah, and his brothers and all his sons—the whole family of the
Rekabites. 4 I brought them into the house of
the LORD, into the room of the sons of Hanan
son of Igdaliah the man of God. It was next to
the room of the officials, which was over that
of Maaseiah son of Shallum the doorkeeper.
5 Then I set bowls full of wine and some cups
before the Rekabites and said to them, "Drink
some wine."

[a] 24 Or *families* [b] 26 Or *will bring them back from captivity* [c] 14 Deut. 15:12

6But they replied, "We do not drink wine,
because our forefather Jehonadab[a] son of
Rekab gave us this command: 'Neither you
nor your descendants must ever drink wine.
7Also you must never build houses, sow seed
or plant vineyards; you must never have any
of these things, but must always live in tents.
Then you will live a long time in the land
where you are nomads.' 8We have obeyed
everything our forefather Jehonadab son of
Rekab commanded us. Neither we nor our
wives nor our sons and daughters have ever
drunk wine 9or built houses to live in or had
vineyards, fields or crops. 10We have lived in
tents and have fully obeyed everything our
forefather Jehonadab commanded us. 11But
when Nebuchadnezzar king of Babylon invaded this land, we said, 'Come, we must go
to Jerusalem to escape the Babylonian[b] and
Aramean armies.' So we have remained in
Jerusalem."

12Then the word of the LORD came to Jeremiah, saying: 13"This is what the LORD Almighty,
the God of Israel, says: Go and tell the people
of Judah and those living in Jerusalem, 'Will
you not learn a lesson and obey my words?'
declares the LORD. 14'Jehonadab son of Rekab
ordered his descendants not to drink wine
and this command has been kept. To this day
they do not drink wine, because they obey
their forefather's command. But I have spoken to you again and again, yet you have not
obeyed me. 15Again and again I sent all my
servants the prophets to you. They said, "Each
of you must turn from your wicked ways and
reform your actions; do not follow other gods
to serve them. Then you will live in the land I
have given to you and your ancestors." But you
have not paid attention or listened to me. 16The
descendants of Jehonadab son of Rekab have
carried out the command their forefather gave
them, but these people have not obeyed me.'

17"Therefore this is what the LORD God Almighty, the God of Israel, says: 'Listen! I am
going to bring on Judah and on everyone living in Jerusalem every disaster I pronounced
against them. I spoke to them, but they did
not listen; I called to them, but they did not
answer.'"

18Then Jeremiah said to the family of the
Rekabites, "This is what the LORD Almighty,
the God of Israel, says: 'You have obeyed the
command of your forefather Jehonadab and
have followed all his instructions and have
done everything he ordered.' 19Therefore this
is what the LORD Almighty, the God of Israel,
says: 'Jehonadab son of Rekab will never fail
to have a descendant to serve me.'"

Jehoiakim Burns Jeremiah's Scroll

36 In the fourth year of Jehoiakim son of
Josiah king of Judah, this word came
to Jeremiah from the LORD: 2"Take a scroll
and write on it all the words I have spoken to
you concerning Israel, Judah and all the other
nations from the time I began speaking to you
in the reign of Josiah till now. 3Perhaps when
the people of Judah hear about every disaster
I plan to inflict on them, they will each turn
from their wicked ways; then I will forgive
their wickedness and their sin."

4So Jeremiah called Baruch son of Neriah,
and while Jeremiah dictated all the words the
LORD had spoken to him, Baruch wrote them
on the scroll. 5Then Jeremiah told Baruch, "I
am restricted; I am not allowed to go to the
LORD's temple. 6So you go to the house of the
LORD on a day of fasting and read to the people
from the scroll the words of the LORD that you
wrote as I dictated. Read them to all the people of Judah who come in from their towns.
7Perhaps they will bring their petition before
the LORD and will each turn from their wicked
ways, for the anger and wrath pronounced
against this people by the LORD are great."

8Baruch son of Neriah did everything Jeremiah the prophet told him to do; at the LORD's
temple he read the words of the LORD from the
scroll. 9In the ninth month of the fifth year of
Jehoiakim son of Josiah king of Judah, a time
of fasting before the LORD was proclaimed for
all the people in Jerusalem and those who
had come from the towns of Judah. 10From
the room of Gemariah son of Shaphan the
secretary, which was in the upper courtyard
at the entrance of the New Gate of the temple,
Baruch read to all the people at the LORD's
temple the words of Jeremiah from the scroll.

11When Micaiah son of Gemariah, the son
of Shaphan, heard all the words of the LORD
from the scroll, 12he went down to the secretary's room in the royal palace, where all the
officials were sitting: Elishama the secretary,
Delaiah son of Shemaiah, Elnathan son of Akbor, Gemariah son of Shaphan, Zedekiah son
of Hananiah, and all the other officials. 13Af-
ter Micaiah told them everything he had heard
Baruch read to the people from the scroll, 14all
the officials sent Jehudi son of Nethaniah, the
son of Shelemiah, the son of Cushi, to say to
Baruch, "Bring the scroll from which you have
read to the people and come." So Baruch son
of Neriah went to them with the scroll in his
hand. 15They said to him, "Sit down, please,
and read it to us."

So Baruch read it to them. 16When they
heard all these words, they looked at each
other in fear and said to Baruch, "We must report all these words to the king." 17Then they
asked Baruch, "Tell us, how did you come to
write all this? Did Jeremiah dictate it?"

18"Yes," Baruch replied, "he dictated all
these words to me, and I wrote them in ink
on the scroll."

19Then the officials said to Baruch, "You
and Jeremiah, go and hide. Don't let anyone
know where you are."

20After they put the scroll in the room of
Elishama the secretary, they went to the king
in the courtyard and reported everything to
him. 21The king sent Jehudi to get the scroll, and
Jehudi brought it from the room of Elishama
the secretary and read it to the king and all the
officials standing beside him. 22It was the ninth

[a] 6 Hebrew *Jonadab*, a variant of *Jehonadab*; here and often in this chapter   [b] 11 Or *Chaldean*

month and the king was sitting in the winter
apartment, with a fire burning in the firepot in
front of him. 23Whenever Jehudi had read three
or four columns of the scroll, the king cut them
off with a scribe's knife and threw them into
the firepot, until the entire scroll was burned in
the fire. 24The king and all his attendants who
heard all these words showed no fear, nor did
they tear their clothes. 25Even though Elnathan,
Delaiah and Gemariah urged the king not to
burn the scroll, he would not listen to them.
26Instead, the king commanded Jerahmeel,
a son of the king, Seraiah son of Azriel and
Shelemiah son of Abdeel to arrest Baruch the
scribe and Jeremiah the prophet. But the LORD
had hidden them.

27After the king burned the scroll containing the words that Baruch had written at Jeremiah's dictation, the word of the LORD came
to Jeremiah: 28"Take another scroll and write
on it all the words that were on the first scroll,
which Jehoiakim king of Judah burned up.
29Also tell Jehoiakim king of Judah, 'This is
what the LORD says: You burned that scroll
and said, "Why did you write on it that the
king of Babylon would certainly come and
destroy this land and wipe from it both man
and beast?" 30Therefore this is what the LORD
says about Jehoiakim king of Judah: He will
have no one to sit on the throne of David; his
body will be thrown out and exposed to the
heat by day and the frost by night. 31I will punish him and his children and his attendants
for their wickedness; I will bring on them and
those living in Jerusalem and the people of
Judah every disaster I pronounced against
them, because they have not listened.'"

32So Jeremiah took another scroll and gave
it to the scribe Baruch son of Neriah, and as
Jeremiah dictated, Baruch wrote on it all the
words of the scroll that Jehoiakim king of Judah had burned in the fire. And many similar
words were added to them.

Jeremiah in Prison

37 Zedekiah son of Josiah was made king
of Judah by Nebuchadnezzar king of
Babylon; he reigned in place of Jehoiachin[a]
son of Jehoiakim. 2Neither he nor his attendants nor the people of the land paid any
attention to the words the LORD had spoken
through Jeremiah the prophet.

3King Zedekiah, however, sent Jehukal son
of Shelemiah with the priest Zephaniah son
of Maaseiah to Jeremiah the prophet with
this message: "Please pray to the LORD our
God for us."

4Now Jeremiah was free to come and go
among the people, for he had not yet been
put in prison. 5Pharaoh's army had marched
out of Egypt, and when the Babylonians[b] who
were besieging Jerusalem heard the report
about them, they withdrew from Jerusalem.

6Then the word of the LORD came to Jeremiah the prophet: 7"This is what the LORD, the
God of Israel, says: Tell the king of Judah, who
sent you to inquire of me, 'Pharaoh's army,
which has marched out to support you, will
go back to its own land, to Egypt. 8Then the
Babylonians will return and attack this city;
they will capture it and burn it down.'

9"This is what the LORD says: Do not deceive
yourselves, thinking, 'The Babylonians will
surely leave us.' They will not! 10Even if you
were to defeat the entire Babylonian[c] army
that is attacking you and only wounded men
were left in their tents, they would come out
and burn this city down."

11After the Babylonian army had withdrawn from Jerusalem because of Pharaoh's
army, 12Jeremiah started to leave the city to
go to the territory of Benjamin to get his share
of the property among the people there. 13But
when he reached the Benjamin Gate, the captain of the guard, whose name was Irijah son
of Shelemiah, the son of Hananiah, arrested
him and said, "You are deserting to the Babylonians!"

14"That's not true!" Jeremiah said. "I am
not deserting to the Babylonians." But Irijah
would not listen to him; instead, he arrested
Jeremiah and brought him to the officials.
15They were angry with Jeremiah and had
him beaten and imprisoned in the house of
Jonathan the secretary, which they had made
into a prison.

16Jeremiah was put into a vaulted cell in
a dungeon, where he remained a long time.
17Then King Zedekiah sent for him and had
him brought to the palace, where he asked
him privately, "Is there any word from the
LORD?"

"Yes," Jeremiah replied, "you will be delivered into the hands of the king of Babylon."

18Then Jeremiah said to King Zedekiah,
"What crime have I committed against you or
your attendants or this people, that you have
put me in prison? 19Where are your prophets
who prophesied to you, 'The king of Babylon
will not attack you or this land'? 20But now,
my lord the king, please listen. Let me bring
my petition before you: Do not send me back
to the house of Jonathan the secretary, or I
will die there."

21King Zedekiah then gave orders for Jeremiah to be placed in the courtyard of the
guard and given a loaf of bread from the street
of the bakers each day until all the bread in
the city was gone. So Jeremiah remained in
the courtyard of the guard.

Jeremiah Thrown Into a Cistern

38 Shephatiah son of Mattan, Gedaliah son
of Pashhur, Jehukal[d] son of Shelemiah,
and Pashhur son of Malkijah heard what Jeremiah was telling all the people when he said,
2"This is what the LORD says: 'Whoever stays
in this city will die by the sword, famine or
plague, but whoever goes over to the Babylonians[e] will live. They will escape with their

[a] *1* Hebrew *Koniah,* a variant of *Jehoiachin* [b] *5* Or *Chaldeans;* also in verses 8, 9, 13 and 14
[c] *10* Or *Chaldean;* also in verse 11 [d] *1* Hebrew *Jukal,* a variant of *Jehukal* [e] *2* Or *Chaldeans;* also
in verses 18, 19 and 23

lives; they will live.' 3And this is what the LORD says: 'This city will certainly be given into the hands of the army of the king of Babylon, who will capture it.'"

4Then the officials said to the king, "This man should be put to death. He is discouraging the soldiers who are left in this city, as well as all the people, by the things he is saying to them. This man is not seeking the good of these people but their ruin."

5"He is in your hands," King Zedekiah answered. "The king can do nothing to oppose you."

6So they took Jeremiah and put him into the cistern of Malkijah, the king's son, which was in the courtyard of the guard. They lowered Jeremiah by ropes into the cistern; it had no water in it, only mud, and Jeremiah sank down into the mud.

7But Ebed-Melek, a Cushite,[a] an official[b] in the royal palace, heard that they had put Jeremiah into the cistern. While the king was sitting in the Benjamin Gate, 8Ebed-Melek went out of the palace and said to him, 9"My lord the king, these men have acted wickedly in all they have done to Jeremiah the prophet. They have thrown him into a cistern, where he will starve to death when there is no longer any bread in the city."

10Then the king commanded Ebed-Melek the Cushite, "Take thirty men from here with you and lift Jeremiah the prophet out of the cistern before he dies."

11So Ebed-Melek took the men with him and went to a room under the treasury in the palace. He took some old rags and worn-out clothes from there and let them down with ropes to Jeremiah in the cistern. 12Ebed-Melek the Cushite said to Jeremiah, "Put these old rags and worn-out clothes under your arms to pad the ropes." Jeremiah did so, 13and they pulled him up with the ropes and lifted him out of the cistern. And Jeremiah remained in the courtyard of the guard.

Zedekiah Questions Jeremiah Again

14Then King Zedekiah sent for Jeremiah the prophet and had him brought to the third entrance to the temple of the LORD. "I am going to ask you something," the king said to Jeremiah. "Do not hide anything from me."

15Jeremiah said to Zedekiah, "If I give you an answer, will you not kill me? Even if I did give you counsel, you would not listen to me."

16But King Zedekiah swore this oath secretly to Jeremiah: "As surely as the LORD lives, who has given us breath, I will neither kill you nor hand you over to those who want to kill you."

17Then Jeremiah said to Zedekiah, "This is what the LORD God Almighty, the God of Israel, says: 'If you surrender to the officers of the king of Babylon, your life will be spared and this city will not be burned down; you and your family will live. 18But if you will not surrender to the officers of the king of Babylon, this city will be given into the hands of the Babylonians and they will burn it down; you yourself will not escape from them.'"

19King Zedekiah said to Jeremiah, "I am afraid of the Jews who have gone over to the Babylonians, for the Babylonians may hand me over to them and they will mistreat me."

20"They will not hand you over," Jeremiah replied. "Obey the LORD by doing what I tell you. Then it will go well with you, and your life will be spared. 21But if you refuse to surrender, this is what the LORD has revealed to me: 22All the women left in the palace of the king of Judah will be brought out to the officials of the king of Babylon. Those women will say to you:

"'They misled you and overcame you—
those trusted friends of yours.
Your feet are sunk in the mud;
your friends have deserted you.'

23"All your wives and children will be brought out to the Babylonians. You yourself will not escape from their hands but will be captured by the king of Babylon; and this city will[c] be burned down."

24Then Zedekiah said to Jeremiah, "Do not let anyone know about this conversation, or you may die. 25If the officials hear that I talked with you, and they come to you and say, 'Tell us what you said to the king and what the king said to you; do not hide it from us or we will kill you,' 26then tell them, 'I was pleading with the king not to send me back to Jonathan's house to die there.'"

27All the officials did come to Jeremiah and question him, and he told them everything the king had ordered him to say. So they said no more to him, for no one had heard his conversation with the king.

28And Jeremiah remained in the courtyard of the guard until the day Jerusalem was captured.

The Fall of Jerusalem

39 This is how Jerusalem was taken: 1In the ninth year of Zedekiah king of Judah, in the tenth month, Nebuchadnezzar king of Babylon marched against Jerusalem with his whole army and laid siege to it. 2And on the ninth day of the fourth month of Zedekiah's eleventh year, the city wall was broken through. 3Then all the officials of the king of Babylon came and took seats in the Middle Gate: Nergal-Sharezer of Samgar, Nebo-Sarsekim a chief officer, Nergal-Sharezer a high official and all the other officials of the king of Babylon. 4When Zedekiah king of Judah and all the soldiers saw them, they fled; they left the city at night by way of the king's garden, through the gate between the two walls, and headed toward the Arabah.[d]

5But the Babylonian[e] army pursued them and overtook Zedekiah in the plains of Jericho. They captured him and took him to Nebuchadnezzar king of Babylon at Riblah

[a] 7 Probably from the upper Nile region [b] 7 Or *a eunuch* [c] 23 Or *and you will cause this city to*
[d] 4 Or *the Jordan Valley* [e] 5 Or *Chaldean*

in the land of Hamath, where he pronounced sentence on him. 6There at Riblah the king of Babylon slaughtered the sons of Zedekiah before his eyes and also killed all the nobles of Judah. 7Then he put out Zedekiah's eyes and bound him with bronze shackles to take him to Babylon.

8The Babylonians[a] set fire to the royal palace and the houses of the people and broke down the walls of Jerusalem. 9Nebuzaradan commander of the imperial guard carried into exile to Babylon the people who remained in the city, along with those who had gone over to him, and the rest of the people. 10But Nebuzaradan the commander of the guard left behind in the land of Judah some of the poor people, who owned nothing; and at that time he gave them vineyards and fields.

11Now Nebuchadnezzar king of Babylon had given these orders about Jeremiah through Nebuzaradan commander of the imperial guard: 12"Take him and look after him; don't harm him but do for him whatever he asks." 13So Nebuzaradan the commander of the guard, Nebushazban a chief officer, Nergal-Sharezer a high official and all the other officers of the king of Babylon 14sent and had Jeremiah taken out of the courtyard of the guard. They turned him over to Gedaliah son of Ahikam, the son of Shaphan, to take him back to his home. So he remained among his own people.

15While Jeremiah had been confined in the courtyard of the guard, the word of the LORD came to him: 16"Go and tell Ebed-Melek the Cushite, 'This is what the LORD Almighty, the God of Israel, says: I am about to fulfill my words against this city—words concerning disaster, not prosperity. At that time they will be fulfilled before your eyes. 17But I will rescue you on that day, declares the LORD; you will not be given into the hands of those you fear. 18I will save you; you will not fall by the sword but will escape with your life, because you trust in me, declares the LORD.'"

Jeremiah Freed

40 The word came to Jeremiah from the LORD after Nebuzaradan commander of the imperial guard had released him at Ramah. He had found Jeremiah bound in chains among all the captives from Jerusalem and Judah who were being carried into exile to Babylon. 2When the commander of the guard found Jeremiah, he said to him, "The LORD your God decreed this disaster for this place. 3And now the LORD has brought it about; he has done just as he said he would. All this happened because you people sinned against the LORD and did not obey him. 4But today I am freeing you from the chains on your wrists. Come with me to Babylon, if you like, and I will look after you; but if you do not want to, then don't come. Look, the whole country lies before you; go wherever you please." 5However, before Jeremiah turned to go,[b] Nebuzaradan added, "Go back to Gedaliah son of Ahikam, the son of Shaphan, whom the king of Babylon has appointed over the towns of Judah, and live with him among the people, or go anywhere else you please."

Then the commander gave him provisions and a present and let him go. 6So Jeremiah went to Gedaliah son of Ahikam at Mizpah and stayed with him among the people who were left behind in the land.

Gedaliah Assassinated

7When all the army officers and their men who were still in the open country heard that the king of Babylon had appointed Gedaliah son of Ahikam as governor over the land and had put him in charge of the men, women and children who were the poorest in the land and who had not been carried into exile to Babylon, 8they came to Gedaliah at Mizpah—Ishmael son of Nethaniah, Johanan and Jonathan the sons of Kareah, Seraiah son of Tanhumeth, the sons of Ephai the Netophathite, and Jaazaniah[c] the son of the Maakathite, and their men. 9Gedaliah son of Ahikam, the son of Shaphan, took an oath to reassure them and their men. "Do not be afraid to serve the Babylonians,[d]" he said. "Settle down in the land and serve the king of Babylon, and it will go well with you. 10I myself will stay at Mizpah to represent you before the Babylonians who come to us, but you are to harvest the wine, summer fruit and olive oil, and put them in your storage jars, and live in the towns you have taken over."

11When all the Jews in Moab, Ammon, Edom and all the other countries heard that the king of Babylon had left a remnant in Judah and had appointed Gedaliah son of Ahikam, the son of Shaphan, as governor over them, 12they all came back to the land of Judah, to Gedaliah at Mizpah, from all the countries where they had been scattered. And they harvested an abundance of wine and summer fruit.

13Johanan son of Kareah and all the army officers still in the open country came to Gedaliah at Mizpah 14and said to him, "Don't you know that Baalis king of the Ammonites has sent Ishmael son of Nethaniah to take your life?" But Gedaliah son of Ahikam did not believe them.

15Then Johanan son of Kareah said privately to Gedaliah in Mizpah, "Let me go and kill Ishmael son of Nethaniah, and no one will know it. Why should he take your life and cause all the Jews who are gathered around you to be scattered and the remnant of Judah to perish?"

16But Gedaliah son of Ahikam said to Johanan son of Kareah, "Don't do such a thing! What you are saying about Ishmael is not true."

41 In the seventh month Ishmael son of Nethaniah, the son of Elishama, who was of royal blood and had been one of the

[a] 8 Or *Chaldeans* [b] 5 Or *Jeremiah answered* [c] 8 Hebrew *Jezaniah*, a variant of *Jaazaniah*
[d] 9 Or *Chaldeans*; also in verse 10

king's officers, came with ten men to Gedaliah
son of Ahikam at Mizpah. While they were
eating together there, 2Ishmael son of Nethaniah and the ten men who were with him got
up and struck down Gedaliah son of Ahikam,
the son of Shaphan, with the sword, killing the
one whom the king of Babylon had appointed
as governor over the land. 3Ishmael also killed
all the men of Judah who were with Gedaliah
at Mizpah, as well as the Babylonian[a] soldiers
who were there.

4The day after Gedaliah's assassination, before anyone knew about it, 5eighty men who
had shaved off their beards, torn their clothes
and cut themselves came from Shechem, Shiloh and Samaria, bringing grain offerings and
incense with them to the house of the LORD.
6Ishmael son of Nethaniah went out from Mizpah to meet them, weeping as he went. When
he met them, he said, "Come to Gedaliah son
of Ahikam." 7When they went into the city,
Ishmael son of Nethaniah and the men who
were with him slaughtered them and threw
them into a cistern. 8But ten of them said to
Ishmael, "Don't kill us! We have wheat and
barley, olive oil and honey, hidden in a field."
So he let them alone and did not kill them
with the others. 9Now the cistern where he
threw all the bodies of the men he had killed
along with Gedaliah was the one King Asa
had made as part of his defense against Baasha king of Israel. Ishmael son of Nethaniah
filled it with the dead.

10Ishmael made captives of all the rest of
the people who were in Mizpah—the king's
daughters along with all the others who were
left there, over whom Nebuzaradan commander of the imperial guard had appointed Gedaliah son of Ahikam. Ishmael son of
Nethaniah took them captive and set out to
cross over to the Ammonites.

11When Johanan son of Kareah and all
the army officers who were with him heard
about all the crimes Ishmael son of Nethaniah
had committed, 12they took all their men and
went to fight Ishmael son of Nethaniah. They
caught up with him near the great pool in Gibeon. 13When all the people Ishmael had with
him saw Johanan son of Kareah and the army
officers who were with him, they were glad.
14All the people Ishmael had taken captive at
Mizpah turned and went over to Johanan son
of Kareah. 15But Ishmael son of Nethaniah
and eight of his men escaped from Johanan
and fled to the Ammonites.

Flight to Egypt

16Then Johanan son of Kareah and all the
army officers who were with him led away
all the people of Mizpah who had survived,
whom Johanan had recovered from Ishmael
son of Nethaniah after Ishmael had assassinated Gedaliah son of Ahikam—the soldiers,
women, children and court officials he had
recovered from Gibeon. 17And they went on,
stopping at Geruth Kimham near Bethlehem
on their way to Egypt 18to escape the Babylonians.[b] They were afraid of them because
Ishmael son of Nethaniah had killed Gedaliah
son of Ahikam, whom the king of Babylon had
appointed as governor over the land.

42 Then all the army officers, including
Johanan son of Kareah and Jezaniah[c]
son of Hoshaiah, and all the people from the
least to the greatest approached 2Jeremiah
the prophet and said to him, "Please hear our
petition and pray to the LORD your God for this
entire remnant. For as you now see, though we
were once many, now only a few are left. 3Pray
that the LORD your God will tell us where we
should go and what we should do."

4"I have heard you," replied Jeremiah the
prophet. "I will certainly pray to the LORD
your God as you have requested; I will tell
you everything the LORD says and will keep
nothing back from you."

5Then they said to Jeremiah, "May the LORD
be a true and faithful witness against us if we
do not act in accordance with everything the
LORD your God sends you to tell us. 6Whether
it is favorable or unfavorable, we will obey the
LORD our God, to whom we are sending you,
so that it will go well with us, for we will obey
the LORD our God."

7Ten days later the word of the LORD came
to Jeremiah. 8So he called together Johanan
son of Kareah and all the army officers who
were with him and all the people from the
least to the greatest. 9He said to them, "This
is what the LORD, the God of Israel, to whom
you sent me to present your petition, says:
10'If you stay in this land, I will build you up
and not tear you down; I will plant you and
not uproot you, for I have relented concerning
the disaster I have inflicted on you. 11Do not
be afraid of the king of Babylon, whom you
now fear. Do not be afraid of him, declares the
LORD, for I am with you and will save you and
deliver you from his hands. 12I will show you
compassion so that he will have compassion
on you and restore you to your land.'

13"However, if you say, 'We will not stay
in this land,' and so disobey the LORD your
God, 14and if you say, 'No, we will go and live
in Egypt, where we will not see war or hear
the trumpet or be hungry for bread,' 15then
hear the word of the LORD, you remnant of
Judah. This is what the LORD Almighty, the
God of Israel, says: 'If you are determined
to go to Egypt and you do go to settle there,
16then the sword you fear will overtake you
there, and the famine you dread will follow
you into Egypt, and there you will die. 17In-
deed, all who are determined to go to Egypt
to settle there will die by the sword, famine
and plague; not one of them will survive or escape the disaster I will bring on them.' 18This
is what the LORD Almighty, the God of Israel, says: 'As my anger and wrath have been
poured out on those who lived in Jerusalem,
so will my wrath be poured out on you when
you go to Egypt. You will be a curse[d] and an

[a] *3* Or *Chaldean* [b] *18* Or *Chaldeans* [c] *1* Hebrew; Septuagint (see also 43:2) *Azariah* [d] *18* That is, your name will be used in cursing (see 29:22); or, others will see that you are cursed.

object of horror, a curse[a] and an object of reproach; you will never see this place again.'
19“Remnant of Judah, the LORD has told you,
'Do not go to Egypt.' Be sure of this: I warn
you today 20that you made a fatal mistake
when you sent me to the LORD your God and
said, 'Pray to the LORD our God for us; tell us
everything he says and we will do it.' 21I have
told you today, but you still have not obeyed
the LORD your God in all he sent me to tell you.
22So now, be sure of this: You will die by the
sword, famine and plague in the place where
you want to go to settle.”

43 When Jeremiah had finished telling the
people all the words of the LORD their
God—everything the LORD had sent him to
tell them— 2Azariah son of Hoshaiah and Johanan son of Kareah and all the arrogant men
said to Jeremiah, “You are lying! The LORD
our God has not sent you to say, 'You must not
go to Egypt to settle there.' 3But Baruch son
of Neriah is inciting you against us to hand
us over to the Babylonians,[b] so they may kill
us or carry us into exile to Babylon.”
4So Johanan son of Kareah and all the army
officers and all the people disobeyed the LORD's
command to stay in the land of Judah. 5Instead,
Johanan son of Kareah and all the army officers led away all the remnant of Judah who
had come back to live in the land of Judah from
all the nations where they had been scattered.
6They also led away all those whom Nebuzaradan commander of the imperial guard had left
with Gedaliah son of Ahikam, the son of Shaphan—the men, the women, the children and
the king's daughters. And they took Jeremiah
the prophet and Baruch son of Neriah along
with them. 7So they entered Egypt in disobedience to the LORD and went as far as Tahpanhes.
8In Tahpanhes the word of the LORD came to
Jeremiah: 9“While the Jews are watching, take
some large stones with you and bury them in
clay in the brick pavement at the entrance to
Pharaoh's palace in Tahpanhes. 10Then say
to them, 'This is what the LORD Almighty, the
God of Israel, says: I will send for my servant
Nebuchadnezzar king of Babylon, and I will
set his throne over these stones I have buried
here; he will spread his royal canopy above
them. 11He will come and attack Egypt, bringing death to those destined for death, captivity
to those destined for captivity, and the sword
to those destined for the sword. 12He will set
fire to the temples of the gods of Egypt; he will
burn their temples and take their gods captive.
As a shepherd picks his garment clean of lice,
so he will pick Egypt clean and depart. 13There
in the temple of the sun[c] in Egypt he will demolish the sacred pillars and will burn down
the temples of the gods of Egypt.' ”

Disaster Because of Idolatry

44 This word came to Jeremiah concerning
all the Jews living in Lower Egypt—in
Migdol, Tahpanhes and Memphis—and in Upper Egypt: 2“This is what the LORD Almighty,
the God of Israel, says: You saw the great disaster I brought on Jerusalem and on all the
towns of Judah. Today they lie deserted and in
ruins 3because of the evil they have done. They
aroused my anger by burning incense to and
worshiping other gods that neither they nor
you nor your ancestors ever knew. 4Again and
again I sent my servants the prophets, who said,
'Do not do this detestable thing that I hate!' 5But
they did not listen or pay attention; they did not
turn from their wickedness or stop burning incense to other gods. 6Therefore, my fierce anger
was poured out; it raged against the towns of
Judah and the streets of Jerusalem and made
them the desolate ruins they are today.
7“Now this is what the LORD God Almighty,
the God of Israel, says: Why bring such great
disaster on yourselves by cutting off from Judah the men and women, the children and
infants, and so leave yourselves without a
remnant? 8Why arouse my anger with what
your hands have made, burning incense to
other gods in Egypt, where you have come to
live? You will destroy yourselves and make
yourselves a curse[d] and an object of reproach
among all the nations on earth. 9Have you
forgotten the wickedness committed by your
ancestors and by the kings and queens of Judah and the wickedness committed by you
and your wives in the land of Judah and the
streets of Jerusalem? 10To this day they have
not humbled themselves or shown reverence,
nor have they followed my law and the decrees
I set before you and your ancestors.
11“Therefore this is what the LORD Almighty, the God of Israel, says: I am determined to bring disaster on you and to destroy
all Judah. 12I will take away the remnant of
Judah who were determined to go to Egypt
to settle there. They will all perish in Egypt;
they will fall by the sword or die from famine.
From the least to the greatest, they will die by
sword or famine. They will become a curse
and an object of horror, a curse and an object
of reproach. 13I will punish those who live in
Egypt with the sword, famine and plague, as I
punished Jerusalem. 14None of the remnant of
Judah who have gone to live in Egypt will escape or survive to return to the land of Judah,
to which they long to return and live; none will
return except a few fugitives.”
15Then all the men who knew that their
wives were burning incense to other gods,
along with all the women who were present—
a large assembly—and all the people living
in Lower and Upper Egypt, said to Jeremiah, 16“We will not listen to the message you
have spoken to us in the name of the LORD!
17We will certainly do everything we said we
would: We will burn incense to the Queen of
Heaven and will pour out drink offerings to
her just as we and our ancestors, our kings
and our officials did in the towns of Judah
and in the streets of Jerusalem. At that time

[a] 18 That is, your name will be used in cursing (see 29:22); or, others will see that you are cursed.
[b] 3 Or *Chaldeans* [c] 13 Or *in Heliopolis* [d] 8 That is, your name will be used in cursing (see 29:22); or, others will see that you are cursed; also in verse 12; similarly in verse 22.

we had plenty of food and were well off and
suffered no harm. 18But ever since we stopped
burning incense to the Queen of Heaven and
pouring out drink offerings to her, we have
had nothing and have been perishing by
sword and famine."

19The women added, "When we burned incense to the Queen of Heaven and poured out
drink offerings to her, did not our husbands
know that we were making cakes impressed
with her image and pouring out drink offerings to her?"

20Then Jeremiah said to all the people, both
men and women, who were answering him,
21"Did not the LORD remember and call to
mind the incense burned in the towns of Judah and the streets of Jerusalem by you and
your ancestors, your kings and your officials
and the people of the land? 22When the LORD
could no longer endure your wicked actions
and the detestable things you did, your land
became a curse and a desolate waste without
inhabitants, as it is today. 23Because you have
burned incense and have sinned against the
LORD and have not obeyed him or followed
his law or his decrees or his stipulations, this
disaster has come upon you, as you now see."

24Then Jeremiah said to all the people, including the women, "Hear the word of the
LORD, all you people of Judah in Egypt. 25This
is what the LORD Almighty, the God of Israel,
says: You and your wives have done what you
said you would do when you promised, 'We
will certainly carry out the vows we made to
burn incense and pour out drink offerings to
the Queen of Heaven.'

"Go ahead then, do what you promised!
Keep your vows! 26But hear the word of the
LORD, all you Jews living in Egypt: 'I swear by
my great name,' says the LORD, 'that no one
from Judah living anywhere in Egypt will ever
again invoke my name or swear, "As surely as
the Sovereign LORD lives." 27For I am watching
over them for harm, not for good; the Jews in
Egypt will perish by sword and famine until
they are all destroyed. 28Those who escape the
sword and return to the land of Judah from
Egypt will be very few. Then the whole remnant of Judah who came to live in Egypt will
know whose word will stand—mine or theirs.

29" 'This will be the sign to you that I will
punish you in this place,' declares the LORD,
'so that you will know that my threats of harm
against you will surely stand.' 30This is what
the LORD says: 'I am going to deliver Pharaoh
Hophra king of Egypt into the hands of his
enemies who want to kill him, just as I gave
Zedekiah king of Judah into the hands of Nebuchadnezzar king of Babylon, the enemy who
wanted to kill him.' "

A Message to Baruch

45 When Baruch son of Neriah wrote on a
scroll the words Jeremiah the prophet
dictated in the fourth year of Jehoiakim son
of Josiah king of Judah, Jeremiah said this to
Baruch: 2"This is what the LORD, the God of
Israel, says to you, Baruch: 3You said, 'Woe to
me! The LORD has added sorrow to my pain; I
am worn out with groaning and find no rest.'
4But the LORD has told me to say to you, 'This
is what the LORD says: I will overthrow what
I have built and uproot what I have planted,
throughout the earth. 5Should you then seek
great things for yourself? Do not seek them.
For I will bring disaster on all people, declares
the LORD, but wherever you go I will let you
escape with your life.' "

A Message About Egypt

46 This is the word of the LORD that came
to Jeremiah the prophet concerning the
nations:

2Concerning Egypt:

This is the message against the army of
Pharaoh Necho king of Egypt, which was defeated at Carchemish on the Euphrates River
by Nebuchadnezzar king of Babylon in the
fourth year of Jehoiakim son of Josiah king
of Judah:

3"Prepare your shields, both large and
small,
and march out for battle!
4Harness the horses,
mount the steeds!
Take your positions
with helmets on!
Polish your spears,
put on your armor!
5What do I see?
They are terrified,
they are retreating,
their warriors are defeated.
They flee in haste
without looking back,
and there is terror on every side,"
declares the LORD.
6"The swift cannot flee
nor the strong escape.
In the north by the River Euphrates
they stumble and fall.

7"Who is this that rises like the Nile,
like rivers of surging waters?
8Egypt rises like the Nile,
like rivers of surging waters.
She says, 'I will rise and cover the earth;
I will destroy cities and their people.'
9Charge, you horses!
Drive furiously, you charioteers!
March on, you warriors—men of Cush[a]
and Put who carry shields,
men of Lydia who draw the bow.
10But that day belongs to the Lord, the
LORD Almighty—
a day of vengeance, for vengeance on
his foes.
The sword will devour till it is satisfied,
till it has quenched its thirst with blood.
For the Lord, the LORD Almighty, will
offer sacrifice
in the land of the north by the River
Euphrates.

[a] 9 That is, the upper Nile region

11 "Go up to Gilead and get balm,
Virgin Daughter Egypt.
But you try many medicines in vain;
there is no healing for you.
12 The nations will hear of your shame;
your cries will fill the earth.
One warrior will stumble over another;
both will fall down together."

13 This is the message the LORD spoke to Jeremiah the prophet about the coming of Nebuchadnezzar king of Babylon to attack Egypt:

14 "Announce this in Egypt, and proclaim it
in Migdol;
proclaim it also in Memphis and
Tahpanhes:
'Take your positions and get ready,
for the sword devours those around
you.'
15 Why will your warriors be laid low?
They cannot stand, for the LORD will
push them down.
16 They will stumble repeatedly;
they will fall over each other.
They will say, 'Get up, let us go back
to our own people and our native lands,
away from the sword of the oppressor.'
17 There they will exclaim,
'Pharaoh king of Egypt is only a loud
noise;
he has missed his opportunity.'

18 "As surely as I live," declares the King,
whose name is the LORD Almighty,
"one will come who is like Tabor among
the mountains,
like Carmel by the sea.
19 Pack your belongings for exile,
you who live in Egypt,
for Memphis will be laid waste
and lie in ruins without inhabitant.

20 "Egypt is a beautiful heifer,
but a gadfly is coming
against her from the north.
21 The mercenaries in her ranks
are like fattened calves.
They too will turn and flee together,
they will not stand their ground,
for the day of disaster is coming upon
them,
the time for them to be punished.
22 Egypt will hiss like a fleeing serpent
as the enemy advances in force;
they will come against her with axes,
like men who cut down trees.
23 They will chop down her forest,"
declares the LORD,
"dense though it be.
They are more numerous than locusts,
they cannot be counted.
24 Daughter Egypt will be put to shame,
given into the hands of the people of the
north."

25 The LORD Almighty, the God of Israel,
says: "I am about to bring punishment on
Amon god of Thebes, on Pharaoh, on Egypt
and her gods and her kings, and on those who
rely on Pharaoh. 26 I will give them into the
hands of those who want to kill them—Nebuchadnezzar king of Babylon and his officers.
Later, however, Egypt will be inhabited as in
times past," declares the LORD.

27 "Do not be afraid, Jacob my servant;
do not be dismayed, Israel.
I will surely save you out of a distant
place,
your descendants from the land of their
exile.
Jacob will again have peace and security,
and no one will make him afraid.
28 Do not be afraid, Jacob my servant,
for I am with you," declares the LORD.
"Though I completely destroy all the
nations
among which I scatter you,
I will not completely destroy you.
I will discipline you but only in due
measure;
I will not let you go entirely
unpunished."

A Message About the Philistines

47 This is the word of the LORD that came
to Jeremiah the prophet concerning the
Philistines before Pharaoh attacked Gaza:

2 This is what the LORD says:

"See how the waters are rising in the north;
they will become an overflowing
torrent.
They will overflow the land and
everything in it,
the towns and those who live in them.
The people will cry out;
all who dwell in the land will wail
3 at the sound of the hooves of galloping
steeds,
at the noise of enemy chariots
and the rumble of their wheels.
Parents will not turn to help their
children;
their hands will hang limp.
4 For the day has come
to destroy all the Philistines
and to remove all survivors
who could help Tyre and Sidon.
The LORD is about to destroy the
Philistines,
the remnant from the coasts of
Caphtor.[a]
5 Gaza will shave her head in mourning;
Ashkelon will be silenced.
You remnant on the plain,
how long will you cut yourselves?

6 " 'Alas, sword of the LORD,
how long till you rest?
Return to your sheath;
cease and be still.'
7 But how can it rest
when the LORD has commanded it,
when he has ordered it
to attack Ashkelon and the coast?"

[a] 4 That is, Crete

A Message About Moab

48 Concerning Moab:

This is what the LORD Almighty, the God of Israel, says:

"Woe to Nebo, for it will be ruined.
Kiriathaim will be disgraced and captured;
the stronghold[a] will be disgraced and shattered.
2 Moab will be praised no more;
in Heshbon[b] people will plot her downfall:
'Come, let us put an end to that nation.'
You, the people of Madmen,[c] will also be silenced;
the sword will pursue you.
3 Cries of anguish arise from Horonaim,
cries of great havoc and destruction.
4 Moab will be broken;
her little ones will cry out.[d]
5 They go up the hill to Luhith,
weeping bitterly as they go;
on the road down to Horonaim
anguished cries over the destruction are heard.
6 Flee! Run for your lives;
become like a bush[e] in the desert.
7 Since you trust in your deeds and riches,
you too will be taken captive,
and Chemosh will go into exile,
together with his priests and officials.
8 The destroyer will come against every town,
and not a town will escape.
The valley will be ruined
and the plateau destroyed,
because the LORD has spoken.
9 Put salt on Moab,
for she will be laid waste[f];
her towns will become desolate,
with no one to live in them.

10 "A curse on anyone who is lax in doing the LORD's work!
A curse on anyone who keeps their sword from bloodshed!

11 "Moab has been at rest from youth,
like wine left on its dregs,
not poured from one jar to another—
she has not gone into exile.
So she tastes as she did,
and her aroma is unchanged.
12 But days are coming,"
declares the LORD,
"when I will send men who pour from pitchers,
and they will pour her out;
they will empty her pitchers
and smash her jars.
13 Then Moab will be ashamed of Chemosh,
as Israel was ashamed
when they trusted in Bethel.

14 "How can you say, 'We are warriors,
men valiant in battle'?
15 Moab will be destroyed and her towns invaded;
her finest young men will go down in the slaughter,"
declares the King, whose name is the LORD Almighty.
16 "The fall of Moab is at hand;
her calamity will come quickly.
17 Mourn for her, all who live around her,
all who know her fame;
say, 'How broken is the mighty scepter,
how broken the glorious staff!'

18 "Come down from your glory
and sit on the parched ground,
you inhabitants of Daughter Dibon,
for the one who destroys Moab
will come up against you
and ruin your fortified cities.
19 Stand by the road and watch,
you who live in Aroer.
Ask the man fleeing and the woman escaping,
ask them, 'What has happened?'
20 Moab is disgraced, for she is shattered.
Wail and cry out!
Announce by the Arnon
that Moab is destroyed.
21 Judgment has come to the plateau—
to Holon, Jahzah and Mephaath,
22 to Dibon, Nebo and Beth Diblathaim,
23 to Kiriathaim, Beth Gamul and Beth Meon,
24 to Kerioth and Bozrah—
to all the towns of Moab, far and near.
25 Moab's horn[g] is cut off;
her arm is broken,"
declares the LORD.

26 "Make her drunk,
for she has defied the LORD.
Let Moab wallow in her vomit;
let her be an object of ridicule.
27 Was not Israel the object of your ridicule?
Was she caught among thieves,
that you shake your head in scorn
whenever you speak of her?
28 Abandon your towns and dwell among the rocks,
you who live in Moab.
Be like a dove that makes its nest
at the mouth of a cave.

29 "We have heard of Moab's pride—
how great is her arrogance!—
of her insolence, her pride, her conceit
and the haughtiness of her heart.
30 I know her insolence but it is futile,"
declares the LORD,
"and her boasts accomplish nothing.
31 Therefore I wail over Moab,
for all Moab I cry out,
I moan for the people of Kir Hareseth.

[a] 1 Or *captured;* / *Misgab* [b] 2 The Hebrew for *Heshbon* sounds like the Hebrew for *plot.* [c] 2 The name of the Moabite town Madmen sounds like the Hebrew for *be silenced.* [d] 4 Hebrew; Septuagint / *proclaim it to Zoar* [e] 6 Or *like Aroer* [f] 9 Or *Give wings to Moab,* / *for she will fly away* [g] 25 *Horn* here symbolizes strength.

32 I weep for you, as Jazer weeps,
you vines of Sibmah.
Your branches spread as far as the sea[a];
they reached as far as[b] Jazer.
The destroyer has fallen
on your ripened fruit and grapes.
33 Joy and gladness are gone
from the orchards and fields of Moab.
I have stopped the flow of wine from the presses;
no one treads them with shouts of joy.
Although there are shouts,
they are not shouts of joy.

34 "The sound of their cry rises
from Heshbon to Elealeh and Jahaz,
from Zoar as far as Horonaim and Eglath Shelishiyah,
for even the waters of Nimrim are dried up.
35 In Moab I will put an end
to those who make offerings on the high places
and burn incense to their gods,"
declares the LORD.
36 "So my heart laments for Moab like the music of a pipe;
it laments like a pipe for the people of Kir Hareseth.
The wealth they acquired is gone.
37 Every head is shaved
and every beard cut off;
every hand is slashed
and every waist is covered with sackcloth.
38 On all the roofs in Moab
and in the public squares
there is nothing but mourning,
for I have broken Moab
like a jar that no one wants,"
declares the LORD.
39 "How shattered she is! How they wail!
How Moab turns her back in shame!
Moab has become an object of ridicule,
an object of horror to all those around her."

40 This is what the LORD says:

"Look! An eagle is swooping down,
spreading its wings over Moab.
41 Kerioth[c] will be captured
and the strongholds taken.
In that day the hearts of Moab's warriors
will be like the heart of a woman in labor.
42 Moab will be destroyed as a nation
because she defied the LORD.
43 Terror and pit and snare await you,
you people of Moab,"
declares the LORD.
44 "Whoever flees from the terror
will fall into a pit,
whoever climbs out of the pit
will be caught in a snare;
for I will bring on Moab
the year of her punishment,"
declares the LORD.

45 "In the shadow of Heshbon
the fugitives stand helpless,
for a fire has gone out from Heshbon,
a blaze from the midst of Sihon;
it burns the foreheads of Moab,
the skulls of the noisy boasters.
46 Woe to you, Moab!
The people of Chemosh are destroyed;
your sons are taken into exile
and your daughters into captivity.

47 "Yet I will restore the fortunes of Moab
in days to come,"
declares the LORD.

Here ends the judgment on Moab.

A Message About Ammon

49 Concerning the Ammonites:

This is what the LORD says:

"Has Israel no sons?
Has Israel no heir?
Why then has Molek[d] taken possession of Gad?
Why do his people live in its towns?
2 But the days are coming,"
declares the LORD,
"when I will sound the battle cry
against Rabbah of the Ammonites;
it will become a mound of ruins,
and its surrounding villages will be set on fire.
Then Israel will drive out
those who drove her out,"
says the LORD.
3 "Wail, Heshbon, for Ai is destroyed!
Cry out, you inhabitants of Rabbah!
Put on sackcloth and mourn;
rush here and there inside the walls,
for Molek will go into exile,
together with his priests and officials.
4 Why do you boast of your valleys,
boast of your valleys so fruitful?
Unfaithful Daughter Ammon,
you trust in your riches and say,
'Who will attack me?'
5 I will bring terror on you
from all those around you,"
declares the Lord,
the LORD Almighty.
"Every one of you will be driven away,
and no one will gather the fugitives.

6 "Yet afterward, I will restore the fortunes of the Ammonites,"
declares the LORD.

A Message About Edom

7 Concerning Edom:

This is what the LORD Almighty says:

"Is there no longer wisdom in Teman?
Has counsel perished from the prudent?
Has their wisdom decayed?

[a] *32* Probably the Dead Sea [b] *32* Two Hebrew manuscripts and Septuagint; most Hebrew manuscripts *as far as the Sea of* [c] *41* Or *The cities* [d] *1* Or *their king*; also in verse 3

8 Turn and flee, hide in deep caves,
you who live in Dedan,
for I will bring disaster on Esau
at the time when I punish him.
9 If grape pickers came to you,
would they not leave a few grapes?
If thieves came during the night,
would they not steal only as much as
they wanted?
10 But I will strip Esau bare;
I will uncover his hiding places,
so that he cannot conceal himself.
His armed men are destroyed,
also his allies and neighbors,
so there is no one to say,
11 'Leave your fatherless children; I will
keep them alive.
Your widows too can depend on me.' "

12 This is what the LORD says: "If those who
do not deserve to drink the cup must drink it,
why should you go unpunished? You will not
go unpunished, but must drink it. 13 I swear
by myself," declares the LORD, "that Bozrah
will become a ruin and a curse,[a] an object of
horror and reproach; and all its towns will be
in ruins forever."

14 I have heard a message from the LORD;
an envoy was sent to the nations to say,
"Assemble yourselves to attack it!
Rise up for battle!"

15 "Now I will make you small among the
nations,
despised by mankind.
16 The terror you inspire
and the pride of your heart have
deceived you,
you who live in the clefts of the rocks,
who occupy the heights of the hill.
Though you build your nest as high as the
eagle's,
from there I will bring you down,"
declares the LORD.
17 "Edom will become an object of horror;
all who pass by will be appalled and
will scoff
because of all its wounds.
18 As Sodom and Gomorrah were
overthrown,
along with their neighboring towns,"
says the LORD,
"so no one will live there;
no people will dwell in it.

19 "Like a lion coming up from Jordan's
thickets
to a rich pastureland,
I will chase Edom from its land in an
instant.
Who is the chosen one I will appoint for
this?
Who is like me and who can challenge me?
And what shepherd can stand against
me?"
20 Therefore, hear what the LORD has
planned against Edom,
what he has purposed against those
who live in Teman:
The young of the flock will be dragged
away;
their pasture will be appalled at their
fate.
21 At the sound of their fall the earth will
tremble;
their cry will resound to the Red Sea.[b]
22 Look! An eagle will soar and swoop
down,
spreading its wings over Bozrah.
In that day the hearts of Edom's warriors
will be like the heart of a woman in
labor.

A Message About Damascus

23 Concerning Damascus:

"Hamath and Arpad are dismayed,
for they have heard bad news.
They are disheartened,
troubled like[c] the restless sea.
24 Damascus has become feeble,
she has turned to flee
and panic has gripped her;
anguish and pain have seized her,
pain like that of a woman in labor.
25 Why has the city of renown not been
abandoned,
the town in which I delight?
26 Surely, her young men will fall in the
streets;
all her soldiers will be silenced in that
day,"
declares the LORD Almighty.
27 "I will set fire to the walls of Damascus;
it will consume the fortresses of Ben-
Hadad."

A Message About Kedar and Hazor

28 Concerning Kedar and the kingdoms of
Hazor, which Nebuchadnezzar king of Babylon attacked:

This is what the LORD says:

"Arise, and attack Kedar
and destroy the people of the East.
29 Their tents and their flocks will be taken;
their shelters will be carried off
with all their goods and camels.
People will shout to them,
'Terror on every side!'

30 "Flee quickly away!
Stay in deep caves, you who live in
Hazor,"
declares the LORD.
"Nebuchadnezzar king of Babylon has
plotted against you;
he has devised a plan against you.
31 "Arise and attack a nation at ease,
which lives in confidence,"
declares the LORD,
"a nation that has neither gates nor bars;
its people live far from danger.

[a] *13* That is, its name will be used in cursing (see 29:22); or, others will see that it is cursed.
[b] *21* Or *the Sea of Reeds* [c] *23* Hebrew *on* or *by*

32 Their camels will become plunder,
and their large herds will be spoils of war.
I will scatter to the winds those who are in distant places[a]
and will bring disaster on them from every side,"
declares the LORD.
33 "Hazor will become a haunt of jackals,
a desolate place forever.
No one will live there;
no people will dwell in it."

A Message About Elam

34 This is the word of the LORD that came to
Jeremiah the prophet concerning Elam, early
in the reign of Zedekiah king of Judah:

35 This is what the LORD Almighty says:

"See, I will break the bow of Elam,
the mainstay of their might.
36 I will bring against Elam the four winds
from the four quarters of heaven;
I will scatter them to the four winds,
and there will not be a nation
where Elam's exiles do not go.
37 I will shatter Elam before their foes,
before those who want to kill them;
I will bring disaster on them,
even my fierce anger,"
declares the LORD.
"I will pursue them with the sword
until I have made an end of them.
38 I will set my throne in Elam
and destroy her king and officials,"
declares the LORD.

39 "Yet I will restore the fortunes of Elam
in days to come,"
declares the LORD.

A Message About Babylon

50 This is the word the LORD spoke through
Jeremiah the prophet concerning Babylon and the land of the Babylonians[b]:

2 "Announce and proclaim among the nations,
lift up a banner and proclaim it;
keep nothing back, but say,
'Babylon will be captured;
Bel will be put to shame,
Marduk filled with terror.
Her images will be put to shame
and her idols filled with terror.'
3 A nation from the north will attack her
and lay waste her land.
No one will live in it;
both people and animals will flee away.

4 "In those days, at that time,"
declares the LORD,
"the people of Israel and the people of Judah together
will go in tears to seek the LORD their God.
5 They will ask the way to Zion
and turn their faces toward it.
They will come and bind themselves to the LORD
in an everlasting covenant
that will not be forgotten.

6 "My people have been lost sheep;
their shepherds have led them astray
and caused them to roam on the mountains.
They wandered over mountain and hill
and forgot their own resting place.
7 Whoever found them devoured them;
their enemies said, 'We are not guilty,
for they sinned against the LORD, their verdant pasture,
the LORD, the hope of their ancestors.'

8 "Flee out of Babylon;
leave the land of the Babylonians,
and be like the goats that lead the flock.
9 For I will stir up and bring against Babylon
an alliance of great nations from the land of the north.
They will take up their positions against her,
and from the north she will be captured.
Their arrows will be like skilled warriors
who do not return empty-handed.
10 So Babylonia[c] will be plundered;
all who plunder her will have their fill,"
declares the LORD.

11 "Because you rejoice and are glad,
you who pillage my inheritance,
because you frolic like a heifer threshing grain
and neigh like stallions,
12 your mother will be greatly ashamed;
she who gave you birth will be disgraced.
She will be the least of the nations—
a wilderness, a dry land, a desert.
13 Because of the LORD's anger she will not be inhabited
but will be completely desolate.
All who pass Babylon will be appalled;
they will scoff because of all her wounds.

14 "Take up your positions around Babylon,
all you who draw the bow.
Shoot at her! Spare no arrows,
for she has sinned against the LORD.
15 Shout against her on every side!
She surrenders, her towers fall,
her walls are torn down.
Since this is the vengeance of the LORD,
take vengeance on her;
do to her as she has done to others.
16 Cut off from Babylon the sower,
and the reaper with his sickle at harvest.
Because of the sword of the oppressor
let everyone return to their own people,
let everyone flee to their own land.

17 "Israel is a scattered flock
that lions have chased away.

[a] 32 Or *who clip the hair by their foreheads* [b] 1 Or *Chaldeans*; also in verses 8, 25, 35 and 45
[c] 10 Or *Chaldea*

The first to devour them
was the king of Assyria;
the last to crush their bones
was Nebuchadnezzar king of Babylon."

18 Therefore this is what the LORD Almighty, the God of Israel, says:

"I will punish the king of Babylon and his land
as I punished the king of Assyria.
19 But I will bring Israel back to their own pasture,
and they will graze on Carmel and Bashan;
their appetite will be satisfied
on the hills of Ephraim and Gilead.
20 In those days, at that time,"
declares the LORD,
"search will be made for Israel's guilt,
but there will be none,
and for the sins of Judah,
but none will be found,
for I will forgive the remnant I spare.

21 "Attack the land of Merathaim
and those who live in Pekod.
Pursue, kill and completely destroy[a] them,"
declares the LORD.
"Do everything I have commanded you.
22 The noise of battle is in the land,
the noise of great destruction!
23 How broken and shattered
is the hammer of the whole earth!
How desolate is Babylon
among the nations!
24 I set a trap for you, Babylon,
and you were caught before you knew it;
you were found and captured
because you opposed the LORD.
25 The LORD has opened his arsenal
and brought out the weapons of his wrath,
for the Sovereign LORD Almighty has work to do
in the land of the Babylonians.
26 Come against her from afar.
Break open her granaries;
pile her up like heaps of grain.
Completely destroy her
and leave her no remnant.
27 Kill all her young bulls;
let them go down to the slaughter!
Woe to them! For their day has come,
the time for them to be punished.
28 Listen to the fugitives and refugees from Babylon
declaring in Zion
how the LORD our God has taken vengeance,
vengeance for his temple.

29 "Summon archers against Babylon,
all those who draw the bow.
Encamp all around her;
let no one escape.
Repay her for her deeds;
do to her as she has done.
For she has defied the LORD,
the Holy One of Israel.
30 Therefore, her young men will fall in the streets;
all her soldiers will be silenced in that day,"
declares the LORD.
31 "See, I am against you, you arrogant one,"
declares the Lord, the LORD Almighty,
"for your day has come,
the time for you to be punished.
32 The arrogant one will stumble and fall
and no one will help her up;
I will kindle a fire in her towns
that will consume all who are around her."

33 This is what the LORD Almighty says:

"The people of Israel are oppressed,
and the people of Judah as well.
All their captors hold them fast,
refusing to let them go.
34 Yet their Redeemer is strong;
the LORD Almighty is his name.
He will vigorously defend their cause
so that he may bring rest to their land,
but unrest to those who live in Babylon.

35 "A sword against the Babylonians!"
declares the LORD—
"against those who live in Babylon
and against her officials and wise men!
36 A sword against her false prophets!
They will become fools.
A sword against her warriors!
They will be filled with terror.
37 A sword against her horses and chariots
and all the foreigners in her ranks!
They will become weaklings.
A sword against her treasures!
They will be plundered.
38 A drought on[b] her waters!
They will dry up.
For it is a land of idols,
idols that will go mad with terror.

39 "So desert creatures and hyenas will live there,
and there the owl will dwell.
It will never again be inhabited
or lived in from generation to generation.
40 As I overthrew Sodom and Gomorrah
along with their neighboring towns,"
declares the LORD,
"so no one will live there;
no people will dwell in it.

41 "Look! An army is coming from the north;
a great nation and many kings
are being stirred up from the ends of the earth.
42 They are armed with bows and spears;
they are cruel and without mercy.

[a] *21* The Hebrew term refers to the irrevocable giving over of things or persons to the LORD, often by totally destroying them; also in verse 26. [b] *38* Or *A sword against*

They sound like the roaring sea
as they ride on their horses;
they come like men in battle formation
to attack you, Daughter Babylon.
43 The king of Babylon has heard reports
about them,
and his hands hang limp.
Anguish has gripped him,
pain like that of a woman in labor.
44 Like a lion coming up from Jordan's
thickets
to a rich pastureland,
I will chase Babylon from its land in an
instant.
Who is the chosen one I will appoint for
this?
Who is like me and who can challenge
me?
And what shepherd can stand against
me?"
45 Therefore, hear what the LORD has
planned against Babylon,
what he has purposed against the land
of the Babylonians:
The young of the flock will be dragged
away;
their pasture will be appalled at their
fate.
46 At the sound of Babylon's capture the
earth will tremble;
its cry will resound among the nations.

51 This is what the LORD says:

"See, I will stir up the spirit of a destroyer
against Babylon and the people of Leb
Kamai.[a]
2 I will send foreigners to Babylon
to winnow her and to devastate her land;
they will oppose her on every side
in the day of her disaster.
3 Let not the archer string his bow,
nor let him put on his armor.
Do not spare her young men;
completely destroy[b] her army.
4 They will fall down slain in Babylon,[c]
fatally wounded in her streets.
5 For Israel and Judah have not been
forsaken
by their God, the LORD Almighty,
though their land[d] is full of guilt
before the Holy One of Israel.

6 "Flee from Babylon!
Run for your lives!
Do not be destroyed because of her
sins.
It is time for the LORD's vengeance;
he will repay her what she deserves.
7 Babylon was a gold cup in the LORD's
hand;
she made the whole earth drunk.
The nations drank her wine;
therefore they have now gone mad.
8 Babylon will suddenly fall and be broken.
Wail over her!
Get balm for her pain;
perhaps she can be healed.

9 " 'We would have healed Babylon,
but she cannot be healed;
let us leave her and each go to our own
land,
for her judgment reaches to the skies,
it rises as high as the heavens.'

10 " 'The LORD has vindicated us;
come, let us tell in Zion
what the LORD our God has done.'

11 "Sharpen the arrows,
take up the shields!
The LORD has stirred up the kings of the
Medes,
because his purpose is to destroy
Babylon.
The LORD will take vengeance,
vengeance for his temple.
12 Lift up a banner against the walls of
Babylon!
Reinforce the guard,
station the watchmen,
prepare an ambush!
The LORD will carry out his purpose,
his decree against the people of Babylon.
13 You who live by many waters
and are rich in treasures,
your end has come,
the time for you to be destroyed.
14 The LORD Almighty has sworn by
himself:
I will surely fill you with troops, as
with a swarm of locusts,
and they will shout in triumph over you.

15 "He made the earth by his power;
he founded the world by his wisdom
and stretched out the heavens by his
understanding.
16 When he thunders, the waters in the
heavens roar;
he makes clouds rise from the ends of
the earth.
He sends lightning with the rain
and brings out the wind from his
storehouses.

17 "Everyone is senseless and without
knowledge;
every goldsmith is shamed by his idols.
The images he makes are a fraud;
they have no breath in them.
18 They are worthless, the objects of
mockery;
when their judgment comes, they will
perish.
19 He who is the Portion of Jacob is not like
these,
for he is the Maker of all things,
including the people of his inheritance—
the LORD Almighty is his name.

20 "You are my war club,
my weapon for battle—

[a] 1 *Leb Kamai* is a cryptogram for Chaldea, that is, Babylonia. [b] 3 The Hebrew term refers to the irrevocable giving over of things or persons to the LORD, often by totally destroying them.
[c] 4 Or *Chaldea* [d] 5 Or *Almighty, / and the land of the Babylonians*

with you I shatter nations,
with you I destroy kingdoms,
21 with you I shatter horse and rider,
with you I shatter chariot and driver,
22 with you I shatter man and woman,
with you I shatter old man and youth,
with you I shatter young man and young woman,
23 with you I shatter shepherd and flock,
with you I shatter farmer and oxen,
with you I shatter governors and officials.

24 "Before your eyes I will repay Babylon and
all who live in Babylonia[a] for all the wrong
they have done in Zion," declares the LORD.

25 "I am against you, you destroying mountain,
you who destroy the whole earth,"
declares the LORD.
"I will stretch out my hand against you,
roll you off the cliffs,
and make you a burned-out mountain.
26 No rock will be taken from you for a cornerstone,
nor any stone for a foundation,
for you will be desolate forever,"
declares the LORD.
27 "Lift up a banner in the land!
Blow the trumpet among the nations!
Prepare the nations for battle against her;
summon against her these kingdoms:
Ararat, Minni and Ashkenaz.
Appoint a commander against her;
send up horses like a swarm of locusts.
28 Prepare the nations for battle against her—
the kings of the Medes,
their governors and all their officials,
and all the countries they rule.
29 The land trembles and writhes,
for the LORD's purposes against Babylon stand—
to lay waste the land of Babylon
so that no one will live there.
30 Babylon's warriors have stopped fighting;
they remain in their strongholds.
Their strength is exhausted;
they have become weaklings.
Her dwellings are set on fire;
the bars of her gates are broken.
31 One courier follows another
and messenger follows messenger
to announce to the king of Babylon
that his entire city is captured,
32 the river crossings seized,
the marshes set on fire,
and the soldiers terrified."

33 This is what the LORD Almighty, the God
of Israel, says:

"Daughter Babylon is like a threshing floor
at the time it is trampled;
the time to harvest her will soon come."

34 "Nebuchadnezzar king of Babylon has devoured us,
he has thrown us into confusion,
he has made us an empty jar.
Like a serpent he has swallowed us
and filled his stomach with our delicacies,
and then has spewed us out.
35 May the violence done to our flesh[b] be on Babylon,"
say the inhabitants of Zion.
"May our blood be on those who live in Babylonia,"
says Jerusalem.

36 Therefore this is what the LORD says:

"See, I will defend your cause
and avenge you;
I will dry up her sea
and make her springs dry.
37 Babylon will be a heap of ruins,
a haunt of jackals,
an object of horror and scorn,
a place where no one lives.
38 Her people all roar like young lions,
they growl like lion cubs.
39 But while they are aroused,
I will set out a feast for them
and make them drunk,
so that they shout with laughter—
then sleep forever and not awake,"
declares the LORD.
40 "I will bring them down
like lambs to the slaughter,
like rams and goats.

41 "How Sheshak[c] will be captured,
the boast of the whole earth seized!
How desolate Babylon will be
among the nations!
42 The sea will rise over Babylon;
its roaring waves will cover her.
43 Her towns will be desolate,
a dry and desert land,
a land where no one lives,
through which no one travels.
44 I will punish Bel in Babylon
and make him spew out what he has swallowed.
The nations will no longer stream to him.
And the wall of Babylon will fall.

45 "Come out of her, my people!
Run for your lives!
Run from the fierce anger of the LORD.
46 Do not lose heart or be afraid
when rumors are heard in the land;
one rumor comes this year, another the next,
rumors of violence in the land
and of ruler against ruler.
47 For the time will surely come
when I will punish the idols of Babylon;
her whole land will be disgraced
and her slain will all lie fallen within her.

[a] 24 Or *Chaldea*; also in verse 35 [b] 35 Or *done to us and to our children* [c] 41 *Sheshak* is a cryptogram for Babylon.

48Then heaven and earth and all that is in
them
will shout for joy over Babylon,
for out of the north
destroyers will attack her,"
declares the LORD.

49"Babylon must fall because of Israel's
slain,
just as the slain in all the earth
have fallen because of Babylon.
50You who have escaped the sword,
leave and do not linger!
Remember the LORD in a distant land,
and call to mind Jerusalem."

51"We are disgraced,
for we have been insulted
and shame covers our faces,
because foreigners have entered
the holy places of the LORD's house."

52"But days are coming," declares the LORD,
"when I will punish her idols,
and throughout her land
the wounded will groan.
53Even if Babylon ascends to the heavens
and fortifies her lofty stronghold,
I will send destroyers against her,"
declares the LORD.

54"The sound of a cry comes from Babylon,
the sound of great destruction
from the land of the Babylonians.[a]
55The LORD will destroy Babylon;
he will silence her noisy din.
Waves of enemies will rage like great
waters;
the roar of their voices will resound.
56A destroyer will come against Babylon;
her warriors will be captured,
and their bows will be broken.
For the LORD is a God of retribution;
he will repay in full.
57I will make her officials and wise men
drunk,
her governors, officers and warriors as
well;
they will sleep forever and not awake,"
declares the King, whose name is the
LORD Almighty.

58This is what the LORD Almighty says:

"Babylon's thick wall will be leveled
and her high gates set on fire;
the peoples exhaust themselves for
nothing,
the nations' labor is only fuel for the
flames."

59This is the message Jeremiah the prophet
gave to the staff officer Seraiah son of Neriah,
the son of Mahseiah, when he went to Babylon
with Zedekiah king of Judah in the fourth
year of his reign. 60Jeremiah had written on a
scroll about all the disasters that would come
upon Babylon—all that had been recorded
concerning Babylon. 61He said to Seraiah,
"When you get to Babylon, see that you read
all these words aloud. 62Then say, 'LORD, you
have said you will destroy this place, so that
neither people nor animals will live in it; it will
be desolate forever.' 63When you finish reading this scroll, tie a stone to it and throw it into
the Euphrates. 64Then say, 'So will Babylon
sink to rise no more because of the disaster I
will bring on her. And her people will fall.'"

The words of Jeremiah end here.

The Fall of Jerusalem

52 Zedekiah was twenty-one years old
when he became king, and he reigned
in Jerusalem eleven years. His mother's name
was Hamutal daughter of Jeremiah; she was
from Libnah. 2He did evil in the eyes of the
LORD, just as Jehoiakim had done. 3It was because of the LORD's anger that all this happened to Jerusalem and Judah, and in the end
he thrust them from his presence.

Now Zedekiah rebelled against the king
of Babylon.

4So in the ninth year of Zedekiah's reign,
on the tenth day of the tenth month, Nebuchadnezzar king of Babylon marched against
Jerusalem with his whole army. They encamped outside the city and built siege works
all around it. 5The city was kept under siege
until the eleventh year of King Zedekiah.

6By the ninth day of the fourth month the
famine in the city had become so severe that
there was no food for the people to eat. 7Then
the city wall was broken through, and the
whole army fled. They left the city at night
through the gate between the two walls near
the king's garden, though the Babylonians[b]
were surrounding the city. They fled toward
the Arabah,[c] 8but the Babylonian[d] army pursued King Zedekiah and overtook him in the
plains of Jericho. All his soldiers were separated from him and scattered, 9and he was
captured.

He was taken to the king of Babylon at
Riblah in the land of Hamath, where he pronounced sentence on him. 10There at Riblah
the king of Babylon killed the sons of Zedekiah before his eyes; he also killed all the
officials of Judah. 11Then he put out Zedekiah's eyes, bound him with bronze shackles
and took him to Babylon, where he put him
in prison till the day of his death.

12On the tenth day of the fifth month, in
the nineteenth year of Nebuchadnezzar king
of Babylon, Nebuzaradan commander of the
imperial guard, who served the king of Babylon, came to Jerusalem. 13He set fire to the
temple of the LORD, the royal palace and all the
houses of Jerusalem. Every important building he burned down. 14The whole Babylonian
army, under the commander of the imperial guard, broke down all the walls around
Jerusalem. 15Nebuzaradan the commander
of the guard carried into exile some of the
poorest people and those who remained in
the city, along with the rest of the craftsmen[e]
and those who had deserted to the king of

[a] 54 Or *Chaldeans* [b] 7 Or *Chaldeans*; also in verse 17 [c] 7 Or *the Jordan Valley*
[d] 8 Or *Chaldean*; also in verse 14 [e] 15 Or *the populace*

Babylon. 16But Nebuzaradan left behind the
rest of the poorest people of the land to work
the vineyards and fields.
17The Babylonians broke up the bronze pillars, the movable stands and the bronze Sea
that were at the temple of the LORD and they
carried all the bronze to Babylon. 18They also
took away the pots, shovels, wick trimmers,
sprinkling bowls, dishes and all the bronze
articles used in the temple service. 19The commander of the imperial guard took away the
basins, censers, sprinkling bowls, pots, lampstands, dishes and bowls used for drink offerings—all that were made of pure gold or silver.
20The bronze from the two pillars, the Sea
and the twelve bronze bulls under it, and the
movable stands, which King Solomon had
made for the temple of the LORD, was more
than could be weighed. 21Each pillar was
eighteen cubits high and twelve cubits in circumference[a]; each was four fingers thick, and
hollow. 22The bronze capital on top of one pillar was five cubits[b] high and was decorated
with a network and pomegranates of bronze
all around. The other pillar, with its pomegranates, was similar. 23There were ninety-six
pomegranates on the sides; the total number
of pomegranates above the surrounding network was a hundred.
24The commander of the guard took as prisoners Seraiah the chief priest, Zephaniah the
priest next in rank and the three doorkeepers.
25Of those still in the city, he took the officer
in charge of the fighting men, and seven royal advisers. He also took the secretary who
was chief officer in charge of conscripting the
people of the land, sixty of whom were found
in the city. 26Nebuzaradan the commander
took them all and brought them to the king
of Babylon at Riblah. 27There at Riblah, in the
land of Hamath, the king had them executed.
So Judah went into captivity, away from
her land. 28This is the number of the people
Nebuchadnezzar carried into exile:

in the seventh year, 3,023 Jews;
29 in Nebuchadnezzar's eighteenth year,
832 people from Jerusalem;
30 in his twenty-third year,
745 Jews taken into exile by Nebuzaradan the commander of the imperial
guard.
There were 4,600 people in all.

Jehoiachin Released

31In the thirty-seventh year of the exile of
Jehoiachin king of Judah, in the year Awel-
Marduk became king of Babylon, on the twenty-fifth day of the twelfth month, he released
Jehoiachin king of Judah and freed him from
prison. 32He spoke kindly to him and gave
him a seat of honor higher than those of the
other kings who were with him in Babylon.
33So Jehoiachin put aside his prison clothes
and for the rest of his life ate regularly at the
king's table. 34Day by day the king of Babylon
gave Jehoiachin a regular allowance as long
as he lived, till the day of his death.

Lamentations

1[c] How deserted lies the city,
once so full of people!
How like a widow is she,
who once was great among the
nations!
She who was queen among the provinces
has now become a slave.

2 Bitterly she weeps at night,
tears are on her cheeks.
Among all her lovers
there is no one to comfort her.
All her friends have betrayed her;
they have become her enemies.

3 After affliction and harsh labor,
Judah has gone into exile.
She dwells among the nations;
she finds no resting place.
All who pursue her have overtaken her
in the midst of her distress.

4 The roads to Zion mourn,
for no one comes to her appointed
festivals.
All her gateways are desolate,
her priests groan,
her young women grieve,
and she is in bitter anguish.

5 Her foes have become her masters;
her enemies are at ease.
The LORD has brought her grief
because of her many sins.
Her children have gone into exile,
captive before the foe.

6 All the splendor has departed
from Daughter Zion.
Her princes are like deer
that find no pasture;
in weakness they have fled
before the pursuer.

[a] *21* That is, about 27 feet high and 18 feet in circumference or about 8.1 meters high and 5.4 meters in circumference [b] *22* That is, about 7 1/2 feet or about 2.3 meters [c] This chapter is an acrostic poem, the verses of which begin with the successive letters of the Hebrew alphabet.

7 In the days of her affliction and
wandering
Jerusalem remembers all the treasures
that were hers in days of old.
When her people fell into enemy hands,
there was no one to help her.
Her enemies looked at her
and laughed at her destruction.

8 Jerusalem has sinned greatly
and so has become unclean.
All who honored her despise her,
for they have all seen her naked;
she herself groans
and turns away.

9 Her filthiness clung to her skirts;
she did not consider her future.
Her fall was astounding;
there was none to comfort her.
"Look, LORD, on my affliction,
for the enemy has triumphed."

10 The enemy laid hands
on all her treasures;
she saw pagan nations
enter her sanctuary—
those you had forbidden
to enter your assembly.

11 All her people groan
as they search for bread;
they barter their treasures for food
to keep themselves alive.
"Look, LORD, and consider,
for I am despised."

12 "Is it nothing to you, all you who pass by?
Look around and see.
Is any suffering like my suffering
that was inflicted on me,
that the LORD brought on me
in the day of his fierce anger?

13 "From on high he sent fire,
sent it down into my bones.
He spread a net for my feet
and turned me back.
He made me desolate,
faint all the day long.

14 "My sins have been bound into a yoke[a];
by his hands they were woven
together.
They have been hung on my neck,
and the Lord has sapped my strength.
He has given me into the hands
of those I cannot withstand.

15 "The Lord has rejected
all the warriors in my midst;
he has summoned an army against me
to[b] crush my young men.
In his winepress the Lord has trampled
Virgin Daughter Judah.

16 "This is why I weep
and my eyes overflow with tears.
No one is near to comfort me,
no one to restore my spirit.
My children are destitute
because the enemy has prevailed."

17 Zion stretches out her hands,
but there is no one to comfort her.
The LORD has decreed for Jacob
that his neighbors become his foes;
Jerusalem has become
an unclean thing among them.

18 "The LORD is righteous,
yet I rebelled against his command.
Listen, all you peoples;
look on my suffering.
My young men and young women
have gone into exile.

19 "I called to my allies
but they betrayed me.
My priests and my elders
perished in the city
while they searched for food
to keep themselves alive.

20 "See, LORD, how distressed I am!
I am in torment within,
and in my heart I am disturbed,
for I have been most rebellious.
Outside, the sword bereaves;
inside, there is only death.

21 "People have heard my groaning,
but there is no one to comfort me.
All my enemies have heard of my
distress;
they rejoice at what you have done.
May you bring the day you have
announced
so they may become like me.

22 "Let all their wickedness come before you;
deal with them
as you have dealt with me
because of all my sins.
My groans are many
and my heart is faint."

2[c] How the Lord has covered Daughter
Zion
with the cloud of his anger[d]!
He has hurled down the splendor of Israel
from heaven to earth;
he has not remembered his footstool
in the day of his anger.

2 Without pity the Lord has swallowed up
all the dwellings of Jacob;
in his wrath he has torn down
the strongholds of Daughter Judah.
He has brought her kingdom and its
princes
down to the ground in dishonor.

3 In fierce anger he has cut off
every horn[e,f] of Israel.

[a] 14 Most Hebrew manuscripts; many Hebrew manuscripts and Septuagint *He kept watch over my sins* [b] 15 Or *has set a time for me / when he will* [c] This chapter is an acrostic poem, the verses of which begin with the successive letters of the Hebrew alphabet. [d] 1 Or *How the Lord in his anger / has treated Daughter Zion with contempt* [e] 3 Or *off / all the strength*; or *every king* [f] 3 *Horn* here symbolizes strength.

He has withdrawn his right hand
at the approach of the enemy.
He has burned in Jacob like a flaming fire
that consumes everything around it.

4 Like an enemy he has strung his bow;
his right hand is ready.
Like a foe he has slain
all who were pleasing to the eye;
he has poured out his wrath like fire
on the tent of Daughter Zion.

5 The Lord is like an enemy;
he has swallowed up Israel.
He has swallowed up all her palaces
and destroyed her strongholds.
He has multiplied mourning and lamentation
for Daughter Judah.

6 He has laid waste his dwelling like a garden;
he has destroyed his place of meeting.
The LORD has made Zion forget
her appointed festivals and her Sabbaths;
in his fierce anger he has spurned
both king and priest.

7 The Lord has rejected his altar
and abandoned his sanctuary.
He has given the walls of her palaces
into the hands of the enemy;
they have raised a shout in the house of the LORD
as on the day of an appointed festival.

8 The LORD determined to tear down
the wall around Daughter Zion.
He stretched out a measuring line
and did not withhold his hand from destroying.
He made ramparts and walls lament;
together they wasted away.

9 Her gates have sunk into the ground;
their bars he has broken and destroyed.
Her king and her princes are exiled
among the nations,
the law is no more,
and her prophets no longer find
visions from the LORD.

10 The elders of Daughter Zion
sit on the ground in silence;
they have sprinkled dust on their heads
and put on sackcloth.
The young women of Jerusalem
have bowed their heads to the ground.

11 My eyes fail from weeping,
I am in torment within;
my heart is poured out on the ground
because my people are destroyed,
because children and infants faint
in the streets of the city.

12 They say to their mothers,
"Where is bread and wine?"
as they faint like the wounded
in the streets of the city,
as their lives ebb away
in their mothers' arms.

13 What can I say for you?
With what can I compare you,
Daughter Jerusalem?
To what can I liken you,
that I may comfort you,
Virgin Daughter Zion?
Your wound is as deep as the sea.
Who can heal you?

14 The visions of your prophets
were false and worthless;
they did not expose your sin
to ward off your captivity.
The prophecies they gave you
were false and misleading.

15 All who pass your way
clap their hands at you;
they scoff and shake their heads
at Daughter Jerusalem:
"Is this the city that was called
the perfection of beauty,
the joy of the whole earth?"

16 All your enemies open their mouths
wide against you;
they scoff and gnash their teeth
and say, "We have swallowed her up.
This is the day we have waited for;
we have lived to see it."

17 The LORD has done what he planned;
he has fulfilled his word,
which he decreed long ago.
He has overthrown you without pity,
he has let the enemy gloat over you,
he has exalted the horn[a] of your foes.

18 The hearts of the people
cry out to the Lord.
You walls of Daughter Zion,
let your tears flow like a river
day and night;
give yourself no relief,
your eyes no rest.

19 Arise, cry out in the night,
as the watches of the night begin;
pour out your heart like water
in the presence of the Lord.
Lift up your hands to him
for the lives of your children,
who faint from hunger
at every street corner.

20 "Look, LORD, and consider:
Whom have you ever treated like this?
Should women eat their offspring,
the children they have cared for?
Should priest and prophet be killed
in the sanctuary of the Lord?

21 "Young and old lie together
in the dust of the streets;
my young men and young women
have fallen by the sword.

[a] 17 *Horn* here symbolizes strength.

You have slain them in the day of your anger;
you have slaughtered them without pity.

22 "As you summon to a feast day,
so you summoned against me terrors on every side.
In the day of the LORD's anger
no one escaped or survived;
those I cared for and reared
my enemy has destroyed."

3[a] I am the man who has seen affliction
by the rod of the LORD's wrath.
2 He has driven me away and made me walk
in darkness rather than light;
3 indeed, he has turned his hand against me
again and again, all day long.

4 He has made my skin and my flesh grow old
and has broken my bones.
5 He has besieged me and surrounded me
with bitterness and hardship.
6 He has made me dwell in darkness
like those long dead.

7 He has walled me in so I cannot escape;
he has weighed me down with chains.
8 Even when I call out or cry for help,
he shuts out my prayer.
9 He has barred my way with blocks of stone;
he has made my paths crooked.

10 Like a bear lying in wait,
like a lion in hiding,
11 he dragged me from the path and mangled me
and left me without help.
12 He drew his bow
and made me the target for his arrows.

13 He pierced my heart
with arrows from his quiver.
14 I became the laughingstock of all my people;
they mock me in song all day long.
15 He has filled me with bitter herbs
and given me gall to drink.

16 He has broken my teeth with gravel;
he has trampled me in the dust.
17 I have been deprived of peace;
I have forgotten what prosperity is.
18 So I say, "My splendor is gone
and all that I had hoped from the LORD."

19 I remember my affliction and my wandering,
the bitterness and the gall.
20 I well remember them,
and my soul is downcast within me.
21 Yet this I call to mind
and therefore I have hope:

22 Because of the LORD's great love we are not consumed,
for his compassions never fail.
23 They are new every morning;
great is your faithfulness.
24 I say to myself, "The LORD is my portion;
therefore I will wait for him."

25 The LORD is good to those whose hope is in him,
to the one who seeks him;
26 it is good to wait quietly
for the salvation of the LORD.
27 It is good for a man to bear the yoke
while he is young.

28 Let him sit alone in silence,
for the LORD has laid it on him.
29 Let him bury his face in the dust—
there may yet be hope.
30 Let him offer his cheek to one who would strike him,
and let him be filled with disgrace.

31 For no one is cast off
by the Lord forever.
32 Though he brings grief, he will show compassion,
so great is his unfailing love.
33 For he does not willingly bring affliction
or grief to anyone.

34 To crush underfoot
all prisoners in the land,
35 to deny people their rights
before the Most High,
36 to deprive them of justice—
would not the Lord see such things?

37 Who can speak and have it happen
if the Lord has not decreed it?
38 Is it not from the mouth of the Most High
that both calamities and good things come?
39 Why should the living complain
when punished for their sins?

40 Let us examine our ways and test them,
and let us return to the LORD.
41 Let us lift up our hearts and our hands
to God in heaven, and say:
42 "We have sinned and rebelled
and you have not forgiven.

43 "You have covered yourself with anger
and pursued us;
you have slain without pity.
44 You have covered yourself with a cloud
so that no prayer can get through.
45 You have made us scum and refuse
among the nations.

46 "All our enemies have opened their mouths
wide against us.
47 We have suffered terror and pitfalls,
ruin and destruction."
48 Streams of tears flow from my eyes
because my people are destroyed.

[a] This chapter is an acrostic poem; the verses of each stanza begin with the successive letters of the Hebrew alphabet, and the verses within each stanza begin with the same letter.

49 My eyes will flow unceasingly,
without relief,
50 until the LORD looks down
from heaven and sees.
51 What I see brings grief to my soul
because of all the women of my city.

52 Those who were my enemies without cause
hunted me like a bird.
53 They tried to end my life in a pit
and threw stones at me;
54 the waters closed over my head,
and I thought I was about to perish.

55 I called on your name, LORD,
from the depths of the pit.
56 You heard my plea: "Do not close your ears
to my cry for relief."
57 You came near when I called you,
and you said, "Do not fear."

58 You, Lord, took up my case;
you redeemed my life.
59 LORD, you have seen the wrong done to me.
Uphold my cause!
60 You have seen the depth of their vengeance,
all their plots against me.

61 LORD, you have heard their insults,
all their plots against me—
62 what my enemies whisper and mutter
against me all day long.
63 Look at them! Sitting or standing,
they mock me in their songs.

64 Pay them back what they deserve, LORD,
for what their hands have done.
65 Put a veil over their hearts,
and may your curse be on them!
66 Pursue them in anger and destroy them
from under the heavens of the LORD.

4 [a] How the gold has lost its luster,
the fine gold become dull!
The sacred gems are scattered
at every street corner.

2 How the precious children of Zion,
once worth their weight in gold,
are now considered as pots of clay,
the work of a potter's hands!

3 Even jackals offer their breasts
to nurse their young,
but my people have become heartless
like ostriches in the desert.

4 Because of thirst the infant's tongue
sticks to the roof of its mouth;
the children beg for bread,
but no one gives it to them.

5 Those who once ate delicacies
are destitute in the streets.
Those brought up in royal purple
now lie on ash heaps.

6 The punishment of my people
is greater than that of Sodom,
which was overthrown in a moment
without a hand turned to help her.

7 Their princes were brighter than snow
and whiter than milk,
their bodies more ruddy than rubies,
their appearance like lapis lazuli.

8 But now they are blacker than soot;
they are not recognized in the streets.
Their skin has shriveled on their bones;
it has become as dry as a stick.

9 Those killed by the sword are better off
than those who die of famine;
racked with hunger, they waste away
for lack of food from the field.

10 With their own hands compassionate women
have cooked their own children,
who became their food
when my people were destroyed.

11 The LORD has given full vent to his wrath;
he has poured out his fierce anger.
He kindled a fire in Zion
that consumed her foundations.

12 The kings of the earth did not believe,
nor did any of the peoples of the world,
that enemies and foes could enter
the gates of Jerusalem.

13 But it happened because of the sins of her prophets
and the iniquities of her priests,
who shed within her
the blood of the righteous.

14 Now they grope through the streets
as if they were blind.
They are so defiled with blood
that no one dares to touch their garments.

15 "Go away! You are unclean!" people cry to them.
"Away! Away! Don't touch us!"
When they flee and wander about,
people among the nations say,
"They can stay here no longer."

16 The LORD himself has scattered them;
he no longer watches over them.
The priests are shown no honor,
the elders no favor.

17 Moreover, our eyes failed,
looking in vain for help;
from our towers we watched
for a nation that could not save us.

18 People stalked us at every step,
so we could not walk in our streets.
Our end was near, our days were numbered,
for our end had come.

19 Our pursuers were swifter
than eagles in the sky;
they chased us over the mountains
and lay in wait for us in the desert.

[a] This chapter is an acrostic poem, the verses of which begin with the successive letters of the Hebrew alphabet.

[20]The LORD's anointed, our very life breath,
was caught in their traps.
We thought that under his shadow
we would live among the nations.

[21]Rejoice and be glad, Daughter Edom,
you who live in the land of Uz.
But to you also the cup will be passed;
you will be drunk and stripped naked.

[22]Your punishment will end, Daughter Zion;
he will not prolong your exile.
But he will punish your sin, Daughter Edom,
and expose your wickedness.

5 Remember, LORD, what has happened
to us;
look, and see our disgrace.
[2]Our inheritance has been turned over to
strangers,
our homes to foreigners.
[3]We have become fatherless,
our mothers are widows.
[4]We must buy the water we drink;
our wood can be had only at a price.
[5]Those who pursue us are at our heels;
we are weary and find no rest.
[6]We submitted to Egypt and Assyria
to get enough bread.
[7]Our ancestors sinned and are no more,
and we bear their punishment.
[8]Slaves rule over us,
and there is no one to free us from their
hands.
[9]We get our bread at the risk of our lives
because of the sword in the desert.
[10]Our skin is hot as an oven,
feverish from hunger.
[11]Women have been violated in Zion,
and virgins in the towns of Judah.
[12]Princes have been hung up by their hands;
elders are shown no respect.
[13]Young men toil at the millstones;
boys stagger under loads of wood.
[14]The elders are gone from the city gate;
the young men have stopped their
music.
[15]Joy is gone from our hearts;
our dancing has turned to mourning.
[16]The crown has fallen from our head.
Woe to us, for we have sinned!
[17]Because of this our hearts are faint,
because of these things our eyes grow
dim
[18]for Mount Zion, which lies desolate,
with jackals prowling over it.

[19]You, LORD, reign forever;
your throne endures from generation to
generation.
[20]Why do you always forget us?
Why do you forsake us so long?
[21]Restore us to yourself, LORD, that we may
return;
renew our days as of old
[22]unless you have utterly rejected us
and are angry with us beyond measure.

Ezekiel

Ezekiel's Inaugural Vision

1 In my thirtieth year, in the fourth month on
the fifth day, while I was among the exiles
by the Kebar River, the heavens were opened
and I saw visions of God.
[2]On the fifth of the month—it was the fifth
year of the exile of King Jehoiachin— [3]the
word of the LORD came to Ezekiel the priest,
the son of Buzi, by the Kebar River in the land
of the Babylonians.[a] There the hand of the
LORD was on him.
[4]I looked, and I saw a windstorm coming out
of the north—an immense cloud with flashing
lightning and surrounded by brilliant light.
The center of the fire looked like glowing metal, [5]and in the fire was what looked like four
living creatures. In appearance their form was
human, [6]but each of them had four faces and
four wings. [7]Their legs were straight; their
feet were like those of a calf and gleamed like
burnished bronze. [8]Under their wings on their
four sides they had human hands. All four of
them had faces and wings, [9]and the wings
of one touched the wings of another. Each
one went straight ahead; they did not turn
as they moved.
[10]Their faces looked like this: Each of the
four had the face of a human being, and on
the right side each had the face of a lion, and
on the left the face of an ox; each also had the
face of an eagle. [11]Such were their faces. They
each had two wings spreading out upward,
each wing touching that of the creature on
either side; and each had two other wings covering its body. [12]Each one went straight ahead.
Wherever the spirit would go, they would go,
without turning as they went. [13]The appearance of the living creatures was like burning
coals of fire or like torches. Fire moved back
and forth among the creatures; it was bright,
and lightning flashed out of it. [14]The creatures
sped back and forth like flashes of lightning.
[15]As I looked at the living creatures, I saw
a wheel on the ground beside each creature
with its four faces. [16]This was the appearance
and structure of the wheels: They sparkled

[a] 3 Or *Chaldeans*

like topaz, and all four looked alike. Each appeared to be made like a wheel intersecting
a wheel. 17As they moved, they would go in
any one of the four directions the creatures
faced; the wheels did not change direction as
the creatures went. 18Their rims were high
and awesome, and all four rims were full of
eyes all around.

19When the living creatures moved, the
wheels beside them moved; and when the
living creatures rose from the ground, the
wheels also rose. 20Wherever the spirit would
go, they would go, and the wheels would rise
along with them, because the spirit of the
living creatures was in the wheels. 21When
the creatures moved, they also moved; when
the creatures stood still, they also stood still;
and when the creatures rose from the ground,
the wheels rose along with them, because the
spirit of the living creatures was in the wheels.

22Spread out above the heads of the living
creatures was what looked something like a
vault, sparkling like crystal, and awesome.
23Under the vault their wings were stretched
out one toward the other, and each had two
wings covering its body. 24When the creatures
moved, I heard the sound of their wings, like
the roar of rushing waters, like the voice of the
Almighty,[a] like the tumult of an army. When
they stood still, they lowered their wings.

25Then there came a voice from above the
vault over their heads as they stood with lowered wings. 26Above the vault over their heads
was what looked like a throne of lapis lazuli,
and high above on the throne was a figure
like that of a man. 27I saw that from what appeared to be his waist up he looked like glowing metal, as if full of fire, and that from there
down he looked like fire; and brilliant light
surrounded him. 28Like the appearance of a
rainbow in the clouds on a rainy day, so was
the radiance around him.

This was the appearance of the likeness of
the glory of the LORD. When I saw it, I fell facedown, and I heard the voice of one speaking.

Ezekiel's Call to Be a Prophet

2 He said to me, "Son of man,[b] stand up on
your feet and I will speak to you." 2As he
spoke, the Spirit came into me and raised me
to my feet, and I heard him speaking to me.

3He said: "Son of man, I am sending you
to the Israelites, to a rebellious nation that
has rebelled against me; they and their ancestors have been in revolt against me to this
very day. 4The people to whom I am sending
you are obstinate and stubborn. Say to them,
'This is what the Sovereign LORD says.' 5And
whether they listen or fail to listen—for they
are a rebellious people—they will know that
a prophet has been among them. 6And you,
son of man, do not be afraid of them or their
words. Do not be afraid, though briers and
thorns are all around you and you live among
scorpions. Do not be afraid of what they say
or be terrified by them, though they are a rebellious people. 7You must speak my words
to them, whether they listen or fail to listen,
for they are rebellious. 8But you, son of man,
listen to what I say to you. Do not rebel like
that rebellious people; open your mouth and
eat what I give you."

9Then I looked, and I saw a hand stretched
out to me. In it was a scroll, 10which he un-
rolled before me. On both sides of it were written words of lament and mourning and woe.

3 And he said to me, "Son of man, eat what
is before you, eat this scroll; then go and
speak to the people of Israel." 2So I opened
my mouth, and he gave me the scroll to eat.

3Then he said to me, "Son of man, eat this
scroll I am giving you and fill your stomach
with it." So I ate it, and it tasted as sweet as
honey in my mouth.

4He then said to me: "Son of man, go now
to the people of Israel and speak my words to
them. 5You are not being sent to a people of
obscure speech and strange language, but to
the people of Israel— 6not to many peoples of
obscure speech and strange language, whose
words you cannot understand. Surely if I had
sent you to them, they would have listened to
you. 7But the people of Israel are not willing
to listen to you because they are not willing
to listen to me, for all the Israelites are hardened and obstinate. 8But I will make you as
unyielding and hardened as they are. 9I will
make your forehead like the hardest stone,
harder than flint. Do not be afraid of them
or terrified by them, though they are a rebellious people."

10And he said to me, "Son of man, listen
carefully and take to heart all the words I
speak to you. 11Go now to your people in exile
and speak to them. Say to them, 'This is what
the Sovereign LORD says,' whether they listen
or fail to listen."

12Then the Spirit lifted me up, and I heard
behind me a loud rumbling sound as the glory
of the LORD rose from the place where it was
standing.[c] 13It was the sound of the wings of
the living creatures brushing against each
other and the sound of the wheels beside them,
a loud rumbling sound. 14The Spirit then lifted me up and took me away, and I went in
bitterness and in the anger of my spirit, with
the strong hand of the LORD on me. 15I came
to the exiles who lived at Tel Aviv near the
Kebar River. And there, where they were living, I sat among them for seven days—deeply
distressed.

Ezekiel's Task as Watchman

16At the end of seven days the word of the
LORD came to me: 17"Son of man, I have made
you a watchman for the people of Israel; so
hear the word I speak and give them warning
from me. 18When I say to a wicked person,

[a] *24* Hebrew *Shaddai* [b] *1* The Hebrew phrase *ben adam* means *human being.* The phrase *son of man* is retained as a form of address here and throughout Ezekiel because of its possible association with "Son of Man" in the New Testament. [c] *12* Probable reading of the original Hebrew text; Masoretic Text *sound—may the glory of the LORD be praised from his place*

‘You will surely die,’ and you do not warn
them or speak out to dissuade them from
their evil ways in order to save their life, that
wicked person will die for[a] their sin, and I will
hold you accountable for their blood. 19But if
you do warn the wicked person and they do
not turn from their wickedness or from their
evil ways, they will die for their sin; but you
will have saved yourself.
20“Again, when a righteous person turns
from their righteousness and does evil, and I
put a stumbling block before them, they will
die. Since you did not warn them, they will die
for their sin. The righteous things that person
did will not be remembered, and I will hold
you accountable for their blood. 21But if you
do warn the righteous person not to sin and
they do not sin, they will surely live because
they took warning, and you will have saved
yourself.”
22The hand of the LORD was on me there,
and he said to me, “Get up and go out to the
plain, and there I will speak to you.” 23So I
got up and went out to the plain. And the glory of the LORD was standing there, like the
glory I had seen by the Kebar River, and I
fell facedown.
24Then the Spirit came into me and raised
me to my feet. He spoke to me and said: “Go,
shut yourself inside your house. 25And you,
son of man, they will tie with ropes; you will
be bound so that you cannot go out among
the people. 26I will make your tongue stick
to the roof of your mouth so that you will be
silent and unable to rebuke them, for they are
a rebellious people. 27But when I speak to you,
I will open your mouth and you shall say to
them, ‘This is what the Sovereign LORD says.’
Whoever will listen let them listen, and whoever will refuse let them refuse; for they are
a rebellious people.

Siege of Jerusalem Symbolized

4 “Now, son of man, take a block of clay,
put it in front of you and draw the city of
Jerusalem on it. 2Then lay siege to it: Erect
siege works against it, build a ramp up to it,
set up camps against it and put battering rams
around it. 3Then take an iron pan, place it as
an iron wall between you and the city and turn
your face toward it. It will be under siege, and
you shall besiege it. This will be a sign to the
people of Israel.
4“Then lie on your left side and put the sin
of the people of Israel upon yourself.[b] You are
to bear their sin for the number of days you lie
on your side. 5I have assigned you the same
number of days as the years of their sin. So
for 390 days you will bear the sin of the people of Israel.
6“After you have finished this, lie down
again, this time on your right side, and bear
the sin of the people of Judah. I have assigned
you 40 days, a day for each year. 7Turn your
face toward the siege of Jerusalem and with
bared arm prophesy against her. 8I will tie you
up with ropes so that you cannot turn from
one side to the other until you have finished
the days of your siege.
9“Take wheat and barley, beans and lentils,
millet and spelt; put them in a storage jar and
use them to make bread for yourself. You are
to eat it during the 390 days you lie on your
side. 10Weigh out twenty shekels[c] of food to eat
each day and eat it at set times. 11Also measure out a sixth of a hin[d] of water and drink
it at set times. 12Eat the food as you would a
loaf of barley bread; bake it in the sight of
the people, using human excrement for fuel.”
13The LORD said, “In this way the people of
Israel will eat defiled food among the nations
where I will drive them.”
14Then I said, “Not so, Sovereign LORD! I
have never defiled myself. From my youth
until now I have never eaten anything found
dead or torn by wild animals. No impure meat
has ever entered my mouth.”
15“Very well,” he said, “I will let you bake
your bread over cow dung instead of human
excrement.”
16He then said to me: “Son of man, I am
about to cut off the food supply in Jerusalem.
The people will eat rationed food in anxiety
and drink rationed water in despair, 17for food
and water will be scarce. They will be appalled at the sight of each other and will waste
away because of[e] their sin.

God’s Razor of Judgment

5 “Now, son of man, take a sharp sword and
use it as a barber’s razor to shave your head
and your beard. Then take a set of scales and
divide up the hair. 2When the days of your siege
come to an end, burn a third of the hair inside the city. Take a third and strike it with the
sword all around the city. And scatter a third
to the wind. For I will pursue them with drawn
sword. 3But take a few hairs and tuck them
away in the folds of your garment. 4Again, take
a few of these and throw them into the fire and
burn them up. A fire will spread from there
to all Israel.
5“This is what the Sovereign LORD says:
This is Jerusalem, which I have set in the center of the nations, with countries all around
her. 6Yet in her wickedness she has rebelled
against my laws and decrees more than the
nations and countries around her. She has
rejected my laws and has not followed my
decrees.
7“Therefore this is what the Sovereign LORD
says: You have been more unruly than the nations around you and have not followed my
decrees or kept my laws. You have not even[f]
conformed to the standards of the nations
around you.
8“Therefore this is what the Sovereign LORD
says: I myself am against you, Jerusalem, and
I will inflict punishment on you in the sight
of the nations. 9Because of all your detestable

[a] *18* Or *in*; also in verses 19 and 20 [b] *4* Or *upon your side* [c] *10* That is, about 8 ounces or about 230 grams [d] *11* That is, about 2/3 quart or about 0.6 liter [e] *17* Or *away in* [f] *7* Most Hebrew manuscripts; some Hebrew manuscripts and Syriac *You have*

idols, I will do to you what I have never done
before and will never do again. 10 Therefore
in your midst parents will eat their children,
and children will eat their parents. I will inflict punishment on you and will scatter all
your survivors to the winds. 11 Therefore as
surely as I live, declares the Sovereign LORD,
because you have defiled my sanctuary with
all your vile images and detestable practices, I myself will shave you; I will not look on
you with pity or spare you. 12 A third of your
people will die of the plague or perish by famine inside you; a third will fall by the sword
outside your walls; and a third I will scatter
to the winds and pursue with drawn sword.
13 "Then my anger will cease and my wrath
against them will subside, and I will be
avenged. And when I have spent my wrath
on them, they will know that I the LORD have
spoken in my zeal.
14 "I will make you a ruin and a reproach
among the nations around you, in the sight of
all who pass by. 15 You will be a reproach and a
taunt, a warning and an object of horror to the
nations around you when I inflict punishment
on you in anger and in wrath and with sting-
ing rebuke. I the LORD have spoken. 16 When I
shoot at you with my deadly and destructive
arrows of famine, I will shoot to destroy you.
I will bring more and more famine upon you
and cut off your supply of food. 17 I will send
famine and wild beasts against you, and they
will leave you childless. Plague and bloodshed
will sweep through you, and I will bring the
sword against you. I the LORD have spoken."

Doom for the Mountains of Israel

6 The word of the LORD came to me: 2 "Son
of man, set your face against the mountains of Israel; prophesy against them 3 and
say: 'You mountains of Israel, hear the word
of the Sovereign LORD. This is what the Sovereign LORD says to the mountains and hills,
to the ravines and valleys: I am about to bring
a sword against you, and I will destroy your
high places. 4 Your altars will be demolished
and your incense altars will be smashed; and
I will slay your people in front of your idols.
5 I will lay the dead bodies of the Israelites
in front of their idols, and I will scatter your
bones around your altars. 6 Wherever you live,
the towns will be laid waste and the high places demolished, so that your altars will be laid
waste and devastated, your idols smashed and
ruined, your incense altars broken down, and
what you have made wiped out. 7 Your people
will fall slain among you, and you will know
that I am the LORD.
8 " 'But I will spare some, for some of you
will escape the sword when you are scattered
among the lands and nations. 9 Then in the
nations where they have been carried captive,
those who escape will remember me—how I
have been grieved by their adulterous hearts,
which have turned away from me, and by their
eyes, which have lusted after their idols. They
will loathe themselves for the evil they have
done and for all their detestable practices.
10 And they will know that I am the LORD; I
did not threaten in vain to bring this calamity on them.
11 " 'This is what the Sovereign LORD says:
Strike your hands together and stamp your
feet and cry out "Alas!" because of all the
wicked and detestable practices of the people of Israel, for they will fall by the sword,
famine and plague. 12 One who is far away
will die of the plague, and one who is near
will fall by the sword, and anyone who survives and is spared will die of famine. So will
I pour out my wrath on them. 13 And they will
know that I am the LORD, when their people lie
slain among their idols around their altars, on
every high hill and on all the mountaintops,
under every spreading tree and every leafy
oak—places where they offered fragrant incense to all their idols. 14 And I will stretch out
my hand against them and make the land a
desolate waste from the desert to Diblah[a]—
wherever they live. Then they will know that
I am the LORD.' "

The End Has Come

7 The word of the LORD came to me: 2 "Son of
man, this is what the Sovereign LORD says
to the land of Israel:

" 'The end! The end has come
upon the four corners of the land!
3 The end is now upon you,
and I will unleash my anger against
you.
I will judge you according to your
conduct
and repay you for all your detestable
practices.
4 I will not look on you with pity;
I will not spare you.
I will surely repay you for your conduct
and for the detestable practices among
you.

" 'Then you will know that I am the LORD.'

5 "This is what the Sovereign LORD says:

" 'Disaster! Unheard-of[b] disaster!
See, it comes!
6 The end has come!
The end has come!
It has roused itself against you.
See, it comes!
7 Doom has come upon you,
upon you who dwell in the land.
The time has come! The day is near!
There is panic, not joy, on the
mountains.
8 I am about to pour out my wrath on you
and spend my anger against you.
I will judge you according to your conduct
and repay you for all your detestable
practices.
9 I will not look on you with pity;
I will not spare you.

[a] 14 Most Hebrew manuscripts; a few Hebrew manuscripts *Riblah* [b] 5 Most Hebrew manuscripts; some Hebrew manuscripts and Syriac *Disaster after*

I will repay you for your conduct
and for the detestable practices among you.

"'Then you will know that it is I the LORD who strikes you.

10 "'See, the day!
See, it comes!
Doom has burst forth,
the rod has budded,
arrogance has blossomed!
11 Violence has arisen,[a]
a rod to punish the wicked.
None of the people will be left,
none of that crowd—
none of their wealth,
nothing of value.
12 The time has come!
The day has arrived!
Let not the buyer rejoice
nor the seller grieve,
for my wrath is on the whole crowd.
13 The seller will not recover
the property that was sold—
as long as both buyer and seller live.
For the vision concerning the whole crowd
will not be reversed.
Because of their sins, not one of them
will preserve their life.

14 "'They have blown the trumpet,
they have made all things ready,
but no one will go into battle,
for my wrath is on the whole crowd.
15 Outside is the sword;
inside are plague and famine.
Those in the country
will die by the sword;
those in the city
will be devoured by famine and plague.
16 The fugitives who escape
will flee to the mountains.
Like doves of the valleys,
they will all moan,
each for their own sins.
17 Every hand will go limp;
every leg will be wet with urine.
18 They will put on sackcloth
and be clothed with terror.
Every face will be covered with shame,
and every head will be shaved.

19 "'They will throw their silver into the streets,
and their gold will be treated as a thing unclean.
Their silver and gold
will not be able to deliver them
in the day of the LORD's wrath.
It will not satisfy their hunger
or fill their stomachs,
for it has caused them to stumble into sin.
20 They took pride in their beautiful jewelry
and used it to make their detestable idols.
They made it into vile images;
therefore I will make it a thing unclean for them.
21 I will give their wealth as plunder to foreigners
and as loot to the wicked of the earth,
who will defile it.
22 I will turn my face away from the people,
and robbers will desecrate the place I treasure.
They will enter it
and will defile it.

23 "'Prepare chains!
For the land is full of bloodshed,
and the city is full of violence.
24 I will bring the most wicked of nations
to take possession of their houses.
I will put an end to the pride of the mighty,
and their sanctuaries will be desecrated.
25 When terror comes,
they will seek peace in vain.
26 Calamity upon calamity will come,
and rumor upon rumor.
They will go searching for a vision from the prophet,
priestly instruction in the law will cease,
the counsel of the elders will come to an end.
27 The king will mourn,
the prince will be clothed with despair,
and the hands of the people of the land will tremble.
I will deal with them according to their conduct,
and by their own standards I will judge them.

"'Then they will know that I am the LORD.'"

Idolatry in the Temple

8 In the sixth year, in the sixth month on the
fifth day, while I was sitting in my house
and the elders of Judah were sitting before
me, the hand of the Sovereign LORD came on
me there. 2 I looked, and I saw a figure like
that of a man.[b] From what appeared to be his
waist down he was like fire, and from there
up his appearance was as bright as glowing
metal. 3 He stretched out what looked like a
hand and took me by the hair of my head.
The Spirit lifted me up between earth and
heaven and in visions of God he took me to
Jerusalem, to the entrance of the north gate of
the inner court, where the idol that provokes
to jealousy stood. 4 And there before me was
the glory of the God of Israel, as in the vision
I had seen in the plain.

5 Then he said to me, "Son of man, look toward the north." So I looked, and in the entrance north of the gate of the altar I saw this
idol of jealousy.

6 And he said to me, "Son of man, do you see
what they are doing—the utterly detestable
things the Israelites are doing here, things

[a] 11 Or *The violent one has become* [b] 2 Or *saw a fiery figure*

that will drive me far from my sanctuary?
But you will see things that are even more
detestable."
7 Then he brought me to the entrance to the
court. I looked, and I saw a hole in the wall.
8 He said to me, "Son of man, now dig into
the wall." So I dug into the wall and saw a
doorway there.
9 And he said to me, "Go in and see the wicked and detestable things they are doing here."
10 So I went in and looked, and I saw portrayed
all over the walls all kinds of crawling things
and unclean animals and all the idols of Israel.
11 In front of them stood seventy elders of Israel,
and Jaazaniah son of Shaphan was standing
among them. Each had a censer in his hand,
and a fragrant cloud of incense was rising.
12 He said to me, "Son of man, have you seen
what the elders of Israel are doing in the darkness, each at the shrine of his own idol? They
say, 'The LORD does not see us; the LORD has
forsaken the land.'" 13 Again, he said, "You
will see them doing things that are even more
detestable."
14 Then he brought me to the entrance of
the north gate of the house of the LORD, and I
saw women sitting there, mourning the god
Tammuz. 15 He said to me, "Do you see this,
son of man? You will see things that are even
more detestable than this."
16 He then brought me into the inner court
of the house of the LORD, and there at the entrance to the temple, between the portico and
the altar, were about twenty-five men. With
their backs toward the temple of the LORD and
their faces toward the east, they were bowing
down to the sun in the east.
17 He said to me, "Have you seen this, son
of man? Is it a trivial matter for the people
of Judah to do the detestable things they are
doing here? Must they also fill the land with
violence and continually arouse my anger?
Look at them putting the branch to their nose!
18 Therefore I will deal with them in anger; I
will not look on them with pity or spare them.
Although they shout in my ears, I will not
listen to them."

Judgment on the Idolaters

9 Then I heard him call out in a loud voice,
"Bring near those who are appointed to execute judgment on the city, each with a weapon in his hand." 2 And I saw six men coming
from the direction of the upper gate, which
faces north, each with a deadly weapon in his
hand. With them was a man clothed in linen
who had a writing kit at his side. They came
in and stood beside the bronze altar.
3 Now the glory of the God of Israel went
up from above the cherubim, where it had
been, and moved to the threshold of the temple. Then the LORD called to the man clothed
in linen who had the writing kit at his side
4 and said to him, "Go throughout the city of
Jerusalem and put a mark on the foreheads
of those who grieve and lament over all the
detestable things that are done in it."
5 As I listened, he said to the others, "Follow him through the city and kill, without
showing pity or compassion. 6 Slaughter the
old men, the young men and women, the mothers and children, but do not touch anyone who
has the mark. Begin at my sanctuary." So they
began with the old men who were in front of
the temple.
7 Then he said to them, "Defile the temple
and fill the courts with the slain. Go!" So they
went out and began killing throughout the
city. 8 While they were killing and I was left
alone, I fell facedown, crying out, "Alas, Sovereign LORD! Are you going to destroy the
entire remnant of Israel in this outpouring
of your wrath on Jerusalem?"
9 He answered me, "The sin of the people
of Israel and Judah is exceedingly great; the
land is full of bloodshed and the city is full of
injustice. They say, 'The LORD has forsaken
the land; the LORD does not see.' 10 So I will
not look on them with pity or spare them, but
I will bring down on their own heads what
they have done."
11 Then the man in linen with the writing kit
at his side brought back word, saying, "I have
done as you commanded."

God's Glory Departs From the Temple

10 I looked, and I saw the likeness of a
throne of lapis lazuli above the vault
that was over the heads of the cherubim. 2 The
LORD said to the man clothed in linen, "Go in
among the wheels beneath the cherubim. Fill
your hands with burning coals from among
the cherubim and scatter them over the city."
And as I watched, he went in.
3 Now the cherubim were standing on the
south side of the temple when the man went
in, and a cloud filled the inner court. 4 Then the
glory of the LORD rose from above the cherubim and moved to the threshold of the temple.
The cloud filled the temple, and the court was
full of the radiance of the glory of the LORD.
5 The sound of the wings of the cherubim could
be heard as far away as the outer court, like
the voice of God Almighty[a] when he speaks.
6 When the LORD commanded the man in
linen, "Take fire from among the wheels,
from among the cherubim," the man went in
and stood beside a wheel. 7 Then one of the
cherubim reached out his hand to the fire that
was among them. He took up some of it and
put it into the hands of the man in linen, who
took it and went out. 8 (Under the wings of
the cherubim could be seen what looked like
human hands.)
9 I looked, and I saw beside the cherubim
four wheels, one beside each of the cherubim;
the wheels sparkled like topaz. 10 As for their
appearance, the four of them looked alike;
each was like a wheel intersecting a wheel.
11 As they moved, they would go in any one of
the four directions the cherubim faced; the
wheels did not turn about[b] as the cherubim
went. The cherubim went in whatever direction the head faced, without turning as they

[a] 5 Hebrew *El-Shaddai* [b] 11 Or *aside*

went. 12Their entire bodies, including their backs, their hands and their wings, were completely full of eyes, as were their four wheels. 13I heard the wheels being called "the whirling wheels." 14Each of the cherubim had four faces: One face was that of a cherub, the second the face of a human being, the third the face of a lion, and the fourth the face of an eagle.

15Then the cherubim rose upward. These were the living creatures I had seen by the Kebar River. 16When the cherubim moved, the wheels beside them moved; and when the cherubim spread their wings to rise from the ground, the wheels did not leave their side. 17When the cherubim stood still, they also stood still; and when the cherubim rose, they rose with them, because the spirit of the living creatures was in them.

18Then the glory of the LORD departed from over the threshold of the temple and stopped above the cherubim. 19While I watched, the cherubim spread their wings and rose from the ground, and as they went, the wheels went with them. They stopped at the entrance of the east gate of the LORD's house, and the glory of the God of Israel was above them.

20These were the living creatures I had seen beneath the God of Israel by the Kebar River, and I realized that they were cherubim. 21Each had four faces and four wings, and under their wings was what looked like human hands. 22Their faces had the same appearance as those I had seen by the Kebar River. Each one went straight ahead.

God's Sure Judgment on Jerusalem

11 Then the Spirit lifted me up and brought me to the gate of the house of the LORD that faces east. There at the entrance of the gate were twenty-five men, and I saw among them Jaazaniah son of Azzur and Pelatiah son of Benaiah, leaders of the people. 2The LORD said to me, "Son of man, these are the men who are plotting evil and giving wicked advice in this city. 3They say, 'Haven't our houses been recently rebuilt? This city is a pot, and we are the meat in it.' 4Therefore prophesy against them; prophesy, son of man."

5Then the Spirit of the LORD came on me, and he told me to say: "This is what the LORD says: That is what you are saying, you leaders in Israel, but I know what is going through your mind. 6You have killed many people in this city and filled its streets with the dead.

7"Therefore this is what the Sovereign LORD says: The bodies you have thrown there are the meat and this city is the pot, but I will drive you out of it. 8You fear the sword, and the sword is what I will bring against you, declares the Sovereign LORD. 9I will drive you out of the city and deliver you into the hands of foreigners and inflict punishment on you. 10You will fall by the sword, and I will execute judgment on you at the borders of Israel. Then you will know that I am the LORD. 11This city will not be a pot for you, nor will you be the meat in it; I will execute judgment on you at the borders of Israel. 12And you will know that I am the LORD, for you have not followed my decrees or kept my laws but have conformed to the standards of the nations around you."

13Now as I was prophesying, Pelatiah son of Benaiah died. Then I fell facedown and cried out in a loud voice, "Alas, Sovereign LORD! Will you completely destroy the remnant of Israel?"

The Promise of Israel's Return

14The word of the LORD came to me: 15"Son of man, the people of Jerusalem have said of your fellow exiles and all the other Israelites, 'They are far away from the LORD; this land was given to us as our possession.'

16"Therefore say: 'This is what the Sovereign LORD says: Although I sent them far away among the nations and scattered them among the countries, yet for a little while I have been a sanctuary for them in the countries where they have gone.'

17"Therefore say: 'This is what the Sovereign LORD says: I will gather you from the nations and bring you back from the countries where you have been scattered, and I will give you back the land of Israel again.'

18"They will return to it and remove all its vile images and detestable idols. 19I will give them an undivided heart and put a new spirit in them; I will remove from them their heart of stone and give them a heart of flesh. 20Then they will follow my decrees and be careful to keep my laws. They will be my people, and I will be their God. 21But as for those whose hearts are devoted to their vile images and detestable idols, I will bring down on their own heads what they have done, declares the Sovereign LORD."

22Then the cherubim, with the wheels beside them, spread their wings, and the glory of the God of Israel was above them. 23The glory of the LORD went up from within the city and stopped above the mountain east of it. 24The Spirit lifted me up and brought me to the exiles in Babylonia[a] in the vision given by the Spirit of God.

Then the vision I had seen went up from me, 25and I told the exiles everything the LORD had shown me.

The Exile Symbolized

12 The word of the LORD came to me: 2"Son of man, you are living among a rebellious people. They have eyes to see but do not see and ears to hear but do not hear, for they are a rebellious people.

3"Therefore, son of man, pack your belongings for exile and in the daytime, as they watch, set out and go from where you are to another place. Perhaps they will understand, though they are a rebellious people. 4During the daytime, while they watch, bring out your belongings packed for exile. Then in the evening, while they are watching, go out like those who go into exile. 5While they

[a] 24 Or *Chaldea*

watch, dig through the wall and take your
belongings out through it. 6Put them on your
shoulder as they are watching and carry them
out at dusk. Cover your face so that you cannot see the land, for I have made you a sign
to the Israelites."
7So I did as I was commanded. During the
day I brought out my things packed for exile.
Then in the evening I dug through the wall
with my hands. I took my belongings out at
dusk, carrying them on my shoulders while
they watched.
8In the morning the word of the LORD came
to me: 9"Son of man, did not the Israelites,
that rebellious people, ask you, 'What are
you doing?'
10"Say to them, 'This is what the Sovereign
LORD says: This prophecy concerns the prince
in Jerusalem and all the Israelites who are
there.' 11Say to them, 'I am a sign to you.'
"As I have done, so it will be done to them.
They will go into exile as captives.
12"The prince among them will put his
things on his shoulder at dusk and leave, and
a hole will be dug in the wall for him to go
through. He will cover his face so that he cannot see the land. 13I will spread my net for him,
and he will be caught in my snare; I will bring
him to Babylonia, the land of the Chaldeans,
but he will not see it, and there he will die.
14I will scatter to the winds all those around
him—his staff and all his troops—and I will
pursue them with drawn sword.
15"They will know that I am the LORD, when
I disperse them among the nations and scatter them through the countries. 16But I will
spare a few of them from the sword, famine
and plague, so that in the nations where they
go they may acknowledge all their detestable
practices. Then they will know that I am the
LORD."
17The word of the LORD came to me: 18"Son
of man, tremble as you eat your food, and
shudder in fear as you drink your water. 19Say
to the people of the land: 'This is what the
Sovereign LORD says about those living in Jerusalem and in the land of Israel: They will
eat their food in anxiety and drink their water
in despair, for their land will be stripped of
everything in it because of the violence of all
who live there. 20The inhabited towns will be
laid waste and the land will be desolate. Then
you will know that I am the LORD.'"

There Will Be No Delay

21The word of the LORD came to me: 22"Son
of man, what is this proverb you have in the
land of Israel: 'The days go by and every vision comes to nothing'? 23Say to them, 'This
is what the Sovereign LORD says: I am going
to put an end to this proverb, and they will
no longer quote it in Israel.' Say to them, 'The
days are near when every vision will be fulfilled. 24For there will be no more false visions
or flattering divinations among the people of
Israel. 25But I the LORD will speak what I will,
and it shall be fulfilled without delay. For in
your days, you rebellious people, I will fulfill
whatever I say, declares the Sovereign LORD.'"
26The word of the LORD came to me: 27"Son
of man, the Israelites are saying, 'The vision
he sees is for many years from now, and he
prophesies about the distant future.'
28"Therefore say to them, 'This is what the
Sovereign LORD says: None of my words will
be delayed any longer; whatever I say will
be fulfilled, declares the Sovereign LORD.'"

False Prophets Condemned

13 The word of the LORD came to me: 2"Son
of man, prophesy against the prophets
of Israel who are now prophesying. Say to
those who prophesy out of their own imagination: 'Hear the word of the LORD! 3This is
what the Sovereign LORD says: Woe to the
foolish[a] prophets who follow their own spirit
and have seen nothing! 4Your prophets, Israel, are like jackals among ruins. 5You have
not gone up to the breaches in the wall to repair it for the people of Israel so that it will
stand firm in the battle on the day of the LORD.
6Their visions are false and their divinations a
lie. Even though the LORD has not sent them,
they say, "The LORD declares," and expect him
to fulfill their words. 7Have you not seen false
visions and uttered lying divinations when
you say, "The LORD declares," though I have
not spoken?
8"'Therefore this is what the Sovereign
LORD says: Because of your false words and
lying visions, I am against you, declares the
Sovereign LORD. 9My hand will be against the
prophets who see false visions and utter lying
divinations. They will not belong to the council of my people or be listed in the records of
Israel, nor will they enter the land of Israel.
Then you will know that I am the Sovereign
LORD.
10"'Because they lead my people astray, saying, "Peace," when there is no peace, and because, when a flimsy wall is built, they cover
it with whitewash, 11therefore tell those who
cover it with whitewash that it is going to fall.
Rain will come in torrents, and I will send
hailstones hurtling down, and violent winds
will burst forth. 12When the wall collapses,
will people not ask you, "Where is the whitewash you covered it with?"
13"'Therefore this is what the Sovereign
LORD says: In my wrath I will unleash a violent wind, and in my anger hailstones and
torrents of rain will fall with destructive fury.
14I will tear down the wall you have covered
with whitewash and will level it to the ground
so that its foundation will be laid bare. When
it[b] falls, you will be destroyed in it; and you
will know that I am the LORD. 15So I will pour
out my wrath against the wall and against
those who covered it with whitewash. I will
say to you, "The wall is gone and so are those
who whitewashed it, 16those prophets of Israel
who prophesied to Jerusalem and saw visions
of peace for her when there was no peace,
declares the Sovereign LORD."'

[a] *3* Or *wicked* [b] *14* Or *the city*

17"Now, son of man, set your face against
the daughters of your people who prophesy out of their own imagination. Prophesy
against them 18and say, 'This is what the Sovereign LORD says: Woe to the women who sew
magic charms on all their wrists and make
veils of various lengths for their heads in order to ensnare people. Will you ensnare the
lives of my people but preserve your own?
19You have profaned me among my people for
a few handfuls of barley and scraps of bread.
By lying to my people, who listen to lies, you
have killed those who should not have died
and have spared those who should not live.

20" 'Therefore this is what the Sovereign
LORD says: I am against your magic charms
with which you ensnare people like birds and
I will tear them from your arms; I will set
free the people that you ensnare like birds.
21I will tear off your veils and save my people
from your hands, and they will no longer fall
prey to your power. Then you will know that I
am the LORD. 22Because you disheartened the
righteous with your lies, when I had brought
them no grief, and because you encouraged
the wicked not to turn from their evil ways
and so save their lives, 23therefore you will
no longer see false visions or practice divination. I will save my people from your hands.
And then you will know that I am the LORD.' "

Idolaters Condemned

14 Some of the elders of Israel came to me
and sat down in front of me. 2Then the
word of the LORD came to me: 3"Son of man,
these men have set up idols in their hearts
and put wicked stumbling blocks before their
faces. Should I let them inquire of me at all?
4Therefore speak to them and tell them, 'This
is what the Sovereign LORD says: When any
of the Israelites set up idols in their hearts
and put a wicked stumbling block before their
faces and then go to a prophet, I the LORD
will answer them myself in keeping with their
great idolatry. 5I will do this to recapture the
hearts of the people of Israel, who have all
deserted me for their idols.'

6"Therefore say to the people of Israel, 'This
is what the Sovereign LORD says: Repent! Turn
from your idols and renounce all your detestable practices!

7" 'When any of the Israelites or any foreigner residing in Israel separate themselves
from me and set up idols in their hearts and
put a wicked stumbling block before their faces and then go to a prophet to inquire of me,
I the LORD will answer them myself. 8I will
set my face against them and make them an
example and a byword. I will remove them
from my people. Then you will know that I
am the LORD.

9" 'And if the prophet is enticed to utter a
prophecy, I the LORD have enticed that prophet, and I will stretch out my hand against him
and destroy him from among my people Israel. 10They will bear their guilt—the prophet will be as guilty as the one who consults
him. 11Then the people of Israel will no longer
stray from me, nor will they defile themselves
anymore with all their sins. They will be my
people, and I will be their God, declares the
Sovereign LORD.' "

Jerusalem's Judgment Inescapable

12The word of the LORD came to me: 13"Son
of man, if a country sins against me by being
unfaithful and I stretch out my hand against
it to cut off its food supply and send famine
upon it and kill its people and their animals,
14even if these three men—Noah, Daniel[a] and
Job—were in it, they could save only themselves by their righteousness, declares the
Sovereign LORD.

15"Or if I send wild beasts through that country and they leave it childless and it becomes
desolate so that no one can pass through it
because of the beasts, 16as surely as I live, declares the Sovereign LORD, even if these three
men were in it, they could not save their own
sons or daughters. They alone would be saved,
but the land would be desolate.

17"Or if I bring a sword against that country
and say, 'Let the sword pass throughout the
land,' and I kill its people and their animals,
18as surely as I live, declares the Sovereign
LORD, even if these three men were in it, they
could not save their own sons or daughters.
They alone would be saved.

19"Or if I send a plague into that land and
pour out my wrath on it through bloodshed,
killing its people and their animals, 20as surely as I live, declares the Sovereign LORD, even
if Noah, Daniel and Job were in it, they could
save neither son nor daughter. They would
save only themselves by their righteousness.

21"For this is what the Sovereign LORD
says: How much worse will it be when I send
against Jerusalem my four dreadful judgments—sword and famine and wild beasts
and plague—to kill its men and their animals!
22Yet there will be some survivors—sons and
daughters who will be brought out of it. They
will come to you, and when you see their conduct and their actions, you will be consoled
regarding the disaster I have brought on Jerusalem—every disaster I have brought on
it. 23You will be consoled when you see their
conduct and their actions, for you will know
that I have done nothing in it without cause,
declares the Sovereign LORD."

Jerusalem as a Useless Vine

15 The word of the LORD came to me: 2"Son
of man, how is the wood of a vine different from that of a branch from any of the
trees in the forest? 3Is wood ever taken from
it to make anything useful? Do they make
pegs from it to hang things on? 4And after it
is thrown on the fire as fuel and the fire burns
both ends and chars the middle, is it then useful for anything? 5If it was not useful for anything when it was whole, how much less can it
be made into something useful when the fire
has burned it and it is charred?

[a] *14* Or *Danel,* a man of renown in ancient literature; also in verse 20

6"Therefore this is what the Sovereign
LORD says: As I have given the wood of the
vine among the trees of the forest as fuel for
the fire, so will I treat the people living in
Jerusalem. 7I will set my face against them.
Although they have come out of the fire, the
fire will yet consume them. And when I set
my face against them, you will know that I
am the LORD. 8I will make the land desolate
because they have been unfaithful, declares
the Sovereign LORD."

Jerusalem as an Adulterous Wife

16 The word of the LORD came to me: 2"Son
of man, confront Jerusalem with her
detestable practices 3and say, 'This is what
the Sovereign LORD says to Jerusalem: Your
ancestry and birth were in the land of the
Canaanites; your father was an Amorite
and your mother a Hittite. 4On the day you
were born your cord was not cut, nor were
you washed with water to make you clean,
nor were you rubbed with salt or wrapped in
cloths. 5No one looked on you with pity or had
compassion enough to do any of these things
for you. Rather, you were thrown out into the
open field, for on the day you were born you
were despised.

6" 'Then I passed by and saw you kicking
about in your blood, and as you lay there in
your blood I said to you, "Live!"[a] 7I made you
grow like a plant of the field. You grew and
developed and entered puberty. Your breasts
had formed and your hair had grown, yet you
were stark naked.

8" 'Later I passed by, and when I looked at
you and saw that you were old enough for
love, I spread the corner of my garment over
you and covered your naked body. I gave you
my solemn oath and entered into a covenant
with you, declares the Sovereign LORD, and
you became mine.

9" 'I bathed you with water and washed the
blood from you and put ointments on you. 10I
clothed you with an embroidered dress and
put sandals of fine leather on you. I dressed
you in fine linen and covered you with costly
garments. 11I adorned you with jewelry: I put
bracelets on your arms and a necklace around
your neck, 12and I put a ring on your nose, earrings on your ears and a beautiful crown on
your head. 13So you were adorned with gold
and silver; your clothes were of fine linen and
costly fabric and embroidered cloth. Your food
was honey, olive oil and the finest flour. You
became very beautiful and rose to be a queen.
14And your fame spread among the nations on
account of your beauty, because the splendor
I had given you made your beauty perfect,
declares the Sovereign LORD.

15" 'But you trusted in your beauty and used
your fame to become a prostitute. You lavished your favors on anyone who passed by
and your beauty became his. 16You took some
of your garments to make gaudy high places,
where you carried on your prostitution. You
went to him, and he possessed your beauty.[b]
17You also took the fine jewelry I gave you, the
jewelry made of my gold and silver, and you
made for yourself male idols and engaged in
prostitution with them. 18And you took your
embroidered clothes to put on them, and you
offered my oil and incense before them. 19Also
the food I provided for you—the flour, olive
oil and honey I gave you to eat—you offered
as fragrant incense before them. That is what
happened, declares the Sovereign LORD.

20" 'And you took your sons and daughters
whom you bore to me and sacrificed them as
food to the idols. Was your prostitution not
enough? 21You slaughtered my children and
sacrificed them to the idols. 22In all your detestable practices and your prostitution you
did not remember the days of your youth,
when you were naked and bare, kicking about
in your blood.

23" 'Woe! Woe to you, declares the Sovereign
LORD. In addition to all your other wickedness,
24you built a mound for yourself and made a
lofty shrine in every public square. 25At every street corner you built your lofty shrines
and degraded your beauty, spreading your
legs with increasing promiscuity to anyone
who passed by. 26You engaged in prostitution
with the Egyptians, your neighbors with large
genitals, and aroused my anger with your increasing promiscuity. 27So I stretched out my
hand against you and reduced your territory; I gave you over to the greed of your enemies, the daughters of the Philistines, who
were shocked by your lewd conduct. 28You
engaged in prostitution with the Assyrians
too, because you were insatiable; and even
after that, you still were not satisfied. 29Then
you increased your promiscuity to include
Babylonia,[c] a land of merchants, but even
with this you were not satisfied.

30" 'I am filled with fury against you,[d] declares the Sovereign LORD, when you do all
these things, acting like a brazen prostitute!
31When you built your mounds at every street
corner and made your lofty shrines in every
public square, you were unlike a prostitute,
because you scorned payment.

32" 'You adulterous wife! You prefer strangers to your own husband! 33All prostitutes receive gifts, but you give gifts to all your lovers,
bribing them to come to you from everywhere
for your illicit favors. 34So in your prostitution
you are the opposite of others; no one runs
after you for your favors. You are the very
opposite, for you give payment and none is
given to you.

35" 'Therefore, you prostitute, hear the word
of the LORD! 36This is what the Sovereign LORD
says: Because you poured out your lust and
exposed your naked body in your promiscuity with your lovers, and because of all your
detestable idols, and because you gave them
your children's blood, 37therefore I am going

[a] 6 A few Hebrew manuscripts, Septuagint and Syriac; most Hebrew manuscripts repeat *and as you lay there in your blood I said to you, "Live!"* [b] 16 The meaning of the Hebrew for this sentence is uncertain. [c] 29 Or *Chaldea* [d] 30 Or *How feverish is your heart,*

to gather all your lovers, with whom you found pleasure, those you loved as well as those you hated. I will gather them against you from all around and will strip you in front of them, and they will see you stark naked. 38I will sentence you to the punishment of women who commit adultery and who shed blood; I will bring on you the blood vengeance of my wrath and jealous anger. 39Then I will deliver you into the hands of your lovers, and they will tear down your mounds and destroy your lofty shrines. They will strip you of your clothes and take your fine jewelry and leave you stark naked. 40They will bring a mob against you, who will stone you and hack you to pieces with their swords. 41They will burn down your houses and inflict punishment on you in the sight of many women. I will put a stop to your prostitution, and you will no longer pay your lovers. 42Then my wrath against you will subside and my jealous anger will turn away from you; I will be calm and no longer angry.

43" 'Because you did not remember the days of your youth but enraged me with all these things, I will surely bring down on your head what you have done, declares the Sovereign LORD. Did you not add lewdness to all your other detestable practices?

44" 'Everyone who quotes proverbs will quote this proverb about you: "Like mother, like daughter." 45You are a true daughter of your mother, who despised her husband and her children; and you are a true sister of your sisters, who despised their husbands and their children. Your mother was a Hittite and your father an Amorite. 46Your older sister was Samaria, who lived to the north of you with her daughters; and your younger sister, who lived to the south of you with her daughters, was Sodom. 47You not only followed their ways and copied their detestable practices, but in all your ways you soon became more depraved than they. 48As surely as I live, declares the Sovereign LORD, your sister Sodom and her daughters never did what you and your daughters have done.

49" 'Now this was the sin of your sister Sodom: She and her daughters were arrogant, overfed and unconcerned; they did not help the poor and needy. 50They were haughty and did detestable things before me. Therefore I did away with them as you have seen. 51Samaria did not commit half the sins you did. You have done more detestable things than they, and have made your sisters seem righteous by all these things you have done. 52Bear your disgrace, for you have furnished some justification for your sisters. Because your sins were more vile than theirs, they appear more righteous than you. So then, be ashamed and bear your disgrace, for you have made your sisters appear righteous.

53" 'However, I will restore the fortunes of Sodom and her daughters and of Samaria and her daughters, and your fortunes along with them, 54so that you may bear your disgrace and be ashamed of all you have done in giving them comfort. 55And your sisters, Sodom with her daughters and Samaria with her daughters, will return to what they were before; and you and your daughters will return to what you were before. 56You would not even mention your sister Sodom in the day of your pride, 57before your wickedness was uncovered. Even so, you are now scorned by the daughters of Edom[a] and all her neighbors and the daughters of the Philistines—all those around you who despise you. 58You will bear the consequences of your lewdness and your detestable practices, declares the LORD.

59" 'This is what the Sovereign LORD says: I will deal with you as you deserve, because you have despised my oath by breaking the covenant. 60Yet I will remember the covenant I made with you in the days of your youth, and I will establish an everlasting covenant with you. 61Then you will remember your ways and be ashamed when you receive your sisters, both those who are older than you and those who are younger. I will give them to you as daughters, but not on the basis of my covenant with you. 62So I will establish my covenant with you, and you will know that I am the LORD. 63Then, when I make atonement for you for all you have done, you will remember and be ashamed and never again open your mouth because of your humiliation, declares the Sovereign LORD.' "

Two Eagles and a Vine

17 The word of the LORD came to me: 2"Son of man, set forth an allegory and tell it to the Israelites as a parable. 3Say to them, 'This is what the Sovereign LORD says: A great eagle with powerful wings, long feathers and full plumage of varied colors came to Lebanon. Taking hold of the top of a cedar, 4he broke off its topmost shoot and carried it away to a land of merchants, where he planted it in a city of traders.

5" 'He took one of the seedlings of the land and put it in fertile soil. He planted it like a willow by abundant water, 6and it sprouted and became a low, spreading vine. Its branches turned toward him, but its roots remained under it. So it became a vine and produced branches and put out leafy boughs.

7" 'But there was another great eagle with powerful wings and full plumage. The vine now sent out its roots toward him from the plot where it was planted and stretched out its branches to him for water. 8It had been planted in good soil by abundant water so that it would produce branches, bear fruit and become a splendid vine.'

9"Say to them, 'This is what the Sovereign LORD says: Will it thrive? Will it not be uprooted and stripped of its fruit so that it withers? All its new growth will wither. It will not take a strong arm or many people to pull it up by the roots. 10It has been planted, but will it thrive? Will it not wither completely when the east wind strikes it—wither away in the plot where it grew?' "

[a] 57 Many Hebrew manuscripts and Syriac; most Hebrew manuscripts, Septuagint and Vulgate *Aram*

11Then the word of the LORD came to me:
12"Say to this rebellious people, 'Do you not
know what these things mean?' Say to them:
'The king of Babylon went to Jerusalem and
carried off her king and her nobles, bringing
them back with him to Babylon. 13Then he
took a member of the royal family and made
a treaty with him, putting him under oath. He
also carried away the leading men of the land,
14so that the kingdom would be brought low,
unable to rise again, surviving only by keeping his treaty. 15But the king rebelled against
him by sending his envoys to Egypt to get
horses and a large army. Will he succeed?
Will he who does such things escape? Will
he break the treaty and yet escape?

16" 'As surely as I live, declares the Sovereign LORD, he shall die in Babylon, in the land
of the king who put him on the throne, whose
oath he despised and whose treaty he broke.
17Pharaoh with his mighty army and great
horde will be of no help to him in war, when
ramps are built and siege works erected to
destroy many lives. 18He despised the oath
by breaking the covenant. Because he had
given his hand in pledge and yet did all these
things, he shall not escape.

19" 'Therefore this is what the Sovereign
LORD says: As surely as I live, I will repay
him for despising my oath and breaking my
covenant. 20I will spread my net for him, and
he will be caught in my snare. I will bring him
to Babylon and execute judgment on him there
because he was unfaithful to me. 21All his
choice troops will fall by the sword, and the
survivors will be scattered to the winds. Then
you will know that I the LORD have spoken.

22" 'This is what the Sovereign LORD says: I
myself will take a shoot from the very top of
a cedar and plant it; I will break off a tender
sprig from its topmost shoots and plant it on
a high and lofty mountain. 23On the mountain heights of Israel I will plant it; it will produce branches and bear fruit and become a
splendid cedar. Birds of every kind will nest
in it; they will find shelter in the shade of its
branches. 24All the trees of the forest will
know that I the LORD bring down the tall tree
and make the low tree grow tall. I dry up the
green tree and make the dry tree flourish.

" 'I the LORD have spoken, and I will do it.' "

The One Who Sins Will Die

18 The word of the LORD came to me:
2"What do you people mean by quoting
this proverb about the land of Israel:

" 'The parents eat sour grapes,
and the children's teeth are set on edge'?

3"As surely as I live, declares the Sovereign
LORD, you will no longer quote this proverb in
Israel. 4For everyone belongs to me, the parent as well as the child—both alike belong to
me. The one who sins is the one who will die.

5"Suppose there is a righteous man
who does what is just and right.
6He does not eat at the mountain shrines
or look to the idols of Israel.
He does not defile his neighbor's wife
or have sexual relations with a woman
during her period.
7He does not oppress anyone,
but returns what he took in pledge for a
loan.
He does not commit robbery
but gives his food to the hungry
and provides clothing for the naked.
8He does not lend to them at interest
or take a profit from them.
He withholds his hand from doing wrong
and judges fairly between two parties.
9He follows my decrees
and faithfully keeps my laws.
That man is righteous;
he will surely live,
declares the Sovereign LORD.

10"Suppose he has a violent son, who sheds
blood or does any of these other things[a]
11(though the father has done none of them):

"He eats at the mountain shrines.
He defiles his neighbor's wife.
12He oppresses the poor and needy.
He commits robbery.
He does not return what he took in
pledge.
He looks to the idols.
He does detestable things.
13He lends at interest and takes a profit.

Will such a man live? He will not! Because he
has done all these detestable things, he is to be
put to death; his blood will be on his own head.

14"But suppose this son has a son who sees
all the sins his father commits, and though he
sees them, he does not do such things:

15"He does not eat at the mountain shrines
or look to the idols of Israel.
He does not defile his neighbor's wife.
16He does not oppress anyone
or require a pledge for a loan.
He does not commit robbery
but gives his food to the hungry
and provides clothing for the naked.
17He withholds his hand from mistreating
the poor
and takes no interest or profit from
them.
He keeps my laws and follows my
decrees.

He will not die for his father's sin; he will surely live. 18But his father will die for his own
sin, because he practiced extortion, robbed
his brother and did what was wrong among
his people.

19"Yet you ask, 'Why does the son not share
the guilt of his father?' Since the son has done
what is just and right and has been careful to
keep all my decrees, he will surely live. 20The
one who sins is the one who will die. The child
will not share the guilt of the parent, nor will
the parent share the guilt of the child. The

[a] 10 Or *things to a brother*

righteousness of the righteous will be credited to them, and the wickedness of the wicked
will be charged against them.
21"But if a wicked person turns away from
all the sins they have committed and keeps all
my decrees and does what is just and right,
that person will surely live; they will not die.
22None of the offenses they have committed
will be remembered against them. Because
of the righteous things they have done, they
will live. 23Do I take any pleasure in the death
of the wicked? declares the Sovereign LORD.
Rather, am I not pleased when they turn from
their ways and live?
24"But if a righteous person turns from their
righteousness and commits sin and does the
same detestable things the wicked person
does, will they live? None of the righteous
things that person has done will be remembered. Because of the unfaithfulness they are
guilty of and because of the sins they have
committed, they will die.
25"Yet you say, 'The way of the Lord is not
just.' Hear, you Israelites: Is my way unjust?
Is it not your ways that are unjust? 26If a righteous person turns from their righteousness
and commits sin, they will die for it; because
of the sin they have committed they will die.
27But if a wicked person turns away from the
wickedness they have committed and does
what is just and right, they will save their life.
28Because they consider all the offenses they
have committed and turn away from them,
that person will surely live; they will not die.
29Yet the Israelites say, 'The way of the Lord is
not just.' Are my ways unjust, people of Israel?
Is it not your ways that are unjust?
30"Therefore, you Israelites, I will judge
each of you according to your own ways,
declares the Sovereign LORD. Repent! Turn
away from all your offenses; then sin will not
be your downfall. 31Rid yourselves of all the
offenses you have committed, and get a new
heart and a new spirit. Why will you die, people of Israel? 32For I take no pleasure in the
death of anyone, declares the Sovereign LORD.
Repent and live!

A Lament Over Israel's Princes

19 "Take up a lament concerning the princes of Israel 2and say:

"'What a lioness was your mother
among the lions!
She lay down among them
and reared her cubs.
3She brought up one of her cubs,
and he became a strong lion.
He learned to tear the prey
and he became a man-eater.
4The nations heard about him,
and he was trapped in their pit.
They led him with hooks
to the land of Egypt.

5"'When she saw her hope unfulfilled,
her expectation gone,
she took another of her cubs
and made him a strong lion.
6He prowled among the lions,
for he was now a strong lion.
He learned to tear the prey
and he became a man-eater.
7He broke down[a] their strongholds
and devastated their towns.
The land and all who were in it
were terrified by his roaring.
8Then the nations came against him,
those from regions round about.
They spread their net for him,
and he was trapped in their pit.
9With hooks they pulled him into a cage
and brought him to the king of
Babylon.
They put him in prison,
so his roar was heard no longer
on the mountains of Israel.

10"'Your mother was like a vine in your
vineyard[b]
planted by the water;
it was fruitful and full of branches
because of abundant water.
11Its branches were strong,
fit for a ruler's scepter.
It towered high
above the thick foliage,
conspicuous for its height
and for its many branches.
12But it was uprooted in fury
and thrown to the ground.
The east wind made it shrivel,
it was stripped of its fruit;
its strong branches withered
and fire consumed them.
13Now it is planted in the desert,
in a dry and thirsty land.
14Fire spread from one of its main[c]
branches
and consumed its fruit.
No strong branch is left on it
fit for a ruler's scepter.'

"This is a lament and is to be used as a lament."

Rebellious Israel Purged

20 In the seventh year, in the fifth month
on the tenth day, some of the elders of
Israel came to inquire of the LORD, and they
sat down in front of me.
2Then the word of the LORD came to me:
3"Son of man, speak to the elders of Israel
and say to them, 'This is what the Sovereign
LORD says: Have you come to inquire of me?
As surely as I live, I will not let you inquire of
me, declares the Sovereign LORD.'
4"Will you judge them? Will you judge them,
son of man? Then confront them with the detestable practices of their ancestors 5and say
to them: 'This is what the Sovereign LORD
says: On the day I chose Israel, I swore with
uplifted hand to the descendants of Jacob
and revealed myself to them in Egypt. With

[a] 7 Targum (see Septuagint); Hebrew *He knew* manuscripts *your blood* [c] 14 Or *from under its* [b] 10 Two Hebrew manuscripts; most Hebrew

uplifted hand I said to them, "I am the LORD your God." 6On that day I swore to them that I would bring them out of Egypt into a land I had searched out for them, a land flowing with milk and honey, the most beautiful of all lands. 7And I said to them, "Each of you, get rid of the vile images you have set your eyes on, and do not defile yourselves with the idols of Egypt. I am the LORD your God."

8" 'But they rebelled against me and would not listen to me; they did not get rid of the vile images they had set their eyes on, nor did they forsake the idols of Egypt. So I said I would pour out my wrath on them and spend my anger against them in Egypt. 9But for the sake of my name, I brought them out of Egypt. I did it to keep my name from being profaned in the eyes of the nations among whom they lived and in whose sight I had revealed myself to the Israelites. 10Therefore I led them out of Egypt and brought them into the wilderness. 11I gave them my decrees and made known to them my laws, by which the person who obeys them will live. 12Also I gave them my Sabbaths as a sign between us, so they would know that I the LORD made them holy.

13" 'Yet the people of Israel rebelled against me in the wilderness. They did not follow my decrees but rejected my laws—by which the person who obeys them will live—and they utterly desecrated my Sabbaths. So I said I would pour out my wrath on them and destroy them in the wilderness. 14But for the sake of my name I did what would keep it from being profaned in the eyes of the nations in whose sight I had brought them out. 15Also with uplifted hand I swore to them in the wilderness that I would not bring them into the land I had given them—a land flowing with milk and honey, the most beautiful of all lands— 16because they rejected my laws and did not follow my decrees and desecrated my Sabbaths. For their hearts were devoted to their idols. 17Yet I looked on them with pity and did not destroy them or put an end to them in the wilderness. 18I said to their children in the wilderness, "Do not follow the statutes of your parents or keep their laws or defile yourselves with their idols. 19I am the LORD your God; follow my decrees and be careful to keep my laws. 20Keep my Sabbaths holy, that they may be a sign between us. Then you will know that I am the LORD your God."

21" 'But the children rebelled against me: They did not follow my decrees, they were not careful to keep my laws, of which I said, "The person who obeys them will live by them," and they desecrated my Sabbaths. So I said I would pour out my wrath on them and spend my anger against them in the wilderness. 22But I withheld my hand, and for the sake of my name I did what would keep it from being profaned in the eyes of the nations in whose sight I had brought them out. 23Also with uplifted hand I swore to them in the wilderness that I would disperse them among the nations and scatter them through the countries, 24because they had not obeyed my laws but had rejected my decrees and desecrated my Sabbaths, and their eyes lusted after their parents' idols. 25So I gave them other statutes that were not good and laws through which they could not live; 26I defiled them through their gifts—the sacrifice of every firstborn—that I might fill them with horror so they would know that I am the LORD.'

27"Therefore, son of man, speak to the people of Israel and say to them, 'This is what the Sovereign LORD says: In this also your ancestors blasphemed me by being unfaithful to me: 28When I brought them into the land I had sworn to give them and they saw any high hill or any leafy tree, there they offered their sacrifices, made offerings that aroused my anger, presented their fragrant incense and poured out their drink offerings. 29Then I said to them: What is this high place you go to?' " (It is called Bamah[a] to this day.)

Rebellious Israel Renewed

30"Therefore say to the Israelites: 'This is what the Sovereign LORD says: Will you defile yourselves the way your ancestors did and lust after their vile images? 31When you offer your gifts—the sacrifice of your children in the fire—you continue to defile yourselves with all your idols to this day. Am I to let you inquire of me, you Israelites? As surely as I live, declares the Sovereign LORD, I will not let you inquire of me.

32" 'You say, "We want to be like the nations, like the peoples of the world, who serve wood and stone." But what you have in mind will never happen. 33As surely as I live, declares the Sovereign LORD, I will reign over you with a mighty hand and an outstretched arm and with outpoured wrath. 34I will bring you from the nations and gather you from the countries where you have been scattered—with a mighty hand and an outstretched arm and with outpoured wrath. 35I will bring you into the wilderness of the nations and there, face to face, I will execute judgment upon you. 36As I judged your ancestors in the wilderness of the land of Egypt, so I will judge you, declares the Sovereign LORD. 37I will take note of you as you pass under my rod, and I will bring you into the bond of the covenant. 38I will purge you of those who revolt and rebel against me. Although I will bring them out of the land where they are living, yet they will not enter the land of Israel. Then you will know that I am the LORD.

39" 'As for you, people of Israel, this is what the Sovereign LORD says: Go and serve your idols, every one of you! But afterward you will surely listen to me and no longer profane my holy name with your gifts and idols. 40For on my holy mountain, the high mountain of Israel, declares the Sovereign LORD, there in the land all the people of Israel will serve me, and there I will accept them. There I will require your offerings and your choice gifts,[b] along with all your holy sacrifices. 41I will

[a] *29* *Bamah* means *high place.* [b] *40* Or *and the gifts of your firstfruits*

accept you as fragrant incense when I bring
you out from the nations and gather you from
the countries where you have been scattered,
and I will be proved holy through you in the
sight of the nations. 42Then you will know
that I am the LORD, when I bring you into the
land of Israel, the land I had sworn with uplifted hand to give to your ancestors. 43There
you will remember your conduct and all the
actions by which you have defiled yourselves,
and you will loathe yourselves for all the evil
you have done. 44You will know that I am the
LORD, when I deal with you for my name's
sake and not according to your evil ways and
your corrupt practices, you people of Israel,
declares the Sovereign LORD.'"

Prophecy Against the South

45The word of the LORD came to me: 46"Son
of man, set your face toward the south; preach
against the south and prophesy against the
forest of the southland. 47Say to the southern
forest: 'Hear the word of the LORD. This is
what the Sovereign LORD says: I am about to
set fire to you, and it will consume all your
trees, both green and dry. The blazing flame
will not be quenched, and every face from
south to north will be scorched by it. 48Every-
one will see that I the LORD have kindled it; it
will not be quenched.'"

49Then I said, "Sovereign LORD, they are
saying of me, 'Isn't he just telling parables?'"[a]

Babylon as God's Sword of Judgment

21[b] The word of the LORD came to me: 2"Son
of man, set your face against Jerusalem
and preach against the sanctuary. Prophesy
against the land of Israel 3and say to her: 'This
is what the LORD says: I am against you. I will
draw my sword from its sheath and cut off from
you both the righteous and the wicked. 4Be-
cause I am going to cut off the righteous and the
wicked, my sword will be unsheathed against
everyone from south to north. 5Then all people will know that I the LORD have drawn my
sword from its sheath; it will not return again.'

6"Therefore groan, son of man! Groan before them with broken heart and bitter grief.
7And when they ask you, 'Why are you groaning?' you shall say, 'Because of the news that
is coming. Every heart will melt with fear and
every hand go limp; every spirit will become
faint and every leg will be wet with urine.' It
is coming! It will surely take place, declares
the Sovereign LORD."

8The word of the LORD came to me: 9"Son
of man, prophesy and say, 'This is what the
Lord says:

"'A sword, a sword,
sharpened and polished—
10sharpened for the slaughter,
polished to flash like lightning!

"'Shall we rejoice in the scepter of my royal son? The sword despises every such stick.

11"'The sword is appointed to be polished,
to be grasped with the hand;
it is sharpened and polished,
made ready for the hand of the slayer.
12Cry out and wail, son of man,
for it is against my people;
it is against all the princes of Israel.
They are thrown to the sword
along with my people.
Therefore beat your breast.

13"'Testing will surely come. And what if
even the scepter, which the sword despises,
does not continue? declares the Sovereign
LORD.'

14"So then, son of man, prophesy
and strike your hands together.
Let the sword strike twice,
even three times.
It is a sword for slaughter—
a sword for great slaughter,
closing in on them from every side.
15So that hearts may melt with fear
and the fallen be many,
I have stationed the sword for slaughter[c]
at all their gates.
Look! It is forged to strike like lightning,
it is grasped for slaughter.
16Slash to the right, you sword,
then to the left,
wherever your blade is turned.
17I too will strike my hands together,
and my wrath will subside.
I the LORD have spoken."

18The word of the LORD came to me: 19"Son
of man, mark out two roads for the sword
of the king of Babylon to take, both starting from the same country. Make a sign-
post where the road branches off to the city.
20Mark out one road for the sword to come
against Rabbah of the Ammonites and another against Judah and fortified Jerusalem.
21For the king of Babylon will stop at the fork
in the road, at the junction of the two roads, to
seek an omen: He will cast lots with arrows,
he will consult his idols, he will examine the
liver. 22Into his right hand will come the lot
for Jerusalem, where he is to set up battering rams, to give the command to slaughter,
to sound the battle cry, to set battering rams
against the gates, to build a ramp and to erect
siege works. 23It will seem like a false omen
to those who have sworn allegiance to him,
but he will remind them of their guilt and
take them captive.

24"Therefore this is what the Sovereign
LORD says: 'Because you people have brought
to mind your guilt by your open rebellion, revealing your sins in all that you do—because
you have done this, you will be taken captive.

25"'You profane and wicked prince of Israel,
whose day has come, whose time of punishment has reached its climax, 26this is what
the Sovereign LORD says: Take off the turban,
remove the crown. It will not be as it was: The
lowly will be exalted and the exalted will be

[a] *49* In Hebrew texts 20:45-49 is numbered 21:1-5. [b] In Hebrew texts 21:1-32 is numbered 21:6-37.
[c] *15* Septuagint; the meaning of the Hebrew for this word is uncertain.

brought low. 27 A ruin! A ruin! I will make it a
ruin! The crown will not be restored until he
to whom it rightfully belongs shall come; to
him I will give it.'
28 "And you, son of man, prophesy and say,
'This is what the Sovereign LORD says about
the Ammonites and their insults:

"'A sword, a sword,
drawn for the slaughter,
polished to consume
and to flash like lightning!
29 Despite false visions concerning you
and lying divinations about you,
it will be laid on the necks
of the wicked who are to be slain,
whose day has come,
whose time of punishment has reached
its climax.
30 "'Let the sword return to its sheath.
In the place where you were created,
in the land of your ancestry,
I will judge you.
31 I will pour out my wrath on you
and breathe out my fiery anger against
you;
I will deliver you into the hands of brutal
men,
men skilled in destruction.
32 You will be fuel for the fire,
your blood will be shed in your land,
you will be remembered no more;
for I the LORD have spoken.'"

Judgment on Jerusalem's Sins

22 The word of the LORD came to me:
2 "Son of man, will you judge her? Will you
judge this city of bloodshed? Then confront
her with all her detestable practices 3 and say:
'This is what the Sovereign LORD says: You
city that brings on herself doom by shedding
blood in her midst and defiles herself by making idols, 4 you have become guilty because
of the blood you have shed and have become
defiled by the idols you have made. You have
brought your days to a close, and the end of
your years has come. Therefore I will make
you an object of scorn to the nations and a
laughingstock to all the countries. 5 Those
who are near and those who are far away will
mock you, you infamous city, full of turmoil.
6 "'See how each of the princes of Israel who
are in you uses his power to shed blood. 7 In
you they have treated father and mother with
contempt; in you they have oppressed the foreigner and mistreated the fatherless and the
widow. 8 You have despised my holy things
and desecrated my Sabbaths. 9 In you are slanderers who are bent on shedding blood; in you
are those who eat at the mountain shrines
and commit lewd acts. 10 In you are those who
dishonor their father's bed; in you are those
who violate women during their period, when
they are ceremonially unclean. 11 In you one
man commits a detestable offense with his
neighbor's wife, another shamefully defiles
his daughter-in-law, and another violates his
sister, his own father's daughter. 12 In you are
people who accept bribes to shed blood; you
take interest and make a profit from the poor.
You extort unjust gain from your neighbors.
And you have forgotten me, declares the Sovereign LORD.
13 "'I will surely strike my hands together
at the unjust gain you have made and at the
blood you have shed in your midst. 14 Will your
courage endure or your hands be strong in the
day I deal with you? I the LORD have spoken,
and I will do it. 15 I will disperse you among
the nations and scatter you through the countries; and I will put an end to your uncleanness. 16 When you have been defiled[a] in the
eyes of the nations, you will know that I am
the LORD.'"
17 Then the word of the LORD came to me:
18 "Son of man, the people of Israel have become dross to me; all of them are the copper,
tin, iron and lead left inside a furnace. They
are but the dross of silver. 19 Therefore this is
what the Sovereign LORD says: 'Because you
have all become dross, I will gather you into
Jerusalem. 20 As silver, copper, iron, lead and
tin are gathered into a furnace to be melted
with a fiery blast, so will I gather you in my
anger and my wrath and put you inside the
city and melt you. 21 I will gather you and I will
blow on you with my fiery wrath, and you will
be melted inside her. 22 As silver is melted in a
furnace, so you will be melted inside her, and
you will know that I the LORD have poured out
my wrath on you.'"
23 Again the word of the LORD came to me:
24 "Son of man, say to the land, 'You are a land
that has not been cleansed or rained on in the
day of wrath.' 25 There is a conspiracy of her
princes[b] within her like a roaring lion tearing
its prey; they devour people, take treasures
and precious things and make many widows
within her. 26 Her priests do violence to my law
and profane my holy things; they do not distinguish between the holy and the common;
they teach that there is no difference between
the unclean and the clean; and they shut their
eyes to the keeping of my Sabbaths, so that
I am profaned among them. 27 Her officials
within her are like wolves tearing their prey;
they shed blood and kill people to make unjust
gain. 28 Her prophets whitewash these deeds
for them by false visions and lying divinations. They say, 'This is what the Sovereign
LORD says'—when the LORD has not spoken.
29 The people of the land practice extortion
and commit robbery; they oppress the poor
and needy and mistreat the foreigner, denying them justice.
30 "I looked for someone among them who
would build up the wall and stand before me
in the gap on behalf of the land so I would not
have to destroy it, but I found no one. 31 So I
will pour out my wrath on them and consume
them with my fiery anger, bringing down on
their own heads all they have done, declares
the Sovereign LORD."

[a] *16* Or *When I have allotted you your inheritance*
[b] *25* Septuagint; Hebrew *prophets*

Two Adulterous Sisters

23 The word of the LORD came to me: 2“Son
of man, there were two women, daughters of the same mother. 3They became prostitutes in Egypt, engaging in prostitution from
their youth. In that land their breasts were
fondled and their virgin bosoms caressed.
4The older was named Oholah, and her sister
was Oholibah. They were mine and gave birth
to sons and daughters. Oholah is Samaria, and
Oholibah is Jerusalem.

5“Oholah engaged in prostitution while
she was still mine; and she lusted after her
lovers, the Assyrians—warriors 6clothed in
blue, governors and commanders, all of them
handsome young men, and mounted horsemen. 7She gave herself as a prostitute to all
the elite of the Assyrians and defiled herself
with all the idols of everyone she lusted after. 8She did not give up the prostitution she
began in Egypt, when during her youth men
slept with her, caressed her virgin bosom and
poured out their lust on her.

9“Therefore I delivered her into the hands
of her lovers, the Assyrians, for whom she
lusted. 10They stripped her naked, took away
her sons and daughters and killed her with the
sword. She became a byword among women,
and punishment was inflicted on her.

11“Her sister Oholibah saw this, yet in her
lust and prostitution she was more depraved
than her sister. 12She too lusted after the Assyrians—governors and commanders, warriors
in full dress, mounted horsemen, all handsome
young men. 13I saw that she too defiled herself;
both of them went the same way.

14“But she carried her prostitution still further. She saw men portrayed on a wall, figures
of Chaldeans[a] portrayed in red, 15with belts
around their waists and flowing turbans on
their heads; all of them looked like Babylonian chariot officers, natives of Chaldea.[b]
16As soon as she saw them, she lusted after
them and sent messengers to them in Chaldea. 17Then the Babylonians came to her, to
the bed of love, and in their lust they defiled
her. After she had been defiled by them, she
turned away from them in disgust. 18When
she carried on her prostitution openly and
exposed her naked body, I turned away from
her in disgust, just as I had turned away from
her sister. 19Yet she became more and more
promiscuous as she recalled the days of her
youth, when she was a prostitute in Egypt.
20There she lusted after her lovers, whose genitals were like those of donkeys and whose
emission was like that of horses. 21So you
longed for the lewdness of your youth, when
in Egypt your bosom was caressed and your
young breasts fondled.[c]

22“Therefore, Oholibah, this is what the
Sovereign LORD says: I will stir up your lovers against you, those you turned away from
in disgust, and I will bring them against you
from every side— 23the Babylonians and all
the Chaldeans, the men of Pekod and Shoa
and Koa, and all the Assyrians with them,
handsome young men, all of them governors
and commanders, chariot officers and men
of high rank, all mounted on horses. 24They
will come against you with weapons,[d] chariots and wagons and with a throng of people;
they will take up positions against you on every side with large and small shields and with
helmets. I will turn you over to them for punishment, and they will punish you according
to their standards. 25I will direct my jealous
anger against you, and they will deal with
you in fury. They will cut off your noses and
your ears, and those of you who are left will
fall by the sword. They will take away your
sons and daughters, and those of you who are
left will be consumed by fire. 26They will also
strip you of your clothes and take your fine
jewelry. 27So I will put a stop to the lewdness
and prostitution you began in Egypt. You will
not look on these things with longing or remember Egypt anymore.

28“For this is what the Sovereign LORD says:
I am about to deliver you into the hands of
those you hate, to those you turned away
from in disgust. 29They will deal with you in
hatred and take away everything you have
worked for. They will leave you stark naked,
and the shame of your prostitution will be exposed. Your lewdness and promiscuity 30have
brought this on you, because you lusted after the nations and defiled yourself with their
idols. 31You have gone the way of your sister;
so I will put her cup into your hand.

32“This is what the Sovereign LORD says:

“You will drink your sister’s cup,
 a cup large and deep;
it will bring scorn and derision,
 for it holds so much.
33 You will be filled with drunkenness and
  sorrow,
 the cup of ruin and desolation,
 the cup of your sister Samaria.
34 You will drink it and drain it dry
 and chew on its pieces—
 and you will tear your breasts.

I have spoken, declares the Sovereign LORD.

35“Therefore this is what the Sovereign
LORD says: Since you have forgotten me and
turned your back on me, you must bear the
consequences of your lewdness and prostitution.”

36The LORD said to me: “Son of man, will
you judge Oholah and Oholibah? Then confront them with their detestable practices,
37for they have committed adultery and blood
is on their hands. They committed adultery
with their idols; they even sacrificed their
children, whom they bore to me, as food for
them. 38They have also done this to me: At
that same time they defiled my sanctuary and
desecrated my Sabbaths. 39On the very day
they sacrificed their children to their idols,
they entered my sanctuary and desecrated it.
That is what they did in my house.

[a] 14 Or *Babylonians* [b] 15 Or *Babylonia*; also in verse 16 [c] 21 Syriac (see also verse 3); Hebrew *caressed because of your young breasts* [d] 24 The meaning of the Hebrew for this word is uncertain.

40“They even sent messengers for men who
came from far away, and when they arrived
you bathed yourself for them, applied eye
makeup and put on your jewelry. 41You sat
on an elegant couch, with a table spread before it on which you had placed the incense
and olive oil that belonged to me.

42“The noise of a carefree crowd was
around her; drunkards were brought from
the desert along with men from the rabble,
and they put bracelets on the wrists of the
woman and her sister and beautiful crowns
on their heads. 43Then I said about the one
worn out by adultery, ‘Now let them use her
as a prostitute, for that is all she is.’ 44And they
slept with her. As men sleep with a prostitute,
so they slept with those lewd women, Oholah
and Oholibah. 45But righteous judges will sentence them to the punishment of women who
commit adultery and shed blood, because they
are adulterous and blood is on their hands.

46“This is what the Sovereign LORD says:
Bring a mob against them and give them over
to terror and plunder. 47The mob will stone
them and cut them down with their swords;
they will kill their sons and daughters and
burn down their houses.

48“So I will put an end to lewdness in the
land, that all women may take warning and
not imitate you. 49You will suffer the penalty
for your lewdness and bear the consequences
of your sins of idolatry. Then you will know
that I am the Sovereign LORD.”

Jerusalem as a Cooking Pot

24 In the ninth year, in the tenth month
on the tenth day, the word of the LORD
came to me: 2“Son of man, record this date,
this very date, because the king of Babylon
has laid siege to Jerusalem this very day. 3Tell
this rebellious people a parable and say to
them: ‘This is what the Sovereign LORD says:

“ ‘Put on the cooking pot; put it on
 and pour water into it.
4Put into it the pieces of meat,
 all the choice pieces—the leg and the
  shoulder.
Fill it with the best of these bones;
5 take the pick of the flock.
Pile wood beneath it for the bones;
 bring it to a boil
 and cook the bones in it.

6“ ‘For this is what the Sovereign LORD says:

“ ‘Woe to the city of bloodshed,
 to the pot now encrusted,
 whose deposit will not go away!
Take the meat out piece by piece
 in whatever order it comes.

7“ ‘For the blood she shed is in her midst:
 She poured it on the bare rock;
she did not pour it on the ground,
 where the dust would cover it.
8To stir up wrath and take revenge
 I put her blood on the bare rock,
 so that it would not be covered.

9“ ‘Therefore this is what the Sovereign LORD
says:

“ ‘Woe to the city of bloodshed!
 I, too, will pile the wood high.
10So heap on the wood
 and kindle the fire.
Cook the meat well,
 mixing in the spices;
 and let the bones be charred.
11Then set the empty pot on the coals
 till it becomes hot and its copper glows,
so that its impurities may be melted
 and its deposit burned away.
12It has frustrated all efforts;
 its heavy deposit has not been removed,
 not even by fire.

13“ ‘Now your impurity is lewdness. Because
I tried to cleanse you but you would not be
cleansed from your impurity, you will not be
clean again until my wrath against you has
subsided.

14“ ‘I the LORD have spoken. The time has
come for me to act. I will not hold back; I will
not have pity, nor will I relent. You will be
judged according to your conduct and your
actions, declares the Sovereign LORD.’ ”

Ezekiel’s Wife Dies

15The word of the LORD came to me: 16“Son
of man, with one blow I am about to take away
from you the delight of your eyes. Yet do not
lament or weep or shed any tears. 17Groan
quietly; do not mourn for the dead. Keep your
turban fastened and your sandals on your feet;
do not cover your mustache and beard or eat
the customary food of mourners.”

18So I spoke to the people in the morning,
and in the evening my wife died. The next
morning I did as I had been commanded.

19Then the people asked me, “Won’t you tell
us what these things have to do with us? Why
are you acting like this?”

20So I said to them, “The word of the LORD
came to me: 21Say to the people of Israel, ‘This
is what the Sovereign LORD says: I am about
to desecrate my sanctuary—the stronghold
in which you take pride, the delight of your
eyes, the object of your affection. The sons
and daughters you left behind will fall by the
sword. 22And you will do as I have done. You
will not cover your mustache and beard or eat
the customary food of mourners. 23You will
keep your turbans on your heads and your
sandals on your feet. You will not mourn or
weep but will waste away because of[a] your
sins and groan among yourselves. 24Ezekiel
will be a sign to you; you will do just as he has
done. When this happens, you will know that
I am the Sovereign LORD.’

25“And you, son of man, on the day I take
away their stronghold, their joy and glory, the
delight of their eyes, their heart’s desire, and
their sons and daughters as well— 26on that
day a fugitive will come to tell you the news.
27At that time your mouth will be opened; you

[a] 23 Or *away in*

will speak with him and will no longer be silent. So you will be a sign to them, and they
will know that I am the LORD."

A Prophecy Against Ammon

25 The word of the LORD came to me: 2"Son
of man, set your face against the Ammonites and prophesy against them. 3Say to
them, 'Hear the word of the Sovereign LORD.
This is what the Sovereign LORD says: Because you said "Aha!" over my sanctuary
when it was desecrated and over the land of
Israel when it was laid waste and over the
people of Judah when they went into exile,
4therefore I am going to give you to the people
of the East as a possession. They will set up
their camps and pitch their tents among you;
they will eat your fruit and drink your milk.
5I will turn Rabbah into a pasture for camels
and Ammon into a resting place for sheep.
Then you will know that I am the LORD. 6For
this is what the Sovereign LORD says: Because
you have clapped your hands and stamped
your feet, rejoicing with all the malice of your
heart against the land of Israel, 7therefore I
will stretch out my hand against you and give
you as plunder to the nations. I will wipe you
out from among the nations and exterminate
you from the countries. I will destroy you, and
you will know that I am the LORD.'"

A Prophecy Against Moab

8"This is what the Sovereign LORD says: 'Because Moab and Seir said, "Look, Judah has
become like all the other nations," 9therefore
I will expose the flank of Moab, beginning
at its frontier towns—Beth Jeshimoth, Baal
Meon and Kiriathaim—the glory of that land.
10I will give Moab along with the Ammonites
to the people of the East as a possession, so
that the Ammonites will not be remembered
among the nations; 11and I will inflict punishment on Moab. Then they will know that
I am the LORD.'"

A Prophecy Against Edom

12"This is what the Sovereign LORD says:
'Because Edom took revenge on Judah and became very guilty by doing so, 13therefore this
is what the Sovereign LORD says: I will stretch
out my hand against Edom and kill both man
and beast. I will lay it waste, and from Teman
to Dedan they will fall by the sword. 14I will
take vengeance on Edom by the hand of my
people Israel, and they will deal with Edom
in accordance with my anger and my wrath;
they will know my vengeance, declares the
Sovereign LORD.'"

A Prophecy Against Philistia

15"This is what the Sovereign LORD says:
'Because the Philistines acted in vengeance
and took revenge with malice in their hearts,
and with ancient hostility sought to destroy
Judah, 16therefore this is what the Sovereign
LORD says: I am about to stretch out my hand
against the Philistines, and I will wipe out the
Kerethites and destroy those remaining along
the coast. 17I will carry out great vengeance
on them and punish them in my wrath. Then
they will know that I am the LORD, when I take
vengeance on them.'"

A Prophecy Against Tyre

26 In the eleventh month of the twelfth[a]
year, on the first day of the month, the
word of the LORD came to me: 2"Son of man,
because Tyre has said of Jerusalem, 'Aha! The
gate to the nations is broken, and its doors
have swung open to me; now that she lies in
ruins I will prosper,' 3therefore this is what
the Sovereign LORD says: I am against you,
Tyre, and I will bring many nations against
you, like the sea casting up its waves. 4They
will destroy the walls of Tyre and pull down
her towers; I will scrape away her rubble and
make her a bare rock. 5Out in the sea she will
become a place to spread fishnets, for I have
spoken, declares the Sovereign LORD. She will
become plunder for the nations, 6and her settlements on the mainland will be ravaged by
the sword. Then they will know that I am the
LORD.

7"For this is what the Sovereign LORD says:
From the north I am going to bring against
Tyre Nebuchadnezzar[b] king of Babylon, king
of kings, with horses and chariots, with horsemen and a great army. 8He will ravage your
settlements on the mainland with the sword;
he will set up siege works against you, build
a ramp up to your walls and raise his shields
against you. 9He will direct the blows of his
battering rams against your walls and demolish your towers with his weapons. 10His horses
will be so many that they will cover you with
dust. Your walls will tremble at the noise of
the warhorses, wagons and chariots when he
enters your gates as men enter a city whose
walls have been broken through. 11The hooves
of his horses will trample all your streets; he
will kill your people with the sword, and your
strong pillars will fall to the ground. 12They
will plunder your wealth and loot your merchandise; they will break down your walls
and demolish your fine houses and throw your
stones, timber and rubble into the sea. 13I will
put an end to your noisy songs, and the music
of your harps will be heard no more. 14I will
make you a bare rock, and you will become
a place to spread fishnets. You will never be
rebuilt, for I the LORD have spoken, declares
the Sovereign LORD.

15"This is what the Sovereign LORD says to
Tyre: Will not the coastlands tremble at the
sound of your fall, when the wounded groan
and the slaughter takes place in you? 16Then
all the princes of the coast will step down from
their thrones and lay aside their robes and
take off their embroidered garments. Clothed

[a] *1* Probable reading of the original Hebrew text; Masoretic Text does not have *month of the twelfth*.
[b] *7* Hebrew *Nebuchadrezzar*, of which *Nebuchadnezzar* is a variant; here and often in Ezekiel and Jeremiah

with terror, they will sit on the ground, trembling every moment, appalled at you. 17Then
they will take up a lament concerning you
and say to you:

"'How you are destroyed, city of renown,
peopled by men of the sea!
You were a power on the seas,
you and your citizens;
you put your terror
on all who lived there.
18Now the coastlands tremble
on the day of your fall;
the islands in the sea
are terrified at your collapse.'

19"This is what the Sovereign LORD says:
When I make you a desolate city, like cities no
longer inhabited, and when I bring the ocean
depths over you and its vast waters cover you,
20then I will bring you down with those who
go down to the pit, to the people of long ago.
I will make you dwell in the earth below, as
in ancient ruins, with those who go down to
the pit, and you will not return or take your
place[a] in the land of the living. 21I will bring
you to a horrible end and you will be no more.
You will be sought, but you will never again
be found, declares the Sovereign LORD."

A Lament Over Tyre

27 The word of the LORD came to me: 2"Son
of man, take up a lament concerning
Tyre. 3Say to Tyre, situated at the gateway to
the sea, merchant of peoples on many coasts,
'This is what the Sovereign LORD says:

"'You say, Tyre,
"I am perfect in beauty."
4Your domain was on the high seas;
your builders brought your beauty to
perfection.
5They made all your timbers
of juniper from Senir[b];
they took a cedar from Lebanon
to make a mast for you.
6Of oaks from Bashan
they made your oars;
of cypress wood[c] from the coasts of
Cyprus
they made your deck, adorned with
ivory.
7Fine embroidered linen from Egypt was
your sail
and served as your banner;
your awnings were of blue and purple
from the coasts of Elishah.
8Men of Sidon and Arvad were your
oarsmen;
your skilled men, Tyre, were aboard as
your sailors.
9Veteran craftsmen of Byblos were on
board
as shipwrights to caulk your seams.
All the ships of the sea and their sailors
came alongside to trade for your wares.
10"'Men of Persia, Lydia and Put
served as soldiers in your army.
They hung their shields and helmets on
your walls,
bringing you splendor.
11Men of Arvad and Helek
guarded your walls on every side;
men of Gammad
were in your towers.
They hung their shields around your
walls;
they brought your beauty to perfection.

12"'Tarshish did business with you because
of your great wealth of goods; they exchanged
silver, iron, tin and lead for your merchandise.
13"'Greece, Tubal and Meshek did business
with you; they traded human beings and articles of bronze for your wares.
14"'Men of Beth Togarmah exchanged chariot horses, cavalry horses and mules for your
merchandise.
15"'The men of Rhodes[d] traded with you,
and many coastlands were your customers;
they paid you with ivory tusks and ebony.
16"'Aram[e] did business with you because
of your many products; they exchanged turquoise, purple fabric, embroidered work, fine
linen, coral and rubies for your merchandise.
17"'Judah and Israel traded with you; they
exchanged wheat from Minnith and con-
fections,[f] honey, olive oil and balm for your
wares.
18"'Damascus did business with you because of your many products and great wealth
of goods. They offered wine from Helbon,
wool from Zahar 19and casks of wine from
Izal in exchange for your wares: wrought iron,
cassia and calamus.
20"'Dedan traded in saddle blankets with
you.
21"'Arabia and all the princes of Kedar were
your customers; they did business with you
in lambs, rams and goats.
22"'The merchants of Sheba and Raamah
traded with you; for your merchandise they
exchanged the finest of all kinds of spices and
precious stones, and gold.
23"'Harran, Kanneh and Eden and merchants of Sheba, Ashur and Kilmad traded
with you. 24In your marketplace they traded
with you beautiful garments, blue fabric, embroidered work and multicolored rugs with
cords twisted and tightly knotted.

25"'The ships of Tarshish serve
as carriers for your wares.
You are filled with heavy cargo
as you sail the sea.
26Your oarsmen take you
out to the high seas.
But the east wind will break you to pieces
far out at sea.
27Your wealth, merchandise and wares,
your mariners, sailors and shipwrights,

[a] *20* Septuagint; Hebrew *return, and I will give glory* [b] *5* That is, Mount Hermon [c] *6* Targum; the Masoretic Text has a different division of the consonants. [d] *15* Septuagint; Hebrew *Dedan* [e] *16* Most Hebrew manuscripts; some Hebrew manuscripts and Syriac *Edom* [f] *17* The meaning of the Hebrew for this word is uncertain.

your merchants and all your soldiers,
and everyone else on board
will sink into the heart of the sea
on the day of your shipwreck.
28 The shorelands will quake
when your sailors cry out.
29 All who handle the oars
will abandon their ships;
the mariners and all the sailors
will stand on the shore.
30 They will raise their voice
and cry bitterly over you;
they will sprinkle dust on their heads
and roll in ashes.
31 They will shave their heads because of you
and will put on sackcloth.
They will weep over you with anguish of soul
and with bitter mourning.
32 As they wail and mourn over you,
they will take up a lament concerning you:
"Who was ever silenced like Tyre,
surrounded by the sea?"
33 When your merchandise went out on the seas,
you satisfied many nations;
with your great wealth and your wares
you enriched the kings of the earth.
34 Now you are shattered by the sea
in the depths of the waters;
your wares and all your company
have gone down with you.
35 All who live in the coastlands
are appalled at you;
their kings shudder with horror
and their faces are distorted with fear.
36 The merchants among the nations scoff at you;
you have come to a horrible end
and will be no more.' "

A Prophecy Against the King of Tyre

28 The word of the LORD came to me: 2"Son
of man, say to the ruler of Tyre, 'This is
what the Sovereign LORD says:

" 'In the pride of your heart
you say, "I am a god;
I sit on the throne of a god
in the heart of the seas."
But you are a mere mortal and not a god,
though you think you are as wise as a god.
3 Are you wiser than Daniel[a]?
Is no secret hidden from you?
4 By your wisdom and understanding
you have gained wealth for yourself
and amassed gold and silver
in your treasuries.
5 By your great skill in trading
you have increased your wealth,
and because of your wealth
your heart has grown proud.

6" 'Therefore this is what the Sovereign
LORD says:

" 'Because you think you are wise,
as wise as a god,
7 I am going to bring foreigners against you,
the most ruthless of nations;
they will draw their swords against your beauty and wisdom
and pierce your shining splendor.
8 They will bring you down to the pit,
and you will die a violent death
in the heart of the seas.
9 Will you then say, "I am a god,"
in the presence of those who kill you?
You will be but a mortal, not a god,
in the hands of those who slay you.
10 You will die the death of the uncircumcised
at the hands of foreigners.
I have spoken, declares the Sovereign LORD.' "

11The word of the LORD came to me: 12"Son
of man, take up a lament concerning the king
of Tyre and say to him: 'This is what the Sovereign LORD says:

" 'You were the seal of perfection,
full of wisdom and perfect in beauty.
13 You were in Eden,
the garden of God;
every precious stone adorned you:
carnelian, chrysolite and emerald,
topaz, onyx and jasper,
lapis lazuli, turquoise and beryl.[b]
Your settings and mountings[c] were made of gold;
on the day you were created they were prepared.
14 You were anointed as a guardian cherub,
for so I ordained you.
You were on the holy mount of God;
you walked among the fiery stones.
15 You were blameless in your ways
from the day you were created
till wickedness was found in you.
16 Through your widespread trade
you were filled with violence,
and you sinned.
So I drove you in disgrace from the mount of God,
and I expelled you, guardian cherub,
from among the fiery stones.
17 Your heart became proud
on account of your beauty,
and you corrupted your wisdom
because of your splendor.
So I threw you to the earth;
I made a spectacle of you before kings.
18 By your many sins and dishonest trade
you have desecrated your sanctuaries.
So I made a fire come out from you,
and it consumed you,
and I reduced you to ashes on the ground
in the sight of all who were watching.
19 All the nations who knew you
are appalled at you;
you have come to a horrible end
and will be no more.' "

[a] *3* Or *Danel,* a man of renown in ancient literature [b] *13* The precise identification of some of these precious stones is uncertain. [c] *13* The meaning of the Hebrew for this phrase is uncertain.

A Prophecy Against Sidon

20The word of the LORD came to me: 21"Son
of man, set your face against Sidon; prophesy against her 22and say: 'This is what the
Sovereign LORD says:

"'I am against you, Sidon,
and among you I will display my glory.
You will know that I am the LORD,
when I inflict punishment on you
and within you am proved to be holy.
23I will send a plague upon you
and make blood flow in your streets.
The slain will fall within you,
with the sword against you on every
side.
Then you will know that I am the LORD.

24"'No longer will the people of Israel have
malicious neighbors who are painful briers
and sharp thorns. Then they will know that I
am the Sovereign LORD.
25"'This is what the Sovereign LORD says:
When I gather the people of Israel from the
nations where they have been scattered, I will
be proved holy through them in the sight of
the nations. Then they will live in their own
land, which I gave to my servant Jacob. 26They
will live there in safety and will build houses
and plant vineyards; they will live in safety
when I inflict punishment on all their neighbors who maligned them. Then they will know
that I am the LORD their God.'"

A Prophecy Against Egypt

Judgment on Pharaoh

29 In the tenth year, in the tenth month on
the twelfth day, the word of the LORD
came to me: 2"Son of man, set your face
against Pharaoh king of Egypt and prophesy against him and against all Egypt. 3Speak
to him and say: 'This is what the Sovereign
LORD says:

"'I am against you, Pharaoh king of Egypt,
you great monster lying among your
streams.
You say, "The Nile belongs to me;
I made it for myself."
4But I will put hooks in your jaws
and make the fish of your streams stick
to your scales.
I will pull you out from among your
streams,
with all the fish sticking to your scales.
5I will leave you in the desert,
you and all the fish of your streams.
You will fall on the open field
and not be gathered or picked up.
I will give you as food
to the beasts of the earth and the birds
of the sky.

6Then all who live in Egypt will know that I
am the LORD.

"'You have been a staff of reed for the people of Israel. 7When they grasped you with
their hands, you splintered and you tore open
their shoulders; when they leaned on you, you
broke and their backs were wrenched.[a]
8"'Therefore this is what the Sovereign
LORD says: I will bring a sword against you
and kill both man and beast. 9Egypt will become a desolate wasteland. Then they will
know that I am the LORD.
"'Because you said, "The Nile is mine; I
made it," 10therefore I am against you and
against your streams, and I will make the
land of Egypt a ruin and a desolate waste
from Migdol to Aswan, as far as the border
of Cush.[b] 11The foot of neither man nor beast
will pass through it; no one will live there for
forty years. 12I will make the land of Egypt
desolate among devastated lands, and her
cities will lie desolate forty years among ruined cities. And I will disperse the Egyptians
among the nations and scatter them through
the countries.
13"'Yet this is what the Sovereign LORD says:
At the end of forty years I will gather the Egyptians from the nations where they were scattered. 14I will bring them back from captivity
and return them to Upper Egypt, the land of
their ancestry. There they will be a lowly kingdom. 15It will be the lowliest of kingdoms and
will never again exalt itself above the other
nations. I will make it so weak that it will never again rule over the nations. 16Egypt will no
longer be a source of confidence for the people
of Israel but will be a reminder of their sin in
turning to her for help. Then they will know
that I am the Sovereign LORD.'"

Nebuchadnezzar's Reward

17In the twenty-seventh year, in the first
month on the first day, the word of the LORD
came to me: 18"Son of man, Nebuchadnezzar
king of Babylon drove his army in a hard campaign against Tyre; every head was rubbed
bare and every shoulder made raw. Yet he and
his army got no reward from the campaign
he led against Tyre. 19Therefore this is what
the Sovereign LORD says: I am going to give
Egypt to Nebuchadnezzar king of Babylon,
and he will carry off its wealth. He will loot
and plunder the land as pay for his army. 20I
have given him Egypt as a reward for his efforts because he and his army did it for me,
declares the Sovereign LORD.
21"On that day I will make a horn[c] grow
for the Israelites, and I will open your mouth
among them. Then they will know that I am
the LORD."

A Lament Over Egypt

30 The word of the LORD came to me: 2"Son
of man, prophesy and say: 'This is what
the Sovereign LORD says:

"'Wail and say,
"Alas for that day!"
3For the day is near,
the day of the LORD is near—

[a] 7 Syriac (see also Septuagint and Vulgate); Hebrew *and you caused their backs to stand* [b] 10 That is, the upper Nile region [c] 21 *Horn* here symbolizes strength.

a day of clouds,
a time of doom for the nations.
4 A sword will come against Egypt,
and anguish will come upon Cush.[a]
When the slain fall in Egypt,
her wealth will be carried away
and her foundations torn down.

5 Cush and Libya, Lydia and all Arabia, Kub
and the people of the covenant land will fall
by the sword along with Egypt.

6 " 'This is what the LORD says:

" 'The allies of Egypt will fall
and her proud strength will fail.
From Migdol to Aswan
they will fall by the sword within her,
declares the Sovereign LORD.
7 " 'They will be desolate
among desolate lands,
and their cities will lie
among ruined cities.
8 Then they will know that I am the LORD,
when I set fire to Egypt
and all her helpers are crushed.

9 " 'On that day messengers will go out from
me in ships to frighten Cush out of her complacency. Anguish will take hold of them on
the day of Egypt's doom, for it is sure to come.

10 " 'This is what the Sovereign LORD says:

" 'I will put an end to the hordes of Egypt
by the hand of Nebuchadnezzar king of
Babylon.
11 He and his army—the most ruthless of
nations—
will be brought in to destroy the land.
They will draw their swords against Egypt
and fill the land with the slain.
12 I will dry up the waters of the Nile
and sell the land to an evil nation;
by the hand of foreigners
I will lay waste the land and everything
in it.

I the LORD have spoken.

13 " 'This is what the Sovereign LORD says:

" 'I will destroy the idols
and put an end to the images in
Memphis.
No longer will there be a prince in Egypt,
and I will spread fear throughout the
land.
14 I will lay waste Upper Egypt,
set fire to Zoan
and inflict punishment on Thebes.
15 I will pour out my wrath on Pelusium,
the stronghold of Egypt,
and wipe out the hordes of Thebes.
16 I will set fire to Egypt;
Pelusium will writhe in agony.
Thebes will be taken by storm;
Memphis will be in constant distress.
17 The young men of Heliopolis and Bubastis
will fall by the sword,
and the cities themselves will go into
captivity.
18 Dark will be the day at Tahpanhes
when I break the yoke of Egypt;
there her proud strength will come to
an end.
She will be covered with clouds,
and her villages will go into captivity.
19 So I will inflict punishment on Egypt,
and they will know that I am the LORD.' "

Pharaoh's Arms Are Broken

20 In the eleventh year, in the first month on
the seventh day, the word of the LORD came to
me: 21 "Son of man, I have broken the arm of
Pharaoh king of Egypt. It has not been bound
up to be healed or put in a splint so that it
may become strong enough to hold a sword.
22 Therefore this is what the Sovereign LORD
says: I am against Pharaoh king of Egypt. I
will break both his arms, the good arm as well
as the broken one, and make the sword fall
from his hand. 23 I will disperse the Egyptians
among the nations and scatter them through
the countries. 24 I will strengthen the arms of
the king of Babylon and put my sword in his
hand, but I will break the arms of Pharaoh,
and he will groan before him like a mortally
wounded man. 25 I will strengthen the arms of
the king of Babylon, but the arms of Pharaoh
will fall limp. Then they will know that I am
the LORD, when I put my sword into the hand
of the king of Babylon and he brandishes it
against Egypt. 26 I will disperse the Egyptians
among the nations and scatter them through
the countries. Then they will know that I am
the LORD."

Pharaoh as a Felled Cedar of Lebanon

31 In the eleventh year, in the third month
on the first day, the word of the LORD
came to me: 2 "Son of man, say to Pharaoh
king of Egypt and to his hordes:

" 'Who can be compared with you in
majesty?
3 Consider Assyria, once a cedar in
Lebanon,
with beautiful branches overshadowing
the forest;
it towered on high,
its top above the thick foliage.
4 The waters nourished it,
deep springs made it grow tall;
their streams flowed
all around its base
and sent their channels
to all the trees of the field.
5 So it towered higher
than all the trees of the field;
its boughs increased
and its branches grew long,
spreading because of abundant waters.
6 All the birds of the sky
nested in its boughs,
all the animals of the wild
gave birth under its branches;
all the great nations
lived in its shade.

[a] *4* That is, the upper Nile region; also in verses 5 and 9

7 It was majestic in beauty,
with its spreading boughs,
for its roots went down
to abundant waters.
8 The cedars in the garden of God
could not rival it,
nor could the junipers
equal its boughs,
nor could the plane trees
compare with its branches—
no tree in the garden of God
could match its beauty.
9 I made it beautiful
with abundant branches,
the envy of all the trees of Eden
in the garden of God.

10 " 'Therefore this is what the Sovereign
LORD says: Because the great cedar towered
over the thick foliage, and because it was
proud of its height, 11 I gave it into the hands
of the ruler of the nations, for him to deal with
according to its wickedness. I cast it aside,
12 and the most ruthless of foreign nations
cut it down and left it. Its boughs fell on the
mountains and in all the valleys; its branches
lay broken in all the ravines of the land. All
the nations of the earth came out from under
its shade and left it. 13 All the birds settled on
the fallen tree, and all the wild animals lived
among its branches. 14 Therefore no other
trees by the waters are ever to tower proudly
on high, lifting their tops above the thick foliage. No other trees so well-watered are ever
to reach such a height; they are all destined
for death, for the earth below, among mortals
who go down to the realm of the dead.
15 " 'This is what the Sovereign LORD says:
On the day it was brought down to the realm
of the dead I covered the deep springs with
mourning for it; I held back its streams, and
its abundant waters were restrained. Because
of it I clothed Lebanon with gloom, and all the
trees of the field withered away. 16 I made the
nations tremble at the sound of its fall when
I brought it down to the realm of the dead to
be with those who go down to the pit. Then
all the trees of Eden, the choicest and best of
Lebanon, the well-watered trees, were consoled in the earth below. 17 They too, like the
great cedar, had gone down to the realm of
the dead, to those killed by the sword, along
with the armed men who lived in its shade
among the nations.
18 " 'Which of the trees of Eden can be compared with you in splendor and majesty? Yet
you, too, will be brought down with the trees
of Eden to the earth below; you will lie among
the uncircumcised, with those killed by the
sword.
" 'This is Pharaoh and all his hordes, declares the Sovereign LORD.' "

A Lament Over Pharaoh

32 In the twelfth year, in the twelfth month
on the first day, the word of the LORD
came to me: 2 "Son of man, take up a lament
concerning Pharaoh king of Egypt and say
to him:

" 'You are like a lion among the nations;
you are like a monster in the seas
thrashing about in your streams,
churning the water with your feet
and muddying the streams.

3 " 'This is what the Sovereign LORD says:

" 'With a great throng of people
I will cast my net over you,
and they will haul you up in my net.
4 I will throw you on the land
and hurl you on the open field.
I will let all the birds of the sky settle on
you
and all the animals of the wild gorge
themselves on you.
5 I will spread your flesh on the mountains
and fill the valleys with your remains.
6 I will drench the land with your flowing
blood
all the way to the mountains,
and the ravines will be filled with your
flesh.
7 When I snuff you out, I will cover the
heavens
and darken their stars;
I will cover the sun with a cloud,
and the moon will not give its light.
8 All the shining lights in the heavens
I will darken over you;
I will bring darkness over your land,
declares the Sovereign LORD.
9 I will trouble the hearts of many peoples
when I bring about your destruction
among the nations,
among[a] lands you have not known.
10 I will cause many peoples to be appalled
at you,
and their kings will shudder with
horror because of you
when I brandish my sword before them.
On the day of your downfall
each of them will tremble
every moment for his life.

11 " 'For this is what the Sovereign LORD says:

" 'The sword of the king of Babylon
will come against you.
12 I will cause your hordes to fall
by the swords of mighty men—
the most ruthless of all nations.
They will shatter the pride of Egypt,
and all her hordes will be overthrown.
13 I will destroy all her cattle
from beside abundant waters
no longer to be stirred by the foot of man
or muddied by the hooves of cattle.
14 Then I will let her waters settle
and make her streams flow like oil,
declares the Sovereign LORD.
15 When I make Egypt desolate
and strip the land of everything in it,
when I strike down all who live there,
then they will know that I am the LORD.'

[a] 9 Hebrew; Septuagint *bring you into captivity among the nations, / to*

16“This is the lament they will chant for her.
The daughters of the nations will chant it; for
Egypt and all her hordes they will chant it,
declares the Sovereign LORD.”

Egypt’s Descent Into the Realm of the Dead

17In the twelfth year, on the fifteenth day of
the month, the word of the LORD came to me:
18“Son of man, wail for the hordes of Egypt
and consign to the earth below both her and
the daughters of mighty nations, along with
those who go down to the pit. 19Say to them,
‘Are you more favored than others? Go down
and be laid among the uncircumcised.’ 20They
will fall among those killed by the sword. The
sword is drawn; let her be dragged off with
all her hordes. 21From within the realm of the
dead the mighty leaders will say of Egypt and
her allies, ‘They have come down and they
lie with the uncircumcised, with those killed
by the sword.’

22“Assyria is there with her whole army; she
is surrounded by the graves of all her slain, all
who have fallen by the sword. 23Their graves
are in the depths of the pit and her army lies
around her grave. All who had spread terror
in the land of the living are slain, fallen by
the sword.

24“Elam is there, with all her hordes around
her grave. All of them are slain, fallen by the
sword. All who had spread terror in the land
of the living went down uncircumcised to the
earth below. They bear their shame with those
who go down to the pit. 25A bed is made for her
among the slain, with all her hordes around
her grave. All of them are uncircumcised,
killed by the sword. Because their terror had
spread in the land of the living, they bear their
shame with those who go down to the pit; they
are laid among the slain.

26“Meshek and Tubal are there, with all
their hordes around their graves. All of them
are uncircumcised, killed by the sword because they spread their terror in the land of
the living. 27But they do not lie with the fallen
warriors of old,[a] who went down to the realm
of the dead with their weapons of war—their
swords placed under their heads and their
shields[b] resting on their bones—though these
warriors also had terrorized the land of the
living.

28“You too, Pharaoh, will be broken and
will lie among the uncircumcised, with those
killed by the sword.

29“Edom is there, her kings and all her
princes; despite their power, they are laid
with those killed by the sword. They lie with
the uncircumcised, with those who go down
to the pit.

30“All the princes of the north and all the
Sidonians are there; they went down with the
slain in disgrace despite the terror caused by
their power. They lie uncircumcised with
those killed by the sword and bear their
shame with those who go down to the pit.

31“Pharaoh—he and all his army—will see
them and he will be consoled for all his hordes
that were killed by the sword, declares the
Sovereign LORD. 32Although I had him spread
terror in the land of the living, Pharaoh and all
his hordes will be laid among the uncircumcised, with those killed by the sword, declares
the Sovereign LORD.”

Renewal of Ezekiel’s Call as Watchman

33 The word of the LORD came to me: 2“Son
of man, speak to your people and say
to them: ‘When I bring the sword against a
land, and the people of the land choose one
of their men and make him their watchman,
3and he sees the sword coming against the
land and blows the trumpet to warn the people, 4then if anyone hears the trumpet but does
not heed the warning and the sword comes
and takes their life, their blood will be on their
own head. 5Since they heard the sound of the
trumpet but did not heed the warning, their
blood will be on their own head. If they had
heeded the warning, they would have saved
themselves. 6But if the watchman sees the
sword coming and does not blow the trumpet to warn the people and the sword comes
and takes someone’s life, that person’s life will
be taken because of their sin, but I will hold
the watchman accountable for their blood.’

7“Son of man, I have made you a watchman
for the people of Israel; so hear the word I
speak and give them warning from me. 8When
I say to the wicked, ‘You wicked person, you
will surely die,’ and you do not speak out to
dissuade them from their ways, that wicked
person will die for[c] their sin, and I will hold
you accountable for their blood. 9But if you
do warn the wicked person to turn from their
ways and they do not do so, they will die for
their sin, though you yourself will be saved.

10“Son of man, say to the Israelites, ‘This is
what you are saying: “Our offenses and sins
weigh us down, and we are wasting away
because of[d] them. How then can we live?”’
11Say to them, ‘As surely as I live, declares
the Sovereign LORD, I take no pleasure in
the death of the wicked, but rather that they
turn from their ways and live. Turn! Turn
from your evil ways! Why will you die, people of Israel?’

12“Therefore, son of man, say to your people, ‘If someone who is righteous disobeys,
that person’s former righteousness will count
for nothing. And if someone who is wicked
repents, that person’s former wickedness will
not bring condemnation. The righteous person who sins will not be allowed to live even
though they were formerly righteous.’ 13If I tell
a righteous person that they will surely live,
but then they trust in their righteousness and
do evil, none of the righteous things that person has done will be remembered; they will
die for the evil they have done. 14And if I say to
a wicked person, ‘You will surely die,’ but they
then turn away from their sin and do what is
just and right— 15if they give back what they

[a] 27 Septuagint; Hebrew *warriors who were uncircumcised* [b] 27 Probable reading of the original Hebrew text; Masoretic Text *punishment* [c] 8 Or *in*; also in verse 9 [d] 10 Or *away in*

took in pledge for a loan, return what they
have stolen, follow the decrees that give life,
and do no evil—that person will surely live;
they will not die. 16None of the sins that person
has committed will be remembered against
them. They have done what is just and right;
they will surely live.
17"Yet your people say, 'The way of the Lord
is not just.' But it is their way that is not just.
18If a righteous person turns from their righteousness and does evil, they will die for it.
19And if a wicked person turns away from
their wickedness and does what is just and
right, they will live by doing so. 20Yet you Israelites say, 'The way of the Lord is not just.'
But I will judge each of you according to your
own ways."

Jerusalem's Fall Explained

21In the twelfth year of our exile, in the tenth
month on the fifth day, a man who had escaped from Jerusalem came to me and said,
"The city has fallen!" 22Now the evening before the man arrived, the hand of the LORD
was on me, and he opened my mouth before
the man came to me in the morning. So my
mouth was opened and I was no longer silent.
23Then the word of the LORD came to me:
24"Son of man, the people living in those ruins
in the land of Israel are saying, 'Abraham was
only one man, yet he possessed the land. But
we are many; surely the land has been given
to us as our possession.' 25Therefore say to
them, 'This is what the Sovereign LORD says:
Since you eat meat with the blood still in it
and look to your idols and shed blood, should
you then possess the land? 26You rely on your
sword, you do detestable things, and each of
you defiles his neighbor's wife. Should you
then possess the land?'
27"Say this to them: 'This is what the Sovereign LORD says: As surely as I live, those
who are left in the ruins will fall by the sword,
those out in the country I will give to the wild
animals to be devoured, and those in strongholds and caves will die of a plague. 28I will
make the land a desolate waste, and her proud
strength will come to an end, and the mountains of Israel will become desolate so that no
one will cross them. 29Then they will know
that I am the LORD, when I have made the land
a desolate waste because of all the detestable
things they have done.'
30"As for you, son of man, your people are
talking together about you by the walls and
at the doors of the houses, saying to each
other, 'Come and hear the message that has
come from the LORD.' 31My people come to
you, as they usually do, and sit before you
to hear your words, but they do not put them
into practice. Their mouths speak of love, but
their hearts are greedy for unjust gain. 32In-
deed, to them you are nothing more than one
who sings love songs with a beautiful voice
and plays an instrument well, for they hear
your words but do not put them into practice.
33"When all this comes true—and it surely
will—then they will know that a prophet has
been among them."

The LORD Will Be Israel's Shepherd

34 The word of the LORD came to me:
2"Son of man, prophesy against the
shepherds of Israel; prophesy and say to
them: 'This is what the Sovereign LORD says:
Woe to you shepherds of Israel who only take
care of yourselves! Should not shepherds take
care of the flock? 3You eat the curds, clothe
yourselves with the wool and slaughter the
choice animals, but you do not take care of
the flock. 4You have not strengthened the
weak or healed the sick or bound up the injured. You have not brought back the strays
or searched for the lost. You have ruled them
harshly and brutally. 5So they were scattered
because there was no shepherd, and when
they were scattered they became food for all
the wild animals. 6My sheep wandered over
all the mountains and on every high hill. They
were scattered over the whole earth, and no
one searched or looked for them.
7" 'Therefore, you shepherds, hear the word
of the LORD: 8As surely as I live, declares the
Sovereign LORD, because my flock lacks a
shepherd and so has been plundered and has
become food for all the wild animals, and because my shepherds did not search for my
flock but cared for themselves rather than for
my flock, 9therefore, you shepherds, hear the
word of the LORD: 10This is what the Sovereign
LORD says: I am against the shepherds and
will hold them accountable for my flock. I will
remove them from tending the flock so that
the shepherds can no longer feed themselves.
I will rescue my flock from their mouths, and
it will no longer be food for them.
11" 'For this is what the Sovereign LORD says:
I myself will search for my sheep and look
after them. 12As a shepherd looks after his
scattered flock when he is with them, so will
I look after my sheep. I will rescue them from
all the places where they were scattered on a
day of clouds and darkness. 13I will bring them
out from the nations and gather them from the
countries, and I will bring them into their own
land. I will pasture them on the mountains of
Israel, in the ravines and in all the settlements
in the land. 14I will tend them in a good pasture, and the mountain heights of Israel will
be their grazing land. There they will lie down
in good grazing land, and there they will feed
in a rich pasture on the mountains of Israel.
15I myself will tend my sheep and have them
lie down, declares the Sovereign LORD. 16I will
search for the lost and bring back the strays.
I will bind up the injured and strengthen the
weak, but the sleek and the strong I will destroy. I will shepherd the flock with justice.
17" 'As for you, my flock, this is what the
Sovereign LORD says: I will judge between
one sheep and another, and between rams
and goats. 18Is it not enough for you to feed
on the good pasture? Must you also trample
the rest of your pasture with your feet? Is it
not enough for you to drink clear water? Must
you also muddy the rest with your feet? 19Must
my flock feed on what you have trampled and
drink what you have muddied with your feet?
20" 'Therefore this is what the Sovereign

LORD says to them: See, I myself will judge between the fat sheep and the lean sheep. 21Be-
cause you shove with flank and shoulder, butt-
ing all the weak sheep with your horns until
you have driven them away, 22I will save my
flock, and they will no longer be plundered.
I will judge between one sheep and another.
23I will place over them one shepherd, my servant David, and he will tend them; he will tend
them and be their shepherd. 24I the LORD will
be their God, and my servant David will be
prince among them. I the LORD have spoken.
25"'I will make a covenant of peace with
them and rid the land of savage beasts so that
they may live in the wilderness and sleep in
the forests in safety. 26I will make them and
the places surrounding my hill a blessing.[a] I
will send down showers in season; there will
be showers of blessing. 27The trees will yield
their fruit and the ground will yield its crops;
the people will be secure in their land. They
will know that I am the LORD, when I break
the bars of their yoke and rescue them from
the hands of those who enslaved them. 28They
will no longer be plundered by the nations, nor
will wild animals devour them. They will live
in safety, and no one will make them afraid.
29I will provide for them a land renowned for
its crops, and they will no longer be victims
of famine in the land or bear the scorn of the
nations. 30Then they will know that I, the LORD
their God, am with them and that they, the
Israelites, are my people, declares the Sovereign LORD. 31You are my sheep, the sheep of
my pasture, and I am your God, declares the
Sovereign LORD.'"

A Prophecy Against Edom

35 The word of the LORD came to me: 2"Son
of man, set your face against Mount
Seir; prophesy against it 3and say: 'This is
what the Sovereign LORD says: I am against
you, Mount Seir, and I will stretch out my
hand against you and make you a desolate
waste. 4I will turn your towns into ruins and
you will be desolate. Then you will know that
I am the LORD.
5"'Because you harbored an ancient hostility and delivered the Israelites over to the
sword at the time of their calamity, the time
their punishment reached its climax, 6there-
fore as surely as I live, declares the Sovereign LORD, I will give you over to bloodshed
and it will pursue you. Since you did not hate
bloodshed, bloodshed will pursue you. 7I will
make Mount Seir a desolate waste and cut off
from it all who come and go. 8I will fill your
mountains with the slain; those killed by the
sword will fall on your hills and in your valleys and in all your ravines. 9I will make you
desolate forever; your towns will not be inhabited. Then you will know that I am the LORD.
10"'Because you have said, "These two nations and countries will be ours and we will
take possession of them," even though I the
LORD was there, 11therefore as surely as I live,
declares the Sovereign LORD, I will treat you
in accordance with the anger and jealousy you
showed in your hatred of them and I will make
myself known among them when I judge you.
12Then you will know that I the LORD have
heard all the contemptible things you have
said against the mountains of Israel. You said,
"They have been laid waste and have been giv-
en over to us to devour." 13You boasted against
me and spoke against me without restraint,
and I heard it. 14This is what the Sovereign
LORD says: While the whole earth rejoices,
I will make you desolate. 15Because you rejoiced when the inheritance of Israel became
desolate, that is how I will treat you. You will
be desolate, Mount Seir, you and all of Edom.
Then they will know that I am the LORD.'"

Hope for the Mountains of Israel

36 "Son of man, prophesy to the mountains
of Israel and say, 'Mountains of Israel, hear the word of the LORD. 2This is what
the Sovereign LORD says: The enemy said of
you, "Aha! The ancient heights have become
our possession."' 3Therefore prophesy and
say, 'This is what the Sovereign LORD says:
Because they ravaged and crushed you from
every side so that you became the possession
of the rest of the nations and the object of
people's malicious talk and slander, 4there-
fore, mountains of Israel, hear the word of the
Sovereign LORD: This is what the Sovereign
LORD says to the mountains and hills, to the
ravines and valleys, to the desolate ruins and
the deserted towns that have been plundered
and ridiculed by the rest of the nations around
you— 5this is what the Sovereign LORD says:
In my burning zeal I have spoken against the
rest of the nations, and against all Edom, for
with glee and with malice in their hearts they
made my land their own possession so that
they might plunder its pastureland.' 6There-
fore prophesy concerning the land of Israel
and say to the mountains and hills, to the ravines and valleys: 'This is what the Sovereign LORD says: I speak in my jealous wrath
because you have suffered the scorn of the
nations. 7Therefore this is what the Sovereign
LORD says: I swear with uplifted hand that
the nations around you will also suffer scorn.
8"'But you, mountains of Israel, will produce branches and fruit for my people Israel,
for they will soon come home. 9I am concerned
for you and will look on you with favor; you
will be plowed and sown, 10and I will cause
many people to live on you—yes, all of Israel. The towns will be inhabited and the ruins
rebuilt. 11I will increase the number of people
and animals living on you, and they will be
fruitful and become numerous. I will settle
people on you as in the past and will make you
prosper more than before. Then you will know
that I am the LORD. 12I will cause people, my
people Israel, to live on you. They will possess
you, and you will be their inheritance; you will
never again deprive them of their children.

[a] 26 Or *I will cause them and the places surrounding my hill to be named in blessings* (see Gen. 48:20); or *I will cause them and the places surrounding my hill to be seen as blessed*

13“‘This is what the Sovereign LORD says:
Because some say to you, “You devour people and deprive your nation of its children,”
14therefore you will no longer devour people
or make your nation childless, declares the
Sovereign LORD. 15No longer will I make you
hear the taunts of the nations, and no longer will you suffer the scorn of the peoples
or cause your nation to fall, declares the Sovereign LORD.’”

Israel's Restoration Assured

16Again the word of the LORD came to me:
17“Son of man, when the people of Israel were
living in their own land, they defiled it by their
conduct and their actions. Their conduct was
like a woman's monthly uncleanness in my
sight. 18So I poured out my wrath on them because they had shed blood in the land and because they had defiled it with their idols. 19I dispersed them among the nations, and they were
scattered through the countries; I judged them
according to their conduct and their actions.
20And wherever they went among the nations
they profaned my holy name, for it was said
of them, ‘These are the LORD's people, and yet
they had to leave his land.’ 21I had concern for
my holy name, which the people of Israel profaned among the nations where they had gone.

22“Therefore say to the Israelites, ‘This is
what the Sovereign LORD says: It is not for
your sake, people of Israel, that I am going to
do these things, but for the sake of my holy
name, which you have profaned among the
nations where you have gone. 23I will show
the holiness of my great name, which has
been profaned among the nations, the name
you have profaned among them. Then the nations will know that I am the LORD, declares
the Sovereign LORD, when I am proved holy
through you before their eyes.

24“‘For I will take you out of the nations;
I will gather you from all the countries and
bring you back into your own land. 25I will
sprinkle clean water on you, and you will be
clean; I will cleanse you from all your impurities and from all your idols. 26I will give you
a new heart and put a new spirit in you; I will
remove from you your heart of stone and give
you a heart of flesh. 27And I will put my Spirit in you and move you to follow my decrees
and be careful to keep my laws. 28Then you
will live in the land I gave your ancestors;
you will be my people, and I will be your God.
29I will save you from all your uncleanness.
I will call for the grain and make it plentiful
and will not bring famine upon you. 30I will
increase the fruit of the trees and the crops
of the field, so that you will no longer suffer
disgrace among the nations because of famine. 31Then you will remember your evil ways
and wicked deeds, and you will loathe yourselves for your sins and detestable practices.
32I want you to know that I am not doing this
for your sake, declares the Sovereign LORD.
Be ashamed and disgraced for your conduct,
people of Israel!

33“‘This is what the Sovereign LORD says:
On the day I cleanse you from all your sins,
I will resettle your towns, and the ruins will
be rebuilt. 34The desolate land will be cultivated instead of lying desolate in the sight
of all who pass through it. 35They will say,
“This land that was laid waste has become
like the garden of Eden; the cities that were
lying in ruins, desolate and destroyed, are
now fortified and inhabited.” 36Then the nations around you that remain will know that
I the LORD have rebuilt what was destroyed
and have replanted what was desolate. I the
LORD have spoken, and I will do it.’

37“This is what the Sovereign LORD says:
Once again I will yield to Israel's plea and do
this for them: I will make their people as numerous as sheep, 38as numerous as the flocks
for offerings at Jerusalem during her appointed festivals. So will the ruined cities be filled
with flocks of people. Then they will know
that I am the LORD.”

The Valley of Dry Bones

37 The hand of the LORD was on me, and
he brought me out by the Spirit of the
LORD and set me in the middle of a valley; it
was full of bones. 2He led me back and forth
among them, and I saw a great many bones
on the floor of the valley, bones that were very
dry. 3He asked me, “Son of man, can these
bones live?”

I said, “Sovereign LORD, you alone know.”

4Then he said to me, “Prophesy to these
bones and say to them, ‘Dry bones, hear the
word of the LORD! 5This is what the Sovereign
LORD says to these bones: I will make breath[a]
enter you, and you will come to life. 6I will
attach tendons to you and make flesh come
upon you and cover you with skin; I will put
breath in you, and you will come to life. Then
you will know that I am the LORD.’”

7So I prophesied as I was commanded. And
as I was prophesying, there was a noise, a
rattling sound, and the bones came together,
bone to bone. 8I looked, and tendons and flesh
appeared on them and skin covered them, but
there was no breath in them.

9Then he said to me, “Prophesy to the
breath; prophesy, son of man, and say to it,
‘This is what the Sovereign LORD says: Come,
breath, from the four winds and breathe into
these slain, that they may live.’” 10So I prophesied as he commanded me, and breath entered
them; they came to life and stood up on their
feet—a vast army.

11Then he said to me: “Son of man, these
bones are the people of Israel. They say, ‘Our
bones are dried up and our hope is gone; we
are cut off.’ 12Therefore prophesy and say to
them: ‘This is what the Sovereign LORD says:
My people, I am going to open your graves and
bring you up from them; I will bring you back
to the land of Israel. 13Then you, my people,
will know that I am the LORD, when I open
your graves and bring you up from them. 14I
will put my Spirit in you and you will live, and

[a] 5 The Hebrew for this word can also mean *wind* or *spirit* (see verses 6-14).

I will settle you in your own land. Then you will know that I the LORD have spoken, and I have done it, declares the LORD.'"

One Nation Under One King

15The word of the LORD came to me: 16"Son of man, take a stick of wood and write on it, 'Belonging to Judah and the Israelites associated with him.' Then take another stick of wood, and write on it, 'Belonging to Joseph (that is, to Ephraim) and all the Israelites associated with him.' 17Join them together into one stick so that they will become one in your hand.

18"When your people ask you, 'Won't you tell us what you mean by this?' 19say to them, 'This is what the Sovereign LORD says: I am going to take the stick of Joseph—which is in Ephraim's hand—and of the Israelite tribes associated with him, and join it to Judah's stick. I will make them into a single stick of wood, and they will become one in my hand.' 20Hold before their eyes the sticks you have written on 21and say to them, 'This is what the Sovereign LORD says: I will take the Israelites out of the nations where they have gone. I will gather them from all around and bring them back into their own land. 22I will make them one nation in the land, on the mountains of Israel. There will be one king over all of them and they will never again be two nations or be divided into two kingdoms. 23They will no longer defile themselves with their idols and vile images or with any of their offenses, for I will save them from all their sinful backsliding,[a] and I will cleanse them. They will be my people, and I will be their God.

24" 'My servant David will be king over them, and they will all have one shepherd. They will follow my laws and be careful to keep my decrees. 25They will live in the land I gave to my servant Jacob, the land where your ancestors lived. They and their children and their children's children will live there forever, and David my servant will be their prince forever. 26I will make a covenant of peace with them; it will be an everlasting covenant. I will establish them and increase their numbers, and I will put my sanctuary among them forever. 27My dwelling place will be with them; I will be their God, and they will be my people. 28Then the nations will know that I the LORD make Israel holy, when my sanctuary is among them forever.'"

The LORD's Great Victory Over the Nations

38 The word of the LORD came to me: 2"Son of man, set your face against Gog, of the land of Magog, the chief prince of[b] Meshek and Tubal; prophesy against him 3and say: 'This is what the Sovereign LORD says: I am against you, Gog, chief prince of[c] Meshek and Tubal. 4I will turn you around, put hooks in your jaws and bring you out with your whole army—your horses, your horsemen fully armed, and a great horde with large and small shields, all of them brandishing their swords. 5Persia, Cush[d] and Put will be with them, all with shields and helmets, 6also Gomer with all its troops, and Beth Togarmah from the far north with all its troops—the many nations with you.

7" 'Get ready; be prepared, you and all the hordes gathered about you, and take command of them. 8After many days you will be called to arms. In future years you will invade a land that has recovered from war, whose people were gathered from many nations to the mountains of Israel, which had long been desolate. They had been brought out from the nations, and now all of them live in safety. 9You and all your troops and the many nations with you will go up, advancing like a storm; you will be like a cloud covering the land.

10" 'This is what the Sovereign LORD says: On that day thoughts will come into your mind and you will devise an evil scheme. 11You will say, "I will invade a land of unwalled villages; I will attack a peaceful and unsuspecting people—all of them living without walls and without gates and bars. 12I will plunder and loot and turn my hand against the resettled ruins and the people gathered from the nations, rich in livestock and goods, living at the center of the land.[e]" 13Sheba and Dedan and the merchants of Tarshish and all her villages[f] will say to you, "Have you come to plunder? Have you gathered your hordes to loot, to carry off silver and gold, to take away livestock and goods and to seize much plunder?"'

14"Therefore, son of man, prophesy and say to Gog: 'This is what the Sovereign LORD says: In that day, when my people Israel are living in safety, will you not take notice of it? 15You will come from your place in the far north, you and many nations with you, all of them riding on horses, a great horde, a mighty army. 16You will advance against my people Israel like a cloud that covers the land. In days to come, Gog, I will bring you against my land, so that the nations may know me when I am proved holy through you before their eyes.

17" 'This is what the Sovereign LORD says: You are the one I spoke of in former days by my servants the prophets of Israel. At that time they prophesied for years that I would bring you against them. 18This is what will happen in that day: When Gog attacks the land of Israel, my hot anger will be aroused, declares the Sovereign LORD. 19In my zeal and fiery wrath I declare that at that time there shall be a great earthquake in the land of Israel. 20The fish in the sea, the birds in the sky, the beasts of the field, every creature that moves along the ground, and all the people on the face of the earth will tremble at my presence. The mountains will be overturned, the cliffs will crumble and every wall will fall to

[a] 23 Many Hebrew manuscripts (see also Septuagint); most Hebrew manuscripts *all their dwelling places where they sinned* [b] 2 Or *the prince of Rosh,* [c] 3 Or *Gog, prince of Rosh,* [d] 5 That is, the upper Nile region [e] 12 The Hebrew for this phrase means *the navel of the earth.* [f] 13 Or *her strong lions*

the ground. 21I will summon a sword against
Gog on all my mountains, declares the Sovereign LORD. Every man's sword will be against
his brother. 22I will execute judgment on him
with plague and bloodshed; I will pour down
torrents of rain, hailstones and burning sulfur on him and on his troops and on the many
nations with him. 23And so I will show my
greatness and my holiness, and I will make
myself known in the sight of many nations.
Then they will know that I am the LORD.'

39 "Son of man, prophesy against Gog and
say: 'This is what the Sovereign LORD
says: I am against you, Gog, chief prince of[a]
Meshek and Tubal. 2I will turn you around
and drag you along. I will bring you from the
far north and send you against the mountains
of Israel. 3Then I will strike your bow from
your left hand and make your arrows drop
from your right hand. 4On the mountains of
Israel you will fall, you and all your troops and
the nations with you. I will give you as food
to all kinds of carrion birds and to the wild
animals. 5You will fall in the open field, for
I have spoken, declares the Sovereign LORD.
6I will send fire on Magog and on those who
live in safety in the coastlands, and they will
know that I am the LORD.

7" 'I will make known my holy name among
my people Israel. I will no longer let my holy
name be profaned, and the nations will know
that I the LORD am the Holy One in Israel. 8It
is coming! It will surely take place, declares
the Sovereign LORD. This is the day I have
spoken of.

9" 'Then those who live in the towns of
Israel will go out and use the weapons for
fuel and burn them up—the small and large
shields, the bows and arrows, the war clubs
and spears. For seven years they will use them
for fuel. 10They will not need to gather wood
from the fields or cut it from the forests, because they will use the weapons for fuel. And
they will plunder those who plundered them
and loot those who looted them, declares the
Sovereign LORD.

11" 'On that day I will give Gog a burial place
in Israel, in the valley of those who travel east
of the Sea. It will block the way of travelers,
because Gog and all his hordes will be buried there. So it will be called the Valley of
Hamon Gog.[b]

12" 'For seven months the Israelites will be
burying them in order to cleanse the land.
13All the people of the land will bury them,
and the day I display my glory will be a mem-
orable day for them, declares the Sovereign
LORD. 14People will be continually employed
in cleansing the land. They will spread out
across the land and, along with others, they
will bury any bodies that are lying on the
ground.

" 'After the seven months they will carry out
a more detailed search. 15As they go through
the land, anyone who sees a human bone will
leave a marker beside it until the gravediggers
bury it in the Valley of Hamon Gog, 16near
a town called Hamonah.[c] And so they will
cleanse the land.'

17"Son of man, this is what the Sovereign
LORD says: Call out to every kind of bird and
all the wild animals: 'Assemble and come together from all around to the sacrifice I am
preparing for you, the great sacrifice on the
mountains of Israel. There you will eat flesh
and drink blood. 18You will eat the flesh of
mighty men and drink the blood of the princes
of the earth as if they were rams and lambs,
goats and bulls—all of them fattened animals
from Bashan. 19At the sacrifice I am preparing for you, you will eat fat till you are glutted
and drink blood till you are drunk. 20At my
table you will eat your fill of horses and riders, mighty men and soldiers of every kind,'
declares the Sovereign LORD.

21"I will display my glory among the nations, and all the nations will see the punishment I inflict and the hand I lay on them.
22From that day forward the people of Israel
will know that I am the LORD their God. 23And
the nations will know that the people of Israel
went into exile for their sin, because they were
unfaithful to me. So I hid my face from them
and handed them over to their enemies, and
they all fell by the sword. 24I dealt with them
according to their uncleanness and their offenses, and I hid my face from them.

25"Therefore this is what the Sovereign
LORD says: I will now restore the fortunes of
Jacob[d] and will have compassion on all the
people of Israel, and I will be zealous for my
holy name. 26They will forget their shame and
all the unfaithfulness they showed toward me
when they lived in safety in their land with
no one to make them afraid. 27When I have
brought them back from the nations and have
gathered them from the countries of their enemies, I will be proved holy through them in
the sight of many nations. 28Then they will
know that I am the LORD their God, for though
I sent them into exile among the nations, I will
gather them to their own land, not leaving any
behind. 29I will no longer hide my face from
them, for I will pour out my Spirit on the people of Israel, declares the Sovereign LORD."

The Temple Area Restored

40 In the twenty-fifth year of our exile, at
the beginning of the year, on the tenth
of the month, in the fourteenth year after the
fall of the city—on that very day the hand of
the LORD was on me and he took me there. 2In
visions of God he took me to the land of Israel
and set me on a very high mountain, on whose
south side were some buildings that looked
like a city. 3He took me there, and I saw a man
whose appearance was like bronze; he was
standing in the gateway with a linen cord and
a measuring rod in his hand. 4The man said
to me, "Son of man, look carefully and listen
closely and pay attention to everything I am
going to show you, for that is why you have

[a] 1 Or *Gog, prince of Rosh,* [b] 11 *Hamon Gog* means *hordes of Gog.* [c] 16 *Hamonah* means *horde.*
[d] 25 Or *now bring Jacob back from captivity*

been brought here. Tell the people of Israel everything you see."

The East Gate to the Outer Court

5 I saw a wall completely surrounding the temple area. The length of the measuring rod in the man's hand was six long cubits,[a] each of which was a cubit and a handbreadth. He measured the wall; it was one measuring rod thick and one rod high.

6 Then he went to the east gate. He climbed its steps and measured the threshold of the gate; it was one rod deep. 7 The alcoves for the guards were one rod long and one rod wide, and the projecting walls between the alcoves were five cubits[b] thick. And the threshold of the gate next to the portico facing the temple was one rod deep.

8 Then he measured the portico of the gateway; 9 it[c] was eight cubits[d] deep and its jambs were two cubits[e] thick. The portico of the gateway faced the temple.

10 Inside the east gate were three alcoves on each side; the three had the same measurements, and the faces of the projecting walls on each side had the same measurements. 11 Then he measured the width of the entrance of the gateway; it was ten cubits and its length was thirteen cubits.[f] 12 In front of each alcove was a wall one cubit high, and the alcoves were six cubits square. 13 Then he measured the gateway from the top of the rear wall of one alcove to the top of the opposite one; the distance was twenty-five cubits[g] from one parapet opening to the opposite one. 14 He measured along the faces of the projecting walls all around the inside of the gateway—sixty cubits.[h] The measurement was up to the portico[i] facing the courtyard.[j] 15 The distance from the entrance of the gateway to the far end of its portico was fifty cubits.[k] 16 The alcoves and the projecting walls inside the gateway were surmounted by narrow parapet openings all around, as was the portico; the openings all around faced inward. The faces of the projecting walls were decorated with palm trees.

The Outer Court

17 Then he brought me into the outer court. There I saw some rooms and a pavement that had been constructed all around the court; there were thirty rooms along the pavement. 18 It abutted the sides of the gateways and was as wide as they were long; this was the lower pavement. 19 Then he measured the distance from the inside of the lower gateway to the outside of the inner court; it was a hundred cubits[l] on the east side as well as on the north.

The North Gate

20 Then he measured the length and width of the north gate, leading into the outer court. 21 Its alcoves—three on each side—its projecting walls and its portico had the same measurements as those of the first gateway. It was fifty cubits long and twenty-five cubits wide. 22 Its openings, its portico and its palm tree decorations had the same measurements as those of the gate facing east. Seven steps led up to it, with its portico opposite them. 23 There was a gate to the inner court facing the north gate, just as there was on the east. He measured from one gate to the opposite one; it was a hundred cubits.

The South Gate

24 Then he led me to the south side and I saw the south gate. He measured its jambs and its portico, and they had the same measurements as the others. 25 The gateway and its portico had narrow openings all around, like the openings of the others. It was fifty cubits long and twenty-five cubits wide. 26 Seven steps led up to it, with its portico opposite them; it had palm tree decorations on the faces of the projecting walls on each side. 27 The inner court also had a gate facing south, and he measured from this gate to the outer gate on the south side; it was a hundred cubits.

The Gates to the Inner Court

28 Then he brought me into the inner court through the south gate, and he measured the south gate; it had the same measurements as the others. 29 Its alcoves, its projecting walls and its portico had the same measurements as the others. The gateway and its portico had openings all around. It was fifty cubits long and twenty-five cubits wide. 30 (The porticoes of the gateways around the inner court were twenty-five cubits wide and five cubits deep.) 31 Its portico faced the outer court; palm trees decorated its jambs, and eight steps led up to it.

32 Then he brought me to the inner court on the east side, and he measured the gateway; it had the same measurements as the others. 33 Its alcoves, its projecting walls and its portico had the same measurements as the others. The gateway and its portico had openings all around. It was fifty cubits long and twenty-five cubits wide. 34 Its portico faced the outer court; palm trees decorated the jambs on either side, and eight steps led up to it.

35 Then he brought me to the north gate and measured it. It had the same measurements as the others, 36 as did its alcoves, its projecting walls and its portico, and it had openings all

[a] *5* That is, about 11 feet or about 3.2 meters; also in verse 12. The long cubit of about 21 inches or about 53 centimeters is the basic unit of measurement of length throughout chapters 40–48. [b] *7* That is, about 8 3/4 feet or about 2.7 meters; also in verse 48 [c] *8,9* Many Hebrew manuscripts, Septuagint, Vulgate and Syriac; most Hebrew manuscripts *gateway facing the temple; it was one rod deep. 9Then he measured the portico of the gateway; it* [d] *9* That is, about 14 feet or about 4.2 meters [e] *9* That is, about 3 1/2 feet or about 1 meter [f] *11* That is, about 18 feet wide and 23 feet long or about 5.3 meters wide and 6.9 meters long [g] *13* That is, about 44 feet or about 13 meters; also in verses 21, 25, 29, 30, 33 and 36 [h] *14* That is, about 105 feet or about 32 meters [i] *14* Septuagint; Hebrew *projecting wall* [j] *14* The meaning of the Hebrew for this verse is uncertain. [k] *15* That is, about 88 feet or about 27 meters; also in verses 21, 25, 29, 33 and 36 [l] *19* That is, about 175 feet or about 53 meters; also in verses 23, 27 and 47

around. It was fifty cubits long and twenty-five cubits wide. 37 Its portico[a] faced the outer court; palm trees decorated the jambs on either side, and eight steps led up to it.

The Rooms for Preparing Sacrifices

38 A room with a doorway was by the portico in each of the inner gateways, where the burnt offerings were washed. 39 In the portico of the gateway were two tables on each side, on which the burnt offerings, sin offerings[b] and guilt offerings were slaughtered. 40 By the outside wall of the portico of the gateway, near the steps at the entrance of the north gateway were two tables, and on the other side of the steps were two tables. 41 So there were four tables on one side of the gateway and four on the other—eight tables in all—on which the sacrifices were slaughtered. 42 There were also four tables of dressed stone for the burnt offerings, each a cubit and a half long, a cubit and a half wide and a cubit high.[c] On them were placed the utensils for slaughtering the burnt offerings and the other sacrifices. 43 And double-pronged hooks, each a handbreadth[d] long, were attached to the wall all around. The tables were for the flesh of the offerings.

The Rooms for the Priests

44 Outside the inner gate, within the inner court, were two rooms, one[e] at the side of the north gate and facing south, and another at the side of the south[f] gate and facing north. 45 He said to me, "The room facing south is for the priests who guard the temple, 46 and the room facing north is for the priests who guard the altar. These are the sons of Zadok, who are the only Levites who may draw near to the LORD to minister before him."

47 Then he measured the court: It was square—a hundred cubits long and a hundred cubits wide. And the altar was in front of the temple.

The New Temple

48 He brought me to the portico of the temple and measured the jambs of the portico; they were five cubits wide on either side. The width of the entrance was fourteen cubits[g] and its projecting walls were[h] three cubits[i] wide on either side. 49 The portico was twenty cubits[j] wide, and twelve[k] cubits[l] from front to back. It was reached by a flight of stairs,[m] and there were pillars on each side of the jambs.

41 Then the man brought me to the main hall and measured the jambs; the width of the jambs was six cubits[n] on each side.[o] 2 The entrance was ten cubits[p] wide, and the projecting walls on each side of it were five cubits[q] wide. He also measured the main hall; it was forty cubits long and twenty cubits wide.[r]

3 Then he went into the inner sanctuary and measured the jambs of the entrance; each was two cubits[s] wide. The entrance was six cubits wide, and the projecting walls on each side of it were seven cubits[t] wide. 4 And he measured the length of the inner sanctuary; it was twenty cubits, and its width was twenty cubits across the end of the main hall. He said to me, "This is the Most Holy Place."

5 Then he measured the wall of the temple; it was six cubits thick, and each side room around the temple was four cubits[u] wide. 6 The side rooms were on three levels, one above another, thirty on each level. There were ledges all around the wall of the temple to serve as supports for the side rooms, so that the supports were not inserted into the wall of the temple. 7 The side rooms all around the temple were wider at each successive level. The structure surrounding the temple was built in ascending stages, so that the rooms widened as one went upward. A stairway went up from the lowest floor to the top floor through the middle floor.

8 I saw that the temple had a raised base all around it, forming the foundation of the side rooms. It was the length of the rod, six long cubits. 9 The outer wall of the side rooms was five cubits thick. The open area between the side rooms of the temple 10 and the priests' rooms was twenty cubits wide all around the temple. 11 There were entrances to the side rooms from the open area, one on the north and another on the south; and the base adjoining the open area was five cubits wide all around.

12 The building facing the temple courtyard on the west side was seventy cubits[v] wide. The wall of the building was five cubits thick all around, and its length was ninety cubits.[w]

13 Then he measured the temple; it was a hundred cubits[x] long, and the temple courtyard and the building with its walls were also a hundred cubits long. 14 The width of the temple courtyard on the east, including the front of the temple, was a hundred cubits.

15 Then he measured the length of the building facing the courtyard at the rear of the

[a] *37* Septuagint (see also verses 31 and 34); Hebrew *jambs* [b] *39* Or *purification offerings* [c] *42* That is, about 2 2/3 feet long and wide and 21 inches high or about 80 centimeters long and wide and 53 centimeters high [d] *43* That is, about 3 1/2 inches or about 9 centimeters [e] *44* Septuagint; Hebrew *were rooms for singers, which were* [f] *44* Septuagint; Hebrew *east* [g] *48* That is, about 25 feet or about 7.4 meters [h] *48* Septuagint; Hebrew *entrance was* [i] *48* That is, about 5 1/4 feet or about 1.6 meters [j] *49* That is, about 35 feet or about 11 meters [k] *49* Septuagint; Hebrew *eleven* [l] *49* That is, about 21 feet or about 6.4 meters [m] *49* Hebrew; Septuagint *Ten steps led up to it* [n] *1* That is, about 11 feet or about 3.2 meters; also in verses 3, 5 and 8 [o] *1* One Hebrew manuscript and Septuagint; most Hebrew manuscripts *side, the width of the tent* [p] *2* That is, about 18 feet or about 5.3 meters [q] *2* That is, about 8 3/4 feet or about 2.7 meters; also in verses 9, 11 and 12 [r] *2* That is, about 70 feet long and 35 feet wide or about 21 meters long and 11 meters wide [s] *3* That is, about 3 1/2 feet or about 1.1 meters; also in verse 22 [t] *3* That is, about 12 feet or about 3.7 meters [u] *5* That is, about 7 feet or about 2.1 meters [v] *12* That is, about 123 feet or about 37 meters [w] *12* That is, about 158 feet or about 48 meters [x] *13* That is, about 175 feet or about 53 meters; also in verses 14 and 15

temple, including its galleries on each side; it
was a hundred cubits.
The main hall, the inner sanctuary and
the portico facing the court, 16as well as the
thresholds and the narrow windows and galleries around the three of them—everything
beyond and including the threshold was covered with wood. The floor, the wall up to the
windows, and the windows were covered. 17In
the space above the outside of the entrance to
the inner sanctuary and on the walls at regular intervals all around the inner and outer
sanctuary 18were carved cherubim and palm
trees. Palm trees alternated with cherubim.
Each cherub had two faces: 19the face of a human being toward the palm tree on one side
and the face of a lion toward the palm tree
on the other. They were carved all around
the whole temple. 20From the floor to the area
above the entrance, cherubim and palm trees
were carved on the wall of the main hall.
21The main hall had a rectangular doorframe, and the one at the front of the Most
Holy Place was similar. 22There was a wood-
en altar three cubits[a] high and two cubits
square[b]; its corners, its base[c] and its sides
were of wood. The man said to me, "This is
the table that is before the LORD." 23Both the
main hall and the Most Holy Place had double doors. 24Each door had two leaves—two
hinged leaves for each door. 25And on the
doors of the main hall were carved cherubim and palm trees like those carved on the
walls, and there was a wooden overhang on
the front of the portico. 26On the sidewalls of
the portico were narrow windows with palm
trees carved on each side. The side rooms of
the temple also had overhangs.

The Rooms for the Priests

42 Then the man led me northward into
the outer court and brought me to the
rooms opposite the temple courtyard and opposite the outer wall on the north side. 2The
building whose door faced north was a hundred cubits long and fifty cubits wide.[d] 3Both
in the section twenty cubits[e] from the inner
court and in the section opposite the pavement of the outer court, gallery faced gallery
at the three levels. 4In front of the rooms was
an inner passageway ten cubits wide and a
hundred cubits[f] long.[g] Their doors were on the
north. 5Now the upper rooms were narrower,
for the galleries took more space from them
than from the rooms on the lower and middle
floors of the building. 6The rooms on the top
floor had no pillars, as the courts had; so they
were smaller in floor space than those on the
lower and middle floors. 7There was an outer
wall parallel to the rooms and the outer court;
it extended in front of the rooms for fifty cubits. 8While the row of rooms on the side next
to the outer court was fifty cubits long, the
row on the side nearest the sanctuary was a
hundred cubits long. 9The lower rooms had an
entrance on the east side as one enters them
from the outer court.
10On the south side[h] along the length of the
wall of the outer court, adjoining the temple
courtyard and opposite the outer wall, were
rooms 11with a passageway in front of them.
These were like the rooms on the north; they
had the same length and width, with similar
exits and dimensions. Similar to the doorways
on the north 12were the doorways of the rooms
on the south. There was a doorway at the beginning of the passageway that was parallel to
the corresponding wall extending eastward,
by which one enters the rooms.
13Then he said to me, "The north and south
rooms facing the temple courtyard are the
priests' rooms, where the priests who approach the LORD will eat the most holy offerings. There they will put the most holy offerings—the grain offerings, the sin offerings[i]
and the guilt offerings—for the place is holy.
14Once the priests enter the holy precincts,
they are not to go into the outer court until
they leave behind the garments in which they
minister, for these are holy. They are to put on
other clothes before they go near the places
that are for the people."
15When he had finished measuring what
was inside the temple area, he led me out
by the east gate and measured the area all
around: 16He measured the east side with
the measuring rod; it was five hundred cubits.[j,k] 17He measured the north side; it was
five hundred cubits[l] by the measuring rod.
18He measured the south side; it was five hundred cubits by the measuring rod. 19Then he
turned to the west side and measured; it was
five hundred cubits by the measuring rod. 20So
he measured the area on all four sides. It had
a wall around it, five hundred cubits long and
five hundred cubits wide, to separate the holy
from the common.

God's Glory Returns to the Temple

43 Then the man brought me to the gate
facing east, 2and I saw the glory of the
God of Israel coming from the east. His voice
was like the roar of rushing waters, and the
land was radiant with his glory. 3The vision
I saw was like the vision I had seen when he[m]
came to destroy the city and like the visions
I had seen by the Kebar River, and I fell facedown. 4The glory of the LORD entered the temple through the gate facing east. 5Then the
Spirit lifted me up and brought me into the

[a] 22 That is, about 5 1/4 feet or about 1.5 meters [b] 22 Septuagint; Hebrew *long* [c] 22 Septuagint; Hebrew *length* [d] 2 That is, about 175 feet long and 88 feet wide or about 53 meters long and 27 meters wide [e] 3 That is, about 35 feet or about 11 meters [f] 4 Septuagint and Syriac; Hebrew *and one cubit* [g] 4 That is, about 18 feet wide and 175 feet long or about 5.3 meters wide and 53 meters long [h] 10 Septuagint; Hebrew *Eastward* [i] 13 Or *purification offerings* [j] 16 See Septuagint of verse 17; Hebrew *rods*; also in verses 18 and 19. [k] 16 Five hundred cubits equal about 875 feet or about 265 meters; also in verses 17, 18 and 19. [l] 17 Septuagint; Hebrew *rods* [m] 3 Some Hebrew manuscripts and Vulgate; most Hebrew manuscripts *I*

inner court, and the glory of the LORD filled
the temple.
6While the man was standing beside me,
I heard someone speaking to me from inside the temple. 7He said: "Son of man, this
is the place of my throne and the place for
the soles of my feet. This is where I will live
among the Israelites forever. The people of
Israel will never again defile my holy name—
neither they nor their kings—by their prostitution and the funeral offerings[a] for their
kings at their death.[b] 8When they placed
their threshold next to my threshold and their
doorposts beside my doorposts, with only a
wall between me and them, they defiled my
holy name by their detestable practices. So I
destroyed them in my anger. 9Now let them
put away from me their prostitution and the
funeral offerings for their kings, and I will
live among them forever.
10"Son of man, describe the temple to the
people of Israel, that they may be ashamed
of their sins. Let them consider its perfection, 11and if they are ashamed of all they
have done, make known to them the design
of the temple—its arrangement, its exits and
entrances—its whole design and all its regulations[c] and laws. Write these down before
them so that they may be faithful to its design
and follow all its regulations.
12"This is the law of the temple: All the surrounding area on top of the mountain will be
most holy. Such is the law of the temple.

The Great Altar Restored

13"These are the measurements of the altar
in long cubits,[d] that cubit being a cubit and
a handbreadth: Its gutter is a cubit deep and
a cubit wide, with a rim of one span[e] around
the edge. And this is the height of the altar:
14From the gutter on the ground up to the lower ledge that goes around the altar it is two
cubits high, and the ledge is a cubit wide.[f]
From this lower ledge to the upper ledge that
goes around the altar it is four cubits high, and
that ledge is also a cubit wide.[g] 15Above that,
the altar hearth is four cubits high, and four
horns project upward from the hearth. 16The
altar hearth is square, twelve cubits[h] long and
twelve cubits wide. 17The upper ledge also is
square, fourteen cubits[i] long and fourteen cubits wide. All around the altar is a gutter of
one cubit with a rim of half a cubit.[e] The steps
of the altar face east."
18Then he said to me, "Son of man, this is
what the Sovereign LORD says: These will be
the regulations for sacrificing burnt offerings
and splashing blood against the altar when it
is built: 19You are to give a young bull as a sin
offering[j] to the Levitical priests of the family
of Zadok, who come near to minister before
me, declares the Sovereign LORD. 20You are
to take some of its blood and put it on the four
horns of the altar and on the four corners of
the upper ledge and all around the rim, and
so purify the altar and make atonement for
it. 21You are to take the bull for the sin offering and burn it in the designated part of the
temple area outside the sanctuary.
22"On the second day you are to offer a male
goat without defect for a sin offering, and the
altar is to be purified as it was purified with
the bull. 23When you have finished purifying
it, you are to offer a young bull and a ram from
the flock, both without defect. 24You are to offer them before the LORD, and the priests are
to sprinkle salt on them and sacrifice them as
a burnt offering to the LORD.
25"For seven days you are to provide a male
goat daily for a sin offering; you are also to
provide a young bull and a ram from the flock,
both without defect. 26For seven days they are
to make atonement for the altar and cleanse it;
thus they will dedicate it. 27At the end of these
days, from the eighth day on, the priests are
to present your burnt offerings and fellowship
offerings on the altar. Then I will accept you,
declares the Sovereign LORD."

The Priesthood Restored

44 Then the man brought me back to the
outer gate of the sanctuary, the one facing east, and it was shut. 2The LORD said to
me, "This gate is to remain shut. It must not
be opened; no one may enter through it. It
is to remain shut because the LORD, the God
of Israel, has entered through it. 3The prince
himself is the only one who may sit inside the
gateway to eat in the presence of the LORD. He
is to enter by way of the portico of the gateway
and go out the same way."
4Then the man brought me by way of the
north gate to the front of the temple. I looked
and saw the glory of the LORD filling the temple of the LORD, and I fell facedown.
5The LORD said to me, "Son of man, look
carefully, listen closely and give attention to
everything I tell you concerning all the regulations and instructions regarding the temple
of the LORD. Give attention to the entrance to
the temple and all the exits of the sanctuary.
6Say to rebellious Israel, 'This is what the Sovereign LORD says: Enough of your detestable
practices, people of Israel! 7In addition to all
your other detestable practices, you brought
foreigners uncircumcised in heart and flesh
into my sanctuary, desecrating my temple
while you offered me food, fat and blood, and
you broke my covenant. 8Instead of carrying
out your duty in regard to my holy things, you
put others in charge of my sanctuary. 9This is
what the Sovereign LORD says: No foreigner

[a] 7 Or *the memorial monuments*; also in verse 9 [b] 7 Or *their high places* [c] 11 Some Hebrew manuscripts and Septuagint; most Hebrew manuscripts *regulations and its whole design* [d] 13 That is, about 21 inches or about 53 centimeters; also in verses 14 and 17. The long cubit is the basic unit for linear measurement throughout Ezekiel 40–48. [e] 13,17 That is, about 11 inches or about 27 centimeters [f] 14 That is, about 3 1/2 feet high and 1 3/4 feet wide or about 105 centimeters high and 53 centimeters wide [g] 14 That is, about 7 feet high and 1 3/4 feet wide or about 2.1 meters high and 53 centimeters wide [h] 16 That is, about 21 feet or about 6.4 meters [i] 17 That is, about 25 feet or about 7.4 meters [j] 19 Or *purification offering*; also in verses 21, 22 and 25

uncircumcised in heart and flesh is to enter my sanctuary, not even the foreigners who live among the Israelites.

10“ ‘The Levites who went far from me when Israel went astray and who wandered from me after their idols must bear the consequences of their sin. 11They may serve in my sanctuary, having charge of the gates of the temple and serving in it; they may slaughter the burnt offerings and sacrifices for the people and stand before the people and serve them. 12But because they served them in the presence of their idols and made the people of Israel fall into sin, therefore I have sworn with uplifted hand that they must bear the consequences of their sin, declares the Sovereign LORD. 13They are not to come near to serve me as priests or come near any of my holy things or my most holy offerings; they must bear the shame of their detestable practices. 14And I will appoint them to guard the temple for all the work that is to be done in it.

15“ ‘But the Levitical priests, who are descendants of Zadok and who guarded my sanctuary when the Israelites went astray from me, are to come near to minister before me; they are to stand before me to offer sacrifices of fat and blood, declares the Sovereign LORD. 16They alone are to enter my sanctuary; they alone are to come near my table to minister before me and serve me as guards.

17“ ‘When they enter the gates of the inner court, they are to wear linen clothes; they must not wear any woolen garment while ministering at the gates of the inner court or inside the temple. 18They are to wear linen turbans on their heads and linen undergarments around their waists. They must not wear anything that makes them perspire. 19When they go out into the outer court where the people are, they are to take off the clothes they have been ministering in and are to leave them in the sacred rooms, and put on other clothes, so that the people are not consecrated through contact with their garments.

20“ ‘They must not shave their heads or let their hair grow long, but they are to keep the hair of their heads trimmed. 21No priest is to drink wine when he enters the inner court. 22They must not marry widows or divorced women; they may marry only virgins of Israelite descent or widows of priests. 23They are to teach my people the difference between the holy and the common and show them how to distinguish between the unclean and the clean.

24“ ‘In any dispute, the priests are to serve as judges and decide it according to my ordinances. They are to keep my laws and my decrees for all my appointed festivals, and they are to keep my Sabbaths holy.

25“ ‘A priest must not defile himself by going near a dead person; however, if the dead person was his father or mother, son or daughter, brother or unmarried sister, then he may defile himself. 26After he is cleansed, he must wait seven days. 27On the day he goes into the inner court of the sanctuary to minister in the sanctuary, he is to offer a sin offering[a] for himself, declares the Sovereign LORD.

28“ ‘I am to be the only inheritance the priests have. You are to give them no possession in Israel; I will be their possession. 29They will eat the grain offerings, the sin offerings and the guilt offerings; and everything in Israel devoted[b] to the LORD will belong to them. 30The best of all the firstfruits and of all your special gifts will belong to the priests. You are to give them the first portion of your ground meal so that a blessing may rest on your household. 31The priests must not eat anything, whether bird or animal, found dead or torn by wild animals.

Israel Fully Restored

45 “ ‘When you allot the land as an inheritance, you are to present to the LORD a portion of the land as a sacred district, 25,000 cubits[c] long and 20,000[d] cubits[e] wide; the entire area will be holy. 2Of this, a section 500 cubits[f] square is to be for the sanctuary, with 50 cubits[g] around it for open land. 3In the sacred district, measure off a section 25,000 cubits long and 10,000 cubits[h] wide. In it will be the sanctuary, the Most Holy Place. 4It will be the sacred portion of the land for the priests, who minister in the sanctuary and who draw near to minister before the LORD. It will be a place for their houses as well as a holy place for the sanctuary. 5An area 25,000 cubits long and 10,000 cubits wide will belong to the Levites, who serve in the temple, as their possession for towns to live in.[i]

6“ ‘You are to give the city as its property an area 5,000 cubits[j] wide and 25,000 cubits long, adjoining the sacred portion; it will belong to all Israel.

7“ ‘The prince will have the land bordering each side of the area formed by the sacred district and the property of the city. It will extend westward from the west side and eastward from the east side, running lengthwise from the western to the eastern border parallel to one of the tribal portions. 8This land will be his possession in Israel. And my princes will no longer oppress my people but will allow the people of Israel to possess the land according to their tribes.

9“ ‘This is what the Sovereign LORD says: You have gone far enough, princes of Israel! Give up your violence and oppression and do what is just and right. Stop dispossessing my people, declares the Sovereign LORD. 10You are

[a] *27* Or *purification offering*; also in verse 29 [b] *29* The Hebrew term refers to the irrevocable giving over of things or persons to the LORD. [c] *1* That is, about 8 miles or about 13 kilometers; also in verses 3, 5 and 6 [d] *1* Septuagint (see also verses 3 and 5 and 48:9); Hebrew *10,000* [e] *1* That is, about 6 1/2 miles or about 11 kilometers [f] *2* That is, about 875 feet or about 265 meters [g] *2* That is, about 88 feet or about 27 meters [h] *3* That is, about 3 1/3 miles or about 5.3 kilometers; also in verse 5 [i] *5* Septuagint; Hebrew *temple; they will have as their possession 20 rooms* [j] *6* That is, about 1 2/3 miles or about 2.7 kilometers

to use accurate scales, an accurate ephah[a] and
an accurate bath.[b] 11The ephah and the bath
are to be the same size, the bath containing a
tenth of a homer and the ephah a tenth of a homer; the homer is to be the standard measure
for both. 12The shekel[c] is to consist of twenty
gerahs. Twenty shekels plus twenty-five shekels plus fifteen shekels equal one mina.[d]
13" 'This is the special gift you are to offer: a
sixth of an ephah[e] from each homer of wheat
and a sixth of an ephah[f] from each homer of
barley. 14The prescribed portion of olive oil,
measured by the bath, is a tenth of a bath[g]
from each cor (which consists of ten baths or
one homer, for ten baths are equivalent to a
homer). 15Also one sheep is to be taken from
every flock of two hundred from the well-watered pastures of Israel. These will be used
for the grain offerings, burnt offerings and
fellowship offerings to make atonement for
the people, declares the Sovereign LORD. 16All
the people of the land will be required to give
this special offering to the prince in Israel.
17It will be the duty of the prince to provide
the burnt offerings, grain offerings and drink
offerings at the festivals, the New Moons and
the Sabbaths—at all the appointed festivals of
Israel. He will provide the sin offerings,[h] grain
offerings, burnt offerings and fellowship offerings to make atonement for the Israelites.
18" 'This is what the Sovereign LORD says:
In the first month on the first day you are to
take a young bull without defect and purify
the sanctuary. 19The priest is to take some
of the blood of the sin offering and put it on
the doorposts of the temple, on the four corners of the upper ledge of the altar and on the
gateposts of the inner court. 20You are to do
the same on the seventh day of the month for
anyone who sins unintentionally or through
ignorance; so you are to make atonement for
the temple.
21" 'In the first month on the fourteenth day
you are to observe the Passover, a festival lasting seven days, during which you shall eat
bread made without yeast. 22On that day the
prince is to provide a bull as a sin offering for
himself and for all the people of the land. 23Ev-
ery day during the seven days of the festival
he is to provide seven bulls and seven rams
without defect as a burnt offering to the LORD,
and a male goat for a sin offering. 24He is to
provide as a grain offering an ephah for each
bull and an ephah for each ram, along with a
hin[i] of olive oil for each ephah.
25" 'During the seven days of the festival,
which begins in the seventh month on the
fifteenth day, he is to make the same provision for sin offerings, burnt offerings, grain
offerings and oil.

46 " 'This is what the Sovereign LORD says:
The gate of the inner court facing east is
to be shut on the six working days, but on the
Sabbath day and on the day of the New Moon
it is to be opened. 2The prince is to enter from
the outside through the portico of the gateway
and stand by the gatepost. The priests are to
sacrifice his burnt offering and his fellowship
offerings. He is to bow down in worship at the
threshold of the gateway and then go out, but
the gate will not be shut until evening. 3On
the Sabbaths and New Moons the people of
the land are to worship in the presence of the
LORD at the entrance of that gateway. 4The
burnt offering the prince brings to the LORD
on the Sabbath day is to be six male lambs and
a ram, all without defect. 5The grain offering
given with the ram is to be an ephah,[j] and the
grain offering with the lambs is to be as much
as he pleases, along with a hin[k] of olive oil for
each ephah. 6On the day of the New Moon he
is to offer a young bull, six lambs and a ram,
all without defect. 7He is to provide as a grain
offering one ephah with the bull, one ephah
with the ram, and with the lambs as much as
he wants to give, along with a hin of oil for
each ephah. 8When the prince enters, he is to
go in through the portico of the gateway, and
he is to come out the same way.
9" 'When the people of the land come before
the LORD at the appointed festivals, whoever enters by the north gate to worship is to
go out the south gate; and whoever enters by
the south gate is to go out the north gate. No
one is to return through the gate by which
they entered, but each is to go out the opposite gate. 10The prince is to be among them,
going in when they go in and going out when
they go out. 11At the feasts and the appointed
festivals, the grain offering is to be an ephah
with a bull, an ephah with a ram, and with
the lambs as much as he pleases, along with
a hin of oil for each ephah.
12" 'When the prince provides a freewill offering to the LORD—whether a burnt offering or fellowship offerings—the gate facing
east is to be opened for him. He shall offer
his burnt offering or his fellowship offerings
as he does on the Sabbath day. Then he shall
go out, and after he has gone out, the gate
will be shut.
13" 'Every day you are to provide a year-old
lamb without defect for a burnt offering to the
LORD; morning by morning you shall provide
it. 14You are also to provide with it morning
by morning a grain offering, consisting of a
sixth of an ephah[e] with a third of a hin[l] of oil to
moisten the flour. The presenting of this grain
offering to the LORD is a lasting ordinance.
15So the lamb and the grain offering and the

[a] *10* An ephah was a dry measure having the capacity of about 3/5 bushel or about 22 liters.
[b] *10* A bath was a liquid measure equaling about 6 gallons or about 22 liters. [c] *12* A shekel weighed about 2/5 ounce or about 12 grams. [d] *12* That is, 60 shekels; the common mina was 50 shekels. Sixty shekels were about 1 1/2 pounds or about 690 grams. [e] *13,14* That is, probably about 6 pounds or about 2.7 kilograms [f] *13* That is, probably about 5 pounds or about 2.3 kilograms [g] *14* That is, about 2 1/2 quarts or about 2.2 liters [h] *17* Or *purification offerings*; also in verses 19, 22, 23 and 25
[i] *24* That is, about 1 gallon or about 3.8 liters [j] *5* That is, probably about 35 pounds or about 16 kilograms; also in verses 7 and 11 [k] *5* That is, about 1 gallon or about 3.8 liters; also in verses 7 and 11 [l] *14* That is, about 1 1/2 quarts or about 1.3 liters

oil shall be provided morning by morning for
a regular burnt offering.

16" 'This is what the Sovereign LORD says:
If the prince makes a gift from his inheritance to one of his sons, it will also belong
to his descendants; it is to be their property by inheritance. 17If, however, he makes a
gift from his inheritance to one of his servants, the servant may keep it until the year
of freedom; then it will revert to the prince.
His inheritance belongs to his sons only; it
is theirs. 18The prince must not take any of
the inheritance of the people, driving them
off their property. He is to give his sons their
inheritance out of his own property, so that
not one of my people will be separated from
their property.' "

19Then the man brought me through the
entrance at the side of the gate to the sacred
rooms facing north, which belonged to the
priests, and showed me a place at the western
end. 20He said to me, "This is the place where
the priests are to cook the guilt offering and
the sin offering[a] and bake the grain offering,
to avoid bringing them into the outer court
and consecrating the people."

21He then brought me to the outer court and
led me around to its four corners, and I saw in
each corner another court. 22In the four corners of the outer court were enclosed[b] courts,
forty cubits long and thirty cubits wide;[c] each
of the courts in the four corners was the same
size. 23Around the inside of each of the four
courts was a ledge of stone, with places for
fire built all around under the ledge. 24He said
to me, "These are the kitchens where those
who minister at the temple are to cook the
sacrifices of the people."

The River From the Temple

47 The man brought me back to the entrance to the temple, and I saw water
coming out from under the threshold of the
temple toward the east (for the temple faced
east). The water was coming down from under the south side of the temple, south of the
altar. 2He then brought me out through the
north gate and led me around the outside to
the outer gate facing east, and the water was
trickling from the south side.

3As the man went eastward with a measuring line in his hand, he measured off a
thousand cubits[d] and then led me through
water that was ankle-deep. 4He measured off
another thousand cubits and led me through
water that was knee-deep. He measured off
another thousand and led me through water
that was up to the waist. 5He measured off
another thousand, but now it was a river that
I could not cross, because the water had ris-
en and was deep enough to swim in—a river
that no one could cross. 6He asked me, "Son
of man, do you see this?"

Then he led me back to the bank of the river.
7When I arrived there, I saw a great number
of trees on each side of the river. 8He said to
me, "This water flows toward the eastern region and goes down into the Arabah,[e] where
it enters the Dead Sea. When it empties into
the sea, the salty water there becomes fresh.
9Swarms of living creatures will live wherever
the river flows. There will be large numbers
of fish, because this water flows there and
makes the salt water fresh; so where the river
flows everything will live. 10Fishermen will
stand along the shore; from En Gedi to En
Eglaim there will be places for spreading nets.
The fish will be of many kinds—like the fish
of the Mediterranean Sea. 11But the swamps
and marshes will not become fresh; they will
be left for salt. 12Fruit trees of all kinds will
grow on both banks of the river. Their leaves
will not wither, nor will their fruit fail. Every
month they will bear fruit, because the water from the sanctuary flows to them. Their
fruit will serve for food and their leaves for
healing."

The Boundaries of the Land

13This is what the Sovereign LORD says:
"These are the boundaries of the land that
you will divide among the twelve tribes of Israel as their inheritance, with two portions for
Joseph. 14You are to divide it equally among
them. Because I swore with uplifted hand to
give it to your ancestors, this land will become
your inheritance.

15"This is to be the boundary of the land:

"On the north side it will run from the Mediterranean Sea by the Hethlon road past
Lebo Hamath to Zedad, 16Berothah[f] and
Sibraim (which lies on the border between Damascus and Hamath), as far as
Hazer Hattikon, which is on the border
of Hauran. 17The boundary will extend
from the sea to Hazar Enan,[g] along the
northern border of Damascus, with the
border of Hamath to the north. This will
be the northern boundary.

18"On the east side the boundary will run between Hauran and Damascus, along the
Jordan between Gilead and the land of
Israel, to the Dead Sea and as far as Tamar.[h] This will be the eastern boundary.

19"On the south side it will run from Tamar
as far as the waters of Meribah Kadesh,
then along the Wadi of Egypt to the Mediterranean Sea. This will be the southern
boundary.

20"On the west side, the Mediterranean Sea
will be the boundary to a point opposite
Lebo Hamath. This will be the western
boundary.

21"You are to distribute this land among
yourselves according to the tribes of Israel.

[a] 20 Or *purification offering* [b] 22 The meaning of the Hebrew for this word is uncertain.
[c] 22 That is, about 70 feet long and 53 feet wide or about 21 meters long and 16 meters wide [d] 3 That
is, about 1,700 feet or about 530 meters [e] 8 Or *the Jordan Valley* [f] 15,16 See Septuagint and 48:1;
Hebrew *road to go into Zedad, 16Hamath, Berothah.* [g] 17 Hebrew *Enon,* a variant of *Enan*
[h] 18 See Syriac; Hebrew *Israel. You will measure to the Dead Sea.*

22You are to allot it as an inheritance for yourselves and for the foreigners residing among
you and who have children. You are to consider them as native-born Israelites; along
with you they are to be allotted an inheritance among the tribes of Israel. 23In whatever tribe a foreigner resides, there you are
to give them their inheritance," declares the
Sovereign LORD.

The Division of the Land

48 "These are the tribes, listed by name: At
the northern frontier, Dan will have one
portion; it will follow the Hethlon road to Lebo
Hamath; Hazar Enan and the northern border
of Damascus next to Hamath will be part of
its border from the east side to the west side.
2"Asher will have one portion; it will border
the territory of Dan from east to west.
3"Naphtali will have one portion; it will border the territory of Asher from east to west.
4"Manasseh will have one portion; it will
border the territory of Naphtali from east to
west.
5"Ephraim will have one portion; it will
border the territory of Manasseh from east
to west.
6"Reuben will have one portion; it will border the territory of Ephraim from east to west.
7"Judah will have one portion; it will border the territory of Reuben from east to west.
8"Bordering the territory of Judah from east
to west will be the portion you are to present
as a special gift. It will be 25,000 cubits[a] wide,
and its length from east to west will equal one
of the tribal portions; the sanctuary will be
in the center of it.
9"The special portion you are to offer to the
LORD will be 25,000 cubits long and 10,000
cubits[b] wide. 10This will be the sacred portion
for the priests. It will be 25,000 cubits long on
the north side, 10,000 cubits wide on the west
side, 10,000 cubits wide on the east side and
25,000 cubits long on the south side. In the
center of it will be the sanctuary of the LORD.
11This will be for the consecrated priests, the
Zadokites, who were faithful in serving me
and did not go astray as the Levites did when
the Israelites went astray. 12It will be a special gift to them from the sacred portion of
the land, a most holy portion, bordering the
territory of the Levites.
13"Alongside the territory of the priests, the
Levites will have an allotment 25,000 cubits
long and 10,000 cubits wide. Its total length
will be 25,000 cubits and its width 10,000 cubits. 14They must not sell or exchange any of
it. This is the best of the land and must not
pass into other hands, because it is holy to
the LORD.
15"The remaining area, 5,000 cubits[c] wide
and 25,000 cubits long, will be for the common use of the city, for houses and for pastureland. The city will be in the center of it
16and will have these measurements: the north
side 4,500 cubits,[d] the south side 4,500 cubits,
the east side 4,500 cubits, and the west side
4,500 cubits. 17The pastureland for the city
will be 250 cubits[e] on the north, 250 cubits
on the south, 250 cubits on the east, and 250
cubits on the west. 18What remains of the area,
bordering on the sacred portion and running
the length of it, will be 10,000 cubits on the
east side and 10,000 cubits on the west side.
Its produce will supply food for the workers
of the city. 19The workers from the city who
farm it will come from all the tribes of Israel.
20The entire portion will be a square, 25,000
cubits on each side. As a special gift you will
set aside the sacred portion, along with the
property of the city.
21"What remains on both sides of the area
formed by the sacred portion and the property of the city will belong to the prince. It
will extend eastward from the 25,000 cubits
of the sacred portion to the eastern border,
and westward from the 25,000 cubits to the
western border. Both these areas running the
length of the tribal portions will belong to the
prince, and the sacred portion with the temple
sanctuary will be in the center of them. 22So
the property of the Levites and the property
of the city will lie in the center of the area that
belongs to the prince. The area belonging to
the prince will lie between the border of Judah
and the border of Benjamin.
23"As for the rest of the tribes: Benjamin
will have one portion; it will extend from the
east side to the west side.
24"Simeon will have one portion; it will
border the territory of Benjamin from east
to west.
25"Issachar will have one portion; it will border the territory of Simeon from east to west.
26"Zebulun will have one portion; it will border the territory of Issachar from east to west.
27"Gad will have one portion; it will border
the territory of Zebulun from east to west.
28"The southern boundary of Gad will run
south from Tamar to the waters of Meribah
Kadesh, then along the Wadi of Egypt to the
Mediterranean Sea.
29"This is the land you are to allot as an
inheritance to the tribes of Israel, and these
will be their portions," declares the Sovereign LORD.

The Gates of the New City

30"These will be the exits of the city: Beginning on the north side, which is 4,500 cubits
long, 31the gates of the city will be named after the tribes of Israel. The three gates on the
north side will be the gate of Reuben, the gate
of Judah and the gate of Levi.
32"On the east side, which is 4,500 cubits
long, will be three gates: the gate of Joseph,
the gate of Benjamin and the gate of Dan.
33"On the south side, which measures 4,500

[a] *8* That is, about 8 miles or about 13 kilometers; also in verses 9, 10, 13, 15, 20 and 21 [b] *9* That is, about 3 1/3 miles or about 5.3 kilometers; also in verses 10, 13 and 18 [c] *15* That is, about 1 2/3 miles or about 2.7 kilometers [d] *16* That is, about 1 1/2 miles or about 2.4 kilometers; also in verses 30, 32, 33 and 34 [e] *17* That is, about 440 feet or about 135 meters

cubits, will be three gates: the gate of Simeon,
the gate of Issachar and the gate of Zebulun.
34"On the west side, which is 4,500 cubits
long, will be three gates: the gate of Gad, the
gate of Asher and the gate of Naphtali.
35"The distance all around will be 18,000
cubits.[a]
"And the name of the city from that time
on will be:

THE LORD IS THERE."

Daniel

Daniel's Training in Babylon

1 In the third year of the reign of Jehoiakim
king of Judah, Nebuchadnezzar king of
Babylon came to Jerusalem and besieged it.
2And the Lord delivered Jehoiakim king of
Judah into his hand, along with some of the
articles from the temple of God. These he carried off to the temple of his god in Babylonia[b]
and put in the treasure house of his god.
3Then the king ordered Ashpenaz, chief
of his court officials, to bring into the king's
service some of the Israelites from the royal
family and the nobility— 4young men without
any physical defect, handsome, showing apti-
tude for every kind of learning, well informed,
quick to understand, and qualified to serve in
the king's palace. He was to teach them the
language and literature of the Babylonians.[c]
5The king assigned them a daily amount of
food and wine from the king's table. They
were to be trained for three years, and after
that they were to enter the king's service.
6Among those who were chosen were some
from Judah: Daniel, Hananiah, Mishael and
Azariah. 7The chief official gave them new
names: to Daniel, the name Belteshazzar; to
Hananiah, Shadrach; to Mishael, Meshach;
and to Azariah, Abednego.
8But Daniel resolved not to defile himself
with the royal food and wine, and he asked
the chief official for permission not to defile
himself this way. 9Now God had caused the
official to show favor and compassion to Daniel, 10but the official told Daniel, "I am afraid
of my lord the king, who has assigned your[d]
food and drink. Why should he see you looking
worse than the other young men your age? The
king would then have my head because of you."
11Daniel then said to the guard whom the
chief official had appointed over Daniel,
Hananiah, Mishael and Azariah, 12"Please
test your servants for ten days: Give us nothing but vegetables to eat and water to drink.
13Then compare our appearance with that of
the young men who eat the royal food, and
treat your servants in accordance with what
you see." 14So he agreed to this and tested
them for ten days.
15At the end of the ten days they looked
healthier and better nourished than any of
the young men who ate the royal food. 16So
the guard took away their choice food and
the wine they were to drink and gave them
vegetables instead.
17To these four young men God gave knowledge and understanding of all kinds of literature and learning. And Daniel could understand visions and dreams of all kinds.
18At the end of the time set by the king to
bring them into his service, the chief official
presented them to Nebuchadnezzar. 19The
king talked with them, and he found none
equal to Daniel, Hananiah, Mishael and Azariah; so they entered the king's service. 20In
every matter of wisdom and understanding
about which the king questioned them, he
found them ten times better than all the magicians and enchanters in his whole kingdom.
21And Daniel remained there until the first
year of King Cyrus.

Nebuchadnezzar's Dream

2 In the second year of his reign, Nebuchadnezzar had dreams; his mind was
troubled and he could not sleep. 2So the king
summoned the magicians, enchanters, sorcerers and astrologers[e] to tell him what he
had dreamed. When they came in and stood
before the king, 3he said to them, "I have had
a dream that troubles me and I want to know
what it means.[f]"
4Then the astrologers answered the king,[g]
"May the king live forever! Tell your servants
the dream, and we will interpret it."
5The king replied to the astrologers, "This
is what I have firmly decided: If you do not
tell me what my dream was and interpret it, I
will have you cut into pieces and your houses turned into piles of rubble. 6But if you tell
me the dream and explain it, you will receive
from me gifts and rewards and great honor.
So tell me the dream and interpret it for me."
7Once more they replied, "Let the king tell
his servants the dream, and we will interpret it."
8Then the king answered, "I am certain that

[a] 35 That is, about 6 miles or about 9.5 kilometers [b] 2 Hebrew *Shinar* [c] 4 Or *Chaldeans*
[d] 10 The Hebrew for *your* and *you* in this verse is plural. [e] 2 Or *Chaldeans*; also in verses 4, 5 and 10
[f] 3 Or *was* [g] 4 At this point the Hebrew text has *in Aramaic*, indicating that the text from here through the end of chapter 7 is in Aramaic.

you are trying to gain time, because you realize that this is what I have firmly decided: 9If
you do not tell me the dream, there is only one
penalty for you. You have conspired to tell me
misleading and wicked things, hoping the situation will change. So then, tell me the dream,
and I will know that you can interpret it for me."
10The astrologers answered the king,
"There is no one on earth who can do what
the king asks! No king, however great and
mighty, has ever asked such a thing of any
magician or enchanter or astrologer. 11What
the king asks is too difficult. No one can reveal it to the king except the gods, and they
do not live among humans."
12This made the king so angry and furious
that he ordered the execution of all the wise
men of Babylon. 13So the decree was issued
to put the wise men to death, and men were
sent to look for Daniel and his friends to put
them to death.
14When Arioch, the commander of the
king's guard, had gone out to put to death
the wise men of Babylon, Daniel spoke to him
with wisdom and tact. 15He asked the king's
officer, "Why did the king issue such a harsh
decree?" Arioch then explained the matter to
Daniel. 16At this, Daniel went in to the king
and asked for time, so that he might interpret
the dream for him.
17Then Daniel returned to his house and
explained the matter to his friends Hananiah, Mishael and Azariah. 18He urged them
to plead for mercy from the God of heaven
concerning this mystery, so that he and his
friends might not be executed with the rest of
the wise men of Babylon. 19During the night
the mystery was revealed to Daniel in a vision. Then Daniel praised the God of heaven
20and said:

"Praise be to the name of God for ever
and ever;
wisdom and power are his.
21 He changes times and seasons;
he deposes kings and raises up others.
He gives wisdom to the wise
and knowledge to the discerning.
22 He reveals deep and hidden things;
he knows what lies in darkness,
and light dwells with him.
23 I thank and praise you, God of my
ancestors:
You have given me wisdom and power,
you have made known to me what we
asked of you,
you have made known to us the dream
of the king."

Daniel Interprets the Dream

24Then Daniel went to Arioch, whom the
king had appointed to execute the wise men
of Babylon, and said to him, "Do not execute
the wise men of Babylon. Take me to the king,
and I will interpret his dream for him."
25Arioch took Daniel to the king at once and
said, "I have found a man among the exiles
from Judah who can tell the king what his
dream means."
26The king asked Daniel (also called Belteshazzar), "Are you able to tell me what I saw
in my dream and interpret it?"
27Daniel replied, "No wise man, enchanter,
magician or diviner can explain to the king
the mystery he has asked about, 28but there
is a God in heaven who reveals mysteries. He
has shown King Nebuchadnezzar what will
happen in days to come. Your dream and the
visions that passed through your mind as you
were lying in bed are these:
29"As Your Majesty was lying there, your
mind turned to things to come, and the revealer of mysteries showed you what is going to
happen. 30As for me, this mystery has been
revealed to me, not because I have greater
wisdom than anyone else alive, but so that
Your Majesty may know the interpretation
and that you may understand what went
through your mind.
31"Your Majesty looked, and there before
you stood a large statue—an enormous, dazzling statue, awesome in appearance. 32The
head of the statue was made of pure gold, its
chest and arms of silver, its belly and thighs
of bronze, 33its legs of iron, its feet partly of
iron and partly of baked clay. 34While you
were watching, a rock was cut out, but not by
human hands. It struck the statue on its feet
of iron and clay and smashed them. 35Then
the iron, the clay, the bronze, the silver and
the gold were all broken to pieces and became
like chaff on a threshing floor in the summer.
The wind swept them away without leaving a
trace. But the rock that struck the statue became a huge mountain and filled the whole
earth.
36"This was the dream, and now we will
interpret it to the king. 37Your Majesty, you
are the king of kings. The God of heaven has
given you dominion and power and might and
glory; 38in your hands he has placed all mankind and the beasts of the field and the birds in
the sky. Wherever they live, he has made you
ruler over them all. You are that head of gold.
39"After you, another kingdom will arise,
inferior to yours. Next, a third kingdom, one
of bronze, will rule over the whole earth. 40Fi-
nally, there will be a fourth kingdom, strong
as iron—for iron breaks and smashes everything—and as iron breaks things to pieces, so
it will crush and break all the others. 41Just
as you saw that the feet and toes were partly
of baked clay and partly of iron, so this will
be a divided kingdom; yet it will have some
of the strength of iron in it, even as you saw
iron mixed with clay. 42As the toes were partly
iron and partly clay, so this kingdom will be
partly strong and partly brittle. 43And just as
you saw the iron mixed with baked clay, so the
people will be a mixture and will not remain
united, any more than iron mixes with clay.
44"In the time of those kings, the God of
heaven will set up a kingdom that will never be destroyed, nor will it be left to another
people. It will crush all those kingdoms and
bring them to an end, but it will itself endure
forever. 45This is the meaning of the vision
of the rock cut out of a mountain, but not by

human hands—a rock that broke the iron,
the bronze, the clay, the silver and the gold
to pieces.
"The great God has shown the king what
will take place in the future. The dream is true
and its interpretation is trustworthy."
[46]Then King Nebuchadnezzar fell prostrate
before Daniel and paid him honor and ordered
that an offering and incense be presented to
him. [47]The king said to Daniel, "Surely your
God is the God of gods and the Lord of kings
and a revealer of mysteries, for you were able
to reveal this mystery."
[48]Then the king placed Daniel in a high
position and lavished many gifts on him. He
made him ruler over the entire province of
Babylon and placed him in charge of all its
wise men. [49]Moreover, at Daniel's request
the king appointed Shadrach, Meshach and
Abednego administrators over the province
of Babylon, while Daniel himself remained
at the royal court.

The Image of Gold and the Blazing Furnace

3 King Nebuchadnezzar made an image
of gold, sixty cubits high and six cubits
wide,[a] and set it up on the plain of Dura in the
province of Babylon. [2]He then summoned the
satraps, prefects, governors, advisers, treasurers, judges, magistrates and all the other
provincial officials to come to the dedication
of the image he had set up. [3]So the satraps,
prefects, governors, advisers, treasurers,
judges, magistrates and all the other provincial officials assembled for the dedication of
the image that King Nebuchadnezzar had set
up, and they stood before it.
[4]Then the herald loudly proclaimed, "Nations and peoples of every language, this is
what you are commanded to do: [5]As soon as
you hear the sound of the horn, flute, zither,
lyre, harp, pipe and all kinds of music, you
must fall down and worship the image of gold
that King Nebuchadnezzar has set up. [6]Who-
ever does not fall down and worship will immediately be thrown into a blazing furnace."
[7]Therefore, as soon as they heard the sound
of the horn, flute, zither, lyre, harp and all
kinds of music, all the nations and peoples
of every language fell down and worshiped
the image of gold that King Nebuchadnezzar
had set up.
[8]At this time some astrologers[b] came forward and denounced the Jews. [9]They said to
King Nebuchadnezzar, "May the king live forever! [10]Your Majesty has issued a decree that
everyone who hears the sound of the horn,
flute, zither, lyre, harp, pipe and all kinds of
music must fall down and worship the image
of gold, [11]and that whoever does not fall down
and worship will be thrown into a blazing
furnace. [12]But there are some Jews whom you
have set over the affairs of the province of
Babylon—Shadrach, Meshach and Abednego—who pay no attention to you, Your Majesty. They neither serve your gods nor worship
the image of gold you have set up."
[13]Furious with rage, Nebuchadnezzar summoned Shadrach, Meshach and Abednego.
So these men were brought before the king,
[14]and Nebuchadnezzar said to them, "Is it true,
Shadrach, Meshach and Abednego, that you
do not serve my gods or worship the image
of gold I have set up? [15]Now when you hear
the sound of the horn, flute, zither, lyre, harp,
pipe and all kinds of music, if you are ready to
fall down and worship the image I made, very
good. But if you do not worship it, you will be
thrown immediately into a blazing furnace.
Then what god will be able to rescue you from
my hand?"
[16]Shadrach, Meshach and Abednego replied to him, "King Nebuchadnezzar, we do
not need to defend ourselves before you in
this matter. [17]If we are thrown into the blazing
furnace, the God we serve is able to deliver
us from it, and he will deliver us[c] from Your
Majesty's hand. [18]But even if he does not, we
want you to know, Your Majesty, that we will
not serve your gods or worship the image of
gold you have set up."
[19]Then Nebuchadnezzar was furious with
Shadrach, Meshach and Abednego, and his
attitude toward them changed. He ordered
the furnace heated seven times hotter than
usual [20]and commanded some of the strongest soldiers in his army to tie up Shadrach,
Meshach and Abednego and throw them into
the blazing furnace. [21]So these men, wearing their robes, trousers, turbans and other
clothes, were bound and thrown into the blazing furnace. [22]The king's command was so
urgent and the furnace so hot that the flames
of the fire killed the soldiers who took up Shadrach, Meshach and Abednego, [23]and these
three men, firmly tied, fell into the blazing
furnace.
[24]Then King Nebuchadnezzar leaped to his
feet in amazement and asked his advisers,
"Weren't there three men that we tied up and
threw into the fire?"
They replied, "Certainly, Your Majesty."
[25]He said, "Look! I see four men walking
around in the fire, unbound and unharmed,
and the fourth looks like a son of the gods."
[26]Nebuchadnezzar then approached the
opening of the blazing furnace and shouted,
"Shadrach, Meshach and Abednego, servants
of the Most High God, come out! Come here!"
So Shadrach, Meshach and Abednego came
out of the fire, [27]and the satraps, prefects, governors and royal advisers crowded around
them. They saw that the fire had not harmed
their bodies, nor was a hair of their heads
singed; their robes were not scorched, and
there was no smell of fire on them.
[28]Then Nebuchadnezzar said, "Praise be
to the God of Shadrach, Meshach and Abednego, who has sent his angel and rescued his
servants! They trusted in him and defied the

[a] *1* That is, about 90 feet high and 9 feet wide or about 27 meters high and 2.7 meters wide
[b] *8* Or *Chaldeans* [c] *17* Or *If the God we serve is able to deliver us, then he will deliver us from the blazing furnace and*

king's command and were willing to give
up their lives rather than serve or worship
any god except their own God. 29Therefore I
decree that the people of any nation or language who say anything against the God of
Shadrach, Meshach and Abednego be cut into
pieces and their houses be turned into piles of
rubble, for no other god can save in this way."
30Then the king promoted Shadrach, Meshach and Abednego in the province of Babylon.

Nebuchadnezzar's Dream of a Tree

4[a] King Nebuchadnezzar,

To the nations and peoples of every language, who live in all the earth:

May you prosper greatly!

2It is my pleasure to tell you about the
miraculous signs and wonders that the
Most High God has performed for me.

3How great are his signs,
how mighty his wonders!
His kingdom is an eternal
kingdom;
his dominion endures from
generation to generation.

4I, Nebuchadnezzar, was at home in
my palace, contented and prosperous. 5I
had a dream that made me afraid. As I
was lying in bed, the images and visions
that passed through my mind terrified
me. 6So I commanded that all the wise
men of Babylon be brought before me to
interpret the dream for me. 7When the
magicians, enchanters, astrologers[b] and
diviners came, I told them the dream, but
they could not interpret it for me. 8Finally,
Daniel came into my presence and I told
him the dream. (He is called Belteshazzar, after the name of my god, and the
spirit of the holy gods is in him.)
9I said, "Belteshazzar, chief of the magicians, I know that the spirit of the holy
gods is in you, and no mystery is too difficult for you. Here is my dream; interpret it
for me. 10These are the visions I saw while
lying in bed: I looked, and there before
me stood a tree in the middle of the land.
Its height was enormous. 11The tree grew
large and strong and its top touched the
sky; it was visible to the ends of the earth.
12Its leaves were beautiful, its fruit abundant, and on it was food for all. Under it
the wild animals found shelter, and the
birds lived in its branches; from it every
creature was fed.
13"In the visions I saw while lying in
bed, I looked, and there before me was
a holy one, a messenger,[c] coming down
from heaven. 14He called in a loud voice:
'Cut down the tree and trim off its branches; strip off its leaves and scatter its fruit.
Let the animals flee from under it and
the birds from its branches. 15But let the
stump and its roots, bound with iron and
bronze, remain in the ground, in the grass
of the field.
"'Let him be drenched with the dew of
heaven, and let him live with the animals
among the plants of the earth. 16Let his
mind be changed from that of a man and
let him be given the mind of an animal,
till seven times[d] pass by for him.
17"'The decision is announced by messengers, the holy ones declare the verdict,
so that the living may know that the Most
High is sovereign over all kingdoms on
earth and gives them to anyone he wishes
and sets over them the lowliest of people.'
18"This is the dream that I, King Nebuchadnezzar, had. Now, Belteshazzar, tell
me what it means, for none of the wise
men in my kingdom can interpret it for
me. But you can, because the spirit of the
holy gods is in you."

Daniel Interprets the Dream

19Then Daniel (also called Belteshazzar) was greatly perplexed for a time, and
his thoughts terrified him. So the king
said, "Belteshazzar, do not let the dream
or its meaning alarm you."
Belteshazzar answered, "My lord, if
only the dream applied to your enemies
and its meaning to your adversaries!
20The tree you saw, which grew large and
strong, with its top touching the sky, visible to the whole earth, 21with beautiful
leaves and abundant fruit, providing food
for all, giving shelter to the wild animals,
and having nesting places in its branches
for the birds— 22Your Majesty, you are
that tree! You have become great and
strong; your greatness has grown until
it reaches the sky, and your dominion extends to distant parts of the earth.
23"Your Majesty saw a holy one, a messenger, coming down from heaven and
saying, 'Cut down the tree and destroy it,
but leave the stump, bound with iron and
bronze, in the grass of the field, while its
roots remain in the ground. Let him be
drenched with the dew of heaven; let him
live with the wild animals, until seven
times pass by for him.'
24"This is the interpretation, Your
Majesty, and this is the decree the Most
High has issued against my lord the king:
25You will be driven away from people
and will live with the wild animals; you
will eat grass like the ox and be drenched
with the dew of heaven. Seven times will
pass by for you until you acknowledge
that the Most High is sovereign over
all kingdoms on earth and gives them
to anyone he wishes. 26The command
to leave the stump of the tree with its
roots means that your kingdom will be
restored to you when you acknowledge

[a] In Aramaic texts 4:1-3 is numbered 3:31-33, and 4:4-37 is numbered 4:1-34. [b] 7 Or *Chaldeans*
[c] *13* Or *watchman*; also in verses 17 and 23 [d] *16* Or *years*; also in verses 23, 25 and 32

that Heaven rules. 27Therefore, Your Majesty, be pleased to accept my advice: Renounce your sins by doing what is right,
and your wickedness by being kind to
the oppressed. It may be that then your
prosperity will continue."

The Dream Is Fulfilled

28All this happened to King Nebuchadnezzar. 29Twelve months later, as the king
was walking on the roof of the royal palace of Babylon, 30he said, "Is not this the
great Babylon I have built as the royal
residence, by my mighty power and for
the glory of my majesty?"

31Even as the words were on his lips, a
voice came from heaven, "This is what is
decreed for you, King Nebuchadnezzar:
Your royal authority has been taken from
you. 32You will be driven away from people and will live with the wild animals;
you will eat grass like the ox. Seven times
will pass by for you until you acknowledge that the Most High is sovereign over
all kingdoms on earth and gives them to
anyone he wishes."

33Immediately what had been said
about Nebuchadnezzar was fulfilled.
He was driven away from people and ate
grass like the ox. His body was drenched
with the dew of heaven until his hair grew
like the feathers of an eagle and his nails
like the claws of a bird.

34At the end of that time, I, Nebuchadnezzar, raised my eyes toward heav-
en, and my sanity was restored. Then
I praised the Most High; I honored and
glorified him who lives forever.

His dominion is an eternal dominion;
his kingdom endures from generation
to generation.
35 All the peoples of the earth
are regarded as nothing.
He does as he pleases
with the powers of heaven
and the peoples of the earth.
No one can hold back his hand
or say to him: "What have you done?"

36At the same time that my sanity was
restored, my honor and splendor were
returned to me for the glory of my kingdom. My advisers and nobles sought me
out, and I was restored to my throne and
became even greater than before. 37Now
I, Nebuchadnezzar, praise and exalt and
glorify the King of heaven, because everything he does is right and all his ways
are just. And those who walk in pride he
is able to humble.

The Writing on the Wall

5 King Belshazzar gave a great banquet for
a thousand of his nobles and drank wine
with them. 2While Belshazzar was drinking
his wine, he gave orders to bring in the gold
and silver goblets that Nebuchadnezzar his
father[a] had taken from the temple in Jerusalem, so that the king and his nobles, his wives
and his concubines might drink from them.
3So they brought in the gold goblets that had
been taken from the temple of God in Jerusalem, and the king and his nobles, his wives
and his concubines drank from them. 4As they
drank the wine, they praised the gods of gold
and silver, of bronze, iron, wood and stone.

5Suddenly the fingers of a human hand appeared and wrote on the plaster of the wall,
near the lampstand in the royal palace. The
king watched the hand as it wrote. 6His face
turned pale and he was so frightened that
his legs became weak and his knees were
knocking.

7The king summoned the enchanters, astrologers[b] and diviners. Then he said to these
wise men of Babylon, "Whoever reads this
writing and tells me what it means will be
clothed in purple and have a gold chain placed
around his neck, and he will be made the third
highest ruler in the kingdom."

8Then all the king's wise men came in, but
they could not read the writing or tell the king
what it meant. 9So King Belshazzar became
even more terrified and his face grew more
pale. His nobles were baffled.

10The queen,[c] hearing the voices of the king
and his nobles, came into the banquet hall.
"May the king live forever!" she said. "Don't
be alarmed! Don't look so pale! 11There is a
man in your kingdom who has the spirit of the
holy gods in him. In the time of your father he
was found to have insight and intelligence and
wisdom like that of the gods. Your father, King
Nebuchadnezzar, appointed him chief of the
magicians, enchanters, astrologers and diviners. 12He did this because Daniel, whom the
king called Belteshazzar, was found to have
a keen mind and knowledge and understanding, and also the ability to interpret dreams,
explain riddles and solve difficult problems.
Call for Daniel, and he will tell you what the
writing means."

13So Daniel was brought before the king,
and the king said to him, "Are you Daniel,
one of the exiles my father the king brought
from Judah? 14I have heard that the spirit of
the gods is in you and that you have insight,
intelligence and outstanding wisdom. 15The
wise men and enchanters were brought before me to read this writing and tell me what
it means, but they could not explain it. 16Now
I have heard that you are able to give inter-
pretations and to solve difficult problems. If
you can read this writing and tell me what
it means, you will be clothed in purple and
have a gold chain placed around your neck,
and you will be made the third highest ruler
in the kingdom."

17Then Daniel answered the king, "You may
keep your gifts for yourself and give your rewards to someone else. Nevertheless, I will

[a] 2 Or *ancestor*; or *predecessor*; also in verses 11, 13 and 18 [b] 7 Or *Chaldeans*; also in verse 11
[c] 10 Or *queen mother*

read the writing for the king and tell him what it means.

18“Your Majesty, the Most High God gave your father Nebuchadnezzar sovereignty and greatness and glory and splendor. 19Because of the high position he gave him, all the nations and peoples of every language dreaded and feared him. Those the king wanted to put to death, he put to death; those he wanted to spare, he spared; those he wanted to promote, he promoted; and those he wanted to humble, he humbled. 20But when his heart became arrogant and hardened with pride, he was deposed from his royal throne and stripped of his glory. 21He was driven away from people and given the mind of an animal; he lived with the wild donkeys and ate grass like the ox; and his body was drenched with the dew of heaven, until he acknowledged that the Most High God is sovereign over all kingdoms on earth and sets over them anyone he wishes.

22“But you, Belshazzar, his son,[a] have not humbled yourself, though you knew all this. 23Instead, you have set yourself up against the Lord of heaven. You had the goblets from his temple brought to you, and you and your nobles, your wives and your concubines drank wine from them. You praised the gods of silver and gold, of bronze, iron, wood and stone, which cannot see or hear or understand. But you did not honor the God who holds in his hand your life and all your ways. 24Therefore he sent the hand that wrote the inscription.

25“This is the inscription that was written:

MENE, MENE, TEKEL, PARSIN

26“Here is what these words mean:

Mene[b]: God has numbered the days of your reign and brought it to an end.

27 *Tekel*[c]: You have been weighed on the scales and found wanting.

28 *Peres*[d]: Your kingdom is divided and given to the Medes and Persians.”

29Then at Belshazzar’s command, Daniel was clothed in purple, a gold chain was placed around his neck, and he was proclaimed the third highest ruler in the kingdom.

30That very night Belshazzar, king of the Babylonians,[e] was slain, 31and Darius the Mede took over the kingdom, at the age of sixty-two.[f]

Daniel in the Den of Lions

6[g] It pleased Darius to appoint 120 satraps to rule throughout the kingdom, 2with three administrators over them, one of whom was Daniel. The satraps were made accountable to them so that the king might not suffer loss. 3Now Daniel so distinguished himself among the administrators and the satraps by his exceptional qualities that the king planned to set him over the whole kingdom. 4At this, the administrators and the satraps tried to find grounds for charges against Daniel in his conduct of government affairs, but they were unable to do so. They could find no corruption in him, because he was trustworthy and neither corrupt nor negligent. 5Finally these men said, “We will never find any basis for charges against this man Daniel unless it has something to do with the law of his God.”

6So these administrators and satraps went as a group to the king and said: “May King Darius live forever! 7The royal administrators, prefects, satraps, advisers and governors have all agreed that the king should issue an edict and enforce the decree that anyone who prays to any god or human being during the next thirty days, except to you, Your Majesty, shall be thrown into the lions’ den. 8Now, Your Majesty, issue the decree and put it in writing so that it cannot be altered—in accordance with the law of the Medes and Persians, which cannot be repealed.” 9So King Darius put the decree in writing.

10Now when Daniel learned that the decree had been published, he went home to his upstairs room where the windows opened toward Jerusalem. Three times a day he got down on his knees and prayed, giving thanks to his God, just as he had done before. 11Then these men went as a group and found Daniel praying and asking God for help. 12So they went to the king and spoke to him about his royal decree: “Did you not publish a decree that during the next thirty days anyone who prays to any god or human being except to you, Your Majesty, would be thrown into the lions’ den?”

The king answered, “The decree stands—in accordance with the law of the Medes and Persians, which cannot be repealed.”

13Then they said to the king, “Daniel, who is one of the exiles from Judah, pays no attention to you, Your Majesty, or to the decree you put in writing. He still prays three times a day.” 14When the king heard this, he was greatly distressed; he was determined to rescue Daniel and made every effort until sundown to save him.

15Then the men went as a group to King Darius and said to him, “Remember, Your Majesty, that according to the law of the Medes and Persians no decree or edict that the king issues can be changed.”

16So the king gave the order, and they brought Daniel and threw him into the lions’ den. The king said to Daniel, “May your God, whom you serve continually, rescue you!”

17A stone was brought and placed over the mouth of the den, and the king sealed it with his own signet ring and with the rings of his nobles, so that Daniel’s situation might not be changed. 18Then the king returned to his palace and spent the night without eating and

[a] 22 Or *descendant*; or *successor* [b] 26 *Mene* can mean *numbered* or *mina* (a unit of money). [c] 27 *Tekel* can mean *weighed* or *shekel*. [d] 28 *Peres* (the singular of *Parsin*) can mean *divided* or *Persia* or *a half mina* or *a half shekel*. [e] 30 Or *Chaldeans* [f] 31 In Aramaic texts this verse (5:31) is numbered 6:1. [g] In Aramaic texts 6:1-28 is numbered 6:2-29.

without any entertainment being brought to him. And he could not sleep.

19At the first light of dawn, the king got up and hurried to the lions' den. 20When he came near the den, he called to Daniel in an anguished voice, "Daniel, servant of the living God, has your God, whom you serve continually, been able to rescue you from the lions?"

21Daniel answered, "May the king live forever! 22My God sent his angel, and he shut the mouths of the lions. They have not hurt me, because I was found innocent in his sight. Nor have I ever done any wrong before you, Your Majesty."

23The king was overjoyed and gave orders to lift Daniel out of the den. And when Daniel was lifted from the den, no wound was found on him, because he had trusted in his God.

24At the king's command, the men who had falsely accused Daniel were brought in and thrown into the lions' den, along with their wives and children. And before they reached the floor of the den, the lions overpowered them and crushed all their bones.

25Then King Darius wrote to all the nations and peoples of every language in all the earth:

"May you prosper greatly!

26"I issue a decree that in every part of my kingdom people must fear and reverence the God of Daniel.

"For he is the living God
and he endures forever;
his kingdom will not be destroyed,
his dominion will never end.
27He rescues and he saves;
he performs signs and wonders
in the heavens and on the earth.
He has rescued Daniel
from the power of the lions."

28So Daniel prospered during the reign of Darius and the reign of Cyrus[a] the Persian.

Daniel's Dream of Four Beasts

7 In the first year of Belshazzar king of Babylon, Daniel had a dream, and visions passed through his mind as he was lying in bed. He wrote down the substance of his dream.

2Daniel said: "In my vision at night I looked, and there before me were the four winds of heaven churning up the great sea. 3Four great beasts, each different from the others, came up out of the sea.

4"The first was like a lion, and it had the wings of an eagle. I watched until its wings were torn off and it was lifted from the ground so that it stood on two feet like a human being, and the mind of a human was given to it.

5"And there before me was a second beast, which looked like a bear. It was raised up on one of its sides, and it had three ribs in its mouth between its teeth. It was told, 'Get up and eat your fill of flesh!'

6"After that, I looked, and there before me was another beast, one that looked like a leopard. And on its back it had four wings like those of a bird. This beast had four heads, and it was given authority to rule.

7"After that, in my vision at night I looked, and there before me was a fourth beast—terrifying and frightening and very powerful. It had large iron teeth; it crushed and devoured its victims and trampled underfoot whatever was left. It was different from all the former beasts, and it had ten horns.

8"While I was thinking about the horns, there before me was another horn, a little one, which came up among them; and three of the first horns were uprooted before it. This horn had eyes like the eyes of a human being and a mouth that spoke boastfully.

9"As I looked,

"thrones were set in place,
and the Ancient of Days took his seat.
His clothing was as white as snow;
the hair of his head was white like wool.
His throne was flaming with fire,
and its wheels were all ablaze.
10A river of fire was flowing,
coming out from before him.
Thousands upon thousands attended him;
ten thousand times ten thousand stood before him.
The court was seated,
and the books were opened.

11"Then I continued to watch because of the boastful words the horn was speaking. I kept looking until the beast was slain and its body destroyed and thrown into the blazing fire. 12(The other beasts had been stripped of their authority, but were allowed to live for a period of time.)

13"In my vision at night I looked, and there before me was one like a son of man,[b] coming with the clouds of heaven. He approached the Ancient of Days and was led into his presence. 14He was given authority, glory and sovereign power; all nations and peoples of every language worshiped him. His dominion is an everlasting dominion that will not pass away, and his kingdom is one that will never be destroyed.

The Interpretation of the Dream

15"I, Daniel, was troubled in spirit, and the visions that passed through my mind disturbed me. 16I approached one of those standing there and asked him the meaning of all this.

"So he told me and gave me the interpretation of these things: 17'The four great beasts are four kings that will rise from the earth. 18But the holy people of the Most High will receive the kingdom and will possess it forever—yes, for ever and ever.'

19"Then I wanted to know the meaning of

[a] *28* Or *Darius, that is, the reign of Cyrus* [b] *13* The Aramaic phrase *bar enash* means *human being.* The phrase *son of man* is retained here because of its use in the New Testament as a title of Jesus, probably based largely on this verse.

the fourth beast, which was different from
all the others and most terrifying, with its
iron teeth and bronze claws—the beast that
crushed and devoured its victims and trampled underfoot whatever was left. 20I also
wanted to know about the ten horns on its
head and about the other horn that came up,
before which three of them fell—the horn that
looked more imposing than the others and
that had eyes and a mouth that spoke boastfully. 21As I watched, this horn was waging
war against the holy people and defeating
them, 22until the Ancient of Days came and
pronounced judgment in favor of the holy people of the Most High, and the time came when
they possessed the kingdom.

23"He gave me this explanation: 'The fourth
beast is a fourth kingdom that will appear on
earth. It will be different from all the other
kingdoms and will devour the whole earth,
trampling it down and crushing it. 24The ten
horns are ten kings who will come from this
kingdom. After them another king will arise,
different from the earlier ones; he will subdue
three kings. 25He will speak against the Most
High and oppress his holy people and try to
change the set times and the laws. The holy
people will be delivered into his hands for a
time, times and half a time.[a]

26" 'But the court will sit, and his power
will be taken away and completely destroyed
forever. 27Then the sovereignty, power and
greatness of all the kingdoms under heaven
will be handed over to the holy people of the
Most High. His kingdom will be an everlasting kingdom, and all rulers will worship and
obey him.'

28"This is the end of the matter. I, Daniel,
was deeply troubled by my thoughts, and my
face turned pale, but I kept the matter to myself."

Daniel's Vision of a Ram and a Goat

8 In the third year of King Belshazzar's
reign, I, Daniel, had a vision, after the one
that had already appeared to me. 2In my vision I saw myself in the citadel of Susa in the
province of Elam; in the vision I was beside
the Ulai Canal. 3I looked up, and there before
me was a ram with two horns, standing beside
the canal, and the horns were long. One of the
horns was longer than the other but grew up
later. 4I watched the ram as it charged toward
the west and the north and the south. No animal could stand against it, and none could
rescue from its power. It did as it pleased and
became great.

5As I was thinking about this, suddenly a
goat with a prominent horn between its eyes
came from the west, crossing the whole earth
without touching the ground. 6It came toward
the two-horned ram I had seen standing beside the canal and charged at it in great rage.
7I saw it attack the ram furiously, striking the
ram and shattering its two horns. The ram
was powerless to stand against it; the goat
knocked it to the ground and trampled on it,
and none could rescue the ram from its power.
8The goat became very great, but at the height
of its power the large horn was broken off,
and in its place four prominent horns grew
up toward the four winds of heaven.

9Out of one of them came another horn,
which started small but grew in power to the
south and to the east and toward the Beautiful
Land. 10It grew until it reached the host of the
heavens, and it threw some of the starry host
down to the earth and trampled on them. 11It
set itself up to be as great as the commander
of the army of the LORD; it took away the daily
sacrifice from the LORD, and his sanctuary
was thrown down. 12Because of rebellion, the
LORD's people[b] and the daily sacrifice were
given over to it. It prospered in everything
it did, and truth was thrown to the ground.

13Then I heard a holy one speaking, and
another holy one said to him, "How long will
it take for the vision to be fulfilled—the vision
concerning the daily sacrifice, the rebellion
that causes desolation, the surrender of the
sanctuary and the trampling underfoot of the
LORD's people?"

14He said to me, "It will take 2,300 evenings
and mornings; then the sanctuary will be re-
consecrated."

The Interpretation of the Vision

15While I, Daniel, was watching the vision
and trying to understand it, there before me
stood one who looked like a man. 16And I
heard a man's voice from the Ulai calling,
"Gabriel, tell this man the meaning of the vision."

17As he came near the place where I was
standing, I was terrified and fell prostrate.
"Son of man,"[c] he said to me, "understand
that the vision concerns the time of the end."

18While he was speaking to me, I was in a
deep sleep, with my face to the ground. Then
he touched me and raised me to my feet.

19He said: "I am going to tell you what will
happen later in the time of wrath, because
the vision concerns the appointed time of the
end.[d] 20The two-horned ram that you saw represents the kings of Media and Persia. 21The
shaggy goat is the king of Greece, and the
large horn between its eyes is the first king.
22The four horns that replaced the one that
was broken off represent four kingdoms that
will emerge from his nation but will not have
the same power.

23"In the latter part of their reign, when
rebels have become completely wicked, a
fierce-looking king, a master of intrigue, will
arise. 24He will become very strong, but not by
his own power. He will cause astounding dev-
astation and will succeed in whatever he does.
He will destroy those who are mighty, the holy

[a] 25 Or *for a year, two years and half a year* [b] 12 Or *rebellion, the armies* [c] 17 The Hebrew phrase *ben adam* means *human being*. The phrase *son of man* is retained as a form of address here because of its possible association with "Son of Man" in the New Testament. [d] 19 Or *because the end will be at the appointed time*

people. 25He will cause deceit to prosper, and he will consider himself superior. When they feel secure, he will destroy many and take his stand against the Prince of princes. Yet he will be destroyed, but not by human power.

26"The vision of the evenings and mornings that has been given you is true, but seal up the vision, for it concerns the distant future."

27I, Daniel, was worn out. I lay exhausted for several days. Then I got up and went about the king's business. I was appalled by the vision; it was beyond understanding.

Daniel's Prayer

9 In the first year of Darius son of Xerxes[a] (a Mede by descent), who was made ruler over the Babylonian[b] kingdom— 2in the first year of his reign, I, Daniel, understood from the Scriptures, according to the word of the LORD given to Jeremiah the prophet, that the desolation of Jerusalem would last seventy years. 3So I turned to the Lord God and pleaded with him in prayer and petition, in fasting, and in sackcloth and ashes.

4I prayed to the LORD my God and confessed:

> "Lord, the great and awesome God, who keeps his covenant of love with those who love him and keep his commandments, 5we have sinned and done wrong. We have been wicked and have rebelled; we have turned away from your commands and laws. 6We have not listened to your servants the prophets, who spoke in your name to our kings, our princes and our ancestors, and to all the people of the land.
>
> 7"Lord, you are righteous, but this day we are covered with shame—the people of Judah and the inhabitants of Jerusalem and all Israel, both near and far, in all the countries where you have scattered us because of our unfaithfulness to you. 8We and our kings, our princes and our ancestors are covered with shame, LORD, because we have sinned against you. 9The Lord our God is merciful and forgiving, even though we have rebelled against him; 10we have not obeyed the LORD our God or kept the laws he gave us through his servants the prophets. 11All Israel has transgressed your law and turned away, refusing to obey you.
>
> "Therefore the curses and sworn judgments written in the Law of Moses, the servant of God, have been poured out on us, because we have sinned against you. 12You have fulfilled the words spoken against us and against our rulers by bringing on us great disaster. Under the whole heaven nothing has ever been done like what has been done to Jerusalem. 13Just as it is written in the Law of Moses, all this disaster has come on us, yet we have not sought the favor of the LORD our God by turning from our sins and giving attention to your truth. 14The LORD did not hesitate to bring the disaster on us, for the LORD our God is righteous in everything he does; yet we have not obeyed him.
>
> 15"Now, Lord our God, who brought your people out of Egypt with a mighty hand and who made for yourself a name that endures to this day, we have sinned, we have done wrong. 16Lord, in keeping with all your righteous acts, turn away your anger and your wrath from Jerusalem, your city, your holy hill. Our sins and the iniquities of our ancestors have made Jerusalem and your people an object of scorn to all those around us.
>
> 17"Now, our God, hear the prayers and petitions of your servant. For your sake, Lord, look with favor on your desolate sanctuary. 18Give ear, our God, and hear; open your eyes and see the desolation of the city that bears your Name. We do not make requests of you because we are righteous, but because of your great mercy. 19Lord, listen! Lord, forgive! Lord, hear and act! For your sake, my God, do not delay, because your city and your people bear your Name."

The Seventy "Sevens"

20While I was speaking and praying, confessing my sin and the sin of my people Israel and making my request to the LORD my God for his holy hill— 21while I was still in prayer, Gabriel, the man I had seen in the earlier vision, came to me in swift flight about the time of the evening sacrifice. 22He instructed me and said to me, "Daniel, I have now come to give you insight and understanding. 23As soon as you began to pray, a word went out, which I have come to tell you, for you are highly esteemed. Therefore, consider the word and understand the vision:

24"Seventy 'sevens'[c] are decreed for your people and your holy city to finish[d] transgression, to put an end to sin, to atone for wickedness, to bring in everlasting righteousness, to seal up vision and prophecy and to anoint the Most Holy Place.[e]

25"Know and understand this: From the time the word goes out to restore and rebuild Jerusalem until the Anointed One,[f] the ruler, comes, there will be seven 'sevens,' and sixty-two 'sevens.' It will be rebuilt with streets and a trench, but in times of trouble. 26After the sixty-two 'sevens,' the Anointed One will be put to death and will have nothing.[g] The people of the ruler who will come will destroy the city and the sanctuary. The end will come like a flood: War will continue until the end, and desolations have been decreed. 27He will confirm a covenant with many for one 'seven.'[h] In the middle of the 'seven'[h] he will put an end to sacrifice and offering. And at the

[a] 1 Hebrew *Ahasuerus* [b] 1 Or *Chaldean* [c] 24 Or *'weeks'*; also in verses 25 and 26
[d] 24 Or *restrain* [e] 24 Or *the most holy One* [f] 25 Or *an anointed one*; also in verse 26
[g] 26 Or *death and will have no one*; or *death, but not for himself* [h] 27 Or *'week'*

temple[a] he will set up an abomination that
causes desolation, until the end that is decreed
is poured out on him.[b]"[c]

Daniel's Vision of a Man

10 In the third year of Cyrus king of Persia, a revelation was given to Daniel
(who was called Belteshazzar). Its message
was true and it concerned a great war.[d] The
understanding of the message came to him
in a vision.
2At that time I, Daniel, mourned for three
weeks. 3I ate no choice food; no meat or wine
touched my lips; and I used no lotions at all
until the three weeks were over.
4On the twenty-fourth day of the first
month, as I was standing on the bank of the
great river, the Tigris, 5I looked up and there
before me was a man dressed in linen, with a
belt of fine gold from Uphaz around his waist.
6His body was like topaz, his face like lightning, his eyes like flaming torches, his arms
and legs like the gleam of burnished bronze,
and his voice like the sound of a multitude.
7I, Daniel, was the only one who saw the
vision; those who were with me did not see it,
but such terror overwhelmed them that they
fled and hid themselves. 8So I was left alone,
gazing at this great vision; I had no strength
left, my face turned deathly pale and I was
helpless. 9Then I heard him speaking, and as
I listened to him, I fell into a deep sleep, my
face to the ground.
10A hand touched me and set me trembling
on my hands and knees. 11He said, "Daniel,
you who are highly esteemed, consider carefully the words I am about to speak to you, and
stand up, for I have now been sent to you." And
when he said this to me, I stood up trembling.
12Then he continued, "Do not be afraid,
Daniel. Since the first day that you set your
mind to gain understanding and to humble
yourself before your God, your words were
heard, and I have come in response to them.
13But the prince of the Persian kingdom resisted me twenty-one days. Then Michael, one
of the chief princes, came to help me, because
I was detained there with the king of Persia.
14Now I have come to explain to you what will
happen to your people in the future, for the
vision concerns a time yet to come."
15While he was saying this to me, I bowed
with my face toward the ground and was
speechless. 16Then one who looked like a
man[e] touched my lips, and I opened my mouth
and began to speak. I said to the one standing before me, "I am overcome with anguish
because of the vision, my lord, and I feel very
weak. 17How can I, your servant, talk with
you, my lord? My strength is gone and I can
hardly breathe."
18Again the one who looked like a man
touched me and gave me strength. 19"Do not
be afraid, you who are highly esteemed," he
said. "Peace! Be strong now; be strong."
When he spoke to me, I was strengthened
and said, "Speak, my lord, since you have giv-
en me strength."
20So he said, "Do you know why I have come
to you? Soon I will return to fight against the
prince of Persia, and when I go, the prince
of Greece will come; 21but first I will tell you
what is written in the Book of Truth. (No one
supports me against them except Michael,
11 your prince. 1And in the first year of Darius the Mede, I took my stand to support
and protect him.)

The Kings of the South and the North

2"Now then, I tell you the truth: Three more
kings will arise in Persia, and then a fourth,
who will be far richer than all the others. When
he has gained power by his wealth, he will stir
up everyone against the kingdom of Greece.
3Then a mighty king will arise, who will rule
with great power and do as he pleases. 4After
he has arisen, his empire will be broken up and
parceled out toward the four winds of heaven.
It will not go to his descendants, nor will it have
the power he exercised, because his empire
will be uprooted and given to others.
5"The king of the South will become strong,
but one of his commanders will become even
stronger than he and will rule his own kingdom with great power. 6After some years, they
will become allies. The daughter of the king
of the South will go to the king of the North to
make an alliance, but she will not retain her
power, and he and his power[f] will not last. In
those days she will be betrayed, together with
her royal escort and her father[g] and the one
who supported her.
7"One from her family line will arise to take
her place. He will attack the forces of the king
of the North and enter his fortress; he will
fight against them and be victorious. 8He will
also seize their gods, their metal images and
their valuable articles of silver and gold and
carry them off to Egypt. For some years he
will leave the king of the North alone. 9Then
the king of the North will invade the realm
of the king of the South but will retreat to
his own country. 10His sons will prepare for
war and assemble a great army, which will
sweep on like an irresistible flood and carry
the battle as far as his fortress.
11"Then the king of the South will march
out in a rage and fight against the king of
the North, who will raise a large army, but it
will be defeated. 12When the army is carried
off, the king of the South will be filled with
pride and will slaughter many thousands, yet
he will not remain triumphant. 13For the king
of the North will muster another army, larger
than the first; and after several years, he will
advance with a huge army fully equipped.

[a] 27 Septuagint and Theodotion; Hebrew *wing* [b] 27 Or *it* [c] 27 Or *And one who causes desolation will come upon the wing of the abominable temple, until the end that is decreed is poured out on the desolated city* [d] 1 Or *true and burdensome* [e] 16 Most manuscripts of the Masoretic Text; one manuscript of the Masoretic Text, Dead Sea Scrolls and Septuagint *Then something that looked like a human hand* [f] 6 Or *offspring* [g] 6 Or *child* (see Vulgate and Syriac)

14“In those times many will rise against
the king of the South. Those who are violent
among your own people will rebel in fulfillment of the vision, but without success.
15Then the king of the North will come and
build up siege ramps and will capture a fortified city. The forces of the South will be
powerless to resist; even their best troops will
not have the strength to stand. 16The invader
will do as he pleases; no one will be able to
stand against him. He will establish himself
in the Beautiful Land and will have the power to destroy it. 17He will determine to come
with the might of his entire kingdom and will
make an alliance with the king of the South.
And he will give him a daughter in marriage
in order to overthrow the kingdom, but his
plans[a] will not succeed or help him. 18Then
he will turn his attention to the coastlands
and will take many of them, but a commander will put an end to his insolence and will
turn his insolence back on him. 19After this,
he will turn back toward the fortresses of his
own country but will stumble and fall, to be
seen no more.

20“His successor will send out a tax collector to maintain the royal splendor. In a few
years, however, he will be destroyed, yet not
in anger or in battle.

21“He will be succeeded by a contemptible
person who has not been given the honor of
royalty. He will invade the kingdom when
its people feel secure, and he will seize it
through intrigue. 22Then an overwhelming
army will be swept away before him; both it
and a prince of the covenant will be destroyed.
23After coming to an agreement with him, he
will act deceitfully, and with only a few people
he will rise to power. 24When the richest provinces feel secure, he will invade them and will
achieve what neither his fathers nor his forefa-
thers did. He will distribute plunder, loot and
wealth among his followers. He will plot the
overthrow of fortresses—but only for a time.

25“With a large army he will stir up his
strength and courage against the king of the
South. The king of the South will wage war
with a large and very powerful army, but he
will not be able to stand because of the plots
devised against him. 26Those who eat from the
king's provisions will try to destroy him; his
army will be swept away, and many will fall
in battle. 27The two kings, with their hearts
bent on evil, will sit at the same table and lie to
each other, but to no avail, because an end will
still come at the appointed time. 28The king of
the North will return to his own country with
great wealth, but his heart will be set against
the holy covenant. He will take action against
it and then return to his own country.

29“At the appointed time he will invade the
South again, but this time the outcome will
be different from what it was before. 30Ships
of the western coastlands will oppose him,
and he will lose heart. Then he will turn back
and vent his fury against the holy covenant.
He will return and show favor to those who
forsake the holy covenant.

31“His armed forces will rise up to desecrate
the temple fortress and will abolish the daily
sacrifice. Then they will set up the abomination that causes desolation. 32With flattery
he will corrupt those who have violated the
covenant, but the people who know their God
will firmly resist him.

33“Those who are wise will instruct many,
though for a time they will fall by the sword or
be burned or captured or plundered. 34When
they fall, they will receive a little help, and
many who are not sincere will join them.
35Some of the wise will stumble, so that they
may be refined, purified and made spotless
until the time of the end, for it will still come
at the appointed time.

The King Who Exalts Himself

36“The king will do as he pleases. He will
exalt and magnify himself above every god
and will say unheard-of things against the
God of gods. He will be successful until the
time of wrath is completed, for what has been
determined must take place. 37He will show
no regard for the gods of his ancestors or for
the one desired by women, nor will he regard
any god, but will exalt himself above them
all. 38Instead of them, he will honor a god of
fortresses; a god unknown to his ancestors he
will honor with gold and silver, with precious
stones and costly gifts. 39He will attack the
mightiest fortresses with the help of a foreign god and will greatly honor those who
acknowledge him. He will make them rulers
over many people and will distribute the land
at a price.[b]

40“At the time of the end the king of the
South will engage him in battle, and the king
of the North will storm out against him with
chariots and cavalry and a great fleet of ships.
He will invade many countries and sweep
through them like a flood. 41He will also invade the Beautiful Land. Many countries will
fall, but Edom, Moab and the leaders of Ammon will be delivered from his hand. 42He will
extend his power over many countries; Egypt
will not escape. 43He will gain control of the
treasures of gold and silver and all the riches
of Egypt, with the Libyans and Cushites[c] in
submission. 44But reports from the east and
the north will alarm him, and he will set out in
a great rage to destroy and annihilate many.
45He will pitch his royal tents between the seas
at[d] the beautiful holy mountain. Yet he will
come to his end, and no one will help him.

The End Times

12 “At that time Michael, the great prince
who protects your people, will arise.
There will be a time of distress such as has
not happened from the beginning of nations
until then. But at that time your people—everyone whose name is found written in the
book—will be delivered. 2Multitudes who

[a] 17 Or *but she* [b] 39 Or *land for a reward* [c] 43 That is, people from the upper Nile region
[d] 45 Or *the sea and*

sleep in the dust of the earth will awake: some
to everlasting life, others to shame and everlasting contempt. 3Those who are wise[a] will
shine like the brightness of the heavens, and
those who lead many to righteousness, like
the stars for ever and ever. 4But you, Daniel,
roll up and seal the words of the scroll until
the time of the end. Many will go here and
there to increase knowledge."

5Then I, Daniel, looked, and there before
me stood two others, one on this bank of the
river and one on the opposite bank. 6One of
them said to the man clothed in linen, who
was above the waters of the river, "How long
will it be before these astonishing things are
fulfilled?"
7The man clothed in linen, who was above
the waters of the river, lifted his right hand
and his left hand toward heaven, and I heard
him swear by him who lives forever, saying, "It
will be for a time, times and half a time.[b] When
the power of the holy people has been finally
broken, all these things will be completed."
8I heard, but I did not understand. So I
asked, "My lord, what will the outcome of all
this be?"
9He replied, "Go your way, Daniel, because
the words are rolled up and sealed until the
time of the end. 10Many will be purified, made
spotless and refined, but the wicked will continue to be wicked. None of the wicked will
understand, but those who are wise will understand.
11"From the time that the daily sacrifice is
abolished and the abomination that causes
desolation is set up, there will be 1,290 days.
12Blessed is the one who waits for and reaches
the end of the 1,335 days.
13"As for you, go your way till the end. You
will rest, and then at the end of the days you
will rise to receive your allotted inheritance."

Hosea

1 The word of the LORD that came to Hosea
son of Beeri during the reigns of Uzziah,
Jotham, Ahaz and Hezekiah, kings of Judah,
and during the reign of Jeroboam son of Jehoash[c] king of Israel:

Hosea's Wife and Children

2When the LORD began to speak through
Hosea, the LORD said to him, "Go, marry a
promiscuous woman and have children with
her, for like an adulterous wife this land is
guilty of unfaithfulness to the LORD." 3So he
married Gomer daughter of Diblaim, and she
conceived and bore him a son.
4Then the LORD said to Hosea, "Call him
Jezreel, because I will soon punish the house
of Jehu for the massacre at Jezreel, and I will
put an end to the kingdom of Israel. 5In that
day I will break Israel's bow in the Valley of
Jezreel."
6Gomer conceived again and gave birth to a
daughter. Then the LORD said to Hosea, "Call
her Lo-Ruhamah (which means "not loved"),
for I will no longer show love to Israel, that I
should at all forgive them. 7Yet I will show love
to Judah; and I will save them—not by bow,
sword or battle, or by horses and horsemen,
but I, the LORD their God, will save them."
8After she had weaned Lo-Ruhamah, Gomer had another son. 9Then the LORD said,
"Call him Lo-Ammi (which means "not my
people"), for you are not my people, and I am
not your God.[d]
10"Yet the Israelites will be like the sand
on the seashore, which cannot be measured
or counted. In the place where it was said to
them, 'You are not my people,' they will be
called 'children of the living God.' 11The people of Judah and the people of Israel will come
together; they will appoint one leader and will
come up out of the land, for great will be the
day of Jezreel.[e]

2[f] "Say of your brothers, 'My people,' and of
your sisters, 'My loved one.'

Israel Punished and Restored

2"Rebuke your mother, rebuke her,
for she is not my wife,
and I am not her husband.
Let her remove the adulterous look from
her face
and the unfaithfulness from between
her breasts.
3Otherwise I will strip her naked
and make her as bare as on the day she
was born;
I will make her like a desert,
turn her into a parched land,
and slay her with thirst.
4I will not show my love to her children,
because they are the children of
adultery.
5Their mother has been unfaithful
and has conceived them in disgrace.
She said, 'I will go after my lovers,
who give me my food and my water,

[a] 3 Or *who impart wisdom* [b] 7 Or *a year, two years and half a year* [c] 1 Hebrew *Joash,* a variant
of *Jehoash* [d] 9 Or *your* I AM [e] 11 In Hebrew texts 1:10,11 is numbered 2:1,2. [f] In Hebrew texts
2:1-23 is numbered 2:3-25.

my wool and my linen, my olive oil and
my drink.'
6 Therefore I will block her path with
thornbushes;
I will wall her in so that she cannot find
her way.
7 She will chase after her lovers but not
catch them;
she will look for them but not find them.
Then she will say,
'I will go back to my husband as at first,
for then I was better off than now.'
8 She has not acknowledged that I was the
one
who gave her the grain, the new wine
and oil,
who lavished on her the silver and gold—
which they used for Baal.

9 "Therefore I will take away my grain
when it ripens,
and my new wine when it is ready.
I will take back my wool and my linen,
intended to cover her naked body.
10 So now I will expose her lewdness
before the eyes of her lovers;
no one will take her out of my hands.
11 I will stop all her celebrations:
her yearly festivals, her New Moons,
her Sabbath days—all her appointed
festivals.
12 I will ruin her vines and her fig trees,
which she said were her pay from her
lovers;
I will make them a thicket,
and wild animals will devour them.
13 I will punish her for the days
she burned incense to the Baals;
she decked herself with rings and
jewelry,
and went after her lovers,
but me she forgot,"
declares the LORD.

14 "Therefore I am now going to allure her;
I will lead her into the wilderness
and speak tenderly to her.
15 There I will give her back her vineyards,
and will make the Valley of Achor[a] a
door of hope.
There she will respond[b] as in the days of
her youth,
as in the day she came up out of Egypt.

16 "In that day," declares the LORD,
"you will call me 'my husband';
you will no longer call me 'my master.[c]'
17 I will remove the names of the Baals from
her lips;
no longer will their names be invoked.
18 In that day I will make a covenant for
them
with the beasts of the field, the birds in
the sky
and the creatures that move along the
ground.
Bow and sword and battle
I will abolish from the land,
so that all may lie down in safety.
19 I will betroth you to me forever;
I will betroth you in[d] righteousness and
justice,
in[d] love and compassion.
20 I will betroth you in[d] faithfulness,
and you will acknowledge the LORD.

21 "In that day I will respond,"
declares the LORD—
"I will respond to the skies,
and they will respond to the earth;
22 and the earth will respond to the grain,
the new wine and the olive oil,
and they will respond to Jezreel.[e]
23 I will plant her for myself in the land;
I will show my love to the one I called
'Not my loved one.[f]'
I will say to those called 'Not my people,[g]'
'You are my people';
and they will say, 'You are my God.'"

Hosea's Reconciliation With His Wife

3 The LORD said to me, "Go, show your love
to your wife again, though she is loved by
another man and is an adulteress. Love her
as the LORD loves the Israelites, though they
turn to other gods and love the sacred raisin
cakes."
2 So I bought her for fifteen shekels[h] of silver and about a homer and a lethek[i] of barley. 3 Then I told her, "You are to live with me
many days; you must not be a prostitute or be
intimate with any man, and I will behave the
same way toward you."
4 For the Israelites will live many days without king or prince, without sacrifice or sacred
stones, without ephod or household gods. 5 Afterward the Israelites will return and seek the
LORD their God and David their king. They
will come trembling to the LORD and to his
blessings in the last days.

The Charge Against Israel

4 Hear the word of the LORD, you
Israelites,
because the LORD has a charge to bring
against you who live in the land:
"There is no faithfulness, no love,
no acknowledgment of God in the land.
2 There is only cursing,[j] lying and murder,
stealing and adultery;
they break all bounds,
and bloodshed follows bloodshed.
3 Because of this the land dries up,
and all who live in it waste away;
the beasts of the field, the birds in the sky
and the fish in the sea are swept away.

4 "But let no one bring a charge,
let no one accuse another,
for your people are like those
who bring charges against a priest.

[a] 15 *Achor* means *trouble.* [b] 15 Or *sing* [c] 16 Hebrew *baal* [d] 19,20 Or *with* [e] 22 *Jezreel* means *God plants.* [f] 23 Hebrew *Lo-Ruhamah* (see 1:6) [g] 23 Hebrew *Lo-Ammi* (see 1:9)
[h] 2 That is, about 6 ounces or about 170 grams [i] 2 A homer and a lethek possibly weighed about 430 pounds or about 195 kilograms. [j] 2 That is, to pronounce a curse on

5 You stumble day and night,
and the prophets stumble with you.
So I will destroy your mother—
6 my people are destroyed from lack of knowledge.

"Because you have rejected knowledge,
I also reject you as my priests;
because you have ignored the law of your God,
I also will ignore your children.
7 The more priests there were,
the more they sinned against me;
they exchanged their glorious God[a] for something disgraceful.
8 They feed on the sins of my people
and relish their wickedness.
9 And it will be: Like people, like priests.
I will punish both of them for their ways
and repay them for their deeds.

10 "They will eat but not have enough;
they will engage in prostitution but not flourish,
because they have deserted the LORD
to give themselves 11 to prostitution;
old wine and new wine
take away their understanding.
12 My people consult a wooden idol,
and a diviner's rod speaks to them.
A spirit of prostitution leads them astray;
they are unfaithful to their God.
13 They sacrifice on the mountaintops
and burn offerings on the hills,
under oak, poplar and terebinth,
where the shade is pleasant.
Therefore your daughters turn to prostitution
and your daughters-in-law to adultery.

14 "I will not punish your daughters
when they turn to prostitution,
nor your daughters-in-law
when they commit adultery,
because the men themselves consort with harlots
and sacrifice with shrine prostitutes—
a people without understanding will come to ruin!

15 "Though you, Israel, commit adultery,
do not let Judah become guilty.

"Do not go to Gilgal;
do not go up to Beth Aven.[b]
And do not swear, 'As surely as the LORD lives!'
16 The Israelites are stubborn,
like a stubborn heifer.
How then can the LORD pasture them
like lambs in a meadow?
17 Ephraim is joined to idols;
leave him alone!
18 Even when their drinks are gone,
they continue their prostitution;
their rulers dearly love shameful ways.
19 A whirlwind will sweep them away,
and their sacrifices will bring them shame.

Judgment Against Israel

5 "Hear this, you priests!
Pay attention, you Israelites!
Listen, royal house!
This judgment is against you:
You have been a snare at Mizpah,
a net spread out on Tabor.
2 The rebels are knee-deep in slaughter.
I will discipline all of them.
3 I know all about Ephraim;
Israel is not hidden from me.
Ephraim, you have now turned to prostitution;
Israel is corrupt.

4 "Their deeds do not permit them
to return to their God.
A spirit of prostitution is in their heart;
they do not acknowledge the LORD.
5 Israel's arrogance testifies against them;
the Israelites, even Ephraim, stumble in their sin;
Judah also stumbles with them.
6 When they go with their flocks and herds
to seek the LORD,
they will not find him;
he has withdrawn himself from them.
7 They are unfaithful to the LORD;
they give birth to illegitimate children.
When they celebrate their New Moon feasts,
he will devour[c] their fields.

8 "Sound the trumpet in Gibeah,
the horn in Ramah.
Raise the battle cry in Beth Aven[b];
lead on, Benjamin.
9 Ephraim will be laid waste
on the day of reckoning.
Among the tribes of Israel
I proclaim what is certain.
10 Judah's leaders are like those
who move boundary stones.
I will pour out my wrath on them
like a flood of water.
11 Ephraim is oppressed,
trampled in judgment,
intent on pursuing idols.[d]
12 I am like a moth to Ephraim,
like rot to the people of Judah.

13 "When Ephraim saw his sickness,
and Judah his sores,
then Ephraim turned to Assyria,
and sent to the great king for help.
But he is not able to cure you,
not able to heal your sores.
14 For I will be like a lion to Ephraim,
like a great lion to Judah.
I will tear them to pieces and go away;
I will carry them off, with no one to rescue them.

[a] 7 Syriac (see also an ancient Hebrew scribal tradition); Masoretic Text *me; / I will exchange their glory* [b] *15,8 Beth Aven* means *house of wickedness* (a derogatory name for Bethel, which means *house of God*). [c] 7 Or *Now their New Moon feasts / will devour them and* [d] *11* The meaning of the Hebrew for this word is uncertain.

15 Then I will return to my lair
until they have borne their guilt
and seek my face—
in their misery
they will earnestly seek me."

Israel Unrepentant

6 "Come, let us return to the LORD.
He has torn us to pieces
but he will heal us;
he has injured us
but he will bind up our wounds.
2 After two days he will revive us;
on the third day he will restore us,
that we may live in his presence.
3 Let us acknowledge the LORD;
let us press on to acknowledge him.
As surely as the sun rises,
he will appear;
he will come to us like the winter rains,
like the spring rains that water the
earth."

4 "What can I do with you, Ephraim?
What can I do with you, Judah?
Your love is like the morning mist,
like the early dew that disappears.
5 Therefore I cut you in pieces with my
prophets,
I killed you with the words of my
mouth—
then my judgments go forth like the
sun.[a]
6 For I desire mercy, not sacrifice,
and acknowledgment of God rather
than burnt offerings.
7 As at Adam,[b] they have broken the
covenant;
they were unfaithful to me there.
8 Gilead is a city of evildoers,
stained with footprints of blood.
9 As marauders lie in ambush for a victim,
so do bands of priests;
they murder on the road to Shechem,
carrying out their wicked schemes.
10 I have seen a horrible thing in Israel:
There Ephraim is given to prostitution,
Israel is defiled.

11 "Also for you, Judah,
a harvest is appointed.

"Whenever I would restore the fortunes
of my people,
7 [1] whenever I would heal Israel,
the sins of Ephraim are exposed
and the crimes of Samaria revealed.
They practice deceit,
thieves break into houses,
bandits rob in the streets;
2 but they do not realize
that I remember all their evil deeds.
Their sins engulf them;
they are always before me.

3 "They delight the king with their
wickedness,
the princes with their lies.
4 They are all adulterers,
burning like an oven
whose fire the baker need not stir
from the kneading of the dough till it
rises.
5 On the day of the festival of our king
the princes become inflamed with wine,
and he joins hands with the mockers.
6 Their hearts are like an oven;
they approach him with intrigue.
Their passion smolders all night;
in the morning it blazes like a flaming
fire.
7 All of them are hot as an oven;
they devour their rulers.
All their kings fall,
and none of them calls on me.

8 "Ephraim mixes with the nations;
Ephraim is a flat loaf not turned over.
9 Foreigners sap his strength,
but he does not realize it.
His hair is sprinkled with gray,
but he does not notice.
10 Israel's arrogance testifies against him,
but despite all this
he does not return to the LORD his God
or search for him.

11 "Ephraim is like a dove,
easily deceived and senseless—
now calling to Egypt,
now turning to Assyria.
12 When they go, I will throw my net over
them;
I will pull them down like the birds in
the sky.
When I hear them flocking together,
I will catch them.
13 Woe to them,
because they have strayed from me!
Destruction to them,
because they have rebelled against me!
I long to redeem them
but they speak about me falsely.
14 They do not cry out to me from their hearts
but wail on their beds.
They slash themselves,[c] appealing to
their gods
for grain and new wine,
but they turn away from me.
15 I trained them and strengthened their
arms,
but they plot evil against me.
16 They do not turn to the Most High;
they are like a faulty bow.
Their leaders will fall by the sword
because of their insolent words.
For this they will be ridiculed
in the land of Egypt.

Israel to Reap the Whirlwind

8 "Put the trumpet to your lips!
An eagle is over the house of the LORD
because the people have broken my
covenant
and rebelled against my law.

[a] 5 The meaning of the Hebrew for this line is uncertain. [b] 7 Or *Like Adam*; or *Like human beings*
[c] 14 Some Hebrew manuscripts and Septuagint; most Hebrew manuscripts *They gather together*

2 Israel cries out to me,
'Our God, we acknowledge you!'
3 But Israel has rejected what is good;
an enemy will pursue him.
4 They set up kings without my consent;
they choose princes without my approval.
With their silver and gold
they make idols for themselves
to their own destruction.
5 Samaria, throw out your calf-idol!
My anger burns against them.
How long will they be incapable of purity?
6 They are from Israel!
This calf—a metalworker has made it;
it is not God.
It will be broken in pieces,
that calf of Samaria.

7 "They sow the wind
and reap the whirlwind.
The stalk has no head;
it will produce no flour.
Were it to yield grain,
foreigners would swallow it up.
8 Israel is swallowed up;
now she is among the nations
like something no one wants.
9 For they have gone up to Assyria
like a wild donkey wandering alone.
Ephraim has sold herself to lovers.
10 Although they have sold themselves
among the nations,
I will now gather them together.
They will begin to waste away
under the oppression of the mighty king.

11 "Though Ephraim built many altars for sin offerings,
these have become altars for sinning.
12 I wrote for them the many things of my law,
but they regarded them as something foreign.
13 Though they offer sacrifices as gifts to me,
and though they eat the meat,
the LORD is not pleased with them.
Now he will remember their wickedness
and punish their sins:
They will return to Egypt.
14 Israel has forgotten their Maker
and built palaces;
Judah has fortified many towns.
But I will send fire on their cities
that will consume their fortresses."

Punishment for Israel

9 Do not rejoice, Israel;
do not be jubilant like the other nations.
For you have been unfaithful to your God;
you love the wages of a prostitute
at every threshing floor.
2 Threshing floors and winepresses will
not feed the people;
the new wine will fail them.
3 They will not remain in the LORD's land;
Ephraim will return to Egypt
and eat unclean food in Assyria.
4 They will not pour out wine offerings to the LORD,
nor will their sacrifices please him.
Such sacrifices will be to them like the bread of mourners;
all who eat them will be unclean.
This food will be for themselves;
it will not come into the temple of the LORD.

5 What will you do on the day of your appointed festivals,
on the feast days of the LORD?
6 Even if they escape from destruction,
Egypt will gather them,
and Memphis will bury them.
Their treasures of silver will be taken over by briers,
and thorns will overrun their tents.
7 The days of punishment are coming,
the days of reckoning are at hand.
Let Israel know this.
Because your sins are so many
and your hostility so great,
the prophet is considered a fool,
the inspired person a maniac.
8 The prophet, along with my God,
is the watchman over Ephraim,[a]
yet snares await him on all his paths,
and hostility in the house of his God.
9 They have sunk deep into corruption,
as in the days of Gibeah.
God will remember their wickedness
and punish them for their sins.

10 "When I found Israel,
it was like finding grapes in the desert;
when I saw your ancestors,
it was like seeing the early fruit on the fig tree.
But when they came to Baal Peor,
they consecrated themselves to that shameful idol
and became as vile as the thing they loved.
11 Ephraim's glory will fly away like a bird—
no birth, no pregnancy, no conception.
12 Even if they rear children,
I will bereave them of every one.
Woe to them
when I turn away from them!
13 I have seen Ephraim, like Tyre,
planted in a pleasant place.
But Ephraim will bring out
their children to the slayer."

14 Give them, LORD—
what will you give them?
Give them wombs that miscarry
and breasts that are dry.

15 "Because of all their wickedness in Gilgal,
I hated them there.
Because of their sinful deeds,
I will drive them out of my house.

[a] 8 Or *The prophet is the watchman over Ephraim, / the people of my God*

I will no longer love them;
all their leaders are rebellious.
16 Ephraim is blighted,
their root is withered,
they yield no fruit.
Even if they bear children,
I will slay their cherished offspring."

17 My God will reject them
because they have not obeyed him;
they will be wanderers among the nations.

10 Israel was a spreading vine;
he brought forth fruit for himself.
As his fruit increased,
he built more altars;
as his land prospered,
he adorned his sacred stones.
2 Their heart is deceitful,
and now they must bear their guilt.
The LORD will demolish their altars
and destroy their sacred stones.

3 Then they will say, "We have no king
because we did not revere the LORD.
But even if we had a king,
what could he do for us?"
4 They make many promises,
take false oaths
and make agreements;
therefore lawsuits spring up
like poisonous weeds in a plowed field.
5 The people who live in Samaria fear
for the calf-idol of Beth Aven.[a]
Its people will mourn over it,
and so will its idolatrous priests,
those who had rejoiced over its splendor,
because it is taken from them into exile.
6 It will be carried to Assyria
as tribute for the great king.
Ephraim will be disgraced;
Israel will be ashamed of its foreign alliances.
7 Samaria's king will be destroyed,
swept away like a twig on the surface of the waters.
8 The high places of wickedness[b] will be destroyed—
it is the sin of Israel.
Thorns and thistles will grow up
and cover their altars.
Then they will say to the mountains,
"Cover us!"
and to the hills, "Fall on us!"

9 "Since the days of Gibeah, you have sinned, Israel,
and there you have remained.[c]
Will not war again overtake
the evildoers in Gibeah?
10 When I please, I will punish them;
nations will be gathered against them
to put them in bonds for their double sin.
11 Ephraim is a trained heifer
that loves to thresh;
so I will put a yoke
on her fair neck.
I will drive Ephraim,
Judah must plow,
and Jacob must break up the ground.
12 Sow righteousness for yourselves,
reap the fruit of unfailing love,
and break up your unplowed ground;
for it is time to seek the LORD,
until he comes
and showers his righteousness on you.
13 But you have planted wickedness,
you have reaped evil,
you have eaten the fruit of deception.
Because you have depended on your own strength
and on your many warriors,
14 the roar of battle will rise against your people,
so that all your fortresses will be devastated—
as Shalman devastated Beth Arbel on the day of battle,
when mothers were dashed to the ground with their children.
15 So will it happen to you, Bethel,
because your wickedness is great.
When that day dawns,
the king of Israel will be completely destroyed.

God's Love for Israel

11 "When Israel was a child, I loved him,
and out of Egypt I called my son.
2 But the more they were called,
the more they went away from me.[d]
They sacrificed to the Baals
and they burned incense to images.
3 It was I who taught Ephraim to walk,
taking them by the arms;
but they did not realize
it was I who healed them.
4 I led them with cords of human kindness,
with ties of love.
To them I was like one who lifts
a little child to the cheek,
and I bent down to feed them.

5 "Will they not return to Egypt
and will not Assyria rule over them
because they refuse to repent?
6 A sword will flash in their cities;
it will devour their false prophets
and put an end to their plans.
7 My people are determined to turn from me.
Even though they call me God Most High,
I will by no means exalt them.

8 "How can I give you up, Ephraim?
How can I hand you over, Israel?
How can I treat you like Admah?
How can I make you like Zeboyim?
My heart is changed within me;
all my compassion is aroused.

[a] 5 *Beth Aven* means *house of wickedness* (a derogatory name for Bethel, which means *house of God*).
[b] 8 Hebrew *aven*, a reference to Beth Aven (a derogatory name for Bethel); see verse 5. [c] 9 Or *there a stand was taken* [d] 2 Septuagint; Hebrew *them*

9 I will not carry out my fierce anger,
nor will I devastate Ephraim again.
For I am God, and not a man—
the Holy One among you.
I will not come against their cities.
10 They will follow the LORD;
he will roar like a lion.
When he roars,
his children will come trembling from the west.
11 They will come from Egypt,
trembling like sparrows,
from Assyria, fluttering like doves.
I will settle them in their homes,"
declares the LORD.

Israel's Sin

12 Ephraim has surrounded me with lies,
Israel with deceit.
And Judah is unruly against God,
even against the faithful Holy One.[a]

12[b] 1 Ephraim feeds on the wind;
he pursues the east wind all day
and multiplies lies and violence.
He makes a treaty with Assyria
and sends olive oil to Egypt.
2 The LORD has a charge to bring against Judah;
he will punish Jacob[c] according to his ways
and repay him according to his deeds.
3 In the womb he grasped his brother's heel;
as a man he struggled with God.
4 He struggled with the angel and overcame him;
he wept and begged for his favor.
He found him at Bethel
and talked with him there—
5 the LORD God Almighty,
the LORD is his name!
6 But you must return to your God;
maintain love and justice,
and wait for your God always.

7 The merchant uses dishonest scales
and loves to defraud.
8 Ephraim boasts,
"I am very rich; I have become wealthy.
With all my wealth they will not find in me
any iniquity or sin."

9 "I have been the LORD your God
ever since you came out of Egypt;
I will make you live in tents again,
as in the days of your appointed festivals.
10 I spoke to the prophets,
gave them many visions
and told parables through them."

11 Is Gilead wicked?
Its people are worthless!
Do they sacrifice bulls in Gilgal?
Their altars will be like piles of stones
on a plowed field.
12 Jacob fled to the country of Aram[d];
Israel served to get a wife,
and to pay for her he tended sheep.
13 The LORD used a prophet to bring Israel up from Egypt,
by a prophet he cared for him.
14 But Ephraim has aroused his bitter anger;
his Lord will leave on him the guilt of his bloodshed
and will repay him for his contempt.

The LORD's Anger Against Israel

13 When Ephraim spoke, people trembled;
he was exalted in Israel.
But he became guilty of Baal worship and died.
2 Now they sin more and more;
they make idols for themselves from their silver,
cleverly fashioned images,
all of them the work of craftsmen.
It is said of these people,
"They offer human sacrifices!
They kiss[e] calf-idols!"
3 Therefore they will be like the morning mist,
like the early dew that disappears,
like chaff swirling from a threshing floor,
like smoke escaping through a window.

4 "But I have been the LORD your God
ever since you came out of Egypt.
You shall acknowledge no God but me,
no Savior except me.
5 I cared for you in the wilderness,
in the land of burning heat.
6 When I fed them, they were satisfied;
when they were satisfied, they became proud;
then they forgot me.
7 So I will be like a lion to them,
like a leopard I will lurk by the path.
8 Like a bear robbed of her cubs,
I will attack them and rip them open;
like a lion I will devour them—
a wild animal will tear them apart.

9 "You are destroyed, Israel,
because you are against me, against your helper.
10 Where is your king, that he may save you?
Where are your rulers in all your towns,
of whom you said,
'Give me a king and princes'?
11 So in my anger I gave you a king,
and in my wrath I took him away.
12 The guilt of Ephraim is stored up,
his sins are kept on record.
13 Pains as of a woman in childbirth come to him,
but he is a child without wisdom;

[a] *12* In Hebrew texts this verse (11:12) is numbered 12:1. [b] In Hebrew texts 12:1-14 is numbered 12:2-15. [c] *2* *Jacob* means *he grasps the heel,* a Hebrew idiom for *he takes advantage of* or *he deceives.*
[d] *12* That is, Northwest Mesopotamia [e] *2* Or *"Men who sacrifice / kiss*

when the time arrives,
he doesn't have the sense to come out of the womb.

14 "I will deliver this people from the power of the grave;
I will redeem them from death.
Where, O death, are your plagues?
Where, O grave, is your destruction?

"I will have no compassion,
15 even though he thrives among his brothers.
An east wind from the LORD will come,
blowing in from the desert;
his spring will fail
and his well dry up.
His storehouse will be plundered
of all its treasures.
16 The people of Samaria must bear their guilt,
because they have rebelled against their God.
They will fall by the sword;
their little ones will be dashed to the ground,
their pregnant women ripped open."[a]

Repentance to Bring Blessing

14 [b] Return, Israel, to the LORD your God.
Your sins have been your downfall!
2 Take words with you
and return to the LORD.
Say to him:
"Forgive all our sins
and receive us graciously,
that we may offer the fruit of our lips.[c]
3 Assyria cannot save us;
we will not mount warhorses.
We will never again say 'Our gods'
to what our own hands have made,
for in you the fatherless find compassion."

4 "I will heal their waywardness
and love them freely,
for my anger has turned away from them.
5 I will be like the dew to Israel;
he will blossom like a lily.
Like a cedar of Lebanon
he will send down his roots;
6 his young shoots will grow.
His splendor will be like an olive tree,
his fragrance like a cedar of Lebanon.
7 People will dwell again in his shade;
they will flourish like the grain,
they will blossom like the vine—
Israel's fame will be like the wine of Lebanon.
8 Ephraim, what more have I[d] to do with idols?
I will answer him and care for him.
I am like a flourishing juniper;
your fruitfulness comes from me."

9 Who is wise? Let them realize these things.
Who is discerning? Let them understand.
The ways of the LORD are right;
the righteous walk in them,
but the rebellious stumble in them.

Joel

1 The word of the LORD that came to Joel son of Pethuel.

An Invasion of Locusts

2 Hear this, you elders;
listen, all who live in the land.
Has anything like this ever happened in your days
or in the days of your ancestors?
3 Tell it to your children,
and let your children tell it to their children,
and their children to the next generation.
4 What the locust swarm has left
the great locusts have eaten;
what the great locusts have left
the young locusts have eaten;
what the young locusts have left
other locusts[e] have eaten.

5 Wake up, you drunkards, and weep!
Wail, all you drinkers of wine;
wail because of the new wine,
for it has been snatched from your lips.
6 A nation has invaded my land,
a mighty army without number;
it has the teeth of a lion,
the fangs of a lioness.
7 It has laid waste my vines
and ruined my fig trees.
It has stripped off their bark
and thrown it away,
leaving their branches white.

8 Mourn like a virgin in sackcloth
grieving for the betrothed of her youth.

[a] *16* In Hebrew texts this verse (13:16) is numbered 14:1. [b] In Hebrew texts 14:1-9 is numbered 14:2-10. [c] *2* Or *offer our lips as sacrifices of bulls* [d] *8* Or Hebrew; Septuagint *What more has Ephraim* [e] *4* The precise meaning of the four Hebrew words used here for locusts is uncertain.

9 Grain offerings and drink offerings
are cut off from the house of the LORD.
The priests are in mourning,
those who minister before the LORD.
10 The fields are ruined,
the ground is dried up;
the grain is destroyed,
the new wine is dried up,
the olive oil fails.

11 Despair, you farmers,
wail, you vine growers;
grieve for the wheat and the barley,
because the harvest of the field is destroyed.
12 The vine is dried up
and the fig tree is withered;
the pomegranate, the palm and the apple[a] tree—
all the trees of the field—are dried up.
Surely the people's joy
is withered away.

A Call to Lamentation

13 Put on sackcloth, you priests, and mourn;
wail, you who minister before the altar.
Come, spend the night in sackcloth,
you who minister before my God;
for the grain offerings and drink offerings
are withheld from the house of your God.
14 Declare a holy fast;
call a sacred assembly.
Summon the elders
and all who live in the land
to the house of the LORD your God,
and cry out to the LORD.

15 Alas for that day!
For the day of the LORD is near;
it will come like destruction from the Almighty.[b]

16 Has not the food been cut off
before our very eyes—
joy and gladness
from the house of our God?
17 The seeds are shriveled
beneath the clods.[c]
The storehouses are in ruins,
the granaries have been broken down,
for the grain has dried up.
18 How the cattle moan!
The herds mill about
because they have no pasture;
even the flocks of sheep are suffering.
19 To you, LORD, I call,
for fire has devoured the pastures in the wilderness
and flames have burned up all the trees of the field.
20 Even the wild animals pant for you;
the streams of water have dried up
and fire has devoured the pastures in the wilderness.

An Army of Locusts

2 Blow the trumpet in Zion;
sound the alarm on my holy hill.

Let all who live in the land tremble,
for the day of the LORD is coming.
It is close at hand—
2 a day of darkness and gloom,
a day of clouds and blackness.
Like dawn spreading across the mountains
a large and mighty army comes,
such as never was in ancient times
nor ever will be in ages to come.

3 Before them fire devours,
behind them a flame blazes.
Before them the land is like the garden of Eden,
behind them, a desert waste—
nothing escapes them.
4 They have the appearance of horses;
they gallop along like cavalry.
5 With a noise like that of chariots
they leap over the mountaintops,
like a crackling fire consuming stubble,
like a mighty army drawn up for battle.

6 At the sight of them, nations are in anguish;
every face turns pale.
7 They charge like warriors;
they scale walls like soldiers.
They all march in line,
not swerving from their course.
8 They do not jostle each other;
each marches straight ahead.
They plunge through defenses
without breaking ranks.
9 They rush upon the city;
they run along the wall.
They climb into the houses;
like thieves they enter through the windows.

10 Before them the earth shakes,
the heavens tremble,
the sun and moon are darkened,
and the stars no longer shine.
11 The LORD thunders
at the head of his army;
his forces are beyond number,
and mighty is the army that obeys his command.
The day of the LORD is great;
it is dreadful.
Who can endure it?

Rend Your Heart

12 "Even now," declares the LORD,
"return to me with all your heart,
with fasting and weeping and mourning."

13 Rend your heart
and not your garments.
Return to the LORD your God,
for he is gracious and compassionate,

[a] 12 Or possibly *apricot* [b] 15 Hebrew *Shaddai* [c] 17 The meaning of the Hebrew for this word is uncertain.

slow to anger and abounding in love,
and he relents from sending calamity.
14 Who knows? He may turn and relent
and leave behind a blessing—
grain offerings and drink offerings
for the LORD your God.

15 Blow the trumpet in Zion,
declare a holy fast,
call a sacred assembly.
16 Gather the people,
consecrate the assembly;
bring together the elders,
gather the children,
those nursing at the breast.
Let the bridegroom leave his room
and the bride her chamber.
17 Let the priests, who minister before the
LORD,
weep between the portico and the altar.
Let them say, "Spare your people, LORD.
Do not make your inheritance an object
of scorn,
a byword among the nations.
Why should they say among the peoples,
'Where is their God?'"

The LORD's Answer

18 Then the LORD was jealous for his land
and took pity on his people.

19 The LORD replied[a] to them:

"I am sending you grain, new wine and
olive oil,
enough to satisfy you fully;
never again will I make you
an object of scorn to the nations.

20 "I will drive the northern horde far from
you,
pushing it into a parched and barren
land;
its eastern ranks will drown in the Dead
Sea
and its western ranks in the
Mediterranean Sea.
And its stench will go up;
its smell will rise."

Surely he has done great things!
21 Do not be afraid, land of Judah;
be glad and rejoice.
Surely the LORD has done great things!
22 Do not be afraid, you wild animals,
for the pastures in the wilderness are
becoming green.
The trees are bearing their fruit;
the fig tree and the vine yield their
riches.
23 Be glad, people of Zion,
rejoice in the LORD your God,
for he has given you the autumn rains
because he is faithful.
He sends you abundant showers,
both autumn and spring rains, as
before.
24 The threshing floors will be filled with
grain;
the vats will overflow with new wine
and oil.

25 "I will repay you for the years the locusts
have eaten—
the great locust and the young locust,
the other locusts and the locust
swarm[b]—
my great army that I sent among you.
26 You will have plenty to eat, until you are
full,
and you will praise the name of the
LORD your God,
who has worked wonders for you;
never again will my people be shamed.
27 Then you will know that I am in Israel,
that I am the LORD your God,
and that there is no other;
never again will my people be shamed.

The Day of the LORD

28 "And afterward,
I will pour out my Spirit on all
people.
Your sons and daughters will prophesy,
your old men will dream dreams,
your young men will see visions.
29 Even on my servants, both men and
women,
I will pour out my Spirit in those days.
30 I will show wonders in the heavens
and on the earth,
blood and fire and billows of smoke.
31 The sun will be turned to darkness
and the moon to blood
before the coming of the great and
dreadful day of the LORD.
32 And everyone who calls
on the name of the LORD will be
saved;
for on Mount Zion and in Jerusalem
there will be deliverance,
as the LORD has said,
even among the survivors
whom the LORD calls.[c]

The Nations Judged

3[d] "In those days and at that time,
when I restore the fortunes of Judah
and Jerusalem,
2 I will gather all nations
and bring them down to the Valley of
Jehoshaphat.[e]
There I will put them on trial
for what they did to my inheritance, my
people Israel,
because they scattered my people among
the nations
and divided up my land.
3 They cast lots for my people
and traded boys for prostitutes;
they sold girls for wine to drink.

[a] 18,19 Or *LORD will be jealous . . . / and take pity . . . / [19]The LORD will reply* [b] 25 The precise meaning of the four Hebrew words used here for locusts is uncertain. [c] 32 In Hebrew texts 2:28-32 is numbered 3:1-5. [d] In Hebrew texts 3:1-21 is numbered 4:1-21. [e] 2 *Jehoshaphat* means *the LORD judges*; also in verse 12.

4"Now what have you against me, Tyre and
Sidon and all you regions of Philistia? Are
you repaying me for something I have done?
If you are paying me back, I will swiftly and
speedily return on your own heads what you
have done. 5For you took my silver and my
gold and carried off my finest treasures to
your temples.[a] 6You sold the people of Judah
and Jerusalem to the Greeks, that you might
send them far from their homeland.

7"See, I am going to rouse them out of the
places to which you sold them, and I will return on your own heads what you have done.
8I will sell your sons and daughters to the
people of Judah, and they will sell them to
the Sabeans, a nation far away." The LORD
has spoken.

9 Proclaim this among the nations:
Prepare for war!
Rouse the warriors!
Let all the fighting men draw near and attack.
10 Beat your plowshares into swords
and your pruning hooks into spears.
Let the weakling say,
"I am strong!"
11 Come quickly, all you nations from every side,
and assemble there.

Bring down your warriors, LORD!

12 "Let the nations be roused;
let them advance into the Valley of Jehoshaphat,
for there I will sit
to judge all the nations on every side.
13 Swing the sickle,
for the harvest is ripe.
Come, trample the grapes,
for the winepress is full
and the vats overflow—
so great is their wickedness!"

14 Multitudes, multitudes
in the valley of decision!
For the day of the LORD is near
in the valley of decision.
15 The sun and moon will be darkened,
and the stars no longer shine.
16 The LORD will roar from Zion
and thunder from Jerusalem;
the earth and the heavens will tremble.
But the LORD will be a refuge for his people,
a stronghold for the people of Israel.

Blessings for God's People

17 "Then you will know that I, the LORD your God,
dwell in Zion, my holy hill.
Jerusalem will be holy;
never again will foreigners invade her.

18 "In that day the mountains will drip new wine,
and the hills will flow with milk;
all the ravines of Judah will run with water.
A fountain will flow out of the LORD's house
and will water the valley of acacias.[b]
19 But Egypt will be desolate,
Edom a desert waste,
because of violence done to the people of Judah,
in whose land they shed innocent blood.
20 Judah will be inhabited forever
and Jerusalem through all generations.
21 Shall I leave their innocent blood unavenged?
No, I will not."

The LORD dwells in Zion!

Amos

1 The words of Amos, one of the shepherds
of Tekoa—the vision he saw concerning
Israel two years before the earthquake, when
Uzziah was king of Judah and Jeroboam son
of Jehoash[c] was king of Israel.
2He said:

"The LORD roars from Zion
and thunders from Jerusalem;
the pastures of the shepherds dry up,
and the top of Carmel withers."

Judgment on Israel's Neighbors

3This is what the LORD says:

"For three sins of Damascus,
even for four, I will not relent.
Because she threshed Gilead
with sledges having iron teeth,
4 I will send fire on the house of Hazael
that will consume the fortresses of Ben-Hadad.
5 I will break down the gate of Damascus;

[a] 5 Or *palaces* [b] 18 Or *Valley of Shittim* [c] 1 Hebrew *Joash,* a variant of *Jehoash*

I will destroy the king who is in[a] the
Valley of Aven[b]
and the one who holds the scepter in Beth
Eden.
The people of Aram will go into exile to
Kir,"
says the LORD.

6This is what the LORD says:

"For three sins of Gaza,
even for four, I will not relent.
Because she took captive whole
communities
and sold them to Edom,
7I will send fire on the walls of Gaza
that will consume her fortresses.
8I will destroy the king[c] of Ashdod
and the one who holds the scepter in
Ashkelon.
I will turn my hand against Ekron,
till the last of the Philistines are dead,"
says the Sovereign LORD.

9This is what the LORD says:

"For three sins of Tyre,
even for four, I will not relent.
Because she sold whole communities of
captives to Edom,
disregarding a treaty of brotherhood,
10I will send fire on the walls of Tyre
that will consume her fortresses."

11This is what the LORD says:

"For three sins of Edom,
even for four, I will not relent.
Because he pursued his brother with a
sword
and slaughtered the women of the land,
because his anger raged continually
and his fury flamed unchecked,
12I will send fire on Teman
that will consume the fortresses of
Bozrah."

13This is what the LORD says:

"For three sins of Ammon,
even for four, I will not relent.
Because he ripped open the pregnant
women of Gilead
in order to extend his borders,
14I will set fire to the walls of Rabbah
that will consume her fortresses
amid war cries on the day of battle,
amid violent winds on a stormy day.
15Her king[d] will go into exile,
he and his officials together,"
says the LORD.

2 This is what the LORD says:

"For three sins of Moab,
even for four, I will not relent.
Because he burned to ashes
the bones of Edom's king,
2I will send fire on Moab
that will consume the fortresses of
Kerioth.[e]
Moab will go down in great tumult
amid war cries and the blast of the
trumpet.
3I will destroy her ruler
and kill all her officials with him,"
says the LORD.

4This is what the LORD says:

"For three sins of Judah,
even for four, I will not relent.
Because they have rejected the law of the
LORD
and have not kept his decrees,
because they have been led astray by
false gods,[f]
the gods[g] their ancestors followed,
5I will send fire on Judah
that will consume the fortresses of
Jerusalem."

Judgment on Israel

6This is what the LORD says:

"For three sins of Israel,
even for four, I will not relent.
They sell the innocent for silver,
and the needy for a pair of sandals.
7They trample on the heads of the poor
as on the dust of the ground
and deny justice to the oppressed.
Father and son use the same girl
and so profane my holy name.
8They lie down beside every altar
on garments taken in pledge.
In the house of their god
they drink wine taken as fines.

9"Yet I destroyed the Amorites before them,
though they were tall as the cedars
and strong as the oaks.
I destroyed their fruit above
and their roots below.
10I brought you up out of Egypt
and led you forty years in the
wilderness
to give you the land of the Amorites.

11"I also raised up prophets from among
your children
and Nazirites from among your youths.
Is this not true, people of Israel?"
declares the LORD.
12"But you made the Nazirites drink wine
and commanded the prophets not to
prophesy.

13"Now then, I will crush you
as a cart crushes when loaded with
grain.
14The swift will not escape,
the strong will not muster their strength,
and the warrior will not save his life.
15The archer will not stand his ground,
the fleet-footed soldier will not get away,
and the horseman will not save his life.
16Even the bravest warriors
will flee naked on that day,"
declares the LORD.

[a] 5 Or *the inhabitants of* [b] 5 *Aven* means *wickedness.* [c] 8 Or *inhabitants* [d] 15 Or */ Molek*
[e] 2 Or *of her cities* [f] 4 Or *by lies* [g] 4 Or *lies*

Witnesses Summoned Against Israel

3 Hear this word, people of Israel, the word
the LORD has spoken against you—against
the whole family I brought up out of Egypt:

2 "You only have I chosen
of all the families of the earth;
therefore I will punish you
for all your sins."
3 Do two walk together
unless they have agreed to do so?
4 Does a lion roar in the thicket
when it has no prey?
Does it growl in its den
when it has caught nothing?
5 Does a bird swoop down to a trap on the ground
when no bait is there?
Does a trap spring up from the ground
if it has not caught anything?
6 When a trumpet sounds in a city,
do not the people tremble?
When disaster comes to a city,
has not the LORD caused it?

7 Surely the Sovereign LORD does nothing
without revealing his plan
to his servants the prophets.

8 The lion has roared—
who will not fear?
The Sovereign LORD has spoken—
who can but prophesy?

9 Proclaim to the fortresses of Ashdod
and to the fortresses of Egypt:
"Assemble yourselves on the mountains of Samaria;
see the great unrest within her
and the oppression among her people."

10 "They do not know how to do right,"
declares the LORD,
"who store up in their fortresses
what they have plundered and looted."

11 Therefore this is what the Sovereign LORD
says:

"An enemy will overrun your land,
pull down your strongholds
and plunder your fortresses."

12 This is what the LORD says:

"As a shepherd rescues from the lion's mouth
only two leg bones or a piece of an ear,
so will the Israelites living in Samaria be rescued,
with only the head of a bed
and a piece of fabric[a] from a couch.[b]"

13 "Hear this and testify against the descendants of Jacob," declares the Lord, the LORD
God Almighty.

14 "On the day I punish Israel for her sins,
I will destroy the altars of Bethel;
the horns of the altar will be cut off
and fall to the ground.
15 I will tear down the winter house
along with the summer house;
the houses adorned with ivory will be destroyed
and the mansions will be demolished,"
declares the LORD.

Israel Has Not Returned to God

4 Hear this word, you cows of Bashan on Mount Samaria,
you women who oppress the poor and crush the needy
and say to your husbands, "Bring us some drinks!"
2 The Sovereign LORD has sworn by his holiness:
"The time will surely come
when you will be taken away with hooks,
the last of you with fishhooks.[c]
3 You will each go straight out
through breaches in the wall,
and you will be cast out toward Harmon,[d]"
declares the LORD.

4 "Go to Bethel and sin;
go to Gilgal and sin yet more.
Bring your sacrifices every morning,
your tithes every three years.[e]
5 Burn leavened bread as a thank offering
and brag about your freewill offerings—
boast about them, you Israelites,
for this is what you love to do,"
declares the Sovereign LORD.

6 "I gave you empty stomachs in every city
and lack of bread in every town,
yet you have not returned to me,"
declares the LORD.

7 "I also withheld rain from you
when the harvest was still three months away.
I sent rain on one town,
but withheld it from another.
One field had rain;
another had none and dried up.
8 People staggered from town to town for water
but did not get enough to drink,
yet you have not returned to me,"
declares the LORD.

9 "Many times I struck your gardens and vineyards,
destroying them with blight and mildew.
Locusts devoured your fig and olive trees,
yet you have not returned to me,"
declares the LORD.

10 "I sent plagues among you
as I did to Egypt.
I killed your young men with the sword,
along with your captured horses.

[a] 12 The meaning of the Hebrew for this phrase is uncertain. [b] 12 Or *Israelites be rescued, / those who sit in Samaria / on the edge of their beds / and in Damascus on their couches.* [c] 2 Or *away in baskets, / the last of you in fish baskets* [d] 3 Masoretic Text; with a different word division of the Hebrew (see Septuagint) *out, you mountain of oppression* [e] 4 Or *days*

I filled your nostrils with the stench of
your camps,
yet you have not returned to me,"
declares the LORD.

11 "I overthrew some of you
as I overthrew Sodom and Gomorrah.
You were like a burning stick snatched
from the fire,
yet you have not returned to me,"
declares the LORD.

12 "Therefore this is what I will do to you,
Israel,
and because I will do this to you, Israel,
prepare to meet your God."

13 He who forms the mountains,
who creates the wind,
and who reveals his thoughts to
mankind,
who turns dawn to darkness,
and treads on the heights of the earth—
the LORD God Almighty is his name.

A Lament and Call to Repentance

5 Hear this word, Israel, this lament I take
up concerning you:

2 "Fallen is Virgin Israel,
never to rise again,
deserted in her own land,
with no one to lift her up."

3 This is what the Sovereign LORD says to
Israel:

"Your city that marches out a thousand
strong
will have only a hundred left;
your town that marches out a hundred
strong
will have only ten left."

4 This is what the LORD says to Israel:

"Seek me and live;
5 do not seek Bethel,
do not go to Gilgal,
do not journey to Beersheba.
For Gilgal will surely go into exile,
and Bethel will be reduced to nothing.[a]"
6 Seek the LORD and live,
or he will sweep through the tribes of
Joseph like a fire;
it will devour them,
and Bethel will have no one to quench it.

7 There are those who turn justice into
bitterness
and cast righteousness to the ground.

8 He who made the Pleiades and Orion,
who turns midnight into dawn
and darkens day into night,
who calls for the waters of the sea
and pours them out over the face of the
land—
the LORD is his name.
9 With a blinding flash he destroys the
stronghold
and brings the fortified city to ruin.

10 There are those who hate the one who
upholds justice in court
and detest the one who tells the truth.

11 You levy a straw tax on the poor
and impose a tax on their grain.
Therefore, though you have built stone
mansions,
you will not live in them;
though you have planted lush vineyards,
you will not drink their wine.
12 For I know how many are your offenses
and how great your sins.

There are those who oppress the innocent
and take bribes
and deprive the poor of justice in the
courts.
13 Therefore the prudent keep quiet in such
times,
for the times are evil.

14 Seek good, not evil,
that you may live.
Then the LORD God Almighty will be with
you,
just as you say he is.
15 Hate evil, love good;
maintain justice in the courts.
Perhaps the LORD God Almighty will
have mercy
on the remnant of Joseph.

16 Therefore this is what the Lord, the LORD
God Almighty, says:

"There will be wailing in all the streets
and cries of anguish in every public
square.
The farmers will be summoned to weep
and the mourners to wail.
17 There will be wailing in all the vineyards,
for I will pass through your midst,"
says the LORD.

The Day of the LORD

18 Woe to you who long
for the day of the LORD!
Why do you long for the day of the LORD?
That day will be darkness, not light.
19 It will be as though a man fled from a lion
only to meet a bear,
as though he entered his house
and rested his hand on the wall
only to have a snake bite him.
20 Will not the day of the LORD be darkness,
not light—
pitch-dark, without a ray of brightness?

21 "I hate, I despise your religious festivals;
your assemblies are a stench to me.
22 Even though you bring me burnt
offerings and grain offerings,
I will not accept them.
Though you bring choice fellowship
offerings,
I will have no regard for them.
23 Away with the noise of your songs!
I will not listen to the music of your
harps.

[a] 5 Hebrew *aven*, a reference to Beth Aven (a derogatory name for Bethel); see Hosea 4:15.

24 But let justice roll on like a river,
righteousness like a never-failing
stream!

25 "Did you bring me sacrifices and
offerings
forty years in the wilderness, people of
Israel?
26 You have lifted up the shrine of your
king,
the pedestal of your idols,
the star of your god[a]—
which you made for yourselves.
27 Therefore I will send you into exile
beyond Damascus,"
says the LORD, whose name is God
Almighty.

Woe to the Complacent

6 Woe to you who are complacent in Zion,
and to you who feel secure on Mount
Samaria,
you notable men of the foremost nation,
to whom the people of Israel come!
2 Go to Kalneh and look at it;
go from there to great Hamath,
and then go down to Gath in Philistia.
Are they better off than your two
kingdoms?
Is their land larger than yours?
3 You put off the day of disaster
and bring near a reign of terror.
4 You lie on beds adorned with ivory
and lounge on your couches.
You dine on choice lambs
and fattened calves.
5 You strum away on your harps like
David
and improvise on musical instruments.
6 You drink wine by the bowlful
and use the finest lotions,
but you do not grieve over the ruin of
Joseph.
7 Therefore you will be among the first to
go into exile;
your feasting and lounging will end.

The LORD Abhors the Pride of Israel

8 The Sovereign LORD has sworn by himself—the LORD God Almighty declares:

"I abhor the pride of Jacob
and detest his fortresses;
I will deliver up the city
and everything in it."

9 If ten people are left in one house, they
too will die. 10 And if the relative who comes
to carry the bodies out of the house to burn
them[b] asks anyone who might be hiding there,
"Is anyone else with you?" and he says, "No,"
then he will go on to say, "Hush! We must not
mention the name of the LORD."

11 For the LORD has given the command,
and he will smash the great house into
pieces
and the small house into bits.

12 Do horses run on the rocky crags?
Does one plow the sea[c] with oxen?
But you have turned justice into poison
and the fruit of righteousness into
bitterness—
13 you who rejoice in the conquest of Lo
Debar[d]
and say, "Did we not take Karnaim[e] by
our own strength?"
14 For the LORD God Almighty declares,
"I will stir up a nation against you,
Israel,
that will oppress you all the way
from Lebo Hamath to the valley of the
Arabah."

Locusts, Fire and a Plumb Line

7 This is what the Sovereign LORD showed
me: He was preparing swarms of locusts
after the king's share had been harvested and
just as the late crops were coming up. 2 When
they had stripped the land clean, I cried out,
"Sovereign LORD, forgive! How can Jacob survive? He is so small!"
3 So the LORD relented.
"This will not happen," the LORD said.
4 This is what the Sovereign LORD showed
me: The Sovereign LORD was calling for judgment by fire; it dried up the great deep and
devoured the land. 5 Then I cried out, "Sovereign LORD, I beg you, stop! How can Jacob
survive? He is so small!"
6 So the LORD relented.
"This will not happen either," the Sovereign
LORD said.

7 This is what he showed me: The Lord was
standing by a wall that had been built true to
plumb,[f] with a plumb line[g] in his hand. 8 And
the LORD asked me, "What do you see, Amos?"
"A plumb line," I replied.
Then the Lord said, "Look, I am setting
a plumb line among my people Israel; I will
spare them no longer.

9 "The high places of Isaac will be
destroyed
and the sanctuaries of Israel will be
ruined;
with my sword I will rise against the
house of Jeroboam."

Amos and Amaziah

10 Then Amaziah the priest of Bethel sent a
message to Jeroboam king of Israel: "Amos is
raising a conspiracy against you in the very
heart of Israel. The land cannot bear all his
words. 11 For this is what Amos is saying:

[a] 26 Or *lifted up Sakkuth your king / and Kaiwan your idols, / your star-gods*; Septuagint *lifted up the shrine of Molek / and the star of your god Rephan, / their idols* [b] 10 Or *to make a funeral fire in honor of the dead* [c] 12 With a different word division of the Hebrew; Masoretic Text *plow there* [d] 13 *Lo Debar* means *nothing.* [e] 13 *Karnaim* means *horns*; *horn* here symbolizes strength. [f] 7 The meaning of the Hebrew for this phrase is uncertain. [g] 7 The meaning of the Hebrew for this phrase is uncertain; also in verse 8.

"'Jeroboam will die by the sword,
and Israel will surely go into exile,
away from their native land.'"

12 Then Amaziah said to Amos, "Get out,
you seer! Go back to the land of Judah. Earn
your bread there and do your prophesying
there. 13 Don't prophesy anymore at Bethel,
because this is the king's sanctuary and the
temple of the kingdom."
14 Amos answered Amaziah, "I was neither
a prophet nor the son of a prophet, but I was a
shepherd, and I also took care of sycamore-fig
trees. 15 But the LORD took me from tending
the flock and said to me, 'Go, prophesy to my
people Israel.' 16 Now then, hear the word of
the LORD. You say,

"'Do not prophesy against Israel,
and stop preaching against the
descendants of Isaac.'

17 "Therefore this is what the LORD says:

"'Your wife will become a prostitute in
the city,
and your sons and daughters will fall
by the sword.
Your land will be measured and divided
up,
and you yourself will die in a pagan[a]
country.
And Israel will surely go into exile,
away from their native land.'"

A Basket of Ripe Fruit

8 This is what the Sovereign LORD showed
me: a basket of ripe fruit. 2 "What do you
see, Amos?" he asked.
"A basket of ripe fruit," I answered.
Then the LORD said to me, "The time is
ripe for my people Israel; I will spare them
no longer.
3 "In that day," declares the Sovereign LORD,
"the songs in the temple will turn to wailing.[b]
Many, many bodies—flung everywhere! Silence!"

4 Hear this, you who trample the needy
and do away with the poor of the land,

5 saying,

"When will the New Moon be over
that we may sell grain,
and the Sabbath be ended
that we may market wheat?"—
skimping on the measure,
boosting the price
and cheating with dishonest scales,
6 buying the poor with silver
and the needy for a pair of sandals,
selling even the sweepings with the
wheat.

7 The LORD has sworn by himself, the Pride
of Jacob: "I will never forget anything they
have done.

8 "Will not the land tremble for this,
and all who live in it mourn?
The whole land will rise like the Nile;
it will be stirred up and then sink
like the river of Egypt.

9 "In that day," declares the Sovereign LORD,

"I will make the sun go down at noon
and darken the earth in broad daylight.
10 I will turn your religious festivals into
mourning
and all your singing into weeping.
I will make all of you wear sackcloth
and shave your heads.
I will make that time like mourning for
an only son
and the end of it like a bitter day.

11 "The days are coming," declares the
Sovereign LORD,
"when I will send a famine through the
land—
not a famine of food or a thirst for water,
but a famine of hearing the words of
the LORD.
12 People will stagger from sea to sea
and wander from north to east,
searching for the word of the LORD,
but they will not find it.

13 "In that day

"the lovely young women and strong
young men
will faint because of thirst.
14 Those who swear by the sin of Samaria—
who say, 'As surely as your god lives,
Dan,'
or, 'As surely as the god[c] of Beersheba
lives'—
they will fall, never to rise again."

Israel to Be Destroyed

9 I saw the Lord standing by the altar, and
he said:

"Strike the tops of the pillars
so that the thresholds shake.
Bring them down on the heads of all the
people;
those who are left I will kill with the
sword.
Not one will get away,
none will escape.
2 Though they dig down to the depths below,
from there my hand will take them.
Though they climb up to the heavens
above,
from there I will bring them down.
3 Though they hide themselves on the top
of Carmel,
there I will hunt them down and seize
them.
Though they hide from my eyes at the
bottom of the sea,
there I will command the serpent to bite
them.
4 Though they are driven into exile by their
enemies,
there I will command the sword to slay
them.

[a] 17 Hebrew *an unclean* [b] 3 Or "*the temple singers will wail* [c] 14 Hebrew *the way*

"I will keep my eye on them
for harm and not for good."

5 The Lord, the LORD Almighty—
he touches the earth and it melts,
and all who live in it mourn;
the whole land rises like the Nile,
then sinks like the river of Egypt;
6 he builds his lofty palace[a] in the heavens
and sets its foundation[b] on the earth;
he calls for the waters of the sea
and pours them out over the face of the land—
the LORD is his name.

7 "Are not you Israelites
the same to me as the Cushites[c]?"
declares the LORD.
"Did I not bring Israel up from Egypt,
the Philistines from Caphtor[d]
and the Arameans from Kir?

8 "Surely the eyes of the Sovereign LORD
are on the sinful kingdom.
I will destroy it
from the face of the earth.
Yet I will not totally destroy
the descendants of Jacob,"
declares the LORD.
9 "For I will give the command,
and I will shake the people of Israel
among all the nations
as grain is shaken in a sieve,
and not a pebble will reach the ground.
10 All the sinners among my people
will die by the sword,
all those who say,
'Disaster will not overtake or meet us.'

Israel's Restoration

11 "In that day

"I will restore David's fallen shelter—
I will repair its broken walls
and restore its ruins—
and will rebuild it as it used to be,
12 so that they may possess the remnant of Edom
and all the nations that bear my name,[e]"
declares the LORD,
who will do these things.

13 "The days are coming," declares the LORD,
"when the reaper will be overtaken by the plowman
and the planter by the one treading grapes.
New wine will drip from the mountains
and flow from all the hills,
14 and I will bring my people Israel back from exile.[f]

"They will rebuild the ruined cities and live in them.
They will plant vineyards and drink their wine;
they will make gardens and eat their fruit.
15 I will plant Israel in their own land,
never again to be uprooted
from the land I have given them,"

says the LORD your God.

Obadiah

Obadiah's Vision

1 The vision of Obadiah.

This is what the Sovereign LORD says about Edom—

We have heard a message from the LORD:
An envoy was sent to the nations to say,
"Rise, let us go against her for battle"—
2 "See, I will make you small among the nations;
you will be utterly despised.
3 The pride of your heart has deceived you,
you who live in the clefts of the rocks[g]
and make your home on the heights,
you who say to yourself,
'Who can bring me down to the ground?'
4 Though you soar like the eagle
and make your nest among the stars,
from there I will bring you down,"
declares the LORD.
5 "If thieves came to you,
if robbers in the night—
oh, what a disaster awaits you!—
would they not steal only as much as they wanted?
If grape pickers came to you,
would they not leave a few grapes?
6 But how Esau will be ransacked,
his hidden treasures pillaged!
7 All your allies will force you to the border;
your friends will deceive and overpower you;
those who eat your bread will set a trap for you,[h]
but you will not detect it.

[a] 6 The meaning of the Hebrew for this phrase is uncertain. [b] 6 The meaning of the Hebrew for this word is uncertain. [c] 7 That is, people from the upper Nile region [d] 7 That is, Crete
[e] 12 Hebrew; Septuagint *so that the remnant of people / and all the nations that bear my name may seek me* [f] 14 Or *will restore the fortunes of my people Israel* [g] 3 Or *of Sela* [h] 7 The meaning of the Hebrew for this clause is uncertain.

8 "In that day," declares the LORD,
"will I not destroy the wise men of Edom,
those of understanding in the
mountains of Esau?
9 Your warriors, Teman, will be terrified,
and everyone in Esau's mountains
will be cut down in the slaughter.
10 Because of the violence against your
brother Jacob,
you will be covered with shame;
you will be destroyed forever.
11 On the day you stood aloof
while strangers carried off his wealth
and foreigners entered his gates
and cast lots for Jerusalem,
you were like one of them.
12 You should not gloat over your brother
in the day of his misfortune,
nor rejoice over the people of Judah
in the day of their destruction,
nor boast so much
in the day of their trouble.
13 You should not march through the gates
of my people
in the day of their disaster,
nor gloat over them in their calamity
in the day of their disaster,
nor seize their wealth
in the day of their disaster.
14 You should not wait at the crossroads
to cut down their fugitives,
nor hand over their survivors
in the day of their trouble.

15 "The day of the LORD is near
for all nations.
As you have done, it will be done to you;
your deeds will return upon your own
head.
16 Just as you drank on my holy hill,
so all the nations will drink continually;
they will drink and drink
and be as if they had never been.
17 But on Mount Zion will be deliverance;
it will be holy,
and Jacob will possess his inheritance.
18 Jacob will be a fire
and Joseph a flame;
Esau will be stubble,
and they will set him on fire and
destroy him.
There will be no survivors
from Esau."
The LORD has spoken.

19 People from the Negev will occupy
the mountains of Esau,
and people from the foothills will possess
the land of the Philistines.
They will occupy the fields of Ephraim
and Samaria,
and Benjamin will possess Gilead.
20 This company of Israelite exiles who are
in Canaan
will possess the land as far as
Zarephath;
the exiles from Jerusalem who are in
Sepharad
will possess the towns of the Negev.
21 Deliverers will go up on[a] Mount Zion
to govern the mountains of Esau.
And the kingdom will be the LORD's.

Jonah

Jonah Flees From the LORD

1 The word of the LORD came to Jonah son of
Amittai: 2 "Go to the great city of Nineveh
and preach against it, because its wickedness
has come up before me."
3 But Jonah ran away from the LORD and
headed for Tarshish. He went down to Joppa,
where he found a ship bound for that port. After paying the fare, he went aboard and sailed
for Tarshish to flee from the LORD.
4 Then the LORD sent a great wind on the sea,
and such a violent storm arose that the ship
threatened to break up. 5 All the sailors were
afraid and each cried out to his own god. And they
threw the cargo into the sea to lighten the ship.
But Jonah had gone below deck, where he
lay down and fell into a deep sleep. 6 The captain went to him and said, "How can you sleep?
Get up and call on your god! Maybe he will
take notice of us so that we will not perish."
7 Then the sailors said to each other, "Come,
let us cast lots to find out who is responsible
for this calamity." They cast lots and the lot
fell on Jonah. 8 So they asked him, "Tell us,
who is responsible for making all this trouble
for us? What kind of work do you do? Where
do you come from? What is your country?
From what people are you?"
9 He answered, "I am a Hebrew and I worship the LORD, the God of heaven, who made
the sea and the dry land."
10 This terrified them and they asked, "What
have you done?" (They knew he was running
away from the LORD, because he had already
told them so.)
11 The sea was getting rougher and rougher.
So they asked him, "What should we do to you
to make the sea calm down for us?"
12 "Pick me up and throw me into the sea,"
he replied, "and it will become calm. I know
that it is my fault that this great storm has
come upon you."

[a] 21 Or *from*

13Instead, the men did their best to row back
to land. But they could not, for the sea grew
even wilder than before. 14Then they cried
out to the LORD, "Please, LORD, do not let us
die for taking this man's life. Do not hold us
accountable for killing an innocent man, for
you, LORD, have done as you pleased." 15Then
they took Jonah and threw him overboard,
and the raging sea grew calm. 16At this the
men greatly feared the LORD, and they offered
a sacrifice to the LORD and made vows to him.

Jonah's Prayer

17Now the LORD provided a huge fish to swallow Jonah, and Jonah was in the belly of the
2[a] fish three days and three nights. 1From
inside the fish Jonah prayed to the LORD
his God. 2He said:

"In my distress I called to the LORD,
  and he answered me.
From deep in the realm of the dead I
    called for help,
  and you listened to my cry.
3 You hurled me into the depths,
  into the very heart of the seas,
  and the currents swirled about me;
all your waves and breakers
  swept over me.
4 I said, 'I have been banished
  from your sight;
yet I will look again
  toward your holy temple.'
5 The engulfing waters threatened me,[b]
  the deep surrounded me;
  seaweed was wrapped around my head.
6 To the roots of the mountains I sank down;
  the earth beneath barred me in forever.
But you, LORD my God,
  brought my life up from the pit.

7 "When my life was ebbing away,
  I remembered you, LORD,
and my prayer rose to you,
  to your holy temple.

8 "Those who cling to worthless idols
  turn away from God's love for them.
9 But I, with shouts of grateful praise,
  will sacrifice to you.
What I have vowed I will make good.
  I will say, 'Salvation comes from the
    LORD.'"

10And the LORD commanded the fish, and
it vomited Jonah onto dry land.

Jonah Goes to Nineveh

3 Then the word of the LORD came to Jonah a
second time: 2"Go to the great city of Nineveh and proclaim to it the message I give you."
3Jonah obeyed the word of the LORD and
went to Nineveh. Now Nineveh was a very
large city; it took three days to go through it.
4Jonah began by going a day's journey into
the city, proclaiming, "Forty more days and
Nineveh will be overthrown." 5The Ninevites
believed God. A fast was proclaimed, and all
of them, from the greatest to the least, put
on sackcloth.

6When Jonah's warning reached the king of
Nineveh, he rose from his throne, took off his
royal robes, covered himself with sackcloth
and sat down in the dust. 7This is the proclamation he issued in Nineveh:

"By the decree of the king and his nobles:

Do not let people or animals, herds or
flocks, taste anything; do not let them
eat or drink. 8But let people and animals
be covered with sackcloth. Let everyone
call urgently on God. Let them give up
their evil ways and their violence. 9Who
knows? God may yet relent and with compassion turn from his fierce anger so that
we will not perish."

10When God saw what they did and how
they turned from their evil ways, he relented
and did not bring on them the destruction he
had threatened.

Jonah's Anger at the LORD's Compassion

4 But to Jonah this seemed very wrong, and
he became angry. 2He prayed to the LORD,
"Isn't this what I said, LORD, when I was still at
home? That is what I tried to forestall by fleeing to Tarshish. I knew that you are a gracious
and compassionate God, slow to anger and
abounding in love, a God who relents from
sending calamity. 3Now, LORD, take away my
life, for it is better for me to die than to live."
4But the LORD replied, "Is it right for you
to be angry?"

5Jonah had gone out and sat down at a place
east of the city. There he made himself a shelter, sat in its shade and waited to see what
would happen to the city. 6Then the LORD God
provided a leafy plant[c] and made it grow up
over Jonah to give shade for his head to ease
his discomfort, and Jonah was very happy
about the plant. 7But at dawn the next day
God provided a worm, which chewed the plant
so that it withered. 8When the sun rose, God
provided a scorching east wind, and the sun
blazed on Jonah's head so that he grew faint.
He wanted to die, and said, "It would be better
for me to die than to live."

9But God said to Jonah, "Is it right for you
to be angry about the plant?"

"It is," he said. "And I'm so angry I wish I
were dead."

10But the LORD said, "You have been concerned about this plant, though you did not
tend it or make it grow. It sprang up overnight and died overnight. 11And should I not
have concern for the great city of Nineveh,
in which there are more than a hundred and
twenty thousand people who cannot tell their
right hand from their left—and also many
animals?"

[a] In Hebrew texts 2:1 is numbered 1:17, and 2:1-10 is numbered 2:2-11. [b] 5 Or *waters were at my throat* [c] 6 The precise identification of this plant is uncertain; also in verses 7, 9 and 10.

Micah

1 The word of the LORD that came to Micah of Moresheth during the reigns of Jotham, Ahaz and Hezekiah, kings of Judah—the vision he saw concerning Samaria and Jerusalem.

2 Hear, you peoples, all of you,
listen, earth and all who live in it,
that the Sovereign LORD may bear witness against you,
the Lord from his holy temple.

Judgment Against Samaria and Jerusalem

3 Look! The LORD is coming from his dwelling place;
he comes down and treads on the heights of the earth.
4 The mountains melt beneath him
and the valleys split apart,
like wax before the fire,
like water rushing down a slope.
5 All this is because of Jacob's transgression,
because of the sins of the people of Israel.
What is Jacob's transgression?
Is it not Samaria?
What is Judah's high place?
Is it not Jerusalem?

6 "Therefore I will make Samaria a heap of rubble,
a place for planting vineyards.
I will pour her stones into the valley
and lay bare her foundations.
7 All her idols will be broken to pieces;
all her temple gifts will be burned with fire;
I will destroy all her images.
Since she gathered her gifts from the wages of prostitutes,
as the wages of prostitutes they will again be used."

Weeping and Mourning

8 Because of this I will weep and wail;
I will go about barefoot and naked.
I will howl like a jackal
and moan like an owl.
9 For Samaria's plague is incurable;
it has spread to Judah.
It has reached the very gate of my people,
even to Jerusalem itself.
10 Tell it not in Gath[a];
weep not at all.
In Beth Ophrah[b]
roll in the dust.
11 Pass by naked and in shame,
you who live in Shaphir.[c]
Those who live in Zaanan[d]
will not come out.
Beth Ezel is in mourning;
it no longer protects you.
12 Those who live in Maroth[e] writhe in pain,
waiting for relief,
because disaster has come from the LORD,
even to the gate of Jerusalem.
13 You who live in Lachish,
harness fast horses to the chariot.
You are where the sin of Daughter Zion began,
for the transgressions of Israel were found in you.
14 Therefore you will give parting gifts
to Moresheth Gath.
The town of Akzib[f] will prove deceptive
to the kings of Israel.
15 I will bring a conqueror against you
who live in Mareshah.[g]
The nobles of Israel
will flee to Adullam.
16 Shave your head in mourning
for the children in whom you delight;
make yourself as bald as the vulture,
for they will go from you into exile.

Human Plans and God's Plans

2 Woe to those who plan iniquity,
to those who plot evil on their beds!
At morning's light they carry it out
because it is in their power to do it.
2 They covet fields and seize them,
and houses, and take them.
They defraud people of their homes,
they rob them of their inheritance.

3 Therefore, the LORD says:

"I am planning disaster against this people,
from which you cannot save yourselves.
You will no longer walk proudly,
for it will be a time of calamity.
4 In that day people will ridicule you;
they will taunt you with this mournful song:
'We are utterly ruined;
my people's possession is divided up.
He takes it from me!
He assigns our fields to traitors.'"

5 Therefore you will have no one in the assembly of the LORD
to divide the land by lot.

False Prophets

6 "Do not prophesy," their prophets say.
"Do not prophesy about these things;
disgrace will not overtake us."

[a] 10 *Gath* sounds like the Hebrew for *tell.* [b] 10 *Beth Ophrah* means *house of dust.* [c] 11 *Shaphir* means *pleasant.* [d] 11 *Zaanan* sounds like the Hebrew for *come out.* [e] 12 *Maroth* sounds like the Hebrew for *bitter.* [f] 14 *Akzib* means *deception.* [g] 15 *Mareshah* sounds like the Hebrew for *conqueror.*

7 You descendants of Jacob, should it be said,
"Does the LORD become[a] impatient?
Does he do such things?"
"Do not my words do good
to the one whose ways are upright?
8 Lately my people have risen up
like an enemy.
You strip off the rich robe
from those who pass by without a care,
like men returning from battle.
9 You drive the women of my people
from their pleasant homes.
You take away my blessing
from their children forever.
10 Get up, go away!
For this is not your resting place,
because it is defiled,
it is ruined, beyond all remedy.
11 If a liar and deceiver comes and says,
'I will prophesy for you plenty of wine and beer,'
that would be just the prophet for this people!

Deliverance Promised

12 "I will surely gather all of you, Jacob;
I will surely bring together the remnant of Israel.
I will bring them together like sheep in a pen,
like a flock in its pasture;
the place will throng with people.
13 The One who breaks open the way will go up before them;
they will break through the gate and go out.
Their King will pass through before them,
the LORD at their head."

Leaders and Prophets Rebuked

3 Then I said,

"Listen, you leaders of Jacob,
you rulers of Israel.
Should you not embrace justice,
2 you who hate good and love evil;
who tear the skin from my people
and the flesh from their bones;
3 who eat my people's flesh,
strip off their skin
and break their bones in pieces;
who chop them up like meat for the pan,
like flesh for the pot?"

4 Then they will cry out to the LORD,
but he will not answer them.
At that time he will hide his face from them
because of the evil they have done.

5 This is what the LORD says:

"As for the prophets
who lead my people astray,
they proclaim 'peace'
if they have something to eat,
but prepare to wage war against anyone
who refuses to feed them.
6 Therefore night will come over you,
without visions,
and darkness, without divination.
The sun will set for the prophets,
and the day will go dark for them.
7 The seers will be ashamed
and the diviners disgraced.
They will all cover their faces
because there is no answer from God."
8 But as for me, I am filled with power,
with the Spirit of the LORD,
and with justice and might,
to declare to Jacob his transgression,
to Israel his sin.

9 Hear this, you leaders of Jacob,
you rulers of Israel,
who despise justice
and distort all that is right;
10 who build Zion with bloodshed,
and Jerusalem with wickedness.
11 Her leaders judge for a bribe,
her priests teach for a price,
and her prophets tell fortunes for money.
Yet they look for the LORD's support and say,
"Is not the LORD among us?
No disaster will come upon us."
12 Therefore because of you,
Zion will be plowed like a field,
Jerusalem will become a heap of rubble,
the temple hill a mound overgrown with thickets.

The Mountain of the LORD

4 In the last days

the mountain of the LORD's temple will be established
as the highest of the mountains;
it will be exalted above the hills,
and peoples will stream to it.

2 Many nations will come and say,

"Come, let us go up to the mountain of the LORD,
to the temple of the God of Jacob.
He will teach us his ways,
so that we may walk in his paths."
The law will go out from Zion,
the word of the LORD from Jerusalem.
3 He will judge between many peoples
and will settle disputes for strong nations far and wide.
They will beat their swords into plowshares
and their spears into pruning hooks.
Nation will not take up sword against nation,
nor will they train for war anymore.
4 Everyone will sit under their own vine
and under their own fig tree,
and no one will make them afraid,
for the LORD Almighty has spoken.

[a] 7 Or *Is the Spirit of the LORD*

5 All the nations may walk
in the name of their gods,
but we will walk in the name of the LORD
our God for ever and ever.

The LORD's Plan

6 "In that day," declares the LORD,

"I will gather the lame;
I will assemble the exiles
and those I have brought to grief.
7 I will make the lame my remnant,
those driven away a strong nation.
The LORD will rule over them in Mount
Zion
from that day and forever.
8 As for you, watchtower of the flock,
stronghold[a] of Daughter Zion,
the former dominion will be restored to
you;
kingship will come to Daughter
Jerusalem."
9 Why do you now cry aloud—
have you no king[b]?
Has your ruler[c] perished,
that pain seizes you like that of a
woman in labor?
10 Writhe in agony, Daughter Zion,
like a woman in labor,
for now you must leave the city
to camp in the open field.
You will go to Babylon;
there you will be rescued.
There the LORD will redeem you
out of the hand of your enemies.

11 But now many nations
are gathered against you.
They say, "Let her be defiled,
let our eyes gloat over Zion!"
12 But they do not know
the thoughts of the LORD;
they do not understand his plan,
that he has gathered them like sheaves
to the threshing floor.
13 "Rise and thresh, Daughter Zion,
for I will give you horns of iron;
I will give you hooves of bronze,
and you will break to pieces many
nations."
You will devote their ill-gotten gains to
the LORD,
their wealth to the Lord of all the
earth.

A Promised Ruler From Bethlehem

5[d] Marshal your troops now, city of troops,
for a siege is laid against us.
They will strike Israel's ruler
on the cheek with a rod.

2 "But you, Bethlehem Ephrathah,
though you are small among the clans[e]
of Judah,
out of you will come for me
one who will be ruler over Israel,
whose origins are from of old,
from ancient times."
3 Therefore Israel will be abandoned
until the time when she who is in labor
bears a son,
and the rest of his brothers return
to join the Israelites.

4 He will stand and shepherd his flock
in the strength of the LORD,
in the majesty of the name of the LORD
his God.
And they will live securely, for then his
greatness
will reach to the ends of the earth.

5 And he will be our peace
when the Assyrians invade our land
and march through our fortresses.
We will raise against them seven
shepherds,
even eight commanders,
6 who will rule[f] the land of Assyria with
the sword,
the land of Nimrod with drawn sword.[g]
He will deliver us from the Assyrians
when they invade our land
and march across our borders.
7 The remnant of Jacob will be
in the midst of many peoples
like dew from the LORD,
like showers on the grass,
which do not wait for anyone
or depend on man.
8 The remnant of Jacob will be among the
nations,
in the midst of many peoples,
like a lion among the beasts of the forest,
like a young lion among flocks of
sheep,
which mauls and mangles as it goes,
and no one can rescue.
9 Your hand will be lifted up in triumph
over your enemies,
and all your foes will be destroyed.

10 "In that day," declares the LORD,

"I will destroy your horses from among
you
and demolish your chariots.
11 I will destroy the cities of your land
and tear down all your strongholds.
12 I will destroy your witchcraft
and you will no longer cast spells.
13 I will destroy your idols
and your sacred stones from among
you;
you will no longer bow down
to the work of your hands.
14 I will uproot from among you your
Asherah poles[h]
when I demolish your cities.
15 I will take vengeance in anger and wrath
on the nations that have not obeyed
me."

[a] 8 Or *hill* [b] 9 Or *King* [c] 9 Or *Ruler* [d] In Hebrew texts 5:1 is numbered 4:14, and 5:2-15 is numbered 5:1-14. [e] 2 Or *rulers* [f] 6 Or *crush* [g] 6 Or *Nimrod in its gates* [h] 14 That is, wooden symbols of the goddess Asherah

The LORD's Case Against Israel

6 Listen to what the LORD says:

"Stand up, plead my case before the
mountains;
let the hills hear what you have to say.
2 "Hear, you mountains, the LORD's
accusation;
listen, you everlasting foundations of
the earth.
For the LORD has a case against his
people;
he is lodging a charge against Israel.
3 "My people, what have I done to you?
How have I burdened you? Answer me.
4 I brought you up out of Egypt
and redeemed you from the land of
slavery.
I sent Moses to lead you,
also Aaron and Miriam.
5 My people, remember
what Balak king of Moab plotted
and what Balaam son of Beor
answered.
Remember your journey from Shittim to
Gilgal,
that you may know the righteous acts
of the LORD."
6 With what shall I come before the LORD
and bow down before the exalted God?
Shall I come before him with burnt
offerings,
with calves a year old?
7 Will the LORD be pleased with thousands
of rams,
with ten thousand rivers of olive oil?
Shall I offer my firstborn for my
transgression,
the fruit of my body for the sin of my
soul?
8 He has shown you, O mortal, what is
good.
And what does the LORD require of
you?
To act justly and to love mercy
and to walk humbly[a] with your God.

Israel's Guilt and Punishment

9 Listen! The LORD is calling to the city—
and to fear your name is wisdom—
"Heed the rod and the One who
appointed it.[b]
10 Am I still to forget your ill-gotten
treasures, you wicked house,
and the short ephah,[c] which is
accursed?
11 Shall I acquit someone with dishonest
scales,
with a bag of false weights?
12 Your rich people are violent;
your inhabitants are liars
and their tongues speak deceitfully.
13 Therefore, I have begun to destroy you,
to ruin[d] you because of your sins.
14 You will eat but not be satisfied;
your stomach will still be empty.[e]
You will store up but save nothing,
because what you save[f] I will give to the
sword.
15 You will plant but not harvest;
you will press olives but not use the oil,
you will crush grapes but not drink the
wine.
16 You have observed the statutes of Omri
and all the practices of Ahab's house;
you have followed their traditions.
Therefore I will give you over to ruin
and your people to derision;
you will bear the scorn of the
nations.[g]"

Israel's Misery

7 What misery is mine!
I am like one who gathers summer fruit
at the gleaning of the vineyard;
there is no cluster of grapes to eat,
none of the early figs that I crave.
2 The faithful have been swept from the
land;
not one upright person remains.
Everyone lies in wait to shed blood;
they hunt each other with nets.
3 Both hands are skilled in doing evil;
the ruler demands gifts,
the judge accepts bribes,
the powerful dictate what they desire—
they all conspire together.
4 The best of them is like a brier,
the most upright worse than a thorn
hedge.
The day God visits you has come,
the day your watchmen sound the
alarm.
Now is the time of your confusion.
5 Do not trust a neighbor;
put no confidence in a friend.
Even with the woman who lies in your
embrace
guard the words of your lips.
6 For a son dishonors his father,
a daughter rises up against her mother,
a daughter-in-law against her mother-in-
law—
a man's enemies are the members of his
own household.

7 But as for me, I watch in hope for the
LORD,
I wait for God my Savior;
my God will hear me.

Israel Will Rise

8 Do not gloat over me, my enemy!
Though I have fallen, I will rise.
Though I sit in darkness,
the LORD will be my light.

[a] 8 Or *prudently* [b] 9 The meaning of the Hebrew for this line is uncertain. [c] 10 An ephah was a dry measure. [d] 13 Or *Therefore, I will make you ill and destroy you; / I will ruin* [e] 14 The meaning of the Hebrew for this word is uncertain. [f] 14 Or *You will press toward birth but not give birth, / and what you bring to birth* [g] 16 Septuagint; Hebrew *scorn due my people*

9 Because I have sinned against him,
I will bear the LORD's wrath,
until he pleads my case
and upholds my cause.
He will bring me out into the light;
I will see his righteousness.
10 Then my enemy will see it
and will be covered with shame,
she who said to me,
"Where is the LORD your God?"
My eyes will see her downfall;
even now she will be trampled
underfoot
like mire in the streets.
11 The day for building your walls will
come,
the day for extending your boundaries.
12 In that day people will come to you
from Assyria and the cities of Egypt,
even from Egypt to the Euphrates
and from sea to sea
and from mountain to mountain.
13 The earth will become desolate because
of its inhabitants,
as the result of their deeds.

Prayer and Praise

14 Shepherd your people with your staff,
the flock of your inheritance,
which lives by itself in a forest,
in fertile pasturelands.[a]
Let them feed in Bashan and Gilead
as in days long ago.
15 "As in the days when you came out of
Egypt,
I will show them my wonders."
16 Nations will see and be ashamed,
deprived of all their power.
They will put their hands over their
mouths
and their ears will become deaf.
17 They will lick dust like a snake,
like creatures that crawl on the ground.
They will come trembling out of their
dens;
they will turn in fear to the LORD our
God
and will be afraid of you.
18 Who is a God like you,
who pardons sin and forgives the
transgression
of the remnant of his inheritance?
You do not stay angry forever
but delight to show mercy.
19 You will again have compassion on us;
you will tread our sins underfoot
and hurl all our iniquities into the
depths of the sea.
20 You will be faithful to Jacob,
and show love to Abraham,
as you pledged on oath to our ancestors
in days long ago.

Nahum

1 A prophecy concerning Nineveh. The book of the vision of Nahum the Elkoshite.

The LORD's Anger Against Nineveh

2 The LORD is a jealous and avenging God;
the LORD takes vengeance and is filled
with wrath.
The LORD takes vengeance on his foes
and vents his wrath against his
enemies.
3 The LORD is slow to anger but great in
power;
the LORD will not leave the guilty
unpunished.
His way is in the whirlwind and the
storm,
and clouds are the dust of his feet.
4 He rebukes the sea and dries it up;
he makes all the rivers run dry.
Bashan and Carmel wither
and the blossoms of Lebanon fade.
5 The mountains quake before him
and the hills melt away.
The earth trembles at his presence,
the world and all who live in it.
6 Who can withstand his indignation?
Who can endure his fierce anger?
His wrath is poured out like fire;
the rocks are shattered before him.

7 The LORD is good,
a refuge in times of trouble.
He cares for those who trust in him,
8 but with an overwhelming flood
he will make an end of Nineveh;
he will pursue his foes into the realm of
darkness.

9 Whatever they plot against the LORD
he will bring[b] to an end;
trouble will not come a second time.
10 They will be entangled among thorns
and drunk from their wine;
they will be consumed like dry stubble.[c]
11 From you, Nineveh, has one come forth
who plots evil against the LORD
and devises wicked plans.

[a] 14 Or *in the middle of Carmel* [b] 9 Or *What do you foes plot against the LORD? / He will bring it*
[c] 10 The meaning of the Hebrew for this verse is uncertain.

12 This is what the LORD says:
"Although they have allies and are
numerous,
they will be destroyed and pass away.
Although I have afflicted you, Judah,
I will afflict you no more.
13 Now I will break their yoke from your neck
and tear your shackles away."

14 The LORD has given a command
concerning you, Nineveh:
"You will have no descendants to bear
your name.
I will destroy the images and idols
that are in the temple of your gods.
I will prepare your grave,
for you are vile."

15 Look, there on the mountains,
the feet of one who brings good news,
who proclaims peace!
Celebrate your festivals, Judah,
and fulfill your vows.
No more will the wicked invade you;
they will be completely destroyed.[a]

Nineveh to Fall

2 [b] An attacker advances against you,
Nineveh.
Guard the fortress,
watch the road,
brace yourselves,
marshal all your strength!

2 The LORD will restore the splendor of
Jacob
like the splendor of Israel,
though destroyers have laid them waste
and have ruined their vines.

3 The shields of the soldiers are red;
the warriors are clad in scarlet.
The metal on the chariots flashes
on the day they are made ready;
the spears of juniper are brandished.[c]
4 The chariots storm through the streets,
rushing back and forth through the
squares.
They look like flaming torches;
they dart about like lightning.

5 Nineveh summons her picked troops,
yet they stumble on their way.
They dash to the city wall;
the protective shield is put in place.
6 The river gates are thrown open
and the palace collapses.
7 It is decreed[d] that Nineveh
be exiled and carried away.
Her female slaves moan like doves
and beat on their breasts.
8 Nineveh is like a pool
whose water is draining away.
"Stop! Stop!" they cry,
but no one turns back.
9 Plunder the silver!
Plunder the gold!
The supply is endless,
the wealth from all its treasures!
10 She is pillaged, plundered, stripped!
Hearts melt, knees give way,
bodies tremble, every face grows pale.

11 Where now is the lions' den,
the place where they fed their young,
where the lion and lioness went,
and the cubs, with nothing to fear?
12 The lion killed enough for his cubs
and strangled the prey for his mate,
filling his lairs with the kill
and his dens with the prey.

13 "I am against you,"
declares the LORD Almighty.
"I will burn up your chariots in smoke,
and the sword will devour your young
lions.
I will leave you no prey on the earth.
The voices of your messengers
will no longer be heard."

Woe to Nineveh

3 Woe to the city of blood,
full of lies,
full of plunder,
never without victims!
2 The crack of whips,
the clatter of wheels,
galloping horses
and jolting chariots!
3 Charging cavalry,
flashing swords
and glittering spears!
Many casualties,
piles of dead,
bodies without number,
people stumbling over the corpses—
4 all because of the wanton lust of a
prostitute,
alluring, the mistress of sorceries,
who enslaved nations by her prostitution
and peoples by her witchcraft.

5 "I am against you," declares the LORD
Almighty.
"I will lift your skirts over your face.
I will show the nations your nakedness
and the kingdoms your shame.
6 I will pelt you with filth,
I will treat you with contempt
and make you a spectacle.
7 All who see you will flee from you and say,
'Nineveh is in ruins—who will mourn
for her?'
Where can I find anyone to comfort you?"

8 Are you better than Thebes,
situated on the Nile,
with water around her?
The river was her defense,
the waters her wall.
9 Cush[e] and Egypt were her boundless
strength;
Put and Libya were among her allies.

[a] *15* In Hebrew texts this verse (1:15) is numbered 2.1. [b] In Hebrew texts 2:1-13 is numbered 2:2-14. [c] *3* Hebrew; Septuagint and Syriac *ready; / the horsemen rush to and fro.* [d] *7* The meaning of the Hebrew for this word is uncertain. [e] *9* That is, the upper Nile region

10 Yet she was taken captive
and went into exile.
Her infants were dashed to pieces
at every street corner.
Lots were cast for her nobles,
and all her great men were put in chains.
11 You too will become drunk;
you will go into hiding
and seek refuge from the enemy.
12 All your fortresses are like fig trees
with their first ripe fruit;
when they are shaken,
the figs fall into the mouth of the eater.
13 Look at your troops—
they are all weaklings.
The gates of your land
are wide open to your enemies;
fire has consumed the bars of your gates.
14 Draw water for the siege,
strengthen your defenses!
Work the clay,
tread the mortar,
repair the brickwork!
15 There the fire will consume you;
the sword will cut you down—
they will devour you like a swarm of locusts.
Multiply like grasshoppers,
multiply like locusts!
16 You have increased the number of your merchants
till they are more numerous than the stars in the sky,
but like locusts they strip the land
and then fly away.
17 Your guards are like locusts,
your officials like swarms of locusts
that settle in the walls on a cold day—
but when the sun appears they fly away,
and no one knows where.
18 King of Assyria, your shepherds[a] slumber;
your nobles lie down to rest.
Your people are scattered on the mountains
with no one to gather them.
19 Nothing can heal you;
your wound is fatal.
All who hear the news about you
clap their hands at your fall,
for who has not felt
your endless cruelty?

Habakkuk

1 The prophecy that Habakkuk the prophet received.

Habakkuk's Complaint

2 How long, LORD, must I call for help,
but you do not listen?
Or cry out to you, "Violence!"
but you do not save?
3 Why do you make me look at injustice?
Why do you tolerate wrongdoing?
Destruction and violence are before me;
there is strife, and conflict abounds.
4 Therefore the law is paralyzed,
and justice never prevails.
The wicked hem in the righteous,
so that justice is perverted.

The LORD's Answer

5 "Look at the nations and watch—
and be utterly amazed.
For I am going to do something in your days
that you would not believe,
even if you were told.
6 I am raising up the Babylonians,[b]
that ruthless and impetuous people,
who sweep across the whole earth
to seize dwellings not their own.
7 They are a feared and dreaded people;
they are a law to themselves
and promote their own honor.
8 Their horses are swifter than leopards,
fiercer than wolves at dusk.
Their cavalry gallops headlong;
their horsemen come from afar.
They fly like an eagle swooping to devour;
9 they all come intent on violence.
Their hordes[c] advance like a desert wind
and gather prisoners like sand.
10 They mock kings
and scoff at rulers.
They laugh at all fortified cities;
by building earthen ramps they capture them.
11 Then they sweep past like the wind and go on—
guilty people, whose own strength is their god."

[a] 18 That is, rulers [b] 6 Or *Chaldeans* [c] 9 The meaning of the Hebrew for this word is uncertain.

Habakkuk's Second Complaint

12 LORD, are you not from everlasting?
My God, my Holy One, you[a] will never die.
You, LORD, have appointed them to execute judgment;
you, my Rock, have ordained them to punish.
13 Your eyes are too pure to look on evil;
you cannot tolerate wrongdoing.
Why then do you tolerate the treacherous?
Why are you silent while the wicked swallow up those more righteous than themselves?
14 You have made people like the fish in the sea,
like the sea creatures that have no ruler.
15 The wicked foe pulls all of them up with hooks,
he catches them in his net,
he gathers them up in his dragnet;
and so he rejoices and is glad.
16 Therefore he sacrifices to his net
and burns incense to his dragnet,
for by his net he lives in luxury
and enjoys the choicest food.
17 Is he to keep on emptying his net,
destroying nations without mercy?

2 I will stand at my watch
and station myself on the ramparts;
I will look to see what he will say to me,
and what answer I am to give to this complaint.[b]

The LORD's Answer

2 Then the LORD replied:

"Write down the revelation
and make it plain on tablets
so that a herald[c] may run with it.
3 For the revelation awaits an appointed time;
it speaks of the end
and will not prove false.
Though it linger, wait for it;
it[d] will certainly come
and will not delay.

4 "See, the enemy is puffed up;
his desires are not upright—
but the righteous person will live by his faithfulness[e]—
5 indeed, wine betrays him;
he is arrogant and never at rest.
Because he is as greedy as the grave
and like death is never satisfied,
he gathers to himself all the nations
and takes captive all the peoples.

6 "Will not all of them taunt him with ridicule and scorn, saying,

" 'Woe to him who piles up stolen goods
and makes himself wealthy by extortion!
How long must this go on?'
7 Will not your creditors suddenly arise?
Will they not wake up and make you tremble?
Then you will become their prey.
8 Because you have plundered many nations,
the peoples who are left will plunder you.
For you have shed human blood;
you have destroyed lands and cities and everyone in them.

9 "Woe to him who builds his house by unjust gain,
setting his nest on high
to escape the clutches of ruin!
10 You have plotted the ruin of many peoples,
shaming your own house and forfeiting your life.
11 The stones of the wall will cry out,
and the beams of the woodwork will echo it.

12 "Woe to him who builds a city with bloodshed
and establishes a town by injustice!
13 Has not the LORD Almighty determined
that the people's labor is only fuel for the fire,
that the nations exhaust themselves for nothing?
14 For the earth will be filled with the knowledge of the glory of the LORD
as the waters cover the sea.

15 "Woe to him who gives drink to his neighbors,
pouring it from the wineskin till they are drunk,
so that he can gaze on their naked bodies!
16 You will be filled with shame instead of glory.
Now it is your turn! Drink and let your nakedness be exposed[f]!
The cup from the LORD's right hand is coming around to you,
and disgrace will cover your glory.
17 The violence you have done to Lebanon
will overwhelm you,
and your destruction of animals will terrify you.
For you have shed human blood;
you have destroyed lands and cities and everyone in them.

18 "Of what value is an idol carved by a craftsman?
Or an image that teaches lies?
For the one who makes it trusts in his own creation;
he makes idols that cannot speak.
19 Woe to him who says to wood, 'Come to life!'
Or to lifeless stone, 'Wake up!'
Can it give guidance?
It is covered with gold and silver;
there is no breath in it."

[a] 12 An ancient Hebrew scribal tradition; Masoretic Text *we* [b] 1 Or *and what to answer when I am rebuked* [c] 2 Or *so that whoever reads it* [d] 3 Or *Though he linger, wait for him; / he* [e] 4 Or *faith*
[f] 16 Masoretic Text; Dead Sea Scrolls, Aquila, Vulgate and Syriac (see also Septuagint) *and stagger*

[20]The LORD is in his holy temple;
let all the earth be silent before him.

Habakkuk's Prayer

3 A prayer of Habakkuk the prophet. On *shigionoth.*[a]

[2]LORD, I have heard of your fame;
I stand in awe of your deeds, LORD.
Repeat them in our day,
in our time make them known;
in wrath remember mercy.

[3]God came from Teman,
the Holy One from Mount Paran.[b]
His glory covered the heavens
and his praise filled the earth.
[4]His splendor was like the sunrise;
rays flashed from his hand,
where his power was hidden.
[5]Plague went before him;
pestilence followed his steps.
[6]He stood, and shook the earth;
he looked, and made the nations tremble.
The ancient mountains crumbled
and the age-old hills collapsed—
but he marches on forever.
[7]I saw the tents of Cushan in distress,
the dwellings of Midian in anguish.

[8]Were you angry with the rivers, LORD?
Was your wrath against the streams?
Did you rage against the sea
when you rode your horses
and your chariots to victory?
[9]You uncovered your bow,
you called for many arrows.
You split the earth with rivers;
[10] the mountains saw you and writhed.
Torrents of water swept by;
the deep roared
and lifted its waves on high.
[11]Sun and moon stood still in the heavens
at the glint of your flying arrows,
at the lightning of your flashing spear.
[12]In wrath you strode through the earth
and in anger you threshed the nations.
[13]You came out to deliver your people,
to save your anointed one.
You crushed the leader of the land of wickedness,
you stripped him from head to foot.
[14]With his own spear you pierced his head
when his warriors stormed out to scatter us,
gloating as though about to devour
the wretched who were in hiding.
[15]You trampled the sea with your horses,
churning the great waters.

[16]I heard and my heart pounded,
my lips quivered at the sound;
decay crept into my bones,
and my legs trembled.
Yet I will wait patiently for the day of calamity
to come on the nation invading us.
[17]Though the fig tree does not bud
and there are no grapes on the vines,
though the olive crop fails
and the fields produce no food,
though there are no sheep in the pen
and no cattle in the stalls,
[18]yet I will rejoice in the LORD,
I will be joyful in God my Savior.

[19]The Sovereign LORD is my strength;
he makes my feet like the feet of a deer,
he enables me to tread on the heights.

For the director of music. On my stringed instruments.

Zephaniah

1 The word of the LORD that came to Zephaniah son of Cushi, the son of Gedaliah, the son of Amariah, the son of Hezekiah, during the reign of Josiah son of Amon king of Judah:

Judgment on the Whole Earth in the Day of the LORD

[2]"I will sweep away everything
from the face of the earth,"
declares the LORD.
[3]"I will sweep away both man and beast;
I will sweep away the birds in the sky
and the fish in the sea—
and the idols that cause the wicked to stumble."[c]

"When I destroy all mankind
on the face of the earth,"
declares the LORD,
[4]"I will stretch out my hand against Judah
and against all who live in Jerusalem.
I will destroy every remnant of Baal worship in this place,
the very names of the idolatrous priests—
[5]those who bow down on the roofs
to worship the starry host,

[a] *1* Probably a literary or musical term [b] *3* The Hebrew has *Selah* (a word of uncertain meaning) here and at the middle of verse 9 and at the end of verse 13. [c] *3* The meaning of the Hebrew for this line is uncertain.

those who bow down and swear by the
LORD
and who also swear by Molek,[a]
6 those who turn back from following the
LORD
and neither seek the LORD nor inquire
of him."

7 Be silent before the Sovereign LORD,
for the day of the LORD is near.
The LORD has prepared a sacrifice;
he has consecrated those he has
invited.

8 "On the day of the LORD's sacrifice
I will punish the officials
and the king's sons
and all those clad
in foreign clothes.
9 On that day I will punish
all who avoid stepping on the
threshold,[b]
who fill the temple of their gods
with violence and deceit.

10 "On that day,"
declares the LORD,
"a cry will go up from the Fish Gate,
wailing from the New Quarter,
and a loud crash from the hills.
11 Wail, you who live in the market
district[c];
all your merchants will be wiped out,
all who trade with[d] silver will be
destroyed.
12 At that time I will search Jerusalem with
lamps
and punish those who are complacent,
who are like wine left on its dregs,
who think, 'The LORD will do nothing,
either good or bad.'
13 Their wealth will be plundered,
their houses demolished.
Though they build houses,
they will not live in them;
though they plant vineyards,
they will not drink the wine."

14 The great day of the LORD is near—
near and coming quickly.
The cry on the day of the LORD is bitter;
the Mighty Warrior shouts his battle
cry.
15 That day will be a day of wrath—
a day of distress and anguish,
a day of trouble and ruin,
a day of darkness and gloom,
a day of clouds and blackness—
16 a day of trumpet and battle cry
against the fortified cities
and against the corner towers.

17 "I will bring such distress on all people
that they will grope about like those
who are blind,
because they have sinned against the
LORD.
Their blood will be poured out like dust
and their entrails like dung.
18 Neither their silver nor their gold
will be able to save them
on the day of the LORD's wrath."

In the fire of his jealousy
the whole earth will be consumed,
for he will make a sudden end
of all who live on the earth.

Judah and Jerusalem Judged Along With the Nations

Judah Summoned to Repent

2 Gather together, gather yourselves
together,
you shameful nation,
2 before the decree takes effect
and that day passes like windblown
chaff,
before the LORD's fierce anger
comes upon you,
before the day of the LORD's wrath
comes upon you.
3 Seek the LORD, all you humble of the land,
you who do what he commands.
Seek righteousness, seek humility;
perhaps you will be sheltered
on the day of the LORD's anger.

Philistia

4 Gaza will be abandoned
and Ashkelon left in ruins.
At midday Ashdod will be emptied
and Ekron uprooted.
5 Woe to you who live by the sea,
you Kerethite people;
the word of the LORD is against you,
Canaan, land of the Philistines.
He says, "I will destroy you,
and none will be left."
6 The land by the sea will become pastures
having wells for shepherds
and pens for flocks.
7 That land will belong
to the remnant of the people of Judah;
there they will find pasture.
In the evening they will lie down
in the houses of Ashkelon.
The LORD their God will care for them;
he will restore their fortunes.[e]

Moab and Ammon

8 "I have heard the insults of Moab
and the taunts of the Ammonites,
who insulted my people
and made threats against their land.
9 Therefore, as surely as I live,"
declares the LORD Almighty,
the God of Israel,
"surely Moab will become like Sodom,
the Ammonites like Gomorrah—
a place of weeds and salt pits,
a wasteland forever.
The remnant of my people will plunder
them;
the survivors of my nation will inherit
their land."

[a] 5 Hebrew *Malkam* [b] 9 See 1 Samuel 5:5. [c] *11* Or *the Mortar* [d] *11* Or *in* [e] 7 Or *will bring back their captives*

10 This is what they will get in return for
their pride,
for insulting and mocking
the people of the LORD Almighty.
11 The LORD will be awesome to them
when he destroys all the gods of the
earth.
Distant nations will bow down to him,
all of them in their own lands.

Cush

12 "You Cushites,[a] too,
will be slain by my sword."

Assyria

13 He will stretch out his hand against the
north
and destroy Assyria,
leaving Nineveh utterly desolate
and dry as the desert.
14 Flocks and herds will lie down there,
creatures of every kind.
The desert owl and the screech owl
will roost on her columns.
Their hooting will echo through the
windows,
rubble will fill the doorways,
the beams of cedar will be exposed.
15 This is the city of revelry
that lived in safety.
She said to herself,
"I am the one! And there is none
besides me."
What a ruin she has become,
a lair for wild beasts!
All who pass by her scoff
and shake their fists.

Jerusalem

3 Woe to the city of oppressors,
rebellious and defiled!
2 She obeys no one,
she accepts no correction.
She does not trust in the LORD,
she does not draw near to her God.
3 Her officials within her
are roaring lions;
her rulers are evening wolves,
who leave nothing for the morning.
4 Her prophets are unprincipled;
they are treacherous people.
Her priests profane the sanctuary
and do violence to the law.
5 The LORD within her is righteous;
he does no wrong.
Morning by morning he dispenses his
justice,
and every new day he does not fail,
yet the unrighteous know no shame.

Jerusalem Remains Unrepentant

6 "I have destroyed nations;
their strongholds are demolished.
I have left their streets deserted,
with no one passing through.
Their cities are laid waste;
they are deserted and empty.
7 Of Jerusalem I thought,
'Surely you will fear me
and accept correction!'
Then her place of refuge[b] would not be
destroyed,
nor all my punishments come upon[c]
her.
But they were still eager
to act corruptly in all they did.
8 Therefore wait for me,"
declares the LORD,
"for the day I will stand up to testify.[d]
I have decided to assemble the nations,
to gather the kingdoms
and to pour out my wrath on them—
all my fierce anger.
The whole world will be consumed
by the fire of my jealous anger.

Restoration of Israel's Remnant

9 "Then I will purify the lips of the
peoples,
that all of them may call on the name of
the LORD
and serve him shoulder to shoulder.
10 From beyond the rivers of Cush[e]
my worshipers, my scattered people,
will bring me offerings.
11 On that day you, Jerusalem, will not be
put to shame
for all the wrongs you have done to me,
because I will remove from you
your arrogant boasters.
Never again will you be haughty
on my holy hill.
12 But I will leave within you
the meek and humble.
The remnant of Israel
will trust in the name of the LORD.
13 They will do no wrong;
they will tell no lies.
A deceitful tongue
will not be found in their mouths.
They will eat and lie down
and no one will make them afraid."
14 Sing, Daughter Zion;
shout aloud, Israel!
Be glad and rejoice with all your heart,
Daughter Jerusalem!
15 The LORD has taken away your
punishment,
he has turned back your enemy.
The LORD, the King of Israel, is with you;
never again will you fear any harm.
16 On that day
they will say to Jerusalem,
"Do not fear, Zion;
do not let your hands hang limp.
17 The LORD your God is with you,
the Mighty Warrior who saves.
He will take great delight in you;
in his love he will no longer rebuke you,
but will rejoice over you with singing."

[a] 12 That is, people from the upper Nile region [b] 7 Or *her sanctuary* [c] 7 Or *all those I appointed over* [d] 8 Septuagint and Syriac; Hebrew *will rise up to plunder* [e] 10 That is, the upper Nile region

18 "I will remove from you
all who mourn over the loss of your
appointed festivals,
which is a burden and reproach for you.
19 At that time I will deal
with all who oppressed you.
I will rescue the lame;
I will gather the exiles.
I will give them praise and honor
in every land where they have suffered
shame.
20 At that time I will gather you;
at that time I will bring you home.
I will give you honor and praise
among all the peoples of the earth
when I restore your fortunes[a]
before your very eyes,"
says the LORD.

Haggai

A Call to Build the House of the LORD

1 In the second year of King Darius, on the
first day of the sixth month, the word of the
LORD came through the prophet Haggai to Zerubbabel son of Shealtiel, governor of Judah,
and to Joshua son of Jozadak,[b] the high priest:
2 This is what the LORD Almighty says:
"These people say, 'The time has not yet come
to rebuild the LORD's house.'"
3 Then the word of the LORD came through
the prophet Haggai: 4 "Is it a time for you yourselves to be living in your paneled houses,
while this house remains a ruin?"
5 Now this is what the LORD Almighty says:
"Give careful thought to your ways. 6 You have
planted much, but harvested little. You eat,
but never have enough. You drink, but never
have your fill. You put on clothes, but are not
warm. You earn wages, only to put them in a
purse with holes in it."
7 This is what the LORD Almighty says: "Give
careful thought to your ways. 8 Go up into the
mountains and bring down timber and build
my house, so that I may take pleasure in it
and be honored," says the LORD. 9 "You expected much, but see, it turned out to be little.
What you brought home, I blew away. Why?"
declares the LORD Almighty. "Because of my
house, which remains a ruin, while each of
you is busy with your own house. 10 Therefore,
because of you the heavens have withheld
their dew and the earth its crops. 11 I called
for a drought on the fields and the mountains,
on the grain, the new wine, the olive oil and
everything else the ground produces, on people and livestock, and on all the labor of your
hands."

12 Then Zerubbabel son of Shealtiel, Joshua son of Jozadak, the high priest, and the
whole remnant of the people obeyed the voice
of the LORD their God and the message of the
prophet Haggai, because the LORD their God
had sent him. And the people feared the LORD.
13 Then Haggai, the LORD's messenger, gave
this message of the LORD to the people: "I am
with you," declares the LORD. 14 So the LORD
stirred up the spirit of Zerubbabel son of
Shealtiel, governor of Judah, and the spirit
of Joshua son of Jozadak, the high priest, and
the spirit of the whole remnant of the people.
They came and began to work on the house of
the LORD Almighty, their God, 15 on the twenty-fourth day of the sixth month.

The Promised Glory of the New House

2 In the second year of King Darius, 1 on the
twenty-first day of the seventh month, the
word of the LORD came through the prophet
Haggai: 2 "Speak to Zerubbabel son of Shealtiel, governor of Judah, to Joshua son of Jozadak,[c] the high priest, and to the remnant of
the people. Ask them, 3 'Who of you is left who
saw this house in its former glory? How does
it look to you now? Does it not seem to you
like nothing? 4 But now be strong, Zerubbabel,' declares the LORD. 'Be strong, Joshua son
of Jozadak, the high priest. Be strong, all you
people of the land,' declares the LORD, 'and
work. For I am with you,' declares the LORD
Almighty. 5 'This is what I covenanted with
you when you came out of Egypt. And my
Spirit remains among you. Do not fear.'
6 "This is what the LORD Almighty says: 'In
a little while I will once more shake the heavens and the earth, the sea and the dry land.
7 I will shake all nations, and what is desired
by all nations will come, and I will fill this
house with glory,' says the LORD Almighty.
8 'The silver is mine and the gold is mine,' declares the LORD Almighty. 9 'The glory of this
present house will be greater than the glory
of the former house,' says the LORD Almighty.
'And in this place I will grant peace,' declares
the LORD Almighty."

Blessings for a Defiled People

10 On the twenty-fourth day of the ninth
month, in the second year of Darius, the
word of the LORD came to the prophet Haggai:
11 "This is what the LORD Almighty says: 'Ask
the priests what the law says: 12 If someone

[a] 20 Or *I bring back your captives* [b] 1 Hebrew *Jehozadak*, a variant of *Jozadak*; also in verses 12 and 14 [c] 2 Hebrew *Jehozadak*, a variant of *Jozadak*; also in verse 4

carries consecrated meat in the fold of their
garment, and that fold touches some bread or
stew, some wine, olive oil or other food, does
it become consecrated?'"
The priests answered, "No."
13Then Haggai said, "If a person defiled by
contact with a dead body touches one of these
things, does it become defiled?"
"Yes," the priests replied, "it becomes defiled."
14Then Haggai said, "'So it is with this people and this nation in my sight,' declares the
LORD. 'Whatever they do and whatever they
offer there is defiled.
15"'Now give careful thought to this from
this day on[a]—consider how things were before one stone was laid on another in the
LORD's temple. 16When anyone came to a
heap of twenty measures, there were only ten.
When anyone went to a wine vat to draw fifty
measures, there were only twenty. 17I struck
all the work of your hands with blight, mildew and hail, yet you did not return to me,'
declares the LORD. 18'From this day on, from
this twenty-fourth day of the ninth month,
give careful thought to the day when the foundation of the LORD's temple was laid. Give
careful thought: 19Is there yet any seed left
in the barn? Until now, the vine and the fig
tree, the pomegranate and the olive tree have
not borne fruit.
"'From this day on I will bless you.'"

Zerubbabel the LORD's Signet Ring

20The word of the LORD came to Haggai a
second time on the twenty-fourth day of the
month: 21"Tell Zerubbabel governor of Judah
that I am going to shake the heavens and the
earth. 22I will overturn royal thrones and shatter the power of the foreign kingdoms. I will
overthrow chariots and their drivers; horses
and their riders will fall, each by the sword
of his brother.
23"'On that day,' declares the LORD Almighty, 'I will take you, my servant Zerubbabel son of Shealtiel,' declares the LORD, 'and
I will make you like my signet ring, for I have
chosen you,' declares the LORD Almighty."

Zechariah

A Call to Return to the LORD

1 In the eighth month of the second year of
Darius, the word of the LORD came to the
prophet Zechariah son of Berekiah, the son
of Iddo:
2"The LORD was very angry with your ancestors. 3Therefore tell the people: This is
what the LORD Almighty says: 'Return to
me,' declares the LORD Almighty, 'and I will
return to you,' says the LORD Almighty. 4Do
not be like your ancestors, to whom the earlier
prophets proclaimed: This is what the LORD
Almighty says: 'Turn from your evil ways
and your evil practices.' But they would not
listen or pay attention to me, declares the
LORD. 5Where are your ancestors now? And
the prophets, do they live forever? 6But did
not my words and my decrees, which I commanded my servants the prophets, overtake
your ancestors?
"Then they repented and said, 'The LORD
Almighty has done to us what our ways and
practices deserve, just as he determined
to do.'"

The Man Among the Myrtle Trees

7On the twenty-fourth day of the eleventh
month, the month of Shebat, in the second
year of Darius, the word of the LORD came to
the prophet Zechariah son of Berekiah, the
son of Iddo.
8During the night I had a vision, and there
before me was a man mounted on a red horse.
He was standing among the myrtle trees in
a ravine. Behind him were red, brown and
white horses.
9I asked, "What are these, my lord?"
The angel who was talking with me answered, "I will show you what they are."
10Then the man standing among the myrtle
trees explained, "They are the ones the LORD
has sent to go throughout the earth."
11And they reported to the angel of the LORD
who was standing among the myrtle trees,
"We have gone throughout the earth and
found the whole world at rest and in peace."
12Then the angel of the LORD said, "LORD
Almighty, how long will you withhold mercy
from Jerusalem and from the towns of Judah,
which you have been angry with these seventy years?" 13So the LORD spoke kind and
comforting words to the angel who talked
with me.
14Then the angel who was speaking to me
said, "Proclaim this word: This is what the
LORD Almighty says: 'I am very jealous for
Jerusalem and Zion, 15and I am very angry
with the nations that feel secure. I was only
a little angry, but they went too far with the
punishment.'
16"Therefore this is what the LORD says: 'I
will return to Jerusalem with mercy, and there
my house will be rebuilt. And the measuring

[a] 15 *Or to the days past*

line will be stretched out over Jerusalem,' declares the LORD Almighty.
17"Proclaim further: This is what the LORD
Almighty says: 'My towns will again overflow
with prosperity, and the LORD will again comfort Zion and choose Jerusalem.'"

Four Horns and Four Craftsmen

18Then I looked up, and there before me
were four horns. 19I asked the angel who was
speaking to me, "What are these?"
He answered me, "These are the horns that
scattered Judah, Israel and Jerusalem."
20Then the LORD showed me four craftsmen.
21I asked, "What are these coming to do?"
He answered, "These are the horns that
scattered Judah so that no one could raise
their head, but the craftsmen have come to
terrify them and throw down these horns of
the nations who lifted up their horns against
the land of Judah to scatter its people."[a]

A Man With a Measuring Line

2[b] Then I looked up, and there before me was
a man with a measuring line in his hand.
2I asked, "Where are you going?"
He answered me, "To measure Jerusalem, to
find out how wide and how long it is."
3While the angel who was speaking to me
was leaving, another angel came to meet him
4and said to him: "Run, tell that young man,
'Jerusalem will be a city without walls because
of the great number of people and animals in it.
5And I myself will be a wall of fire around it,' declares the LORD, 'and I will be its glory within.'
6"Come! Come! Flee from the land of the
north," declares the LORD, "for I have scattered you to the four winds of heaven," declares the LORD.
7"Come, Zion! Escape, you who live in
Daughter Babylon!" 8For this is what the LORD
Almighty says: "After the Glorious One has
sent me against the nations that have plundered you—for whoever touches you touches
the apple of his eye— 9I will surely raise my
hand against them so that their slaves will
plunder them.[c] Then you will know that the
LORD Almighty has sent me.
10"Shout and be glad, Daughter Zion. For
I am coming, and I will live among you,"
declares the LORD. 11"Many nations will be
joined with the LORD in that day and will become my people. I will live among you and
you will know that the LORD Almighty has
sent me to you. 12The LORD will inherit Judah
as his portion in the holy land and will again
choose Jerusalem. 13Be still before the LORD,
all mankind, because he has roused himself
from his holy dwelling."

Clean Garments for the High Priest

3 Then he showed me Joshua the high priest
standing before the angel of the LORD, and
Satan[d] standing at his right side to accuse
him. 2The LORD said to Satan, "The LORD rebuke you, Satan! The LORD, who has chosen
Jerusalem, rebuke you! Is not this man a burning stick snatched from the fire?"
3Now Joshua was dressed in filthy clothes
as he stood before the angel. 4The angel said
to those who were standing before him, "Take
off his filthy clothes."
Then he said to Joshua, "See, I have taken
away your sin, and I will put fine garments
on you."
5Then I said, "Put a clean turban on his
head." So they put a clean turban on his head
and clothed him, while the angel of the LORD
stood by.
6The angel of the LORD gave this charge
to Joshua: 7"This is what the LORD Almighty
says: 'If you will walk in obedience to me and
keep my requirements, then you will govern
my house and have charge of my courts, and
I will give you a place among these standing here.
8"'Listen, High Priest Joshua, you and your
associates seated before you, who are men
symbolic of things to come: I am going to
bring my servant, the Branch. 9See, the stone
I have set in front of Joshua! There are seven
eyes[e] on that one stone, and I will engrave
an inscription on it,' says the LORD Almighty,
'and I will remove the sin of this land in a
single day.
10"'In that day each of you will invite your
neighbor to sit under your vine and fig tree,'
declares the LORD Almighty."

The Gold Lampstand and the Two Olive Trees

4 Then the angel who talked with me returned and woke me up, like someone
awakened from sleep. 2He asked me, "What
do you see?"
I answered, "I see a solid gold lampstand
with a bowl at the top and seven lamps on it,
with seven channels to the lamps. 3Also there
are two olive trees by it, one on the right of
the bowl and the other on its left."
4I asked the angel who talked with me,
"What are these, my lord?"
5He answered, "Do you not know what
these are?"
"No, my lord," I replied.
6So he said to me, "This is the word of the
LORD to Zerubbabel: 'Not by might nor by
power, but by my Spirit,' says the LORD Almighty.
7"What are you, mighty mountain? Before
Zerubbabel you will become level ground.
Then he will bring out the capstone to shouts
of 'God bless it! God bless it!'"
8Then the word of the LORD came to me:
9"The hands of Zerubbabel have laid the foundation of this temple; his hands will also complete it. Then you will know that the LORD
Almighty has sent me to you.
10"Who dares despise the day of small
things, since the seven eyes of the LORD that

[a] *21* In Hebrew texts 1:18-21 is numbered 2:1-4. [b] In Hebrew texts 2:1-13 is numbered 2:5-17
[c] *8,9* Or *says after . . . eye:* 9"*I . . . plunder them.*" [d] *1* Hebrew *satan* means *adversary.*
[e] *9* Or *facets*

range throughout the earth will rejoice when they see the chosen capstone[a] in the hand of Zerubbabel?"

11Then I asked the angel, "What are these two olive trees on the right and the left of the lampstand?"

12Again I asked him, "What are these two olive branches beside the two gold pipes that pour out golden oil?"

13He replied, "Do you not know what these are?"

"No, my lord," I said.

14So he said, "These are the two who are anointed to[b] serve the Lord of all the earth."

The Flying Scroll

5 I looked again, and there before me was a flying scroll.

2He asked me, "What do you see?"

I answered, "I see a flying scroll, twenty cubits long and ten cubits wide.[c]"

3And he said to me, "This is the curse that is going out over the whole land; for according to what it says on one side, every thief will be banished, and according to what it says on the other, everyone who swears falsely will be banished. 4The LORD Almighty declares, 'I will send it out, and it will enter the house of the thief and the house of anyone who swears falsely by my name. It will remain in that house and destroy it completely, both its timbers and its stones.'"

The Woman in a Basket

5Then the angel who was speaking to me came forward and said to me, "Look up and see what is appearing."

6I asked, "What is it?"

He replied, "It is a basket." And he added, "This is the iniquity[d] of the people throughout the land."

7Then the cover of lead was raised, and there in the basket sat a woman! 8He said, "This is wickedness," and he pushed her back into the basket and pushed its lead cover down on it.

9Then I looked up—and there before me were two women, with the wind in their wings! They had wings like those of a stork, and they lifted up the basket between heaven and earth.

10"Where are they taking the basket?" I asked the angel who was speaking to me.

11He replied, "To the country of Babylonia[e] to build a house for it. When the house is ready, the basket will be set there in its place."

Four Chariots

6 I looked up again, and there before me were four chariots coming out from between two mountains—mountains of bronze. 2The first chariot had red horses, the second black, 3the third white, and the fourth dappled—all of them powerful. 4I asked the angel who was speaking to me, "What are these, my lord?"

5The angel answered me, "These are the four spirits[f] of heaven, going out from standing in the presence of the Lord of the whole world. 6The one with the black horses is going toward the north country, the one with the white horses toward the west,[g] and the one with the dappled horses toward the south."

7When the powerful horses went out, they were straining to go throughout the earth. And he said, "Go throughout the earth!" So they went throughout the earth.

8Then he called to me, "Look, those going toward the north country have given my Spirit[h] rest in the land of the north."

A Crown for Joshua

9The word of the LORD came to me: 10"Take silver and gold from the exiles Heldai, Tobijah and Jedaiah, who have arrived from Babylon. Go the same day to the house of Josiah son of Zephaniah. 11Take the silver and gold and make a crown, and set it on the head of the high priest, Joshua son of Jozadak.[i] 12Tell him this is what the LORD Almighty says: 'Here is the man whose name is the Branch, and he will branch out from his place and build the temple of the LORD. 13It is he who will build the temple of the LORD, and he will be clothed with majesty and will sit and rule on his throne. And he[j] will be a priest on his throne. And there will be harmony between the two.' 14The crown will be given to Heldai,[k] Tobijah, Jedaiah and Hen[l] son of Zephaniah as a memorial in the temple of the LORD. 15Those who are far away will come and help to build the temple of the LORD, and you will know that the LORD Almighty has sent me to you. This will happen if you diligently obey the LORD your God."

Justice and Mercy, Not Fasting

7 In the fourth year of King Darius, the word of the LORD came to Zechariah on the fourth day of the ninth month, the month of Kislev. 2The people of Bethel had sent Sharezer and Regem-Melek, together with their men, to entreat the LORD 3by asking the priests of the house of the LORD Almighty and the prophets, "Should I mourn and fast in the fifth month, as I have done for so many years?"

4Then the word of the LORD Almighty came to me: 5"Ask all the people of the land and the priests, 'When you fasted and mourned in the fifth and seventh months for the past seventy years, was it really for me that you fasted? 6And when you were eating and drinking, were you not just feasting for yourselves? 7Are these not the words the LORD proclaimed through the earlier prophets when Jerusalem and its surrounding towns were at rest and prosperous, and the Negev and the western foothills were settled?'"

8And the word of the LORD came again to

[a] 10 Or *the plumb line* [b] 14 Or *two who bring oil and* [c] 2 That is, about 30 feet long and 15 feet wide or about 9 meters long and 4.5 meters wide [d] 6 Or *appearance* [e] 11 Hebrew *Shinar* [f] 5 Or *winds* [g] 6 Or *horses after them* [h] 8 Or *spirit* [i] 11 Hebrew *Jehozadak*, a variant of *Jozadak* [j] 13 Or *there* [k] 14 Syriac; Hebrew *Helem* [l] 14 Or *and the gracious one, the*

Zechariah: 9“This is what the LORD Almighty
said: ‘Administer true justice; show mercy and
compassion to one another. 10Do not oppress
the widow or the fatherless, the foreigner or
the poor. Do not plot evil against each other.’
11“But they refused to pay attention; stubbornly they turned their backs and covered
their ears. 12They made their hearts as hard
as flint and would not listen to the law or to
the words that the LORD Almighty had sent
by his Spirit through the earlier prophets. So
the LORD Almighty was very angry.
13“ ‘When I called, they did not listen; so
when they called, I would not listen,’ says
the LORD Almighty. 14‘I scattered them with
a whirlwind among all the nations, where
they were strangers. The land they left behind them was so desolate that no one traveled
through it. This is how they made the pleasant
land desolate.’ ”

The LORD Promises to Bless Jerusalem

8 The word of the LORD Almighty came to
me.
2This is what the LORD Almighty says: “I
am very jealous for Zion; I am burning with
jealousy for her.”
3This is what the LORD says: “I will return
to Zion and dwell in Jerusalem. Then Jerusalem will be called the Faithful City, and the
mountain of the LORD Almighty will be called
the Holy Mountain.”
4This is what the LORD Almighty says:
“Once again men and women of ripe old age
will sit in the streets of Jerusalem, each of
them with cane in hand because of their age.
5The city streets will be filled with boys and
girls playing there.”
6This is what the LORD Almighty says: “It
may seem marvelous to the remnant of this
people at that time, but will it seem marvelous
to me?” declares the LORD Almighty.
7This is what the LORD Almighty says: “I
will save my people from the countries of the
east and the west. 8I will bring them back to
live in Jerusalem; they will be my people,
and I will be faithful and righteous to them
as their God.”
9This is what the LORD Almighty says: “Now
hear these words, ‘Let your hands be strong so
that the temple may be built.’ This is also what
the prophets said who were present when the
foundation was laid for the house of the LORD
Almighty. 10Before that time there were no
wages for people or hire for animals. No one
could go about their business safely because
of their enemies, since I had turned everyone against their neighbor. 11But now I will
not deal with the remnant of this people as I
did in the past,” declares the LORD Almighty.
12“The seed will grow well, the vine will
yield its fruit, the ground will produce its
crops, and the heavens will drop their dew.
I will give all these things as an inheritance
to the remnant of this people. 13Just as you,
Judah and Israel, have been a curse[a] among
the nations, so I will save you, and you will
be a blessing.[b] Do not be afraid, but let your
hands be strong.”
14This is what the LORD Almighty says: “Just
as I had determined to bring disaster on you
and showed no pity when your ancestors angered me,” says the LORD Almighty, 15“so now
I have determined to do good again to Jerusalem and Judah. Do not be afraid. 16These are
the things you are to do: Speak the truth to
each other, and render true and sound judgment in your courts; 17do not plot evil against
each other, and do not love to swear falsely. I
hate all this,” declares the LORD.
18The word of the LORD Almighty came to
me.
19This is what the LORD Almighty says: “The
fasts of the fourth, fifth, seventh and tenth
months will become joyful and glad occasions
and happy festivals for Judah. Therefore love
truth and peace.”
20This is what the LORD Almighty says:
“Many peoples and the inhabitants of many
cities will yet come, 21and the inhabitants of
one city will go to another and say, ‘Let us go
at once to entreat the LORD and seek the LORD
Almighty. I myself am going.’ 22And many
peoples and powerful nations will come to
Jerusalem to seek the LORD Almighty and to
entreat him.”
23This is what the LORD Almighty says: “In
those days ten people from all languages and
nations will take firm hold of one Jew by the
hem of his robe and say, ‘Let us go with you,
because we have heard that God is with you.’ ”

Judgment on Israel’s Enemies

9 A prophecy:

The word of the LORD is against the land
of Hadrak
and will come to rest on Damascus—
for the eyes of all people and all the tribes
of Israel
are on the LORD—[c]
2 and on Hamath too, which borders on it,
and on Tyre and Sidon, though they are
very skillful.
3 Tyre has built herself a stronghold;
she has heaped up silver like dust,
and gold like the dirt of the streets.
4 But the Lord will take away her
possessions
and destroy her power on the sea,
and she will be consumed by fire.
5 Ashkelon will see it and fear;
Gaza will writhe in agony,
and Ekron too, for her hope will
wither.
Gaza will lose her king
and Ashkelon will be deserted.
6 A mongrel people will occupy Ashdod,
and I will put an end to the pride of the
Philistines.

[a] 13 That is, your name has been used in cursing (see Jer. 29:22); or, you have been regarded as under a curse. [b] 13 Or *and your name will be used in blessings* (see Gen. 48:20); or *and you will be seen as blessed* [c] 1 Or *Damascus. / For the eye of the LORD is on all people, / as well as on the tribes of Israel,*

[7] I will take the blood from their mouths,
the forbidden food from between their teeth.
Those who are left will belong to our God
and become a clan in Judah,
and Ekron will be like the Jebusites.
[8] But I will encamp at my temple
to guard it against marauding forces.
Never again will an oppressor overrun my people,
for now I am keeping watch.

The Coming of Zion's King

[9] Rejoice greatly, Daughter Zion!
Shout, Daughter Jerusalem!
See, your king comes to you,
righteous and victorious,
lowly and riding on a donkey,
on a colt, the foal of a donkey.
[10] I will take away the chariots from Ephraim
and the warhorses from Jerusalem,
and the battle bow will be broken.
He will proclaim peace to the nations.
His rule will extend from sea to sea
and from the River[a] to the ends of the earth.
[11] As for you, because of the blood of my covenant with you,
I will free your prisoners from the waterless pit.
[12] Return to your fortress, you prisoners of hope;
even now I announce that I will restore twice as much to you.
[13] I will bend Judah as I bend my bow
and fill it with Ephraim.
I will rouse your sons, Zion,
against your sons, Greece,
and make you like a warrior's sword.

The LORD Will Appear

[14] Then the LORD will appear over them;
his arrow will flash like lightning.
The Sovereign LORD will sound the trumpet;
he will march in the storms of the south,
[15] and the LORD Almighty will shield them.
They will destroy
and overcome with slingstones.
They will drink and roar as with wine;
they will be full like a bowl
used for sprinkling[b] the corners of the altar.
[16] The LORD their God will save his people on that day
as a shepherd saves his flock.
They will sparkle in his land
like jewels in a crown.
[17] How attractive and beautiful they will be!
Grain will make the young men thrive,
and new wine the young women.

The LORD Will Care for Judah

10 Ask the LORD for rain in the springtime;
it is the LORD who sends the thunderstorms.
He gives showers of rain to all people,
and plants of the field to everyone.
[2] The idols speak deceitfully,
diviners see visions that lie;
they tell dreams that are false,
they give comfort in vain.
Therefore the people wander like sheep
oppressed for lack of a shepherd.

[3] "My anger burns against the shepherds,
and I will punish the leaders;
for the LORD Almighty will care
for his flock, the people of Judah,
and make them like a proud horse in battle.
[4] From Judah will come the cornerstone,
from him the tent peg,
from him the battle bow,
from him every ruler.
[5] Together they[c] will be like warriors in battle
trampling their enemy into the mud of the streets.
They will fight because the LORD is with them,
and they will put the enemy horsemen to shame.

[6] "I will strengthen Judah
and save the tribes of Joseph.
I will restore them
because I have compassion on them.
They will be as though
I had not rejected them,
for I am the LORD their God
and I will answer them.
[7] The Ephraimites will become like warriors,
and their hearts will be glad as with wine.
Their children will see it and be joyful;
their hearts will rejoice in the LORD.
[8] I will signal for them
and gather them in.
Surely I will redeem them;
they will be as numerous as before.
[9] Though I scatter them among the peoples,
yet in distant lands they will remember me.
They and their children will survive,
and they will return.
[10] I will bring them back from Egypt
and gather them from Assyria.
I will bring them to Gilead and Lebanon,
and there will not be room enough for them.
[11] They will pass through the sea of trouble;
the surging sea will be subdued
and all the depths of the Nile will dry up.
Assyria's pride will be brought down
and Egypt's scepter will pass away.

[a] *10* That is, the Euphrates [b] *15* Or *bowl, / like* [c] *4,5* Or *ruler, all of them together. / [5]They*

[12]I will strengthen them in the LORD
and in his name they will live securely,"
declares the LORD.

11 Open your doors, Lebanon,
so that fire may devour your cedars!
[2]Wail, you juniper, for the cedar has fallen;
the stately trees are ruined!
Wail, oaks of Bashan;
the dense forest has been cut down!
[3]Listen to the wail of the shepherds;
their rich pastures are destroyed!
Listen to the roar of the lions;
the lush thicket of the Jordan is ruined!

Two Shepherds

[4]This is what the LORD my God says: "Shepherd the flock marked for slaughter. [5]Their
buyers slaughter them and go unpunished.
Those who sell them say, 'Praise the LORD, I
am rich!' Their own shepherds do not spare
them. [6]For I will no longer have pity on the
people of the land," declares the LORD. "I will
give everyone into the hands of their neighbors and their king. They will devastate the
land, and I will not rescue anyone from their
hands."

[7]So I shepherded the flock marked for
slaughter, particularly the oppressed of the
flock. Then I took two staffs and called one
Favor and the other Union, and I shepherded
the flock. [8]In one month I got rid of the three
shepherds.

The flock detested me, and I grew weary of
them [9]and said, "I will not be your shepherd.
Let the dying die, and the perishing perish.
Let those who are left eat one another's flesh."

[10]Then I took my staff called Favor and
broke it, revoking the covenant I had made
with all the nations. [11]It was revoked on that
day, and so the oppressed of the flock who
were watching me knew it was the word of
the LORD.

[12]I told them, "If you think it best, give me
my pay; but if not, keep it." So they paid me
thirty pieces of silver.

[13]And the LORD said to me, "Throw it to the
potter"—the handsome price at which they
valued me! So I took the thirty pieces of silver and threw them to the potter at the house
of the LORD.

[14]Then I broke my second staff called
Union, breaking the family bond between
Judah and Israel.

[15]Then the LORD said to me, "Take again the
equipment of a foolish shepherd. [16]For I am
going to raise up a shepherd over the land who
will not care for the lost, or seek the young,
or heal the injured, or feed the healthy, but
will eat the meat of the choice sheep, tearing
off their hooves.

[17]"Woe to the worthless shepherd,
who deserts the flock!
May the sword strike his arm and his
right eye!
May his arm be completely withered,
his right eye totally blinded!"

Jerusalem's Enemies to Be Destroyed

12 A prophecy: The word of the LORD concerning Israel.

The LORD, who stretches out the heavens,
who lays the foundation of the earth, and
who forms the human spirit within a person,
declares: [2]"I am going to make Jerusalem a
cup that sends all the surrounding peoples
reeling. Judah will be besieged as well as Jerusalem. [3]On that day, when all the nations
of the earth are gathered against her, I will
make Jerusalem an immovable rock for all
the nations. All who try to move it will injure
themselves. [4]On that day I will strike every
horse with panic and its rider with madness,"
declares the LORD. "I will keep a watchful eye
over Judah, but I will blind all the horses of
the nations. [5]Then the clans of Judah will say
in their hearts, 'The people of Jerusalem are
strong, because the LORD Almighty is their
God.'

[6]"On that day I will make the clans of Judah
like a firepot in a woodpile, like a flaming
torch among sheaves. They will consume all
the surrounding peoples right and left, but
Jerusalem will remain intact in her place.

[7]"The LORD will save the dwellings of Judah
first, so that the honor of the house of David
and of Jerusalem's inhabitants may not be
greater than that of Judah. [8]On that day the
LORD will shield those who live in Jerusalem,
so that the feeblest among them will be like
David, and the house of David will be like
God, like the angel of the LORD going before
them. [9]On that day I will set out to destroy all
the nations that attack Jerusalem.

Mourning for the One They Pierced

[10]"And I will pour out on the house of David and the inhabitants of Jerusalem a spirit[a] of grace and supplication. They will look
on[b] me, the one they have pierced, and they
will mourn for him as one mourns for an
only child, and grieve bitterly for him as one
grieves for a firstborn son. [11]On that day the
weeping in Jerusalem will be as great as the
weeping of Hadad Rimmon in the plain of Megiddo. [12]The land will mourn, each clan by
itself, with their wives by themselves: the clan
of the house of David and their wives, the clan
of the house of Nathan and their wives, [13]the
clan of the house of Levi and their wives, the
clan of Shimei and their wives, [14]and all the
rest of the clans and their wives.

Cleansing From Sin

13 "On that day a fountain will be opened
to the house of David and the inhabitants of Jerusalem, to cleanse them from sin
and impurity.

[2]"On that day, I will banish the names of the
idols from the land, and they will be remembered no more," declares the LORD Almighty.
"I will remove both the prophets and the spirit
of impurity from the land. [3]And if anyone still
prophesies, their father and mother, to whom

[a] 10 Or *the Spirit* [b] 10 Or *to*

they were born, will say to them, 'You must
die, because you have told lies in the LORD's
name.' Then their own parents will stab the
one who prophesies.
4"On that day every prophet will be
ashamed of their prophetic vision. They will
not put on a prophet's garment of hair in order
to deceive. 5Each will say, 'I am not a prophet.
I am a farmer; the land has been my livelihood
since my youth.[a]' 6If someone asks, 'What are
these wounds on your body[b]?' they will answer, 'The wounds I was given at the house
of my friends.'

The Shepherd Struck, the Sheep Scattered

7"Awake, sword, against my shepherd,
  against the man who is close to me!"
  declares the LORD Almighty.
"Strike the shepherd,
  and the sheep will be scattered,
  and I will turn my hand against the
    little ones.
8In the whole land," declares the LORD,
  "two-thirds will be struck down and
    perish;
  yet one-third will be left in it.
9This third I will put into the fire;
  I will refine them like silver
  and test them like gold.
They will call on my name
  and I will answer them;
I will say, 'They are my people,'
  and they will say, 'The LORD is our
    God.'"

The LORD Comes and Reigns

14 A day of the LORD is coming, Jerusalem, when your possessions will be plundered and divided up within your very walls.
2I will gather all the nations to Jerusalem
to fight against it; the city will be captured,
the houses ransacked, and the women raped.
Half of the city will go into exile, but the rest
of the people will not be taken from the city.
3Then the LORD will go out and fight against
those nations, as he fights on a day of battle. 4On that day his feet will stand on the
Mount of Olives, east of Jerusalem, and the
Mount of Olives will be split in two from east
to west, forming a great valley, with half of
the mountain moving north and half moving
south. 5You will flee by my mountain valley,
for it will extend to Azel. You will flee as you
fled from the earthquake[c] in the days of Uzziah king of Judah. Then the LORD my God will
come, and all the holy ones with him.
6On that day there will be neither sunlight
nor cold, frosty darkness. 7It will be a unique
day—a day known only to the LORD—with
no distinction between day and night. When
evening comes, there will be light.
8On that day living water will flow out from
Jerusalem, half of it east to the Dead Sea and
half of it west to the Mediterranean Sea, in
summer and in winter.
9The LORD will be king over the whole
earth. On that day there will be one LORD,
and his name the only name.
10The whole land, from Geba to Rimmon,
south of Jerusalem, will become like the Arabah. But Jerusalem will be raised up high
from the Benjamin Gate to the site of the First
Gate, to the Corner Gate, and from the Tower of Hananel to the royal winepresses, and
will remain in its place. 11It will be inhabited;
never again will it be destroyed. Jerusalem
will be secure.
12This is the plague with which the LORD
will strike all the nations that fought against
Jerusalem: Their flesh will rot while they are
still standing on their feet, their eyes will rot
in their sockets, and their tongues will rot
in their mouths. 13On that day people will be
stricken by the LORD with great panic. They
will seize each other by the hand and attack
one another. 14Judah too will fight at Jerusalem. The wealth of all the surrounding nations
will be collected—great quantities of gold and
silver and clothing. 15A similar plague will
strike the horses and mules, the camels and
donkeys, and all the animals in those camps.
16Then the survivors from all the nations
that have attacked Jerusalem will go up year
after year to worship the King, the LORD Almighty, and to celebrate the Festival of Tabernacles. 17If any of the peoples of the earth do
not go up to Jerusalem to worship the King,
the LORD Almighty, they will have no rain.
18If the Egyptian people do not go up and take
part, they will have no rain. The LORD[d] will
bring on them the plague he inflicts on the nations that do not go up to celebrate the Festival
of Tabernacles. 19This will be the punishment
of Egypt and the punishment of all the nations
that do not go up to celebrate the Festival of
Tabernacles.
20On that day HOLY TO THE LORD will be inscribed on the bells of the horses, and the
cooking pots in the LORD's house will be like
the sacred bowls in front of the altar. 21Every
pot in Jerusalem and Judah will be holy to the
LORD Almighty, and all who come to sacrifice
will take some of the pots and cook in them.
And on that day there will no longer be a Canaanite[e] in the house of the LORD Almighty.

[a] 5 Or *farmer; a man sold me in my youth* [b] 6 Or *wounds between your hands* [c] 5 Or [5]*My mountain valley will be blocked and will extend to Azel. It will be blocked as it was blocked because of the earthquake* [d] 18 Or *part, then the* LORD [e] 21 Or *merchant*

Malachi

1 A prophecy: The word of the LORD to Israel through Malachi.[a]

Israel Doubts God's Love

2“I have loved you,” says the LORD.

“But you ask, ‘How have you loved us?’

“Was not Esau Jacob's brother?” declares the LORD. “Yet I have loved Jacob, 3but Esau I have hated, and I have turned his hill country into a wasteland and left his inheritance to the desert jackals.”

4Edom may say, “Though we have been crushed, we will rebuild the ruins.”

But this is what the LORD Almighty says: “They may build, but I will demolish. They will be called the Wicked Land, a people always under the wrath of the LORD. 5You will see it with your own eyes and say, ‘Great is the LORD—even beyond the borders of Israel!’

Breaking Covenant Through Blemished Sacrifices

6“A son honors his father, and a slave his master. If I am a father, where is the honor due me? If I am a master, where is the respect due me?” says the LORD Almighty.

“It is you priests who show contempt for my name.

“But you ask, ‘How have we shown contempt for your name?’

7“By offering defiled food on my altar.

“But you ask, ‘How have we defiled you?’

“By saying that the LORD's table is contemptible. 8When you offer blind animals for sacrifice, is that not wrong? When you sacrifice lame or diseased animals, is that not wrong? Try offering them to your governor! Would he be pleased with you? Would he accept you?” says the LORD Almighty.

9“Now plead with God to be gracious to us. With such offerings from your hands, will he accept you?”—says the LORD Almighty.

10“Oh, that one of you would shut the temple doors, so that you would not light useless fires on my altar! I am not pleased with you,” says the LORD Almighty, “and I will accept no offering from your hands. 11My name will be great among the nations, from where the sun rises to where it sets. In every place incense and pure offerings will be brought to me, because my name will be great among the nations,” says the LORD Almighty.

12“But you profane it by saying, ‘The Lord's table is defiled,’ and, ‘Its food is contemptible.’ 13And you say, ‘What a burden!’ and you sniff at it contemptuously,” says the LORD Almighty.

“When you bring injured, lame or diseased animals and offer them as sacrifices, should I accept them from your hands?” says the LORD. 14“Cursed is the cheat who has an acceptable male in his flock and vows to give it, but then sacrifices a blemished animal to the Lord. For I am a great king,” says the LORD Almighty, “and my name is to be feared among the nations.

Additional Warning to the Priests

2 “And now, you priests, this warning is for you. 2If you do not listen, and if you do not resolve to honor my name,” says the LORD Almighty, “I will send a curse on you, and I will curse your blessings. Yes, I have already cursed them, because you have not resolved to honor me.

3“Because of you I will rebuke your descendants[b]; I will smear on your faces the dung from your festival sacrifices, and you will be carried off with it. 4And you will know that I have sent you this warning so that my covenant with Levi may continue,” says the LORD Almighty. 5“My covenant was with him, a covenant of life and peace, and I gave them to him; this called for reverence and he revered me and stood in awe of my name. 6True instruction was in his mouth and nothing false was found on his lips. He walked with me in peace and uprightness, and turned many from sin.

7“For the lips of a priest ought to preserve knowledge, because he is the messenger of the LORD Almighty and people seek instruction from his mouth. 8But you have turned from the way and by your teaching have caused many to stumble; you have violated the covenant with Levi,” says the LORD Almighty. 9“So I have caused you to be despised and humiliated before all the people, because you have not followed my ways but have shown partiality in matters of the law.”

Breaking Covenant Through Divorce

10Do we not all have one Father[c]? Did not one God create us? Why do we profane the covenant of our ancestors by being unfaithful to one another?

11Judah has been unfaithful. A detestable thing has been committed in Israel and in Jerusalem: Judah has desecrated the sanctuary the LORD loves by marrying women who worship a foreign god. 12As for the man who does this, whoever he may be, may the LORD remove him from the tents of Jacob[d]—even though he brings an offering to the LORD Almighty.

13Another thing you do: You flood the LORD's altar with tears. You weep and wail because he no longer looks with favor on your

[a] 1 *Malachi* means *my messenger.* [b] 3 Or *will blight your grain* [c] 10 Or *father* [d] 12 Or *12May the LORD remove from the tents of Jacob anyone who gives testimony in behalf of the man who does this*

offerings or accepts them with pleasure from your hands. 14You ask, "Why?" It is because the LORD is the witness between you and the wife of your youth. You have been unfaithful to her, though she is your partner, the wife of your marriage covenant.

15Has not the one God made you? You belong to him in body and spirit. And what does the one God seek? Godly offspring.[a] So be on your guard, and do not be unfaithful to the wife of your youth.

16"The man who hates and divorces his wife," says the LORD, the God of Israel, "does violence to the one he should protect,"[b] says the LORD Almighty.

So be on your guard, and do not be unfaithful.

Breaking Covenant Through Injustice

17You have wearied the LORD with your words.

"How have we wearied him?" you ask.

By saying, "All who do evil are good in the eyes of the LORD, and he is pleased with them" or "Where is the God of justice?"

3 "I will send my messenger, who will prepare the way before me. Then suddenly the Lord you are seeking will come to his temple; the messenger of the covenant, whom you desire, will come," says the LORD Almighty.

2But who can endure the day of his coming? Who can stand when he appears? For he will be like a refiner's fire or a launderer's soap. 3He will sit as a refiner and purifier of silver; he will purify the Levites and refine them like gold and silver. Then the LORD will have men who will bring offerings in righteousness, 4and the offerings of Judah and Jerusalem will be acceptable to the LORD, as in days gone by, as in former years.

5"So I will come to put you on trial. I will be quick to testify against sorcerers, adulterers and perjurers, against those who defraud laborers of their wages, who oppress the widows and the fatherless, and deprive the foreigners among you of justice, but do not fear me," says the LORD Almighty.

Breaking Covenant by Withholding Tithes

6"I the LORD do not change. So you, the descendants of Jacob, are not destroyed. 7Ever since the time of your ancestors you have turned away from my decrees and have not kept them. Return to me, and I will return to you," says the LORD Almighty.

"But you ask, 'How are we to return?'

8"Will a mere mortal rob God? Yet you rob me.

"But you ask, 'How are we robbing you?'

"In tithes and offerings. 9You are under a curse—your whole nation—because you are robbing me. 10Bring the whole tithe into the storehouse, that there may be food in my house. Test me in this," says the LORD Almighty, "and see if I will not throw open the floodgates of heaven and pour out so much blessing that there will not be room enough to store it. 11I will prevent pests from devouring your crops, and the vines in your fields will not drop their fruit before it is ripe," says the LORD Almighty. 12"Then all the nations will call you blessed, for yours will be a delightful land," says the LORD Almighty.

Israel Speaks Arrogantly Against God

13"You have spoken arrogantly against me," says the LORD.

"Yet you ask, 'What have we said against you?'

14"You have said, 'It is futile to serve God. What do we gain by carrying out his requirements and going about like mourners before the LORD Almighty? 15But now we call the arrogant blessed. Certainly evildoers prosper, and even when they put God to the test, they get away with it.' "

The Faithful Remnant

16Then those who feared the LORD talked with each other, and the LORD listened and heard. A scroll of remembrance was written in his presence concerning those who feared the LORD and honored his name.

17"On the day when I act," says the LORD Almighty, "they will be my treasured possession. I will spare them, just as a father has compassion and spares his son who serves him. 18And you will again see the distinction between the righteous and the wicked, between those who serve God and those who do not.

Judgment and Covenant Renewal

4[c] "Surely the day is coming; it will burn like a furnace. All the arrogant and every evildoer will be stubble, and the day that is coming will set them on fire," says the LORD Almighty. "Not a root or a branch will be left to them. 2But for you who revere my name, the sun of righteousness will rise with healing in its rays. And you will go out and frolic like well-fed calves. 3Then you will trample on the wicked; they will be ashes under the soles of your feet on the day when I act," says the LORD Almighty.

4"Remember the law of my servant Moses, the decrees and laws I gave him at Horeb for all Israel.

5"See, I will send the prophet Elijah to you before that great and dreadful day of the LORD comes. 6He will turn the hearts of the parents to their children, and the hearts of the children to their parents; or else I will come and strike the land with total destruction."

[a] *15* The meaning of the Hebrew for the first part of this verse is uncertain. [b] *16* Or *"I hate divorce," says the LORD, the God of Israel, "because the man who divorces his wife covers his garment with violence,"* [c] In Hebrew texts 4:1-6 is numbered 3:19-24.

The
New Testament

Matthew

The Genealogy of Jesus the Messiah

1 This is the genealogy[a] of Jesus the Messiah[b] the son of David, the son of Abraham:

2 Abraham was the father of Isaac,
Isaac the father of Jacob,
Jacob the father of Judah and his brothers,
3 Judah the father of Perez and Zerah, whose mother was Tamar,
Perez the father of Hezron,
Hezron the father of Ram,
4 Ram the father of Amminadab,
Amminadab the father of Nahshon,
Nahshon the father of Salmon,
5 Salmon the father of Boaz, whose mother was Rahab,
Boaz the father of Obed, whose mother was Ruth,
Obed the father of Jesse,
6 and Jesse the father of King David.

David was the father of Solomon, whose mother had been Uriah's wife,
7 Solomon the father of Rehoboam,
Rehoboam the father of Abijah,
Abijah the father of Asa,
8 Asa the father of Jehoshaphat,
Jehoshaphat the father of Jehoram,
Jehoram the father of Uzziah,
9 Uzziah the father of Jotham,
Jotham the father of Ahaz,
Ahaz the father of Hezekiah,
10 Hezekiah the father of Manasseh,
Manasseh the father of Amon,
Amon the father of Josiah,
11 and Josiah the father of Jeconiah[c] and his brothers at the time of the exile to Babylon.

12 After the exile to Babylon:
Jeconiah was the father of Shealtiel,
Shealtiel the father of Zerubbabel,
13 Zerubbabel the father of Abihud,
Abihud the father of Eliakim,
Eliakim the father of Azor,
14 Azor the father of Zadok,
Zadok the father of Akim,
Akim the father of Elihud,
15 Elihud the father of Eleazar,
Eleazar the father of Matthan,
Matthan the father of Jacob,
16 and Jacob the father of Joseph, the husband of Mary, and Mary was the mother of Jesus who is called the Messiah.

17 Thus there were fourteen generations in all from Abraham to David, fourteen from David to the exile to Babylon, and fourteen from the exile to the Messiah.

Joseph Accepts Jesus as His Son

18 This is how the birth of Jesus the Messiah came about[d]: His mother Mary was pledged to be married to Joseph, but before they came together, she was found to be pregnant through the Holy Spirit. 19 Because Joseph her husband was faithful to the law, and yet[e] did not want to expose her to public disgrace, he had in mind to divorce her quietly.

20 But after he had considered this, an angel of the Lord appeared to him in a dream and said, "Joseph son of David, do not be afraid to take Mary home as your wife, because what is conceived in her is from the Holy Spirit. 21 She will give birth to a son, and you are to give him the name Jesus,[f] because he will save his people from their sins."

22 All this took place to fulfill what the Lord had said through the prophet: 23 "The virgin will conceive and give birth to a son, and they will call him Immanuel"[g] (which means "God with us").

24 When Joseph woke up, he did what the angel of the Lord had commanded him and took Mary home as his wife. 25 But he did not consummate their marriage until she gave birth to a son. And he gave him the name Jesus.

The Magi Visit the Messiah

2 After Jesus was born in Bethlehem in Judea, during the time of King Herod, Magi[h] from the east came to Jerusalem 2 and asked, "Where is the one who has been born king of the Jews? We saw his star when it rose and have come to worship him."

3 When King Herod heard this he was disturbed, and all Jerusalem with him. 4 When he had called together all the people's chief priests and teachers of the law, he asked them where the Messiah was to be born. 5 "In Bethlehem in Judea," they replied, "for this is what the prophet has written:

6 " 'But you, Bethlehem, in the land of Judah,
are by no means least among the rulers of Judah;
for out of you will come a ruler
who will shepherd my people Israel.'[i]"

7 Then Herod called the Magi secretly and found out from them the exact time the star had appeared. 8 He sent them to Bethlehem and said, "Go and search carefully for the child. As soon as you find him, report to me, so that I too may go and worship him."

[a] 1 Or *is an account of the origin* [b] 1 Or *Jesus Christ. Messiah* (Hebrew) and *Christ* (Greek) both mean *Anointed One*; also in verse 18. [c] 11 That is, Jehoiachin; also in verse 12 [d] 18 Or *The origin of Jesus the Messiah was like this* [e] 19 Or *was a righteous man and* [f] 21 *Jesus* is the Greek form of *Joshua*, which means *the LORD saves*. [g] 23 Isaiah 7:14 [h] 1 Traditionally *wise men* [i] 6 Micah 5:2,4

9After they had heard the king, they went
on their way, and the star they had seen when
it rose went ahead of them until it stopped
over the place where the child was. 10When
they saw the star, they were overjoyed. 11On
coming to the house, they saw the child with
his mother Mary, and they bowed down and
worshiped him. Then they opened their treasures and presented him with gifts of gold,
frankincense and myrrh. 12And having been
warned in a dream not to go back to Herod,
they returned to their country by another
route.

The Escape to Egypt

13When they had gone, an angel of the Lord
appeared to Joseph in a dream. "Get up," he
said, "take the child and his mother and escape to Egypt. Stay there until I tell you, for
Herod is going to search for the child to kill
him."

14So he got up, took the child and his mother
during the night and left for Egypt, 15where
he stayed until the death of Herod. And so
was fulfilled what the Lord had said through
the prophet: "Out of Egypt I called my son."[a]

16When Herod realized that he had been
outwitted by the Magi, he was furious, and he
gave orders to kill all the boys in Bethlehem
and its vicinity who were two years old and
under, in accordance with the time he had
learned from the Magi. 17Then what was said
through the prophet Jeremiah was fulfilled:

18"A voice is heard in Ramah,
weeping and great mourning,
Rachel weeping for her children
and refusing to be comforted,
because they are no more."[b]

The Return to Nazareth

19After Herod died, an angel of the Lord
appeared in a dream to Joseph in Egypt 20and
said, "Get up, take the child and his mother
and go to the land of Israel, for those who
were trying to take the child's life are dead."

21So he got up, took the child and his mother
and went to the land of Israel. 22But when he
heard that Archelaus was reigning in Judea
in place of his father Herod, he was afraid to
go there. Having been warned in a dream,
he withdrew to the district of Galilee, 23and
he went and lived in a town called Nazareth.
So was fulfilled what was said through the
prophets, that he would be called a Nazarene.

John the Baptist Prepares the Way

3 In those days John the Baptist came,
preaching in the wilderness of Judea 2and
saying, "Repent, for the kingdom of heaven
has come near." 3This is he who was spoken
of through the prophet Isaiah:

"A voice of one calling in the wilderness,
'Prepare the way for the Lord,
make straight paths for him.'"[c]

4John's clothes were made of camel's hair,
and he had a leather belt around his waist. His
food was locusts and wild honey. 5People went
out to him from Jerusalem and all Judea and
the whole region of the Jordan. 6Confessing
their sins, they were baptized by him in the
Jordan River.

7But when he saw many of the Pharisees
and Sadducees coming to where he was baptizing, he said to them: "You brood of vipers!
Who warned you to flee from the coming
wrath? 8Produce fruit in keeping with repentance. 9And do not think you can say to yourselves, 'We have Abraham as our father.' I tell
you that out of these stones God can raise up
children for Abraham. 10The ax is already at
the root of the trees, and every tree that does
not produce good fruit will be cut down and
thrown into the fire.

11"I baptize you with[d] water for repentance.
But after me comes one who is more powerful
than I, whose sandals I am not worthy to carry. He will baptize you with[d] the Holy Spirit
and fire. 12His winnowing fork is in his hand,
and he will clear his threshing floor, gathering his wheat into the barn and burning up
the chaff with unquenchable fire."

The Baptism of Jesus

13Then Jesus came from Galilee to the Jordan to be baptized by John. 14But John tried
to deter him, saying, "I need to be baptized by
you, and do you come to me?"

15Jesus replied, "Let it be so now; it is proper
for us to do this to fulfill all righteousness."
Then John consented.

16As soon as Jesus was baptized, he went
up out of the water. At that moment heaven
was opened, and he saw the Spirit of God descending like a dove and alighting on him.
17And a voice from heaven said, "This is my
Son, whom I love; with him I am well pleased."

Jesus Is Tested in the Wilderness

4 Then Jesus was led by the Spirit into the
wilderness to be tempted[e] by the devil. 2Af-
ter fasting forty days and forty nights, he was
hungry. 3The tempter came to him and said,
"If you are the Son of God, tell these stones
to become bread."

4Jesus answered, "It is written: 'Man shall
not live on bread alone, but on every word that
comes from the mouth of God.'[f]"

5Then the devil took him to the holy city
and had him stand on the highest point of
the temple. 6"If you are the Son of God," he
said, "throw yourself down. For it is written:

"'He will command his angels concerning
you,
and they will lift you up in their hands,
so that you will not strike your foot
against a stone.'[g]"

7Jesus answered him, "It is also written:
'Do not put the Lord your God to the test.'[h]"

[a] *15* Hosea 11:1 [b] *18* Jer. 31:15 [c] *3* Isaiah 40:3 [d] *11* Or *in* [e] *1* The Greek for *tempted* can also mean *tested.* [f] *4* Deut. 8:3 [g] *6* Psalm 91:11,12 [h] *7* Deut. 6:16

8Again, the devil took him to a very high
mountain and showed him all the kingdoms
of the world and their splendor. 9"All this I
will give you," he said, "if you will bow down
and worship me."
10Jesus said to him, "Away from me, Satan!
For it is written: 'Worship the Lord your God,
and serve him only.'[a]"
11Then the devil left him, and angels came
and attended him.

Jesus Begins to Preach

12When Jesus heard that John had been put
in prison, he withdrew to Galilee. 13Leaving
Nazareth, he went and lived in Capernaum,
which was by the lake in the area of Zebulun and Naphtali— 14to fulfill what was said
through the prophet Isaiah:

15"Land of Zebulun and land of Naphtali,
the Way of the Sea, beyond the
Jordan,
Galilee of the Gentiles—
16the people living in darkness
have seen a great light;
on those living in the land of the shadow
of death
a light has dawned."[b]

17From that time on Jesus began to preach,
"Repent, for the kingdom of heaven has come
near."

Jesus Calls His First Disciples

18As Jesus was walking beside the Sea of
Galilee, he saw two brothers, Simon called Peter and his brother Andrew. They were casting
a net into the lake, for they were fishermen.
19"Come, follow me," Jesus said, "and I will
send you out to fish for people." 20At once they
left their nets and followed him.
21Going on from there, he saw two other
brothers, James son of Zebedee and his brother John. They were in a boat with their father
Zebedee, preparing their nets. Jesus called
them, 22and immediately they left the boat and
their father and followed him.

Jesus Heals the Sick

23Jesus went throughout Galilee, teaching
in their synagogues, proclaiming the good
news of the kingdom, and healing every disease and sickness among the people. 24News
about him spread all over Syria, and people
brought to him all who were ill with various
diseases, those suffering severe pain, the demon-possessed, those having seizures, and
the paralyzed; and he healed them. 25Large
crowds from Galilee, the Decapolis,[c] Jerusalem, Judea and the region across the Jordan
followed him.

Introduction to the Sermon on the Mount

5 Now when Jesus saw the crowds, he went
up on a mountainside and sat down. His
disciples came to him, 2and he began to teach
them.

The Beatitudes

He said:

3"Blessed are the poor in spirit,
for theirs is the kingdom of heaven.
4Blessed are those who mourn,
for they will be comforted.
5Blessed are the meek,
for they will inherit the earth.
6Blessed are those who hunger and thirst
for righteousness,
for they will be filled.
7Blessed are the merciful,
for they will be shown mercy.
8Blessed are the pure in heart,
for they will see God.
9Blessed are the peacemakers,
for they will be called children of God.
10Blessed are those who are persecuted
because of righteousness,
for theirs is the kingdom of heaven.

11"Blessed are you when people insult you,
persecute you and falsely say all kinds of evil
against you because of me. 12Rejoice and be
glad, because great is your reward in heav-
en, for in the same way they persecuted the
prophets who were before you.

Salt and Light

13"You are the salt of the earth. But if the
salt loses its saltiness, how can it be made
salty again? It is no longer good for anything,
except to be thrown out and trampled underfoot.
14"You are the light of the world. A town
built on a hill cannot be hidden. 15Neither do
people light a lamp and put it under a bowl.
Instead they put it on its stand, and it gives
light to everyone in the house. 16In the same
way, let your light shine before others, that
they may see your good deeds and glorify
your Father in heaven.

The Fulfillment of the Law

17"Do not think that I have come to abolish
the Law or the Prophets; I have not come to
abolish them but to fulfill them. 18For truly I
tell you, until heaven and earth disappear,
not the smallest letter, not the least stroke
of a pen, will by any means disappear from
the Law until everything is accomplished.
19Therefore anyone who sets aside one of the
least of these commands and teaches others
accordingly will be called least in the kingdom of heaven, but whoever practices and
teaches these commands will be called great
in the kingdom of heaven. 20For I tell you that
unless your righteousness surpasses that of
the Pharisees and the teachers of the law,
you will certainly not enter the kingdom of
heaven.

Murder

21"You have heard that it was said to the
people long ago, 'You shall not murder,[d]
and anyone who murders will be subject to

[a] 10 Deut. 6:13 [b] 16 Isaiah 9:1,2 [c] 25 That is, the Ten Cities [d] 21 Exodus 20:13

judgment.’ 22But I tell you that anyone who is
angry with a brother or sister[a,b] will be subject to judgment. Again, anyone who says to
a brother or sister, ‘Raca,’[c] is answerable to
the court. And anyone who says, ‘You fool!’
will be in danger of the fire of hell.
23“Therefore, if you are offering your gift at
the altar and there remember that your brother or sister has something against you, 24leave
your gift there in front of the altar. First go
and be reconciled to them; then come and offer your gift.
25“Settle matters quickly with your adversary who is taking you to court. Do it while
you are still together on the way, or your adversary may hand you over to the judge, and
the judge may hand you over to the officer,
and you may be thrown into prison. 26Truly
I tell you, you will not get out until you have
paid the last penny.

Adultery

27“You have heard that it was said, ‘You
shall not commit adultery.’[d] 28But I tell you
that anyone who looks at a woman lustfully
has already committed adultery with her in
his heart. 29If your right eye causes you to
stumble, gouge it out and throw it away. It is
better for you to lose one part of your body
than for your whole body to be thrown into
hell. 30And if your right hand causes you to
stumble, cut it off and throw it away. It is better for you to lose one part of your body than
for your whole body to go into hell.

Divorce

31“It has been said, ‘Anyone who divorces
his wife must give her a certificate of divorce.’[e]
32But I tell you that anyone who divorces his
wife, except for sexual immorality, makes
her the victim of adultery, and anyone who
marries a divorced woman commits adultery.

Oaths

33“Again, you have heard that it was said to
the people long ago, ‘Do not break your oath,
but fulfill to the Lord the vows you have made.’
34But I tell you, do not swear an oath at all:
either by heaven, for it is God’s throne; 35or by
the earth, for it is his footstool; or by Jerusalem, for it is the city of the Great King. 36And
do not swear by your head, for you cannot
make even one hair white or black. 37All you
need to say is simply ‘Yes’ or ‘No’; anything
beyond this comes from the evil one.[f]

Eye for Eye

38“You have heard that it was said, ‘Eye for
eye, and tooth for tooth.’[g] 39But I tell you, do
not resist an evil person. If anyone slaps you
on the right cheek, turn to them the other
cheek also. 40And if anyone wants to sue you
and take your shirt, hand over your coat as
well. 41If anyone forces you to go one mile, go
with them two miles. 42Give to the one who
asks you, and do not turn away from the one
who wants to borrow from you.

Love for Enemies

43“You have heard that it was said, ‘Love
your neighbor[h] and hate your enemy.’ 44But I
tell you, love your enemies and pray for those
who persecute you, 45that you may be children
of your Father in heaven. He causes his sun to
rise on the evil and the good, and sends rain
on the righteous and the unrighteous. 46If you
love those who love you, what reward will
you get? Are not even the tax collectors doing
that? 47And if you greet only your own people,
what are you doing more than others? Do not
even pagans do that? 48Be perfect, therefore,
as your heavenly Father is perfect.

Giving to the Needy

6 “Be careful not to practice your righteousness in front of others to be seen by them.
If you do, you will have no reward from your
Father in heaven.
2“So when you give to the needy, do not announce it with trumpets, as the hypocrites do
in the synagogues and on the streets, to be honored by others. Truly I tell you, they have received their reward in full. 3But when you give
to the needy, do not let your left hand know
what your right hand is doing, 4so that your
giving may be in secret. Then your Father, who
sees what is done in secret, will reward you.

Prayer

5“And when you pray, do not be like the
hypocrites, for they love to pray standing in
the synagogues and on the street corners to
be seen by others. Truly I tell you, they have
received their reward in full. 6But when you
pray, go into your room, close the door and
pray to your Father, who is unseen. Then your
Father, who sees what is done in secret, will
reward you. 7And when you pray, do not keep
on babbling like pagans, for they think they
will be heard because of their many words.
8Do not be like them, for your Father knows
what you need before you ask him.
9“This, then, is how you should pray:

“ ‘Our Father in heaven,
hallowed be your name,
10your kingdom come,
your will be done,
on earth as it is in heaven.
11Give us today our daily bread.
12And forgive us our debts,
as we also have forgiven our debtors.
13And lead us not into temptation,[i]
but deliver us from the evil one.’[j]

[a] 22 The Greek word for *brother or sister* (*adelphos*) refers here to a fellow disciple, whether man or woman; also in verse 23. [b] 22 Some manuscripts *brother or sister without cause*
[c] 22 An Aramaic term of contempt [d] 27 Exodus 20:14 [e] 31 Deut. 24:1 [f] 37 Or *from evil*
[g] 38 Exodus 21:24; Lev. 24:20; Deut. 19:21 [h] 43 Lev. 19:18 [i] 13 The Greek for *temptation* can also mean *testing.* [j] 13 Or *from evil*; some late manuscripts *one, / for yours is the kingdom and the power and the glory forever. Amen.*

14For if you forgive other people when they
sin against you, your heavenly Father will
also forgive you. 15But if you do not forgive
others their sins, your Father will not forgive
your sins.

Fasting

16“When you fast, do not look somber as the
hypocrites do, for they disfigure their faces to
show others they are fasting. Truly I tell you,
they have received their reward in full. 17But
when you fast, put oil on your head and wash
your face, 18so that it will not be obvious to
others that you are fasting, but only to your
Father, who is unseen; and your Father, who
sees what is done in secret, will reward you.

Treasures in Heaven

19“Do not store up for yourselves treasures
on earth, where moths and vermin destroy,
and where thieves break in and steal. 20But
store up for yourselves treasures in heaven,
where moths and vermin do not destroy, and
where thieves do not break in and steal. 21For
where your treasure is, there your heart will
be also.

22“The eye is the lamp of the body. If your
eyes are healthy,[a] your whole body will be full
of light. 23But if your eyes are unhealthy,[b] your
whole body will be full of darkness. If then
the light within you is darkness, how great
is that darkness!

24“No one can serve two masters. Either you
will hate the one and love the other, or you will
be devoted to the one and despise the other.
You cannot serve both God and money.

Do Not Worry

25“Therefore I tell you, do not worry about
your life, what you will eat or drink; or about
your body, what you will wear. Is not life more
than food, and the body more than clothes?
26Look at the birds of the air; they do not sow
or reap or store away in barns, and yet your
heavenly Father feeds them. Are you not much
more valuable than they? 27Can any one of you
by worrying add a single hour to your life[c]?

28“And why do you worry about clothes?
See how the flowers of the field grow. They
do not labor or spin. 29Yet I tell you that not
even Solomon in all his splendor was dressed
like one of these. 30If that is how God clothes
the grass of the field, which is here today and
tomorrow is thrown into the fire, will he not
much more clothe you—you of little faith?
31So do not worry, saying, ‘What shall we eat?’
or ‘What shall we drink?’ or ‘What shall we
wear?’ 32For the pagans run after all these
things, and your heavenly Father knows that
you need them. 33But seek first his kingdom
and his righteousness, and all these things
will be given to you as well. 34Therefore do
not worry about tomorrow, for tomorrow will
worry about itself. Each day has enough trouble of its own.

Judging Others

7 “Do not judge, or you too will be judged.
2For in the same way you judge others, you
will be judged, and with the measure you use,
it will be measured to you.

3“Why do you look at the speck of sawdust
in your brother’s eye and pay no attention to
the plank in your own eye? 4How can you say
to your brother, ‘Let me take the speck out of
your eye,’ when all the time there is a plank
in your own eye? 5You hypocrite, first take
the plank out of your own eye, and then you
will see clearly to remove the speck from your
brother’s eye.

6“Do not give dogs what is sacred; do not
throw your pearls to pigs. If you do, they may
trample them under their feet, and turn and
tear you to pieces.

Ask, Seek, Knock

7“Ask and it will be given to you; seek and
you will find; knock and the door will be
opened to you. 8For everyone who asks receives; the one who seeks finds; and to the one
who knocks, the door will be opened.

9“Which of you, if your son asks for bread,
will give him a stone? 10Or if he asks for a fish,
will give him a snake? 11If you, then, though
you are evil, know how to give good gifts to
your children, how much more will your Father in heaven give good gifts to those who
ask him! 12So in everything, do to others what
you would have them do to you, for this sums
up the Law and the Prophets.

The Narrow and Wide Gates

13“Enter through the narrow gate. For wide
is the gate and broad is the road that leads to
destruction, and many enter through it. 14But
small is the gate and narrow the road that
leads to life, and only a few find it.

True and False Prophets

15“Watch out for false prophets. They come
to you in sheep’s clothing, but inwardly they
are ferocious wolves. 16By their fruit you will
recognize them. Do people pick grapes from
thornbushes, or figs from thistles? 17Likewise,
every good tree bears good fruit, but a bad
tree bears bad fruit. 18A good tree cannot bear
bad fruit, and a bad tree cannot bear good
fruit. 19Every tree that does not bear good fruit
is cut down and thrown into the fire. 20Thus,
by their fruit you will recognize them.

True and False Disciples

21“Not everyone who says to me, ‘Lord,
Lord,’ will enter the kingdom of heaven, but
only the one who does the will of my Father
who is in heaven. 22Many will say to me on
that day, ‘Lord, Lord, did we not prophesy in
your name and in your name drive out demons
and in your name perform many miracles?’
23Then I will tell them plainly, ‘I never knew
you. Away from me, you evildoers!’

[a] 22 The Greek for *healthy* here implies *generous.*
[b] 23 The Greek for *unhealthy* here implies *stingy.*
[c] 27 Or *single cubit to your height*

The Wise and Foolish Builders

24“Therefore everyone who hears these
words of mine and puts them into practice is
like a wise man who built his house on the rock.
25The rain came down, the streams rose, and
the winds blew and beat against that house;
yet it did not fall, because it had its foundation
on the rock. 26But everyone who hears these
words of mine and does not put them into practice is like a foolish man who built his house
on sand. 27The rain came down, the streams
rose, and the winds blew and beat against that
house, and it fell with a great crash.”

28When Jesus had finished saying these
things, the crowds were amazed at his teaching, 29because he taught as one who had authority, and not as their teachers of the law.

Jesus Heals a Man With Leprosy

8 When Jesus came down from the mountainside, large crowds followed him. 2A
man with leprosy[a] came and knelt before him
and said, “Lord, if you are willing, you can
make me clean.”

3Jesus reached out his hand and touched
the man. “I am willing,” he said. “Be clean!”
Immediately he was cleansed of his leprosy.
4Then Jesus said to him, “See that you don’t
tell anyone. But go, show yourself to the priest
and offer the gift Moses commanded, as a
testimony to them.”

The Faith of the Centurion

5When Jesus had entered Capernaum,
a centurion came to him, asking for help.
6“Lord,” he said, “my servant lies at home
paralyzed, suffering terribly.”

7Jesus said to him, “Shall I come and heal
him?”

8The centurion replied, “Lord, I do not deserve to have you come under my roof. But just
say the word, and my servant will be healed.
9For I myself am a man under authority, with
soldiers under me. I tell this one, ‘Go,’ and he
goes; and that one, ‘Come,’ and he comes. I
say to my servant, ‘Do this,’ and he does it.”

10When Jesus heard this, he was amazed
and said to those following him, “Truly I tell
you, I have not found anyone in Israel with
such great faith. 11I say to you that many will
come from the east and the west, and will take
their places at the feast with Abraham, Isaac
and Jacob in the kingdom of heaven. 12But
the subjects of the kingdom will be thrown
outside, into the darkness, where there will
be weeping and gnashing of teeth.”

13Then Jesus said to the centurion, “Go! Let
it be done just as you believed it would.” And
his servant was healed at that moment.

Jesus Heals Many

14When Jesus came into Peter’s house, he
saw Peter’s mother-in-law lying in bed with a
fever. 15He touched her hand and the fever left
her, and she got up and began to wait on him.

16When evening came, many who were demon-possessed were brought to him, and he
drove out the spirits with a word and healed
all the sick. 17This was to fulfill what was spoken through the prophet Isaiah:

> “He took up our infirmities
> and bore our diseases.”[b]

The Cost of Following Jesus

18When Jesus saw the crowd around him,
he gave orders to cross to the other side of
the lake. 19Then a teacher of the law came
to him and said, “Teacher, I will follow you
wherever you go.”

20Jesus replied, “Foxes have dens and birds
have nests, but the Son of Man has no place
to lay his head.”

21Another disciple said to him, “Lord, first
let me go and bury my father.”

22But Jesus told him, “Follow me, and let the
dead bury their own dead.”

Jesus Calms the Storm

23Then he got into the boat and his disciples followed him. 24Suddenly a furious storm
came up on the lake, so that the waves swept
over the boat. But Jesus was sleeping. 25The
disciples went and woke him, saying, “Lord,
save us! We’re going to drown!”

26He replied, “You of little faith, why are you
so afraid?” Then he got up and rebuked the
winds and the waves, and it was completely
calm.

27The men were amazed and asked, “What
kind of man is this? Even the winds and the
waves obey him!”

Jesus Restores Two Demon-Possessed Men

28When he arrived at the other side in the
region of the Gadarenes,[c] two demon-possessed men coming from the tombs met him.
They were so violent that no one could pass
that way. 29“What do you want with us, Son of
God?” they shouted. “Have you come here to
torture us before the appointed time?”

30Some distance from them a large herd
of pigs was feeding. 31The demons begged
Jesus, “If you drive us out, send us into the
herd of pigs.”

32He said to them, “Go!” So they came out
and went into the pigs, and the whole herd
rushed down the steep bank into the lake and
died in the water. 33Those tending the pigs ran
off, went into the town and reported all this,
including what had happened to the demon-
possessed men. 34Then the whole town went
out to meet Jesus. And when they saw him,
they pleaded with him to leave their region.

Jesus Forgives and Heals a Paralyzed Man

9 Jesus stepped into a boat, crossed over and
came to his own town. 2Some men brought
to him a paralyzed man, lying on a mat. When
Jesus saw their faith, he said to the man, “Take
heart, son; your sins are forgiven.”

[a] 2 The Greek word traditionally translated *leprosy* was used for various diseases affecting the skin.
[b] 17 Isaiah 53:4 (see Septuagint) [c] 28 Some manuscripts *Gergesenes*; other manuscripts *Gerasenes*

3At this, some of the teachers of the law said to themselves, "This fellow is blaspheming!"

4Knowing their thoughts, Jesus said, "Why do you entertain evil thoughts in your hearts? 5Which is easier: to say, 'Your sins are forgiven,' or to say, 'Get up and walk'? 6But I want you to know that the Son of Man has authority on earth to forgive sins." So he said to the paralyzed man, "Get up, take your mat and go home." 7Then the man got up and went home. 8When the crowd saw this, they were filled with awe; and they praised God, who had given such authority to man.

The Calling of Matthew

9As Jesus went on from there, he saw a man named Matthew sitting at the tax collector's booth. "Follow me," he told him, and Matthew got up and followed him.

10While Jesus was having dinner at Matthew's house, many tax collectors and sinners came and ate with him and his disciples. 11When the Pharisees saw this, they asked his disciples, "Why does your teacher eat with tax collectors and sinners?"

12On hearing this, Jesus said, "It is not the healthy who need a doctor, but the sick. 13But go and learn what this means: 'I desire mercy, not sacrifice.'[a] For I have not come to call the righteous, but sinners."

Jesus Questioned About Fasting

14Then John's disciples came and asked him, "How is it that we and the Pharisees fast often, but your disciples do not fast?"

15Jesus answered, "How can the guests of the bridegroom mourn while he is with them? The time will come when the bridegroom will be taken from them; then they will fast.

16"No one sews a patch of unshrunk cloth on an old garment, for the patch will pull away from the garment, making the tear worse. 17Neither do people pour new wine into old wineskins. If they do, the skins will burst; the wine will run out and the wineskins will be ruined. No, they pour new wine into new wineskins, and both are preserved."

Jesus Raises a Dead Girl and Heals a Sick Woman

18While he was saying this, a synagogue leader came and knelt before him and said, "My daughter has just died. But come and put your hand on her, and she will live." 19Jesus got up and went with him, and so did his disciples.

20Just then a woman who had been subject to bleeding for twelve years came up behind him and touched the edge of his cloak. 21She said to herself, "If I only touch his cloak, I will be healed."

22Jesus turned and saw her. "Take heart, daughter," he said, "your faith has healed you." And the woman was healed at that moment.

23When Jesus entered the synagogue leader's house and saw the noisy crowd and people playing pipes, 24he said, "Go away. The girl is not dead but asleep." But they laughed at him. 25After the crowd had been put outside, he went in and took the girl by the hand, and she got up. 26News of this spread through all that region.

Jesus Heals the Blind and the Mute

27As Jesus went on from there, two blind men followed him, calling out, "Have mercy on us, Son of David!"

28When he had gone indoors, the blind men came to him, and he asked them, "Do you believe that I am able to do this?"

"Yes, Lord," they replied.

29Then he touched their eyes and said, "According to your faith let it be done to you"; 30and their sight was restored. Jesus warned them sternly, "See that no one knows about this." 31But they went out and spread the news about him all over that region.

32While they were going out, a man who was demon-possessed and could not talk was brought to Jesus. 33And when the demon was driven out, the man who had been mute spoke. The crowd was amazed and said, "Nothing like this has ever been seen in Israel."

34But the Pharisees said, "It is by the prince of demons that he drives out demons."

The Workers Are Few

35Jesus went through all the towns and villages, teaching in their synagogues, proclaiming the good news of the kingdom and healing every disease and sickness. 36When he saw the crowds, he had compassion on them, because they were harassed and helpless, like sheep without a shepherd. 37Then he said to his disciples, "The harvest is plentiful but the workers are few. 38Ask the Lord of the harvest, therefore, to send out workers into his harvest field."

Jesus Sends Out the Twelve

10 Jesus called his twelve disciples to him and gave them authority to drive out impure spirits and to heal every disease and sickness.

2These are the names of the twelve apostles: first, Simon (who is called Peter) and his brother Andrew; James son of Zebedee, and his brother John; 3Philip and Bartholomew; Thomas and Matthew the tax collector; James son of Alphaeus, and Thaddaeus; 4Simon the Zealot and Judas Iscariot, who betrayed him.

5These twelve Jesus sent out with the following instructions: "Do not go among the Gentiles or enter any town of the Samaritans. 6Go rather to the lost sheep of Israel. 7As you go, proclaim this message: 'The kingdom of heaven has come near.' 8Heal the sick, raise the dead, cleanse those who have leprosy,[b] drive out demons. Freely you have received; freely give.

[a] *13* Hosea 6:6 [b] *8* The Greek word traditionally translated *leprosy* was used for various diseases affecting the skin.

9“Do not get any gold or silver or copper to
take with you in your belts— 10no bag for the
journey or extra shirt or sandals or a staff, for
the worker is worth his keep. 11Whatever town
or village you enter, search there for some worthy person and stay at their house until you
leave. 12As you enter the home, give it your
greeting. 13If the home is deserving, let your
peace rest on it; if it is not, let your peace return
to you. 14If anyone will not welcome you or listen to your words, leave that home or town and
shake the dust off your feet. 15Truly I tell you, it
will be more bearable for Sodom and Gomorrah on the day of judgment than for that town.

16“I am sending you out like sheep among
wolves. Therefore be as shrewd as snakes and
as innocent as doves. 17Be on your guard; you
will be handed over to the local councils and
be flogged in the synagogues. 18On my account you will be brought before governors
and kings as witnesses to them and to the
Gentiles. 19But when they arrest you, do not
worry about what to say or how to say it. At
that time you will be given what to say, 20for
it will not be you speaking, but the Spirit of
your Father speaking through you.

21“Brother will betray brother to death, and
a father his child; children will rebel against
their parents and have them put to death.
22You will be hated by everyone because of
me, but the one who stands firm to the end will
be saved. 23When you are persecuted in one
place, flee to another. Truly I tell you, you will
not finish going through the towns of Israel
before the Son of Man comes.

24“The student is not above the teacher, nor
a servant above his master. 25It is enough for
students to be like their teachers, and servants
like their masters. If the head of the house has
been called Beelzebul, how much more the
members of his household!

26“So do not be afraid of them, for there is
nothing concealed that will not be disclosed,
or hidden that will not be made known.
27What I tell you in the dark, speak in the
daylight; what is whispered in your ear, proclaim from the roofs. 28Do not be afraid of
those who kill the body but cannot kill the
soul. Rather, be afraid of the One who can destroy both soul and body in hell. 29Are not two
sparrows sold for a penny? Yet not one of them
will fall to the ground outside your Father's
care.[a] 30And even the very hairs of your head
are all numbered. 31So don't be afraid; you are
worth more than many sparrows.

32“Whoever acknowledges me before others, I will also acknowledge before my Father
in heaven. 33But whoever disowns me before
others, I will disown before my Father in
heaven.

34“Do not suppose that I have come to bring
peace to the earth. I did not come to bring
peace, but a sword. 35For I have come to turn

“ ‘a man against his father,
a daughter against her mother,
a daughter-in-law against her mother-in-
law—
36 a man's enemies will be the members of
his own household.’[b]

37“Anyone who loves their father or mother
more than me is not worthy of me; anyone
who loves their son or daughter more than
me is not worthy of me. 38Whoever does not
take up their cross and follow me is not worthy of me. 39Whoever finds their life will lose
it, and whoever loses their life for my sake
will find it.

40“Anyone who welcomes you welcomes
me, and anyone who welcomes me welcomes
the one who sent me. 41Whoever welcomes a
prophet as a prophet will receive a prophet's reward, and whoever welcomes a righteous person as a righteous person will receive a righteous person's reward. 42And if anyone gives
even a cup of cold water to one of these little
ones who is my disciple, truly I tell you, that
person will certainly not lose their reward.”

Jesus and John the Baptist

11 After Jesus had finished instructing his
twelve disciples, he went on from there
to teach and preach in the towns of Galilee.[c]

2When John, who was in prison, heard
about the deeds of the Messiah, he sent his
disciples 3to ask him, “Are you the one who is
to come, or should we expect someone else?”

4Jesus replied, “Go back and report to John
what you hear and see: 5The blind receive
sight, the lame walk, those who have leprosy[d] are cleansed, the deaf hear, the dead are
raised, and the good news is proclaimed to the
poor. 6Blessed is anyone who does not stumble
on account of me.”

7As John's disciples were leaving, Jesus began to speak to the crowd about John: “What
did you go out into the wilderness to see? A
reed swayed by the wind? 8If not, what did you
go out to see? A man dressed in fine clothes?
No, those who wear fine clothes are in kings'
palaces. 9Then what did you go out to see?
A prophet? Yes, I tell you, and more than a
prophet. 10This is the one about whom it is
written:

“ ‘I will send my messenger ahead of you,
who will prepare your way before you.’[e]

11Truly I tell you, among those born of women
there has not risen anyone greater than John
the Baptist; yet whoever is least in the kingdom of heaven is greater than he. 12From the
days of John the Baptist until now, the kingdom of heaven has been subjected to violence,[f]
and violent people have been raiding it. 13For
all the Prophets and the Law prophesied until
John. 14And if you are willing to accept it, he
is the Elijah who was to come. 15Whoever has
ears, let them hear.

16“To what can I compare this generation?
They are like children sitting in the marketplaces and calling out to others:

[a] 29 Or *will*; or *knowledge* [b] 36 Micah 7:6 [c] 1 Greek *in their towns* [d] 5 The Greek word traditionally translated *leprosy* was used for various diseases affecting the skin. [e] 10 Mal. 3:1
[f] 12 Or *been forcefully advancing*

17"'We played the pipe for you,
and you did not dance;
we sang a dirge,
and you did not mourn.'

18For John came neither eating nor drinking,
and they say, 'He has a demon.' 19The Son of
Man came eating and drinking, and they say,
'Here is a glutton and a drunkard, a friend
of tax collectors and sinners.' But wisdom is
proved right by her deeds."

Woe on Unrepentant Towns

20Then Jesus began to denounce the towns
in which most of his miracles had been performed, because they did not repent. 21"Woe
to you, Chorazin! Woe to you, Bethsaida! For
if the miracles that were performed in you had
been performed in Tyre and Sidon, they would
have repented long ago in sackcloth and ashes. 22But I tell you, it will be more bearable for
Tyre and Sidon on the day of judgment than
for you. 23And you, Capernaum, will you be
lifted to the heavens? No, you will go down
to Hades.[a] For if the miracles that were performed in you had been performed in Sodom,
it would have remained to this day. 24But I tell
you that it will be more bearable for Sodom
on the day of judgment than for you."

The Father Revealed in the Son

25At that time Jesus said, "I praise you, Father, Lord of heaven and earth, because you
have hidden these things from the wise and
learned, and revealed them to little children.
26Yes, Father, for this is what you were pleased
to do.

27"All things have been committed to me by
my Father. No one knows the Son except the
Father, and no one knows the Father except
the Son and those to whom the Son chooses
to reveal him.

28"Come to me, all you who are weary and
burdened, and I will give you rest. 29Take my
yoke upon you and learn from me, for I am
gentle and humble in heart, and you will find
rest for your souls. 30For my yoke is easy and
my burden is light."

Jesus Is Lord of the Sabbath

12 At that time Jesus went through the
grainfields on the Sabbath. His disciples
were hungry and began to pick some heads of
grain and eat them. 2When the Pharisees saw
this, they said to him, "Look! Your disciples
are doing what is unlawful on the Sabbath."

3He answered, "Haven't you read what David did when he and his companions were
hungry? 4He entered the house of God, and
he and his companions ate the consecrated
bread—which was not lawful for them to do,
but only for the priests. 5Or haven't you read
in the Law that the priests on Sabbath duty in
the temple desecrate the Sabbath and yet are
innocent? 6I tell you that something greater
than the temple is here. 7If you had known
what these words mean, 'I desire mercy, not
sacrifice,'[b] you would not have condemned
the innocent. 8For the Son of Man is Lord of
the Sabbath."

9Going on from that place, he went into
their synagogue, 10and a man with a shriveled hand was there. Looking for a reason to
bring charges against Jesus, they asked him,
"Is it lawful to heal on the Sabbath?"

11He said to them, "If any of you has a sheep
and it falls into a pit on the Sabbath, will you
not take hold of it and lift it out? 12How much
more valuable is a person than a sheep! Therefore it is lawful to do good on the Sabbath."

13Then he said to the man, "Stretch out your
hand." So he stretched it out and it was completely restored, just as sound as the other.
14But the Pharisees went out and plotted how
they might kill Jesus.

God's Chosen Servant

15Aware of this, Jesus withdrew from that
place. A large crowd followed him, and he
healed all who were ill. 16He warned them not
to tell others about him. 17This was to fulfill
what was spoken through the prophet Isaiah:

18"Here is my servant whom I have chosen,
the one I love, in whom I delight;
I will put my Spirit on him,
and he will proclaim justice to the
nations.
19He will not quarrel or cry out;
no one will hear his voice in the streets.
20A bruised reed he will not break,
and a smoldering wick he will not snuff
out,
till he has brought justice through to
victory.
21 In his name the nations will put their
hope."[c]

Jesus and Beelzebul

22Then they brought him a demon-possessed man who was blind and mute, and
Jesus healed him, so that he could both talk
and see. 23All the people were astonished and
said, "Could this be the Son of David?"

24But when the Pharisees heard this, they
said, "It is only by Beelzebul, the prince of
demons, that this fellow drives out demons."

25Jesus knew their thoughts and said to
them, "Every kingdom divided against itself
will be ruined, and every city or household
divided against itself will not stand. 26If Satan
drives out Satan, he is divided against himself. How then can his kingdom stand? 27And
if I drive out demons by Beelzebul, by whom
do your people drive them out? So then, they
will be your judges. 28But if it is by the Spirit
of God that I drive out demons, then the kingdom of God has come upon you.

29"Or again, how can anyone enter a strong
man's house and carry off his possessions unless he first ties up the strong man? Then he
can plunder his house.

30"Whoever is not with me is against me,
and whoever does not gather with me scatters.

[a] *23* That is, the realm of the dead [b] *7* Hosea 6:6 [c] *21* Isaiah 42:1-4

31And so I tell you, every kind of sin and slander can be forgiven, but blasphemy against the Spirit will not be forgiven. 32Anyone who speaks a word against the Son of Man will be forgiven, but anyone who speaks against the Holy Spirit will not be forgiven, either in this age or in the age to come.

33"Make a tree good and its fruit will be good, or make a tree bad and its fruit will be bad, for a tree is recognized by its fruit. 34You brood of vipers, how can you who are evil say anything good? For the mouth speaks what the heart is full of. 35A good man brings good things out of the good stored up in him, and an evil man brings evil things out of the evil stored up in him. 36But I tell you that everyone will have to give account on the day of judgment for every empty word they have spoken. 37For by your words you will be acquitted, and by your words you will be condemned."

The Sign of Jonah

38Then some of the Pharisees and teachers of the law said to him, "Teacher, we want to see a sign from you."

39He answered, "A wicked and adulterous generation asks for a sign! But none will be given it except the sign of the prophet Jonah. 40For as Jonah was three days and three nights in the belly of a huge fish, so the Son of Man will be three days and three nights in the heart of the earth. 41The men of Nineveh will stand up at the judgment with this generation and condemn it; for they repented at the preaching of Jonah, and now something greater than Jonah is here. 42The Queen of the South will rise at the judgment with this generation and condemn it; for she came from the ends of the earth to listen to Solomon's wisdom, and now something greater than Solomon is here.

43"When an impure spirit comes out of a person, it goes through arid places seeking rest and does not find it. 44Then it says, 'I will return to the house I left.' When it arrives, it finds the house unoccupied, swept clean and put in order. 45Then it goes and takes with it seven other spirits more wicked than itself, and they go in and live there. And the final condition of that person is worse than the first. That is how it will be with this wicked generation."

Jesus' Mother and Brothers

46While Jesus was still talking to the crowd, his mother and brothers stood outside, wanting to speak to him. 47Someone told him, "Your mother and brothers are standing outside, wanting to speak to you."

48He replied to him, "Who is my mother, and who are my brothers?" 49Pointing to his disciples, he said, "Here are my mother and my brothers. 50For whoever does the will of my Father in heaven is my brother and sister and mother."

The Parable of the Sower

13 That same day Jesus went out of the house and sat by the lake. 2Such large crowds gathered around him that he got into a boat and sat in it, while all the people stood on the shore. 3Then he told them many things in parables, saying: "A farmer went out to sow his seed. 4As he was scattering the seed, some fell along the path, and the birds came and ate it up. 5Some fell on rocky places, where it did not have much soil. It sprang up quickly, because the soil was shallow. 6But when the sun came up, the plants were scorched, and they withered because they had no root. 7Other seed fell among thorns, which grew up and choked the plants. 8Still other seed fell on good soil, where it produced a crop—a hundred, sixty or thirty times what was sown. 9Whoever has ears, let them hear."

10The disciples came to him and asked, "Why do you speak to the people in parables?"

11He replied, "Because the knowledge of the secrets of the kingdom of heaven has been given to you, but not to them. 12Whoever has will be given more, and they will have an abundance. Whoever does not have, even what they have will be taken from them. 13This is why I speak to them in parables:

"Though seeing, they do not see;
  though hearing, they do not hear or
    understand.

14In them is fulfilled the prophecy of Isaiah:

"'You will be ever hearing but never
    understanding;
  you will be ever seeing but never
    perceiving.
15For this people's heart has become
    calloused;
  they hardly hear with their ears,
  and they have closed their eyes.
Otherwise they might see with their eyes,
  hear with their ears,
  understand with their hearts
and turn, and I would heal them.'[a]

16But blessed are your eyes because they see, and your ears because they hear. 17For truly I tell you, many prophets and righteous people longed to see what you see but did not see it, and to hear what you hear but did not hear it.

18"Listen then to what the parable of the sower means: 19When anyone hears the message about the kingdom and does not understand it, the evil one comes and snatches away what was sown in their heart. This is the seed sown along the path. 20The seed falling on rocky ground refers to someone who hears the word and at once receives it with joy. 21But since they have no root, they last only a short time. When trouble or persecution comes because of the word, they quickly fall away. 22The seed falling among the thorns refers to someone who hears the word, but the worries of this life and the deceitfulness of wealth choke the word, making it unfruitful. 23But the seed falling on good soil refers

[a] *15* Isaiah 6:9,10 (see Septuagint)

to someone who hears the word and understands it. This is the one who produces a crop,
yielding a hundred, sixty or thirty times what
was sown."

The Parable of the Weeds

24Jesus told them another parable: "The
kingdom of heaven is like a man who sowed
good seed in his field. 25But while everyone
was sleeping, his enemy came and sowed
weeds among the wheat, and went away.
26When the wheat sprouted and formed heads,
then the weeds also appeared.

27"The owner's servants came to him and
said, 'Sir, didn't you sow good seed in your
field? Where then did the weeds come from?'

28" 'An enemy did this,' he replied.

"The servants asked him, 'Do you want us
to go and pull them up?'

29" 'No,' he answered, 'because while you
are pulling the weeds, you may uproot the
wheat with them. 30Let both grow together until the harvest. At that time I will tell the harvesters: First collect the weeds and tie them in
bundles to be burned; then gather the wheat
and bring it into my barn.' "

The Parables of the Mustard Seed and the Yeast

31He told them another parable: "The kingdom of heaven is like a mustard seed, which a
man took and planted in his field. 32Though it
is the smallest of all seeds, yet when it grows,
it is the largest of garden plants and becomes
a tree, so that the birds come and perch in its
branches."

33He told them still another parable: "The
kingdom of heaven is like yeast that a woman
took and mixed into about sixty pounds[a] of
flour until it worked all through the dough."

34Jesus spoke all these things to the crowd
in parables; he did not say anything to them
without using a parable. 35So was fulfilled
what was spoken through the prophet:

"I will open my mouth in parables,
  I will utter things hidden since the
    creation of the world."[b]

The Parable of the Weeds Explained

36Then he left the crowd and went into the
house. His disciples came to him and said,
"Explain to us the parable of the weeds in
the field."

37He answered, "The one who sowed the
good seed is the Son of Man. 38The field is the
world, and the good seed stands for the people
of the kingdom. The weeds are the people of
the evil one, 39and the enemy who sows them
is the devil. The harvest is the end of the age,
and the harvesters are angels.

40"As the weeds are pulled up and burned
in the fire, so it will be at the end of the age.
41The Son of Man will send out his angels, and
they will weed out of his kingdom everything
that causes sin and all who do evil. 42They will
throw them into the blazing furnace, where
there will be weeping and gnashing of teeth.
43Then the righteous will shine like the sun
in the kingdom of their Father. Whoever has
ears, let them hear.

The Parables of the Hidden Treasure and the Pearl

44"The kingdom of heaven is like treasure
hidden in a field. When a man found it, he hid
it again, and then in his joy went and sold all
he had and bought that field.

45"Again, the kingdom of heaven is like a
merchant looking for fine pearls. 46When he
found one of great value, he went away and
sold everything he had and bought it.

The Parable of the Net

47"Once again, the kingdom of heaven is
like a net that was let down into the lake and
caught all kinds of fish. 48When it was full,
the fishermen pulled it up on the shore. Then
they sat down and collected the good fish in
baskets, but threw the bad away. 49This is how
it will be at the end of the age. The angels
will come and separate the wicked from the
righteous 50and throw them into the blazing
furnace, where there will be weeping and
gnashing of teeth.

51"Have you understood all these things?"
Jesus asked.

"Yes," they replied.

52He said to them, "Therefore every teacher of the law who has become a disciple in
the kingdom of heaven is like the owner of a
house who brings out of his storeroom new
treasures as well as old."

A Prophet Without Honor

53When Jesus had finished these parables, he moved on from there. 54Coming to
his hometown, he began teaching the people
in their synagogue, and they were amazed.
"Where did this man get this wisdom and
these miraculous powers?" they asked. 55"Isn't
this the carpenter's son? Isn't his mother's
name Mary, and aren't his brothers James,
Joseph, Simon and Judas? 56Aren't all his sisters with us? Where then did this man get all
these things?" 57And they took offense at him.

But Jesus said to them, "A prophet is not
without honor except in his own town and in
his own home."

58And he did not do many miracles there
because of their lack of faith.

John the Baptist Beheaded

14 At that time Herod the tetrarch heard the
reports about Jesus, 2and he said to his
attendants, "This is John the Baptist; he has
risen from the dead! That is why miraculous
powers are at work in him."

3Now Herod had arrested John and bound
him and put him in prison because of Herodias, his brother Philip's wife, 4for John had

[a] *33* Or about 27 kilograms [b] *35* Psalm 78:2

been saying to him: "It is not lawful for you to
have her." 5Herod wanted to kill John, but he
was afraid of the people, because they considered John a prophet.
6On Herod's birthday the daughter of Herodias danced for the guests and pleased Herod
so much 7that he promised with an oath to give
her whatever she asked. 8Prompted by her
mother, she said, "Give me here on a platter
the head of John the Baptist." 9The king was
distressed, but because of his oaths and his
dinner guests, he ordered that her request be
granted 10and had John beheaded in the prison. 11His head was brought in on a platter and
given to the girl, who carried it to her mother.
12John's disciples came and took his body and
buried it. Then they went and told Jesus.

Jesus Feeds the Five Thousand

13When Jesus heard what had happened, he
withdrew by boat privately to a solitary place.
Hearing of this, the crowds followed him on
foot from the towns. 14When Jesus landed
and saw a large crowd, he had compassion
on them and healed their sick.
15As evening approached, the disciples
came to him and said, "This is a remote place,
and it's already getting late. Send the crowds
away, so they can go to the villages and buy
themselves some food."
16Jesus replied, "They do not need to go
away. You give them something to eat."
17"We have here only five loaves of bread
and two fish," they answered.
18"Bring them here to me," he said. 19And he
directed the people to sit down on the grass.
Taking the five loaves and the two fish and
looking up to heaven, he gave thanks and
broke the loaves. Then he gave them to the
disciples, and the disciples gave them to the
people. 20They all ate and were satisfied, and
the disciples picked up twelve basketfuls of
broken pieces that were left over. 21The number of those who ate was about five thousand
men, besides women and children.

Jesus Walks on the Water

22Immediately Jesus made the disciples get
into the boat and go on ahead of him to the other side, while he dismissed the crowd. 23After
he had dismissed them, he went up on a mountainside by himself to pray. Later that night,
he was there alone, 24and the boat was already
a considerable distance from land, buffeted
by the waves because the wind was against it.
25Shortly before dawn Jesus went out to
them, walking on the lake. 26When the disciples saw him walking on the lake, they were
terrified. "It's a ghost," they said, and cried
out in fear.
27But Jesus immediately said to them: "Take
courage! It is I. Don't be afraid."
28"Lord, if it's you," Peter replied, "tell me
to come to you on the water."
29"Come," he said.
Then Peter got down out of the boat, walked
on the water and came toward Jesus. 30But
when he saw the wind, he was afraid and,
beginning to sink, cried out, "Lord, save me!"
31Immediately Jesus reached out his hand
and caught him. "You of little faith," he said,
"why did you doubt?"
32And when they climbed into the boat, the
wind died down. 33Then those who were in the
boat worshiped him, saying, "Truly you are
the Son of God."
34When they had crossed over, they landed
at Gennesaret. 35And when the men of that
place recognized Jesus, they sent word to all
the surrounding country. People brought all
their sick to him 36and begged him to let the
sick just touch the edge of his cloak, and all
who touched it were healed.

That Which Defiles

15 Then some Pharisees and teachers of
the law came to Jesus from Jerusalem
and asked, 2"Why do your disciples break the
tradition of the elders? They don't wash their
hands before they eat!"
3Jesus replied, "And why do you break the
command of God for the sake of your tradition? 4For God said, 'Honor your father and
mother'[a] and 'Anyone who curses their father
or mother is to be put to death.'[b] 5But you say
that if anyone declares that what might have
been used to help their father or mother is
'devoted to God,' 6they are not to 'honor their
father or mother' with it. Thus you nullify the
word of God for the sake of your tradition.
7You hypocrites! Isaiah was right when he
prophesied about you:

8" 'These people honor me with their lips,
but their hearts are far from me.
9They worship me in vain;
their teachings are merely human
rules.'[c]"

10Jesus called the crowd to him and said,
"Listen and understand. 11What goes into
someone's mouth does not defile them, but
what comes out of their mouth, that is what
defiles them."
12Then the disciples came to him and asked,
"Do you know that the Pharisees were offend-
ed when they heard this?"
13He replied, "Every plant that my heavenly
Father has not planted will be pulled up by the
roots. 14Leave them; they are blind guides.[d]
If the blind lead the blind, both will fall into
a pit."
15Peter said, "Explain the parable to us."
16"Are you still so dull?" Jesus asked them.
17"Don't you see that whatever enters the
mouth goes into the stomach and then out
of the body? 18But the things that come out
of a person's mouth come from the heart,
and these defile them. 19For out of the heart
come evil thoughts—murder, adultery, sexual immorality, theft, false testimony, slander.
20These are what defile a person; but eating
with unwashed hands does not defile them."

[a] *4* Exodus 20:12; Deut. 5:16 [b] *4* Exodus 21:17; Lev. 20:9 [c] *9* Isaiah 29:13 [d] *14* Some manuscripts *blind guides of the blind*

The Faith of a Canaanite Woman

21 Leaving that place, Jesus withdrew to the
region of Tyre and Sidon. 22 A Canaanite woman from that vicinity came to him, crying out,
"Lord, Son of David, have mercy on me! My
daughter is demon-possessed and suffering
terribly."

23 Jesus did not answer a word. So his disciples came to him and urged him, "Send her
away, for she keeps crying out after us."

24 He answered, "I was sent only to the lost
sheep of Israel."

25 The woman came and knelt before him.
"Lord, help me!" she said.

26 He replied, "It is not right to take the children's bread and toss it to the dogs."

27 "Yes it is, Lord," she said. "Even the dogs
eat the crumbs that fall from their master's
table."

28 Then Jesus said to her, "Woman, you have
great faith! Your request is granted." And her
daughter was healed at that moment.

Jesus Feeds the Four Thousand

29 Jesus left there and went along the Sea of
Galilee. Then he went up on a mountainside
and sat down. 30 Great crowds came to him,
bringing the lame, the blind, the crippled, the
mute and many others, and laid them at his
feet; and he healed them. 31 The people were
amazed when they saw the mute speaking,
the crippled made well, the lame walking and
the blind seeing. And they praised the God
of Israel.

32 Jesus called his disciples to him and said,
"I have compassion for these people; they have
already been with me three days and have
nothing to eat. I do not want to send them
away hungry, or they may collapse on the
way."

33 His disciples answered, "Where could we
get enough bread in this remote place to feed
such a crowd?"

34 "How many loaves do you have?" Jesus
asked.

"Seven," they replied, "and a few small fish."

35 He told the crowd to sit down on the
ground. 36 Then he took the seven loaves and
the fish, and when he had given thanks, he
broke them and gave them to the disciples,
and they in turn to the people. 37 They all ate
and were satisfied. Afterward the disciples
picked up seven basketfuls of broken pieces
that were left over. 38 The number of those who
ate was four thousand men, besides women
and children. 39 After Jesus had sent the crowd
away, he got into the boat and went to the vicinity of Magadan.

The Demand for a Sign

16 The Pharisees and Sadducees came to
Jesus and tested him by asking him to
show them a sign from heaven.

2 He replied, "When evening comes, you say,
'It will be fair weather, for the sky is red,' 3 and
in the morning, 'Today it will be stormy, for
the sky is red and overcast.' You know how to
interpret the appearance of the sky, but you
cannot interpret the signs of the times.[a] 4 A
wicked and adulterous generation looks for a
sign, but none will be given it except the sign
of Jonah." Jesus then left them and went away.

The Yeast of the Pharisees and Sadducees

5 When they went across the lake, the disciples forgot to take bread. 6 "Be careful," Jesus
said to them. "Be on your guard against the
yeast of the Pharisees and Sadducees."

7 They discussed this among themselves and
said, "It is because we didn't bring any bread."

8 Aware of their discussion, Jesus asked,
"You of little faith, why are you talking among
yourselves about having no bread? 9 Do you
still not understand? Don't you remember
the five loaves for the five thousand, and
how many basketfuls you gathered? 10 Or the
seven loaves for the four thousand, and how
many basketfuls you gathered? 11 How is it you
don't understand that I was not talking to you
about bread? But be on your guard against
the yeast of the Pharisees and Sadducees."
12 Then they understood that he was not telling
them to guard against the yeast used in bread,
but against the teaching of the Pharisees and
Sadducees.

Peter Declares That Jesus Is the Messiah

13 When Jesus came to the region of Caesarea Philippi, he asked his disciples, "Who do
people say the Son of Man is?"

14 They replied, "Some say John the Baptist;
others say Elijah; and still others, Jeremiah
or one of the prophets."

15 "But what about you?" he asked. "Who do
you say I am?"

16 Simon Peter answered, "You are the Messiah, the Son of the living God."

17 Jesus replied, "Blessed are you, Simon son
of Jonah, for this was not revealed to you by
flesh and blood, but by my Father in heav-
en. 18 And I tell you that you are Peter,[b] and
on this rock I will build my church, and the
gates of Hades[c] will not overcome it. 19 I will
give you the keys of the kingdom of heaven;
whatever you bind on earth will be[d] bound
in heaven, and whatever you loose on earth
will be[d] loosed in heaven." 20 Then he ordered
his disciples not to tell anyone that he was
the Messiah.

Jesus Predicts His Death

21 From that time on Jesus began to explain
to his disciples that he must go to Jerusalem
and suffer many things at the hands of the
elders, the chief priests and the teachers of
the law, and that he must be killed and on the
third day be raised to life.

22 Peter took him aside and began to rebuke
him. "Never, Lord!" he said. "This shall never
happen to you!"

[a] 2,3 Some early manuscripts do not have *When evening comes . . . of the times.* [b] 18 The Greek word for *Peter* means *rock.* [c] 18 That is, the realm of the dead [d] 19 Or *will have been*

23 Jesus turned and said to Peter, "Get behind me, Satan! You are a stumbling block to me; you do not have in mind the concerns of God, but merely human concerns."

24 Then Jesus said to his disciples, "Whoever wants to be my disciple must deny themselves and take up their cross and follow me. 25 For whoever wants to save their life[a] will lose it, but whoever loses their life for me will find it. 26 What good will it be for someone to gain the whole world, yet forfeit their soul? Or what can anyone give in exchange for their soul? 27 For the Son of Man is going to come in his Father's glory with his angels, and then he will reward each person according to what they have done.

28 "Truly I tell you, some who are standing here will not taste death before they see the Son of Man coming in his kingdom."

The Transfiguration

17 After six days Jesus took with him Peter, James and John the brother of James, and led them up a high mountain by themselves. 2 There he was transfigured before them. His face shone like the sun, and his clothes became as white as the light. 3 Just then there appeared before them Moses and Elijah, talking with Jesus.

4 Peter said to Jesus, "Lord, it is good for us to be here. If you wish, I will put up three shelters—one for you, one for Moses and one for Elijah."

5 While he was still speaking, a bright cloud covered them, and a voice from the cloud said, "This is my Son, whom I love; with him I am well pleased. Listen to him!"

6 When the disciples heard this, they fell facedown to the ground, terrified. 7 But Jesus came and touched them. "Get up," he said. "Don't be afraid." 8 When they looked up, they saw no one except Jesus.

9 As they were coming down the mountain, Jesus instructed them, "Don't tell anyone what you have seen, until the Son of Man has been raised from the dead."

10 The disciples asked him, "Why then do the teachers of the law say that Elijah must come first?"

11 Jesus replied, "To be sure, Elijah comes and will restore all things. 12 But I tell you, Elijah has already come, and they did not recognize him, but have done to him everything they wished. In the same way the Son of Man is going to suffer at their hands." 13 Then the disciples understood that he was talking to them about John the Baptist.

Jesus Heals a Demon-Possessed Boy

14 When they came to the crowd, a man approached Jesus and knelt before him. 15 "Lord, have mercy on my son," he said. "He has seizures and is suffering greatly. He often falls into the fire or into the water. 16 I brought him to your disciples, but they could not heal him."

17 "You unbelieving and perverse generation," Jesus replied, "how long shall I stay with you? How long shall I put up with you? Bring the boy here to me." 18 Jesus rebuked the demon, and it came out of the boy, and he was healed at that moment.

19 Then the disciples came to Jesus in private and asked, "Why couldn't we drive it out?"

20 He replied, "Because you have so little faith. Truly I tell you, if you have faith as small as a mustard seed, you can say to this mountain, 'Move from here to there,' and it will move. Nothing will be impossible for you." [21][b]

Jesus Predicts His Death a Second Time

22 When they came together in Galilee, he said to them, "The Son of Man is going to be delivered into the hands of men. 23 They will kill him, and on the third day he will be raised to life." And the disciples were filled with grief.

The Temple Tax

24 After Jesus and his disciples arrived in Capernaum, the collectors of the two-drachma temple tax came to Peter and asked, "Doesn't your teacher pay the temple tax?"

25 "Yes, he does," he replied.

When Peter came into the house, Jesus was the first to speak. "What do you think, Simon?" he asked. "From whom do the kings of the earth collect duty and taxes—from their own children or from others?"

26 "From others," Peter answered.

"Then the children are exempt," Jesus said to him. 27 "But so that we may not cause offense, go to the lake and throw out your line. Take the first fish you catch; open its mouth and you will find a four-drachma coin. Take it and give it to them for my tax and yours."

The Greatest in the Kingdom of Heaven

18 At that time the disciples came to Jesus and asked, "Who, then, is the greatest in the kingdom of heaven?"

2 He called a little child to him, and placed the child among them. 3 And he said: "Truly I tell you, unless you change and become like little children, you will never enter the kingdom of heaven. 4 Therefore, whoever takes the lowly position of this child is the greatest in the kingdom of heaven. 5 And whoever welcomes one such child in my name welcomes me.

Causing to Stumble

6 "If anyone causes one of these little ones—those who believe in me—to stumble, it would be better for them to have a large millstone hung around their neck and to be drowned in the depths of the sea. 7 Woe to the world because of the things that cause people to stumble! Such things must come, but woe to the person through whom they come! 8 If your hand or your foot causes you to stumble, cut it off and throw it away. It is better for you to

[a] *25* The Greek word means either *life* or *soul*; also in verse 26. [b] *21* Some manuscripts include here words similar to Mark 9:29.

enter life maimed or crippled than to have two
hands or two feet and be thrown into eternal
fire. 9And if your eye causes you to stumble,
gouge it out and throw it away. It is better for
you to enter life with one eye than to have
two eyes and be thrown into the fire of hell.

The Parable of the Wandering Sheep

10"See that you do not despise one of these
little ones. For I tell you that their angels in
heaven always see the face of my Father in
heaven. [11][a]
12"What do you think? If a man owns a hundred sheep, and one of them wanders away,
will he not leave the ninety-nine on the hills
and go to look for the one that wandered off?
13And if he finds it, truly I tell you, he is happier about that one sheep than about the ninety-nine that did not wander off. 14In the same
way your Father in heaven is not willing that
any of these little ones should perish.

Dealing With Sin in the Church

15"If your brother or sister[b] sins,[c] go and
point out their fault, just between the two of
you. If they listen to you, you have won them
over. 16But if they will not listen, take one or
two others along, so that 'every matter may be
established by the testimony of two or three
witnesses.'[d] 17If they still refuse to listen, tell
it to the church; and if they refuse to listen
even to the church, treat them as you would
a pagan or a tax collector.
18"Truly I tell you, whatever you bind on
earth will be[e] bound in heaven, and whatever
you loose on earth will be[e] loosed in heaven.
19"Again, truly I tell you that if two of you
on earth agree about anything they ask for, it
will be done for them by my Father in heaven.
20For where two or three gather in my name,
there am I with them."

The Parable of the Unmerciful Servant

21Then Peter came to Jesus and asked,
"Lord, how many times shall I forgive my
brother or sister who sins against me? Up to
seven times?"
22Jesus answered, "I tell you, not seven
times, but seventy-seven times.[f]
23"Therefore, the kingdom of heaven is like
a king who wanted to settle accounts with
his servants. 24As he began the settlement,
a man who owed him ten thousand bags of
gold[g] was brought to him. 25Since he was not
able to pay, the master ordered that he and
his wife and his children and all that he had
be sold to repay the debt.
26"At this the servant fell on his knees before him. 'Be patient with me,' he begged, 'and
I will pay back everything.' 27The servant's
master took pity on him, canceled the debt
and let him go.
28"But when that servant went out, he found
one of his fellow servants who owed him a
hundred silver coins.[h] He grabbed him and
began to choke him. 'Pay back what you owe
me!' he demanded.
29"His fellow servant fell to his knees and
begged him, 'Be patient with me, and I will
pay it back.'
30"But he refused. Instead, he went off and
had the man thrown into prison until he could
pay the debt. 31When the other servants saw
what had happened, they were outraged and
went and told their master everything that
had happened.
32"Then the master called the servant in.
'You wicked servant,' he said, 'I canceled all
that debt of yours because you begged me to.
33Shouldn't you have had mercy on your fellow servant just as I had on you?' 34In anger
his master handed him over to the jailers to be
tortured, until he should pay back all he owed.
35"This is how my heavenly Father will treat
each of you unless you forgive your brother
or sister from your heart."

Divorce

19 When Jesus had finished saying these
things, he left Galilee and went into the
region of Judea to the other side of the Jordan.
2Large crowds followed him, and he healed
them there.
3Some Pharisees came to him to test him.
They asked, "Is it lawful for a man to divorce
his wife for any and every reason?"
4"Haven't you read," he replied, "that at the
beginning the Creator 'made them male and
female,'[i] 5and said, 'For this reason a man
will leave his father and mother and be united to his wife, and the two will become one
flesh'[j]? 6So they are no longer two, but one
flesh. Therefore what God has joined together,
let no one separate."
7"Why then," they asked, "did Moses command that a man give his wife a certificate of
divorce and send her away?"
8Jesus replied, "Moses permitted you to divorce your wives because your hearts were
hard. But it was not this way from the beginning. 9I tell you that anyone who divorces
his wife, except for sexual immorality, and
marries another woman commits adultery."
10The disciples said to him, "If this is the
situation between a husband and wife, it is
better not to marry."
11Jesus replied, "Not everyone can accept
this word, but only those to whom it has been
given. 12For there are eunuchs who were born
that way, and there are eunuchs who have
been made eunuchs by others—and there are
those who choose to live like eunuchs for the
sake of the kingdom of heaven. The one who
can accept this should accept it."

[a] *11* Some manuscripts include here the words of Luke 19:10. [b] *15* The Greek word for *brother or sister* (*adelphos*) refers here to a fellow disciple, whether man or woman; also in verses 21 and 35. [c] *15* Some manuscripts *sins against you* [d] *16* Deut. 19:15 [e] *18* Or *will have been* [f] *22* Or *seventy times seven* [g] *24* Greek *ten thousand talents*; a talent was worth about 20 years of a day laborer's wages. [h] *28* Greek *a hundred denarii*; a denarius was the usual daily wage of a day laborer (see 20:2). [i] *4* Gen. 1:27 [j] *5* Gen. 2:24

The Little Children and Jesus

13Then people brought little children to
Jesus for him to place his hands on them and
pray for them. But the disciples rebuked them.
14Jesus said, "Let the little children come to
me, and do not hinder them, for the kingdom
of heaven belongs to such as these." 15When
he had placed his hands on them, he went on
from there.

The Rich and the Kingdom of God

16Just then a man came up to Jesus and
asked, "Teacher, what good thing must I do
to get eternal life?"
17"Why do you ask me about what is good?"
Jesus replied. "There is only One who is good.
If you want to enter life, keep the commandments."
18"Which ones?" he inquired.
Jesus replied, "'You shall not murder, you
shall not commit adultery, you shall not steal,
you shall not give false testimony, 19hon-
or your father and mother,'[a] and 'love your
neighbor as yourself.'[b]"
20"All these I have kept," the young man
said. "What do I still lack?"
21Jesus answered, "If you want to be perfect,
go, sell your possessions and give to the poor,
and you will have treasure in heaven. Then
come, follow me."
22When the young man heard this, he went
away sad, because he had great wealth.
23Then Jesus said to his disciples, "Truly I
tell you, it is hard for someone who is rich to
enter the kingdom of heaven. 24Again I tell
you, it is easier for a camel to go through the
eye of a needle than for someone who is rich
to enter the kingdom of God."
25When the disciples heard this, they were
greatly astonished and asked, "Who then can
be saved?"
26Jesus looked at them and said, "With man
this is impossible, but with God all things are
possible."
27Peter answered him, "We have left everything to follow you! What then will there be
for us?"
28Jesus said to them, "Truly I tell you, at the
renewal of all things, when the Son of Man
sits on his glorious throne, you who have followed me will also sit on twelve thrones, judging the twelve tribes of Israel. 29And everyone
who has left houses or brothers or sisters or
father or mother or wife[c] or children or fields
for my sake will receive a hundred times as
much and will inherit eternal life. 30But many
who are first will be last, and many who are
last will be first.

The Parable of the Workers in the Vineyard

20 "For the kingdom of heaven is like a
landowner who went out early in the
morning to hire workers for his vineyard. 2He
agreed to pay them a denarius[d] for the day
and sent them into his vineyard.
3"About nine in the morning he went out
and saw others standing in the marketplace
doing nothing. 4He told them, 'You also go
and work in my vineyard, and I will pay you
whatever is right.' 5So they went.
"He went out again about noon and about
three in the afternoon and did the same thing.
6About five in the afternoon he went out and
found still others standing around. He asked
them, 'Why have you been standing here all
day long doing nothing?'
7"'Because no one has hired us,' they answered.
"He said to them, 'You also go and work in
my vineyard.'
8"When evening came, the owner of the
vineyard said to his foreman, 'Call the workers and pay them their wages, beginning with
the last ones hired and going on to the first.'
9"The workers who were hired about five
in the afternoon came and each received a
denarius. 10So when those came who were
hired first, they expected to receive more. But
each one of them also received a denarius.
11When they received it, they began to grumble against the landowner. 12'These who were
hired last worked only one hour,' they said,
'and you have made them equal to us who
have borne the burden of the work and the
heat of the day.'
13"But he answered one of them, 'I am not
being unfair to you, friend. Didn't you agree
to work for a denarius? 14Take your pay and
go. I want to give the one who was hired last
the same as I gave you. 15Don't I have the right
to do what I want with my own money? Or are
you envious because I am generous?'
16"So the last will be first, and the first will
be last."

Jesus Predicts His Death a Third Time

17Now Jesus was going up to Jerusalem. On
the way, he took the Twelve aside and said to
them, 18"We are going up to Jerusalem, and
the Son of Man will be delivered over to the
chief priests and the teachers of the law. They
will condemn him to death 19and will hand
him over to the Gentiles to be mocked and
flogged and crucified. On the third day he
will be raised to life!"

A Mother's Request

20Then the mother of Zebedee's sons came
to Jesus with her sons and, kneeling down,
asked a favor of him.
21"What is it you want?" he asked.
She said, "Grant that one of these two sons
of mine may sit at your right and the other at
your left in your kingdom."
22"You don't know what you are asking,"
Jesus said to them. "Can you drink the cup I
am going to drink?"
"We can," they answered.
23Jesus said to them, "You will indeed drink
from my cup, but to sit at my right or left is
not for me to grant. These places belong to

[a] *19* Exodus 20:12-16; Deut. 5:16-20 [b] *19* Lev. 19:18 [c] *29* Some manuscripts do not have *or wife.*
[d] 2 A denarius was the usual daily wage of a day laborer.

those for whom they have been prepared by my Father."

24When the ten heard about this, they were indignant with the two brothers. 25Jesus called them together and said, "You know that the rulers of the Gentiles lord it over them, and their high officials exercise authority over them. 26Not so with you. Instead, whoever wants to become great among you must be your servant, 27and whoever wants to be first must be your slave— 28just as the Son of Man did not come to be served, but to serve, and to give his life as a ransom for many."

Two Blind Men Receive Sight

29As Jesus and his disciples were leaving Jericho, a large crowd followed him. 30Two blind men were sitting by the roadside, and when they heard that Jesus was going by, they shouted, "Lord, Son of David, have mercy on us!"

31The crowd rebuked them and told them to be quiet, but they shouted all the louder, "Lord, Son of David, have mercy on us!"

32Jesus stopped and called them. "What do you want me to do for you?" he asked.

33"Lord," they answered, "we want our sight."

34Jesus had compassion on them and touched their eyes. Immediately they received their sight and followed him.

Jesus Comes to Jerusalem as King

21 As they approached Jerusalem and came to Bethphage on the Mount of Olives, Jesus sent two disciples, 2saying to them, "Go to the village ahead of you, and at once you will find a donkey tied there, with her colt by her. Untie them and bring them to me. 3If anyone says anything to you, say that the Lord needs them, and he will send them right away."

4This took place to fulfill what was spoken through the prophet:

5"Say to Daughter Zion,
'See, your king comes to you,
gentle and riding on a donkey,
and on a colt, the foal of a donkey.'"[a]

6The disciples went and did as Jesus had instructed them. 7They brought the donkey and the colt and placed their cloaks on them for Jesus to sit on. 8A very large crowd spread their cloaks on the road, while others cut branches from the trees and spread them on the road. 9The crowds that went ahead of him and those that followed shouted,

"Hosanna[b] to the Son of David!"

"Blessed is he who comes in the name of the Lord!"[c]

"Hosanna[b] in the highest heaven!"

10When Jesus entered Jerusalem, the whole city was stirred and asked, "Who is this?"

11The crowds answered, "This is Jesus, the prophet from Nazareth in Galilee."

Jesus at the Temple

12Jesus entered the temple courts and drove out all who were buying and selling there. He overturned the tables of the money changers and the benches of those selling doves. 13"It is written," he said to them, "'My house will be called a house of prayer,'[d] but you are making it 'a den of robbers.'[e]"

14The blind and the lame came to him at the temple, and he healed them. 15But when the chief priests and the teachers of the law saw the wonderful things he did and the children shouting in the temple courts, "Hosanna to the Son of David," they were indignant.

16"Do you hear what these children are saying?" they asked him.

"Yes," replied Jesus, "have you never read,

"'From the lips of children and infants
you, Lord, have called forth your
praise'[f]?"

17And he left them and went out of the city to Bethany, where he spent the night.

Jesus Curses a Fig Tree

18Early in the morning, as Jesus was on his way back to the city, he was hungry. 19Seeing a fig tree by the road, he went up to it but found nothing on it except leaves. Then he said to it, "May you never bear fruit again!" Immediately the tree withered.

20When the disciples saw this, they were amazed. "How did the fig tree wither so quickly?" they asked.

21Jesus replied, "Truly I tell you, if you have faith and do not doubt, not only can you do what was done to the fig tree, but also you can say to this mountain, 'Go, throw yourself into the sea,' and it will be done. 22If you believe, you will receive whatever you ask for in prayer."

The Authority of Jesus Questioned

23Jesus entered the temple courts, and, while he was teaching, the chief priests and the elders of the people came to him. "By what authority are you doing these things?" they asked. "And who gave you this authority?"

24Jesus replied, "I will also ask you one question. If you answer me, I will tell you by what authority I am doing these things. 25John's baptism—where did it come from? Was it from heaven, or of human origin?"

They discussed it among themselves and said, "If we say, 'From heaven,' he will ask, 'Then why didn't you believe him?' 26But if we say, 'Of human origin'—we are afraid of the people, for they all hold that John was a prophet."

27So they answered Jesus, "We don't know."

Then he said, "Neither will I tell you by what authority I am doing these things.

[a] *5* Zech. 9:9 [b] *9* A Hebrew expression meaning "Save!" which became an exclamation of praise; also in verse 15 [c] *9* Psalm 118:25,26 [d] *13* Isaiah 56:7 [e] *13* Jer. 7:11 [f] *16* Psalm 8:2 (see Septuagint)

The Parable of the Two Sons

28"What do you think? There was a man who had two sons. He went to the first and said, 'Son, go and work today in the vineyard.'

29" 'I will not,' he answered, but later he changed his mind and went.

30"Then the father went to the other son and said the same thing. He answered, 'I will, sir,' but he did not go.

31"Which of the two did what his father wanted?"

"The first," they answered.

Jesus said to them, "Truly I tell you, the tax collectors and the prostitutes are entering the kingdom of God ahead of you. 32For John came to you to show you the way of righteousness, and you did not believe him, but the tax collectors and the prostitutes did. And even after you saw this, you did not repent and believe him.

The Parable of the Tenants

33"Listen to another parable: There was a landowner who planted a vineyard. He put a wall around it, dug a winepress in it and built a watchtower. Then he rented the vineyard to some farmers and moved to another place. 34When the harvest time approached, he sent his servants to the tenants to collect his fruit.

35"The tenants seized his servants; they beat one, killed another, and stoned a third. 36Then he sent other servants to them, more than the first time, and the tenants treated them the same way. 37Last of all, he sent his son to them. 'They will respect my son,' he said.

38"But when the tenants saw the son, they said to each other, 'This is the heir. Come, let's kill him and take his inheritance.' 39So they took him and threw him out of the vineyard and killed him.

40"Therefore, when the owner of the vineyard comes, what will he do to those tenants?"

41"He will bring those wretches to a wretched end," they replied, "and he will rent the vineyard to other tenants, who will give him his share of the crop at harvest time."

42Jesus said to them, "Have you never read in the Scriptures:

" 'The stone the builders rejected
has become the cornerstone;
the Lord has done this,
and it is marvelous in our eyes'[a]?

43"Therefore I tell you that the kingdom of God will be taken away from you and given to a people who will produce its fruit. 44Anyone who falls on this stone will be broken to pieces; anyone on whom it falls will be crushed."[b]

45When the chief priests and the Pharisees heard Jesus' parables, they knew he was talking about them. 46They looked for a way to arrest him, but they were afraid of the crowd because the people held that he was a prophet.

The Parable of the Wedding Banquet

22 Jesus spoke to them again in parables, saying: 2"The kingdom of heaven is like a king who prepared a wedding banquet for his son. 3He sent his servants to those who had been invited to the banquet to tell them to come, but they refused to come.

4"Then he sent some more servants and said, 'Tell those who have been invited that I have prepared my dinner: My oxen and fattened cattle have been butchered, and everything is ready. Come to the wedding banquet.'

5"But they paid no attention and went off—one to his field, another to his business. 6The rest seized his servants, mistreated them and killed them. 7The king was enraged. He sent his army and destroyed those murderers and burned their city.

8"Then he said to his servants, 'The wedding banquet is ready, but those I invited did not deserve to come. 9So go to the street corners and invite to the banquet anyone you find.' 10So the servants went out into the streets and gathered all the people they could find, the bad as well as the good, and the wedding hall was filled with guests.

11"But when the king came in to see the guests, he noticed a man there who was not wearing wedding clothes. 12He asked, 'How did you get in here without wedding clothes, friend?' The man was speechless.

13"Then the king told the attendants, 'Tie him hand and foot, and throw him outside, into the darkness, where there will be weeping and gnashing of teeth.'

14"For many are invited, but few are chosen."

Paying the Imperial Tax to Caesar

15Then the Pharisees went out and laid plans to trap him in his words. 16They sent their disciples to him along with the Herodians. "Teacher," they said, "we know that you are a man of integrity and that you teach the way of God in accordance with the truth. You aren't swayed by others, because you pay no attention to who they are. 17Tell us then, what is your opinion? Is it right to pay the imperial tax[c] to Caesar or not?"

18But Jesus, knowing their evil intent, said, "You hypocrites, why are you trying to trap me? 19Show me the coin used for paying the tax." They brought him a denarius, 20and he asked them, "Whose image is this? And whose inscription?"

21"Caesar's," they replied.

Then he said to them, "So give back to Caesar what is Caesar's, and to God what is God's."

22When they heard this, they were amazed. So they left him and went away.

Marriage at the Resurrection

23That same day the Sadducees, who say there is no resurrection, came to him with a

[a] *42* Psalm 118:22,23 [b] *44* Some manuscripts do not have verse 44. [c] *17* A special tax levied on subject peoples, not on Roman citizens

question. 24“Teacher,” they said, “Moses told
us that if a man dies without having children,
his brother must marry the widow and raise
up offspring for him. 25Now there were sev-
en brothers among us. The first one married
and died, and since he had no children, he left
his wife to his brother. 26The same thing happened to the second and third brother, right
on down to the seventh. 27Finally, the woman
died. 28Now then, at the resurrection, whose
wife will she be of the seven, since all of them
were married to her?”

29Jesus replied, “You are in error because
you do not know the Scriptures or the power of God. 30At the resurrection people will
neither marry nor be given in marriage; they
will be like the angels in heaven. 31But about
the resurrection of the dead—have you not
read what God said to you, 32‘I am the God
of Abraham, the God of Isaac, and the God
of Jacob’[a]? He is not the God of the dead but
of the living.”

33When the crowds heard this, they were
astonished at his teaching.

The Greatest Commandment

34Hearing that Jesus had silenced the Sadducees, the Pharisees got together. 35One of
them, an expert in the law, tested him with
this question: 36“Teacher, which is the greatest
commandment in the Law?”

37Jesus replied: “ ‘Love the Lord your God
with all your heart and with all your soul and
with all your mind.’[b] 38This is the first and
greatest commandment. 39And the second is
like it: ‘Love your neighbor as yourself.’[c] 40All
the Law and the Prophets hang on these two
commandments.”

Whose Son Is the Messiah?

41While the Pharisees were gathered together, Jesus asked them, 42“What do you think
about the Messiah? Whose son is he?”

“The son of David,” they replied.

43He said to them, “How is it then that David, speaking by the Spirit, calls him ‘Lord’?
For he says,

44“ ‘The Lord said to my Lord:
“Sit at my right hand
until I put your enemies
under your feet.” ’[d]

45If then David calls him ‘Lord,’ how can he be
his son?” 46No one could say a word in reply,
and from that day on no one dared to ask him
any more questions.

A Warning Against Hypocrisy

23 Then Jesus said to the crowds and to
his disciples: 2“The teachers of the law
and the Pharisees sit in Moses’ seat. 3So you
must be careful to do everything they tell you.
But do not do what they do, for they do not
practice what they preach. 4They tie up heavy,
cumbersome loads and put them on other people’s shoulders, but they themselves are not
willing to lift a finger to move them.

5“Everything they do is done for people to
see: They make their phylacteries[e] wide and
the tassels on their garments long; 6they love
the place of honor at banquets and the most
important seats in the synagogues; 7they love
to be greeted with respect in the marketplaces
and to be called ‘Rabbi’ by others.

8“But you are not to be called ‘Rabbi,’ for
you have one Teacher, and you are all brothers. 9And do not call anyone on earth ‘father,’
for you have one Father, and he is in heav-
en. 10Nor are you to be called instructors, for
you have one Instructor, the Messiah. 11The
greatest among you will be your servant. 12For
those who exalt themselves will be humbled,
and those who humble themselves will be
exalted.

Seven Woes on the Teachers of the Law and the Pharisees

13“Woe to you, teachers of the law and Pharisees, you hypocrites! You shut the door of
the kingdom of heaven in people’s faces. You
yourselves do not enter, nor will you let those
enter who are trying to. [14][f]

15“Woe to you, teachers of the law and Pharisees, you hypocrites! You travel over land
and sea to win a single convert, and when
you have succeeded, you make them twice
as much a child of hell as you are.

16“Woe to you, blind guides! You say, ‘If anyone swears by the temple, it means nothing;
but anyone who swears by the gold of the temple is bound by that oath.’ 17You blind fools!
Which is greater: the gold, or the temple that
makes the gold sacred? 18You also say, ‘If anyone swears by the altar, it means nothing; but
anyone who swears by the gift on the altar is
bound by that oath.’ 19You blind men! Which
is greater: the gift, or the altar that makes the
gift sacred? 20Therefore, anyone who swears
by the altar swears by it and by everything
on it. 21And anyone who swears by the temple
swears by it and by the one who dwells in it.
22And anyone who swears by heaven swears
by God’s throne and by the one who sits on it.

23“Woe to you, teachers of the law and Pharisees, you hypocrites! You give a tenth of your
spices—mint, dill and cumin. But you have
neglected the more important matters of the
law—justice, mercy and faithfulness. You
should have practiced the latter, without ne-
glecting the former. 24You blind guides! You
strain out a gnat but swallow a camel.

25“Woe to you, teachers of the law and Pharisees, you hypocrites! You clean the outside
of the cup and dish, but inside they are full of
greed and self-indulgence. 26Blind Pharisee!
First clean the inside of the cup and dish, and
then the outside also will be clean.

27“Woe to you, teachers of the law and
Pharisees, you hypocrites! You are like

[a] *32* Exodus 3:6 [b] *37* Deut. 6:5 [c] *39* Lev. 19:18 [d] *44* Psalm 110:1 [e] *5* That is, boxes containing Scripture verses, worn on forehead and arm [f] *14* Some manuscripts include here words similar to Mark 12:40 and Luke 20:47.

whitewashed tombs, which look beautiful on
the outside but on the inside are full of the
bones of the dead and everything unclean.
28In the same way, on the outside you appear
to people as righteous but on the inside you
are full of hypocrisy and wickedness.

29"Woe to you, teachers of the law and Pharisees, you hypocrites! You build tombs for
the prophets and decorate the graves of the
righteous. 30And you say, 'If we had lived in
the days of our ancestors, we would not have
taken part with them in shedding the blood
of the prophets.' 31So you testify against yourselves that you are the descendants of those
who murdered the prophets. 32Go ahead, then,
and complete what your ancestors started!

33"You snakes! You brood of vipers! How
will you escape being condemned to hell?
34Therefore I am sending you prophets and
sages and teachers. Some of them you will
kill and crucify; others you will flog in your
synagogues and pursue from town to town.
35And so upon you will come all the righteous
blood that has been shed on earth, from the
blood of righteous Abel to the blood of Zechariah son of Berekiah, whom you murdered
between the temple and the altar. 36Truly I
tell you, all this will come on this generation.

37"Jerusalem, Jerusalem, you who kill the
prophets and stone those sent to you, how
often I have longed to gather your children
together, as a hen gathers her chicks under
her wings, and you were not willing. 38Look,
your house is left to you desolate. 39For I tell
you, you will not see me again until you say,
'Blessed is he who comes in the name of the
Lord.'[a]"

The Destruction of the Temple and Signs of the End Times

24 Jesus left the temple and was walking
away when his disciples came up to him
to call his attention to its buildings. 2"Do you
see all these things?" he asked. "Truly I tell
you, not one stone here will be left on another;
every one will be thrown down."

3As Jesus was sitting on the Mount of Olives, the disciples came to him privately. "Tell
us," they said, "when will this happen, and
what will be the sign of your coming and of
the end of the age?"

4Jesus answered: "Watch out that no one deceives you. 5For many will come in my name,
claiming, 'I am the Messiah,' and will deceive
many. 6You will hear of wars and rumors of
wars, but see to it that you are not alarmed.
Such things must happen, but the end is still
to come. 7Nation will rise against nation, and
kingdom against kingdom. There will be famines and earthquakes in various places. 8All
these are the beginning of birth pains.

9"Then you will be handed over to be persecuted and put to death, and you will be
hated by all nations because of me. 10At that
time many will turn away from the faith and
will betray and hate each other, 11and many
false prophets will appear and deceive many
people. 12Because of the increase of wickedness, the love of most will grow cold, 13but
the one who stands firm to the end will be
saved. 14And this gospel of the kingdom will
be preached in the whole world as a testimony to all nations, and then the end will come.

15"So when you see standing in the holy
place 'the abomination that causes desolation,'[b] spoken of through the prophet Daniel—let the reader understand— 16then let
those who are in Judea flee to the mountains.
17Let no one on the housetop go down to take
anything out of the house. 18Let no one in the
field go back to get their cloak. 19How dreadful
it will be in those days for pregnant women
and nursing mothers! 20Pray that your flight
will not take place in winter or on the Sabbath. 21For then there will be great distress,
unequaled from the beginning of the world
until now—and never to be equaled again.

22"If those days had not been cut short, no
one would survive, but for the sake of the elect
those days will be shortened. 23At that time
if anyone says to you, 'Look, here is the Messiah!' or, 'There he is!' do not believe it. 24For
false messiahs and false prophets will appear
and perform great signs and wonders to deceive, if possible, even the elect. 25See, I have
told you ahead of time.

26"So if anyone tells you, 'There he is, out in
the wilderness,' do not go out; or, 'Here he is,
in the inner rooms,' do not believe it. 27For as
lightning that comes from the east is visible
even in the west, so will be the coming of the
Son of Man. 28Wherever there is a carcass,
there the vultures will gather.

29"Immediately after the distress of those
days

"'the sun will be darkened,
  and the moon will not give its light;
the stars will fall from the sky,
  and the heavenly bodies will be
    shaken.'[c]

30"Then will appear the sign of the Son of
Man in heaven. And then all the peoples of
the earth[d] will mourn when they see the Son
of Man coming on the clouds of heaven, with
power and great glory.[e] 31And he will send his
angels with a loud trumpet call, and they will
gather his elect from the four winds, from one
end of the heavens to the other.

32"Now learn this lesson from the fig tree:
As soon as its twigs get tender and its leaves
come out, you know that summer is near.
33Even so, when you see all these things, you
know that it[f] is near, right at the door. 34Truly I
tell you, this generation will certainly not pass
away until all these things have happened.
35Heaven and earth will pass away, but my
words will never pass away.

The Day and Hour Unknown

36"But about that day or hour no one knows,
not even the angels in heaven, nor the Son,[g]

[a] *39* Psalm 118:26 [b] *15* Daniel 9:27; 11:31; 12:11 [c] *29* Isaiah 13:10; 34:4 [d] *30* Or *the tribes of the land* [e] *30* See Daniel 7:13-14. [f] *33* Or *he* [g] *36* Some manuscripts do not have *nor the Son.*

but only the Father. 37As it was in the days of Noah, so it will be at the coming of the Son of Man. 38For in the days before the flood, people were eating and drinking, marrying and giving in marriage, up to the day Noah entered the ark; 39and they knew nothing about what would happen until the flood came and took them all away. That is how it will be at the coming of the Son of Man. 40Two men will be in the field; one will be taken and the other left. 41Two women will be grinding with a hand mill; one will be taken and the other left.

42"Therefore keep watch, because you do not know on what day your Lord will come. 43But understand this: If the owner of the house had known at what time of night the thief was coming, he would have kept watch and would not have let his house be broken into. 44So you also must be ready, because the Son of Man will come at an hour when you do not expect him.

45"Who then is the faithful and wise servant, whom the master has put in charge of the servants in his household to give them their food at the proper time? 46It will be good for that servant whose master finds him doing so when he returns. 47Truly I tell you, he will put him in charge of all his possessions. 48But suppose that servant is wicked and says to himself, 'My master is staying away a long time,' 49and he then begins to beat his fellow servants and to eat and drink with drunkards. 50The master of that servant will come on a day when he does not expect him and at an hour he is not aware of. 51He will cut him to pieces and assign him a place with the hypocrites, where there will be weeping and gnashing of teeth.

The Parable of the Ten Virgins

25 "At that time the kingdom of heaven will be like ten virgins who took their lamps and went out to meet the bridegroom. 2Five of them were foolish and five were wise. 3The foolish ones took their lamps but did not take any oil with them. 4The wise ones, however, took oil in jars along with their lamps. 5The bridegroom was a long time in coming, and they all became drowsy and fell asleep.

6"At midnight the cry rang out: 'Here's the bridegroom! Come out to meet him!'

7"Then all the virgins woke up and trimmed their lamps. 8The foolish ones said to the wise, 'Give us some of your oil; our lamps are going out.'

9" 'No,' they replied, 'there may not be enough for both us and you. Instead, go to those who sell oil and buy some for yourselves.'

10"But while they were on their way to buy the oil, the bridegroom arrived. The virgins who were ready went in with him to the wedding banquet. And the door was shut.

11"Later the others also came. 'Lord, Lord,' they said, 'open the door for us!'

12"But he replied, 'Truly I tell you, I don't know you.'

13"Therefore keep watch, because you do not know the day or the hour.

The Parable of the Bags of Gold

14"Again, it will be like a man going on a journey, who called his servants and entrusted his wealth to them. 15To one he gave five bags of gold, to another two bags, and to another one bag,[a] each according to his ability. Then he went on his journey. 16The man who had received five bags of gold went at once and put his money to work and gained five bags more. 17So also, the one with two bags of gold gained two more. 18But the man who had received one bag went off, dug a hole in the ground and hid his master's money.

19"After a long time the master of those servants returned and settled accounts with them. 20The man who had received five bags of gold brought the other five. 'Master,' he said, 'you entrusted me with five bags of gold. See, I have gained five more.'

21"His master replied, 'Well done, good and faithful servant! You have been faithful with a few things; I will put you in charge of many things. Come and share your master's happiness!'

22"The man with two bags of gold also came. 'Master,' he said, 'you entrusted me with two bags of gold; see, I have gained two more.'

23"His master replied, 'Well done, good and faithful servant! You have been faithful with a few things; I will put you in charge of many things. Come and share your master's happiness!'

24"Then the man who had received one bag of gold came. 'Master,' he said, 'I knew that you are a hard man, harvesting where you have not sown and gathering where you have not scattered seed. 25So I was afraid and went out and hid your gold in the ground. See, here is what belongs to you.'

26"His master replied, 'You wicked, lazy servant! So you knew that I harvest where I have not sown and gather where I have not scattered seed? 27Well then, you should have put my money on deposit with the bankers, so that when I returned I would have received it back with interest.

28" 'So take the bag of gold from him and give it to the one who has ten bags. 29For whoever has will be given more, and they will have an abundance. Whoever does not have, even what they have will be taken from them. 30And throw that worthless servant outside, into the darkness, where there will be weeping and gnashing of teeth.'

The Sheep and the Goats

31"When the Son of Man comes in his glory, and all the angels with him, he will sit on his glorious throne. 32All the nations will be gathered before him, and he will separate the people one from another as a shepherd separates the sheep from the goats. 33He will

[a] 15 Greek *five talents . . . two talents . . . one talent*; also throughout this parable; a talent was worth about 20 years of a day laborer's wage.

put the sheep on his right and the goats on his left.

34“Then the King will say to those on his right, ‘Come, you who are blessed by my Father; take your inheritance, the kingdom prepared for you since the creation of the world. 35For I was hungry and you gave me something to eat, I was thirsty and you gave me something to drink, I was a stranger and you invited me in, 36I needed clothes and you clothed me, I was sick and you looked after me, I was in prison and you came to visit me.’

37“Then the righteous will answer him, ‘Lord, when did we see you hungry and feed you, or thirsty and give you something to drink? 38When did we see you a stranger and invite you in, or needing clothes and clothe you? 39When did we see you sick or in prison and go to visit you?’

40“The King will reply, ‘Truly I tell you, whatever you did for one of the least of these brothers and sisters of mine, you did for me.’

41“Then he will say to those on his left, ‘Depart from me, you who are cursed, into the eternal fire prepared for the devil and his angels. 42For I was hungry and you gave me nothing to eat, I was thirsty and you gave me nothing to drink, 43I was a stranger and you did not invite me in, I needed clothes and you did not clothe me, I was sick and in prison and you did not look after me.’

44“They also will answer, ‘Lord, when did we see you hungry or thirsty or a stranger or needing clothes or sick or in prison, and did not help you?’

45“He will reply, ‘Truly I tell you, whatever you did not do for one of the least of these, you did not do for me.’

46“Then they will go away to eternal punishment, but the righteous to eternal life.”

The Plot Against Jesus

26 When Jesus had finished saying all these things, he said to his disciples, 2“As you know, the Passover is two days away—and the Son of Man will be handed over to be crucified.”

3Then the chief priests and the elders of the people assembled in the palace of the high priest, whose name was Caiaphas, 4and they schemed to arrest Jesus secretly and kill him. 5“But not during the festival,” they said, “or there may be a riot among the people.”

Jesus Anointed at Bethany

6While Jesus was in Bethany in the home of Simon the Leper, 7a woman came to him with an alabaster jar of very expensive perfume, which she poured on his head as he was reclining at the table.

8When the disciples saw this, they were indignant. “Why this waste?” they asked. 9“This perfume could have been sold at a high price and the money given to the poor.”

10Aware of this, Jesus said to them, “Why are you bothering this woman? She has done a beautiful thing to me. 11The poor you will always have with you,[a] but you will not always have me. 12When she poured this perfume on my body, she did it to prepare me for burial. 13Truly I tell you, wherever this gospel is preached throughout the world, what she has done will also be told, in memory of her.”

Judas Agrees to Betray Jesus

14Then one of the Twelve—the one called Judas Iscariot—went to the chief priests 15and asked, “What are you willing to give me if I deliver him over to you?” So they counted out for him thirty pieces of silver. 16From then on Judas watched for an opportunity to hand him over.

The Last Supper

17On the first day of the Festival of Unleavened Bread, the disciples came to Jesus and asked, “Where do you want us to make preparations for you to eat the Passover?”

18He replied, “Go into the city to a certain man and tell him, ‘The Teacher says: My appointed time is near. I am going to celebrate the Passover with my disciples at your house.’ ” 19So the disciples did as Jesus had directed them and prepared the Passover.

20When evening came, Jesus was reclining at the table with the Twelve. 21And while they were eating, he said, “Truly I tell you, one of you will betray me.”

22They were very sad and began to say to him one after the other, “Surely you don’t mean me, Lord?”

23Jesus replied, “The one who has dipped his hand into the bowl with me will betray me. 24The Son of Man will go just as it is written about him. But woe to that man who betrays the Son of Man! It would be better for him if he had not been born.”

25Then Judas, the one who would betray him, said, “Surely you don’t mean me, Rabbi?”

Jesus answered, “You have said so.”

26While they were eating, Jesus took bread, and when he had given thanks, he broke it and gave it to his disciples, saying, “Take and eat; this is my body.”

27Then he took a cup, and when he had given thanks, he gave it to them, saying, “Drink from it, all of you. 28This is my blood of the[b] covenant, which is poured out for many for the forgiveness of sins. 29I tell you, I will not drink from this fruit of the vine from now on until that day when I drink it new with you in my Father’s kingdom.”

30When they had sung a hymn, they went out to the Mount of Olives.

Jesus Predicts Peter’s Denial

31Then Jesus told them, “This very night you will all fall away on account of me, for it is written:

> “ ‘I will strike the shepherd,
> and the sheep of the flock will be
> scattered.’[c]

[a] 11 See Deut. 15:11. [b] 28 Some manuscripts *the new* [c] 31 Zech. 13:7

32But after I have risen, I will go ahead of you
into Galilee."
33Peter replied, "Even if all fall away on account of you, I never will."
34"Truly I tell you," Jesus answered, "this
very night, before the rooster crows, you will
disown me three times."
35But Peter declared, "Even if I have to die
with you, I will never disown you." And all
the other disciples said the same.

Gethsemane

36Then Jesus went with his disciples to a
place called Gethsemane, and he said to them,
"Sit here while I go over there and pray." 37He
took Peter and the two sons of Zebedee along
with him, and he began to be sorrowful and
troubled. 38Then he said to them, "My soul
is overwhelmed with sorrow to the point of
death. Stay here and keep watch with me."
39Going a little farther, he fell with his face
to the ground and prayed, "My Father, if it is
possible, may this cup be taken from me. Yet
not as I will, but as you will."
40Then he returned to his disciples and
found them sleeping. "Couldn't you men keep
watch with me for one hour?" he asked Peter.
41"Watch and pray so that you will not fall
into temptation. The spirit is willing, but the
flesh is weak."
42He went away a second time and prayed,
"My Father, if it is not possible for this cup
to be taken away unless I drink it, may your
will be done."
43When he came back, he again found them
sleeping, because their eyes were heavy. 44So
he left them and went away once more and
prayed the third time, saying the same thing.
45Then he returned to the disciples and said
to them, "Are you still sleeping and resting?
Look, the hour has come, and the Son of Man
is delivered into the hands of sinners. 46Rise!
Let us go! Here comes my betrayer!"

Jesus Arrested

47While he was still speaking, Judas, one
of the Twelve, arrived. With him was a large
crowd armed with swords and clubs, sent
from the chief priests and the elders of the
people. 48Now the betrayer had arranged a
signal with them: "The one I kiss is the man;
arrest him." 49Going at once to Jesus, Judas
said, "Greetings, Rabbi!" and kissed him.
50Jesus replied, "Do what you came for,
friend."[a]
Then the men stepped forward, seized Jesus
and arrested him. 51With that, one of Jesus'
companions reached for his sword, drew it
out and struck the servant of the high priest,
cutting off his ear.
52"Put your sword back in its place," Jesus
said to him, "for all who draw the sword will
die by the sword. 53Do you think I cannot call
on my Father, and he will at once put at my
disposal more than twelve legions of angels?
54But how then would the Scriptures be fulfilled that say it must happen in this way?"
55In that hour Jesus said to the crowd, "Am I
leading a rebellion, that you have come out
with swords and clubs to capture me? Every
day I sat in the temple courts teaching, and
you did not arrest me. 56But this has all taken
place that the writings of the prophets might
be fulfilled." Then all the disciples deserted
him and fled.

Jesus Before the Sanhedrin

57Those who had arrested Jesus took him
to Caiaphas the high priest, where the teachers of the law and the elders had assembled.
58But Peter followed him at a distance, right
up to the courtyard of the high priest. He entered and sat down with the guards to see
the outcome.
59The chief priests and the whole Sanhedrin
were looking for false evidence against Jesus
so that they could put him to death. 60But they
did not find any, though many false witnesses
came forward.
Finally two came forward 61and declared,
"This fellow said, 'I am able to destroy the
temple of God and rebuild it in three days.'"
62Then the high priest stood up and said to
Jesus, "Are you not going to answer? What
is this testimony that these men are bringing against you?" 63But Jesus remained silent.
The high priest said to him, "I charge you
under oath by the living God: Tell us if you
are the Messiah, the Son of God."
64"You have said so," Jesus replied. "But I
say to all of you: From now on you will see
the Son of Man sitting at the right hand of
the Mighty One and coming on the clouds
of heaven."[b]
65Then the high priest tore his clothes and
said, "He has spoken blasphemy! Why do we
need any more witnesses? Look, now you
have heard the blasphemy. 66What do you
think?"
"He is worthy of death," they answered.
67Then they spit in his face and struck him
with their fists. Others slapped him 68and said,
"Prophesy to us, Messiah. Who hit you?"

Peter Disowns Jesus

69Now Peter was sitting out in the courtyard, and a servant girl came to him. "You
also were with Jesus of Galilee," she said.
70But he denied it before them all. "I don't
know what you're talking about," he said.
71Then he went out to the gateway, where
another servant girl saw him and said to the
people there, "This fellow was with Jesus of
Nazareth."
72He denied it again, with an oath: "I don't
know the man!"
73After a little while, those standing there
went up to Peter and said, "Surely you are one
of them; your accent gives you away."
74Then he began to call down curses, and
he swore to them, "I don't know the man!"
Immediately a rooster crowed. 75Then Peter remembered the word Jesus had spoken:
"Before the rooster crows, you will disown

[a] *50* Or *"Why have you come, friend?"* [b] *64* See Psalm 110:1; Daniel 7:13.

me three times." And he went outside and
wept bitterly.

Judas Hangs Himself

27 Early in the morning, all the chief
priests and the elders of the people
made their plans how to have Jesus executed.
2So they bound him, led him away and handed
him over to Pilate the governor.
3When Judas, who had betrayed him, saw
that Jesus was condemned, he was seized
with remorse and returned the thirty pieces
of silver to the chief priests and the elders.
4"I have sinned," he said, "for I have betrayed
innocent blood."
"What is that to us?" they replied. "That's
your responsibility."
5So Judas threw the money into the temple and left. Then he went away and hanged
himself.
6The chief priests picked up the coins and
said, "It is against the law to put this into the
treasury, since it is blood money." 7So they
decided to use the money to buy the potter's
field as a burial place for foreigners. 8That is
why it has been called the Field of Blood to this
day. 9Then what was spoken by Jeremiah the
prophet was fulfilled: "They took the thirty
pieces of silver, the price set on him by the people of Israel, 10and they used them to buy the
potter's field, as the Lord commanded me."[a]

Jesus Before Pilate

11Meanwhile Jesus stood before the governor, and the governor asked him, "Are you the
king of the Jews?"
"You have said so," Jesus replied.
12When he was accused by the chief priests
and the elders, he gave no answer. 13Then Pilate asked him, "Don't you hear the testimony
they are bringing against you?" 14But Jesus
made no reply, not even to a single charge—to
the great amazement of the governor.
15Now it was the governor's custom at the
festival to release a prisoner chosen by the
crowd. 16At that time they had a well-known
prisoner whose name was Jesus[b] Barabbas.
17So when the crowd had gathered, Pilate
asked them, "Which one do you want me to
release to you: Jesus Barabbas, or Jesus who
is called the Messiah?" 18For he knew it was
out of self-interest that they had handed Jesus
over to him.
19While Pilate was sitting on the judge's
seat, his wife sent him this message: "Don't
have anything to do with that innocent man,
for I have suffered a great deal today in a
dream because of him."
20But the chief priests and the elders persuaded the crowd to ask for Barabbas and to
have Jesus executed.
21"Which of the two do you want me to release to you?" asked the governor.
"Barabbas," they answered.
22"What shall I do, then, with Jesus who is
called the Messiah?" Pilate asked.
They all answered, "Crucify him!"
23"Why? What crime has he committed?"
asked Pilate.
But they shouted all the louder, "Crucify
him!"
24When Pilate saw that he was getting nowhere, but that instead an uproar was starting, he took water and washed his hands in
front of the crowd. "I am innocent of this
man's blood," he said. "It is your responsibility!"
25All the people answered, "His blood is on
us and on our children!"
26Then he released Barabbas to them. But
he had Jesus flogged, and handed him over
to be crucified.

The Soldiers Mock Jesus

27Then the governor's soldiers took Jesus
into the Praetorium and gathered the whole
company of soldiers around him. 28They
stripped him and put a scarlet robe on him,
29and then twisted together a crown of thorns
and set it on his head. They put a staff in his
right hand. Then they knelt in front of him
and mocked him. "Hail, king of the Jews!"
they said. 30They spit on him, and took the
staff and struck him on the head again and
again. 31After they had mocked him, they took
off the robe and put his own clothes on him.
Then they led him away to crucify him.

The Crucifixion of Jesus

32As they were going out, they met a man
from Cyrene, named Simon, and they forced
him to carry the cross. 33They came to a place
called Golgotha (which means "the place of
the skull"). 34There they offered Jesus wine to
drink, mixed with gall; but after tasting it, he
refused to drink it. 35When they had crucified
him, they divided up his clothes by casting
lots. 36And sitting down, they kept watch over
him there. 37Above his head they placed the
written charge against him: THIS IS JESUS, THE
KING OF THE JEWS.
38Two rebels were crucified with him, one
on his right and one on his left. 39Those who
passed by hurled insults at him, shaking their
heads 40and saying, "You who are going to
destroy the temple and build it in three days,
save yourself! Come down from the cross, if
you are the Son of God!" 41In the same way the
chief priests, the teachers of the law and the
elders mocked him. 42"He saved others," they
said, "but he can't save himself! He's the king
of Israel! Let him come down now from the
cross, and we will believe in him. 43He trusts
in God. Let God rescue him now if he wants
him, for he said, 'I am the Son of God.'" 44In
the same way the rebels who were crucified
with him also heaped insults on him.

The Death of Jesus

45From noon until three in the afternoon
darkness came over all the land. 46About
three in the afternoon Jesus cried out in a loud

[a] *10* See Zech. 11:12,13; Jer. 19:1-13; 32:6-9. [b] *16* Many manuscripts do not have *Jesus*; also in verse 17.

voice, "*Eli, Eli,*[a] *lema sabachthani?*" (which means "My God, my God, why have you forsaken me?").[b]

47 When some of those standing there heard this, they said, "He's calling Elijah."

48 Immediately one of them ran and got a sponge. He filled it with wine vinegar, put it on a staff, and offered it to Jesus to drink. 49 The rest said, "Now leave him alone. Let's see if Elijah comes to save him."

50 And when Jesus had cried out again in a loud voice, he gave up his spirit.

51 At that moment the curtain of the temple was torn in two from top to bottom. The earth shook, the rocks split 52 and the tombs broke open. The bodies of many holy people who had died were raised to life. 53 They came out of the tombs after Jesus' resurrection and[c] went into the holy city and appeared to many people.

54 When the centurion and those with him who were guarding Jesus saw the earthquake and all that had happened, they were terrified, and exclaimed, "Surely he was the Son of God!"

55 Many women were there, watching from a distance. They had followed Jesus from Galilee to care for his needs. 56 Among them were Mary Magdalene, Mary the mother of James and Joseph,[d] and the mother of Zebedee's sons.

The Burial of Jesus

57 As evening approached, there came a rich man from Arimathea, named Joseph, who had himself become a disciple of Jesus. 58 Going to Pilate, he asked for Jesus' body, and Pilate ordered that it be given to him. 59 Joseph took the body, wrapped it in a clean linen cloth, 60 and placed it in his own new tomb that he had cut out of the rock. He rolled a big stone in front of the entrance to the tomb and went away. 61 Mary Magdalene and the other Mary were sitting there opposite the tomb.

The Guard at the Tomb

62 The next day, the one after Preparation Day, the chief priests and the Pharisees went to Pilate. 63 "Sir," they said, "we remember that while he was still alive that deceiver said, 'After three days I will rise again.' 64 So give the order for the tomb to be made secure until the third day. Otherwise, his disciples may come and steal the body and tell the people that he has been raised from the dead. This last deception will be worse than the first."

65 "Take a guard," Pilate answered. "Go, make the tomb as secure as you know how." 66 So they went and made the tomb secure by putting a seal on the stone and posting the guard.

Jesus Has Risen

28 After the Sabbath, at dawn on the first day of the week, Mary Magdalene and the other Mary went to look at the tomb.

2 There was a violent earthquake, for an angel of the Lord came down from heaven and, going to the tomb, rolled back the stone and sat on it. 3 His appearance was like lightning, and his clothes were white as snow. 4 The guards were so afraid of him that they shook and became like dead men.

5 The angel said to the women, "Do not be afraid, for I know that you are looking for Jesus, who was crucified. 6 He is not here; he has risen, just as he said. Come and see the place where he lay. 7 Then go quickly and tell his disciples: 'He has risen from the dead and is going ahead of you into Galilee. There you will see him.' Now I have told you."

8 So the women hurried away from the tomb, afraid yet filled with joy, and ran to tell his disciples. 9 Suddenly Jesus met them. "Greetings," he said. They came to him, clasped his feet and worshiped him. 10 Then Jesus said to them, "Do not be afraid. Go and tell my brothers to go to Galilee; there they will see me."

The Guards' Report

11 While the women were on their way, some of the guards went into the city and reported to the chief priests everything that had happened. 12 When the chief priests had met with the elders and devised a plan, they gave the soldiers a large sum of money, 13 telling them, "You are to say, 'His disciples came during the night and stole him away while we were asleep.' 14 If this report gets to the governor, we will satisfy him and keep you out of trouble." 15 So the soldiers took the money and did as they were instructed. And this story has been widely circulated among the Jews to this very day.

The Great Commission

16 Then the eleven disciples went to Galilee, to the mountain where Jesus had told them to go. 17 When they saw him, they worshiped him; but some doubted. 18 Then Jesus came to them and said, "All authority in heaven and on earth has been given to me. 19 Therefore go and make disciples of all nations, baptizing them in the name of the Father and of the Son and of the Holy Spirit, 20 and teaching them to obey everything I have commanded you. And surely I am with you always, to the very end of the age."

[a] *46* Some manuscripts *Eloi, Eloi* [b] *46* Psalm 22:1 [c] *53* Or *tombs, and after Jesus' resurrection they* [d] *56* Greek *Joses,* a variant of *Joseph*

Mark

John the Baptist Prepares the Way

1 The beginning of the good news about Jesus the Messiah,[a] the Son of God,[b] 2as it is written in Isaiah the prophet:

> "I will send my messenger ahead of you,
> who will prepare your way"[c]—
> 3"a voice of one calling in the wilderness,
> 'Prepare the way for the Lord,
> make straight paths for him.'"[d]

4And so John the Baptist appeared in the wilderness, preaching a baptism of repentance for the forgiveness of sins. 5The whole Judean countryside and all the people of Jerusalem went out to him. Confessing their sins, they were baptized by him in the Jordan River. 6John wore clothing made of camel's hair, with a leather belt around his waist, and he ate locusts and wild honey. 7And this was his message: "After me comes the one more powerful than I, the straps of whose sandals I am not worthy to stoop down and untie. 8I baptize you with[e] water, but he will baptize you with[e] the Holy Spirit."

The Baptism and Testing of Jesus

9At that time Jesus came from Nazareth in Galilee and was baptized by John in the Jordan. 10Just as Jesus was coming up out of the water, he saw heaven being torn open and the Spirit descending on him like a dove. 11And a voice came from heaven: "You are my Son, whom I love; with you I am well pleased."

12At once the Spirit sent him out into the wilderness, 13and he was in the wilderness forty days, being tempted[f] by Satan. He was with the wild animals, and angels attended him.

Jesus Announces the Good News

14After John was put in prison, Jesus went into Galilee, proclaiming the good news of God. 15"The time has come," he said. "The kingdom of God has come near. Repent and believe the good news!"

Jesus Calls His First Disciples

16As Jesus walked beside the Sea of Galilee, he saw Simon and his brother Andrew casting a net into the lake, for they were fishermen. 17"Come, follow me," Jesus said, "and I will send you out to fish for people." 18At once they left their nets and followed him.

19When he had gone a little farther, he saw James son of Zebedee and his brother John in a boat, preparing their nets. 20Without delay he called them, and they left their father Zebedee in the boat with the hired men and followed him.

Jesus Drives Out an Impure Spirit

21They went to Capernaum, and when the Sabbath came, Jesus went into the synagogue and began to teach. 22The people were amazed at his teaching, because he taught them as one who had authority, not as the teachers of the law. 23Just then a man in their synagogue who was possessed by an impure spirit cried out, 24"What do you want with us, Jesus of Nazareth? Have you come to destroy us? I know who you are—the Holy One of God!"

25"Be quiet!" said Jesus sternly. "Come out of him!" 26The impure spirit shook the man violently and came out of him with a shriek.

27The people were all so amazed that they asked each other, "What is this? A new teaching—and with authority! He even gives orders to impure spirits and they obey him." 28News about him spread quickly over the whole region of Galilee.

Jesus Heals Many

29As soon as they left the synagogue, they went with James and John to the home of Simon and Andrew. 30Simon's mother-in-law was in bed with a fever, and they immediately told Jesus about her. 31So he went to her, took her hand and helped her up. The fever left her and she began to wait on them.

32That evening after sunset the people brought to Jesus all the sick and demon-possessed. 33The whole town gathered at the door, 34and Jesus healed many who had various diseases. He also drove out many demons, but he would not let the demons speak because they knew who he was.

Jesus Prays in a Solitary Place

35Very early in the morning, while it was still dark, Jesus got up, left the house and went off to a solitary place, where he prayed. 36Simon and his companions went to look for him, 37and when they found him, they exclaimed: "Everyone is looking for you!"

38Jesus replied, "Let us go somewhere else—to the nearby villages—so I can preach there also. That is why I have come." 39So he traveled throughout Galilee, preaching in their synagogues and driving out demons.

Jesus Heals a Man With Leprosy

40A man with leprosy[g] came to him and begged him on his knees, "If you are willing, you can make me clean."

[a] 1 Or *Jesus Christ. Messiah* (Hebrew) and *Christ* (Greek) both mean *Anointed One*. [b] 1 Some manuscripts do not have *the Son of God*. [c] 2 Mal. 3:1 [d] 3 Isaiah 40:3 [e] 8 Or *in* [f] 13 The Greek for *tempted* can also mean *tested*. [g] 40 The Greek word traditionally translated *leprosy* was used for various diseases affecting the skin.

41 Jesus was indignant.[a] He reached out his hand and touched the man. "I am willing," he said. "Be clean!" 42 Immediately the leprosy left him and he was cleansed.

43 Jesus sent him away at once with a strong warning: 44 "See that you don't tell this to anyone. But go, show yourself to the priest and offer the sacrifices that Moses commanded for your cleansing, as a testimony to them." 45 Instead he went out and began to talk freely, spreading the news. As a result, Jesus could no longer enter a town openly but stayed outside in lonely places. Yet the people still came to him from everywhere.

Jesus Forgives and Heals a Paralyzed Man

2 A few days later, when Jesus again entered Capernaum, the people heard that he had come home. 2 They gathered in such large numbers that there was no room left, not even outside the door, and he preached the word to them. 3 Some men came, bringing to him a paralyzed man, carried by four of them. 4 Since they could not get him to Jesus because of the crowd, they made an opening in the roof above Jesus by digging through it and then lowered the mat the man was lying on. 5 When Jesus saw their faith, he said to the paralyzed man, "Son, your sins are forgiven."

6 Now some teachers of the law were sitting there, thinking to themselves, 7 "Why does this fellow talk like that? He's blaspheming! Who can forgive sins but God alone?"

8 Immediately Jesus knew in his spirit that this was what they were thinking in their hearts, and he said to them, "Why are you thinking these things? 9 Which is easier: to say to this paralyzed man, 'Your sins are forgiven,' or to say, 'Get up, take your mat and walk'? 10 But I want you to know that the Son of Man has authority on earth to forgive sins." So he said to the man, 11 "I tell you, get up, take your mat and go home." 12 He got up, took his mat and walked out in full view of them all. This amazed everyone and they praised God, saying, "We have never seen anything like this!"

Jesus Calls Levi and Eats With Sinners

13 Once again Jesus went out beside the lake. A large crowd came to him, and he began to teach them. 14 As he walked along, he saw Levi son of Alphaeus sitting at the tax collector's booth. "Follow me," Jesus told him, and Levi got up and followed him.

15 While Jesus was having dinner at Levi's house, many tax collectors and sinners were eating with him and his disciples, for there were many who followed him. 16 When the teachers of the law who were Pharisees saw him eating with the sinners and tax collectors, they asked his disciples: "Why does he eat with tax collectors and sinners?"

17 On hearing this, Jesus said to them, "It is not the healthy who need a doctor, but the sick. I have not come to call the righteous, but sinners."

Jesus Questioned About Fasting

18 Now John's disciples and the Pharisees were fasting. Some people came and asked Jesus, "How is it that John's disciples and the disciples of the Pharisees are fasting, but yours are not?"

19 Jesus answered, "How can the guests of the bridegroom fast while he is with them? They cannot, so long as they have him with them. 20 But the time will come when the bridegroom will be taken from them, and on that day they will fast.

21 "No one sews a patch of unshrunk cloth on an old garment. Otherwise, the new piece will pull away from the old, making the tear worse. 22 And no one pours new wine into old wineskins. Otherwise, the wine will burst the skins, and both the wine and the wineskins will be ruined. No, they pour new wine into new wineskins."

Jesus Is Lord of the Sabbath

23 One Sabbath Jesus was going through the grainfields, and as his disciples walked along, they began to pick some heads of grain. 24 The Pharisees said to him, "Look, why are they doing what is unlawful on the Sabbath?"

25 He answered, "Have you never read what David did when he and his companions were hungry and in need? 26 In the days of Abiathar the high priest, he entered the house of God and ate the consecrated bread, which is lawful only for priests to eat. And he also gave some to his companions."

27 Then he said to them, "The Sabbath was made for man, not man for the Sabbath. 28 So the Son of Man is Lord even of the Sabbath."

Jesus Heals on the Sabbath

3 Another time Jesus went into the synagogue, and a man with a shriveled hand was there. 2 Some of them were looking for a reason to accuse Jesus, so they watched him closely to see if he would heal him on the Sabbath. 3 Jesus said to the man with the shriveled hand, "Stand up in front of everyone."

4 Then Jesus asked them, "Which is lawful on the Sabbath: to do good or to do evil, to save life or to kill?" But they remained silent.

5 He looked around at them in anger and, deeply distressed at their stubborn hearts, said to the man, "Stretch out your hand." He stretched it out, and his hand was completely restored. 6 Then the Pharisees went out and began to plot with the Herodians how they might kill Jesus.

Crowds Follow Jesus

7 Jesus withdrew with his disciples to the lake, and a large crowd from Galilee followed. 8 When they heard about all he was doing, many people came to him from Judea, Jerusalem, Idumea, and the regions across the

[a] 41 Many manuscripts *Jesus was filled with compassion*

Jordan and around Tyre and Sidon. 9Because
of the crowd he told his disciples to have a
small boat ready for him, to keep the people
from crowding him. 10For he had healed many,
so that those with diseases were pushing forward to touch him. 11Whenever the impure
spirits saw him, they fell down before him
and cried out, "You are the Son of God." 12But
he gave them strict orders not to tell others
about him.

Jesus Appoints the Twelve

13Jesus went up on a mountainside and
called to him those he wanted, and they came
to him. 14He appointed twelve[a] that they might
be with him and that he might send them out
to preach 15and to have authority to drive out
demons. 16These are the twelve he appointed: Simon (to whom he gave the name Peter),
17James son of Zebedee and his brother John
(to them he gave the name Boanerges, which
means "sons of thunder"), 18Andrew, Philip,
Bartholomew, Matthew, Thomas, James son
of Alphaeus, Thaddaeus, Simon the Zealot
19and Judas Iscariot, who betrayed him.

Jesus Accused by His Family and by Teachers of the Law

20Then Jesus entered a house, and again a
crowd gathered, so that he and his disciples
were not even able to eat. 21When his family[b]
heard about this, they went to take charge
of him, for they said, "He is out of his mind."
22And the teachers of the law who came
down from Jerusalem said, "He is possessed
by Beelzebul! By the prince of demons he is
driving out demons."
23So Jesus called them over to him and
began to speak to them in parables: "How
can Satan drive out Satan? 24If a kingdom is
divided against itself, that kingdom cannot
stand. 25If a house is divided against itself,
that house cannot stand. 26And if Satan opposes himself and is divided, he cannot stand;
his end has come. 27In fact, no one can enter a
strong man's house without first tying him up.
Then he can plunder the strong man's house.
28Truly I tell you, people can be forgiven all
their sins and every slander they utter, 29but
whoever blasphemes against the Holy Spirit
will never be forgiven; they are guilty of an
eternal sin."
30He said this because they were saying,
"He has an impure spirit."
31Then Jesus' mother and brothers arrived.
Standing outside, they sent someone in to call
him. 32A crowd was sitting around him, and
they told him, "Your mother and brothers are
outside looking for you."
33"Who are my mother and my brothers?"
he asked.
34Then he looked at those seated in a circle
around him and said, "Here are my mother
and my brothers! 35Whoever does God's will
is my brother and sister and mother."

The Parable of the Sower

4 Again Jesus began to teach by the lake.
The crowd that gathered around him was
so large that he got into a boat and sat in it out
on the lake, while all the people were along
the shore at the water's edge. 2He taught them
many things by parables, and in his teaching
said: 3"Listen! A farmer went out to sow his
seed. 4As he was scattering the seed, some
fell along the path, and the birds came and
ate it up. 5Some fell on rocky places, where
it did not have much soil. It sprang up quickly, because the soil was shallow. 6But when
the sun came up, the plants were scorched,
and they withered because they had no root.
7Other seed fell among thorns, which grew
up and choked the plants, so that they did
not bear grain. 8Still other seed fell on good
soil. It came up, grew and produced a crop,
some multiplying thirty, some sixty, some a
hundred times."
9Then Jesus said, "Whoever has ears to
hear, let them hear."
10When he was alone, the Twelve and the
others around him asked him about the parables. 11He told them, "The secret of the kingdom of God has been given to you. But to those
on the outside everything is said in parables
12so that,

"'they may be ever seeing but never
perceiving,
and ever hearing but never
understanding;
otherwise they might turn and be
forgiven!'[c]"

13Then Jesus said to them, "Don't you understand this parable? How then will you understand any parable? 14The farmer sows the
word. 15Some people are like seed along the
path, where the word is sown. As soon as they
hear it, Satan comes and takes away the word
that was sown in them. 16Others, like seed
sown on rocky places, hear the word and at
once receive it with joy. 17But since they have
no root, they last only a short time. When trouble or persecution comes because of the word,
they quickly fall away. 18Still others, like seed
sown among thorns, hear the word; 19but the
worries of this life, the deceitfulness of wealth
and the desires for other things come in and
choke the word, making it unfruitful. 20Oth-
ers, like seed sown on good soil, hear the
word, accept it, and produce a crop—some
thirty, some sixty, some a hundred times what
was sown."

A Lamp on a Stand

21He said to them, "Do you bring in a lamp
to put it under a bowl or a bed? Instead, don't
you put it on its stand? 22For whatever is hidden is meant to be disclosed, and whatever is
concealed is meant to be brought out into the
open. 23If anyone has ears to hear, let them
hear."
24"Consider carefully what you hear," he

[a] *14* Some manuscripts *twelve—designating them apostles—* [b] *21* Or *his associates* [c] *12* Isaiah 6:9,10

continued. "With the measure you use, it will
be measured to you—and even more. 25Who-
ever has will be given more; whoever does
not have, even what they have will be taken
from them."

The Parable of the Growing Seed

26He also said, "This is what the kingdom
of God is like. A man scatters seed on the
ground. 27Night and day, whether he sleeps or
gets up, the seed sprouts and grows, though
he does not know how. 28All by itself the soil
produces grain—first the stalk, then the head,
then the full kernel in the head. 29As soon as
the grain is ripe, he puts the sickle to it, because the harvest has come."

The Parable of the Mustard Seed

30Again he said, "What shall we say the
kingdom of God is like, or what parable shall
we use to describe it? 31It is like a mustard
seed, which is the smallest of all seeds on
earth. 32Yet when planted, it grows and becomes the largest of all garden plants, with
such big branches that the birds can perch
in its shade."

33With many similar parables Jesus spoke
the word to them, as much as they could understand. 34He did not say anything to them
without using a parable. But when he was
alone with his own disciples, he explained
everything.

Jesus Calms the Storm

35That day when evening came, he said to
his disciples, "Let us go over to the other side."
36Leaving the crowd behind, they took him
along, just as he was, in the boat. There were
also other boats with him. 37A furious squall
came up, and the waves broke over the boat,
so that it was nearly swamped. 38Jesus was in
the stern, sleeping on a cushion. The disciples
woke him and said to him, "Teacher, don't you
care if we drown?"

39He got up, rebuked the wind and said to
the waves, "Quiet! Be still!" Then the wind
died down and it was completely calm.

40He said to his disciples, "Why are you so
afraid? Do you still have no faith?"

41They were terrified and asked each other,
"Who is this? Even the wind and the waves
obey him!"

Jesus Restores a Demon-Possessed Man

5 They went across the lake to the region of
the Gerasenes.[a] 2When Jesus got out of the
boat, a man with an impure spirit came from
the tombs to meet him. 3This man lived in the
tombs, and no one could bind him anymore,
not even with a chain. 4For he had often been
chained hand and foot, but he tore the chains
apart and broke the irons on his feet. No one
was strong enough to subdue him. 5Night and
day among the tombs and in the hills he would
cry out and cut himself with stones.

6When he saw Jesus from a distance, he
ran and fell on his knees in front of him. 7He
shouted at the top of his voice, "What do you
want with me, Jesus, Son of the Most High
God? In God's name don't torture me!" 8For
Jesus had said to him, "Come out of this man,
you impure spirit!"

9Then Jesus asked him, "What is your
name?"

"My name is Legion," he replied, "for we
are many." 10And he begged Jesus again and
again not to send them out of the area.

11A large herd of pigs was feeding on the
nearby hillside. 12The demons begged Jesus,
"Send us among the pigs; allow us to go into
them." 13He gave them permission, and the
impure spirits came out and went into the
pigs. The herd, about two thousand in number, rushed down the steep bank into the lake
and were drowned.

14Those tending the pigs ran off and reported this in the town and countryside, and the
people went out to see what had happened.
15When they came to Jesus, they saw the man
who had been possessed by the legion of demons, sitting there, dressed and in his right
mind; and they were afraid. 16Those who had
seen it told the people what had happened to
the demon-possessed man—and told about
the pigs as well. 17Then the people began to
plead with Jesus to leave their region.

18As Jesus was getting into the boat, the
man who had been demon-possessed begged
to go with him. 19Jesus did not let him, but
said, "Go home to your own people and tell
them how much the Lord has done for you,
and how he has had mercy on you." 20So the
man went away and began to tell in the Decapolis[b] how much Jesus had done for him.
And all the people were amazed.

Jesus Raises a Dead Girl and Heals a Sick Woman

21When Jesus had again crossed over by
boat to the other side of the lake, a large crowd
gathered around him while he was by the lake.
22Then one of the synagogue leaders, named
Jairus, came, and when he saw Jesus, he fell at
his feet. 23He pleaded earnestly with him, "My
little daughter is dying. Please come and put
your hands on her so that she will be healed
and live." 24So Jesus went with him.

A large crowd followed and pressed around
him. 25And a woman was there who had been
subject to bleeding for twelve years. 26She had
suffered a great deal under the care of many
doctors and had spent all she had, yet instead
of getting better she grew worse. 27When she
heard about Jesus, she came up behind him
in the crowd and touched his cloak, 28be-
cause she thought, "If I just touch his clothes,
I will be healed." 29Immediately her bleeding
stopped and she felt in her body that she was
freed from her suffering.

30At once Jesus realized that power had
gone out from him. He turned around in the
crowd and asked, "Who touched my clothes?"

31"You see the people crowding against

[a] *1* Some manuscripts *Gadarenes*; other manuscripts *Gergesenes* [b] *20* That is, the Ten Cities

you," his disciples answered, "and yet you
can ask, 'Who touched me?' "
32But Jesus kept looking around to see who
had done it. 33Then the woman, knowing what
had happened to her, came and fell at his feet
and, trembling with fear, told him the whole
truth. 34He said to her, "Daughter, your faith
has healed you. Go in peace and be freed from
your suffering."
35While Jesus was still speaking, some people came from the house of Jairus, the synagogue leader. "Your daughter is dead," they
said. "Why bother the teacher anymore?"
36Overhearing[a] what they said, Jesus told
him, "Don't be afraid; just believe."
37He did not let anyone follow him except
Peter, James and John the brother of James.
38When they came to the home of the synagogue leader, Jesus saw a commotion, with
people crying and wailing loudly. 39He went
in and said to them, "Why all this commotion
and wailing? The child is not dead but asleep."
40But they laughed at him.
After he put them all out, he took the child's
father and mother and the disciples who were
with him, and went in where the child was.
41He took her by the hand and said to her,
"*Talitha koum!*" (which means "Little girl, I
say to you, get up!"). 42Immediately the girl
stood up and began to walk around (she was
twelve years old). At this they were completely
astonished. 43He gave strict orders not to let
anyone know about this, and told them to give
her something to eat.

A Prophet Without Honor

6 Jesus left there and went to his hometown,
accompanied by his disciples. 2When
the Sabbath came, he began to teach in the
synagogue, and many who heard him were
amazed.
"Where did this man get these things?" they
asked. "What's this wisdom that has been giv-
en him? What are these remarkable miracles
he is performing? 3Isn't this the carpenter?
Isn't this Mary's son and the brother of James,
Joseph,[b] Judas and Simon? Aren't his sisters
here with us?" And they took offense at him.
4Jesus said to them, "A prophet is not without honor except in his own town, among his
relatives and in his own home." 5He could not
do any miracles there, except lay his hands
on a few sick people and heal them. 6He was
amazed at their lack of faith.

Jesus Sends Out the Twelve

Then Jesus went around teaching from village to village. 7Calling the Twelve to him, he
began to send them out two by two and gave
them authority over impure spirits.
8These were his instructions: "Take nothing
for the journey except a staff—no bread, no
bag, no money in your belts. 9Wear sandals
but not an extra shirt. 10Whenever you enter
a house, stay there until you leave that town.
11And if any place will not welcome you or listen to you, leave that place and shake the dust
off your feet as a testimony against them."
12They went out and preached that people
should repent. 13They drove out many demons
and anointed many sick people with oil and
healed them.

John the Baptist Beheaded

14King Herod heard about this, for Jesus'
name had become well known. Some were
saying,[c] "John the Baptist has been raised
from the dead, and that is why miraculous
powers are at work in him."
15Others said, "He is Elijah."
And still others claimed, "He is a prophet,
like one of the prophets of long ago."
16But when Herod heard this, he said, "John,
whom I beheaded, has been raised from the
dead!"
17For Herod himself had given orders to
have John arrested, and he had him bound
and put in prison. He did this because of Herodias, his brother Philip's wife, whom he had
married. 18For John had been saying to Herod,
"It is not lawful for you to have your brother's
wife." 19So Herodias nursed a grudge against
John and wanted to kill him. But she was not
able to, 20because Herod feared John and protected him, knowing him to be a righteous and
holy man. When Herod heard John, he was
greatly puzzled[d]; yet he liked to listen to him.
21Finally the opportune time came. On his
birthday Herod gave a banquet for his high
officials and military commanders and the
leading men of Galilee. 22When the daughter
of[e] Herodias came in and danced, she pleased
Herod and his dinner guests.
The king said to the girl, "Ask me for anything you want, and I'll give it to you." 23And
he promised her with an oath, "Whatever you
ask I will give you, up to half my kingdom."
24She went out and said to her mother,
"What shall I ask for?"
"The head of John the Baptist," she answered.
25At once the girl hurried in to the king with
the request: "I want you to give me right now
the head of John the Baptist on a platter."
26The king was greatly distressed, but because of his oaths and his dinner guests, he
did not want to refuse her. 27So he immediately sent an executioner with orders to bring
John's head. The man went, beheaded John
in the prison, 28and brought back his head on
a platter. He presented it to the girl, and she
gave it to her mother. 29On hearing of this,
John's disciples came and took his body and
laid it in a tomb.

Jesus Feeds the Five Thousand

30The apostles gathered around Jesus and
reported to him all they had done and taught.
31Then, because so many people were coming
and going that they did not even have a chance
to eat, he said to them, "Come with me by
yourselves to a quiet place and get some rest."

[a] *36* Or *Ignoring* [b] *3* Greek *Joses,* a variant of *Joseph* [c] *14* Some early manuscripts *He was saying*
[d] *20* Some early manuscripts *he did many things* [e] *22* Some early manuscripts *When his daughter*

32So they went away by themselves in a boat
to a solitary place. 33But many who saw them
leaving recognized them and ran on foot from
all the towns and got there ahead of them.
34When Jesus landed and saw a large crowd,
he had compassion on them, because they
were like sheep without a shepherd. So he
began teaching them many things.
35By this time it was late in the day, so
his disciples came to him. "This is a remote
place," they said, "and it's already very late.
36Send the people away so that they can go to
the surrounding countryside and villages and
buy themselves something to eat."
37But he answered, "You give them something to eat."
They said to him, "That would take more
than half a year's wages[a]! Are we to go and
spend that much on bread and give it to them
to eat?"
38"How many loaves do you have?" he
asked. "Go and see."
When they found out, they said, "Five—and
two fish."
39Then Jesus directed them to have all the
people sit down in groups on the green grass.
40So they sat down in groups of hundreds and
fifties. 41Taking the five loaves and the two
fish and looking up to heaven, he gave thanks
and broke the loaves. Then he gave them to his
disciples to distribute to the people. He also
divided the two fish among them all. 42They
all ate and were satisfied, 43and the disciples
picked up twelve basketfuls of broken pieces
of bread and fish. 44The number of the men
who had eaten was five thousand.

Jesus Walks on the Water

45Immediately Jesus made his disciples get
into the boat and go on ahead of him to Bethsaida,
while he dismissed the crowd. 46After
leaving them, he went up on a mountainside
to pray.
47Later that night, the boat was in the middle
of the lake, and he was alone on land.
48He saw the disciples straining at the oars,
because the wind was against them. Shortly
before dawn he went out to them, walking
on the lake. He was about to pass by them,
49but when they saw him walking on the lake,
they thought he was a ghost. They cried out,
50because they all saw him and were terrified.
Immediately he spoke to them and said,
"Take courage! It is I. Don't be afraid." 51Then
he climbed into the boat with them, and the
wind died down. They were completely
amazed, 52for they had not understood about
the loaves; their hearts were hardened.
53When they had crossed over, they landed
at Gennesaret and anchored there. 54As soon
as they got out of the boat, people recognized
Jesus. 55They ran throughout that whole region
and carried the sick on mats to wherever
they heard he was. 56And wherever he
went—into villages, towns or countryside—
they placed the sick in the marketplaces. They
begged him to let them touch even the edge of
his cloak, and all who touched it were healed.

That Which Defiles

7 The Pharisees and some of the teachers
of the law who had come from Jerusalem
gathered around Jesus 2and saw some of his
disciples eating food with hands that were
defiled, that is, unwashed. 3(The Pharisees
and all the Jews do not eat unless they give
their hands a ceremonial washing, holding to
the tradition of the elders. 4When they come
from the marketplace they do not eat unless
they wash. And they observe many other traditions,
such as the washing of cups, pitchers
and kettles.[b])
5So the Pharisees and teachers of the law
asked Jesus, "Why don't your disciples live
according to the tradition of the elders instead
of eating their food with defiled hands?"
6He replied, "Isaiah was right when he
prophesied about you hypocrites; as it is
written:

> "'These people honor me with their lips,
> but their hearts are far from me.
> 7They worship me in vain;
> their teachings are merely human rules.'[c]

8You have let go of the commands of God and
are holding on to human traditions."
9And he continued, "You have a fine way of
setting aside the commands of God in order
to observe[d] your own traditions! 10For Moses
said, 'Honor your father and mother,'[e] and,
'Anyone who curses their father or mother is
to be put to death.'[f] 11But you say that if anyone
declares that what might have been used
to help their father or mother is Corban (that
is, devoted to God)— 12then you no longer let
them do anything for their father or mother.
13Thus you nullify the word of God by your
tradition that you have handed down. And
you do many things like that."
14Again Jesus called the crowd to him and
said, "Listen to me, everyone, and understand
this. 15Nothing outside a person can defile
them by going into them. Rather, it is what
comes out of a person that defiles them." [16][g]
17After he had left the crowd and entered
the house, his disciples asked him about this
parable. 18"Are you so dull?" he asked. "Don't
you see that nothing that enters a person from
the outside can defile them? 19For it doesn't
go into their heart but into their stomach, and
then out of the body." (In saying this, Jesus
declared all foods clean.)
20He went on: "What comes out of a person
is what defiles them. 21For it is from within,
out of a person's heart, that evil thoughts
come—sexual immorality, theft, murder,
22adultery, greed, malice, deceit, lewdness,
envy, slander, arrogance and folly. 23All these
evils come from inside and defile a person."

[a] 37 Greek *take two hundred denarii* [b] 4 Some early manuscripts *pitchers, kettles and dining couches* [c] 6,7 Isaiah 29:13 [d] 9 Some manuscripts *set up* [e] 10 Exodus 20:12; Deut. 5:16 [f] 10 Exodus 21:17; Lev. 20:9 [g] 16 Some manuscripts include here the words of 4:23.

Jesus Honors a Syrophoenician Woman's Faith

24 Jesus left that place and went to the vicinity of Tyre.[a] He entered a house and did
not want anyone to know it; yet he could not
keep his presence secret. 25 In fact, as soon as
she heard about him, a woman whose little
daughter was possessed by an impure spirit
came and fell at his feet. 26 The woman was a
Greek, born in Syrian Phoenicia. She begged
Jesus to drive the demon out of her daughter.
27 "First let the children eat all they want,"
he told her, "for it is not right to take the children's bread and toss it to the dogs."
28 "Lord," she replied, "even the dogs under
the table eat the children's crumbs."
29 Then he told her, "For such a reply, you
may go; the demon has left your daughter."
30 She went home and found her child lying
on the bed, and the demon gone.

Jesus Heals a Deaf and Mute Man

31 Then Jesus left the vicinity of Tyre and
went through Sidon, down to the Sea of Galilee and into the region of the Decapolis.[b]
32 There some people brought to him a man
who was deaf and could hardly talk, and they
begged Jesus to place his hand on him.
33 After he took him aside, away from the
crowd, Jesus put his fingers into the man's
ears. Then he spit and touched the man's
tongue. 34 He looked up to heaven and with a
deep sigh said to him, *"Ephphatha!"* (which
means "Be opened!"). 35 At this, the man's ears
were opened, his tongue was loosened and he
began to speak plainly.
36 Jesus commanded them not to tell anyone.
But the more he did so, the more they kept
talking about it. 37 People were overwhelmed
with amazement. "He has done everything
well," they said. "He even makes the deaf hear
and the mute speak."

Jesus Feeds the Four Thousand

8 During those days another large crowd
gathered. Since they had nothing to eat,
Jesus called his disciples to him and said, 2 "I
have compassion for these people; they have
already been with me three days and have
nothing to eat. 3 If I send them home hungry,
they will collapse on the way, because some
of them have come a long distance."
4 His disciples answered, "But where in this
remote place can anyone get enough bread to
feed them?"
5 "How many loaves do you have?" Jesus
asked.
"Seven," they replied.
6 He told the crowd to sit down on the
ground. When he had taken the seven loaves
and given thanks, he broke them and gave
them to his disciples to distribute to the people, and they did so. 7 They had a few small fish
as well; he gave thanks for them also and told
the disciples to distribute them. 8 The people
ate and were satisfied. Afterward the disciples
picked up seven basketfuls of broken pieces
that were left over. 9 About four thousand were
present. After he had sent them away, 10 he got
into the boat with his disciples and went to the
region of Dalmanutha.
11 The Pharisees came and began to question
Jesus. To test him, they asked him for a sign
from heaven. 12 He sighed deeply and said,
"Why does this generation ask for a sign?
Truly I tell you, no sign will be given to it."
13 Then he left them, got back into the boat
and crossed to the other side.

The Yeast of the Pharisees and Herod

14 The disciples had forgotten to bring bread,
except for one loaf they had with them in the
boat. 15 "Be careful," Jesus warned them.
"Watch out for the yeast of the Pharisees and
that of Herod."
16 They discussed this with one another and
said, "It is because we have no bread."
17 Aware of their discussion, Jesus asked
them: "Why are you talking about having no
bread? Do you still not see or understand? Are
your hearts hardened? 18 Do you have eyes but
fail to see, and ears but fail to hear? And don't
you remember? 19 When I broke the five loaves
for the five thousand, how many basketfuls
of pieces did you pick up?"
"Twelve," they replied.
20 "And when I broke the seven loaves for
the four thousand, how many basketfuls of
pieces did you pick up?"
They answered, "Seven."
21 He said to them, "Do you still not understand?"

Jesus Heals a Blind Man at Bethsaida

22 They came to Bethsaida, and some people brought a blind man and begged Jesus
to touch him. 23 He took the blind man by the
hand and led him outside the village. When he
had spit on the man's eyes and put his hands
on him, Jesus asked, "Do you see anything?"
24 He looked up and said, "I see people; they
look like trees walking around."
25 Once more Jesus put his hands on the
man's eyes. Then his eyes were opened, his
sight was restored, and he saw everything
clearly. 26 Jesus sent him home, saying, "Don't
even go into[c] the village."

Peter Declares That Jesus Is the Messiah

27 Jesus and his disciples went on to the villages around Caesarea Philippi. On the way
he asked them, "Who do people say I am?"
28 They replied, "Some say John the Baptist;
others say Elijah; and still others, one of the
prophets."
29 "But what about you?" he asked. "Who
do you say I am?"
Peter answered, "You are the Messiah."
30 Jesus warned them not to tell anyone
about him.

[a] 24 Many early manuscripts *Tyre and Sidon* [b] 31 That is, the Ten Cities [c] 26 Some manuscripts *go and tell anyone in*

Jesus Predicts His Death

31He then began to teach them that the Son of Man must suffer many things and be rejected by the elders, the chief priests and the teachers of the law, and that he must be killed and after three days rise again. 32He spoke plainly about this, and Peter took him aside and began to rebuke him.

33But when Jesus turned and looked at his disciples, he rebuked Peter. "Get behind me, Satan!" he said. "You do not have in mind the concerns of God, but merely human concerns."

The Way of the Cross

34Then he called the crowd to him along with his disciples and said: "Whoever wants to be my disciple must deny themselves and take up their cross and follow me. 35For whoever wants to save their life[a] will lose it, but whoever loses their life for me and for the gospel will save it. 36What good is it for someone to gain the whole world, yet forfeit their soul? 37Or what can anyone give in exchange for their soul? 38If anyone is ashamed of me and my words in this adulterous and sinful generation, the Son of Man will be ashamed of them when he comes in his Father's glory with the holy angels."

9 And he said to them, "Truly I tell you, some who are standing here will not taste death before they see that the kingdom of God has come with power."

The Transfiguration

2After six days Jesus took Peter, James and John with him and led them up a high mountain, where they were all alone. There he was transfigured before them. 3His clothes became dazzling white, whiter than anyone in the world could bleach them. 4And there appeared before them Elijah and Moses, who were talking with Jesus.

5Peter said to Jesus, "Rabbi, it is good for us to be here. Let us put up three shelters—one for you, one for Moses and one for Elijah." 6(He did not know what to say, they were so frightened.)

7Then a cloud appeared and covered them, and a voice came from the cloud: "This is my Son, whom I love. Listen to him!"

8Suddenly, when they looked around, they no longer saw anyone with them except Jesus.

9As they were coming down the mountain, Jesus gave them orders not to tell anyone what they had seen until the Son of Man had risen from the dead. 10They kept the matter to themselves, discussing what "rising from the dead" meant.

11And they asked him, "Why do the teachers of the law say that Elijah must come first?"

12Jesus replied, "To be sure, Elijah does come first, and restores all things. Why then is it written that the Son of Man must suffer much and be rejected? 13But I tell you, Elijah has come, and they have done to him everything they wished, just as it is written about him."

Jesus Heals a Boy Possessed by an Impure Spirit

14When they came to the other disciples, they saw a large crowd around them and the teachers of the law arguing with them. 15As soon as all the people saw Jesus, they were overwhelmed with wonder and ran to greet him.

16"What are you arguing with them about?" he asked.

17A man in the crowd answered, "Teacher, I brought you my son, who is possessed by a spirit that has robbed him of speech. 18Whenever it seizes him, it throws him to the ground. He foams at the mouth, gnashes his teeth and becomes rigid. I asked your disciples to drive out the spirit, but they could not."

19"You unbelieving generation," Jesus replied, "how long shall I stay with you? How long shall I put up with you? Bring the boy to me."

20So they brought him. When the spirit saw Jesus, it immediately threw the boy into a convulsion. He fell to the ground and rolled around, foaming at the mouth.

21Jesus asked the boy's father, "How long has he been like this?"

"From childhood," he answered. 22"It has often thrown him into fire or water to kill him. But if you can do anything, take pity on us and help us."

23" 'If you can'?" said Jesus. "Everything is possible for one who believes."

24Immediately the boy's father exclaimed, "I do believe; help me overcome my unbelief!"

25When Jesus saw that a crowd was running to the scene, he rebuked the impure spirit. "You deaf and mute spirit," he said, "I command you, come out of him and never enter him again."

26The spirit shrieked, convulsed him violently and came out. The boy looked so much like a corpse that many said, "He's dead." 27But Jesus took him by the hand and lifted him to his feet, and he stood up.

28After Jesus had gone indoors, his disciples asked him privately, "Why couldn't we drive it out?"

29He replied, "This kind can come out only by prayer.[b]"

Jesus Predicts His Death a Second Time

30They left that place and passed through Galilee. Jesus did not want anyone to know where they were, 31because he was teaching his disciples. He said to them, "The Son of Man is going to be delivered into the hands of men. They will kill him, and after three days he will rise." 32But they did not understand what he meant and were afraid to ask him about it.

[a] *35* The Greek word means either *life* or *soul*; also in verses 36 and 37. [b] *29* Some manuscripts *prayer and fasting*

33 They came to Capernaum. When he was
in the house, he asked them, "What were you
arguing about on the road?" 34 But they kept
quiet because on the way they had argued
about who was the greatest.
35 Sitting down, Jesus called the Twelve and
said, "Anyone who wants to be first must be
the very last, and the servant of all."
36 He took a little child whom he placed
among them. Taking the child in his arms,
he said to them, 37 "Whoever welcomes one of
these little children in my name welcomes me;
and whoever welcomes me does not welcome
me but the one who sent me."

Whoever Is Not Against Us Is for Us

38 "Teacher," said John, "we saw someone
driving out demons in your name and we told
him to stop, because he was not one of us."
39 "Do not stop him," Jesus said. "For no one
who does a miracle in my name can in the
next moment say anything bad about me, 40 for
whoever is not against us is for us. 41 Truly I tell
you, anyone who gives you a cup of water in
my name because you belong to the Messiah
will certainly not lose their reward.

Causing to Stumble

42 "If anyone causes one of these little ones—
those who believe in me—to stumble, it would
be better for them if a large millstone were
hung around their neck and they were thrown
into the sea. 43 If your hand causes you to stumble, cut it off. It is better for you to enter life
maimed than with two hands to go into hell,
where the fire never goes out. [44][a] 45 And if
your foot causes you to stumble, cut it off.
It is better for you to enter life crippled than
to have two feet and be thrown into hell. [46][a]
47 And if your eye causes you to stumble, pluck
it out. It is better for you to enter the kingdom
of God with one eye than to have two eyes and
be thrown into hell, 48 where

> " 'the worms that eat them do not die,
> and the fire is not quenched.'[b]

49 Everyone will be salted with fire.
50 "Salt is good, but if it loses its saltiness,
how can you make it salty again? Have salt
among yourselves, and be at peace with each
other."

Divorce

10 Jesus then left that place and went into
the region of Judea and across the Jordan. Again crowds of people came to him, and
as was his custom, he taught them.
2 Some Pharisees came and tested him by
asking, "Is it lawful for a man to divorce his
wife?"
3 "What did Moses command you?" he replied.
4 They said, "Moses permitted a man to write
a certificate of divorce and send her away."
5 "It was because your hearts were hard that
Moses wrote you this law," Jesus replied. 6 "But
at the beginning of creation God 'made them
male and female.'[c] 7 'For this reason a man
will leave his father and mother and be united to his wife,[d] 8 and the two will become one
flesh.'[e] So they are no longer two, but one
flesh. 9 Therefore what God has joined together, let no one separate."
10 When they were in the house again, the
disciples asked Jesus about this. 11 He answered, "Anyone who divorces his wife and
marries another woman commits adultery
against her. 12 And if she divorces her husband and marries another man, she commits
adultery."

The Little Children and Jesus

13 People were bringing little children to
Jesus for him to place his hands on them, but
the disciples rebuked them. 14 When Jesus saw
this, he was indignant. He said to them, "Let
the little children come to me, and do not hinder them, for the kingdom of God belongs to
such as these. 15 Truly I tell you, anyone who
will not receive the kingdom of God like a
little child will never enter it." 16 And he took
the children in his arms, placed his hands on
them and blessed them.

The Rich and the Kingdom of God

17 As Jesus started on his way, a man ran
up to him and fell on his knees before him.
"Good teacher," he asked, "what must I do to
inherit eternal life?"
18 "Why do you call me good?" Jesus answered. "No one is good—except God alone.
19 You know the commandments: 'You shall
not murder, you shall not commit adultery,
you shall not steal, you shall not give false
testimony, you shall not defraud, honor your
father and mother.'[f]"
20 "Teacher," he declared, "all these I have
kept since I was a boy."
21 Jesus looked at him and loved him. "One
thing you lack," he said. "Go, sell everything
you have and give to the poor, and you will
have treasure in heaven. Then come, follow me."
22 At this the man's face fell. He went away
sad, because he had great wealth.
23 Jesus looked around and said to his disciples, "How hard it is for the rich to enter the
kingdom of God!"
24 The disciples were amazed at his words.
But Jesus said again, "Children, how hard it
is[g] to enter the kingdom of God! 25 It is easier
for a camel to go through the eye of a needle than for someone who is rich to enter the
kingdom of God."
26 The disciples were even more amazed,
and said to each other, "Who then can be
saved?"
27 Jesus looked at them and said, "With man

[a] *44,46* Some manuscripts include here the words of verse 48. [b] *48* Isaiah 66:24 [c] *6* Gen. 1:27
[d] *7* Some early manuscripts do not have *and be united to his wife.* [e] *8* Gen. 2:24 [f] *19* Exodus
20:12-16; Deut. 5:16-20 [g] *24* Some manuscripts *is for those who trust in riches*

this is impossible, but not with God; all things are possible with God."

28 Then Peter spoke up, "We have left everything to follow you!"

29 "Truly I tell you," Jesus replied, "no one who has left home or brothers or sisters or mother or father or children or fields for me and the gospel 30 will fail to receive a hundred times as much in this present age: homes, brothers, sisters, mothers, children and fields—along with persecutions—and in the age to come eternal life. 31 But many who are first will be last, and the last first."

Jesus Predicts His Death a Third Time

32 They were on their way up to Jerusalem, with Jesus leading the way, and the disciples were astonished, while those who followed were afraid. Again he took the Twelve aside and told them what was going to happen to him. 33 "We are going up to Jerusalem," he said, "and the Son of Man will be delivered over to the chief priests and the teachers of the law. They will condemn him to death and will hand him over to the Gentiles, 34 who will mock him and spit on him, flog him and kill him. Three days later he will rise."

The Request of James and John

35 Then James and John, the sons of Zebedee, came to him. "Teacher," they said, "we want you to do for us whatever we ask."

36 "What do you want me to do for you?" he asked.

37 They replied, "Let one of us sit at your right and the other at your left in your glory."

38 "You don't know what you are asking," Jesus said. "Can you drink the cup I drink or be baptized with the baptism I am baptized with?"

39 "We can," they answered.

Jesus said to them, "You will drink the cup I drink and be baptized with the baptism I am baptized with, 40 but to sit at my right or left is not for me to grant. These places belong to those for whom they have been prepared."

41 When the ten heard about this, they became indignant with James and John. 42 Jesus called them together and said, "You know that those who are regarded as rulers of the Gentiles lord it over them, and their high officials exercise authority over them. 43 Not so with you. Instead, whoever wants to become great among you must be your servant, 44 and whoever wants to be first must be slave of all. 45 For even the Son of Man did not come to be served, but to serve, and to give his life as a ransom for many."

Blind Bartimaeus Receives His Sight

46 Then they came to Jericho. As Jesus and his disciples, together with a large crowd, were leaving the city, a blind man, Bartimaeus (which means "son of Timaeus"), was sitting by the roadside begging. 47 When he heard that it was Jesus of Nazareth, he began to shout, "Jesus, Son of David, have mercy on me!"

48 Many rebuked him and told him to be quiet, but he shouted all the more, "Son of David, have mercy on me!"

49 Jesus stopped and said, "Call him."

So they called to the blind man, "Cheer up! On your feet! He's calling you." 50 Throwing his cloak aside, he jumped to his feet and came to Jesus.

51 "What do you want me to do for you?" Jesus asked him.

The blind man said, "Rabbi, I want to see."

52 "Go," said Jesus, "your faith has healed you." Immediately he received his sight and followed Jesus along the road.

Jesus Comes to Jerusalem as King

11 As they approached Jerusalem and came to Bethphage and Bethany at the Mount of Olives, Jesus sent two of his disciples, 2 saying to them, "Go to the village ahead of you, and just as you enter it, you will find a colt tied there, which no one has ever ridden. Untie it and bring it here. 3 If anyone asks you, 'Why are you doing this?' say, 'The Lord needs it and will send it back here shortly.'"

4 They went and found a colt outside in the street, tied at a doorway. As they untied it, 5 some people standing there asked, "What are you doing, untying that colt?" 6 They answered as Jesus had told them to, and the people let them go. 7 When they brought the colt to Jesus and threw their cloaks over it, he sat on it. 8 Many people spread their cloaks on the road, while others spread branches they had cut in the fields. 9 Those who went ahead and those who followed shouted,

"Hosanna![a]"

"Blessed is he who comes in the name of
the Lord!"[b]

10 "Blessed is the coming kingdom of our
father David!"

"Hosanna in the highest heaven!"

11 Jesus entered Jerusalem and went into the temple courts. He looked around at everything, but since it was already late, he went out to Bethany with the Twelve.

Jesus Curses a Fig Tree and Clears the Temple Courts

12 The next day as they were leaving Bethany, Jesus was hungry. 13 Seeing in the distance a fig tree in leaf, he went to find out if it had any fruit. When he reached it, he found nothing but leaves, because it was not the season for figs. 14 Then he said to the tree, "May no one ever eat fruit from you again." And his disciples heard him say it.

15 On reaching Jerusalem, Jesus entered the temple courts and began driving out those who were buying and selling there. He overturned the tables of the money changers and

[a] 9 A Hebrew expression meaning "Save!" which became an exclamation of praise; also in verse 10
[b] 9 Psalm 118:25,26

the benches of those selling doves, 16and
would not allow anyone to carry merchandise
through the temple courts. 17And as he taught
them, he said, "Is it not written: 'My house will
be called a house of prayer for all nations'[a]?
But you have made it 'a den of robbers.'[b]"
18The chief priests and the teachers of the
law heard this and began looking for a way
to kill him, for they feared him, because the
whole crowd was amazed at his teaching.
19When evening came, Jesus and his disciples[c] went out of the city.
20In the morning, as they went along, they
saw the fig tree withered from the roots. 21Pe-
ter remembered and said to Jesus, "Rabbi,
look! The fig tree you cursed has withered!"
22"Have faith in God," Jesus answered.
23"Truly[d] I tell you, if anyone says to this
mountain, 'Go, throw yourself into the sea,'
and does not doubt in their heart but believes
that what they say will happen, it will be done
for them. 24Therefore I tell you, whatever you
ask for in prayer, believe that you have received it, and it will be yours. 25And when you
stand praying, if you hold anything against
anyone, forgive them, so that your Father in
heaven may forgive you your sins." [26][e]

The Authority of Jesus Questioned

27They arrived again in Jerusalem, and
while Jesus was walking in the temple courts,
the chief priests, the teachers of the law and
the elders came to him. 28"By what authority
are you doing these things?" they asked. "And
who gave you authority to do this?"
29Jesus replied, "I will ask you one question. Answer me, and I will tell you by what
authority I am doing these things. 30John's
baptism—was it from heaven, or of human
origin? Tell me!"
31They discussed it among themselves and
said, "If we say, 'From heaven,' he will ask,
'Then why didn't you believe him?' 32But if
we say, 'Of human origin' . . ." (They feared
the people, for everyone held that John really
was a prophet.)
33So they answered Jesus, "We don't know."
Jesus said, "Neither will I tell you by what
authority I am doing these things."

The Parable of the Tenants

12 Jesus then began to speak to them in
parables: "A man planted a vineyard.
He put a wall around it, dug a pit for the winepress and built a watchtower. Then he rented the vineyard to some farmers and moved
to another place. 2At harvest time he sent a
servant to the tenants to collect from them
some of the fruit of the vineyard. 3But they
seized him, beat him and sent him away empty-handed. 4Then he sent another servant to
them; they struck this man on the head and
treated him shamefully. 5He sent still another, and that one they killed. He sent many
others; some of them they beat, others they
killed.
6"He had one left to send, a son, whom he
loved. He sent him last of all, saying, 'They
will respect my son.'
7"But the tenants said to one another, 'This
is the heir. Come, let's kill him, and the inheritance will be ours.' 8So they took him and
killed him, and threw him out of the vineyard.
9"What then will the owner of the vineyard
do? He will come and kill those tenants and
give the vineyard to others. 10Haven't you read
this passage of Scripture:

"'The stone the builders rejected
has become the cornerstone;
11the Lord has done this,
and it is marvelous in our eyes'[f]?"

12Then the chief priests, the teachers of the
law and the elders looked for a way to arrest
him because they knew he had spoken the
parable against them. But they were afraid
of the crowd; so they left him and went away.

Paying the Imperial Tax to Caesar

13Later they sent some of the Pharisees and
Herodians to Jesus to catch him in his words.
14They came to him and said, "Teacher, we
know that you are a man of integrity. You
aren't swayed by others, because you pay no
attention to who they are; but you teach the
way of God in accordance with the truth. Is
it right to pay the imperial tax[g] to Caesar or
not? 15Should we pay or shouldn't we?"
But Jesus knew their hypocrisy. "Why are
you trying to trap me?" he asked. "Bring me a
denarius and let me look at it." 16They brought
the coin, and he asked them, "Whose image
is this? And whose inscription?"
"Caesar's," they replied.
17Then Jesus said to them, "Give back to
Caesar what is Caesar's and to God what is
God's."
And they were amazed at him.

Marriage at the Resurrection

18Then the Sadducees, who say there is no
resurrection, came to him with a question.
19"Teacher," they said, "Moses wrote for us
that if a man's brother dies and leaves a wife
but no children, the man must marry the widow and raise up offspring for his brother.
20Now there were seven brothers. The first one
married and died without leaving any children. 21The second one married the widow, but
he also died, leaving no child. It was the same
with the third. 22In fact, none of the seven left
any children. Last of all, the woman died too.
23At the resurrection[h] whose wife will she be,
since the seven were married to her?"
24Jesus replied, "Are you not in error because you do not know the Scriptures or the
power of God? 25When the dead rise, they
will neither marry nor be given in marriage;

[a] *17* Isaiah 56:7 [b] *17* Jer. 7:11 [c] *19* Some early manuscripts *came, Jesus* [d] *22,23* Some early manuscripts *"If you have faith in God," Jesus answered, 23"truly* [e] *26* Some manuscripts include here words similar to Matt. 6:15. [f] *11* Psalm 118:22,23 [g] *14* A special tax levied on subject peoples, not on Roman citizens [h] *23* Some manuscripts *resurrection, when people rise from the dead,*

they will be like the angels in heaven. 26Now
about the dead rising—have you not read in
the Book of Moses, in the account of the burning bush, how God said to him, 'I am the God
of Abraham, the God of Isaac, and the God of
Jacob'[a]? 27He is not the God of the dead, but of
the living. You are badly mistaken!"

The Greatest Commandment

28One of the teachers of the law came and
heard them debating. Noticing that Jesus had
given them a good answer, he asked him, "Of
all the commandments, which is the most important?"
29"The most important one," answered
Jesus, "is this: 'Hear, O Israel: The Lord our
God, the Lord is one.[b] 30Love the Lord your
God with all your heart and with all your
soul and with all your mind and with all your
strength.'[c] 31The second is this: 'Love your
neighbor as yourself.'[d] There is no commandment greater than these."
32"Well said, teacher," the man replied. "You
are right in saying that God is one and there is
no other but him. 33To love him with all your
heart, with all your understanding and with
all your strength, and to love your neighbor
as yourself is more important than all burnt
offerings and sacrifices."
34When Jesus saw that he had answered
wisely, he said to him, "You are not far from
the kingdom of God." And from then on no
one dared ask him any more questions.

Whose Son Is the Messiah?

35While Jesus was teaching in the temple
courts, he asked, "Why do the teachers of the
law say that the Messiah is the son of David?
36David himself, speaking by the Holy Spirit,
declared:

"'The Lord said to my Lord:
"Sit at my right hand
until I put your enemies
under your feet."'[e]

37David himself calls him 'Lord.' How then
can he be his son?"
The large crowd listened to him with delight.

Warning Against the Teachers of the Law

38As he taught, Jesus said, "Watch out for
the teachers of the law. They like to walk
around in flowing robes and be greeted with
respect in the marketplaces, 39and have the
most important seats in the synagogues and
the places of honor at banquets. 40They devour widows' houses and for a show make
lengthy prayers. These men will be punished
most severely."

The Widow's Offering

41Jesus sat down opposite the place where
the offerings were put and watched the crowd
putting their money into the temple treasury.
Many rich people threw in large amounts.
42But a poor widow came and put in two very
small copper coins, worth only a few cents.
43Calling his disciples to him, Jesus said,
"Truly I tell you, this poor widow has put more
into the treasury than all the others. 44They
all gave out of their wealth; but she, out of
her poverty, put in everything—all she had
to live on."

The Destruction of the Temple and Signs of the End Times

13 As Jesus was leaving the temple, one of
his disciples said to him, "Look, Teacher! What massive stones! What magnificent
buildings!"
2"Do you see all these great buildings?" replied Jesus. "Not one stone here will be left
on another; every one will be thrown down."
3As Jesus was sitting on the Mount of Olives
opposite the temple, Peter, James, John and
Andrew asked him privately, 4"Tell us, when
will these things happen? And what will be
the sign that they are all about to be fulfilled?"
5Jesus said to them: "Watch out that no one
deceives you. 6Many will come in my name,
claiming, 'I am he,' and will deceive many.
7When you hear of wars and rumors of wars,
do not be alarmed. Such things must happen,
but the end is still to come. 8Nation will rise
against nation, and kingdom against kingdom. There will be earthquakes in various
places, and famines. These are the beginning
of birth pains.
9"You must be on your guard. You will be
handed over to the local councils and flogged
in the synagogues. On account of me you will
stand before governors and kings as witnesses to them. 10And the gospel must first be
preached to all nations. 11Whenever you are
arrested and brought to trial, do not worry
beforehand about what to say. Just say whatever is given you at the time, for it is not you
speaking, but the Holy Spirit.
12"Brother will betray brother to death, and
a father his child. Children will rebel against
their parents and have them put to death. 13Ev-
eryone will hate you because of me, but the
one who stands firm to the end will be saved.
14"When you see 'the abomination that
causes desolation'[f] standing where it[g] does not
belong—let the reader understand—then let
those who are in Judea flee to the mountains.
15Let no one on the housetop go down or enter
the house to take anything out. 16Let no one
in the field go back to get their cloak. 17How
dreadful it will be in those days for pregnant
women and nursing mothers! 18Pray that this
will not take place in winter, 19because those
will be days of distress unequaled from the
beginning, when God created the world, until
now—and never to be equaled again.
20"If the Lord had not cut short those days,
no one would survive. But for the sake of the
elect, whom he has chosen, he has shortened
them. 21At that time if anyone says to you,

[a] *26* Exodus 3:6 [b] *29* Or *The Lord our God is one Lord* [c] *30* Deut. 6:4,5 [d] *31* Lev. 19:18
[e] *36* Psalm 110:1 [f] *14* Daniel 9:27; 11:31; 12:11 [g] *14* Or *he*

'Look, here is the Messiah!' or, 'Look, there
he is!' do not believe it. 22For false messiahs
and false prophets will appear and perform
signs and wonders to deceive, if possible, even
the elect. 23So be on your guard; I have told
you everything ahead of time.

24"But in those days, following that distress,

"'the sun will be darkened,
and the moon will not give its light;
25the stars will fall from the sky,
and the heavenly bodies will be
shaken.'[a]

26"At that time people will see the Son of
Man coming in clouds with great power and
glory. 27And he will send his angels and gather
his elect from the four winds, from the ends of
the earth to the ends of the heavens.

28"Now learn this lesson from the fig tree:
As soon as its twigs get tender and its leaves
come out, you know that summer is near.
29Even so, when you see these things happening, you know that it[b] is near, right at the
door. 30Truly I tell you, this generation will
certainly not pass away until all these things
have happened. 31Heaven and earth will pass
away, but my words will never pass away.

The Day and Hour Unknown

32"But about that day or hour no one knows,
not even the angels in heaven, nor the Son,
but only the Father. 33Be on guard! Be alert[c]!
You do not know when that time will come.
34It's like a man going away: He leaves his
house and puts his servants in charge, each
with their assigned task, and tells the one at
the door to keep watch.

35"Therefore keep watch because you do not
know when the owner of the house will come
back—whether in the evening, or at midnight,
or when the rooster crows, or at dawn. 36If
he comes suddenly, do not let him find you
sleeping. 37What I say to you, I say to everyone: 'Watch!'"

Jesus Anointed at Bethany

14 Now the Passover and the Festival of
Unleavened Bread were only two days
away, and the chief priests and the teachers of
the law were scheming to arrest Jesus secretly
and kill him. 2"But not during the festival,"
they said, "or the people may riot."

3While he was in Bethany, reclining at the
table in the home of Simon the Leper, a woman came with an alabaster jar of very expensive perfume, made of pure nard. She broke
the jar and poured the perfume on his head.

4Some of those present were saying indig-
nantly to one another, "Why this waste of perfume? 5It could have been sold for more than
a year's wages[d] and the money given to the
poor." And they rebuked her harshly.

6"Leave her alone," said Jesus. "Why are
you bothering her? She has done a beautiful
thing to me. 7The poor you will always have
with you,[e] and you can help them any time you
want. But you will not always have me. 8She
did what she could. She poured perfume on
my body beforehand to prepare for my burial. 9Truly I tell you, wherever the gospel is
preached throughout the world, what she has
done will also be told, in memory of her."

10Then Judas Iscariot, one of the Twelve,
went to the chief priests to betray Jesus to
them. 11They were delighted to hear this and
promised to give him money. So he watched
for an opportunity to hand him over.

The Last Supper

12On the first day of the Festival of Unleavened Bread, when it was customary to sacrifice the Passover lamb, Jesus' disciples asked
him, "Where do you want us to go and make
preparations for you to eat the Passover?"

13So he sent two of his disciples, telling
them, "Go into the city, and a man carrying a jar of water will meet you. Follow him.
14Say to the owner of the house he enters, 'The
Teacher asks: Where is my guest room, where
I may eat the Passover with my disciples?'
15He will show you a large room upstairs,
furnished and ready. Make preparations for
us there."

16The disciples left, went into the city and
found things just as Jesus had told them. So
they prepared the Passover.

17When evening came, Jesus arrived with
the Twelve. 18While they were reclining at
the table eating, he said, "Truly I tell you,
one of you will betray me—one who is eating with me."

19They were saddened, and one by one they
said to him, "Surely you don't mean me?"

20"It is one of the Twelve," he replied, "one
who dips bread into the bowl with me. 21The
Son of Man will go just as it is written about
him. But woe to that man who betrays the Son
of Man! It would be better for him if he had
not been born."

22While they were eating, Jesus took bread,
and when he had given thanks, he broke it
and gave it to his disciples, saying, "Take it;
this is my body."

23Then he took a cup, and when he had giv-
en thanks, he gave it to them, and they all
drank from it.

24"This is my blood of the[f] covenant, which
is poured out for many," he said to them.
25"Truly I tell you, I will not drink again from
the fruit of the vine until that day when I drink
it new in the kingdom of God."

26When they had sung a hymn, they went
out to the Mount of Olives.

Jesus Predicts Peter's Denial

27"You will all fall away," Jesus told them,
"for it is written:

"'I will strike the shepherd,
and the sheep will be scattered.'[g]

28But after I have risen, I will go ahead of you
into Galilee."

[a] 25 Isaiah 13:10; 34:4 [b] 29 Or *he* [c] 33 Some manuscripts *alert and pray* [d] 5 Greek *than three hundred denarii* [e] 7 See Deut. 15:11. [f] 24 Some manuscripts *the new* [g] 27 Zech. 13:7

29Peter declared, "Even if all fall away, I
will not."
30"Truly I tell you," Jesus answered, "today—
yes, tonight—before the rooster crows twice[a]
you yourself will disown me three times."
31But Peter insisted emphatically, "Even if I
have to die with you, I will never disown you."
And all the others said the same.

Gethsemane

32They went to a place called Gethsemane, and Jesus said to his disciples, "Sit here
while I pray." 33He took Peter, James and John
along with him, and he began to be deeply
distressed and troubled. 34"My soul is overwhelmed with sorrow to the point of death,"
he said to them. "Stay here and keep watch."
35Going a little farther, he fell to the ground
and prayed that if possible the hour might pass
from him. 36"*Abba*,[b] Father," he said, "everything is possible for you. Take this cup from
me. Yet not what I will, but what you will."
37Then he returned to his disciples and
found them sleeping. "Simon," he said to Peter,
"are you asleep? Couldn't you keep watch for
one hour? 38Watch and pray so that you will
not fall into temptation. The spirit is willing,
but the flesh is weak."
39Once more he went away and prayed the
same thing. 40When he came back, he again
found them sleeping, because their eyes were
heavy. They did not know what to say to him.
41Returning the third time, he said to them,
"Are you still sleeping and resting? Enough!
The hour has come. Look, the Son of Man is
delivered into the hands of sinners. 42Rise! Let
us go! Here comes my betrayer!"

Jesus Arrested

43Just as he was speaking, Judas, one of the
Twelve, appeared. With him was a crowd armed
with swords and clubs, sent from the chief
priests, the teachers of the law, and the elders.
44Now the betrayer had arranged a signal
with them: "The one I kiss is the man; arrest
him and lead him away under guard." 45Go-
ing at once to Jesus, Judas said, "Rabbi!" and
kissed him. 46The men seized Jesus and arrested him. 47Then one of those standing near
drew his sword and struck the servant of the
high priest, cutting off his ear.
48"Am I leading a rebellion," said Jesus, "that
you have come out with swords and clubs to
capture me? 49Every day I was with you, teaching in the temple courts, and you did not arrest me. But the Scriptures must be fulfilled."
50Then everyone deserted him and fled.
51A young man, wearing nothing but a lin-
en garment, was following Jesus. When they
seized him, 52he fled naked, leaving his garment behind.

Jesus Before the Sanhedrin

53They took Jesus to the high priest, and all
the chief priests, the elders and the teachers
of the law came together. 54Peter followed him
at a distance, right into the courtyard of the
high priest. There he sat with the guards and
warmed himself at the fire.
55The chief priests and the whole Sanhedrin
were looking for evidence against Jesus so
that they could put him to death, but they did
not find any. 56Many testified falsely against
him, but their statements did not agree.
57Then some stood up and gave this false
testimony against him: 58"We heard him say,
'I will destroy this temple made with human
hands and in three days will build another,
not made with hands.'" 59Yet even then their
testimony did not agree.
60Then the high priest stood up before them
and asked Jesus, "Are you not going to answer? What is this testimony that these men
are bringing against you?" 61But Jesus remained silent and gave no answer.
Again the high priest asked him, "Are you
the Messiah, the Son of the Blessed One?"
62"I am," said Jesus. "And you will see the
Son of Man sitting at the right hand of the
Mighty One and coming on the clouds of
heaven."
63The high priest tore his clothes. "Why
do we need any more witnesses?" he asked.
64"You have heard the blasphemy. What do
you think?"
They all condemned him as worthy of
death. 65Then some began to spit at him; they
blindfolded him, struck him with their fists,
and said, "Prophesy!" And the guards took
him and beat him.

Peter Disowns Jesus

66While Peter was below in the courtyard,
one of the servant girls of the high priest came
by. 67When she saw Peter warming himself,
she looked closely at him.
"You also were with that Nazarene, Jesus,"
she said.
68But he denied it. "I don't know or understand what you're talking about," he said, and
went out into the entryway.[c]
69When the servant girl saw him there, she
said again to those standing around, "This
fellow is one of them." 70Again he denied it.
After a little while, those standing near said
to Peter, "Surely you are one of them, for you
are a Galilean."
71He began to call down curses, and he
swore to them, "I don't know this man you're
talking about."
72Immediately the rooster crowed the second time.[d] Then Peter remembered the word
Jesus had spoken to him: "Before the rooster
crows twice[a] you will disown me three times."
And he broke down and wept.

Jesus Before Pilate

15 Very early in the morning, the chief
priests, with the elders, the teachers of
the law and the whole Sanhedrin, made their

[a] 30,72 Some early manuscripts do not have *twice*. [b] 36 Aramaic for *father* [c] 68 Some early manuscripts *entryway and the rooster crowed* [d] 72 Some early manuscripts do not have *the second time*.

plans. So they bound Jesus, led him away and handed him over to Pilate.

2“Are you the king of the Jews?” asked Pilate.

“You have said so,” Jesus replied.

3The chief priests accused him of many things. 4So again Pilate asked him, “Aren’t you going to answer? See how many things they are accusing you of.”

5But Jesus still made no reply, and Pilate was amazed.

6Now it was the custom at the festival to release a prisoner whom the people requested. 7A man called Barabbas was in prison with the insurrectionists who had committed murder in the uprising. 8The crowd came up and asked Pilate to do for them what he usually did.

9“Do you want me to release to you the king of the Jews?” asked Pilate, 10knowing it was out of self-interest that the chief priests had handed Jesus over to him. 11But the chief priests stirred up the crowd to have Pilate release Barabbas instead.

12“What shall I do, then, with the one you call the king of the Jews?” Pilate asked them.

13“Crucify him!” they shouted.

14“Why? What crime has he committed?” asked Pilate.

But they shouted all the louder, “Crucify him!”

15Wanting to satisfy the crowd, Pilate released Barabbas to them. He had Jesus flogged, and handed him over to be crucified.

The Soldiers Mock Jesus

16The soldiers led Jesus away into the palace (that is, the Praetorium) and called together the whole company of soldiers. 17They put a purple robe on him, then twisted together a crown of thorns and set it on him. 18And they began to call out to him, “Hail, king of the Jews!” 19Again and again they struck him on the head with a staff and spit on him. Falling on their knees, they paid homage to him. 20And when they had mocked him, they took off the purple robe and put his own clothes on him. Then they led him out to crucify him.

The Crucifixion of Jesus

21A certain man from Cyrene, Simon, the father of Alexander and Rufus, was passing by on his way in from the country, and they forced him to carry the cross. 22They brought Jesus to the place called Golgotha (which means “the place of the skull”). 23Then they offered him wine mixed with myrrh, but he did not take it. 24And they crucified him. Dividing up his clothes, they cast lots to see what each would get.

25It was nine in the morning when they crucified him. 26The written notice of the charge against him read: THE KING OF THE JEWS.

27They crucified two rebels with him, one on his right and one on his left. [28][a] 29Those who passed by hurled insults at him, shaking their heads and saying, “So! You who are going to destroy the temple and build it in three days, 30come down from the cross and save yourself!” 31In the same way the chief priests and the teachers of the law mocked him among themselves. “He saved others,” they said, “but he can’t save himself! 32Let this Messiah, this king of Israel, come down now from the cross, that we may see and believe.” Those crucified with him also heaped insults on him.

The Death of Jesus

33At noon, darkness came over the whole land until three in the afternoon. 34And at three in the afternoon Jesus cried out in a loud voice, *“Eloi, Eloi, lema sabachthani?”* (which means “My God, my God, why have you forsaken me?”).[b]

35When some of those standing near heard this, they said, “Listen, he’s calling Elijah.”

36Someone ran, filled a sponge with wine vinegar, put it on a staff, and offered it to Jesus to drink. “Now leave him alone. Let’s see if Elijah comes to take him down,” he said.

37With a loud cry, Jesus breathed his last.

38The curtain of the temple was torn in two from top to bottom. 39And when the centurion, who stood there in front of Jesus, saw how he died,[c] he said, “Surely this man was the Son of God!”

40Some women were watching from a distance. Among them were Mary Magdalene, Mary the mother of James the younger and of Joseph,[d] and Salome. 41In Galilee these women had followed him and cared for his needs. Many other women who had come up with him to Jerusalem were also there.

The Burial of Jesus

42It was Preparation Day (that is, the day before the Sabbath). So as evening approached, 43Joseph of Arimathea, a prominent member of the Council, who was himself waiting for the kingdom of God, went boldly to Pilate and asked for Jesus’ body. 44Pilate was surprised to hear that he was already dead. Summoning the centurion, he asked him if Jesus had already died. 45When he learned from the centurion that it was so, he gave the body to Joseph. 46So Joseph bought some linen cloth, took down the body, wrapped it in the linen, and placed it in a tomb cut out of rock. Then he rolled a stone against the entrance of the tomb. 47Mary Magdalene and Mary the mother of Joseph saw where he was laid.

Jesus Has Risen

16 When the Sabbath was over, Mary Magdalene, Mary the mother of James, and Salome bought spices so that they might go to anoint Jesus’ body. 2Very early on the first day of the week, just after sunrise, they were on their way to the tomb 3and they asked each other, “Who will roll the stone away from the entrance of the tomb?”

[a] *28* Some manuscripts include here words similar to Luke 22:37. [b] *34* Psalm 22:1 [c] *39* Some manuscripts *saw that he died with such a cry* [d] *40* Greek *Joses,* a variant of *Joseph;* also in verse 47

[4]But when they looked up, they saw that the stone, which was very large, had been rolled away. [5]As they entered the tomb, they saw a young man dressed in a white robe sitting on the right side, and they were alarmed.

[6]"Don't be alarmed," he said. "You are looking for Jesus the Nazarene, who was crucified. He has risen! He is not here. See the place where they laid him. [7]But go, tell his disciples and Peter, 'He is going ahead of you into Galilee. There you will see him, just as he told you.'"

[8]Trembling and bewildered, the women went out and fled from the tomb. They said nothing to anyone, because they were afraid.[a]

[The earliest manuscripts and some other ancient witnesses do not have verses 9–20.]

[9]When Jesus rose early on the first day of the week, he appeared first to Mary Magdalene, out of whom he had driven seven demons. [10]She went and told those who had been with him and who were mourning and weeping. [11]When they heard that Jesus was alive and that she had seen him, they did not believe it.

[12]Afterward Jesus appeared in a different form to two of them while they were walking in the country. [13]These returned and reported it to the rest; but they did not believe them either.

[14]Later Jesus appeared to the Eleven as they were eating; he rebuked them for their lack of faith and their stubborn refusal to believe those who had seen him after he had risen.

[15]He said to them, "Go into all the world and preach the gospel to all creation. [16]Whoever believes and is baptized will be saved, but whoever does not believe will be condemned. [17]And these signs will accompany those who believe: In my name they will drive out demons; they will speak in new tongues; [18]they will pick up snakes with their hands; and when they drink deadly poison, it will not hurt them at all; they will place their hands on sick people, and they will get well."

[19]After the Lord Jesus had spoken to them, he was taken up into heaven and he sat at the right hand of God. [20]Then the disciples went out and preached everywhere, and the Lord worked with them and confirmed his word by the signs that accompanied it.

Luke

Introduction

1 Many have undertaken to draw up an account of the things that have been fulfilled[b] among us, [2]just as they were handed down to us by those who from the first were eyewitnesses and servants of the word. [3]With this in mind, since I myself have carefully investigated everything from the beginning, I too decided to write an orderly account for you, most excellent Theophilus, [4]so that you may know the certainty of the things you have been taught.

The Birth of John the Baptist Foretold

[5]In the time of Herod king of Judea there was a priest named Zechariah, who belonged to the priestly division of Abijah; his wife Elizabeth was also a descendant of Aaron. [6]Both of them were righteous in the sight of God, observing all the Lord's commands and decrees blamelessly. [7]But they were childless because Elizabeth was not able to conceive, and they were both very old.

[8]Once when Zechariah's division was on duty and he was serving as priest before God, [9]he was chosen by lot, according to the custom of the priesthood, to go into the temple of the Lord and burn incense. [10]And when the time for the burning of incense came, all the assembled worshipers were praying outside.

[11]Then an angel of the Lord appeared to him, standing at the right side of the altar of incense. [12]When Zechariah saw him, he was startled and was gripped with fear. [13]But the angel said to him: "Do not be afraid, Zechariah; your prayer has been heard. Your wife Elizabeth will bear you a son, and you are to call him John. [14]He will be a joy and delight to you, and many will rejoice because of his birth, [15]for he will be great in the sight of the Lord. He is never to take wine or other fermented drink, and he will be filled with the Holy Spirit even before he is born. [16]He will bring back many of the people of Israel to the Lord their God. [17]And he will go on before the Lord, in the spirit and power of Elijah, to turn the hearts of the parents to their children and the disobedient to the wisdom of the righteous—to make ready a people prepared for the Lord."

[18]Zechariah asked the angel, "How can I be sure of this? I am an old man and my wife is well along in years."

[19]The angel said to him, "I am Gabriel. I

[a] 8 Some manuscripts have the following ending between verses 8 and 9, and one manuscript has it after verse 8 (omitting verses 9-20): *Then they quickly reported all these instructions to those around Peter. After this, Jesus himself also sent out through them from east to west the sacred and imperishable proclamation of eternal salvation. Amen.* [b] 1 *Or been surely believed*

stand in the presence of God, and I have been
sent to speak to you and to tell you this good
news. 20And now you will be silent and not
able to speak until the day this happens, because you did not believe my words, which
will come true at their appointed time."
21Meanwhile, the people were waiting for
Zechariah and wondering why he stayed so
long in the temple. 22When he came out, he
could not speak to them. They realized he had
seen a vision in the temple, for he kept making
signs to them but remained unable to speak.
23When his time of service was completed,
he returned home. 24After this his wife Elizabeth became pregnant and for five months
remained in seclusion. 25"The Lord has done
this for me," she said. "In these days he has
shown his favor and taken away my disgrace
among the people."

The Birth of Jesus Foretold

26In the sixth month of Elizabeth's pregnancy, God sent the angel Gabriel to Nazareth,
a town in Galilee, 27to a virgin pledged to be
married to a man named Joseph, a descendant
of David. The virgin's name was Mary. 28The
angel went to her and said, "Greetings, you
who are highly favored! The Lord is with you."
29Mary was greatly troubled at his words
and wondered what kind of greeting this
might be. 30But the angel said to her, "Do not
be afraid, Mary; you have found favor with
God. 31You will conceive and give birth to a
son, and you are to call him Jesus. 32He will
be great and will be called the Son of the Most
High. The Lord God will give him the throne
of his father David, 33and he will reign over
Jacob's descendants forever; his kingdom will
never end."
34"How will this be," Mary asked the angel,
"since I am a virgin?"
35The angel answered, "The Holy Spirit will
come on you, and the power of the Most High
will overshadow you. So the holy one to be
born will be called[a] the Son of God. 36Even
Elizabeth your relative is going to have a child
in her old age, and she who was said to be unable to conceive is in her sixth month. 37For
no word from God will ever fail."
38"I am the Lord's servant," Mary answered.
"May your word to me be fulfilled." Then the
angel left her.

Mary Visits Elizabeth

39At that time Mary got ready and hurried
to a town in the hill country of Judea, 40where
she entered Zechariah's home and greeted
Elizabeth. 41When Elizabeth heard Mary's
greeting, the baby leaped in her womb, and
Elizabeth was filled with the Holy Spirit. 42In
a loud voice she exclaimed: "Blessed are you
among women, and blessed is the child you
will bear! 43But why am I so favored, that the
mother of my Lord should come to me? 44As
soon as the sound of your greeting reached
my ears, the baby in my womb leaped for joy.
45Blessed is she who has believed that the Lord
would fulfill his promises to her!"

Mary's Song

46And Mary said:

"My soul glorifies the Lord
47 and my spirit rejoices in God my
Savior,
48 for he has been mindful
of the humble state of his servant.
From now on all generations will call me
blessed,
49 for the Mighty One has done great
things for me—
holy is his name.
50 His mercy extends to those who fear him,
from generation to generation.
51 He has performed mighty deeds with his
arm;
he has scattered those who are proud in
their inmost thoughts.
52 He has brought down rulers from their
thrones
but has lifted up the humble.
53 He has filled the hungry with good things
but has sent the rich away empty.
54 He has helped his servant Israel,
remembering to be merciful
55 to Abraham and his descendants forever,
just as he promised our ancestors."

56Mary stayed with Elizabeth for about
three months and then returned home.

The Birth of John the Baptist

57When it was time for Elizabeth to have her
baby, she gave birth to a son. 58Her neighbors
and relatives heard that the Lord had shown
her great mercy, and they shared her joy.
59On the eighth day they came to circumcise the child, and they were going to name
him after his father Zechariah, 60but his mother spoke up and said, "No! He is to be called
John."
61They said to her, "There is no one among
your relatives who has that name."
62Then they made signs to his father, to find
out what he would like to name the child. 63He
asked for a writing tablet, and to everyone's
astonishment he wrote, "His name is John."
64Immediately his mouth was opened and his
tongue set free, and he began to speak, praising God. 65All the neighbors were filled with
awe, and throughout the hill country of Judea
people were talking about all these things.
66Everyone who heard this wondered about it,
asking, "What then is this child going to be?"
For the Lord's hand was with him.

Zechariah's Song

67His father Zechariah was filled with the
Holy Spirit and prophesied:

68 "Praise be to the Lord, the God of Israel,
because he has come to his people and
redeemed them.

[a] 35 Or *So the child to be born will be called holy,*

69 He has raised up a horn[a] of salvation
for us
in the house of his servant David
70 (as he said through his holy prophets of
long ago),
71 salvation from our enemies
and from the hand of all who hate us—
72 to show mercy to our ancestors
and to remember his holy covenant,
73 the oath he swore to our father
Abraham:
74 to rescue us from the hand of our
enemies,
and to enable us to serve him without
fear
75 in holiness and righteousness before
him all our days.

76 And you, my child, will be called a
prophet of the Most High;
for you will go on before the Lord to
prepare the way for him,
77 to give his people the knowledge of
salvation
through the forgiveness of their sins,
78 because of the tender mercy of our God,
by which the rising sun will come to us
from heaven
79 to shine on those living in darkness
and in the shadow of death,
to guide our feet into the path of peace."

80 And the child grew and became strong in
spirit[b]; and he lived in the wilderness until he
appeared publicly to Israel.

The Birth of Jesus

2 In those days Caesar Augustus issued a
decree that a census should be taken of
the entire Roman world. 2 (This was the first
census that took place while[c] Quirinius was
governor of Syria.) 3 And everyone went to
their own town to register.

4 So Joseph also went up from the town of
Nazareth in Galilee to Judea, to Bethlehem
the town of David, because he belonged to
the house and line of David. 5 He went there
to register with Mary, who was pledged to be
married to him and was expecting a child.
6 While they were there, the time came for the
baby to be born, 7 and she gave birth to her
firstborn, a son. She wrapped him in cloths
and placed him in a manger, because there
was no guest room available for them.

8 And there were shepherds living out in the
fields nearby, keeping watch over their flocks
at night. 9 An angel of the Lord appeared to
them, and the glory of the Lord shone around
them, and they were terrified. 10 But the angel
said to them, "Do not be afraid. I bring you
good news that will cause great joy for all the
people. 11 Today in the town of David a Savior
has been born to you; he is the Messiah, the
Lord. 12 This will be a sign to you: You will
find a baby wrapped in cloths and lying in
a manger."

13 Suddenly a great company of the heavenly host appeared with the angel, praising
God and saying,

14 "Glory to God in the highest heaven,
and on earth peace to those on whom
his favor rests."

15 When the angels had left them and gone
into heaven, the shepherds said to one another, "Let's go to Bethlehem and see this thing
that has happened, which the Lord has told
us about."

16 So they hurried off and found Mary and
Joseph, and the baby, who was lying in the
manger. 17 When they had seen him, they
spread the word concerning what had been
told them about this child, 18 and all who heard
it were amazed at what the shepherds said to
them. 19 But Mary treasured up all these things
and pondered them in her heart. 20 The shepherds returned, glorifying and praising God
for all the things they had heard and seen,
which were just as they had been told.

21 On the eighth day, when it was time to
circumcise the child, he was named Jesus,
the name the angel had given him before he
was conceived.

Jesus Presented in the Temple

22 When the time came for the purification
rites required by the Law of Moses, Joseph
and Mary took him to Jerusalem to present
him to the Lord 23 (as it is written in the Law of
the Lord, "Every firstborn male is to be consecrated to the Lord"[d]), 24 and to offer a sacrifice
in keeping with what is said in the Law of the
Lord: "a pair of doves or two young pigeons."[e]

25 Now there was a man in Jerusalem called
Simeon, who was righteous and devout. He
was waiting for the consolation of Israel, and
the Holy Spirit was on him. 26 It had been revealed to him by the Holy Spirit that he would
not die before he had seen the Lord's Messiah.
27 Moved by the Spirit, he went into the temple courts. When the parents brought in the
child Jesus to do for him what the custom of
the Law required, 28 Simeon took him in his
arms and praised God, saying:

29 "Sovereign Lord, as you have promised,
you may now dismiss[f] your servant in
peace.
30 For my eyes have seen your salvation,
31 which you have prepared in the sight of
all nations:
32 a light for revelation to the Gentiles,
and the glory of your people Israel."

33 The child's father and mother marveled
at what was said about him. 34 Then Simeon
blessed them and said to Mary, his mother:
"This child is destined to cause the falling and
rising of many in Israel, and to be a sign that
will be spoken against, 35 so that the thoughts
of many hearts will be revealed. And a sword
will pierce your own soul too."

36 There was also a prophet, Anna, the

[a] 69 *Horn* here symbolizes a strong king. [b] 80 Or *in the Spirit* [c] 2 Or *This census took place before* [d] 23 Exodus 13:2,12 [e] 24 Lev. 12:8 [f] 29 Or *promised, / now dismiss*

daughter of Penuel, of the tribe of Asher. She
was very old; she had lived with her husband
seven years after her marriage, 37and then
was a widow until she was eighty-four.[a] She
never left the temple but worshiped night
and day, fasting and praying. 38Coming up
to them at that very moment, she gave thanks
to God and spoke about the child to all who
were looking forward to the redemption of
Jerusalem.

39When Joseph and Mary had done everything required by the Law of the Lord, they
returned to Galilee to their own town of Nazareth. 40And the child grew and became strong;
he was filled with wisdom, and the grace of
God was on him.

The Boy Jesus at the Temple

41Every year Jesus' parents went to Jerusalem for the Festival of the Passover. 42When
he was twelve years old, they went up to the
festival, according to the custom. 43After the
festival was over, while his parents were returning home, the boy Jesus stayed behind
in Jerusalem, but they were unaware of it.
44Thinking he was in their company, they
traveled on for a day. Then they began looking for him among their relatives and friends.
45When they did not find him, they went back
to Jerusalem to look for him. 46After three
days they found him in the temple courts, sitting among the teachers, listening to them
and asking them questions. 47Everyone who
heard him was amazed at his understanding
and his answers. 48When his parents saw him,
they were astonished. His mother said to him,
"Son, why have you treated us like this? Your
father and I have been anxiously searching
for you."

49"Why were you searching for me?" he
asked. "Didn't you know I had to be in my
Father's house?"[b] 50But they did not understand what he was saying to them.

51Then he went down to Nazareth with them
and was obedient to them. But his mother
treasured all these things in her heart. 52And
Jesus grew in wisdom and stature, and in favor with God and man.

John the Baptist Prepares the Way

3 In the fifteenth year of the reign of Tiberius
Caesar—when Pontius Pilate was governor of Judea, Herod tetrarch of Galilee, his
brother Philip tetrarch of Iturea and Traconi-
tis, and Lysanias tetrarch of Abilene— 2dur-
ing the high-priesthood of Annas and Caiaphas, the word of God came to John son of
Zechariah in the wilderness. 3He went into all
the country around the Jordan, preaching a
baptism of repentance for the forgiveness of
sins. 4As it is written in the book of the words
of Isaiah the prophet:

"A voice of one calling in the wilderness,
'Prepare the way for the Lord,
make straight paths for him.
5Every valley shall be filled in,
every mountain and hill made low.
The crooked roads shall become straight,
the rough ways smooth.
6And all people will see God's salvation.'"[c]

7John said to the crowds coming out to be
baptized by him, "You brood of vipers! Who
warned you to flee from the coming wrath?
8Produce fruit in keeping with repentance.
And do not begin to say to yourselves, 'We
have Abraham as our father.' For I tell you that
out of these stones God can raise up children
for Abraham. 9The ax is already at the root
of the trees, and every tree that does not produce good fruit will be cut down and thrown
into the fire."

10"What should we do then?" the crowd
asked.

11John answered, "Anyone who has two
shirts should share with the one who has
none, and anyone who has food should do
the same."

12Even tax collectors came to be baptized.
"Teacher," they asked, "what should we do?"

13"Don't collect any more than you are required to," he told them.

14Then some soldiers asked him, "And what
should we do?"

He replied, "Don't extort money and don't
accuse people falsely—be content with your
pay."

15The people were waiting expectantly and
were all wondering in their hearts if John
might possibly be the Messiah. 16John answered them all, "I baptize you with[d] water.
But one who is more powerful than I will come,
the straps of whose sandals I am not worthy
to untie. He will baptize you with[d] the Holy
Spirit and fire. 17His winnowing fork is in his
hand to clear his threshing floor and to gather the wheat into his barn, but he will burn up
the chaff with unquenchable fire." 18And with
many other words John exhorted the people
and proclaimed the good news to them.

19But when John rebuked Herod the tetrarch because of his marriage to Herodias,
his brother's wife, and all the other evil things
he had done, 20Herod added this to them all:
He locked John up in prison.

The Baptism and Genealogy of Jesus

21When all the people were being baptized,
Jesus was baptized too. And as he was pray-
ing, heaven was opened 22and the Holy Spirit
descended on him in bodily form like a dove.
And a voice came from heaven: "You are my
Son, whom I love; with you I am well pleased."

23Now Jesus himself was about thirty years
old when he began his ministry. He was the
son, so it was thought, of Joseph,

the son of Heli, 24the son of Matthat,
the son of Levi, the son of Melki,
the son of Jannai, the son of Joseph,
25the son of Mattathias, the son of Amos,
the son of Nahum, the son of Esli,

[a] 37 Or *then had been a widow for eighty-four years.* [b] 49 Or *be about my Father's business*
[c] 6 Isaiah 40:3-5 [d] 16 Or *in*

the son of Naggai, 26the son of Maath,
the son of Mattathias, the son of Semein,
the son of Josek, the son of Joda,
27the son of Joanan, the son of Rhesa,
the son of Zerubbabel, the son of Shealtiel,
the son of Neri, 28the son of Melki,
the son of Addi, the son of Cosam,
the son of Elmadam, the son of Er,
29the son of Joshua, the son of Eliezer,
the son of Jorim, the son of Matthat,
the son of Levi, 30the son of Simeon,
the son of Judah, the son of Joseph,
the son of Jonam, the son of Eliakim,
31the son of Melea, the son of Menna,
the son of Mattatha, the son of Nathan,
the son of David, 32the son of Jesse,
the son of Obed, the son of Boaz,
the son of Salmon,[a] the son of Nahshon,
33the son of Amminadab, the son of Ram,[b]
the son of Hezron, the son of Perez,
the son of Judah, 34the son of Jacob,
the son of Isaac, the son of Abraham,
the son of Terah, the son of Nahor,
35the son of Serug, the son of Reu,
the son of Peleg, the son of Eber,
the son of Shelah, 36the son of Cainan,
the son of Arphaxad, the son of Shem,
the son of Noah, the son of Lamech,
37the son of Methuselah, the son of Enoch,
the son of Jared, the son of Mahalalel,
the son of Kenan, 38the son of Enosh,
the son of Seth, the son of Adam,
the son of God.

Jesus Is Tested in the Wilderness

4 Jesus, full of the Holy Spirit, left the Jordan
and was led by the Spirit into the wilderness, 2where for forty days he was tempted[c]
by the devil. He ate nothing during those days,
and at the end of them he was hungry.
3The devil said to him, "If you are the Son of
God, tell this stone to become bread."
4Jesus answered, "It is written: 'Man shall
not live on bread alone.'[d]"
5The devil led him up to a high place and
showed him in an instant all the kingdoms of
the world. 6And he said to him, "I will give you
all their authority and splendor; it has been
given to me, and I can give it to anyone I want
to. 7If you worship me, it will all be yours."
8Jesus answered, "It is written: 'Worship the
Lord your God and serve him only.'[e]"
9The devil led him to Jerusalem and had
him stand on the highest point of the temple.
"If you are the Son of God," he said, "throw
yourself down from here. 10For it is written:

"'He will command his angels concerning
you
to guard you carefully;
11they will lift you up in their hands,
so that you will not strike your foot
against a stone.'[f]"

12Jesus answered, "It is said: 'Do not put the
Lord your God to the test.'[g]"
13When the devil had finished all this tempting, he left him until an opportune time.

Jesus Rejected at Nazareth

14Jesus returned to Galilee in the power of
the Spirit, and news about him spread through
the whole countryside. 15He was teaching in
their synagogues, and everyone praised him.
16He went to Nazareth, where he had been
brought up, and on the Sabbath day he went
into the synagogue, as was his custom. He
stood up to read, 17and the scroll of the prophet Isaiah was handed to him. Unrolling it, he
found the place where it is written:

18"The Spirit of the Lord is on me,
because he has anointed me
to proclaim good news to the poor.
He has sent me to proclaim freedom for
the prisoners
and recovery of sight for the blind,
to set the oppressed free,
19 to proclaim the year of the Lord's
favor."[h]

20Then he rolled up the scroll, gave it back
to the attendant and sat down. The eyes of
everyone in the synagogue were fastened on
him. 21He began by saying to them, "Today
this scripture is fulfilled in your hearing."
22All spoke well of him and were amazed
at the gracious words that came from his lips.
"Isn't this Joseph's son?" they asked.
23Jesus said to them, "Surely you will quote
this proverb to me: 'Physician, heal yourself!'
And you will tell me, 'Do here in your hometown what we have heard that you did in Capernaum.'"
24"Truly I tell you," he continued, "no prophet is accepted in his hometown. 25I assure you
that there were many widows in Israel in Elijah's time, when the sky was shut for three and
a half years and there was a severe famine
throughout the land. 26Yet Elijah was not sent
to any of them, but to a widow in Zarephath
in the region of Sidon. 27And there were many
in Israel with leprosy[i] in the time of Elisha the
prophet, yet not one of them was cleansed—
only Naaman the Syrian."
28All the people in the synagogue were furious when they heard this. 29They got up, drove
him out of the town, and took him to the brow
of the hill on which the town was built, in order to throw him off the cliff. 30But he walked
right through the crowd and went on his way.

Jesus Drives Out an Impure Spirit

31Then he went down to Capernaum, a town
in Galilee, and on the Sabbath he taught the
people. 32They were amazed at his teaching,
because his words had authority.
33In the synagogue there was a man

[a] *32* Some early manuscripts *Sala* [b] *33* Some manuscripts *Amminadab, the son of Admin, the son of Arni*; other manuscripts vary widely. [c] *2* The Greek for *tempted* can also mean *tested*. [d] *4* Deut. 8:3 [e] *8* Deut. 6:13 [f] *11* Psalm 91:11,12 [g] *12* Deut. 6:16 [h] *19* Isaiah 61:1,2 (see Septuagint); Isaiah 58:6 [i] *27* The Greek word traditionally translated *leprosy* was used for various diseases affecting the skin.

possessed by a demon, an impure spirit. He cried out at the top of his voice, 34“Go away! What do you want with us, Jesus of Nazareth? Have you come to destroy us? I know who you are—the Holy One of God!”

35“Be quiet!” Jesus said sternly. “Come out of him!” Then the demon threw the man down before them all and came out without injuring him.

36All the people were amazed and said to each other, “What words these are! With authority and power he gives orders to impure spirits and they come out!” 37And the news about him spread throughout the surrounding area.

Jesus Heals Many

38Jesus left the synagogue and went to the home of Simon. Now Simon’s mother-in-law was suffering from a high fever, and they asked Jesus to help her. 39So he bent over her and rebuked the fever, and it left her. She got up at once and began to wait on them.

40At sunset, the people brought to Jesus all who had various kinds of sickness, and laying his hands on each one, he healed them. 41Moreover, demons came out of many people, shouting, “You are the Son of God!” But he rebuked them and would not allow them to speak, because they knew he was the Messiah.

42At daybreak, Jesus went out to a solitary place. The people were looking for him and when they came to where he was, they tried to keep him from leaving them. 43But he said, “I must proclaim the good news of the kingdom of God to the other towns also, because that is why I was sent.” 44And he kept on preaching in the synagogues of Judea.

Jesus Calls His First Disciples

5 One day as Jesus was standing by the Lake of Gennesaret,[a] the people were crowding around him and listening to the word of God. 2He saw at the water’s edge two boats, left there by the fishermen, who were washing their nets. 3He got into one of the boats, the one belonging to Simon, and asked him to put out a little from shore. Then he sat down and taught the people from the boat.

4When he had finished speaking, he said to Simon, “Put out into deep water, and let down the nets for a catch.”

5Simon answered, “Master, we’ve worked hard all night and haven’t caught anything. But because you say so, I will let down the nets.”

6When they had done so, they caught such a large number of fish that their nets began to break. 7So they signaled their partners in the other boat to come and help them, and they came and filled both boats so full that they began to sink.

8When Simon Peter saw this, he fell at Jesus’ knees and said, “Go away from me, Lord; I am a sinful man!” 9For he and all his companions were astonished at the catch of fish they had taken, 10and so were James and John, the sons of Zebedee, Simon’s partners.

Then Jesus said to Simon, “Don’t be afraid; from now on you will fish for people.” 11So they pulled their boats up on shore, left everything and followed him.

Jesus Heals a Man With Leprosy

12While Jesus was in one of the towns, a man came along who was covered with leprosy.[b] When he saw Jesus, he fell with his face to the ground and begged him, “Lord, if you are willing, you can make me clean.”

13Jesus reached out his hand and touched the man. “I am willing,” he said. “Be clean!” And immediately the leprosy left him.

14Then Jesus ordered him, “Don’t tell anyone, but go, show yourself to the priest and offer the sacrifices that Moses commanded for your cleansing, as a testimony to them.”

15Yet the news about him spread all the more, so that crowds of people came to hear him and to be healed of their sicknesses. 16But Jesus often withdrew to lonely places and prayed.

Jesus Forgives and Heals a Paralyzed Man

17One day Jesus was teaching, and Pharisees and teachers of the law were sitting there. They had come from every village of Galilee and from Judea and Jerusalem. And the power of the Lord was with Jesus to heal the sick. 18Some men came carrying a paralyzed man on a mat and tried to take him into the house to lay him before Jesus. 19When they could not find a way to do this because of the crowd, they went up on the roof and lowered him on his mat through the tiles into the middle of the crowd, right in front of Jesus.

20When Jesus saw their faith, he said, “Friend, your sins are forgiven.”

21The Pharisees and the teachers of the law began thinking to themselves, “Who is this fellow who speaks blasphemy? Who can forgive sins but God alone?”

22Jesus knew what they were thinking and asked, “Why are you thinking these things in your hearts? 23Which is easier: to say, ‘Your sins are forgiven,’ or to say, ‘Get up and walk’? 24But I want you to know that the Son of Man has authority on earth to forgive sins.” So he said to the paralyzed man, “I tell you, get up, take your mat and go home.” 25Immediately he stood up in front of them, took what he had been lying on and went home praising God. 26Everyone was amazed and gave praise to God. They were filled with awe and said, “We have seen remarkable things today.”

Jesus Calls Levi and Eats With Sinners

27After this, Jesus went out and saw a tax collector by the name of Levi sitting at his tax booth. “Follow me,” Jesus said to him, 28and Levi got up, left everything and followed him.

[a] *1* That is, the Sea of Galilee [b] *12* The Greek word traditionally translated *leprosy* was used for various diseases affecting the skin.

29 Then Levi held a great banquet for Jesus
at his house, and a large crowd of tax collectors and others were eating with them. 30 But
the Pharisees and the teachers of the law who
belonged to their sect complained to his disciples, "Why do you eat and drink with tax
collectors and sinners?"
31 Jesus answered them, "It is not the healthy
who need a doctor, but the sick. 32 I have not
come to call the righteous, but sinners to repentance."

Jesus Questioned About Fasting

33 They said to him, "John's disciples often
fast and pray, and so do the disciples of the
Pharisees, but yours go on eating and drinking."
34 Jesus answered, "Can you make the
friends of the bridegroom fast while he is
with them? 35 But the time will come when
the bridegroom will be taken from them; in
those days they will fast."
36 He told them this parable: "No one tears
a piece out of a new garment to patch an old
one. Otherwise, they will have torn the new
garment, and the patch from the new will not
match the old. 37 And no one pours new wine
into old wineskins. Otherwise, the new wine
will burst the skins; the wine will run out and
the wineskins will be ruined. 38 No, new wine
must be poured into new wineskins. 39 And no
one after drinking old wine wants the new,
for they say, 'The old is better.'"

Jesus Is Lord of the Sabbath

6 One Sabbath Jesus was going through the
grainfields, and his disciples began to pick
some heads of grain, rub them in their hands
and eat the kernels. 2 Some of the Pharisees
asked, "Why are you doing what is unlawful
on the Sabbath?"
3 Jesus answered them, "Have you never
read what David did when he and his companions were hungry? 4 He entered the house
of God, and taking the consecrated bread, he
ate what is lawful only for priests to eat. And
he also gave some to his companions." 5 Then
Jesus said to them, "The Son of Man is Lord
of the Sabbath."
6 On another Sabbath he went into the synagogue and was teaching, and a man was
there whose right hand was shriveled. 7 The
Pharisees and the teachers of the law were
looking for a reason to accuse Jesus, so they
watched him closely to see if he would heal
on the Sabbath. 8 But Jesus knew what they
were thinking and said to the man with the
shriveled hand, "Get up and stand in front
of everyone." So he got up and stood there.
9 Then Jesus said to them, "I ask you, which
is lawful on the Sabbath: to do good or to do
evil, to save life or to destroy it?"
10 He looked around at them all, and then
said to the man, "Stretch out your hand." He
did so, and his hand was completely restored.
11 But the Pharisees and the teachers of the law
were furious and began to discuss with one
another what they might do to Jesus.

The Twelve Apostles

12 One of those days Jesus went out to a
mountainside to pray, and spent the night
praying to God. 13 When morning came, he
called his disciples to him and chose twelve
of them, whom he also designated apostles:
14 Simon (whom he named Peter), his brother
Andrew, James, John, Philip, Bartholomew,
15 Matthew, Thomas, James son of Alphaeus,
Simon who was called the Zealot, 16 Judas son
of James, and Judas Iscariot, who became a
traitor.

Blessings and Woes

17 He went down with them and stood on
a level place. A large crowd of his disciples
was there and a great number of people from
all over Judea, from Jerusalem, and from the
coastal region around Tyre and Sidon, 18 who
had come to hear him and to be healed of their
diseases. Those troubled by impure spirits
were cured, 19 and the people all tried to touch
him, because power was coming from him
and healing them all.
20 Looking at his disciples, he said:

"Blessed are you who are poor,
for yours is the kingdom of God.
21 Blessed are you who hunger now,
for you will be satisfied.
Blessed are you who weep now,
for you will laugh.
22 Blessed are you when people hate you,
when they exclude you and insult you
and reject your name as evil,
because of the Son of Man.

23 "Rejoice in that day and leap for joy, because great is your reward in heaven. For that
is how their ancestors treated the prophets.

24 "But woe to you who are rich,
for you have already received your
comfort.
25 Woe to you who are well fed now,
for you will go hungry.
Woe to you who laugh now,
for you will mourn and weep.
26 Woe to you when everyone speaks well of
you,
for that is how their ancestors treated
the false prophets.

Love for Enemies

27 "But to you who are listening I say: Love
your enemies, do good to those who hate you,
28 bless those who curse you, pray for those
who mistreat you. 29 If someone slaps you
on one cheek, turn to them the other also.
If someone takes your coat, do not withhold
your shirt from them. 30 Give to everyone who
asks you, and if anyone takes what belongs
to you, do not demand it back. 31 Do to others
as you would have them do to you.
32 "If you love those who love you, what
credit is that to you? Even sinners love those
who love them. 33 And if you do good to those
who are good to you, what credit is that to
you? Even sinners do that. 34 And if you lend
to those from whom you expect repayment,

what credit is that to you? Even sinners lend to sinners, expecting to be repaid in full. 35But love your enemies, do good to them, and lend to them without expecting to get anything back. Then your reward will be great, and you will be children of the Most High, because he is kind to the ungrateful and wicked. 36Be merciful, just as your Father is merciful.

Judging Others

37"Do not judge, and you will not be judged. Do not condemn, and you will not be condemned. Forgive, and you will be forgiven. 38Give, and it will be given to you. A good measure, pressed down, shaken together and running over, will be poured into your lap. For with the measure you use, it will be measured to you."

39He also told them this parable: "Can the blind lead the blind? Will they not both fall into a pit? 40The student is not above the teacher, but everyone who is fully trained will be like their teacher.

41"Why do you look at the speck of sawdust in your brother's eye and pay no attention to the plank in your own eye? 42How can you say to your brother, 'Brother, let me take the speck out of your eye,' when you yourself fail to see the plank in your own eye? You hypocrite, first take the plank out of your eye, and then you will see clearly to remove the speck from your brother's eye.

A Tree and Its Fruit

43"No good tree bears bad fruit, nor does a bad tree bear good fruit. 44Each tree is recognized by its own fruit. People do not pick figs from thornbushes, or grapes from briers. 45A good man brings good things out of the good stored up in his heart, and an evil man brings evil things out of the evil stored up in his heart. For the mouth speaks what the heart is full of.

The Wise and Foolish Builders

46"Why do you call me, 'Lord, Lord,' and do not do what I say? 47As for everyone who comes to me and hears my words and puts them into practice, I will show you what they are like. 48They are like a man building a house, who dug down deep and laid the foundation on rock. When a flood came, the torrent struck that house but could not shake it, because it was well built. 49But the one who hears my words and does not put them into practice is like a man who built a house on the ground without a foundation. The moment the torrent struck that house, it collapsed and its destruction was complete."

The Faith of the Centurion

7 When Jesus had finished saying all this to the people who were listening, he entered Capernaum. 2There a centurion's servant, whom his master valued highly, was sick and about to die. 3The centurion heard of Jesus and sent some elders of the Jews to him, asking him to come and heal his servant. 4When they came to Jesus, they pleaded earnestly with him, "This man deserves to have you do this, 5because he loves our nation and has built our synagogue." 6So Jesus went with them.

He was not far from the house when the centurion sent friends to say to him: "Lord, don't trouble yourself, for I do not deserve to have you come under my roof. 7That is why I did not even consider myself worthy to come to you. But say the word, and my servant will be healed. 8For I myself am a man under authority, with soldiers under me. I tell this one, 'Go,' and he goes; and that one, 'Come,' and he comes. I say to my servant, 'Do this,' and he does it."

9When Jesus heard this, he was amazed at him, and turning to the crowd following him, he said, "I tell you, I have not found such great faith even in Israel." 10Then the men who had been sent returned to the house and found the servant well.

Jesus Raises a Widow's Son

11Soon afterward, Jesus went to a town called Nain, and his disciples and a large crowd went along with him. 12As he approached the town gate, a dead person was being carried out—the only son of his mother, and she was a widow. And a large crowd from the town was with her. 13When the Lord saw her, his heart went out to her and he said, "Don't cry."

14Then he went up and touched the bier they were carrying him on, and the bearers stood still. He said, "Young man, I say to you, get up!" 15The dead man sat up and began to talk, and Jesus gave him back to his mother.

16They were all filled with awe and praised God. "A great prophet has appeared among us," they said. "God has come to help his people." 17This news about Jesus spread throughout Judea and the surrounding country.

Jesus and John the Baptist

18John's disciples told him about all these things. Calling two of them, 19he sent them to the Lord to ask, "Are you the one who is to come, or should we expect someone else?"

20When the men came to Jesus, they said, "John the Baptist sent us to you to ask, 'Are you the one who is to come, or should we expect someone else?'"

21At that very time Jesus cured many who had diseases, sicknesses and evil spirits, and gave sight to many who were blind. 22So he replied to the messengers, "Go back and report to John what you have seen and heard: The blind receive sight, the lame walk, those who have leprosy[a] are cleansed, the deaf hear, the dead are raised, and the good news is proclaimed to the poor. 23Blessed is anyone who does not stumble on account of me."

24After John's messengers left, Jesus began

[a] *22* The Greek word traditionally translated *leprosy* was used for various diseases affecting the skin.

to speak to the crowd about John: "What did
you go out into the wilderness to see? A reed
swayed by the wind? 25 If not, what did you go
out to see? A man dressed in fine clothes? No,
those who wear expensive clothes and indulge
in luxury are in palaces. 26 But what did you
go out to see? A prophet? Yes, I tell you, and
more than a prophet. 27 This is the one about
whom it is written:

"'I will send my messenger ahead of you,
who will prepare your way before you.'[a]

28 I tell you, among those born of women there
is no one greater than John; yet the one who
is least in the kingdom of God is greater
than he."

29 (All the people, even the tax collectors,
when they heard Jesus' words, acknowledged
that God's way was right, because they had
been baptized by John. 30 But the Pharisees
and the experts in the law rejected God's
purpose for themselves, because they had
not been baptized by John.)

31 Jesus went on to say, "To what, then, can I
compare the people of this generation? What
are they like? 32 They are like children sitting
in the marketplace and calling out to each
other:

"'We played the pipe for you,
and you did not dance;
we sang a dirge,
and you did not cry.'

33 For John the Baptist came neither eating
bread nor drinking wine, and you say, 'He
has a demon.' 34 The Son of Man came eating
and drinking, and you say, 'Here is a glutton
and a drunkard, a friend of tax collectors and
sinners.' 35 But wisdom is proved right by all
her children."

Jesus Anointed by a Sinful Woman

36 When one of the Pharisees invited Jesus
to have dinner with him, he went to the Pharisee's house and reclined at the table. 37 A woman in that town who lived a sinful life learned
that Jesus was eating at the Pharisee's house,
so she came there with an alabaster jar of
perfume. 38 As she stood behind him at his
feet weeping, she began to wet his feet with
her tears. Then she wiped them with her hair,
kissed them and poured perfume on them.

39 When the Pharisee who had invited him
saw this, he said to himself, "If this man were
a prophet, he would know who is touching
him and what kind of woman she is—that
she is a sinner."

40 Jesus answered him, "Simon, I have something to tell you."

"Tell me, teacher," he said.

41 "Two people owed money to a certain
moneylender. One owed him five hundred denarii,[b] and the other fifty. 42 Neither of them
had the money to pay him back, so he forgave
the debts of both. Now which of them will
love him more?"

43 Simon replied, "I suppose the one who had
the bigger debt forgiven."

"You have judged correctly," Jesus said.

44 Then he turned toward the woman and
said to Simon, "Do you see this woman? I
came into your house. You did not give me
any water for my feet, but she wet my feet with
her tears and wiped them with her hair. 45 You
did not give me a kiss, but this woman, from
the time I entered, has not stopped kissing my
feet. 46 You did not put oil on my head, but she
has poured perfume on my feet. 47 Therefore, I
tell you, her many sins have been forgiven—
as her great love has shown. But whoever has
been forgiven little loves little."

48 Then Jesus said to her, "Your sins are forgiven."

49 The other guests began to say among
themselves, "Who is this who even forgives
sins?"

50 Jesus said to the woman, "Your faith has
saved you; go in peace."

The Parable of the Sower

8 After this, Jesus traveled about from one
town and village to another, proclaiming the good news of the kingdom of God.
The Twelve were with him, 2 and also some
women who had been cured of evil spirits
and diseases: Mary (called Magdalene) from
whom seven demons had come out; 3 Joanna
the wife of Chuza, the manager of Herod's
household; Susanna; and many others. These
women were helping to support them out of
their own means.

4 While a large crowd was gathering and
people were coming to Jesus from town after
town, he told this parable: 5 "A farmer went out
to sow his seed. As he was scattering the seed,
some fell along the path; it was trampled on,
and the birds ate it up. 6 Some fell on rocky
ground, and when it came up, the plants withered because they had no moisture. 7 Other
seed fell among thorns, which grew up with
it and choked the plants. 8 Still other seed fell
on good soil. It came up and yielded a crop, a
hundred times more than was sown."

When he said this, he called out, "Whoever
has ears to hear, let them hear."

9 His disciples asked him what this parable
meant. 10 He said, "The knowledge of the secrets of the kingdom of God has been given to
you, but to others I speak in parables, so that,

"'though seeing, they may not see;
though hearing, they may not
understand.'[c]

11 "This is the meaning of the parable: The
seed is the word of God. 12 Those along the
path are the ones who hear, and then the devil
comes and takes away the word from their
hearts, so that they may not believe and be
saved. 13 Those on the rocky ground are the
ones who receive the word with joy when they
hear it, but they have no root. They believe
for a while, but in the time of testing they

[a] *27* Mal. 3:1 [b] *41* A denarius was the usual daily wage of a day laborer (see Matt. 20:2).
[c] *10* Isaiah 6:9

fall away. 14The seed that fell among thorns stands for those who hear, but as they go on their way they are choked by life's worries, riches and pleasures, and they do not mature. 15But the seed on good soil stands for those with a noble and good heart, who hear the word, retain it, and by persevering produce a crop.

A Lamp on a Stand

16"No one lights a lamp and hides it in a clay jar or puts it under a bed. Instead, they put it on a stand, so that those who come in can see the light. 17For there is nothing hidden that will not be disclosed, and nothing concealed that will not be known or brought out into the open. 18Therefore consider carefully how you listen. Whoever has will be given more; whoever does not have, even what they think they have will be taken from them."

Jesus' Mother and Brothers

19Now Jesus' mother and brothers came to see him, but they were not able to get near him because of the crowd. 20Someone told him, "Your mother and brothers are standing outside, wanting to see you."

21He replied, "My mother and brothers are those who hear God's word and put it into practice."

Jesus Calms the Storm

22One day Jesus said to his disciples, "Let us go over to the other side of the lake." So they got into a boat and set out. 23As they sailed, he fell asleep. A squall came down on the lake, so that the boat was being swamped, and they were in great danger.

24The disciples went and woke him, saying, "Master, Master, we're going to drown!"

He got up and rebuked the wind and the raging waters; the storm subsided, and all was calm. 25"Where is your faith?" he asked his disciples.

In fear and amazement they asked one another, "Who is this? He commands even the winds and the water, and they obey him."

Jesus Restores a Demon-Possessed Man

26They sailed to the region of the Gerasenes,[a] which is across the lake from Galilee. 27When Jesus stepped ashore, he was met by a demon-possessed man from the town. For a long time this man had not worn clothes or lived in a house, but had lived in the tombs. 28When he saw Jesus, he cried out and fell at his feet, shouting at the top of his voice, "What do you want with me, Jesus, Son of the Most High God? I beg you, don't torture me!" 29For Jesus had commanded the impure spirit to come out of the man. Many times it had seized him, and though he was chained hand and foot and kept under guard, he had broken his chains and had been driven by the demon into solitary places.

30Jesus asked him, "What is your name?"

"Legion," he replied, because many demons had gone into him. 31And they begged Jesus repeatedly not to order them to go into the Abyss.

32A large herd of pigs was feeding there on the hillside. The demons begged Jesus to let them go into the pigs, and he gave them permission. 33When the demons came out of the man, they went into the pigs, and the herd rushed down the steep bank into the lake and was drowned.

34When those tending the pigs saw what had happened, they ran off and reported this in the town and countryside, 35and the people went out to see what had happened. When they came to Jesus, they found the man from whom the demons had gone out, sitting at Jesus' feet, dressed and in his right mind; and they were afraid. 36Those who had seen it told the people how the demon-possessed man had been cured. 37Then all the people of the region of the Gerasenes asked Jesus to leave them, because they were overcome with fear. So he got into the boat and left.

38The man from whom the demons had gone out begged to go with him, but Jesus sent him away, saying, 39"Return home and tell how much God has done for you." So the man went away and told all over town how much Jesus had done for him.

Jesus Raises a Dead Girl and Heals a Sick Woman

40Now when Jesus returned, a crowd welcomed him, for they were all expecting him. 41Then a man named Jairus, a synagogue leader, came and fell at Jesus' feet, pleading with him to come to his house 42because his only daughter, a girl of about twelve, was dying.

As Jesus was on his way, the crowds almost crushed him. 43And a woman was there who had been subject to bleeding for twelve years,[b] but no one could heal her. 44She came up behind him and touched the edge of his cloak, and immediately her bleeding stopped.

45"Who touched me?" Jesus asked.

When they all denied it, Peter said, "Master, the people are crowding and pressing against you."

46But Jesus said, "Someone touched me; I know that power has gone out from me."

47Then the woman, seeing that she could not go unnoticed, came trembling and fell at his feet. In the presence of all the people, she told why she had touched him and how she had been instantly healed. 48Then he said to her, "Daughter, your faith has healed you. Go in peace."

49While Jesus was still speaking, someone came from the house of Jairus, the synagogue leader. "Your daughter is dead," he said. "Don't bother the teacher anymore."

50Hearing this, Jesus said to Jairus, "Don't be afraid; just believe, and she will be healed."

[a] *26* Some manuscripts *Gadarenes*; other manuscripts *Gergesenes*; also in verse 37 [b] *43* Many manuscripts *years, and she had spent all she had on doctors*

51When he arrived at the house of Jairus,
he did not let anyone go in with him except
Peter, John and James, and the child's father
and mother. 52Meanwhile, all the people were
wailing and mourning for her. "Stop wailing,"
Jesus said. "She is not dead but asleep."
53They laughed at him, knowing that she
was dead. 54But he took her by the hand and
said, "My child, get up!" 55Her spirit returned,
and at once she stood up. Then Jesus told them
to give her something to eat. 56Her parents
were astonished, but he ordered them not to
tell anyone what had happened.

Jesus Sends Out the Twelve

9 When Jesus had called the Twelve together, he gave them power and authority to
drive out all demons and to cure diseases,
2and he sent them out to proclaim the kingdom of God and to heal the sick. 3He told them:
"Take nothing for the journey—no staff, no
bag, no bread, no money, no extra shirt.
4Whatever house you enter, stay there until
you leave that town. 5If people do not welcome
you, leave their town and shake the dust off
your feet as a testimony against them." 6So
they set out and went from village to village,
proclaiming the good news and healing people everywhere.
7Now Herod the tetrarch heard about all
that was going on. And he was perplexed because some were saying that John had been
raised from the dead, 8others that Elijah had
appeared, and still others that one of the
prophets of long ago had come back to life.
9But Herod said, "I beheaded John. Who, then,
is this I hear such things about?" And he tried
to see him.

Jesus Feeds the Five Thousand

10When the apostles returned, they reported to Jesus what they had done. Then he took
them with him and they withdrew by themselves to a town called Bethsaida, 11but the
crowds learned about it and followed him.
He welcomed them and spoke to them about
the kingdom of God, and healed those who
needed healing.
12Late in the afternoon the Twelve came to
him and said, "Send the crowd away so they
can go to the surrounding villages and countryside and find food and lodging, because we
are in a remote place here."
13He replied, "You give them something to
eat."
They answered, "We have only five loaves
of bread and two fish—unless we go and buy
food for all this crowd." 14(About five thousand men were there.)
But he said to his disciples, "Have them sit
down in groups of about fifty each." 15The
disciples did so, and everyone sat down.
16Taking the five loaves and the two fish
and looking up to heaven, he gave thanks
and broke them. Then he gave them to the
disciples to distribute to the people. 17They
all ate and were satisfied, and the disciples
picked up twelve basketfuls of broken pieces
that were left over.

Peter Declares That Jesus Is the Messiah

18Once when Jesus was praying in private
and his disciples were with him, he asked
them, "Who do the crowds say I am?"
19They replied, "Some say John the Baptist;
others say Elijah; and still others, that one
of the prophets of long ago has come back
to life."
20"But what about you?" he asked. "Who
do you say I am?"
Peter answered, "God's Messiah."

Jesus Predicts His Death

21Jesus strictly warned them not to tell this
to anyone. 22And he said, "The Son of Man
must suffer many things and be rejected by
the elders, the chief priests and the teachers
of the law, and he must be killed and on the
third day be raised to life."
23Then he said to them all: "Whoever wants
to be my disciple must deny themselves and
take up their cross daily and follow me. 24For
whoever wants to save their life will lose it,
but whoever loses their life for me will save
it. 25What good is it for someone to gain the
whole world, and yet lose or forfeit their very
self? 26Whoever is ashamed of me and my
words, the Son of Man will be ashamed of
them when he comes in his glory and in the
glory of the Father and of the holy angels.
27"Truly I tell you, some who are standing
here will not taste death before they see the
kingdom of God."

The Transfiguration

28About eight days after Jesus said this,
he took Peter, John and James with him and
went up onto a mountain to pray. 29As he was
praying, the appearance of his face changed,
and his clothes became as bright as a flash
of lightning. 30Two men, Moses and Elijah,
appeared in glorious splendor, talking with
Jesus. 31They spoke about his departure,[a]
which he was about to bring to fulfillment
at Jerusalem. 32Peter and his companions
were very sleepy, but when they became
fully awake, they saw his glory and the two
men standing with him. 33As the men were
leaving Jesus, Peter said to him, "Master, it
is good for us to be here. Let us put up three
shelters—one for you, one for Moses and
one for Elijah." (He did not know what he
was saying.)
34While he was speaking, a cloud appeared
and covered them, and they were afraid as
they entered the cloud. 35A voice came from
the cloud, saying, "This is my Son, whom I
have chosen; listen to him." 36When the voice
had spoken, they found that Jesus was alone.
The disciples kept this to themselves and did
not tell anyone at that time what they had
seen.

[a] *31* Greek *exodos*

Jesus Heals a Demon-Possessed Boy

37The next day, when they came down from the mountain, a large crowd met him. 38A man in the crowd called out, "Teacher, I beg you to look at my son, for he is my only child. 39A spirit seizes him and he suddenly screams; it throws him into convulsions so that he foams at the mouth. It scarcely ever leaves him and is destroying him. 40I begged your disciples to drive it out, but they could not."

41"You unbelieving and perverse generation," Jesus replied, "how long shall I stay with you and put up with you? Bring your son here."

42Even while the boy was coming, the demon threw him to the ground in a convulsion. But Jesus rebuked the impure spirit, healed the boy and gave him back to his father. 43And they were all amazed at the greatness of God.

Jesus Predicts His Death a Second Time

While everyone was marveling at all that Jesus did, he said to his disciples, 44"Listen carefully to what I am about to tell you: The Son of Man is going to be delivered into the hands of men." 45But they did not understand what this meant. It was hidden from them, so that they did not grasp it, and they were afraid to ask him about it.

46An argument started among the disciples as to which of them would be the greatest. 47Jesus, knowing their thoughts, took a little child and had him stand beside him. 48Then he said to them, "Whoever welcomes this little child in my name welcomes me; and whoever welcomes me welcomes the one who sent me. For it is the one who is least among you all who is the greatest."

49"Master," said John, "we saw someone driving out demons in your name and we tried to stop him, because he is not one of us."

50"Do not stop him," Jesus said, "for whoever is not against you is for you."

Samaritan Opposition

51As the time approached for him to be taken up to heaven, Jesus resolutely set out for Jerusalem. 52And he sent messengers on ahead, who went into a Samaritan village to get things ready for him; 53but the people there did not welcome him, because he was heading for Jerusalem. 54When the disciples James and John saw this, they asked, "Lord, do you want us to call fire down from heaven to destroy them[a]?" 55But Jesus turned and rebuked them. 56Then he and his disciples went to another village.

The Cost of Following Jesus

57As they were walking along the road, a man said to him, "I will follow you wherever you go."

58Jesus replied, "Foxes have dens and birds have nests, but the Son of Man has no place to lay his head."

59He said to another man, "Follow me."

But he replied, "Lord, first let me go and bury my father."

60Jesus said to him, "Let the dead bury their own dead, but you go and proclaim the kingdom of God."

61Still another said, "I will follow you, Lord; but first let me go back and say goodbye to my family."

62Jesus replied, "No one who puts a hand to the plow and looks back is fit for service in the kingdom of God."

Jesus Sends Out the Seventy-Two

10 After this the Lord appointed seventy-two[b] others and sent them two by two ahead of him to every town and place where he was about to go. 2He told them, "The harvest is plentiful, but the workers are few. Ask the Lord of the harvest, therefore, to send out workers into his harvest field. 3Go! I am sending you out like lambs among wolves. 4Do not take a purse or bag or sandals; and do not greet anyone on the road.

5"When you enter a house, first say, 'Peace to this house.' 6If someone who promotes peace is there, your peace will rest on them; if not, it will return to you. 7Stay there, eating and drinking whatever they give you, for the worker deserves his wages. Do not move around from house to house.

8"When you enter a town and are welcomed, eat what is offered to you. 9Heal the sick who are there and tell them, 'The kingdom of God has come near to you.' 10But when you enter a town and are not welcomed, go into its streets and say, 11'Even the dust of your town we wipe from our feet as a warning to you. Yet be sure of this: The kingdom of God has come near.' 12I tell you, it will be more bearable on that day for Sodom than for that town.

13"Woe to you, Chorazin! Woe to you, Bethsaida! For if the miracles that were performed in you had been performed in Tyre and Sidon, they would have repented long ago, sitting in sackcloth and ashes. 14But it will be more bearable for Tyre and Sidon at the judgment than for you. 15And you, Capernaum, will you be lifted to the heavens? No, you will go down to Hades.[c]

16"Whoever listens to you listens to me; whoever rejects you rejects me; but whoever rejects me rejects him who sent me."

17The seventy-two returned with joy and said, "Lord, even the demons submit to us in your name."

18He replied, "I saw Satan fall like lightning from heaven. 19I have given you authority to trample on snakes and scorpions and to overcome all the power of the enemy; nothing will harm you. 20However, do not rejoice that the spirits submit to you, but rejoice that your names are written in heaven."

21At that time Jesus, full of joy through the Holy Spirit, said, "I praise you, Father, Lord of heaven and earth, because you have hidden

[a] *54* Some manuscripts *them, just as Elijah did*
[b] *1* Some manuscripts *seventy;* also in verse 17
[c] *15* That is, the realm of the dead

these things from the wise and learned, and revealed them to little children. Yes, Father, for this is what you were pleased to do.

22“All things have been committed to me by my Father. No one knows who the Son is except the Father, and no one knows who the Father is except the Son and those to whom the Son chooses to reveal him.”

23Then he turned to his disciples and said privately, “Blessed are the eyes that see what you see. 24For I tell you that many prophets and kings wanted to see what you see but did not see it, and to hear what you hear but did not hear it.”

The Parable of the Good Samaritan

25On one occasion an expert in the law stood up to test Jesus. “Teacher,” he asked, “what must I do to inherit eternal life?”

26“What is written in the Law?” he replied. “How do you read it?”

27He answered, “ ‘Love the Lord your God with all your heart and with all your soul and with all your strength and with all your mind’[a]; and, ‘Love your neighbor as yourself.’[b]”

28“You have answered correctly,” Jesus replied. “Do this and you will live.”

29But he wanted to justify himself, so he asked Jesus, “And who is my neighbor?”

30In reply Jesus said: “A man was going down from Jerusalem to Jericho, when he was attacked by robbers. They stripped him of his clothes, beat him and went away, leaving him half dead. 31A priest happened to be going down the same road, and when he saw the man, he passed by on the other side. 32So too, a Levite, when he came to the place and saw him, passed by on the other side. 33But a Samaritan, as he traveled, came where the man was; and when he saw him, he took pity on him. 34He went to him and bandaged his wounds, pouring on oil and wine. Then he put the man on his own donkey, brought him to an inn and took care of him. 35The next day he took out two denarii[c] and gave them to the innkeeper. ‘Look after him,’ he said, ‘and when I return, I will reimburse you for any extra expense you may have.’

36“Which of these three do you think was a neighbor to the man who fell into the hands of robbers?”

37The expert in the law replied, “The one who had mercy on him.”

Jesus told him, “Go and do likewise.”

At the Home of Martha and Mary

38As Jesus and his disciples were on their way, he came to a village where a woman named Martha opened her home to him. 39She had a sister called Mary, who sat at the Lord’s feet listening to what he said. 40But Martha was distracted by all the preparations that had to be made. She came to him and asked, “Lord, don’t you care that my sister has left me to do the work by myself? Tell her to help me!”

41“Martha, Martha,” the Lord answered, “you are worried and upset about many things, 42but few things are needed—or indeed only one.[d] Mary has chosen what is better, and it will not be taken away from her.”

Jesus’ Teaching on Prayer

11 One day Jesus was praying in a certain place. When he finished, one of his disciples said to him, “Lord, teach us to pray, just as John taught his disciples.”

2He said to them, “When you pray, say:

“ ‘Father,[e]
hallowed be your name,
your kingdom come.[f]
3Give us each day our daily bread.
4Forgive us our sins,
for we also forgive everyone who sins against us.[g]
And lead us not into temptation.[h]’ ”

5Then Jesus said to them, “Suppose you have a friend, and you go to him at midnight and say, ‘Friend, lend me three loaves of bread; 6a friend of mine on a journey has come to me, and I have no food to offer him.’ 7And suppose the one inside answers, ‘Don’t bother me. The door is already locked, and my children and I are in bed. I can’t get up and give you anything.’ 8I tell you, even though he will not get up and give you the bread because of friendship, yet because of your shameless audacity[i] he will surely get up and give you as much as you need.

9“So I say to you: Ask and it will be given to you; seek and you will find; knock and the door will be opened to you. 10For everyone who asks receives; the one who seeks finds; and to the one who knocks, the door will be opened.

11“Which of you fathers, if your son asks for[j] a fish, will give him a snake instead? 12Or if he asks for an egg, will give him a scorpion? 13If you then, though you are evil, know how to give good gifts to your children, how much more will your Father in heaven give the Holy Spirit to those who ask him!”

Jesus and Beelzebul

14Jesus was driving out a demon that was mute. When the demon left, the man who had been mute spoke, and the crowd was amazed. 15But some of them said, “By Beelzebul, the prince of demons, he is driving out demons.” 16Others tested him by asking for a sign from heaven.

17Jesus knew their thoughts and said to them: “Any kingdom divided against itself

[a] 27 Deut. 6:5 [b] 27 Lev. 19:18 [c] 35 A denarius was the usual daily wage of a day laborer (see Matt. 20:2). [d] 42 Some manuscripts *but only one thing is needed* [e] 2 Some manuscripts *Our Father in heaven* [f] 2 Some manuscripts *come. May your will be done on earth as it is in heaven.* [g] 4 Greek *everyone who is indebted to us* [h] 4 Some manuscripts *temptation, but deliver us from the evil one* [i] 8 Or *yet to preserve his good name* [j] 11 Some manuscripts *for bread, will give him a stone? Or if he asks for*

will be ruined, and a house divided against
itself will fall. 18If Satan is divided against
himself, how can his kingdom stand? I say
this because you claim that I drive out demons
by Beelzebul. 19Now if I drive out demons by
Beelzebul, by whom do your followers drive
them out? So then, they will be your judges.
20But if I drive out demons by the finger of God,
then the kingdom of God has come upon you.
21"When a strong man, fully armed, guards
his own house, his possessions are safe. 22But
when someone stronger attacks and overpow-
ers him, he takes away the armor in which
the man trusted and divides up his plunder.
23"Whoever is not with me is against me,
and whoever does not gather with me scatters.
24"When an impure spirit comes out of a
person, it goes through arid places seeking
rest and does not find it. Then it says, 'I will
return to the house I left.' 25When it arrives, it
finds the house swept clean and put in order.
26Then it goes and takes seven other spirits
more wicked than itself, and they go in and
live there. And the final condition of that person is worse than the first."
27As Jesus was saying these things, a woman in the crowd called out, "Blessed is the
mother who gave you birth and nursed you."
28He replied, "Blessed rather are those who
hear the word of God and obey it."

The Sign of Jonah

29As the crowds increased, Jesus said, "This
is a wicked generation. It asks for a sign, but
none will be given it except the sign of Jonah.
30For as Jonah was a sign to the Ninevites, so
also will the Son of Man be to this generation.
31The Queen of the South will rise at the judgment with the people of this generation and
condemn them, for she came from the ends of
the earth to listen to Solomon's wisdom; and
now something greater than Solomon is here.
32The men of Nineveh will stand up at the judgment with this generation and condemn it, for
they repented at the preaching of Jonah; and
now something greater than Jonah is here.

The Lamp of the Body

33"No one lights a lamp and puts it in a place
where it will be hidden, or under a bowl. Instead they put it on its stand, so that those
who come in may see the light. 34Your eye is
the lamp of your body. When your eyes are
healthy,[a] your whole body also is full of light.
But when they are unhealthy,[b] your body also
is full of darkness. 35See to it, then, that the
light within you is not darkness. 36Therefore,
if your whole body is full of light, and no part
of it dark, it will be just as full of light as when
a lamp shines its light on you."

Woes on the Pharisees and the Experts in the Law

37When Jesus had finished speaking, a
Pharisee invited him to eat with him; so he
went in and reclined at the table. 38But the
Pharisee was surprised when he noticed that
Jesus did not first wash before the meal.
39Then the Lord said to him, "Now then,
you Pharisees clean the outside of the cup
and dish, but inside you are full of greed and
wickedness. 40You foolish people! Did not the
one who made the outside make the inside
also? 41But now as for what is inside you—be
generous to the poor, and everything will be
clean for you.
42"Woe to you Pharisees, because you give
God a tenth of your mint, rue and all other
kinds of garden herbs, but you neglect justice
and the love of God. You should have practiced the latter without leaving the former
undone.
43"Woe to you Pharisees, because you love
the most important seats in the synagogues
and respectful greetings in the marketplaces.
44"Woe to you, because you are like un-
marked graves, which people walk over without knowing it."
45One of the experts in the law answered
him, "Teacher, when you say these things, you
insult us also."
46Jesus replied, "And you experts in the law,
woe to you, because you load people down
with burdens they can hardly carry, and you
yourselves will not lift one finger to help them.
47"Woe to you, because you build tombs for
the prophets, and it was your ancestors who
killed them. 48So you testify that you approve
of what your ancestors did; they killed the
prophets, and you build their tombs. 49Because
of this, God in his wisdom said, 'I will send
them prophets and apostles, some of whom
they will kill and others they will persecute.'
50Therefore this generation will be held responsible for the blood of all the prophets
that has been shed since the beginning of the
world, 51from the blood of Abel to the blood of
Zechariah, who was killed between the altar
and the sanctuary. Yes, I tell you, this generation will be held responsible for it all.
52"Woe to you experts in the law, because
you have taken away the key to knowledge.
You yourselves have not entered, and you have
hindered those who were entering."
53When Jesus went outside, the Pharisees
and the teachers of the law began to oppose
him fiercely and to besiege him with questions, 54waiting to catch him in something he
might say.

Warnings and Encouragements

12 Meanwhile, when a crowd of many thousands had gathered, so that they were
trampling on one another, Jesus began to
speak first to his disciples, saying: "Be[c] on
your guard against the yeast of the Pharisees,
which is hypocrisy. 2There is nothing concealed that will not be disclosed, or hidden
that will not be made known. 3What you have
said in the dark will be heard in the daylight,
and what you have whispered in the ear in

[a] 34 The Greek for *healthy* here implies *generous.*
[b] 34 The Greek for *unhealthy* here implies *stingy.*
[c] 1 Or *speak to his disciples, saying: "First of all, be*

the inner rooms will be proclaimed from the
roofs.
4"I tell you, my friends, do not be afraid of
those who kill the body and after that can
do no more. 5But I will show you whom you
should fear: Fear him who, after your body
has been killed, has authority to throw you
into hell. Yes, I tell you, fear him. 6Are not five
sparrows sold for two pennies? Yet not one of
them is forgotten by God. 7Indeed, the very
hairs of your head are all numbered. Don't
be afraid; you are worth more than many
sparrows.
8"I tell you, whoever publicly acknowledges me before others, the Son of Man will also
acknowledge before the angels of God. 9But
whoever disowns me before others will be
disowned before the angels of God. 10And
everyone who speaks a word against the
Son of Man will be forgiven, but anyone who
blasphemes against the Holy Spirit will not
be forgiven.
11"When you are brought before synagogues, rulers and authorities, do not worry
about how you will defend yourselves or what
you will say, 12for the Holy Spirit will teach
you at that time what you should say."

The Parable of the Rich Fool

13Someone in the crowd said to him, "Teacher, tell my brother to divide the inheritance
with me."
14Jesus replied, "Man, who appointed me a
judge or an arbiter between you?" 15Then he
said to them, "Watch out! Be on your guard
against all kinds of greed; life does not consist
in an abundance of possessions."
16And he told them this parable: "The
ground of a certain rich man yielded an abundant harvest. 17He thought to himself, 'What
shall I do? I have no place to store my crops.'
18"Then he said, 'This is what I'll do. I will
tear down my barns and build bigger ones,
and there I will store my surplus grain. 19And
I'll say to myself, "You have plenty of grain
laid up for many years. Take life easy; eat,
drink and be merry."'
20"But God said to him, 'You fool! This very
night your life will be demanded from you.
Then who will get what you have prepared
for yourself?'
21"This is how it will be with whoever stores
up things for themselves but is not rich toward God."

Do Not Worry

22Then Jesus said to his disciples: "Therefore I tell you, do not worry about your life,
what you will eat; or about your body, what
you will wear. 23For life is more than food,
and the body more than clothes. 24Consider
the ravens: They do not sow or reap, they have
no storeroom or barn; yet God feeds them.
And how much more valuable you are than
birds! 25Who of you by worrying can add a
single hour to your life[a]? 26Since you cannot
do this very little thing, why do you worry
about the rest?
27"Consider how the wild flowers grow.
They do not labor or spin. Yet I tell you, not
even Solomon in all his splendor was dressed
like one of these. 28If that is how God clothes
the grass of the field, which is here today, and
tomorrow is thrown into the fire, how much
more will he clothe you—you of little faith!
29And do not set your heart on what you will
eat or drink; do not worry about it. 30For the
pagan world runs after all such things, and
your Father knows that you need them. 31But
seek his kingdom, and these things will be
given to you as well.
32"Do not be afraid, little flock, for your Father has been pleased to give you the kingdom. 33Sell your possessions and give to the
poor. Provide purses for yourselves that will
not wear out, a treasure in heaven that will
never fail, where no thief comes near and no
moth destroys. 34For where your treasure is,
there your heart will be also.

Watchfulness

35"Be dressed ready for service and keep
your lamps burning, 36like servants waiting
for their master to return from a wedding banquet, so that when he comes and knocks they
can immediately open the door for him. 37It
will be good for those servants whose master
finds them watching when he comes. Truly I
tell you, he will dress himself to serve, will
have them recline at the table and will come
and wait on them. 38It will be good for those
servants whose master finds them ready, even
if he comes in the middle of the night or toward daybreak. 39But understand this: If the
owner of the house had known at what hour
the thief was coming, he would not have let
his house be broken into. 40You also must be
ready, because the Son of Man will come at
an hour when you do not expect him."
41Peter asked, "Lord, are you telling this
parable to us, or to everyone?"
42The Lord answered, "Who then is the
faithful and wise manager, whom the master puts in charge of his servants to give them
their food allowance at the proper time? 43It
will be good for that servant whom the master finds doing so when he returns. 44Truly I
tell you, he will put him in charge of all his
possessions. 45But suppose the servant says
to himself, 'My master is taking a long time
in coming,' and he then begins to beat the
other servants, both men and women, and to
eat and drink and get drunk. 46The master of
that servant will come on a day when he does
not expect him and at an hour he is not aware
of. He will cut him to pieces and assign him a
place with the unbelievers.
47"The servant who knows the master's will
and does not get ready or does not do what
the master wants will be beaten with many
blows. 48But the one who does not know and
does things deserving punishment will be
beaten with few blows. From everyone who

[a] 25 Or *single cubit to your height*

has been given much, much will be demanded;
and from the one who has been entrusted with
much, much more will be asked.

Not Peace but Division

49"I have come to bring fire on the earth,
and how I wish it were already kindled! 50But
I have a baptism to undergo, and what con-
straint I am under until it is completed! 51Do
you think I came to bring peace on earth? No, I
tell you, but division. 52From now on there will
be five in one family divided against each other, three against two and two against three.
53They will be divided, father against son and
son against father, mother against daughter
and daughter against mother, mother-in-law
against daughter-in-law and daughter-in-law
against mother-in-law."

Interpreting the Times

54He said to the crowd: "When you see a
cloud rising in the west, immediately you say,
'It's going to rain,' and it does. 55And when
the south wind blows, you say, 'It's going to
be hot,' and it is. 56Hypocrites! You know how
to interpret the appearance of the earth and
the sky. How is it that you don't know how to
interpret this present time?

57"Why don't you judge for yourselves what
is right? 58As you are going with your adversary to the magistrate, try hard to be reconciled on the way, or your adversary may drag
you off to the judge, and the judge turn you
over to the officer, and the officer throw you
into prison. 59I tell you, you will not get out
until you have paid the last penny."

Repent or Perish

13 Now there were some present at that
time who told Jesus about the Galileans whose blood Pilate had mixed with their
sacrifices. 2Jesus answered, "Do you think
that these Galileans were worse sinners than
all the other Galileans because they suffered
this way? 3I tell you, no! But unless you repent,
you too will all perish. 4Or those eighteen who
died when the tower in Siloam fell on them—
do you think they were more guilty than all
the others living in Jerusalem? 5I tell you, no!
But unless you repent, you too will all perish."

6Then he told this parable: "A man had a fig
tree growing in his vineyard, and he went to
look for fruit on it but did not find any. 7So he
said to the man who took care of the vineyard,
'For three years now I've been coming to look
for fruit on this fig tree and haven't found any.
Cut it down! Why should it use up the soil?'

8" 'Sir,' the man replied, 'leave it alone for
one more year, and I'll dig around it and fer-
tilize it. 9If it bears fruit next year, fine! If not,
then cut it down.' "

Jesus Heals a Crippled Woman on the Sabbath

10On a Sabbath Jesus was teaching in one
of the synagogues, 11and a woman was there
who had been crippled by a spirit for eighteen years. She was bent over and could not
straighten up at all. 12When Jesus saw her, he
called her forward and said to her, "Woman,
you are set free from your infirmity." 13Then
he put his hands on her, and immediately she
straightened up and praised God.

14Indignant because Jesus had healed on the
Sabbath, the synagogue leader said to the people, "There are six days for work. So come and
be healed on those days, not on the Sabbath."

15The Lord answered him, "You hypocrites!
Doesn't each of you on the Sabbath untie your
ox or donkey from the stall and lead it out to
give it water? 16Then should not this woman,
a daughter of Abraham, whom Satan has kept
bound for eighteen long years, be set free on
the Sabbath day from what bound her?"

17When he said this, all his opponents were
humiliated, but the people were delighted with
all the wonderful things he was doing.

The Parables of the Mustard Seed and the Yeast

18Then Jesus asked, "What is the kingdom
of God like? What shall I compare it to? 19It
is like a mustard seed, which a man took and
planted in his garden. It grew and became a
tree, and the birds perched in its branches."

20Again he asked, "What shall I compare the
kingdom of God to? 21It is like yeast that a woman took and mixed into about sixty pounds[a] of
flour until it worked all through the dough."

The Narrow Door

22Then Jesus went through the towns and
villages, teaching as he made his way to Jerusalem. 23Someone asked him, "Lord, are only
a few people going to be saved?"

He said to them, 24"Make every effort to enter through the narrow door, because many, I
tell you, will try to enter and will not be able
to. 25Once the owner of the house gets up and
closes the door, you will stand outside knocking and pleading, 'Sir, open the door for us.'

"But he will answer, 'I don't know you or
where you come from.'

26"Then you will say, 'We ate and drank
with you, and you taught in our streets.'

27"But he will reply, 'I don't know you or
where you come from. Away from me, all you
evildoers!'

28"There will be weeping there, and gnashing of teeth, when you see Abraham, Isaac and
Jacob and all the prophets in the kingdom of
God, but you yourselves thrown out. 29People
will come from east and west and north and
south, and will take their places at the feast in
the kingdom of God. 30Indeed there are those
who are last who will be first, and first who
will be last."

Jesus' Sorrow for Jerusalem

31At that time some Pharisees came to
Jesus and said to him, "Leave this place and
go somewhere else. Herod wants to kill you."

[a] *21* Or about 27 kilograms

32He replied, "Go tell that fox, 'I will keep on driving out demons and healing people today and tomorrow, and on the third day I will reach my goal.' 33In any case, I must press on today and tomorrow and the next day—for surely no prophet can die outside Jerusalem!

34"Jerusalem, Jerusalem, you who kill the prophets and stone those sent to you, how often I have longed to gather your children together, as a hen gathers her chicks under her wings, and you were not willing. 35Look, your house is left to you desolate. I tell you, you will not see me again until you say, 'Blessed is he who comes in the name of the Lord.'[a]"

Jesus at a Pharisee's House

14 One Sabbath, when Jesus went to eat in the house of a prominent Pharisee, he was being carefully watched. 2There in front of him was a man suffering from abnormal swelling of his body. 3Jesus asked the Pharisees and experts in the law, "Is it lawful to heal on the Sabbath or not?" 4But they remained silent. So taking hold of the man, he healed him and sent him on his way.

5Then he asked them, "If one of you has a child[b] or an ox that falls into a well on the Sabbath day, will you not immediately pull it out?" 6And they had nothing to say.

7When he noticed how the guests picked the places of honor at the table, he told them this parable: 8"When someone invites you to a wedding feast, do not take the place of honor, for a person more distinguished than you may have been invited. 9If so, the host who invited both of you will come and say to you, 'Give this person your seat.' Then, humiliated, you will have to take the least important place. 10But when you are invited, take the lowest place, so that when your host comes, he will say to you, 'Friend, move up to a better place.' Then you will be honored in the presence of all the other guests. 11For all those who exalt themselves will be humbled, and those who humble themselves will be exalted."

12Then Jesus said to his host, "When you give a luncheon or dinner, do not invite your friends, your brothers or sisters, your relatives, or your rich neighbors; if you do, they may invite you back and so you will be repaid. 13But when you give a banquet, invite the poor, the crippled, the lame, the blind, 14and you will be blessed. Although they cannot repay you, you will be repaid at the resurrection of the righteous."

The Parable of the Great Banquet

15When one of those at the table with him heard this, he said to Jesus, "Blessed is the one who will eat at the feast in the kingdom of God."

16Jesus replied: "A certain man was preparing a great banquet and invited many guests. 17At the time of the banquet he sent his servant to tell those who had been invited, 'Come, for everything is now ready.'

18"But they all alike began to make excuses. The first said, 'I have just bought a field, and I must go and see it. Please excuse me.'

19"Another said, 'I have just bought five yoke of oxen, and I'm on my way to try them out. Please excuse me.'

20"Still another said, 'I just got married, so I can't come.'

21"The servant came back and reported this to his master. Then the owner of the house became angry and ordered his servant, 'Go out quickly into the streets and alleys of the town and bring in the poor, the crippled, the blind and the lame.'

22"'Sir,' the servant said, 'what you ordered has been done, but there is still room.'

23"Then the master told his servant, 'Go out to the roads and country lanes and compel them to come in, so that my house will be full. 24I tell you, not one of those who were invited will get a taste of my banquet.'"

The Cost of Being a Disciple

25Large crowds were traveling with Jesus, and turning to them he said: 26"If anyone comes to me and does not hate father and mother, wife and children, brothers and sisters—yes, even their own life—such a person cannot be my disciple. 27And whoever does not carry their cross and follow me cannot be my disciple.

28"Suppose one of you wants to build a tower. Won't you first sit down and estimate the cost to see if you have enough money to complete it? 29For if you lay the foundation and are not able to finish it, everyone who sees it will ridicule you, 30saying, 'This person began to build and wasn't able to finish.'

31"Or suppose a king is about to go to war against another king. Won't he first sit down and consider whether he is able with ten thousand men to oppose the one coming against him with twenty thousand? 32If he is not able, he will send a delegation while the other is still a long way off and will ask for terms of peace. 33In the same way, those of you who do not give up everything you have cannot be my disciples.

34"Salt is good, but if it loses its saltiness, how can it be made salty again? 35It is fit neither for the soil nor for the manure pile; it is thrown out.

"Whoever has ears to hear, let them hear."

The Parable of the Lost Sheep

15 Now the tax collectors and sinners were all gathering around to hear Jesus. 2But the Pharisees and the teachers of the law muttered, "This man welcomes sinners and eats with them."

3Then Jesus told them this parable: 4"Suppose one of you has a hundred sheep and loses one of them. Doesn't he leave the ninety-nine in the open country and go after the lost sheep until he finds it? 5And when he finds it, he joyfully puts it on his shoulders 6and goes

[a] 35 Psalm 118:26 [b] 5 Some manuscripts *donkey*

home. Then he calls his friends and neighbors together and says, 'Rejoice with me; I have found my lost sheep.' 7I tell you that in the same way there will be more rejoicing in heaven over one sinner who repents than over ninety-nine righteous persons who do not need to repent.

The Parable of the Lost Coin

8"Or suppose a woman has ten silver coins[a] and loses one. Doesn't she light a lamp, sweep the house and search carefully until she finds it? 9And when she finds it, she calls her friends and neighbors together and says, 'Rejoice with me; I have found my lost coin.' 10In the same way, I tell you, there is rejoicing in the presence of the angels of God over one sinner who repents."

The Parable of the Lost Son

11Jesus continued: "There was a man who had two sons. 12The younger one said to his father, 'Father, give me my share of the estate.' So he divided his property between them.

13"Not long after that, the younger son got together all he had, set off for a distant country and there squandered his wealth in wild living. 14After he had spent everything, there was a severe famine in that whole country, and he began to be in need. 15So he went and hired himself out to a citizen of that country, who sent him to his fields to feed pigs. 16He longed to fill his stomach with the pods that the pigs were eating, but no one gave him anything.

17"When he came to his senses, he said, 'How many of my father's hired servants have food to spare, and here I am starving to death! 18I will set out and go back to my father and say to him: Father, I have sinned against heaven and against you. 19I am no longer worthy to be called your son; make me like one of your hired servants.' 20So he got up and went to his father.

"But while he was still a long way off, his father saw him and was filled with compassion for him; he ran to his son, threw his arms around him and kissed him.

21"The son said to him, 'Father, I have sinned against heaven and against you. I am no longer worthy to be called your son.'

22"But the father said to his servants, 'Quick! Bring the best robe and put it on him. Put a ring on his finger and sandals on his feet. 23Bring the fattened calf and kill it. Let's have a feast and celebrate. 24For this son of mine was dead and is alive again; he was lost and is found.' So they began to celebrate.

25"Meanwhile, the older son was in the field. When he came near the house, he heard music and dancing. 26So he called one of the servants and asked him what was going on. 27'Your brother has come,' he replied, 'and your father has killed the fattened calf because he has him back safe and sound.'

28"The older brother became angry and refused to go in. So his father went out and pleaded with him. 29But he answered his father, 'Look! All these years I've been slaving for you and never disobeyed your orders. Yet you never gave me even a young goat so I could celebrate with my friends. 30But when this son of yours who has squandered your property with prostitutes comes home, you kill the fattened calf for him!'

31" 'My son,' the father said, 'you are always with me, and everything I have is yours. 32But we had to celebrate and be glad, because this brother of yours was dead and is alive again; he was lost and is found.' "

The Parable of the Shrewd Manager

16 Jesus told his disciples: "There was a rich man whose manager was accused of wasting his possessions. 2So he called him in and asked him, 'What is this I hear about you? Give an account of your management, because you cannot be manager any longer.'

3"The manager said to himself, 'What shall I do now? My master is taking away my job. I'm not strong enough to dig, and I'm ashamed to beg— 4I know what I'll do so that, when I lose my job here, people will welcome me into their houses.'

5"So he called in each one of his master's debtors. He asked the first, 'How much do you owe my master?'

6" 'Nine hundred gallons[b] of olive oil,' he replied.

"The manager told him, 'Take your bill, sit down quickly, and make it four hundred and fifty.'

7"Then he asked the second, 'And how much do you owe?'

" 'A thousand bushels[c] of wheat,' he replied.

"He told him, 'Take your bill and make it eight hundred.'

8"The master commended the dishonest manager because he had acted shrewdly. For the people of this world are more shrewd in dealing with their own kind than are the people of the light. 9I tell you, use worldly wealth to gain friends for yourselves, so that when it is gone, you will be welcomed into eternal dwellings.

10"Whoever can be trusted with very little can also be trusted with much, and whoever is dishonest with very little will also be dishonest with much. 11So if you have not been trustworthy in handling worldly wealth, who will trust you with true riches? 12And if you have not been trustworthy with someone else's property, who will give you property of your own?

13"No one can serve two masters. Either you will hate the one and love the other, or you will be devoted to the one and despise the other. You cannot serve both God and money."

14The Pharisees, who loved money, heard all this and were sneering at Jesus. 15He said to them, "You are the ones who justify your-

[a] 8 Greek *ten drachmas*, each worth about a day's wages [b] 6 Or about 3,000 liters [c] 7 Or about 30 tons

selves in the eyes of others, but God knows
your hearts. What people value highly is detestable in God's sight.

Additional Teachings

16"The Law and the Prophets were proclaimed until John. Since that time, the
good news of the kingdom of God is being
preached, and everyone is forcing their way
into it. 17It is easier for heaven and earth to
disappear than for the least stroke of a pen
to drop out of the Law.

18"Anyone who divorces his wife and marries another woman commits adultery, and
the man who marries a divorced woman commits adultery.

The Rich Man and Lazarus

19"There was a rich man who was dressed in
purple and fine linen and lived in luxury every
day. 20At his gate was laid a beggar named
Lazarus, covered with sores 21and longing to
eat what fell from the rich man's table. Even
the dogs came and licked his sores.

22"The time came when the beggar died and
the angels carried him to Abraham's side. The
rich man also died and was buried. 23In Hades,
where he was in torment, he looked up and
saw Abraham far away, with Lazarus by his
side. 24So he called to him, 'Father Abraham,
have pity on me and send Lazarus to dip the
tip of his finger in water and cool my tongue,
because I am in agony in this fire.'

25"But Abraham replied, 'Son, remember
that in your lifetime you received your good
things, while Lazarus received bad things, but
now he is comforted here and you are in agony. 26And besides all this, between us and you
a great chasm has been set in place, so that
those who want to go from here to you cannot,
nor can anyone cross over from there to us.'

27"He answered, 'Then I beg you, father,
send Lazarus to my family, 28for I have five
brothers. Let him warn them, so that they will
not also come to this place of torment.'

29"Abraham replied, 'They have Moses and
the Prophets; let them listen to them.'

30"'No, father Abraham,' he said, 'but if
someone from the dead goes to them, they
will repent.'

31"He said to him, 'If they do not listen to
Moses and the Prophets, they will not be convinced even if someone rises from the dead.'"

Sin, Faith, Duty

17 Jesus said to his disciples: "Things that
cause people to stumble are bound to
come, but woe to anyone through whom
they come. 2It would be better for them to
be thrown into the sea with a millstone tied
around their neck than to cause one of these
little ones to stumble. 3So watch yourselves.

"If your brother or sister[a] sins against you,
rebuke them; and if they repent, forgive them.
4Even if they sin against you seven times in a
day and seven times come back to you saying
'I repent,' you must forgive them."

5The apostles said to the Lord, "Increase
our faith!"

6He replied, "If you have faith as small as
a mustard seed, you can say to this mulberry
tree, 'Be uprooted and planted in the sea,' and
it will obey you.

7"Suppose one of you has a servant plowing or looking after the sheep. Will he say to
the servant when he comes in from the field,
'Come along now and sit down to eat'? 8Won't
he rather say, 'Prepare my supper, get yourself
ready and wait on me while I eat and drink;
after that you may eat and drink'? 9Will he
thank the servant because he did what he
was told to do? 10So you also, when you have
done everything you were told to do, should
say, 'We are unworthy servants; we have only
done our duty.'"

Jesus Heals Ten Men With Leprosy

11Now on his way to Jerusalem, Jesus traveled along the border between Samaria and
Galilee. 12As he was going into a village, ten
men who had leprosy[b] met him. They stood
at a distance 13and called out in a loud voice,
"Jesus, Master, have pity on us!"

14When he saw them, he said, "Go, show
yourselves to the priests." And as they went,
they were cleansed.

15One of them, when he saw he was healed,
came back, praising God in a loud voice. 16He
threw himself at Jesus' feet and thanked
him—and he was a Samaritan.

17Jesus asked, "Were not all ten cleansed?
Where are the other nine? 18Has no one returned to give praise to God except this foreigner?" 19Then he said to him, "Rise and go;
your faith has made you well."

The Coming of the Kingdom of God

20Once, on being asked by the Pharisees
when the kingdom of God would come, Jesus
replied, "The coming of the kingdom of God
is not something that can be observed, 21nor
will people say, 'Here it is,' or 'There it is,' because the kingdom of God is in your midst."[c]

22Then he said to his disciples, "The time
is coming when you will long to see one of
the days of the Son of Man, but you will not
see it. 23People will tell you, 'There he is!' or
'Here he is!' Do not go running off after them.
24For the Son of Man in his day[d] will be like
the lightning, which flashes and lights up the
sky from one end to the other. 25But first he
must suffer many things and be rejected by
this generation.

26"Just as it was in the days of Noah, so
also will it be in the days of the Son of Man.
27People were eating, drinking, marrying and
being given in marriage up to the day Noah
entered the ark. Then the flood came and destroyed them all.

[a] *3* The Greek word for *brother or sister* (*adelphos*) refers here to a fellow disciple, whether man or woman. [b] *12* The Greek word traditionally translated *leprosy* was used for various diseases affecting the skin. [c] *21* Or *is within you* [d] *24* Some manuscripts do not have *in his day.*

28"It was the same in the days of Lot. People were eating and drinking, buying and selling, planting and building. 29But the day Lot left Sodom, fire and sulfur rained down from heaven and destroyed them all.

30"It will be just like this on the day the Son of Man is revealed. 31On that day no one who is on the housetop, with possessions inside, should go down to get them. Likewise, no one in the field should go back for anything. 32Remember Lot's wife! 33Whoever tries to keep their life will lose it, and whoever loses their life will preserve it. 34I tell you, on that night two people will be in one bed; one will be taken and the other left. 35Two women will be grinding grain together; one will be taken and the other left." [36][a]

37"Where, Lord?" they asked.

He replied, "Where there is a dead body, there the vultures will gather."

The Parable of the Persistent Widow

18 Then Jesus told his disciples a parable to show them that they should always pray and not give up. 2He said: "In a certain town there was a judge who neither feared God nor cared what people thought. 3And there was a widow in that town who kept coming to him with the plea, 'Grant me justice against my adversary.'

4"For some time he refused. But finally he said to himself, 'Even though I don't fear God or care what people think, 5yet because this widow keeps bothering me, I will see that she gets justice, so that she won't eventually come and attack me!'"

6And the Lord said, "Listen to what the unjust judge says. 7And will not God bring about justice for his chosen ones, who cry out to him day and night? Will he keep putting them off? 8I tell you, he will see that they get justice, and quickly. However, when the Son of Man comes, will he find faith on the earth?"

The Parable of the Pharisee and the Tax Collector

9To some who were confident of their own righteousness and looked down on everyone else, Jesus told this parable: 10"Two men went up to the temple to pray, one a Pharisee and the other a tax collector. 11The Pharisee stood by himself and prayed: 'God, I thank you that I am not like other people—robbers, evildoers, adulterers—or even like this tax collector. 12I fast twice a week and give a tenth of all I get.'

13"But the tax collector stood at a distance. He would not even look up to heaven, but beat his breast and said, 'God, have mercy on me, a sinner.'

14"I tell you that this man, rather than the other, went home justified before God. For all those who exalt themselves will be humbled, and those who humble themselves will be exalted."

The Little Children and Jesus

15People were also bringing babies to Jesus for him to place his hands on them. When the disciples saw this, they rebuked them. 16But Jesus called the children to him and said, "Let the little children come to me, and do not hinder them, for the kingdom of God belongs to such as these. 17Truly I tell you, anyone who will not receive the kingdom of God like a little child will never enter it."

The Rich and the Kingdom of God

18A certain ruler asked him, "Good teacher, what must I do to inherit eternal life?"

19"Why do you call me good?" Jesus answered. "No one is good—except God alone. 20You know the commandments: 'You shall not commit adultery, you shall not murder, you shall not steal, you shall not give false testimony, honor your father and mother.'[b]"

21"All these I have kept since I was a boy," he said.

22When Jesus heard this, he said to him, "You still lack one thing. Sell everything you have and give to the poor, and you will have treasure in heaven. Then come, follow me."

23When he heard this, he became very sad, because he was very wealthy. 24Jesus looked at him and said, "How hard it is for the rich to enter the kingdom of God! 25Indeed, it is easier for a camel to go through the eye of a needle than for someone who is rich to enter the kingdom of God."

26Those who heard this asked, "Who then can be saved?"

27Jesus replied, "What is impossible with man is possible with God."

28Peter said to him, "We have left all we had to follow you!"

29"Truly I tell you," Jesus said to them, "no one who has left home or wife or brothers or sisters or parents or children for the sake of the kingdom of God 30will fail to receive many times as much in this age, and in the age to come eternal life."

Jesus Predicts His Death a Third Time

31Jesus took the Twelve aside and told them, "We are going up to Jerusalem, and everything that is written by the prophets about the Son of Man will be fulfilled. 32He will be delivered over to the Gentiles. They will mock him, insult him and spit on him; 33they will flog him and kill him. On the third day he will rise again."

34The disciples did not understand any of this. Its meaning was hidden from them, and they did not know what he was talking about.

A Blind Beggar Receives His Sight

35As Jesus approached Jericho, a blind man was sitting by the roadside begging. 36When he heard the crowd going by, he asked what was happening. 37They told him, "Jesus of Nazareth is passing by."

[a] *36* Some manuscripts include here words similar to Matt. 24:40. [b] *20* Exodus 20:12-16; Deut. 5:16-20

38He called out, "Jesus, Son of David, have
mercy on me!"
39Those who led the way rebuked him and
told him to be quiet, but he shouted all the
more, "Son of David, have mercy on me!"
40Jesus stopped and ordered the man to be
brought to him. When he came near, Jesus
asked him, 41"What do you want me to do for
you?"
"Lord, I want to see," he replied.
42Jesus said to him, "Receive your sight;
your faith has healed you." 43Immediately he
received his sight and followed Jesus, praising God. When all the people saw it, they also
praised God.

Zacchaeus the Tax Collector

19 Jesus entered Jericho and was passing
through. 2A man was there by the name
of Zacchaeus; he was a chief tax collector and
was wealthy. 3He wanted to see who Jesus
was, but because he was short he could not see
over the crowd. 4So he ran ahead and climbed
a sycamore-fig tree to see him, since Jesus
was coming that way.
5When Jesus reached the spot, he looked
up and said to him, "Zacchaeus, come down
immediately. I must stay at your house today."
6So he came down at once and welcomed him
gladly.
7All the people saw this and began to mutter, "He has gone to be the guest of a sinner."
8But Zacchaeus stood up and said to the
Lord, "Look, Lord! Here and now I give half
of my possessions to the poor, and if I have
cheated anybody out of anything, I will pay
back four times the amount."
9Jesus said to him, "Today salvation has
come to this house, because this man, too, is
a son of Abraham. 10For the Son of Man came
to seek and to save the lost."

The Parable of the Ten Minas

11While they were listening to this, he went
on to tell them a parable, because he was near
Jerusalem and the people thought that the
kingdom of God was going to appear at once.
12He said: "A man of noble birth went to a distant country to have himself appointed king
and then to return. 13So he called ten of his
servants and gave them ten minas.[a] 'Put this
money to work,' he said, 'until I come back.'
14"But his subjects hated him and sent a delegation after him to say, 'We don't want this
man to be our king.'
15"He was made king, however, and returned home. Then he sent for the servants
to whom he had given the money, in order to
find out what they had gained with it.
16"The first one came and said, 'Sir, your
mina has earned ten more.'
17" 'Well done, my good servant!' his master
replied. 'Because you have been trustworthy in
a very small matter, take charge of ten cities.'
18"The second came and said, 'Sir, your
mina has earned five more.'
19"His master answered, 'You take charge
of five cities.'
20"Then another servant came and said, 'Sir,
here is your mina; I have kept it laid away in
a piece of cloth. 21I was afraid of you, because
you are a hard man. You take out what you
did not put in and reap what you did not sow.'
22"His master replied, 'I will judge you by
your own words, you wicked servant! You
knew, did you, that I am a hard man, taking
out what I did not put in, and reaping what
I did not sow? 23Why then didn't you put my
money on deposit, so that when I came back,
I could have collected it with interest?'
24"Then he said to those standing by, 'Take
his mina away from him and give it to the one
who has ten minas.'
25" 'Sir,' they said, 'he already has ten!'
26"He replied, 'I tell you that to everyone
who has, more will be given, but as for the one
who has nothing, even what they have will be
taken away. 27But those enemies of mine who
did not want me to be king over them—bring
them here and kill them in front of me.' "

Jesus Comes to Jerusalem as King

28After Jesus had said this, he went on
ahead, going up to Jerusalem. 29As he approached Bethphage and Bethany at the hill
called the Mount of Olives, he sent two of his
disciples, saying to them, 30"Go to the village
ahead of you, and as you enter it, you will
find a colt tied there, which no one has ever
ridden. Untie it and bring it here. 31If anyone
asks you, 'Why are you untying it?' say, 'The
Lord needs it.' "
32Those who were sent ahead went and
found it just as he had told them. 33As they
were untying the colt, its owners asked them,
"Why are you untying the colt?"
34They replied, "The Lord needs it."
35They brought it to Jesus, threw their
cloaks on the colt and put Jesus on it. 36As
he went along, people spread their cloaks on
the road.
37When he came near the place where the
road goes down the Mount of Olives, the whole
crowd of disciples began joyfully to praise
God in loud voices for all the miracles they
had seen:

38"Blessed is the king who comes in the
name of the Lord!"[b]

"Peace in heaven and glory in the
highest!"

39Some of the Pharisees in the crowd said
to Jesus, "Teacher, rebuke your disciples!"
40"I tell you," he replied, "if they keep quiet,
the stones will cry out."
41As he approached Jerusalem and saw the
city, he wept over it 42and said, "If you, even
you, had only known on this day what would
bring you peace—but now it is hidden from
your eyes. 43The days will come upon you
when your enemies will build an embank-
ment against you and encircle you and hem

[a] *13* A mina was about three months' wages. [b] *38* Psalm 118:26

you in on every side. 44They will dash you to
the ground, you and the children within your
walls. They will not leave one stone on another, because you did not recognize the time of
God's coming to you."

Jesus at the Temple

45When Jesus entered the temple courts, he
began to drive out those who were selling. 46"It
is written," he said to them, "'My house will
be a house of prayer'[a]; but you have made it
'a den of robbers.'[b]"

47Every day he was teaching at the temple.
But the chief priests, the teachers of the law
and the leaders among the people were trying to kill him. 48Yet they could not find any
way to do it, because all the people hung on
his words.

The Authority of Jesus Questioned

20 One day as Jesus was teaching the people in the temple courts and proclaiming the good news, the chief priests and the
teachers of the law, together with the elders,
came up to him. 2"Tell us by what authority
you are doing these things," they said. "Who
gave you this authority?"

3He replied, "I will also ask you a question.
Tell me: 4John's baptism—was it from heaven,
or of human origin?"

5They discussed it among themselves and
said, "If we say, 'From heaven,' he will ask,
'Why didn't you believe him?' 6But if we say,
'Of human origin,' all the people will stone
us, because they are persuaded that John was
a prophet."

7So they answered, "We don't know where
it was from."

8Jesus said, "Neither will I tell you by what
authority I am doing these things."

The Parable of the Tenants

9He went on to tell the people this parable:
"A man planted a vineyard, rented it to some
farmers and went away for a long time. 10At
harvest time he sent a servant to the tenants
so they would give him some of the fruit of the
vineyard. But the tenants beat him and sent
him away empty-handed. 11He sent another
servant, but that one also they beat and treated shamefully and sent away empty-handed.
12He sent still a third, and they wounded him
and threw him out.

13"Then the owner of the vineyard said,
'What shall I do? I will send my son, whom I
love; perhaps they will respect him.'

14"But when the tenants saw him, they
talked the matter over. 'This is the heir,' they
said. 'Let's kill him, and the inheritance will
be ours.' 15So they threw him out of the vineyard and killed him.

"What then will the owner of the vineyard
do to them? 16He will come and kill those tenants and give the vineyard to others."

When the people heard this, they said, "God
forbid!"

17Jesus looked directly at them and asked,
"Then what is the meaning of that which is
written:

"'The stone the builders rejected
has become the cornerstone'[c]?

18Everyone who falls on that stone will be broken to pieces; anyone on whom it falls will
be crushed."

19The teachers of the law and the chief
priests looked for a way to arrest him immediately, because they knew he had spoken this
parable against them. But they were afraid
of the people.

Paying Taxes to Caesar

20Keeping a close watch on him, they sent
spies, who pretended to be sincere. They
hoped to catch Jesus in something he said,
so that they might hand him over to the power
and authority of the governor. 21So the spies
questioned him: "Teacher, we know that you
speak and teach what is right, and that you do
not show partiality but teach the way of God
in accordance with the truth. 22Is it right for
us to pay taxes to Caesar or not?"

23He saw through their duplicity and said to
them, 24"Show me a denarius. Whose image
and inscription are on it?"

"Caesar's," they replied.

25He said to them, "Then give back to Caesar
what is Caesar's, and to God what is God's."

26They were unable to trap him in what he
had said there in public. And astonished by
his answer, they became silent.

The Resurrection and Marriage

27Some of the Sadducees, who say there is
no resurrection, came to Jesus with a question. 28"Teacher," they said, "Moses wrote for
us that if a man's brother dies and leaves
a wife but no children, the man must marry the widow and raise up offspring for his
brother. 29Now there were seven brothers.
The first one married a woman and died
childless. 30The second 31and then the third
married her, and in the same way the seven
died, leaving no children. 32Finally, the woman died too. 33Now then, at the resurrection
whose wife will she be, since the seven were
married to her?"

34Jesus replied, "The people of this age marry and are given in marriage. 35But those who
are considered worthy of taking part in the
age to come and in the resurrection from the
dead will neither marry nor be given in marriage, 36and they can no longer die; for they
are like the angels. They are God's children,
since they are children of the resurrection.
37But in the account of the burning bush, even
Moses showed that the dead rise, for he calls
the Lord 'the God of Abraham, and the God
of Isaac, and the God of Jacob.'[d] 38He is not
the God of the dead, but of the living, for to
him all are alive."

39Some of the teachers of the law respond-

[a] *46* Isaiah 56:7 [b] *46* Jer. 7:11 [c] *17* Psalm 118:22 [d] *37* Exodus 3:6

ed, "Well said, teacher!" 40And no one dared
to ask him any more questions.

Whose Son Is the Messiah?

41Then Jesus said to them, "Why is it said
that the Messiah is the son of David? 42David
himself declares in the Book of Psalms:

"'The Lord said to my Lord:
"Sit at my right hand
43until I make your enemies
a footstool for your feet." '[a]

44David calls him 'Lord.' How then can he be
his son?"

Warning Against the Teachers of the Law

45While all the people were listening, Jesus
said to his disciples, 46"Beware of the teachers
of the law. They like to walk around in flowing
robes and love to be greeted with respect in
the marketplaces and have the most important seats in the synagogues and the places
of honor at banquets. 47They devour widows'
houses and for a show make lengthy prayers.
These men will be punished most severely."

The Widow's Offering

21 As Jesus looked up, he saw the rich putting their gifts into the temple treasury.
2He also saw a poor widow put in two very
small copper coins. 3"Truly I tell you," he said,
"this poor widow has put in more than all the
others. 4All these people gave their gifts out
of their wealth; but she out of her poverty put
in all she had to live on."

The Destruction of the Temple and Signs of the End Times

5Some of his disciples were remarking
about how the temple was adorned with beautiful stones and with gifts dedicated to God.
But Jesus said, 6"As for what you see here,
the time will come when not one stone will
be left on another; every one of them will be
thrown down."

7"Teacher," they asked, "when will these
things happen? And what will be the sign
that they are about to take place?"

8He replied: "Watch out that you are not
deceived. For many will come in my name,
claiming, 'I am he,' and, 'The time is near.'
Do not follow them. 9When you hear of wars
and uprisings, do not be frightened. These
things must happen first, but the end will not
come right away."

10Then he said to them: "Nation will rise
against nation, and kingdom against kingdom. 11There will be great earthquakes, famines and pestilences in various places, and
fearful events and great signs from heaven.

12"But before all this, they will seize you
and persecute you. They will hand you over
to synagogues and put you in prison, and you
will be brought before kings and governors,
and all on account of my name. 13And so you
will bear testimony to me. 14But make up your
mind not to worry beforehand how you will
defend yourselves. 15For I will give you words
and wisdom that none of your adversaries will
be able to resist or contradict. 16You will be
betrayed even by parents, brothers and sisters, relatives and friends, and they will put
some of you to death. 17Everyone will hate you
because of me. 18But not a hair of your head
will perish. 19Stand firm, and you will win life.

20"When you see Jerusalem being surrounded by armies, you will know that its desolation
is near. 21Then let those who are in Judea flee
to the mountains, let those in the city get out,
and let those in the country not enter the city.
22For this is the time of punishment in fulfillment of all that has been written. 23How
dreadful it will be in those days for pregnant
women and nursing mothers! There will be
great distress in the land and wrath against
this people. 24They will fall by the sword and
will be taken as prisoners to all the nations.
Jerusalem will be trampled on by the Gentiles
until the times of the Gentiles are fulfilled.

25"There will be signs in the sun, moon and
stars. On the earth, nations will be in anguish
and perplexity at the roaring and tossing of
the sea. 26People will faint from terror, appre-
hensive of what is coming on the world, for
the heavenly bodies will be shaken. 27At that
time they will see the Son of Man coming in
a cloud with power and great glory. 28When
these things begin to take place, stand up and
lift up your heads, because your redemption
is drawing near."

29He told them this parable: "Look at the
fig tree and all the trees. 30When they sprout
leaves, you can see for yourselves and know
that summer is near. 31Even so, when you see
these things happening, you know that the
kingdom of God is near.

32"Truly I tell you, this generation will certainly not pass away until all these things
have happened. 33Heaven and earth will pass
away, but my words will never pass away.

34"Be careful, or your hearts will be weighed
down with carousing, drunkenness and the
anxieties of life, and that day will close on you
suddenly like a trap. 35For it will come on all
those who live on the face of the whole earth.
36Be always on the watch, and pray that you
may be able to escape all that is about to happen, and that you may be able to stand before
the Son of Man."

37Each day Jesus was teaching at the temple, and each evening he went out to spend the
night on the hill called the Mount of Olives,
38and all the people came early in the morning
to hear him at the temple.

Judas Agrees to Betray Jesus

22 Now the Festival of Unleavened Bread,
called the Passover, was approaching,
2and the chief priests and the teachers of the
law were looking for some way to get rid of
Jesus, for they were afraid of the people. 3Then
Satan entered Judas, called Iscariot, one of the

[a] *43* Psalm 110:1

Twelve. 4And Judas went to the chief priests and the officers of the temple guard and discussed with them how he might betray Jesus. 5They were delighted and agreed to give him money. 6He consented, and watched for an opportunity to hand Jesus over to them when no crowd was present.

The Last Supper

7Then came the day of Unleavened Bread on which the Passover lamb had to be sacrificed. 8Jesus sent Peter and John, saying, "Go and make preparations for us to eat the Passover."

9"Where do you want us to prepare for it?" they asked.

10He replied, "As you enter the city, a man carrying a jar of water will meet you. Follow him to the house that he enters, 11and say to the owner of the house, 'The Teacher asks: Where is the guest room, where I may eat the Passover with my disciples?' 12He will show you a large room upstairs, all furnished. Make preparations there."

13They left and found things just as Jesus had told them. So they prepared the Passover.

14When the hour came, Jesus and his apostles reclined at the table. 15And he said to them, "I have eagerly desired to eat this Passover with you before I suffer. 16For I tell you, I will not eat it again until it finds fulfillment in the kingdom of God."

17After taking the cup, he gave thanks and said, "Take this and divide it among you. 18For I tell you I will not drink again from the fruit of the vine until the kingdom of God comes."

19And he took bread, gave thanks and broke it, and gave it to them, saying, "This is my body given for you; do this in remembrance of me."

20In the same way, after the supper he took the cup, saying, "This cup is the new covenant in my blood, which is poured out for you.[a] 21But the hand of him who is going to betray me is with mine on the table. 22The Son of Man will go as it has been decreed. But woe to that man who betrays him!" 23They began to question among themselves which of them it might be who would do this.

24A dispute also arose among them as to which of them was considered to be greatest. 25Jesus said to them, "The kings of the Gentiles lord it over them; and those who exercise authority over them call themselves Benefactors. 26But you are not to be like that. Instead, the greatest among you should be like the youngest, and the one who rules like the one who serves. 27For who is greater, the one who is at the table or the one who serves? Is it not the one who is at the table? But I am among you as one who serves. 28You are those who have stood by me in my trials. 29And I confer on you a kingdom, just as my Father conferred one on me, 30so that you may eat and drink at my table in my kingdom and sit on thrones, judging the twelve tribes of Israel.

31"Simon, Simon, Satan has asked to sift all of you as wheat. 32But I have prayed for you, Simon, that your faith may not fail. And when you have turned back, strengthen your brothers."

33But he replied, "Lord, I am ready to go with you to prison and to death."

34Jesus answered, "I tell you, Peter, before the rooster crows today, you will deny three times that you know me."

35Then Jesus asked them, "When I sent you without purse, bag or sandals, did you lack anything?"

"Nothing," they answered.

36He said to them, "But now if you have a purse, take it, and also a bag; and if you don't have a sword, sell your cloak and buy one. 37It is written: 'And he was numbered with the transgressors'[b]; and I tell you that this must be fulfilled in me. Yes, what is written about me is reaching its fulfillment."

38The disciples said, "See, Lord, here are two swords."

"That's enough!" he replied.

Jesus Prays on the Mount of Olives

39Jesus went out as usual to the Mount of Olives, and his disciples followed him. 40On reaching the place, he said to them, "Pray that you will not fall into temptation." 41He withdrew about a stone's throw beyond them, knelt down and prayed, 42"Father, if you are willing, take this cup from me; yet not my will, but yours be done." 43An angel from heaven appeared to him and strengthened him. 44And being in anguish, he prayed more earnestly, and his sweat was like drops of blood falling to the ground.[c]

45When he rose from prayer and went back to the disciples, he found them asleep, exhausted from sorrow. 46"Why are you sleeping?" he asked them. "Get up and pray so that you will not fall into temptation."

Jesus Arrested

47While he was still speaking a crowd came up, and the man who was called Judas, one of the Twelve, was leading them. He approached Jesus to kiss him, 48but Jesus asked him, "Judas, are you betraying the Son of Man with a kiss?"

49When Jesus' followers saw what was going to happen, they said, "Lord, should we strike with our swords?" 50And one of them struck the servant of the high priest, cutting off his right ear.

51But Jesus answered, "No more of this!" And he touched the man's ear and healed him.

52Then Jesus said to the chief priests, the officers of the temple guard, and the elders, who had come for him, "Am I leading a rebellion, that you have come with swords and clubs? 53Every day I was with you in the temple courts, and you did not lay a hand on me. But this is your hour—when darkness reigns."

[a] *19,20* Some manuscripts do not have *given for you . . . poured out for you.* [b] *37* Isaiah 53:12
[c] *43,44* Many early manuscripts do not have verses 43 and 44.

Peter Disowns Jesus

54 Then seizing him, they led him away and
took him into the house of the high priest. Peter followed at a distance. 55 And when some
there had kindled a fire in the middle of the
courtyard and had sat down together, Peter
sat down with them. 56 A servant girl saw him
seated there in the firelight. She looked closely at him and said, "This man was with him."
57 But he denied it. "Woman, I don't know
him," he said.
58 A little later someone else saw him and
said, "You also are one of them."
"Man, I am not!" Peter replied.
59 About an hour later another asserted,
"Certainly this fellow was with him, for he
is a Galilean."
60 Peter replied, "Man, I don't know what
you're talking about!" Just as he was speaking, the rooster crowed. 61 The Lord turned
and looked straight at Peter. Then Peter remembered the word the Lord had spoken to
him: "Before the rooster crows today, you will
disown me three times." 62 And he went outside
and wept bitterly.

The Guards Mock Jesus

63 The men who were guarding Jesus began
mocking and beating him. 64 They blindfolded him and demanded, "Prophesy! Who hit
you?" 65 And they said many other insulting
things to him.

Jesus Before Pilate and Herod

66 At daybreak the council of the elders
of the people, both the chief priests and the
teachers of the law, met together, and Jesus
was led before them. 67 "If you are the Messiah," they said, "tell us."
Jesus answered, "If I tell you, you will not
believe me, 68 and if I asked you, you would
not answer. 69 But from now on, the Son of
Man will be seated at the right hand of the
mighty God."
70 They all asked, "Are you then the Son of
God?"
He replied, "You say that I am."
71 Then they said, "Why do we need any
more testimony? We have heard it from his
own lips."

23 Then the whole assembly rose and led
him off to Pilate. 2 And they began to
accuse him, saying, "We have found this man
subverting our nation. He opposes payment
of taxes to Caesar and claims to be Messiah,
a king."
3 So Pilate asked Jesus, "Are you the king
of the Jews?"
"You have said so," Jesus replied.
4 Then Pilate announced to the chief priests
and the crowd, "I find no basis for a charge
against this man."
5 But they insisted, "He stirs up the people
all over Judea by his teaching. He started in
Galilee and has come all the way here."
6 On hearing this, Pilate asked if the man
was a Galilean. 7 When he learned that Jesus
was under Herod's jurisdiction, he sent him to
Herod, who was also in Jerusalem at that time.
8 When Herod saw Jesus, he was greatly
pleased, because for a long time he had been
wanting to see him. From what he had heard
about him, he hoped to see him perform a sign
of some sort. 9 He plied him with many questions, but Jesus gave him no answer. 10 The
chief priests and the teachers of the law were
standing there, vehemently accusing him.
11 Then Herod and his soldiers ridiculed and
mocked him. Dressing him in an elegant robe,
they sent him back to Pilate. 12 That day Herod
and Pilate became friends—before this they
had been enemies.
13 Pilate called together the chief priests, the
rulers and the people, 14 and said to them, "You
brought me this man as one who was inciting the people to rebellion. I have examined
him in your presence and have found no basis
for your charges against him. 15 Neither has
Herod, for he sent him back to us; as you can
see, he has done nothing to deserve death.
16 Therefore, I will punish him and then release him." [17][a]
18 But the whole crowd shouted, "Away with
this man! Release Barabbas to us!" 19 (Barabbas had been thrown into prison for an insurrection in the city, and for murder.)
20 Wanting to release Jesus, Pilate appealed
to them again. 21 But they kept shouting, "Crucify him! Crucify him!"
22 For the third time he spoke to them:
"Why? What crime has this man committed?
I have found in him no grounds for the death
penalty. Therefore I will have him punished
and then release him."
23 But with loud shouts they insistently demanded that he be crucified, and their shouts
prevailed. 24 So Pilate decided to grant their
demand. 25 He released the man who had been
thrown into prison for insurrection and murder, the one they asked for, and surrendered
Jesus to their will.

The Crucifixion of Jesus

26 As the soldiers led him away, they seized
Simon from Cyrene, who was on his way in
from the country, and put the cross on him
and made him carry it behind Jesus. 27 A large
number of people followed him, including
women who mourned and wailed for him.
28 Jesus turned and said to them, "Daughters of
Jerusalem, do not weep for me; weep for yourselves and for your children. 29 For the time
will come when you will say, 'Blessed are the
childless women, the wombs that never bore
and the breasts that never nursed!' 30 Then

"'they will say to the mountains, "Fall on
us!"
and to the hills, "Cover us!"'[b]

31 For if people do these things when the tree
is green, what will happen when it is dry?"
32 Two other men, both criminals, were also
led out with him to be executed. 33 When they

[a] *17* Some manuscripts include here words similar to Matt. 27:15 and Mark 15:6. [b] *30* Hosea 10:8

came to the place called the Skull, they crucified him there, along with the criminals—one
on his right, the other on his left. [34]Jesus said,
"Father, forgive them, for they do not know
what they are doing."[a] And they divided up
his clothes by casting lots.

[35]The people stood watching, and the rulers
even sneered at him. They said, "He saved
others; let him save himself if he is God's Messiah, the Chosen One."

[36]The soldiers also came up and mocked
him. They offered him wine vinegar [37]and
said, "If you are the king of the Jews, save
yourself."

[38]There was a written notice above him,
which read: THIS IS THE KING OF THE JEWS.

[39]One of the criminals who hung there
hurled insults at him: "Aren't you the Messiah? Save yourself and us!"

[40]But the other criminal rebuked him.
"Don't you fear God," he said, "since you are
under the same sentence? [41]We are punished
justly, for we are getting what our deeds deserve. But this man has done nothing wrong."

[42]Then he said, "Jesus, remember me when
you come into your kingdom.[b]"

[43]Jesus answered him, "Truly I tell you, today you will be with me in paradise."

The Death of Jesus

[44]It was now about noon, and darkness
came over the whole land until three in the
afternoon, [45]for the sun stopped shining. And
the curtain of the temple was torn in two.
[46]Jesus called out with a loud voice, "Father,
into your hands I commit my spirit."[c] When
he had said this, he breathed his last.

[47]The centurion, seeing what had happened, praised God and said, "Surely this
was a righteous man." [48]When all the people
who had gathered to witness this sight saw
what took place, they beat their breasts and
went away. [49]But all those who knew him,
including the women who had followed him
from Galilee, stood at a distance, watching
these things.

The Burial of Jesus

[50]Now there was a man named Joseph, a
member of the Council, a good and upright
man, [51]who had not consented to their decision
and action. He came from the Judean town
of Arimathea, and he himself was waiting
for the kingdom of God. [52]Going to Pilate, he
asked for Jesus' body. [53]Then he took it down,
wrapped it in linen cloth and placed it in a
tomb cut in the rock, one in which no one had
yet been laid. [54]It was Preparation Day, and
the Sabbath was about to begin.

[55]The women who had come with Jesus
from Galilee followed Joseph and saw the
tomb and how his body was laid in it. [56]Then
they went home and prepared spices and perfumes. But they rested on the Sabbath in obedience to the commandment.

Jesus Has Risen

24 On the first day of the week, very early in the morning, the women took the
spices they had prepared and went to the
tomb. [2]They found the stone rolled away from
the tomb, [3]but when they entered, they did not
find the body of the Lord Jesus. [4]While they
were wondering about this, suddenly two men
in clothes that gleamed like lightning stood
beside them. [5]In their fright the women bowed
down with their faces to the ground, but the
men said to them, "Why do you look for the
living among the dead? [6]He is not here; he has
risen! Remember how he told you, while he
was still with you in Galilee: [7]'The Son of Man
must be delivered over to the hands of sinners,
be crucified and on the third day be raised
again.' " [8]Then they remembered his words.

[9]When they came back from the tomb, they
told all these things to the Eleven and to all
the others. [10]It was Mary Magdalene, Joanna,
Mary the mother of James, and the others
with them who told this to the apostles. [11]But
they did not believe the women, because their
words seemed to them like nonsense. [12]Peter,
however, got up and ran to the tomb. Bend-
ing over, he saw the strips of linen lying by
themselves, and he went away, wondering to
himself what had happened.

On the Road to Emmaus

[13]Now that same day two of them were going to a village called Emmaus, about seven
miles[d] from Jerusalem. [14]They were talking
with each other about everything that had
happened. [15]As they talked and discussed
these things with each other, Jesus himself
came up and walked along with them; [16]but
they were kept from recognizing him.

[17]He asked them, "What are you discussing
together as you walk along?"

They stood still, their faces downcast. [18]One
of them, named Cleopas, asked him, "Are you
the only one visiting Jerusalem who does not
know the things that have happened there in
these days?"

[19]"What things?" he asked.

"About Jesus of Nazareth," they replied. "He
was a prophet, powerful in word and deed
before God and all the people. [20]The chief
priests and our rulers handed him over to be
sentenced to death, and they crucified him;
[21]but we had hoped that he was the one who
was going to redeem Israel. And what is more,
it is the third day since all this took place.
[22]In addition, some of our women amazed
us. They went to the tomb early this morning
[23]but didn't find his body. They came and told
us that they had seen a vision of angels, who
said he was alive. [24]Then some of our companions went to the tomb and found it just as the
women had said, but they did not see Jesus."

[25]He said to them, "How foolish you are, and
how slow to believe all that the prophets have
spoken! [26]Did not the Messiah have to suffer
these things and then enter his glory?" [27]And

[a] *34* Some early manuscripts do not have this sentence. [b] *42* Some manuscripts *come with your kingly power* [c] *46* Psalm 31:5 [d] *13* Or about 11 kilometers

beginning with Moses and all the Prophets,
he explained to them what was said in all the
Scriptures concerning himself.
28As they approached the village to which
they were going, Jesus continued on as if
he were going farther. 29But they urged him
strongly, “Stay with us, for it is nearly evening; the day is almost over.” So he went in
to stay with them.
30When he was at the table with them, he
took bread, gave thanks, broke it and began to
give it to them. 31Then their eyes were opened
and they recognized him, and he disappeared
from their sight. 32They asked each other,
“Were not our hearts burning within us while
he talked with us on the road and opened the
Scriptures to us?”
33They got up and returned at once to Jerusalem. There they found the Eleven and those
with them, assembled together 34and saying,
“It is true! The Lord has risen and has appeared to Simon.” 35Then the two told what
had happened on the way, and how Jesus was
recognized by them when he broke the bread.

Jesus Appears to the Disciples

36While they were still talking about this,
Jesus himself stood among them and said to
them, “Peace be with you.”
37They were startled and frightened, thinking they saw a ghost. 38He said to them, “Why
are you troubled, and why do doubts rise in
your minds? 39Look at my hands and my feet.
It is I myself! Touch me and see; a ghost does
not have flesh and bones, as you see I have.”
40When he had said this, he showed them
his hands and feet. 41And while they still did
not believe it because of joy and amazement,
he asked them, “Do you have anything here to
eat?” 42They gave him a piece of broiled fish,
43and he took it and ate it in their presence.
44He said to them, “This is what I told you
while I was still with you: Everything must
be fulfilled that is written about me in the
Law of Moses, the Prophets and the Psalms.”
45Then he opened their minds so they could
understand the Scriptures. 46He told them,
“This is what is written: The Messiah will suffer and rise from the dead on the third day,
47and repentance for the forgiveness of sins will
be preached in his name to all nations, beginning at Jerusalem. 48You are witnesses of these
things. 49I am going to send you what my Father
has promised; but stay in the city until you have
been clothed with power from on high.”

The Ascension of Jesus

50When he had led them out to the vicinity
of Bethany, he lifted up his hands and blessed
them. 51While he was blessing them, he left
them and was taken up into heaven. 52Then
they worshiped him and returned to Jerusalem with great joy. 53And they stayed continually at the temple, praising God.

John

The Word Became Flesh

1 In the beginning was the Word, and the
Word was with God, and the Word was
God. 2He was with God in the beginning.
3Through him all things were made; without
him nothing was made that has been made.
4In him was life, and that life was the light of
all mankind. 5The light shines in the darkness, and the darkness has not overcome[a] it.
6There was a man sent from God whose
name was John. 7He came as a witness to
testify concerning that light, so that through
him all might believe. 8He himself was not the
light; he came only as a witness to the light.
9The true light that gives light to everyone was coming into the world. 10He was in
the world, and though the world was made
through him, the world did not recognize
him. 11He came to that which was his own,
but his own did not receive him. 12Yet to all
who did receive him, to those who believed
in his name, he gave the right to become children of God— 13children born not of natural
descent, nor of human decision or a husband’s
will, but born of God.
14The Word became flesh and made his
dwelling among us. We have seen his glory,
the glory of the one and only Son, who came
from the Father, full of grace and truth.
15(John testified concerning him. He cried
out, saying, “This is the one I spoke about
when I said, ‘He who comes after me has surpassed me because he was before me.’ ”) 16Out
of his fullness we have all received grace in
place of grace already given. 17For the law was
given through Moses; grace and truth came
through Jesus Christ. 18No one has ever seen
God, but the one and only Son, who is himself
God and[b] is in closest relationship with the
Father, has made him known.

John the Baptist Denies Being the Messiah

19Now this was John’s testimony when the
Jewish leaders[c] in Jerusalem sent priests and

[a] 5 Or *understood* [b] 18 Some manuscripts *but the only Son, who* [c] 19 The Greek term traditionally translated *the Jews* (*hoi Ioudaioi*) refers here and elsewhere in John’s Gospel to those Jewish leaders who opposed Jesus; also in 5:10, 15, 16; 7:1, 11, 13; 9:22; 18:14, 28, 36; 19:7, 12, 31, 38; 20:19.

Levites to ask him who he was. 20He did not
fail to confess, but confessed freely, "I am not
the Messiah."
21They asked him, "Then who are you? Are
you Elijah?"
He said, "I am not."
"Are you the Prophet?"
He answered, "No."
22Finally they said, "Who are you? Give us
an answer to take back to those who sent us.
What do you say about yourself?"
23John replied in the words of Isaiah the
prophet, "I am the voice of one calling in the
wilderness, 'Make straight the way for the
Lord.'"[a]
24Now the Pharisees who had been sent
25questioned him, "Why then do you baptize
if you are not the Messiah, nor Elijah, nor
the Prophet?"
26"I baptize with[b] water," John replied, "but
among you stands one you do not know. 27He
is the one who comes after me, the straps of
whose sandals I am not worthy to untie."
28This all happened at Bethany on the other
side of the Jordan, where John was baptizing.

John Testifies About Jesus

29The next day John saw Jesus coming toward him and said, "Look, the Lamb of God,
who takes away the sin of the world! 30This
is the one I meant when I said, 'A man who
comes after me has surpassed me because he
was before me.' 31I myself did not know him,
but the reason I came baptizing with water
was that he might be revealed to Israel."
32Then John gave this testimony: "I saw the
Spirit come down from heaven as a dove and
remain on him. 33And I myself did not know
him, but the one who sent me to baptize with
water told me, 'The man on whom you see the
Spirit come down and remain is the one who
will baptize with the Holy Spirit.' 34I have seen
and I testify that this is God's Chosen One."[c]

John's Disciples Follow Jesus

35The next day John was there again with
two of his disciples. 36When he saw Jesus
passing by, he said, "Look, the Lamb of God!"
37When the two disciples heard him say
this, they followed Jesus. 38Turning around,
Jesus saw them following and asked, "What
do you want?"
They said, "Rabbi" (which means "Teacher"), "where are you staying?"
39"Come," he replied, "and you will see."
So they went and saw where he was staying, and they spent that day with him. It was
about four in the afternoon.
40Andrew, Simon Peter's brother, was one
of the two who heard what John had said and
who had followed Jesus. 41The first thing Andrew did was to find his brother Simon and
tell him, "We have found the Messiah" (that
is, the Christ). 42And he brought him to Jesus.
Jesus looked at him and said, "You are Simon son of John. You will be called Cephas"
(which, when translated, is Peter[d]).

Jesus Calls Philip and Nathanael

43The next day Jesus decided to leave for
Galilee. Finding Philip, he said to him, "Follow me."
44Philip, like Andrew and Peter, was from
the town of Bethsaida. 45Philip found Nathanael and told him, "We have found the one Moses wrote about in the Law, and about whom
the prophets also wrote—Jesus of Nazareth,
the son of Joseph."
46"Nazareth! Can anything good come from
there?" Nathanael asked.
"Come and see," said Philip.
47When Jesus saw Nathanael approaching,
he said of him, "Here truly is an Israelite in
whom there is no deceit."
48"How do you know me?" Nathanael asked.
Jesus answered, "I saw you while you were
still under the fig tree before Philip called
you."
49Then Nathanael declared, "Rabbi, you are
the Son of God; you are the king of Israel."
50Jesus said, "You believe[e] because I told
you I saw you under the fig tree. You will see
greater things than that." 51He then added,
"Very truly I tell you,[f] you[f] will see 'heaven
open, and the angels of God ascending and
descending on'[g] the Son of Man."

Jesus Changes Water Into Wine

2 On the third day a wedding took place at
Cana in Galilee. Jesus' mother was there,
2and Jesus and his disciples had also been
invited to the wedding. 3When the wine was
gone, Jesus' mother said to him, "They have
no more wine."
4"Woman,[h] why do you involve me?" Jesus
replied. "My hour has not yet come."
5His mother said to the servants, "Do whatever he tells you."
6Nearby stood six stone water jars, the kind
used by the Jews for ceremonial washing,
each holding from twenty to thirty gallons.[i]
7Jesus said to the servants, "Fill the jars
with water"; so they filled them to the brim.
8Then he told them, "Now draw some out
and take it to the master of the banquet."
They did so, 9and the master of the banquet
tasted the water that had been turned into
wine. He did not realize where it had come
from, though the servants who had drawn the
water knew. Then he called the bridegroom
aside 10and said, "Everyone brings out the
choice wine first and then the cheaper wine
after the guests have had too much to drink;
but you have saved the best till now."
11What Jesus did here in Cana of Galilee
was the first of the signs through which he
revealed his glory; and his disciples believed
in him.

[a] *23* Isaiah 40:3 [b] *26* Or *in*; also in verses 31 and 33 (twice) [c] *34* See Isaiah 42:1; many manuscripts *is the Son of God.* [d] *42* *Cephas* (Aramaic) and *Peter* (Greek) both mean *rock.* [e] *50* Or *Do you believe . . . ?* [f] *51* The Greek is plural. [g] *51* Gen. 28:12 [h] *4* The Greek for *Woman* does not denote any disrespect. [i] *6* Or from about 75 to about 115 liters

12After this he went down to Capernaum with his mother and brothers and his disciples. There they stayed for a few days.

Jesus Clears the Temple Courts

13When it was almost time for the Jewish Passover, Jesus went up to Jerusalem. 14In the temple courts he found people selling cattle, sheep and doves, and others sitting at tables exchanging money. 15So he made a whip out of cords, and drove all from the temple courts, both sheep and cattle; he scattered the coins of the money changers and overturned their tables. 16To those who sold doves he said, "Get these out of here! Stop turning my Father's house into a market!" 17His disciples remembered that it is written: "Zeal for your house will consume me."[a]

18The Jews then responded to him, "What sign can you show us to prove your authority to do all this?"

19Jesus answered them, "Destroy this temple, and I will raise it again in three days."

20They replied, "It has taken forty-six years to build this temple, and you are going to raise it in three days?" 21But the temple he had spoken of was his body. 22After he was raised from the dead, his disciples recalled what he had said. Then they believed the scripture and the words that Jesus had spoken.

23Now while he was in Jerusalem at the Passover Festival, many people saw the signs he was performing and believed in his name.[b] 24But Jesus would not entrust himself to them, for he knew all people. 25He did not need any testimony about mankind, for he knew what was in each person.

Jesus Teaches Nicodemus

3 Now there was a Pharisee, a man named Nicodemus who was a member of the Jewish ruling council. 2He came to Jesus at night and said, "Rabbi, we know that you are a teacher who has come from God. For no one could perform the signs you are doing if God were not with him."

3Jesus replied, "Very truly I tell you, no one can see the kingdom of God unless they are born again.[c]"

4"How can someone be born when they are old?" Nicodemus asked. "Surely they cannot enter a second time into their mother's womb to be born!"

5Jesus answered, "Very truly I tell you, no one can enter the kingdom of God unless they are born of water and the Spirit. 6Flesh gives birth to flesh, but the Spirit[d] gives birth to spirit. 7You should not be surprised at my saying, 'You[e] must be born again.' 8The wind blows wherever it pleases. You hear its sound, but you cannot tell where it comes from or where it is going. So it is with everyone born of the Spirit."[f]

9"How can this be?" Nicodemus asked.

10"You are Israel's teacher," said Jesus, "and do you not understand these things? 11Very truly I tell you, we speak of what we know, and we testify to what we have seen, but still you people do not accept our testimony. 12I have spoken to you of earthly things and you do not believe; how then will you believe if I speak of heavenly things? 13No one has ever gone into heaven except the one who came from heaven—the Son of Man.[g] 14Just as Moses lifted up the snake in the wilderness, so the Son of Man must be lifted up,[h] 15that everyone who believes may have eternal life in him."[i]

16For God so loved the world that he gave his one and only Son, that whoever believes in him shall not perish but have eternal life. 17For God did not send his Son into the world to condemn the world, but to save the world through him. 18Whoever believes in him is not condemned, but whoever does not believe stands condemned already because they have not believed in the name of God's one and only Son. 19This is the verdict: Light has come into the world, but people loved darkness instead of light because their deeds were evil. 20Everyone who does evil hates the light, and will not come into the light for fear that their deeds will be exposed. 21But whoever lives by the truth comes into the light, so that it may be seen plainly that what they have done has been done in the sight of God.

John Testifies Again About Jesus

22After this, Jesus and his disciples went out into the Judean countryside, where he spent some time with them, and baptized. 23Now John also was baptizing at Aenon near Salim, because there was plenty of water, and people were coming and being baptized. 24(This was before John was put in prison.) 25An argument developed between some of John's disciples and a certain Jew over the matter of ceremonial washing. 26They came to John and said to him, "Rabbi, that man who was with you on the other side of the Jordan—the one you testified about—look, he is baptizing, and everyone is going to him."

27To this John replied, "A person can receive only what is given them from heaven. 28You yourselves can testify that I said, 'I am not the Messiah but am sent ahead of him.' 29The bride belongs to the bridegroom. The friend who attends the bridegroom waits and listens for him, and is full of joy when he hears the bridegroom's voice. That joy is mine, and it is now complete. 30He must become greater; I must become less."[j]

31The one who comes from above is above all; the one who is from the earth belongs to the earth, and speaks as one from the earth. The one who comes from heaven is above all. 32He testifies to what he has seen and heard,

[a] *17* Psalm 69:9 [b] *23* Or *in him* [c] *3* The Greek for *again* also means *from above*; also in verse 7.
[d] *6* Or *but spirit* [e] *7* The Greek is plural. [f] *8* The Greek for *Spirit* is the same as that for *wind*.
[g] *13* Some manuscripts *Man, who is in heaven* [h] *14* The Greek for *lifted up* also means *exalted*.
[i] *15* Some interpreters end the quotation with verse 21. [j] *30* Some interpreters end the quotation with verse 36.

but no one accepts his testimony. 33Whoever
has accepted it has certified that God is truthful. 34For the one whom God has sent speaks
the words of God, for God[a] gives the Spirit
without limit. 35The Father loves the Son and
has placed everything in his hands. 36Who-
ever believes in the Son has eternal life, but
whoever rejects the Son will not see life, for
God's wrath remains on them.

Jesus Talks With a Samaritan Woman

4 Now Jesus learned that the Pharisees had
heard that he was gaining and baptizing
more disciples than John— 2although in fact
it was not Jesus who baptized, but his disciples. 3So he left Judea and went back once
more to Galilee.

4Now he had to go through Samaria. 5So
he came to a town in Samaria called Sychar,
near the plot of ground Jacob had given to
his son Joseph. 6Jacob's well was there, and
Jesus, tired as he was from the journey, sat
down by the well. It was about noon.

7When a Samaritan woman came to draw
water, Jesus said to her, "Will you give me a
drink?" 8(His disciples had gone into the town
to buy food.)

9The Samaritan woman said to him, "You
are a Jew and I am a Samaritan woman. How
can you ask me for a drink?" (For Jews do not
associate with Samaritans.[b])

10Jesus answered her, "If you knew the gift
of God and who it is that asks you for a drink,
you would have asked him and he would have
given you living water."

11"Sir," the woman said, "you have nothing
to draw with and the well is deep. Where can
you get this living water? 12Are you greater
than our father Jacob, who gave us the well
and drank from it himself, as did also his sons
and his livestock?"

13Jesus answered, "Everyone who drinks
this water will be thirsty again, 14but whoever drinks the water I give them will never
thirst. Indeed, the water I give them will become in them a spring of water welling up to
eternal life."

15The woman said to him, "Sir, give me this
water so that I won't get thirsty and have to
keep coming here to draw water."

16He told her, "Go, call your husband and
come back."

17"I have no husband," she replied.

Jesus said to her, "You are right when you
say you have no husband. 18The fact is, you
have had five husbands, and the man you now
have is not your husband. What you have just
said is quite true."

19"Sir," the woman said, "I can see that you
are a prophet. 20Our ancestors worshiped on
this mountain, but you Jews claim that the
place where we must worship is in Jerusalem."

21"Woman," Jesus replied, "believe me, a
time is coming when you will worship the
Father neither on this mountain nor in Jerusalem. 22You Samaritans worship what you
do not know; we worship what we do know,
for salvation is from the Jews. 23Yet a time
is coming and has now come when the true
worshipers will worship the Father in the
Spirit and in truth, for they are the kind of
worshipers the Father seeks. 24God is spirit,
and his worshipers must worship in the Spirit
and in truth."

25The woman said, "I know that Messiah"
(called Christ) "is coming. When he comes,
he will explain everything to us."

26Then Jesus declared, "I, the one speaking
to you—I am he."

The Disciples Rejoin Jesus

27Just then his disciples returned and were
surprised to find him talking with a woman.
But no one asked, "What do you want?" or
"Why are you talking with her?"

28Then, leaving her water jar, the woman
went back to the town and said to the people,
29"Come, see a man who told me everything I
ever did. Could this be the Messiah?" 30They
came out of the town and made their way toward him.

31Meanwhile his disciples urged him, "Rabbi, eat something."

32But he said to them, "I have food to eat
that you know nothing about."

33Then his disciples said to each other,
"Could someone have brought him food?"

34"My food," said Jesus, "is to do the will of
him who sent me and to finish his work. 35Don't
you have a saying, 'It's still four months until
harvest'? I tell you, open your eyes and look
at the fields! They are ripe for harvest. 36Even
now the one who reaps draws a wage and harvests a crop for eternal life, so that the sower
and the reaper may be glad together. 37Thus the
saying 'One sows and another reaps' is true.
38I sent you to reap what you have not worked
for. Others have done the hard work, and you
have reaped the benefits of their labor."

Many Samaritans Believe

39Many of the Samaritans from that town
believed in him because of the woman's testimony, "He told me everything I ever did."
40So when the Samaritans came to him, they
urged him to stay with them, and he stayed
two days. 41And because of his words many
more became believers.

42They said to the woman, "We no longer
believe just because of what you said; now we
have heard for ourselves, and we know that
this man really is the Savior of the world."

Jesus Heals an Official's Son

43After the two days he left for Galilee.
44(Now Jesus himself had pointed out that a
prophet has no honor in his own country.)
45When he arrived in Galilee, the Galileans
welcomed him. They had seen all that he had
done in Jerusalem at the Passover Festival,
for they also had been there.

46Once more he visited Cana in Galilee,
where he had turned the water into wine.

[a] 34 Greek *he* [b] 9 Or *do not use dishes Samaritans have used*

And there was a certain royal official whose
son lay sick at Capernaum. 47When this man
heard that Jesus had arrived in Galilee from
Judea, he went to him and begged him to come
and heal his son, who was close to death.
48"Unless you people see signs and wonders," Jesus told him, "you will never believe."
49The royal official said, "Sir, come down
before my child dies."
50"Go," Jesus replied, "your son will live."
The man took Jesus at his word and departed. 51While he was still on the way, his servants met him with the news that his boy was
living. 52When he inquired as to the time when
his son got better, they said to him, "Yesterday,
at one in the afternoon, the fever left him."
53Then the father realized that this was the
exact time at which Jesus had said to him,
"Your son will live." So he and his whole
household believed.
54This was the second sign Jesus performed
after coming from Judea to Galilee.

The Healing at the Pool

5 Some time later, Jesus went up to Jerusalem for one of the Jewish festivals. 2Now
there is in Jerusalem near the Sheep Gate a
pool, which in Aramaic is called Bethesda[a]
and which is surrounded by five covered col-
onnades. 3Here a great number of disabled
people used to lie—the blind, the lame, the
paralyzed. [4][b] 5One who was there had been
an invalid for thirty-eight years. 6When Jesus
saw him lying there and learned that he had
been in this condition for a long time, he asked
him, "Do you want to get well?"
7"Sir," the invalid replied, "I have no one to
help me into the pool when the water is stirred.
While I am trying to get in, someone else goes
down ahead of me."
8Then Jesus said to him, "Get up! Pick up
your mat and walk." 9At once the man was
cured; he picked up his mat and walked.
The day on which this took place was a Sabbath, 10and so the Jewish leaders said to the
man who had been healed, "It is the Sabbath;
the law forbids you to carry your mat."
11But he replied, "The man who made me
well said to me, 'Pick up your mat and walk.'"
12So they asked him, "Who is this fellow
who told you to pick it up and walk?"
13The man who was healed had no idea who
it was, for Jesus had slipped away into the
crowd that was there.
14Later Jesus found him at the temple and
said to him, "See, you are well again. Stop
sinning or something worse may happen to
you." 15The man went away and told the Jewish leaders that it was Jesus who had made
him well.

The Authority of the Son

16So, because Jesus was doing these things
on the Sabbath, the Jewish leaders began to
persecute him. 17In his defense Jesus said to
them, "My Father is always at his work to this
very day, and I too am working." 18For this
reason they tried all the more to kill him; not
only was he breaking the Sabbath, but he was
even calling God his own Father, making himself equal with God.
19Jesus gave them this answer: "Very truly
I tell you, the Son can do nothing by himself;
he can do only what he sees his Father doing,
because whatever the Father does the Son also
does. 20For the Father loves the Son and shows
him all he does. Yes, and he will show him
even greater works than these, so that you
will be amazed. 21For just as the Father raises the dead and gives them life, even so the
Son gives life to whom he is pleased to give
it. 22Moreover, the Father judges no one, but
has entrusted all judgment to the Son, 23that
all may honor the Son just as they honor the
Father. Whoever does not honor the Son does
not honor the Father, who sent him.
24"Very truly I tell you, whoever hears my
word and believes him who sent me has eternal life and will not be judged but has crossed
over from death to life. 25Very truly I tell you,
a time is coming and has now come when the
dead will hear the voice of the Son of God and
those who hear will live. 26For as the Father
has life in himself, so he has granted the Son
also to have life in himself. 27And he has giv-
en him authority to judge because he is the
Son of Man.
28"Do not be amazed at this, for a time is
coming when all who are in their graves will
hear his voice 29and come out—those who
have done what is good will rise to live, and
those who have done what is evil will rise to
be condemned. 30By myself I can do nothing;
I judge only as I hear, and my judgment is
just, for I seek not to please myself but him
who sent me.

Testimonies About Jesus

31"If I testify about myself, my testimony
is not true. 32There is another who testifies
in my favor, and I know that his testimony
about me is true.
33"You have sent to John and he has testified
to the truth. 34Not that I accept human testimony; but I mention it that you may be saved.
35John was a lamp that burned and gave light,
and you chose for a time to enjoy his light.
36"I have testimony weightier than that of
John. For the works that the Father has given
me to finish—the very works that I am doing—testify that the Father has sent me. 37And
the Father who sent me has himself testified
concerning me. You have never heard his
voice nor seen his form, 38nor does his word
dwell in you, for you do not believe the one
he sent. 39You study[c] the Scriptures diligently because you think that in them you have
eternal life. These are the very Scriptures that

[a] 2 Some manuscripts *Bethzatha*; other manuscripts *Bethsaida* [b] 3,4 Some manuscripts include here, wholly or in part, *paralyzed—and they waited for the moving of the waters.* [4]*From time to time an angel of the Lord would come down and stir up the waters. The first one into the pool after each such disturbance would be cured of whatever disease they had.* [c] 39 Or [39]*Study*

testify about me, 40yet you refuse to come to me to have life.

41"I do not accept glory from human beings, 42but I know you. I know that you do not have the love of God in your hearts. 43I have come in my Father's name, and you do not accept me; but if someone else comes in his own name, you will accept him. 44How can you believe since you accept glory from one another but do not seek the glory that comes from the only God[a]?

45"But do not think I will accuse you before the Father. Your accuser is Moses, on whom your hopes are set. 46If you believed Moses, you would believe me, for he wrote about me. 47But since you do not believe what he wrote, how are you going to believe what I say?"

Jesus Feeds the Five Thousand

6 Some time after this, Jesus crossed to the far shore of the Sea of Galilee (that is, the Sea of Tiberias), 2and a great crowd of people followed him because they saw the signs he had performed by healing the sick. 3Then Jesus went up on a mountainside and sat down with his disciples. 4The Jewish Passover Festival was near.

5When Jesus looked up and saw a great crowd coming toward him, he said to Philip, "Where shall we buy bread for these people to eat?" 6He asked this only to test him, for he already had in mind what he was going to do.

7Philip answered him, "It would take more than half a year's wages[b] to buy enough bread for each one to have a bite!"

8Another of his disciples, Andrew, Simon Peter's brother, spoke up, 9"Here is a boy with five small barley loaves and two small fish, but how far will they go among so many?"

10Jesus said, "Have the people sit down." There was plenty of grass in that place, and they sat down (about five thousand men were there). 11Jesus then took the loaves, gave thanks, and distributed to those who were seated as much as they wanted. He did the same with the fish.

12When they had all had enough to eat, he said to his disciples, "Gather the pieces that are left over. Let nothing be wasted." 13So they gathered them and filled twelve baskets with the pieces of the five barley loaves left over by those who had eaten.

14After the people saw the sign Jesus performed, they began to say, "Surely this is the Prophet who is to come into the world." 15Jesus, knowing that they intended to come and make him king by force, withdrew again to a mountain by himself.

Jesus Walks on the Water

16When evening came, his disciples went down to the lake, 17where they got into a boat and set off across the lake for Capernaum. By now it was dark, and Jesus had not yet joined them. 18A strong wind was blowing and the waters grew rough. 19When they had rowed about three or four miles,[c] they saw Jesus approaching the boat, walking on the water; and they were frightened. 20But he said to them, "It is I; don't be afraid." 21Then they were willing to take him into the boat, and immediately the boat reached the shore where they were heading.

22The next day the crowd that had stayed on the opposite shore of the lake realized that only one boat had been there, and that Jesus had not entered it with his disciples, but that they had gone away alone. 23Then some boats from Tiberias landed near the place where the people had eaten the bread after the Lord had given thanks. 24Once the crowd realized that neither Jesus nor his disciples were there, they got into the boats and went to Capernaum in search of Jesus.

Jesus the Bread of Life

25When they found him on the other side of the lake, they asked him, "Rabbi, when did you get here?"

26Jesus answered, "Very truly I tell you, you are looking for me, not because you saw the signs I performed but because you ate the loaves and had your fill. 27Do not work for food that spoils, but for food that endures to eternal life, which the Son of Man will give you. For on him God the Father has placed his seal of approval."

28Then they asked him, "What must we do to do the works God requires?"

29Jesus answered, "The work of God is this: to believe in the one he has sent."

30So they asked him, "What sign then will you give that we may see it and believe you? What will you do? 31Our ancestors ate the manna in the wilderness; as it is written: 'He gave them bread from heaven to eat.'[d]"

32Jesus said to them, "Very truly I tell you, it is not Moses who has given you the bread from heaven, but it is my Father who gives you the true bread from heaven. 33For the bread of God is the bread that comes down from heaven and gives life to the world."

34"Sir," they said, "always give us this bread."

35Then Jesus declared, "I am the bread of life. Whoever comes to me will never go hungry, and whoever believes in me will never be thirsty. 36But as I told you, you have seen me and still you do not believe. 37All those the Father gives me will come to me, and whoever comes to me I will never drive away. 38For I have come down from heaven not to do my will but to do the will of him who sent me. 39And this is the will of him who sent me, that I shall lose none of all those he has given me, but raise them up at the last day. 40For my Father's will is that everyone who looks to the Son and believes in him shall have eternal life, and I will raise them up at the last day."

41At this the Jews there began to grumble about him because he said, "I am the bread

[a] *44* Some early manuscripts *the Only One* [b] *7* Greek *take two hundred denarii* [c] *19* Or about 5 or 6 kilometers [d] *31* Exodus 16:4; Neh. 9:15; Psalm 78:24,25

that came down from heaven." 42They said,
"Is this not Jesus, the son of Joseph, whose
father and mother we know? How can he now
say, 'I came down from heaven'?"
43"Stop grumbling among yourselves,"
Jesus answered. 44"No one can come to me
unless the Father who sent me draws them,
and I will raise them up at the last day. 45It
is written in the Prophets: 'They will all be
taught by God.'[a] Everyone who has heard the
Father and learned from him comes to me.
46No one has seen the Father except the one
who is from God; only he has seen the Father.
47Very truly I tell you, the one who believes
has eternal life. 48I am the bread of life. 49Your
ancestors ate the manna in the wilderness, yet
they died. 50But here is the bread that comes
down from heaven, which anyone may eat
and not die. 51I am the living bread that came
down from heaven. Whoever eats this bread
will live forever. This bread is my flesh, which
I will give for the life of the world."
52Then the Jews began to argue sharply
among themselves, "How can this man give
us his flesh to eat?"
53Jesus said to them, "Very truly I tell you,
unless you eat the flesh of the Son of Man
and drink his blood, you have no life in you.
54Whoever eats my flesh and drinks my blood
has eternal life, and I will raise them up at the
last day. 55For my flesh is real food and my
blood is real drink. 56Whoever eats my flesh
and drinks my blood remains in me, and I in
them. 57Just as the living Father sent me and
I live because of the Father, so the one who
feeds on me will live because of me. 58This is
the bread that came down from heaven. Your
ancestors ate manna and died, but whoever
feeds on this bread will live forever." 59He said
this while teaching in the synagogue in Capernaum.

Many Disciples Desert Jesus

60On hearing it, many of his disciples said,
"This is a hard teaching. Who can accept it?"
61Aware that his disciples were grumbling
about this, Jesus said to them, "Does this offend you? 62Then what if you see the Son of
Man ascend to where he was before! 63The
Spirit gives life; the flesh counts for nothing. The words I have spoken to you—they
are full of the Spirit[b] and life. 64Yet there are
some of you who do not believe." For Jesus had
known from the beginning which of them did
not believe and who would betray him. 65He
went on to say, "This is why I told you that
no one can come to me unless the Father has
enabled them."
66From this time many of his disciples
turned back and no longer followed him.
67"You do not want to leave too, do you?"
Jesus asked the Twelve.
68Simon Peter answered him, "Lord, to
whom shall we go? You have the words of
eternal life. 69We have come to believe and
to know that you are the Holy One of God."
70Then Jesus replied, "Have I not chosen
you, the Twelve? Yet one of you is a devil!"
71(He meant Judas, the son of Simon Iscariot,
who, though one of the Twelve, was later to
betray him.)

Jesus Goes to the Festival of Tabernacles

7 After this, Jesus went around in Galilee. He
did not want[c] to go about in Judea because
the Jewish leaders there were looking for a
way to kill him. 2But when the Jewish Festival of Tabernacles was near, 3Jesus' brothers
said to him, "Leave Galilee and go to Judea,
so that your disciples there may see the works
you do. 4No one who wants to become a public figure acts in secret. Since you are doing
these things, show yourself to the world." 5For
even his own brothers did not believe in him.
6Therefore Jesus told them, "My time is not
yet here; for you any time will do. 7The world
cannot hate you, but it hates me because I
testify that its works are evil. 8You go to the
festival. I am not[d] going up to this festival, because my time has not yet fully come." 9After
he had said this, he stayed in Galilee.
10However, after his brothers had left for
the festival, he went also, not publicly, but in
secret. 11Now at the festival the Jewish leaders
were watching for Jesus and asking, "Where
is he?"
12Among the crowds there was widespread
whispering about him. Some said, "He is a
good man."
Others replied, "No, he deceives the people." 13But no one would say anything publicly
about him for fear of the leaders.

Jesus Teaches at the Festival

14Not until halfway through the festival did
Jesus go up to the temple courts and begin
to teach. 15The Jews there were amazed and
asked, "How did this man get such learning
without having been taught?"
16Jesus answered, "My teaching is not my
own. It comes from the one who sent me.
17Anyone who chooses to do the will of God
will find out whether my teaching comes from
God or whether I speak on my own. 18Who-
ever speaks on their own does so to gain personal glory, but he who seeks the glory of the
one who sent him is a man of truth; there is
nothing false about him. 19Has not Moses giv-
en you the law? Yet not one of you keeps the
law. Why are you trying to kill me?"
20"You are demon-possessed," the crowd
answered. "Who is trying to kill you?"
21Jesus said to them, "I did one miracle, and
you are all amazed. 22Yet, because Moses gave
you circumcision (though actually it did not
come from Moses, but from the patriarchs),
you circumcise a boy on the Sabbath. 23Now
if a boy can be circumcised on the Sabbath so
that the law of Moses may not be broken, why
are you angry with me for healing a man's
whole body on the Sabbath? 24Stop judging

[a] 45 Isaiah 54:13 [b] 63 Or *are Spirit*; or *are spirit*
[d] 8 Some manuscripts *not yet*
[c] 1 Some manuscripts *not have authority*

by mere appearances, but instead judge correctly."

Division Over Who Jesus Is

25At that point some of the people of Jerusalem began to ask, "Isn't this the man they are trying to kill? 26Here he is, speaking publicly, and they are not saying a word to him. Have the authorities really concluded that he is the Messiah? 27But we know where this man is from; when the Messiah comes, no one will know where he is from."

28Then Jesus, still teaching in the temple courts, cried out, "Yes, you know me, and you know where I am from. I am not here on my own authority, but he who sent me is true. You do not know him, 29but I know him because I am from him and he sent me."

30At this they tried to seize him, but no one laid a hand on him, because his hour had not yet come. 31Still, many in the crowd believed in him. They said, "When the Messiah comes, will he perform more signs than this man?"

32The Pharisees heard the crowd whispering such things about him. Then the chief priests and the Pharisees sent temple guards to arrest him.

33Jesus said, "I am with you for only a short time, and then I am going to the one who sent me. 34You will look for me, but you will not find me; and where I am, you cannot come."

35The Jews said to one another, "Where does this man intend to go that we cannot find him? Will he go where our people live scattered among the Greeks, and teach the Greeks? 36What did he mean when he said, 'You will look for me, but you will not find me,' and 'Where I am, you cannot come'?"

37On the last and greatest day of the festival, Jesus stood and said in a loud voice, "Let anyone who is thirsty come to me and drink. 38Whoever believes in me, as Scripture has said, rivers of living water will flow from within them."[a] 39By this he meant the Spirit, whom those who believed in him were later to receive. Up to that time the Spirit had not been given, since Jesus had not yet been glorified.

40On hearing his words, some of the people said, "Surely this man is the Prophet."

41Others said, "He is the Messiah."

Still others asked, "How can the Messiah come from Galilee? 42Does not Scripture say that the Messiah will come from David's descendants and from Bethlehem, the town where David lived?" 43Thus the people were divided because of Jesus. 44Some wanted to seize him, but no one laid a hand on him.

Unbelief of the Jewish Leaders

45Finally the temple guards went back to the chief priests and the Pharisees, who asked them, "Why didn't you bring him in?"

46"No one ever spoke the way this man does," the guards replied.

47"You mean he has deceived you also?" the Pharisees retorted. 48"Have any of the rulers or of the Pharisees believed in him? 49No! But this mob that knows nothing of the law—there is a curse on them."

50Nicodemus, who had gone to Jesus earlier and who was one of their own number, asked, 51"Does our law condemn a man without first hearing him to find out what he has been doing?"

52They replied, "Are you from Galilee, too? Look into it, and you will find that a prophet does not come out of Galilee."

[The earliest manuscripts and many other ancient witnesses do not have John 7:53—8:11. A few manuscripts include these verses, wholly or in part, after John 7:36, John 21:25, Luke 21:38 or Luke 24:53.]

8 *53Then they all went home, 1but Jesus went to the Mount of Olives.*

2At dawn he appeared again in the temple courts, where all the people gathered around him, and he sat down to teach them. 3The teachers of the law and the Pharisees brought in a woman caught in adultery. They made her stand before the group 4and said to Jesus, "Teacher, this woman was caught in the act of adultery. 5In the Law Moses commanded us to stone such women. Now what do you say?" 6They were using this question as a trap, in order to have a basis for accusing him.

But Jesus bent down and started to write on the ground with his finger. 7When they kept on questioning him, he straightened up and said to them, "Let any one of you who is without sin be the first to throw a stone at her." 8Again he stooped down and wrote on the ground.

9At this, those who heard began to go away one at a time, the older ones first, until only Jesus was left, with the woman still standing there. 10Jesus straightened up and asked her, "Woman, where are they? Has no one condemned you?"

11"No one, sir," she said.

"Then neither do I condemn you," Jesus declared. "Go now and leave your life of sin."

Dispute Over Jesus' Testimony

12When Jesus spoke again to the people, he said, "I am the light of the world. Whoever follows me will never walk in darkness, but will have the light of life."

13The Pharisees challenged him, "Here you are, appearing as your own witness; your testimony is not valid."

14Jesus answered, "Even if I testify on my own behalf, my testimony is valid, for I know where I came from and where I am going. But you have no idea where I come from or where I am going. 15You judge by human standards; I pass judgment on no one. 16But if I do judge, my decisions are true, because I am not alone. I stand with the Father, who sent me. 17In your own Law it is written that the testimony of two

[a] *37,38* Or *me. And let anyone drink 38who believes in me." As Scripture has said, "Out of him* (or *them*) *will flow rivers of living water."*

witnesses is true. 18I am one who testifies for
myself; my other witness is the Father, who
sent me."

19Then they asked him, "Where is your father?"

"You do not know me or my Father," Jesus
replied. "If you knew me, you would know
my Father also." 20He spoke these words
while teaching in the temple courts near the
place where the offerings were put. Yet no
one seized him, because his hour had not yet
come.

Dispute Over Who Jesus Is

21Once more Jesus said to them, "I am going
away, and you will look for me, and you will
die in your sin. Where I go, you cannot come."

22This made the Jews ask, "Will he kill himself? Is that why he says, 'Where I go, you
cannot come'?"

23But he continued, "You are from below;
I am from above. You are of this world; I am
not of this world. 24I told you that you would
die in your sins; if you do not believe that I am
he, you will indeed die in your sins."

25"Who are you?" they asked.

"Just what I have been telling you from the
beginning," Jesus replied. 26"I have much to
say in judgment of you. But he who sent me
is trustworthy, and what I have heard from
him I tell the world."

27They did not understand that he was telling them about his Father. 28So Jesus said,
"When you have lifted up[a] the Son of Man,
then you will know that I am he and that I
do nothing on my own but speak just what
the Father has taught me. 29The one who sent
me is with me; he has not left me alone, for
I always do what pleases him." 30Even as he
spoke, many believed in him.

Dispute Over Whose Children Jesus' Opponents Are

31To the Jews who had believed him, Jesus
said, "If you hold to my teaching, you are
really my disciples. 32Then you will know the
truth, and the truth will set you free."

33They answered him, "We are Abraham's
descendants and have never been slaves of
anyone. How can you say that we shall be
set free?"

34Jesus replied, "Very truly I tell you, everyone who sins is a slave to sin. 35Now a slave
has no permanent place in the family, but a
son belongs to it forever. 36So if the Son sets
you free, you will be free indeed. 37I know
that you are Abraham's descendants. Yet you
are looking for a way to kill me, because you
have no room for my word. 38I am telling you
what I have seen in the Father's presence, and
you are doing what you have heard from your
father.[b]"

39"Abraham is our father," they answered.

"If you were Abraham's children," said
Jesus, "then you would[c] do what Abraham
did. 40As it is, you are looking for a way to kill
me, a man who has told you the truth that I
heard from God. Abraham did not do such
things. 41You are doing the works of your
own father."

"We are not illegitimate children," they
protested. "The only Father we have is God
himself."

42Jesus said to them, "If God were your Father, you would love me, for I have come here
from God. I have not come on my own; God
sent me. 43Why is my language not clear to
you? Because you are unable to hear what
I say. 44You belong to your father, the devil,
and you want to carry out your father's desires. He was a murderer from the beginning,
not holding to the truth, for there is no truth
in him. When he lies, he speaks his native
language, for he is a liar and the father of
lies. 45Yet because I tell the truth, you do not
believe me! 46Can any of you prove me guilty
of sin? If I am telling the truth, why don't you
believe me? 47Whoever belongs to God hears
what God says. The reason you do not hear
is that you do not belong to God."

Jesus' Claims About Himself

48The Jews answered him, "Aren't we right
in saying that you are a Samaritan and demon-possessed?"

49"I am not possessed by a demon," said
Jesus, "but I honor my Father and you dishonor me. 50I am not seeking glory for myself;
but there is one who seeks it, and he is the
judge. 51Very truly I tell you, whoever obeys
my word will never see death."

52At this they exclaimed, "Now we know
that you are demon-possessed! Abraham died
and so did the prophets, yet you say that whoever obeys your word will never taste death.
53Are you greater than our father Abraham?
He died, and so did the prophets. Who do you
think you are?"

54Jesus replied, "If I glorify myself, my
glory means nothing. My Father, whom you
claim as your God, is the one who glorifies
me. 55Though you do not know him, I know
him. If I said I did not, I would be a liar like
you, but I do know him and obey his word.
56Your father Abraham rejoiced at the thought
of seeing my day; he saw it and was glad."

57"You are not yet fifty years old," they said
to him, "and you have seen Abraham!"

58"Very truly I tell you," Jesus answered,
"before Abraham was born, I am!" 59At this,
they picked up stones to stone him, but Jesus
hid himself, slipping away from the temple
grounds.

Jesus Heals a Man Born Blind

9 As he went along, he saw a man blind from
birth. 2His disciples asked him, "Rabbi,
who sinned, this man or his parents, that he
was born blind?"

3"Neither this man nor his parents sinned,"

[a] 28 The Greek for *lifted up* also means *exalted.* [b] 38 Or *presence. Therefore do what you have heard from the Father.* [c] 39 Some early manuscripts *"If you are Abraham's children," said Jesus, "then*

said Jesus, "but this happened so that the works of God might be displayed in him. 4As long as it is day, we must do the works of him who sent me. Night is coming, when no one can work. 5While I am in the world, I am the light of the world."

6After saying this, he spit on the ground, made some mud with the saliva, and put it on the man's eyes. 7"Go," he told him, "wash in the Pool of Siloam" (this word means "Sent"). So the man went and washed, and came home seeing.

8His neighbors and those who had formerly seen him begging asked, "Isn't this the same man who used to sit and beg?" 9Some claimed that he was.

Others said, "No, he only looks like him."

But he himself insisted, "I am the man."

10"How then were your eyes opened?" they asked.

11He replied, "The man they call Jesus made some mud and put it on my eyes. He told me to go to Siloam and wash. So I went and washed, and then I could see."

12"Where is this man?" they asked him.

"I don't know," he said.

The Pharisees Investigate the Healing

13They brought to the Pharisees the man who had been blind. 14Now the day on which Jesus had made the mud and opened the man's eyes was a Sabbath. 15Therefore the Pharisees also asked him how he had received his sight. "He put mud on my eyes," the man replied, "and I washed, and now I see."

16Some of the Pharisees said, "This man is not from God, for he does not keep the Sabbath."

But others asked, "How can a sinner perform such signs?" So they were divided.

17Then they turned again to the blind man, "What have you to say about him? It was your eyes he opened."

The man replied, "He is a prophet."

18They still did not believe that he had been blind and had received his sight until they sent for the man's parents. 19"Is this your son?" they asked. "Is this the one you say was born blind? How is it that now he can see?"

20"We know he is our son," the parents answered, "and we know he was born blind. 21But how he can see now, or who opened his eyes, we don't know. Ask him. He is of age; he will speak for himself." 22His parents said this because they were afraid of the Jewish leaders, who already had decided that anyone who acknowledged that Jesus was the Messiah would be put out of the synagogue. 23That was why his parents said, "He is of age; ask him."

24A second time they summoned the man who had been blind. "Give glory to God by telling the truth," they said. "We know this man is a sinner."

25He replied, "Whether he is a sinner or not, I don't know. One thing I do know. I was blind but now I see!"

26Then they asked him, "What did he do to you? How did he open your eyes?"

27He answered, "I have told you already and you did not listen. Why do you want to hear it again? Do you want to become his disciples too?"

28Then they hurled insults at him and said, "You are this fellow's disciple! We are disciples of Moses! 29We know that God spoke to Moses, but as for this fellow, we don't even know where he comes from."

30The man answered, "Now that is remarkable! You don't know where he comes from, yet he opened my eyes. 31We know that God does not listen to sinners. He listens to the godly person who does his will. 32Nobody has ever heard of opening the eyes of a man born blind. 33If this man were not from God, he could do nothing."

34To this they replied, "You were steeped in sin at birth; how dare you lecture us!" And they threw him out.

Spiritual Blindness

35Jesus heard that they had thrown him out, and when he found him, he said, "Do you believe in the Son of Man?"

36"Who is he, sir?" the man asked. "Tell me so that I may believe in him."

37Jesus said, "You have now seen him; in fact, he is the one speaking with you."

38Then the man said, "Lord, I believe," and he worshiped him.

39Jesus said,[a] "For judgment I have come into this world, so that the blind will see and those who see will become blind."

40Some Pharisees who were with him heard him say this and asked, "What? Are we blind too?"

41Jesus said, "If you were blind, you would not be guilty of sin; but now that you claim you can see, your guilt remains."

The Good Shepherd and His Sheep

10 "Very truly I tell you Pharisees, anyone who does not enter the sheep pen by the gate, but climbs in by some other way, is a thief and a robber. 2The one who enters by the gate is the shepherd of the sheep. 3The gatekeeper opens the gate for him, and the sheep listen to his voice. He calls his own sheep by name and leads them out. 4When he has brought out all his own, he goes on ahead of them, and his sheep follow him because they know his voice. 5But they will never follow a stranger; in fact, they will run away from him because they do not recognize a stranger's voice." 6Jesus used this figure of speech, but the Pharisees did not understand what he was telling them.

7Therefore Jesus said again, "Very truly I tell you, I am the gate for the sheep. 8All who have come before me are thieves and robbers, but the sheep have not listened to them. 9I am the gate; whoever enters through me will be saved.[b] They will come in and go out, and find

[a] *38,39* Some early manuscripts do not have *Then the man said . . . 39Jesus said.* [b] *9* Or *kept safe*

pasture. 10The thief comes only to steal and kill and destroy; I have come that they may have life, and have it to the full.

11"I am the good shepherd. The good shepherd lays down his life for the sheep. 12The hired hand is not the shepherd and does not own the sheep. So when he sees the wolf coming, he abandons the sheep and runs away. Then the wolf attacks the flock and scatters it. 13The man runs away because he is a hired hand and cares nothing for the sheep.

14"I am the good shepherd; I know my sheep and my sheep know me— 15just as the Father knows me and I know the Father—and I lay down my life for the sheep. 16I have other sheep that are not of this sheep pen. I must bring them also. They too will listen to my voice, and there shall be one flock and one shepherd. 17The reason my Father loves me is that I lay down my life—only to take it up again. 18No one takes it from me, but I lay it down of my own accord. I have authority to lay it down and authority to take it up again. This command I received from my Father."

19The Jews who heard these words were again divided. 20Many of them said, "He is demon-possessed and raving mad. Why listen to him?"

21But others said, "These are not the sayings of a man possessed by a demon. Can a demon open the eyes of the blind?"

Further Conflict Over Jesus' Claims

22Then came the Festival of Dedication[a] at Jerusalem. It was winter, 23and Jesus was in the temple courts walking in Solomon's Colonnade. 24The Jews who were there gathered around him, saying, "How long will you keep us in suspense? If you are the Messiah, tell us plainly."

25Jesus answered, "I did tell you, but you do not believe. The works I do in my Father's name testify about me, 26but you do not believe because you are not my sheep. 27My sheep listen to my voice; I know them, and they follow me. 28I give them eternal life, and they shall never perish; no one will snatch them out of my hand. 29My Father, who has given them to me, is greater than all[b]; no one can snatch them out of my Father's hand. 30I and the Father are one."

31Again his Jewish opponents picked up stones to stone him, 32but Jesus said to them, "I have shown you many good works from the Father. For which of these do you stone me?"

33"We are not stoning you for any good work," they replied, "but for blasphemy, because you, a mere man, claim to be God."

34Jesus answered them, "Is it not written in your Law, 'I have said you are "gods"'[c]? 35If he called them 'gods,' to whom the word of God came—and Scripture cannot be set aside— 36what about the one whom the Father set apart as his very own and sent into the world? Why then do you accuse me of blasphemy because I said, 'I am God's Son'? 37Do not believe me unless I do the works of my Father. 38But if I do them, even though you do not believe me, believe the works, that you may know and understand that the Father is in me, and I in the Father." 39Again they tried to seize him, but he escaped their grasp.

40Then Jesus went back across the Jordan to the place where John had been baptizing in the early days. There he stayed, 41and many people came to him. They said, "Though John never performed a sign, all that John said about this man was true." 42And in that place many believed in Jesus.

The Death of Lazarus

11 Now a man named Lazarus was sick. He was from Bethany, the village of Mary and her sister Martha. 2(This Mary, whose brother Lazarus now lay sick, was the same one who poured perfume on the Lord and wiped his feet with her hair.) 3So the sisters sent word to Jesus, "Lord, the one you love is sick."

4When he heard this, Jesus said, "This sickness will not end in death. No, it is for God's glory so that God's Son may be glorified through it." 5Now Jesus loved Martha and her sister and Lazarus. 6So when he heard that Lazarus was sick, he stayed where he was two more days, 7and then he said to his disciples, "Let us go back to Judea."

8"But Rabbi," they said, "a short while ago the Jews there tried to stone you, and yet you are going back?"

9Jesus answered, "Are there not twelve hours of daylight? Anyone who walks in the daytime will not stumble, for they see by this world's light. 10It is when a person walks at night that they stumble, for they have no light."

11After he had said this, he went on to tell them, "Our friend Lazarus has fallen asleep; but I am going there to wake him up."

12His disciples replied, "Lord, if he sleeps, he will get better." 13Jesus had been speaking of his death, but his disciples thought he meant natural sleep.

14So then he told them plainly, "Lazarus is dead, 15and for your sake I am glad I was not there, so that you may believe. But let us go to him."

16Then Thomas (also known as Didymus[d]) said to the rest of the disciples, "Let us also go, that we may die with him."

Jesus Comforts the Sisters of Lazarus

17On his arrival, Jesus found that Lazarus had already been in the tomb for four days. 18Now Bethany was less than two miles[e] from Jerusalem, 19and many Jews had come to Martha and Mary to comfort them in the loss of their brother. 20When Martha heard that Jesus was coming, she went out to meet him, but Mary stayed at home.

21"Lord," Martha said to Jesus, "if you had

[a] *22* That is, Hanukkah [b] *29* Many early manuscripts *What my Father has given me is greater than all* [c] *34* Psalm 82:6 [d] *16* *Thomas* (Aramaic) and *Didymus* (Greek) both mean *twin.*
[e] *18* Or about 3 kilometers

been here, my brother would not have died.
22But I know that even now God will give you
whatever you ask."

23Jesus said to her, "Your brother will rise
again."

24Martha answered, "I know he will rise
again in the resurrection at the last day."

25Jesus said to her, "I am the resurrection
and the life. The one who believes in me will
live, even though they die; 26and whoever lives
by believing in me will never die. Do you believe this?"

27"Yes, Lord," she replied, "I believe that
you are the Messiah, the Son of God, who is
to come into the world."

28After she had said this, she went back
and called her sister Mary aside. "The Teacher is here," she said, "and is asking for you."
29When Mary heard this, she got up quickly and went to him. 30Now Jesus had not yet
entered the village, but was still at the place
where Martha had met him. 31When the Jews
who had been with Mary in the house, comforting her, noticed how quickly she got up
and went out, they followed her, supposing
she was going to the tomb to mourn there.

32When Mary reached the place where
Jesus was and saw him, she fell at his feet and
said, "Lord, if you had been here, my brother
would not have died."

33When Jesus saw her weeping, and the
Jews who had come along with her also weeping, he was deeply moved in spirit and troubled. 34"Where have you laid him?" he asked.

"Come and see, Lord," they replied.

35Jesus wept.

36Then the Jews said, "See how he loved him!"

37But some of them said, "Could not he who
opened the eyes of the blind man have kept
this man from dying?"

Jesus Raises Lazarus From the Dead

38Jesus, once more deeply moved, came to
the tomb. It was a cave with a stone laid across
the entrance. 39"Take away the stone," he said.

"But, Lord," said Martha, the sister of the
dead man, "by this time there is a bad odor,
for he has been there four days."

40Then Jesus said, "Did I not tell you that if
you believe, you will see the glory of God?"

41So they took away the stone. Then Jesus
looked up and said, "Father, I thank you that
you have heard me. 42I knew that you always
hear me, but I said this for the benefit of the
people standing here, that they may believe
that you sent me."

43When he had said this, Jesus called in a
loud voice, "Lazarus, come out!" 44The dead
man came out, his hands and feet wrapped
with strips of linen, and a cloth around his face.

Jesus said to them, "Take off the grave
clothes and let him go."

The Plot to Kill Jesus

45Therefore many of the Jews who had come
to visit Mary, and had seen what Jesus did,
believed in him. 46But some of them went to
the Pharisees and told them what Jesus had
done. 47Then the chief priests and the Pharisees called a meeting of the Sanhedrin.

"What are we accomplishing?" they asked.
"Here is this man performing many signs. 48If
we let him go on like this, everyone will believe in him, and then the Romans will come
and take away both our temple and our nation."

49Then one of them, named Caiaphas, who
was high priest that year, spoke up, "You
know nothing at all! 50You do not realize
that it is better for you that one man die for
the people than that the whole nation perish."

51He did not say this on his own, but as
high priest that year he prophesied that Jesus
would die for the Jewish nation, 52and not only
for that nation but also for the scattered children of God, to bring them together and make
them one. 53So from that day on they plotted
to take his life.

54Therefore Jesus no longer moved about
publicly among the people of Judea. Instead
he withdrew to a region near the wilderness,
to a village called Ephraim, where he stayed
with his disciples.

55When it was almost time for the Jewish
Passover, many went up from the country
to Jerusalem for their ceremonial cleansing
before the Passover. 56They kept looking for
Jesus, and as they stood in the temple courts
they asked one another, "What do you think?
Isn't he coming to the festival at all?" 57But
the chief priests and the Pharisees had giv-
en orders that anyone who found out where
Jesus was should report it so that they might
arrest him.

Jesus Anointed at Bethany

12 Six days before the Passover, Jesus came
to Bethany, where Lazarus lived, whom
Jesus had raised from the dead. 2Here a dinner was given in Jesus' honor. Martha served,
while Lazarus was among those reclining at
the table with him. 3Then Mary took about
a pint[a] of pure nard, an expensive perfume;
she poured it on Jesus' feet and wiped his feet
with her hair. And the house was filled with
the fragrance of the perfume.

4But one of his disciples, Judas Iscariot,
who was later to betray him, objected, 5"Why
wasn't this perfume sold and the money given
to the poor? It was worth a year's wages.[b]"
6He did not say this because he cared about
the poor but because he was a thief; as keeper
of the money bag, he used to help himself to
what was put into it.

7"Leave her alone," Jesus replied. "It was
intended that she should save this perfume for
the day of my burial. 8You will always have
the poor among you,[c] but you will not always
have me."

9Meanwhile a large crowd of Jews found out
that Jesus was there and came, not only because of him but also to see Lazarus, whom he
had raised from the dead. 10So the chief priests

[a] 3 Or about 0.5 liter [b] 5 Greek *three hundred denarii* [c] 8 See Deut. 15:11.

made plans to kill Lazarus as well, 11for on
account of him many of the Jews were going
over to Jesus and believing in him.

Jesus Comes to Jerusalem as King

12The next day the great crowd that had
come for the festival heard that Jesus was
on his way to Jerusalem. 13They took palm
branches and went out to meet him, shouting,

"Hosanna![a]"

"Blessed is he who comes in the name of
the Lord!"[b]

"Blessed is the king of Israel!"

14Jesus found a young donkey and sat on it,
as it is written:

15"Do not be afraid, Daughter Zion;
see, your king is coming,
seated on a donkey's colt."[c]

16At first his disciples did not understand
all this. Only after Jesus was glorified did
they realize that these things had been written about him and that these things had been
done to him.

17Now the crowd that was with him when he
called Lazarus from the tomb and raised him
from the dead continued to spread the word.
18Many people, because they had heard that
he had performed this sign, went out to meet
him. 19So the Pharisees said to one another,
"See, this is getting us nowhere. Look how the
whole world has gone after him!"

Jesus Predicts His Death

20Now there were some Greeks among those
who went up to worship at the festival. 21They
came to Philip, who was from Bethsaida in
Galilee, with a request. "Sir," they said, "we
would like to see Jesus." 22Philip went to tell
Andrew; Andrew and Philip in turn told Jesus.

23Jesus replied, "The hour has come for
the Son of Man to be glorified. 24Very truly
I tell you, unless a kernel of wheat falls to
the ground and dies, it remains only a single
seed. But if it dies, it produces many seeds.
25Anyone who loves their life will lose it, while
anyone who hates their life in this world will
keep it for eternal life. 26Whoever serves me
must follow me; and where I am, my servant
also will be. My Father will honor the one
who serves me.

27"Now my soul is troubled, and what shall
I say? 'Father, save me from this hour'? No, it
was for this very reason I came to this hour.
28Father, glorify your name!"

Then a voice came from heaven, "I have
glorified it, and will glorify it again." 29The
crowd that was there and heard it said it had
thundered; others said an angel had spoken
to him.

30Jesus said, "This voice was for your benefit, not mine. 31Now is the time for judgment
on this world; now the prince of this world
will be driven out. 32And I, when I am lifted
up[d] from the earth, will draw all people to
myself." 33He said this to show the kind of
death he was going to die.

34The crowd spoke up, "We have heard from
the Law that the Messiah will remain forever,
so how can you say, 'The Son of Man must be
lifted up'? Who is this 'Son of Man'?"

35Then Jesus told them, "You are going to
have the light just a little while longer. Walk
while you have the light, before darkness
overtakes you. Whoever walks in the dark
does not know where they are going. 36Be-
lieve in the light while you have the light, so
that you may become children of light." When
he had finished speaking, Jesus left and hid
himself from them.

Belief and Unbelief Among the Jews

37Even after Jesus had performed so many
signs in their presence, they still would not
believe in him. 38This was to fulfill the word
of Isaiah the prophet:

"Lord, who has believed our message
and to whom has the arm of the Lord
been revealed?"[e]

39For this reason they could not believe, because, as Isaiah says elsewhere:

40"He has blinded their eyes
and hardened their hearts,
so they can neither see with their eyes,
nor understand with their hearts,
nor turn—and I would heal them."[f]

41Isaiah said this because he saw Jesus' glory
and spoke about him.

42Yet at the same time many even among
the leaders believed in him. But because of the
Pharisees they would not openly acknowledge
their faith for fear they would be put out of
the synagogue; 43for they loved human praise
more than praise from God.

44Then Jesus cried out, "Whoever believes
in me does not believe in me only, but in the
one who sent me. 45The one who looks at me
is seeing the one who sent me. 46I have come
into the world as a light, so that no one who
believes in me should stay in darkness.

47"If anyone hears my words but does not
keep them, I do not judge that person. For I
did not come to judge the world, but to save
the world. 48There is a judge for the one who
rejects me and does not accept my words; the
very words I have spoken will condemn them
at the last day. 49For I did not speak on my
own, but the Father who sent me commanded
me to say all that I have spoken. 50I know that
his command leads to eternal life. So whatever
I say is just what the Father has told me to say."

Jesus Washes His Disciples' Feet

13 It was just before the Passover Festival.
Jesus knew that the hour had come for
him to leave this world and go to the Father.

[a] *13* A Hebrew expression meaning "Save!" which became an exclamation of praise
[b] *13* Psalm 118:25,26 [c] *15* Zech. 9:9 [d] *32* The Greek for *lifted up* also means *exalted.*
[e] *38* Isaiah 53:1 [f] *40* Isaiah 6:10

Having loved his own who were in the world, he loved them to the end.

2The evening meal was in progress, and the devil had already prompted Judas, the son of Simon Iscariot, to betray Jesus. 3Jesus knew that the Father had put all things under his power, and that he had come from God and was returning to God; 4so he got up from the meal, took off his outer clothing, and wrapped a towel around his waist. 5After that, he poured water into a basin and began to wash his disciples' feet, drying them with the towel that was wrapped around him.

6He came to Simon Peter, who said to him, “Lord, are you going to wash my feet?”

7Jesus replied, “You do not realize now what I am doing, but later you will understand.”

8“No,” said Peter, “you shall never wash my feet.”

Jesus answered, “Unless I wash you, you have no part with me.”

9“Then, Lord,” Simon Peter replied, “not just my feet but my hands and my head as well!”

10Jesus answered, “Those who have had a bath need only to wash their feet; their whole body is clean. And you are clean, though not every one of you.” 11For he knew who was going to betray him, and that was why he said not every one was clean.

12When he had finished washing their feet, he put on his clothes and returned to his place. “Do you understand what I have done for you?” he asked them. 13“You call me ‘Teacher’ and ‘Lord,’ and rightly so, for that is what I am. 14Now that I, your Lord and Teacher, have washed your feet, you also should wash one another's feet. 15I have set you an example that you should do as I have done for you. 16Very truly I tell you, no servant is greater than his master, nor is a messenger greater than the one who sent him. 17Now that you know these things, you will be blessed if you do them.

Jesus Predicts His Betrayal

18“I am not referring to all of you; I know those I have chosen. But this is to fulfill this passage of Scripture: ‘He who shared my bread has turned[a] against me.’[b]

19“I am telling you now before it happens, so that when it does happen you will believe that I am who I am. 20Very truly I tell you, whoever accepts anyone I send accepts me; and whoever accepts me accepts the one who sent me.”

21After he had said this, Jesus was troubled in spirit and testified, “Very truly I tell you, one of you is going to betray me.”

22His disciples stared at one another, at a loss to know which of them he meant. 23One of them, the disciple whom Jesus loved, was reclining next to him. 24Simon Peter motioned to this disciple and said, “Ask him which one he means.”

25Leaning back against Jesus, he asked him, “Lord, who is it?”

26Jesus answered, “It is the one to whom I will give this piece of bread when I have dipped it in the dish.” Then, dipping the piece of bread, he gave it to Judas, the son of Simon Iscariot. 27As soon as Judas took the bread, Satan entered into him.

So Jesus told him, “What you are about to do, do quickly.” 28But no one at the meal understood why Jesus said this to him. 29Since Judas had charge of the money, some thought Jesus was telling him to buy what was needed for the festival, or to give something to the poor. 30As soon as Judas had taken the bread, he went out. And it was night.

Jesus Predicts Peter's Denial

31When he was gone, Jesus said, “Now the Son of Man is glorified and God is glorified in him. 32If God is glorified in him,[c] God will glorify the Son in himself, and will glorify him at once.

33“My children, I will be with you only a little longer. You will look for me, and just as I told the Jews, so I tell you now: Where I am going, you cannot come.

34“A new command I give you: Love one another. As I have loved you, so you must love one another. 35By this everyone will know that you are my disciples, if you love one another.”

36Simon Peter asked him, “Lord, where are you going?”

Jesus replied, “Where I am going, you cannot follow now, but you will follow later.”

37Peter asked, “Lord, why can't I follow you now? I will lay down my life for you.”

38Then Jesus answered, “Will you really lay down your life for me? Very truly I tell you, before the rooster crows, you will disown me three times!

Jesus Comforts His Disciples

14 “Do not let your hearts be troubled. You believe in God[d]; believe also in me. 2My Father's house has many rooms; if that were not so, would I have told you that I am going there to prepare a place for you? 3And if I go and prepare a place for you, I will come back and take you to be with me that you also may be where I am. 4You know the way to the place where I am going.”

Jesus the Way to the Father

5Thomas said to him, “Lord, we don't know where you are going, so how can we know the way?”

6Jesus answered, “I am the way and the truth and the life. No one comes to the Father except through me. 7If you really know me, you will know[e] my Father as well. From now on, you do know him and have seen him.”

8Philip said, “Lord, show us the Father and that will be enough for us.”

9Jesus answered: “Don't you know me, Philip, even after I have been among you such

[a] *18* Greek *has lifted up his heel* [b] *18* Psalm 41:9 [c] *32* Many early manuscripts do not have *If God is glorified in him.* [d] *1* Or *Believe in God* [e] *7* Some manuscripts *If you really knew me, you would know*

a long time? Anyone who has seen me has
seen the Father. How can you say, 'Show us
the Father'? 10Don't you believe that I am in
the Father, and that the Father is in me? The
words I say to you I do not speak on my own
authority. Rather, it is the Father, living in me,
who is doing his work. 11Believe me when I
say that I am in the Father and the Father is
in me; or at least believe on the evidence of
the works themselves. 12Very truly I tell you,
whoever believes in me will do the works I
have been doing, and they will do even greater
things than these, because I am going to the
Father. 13And I will do whatever you ask in
my name, so that the Father may be glorified
in the Son. 14You may ask me for anything in
my name, and I will do it.

Jesus Promises the Holy Spirit

15"If you love me, keep my commands.
16And I will ask the Father, and he will give
you another advocate to help you and be
with you forever— 17the Spirit of truth. The
world cannot accept him, because it neither
sees him nor knows him. But you know him,
for he lives with you and will be[a] in you. 18I
will not leave you as orphans; I will come
to you. 19Before long, the world will not see
me anymore, but you will see me. Because
I live, you also will live. 20On that day you
will realize that I am in my Father, and you
are in me, and I am in you. 21Whoever has
my commands and keeps them is the one
who loves me. The one who loves me will be
loved by my Father, and I too will love them
and show myself to them."

22Then Judas (not Judas Iscariot) said, "But,
Lord, why do you intend to show yourself to
us and not to the world?"

23Jesus replied, "Anyone who loves me will
obey my teaching. My Father will love them,
and we will come to them and make our home
with them. 24Anyone who does not love me
will not obey my teaching. These words you
hear are not my own; they belong to the Father who sent me.

25"All this I have spoken while still with you.
26But the Advocate, the Holy Spirit, whom the
Father will send in my name, will teach you
all things and will remind you of everything
I have said to you. 27Peace I leave with you;
my peace I give you. I do not give to you as the
world gives. Do not let your hearts be troubled
and do not be afraid.

28"You heard me say, 'I am going away and
I am coming back to you.' If you loved me, you
would be glad that I am going to the Father,
for the Father is greater than I. 29I have told
you now before it happens, so that when it
does happen you will believe. 30I will not say
much more to you, for the prince of this world
is coming. He has no hold over me, 31but he
comes so that the world may learn that I love
the Father and do exactly what my Father has
commanded me.

"Come now; let us leave.

The Vine and the Branches

15 "I am the true vine, and my Father is the
gardener. 2He cuts off every branch in
me that bears no fruit, while every branch
that does bear fruit he prunes[b] so that it will
be even more fruitful. 3You are already clean
because of the word I have spoken to you.
4Remain in me, as I also remain in you. No
branch can bear fruit by itself; it must remain
in the vine. Neither can you bear fruit unless
you remain in me.

5"I am the vine; you are the branches. If
you remain in me and I in you, you will bear
much fruit; apart from me you can do nothing. 6If you do not remain in me, you are like
a branch that is thrown away and withers;
such branches are picked up, thrown into the
fire and burned. 7If you remain in me and my
words remain in you, ask whatever you wish,
and it will be done for you. 8This is to my Father's glory, that you bear much fruit, showing
yourselves to be my disciples.

9"As the Father has loved me, so have I
loved you. Now remain in my love. 10If you
keep my commands, you will remain in my
love, just as I have kept my Father's commands and remain in his love. 11I have told
you this so that my joy may be in you and that
your joy may be complete. 12My command
is this: Love each other as I have loved you.
13Greater love has no one than this: to lay
down one's life for one's friends. 14You are
my friends if you do what I command. 15I no
longer call you servants, because a servant
does not know his master's business. Instead,
I have called you friends, for everything that
I learned from my Father I have made known
to you. 16You did not choose me, but I chose
you and appointed you so that you might go
and bear fruit—fruit that will last—and so
that whatever you ask in my name the Father
will give you. 17This is my command: Love
each other.

The World Hates the Disciples

18"If the world hates you, keep in mind
that it hated me first. 19If you belonged to the
world, it would love you as its own. As it is, you
do not belong to the world, but I have chosen
you out of the world. That is why the world
hates you. 20Remember what I told you: 'A servant is not greater than his master.'[c] If they
persecuted me, they will persecute you also. If
they obeyed my teaching, they will obey yours
also. 21They will treat you this way because
of my name, for they do not know the one
who sent me. 22If I had not come and spoken
to them, they would not be guilty of sin; but
now they have no excuse for their sin. 23Who-
ever hates me hates my Father as well. 24If I
had not done among them the works no one
else did, they would not be guilty of sin. As
it is, they have seen, and yet they have hated
both me and my Father. 25But this is to fulfill
what is written in their Law: 'They hated me
without reason.'[d]

[a] *17* Some early manuscripts *and is* [b] *2* The Greek for *he prunes* also means *he cleans.* [c] *20* John 13:16 [d] *25* Psalms 35:19; 69:4

The Work of the Holy Spirit

26“When the Advocate comes, whom I will
send to you from the Father—the Spirit of
truth who goes out from the Father—he will
testify about me. 27And you also must testify,
for you have been with me from the beginning.

16 “All this I have told you so that you will
not fall away. 2They will put you out of
the synagogue; in fact, the time is coming
when anyone who kills you will think they
are offering a service to God. 3They will do
such things because they have not known the
Father or me. 4I have told you this, so that
when their time comes you will remember
that I warned you about them. I did not tell
you this from the beginning because I was
with you, 5but now I am going to him who
sent me. None of you asks me, ‘Where are you
going?’ 6Rather, you are filled with grief because I have said these things. 7But very truly
I tell you, it is for your good that I am going
away. Unless I go away, the Advocate will not
come to you; but if I go, I will send him to you.
8When he comes, he will prove the world to be
in the wrong about sin and righteousness and
judgment: 9about sin, because people do not
believe in me; 10about righteousness, because I
am going to the Father, where you can see me
no longer; 11and about judgment, because the
prince of this world now stands condemned.

12“I have much more to say to you, more
than you can now bear. 13But when he, the
Spirit of truth, comes, he will guide you into
all the truth. He will not speak on his own;
he will speak only what he hears, and he will
tell you what is yet to come. 14He will glorify
me because it is from me that he will receive
what he will make known to you. 15All that
belongs to the Father is mine. That is why I
said the Spirit will receive from me what he
will make known to you.”

The Disciples’ Grief Will Turn to Joy

16Jesus went on to say, “In a little while you
will see me no more, and then after a little
while you will see me.”

17At this, some of his disciples said to one
another, “What does he mean by saying, ‘In
a little while you will see me no more, and
then after a little while you will see me,’ and
‘Because I am going to the Father’?” 18They
kept asking, “What does he mean by ‘a little while’? We don’t understand what he is
saying.”

19Jesus saw that they wanted to ask him
about this, so he said to them, “Are you asking
one another what I meant when I said, ‘In a
little while you will see me no more, and then
after a little while you will see me’? 20Very truly I tell you, you will weep and mourn while
the world rejoices. You will grieve, but your
grief will turn to joy. 21A woman giving birth
to a child has pain because her time has come;
but when her baby is born she forgets the anguish because of her joy that a child is born
into the world. 22So with you: Now is your
time of grief, but I will see you again and you
will rejoice, and no one will take away your
joy. 23In that day you will no longer ask me
anything. Very truly I tell you, my Father will
give you whatever you ask in my name. 24Until
now you have not asked for anything in my
name. Ask and you will receive, and your joy
will be complete.

25“Though I have been speaking figuratively, a time is coming when I will no longer use
this kind of language but will tell you plainly
about my Father. 26In that day you will ask
in my name. I am not saying that I will ask
the Father on your behalf. 27No, the Father
himself loves you because you have loved me
and have believed that I came from God. 28I
came from the Father and entered the world;
now I am leaving the world and going back
to the Father.”

29Then Jesus’ disciples said, “Now you
are speaking clearly and without figures of
speech. 30Now we can see that you know all
things and that you do not even need to have
anyone ask you questions. This makes us believe that you came from God.”

31“Do you now believe?” Jesus replied. 32“A
time is coming and in fact has come when you
will be scattered, each to your own home. You
will leave me all alone. Yet I am not alone, for
my Father is with me.

33“I have told you these things, so that in
me you may have peace. In this world you
will have trouble. But take heart! I have overcome the world.”

Jesus Prays to Be Glorified

17 After Jesus said this, he looked toward
heaven and prayed:

“Father, the hour has come. Glorify
your Son, that your Son may glorify you.
2For you granted him authority over all
people that he might give eternal life to
all those you have given him. 3Now this
is eternal life: that they know you, the
only true God, and Jesus Christ, whom
you have sent. 4I have brought you glory
on earth by finishing the work you gave
me to do. 5And now, Father, glorify me in
your presence with the glory I had with
you before the world began.

Jesus Prays for His Disciples

6“I have revealed you[a] to those whom
you gave me out of the world. They were
yours; you gave them to me and they have
obeyed your word. 7Now they know that
everything you have given me comes
from you. 8For I gave them the words you
gave me and they accepted them. They
knew with certainty that I came from
you, and they believed that you sent me.
9I pray for them. I am not praying for the
world, but for those you have given me,
for they are yours. 10All I have is yours,
and all you have is mine. And glory has

[a] 6 Greek *your name*

come to me through them. [11]I will remain
in the world no longer, but they are still
in the world, and I am coming to you.
Holy Father, protect them by the power
of[a] your name, the name you gave me,
so that they may be one as we are one.
[12]While I was with them, I protected them
and kept them safe by[b] that name you
gave me. None has been lost except the
one doomed to destruction so that Scripture would be fulfilled.

[13]"I am coming to you now, but I say
these things while I am still in the world,
so that they may have the full measure of
my joy within them. [14]I have given them
your word and the world has hated them,
for they are not of the world any more
than I am of the world. [15]My prayer is not
that you take them out of the world but
that you protect them from the evil one.
[16]They are not of the world, even as I am
not of it. [17]Sanctify them by[c] the truth;
your word is truth. [18]As you sent me into
the world, I have sent them into the world.
[19]For them I sanctify myself, that they too
may be truly sanctified.

Jesus Prays for All Believers

[20]"My prayer is not for them alone. I
pray also for those who will believe in
me through their message, [21]that all of
them may be one, Father, just as you are
in me and I am in you. May they also be
in us so that the world may believe that
you have sent me. [22]I have given them the
glory that you gave me, that they may be
one as we are one— [23]I in them and you
in me—so that they may be brought to
complete unity. Then the world will know
that you sent me and have loved them
even as you have loved me.

[24]"Father, I want those you have given
me to be with me where I am, and to see
my glory, the glory you have given me
because you loved me before the creation
of the world.

[25]"Righteous Father, though the world
does not know you, I know you, and they
know that you have sent me. [26]I have
made you[d] known to them, and will continue to make you known in order that the
love you have for me may be in them and
that I myself may be in them."

Jesus Arrested

18 When he had finished praying, Jesus
left with his disciples and crossed the
Kidron Valley. On the other side there was a
garden, and he and his disciples went into it.
[2]Now Judas, who betrayed him, knew the
place, because Jesus had often met there with
his disciples. [3]So Judas came to the garden,
guiding a detachment of soldiers and some
officials from the chief priests and the Pharisees. They were carrying torches, lanterns
and weapons.

[4]Jesus, knowing all that was going to happen to him, went out and asked them, "Who
is it you want?"

[5]"Jesus of Nazareth," they replied.

"I am he," Jesus said. (And Judas the traitor
was standing there with them.) [6]When Jesus
said, "I am he," they drew back and fell to
the ground.

[7]Again he asked them, "Who is it you
want?"

"Jesus of Nazareth," they said.

[8]Jesus answered, "I told you that I am he.
If you are looking for me, then let these men
go." [9]This happened so that the words he had
spoken would be fulfilled: "I have not lost one
of those you gave me."[e]

[10]Then Simon Peter, who had a sword, drew
it and struck the high priest's servant, cutting off his right ear. (The servant's name
was Malchus.)

[11]Jesus commanded Peter, "Put your sword
away! Shall I not drink the cup the Father has
given me?"

[12]Then the detachment of soldiers with its
commander and the Jewish officials arrested Jesus. They bound him [13]and brought him
first to Annas, who was the father-in-law of
Caiaphas, the high priest that year. [14]Caia-
phas was the one who had advised the Jewish
leaders that it would be good if one man died
for the people.

Peter's First Denial

[15]Simon Peter and another disciple were
following Jesus. Because this disciple was
known to the high priest, he went with Jesus
into the high priest's courtyard, [16]but Peter
had to wait outside at the door. The other disciple, who was known to the high priest, came
back, spoke to the servant girl on duty there
and brought Peter in.

[17]"You aren't one of this man's disciples too,
are you?" she asked Peter.

He replied, "I am not."

[18]It was cold, and the servants and officials
stood around a fire they had made to keep
warm. Peter also was standing with them,
warming himself.

The High Priest Questions Jesus

[19]Meanwhile, the high priest questioned
Jesus about his disciples and his teaching.

[20]"I have spoken openly to the world," Jesus
replied. "I always taught in synagogues or at
the temple, where all the Jews come together.
I said nothing in secret. [21]Why question me?
Ask those who heard me. Surely they know
what I said."

[22]When Jesus said this, one of the officials
nearby slapped him in the face. "Is this the
way you answer the high priest?" he demanded.

[23]"If I said something wrong," Jesus replied,
"testify as to what is wrong. But if I spoke the
truth, why did you strike me?" [24]Then Annas
sent him bound to Caiaphas the high priest.

[a] 11 Or *Father, keep them faithful to* [b] 12 Or *kept them faithful to* [c] 17 Or *them to live in accordance with* [d] 26 Greek *your name* [e] 9 John 6:39

Peter's Second and Third Denials

25 Meanwhile, Simon Peter was still standing there warming himself. So they asked him, "You aren't one of his disciples too, are you?"

He denied it, saying, "I am not."

26 One of the high priest's servants, a relative of the man whose ear Peter had cut off, challenged him, "Didn't I see you with him in the garden?" 27 Again Peter denied it, and at that moment a rooster began to crow.

Jesus Before Pilate

28 Then the Jewish leaders took Jesus from Caiaphas to the palace of the Roman governor. By now it was early morning, and to avoid ceremonial uncleanness they did not enter the palace, because they wanted to be able to eat the Passover. 29 So Pilate came out to them and asked, "What charges are you bringing against this man?"

30 "If he were not a criminal," they replied, "we would not have handed him over to you."

31 Pilate said, "Take him yourselves and judge him by your own law."

"But we have no right to execute anyone," they objected. 32 This took place to fulfill what Jesus had said about the kind of death he was going to die.

33 Pilate then went back inside the palace, summoned Jesus and asked him, "Are you the king of the Jews?"

34 "Is that your own idea," Jesus asked, "or did others talk to you about me?"

35 "Am I a Jew?" Pilate replied. "Your own people and chief priests handed you over to me. What is it you have done?"

36 Jesus said, "My kingdom is not of this world. If it were, my servants would fight to prevent my arrest by the Jewish leaders. But now my kingdom is from another place."

37 "You are a king, then!" said Pilate.

Jesus answered, "You say that I am a king. In fact, the reason I was born and came into the world is to testify to the truth. Everyone on the side of truth listens to me."

38 "What is truth?" retorted Pilate. With this he went out again to the Jews gathered there and said, "I find no basis for a charge against him. 39 But it is your custom for me to release to you one prisoner at the time of the Passover. Do you want me to release 'the king of the Jews'?"

40 They shouted back, "No, not him! Give us Barabbas!" Now Barabbas had taken part in an uprising.

Jesus Sentenced to Be Crucified

19 Then Pilate took Jesus and had him flogged. 2 The soldiers twisted together a crown of thorns and put it on his head. They clothed him in a purple robe 3 and went up to him again and again, saying, "Hail, king of the Jews!" And they slapped him in the face.

4 Once more Pilate came out and said to the Jews gathered there, "Look, I am bringing him out to you to let you know that I find no basis for a charge against him." 5 When Jesus came out wearing the crown of thorns and the purple robe, Pilate said to them, "Here is the man!"

6 As soon as the chief priests and their officials saw him, they shouted, "Crucify! Crucify!"

But Pilate answered, "You take him and crucify him. As for me, I find no basis for a charge against him."

7 The Jewish leaders insisted, "We have a law, and according to that law he must die, because he claimed to be the Son of God."

8 When Pilate heard this, he was even more afraid, 9 and he went back inside the palace. "Where do you come from?" he asked Jesus, but Jesus gave him no answer. 10 "Do you refuse to speak to me?" Pilate said. "Don't you realize I have power either to free you or to crucify you?"

11 Jesus answered, "You would have no power over me if it were not given to you from above. Therefore the one who handed me over to you is guilty of a greater sin."

12 From then on, Pilate tried to set Jesus free, but the Jewish leaders kept shouting, "If you let this man go, you are no friend of Caesar. Anyone who claims to be a king opposes Caesar."

13 When Pilate heard this, he brought Jesus out and sat down on the judge's seat at a place known as the Stone Pavement (which in Aramaic is Gabbatha). 14 It was the day of Preparation of the Passover; it was about noon.

"Here is your king," Pilate said to the Jews.

15 But they shouted, "Take him away! Take him away! Crucify him!"

"Shall I crucify your king?" Pilate asked.

"We have no king but Caesar," the chief priests answered.

16 Finally Pilate handed him over to them to be crucified.

The Crucifixion of Jesus

So the soldiers took charge of Jesus. 17 Carrying his own cross, he went out to the place of the Skull (which in Aramaic is called Golgotha). 18 There they crucified him, and with him two others—one on each side and Jesus in the middle.

19 Pilate had a notice prepared and fastened to the cross. It read: JESUS OF NAZARETH, THE KING OF THE JEWS. 20 Many of the Jews read this sign, for the place where Jesus was crucified was near the city, and the sign was written in Aramaic, Latin and Greek. 21 The chief priests of the Jews protested to Pilate, "Do not write 'The King of the Jews,' but that this man claimed to be king of the Jews."

22 Pilate answered, "What I have written, I have written."

23 When the soldiers crucified Jesus, they took his clothes, dividing them into four shares, one for each of them, with the undergarment remaining. This garment was seamless, woven in one piece from top to bottom.

24 "Let's not tear it," they said to one another. "Let's decide by lot who will get it."

This happened that the scripture might be fulfilled that said,

> "They divided my clothes among them
> and cast lots for my garment."[a]

So this is what the soldiers did.

25Near the cross of Jesus stood his mother, his mother's sister, Mary the wife of Clopas, and Mary Magdalene. 26When Jesus saw his mother there, and the disciple whom he loved standing nearby, he said to her, "Woman,[b] here is your son," 27and to the disciple, "Here is your mother." From that time on, this disciple took her into his home.

The Death of Jesus

28Later, knowing that everything had now been finished, and so that Scripture would be fulfilled, Jesus said, "I am thirsty." 29A jar of wine vinegar was there, so they soaked a sponge in it, put the sponge on a stalk of the hyssop plant, and lifted it to Jesus' lips. 30When he had received the drink, Jesus said, "It is finished." With that, he bowed his head and gave up his spirit.

31Now it was the day of Preparation, and the next day was to be a special Sabbath. Because the Jewish leaders did not want the bodies left on the crosses during the Sabbath, they asked Pilate to have the legs broken and the bodies taken down. 32The soldiers therefore came and broke the legs of the first man who had been crucified with Jesus, and then those of the other. 33But when they came to Jesus and found that he was already dead, they did not break his legs. 34Instead, one of the soldiers pierced Jesus' side with a spear, bringing a sudden flow of blood and water. 35The man who saw it has given testimony, and his testimony is true. He knows that he tells the truth, and he testifies so that you also may believe. 36These things happened so that the scripture would be fulfilled: "Not one of his bones will be broken,"[c] 37and, as another scripture says, "They will look on the one they have pierced."[d]

The Burial of Jesus

38Later, Joseph of Arimathea asked Pilate for the body of Jesus. Now Joseph was a disciple of Jesus, but secretly because he feared the Jewish leaders. With Pilate's permission, he came and took the body away. 39He was accompanied by Nicodemus, the man who earlier had visited Jesus at night. Nicodemus brought a mixture of myrrh and aloes, about seventy-five pounds.[e] 40Taking Jesus' body, the two of them wrapped it, with the spices, in strips of linen. This was in accordance with Jewish burial customs. 41At the place where Jesus was crucified, there was a garden, and in the garden a new tomb, in which no one had ever been laid. 42Because it was the Jewish day of Preparation and since the tomb was nearby, they laid Jesus there.

The Empty Tomb

20 Early on the first day of the week, while it was still dark, Mary Magdalene went to the tomb and saw that the stone had been removed from the entrance. 2So she came running to Simon Peter and the other disciple, the one Jesus loved, and said, "They have taken the Lord out of the tomb, and we don't know where they have put him!"

3So Peter and the other disciple started for the tomb. 4Both were running, but the other disciple outran Peter and reached the tomb first. 5He bent over and looked in at the strips of linen lying there but did not go in. 6Then Simon Peter came along behind him and went straight into the tomb. He saw the strips of linen lying there, 7as well as the cloth that had been wrapped around Jesus' head. The cloth was still lying in its place, separate from the linen. 8Finally the other disciple, who had reached the tomb first, also went inside. He saw and believed. 9(They still did not understand from Scripture that Jesus had to rise from the dead.) 10Then the disciples went back to where they were staying.

Jesus Appears to Mary Magdalene

11Now Mary stood outside the tomb crying. As she wept, she bent over to look into the tomb 12and saw two angels in white, seated where Jesus' body had been, one at the head and the other at the foot.

13They asked her, "Woman, why are you crying?"

"They have taken my Lord away," she said, "and I don't know where they have put him." 14At this, she turned around and saw Jesus standing there, but she did not realize that it was Jesus.

15He asked her, "Woman, why are you crying? Who is it you are looking for?"

Thinking he was the gardener, she said, "Sir, if you have carried him away, tell me where you have put him, and I will get him."

16Jesus said to her, "Mary."

She turned toward him and cried out in Aramaic, "Rabboni!" (which means "Teacher").

17Jesus said, "Do not hold on to me, for I have not yet ascended to the Father. Go instead to my brothers and tell them, 'I am ascending to my Father and your Father, to my God and your God.'"

18Mary Magdalene went to the disciples with the news: "I have seen the Lord!" And she told them that he had said these things to her.

Jesus Appears to His Disciples

19On the evening of that first day of the week, when the disciples were together, with the doors locked for fear of the Jewish leaders, Jesus came and stood among them and said, "Peace be with you!" 20After he said this, he showed them his hands and side. The disciples were overjoyed when they saw the Lord.

21Again Jesus said, "Peace be with you! As the Father has sent me, I am sending you." 22And with that he breathed on them and said, "Receive the Holy Spirit. 23If you forgive anyone's sins, their sins are forgiven; if you do not forgive them, they are not forgiven."

[a] *24* Psalm 22:18 [b] *26* The Greek for *Woman* does not denote any disrespect. [c] *36* Exodus 12:46; Num. 9:12; Psalm 34:20 [d] *37* Zech. 12:10 [e] *39* Or about 34 kilograms

Jesus Appears to Thomas

24 Now Thomas (also known as Didymus[a]), one of the Twelve, was not with the disciples when Jesus came. 25 So the other disciples told him, "We have seen the Lord!"

But he said to them, "Unless I see the nail marks in his hands and put my finger where the nails were, and put my hand into his side, I will not believe."

26 A week later his disciples were in the house again, and Thomas was with them. Though the doors were locked, Jesus came and stood among them and said, "Peace be with you!" 27 Then he said to Thomas, "Put your finger here; see my hands. Reach out your hand and put it into my side. Stop doubting and believe."

28 Thomas said to him, "My Lord and my God!"

29 Then Jesus told him, "Because you have seen me, you have believed; blessed are those who have not seen and yet have believed."

The Purpose of John's Gospel

30 Jesus performed many other signs in the presence of his disciples, which are not recorded in this book. 31 But these are written that you may believe[b] that Jesus is the Messiah, the Son of God, and that by believing you may have life in his name.

Jesus and the Miraculous Catch of Fish

21 Afterward Jesus appeared again to his disciples, by the Sea of Galilee.[c] It happened this way: 2 Simon Peter, Thomas (also known as Didymus[a]), Nathanael from Cana in Galilee, the sons of Zebedee, and two other disciples were together. 3 "I'm going out to fish," Simon Peter told them, and they said, "We'll go with you." So they went out and got into the boat, but that night they caught nothing.

4 Early in the morning, Jesus stood on the shore, but the disciples did not realize that it was Jesus.

5 He called out to them, "Friends, haven't you any fish?"

"No," they answered.

6 He said, "Throw your net on the right side of the boat and you will find some." When they did, they were unable to haul the net in because of the large number of fish.

7 Then the disciple whom Jesus loved said to Peter, "It is the Lord!" As soon as Simon Peter heard him say, "It is the Lord," he wrapped his outer garment around him (for he had taken it off) and jumped into the water. 8 The other disciples followed in the boat, towing the net full of fish, for they were not far from shore, about a hundred yards.[d] 9 When they landed, they saw a fire of burning coals there with fish on it, and some bread.

10 Jesus said to them, "Bring some of the fish you have just caught." 11 So Simon Peter climbed back into the boat and dragged the net ashore. It was full of large fish, 153, but even with so many the net was not torn. 12 Jesus said to them, "Come and have breakfast." None of the disciples dared ask him, "Who are you?" They knew it was the Lord. 13 Jesus came, took the bread and gave it to them, and did the same with the fish. 14 This was now the third time Jesus appeared to his disciples after he was raised from the dead.

Jesus Reinstates Peter

15 When they had finished eating, Jesus said to Simon Peter, "Simon son of John, do you love me more than these?"

"Yes, Lord," he said, "you know that I love you."

Jesus said, "Feed my lambs."

16 Again Jesus said, "Simon son of John, do you love me?"

He answered, "Yes, Lord, you know that I love you."

Jesus said, "Take care of my sheep."

17 The third time he said to him, "Simon son of John, do you love me?"

Peter was hurt because Jesus asked him the third time, "Do you love me?" He said, "Lord, you know all things; you know that I love you."

Jesus said, "Feed my sheep. 18 Very truly I tell you, when you were younger you dressed yourself and went where you wanted; but when you are old you will stretch out your hands, and someone else will dress you and lead you where you do not want to go." 19 Jesus said this to indicate the kind of death by which Peter would glorify God. Then he said to him, "Follow me!"

20 Peter turned and saw that the disciple whom Jesus loved was following them. (This was the one who had leaned back against Jesus at the supper and had said, "Lord, who is going to betray you?") 21 When Peter saw him, he asked, "Lord, what about him?"

22 Jesus answered, "If I want him to remain alive until I return, what is that to you? You must follow me." 23 Because of this, the rumor spread among the believers that this disciple would not die. But Jesus did not say that he would not die; he only said, "If I want him to remain alive until I return, what is that to you?"

24 This is the disciple who testifies to these things and who wrote them down. We know that his testimony is true.

25 Jesus did many other things as well. If every one of them were written down, I suppose that even the whole world would not have room for the books that would be written.

[a] *24,2 Thomas* (Aramaic) and *Didymus* (Greek) both mean *twin.* [b] *31* Or *may continue to believe*
[c] *1* Greek *Tiberias* [d] *8* Or about 90 meters

Acts

Jesus Taken Up Into Heaven

1 In my former book, Theophilus, I wrote
about all that Jesus began to do and to
teach 2until the day he was taken up to heav-
en, after giving instructions through the Holy
Spirit to the apostles he had chosen. 3After
his suffering, he presented himself to them
and gave many convincing proofs that he was
alive. He appeared to them over a period of
forty days and spoke about the kingdom of
God. 4On one occasion, while he was eating
with them, he gave them this command: "Do
not leave Jerusalem, but wait for the gift my
Father promised, which you have heard me
speak about. 5For John baptized with[a] water,
but in a few days you will be baptized with[a]
the Holy Spirit."

6Then they gathered around him and asked
him, "Lord, are you at this time going to restore the kingdom to Israel?"

7He said to them: "It is not for you to know
the times or dates the Father has set by his
own authority. 8But you will receive power
when the Holy Spirit comes on you; and you
will be my witnesses in Jerusalem, and in all
Judea and Samaria, and to the ends of the
earth."

9After he said this, he was taken up before
their very eyes, and a cloud hid him from their
sight.

10They were looking intently up into the
sky as he was going, when suddenly two men
dressed in white stood beside them. 11"Men of
Galilee," they said, "why do you stand here
looking into the sky? This same Jesus, who
has been taken from you into heaven, will
come back in the same way you have seen
him go into heaven."

Matthias Chosen to Replace Judas

12Then the apostles returned to Jerusalem
from the hill called the Mount of Olives, a
Sabbath day's walk[b] from the city. 13When
they arrived, they went upstairs to the room
where they were staying. Those present were
Peter, John, James and Andrew; Philip and
Thomas, Bartholomew and Matthew; James
son of Alphaeus and Simon the Zealot, and
Judas son of James. 14They all joined together
constantly in prayer, along with the women
and Mary the mother of Jesus, and with his
brothers.

15In those days Peter stood up among the
believers (a group numbering about a hundred and twenty) 16and said, "Brothers and
sisters,[c] the Scripture had to be fulfilled in
which the Holy Spirit spoke long ago through
David concerning Judas, who served as guide
for those who arrested Jesus. 17He was one
of our number and shared in our ministry."

18(With the payment he received for his
wickedness, Judas bought a field; there he
fell headlong, his body burst open and all his
intestines spilled out. 19Everyone in Jerusalem heard about this, so they called that field
in their language Akeldama, that is, Field of
Blood.)

20"For," said Peter, "it is written in the Book
of Psalms:

> " 'May his place be deserted;
> let there be no one to dwell in it,'[d]

and,

> " 'May another take his place of
> leadership.'[e]

21Therefore it is necessary to choose one of the
men who have been with us the whole time the
Lord Jesus was living among us, 22beginning
from John's baptism to the time when Jesus
was taken up from us. For one of these must
become a witness with us of his resurrection."

23So they nominated two men: Joseph called
Barsabbas (also known as Justus) and Matthias. 24Then they prayed, "Lord, you know
everyone's heart. Show us which of these two
you have chosen 25to take over this apostolic
ministry, which Judas left to go where he belongs." 26Then they cast lots, and the lot fell
to Matthias; so he was added to the eleven
apostles.

The Holy Spirit Comes at Pentecost

2 When the day of Pentecost came, they
were all together in one place. 2Suddenly a
sound like the blowing of a violent wind came
from heaven and filled the whole house where
they were sitting. 3They saw what seemed to
be tongues of fire that separated and came
to rest on each of them. 4All of them were
filled with the Holy Spirit and began to speak
in other tongues[f] as the Spirit enabled them.

5Now there were staying in Jerusalem God-
fearing Jews from every nation under heaven.
6When they heard this sound, a crowd came
together in bewilderment, because each one
heard their own language being spoken. 7Ut-
terly amazed, they asked: "Aren't all these
who are speaking Galileans? 8Then how is it
that each of us hears them in our native language? 9Parthians, Medes and Elamites; residents of Mesopotamia, Judea and Cappadocia,
Pontus and Asia,[g] 10Phrygia and Pamphylia,
Egypt and the parts of Libya near Cyrene;
visitors from Rome 11(both Jews and converts
to Judaism); Cretans and Arabs—we hear

[a] *5* Or *in* [b] *12* That is, about 5/8 mile or about 1 kilometer [c] *16* The Greek word for *brothers and sisters* (*adelphoi*) refers here to believers, both men and women, as part of God's family; also in 6:3; 11:29; 12:17; 16:40; 18:18, 27; 21:7, 17; 28:14, 15. [d] *20* Psalm 69:25 [e] *20* Psalm 109:8 [f] *4* Or *languages*; also in verse 11 [g] *9* That is, the Roman province by that name

them declaring the wonders of God in our
own tongues!" 12Amazed and perplexed, they
asked one another, "What does this mean?"
13Some, however, made fun of them and
said, "They have had too much wine."

Peter Addresses the Crowd

14Then Peter stood up with the Eleven,
raised his voice and addressed the crowd:
"Fellow Jews and all of you who live in Jerusalem, let me explain this to you; listen
carefully to what I say. 15These people are
not drunk, as you suppose. It's only nine in
the morning! 16No, this is what was spoken
by the prophet Joel:

17" 'In the last days, God says,
I will pour out my Spirit on all people.
Your sons and daughters will prophesy,
your young men will see visions,
your old men will dream dreams.
18Even on my servants, both men and
women,
I will pour out my Spirit in those days,
and they will prophesy.
19I will show wonders in the heavens above
and signs on the earth below,
blood and fire and billows of smoke.
20The sun will be turned to darkness
and the moon to blood
before the coming of the great and
glorious day of the Lord.
21And everyone who calls
on the name of the Lord will be saved.'[a]

22"Fellow Israelites, listen to this: Jesus of
Nazareth was a man accredited by God to
you by miracles, wonders and signs, which
God did among you through him, as you yourselves know. 23This man was handed over to
you by God's deliberate plan and foreknowledge; and you, with the help of wicked men,[b]
put him to death by nailing him to the cross.
24But God raised him from the dead, freeing
him from the agony of death, because it was
impossible for death to keep its hold on him.
25David said about him:

" 'I saw the Lord always before me.
Because he is at my right hand,
I will not be shaken.
26Therefore my heart is glad and my tongue
rejoices;
my body also will rest in hope,
27because you will not abandon me to the
realm of the dead,
you will not let your holy one see decay.
28You have made known to me the paths of
life;
you will fill me with joy in your
presence.'[c]

29"Fellow Israelites, I can tell you confidently that the patriarch David died and was buried, and his tomb is here to this day. 30But he
was a prophet and knew that God had promised him on oath that he would place one of
his descendants on his throne. 31Seeing what
was to come, he spoke of the resurrection of
the Messiah, that he was not abandoned to
the realm of the dead, nor did his body see
decay. 32God has raised this Jesus to life, and
we are all witnesses of it. 33Exalted to the right
hand of God, he has received from the Father
the promised Holy Spirit and has poured out
what you now see and hear. 34For David did
not ascend to heaven, and yet he said,

" 'The Lord said to my Lord:
"Sit at my right hand
35until I make your enemies
a footstool for your feet." '[d]

36"Therefore let all Israel be assured of this:
God has made this Jesus, whom you crucified,
both Lord and Messiah."
37When the people heard this, they were cut
to the heart and said to Peter and the other
apostles, "Brothers, what shall we do?"
38Peter replied, "Repent and be baptized,
every one of you, in the name of Jesus Christ
for the forgiveness of your sins. And you will
receive the gift of the Holy Spirit. 39The promise is for you and your children and for all
who are far off—for all whom the Lord our
God will call."
40With many other words he warned them;
and he pleaded with them, "Save yourselves
from this corrupt generation." 41Those who accepted his message were baptized, and about
three thousand were added to their number
that day.

The Fellowship of the Believers

42They devoted themselves to the apostles'
teaching and to fellowship, to the breaking
of bread and to prayer. 43Everyone was filled
with awe at the many wonders and signs performed by the apostles. 44All the believers
were together and had everything in common. 45They sold property and possessions
to give to anyone who had need. 46Every day
they continued to meet together in the temple courts. They broke bread in their homes
and ate together with glad and sincere hearts,
47praising God and enjoying the favor of all
the people. And the Lord added to their number daily those who were being saved.

Peter Heals a Lame Beggar

3 One day Peter and John were going up to
the temple at the time of prayer—at three
in the afternoon. 2Now a man who was lame
from birth was being carried to the temple
gate called Beautiful, where he was put every
day to beg from those going into the temple
courts. 3When he saw Peter and John about to
enter, he asked them for money. 4Peter looked
straight at him, as did John. Then Peter said,
"Look at us!" 5So the man gave them his attention, expecting to get something from them.
6Then Peter said, "Silver or gold I do not
have, but what I do have I give you. In the
name of Jesus Christ of Nazareth, walk."
7Taking him by the right hand, he helped him

[a] *21* Joel 2:28-32 [b] *23* Or *of those not having the law* (that is, Gentiles) [c] *28* Psalm 16:8-11 (see Septuagint) [d] *35* Psalm 110:1

up, and instantly the man's feet and ankles became strong. 8He jumped to his feet and began to walk. Then he went with them into the temple courts, walking and jumping, and praising God. 9When all the people saw him walking and praising God, 10they recognized him as the same man who used to sit begging at the temple gate called Beautiful, and they were filled with wonder and amazement at what had happened to him.

Peter Speaks to the Onlookers

11While the man held on to Peter and John, all the people were astonished and came running to them in the place called Solomon's Colonnade. 12When Peter saw this, he said to them: "Fellow Israelites, why does this surprise you? Why do you stare at us as if by our own power or godliness we had made this man walk? 13The God of Abraham, Isaac and Jacob, the God of our fathers, has glorified his servant Jesus. You handed him over to be killed, and you disowned him before Pilate, though he had decided to let him go. 14You disowned the Holy and Righteous One and asked that a murderer be released to you. 15You killed the author of life, but God raised him from the dead. We are witnesses of this. 16By faith in the name of Jesus, this man whom you see and know was made strong. It is Jesus' name and the faith that comes through him that has completely healed him, as you can all see.

17"Now, fellow Israelites, I know that you acted in ignorance, as did your leaders. 18But this is how God fulfilled what he had foretold through all the prophets, saying that his Messiah would suffer. 19Repent, then, and turn to God, so that your sins may be wiped out, that times of refreshing may come from the Lord, 20and that he may send the Messiah, who has been appointed for you—even Jesus. 21Heaven must receive him until the time comes for God to restore everything, as he promised long ago through his holy prophets. 22For Moses said, 'The Lord your God will raise up for you a prophet like me from among your own people; you must listen to everything he tells you. 23Anyone who does not listen to him will be completely cut off from their people.'[a]

24"Indeed, beginning with Samuel, all the prophets who have spoken have foretold these days. 25And you are heirs of the prophets and of the covenant God made with your fathers. He said to Abraham, 'Through your offspring all peoples on earth will be blessed.'[b] 26When God raised up his servant, he sent him first to you to bless you by turning each of you from your wicked ways."

Peter and John Before the Sanhedrin

4 The priests and the captain of the temple guard and the Sadducees came up to Peter and John while they were speaking to the people. 2They were greatly disturbed because the apostles were teaching the people, proclaiming in Jesus the resurrection of the dead. 3They seized Peter and John and, because it was evening, they put them in jail until the next day. 4But many who heard the message believed; so the number of men who believed grew to about five thousand.

5The next day the rulers, the elders and the teachers of the law met in Jerusalem. 6Annas the high priest was there, and so were Caiaphas, John, Alexander and others of the high priest's family. 7They had Peter and John brought before them and began to question them: "By what power or what name did you do this?"

8Then Peter, filled with the Holy Spirit, said to them: "Rulers and elders of the people! 9If we are being called to account today for an act of kindness shown to a man who was lame and are being asked how he was healed, 10then know this, you and all the people of Israel: It is by the name of Jesus Christ of Nazareth, whom you crucified but whom God raised from the dead, that this man stands before you healed. 11Jesus is

"'the stone you builders rejected,
which has become the cornerstone.'[c]

12Salvation is found in no one else, for there is no other name under heaven given to mankind by which we must be saved."

13When they saw the courage of Peter and John and realized that they were unschooled, ordinary men, they were astonished and they took note that these men had been with Jesus. 14But since they could see the man who had been healed standing there with them, there was nothing they could say. 15So they ordered them to withdraw from the Sanhedrin and then conferred together. 16"What are we going to do with these men?" they asked. "Everyone living in Jerusalem knows they have performed a notable sign, and we cannot deny it. 17But to stop this thing from spreading any further among the people, we must warn them to speak no longer to anyone in this name."

18Then they called them in again and commanded them not to speak or teach at all in the name of Jesus. 19But Peter and John replied, "Which is right in God's eyes: to listen to you, or to him? You be the judges! 20As for us, we cannot help speaking about what we have seen and heard."

21After further threats they let them go. They could not decide how to punish them, because all the people were praising God for what had happened. 22For the man who was miraculously healed was over forty years old.

The Believers Pray

23On their release, Peter and John went back to their own people and reported all that the chief priests and the elders had said to them. 24When they heard this, they raised their voices together in prayer to God. "Sovereign Lord," they said, "you made the heavens and the earth and the sea, and everything in

[a] *23* Deut. 18:15,18,19 [b] *25* Gen. 22:18; 26:4 [c] *11* Psalm 118:22

them. 25You spoke by the Holy Spirit through
the mouth of your servant, our father David:

"'Why do the nations rage
and the peoples plot in vain?
26The kings of the earth rise up
and the rulers band together
against the Lord
and against his anointed one.'[a][b]

27Indeed Herod and Pontius Pilate met together with the Gentiles and the people of Israel in
this city to conspire against your holy servant
Jesus, whom you anointed. 28They did what
your power and will had decided beforehand
should happen. 29Now, Lord, consider their
threats and enable your servants to speak
your word with great boldness. 30Stretch out
your hand to heal and perform signs and wonders through the name of your holy servant
Jesus."
31After they prayed, the place where they
were meeting was shaken. And they were all
filled with the Holy Spirit and spoke the word
of God boldly.

The Believers Share Their Possessions

32All the believers were one in heart and
mind. No one claimed that any of their possessions was their own, but they shared everything they had. 33With great power the
apostles continued to testify to the resurrection of the Lord Jesus. And God's grace was
so powerfully at work in them all 34that there
were no needy persons among them. For from
time to time those who owned land or houses
sold them, brought the money from the sales
35and put it at the apostles' feet, and it was
distributed to anyone who had need.
36Joseph, a Levite from Cyprus, whom the
apostles called Barnabas (which means "son
of encouragement"), 37sold a field he owned
and brought the money and put it at the apostles' feet.

Ananias and Sapphira

5 Now a man named Ananias, together
with his wife Sapphira, also sold a piece
of property. 2With his wife's full knowledge he
kept back part of the money for himself, but
brought the rest and put it at the apostles' feet.
3Then Peter said, "Ananias, how is it that
Satan has so filled your heart that you have
lied to the Holy Spirit and have kept for yourself some of the money you received for the
land? 4Didn't it belong to you before it was
sold? And after it was sold, wasn't the money at your disposal? What made you think of
doing such a thing? You have not lied just to
human beings but to God."
5When Ananias heard this, he fell down and
died. And great fear seized all who heard what
had happened. 6Then some young men came
forward, wrapped up his body, and carried
him out and buried him.
7About three hours later his wife came in,
not knowing what had happened. 8Peter asked
her, "Tell me, is this the price you and Ananias
got for the land?"
"Yes," she said, "that is the price."
9Peter said to her, "How could you conspire
to test the Spirit of the Lord? Listen! The feet
of the men who buried your husband are at
the door, and they will carry you out also."
10At that moment she fell down at his feet
and died. Then the young men came in and,
finding her dead, carried her out and buried
her beside her husband. 11Great fear seized
the whole church and all who heard about
these events.

The Apostles Heal Many

12The apostles performed many signs and
wonders among the people. And all the believers used to meet together in Solomon's
Colonnade. 13No one else dared join them,
even though they were highly regarded by
the people. 14Nevertheless, more and more
men and women believed in the Lord and
were added to their number. 15As a result,
people brought the sick into the streets and
laid them on beds and mats so that at least
Peter's shadow might fall on some of them as
he passed by. 16Crowds gathered also from
the towns around Jerusalem, bringing their
sick and those tormented by impure spirits,
and all of them were healed.

The Apostles Persecuted

17Then the high priest and all his associates,
who were members of the party of the Sadducees, were filled with jealousy. 18They arrested the apostles and put them in the public jail.
19But during the night an angel of the Lord
opened the doors of the jail and brought them
out. 20"Go, stand in the temple courts," he said,
"and tell the people all about this new life."
21At daybreak they entered the temple
courts, as they had been told, and began to
teach the people.
When the high priest and his associates arrived, they called together the Sanhedrin—
the full assembly of the elders of Israel—and
sent to the jail for the apostles. 22But on arriving at the jail, the officers did not find them
there. So they went back and reported, 23"We
found the jail securely locked, with the guards
standing at the doors; but when we opened
them, we found no one inside." 24On hearing
this report, the captain of the temple guard
and the chief priests were at a loss, wondering
what this might lead to.
25Then someone came and said, "Look! The
men you put in jail are standing in the temple courts teaching the people." 26At that, the
captain went with his officers and brought
the apostles. They did not use force, because
they feared that the people would stone them.
27The apostles were brought in and made to
appear before the Sanhedrin to be questioned
by the high priest. 28"We gave you strict orders not to teach in this name," he said. "Yet
you have filled Jerusalem with your teaching

[a] *26* That is, Messiah or Christ [b] *26* Psalm 2:1,2

and are determined to make us guilty of this
man's blood."
29 Peter and the other apostles replied: "We
must obey God rather than human beings!
30 The God of our ancestors raised Jesus from
the dead—whom you killed by hanging him
on a cross. 31 God exalted him to his own right
hand as Prince and Savior that he might bring
Israel to repentance and forgive their sins.
32 We are witnesses of these things, and so is
the Holy Spirit, whom God has given to those
who obey him."
33 When they heard this, they were furious
and wanted to put them to death. 34 But a Pharisee named Gamaliel, a teacher of the law, who
was honored by all the people, stood up in the
Sanhedrin and ordered that the men be put
outside for a little while. 35 Then he addressed
the Sanhedrin: "Men of Israel, consider carefully what you intend to do to these men.
36 Some time ago Theudas appeared, claiming
to be somebody, and about four hundred men
rallied to him. He was killed, all his followers
were dispersed, and it all came to nothing.
37 After him, Judas the Galilean appeared in
the days of the census and led a band of people in revolt. He too was killed, and all his
followers were scattered. 38 Therefore, in the
present case I advise you: Leave these men
alone! Let them go! For if their purpose or
activity is of human origin, it will fail. 39 But
if it is from God, you will not be able to stop
these men; you will only find yourselves fighting against God."
40 His speech persuaded them. They called
the apostles in and had them flogged. Then
they ordered them not to speak in the name
of Jesus, and let them go.
41 The apostles left the Sanhedrin, rejoicing
because they had been counted worthy of suffering disgrace for the Name. 42 Day after day,
in the temple courts and from house to house,
they never stopped teaching and proclaiming
the good news that Jesus is the Messiah.

The Choosing of the Seven

6 In those days when the number of disciples was increasing, the Hellenistic Jews[a]
among them complained against the Hebraic
Jews because their widows were being overlooked in the daily distribution of food. 2 So
the Twelve gathered all the disciples together
and said, "It would not be right for us to neglect the ministry of the word of God in order
to wait on tables. 3 Brothers and sisters, choose
seven men from among you who are known
to be full of the Spirit and wisdom. We will
turn this responsibility over to them 4 and will
give our attention to prayer and the ministry
of the word."
5 This proposal pleased the whole group.
They chose Stephen, a man full of faith and of
the Holy Spirit; also Philip, Procorus, Nicanor,
Timon, Parmenas, and Nicolas from Antioch,
a convert to Judaism. 6 They presented these
men to the apostles, who prayed and laid their
hands on them.
7 So the word of God spread. The number
of disciples in Jerusalem increased rapidly,
and a large number of priests became obedient to the faith.

Stephen Seized

8 Now Stephen, a man full of God's grace
and power, performed great wonders and
signs among the people. 9 Opposition arose,
however, from members of the Synagogue of
the Freedmen (as it was called)—Jews of Cyrene and Alexandria as well as the provinces
of Cilicia and Asia—who began to argue with
Stephen. 10 But they could not stand up against
the wisdom the Spirit gave him as he spoke.
11 Then they secretly persuaded some men to
say, "We have heard Stephen speak blasphemous words against Moses and against God."
12 So they stirred up the people and the elders and the teachers of the law. They seized
Stephen and brought him before the Sanhedrin. 13 They produced false witnesses, who
testified, "This fellow never stops speaking
against this holy place and against the law.
14 For we have heard him say that this Jesus of
Nazareth will destroy this place and change
the customs Moses handed down to us."
15 All who were sitting in the Sanhedrin
looked intently at Stephen, and they saw that
his face was like the face of an angel.

Stephen's Speech to the Sanhedrin

7 Then the high priest asked Stephen, "Are
these charges true?"
2 To this he replied: "Brothers and fathers,
listen to me! The God of glory appeared to our
father Abraham while he was still in Mesopotamia, before he lived in Harran. 3 'Leave
your country and your people,' God said, 'and
go to the land I will show you.'[b]
4 "So he left the land of the Chaldeans and
settled in Harran. After the death of his father, God sent him to this land where you
are now living. 5 He gave him no inheritance
here, not even enough ground to set his foot
on. But God promised him that he and his descendants after him would possess the land,
even though at that time Abraham had no
child. 6 God spoke to him in this way: 'For
four hundred years your descendants will be
strangers in a country not their own, and they
will be enslaved and mistreated. 7 But I will
punish the nation they serve as slaves,' God
said, 'and afterward they will come out of
that country and worship me in this place.'[c]
8 Then he gave Abraham the covenant of circumcision. And Abraham became the father
of Isaac and circumcised him eight days after
his birth. Later Isaac became the father of
Jacob, and Jacob became the father of the
twelve patriarchs.
9 "Because the patriarchs were jealous of
Joseph, they sold him as a slave into Egypt.
But God was with him 10 and rescued him from
all his troubles. He gave Joseph wisdom and
enabled him to gain the goodwill of Pharaoh

[a] *1* That is, Jews who had adopted the Greek language and culture [b] *3* Gen. 12:1 [c] *7* Gen. 15:13,14

king of Egypt. So Pharaoh made him ruler
over Egypt and all his palace.

11“Then a famine struck all Egypt and Canaan, bringing great suffering, and our ancestors could not find food. 12When Jacob heard
that there was grain in Egypt, he sent our fore-
fathers on their first visit. 13On their second
visit, Joseph told his brothers who he was, and
Pharaoh learned about Joseph's family. 14Af-
ter this, Joseph sent for his father Jacob and
his whole family, seventy-five in all. 15Then
Jacob went down to Egypt, where he and our
ancestors died. 16Their bodies were brought
back to Shechem and placed in the tomb that
Abraham had bought from the sons of Hamor
at Shechem for a certain sum of money.

17“As the time drew near for God to fulfill
his promise to Abraham, the number of our
people in Egypt had greatly increased. 18Then
‘a new king, to whom Joseph meant nothing,
came to power in Egypt.’[a] 19He dealt treacherously with our people and oppressed our
ancestors by forcing them to throw out their
newborn babies so that they would die.

20“At that time Moses was born, and he
was no ordinary child.[b] For three months he
was cared for by his family. 21When he was
placed outside, Pharaoh's daughter took him
and brought him up as her own son. 22Moses
was educated in all the wisdom of the Egyptians and was powerful in speech and action.

23“When Moses was forty years old, he decided to visit his own people, the Israelites.
24He saw one of them being mistreated by
an Egyptian, so he went to his defense and
avenged him by killing the Egyptian. 25Moses
thought that his own people would realize that
God was using him to rescue them, but they
did not. 26The next day Moses came upon two
Israelites who were fighting. He tried to reconcile them by saying, ‘Men, you are brothers;
why do you want to hurt each other?’

27“But the man who was mistreating the
other pushed Moses aside and said, ‘Who
made you ruler and judge over us? 28Are you
thinking of killing me as you killed the Egyptian yesterday?’[c] 29When Moses heard this, he
fled to Midian, where he settled as a foreigner
and had two sons.

30“After forty years had passed, an angel
appeared to Moses in the flames of a burning
bush in the desert near Mount Sinai. 31When
he saw this, he was amazed at the sight. As
he went over to get a closer look, he heard the
Lord say: 32‘I am the God of your fathers, the
God of Abraham, Isaac and Jacob.’[d] Moses
trembled with fear and did not dare to look.

33“Then the Lord said to him, ‘Take off your
sandals, for the place where you are standing
is holy ground. 34I have indeed seen the oppression of my people in Egypt. I have heard
their groaning and have come down to set
them free. Now come, I will send you back
to Egypt.’[e]

35“This is the same Moses they had rejected with the words, ‘Who made you ruler and
judge?’ He was sent to be their ruler and deliverer by God himself, through the angel who
appeared to him in the bush. 36He led them out
of Egypt and performed wonders and signs
in Egypt, at the Red Sea and for forty years
in the wilderness.

37“This is the Moses who told the Israelites, ‘God will raise up for you a prophet like
me from your own people.’[f] 38He was in the
assembly in the wilderness, with the angel
who spoke to him on Mount Sinai, and with
our ancestors; and he received living words
to pass on to us.

39“But our ancestors refused to obey him.
Instead, they rejected him and in their hearts
turned back to Egypt. 40They told Aaron,
‘Make us gods who will go before us. As for
this fellow Moses who led us out of Egypt—
we don't know what has happened to him!’[g]
41That was the time they made an idol in the
form of a calf. They brought sacrifices to it and
reveled in what their own hands had made.
42But God turned away from them and gave
them over to the worship of the sun, moon and
stars. This agrees with what is written in the
book of the prophets:

“ ‘Did you bring me sacrifices and
offerings
forty years in the wilderness, people of
Israel?
43You have taken up the tabernacle of
Molek
and the star of your god Rephan,
the idols you made to worship.
Therefore I will send you into exile’[h]
beyond Babylon.

44“Our ancestors had the tabernacle of the
covenant law with them in the wilderness. It
had been made as God directed Moses, according to the pattern he had seen. 45After
receiving the tabernacle, our ancestors under
Joshua brought it with them when they took
the land from the nations God drove out before them. It remained in the land until the
time of David, 46who enjoyed God's favor and
asked that he might provide a dwelling place
for the God of Jacob.[i] 47But it was Solomon
who built a house for him.

48“However, the Most High does not live in
houses made by human hands. As the prophet says:

49“ ‘Heaven is my throne,
and the earth is my footstool.
What kind of house will you build for me?
says the Lord.
Or where will my resting place be?
50Has not my hand made all these things?’[j]

51“You stiff-necked people! Your hearts and
ears are still uncircumcised. You are just like
your ancestors: You always resist the Holy
Spirit! 52Was there ever a prophet your ancestors did not persecute? They even killed

[a] *18* Exodus 1:8 [b] *20* Or *was fair in the sight of God* [c] *28* Exodus 2:14 [d] *32* Exodus 3:6
[e] *34* Exodus 3:5,7,8,10 [f] *37* Deut. 18:15 [g] *40* Exodus 32:1 [h] *43* Amos 5:25-27 (see Septuagint)
[i] *46* Some early manuscripts *the house of Jacob* [j] *50* Isaiah 66:1,2

those who predicted the coming of the Righteous One. And now you have betrayed and
murdered him— 53you who have received the
law that was given through angels but have
not obeyed it."

The Stoning of Stephen

54When the members of the Sanhedrin
heard this, they were furious and gnashed
their teeth at him. 55But Stephen, full of the
Holy Spirit, looked up to heaven and saw the
glory of God, and Jesus standing at the right
hand of God. 56"Look," he said, "I see heaven
open and the Son of Man standing at the right
hand of God."

57At this they covered their ears and, yell-
ing at the top of their voices, they all rushed at
him, 58dragged him out of the city and began to
stone him. Meanwhile, the witnesses laid their
coats at the feet of a young man named Saul.

59While they were stoning him, Stephen
prayed, "Lord Jesus, receive my spirit." 60Then
he fell on his knees and cried out, "Lord, do
not hold this sin against them." When he had
said this, he fell asleep.

8 And Saul approved of their killing him.

The Church Persecuted and Scattered

On that day a great persecution broke out
against the church in Jerusalem, and all except the apostles were scattered throughout
Judea and Samaria. 2Godly men buried Stephen and mourned deeply for him. 3But Saul
began to destroy the church. Going from
house to house, he dragged off both men and
women and put them in prison.

Philip in Samaria

4Those who had been scattered preached
the word wherever they went. 5Philip went
down to a city in Samaria and proclaimed
the Messiah there. 6When the crowds heard
Philip and saw the signs he performed, they
all paid close attention to what he said. 7For
with shrieks, impure spirits came out of many,
and many who were paralyzed or lame were
healed. 8So there was great joy in that city.

Simon the Sorcerer

9Now for some time a man named Simon
had practiced sorcery in the city and amazed
all the people of Samaria. He boasted that he
was someone great, 10and all the people, both
high and low, gave him their attention and exclaimed, "This man is rightly called the Great
Power of God." 11They followed him because
he had amazed them for a long time with his
sorcery. 12But when they believed Philip as
he proclaimed the good news of the kingdom
of God and the name of Jesus Christ, they
were baptized, both men and women. 13Simon
himself believed and was baptized. And he
followed Philip everywhere, astonished by
the great signs and miracles he saw.

14When the apostles in Jerusalem heard
that Samaria had accepted the word of God,
they sent Peter and John to Samaria. 15When
they arrived, they prayed for the new believers
there that they might receive the Holy Spirit,
16because the Holy Spirit had not yet come on
any of them; they had simply been baptized in
the name of the Lord Jesus. 17Then Peter and
John placed their hands on them, and they
received the Holy Spirit.

18When Simon saw that the Spirit was giv-
en at the laying on of the apostles' hands, he
offered them money 19and said, "Give me also
this ability so that everyone on whom I lay my
hands may receive the Holy Spirit."

20Peter answered: "May your money perish
with you, because you thought you could buy
the gift of God with money! 21You have no part
or share in this ministry, because your heart
is not right before God. 22Repent of this wickedness and pray to the Lord in the hope that
he may forgive you for having such a thought
in your heart. 23For I see that you are full of
bitterness and captive to sin."

24Then Simon answered, "Pray to the Lord
for me so that nothing you have said may happen to me."

25After they had further proclaimed the
word of the Lord and testified about Jesus,
Peter and John returned to Jerusalem, preaching the gospel in many Samaritan villages.

Philip and the Ethiopian

26Now an angel of the Lord said to Philip,
"Go south to the road—the desert road—that
goes down from Jerusalem to Gaza." 27So he
started out, and on his way he met an Ethiopian[a] eunuch, an important official in charge of
all the treasury of the Kandake (which means
"queen of the Ethiopians"). This man had gone
to Jerusalem to worship, 28and on his way
home was sitting in his chariot reading the
Book of Isaiah the prophet. 29The Spirit told
Philip, "Go to that chariot and stay near it."

30Then Philip ran up to the chariot and
heard the man reading Isaiah the prophet.
"Do you understand what you are reading?"
Philip asked.

31"How can I," he said, "unless someone ex-
plains it to me?" So he invited Philip to come
up and sit with him.

32This is the passage of Scripture the eunuch was reading:

"He was led like a sheep to the slaughter,
and as a lamb before its shearer is
silent,
so he did not open his mouth.
33In his humiliation he was deprived of
justice.
Who can speak of his descendants?
For his life was taken from the earth."[b]

34The eunuch asked Philip, "Tell me, please,
who is the prophet talking about, himself or
someone else?" 35Then Philip began with that
very passage of Scripture and told him the
good news about Jesus.

36As they traveled along the road, they came
to some water and the eunuch said, "Look,

[a] 27 That is, from the southern Nile region [b] 33 Isaiah 53:7,8 (see Septuagint)

here is water. What can stand in the way of my being baptized?" [37][a] 38And he gave orders to stop the chariot. Then both Philip and the eunuch went down into the water and Philip baptized him. 39When they came up out of the water, the Spirit of the Lord suddenly took Philip away, and the eunuch did not see him again, but went on his way rejoicing. 40Philip, however, appeared at Azotus and traveled about, preaching the gospel in all the towns until he reached Caesarea.

Saul's Conversion

9 Meanwhile, Saul was still breathing out murderous threats against the Lord's disciples. He went to the high priest 2and asked him for letters to the synagogues in Damascus, so that if he found any there who belonged to the Way, whether men or women, he might take them as prisoners to Jerusalem. 3As he neared Damascus on his journey, suddenly a light from heaven flashed around him. 4He fell to the ground and heard a voice say to him, "Saul, Saul, why do you persecute me?"

5"Who are you, Lord?" Saul asked.

"I am Jesus, whom you are persecuting," he replied. 6"Now get up and go into the city, and you will be told what you must do."

7The men traveling with Saul stood there speechless; they heard the sound but did not see anyone. 8Saul got up from the ground, but when he opened his eyes he could see nothing. So they led him by the hand into Damascus. 9For three days he was blind, and did not eat or drink anything.

10In Damascus there was a disciple named Ananias. The Lord called to him in a vision, "Ananias!"

"Yes, Lord," he answered.

11The Lord told him, "Go to the house of Judas on Straight Street and ask for a man from Tarsus named Saul, for he is praying. 12In a vision he has seen a man named Ananias come and place his hands on him to restore his sight."

13"Lord," Ananias answered, "I have heard many reports about this man and all the harm he has done to your holy people in Jerusalem. 14And he has come here with authority from the chief priests to arrest all who call on your name."

15But the Lord said to Ananias, "Go! This man is my chosen instrument to proclaim my name to the Gentiles and their kings and to the people of Israel. 16I will show him how much he must suffer for my name."

17Then Ananias went to the house and entered it. Placing his hands on Saul, he said, "Brother Saul, the Lord—Jesus, who appeared to you on the road as you were coming here—has sent me so that you may see again and be filled with the Holy Spirit." 18Immediately, something like scales fell from Saul's eyes, and he could see again. He got up and was baptized, 19and after taking some food, he regained his strength.

Saul in Damascus and Jerusalem

Saul spent several days with the disciples in Damascus. 20At once he began to preach in the synagogues that Jesus is the Son of God. 21All those who heard him were astonished and asked, "Isn't he the man who raised havoc in Jerusalem among those who call on this name? And hasn't he come here to take them as prisoners to the chief priests?" 22Yet Saul grew more and more powerful and baffled the Jews living in Damascus by proving that Jesus is the Messiah.

23After many days had gone by, there was a conspiracy among the Jews to kill him, 24but Saul learned of their plan. Day and night they kept close watch on the city gates in order to kill him. 25But his followers took him by night and lowered him in a basket through an opening in the wall.

26When he came to Jerusalem, he tried to join the disciples, but they were all afraid of him, not believing that he really was a disciple. 27But Barnabas took him and brought him to the apostles. He told them how Saul on his journey had seen the Lord and that the Lord had spoken to him, and how in Damascus he had preached fearlessly in the name of Jesus. 28So Saul stayed with them and moved about freely in Jerusalem, speaking boldly in the name of the Lord. 29He talked and debated with the Hellenistic Jews,[b] but they tried to kill him. 30When the believers learned of this, they took him down to Caesarea and sent him off to Tarsus.

31Then the church throughout Judea, Galilee and Samaria enjoyed a time of peace and was strengthened. Living in the fear of the Lord and encouraged by the Holy Spirit, it increased in numbers.

Aeneas and Dorcas

32As Peter traveled about the country, he went to visit the Lord's people who lived in Lydda. 33There he found a man named Aeneas, who was paralyzed and had been bedridden for eight years. 34"Aeneas," Peter said to him, "Jesus Christ heals you. Get up and roll up your mat." Immediately Aeneas got up. 35All those who lived in Lydda and Sharon saw him and turned to the Lord.

36In Joppa there was a disciple named Tabitha (in Greek her name is Dorcas); she was always doing good and helping the poor. 37About that time she became sick and died, and her body was washed and placed in an upstairs room. 38Lydda was near Joppa; so when the disciples heard that Peter was in Lydda, they sent two men to him and urged him, "Please come at once!"

39Peter went with them, and when he arrived he was taken upstairs to the room. All the widows stood around him, crying and

[a] 37 Some manuscripts include here *Philip said, "If you believe with all your heart, you may." The eunuch answered, "I believe that Jesus Christ is the Son of God."* [b] 29 That is, Jews who had adopted the Greek language and culture

showing him the robes and other clothing
that Dorcas had made while she was still
with them.
40Peter sent them all out of the room; then
he got down on his knees and prayed. Turning
toward the dead woman, he said, "Tabitha, get
up." She opened her eyes, and seeing Peter she
sat up. 41He took her by the hand and helped
her to her feet. Then he called for the believers, especially the widows, and presented her
to them alive. 42This became known all over
Joppa, and many people believed in the Lord.
43Peter stayed in Joppa for some time with a
tanner named Simon.

Cornelius Calls for Peter

10 At Caesarea there was a man named
Cornelius, a centurion in what was
known as the Italian Regiment. 2He and all
his family were devout and God-fearing; he
gave generously to those in need and prayed
to God regularly. 3One day at about three in
the afternoon he had a vision. He distinctly
saw an angel of God, who came to him and
said, "Cornelius!"
4Cornelius stared at him in fear. "What is
it, Lord?" he asked.
The angel answered, "Your prayers and
gifts to the poor have come up as a memorial
offering before God. 5Now send men to Joppa to bring back a man named Simon who is
called Peter. 6He is staying with Simon the
tanner, whose house is by the sea."
7When the angel who spoke to him had
gone, Cornelius called two of his servants
and a devout soldier who was one of his attendants. 8He told them everything that had
happened and sent them to Joppa.

Peter's Vision

9About noon the following day as they were
on their journey and approaching the city, Peter went up on the roof to pray. 10He became
hungry and wanted something to eat, and
while the meal was being prepared, he fell
into a trance. 11He saw heaven opened and
something like a large sheet being let down
to earth by its four corners. 12It contained all
kinds of four-footed animals, as well as reptiles and birds. 13Then a voice told him, "Get
up, Peter. Kill and eat."
14"Surely not, Lord!" Peter replied. "I have
never eaten anything impure or unclean."
15The voice spoke to him a second time,
"Do not call anything impure that God has
made clean."
16This happened three times, and immediately the sheet was taken back to heaven.
17While Peter was wondering about the
meaning of the vision, the men sent by Cornelius found out where Simon's house was
and stopped at the gate. 18They called out,
asking if Simon who was known as Peter was
staying there.
19While Peter was still thinking about the
vision, the Spirit said to him, "Simon, three[a]
men are looking for you. 20So get up and go
downstairs. Do not hesitate to go with them,
for I have sent them."
21Peter went down and said to the men,
"I'm the one you're looking for. Why have
you come?"
22The men replied, "We have come from
Cornelius the centurion. He is a righteous and
God-fearing man, who is respected by all the
Jewish people. A holy angel told him to ask
you to come to his house so that he could hear
what you have to say." 23Then Peter invited the
men into the house to be his guests.

Peter at Cornelius's House

The next day Peter started out with them,
and some of the believers from Joppa went
along. 24The following day he arrived in Caesarea. Cornelius was expecting them and had
called together his relatives and close friends.
25As Peter entered the house, Cornelius met
him and fell at his feet in reverence. 26But Peter made him get up. "Stand up," he said, "I
am only a man myself."
27While talking with him, Peter went inside
and found a large gathering of people. 28He
said to them: "You are well aware that it is
against our law for a Jew to associate with
or visit a Gentile. But God has shown me that
I should not call anyone impure or unclean.
29So when I was sent for, I came without raising any objection. May I ask why you sent
for me?"
30Cornelius answered: "Three days ago I
was in my house praying at this hour, at three
in the afternoon. Suddenly a man in shining
clothes stood before me 31and said, 'Cornelius,
God has heard your prayer and remembered
your gifts to the poor. 32Send to Joppa for Simon who is called Peter. He is a guest in the
home of Simon the tanner, who lives by the
sea.' 33So I sent for you immediately, and it
was good of you to come. Now we are all here
in the presence of God to listen to everything
the Lord has commanded you to tell us."
34Then Peter began to speak: "I now realize
how true it is that God does not show favoritism 35but accepts from every nation the one
who fears him and does what is right. 36You
know the message God sent to the people of
Israel, announcing the good news of peace
through Jesus Christ, who is Lord of all.
37You know what has happened throughout
the province of Judea, beginning in Galilee
after the baptism that John preached— 38how
God anointed Jesus of Nazareth with the Holy
Spirit and power, and how he went around doing good and healing all who were under the
power of the devil, because God was with him.
39"We are witnesses of everything he did
in the country of the Jews and in Jerusalem.
They killed him by hanging him on a cross,
40but God raised him from the dead on the
third day and caused him to be seen. 41He was
not seen by all the people, but by witnesses
whom God had already chosen—by us who
ate and drank with him after he rose from the

[a] *19* One early manuscript *two*; other manuscripts do not have the number.

dead. 42 He commanded us to preach to the people and to testify that he is the one whom God appointed as judge of the living and the dead. 43 All the prophets testify about him that everyone who believes in him receives forgiveness of sins through his name."

44 While Peter was still speaking these words, the Holy Spirit came on all who heard the message. 45 The circumcised believers who had come with Peter were astonished that the gift of the Holy Spirit had been poured out even on Gentiles. 46 For they heard them speaking in tongues[a] and praising God.

Then Peter said, 47 "Surely no one can stand in the way of their being baptized with water. They have received the Holy Spirit just as we have." 48 So he ordered that they be baptized in the name of Jesus Christ. Then they asked Peter to stay with them for a few days.

Peter Explains His Actions

11 The apostles and the believers throughout Judea heard that the Gentiles also had received the word of God. 2 So when Peter went up to Jerusalem, the circumcised believers criticized him 3 and said, "You went into the house of uncircumcised men and ate with them."

4 Starting from the beginning, Peter told them the whole story: 5 "I was in the city of Joppa praying, and in a trance I saw a vision. I saw something like a large sheet being let down from heaven by its four corners, and it came down to where I was. 6 I looked into it and saw four-footed animals of the earth, wild beasts, reptiles and birds. 7 Then I heard a voice telling me, 'Get up, Peter. Kill and eat.'

8 "I replied, 'Surely not, Lord! Nothing impure or unclean has ever entered my mouth.'

9 "The voice spoke from heaven a second time, 'Do not call anything impure that God has made clean.' 10 This happened three times, and then it was all pulled up to heaven again.

11 "Right then three men who had been sent to me from Caesarea stopped at the house where I was staying. 12 The Spirit told me to have no hesitation about going with them. These six brothers also went with me, and we entered the man's house. 13 He told us how he had seen an angel appear in his house and say, 'Send to Joppa for Simon who is called Peter. 14 He will bring you a message through which you and all your household will be saved.'

15 "As I began to speak, the Holy Spirit came on them as he had come on us at the beginning. 16 Then I remembered what the Lord had said: 'John baptized with[b] water, but you will be baptized with[b] the Holy Spirit.' 17 So if God gave them the same gift he gave us who believed in the Lord Jesus Christ, who was I to think that I could stand in God's way?"

18 When they heard this, they had no further objections and praised God, saying, "So then, even to Gentiles God has granted repentance that leads to life."

The Church in Antioch

19 Now those who had been scattered by the persecution that broke out when Stephen was killed traveled as far as Phoenicia, Cyprus and Antioch, spreading the word only among Jews. 20 Some of them, however, men from Cyprus and Cyrene, went to Antioch and began to speak to Greeks also, telling them the good news about the Lord Jesus. 21 The Lord's hand was with them, and a great number of people believed and turned to the Lord.

22 News of this reached the church in Jerusalem, and they sent Barnabas to Antioch. 23 When he arrived and saw what the grace of God had done, he was glad and encouraged them all to remain true to the Lord with all their hearts. 24 He was a good man, full of the Holy Spirit and faith, and a great number of people were brought to the Lord.

25 Then Barnabas went to Tarsus to look for Saul, 26 and when he found him, he brought him to Antioch. So for a whole year Barnabas and Saul met with the church and taught great numbers of people. The disciples were called Christians first at Antioch.

27 During this time some prophets came down from Jerusalem to Antioch. 28 One of them, named Agabus, stood up and through the Spirit predicted that a severe famine would spread over the entire Roman world. (This happened during the reign of Claudius.) 29 The disciples, as each one was able, decided to provide help for the brothers and sisters living in Judea. 30 This they did, sending their gift to the elders by Barnabas and Saul.

Peter's Miraculous Escape From Prison

12 It was about this time that King Herod arrested some who belonged to the church, intending to persecute them. 2 He had James, the brother of John, put to death with the sword. 3 When he saw that this met with approval among the Jews, he proceeded to seize Peter also. This happened during the Festival of Unleavened Bread. 4 After arresting him, he put him in prison, handing him over to be guarded by four squads of four soldiers each. Herod intended to bring him out for public trial after the Passover.

5 So Peter was kept in prison, but the church was earnestly praying to God for him.

6 The night before Herod was to bring him to trial, Peter was sleeping between two soldiers, bound with two chains, and sentries stood guard at the entrance. 7 Suddenly an angel of the Lord appeared and a light shone in the cell. He struck Peter on the side and woke him up. "Quick, get up!" he said, and the chains fell off Peter's wrists.

8 Then the angel said to him, "Put on your clothes and sandals." And Peter did so. "Wrap your cloak around you and follow me," the angel told him. 9 Peter followed him out of the prison, but he had no idea that what the angel was doing was really happening; he thought he was seeing a vision. 10 They passed the first

[a] 46 Or *other languages* [b] 16 Or *in*

and second guards and came to the iron gate
leading to the city. It opened for them by itself, and they went through it. When they had
walked the length of one street, suddenly the
angel left him.
11Then Peter came to himself and said,
"Now I know without a doubt that the Lord
has sent his angel and rescued me from Herod's clutches and from everything the Jewish
people were hoping would happen."
12When this had dawned on him, he went
to the house of Mary the mother of John, also
called Mark, where many people had gathered
and were praying. 13Peter knocked at the outer
entrance, and a servant named Rhoda came
to answer the door. 14When she recognized
Peter's voice, she was so overjoyed she ran
back without opening it and exclaimed, "Peter
is at the door!"
15"You're out of your mind," they told her.
When she kept insisting that it was so, they
said, "It must be his angel."
16But Peter kept on knocking, and when
they opened the door and saw him, they were
astonished. 17Peter motioned with his hand for
them to be quiet and described how the Lord
had brought him out of prison. "Tell James
and the other brothers and sisters about this,"
he said, and then he left for another place.
18In the morning, there was no small commotion among the soldiers as to what had become of Peter. 19After Herod had a thorough
search made for him and did not find him, he
cross-examined the guards and ordered that
they be executed.

Herod's Death

Then Herod went from Judea to Caesarea
and stayed there. 20He had been quarreling
with the people of Tyre and Sidon; they now
joined together and sought an audience with
him. After securing the support of Blastus,
a trusted personal servant of the king, they
asked for peace, because they depended on
the king's country for their food supply.
21On the appointed day Herod, wearing his
royal robes, sat on his throne and delivered a
public address to the people. 22They shouted,
"This is the voice of a god, not of a man." 23Im-
mediately, because Herod did not give praise
to God, an angel of the Lord struck him down,
and he was eaten by worms and died.
24But the word of God continued to spread
and flourish.

Barnabas and Saul Sent Off

25When Barnabas and Saul had finished
their mission, they returned from[a] Jerusalem, taking with them John, also called Mark.
13 1Now in the church at Antioch there
were prophets and teachers: Barnabas,
Simeon called Niger, Lucius of Cyrene, Man-
aen (who had been brought up with Herod the
tetrarch) and Saul. 2While they were worshiping the Lord and fasting, the Holy Spirit said,
"Set apart for me Barnabas and Saul for the
work to which I have called them." 3So after
they had fasted and prayed, they placed their
hands on them and sent them off.

On Cyprus

4The two of them, sent on their way by the
Holy Spirit, went down to Seleucia and sailed
from there to Cyprus. 5When they arrived at
Salamis, they proclaimed the word of God in
the Jewish synagogues. John was with them
as their helper.
6They traveled through the whole island
until they came to Paphos. There they met
a Jewish sorcerer and false prophet named
Bar-Jesus, 7who was an attendant of the proconsul, Sergius Paulus. The proconsul, an
intelligent man, sent for Barnabas and Saul
because he wanted to hear the word of God.
8But Elymas the sorcerer (for that is what
his name means) opposed them and tried to
turn the proconsul from the faith. 9Then Saul,
who was also called Paul, filled with the Holy
Spirit, looked straight at Elymas and said,
10"You are a child of the devil and an enemy
of everything that is right! You are full of all
kinds of deceit and trickery. Will you never
stop perverting the right ways of the Lord?
11Now the hand of the Lord is against you.
You are going to be blind for a time, not even
able to see the light of the sun."
Immediately mist and darkness came over
him, and he groped about, seeking someone to
lead him by the hand. 12When the proconsul
saw what had happened, he believed, for he
was amazed at the teaching about the Lord.

In Pisidian Antioch

13From Paphos, Paul and his companions
sailed to Perga in Pamphylia, where John
left them to return to Jerusalem. 14From Perga they went on to Pisidian Antioch. On the
Sabbath they entered the synagogue and sat
down. 15After the reading from the Law and
the Prophets, the leaders of the synagogue
sent word to them, saying, "Brothers, if you
have a word of exhortation for the people,
please speak."
16Standing up, Paul motioned with his hand
and said: "Fellow Israelites and you Gentiles
who worship God, listen to me! 17The God of
the people of Israel chose our ancestors; he
made the people prosper during their stay in
Egypt; with mighty power he led them out of
that country; 18for about forty years he endured their conduct[b] in the wilderness; 19and
he overthrew seven nations in Canaan, giving
their land to his people as their inheritance.
20All this took about 450 years.
"After this, God gave them judges until the
time of Samuel the prophet. 21Then the people
asked for a king, and he gave them Saul son
of Kish, of the tribe of Benjamin, who ruled
forty years. 22After removing Saul, he made
David their king. God testified concerning
him: 'I have found David son of Jesse, a man
after my own heart; he will do everything I
want him to do.'

[a] *25* Some manuscripts *to* [b] *18* Some manuscripts *he cared for them*

23“From this man’s descendants God has
brought to Israel the Savior Jesus, as he
promised. 24Before the coming of Jesus, John
preached repentance and baptism to all the
people of Israel. 25As John was completing his
work, he said: ‘Who do you suppose I am? I
am not the one you are looking for. But there
is one coming after me whose sandals I am
not worthy to untie.’

26“Fellow children of Abraham and you
God-fearing Gentiles, it is to us that this
message of salvation has been sent. 27The
people of Jerusalem and their rulers did not
recognize Jesus, yet in condemning him they
fulfilled the words of the prophets that are
read every Sabbath. 28Though they found
no proper ground for a death sentence, they
asked Pilate to have him executed. 29When
they had carried out all that was written about
him, they took him down from the cross and
laid him in a tomb. 30But God raised him from
the dead, 31and for many days he was seen by
those who had traveled with him from Galilee
to Jerusalem. They are now his witnesses to
our people.

32“We tell you the good news: What God
promised our ancestors 33he has fulfilled for
us, their children, by raising up Jesus. As it
is written in the second Psalm:

“ ‘You are my son;
today I have become your father.’[a]

34God raised him from the dead so that he will
never be subject to decay. As God has said,

“ ‘I will give you the holy and sure
blessings promised to David.’[b]

35So it is also stated elsewhere:

“ ‘You will not let your holy one see
decay.’[c]

36“Now when David had served God’s purpose in his own generation, he fell asleep; he
was buried with his ancestors and his body
decayed. 37But the one whom God raised from
the dead did not see decay.

38“Therefore, my friends, I want you to
know that through Jesus the forgiveness of
sins is proclaimed to you. 39Through him everyone who believes is set free from every
sin, a justification you were not able to obtain
under the law of Moses. 40Take care that what
the prophets have said does not happen to you:

41“ ‘Look, you scoffers,
wonder and perish,
for I am going to do something in your
days
that you would never believe,
even if someone told you.’[d]”

42As Paul and Barnabas were leaving
the synagogue, the people invited them to
speak further about these things on the next
Sabbath. 43When the congregation was dismissed, many of the Jews and devout converts
to Judaism followed Paul and Barnabas, who
talked with them and urged them to continue
in the grace of God.

44On the next Sabbath almost the whole city
gathered to hear the word of the Lord. 45When
the Jews saw the crowds, they were filled with
jealousy. They began to contradict what Paul
was saying and heaped abuse on him.

46Then Paul and Barnabas answered them
boldly: “We had to speak the word of God to
you first. Since you reject it and do not consider yourselves worthy of eternal life, we now
turn to the Gentiles. 47For this is what the Lord
has commanded us:

“ ‘I have made you[e] a light for the
Gentiles,
that you[e] may bring salvation to the
ends of the earth.’[f]”

48When the Gentiles heard this, they were
glad and honored the word of the Lord; and all
who were appointed for eternal life believed.

49The word of the Lord spread through the
whole region. 50But the Jewish leaders incited the God-fearing women of high standing
and the leading men of the city. They stirred
up persecution against Paul and Barnabas,
and expelled them from their region. 51So they
shook the dust off their feet as a warning to
them and went to Iconium. 52And the disciples
were filled with joy and with the Holy Spirit.

In Iconium

14 At Iconium Paul and Barnabas went as
usual into the Jewish synagogue. There
they spoke so effectively that a great number
of Jews and Greeks believed. 2But the Jews
who refused to believe stirred up the other
Gentiles and poisoned their minds against
the brothers. 3So Paul and Barnabas spent
considerable time there, speaking boldly for
the Lord, who confirmed the message of his
grace by enabling them to perform signs and
wonders. 4The people of the city were divided; some sided with the Jews, others with the
apostles. 5There was a plot afoot among both
Gentiles and Jews, together with their leaders, to mistreat them and stone them. 6But
they found out about it and fled to the Lycaonian cities of Lystra and Derbe and to the
surrounding country, 7where they continued
to preach the gospel.

In Lystra and Derbe

8In Lystra there sat a man who was lame. He
had been that way from birth and had never
walked. 9He listened to Paul as he was speaking. Paul looked directly at him, saw that he
had faith to be healed 10and called out, “Stand
up on your feet!” At that, the man jumped up
and began to walk.

11When the crowd saw what Paul had done,
they shouted in the Lycaonian language,
“The gods have come down to us in human
form!” 12Barnabas they called Zeus, and Paul
they called Hermes because he was the chief
speaker. 13The priest of Zeus, whose temple

[a] *33* Psalm 2:7 [b] *34* Isaiah 55:3 [c] *35* Psalm 16:10 (see Septuagint) [d] *41* Hab. 1:5
[e] *47* The Greek is singular. [f] *47* Isaiah 49:6

was just outside the city, brought bulls and
wreaths to the city gates because he and the
crowd wanted to offer sacrifices to them.
14But when the apostles Barnabas and
Paul heard of this, they tore their clothes
and rushed out into the crowd, shouting:
15"Friends, why are you doing this? We too
are only human, like you. We are bringing
you good news, telling you to turn from these
worthless things to the living God, who made
the heavens and the earth and the sea and
everything in them. 16In the past, he let all
nations go their own way. 17Yet he has not
left himself without testimony: He has shown
kindness by giving you rain from heaven and
crops in their seasons; he provides you with
plenty of food and fills your hearts with joy."
18Even with these words, they had difficulty
keeping the crowd from sacrificing to them.
19Then some Jews came from Antioch and
Iconium and won the crowd over. They stoned
Paul and dragged him outside the city, thinking he was dead. 20But after the disciples had
gathered around him, he got up and went back
into the city. The next day he and Barnabas
left for Derbe.

The Return to Antioch in Syria

21They preached the gospel in that city and
won a large number of disciples. Then they
returned to Lystra, Iconium and Antioch,
22strengthening the disciples and encouraging them to remain true to the faith. "We must
go through many hardships to enter the kingdom of God," they said. 23Paul and Barnabas
appointed elders[a] for them in each church and,
with prayer and fasting, committed them to
the Lord, in whom they had put their trust.
24After going through Pisidia, they came into
Pamphylia, 25and when they had preached the
word in Perga, they went down to Attalia.
26From Attalia they sailed back to Antioch,
where they had been committed to the grace
of God for the work they had now completed.
27On arriving there, they gathered the church
together and reported all that God had done
through them and how he had opened a door
of faith to the Gentiles. 28And they stayed
there a long time with the disciples.

The Council at Jerusalem

15 Certain people came down from Judea to Antioch and were teaching the
believers: "Unless you are circumcised, according to the custom taught by Moses, you
cannot be saved." 2This brought Paul and
Barnabas into sharp dispute and debate with
them. So Paul and Barnabas were appointed,
along with some other believers, to go up
to Jerusalem to see the apostles and elders
about this question. 3The church sent them
on their way, and as they traveled through
Phoenicia and Samaria, they told how the
Gentiles had been converted. This news
made all the believers very glad. 4When they
came to Jerusalem, they were welcomed by
the church and the apostles and elders, to
whom they reported everything God had
done through them.
5Then some of the believers who belonged
to the party of the Pharisees stood up and
said, "The Gentiles must be circumcised and
required to keep the law of Moses."
6The apostles and elders met to consider
this question. 7After much discussion, Peter
got up and addressed them: "Brothers, you
know that some time ago God made a choice
among you that the Gentiles might hear from
my lips the message of the gospel and believe.
8God, who knows the heart, showed that he
accepted them by giving the Holy Spirit to
them, just as he did to us. 9He did not discrim-
inate between us and them, for he purified
their hearts by faith. 10Now then, why do you
try to test God by putting on the necks of Gentiles a yoke that neither we nor our ancestors
have been able to bear? 11No! We believe it is
through the grace of our Lord Jesus that we
are saved, just as they are."
12The whole assembly became silent as they
listened to Barnabas and Paul telling about
the signs and wonders God had done among
the Gentiles through them. 13When they finished, James spoke up. "Brothers," he said,
"listen to me. 14Simon[b] has described to us
how God first intervened to choose a people
for his name from the Gentiles. 15The words
of the prophets are in agreement with this,
as it is written:

16" 'After this I will return
and rebuild David's fallen tent.
Its ruins I will rebuild,
and I will restore it,
17that the rest of mankind may seek the
Lord,
even all the Gentiles who bear my
name,
says the Lord, who does these
things'[c]—
18 things known from long ago.[d]

19"It is my judgment, therefore, that we
should not make it difficult for the Gentiles
who are turning to God. 20Instead we should
write to them, telling them to abstain from
food polluted by idols, from sexual immorality, from the meat of strangled animals and
from blood. 21For the law of Moses has been
preached in every city from the earliest times
and is read in the synagogues on every Sabbath."

The Council's Letter to Gentile Believers

22Then the apostles and elders, with the
whole church, decided to choose some of
their own men and send them to Antioch with
Paul and Barnabas. They chose Judas (called
Barsabbas) and Silas, men who were leaders
among the believers. 23With them they sent
the following letter:

[a] 23 Or *Barnabas ordained elders*; or *Barnabas had elders elected* [b] 14 Greek *Simeon*, a variant of *Simon*; that is, Peter [c] 17 Amos 9:11,12 (see Septuagint) [d] 17,18 Some manuscripts *things'— / 18the Lord's work is known to him from long ago*

The apostles and elders, your brothers,

To the Gentile believers in Antioch, Syria and Cilicia:

Greetings.

24We have heard that some went out from us without our authorization and disturbed you, troubling your minds by what they said. 25So we all agreed to choose some men and send them to you with our dear friends Barnabas and Paul— 26men who have risked their lives for the name of our Lord Jesus Christ. 27Therefore we are sending Judas and Silas to confirm by word of mouth what we are writing. 28It seemed good to the Holy Spirit and to us not to burden you with anything beyond the following requirements: 29You are to abstain from food sacrificed to idols, from blood, from the meat of strangled animals and from sexual immorality. You will do well to avoid these things.

Farewell.

30So the men were sent off and went down to Antioch, where they gathered the church together and delivered the letter. 31The people read it and were glad for its encouraging message. 32Judas and Silas, who themselves were prophets, said much to encourage and strengthen the believers. 33After spending some time there, they were sent off by the believers with the blessing of peace to return to those who had sent them. [34][a] 35But Paul and Barnabas remained in Antioch, where they and many others taught and preached the word of the Lord.

Disagreement Between Paul and Barnabas

36Some time later Paul said to Barnabas, "Let us go back and visit the believers in all the towns where we preached the word of the Lord and see how they are doing." 37Barnabas wanted to take John, also called Mark, with them, 38but Paul did not think it wise to take him, because he had deserted them in Pamphylia and had not continued with them in the work. 39They had such a sharp disagreement that they parted company. Barnabas took Mark and sailed for Cyprus, 40but Paul chose Silas and left, commended by the believers to the grace of the Lord. 41He went through Syria and Cilicia, strengthening the churches.

Timothy Joins Paul and Silas

16 Paul came to Derbe and then to Lystra, where a disciple named Timothy lived, whose mother was Jewish and a believer but whose father was a Greek. 2The believers at Lystra and Iconium spoke well of him. 3Paul wanted to take him along on the journey, so he circumcised him because of the Jews who lived in that area, for they all knew that his father was a Greek. 4As they traveled from town to town, they delivered the decisions reached by the apostles and elders in Jerusalem for the people to obey. 5So the churches were strengthened in the faith and grew daily in numbers.

Paul's Vision of the Man of Macedonia

6Paul and his companions traveled throughout the region of Phrygia and Galatia, having been kept by the Holy Spirit from preaching the word in the province of Asia. 7When they came to the border of Mysia, they tried to enter Bithynia, but the Spirit of Jesus would not allow them to. 8So they passed by Mysia and went down to Troas. 9During the night Paul had a vision of a man of Macedonia standing and begging him, "Come over to Macedonia and help us." 10After Paul had seen the vision, we got ready at once to leave for Macedonia, concluding that God had called us to preach the gospel to them.

Lydia's Conversion in Philippi

11From Troas we put out to sea and sailed straight for Samothrace, and the next day we went on to Neapolis. 12From there we traveled to Philippi, a Roman colony and the leading city of that district[b] of Macedonia. And we stayed there several days.

13On the Sabbath we went outside the city gate to the river, where we expected to find a place of prayer. We sat down and began to speak to the women who had gathered there. 14One of those listening was a woman from the city of Thyatira named Lydia, a dealer in purple cloth. She was a worshiper of God. The Lord opened her heart to respond to Paul's message. 15When she and the members of her household were baptized, she invited us to her home. "If you consider me a believer in the Lord," she said, "come and stay at my house." And she persuaded us.

Paul and Silas in Prison

16Once when we were going to the place of prayer, we were met by a female slave who had a spirit by which she predicted the future. She earned a great deal of money for her owners by fortune-telling. 17She followed Paul and the rest of us, shouting, "These men are servants of the Most High God, who are telling you the way to be saved." 18She kept this up for many days. Finally Paul became so annoyed that he turned around and said to the spirit, "In the name of Jesus Christ I command you to come out of her!" At that moment the spirit left her.

19When her owners realized that their hope of making money was gone, they seized Paul and Silas and dragged them into the marketplace to face the authorities. 20They brought them before the magistrates and said, "These men are Jews, and are throwing our city into an uproar 21by advocating customs unlawful for us Romans to accept or practice."

[a] *34* Some manuscripts include here *But Silas decided to remain there.* [b] *12* The text and meaning of the Greek for *the leading city of that district* are uncertain.

22The crowd joined in the attack against
Paul and Silas, and the magistrates ordered
them to be stripped and beaten with rods.
23After they had been severely flogged, they
were thrown into prison, and the jailer was
commanded to guard them carefully. 24When
he received these orders, he put them in the
inner cell and fastened their feet in the stocks.
25About midnight Paul and Silas were praying and singing hymns to God, and the other
prisoners were listening to them. 26Sudden-
ly there was such a violent earthquake that
the foundations of the prison were shaken.
At once all the prison doors flew open, and
everyone's chains came loose. 27The jailer
woke up, and when he saw the prison doors
open, he drew his sword and was about to
kill himself because he thought the prisoners
had escaped. 28But Paul shouted, "Don't harm
yourself! We are all here!"
29The jailer called for lights, rushed in and
fell trembling before Paul and Silas. 30He then
brought them out and asked, "Sirs, what must
I do to be saved?"
31They replied, "Believe in the Lord Jesus,
and you will be saved—you and your household." 32Then they spoke the word of the Lord
to him and to all the others in his house. 33At
that hour of the night the jailer took them and
washed their wounds; then immediately he
and all his household were baptized. 34The
jailer brought them into his house and set a
meal before them; he was filled with joy because he had come to believe in God—he and
his whole household.
35When it was daylight, the magistrates sent
their officers to the jailer with the order: "Release those men." 36The jailer told Paul, "The
magistrates have ordered that you and Silas
be released. Now you can leave. Go in peace."
37But Paul said to the officers: "They beat us
publicly without a trial, even though we are
Roman citizens, and threw us into prison. And
now do they want to get rid of us quietly? No!
Let them come themselves and escort us out."
38The officers reported this to the magistrates, and when they heard that Paul and Silas were Roman citizens, they were alarmed.
39They came to appease them and escorted
them from the prison, requesting them to
leave the city. 40After Paul and Silas came
out of the prison, they went to Lydia's house,
where they met with the brothers and sisters
and encouraged them. Then they left.

In Thessalonica

17 When Paul and his companions had
passed through Amphipolis and Apol-
lonia, they came to Thessalonica, where there
was a Jewish synagogue. 2As was his custom,
Paul went into the synagogue, and on three
Sabbath days he reasoned with them from
the Scriptures, 3explaining and proving that
the Messiah had to suffer and rise from the
dead. "This Jesus I am proclaiming to you is
the Messiah," he said. 4Some of the Jews were
persuaded and joined Paul and Silas, as did
a large number of God-fearing Greeks and
quite a few prominent women.
5But other Jews were jealous; so they rounded up some bad characters from the marketplace, formed a mob and started a riot in the
city. They rushed to Jason's house in search
of Paul and Silas in order to bring them out
to the crowd.[a] 6But when they did not find
them, they dragged Jason and some other
believers before the city officials, shouting:
"These men who have caused trouble all over
the world have now come here, 7and Jason has
welcomed them into his house. They are all
defying Caesar's decrees, saying that there
is another king, one called Jesus." 8When
they heard this, the crowd and the city officials were thrown into turmoil. 9Then they
made Jason and the others post bond and let
them go.

In Berea

10As soon as it was night, the believers sent
Paul and Silas away to Berea. On arriving
there, they went to the Jewish synagogue.
11Now the Berean Jews were of more noble
character than those in Thessalonica, for they
received the message with great eagerness
and examined the Scriptures every day to
see if what Paul said was true. 12As a result,
many of them believed, as did also a number
of prominent Greek women and many Greek
men.
13But when the Jews in Thessalonica
learned that Paul was preaching the word of
God at Berea, some of them went there too,
agitating the crowds and stirring them up.
14The believers immediately sent Paul to the
coast, but Silas and Timothy stayed at Berea. 15Those who escorted Paul brought him
to Athens and then left with instructions for
Silas and Timothy to join him as soon as possible.

In Athens

16While Paul was waiting for them in Athens, he was greatly distressed to see that the
city was full of idols. 17So he reasoned in the
synagogue with both Jews and God-fearing
Greeks, as well as in the marketplace day by
day with those who happened to be there. 18A
group of Epicurean and Stoic philosophers began to debate with him. Some of them asked,
"What is this babbler trying to say?" Others
remarked, "He seems to be advocating foreign gods." They said this because Paul was
preaching the good news about Jesus and
the resurrection. 19Then they took him and
brought him to a meeting of the Areopagus,
where they said to him, "May we know what
this new teaching is that you are presenting?
20You are bringing some strange ideas to our
ears, and we would like to know what they
mean." 21(All the Athenians and the foreigners
who lived there spent their time doing nothing
but talking about and listening to the latest
ideas.)

[a] 5 Or *the assembly of the people*

22Paul then stood up in the meeting of the Areopagus and said: "People of Athens! I see that in every way you are very religious. 23For as I walked around and looked carefully at your objects of worship, I even found an altar with this inscription: TO AN UNKNOWN GOD. So you are ignorant of the very thing you worship—and this is what I am going to proclaim to you.

24"The God who made the world and everything in it is the Lord of heaven and earth and does not live in temples built by human hands. 25And he is not served by human hands, as if he needed anything. Rather, he himself gives everyone life and breath and everything else. 26From one man he made all the nations, that they should inhabit the whole earth; and he marked out their appointed times in history and the boundaries of their lands. 27God did this so that they would seek him and perhaps reach out for him and find him, though he is not far from any one of us. 28'For in him we live and move and have our being.'[a] As some of your own poets have said, 'We are his offspring.'[b]

29"Therefore since we are God's offspring, we should not think that the divine being is like gold or silver or stone—an image made by human design and skill. 30In the past God overlooked such ignorance, but now he commands all people everywhere to repent. 31For he has set a day when he will judge the world with justice by the man he has appointed. He has given proof of this to everyone by raising him from the dead."

32When they heard about the resurrection of the dead, some of them sneered, but others said, "We want to hear you again on this subject." 33At that, Paul left the Council. 34Some of the people became followers of Paul and believed. Among them was Dionysius, a member of the Areopagus, also a woman named Damaris, and a number of others.

In Corinth

18 After this, Paul left Athens and went to Corinth. 2There he met a Jew named Aquila, a native of Pontus, who had recently come from Italy with his wife Priscilla, because Claudius had ordered all Jews to leave Rome. Paul went to see them, 3and because he was a tentmaker as they were, he stayed and worked with them. 4Every Sabbath he reasoned in the synagogue, trying to persuade Jews and Greeks.

5When Silas and Timothy came from Macedonia, Paul devoted himself exclusively to preaching, testifying to the Jews that Jesus was the Messiah. 6But when they opposed Paul and became abusive, he shook out his clothes in protest and said to them, "Your blood be on your own heads! I am innocent of it. From now on I will go to the Gentiles."

7Then Paul left the synagogue and went next door to the house of Titius Justus, a worshiper of God. 8Crispus, the synagogue leader, and his entire household believed in the Lord; and many of the Corinthians who heard Paul believed and were baptized.

9One night the Lord spoke to Paul in a vision: "Do not be afraid; keep on speaking, do not be silent. 10For I am with you, and no one is going to attack and harm you, because I have many people in this city." 11So Paul stayed in Corinth for a year and a half, teaching them the word of God.

12While Gallio was proconsul of Achaia, the Jews of Corinth made a united attack on Paul and brought him to the place of judgment. 13"This man," they charged, "is persuading the people to worship God in ways contrary to the law."

14Just as Paul was about to speak, Gallio said to them, "If you Jews were making a complaint about some misdemeanor or serious crime, it would be reasonable for me to listen to you. 15But since it involves questions about words and names and your own law—settle the matter yourselves. I will not be a judge of such things." 16So he drove them off. 17Then the crowd there turned on Sosthenes the synagogue leader and beat him in front of the proconsul; and Gallio showed no concern whatever.

Priscilla, Aquila and Apollos

18Paul stayed on in Corinth for some time. Then he left the brothers and sisters and sailed for Syria, accompanied by Priscilla and Aquila. Before he sailed, he had his hair cut off at Cenchreae because of a vow he had taken. 19They arrived at Ephesus, where Paul left Priscilla and Aquila. He himself went into the synagogue and reasoned with the Jews. 20When they asked him to spend more time with them, he declined. 21But as he left, he promised, "I will come back if it is God's will." Then he set sail from Ephesus. 22When he landed at Caesarea, he went up to Jerusalem and greeted the church and then went down to Antioch.

23After spending some time in Antioch, Paul set out from there and traveled from place to place throughout the region of Galatia and Phrygia, strengthening all the disciples.

24Meanwhile a Jew named Apollos, a native of Alexandria, came to Ephesus. He was a learned man, with a thorough knowledge of the Scriptures. 25He had been instructed in the way of the Lord, and he spoke with great fervor[c] and taught about Jesus accurately, though he knew only the baptism of John. 26He began to speak boldly in the synagogue. When Priscilla and Aquila heard him, they invited him to their home and explained to him the way of God more adequately.

27When Apollos wanted to go to Achaia, the brothers and sisters encouraged him and wrote to the disciples there to welcome him. When he arrived, he was a great help to those who by grace had believed. 28For he vigorously refuted his Jewish opponents in public

[a] *28* From the Cretan philosopher Epimenides [b] *28* From the Cilician Stoic philosopher Aratus
[c] *25* Or *with fervor in the Spirit*

debate, proving from the Scriptures that Jesus was the Messiah.

Paul in Ephesus

19 While Apollos was at Corinth, Paul took the road through the interior and arrived at Ephesus. There he found some disciples 2and asked them, "Did you receive the Holy Spirit when[a] you believed?"

They answered, "No, we have not even heard that there is a Holy Spirit."

3So Paul asked, "Then what baptism did you receive?"

"John's baptism," they replied.

4Paul said, "John's baptism was a baptism of repentance. He told the people to believe in the one coming after him, that is, in Jesus." 5On hearing this, they were baptized in the name of the Lord Jesus. 6When Paul placed his hands on them, the Holy Spirit came on them, and they spoke in tongues[b] and prophesied. 7There were about twelve men in all.

8Paul entered the synagogue and spoke boldly there for three months, arguing persuasively about the kingdom of God. 9But some of them became obstinate; they refused to believe and publicly maligned the Way. So Paul left them. He took the disciples with him and had discussions daily in the lecture hall of Tyrannus. 10This went on for two years, so that all the Jews and Greeks who lived in the province of Asia heard the word of the Lord.

11God did extraordinary miracles through Paul, 12so that even handkerchiefs and aprons that had touched him were taken to the sick, and their illnesses were cured and the evil spirits left them.

13Some Jews who went around driving out evil spirits tried to invoke the name of the Lord Jesus over those who were demon-possessed. They would say, "In the name of the Jesus whom Paul preaches, I command you to come out." 14Seven sons of Sceva, a Jewish chief priest, were doing this. 15One day the evil spirit answered them, "Jesus I know, and Paul I know about, but who are you?" 16Then the man who had the evil spirit jumped on them and overpowered them all. He gave them such a beating that they ran out of the house naked and bleeding.

17When this became known to the Jews and Greeks living in Ephesus, they were all seized with fear, and the name of the Lord Jesus was held in high honor. 18Many of those who believed now came and openly confessed what they had done. 19A number who had practiced sorcery brought their scrolls together and burned them publicly. When they calculated the value of the scrolls, the total came to fifty thousand drachmas.[c] 20In this way the word of the Lord spread widely and grew in power.

21After all this had happened, Paul decided[d] to go to Jerusalem, passing through Macedonia and Achaia. "After I have been there," he said, "I must visit Rome also." 22He sent two of his helpers, Timothy and Erastus, to Macedonia, while he stayed in the province of Asia a little longer.

The Riot in Ephesus

23About that time there arose a great disturbance about the Way. 24A silversmith named Demetrius, who made silver shrines of Artemis, brought in a lot of business for the craftsmen there. 25He called them together, along with the workers in related trades, and said: "You know, my friends, that we receive a good income from this business. 26And you see and hear how this fellow Paul has convinced and led astray large numbers of people here in Ephesus and in practically the whole province of Asia. He says that gods made by human hands are no gods at all. 27There is danger not only that our trade will lose its good name, but also that the temple of the great goddess Artemis will be discredited; and the goddess herself, who is worshiped throughout the province of Asia and the world, will be robbed of her divine majesty."

28When they heard this, they were furious and began shouting: "Great is Artemis of the Ephesians!" 29Soon the whole city was in an uproar. The people seized Gaius and Aristarchus, Paul's traveling companions from Macedonia, and all of them rushed into the theater together. 30Paul wanted to appear before the crowd, but the disciples would not let him. 31Even some of the officials of the province, friends of Paul, sent him a message begging him not to venture into the theater.

32The assembly was in confusion: Some were shouting one thing, some another. Most of the people did not even know why they were there. 33The Jews in the crowd pushed Alexander to the front, and they shouted instructions to him. He motioned for silence in order to make a defense before the people. 34But when they realized he was a Jew, they all shouted in unison for about two hours: "Great is Artemis of the Ephesians!"

35The city clerk quieted the crowd and said: "Fellow Ephesians, doesn't all the world know that the city of Ephesus is the guardian of the temple of the great Artemis and of her image, which fell from heaven? 36Therefore, since these facts are undeniable, you ought to calm down and not do anything rash. 37You have brought these men here, though they have neither robbed temples nor blasphemed our goddess. 38If, then, Demetrius and his fellow craftsmen have a grievance against anybody, the courts are open and there are proconsuls. They can press charges. 39If there is anything further you want to bring up, it must be settled in a legal assembly. 40As it is, we are in danger of being charged with rioting because of what happened today. In that case we would not be able to account for this commotion, since there is no reason for it." 41After he had said this, he dismissed the assembly.

[a] 2 Or *after* [b] 6 Or *other languages* [c] 19 A drachma was a silver coin worth about a day's wages.
[d] 21 Or *decided in the Spirit*

Through Macedonia and Greece

20 When the uproar had ended, Paul sent for the disciples and, after encouraging them, said goodbye and set out for Macedonia. 2He traveled through that area, speaking many words of encouragement to the people, and finally arrived in Greece, 3where he stayed three months. Because some Jews had plotted against him just as he was about to sail for Syria, he decided to go back through Macedonia. 4He was accompanied by Sopater son of Pyrrhus from Berea, Aristarchus and Secundus from Thessalonica, Gaius from Derbe, Timothy also, and Tychicus and Trophimus from the province of Asia. 5These men went on ahead and waited for us at Troas. 6But we sailed from Philippi after the Festival of Unleavened Bread, and five days later joined the others at Troas, where we stayed seven days.

Eutychus Raised From the Dead at Troas

7On the first day of the week we came together to break bread. Paul spoke to the people and, because he intended to leave the next day, kept on talking until midnight. 8There were many lamps in the upstairs room where we were meeting. 9Seated in a window was a young man named Eutychus, who was sinking into a deep sleep as Paul talked on and on. When he was sound asleep, he fell to the ground from the third story and was picked up dead. 10Paul went down, threw himself on the young man and put his arms around him. "Don't be alarmed," he said. "He's alive!" 11Then he went upstairs again and broke bread and ate. After talking until daylight, he left. 12The people took the young man home alive and were greatly comforted.

Paul's Farewell to the Ephesian Elders

13We went on ahead to the ship and sailed for Assos, where we were going to take Paul aboard. He had made this arrangement because he was going there on foot. 14When he met us at Assos, we took him aboard and went on to Mitylene. 15The next day we set sail from there and arrived off Chios. The day after that we crossed over to Samos, and on the following day arrived at Miletus. 16Paul had decided to sail past Ephesus to avoid spending time in the province of Asia, for he was in a hurry to reach Jerusalem, if possible, by the day of Pentecost.

17From Miletus, Paul sent to Ephesus for the elders of the church. 18When they arrived, he said to them: "You know how I lived the whole time I was with you, from the first day I came into the province of Asia. 19I served the Lord with great humility and with tears and in the midst of severe testing by the plots of my Jewish opponents. 20You know that I have not hesitated to preach anything that would be helpful to you but have taught you publicly and from house to house. 21I have declared to both Jews and Greeks that they must turn to God in repentance and have faith in our Lord Jesus.

22"And now, compelled by the Spirit, I am going to Jerusalem, not knowing what will happen to me there. 23I only know that in every city the Holy Spirit warns me that prison and hardships are facing me. 24However, I consider my life worth nothing to me; my only aim is to finish the race and complete the task the Lord Jesus has given me—the task of testifying to the good news of God's grace.

25"Now I know that none of you among whom I have gone about preaching the kingdom will ever see me again. 26Therefore, I declare to you today that I am innocent of the blood of any of you. 27For I have not hesitated to proclaim to you the whole will of God. 28Keep watch over yourselves and all the flock of which the Holy Spirit has made you overseers. Be shepherds of the church of God,[a] which he bought with his own blood.[b] 29I know that after I leave, savage wolves will come in among you and will not spare the flock. 30Even from your own number men will arise and distort the truth in order to draw away disciples after them. 31So be on your guard! Remember that for three years I never stopped warning each of you night and day with tears.

32"Now I commit you to God and to the word of his grace, which can build you up and give you an inheritance among all those who are sanctified. 33I have not coveted anyone's silver or gold or clothing. 34You yourselves know that these hands of mine have supplied my own needs and the needs of my companions. 35In everything I did, I showed you that by this kind of hard work we must help the weak, remembering the words the Lord Jesus himself said: 'It is more blessed to give than to receive.' "

36When Paul had finished speaking, he knelt down with all of them and prayed. 37They all wept as they embraced him and kissed him. 38What grieved them most was his statement that they would never see his face again. Then they accompanied him to the ship.

On to Jerusalem

21 After we had torn ourselves away from them, we put out to sea and sailed straight to Kos. The next day we went to Rhodes and from there to Patara. 2We found a ship crossing over to Phoenicia, went on board and set sail. 3After sighting Cyprus and passing to the south of it, we sailed on to Syria. We landed at Tyre, where our ship was to unload its cargo. 4We sought out the disciples there and stayed with them seven days. Through the Spirit they urged Paul not to go on to Jerusalem. 5When it was time to leave, we left and continued on our way. All of them, including wives and children, accompanied us out of the city, and there on the beach we knelt to pray. 6After saying goodbye to each other, we went aboard the ship, and they returned home.

7We continued our voyage from Tyre and landed at Ptolemais, where we greeted the

[a] 28 Many manuscripts *of the Lord* [b] 28 Or *with the blood of his own Son*

brothers and sisters and stayed with them
for a day. 8Leaving the next day, we reached
Caesarea and stayed at the house of Philip
the evangelist, one of the Seven. 9He had four
unmarried daughters who prophesied.
10After we had been there a number of days,
a prophet named Agabus came down from Judea. 11Coming over to us, he took Paul's belt,
tied his own hands and feet with it and said,
"The Holy Spirit says, 'In this way the Jewish
leaders in Jerusalem will bind the owner of this
belt and will hand him over to the Gentiles.'"
12When we heard this, we and the people
there pleaded with Paul not to go up to Jerusalem. 13Then Paul answered, "Why are you
weeping and breaking my heart? I am ready
not only to be bound, but also to die in Jerusalem for the name of the Lord Jesus." 14When
he would not be dissuaded, we gave up and
said, "The Lord's will be done."
15After this, we started on our way up to
Jerusalem. 16Some of the disciples from Caesarea accompanied us and brought us to the
home of Mnason, where we were to stay. He
was a man from Cyprus and one of the early
disciples.

Paul's Arrival at Jerusalem

17When we arrived at Jerusalem, the brothers and sisters received us warmly. 18The next
day Paul and the rest of us went to see James,
and all the elders were present. 19Paul greeted them and reported in detail what God had
done among the Gentiles through his ministry.
20When they heard this, they praised God.
Then they said to Paul: "You see, brother, how
many thousands of Jews have believed, and
all of them are zealous for the law. 21They have
been informed that you teach all the Jews who
live among the Gentiles to turn away from
Moses, telling them not to circumcise their
children or live according to our customs.
22What shall we do? They will certainly hear
that you have come, 23so do what we tell you.
There are four men with us who have made a
vow. 24Take these men, join in their purification rites and pay their expenses, so that they
can have their heads shaved. Then everyone
will know there is no truth in these reports
about you, but that you yourself are living in
obedience to the law. 25As for the Gentile believers, we have written to them our decision
that they should abstain from food sacrificed
to idols, from blood, from the meat of strangled animals and from sexual immorality."
26The next day Paul took the men and purified himself along with them. Then he went to
the temple to give notice of the date when the
days of purification would end and the offering would be made for each of them.

Paul Arrested

27When the seven days were nearly over,
some Jews from the province of Asia saw
Paul at the temple. They stirred up the whole
crowd and seized him, 28shouting, "Fellow Israelites, help us! This is the man who teaches
everyone everywhere against our people and
our law and this place. And besides, he has
brought Greeks into the temple and defiled
this holy place." 29(They had previously seen
Trophimus the Ephesian in the city with Paul
and assumed that Paul had brought him into
the temple.)
30The whole city was aroused, and the people came running from all directions. Seizing
Paul, they dragged him from the temple, and
immediately the gates were shut. 31While they
were trying to kill him, news reached the commander of the Roman troops that the whole
city of Jerusalem was in an uproar. 32He at
once took some officers and soldiers and ran
down to the crowd. When the rioters saw the
commander and his soldiers, they stopped
beating Paul.
33The commander came up and arrested
him and ordered him to be bound with two
chains. Then he asked who he was and what
he had done. 34Some in the crowd shouted
one thing and some another, and since the
commander could not get at the truth because
of the uproar, he ordered that Paul be taken
into the barracks. 35When Paul reached the
steps, the violence of the mob was so great he
had to be carried by the soldiers. 36The crowd
that followed kept shouting, "Get rid of him!"

Paul Speaks to the Crowd

37As the soldiers were about to take Paul
into the barracks, he asked the commander,
"May I say something to you?"
"Do you speak Greek?" he replied. 38"Aren't
you the Egyptian who started a revolt and led
four thousand terrorists out into the wilderness some time ago?"
39Paul answered, "I am a Jew, from Tarsus
in Cilicia, a citizen of no ordinary city. Please
let me speak to the people."
40After receiving the commander's permission, Paul stood on the steps and motioned to
the crowd. When they were all silent, he said
22 to them in Aramaic[a]: 1"Brothers and fathers, listen now to my defense."
2When they heard him speak to them in
Aramaic, they became very quiet.
Then Paul said: 3"I am a Jew, born in Tarsus of Cilicia, but brought up in this city. I
studied under Gamaliel and was thoroughly
trained in the law of our ancestors. I was just
as zealous for God as any of you are today. 4I
persecuted the followers of this Way to their
death, arresting both men and women and
throwing them into prison, 5as the high priest
and all the Council can themselves testify. I
even obtained letters from them to their associates in Damascus, and went there to bring
these people as prisoners to Jerusalem to be
punished.
6"About noon as I came near Damascus,
suddenly a bright light from heaven flashed
around me. 7I fell to the ground and heard

[a] *40* Or possibly *Hebrew*; also in 22:2

a voice say to me, ‘Saul! Saul! Why do you
persecute me?’
8“ ‘Who are you, Lord?’ I asked.
“ ‘I am Jesus of Nazareth, whom you are
persecuting,’ he replied. 9My companions saw
the light, but they did not understand the voice
of him who was speaking to me.
10“ ‘What shall I do, Lord?’ I asked.
“ ‘Get up,’ the Lord said, ‘and go into Damascus. There you will be told all that you have
been assigned to do.’ 11My companions led
me by the hand into Damascus, because the
brilliance of the light had blinded me.
12“A man named Ananias came to see me.
He was a devout observer of the law and highly respected by all the Jews living there. 13He
stood beside me and said, ‘Brother Saul, receive your sight!’ And at that very moment I
was able to see him.
14“Then he said: ‘The God of our ancestors
has chosen you to know his will and to see the
Righteous One and to hear words from his
mouth. 15You will be his witness to all people of what you have seen and heard. 16And
now what are you waiting for? Get up, be
baptized and wash your sins away, calling
on his name.’
17“When I returned to Jerusalem and was
praying at the temple, I fell into a trance 18and
saw the Lord speaking to me. ‘Quick!’ he said.
‘Leave Jerusalem immediately, because the
people here will not accept your testimony
about me.’
19“ ‘Lord,’ I replied, ‘these people know
that I went from one synagogue to another
to imprison and beat those who believe in
you. 20And when the blood of your martyr[a]
Stephen was shed, I stood there giving my
approval and guarding the clothes of those
who were killing him.’
21“Then the Lord said to me, ‘Go; I will send
you far away to the Gentiles.’ ”

Paul the Roman Citizen

22The crowd listened to Paul until he said
this. Then they raised their voices and shouted, “Rid the earth of him! He’s not fit to live!”
23As they were shouting and throwing off
their cloaks and flinging dust into the air,
24the commander ordered that Paul be tak-
en into the barracks. He directed that he be
flogged and interrogated in order to find out
why the people were shouting at him like this.
25As they stretched him out to flog him, Paul
said to the centurion standing there, “Is it legal for you to flog a Roman citizen who hasn’t
even been found guilty?”
26When the centurion heard this, he went
to the commander and reported it. “What are
you going to do?” he asked. “This man is a
Roman citizen.”
27The commander went to Paul and asked,
“Tell me, are you a Roman citizen?”
“Yes, I am,” he answered.
28Then the commander said, “I had to pay
a lot of money for my citizenship.”
“But I was born a citizen,” Paul replied.
29Those who were about to interrogate him
withdrew immediately. The commander himself was alarmed when he realized that he had
put Paul, a Roman citizen, in chains.

Paul Before the Sanhedrin

30The commander wanted to find out exactly why Paul was being accused by the Jews.
So the next day he released him and ordered
the chief priests and all the members of the
Sanhedrin to assemble. Then he brought Paul
and had him stand before them.

23 Paul looked straight at the Sanhedrin
and said, “My brothers, I have fulfilled
my duty to God in all good conscience to this
day.” 2At this the high priest Ananias ordered those standing near Paul to strike him
on the mouth. 3Then Paul said to him, “God
will strike you, you whitewashed wall! You
sit there to judge me according to the law, yet
you yourself violate the law by commanding
that I be struck!”
4Those who were standing near Paul said,
“How dare you insult God’s high priest!”
5Paul replied, “Brothers, I did not realize
that he was the high priest; for it is written:
‘Do not speak evil about the ruler of your
people.’[b]”
6Then Paul, knowing that some of them
were Sadducees and the others Pharisees,
called out in the Sanhedrin, “My brothers, I
am a Pharisee, descended from Pharisees. I
stand on trial because of the hope of the resurrection of the dead.” 7When he said this,
a dispute broke out between the Pharisees
and the Sadducees, and the assembly was
divided. 8(The Sadducees say that there is
no resurrection, and that there are neither
angels nor spirits, but the Pharisees believe
all these things.)
9There was a great uproar, and some of the
teachers of the law who were Pharisees stood
up and argued vigorously. “We find nothing
wrong with this man,” they said. “What if a
spirit or an angel has spoken to him?” 10The
dispute became so violent that the commander was afraid Paul would be torn to pieces by
them. He ordered the troops to go down and
take him away from them by force and bring
him into the barracks.
11The following night the Lord stood near
Paul and said, “Take courage! As you have
testified about me in Jerusalem, so you must
also testify in Rome.”

The Plot to Kill Paul

12The next morning some Jews formed a
conspiracy and bound themselves with an
oath not to eat or drink until they had killed
Paul. 13More than forty men were involved in
this plot. 14They went to the chief priests and
the elders and said, “We have taken a solemn
oath not to eat anything until we have killed
Paul. 15Now then, you and the Sanhedrin petition the commander to bring him before you
on the pretext of wanting more accurate in-

[a] 20 Or *witness* [b] 5 Exodus 22:28

formation about his case. We are ready to kill
him before he gets here."
16But when the son of Paul's sister heard
of this plot, he went into the barracks and
told Paul.
17Then Paul called one of the centurions
and said, "Take this young man to the commander; he has something to tell him." 18So
he took him to the commander.
The centurion said, "Paul, the prisoner, sent
for me and asked me to bring this young man
to you because he has something to tell you."
19The commander took the young man by
the hand, drew him aside and asked, "What
is it you want to tell me?"
20He said: "Some Jews have agreed to ask
you to bring Paul before the Sanhedrin tomorrow on the pretext of wanting more accurate information about him. 21Don't give in
to them, because more than forty of them are
waiting in ambush for him. They have taken
an oath not to eat or drink until they have
killed him. They are ready now, waiting for
your consent to their request."
22The commander dismissed the young man
with this warning: "Don't tell anyone that you
have reported this to me."

Paul Transferred to Caesarea

23Then he called two of his centurions and
ordered them, "Get ready a detachment of two
hundred soldiers, seventy horsemen and two
hundred spearmen[a] to go to Caesarea at nine
tonight. 24Provide horses for Paul so that he
may be taken safely to Governor Felix."
25He wrote a letter as follows:

26Claudius Lysias,

To His Excellency, Governor Felix:

Greetings.

27This man was seized by the Jews and
they were about to kill him, but I came
with my troops and rescued him, for I
had learned that he is a Roman citizen. 28I
wanted to know why they were accusing
him, so I brought him to their Sanhedrin.
29I found that the accusation had to do
with questions about their law, but there
was no charge against him that deserved
death or imprisonment. 30When I was informed of a plot to be carried out against
the man, I sent him to you at once. I also
ordered his accusers to present to you
their case against him.

31So the soldiers, carrying out their orders,
took Paul with them during the night and
brought him as far as Antipatris. 32The next
day they let the cavalry go on with him, while
they returned to the barracks. 33When the cavalry arrived in Caesarea, they delivered the
letter to the governor and handed Paul over to
him. 34The governor read the letter and asked
what province he was from. Learning that
he was from Cilicia, 35he said, "I will hear
your case when your accusers get here." Then
he ordered that Paul be kept under guard in
Herod's palace.

Paul's Trial Before Felix

24 Five days later the high priest Ananias
went down to Caesarea with some of the
elders and a lawyer named Tertullus, and they
brought their charges against Paul before the
governor. 2When Paul was called in, Tertullus
presented his case before Felix: "We have enjoyed a long period of peace under you, and
your foresight has brought about reforms in
this nation. 3Everywhere and in every way,
most excellent Felix, we acknowledge this
with profound gratitude. 4But in order not to
weary you further, I would request that you
be kind enough to hear us briefly.
5"We have found this man to be a troublemaker, stirring up riots among the Jews all
over the world. He is a ringleader of the Nazarene sect 6and even tried to desecrate the
temple; so we seized him. [7][b] 8By examining
him yourself you will be able to learn the
truth about all these charges we are bringing against him."
9The other Jews joined in the accusation,
asserting that these things were true.
10When the governor motioned for him to
speak, Paul replied: "I know that for a number of years you have been a judge over this
nation; so I gladly make my defense. 11You
can easily verify that no more than twelve
days ago I went up to Jerusalem to worship.
12My accusers did not find me arguing with
anyone at the temple, or stirring up a crowd in
the synagogues or anywhere else in the city.
13And they cannot prove to you the charges
they are now making against me. 14However,
I admit that I worship the God of our ancestors as a follower of the Way, which they call
a sect. I believe everything that is in accordance with the Law and that is written in the
Prophets, 15and I have the same hope in God
as these men themselves have, that there will
be a resurrection of both the righteous and
the wicked. 16So I strive always to keep my
conscience clear before God and man.
17"After an absence of several years, I came
to Jerusalem to bring my people gifts for the
poor and to present offerings. 18I was ceremonially clean when they found me in the temple
courts doing this. There was no crowd with
me, nor was I involved in any disturbance.
19But there are some Jews from the province
of Asia, who ought to be here before you and
bring charges if they have anything against
me. 20Or these who are here should state what
crime they found in me when I stood before
the Sanhedrin— 21unless it was this one thing
I shouted as I stood in their presence: 'It is
concerning the resurrection of the dead that
I am on trial before you today.'"

[a] 23 The meaning of the Greek for this word is uncertain. [b] 6-8 Some manuscripts include here *him, and we would have judged him in accordance with our law. 7But the commander Lysias came and took him from us with much violence, 8ordering his accusers to come before you.*

22Then Felix, who was well acquainted with
the Way, adjourned the proceedings. "When
Lysias the commander comes," he said, "I will
decide your case." 23He ordered the centurion to keep Paul under guard but to give him
some freedom and permit his friends to take
care of his needs.

24Several days later Felix came with his
wife Drusilla, who was Jewish. He sent for
Paul and listened to him as he spoke about
faith in Christ Jesus. 25As Paul talked about
righteousness, self-control and the judgment
to come, Felix was afraid and said, "That's
enough for now! You may leave. When I find
it convenient, I will send for you." 26At the
same time he was hoping that Paul would offer him a bribe, so he sent for him frequently
and talked with him.

27When two years had passed, Felix was
succeeded by Porcius Festus, but because Felix wanted to grant a favor to the Jews, he left
Paul in prison.

Paul's Trial Before Festus

25 Three days after arriving in the province, Festus went up from Caesarea to
Jerusalem, 2where the chief priests and the
Jewish leaders appeared before him and
presented the charges against Paul. 3They
requested Festus, as a favor to them, to have
Paul transferred to Jerusalem, for they were
preparing an ambush to kill him along the
way. 4Festus answered, "Paul is being held at
Caesarea, and I myself am going there soon.
5Let some of your leaders come with me, and
if the man has done anything wrong, they can
press charges against him there."

6After spending eight or ten days with them,
Festus went down to Caesarea. The next day
he convened the court and ordered that Paul
be brought before him. 7When Paul came in,
the Jews who had come down from Jerusalem stood around him. They brought many
serious charges against him, but they could
not prove them.

8Then Paul made his defense: "I have done
nothing wrong against the Jewish law or
against the temple or against Caesar."

9Festus, wishing to do the Jews a favor, said
to Paul, "Are you willing to go up to Jerusalem and stand trial before me there on these
charges?"

10Paul answered: "I am now standing before
Caesar's court, where I ought to be tried. I
have not done any wrong to the Jews, as you
yourself know very well. 11If, however, I am
guilty of doing anything deserving death, I do
not refuse to die. But if the charges brought
against me by these Jews are not true, no one
has the right to hand me over to them. I appeal to Caesar!"

12After Festus had conferred with his council, he declared: "You have appealed to Caesar.
To Caesar you will go!"

Festus Consults King Agrippa

13A few days later King Agrippa and Bernice arrived at Caesarea to pay their respects
to Festus. 14Since they were spending many
days there, Festus discussed Paul's case with
the king. He said: "There is a man here whom
Felix left as a prisoner. 15When I went to Jerusalem, the chief priests and the elders of the
Jews brought charges against him and asked
that he be condemned.

16"I told them that it is not the Roman custom to hand over anyone before they have
faced their accusers and have had an opportunity to defend themselves against the charges. 17When they came here with me, I did not
delay the case, but convened the court the
next day and ordered the man to be brought
in. 18When his accusers got up to speak, they
did not charge him with any of the crimes I
had expected. 19Instead, they had some points
of dispute with him about their own religion
and about a dead man named Jesus who Paul
claimed was alive. 20I was at a loss how to investigate such matters; so I asked if he would
be willing to go to Jerusalem and stand trial
there on these charges. 21But when Paul made
his appeal to be held over for the Emperor's
decision, I ordered him held until I could send
him to Caesar."

22Then Agrippa said to Festus, "I would like
to hear this man myself."

He replied, "Tomorrow you will hear him."

Paul Before Agrippa

23The next day Agrippa and Bernice came
with great pomp and entered the audience
room with the high-ranking military officers and the prominent men of the city. At
the command of Festus, Paul was brought
in. 24Festus said: "King Agrippa, and all who
are present with us, you see this man! The
whole Jewish community has petitioned me
about him in Jerusalem and here in Caesarea,
shouting that he ought not to live any longer.
25I found he had done nothing deserving of
death, but because he made his appeal to the
Emperor I decided to send him to Rome. 26But
I have nothing definite to write to His Majesty about him. Therefore I have brought him
before all of you, and especially before you,
King Agrippa, so that as a result of this investigation I may have something to write. 27For
I think it is unreasonable to send a prisoner
on to Rome without specifying the charges
against him."

26 Then Agrippa said to Paul, "You have
permission to speak for yourself."

So Paul motioned with his hand and began
his defense: 2"King Agrippa, I consider myself
fortunate to stand before you today as I make
my defense against all the accusations of the
Jews, 3and especially so because you are well
acquainted with all the Jewish customs and
controversies. Therefore, I beg you to listen
to me patiently.

4"The Jewish people all know the way I have
lived ever since I was a child, from the beginning of my life in my own country, and also in
Jerusalem. 5They have known me for a long
time and can testify, if they are willing, that I
conformed to the strictest sect of our religion,
living as a Pharisee. 6And now it is because

of my hope in what God has promised our
ancestors that I am on trial today. 7This is
the promise our twelve tribes are hoping to
see fulfilled as they earnestly serve God day
and night. King Agrippa, it is because of this
hope that these Jews are accusing me. 8Why
should any of you consider it incredible that
God raises the dead?
9"I too was convinced that I ought to do all
that was possible to oppose the name of Jesus
of Nazareth. 10And that is just what I did in Jerusalem. On the authority of the chief priests
I put many of the Lord's people in prison, and
when they were put to death, I cast my vote
against them. 11Many a time I went from one
synagogue to another to have them punished,
and I tried to force them to blaspheme. I was
so obsessed with persecuting them that I even
hunted them down in foreign cities.
12"On one of these journeys I was going to
Damascus with the authority and commission of the chief priests. 13About noon, King
Agrippa, as I was on the road, I saw a light
from heaven, brighter than the sun, blazing
around me and my companions. 14We all fell
to the ground, and I heard a voice saying to
me in Aramaic,[a] 'Saul, Saul, why do you persecute me? It is hard for you to kick against
the goads.'
15"Then I asked, 'Who are you, Lord?'
"'I am Jesus, whom you are persecuting,'
the Lord replied. 16'Now get up and stand on
your feet. I have appeared to you to appoint
you as a servant and as a witness of what
you have seen and will see of me. 17I will rescue you from your own people and from the
Gentiles. I am sending you to them 18to open
their eyes and turn them from darkness to
light, and from the power of Satan to God,
so that they may receive forgiveness of sins
and a place among those who are sanctified
by faith in me.'
19"So then, King Agrippa, I was not disobedient to the vision from heaven. 20First to
those in Damascus, then to those in Jerusalem and in all Judea, and then to the Gentiles,
I preached that they should repent and turn
to God and demonstrate their repentance by
their deeds. 21That is why some Jews seized
me in the temple courts and tried to kill me.
22But God has helped me to this very day; so I
stand here and testify to small and great alike.
I am saying nothing beyond what the prophets
and Moses said would happen— 23that the
Messiah would suffer and, as the first to rise
from the dead, would bring the message of
light to his own people and to the Gentiles."
24At this point Festus interrupted Paul's
defense. "You are out of your mind, Paul!"
he shouted. "Your great learning is driving
you insane."
25"I am not insane, most excellent Festus,"
Paul replied. "What I am saying is true and
reasonable. 26The king is familiar with these
things, and I can speak freely to him. I am
convinced that none of this has escaped his
notice, because it was not done in a corner.
27King Agrippa, do you believe the prophets?
I know you do."
28Then Agrippa said to Paul, "Do you think
that in such a short time you can persuade me
to be a Christian?"
29Paul replied, "Short time or long—I pray
to God that not only you but all who are listening to me today may become what I am,
except for these chains."
30The king rose, and with him the governor and Bernice and those sitting with them.
31After they left the room, they began saying
to one another, "This man is not doing anything that deserves death or imprisonment."
32Agrippa said to Festus, "This man could
have been set free if he had not appealed to
Caesar."

Paul Sails for Rome

27 When it was decided that we would sail
for Italy, Paul and some other prisoners were handed over to a centurion named
Julius, who belonged to the Imperial Regiment. 2We boarded a ship from Adramyttium
about to sail for ports along the coast of the
province of Asia, and we put out to sea. Aristarchus, a Macedonian from Thessalonica,
was with us.
3The next day we landed at Sidon; and Julius, in kindness to Paul, allowed him to go
to his friends so they might provide for his
needs. 4From there we put out to sea again
and passed to the lee of Cyprus because the
winds were against us. 5When we had sailed
across the open sea off the coast of Cilicia
and Pamphylia, we landed at Myra in Lycia.
6There the centurion found an Alexandrian
ship sailing for Italy and put us on board.
7We made slow headway for many days and
had difficulty arriving off Cnidus. When the
wind did not allow us to hold our course, we
sailed to the lee of Crete, opposite Salmone.
8We moved along the coast with difficulty
and came to a place called Fair Havens, near
the town of Lasea.
9Much time had been lost, and sailing had
already become dangerous because by now
it was after the Day of Atonement.[b] So Paul
warned them, 10"Men, I can see that our voyage is going to be disastrous and bring great
loss to ship and cargo, and to our own lives
also." 11But the centurion, instead of listening
to what Paul said, followed the advice of the
pilot and of the owner of the ship. 12Since the
harbor was unsuitable to winter in, the majority decided that we should sail on, hoping
to reach Phoenix and winter there. This was
a harbor in Crete, facing both southwest and
northwest.

The Storm

13When a gentle south wind began to blow,
they saw their opportunity; so they weighed
anchor and sailed along the shore of Crete.
14Before very long, a wind of hurricane force,
called the Northeaster, swept down from the

[a] *14* Or *Hebrew* [b] *9* That is, Yom Kippur

island. 15The ship was caught by the storm and could not head into the wind; so we gave way to it and were driven along. 16As we passed to the lee of a small island called Cauda, we were hardly able to make the lifeboat secure, 17so the men hoisted it aboard. Then they passed ropes under the ship itself to hold it together. Because they were afraid they would run aground on the sandbars of Syrtis, they lowered the sea anchor[a] and let the ship be driven along. 18We took such a violent battering from the storm that the next day they began to throw the cargo overboard. 19On the third day, they threw the ship's tackle overboard with their own hands. 20When neither sun nor stars appeared for many days and the storm continued raging, we finally gave up all hope of being saved.

21After they had gone a long time without food, Paul stood up before them and said: "Men, you should have taken my advice not to sail from Crete; then you would have spared yourselves this damage and loss. 22But now I urge you to keep up your courage, because not one of you will be lost; only the ship will be destroyed. 23Last night an angel of the God to whom I belong and whom I serve stood beside me 24and said, 'Do not be afraid, Paul. You must stand trial before Caesar; and God has graciously given you the lives of all who sail with you.' 25So keep up your courage, men, for I have faith in God that it will happen just as he told me. 26Nevertheless, we must run aground on some island."

The Shipwreck

27On the fourteenth night we were still being driven across the Adriatic[b] Sea, when about midnight the sailors sensed they were approaching land. 28They took soundings and found that the water was a hundred and twenty feet[c] deep. A short time later they took soundings again and found it was ninety feet[d] deep. 29Fearing that we would be dashed against the rocks, they dropped four anchors from the stern and prayed for daylight. 30In an attempt to escape from the ship, the sailors let the lifeboat down into the sea, pretending they were going to lower some anchors from the bow. 31Then Paul said to the centurion and the soldiers, "Unless these men stay with the ship, you cannot be saved." 32So the soldiers cut the ropes that held the lifeboat and let it drift away.

33Just before dawn Paul urged them all to eat. "For the last fourteen days," he said, "you have been in constant suspense and have gone without food—you haven't eaten anything. 34Now I urge you to take some food. You need it to survive. Not one of you will lose a single hair from his head." 35After he said this, he took some bread and gave thanks to God in front of them all. Then he broke it and began to eat. 36They were all encouraged and ate some food themselves. 37Altogether there were 276 of us on board. 38When they had eaten as much as they wanted, they lightened the ship by throwing the grain into the sea.

39When daylight came, they did not recognize the land, but they saw a bay with a sandy beach, where they decided to run the ship aground if they could. 40Cutting loose the anchors, they left them in the sea and at the same time untied the ropes that held the rudders. Then they hoisted the foresail to the wind and made for the beach. 41But the ship struck a sandbar and ran aground. The bow stuck fast and would not move, and the stern was broken to pieces by the pounding of the surf.

42The soldiers planned to kill the prisoners to prevent any of them from swimming away and escaping. 43But the centurion wanted to spare Paul's life and kept them from carrying out their plan. He ordered those who could swim to jump overboard first and get to land. 44The rest were to get there on planks or on other pieces of the ship. In this way everyone reached land safely.

Paul Ashore on Malta

28 Once safely on shore, we found out that the island was called Malta. 2The islanders showed us unusual kindness. They built a fire and welcomed us all because it was raining and cold. 3Paul gathered a pile of brushwood and, as he put it on the fire, a viper, driven out by the heat, fastened itself on his hand. 4When the islanders saw the snake hanging from his hand, they said to each other, "This man must be a murderer; for though he escaped from the sea, the goddess Justice has not allowed him to live." 5But Paul shook the snake off into the fire and suffered no ill effects. 6The people expected him to swell up or suddenly fall dead; but after waiting a long time and seeing nothing unusual happen to him, they changed their minds and said he was a god.

7There was an estate nearby that belonged to Publius, the chief official of the island. He welcomed us to his home and showed us generous hospitality for three days. 8His father was sick in bed, suffering from fever and dysentery. Paul went in to see him and, after prayer, placed his hands on him and healed him. 9When this had happened, the rest of the sick on the island came and were cured. 10They honored us in many ways; and when we were ready to sail, they furnished us with the supplies we needed.

Paul's Arrival at Rome

11After three months we put out to sea in a ship that had wintered in the island—it was an Alexandrian ship with the figurehead of the twin gods Castor and Pollux. 12We put in at Syracuse and stayed there three days. 13From there we set sail and arrived at Rhegium. The next day the south wind came up, and on the following day we reached Puteoli. 14There we found some brothers and sisters who invited

[a] 17 Or *the sails* [b] 27 In ancient times the name referred to an area extending well south of Italy.
[c] 28 Or about 37 meters [d] 28 Or about 27 meters

us to spend a week with them. And so we came to Rome. 15The brothers and sisters there had heard that we were coming, and they traveled as far as the Forum of Appius and the Three Taverns to meet us. At the sight of these people Paul thanked God and was encouraged. 16When we got to Rome, Paul was allowed to live by himself, with a soldier to guard him.

Paul Preaches at Rome Under Guard

17Three days later he called together the local Jewish leaders. When they had assembled, Paul said to them: "My brothers, although I have done nothing against our people or against the customs of our ancestors, I was arrested in Jerusalem and handed over to the Romans. 18They examined me and wanted to release me, because I was not guilty of any crime deserving death. 19The Jews objected, so I was compelled to make an appeal to Caesar. I certainly did not intend to bring any charge against my own people. 20For this reason I have asked to see you and talk with you. It is because of the hope of Israel that I am bound with this chain."

21They replied, "We have not received any letters from Judea concerning you, and none of our people who have come from there has reported or said anything bad about you. 22But we want to hear what your views are, for we know that people everywhere are talking against this sect."

23They arranged to meet Paul on a certain day, and came in even larger numbers to the place where he was staying. He witnessed to them from morning till evening, explaining about the kingdom of God, and from the Law of Moses and from the Prophets he tried to persuade them about Jesus. 24Some were convinced by what he said, but others would not believe. 25They disagreed among themselves and began to leave after Paul had made this final statement: "The Holy Spirit spoke the truth to your ancestors when he said through Isaiah the prophet:

26"'Go to this people and say,
"You will be ever hearing but never
understanding;
you will be ever seeing but never
perceiving."
27For this people's heart has become
calloused;
they hardly hear with their ears,
and they have closed their eyes.
Otherwise they might see with their eyes,
hear with their ears,
understand with their hearts
and turn, and I would heal them.'[a]

28"Therefore I want you to know that God's salvation has been sent to the Gentiles, and they will listen!" [29][b]

30For two whole years Paul stayed there in his own rented house and welcomed all who came to see him. 31He proclaimed the kingdom of God and taught about the Lord Jesus Christ—with all boldness and without hindrance!

Romans

1 Paul, a servant of Christ Jesus, called to be an apostle and set apart for the gospel of God— 2the gospel he promised beforehand through his prophets in the Holy Scriptures 3regarding his Son, who as to his earthly life[c] was a descendant of David, 4and who through the Spirit of holiness was appointed the Son of God in power[d] by his resurrection from the dead: Jesus Christ our Lord. 5Through him we received grace and apostleship to call all the Gentiles to the obedience that comes from[e] faith for his name's sake. 6And you also are among those Gentiles who are called to belong to Jesus Christ.

7To all in Rome who are loved by God and called to be his holy people:

Grace and peace to you from God our Father and from the Lord Jesus Christ.

Paul's Longing to Visit Rome

8First, I thank my God through Jesus Christ for all of you, because your faith is being reported all over the world. 9God, whom I serve in my spirit in preaching the gospel of his Son, is my witness how constantly I remember you 10in my prayers at all times; and I pray that now at last by God's will the way may be opened for me to come to you.

11I long to see you so that I may impart to you some spiritual gift to make you strong— 12that is, that you and I may be mutually encouraged by each other's faith. 13I do not want you to be unaware, brothers and sisters,[f] that I planned many times to come to you (but have been prevented from doing so until now) in order that I might have a harvest among you, just as I have had among the other Gentiles.

[a] 27 Isaiah 6:9,10 (see Septuagint) [b] 29 Some manuscripts include here *After he said this, the Jews left, arguing vigorously among themselves.* [c] 3 Or *who according to the flesh* [d] 4 Or *was declared with power to be the Son of God* [e] 5 Or *that is* [f] 13 The Greek word for *brothers and sisters* (*adelphoi*) refers here to believers, both men and women, as part of God's family; also in 7:1, 4; 8:12, 29; 10:1; 11:25; 12:1; 15:14, 30; 16:14, 17.

14I am obligated both to Greeks and
non-Greeks, both to the wise and the foolish. 15That is why I am so eager to preach the
gospel also to you who are in Rome.
16For I am not ashamed of the gospel, because it is the power of God that brings salvation to everyone who believes: first to the
Jew, then to the Gentile. 17For in the gospel
the righteousness of God is revealed—a righteousness that is by faith from first to last,[a]
just as it is written: "The righteous will live
by faith."[b]

God's Wrath Against Sinful Humanity

18The wrath of God is being revealed from
heaven against all the godlessness and wickedness of people, who suppress the truth by
their wickedness, 19since what may be known
about God is plain to them, because God has
made it plain to them. 20For since the creation
of the world God's invisible qualities—his
eternal power and divine nature—have been
clearly seen, being understood from what
has been made, so that people are without
excuse.
21For although they knew God, they neither
glorified him as God nor gave thanks to him,
but their thinking became futile and their
foolish hearts were darkened. 22Although
they claimed to be wise, they became fools
23and exchanged the glory of the immortal
God for images made to look like a mortal
human being and birds and animals and
reptiles.
24Therefore God gave them over in the sinful desires of their hearts to sexual impurity
for the degrading of their bodies with one another. 25They exchanged the truth about God
for a lie, and worshiped and served created
things rather than the Creator—who is forever praised. Amen.
26Because of this, God gave them over to
shameful lusts. Even their women exchanged
natural sexual relations for unnatural ones.
27In the same way the men also abandoned
natural relations with women and were inflamed with lust for one another. Men committed shameful acts with other men, and
received in themselves the due penalty for
their error.
28Furthermore, just as they did not think it
worthwhile to retain the knowledge of God,
so God gave them over to a depraved mind,
so that they do what ought not to be done.
29They have become filled with every kind
of wickedness, evil, greed and depravity.
They are full of envy, murder, strife, deceit
and malice. They are gossips, 30slanderers,
God-haters, insolent, arrogant and boastful;
they invent ways of doing evil; they disobey
their parents; 31they have no understanding,
no fidelity, no love, no mercy. 32Although they
know God's righteous decree that those who
do such things deserve death, they not only
continue to do these very things but also approve of those who practice them.

God's Righteous Judgment

2 You, therefore, have no excuse, you who
pass judgment on someone else, for at
whatever point you judge another, you are
condemning yourself, because you who
pass judgment do the same things. 2Now we
know that God's judgment against those who
do such things is based on truth. 3So when
you, a mere human being, pass judgment on
them and yet do the same things, do you think
you will escape God's judgment? 4Or do you
show contempt for the riches of his kindness,
forbearance and patience, not realizing that
God's kindness is intended to lead you to repentance?
5But because of your stubbornness and your
unrepentant heart, you are storing up wrath
against yourself for the day of God's wrath,
when his righteous judgment will be revealed.
6God "will repay each person according to
what they have done."[c] 7To those who by per-
sistence in doing good seek glory, honor and
immortality, he will give eternal life. 8But for
those who are self-seeking and who reject the
truth and follow evil, there will be wrath and
anger. 9There will be trouble and distress for
every human being who does evil: first for the
Jew, then for the Gentile; 10but glory, honor
and peace for everyone who does good: first
for the Jew, then for the Gentile. 11For God
does not show favoritism.
12All who sin apart from the law will also
perish apart from the law, and all who sin under the law will be judged by the law. 13For it is
not those who hear the law who are righteous
in God's sight, but it is those who obey the
law who will be declared righteous. 14(Indeed,
when Gentiles, who do not have the law, do by
nature things required by the law, they are a
law for themselves, even though they do not
have the law. 15They show that the requirements of the law are written on their hearts,
their consciences also bearing witness, and
their thoughts sometimes accusing them and
at other times even defending them.) 16This
will take place on the day when God judges
people's secrets through Jesus Christ, as my
gospel declares.

The Jews and the Law

17Now you, if you call yourself a Jew; if you
rely on the law and boast in God; 18if you know
his will and approve of what is superior because you are instructed by the law; 19if you
are convinced that you are a guide for the
blind, a light for those who are in the dark,
20an instructor of the foolish, a teacher of little children, because you have in the law the
embodiment of knowledge and truth— 21you,
then, who teach others, do you not teach yourself? You who preach against stealing, do you
steal? 22You who say that people should not
commit adultery, do you commit adultery?
You who abhor idols, do you rob temples?
23You who boast in the law, do you dishonor
God by breaking the law? 24As it is written:

[a] *17* Or *is from faith to faith* [b] *17* Hab. 2:4 [c] *6* Psalm 62:12; Prov. 24:12

"God's name is blasphemed among the Gentiles because of you."[a]

25 Circumcision has value if you observe the law, but if you break the law, you have become as though you had not been circumcised. 26 So then, if those who are not circumcised keep the law's requirements, will they not be regarded as though they were circumcised? 27 The one who is not circumcised physically and yet obeys the law will condemn you who, even though you have the[b] written code and circumcision, are a lawbreaker.

28 A person is not a Jew who is one only outwardly, nor is circumcision merely outward and physical. 29 No, a person is a Jew who is one inwardly; and circumcision is circumcision of the heart, by the Spirit, not by the written code. Such a person's praise is not from other people, but from God.

God's Faithfulness

3 What advantage, then, is there in being a Jew, or what value is there in circumcision? 2 Much in every way! First of all, the Jews have been entrusted with the very words of God.

3 What if some were unfaithful? Will their unfaithfulness nullify God's faithfulness? 4 Not at all! Let God be true, and every human being a liar. As it is written:

"So that you may be proved right when
you speak
and prevail when you judge."[c]

5 But if our unrighteousness brings out God's righteousness more clearly, what shall we say? That God is unjust in bringing his wrath on us? (I am using a human argument.) 6 Certainly not! If that were so, how could God judge the world? 7 Someone might argue, "If my falsehood enhances God's truthfulness and so increases his glory, why am I still condemned as a sinner?" 8 Why not say—as some slanderously claim that we say—"Let us do evil that good may result"? Their condemnation is just!

No One Is Righteous

9 What shall we conclude then? Do we have any advantage? Not at all! For we have already made the charge that Jews and Gentiles alike are all under the power of sin. 10 As it is written:

"There is no one righteous, not even one;
11 there is no one who understands;
there is no one who seeks God.
12 All have turned away,
they have together become worthless;
there is no one who does good,
not even one."[d]
13 "Their throats are open graves;
their tongues practice deceit."[e]
"The poison of vipers is on their lips."[f]
14 "Their mouths are full of cursing and
bitterness."[g]
15 "Their feet are swift to shed blood;
16 ruin and misery mark their ways,
17 and the way of peace they do not know."[h]
18 "There is no fear of God before their
eyes."[i]

19 Now we know that whatever the law says, it says to those who are under the law, so that every mouth may be silenced and the whole world held accountable to God. 20 Therefore no one will be declared righteous in God's sight by the works of the law; rather, through the law we become conscious of our sin.

Righteousness Through Faith

21 But now apart from the law the righteousness of God has been made known, to which the Law and the Prophets testify. 22 This righteousness is given through faith in[j] Jesus Christ to all who believe. There is no difference between Jew and Gentile, 23 for all have sinned and fall short of the glory of God, 24 and all are justified freely by his grace through the redemption that came by Christ Jesus. 25 God presented Christ as a sacrifice of atonement,[k] through the shedding of his blood—to be received by faith. He did this to demonstrate his righteousness, because in his forbearance he had left the sins committed beforehand unpunished— 26 he did it to demonstrate his righteousness at the present time, so as to be just and the one who justifies those who have faith in Jesus.

27 Where, then, is boasting? It is excluded. Because of what law? The law that requires works? No, because of the law that requires faith. 28 For we maintain that a person is justified by faith apart from the works of the law. 29 Or is God the God of Jews only? Is he not the God of Gentiles too? Yes, of Gentiles too, 30 since there is only one God, who will justify the circumcised by faith and the uncircumcised through that same faith. 31 Do we, then, nullify the law by this faith? Not at all! Rather, we uphold the law.

Abraham Justified by Faith

4 What then shall we say that Abraham, our forefather according to the flesh, discovered in this matter? 2 If, in fact, Abraham was justified by works, he had something to boast about—but not before God. 3 What does Scripture say? "Abraham believed God, and it was credited to him as righteousness."[l]

4 Now to the one who works, wages are not credited as a gift but as an obligation. 5 However, to the one who does not work but trusts God who justifies the ungodly, their faith is credited as righteousness. 6 David says the same thing when he speaks of the blessedness

[a] *24* Isaiah 52:5 (see Septuagint); Ezek. 36:20,22 [b] *27* Or *who, by means of a* [c] *4* Psalm 51:4 [d] *12* Psalms 14:1-3; 53:1-3; Eccles. 7:20 [e] *13* Psalm 5:9 [f] *13* Psalm 140:3 [g] *14* Psalm 10:7 (see Septuagint) [h] *17* Isaiah 59:7,8 [i] *18* Psalm 36:1 [j] *22* Or *through the faithfulness of* [k] *25* The Greek for *sacrifice of atonement* refers to the atonement cover on the ark of the covenant (see Lev. 16:15,16). [l] *3* Gen. 15:6; also in verse 22

of the one to whom God credits righteousness
apart from works:

7 "Blessed are those
whose transgressions are forgiven,
whose sins are covered.
8 Blessed is the one
whose sin the Lord will never count
against them."[a]

9 Is this blessedness only for the circumcised, or also for the uncircumcised? We have
been saying that Abraham's faith was credited to him as righteousness. 10 Under what
circumstances was it credited? Was it after he
was circumcised, or before? It was not after,
but before! 11 And he received circumcision
as a sign, a seal of the righteousness that he
had by faith while he was still uncircumcised.
So then, he is the father of all who believe but
have not been circumcised, in order that righteousness might be credited to them. 12 And
he is then also the father of the circumcised
who not only are circumcised but who also
follow in the footsteps of the faith that our father Abraham had before he was circumcised.

13 It was not through the law that Abraham
and his offspring received the promise that
he would be heir of the world, but through
the righteousness that comes by faith. 14 For if
those who depend on the law are heirs, faith
means nothing and the promise is worthless,
15 because the law brings wrath. And where
there is no law there is no transgression.

16 Therefore, the promise comes by faith, so
that it may be by grace and may be guaranteed to all Abraham's offspring—not only to
those who are of the law but also to those who
have the faith of Abraham. He is the father of
us all. 17 As it is written: "I have made you a
father of many nations."[b] He is our father in
the sight of God, in whom he believed—the
God who gives life to the dead and calls into
being things that were not.

18 Against all hope, Abraham in hope believed and so became the father of many nations, just as it had been said to him, "So shall
your offspring be."[c] 19 Without weakening in
his faith, he faced the fact that his body was
as good as dead—since he was about a hundred years old—and that Sarah's womb was
also dead. 20 Yet he did not waver through unbelief regarding the promise of God, but was
strengthened in his faith and gave glory to
God, 21 being fully persuaded that God had
power to do what he had promised. 22 This is
why "it was credited to him as righteousness."
23 The words "it was credited to him" were written not for him alone, 24 but also for us, to whom
God will credit righteousness—for us who believe in him who raised Jesus our Lord from the
dead. 25 He was delivered over to death for our
sins and was raised to life for our justification.

Peace and Hope

5 Therefore, since we have been justified
through faith, we[d] have peace with God
through our Lord Jesus Christ, 2 through
whom we have gained access by faith into this
grace in which we now stand. And we[e] boast
in the hope of the glory of God. 3 Not only so,
but we[e] also glory in our sufferings, because
we know that suffering produces perseverance; 4 perseverance, character; and character,
hope. 5 And hope does not put us to shame,
because God's love has been poured out into
our hearts through the Holy Spirit, who has
been given to us.

6 You see, at just the right time, when we
were still powerless, Christ died for the
ungodly. 7 Very rarely will anyone die for
a righteous person, though for a good person someone might possibly dare to die.
8 But God demonstrates his own love for us
in this: While we were still sinners, Christ
died for us.

9 Since we have now been justified by his
blood, how much more shall we be saved from
God's wrath through him! 10 For if, while we
were God's enemies, we were reconciled to
him through the death of his Son, how much
more, having been reconciled, shall we be
saved through his life! 11 Not only is this so,
but we also boast in God through our Lord
Jesus Christ, through whom we have now received reconciliation.

Death Through Adam, Life Through Christ

12 Therefore, just as sin entered the world
through one man, and death through sin, and
in this way death came to all people, because
all sinned—

13 To be sure, sin was in the world before the
law was given, but sin is not charged against
anyone's account where there is no law. 14 Nevertheless, death reigned from the time of
Adam to the time of Moses, even over those
who did not sin by breaking a command, as
did Adam, who is a pattern of the one to come.

15 But the gift is not like the trespass. For
if the many died by the trespass of the one
man, how much more did God's grace and the
gift that came by the grace of the one man,
Jesus Christ, overflow to the many! 16 Nor can
the gift of God be compared with the result
of one man's sin: The judgment followed one
sin and brought condemnation, but the gift
followed many trespasses and brought justification. 17 For if, by the trespass of the one
man, death reigned through that one man,
how much more will those who receive God's
abundant provision of grace and of the gift of
righteousness reign in life through the one
man, Jesus Christ!

18 Consequently, just as one trespass resulted in condemnation for all people, so also one
righteous act resulted in justification and life
for all people. 19 For just as through the disobedience of the one man the many were made
sinners, so also through the obedience of the
one man the many will be made righteous.

20 The law was brought in so that the trespass might increase. But where sin increased,
grace increased all the more, 21 so that, just
as sin reigned in death, so also grace might

[a] *8* Psalm 32:1,2 [b] *17* Gen. 17:5 [c] *18* Gen. 15:5 [d] *1* Many manuscripts *let us* [e] *2,3* Or *let us*

reign through righteousness to bring eternal life through Jesus Christ our Lord.

Dead to Sin, Alive in Christ

6 What shall we say, then? Shall we go on sinning so that grace may increase? [2]By no means! We are those who have died to sin; how can we live in it any longer? [3]Or don't you know that all of us who were baptized into Christ Jesus were baptized into his death? [4]We were therefore buried with him through baptism into death in order that, just as Christ was raised from the dead through the glory of the Father, we too may live a new life.

[5]For if we have been united with him in a death like his, we will certainly also be united with him in a resurrection like his. [6]For we know that our old self was crucified with him so that the body ruled by sin might be done away with,[a] that we should no longer be slaves to sin— [7]because anyone who has died has been set free from sin.

[8]Now if we died with Christ, we believe that we will also live with him. [9]For we know that since Christ was raised from the dead, he cannot die again; death no longer has mastery over him. [10]The death he died, he died to sin once for all; but the life he lives, he lives to God.

[11]In the same way, count yourselves dead to sin but alive to God in Christ Jesus. [12]Therefore do not let sin reign in your mortal body so that you obey its evil desires. [13]Do not offer any part of yourself to sin as an instrument of wickedness, but rather offer yourselves to God as those who have been brought from death to life; and offer every part of yourself to him as an instrument of righteousness. [14]For sin shall no longer be your master, because you are not under the law, but under grace.

Slaves to Righteousness

[15]What then? Shall we sin because we are not under the law but under grace? By no means! [16]Don't you know that when you offer yourselves to someone as obedient slaves, you are slaves of the one you obey—whether you are slaves to sin, which leads to death, or to obedience, which leads to righteousness? [17]But thanks be to God that, though you used to be slaves to sin, you have come to obey from your heart the pattern of teaching that has now claimed your allegiance. [18]You have been set free from sin and have become slaves to righteousness.

[19]I am using an example from everyday life because of your human limitations. Just as you used to offer yourselves as slaves to impurity and to ever-increasing wickedness, so now offer yourselves as slaves to righteousness leading to holiness. [20]When you were slaves to sin, you were free from the control of righteousness. [21]What benefit did you reap at that time from the things you are now ashamed of? Those things result in death! [22]But now that you have been set free from sin and have become slaves of God, the benefit you reap leads to holiness, and the result is eternal life. [23]For the wages of sin is death, but the gift of God is eternal life in[b] Christ Jesus our Lord.

Released From the Law, Bound to Christ

7 Do you not know, brothers and sisters—for I am speaking to those who know the law—that the law has authority over someone only as long as that person lives? [2]For example, by law a married woman is bound to her husband as long as he is alive, but if her husband dies, she is released from the law that binds her to him. [3]So then, if she has sexual relations with another man while her husband is still alive, she is called an adulteress. But if her husband dies, she is released from that law and is not an adulteress if she marries another man.

[4]So, my brothers and sisters, you also died to the law through the body of Christ, that you might belong to another, to him who was raised from the dead, in order that we might bear fruit for God. [5]For when we were in the realm of the flesh,[c] the sinful passions aroused by the law were at work in us, so that we bore fruit for death. [6]But now, by dying to what once bound us, we have been released from the law so that we serve in the new way of the Spirit, and not in the old way of the written code.

The Law and Sin

[7]What shall we say, then? Is the law sinful? Certainly not! Nevertheless, I would not have known what sin was had it not been for the law. For I would not have known what coveting really was if the law had not said, "You shall not covet."[d] [8]But sin, seizing the opportunity afforded by the commandment, produced in me every kind of coveting. For apart from the law, sin was dead. [9]Once I was alive apart from the law; but when the commandment came, sin sprang to life and I died. [10]I found that the very commandment that was intended to bring life actually brought death. [11]For sin, seizing the opportunity afforded by the commandment, deceived me, and through the commandment put me to death. [12]So then, the law is holy, and the commandment is holy, righteous and good.

[13]Did that which is good, then, become death to me? By no means! Nevertheless, in order that sin might be recognized as sin, it used what is good to bring about my death, so that through the commandment sin might become utterly sinful.

[14]We know that the law is spiritual; but I am unspiritual, sold as a slave to sin. [15]I do not understand what I do. For what I want to do I do not do, but what I hate I do. [16]And if I do what I do not want to do, I agree that the law is good. [17]As it is, it is no longer I myself who

[a] *6* Or *be rendered powerless* [b] *23* Or *through* [c] *5* In contexts like this, the Greek word for *flesh* (*sarx*) refers to the sinful state of human beings, often presented as a power in opposition to the Spirit.
[d] *7* Exodus 20:17; Deut. 5:21

do it, but it is sin living in me. 18For I know that good itself does not dwell in me, that is, in my sinful nature.[a] For I have the desire to do what is good, but I cannot carry it out. 19For I do not do the good I want to do, but the evil I do not want to do—this I keep on doing. 20Now if I do what I do not want to do, it is no longer I who do it, but it is sin living in me that does it.

21So I find this law at work: Although I want to do good, evil is right there with me. 22For in my inner being I delight in God's law; 23but I see another law at work in me, waging war against the law of my mind and making me a prisoner of the law of sin at work within me. 24What a wretched man I am! Who will rescue me from this body that is subject to death? 25Thanks be to God, who delivers me through Jesus Christ our Lord!

So then, I myself in my mind am a slave to God's law, but in my sinful nature[b] a slave to the law of sin.

Life Through the Spirit

8 Therefore, there is now no condemnation for those who are in Christ Jesus, 2because through Christ Jesus the law of the Spirit who gives life has set you[c] free from the law of sin and death. 3For what the law was powerless to do because it was weakened by the flesh,[d] God did by sending his own Son in the likeness of sinful flesh to be a sin offering.[e] And so he condemned sin in the flesh, 4in order that the righteous requirement of the law might be fully met in us, who do not live according to the flesh but according to the Spirit.

5Those who live according to the flesh have their minds set on what the flesh desires; but those who live in accordance with the Spirit have their minds set on what the Spirit desires. 6The mind governed by the flesh is death, but the mind governed by the Spirit is life and peace. 7The mind governed by the flesh is hostile to God; it does not submit to God's law, nor can it do so. 8Those who are in the realm of the flesh cannot please God.

9You, however, are not in the realm of the flesh but are in the realm of the Spirit, if indeed the Spirit of God lives in you. And if anyone does not have the Spirit of Christ, they do not belong to Christ. 10But if Christ is in you, then even though your body is subject to death because of sin, the Spirit gives life[f] because of righteousness. 11And if the Spirit of him who raised Jesus from the dead is living in you, he who raised Christ from the dead will also give life to your mortal bodies because of[g] his Spirit who lives in you.

12Therefore, brothers and sisters, we have an obligation—but it is not to the flesh, to live according to it. 13For if you live according to the flesh, you will die; but if by the Spirit you put to death the misdeeds of the body, you will live.

14For those who are led by the Spirit of God are the children of God. 15The Spirit you received does not make you slaves, so that you live in fear again; rather, the Spirit you received brought about your adoption to sonship.[h] And by him we cry, "*Abba,*[i] Father." 16The Spirit himself testifies with our spirit that we are God's children. 17Now if we are children, then we are heirs—heirs of God and co-heirs with Christ, if indeed we share in his sufferings in order that we may also share in his glory.

Present Suffering and Future Glory

18I consider that our present sufferings are not worth comparing with the glory that will be revealed in us. 19For the creation waits in eager expectation for the children of God to be revealed. 20For the creation was subjected to frustration, not by its own choice, but by the will of the one who subjected it, in hope 21that[j] the creation itself will be liberated from its bondage to decay and brought into the freedom and glory of the children of God.

22We know that the whole creation has been groaning as in the pains of childbirth right up to the present time. 23Not only so, but we ourselves, who have the firstfruits of the Spirit, groan inwardly as we wait eagerly for our adoption to sonship, the redemption of our bodies. 24For in this hope we were saved. But hope that is seen is no hope at all. Who hopes for what they already have? 25But if we hope for what we do not yet have, we wait for it patiently.

26In the same way, the Spirit helps us in our weakness. We do not know what we ought to pray for, but the Spirit himself intercedes for us through wordless groans. 27And he who searches our hearts knows the mind of the Spirit, because the Spirit intercedes for God's people in accordance with the will of God.

28And we know that in all things God works for the good of those who love him, who[k] have been called according to his purpose. 29For those God foreknew he also predestined to be conformed to the image of his Son, that he might be the firstborn among many brothers and sisters. 30And those he predestined, he also called; those he called, he also justified; those he justified, he also glorified.

More Than Conquerors

31What, then, shall we say in response to these things? If God is for us, who can be against us? 32He who did not spare his own

[a] 18 Or *my flesh* [b] 25 Or *in the flesh* [c] 2 The Greek is singular; some manuscripts *me* [d] 3 In contexts like this, the Greek word for *flesh* (*sarx*) refers to the sinful state of human beings, often presented as a power in opposition to the Spirit; also in verses 4-13. [e] 3 Or *flesh, for sin*
[f] 10 Or *you, your body is dead because of sin, yet your spirit is alive* [g] 11 Some manuscripts *bodies through* [h] 15 The Greek word for *adoption to sonship* is a term referring to the full legal standing of an adopted male heir in Roman culture; also in verse 23. [i] 15 Aramaic for *father*
[j] 20,21 Or *subjected it in hope.* 21*For* [k] 28 Or *that all things work together for good to those who love God, who*; or *that in all things God works together with those who love him to bring about what is good—with those who*

Son, but gave him up for us all—how will
he not also, along with him, graciously give
us all things? 33Who will bring any charge
against those whom God has chosen? It is God
who justifies. 34Who then is the one who condemns? No one. Christ Jesus who died—more
than that, who was raised to life—is at the
right hand of God and is also interceding for
us. 35Who shall separate us from the love of
Christ? Shall trouble or hardship or persecution or famine or nakedness or danger or
sword? 36As it is written:

"For your sake we face death all day
long;
we are considered as sheep to be
slaughtered."[a]

37No, in all these things we are more than con-
querors through him who loved us. 38For I am
convinced that neither death nor life, neither
angels nor demons,[b] neither the present nor
the future, nor any powers, 39neither height
nor depth, nor anything else in all creation,
will be able to separate us from the love of
God that is in Christ Jesus our Lord.

Paul's Anguish Over Israel

9 I speak the truth in Christ—I am not lying, my conscience confirms it through
the Holy Spirit— 2I have great sorrow and
unceasing anguish in my heart. 3For I could
wish that I myself were cursed and cut off
from Christ for the sake of my people, those
of my own race, 4the people of Israel. Theirs
is the adoption to sonship; theirs the divine
glory, the covenants, the receiving of the law,
the temple worship and the promises. 5Theirs
are the patriarchs, and from them is traced the
human ancestry of the Messiah, who is God
over all, forever praised![c] Amen.

God's Sovereign Choice

6It is not as though God's word had failed.
For not all who are descended from Israel
are Israel. 7Nor because they are his descendants are they all Abraham's children. On
the contrary, "It is through Isaac that your
offspring will be reckoned."[d] 8In other words,
it is not the children by physical descent who
are God's children, but it is the children of
the promise who are regarded as Abraham's
offspring. 9For this was how the promise was
stated: "At the appointed time I will return,
and Sarah will have a son."[e]

10Not only that, but Rebekah's children
were conceived at the same time by our father Isaac. 11Yet, before the twins were born or
had done anything good or bad—in order that
God's purpose in election might stand: 12not
by works but by him who calls—she was told,
"The older will serve the younger."[f] 13Just as it
is written: "Jacob I loved, but Esau I hated."[g]

14What then shall we say? Is God unjust?
Not at all! 15For he says to Moses,

"I will have mercy on whom I have mercy,
and I will have compassion on whom I
have compassion."[h]

16It does not, therefore, depend on human desire or effort, but on God's mercy. 17For Scripture says to Pharaoh: "I raised you up for this
very purpose, that I might display my power
in you and that my name might be proclaimed
in all the earth."[i] 18Therefore God has mercy on whom he wants to have mercy, and he
hardens whom he wants to harden.

19One of you will say to me: "Then why does
God still blame us? For who is able to resist
his will?" 20But who are you, a human being,
to talk back to God? "Shall what is formed say
to the one who formed it, 'Why did you make
me like this?'"[j] 21Does not the potter have the
right to make out of the same lump of clay
some pottery for special purposes and some
for common use?

22What if God, although choosing to show
his wrath and make his power known, bore
with great patience the objects of his wrath—
prepared for destruction? 23What if he did this
to make the riches of his glory known to the
objects of his mercy, whom he prepared in
advance for glory— 24even us, whom he also
called, not only from the Jews but also from
the Gentiles? 25As he says in Hosea:

"I will call them 'my people' who are not
my people;
and I will call her 'my loved one' who is
not my loved one,"[k]

26and,

"In the very place where it was said to
them,
'You are not my people,'
there they will be called 'children of the
living God.'"[l]

27Isaiah cries out concerning Israel:

"Though the number of the Israelites be
like the sand by the sea,
only the remnant will be saved.
28For the Lord will carry out
his sentence on earth with speed and
finality."[m]

29It is just as Isaiah said previously:

"Unless the Lord Almighty
had left us descendants,
we would have become like Sodom,
we would have been like Gomorrah."[n]

Israel's Unbelief

30What then shall we say? That the Gentiles,
who did not pursue righteousness, have obtained it, a righteousness that is by faith; 31but
the people of Israel, who pursued the law as
the way of righteousness, have not attained
their goal. 32Why not? Because they pursued
it not by faith but as if it were by works. They

[a] *36* Psalm 44:22 [b] *38* Or *nor heavenly rulers* [c] *5* Or *Messiah, who is over all. God be forever praised!* Or *Messiah. God who is over all be forever praised!* [d] *7* Gen. 21:12 [e] *9* Gen. 18:10,14 [f] *12* Gen. 25:23 [g] *13* Mal. 1:2,3 [h] *15* Exodus 33:19 [i] *17* Exodus 9:16 [j] *20* Isaiah 29:16; 45:9 [k] *25* Hosea 2:23 [l] *26* Hosea 1:10 [m] *28* Isaiah 10:22,23 (see Septuagint) [n] *29* Isaiah 1:9

stumbled over the stumbling stone. 33As it is written:

> "See, I lay in Zion a stone that causes people to stumble
> and a rock that makes them fall,
> and the one who believes in him will never be put to shame."[a]

10 Brothers and sisters, my heart's desire and prayer to God for the Israelites is that they may be saved. 2For I can testify about them that they are zealous for God, but their zeal is not based on knowledge. 3Since they did not know the righteousness of God and sought to establish their own, they did not submit to God's righteousness. 4Christ is the culmination of the law so that there may be righteousness for everyone who believes.

5Moses writes this about the righteousness that is by the law: "The person who does these things will live by them."[b] 6But the righteousness that is by faith says: "Do not say in your heart, 'Who will ascend into heaven?'"[c] (that is, to bring Christ down) 7"or 'Who will descend into the deep?'"[d] (that is, to bring Christ up from the dead). 8But what does it say? "The word is near you; it is in your mouth and in your heart,"[e] that is, the message concerning faith that we proclaim: 9If you declare with your mouth, "Jesus is Lord," and believe in your heart that God raised him from the dead, you will be saved. 10For it is with your heart that you believe and are justified, and it is with your mouth that you profess your faith and are saved. 11As Scripture says, "Anyone who believes in him will never be put to shame."[f] 12For there is no difference between Jew and Gentile—the same Lord is Lord of all and richly blesses all who call on him, 13for, "Everyone who calls on the name of the Lord will be saved."[g]

14How, then, can they call on the one they have not believed in? And how can they believe in the one of whom they have not heard? And how can they hear without someone preaching to them? 15And how can anyone preach unless they are sent? As it is written: "How beautiful are the feet of those who bring good news!"[h]

16But not all the Israelites accepted the good news. For Isaiah says, "Lord, who has believed our message?"[i] 17Consequently, faith comes from hearing the message, and the message is heard through the word about Christ. 18But I ask: Did they not hear? Of course they did:

> "Their voice has gone out into all the earth,
> their words to the ends of the world."[j]

19Again I ask: Did Israel not understand? First, Moses says,

> "I will make you envious by those who are not a nation;
> I will make you angry by a nation that has no understanding."[k]

20And Isaiah boldly says,

> "I was found by those who did not seek me;
> I revealed myself to those who did not ask for me."[l]

21But concerning Israel he says,

> "All day long I have held out my hands
> to a disobedient and obstinate people."[m]

The Remnant of Israel

11 I ask then: Did God reject his people? By no means! I am an Israelite myself, a descendant of Abraham, from the tribe of Benjamin. 2God did not reject his people, whom he foreknew. Don't you know what Scripture says in the passage about Elijah—how he appealed to God against Israel: 3"Lord, they have killed your prophets and torn down your altars; I am the only one left, and they are trying to kill me"[n]? 4And what was God's answer to him? "I have reserved for myself seven thousand who have not bowed the knee to Baal."[o] 5So too, at the present time there is a remnant chosen by grace. 6And if by grace, then it cannot be based on works; if it were, grace would no longer be grace.

7What then? What the people of Israel sought so earnestly they did not obtain. The elect among them did, but the others were hardened, 8as it is written:

> "God gave them a spirit of stupor,
> eyes that could not see
> and ears that could not hear,
> to this very day."[p]

9And David says:

> "May their table become a snare and a trap,
> a stumbling block and a retribution for them.
> 10May their eyes be darkened so they cannot see,
> and their backs be bent forever."[q]

Ingrafted Branches

11Again I ask: Did they stumble so as to fall beyond recovery? Not at all! Rather, because of their transgression, salvation has come to the Gentiles to make Israel envious. 12But if their transgression means riches for the world, and their loss means riches for the Gentiles, how much greater riches will their full inclusion bring!

13I am talking to you Gentiles. Inasmuch as I am the apostle to the Gentiles, I take pride in my ministry 14in the hope that I may somehow arouse my own people to envy and save some of them. 15For if their rejection brought reconciliation to the world, what will their acceptance be but life from the dead? 16If the part of the dough offered as firstfruits is holy,

[a] *33* Isaiah 8:14; 28:16 [b] *5* Lev. 18:5 [c] *6* Deut. 30:12 [d] *7* Deut. 30:13 [e] *8* Deut. 30:14
[f] *11* Isaiah 28:16 (see Septuagint) [g] *13* Joel 2:32 [h] *15* Isaiah 52:7 [i] *16* Isaiah 53:1
[j] *18* Psalm 19:4 [k] *19* Deut. 32:21 [l] *20* Isaiah 65:1 [m] *21* Isaiah 65:2 [n] *3* 1 Kings 19:10,14
[o] *4* 1 Kings 19:18 [p] *8* Deut. 29:4; Isaiah 29:10 [q] *10* Psalm 69:22,23

then the whole batch is holy; if the root is holy,
so are the branches.
17If some of the branches have been broken
off, and you, though a wild olive shoot, have
been grafted in among the others and now
share in the nourishing sap from the olive
root, 18do not consider yourself to be superior
to those other branches. If you do, consider
this: You do not support the root, but the root
supports you. 19You will say then, "Branches
were broken off so that I could be grafted in."
20Granted. But they were broken off because
of unbelief, and you stand by faith. Do not
be arrogant, but tremble. 21For if God did not
spare the natural branches, he will not spare
you either.
22Consider therefore the kindness and
sternness of God: sternness to those who
fell, but kindness to you, provided that you
continue in his kindness. Otherwise, you also
will be cut off. 23And if they do not persist in
unbelief, they will be grafted in, for God is
able to graft them in again. 24After all, if you
were cut out of an olive tree that is wild by
nature, and contrary to nature were grafted
into a cultivated olive tree, how much more
readily will these, the natural branches, be
grafted into their own olive tree!

All Israel Will Be Saved

25I do not want you to be ignorant of this
mystery, brothers and sisters, so that you
may not be conceited: Israel has experienced
a hardening in part until the full number of
the Gentiles has come in, 26and in this way[a]
all Israel will be saved. As it is written:

"The deliverer will come from Zion;
he will turn godlessness away from
Jacob.
27And this is[b] my covenant with them
when I take away their sins."[c]

28As far as the gospel is concerned, they are
enemies for your sake; but as far as election
is concerned, they are loved on account of the
patriarchs, 29for God's gifts and his call are
irrevocable. 30Just as you who were at one
time disobedient to God have now received
mercy as a result of their disobedience, 31so
they too have now become disobedient in order that they too may now[d] receive mercy as
a result of God's mercy to you. 32For God has
bound everyone over to disobedience so that
he may have mercy on them all.

Doxology

33Oh, the depth of the riches of the wisdom
and[e] knowledge of God!
How unsearchable his judgments,
and his paths beyond tracing out!
34"Who has known the mind of the Lord?
Or who has been his counselor?"[f]
35"Who has ever given to God,
that God should repay them?"[g]
36For from him and through him and for
him are all things.
To him be the glory forever! Amen.

A Living Sacrifice

12 Therefore, I urge you, brothers and sisters, in view of God's mercy, to offer your
bodies as a living sacrifice, holy and pleasing
to God—this is your true and proper worship.
2Do not conform to the pattern of this world,
but be transformed by the renewing of your
mind. Then you will be able to test and approve what God's will is—his good, pleasing
and perfect will.

Humble Service in the Body of Christ

3For by the grace given me I say to every one
of you: Do not think of yourself more highly
than you ought, but rather think of yourself
with sober judgment, in accordance with the
faith God has distributed to each of you. 4For
just as each of us has one body with many
members, and these members do not all have
the same function, 5so in Christ we, though
many, form one body, and each member belongs to all the others. 6We have different
gifts, according to the grace given to each of
us. If your gift is prophesying, then prophesy
in accordance with your[h] faith; 7if it is serving, then serve; if it is teaching, then teach; 8if
it is to encourage, then give encouragement;
if it is giving, then give generously; if it is to
lead,[i] do it diligently; if it is to show mercy,
do it cheerfully.

Love in Action

9Love must be sincere. Hate what is evil;
cling to what is good. 10Be devoted to one another in love. Honor one another above yourselves. 11Never be lacking in zeal, but keep
your spiritual fervor, serving the Lord. 12Be
joyful in hope, patient in affliction, faithful
in prayer. 13Share with the Lord's people who
are in need. Practice hospitality.
14Bless those who persecute you; bless and
do not curse. 15Rejoice with those who rejoice;
mourn with those who mourn. 16Live in harmony with one another. Do not be proud, but
be willing to associate with people of low position.[j] Do not be conceited.
17Do not repay anyone evil for evil. Be careful to do what is right in the eyes of everyone.
18If it is possible, as far as it depends on you,
live at peace with everyone. 19Do not take revenge, my dear friends, but leave room for
God's wrath, for it is written: "It is mine to
avenge; I will repay,"[k] says the Lord. 20On the
contrary:

"If your enemy is hungry, feed him;
if he is thirsty, give him something to
drink.
In doing this, you will heap burning coals
on his head."[l]

[a] 26 Or *and so* [b] 27 Or *will be* [c] 27 Isaiah 59:20,21; 27:9 (see Septuagint); Jer. 31:33,34
[d] 31 Some manuscripts do not have *now.* [e] 33 Or *riches and the wisdom and the* [f] 34 Isaiah 40:13
[g] 35 Job 41:11 [h] 6 Or *the* [i] 8 Or *to provide for others* [j] 16 Or *willing to do menial work*
[k] 19 Deut. 32:35 [l] 20 Prov. 25:21,22

21Do not be overcome by evil, but overcome evil with good.

Submission to Governing Authorities

13 Let everyone be subject to the governing authorities, for there is no authority except that which God has established. The authorities that exist have been established by God. 2Consequently, whoever rebels against the authority is rebelling against what God has instituted, and those who do so will bring judgment on themselves. 3For rulers hold no terror for those who do right, but for those who do wrong. Do you want to be free from fear of the one in authority? Then do what is right and you will be commended. 4For the one in authority is God's servant for your good. But if you do wrong, be afraid, for rulers do not bear the sword for no reason. They are God's servants, agents of wrath to bring punishment on the wrongdoer. 5Therefore, it is necessary to submit to the authorities, not only because of possible punishment but also as a matter of conscience.

6This is also why you pay taxes, for the authorities are God's servants, who give their full time to governing. 7Give to everyone what you owe them: If you owe taxes, pay taxes; if revenue, then revenue; if respect, then respect; if honor, then honor.

Love Fulfills the Law

8Let no debt remain outstanding, except the continuing debt to love one another, for whoever loves others has fulfilled the law. 9The commandments, "You shall not commit adultery," "You shall not murder," "You shall not steal," "You shall not covet,"[a] and whatever other command there may be, are summed up in this one command: "Love your neighbor as yourself."[b] 10Love does no harm to a neighbor. Therefore love is the fulfillment of the law.

The Day Is Near

11And do this, understanding the present time: The hour has already come for you to wake up from your slumber, because our salvation is nearer now than when we first believed. 12The night is nearly over; the day is almost here. So let us put aside the deeds of darkness and put on the armor of light. 13Let us behave decently, as in the daytime, not in carousing and drunkenness, not in sexual immorality and debauchery, not in dissension and jealousy. 14Rather, clothe yourselves with the Lord Jesus Christ, and do not think about how to gratify the desires of the flesh.[c]

The Weak and the Strong

14 Accept the one whose faith is weak, without quarreling over disputable matters. 2One person's faith allows them to eat anything, but another, whose faith is weak, eats only vegetables. 3The one who eats everything must not treat with contempt the one who does not, and the one who does not eat everything must not judge the one who does, for God has accepted them. 4Who are you to judge someone else's servant? To their own master, servants stand or fall. And they will stand, for the Lord is able to make them stand.

5One person considers one day more sacred than another; another considers every day alike. Each of them should be fully convinced in their own mind. 6Whoever regards one day as special does so to the Lord. Whoever eats meat does so to the Lord, for they give thanks to God; and whoever abstains does so to the Lord and gives thanks to God. 7For none of us lives for ourselves alone, and none of us dies for ourselves alone. 8If we live, we live for the Lord; and if we die, we die for the Lord. So, whether we live or die, we belong to the Lord. 9For this very reason, Christ died and returned to life so that he might be the Lord of both the dead and the living.

10You, then, why do you judge your brother or sister[d]? Or why do you treat them with contempt? For we will all stand before God's judgment seat. 11It is written:

"'As surely as I live,' says the Lord,
'every knee will bow before me;
every tongue will acknowledge God.'"[e]

12So then, each of us will give an account of ourselves to God.

13Therefore let us stop passing judgment on one another. Instead, make up your mind not to put any stumbling block or obstacle in the way of a brother or sister. 14I am convinced, being fully persuaded in the Lord Jesus, that nothing is unclean in itself. But if anyone regards something as unclean, then for that person it is unclean. 15If your brother or sister is distressed because of what you eat, you are no longer acting in love. Do not by your eating destroy someone for whom Christ died. 16Therefore do not let what you know is good be spoken of as evil. 17For the kingdom of God is not a matter of eating and drinking, but of righteousness, peace and joy in the Holy Spirit, 18because anyone who serves Christ in this way is pleasing to God and receives human approval.

19Let us therefore make every effort to do what leads to peace and to mutual edification. 20Do not destroy the work of God for the sake of food. All food is clean, but it is wrong for a person to eat anything that causes someone else to stumble. 21It is better not to eat meat or drink wine or to do anything else that will cause your brother or sister to fall.

22So whatever you believe about these things keep between yourself and God. Blessed is the one who does not condemn himself by what he approves. 23But whoever has doubts is condemned if they eat, because

[a] *9* Exodus 20:13-15,17; Deut. 5:17-19,21 [b] *9* Lev. 19:18 [c] *14* In contexts like this, the Greek word for *flesh* (*sarx*) refers to the sinful state of human beings, often presented as a power in opposition to the Spirit. [d] *10* The Greek word for *brother or sister* (*adelphos*) refers here to a believer, whether man or woman, as part of God's family; also in verses 13, 15 and 21. [e] *11* Isaiah 45:23

their eating is not from faith; and everything
that does not come from faith is sin.[a]
15 We who are strong ought to bear with
the failings of the weak and not to
please ourselves. 2Each of us should please
our neighbors for their good, to build them up.
3For even Christ did not please himself but, as
it is written: "The insults of those who insult
you have fallen on me."[b] 4For everything that
was written in the past was written to teach
us, so that through the endurance taught in
the Scriptures and the encouragement they
provide we might have hope.
5May the God who gives endurance and
encouragement give you the same attitude
of mind toward each other that Christ Jesus
had, 6so that with one mind and one voice you
may glorify the God and Father of our Lord
Jesus Christ.
7Accept one another, then, just as Christ
accepted you, in order to bring praise to God.
8For I tell you that Christ has become a servant of the Jews[c] on behalf of God's truth,
so that the promises made to the patriarchs
might be confirmed 9and, moreover, that the
Gentiles might glorify God for his mercy. As
it is written:

"Therefore I will praise you among the
Gentiles;
I will sing the praises of your name."[d]

10Again, it says,

"Rejoice, you Gentiles, with his people."[e]

11And again,

"Praise the Lord, all you Gentiles;
let all the peoples extol him."[f]

12And again, Isaiah says,

"The Root of Jesse will spring up,
one who will arise to rule over the
nations;
in him the Gentiles will hope."[g]

13May the God of hope fill you with all joy
and peace as you trust in him, so that you
may overflow with hope by the power of the
Holy Spirit.

Paul the Minister to the Gentiles

14I myself am convinced, my brothers and
sisters, that you yourselves are full of goodness, filled with knowledge and competent
to instruct one another. 15Yet I have written
you quite boldly on some points to remind
you of them again, because of the grace God
gave me 16to be a minister of Christ Jesus to
the Gentiles. He gave me the priestly duty of
proclaiming the gospel of God, so that the
Gentiles might become an offering acceptable
to God, sanctified by the Holy Spirit.
17Therefore I glory in Christ Jesus in my
service to God. 18I will not venture to speak
of anything except what Christ has accomplished through me in leading the Gentiles to
obey God by what I have said and done— 19by
the power of signs and wonders, through the
power of the Spirit of God. So from Jerusalem
all the way around to Illyricum, I have fully
proclaimed the gospel of Christ. 20It has always been my ambition to preach the gospel
where Christ was not known, so that I would
not be building on someone else's foundation.
21Rather, as it is written:

"Those who were not told about him will
see,
and those who have not heard will
understand."[h]

22This is why I have often been hindered from
coming to you.

Paul's Plan to Visit Rome

23But now that there is no more place for
me to work in these regions, and since I have
been longing for many years to visit you, 24I
plan to do so when I go to Spain. I hope to see
you while passing through and to have you
assist me on my journey there, after I have
enjoyed your company for a while. 25Now,
however, I am on my way to Jerusalem in
the service of the Lord's people there. 26For
Macedonia and Achaia were pleased to make
a contribution for the poor among the Lord's
people in Jerusalem. 27They were pleased to
do it, and indeed they owe it to them. For if
the Gentiles have shared in the Jews' spiritual blessings, they owe it to the Jews to share
with them their material blessings. 28So after
I have completed this task and have made
sure that they have received this contribution, I will go to Spain and visit you on the
way. 29I know that when I come to you, I will
come in the full measure of the blessing of
Christ.
30I urge you, brothers and sisters, by our
Lord Jesus Christ and by the love of the Spirit,
to join me in my struggle by praying to God
for me. 31Pray that I may be kept safe from
the unbelievers in Judea and that the contribution I take to Jerusalem may be favorably
received by the Lord's people there, 32so that
I may come to you with joy, by God's will, and
in your company be refreshed. 33The God of
peace be with you all. Amen.

Personal Greetings

16 I commend to you our sister Phoebe, a
deacon[i,j] of the church in Cenchreae. 2I
ask you to receive her in the Lord in a way
worthy of his people and to give her any help
she may need from you, for she has been the
benefactor of many people, including me.

3Greet Priscilla[k] and Aquila, my co-workers
in Christ Jesus. 4They risked their lives

[a] *23* Some manuscripts place 16:25-27 here; others after 15:33. [b] *3* Psalm 69:9 [c] *8* Greek *circumcision* [d] *9* 2 Samuel 22:50; Psalm 18:49 [e] *10* Deut. 32:43 [f] *11* Psalm 117:1 [g] *12* Isaiah 11:10 (see Septuagint) [h] *21* Isaiah 52:15 (see Septuagint) [i] *1* Or *servant* [j] *1* The word *deacon* refers here to a Christian designated to serve with the overseers/elders of the church in a variety of ways; similarly in Phil. 1:1 and 1 Tim. 3:8,12. [k] *3* Greek *Prisca*, a variant of *Priscilla*

for me. Not only I but all the churches of
the Gentiles are grateful to them.
5 Greet also the church that meets at their
house.
Greet my dear friend Epenetus, who was
the first convert to Christ in the province
of Asia.
6 Greet Mary, who worked very hard for you.
7 Greet Andronicus and Junia, my fellow
Jews who have been in prison with me.
They are outstanding among[a] the apostles, and they were in Christ before I was.
8 Greet Ampliatus, my dear friend in the
Lord.
9 Greet Urbanus, our co-worker in Christ, and
my dear friend Stachys.
10 Greet Apelles, whose fidelity to Christ has
stood the test.
Greet those who belong to the household of
Aristobulus.
11 Greet Herodion, my fellow Jew.
Greet those in the household of Narcissus
who are in the Lord.
12 Greet Tryphena and Tryphosa, those wom-
en who work hard in the Lord.
Greet my dear friend Persis, another woman who has worked very hard in the Lord.
13 Greet Rufus, chosen in the Lord, and his
mother, who has been a mother to me,
too.
14 Greet Asyncritus, Phlegon, Hermes, Patro-
bas, Hermas and the other brothers and
sisters with them.
15 Greet Philologus, Julia, Nereus and his sister, and Olympas and all the Lord's people
who are with them.
16 Greet one another with a holy kiss.
All the churches of Christ send greetings.

17 I urge you, brothers and sisters, to watch
out for those who cause divisions and put
obstacles in your way that are contrary to
the teaching you have learned. Keep away
from them. 18 For such people are not serving our Lord Christ, but their own appetites.
By smooth talk and flattery they deceive the
minds of naive people. 19 Everyone has heard
about your obedience, so I rejoice because of
you; but I want you to be wise about what is
good, and innocent about what is evil.
20 The God of peace will soon crush Satan
under your feet.
The grace of our Lord Jesus be with you.
21 Timothy, my co-worker, sends his greetings to you, as do Lucius, Jason and Sosipater,
my fellow Jews.
22 I, Tertius, who wrote down this letter,
greet you in the Lord.
23 Gaius, whose hospitality I and the whole
church here enjoy, sends you his greetings.
Erastus, who is the city's director of public works, and our brother Quartus send you
their greetings. [24][b]

25 Now to him who is able to establish you
in accordance with my gospel, the message
I proclaim about Jesus Christ, in keeping
with the revelation of the mystery hidden
for long ages past, 26 but now revealed and
made known through the prophetic writings
by the command of the eternal God, so that
all the Gentiles might come to the obedience
that comes from[c] faith— 27 to the only wise
God be glory forever through Jesus Christ!
Amen.

1 Corinthians

1 Paul, called to be an apostle of Christ Jesus
by the will of God, and our brother Sosthenes,

2 To the church of God in Corinth, to those
sanctified in Christ Jesus and called to be
his holy people, together with all those everywhere who call on the name of our Lord
Jesus Christ—their Lord and ours:

3 Grace and peace to you from God our Father and the Lord Jesus Christ.

Thanksgiving

4 I always thank my God for you because of
his grace given you in Christ Jesus. 5 For in
him you have been enriched in every way—
with all kinds of speech and with all knowledge— 6 God thus confirming our testimony
about Christ among you. 7 Therefore you do
not lack any spiritual gift as you eagerly wait
for our Lord Jesus Christ to be revealed. 8 He
will also keep you firm to the end, so that
you will be blameless on the day of our Lord
Jesus Christ. 9 God is faithful, who has called
you into fellowship with his Son, Jesus Christ
our Lord.

A Church Divided Over Leaders

10 I appeal to you, brothers and sisters,[d] in
the name of our Lord Jesus Christ, that all
of you agree with one another in what you
say and that there be no divisions among

[a] 7 Or *are esteemed by* [b] 24 Some manuscripts include here *May the grace of our Lord Jesus Christ be with all of you. Amen.* [c] 26 Or *that is* [d] 10 The Greek word for *brothers and sisters* (*adelphoi*) refers here to believers, both men and women, as part of God's family; also in verses 11 and 26; and in 2:1; 3:1; 4:6; 6:8; 7:24, 29; 10:1; 11:33; 12:1; 14:6, 20, 26, 39; 15:1, 6, 50, 58; 16:15, 20.

you, but that you be perfectly united in mind and thought. 11My brothers and sisters, some from Chloe's household have informed me that there are quarrels among you. 12What I mean is this: One of you says, "I follow Paul"; another, "I follow Apollos"; another, "I follow Cephas[a]"; still another, "I follow Christ."

13Is Christ divided? Was Paul crucified for you? Were you baptized in the name of Paul? 14I thank God that I did not baptize any of you except Crispus and Gaius, 15so no one can say that you were baptized in my name. 16(Yes, I also baptized the household of Stephanas; beyond that, I don't remember if I baptized anyone else.) 17For Christ did not send me to baptize, but to preach the gospel—not with wisdom and eloquence, lest the cross of Christ be emptied of its power.

Christ Crucified Is God's Power and Wisdom

18For the message of the cross is foolishness to those who are perishing, but to us who are being saved it is the power of God. 19For it is written:

> "I will destroy the wisdom of the wise;
> the intelligence of the intelligent I will frustrate."[b]

20Where is the wise person? Where is the teacher of the law? Where is the philosopher of this age? Has not God made foolish the wisdom of the world? 21For since in the wisdom of God the world through its wisdom did not know him, God was pleased through the foolishness of what was preached to save those who believe. 22Jews demand signs and Greeks look for wisdom, 23but we preach Christ crucified: a stumbling block to Jews and foolishness to Gentiles, 24but to those whom God has called, both Jews and Greeks, Christ the power of God and the wisdom of God. 25For the foolishness of God is wiser than human wisdom, and the weakness of God is stronger than human strength.

26Brothers and sisters, think of what you were when you were called. Not many of you were wise by human standards; not many were influential; not many were of noble birth. 27But God chose the foolish things of the world to shame the wise; God chose the weak things of the world to shame the strong. 28God chose the lowly things of this world and the despised things—and the things that are not—to nullify the things that are, 29so that no one may boast before him. 30It is because of him that you are in Christ Jesus, who has become for us wisdom from God—that is, our righteousness, holiness and redemption. 31Therefore, as it is written: "Let the one who boasts boast in the Lord."[c]

2 And so it was with me, brothers and sisters. When I came to you, I did not come with eloquence or human wisdom as I proclaimed to you the testimony about God.[d] 2For I resolved to know nothing while I was with you except Jesus Christ and him crucified. 3I came to you in weakness with great fear and trembling. 4My message and my preaching were not with wise and persuasive words, but with a demonstration of the Spirit's power, 5so that your faith might not rest on human wisdom, but on God's power.

God's Wisdom Revealed by the Spirit

6We do, however, speak a message of wisdom among the mature, but not the wisdom of this age or of the rulers of this age, who are coming to nothing. 7No, we declare God's wisdom, a mystery that has been hidden and that God destined for our glory before time began. 8None of the rulers of this age understood it, for if they had, they would not have crucified the Lord of glory. 9However, as it is written:

> "What no eye has seen,
> what no ear has heard,
> and what no human mind has conceived"[e]—
> the things God has prepared for those who love him—

10these are the things God has revealed to us by his Spirit.

The Spirit searches all things, even the deep things of God. 11For who knows a person's thoughts except their own spirit within them? In the same way no one knows the thoughts of God except the Spirit of God. 12What we have received is not the spirit of the world, but the Spirit who is from God, so that we may understand what God has freely given us. 13This is what we speak, not in words taught us by human wisdom but in words taught by the Spirit, explaining spiritual realities with Spirit-taught words.[f] 14The person without the Spirit does not accept the things that come from the Spirit of God but considers them foolishness, and cannot understand them because they are discerned only through the Spirit. 15The person with the Spirit makes judgments about all things, but such a person is not subject to merely human judgments, 16for,

> "Who has known the mind of the Lord
> so as to instruct him?"[g]

But we have the mind of Christ.

The Church and Its Leaders

3 Brothers and sisters, I could not address you as people who live by the Spirit but as people who are still worldly—mere infants in Christ. 2I gave you milk, not solid food, for you were not yet ready for it. Indeed, you are still not ready. 3You are still worldly. For since there is jealousy and quarreling among you, are you not worldly? Are you not acting like mere humans? 4For when one says, "I follow Paul," and another, "I follow Apollos," are you not mere human beings?

5What, after all, is Apollos? And what is Paul? Only servants, through whom you came

a *12* That is, Peter *b* *19* Isaiah 29:14 *c* *31* Jer. 9:24 *d* *1* Some manuscripts *proclaimed to you God's mystery* *e* *9* Isaiah 64:4 *f* *13* Or *Spirit, interpreting spiritual truths to those who are spiritual* *g* *16* Isaiah 40:13

to believe—as the Lord has assigned to each his task. 6I planted the seed, Apollos watered it, but God has been making it grow. 7So neither the one who plants nor the one who waters is anything, but only God, who makes things grow. 8The one who plants and the one who waters have one purpose, and they will each be rewarded according to their own labor. 9For we are co-workers in God's service; you are God's field, God's building.

10By the grace God has given me, I laid a foundation as a wise builder, and someone else is building on it. But each one should build with care. 11For no one can lay any foundation other than the one already laid, which is Jesus Christ. 12If anyone builds on this foundation using gold, silver, costly stones, wood, hay or straw, 13their work will be shown for what it is, because the Day will bring it to light. It will be revealed with fire, and the fire will test the quality of each person's work. 14If what has been built survives, the builder will receive a reward. 15If it is burned up, the builder will suffer loss but yet will be saved—even though only as one escaping through the flames.

16Don't you know that you yourselves are God's temple and that God's Spirit dwells in your midst? 17If anyone destroys God's temple, God will destroy that person; for God's temple is sacred, and you together are that temple.

18Do not deceive yourselves. If any of you think you are wise by the standards of this age, you should become "fools" so that you may become wise. 19For the wisdom of this world is foolishness in God's sight. As it is written: "He catches the wise in their craftiness"[a]; 20and again, "The Lord knows that the thoughts of the wise are futile."[b] 21So then, no more boasting about human leaders! All things are yours, 22whether Paul or Apollos or Cephas[c] or the world or life or death or the present or the future—all are yours, 23and you are of Christ, and Christ is of God.

The Nature of True Apostleship

4 This, then, is how you ought to regard us: as servants of Christ and as those entrusted with the mysteries God has revealed. 2Now it is required that those who have been given a trust must prove faithful. 3I care very little if I am judged by you or by any human court; indeed, I do not even judge myself. 4My conscience is clear, but that does not make me innocent. It is the Lord who judges me. 5Therefore judge nothing before the appointed time; wait until the Lord comes. He will bring to light what is hidden in darkness and will expose the motives of the heart. At that time each will receive their praise from God.

6Now, brothers and sisters, I have applied these things to myself and Apollos for your benefit, so that you may learn from us the meaning of the saying, "Do not go beyond what is written." Then you will not be puffed up in being a follower of one of us over against the other. 7For who makes you different from anyone else? What do you have that you did not receive? And if you did receive it, why do you boast as though you did not?

8Already you have all you want! Already you have become rich! You have begun to reign—and that without us! How I wish that you really had begun to reign so that we also might reign with you! 9For it seems to me that God has put us apostles on display at the end of the procession, like those condemned to die in the arena. We have been made a spectacle to the whole universe, to angels as well as to human beings. 10We are fools for Christ, but you are so wise in Christ! We are weak, but you are strong! You are honored, we are dishonored! 11To this very hour we go hungry and thirsty, we are in rags, we are brutally treated, we are homeless. 12We work hard with our own hands. When we are cursed, we bless; when we are persecuted, we endure it; 13when we are slandered, we answer kindly. We have become the scum of the earth, the garbage of the world—right up to this moment.

Paul's Appeal and Warning

14I am writing this not to shame you but to warn you as my dear children. 15Even if you had ten thousand guardians in Christ, you do not have many fathers, for in Christ Jesus I became your father through the gospel. 16Therefore I urge you to imitate me. 17For this reason I have sent to you Timothy, my son whom I love, who is faithful in the Lord. He will remind you of my way of life in Christ Jesus, which agrees with what I teach everywhere in every church.

18Some of you have become arrogant, as if I were not coming to you. 19But I will come to you very soon, if the Lord is willing, and then I will find out not only how these arrogant people are talking, but what power they have. 20For the kingdom of God is not a matter of talk but of power. 21What do you prefer? Shall I come to you with a rod of discipline, or shall I come in love and with a gentle spirit?

Dealing With a Case of Incest

5 It is actually reported that there is sexual immorality among you, and of a kind that even pagans do not tolerate: A man is sleeping with his father's wife. 2And you are proud! Shouldn't you rather have gone into mourning and have put out of your fellowship the man who has been doing this? 3For my part, even though I am not physically present, I am with you in spirit. As one who is present with you in this way, I have already passed judgment in the name of our Lord Jesus on the one who has been doing this. 4So when you are assembled and I am with you in spirit, and the power of our Lord Jesus is present, 5hand this man over to Satan for the destruction of the flesh,[d,e] so that his spirit may be saved on the day of the Lord.

[a] *19* Job 5:13 [b] *20* Psalm 94:11 [c] *22* That is, Peter [d] *5* In contexts like this, the Greek word for *flesh* (*sarx*) refers to the sinful state of human beings, often presented as a power in opposition to the Spirit. [e] *5* Or *of his body*

6Your boasting is not good. Don't you know
that a little yeast leavens the whole batch of
dough? 7Get rid of the old yeast, so that you
may be a new unleavened batch—as you really are. For Christ, our Passover lamb, has been
sacrificed. 8Therefore let us keep the Festival,
not with the old bread leavened with malice
and wickedness, but with the unleavened
bread of sincerity and truth.
9I wrote to you in my letter not to associate with sexually immoral people— 10not at
all meaning the people of this world who are
immoral, or the greedy and swindlers, or idolaters. In that case you would have to leave this
world. 11But now I am writing to you that you
must not associate with anyone who claims to
be a brother or sister[a] but is sexually immoral
or greedy, an idolater or slanderer, a drunkard
or swindler. Do not even eat with such people.
12What business is it of mine to judge those
outside the church? Are you not to judge those
inside? 13God will judge those outside. "Expel
the wicked person from among you."[b]

Lawsuits Among Believers

6 If any of you has a dispute with another, do
you dare to take it before the ungodly for
judgment instead of before the Lord's people?
2Or do you not know that the Lord's people
will judge the world? And if you are to judge
the world, are you not competent to judge trivial cases? 3Do you not know that we will judge
angels? How much more the things of this life!
4Therefore, if you have disputes about such
matters, do you ask for a ruling from those
whose way of life is scorned in the church? 5I
say this to shame you. Is it possible that there
is nobody among you wise enough to judge a
dispute between believers? 6But instead, one
brother takes another to court—and this in
front of unbelievers!
7The very fact that you have lawsuits among
you means you have been completely defeated
already. Why not rather be wronged? Why not
rather be cheated? 8Instead, you yourselves
cheat and do wrong, and you do this to your
brothers and sisters. 9Or do you not know that
wrongdoers will not inherit the kingdom of
God? Do not be deceived: Neither the sexually immoral nor idolaters nor adulterers nor
men who have sex with men[c] 10nor thieves nor
the greedy nor drunkards nor slanderers nor
swindlers will inherit the kingdom of God.
11And that is what some of you were. But you
were washed, you were sanctified, you were
justified in the name of the Lord Jesus Christ
and by the Spirit of our God.

Sexual Immorality

12"I have the right to do anything," you
say—but not everything is beneficial. "I have
the right to do anything"—but I will not be
mastered by anything. 13You say, "Food for the
stomach and the stomach for food, and God
will destroy them both." The body, however,
is not meant for sexual immorality but for
the Lord, and the Lord for the body. 14By his
power God raised the Lord from the dead, and
he will raise us also. 15Do you not know that
your bodies are members of Christ himself?
Shall I then take the members of Christ and
unite them with a prostitute? Never! 16Do you
not know that he who unites himself with a
prostitute is one with her in body? For it is
said, "The two will become one flesh."[d] 17But
whoever is united with the Lord is one with
him in spirit.[e]
18Flee from sexual immorality. All other
sins a person commits are outside the body,
but whoever sins sexually, sins against their
own body. 19Do you not know that your bodies
are temples of the Holy Spirit, who is in you,
whom you have received from God? You are
not your own; 20you were bought at a price.
Therefore honor God with your bodies.

Concerning Married Life

7 Now for the matters you wrote about: "It
is good for a man not to have sexual relations with a woman." 2But since sexual immorality is occurring, each man should have
sexual relations with his own wife, and each
woman with her own husband. 3The husband
should fulfill his marital duty to his wife, and
likewise the wife to her husband. 4The wife
does not have authority over her own body
but yields it to her husband. In the same way,
the husband does not have authority over his
own body but yields it to his wife. 5Do not
deprive each other except perhaps by mutual consent and for a time, so that you may
devote yourselves to prayer. Then come together again so that Satan will not tempt you
because of your lack of self-control. 6I say
this as a concession, not as a command. 7I
wish that all of you were as I am. But each
of you has your own gift from God; one has
this gift, another has that.
8Now to the unmarried[f] and the widows I
say: It is good for them to stay unmarried, as
I do. 9But if they cannot control themselves,
they should marry, for it is better to marry
than to burn with passion.
10To the married I give this command (not I,
but the Lord): A wife must not separate from
her husband. 11But if she does, she must remain unmarried or else be reconciled to her
husband. And a husband must not divorce
his wife.
12To the rest I say this (I, not the Lord): If
any brother has a wife who is not a believer
and she is willing to live with him, he must
not divorce her. 13And if a woman has a husband who is not a believer and he is willing to
live with her, she must not divorce him. 14For
the unbelieving husband has been sanctified
through his wife, and the unbelieving wife
has been sanctified through her believing

[a] *11* The Greek word for *brother or sister* (*adelphos*) refers here to a believer, whether man or woman, as part of God's family; also in 8:11, 13. [b] *13* Deut. 13:5; 17:7; 19:19; 21:21; 22:21,24; 24:7 [c] *9* The words *men who have sex with men* translate two Greek words that refer to the passive and active participants in homosexual acts. [d] *16* Gen. 2:24 [e] *17* Or *in the Spirit* [f] *8* Or *widowers*

husband. Otherwise your children would be unclean, but as it is, they are holy.

[15]But if the unbeliever leaves, let it be so. The brother or the sister is not bound in such circumstances; God has called us to live in peace. [16]How do you know, wife, whether you will save your husband? Or, how do you know, husband, whether you will save your wife?

Concerning Change of Status

[17]Nevertheless, each person should live as a believer in whatever situation the Lord has assigned to them, just as God has called them. This is the rule I lay down in all the churches. [18]Was a man already circumcised when he was called? He should not become uncircumcised. Was a man uncircumcised when he was called? He should not be circumcised. [19]Circumcision is nothing and uncircumcision is nothing. Keeping God's commands is what counts. [20]Each person should remain in the situation they were in when God called them.

[21]Were you a slave when you were called? Don't let it trouble you—although if you can gain your freedom, do so. [22]For the one who was a slave when called to faith in the Lord is the Lord's freed person; similarly, the one who was free when called is Christ's slave. [23]You were bought at a price; do not become slaves of human beings. [24]Brothers and sisters, each person, as responsible to God, should remain in the situation they were in when God called them.

Concerning the Unmarried

[25]Now about virgins: I have no command from the Lord, but I give a judgment as one who by the Lord's mercy is trustworthy. [26]Because of the present crisis, I think that it is good for a man to remain as he is. [27]Are you pledged to a woman? Do not seek to be released. Are you free from such a commitment? Do not look for a wife. [28]But if you do marry, you have not sinned; and if a virgin marries, she has not sinned. But those who marry will face many troubles in this life, and I want to spare you this.

[29]What I mean, brothers and sisters, is that the time is short. From now on those who have wives should live as if they do not; [30]those who mourn, as if they did not; those who are happy, as if they were not; those who buy something, as if it were not theirs to keep; [31]those who use the things of the world, as if not engrossed in them. For this world in its present form is passing away.

[32]I would like you to be free from concern. An unmarried man is concerned about the Lord's affairs—how he can please the Lord. [33]But a married man is concerned about the affairs of this world—how he can please his wife— [34]and his interests are divided. An unmarried woman or virgin is concerned about the Lord's affairs: Her aim is to be devoted to the Lord in both body and spirit. But a married woman is concerned about the affairs of this world—how she can please her husband. [35]I am saying this for your own good, not to restrict you, but that you may live in a right way in undivided devotion to the Lord.

[36]If anyone is worried that he might not be acting honorably toward the virgin he is engaged to, and if his passions are too strong[a] and he feels he ought to marry, he should do as he wants. He is not sinning. They should get married. [37]But the man who has settled the matter in his own mind, who is under no compulsion but has control over his own will, and who has made up his mind not to marry the virgin—this man also does the right thing. [38]So then, he who marries the virgin does right, but he who does not marry her does better.[b]

[39]A woman is bound to her husband as long as he lives. But if her husband dies, she is free to marry anyone she wishes, but he must belong to the Lord. [40]In my judgment, she is happier if she stays as she is—and I think that I too have the Spirit of God.

Concerning Food Sacrificed to Idols

8 Now about food sacrificed to idols: We know that "We all possess knowledge." But knowledge puffs up while love builds up. [2]Those who think they know something do not yet know as they ought to know. [3]But whoever loves God is known by God.[c]

[4]So then, about eating food sacrificed to idols: We know that "An idol is nothing at all in the world" and that "There is no God but one." [5]For even if there are so-called gods, whether in heaven or on earth (as indeed there are many "gods" and many "lords"), [6]yet for us there is but one God, the Father, from whom all things came and for whom we live; and there is but one Lord, Jesus Christ, through whom all things came and through whom we live.

[7]But not everyone possesses this knowledge. Some people are still so accustomed to idols that when they eat sacrificial food they think of it as having been sacrificed to a god, and since their conscience is weak, it is defiled. [8]But food does not bring us near to God; we are no worse if we do not eat, and no better if we do.

[9]Be careful, however, that the exercise of your rights does not become a stumbling block to the weak. [10]For if someone with a weak conscience sees you, with all your

[a] 36 Or *if she is getting beyond the usual age for marriage* [b] 36-38 Or [36]*If anyone thinks he is not treating his daughter properly, and if she is getting along in years* (or *if her passions are too strong*), *and he feels she ought to marry, he should do as he wants. He is not sinning. He should let her get married.* [37]*But the man who has settled the matter in his own mind, who is under no compulsion but has control over his own will, and who has made up his mind to keep the virgin unmarried—this man also does the right thing.* [38]*So then, he who gives his virgin in marriage does right, but he who does not give her in marriage does better.* [c] 2,3 An early manuscript and another ancient witness *think they have knowledge do not yet know as they ought to know.* [3]*But whoever loves truly knows.*

knowledge, eating in an idol's temple, won't
that person be emboldened to eat what is sacrificed to idols? 11So this weak brother or sister, for whom Christ died, is destroyed by your
knowledge. 12When you sin against them in
this way and wound their weak conscience,
you sin against Christ. 13Therefore, if what I
eat causes my brother or sister to fall into sin,
I will never eat meat again, so that I will not
cause them to fall.

Paul's Rights as an Apostle

9 Am I not free? Am I not an apostle? Have
I not seen Jesus our Lord? Are you not the
result of my work in the Lord? 2Even though
I may not be an apostle to others, surely I am
to you! For you are the seal of my apostleship
in the Lord.

3This is my defense to those who sit in judgment on me. 4Don't we have the right to food
and drink? 5Don't we have the right to take a
believing wife along with us, as do the other
apostles and the Lord's brothers and Cephas[a]?
6Or is it only I and Barnabas who lack the
right to not work for a living?

7Who serves as a soldier at his own expense? Who plants a vineyard and does not
eat its grapes? Who tends a flock and does
not drink the milk? 8Do I say this merely
on human authority? Doesn't the Law say
the same thing? 9For it is written in the Law
of Moses: "Do not muzzle an ox while it is
treading out the grain."[b] Is it about oxen that
God is concerned? 10Surely he says this for
us, doesn't he? Yes, this was written for us,
because whoever plows and threshes should
be able to do so in the hope of sharing in
the harvest. 11If we have sown spiritual seed
among you, is it too much if we reap a material harvest from you? 12If others have this
right of support from you, shouldn't we have
it all the more?

But we did not use this right. On the contrary, we put up with anything rather than
hinder the gospel of Christ.

13Don't you know that those who serve in
the temple get their food from the temple, and
that those who serve at the altar share in what
is offered on the altar? 14In the same way, the
Lord has commanded that those who preach
the gospel should receive their living from
the gospel.

15But I have not used any of these rights.
And I am not writing this in the hope that
you will do such things for me, for I would
rather die than allow anyone to deprive me
of this boast. 16For when I preach the gospel, I cannot boast, since I am compelled to
preach. Woe to me if I do not preach the gospel! 17If I preach voluntarily, I have a reward;
if not voluntarily, I am simply discharging
the trust committed to me. 18What then is
my reward? Just this: that in preaching the
gospel I may offer it free of charge, and so
not make full use of my rights as a preacher
of the gospel.

Paul's Use of His Freedom

19Though I am free and belong to no one, I
have made myself a slave to everyone, to win
as many as possible. 20To the Jews I became
like a Jew, to win the Jews. To those under the
law I became like one under the law (though
I myself am not under the law), so as to win
those under the law. 21To those not having
the law I became like one not having the law
(though I am not free from God's law but am
under Christ's law), so as to win those not having the law. 22To the weak I became weak, to
win the weak. I have become all things to all
people so that by all possible means I might
save some. 23I do all this for the sake of the
gospel, that I may share in its blessings.

The Need for Self-Discipline

24Do you not know that in a race all the
runners run, but only one gets the prize? Run
in such a way as to get the prize. 25Everyone
who competes in the games goes into strict
training. They do it to get a crown that will not
last, but we do it to get a crown that will last
forever. 26Therefore I do not run like someone running aimlessly; I do not fight like a
boxer beating the air. 27No, I strike a blow to
my body and make it my slave so that after I
have preached to others, I myself will not be
disqualified for the prize.

Warnings From Israel's History

10 For I do not want you to be ignorant of
the fact, brothers and sisters, that our
ancestors were all under the cloud and that
they all passed through the sea. 2They were
all baptized into Moses in the cloud and in the
sea. 3They all ate the same spiritual food 4and
drank the same spiritual drink; for they drank
from the spiritual rock that accompanied
them, and that rock was Christ. 5Neverthe-
less, God was not pleased with most of them;
their bodies were scattered in the wilderness.

6Now these things occurred as examples to
keep us from setting our hearts on evil things
as they did. 7Do not be idolaters, as some of
them were; as it is written: "The people sat
down to eat and drink and got up to indulge
in revelry."[c] 8We should not commit sexual
immorality, as some of them did—and in one
day twenty-three thousand of them died. 9We
should not test Christ,[d] as some of them did—
and were killed by snakes. 10And do not grumble, as some of them did—and were killed by
the destroying angel.

11These things happened to them as examples and were written down as warnings for
us, on whom the culmination of the ages has
come. 12So, if you think you are standing firm,
be careful that you don't fall! 13No temptation[e]
has overtaken you except what is common to
mankind. And God is faithful; he will not let
you be tempted[e] beyond what you can bear.
But when you are tempted,[e] he will also provide a way out so that you can endure it.

[a] 5 That is, Peter [b] 9 Deut. 25:4 [c] 7 Exodus 32:6 [d] 9 Some manuscripts *test the Lord*
[e] *13* The Greek for *temptation* and *tempted* can also mean *testing* and *tested.*

Idol Feasts and the Lord's Supper

14 Therefore, my dear friends, flee from idolatry. 15 I speak to sensible people; judge for yourselves what I say. 16 Is not the cup of thanksgiving for which we give thanks a participation in the blood of Christ? And is not the bread that we break a participation in the body of Christ? 17 Because there is one loaf, we, who are many, are one body, for we all share the one loaf.

18 Consider the people of Israel: Do not those who eat the sacrifices participate in the altar? 19 Do I mean then that food sacrificed to an idol is anything, or that an idol is anything? 20 No, but the sacrifices of pagans are offered to demons, not to God, and I do not want you to be participants with demons. 21 You cannot drink the cup of the Lord and the cup of demons too; you cannot have a part in both the Lord's table and the table of demons. 22 Are we trying to arouse the Lord's jealousy? Are we stronger than he?

The Believer's Freedom

23 "I have the right to do anything," you say—but not everything is beneficial. "I have the right to do anything"—but not everything is constructive. 24 No one should seek their own good, but the good of others.

25 Eat anything sold in the meat market without raising questions of conscience, 26 for, "The earth is the Lord's, and everything in it."[a]

27 If an unbeliever invites you to a meal and you want to go, eat whatever is put before you without raising questions of conscience. 28 But if someone says to you, "This has been offered in sacrifice," then do not eat it, both for the sake of the one who told you and for the sake of conscience. 29 I am referring to the other person's conscience, not yours. For why is my freedom being judged by another's conscience? 30 If I take part in the meal with thankfulness, why am I denounced because of something I thank God for?

31 So whether you eat or drink or whatever you do, do it all for the glory of God. 32 Do not cause anyone to stumble, whether Jews, Greeks or the church of God— 33 even as I try to please everyone in every way. For I am not seeking my own good but the good of many, so that they may be saved.

11 1 Follow my example, as I follow the example of Christ.

On Covering the Head in Worship

2 I praise you for remembering me in everything and for holding to the traditions just as I passed them on to you. 3 But I want you to realize that the head of every man is Christ, and the head of the woman is man,[b] and the head of Christ is God. 4 Every man who prays or prophesies with his head covered dishonors his head. 5 But every woman who prays or prophesies with her head uncovered dishonors her head—it is the same as having her head shaved. 6 For if a woman does not cover her head, she might as well have her hair cut off; but if it is a disgrace for a woman to have her hair cut off or her head shaved, then she should cover her head.

7 A man ought not to cover his head,[c] since he is the image and glory of God; but woman is the glory of man. 8 For man did not come from woman, but woman from man; 9 neither was man created for woman, but woman for man. 10 It is for this reason that a woman ought to have authority over her own[d] head, because of the angels. 11 Nevertheless, in the Lord woman is not independent of man, nor is man independent of woman. 12 For as woman came from man, so also man is born of woman. But everything comes from God.

13 Judge for yourselves: Is it proper for a woman to pray to God with her head uncovered? 14 Does not the very nature of things teach you that if a man has long hair, it is a disgrace to him, 15 but that if a woman has long hair, it is her glory? For long hair is given to her as a covering. 16 If anyone wants to be contentious about this, we have no other practice—nor do the churches of God.

Correcting an Abuse of the Lord's Supper

17 In the following directives I have no praise for you, for your meetings do more harm than good. 18 In the first place, I hear that when you come together as a church, there are divisions among you, and to some extent I believe it. 19 No doubt there have to be differences among you to show which of you have God's approval. 20 So then, when you come together, it is not the Lord's Supper you eat, 21 for when you are eating, some of you go ahead with your own private suppers. As a result, one person remains hungry and another gets drunk. 22 Don't you have homes to eat and drink in? Or do you despise the church of God by humiliating those who have nothing? What shall I say to you? Shall I praise you? Certainly not in this matter!

23 For I received from the Lord what I also passed on to you: The Lord Jesus, on the night he was betrayed, took bread, 24 and when he had given thanks, he broke it and said, "This is my body, which is for you; do this in remembrance of me." 25 In the same way, after supper he took the cup, saying, "This cup is the new covenant in my blood; do this, whenever you drink it, in remembrance of me." 26 For whenever you eat this bread and drink this cup, you proclaim the Lord's death until he comes.

27 So then, whoever eats the bread or drinks the cup of the Lord in an unworthy manner will be guilty of sinning against the body and blood of the Lord. 28 Everyone ought to examine themselves before they eat of the

[a] *26* Psalm 24:1 [b] *3* Or *of the wife is her husband* [c] *4-7* Or *4Every man who prays or prophesies with long hair dishonors his head. 5But every woman who prays or prophesies with no covering of hair dishonors her head—she is just like one of the "shorn women." 6If a woman has no covering, let her be for now with short hair; but since it is a disgrace for a woman to have her hair shorn or shaved, she should grow it again. 7A man ought not to have long hair* [d] *10* Or *have a sign of authority on her*

bread and drink from the cup. [29]For those who eat and drink without discerning the body of Christ eat and drink judgment on themselves. [30]That is why many among you are weak and sick, and a number of you have fallen asleep. [31]But if we were more discerning with regard to ourselves, we would not come under such judgment. [32]Nevertheless, when we are judged in this way by the Lord, we are being disciplined so that we will not be finally condemned with the world.

[33]So then, my brothers and sisters, when you gather to eat, you should all eat together. [34]Anyone who is hungry should eat something at home, so that when you meet together it may not result in judgment.

And when I come I will give further directions.

Concerning Spiritual Gifts

12 Now about the gifts of the Spirit, brothers and sisters, I do not want you to be uninformed. [2]You know that when you were pagans, somehow or other you were influenced and led astray to mute idols. [3]Therefore I want you to know that no one who is speaking by the Spirit of God says, "Jesus be cursed," and no one can say, "Jesus is Lord," except by the Holy Spirit.

[4]There are different kinds of gifts, but the same Spirit distributes them. [5]There are different kinds of service, but the same Lord. [6]There are different kinds of working, but in all of them and in everyone it is the same God at work.

[7]Now to each one the manifestation of the Spirit is given for the common good. [8]To one there is given through the Spirit a message of wisdom, to another a message of knowledge by means of the same Spirit, [9]to another faith by the same Spirit, to another gifts of healing by that one Spirit, [10]to another miraculous powers, to another prophecy, to another distinguishing between spirits, to another speaking in different kinds of tongues,[a] and to still another the interpretation of tongues.[a] [11]All these are the work of one and the same Spirit, and he distributes them to each one, just as he determines.

Unity and Diversity in the Body

[12]Just as a body, though one, has many parts, but all its many parts form one body, so it is with Christ. [13]For we were all baptized by[b] one Spirit so as to form one body—whether Jews or Gentiles, slave or free—and we were all given the one Spirit to drink. [14]Even so the body is not made up of one part but of many.

[15]Now if the foot should say, "Because I am not a hand, I do not belong to the body," it would not for that reason stop being part of the body. [16]And if the ear should say, "Because I am not an eye, I do not belong to the body," it would not for that reason stop being part of the body. [17]If the whole body were an eye, where would the sense of hearing be? If the whole body were an ear, where would the sense of smell be? [18]But in fact God has placed the parts in the body, every one of them, just as he wanted them to be. [19]If they were all one part, where would the body be? [20]As it is, there are many parts, but one body.

[21]The eye cannot say to the hand, "I don't need you!" And the head cannot say to the feet, "I don't need you!" [22]On the contrary, those parts of the body that seem to be weaker are indispensable, [23]and the parts that we think are less honorable we treat with special honor. And the parts that are unpresentable are treated with special modesty, [24]while our presentable parts need no special treatment. But God has put the body together, giving greater honor to the parts that lacked it, [25]so that there should be no division in the body, but that its parts should have equal concern for each other. [26]If one part suffers, every part suffers with it; if one part is honored, every part rejoices with it.

[27]Now you are the body of Christ, and each one of you is a part of it. [28]And God has placed in the church first of all apostles, second prophets, third teachers, then miracles, then gifts of healing, of helping, of guidance, and of different kinds of tongues. [29]Are all apostles? Are all prophets? Are all teachers? Do all work miracles? [30]Do all have gifts of healing? Do all speak in tongues[c]? Do all interpret? [31]Now eagerly desire the greater gifts.

Love Is Indispensable

And yet I will show you the most excellent way.

13 If I speak in the tongues[d] of men or of angels, but do not have love, I am only a resounding gong or a clanging cymbal. [2]If I have the gift of prophecy and can fathom all mysteries and all knowledge, and if I have a faith that can move mountains, but do not have love, I am nothing. [3]If I give all I possess to the poor and give over my body to hardship that I may boast,[e] but do not have love, I gain nothing.

[4]Love is patient, love is kind. It does not envy, it does not boast, it is not proud. [5]It does not dishonor others, it is not self-seeking, it is not easily angered, it keeps no record of wrongs. [6]Love does not delight in evil but rejoices with the truth. [7]It always protects, always trusts, always hopes, always perseveres.

[8]Love never fails. But where there are prophecies, they will cease; where there are tongues, they will be stilled; where there is knowledge, it will pass away. [9]For we know in part and we prophesy in part, [10]but when completeness comes, what is in part disappears. [11]When I was a child, I talked like a child, I thought like a child, I reasoned like a child. When I became a man, I put the ways of childhood behind me. [12]For now we see only a reflection as in a mirror; then we shall see face to face. Now I know in part; then I shall know fully, even as I am fully known.

[a] *10* Or *languages*; also in verse 28 [b] *13* Or *with*; or *in* [c] *30* Or *other languages*
[d] *1* Or *languages* [e] *3* Some manuscripts *body to the flames*

13And now these three remain: faith, hope and love. But the greatest of these is love.

Intelligibility in Worship

14 Follow the way of love and eagerly desire gifts of the Spirit, especially prophecy. 2For anyone who speaks in a tongue[a] does not speak to people but to God. Indeed, no one understands them; they utter mysteries by the Spirit. 3But the one who prophesies speaks to people for their strengthening, encouraging and comfort. 4Anyone who speaks in a tongue edifies themselves, but the one who prophesies edifies the church. 5I would like every one of you to speak in tongues,[b] but I would rather have you prophesy. The one who prophesies is greater than the one who speaks in tongues,[b] unless someone interprets, so that the church may be edified.

6Now, brothers and sisters, if I come to you and speak in tongues, what good will I be to you, unless I bring you some revelation or knowledge or prophecy or word of instruction? 7Even in the case of lifeless things that make sounds, such as the pipe or harp, how will anyone know what tune is being played unless there is a distinction in the notes? 8Again, if the trumpet does not sound a clear call, who will get ready for battle? 9So it is with you. Unless you speak intelligible words with your tongue, how will anyone know what you are saying? You will just be speaking into the air. 10Undoubtedly there are all sorts of languages in the world, yet none of them is without meaning. 11If then I do not grasp the meaning of what someone is saying, I am a foreigner to the speaker, and the speaker is a foreigner to me. 12So it is with you. Since you are eager for gifts of the Spirit, try to excel in those that build up the church.

13For this reason the one who speaks in a tongue should pray that they may interpret what they say. 14For if I pray in a tongue, my spirit prays, but my mind is unfruitful. 15So what shall I do? I will pray with my spirit, but I will also pray with my understanding; I will sing with my spirit, but I will also sing with my understanding. 16Otherwise when you are praising God in the Spirit, how can someone else, who is now put in the position of an inquirer,[c] say "Amen" to your thanksgiving, since they do not know what you are saying? 17You are giving thanks well enough, but no one else is edified.

18I thank God that I speak in tongues more than all of you. 19But in the church I would rather speak five intelligible words to instruct others than ten thousand words in a tongue.

20Brothers and sisters, stop thinking like children. In regard to evil be infants, but in your thinking be adults. 21In the Law it is written:

"With other tongues
  and through the lips of foreigners
I will speak to this people,
  but even then they will not listen to me,
    says the Lord."[d]

22Tongues, then, are a sign, not for believers but for unbelievers; prophecy, however, is not for unbelievers but for believers. 23So if the whole church comes together and everyone speaks in tongues, and inquirers or unbelievers come in, will they not say that you are out of your mind? 24But if an unbeliever or an inquirer comes in while everyone is prophesying, they are convicted of sin and are brought under judgment by all, 25as the secrets of their hearts are laid bare. So they will fall down and worship God, exclaiming, "God is really among you!"

Good Order in Worship

26What then shall we say, brothers and sisters? When you come together, each of you has a hymn, or a word of instruction, a revelation, a tongue or an interpretation. Everything must be done so that the church may be built up. 27If anyone speaks in a tongue, two—or at the most three—should speak, one at a time, and someone must interpret. 28If there is no interpreter, the speaker should keep quiet in the church and speak to himself and to God.

29Two or three prophets should speak, and the others should weigh carefully what is said. 30And if a revelation comes to someone who is sitting down, the first speaker should stop. 31For you can all prophesy in turn so that everyone may be instructed and encouraged. 32The spirits of prophets are subject to the control of prophets. 33For God is not a God of disorder but of peace—as in all the congregations of the Lord's people.

34Women[e] should remain silent in the churches. They are not allowed to speak, but must be in submission, as the law says. 35If they want to inquire about something, they should ask their own husbands at home; for it is disgraceful for a woman to speak in the church.[f]

36Or did the word of God originate with you? Or are you the only people it has reached? 37If anyone thinks they are a prophet or otherwise gifted by the Spirit, let them acknowledge that what I am writing to you is the Lord's command. 38But if anyone ignores this, they will themselves be ignored.[g]

39Therefore, my brothers and sisters, be eager to prophesy, and do not forbid speaking in tongues. 40But everything should be done in a fitting and orderly way.

The Resurrection of Christ

15 Now, brothers and sisters, I want to remind you of the gospel I preached to you, which you received and on which you have taken your stand. 2By this gospel you

[a] *2* Or *in another language*; also in verses 4, 13, 14, 19, 26 and 27 [b] *5* Or *in other languages*; also in verses 6, 18, 22, 23 and 39 [c] *16* The Greek word for *inquirer* is a technical term for someone not fully initiated into a religion; also in verses 23 and 24. [d] *21* Isaiah 28:11,12 [e] *33,34* Or *peace. As in all the congregations of the Lord's people, 34women* [f] *34,35* In a few manuscripts these verses come after verse 40. [g] *38* Some manuscripts *But anyone who is ignorant of this will be ignorant*

are saved, if you hold firmly to the word I
preached to you. Otherwise, you have believed
in vain.
3For what I received I passed on to you as
of first importance[a]: that Christ died for our
sins according to the Scriptures, 4that he was
buried, that he was raised on the third day
according to the Scriptures, 5and that he appeared to Cephas,[b] and then to the Twelve.
6After that, he appeared to more than five
hundred of the brothers and sisters at the
same time, most of whom are still living,
though some have fallen asleep. 7Then he
appeared to James, then to all the apostles,
8and last of all he appeared to me also, as to
one abnormally born.
9For I am the least of the apostles and do not
even deserve to be called an apostle, because
I persecuted the church of God. 10But by the
grace of God I am what I am, and his grace to
me was not without effect. No, I worked harder than all of them—yet not I, but the grace
of God that was with me. 11Whether, then, it
is I or they, this is what we preach, and this
is what you believed.

The Resurrection of the Dead

12But if it is preached that Christ has been
raised from the dead, how can some of you
say that there is no resurrection of the dead?
13If there is no resurrection of the dead, then
not even Christ has been raised. 14And if
Christ has not been raised, our preaching is
useless and so is your faith. 15More than that,
we are then found to be false witnesses about
God, for we have testified about God that he
raised Christ from the dead. But he did not
raise him if in fact the dead are not raised.
16For if the dead are not raised, then Christ
has not been raised either. 17And if Christ has
not been raised, your faith is futile; you are
still in your sins. 18Then those also who have
fallen asleep in Christ are lost. 19If only for
this life we have hope in Christ, we are of all
people most to be pitied.
20But Christ has indeed been raised from
the dead, the firstfruits of those who have fall-
en asleep. 21For since death came through a
man, the resurrection of the dead comes also
through a man. 22For as in Adam all die, so
in Christ all will be made alive. 23But each
in turn: Christ, the firstfruits; then, when he
comes, those who belong to him. 24Then the
end will come, when he hands over the kingdom to God the Father after he has destroyed
all dominion, authority and power. 25For he
must reign until he has put all his enemies under his feet. 26The last enemy to be destroyed
is death. 27For he "has put everything under
his feet."[c] Now when it says that "everything"
has been put under him, it is clear that this
does not include God himself, who put everything under Christ. 28When he has done this,
then the Son himself will be made subject to
him who put everything under him, so that
God may be all in all.
29Now if there is no resurrection, what will
those do who are baptized for the dead? If
the dead are not raised at all, why are people
baptized for them? 30And as for us, why do we
endanger ourselves every hour? 31I face death
every day—yes, just as surely as I boast about
you in Christ Jesus our Lord. 32If I fought wild
beasts in Ephesus with no more than human
hopes, what have I gained? If the dead are
not raised,

"Let us eat and drink,
for tomorrow we die."[d]

33Do not be misled: "Bad company corrupts
good character."[e] 34Come back to your senses
as you ought, and stop sinning; for there are
some who are ignorant of God—I say this to
your shame.

The Resurrection Body

35But someone will ask, "How are the
dead raised? With what kind of body will
they come?" 36How foolish! What you sow
does not come to life unless it dies. 37When
you sow, you do not plant the body that will
be, but just a seed, perhaps of wheat or of
something else. 38But God gives it a body as
he has determined, and to each kind of seed
he gives its own body. 39Not all flesh is the
same: People have one kind of flesh, animals
have another, birds another and fish another.
40There are also heavenly bodies and there
are earthly bodies; but the splendor of the
heavenly bodies is one kind, and the splendor
of the earthly bodies is another. 41The sun
has one kind of splendor, the moon another
and the stars another; and star differs from
star in splendor.
42So will it be with the resurrection of the
dead. The body that is sown is perishable, it is
raised imperishable; 43it is sown in dishonor,
it is raised in glory; it is sown in weakness, it
is raised in power; 44it is sown a natural body,
it is raised a spiritual body.
If there is a natural body, there is also a
spiritual body. 45So it is written: "The first
man Adam became a living being"[f]; the last
Adam, a life-giving spirit. 46The spiritual did
not come first, but the natural, and after that
the spiritual. 47The first man was of the dust
of the earth; the second man is of heaven. 48As
was the earthly man, so are those who are of
the earth; and as is the heavenly man, so also
are those who are of heaven. 49And just as we
have borne the image of the earthly man, so
shall we[g] bear the image of the heavenly man.
50I declare to you, brothers and sisters, that
flesh and blood cannot inherit the kingdom of
God, nor does the perishable inherit the imperishable. 51Listen, I tell you a mystery: We
will not all sleep, but we will all be changed—
52in a flash, in the twinkling of an eye, at the
last trumpet. For the trumpet will sound, the
dead will be raised imperishable, and we will
be changed. 53For the perishable must clothe
itself with the imperishable, and the mortal

[a] *3* Or *you at the first* [b] *5* That is, Peter [c] *27* Psalm 8:6 [d] *32* Isaiah 22:13 [e] *33* From the Greek poet Menander [f] *45* Gen. 2:7 [g] *49* Some early manuscripts *so let us*

with immortality. 54When the perishable has been clothed with the imperishable, and the mortal with immortality, then the saying that is written will come true: "Death has been swallowed up in victory."[a]

55"Where, O death, is your victory?
Where, O death, is your sting?"[b]

56The sting of death is sin, and the power of sin is the law. 57But thanks be to God! He gives us the victory through our Lord Jesus Christ.

58Therefore, my dear brothers and sisters, stand firm. Let nothing move you. Always give yourselves fully to the work of the Lord, because you know that your labor in the Lord is not in vain.

The Collection for the Lord's People

16 Now about the collection for the Lord's people: Do what I told the Galatian churches to do. 2On the first day of every week, each one of you should set aside a sum of money in keeping with your income, saving it up, so that when I come no collections will have to be made. 3Then, when I arrive, I will give letters of introduction to the men you approve and send them with your gift to Jerusalem. 4If it seems advisable for me to go also, they will accompany me.

Personal Requests

5After I go through Macedonia, I will come to you—for I will be going through Macedonia. 6Perhaps I will stay with you for a while, or even spend the winter, so that you can help me on my journey, wherever I go. 7For I do not want to see you now and make only a passing visit; I hope to spend some time with you, if the Lord permits. 8But I will stay on at Ephesus until Pentecost, 9because a great door for effective work has opened to me, and there are many who oppose me.

10When Timothy comes, see to it that he has nothing to fear while he is with you, for he is carrying on the work of the Lord, just as I am. 11No one, then, should treat him with contempt. Send him on his way in peace so that he may return to me. I am expecting him along with the brothers.

12Now about our brother Apollos: I strongly urged him to go to you with the brothers. He was quite unwilling to go now, but he will go when he has the opportunity.

13Be on your guard; stand firm in the faith; be courageous; be strong. 14Do everything in love.

15You know that the household of Stephanas were the first converts in Achaia, and they have devoted themselves to the service of the Lord's people. I urge you, brothers and sisters, 16to submit to such people and to everyone who joins in the work and labors at it. 17I was glad when Stephanas, Fortunatus and Achaicus arrived, because they have supplied what was lacking from you. 18For they refreshed my spirit and yours also. Such men deserve recognition.

Final Greetings

19The churches in the province of Asia send you greetings. Aquila and Priscilla[c] greet you warmly in the Lord, and so does the church that meets at their house. 20All the brothers and sisters here send you greetings. Greet one another with a holy kiss.

21I, Paul, write this greeting in my own hand.

22If anyone does not love the Lord, let that person be cursed! Come, Lord[d]!

23The grace of the Lord Jesus be with you.

24My love to all of you in Christ Jesus. Amen.[e]

2 Corinthians

1 Paul, an apostle of Christ Jesus by the will of God, and Timothy our brother,

To the church of God in Corinth, together with all his holy people throughout Achaia:

2Grace and peace to you from God our Father and the Lord Jesus Christ.

Praise to the God of All Comfort

3Praise be to the God and Father of our Lord Jesus Christ, the Father of compassion and the God of all comfort, 4who comforts us in all our troubles, so that we can comfort those in any trouble with the comfort we ourselves receive from God. 5For just as we share abundantly in the sufferings of Christ, so also our comfort abounds through Christ. 6If we are distressed, it is for your comfort and salvation; if we are comforted, it is for your comfort, which produces in you patient endurance of the same sufferings we suffer. 7And our hope for you is firm, because we know that just as you share in our sufferings, so also you share in our comfort.

8We do not want you to be uninformed, brothers and sisters,[f] about the troubles we experi-

[a] 54 Isaiah 25:8 [b] 55 Hosea 13:14 [c] 19 Greek *Prisca*, a variant of *Priscilla* [d] 22 The Greek for *Come, Lord* reproduces an Aramaic expression (*Marana tha*) used by early Christians. [e] 24 Some manuscripts do not have *Amen*. [f] 8 The Greek word for *brothers and sisters* (*adelphoi*) refers here to believers, both men and women, as part of God's family; also in 8:1; 13:11.

enced in the province of Asia. We were under great pressure, far beyond our ability to endure, so that we despaired of life itself. [9]Indeed, we felt we had received the sentence of death. But this happened that we might not rely on ourselves but on God, who raises the dead. [10]He has delivered us from such a deadly peril, and he will deliver us again. On him we have set our hope that he will continue to deliver us, [11]as you help us by your prayers. Then many will give thanks on our behalf for the gracious favor granted us in answer to the prayers of many.

Paul's Change of Plans

[12]Now this is our boast: Our conscience testifies that we have conducted ourselves in the world, and especially in our relations with you, with integrity[a] and godly sincerity. We have done so, relying not on worldly wisdom but on God's grace. [13]For we do not write you anything you cannot read or understand. And I hope that, [14]as you have understood us in part, you will come to understand fully that you can boast of us just as we will boast of you in the day of the Lord Jesus.

[15]Because I was confident of this, I wanted to visit you first so that you might benefit twice. [16]I wanted to visit you on my way to Macedonia and to come back to you from Macedonia, and then to have you send me on my way to Judea. [17]Was I fickle when I intended to do this? Or do I make my plans in a worldly manner so that in the same breath I say both "Yes, yes" and "No, no"?

[18]But as surely as God is faithful, our message to you is not "Yes" and "No." [19]For the Son of God, Jesus Christ, who was preached among you by us—by me and Silas[b] and Timothy—was not "Yes" and "No," but in him it has always been "Yes." [20]For no matter how many promises God has made, they are "Yes" in Christ. And so through him the "Amen" is spoken by us to the glory of God. [21]Now it is God who makes both us and you stand firm in Christ. He anointed us, [22]set his seal of ownership on us, and put his Spirit in our hearts as a deposit, guaranteeing what is to come.

[23]I call God as my witness—and I stake my life on it—that it was in order to spare you that I did not return to Corinth. [24]Not that we lord it over your faith, but we work with you for your joy, because it is by faith you stand firm.

2 [1]So I made up my mind that I would not make another painful visit to you. [2]For if I grieve you, who is left to make me glad but you whom I have grieved? [3]I wrote as I did, so that when I came I would not be distressed by those who should have made me rejoice. I had confidence in all of you, that you would all share my joy. [4]For I wrote you out of great distress and anguish of heart and with many tears, not to grieve you but to let you know the depth of my love for you.

Forgiveness for the Offender

[5]If anyone has caused grief, he has not so much grieved me as he has grieved all of you to some extent—not to put it too severely. [6]The punishment inflicted on him by the majority is sufficient. [7]Now instead, you ought to forgive and comfort him, so that he will not be overwhelmed by excessive sorrow. [8]I urge you, therefore, to reaffirm your love for him. [9]Another reason I wrote you was to see if you would stand the test and be obedient in everything. [10]Anyone you forgive, I also forgive. And what I have forgiven—if there was anything to forgive—I have forgiven in the sight of Christ for your sake, [11]in order that Satan might not outwit us. For we are not unaware of his schemes.

Ministers of the New Covenant

[12]Now when I went to Troas to preach the gospel of Christ and found that the Lord had opened a door for me, [13]I still had no peace of mind, because I did not find my brother Titus there. So I said goodbye to them and went on to Macedonia.

[14]But thanks be to God, who always leads us as captives in Christ's triumphal procession and uses us to spread the aroma of the knowledge of him everywhere. [15]For we are to God the pleasing aroma of Christ among those who are being saved and those who are perishing. [16]To the one we are an aroma that brings death; to the other, an aroma that brings life. And who is equal to such a task? [17]Unlike so many, we do not peddle the word of God for profit. On the contrary, in Christ we speak before God with sincerity, as those sent from God.

3 Are we beginning to commend ourselves again? Or do we need, like some people, letters of recommendation to you or from you? [2]You yourselves are our letter, written on our hearts, known and read by everyone. [3]You show that you are a letter from Christ, the result of our ministry, written not with ink but with the Spirit of the living God, not on tablets of stone but on tablets of human hearts.

[4]Such confidence we have through Christ before God. [5]Not that we are competent in ourselves to claim anything for ourselves, but our competence comes from God. [6]He has made us competent as ministers of a new covenant—not of the letter but of the Spirit; for the letter kills, but the Spirit gives life.

The Greater Glory of the New Covenant

[7]Now if the ministry that brought death, which was engraved in letters on stone, came with glory, so that the Israelites could not look steadily at the face of Moses because of its glory, transitory though it was, [8]will not the ministry of the Spirit be even more glorious? [9]If the ministry that brought condemnation was glorious, how much more glorious is the ministry that brings righteousness! [10]For what was glorious has no glory now in comparison with the surpassing glory. [11]And if what was transitory came with glory, how much greater is the glory of that which lasts!

[a] *12* Many manuscripts *holiness* [b] *19* Greek *Silvanus*, a variant of *Silas*

[12]Therefore, since we have such a hope, we are very bold. [13]We are not like Moses, who would put a veil over his face to prevent the Israelites from seeing the end of what was passing away. [14]But their minds were made dull, for to this day the same veil remains when the old covenant is read. It has not been removed, because only in Christ is it taken away. [15]Even to this day when Moses is read, a veil covers their hearts. [16]But whenever anyone turns to the Lord, the veil is taken away. [17]Now the Lord is the Spirit, and where the Spirit of the Lord is, there is freedom. [18]And we all, who with unveiled faces contemplate[a] the Lord's glory, are being transformed into his image with ever-increasing glory, which comes from the Lord, who is the Spirit.

Present Weakness and Resurrection Life

4 Therefore, since through God's mercy we have this ministry, we do not lose heart. [2]Rather, we have renounced secret and shameful ways; we do not use deception, nor do we distort the word of God. On the contrary, by setting forth the truth plainly we commend ourselves to everyone's conscience in the sight of God. [3]And even if our gospel is veiled, it is veiled to those who are perishing. [4]The god of this age has blinded the minds of unbelievers, so that they cannot see the light of the gospel that displays the glory of Christ, who is the image of God. [5]For what we preach is not ourselves, but Jesus Christ as Lord, and ourselves as your servants for Jesus' sake. [6]For God, who said, "Let light shine out of darkness,"[b] made his light shine in our hearts to give us the light of the knowledge of God's glory displayed in the face of Christ.

[7]But we have this treasure in jars of clay to show that this all-surpassing power is from God and not from us. [8]We are hard pressed on every side, but not crushed; perplexed, but not in despair; [9]persecuted, but not abandoned; struck down, but not destroyed. [10]We always carry around in our body the death of Jesus, so that the life of Jesus may also be revealed in our body. [11]For we who are alive are always being given over to death for Jesus' sake, so that his life may also be revealed in our mortal body. [12]So then, death is at work in us, but life is at work in you.

[13]It is written: "I believed; therefore I have spoken."[c] Since we have that same spirit of[d] faith, we also believe and therefore speak, [14]because we know that the one who raised the Lord Jesus from the dead will also raise us with Jesus and present us with you to himself. [15]All this is for your benefit, so that the grace that is reaching more and more people may cause thanksgiving to overflow to the glory of God.

[16]Therefore we do not lose heart. Though outwardly we are wasting away, yet inwardly we are being renewed day by day. [17]For our light and momentary troubles are achieving for us an eternal glory that far outweighs them all. [18]So we fix our eyes not on what is seen, but on what is unseen, since what is seen is temporary, but what is unseen is eternal.

Awaiting the New Body

5 For we know that if the earthly tent we live in is destroyed, we have a building from God, an eternal house in heaven, not built by human hands. [2]Meanwhile we groan, longing to be clothed instead with our heavenly dwelling, [3]because when we are clothed, we will not be found naked. [4]For while we are in this tent, we groan and are burdened, because we do not wish to be unclothed but to be clothed instead with our heavenly dwelling, so that what is mortal may be swallowed up by life. [5]Now the one who has fashioned us for this very purpose is God, who has given us the Spirit as a deposit, guaranteeing what is to come.

[6]Therefore we are always confident and know that as long as we are at home in the body we are away from the Lord. [7]For we live by faith, not by sight. [8]We are confident, I say, and would prefer to be away from the body and at home with the Lord. [9]So we make it our goal to please him, whether we are at home in the body or away from it. [10]For we must all appear before the judgment seat of Christ, so that each of us may receive what is due us for the things done while in the body, whether good or bad.

The Ministry of Reconciliation

[11]Since, then, we know what it is to fear the Lord, we try to persuade others. What we are is plain to God, and I hope it is also plain to your conscience. [12]We are not trying to commend ourselves to you again, but are giving you an opportunity to take pride in us, so that you can answer those who take pride in what is seen rather than in what is in the heart. [13]If we are "out of our mind," as some say, it is for God; if we are in our right mind, it is for you. [14]For Christ's love compels us, because we are convinced that one died for all, and therefore all died. [15]And he died for all, that those who live should no longer live for themselves but for him who died for them and was raised again.

[16]So from now on we regard no one from a worldly point of view. Though we once regarded Christ in this way, we do so no longer. [17]Therefore, if anyone is in Christ, the new creation has come:[e] The old has gone, the new is here! [18]All this is from God, who reconciled us to himself through Christ and gave us the ministry of reconciliation: [19]that God was reconciling the world to himself in Christ, not counting people's sins against them. And he has committed to us the message of reconciliation. [20]We are therefore Christ's ambassadors, as though God were making his appeal through us. We implore you on Christ's behalf: Be reconciled to God. [21]God made him who had no sin to be sin[f] for us, so that in him we might become the righteousness of God.

[a] *18* Or *reflect* [b] *6* Gen. 1:3 [c] *13* Psalm 116:10 (see Septuagint) [d] *13* Or *Spirit-given*
[e] *17* Or *Christ, that person is a new creation.* [f] *21* Or *be a sin offering*

6 As God's co-workers we urge you not to
receive God's grace in vain. 2For he says,

> "In the time of my favor I heard you,
> and in the day of salvation I helped
> you."[a]

I tell you, now is the time of God's favor, now
is the day of salvation.

Paul's Hardships

3We put no stumbling block in anyone's
path, so that our ministry will not be discredited. 4Rather, as servants of God we commend
ourselves in every way: in great endurance; in
troubles, hardships and distresses; 5in beatings, imprisonments and riots; in hard work,
sleepless nights and hunger; 6in purity, understanding, patience and kindness; in the
Holy Spirit and in sincere love; 7in truthful
speech and in the power of God; with weapons
of righteousness in the right hand and in the
left; 8through glory and dishonor, bad report
and good report; genuine, yet regarded as impostors; 9known, yet regarded as unknown;
dying, and yet we live on; beaten, and yet not
killed; 10sorrowful, yet always rejoicing; poor,
yet making many rich; having nothing, and
yet possessing everything.

11We have spoken freely to you, Corinthians, and opened wide our hearts to you. 12We
are not withholding our affection from you,
but you are withholding yours from us. 13As
a fair exchange—I speak as to my children—
open wide your hearts also.

Warning Against Idolatry

14Do not be yoked together with unbelievers. For what do righteousness and wickedness have in common? Or what fellowship can
light have with darkness? 15What harmony
is there between Christ and Belial[b]? Or what
does a believer have in common with an unbeliever? 16What agreement is there between
the temple of God and idols? For we are the
temple of the living God. As God has said:

> "I will live with them
> and walk among them,
> and I will be their God,
> and they will be my people."[c]

17Therefore,

> "Come out from them
> and be separate,
> says the Lord.
> Touch no unclean thing,
> and I will receive you."[d]

18And,

> "I will be a Father to you,
> and you will be my sons and daughters,
> says the Lord Almighty."[e]

7 Therefore, since we have these promises,
dear friends, let us purify ourselves from
everything that contaminates body and spirit,
perfecting holiness out of reverence for God.

Paul's Joy Over the Church's Repentance

2Make room for us in your hearts. We have
wronged no one, we have corrupted no one,
we have exploited no one. 3I do not say this
to condemn you; I have said before that you
have such a place in our hearts that we would
live or die with you. 4I have spoken to you with
great frankness; I take great pride in you. I
am greatly encouraged; in all our troubles my
joy knows no bounds.

5For when we came into Macedonia, we
had no rest, but we were harassed at every
turn—conflicts on the outside, fears within.
6But God, who comforts the downcast, comforted us by the coming of Titus, 7and not only
by his coming but also by the comfort you had
given him. He told us about your longing for
me, your deep sorrow, your ardent concern
for me, so that my joy was greater than ever.

8Even if I caused you sorrow by my letter, I
do not regret it. Though I did regret it—I see
that my letter hurt you, but only for a little
while— 9yet now I am happy, not because you
were made sorry, but because your sorrow led
you to repentance. For you became sorrowful as God intended and so were not harmed
in any way by us. 10Godly sorrow brings repentance that leads to salvation and leaves
no regret, but worldly sorrow brings death.
11See what this godly sorrow has produced
in you: what earnestness, what eagerness
to clear yourselves, what indignation, what
alarm, what longing, what concern, what
readiness to see justice done. At every point
you have proved yourselves to be innocent in
this matter. 12So even though I wrote to you,
it was neither on account of the one who did
the wrong nor on account of the injured party,
but rather that before God you could see for
yourselves how devoted to us you are. 13By all
this we are encouraged.

In addition to our own encouragement, we
were especially delighted to see how happy Titus was, because his spirit has been refreshed
by all of you. 14I had boasted to him about
you, and you have not embarrassed me. But
just as everything we said to you was true, so
our boasting about you to Titus has proved to
be true as well. 15And his affection for you is
all the greater when he remembers that you
were all obedient, receiving him with fear and
trembling. 16I am glad I can have complete
confidence in you.

The Collection for the Lord's People

8 And now, brothers and sisters, we want
you to know about the grace that God
has given the Macedonian churches. 2In the
midst of a very severe trial, their overflowing
joy and their extreme poverty welled up in
rich generosity. 3For I testify that they gave
as much as they were able, and even beyond
their ability. Entirely on their own, 4they urgently pleaded with us for the privilege of
sharing in this service to the Lord's people.
5And they exceeded our expectations: They

[a] *2* Isaiah 49:8 [b] *15* Greek *Beliar,* a variant of *Belial* [c] *16* Lev. 26:12; Jer. 32:38; Ezek. 37:27
[d] *17* Isaiah 52:11; Ezek. 20:34,41 [e] *18* 2 Samuel 7:14; 7:8

gave themselves first of all to the Lord, and then by the will of God also to us. 6So we urged Titus, just as he had earlier made a beginning, to bring also to completion this act of grace on your part. 7But since you excel in everything—in faith, in speech, in knowledge, in complete earnestness and in the love we have kindled in you[a]—see that you also excel in this grace of giving.

8I am not commanding you, but I want to test the sincerity of your love by comparing it with the earnestness of others. 9For you know the grace of our Lord Jesus Christ, that though he was rich, yet for your sake he became poor, so that you through his poverty might become rich.

10And here is my judgment about what is best for you in this matter. Last year you were the first not only to give but also to have the desire to do so. 11Now finish the work, so that your eager willingness to do it may be matched by your completion of it, according to your means. 12For if the willingness is there, the gift is acceptable according to what one has, not according to what one does not have.

13Our desire is not that others might be relieved while you are hard pressed, but that there might be equality. 14At the present time your plenty will supply what they need, so that in turn their plenty will supply what you need. The goal is equality, 15as it is written: "The one who gathered much did not have too much, and the one who gathered little did not have too little."[b]

Titus Sent to Receive the Collection

16Thanks be to God, who put into the heart of Titus the same concern I have for you. 17For Titus not only welcomed our appeal, but he is coming to you with much enthusiasm and on his own initiative. 18And we are sending along with him the brother who is praised by all the churches for his service to the gospel. 19What is more, he was chosen by the churches to accompany us as we carry the offering, which we administer in order to honor the Lord himself and to show our eagerness to help. 20We want to avoid any criticism of the way we administer this liberal gift. 21For we are taking pains to do what is right, not only in the eyes of the Lord but also in the eyes of man.

22In addition, we are sending with them our brother who has often proved to us in many ways that he is zealous, and now even more so because of his great confidence in you. 23As for Titus, he is my partner and coworker among you; as for our brothers, they are representatives of the churches and an honor to Christ. 24Therefore show these men the proof of your love and the reason for our pride in you, so that the churches can see it.

9 There is no need for me to write to you about this service to the Lord's people. 2For I know your eagerness to help, and I have been boasting about it to the Macedonians, telling them that since last year you in Achaia were ready to give; and your enthusiasm has stirred most of them to action. 3But I am sending the brothers in order that our boasting about you in this matter should not prove hollow, but that you may be ready, as I said you would be. 4For if any Macedonians come with me and find you unprepared, we—not to say anything about you—would be ashamed of having been so confident. 5So I thought it necessary to urge the brothers to visit you in advance and finish the arrangements for the generous gift you had promised. Then it will be ready as a generous gift, not as one grudgingly given.

Generosity Encouraged

6Remember this: Whoever sows sparingly will also reap sparingly, and whoever sows generously will also reap generously. 7Each of you should give what you have decided in your heart to give, not reluctantly or under compulsion, for God loves a cheerful giver. 8And God is able to bless you abundantly, so that in all things at all times, having all that you need, you will abound in every good work. 9As it is written:

> "They have freely scattered their gifts to
> the poor;
> their righteousness endures forever."[c]

10Now he who supplies seed to the sower and bread for food will also supply and increase your store of seed and will enlarge the harvest of your righteousness. 11You will be enriched in every way so that you can be generous on every occasion, and through us your generosity will result in thanksgiving to God.

12This service that you perform is not only supplying the needs of the Lord's people but is also overflowing in many expressions of thanks to God. 13Because of the service by which you have proved yourselves, others will praise God for the obedience that accompanies your confession of the gospel of Christ, and for your generosity in sharing with them and with everyone else. 14And in their prayers for you their hearts will go out to you, because of the surpassing grace God has given you. 15Thanks be to God for his indescribable gift!

Paul's Defense of His Ministry

10 By the humility and gentleness of Christ, I appeal to you—I, Paul, who am "timid" when face to face with you, but "bold" toward you when away! 2I beg you that when I come I may not have to be as bold as I expect to be toward some people who think that we live by the standards of this world. 3For though we live in the world, we do not wage war as the world does. 4The weapons we fight with are not the weapons of the world. On the contrary, they have divine power to demolish strongholds. 5We demolish arguments and every pretension that sets itself up against the knowledge of God, and we take captive every thought to make it obedient to Christ. 6And we will be ready to punish every act of disobedience, once your obedience is complete.

[a] 7 Some manuscripts *and in your love for us* [b] *15* Exodus 16:18 [c] *9* Psalm 112:9

7You are judging by appearances.[a] If anyone is confident that they belong to Christ, they should consider again that we belong to Christ just as much as they do. 8So even if I boast somewhat freely about the authority the Lord gave us for building you up rather than tearing you down, I will not be ashamed of it. 9I do not want to seem to be trying to frighten you with my letters. 10For some say, "His letters are weighty and forceful, but in person he is unimpressive and his speaking amounts to nothing." 11Such people should realize that what we are in our letters when we are absent, we will be in our actions when we are present.

12We do not dare to classify or compare ourselves with some who commend themselves. When they measure themselves by themselves and compare themselves with themselves, they are not wise. 13We, however, will not boast beyond proper limits, but will confine our boasting to the sphere of service God himself has assigned to us, a sphere that also includes you. 14We are not going too far in our boasting, as would be the case if we had not come to you, for we did get as far as you with the gospel of Christ. 15Neither do we go beyond our limits by boasting of work done by others. Our hope is that, as your faith continues to grow, our sphere of activity among you will greatly expand, 16so that we can preach the gospel in the regions beyond you. For we do not want to boast about work already done in someone else's territory. 17But, "Let the one who boasts boast in the Lord."[b] 18For it is not the one who commends himself who is approved, but the one whom the Lord commends.

Paul and the False Apostles

11 I hope you will put up with me in a little foolishness. Yes, please put up with me! 2I am jealous for you with a godly jealousy. I promised you to one husband, to Christ, so that I might present you as a pure virgin to him. 3But I am afraid that just as Eve was deceived by the serpent's cunning, your minds may somehow be led astray from your sincere and pure devotion to Christ. 4For if someone comes to you and preaches a Jesus other than the Jesus we preached, or if you receive a different spirit from the Spirit you received, or a different gospel from the one you accepted, you put up with it easily enough.

5I do not think I am in the least inferior to those "super-apostles."[c] 6I may indeed be untrained as a speaker, but I do have knowledge. We have made this perfectly clear to you in every way. 7Was it a sin for me to lower myself in order to elevate you by preaching the gospel of God to you free of charge? 8I robbed other churches by receiving support from them so as to serve you. 9And when I was with you and needed something, I was not a burden to anyone, for the brothers who came from Macedonia supplied what I needed. I have kept myself from being a burden to you in any way, and will continue to do so. 10As surely as the truth of Christ is in me, nobody in the regions of Achaia will stop this boasting of mine. 11Why? Because I do not love you? God knows I do!

12And I will keep on doing what I am doing in order to cut the ground from under those who want an opportunity to be considered equal with us in the things they boast about. 13For such people are false apostles, deceitful workers, masquerading as apostles of Christ. 14And no wonder, for Satan himself masquerades as an angel of light. 15It is not surprising, then, if his servants also masquerade as servants of righteousness. Their end will be what their actions deserve.

Paul Boasts About His Sufferings

16I repeat: Let no one take me for a fool. But if you do, then tolerate me just as you would a fool, so that I may do a little boasting. 17In this self-confident boasting I am not talking as the Lord would, but as a fool. 18Since many are boasting in the way the world does, I too will boast. 19You gladly put up with fools since you are so wise! 20In fact, you even put up with anyone who enslaves you or exploits you or takes advantage of you or puts on airs or slaps you in the face. 21To my shame I admit that we were too weak for that!

Whatever anyone else dares to boast about—I am speaking as a fool—I also dare to boast about. 22Are they Hebrews? So am I. Are they Israelites? So am I. Are they Abraham's descendants? So am I. 23Are they servants of Christ? (I am out of my mind to talk like this.) I am more. I have worked much harder, been in prison more frequently, been flogged more severely, and been exposed to death again and again. 24Five times I received from the Jews the forty lashes minus one. 25Three times I was beaten with rods, once I was pelted with stones, three times I was shipwrecked, I spent a night and a day in the open sea, 26I have been constantly on the move. I have been in danger from rivers, in danger from bandits, in danger from my fellow Jews, in danger from Gentiles; in danger in the city, in danger in the country, in danger at sea; and in danger from false believers. 27I have labored and toiled and have often gone without sleep; I have known hunger and thirst and have often gone without food; I have been cold and naked. 28Besides everything else, I face daily the pressure of my concern for all the churches. 29Who is weak, and I do not feel weak? Who is led into sin, and I do not inwardly burn?

30If I must boast, I will boast of the things that show my weakness. 31The God and Father of the Lord Jesus, who is to be praised forever, knows that I am not lying. 32In Damascus the governor under King Aretas had the city of the Damascenes guarded in order to arrest me. 33But I was lowered in a basket from a window in the wall and slipped through his hands.

[a] 7 Or *Look at the obvious facts* [b] 17 Jer. 9:24 [c] 5 Or *to the most eminent apostles*

Paul's Vision and His Thorn

12 I must go on boasting. Although there is nothing to be gained, I will go on to visions and revelations from the Lord. 2I know a man in Christ who fourteen years ago was caught up to the third heaven. Whether it was in the body or out of the body I do not know—God knows. 3And I know that this man—whether in the body or apart from the body I do not know, but God knows— 4was caught up to paradise and heard inexpressible things, things that no one is permitted to tell. 5I will boast about a man like that, but I will not boast about myself, except about my weaknesses. 6Even if I should choose to boast, I would not be a fool, because I would be speaking the truth. But I refrain, so no one will think more of me than is warranted by what I do or say, 7or because of these surpassingly great revelations. Therefore, in order to keep me from becoming conceited, I was given a thorn in my flesh, a messenger of Satan, to torment me. 8Three times I pleaded with the Lord to take it away from me. 9But he said to me, "My grace is sufficient for you, for my power is made perfect in weakness." Therefore I will boast all the more gladly about my weaknesses, so that Christ's power may rest on me. 10That is why, for Christ's sake, I delight in weaknesses, in insults, in hardships, in persecutions, in difficulties. For when I am weak, then I am strong.

Paul's Concern for the Corinthians

11I have made a fool of myself, but you drove me to it. I ought to have been commended by you, for I am not in the least inferior to the "super-apostles,"[a] even though I am nothing. 12I persevered in demonstrating among you the marks of a true apostle, including signs, wonders and miracles. 13How were you inferior to the other churches, except that I was never a burden to you? Forgive me this wrong!

14Now I am ready to visit you for the third time, and I will not be a burden to you, because what I want is not your possessions but you. After all, children should not have to save up for their parents, but parents for their children. 15So I will very gladly spend for you everything I have and expend myself as well. If I love you more, will you love me less? 16Be that as it may, I have not been a burden to you. Yet, crafty fellow that I am, I caught you by trickery! 17Did I exploit you through any of the men I sent to you? 18I urged Titus to go to you and I sent our brother with him. Titus did not exploit you, did he? Did we not walk in the same footsteps by the same Spirit?

19Have you been thinking all along that we have been defending ourselves to you? We have been speaking in the sight of God as those in Christ; and everything we do, dear friends, is for your strengthening. 20For I am afraid that when I come I may not find you as I want you to be, and you may not find me as you want me to be. I fear that there may be discord, jealousy, fits of rage, selfish ambition, slander, gossip, arrogance and disorder. 21I am afraid that when I come again my God will humble me before you, and I will be grieved over many who have sinned earlier and have not repented of the impurity, sexual sin and debauchery in which they have indulged.

Final Warnings

13 This will be my third visit to you. "Every matter must be established by the testimony of two or three witnesses."[b] 2I already gave you a warning when I was with you the second time. I now repeat it while absent: On my return I will not spare those who sinned earlier or any of the others, 3since you are demanding proof that Christ is speaking through me. He is not weak in dealing with you, but is powerful among you. 4For to be sure, he was crucified in weakness, yet he lives by God's power. Likewise, we are weak in him, yet by God's power we will live with him in our dealing with you.

5Examine yourselves to see whether you are in the faith; test yourselves. Do you not realize that Christ Jesus is in you—unless, of course, you fail the test? 6And I trust that you will discover that we have not failed the test. 7Now we pray to God that you will not do anything wrong—not so that people will see that we have stood the test but so that you will do what is right even though we may seem to have failed. 8For we cannot do anything against the truth, but only for the truth. 9We are glad whenever we are weak but you are strong; and our prayer is that you may be fully restored. 10This is why I write these things when I am absent, that when I come I may not have to be harsh in my use of authority—the authority the Lord gave me for building you up, not for tearing you down.

Final Greetings

11Finally, brothers and sisters, rejoice! Strive for full restoration, encourage one another, be of one mind, live in peace. And the God of love and peace will be with you.

12Greet one another with a holy kiss. 13All God's people here send their greetings.

14May the grace of the Lord Jesus Christ, and the love of God, and the fellowship of the Holy Spirit be with you all.

[a] *11* Or *the most eminent apostles* [b] *1* Deut. 19:15

Galatians

1 Paul, an apostle—sent not from men nor
by a man, but by Jesus Christ and God the
Father, who raised him from the dead— 2and
all the brothers and sisters[a] with me,

To the churches in Galatia:

3Grace and peace to you from God our Father and the Lord Jesus Christ, 4who gave
himself for our sins to rescue us from the
present evil age, according to the will of our
God and Father, 5to whom be glory for ever
and ever. Amen.

No Other Gospel

6I am astonished that you are so quickly
deserting the one who called you to live in
the grace of Christ and are turning to a different gospel— 7which is really no gospel at
all. Evidently some people are throwing you
into confusion and are trying to pervert the
gospel of Christ. 8But even if we or an angel
from heaven should preach a gospel other
than the one we preached to you, let them be
under God's curse! 9As we have already said,
so now I say again: If anybody is preaching
to you a gospel other than what you accepted,
let them be under God's curse!

10Am I now trying to win the approval of
human beings, or of God? Or am I trying to
please people? If I were still trying to please
people, I would not be a servant of Christ.

Paul Called by God

11I want you to know, brothers and sisters,
that the gospel I preached is not of human
origin. 12I did not receive it from any man,
nor was I taught it; rather, I received it by revelation from Jesus Christ.

13For you have heard of my previous way
of life in Judaism, how intensely I persecuted
the church of God and tried to destroy it. 14I
was advancing in Judaism beyond many of my
own age among my people and was extremely
zealous for the traditions of my fathers. 15But
when God, who set me apart from my mother's
womb and called me by his grace, was pleased
16to reveal his Son in me so that I might preach
him among the Gentiles, my immediate response was not to consult any human being.
17I did not go up to Jerusalem to see those who
were apostles before I was, but I went into Arabia. Later I returned to Damascus.

18Then after three years, I went up to Jerusalem to get acquainted with Cephas[b] and
stayed with him fifteen days. 19I saw none of
the other apostles—only James, the Lord's
brother. 20I assure you before God that what
I am writing you is no lie.
21Then I went to Syria and Cilicia. 22I was
personally unknown to the churches of Judea
that are in Christ. 23They only heard the report: "The man who formerly persecuted us
is now preaching the faith he once tried to destroy." 24And they praised God because of me.

Paul Accepted by the Apostles

2 Then after fourteen years, I went up again
to Jerusalem, this time with Barnabas. I
took Titus along also. 2I went in response
to a revelation and, meeting privately with
those esteemed as leaders, I presented to them
the gospel that I preach among the Gentiles.
I wanted to be sure I was not running and
had not been running my race in vain. 3Yet
not even Titus, who was with me, was compelled to be circumcised, even though he was
a Greek. 4This matter arose because some
false believers had infiltrated our ranks to
spy on the freedom we have in Christ Jesus
and to make us slaves. 5We did not give in to
them for a moment, so that the truth of the
gospel might be preserved for you.

6As for those who were held in high esteem—whatever they were makes no difference to me; God does not show favoritism—
they added nothing to my message. 7On the
contrary, they recognized that I had been
entrusted with the task of preaching the gospel to the uncircumcised,[c] just as Peter had
been to the circumcised.[d] 8For God, who was
at work in Peter as an apostle to the circumcised, was also at work in me as an apostle to
the Gentiles. 9James, Cephas[e] and John, those
esteemed as pillars, gave me and Barnabas
the right hand of fellowship when they recognized the grace given to me. They agreed
that we should go to the Gentiles, and they
to the circumcised. 10All they asked was that
we should continue to remember the poor, the
very thing I had been eager to do all along.

Paul Opposes Cephas

11When Cephas came to Antioch, I opposed
him to his face, because he stood condemned.
12For before certain men came from James, he
used to eat with the Gentiles. But when they
arrived, he began to draw back and separate
himself from the Gentiles because he was
afraid of those who belonged to the circumcision group. 13The other Jews joined him in
his hypocrisy, so that by their hypocrisy even
Barnabas was led astray.

14When I saw that they were not acting in
line with the truth of the gospel, I said to Cephas in front of them all, "You are a Jew, yet
you live like a Gentile and not like a Jew. How

[a] *2* The Greek word for *brothers and sisters* (*adelphoi*) refers here to believers, both men and women, as part of God's family; also in verse 11; and in 3:15; 4:12, 28, 31; 5:11, 13; 6:1, 18. [b] *18* That is, Peter [c] *7* That is, Gentiles [d] *7* That is, Jews; also in verses 8 and 9 [e] *9* That is, Peter; also in verses 11 and 14

is it, then, that you force Gentiles to follow Jewish customs?

15 “We who are Jews by birth and not sinful Gentiles 16 know that a person is not justified by the works of the law, but by faith in Jesus Christ. So we, too, have put our faith in Christ Jesus that we may be justified by faith in[a] Christ and not by the works of the law, because by the works of the law no one will be justified.

17 “But if, in seeking to be justified in Christ, we Jews find ourselves also among the sinners, doesn't that mean that Christ promotes sin? Absolutely not! 18 If I rebuild what I destroyed, then I really would be a lawbreaker.

19 “For through the law I died to the law so that I might live for God. 20 I have been crucified with Christ and I no longer live, but Christ lives in me. The life I now live in the body, I live by faith in the Son of God, who loved me and gave himself for me. 21 I do not set aside the grace of God, for if righteousness could be gained through the law, Christ died for nothing!”[b]

Faith or Works of the Law

3 You foolish Galatians! Who has bewitched you? Before your very eyes Jesus Christ was clearly portrayed as crucified. 2 I would like to learn just one thing from you: Did you receive the Spirit by the works of the law, or by believing what you heard? 3 Are you so foolish? After beginning by means of the Spirit, are you now trying to finish by means of the flesh?[c] 4 Have you experienced[d] so much in vain—if it really was in vain? 5 So again I ask, does God give you his Spirit and work miracles among you by the works of the law, or by your believing what you heard? 6 So also Abraham “believed God, and it was credited to him as righteousness.”[e]

7 Understand, then, that those who have faith are children of Abraham. 8 Scripture foresaw that God would justify the Gentiles by faith, and announced the gospel in advance to Abraham: “All nations will be blessed through you.”[f] 9 So those who rely on faith are blessed along with Abraham, the man of faith.

10 For all who rely on the works of the law are under a curse, as it is written: “Cursed is everyone who does not continue to do everything written in the Book of the Law.”[g] 11 Clearly no one who relies on the law is justified before God, because “the righteous will live by faith.”[h] 12 The law is not based on faith; on the contrary, it says, “The person who does these things will live by them.”[i] 13 Christ redeemed us from the curse of the law by becoming a curse for us, for it is written: “Cursed is everyone who is hung on a pole.”[j] 14 He redeemed us in order that the blessing given to Abraham might come to the Gentiles through Christ Jesus, so that by faith we might receive the promise of the Spirit.

The Law and the Promise

15 Brothers and sisters, let me take an example from everyday life. Just as no one can set aside or add to a human covenant that has been duly established, so it is in this case. 16 The promises were spoken to Abraham and to his seed. Scripture does not say “and to seeds,” meaning many people, but “and to your seed,”[k] meaning one person, who is Christ. 17 What I mean is this: The law, introduced 430 years later, does not set aside the covenant previously established by God and thus do away with the promise. 18 For if the inheritance depends on the law, then it no longer depends on the promise; but God in his grace gave it to Abraham through a promise.

19 Why, then, was the law given at all? It was added because of transgressions until the Seed to whom the promise referred had come. The law was given through angels and entrusted to a mediator. 20 A mediator, however, implies more than one party; but God is one.

21 Is the law, therefore, opposed to the promises of God? Absolutely not! For if a law had been given that could impart life, then righteousness would certainly have come by the law. 22 But Scripture has locked up everything under the control of sin, so that what was promised, being given through faith in Jesus Christ, might be given to those who believe.

Children of God

23 Before the coming of this faith,[l] we were held in custody under the law, locked up until the faith that was to come would be revealed. 24 So the law was our guardian until Christ came that we might be justified by faith. 25 Now that this faith has come, we are no longer under a guardian.

26 So in Christ Jesus you are all children of God through faith, 27 for all of you who were baptized into Christ have clothed yourselves with Christ. 28 There is neither Jew nor Gentile, neither slave nor free, nor is there male and female, for you are all one in Christ Jesus. 29 If you belong to Christ, then you are Abraham's seed, and heirs according to the promise.

4 What I am saying is that as long as an heir is underage, he is no different from a slave, although he owns the whole estate. 2 The heir is subject to guardians and trustees until the time set by his father. 3 So also, when we were underage, we were in slavery under the elemental spiritual forces[m] of the world. 4 But when the set time had fully come, God sent his Son, born of a woman, born under the law, 5 to redeem those under the law, that we might receive adoption to sonship.[n] 6 Be-

[a] *16* Or *but through the faithfulness of . . . justified on the basis of the faithfulness of* [b] *21* Some interpreters end the quotation after verse 14. [c] *3* In contexts like this, the Greek word for *flesh* (*sarx*) refers to the sinful state of human beings, often presented as a power in opposition to the Spirit. [d] *4* Or *suffered* [e] *6* Gen. 15:6 [f] *8* Gen. 12:3; 18:18; 22:18 [g] *10* Deut. 27:26 [h] *11* Hab. 2:4 [i] *12* Lev. 18:5 [j] *13* Deut. 21:23 [k] *16* Gen. 12:7; 13:15; 24:7 [l] *22,23* Or *through the faithfulness of Jesus . . . ²³Before faith came* [m] *3* Or *under the basic principles* [n] *5* The Greek word for *adoption to sonship* is a legal term referring to the full legal standing of an adopted male heir in Roman culture.

cause you are his sons, God sent the Spirit of
his Son into our hearts, the Spirit who calls
out, *"Abba,*[a] Father." 7So you are no longer a
slave, but God's child; and since you are his
child, God has made you also an heir.

Paul's Concern for the Galatians

8Formerly, when you did not know God,
you were slaves to those who by nature are
not gods. 9But now that you know God—or
rather are known by God—how is it that you
are turning back to those weak and miserable
forces[b]? Do you wish to be enslaved by them
all over again? 10You are observing special
days and months and seasons and years! 11I
fear for you, that somehow I have wasted my
efforts on you.

12I plead with you, brothers and sisters, become like me, for I became like you. You did
me no wrong. 13As you know, it was because
of an illness that I first preached the gospel
to you, 14and even though my illness was a
trial to you, you did not treat me with contempt or scorn. Instead, you welcomed me as
if I were an angel of God, as if I were Christ
Jesus himself. 15Where, then, is your blessing
of me now? I can testify that, if you could have
done so, you would have torn out your eyes
and given them to me. 16Have I now become
your enemy by telling you the truth?

17Those people are zealous to win you over,
but for no good. What they want is to alienate
you from us, so that you may have zeal for
them. 18It is fine to be zealous, provided the
purpose is good, and to be so always, not just
when I am with you. 19My dear children, for
whom I am again in the pains of childbirth
until Christ is formed in you, 20how I wish I
could be with you now and change my tone,
because I am perplexed about you!

Hagar and Sarah

21Tell me, you who want to be under the
law, are you not aware of what the law says?
22For it is written that Abraham had two sons,
one by the slave woman and the other by the
free woman. 23His son by the slave woman
was born according to the flesh, but his son
by the free woman was born as the result of
a divine promise.

24These things are being taken figuratively: The women represent two covenants.
One covenant is from Mount Sinai and bears
children who are to be slaves: This is Hagar.
25Now Hagar stands for Mount Sinai in Arabia and corresponds to the present city of Jerusalem, because she is in slavery with her
children. 26But the Jerusalem that is above is
free, and she is our mother. 27For it is written:

"Be glad, barren woman,
  you who never bore a child;
shout for joy and cry aloud,
  you who were never in labor;
because more are the children of the
  desolate woman
  than of her who has a husband."[c]

28Now you, brothers and sisters, like Isaac,
are children of promise. 29At that time the son
born according to the flesh persecuted the son
born by the power of the Spirit. It is the same
now. 30But what does Scripture say? "Get rid
of the slave woman and her son, for the slave
woman's son will never share in the inheritance with the free woman's son."[d] 31There-
fore, brothers and sisters, we are not children
of the slave woman, but of the free woman.

Freedom in Christ

5 It is for freedom that Christ has set us free.
Stand firm, then, and do not let yourselves
be burdened again by a yoke of slavery.

2Mark my words! I, Paul, tell you that if you
let yourselves be circumcised, Christ will be of
no value to you at all. 3Again I declare to every
man who lets himself be circumcised that he
is obligated to obey the whole law. 4You who
are trying to be justified by the law have been
alienated from Christ; you have fallen away
from grace. 5For through the Spirit we eagerly
await by faith the righteousness for which we
hope. 6For in Christ Jesus neither circumcision nor uncircumcision has any value. The
only thing that counts is faith expressing itself
through love.

7You were running a good race. Who cut in
on you to keep you from obeying the truth?
8That kind of persuasion does not come from
the one who calls you. 9"A little yeast works
through the whole batch of dough." 10I am
confident in the Lord that you will take no
other view. The one who is throwing you into
confusion, whoever that may be, will have to
pay the penalty. 11Brothers and sisters, if I am
still preaching circumcision, why am I still
being persecuted? In that case the offense of
the cross has been abolished. 12As for those
agitators, I wish they would go the whole way
and emasculate themselves!

Life by the Spirit

13You, my brothers and sisters, were called
to be free. But do not use your freedom to
indulge the flesh[e]; rather, serve one another humbly in love. 14For the entire law is fulfilled in keeping this one command: "Love
your neighbor as yourself."[f] 15If you bite and
devour each other, watch out or you will be
destroyed by each other.

16So I say, walk by the Spirit, and you will
not gratify the desires of the flesh. 17For the
flesh desires what is contrary to the Spirit,
and the Spirit what is contrary to the flesh.
They are in conflict with each other, so that
you are not to do whatever[g] you want. 18But
if you are led by the Spirit, you are not under
the law.

[a] *6* Aramaic for *Father* [b] *9* Or *principles* [c] *27* Isaiah 54:1 [d] *30* Gen. 21:10 [e] *13* In contexts like this, the Greek word for *flesh* (*sarx*) refers to the sinful state of human beings, often presented as a power in opposition to the Spirit; also in verses 16, 17, 19 and 24; and in 6:8. [f] *14* Lev. 19:18
[g] *17* Or *you do not do what*

19 The acts of the flesh are obvious: sexual immorality, impurity and debauchery; 20 idolatry and witchcraft; hatred, discord, jealousy, fits of rage, selfish ambition, dissensions, factions 21 and envy; drunkenness, orgies, and the like. I warn you, as I did before, that those who live like this will not inherit the kingdom of God.

22 But the fruit of the Spirit is love, joy, peace, forbearance, kindness, goodness, faithfulness, 23 gentleness and self-control. Against such things there is no law. 24 Those who belong to Christ Jesus have crucified the flesh with its passions and desires. 25 Since we live by the Spirit, let us keep in step with the Spirit. 26 Let us not become conceited, provoking and envying each other.

Doing Good to All

6 Brothers and sisters, if someone is caught in a sin, you who live by the Spirit should restore that person gently. But watch yourselves, or you also may be tempted. 2 Carry each other's burdens, and in this way you will fulfill the law of Christ. 3 If anyone thinks they are something when they are not, they deceive themselves. 4 Each one should test their own actions. Then they can take pride in themselves alone, without comparing themselves to someone else, 5 for each one should carry their own load. 6 Nevertheless, the one who receives instruction in the word should share all good things with their instructor.

7 Do not be deceived: God cannot be mocked. A man reaps what he sows. 8 Whoever sows to please their flesh, from the flesh will reap destruction; whoever sows to please the Spirit, from the Spirit will reap eternal life. 9 Let us not become weary in doing good, for at the proper time we will reap a harvest if we do not give up. 10 Therefore, as we have opportunity, let us do good to all people, especially to those who belong to the family of believers.

Not Circumcision but the New Creation

11 See what large letters I use as I write to you with my own hand!

12 Those who want to impress people by means of the flesh are trying to compel you to be circumcised. The only reason they do this is to avoid being persecuted for the cross of Christ. 13 Not even those who are circumcised keep the law, yet they want you to be circumcised that they may boast about your circumcision in the flesh. 14 May I never boast except in the cross of our Lord Jesus Christ, through which[a] the world has been crucified to me, and I to the world. 15 Neither circumcision nor uncircumcision means anything; what counts is the new creation. 16 Peace and mercy to all who follow this rule—to[b] the Israel of God.

17 From now on, let no one cause me trouble, for I bear on my body the marks of Jesus.

18 The grace of our Lord Jesus Christ be with your spirit, brothers and sisters. Amen.

Ephesians

1 Paul, an apostle of Christ Jesus by the will of God,

To God's holy people in Ephesus,[c] the faithful in Christ Jesus:

2 Grace and peace to you from God our Father and the Lord Jesus Christ.

Praise for Spiritual Blessings in Christ

3 Praise be to the God and Father of our Lord Jesus Christ, who has blessed us in the heavenly realms with every spiritual blessing in Christ. 4 For he chose us in him before the creation of the world to be holy and blameless in his sight. In love 5 he[d] predestined us for adoption to sonship[e] through Jesus Christ, in accordance with his pleasure and will— 6 to the praise of his glorious grace, which he has freely given us in the One he loves. 7 In him we have redemption through his blood, the forgiveness of sins, in accordance with the riches of God's grace 8 that he lavished on us. With all wisdom and understanding, 9 he[f] made known to us the mystery of his will according to his good pleasure, which he purposed in Christ, 10 to be put into effect when the times reach their fulfillment—to bring unity to all things in heaven and on earth under Christ.

11 In him we were also chosen,[g] having been predestined according to the plan of him who works out everything in conformity with the purpose of his will, 12 in order that we, who were the first to put our hope in Christ, might be for the praise of his glory. 13 And you also were included in Christ when you heard the message of truth, the gospel of your salvation. When you believed, you were marked in him with a seal, the promised Holy Spirit, 14 who is a deposit guaranteeing our inheritance until

[a] 14 Or *whom* [b] 16 Or *rule and to* [c] 1 Some early manuscripts do not have *in Ephesus.* [d] 4,5 Or *sight in love.* 5*He* [e] 5 The Greek word for *adoption to sonship* is a legal term referring to the full legal standing of an adopted male heir in Roman culture. [f] 8,9 Or *us with all wisdom and understanding.* 9*And he* [g] 11 Or *were made heirs*

the redemption of those who are God's possession—to the praise of his glory.

Thanksgiving and Prayer

15 For this reason, ever since I heard about
your faith in the Lord Jesus and your love
for all God's people, 16 I have not stopped giving thanks for you, remembering you in my
prayers. 17 I keep asking that the God of our
Lord Jesus Christ, the glorious Father, may
give you the Spirit[a] of wisdom and revelation,
so that you may know him better. 18 I pray that
the eyes of your heart may be enlightened in
order that you may know the hope to which
he has called you, the riches of his glorious
inheritance in his holy people, 19 and his in-
comparably great power for us who believe.
That power is the same as the mighty strength
20 he exerted when he raised Christ from the
dead and seated him at his right hand in the
heavenly realms, 21 far above all rule and authority, power and dominion, and every name
that is invoked, not only in the present age but
also in the one to come. 22 And God placed all
things under his feet and appointed him to be
head over everything for the church, 23 which
is his body, the fullness of him who fills everything in every way.

Made Alive in Christ

2 As for you, you were dead in your transgressions and sins, 2 in which you used to
live when you followed the ways of this world
and of the ruler of the kingdom of the air, the
spirit who is now at work in those who are disobedient. 3 All of us also lived among them at
one time, gratifying the cravings of our flesh[b]
and following its desires and thoughts. Like the
rest, we were by nature deserving of wrath.
4 But because of his great love for us, God, who
is rich in mercy, 5 made us alive with Christ
even when we were dead in transgressions—it
is by grace you have been saved. 6 And God
raised us up with Christ and seated us with him
in the heavenly realms in Christ Jesus, 7 in order that in the coming ages he might show the
incomparable riches of his grace, expressed in
his kindness to us in Christ Jesus. 8 For it is by
grace you have been saved, through faith—
and this is not from yourselves, it is the gift
of God— 9 not by works, so that no one can
boast. 10 For we are God's handiwork, created
in Christ Jesus to do good works, which God
prepared in advance for us to do.

Jew and Gentile Reconciled Through Christ

11 Therefore, remember that formerly you
who are Gentiles by birth and called "uncircumcised" by those who call themselves
"the circumcision" (which is done in the body
by human hands)— 12 remember that at that
time you were separate from Christ, excluded
from citizenship in Israel and foreigners to the
covenants of the promise, without hope and
without God in the world. 13 But now in Christ
Jesus you who once were far away have been
brought near by the blood of Christ.
14 For he himself is our peace, who has made
the two groups one and has destroyed the barrier, the dividing wall of hostility, 15 by setting
aside in his flesh the law with its commands
and regulations. His purpose was to create
in himself one new humanity out of the two,
thus making peace, 16 and in one body to reconcile both of them to God through the cross,
by which he put to death their hostility. 17 He
came and preached peace to you who were
far away and peace to those who were near.
18 For through him we both have access to the
Father by one Spirit.
19 Consequently, you are no longer foreigners and strangers, but fellow citizens with
God's people and also members of his household, 20 built on the foundation of the apostles
and prophets, with Christ Jesus himself as the
chief cornerstone. 21 In him the whole building
is joined together and rises to become a holy
temple in the Lord. 22 And in him you too are
being built together to become a dwelling in
which God lives by his Spirit.

God's Marvelous Plan for the Gentiles

3 For this reason I, Paul, the prisoner of
Christ Jesus for the sake of you Gentiles—
2 Surely you have heard about the administration of God's grace that was given to me
for you, 3 that is, the mystery made known to
me by revelation, as I have already written
briefly. 4 In reading this, then, you will be able
to understand my insight into the mystery of
Christ, 5 which was not made known to people
in other generations as it has now been revealed by the Spirit to God's holy apostles and
prophets. 6 This mystery is that through the
gospel the Gentiles are heirs together with Israel, members together of one body, and shar-
ers together in the promise in Christ Jesus.
7 I became a servant of this gospel by the gift
of God's grace given me through the working of his power. 8 Although I am less than
the least of all the Lord's people, this grace
was given me: to preach to the Gentiles the
boundless riches of Christ, 9 and to make plain
to everyone the administration of this mystery, which for ages past was kept hidden in
God, who created all things. 10 His intent was
that now, through the church, the manifold
wisdom of God should be made known to the
rulers and authorities in the heavenly realms,
11 according to his eternal purpose that he accomplished in Christ Jesus our Lord. 12 In him
and through faith in him we may approach
God with freedom and confidence. 13 I ask you,
therefore, not to be discouraged because of
my sufferings for you, which are your glory.

A Prayer for the Ephesians

14 For this reason I kneel before the Father,
15 from whom every family[c] in heaven and on

[a] *17* Or *a spirit* [b] *3* In contexts like this, the Greek word for *flesh* (*sarx*) refers to the sinful state of human beings, often presented as a power in opposition to the Spirit. [c] *15* The Greek for *family* (*patria*) is derived from the Greek for *father* (*pater*).

earth derives its name. [16]I pray that out of his
glorious riches he may strengthen you with
power through his Spirit in your inner being, [17]so that Christ may dwell in your hearts
through faith. And I pray that you, being rooted and established in love, [18]may have power,
together with all the Lord's holy people, to
grasp how wide and long and high and deep
is the love of Christ, [19]and to know this love
that surpasses knowledge—that you may be
filled to the measure of all the fullness of God.

[20]Now to him who is able to do immeasur-
ably more than all we ask or imagine, according to his power that is at work within us,
[21]to him be glory in the church and in Christ
Jesus throughout all generations, for ever and
ever! Amen.

Unity and Maturity in the Body of Christ

4 As a prisoner for the Lord, then, I urge you
to live a life worthy of the calling you have
received. [2]Be completely humble and gentle;
be patient, bearing with one another in love.
[3]Make every effort to keep the unity of the
Spirit through the bond of peace. [4]There is one
body and one Spirit, just as you were called
to one hope when you were called; [5]one Lord,
one faith, one baptism; [6]one God and Father of
all, who is over all and through all and in all.

[7]But to each one of us grace has been given
as Christ apportioned it. [8]This is why it[a] says:

"When he ascended on high,
he took many captives
and gave gifts to his people."[b]

[9](What does "he ascended" mean except that
he also descended to the lower, earthly regions[c]? [10]He who descended is the very one
who ascended higher than all the heavens, in
order to fill the whole universe.) [11]So Christ
himself gave the apostles, the prophets, the
evangelists, the pastors and teachers, [12]to equip
his people for works of service, so that the body
of Christ may be built up [13]until we all reach
unity in the faith and in the knowledge of the
Son of God and become mature, attaining to
the whole measure of the fullness of Christ.

[14]Then we will no longer be infants, tossed
back and forth by the waves, and blown here
and there by every wind of teaching and by
the cunning and craftiness of people in their
deceitful scheming. [15]Instead, speaking the
truth in love, we will grow to become in every
respect the mature body of him who is the
head, that is, Christ. [16]From him the whole
body, joined and held together by every supporting ligament, grows and builds itself up
in love, as each part does its work.

Instructions for Christian Living

[17]So I tell you this, and insist on it in the
Lord, that you must no longer live as the
Gentiles do, in the futility of their thinking.
[18]They are darkened in their understanding
and separated from the life of God because
of the ignorance that is in them due to the
hardening of their hearts. [19]Having lost all
sensitivity, they have given themselves over
to sensuality so as to indulge in every kind of
impurity, and they are full of greed.

[20]That, however, is not the way of life you
learned [21]when you heard about Christ and
were taught in him in accordance with the
truth that is in Jesus. [22]You were taught, with
regard to your former way of life, to put off
your old self, which is being corrupted by its
deceitful desires; [23]to be made new in the attitude of your minds; [24]and to put on the new
self, created to be like God in true righteousness and holiness.

[25]Therefore each of you must put off falsehood and speak truthfully to your neighbor,
for we are all members of one body. [26]"In your
anger do not sin"[d]: Do not let the sun go down
while you are still angry, [27]and do not give
the devil a foothold. [28]Anyone who has been
stealing must steal no longer, but must work,
doing something useful with their own hands,
that they may have something to share with
those in need.

[29]Do not let any unwholesome talk come
out of your mouths, but only what is helpful for building others up according to their
needs, that it may benefit those who listen.
[30]And do not grieve the Holy Spirit of God,
with whom you were sealed for the day of redemption. [31]Get rid of all bitterness, rage and
anger, brawling and slander, along with every
form of malice. [32]Be kind and compassionate
to one another, forgiving each other, just as
in Christ God forgave you.

5 [1]Follow God's
example, therefore, as dearly loved children [2]and walk in the way of love, just as
Christ loved us and gave himself up for us
as a fragrant offering and sacrifice to God.

[3]But among you there must not be even a hint
of sexual immorality, or of any kind of impurity, or of greed, because these are improper
for God's holy people. [4]Nor should there be
obscenity, foolish talk or coarse joking, which
are out of place, but rather thanksgiving. [5]For
of this you can be sure: No immoral, impure
or greedy person—such a person is an idolater—has any inheritance in the kingdom of
Christ and of God.[e] [6]Let no one deceive you
with empty words, for because of such things
God's wrath comes on those who are disobedient. [7]Therefore do not be partners with them.

[8]For you were once darkness, but now you
are light in the Lord. Live as children of light
[9](for the fruit of the light consists in all goodness, righteousness and truth) [10]and find out
what pleases the Lord. [11]Have nothing to do
with the fruitless deeds of darkness, but rather expose them. [12]It is shameful even to mention what the disobedient do in secret. [13]But
everything exposed by the light becomes
visible—and everything that is illuminated
becomes a light. [14]This is why it is said:

"Wake up, sleeper,
rise from the dead,
and Christ will shine on you."

[a] 8 Or *God* [b] 8 Psalm 68:18 [c] 9 Or *the depths of the earth* [d] 26 Psalm 4:4 (see Septuagint)
[e] 5 Or *kingdom of the Messiah and God*

[15]Be very careful, then, how you live—not
as unwise but as wise, [16]making the most of
every opportunity, because the days are evil.
[17]Therefore do not be foolish, but understand
what the Lord's will is. [18]Do not get drunk on
wine, which leads to debauchery. Instead, be
filled with the Spirit, [19]speaking to one another with psalms, hymns, and songs from the
Spirit. Sing and make music from your heart
to the Lord, [20]always giving thanks to God
the Father for everything, in the name of our
Lord Jesus Christ.

Instructions for Christian Households

[21]Submit to one another out of reverence
for Christ.
[22]Wives, submit yourselves to your own husbands as you do to the Lord. [23]For the husband
is the head of the wife as Christ is the head of
the church, his body, of which he is the Savior. [24]Now as the church submits to Christ, so
also wives should submit to their husbands
in everything.
[25]Husbands, love your wives, just as Christ
loved the church and gave himself up for her
[26]to make her holy, cleansing[a] her by the
washing with water through the word, [27]and
to present her to himself as a radiant church,
without stain or wrinkle or any other blemish, but holy and blameless. [28]In this same
way, husbands ought to love their wives as
their own bodies. He who loves his wife loves
himself. [29]After all, no one ever hated their
own body, but they feed and care for their
body, just as Christ does the church— [30]for
we are members of his body. [31]"For this reason a man will leave his father and mother
and be united to his wife, and the two will
become one flesh."[b] [32]This is a profound mystery—but I am talking about Christ and the
church. [33]However, each one of you also must
love his wife as he loves himself, and the wife
must respect her husband.
6 Children, obey your parents in the Lord,
for this is right. [2]"Honor your father and
mother"—which is the first commandment
with a promise— [3]"so that it may go well with
you and that you may enjoy long life on the
earth."[c]
[4]Fathers,[d] do not exasperate your children;
instead, bring them up in the training and
instruction of the Lord.
[5]Slaves, obey your earthly masters with
respect and fear, and with sincerity of heart,
just as you would obey Christ. [6]Obey them not
only to win their favor when their eye is on
you, but as slaves of Christ, doing the will of
God from your heart. [7]Serve wholeheartedly,
as if you were serving the Lord, not people,
[8]because you know that the Lord will reward
each one for whatever good they do, whether
they are slave or free.
[9]And masters, treat your slaves in the same
way. Do not threaten them, since you know
that he who is both their Master and yours is
in heaven, and there is no favoritism with him.

The Armor of God

[10]Finally, be strong in the Lord and in his
mighty power. [11]Put on the full armor of God,
so that you can take your stand against the
devil's schemes. [12]For our struggle is not
against flesh and blood, but against the rulers, against the authorities, against the powers of this dark world and against the spiritual forces of evil in the heavenly realms.
[13]Therefore put on the full armor of God, so
that when the day of evil comes, you may be
able to stand your ground, and after you have
done everything, to stand. [14]Stand firm then,
with the belt of truth buckled around your
waist, with the breastplate of righteousness
in place, [15]and with your feet fitted with the
readiness that comes from the gospel of peace.
[16]In addition to all this, take up the shield of
faith, with which you can extinguish all the
flaming arrows of the evil one. [17]Take the helmet of salvation and the sword of the Spirit,
which is the word of God.
[18]And pray in the Spirit on all occasions
with all kinds of prayers and requests. With
this in mind, be alert and always keep on
praying for all the Lord's people. [19]Pray also
for me, that whenever I speak, words may be
given me so that I will fearlessly make known
the mystery of the gospel, [20]for which I am an
ambassador in chains. Pray that I may declare
it fearlessly, as I should.

Final Greetings

[21]Tychicus, the dear brother and faithful
servant in the Lord, will tell you everything,
so that you also may know how I am and what
I am doing. [22]I am sending him to you for this
very purpose, that you may know how we are,
and that he may encourage you.
[23]Peace to the brothers and sisters,[e] and love
with faith from God the Father and the Lord
Jesus Christ. [24]Grace to all who love our Lord
Jesus Christ with an undying love.[f]

[a] *26* Or *having cleansed* [b] *31* Gen. 2:24 [c] *3* Deut. 5:16 [d] *4* Or *Parents* [e] *23* The Greek word for *brothers and sisters* (*adelphoi*) refers here to believers, both men and women, as part of God's family. [f] *24* Or *Grace and immortality to all who love our Lord Jesus Christ.*

Philippians

1 Paul and Timothy, servants of Christ Jesus,
To all God's holy people in Christ Jesus
at Philippi, together with the overseers and
deacons[a]:
2 Grace and peace to you from God our Father and the Lord Jesus Christ.

Thanksgiving and Prayer

3 I thank my God every time I remember
you. 4 In all my prayers for all of you, I always
pray with joy 5 because of your partnership in
the gospel from the first day until now, 6 being
confident of this, that he who began a good
work in you will carry it on to completion until
the day of Christ Jesus.
7 It is right for me to feel this way about all of
you, since I have you in my heart and, whether
I am in chains or defending and confirming
the gospel, all of you share in God's grace with
me. 8 God can testify how I long for all of you
with the affection of Christ Jesus.
9 And this is my prayer: that your love may
abound more and more in knowledge and
depth of insight, 10 so that you may be able
to discern what is best and may be pure and
blameless for the day of Christ, 11 filled with
the fruit of righteousness that comes through
Jesus Christ—to the glory and praise of God.

Paul's Chains Advance the Gospel

12 Now I want you to know, brothers and
sisters,[b] that what has happened to me has
actually served to advance the gospel. 13 As
a result, it has become clear throughout the
whole palace guard[c] and to everyone else that
I am in chains for Christ. 14 And because of my
chains, most of the brothers and sisters have
become confident in the Lord and dare all
the more to proclaim the gospel without fear.
15 It is true that some preach Christ out of
envy and rivalry, but others out of goodwill.
16 The latter do so out of love, knowing that
I am put here for the defense of the gospel.
17 The former preach Christ out of selfish ambition, not sincerely, supposing that they can
stir up trouble for me while I am in chains.
18 But what does it matter? The important
thing is that in every way, whether from false
motives or true, Christ is preached. And because of this I rejoice.
Yes, and I will continue to rejoice, 19 for I
know that through your prayers and God's
provision of the Spirit of Jesus Christ what
has happened to me will turn out for my deliverance.[d] 20 I eagerly expect and hope that I
will in no way be ashamed, but will have sufficient courage so that now as always Christ
will be exalted in my body, whether by life
or by death. 21 For to me, to live is Christ and
to die is gain. 22 If I am to go on living in the
body, this will mean fruitful labor for me. Yet
what shall I choose? I do not know! 23 I am
torn between the two: I desire to depart and
be with Christ, which is better by far; 24 but
it is more necessary for you that I remain in
the body. 25 Convinced of this, I know that I
will remain, and I will continue with all of
you for your progress and joy in the faith,
26 so that through my being with you again
your boasting in Christ Jesus will abound on
account of me.

Life Worthy of the Gospel

27 Whatever happens, conduct yourselves
in a manner worthy of the gospel of Christ.
Then, whether I come and see you or only hear
about you in my absence, I will know that you
stand firm in the one Spirit,[e] striving together as one for the faith of the gospel 28 without
being frightened in any way by those who oppose you. This is a sign to them that they will
be destroyed, but that you will be saved—and
that by God. 29 For it has been granted to you
on behalf of Christ not only to believe in him,
but also to suffer for him, 30 since you are going
through the same struggle you saw I had, and
now hear that I still have.

Imitating Christ's Humility

2 Therefore if you have any encouragement
from being united with Christ, if any comfort from his love, if any common sharing in
the Spirit, if any tenderness and compassion,
2 then make my joy complete by being like-
minded, having the same love, being one in
spirit and of one mind. 3 Do nothing out of
selfish ambition or vain conceit. Rather, in
humility value others above yourselves, 4 not
looking to your own interests but each of you
to the interests of the others.
5 In your relationships with one another,
have the same mindset as Christ Jesus:

6 Who, being in very nature[f] God,
did not consider equality with God
something to be used to his own
advantage;
7 rather, he made himself nothing
by taking the very nature[g] of a servant,
being made in human likeness.
8 And being found in appearance as a man,
he humbled himself
by becoming obedient to death—
even death on a cross!

[a] *1* The word *deacons* refers here to Christians designated to serve with the overseers/elders of the church in a variety of ways; similarly in Romans 16:1 and 1 Tim. 3:8,12. [b] *12* The Greek word for *brothers and sisters (adelphoi)* refers here to believers, both men and women, as part of God's family; also in verse 14; and in 3:1, 13, 17; 4:1, 8, 21. [c] *13* Or *whole palace* [d] *19* Or *vindication*; or *salvation* [e] *27* Or *in one spirit* [f] *6* Or *in the form of* [g] *7* Or *the form*

9Therefore God exalted him to the highest
place
and gave him the name that is above
every name,
10that at the name of Jesus every knee
should bow,
in heaven and on earth and under the
earth,
11and every tongue acknowledge that Jesus
Christ is Lord,
to the glory of God the Father.

Do Everything Without Grumbling

12Therefore, my dear friends, as you have
always obeyed—not only in my presence, but
now much more in my absence—continue to
work out your salvation with fear and trembling, 13for it is God who works in you to will
and to act in order to fulfill his good purpose.
14Do everything without grumbling or arguing, 15so that you may become blameless
and pure, "children of God without fault in a
warped and crooked generation."[a] Then you
will shine among them like stars in the sky
16as you hold firmly to the word of life. And
then I will be able to boast on the day of Christ
that I did not run or labor in vain. 17But even
if I am being poured out like a drink offering
on the sacrifice and service coming from your
faith, I am glad and rejoice with all of you. 18So
you too should be glad and rejoice with me.

Timothy and Epaphroditus

19I hope in the Lord Jesus to send Timothy to
you soon, that I also may be cheered when I receive news about you. 20I have no one else like
him, who will show genuine concern for your
welfare. 21For everyone looks out for their own
interests, not those of Jesus Christ. 22But you
know that Timothy has proved himself, because as a son with his father he has served
with me in the work of the gospel. 23I hope,
therefore, to send him as soon as I see how
things go with me. 24And I am confident in the
Lord that I myself will come soon.
25But I think it is necessary to send back
to you Epaphroditus, my brother, co-worker
and fellow soldier, who is also your messenger, whom you sent to take care of my needs.
26For he longs for all of you and is distressed
because you heard he was ill. 27Indeed he was
ill, and almost died. But God had mercy on
him, and not on him only but also on me, to
spare me sorrow upon sorrow. 28Therefore
I am all the more eager to send him, so that
when you see him again you may be glad and
I may have less anxiety. 29So then, welcome
him in the Lord with great joy, and honor people like him, 30because he almost died for the
work of Christ. He risked his life to make up
for the help you yourselves could not give me.

No Confidence in the Flesh

3 Further, my brothers and sisters, rejoice in the Lord! It is no trouble for me
to write the same things to you again, and it
is a safeguard for you. 2Watch out for those
dogs, those evildoers, those mutilators of the
flesh. 3For it is we who are the circumcision,
we who serve God by his Spirit, who boast in
Christ Jesus, and who put no confidence in
the flesh— 4though I myself have reasons for
such confidence.
If someone else thinks they have reasons to
put confidence in the flesh, I have more: 5cir-
cumcised on the eighth day, of the people of
Israel, of the tribe of Benjamin, a Hebrew of
Hebrews; in regard to the law, a Pharisee; 6as
for zeal, persecuting the church; as for righteousness based on the law, faultless.
7But whatever were gains to me I now consider loss for the sake of Christ. 8What is more,
I consider everything a loss because of the
surpassing worth of knowing Christ Jesus my
Lord, for whose sake I have lost all things. I
consider them garbage, that I may gain Christ
9and be found in him, not having a righteousness of my own that comes from the law, but
that which is through faith in[b] Christ—the
righteousness that comes from God on the basis of faith. 10I want to know Christ—yes, to
know the power of his resurrection and participation in his sufferings, becoming like him
in his death, 11and so, somehow, attaining to
the resurrection from the dead.
12Not that I have already obtained all this,
or have already arrived at my goal, but I press
on to take hold of that for which Christ Jesus
took hold of me. 13Brothers and sisters, I do
not consider myself yet to have taken hold
of it. But one thing I do: Forgetting what is
behind and straining toward what is ahead,
14I press on toward the goal to win the prize
for which God has called me heavenward in
Christ Jesus.

Following Paul's Example

15All of us, then, who are mature should
take such a view of things. And if on some
point you think differently, that too God will
make clear to you. 16Only let us live up to what
we have already attained.
17Join together in following my example,
brothers and sisters, and just as you have us
as a model, keep your eyes on those who live as
we do. 18For, as I have often told you before and
now tell you again even with tears, many live
as enemies of the cross of Christ. 19Their destiny is destruction, their god is their stomach,
and their glory is in their shame. Their mind
is set on earthly things. 20But our citizenship is
in heaven. And we eagerly await a Savior from
there, the Lord Jesus Christ, 21who, by the power that enables him to bring everything under
his control, will transform our lowly bodies so
that they will be like his glorious body.

Closing Appeal for Steadfastness and Unity

4 Therefore, my brothers and sisters, you
whom I love and long for, my joy and
crown, stand firm in the Lord in this way,
dear friends!

[a] *15* Deut. 32:5 [b] *9* Or *through the faithfulness of*

[2]I plead with Euodia and I plead with Synty-
che to be of the same mind in the Lord. [3]Yes,
and I ask you, my true companion, help these
women since they have contended at my side
in the cause of the gospel, along with Clement
and the rest of my co-workers, whose names
are in the book of life.

Final Exhortations

[4]Rejoice in the Lord always. I will say it
again: Rejoice! [5]Let your gentleness be evident to all. The Lord is near. [6]Do not be anxious about anything, but in every situation,
by prayer and petition, with thanksgiving,
present your requests to God. [7]And the peace
of God, which transcends all understanding,
will guard your hearts and your minds in
Christ Jesus.

[8]Finally, brothers and sisters, whatever is
true, whatever is noble, whatever is right,
whatever is pure, whatever is lovely, whatever is admirable—if anything is excellent
or praiseworthy—think about such things.
[9]Whatever you have learned or received or
heard from me, or seen in me—put it into practice. And the God of peace will be with you.

Thanks for Their Gifts

[10]I rejoiced greatly in the Lord that at last
you renewed your concern for me. Indeed, you
were concerned, but you had no opportunity
to show it. [11]I am not saying this because I
am in need, for I have learned to be content
whatever the circumstances. [12]I know what
it is to be in need, and I know what it is to
have plenty. I have learned the secret of being
content in any and every situation, whether
well fed or hungry, whether living in plenty
or in want. [13]I can do all this through him who
gives me strength.

[14]Yet it was good of you to share in my troubles. [15]Moreover, as you Philippians know, in
the early days of your acquaintance with the
gospel, when I set out from Macedonia, not
one church shared with me in the matter of
giving and receiving, except you only; [16]for
even when I was in Thessalonica, you sent
me aid more than once when I was in need.
[17]Not that I desire your gifts; what I desire
is that more be credited to your account. [18]I
have received full payment and have more
than enough. I am amply supplied, now that
I have received from Epaphroditus the gifts
you sent. They are a fragrant offering, an acceptable sacrifice, pleasing to God. [19]And my
God will meet all your needs according to the
riches of his glory in Christ Jesus.

[20]To our God and Father be glory for ever
and ever. Amen.

Final Greetings

[21]Greet all God's people in Christ Jesus. The
brothers and sisters who are with me send
greetings. [22]All God's people here send you
greetings, especially those who belong to Caesar's household.

[23]The grace of the Lord Jesus Christ be with
your spirit. Amen.[a]

Colossians

1 Paul, an apostle of Christ Jesus by the will
of God, and Timothy our brother,

[2]To God's holy people in Colossae, the faithful brothers and sisters[b] in Christ:

Grace and peace to you from God our Father.[c]

Thanksgiving and Prayer

[3]We always thank God, the Father of our
Lord Jesus Christ, when we pray for you, [4]be-
cause we have heard of your faith in Christ
Jesus and of the love you have for all God's
people— [5]the faith and love that spring from
the hope stored up for you in heaven and about
which you have already heard in the true message of the gospel [6]that has come to you. In
the same way, the gospel is bearing fruit and
growing throughout the whole world—just
as it has been doing among you since the day
you heard it and truly understood God's grace.
[7]You learned it from Epaphras, our dear fellow servant,[d] who is a faithful minister of
Christ on our[e] behalf, [8]and who also told us
of your love in the Spirit.

[9]For this reason, since the day we heard
about you, we have not stopped praying for
you. We continually ask God to fill you with
the knowledge of his will through all the wisdom and understanding that the Spirit gives,[f]
[10]so that you may live a life worthy of the Lord
and please him in every way: bearing fruit in
every good work, growing in the knowledge
of God, [11]being strengthened with all power
according to his glorious might so that you
may have great endurance and patience, [12]and
giving joyful thanks to the Father, who has
qualified you[g] to share in the inheritance of

[a] 23 Some manuscripts do not have *Amen.* [b] 2 The Greek word for *brothers and sisters (adelphoi)* refers here to believers, both men and women, as part of God's family; also in 4:15. [c] 2 Some manuscripts *Father and the Lord Jesus Christ* [d] 7 Or *slave* [e] 7 Some manuscripts *your* [f] 9 Or *all spiritual wisdom and understanding* [g] 12 Some manuscripts *us*

his holy people in the kingdom of light. 13For
he has rescued us from the dominion of darkness and brought us into the kingdom of the
Son he loves, 14in whom we have redemption,
the forgiveness of sins.

The Supremacy of the Son of God

15The Son is the image of the invisible God,
the firstborn over all creation. 16For in him
all things were created: things in heaven
and on earth, visible and invisible, whether
thrones or powers or rulers or authorities; all
things have been created through him and for
him. 17He is before all things, and in him all
things hold together. 18And he is the head of
the body, the church; he is the beginning and
the firstborn from among the dead, so that
in everything he might have the supremacy.
19For God was pleased to have all his fullness
dwell in him, 20and through him to reconcile
to himself all things, whether things on earth
or things in heaven, by making peace through
his blood, shed on the cross.

21Once you were alienated from God and
were enemies in your minds because of[a] your
evil behavior. 22But now he has reconciled you
by Christ's physical body through death to
present you holy in his sight, without blemish
and free from accusation— 23if you continue
in your faith, established and firm, and do
not move from the hope held out in the gospel. This is the gospel that you heard and that
has been proclaimed to every creature under
heaven, and of which I, Paul, have become a
servant.

Paul's Labor for the Church

24Now I rejoice in what I am suffering for
you, and I fill up in my flesh what is still lacking in regard to Christ's afflictions, for the
sake of his body, which is the church. 25I have
become its servant by the commission God
gave me to present to you the word of God
in its fullness— 26the mystery that has been
kept hidden for ages and generations, but is
now disclosed to the Lord's people. 27To them
God has chosen to make known among the
Gentiles the glorious riches of this mystery,
which is Christ in you, the hope of glory.

28He is the one we proclaim, admonishing
and teaching everyone with all wisdom, so
that we may present everyone fully mature
in Christ. 29To this end I strenuously contend
with all the energy Christ so powerfully
works in me.

2 I want you to know how hard I am contend-
ing for you and for those at Laodicea, and
for all who have not met me personally. 2My
goal is that they may be encouraged in heart
and united in love, so that they may have the
full riches of complete understanding, in order that they may know the mystery of God,
namely, Christ, 3in whom are hidden all the
treasures of wisdom and knowledge. 4I tell
you this so that no one may deceive you by
fine-sounding arguments. 5For though I am
absent from you in body, I am present with
you in spirit and delight to see how disciplined
you are and how firm your faith in Christ is.

Spiritual Fullness in Christ

6So then, just as you received Christ Jesus
as Lord, continue to live your lives in him,
7rooted and built up in him, strengthened in
the faith as you were taught, and overflowing
with thankfulness.

8See to it that no one takes you captive
through hollow and deceptive philosophy,
which depends on human tradition and the
elemental spiritual forces[b] of this world rather
than on Christ.

9For in Christ all the fullness of the Dei-
ty lives in bodily form, 10and in Christ you
have been brought to fullness. He is the head
over every power and authority. 11In him you
were also circumcised with a circumcision
not performed by human hands. Your whole
self ruled by the flesh[c] was put off when you
were circumcised by[d] Christ, 12having been
buried with him in baptism, in which you were
also raised with him through your faith in
the working of God, who raised him from
the dead.

13When you were dead in your sins and in
the uncircumcision of your flesh, God made
you[e] alive with Christ. He forgave us all our
sins, 14having canceled the charge of our legal
indebtedness, which stood against us and condemned us; he has taken it away, nailing it to
the cross. 15And having disarmed the powers
and authorities, he made a public spectacle
of them, triumphing over them by the cross.[f]

Freedom From Human Rules

16Therefore do not let anyone judge you by
what you eat or drink, or with regard to a religious festival, a New Moon celebration or
a Sabbath day. 17These are a shadow of the
things that were to come; the reality, however,
is found in Christ. 18Do not let anyone who
delights in false humility and the worship of
angels disqualify you. Such a person also goes
into great detail about what they have seen;
they are puffed up with idle notions by their
unspiritual mind. 19They have lost connection
with the head, from whom the whole body,
supported and held together by its ligaments
and sinews, grows as God causes it to grow.

20Since you died with Christ to the elemental spiritual forces of this world, why, as
though you still belonged to the world, do you
submit to its rules: 21"Do not handle! Do not
taste! Do not touch!"? 22These rules, which
have to do with things that are all destined
to perish with use, are based on merely human commands and teachings. 23Such regulations indeed have an appearance of wisdom,
with their self-imposed worship, their false

[a] *21* Or *minds, as shown by* [b] *8* Or *the basic principles*; also in verse 20 [c] *11* In contexts like this, the Greek word for *flesh* (*sarx*) refers to the sinful state of human beings, often presented as a power in opposition to the Spirit; also in verse 13. [d] *11* Or *put off in the circumcision of* [e] *13* Some manuscripts *us* [f] *15* Or *them in him*

humility and their harsh treatment of the body, but they lack any value in restraining sensual indulgence.

Living as Those Made Alive in Christ

3 Since, then, you have been raised with Christ, set your hearts on things above, where Christ is, seated at the right hand of God. 2Set your minds on things above, not on earthly things. 3For you died, and your life is now hidden with Christ in God. 4When Christ, who is your[a] life, appears, then you also will appear with him in glory.

5Put to death, therefore, whatever belongs to your earthly nature: sexual immorality, impurity, lust, evil desires and greed, which is idolatry. 6Because of these, the wrath of God is coming.[b] 7You used to walk in these ways, in the life you once lived. 8But now you must also rid yourselves of all such things as these: anger, rage, malice, slander, and filthy language from your lips. 9Do not lie to each other, since you have taken off your old self with its practices 10and have put on the new self, which is being renewed in knowledge in the image of its Creator. 11Here there is no Gentile or Jew, circumcised or uncircumcised, barbarian, Scythian, slave or free, but Christ is all, and is in all.

12Therefore, as God's chosen people, holy and dearly loved, clothe yourselves with compassion, kindness, humility, gentleness and patience. 13Bear with each other and forgive one another if any of you has a grievance against someone. Forgive as the Lord forgave you. 14And over all these virtues put on love, which binds them all together in perfect unity.

15Let the peace of Christ rule in your hearts, since as members of one body you were called to peace. And be thankful. 16Let the message of Christ dwell among you richly as you teach and admonish one another with all wisdom through psalms, hymns, and songs from the Spirit, singing to God with gratitude in your hearts. 17And whatever you do, whether in word or deed, do it all in the name of the Lord Jesus, giving thanks to God the Father through him.

Instructions for Christian Households

18Wives, submit yourselves to your husbands, as is fitting in the Lord.

19Husbands, love your wives and do not be harsh with them.

20Children, obey your parents in everything, for this pleases the Lord.

21Fathers,[c] do not embitter your children, or they will become discouraged.

22Slaves, obey your earthly masters in everything; and do it, not only when their eye is on you and to curry their favor, but with sincerity of heart and reverence for the Lord. 23Whatever you do, work at it with all your heart, as working for the Lord, not for human masters, 24since you know that you will receive an inheritance from the Lord as a reward. It is the Lord Christ you are serving. 25Anyone who does wrong will be repaid for their wrongs, and there is no favoritism.

4 Masters, provide your slaves with what is right and fair, because you know that you also have a Master in heaven.

Further Instructions

2Devote yourselves to prayer, being watchful and thankful. 3And pray for us, too, that God may open a door for our message, so that we may proclaim the mystery of Christ, for which I am in chains. 4Pray that I may proclaim it clearly, as I should. 5Be wise in the way you act toward outsiders; make the most of every opportunity. 6Let your conversation be always full of grace, seasoned with salt, so that you may know how to answer everyone.

Final Greetings

7Tychicus will tell you all the news about me. He is a dear brother, a faithful minister and fellow servant[d] in the Lord. 8I am sending him to you for the express purpose that you may know about our[e] circumstances and that he may encourage your hearts. 9He is coming with Onesimus, our faithful and dear brother, who is one of you. They will tell you everything that is happening here.

10My fellow prisoner Aristarchus sends you his greetings, as does Mark, the cousin of Barnabas. (You have received instructions about him; if he comes to you, welcome him.) 11Jesus, who is called Justus, also sends greetings. These are the only Jews[f] among my co-workers for the kingdom of God, and they have proved a comfort to me. 12Epaphras, who is one of you and a servant of Christ Jesus, sends greetings. He is always wrestling in prayer for you, that you may stand firm in all the will of God, mature and fully assured. 13I vouch for him that he is working hard for you and for those at Laodicea and Hierapolis. 14Our dear friend Luke, the doctor, and Demas send greetings. 15Give my greetings to the brothers and sisters at Laodicea, and to Nympha and the church in her house.

16After this letter has been read to you, see that it is also read in the church of the Laodiceans and that you in turn read the letter from Laodicea.

17Tell Archippus: "See to it that you complete the ministry you have received in the Lord."

18I, Paul, write this greeting in my own hand. Remember my chains. Grace be with you.

[a] *4* Some manuscripts *our* [b] *6* Some early manuscripts *coming on those who are disobedient* [c] *21* Or *Parents* [d] *7* Or *slave*; also in verse 12 [e] *8* Some manuscripts *that he may know about your* [f] *11* Greek *only ones of the circumcision group*

1 Thessalonians

1 Paul, Silas[a] and Timothy,

To the church of the Thessalonians in God the Father and the Lord Jesus Christ:

Grace and peace to you.

Thanksgiving for the Thessalonians' Faith

2We always thank God for all of you and continually mention you in our prayers. 3We remember before our God and Father your work produced by faith, your labor prompted by love, and your endurance inspired by hope in our Lord Jesus Christ.

4For we know, brothers and sisters[b] loved by God, that he has chosen you, 5because our gospel came to you not simply with words but also with power, with the Holy Spirit and deep conviction. You know how we lived among you for your sake. 6You became imitators of us and of the Lord, for you welcomed the message in the midst of severe suffering with the joy given by the Holy Spirit. 7And so you became a model to all the believers in Macedonia and Achaia. 8The Lord's message rang out from you not only in Macedonia and Achaia—your faith in God has become known everywhere. Therefore we do not need to say anything about it, 9for they themselves report what kind of reception you gave us. They tell how you turned to God from idols to serve the living and true God, 10and to wait for his Son from heaven, whom he raised from the dead—Jesus, who rescues us from the coming wrath.

Paul's Ministry in Thessalonica

2 You know, brothers and sisters, that our visit to you was not without results. 2We had previously suffered and been treated outrageously in Philippi, as you know, but with the help of our God we dared to tell you his gospel in the face of strong opposition. 3For the appeal we make does not spring from error or impure motives, nor are we trying to trick you. 4On the contrary, we speak as those approved by God to be entrusted with the gospel. We are not trying to please people but God, who tests our hearts. 5You know we never used flattery, nor did we put on a mask to cover up greed—God is our witness. 6We were not looking for praise from people, not from you or anyone else, even though as apostles of Christ we could have asserted our authority. 7Instead, we were like young children[c] among you.

Just as a nursing mother cares for her children, 8so we cared for you. Because we loved you so much, we were delighted to share with you not only the gospel of God but our lives as well. 9Surely you remember, brothers and sisters, our toil and hardship; we worked night and day in order not to be a burden to anyone while we preached the gospel of God to you. 10You are witnesses, and so is God, of how holy, righteous and blameless we were among you who believed. 11For you know that we dealt with each of you as a father deals with his own children, 12encouraging, comforting and urging you to live lives worthy of God, who calls you into his kingdom and glory.

13And we also thank God continually because, when you received the word of God, which you heard from us, you accepted it not as a human word, but as it actually is, the word of God, which is indeed at work in you who believe. 14For you, brothers and sisters, became imitators of God's churches in Judea, which are in Christ Jesus: You suffered from your own people the same things those churches suffered from the Jews 15who killed the Lord Jesus and the prophets and also drove us out. They displease God and are hostile to everyone 16in their effort to keep us from speaking to the Gentiles so that they may be saved. In this way they always heap up their sins to the limit. The wrath of God has come upon them at last.[d]

Paul's Longing to See the Thessalonians

17But, brothers and sisters, when we were orphaned by being separated from you for a short time (in person, not in thought), out of our intense longing we made every effort to see you. 18For we wanted to come to you—certainly I, Paul, did, again and again—but Satan blocked our way. 19For what is our hope, our joy, or the crown in which we will glory in the presence of our Lord Jesus when he comes? Is it not you? 20Indeed, you are our glory and joy.

3 So when we could stand it no longer, we thought it best to be left by ourselves in Athens. 2We sent Timothy, who is our brother and co-worker in God's service in spreading the gospel of Christ, to strengthen and encourage you in your faith, 3so that no one would be unsettled by these trials. For you know quite well that we are destined for them. 4In fact, when we were with you, we kept telling you that we would be persecuted. And it turned out that way, as you well know. 5For this reason, when I could stand it no longer, I sent to find out about your faith. I was afraid that in some way the tempter had tempted you and that our labors might have been in vain.

[a] *1* Greek *Silvanus*, a variant of *Silas* [b] *4* The Greek word for *brothers and sisters* (*adelphoi*) refers here to believers, both men and women, as part of God's family; also in 2:1, 9, 14, 17; 3:7; 4:1, 10, 13; 5:1, 4, 12, 14, 25, 27. [c] *7* Some manuscripts *were gentle* [d] *16* Or *them fully*

Timothy's Encouraging Report

6But Timothy has just now come to us from you and has brought good news about your faith and love. He has told us that you always have pleasant memories of us and that you long to see us, just as we also long to see you. 7Therefore, brothers and sisters, in all our distress and persecution we were encouraged about you because of your faith. 8For now we really live, since you are standing firm in the Lord. 9How can we thank God enough for you in return for all the joy we have in the presence of our God because of you? 10Night and day we pray most earnestly that we may see you again and supply what is lacking in your faith.

11Now may our God and Father himself and our Lord Jesus clear the way for us to come to you. 12May the Lord make your love increase and overflow for each other and for everyone else, just as ours does for you. 13May he strengthen your hearts so that you will be blameless and holy in the presence of our God and Father when our Lord Jesus comes with all his holy ones.

Living to Please God

4 As for other matters, brothers and sisters, we instructed you how to live in order to please God, as in fact you are living. Now we ask you and urge you in the Lord Jesus to do this more and more. 2For you know what instructions we gave you by the authority of the Lord Jesus.

3It is God's will that you should be sanctified: that you should avoid sexual immorality; 4that each of you should learn to control your own body[a] in a way that is holy and honorable, 5not in passionate lust like the pagans, who do not know God; 6and that in this matter no one should wrong or take advantage of a brother or sister.[b] The Lord will punish all those who commit such sins, as we told you and warned you before. 7For God did not call us to be impure, but to live a holy life. 8Therefore, anyone who rejects this instruction does not reject a human being but God, the very God who gives you his Holy Spirit.

9Now about your love for one another we do not need to write to you, for you yourselves have been taught by God to love each other. 10And in fact, you do love all of God's family throughout Macedonia. Yet we urge you, brothers and sisters, to do so more and more, 11and to make it your ambition to lead a quiet life: You should mind your own business and work with your hands, just as we told you, 12so that your daily life may win the respect of outsiders and so that you will not be dependent on anybody.

Believers Who Have Died

13Brothers and sisters, we do not want you to be uninformed about those who sleep in death, so that you do not grieve like the rest of mankind, who have no hope. 14For we believe that Jesus died and rose again, and so we believe that God will bring with Jesus those who have fallen asleep in him. 15According to the Lord's word, we tell you that we who are still alive, who are left until the coming of the Lord, will certainly not precede those who have fallen asleep. 16For the Lord himself will come down from heaven, with a loud command, with the voice of the archangel and with the trumpet call of God, and the dead in Christ will rise first. 17After that, we who are still alive and are left will be caught up together with them in the clouds to meet the Lord in the air. And so we will be with the Lord forever. 18Therefore encourage one another with these words.

The Day of the Lord

5 Now, brothers and sisters, about times and dates we do not need to write to you, 2for you know very well that the day of the Lord will come like a thief in the night. 3While people are saying, "Peace and safety," destruction will come on them suddenly, as labor pains on a pregnant woman, and they will not escape.

4But you, brothers and sisters, are not in darkness so that this day should surprise you like a thief. 5You are all children of the light and children of the day. We do not belong to the night or to the darkness. 6So then, let us not be like others, who are asleep, but let us be awake and sober. 7For those who sleep, sleep at night, and those who get drunk, get drunk at night. 8But since we belong to the day, let us be sober, putting on faith and love as a breastplate, and the hope of salvation as a helmet. 9For God did not appoint us to suffer wrath but to receive salvation through our Lord Jesus Christ. 10He died for us so that, whether we are awake or asleep, we may live together with him. 11Therefore encourage one another and build each other up, just as in fact you are doing.

Final Instructions

12Now we ask you, brothers and sisters, to acknowledge those who work hard among you, who care for you in the Lord and who admonish you. 13Hold them in the highest regard in love because of their work. Live in peace with each other. 14And we urge you, brothers and sisters, warn those who are idle and disruptive, encourage the disheartened, help the weak, be patient with everyone. 15Make sure that nobody pays back wrong for wrong, but always strive to do what is good for each other and for everyone else.

16Rejoice always, 17pray continually, 18give thanks in all circumstances; for this is God's will for you in Christ Jesus.

19Do not quench the Spirit. 20Do not treat prophecies with contempt 21but test them all; hold on to what is good, 22reject every kind of evil.

[a] 4 Or *learn to live with your own wife*; or *learn to acquire a wife* [b] 6 The Greek word for *brother or sister* (*adelphos*) refers here to a believer, whether man or woman, as part of God's family.

23May God himself, the God of peace, sanctify you through and through. May your
whole spirit, soul and body be kept blameless
at the coming of our Lord Jesus Christ. 24The
one who calls you is faithful, and he will
do it.

25Brothers and sisters, pray for us. 26Greet
all God's people with a holy kiss. 27I charge
you before the Lord to have this letter read to
all the brothers and sisters.

28The grace of our Lord Jesus Christ be
with you.

2 Thessalonians

1 Paul, Silas[a] and Timothy,

To the church of the Thessalonians in God
our Father and the Lord Jesus Christ:

2Grace and peace to you from God the Father and the Lord Jesus Christ.

Thanksgiving and Prayer

3We ought always to thank God for you,
brothers and sisters,[b] and rightly so, because
your faith is growing more and more, and the
love all of you have for one another is increasing. 4Therefore, among God's churches we
boast about your perseverance and faith in all
the persecutions and trials you are enduring.

5All this is evidence that God's judgment is
right, and as a result you will be counted worthy of the kingdom of God, for which you are
suffering. 6God is just: He will pay back trouble
to those who trouble you 7and give relief to you
who are troubled, and to us as well. This will
happen when the Lord Jesus is revealed from
heaven in blazing fire with his powerful angels. 8He will punish those who do not know
God and do not obey the gospel of our Lord
Jesus. 9They will be punished with everlasting
destruction and shut out from the presence of
the Lord and from the glory of his might 10on
the day he comes to be glorified in his holy
people and to be marveled at among all those
who have believed. This includes you, because
you believed our testimony to you.

11With this in mind, we constantly pray for
you, that our God may make you worthy of his
calling, and that by his power he may bring to
fruition your every desire for goodness and
your every deed prompted by faith. 12We pray
this so that the name of our Lord Jesus may
be glorified in you, and you in him, according
to the grace of our God and the Lord Jesus
Christ.[c]

The Man of Lawlessness

2 Concerning the coming of our Lord Jesus
Christ and our being gathered to him, we
ask you, brothers and sisters, 2not to become
easily unsettled or alarmed by the teaching
allegedly from us—whether by a prophecy or
by word of mouth or by letter—asserting that
the day of the Lord has already come. 3Don't
let anyone deceive you in any way, for that
day will not come until the rebellion occurs
and the man of lawlessness[d] is revealed, the
man doomed to destruction. 4He will oppose
and will exalt himself over everything that
is called God or is worshiped, so that he sets
himself up in God's temple, proclaiming himself to be God.

5Don't you remember that when I was with
you I used to tell you these things? 6And now
you know what is holding him back, so that
he may be revealed at the proper time. 7For
the secret power of lawlessness is already at
work; but the one who now holds it back will
continue to do so till he is taken out of the
way. 8And then the lawless one will be revealed, whom the Lord Jesus will overthrow
with the breath of his mouth and destroy by
the splendor of his coming. 9The coming of the
lawless one will be in accordance with how
Satan works. He will use all sorts of displays
of power through signs and wonders that
serve the lie, 10and all the ways that wickedness deceives those who are perishing. They
perish because they refused to love the truth
and so be saved. 11For this reason God sends
them a powerful delusion so that they will
believe the lie 12and so that all will be condemned who have not believed the truth but
have delighted in wickedness.

Stand Firm

13But we ought always to thank God for you,
brothers and sisters loved by the Lord, because God chose you as firstfruits[e] to be saved
through the sanctifying work of the Spirit and
through belief in the truth. 14He called you to
this through our gospel, that you might share
in the glory of our Lord Jesus Christ.

15So then, brothers and sisters, stand firm
and hold fast to the teachings[f] we passed on
to you, whether by word of mouth or by letter.

16May our Lord Jesus Christ himself and

[a] 1 Greek *Silvanus*, a variant of *Silas* [b] 3 The Greek word for *brothers and sisters* (*adelphoi*) refers here to believers, both men and women, as part of God's family; also in 2:1, 13, 15; 3:1, 6, 13.
[c] 12 Or *God and Lord, Jesus Christ* [d] 3 Some manuscripts *sin* [e] 13 Some manuscripts *because from the beginning God chose you* [f] 15 Or *traditions*

God our Father, who loved us and by his grace gave us eternal encouragement and good hope, 17encourage your hearts and strengthen you in every good deed and word.

Request for Prayer

3 As for other matters, brothers and sisters, pray for us that the message of the Lord may spread rapidly and be honored, just as it was with you. 2And pray that we may be delivered from wicked and evil people, for not everyone has faith. 3But the Lord is faithful, and he will strengthen you and protect you from the evil one. 4We have confidence in the Lord that you are doing and will continue to do the things we command. 5May the Lord direct your hearts into God's love and Christ's perseverance.

Warning Against Idleness

6In the name of the Lord Jesus Christ, we command you, brothers and sisters, to keep away from every believer who is idle and disruptive and does not live according to the teaching[a] you received from us. 7For you yourselves know how you ought to follow our example. We were not idle when we were with you, 8nor did we eat anyone's food without paying for it. On the contrary, we worked night and day, laboring and toiling so that we would not be a burden to any of you. 9We did this, not because we do not have the right to such help, but in order to offer ourselves as a model for you to imitate. 10For even when we were with you, we gave you this rule: "The one who is unwilling to work shall not eat."

11We hear that some among you are idle and disruptive. They are not busy; they are busybodies. 12Such people we command and urge in the Lord Jesus Christ to settle down and earn the food they eat. 13And as for you, brothers and sisters, never tire of doing what is good.

14Take special note of anyone who does not obey our instruction in this letter. Do not associate with them, in order that they may feel ashamed. 15Yet do not regard them as an enemy, but warn them as you would a fellow believer.

Final Greetings

16Now may the Lord of peace himself give you peace at all times and in every way. The Lord be with all of you.

17I, Paul, write this greeting in my own hand, which is the distinguishing mark in all my letters. This is how I write.

18The grace of our Lord Jesus Christ be with you all.

1 Timothy

1 Paul, an apostle of Christ Jesus by the command of God our Savior and of Christ Jesus our hope,

2To Timothy my true son in the faith:

Grace, mercy and peace from God the Father and Christ Jesus our Lord.

Timothy Charged to Oppose False Teachers

3As I urged you when I went into Macedonia, stay there in Ephesus so that you may command certain people not to teach false doctrines any longer 4or to devote themselves to myths and endless genealogies. Such things promote controversial speculations rather than advancing God's work—which is by faith. 5The goal of this command is love, which comes from a pure heart and a good conscience and a sincere faith. 6Some have departed from these and have turned to meaningless talk. 7They want to be teachers of the law, but they do not know what they are talking about or what they so confidently affirm.

8We know that the law is good if one uses it properly. 9We also know that the law is made not for the righteous but for lawbreakers and rebels, the ungodly and sinful, the unholy and irreligious, for those who kill their fathers or mothers, for murderers, 10for the sexually immoral, for those practicing homosexuality, for slave traders and liars and perjurers—and for whatever else is contrary to the sound doctrine 11that conforms to the gospel concerning the glory of the blessed God, which he entrusted to me.

The Lord's Grace to Paul

12I thank Christ Jesus our Lord, who has given me strength, that he considered me trustworthy, appointing me to his service. 13Even though I was once a blasphemer and a persecutor and a violent man, I was shown mercy because I acted in ignorance and unbelief. 14The grace of our Lord was poured out on me abundantly, along with the faith and love that are in Christ Jesus.

15Here is a trustworthy saying that deserves full acceptance: Christ Jesus came into the world to save sinners—of whom I am the worst. 16But for that very reason I was shown mercy so that in me, the worst of sinners, Christ Jesus might display his immense

[a] 6 Or *tradition*

patience as an example for those who would believe in him and receive eternal life. 17Now to the King eternal, immortal, invisible, the only God, be honor and glory for ever and ever. Amen.

The Charge to Timothy Renewed

18Timothy, my son, I am giving you this command in keeping with the prophecies once made about you, so that by recalling them you may fight the battle well, 19holding on to faith and a good conscience, which some have rejected and so have suffered shipwreck with regard to the faith. 20Among them are Hymenaeus and Alexander, whom I have handed over to Satan to be taught not to blaspheme.

Instructions on Worship

2 I urge, then, first of all, that petitions, prayers, intercession and thanksgiving be made for all people— 2for kings and all those in authority, that we may live peaceful and quiet lives in all godliness and holiness. 3This is good, and pleases God our Savior, 4who wants all people to be saved and to come to a knowledge of the truth. 5For there is one God and one mediator between God and mankind, the man Christ Jesus, 6who gave himself as a ransom for all people. This has now been witnessed to at the proper time. 7And for this purpose I was appointed a herald and an apostle—I am telling the truth, I am not lying—and a true and faithful teacher of the Gentiles.

8Therefore I want the men everywhere to pray, lifting up holy hands without anger or disputing. 9I also want the women to dress modestly, with decency and propriety, adorning themselves, not with elaborate hairstyles or gold or pearls or expensive clothes, 10but with good deeds, appropriate for women who profess to worship God.

11A woman[a] should learn in quietness and full submission. 12I do not permit a woman to teach or to assume authority over a man;[b] she must be quiet. 13For Adam was formed first, then Eve. 14And Adam was not the one deceived; it was the woman who was deceived and became a sinner. 15But women[c] will be saved through childbearing—if they continue in faith, love and holiness with propriety.

Qualifications for Overseers and Deacons

3 Here is a trustworthy saying: Whoever aspires to be an overseer desires a noble task. 2Now the overseer is to be above reproach, faithful to his wife, temperate, self-controlled, respectable, hospitable, able to teach, 3not given to drunkenness, not violent but gentle, not quarrelsome, not a lover of money. 4He must manage his own family well and see that his children obey him, and he must do so in a manner worthy of full[d] respect. 5(If anyone does not know how to manage his own family, how can he take care of God's church?) 6He must not be a recent convert, or he may become conceited and fall under the same judgment as the devil. 7He must also have a good reputation with outsiders, so that he will not fall into disgrace and into the devil's trap.

8In the same way, deacons[e] are to be worthy of respect, sincere, not indulging in much wine, and not pursuing dishonest gain. 9They must keep hold of the deep truths of the faith with a clear conscience. 10They must first be tested; and then if there is nothing against them, let them serve as deacons.

11In the same way, the women[f] are to be worthy of respect, not malicious talkers but temperate and trustworthy in everything.

12A deacon must be faithful to his wife and must manage his children and his household well. 13Those who have served well gain an excellent standing and great assurance in their faith in Christ Jesus.

Reasons for Paul's Instructions

14Although I hope to come to you soon, I am writing you these instructions so that, 15if I am delayed, you will know how people ought to conduct themselves in God's household, which is the church of the living God, the pillar and foundation of the truth. 16Beyond all question, the mystery from which true godliness springs is great:

He appeared in the flesh,
  was vindicated by the Spirit,[g]
was seen by angels,
  was preached among the nations,
was believed on in the world,
  was taken up in glory.

4 The Spirit clearly says that in later times some will abandon the faith and follow deceiving spirits and things taught by demons. 2Such teachings come through hypocritical liars, whose consciences have been seared as with a hot iron. 3They forbid people to marry and order them to abstain from certain foods, which God created to be received with thanksgiving by those who believe and who know the truth. 4For everything God created is good, and nothing is to be rejected if it is received with thanksgiving, 5because it is consecrated by the word of God and prayer.

6If you point these things out to the brothers and sisters,[h] you will be a good minister of Christ Jesus, nourished on the truths of the faith and of the good teaching that you have followed. 7Have nothing to do with godless myths and old wives' tales; rather, train yourself to be godly. 8For physical training is of some value, but godliness has value for all things, holding promise for both the present life and the life to come. 9This is a trustworthy

[a] *11* Or *wife*; also in verse 12 [b] *12* Or *over her husband* [c] *15* Greek *she* [d] *4* Or *him with proper* [e] *8* The word *deacons* refers here to Christians designated to serve with the overseers/elders of the church in a variety of ways; similarly in verse 12; and in Romans 16:1 and Phil. 1:1. [f] *11* Possibly deacons' wives or women who are deacons [g] *16* Or *vindicated in spirit* [h] *6* The Greek word for *brothers and sisters* (*adelphoi*) refers here to believers, both men and women, as part of God's family.

saying that deserves full acceptance. 10That is why we labor and strive, because we have put our hope in the living God, who is the Savior of all people, and especially of those who believe.

11Command and teach these things. 12Don't let anyone look down on you because you are young, but set an example for the believers in speech, in conduct, in love, in faith and in purity. 13Until I come, devote yourself to the public reading of Scripture, to preaching and to teaching. 14Do not neglect your gift, which was given you through prophecy when the body of elders laid their hands on you.

15Be diligent in these matters; give yourself wholly to them, so that everyone may see your progress. 16Watch your life and doctrine closely. Persevere in them, because if you do, you will save both yourself and your hearers.

Widows, Elders and Slaves

5 Do not rebuke an older man harshly, but exhort him as if he were your father. Treat younger men as brothers, 2older women as mothers, and younger women as sisters, with absolute purity.

3Give proper recognition to those widows who are really in need. 4But if a widow has children or grandchildren, these should learn first of all to put their religion into practice by caring for their own family and so repaying their parents and grandparents, for this is pleasing to God. 5The widow who is really in need and left all alone puts her hope in God and continues night and day to pray and to ask God for help. 6But the widow who lives for pleasure is dead even while she lives. 7Give the people these instructions, so that no one may be open to blame. 8Anyone who does not provide for their relatives, and especially for their own household, has denied the faith and is worse than an unbeliever.

9No widow may be put on the list of widows unless she is over sixty, has been faithful to her husband, 10and is well known for her good deeds, such as bringing up children, showing hospitality, washing the feet of the Lord's people, helping those in trouble and devoting herself to all kinds of good deeds.

11As for younger widows, do not put them on such a list. For when their sensual desires overcome their dedication to Christ, they want to marry. 12Thus they bring judgment on themselves, because they have broken their first pledge. 13Besides, they get into the habit of being idle and going about from house to house. And not only do they become idlers, but also busybodies who talk nonsense, saying things they ought not to. 14So I counsel younger widows to marry, to have children, to manage their homes and to give the enemy no opportunity for slander. 15Some have in fact already turned away to follow Satan.

16If any woman who is a believer has widows in her care, she should continue to help them and not let the church be burdened with them, so that the church can help those widows who are really in need.

17The elders who direct the affairs of the church well are worthy of double honor, especially those whose work is preaching and teaching. 18For Scripture says, "Do not muzzle an ox while it is treading out the grain,"[a] and "The worker deserves his wages."[b] 19Do not entertain an accusation against an elder unless it is brought by two or three witnesses. 20But those elders who are sinning you are to reprove before everyone, so that the others may take warning. 21I charge you, in the sight of God and Christ Jesus and the elect angels, to keep these instructions without partiality, and to do nothing out of favoritism.

22Do not be hasty in the laying on of hands, and do not share in the sins of others. Keep yourself pure.

23Stop drinking only water, and use a little wine because of your stomach and your frequent illnesses.

24The sins of some are obvious, reaching the place of judgment ahead of them; the sins of others trail behind them. 25In the same way, good deeds are obvious, and even those that are not obvious cannot remain hidden forever.

6 All who are under the yoke of slavery should consider their masters worthy of full respect, so that God's name and our teaching may not be slandered. 2Those who have believing masters should not show them disrespect just because they are fellow believers. Instead, they should serve them even better because their masters are dear to them as fellow believers and are devoted to the welfare[c] of their slaves.

False Teachers and the Love of Money

These are the things you are to teach and insist on. 3If anyone teaches otherwise and does not agree to the sound instruction of our Lord Jesus Christ and to godly teaching, 4they are conceited and understand nothing. They have an unhealthy interest in controversies and quarrels about words that result in envy, strife, malicious talk, evil suspicions 5and constant friction between people of corrupt mind, who have been robbed of the truth and who think that godliness is a means to financial gain.

6But godliness with contentment is great gain. 7For we brought nothing into the world, and we can take nothing out of it. 8But if we have food and clothing, we will be content with that. 9Those who want to get rich fall into temptation and a trap and into many foolish and harmful desires that plunge people into ruin and destruction. 10For the love of money is a root of all kinds of evil. Some people, eager for money, have wandered from the faith and pierced themselves with many griefs.

Final Charge to Timothy

11But you, man of God, flee from all this, and pursue righteousness, godliness, faith,

[a] *18* Deut. 25:4 [b] *18* Luke 10:7 [c] *2* Or *and benefit from the service*

love, endurance and gentleness. 12Fight the
good fight of the faith. Take hold of the eternal
life to which you were called when you made
your good confession in the presence of many
witnesses. 13In the sight of God, who gives
life to everything, and of Christ Jesus, who
while testifying before Pontius Pilate made
the good confession, I charge you 14to keep
this command without spot or blame until the
appearing of our Lord Jesus Christ, 15which
God will bring about in his own time—God,
the blessed and only Ruler, the King of kings
and Lord of lords, 16who alone is immortal and
who lives in unapproachable light, whom no
one has seen or can see. To him be honor and
might forever. Amen.

17Command those who are rich in this present world not to be arrogant nor to put their
hope in wealth, which is so uncertain, but to put
their hope in God, who richly provides us with
everything for our enjoyment. 18Command
them to do good, to be rich in good deeds, and
to be generous and willing to share. 19In this
way they will lay up treasure for themselves as
a firm foundation for the coming age, so that
they may take hold of the life that is truly life.

20Timothy, guard what has been entrusted
to your care. Turn away from godless chatter
and the opposing ideas of what is falsely called
knowledge, 21which some have professed and
in so doing have departed from the faith.

Grace be with you all.

2 Timothy

1 Paul, an apostle of Christ Jesus by the will
of God, in keeping with the promise of life
that is in Christ Jesus,

2To Timothy, my dear son:

Grace, mercy and peace from God the Father and Christ Jesus our Lord.

Thanksgiving

3I thank God, whom I serve, as my ancestors did, with a clear conscience, as night and
day I constantly remember you in my prayers.
4Recalling your tears, I long to see you, so
that I may be filled with joy. 5I am reminded
of your sincere faith, which first lived in your
grandmother Lois and in your mother Eunice
and, I am persuaded, now lives in you also.

Appeal for Loyalty to Paul and the Gospel

6For this reason I remind you to fan into
flame the gift of God, which is in you through
the laying on of my hands. 7For the Spirit God
gave us does not make us timid, but gives us
power, love and self-discipline. 8So do not be
ashamed of the testimony about our Lord
or of me his prisoner. Rather, join with me
in suffering for the gospel, by the power of
God. 9He has saved us and called us to a holy
life—not because of anything we have done
but because of his own purpose and grace.
This grace was given us in Christ Jesus before the beginning of time, 10but it has now
been revealed through the appearing of our
Savior, Christ Jesus, who has destroyed death
and has brought life and immortality to light
through the gospel. 11And of this gospel I was
appointed a herald and an apostle and a teacher. 12That is why I am suffering as I am. Yet
this is no cause for shame, because I know
whom I have believed, and am convinced that
he is able to guard what I have entrusted to
him until that day.

13What you heard from me, keep as the pattern of sound teaching, with faith and love in
Christ Jesus. 14Guard the good deposit that
was entrusted to you—guard it with the help
of the Holy Spirit who lives in us.

Examples of Disloyalty and Loyalty

15You know that everyone in the province
of Asia has deserted me, including Phygelus
and Hermogenes.

16May the Lord show mercy to the household of Onesiphorus, because he often refreshed me and was not ashamed of my
chains. 17On the contrary, when he was in
Rome, he searched hard for me until he found
me. 18May the Lord grant that he will find
mercy from the Lord on that day! You know
very well in how many ways he helped me
in Ephesus.

The Appeal Renewed

2 You then, my son, be strong in the grace
that is in Christ Jesus. 2And the things you
have heard me say in the presence of many
witnesses entrust to reliable people who will
also be qualified to teach others. 3Join with
me in suffering, like a good soldier of Christ
Jesus. 4No one serving as a soldier gets entangled in civilian affairs, but rather tries to
please his commanding officer. 5Similarly,
anyone who competes as an athlete does not
receive the victor's crown except by compet-
ing according to the rules. 6The hardworking
farmer should be the first to receive a share
of the crops. 7Reflect on what I am saying,
for the Lord will give you insight into all this.

8Remember Jesus Christ, raised from the
dead, descended from David. This is my gospel, 9for which I am suffering even to the point
of being chained like a criminal. But God's
word is not chained. 10Therefore I endure everything for the sake of the elect, that they

too may obtain the salvation that is in Christ
Jesus, with eternal glory.
11Here is a trustworthy saying:

If we died with him,
we will also live with him;
12if we endure,
we will also reign with him.
If we disown him,
he will also disown us;
13if we are faithless,
he remains faithful,
for he cannot disown himself.

Dealing With False Teachers

14Keep reminding God's people of these
things. Warn them before God against quarreling about words; it is of no value, and only
ruins those who listen. 15Do your best to present yourself to God as one approved, a worker who does not need to be ashamed and who
correctly handles the word of truth. 16Avoid
godless chatter, because those who indulge
in it will become more and more ungodly.
17Their teaching will spread like gangrene.
Among them are Hymenaeus and Philetus,
18who have departed from the truth. They say
that the resurrection has already taken place,
and they destroy the faith of some. 19Never-
theless, God's solid foundation stands firm,
sealed with this inscription: "The Lord knows
those who are his," and, "Everyone who confesses the name of the Lord must turn away
from wickedness."

20In a large house there are articles not only
of gold and silver, but also of wood and clay;
some are for special purposes and some for
common use. 21Those who cleanse themselves
from the latter will be instruments for special
purposes, made holy, useful to the Master and
prepared to do any good work.

22Flee the evil desires of youth and pursue
righteousness, faith, love and peace, along
with those who call on the Lord out of a pure
heart. 23Don't have anything to do with foolish
and stupid arguments, because you know they
produce quarrels. 24And the Lord's servant
must not be quarrelsome but must be kind to
everyone, able to teach, not resentful. 25Oppo-
nents must be gently instructed, in the hope
that God will grant them repentance leading
them to a knowledge of the truth, 26and that
they will come to their senses and escape from
the trap of the devil, who has taken them captive to do his will.

3 But mark this: There will be terrible times
in the last days. 2People will be lovers of
themselves, lovers of money, boastful, proud,
abusive, disobedient to their parents, ungrateful, unholy, 3without love, unforgiving, slan-
derous, without self-control, brutal, not lovers
of the good, 4treacherous, rash, conceited, lovers of pleasure rather than lovers of God—
5having a form of godliness but denying its
power. Have nothing to do with such people.

6They are the kind who worm their way into
homes and gain control over gullible wom-
en, who are loaded down with sins and are
swayed by all kinds of evil desires, 7always
learning but never able to come to a knowledge of the truth. 8Just as Jannes and Jambres
opposed Moses, so also these teachers oppose
the truth. They are men of depraved minds,
who, as far as the faith is concerned, are rejected. 9But they will not get very far because,
as in the case of those men, their folly will be
clear to everyone.

A Final Charge to Timothy

10You, however, know all about my teaching, my way of life, my purpose, faith, patience, love, endurance, 11persecutions, sufferings—what kinds of things happened to me in
Antioch, Iconium and Lystra, the persecutions
I endured. Yet the Lord rescued me from all of
them. 12In fact, everyone who wants to live a
godly life in Christ Jesus will be persecuted,
13while evildoers and impostors will go from
bad to worse, deceiving and being deceived.
14But as for you, continue in what you have
learned and have become convinced of, because you know those from whom you learned
it, 15and how from infancy you have known
the Holy Scriptures, which are able to make
you wise for salvation through faith in Christ
Jesus. 16All Scripture is God-breathed and is
useful for teaching, rebuking, correcting and
training in righteousness, 17so that the servant
of God[a] may be thoroughly equipped for every good work.

4 In the presence of God and of Christ Jesus,
who will judge the living and the dead, and
in view of his appearing and his kingdom, I
give you this charge: 2Preach the word; be prepared in season and out of season; correct, rebuke and encourage—with great patience and
careful instruction. 3For the time will come
when people will not put up with sound doctrine. Instead, to suit their own desires, they
will gather around them a great number of
teachers to say what their itching ears want
to hear. 4They will turn their ears away from
the truth and turn aside to myths. 5But you,
keep your head in all situations, endure hardship, do the work of an evangelist, discharge
all the duties of your ministry.

6For I am already being poured out like a
drink offering, and the time for my departure is near. 7I have fought the good fight, I
have finished the race, I have kept the faith.
8Now there is in store for me the crown of
righteousness, which the Lord, the righteous
Judge, will award to me on that day—and not
only to me, but also to all who have longed for
his appearing.

Personal Remarks

9Do your best to come to me quickly, 10for
Demas, because he loved this world, has
deserted me and has gone to Thessalonica.
Crescens has gone to Galatia, and Titus to
Dalmatia. 11Only Luke is with me. Get Mark
and bring him with you, because he is helpful

[a] 17 Or *that you, a man of God,*

to me in my ministry. 12I sent Tychicus to Ephesus. 13When you come, bring the cloak that I left with Carpus at Troas, and my scrolls, especially the parchments.

14Alexander the metalworker did me a great deal of harm. The Lord will repay him for what he has done. 15You too should be on your guard against him, because he strongly opposed our message.

16At my first defense, no one came to my support, but everyone deserted me. May it not be held against them. 17But the Lord stood at my side and gave me strength, so that through me the message might be fully proclaimed and all the Gentiles might hear it. And I was delivered from the lion's mouth. 18The Lord will rescue me from every evil attack and will bring me safely to his heavenly kingdom. To him be glory for ever and ever. Amen.

Final Greetings

19Greet Priscilla[a] and Aquila and the household of Onesiphorus. 20Erastus stayed in Corinth, and I left Trophimus sick in Miletus. 21Do your best to get here before winter. Eubulus greets you, and so do Pudens, Linus, Claudia and all the brothers and sisters.[b]

22The Lord be with your spirit. Grace be with you all.

Titus

1 Paul, a servant of God and an apostle of Jesus Christ to further the faith of God's elect and their knowledge of the truth that leads to godliness— 2in the hope of eternal life, which God, who does not lie, promised before the beginning of time, 3and which now at his appointed season he has brought to light through the preaching entrusted to me by the command of God our Savior,

4To Titus, my true son in our common faith:

Grace and peace from God the Father and Christ Jesus our Savior.

Appointing Elders Who Love What Is Good

5The reason I left you in Crete was that you might put in order what was left unfinished and appoint[c] elders in every town, as I directed you. 6An elder must be blameless, faithful to his wife, a man whose children believe[d] and are not open to the charge of being wild and disobedient. 7Since an overseer manages God's household, he must be blameless—not overbearing, not quick-tempered, not given to drunkenness, not violent, not pursuing dishonest gain. 8Rather, he must be hospitable, one who loves what is good, who is self-controlled, upright, holy and disciplined. 9He must hold firmly to the trustworthy message as it has been taught, so that he can encourage others by sound doctrine and refute those who oppose it.

Rebuking Those Who Fail to Do Good

10For there are many rebellious people, full of meaningless talk and deception, especially those of the circumcision group. 11They must be silenced, because they are disrupting whole households by teaching things they ought not to teach—and that for the sake of dishonest gain. 12One of Crete's own prophets has said it: "Cretans are always liars, evil brutes, lazy gluttons."[e] 13This saying is true. Therefore rebuke them sharply, so that they will be sound in the faith 14and will pay no attention to Jewish myths or to the merely human commands of those who reject the truth. 15To the pure, all things are pure, but to those who are corrupted and do not believe, nothing is pure. In fact, both their minds and consciences are corrupted. 16They claim to know God, but by their actions they deny him. They are detestable, disobedient and unfit for doing anything good.

Doing Good for the Sake of the Gospel

2 You, however, must teach what is appropriate to sound doctrine. 2Teach the older men to be temperate, worthy of respect, self-controlled, and sound in faith, in love and in endurance.

3Likewise, teach the older women to be reverent in the way they live, not to be slanderers or addicted to much wine, but to teach what is good. 4Then they can urge the younger women to love their husbands and children, 5to be self-controlled and pure, to be busy at home, to be kind, and to be subject to their husbands, so that no one will malign the word of God.

6Similarly, encourage the young men to be self-controlled. 7In everything set them an example by doing what is good. In your teaching show integrity, seriousness 8and soundness of speech that cannot be condemned, so that those who oppose you may be ashamed because they have nothing bad to say about us.

9Teach slaves to be subject to their masters

[a] 10 Greek *Prisca*, a variant of *Priscilla* [b] 21 The Greek word for *brothers and sisters* (*adelphoi*) refers here to believers, both men and women, as part of God's family. [c] 5 Or *ordain* [d] 6 Or *children are trustworthy* [e] 12 From the Cretan philosopher Epimenides

in everything, to try to please them, not to talk
back to them, 10and not to steal from them,
but to show that they can be fully trusted, so
that in every way they will make the teaching
about God our Savior attractive.
11For the grace of God has appeared that
offers salvation to all people. 12It teaches us
to say "No" to ungodliness and worldly passions, and to live self-controlled, upright and
godly lives in this present age, 13while we
wait for the blessed hope—the appearing of
the glory of our great God and Savior, Jesus
Christ, 14who gave himself for us to redeem
us from all wickedness and to purify for himself a people that are his very own, eager to
do what is good.
15These, then, are the things you should
teach. Encourage and rebuke with all authority. Do not let anyone despise you.

Saved in Order to Do Good

3 Remind the people to be subject to rulers
and authorities, to be obedient, to be ready
to do whatever is good, 2to slander no one, to
be peaceable and considerate, and always to
be gentle toward everyone.
3At one time we too were foolish, disobedient, deceived and enslaved by all kinds of
passions and pleasures. We lived in malice
and envy, being hated and hating one another.
4But when the kindness and love of God our
Savior appeared, 5he saved us, not because of
righteous things we had done, but because of
his mercy. He saved us through the washing of
rebirth and renewal by the Holy Spirit, 6whom
he poured out on us generously through Jesus
Christ our Savior, 7so that, having been justified by his grace, we might become heirs
having the hope of eternal life. 8This is a trustworthy saying. And I want you to stress these
things, so that those who have trusted in God
may be careful to devote themselves to doing
what is good. These things are excellent and
profitable for everyone.
9But avoid foolish controversies and genealogies and arguments and quarrels about the
law, because these are unprofitable and useless. 10Warn a divisive person once, and then
warn them a second time. After that, have
nothing to do with them. 11You may be sure
that such people are warped and sinful; they
are self-condemned.

Final Remarks

12As soon as I send Artemas or Tychicus to
you, do your best to come to me at Nicopolis,
because I have decided to winter there. 13Do
everything you can to help Zenas the lawyer
and Apollos on their way and see that they
have everything they need. 14Our people must
learn to devote themselves to doing what is
good, in order to provide for urgent needs and
not live unproductive lives.
15Everyone with me sends you greetings.
Greet those who love us in the faith.
Grace be with you all.

Philemon

1Paul, a prisoner of Christ Jesus, and Timothy our brother,

To Philemon our dear friend and fellow
worker— 2also to Apphia our sister and Archippus our fellow soldier—and to the church
that meets in your home:

3Grace and peace to you[a] from God our Father and the Lord Jesus Christ.

Thanksgiving and Prayer

4I always thank my God as I remember you
in my prayers, 5because I hear about your love
for all his holy people and your faith in the
Lord Jesus. 6I pray that your partnership with
us in the faith may be effective in deepening
your understanding of every good thing we
share for the sake of Christ. 7Your love has
given me great joy and encouragement, because you, brother, have refreshed the hearts
of the Lord's people.

Paul's Plea for Onesimus

8Therefore, although in Christ I could be
bold and order you to do what you ought to
do, 9yet I prefer to appeal to you on the basis
of love. It is as none other than Paul—an old
man and now also a prisoner of Christ Jesus—
10that I appeal to you for my son Onesimus,[b]
who became my son while I was in chains.
11Formerly he was useless to you, but now he
has become useful both to you and to me.
12I am sending him—who is my very
heart—back to you. 13I would have liked to
keep him with me so that he could take your
place in helping me while I am in chains for
the gospel. 14But I did not want to do anything without your consent, so that any favor
you do would not seem forced but would be
voluntary. 15Perhaps the reason he was separated from you for a little while was that you
might have him back forever— 16no longer
as a slave, but better than a slave, as a dear

[a] *3* The Greek is plural; also in verses 22 and 25; elsewhere in this letter "you" is singular.
[b] *10 Onesimus* means *useful.*

brother. He is very dear to me but even dearer
to you, both as a fellow man and as a brother
in the Lord.
17So if you consider me a partner, welcome
him as you would welcome me. 18If he has
done you any wrong or owes you anything,
charge it to me. 19I, Paul, am writing this
with my own hand. I will pay it back—not to
mention that you owe me your very self. 20I
do wish, brother, that I may have some benefit from you in the Lord; refresh my heart
in Christ. 21Confident of your obedience, I
write to you, knowing that you will do even
more than I ask.
22And one thing more: Prepare a guest room
for me, because I hope to be restored to you
in answer to your prayers.

23Epaphras, my fellow prisoner in Christ
Jesus, sends you greetings. 24And so do Mark,
Aristarchus, Demas and Luke, my fellow
workers.
25The grace of the Lord Jesus Christ be with
your spirit.

Hebrews

God's Final Word: His Son

1 In the past God spoke to our ancestors
through the prophets at many times and
in various ways, 2but in these last days he has
spoken to us by his Son, whom he appointed
heir of all things, and through whom also he
made the universe. 3The Son is the radiance
of God's glory and the exact representation of
his being, sustaining all things by his powerful word. After he had provided purification
for sins, he sat down at the right hand of the
Majesty in heaven. 4So he became as much
superior to the angels as the name he has inherited is superior to theirs.

The Son Superior to Angels

5For to which of the angels did God ever say,

"You are my Son;
today I have become your Father"[a]?

Or again,

"I will be his Father,
and he will be my Son"[b]?

6And again, when God brings his firstborn
into the world, he says,

"Let all God's angels worship him."[c]

7In speaking of the angels he says,

"He makes his angels spirits,
and his servants flames of fire."[d]

8But about the Son he says,

"Your throne, O God, will last for ever
and ever;
a scepter of justice will be the scepter of
your kingdom.
9You have loved righteousness and hated
wickedness;
therefore God, your God, has set you
above your companions
by anointing you with the oil of joy."[e]

10He also says,

"In the beginning, Lord, you laid the
foundations of the earth,
and the heavens are the work of your
hands.
11They will perish, but you remain;
they will all wear out like a garment.
12You will roll them up like a robe;
like a garment they will be changed.
But you remain the same,
and your years will never end."[f]

13To which of the angels did God ever say,

"Sit at my right hand
until I make your enemies
a footstool for your feet"[g]?

14Are not all angels ministering spirits sent to
serve those who will inherit salvation?

Warning to Pay Attention

2 We must pay the most careful attention,
therefore, to what we have heard, so that
we do not drift away. 2For since the message
spoken through angels was binding, and every violation and disobedience received its
just punishment, 3how shall we escape if we
ignore so great a salvation? This salvation,
which was first announced by the Lord, was
confirmed to us by those who heard him. 4God
also testified to it by signs, wonders and various miracles, and by gifts of the Holy Spirit
distributed according to his will.

Jesus Made Fully Human

5It is not to angels that he has subjected the
world to come, about which we are speaking. 6But there is a place where someone has
testified:

"What is mankind that you are mindful
of them,
a son of man that you care for him?

[a] 5 Psalm 2:7 [b] 5 2 Samuel 7:14; 1 Chron. 17:13 [c] 6 Deut. 32:43 (see Dead Sea Scrolls and Septuagint) [d] 7 Psalm 104:4 [e] 9 Psalm 45:6,7 [f] 12 Psalm 102:25-27 [g] 13 Psalm 110:1

7You made them a little[a] lower than the
angels;
you crowned them with glory and
honor
8 and put everything under their feet."[b,c]

In putting everything under them,[d] God left
nothing that is not subject to them.[d] Yet at
present we do not see everything subject to
them.[d] 9But we do see Jesus, who was made
lower than the angels for a little while, now
crowned with glory and honor because he
suffered death, so that by the grace of God
he might taste death for everyone.

10In bringing many sons and daughters to
glory, it was fitting that God, for whom and
through whom everything exists, should
make the pioneer of their salvation perfect
through what he suffered. 11Both the one who
makes people holy and those who are made
holy are of the same family. So Jesus is not
ashamed to call them brothers and sisters.[e]
12He says,

"I will declare your name to my brothers
and sisters;
in the assembly I will sing your
praises."[f]

13And again,

"I will put my trust in him."[g]

And again he says,

"Here am I, and the children God has
given me."[h]

14Since the children have flesh and blood,
he too shared in their humanity so that by his
death he might break the power of him who
holds the power of death—that is, the devil— 15and free those who all their lives were
held in slavery by their fear of death. 16For
surely it is not angels he helps, but Abraham's
descendants. 17For this reason he had to be
made like them,[i] fully human in every way,
in order that he might become a merciful and
faithful high priest in service to God, and that
he might make atonement for the sins of the
people. 18Because he himself suffered when
he was tempted, he is able to help those who
are being tempted.

Jesus Greater Than Moses

3 Therefore, holy brothers and sisters, who
share in the heavenly calling, fix your
thoughts on Jesus, whom we acknowledge as
our apostle and high priest. 2He was faithful
to the one who appointed him, just as Moses
was faithful in all God's house. 3Jesus has
been found worthy of greater honor than Moses, just as the builder of a house has greater
honor than the house itself. 4For every house
is built by someone, but God is the builder of
everything. 5"Moses was faithful as a servant
in all God's house,"[j] bearing witness to what
would be spoken by God in the future. 6But
Christ is faithful as the Son over God's house.
And we are his house, if indeed we hold firmly to our confidence and the hope in which we
glory.

Warning Against Unbelief

7So, as the Holy Spirit says:

"Today, if you hear his voice,
8 do not harden your hearts
as you did in the rebellion,
during the time of testing in the
wilderness,
9where your ancestors tested and tried me,
though for forty years they saw what I
did.
10That is why I was angry with that
generation;
I said, 'Their hearts are always going
astray,
and they have not known my ways.'
11So I declared on oath in my anger,
'They shall never enter my rest.'"[k]

12See to it, brothers and sisters, that none of
you has a sinful, unbelieving heart that turns
away from the living God. 13But encourage
one another daily, as long as it is called "Today," so that none of you may be hardened by
sin's deceitfulness. 14We have come to share
in Christ, if indeed we hold our original conviction firmly to the very end. 15As has just
been said:

"Today, if you hear his voice,
do not harden your hearts
as you did in the rebellion."[l]

16Who were they who heard and rebelled?
Were they not all those Moses led out of
Egypt? 17And with whom was he angry
for forty years? Was it not with those who
sinned, whose bodies perished in the wilderness? 18And to whom did God swear that they
would never enter his rest if not to those who
disobeyed? 19So we see that they were not able
to enter, because of their unbelief.

A Sabbath-Rest for the People of God

4 Therefore, since the promise of entering
his rest still stands, let us be careful that
none of you be found to have fallen short of
it. 2For we also have had the good news proclaimed to us, just as they did; but the message
they heard was of no value to them, because
they did not share the faith of those who
obeyed.[m] 3Now we who have believed enter
that rest, just as God has said,

"So I declared on oath in my anger,
'They shall never enter my rest.'"[n]

[a] 7 Or *them for a little while* [b] 6-8 Psalm 8:4-6 [c] 7,8 Or *7You made him a little lower than the angels;/ you crowned him with glory and honor/ 8and put everything under his feet."* [d] 8 Or *him*
[e] 11 The Greek word for *brothers and sisters* (*adelphoi*) refers here to believers, both men and women, as part of God's family; also in verse 12; and in 3:1, 12; 10:19; 13:22. [f] 12 Psalm 22:22
[g] 13 Isaiah 8:17 [h] 13 Isaiah 8:18 [i] 17 Or *like his brothers* [j] 5 Num. 12:7 [k] 11 Psalm 95:7-11
[l] 15 Psalm 95:7,8 [m] 2 Some manuscripts *because those who heard did not combine it with faith*
[n] 3 Psalm 95:11; also in verse 5

And yet his works have been finished since
the creation of the world. 4For somewhere he
has spoken about the seventh day in these
words: "On the seventh day God rested from
all his works."[a] 5And again in the passage
above he says, "They shall never enter my
rest."

6Therefore since it still remains for some
to enter that rest, and since those who formerly had the good news proclaimed to them
did not go in because of their disobedience,
7God again set a certain day, calling it "Today." This he did when a long time later he
spoke through David, as in the passage already quoted:

> "Today, if you hear his voice,
> do not harden your hearts."[b]

8For if Joshua had given them rest, God would
not have spoken later about another day.
9There remains, then, a Sabbath-rest for the
people of God; 10for anyone who enters God's
rest also rests from their works,[c] just as God
did from his. 11Let us, therefore, make every
effort to enter that rest, so that no one will
perish by following their example of disobedience.

12For the word of God is alive and active.
Sharper than any double-edged sword, it pen-
etrates even to dividing soul and spirit, joints
and marrow; it judges the thoughts and atti-
tudes of the heart. 13Nothing in all creation
is hidden from God's sight. Everything is uncovered and laid bare before the eyes of him
to whom we must give account.

Jesus the Great High Priest

14Therefore, since we have a great high
priest who has ascended into heaven,[d] Jesus
the Son of God, let us hold firmly to the faith
we profess. 15For we do not have a high priest
who is unable to empathize with our weaknesses, but we have one who has been tempted in every way, just as we are—yet he did
not sin. 16Let us then approach God's throne
of grace with confidence, so that we may receive mercy and find grace to help us in our
time of need.

5 Every high priest is selected from among
the people and is appointed to represent
the people in matters related to God, to offer
gifts and sacrifices for sins. 2He is able to deal
gently with those who are ignorant and are
going astray, since he himself is subject to
weakness. 3This is why he has to offer sacrifices for his own sins, as well as for the sins
of the people. 4And no one takes this honor
on himself, but he receives it when called by
God, just as Aaron was.

5In the same way, Christ did not take on
himself the glory of becoming a high priest.
But God said to him,

> "You are my Son;
> today I have become your Father."[e]

6And he says in another place,

> "You are a priest forever,
> in the order of Melchizedek."[f]

7During the days of Jesus' life on earth,
he offered up prayers and petitions with fervent cries and tears to the one who could save
him from death, and he was heard because
of his reverent submission. 8Son though he
was, he learned obedience from what he suffered 9and, once made perfect, he became the
source of eternal salvation for all who obey
him 10and was designated by God to be high
priest in the order of Melchizedek.

Warning Against Falling Away

11We have much to say about this, but it is
hard to make it clear to you because you no
longer try to understand. 12In fact, though by
this time you ought to be teachers, you need
someone to teach you the elementary truths of
God's word all over again. You need milk, not
solid food! 13Anyone who lives on milk, being
still an infant, is not acquainted with the teaching about righteousness. 14But solid food is for
the mature, who by constant use have trained
themselves to distinguish good from evil.

6 Therefore let us move beyond the elementary teachings about Christ and be tak-
en forward to maturity, not laying again the
foundation of repentance from acts that lead
to death,[g] and of faith in God, 2instruction
about cleansing rites,[h] the laying on of hands,
the resurrection of the dead, and eternal judgment. 3And God permitting, we will do so.

4It is impossible for those who have once been
enlightened, who have tasted the heavenly gift,
who have shared in the Holy Spirit, 5who have
tasted the goodness of the word of God and the
powers of the coming age 6and who have fallen[i]
away, to be brought back to repentance. To their
loss they are crucifying the Son of God all over
again and subjecting him to public disgrace.
7Land that drinks in the rain often falling on
it and that produces a crop useful to those for
whom it is farmed receives the blessing of God.
8But land that produces thorns and thistles is
worthless and is in danger of being cursed. In
the end it will be burned.

9Even though we speak like this, dear
friends, we are convinced of better things in
your case—the things that have to do with salvation. 10God is not unjust; he will not forget
your work and the love you have shown him
as you have helped his people and continue to
help them. 11We want each of you to show this
same diligence to the very end, so that what
you hope for may be fully realized. 12We do
not want you to become lazy, but to imitate
those who through faith and patience inherit
what has been promised.

The Certainty of God's Promise

13When God made his promise to Abraham, since there was no one greater for him

[a] 4 Gen. 2:2 [b] 7 Psalm 95:7,8 [c] *10* Or *labor* [d] *14* Greek *has gone through the heavens*
[e] 5 Psalm 2:7 [f] 6 Psalm 110:4 [g] *1* Or *from useless rituals* [h] *2* Or *about baptisms* [i] *6* Or *age,*
6if they fall

to swear by, he swore by himself, 14saying, "I
will surely bless you and give you many descendants."[a] 15And so after waiting patiently,
Abraham received what was promised.
16People swear by someone greater than
themselves, and the oath confirms what is
said and puts an end to all argument. 17Be-
cause God wanted to make the unchanging
nature of his purpose very clear to the heirs
of what was promised, he confirmed it with
an oath. 18God did this so that, by two un-
changeable things in which it is impossible
for God to lie, we who have fled to take hold
of the hope set before us may be greatly encouraged. 19We have this hope as an anchor
for the soul, firm and secure. It enters the inner sanctuary behind the curtain, 20where our
forerunner, Jesus, has entered on our behalf.
He has become a high priest forever, in the
order of Melchizedek.

Melchizedek the Priest

7 This Melchizedek was king of Salem and
priest of God Most High. He met Abraham returning from the defeat of the kings
and blessed him, 2and Abraham gave him
a tenth of everything. First, the name Melchizedek means "king of righteousness"; then
also, "king of Salem" means "king of peace."
3Without father or mother, without genealogy,
without beginning of days or end of life, re-
sembling the Son of God, he remains a priest
forever.
4Just think how great he was: Even the
patriarch Abraham gave him a tenth of the
plunder! 5Now the law requires the descendants of Levi who become priests to collect
a tenth from the people—that is, from their
fellow Israelites—even though they also are
descended from Abraham. 6This man, however, did not trace his descent from Levi, yet he
collected a tenth from Abraham and blessed
him who had the promises. 7And without
doubt the lesser is blessed by the greater. 8In
the one case, the tenth is collected by people
who die; but in the other case, by him who is
declared to be living. 9One might even say that
Levi, who collects the tenth, paid the tenth
through Abraham, 10because when Melchizedek met Abraham, Levi was still in the body
of his ancestor.

Jesus Like Melchizedek

11If perfection could have been attained
through the Levitical priesthood—and indeed the law given to the people established
that priesthood—why was there still need for
another priest to come, one in the order of
Melchizedek, not in the order of Aaron? 12For
when the priesthood is changed, the law must
be changed also. 13He of whom these things
are said belonged to a different tribe, and no
one from that tribe has ever served at the altar. 14For it is clear that our Lord descended
from Judah, and in regard to that tribe Moses said nothing about priests. 15And what we
have said is even more clear if another priest
like Melchizedek appears, 16one who has become a priest not on the basis of a regulation
as to his ancestry but on the basis of the power
of an indestructible life. 17For it is declared:

> "You are a priest forever,
> in the order of Melchizedek."[b]

18The former regulation is set aside because
it was weak and useless 19(for the law made
nothing perfect), and a better hope is introduced, by which we draw near to God.
20And it was not without an oath! Others
became priests without any oath, 21but he
became a priest with an oath when God said
to him:

> "The Lord has sworn
> and will not change his mind:
> 'You are a priest forever.'"[b]

22Because of this oath, Jesus has become the
guarantor of a better covenant.
23Now there have been many of those
priests, since death prevented them from continuing in office; 24but because Jesus lives forever, he has a permanent priesthood. 25There-
fore he is able to save completely[c] those who
come to God through him, because he always
lives to intercede for them.
26Such a high priest truly meets our need—
one who is holy, blameless, pure, set apart
from sinners, exalted above the heavens.
27Unlike the other high priests, he does not
need to offer sacrifices day after day, first
for his own sins, and then for the sins of the
people. He sacrificed for their sins once for
all when he offered himself. 28For the law appoints as high priests men in all their weakness; but the oath, which came after the law,
appointed the Son, who has been made perfect forever.

The High Priest of a New Covenant

8 Now the main point of what we are saying is this: We do have such a high priest,
who sat down at the right hand of the throne
of the Majesty in heaven, 2and who serves in
the sanctuary, the true tabernacle set up by
the Lord, not by a mere human being.
3Every high priest is appointed to offer both
gifts and sacrifices, and so it was necessary
for this one also to have something to offer. 4If
he were on earth, he would not be a priest, for
there are already priests who offer the gifts
prescribed by the law. 5They serve at a sanctuary that is a copy and shadow of what is in
heaven. This is why Moses was warned when
he was about to build the tabernacle: "See to
it that you make everything according to the
pattern shown you on the mountain."[d] 6But
in fact the ministry Jesus has received is as
superior to theirs as the covenant of which he
is mediator is superior to the old one, since
the new covenant is established on better
promises.
7For if there had been nothing wrong with
that first covenant, no place would have been

[a] *14* Gen. 22:17 [b] *17,21* Psalm 110:4 [c] *25* Or *forever* [d] *5* Exodus 25:40

sought for another. 8But God found fault with
the people and said[a]:

"The days are coming, declares the
Lord,
when I will make a new covenant
with the people of Israel
and with the people of Judah.
9 It will not be like the covenant
I made with their ancestors
when I took them by the hand
to lead them out of Egypt,
because they did not remain faithful to
my covenant,
and I turned away from them,
declares the Lord.
10 This is the covenant I will establish with
the people of Israel
after that time, declares the Lord.
I will put my laws in their minds
and write them on their hearts.
I will be their God,
and they will be my people.
11 No longer will they teach their neighbor,
or say to one another, 'Know the
Lord,'
because they will all know me,
from the least of them to the greatest.
12 For I will forgive their wickedness
and will remember their sins no
more."[b]

13By calling this covenant "new," he has
made the first one obsolete; and what is obsolete and outdated will soon disappear.

Worship in the Earthly Tabernacle

9 Now the first covenant had regulations for
worship and also an earthly sanctuary. 2A
tabernacle was set up. In its first room were
the lampstand and the table with its consecrated bread; this was called the Holy Place.
3Behind the second curtain was a room called
the Most Holy Place, 4which had the golden
altar of incense and the gold-covered ark of
the covenant. This ark contained the gold jar
of manna, Aaron's staff that had budded, and
the stone tablets of the covenant. 5Above the
ark were the cherubim of the Glory, overshadowing the atonement cover. But we cannot
discuss these things in detail now.

6When everything had been arranged like
this, the priests entered regularly into the
outer room to carry on their ministry. 7But
only the high priest entered the inner room,
and that only once a year, and never without
blood, which he offered for himself and for the
sins the people had committed in ignorance.
8The Holy Spirit was showing by this that the
way into the Most Holy Place had not yet been
disclosed as long as the first tabernacle was
still functioning. 9This is an illustration for
the present time, indicating that the gifts and
sacrifices being offered were not able to clear
the conscience of the worshiper. 10They are
only a matter of food and drink and various
ceremonial washings—external regulations
applying until the time of the new order.

The Blood of Christ

11But when Christ came as high priest of
the good things that are now already here,[c]
he went through the greater and more perfect tabernacle that is not made with human
hands, that is to say, is not a part of this creation. 12He did not enter by means of the blood
of goats and calves; but he entered the Most
Holy Place once for all by his own blood, thus
obtaining[d] eternal redemption. 13The blood
of goats and bulls and the ashes of a heifer
sprinkled on those who are ceremonially unclean sanctify them so that they are outwardly
clean. 14How much more, then, will the blood
of Christ, who through the eternal Spirit offered himself unblemished to God, cleanse our
consciences from acts that lead to death,[e] so
that we may serve the living God!

15For this reason Christ is the mediator of a
new covenant, that those who are called may
receive the promised eternal inheritance—
now that he has died as a ransom to set them
free from the sins committed under the first
covenant.

16In the case of a will,[f] it is necessary to
prove the death of the one who made it, 17be-
cause a will is in force only when somebody
has died; it never takes effect while the one
who made it is living. 18This is why even the
first covenant was not put into effect without blood. 19When Moses had proclaimed
every command of the law to all the people,
he took the blood of calves, together with
water, scarlet wool and branches of hyssop,
and sprinkled the scroll and all the people.
20He said, "This is the blood of the covenant,
which God has commanded you to keep."[g] 21In
the same way, he sprinkled with the blood
both the tabernacle and everything used in
its ceremonies. 22In fact, the law requires that
nearly everything be cleansed with blood,
and without the shedding of blood there is
no forgiveness.

23It was necessary, then, for the copies of
the heavenly things to be purified with these
sacrifices, but the heavenly things themselves
with better sacrifices than these. 24For Christ
did not enter a sanctuary made with human
hands that was only a copy of the true one;
he entered heaven itself, now to appear for us
in God's presence. 25Nor did he enter heaven
to offer himself again and again, the way the
high priest enters the Most Holy Place every
year with blood that is not his own. 26Other-
wise Christ would have had to suffer many
times since the creation of the world. But he
has appeared once for all at the culmination
of the ages to do away with sin by the sacrifice of himself. 27Just as people are destined
to die once, and after that to face judgment,
28so Christ was sacrificed once to take away
the sins of many; and he will appear a second

[a] *8* Some manuscripts may be translated *fault and said to the people.* [b] *12* Jer. 31:31-34 [c] *11* Some early manuscripts *are to come* [d] *12* Or *blood, having obtained* [e] *14* Or *from useless rituals*
[f] *16* Same Greek word as *covenant*; also in verse 17 [g] *20* Exodus 24:8

time, not to bear sin, but to bring salvation to those who are waiting for him.

Christ's Sacrifice Once for All

10 The law is only a shadow of the good things that are coming—not the realities themselves. For this reason it can never, by the same sacrifices repeated endlessly year after year, make perfect those who draw near to worship. 2Otherwise, would they not have stopped being offered? For the worshipers would have been cleansed once for all, and would no longer have felt guilty for their sins. 3But those sacrifices are an annual reminder of sins. 4It is impossible for the blood of bulls and goats to take away sins.

5Therefore, when Christ came into the world, he said:

"Sacrifice and offering you did not desire,
 but a body you prepared for me;
6with burnt offerings and sin offerings
 you were not pleased.
7Then I said, 'Here I am—it is written
 about me in the scroll—
 I have come to do your will, my God.' "[a]

8First he said, "Sacrifices and offerings, burnt offerings and sin offerings you did not desire, nor were you pleased with them"—though they were offered in accordance with the law. 9Then he said, "Here I am, I have come to do your will." He sets aside the first to establish the second. 10And by that will, we have been made holy through the sacrifice of the body of Jesus Christ once for all.

11Day after day every priest stands and performs his religious duties; again and again he offers the same sacrifices, which can never take away sins. 12But when this priest had offered for all time one sacrifice for sins, he sat down at the right hand of God, 13and since that time he waits for his enemies to be made his footstool. 14For by one sacrifice he has made perfect forever those who are being made holy.

15The Holy Spirit also testifies to us about this. First he says:

16"This is the covenant I will make with
 them
 after that time, says the Lord.
I will put my laws in their hearts,
 and I will write them on their minds."[b]

17Then he adds:

"Their sins and lawless acts
 I will remember no more."[c]

18And where these have been forgiven, sacrifice for sin is no longer necessary.

A Call to Persevere in Faith

19Therefore, brothers and sisters, since we have confidence to enter the Most Holy Place by the blood of Jesus, 20by a new and living way opened for us through the curtain, that is, his body, 21and since we have a great priest over the house of God, 22let us draw near to God with a sincere heart and with the full assurance that faith brings, having our hearts sprinkled to cleanse us from a guilty conscience and having our bodies washed with pure water. 23Let us hold unswervingly to the hope we profess, for he who promised is faithful. 24And let us consider how we may spur one another on toward love and good deeds, 25not giving up meeting together, as some are in the habit of doing, but encouraging one another—and all the more as you see the Day approaching.

26If we deliberately keep on sinning after we have received the knowledge of the truth, no sacrifice for sins is left, 27but only a fearful expectation of judgment and of raging fire that will consume the enemies of God. 28Anyone who rejected the law of Moses died without mercy on the testimony of two or three witnesses. 29How much more severely do you think someone deserves to be punished who has trampled the Son of God underfoot, who has treated as an unholy thing the blood of the covenant that sanctified them, and who has insulted the Spirit of grace? 30For we know him who said, "It is mine to avenge; I will repay,"[d] and again, "The Lord will judge his people."[e] 31It is a dreadful thing to fall into the hands of the living God.

32Remember those earlier days after you had received the light, when you endured in a great conflict full of suffering. 33Sometimes you were publicly exposed to insult and persecution; at other times you stood side by side with those who were so treated. 34You suffered along with those in prison and joyfully accepted the confiscation of your property, because you knew that you yourselves had better and lasting possessions. 35So do not throw away your confidence; it will be richly rewarded.

36You need to persevere so that when you have done the will of God, you will receive what he has promised. 37For,

"In just a little while,
 he who is coming will come
 and will not delay."[f]

38And,

"But my righteous[g] one will live by faith.
 And I take no pleasure
 in the one who shrinks back."[h]

39But we do not belong to those who shrink back and are destroyed, but to those who have faith and are saved.

Faith in Action

11 Now faith is confidence in what we hope for and assurance about what we do not see. 2This is what the ancients were commended for.

3By faith we understand that the universe was formed at God's command, so that what is seen was not made out of what was visible.

[a] *7* Psalm 40:6-8 (see Septuagint) [b] *16* Jer. 31:33 [c] *17* Jer. 31:34 [d] *30* Deut. 32:35 [e] *30* Deut. 32:36; Psalm 135:14 [f] *37* Isaiah 26:20; Hab. 2:3 [g] *38* Some early manuscripts *But the righteous* [h] *38* Hab. 2:4 (see Septuagint)

4By faith Abel brought God a better offering
than Cain did. By faith he was commended
as righteous, when God spoke well of his offerings. And by faith Abel still speaks, even
though he is dead.
5By faith Enoch was taken from this life,
so that he did not experience death: "He
could not be found, because God had taken
him away."[a] For before he was taken, he was
commended as one who pleased God. 6And
without faith it is impossible to please God,
because anyone who comes to him must believe that he exists and that he rewards those
who earnestly seek him.
7By faith Noah, when warned about things
not yet seen, in holy fear built an ark to save
his family. By his faith he condemned the
world and became heir of the righteousness
that is in keeping with faith.
8By faith Abraham, when called to go to
a place he would later receive as his inheritance, obeyed and went, even though he did
not know where he was going. 9By faith he
made his home in the promised land like a
stranger in a foreign country; he lived in tents,
as did Isaac and Jacob, who were heirs with
him of the same promise. 10For he was looking
forward to the city with foundations, whose
architect and builder is God. 11And by faith
even Sarah, who was past childbearing age,
was enabled to bear children because she[b]
considered him faithful who had made the
promise. 12And so from this one man, and he
as good as dead, came descendants as numerous as the stars in the sky and as countless as
the sand on the seashore.
13All these people were still living by faith
when they died. They did not receive the
things promised; they only saw them and
welcomed them from a distance, admitting
that they were foreigners and strangers on
earth. 14People who say such things show that
they are looking for a country of their own.
15If they had been thinking of the country they
had left, they would have had opportunity to
return. 16Instead, they were longing for a better country—a heavenly one. Therefore God
is not ashamed to be called their God, for he
has prepared a city for them.
17By faith Abraham, when God tested him,
offered Isaac as a sacrifice. He who had embraced the promises was about to sacrifice his
one and only son, 18even though God had said
to him, "It is through Isaac that your offspring
will be reckoned."[c] 19Abraham reasoned that
God could even raise the dead, and so in a
manner of speaking he did receive Isaac back
from death.
20By faith Isaac blessed Jacob and Esau in
regard to their future.
21By faith Jacob, when he was dying,
blessed each of Joseph's sons, and worshiped
as he leaned on the top of his staff.
22By faith Joseph, when his end was near,
spoke about the exodus of the Israelites from
Egypt and gave instructions concerning the
burial of his bones.
23By faith Moses' parents hid him for three
months after he was born, because they saw
he was no ordinary child, and they were not
afraid of the king's edict.
24By faith Moses, when he had grown up,
refused to be known as the son of Pharaoh's
daughter. 25He chose to be mistreated along
with the people of God rather than to enjoy
the fleeting pleasures of sin. 26He regarded
disgrace for the sake of Christ as of greater
value than the treasures of Egypt, because he
was looking ahead to his reward. 27By faith
he left Egypt, not fearing the king's anger; he
persevered because he saw him who is invisible. 28By faith he kept the Passover and the
application of blood, so that the destroyer of
the firstborn would not touch the firstborn
of Israel.
29By faith the people passed through the
Red Sea as on dry land; but when the Egyptians tried to do so, they were drowned.
30By faith the walls of Jericho fell, after
the army had marched around them for sev-
en days.
31By faith the prostitute Rahab, because she
welcomed the spies, was not killed with those
who were disobedient.[d]
32And what more shall I say? I do not have
time to tell about Gideon, Barak, Samson
and Jephthah, about David and Samuel and
the prophets, 33who through faith conquered
kingdoms, administered justice, and gained
what was promised; who shut the mouths
of lions, 34quenched the fury of the flames,
and escaped the edge of the sword; whose
weakness was turned to strength; and who
became powerful in battle and routed foreign armies. 35Women received back their
dead, raised to life again. There were others
who were tortured, refusing to be released
so that they might gain an even better resurrection. 36Some faced jeers and flogging, and
even chains and imprisonment. 37They were
put to death by stoning;[e] they were sawed in
two; they were killed by the sword. They went
about in sheepskins and goatskins, destitute,
persecuted and mistreated— 38the world was
not worthy of them. They wandered in deserts
and mountains, living in caves and in holes
in the ground.
39These were all commended for their faith,
yet none of them received what had been
promised, 40since God had planned something better for us so that only together with
us would they be made perfect.

12 Therefore, since we are surrounded by
such a great cloud of witnesses, let us
throw off everything that hinders and the
sin that so easily entangles. And let us run
with perseverance the race marked out for
us, 2fixing our eyes on Jesus, the pioneer and
perfecter of faith. For the joy set before him he
endured the cross, scorning its shame, and sat

[a] 5 Gen. 5:24 [b] 11 Or *By faith Abraham, even though he was too old to have children—and Sarah herself was not able to conceive—was enabled to become a father because he* [c] 18 Gen. 21:12
[d] 31 Or *unbelieving* [e] 37 Some early manuscripts *stoning; they were put to the test;*

down at the right hand of the throne of God. 3Consider him who endured such opposition from sinners, so that you will not grow weary and lose heart.

God Disciplines His Children

4In your struggle against sin, you have not yet resisted to the point of shedding your blood. 5And have you completely forgotten this word of encouragement that addresses you as a father addresses his son? It says,

> "My son, do not make light of the Lord's discipline,
> and do not lose heart when he rebukes you,
> 6because the Lord disciplines the one he loves,
> and he chastens everyone he accepts as his son."[a]

7Endure hardship as discipline; God is treating you as his children. For what children are not disciplined by their father? 8If you are not disciplined—and everyone undergoes discipline—then you are not legitimate, not true sons and daughters at all. 9Moreover, we have all had human fathers who disciplined us and we respected them for it. How much more should we submit to the Father of spirits and live! 10They disciplined us for a little while as they thought best; but God disciplines us for our good, in order that we may share in his holiness. 11No discipline seems pleasant at the time, but painful. Later on, however, it produces a harvest of righteousness and peace for those who have been trained by it.

12Therefore, strengthen your feeble arms and weak knees. 13"Make level paths for your feet,"[b] so that the lame may not be disabled, but rather healed.

Warning and Encouragement

14Make every effort to live in peace with everyone and to be holy; without holiness no one will see the Lord. 15See to it that no one falls short of the grace of God and that no bitter root grows up to cause trouble and defile many. 16See that no one is sexually immoral, or is godless like Esau, who for a single meal sold his inheritance rights as the oldest son. 17Afterward, as you know, when he wanted to inherit this blessing, he was rejected. Even though he sought the blessing with tears, he could not change what he had done.

The Mountain of Fear and the Mountain of Joy

18You have not come to a mountain that can be touched and that is burning with fire; to darkness, gloom and storm; 19to a trumpet blast or to such a voice speaking words that those who heard it begged that no further word be spoken to them, 20because they could not bear what was commanded: "If even an animal touches the mountain, it must be stoned to death."[c] 21The sight was so terrifying that Moses said, "I am trembling with fear."[d]

22But you have come to Mount Zion, to the city of the living God, the heavenly Jerusalem. You have come to thousands upon thousands of angels in joyful assembly, 23to the church of the firstborn, whose names are written in heaven. You have come to God, the Judge of all, to the spirits of the righteous made perfect, 24to Jesus the mediator of a new covenant, and to the sprinkled blood that speaks a better word than the blood of Abel.

25See to it that you do not refuse him who speaks. If they did not escape when they refused him who warned them on earth, how much less will we, if we turn away from him who warns us from heaven? 26At that time his voice shook the earth, but now he has promised, "Once more I will shake not only the earth but also the heavens."[e] 27The words "once more" indicate the removing of what can be shaken—that is, created things—so that what cannot be shaken may remain.

28Therefore, since we are receiving a kingdom that cannot be shaken, let us be thankful, and so worship God acceptably with reverence and awe, 29for our "God is a consuming fire."[f]

Concluding Exhortations

13 Keep on loving one another as brothers and sisters. 2Do not forget to show hospitality to strangers, for by so doing some people have shown hospitality to angels without knowing it. 3Continue to remember those in prison as if you were together with them in prison, and those who are mistreated as if you yourselves were suffering.

4Marriage should be honored by all, and the marriage bed kept pure, for God will judge the adulterer and all the sexually immoral. 5Keep your lives free from the love of money and be content with what you have, because God has said,

> "Never will I leave you;
> never will I forsake you."[g]

6So we say with confidence,

> "The Lord is my helper; I will not be afraid.
> What can mere mortals do to me?"[h]

7Remember your leaders, who spoke the word of God to you. Consider the outcome of their way of life and imitate their faith. 8Jesus Christ is the same yesterday and today and forever.

9Do not be carried away by all kinds of strange teachings. It is good for our hearts to be strengthened by grace, not by eating ceremonial foods, which is of no benefit to those who do so. 10We have an altar from which those who minister at the tabernacle have no right to eat.

11The high priest carries the blood of an-

[a] *5,6* Prov. 3:11,12 (see Septuagint) [b] *13* Prov. 4:26 [c] *20* Exodus 19:12,13 [d] *21* See Deut. 9:19. [e] *26* Haggai 2:6 [f] *29* Deut. 4:24 [g] *5* Deut. 31:6 [h] *6* Psalm 118:6,7

imals into the Most Holy Place as a sin offering, but the bodies are burned outside the
camp. 12And so Jesus also suffered outside the
city gate to make the people holy through his
own blood. 13Let us, then, go to him outside
the camp, bearing the disgrace he bore. 14For
here we do not have an enduring city, but we
are looking for the city that is to come.
15Through Jesus, therefore, let us continually offer to God a sacrifice of praise—the fruit
of lips that openly profess his name. 16And do
not forget to do good and to share with others,
for with such sacrifices God is pleased.
17Have confidence in your leaders and
submit to their authority, because they keep
watch over you as those who must give an
account. Do this so that their work will be
a joy, not a burden, for that would be of no
benefit to you.
18Pray for us. We are sure that we have a
clear conscience and desire to live honorably
in every way. 19I particularly urge you to pray
so that I may be restored to you soon.

Benediction and Final Greetings

20Now may the God of peace, who through
the blood of the eternal covenant brought back
from the dead our Lord Jesus, that great Shepherd of the sheep, 21equip you with everything
good for doing his will, and may he work in us
what is pleasing to him, through Jesus Christ,
to whom be glory for ever and ever. Amen.

22Brothers and sisters, I urge you to bear
with my word of exhortation, for in fact I have
written to you quite briefly.
23I want you to know that our brother Timothy has been released. If he arrives soon, I
will come with him to see you.
24Greet all your leaders and all the Lord's people. Those from Italy send you their greetings.
25Grace be with you all.

James

1 James, a servant of God and of the Lord
Jesus Christ,

To the twelve tribes scattered among the
nations:

Greetings.

Trials and Temptations

2Consider it pure joy, my brothers and sisters,[a] whenever you face trials of many kinds,
3because you know that the testing of your
faith produces perseverance. 4Let perseverance finish its work so that you may be mature
and complete, not lacking anything. 5If any of
you lacks wisdom, you should ask God, who
gives generously to all without finding fault,
and it will be given to you. 6But when you
ask, you must believe and not doubt, because
the one who doubts is like a wave of the sea,
blown and tossed by the wind. 7That person
should not expect to receive anything from
the Lord. 8Such a person is double-minded
and unstable in all they do.
9Believers in humble circumstances ought
to take pride in their high position. 10But the
rich should take pride in their humiliation—
since they will pass away like a wild flower.
11For the sun rises with scorching heat and
withers the plant; its blossom falls and its
beauty is destroyed. In the same way, the
rich will fade away even while they go about
their business.
12Blessed is the one who perseveres under
trial because, having stood the test, that person will receive the crown of life that the Lord
has promised to those who love him.
13When tempted, no one should say, "God is
tempting me." For God cannot be tempted by
evil, nor does he tempt anyone; 14but each person is tempted when they are dragged away by
their own evil desire and enticed. 15Then, after
desire has conceived, it gives birth to sin; and
sin, when it is full-grown, gives birth to death.
16Don't be deceived, my dear brothers and
sisters. 17Every good and perfect gift is from
above, coming down from the Father of the
heavenly lights, who does not change like
shifting shadows. 18He chose to give us birth
through the word of truth, that we might be
a kind of firstfruits of all he created.

Listening and Doing

19My dear brothers and sisters, take note of
this: Everyone should be quick to listen, slow
to speak and slow to become angry, 20because
human anger does not produce the righteousness that God desires. 21Therefore, get rid of
all moral filth and the evil that is so prevalent
and humbly accept the word planted in you,
which can save you.
22Do not merely listen to the word, and so
deceive yourselves. Do what it says. 23Anyone
who listens to the word but does not do what it
says is like someone who looks at his face in
a mirror 24and, after looking at himself, goes
away and immediately forgets what he looks
like. 25But whoever looks intently into the perfect law that gives freedom, and continues in

[a] 2 The Greek word for *brothers and sisters* (*adelphoi*) refers here to believers, both men and women, as part of God's family; also in verses 16 and 19; and in 2:1, 5, 14; 3:10, 12; 4:11; 5:7, 9, 10, 12, 19.

it—not forgetting what they have heard, but doing it—they will be blessed in what they do.

26Those who consider themselves religious and yet do not keep a tight rein on their tongues deceive themselves, and their religion is worthless. 27Religion that God our Father accepts as pure and faultless is this: to look after orphans and widows in their distress and to keep oneself from being polluted by the world.

Favoritism Forbidden

2 My brothers and sisters, believers in our glorious Lord Jesus Christ must not show favoritism. 2Suppose a man comes into your meeting wearing a gold ring and fine clothes, and a poor man in filthy old clothes also comes in. 3If you show special attention to the man wearing fine clothes and say, "Here's a good seat for you," but say to the poor man, "You stand there" or "Sit on the floor by my feet," 4have you not discriminated among yourselves and become judges with evil thoughts?

5Listen, my dear brothers and sisters: Has not God chosen those who are poor in the eyes of the world to be rich in faith and to inherit the kingdom he promised those who love him? 6But you have dishonored the poor. Is it not the rich who are exploiting you? Are they not the ones who are dragging you into court? 7Are they not the ones who are blaspheming the noble name of him to whom you belong?

8If you really keep the royal law found in Scripture, "Love your neighbor as yourself,"[a] you are doing right. 9But if you show favoritism, you sin and are convicted by the law as lawbreakers. 10For whoever keeps the whole law and yet stumbles at just one point is guilty of breaking all of it. 11For he who said, "You shall not commit adultery,"[b] also said, "You shall not murder."[c] If you do not commit adultery but do commit murder, you have become a lawbreaker.

12Speak and act as those who are going to be judged by the law that gives freedom, 13because judgment without mercy will be shown to anyone who has not been merciful. Mercy triumphs over judgment.

Faith and Deeds

14What good is it, my brothers and sisters, if someone claims to have faith but has no deeds? Can such faith save them? 15Suppose a brother or a sister is without clothes and daily food. 16If one of you says to them, "Go in peace; keep warm and well fed," but does nothing about their physical needs, what good is it? 17In the same way, faith by itself, if it is not accompanied by action, is dead.

18But someone will say, "You have faith; I have deeds."

Show me your faith without deeds, and I will show you my faith by my deeds. 19You believe that there is one God. Good! Even the demons believe that—and shudder.

20You foolish person, do you want evidence that faith without deeds is useless[d]? 21Was not our father Abraham considered righteous for what he did when he offered his son Isaac on the altar? 22You see that his faith and his actions were working together, and his faith was made complete by what he did. 23And the scripture was fulfilled that says, "Abraham believed God, and it was credited to him as righteousness,"[e] and he was called God's friend. 24You see that a person is considered righteous by what they do and not by faith alone.

25In the same way, was not even Rahab the prostitute considered righteous for what she did when she gave lodging to the spies and sent them off in a different direction? 26As the body without the spirit is dead, so faith without deeds is dead.

Taming the Tongue

3 Not many of you should become teachers, my fellow believers, because you know that we who teach will be judged more strictly. 2We all stumble in many ways. Anyone who is never at fault in what they say is perfect, able to keep their whole body in check.

3When we put bits into the mouths of horses to make them obey us, we can turn the whole animal. 4Or take ships as an example. Although they are so large and are driven by strong winds, they are steered by a very small rudder wherever the pilot wants to go. 5Likewise, the tongue is a small part of the body, but it makes great boasts. Consider what a great forest is set on fire by a small spark. 6The tongue also is a fire, a world of evil among the parts of the body. It corrupts the whole body, sets the whole course of one's life on fire, and is itself set on fire by hell.

7All kinds of animals, birds, reptiles and sea creatures are being tamed and have been tamed by mankind, 8but no human being can tame the tongue. It is a restless evil, full of deadly poison.

9With the tongue we praise our Lord and Father, and with it we curse human beings, who have been made in God's likeness. 10Out of the same mouth come praise and cursing. My brothers and sisters, this should not be. 11Can both fresh water and salt water flow from the same spring? 12My brothers and sisters, can a fig tree bear olives, or a grapevine bear figs? Neither can a salt spring produce fresh water.

Two Kinds of Wisdom

13Who is wise and understanding among you? Let them show it by their good life, by deeds done in the humility that comes from wisdom. 14But if you harbor bitter envy and selfish ambition in your hearts, do not boast about it or deny the truth. 15Such "wisdom" does not come down from heaven but is earthly, unspiritual, demonic. 16For where you have envy and selfish ambition, there you find disorder and every evil practice.

[a] *8* Lev. 19:18 [b] *11* Exodus 20:14; Deut. 5:18 [c] *11* Exodus 20:13; Deut. 5:17 [d] *20* Some early manuscripts *dead* [e] *23* Gen. 15:6

17But the wisdom that comes from heaven is
first of all pure; then peace-loving, considerate, submissive, full of mercy and good fruit,
impartial and sincere. 18Peacemakers who
sow in peace reap a harvest of righteousness.

Submit Yourselves to God

4 What causes fights and quarrels among
you? Don't they come from your desires
that battle within you? 2You desire but do not
have, so you kill. You covet but you cannot
get what you want, so you quarrel and fight.
You do not have because you do not ask God.
3When you ask, you do not receive, because
you ask with wrong motives, that you may
spend what you get on your pleasures.
4You adulterous people,[a] don't you know
that friendship with the world means enmity
against God? Therefore, anyone who chooses
to be a friend of the world becomes an enemy
of God. 5Or do you think Scripture says without reason that he jealously longs for the spirit
he has caused to dwell in us[b]? 6But he gives
us more grace. That is why Scripture says:

"God opposes the proud
but shows favor to the humble."[c]

7Submit yourselves, then, to God. Resist the
devil, and he will flee from you. 8Come near to
God and he will come near to you. Wash your
hands, you sinners, and purify your hearts,
you double-minded. 9Grieve, mourn and wail.
Change your laughter to mourning and your
joy to gloom. 10Humble yourselves before the
Lord, and he will lift you up.
11Brothers and sisters, do not slander one
another. Anyone who speaks against a brother or sister[d] or judges them speaks against the
law and judges it. When you judge the law, you
are not keeping it, but sitting in judgment on
it. 12There is only one Lawgiver and Judge,
the one who is able to save and destroy. But
you—who are you to judge your neighbor?

Boasting About Tomorrow

13Now listen, you who say, "Today or tomorrow we will go to this or that city, spend a year
there, carry on business and make money."
14Why, you do not even know what will happen tomorrow. What is your life? You are a
mist that appears for a little while and then
vanishes. 15Instead, you ought to say, "If it
is the Lord's will, we will live and do this or
that." 16As it is, you boast in your arrogant
schemes. All such boasting is evil. 17If anyone, then, knows the good they ought to do
and doesn't do it, it is sin for them.

Warning to Rich Oppressors

5 Now listen, you rich people, weep and
wail because of the misery that is coming on you. 2Your wealth has rotted, and
moths have eaten your clothes. 3Your gold
and silver are corroded. Their corrosion
will testify against you and eat your flesh
like fire. You have hoarded wealth in the
last days. 4Look! The wages you failed to
pay the workers who mowed your fields are
crying out against you. The cries of the harvesters have reached the ears of the Lord
Almighty. 5You have lived on earth in luxury and self-indulgence. You have fattened
yourselves in the day of slaughter.[e] 6You have
condemned and murdered the innocent one,
who was not opposing you.

Patience in Suffering

7Be patient, then, brothers and sisters, until
the Lord's coming. See how the farmer waits
for the land to yield its valuable crop, patiently waiting for the autumn and spring rains.
8You too, be patient and stand firm, because
the Lord's coming is near. 9Don't grumble
against one another, brothers and sisters, or
you will be judged. The Judge is standing
at the door!
10Brothers and sisters, as an example of patience in the face of suffering, take the prophets who spoke in the name of the Lord. 11As
you know, we count as blessed those who have
persevered. You have heard of Job's perseverance and have seen what the Lord finally
brought about. The Lord is full of compassion
and mercy.
12Above all, my brothers and sisters, do
not swear—not by heaven or by earth or by
anything else. All you need to say is a simple "Yes" or "No." Otherwise you will be condemned.

The Prayer of Faith

13Is anyone among you in trouble? Let them
pray. Is anyone happy? Let them sing songs
of praise. 14Is anyone among you sick? Let
them call the elders of the church to pray over
them and anoint them with oil in the name
of the Lord. 15And the prayer offered in faith
will make the sick person well; the Lord will
raise them up. If they have sinned, they will
be forgiven. 16Therefore confess your sins to
each other and pray for each other so that
you may be healed. The prayer of a righteous
person is powerful and effective.
17Elijah was a human being, even as we are.
He prayed earnestly that it would not rain,
and it did not rain on the land for three and a
half years. 18Again he prayed, and the heavens
gave rain, and the earth produced its crops.
19My brothers and sisters, if one of you
should wander from the truth and someone
should bring that person back, 20remember
this: Whoever turns a sinner from the error
of their way will save them from death and
cover over a multitude of sins.

[a] *4* An allusion to covenant unfaithfulness; see Hosea 3:1. [b] *5* Or *that the spirit he caused to dwell in us envies intensely;* or *that the Spirit he caused to dwell in us longs jealously* [c] *6* Prov. 3:34
[d] *11* The Greek word for *brother or sister* (*adelphos*) refers here to a believer, whether man or woman, as part of God's family. [e] *5* Or *yourselves as in a day of feasting*

1 Peter

1 Peter, an apostle of Jesus Christ,

To God's elect, exiles scattered throughout the provinces of Pontus, Galatia, Cappadocia, Asia and Bithynia, 2who have been chosen according to the foreknowledge of God the Father, through the sanctifying work of the Spirit, to be obedient to Jesus Christ and sprinkled with his blood:

Grace and peace be yours in abundance.

Praise to God for a Living Hope

3Praise be to the God and Father of our Lord Jesus Christ! In his great mercy he has given us new birth into a living hope through the resurrection of Jesus Christ from the dead, 4and into an inheritance that can never perish, spoil or fade. This inheritance is kept in heaven for you, 5who through faith are shielded by God's power until the coming of the salvation that is ready to be revealed in the last time. 6In all this you greatly rejoice, though now for a little while you may have had to suffer grief in all kinds of trials. 7These have come so that the proven genuineness of your faith—of greater worth than gold, which perishes even though refined by fire—may result in praise, glory and honor when Jesus Christ is revealed. 8Though you have not seen him, you love him; and even though you do not see him now, you believe in him and are filled with an inexpressible and glorious joy, 9for you are receiving the end result of your faith, the salvation of your souls.

10Concerning this salvation, the prophets, who spoke of the grace that was to come to you, searched intently and with the greatest care, 11trying to find out the time and circumstances to which the Spirit of Christ in them was pointing when he predicted the sufferings of the Messiah and the glories that would follow. 12It was revealed to them that they were not serving themselves but you, when they spoke of the things that have now been told you by those who have preached the gospel to you by the Holy Spirit sent from heaven. Even angels long to look into these things.

Be Holy

13Therefore, with minds that are alert and fully sober, set your hope on the grace to be brought to you when Jesus Christ is revealed at his coming. 14As obedient children, do not conform to the evil desires you had when you lived in ignorance. 15But just as he who called you is holy, so be holy in all you do; 16for it is written: "Be holy, because I am holy."[a]

17Since you call on a Father who judges each person's work impartially, live out your time as foreigners here in reverent fear. 18For you know that it was not with perishable things such as silver or gold that you were redeemed from the empty way of life handed down to you from your ancestors, 19but with the precious blood of Christ, a lamb without blemish or defect. 20He was chosen before the creation of the world, but was revealed in these last times for your sake. 21Through him you believe in God, who raised him from the dead and glorified him, and so your faith and hope are in God.

22Now that you have purified yourselves by obeying the truth so that you have sincere love for each other, love one another deeply, from the heart.[b] 23For you have been born again, not of perishable seed, but of imperishable, through the living and enduring word of God. 24For,

"All people are like grass,
  and all their glory is like the flowers of the field;
the grass withers and the flowers fall,
25 but the word of the Lord endures forever."[c]

And this is the word that was preached to you.

2 Therefore, rid yourselves of all malice and all deceit, hypocrisy, envy, and slander of every kind. 2Like newborn babies, crave pure spiritual milk, so that by it you may grow up in your salvation, 3now that you have tasted that the Lord is good.

The Living Stone and a Chosen People

4As you come to him, the living Stone—rejected by humans but chosen by God and precious to him— 5you also, like living stones, are being built into a spiritual house[d] to be a holy priesthood, offering spiritual sacrifices acceptable to God through Jesus Christ. 6For in Scripture it says:

"See, I lay a stone in Zion,
  a chosen and precious cornerstone,
and the one who trusts in him
  will never be put to shame."[e]

7Now to you who believe, this stone is precious. But to those who do not believe,

"The stone the builders rejected
  has become the cornerstone,"[f]

8and,

"A stone that causes people to stumble
  and a rock that makes them fall."[g]

They stumble because they disobey the message—which is also what they were destined for.

9But you are a chosen people, a royal priesthood, a holy nation, God's special possession, that you may declare the praises of him who called you out of darkness into his wonderful light. 10Once you were not a people, but now

[a] *16* Lev. 11:44,45; 19:2 [b] *22* Some early manuscripts *from a pure heart* [c] *25* Isaiah 40:6-8 (see Septuagint) [d] *5* Or *into a temple of the Spirit* [e] *6* Isaiah 28:16 [f] *7* Psalm 118:22 [g] *8* Isaiah 8:14

you are the people of God; once you had not received mercy, but now you have received mercy.

Living Godly Lives in a Pagan Society

[11]Dear friends, I urge you, as foreigners and
exiles, to abstain from sinful desires, which
wage war against your soul. [12]Live such good
lives among the pagans that, though they accuse
you of doing wrong, they may see your good
deeds and glorify God on the day he visits us.
[13]Submit yourselves for the Lord's sake to every human authority: whether to the emperor,
as the supreme authority, [14]or to governors, who
are sent by him to punish those who do wrong
and to commend those who do right. [15]For it is
God's will that by doing good you should silence the ignorant talk of foolish people. [16]Live
as free people, but do not use your freedom as
a cover-up for evil; live as God's slaves. [17]Show
proper respect to everyone, love the family of
believers, fear God, honor the emperor.
[18]Slaves, in reverent fear of God submit
yourselves to your masters, not only to those
who are good and considerate, but also to
those who are harsh. [19]For it is commendable
if someone bears up under the pain of unjust
suffering because they are conscious of God.
[20]But how is it to your credit if you receive a
beating for doing wrong and endure it? But
if you suffer for doing good and you endure
it, this is commendable before God. [21]To this
you were called, because Christ suffered for
you, leaving you an example, that you should
follow in his steps.

[22]"He committed no sin,
and no deceit was found in his mouth."[a]

[23]When they hurled their insults at him, he
did not retaliate; when he suffered, he made
no threats. Instead, he entrusted himself to
him who judges justly. [24]"He himself bore
our sins" in his body on the cross, so that we
might die to sins and live for righteousness;
"by his wounds you have been healed." [25]For
"you were like sheep going astray,"[b] but now
you have returned to the Shepherd and Overseer of your souls.

3 Wives, in the same way submit yourselves
to your own husbands so that, if any of
them do not believe the word, they may be
won over without words by the behavior of
their wives, [2]when they see the purity and
reverence of your lives. [3]Your beauty should
not come from outward adornment, such as
elaborate hairstyles and the wearing of gold
jewelry or fine clothes. [4]Rather, it should be
that of your inner self, the unfading beauty
of a gentle and quiet spirit, which is of great
worth in God's sight. [5]For this is the way the
holy women of the past who put their hope in
God used to adorn themselves. They submitted themselves to their own husbands, [6]like
Sarah, who obeyed Abraham and called him
her lord. You are her daughters if you do what
is right and do not give way to fear.

[7]Husbands, in the same way be considerate
as you live with your wives, and treat them
with respect as the weaker partner and as
heirs with you of the gracious gift of life, so
that nothing will hinder your prayers.

Suffering for Doing Good

[8]Finally, all of you, be like-minded, be sym-
pathetic, love one another, be compassionate
and humble. [9]Do not repay evil with evil or
insult with insult. On the contrary, repay evil
with blessing, because to this you were called
so that you may inherit a blessing. [10]For,

"Whoever would love life
and see good days
must keep their tongue from evil
and their lips from deceitful speech.
[11]They must turn from evil and do good;
they must seek peace and pursue it.
[12]For the eyes of the Lord are on the
righteous
and his ears are attentive to their prayer,
but the face of the Lord is against those
who do evil."[c]

[13]Who is going to harm you if you are eager
to do good? [14]But even if you should suffer for
what is right, you are blessed. "Do not fear their
threats[d]; do not be frightened."[e] [15]But in your
hearts revere Christ as Lord. Always be prepared to give an answer to everyone who asks
you to give the reason for the hope that you
have. But do this with gentleness and respect,
[16]keeping a clear conscience, so that those who
speak maliciously against your good behavior in Christ may be ashamed of their slander.
[17]For it is better, if it is God's will, to suffer for
doing good than for doing evil. [18]For Christ
also suffered once for sins, the righteous for
the unrighteous, to bring you to God. He was
put to death in the body but made alive in the
Spirit. [19]After being made alive,[f] he went and
made proclamation to the imprisoned spirits— [20]to those who were disobedient long ago
when God waited patiently in the days of Noah
while the ark was being built. In it only a few
people, eight in all, were saved through water,
[21]and this water symbolizes baptism that now
saves you also—not the removal of dirt from
the body but the pledge of a clear conscience
toward God.[g] It saves you by the resurrection of
Jesus Christ, [22]who has gone into heaven and is
at God's right hand—with angels, authorities
and powers in submission to him.

Living for God

4 Therefore, since Christ suffered in his body,
arm yourselves also with the same attitude,
because whoever suffers in the body is done
with sin. [2]As a result, they do not live the rest
of their earthly lives for evil human desires,
but rather for the will of God. [3]For you have
spent enough time in the past doing what pagans choose to do—living in debauchery, lust,
drunkenness, orgies, carousing and detestable

[a] *22* Isaiah 53:9 [b] *24,25* Isaiah 53:4,5,6 (see Septuagint) [c] *12* Psalm 34:12-16 [d] *14* Or *fear what they fear* [e] *14* Isaiah 8:12 [f] *18,19* Or *but made alive in the spirit,* [19]*in which also* [g] *21* Or *but an appeal to God for a clear conscience*

idolatry. 4They are surprised that you do not
join them in their reckless, wild living, and
they heap abuse on you. 5But they will have
to give account to him who is ready to judge
the living and the dead. 6For this is the reason
the gospel was preached even to those who are
now dead, so that they might be judged according to human standards in regard to the body,
but live according to God in regard to the spirit.
7The end of all things is near. Therefore be
alert and of sober mind so that you may pray.
8Above all, love each other deeply, because
love covers over a multitude of sins. 9Offer
hospitality to one another without grumbling. 10Each of you should use whatever gift
you have received to serve others, as faithful
stewards of God's grace in its various forms.
11If anyone speaks, they should do so as one
who speaks the very words of God. If anyone
serves, they should do so with the strength
God provides, so that in all things God may
be praised through Jesus Christ. To him be the
glory and the power for ever and ever. Amen.

Suffering for Being a Christian

12Dear friends, do not be surprised at the fiery ordeal that has come on you to test you, as
though something strange were happening to
you. 13But rejoice inasmuch as you participate
in the sufferings of Christ, so that you may be
overjoyed when his glory is revealed. 14If you
are insulted because of the name of Christ,
you are blessed, for the Spirit of glory and of
God rests on you. 15If you suffer, it should not
be as a murderer or thief or any other kind of
criminal, or even as a meddler. 16However, if
you suffer as a Christian, do not be ashamed,
but praise God that you bear that name. 17For
it is time for judgment to begin with God's
household; and if it begins with us, what will
the outcome be for those who do not obey the
gospel of God? 18And,

"If it is hard for the righteous to be saved,
what will become of the ungodly and
the sinner?"[a]

19So then, those who suffer according to
God's will should commit themselves to their
faithful Creator and continue to do good.

To the Elders and the Flock

5 To the elders among you, I appeal as a
fellow elder and a witness of Christ's sufferings who also will share in the glory to be
revealed: 2Be shepherds of God's flock that is
under your care, watching over them—not because you must, but because you are willing,
as God wants you to be; not pursuing dishonest gain, but eager to serve; 3not lording it over
those entrusted to you, but being examples
to the flock. 4And when the Chief Shepherd
appears, you will receive the crown of glory
that will never fade away.
5In the same way, you who are younger,
submit yourselves to your elders. All of you,
clothe yourselves with humility toward one
another, because,

"God opposes the proud
but shows favor to the humble."[b]

6Humble yourselves, therefore, under God's
mighty hand, that he may lift you up in due
time. 7Cast all your anxiety on him because
he cares for you.
8Be alert and of sober mind. Your enemy
the devil prowls around like a roaring lion
looking for someone to devour. 9Resist him,
standing firm in the faith, because you know
that the family of believers throughout the
world is undergoing the same kind of sufferings.
10And the God of all grace, who called you
to his eternal glory in Christ, after you have
suffered a little while, will himself restore
you and make you strong, firm and steadfast. 11To him be the power for ever and ever.
Amen.

Final Greetings

12With the help of Silas,[c] whom I regard as a
faithful brother, I have written to you briefly,
encouraging you and testifying that this is the
true grace of God. Stand fast in it.
13She who is in Babylon, chosen together
with you, sends you her greetings, and so
does my son Mark. 14Greet one another with
a kiss of love.
Peace to all of you who are in Christ.

2 Peter

1 Simon Peter, a servant and apostle of Jesus
Christ,

To those who through the righteousness
of our God and Savior Jesus Christ have received a faith as precious as ours:

2Grace and peace be yours in abundance
through the knowledge of God and of Jesus
our Lord.

Confirming One's Calling and Election

3His divine power has given us everything
we need for a godly life through our knowledge of him who called us by his own glory
and goodness. 4Through these he has given
us his very great and precious promises, so
that through them you may participate in the
divine nature, having escaped the corruption
in the world caused by evil desires.

[a] *18* Prov. 11:31 (see Septuagint) [b] *5* Prov. 3:34 [c] *12* Greek *Silvanus*, a variant of *Silas*

5For this very reason, make every effort to add to your faith goodness; and to goodness, knowledge; 6and to knowledge, self-control; and to self-control, perseverance; and to perseverance, godliness; 7and to godliness, mutual affection; and to mutual affection, love. 8For if you possess these qualities in increasing measure, they will keep you from being ineffective and unproductive in your knowledge of our Lord Jesus Christ. 9But whoever does not have them is nearsighted and blind, forgetting that they have been cleansed from their past sins.

10Therefore, my brothers and sisters,[a] make every effort to confirm your calling and election. For if you do these things, you will never stumble, 11and you will receive a rich welcome into the eternal kingdom of our Lord and Savior Jesus Christ.

Prophecy of Scripture

12So I will always remind you of these things, even though you know them and are firmly established in the truth you now have. 13I think it is right to refresh your memory as long as I live in the tent of this body, 14because I know that I will soon put it aside, as our Lord Jesus Christ has made clear to me. 15And I will make every effort to see that after my departure you will always be able to remember these things.

16For we did not follow cleverly devised stories when we told you about the coming of our Lord Jesus Christ in power, but we were eyewitnesses of his majesty. 17He received honor and glory from God the Father when the voice came to him from the Majestic Glory, saying, "This is my Son, whom I love; with him I am well pleased."[b] 18We ourselves heard this voice that came from heaven when we were with him on the sacred mountain.

19We also have the prophetic message as something completely reliable, and you will do well to pay attention to it, as to a light shining in a dark place, until the day dawns and the morning star rises in your hearts. 20Above all, you must understand that no prophecy of Scripture came about by the prophet's own interpretation of things. 21For prophecy never had its origin in the human will, but prophets, though human, spoke from God as they were carried along by the Holy Spirit.

False Teachers and Their Destruction

2 But there were also false prophets among the people, just as there will be false teachers among you. They will secretly introduce destructive heresies, even denying the sovereign Lord who bought them—bringing swift destruction on themselves. 2Many will follow their depraved conduct and will bring the way of truth into disrepute. 3In their greed these teachers will exploit you with fabricated stories. Their condemnation has long been hanging over them, and their destruction has not been sleeping.

4For if God did not spare angels when they sinned, but sent them to hell,[c] putting them in chains of darkness[d] to be held for judgment; 5if he did not spare the ancient world when he brought the flood on its ungodly people, but protected Noah, a preacher of righteousness, and seven others; 6if he condemned the cities of Sodom and Gomorrah by burning them to ashes, and made them an example of what is going to happen to the ungodly; 7and if he rescued Lot, a righteous man, who was distressed by the depraved conduct of the lawless 8(for that righteous man, living among them day after day, was tormented in his righteous soul by the lawless deeds he saw and heard)— 9if this is so, then the Lord knows how to rescue the godly from trials and to hold the unrighteous for punishment on the day of judgment. 10This is especially true of those who follow the corrupt desire of the flesh[e] and despise authority.

Bold and arrogant, they are not afraid to heap abuse on celestial beings; 11yet even angels, although they are stronger and more powerful, do not heap abuse on such beings when bringing judgment on them from[f] the Lord. 12But these people blaspheme in matters they do not understand. They are like unreasoning animals, creatures of instinct, born only to be caught and destroyed, and like animals they too will perish.

13They will be paid back with harm for the harm they have done. Their idea of pleasure is to carouse in broad daylight. They are blots and blemishes, reveling in their pleasures while they feast with you.[g] 14With eyes full of adultery, they never stop sinning; they seduce the unstable; they are experts in greed—an accursed brood! 15They have left the straight way and wandered off to follow the way of Balaam son of Bezer,[h] who loved the wages of wickedness. 16But he was rebuked for his wrongdoing by a donkey—an animal without speech—who spoke with a human voice and restrained the prophet's madness.

17These people are springs without water and mists driven by a storm. Blackest darkness is reserved for them. 18For they mouth empty, boastful words and, by appealing to the lustful desires of the flesh, they entice people who are just escaping from those who live in error. 19They promise them freedom, while they themselves are slaves of depravity—for "people are slaves to whatever has mastered them." 20If they have escaped the corruption of the world by knowing our Lord and Savior Jesus Christ and are again entangled in it and are overcome, they are worse off at the end than they were at the beginning. 21It would

[a] *10* The Greek word for *brothers and sisters* (*adelphoi*) refers here to believers, both men and women, as part of God's family. [b] *17* Matt. 17:5; Mark 9:7; Luke 9:35 [c] *4* Greek *Tartarus* [d] *4* Some manuscripts *in gloomy dungeons* [e] *10* In contexts like this, the Greek word for *flesh* (*sarx*) refers to the sinful state of human beings, often presented as a power in opposition to the Spirit; also in verse 18. [f] *11* Many manuscripts *beings in the presence of* [g] *13* Some manuscripts *in their love feasts* [h] *15* Greek *Bosor*

have been better for them not to have known
the way of righteousness, than to have known
it and then to turn their backs on the sacred
command that was passed on to them. 22Of
them the proverbs are true: "A dog returns to
its vomit,"[a] and, "A sow that is washed returns
to her wallowing in the mud."

The Day of the Lord

3 Dear friends, this is now my second letter
to you. I have written both of them as re-
minders to stimulate you to wholesome thinking. 2I want you to recall the words spoken in
the past by the holy prophets and the command given by our Lord and Savior through
your apostles.
3Above all, you must understand that in the
last days scoffers will come, scoffing and following their own evil desires. 4They will say,
"Where is this 'coming' he promised? Ever
since our ancestors died, everything goes
on as it has since the beginning of creation."
5But they deliberately forget that long ago
by God's word the heavens came into being
and the earth was formed out of water and
by water. 6By these waters also the world of
that time was deluged and destroyed. 7By the
same word the present heavens and earth are
reserved for fire, being kept for the day of
judgment and destruction of the ungodly.
8But do not forget this one thing, dear
friends: With the Lord a day is like a thousand years, and a thousand years are like
a day. 9The Lord is not slow in keeping his
promise, as some understand slowness. Instead he is patient with you, not wanting
anyone to perish, but everyone to come to
repentance.
10But the day of the Lord will come like a
thief. The heavens will disappear with a roar;
the elements will be destroyed by fire, and
the earth and everything done in it will be
laid bare.[b]
11Since everything will be destroyed in this
way, what kind of people ought you to be? You
ought to live holy and godly lives 12as you
look forward to the day of God and speed its
coming.[c] That day will bring about the destruction of the heavens by fire, and the elements will melt in the heat. 13But in keeping
with his promise we are looking forward to
a new heaven and a new earth, where righteousness dwells.
14So then, dear friends, since you are looking forward to this, make every effort to be
found spotless, blameless and at peace with
him. 15Bear in mind that our Lord's patience
means salvation, just as our dear brother Paul
also wrote you with the wisdom that God gave
him. 16He writes the same way in all his letters, speaking in them of these matters. His
letters contain some things that are hard to
understand, which ignorant and unstable people distort, as they do the other Scriptures, to
their own destruction.
17Therefore, dear friends, since you have
been forewarned, be on your guard so that
you may not be carried away by the error of
the lawless and fall from your secure position.
18But grow in the grace and knowledge of our
Lord and Savior Jesus Christ. To him be glory
both now and forever! Amen.

1 John

The Incarnation of the Word of Life

1 That which was from the beginning, which
we have heard, which we have seen with
our eyes, which we have looked at and our
hands have touched—this we proclaim concerning the Word of life. 2The life appeared;
we have seen it and testify to it, and we proclaim to you the eternal life, which was with
the Father and has appeared to us. 3We proclaim to you what we have seen and heard,
so that you also may have fellowship with us.
And our fellowship is with the Father and with
his Son, Jesus Christ. 4We write this to make
our[d] joy complete.

Light and Darkness, Sin and Forgiveness

5This is the message we have heard from him
and declare to you: God is light; in him there is
no darkness at all. 6If we claim to have fellowship with him and yet walk in the darkness,
we lie and do not live out the truth. 7But if we
walk in the light, as he is in the light, we have
fellowship with one another, and the blood of
Jesus, his Son, purifies us from all[e] sin.
8If we claim to be without sin, we deceive
ourselves and the truth is not in us. 9If we
confess our sins, he is faithful and just and
will forgive us our sins and purify us from all
unrighteousness. 10If we claim we have not
sinned, we make him out to be a liar and his
word is not in us.

2 My dear children, I write this to you so that
you will not sin. But if anybody does sin,
we have an advocate with the Father—Jesus
Christ, the Righteous One. 2He is the atoning
sacrifice for our sins, and not only for ours but
also for the sins of the whole world.

[a] 22 Prov. 26:11 [b] *10* Some manuscripts *be burned up* [c] *12* Or *as you wait eagerly for the day of God to come* [d] *4* Some manuscripts *your* [e] *7* Or *every*

Love and Hatred for Fellow Believers

3We know that we have come to know him if we keep his commands. 4Whoever says, "I know him," but does not do what he commands is a liar, and the truth is not in that person. 5But if anyone obeys his word, love for God[a] is truly made complete in them. This is how we know we are in him: 6Whoever claims to live in him must live as Jesus did.

7Dear friends, I am not writing you a new command but an old one, which you have had since the beginning. This old command is the message you have heard. 8Yet I am writing you a new command; its truth is seen in him and in you, because the darkness is passing and the true light is already shining.

9Anyone who claims to be in the light but hates a brother or sister[b] is still in the darkness. 10Anyone who loves their brother and sister[c] lives in the light, and there is nothing in them to make them stumble. 11But anyone who hates a brother or sister is in the darkness and walks around in the darkness. They do not know where they are going, because the darkness has blinded them.

Reasons for Writing

12I am writing to you, dear children,
because your sins have been forgiven
on account of his name.
13I am writing to you, fathers,
because you know him who is from the
beginning.
I am writing to you, young men,
because you have overcome the evil
one.

14I write to you, dear children,
because you know the Father.
I write to you, fathers,
because you know him who is from the
beginning.
I write to you, young men,
because you are strong,
and the word of God lives in you,
and you have overcome the evil one.

On Not Loving the World

15Do not love the world or anything in the world. If anyone loves the world, love for the Father[d] is not in them. 16For everything in the world—the lust of the flesh, the lust of the eyes, and the pride of life—comes not from the Father but from the world. 17The world and its desires pass away, but whoever does the will of God lives forever.

Warnings Against Denying the Son

18Dear children, this is the last hour; and as you have heard that the antichrist is coming, even now many antichrists have come. This is how we know it is the last hour. 19They went out from us, but they did not really belong to us. For if they had belonged to us, they would have remained with us; but their going showed that none of them belonged to us.

20But you have an anointing from the Holy One, and all of you know the truth.[e] 21I do not write to you because you do not know the truth, but because you do know it and because no lie comes from the truth. 22Who is the liar? It is whoever denies that Jesus is the Christ. Such a person is the antichrist—denying the Father and the Son. 23No one who denies the Son has the Father; whoever acknowledges the Son has the Father also.

24As for you, see that what you have heard from the beginning remains in you. If it does, you also will remain in the Son and in the Father. 25And this is what he promised us—eternal life.

26I am writing these things to you about those who are trying to lead you astray. 27As for you, the anointing you received from him remains in you, and you do not need anyone to teach you. But as his anointing teaches you about all things and as that anointing is real, not counterfeit—just as it has taught you, remain in him.

God's Children and Sin

28And now, dear children, continue in him, so that when he appears we may be confident and unashamed before him at his coming.

29If you know that he is righteous, you know that everyone who does what is right has been born of him.

3 See what great love the Father has lavished on us, that we should be called children of God! And that is what we are! The reason the world does not know us is that it did not know him. 2Dear friends, now we are children of God, and what we will be has not yet been made known. But we know that when Christ appears,[f] we shall be like him, for we shall see him as he is. 3All who have this hope in him purify themselves, just as he is pure.

4Everyone who sins breaks the law; in fact, sin is lawlessness. 5But you know that he appeared so that he might take away our sins. And in him is no sin. 6No one who lives in him keeps on sinning. No one who continues to sin has either seen him or known him.

7Dear children, do not let anyone lead you astray. The one who does what is right is righteous, just as he is righteous. 8The one who does what is sinful is of the devil, because the devil has been sinning from the beginning. The reason the Son of God appeared was to destroy the devil's work. 9No one who is born of God will continue to sin, because God's seed remains in them; they cannot go on sinning, because they have been born of God. 10This is how we know who the children of God are and who the children of the devil are: Anyone who does not do what is right is

[a] 5 Or *word, God's love* [b] 9 The Greek word for *brother or sister* (*adelphos*) refers here to a believer, whether man or woman, as part of God's family; also in verse 11; and in 3:15, 17; 4:20; 5:16. [c] 10 The Greek word for *brother and sister* (*adelphos*) refers here to a believer, whether man or woman, as part of God's family; also in 3:10; 4:20, 21. [d] 15 Or *world, the Father's love* [e] 20 Some manuscripts *and you know all things* [f] 2 Or *when it is made known*

not God's child, nor is anyone who does not
love their brother and sister.

More on Love and Hatred

11For this is the message you heard from
the beginning: We should love one another.
12Do not be like Cain, who belonged to the
evil one and murdered his brother. And why
did he murder him? Because his own actions
were evil and his brother's were righteous.
13Do not be surprised, my brothers and sisters,[a] if the world hates you. 14We know that
we have passed from death to life, because
we love each other. Anyone who does not
love remains in death. 15Anyone who hates
a brother or sister is a murderer, and you
know that no murderer has eternal life residing in him.

16This is how we know what love is: Jesus
Christ laid down his life for us. And we ought
to lay down our lives for our brothers and sisters. 17If anyone has material possessions and
sees a brother or sister in need but has no pity
on them, how can the love of God be in that
person? 18Dear children, let us not love with
words or speech but with actions and in truth.

19This is how we know that we belong to
the truth and how we set our hearts at rest
in his presence: 20If our hearts condemn us,
we know that God is greater than our hearts,
and he knows everything. 21Dear friends, if
our hearts do not condemn us, we have confidence before God 22and receive from him
anything we ask, because we keep his commands and do what pleases him. 23And this
is his command: to believe in the name of his
Son, Jesus Christ, and to love one another as
he commanded us. 24The one who keeps God's
commands lives in him, and he in them. And
this is how we know that he lives in us: We
know it by the Spirit he gave us.

On Denying the Incarnation

4 Dear friends, do not believe every spirit,
but test the spirits to see whether they are
from God, because many false prophets have
gone out into the world. 2This is how you can
recognize the Spirit of God: Every spirit that
acknowledges that Jesus Christ has come in
the flesh is from God, 3but every spirit that
does not acknowledge Jesus is not from God.
This is the spirit of the antichrist, which you
have heard is coming and even now is already
in the world.

4You, dear children, are from God and have
overcome them, because the one who is in you
is greater than the one who is in the world.
5They are from the world and therefore speak
from the viewpoint of the world, and the world
listens to them. 6We are from God, and whoever knows God listens to us; but whoever
is not from God does not listen to us. This is
how we recognize the Spirit[b] of truth and the
spirit of falsehood.

God's Love and Ours

7Dear friends, let us love one another, for
love comes from God. Everyone who loves has
been born of God and knows God. 8Whoever
does not love does not know God, because
God is love. 9This is how God showed his love
among us: He sent his one and only Son into
the world that we might live through him.
10This is love: not that we loved God, but that
he loved us and sent his Son as an atoning
sacrifice for our sins. 11Dear friends, since
God so loved us, we also ought to love one
another. 12No one has ever seen God; but if
we love one another, God lives in us and his
love is made complete in us.

13This is how we know that we live in him
and he in us: He has given us of his Spirit.
14And we have seen and testify that the Father has sent his Son to be the Savior of the
world. 15If anyone acknowledges that Jesus is
the Son of God, God lives in them and they in
God. 16And so we know and rely on the love
God has for us.

God is love. Whoever lives in love lives in
God, and God in them. 17This is how love is
made complete among us so that we will have
confidence on the day of judgment: In this
world we are like Jesus. 18There is no fear in
love. But perfect love drives out fear, because
fear has to do with punishment. The one who
fears is not made perfect in love.

19We love because he first loved us. 20Who-
ever claims to love God yet hates a brother
or sister is a liar. For whoever does not love
their brother and sister, whom they have seen,
cannot love God, whom they have not seen.
21And he has given us this command: Anyone
who loves God must also love their brother
and sister.

Faith in the Incarnate Son of God

5 Everyone who believes that Jesus is the
Christ is born of God, and everyone who
loves the father loves his child as well. 2This
is how we know that we love the children of
God: by loving God and carrying out his commands. 3In fact, this is love for God: to keep
his commands. And his commands are not
burdensome, 4for everyone born of God overcomes the world. This is the victory that has
overcome the world, even our faith. 5Who is it
that overcomes the world? Only the one who
believes that Jesus is the Son of God.

6This is the one who came by water and
blood—Jesus Christ. He did not come by water only, but by water and blood. And it is the
Spirit who testifies, because the Spirit is the
truth. 7For there are three that testify: 8the[c]
Spirit, the water and the blood; and the three
are in agreement. 9We accept human testimony, but God's testimony is greater because it
is the testimony of God, which he has given
about his Son. 10Whoever believes in the Son
of God accepts this testimony. Whoever does

[a] 13 The Greek word for *brothers and sisters* (*adelphoi*) refers here to believers, both men and women, as part of God's family; also in verse 16. [b] 6 Or *spirit* [c] 7,8 Late manuscripts of the Vulgate *testify in heaven: the Father, the Word and the Holy Spirit, and these three are one. 8And there are three that testify on earth: the* (not found in any Greek manuscript before the fourteenth century)

not believe God has made him out to be a liar,
because they have not believed the testimony
God has given about his Son. 11And this is
the testimony: God has given us eternal life,
and this life is in his Son. 12Whoever has the
Son has life; whoever does not have the Son
of God does not have life.

Concluding Affirmations

13I write these things to you who believe
in the name of the Son of God so that you
may know that you have eternal life. 14This is
the confidence we have in approaching God:
that if we ask anything according to his will,
he hears us. 15And if we know that he hears
us—whatever we ask—we know that we have
what we asked of him.

16If you see any brother or sister commit
a sin that does not lead to death, you should
pray and God will give them life. I refer to
those whose sin does not lead to death. There
is a sin that leads to death. I am not saying
that you should pray about that. 17All wrongdoing is sin, and there is sin that does not
lead to death.

18We know that anyone born of God does not
continue to sin; the One who was born of God
keeps them safe, and the evil one cannot harm
them. 19We know that we are children of God,
and that the whole world is under the control
of the evil one. 20We know also that the Son of
God has come and has given us understanding,
so that we may know him who is true. And we
are in him who is true by being in his Son Jesus
Christ. He is the true God and eternal life.

21Dear children, keep yourselves from idols.

2 John

1The elder,

To the lady chosen by God and to her children, whom I love in the truth—and not I only,
but also all who know the truth— 2because of
the truth, which lives in us and will be with
us forever:

3Grace, mercy and peace from God the Father and from Jesus Christ, the Father's Son,
will be with us in truth and love.

4It has given me great joy to find some of
your children walking in the truth, just as the
Father commanded us. 5And now, dear lady, I
am not writing you a new command but one
we have had from the beginning. I ask that
we love one another. 6And this is love: that we
walk in obedience to his commands. As you
have heard from the beginning, his command
is that you walk in love.

7I say this because many deceivers, who do
not acknowledge Jesus Christ as coming in
the flesh, have gone out into the world. Any
such person is the deceiver and the antichrist.
8Watch out that you do not lose what we[a] have
worked for, but that you may be rewarded
fully. 9Anyone who runs ahead and does not
continue in the teaching of Christ does not
have God; whoever continues in the teaching
has both the Father and the Son. 10If anyone
comes to you and does not bring this teaching,
do not take them into your house or welcome
them. 11Anyone who welcomes them shares
in their wicked work.

12I have much to write to you, but I do not
want to use paper and ink. Instead, I hope to
visit you and talk with you face to face, so that
our joy may be complete.

13The children of your sister, who is chosen
by God, send their greetings.

3 John

1The elder,

To my dear friend Gaius, whom I love in
the truth.

2Dear friend, I pray that you may enjoy
good health and that all may go well with you,
even as your soul is getting along well. 3It gave
me great joy when some believers came and
testified about your faithfulness to the truth,
telling how you continue to walk in it. 4I have
no greater joy than to hear that my children
are walking in the truth.

5Dear friend, you are faithful in what you

[a] 8 Some manuscripts *you*

are doing for the brothers and sisters,[a] even
though they are strangers to you. 6They have
told the church about your love. Please send
them on their way in a manner that honors
God. 7It was for the sake of the Name that
they went out, receiving no help from the pagans. 8We ought therefore to show hospitality
to such people so that we may work together
for the truth.

9I wrote to the church, but Diotrephes, who
loves to be first, will not welcome us. 10So
when I come, I will call attention to what he
is doing, spreading malicious nonsense about
us. Not satisfied with that, he even refuses to
welcome other believers. He also stops those
who want to do so and puts them out of the
church.

11Dear friend, do not imitate what is evil but
what is good. Anyone who does what is good
is from God. Anyone who does what is evil
has not seen God. 12Demetrius is well spoken
of by everyone—and even by the truth itself.
We also speak well of him, and you know that
our testimony is true.

13I have much to write you, but I do not want
to do so with pen and ink. 14I hope to see you
soon, and we will talk face to face.

15Peace to you. The friends here send their
greetings. Greet the friends there by name.

Jude

1Jude, a servant of Jesus Christ and a brother of James,

To those who have been called, who are
loved in God the Father and kept for[b] Jesus
Christ:

2Mercy, peace and love be yours in abundance.

The Sin and Doom of Ungodly People

3Dear friends, although I was very eager to
write to you about the salvation we share, I felt
compelled to write and urge you to contend
for the faith that was once for all entrusted
to God's holy people. 4For certain individuals
whose condemnation was written about[c] long
ago have secretly slipped in among you. They
are ungodly people, who pervert the grace
of our God into a license for immorality and
deny Jesus Christ our only Sovereign and
Lord.

5Though you already know all this, I want
to remind you that the Lord[d] at one time delivered his people out of Egypt, but later destroyed those who did not believe. 6And the
angels who did not keep their positions of authority but abandoned their proper dwelling—
these he has kept in darkness, bound with
everlasting chains for judgment on the great
Day. 7In a similar way, Sodom and Gomorrah
and the surrounding towns gave themselves
up to sexual immorality and perversion. They
serve as an example of those who suffer the
punishment of eternal fire.

8In the very same way, on the strength of
their dreams these ungodly people pollute
their own bodies, reject authority and heap
abuse on celestial beings. 9But even the archangel Michael, when he was disputing with
the devil about the body of Moses, did not
himself dare to condemn him for slander but
said, "The Lord rebuke you!"[e] 10Yet these people slander whatever they do not understand,
and the very things they do understand by
instinct—as irrational animals do—will destroy them.

11Woe to them! They have taken the way
of Cain; they have rushed for profit into Balaam's error; they have been destroyed in Korah's rebellion.

12These people are blemishes at your love
feasts, eating with you without the slightest
qualm—shepherds who feed only themselves.
They are clouds without rain, blown along by
the wind; autumn trees, without fruit and uprooted—twice dead. 13They are wild waves of
the sea, foaming up their shame; wandering
stars, for whom blackest darkness has been
reserved forever.

14Enoch, the seventh from Adam, prophesied about them: "See, the Lord is coming with
thousands upon thousands of his holy ones
15to judge everyone, and to convict all of them
of all the ungodly acts they have committed in
their ungodliness, and of all the defiant words
ungodly sinners have spoken against him."[f]
16These people are grumblers and faultfind-
ers; they follow their own evil desires; they
boast about themselves and flatter others for
their own advantage.

A Call to Persevere

17But, dear friends, remember what the
apostles of our Lord Jesus Christ foretold.

[a] 5 The Greek word for *brothers and sisters* (*adelphoi*) refers here to believers, both men and women, as part of God's family. [b] *1* Or *by*; or *in* [c] *4* Or *individuals who were marked out for condemnation* [d] 5 Some early manuscripts *Jesus* [e] *9* Jude is alluding to the Jewish *Testament of Moses* (approximately the first century A.D.). [f] *14,15* From the Jewish *First Book of Enoch* (approximately the first century B.C.)

18They said to you, "In the last times there will
be scoffers who will follow their own ungodly
desires." 19These are the people who divide
you, who follow mere natural instincts and
do not have the Spirit.
20But you, dear friends, by building yourselves up in your most holy faith and praying
in the Holy Spirit, 21keep yourselves in God's
love as you wait for the mercy of our Lord
Jesus Christ to bring you to eternal life.
22Be merciful to those who doubt; 23save others by snatching them from the fire; to others
show mercy, mixed with fear—hating even
the clothing stained by corrupted flesh.[a]

Doxology

24To him who is able to keep you from stumbling and to present you before his glorious
presence without fault and with great joy—
25to the only God our Savior be glory, majesty,
power and authority, through Jesus Christ
our Lord, before all ages, now and forevermore! Amen.

Revelation

Prologue

1 The revelation from Jesus Christ, which
God gave him to show his servants what
must soon take place. He made it known by
sending his angel to his servant John, 2who
testifies to everything he saw—that is, the
word of God and the testimony of Jesus
Christ. 3Blessed is the one who reads aloud
the words of this prophecy, and blessed are
those who hear it and take to heart what is
written in it, because the time is near.

Greetings and Doxology

4John,

To the seven churches in the province of Asia:

Grace and peace to you from him who is,
and who was, and who is to come, and from
the seven spirits[b] before his throne, 5and from
Jesus Christ, who is the faithful witness, the
firstborn from the dead, and the ruler of the
kings of the earth.

To him who loves us and has freed us from
our sins by his blood, 6and has made us to be
a kingdom and priests to serve his God and
Father—to him be glory and power for ever
and ever! Amen.

7"Look, he is coming with the clouds,"[c]
and "every eye will see him,
even those who pierced him";
and all peoples on earth "will mourn
because of him."[d]
So shall it be! Amen.

8"I am the Alpha and the Omega," says the
Lord God, "who is, and who was, and who is
to come, the Almighty."

John's Vision of Christ

9I, John, your brother and companion in the
suffering and kingdom and patient endurance
that are ours in Jesus, was on the island of
Patmos because of the word of God and the
testimony of Jesus. 10On the Lord's Day I was
in the Spirit, and I heard behind me a loud
voice like a trumpet, 11which said: "Write on
a scroll what you see and send it to the seven
churches: to Ephesus, Smyrna, Pergamum,
Thyatira, Sardis, Philadelphia and Laodicea."
12I turned around to see the voice that was
speaking to me. And when I turned I saw
seven golden lampstands, 13and among the
lampstands was someone like a son of man,[e]
dressed in a robe reaching down to his feet
and with a golden sash around his chest.
14The hair on his head was white like wool,
as white as snow, and his eyes were like blazing fire. 15His feet were like bronze glowing
in a furnace, and his voice was like the sound
of rushing waters. 16In his right hand he held
seven stars, and coming out of his mouth was
a sharp, double-edged sword. His face was
like the sun shining in all its brilliance.
17When I saw him, I fell at his feet as though
dead. Then he placed his right hand on me and
said: "Do not be afraid. I am the First and the
Last. 18I am the Living One; I was dead, and
now look, I am alive for ever and ever! And I
hold the keys of death and Hades.
19"Write, therefore, what you have seen,
what is now and what will take place later.
20The mystery of the seven stars that you
saw in my right hand and of the seven gold-
en lampstands is this: The seven stars are the
angels[f] of the seven churches, and the seven
lampstands are the seven churches.

To the Church in Ephesus

2 "To the angel[g] of the church in Ephesus
write:

These are the words of him who holds
the seven stars in his right hand and walks
among the seven golden lampstands.

[a] *22,23* The Greek manuscripts of these verses vary at several points. [b] *4* That is, the sevenfold Spirit [c] *7* Daniel 7:13 [d] *7* Zech. 12:10 [e] *13* See Daniel 7:13. [f] *20* Or *messengers*
[g] *1* Or *messenger*; also in verses 8, 12 and 18

2I know your deeds, your hard work and
your perseverance. I know that you cannot tolerate wicked people, that you have
tested those who claim to be apostles but
are not, and have found them false. 3You
have persevered and have endured hardships for my name, and have not grown
weary.
4Yet I hold this against you: You have
forsaken the love you had at first. 5Con-
sider how far you have fallen! Repent and
do the things you did at first. If you do
not repent, I will come to you and remove
your lampstand from its place. 6But you
have this in your favor: You hate the practices of the Nicolaitans, which I also hate.
7Whoever has ears, let them hear what
the Spirit says to the churches. To the one
who is victorious, I will give the right to
eat from the tree of life, which is in the
paradise of God.

To the Church in Smyrna

8"To the angel of the church in Smyrna write:

These are the words of him who is the
First and the Last, who died and came to
life again. 9I know your afflictions and
your poverty—yet you are rich! I know
about the slander of those who say they
are Jews and are not, but are a synagogue
of Satan. 10Do not be afraid of what you
are about to suffer. I tell you, the devil will
put some of you in prison to test you, and
you will suffer persecution for ten days.
Be faithful, even to the point of death, and
I will give you life as your victor's crown.
11Whoever has ears, let them hear what
the Spirit says to the churches. The one
who is victorious will not be hurt at all
by the second death.

To the Church in Pergamum

12"To the angel of the church in Pergamum
write:

These are the words of him who has
the sharp, double-edged sword. 13I know
where you live—where Satan has his
throne. Yet you remain true to my name.
You did not renounce your faith in me, not
even in the days of Antipas, my faithful
witness, who was put to death in your
city—where Satan lives.
14Nevertheless, I have a few things
against you: There are some among
you who hold to the teaching of Balaam,
who taught Balak to entice the Israelites
to sin so that they ate food sacrificed to
idols and committed sexual immorality.
15Likewise, you also have those who hold
to the teaching of the Nicolaitans. 16Re-
pent therefore! Otherwise, I will soon
come to you and will fight against them
with the sword of my mouth.
17Whoever has ears, let them hear what
the Spirit says to the churches. To the one
who is victorious, I will give some of the
hidden manna. I will also give that person
a white stone with a new name written on
it, known only to the one who receives it.

To the Church in Thyatira

18"To the angel of the church in Thyatira write:

These are the words of the Son of God,
whose eyes are like blazing fire and
whose feet are like burnished bronze.
19I know your deeds, your love and faith,
your service and perseverance, and that
you are now doing more than you did at
first.
20Nevertheless, I have this against you:
You tolerate that woman Jezebel, who
calls herself a prophet. By her teaching
she misleads my servants into sexual immorality and the eating of food sacrificed
to idols. 21I have given her time to repent
of her immorality, but she is unwilling.
22So I will cast her on a bed of suffering, and I will make those who commit
adultery with her suffer intensely, unless
they repent of her ways. 23I will strike her
children dead. Then all the churches will
know that I am he who searches hearts
and minds, and I will repay each of you
according to your deeds.
24Now I say to the rest of you in Thyatira, to you who do not hold to her teaching
and have not learned Satan's so-called
deep secrets, 'I will not impose any other
burden on you, 25except to hold on to what
you have until I come.'
26To the one who is victorious and does
my will to the end, I will give authority
over the nations— 27that one 'will rule
them with an iron scepter and will dash
them to pieces like pottery'[a]—just as I
have received authority from my Father.
28I will also give that one the morning
star. 29Whoever has ears, let them hear
what the Spirit says to the churches.

To the Church in Sardis

3 "To the angel[b] of the church in Sardis
write:

These are the words of him who holds
the seven spirits[c] of God and the seven
stars. I know your deeds; you have a reputation of being alive, but you are dead.
2Wake up! Strengthen what remains
and is about to die, for I have found your
deeds unfinished in the sight of my God.
3Remember, therefore, what you have received and heard; hold it fast, and repent.
But if you do not wake up, I will come like
a thief, and you will not know at what
time I will come to you.
4Yet you have a few people in Sardis
who have not soiled their clothes. They
will walk with me, dressed in white, for
they are worthy. 5The one who is victorious will, like them, be dressed in white. I

[a] *27* Psalm 2:9 [b] *1* Or *messenger*; also in verses 7 and 14 [c] *1* That is, the sevenfold Spirit

will never blot out the name of that person from the book of life, but will acknowledge that name before my Father and his angels. 6Whoever has ears, let them hear what the Spirit says to the churches.

To the Church in Philadelphia

7"To the angel of the church in Philadelphia write:

These are the words of him who is holy and true, who holds the key of David. What he opens no one can shut, and what he shuts no one can open. 8I know your deeds. See, I have placed before you an open door that no one can shut. I know that you have little strength, yet you have kept my word and have not denied my name. 9I will make those who are of the synagogue of Satan, who claim to be Jews though they are not, but are liars—I will make them come and fall down at your feet and acknowledge that I have loved you. 10Since you have kept my command to endure patiently, I will also keep you from the hour of trial that is going to come on the whole world to test the inhabitants of the earth.

11I am coming soon. Hold on to what you have, so that no one will take your crown. 12The one who is victorious I will make a pillar in the temple of my God. Never again will they leave it. I will write on them the name of my God and the name of the city of my God, the new Jerusalem, which is coming down out of heaven from my God; and I will also write on them my new name. 13Whoever has ears, let them hear what the Spirit says to the churches.

To the Church in Laodicea

14"To the angel of the church in Laodicea write:

These are the words of the Amen, the faithful and true witness, the ruler of God's creation. 15I know your deeds, that you are neither cold nor hot. I wish you were either one or the other! 16So, because you are lukewarm—neither hot nor cold—I am about to spit you out of my mouth. 17You say, 'I am rich; I have acquired wealth and do not need a thing.' But you do not realize that you are wretched, pitiful, poor, blind and naked. 18I counsel you to buy from me gold refined in the fire, so you can become rich; and white clothes to wear, so you can cover your shameful nakedness; and salve to put on your eyes, so you can see.

19Those whom I love I rebuke and discipline. So be earnest and repent. 20Here I am! I stand at the door and knock. If anyone hears my voice and opens the door, I will come in and eat with that person, and they with me.

21To the one who is victorious, I will give the right to sit with me on my throne, just as I was victorious and sat down with my Father on his throne. 22Whoever has ears, let them hear what the Spirit says to the churches."

The Throne in Heaven

4 After this I looked, and there before me was a door standing open in heaven. And the voice I had first heard speaking to me like a trumpet said, "Come up here, and I will show you what must take place after this." 2At once I was in the Spirit, and there before me was a throne in heaven with someone sitting on it. 3And the one who sat there had the appearance of jasper and ruby. A rainbow that shone like an emerald encircled the throne. 4Surrounding the throne were twenty-four other thrones, and seated on them were twenty-four elders. They were dressed in white and had crowns of gold on their heads. 5From the throne came flashes of lightning, rumblings and peals of thunder. In front of the throne, seven lamps were blazing. These are the seven spirits[a] of God. 6Also in front of the throne there was what looked like a sea of glass, clear as crystal.

In the center, around the throne, were four living creatures, and they were covered with eyes, in front and in back. 7The first living creature was like a lion, the second was like an ox, the third had a face like a man, the fourth was like a flying eagle. 8Each of the four living creatures had six wings and was covered with eyes all around, even under its wings. Day and night they never stop saying:

"'Holy, holy, holy
is the Lord God Almighty,'[b]
who was, and is, and is to come."

9Whenever the living creatures give glory, honor and thanks to him who sits on the throne and who lives for ever and ever, 10the twenty-four elders fall down before him who sits on the throne and worship him who lives for ever and ever. They lay their crowns before the throne and say:

11"You are worthy, our Lord and God,
to receive glory and honor and power,
for you created all things,
and by your will they were created
and have their being."

The Scroll and the Lamb

5 Then I saw in the right hand of him who sat on the throne a scroll with writing on both sides and sealed with seven seals. 2And I saw a mighty angel proclaiming in a loud voice, "Who is worthy to break the seals and open the scroll?" 3But no one in heaven or on earth or under the earth could open the scroll or even look inside it. 4I wept and wept because no one was found who was worthy to open the scroll or look inside. 5Then one of the elders said to me, "Do not weep! See, the

[a] 5 That is, the sevenfold Spirit [b] 8 Isaiah 6:3

Lion of the tribe of Judah, the Root of David,
has triumphed. He is able to open the scroll
and its seven seals."
6 Then I saw a Lamb, looking as if it had
been slain, standing at the center of the
throne, encircled by the four living creatures
and the elders. The Lamb had seven horns and
seven eyes, which are the seven spirits[a] of God
sent out into all the earth. 7 He went and took
the scroll from the right hand of him who sat
on the throne. 8 And when he had taken it, the
four living creatures and the twenty-four elders fell down before the Lamb. Each one had
a harp and they were holding golden bowls
full of incense, which are the prayers of God's
people. 9 And they sang a new song, saying:

"You are worthy to take the scroll
  and to open its seals,
because you were slain,
  and with your blood you purchased for God
  persons from every tribe and language
    and people and nation.
10 You have made them to be a kingdom and
    priests to serve our God,
  and they will reign[b] on the earth."

11 Then I looked and heard the voice of
many angels, numbering thousands upon
thousands, and ten thousand times ten thousand. They encircled the throne and the living
creatures and the elders. 12 In a loud voice they
were saying:

"Worthy is the Lamb, who was slain,
  to receive power and wealth and
    wisdom and strength
  and honor and glory and praise!"

13 Then I heard every creature in heaven and
on earth and under the earth and on the sea,
and all that is in them, saying:

"To him who sits on the throne and to the Lamb
  be praise and honor and glory and power,
    for ever and ever!"

14 The four living creatures said, "Amen," and
the elders fell down and worshiped.

The Seals

6 I watched as the Lamb opened the first of
the seven seals. Then I heard one of the
four living creatures say in a voice like thunder, "Come!" 2 I looked, and there before me
was a white horse! Its rider held a bow, and
he was given a crown, and he rode out as a
conqueror bent on conquest.
3 When the Lamb opened the second seal, I
heard the second living creature say, "Come!"
4 Then another horse came out, a fiery red one.
Its rider was given power to take peace from
the earth and to make people kill each other.
To him was given a large sword.
5 When the Lamb opened the third seal, I
heard the third living creature say, "Come!"
I looked, and there before me was a black
horse! Its rider was holding a pair of scales
in his hand. 6 Then I heard what sounded like a
voice among the four living creatures, saying,
"Two pounds[c] of wheat for a day's wages,[d] and
six pounds[e] of barley for a day's wages,[d] and
do not damage the oil and the wine!"
7 When the Lamb opened the fourth seal, I
heard the voice of the fourth living creature
say, "Come!" 8 I looked, and there before me
was a pale horse! Its rider was named Death,
and Hades was following close behind him.
They were given power over a fourth of the
earth to kill by sword, famine and plague, and
by the wild beasts of the earth.
9 When he opened the fifth seal, I saw under
the altar the souls of those who had been slain
because of the word of God and the testimony
they had maintained. 10 They called out in a
loud voice, "How long, Sovereign Lord, holy
and true, until you judge the inhabitants of the
earth and avenge our blood?" 11 Then each of
them was given a white robe, and they were
told to wait a little longer, until the full number of their fellow servants, their brothers
and sisters,[f] were killed just as they had been.
12 I watched as he opened the sixth seal.
There was a great earthquake. The sun turned
black like sackcloth made of goat hair, the
whole moon turned blood red, 13 and the stars
in the sky fell to earth, as figs drop from a
fig tree when shaken by a strong wind. 14 The
heavens receded like a scroll being rolled up,
and every mountain and island was removed
from its place.
15 Then the kings of the earth, the princes,
the generals, the rich, the mighty, and everyone else, both slave and free, hid in caves
and among the rocks of the mountains. 16 They
called to the mountains and the rocks, "Fall
on us and hide us[g] from the face of him who
sits on the throne and from the wrath of the
Lamb! 17 For the great day of their[h] wrath has
come, and who can withstand it?"

144,000 Sealed

7 After this I saw four angels standing at the
four corners of the earth, holding back the
four winds of the earth to prevent any wind
from blowing on the land or on the sea or on
any tree. 2 Then I saw another angel coming
up from the east, having the seal of the living
God. He called out in a loud voice to the four
angels who had been given power to harm the
land and the sea: 3 "Do not harm the land or
the sea or the trees until we put a seal on the
foreheads of the servants of our God." 4 Then
I heard the number of those who were sealed:
144,000 from all the tribes of Israel.

5 From the tribe of Judah 12,000 were
    sealed,
  from the tribe of Reuben 12,000,

[a] *6* That is, the sevenfold Spirit [b] *10* Some manuscripts *they reign* [c] *6* Or about 1 kilogram
[d] *6* Greek *a denarius* [e] *6* Or about 3 kilograms [f] *11* The Greek word for *brothers and sisters*
(*adelphoi*) refers here to believers, both men and women, as part of God's family; also in 12:10; 19:10.
[g] *16* See Hosea 10:8. [h] *17* Some manuscripts *his*

from the tribe of Gad 12,000,
6 from the tribe of Asher 12,000,
from the tribe of Naphtali 12,000,
from the tribe of Manasseh 12,000,
7 from the tribe of Simeon 12,000,
from the tribe of Levi 12,000,
from the tribe of Issachar 12,000,
8 from the tribe of Zebulun 12,000,
from the tribe of Joseph 12,000,
from the tribe of Benjamin 12,000.

The Great Multitude in White Robes

9 After this I looked, and there before me
was a great multitude that no one could count,
from every nation, tribe, people and language,
standing before the throne and before the
Lamb. They were wearing white robes and
were holding palm branches in their hands.
10 And they cried out in a loud voice:

"Salvation belongs to our God,
who sits on the throne,
and to the Lamb."

11 All the angels were standing around the
throne and around the elders and the four
living creatures. They fell down on their
faces before the throne and worshiped God,
12 saying:

"Amen!
Praise and glory
and wisdom and thanks and honor
and power and strength
be to our God for ever and ever.
Amen!"

13 Then one of the elders asked me, "These
in white robes—who are they, and where did
they come from?"
14 I answered, "Sir, you know."
And he said, "These are they who have
come out of the great tribulation; they have
washed their robes and made them white in
the blood of the Lamb. 15 Therefore,

"they are before the throne of God
and serve him day and night in his
temple;
and he who sits on the throne
will shelter them with his presence.
16 'Never again will they hunger;
never again will they thirst.
The sun will not beat down on them,'[a]
nor any scorching heat.
17 For the Lamb at the center of the throne
will be their shepherd;
'he will lead them to springs of living
water.'[a]
'And God will wipe away every tear
from their eyes.'[b]"

The Seventh Seal and the Golden Censer

8 When he opened the seventh seal, there
was silence in heaven for about half an
hour.
2 And I saw the seven angels who stand before God, and seven trumpets were given to
them.
3 Another angel, who had a golden censer,
came and stood at the altar. He was given
much incense to offer, with the prayers of all
God's people, on the golden altar in front of
the throne. 4 The smoke of the incense, together with the prayers of God's people, went up
before God from the angel's hand. 5 Then the
angel took the censer, filled it with fire from
the altar, and hurled it on the earth; and there
came peals of thunder, rumblings, flashes of
lightning and an earthquake.

The Trumpets

6 Then the seven angels who had the seven
trumpets prepared to sound them.
7 The first angel sounded his trumpet, and
there came hail and fire mixed with blood,
and it was hurled down on the earth. A third
of the earth was burned up, a third of the trees
were burned up, and all the green grass was
burned up.
8 The second angel sounded his trumpet,
and something like a huge mountain, all
ablaze, was thrown into the sea. A third of
the sea turned into blood, 9 a third of the living
creatures in the sea died, and a third of the
ships were destroyed.
10 The third angel sounded his trumpet, and
a great star, blazing like a torch, fell from the
sky on a third of the rivers and on the springs
of water— 11 the name of the star is Wormwood.[c] A third of the waters turned bitter, and
many people died from the waters that had
become bitter.
12 The fourth angel sounded his trumpet,
and a third of the sun was struck, a third of the
moon, and a third of the stars, so that a third
of them turned dark. A third of the day was
without light, and also a third of the night.
13 As I watched, I heard an eagle that was
flying in midair call out in a loud voice: "Woe!
Woe! Woe to the inhabitants of the earth, because of the trumpet blasts about to be sounded by the other three angels!"
9 The fifth angel sounded his trumpet, and
I saw a star that had fallen from the sky
to the earth. The star was given the key to
the shaft of the Abyss. 2 When he opened the
Abyss, smoke rose from it like the smoke
from a gigantic furnace. The sun and sky
were darkened by the smoke from the Abyss.
3 And out of the smoke locusts came down on
the earth and were given power like that of
scorpions of the earth. 4 They were told not to
harm the grass of the earth or any plant or
tree, but only those people who did not have
the seal of God on their foreheads. 5 They were
not allowed to kill them but only to torture
them for five months. And the agony they suffered was like that of the sting of a scorpion
when it strikes. 6 During those days people
will seek death but will not find it; they will
long to die, but death will elude them.
7 The locusts looked like horses prepared
for battle. On their heads they wore something like crowns of gold, and their faces resembled human faces. 8 Their hair was like

[a] *16,17* Isaiah 49:10 [b] *17* Isaiah 25:8 [c] *11* Wormwood is a bitter substance.

women's hair, and their teeth were like lions' teeth. 9They had breastplates like breastplates of iron, and the sound of their wings was like the thundering of many horses and chariots rushing into battle. 10They had tails with stingers, like scorpions, and in their tails they had power to torment people for five months. 11They had as king over them the angel of the Abyss, whose name in Hebrew is Abaddon and in Greek is Apollyon (that is, Destroyer).

12The first woe is past; two other woes are yet to come.

13The sixth angel sounded his trumpet, and I heard a voice coming from the four horns of the golden altar that is before God. 14It said to the sixth angel who had the trumpet, "Release the four angels who are bound at the great river Euphrates." 15And the four angels who had been kept ready for this very hour and day and month and year were released to kill a third of mankind. 16The number of the mounted troops was twice ten thousand times ten thousand. I heard their number.

17The horses and riders I saw in my vision looked like this: Their breastplates were fiery red, dark blue, and yellow as sulfur. The heads of the horses resembled the heads of lions, and out of their mouths came fire, smoke and sulfur. 18A third of mankind was killed by the three plagues of fire, smoke and sulfur that came out of their mouths. 19The power of the horses was in their mouths and in their tails; for their tails were like snakes, having heads with which they inflict injury.

20The rest of mankind who were not killed by these plagues still did not repent of the work of their hands; they did not stop worshiping demons, and idols of gold, silver, bronze, stone and wood—idols that cannot see or hear or walk. 21Nor did they repent of their murders, their magic arts, their sexual immorality or their thefts.

The Angel and the Little Scroll

10 Then I saw another mighty angel coming down from heaven. He was robed in a cloud, with a rainbow above his head; his face was like the sun, and his legs were like fiery pillars. 2He was holding a little scroll, which lay open in his hand. He planted his right foot on the sea and his left foot on the land, 3and he gave a loud shout like the roar of a lion. When he shouted, the voices of the seven thunders spoke. 4And when the seven thunders spoke, I was about to write; but I heard a voice from heaven say, "Seal up what the seven thunders have said and do not write it down."

5Then the angel I had seen standing on the sea and on the land raised his right hand to heaven. 6And he swore by him who lives for ever and ever, who created the heavens and all that is in them, the earth and all that is in it, and the sea and all that is in it, and said, "There will be no more delay! 7But in the days when the seventh angel is about to sound his trumpet, the mystery of God will be accomplished, just as he announced to his servants the prophets."

8Then the voice that I had heard from heaven spoke to me once more: "Go, take the scroll that lies open in the hand of the angel who is standing on the sea and on the land."

9So I went to the angel and asked him to give me the little scroll. He said to me, "Take it and eat it. It will turn your stomach sour, but 'in your mouth it will be as sweet as honey.'[a]" 10I took the little scroll from the angel's hand and ate it. It tasted as sweet as honey in my mouth, but when I had eaten it, my stomach turned sour. 11Then I was told, "You must prophesy again about many peoples, nations, languages and kings."

The Two Witnesses

11 I was given a reed like a measuring rod and was told, "Go and measure the temple of God and the altar, with its worshipers. 2But exclude the outer court; do not measure it, because it has been given to the Gentiles. They will trample on the holy city for 42 months. 3And I will appoint my two witnesses, and they will prophesy for 1,260 days, clothed in sackcloth." 4They are "the two olive trees" and the two lampstands, and "they stand before the Lord of the earth."[b] 5If anyone tries to harm them, fire comes from their mouths and devours their enemies. This is how anyone who wants to harm them must die. 6They have power to shut up the heavens so that it will not rain during the time they are prophesying; and they have power to turn the waters into blood and to strike the earth with every kind of plague as often as they want.

7Now when they have finished their testimony, the beast that comes up from the Abyss will attack them, and overpower and kill them. 8Their bodies will lie in the public square of the great city—which is figuratively called Sodom and Egypt—where also their Lord was crucified. 9For three and a half days some from every people, tribe, language and nation will gaze on their bodies and refuse them burial. 10The inhabitants of the earth will gloat over them and will celebrate by sending each other gifts, because these two prophets had tormented those who live on the earth.

11But after the three and a half days the breath[c] of life from God entered them, and they stood on their feet, and terror struck those who saw them. 12Then they heard a loud voice from heaven saying to them, "Come up here." And they went up to heaven in a cloud, while their enemies looked on.

13At that very hour there was a severe earthquake and a tenth of the city collapsed. Seven thousand people were killed in the earthquake, and the survivors were terrified and gave glory to the God of heaven.

14The second woe has passed; the third woe is coming soon.

[a] *9* Ezek. 3:3 [b] *4* See Zech. 4:3,11,14. [c] *11* Or *Spirit* (see Ezek. 37:5,14)

The Seventh Trumpet

[15]The seventh angel sounded his trumpet, and there were loud voices in heaven, which said:

"The kingdom of the world has become
the kingdom of our Lord and of his
Messiah,
and he will reign for ever and ever."

[16]And the twenty-four elders, who were seated on their thrones before God, fell on their faces and worshiped God, [17]saying:

"We give thanks to you, Lord God
Almighty,
the One who is and who was,
because you have taken your great
power
and have begun to reign.
[18]The nations were angry,
and your wrath has come.
The time has come for judging the dead,
and for rewarding your servants the
prophets
and your people who revere your name,
both great and small—
and for destroying those who destroy the
earth."

[19]Then God's temple in heaven was opened, and within his temple was seen the ark of his covenant. And there came flashes of lightning, rumblings, peals of thunder, an earthquake and a severe hailstorm.

The Woman and the Dragon

12 A great sign appeared in heaven: a woman clothed with the sun, with the moon under her feet and a crown of twelve stars on
her head. [2]She was pregnant and cried out in
pain as she was about to give birth. [3]Then another sign appeared in heaven: an enormous red dragon with seven heads and ten horns
and seven crowns on its heads. [4]Its tail swept
a third of the stars out of the sky and flung them to the earth. The dragon stood in front of the woman who was about to give birth, so that it might devour her child the moment
he was born. [5]She gave birth to a son, a male
child, who "will rule all the nations with an iron scepter."[a] And her child was snatched up
to God and to his throne. [6]The woman fled into
the wilderness to a place prepared for her by God, where she might be taken care of for 1,260 days.

[7]Then war broke out in heaven. Michael and his angels fought against the dragon, and the
dragon and his angels fought back. [8]But he
was not strong enough, and they lost their
place in heaven. [9]The great dragon was hurled
down—that ancient serpent called the devil, or Satan, who leads the whole world astray. He was hurled to the earth, and his angels with him.

[10]Then I heard a loud voice in heaven say:

"Now have come the salvation and the
power
and the kingdom of our God,
and the authority of his Messiah.
For the accuser of our brothers and
sisters,
who accuses them before our God day
and night,
has been hurled down.
[11]They triumphed over him
by the blood of the Lamb
and by the word of their testimony;
they did not love their lives so much
as to shrink from death.
[12]Therefore rejoice, you heavens
and you who dwell in them!
But woe to the earth and the sea,
because the devil has gone down to
you!
He is filled with fury,
because he knows that his time is
short."

[13]When the dragon saw that he had been hurled to the earth, he pursued the woman
who had given birth to the male child. [14]The
woman was given the two wings of a great eagle, so that she might fly to the place prepared for her in the wilderness, where she would be taken care of for a time, times and
half a time, out of the serpent's reach. [15]Then
from his mouth the serpent spewed water like a river, to overtake the woman and sweep her
away with the torrent. [16]But the earth helped
the woman by opening its mouth and swallowing the river that the dragon had spewed
out of his mouth. [17]Then the dragon was enraged at the woman and went off to wage war against the rest of her offspring—those who keep God's commands and hold fast their testimony about Jesus.

The Beast out of the Sea

13 The dragon[b] stood on the shore of the sea. And I saw a beast coming out of the sea. It had ten horns and seven heads, with ten crowns on its horns, and on each head a
blasphemous name. [2]The beast I saw resembled a leopard, but had feet like those of a bear and a mouth like that of a lion. The dragon gave the beast his power and his throne
and great authority. [3]One of the heads of the
beast seemed to have had a fatal wound, but the fatal wound had been healed. The whole world was filled with wonder and followed the
beast. [4]People worshiped the dragon because
he had given authority to the beast, and they also worshiped the beast and asked, "Who is like the beast? Who can wage war against it?"

[5]The beast was given a mouth to utter proud words and blasphemies and to exercise its authority for forty-two months. [6]It opened its
mouth to blaspheme God, and to slander his name and his dwelling place and those who
live in heaven. [7]It was given power to wage
war against God's holy people and to conquer them. And it was given authority over every
tribe, people, language and nation. [8]All inhab-
itants of the earth will worship the beast—all

[a] 5 Psalm 2:9 [b] 1 Some manuscripts *And I*

whose names have not been written in the Lamb's book of life, the Lamb who was slain from the creation of the world.[a]

9 Whoever has ears, let them hear.

10 "If anyone is to go into captivity,
into captivity they will go.
If anyone is to be killed[b] with the sword,
with the sword they will be killed."[c]

This calls for patient endurance and faithfulness on the part of God's people.

The Beast out of the Earth

11 Then I saw a second beast, coming out of the earth. It had two horns like a lamb, but it spoke like a dragon. 12 It exercised all the authority of the first beast on its behalf, and made the earth and its inhabitants worship the first beast, whose fatal wound had been healed. 13 And it performed great signs, even causing fire to come down from heaven to the earth in full view of the people. 14 Because of the signs it was given power to perform on behalf of the first beast, it deceived the inhabitants of the earth. It ordered them to set up an image in honor of the beast who was wounded by the sword and yet lived. 15 The second beast was given power to give breath to the image of the first beast, so that the image could speak and cause all who refused to worship the image to be killed. 16 It also forced all people, great and small, rich and poor, free and slave, to receive a mark on their right hands or on their foreheads, 17 so that they could not buy or sell unless they had the mark, which is the name of the beast or the number of its name.

18 This calls for wisdom. Let the person who has insight calculate the number of the beast, for it is the number of a man.[d] That number is 666.

The Lamb and the 144,000

14 Then I looked, and there before me was the Lamb, standing on Mount Zion, and with him 144,000 who had his name and his Father's name written on their foreheads. 2 And I heard a sound from heaven like the roar of rushing waters and like a loud peal of thunder. The sound I heard was like that of harpists playing their harps. 3 And they sang a new song before the throne and before the four living creatures and the elders. No one could learn the song except the 144,000 who had been redeemed from the earth. 4 These are those who did not defile themselves with women, for they remained virgins. They follow the Lamb wherever he goes. They were purchased from among mankind and offered as firstfruits to God and the Lamb. 5 No lie was found in their mouths; they are blameless.

The Three Angels

6 Then I saw another angel flying in midair, and he had the eternal gospel to proclaim to those who live on the earth—to every nation, tribe, language and people. 7 He said in a loud voice, "Fear God and give him glory, because the hour of his judgment has come. Worship him who made the heavens, the earth, the sea and the springs of water."

8 A second angel followed and said, "'Fallen! Fallen is Babylon the Great,'[e] which made all the nations drink the maddening wine of her adulteries."

9 A third angel followed them and said in a loud voice: "If anyone worships the beast and its image and receives its mark on their forehead or on their hand, 10 they, too, will drink the wine of God's fury, which has been poured full strength into the cup of his wrath. They will be tormented with burning sulfur in the presence of the holy angels and of the Lamb. 11 And the smoke of their torment will rise for ever and ever. There will be no rest day or night for those who worship the beast and its image, or for anyone who receives the mark of its name." 12 This calls for patient endurance on the part of the people of God who keep his commands and remain faithful to Jesus.

13 Then I heard a voice from heaven say, "Write this: Blessed are the dead who die in the Lord from now on."

"Yes," says the Spirit, "they will rest from their labor, for their deeds will follow them."

Harvesting the Earth and Trampling the Winepress

14 I looked, and there before me was a white cloud, and seated on the cloud was one like a son of man[f] with a crown of gold on his head and a sharp sickle in his hand. 15 Then another angel came out of the temple and called in a loud voice to him who was sitting on the cloud, "Take your sickle and reap, because the time to reap has come, for the harvest of the earth is ripe." 16 So he who was seated on the cloud swung his sickle over the earth, and the earth was harvested.

17 Another angel came out of the temple in heaven, and he too had a sharp sickle. 18 Still another angel, who had charge of the fire, came from the altar and called in a loud voice to him who had the sharp sickle, "Take your sharp sickle and gather the clusters of grapes from the earth's vine, because its grapes are ripe." 19 The angel swung his sickle on the earth, gathered its grapes and threw them into the great winepress of God's wrath. 20 They were trampled in the winepress outside the city, and blood flowed out of the press, rising as high as the horses' bridles for a distance of 1,600 stadia.[g]

Seven Angels With Seven Plagues

15 I saw in heaven another great and marvelous sign: seven angels with the seven last plagues—last, because with them God's wrath is completed. 2 And I saw what

[a] 8 Or *written from the creation of the world in the book of life belonging to the Lamb who was slain*
[b] 10 Some manuscripts *anyone kills* [c] 10 Jer. 15:2 [d] 18 Or *is humanity's number* [e] 8 Isaiah 21:9
[f] 14 See Daniel 7:13. [g] 20 That is, about 180 miles or about 300 kilometers

looked like a sea of glass glowing with fire
and, standing beside the sea, those who had
been victorious over the beast and its image
and over the number of its name. They held
harps given them by God 3and sang the song
of God's servant Moses and of the Lamb:

"Great and marvelous are your deeds,
  Lord God Almighty.
Just and true are your ways,
  King of the nations.[a]
4Who will not fear you, Lord,
  and bring glory to your name?
For you alone are holy.
All nations will come
  and worship before you,
for your righteous acts have been
    revealed."[b]

5After this I looked, and I saw in heaven
the temple—that is, the tabernacle of the
covenant law—and it was opened. 6Out of
the temple came the seven angels with the
seven plagues. They were dressed in clean,
shining linen and wore golden sashes around
their chests. 7Then one of the four living creatures gave to the seven angels seven golden
bowls filled with the wrath of God, who lives
for ever and ever. 8And the temple was filled
with smoke from the glory of God and from
his power, and no one could enter the temple
until the seven plagues of the seven angels
were completed.

The Seven Bowls of God's Wrath

16 Then I heard a loud voice from the temple saying to the seven angels, "Go, pour
out the seven bowls of God's wrath on the
earth."

2The first angel went and poured out his
bowl on the land, and ugly, festering sores
broke out on the people who had the mark of
the beast and worshiped its image.

3The second angel poured out his bowl on
the sea, and it turned into blood like that of
a dead person, and every living thing in the
sea died.

4The third angel poured out his bowl on the
rivers and springs of water, and they became
blood. 5Then I heard the angel in charge of
the waters say:

"You are just in these judgments, O Holy
    One,
  you who are and who were;
6for they have shed the blood of your holy
    people and your prophets,
  and you have given them blood to drink
    as they deserve."

7And I heard the altar respond:

"Yes, Lord God Almighty,
  true and just are your judgments."

8The fourth angel poured out his bowl on
the sun, and the sun was allowed to scorch
people with fire. 9They were seared by the
intense heat and they cursed the name of God,
who had control over these plagues, but they
refused to repent and glorify him.

10The fifth angel poured out his bowl on
the throne of the beast, and its kingdom was
plunged into darkness. People gnawed their
tongues in agony 11and cursed the God of heav-
en because of their pains and their sores, but
they refused to repent of what they had done.

12The sixth angel poured out his bowl on
the great river Euphrates, and its water was
dried up to prepare the way for the kings from
the East. 13Then I saw three impure spirits
that looked like frogs; they came out of the
mouth of the dragon, out of the mouth of the
beast and out of the mouth of the false prophet. 14They are demonic spirits that perform
signs, and they go out to the kings of the whole
world, to gather them for the battle on the
great day of God Almighty.

15"Look, I come like a thief! Blessed is
the one who stays awake and remains
clothed, so as not to go naked and be
shamefully exposed."

16Then they gathered the kings together to the
place that in Hebrew is called Armageddon.

17The seventh angel poured out his bowl
into the air, and out of the temple came a loud
voice from the throne, saying, "It is done!"
18Then there came flashes of lightning, rumblings, peals of thunder and a severe earthquake. No earthquake like it has ever occurred since mankind has been on earth, so
tremendous was the quake. 19The great city
split into three parts, and the cities of the nations collapsed. God remembered Babylon the
Great and gave her the cup filled with the wine
of the fury of his wrath. 20Every island fled
away and the mountains could not be found.
21From the sky huge hailstones, each weighing about a hundred pounds,[c] fell on people.
And they cursed God on account of the plague
of hail, because the plague was so terrible.

Babylon, the Prostitute on the Beast

17 One of the seven angels who had the sev-
en bowls came and said to me, "Come,
I will show you the punishment of the great
prostitute, who sits by many waters. 2With her
the kings of the earth committed adultery, and
the inhabitants of the earth were intoxicated
with the wine of her adulteries."

3Then the angel carried me away in the
Spirit into a wilderness. There I saw a woman sitting on a scarlet beast that was covered
with blasphemous names and had seven heads
and ten horns. 4The woman was dressed in
purple and scarlet, and was glittering with
gold, precious stones and pearls. She held a
golden cup in her hand, filled with abominable things and the filth of her adulteries. 5The
name written on her forehead was a mystery:

BABYLON THE GREAT
THE MOTHER OF PROSTITUTES
AND OF THE ABOMINATIONS OF THE EARTH.

[a] *3* Some manuscripts *ages* [b] *3,4* Phrases in this song are drawn from Psalm 111:2,3; Deut. 32:4; Jer. 10:7; Psalms 86:9; 98:2. [c] *21* Or about 45 kilograms

6I saw that the woman was drunk with the
blood of God's holy people, the blood of those
who bore testimony to Jesus.
When I saw her, I was greatly astonished.
7Then the angel said to me: "Why are you astonished? I will explain to you the mystery of
the woman and of the beast she rides, which
has the seven heads and ten horns. 8The beast,
which you saw, once was, now is not, and yet
will come up out of the Abyss and go to its destruction. The inhabitants of the earth whose
names have not been written in the book of
life from the creation of the world will be astonished when they see the beast, because it
once was, now is not, and yet will come.
9"This calls for a mind with wisdom. The
seven heads are seven hills on which the woman sits. 10They are also seven kings. Five have
fallen, one is, the other has not yet come; but
when he does come, he must remain for only
a little while. 11The beast who once was, and
now is not, is an eighth king. He belongs to the
seven and is going to his destruction.
12"The ten horns you saw are ten kings who
have not yet received a kingdom, but who for
one hour will receive authority as kings along
with the beast. 13They have one purpose and
will give their power and authority to the beast.
14They will wage war against the Lamb, but the
Lamb will triumph over them because he is Lord
of lords and King of kings—and with him will
be his called, chosen and faithful followers."
15Then the angel said to me, "The waters
you saw, where the prostitute sits, are peoples, multitudes, nations and languages.
16The beast and the ten horns you saw will
hate the prostitute. They will bring her to ruin
and leave her naked; they will eat her flesh
and burn her with fire. 17For God has put it
into their hearts to accomplish his purpose
by agreeing to hand over to the beast their
royal authority, until God's words are fulfilled. 18The woman you saw is the great city
that rules over the kings of the earth."

Lament Over Fallen Babylon

18 After this I saw another angel coming
down from heaven. He had great authority, and the earth was illuminated by his
splendor. 2With a mighty voice he shouted:

"'Fallen! Fallen is Babylon the Great!'[a]
She has become a dwelling for demons
and a haunt for every impure spirit,
a haunt for every unclean bird,
a haunt for every unclean and
detestable animal.
3For all the nations have drunk
the maddening wine of her adulteries.
The kings of the earth committed
adultery with her,
and the merchants of the earth grew
rich from her excessive luxuries."

Warning to Escape Babylon's Judgment

4Then I heard another voice from heaven
say:

"'Come out of her, my people,'[b]
so that you will not share in her sins,
so that you will not receive any of her
plagues;
5for her sins are piled up to heaven,
and God has remembered her crimes.
6Give back to her as she has given;
pay her back double for what she has
done.
Pour her a double portion from her own
cup.
7Give her as much torment and grief
as the glory and luxury she gave
herself.
In her heart she boasts,
'I sit enthroned as queen.
I am not a widow;[c]
I will never mourn.'
8Therefore in one day her plagues will
overtake her:
death, mourning and famine.
She will be consumed by fire,
for mighty is the Lord God who judges
her.

Threefold Woe Over Babylon's Fall

9"When the kings of the earth who committed adultery with her and shared her luxury
see the smoke of her burning, they will weep
and mourn over her. 10Terrified at her torment,
they will stand far off and cry:

"'Woe! Woe to you, great city,
you mighty city of Babylon!
In one hour your doom has come!'

11"The merchants of the earth will weep and
mourn over her because no one buys their
cargoes anymore— 12cargoes of gold, silver,
precious stones and pearls; fine linen, purple, silk and scarlet cloth; every sort of cit-
ron wood, and articles of every kind made of
ivory, costly wood, bronze, iron and marble;
13cargoes of cinnamon and spice, of incense,
myrrh and frankincense, of wine and olive
oil, of fine flour and wheat; cattle and sheep;
horses and carriages; and human beings sold
as slaves.
14"They will say, 'The fruit you longed for is
gone from you. All your luxury and splendor
have vanished, never to be recovered.' 15The
merchants who sold these things and gained
their wealth from her will stand far off, terrified at her torment. They will weep and mourn
16and cry out:

"'Woe! Woe to you, great city,
dressed in fine linen, purple and
scarlet,
and glittering with gold, precious
stones and pearls!
17In one hour such great wealth has been
brought to ruin!'

"Every sea captain, and all who travel by
ship, the sailors, and all who earn their living from the sea, will stand far off. 18When
they see the smoke of her burning, they will
exclaim, 'Was there ever a city like this great

[a] 2 Isaiah 21:9 [b] 4 Jer. 51:45 [c] 7 See Isaiah 47:7,8.

city?' [19]They will throw dust on their heads, and with weeping and mourning cry out:

"'Woe! Woe to you, great city,
where all who had ships on the sea
became rich through her wealth!
In one hour she has been brought to ruin!'

[20]"Rejoice over her, you heavens!
Rejoice, you people of God!
Rejoice, apostles and prophets!
For God has judged her
with the judgment she imposed on
you."

The Finality of Babylon's Doom

[21]Then a mighty angel picked up a boulder
the size of a large millstone and threw it into
the sea, and said:

"With such violence
the great city of Babylon will be thrown
down,
never to be found again.
[22]The music of harpists and musicians,
pipers and trumpeters,
will never be heard in you again.
No worker of any trade
will ever be found in you again.
The sound of a millstone
will never be heard in you again.
[23]The light of a lamp
will never shine in you again.
The voice of bridegroom and bride
will never be heard in you again.
Your merchants were the world's
important people.
By your magic spell all the nations
were led astray.
[24]In her was found the blood of prophets
and of God's holy people,
of all who have been slaughtered on the
earth."

Threefold Hallelujah Over Babylon's Fall

19 After this I heard what sounded like
the roar of a great multitude in heaven
shouting:

"Hallelujah!
Salvation and glory and power belong to
our God,
[2] for true and just are his judgments.
He has condemned the great prostitute
who corrupted the earth by her
adulteries.
He has avenged on her the blood of his
servants."

[3]And again they shouted:

"Hallelujah!
The smoke from her goes up for ever and
ever."

[4]The twenty-four elders and the four living
creatures fell down and worshiped God, who
was seated on the throne. And they cried:

"Amen, Hallelujah!"

[5]Then a voice came from the throne, saying:

"Praise our God,
all you his servants,
you who fear him,
both great and small!"

[6]Then I heard what sounded like a great
multitude, like the roar of rushing waters and
like loud peals of thunder, shouting:

"Hallelujah!
For our Lord God Almighty reigns.
[7]Let us rejoice and be glad
and give him glory!
For the wedding of the Lamb has come,
and his bride has made herself ready.
[8]Fine linen, bright and clean,
was given her to wear."
(Fine linen stands for the righteous acts of
God's holy people.)

[9]Then the angel said to me, "Write this:
Blessed are those who are invited to the
wedding supper of the Lamb!" And he added, "These are the true words of God."
[10]At this I fell at his feet to worship him.
But he said to me, "Don't do that! I am a fellow servant with you and with your brothers
and sisters who hold to the testimony of Jesus.
Worship God! For it is the Spirit of prophecy
who bears testimony to Jesus."

The Heavenly Warrior Defeats the Beast

[11]I saw heaven standing open and there
before me was a white horse, whose rider is
called Faithful and True. With justice he judges and wages war. [12]His eyes are like blazing
fire, and on his head are many crowns. He has
a name written on him that no one knows but
he himself. [13]He is dressed in a robe dipped in
blood, and his name is the Word of God. [14]The
armies of heaven were following him, riding
on white horses and dressed in fine linen,
white and clean. [15]Coming out of his mouth
is a sharp sword with which to strike down
the nations. "He will rule them with an iron
scepter."[a] He treads the winepress of the fury
of the wrath of God Almighty. [16]On his robe
and on his thigh he has this name written:

KING OF KINGS AND LORD OF LORDS.

[17]And I saw an angel standing in the sun,
who cried in a loud voice to all the birds flying
in midair, "Come, gather together for the great
supper of God, [18]so that you may eat the flesh
of kings, generals, and the mighty, of horses
and their riders, and the flesh of all people,
free and slave, great and small."
[19]Then I saw the beast and the kings of the
earth and their armies gathered together to
wage war against the rider on the horse and
his army. [20]But the beast was captured, and
with it the false prophet who had performed
the signs on its behalf. With these signs he had
deluded those who had received the mark of
the beast and worshiped its image. The two
of them were thrown alive into the fiery lake

[a] *15* Psalm 2:9

of burning sulfur. 21The rest were killed with the sword coming out of the mouth of the rider on the horse, and all the birds gorged themselves on their flesh.

The Thousand Years

20 And I saw an angel coming down out of heaven, having the key to the Abyss and holding in his hand a great chain. 2He seized the dragon, that ancient serpent, who is the devil, or Satan, and bound him for a thousand years. 3He threw him into the Abyss, and locked and sealed it over him, to keep him from deceiving the nations anymore until the thousand years were ended. After that, he must be set free for a short time.

4I saw thrones on which were seated those who had been given authority to judge. And I saw the souls of those who had been beheaded because of their testimony about Jesus and because of the word of God. They[a] had not worshiped the beast or its image and had not received its mark on their foreheads or their hands. They came to life and reigned with Christ a thousand years. 5(The rest of the dead did not come to life until the thousand years were ended.) This is the first resurrection. 6Blessed and holy are those who share in the first resurrection. The second death has no power over them, but they will be priests of God and of Christ and will reign with him for a thousand years.

The Judgment of Satan

7When the thousand years are over, Satan will be released from his prison 8and will go out to deceive the nations in the four corners of the earth—Gog and Magog—and to gather them for battle. In number they are like the sand on the seashore. 9They marched across the breadth of the earth and surrounded the camp of God's people, the city he loves. But fire came down from heaven and devoured them. 10And the devil, who deceived them, was thrown into the lake of burning sulfur, where the beast and the false prophet had been thrown. They will be tormented day and night for ever and ever.

The Judgment of the Dead

11Then I saw a great white throne and him who was seated on it. The earth and the heavens fled from his presence, and there was no place for them. 12And I saw the dead, great and small, standing before the throne, and books were opened. Another book was opened, which is the book of life. The dead were judged according to what they had done as recorded in the books. 13The sea gave up the dead that were in it, and death and Hades gave up the dead that were in them, and each person was judged according to what they had done. 14Then death and Hades were thrown into the lake of fire. The lake of fire is the second death. 15Anyone whose name was not found written in the book of life was thrown into the lake of fire.

A New Heaven and a New Earth

21 Then I saw "a new heaven and a new earth,"[b] for the first heaven and the first earth had passed away, and there was no longer any sea. 2I saw the Holy City, the new Jerusalem, coming down out of heaven from God, prepared as a bride beautifully dressed for her husband. 3And I heard a loud voice from the throne saying, "Look! God's dwelling place is now among the people, and he will dwell with them. They will be his people, and God himself will be with them and be their God. 4'He will wipe every tear from their eyes. There will be no more death'[c] or mourning or crying or pain, for the old order of things has passed away."

5He who was seated on the throne said, "I am making everything new!" Then he said, "Write this down, for these words are trustworthy and true."

6He said to me: "It is done. I am the Alpha and the Omega, the Beginning and the End. To the thirsty I will give water without cost from the spring of the water of life. 7Those who are victorious will inherit all this, and I will be their God and they will be my children. 8But the cowardly, the unbelieving, the vile, the murderers, the sexually immoral, those who practice magic arts, the idolaters and all liars—they will be consigned to the fiery lake of burning sulfur. This is the second death."

The New Jerusalem, the Bride of the Lamb

9One of the seven angels who had the seven bowls full of the seven last plagues came and said to me, "Come, I will show you the bride, the wife of the Lamb." 10And he carried me away in the Spirit to a mountain great and high, and showed me the Holy City, Jerusalem, coming down out of heaven from God. 11It shone with the glory of God, and its brilliance was like that of a very precious jewel, like a jasper, clear as crystal. 12It had a great, high wall with twelve gates, and with twelve angels at the gates. On the gates were written the names of the twelve tribes of Israel. 13There were three gates on the east, three on the north, three on the south and three on the west. 14The wall of the city had twelve foundations, and on them were the names of the twelve apostles of the Lamb.

15The angel who talked with me had a measuring rod of gold to measure the city, its gates and its walls. 16The city was laid out like a square, as long as it was wide. He measured the city with the rod and found it to be 12,000 stadia[d] in length, and as wide and high as it is long. 17The angel measured the wall using human measurement, and it was 144 cubits[e] thick.[f] 18The wall was made of jasper, and the city of pure gold, as pure as glass. 19The foundations of the city walls were decorated with every kind of precious stone. The first

[a] *4* Or *God; I also saw those who* [b] *1* Isaiah 65:17 [c] *4* Isaiah 25:8 [d] *16* That is, about 1,400 miles or about 2,200 kilometers [e] *17* That is, about 200 feet or about 65 meters [f] *17* Or *high*

foundation was jasper, the second sapphire,
the third agate, the fourth emerald, 20the fifth
onyx, the sixth ruby, the seventh chrysolite,
the eighth beryl, the ninth topaz, the tenth turquoise, the eleventh jacinth, and the twelfth
amethyst.[a] 21The twelve gates were twelve
pearls, each gate made of a single pearl. The
great street of the city was of gold, as pure as
transparent glass.

22I did not see a temple in the city, because
the Lord God Almighty and the Lamb are its
temple. 23The city does not need the sun or
the moon to shine on it, for the glory of God
gives it light, and the Lamb is its lamp. 24The
nations will walk by its light, and the kings
of the earth will bring their splendor into it.
25On no day will its gates ever be shut, for
there will be no night there. 26The glory and
honor of the nations will be brought into it.
27Nothing impure will ever enter it, nor will
anyone who does what is shameful or deceitful, but only those whose names are written
in the Lamb's book of life.

Eden Restored

22 Then the angel showed me the river
of the water of life, as clear as crystal,
flowing from the throne of God and of the
Lamb 2down the middle of the great street of
the city. On each side of the river stood the tree
of life, bearing twelve crops of fruit, yielding
its fruit every month. And the leaves of the
tree are for the healing of the nations. 3No
longer will there be any curse. The throne of
God and of the Lamb will be in the city, and
his servants will serve him. 4They will see his
face, and his name will be on their foreheads.
5There will be no more night. They will not
need the light of a lamp or the light of the sun,
for the Lord God will give them light. And
they will reign for ever and ever.

John and the Angel

6The angel said to me, "These words are
trustworthy and true. The Lord, the God who
inspires the prophets, sent his angel to show
his servants the things that must soon take
place."

7"Look, I am coming soon! Blessed is the
one who keeps the words of the prophecy written in this scroll."

8I, John, am the one who heard and saw
these things. And when I had heard and seen
them, I fell down to worship at the feet of the
angel who had been showing them to me. 9But
he said to me, "Don't do that! I am a fellow servant with you and with your fellow prophets
and with all who keep the words of this scroll.
Worship God!"

10Then he told me, "Do not seal up the
words of the prophecy of this scroll, because the time is near. 11Let the one who does
wrong continue to do wrong; let the vile person continue to be vile; let the one who does
right continue to do right; and let the holy
person continue to be holy."

Epilogue: Invitation and Warning

12"Look, I am coming soon! My reward is
with me, and I will give to each person according to what they have done. 13I am the Alpha
and the Omega, the First and the Last, the
Beginning and the End.

14"Blessed are those who wash their robes,
that they may have the right to the tree of life
and may go through the gates into the city.
15Outside are the dogs, those who practice
magic arts, the sexually immoral, the murderers, the idolaters and everyone who loves
and practices falsehood.

16"I, Jesus, have sent my angel to give you[b]
this testimony for the churches. I am the Root
and the Offspring of David, and the bright
Morning Star."

17The Spirit and the bride say, "Come!" And
let the one who hears say, "Come!" Let the
one who is thirsty come; and let the one who
wishes take the free gift of the water of life.

18I warn everyone who hears the words of
the prophecy of this scroll: If anyone adds
anything to them, God will add to that person the plagues described in this scroll. 19And
if anyone takes words away from this scroll
of prophecy, God will take away from that
person any share in the tree of life and in the
Holy City, which are described in this scroll.

20He who testifies to these things says, "Yes,
I am coming soon."

Amen. Come, Lord Jesus.

21The grace of the Lord Jesus be with God's
people. Amen.

[a] *20* The precise identification of some of these precious stones is uncertain. [b] *16* The Greek is plural.

Table of Weights and Measures

	Biblical Unit	Approximate American Equivalent	Approximate Metric Equivalent
Weights	talent (60 minas)	75 pounds	34 kilograms
	mina (50 shekels)	1 1/4 pounds	560 grams
	shekel (2 bekas)	2/5 ounce	11.5 grams
	pim (2/3 shekel)	1/4 ounce	7.8 grams
	beka (10 gerahs)	1/5 ounce	5.7 grams
	gerah	1/50 ounce	0.6 gram
	daric	1/3 ounce	8.4 grams
Length	cubit	18 inches	45 centimeters
	span	9 inches	23 centimeters
	handbreadth	3 inches	7.5 centimeters
	stadion (pl. stadia)	600 feet	183 meters
Capacity			
Dry Measure	cor [homer] (10 ephahs)	6 bushels	220 liters
	lethek (5 ephahs)	3 bushels	110 liters
	ephah (10 omers)	3/5 bushel	22 liters
	seah (1/3 ephah)	7 quarts	7.5 liters
	omer (1/10 ephah)	2 quarts	2 liters
	cab (1/18 ephah)	1 quart	1 liter
Liquid Measure	bath (1 ephah)	6 gallons	22 liters
	hin (1/6 bath)	1 gallon	3.8 liters
	log (1/72 bath)	1/3 quart	0.3 liter

The figures of the table are calculated on the basis of a shekel equaling 11.5 grams, a cubit equaling 18 inches and an ephah equaling 22 liters. The quart referred to is either a dry quart (slightly larger than a liter) or a liquid quart (slightly smaller than a liter), whichever is applicable. The ton referred to in the footnotes is the American ton of 2,000 pounds. These weights are calculated relative to the particular commodity involved. Accordingly, the same measure of capacity in the text may be converted into different weights in the footnotes.

This table is based upon the best available information, but it is not intended to be mathematically precise; like the measurement equivalents in the footnotes, it merely gives approximate amounts and distances. Weights and measures differed somewhat at various times and places in the ancient world. There is uncertainty particularly about the ephah and the bath; further discoveries may shed more light on these units of capacity.

Getting to Know God

God created you because he wants a relationship with you. He loves you. He wants you to know him personally and intimately, not just know about him. Through God's written Word (the Bible), and through his only Son (Jesus), God reveals that he wants you to enjoy a life that's in line with his purpose and destiny for you. He wants to be a nurturing and powerful presence in your life, not just an idea in your head. Knowing him means receiving his love. Following him means following his leadership. And let's tell it like it is: Accepting that leadership will affect your lifestyle. As you come to know God, he no longer is a concept simply to be believed or disbelieved; he is a living reality who is known and followed along a pathway that leads to freedom.

According to the Bible, until you come to terms with Jesus, you haven't dealt with the issue that's most important in getting to know God. In John 14:6, Jesus said, "I am the way and the truth and the life. No one comes to the Father except through me." Through him, countless millions have come to know the Father, transforming their lives as well as the entire course of human history.

And Jesus continues to change history — one person at a time. He wants to change your life too. But he will not do so unless you ask him. It's not enough simply to agree intellectually with Jesus' claims. You must believe in him — believe that he is the Son of God sent to earth to pay the penalty for all sin, once for all, through his death on the cross — and ask him to come into your life.

Receiving this free gift of salvation is as simple as saying, "Jesus, I acknowledge my sin and your payment for it on the cross. I now ask you to forgive me, and I willingly give my life to you." At that moment, he will come into your innermost being and start you on a wonderful journey toward intimacy with God.

Another way to explain this is through a step-by-step "path of salvation." Many people find this sort of process helpful as they consider the important decision to give their life to Jesus. Here is a brief four-step system explaining why we all need the Lord and how we can go about making that decision. It includes key Scripture passages supporting each statement. You can look up these verses in the Bible if you'd like to read more of the context.

First:

Realize that everyone needs to be saved. No one is righteous. We are all guilty of breaking God's law in some way and therefore already condemned and sentenced.

> **Romans 3:19–20** "Now we know that whatever the law says, it says to those who are under the law, so that every mouth may be silenced and the whole world held accountable to God. Therefore no one will be declared righteous in God's sight by the works of the law; rather, through the law we become conscious of our sin."

Second:

Understand that there is hope in Christ. Salvation does not come by keeping laws or being good or doing good works, but only through faith in Christ. All have sinned, but anyone who receives Christ can be forgiven and accepted by God as righteous.

> **Romans 3:21–25** "But now apart from the law the righteousness of God has been made known, to which the Law and the Prophets testify. This righteousness is given through faith in Jesus Christ to all who believe. There is no difference between Jew and Gentile, for all have sinned and fall short of the glory of God, and all are justified freely by his grace through the redemption that came by Christ Jesus. God presented Christ as a sacrifice of atonement, through the shedding of his blood — to be received by faith. He did this to demonstrate his righteousness, because in his forbearance he had left the sins committed beforehand unpunished."

> **Romans 5:8** "But God demonstrates his own love for us in this: While we were still sinners, Christ died for us."

> **Romans 6:23** "For the wages of sin is death, but the gift of God is eternal life in Christ Jesus our Lord."

Third:

Know that God forgives and accepts unconditionally anyone who believes in Christ.

> **Romans 8:1–2** "Therefore, there is now no condemnation for those who are in Christ Jesus, because through Christ Jesus the law of the Spirit who gives life has set you free from the law of sin and death."

Finally:

Trust Christ in your heart and confess him as Lord with your mouth.

> **Romans 10:9–10** "If you declare with your mouth, 'Jesus is Lord,' and believe in your heart that God raised him from the dead, you will be saved. For it is with your heart that you believe and are justified, and it is with your mouth that you profess your faith and are saved."

Repeat aloud this prayer (or something similar—what you mean is what matters, not the exact words you use):

> *I thank you, heavenly Father, for sending your own Son, Jesus Christ, to die on the cross and pay the penalty for sin. I now believe in him and accept him as my Lord. Thank you that I am saved in him.*
>
> *In Jesus' name, Amen.*

Some other helpful passages relating to the topic of salvation:

> **Luke 18:9–14** "To some who were confident of their own righteousness and looked down on everyone else, Jesus told this parable: 'Two men went up to the temple to pray, one a Pharisee and the other a tax collector. The Pharisee stood by himself and prayed: "God, I thank you that I am not like other people—robbers, evildoers, adulterers—or even like this tax collector. I fast twice a week and give a tenth of all I get."
>
> "'But the tax collector stood at a distance. He would not even look up to heaven, but beat his breast and said, "God, have mercy on me, a sinner."
>
> "'I tell you that this man, rather than the other, went home justified before God. For all those who exalt themselves will be humbled, and those who humble themselves will be exalted.'"
>
> **John 1:12** "Yet to all who did receive him, to those who believed in his name, he gave the right to become children of God."
>
> **John 3:16–18** "For God so loved the world that he gave his one and only Son, that whoever believes in him shall not perish but have eternal life. For God did not send his Son into the world to condemn the world, but to save the world through him. Whoever believes in him is not condemned, but whoever does not believe stands condemned already because they have not believed in the name of God's one and only Son."
>
> **John 5:24** "Very truly I tell you, whoever hears my word and believes him who sent me has eternal life and will not be judged but has crossed over from death to life."
>
> **John 20:31** "But these are written that you may believe that Jesus is the Messiah, the Son of God, and that by believing you may have life in his name."
>
> **Acts 10:43** "All the prophets testify about him that everyone who believes in him receives forgiveness of sins through his name."
>
> **2 Corinthians 6:2** "For he says, 'In the time of my favor I heard you, and in the day of salvation I helped you.' I tell you, now is the time of God's favor, now is the day of salvation."
>
> **Hebrews 11:6** "And without faith it is impossible to please God, because anyone who comes to him must believe that he exists and that he rewards those who earnestly seek him."

1 John 1:9 "If we confess our sins, he is faithful and just and will forgive us our sins and purify us from all unrighteousness."

1 John 5:13 "I write these things to you who believe in the name of the Son of God so that you may know that you have eternal life."

Revelation 3:20 "'Here I am! I stand at the door and knock. If anyone hears my voice and opens the door, I will come in and eat with that person, and they with me.'"

You may be wondering what kinds of practical steps you might take to guide you as you discover your personal path toward knowing God. Consider some of these ideas:

- Ask God to reveal himself to you if you're not sure he's there.
- Talk to people who display a genuine relationship with God—those who obviously love him and who live by a different set of principles.
- Spend time enjoying God's creation.
- Listen to the stories of older people who have walked with God for a long time.
- Be a lover of truth, and don't hesitate to raise questions about things many others seem to take for granted.
- Follow the leading of the Holy Spirit. You can trust God's "gentle whisper" to give you direction. If you lack understanding, ask him for it.
- Read what other believers have said about Christianity. Ask your Christian friends for a list of authors who have inspired them in their walk with God.
- Write down your questions, including those that occur to you as you read the Bible, and take them to a believer who will respect your search for the truth.
- Be aware that moments of doubts and questions are normal and legitimate as you discover your personal path of faith.
- Be alert to your presuppositions—the things you already believe—and your personal roadblocks, and try not to let them stand in the way of your discovery process.
- Keep a journal of your thoughts and feelings during your search.
- Determine to spend a specified time each day walking the pathway toward faith, and keep evaluating your progress.
- Act on what you decide.

Deepen your Experience with God's Word through these Best-Selling NIV Bibles from Zondervan

AVAILABLE WHEREVER BIBLES ARE SOLD

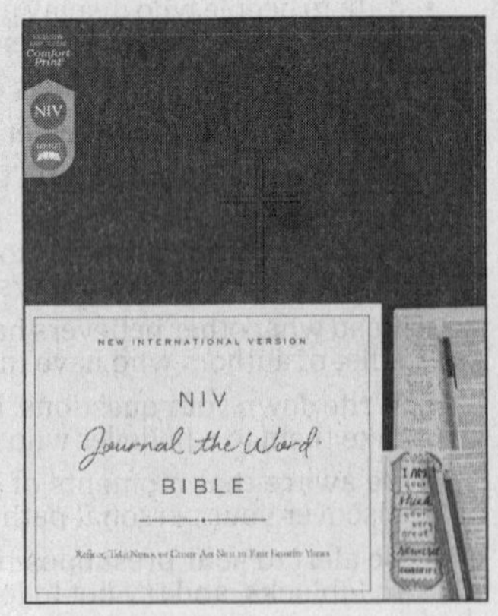

NIV Study Bible, Fully Revised Edition

A comprehensive study Bible that features over 20,000 study notes and a stunning four-color interior with photographs, maps, charts, and illustrations.

ISBN: 9780310448945

NIV Biblical Theology Study Bible

With helpful articles, introductions to books and sections of the Bible, and 20,000 verse-by-verse study notes, you will gain a clearer understanding of every portion of Scripture.

ISBN: 9780310450405

NIV Journal the Word Bible

This Bible allows you to creatively express yourself every day with plenty of room for journaling or creating Bible art next to your treasured verses.

ISBN: 9780310450276